I thank my God every time I remember you,

constantly praying with joy

in every one of my prayers for all of you.

Philippians 1:3-4

Presented To

Kayla Krzewinski

By

On

This book can change your life.

The Bible's essential message is this: God loves us and wants to be in a lifelong **friendship** with us. The Bible tells the story of God's love, revealed most perfectly in Jesus' **life**, death, and Resurrection. Through Christ, God offers us forgiveness, freedom, companionship, and **new** life. It is a wonderful gift, but we must choose to accept it. How will you respond to that invitation?

Lord God, here I am!
You created me and know me completely.
You know all about my life—my joys and my
sufferings, my questions and my dreams.
I know you love me, even when I feel my sins
and mistakes make me unlovable.
Help me to love you, God, with all my heart,
mind, and soul, and to love all people,
even as I love myself.

Jesus, thank you for showing me how to live.
I know you want only the best for my life,
and I believe following you is the way to a
full and abundant life.

Holy Spirit, give me the courage and wisdom
to be Jesus' follower, even when it isn't easy.
Fill me with the joy and peace that comes
from doing your will.

Amen.

THE Catholic Youth Bible® Third Edition

Pray It! Study It! Live It!®
resources offer a holistic approach
to learning, living, and passing on the
Catholic faith

For the text of the articles and introductions

Nihil Obstat: Rev. William M. Becker, STD
                Censor Librorum
                September 22, 2009
Imprimatur: †Most Rev. John M. Quinn
                Bishop of Winona
                September 22, 2009

The nihil obstat and imprimatur are official declarations that a book or pamphlet is free doctrinal or moral error. No implication is contained therein that those who have granted the nihil obstat imprimatur agree with the contents, opinions, or statements expressed, nor do they assume any legal responsibility associated with publication.

For the text of the New Revised Standard Version (NRSV): Catholic Edition

Nihil Obstat: †Most Rev. Daniel E. Pilarczyk
                President, National Conference of Catholic Bishops
                Washington, DC, 12 September 1991
Imprimatur: Canadian Conference of Catholic Bishops
                Ottawa, 15 October 1991

Third edition reviewers and article writers: Catherine Cory, Marissa Esparza-Garcia, Dennis Kurtz, Paula Norbert, Margaret Nutting Ralph, Larry Schatz, FSC, James Spillman, Alan Talley, Michael Theisen

Interior Design: Laurie Nelson; Illustrations: Vicki Shuck; Typesetting: Blue Heron Bookcraft; Proofreading: Peachtree Editorial and Proofreading Services

The acknowledgments continue on page 1515.

The publishing team included Virginia Halbur, development editor; prepress and manufacturing coordinated by the production departments of Saint Mary's Press.

Copyright © 2010 by Saint Mary's Press, Christian Brothers Publications, 702 Terrace Heights, Winona, MN 55987-1320, www.smp.org. All rights reserved. No part of this book may be reproduced by any means without the written permission of the publisher.

Printed in the United States of America

4130   (PO4333)

ISBN 978-0-88489-787-3, paper
ISBN 978-0-88489-788-0, hardcover
ISBN 978-0-88489-791-0, leatherette

Library of Congress Cataloging-in-Publication Data

Bible. English. New Revised Standard. 2010.
    The Catholic youth Bible : New Revised Standard Version, Catholic edition. — 3rd ed.
        p. cm.
Includes index.
ISBN 978-0-88489-788-0 (hardcover) — ISBN 978-0-88489-787-3 (pbk.) — ISBN 978-0-88489-791-0 (faux leather)
    1. Bible—Study and teaching—Catholic Church. 2. Catholic youth—Religious life. I. Saint Mary's Press. II. Title.
BS191.5.A12010 W56 2010
220.5'20434—dc22

                                2009023605

THE
Catholic
Youth
Bible® Third Edition

New Revised Standard Version:
Catholic Edition

saint mary's press

Contents

The Old Testament

The New Testament

v

Welcome!

This Unique Bible Is for YOU!

The *Catholic Youth Bible® (CYB)* is filled with things that will make it easier for you to understand the Bible's message. The authors, editors, designers, and artists involved in creating its special features were focused on you — a young person seeking answers to life's important questions. The *CYB* can be a true companion, helping you find the answers you seek and perhaps raising new questions along the way. It will help you see yourself in God's image and likeness...

a vital part of God's saving work in the world.

What Makes this Youth Bible CATHOLIC?

For starters, its introductions and articles reflect Catholic inter-pretation of the Bible and make connections to Catholic beliefs and traditions. In addition, this Biblecontains all seventy-three books and letters that form a complete Catholic Bible, seven more than most other Bibles (see "The Case of the Missing Books," near Tob 1:16). Does this mean that other Christians cannot use ***The Catholic Youth Bible?*** Not at all. When it comes to the Scrip-tures, Christians from all cultures and denominations have more in common than they have differences.

As You Use this Bible, keep in mind two important points. The first is that the Bible is for everyone. Wherever you are in your relationship with God, *the Bible can speak to you.* The articles in the ***CYB*** invite you to consider what the church teaches about God's message in the Bible, whether you are a committed Christian or a searcher with lots of questions.

The second point is that all the special features in ***The Catholic Youth Bible*** are designed to encourage you *to read the Bible itself.* It is the Bible's stories, poems, prophecies, and letters that carry this central message: *God desires a loving relationship with us.* The special features of this Bible can help you understand God's message. **But it is God's word in the Bible that can CHANGE YOUR LIFE!**

Special Features

The *Catholic Youth Bible* is loaded with special features to help make it easier for you to read and understand the Bible. Here is a list of some of those features and where to find them.

SECTION INTRODUCTIONS

Each major section of the Bible (the Pentateuch, the historical books, the wisdom books, the prophetic books, the Gospels and the Acts of the Apostles, and the Letters and Revelation) begins with background on the books in that section.

BOOK INTRODUCTIONS

Introductions at the beginning of most books (sometimes two or three books share a single introduction) give insight into each book's central message and an overview of its contents.

COLOR INSERTS

The five sections of color inserts cover how to read and study the Bible; how to pray with the Scriptures; how to apply biblical principles to daily life and six saints who illustrate the principles, including a list of the seven principles of Catholic social teaching; photos and charts highlighting biblical people, places, and events; and an overview of Catholic practices and prayers.

 The **"Live It!"** articles apply the Bible's messages to situations you may be facing now or will face in the future.

 The **"Pray It!"** articles can help you use the Bible for personal prayer. They show the biblical basis for the prayer and sacramental life of the Catholic Church.

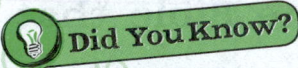 The **"Did You Know?"** articles provide background from biblical scholars to help you understand the culture and traditions of biblical times, or the Church's interpretation of certain passages.

 The **"Introducing . . ."** articles give a quick introduction to the lives of important biblical people.

 The **"Catholic Connection"** articles are full-page articles that show the biblical basis for many Catholic Christian beliefs and practices.

 The **"Cultural Connection"** articles explain how people in different cultures have understood and lived out God's revelation in the Bible. The articles represent many of the diverse cultures that have found their home in the United States.

 These articles focus on the seven principles of Catholic social teaching and help the reader to understand their biblical basis.

WHERE DO I FIND IT?

Several indexes are located at the back of the Bible. The first index helps you locate Bible passages on events, people, and teachings of Jesus. The second index helps you find Bible passages related to Catholic teaching. The third index helps you find Bible passages related to each sacrament. The fourth index helps you find Bible passages related to life and faith issues. The fifth index leads you to articles on specific topics.

STUDY AIDS

A calendar of the Church year and Sunday readings, a glossary of Scripture-related terms, color maps, pictures, and a timeline are found at the back of the Bible. The timeline and maps will help you locate where and when different biblical events occurred.

The Bible Is
Multicultural

The Bible developed in the midst of great cultural diversity. In fact, the Bible was originally written in at least two languages, Hebrew and Greek. The people of the Old Testament were influenced by Arabic, Egyptian, and other Middle Eastern cultures that surrounded them. Later, they and the early Christian church were influenced by the Greek and Roman cultures. In the Bible, God is revealed as the God of all nations and all cultures.

As the Word of God, the Bible's core message of God's love for human beings speaks to people of any culture. That is one reason the Bible has been translated into more languages than any other book in the world. Christians also believe that God is at work in the lives of people of every culture, whether or not they have been formally introduced to the Christian message. Listening to other cultures' experience of God can deepen Christian people's appreciation of God's message present in the Bible.

We also live in a multicultural world. **The Catholic Youth Bible** responds to this reality in two main ways. First, all the articles attempt to speak in a way that people of all cultures can appreciate and understand. Second, some articles have been specially written to represent distinct cultural perspectives. Most of these articles represent African American, Asian American, Hispanic and Latino, and Native American perspectives. The revised edition of **The Catholic Youth Bible, Third Edition** also includes additional articles representing cultural perspectives from around the world.

All the articles share cultural experiences and traditions, religious symbols, prayers, and poetry, and they connect all these elements to the Bible. If you would like to read articles from one of the four major cultural perspectives mentioned above, the subject index contains entries for those.

The cultural perspectives represented in **The Catholic Youth Bible** are a small sampling of the many unique cultures in the world. Because of space restrictions, articles on many cultures could not be included. Despite these limitations, the multicultural articles can deepen your appreciation of the Bible's message and of the rich ways different cultures live that message.

Navigating
The Catholic Youth Bible

The Catholic Youth Bible has several aids to help you locate references to Bible books and the Bible's special features. The contents on pages iv–v will be your main guide in locating the different books and features. However, the last page in the color section (facing the back cover) lists all the Bible books alphabetically and gives their abbreviations and beginning page numbers. You will find this a useful and easy-to-locate guide. Also, the section "Where Do I Find It?" offers several types of indexes to help you locate specific passages and articles.

Throughout **The Catholic Youth Bible,** there are many references to specific Bible passages. These references are given in shorthand form, such as Jn 3:16–17. The initial letters are the abbreviation for (or, in a few cases, the full name of) the Bible book. The number before the colon stands for the chapter, and the number(s) after the colon stands for the verse(s). So Jn 3:16–17 refers to the Gospel According to John, chapter 3, verses 16 to 17.

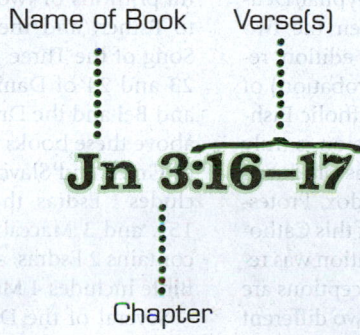

Name of Book   Verse(s)

Jn 3:16–17

Chapter

Most of the articles end with a citation identifying the Bible passage the article is based on. It is important to read the passage before reading the article.

Preface
to the NRSV: Catholic Edition

This Catholic edition of the New Revised Standard Version of the Bible has been authorized by the National Conference of Catholic Bishops in the U.S.A. and by the National Council of the Churches of Christ in the U.S.A. It has received the ecclesiastical approval of the Catholic Bishops of both the United States and Canada. The undersigned, who prepared this edition, is a member of the Revised Standard Version Bible Translation Committee as well as an active member and past president of the Catholic Biblical Association of America.

Roman Catholics are already familiar with the accuracy and elegance of the New Revised Standard Version, first published in 1990. It has previously appeared in two major types of edition: an edition of the Old and New Testaments alone, the Bible of most Protestants; and an edition of the Old and New Testaments with the Apocryphal/Deuterocanonical Books placed between the two Testaments. The text of the latter edition received the Imprimatur (official approbation) of the United States and Canadian Catholic Bishops. The New Revised Standard Version is truly an ecumenical translation, for it was produced by Roman Catholic, Eastern Orthodox, Protestant, and Jewish scholars. Because of this Catholic presence no change in the translation was requested for this edition. The only exceptions are the Book of Esther, which exists in two different forms that are explained below, and the Book of Daniel, which includes the deuterocanonical portions that are listed below.

Regarding the number of the books of the Old Testament canon and their arrangement, however, Protestants and Jews on the one hand, and Roman Catholics and Orthodox Christians on the other, hold different beliefs. From the time of the Reformation in the sixteenth century, Protestants have adopted the Jewish canon of the Old Testament, which was established by the rabbis at the end of the first century of the Common Era. This canon includes only those books that were written in Hebrew and Aramaic.

In addition to these books, however, Roman Catholics, following the ancient tradition of the Christian church, also hold the Deuterocanonical Books of the Old Testament to be sacred and inspired, and therefore canonical. Protestants and Jews call these books Apocrypha, a word that means "hidden or concealed," an inappropriate title for works that were part of the Greek Old Testament (the Septuagint) from pre-Christian times. The Roman Catholic canon, which was fixed by the time of the Council of Hippo in 393 and reaffirmed by the two Councils of Carthage in 397 and 419, was formally defined by the Council of Trent in 1546. This canon contains seven Deuterocanonical Books: Tobit, Judith, the Wisdom of Solomon, Sirach (the Wisdom of Ben Sira, also known as Ecclesiasticus), Baruch including the Letter of Jeremiah as chapter 6, and 1 and 2 Maccabees; and extra portions of two other books: the Additions to Esther; and the Prayer of Azariah and the Song of the Three Jews inserted between verses 23 and 24 of Daniel 3, Susanna as Daniel 13, and Bel and the Dragon as Daniel 14. Over and above these books and extra portions, the Bible of Greek and Slavonic Orthodox Christians includes 1 Esdras, the Prayer of Manasseh, Psalm 151, and 3 Maccabees. The Slavonic Bible also contains 2 Esdras, and an appendix to the Greek Bible includes 4 Maccabees.

Several of the Deuterocanonical Books were written originally in Hebrew or Aramaic, the rest in Greek. More than two-thirds of the Book of Sirach is now extant in Hebrew, and four fragments of the Book of Tobit in Hebrew and Aramaic were recovered from Qumran Cave IV. It seems certain that Judith and the additions to Daniel were also written originally in Hebrew. Hebrew is the original language of the prose parts of Baruch; the poetic parts were composed in Greek. The Wisdom of Solomon was written completely in Greek. The original language of 1 Maccabees was Hebrew while 2 Maccabees was composed in Greek.

The Book of Esther has two different forms: the short Hebrew original; and the longer Greek version that contains one hundred and seven additional verses comprising six distinct portions, A through F. It is the translation of the entire Greek version that appears in the Deuterocanonical section of the New Revised Standard Version. In this Catholic edition, however, the translation of the Greek portions has been inserted at the appropriate places of the translation of the Hebrew form of the book. Some of the Greek portions apparently had a Hebrew origin; the others were written in Greek.

What is distinctive about this Catholic edition—as well as every other edition published by Roman Catholics—is that the Deuterocanonical Books and portions are placed in their proper order among the other books of the Old Testament. Thus, Tobit, Judith, the long form of Esther, and 1 and 2 Maccabees are found among the so-called historical books directly after Nehemiah. The Wisdom of Solomon and the Book of Sirach follow after the Song of Solomon among the wisdom books. Because Baruch, the well-known secretary of Jeremiah, is said to be the author of the work that bears his name, the book is placed after Jeremiah and Lamentations. This order of books comes from the Latin Vulgate translated by St. Jerome in the late fourth and early fifth centuries. It is essentially the same order as that found in the fourth-century Codex Vaticanus, one of the oldest extant manuscripts of the Septuagint.

Roman Catholics will welcome this edition of the New Revised Standard Version of the Bible for personal reading and study as well as liturgical usage. Based on the latest manuscript discoveries and critical editions, it offers the fruits of the best biblical scholarship in the idiom of today while being sensitive to the contemporary concern for inclusive language when referring to human beings.

ALEXANDER A. DI LELLA, O.F.M.
Andrews-Kelly-Ryan Distinguished Professor of Biblical Studies
The Catholic University of America

September 30, 1992
Feast of St. Jerome

To the Reader

This preface is addressed to you by the Committee of translators, who wish to explain, as briefly as possible, the origin and character of our work. The publication of our revision is yet another step in the long, continual process of making the Bible available in the form of the English language that is most widely current in our day. To summarize in a single sentence: the New Revised Standard Version of the Bible is an authorized revision of the Revised Standard Version, published in 1952, which was a revision of the American Standard Version, published in 1901, which, in turn, embodied earlier revisions of the King James Version, published in 1611.

In the course of time, the King James Version came to be regarded as "the Authorized Version." With good reason it has been termed "the noblest monument of English prose," and it has entered, as no other book has, into the making of the personal character and the public institutions of the English-speaking peoples. We owe to it an incalculable debt.

Yet the King James Version has serious defects. By the middle of the nineteenth century, the development of biblical studies and the discovery of many biblical manuscripts more ancient than those on which the King James Version was based made it apparent that these defects were so many as to call for revision. The task was begun, by authority of the Church of England, in 1870. The (British) Revised Version of the Bible was published in 1881–1885; and the American Standard Version, its variant embodying the preferences of the American scholars associated with the work, was published, as was mentioned above, in 1901. In 1928 the copyright of the latter was acquired by the International Council of Religious Education and thus passed into the ownership of the churches of the United States and Canada that were associated in this Council through their boards of education and publication.

The Council appointed a committee of scholars to have charge of the text of the American Standard Version and to undertake inquiry concerning the need for further revision. After studying the questions whether or not revision should be undertaken, and if so, what its nature and extent should be, in 1937 the Council authorized a revision. The scholars who served as members of the Committee worked in two sections, one dealing with the Old Testament and one with the New Testament. In 1946 the Revised Standard Version of the New Testament was published. The publication of the Revised Standard Version of the Bible, containing the Old and New Testaments, took place on September 30, 1952. A translation of the Apocryphal/Deuterocanonical Books of the Old Testament followed in 1957. In 1977 this collection was issued in an expanded edition, containing three additional texts received by Eastern Orthodox communions (3 and 4 Maccabees and Psalm 151). Thereafter the Revised Standard Version gained the distinction of being officially authorized for use by all major Christian churches: Protestant, Anglican, Roman Catholic, and Eastern Orthodox.

The Revised Standard Version Bible Committee is a continuing body, comprising about thirty members, both men and women. Ecumenical in representation, it includes scholars affiliated with various Protestant denominations, as well as several Roman Catholic members, an Eastern Orthodox member, and a Jewish member who serves in the Old Testament section. For a period of time the Committee included several members from Canada and from England.

Because no translation of the Bible is perfect or is acceptable to all groups of readers, and because discoveries of older manuscripts and further investigation of linguistic features of the text continue to become available, renderings of the Bible have proliferated. During the years following the publication of the Revised Standard Version, twenty-six other English translations and revisions of the Bible were produced by committees and by individual scholars—not to mention twenty-five other translations and revisions of the New Testament alone. One of the latter was the second edition of the RSV New Testament, issued in 1971, twenty-five years after its initial publication.

Following the publication of the RSV Old Testament in 1952, significant advances were made in the discovery and interpretation of documents in Semitic languages related to Hebrew. In addition to the information that had become available in the late 1940s from the Dead Sea texts of Isaiah and Habakkuk, subsequent acquisitions from the same area brought to light many other early copies of all the books of the Hebrew Scriptures (except Esther), though most of these copies are fragmentary. During the same period early Greek manuscript copies of books of the New Testament also became available.

In order to take these discoveries into account, along with recent studies of documents in Semitic languages related to Hebrew, in 1974 the Policies Committee of the Revised Standard Version, which is a standing committee of the National Council of the Churches of Christ in the U.S.A., authorized the preparation of a revision of the entire RSV Bible.

For the Old Testament the Committee has made use of the *Biblia Hebraica Stuttgartensia* (1977; ed. sec. emendata, 1983). This is an edition of the Hebrew and Aramaic text as current early in the Christian era and fixed by Jewish scholars (the "Masoretes") of the sixth to the ninth centuries. The vowel signs, which were added by the Masoretes, are accepted in the main, but where a more probable and convincing reading can be obtained by assuming different vowels this has been done. No notes are given in such cases, because the vowel points are less ancient and reliable than the consonants. When an alternative reading given by the Masoretes is translated in a footnote, this is identified by the words "Another reading is."

Departures from the consonantal text of the best manuscripts have been made only where it seems clear that errors in copying had been made before the text was standardized. Most of the corrections adopted are based on the ancient versions (translations into Greek, Aramaic, Syriac, and Latin), which were made prior to the time of the work of the Masoretes and which therefore may reflect earlier forms of the Hebrew text. In such instances a footnote specifies the version or versions from which the correction has been derived and also gives a translation of the Masoretic Text. Where it was deemed appropriate to do so, information is supplied in footnotes from subsidiary Jewish traditions concerning other textual readings (the *Tiqqune Sopherim*, "emendations of the scribes"). These are identified in the footnotes as "Ancient Heb tradition."

Occasionally it is evident that the text has suffered in transmission and that none of the versions provides a satisfactory restoration. Here we can only follow the best judgment of competent scholars as to the most probable reconstruction of the original text. Such reconstructions are indicated in footnotes by the abbreviation Cn ("Correction"), and a translation of the Masoretic Text is added.

For the Apocryphal/Deuterocanonical Books of the Old Testament the Committee has made use of a number of texts. For most of these books the basic Greek text from which the present translation was made is the edition of the Septuagint prepared by Alfred Rahlfs and published by the Württemberg Bible Society (Stuttgart, 1935). For several of the books the more recently published individual volumes of the Göttingen Septuagint project were utilized. For the Book of Tobit it was decided to follow the form of the Greek text found in codex Sinaiticus (supported as it is by evidence from Qumran); where this text is defective, it was supplemented and corrected by other Greek manuscripts. For the three Additions to Daniel (namely, Susanna, the Prayer of Azariah and the Song of the Three Jews, and Bel and the Dragon) the Committee continued to use the Greek version attributed to Theodotion (the so-called "Theodotion-Daniel"). In translating Ecclesiasticus (Sirach), while constant reference was made to the Hebrew fragments of a large portion of this book (those discovered at Qumran and Masada as well as those recovered from the Cairo Geniza) the Committee generally followed the Greek text (including verse numbers) published by Joseph Ziegler in the Göttingen Septuagint (1965). But in many places the Committee has translated the Hebrew text when this provides a reading that is clearly superior to the Greek; the Syriac and Latin versions were also consulted throughout and occasionally adopted.

Finally, in the Book of Esther we have placed the deuterocanonical portions, translated from Robert Hanhart's Göttingen edition of the Greek (1983), in their original context within the translation of the Hebrew text.

For the New Testament the Committee has based its work on the most recent edition of *The Greek New Testament*, prepared by an interconfessional and international committee and published by the United Bible Societies (1966, 3rd ed. corrected, 1983; information concerning changes to be introduced into the critical apparatus of the forthcoming 4th edition was available to the Committee). As in that edition, double brackets are used to enclose a few passages that are generally regarded to be later additions to the text, but which we have retained because of their evident antiquity and their importance in the textual tradition. Only in very rare instances have we replaced the text or the punctuation of the Bible Societies' edition by an alternative that seemed to us to be superior. Here and there in the footnotes the phrase, "Other ancient authorities read," identifies alternative readings preserved by Greek manuscripts and early versions. In both Testaments, alternative renderings of the text are indicated by the word "Or."

As for the style of English adopted for the present revision, among the mandates given to the Committee in 1980 by the Division of Education and Ministry of the National Council of the Churches of Christ (which now holds the copyright of the RSV Bible) was the directive to continue in the tradition of the King James Bible, but to introduce such changes as are warranted on the basis of accuracy, clarity, euphony, and current English usage. Within the constraints set by the original texts and by the mandates of the Division, the Committee has followed the maxim, "As literal as possible, as free as necessary." As a consequence, the New Revised Standard Version (NRSV) remains essentially a literal translation. Paraphrastic renderings have been adopted only sparingly, and then chiefly to compensate for a deficiency in the English language—the lack of a common gender third person singular pronoun.

During the almost half a century since the publication of the RSV, many in the churches have become sensitive to the danger of linguistic sexism arising from the inherent bias of the English language towards the masculine gender, a bias that in the case of the Bible has often restricted or obscured the meaning of the original text. The mandates from the Division specified that, in references to men and women, masculine-oriented language should be eliminated as far as this can be done without altering passages that reflect the historical situation of ancient patriarchal culture. As can be appreciated, more than once the Committee found that the several mandates stood in tension and even in conflict. The various concerns had to be balanced case by case in order to provide a faithful and acceptable rendering without using contrived English. Only very occasionally has the pronoun "he" or "him" been retained in passages where the reference may have been to a woman as well as to a man; for example, in several legal texts in Leviticus and Deuteronomy. In such instances of formal, legal language, the options of either putting the passage in the plural or of introducing additional nouns to avoid masculine pronouns in English seemed to the Committee to obscure the historic structure and literary character of the original. In the vast majority of cases, however, inclusiveness has been attained by simple rephrasing or by introducing plural forms when this does not distort the meaning of the passage. Of course, in narrative and in parable no attempt was made to generalize the sex of individual persons.

Another aspect of style will be detected by readers who compare the more stately English rendering of the Old Testament with the less formal rendering adopted for the New Testament. For example, the traditional distinction between *shall* and *will* in English has been retained in the Old Testament as appropriate in rendering a document that embodies what may be termed the classic form of Hebrew, while in the New Testament the abandonment of such distinctions in the usage of the future tense in English reflects the more colloquial nature of the koine Greek used by most New Testament authors except when they are quoting the Old Testament.

Careful readers will notice that here and there in the Old Testament the word LORD (or in certain cases GOD) is printed in capital letters. This represents the traditional manner in English versions of rendering the Divine Name, the "Tetragrammaton" (see the notes on Exodus 3:14, 15), following the precedent of the ancient Greek and Latin translators and the long established practice in the reading of the Hebrew Scriptures in the synagogue. While it is almost if not quite certain that the Name was originally pronounced "Yahweh," this pronunciation was not indicated when the Masoretes added vowel sounds to the consonantal Hebrew text. To the four consonants YHWH of the Name, which had come to be regarded as too sacred to be pronounced, they attached vowel signs indicating that in its place should be read the Hebrew word *Adonai* meaning "Lord" (or *Elohim* meaning "God"). Ancient Greek translators employed the word *Kyrios* ("Lord") for the Name. The Vulgate likewise used the Latin word *Dominus* ("Lord"). The form "Jehovah" is of late medieval origin; it is a combination of the consonants of the Divine Name and the vowels attached to it by the Masoretes but belonging to an entirely different word. Although the American Standard Version (1901) had used "Jehovah" to render the Tetragrammaton (the sound of Y being represented by J and the sound of W by V, as in Latin), for two reasons the Committees that produced the RSV and the NRSV returned to the more familiar usage of the King James Version. (1) The word "Jehovah" does not accurately represent any form of the Name ever used in Hebrew. (2) The use of any proper name for the one and only God, as though there were other gods from whom the true God had to be distinguished, began to be discontinued in Judaism before the Christian era and is inappropriate for the universal faith of the Christian Church.

It will be seen that in the Psalms and in other prayers addressed to God the archaic second person singular pronouns (*thee, thou, thine*) and verb forms (*art, hast, hadst*) are no longer used. Although some readers may regret this change, it should be pointed out that in the original languages neither the Old Testament nor the New makes any linguistic distinction between addressing a human being and addressing the Deity. Furthermore, in the tradition of the King James Version one will not expect to find the use of capital letters for pronouns that refer to the Deity—such capitalization is an unnecessary innovation that has only recently been introduced into a few English translations of the Bible. Finally, we have left to the discretion of the licensed publishers such matters as section headings, cross-references, and clues to the pronunciation of proper names.

This new version seeks to preserve all that is best in the English Bible as it has been known and used through the years. It is intended for use in public reading and congregational worship, as well as in private study, instruction, and meditation. We have resisted the temptation to introduce terms and phrases that merely reflect current moods, and have tried to put the message of the Scriptures in simple, enduring words and expressions that are worthy to stand in the great tradition of the King James Bible and its predecessors.

In traditional Judaism and Christianity, the Bible has been more than a historical document to be preserved or a classic of literature to be cherished and admired; it is recognized as the unique record of God's dealings with people over the ages. The Old Testament sets forth the call of a special people to enter into covenant relation with the God of justice and steadfast love and to bring God's law to the nations. The New Testament records the life and work of Jesus Christ, the one in whom "the Word became flesh," as well as describes the rise and spread of the early Christian Church. The Bible carries its full message, not to those who regard it simply as a noble literary heritage of the past or who wish to use it to enhance political purposes and advance otherwise desirable goals, but to all persons and communities who read it so that they may discern and understand what God is saying to them. That message must not be disguised in phrases that are no longer clear, or hidden under words that have changed or lost their meaning; it must be presented in language that is direct and plain and meaningful to people today. It is the hope and prayer of the translators that this version of the Bible may continue to hold a large place in congregational life and to speak to all readers, young and old alike, helping them to understand and believe and respond to its message.

For the Committee,
BRUCE M. METZGER

Guide to . . .

Pronunciation of Proper Names

This edition of the New Revised Standard Version includes a simplified self-pronunciation system for proper names. The system is designed to provide assistance to the reader without filling the text with a complicated variety of symbols, many of which provide unneeded pronunciation clues.

Well-known proper names such as Moses, Nazareth, and Timothy are printed without pronunciation marks of any kind. Such names are a familiar part of our cultural heritage, and they are instantly recognizable to most readers.

More difficult proper names (as well as certain transliterated non-English words) are shown in the text with simplified pronunciation markings. (Two notes of caution: The anglicized pronunciation of a name differs at times from that of the ancient language. Also, there are differences of opinion among speakers of English concerning the most desirable pronunciation of certain names.)

Three kinds of marks are used:

ʹ   The acute accent mark: shows which syllable of a name is to be stressed. A compound name—with parts separated by a hyphen—has an accent mark in each part having more than one syllable.

.   The centered dot: shows where an unaccented syllable ends and another syllable begins.

¯   The macron: printed over a vowel that has a "long" sound. The macron is shown over the following vowels when they are sounded as indicated:

> *a* as in g*a*te
> *e* as in k*e*y
> *i* as in *i*ce
> *o* as in h*o*pe
> *u* as in *u*se or r*u*le
> *y* as in t*y*pe

The macron also indicates the pronunciation of certain diphthongs, or vowel combinations:

> over the *a* in *ai* as in p*ai*l
> over the *i* in *ai* as in *ai*sle

A vowel that does not have a "long" sound is printed with no pronunciation mark. In most cases the sound of such a vowel can be determined closely enough by observing how the name is spelled, divided into syllables, and accented.

Abbreviations Used in the Notes

In the notes to the books of the Old Testament the following abbreviations are used:

Ant.	Josephus, *Antiquities of the Jews*
Aram	Aramaic
Ch, chs	Chapter, chapters
Cn	Correction; made where the text has suffered in transmission and the versions provide no satisfactory restoration but where the Standard Bible Committee agrees with the judgment of competent scholars as to the most probable reconstruction of the original text
Gk	Septuagint, Greek version of the Old Testament
Heb	Hebrew of the consonantal Masoretic Text of the Old Testament
Josephus	Flavius Josephus (Jewish historian, about A.D. 37 to about 95)
Macc.	The book(s) of the Maccabees
Ms(s)	Manuscript(s)
MT	The Hebrew of the pointed Masoretic Text of the Old Testament
OL	Old Latin
Q Ms(s)	Manuscript(s) found at Qumran by the Dead Sea
Sam	Samaritan Hebrew text of the Old Testament
Syr	Syriac Version of the Old Testament
Syr H	Syriac Version of Origen's Hexapla
Tg	Targum
Vg	Vulgate, Latin Version of the Old Testament

ā   as in gate
ē   as in key
ī   as in ice
ō   as in hope
ū   as in use or fuse
ȳ   as in type

over the ü as in pull
over the ü as in rule

The Old Testament

Introduction to
the Pentateuch

Have you ever been late to a movie? You probably spent a few minutes trying to figure out what you missed and hoped it wasn't too important to the plot. Like the first crucial minutes of a movie, the five books of the Pentateuch set the stage for much of what happens in the rest of the Bible. If you don't know the people involved and their wonderful stories, when you read later books, you might find yourself asking: What's going on? Why is he doing this? What does she mean by that?

In Depth

The name *Pentateuch* literally means "five-part writing." Thus, the Pentateuch is the first five books of the Old Testament: Genesis, Exodus, Leviticus, Numbers, and Deuteronomy. These books are special to Jewish and Christian believers because they are God's word, reveal who God is, and tell of the origins of God's People and their unique relationship with God—sometimes called salvation history. They are the blueprint needed for properly understanding the rest of the Bible. The Pentateuch introduces the idea of a single God who is responsible for all creation. It also tells that this God is active in the world and in the lives of its people, and that the Israelites have been called into a special relationship with this God.

One of the central elements of the special relationship between God and the Israelites described in the Pentateuch is the Sinai Covenant. A covenant establishes a new relationship between two parties and is marked by a solemn promise, where both parties agree to fulfill certain obligations. The Sinai Covenant is the most famous one between God and Israel, with Moses as the mediator, which you will read about in Exodus. In Genesis, you will read about the covenant God makes with Noah, Abraham, and Jacob, which lead to the Sinai Covenant.

Reading the Pentateuch is like appreciating a fine tapestry. When you view a tapestry from the front, all the threads combine to make a beautiful, coherent image. In the same way, an overall look at the covenant, stories, and laws in the Pentateuch combines them to form a picture of the love relationship between God and the people of Israel. A close look at the back of a tapestry shows a more chaotic mix of colors and yarn. So too a closer look at the writings in the Pentateuch reveals not one story but many.

Biblical scholars speak of four primary sources for the stories and traditions in the Pentateuch. The sources reflect four different schools of thought about Israel's relationship with God. For convenience, each source is referred to as an individual author.

The Yahwist used Yahweh as God's name. This writer focused on the southern kingdom of Judah, used lots of stories, emphasized God's closeness to humanity, and portrayed God acting as a human person.

The Elohist referred to God as Elohim or Lord. The Elohist wrote about the northern kingdom of Israel and was concerned about idolatry and morality. The writings of the Elohist present God's presence as mediated, such as through a burning bush.

The Deuteronomist emphasized the Law as the foundation of the kingdom of Judah. The Deuteronomist emerged toward the end of the monarchy (the time of the Israelite kings), when the Covenant Law seemed to have been forgotten.

Finally, the Priestly writer emphasized religious rituals and the role of the priesthood. This writer portrayed God as more distant and used a more formal style. This source was written after the Babylonian Exile.

Knowing that these four sources contributed to the final form of the Pentateuch can help us understand that the Pentateuch books are not simply records of events as they occurred but rather faith accounts about the Israelites' growing relationship with God, inspired by God and told from different perspectives.

In the Pentateuch, God reveals how much God loves the human race collectively and how much God loves us personally. God wishes to be in a relationship with us today just as much as God did back then. The Pentateuch reminds us that we are all children of God.

Other Background

Some of the most familiar stories and people of the Old Testament are found in Genesis and Exodus. Genesis includes the stories of Creation, Adam and Eve, Noah and the Flood, Abraham and Sarah, and Joseph and his brothers. Exodus contains the stories of Moses and the burning bush, Pharaoh and the ten plagues, the parting of the Red Sea, the Exodus out of Egypt, and the Ten Commandments.

The Jewish people also refer to the five books of the Pentateuch as the Torah, meaning "teaching" or "instruction."

An ancient tradition named Moses as the original writer of the Pentateuch. This was no doubt due to Moses' importance in the Pentateuch itself. But evidence suggests that most of the Pentateuch was written hundreds of years after Moses' death.

The two types of writing in the Pentateuch are narratives and laws. Genesis is all inspired narratives, Leviticus and Deuteronomy are mostly laws, and Exodus and Numbers are approximately half stories and half laws.

Displays of awesome cosmic power, tender love stories, tearful family reunions, and tales of deceit, rape, murder, and worldwide destruction. Does this sound like the script for next summer's blockbuster movie? No, it's the Book of Genesis! It is the story of how a world created for love and harmony goes astray because of human sin. Through it all, God is at work, forming a people to restore what was lost.

In Depth

Genesis gathers together inspired stories and traditions that reveal Israel's understanding of God's nature and purpose, and the beginning of the Israelites' special relationship with God. Genesis has two main sections. The first section (1:1—11:32) contains some of the Bible's most memorable stories about Creation and the effect of sin. Chapters 1–2 tell two accounts of Creation that portray the beauty and wonder of the natural world and emphasize the goodness and harmony that God intended in Creation. Creation culminates in human beings, made in God's own image. Those human beings, symbolic of us all, live in a wonderful garden in harmony with God, Creation, and each other. But in chapter 3, sin enters the world, and as a result, Adam and Eve will experience separation, suffering, and ultimately death.

And first sin spreads, first to the family (Cain and Abel in chapter 4), then to all society (Noah and the Flood in chapters 6–9). Even after the Flood and God's covenant with Noah, the story of the tower of Babel demonstrates that sin pits nation against nation. As you read these chapters, remember that they were written not as historical accounts or scientific explanations but as inspired stories that share a faith perspective and teach important religious truths.

The second section of Genesis (12:1—50:26) tells the story of the origins of the Israelite people. The story begins with Abraham and Sarah (originally called Abram and Sarai) and continues with Ishmael and Isaac and with Isaac and Rebekah's children, Esau and Jacob. Genesis ends with Joseph, one of Jacob's twelve sons, cleverly saving Egypt and Israel from famine. This section introduces the covenant God makes with Abraham and the Israelite people and reminds the reader that God's plans will overcome human sin and weakness.

◉ At a Glance

- 1:1—11:32. the creation of the world and human beings by God
- 12:1—50:26. stories of the ancestors (matriarchs and patriarchs) of Israel

★ Quick Facts

Period Covered: The stories in the first eleven chapters are primeval history. Genesis 12:1—50:26 covers the period of the ancestors, or patriarchs and matriarchs (from 2000 to 1500 BC).

Inspired Author: Stories were gathered from the oral tradition of tribal peoples in the period around 1225 to 1000 BC (see Introduction to the Pentateuch).

Themes: the goodness of Creation, human responsibility, the effects of sin, covenant, God's bringing good out of evil

The Book of
Genesis

Genesis

Six Days of Creation and the Sabbath

1 In the beginning when God created*a* the heavens and the earth, ²the earth was a formless void and darkness covered the face of the deep, while a wind from God*b* swept over the face of the waters. ³Then God said, "Let there be light"; and there was light. ⁴And God saw that the light was good; and God separated the light from the darkness. ⁵God called the light Day, and the darkness he called Night. And there was evening and there was morning, the first day.

6 And God said, "Let there be a dome in the midst of the waters, and let it separate the waters from the waters." ⁷So God made the dome and separated the waters that were under the dome from the waters that were above the dome. And it was so. ⁸God called the dome Sky. And there was evening and there was morning, the second day.

9 And God said, "Let the waters under the sky be gathered together into one place, and let the dry land appear." And it was so. ¹⁰God called the dry land Earth, and the waters that were gathered together he called Seas. And God saw that it was good. ¹¹Then God said, "Let the earth put forth vegetation: plants yielding seed, and fruit trees of every kind on earth that bear fruit with the seed in it." And it was so. ¹²The earth brought forth vegetation: plants yielding seed of every kind, and trees of every kind bearing fruit with the seed in it. And God saw that it was good. ¹³And there was evening and there was morning, the third day.

14 And God said, "Let there be lights in the dome of the sky to separate the day from the night; and let them be for signs and for seasons and for days and years, ¹⁵and let them be lights in the dome of the sky to give light upon the earth." And it was so. ¹⁶God made the two great lights— the greater light to rule the day and the lesser light to rule the night—and the stars. ¹⁷God set them in the dome of the sky to give light upon the earth, ¹⁸to rule over the day and over the night, and to separate the light from the darkness. And God saw that it was good. ¹⁹And there was evening and there was morning, the fourth day.

20 And God said, "Let the waters bring forth swarms of living creatures, and let birds fly above the earth across the dome of the sky." ²¹So God created the great sea monsters and every living creature that moves, of every kind, with which the waters swarm, and every winged bird of every kind. And God saw that it was good. ²²God blessed them, saying, "Be fruitful and multiply and fill the waters in the seas, and let birds multiply on the earth." ²³And there was evening and there was morning, the fifth day.

24 And God said, "Let the earth bring forth living creatures of every kind: cattle and creeping things and wild animals of the earth of every kind." And it was so. ²⁵God made the wild animals of the earth of every kind, and the cattle of every kind, and everything that creeps upon the ground of every kind. And God saw that it was good.

---

a Or *when God began to create* or *In the beginning God created*
b Or *while the spirit of God* or *while a mighty wind*

26 Then God said, "Let us make humankind*a* in our image, according to our likeness; and let them have dominion over the fish of the sea, and over the birds of the air, and over the cattle, and over all the wild animals of the earth,*b* and over every creeping thing that creeps upon the earth."
27 So God created humankind*a* in his image,
in the image of God he created them;*c*
male and female he created them.
28God blessed them, and God said to them, "Be fruitful and multiply, and fill the earth and subdue it; and have dominion over the fish of the sea and over the birds of the air and over every living thing that moves upon the earth." 29God said, "See, I have given you every plant yielding seed that is upon the face of all the earth, and every

tree with seed in its fruit; you shall have them for food. 30And to every beast of the earth, and to every bird of the air, and to everything that creeps on the earth, everything that has the breath of life, I have given every green plant for food." And it was so. 31God saw everything that he had made, and indeed, it was very good. And there was evening and there was morning, the sixth day.

2 Thus the heavens and the earth were finished, and all their multitude. 2And on the seventh day God finished the work that he had done, and he rested on the seventh day from all the work that he had done. 3So God blessed the seventh day and hallowed it, because on it God rested from all the work that he had done in creation.

4 These are the generations of the heavens and the earth when they were created.

a Heb *adam*   *b* Syr: Heb *and over all the earth*   *c* Heb *him*

In the Beginning

"In the beginning when God created the heavens and the earth . . ." (Gen 1:1). This simple verse is one of the foundational beliefs of Christianity. We are not a random collection of atoms. The world is not a lucky combination of cosmic circumstances. The universe did not just accidentally happen.

The beginning of wisdom is acknowledging that a higher power is at work in our lives, that the universe has purpose, and that everything was created by God. The ancient writers and editors of Genesis expressed these ideas in the Creation stories. The Church affirms these beliefs. They are expressed in a prayer called the Apostles' Creed, which begins, "I believe in God, the Father almighty, Creator of heaven and earth."

Genesis expresses another foundational belief: God created everything good! Read the story in chapter 1, and see how this belief is constantly repeated: And humankind is "very good," created in God's own image. This is God's message to you in the first chapter of the Bible: You carry God's image within you. You are very good! Don't let anyone ever try to convince you otherwise.

▶ **Gen 1:1—2:4**

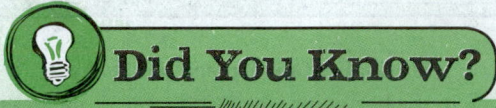

Did You Know?

Literary Genres

Some Christians believe that God actually created the world in seven twenty-four-hour days. Such a belief comes from a literal reading of the first chapter of Genesis, as though it were a scientific textbook. However, Genesis was written not as a science article but as a series of symbolic stories, sometimes called mythic stories, that convey great moral and spiritual truths. We should not try to come to any scientific conclusions about the creation of the world from reading these stories.

Mythic stories are one literary type, or genre. You just have to look in a newspaper to see examples of different literary genres: news stories, advice columns, editorials, and comics. Each genre has different rules for interpreting its meaning. The Bible also contains many types of literary genres, including hero stories, poetry, laws, legends, fictional satire, debates, and letters. To properly understand the Bible, pay attention to the literary genre—otherwise, you might believe the Bible is saying something God doesn't intend.

▶ **Gen 1:1—2:4**

Catholic Social Teaching

Coworkers with God

In the opening chapters of the Book of Genesis, we read the wonderful story of God's creation of the universe. With each new day, God creates the light and darkness, the earth and sea, the plants and animals, and ultimately humankind. On the seventh day, God observes the amazing creation and we read, "God saw everything, . . . and it was very good" (Gen 1:31).

After God creates the man and woman, he commands them to "fill the earth and subdue it" (Gen 1:28). In other words, human beings are to cooperate with God in the completion and care of creation. With God's grace, we participate in laying the foundation for God's reign on earth.

Catholic social teaching tells us that as coworkers with God in caring for and sustaining the world, we have a responsibility to protect both the dignity of the human person as well as the planet. Amazing breakthroughs are happening in our world all the time, and yet, as Christians, we are asked to consider whether such developments are in keeping with the teachings of our Church. For example, we now have the ability to clone animals and genetically alter agricultural products, but will these practices sustain our world or ultimately destroy it? Do these practices really revere and value human life and the created order?

God has given us the amazing gift of intellectual inquiry, which can lead to wonderful advancements for our world, but we must always ask ourselves how we might help promote ethical approaches to research so that future generations may continue to enjoy the beauty of creation and thrive in the universe.

● As a coworker with God, how do I sustain and care for God's creation?

● How might I use my gifts of knowledge and education to really improve the world and help bring about God's reign on earth?

▶ **Genesis, chapters 1–2**
Caring for God's Creation

Another Account of the Creation

In the day that the Lord[a] God made the earth and the heavens, ⁵when no plant of the field was yet in the earth and no herb of the field had yet sprung up—for the Lord God had not caused it to rain upon the earth, and there was no one to till the ground; ⁶but a stream would rise from the earth, and water the whole face of the ground— ⁷then the Lord God formed man from the dust of the ground,[b] and breathed into his nostrils the breath of life; and the man became a living being. ⁸And the Lord God planted a garden in Eden, in the east; and there he put the man whom he had formed. ⁹Out of the ground the Lord God made to grow every tree that is pleasant to the sight and good for food, the tree of life also in the midst of the garden, and the tree of the knowledge of good and evil.

10 A river flows out of Eden to water the garden, and from there it divides and becomes four branches. ¹¹The name of the first is Pishon; it is the one that flows around the whole land of Havilah, where there is gold; ¹²and the gold of that land is good; bdellium and onyx stone are there. ¹³The name of the second river is Gihon; it is the one that flows around the whole land of Cush. ¹⁴The name of the third river is Tigris, which flows east of Assyria. And the fourth river is the Euphrates.

15 The Lord God took the man and put him in the garden of Eden to till it and keep it. ¹⁶And the Lord God commanded the man, "You may freely eat of every tree of the garden; ¹⁷but of the tree of the knowledge of good and evil you shall not eat, for in the day that you eat of it you shall die."

18 Then the Lord God said, "It is not good that the man should be alone; I will make him a helper as his partner." ¹⁹So out of the ground the Lord God formed every animal of the field and every bird of the air, and brought them to the man to see what he would call them; and whatever the man called every living creature,

a Heb YHWH, as in other places where "Lord" is spelled with capital letters (see also Ex 3.14–15 with notes).   b Or *formed a man* (Heb *adam*) *of dust from the ground* (Heb *adamah*)

Cultural Connection

God Is Our Creator

According to Genesis, chapters 1–2, God created the universe and is the source of order in all creation. Creation is good, and its goodness is reflected in the harmony, peace, and love between the Creator and his creatures, and among the creatures themselves. In Hispanic theological traditions, this ideal relationship—symbolized by the way God and Adam and Eve relate in the Garden of Eden—is considered the foundation in which salvation history is rooted.

● How are your relationships with God, your friends, your family, and nature characterized by harmony, peace, and love?

● Reflect on how you can improve some of your strained relationships, and ask God's help to do it.

Human beings are created in God's image and likeness and share God's attributes: freedom, love, knowledge, and the ability to create. With these gifts comes the responsibility of caring for all creation.

● Give thanks and praise to God for creation, especially for your own life and the lives of the people around you.

● Think of how you, your family, and your community can take better care of all creation. Pray that you fully develop your capacity to love, to know the truth, and to use your freedom wisely.

God established a covenant with us at the moment of our creation, and we keep this covenant by freely placing ourselves in God's hands and being responsive to God's invitation to live in communion with God and people.

● How do you use your freedom to respond to God's invitation?

● Think about the aspects of your life for which you most need God's wisdom to live in harmony and love. Put yourself in God's hands, and let God help and direct you.

▶ **Genesis, chapters 1–2**

---

that was its name. ²⁰The man gave names to all cattle, and to the birds of the air, and to every animal of the field; but for the man*ᵃ* there was not found a helper as his partner. ²¹So the LORD God caused a deep sleep to fall upon the man, and he slept; then he took one of his ribs and closed up its place with flesh. ²²And the rib that the LORD God had taken from the man he made into a woman and brought her to the man. ²³Then the man said,

"This at last is bone of my bones
and flesh of my flesh;
this one shall be called Woman,*ᵇ*
for out of Man*ᶜ* this one was taken."

²⁴Therefore a man leaves his father and his mother and clings to his wife, and they become one flesh. ²⁵And the man and his wife were both naked, and were not ashamed.

The First Sin and Its Punishment

3 Now the serpent was more crafty than any other wild animal that the LORD God had made. He said to the woman, "Did God say, 'You shall not eat from any tree in the garden'?" ²The woman said to the serpent, "We may eat of the fruit of the trees in the garden; ³but God said,

'You shall not eat of the fruit of the tree that is in the middle of the garden, nor shall you touch it, or you shall die.' " ⁴But the serpent said to the woman, "You will not die; ⁵for God knows that when you eat of it your eyes will be opened, and you will be like God,*ᵈ* knowing good and evil." ⁶So when the woman saw that the tree was good for food, and that it was a delight to the eyes, and that the tree was to be desired to make one wise, she took of its fruit and ate; and she also gave some to her husband, who was with her, and he ate. ⁷Then the eyes of both were opened, and they knew that they were naked; and they sewed fig leaves together and made loincloths for themselves.

8 They heard the sound of the LORD God walking in the garden at the time of the evening breeze, and the man and his wife hid themselves from the presence of the LORD God among the trees of the garden. ⁹But the LORD God called to the man, and said to him, "Where are you?" ¹⁰He said, "I heard the sound of you in the garden, and I was afraid, because I was naked; and I hid myself." ¹¹He said,

a Or for Adam   *b* Heb *ishshah*   *c* Heb *ish*   *d* Or *gods*

"Who told you that you were naked? Have you eaten from the tree of which I commanded you not to eat?" ¹²The man said, "The woman whom you gave to be with me, she gave me fruit from the tree, and I ate." ¹³Then the Lᴏʀᴅ God said to the woman, "What is this that you have done?" The woman said, "The serpent tricked me, and I ate." ¹⁴The Lᴏʀᴅ God said to the serpent,

"Because you have done this,
    cursed are you among all animals
    and among all wild creatures;
upon your belly you shall go,
    and dust you shall eat
    all the days of your life.
¹⁵ I will put enmity between you and the woman,
    and between your offspring and hers;
he will strike your head,
    and you will strike his heel."

¹⁶To the woman he said,

"I will greatly increase your pangs in childbearing;
    in pain you shall bring forth children,
yet your desire shall be for your husband,
    and he shall rule over you."

¹⁷And to the man[a] he said,

"Because you have listened to the voice of your wife,
    and have eaten of the tree
about which I commanded you,
    'You shall not eat of it,'

cursed is the ground because of you;
    in toil you shall eat of it all the days of your life;
¹⁸ thorns and thistles it shall bring forth for you;
    and you shall eat the plants of the field.
¹⁹ By the sweat of your face
    you shall eat bread
until you return to the ground,
    for out of it you were taken;
you are dust,
    and to dust you shall return."

20 The man named his wife Eve,[b] because she was the mother of all living. ²¹And the Lᴏʀᴅ God made garments of skins for the man[c] and for his wife, and clothed them.

22 Then the Lᴏʀᴅ God said, "See, the man has become like one of us, knowing good and evil;

a Or to Adam   b In Heb Eve resembles the word for *living*
c Or for Adam

Live It!

In God's Image

God does not make mistakes; people do. Some people might be tempted to deny their racial heritage, even to change their physical appearance in order to conform to the latest fad or fit the dominant cultural image of beauty. We must remember that physical features are not accidents. God planned for them—we are all made in God's image, inside and out.

If we are to authentically love ourselves, we must love our whole selves. This includes a love for dark skin or light skin, straight hair or curly hair, wide nose or pug nose, and all the variations in between. Whatever our appearance, we are all blessed by God.

▶ Gen 1:26–27

The Sabbath

Even God needed to take a rest. The writer of Genesis makes this point to remind readers to set aside a day for rest and prayer, which Jewish people call the Sabbath. Honoring the Sabbath is an act of trust in God. It means we believe that the world will not fall apart if we stop our activity. The world is in God's hands. We can hear this truth echoed in Jesus' words:

Consider the lilies, how they grow: they neither toil nor spin; yet I tell you, even Solomon in all his glory was not clothed like one of these. But if God so clothes the grass of the field, which is alive today and tomorrow is thrown into the oven, how much more will he clothe you. (Lk 12:27–28)

Traditionally, Christians rest and pray on Sunday because it is the day on which Jesus was resurrected. In our culture today, it seems that many people are losing this practice. What could we gain if we recommitted ourselves to a day of rest, celebration, and prayer? What can you do personally to more fully honor the concept of Sabbath rest?

▶ Gen 2:1–3

✝ Catholic Connection

Original Sin

Before the Fall, Adam and Eve had it all. God gave them freedom and established a close friendship with them. They could simply walk about the garden tending to it alongside of God. They lived in perfect harmony with each other and all of creation without fear, suffering, or death. Yet, Adam and Eve wanted more. By believing the serpent's lie, Adam and Eve sought to make themselves equal to God. They distrusted God's goodness, directly disobeyed God, and abused the freedom God had given them. The results were tragic. Adam and Eve's friendship with God turned into fear as they hid in the garden. After being expelled from the garden, tension and strife entered Adam and Eve's once harmonious relationship. The creation they once helped tend with God became hazardous and difficult to manage. Ultimately, through their sin, death became a reality for Adam and Eve. Though this account in chapter three of Genesis uses figurative language, it points to the reality that all of humanity has been affected by the sin our first parents freely chose to commit.

This original sin and its consequences have been handed down to every generation throughout all of history, with the exception of Jesus and his mother, Mary. Although we are not personally responsible for it, our nature also has been wounded by this sin. As a result, we do not have the original holiness and justice God intended for us, but are inclined to sin and subject to death. Fortunately, Jesus Christ, unlike Adam and Eve, came in total obedience to the will of God. As a result, the sin brought into the world by Adam and Eve has been overcome by the Passion, death, and Resurrection of Jesus Christ. (Read Romans 5:12–21 to learn more about the relationship between Adam and Jesus.) Through the grace of the sacrament of Baptism, we are freed from original sin and turned back toward God. And the graces we receive through Christ will surpass those that Adam and Eve ever knew before the Fall!

▶ **Gen 3:1–24**
Catechism, nos. 369–421

and now, he might reach out his hand and take also from the tree of life, and eat, and live forever"— [23]therefore the Lord God sent him forth from the garden of Eden, to till the ground from which he was taken. [24]He drove out the man; and at the east of the garden of Eden he placed the cherubim, and a sword flaming and turning to guard the way to the tree of life.

Cain Murders Abel

4 Now the man knew his wife Eve, and she conceived and bore Cain, saying, "I have produced[a] a man with the help of the Lord." [2]Next she bore his brother Abel. Now Abel was a keeper of sheep, and Cain a tiller of the ground. [3]In the course of time Cain brought to the Lord an offering of the fruit of the ground, [4]and Abel for his part brought of the firstlings of his flock, their fat portions. And the Lord had regard for Abel and his offering, [5]but for Cain and his offering he had no regard. So Cain was very angry, and his countenance fell. [6]The Lord said to Cain, "Why are you angry, and why has your countenance fallen? [7]If you do well, will you not be accepted? And if you do not do well, sin is lurking at the door; its desire is for you, but you must master it."

[8] Cain said to his brother Abel, "Let us go out to the field."[b] And when they were in the field, Cain rose up against his brother Abel, and killed him. [9]Then the Lord said to Cain, "Where is your brother Abel?" He said, "I do not know; am I my brother's keeper?" [10]And the Lord said, "What have you done? Listen; your brother's blood is crying out to me from the ground! [11]And now you are cursed from the ground, which has opened its mouth to receive your brother's blood from your hand. [12]When you till the ground, it will no longer yield to you its strength; you will be a fugitive and a wanderer on the earth." [13]Cain said to the Lord, "My punishment is greater than I can bear! [14]Today you have driven me away from the soil, and I shall be hidden from your face; I shall be a fugitive and a wanderer on the earth, and anyone who meets me may kill me." [15]Then the Lord said to him, "Not so![c] Whoever kills Cain will suffer a sevenfold vengeance." And the Lord put a mark on Cain, so that no one who came upon him would kill him. [16]Then Cain went away from the presence of the Lord, and settled in the land of Nod,[d] east of Eden.

Beginnings of Civilization

[17] Cain knew his wife, and she conceived and bore Enoch; and he built a city, and named it Enoch after his son Enoch. [18]To Enoch was born

Irad; and Irad was the father of Mehujael, and Mehujael the father of Methushael, and Methushael the father of Lamech. [19]Lamech took two wives; the name of the one was Adah, and the name of the other Zillah. [20]Adah bore Jabal; he was the ancestor of those who live in tents and have livestock. [21]His brother's name was Jubal; he was the ancestor of all those who play the lyre and pipe. [22]Zillah bore Tubal-cain, who made all kinds of bronze and iron tools. The sister of Tubal-cain was Naamah.

[23] Lamech said to his wives:
"Adah and Zillah, hear my voice;
    you wives of Lamech, listen to what I say:
I have killed a man for wounding me,
    a young man for striking me.
[24] If Cain is avenged sevenfold,
    truly Lamech seventy-sevenfold."

[25] Adam knew his wife again, and she bore a son and named him Seth, for she said, "God has appointed[e] for me another child instead of Abel, because Cain killed him." [26]To Seth also a son was born, and he named him Enosh. At that time people began to invoke the name of the Lord.

---

a The verb in Heb resembles the word for *Cain*   b Sam Gk Syr Compare Vg: MT lacks *Let us go out to the field*   c Gk Syr Vg: Heb *Therefore*   d That is *Wandering*   e The verb in Heb resembles the word for *Seth*

Brothers and Sisters

"**A**m I my brother's keeper?" (Gen 4:9). With that famous question, Cain pretends he does not know where his brother is. God does not answer Cain's question directly, but each of us knows the response. We are— each of us and all of us—responsible for one another: family, friends, and strangers. We are brothers and sisters because God has created us that way. We cannot avoid our obligation to watch out for one another.

● Are there people in your life who need you to be a brother or sister to them? How can you reach out to them?

▶ **Gen 4:9**

Catholic Social Teaching

The Cycle of Violence

Cain was a murderer. Some might say that he deserved the death penalty. But in Genesis 4:15, God marks Cain so that he is protected from being killed. God seeks to stop the cycle of violence. Why kill someone to show that it is wrong to kill someone?

Catholic social teaching echoes this sentiment, asserting that all life—even the life of a violent criminal—has a God-given sense of dignity that must be protected at all times. This can sometimes be a difficult teaching to understand. It's easy to see why we should work to protect the dignity of the

poor, the dying, and the unborn—but murderers too? Why should we respect someone whose actions have not shown any concern for life?

The Scriptures have taught us to believe that justice cannot be achieved through vengeance and that forgiveness, reconciliation, and conversion are always possible, even for the greatest of sinners. Capital punishment has proven to be unnecessary, ineffective, and unacceptable in today's world, given the alternative options that are available for achieving retribution. When we choose

to support capital punishment, we feed the cycle of violence and risk becoming less sensitive to the preciousness of every human life; we forget that all of us—even grave sinners—have been created in the image and likeness of God.

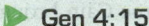 **Gen 4:15**

Life and Dignity of the Human Person

Adam's Descendants to Noah and His Sons

5 This is the list of the descendants of Adam. When God created humankind,*a* he made them*b* in the likeness of God. ²Male and female he created them, and he blessed them and named them "Humankind"*a* when they were created.

3 When Adam had lived one hundred thirty years, he became the father of a son in his likeness, according to his image, and named him Seth. ⁴The days of Adam after he became the father of Seth were eight hundred years; and he had other sons and daughters. ⁵Thus all the days that Adam lived were nine hundred thirty years; and he died.

6 When Seth had lived one hundred five years, he became the father of Enosh. ⁷Seth lived after the birth of Enosh eight hundred seven years, and had other sons and daughters. ⁸Thus all the days of Seth were nine hundred twelve years; and he died.

9 When Enosh had lived ninety years, he became the father of Kenan. ¹⁰Enosh lived after the birth of Kenan eight hundred fifteen years, and had other sons and daughters. ¹¹Thus all the days of Enosh were nine hundred five years; and he died.

12 When Kenan had lived seventy years, he

became the father of Mahalalel. ¹³Kenan lived after the birth of Mahalalel eight hundred and forty years, and had other sons and daughters. ¹⁴Thus all the days of Kenan were nine hundred and ten years; and he died.

15 When Mahalalel had lived sixty-five years, he became the father of Jared. ¹⁶Mahalalel lived after the birth of Jared eight hundred thirty years, and had other sons and daughters. ¹⁷Thus all the days of Mahalalel were eight hundred ninety-five years; and he died.

18 When Jared had lived one hundred sixty-two years he became the father of Enoch. ¹⁹Jared lived after the birth of Enoch eight hundred years, and had other sons and daughters. ²⁰Thus all the days of Jared were nine hundred sixty-two years; and he died.

21 When Enoch had lived sixty-five years, he became the father of Methuselah. ²²Enoch walked with God after the birth of Methuselah three hundred years, and had other sons and daughters. ²³Thus all the days of Enoch were three hundred sixty-five years. ²⁴Enoch walked with God; then he was no more, because God took him.

25 When Methuselah had lived one hundred eighty-seven years, he became the father of

a Heb *adam*   *b* Heb *him*

Lamech. ²⁶Methuselah lived after the birth of Lamech seven hundred eighty-two years, and had
other sons and daughters. ²⁷Thus all the days of
Methuselah were nine hundred sixty-nine years;
and he died.

28 When Lamech had lived one hundred
eighty-two years, he became the father of a son;
²⁹he named him Noah, saying, "Out of the
ground that the LORD has cursed this one shall
bring us relief from our work and from the toil
of our hands." ³⁰Lamech lived after the birth of
Noah five hundred ninety-five years, and had
other sons and daughters. ³¹Thus all the days of
Lamech were seven hundred seventy-seven years;
and he died.

32 After Noah was five hundred years old,
Noah became the father of Shem, Ham, and
Japheth.

The Wickedness of Humankind

6 When people began to multiply on the face
of the ground, and daughters were born to
them, ²the sons of God saw that they were fair;
and they took wives for themselves of all that
they chose. ³Then the LORD said, "My spirit shall
not abide*ᵃ* in mortals forever, for they are flesh;
their days shall be one hundred twenty years."
⁴The Nephilim were on the earth in those days—
and also afterward—when the sons of God went
in to the daughters of humans, who bore children to them. These were the heroes that were of
old, warriors of renown.

5 The LORD saw that the wickedness of humankind was great in the earth, and that every
inclination of the thoughts of their hearts was
only evil continually. ⁶And the LORD was sorry
that he had made humankind on the earth, and
it grieved him to his heart. ⁷So the LORD said, "I
will blot out from the earth the human beings
I have created—people together with animals
and creeping things and birds of the air, for I am
sorry that I have made them." ⁸But Noah found
favor in the sight of the LORD.

Noah Pleases God

9 These are the descendants of Noah. Noah
was a righteous man, blameless in his generation; Noah walked with God. ¹⁰And Noah had
three sons, Shem, Ham, and Japheth.

11 Now the earth was corrupt in God's sight,
and the earth was filled with violence. ¹²And God
saw that the earth was corrupt; for all flesh had
corrupted its ways upon the earth. ¹³And God
said to Noah, "I have determined to make an end
of all flesh, for the earth is filled with violence
because of them; now I am going to destroy

them along with the earth. ¹⁴Make yourself an
ark of cypress*ᵃ* wood; make rooms in the ark,
and cover it inside and out with pitch. ¹⁵This
is how you are to make it: the length of the ark
three hundred cubits, its width fifty cubits, and
its height thirty cubits. ¹⁶Make a roof*ᵇ* for the ark,
and finish it to a cubit above; and put the door
of the ark in its side; make it with lower, second,
and third decks. ¹⁷For my part, I am going to
bring a flood of waters on the earth, to destroy
from under heaven all flesh in which is the
breath of life; everything that is on the earth shall
die. ¹⁸But I will establish my covenant with you;
and you shall come into the ark, you, your sons,
your wife, and your sons' wives with you. ¹⁹And
of every living thing, of all flesh, you shall bring
two of every kind into the ark, to keep them alive
with you; they shall be male and female. ²⁰Of the

---

a Meaning of Heb uncertain   *b* Or *window*

Sin Has Social Consequences

At the beginning of the Noah story, sin has
continued to spread so that it has become
an accepted part of society. The Great Flood,
which wipes out a whole civilization, symbolizes
the consequences of widespread sin. Later in
Genesis, the story of the tower of Babel (11:1–
9) symbolizes another consequence of the insti-
tutionalized sin of disobedience and pride.

When sin becomes part of our social systems
and our institutions, the Church calls it social
sin. Social sin is a result of personal sin, but it
is bigger than any one person's choice. Examples of social sin are the unequal distribution of
the world's wealth, the exploitation of workers by
corporations, and discrimination based on race
or gender. The good news is that God's saving
power is greater than social sin!

● What are the effects of social sin in your community? in your country? in the world?
● How are Christians in your church or community organizing to stand against social sin?

▶ **Gen 6:1—9:17**

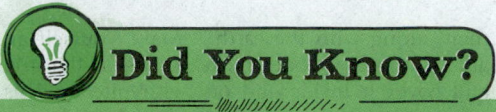

Did You Know?

The Flood

The sin of Adam and Eve in the garden starts a disastrous trend in which each generation adds to sin in the world. This sin leads to the corruption of the world and the destruction of human beings. The Great Flood illustrates the ancient belief that God washed the world clean of this sinfulness and gave another chance to those who were faithful to God.

Other ancient cultures had stories about great floods. But in those stories, vindictive gods caused the floods for petty reasons. These gods had no real love for humanity. The Bible's Flood story is unique because it insists that God acted out of justice and in response to great evil.

God takes great care to save Noah and his family because they are faithful to God. After the Flood, God makes a covenant with Noah, promising never to destroy the earth by flood again—another unique element not found in the stories of other cultures.

▶ **Gen 6:1—9:17**

birds according to their kinds, and of the animals according to their kinds, of every creeping thing of the ground according to its kind, two of every kind shall come in to you, to keep them alive. ²¹Also take with you every kind of food that is eaten, and store it up; and it shall serve as food for you and for them." ²²Noah did this; he did all that God commanded him.

The Great Flood

7 Then the LORD said to Noah, "Go into the ark, you and all your household, for I have seen that you alone are righteous before me in this generation. ²Take with you seven pairs of all clean animals, the male and its mate; and a pair of the animals that are not clean, the male and its mate; ³and seven pairs of the birds of the air also, male and female, to keep their kind alive on the face of all the earth. ⁴For in seven days I will send rain on the earth for forty days and forty nights; and every living thing that I have made I will blot out from the face of the ground." ⁵And Noah did all that the LORD had commanded him.

6 Noah was six hundred years old when the flood of waters came on the earth. ⁷And Noah with his sons and his wife and his sons' wives went into the ark to escape the waters of the flood. ⁸Of clean animals, and of animals that are not clean, and of birds, and of everything that creeps on the ground, ⁹two and two, male and female, went into the ark with Noah, as God had commanded Noah. ¹⁰And after seven days the waters of the flood came on the earth.

11 In the six hundredth year of Noah's life, in the second month, on the seventeenth day of the month, on that day all the fountains of the great deep burst forth, and the windows of the heavens were opened. ¹²The rain fell on the earth forty days and forty nights. ¹³On the very same day Noah with his sons, Shem and Ham and Japheth, and Noah's wife and the three wives of his sons entered the ark, ¹⁴they and every wild animal of every kind, and all domestic animals of every kind, and every creeping thing that creeps on the earth, and every bird of every kind—every bird, every winged creature. ¹⁵They went into the ark with Noah, two and two of all flesh in which there was the breath of life. ¹⁶And those that entered, male and female of all flesh, went in as God had commanded him; and the LORD shut him in.

17 The flood continued forty days on the earth; and the waters increased, and bore up the ark, and it rose high above the earth. ¹⁸The waters swelled and increased greatly on the earth; and the ark floated on the face of the waters. ¹⁹The waters swelled so mightily on the earth that all the high mountains under the whole heaven were covered; ²⁰the waters swelled above the mountains, covering them fifteen cubits deep. ²¹And all flesh died that moved on the earth, birds, domestic animals, wild animals, all swarming creatures that swarm on the earth, and all human beings; ²²everything on dry land in whose nostrils was the breath of life died. ²³He blotted out every living thing that was on the face of the ground, human beings and animals and creeping things and birds of the air; they were blotted out from the earth. Only Noah was left, and those that were with him in the ark. ²⁴And the waters swelled on the earth for one hundred fifty days.

The Flood Subsides

8 But God remembered Noah and all the wild animals and all the domestic animals that were with him in the ark. And God made a wind blow over the earth, and the waters subsided; ²the fountains of the deep and the windows of the heavens were closed, the rain from the heavens was restrained, ³and the waters gradually receded from the earth. At the end of one hundred fifty days the waters had abated; ⁴and in the seventh month, on the seventeenth day of the month, the ark came to rest on the mountains of Ararat. ⁵The waters continued to abate until the tenth month; in the tenth month, on the first day of the month, the tops of the mountains appeared.

6 At the end of forty days Noah opened the window of the ark that he had made ⁷and sent out the raven; and it went to and fro until the waters were dried up from the earth. ⁸Then he sent out the dove from him, to see if the waters had subsided from the face of the ground; ⁹but the dove found no place to set its foot, and it returned to him to the ark, for the waters were still on the face of the whole earth. So he put out his hand and took it and brought it into the ark with him. ¹⁰He waited another seven days, and again he sent out the dove from the ark; ¹¹and the dove came back to him in the evening, and there in its beak was a freshly plucked olive leaf; so Noah knew that the waters had subsided from the earth. ¹²Then he waited another seven days, and sent out the dove; and it did not return to him any more.

13 In the six hundred first year, in the first month, on the first day of the month, the waters were dried up from the earth; and Noah removed the covering of the ark, and looked, and saw that the face of the ground was drying. ¹⁴In the second month, on the twenty-seventh day of the month, the earth was dry. ¹⁵Then God said to Noah, ¹⁶"Go out of the ark, you and your wife, and your sons and your sons' wives with you. ¹⁷Bring out with you every living thing that is with you of all flesh—birds and animals and every creeping thing that creeps on the earth—so that they may abound on the earth, and be fruitful and multiply on the earth." ¹⁸So Noah went out with his sons and his wife and his sons' wives. ¹⁹And every animal, every creeping thing, and every bird, everything that moves on the earth, went out of the ark by families.

God's Promise to Noah

20 Then Noah built an altar to the LORD, and took of every clean animal and of every clean bird, and offered burnt offerings on the altar. ²¹And when the LORD smelled the pleasing odor, the LORD said in his heart, "I will never again curse the ground because of humankind, for the inclination of the human heart is evil from youth; nor will I ever again destroy every living creature as I have done.

²² As long as the earth endures,
    seedtime and harvest, cold and heat,
    summer and winter, day and night,
        shall not cease."

The Covenant with Noah

9 God blessed Noah and his sons, and said to them, "Be fruitful and multiply, and fill the earth. ²The fear and dread of you shall rest on

8:11

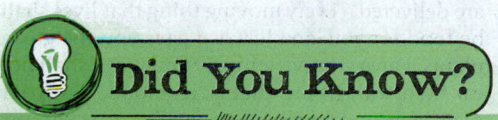

Did You Know?

Water in the Bible

For the ancient Hebrews, although water often represented a source of life, it also represented forces of destruction over which God triumphs. In the story of Creation, God is portrayed as mastering the waters that represent chaos (see Gen 1:1–2)—God constructs the upper and lower firmaments to hold back the waters. At the time of the Great Flood, God releases the waters, and they destroy life on the earth. At the time of the Exodus, God will once again display the divine mastery of the waters, as will Jesus Christ later on.

Pray It!

The Rainbow

What do you see when you see a rainbow? Do you see a multicolored arc caused by the refraction of sunlight through droplets of water? or do you see a wonder of nature that causes you to stop and stare in awe? Something as remarkable as a rainbow is more than just science. It's no wonder the writer of Genesis used it as a symbol of God's covenant promise— a sign of God's faithfulness and love. When God and Israel see the rainbow in the clouds, they will recall their covenant together.

God of imagination and color, only you could come up with the idea of a rainbow! Rainstorm and sunshine, harmony and diversity, mercy and hope, promise and joy, wonder and awe, faithfulness and love. Are these inside me, the wondrous creation you delight in? Guide me to the rainbows in my life!

▶ Gen 9:8–17

every animal of the earth, and on every bird of the air, on everything that creeps on the ground, and on all the fish of the sea; into your hand they are delivered. ³Every moving thing that lives shall be food for you; and just as I gave you the green plants, I give you everything. ⁴Only, you shall not eat flesh with its life, that is, its blood. ⁵For your own lifeblood I will surely require a reckoning: from every animal I will require it and from human beings, each one for the blood of another, I will require a reckoning for human life.

⁶ Whoever sheds the blood of a human,
    by a human shall that person's blood be shed;
  for in his own image
    God made humankind.

⁷And you, be fruitful and multiply, abound on the earth and multiply in it."

8 Then God said to Noah and to his sons with him, ⁹"As for me, I am establishing my covenant with you and your descendants after you, ¹⁰and with every living creature that is with you, the birds, the domestic animals, and every animal of the earth with you, as many as came out of the ark.ᵃ ¹¹I establish my covenant with you, that never again shall all flesh be cut off by the waters

of a flood, and never again shall there be a flood to destroy the earth." ¹²God said, "This is the sign of the covenant that I make between me and you and every living creature that is with you, for all future generations: ¹³I have set my bow in the clouds, and it shall be a sign of the covenant between me and the earth. ¹⁴When I bring clouds over the earth and the bow is seen in the clouds, ¹⁵I will remember my covenant that is between me and you and every living creature of all flesh; and the waters shall never again become a flood to destroy all flesh. ¹⁶When the bow is in the clouds, I will see it and remember the everlasting covenant between God and every living creature of all flesh that is on the earth." ¹⁷God said to Noah, "This is the sign of the covenant that I have established between me and all flesh that is on the earth."

Noah and His Sons

18 The sons of Noah who went out of the ark were Shem, Ham, and Japheth. Ham was the father of Canaan. ¹⁹These three were the sons of Noah; and from these the whole earth was peopled.

20 Noah, a man of the soil, was the first to plant a vineyard. ²¹He drank some of the wine and became drunk, and he lay uncovered in his tent. ²²And Ham, the father of Canaan, saw the nakedness of his father, and told his two brothers outside. ²³Then Shem and Japheth took a garment, laid it on both their shoulders, and walked backward and covered the nakedness of their father; their faces were turned away, and they did not see their father's nakedness. ²⁴When Noah awoke from his wine and knew what his youngest son had done to him, ²⁵he said,

"Cursed be Canaan;
  lowest of slaves shall he be to his brothers."

²⁶He also said,

"Blessed by the Lᴏʀᴅ my God be Shem;
  and let Canaan be his slave.

²⁷ May God make space forᵇ Japheth,
  and let him live in the tents of Shem;
  and let Canaan be his slave."

28 After the flood Noah lived three hundred fifty years. ²⁹All the days of Noah were nine hundred fifty years; and he died.

Nations Descended from Noah

10 These are the descendants of Noah's sons, Shem, Ham, and Japheth; children were born to them after the flood.

a Gk: Heb adds *every animal of the earth*   b Heb *yapht*, a play on *Japheth*

2 The descendants of Japheth: Gomer, Magog, Madai, Javan, Tubal, Meshech, and Tiras. ³The descendants of Gomer: Ashkenaz, Riphath, and Togarmah. ⁴The descendants of Javan: Elishah, Tarshish, Kittim, and Rodanim.ᵃ ⁵From these the coastland peoples spread. These are the descendants of Japhethᵇ in their lands, with their own language, by their families, in their nations.

6 The descendants of Ham: Cush, Egypt, Put, and Canaan. ⁷The descendants of Cush: Seba, Havilah, Sabtah, Raamah, and Sabteca. The descendants of Raamah: Sheba and Dedan. ⁸Cush became the father of Nimrod; he was the first on earth to become a mighty warrior. ⁹He was a mighty hunter before the Lᴏʀᴅ; therefore it is said, "Like Nimrod a mighty hunter before the Lᴏʀᴅ." ¹⁰The beginning of his kingdom was Babel, Erech, and Accad, all of them in the land of Shinar. ¹¹From that land he went into Assyria, and built Nineveh, Rehoboth-ir, Calah, and ¹²Resen between Nineveh and Calah; that is the great city. ¹³Egypt became the father of Ludim, Anamim, Lehabim, Naphtuhim, ¹⁴Pathrusim, Casluhim, and Caphtorim, from which the Philistines come.ᶜ

15 Canaan became the father of Sidon his firstborn, and Heth, ¹⁶and the Jebusites, the Amorites, the Girgashites, ¹⁷the Hivites, the Arkites, the Sinites, ¹⁸the Arvadites, the Zemarites, and the Hamathites. Afterward the families of the Canaanites spread abroad. ¹⁹And the territory of the Canaanites extended from Sidon, in the direction of Gerar, as far as Gaza, and in the direction of Sodom, Gomorrah, Admah, and Zeboiim, as far as Lasha. ²⁰These are the descendants of Ham, by their families, their languages, their lands, and their nations.

21 To Shem also, the father of all the children of Eber, the elder brother of Japheth, children were born. ²²The descendants of Shem: Elam, Asshur, Arpachshad, Lud, and Aram. ²³The descendants of Aram: Uz, Hul, Gether, and Mash. ²⁴Arpachshad became the father of Shelah; and Shelah became the father of Eber. ²⁵To Eber were born two sons: the name of the one was Peleg,ᵈ for in his days the earth was divided, and his brother's name was Joktan. ²⁶Joktan became the father of Almodad, Sheleph, Hazarmaveth, Jerah, ²⁷Hadoram, Uzal, Diklah, ²⁸Obal, Abimael, Sheba, ²⁹Ophir, Havilah, and Jobab; all these were the descendants of Joktan. ³⁰The territory in which they lived extended from Mesha in the direction of Sephar, the hill country of the east. ³¹These are the descendants of Shem, by their families, their languages, their lands, and their nations.

32 These are the families of Noah's sons, according to their genealogies, in their nations; and from these the nations spread abroad on the earth after the flood.

The Tower of Babel

11 Now the whole earth had one language and the same words. ²And as they migrated from the east,ᵉ they came upon a plain in the land of Shinar and settled there. ³And they said to one another, "Come, let us make bricks, and

ᵃ Heb Mss Sam Gk See 1 Chr 1.7: MT *Dodanim*   ᵇ Compare verses 20, 31. Heb lacks *These are the descendants of Japheth*   ᶜ Cn: Heb *Casluhim, from which the Philistines come, and Caphtorim*   ᵈ That is *Division*   ᵉ Or *migrated eastward*

A Barrier or a Bridge?

Language can be either a barrier or a bridge. Through our speech, we connect with other people. And we often hear that love, music, and a smile are universal languages. Yet, languages also separate, symbolizing differences between cultures and nations, which can cause wars and other atrocities to erupt.

The story of the tower of Babel is an ancient explanation of why the separation between people, symbolized by different languages, occurs. The people ignore God's command to "fill the earth" (Gen 1:28). Instead, they gather in one place to try to build a tower reaching to heaven, a sin of pride and arrogance. God confuses their language to foil their plan. It is not language but pride that separates us.

In the Acts of the Apostles, chapter 2, language serves as a bridge. The Holy Spirit enables the people from many different lands to hear the Apostles speaking in their own languages. The Spirit serves to unify us, no matter what earthly language we speak. Anyone who has attended a World Youth Day knows that when we live by the Spirit, we can rise above the differences of language and culture. The Good News is universal and unites us!

▶ Gen 11:1–9

burn them thoroughly." And they had brick for stone, and bitumen for mortar. 4Then they said, "Come, let us build ourselves a city, and a tower with its top in the heavens, and let us make a name for ourselves; otherwise we shall be scattered abroad upon the face of the whole earth." 5The LORD came down to see the city and the tower, which mortals had built. 6And the LORD said, "Look, they are one people, and they have all one language; and this is only the beginning of what they will do; nothing that they propose to do will now be impossible for them. 7Come, let us go down, and confuse their language there, so that they will not understand one another's speech." 8So the LORD scattered them abroad from there over the face of all the earth, and they left off building the city. 9Therefore it was called Babel, because there the LORD confused*a* the language of all the earth; and from there the LORD scattered them abroad over the face of all the earth.

Descendants of Shem

10 These are the descendants of Shem. When Shem was one hundred years old, he became the father of Arpachshad two years after the flood; 11and Shem lived after the birth of Arpachshad five hundred years, and had other sons and daughters.

12 When Arpachshad had lived thirty-five years, he became the father of Shelah; 13and Arpachshad lived after the birth of Shelah four hundred three years, and had other sons and daughters.

14 When Shelah had lived thirty years, he became the father of Eber; 15and Shelah lived after the birth of Eber four hundred three years, and had other sons and daughters.

16 When Eber had lived thirty-four years, he became the father of Peleg; 17and Eber lived after the birth of Peleg four hundred thirty years, and had other sons and daughters.

18 When Peleg had lived thirty years, he became the father of Reu; 19and Peleg lived after the birth of Reu two hundred nine years, and had other sons and daughters.

20 When Reu had lived thirty-two years, he became the father of Serug; 21and Reu lived after the birth of Serug two hundred seven years, and had other sons and daughters.

22 When Serug had lived thirty years, he became the father of Nahor; 23and Serug lived after the birth of Nahor two hundred years, and had other sons and daughters.

24 When Nahor had lived twenty-nine years, he became the father of Terah; 25and Nahor lived after the birth of Terah one hundred nineteen years, and had other sons and daughters.

26 When Terah had lived seventy years, he became the father of Abram, Nahor, and Haran.

Descendants of Terah

27 Now these are the descendants of Terah. Terah was the father of Abram, Nahor, and Haran; and Haran was the father of Lot. 28Haran died before his father Terah in the land of his birth, in Ur of the Chaldeans. 29Abram and Nahor took wives; the name of Abram's wife was Sarai, and the name of Nahor's wife was Milcah. She was the daughter of Haran the father of Milcah and Iscah. 30Now Sarai was barren; she had no child.

31 Terah took his son Abram and his grandson Lot son of Haran, and his daughter-in-law Sarai, his son Abram's wife, and they went out together from Ur of the Chaldeans to go into the land of Canaan; but when they came to Haran, they settled there. 32The days of Terah were two hundred five years; and Terah died in Haran.

The Call of Abram

12 Now the LORD said to Abram, "Go from your country and your kindred and your father's house to the land that I will show you. 2I will make of you a great nation, and I will bless you, and make your name great, so that you will be a blessing. 3I will bless those who bless you, and the one who curses you I will curse; and in you all the families of the earth shall be blessed."*b*

4 So Abram went, as the LORD had told him; and Lot went with him. Abram was seventy-five years old when he departed from Haran. 5Abram took his wife Sarai and his brother's son Lot, and all the possessions that they had gathered, and the persons whom they had acquired in Haran; and they set forth to go to the land of Canaan. When they had come to the land of Canaan, 6Abram passed through the land to the place at Shechem, to the oak*c* of Moreh. At that time the Canaanites were in the land. 7Then the LORD appeared to Abram, and said, "To your offspring*d* I will give this land." So he built there an altar to the LORD, who had appeared to him. 8From there he moved on to the hill country on the east of Bethel, and pitched his tent, with Bethel on the west and Ai on the east; and there he built an altar to the LORD and invoked the name of the LORD. 9And Abram journeyed on by stages toward the Negeb.

---

a Heb balal, meaning to confuse   b Or by you all the families of the earth shall bless themselves   c Or terebinth   d Heb seed

Abram and Sarai in Egypt

10 Now there was a famine in the land. So Abram went down to Egypt to reside there as an alien, for the famine was severe in the land. ¹¹When he was about to enter Egypt, he said to his wife Sarai, "I know well that you are a woman beautiful in appearance; ¹²and when the Egyptians see you, they will say, 'This is his wife'; then they will kill me, but they will let you live. ¹³Say you are my sister, so that it may go well with me because of you, and that my life may be spared on your account." ¹⁴When Abram entered Egypt the Egyptians saw that the woman was very beautiful. ¹⁵When the officials of Pharaoh saw her, they praised her to Pharaoh. And the woman was taken into Pharaoh's house. ¹⁶And for her sake he dealt well with Abram; and he had sheep, oxen, male donkeys, male and female slaves, female donkeys, and camels.

17 But the LORD afflicted Pharaoh and his house with great plagues because of Sarai, Abram's wife. ¹⁸So Pharaoh called Abram, and said, "What is this you have done to me? Why did you not tell me that she was your wife? ¹⁹Why did you say, 'She is my sister,' so that I took her for my wife? Now then, here is your wife, take her, and be gone." ²⁰And Pharaoh gave his men orders concerning him; and they set him on the way, with his wife and all that he had.

Abram and Lot Separate

13 So Abram went up from Egypt, he and his wife, and all that he had, and Lot with him, into the Negeb.

2 Now Abram was very rich in livestock, in silver, and in gold. ³He journeyed on by stages from the Negeb as far as Bethel, to the place where his tent had been at the beginning, between Bethel and Ai, ⁴to the place where he had made an altar at the first; and there Abram called on the name of the LORD. ⁵Now Lot, who went with Abram, also had flocks and herds and tents, ⁶so that the land could not support both of them living together; for their possessions were so great that they could not live together, ⁷and there was strife between the herders of Abram's livestock and the herders of Lot's livestock. At that time the Canaanites and the Perizzites lived in the land.

8 Then Abram said to Lot, "Let there be no strife between you and me, and between your herders and my herders; for we are kindred. ⁹Is not the whole land before you? Separate yourself from me. If you take the left hand, then I will go to the right; or if you take the right hand, then I will go to the left." ¹⁰Lot looked about him, and saw that the plain of the Jordan was well watered everywhere like the garden of the LORD, like the land of Egypt, in the direction of Zoar; this was before the LORD had destroyed Sodom and Gomorrah. ¹¹So Lot chose for himself all the plain of the Jordan, and Lot journeyed eastward; thus they separated from each other. ¹²Abram settled in the land of Canaan, while Lot settled among the cities of the Plain and moved his tent as far as Sodom. ¹³Now the people of Sodom were wicked, great sinners against the LORD.

14 The LORD said to Abram, after Lot had separated from him, "Raise your eyes now, and look from the place where you are, northward and southward and eastward and westward; ¹⁵for all the land that you see I will give to you

Introducing...

Abraham and Sarah

Abraham, whose name was originally Abram, is an important figure for three major world religions: Judaism, Christianity, and Islam. Abraham is regarded as the great example of faith in God. He first appears in Genesis 11:26. For many years, Abram lives in Haran in northern Mesopotamia (see map 1, "The World of the Patriarchs") with his wife, Sarai. God calls Abram and Sarai to leave their home, seals a covenant with them, and changes their names to Abraham and Sarah. God's covenant promises that they will be the parents "of a multitude of nations" (17:5) and their descendants will be as numerous as the "stars of heaven" (22:17).

Later, God requests that Abraham sacrifice his son Isaac. God stops him from going through with it, but Abraham's willingness to cooperate with God and his complete trust in God become the foundation for Israel's faith. Not surprisingly, in the Old Testament, when a prophet or teacher needed an example of someone with unwavering trust in God, Abraham was often cited.

In the New Testament, Abraham is revered as the first patriarch to enter into a covenant with God (see Mt 1:1, Lk 16:19–31) and the great pioneer of Israel's faith (see Acts 7:2–50, Rom 4:1–25, Heb 7:1–10).

▶ **Gen 12:1—25:11**

GEN

and to your offspring[a] forever. ¹⁶I will make your offspring like the dust of the earth; so that if one can count the dust of the earth, your offspring also can be counted. ¹⁷Rise up, walk through the length and the breadth of the land, for I will give it to you." ¹⁸So Abram moved his tent, and came and settled by the oaks[b] of Mamre, which are at Hebron; and there he built an altar to the LORD.

Lot's Captivity and Rescue

14 In the days of King Amraphel of Shinar, King Arioch of Ellasar, King Chedorlaomer of Elam, and King Tidal of Goiim, ²these kings made war with King Bera of Sodom, King Birsha of Gomorrah, King Shinab of Admah, King Shemeber of Zeboiim, and the king of Bela (that is, Zoar). ³All these joined forces in the Valley of Siddim (that is, the Dead Sea).[c] ⁴Twelve years they had served Chedorlaomer, but in the thirteenth year they rebelled. ⁵In the fourteenth year Chedorlaomer and the kings who were with him came and subdued the Rephaim in Ashteroth-karnaim, the Zuzim in Ham, the Emim in Shaveh-kiriathaim, ⁶and the Horites in the hill country of Seir as far as El-paran on the edge of the wilderness; ⁷then they turned back and came to En-mishpat (that is, Kadesh), and subdued all the country of the Amalekites, and also the Amorites who lived in Hazazon-tamar. ⁸Then the king of Sodom, the king of Gomorrah, the king of Admah, the king of Zeboiim, and the king of Bela (that is, Zoar) went out, and they joined battle in the Valley of Siddim ⁹with King Chedorlaomer of Elam, King Tidal of Goiim, King Amraphel of Shinar, and King Arioch of Ellasar, four kings against five. ¹⁰Now the Valley of Siddim was full of bitumen pits; and as the kings of Sodom and Gomorrah fled, some fell into them, and the rest fled to the hill country. ¹¹So the enemy took all the goods of Sodom and Gomorrah, and all their provisions, and went their way; ¹²they also took Lot, the son of Abram's brother, who lived in Sodom, and his goods, and departed.

13 Then one who had escaped came and told Abram the Hebrew, who was living by the oaks[b] of Mamre the Amorite, brother of Eshcol and of Aner; these were allies of Abram. ¹⁴When Abram heard that his nephew had been taken captive, he led forth his trained men, born in his house, three hundred eighteen of them, and went in pursuit as far as Dan. ¹⁵He divided his forces against them by night, he and his servants, and routed them and pursued them to Hobah, north of Damascus. ¹⁶Then he brought back all the goods, and also brought back his nephew Lot with his goods, and the women and the people.

Abram Blessed by Melchizedek

17 After his return from the defeat of Chedorlaomer and the kings who were with him, the king of Sodom went out to meet him at the Valley of Shaveh (that is, the King's Valley). ¹⁸And King Melchizedek of Salem brought out bread and wine; he was priest of God Most High.[d] ¹⁹He blessed him and said,

"Blessed be Abram by God Most High,[d]
    maker of heaven and earth;
²⁰ and blessed be God Most High,[d]
    who has delivered your enemies into your
        hand!"
And Abram gave him one-tenth of everything. ²¹Then the king of Sodom said to Abram, "Give me the persons, but take the goods for yourself." ²²But Abram said to the king of Sodom, "I have sworn to the LORD, God Most High,[d] maker of heaven and earth, ²³that I would not take a thread or a sandal-thong or anything that is yours, so that you might not say, 'I have made Abram rich.' ²⁴I will take nothing but what the young men have eaten, and the share of the men who went with me—Aner, Eshcol, and Mamre. Let them take their share."

God's Covenant with Abram

15 After these things the word of the LORD came to Abram in a vision, "Do not be afraid, Abram, I am your shield; your reward shall be very great." ²But Abram said, "O Lord GOD, what will you give me, for I continue childless, and the heir of my house is Eliezer of Damascus?"[e] ³And Abram said, "You have given me no offspring, and so a slave born in my house is to be my heir." ⁴But the word of the LORD came to him, "This man shall not be your heir; no one but your very own issue shall be your heir." ⁵He brought him outside and said, "Look toward heaven and count the stars, if you are able to count them." Then he said to him, "So shall your descendants be." ⁶And he believed the LORD; and the LORD[f] reckoned it to him as righteousness.

7 Then he said to him, "I am the LORD who brought you from Ur of the Chaldeans, to give you this land to possess." ⁸But he said, "O Lord GOD, how am I to know that I shall possess it?" ⁹He said to him, "Bring me a heifer three years old, a female goat three years old, a ram three years old, a turtledove, and a young pigeon." ¹⁰He

---

a Heb *seed*   b Or *terebinths*   c Heb *Salt Sea*   d Heb *El Elyon*
e Meaning of Heb uncertain   f Heb *he*

✝ Catholic Connection

Sacramental Symbols

Sometimes words alone are not enough. Consider the inexpressible joy and relief of Abram in Genesis 14:17–20. Abram's nephew Lot has been captured by foreign invaders and Abram takes his men to battle and returns Lot safely. Upon Abram's return, Melchizedek, a king and priest, meets with Abram to rejoice in their great victory. As part of their celebration, Melchizedek uses not only words but the everyday objects of bread and wine in a ritual to offer a blessing on Abram and to give praise to God.

The use of symbols, like bread and wine, even today enable us to express and deepen our relationship with God. In the Catholic Church, this is most evident when we celebrate the sacraments. The symbols used in the sacraments find their roots in three areas.

The first area is from Creation. Because God created the world, it is natural that we can find and express meaning through symbols like fire and water. For example, during the sacrament of Baptism, we use water as a sign of purification and new birth and a lit candle as a sign of our desire to walk in the light of Christ.

The second area from which sacramental symbols come is everyday human life. These are things we commonly do, like rubbing oils or lotion on our bodies or placing a reassuring hand on a friend. For example, in the sacrament of the Anointing of the Sick, the priest uses oil to bless and strengthen the sick and places or lays a hand upon them as a sign of blessing.

The third source of sacramental symbols is from events in the history of God's people, especially the Passover. We see this most clearly when we celebrate the Eucharist; we use the symbols of bread and wine along with words and gestures that Jesus used when he celebrated the Passover with his disciples on the eve of his Crucifixion.

When the Church celebrates the sacraments, it combines words with symbols; through faith and the power of the Holy Spirit, the sacraments express and make present to us the graces offered by Christ.

▶ **Gen 14:17–20**

Catechism, nos. 1145–1152

brought him all these and cut them in two, laying each half over against the other; but he did not cut the birds in two. ¹¹And when birds of prey came down on the carcasses, Abram drove them away.

12 As the sun was going down, a deep sleep fell upon Abram, and a deep and terrifying darkness descended upon him. ¹³Then the Lord*ᵃ* said to Abram, "Know this for certain, that your offspring shall be aliens in a land that is not theirs, and shall be slaves there, and they shall be oppressed for four hundred years; ¹⁴but I will bring judgment on the nation that they serve, and afterward they shall come out with great possessions. ¹⁵As for yourself, you shall go to your ancestors in peace; you shall be buried in a good old age. ¹⁶And they shall come back here in the fourth generation; for the iniquity of the Amorites is not yet complete."

17 When the sun had gone down and it was dark, a smoking fire pot and a flaming torch passed between these pieces. ¹⁸On that day the Lord made a covenant with Abram, saying, "To your descendants I give this land, from the river of Egypt to the great river, the river Euphrates, ¹⁹the land of the Kenites, the Kenizzites, the Kadmonites, ²⁰the Hittites, the Perizzites, the Rephaim, ²¹the Amorites, the Canaanites, the Girgashites, and the Jebusites."

The Birth of Ishmael

16 Now Sarai, Abram's wife, bore him no children. She had an Egyptian slave-girl whose name was Hagar, ²and Sarai said to

Abram, "You see that the Lord has prevented me from bearing children; go in to my slave-girl; it may be that I shall obtain children by her." And Abram listened to the voice of Sarai. ³So, after Abram had lived ten years in the land of Canaan, Sarai, Abram's wife, took Hagar the Egyptian, her slave-girl, and gave her to her husband Abram as a wife. ⁴He went in to Hagar, and she conceived; and when she saw that she had conceived, she looked with contempt on her mistress. ⁵Then Sarai said to Abram, "May the wrong done to me be on you! I gave my slave-girl to your embrace, and when she saw that she had conceived, she looked on me with contempt. May the Lord judge between you and me!" ⁶But Abram said to Sarai, "Your slave-girl is in your power; do to her

a Heb *he*

Love and Jealousy

A love triangle in the Bible! The relationship between Abram, Sarai, and Hagar is shocking by Christian moral standards but would not have been unusual in their time. A patriarch like Abram would often have children by several wives, slaves, and concubines (something like mistresses who lived with the household). It's not surprising that such relationships would have fostered jealousy and tension. The conflict between Hagar and Sarai must have been fierce, to cause Hagar to leave the security of Abram's household.

Today, we encourage victims of abuse and harassment to speak out and take action, so it may seem strange to us that God's angel seeks out Hagar and asks her to return to a place where she is likely to be mistreated. When we encounter people who have been abused or harassed, we need to help them seek justice and set things right. Remember the larger message in Genesis—that every person is created in God's image and is to be treated with the utmost dignity and respect. Carrying out this message is our responsibility as brothers and sisters to one another.

▶ **Gen 16:1–16**

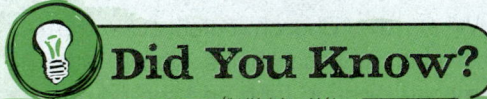

Fire in the Bible

Fire appears frequently throughout the Old Testament, symbolizing two aspects of God: presence and holiness. Fire symbolizes a special presence of God in the sealing of the covenant with Abraham (see Gen 15:17), in the burning bush (see Ex 3:2), and in the pillar of fire leading Israel through the desert (see Ex 13:21). Fire also symbolizes God's holiness appearing to purge and purify those who deviate from God's ways, as in Sodom and Gomorrah (see Gen 19:24) and the seventh plague against Egypt (see Ex 9:23).

▶ **Gen 15:17**

as you please." Then Sarai dealt harshly with her, and she ran away from her.

7 The angel of the Lord found her by a spring of water in the wilderness, the spring on the way to Shur. 8And he said, "Hagar, slave-girl of Sarai, where have you come from and where are you going?" She said, "I am running away from my mistress Sarai." 9The angel of the Lord said to her, "Return to your mistress, and submit to her." 10The angel of the Lord also said to her, "I will so greatly multiply your offspring that they cannot be counted for multitude." 11And the angel of the Lord said to her,

"Now you have conceived and shall bear a son;
　you shall call him Ishmael,^a
　for the Lord has given heed to your affliction.
12 He shall be a wild ass of a man,
　with his hand against everyone,
　and everyone's hand against him;
　and he shall live at odds with all his kin."

13So she named the Lord who spoke to her, "You are El-roi";^b for she said, "Have I really seen God and remained alive after seeing him?"^c 14Therefore the well was called Beer-lahai-roi;^d it lies between Kadesh and Bered.

15 Hagar bore Abram a son; and Abram named his son, whom Hagar bore, Ishmael. 16Abram was eighty-six years old when Hagar bore him^e Ishmael.

The Sign of the Covenant

17 When Abram was ninety-nine years old, the Lord appeared to Abram, and said to him, "I am God Almighty;^f walk before me, and be blameless. 2And I will make my covenant between me and you, and will make you exceedingly numerous." 3Then Abram fell on his face; and God said to him, 4"As for me, this is my covenant with you: You shall be the ancestor of a multitude of nations. 5No longer shall your name be Abram,^g but your name shall be Abraham;^h for I have made you the ancestor of a multitude of nations. 6I will make you exceedingly fruitful; and I will make nations of you, and kings shall come from you. 7I will establish my covenant between me and you, and your offspring after you throughout their generations, for an everlasting covenant, to be God to you and to your offspringⁱ after you. 8And I will give to you, and to your offspring after you, the land where you are now an alien, all the land of Canaan, for a perpetual holding; and I will be their God."

9 God said to Abraham, "As for you, you shall keep my covenant, you and your offspring after you throughout their generations. 10This is my covenant, which you shall keep, between me

Live It!

Covenant

Covenant is a powerful word in the Bible, with deep religious significance because it expresses the intimate relationship between God and God's people. At its most basic level, a covenant is a promise, made by both parties involved, to do certain things. In the covenant God makes with Noah, God promises never to destroy the earth again, and Noah's family promises to fill the earth and subdue it (see Gen 9:1–17). In the covenant with Abraham, God promises that Abram's descendants will be numerous and become a great nation. In return, Abram and all the male members of his household and their male descendants must practice circumcision to mark that they belong to God (see 17:1–27). In the covenant made at Mount Sinai with Moses (see Ex 19:1–9) and the Hebrew people, God promises to give them the Promised Land. In return, they promise to follow the laws God gives to them.

We are, each of us, part of these ancient promises. Like the many faithful people who have gone before us, we too are the descendants of Abraham and Sarah, believers in the one God and members of God's family. We too are heirs to a special, intimate relationship with the Holy One through Jesus.

▶ Gen 17:1–27

and you and your offspring after you: Every male among you shall be circumcised. 11You shall circumcise the flesh of your foreskins, and it shall be a sign of the covenant between me and you. 12Throughout your generations every male among you shall be circumcised when he is eight days old, including the slave born in your house and the one bought with your money from any foreigner who is not of your offspring. 13Both the slave born in your house and the one bought with

---

a That is *God hears*　b Perhaps *God of seeing* or *God who sees*　c Meaning of Heb uncertain　d That is *the Well of the Living One who sees me*　e Heb *Abram*　f Traditional rendering of Heb *El Shaddai*　g That is *exalted ancestor*　h Here taken to mean *ancestor of a multitude*　i Heb *seed*

your money must be circumcised. So shall my covenant be in your flesh an everlasting covenant. [14]Any uncircumcised male who is not circumcised in the flesh of his foreskin shall be cut off from his people; he has broken my covenant."

15 God said to Abraham, "As for Sarai your wife, you shall not call her Sarai, but Sarah shall be her name. [16]I will bless her, and moreover I will give you a son by her. I will bless her, and she shall give rise to nations; kings of peoples shall come from her." [17]Then Abraham fell on his face and laughed, and said to himself, "Can a child be born to a man who is a hundred years old? Can Sarah, who is ninety years old, bear a child?" [18]And Abraham said to God, "O that Ishmael might live in your sight!" [19]God said, "No, but your wife Sarah shall bear you a son, and you shall name him Isaac.[a] I will establish my covenant with him as an everlasting covenant for his offspring after him. [20]As for Ishmael, I have heard you; I will bless him and make him fruitful and exceedingly numerous; he shall be the father of twelve princes, and I will make him a great nation. [21]But my covenant I will establish with Isaac, whom Sarah shall bear to you at this season next year." [22]And when he had finished talking with him, God went up from Abraham.

23 Then Abraham took his son Ishmael and all the slaves born in his house or bought with his money, every male among the men of Abraham's house, and he circumcised the flesh of their foreskins that very day, as God had said to him. [24]Abraham was ninety-nine years old when he was circumcised in the flesh of his foreskin. [25]And his son Ishmael was thirteen years old when he was circumcised in the flesh of his foreskin. [26]That very day Abraham and his son Ishmael were circumcised; [27]and all the men of his house, slaves born in the house and those bought with money from a foreigner, were circumcised with him.

A Son Promised to Abraham and Sarah

18 The Lord appeared to Abraham[b] by the oaks[c] of Mamre, as he sat at the entrance of his tent in the heat of the day. [2]He looked up

---

a That is *he laughs*   b Heb *him*   c Or *terebinths*

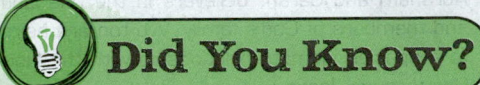

Did You Know?

Circumcision

Circumcision, the removal of the foreskin of the penis, was practiced by many peoples in the ancient world. In Israel circumcision was performed shortly after birth. It symbolized that this person belonged to the people of God, and was required by the Covenant that God made first with Abraham and then with Moses and all of Israel. Today most Jews continue circumcision as a religious practice, and other people may be circumcised for personal reasons.

In the early Church, circumcision became the center of a controversy about whether Gentiles who wanted to become Christians had to first become Jews (see the Acts of the Apostles, chapter 15; Phil 3:2–9).

▶ **Gen 17:9–14**

Live It!

What's So Funny?

Laughter is not a word we usually associate with the Bible, and certainly not with the Old Testament. Most of the stories are serious, filled with accounts of sacrifice, battles, and the Covenant. But here is Sarah, an old woman, long past childbearing age. She overhears one of Abraham's mysterious guests tell him that in a year he and Sarah will have a son (see Gen 18:10). How can she help but laugh? She and Abraham do produce, of course, a son called Isaac, whose Hebrew name, *Yishaq*, means "laughed." Sarah's cynical chuckles must have turned to joyful laughs at the birth of her beloved son. Laughter is a wonderful response to the gift of life and is a natural and often spontaneous response to God's presence within us and around us.

"Is anything too wonderful for the Lord?" (verse 14). We are all tempted to laugh at the notion that miracles can happen to us. As we grow in faith and open ourselves to God's goodness, our laughter will change from skeptical laughter to joyful laughter.

▶ **Gen 18:9–15**

and saw three men standing near him. When he saw them, he ran from the tent entrance to meet them, and bowed down to the ground. [3]He said, "My lord, if I find favor with you, do not pass by your servant. [4]Let a little water be brought, and wash your feet, and rest yourselves under the tree. [5]Let me bring a little bread, that you may refresh yourselves, and after that you may pass on—since you have come to your servant." So they said, "Do as you have said." [6]And Abraham hastened into the tent to Sarah, and said, "Make ready quickly three measures[a] of choice flour, knead it, and make cakes." [7]Abraham ran to the herd, and took a calf, tender and good, and gave it to the servant, who hastened to prepare it. [8]Then he took curds and milk and the calf that he had prepared, and set it before them; and he stood by them under the tree while they ate.

9 They said to him, "Where is your wife Sarah?" And he said, "There, in the tent." [10]Then one said, "I will surely return to you in due season, and your wife Sarah shall have a son." And Sarah was listening at the tent entrance behind him. [11]Now Abraham and Sarah were old, advanced in age; it had ceased to be with Sarah after the manner of women. [12]So Sarah laughed to herself, saying, "After I have grown old, and my husband is old, shall I have pleasure?" [13]The LORD said to Abraham, "Why did Sarah laugh, and say, 'Shall I indeed bear a child, now that I am old?' [14]Is anything too wonderful for the LORD? At the set time I will return to you, in due season, and Sarah shall have a son." [15]But Sarah denied, saying, "I did not laugh"; for she was afraid. He said, "Oh yes, you did laugh."

Judgment Pronounced on Sodom

16 Then the men set out from there, and they looked toward Sodom; and Abraham went with them to set them on their way. [17]The LORD said, "Shall I hide from Abraham what I am about to do, [18]seeing that Abraham shall become a great and mighty nation, and all the nations of the earth shall be blessed in him?[b] [19]No, for I have chosen[c] him, that he may charge his children and his household after him to keep the way of the LORD by doing righteousness and justice; so that the LORD may bring about for Abraham what he has promised him." [20]Then the LORD said, "How great is the outcry against Sodom and Gomorrah and how very grave their sin! [21]I must go down and see whether they have done altogether according to the outcry that has come to me; and if not, I will know."

22 So the men turned from there, and went toward Sodom, while Abraham remained

Pray It!

Get Close to God

Our prayers reveal what we believe about God and what we value. Abraham's bargaining for the inhabitants of Sodom and Gomorrah shows his faith, his care for others, and his closeness with God. Although he is humble, he deals with God as a friend whom he is not afraid to be honest with.

We too must be honest with God in our prayer. Many Christians simply do not trust God enough to be completely themselves with God. They are afraid to share their doubts, anger, grief, and frustrations. But God is big enough to handle it all. Find a way in your prayer time to share your innermost thoughts and feelings with God. For some people, journaling helps; others yell and shout aloud at the Lord. Remember that love requires freedom and God wants to be invited in. Tell God what is on your mind right now. Don't hold back.

▶ **Gen 18:22–33**

standing before the LORD.[d] [23]Then Abraham came near and said, "Will you indeed sweep away the righteous with the wicked? [24]Suppose there are fifty righteous within the city; will you then sweep away the place and not forgive it for the fifty righteous who are in it? [25]Far be it from you to do such a thing, to slay the righteous with the wicked, so that the righteous fare as the wicked! Far be that from you! Shall not the Judge of all the earth do what is just?" [26]And the LORD said, "If I find at Sodom fifty righteous in the city, I will forgive the whole place for their sake." [27]Abraham answered, "Let me take it upon myself to speak to the Lord, I who am but dust and ashes. [28]Suppose five of the fifty righteous are lacking? Will you destroy the whole city for

---

a Heb *seahs*   b Or *and all the nations of the earth shall bless themselves by him*   c Heb *known*   d Another ancient tradition reads *while the* LORD *remained standing before Abraham*

Be Kind to Strangers

If our first gesture to outsiders were one of respect, kindness, and gracious hospitality, what might our world be like? The story of Sodom and Gomorrah shows us the results of disrespect, inhospitality, and the attempted sexual abuse of strangers. Like Abraham, Lot is a wonderful host. But the people of Sodom want Lot's visitors for their own sexual pleasure; being welcoming and hospitable is clearly the last thing on their minds.

As children of God, we have a responsibility to extend our kindness to stranger and friend alike.

How are visitors or new students treated in your school? How are guests treated in your home?

▶ Gen 19:1–11

lack of five?" And he said, "I will not destroy it if I find forty-five there." ²⁹Again he spoke to him, "Suppose forty are found there." He answered, "For the sake of forty I will not do it." ³⁰Then he said, "Oh do not let the Lord be angry if I speak. Suppose thirty are found there." He answered, "I will not do it, if I find thirty there." ³¹He said, "Let me take it upon myself to speak to the Lord. Suppose twenty are found there." He answered, "For the sake of twenty I will not destroy it." ³²Then he said, "Oh do not let the Lord be angry if I speak just once more. Suppose ten are found there." He answered, "For the sake of ten I will not destroy it." ³³And the LORD went his way, when he had finished speaking to Abraham; and Abraham returned to his place.

The Depravity of Sodom

19 The two angels came to Sodom in the evening, and Lot was sitting in the gateway of Sodom. When Lot saw them, he rose to meet them, and bowed down with his face to the ground. ²He said, "Please, my lords, turn aside to your servant's house and spend the night, and wash your feet; then you can rise early and go on your way." They said, "No; we will spend the night in the square." ³But he urged them

strongly; so they turned aside to him and entered his house; and he made them a feast, and baked unleavened bread, and they ate. ⁴But before they lay down, the men of the city, the men of Sodom, both young and old, all the people to the last man, surrounded the house; ⁵and they called to Lot, "Where are the men who came to you tonight? Bring them out to us, so that we may know them." ⁶Lot went out of the door to the men, shut the door after him, ⁷and said, "I beg you, my brothers, do not act so wickedly. ⁸Look, I have two daughters who have not known a man; let me bring them out to you, and do to them as you please; only do nothing to these men, for they have come under the shelter of my roof." ⁹But they replied, "Stand back!" And they said, "This fellow came here as an alien, and he would play the judge! Now we will deal worse with you than with them." Then they pressed hard against the man Lot, and came near the door to break it down. ¹⁰But the men inside reached out their hands and brought Lot into the house with them, and shut the door. ¹¹And they struck with blindness the men who were at the door of the house, both small and great, so that they were unable to find the door.

Sodom and Gomorrah Destroyed

12 Then the men said to Lot, "Have you anyone else here? Sons-in-law, sons, daughters, or anyone you have in the city—bring them out of the place. ¹³For we are about to destroy this place, because the outcry against its people has become great before the LORD, and the LORD has sent us to destroy it." ¹⁴So Lot went out and said to his sons-in-law, who were to marry his daughters, "Up, get out of this place; for the LORD is about to destroy the city." But he seemed to his sons-in-law to be jesting.

15 When morning dawned, the angels urged Lot, saying, "Get up, take your wife and your two daughters who are here, or else you will be consumed in the punishment of the city." ¹⁶But he lingered; so the men seized him and his wife and his two daughters by the hand, the LORD being merciful to him, and they brought him out and left them outside the city. ¹⁷When they had brought them outside, theyᵃ said, "Flee for your life; do not look back or stop anywhere in the Plain; flee to the hills, or else you will be consumed." ¹⁸And Lot said to them, "Oh, no, my lords; ¹⁹your servant has found favor with you, and you have shown me great kindness in saving my life; but I cannot flee to the hills, for fear the

---

a Gk Syr Vg: Heb *he*

disaster will overtake me and I die. ²⁰Look, that city is near enough to flee to, and it is a little one. Let me escape there—is it not a little one?—and my life will be saved!" ²¹He said to him, "Very well, I grant you this favor too, and will not overthrow the city of which you have spoken. ²²Hurry, escape there, for I can do nothing until you arrive there." Therefore the city was called Zoar.ᵃ ²³The sun had risen on the earth when Lot came to Zoar.

24 Then the Lord rained on Sodom and Gomorrah sulfur and fire from the Lord out of heaven; ²⁵and he overthrew those cities, and all the Plain, and all the inhabitants of the cities, and what grew on the ground. ²⁶But Lot's wife, behind him, looked back, and she became a pillar of salt.

27 Abraham went early in the morning to the place where he had stood before the Lord; ²⁸and he looked down toward Sodom and Gomorrah and toward all the land of the Plain and saw the smoke of the land going up like the smoke of a furnace.

29 So it was that, when God destroyed the cities of the Plain, God remembered Abraham, and sent Lot out of the midst of the overthrow, when he overthrew the cities in which Lot had settled.

The Shameful Origin of Moab and Ammon

30 Now Lot went up out of Zoar and settled in the hills with his two daughters, for he was afraid to stay in Zoar; so he lived in a cave with his two daughters. ³¹And the firstborn said to the younger, "Our father is old, and there is not a man on earth to come in to us after the manner of all the world. ³²Come, let us make our father drink wine, and we will lie with him, so that we may preserve offspring through our father." ³³So they made their father drink wine that night; and the firstborn went in, and lay with her father; he did not know when she lay down or when she rose. ³⁴On the next day, the firstborn said to the younger, "Look, I lay last night with my father; let us make him drink wine tonight also; then you go in and lie with him, so that we may preserve offspring through our father." ³⁵So they made their father drink wine that night also; and the younger rose, and lay with him; and he did not know when she lay down or when she rose. ³⁶Thus both the daughters of Lot became pregnant by their father. ³⁷The firstborn bore a son, and named him Moab; he is the ancestor of the Moabites to this day. ³⁸The younger also bore a son and named him Ben-ammi; he is the ancestor of the Ammonites to this day.

Abraham and Sarah at Gerar

20 From there Abraham journeyed toward the region of the Negeb, and settled between Kadesh and Shur. While residing in Gerar as an alien, ²Abraham said of his wife Sarah, "She is my sister." And King Abimelech of Gerar sent and took Sarah. ³But God came to Abimelech in a dream by night, and said to him, "You are about to die because of the woman whom you have taken; for she is a married woman." ⁴Now Abimelech had not approached her; so he said, "Lord, will you destroy an innocent people? ⁵Did he not himself say to me, 'She is my sister'? And she herself said, 'He is my brother.' I did this in the integrity of my heart and the innocence of my hands." ⁶Then God said to him in the dream, "Yes, I know that you did this in the integrity of your heart; furthermore it was I who kept you from sinning against me. Therefore I did not let you touch her. ⁷Now then, return the man's wife; for he is a prophet, and he will pray for you and you shall live. But if you do not restore her, know that you shall surely die, you and all that are yours."

8 So Abimelech rose early in the morning, and called all his servants and told them all these things; and the men were very much afraid. ⁹Then Abimelech called Abraham, and said to him, "What have you done to us? How have I sinned against you, that you have brought such great guilt on me and my kingdom? You have done things to me that ought not to be done." ¹⁰And Abimelech said to Abraham, "What were you thinking of, that you did this thing?" ¹¹Abraham said, "I did it because I thought, There is no fear of God at all in this place, and they will kill me because of my wife. ¹²Besides, she is indeed my sister, the daughter of my father but not the daughter of my mother; and she became my wife. ¹³And when God caused me to wander from my father's house, I said to her, 'This is the kindness you must do me: at every place to which we come, say of me, He is my brother.' " ¹⁴Then Abimelech took sheep and oxen, and male and female slaves, and gave them to Abraham, and restored his wife Sarah to him. ¹⁵Abimelech said, "My land is before you; settle where it pleases you." ¹⁶To Sarah he said, "Look, I have given your brother a thousand pieces of silver; it is your exoneration before all who are with you; you are completely vindicated." ¹⁷Then Abraham prayed to God; and God healed Abimelech, and also healed his wife and female slaves so that they

---

ᵃ That is *Little*

GEN

Pray It!

Hagar's Rescue

Genesis 21:8–21 is part two of the Hagar and Ishmael story begun in 16:1–16. Once again, Hagar is the victim of Sarah's jealousy. But this time God does not send her back. Seemingly facing certain death, Hagar receives from God the ability to see the opportunity for life in front of her. This time the writer of Genesis makes the point that God rescues the oppressed and abandoned. Hagar and Ishmael survive, and from their descendants, a great people emerges.

Hagar's story reminds us that God wants to rescue us from oppression and injustice. Often we want to ask God to magically take these things away. But because God has given human beings free will, we cannot always be spared from the injustice of others. In your prayer, you can always ask God to rescue you, to give you the vision to see the healthy choices you can make to improve your situation. Do that right now if you are in an unjust situation. God's grace can be found in all things, even during our darkest times.

▶ **Gen 21:8–21**

bore children. ¹⁸For the LORD had closed fast all the wombs of the house of Abimelech because of Sarah, Abraham's wife.

The Birth of Isaac

21 The LORD dealt with Sarah as he had said, and the LORD did for Sarah as he had promised. ²Sarah conceived and bore Abraham a son in his old age, at the time of which God had spoken to him. ³Abraham gave the name Isaac to his son whom Sarah bore him. ⁴And Abraham circumcised his son Isaac when he was eight days old, as God had commanded him. ⁵Abraham was a hundred years old when his son Isaac was born to him. ⁶Now Sarah said, "God has brought laughter for me; everyone who hears will laugh with me." ⁷And she said, "Who would ever have said to Abraham that Sarah would

nurse children? Yet I have borne him a son in his old age."

Hagar and Ishmael Sent Away

8 The child grew, and was weaned; and Abraham made a great feast on the day that Isaac was weaned. ⁹But Sarah saw the son of Hagar the Egyptian, whom she had borne to Abraham, playing with her son Isaac.^a ¹⁰So she said to Abraham, "Cast out this slave woman with her son; for the son of this slave woman shall not inherit along with my son Isaac." ¹¹The matter was very distressing to Abraham on account of his son. ¹²But God said to Abraham, "Do not be distressed because of the boy and because of your slave woman; whatever Sarah says to you, do as she tells you, for it is through Isaac that offspring shall be named for you. ¹³As for the son of the slave woman, I will make a nation of him also, because he is your offspring." ¹⁴So Abraham rose early in the morning, and took bread and a skin of water, and gave it to Hagar, putting it on her shoulder, along with the child, and sent her away. And she departed, and wandered about in the wilderness of Beer-sheba.

15 When the water in the skin was gone, she cast the child under one of the bushes. ¹⁶Then she went and sat down opposite him a good way off, about the distance of a bowshot; for she said, "Do not let me look on the death of the child." And as she sat opposite him, she lifted up her voice and wept. ¹⁷And God heard the voice of the boy; and the angel of God called to Hagar from heaven, and said to her, "What troubles you, Hagar? Do not be afraid; for God has heard the voice of the boy where he is. ¹⁸Come, lift up the boy and hold him fast with your hand, for I will make a great nation of him." ¹⁹Then God opened her eyes and she saw a well of water. She went, and filled the skin with water, and gave the boy a drink.

20 God was with the boy, and he grew up; he lived in the wilderness, and became an expert with the bow. ²¹He lived in the wilderness of Paran; and his mother got a wife for him from the land of Egypt.

Abraham and Abimelech Make a Covenant

22 At that time Abimelech, with Phicol the commander of his army, said to Abraham, "God is with you in all that you do; ²³now therefore swear to me here by God that you will not deal falsely with me or with my offspring or with my posterity, but as I have dealt loyally with you,

---

a Gk Vg: Heb lacks *with her son Isaac*

you will deal with me and with the land where you have resided as an alien." [24]And Abraham said, "I swear it."

25 When Abraham complained to Abimelech about a well of water that Abimelech's servants had seized, [26]Abimelech said, "I do not know who has done this; you did not tell me, and I have not heard of it until today." [27]So Abraham took sheep and oxen and gave them to Abimelech, and the two men made a covenant. [28]Abraham set apart seven ewe lambs of the flock. [29]And Abimelech said to Abraham, "What is the meaning of these seven ewe lambs that you have set apart?" [30]He said, "These seven ewe lambs you shall accept from my hand, in order that you may be a witness for me that I dug this well." [31]Therefore that place was called Beer-sheba;[a] because there both of them swore an oath. [32]When they had made a covenant at Beer-sheba, Abimelech, with Phicol the commander of his army, left and returned to the land of the Philistines. [33]Abraham[b] planted a tamarisk tree in Beer-sheba, and called there on the name of the LORD, the Everlasting God.[c] [34]And Abraham resided as an alien many days in the land of the Philistines.

The Command to Sacrifice Isaac

22 After these things God tested Abraham. He said to him, "Abraham!" And he said, "Here I am." [2]He said, "Take your son, your only son Isaac, whom you love, and go to the land of Moriah, and offer him there as a burnt offering on one of the mountains that I shall show you." [3]So Abraham rose early in the morning, saddled his donkey, and took two of his young men with him, and his son Isaac; he cut the wood for the burnt offering, and set out and went to the place in the distance that God had shown him. [4]On the third day Abraham looked up and saw the place far away. [5]Then Abraham said to his young men, "Stay here with the donkey; the boy and I will go over there; we will worship, and then we will come back to you." [6]Abraham took the wood of the burnt offering and laid it on his son Isaac, and he himself carried the fire and the knife. So the two of them walked on together. [7]Isaac said to his father Abraham, "Father!" And he said, "Here I am, my son." He said, "The fire and the wood are here, but where is the lamb for a burnt offering?" [8]Abraham said, "God himself will provide the lamb for a burnt offering, my son." So the two of them walked on together.

9 When they came to the place that God had shown him, Abraham built an altar there and laid the wood in order. He bound his son Isaac, and laid him on the altar, on top of the wood.

[10]Then Abraham reached out his hand and took the knife to kill[d] his son. [11]But the angel of the LORD called to him from heaven, and said, "Abraham, Abraham!" And he said, "Here I am." [12]He said, "Do not lay your hand on the boy or do anything to him; for now I know that you fear God, since you have not withheld your son, your only son, from me." [13]And Abraham looked up and saw a ram, caught in a thicket by its horns. Abraham went and took the ram and offered it up as a burnt offering instead of his son. [14]So Abraham called that place "The LORD will provide";[e] as it is said to this day, "On the mount of the LORD it shall be provided."[f]

---

a That is *Well of seven* or *Well of the oath*   b Heb *He*   c Or *the LORD, El Olam*   d Or *to slaughter*   e Or *will see;* Heb traditionally transliterated *Jehovah Jireh*   f Or *he shall be seen*

Ultimate Trust in God!

To us it seems horrible that God would ask Abraham to sacrifice his son Isaac. But this story is meant to be a sign of Abraham's complete trust in God. Ultimately, God prevented the sacrifice because God wanted not Isaac's death but Abraham's faith. Because of his willingness to respond to God's demand, Abraham is recognized as the father of our faith. Our trust in God should be as total as Abraham's trust was.

We probably won't ever be faced with the test of Abraham, but perhaps we will be faced with different, though equally difficult, tests of faith in our own lives. The story of Abraham shows us the power of faith. Because of Abraham's faith in God's promise, Isaac lived and became the father of Jacob, whose twelve sons became the twelve Tribes of Israel. In your prayer time, reflect or journal on the following questions:

● Because of your beliefs, have you ever had to give up someone or something that was precious to you?

● How has your life been enriched as a result of your trust in God in a difficult situation?

▶ Gen 22:1–19

GEN

15 The angel of the LORD called to Abraham a second time from heaven, ¹⁶and said, "By myself I have sworn, says the LORD: Because you have done this, and have not withheld your son, your only son, ¹⁷I will indeed bless you, and I will make your offspring as numerous as the stars of heaven and as the sand that is on the seashore. And your offspring shall possess the gate of their enemies, ¹⁸and by your offspring shall all the nations of the earth gain blessing for themselves, because you have obeyed my voice." ¹⁹So Abraham returned to his young men, and they arose and went together to Beer-sheba; and Abraham lived at Beer-sheba.

The Children of Nahor

20 Now after these things it was told Abraham, "Milcah also has borne children, to your brother Nahor: ²¹Uz the firstborn, Buz his brother, Kemuel the father of Aram, ²²Chesed, Hazo, Pildash, Jidlaph, and Bethuel." ²³Bethuel became the father of Rebekah. These eight Milcah bore to Nahor, Abraham's brother. ²⁴Moreover, his concubine, whose name was Reumah, bore Tebah, Gaham, Tahash, and Maacah.

Sarah's Death and Burial

23 Sarah lived one hundred twenty-seven years; this was the length of Sarah's life. ²And Sarah died at Kiriath-arba (that is, Hebron) in the land of Canaan; and Abraham went in to mourn for Sarah and to weep for her. ³Abraham rose up from beside his dead, and said to the Hittites, ⁴"I am a stranger and an alien residing among you; give me property among you for a burying place, so that I may bury my dead out of my sight." ⁵The Hittites answered Abraham, ⁶"Hear us, my lord; you are a mighty prince among us. Bury your dead in the choicest of our burial places; none of us will withhold from you any burial ground for burying your dead." ⁷Abraham rose and bowed to the Hittites, the people of the land. ⁸He said to them, "If you are willing that I should bury my dead out of my sight, hear me, and entreat for me Ephron son of Zohar, ⁹so that he may give me the cave of Machpelah, which he owns; it is at the end of his field. For the full price let him give it to me in your presence as a possession for a burying place." ¹⁰Now Ephron was sitting among the Hittites; and Ephron the Hittite answered Abraham in the hearing of the Hittites, of all who went in at the gate of his city, ¹¹"No, my lord, hear me; I give you the field, and I give you the cave that is in it; in the presence of my people I give it to you; bury your dead." ¹²Then Abraham bowed down before the people

of the land. ¹³He said to Ephron in the hearing of the people of the land, "If you only will listen to me! I will give the price of the field; accept it from me, so that I may bury my dead there." ¹⁴Ephron answered Abraham, ¹⁵"My lord, listen to me; a piece of land worth four hundred shekels of silver—what is that between you and me? Bury your dead." ¹⁶Abraham agreed with Ephron; and Abraham weighed out for Ephron the silver that he had named in the hearing of the Hittites, four hundred shekels of silver, according to the weights current among the merchants.

17 So the field of Ephron in Machpelah, which was to the east of Mamre, the field with the cave that was in it and all the trees that were in the field, throughout its whole area, passed ¹⁸to Abraham as a possession in the presence of the Hittites, in the presence of all who went in at the gate of his city. ¹⁹After this, Abraham buried Sarah his wife in the cave of the field of Machpelah facing Mamre (that is, Hebron) in the land of Canaan. ²⁰The field and the cave that is in it passed from the Hittites into Abraham's possession as a burying place.

The Marriage of Isaac and Rebekah

24 Now Abraham was old, well advanced in years; and the LORD had blessed Abraham in all things. ²Abraham said to his servant, the oldest of his house, who had charge of all that he had, "Put your hand under my thigh ³and I will make you swear by the LORD, the God of heaven and earth, that you will not get a wife for my son from the daughters of the Canaanites, among whom I live, ⁴but will go to my country and to my kindred and get a wife for my son Isaac." ⁵The servant said to him, "Perhaps the woman may not be willing to follow me to this land; must I then take your son back to the land from which you came?" ⁶Abraham said to him, "See to it that you do not take my son back there. ⁷The LORD, the God of heaven, who took me from my father's house and from the land of my birth, and who spoke to me and swore to me, 'To your offspring I will give this land,' he will send his angel before you, and you shall take a wife for my son from there. ⁸But if the woman is not willing to follow you, then you will be free from this oath of mine; only you must not take my son back there." ⁹So the servant put his hand under the thigh of Abraham his master and swore to him concerning this matter.

10 Then the servant took ten of his master's camels and departed, taking all kinds of choice gifts from his master; and he set out and went to Aram-naharaim, to the city of Nahor. ¹¹He

made the camels kneel down outside the city by the well of water; it was toward evening, the time when women go out to draw water. ¹²And he said, "O Lᴏʀᴅ, God of my master Abraham, please grant me success today and show steadfast love to my master Abraham. ¹³I am standing here by the spring of water, and the daughters of the townspeople are coming out to draw water. ¹⁴Let the girl to whom I shall say, 'Please offer your jar that I may drink,' and who shall say, 'Drink, and I will water your camels'—let her be the one whom you have appointed for your servant Isaac. By this I shall know that you have shown steadfast love to my master."

15 Before he had finished speaking, there was Rebekah, who was born to Bethuel son of Milcah, the wife of Nahor, Abraham's brother, coming out with her water jar on her shoulder. ¹⁶The girl was very fair to look upon, a virgin, whom no man had known. She went down to the spring, filled her jar, and came up. ¹⁷Then the servant ran to meet her and said, "Please let me sip a little water from your jar." ¹⁸"Drink, my lord," she said, and quickly lowered her jar upon her hand and gave him a drink. ¹⁹When she had finished giving him a drink, she said, "I will draw for your camels also, until they have finished drinking." ²⁰So she quickly emptied her jar into the trough and ran again to the well to draw, and she drew for all his camels. ²¹The man gazed at her in silence to learn whether or not the Lᴏʀᴅ had made his journey successful.

22 When the camels had finished drinking, the man took a gold nose-ring weighing a half shekel, and two bracelets for her arms weighing ten gold shekels, ²³and said, "Tell me whose daughter you are. Is there room in your father's house for us to spend the night?" ²⁴She said to him, "I am the daughter of Bethuel son of Milcah, whom she bore to Nahor." ²⁵She added, "We have plenty of straw and fodder and a place to spend the night." ²⁶The man bowed his head and worshiped the Lᴏʀᴅ ²⁷and said, "Blessed be the Lᴏʀᴅ, the God of my master Abraham, who has not forsaken his steadfast love and his faithfulness toward my master. As for me, the Lᴏʀᴅ has led me on the way to the house of my master's kin."

28 Then the girl ran and told her mother's household about these things. ²⁹Rebekah had a brother whose name was Laban; and Laban ran out to the man, to the spring. ³⁰As soon as he had seen the nose-ring, and the bracelets on his sister's arms, and when he heard the words of his sister Rebekah, "Thus the man spoke to me," he went to the man; and there he was, standing by the camels at the spring. ³¹He said, "Come in,

O blessed of the Lᴏʀᴅ. Why do you stand outside when I have prepared the house and a place for the camels?" ³²So the man came into the house; and Laban unloaded the camels, and gave him straw and fodder for the camels, and water to wash his feet and the feet of the men who were with him. ³³Then food was set before him to eat; but he said, "I will not eat until I have told my errand." He said, "Speak on."

34 So he said, "I am Abraham's servant. ³⁵The Lᴏʀᴅ has greatly blessed my master, and he has become wealthy; he has given him flocks and herds, silver and gold, male and female slaves, camels and donkeys. ³⁶And Sarah my master's wife bore a son to my master when she was old; and he has given him all that he has. ³⁷My master made me swear, saying, 'You shall not take a wife for my son from the daughters of the Canaanites, in whose land I live; ³⁸but you shall go to my father's house, to my kindred, and get a wife for my son.' ³⁹I said to my master, 'Perhaps the woman will not follow me.' ⁴⁰But he said to me, 'The Lᴏʀᴅ, before whom I walk, will send his angel with you and make your way successful. You shall get a wife for my son from my kindred, from my father's house. ⁴¹Then you will be free from my oath, when you come to my kindred; even if they will not give her to you, you will be free from my oath.'

42 "I came today to the spring, and said, 'O Lᴏʀᴅ, the God of my master Abraham, if now you will only make successful the way I am going! ⁴³I am standing here by the spring of water; let the young woman who comes out to draw, to whom I shall say, "Please give me a little water from your jar to drink," ⁴⁴and who will say to me, "Drink, and I will draw for your camels also"—let her be the woman whom the Lᴏʀᴅ has appointed for my master's son.'

45 "Before I had finished speaking in my heart, there was Rebekah coming out with her water jar on her shoulder; and she went down to the spring, and drew. I said to her, 'Please let me drink.' ⁴⁶She quickly let down her jar from her shoulder, and said, 'Drink, and I will also water your camels.' So I drank, and she also watered the camels. ⁴⁷Then I asked her, 'Whose daughter are you?' She said, 'The daughter of Bethuel, Nahor's son, whom Milcah bore to him.' So I put the ring on her nose, and the bracelets on her arms. ⁴⁸Then I bowed my head and worshiped the Lᴏʀᴅ, and blessed the Lᴏʀᴅ, the God of my master Abraham, who had led me by the right way to obtain the daughter of my master's kinsman for his son. ⁴⁹Now then, if you will deal loyally and truly with my master, tell me; and if

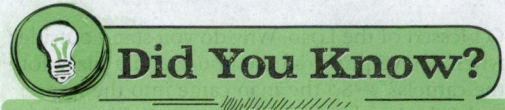

Did You Know?

Abraham's Descendants

God promised Hagar that her son Ishmael would be made "a great nation" (Gen 21:18). The Old Testament lists twelve princely tribes that descended from Abraham's older son (see 25:13–16), tribes traditionally associated with the people of ancient Edom. A much later Islamic tradition identifies Muhammad and his descendants—the Muslims—as "children of Ishmael."

Abraham's younger son, Isaac, was the father of Jacob. The Jewish people trace their lineage to Jacob and his twelve sons. Because Jesus was a Jew, Christians ultimately trace their ancestry through Jacob to Abraham as well.

Thus, three major world religions—Judaism, Christianity, and Islam—all see Abraham as their "father in faith."

▶ **Gen 25:12–18**

not, tell me, so that I may turn either to the right hand or to the left."

50 Then Laban and Bethuel answered, "The thing comes from the Lord; we cannot speak to you anything bad or good. ⁵¹Look, Rebekah is before you, take her and go, and let her be the wife of your master's son, as the Lord has spoken."

52 When Abraham's servant heard their words, he bowed himself to the ground before the Lord. ⁵³And the servant brought out jewelry of silver and of gold, and garments, and gave them to Rebekah; he also gave to her brother and to her mother costly ornaments. ⁵⁴Then he and the men who were with him ate and drank, and they spent the night there. When they rose in the morning, he said, "Send me back to my master." ⁵⁵Her brother and her mother said, "Let the girl remain with us a while, at least ten days; after that she may go." ⁵⁶But he said to them, "Do not delay me, since the Lord has made my journey successful; let me go that I may go to my master." ⁵⁷They said, "We will call the girl, and ask her." ⁵⁸And they called Rebekah, and said to her, "Will you go with this man?" She said, "I will." ⁵⁹So they sent away their sister Rebekah and her nurse along with Abraham's servant and his men. ⁶⁰And they blessed Rebekah and said to her,

"May you, our sister, become
   thousands of myriads;
may your offspring gain possession
   of the gates of their foes."

⁶¹Then Rebekah and her maids rose up, mounted the camels, and followed the man; thus the servant took Rebekah, and went his way.

62 Now Isaac had come from*ᵃ* Beer-lahai-roi, and was settled in the Negeb. ⁶³Isaac went out in the evening to walk*ᵇ* in the field; and looking up, he saw camels coming. ⁶⁴And Rebekah looked up, and when she saw Isaac, she slipped quickly from the camel, ⁶⁵and said to the servant, "Who is the man over there, walking in the field to meet us?" The servant said, "It is my master." So she took her veil and covered herself. ⁶⁶And the servant told Isaac all the things that he had done. ⁶⁷Then Isaac brought her into his mother Sarah's tent. He took Rebekah, and she became his wife; and he loved her. So Isaac was comforted after his mother's death.

Abraham Marries Keturah

25 Abraham took another wife, whose name was Keturah. ²She bore him Zimran, Jokshan, Medan, Midian, Ishbak, and Shuah. ³Jokshan was the father of Sheba and Dedan. The sons of Dedan were Asshurim, Letushim, and Leummim. ⁴The sons of Midian were Ephah, Epher, Hanoch, Abida, and Eldaah. All these were the children of Keturah. ⁵Abraham gave all he had to Isaac. ⁶But to the sons of his concubines Abraham gave gifts, while he was still living, and he sent them away from his son Isaac, eastward to the east country.

The Death of Abraham

7 This is the length of Abraham's life, one hundred seventy-five years. ⁸Abraham breathed his last and died in a good old age, an old man and full of years, and was gathered to his people. ⁹His sons Isaac and Ishmael buried him in the cave of Machpelah, in the field of Ephron son of Zohar the Hittite, east of Mamre, ¹⁰the field that Abraham purchased from the Hittites. There Abraham was buried, with his wife Sarah. ¹¹After the death of Abraham God blessed his son Isaac. And Isaac settled at Beer-lahai-roi.

Ishmael's Descendants

12 These are the descendants of Ishmael, Abraham's son, whom Hagar the Egyptian, Sarah's slave-girl, bore to Abraham. ¹³These are the

---
a Syr Tg: Heb *from coming to*   *b* Meaning of Heb word is uncertain

names of the sons of Ishmael, named in the order of their birth: Nebaioth, the firstborn of Ishmael; and Kedar, Adbeel, Mibsam, ¹⁴Mishma, Dumah, Massa, ¹⁵Hadad, Tema, Jetur, Naphish, and Kedemah. ¹⁶These are the sons of Ishmael and these are their names, by their villages and by their encampments, twelve princes according to their tribes. ¹⁷(This is the length of the life of Ishmael, one hundred thirty-seven years; he breathed his last and died, and was gathered to his people.) ¹⁸They settled from Havilah to Shur, which is opposite Egypt in the direction of Assyria; he settled down*a* alongside of*b* all his people.

The Birth and Youth of Esau and Jacob

19 These are the descendants of Isaac, Abraham's son: Abraham was the father of Isaac, ²⁰and Isaac was forty years old when he married Rebekah, daughter of Bethuel the Aramean of Paddan-aram, sister of Laban the Aramean. ²¹Isaac prayed to the LORD for his wife, because she was barren; and the LORD granted his prayer, and his wife Rebekah conceived. ²²The children struggled together within her; and she said, "If it is to be this way, why do I live?"*c* So she went to inquire of the LORD. ²³And the LORD said to her,

"Two nations are in your womb,
   and two peoples born of you shall be divided;
the one shall be stronger than the other,
   the elder shall serve the younger."

²⁴When her time to give birth was at hand, there were twins in her womb. ²⁵The first came out red, all his body like a hairy mantle; so they named him Esau. ²⁶Afterward his brother came out, with his hand gripping Esau's heel; so he was named Jacob.*d* Isaac was sixty years old when she bore them.

27 When the boys grew up, Esau was a skillful hunter, a man of the field, while Jacob was a quiet man, living in tents. ²⁸Isaac loved Esau, because he was fond of game; but Rebekah loved Jacob.

Esau Sells His Birthright

29 Once when Jacob was cooking a stew, Esau came in from the field, and he was famished. ³⁰Esau said to Jacob, "Let me eat some of that red stuff, for I am famished!" (Therefore he was called Edom.*e*) ³¹Jacob said, "First sell me your birthright." ³²Esau said, "I am about to die; of what use is a birthright to me?" ³³Jacob said, "Swear to me first."*f* So he swore to him, and sold his birthright to Jacob. ³⁴Then Jacob gave Esau bread and lentil stew, and he ate and drank, and rose and went his way. Thus Esau despised his birthright.

Isaac and Abimelech

26 Now there was a famine in the land, besides the former famine that had occurred in the days of Abraham. And Isaac went to Gerar, to King Abimelech of the Philistines. ²The LORD appeared to Isaac*g* and said, "Do not go down to Egypt; settle in the land that I shall show you. ³Reside in this land as an alien, and I will be with you, and will bless you; for to you and to your descendants I will give all these lands, and I will fulfill the oath that I swore to your father Abraham. ⁴I will make your offspring as numerous as the stars of heaven, and will give to your offspring all these lands; and all the nations of the earth shall gain blessing for themselves through

Sibling Rivalry

It is common for siblings to have conflict in their relationship, but with Jacob and Esau, the conflict becomes extreme. Follow their story in Genesis, chapters 27–28, 33.

For another story of extreme sibling rivalry, see Genesis 37:12–36. Joseph's brothers (all sons of Jacob) are so jealous of him that they plot to kill him. But instead, he gets sold as a slave—and that turns out to be a great career move for him.

The story of the prodigal son in Luke 15:11–32 is yet another example of sibling rivalry.

Do you have any brothers or sisters? If so, how do you treat them? Do you ever pray for them? Do you ever tell them that you care about them—even if they drive you crazy at times?

If you don't have any brothers or sisters, how about cousins, neighbors, or friends? All relationships get better with prayer and care. Take a moment to pray for your siblings, a close cousin, or friend by name.

▶ **Gen 25:19–34**

GEN

your offspring, 5because Abraham obeyed my voice and kept my charge, my commandments, my statutes, and my laws."

6 So Isaac settled in Gerar. 7When the men of the place asked him about his wife, he said, "She is my sister"; for he was afraid to say, "My wife," thinking, "or else the men of the place might kill me for the sake of Rebekah, because she is attractive in appearance." 8When Isaac had been there a long time, King Abimelech of the Philistines looked out of a window and saw him fondling his wife Rebekah. 9So Abimelech called for Isaac, and said, "So she is your wife! Why then did you say, 'She is my sister'?" Isaac said to him, "Because I thought I might die because of her." 10Abimelech said, "What is this you have done to us? One of the people might easily have lain with your wife, and you would have brought guilt upon us." 11So Abimelech warned all the people, saying, "Whoever touches this man or his wife shall be put to death."

Introducing...

Jacob

According to the Bible, Abraham was the father of Isaac, and Isaac was the father of Jacob, and Jacob was the father of twelve sons who became the leaders of the twelve Tribes of Israel. Jacob, like his ancestors, participated in the covenant with God that promised a great land and many descendants. He is portrayed as a very human character with a wide range of emotions and actions, both good and bad. Jacob is a repentant brother, a kind father, and a successful herder, but he is also a trickster who steals his brother Esau's birthright and his father's blessing (see Gen 25:29–34, 27:1–29). It is no wonder that Jacob's name means "supplanter" or "heel grabber."

In a dream, God renews the covenant promises to Jacob (see 28:10–17), and in another dream (see 35:9–15), God changes Jacob's name to Israel (see Gen 32:22–32). Jacob's descendants become known as the Israelites. His story reveals that God's blessing continues to work even through flawed human beings.

▶ Gen 25:19—50:14

12 Isaac sowed seed in that land, and in the same year reaped a hundredfold. The LORD blessed him, 13and the man became rich; he prospered more and more until he became very wealthy. 14He had possessions of flocks and herds, and a great household, so that the Philistines envied him. 15(Now the Philistines had stopped up and filled with earth all the wells that his father's servants had dug in the days of his father Abraham.) 16And Abimelech said to Isaac, "Go away from us; you have become too powerful for us."

17 So Isaac departed from there and camped in the valley of Gerar and settled there. 18Isaac dug again the wells of water that had been dug in the days of his father Abraham; for the Philistines had stopped them up after the death of Abraham; and he gave them the names that his father had given them. 19But when Isaac's servants dug in the valley and found there a well of spring water, 20the herders of Gerar quarreled with Isaac's herders, saying, "The water is ours." So he called the well Esek,a because they contended with him. 21Then they dug another well, and they quarreled over that one also; so he called it Sitnah.b 22He moved from there and dug another well, and they did not quarrel over it; so he called it Rehoboth,c saying, "Now the LORD has made room for us, and we shall be fruitful in the land."

23 From there he went up to Beer-sheba. 24And that very night the LORD appeared to him and said, "I am the God of your father Abraham; do not be afraid, for I am with you and will bless you and make your offspring numerous for my servant Abraham's sake." 25So he built an altar there, called on the name of the LORD, and pitched his tent there. And there Isaac's servants dug a well.

26 Then Abimelech went to him from Gerar, with Ahuzzath his adviser and Phicol the commander of his army. 27Isaac said to them, "Why have you come to me, seeing that you hate me and have sent me away from you?" 28They said, "We see plainly that the LORD has been with you; so we say, let there be an oath between you and us, and let us make a covenant with you 29so that you will do us no harm, just as we have not touched you and have done to you nothing but good and have sent you away in peace. You are now the blessed of the LORD." 30So he made them a feast, and they ate and drank. 31In the morning they rose early and exchanged oaths; and Isaac

---

a That is Contention   b That is Enmity   c That is Broad places or Room

set them on their way, and they departed from him in peace. [32]That same day Isaac's servants came and told him about the well that they had dug, and said to him, "We have found water!" [33]He called it Shibah;[a] therefore the name of the city is Beer-sheba[b] to this day.

Esau's Hittite Wives

34 When Esau was forty years old, he married Judith daughter of Beeri the Hittite, and Basemath daughter of Elon the Hittite; [35]and they made life bitter for Isaac and Rebekah.

Isaac Blesses Jacob

27 When Isaac was old and his eyes were dim so that he could not see, he called his elder son Esau and said to him, "My son"; and he answered, "Here I am." [2]He said, "See, I am old; I do not know the day of my death. [3]Now then, take your weapons, your quiver and your bow, and go out to the field, and hunt game for me. [4]Then prepare for me savory food, such as I like, and bring it to me to eat, so that I may bless you before I die."

5 Now Rebekah was listening when Isaac spoke to his son Esau. So when Esau went to the field to hunt for game and bring it, [6]Rebekah said to her son Jacob, "I heard your father say to your brother Esau, [7]'Bring me game, and prepare for me savory food to eat, that I may bless you before the LORD before I die.' [8]Now therefore, my son, obey my word as I command you. [9]Go to the flock, and get me two choice kids, so that I may prepare from them savory food for your father, such as he likes; [10]and you shall take it to your father to eat, so that he may bless you before he dies." [11]But Jacob said to his mother Rebekah, "Look, my brother Esau is a hairy man, and I am a man of smooth skin. [12]Perhaps my father will feel me, and I shall seem to be mocking him, and bring a curse on myself and not a blessing." [13]His mother said to him, "Let your curse be on me, my son; only obey my word, and go, get them for me." [14]So he went and got them and brought them to his mother; and his mother prepared savory food, such as his father loved. [15]Then Rebekah took the best garments of her elder son Esau, which were with her in the house, and put them on her younger son Jacob; [16]and she put the skins of the kids on his hands and on the smooth part of his neck. [17]Then she handed the savory food, and the bread that she had prepared, to her son Jacob.

18 So he went in to his father, and said, "My father"; and he said, "Here I am; who are you, my son?" [19]Jacob said to his father, "I am Esau your

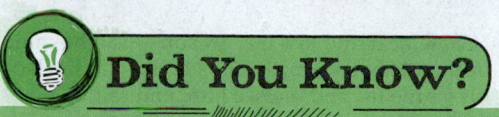

Did You Know?

God's Surprising Choice

In most ancient cultures, including Israel's, the oldest son of the family was expected to inherit his father's property (the birthright) and authority (the blessing). In the story of Esau and Jacob, Jacob tricks Esau (the oldest son) out of his birthright (see Gen 25:29–34) and deceives his blind father into giving him the blessing (see 27:1–29).

It is surprising that Genesis makes no comment on Jacob's actions. Ultimately, the story is not a commentary on Jacob's morality but about God's justice. God is not bound by cultural expectations. Again and again in the Old Testament, God defies human norms by choosing the "little ones" for big responsibilities: Jacob, Joseph, Ruth, David, and Esther, for example. Even the Israelites themselves were an unlikely choice on God's part. Why didn't God choose a nation of great wealth and power instead of a group that was enslaved?

The story of Jacob and Esau reminds us that God does not bow to human expectations or plans. God's ways are often surprising!

▶ **Gen 27:1–40**

firstborn. I have done as you told me; now sit up and eat of my game, so that you may bless me." [20]But Isaac said to his son, "How is it that you have found it so quickly, my son?" He answered, "Because the LORD your God granted me success." [21]Then Isaac said to Jacob, "Come near, that I may feel you, my son, to know whether you are really my son Esau or not." [22]So Jacob went up to his father Isaac, who felt him and said, "The voice is Jacob's voice, but the hands are the hands of Esau." [23]He did not recognize him, because his hands were hairy like his brother Esau's hands; so he blessed him. [24]He said, "Are you really my son Esau?" He answered, "I am." [25]Then he said, "Bring it to me, that I may eat of my son's game and bless you." So he brought it to him, and he ate; and he brought him wine, and he drank. [26]Then his father Isaac said to him,

---

a A word resembling the word for *oath*   *b* That is *Well of the oath* or *Well of seven*

"Come near and kiss me, my son." 27So he came near and kissed him; and he smelled the smell of his garments, and blessed him, and said,

"Ah, the smell of my son
is like the smell of a field that the LORD has blessed.
28 May God give you of the dew of heaven,
and of the fatness of the earth,
and plenty of grain and wine.
29 Let peoples serve you,
and nations bow down to you.
Be lord over your brothers,
and may your mother's sons bow down to you.
Cursed be everyone who curses you,
and blessed be everyone who blesses you!"

Esau's Lost Blessing

30 As soon as Isaac had finished blessing Jacob, when Jacob had scarcely gone out from the presence of his father Isaac, his brother Esau came in from his hunting. 31He also prepared savory food, and brought it to his father. And he said to his father, "Let my father sit up and eat of his son's game, so that you may bless me." 32His father Isaac said to him, "Who are you?" He answered, "I am your firstborn son, Esau." 33Then Isaac trembled violently, and said, "Who was it then that hunted game and brought it to me, and I ate it all[a] before you came, and I have blessed him?—yes, and blessed he shall be!" 34When Esau heard his father's words, he cried out with an exceedingly great and bitter cry, and said to his father, "Bless me, me also, father!" 35But he said, "Your brother came deceitfully, and he has taken away your blessing." 36Esau said, "Is he not rightly named Jacob?[b] For he has supplanted me these two times. He took away my birthright; and look, now he has taken away my blessing." Then he said, "Have you not reserved a blessing for me?" 37Isaac answered Esau, "I have already made him your lord, and I have given him all his brothers as servants, and with grain and wine I have sustained him. What then can I do for you, my son?" 38Esau said to his father, "Have you only one blessing, father? Bless me, me also, father!" And Esau lifted up his voice and wept.

39 Then his father Isaac answered him:

"See, away from[c] the fatness of the earth shall your home be,
and away from[d] the dew of heaven on high.
40 By your sword you shall live,
and you shall serve your brother;
but when you break loose,[e]
you shall break his yoke from your neck."

Jacob Escapes Esau's Fury

41 Now Esau hated Jacob because of the blessing with which his father had blessed him, and Esau said to himself, "The days of mourning for my father are approaching; then I will kill my brother Jacob." 42But the words of her elder son Esau were told to Rebekah; so she sent and called her younger son Jacob and said to him, "Your brother Esau is consoling himself by planning to kill you. 43Now therefore, my son, obey my voice; flee at once to my brother Laban in Haran, 44and stay with him a while, until your brother's fury turns away— 45until your brother's anger against you turns away, and he forgets what you have done to him; then I will send, and bring you back from there. Why should I lose both of you in one day?"

46 Then Rebekah said to Isaac, "I am weary of my life because of the Hittite women. If Jacob marries one of the Hittite women such as these, one of the women of the land, what good will my life be to me?"

28 Then Isaac called Jacob and blessed him, and charged him, "You shall not marry one of the Canaanite women. 2Go at once to Paddan-aram to the house of Bethuel, your mother's father; and take as wife from there one of the daughters of Laban, your mother's brother. 3May God Almighty[f] bless you and make you fruitful and numerous, that you may become a company of peoples. 4May he give to you the blessing of Abraham, to you and to your offspring with you, so that you may take possession of the land where you now live as an alien—land that God gave to Abraham." 5Thus Isaac sent Jacob away; and he went to Paddan-aram, to Laban son of Bethuel the Aramean, the brother of Rebekah, Jacob's and Esau's mother.

Esau Marries Ishmael's Daughter

6 Now Esau saw that Isaac had blessed Jacob and sent him away to Paddan-aram to take a wife from there, and that as he blessed him, charged him, "You shall not marry one of the Canaanite women," 7and that Jacob had obeyed his father and his mother and gone to Paddan-aram. 8So when Esau saw that the Canaanite women did not please his father Isaac, 9Esau went to Ishmael and took Mahalath daughter of Abraham's son Ishmael, and sister of Nebaioth, to be his wife in addition to the wives he had.

---

a Cn: Heb *of all*   b That is *He supplants* or *He takes by the heel*   c Or *See, of*   d Or *and of*   e Meaning of Heb uncertain   f Traditional rendering of Heb *El Shaddai*

Jacob's Dream at Bethel

10 Jacob left Beer-sheba and went toward Haran. [11]He came to a certain place and stayed there for the night, because the sun had set. Taking one of the stones of the place, he put it under his head and lay down in that place. [12]And he dreamed that there was a ladder[a] set up on the earth, the top of it reaching to heaven; and the angels of God were ascending and descending on it. [13]And the LORD stood beside him[b] and said, "I am the LORD, the God of Abraham your father and the God of Isaac; the land on which you lie I will give to you and to your offspring; [14]and your offspring shall be like the dust of the earth, and you shall spread abroad to the west and to the east and to the north and to the south; and all the families of the earth shall be blessed[c] in you and in your offspring. [15]Know that I am with you and will keep you wherever you go, and will bring you back to this land; for I will not leave you until I have done what I have promised you." [16]Then Jacob woke from his sleep and said, "Surely the LORD is in this place—and I did not know it!" [17]And he was afraid, and said, "How awesome is this place! This is none other than the house of God, and this is the gate of heaven."

18 So Jacob rose early in the morning, and he took the stone that he had put under his head and set it up for a pillar and poured oil on the top of it. [19]He called that place Bethel;[d] but the name of the city was Luz at the first. [20]Then Jacob made a vow, saying, "If God will be with me, and will keep me in this way that I go, and will give me bread to eat and clothing to wear, [21]so that I come again to my father's house in peace, then the LORD shall be my God, [22]and this stone, which I have set up for a pillar, shall be God's house; and of all that you give me I will surely give one-tenth to you."

Jacob Meets Rachel

29 Then Jacob went on his journey, and came to the land of the people of the east. [2]As he looked, he saw a well in the field and three flocks of sheep lying there beside it; for out of that well the flocks were watered. The stone on the well's mouth was large, [3]and when all the flocks were gathered there, the shepherds would roll the stone from the mouth of the well, and water the sheep, and put the stone back in its place on the mouth of the well.

4 Jacob said to them, "My brothers, where do you come from?" They said, "We are from Haran." [5]He said to them, "Do you know Laban son of Nahor?" They said, "We do." [6]He said to them, "Is it well with him?" "Yes," they replied,

Pray It!

Friendship with God

Just as Jacob is leaving his home and everything he knows, God establishes a personal relationship with him through a dream. In this relationship, God and Jacob interact personally, are accountable to each other, and trust each other. Jacob will need this relationship to help him through the tough times ahead. See Genesis 32:22–32 for further developments in Jacob's relationship with God.

God, I want to know your presence. Use my dreams and my waking thoughts; use my family, friends, and neighbors; use your holy word. Use them all to reach me. For I know your presence will sustain me on my most difficult journeys, as it did Jacob.

▶ Gen 28:10–22

"and here is his daughter Rachel, coming with the sheep." [7]He said, "Look, it is still broad daylight; it is not time for the animals to be gathered together. Water the sheep, and go, pasture them." [8]But they said, "We cannot until all the flocks are gathered together, and the stone is rolled from the mouth of the well; then we water the sheep."

9 While he was still speaking with them, Rachel came with her father's sheep; for she kept them. [10]Now when Jacob saw Rachel, the daughter of his mother's brother Laban, and the sheep of his mother's brother Laban, Jacob went up and rolled the stone from the well's mouth, and watered the flock of his mother's brother Laban. [11]Then Jacob kissed Rachel, and wept aloud. [12]And Jacob told Rachel that he was her father's kinsman, and that he was Rebekah's son; and she ran and told her father.

13 When Laban heard the news about his sister's son Jacob, he ran to meet him; he embraced him and kissed him, and brought him to his house. Jacob[e] told Laban all these things, [14]and Laban said to him, "Surely you are my bone and my flesh!" And he stayed with him a month.

---

a Or stairway or ramp   b Or stood above it   c Or shall bless themselves   d That is House of God   e Heb He

GEN

When Lies Boomerang

Predictably, Jacob becomes upset when he finds out he has been deceived by Laban (see Gen 29:25). Yet, the very reason Jacob is working for his uncle Laban is because he has fled from his brother Esau, whom he deceived several years earlier (see 27:1–40). Jacob's lies and deceit have boomeranged, so now he is the victim.

Just as the good deeds we do often come back to us, sometimes in surprising ways, so it is with the bad deeds. Think about your bad deeds as slow-moving boomerangs. Sooner or later, they will come back to you and the situation probably won't be too pleasant. Is that what you want? Reflect on a lie you told that has come back to haunt you.

▶ Gen 29:15–30

Jacob Marries Laban's Daughters

15 Then Laban said to Jacob, "Because you are my kinsman, should you therefore serve me for nothing? Tell me, what shall your wages be?" 16Now Laban had two daughters; the name of the elder was Leah, and the name of the younger was Rachel. 17Leah's eyes were lovely,[a] and Rachel was graceful and beautiful. 18Jacob loved Rachel; so he said, "I will serve you seven years for your younger daughter Rachel." 19Laban said, "It is better that I give her to you than that I should give her to any other man; stay with me." 20So Jacob served seven years for Rachel, and they seemed to him but a few days because of the love he had for her.

21 Then Jacob said to Laban, "Give me my wife that I may go in to her, for my time is completed." 22So Laban gathered together all the people of the place, and made a feast. 23But in the evening he took his daughter Leah and brought her to Jacob; and he went in to her. 24(Laban gave his maid Zilpah to his daughter Leah to be her maid.) 25When morning came, it was Leah! And Jacob said to Laban, "What is this you have done to me? Did I not serve with you for Rachel? Why

then have you deceived me?" 26Laban said, "This is not done in our country—giving the younger before the firstborn. 27Complete the week of this one, and we will give you the other also in return for serving me another seven years." 28Jacob did so, and completed her week; then Laban gave him his daughter Rachel as a wife. 29(Laban gave his maid Bilhah to his daughter Rachel to be her maid.) 30So Jacob went in to Rachel also, and he loved Rachel more than Leah. He served Laban[b] for another seven years.

31 When the LORD saw that Leah was unloved, he opened her womb; but Rachel was barren. 32Leah conceived and bore a son, and she named him Reuben;[c] for she said, "Because the LORD has looked on my affliction; surely now my husband will love me." 33She conceived again and bore a son, and said, "Because the LORD has heard[d] that I am hated, he has given me this son also"; and she named him Simeon. 34Again she conceived and bore a son, and said, "Now this time my husband will be joined[e] to me, because I have borne him three sons"; therefore he was named Levi. 35She conceived again and bore a son, and said, "This time I will praise[f] the LORD"; therefore she named him Judah; then she ceased bearing.

30 When Rachel saw that she bore Jacob no children, she envied her sister; and she said to Jacob, "Give me children, or I shall die!" 2Jacob became very angry with Rachel and said, "Am I in the place of God, who has withheld from you the fruit of the womb?" 3Then she said, "Here is my maid Bilhah; go in to her, that she may bear upon my knees and that I too may have children through her." 4So she gave him her maid Bilhah as a wife; and Jacob went in to her. 5And Bilhah conceived and bore Jacob a son. 6Then Rachel said, "God has judged me, and has also heard my voice and given me a son"; therefore she named him Dan.[g] 7Rachel's maid Bilhah conceived again and bore Jacob a second son. 8Then Rachel said, "With mighty wrestlings I have wrestled[h] with my sister, and have prevailed"; so she named him Naphtali.

9 When Leah saw that she had ceased bearing children, she took her maid Zilpah and gave her to Jacob as a wife. 10Then Leah's maid Zilpah bore Jacob a son. 11And Leah said, "Good fortune!" so she named him Gad.[i] 12Leah's maid Zilpah bore Jacob a second son. 13And Leah said, "Happy am I! For the women will call me happy"; so she named him Asher.[j]

---

a Meaning of Heb uncertain   b Heb *him*   c That is *See, a son*   d Heb *shama*   e Heb *lawah*   f Heb *hodah*   g That is *He judged*   h Heb *niphtal*   i That is *Fortune*   j That is *Happy*

14 In the days of wheat harvest Reuben went and found mandrakes in the field, and brought them to his mother Leah. Then Rachel said to Leah, "Please give me some of your son's mandrakes." ¹⁵But she said to her, "Is it a small matter that you have taken away my husband? Would you take away my son's mandrakes also?" Rachel said, "Then he may lie with you tonight for your son's mandrakes." ¹⁶When Jacob came from the field in the evening, Leah went out to meet him, and said, "You must come in to me; for I have hired you with my son's mandrakes." So he lay with her that night. ¹⁷And God heeded Leah, and she conceived and bore Jacob a fifth son. ¹⁸Leah said, "God has given me my hire[a] because I gave my maid to my husband"; so she named him Issachar. ¹⁹And Leah conceived again, and she bore Jacob a sixth son. ²⁰Then Leah said, "God has endowed me with a good dowry; now my husband will honor[b] me, because I have borne him six sons"; so she named him Zebulun. ²¹Afterwards she bore a daughter, and named her Dinah.

22 Then God remembered Rachel, and God heeded her and opened her womb. ²³She conceived and bore a son, and said, "God has taken away my reproach"; ²⁴and she named him Joseph,[c] saying, "May the LORD add to me another son!"

Jacob Prospers at Laban's Expense

25 When Rachel had borne Joseph, Jacob said to Laban, "Send me away, that I may go to my own home and country. ²⁶Give me my wives and my children for whom I have served you, and let me go; for you know very well the service I have given you." ²⁷But Laban said to him, "If you will allow me to say so, I have learned by divination that the LORD has blessed me because of you; ²⁸name your wages, and I will give it." ²⁹Jacob said to him, "You yourself know how I have served you, and how your cattle have fared with me. ³⁰For you had little before I came, and it has increased abundantly; and the LORD has blessed you wherever I turned. But now when shall I provide for my own household also?" ³¹He said, "What shall I give you?" Jacob said, "You shall not give me anything; if you will do this for me, I will again feed your flock and keep it: ³²let me pass through all your flock today, removing from it every speckled and spotted sheep and every black lamb, and the spotted and speckled among the goats; and such shall be my wages. ³³So my honesty will answer for me later, when you come to look into my wages with you. Every one that is not speckled and spotted among the goats and black among the lambs, if found with me, shall

be counted stolen." ³⁴Laban said, "Good! Let it be as you have said." ³⁵But that day Laban removed the male goats that were striped and spotted, and all the female goats that were speckled and spotted, every one that had white on it, and every lamb that was black, and put them in charge of his sons; ³⁶and he set a distance of three days' journey between himself and Jacob, while Jacob was pasturing the rest of Laban's flock.

37 Then Jacob took fresh rods of poplar and almond and plane, and peeled white streaks in them, exposing the white of the rods. ³⁸He set the rods that he had peeled in front of the flocks in the troughs, that is, the watering places, where the flocks came to drink. And since they bred when they came to drink, ³⁹the flocks bred in front of the rods, and so the flocks produced young that were striped, speckled, and spotted. ⁴⁰Jacob separated the lambs, and set the faces of the flocks toward the striped and the completely black animals in the flock of Laban; and he put his own droves apart, and did not put them with Laban's flock. ⁴¹Whenever the stronger of the flock were breeding, Jacob laid the rods in the troughs before the eyes of the flock, that they might breed among the rods, ⁴²but for the feebler of the flock he did not lay them there; so the feebler were Laban's, and the stronger Jacob's. ⁴³Thus the man grew exceedingly rich, and had large flocks, and male and female slaves, and camels and donkeys.

Jacob Flees with Family and Flocks

31 Now Jacob heard that the sons of Laban were saying, "Jacob has taken all that was our father's; he has gained all this wealth from what belonged to our father." ²And Jacob saw that Laban did not regard him as favorably as he did before. ³Then the LORD said to Jacob, "Return to the land of your ancestors and to your kindred, and I will be with you." ⁴So Jacob sent and called Rachel and Leah into the field where his flock was, ⁵and said to them, "I see that your father does not regard me as favorably as he did before. But the God of my father has been with me. ⁶You know that I have served your father with all my strength, ⁷yet your father has cheated me and changed my wages ten times, but God did not permit him to harm me. ⁸If he said, 'The speckled shall be your wages,' then all the flock bore speckled; and if he said, 'The striped shall be your wages,' then all the flock bore striped. ⁹Thus God has taken away the livestock of your father, and given them to me.

---

a Heb *sakar*   b Heb *zabal*   c That is *He adds*

GEN

10 "During the mating of the flock I once had a dream in which I looked up and saw that the male goats that leaped upon the flock were striped, speckled, and mottled. 11Then the angel of God said to me in the dream, 'Jacob,' and I said, 'Here I am!' 12And he said, 'Look up and see that all the goats that leap on the flock are striped, speckled, and mottled; for I have seen all that Laban is doing to you. 13I am the God of Bethel,ᵃ where you anointed a pillar and made a vow to me. Now leave this land at once and return to the land of your birth.' " 14Then Rachel and Leah answered him, "Is there any portion or inheritance left to us in our father's house? 15Are we not regarded by him as foreigners? For he has sold us, and he has been using up the money given for us. 16All the property that God has taken away from our father belongs to us and to our children; now then, do whatever God has said to you."

17 So Jacob arose, and set his children and his wives on camels; 18and he drove away all his livestock, all the property that he had gained, the livestock in his possession that he had acquired in Paddan-aram, to go to his father Isaac in the land of Canaan.

19 Now Laban had gone to shear his sheep, and Rachel stole her father's household gods. 20And Jacob deceived Laban the Aramean, in that he did not tell him that he intended to flee. 21So he fled with all that he had; starting out he crossed the Euphrates,ᵇ and set his face toward the hill country of Gilead.

Laban Overtakes Jacob

22 On the third day Laban was told that Jacob had fled. 23So he took his kinsfolk with him and pursued him for seven days until he caught up with him in the hill country of Gilead. 24But God came to Laban the Aramean in a dream by night, and said to him, "Take heed that you say not a word to Jacob, either good or bad."

25 Laban overtook Jacob. Now Jacob had pitched his tent in the hill country, and Laban with his kinsfolk camped in the hill country of Gilead. 26Laban said to Jacob, "What have you done? You have deceived me, and carried away my daughters like captives of the sword. 27Why did you flee secretly and deceive me and not tell me? I would have sent you away with mirth and songs, with tambourine and lyre. 28And why did you not permit me to kiss my sons and my daughters farewell? What you have done is foolish. 29It is in my power to do you harm; but the God of your father spoke to me last night, saying, 'Take heed that you speak to Jacob neither good nor bad.' 30Even though you had to go because you longed

greatly for your father's house, why did you steal my gods?" 31Jacob answered Laban, "Because I was afraid, for I thought that you would take your daughters from me by force. 32But anyone with whom you find your gods shall not live. In the presence of our kinsfolk, point out what I have that is yours, and take it." Now Jacob did not know that Rachel had stolen the gods.ᶜ

33 So Laban went into Jacob's tent, and into Leah's tent, and into the tent of the two maids, but he did not find them. And he went out of Leah's tent, and entered Rachel's. 34Now Rachel had taken the household gods and put them in the camel's saddle, and sat on them. Laban felt all about in the tent, but did not find them. 35And she said to her father, "Let not my lord be angry that I cannot rise before you, for the way of women is upon me." So he searched, but did not find the household gods.

36 Then Jacob became angry, and upbraided Laban. Jacob said to Laban, "What is my offense? What is my sin, that you have hotly pursued me? 37Although you have felt about through all my goods, what have you found of all your household goods? Set it here before my kinsfolk and your kinsfolk, so that they may decide between us two. 38These twenty years I have been with you; your ewes and your female goats have not miscarried, and I have not eaten the rams of your flocks. 39That which was torn by wild beasts I did not bring to you; I bore the loss of it myself; of my hand you required it, whether stolen by day or stolen by night. 40It was like this with me: by day the heat consumed me, and the cold by night, and my sleep fled from my eyes. 41These twenty years I have been in your house; I served you fourteen years for your two daughters, and six years for your flock, and you have changed my wages ten times. 42If the God of my father, the God of Abraham and the Fearᵈ of Isaac, had not been on my side, surely now you would have sent me away empty-handed. God saw my affliction and the labor of my hands, and rebuked you last night."

Laban and Jacob Make a Covenant

43 Then Laban answered and said to Jacob, "The daughters are my daughters, the children are my children, the flocks are my flocks, and all that you see is mine. But what can I do today about these daughters of mine, or about their children whom they have borne? 44Come now, let us make a covenant, you and I; and let it be a witness between you and me." 45So Jacob took a

---

ᵃ Cn: Meaning of Heb uncertain   ᵇ Heb *the river*   ᶜ Heb *them*
ᵈ Meaning of Heb uncertain

stone, and set it up as a pillar. ⁴⁶And Jacob said to his kinsfolk, "Gather stones," and they took stones, and made a heap; and they ate there by the heap. ⁴⁷Laban called it Jegar-sahadutha:ᵈ but Jacob called it Galeed.ᵇ ⁴⁸Laban said, "This heap is a witness between you and me today." Therefore he called it Galeed, ⁴⁹and the pillarᶜ Mizpah,ᵈ for he said, "The LORD watch between you and me, when we are absent one from the other. ⁵⁰If you ill-treat my daughters, or if you take wives in addition to my daughters, though no one else is with us, remember that God is witness between you and me."

51 Then Laban said to Jacob, "See this heap and see the pillar, which I have set between you and me. ⁵²This heap is a witness, and the pillar is a witness, that I will not pass beyond this heap to you, and you will not pass beyond this heap and this pillar to me, for harm. ⁵³May the God of Abraham and the God of Nahor"—the God of their father—"judge between us." So Jacob swore by the Fearᵉ of his father Isaac, ⁵⁴and Jacob offered a sacrifice on the height and called his kinsfolk to eat bread; and they ate bread and tarried all night in the hill country.

55ᶠ Early in the morning Laban rose up, and kissed his grandchildren and his daughters and blessed them; then he departed and returned home.

32 Jacob went on his way and the angels of God met him; ²and when Jacob saw them he said, "This is God's camp!" So he called that place Mahanaim.ᵍ

Jacob Sends Presents to Appease Esau

3 Jacob sent messengers before him to his brother Esau in the land of Seir, the country of Edom, ⁴instructing them, "Thus you shall say to my lord Esau: Thus says your servant Jacob, 'I have lived with Laban as an alien, and stayed until now; ⁵and I have oxen, donkeys, flocks, male and female slaves; and I have sent to tell my lord, in order that I may find favor in your sight.' "

6 The messengers returned to Jacob, saying, "We came to your brother Esau, and he is coming to meet you, and four hundred men are with him." ⁷Then Jacob was greatly afraid and distressed; and he divided the people that were with him, and the flocks and herds and camels, into two companies, ⁸thinking, "If Esau comes to the one company and destroys it, then the company that is left will escape."

9 And Jacob said, "O God of my father Abraham and God of my father Isaac, O LORD who said to me, 'Return to your country and to your kindred, and I will do you good,' ¹⁰I am not worthy

of the least of all the steadfast love and all the faithfulness that you have shown to your servant, for with only my staff I crossed this Jordan; and now I have become two companies. ¹¹Deliver me, please, from the hand of my brother, from the hand of Esau, for I am afraid of him; he may come and kill us all, the mothers with the children. ¹²Yet you have said, 'I will surely do you good, and make your offspring as the sand of the sea, which cannot be counted because of their number.' "

13 So he spent that night there, and from what he had with him he took a present for his brother Esau, ¹⁴two hundred female goats and twenty male goats, two hundred ewes and twenty

a In Aramaic *The heap of witness*   b In Hebrew *The heap of witness*   c Compare Sam: MT lacks *the pillar*   d That is *Watchpost*   e Meaning of Heb uncertain   f Ch 32.1 in Heb   g Here taken to mean *Two camps*

Pray It!

Wrestling with God

Even after twenty years, Jacob is anxious about meeting Esau again. This time Jacob uses his craftiness not to deceive Esau but to gain Esau's good graces. Then, while on the way home, he has an amazing religious experience. Many Scripture scholars believe the strange wrestling encounter is a symbol that Jacob has become a changed person. He finally realizes that in all his troubles, God was his true opponent.

Perhaps at times you have wrestled with yourself or with God. It is not so much that God is your opponent or that you are in a contest. It is the wrestling itself that matters. When you face challenges, especially the big ones, you wrestle between the person you are now and the person God is calling you to be.

In your prayer time, reflect or journal on the following questions:

- When does it seem like God is trying to wrestle with you? What does it feel like?
- Is God challenging you about something in your life right now?
- What blessings might you gain in accepting God's challenge and changing your life?

▶ Gen 32:22–32

GEN

rams, ¹⁵thirty milch camels and their colts, forty cows and ten bulls, twenty female donkeys and ten male donkeys. ¹⁶These he delivered into the hand of his servants, every drove by itself, and said to his servants, "Pass on ahead of me, and put a space between drove and drove." ¹⁷He instructed the foremost, "When Esau my brother meets you, and asks you, 'To whom do you belong? Where are you going? And whose are these ahead of you?' ¹⁸then you shall say, 'They belong to your servant Jacob; they are a present sent to my lord Esau; and moreover he is behind us.' " ¹⁹He likewise instructed the second and the third and all who followed the droves, "You shall say the same thing to Esau when you meet him, ²⁰and you shall say, 'Moreover your servant Jacob is behind us.' " For he thought, "I may appease him with the present that goes ahead of me, and afterwards I shall see his face; perhaps

Letting Go of the Past

Jacob is understandably apprehensive as he approaches his long-estranged twin brother. How will Esau react? But Esau, who was wronged by Jacob, runs to meet him and gives him a hug. All is forgiven, and the two are reconciled at last. This story is like the parable of the prodigal son in Luke 15:11–32.

All of us have wronged others, especially the people we care about most. All of us have also experienced forgiveness. Nothing is quite like the freedom that comes with genuine forgiveness and reconciliation. A burden is lifted. A heavy heart is made lighter. A vengeful attitude is transformed into a feeling of inner peace and harmony. This is the work of God's grace. Forgiveness and reconciliation are powerful signs of the presence of God. We can almost feel the enormous sense of relief Jacob experiences as he realizes that his brother holds no grudge.

● Does a relationship in your life need forgiveness and reconciliation? If so, what can you do to bring about healing in this relationship?

▶ Gen 33:1–17

he will accept me." ²¹So the present passed on ahead of him; and he himself spent that night in the camp.

Jacob Wrestles at Peniel

22 The same night he got up and took his two wives, his two maids, and his eleven children, and crossed the ford of the Jabbok. ²³He took them and sent them across the stream, and likewise everything that he had. ²⁴Jacob was left alone; and a man wrestled with him until daybreak. ²⁵When the man saw that he did not prevail against Jacob, he struck him on the hip socket; and Jacob's hip was put out of joint as he wrestled with him. ²⁶Then he said, "Let me go, for the day is breaking." But Jacob said, "I will not let you go, unless you bless me." ²⁷So he said to him, "What is your name?" And he said, "Jacob." ²⁸Then the manᵃ said, "You shall no longer be called Jacob, but Israel,ᵇ for you have striven with God and with humans,ᶜ and have prevailed." ²⁹Then Jacob asked him, "Please tell me your name." But he said, "Why is it that you ask my name?" And there he blessed him. ³⁰So Jacob called the place Peniel,ᵈ saying, "For I have seen God face to face, and yet my life is preserved." ³¹The sun rose upon him as he passed Penuel, limping because of his hip. ³²Therefore to this day the Israelites do not eat the thigh muscle that is on the hip socket, because he struck Jacob on the hip socket at the thigh muscle.

Jacob and Esau Meet

33 Now Jacob looked up and saw Esau coming, and four hundred men with him. So he divided the children among Leah and Rachel and the two maids. ²He put the maids with their children in front, then Leah with her children, and Rachel and Joseph last of all. ³He himself went on ahead of them, bowing himself to the ground seven times, until he came near his brother.

4 But Esau ran to meet him, and embraced him, and fell on his neck and kissed him, and they wept. ⁵When Esau looked up and saw the women and children, he said, "Who are these with you?" Jacob said, "The children whom God has graciously given your servant." ⁶Then the maids drew near, they and their children, and bowed down; ⁷Leah likewise and her children drew near and bowed down; and finally Joseph and Rachel drew near, and they bowed down. ⁸Esau said, "What do you mean by all this company that I met?" Jacob answered, "To find favor

---

a Heb *he*   b That is *The one who strives with God* or *God strives*
c Or *with divine and human beings*   d That is *The face of God*

with my lord." [9]But Esau said, "I have enough, my brother; keep what you have for yourself." [10]Jacob said, "No, please; if I find favor with you, then accept my present from my hand; for truly to see your face is like seeing the face of God—since you have received me with such favor. [11]Please accept my gift that is brought to you, because God has dealt graciously with me, and because I have everything I want." So he urged him, and he took it.

12 Then Esau said, "Let us journey on our way, and I will go alongside you." [13]But Jacob said to him, "My lord knows that the children are frail and that the flocks and herds, which are nursing, are a care to me; and if they are over-driven for one day, all the flocks will die. [14]Let my lord pass on ahead of his servant, and I will lead on slowly, according to the pace of the cattle that are before me and according to the pace of the children, until I come to my lord in Seir."

15 So Esau said, "Let me leave with you some of the people who are with me." But he said, "Why should my lord be so kind to me?" [16]So Esau returned that day on his way to Seir. [17]But Jacob journeyed to Succoth,[a] and built himself a house, and made booths for his cattle; therefore the place is called Succoth.

Jacob Reaches Shechem

18 Jacob came safely to the city of Shechem, which is in the land of Canaan, on his way from Paddan-aram; and he camped before the city. [19]And from the sons of Hamor, Shechem's father, he bought for one hundred pieces of money[b] the plot of land on which he had pitched his tent. [20]There he erected an altar and called it El-Elohe-Israel.[c]

The Rape of Dinah

34 Now Dinah the daughter of Leah, whom she had borne to Jacob, went out to visit the women of the region. [2]When Shechem son of Hamor the Hivite, prince of the region, saw her, he seized her and lay with her by force. [3]And his soul was drawn to Dinah daughter of Jacob; he loved the girl, and spoke tenderly to her. [4]So Shechem spoke to his father Hamor, saying, "Get me this girl to be my wife."

5 Now Jacob heard that Shechem[d] had defiled his daughter Dinah; but his sons were with his cattle in the field, so Jacob held his peace until they came. [6]And Hamor the father of Shechem went out to Jacob to speak with him, [7]just as the sons of Jacob came in from the field. When they heard of it, the men were indignant and very angry, because he had committed an outrage in

Live It!

No Way, Shechem!

Every now and then there will be a news story about someone being attacked by another person or one ethnic group attacking another group, and sometimes part of their domination and victory includes rape. This is an especially evil act because it combines brutal violence with sex. Any time a woman is raped, she is violated against her will, and she can never be the same. Males can also be victims of rape.

The story in Genesis, chapter 34, tells us of Shechem, a local prince, who rapes Dinah. Because of his power, Shechem figures he can do what he wants to her. But in the end, his life is taken.

Rape is a violent and sinful act, no matter what the context. We are to respect one another, no matter what. Position or power does not give us the right to commit sexual violence. Rape and any other sexual abuse are an outrage to God.

▶ Gen 34:1–31

Israel by lying with Jacob's daughter, for such a thing ought not to be done.

8 But Hamor spoke with them, saying, "The heart of my son Shechem longs for your daughter; please give her to him in marriage. [9]Make marriages with us; give your daughters to us, and take our daughters for yourselves. [10]You shall live with us; and the land shall be open to you; live and trade in it, and get property in it." [11]Shechem also said to her father and to her brothers, "Let me find favor with you, and whatever you say to me I will give. [12]Put the marriage present and gift as high as you like, and I will give whatever you ask me; only give me the girl to be my wife."

13 The sons of Jacob answered Shechem and his father Hamor deceitfully, because he had defiled their sister Dinah. [14]They said to them, "We cannot do this thing, to give our sister to one who is uncircumcised, for that would be a disgrace to

---

a That is *Booths*   *b* Heb one hundred *qesitah*   *c* That is *God, the God of Israel*   *d* Heb he

us. 15Only on this condition will we consent to you: that you will become as we are and every male among you be circumcised. 16Then we will give our daughters to you, and we will take your daughters for ourselves, and we will live among you and become one people. 17But if you will not listen to us and be circumcised, then we will take our daughter and be gone."

18 Their words pleased Hamor and Hamor's son Shechem. 19And the young man did not delay to do the thing, because he was delighted with Jacob's daughter. Now he was the most honored of all his family. 20So Hamor and his son Shechem came to the gate of their city and spoke to the men of their city, saying, 21"These people are friendly with us; let them live in the land and trade in it, for the land is large enough for them; let us take their daughters in marriage, and let us give them our daughters. 22Only on this condition will they agree to live among us, to become one people: that every male among us be circumcised as they are circumcised. 23Will not their livestock, their property, and all their animals be ours? Only let us agree with them, and they will live among us." 24And all who went out of the city gate heeded Hamor and his son Shechem; and every male was circumcised, all who went out of the gate of his city.

Dinah's Brothers Avenge Their Sister

25 On the third day, when they were still in pain, two of the sons of Jacob, Simeon and Levi, Dinah's brothers, took their swords and came against the city unawares, and killed all the males. 26They killed Hamor and his son Shechem with the sword, and took Dinah out of Shechem's house, and went away. 27And the other sons of Jacob came upon the slain, and plundered the city, because their sister had been defiled. 28They took their flocks and their herds, their donkeys, and whatever was in the city and in the field. 29All their wealth, all their little ones and their wives, all that was in the houses, they captured and made their prey. 30Then Jacob said to Simeon and Levi, "You have brought trouble on me by making me odious to the inhabitants of the land, the Canaanites and the Perizzites; my numbers are few, and if they gather themselves against me and attack me, I shall be destroyed, both I and my household." 31But they said, "Should our sister be treated like a whore?"

Jacob Returns to Bethel

35 God said to Jacob, "Arise, go up to Bethel, and settle there. Make an altar there to the God who appeared to you when you fled from your brother Esau." 2So Jacob said to his household and to all who were with him, "Put away the foreign gods that are among you, and purify yourselves, and change your clothes; 3then come, let us go up to Bethel, that I may make an altar there to the God who answered me in the day of my distress and has been with me wherever I have gone." 4So they gave to Jacob all the foreign gods that they had, and the rings that were in their ears; and Jacob hid them under the oak that was near Shechem.

5 As they journeyed, a terror from God fell upon the cities all around them, so that no one pursued them. 6Jacob came to Luz (that is, Bethel), which is in the land of Canaan, he and all the people who were with him, 7and there he built an altar and called the place El-bethel,a because it was there that God had revealed himself to him when he fled from his brother. 8And Deborah, Rebekah's nurse, died, and she was buried under an oak below Bethel. So it was called Allon-bacuth.b

9 God appeared to Jacob again when he came from Paddan-aram, and he blessed him. 10God said to him, "Your name is Jacob; no longer shall you be called Jacob, but Israel shall be your name." So he was called Israel. 11God said to him, "I am God Almighty:c be fruitful and multiply; a nation and a company of nations shall come from you, and kings shall spring from you. 12The land that I gave to Abraham and Isaac I will give to you, and I will give the land to your offspring after you." 13Then God went up from him at the place where he had spoken with him. 14Jacob set up a pillar in the place where he had spoken with him, a pillar of stone; and he poured out a drink offering on it, and poured oil on it. 15So Jacob called the place where God had spoken with him Bethel.

The Birth of Benjamin and the Death of Rachel

16 Then they journeyed from Bethel; and when they were still some distance from Ephrath, Rachel was in childbirth, and she had hard labor. 17When she was in her hard labor, the midwife said to her, "Do not be afraid; for now you will have another son." 18As her soul was departing (for she died), she named him Ben-oni;d but his father called him Benjamin.e 19So Rachel died, and she was buried on the way to Ephrath (that is, Bethlehem), 20and Jacob set up a pillar at her grave; it is the pillar of Rachel's tomb, which is there to this day. 21Israel journeyed on, and pitched his tent beyond the tower of Eder.

---

a That is *God of Bethel*   b That is *Oak of weeping*
c Traditional rendering of Heb *El Shaddai*   d That is *Son of my sorrow*   e That is *Son of the right hand* or *Son of the South*

22 While Israel lived in that land, Reuben went and lay with Bilhah his father's concubine; and Israel heard of it.

Now the sons of Jacob were twelve. 23The sons of Leah: Reuben (Jacob's firstborn), Simeon, Levi, Judah, Issachar, and Zebulun. 24The sons of Rachel: Joseph and Benjamin. 25The sons of Bilhah, Rachel's maid: Dan and Naphtali. 26The sons of Zilpah, Leah's maid: Gad and Asher. These were the sons of Jacob who were born to him in Paddan-aram.

The Death of Isaac

27 Jacob came to his father Isaac at Mamre, or Kiriath-arba (that is, Hebron), where Abraham and Isaac had resided as aliens. 28Now the days of Isaac were one hundred eighty years. 29And Isaac breathed his last; he died and was gathered to his people, old and full of days; and his sons Esau and Jacob buried him.

Esau's Descendants

36 These are the descendants of Esau (that is, Edom). 2Esau took his wives from the Canaanites: Adah daughter of Elon the Hittite, Oholibamah daughter of Anah son^a of Zibeon the Hivite, 3and Basemath, Ishmael's daughter, sister of Nebaioth. 4Adah bore Eliphaz to Esau; Basemath bore Reuel; 5and Oholibamah bore Jeush, Jalam, and Korah. These are the sons of Esau who were born to him in the land of Canaan.

6 Then Esau took his wives, his sons, his daughters, and all the members of his household, his cattle, all his livestock, and all the property he had acquired in the land of Canaan; and he moved to a land some distance from his brother Jacob. 7For their possessions were too great for them to live together; the land where they were staying could not support them because of their livestock. 8So Esau settled in the hill country of Seir; Esau is Edom.

9 These are the descendants of Esau, ancestor of the Edomites, in the hill country of Seir. 10These are the names of Esau's sons: Eliphaz son of Adah the wife of Esau; Reuel, the son of Esau's wife Basemath. 11The sons of Eliphaz were Teman, Omar, Zepho, Gatam, and Kenaz. 12(Timna was a concubine of Eliphaz, Esau's son; she bore Amalek to Eliphaz.) These were the sons of Adah, Esau's wife. 13These were the sons of Reuel: Nahath, Zerah, Shammah, and Mizzah. These were the sons of Esau's wife, Basemath. 14These were the sons of Esau's wife Oholibamah, daughter of Anah son^b of Zibeon: she bore to Esau Jeush, Jalam, and Korah.

Clans and Kings of Edom

15 These are the clans^c of the sons of Esau. The sons of Eliphaz the firstborn of Esau: the clans^c Teman, Omar, Zepho, Kenaz, 16Korah, Gatam, and Amalek; these are the clans^c of Eliphaz in the land of Edom; they are the sons of Adah. 17These are the sons of Esau's son Reuel: the clans^c Nahath, Zerah, Shammah, and Mizzah; these are the clans^c of Reuel in the land of Edom; they are the sons of Esau's wife Basemath. 18These are the sons of Esau's wife Oholibamah: the clans^c Jeush, Jalam, and Korah; these are the clans^c born of Esau's wife Oholibamah, the daughter of Anah. 19These are the sons of Esau (that is, Edom), and these are their clans.^c

20 These are the sons of Seir the Horite, the inhabitants of the land: Lotan, Shobal, Zibeon, Anah, 21Dishon, Ezer, and Dishan; these are the clans^c of the Horites, the sons of Seir in the land of Edom. 22The sons of Lotan were Hori and Heman; and Lotan's sister was Timna. 23These are the sons of Shobal: Alvan, Manahath, Ebal, Shepho, and Onam. 24These are the sons of Zibeon: Aiah and Anah; he is the Anah who found the springs^d in the wilderness, as he pastured the donkeys of his father Zibeon. 25These are the children of Anah: Dishon and Oholibamah daughter of Anah. 26These are the sons of Dishon: Hemdan, Eshban, Ithran, and Cheran. 27These are the sons of Ezer: Bilhan, Zaavan, and Akan. 28These are the sons of Dishan: Uz and Aran. 29These are the clans^c of the Horites: the clans^c Lotan, Shobal, Zibeon, Anah, 30Dishon, Ezer, and Dishan; these are the clans^c of the Horites, clan by clan^e in the land of Seir.

31 These are the kings who reigned in the land of Edom, before any king reigned over the Israelites. 32Bela son of Beor reigned in Edom, the name of his city being Dinhabah. 33Bela died, and Jobab son of Zerah of Bozrah succeeded him as king. 34Jobab died, and Husham of the land of the Temanites succeeded him as king. 35Husham died, and Hadad son of Bedad, who defeated Midian in the country of Moab, succeeded him as king, the name of his city being Avith. 36Hadad died, and Samlah of Masrekah succeeded him as king. 37Samlah died, and Shaul of Rehoboth on the Euphrates succeeded him as king. 38Shaul died, and Baal-hanan son of Achbor succeeded him as king. 39Baal-hanan son of Achbor died, and Hadar succeeded him as king, the name of his city being Pau; his wife's name

---

^a Sam Gk Syr: Heb *daughter*   ^b Gk Syr: Heb *daughter*
^c Or *chiefs*   ^d Meaning of Heb uncertain   ^e Or *chief by chief*

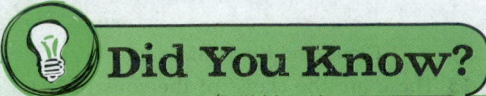

Did You Know?

Dreams

In the ancient world, belief in the reality and significance of dreams was widespread. The ancients believed that dreams and visions revealed messages, prophecies, and healing from their gods. Israel shared this view of the importance of dreams. Joseph is described as an interpreter of dreams, and this skill earns him Pharaoh's respect (see Gen 41:37–45), as well as his brothers' jealousy (see 37:5–11).

In the Old Testament, the prophets are often referred to as seers because the word of God so often comes to them through dreams and visions. The focus, however, is always on the word of God and its meaning, not on the dream itself. In fact, a character in the story, inspired by God, usually interprets the dream, which aims to lead the people to more faithful observance of the covenant. If the dream does not do this, it is to be considered a false dream. (See other references to dreams in Genesis 28:10–22; Deuteronomy 13:2–6; Sirach 34:1–4; Jeremiah 27:9–10, 29:8–9; Joel 2:28; Zechariah 1:8; and Matthew 1:20, 2:13.)

▶ **Gen 37:1–11; 40:1—41:36**

was Mehetabel, the daughter of Matred, daughter of Me-zahab.

40 These are the names of the clans[a] of Esau, according to their families and their localities by their names: the clans[a] Timna, Alvah, Jetheth, 41Oholibamah, Elah, Pinon, 42Kenaz, Teman, Mibzar, 43Magdiel, and Iram; these are the clans[a] of Edom (that is, Esau, the father of Edom), according to their settlements in the land that they held.

Joseph Dreams of Greatness

37 Jacob settled in the land where his father had lived as an alien, the land of Canaan. 2This is the story of the family of Jacob.

Joseph, being seventeen years old, was shepherding the flock with his brothers; he was a helper to the sons of Bilhah and Zilpah, his father's wives; and Joseph brought a bad report of them to their father. 3Now Israel loved Joseph more than any other of his children, because he was the son of his old age; and he had made him a long robe with sleeves.[b] 4But when his brothers saw that their father loved him more than all his brothers, they hated him, and could not speak peaceably to him.

5 Once Joseph had a dream, and when he told it to his brothers, they hated him even more. 6He said to them, "Listen to this dream that I dreamed. 7There we were, binding sheaves in the field. Suddenly my sheaf rose and stood upright; then your sheaves gathered around it, and bowed down to my sheaf." 8His brothers said to him, "Are you indeed to reign over us? Are you indeed to have dominion over us?" So they hated him even more because of his dreams and his words.

9 He had another dream, and told it to his brothers, saying, "Look, I have had another dream: the sun, the moon, and eleven stars were bowing down to me." 10But when he told it to his father and to his brothers, his father rebuked him, and said to him, "What kind of dream is this that you have had? Shall we indeed come, I and your mother and your brothers, and bow to the ground before you?" 11So his brothers were jealous of him, but his father kept the matter in mind.

Joseph Is Sold by His Brothers

12 Now his brothers went to pasture their father's flock near Shechem. 13And Israel said to Joseph, "Are not your brothers pasturing the flock at Shechem? Come, I will send you to them." He answered, "Here I am." 14So he said to him, "Go now, see if it is well with your brothers and with the flock; and bring word back to me." So he sent him from the valley of Hebron.

He came to Shechem, 15and a man found him wandering in the fields; the man asked him, "What are you seeking?" 16"I am seeking my brothers," he said; "tell me, please, where they are pasturing the flock." 17The man said, "They have gone away, for I heard them say, 'Let us go to Dothan.' " So Joseph went after his brothers, and found them at Dothan. 18They saw him from a distance, and before he came near to them, they conspired to kill him. 19They said to one another, "Here comes this dreamer. 20Come now, let us kill him and throw him into one of the pits; then we shall say that a wild animal has devoured him, and we shall see what will become of his dreams." 21But when Reuben heard it, he delivered him out of their hands, saying, "Let us not take his life." 22Reuben said to them, "Shed

---

a Or chiefs   b Traditional rendering (compare Gk): a coat of many colors; meaning of Heb uncertain

no blood; throw him into this pit here in the wilderness, but lay no hand on him"—that he might rescue him out of their hand and restore him to his father. ²³So when Joseph came to his brothers, they stripped him of his robe, the long robe with sleeves*a* that he wore; ²⁴and they took him and threw him into a pit. The pit was empty; there was no water in it.

25 Then they sat down to eat; and looking up they saw a caravan of Ishmaelites coming from Gilead, with their camels carrying gum, balm, and resin, on their way to carry it down to Egypt. ²⁶Then Judah said to his brothers, "What profit is it if we kill our brother and conceal his blood? ²⁷Come, let us sell him to the Ishmaelites, and not lay our hands on him, for he is our brother, our own flesh." And his brothers agreed. ²⁸When some Midianite traders passed by, they drew Joseph up, lifting him out of the pit, and sold him to the Ishmaelites for twenty pieces of silver. And they took Joseph to Egypt.

29 When Reuben returned to the pit and saw that Joseph was not in the pit, he tore his clothes. ³⁰He returned to his brothers, and said, "The boy is gone; and I, where can I turn?" ³¹Then they took Joseph's robe, slaughtered a goat, and dipped the robe in the blood. ³²They had the long robe with sleeves*a* taken to their father, and they said, "This we have found; see now whether it is your son's robe or not." ³³He recognized it, and said, "It is my son's robe! A wild animal has devoured him; Joseph is without doubt torn to pieces." ³⁴Then Jacob tore his garments, and put sackcloth on his loins, and mourned for his son many days. ³⁵All his sons and all his daughters sought to comfort him; but he refused to be comforted, and said, "No, I shall go down to Sheol to my son, mourning." Thus his father bewailed him. ³⁶Meanwhile the Midianites had sold him in Egypt to Potiphar, one of Pharaoh's officials, the captain of the guard.

Judah and Tamar

38 It happened at that time that Judah went down from his brothers and settled near a certain Adullamite whose name was Hirah. ²There Judah saw the daughter of a certain Canaanite whose name was Shua; he married her and went in to her. ³She conceived and bore a son; and he named him Er. ⁴Again she conceived and bore a son whom she named Onan. ⁵Yet again she bore a son, and she named him Shelah. She*b* was in Chezib when she bore him. ⁶Judah took a wife for Er his firstborn; her name was Tamar. ⁷But Er, Judah's firstborn, was wicked in the sight of the LORD, and the LORD put him

to death. ⁸Then Judah said to Onan, "Go in to your brother's wife and perform the duty of a brother-in-law to her; raise up offspring for your brother." ⁹But since Onan knew that the offspring would not be his, he spilled his semen on the ground whenever he went in to his brother's wife, so that he would not give offspring to his brother. ¹⁰What he did was displeasing in the sight of the LORD, and he put him to death also. ¹¹Then Judah said to his daughter-in-law Tamar, "Remain a widow in your father's house until my son Shelah grows up"—for he feared that he too would die, like his brothers. So Tamar went to live in her father's house.

12 In course of time the wife of Judah, Shua's daughter, died; when Judah's time of mourning

---

a See note on 37.3   *b* Gk: Heb *He*

Joseph

The timeless power of Joseph's story is reaffirmed by the long and successful run of the Broadway play *Joseph and the Amazing Technicolor Dreamcoat.* (In other Bible versions, the "long robe with sleeves" in Genesis 37:3 is translated as a "coat of many colors.") The play is based on chapters 37–50 of Genesis, which contain one of the world's greatest stories of family, jealousy, betrayal, and forgiveness.

A son of Jacob and Rachel, Joseph carries to Egypt the divine promises of land and descendants, and eventually becomes the link with the story of Moses and the Exodus. As Jacob's favorite son, Joseph experiences the jealousy of his brothers, who sell him to Egyptian merchants. In Egypt, Joseph rises to power, becoming second in command to the pharaoh. Later, when Joseph's brothers come to Egypt looking for food, he forgives them and becomes reconciled with them.

Joseph's story encourages us to forgive others, even when we have been unjustly treated by them. Whenever we have been greatly wronged, remembering Joseph will offer us hope and courage.

▶ **Gen 37:1—50:26**

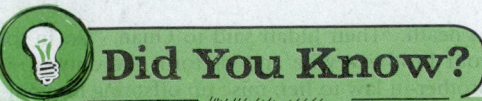

Did You Know?

Levirate Marriage

Why does Onan have to marry his dead brother's wife and have a son by her? One of the laws specified in Deuteronomy 25:5–10 regulates what is called levirate marriage. *Levirate* means "brother-in-law." When a man's married brother dies without a son, that man is obligated to marry the wife who was left, and the first son whom she bears shall "succeed to the name of the deceased" (verse 6). This marriage practice seems to have developed in Israel for several reasons:

- A male child was needed to be heir to the dead man's property because women generally did not own property.
- The dead man's widow needed support and protection.
- A male heir ensured that the family property was kept within the immediate family.

▶ **Gen 38:8**

---

was over,[a] he went up to Timnah to his sheep-shearers, he and his friend Hirah the Adullamite. [13]When Tamar was told, "Your father-in-law is going up to Timnah to shear his sheep," [14]she put off her widow's garments, put on a veil, wrapped herself up, and sat down at the entrance to Enaim, which is on the road to Timnah. She saw that Shelah was grown up, yet she had not been given to him in marriage. [15]When Judah saw her, he thought her to be a prostitute, for she had covered her face. [16]He went over to her at the roadside, and said, "Come, let me come in to you," for he did not know that she was his daughter-in-law. She said, "What will you give me, that you may come in to me?" [17]He answered, "I will send you a kid from the flock." And she said, "Only if you give me a pledge, until you send it." [18]He said, "What pledge shall I give you?" She replied, "Your signet and your cord, and the staff that is in your hand." So he gave them to her, and went in to her, and she conceived by him. [19]Then she got up and went away, and taking off her veil she put on the garments of her widowhood.

20 When Judah sent the kid by his friend the Adullamite, to recover the pledge from the woman, he could not find her. [21]He asked the townspeople, "Where is the temple prostitute who was at Enaim by the wayside?" But they said, "No prostitute has been here." [22]So he returned to Judah, and said, "I have not found her; moreover the townspeople said, 'No prostitute has been here.'" [23]Judah replied, "Let her keep the things as her own, otherwise we will be laughed at; you see, I sent this kid, and you could not find her."

24 About three months later Judah was told, "Your daughter-in-law Tamar has played the whore; moreover she is pregnant as a result of whoredom." And Judah said, "Bring her out, and let her be burned." [25]As she was being brought out, she sent word to her father-in-law, "It was the owner of these who made me pregnant." And she said, "Take note, please, whose these are, the signet and the cord and the staff." [26]Then Judah acknowledged them and said, "She is more in the right than I, since I did not give her to my son Shelah." And he did not lie with her again.

27 When the time of her delivery came, there were twins in her womb. [28]While she was in labor, one put out a hand; and the midwife took and bound on his hand a crimson thread, saying, "This one came out first." [29]But just then he drew back his hand, and out came his brother; and she said, "What a breach you have made for yourself!" Therefore he was named Perez.[b] [30]Afterward his brother came out with the crimson thread on his hand; and he was named Zerah.[c]

Joseph and Potiphar's Wife

39 Now Joseph was taken down to Egypt, and Potiphar, an officer of Pharaoh, the captain of the guard, an Egyptian, bought him from the Ishmaelites who had brought him down there. [2]The LORD was with Joseph, and he became a successful man; he was in the house of his Egyptian master. [3]His master saw that the LORD was with him, and that the LORD caused all that he did to prosper in his hands. [4]So Joseph found favor in his sight and attended him; he made him overseer of his house and put him in charge of all that he had. [5]From the time that he made him overseer in his house and over all that he had, the LORD blessed the Egyptian's house for Joseph's sake; the blessing of the LORD was on all that he had, in house and field. [6]So he left all that he had in Joseph's charge; and, with him there, he had no concern for anything but the food that he ate.

---

a Heb *when Judah was comforted*   b That is *A breach*   c That is *Brightness*; perhaps alluding to the crimson thread

Now Joseph was handsome and good-looking. [7]And after a time his master's wife cast her eyes on Joseph and said, "Lie with me." [8]But he refused and said to his master's wife, "Look, with me here, my master has no concern about anything in the house, and he has put everything that he has in my hand. [9]He is not greater in this house than I am, nor has he kept back anything from me except yourself, because you are his wife. How then could I do this great wickedness, and sin against God?" [10]And although she spoke to Joseph day after day, he would not consent to lie beside her or to be with her. [11]One day, however, when he went into the house to do his work, and while no one else was in the house, [12]she caught hold of his garment, saying, "Lie with me!" But he left his garment in her hand, and fled and ran outside. [13]When she saw that he had left his garment in her hand and had fled outside, [14]she called out to the members of her household and said to them, "See, my husband[a] has brought among us a Hebrew to insult us! He came in to me to lie with me, and I cried out with a loud voice; [15]and when he heard me raise my voice and cry out, he left his garment beside me, and fled outside." [16]Then she kept his garment by her until his master came home, [17]and she told him the same story, saying, "The Hebrew servant, whom you have brought among us, came in to me to insult me; [18]but as soon as I raised my voice and cried out, he left his garment beside me, and fled outside."

19 When his master heard the words that his wife spoke to him, saying, "This is the way your servant treated me," he became enraged. [20]And Joseph's master took him and put him into the prison, the place where the king's prisoners were confined; he remained there in prison. [21]But the LORD was with Joseph and showed him steadfast love; he gave him favor in the sight of the chief jailer. [22]The chief jailer committed to Joseph's care all the prisoners who were in the prison, and whatever was done there, he was the one who did it. [23]The chief jailer paid no heed to anything that was in Joseph's care, because the LORD was with him; and whatever he did, the LORD made it prosper.

The Dreams of Two Prisoners

40 Some time after this, the cupbearer of the king of Egypt and his baker offended their lord the king of Egypt. [2]Pharaoh was angry with his two officers, the chief cupbearer and the chief baker, [3]and he put them in custody in the house of the captain of the guard, in the prison where Joseph was confined. [4]The captain of the guard charged Joseph with them, and he waited on them; and they continued for some time in custody. [5]One night they both dreamed—the cupbearer and the baker of the king of Egypt, who were confined in the prison—each his own dream, and each dream with its own meaning. [6]When Joseph came to them in the morning, he saw that they were troubled. [7]So he asked Pharaoh's officers, who were with him in custody in his master's house, "Why are your faces downcast today?" [8]They said to him, "We have had dreams, and there is no one to interpret them." And Joseph said to them, "Do not interpretations belong to God? Please tell them to me."

9 So the chief cupbearer told his dream to Joseph, and said to him, "In my dream there was a vine before me, [10]and on the vine there were three branches. As soon as it budded, its blossoms came out and the clusters ripened into grapes. [11]Pharaoh's cup was in my hand; and I took the grapes and pressed them into Pharaoh's cup, and placed the cup in Pharaoh's hand." [12]Then Joseph said to him, "This is its interpretation: the three branches are three days; [13]within three days Pharaoh will lift up your head and restore you to your office; and you shall place Pharaoh's cup in his hand, just as you used to do when you were his cupbearer. [14]But remember me when it is well with you; please do me the kindness to make mention of me to Pharaoh, and so get me out of this place. [15]For in fact I was stolen out of the land of the Hebrews; and here also I have done nothing that they should have put me into the dungeon."

16 When the chief baker saw that the interpretation was favorable, he said to Joseph, "I also had a dream: there were three cake baskets on my head, [17]and in the uppermost basket there were all sorts of baked food for Pharaoh, but the birds were eating it out of the basket on my head." [18]And Joseph answered, "This is its interpretation: the three baskets are three days; [19]within three days Pharaoh will lift up your head—from you!—and hang you on a pole; and the birds will eat the flesh from you."

20 On the third day, which was Pharaoh's birthday, he made a feast for all his servants, and lifted up the head of the chief cupbearer and the head of the chief baker among his servants. [21]He restored the chief cupbearer to his cupbearing, and he placed the cup in Pharaoh's hand; [22]but the chief baker he hanged, just as Joseph had interpreted to them. [23]Yet the chief cupbearer did not remember Joseph, but forgot him.

a Heb *he*

GEN

Joseph Interprets Pharaoh's Dream

41 After two whole years, Pharaoh dreamed that he was standing by the Nile, ²and there came up out of the Nile seven sleek and fat cows, and they grazed in the reed grass. ³Then seven other cows, ugly and thin, came up out of the Nile after them, and stood by the other cows on the bank of the Nile. ⁴The ugly and thin cows ate up the seven sleek and fat cows. And Pharaoh awoke. ⁵Then he fell asleep and dreamed a second time; seven ears of grain, plump and good, were growing on one stalk. ⁶Then seven ears, thin and blighted by the east wind, sprouted after them. ⁷The thin ears swallowed up the seven plump and full ears. Pharaoh awoke, and it was a dream. ⁸In the morning his spirit was troubled; so he sent and called for all the magicians of Egypt and all its wise men. Pharaoh told them his dreams, but there was no one who could interpret them to Pharaoh.

9 Then the chief cupbearer said to Pharaoh, "I remember my faults today. ¹⁰Once Pharaoh was angry with his servants, and put me and the chief baker in custody in the house of the captain of the guard. ¹¹We dreamed on the same night, he and I, each having a dream with its own meaning. ¹²A young Hebrew was there with us, a servant of the captain of the guard. When we told him, he interpreted our dreams to us, giving an interpretation to each according to his dream. ¹³As he interpreted to us, so it turned out; I was restored to my office, and the baker was hanged."

14 Then Pharaoh sent for Joseph, and he was hurriedly brought out of the dungeon. When he had shaved himself and changed his clothes, he came in before Pharaoh. ¹⁵And Pharaoh said to Joseph, "I have had a dream, and there is no one who can interpret it. I have heard it said of you that when you hear a dream you can interpret it." ¹⁶Joseph answered Pharaoh, "It is not I; God will give Pharaoh a favorable answer." ¹⁷Then Pharaoh said to Joseph, "In my dream I was standing on the banks of the Nile; ¹⁸and seven cows, fat and sleek, came up out of the Nile and fed in the reed grass. ¹⁹Then seven other cows came up after them, poor, very ugly, and thin. Never had I seen such ugly ones in all the land of Egypt. ²⁰The thin and ugly cows ate up the first seven fat cows, ²¹but when they had eaten them no one would have known that they had done so, for they were still as ugly as before. Then I awoke. ²²I fell asleep a second time[a] and I saw in my dream seven ears of grain, full and good, growing on one stalk, ²³and seven ears,

withered, thin, and blighted by the east wind, sprouting after them; ²⁴and the thin ears swallowed up the seven good ears. But when I told it to the magicians, there was no one who could explain it to me."

25 Then Joseph said to Pharaoh, "Pharaoh's dreams are one and the same; God has revealed to Pharaoh what he is about to do. ²⁶The seven good cows are seven years, and the seven good ears are seven years; the dreams are one. ²⁷The seven lean and ugly cows that came up after them are seven years, as are the seven empty ears blighted by the east wind. They are seven years of famine. ²⁸It is as I told Pharaoh; God has shown to Pharaoh what he is about to do. ²⁹There will come seven years of great plenty throughout all the land of Egypt. ³⁰After them there will arise seven years of famine, and all the plenty will be forgotten in the land of Egypt; the famine will consume the land. ³¹The plenty will no longer be known in the land because of the famine that will follow, for it will be very grievous. ³²And the doubling of Pharaoh's dream means that the thing is fixed by God, and God will shortly bring it about. ³³Now therefore let Pharaoh select a man who is discerning and wise, and set him over the land of Egypt. ³⁴Let Pharaoh proceed to appoint overseers over the land, and take one-fifth of the produce of the land of Egypt during the seven plenteous years. ³⁵Let them gather all the food of these good years that are coming, and lay up grain under the authority of Pharaoh for food in the cities, and let them keep it. ³⁶That food shall be a reserve for the land against the seven years of famine that are to befall the land of Egypt, so that the land may not perish through the famine."

Joseph's Rise to Power

37 The proposal pleased Pharaoh and all his servants. ³⁸Pharaoh said to his servants, "Can we find anyone else like this—one in whom is the spirit of God?" ³⁹So Pharaoh said to Joseph, "Since God has shown you all this, there is no one so discerning and wise as you. ⁴⁰You shall be over my house, and all my people shall order themselves as you command; only with regard to the throne will I be greater than you." ⁴¹And Pharaoh said to Joseph, "See, I have set you over all the land of Egypt." ⁴²Removing his signet ring from his hand, Pharaoh put it on Joseph's hand; he arrayed him in garments of fine linen, and put a gold chain around his neck. ⁴³He had him ride in the chariot of his second-in-command; and

---

a Gk Syr Vg: Heb lacks *I fell asleep a second time*

they cried out in front of him, "Bow the knee!"*a* Thus he set him over all the land of Egypt. [44]Moreover Pharaoh said to Joseph, "I am Pharaoh, and without your consent no one shall lift up hand or foot in all the land of Egypt." [45]Pharaoh gave Joseph the name Zaphenath-paneah; and he gave him Asenath daughter of Potiphera, priest of On, as his wife. Thus Joseph gained authority over the land of Egypt.

[46] Joseph was thirty years old when he entered the service of Pharaoh king of Egypt. And Joseph went out from the presence of Pharaoh, and went through all the land of Egypt. [47]During the seven plenteous years the earth produced abundantly. [48]He gathered up all the food of the seven years when there was plenty*b* in the land of Egypt, and stored up food in the cities; he stored up in every city the food from the fields around it. [49]So Joseph stored up grain in such abundance—like the sand of the sea—that he stopped measuring it; it was beyond measure.

[50] Before the years of famine came, Joseph had two sons, whom Asenath daughter of Potiphera, priest of On, bore to him. [51]Joseph named the firstborn Manasseh,*c* "For," he said, "God has made me forget all my hardship and all my father's house." [52]The second he named Ephraim,*d* "For God has made me fruitful in the land of my misfortunes."

[53] The seven years of plenty that prevailed in the land of Egypt came to an end; [54]and the seven years of famine began to come, just as Joseph had said. There was famine in every country, but throughout the land of Egypt there was bread. [55]When all the land of Egypt was famished, the people cried to Pharaoh for bread. Pharaoh said to all the Egyptians, "Go to Joseph; what he says to you, do." [56]And since the famine had spread over all the land, Joseph opened all the storehouses,*e* and sold to the Egyptians, for the famine was severe in the land of Egypt. [57]Moreover, all the world came to Joseph in Egypt to buy grain, because the famine became severe throughout the world.

Joseph's Brothers Go to Egypt

42 When Jacob learned that there was grain in Egypt, he said to his sons, "Why do you keep looking at one another? [2]I have heard," he said, "that there is grain in Egypt; go down and buy grain for us there, that we may live and not die." [3]So ten of Joseph's brothers went down to buy grain in Egypt. [4]But Jacob did not send Joseph's brother Benjamin with his brothers, for he feared that harm might come to him. [5]Thus the sons of Israel were among the other people who came to buy grain, for the famine had reached the land of Canaan.

[6] Now Joseph was governor over the land; it was he who sold to all the people of the land. And Joseph's brothers came and bowed themselves before him with their faces to the ground. [7]When Joseph saw his brothers, he recognized them, but he treated them like strangers and spoke harshly to them. "Where do you come from?" he said. They said, "From the land of Canaan, to buy food." [8]Although Joseph had recognized his brothers, they did not recognize him. [9]Joseph also remembered the dreams that he had dreamed about them. He said to them, "You are spies; you have come to see the nakedness of the land!" [10]They said to him, "No, my lord; your servants have come to buy food. [11]We are all sons of one man; we are honest men; your servants have never been spies." [12]But he said to them, "No, you have come to see the nakedness of the land!" [13]They said, "We, your servants, are twelve brothers, the sons of a certain man in the land of Canaan; the youngest, however, is now with our father, and one is no more." [14]But Joseph said to them, "It is just as I have said to you; you are spies! [15]Here is how you shall be tested: as Pharaoh lives, you shall not leave this place unless your youngest brother comes here! [16]Let one of you go and bring your brother, while the rest of you remain in prison, in order that your words may be tested, whether there is truth in you; or else, as Pharaoh lives, surely you are spies." [17]And he put them all together in prison for three days.

[18] On the third day Joseph said to them, "Do this and you will live, for I fear God: [19]if you are honest men, let one of your brothers stay here where you are imprisoned. The rest of you shall go and carry grain for the famine of your households, [20]and bring your youngest brother to me. Thus your words will be verified, and you shall not die." And they agreed to do so. [21]They said to one another, "Alas, we are paying the penalty for what we did to our brother; we saw his anguish when he pleaded with us, but we would not listen. That is why this anguish has come upon us." [22]Then Reuben answered them, "Did I not tell you not to wrong the boy? But you would not listen. So now there comes a reckoning for his blood." [23]They did not know that Joseph understood them, since he spoke with them through

---

a Abrek, apparently an Egyptian word similar in sound to the Hebrew word meaning *to kneel*   *b* Sam Gk: MT *the seven years that were*   *c* That is *Making to forget*   *d* From a Hebrew word meaning *to be fruitful*   *e* Gk Vg Compare Syr: Heb *opened all that was in* (or, *among*) *them*

an interpreter. ²⁴He turned away from them and wept; then he returned and spoke to them. And he picked out Simeon and had him bound before their eyes. ²⁵Joseph then gave orders to fill their bags with grain, to return every man's money to his sack, and to give them provisions for their journey. This was done for them.

Joseph's Brothers Return to Canaan

26 They loaded their donkeys with their grain, and departed. ²⁷When one of them opened his sack to give his donkey fodder at the lodging place, he saw his money at the top of the sack. ²⁸He said to his brothers, "My money has been put back; here it is in my sack!" At this they lost heart and turned trembling to one another, saying, "What is this that God has done to us?"

29 When they came to their father Jacob in the land of Canaan, they told him all that had happened to them, saying, ³⁰"The man, the lord of the land, spoke harshly to us, and charged us with spying on the land. ³¹But we said to him, 'We are honest men, we are not spies. ³²We are twelve brothers, sons of our father; one is no more, and the youngest is now with our father in the land of Canaan.' ³³Then the man, the lord of the land, said to us, 'By this I shall know that you are honest men: leave one of your brothers with me, take grain for the famine of your households, and go your way. ³⁴Bring your youngest brother to me, and I shall know that you are not spies but honest men. Then I will release your brother to you, and you may trade in the land.'"

35 As they were emptying their sacks, there in each one's sack was his bag of money. When they and their father saw their bundles of money, they were dismayed. ³⁶And their father Jacob said to them, "I am the one you have bereaved of children: Joseph is no more, and Simeon is no more, and now you would take Benjamin. All this has happened to me!" ³⁷Then Reuben said to his father, "You may kill my two sons if I do not bring him back to you. Put him in my hands, and I will bring him back to you." ³⁸But he said, "My son shall not go down with you, for his brother is dead, and he alone is left. If harm should come to him on the journey that you are to make, you would bring down my gray hairs with sorrow to Sheol."

The Brothers Come Again, Bringing Benjamin

43 Now the famine was severe in the land. ²And when they had eaten up the grain that they had brought from Egypt, their father said to them, "Go again, buy us a little more food." ³But Judah said to him, "The man

solemnly warned us, saying, 'You shall not see my face unless your brother is with you.' ⁴If you will send our brother with us, we will go down and buy you food; ⁵but if you will not send him, we will not go down, for the man said to us, 'You shall not see my face, unless your brother is with you.'" ⁶Israel said, "Why did you treat me so badly as to tell the man that you had another brother?" ⁷They replied, "The man questioned us carefully about ourselves and our kindred, saying, 'Is your father still alive? Have you another brother?' What we told him was in answer to these questions. Could we in any way know that he would say, 'Bring your brother down'?" ⁸Then Judah said to his father Israel, "Send the boy with me, and let us be on our way, so that we may live and not die—you and we and also our little ones. ⁹I myself will be surety for him; you can hold me accountable for him. If I do not bring him back to you and set him before you, then let me bear the blame forever. ¹⁰If we had not delayed, we would now have returned twice."

11 Then their father Israel said to them, "If it must be so, then do this: take some of the choice fruits of the land in your bags, and carry them down as a present to the man—a little balm and a little honey, gum, resin, pistachio nuts, and almonds. ¹²Take double the money with you. Carry back with you the money that was returned in the top of your sacks; perhaps it was an oversight. ¹³Take your brother also, and be on your way again to the man; ¹⁴may God Almighty[a] grant you mercy before the man, so that he may send back your other brother and Benjamin. As for me, if I am bereaved of my children, I am bereaved." ¹⁵So the men took the present, and they took double the money with them, as well as Benjamin. Then they went on their way down to Egypt, and stood before Joseph.

16 When Joseph saw Benjamin with them, he said to the steward of his house, "Bring the men into the house, and slaughter an animal and make ready, for the men are to dine with me at noon." ¹⁷The man did as Joseph said, and brought the men to Joseph's house. ¹⁸Now the men were afraid because they were brought to Joseph's house, and they said, "It is because of the money, replaced in our sacks the first time, that we have been brought in, so that he may have an opportunity to fall upon us, to make slaves of us and take our donkeys." ¹⁹So they went up to the steward of Joseph's house and spoke with him at the entrance to the house. ²⁰They said, "Oh, my lord, we came down the first time to

a Traditional rendering of Heb *El Shaddai*

buy food; ²¹and when we came to the lodging place we opened our sacks, and there was each one's money in the top of his sack, our money in full weight. So we have brought it back with us. ²²Moreover we have brought down with us additional money to buy food. We do not know who put our money in our sacks." ²³He replied, "Rest assured, do not be afraid; your God and the God of your father must have put treasure in your sacks for you; I received your money." Then he brought Simeon out to them. ²⁴When the steward[a] had brought the men into Joseph's house, and given them water, and they had washed their feet, and when he had given their donkeys fodder, ²⁵they made the present ready for Joseph's coming at noon, for they had heard that they would dine there.

26 When Joseph came home, they brought him the present that they had carried into the house, and bowed to the ground before him. ²⁷He inquired about their welfare, and said, "Is your father well, the old man of whom you spoke? Is he still alive?" ²⁸They said, "Your servant our father is well; he is still alive." And they bowed their heads and did obeisance. ²⁹Then he looked up and saw his brother Benjamin, his mother's son, and said, "Is this your youngest brother, of whom you spoke to me? God be gracious to you, my son!" ³⁰With that, Joseph hurried out, because he was overcome with affection for his brother, and he was about to weep. So he went into a private room and wept there. ³¹Then he washed his face and came out; and controlling himself he said, "Serve the meal." ³²They served him by himself, and them by themselves, and the Egyptians who ate with him by themselves, because the Egyptians could not eat with the Hebrews, for that is an abomination to the Egyptians. ³³When they were seated before him, the firstborn according to his birthright and the youngest according to his youth, the men looked at one another in amazement. ³⁴Portions were taken to them from Joseph's table, but Benjamin's portion was five times as much as any of theirs. So they drank and were merry with him.

Joseph Detains Benjamin

44 Then he commanded the steward of his house, "Fill the men's sacks with food, as much as they can carry, and put each man's money in the top of his sack. ²Put my cup, the silver cup, in the top of the sack of the youngest, with his money for the grain." And he did as Joseph told him. ³As soon as the morning was light, the men were sent away with their donkeys. ⁴When they had gone only a short distance from the city, Joseph said to his steward, "Go, follow after the men; and when you overtake them, say to them, 'Why have you returned evil for good? Why have you stolen my silver cup?[b] ⁵Is it not from this that my lord drinks? Does he not indeed use it for divination? You have done wrong in doing this.' "

6 When he overtook them, he repeated these words to them. ⁷They said to him, "Why does my lord speak such words as these? Far be it from your servants that they should do such a thing! ⁸Look, the money that we found at the top of our sacks, we brought back to you from the land of Canaan; why then would we steal silver or gold from your lord's house? ⁹Should it be found with any one of your servants, let him die; moreover the rest of us will become my lord's slaves." ¹⁰He said, "Even so; in accordance with your words, let it be: he with whom it is found shall become my slave, but the rest of you shall go free." ¹¹Then each one quickly lowered his sack to the ground, and each opened his sack. ¹²He searched, beginning with the eldest and ending with the youngest; and the cup was found in Benjamin's sack. ¹³At this they tore their clothes. Then each one loaded his donkey, and they returned to the city.

14 Judah and his brothers came to Joseph's house while he was still there; and they fell to the ground before him. ¹⁵Joseph said to them, "What deed is this that you have done? Do you not know that one such as I can practice divination?" ¹⁶And Judah said, "What can we say to my lord? What can we speak? How can we clear ourselves? God has found out the guilt of your servants; here we are then, my lord's slaves, both we and also the one in whose possession the cup has been found." ¹⁷But he said, "Far be it from me that I should do so! Only the one in whose possession the cup was found shall be my slave; but as for you, go up in peace to your father."

Judah Pleads for Benjamin's Release

18 Then Judah stepped up to him and said, "O my lord, let your servant please speak a word in my lord's ears, and do not be angry with your servant; for you are like Pharaoh himself. ¹⁹My lord asked his servants, saying, 'Have you a father or a brother?' ²⁰And we said to my lord, 'We have a father, an old man, and a young brother, the child of his old age. His brother is dead; he alone is left of his mother's children, and his father loves him.' ²¹Then you said to your servants,

---

a Heb *the man*   *b* Gk Compare Vg: Heb lacks *Why have you stolen my silver cup?*

God's Master Plan

After Joseph's tearful reconciliation with his brothers, he tells them that their past treatment of him enabled him to save them from the famine. Because he ended up in Egypt and rose to power, he can now invite them to stay as guests of the pharaoh.

Joseph realizes that good has come out of an evil act. He sees the events of his family's life as part of God's plan to preserve life and to make sure the Covenant continues. Joseph's insight does not justify what his brothers did, but it does help us realize that good can come out of a tragic event. It is often hard for us to understand why something bad is happening, but as time passes, we often gain perspective and insight. These are the rewards of trust and faith. Joseph remained faithful, despite many difficulties. Let us strive to do the same, assured that not even our sinfulness can thwart God's saving plans.

When have you experienced good things coming out of a bad situation? Has it ever seemed like God has upset part of your life, only to result in something better than you expected?

▶ **Gen 45:5–8**

'Bring him down to me, so that I may set my eyes on him.' ²²We said to my lord, 'The boy cannot leave his father, for if he should leave his father, his father would die.' ²³Then you said to your servants, 'Unless your youngest brother comes down with you, you shall see my face no more.' ²⁴When we went back to your servant my father we told him the words of my lord. ²⁵And when our father said, 'Go again, buy us a little food,' ²⁶we said, 'We cannot go down. Only if our youngest brother goes with us, will we go down; for we cannot see the man's face unless our youngest brother is with us.' ²⁷Then your servant my father said to us, 'You know that my wife bore me two sons; ²⁸one left me, and I said, Surely he has been torn to pieces; and I have never seen him since. ²⁹If you take this one also from me, and harm comes to him, you will bring down my gray hairs in sorrow to Sheol.' ³⁰Now

therefore, when I come to your servant my father and the boy is not with us, then, as his life is bound up in the boy's life, ³¹when he sees that the boy is not with us, he will die; and your servants will bring down the gray hairs of your servant our father with sorrow to Sheol. ³²For your servant became surety for the boy to my father, saying, 'If I do not bring him back to you, then I will bear the blame in the sight of my father all my life.' ³³Now therefore, please let your servant remain as a slave to my lord in place of the boy; and let the boy go back with his brothers. ³⁴For how can I go back to my father if the boy is not with me? I fear to see the suffering that would come upon my father."

Joseph Reveals Himself to His Brothers

45 Then Joseph could no longer control himself before all those who stood by him, and he cried out, "Send everyone away from me." So no one stayed with him when Joseph made himself known to his brothers. ²And he wept so loudly that the Egyptians heard it, and the household of Pharaoh heard it. ³Joseph said to his brothers, "I am Joseph. Is my father still alive?" But his brothers could not answer him, so dismayed were they at his presence.

4 Then Joseph said to his brothers, "Come closer to me." And they came closer. He said, "I am your brother, Joseph, whom you sold into Egypt. ⁵And now do not be distressed, or angry with yourselves, because you sold me here; for God sent me before you to preserve life. ⁶For the famine has been in the land these two years; and there are five more years in which there will be neither plowing nor harvest. ⁷God sent me before you to preserve for you a remnant on earth, and to keep alive for you many survivors. ⁸So it was not you who sent me here, but God; he has made me a father to Pharaoh, and lord of all his house and ruler over all the land of Egypt. ⁹Hurry and go up to my father and say to him, 'Thus says your son Joseph, God has made me lord of all Egypt; come down to me, do not delay. ¹⁰You shall settle in the land of Goshen, and you shall be near me, you and your children and your children's children, as well as your flocks, your herds, and all that you have. ¹¹I will provide for you there—since there are five more years of famine to come—so that you and your household, and all that you have, will not come to poverty.' ¹²And now your eyes and the eyes of my brother Benjamin see that it is my own mouth that speaks to you. ¹³You must tell my father how greatly I am honored in Egypt, and all that you have seen. Hurry and bring my father

down here." [14]Then he fell upon his brother Benjamin's neck and wept, while Benjamin wept upon his neck. [15]And he kissed all his brothers and wept upon them; and after that his brothers talked with him.

16 When the report was heard in Pharaoh's house, "Joseph's brothers have come," Pharaoh and his servants were pleased. [17]Pharaoh said to Joseph, "Say to your brothers, 'Do this: load your animals and go back to the land of Canaan. [18]Take your father and your households and come to me, so that I may give you the best of the land of Egypt, and you may enjoy the fat of the land.' [19]You are further charged to say, 'Do this: take wagons from the land of Egypt for your little ones and for your wives, and bring your father, and come. [20]Give no thought to your possessions, for the best of all the land of Egypt is yours.' "

21 The sons of Israel did so. Joseph gave them wagons according to the instruction of Pharaoh, and he gave them provisions for the journey. [22]To each one of them he gave a set of garments; but to Benjamin he gave three hundred pieces of silver and five sets of garments. [23]To his father he sent the following: ten donkeys loaded with the good things of Egypt, and ten female donkeys loaded with grain, bread, and provision for his father on the journey. [24]Then he sent his brothers on their way, and as they were leaving he said to them, "Do not quarrel[d] along the way."

25 So they went up out of Egypt and came to their father Jacob in the land of Canaan. [26]And they told him, "Joseph is still alive! He is even ruler over all the land of Egypt." He was stunned; he could not believe them. [27]But when they told him all the words of Joseph that he had said to them, and when he saw the wagons that Joseph had sent to carry him, the spirit of their father Jacob revived. [28]Israel said, "Enough! My son Joseph is still alive. I must go and see him before I die."

Jacob Brings His Whole Family to Egypt

46 When Israel set out on his journey with all that he had and came to Beer-sheba, he offered sacrifices to the God of his father Isaac. [2]God spoke to Israel in visions of the night, and said, "Jacob, Jacob." And he said, "Here I am." [3]Then he said, "I am God,[b] the God of your father; do not be afraid to go down to Egypt, for I will make of you a great nation there. [4]I myself will go down with you to Egypt, and I will also bring you up again; and Joseph's own hand shall close your eyes."

5 Then Jacob set out from Beer-sheba; and the sons of Israel carried their father Jacob, their little ones, and their wives, in the wagons that Pharaoh had sent to carry him. [6]They also took their livestock and the goods that they had acquired in the land of Canaan, and they came into Egypt, Jacob and all his offspring with him, [7]his sons, and his sons' sons with him, his daughters, and his sons' daughters; all his offspring he brought with him into Egypt.

8 Now these are the names of the Israelites, Jacob and his offspring, who came to Egypt. Reuben, Jacob's firstborn, [9]and the children of Reuben: Hanoch, Pallu, Hezron, and Carmi. [10]The children of Simeon: Jemuel, Jamin, Ohad, Jachin, Zohar, and Shaul,[c] the son of a Canaanite woman. [11]The children of Levi: Gershon, Kohath, and Merari. [12]The children of Judah: Er, Onan, Shelah, Perez, and Zerah (but Er and Onan died in the land of Canaan); and the children of Perez were Hezron and Hamul. [13]The children of Issachar: Tola, Puvah, Jashub,[d] and Shimron. [14]The children of Zebulun: Sered, Elon, and Jahleel [15](these are the sons of Leah, whom she bore to Jacob in Paddan-aram, together with his daughter Dinah; in all his sons and his daughters numbered thirty-three). [16]The children of Gad: Ziphion, Haggi, Shuni, Ezbon, Eri, Arodi, and Areli. [17]The children of Asher: Imnah, Ishvah, Ishvi, Beriah, and their sister Serah. The children of Beriah: Heber and Malchiel [18](these are the children of Zilpah, whom Laban gave to his daughter Leah; and these she bore to Jacob—sixteen persons). [19]The children of Jacob's wife Rachel: Joseph and Benjamin. [20]To Joseph in the land of Egypt were born Manasseh and Ephraim, whom Asenath daughter of Potiphera, priest of On, bore to him. [21]The children of Benjamin: Bela, Becher, Ashbel, Gera, Naaman, Ehi, Rosh, Muppim, Huppim, and Ard [22](these are the children of Rachel, who were born to Jacob—fourteen persons in all). [23]The children of Dan: Hashum.[e] [24]The children of Naphtali: Jahzeel, Guni, Jezer, and Shillem [25](these are the children of Bilhah, whom Laban gave to his daughter Rachel, and these she bore to Jacob—seven persons in all). [26]All the persons belonging to Jacob who came into Egypt, who were his own offspring, not including the wives of his sons, were sixty-six persons in all. [27]The children of Joseph, who were born to him in Egypt, were two; all the persons of the house of Jacob who came into Egypt were seventy.

---

a Or *be agitated*   *b* Heb *the God*   *c* Or *Saul*   *d* Compare Sam Gk Num 26.24; 1 Chr 7.1: MT *Iob*   *e* Gk: Heb *Hushim*

GEN

Did You Know?

Israel's Ancestry

Although the Israelites descended from many different kin, the Book of Genesis traces their origins back to a series of common ancestors, which served to unite them as a people. Genesis tells the stories of those great ancestors, men and women called patriarchs and matriarchs, who were the founders of what later became the people of Israel. The twelve Tribes of Israel are understood to be descendants from Jacob's twelve sons (see Jacob's last words in Genesis, chapter 49, for a description of those tribes). Twelve becomes an important number that comes up again and again in the Bible. For example, the twelve Apostles are Jesus' closest followers in the New Testament.

It can be confusing to remember who is related to whom, so here's a chart to keep everyone straight:

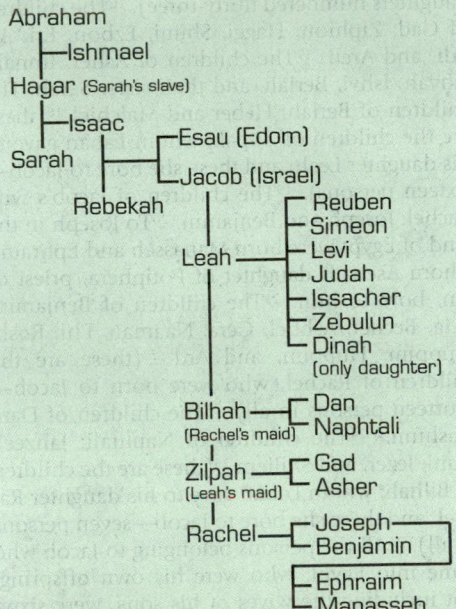

- Levi's tribe was set aside as priests and was not assigned land after the conquest of Canaan.
- Because Jacob adopted Joseph's sons Ephraim and Manasseh, Joseph is the father of two tribes.

Jacob Settles in Goshen

28 Israel[a] sent Judah ahead to Joseph to lead the way before him into Goshen. When they came to the land of Goshen, 29Joseph made ready his chariot and went up to meet his father Israel in Goshen. He presented himself to him, fell on his neck, and wept on his neck a good while. 30Israel said to Joseph, "I can die now, having seen for myself that you are still alive." 31Joseph said to his brothers and to his father's household, "I will go up and tell Pharaoh, and will say to him, 'My brothers and my father's household, who were in the land of Canaan, have come to me. 32The men are shepherds, for they have been keepers of livestock; and they have brought their flocks, and their herds, and all that they have.' 33When Pharaoh calls you, and says, 'What is your occupation?' 34you shall say, 'Your servants have been keepers of livestock from our youth even until now, both we and our ancestors'—in order that you may settle in the land of Goshen, because all shepherds are abhorrent to the Egyptians."

47 So Joseph went and told Pharaoh, "My father and my brothers, with their flocks and herds and all that they possess, have come from the land of Canaan; they are now in the land of Goshen." 2From among his brothers he took five men and presented them to Pharaoh. 3Pharaoh said to his brothers, "What is your occupation?" And they said to Pharaoh, "Your servants are shepherds, as our ancestors were." 4They said to Pharaoh, "We have come to reside as aliens in the land; for there is no pasture for your servants' flocks because the famine is severe in the land of Canaan. Now, we ask you, let your servants settle in the land of Goshen." 5Then Pharaoh said to Joseph, "Your father and your brothers have come to you. 6The land of Egypt is before you; settle your father and your brothers in the best part of the land; let them live in the land of Goshen; and if you know that there are capable men among them, put them in charge of my livestock."

7 Then Joseph brought in his father Jacob, and presented him before Pharaoh, and Jacob blessed Pharaoh. 8Pharaoh said to Jacob, "How many are the years of your life?" 9Jacob said to Pharaoh, "The years of my earthly sojourn are one hundred thirty; few and hard have been the years of my life. They do not compare with the years of the life of my ancestors during their long sojourn." 10Then Jacob blessed Pharaoh, and

went out from the presence of Pharaoh. [11]Joseph settled his father and his brothers, and granted them a holding in the land of Egypt, in the best part of the land, in the land of Rameses, as Pharaoh had instructed. [12]And Joseph provided his father, his brothers, and all his father's household with food, according to the number of their dependents.

The Famine in Egypt

13 Now there was no food in all the land, for the famine was very severe. The land of Egypt and the land of Canaan languished because of the famine. [14]Joseph collected all the money to be found in the land of Egypt and in the land of Canaan, in exchange for the grain that they bought; and Joseph brought the money into Pharaoh's house. [15]When the money from the land of Egypt and from the land of Canaan was spent, all the Egyptians came to Joseph, and said, "Give us food! Why should we die before your eyes? For our money is gone." [16]And Joseph answered, "Give me your livestock, and I will give you food in exchange for your livestock, if your money is gone." [17]So they brought their livestock to Joseph; and Joseph gave them food in exchange for the horses, the flocks, the herds, and the donkeys. That year he supplied them with food in exchange for all their livestock. [18]When that year was ended, they came to him the following year, and said to him, "We can not hide from my lord that our money is all spent; and the herds of cattle are my lord's. There is nothing left in the sight of my lord but our bodies and our lands. [19]Shall we die before your eyes, both we and our land? Buy us and our land in exchange for food. We with our land will become slaves to Pharaoh; just give us seed, so that we may live and not die, and that the land may not become desolate."

20 So Joseph bought all the land of Egypt for Pharaoh. All the Egyptians sold their fields, because the famine was severe upon them; and the land became Pharaoh's. [21]As for the people, he made slaves of them[a] from one end of Egypt to the other. [22]Only the land of the priests he did not buy; for the priests had a fixed allowance from Pharaoh, and lived on the allowance that Pharaoh gave them; therefore they did not sell their land. [23]Then Joseph said to the people, "Now that I have this day bought you and your land for Pharaoh, here is seed for you; sow the land. [24]And at the harvests you shall give one-fifth to Pharaoh, and four-fifths shall be your own, as seed for the field and as food for yourselves and your households, and as food for your

little ones." [25]They said, "You have saved our lives; may it please my lord, we will be slaves to Pharaoh." [26]So Joseph made it a statute concerning the land of Egypt, and it stands to this day, that Pharaoh should have the fifth. The land of the priests alone did not become Pharaoh's.

The Last Days of Jacob

27 Thus Israel settled in the land of Egypt, in the region of Goshen; and they gained possessions in it, and were fruitful and multiplied exceedingly. [28]Jacob lived in the land of Egypt seventeen years; so the days of Jacob, the years of his life, were one hundred forty-seven years.

29 When the time of Israel's death drew near, he called his son Joseph and said to him, "If I have found favor with you, put your hand under my thigh and promise to deal loyally and truly with me. Do not bury me in Egypt. [30]When I lie down with my ancestors, carry me out of Egypt and bury me in their burial place." He answered, "I will do as you have said." [31]And he said, "Swear to me"; and he swore to him. Then Israel bowed himself on the head of his bed.

Jacob Blesses Joseph's Sons

48 After this Joseph was told, "Your father is ill." So he took with him his two sons, Manasseh and Ephraim. [2]When Jacob was told, "Your son Joseph has come to you," he[b] summoned his strength and sat up in bed. [3]And Jacob said to Joseph, "God Almighty[c] appeared to me at Luz in the land of Canaan, and he blessed me, [4]and said to me, 'I am going to make you fruitful and increase your numbers; I will make of you a company of peoples, and will give this land to your offspring after you for a perpetual holding.' [5]Therefore your two sons, who were born to you in the land of Egypt before I came to you in Egypt, are now mine; Ephraim and Manasseh shall be mine, just as Reuben and Simeon are. [6]As for the offspring born to you after them, they shall be yours. They shall be recorded under the names of their brothers with regard to their inheritance. [7]For when I came from Paddan, Rachel, alas, died in the land of Canaan on the way, while there was still some distance to go to Ephrath; and I buried her there on the way to Ephrath" (that is, Bethlehem).

8 When Israel saw Joseph's sons, he said, "Who are these?" [9]Joseph said to his father, "They are my sons, whom God has given me here." And he said, "Bring them to me, please, that I may

---

a Sam Gk Compare Vg: MT *He removed them to the cities*
b Heb *Israel* c Traditional rendering of Heb *El Shaddai*

GEN

Cultural Connection

Assemble and Hear!

Genesis 49:1–2 is the first reading at Mass on the ninth day before Christmas. This is an important day for Filipino Catholics because it marks the beginning of Simbang Gabi, or Dawn Worship.

On the nine days before Christmas, people gather to celebrate Mass in the dark of the pre-dawn—usually between four and five o'clock in the morning. Mass ends with chocolate and buns and socializing. In fact, this is such a popular custom that even people who don't come to Mass all year will make it for the nine Masses of Simbang Gabi! It is a special celebration of thankfulness for the gift of their Catholic faith.

This Philippine tradition is an example of a Catholic custom called a novena. A novena is a public or private prayer repeated nine times. It can be a prayer said every day for nine days, one day a week for nine weeks, one day a month for nine months, or in any other pattern of nine. Why not make up your own personal novena? Just think of a prayer in a form you find meaningful (journaling, singing, reading the Scriptures, or even praying silently), and repeat it once a day for nine days or once a week for nine weeks. Happy praying!

▶ Gen 49:1–2

bless them." ¹⁰Now the eyes of Israel were dim with age, and he could not see well. So Joseph brought them near him; and he kissed them and embraced them. ¹¹Israel said to Joseph, "I did not expect to see your face; and here God has let me see your children also." ¹²Then Joseph removed them from his father's knees,ᵃ and he bowed himself with his face to the earth. ¹³Joseph took them both, Ephraim in his right hand toward Israel's left, and Manasseh in his left hand toward Israel's right, and brought them near him. ¹⁴But Israel stretched out his right hand and laid it on the head of Ephraim, who was the younger, and his left hand on the head of Manasseh, crossing his hands, for Manasseh was the firstborn. ¹⁵He blessed Joseph, and said,

"The God before whom my ancestors Abraham
    and Isaac walked,
the God who has been my shepherd all my life
    to this day,
¹⁶ the angel who has redeemed me from all harm,
    bless the boys;
and in them let my name be perpetuated, and
    the name of my ancestors Abraham and
    Isaac;
and let them grow into a multitude on the
    earth."

17 When Joseph saw that his father laid his right hand on the head of Ephraim, it displeased him; so he took his father's hand, to remove it from Ephraim's head to Manasseh's head. ¹⁸Joseph said to his father, "Not so, my father! Since this one is the firstborn, put your right hand on his head." ¹⁹But his father refused, and said, "I know, my son, I know; he also shall become a people, and he also shall be great. Nevertheless his younger brother shall be greater than he, and his offspring shall become a multitude of nations." ²⁰So he blessed them that day, saying,

"By youᵇ Israel will invoke blessings, saying,
    'God make youᵇ like Ephraim and like
        Manasseh.' "

So he put Ephraim ahead of Manasseh. ²¹Then Israel said to Joseph, "I am about to die, but God will be with you and will bring you again to the land of your ancestors. ²²I now give to you one portionᶜ more than to your brothers, the portionᶜ that I took from the hand of the Amorites with my sword and with my bow."

Jacob's Last Words to His Sons

49 Then Jacob called his sons, and said: "Gather around, that I may tell you what will happen to you in days to come.
² Assemble and hear, O sons of Jacob;
    listen to Israel your father.

³ Reuben, you are my firstborn,
    my might and the first fruits of my vigor,
    excelling in rank and excelling in power.

ᵃ Heb *from his knees*   ᵇ *you* here is singular in Heb
ᶜ Or *mountain slope* (Heb *shekem*, a play on the name of the town and district of Shechem)

⁴ Unstable as water, you shall no longer excel
    because you went up onto your father's bed;
  then you defiled it—you*a* went up onto my
    couch!

⁵ Simeon and Levi are brothers;
    weapons of violence are their swords.
⁶ May I never come into their council;
    may I not be joined to their company—
for in their anger they killed men,
    and at their whim they hamstrung oxen.
⁷ Cursed be their anger, for it is fierce,
    and their wrath, for it is cruel!
I will divide them in Jacob,
    and scatter them in Israel.

⁸ Judah, your brothers shall praise you;
    your hand shall be on the neck of your enemies;
    your father's sons shall bow down before you.
⁹ Judah is a lion's whelp;
    from the prey, my son, you have gone up.
He crouches down, he stretches out like a lion,
    like a lioness—who dares rouse him up?
¹⁰ The scepter shall not depart from Judah,
    nor the ruler's staff from between his feet,
until tribute comes to him;*b*
    and the obedience of the peoples is his.
¹¹ Binding his foal to the vine
    and his donkey's colt to the choice vine,
he washes his garments in wine
    and his robe in the blood of grapes;
¹² his eyes are darker than wine,
    and his teeth whiter than milk.

¹³ Zebulun shall settle at the shore of the sea;
    he shall be a haven for ships,
    and his border shall be at Sidon.

¹⁴ Issachar is a strong donkey,
    lying down between the sheepfolds;
¹⁵ he saw that a resting place was good,
    and that the land was pleasant;
so he bowed his shoulder to the burden,
    and became a slave at forced labor.

¹⁶ Dan shall judge his people
    as one of the tribes of Israel.
¹⁷ Dan shall be a snake by the roadside,
    a viper along the path,
that bites the horse's heels
    so that its rider falls backward.

¹⁸ I wait for your salvation, O Lᴏʀᴅ.

¹⁹ Gad shall be raided by raiders,
    but he shall raid at their heels.

²⁰ Asher's*c* food shall be rich,
    and he shall provide royal delicacies.

²¹ Naphtali is a doe let loose
    that bears lovely fawns.*d*

²² Joseph is a fruitful bough,
    a fruitful bough by a spring;
    his branches run over the wall.*e*
²³ The archers fiercely attacked him;
    they shot at him and pressed him hard.
²⁴ Yet his bow remained taut,
    and his arms*f* were made agile
by the hands of the Mighty One of Jacob,
    by the name of the Shepherd, the Rock of
      Israel,
²⁵ by the God of your father, who will help you,
    by the Almighty*g* who will bless you
    with blessings of heaven above,
blessings of the deep that lies beneath,
    blessings of the breasts and of the womb.
²⁶ The blessings of your father
    are stronger than the blessings of the eternal
      mountains,
    the bounties*h* of the everlasting hills;
may they be on the head of Joseph,
    on the brow of him who was set apart from
      his brothers.

²⁷ Benjamin is a ravenous wolf,
    in the morning devouring the prey,
    and at evening dividing the spoil."

28 All these are the twelve tribes of Israel, and this is what their father said to them when he blessed them, blessing each one of them with a suitable blessing.

Jacob's Death and Burial

29 Then he charged them, saying to them, "I am about to be gathered to my people. Bury me with my ancestors—in the cave in the field of Ephron the Hittite, ³⁰in the cave in the field at Machpelah, near Mamre, in the land of Canaan, in the field that Abraham bought from Ephron the Hittite as a burial site ³¹There Abraham and his wife Sarah were buried; there Isaac and his wife Rebekah were buried; and there I buried Leah— ³²the field and the cave that is in it were purchased from the Hittites." ³³When Jacob

---

a Gk Syr Tg: Heb *he*   *b* Or *until Shiloh comes* or *until he comes to Shiloh* or (with Syr) *until he comes to whom it belongs*
c Gk Vg Syr: Heb *From Asher*   *d* Or *that gives beautiful words*
e Meaning of Heb uncertain   *f* Heb *the arms of his hands*
g Traditional rendering of Heb *Shaddai*   *h* Cn Compare Gk: Heb *of my progenitors to the boundaries*

ended his charge to his sons, he drew up his feet into the bed, breathed his last, and was gathered to his people.

50 Then Joseph threw himself on his father's face and wept over him and kissed him. 2Joseph commanded the physicians in his service to embalm his father. So the physicians embalmed Israel; 3they spent forty days in doing this, for that is the time required for embalming. And the Egyptians wept for him seventy days.

4 When the days of weeping for him were past, Joseph addressed the household of Pharaoh, "If now I have found favor with you, please speak to Pharaoh as follows: 5My father made me swear an oath; he said, 'I am about to die. In the tomb that I hewed out for myself in the land of Canaan, there you shall bury me.' Now therefore let me go up, so that I may bury my father; then I will return." 6Pharaoh answered, "Go up, and bury your father, as he made you swear to do."

7 So Joseph went up to bury his father. With him went up all the servants of Pharaoh, the elders of his household, and all the elders of the land of Egypt, 8as well as all the household of Joseph, his brothers, and his father's household. Only their children, their flocks, and their herds were left in the land of Goshen. 9Both chariots and charioteers went up with him. It was a very great company. 10When they came to the threshing floor of Atad, which is beyond the Jordan, they held there a very great and sorrowful lamentation; and he observed a time of mourning for his father seven days. 11When the Canaanite inhabitants of the land saw the mourning on the threshing floor of Atad, they said, "This is a grievous mourning on the part of the Egyptians." Therefore the place was named Abel-mizraim;a it is beyond the Jordan. 12Thus his sons did for him as he had instructed them. 13They carried him to the land of Canaan and buried him in the cave of the field at Machpelah, the field near Mamre, which Abraham bought as a burial site from Ephron the Hittite. 14After he had buried his father, Joseph returned to Egypt with his brothers and all who had gone up with him to bury his father.

Joseph Forgives His Brothers

15 Realizing that their father was dead, Joseph's brothers said, "What if Joseph still bears a grudge against us and pays us back in full for all the wrong that we did to him?" 16So they approachedb Joseph, saying, "Your father gave this instruction before he died, 17'Say to Joseph: I beg you, forgive the crime of your brothers and the wrong they did in harming you.' Now therefore please forgive the crime of the servants of the God of your father." Joseph wept when they spoke to him. 18Then his brothers also wept,c fell down before him, and said, "We are here as your slaves." 19But Joseph said to them, "Do not be afraid! Am I in the place of God? 20Even though you intended to do harm to me, God intended it for good, in order to preserve a numerous people, as he is doing today. 21So have no fear; I myself will provide for you and your little ones." In this way he reassured them, speaking kindly to them.

Joseph's Last Days and Death

22 So Joseph remained in Egypt, he and his father's household; and Joseph lived one hundred ten years. 23Joseph saw Ephraim's children of the third generation; the children of Machir son of Manasseh were also born on Joseph's knees.

24 Then Joseph said to his brothers, "I am about to die; but God will surely come to you, and bring you up out of this land to the land that he swore to Abraham, to Isaac, and to Jacob." 25So Joseph made the Israelites swear, saying, "When God comes to you, you shall carry up my bones from here." 26And Joseph died, being one hundred ten years old; he was embalmed and placed in a coffin in Egypt.

a That is mourning (or meadow) of Egypt   b Gk Syr: Heb they commanded   c Cn: Heb also came

Click! Chains snap shut around your ankles. Crack! The tip of a whip whistles past your head. Bang! A door shuts, leaving you in darkness. These are the sounds of slavery, and they come as a surprise at the beginning of the Book of Exodus. What happened after the happy ending in Genesis? Like an action-packed drama, Exodus tells a story of deceit and broken promises, and of how God's miraculous interventions delivered the Israelites from their slavery in Egypt.

At a Glance

- Chapters 1–10. Pharaoh's oppression, the call of Moses, the plagues
- 11:1—15:21. the Passover and Exodus, deliverance at the Red Sea
- 15:22—18:27. the journey through the wilderness
- 19:1—35:3. the Covenant at Mount Sinai, difficulty living the Covenant
- 35:4—40:38. construction of the tabernacle

Quick Facts

Period Covered: sometime from 1500 to 1250 BC
Inspired Author: unknown author gathering oral tradition and stories from various tribal peoples
Themes: God liberates people from slavery and oppression. God sustains the Israelites in the wilderness. God forms a covenant marked by laws and rituals.

In Depth

The Book of Exodus is the ultimate story of Israel's liberation. *Exodus* literally means "departure," and this book's central event is of how God liberates the Israelite people from slavery in Egypt (an event called the Exodus). Its central character is Moses, who is chosen by God to become God's messenger and the instrument of God's power. Exodus was written hundreds of years after these events, using oral tradition that described the origin of many of the Israelites' beliefs and religious rituals.

Exodus is divided into two main sections. The first section, chapters 1–18, begins with the Israelites enslaved in Egypt and prohibited from worshiping their God. Israel cries out to God, and God answers by sending Moses. When Pharaoh refuses to let the Israelites go, God sends ten devastating plagues, and Pharaoh finally gives in. Later, Pharaoh changes his mind and chases the Israelites, only to have his army destroyed after the Israelites' escape through the Red Sea. This section ends with the people wandering through the wilderness, sustained by food and water miraculously provided by God.

Section two of Exodus, chapters 19–40, occurs at Mount Sinai. There God enters into a covenant with all the people. God's part of the Sinai Covenant is to guarantee continued protection. Israel's part is to be faithful to God alone, a faithfulness marked by special laws (chapters 20–23) and special worship (chapters 24–31) that unite them as a people. Exodus ends with Israel still encamped at Mount Sinai, struggling to become a people of the Covenant.

The stories and laws in Exodus are at the heart of both Jewish and Christian belief in a God who saves, a God of freedom. You cannot fully appreciate the meaning of Jesus' life, death, and Resurrection without knowing these stories.

The Book of Exodus

Exodus

1 These are the names of the sons of Israel who came to Egypt with Jacob, each with his household: ²Reuben, Simeon, Levi, and Judah, ³Issachar, Zebulun, and Benjamin, ⁴Dan and Naphtali, Gad and Asher. ⁵The total number of people born to Jacob was seventy. Joseph was already in Egypt. ⁶Then Joseph died, and all his brothers, and that whole generation. ⁷But the Israelites were fruitful and prolific; they multiplied and grew exceedingly strong, so that the land was filled with them.

The Israelites Are Oppressed

8 Now a new king arose over Egypt, who did not know Joseph. ⁹He said to his people, "Look, the Israelite people are more numerous and more powerful than we. ¹⁰Come, let us deal shrewdly with them, or they will increase and, in the event of war, join our enemies and fight against us and escape from the land." ¹¹Therefore they set taskmasters over them to oppress them with forced labor. They built supply cities, Pithom and Rameses, for Pharaoh. ¹²But the more they were oppressed, the more they multiplied and spread, so that the Egyptians came to dread the Israelites. ¹³The Egyptians became ruthless in imposing tasks on the Israelites, ¹⁴and made their lives bitter with hard service in mortar and brick and in every kind of field labor. They were ruthless in all the tasks that they imposed on them.

15 The king of Egypt said to the Hebrew midwives, one of whom was named Shiphrah and the other Puah, ¹⁶"When you act as midwives to the Hebrew women, and see them on the birthstool, if it is a boy, kill him; but if it is a girl, she shall live." ¹⁷But the midwives feared God; they did not do as the king of Egypt commanded them, but they let the boys live. ¹⁸So the king of Egypt summoned the midwives and said to them, "Why have you done this, and allowed the boys to live?" ¹⁹The midwives said to Pharaoh, "Because the Hebrew women are not like the Egyptian women; for they are vigorous and give birth before the midwife comes to them." ²⁰So God dealt well with the midwives; and the people multiplied and became very strong. ²¹And because the midwives feared God, he gave them families. ²²Then Pharaoh commanded all his people, "Every boy that is born to the Hebrews*a* you shall throw into the Nile, but you shall let every girl live."

Birth and Youth of Moses

2 Now a man from the house of Levi went and married a Levite woman. ²The woman conceived and bore a son; and when she saw that he was a fine baby, she hid him three months. ³When she could hide him no longer she got a papyrus basket for him, and plastered it with bitumen and pitch; she put the child in it and placed it among the reeds on the bank of the river. ⁴His sister stood at a distance, to see what would happen to him.

5 The daughter of Pharaoh came down to bathe at the river, while her attendants walked beside the river. She saw the basket among the

a Sam Gk Tg: Heb lacks *to the Hebrews*

reeds and sent her maid to bring it. ⁶When she opened it, she saw the child. He was crying, and she took pity on him. "This must be one of the Hebrews' children," she said. ⁷Then his sister said to Pharaoh's daughter, "Shall I go and get you a nurse from the Hebrew women to nurse the child for you?" ⁸Pharaoh's daughter said to her, "Yes." So the girl went and called the child's mother. ⁹Pharaoh's daughter said to her, "Take this child and nurse it for me, and I will give you your wages." So the woman took the child and nursed it. ¹⁰When the child grew up, she brought him to Pharaoh's daughter, and she took him as her son. She named him Moses,*a* "because," she said, "I drew him out*b* of the water."

Moses Flees to Midian

11 One day, after Moses had grown up, he went out to his people and saw their forced labor. He saw an Egyptian beating a Hebrew, one of his kinsfolk. ¹²He looked this way and that, and seeing no one he killed the Egyptian and hid him in the sand. ¹³When he went out the next day, he saw two Hebrews fighting; and he said to the one who was in the wrong, "Why do you strike your fellow Hebrew?" ¹⁴He answered, "Who made you a ruler and judge over us? Do you mean to kill me as you killed the Egyptian?" Then Moses was afraid and thought, "Surely the thing is known." ¹⁵When Pharaoh heard of it, he sought to kill Moses.

But Moses fled from Pharaoh. He settled in the land of Midian, and sat down by a well. ¹⁶The priest of Midian had seven daughters. They came to draw water, and filled the troughs to water their father's flock. ¹⁷But some shepherds came and drove them away. Moses got up and came to their defense and watered their flock. ¹⁸When they returned to their father Reuel, he said, "How is it that you have come back so soon today?" ¹⁹They said, "An Egyptian helped us against the shepherds; he even drew water for us and watered the flock." ²⁰He said to his daughters, "Where is he? Why did you leave the man? Invite him to break bread." ²¹Moses agreed to stay with the man, and he gave Moses his daughter Zipporah in marriage. ²²She bore a son, and he named him Gershom; for he said, "I have been an alien*c* residing in a foreign land."

23 After a long time the king of Egypt died. The Israelites groaned under their slavery, and cried out. Out of the slavery their cry for help rose up to God. ²⁴God heard their groaning, and God remembered his covenant with Abraham, Isaac, and Jacob. ²⁵God looked upon the Israelites, and God took notice of them.

Saving Lives

In the story of the birth of Moses, Pharaoh orders the Egyptian midwives to kill all the male Israelite babies at birth. The midwives recognize such killing as an atrocity and refuse to obey Pharaoh. Their actions might be considered civil disobedience against unjust laws.

Some people claim that the right to have an abortion is a just law. Most of us have seen the images of an unborn baby resting within its mother's womb, thanks to the technology of ultrasounds. Clearly, there is a living human being there, who only needs a safe and protective environment in which to grow. Doesn't society have an obligation to protect this completely defenseless life? Where is the justice for the unborn child?

As the Egyptian midwives knew, all human life is sacred, no matter where or in what stage of development it exists.

▶ Ex 1:15–22

Moses at the Burning Bush

3 Moses was keeping the flock of his father-in-law Jethro, the priest of Midian; he led his flock beyond the wilderness, and came to Horeb, the mountain of God. ²There the angel of the LORD appeared to him in a flame of fire out of a bush; he looked, and the bush was blazing, yet it was not consumed. ³Then Moses said, "I must turn aside and look at this great sight, and see why the bush is not burned up." ⁴When the LORD saw that he had turned aside to see, God called to him out of the bush, "Moses, Moses!" And he said, "Here I am." ⁵Then he said, "Come no closer! Remove the sandals from your feet, for the place on which you are standing is holy ground." ⁶He said further, "I am the God of your father, the God of Abraham, the God of Isaac, and the God of Jacob." And Moses hid his face, for he was afraid to look at God.

7 Then the LORD said, "I have observed the

---

a Heb *Mosheh*   *b* Heb *mashah*   *c* Heb *ger*

Cultural Connection

Holy Ground

In many Asian cultures, before people enter a home, they remove their shoes. People do this before entering a mosque too. Perhaps you remove your shoes before entering your home as well. Removing one's shoes is a common sign of respect. Moses is commanded to remove his sandals in Exodus 3:5. Why? Because he is standing on holy ground. Why is the ground holy? Because God is present.

Moses is awestruck and humbled by his experience of God's presence. In today's multimedia culture, we are rarely awed by anything. Even the burning bush would be just another special effect. How can we regain our sense of awe at God's majesty? Some people experience it in nature, looking at a star-filled sky or the waves rolling in on the ocean. Others experience it in getting to know other people deeply. Still others find it in the amazing patterns that science reveals. The one common element to experiencing awe seems to be the ability to slow down, look closely, and appreciate what we discover.

So, slow down, find your own holy ground, take your shoes off, and let God fill you with awe!

▶ Ex 3:1–6

---

misery of my people who are in Egypt; I have heard their cry on account of their taskmasters. Indeed, I know their sufferings, ⁸and I have come down to deliver them from the Egyptians, and to bring them up out of that land to a good and broad land, a land flowing with milk and honey, to the country of the Canaanites, the Hittites, the Amorites, the Perizzites, the Hivites, and the Jebusites. ⁹The cry of the Israelites has now come to me; I have also seen how the Egyptians oppress them. ¹⁰So come, I will send you to Pharaoh to bring my people, the Israelites, out of Egypt." ¹¹But Moses said to God, "Who am I that I should go to Pharaoh, and bring the Israelites out of Egypt?" ¹²He said, "I will be with you; and this shall be the sign for you that it is I who sent you: when you have brought the people out of Egypt, you shall worship God on this mountain."

The Divine Name Revealed

13 But Moses said to God, "If I come to the Israelites and say to them, 'The God of your ancestors has sent me to you,' and they ask me, 'What is his name?' what shall I say to them?" ¹⁴God said to Moses, "I AM WHO I AM."[a] He said further, "Thus you shall say to the Israelites, 'I AM has sent me to you.'" ¹⁵God also said to Moses, "Thus you shall say to the Israelites, 'The LORD,[b] the God of your ancestors, the God of Abraham, the God of Isaac, and the God of Jacob, has sent me to you':

This is my name forever,
and this my title for all generations.

¹⁶Go and assemble the elders of Israel, and say to them, 'The LORD, the God of your ancestors, the God of Abraham, of Isaac, and of Jacob, has appeared to me, saying: I have given heed to you and to what has been done to you in Egypt. ¹⁷I declare that I will bring you up out of the misery of Egypt, to the land of the Canaanites, the Hittites, the Amorites, the Perizzites, the Hivites, and the Jebusites, a land flowing with milk and honey.' ¹⁸They will listen to your voice; and you and the elders of Israel shall go to the king of Egypt and say to him, 'The LORD, the God of the Hebrews, has met with us; let us now go a three days' journey into the wilderness, so that we may sacrifice to the LORD our God.' ¹⁹I know, however, that the king of Egypt will not let you go unless compelled by a mighty hand.[c] ²⁰So I will stretch out my hand and strike Egypt with all my wonders that I will perform in it; after that he will let you go. ²¹I will bring this people into such favor with the Egyptians that, when you go, you will not go empty-handed; ²²each woman shall ask her neighbor and any woman living in the neighbor's house for jewelry of silver and of gold, and clothing, and you shall put them on your sons and on your daughters; and so you shall plunder the Egyptians."

---

a Or *I AM WHAT I AM* or *I WILL BE WHAT I WILL BE* b The word "LORD" when spelled with capital letters stands for the divine name, YHWH, which is here connected with the verb *hayah*, "to be"
c Gk Vg: Heb *no, not by a mighty hand*

Cultural Connection

Many Native American peoples, such as the Lakota and the Sioux, have several names for God. *Wakan-Tanka* and *Tun-ka-shi-la* are still commonly used today. These words for God are often translated as "Great Spirit."

This is a good translation because *Wakan* is a word that brings together the concepts of mystery, sacredness, holiness, awe, and inspiration. *Tanka* describes something that is great.

Tun-ka-shi-la is often used the same way as *Wakan-Tanka*, but its meaning is slightly different. *Tun-ka-shi-la* is often translated as "Grandfather or Great Grandfather," but it means the "one who is the oldest, so old that nothing or no one is older." *Tun-ka-shi-la* is a name that reflects the Great Spirit as the source of all things, the one who has existed from the beginning.

▶ **Ex 3:13–15**

Moses' Miraculous Power

4 Then Moses answered, "But suppose they do not believe me or listen to me, but say, 'The LORD did not appear to you.' " ²The LORD said to him, "What is that in your hand?" He said, "A staff." ³And he said, "Throw it on the ground." So he threw the staff on the ground, and it became a snake; and Moses drew back from it. ⁴Then the LORD said to Moses, "Reach out your hand, and seize it by the tail"—so he reached out his hand and grasped it, and it became a staff in his hand— ⁵ "so that they may believe that the LORD, the God of their ancestors, the God of Abraham, the God of Isaac, and the God of Jacob, has appeared to you."

6 Again, the LORD said to him, "Put your hand inside your cloak." He put his hand into his cloak; and when he took it out, his hand was leprous,ᵃ as white as snow. ⁷Then God said, "Put your hand back into your cloak"—so he put his hand back into his cloak, and when he took it out, it was restored like the rest of his body— ⁸ "If they will not believe you or heed the first sign, they may believe the second sign ⁹If they will not believe even these two signs or heed you, you shall take some water from the Nile and pour it on the dry ground; and the water that you shall take from the Nile will become blood on the dry ground."

10 But Moses said to the LORD, "O my Lord, I have never been eloquent, neither in the past nor even now that you have spoken to your servant; but I am slow of speech and slow of tongue." ¹¹Then the LORD said to him, "Who gives speech to mortals? Who makes them mute or deaf, seeing or blind? Is it not I, the LORD? ¹²Now go, and I will be with your mouth and teach you what you are to speak." ¹³But he said, "O my Lord, please send someone else." ¹⁴Then the anger of the LORD was kindled against Moses and he said,

---

ᵃ A term for several skin diseases; precise meaning uncertain

Did You Know?

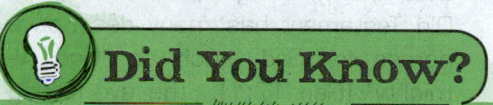

God's Mysterious Name

"I AM WHO I AM"—one possible translation of *Yahweh* from Exodus 3:14—seems more like a definition than a name. Some scholars have suggested *Yahweh* might be better translated "he causes to be what exists." In any case, the four Hebrew letters *YHWH* (or *Yahweh* in English) are difficult to translate. Over the centuries, the Jewish people stopped pronouncing the four letters out of reverence for God and replaced them with the word *Adonai*, meaning "my Lord." Most English translations of the Bible respect this long-standing tradition, translating the original *YHWH* as "LORD." This mysterious name of God reminds us that no name or symbol can fully express who God is.

▶ **Ex 3:13–15**

✝ Catholic Connection

God the Father

Have you ever asked your parents what your name means or why they chose it for you? Generally, behind each name is a story or a meaning that says something about the individual. The same is true about God's own name, which was revealed to Moses from the burning bush. God tells Moses that his name in Hebrew is "Yahweh," which can be translated as "I AM WHO I AM" or "he causes to be what exists." From this name we learn that God alone is the source of all things.

But the meaning from one name alone cannot be enough to truly encompass all that God is. Perhaps that is why, along with Yahweh, the Old Testament has many descriptive names for God, such as "God Almighty" (Gen 17:1), "the everlasting God" (Isa 40:28) and "the Most High" (Isa 14:14).

One name the Israelites often used was Father (see Deut 32:6) in reference to God as the creator of all things. But it was not until Jesus came into the world that we learned the true meaning of the name Father for God. By revealing himself as God's only Son, Jesus also revealed his relationship with God as Father. (See "The Trinity," near Jn 17:20–26, for more information about the relationship between God the Father and Jesus.) From the name Father, we are reminded of our role as God's adopted daughters and sons and the endless love the Father has for each one of us. The name Father also helps us to remember God's authority and power over us and all of creation. Jesus taught us to pray calling God Father, and so we are able to address God intimately and realize that God desires a loving and personal relationship with us.

▶ **Ex 3:13–15**
Catechism, nos. 232–242

Cultural Connection

God Sends Prophets to Liberate His People

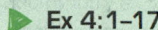

God responded to the cry of his people, choosing Moses as a prophet and commissioning him to lead the Israelites to freedom. Despite Moses' first doubts, with God's assistance, Moses became an effective and powerful leader. God would not let Moses' excuses stand in the way of God's mission of liberation.

Christians share in Jesus Christ's prophetic work as well. We too need to speak out against injustice and help the victims of oppression. Like the prophets before us, we can succeed only with God's help.

In our time, great spiritual leaders have risen up to lead people to freedom: Mohandas Gandhi, Martin Luther King Jr., Dorothy Day, Archbishop Oscar Romero, and César Chávez are just a few. As in the case of Moses, God inspired these leaders to see their people experiencing injustice and to seek to liberate them from oppressive powers. You can be sure that these people also had their doubts and relied on God for their strength and hope.

- Are you aware of any group that is being oppressed today? How might God be calling you to help?
- Ask God for wisdom, strength, and help in your mission.

▶ Ex 4:1–17

EX

"What of your brother Aaron the Levite? I know that he can speak fluently; even now he is coming out to meet you, and when he sees you his heart will be glad. ¹⁵You shall speak to him and put the words in his mouth; and I will be with your mouth and with his mouth, and will teach you what you shall do. ¹⁶He indeed shall speak for you to the people; he shall serve as a mouth for you, and you shall serve as God for him. ¹⁷Take in your hand this staff, with which you shall perform the signs."

Moses Returns to Egypt

18 Moses went back to his father-in-law Jethro and said to him, "Please let me go back to my kindred in Egypt and see whether they are still living." And Jethro said to Moses, "Go in peace." ¹⁹The LORD said to Moses in Midian, "Go back to Egypt; for all those who were seeking your life are dead." ²⁰So Moses took his wife and his sons, put them on a donkey, and went back to the land of Egypt; and Moses carried the staff of God in his hand.

21 And the LORD said to Moses, "When you go back to Egypt, see that you perform before Pharaoh all the wonders that I have put in your power; but I will harden his heart, so that he will not let the people go. ²²Then you shall say to Pharaoh, 'Thus says the LORD: Israel is my firstborn son. ²³I said to you, "Let my son go that he may worship me." But you refused to let him go; now I will kill your firstborn son.'"

24 On the way, at a place where they spent the night, the LORD met him and tried to kill him. ²⁵But Zipporah took a flint and cut off her son's foreskin, and touched Moses'ᵃ feet with it, and said, "Truly you are a bridegroom of blood to me!" ²⁶So he let him alone. It was then she said, "A bridegroom of blood by circumcision."

27 The LORD said to Aaron, "Go into the wilderness to meet Moses." So he went; and he met him at the mountain of God and kissed him. ²⁸Moses told Aaron all the words of the LORD with which he had sent him, and all the signs with which he had charged him. ²⁹Then Moses and Aaron went and assembled all the elders of the Israelites. ³⁰Aaron spoke all the words that the LORD had spoken to Moses, and performed the signs in the sight of the people. ³¹The people believed; and when they heard that the LORD had given heed to the Israelites and that he had seen their misery, they bowed down and worshiped.

Bricks without Straw

5 Afterward Moses and Aaron went to Pharaoh and said, "Thus says the LORD, the God of Israel, 'Let my people go, so that they may celebrate a festival to me in the wilderness.'" ²But Pharaoh said, "Who is the LORD, that I should heed him and let Israel go? I do not know the LORD, and I will not let Israel go." ³Then they said, "The God of the Hebrews has revealed himself to us; let us

---

ᵃ Heb his

Catholic Social Teaching

Slave Labor

Demanding bosses. Long hours. Poor working conditions. Although this story details Pharaoh's unjust treatment of the Israelites almost 3,500 years ago, it is a story that is unfortunately and remarkably similar to the work lives of many laborers throughout the world today. The word *sweatshop* is commonly used to describe a working environment with dangerous and unjust working conditions. Workers in sweatshops typically have very few rights and are often made to work long hours for low wages. The companies that use sweat-

shops to produce their goods are familiar names to us all. You may even be wearing clothes right now that have been manufactured under unjust conditions, without even knowing it!

Catholic social teaching, however, demands that we become more aware of the origins of the things we buy. If we ignore the conditions under which these products were produced, then in a small way, we contribute to the injustice. But if we refuse to buy these products and stand up in a unified way against those companies that continue to use sweat-

shop labor, we will emphatically assert that all workers deserve to be treated with dignity and that low wages, unfair labor practices, and dangerous working conditions are unjust and unacceptable in our world today.

▶ **Exodus, chapter 5**

The Dignity of Work and the Rights of Workers

go a three days' journey into the wilderness to sacrifice to the LORD our God, or he will fall upon us with pestilence or sword." ⁴But the king of Egypt said to them, "Moses and Aaron, why are you taking the people away from their work? Get to your labors!" ⁵Pharaoh continued, "Now they are more numerous than the people of the land*ᵃ* and yet you want them to stop working!" ⁶That same day Pharaoh commanded the taskmasters of the people, as well as their supervisors, ⁷"You shall no longer give the people straw to make bricks, as before; let them go and gather straw for themselves. ⁸But you shall require of them the same quantity of bricks as they have made previously; do not diminish it, for they are lazy; that is why they cry, 'Let us go and offer sacrifice to our God.' ⁹Let heavier work be laid on them; then they will labor at it and pay no attention to deceptive words."

10 So the taskmasters and the supervisors of the people went out and said to the people, "Thus says Pharaoh, 'I will not give you straw. ¹¹Go and get straw yourselves, wherever you can find it; but your work will not be lessened in the least.' " ¹²So the people scattered throughout the land of Egypt, to gather stubble for straw. ¹³The taskmasters were urgent, saying, "Complete your work, the same daily assignment as when you were given straw." ¹⁴And the supervisors of the

Israelites, whom Pharaoh's taskmasters had set over them, were beaten, and were asked, "Why did you not finish the required quantity of bricks yesterday and today, as you did before?"

15 Then the Israelite supervisors came to Pharaoh and cried, "Why do you treat your servants like this? ¹⁶No straw is given to your servants, yet they say to us, 'Make bricks!' Look how your servants are beaten! You are unjust to your own people."*ᵇ* ¹⁷He said, "You are lazy, lazy; that is why you say, 'Let us go and sacrifice to the LORD.' ¹⁸Go now, and work; for no straw shall be given you, but you shall still deliver the same number of bricks." ¹⁹The Israelite supervisors saw that they were in trouble when they were told, "You shall not lessen your daily number of bricks." ²⁰As they left Pharaoh, they came upon Moses and Aaron who were waiting to meet them. ²¹They said to them, "The LORD look upon you and judge! You have brought us into bad odor with Pharaoh and his officials, and have put a sword in their hand to kill us."

22 Then Moses turned again to the LORD and said, "O LORD, why have you mistreated this people? Why did you ever send me? ²³Since I first came to Pharaoh to speak in your name, he has

a Sam: Heb *The people of the land are now many*
b Gk Compare Syr Vg: Heb *beaten, and the sin of your people*

mistreated this people, and you have done nothing at all to deliver your people."

Israel's Deliverance Assured

6 Then the LORD said to Moses, "Now you shall see what I will do to Pharaoh: Indeed, by a mighty hand he will let them go; by a mighty hand he will drive them out of his land."

2 God also spoke to Moses and said to him: "I am the LORD. ³I appeared to Abraham, Isaac, and Jacob as God Almighty,ᵃ but by my name 'The LORD'ᵇ I did not make myself known to them. ⁴I also established my covenant with them, to give them the land of Canaan, the land in which they resided as aliens. ⁵I have also heard the groaning of the Israelites whom the Egyptians are holding as slaves, and I have remembered my covenant. ⁶Say therefore to the Israelites, 'I am the LORD, and I will free you from the burdens of the Egyptians and deliver you from slavery to them. I will redeem you with an outstretched arm and with mighty acts of judgment. ⁷I will take you as my people, and I will be your God. You shall know that I am the LORD your God, who has freed you from the burdens of the Egyptians. ⁸I will bring you into the land that I swore to give to Abraham, Isaac, and Jacob; I will give it to you for a possession. I am the LORD.' " ⁹Moses told this to the Israelites; but they would not listen to Moses, because of their broken spirit and their cruel slavery.

10 Then the LORD spoke to Moses, ¹¹"Go and tell Pharaoh king of Egypt to let the Israelites go out of his land." ¹²But Moses spoke to the LORD, "The Israelites have not listened to me; how then shall Pharaoh listen to me, poor speaker that I am?"ᶜ ¹³Thus the LORD spoke to Moses and Aaron, and gave them orders regarding the Israelites and Pharaoh king of Egypt, charging them to free the Israelites from the land of Egypt.

The Genealogy of Moses and Aaron

14 The following are the heads of their ancestral houses: the sons of Reuben, the firstborn of Israel: Hanoch, Pallu, Hezron, and Carmi; these are the families of Reuben. ¹⁵The sons of Simeon: Jemuel, Jamin, Ohad, Jachin, Zohar, and Shaul,ᵈ the son of a Canaanite woman; these are the families of Simeon. ¹⁶The following are the names of the sons of Levi according to their genealogies: Gershon,ᵉ Kohath, and Merari, and the length of Levi's life was one hundred thirty-seven years. ¹⁷The sons of Gershon:ᵉ Libni and Shimei, by their families. ¹⁸The sons of Kohath: Amram, Izhar, Hebron, and Uzziel, and the length of Kohath's life was one hundred thirty-three

Pray It!

Why Me?

Read Exodus 5:22–23. Can you imagine how Moses must have felt? He did what God told him to do, and things only got worse for the Israelites. But Moses was still able to talk to God, even if only to say, "Why did you ever send me?" (verse 22).

Thomas Merton, a famous Trappist monk and spiritual writer, knew that Christians sometimes feel like Moses did:

The Christian
must have the courage
to follow Christ.
The Christian
who is risen in Christ
must dare
to be like Christ:
he must dare
to follow conscience
even in unpopular causes.
He must, if necessary,
be able to disagree with the majority
and make decisions
that he knows
to be according to the Gospel
and teaching of Christ,
even when others
do not understand
why he is acting this way.

[*He Is Risen*, p. 22]

The next time you are feeling a little like Moses and wondering, Why me? try this prayer:

Faithful God, help me to trust in you during times of disappointment and disillusion. I want to believe you are working in ways I cannot see. Please help my disbelief, for I know that you will honor my best efforts and make things come out right in the end. Amen.

▶ Ex 5:22–23

years. ¹⁹The sons of Merari: Mahli and Mushi. These are the families of the Levites according to their genealogies. ²⁰Amram married Jochebed his father's sister and she bore him Aaron and

---

a Traditional rendering of Heb *El Shaddai*   *b* Heb *YHWH*; see note at 3.15   *c* Heb *me? I am uncircumcised of lips*   *d* Or *Saul*
e Also spelled *Gershom*; see 2.22

Moses, and the length of Amram's life was one hundred thirty-seven years. ²¹The sons of Izhar: Korah, Nepheg, and Zichri. ²²The sons of Uzziel: Mishael, Elzaphan, and Sithri. ²³Aaron married Elisheba, daughter of Amminadab and sister of Nahshon, and she bore him Nadab, Abihu, Eleazar, and Ithamar. ²⁴The sons of Korah: Assir, Elkanah, and Abiasaph; these are the families of the Korahites. ²⁵Aaron's son Eleazar married one of the daughters of Putiel, and she bore him Phinehas. These are the heads of the ancestral houses of the Levites by their families.

26 It was this same Aaron and Moses to whom the LORD said, "Bring the Israelites out of the land of Egypt, company by company." ²⁷It was they who spoke to Pharaoh king of Egypt to bring the Israelites out of Egypt, the same Moses and Aaron.

Moses and Aaron Obey God's Commands

28 On the day when the LORD spoke to Moses in the land of Egypt, ²⁹he said to him, "I am the LORD; tell Pharaoh king of Egypt all that I

You Promised, God

The Israelite people had been slaves for so long, they were discouraged and did not believe Moses' liberating message in Exodus 6:1–9. Moses probably sounded crazy to them. The writer of Exodus reminds us of God's faithfulness to God's promises and that God's plans cannot be stopped by human weakness. We too may find it hard to believe in God's power in our lives when we feel burdened and oppressed, especially over a long time.

In your prayer time, reflect or journal on the following questions and suggestion:
- When do you find it hard to believe in God's promises?
- What people do you know who find it hard to accept God's power in their lives?
- What barriers are keeping them from accepting God?
- Make up your own prayer expressing your desire to count on God's promises.

▶ Ex 6:1–9

am speaking to you." ³⁰But Moses said in the LORD's presence, "Since I am a poor speaker,ᵃ why would Pharaoh listen to me?"

7 The LORD said to Moses, "See, I have made you like God to Pharaoh, and your brother Aaron shall be your prophet. ²You shall speak all that I command you, and your brother Aaron shall tell Pharaoh to let the Israelites go out of his land. ³But I will harden Pharaoh's heart, and I will multiply my signs and wonders in the land of Egypt. ⁴When Pharaoh does not listen to you, I will lay my hand upon Egypt and bring my people the Israelites, company by company, out of the land of Egypt by great acts of judgment. ⁵The Egyptians shall know that I am the LORD, when I stretch out my hand against Egypt and bring the Israelites out from among them." ⁶Moses and Aaron did so; they did just as the LORD commanded them. ⁷Moses was eighty years old and Aaron eighty-three when they spoke to Pharaoh.

Aaron's Miraculous Rod

8 The LORD said to Moses and Aaron, ⁹"When Pharaoh says to you, 'Perform a wonder,' then you shall say to Aaron, 'Take your staff and throw it down before Pharaoh, and it will become a snake.'" ¹⁰So Moses and Aaron went to Pharaoh and did as the LORD had commanded; Aaron threw down his staff before Pharaoh and his officials, and it became a snake. ¹¹Then Pharaoh summoned the wise men and the sorcerers; and they also, the magicians of Egypt, did the same by their secret arts. ¹²Each one threw down his staff, and they became snakes; but Aaron's staff swallowed up theirs. ¹³Still Pharaoh's heart was hardened, and he would not listen to them, as the LORD had said.

The First Plague: Water Turned to Blood

14 Then the LORD said to Moses, "Pharaoh's heart is hardened; he refuses to let the people go. ¹⁵Go to Pharaoh in the morning, as he is going out to the water; stand by at the river bank to meet him, and take in your hand the staff that was turned into a snake. ¹⁶Say to him, 'The LORD, the God of the Hebrews, sent me to you to say, "Let my people go, so that they may worship me in the wilderness." But until now you have not listened. ¹⁷Thus says the LORD, "By this you shall know that I am the LORD." See, with the staff that is in my hand I will strike the water that is in the Nile, and it shall be turned to blood. ¹⁸The fish in the river shall die, the river itself

---

ᵃ Heb *am uncircumcised of lips*; see 6.12

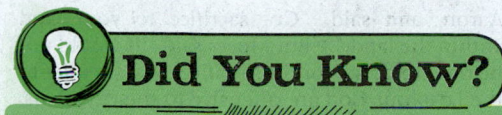

Did You Know?

Plagues and the Crossing of the Red Sea

The writer of Exodus combines several versions of what happened in describing the ten plagues and the crossing of the Red Sea. Like in a fine tapestry, the different strands are carefully woven together to produce a suspenseful story. When Pharaoh refuses to let the Israelites go, God sends ten plagues to convince Pharaoh to cooperate. The first nine plagues are religious interpretations of naturally occurring events. For example, Exodus says that the first plague is the water of the Nile turning to blood. At times silt and microbes pollute and redden the Nile, making the water undrinkable. The Israelite people see God at work in the miraculous timing of these natural events.

Finally, God must resort to drastic measures. For the tenth plague, God sends the angel of death to kill the firstborn children of the Egyptians. Moses has the Israelites mark their doorposts with the blood of a lamb so that the angel of death "passes over" their homes. Pharaoh is now eager to get rid of the Israelites and releases them from service. They gladly begin their journey to God's Promised Land.

After the Israelites leave, Pharaoh regrets his decision and sends his army after them. As the Egyptians close in, the Israelites seem to be trapped at the marshlands by the Red Sea (see map 2, "The Exodus from Egypt"). Although the prose version of this situation in Exodus, chapter 14, and the poetic version in chapter 15 differ in many details, both stress that the Israelites are able to pass through a section of wetlands that was made nearly dry by a strong east wind. The chariot wheels of the Egyptians get stuck in the mud, and as the water returns, they drown. Again, it is the timing of God's help that enables the miraculous escape. God hears God's people and sets them free!

▶ Ex 7:1—14:31

shall stink, and the Egyptians shall be unable to drink water from the Nile.' " ¹⁹The Lord said to Moses, "Say to Aaron, 'Take your staff and stretch out your hand over the waters of Egypt—over its rivers, its canals, and its ponds, and all its pools of water—so that they may become blood; and there shall be blood throughout the whole land of Egypt, even in vessels of wood and in vessels of stone.' "

20 Moses and Aaron did just as the Lord commanded. In the sight of Pharaoh and of his officials he lifted up the staff and struck the water in the river, and all the water in the river was turned into blood, ²¹and the fish in the river died. The river stank so that the Egyptians could not drink its water, and there was blood throughout the whole land of Egypt. ²²But the magicians of Egypt did the same by their secret arts; so Pharaoh's heart remained hardened, and he would not listen to them, as the Lord had said. ²³Pharaoh turned and went into his house, and he did not take even this to heart. ²⁴And all the Egyptians had to dig along the Nile for water to drink, for they could not drink the water of the river.

25 Seven days passed after the Lord had struck the Nile.

The Second Plague: Frogs

8 ᵃ Then the Lord said to Moses, "Go to Pharaoh and say to him, 'Thus says the Lord: Let my people go, so that they may worship me. ²If you refuse to let them go, I will plague your whole country with frogs. ³The river shall swarm with frogs; they shall come up into your palace, into your bedchamber and your bed, and into the houses of your officials and of your people,ᵇ and into your ovens and your kneading bowls. ⁴The frogs shall come up on you and on your people and on all your officials.' " ⁵ᶜ And the Lord said to Moses, "Say to Aaron, 'Stretch out your hand with your staff over the rivers, the canals, and the pools, and make frogs come up on the land of Egypt.' " ⁶So Aaron stretched out his hand over the waters of Egypt; and the frogs came up and covered the land of Egypt. ⁷But the magicians did the same by their secret arts, and brought frogs up on the land of Egypt.

8 Then Pharaoh called Moses and Aaron, and said, "Pray to the Lord to take away the frogs from me and my people, and I will let the people go to sacrifice to the Lord." ⁹Moses said to Pharaoh, "Kindly tell me when I am to pray for you

---

ᵃ Ch 7.26 in Heb   ᵇ Gk: Heb *upon your people*   ᶜ Ch 8.1 in Heb

EX

and for your officials and for your people, that the frogs may be removed from you and your houses and be left only in the Nile." [10]And he said, "Tomorrow." Moses said, "As you say! So that you may know that there is no one like the LORD our God, [11]the frogs shall leave you and your houses and your officials and your people; they shall be left only in the Nile." [12]Then Moses and Aaron went out from Pharaoh; and Moses cried out to the LORD concerning the frogs that he had brought upon Pharaoh.[a] [13]And the LORD did as Moses requested: the frogs died in the houses, the courtyards, and the fields. [14]And they gathered them together in heaps, and the land stank. [15]But when Pharaoh saw that there was a respite, he hardened his heart, and would not listen to them, just as the LORD had said.

The Third Plague: Gnats

[16] Then the LORD said to Moses, "Say to Aaron, 'Stretch out your staff and strike the dust of the earth, so that it may become gnats throughout the whole land of Egypt.'" [17]And they did so; Aaron stretched out his hand with his staff and struck the dust of the earth, and gnats came on humans and animals alike; all the dust of the earth turned into gnats throughout the whole land of Egypt. [18]The magicians tried to produce gnats by their secret arts, but they could not. There were gnats on both humans and animals. [19]And the magicians said to Pharaoh, "This is the finger of God!" But Pharaoh's heart was hardened, and he would not listen to them, just as the LORD had said.

The Fourth Plague: Flies

[20] Then the LORD said to Moses, "Rise early in the morning and present yourself before Pharaoh, as he goes out to the water, and say to him, 'Thus says the LORD: Let my people go, so that they may worship me. [21]For if you will not let my people go, I will send swarms of flies on you, your officials, and your people, and into your houses; and the houses of the Egyptians shall be filled with swarms of flies; so also the land where they live. [22]But on that day I will set apart the land of Goshen, where my people live, so that no swarms of flies shall be there, that you may know that I the LORD am in this land. [23]Thus I will make a distinction[b] between my people and your people. This sign shall appear tomorrow.'" [24]The LORD did so, and great swarms of flies came into the house of Pharaoh and into his officials' houses; in all of Egypt the land was ruined because of the flies.

[25] Then Pharaoh summoned Moses and Aaron, and said, "Go, sacrifice to your God within the land." [26]But Moses said, "It would not be right to do so; for the sacrifices that we offer to the LORD our God are offensive to the Egyptians. If we offer in the sight of the Egyptians sacrifices that are offensive to them, will they not stone us? [27]We must go a three days' journey into the wilderness and sacrifice to the LORD our God as he commands us." [28]So Pharaoh said, "I will let you go to sacrifice to the LORD your God in the wilderness, provided you do not go very far away. Pray for me." [29]Then Moses said, "As soon as I leave you, I will pray to the LORD that the swarms of flies may depart tomorrow from Pharaoh, from his officials, and from his people; only do not let Pharaoh again deal falsely by not letting the people go to sacrifice to the LORD."

[30] So Moses went out from Pharaoh and prayed to the LORD. [31]And the LORD did as Moses asked: he removed the swarms of flies from Pharaoh, from his officials, and from his people; not one remained. [32]But Pharaoh hardened his heart this time also, and would not let the people go.

The Fifth Plague: Livestock Diseased

9 Then the LORD said to Moses, "Go to Pharaoh, and say to him, 'Thus says the LORD, the God of the Hebrews: Let my people go, so that they may worship me. [2]For if you refuse to let them go and still hold them, [3]the hand of the LORD will strike with a deadly pestilence your livestock in the field: the horses, the donkeys, the camels, the herds, and the flocks. [4]But the LORD will make a distinction between the livestock of Israel and the livestock of Egypt, so that nothing shall die of all that belongs to the Israelites.'" [5]The LORD set a time, saying, "Tomorrow the LORD will do this thing in the land." [6]And on the next day the LORD did so; all the livestock of the Egyptians died, but of the livestock of the Israelites not one died. [7]Pharaoh inquired and found that not one of the livestock of the Israelites was dead. But the heart of Pharaoh was hardened, and he would not let the people go.

The Sixth Plague: Boils

[8] Then the LORD said to Moses and Aaron, "Take handfuls of soot from the kiln, and let Moses throw it in the air in the sight of Pharaoh. [9]It shall become fine dust all over the land of Egypt, and shall cause festering boils on humans and animals throughout the whole land of Egypt." [10]So they took soot from the kiln, and

---

a Or frogs, as he had agreed with Pharaoh   *b* Gk Vg: Heb *will set redemption*

stood before Pharaoh, and Moses threw it in the air, and it caused festering boils on humans and animals. ¹¹The magicians could not stand before Moses because of the boils, for the boils afflicted the magicians as well as all the Egyptians. ¹²But the LORD hardened the heart of Pharaoh, and he would not listen to them, just as the LORD had spoken to Moses.

The Seventh Plague: Thunder and Hail

13 Then the LORD said to Moses, "Rise up early in the morning and present yourself before Pharaoh, and say to him, 'Thus says the LORD, the God of the Hebrews: Let my people go, so that they may worship me. ¹⁴For this time I will send all my plagues upon you yourself, and upon your officials, and upon your people, so that you may know that there is no one like me in all the earth. ¹⁵For by now I could have stretched out my hand and struck you and your people with pestilence, and you would have been cut off from the earth. ¹⁶But this is why I have let you live: to show you my power, and to make my name resound through all the earth. ¹⁷You are still exalting yourself against my people, and will not let them go. ¹⁸Tomorrow at this time I will cause the heaviest hail to fall that has ever fallen in Egypt from the day it was founded until now. ¹⁹Send, therefore, and have your livestock and everything that you have in the open field brought to a secure place; every human or animal that is in the open field and is not brought under shelter will die when the hail comes down upon them.'" ²⁰Those officials of Pharaoh who feared the word of the LORD hurried their slaves and livestock off to a secure place. ²¹Those who did not regard the word of the LORD left their slaves and livestock in the open field.

22 The LORD said to Moses, "Stretch out your hand toward heaven so that hail may fall on the whole land of Egypt, on humans and animals and all the plants of the field in the land of Egypt." ²³Then Moses stretched out his staff toward heaven, and the LORD sent thunder and hail, and fire came down on the earth. And the LORD rained hail on the land of Egypt; ²⁴there was hail with fire flashing continually in the midst of it, such heavy hail as had never fallen in all the land of Egypt since it became a nation. ²⁵The hail struck down everything that was in the open field throughout all the land of Egypt, both human and animal; the hail also struck down all the plants of the field, and shattered every tree in the field. ²⁶Only in the land of Goshen, where the Israelites were, there was no hail.

27 Then Pharaoh summoned Moses and Aaron, and said to them, "This time I have sinned; the LORD is in the right, and I and my people are in the wrong. ²⁸Pray to the LORD! Enough of God's thunder and hail! I will let you go; you need stay no longer." ²⁹Moses said to him, "As soon as I have gone out of the city, I will stretch out my hands to the LORD; the thunder will cease, and there will be no more hail, so that you may know that the earth is the LORD's. ³⁰But as for you and your officials, I know that you do not yet fear the LORD God." ³¹(Now the flax and the barley were ruined, for the barley was in the ear and the flax was in bud. ³²But the wheat and the spelt were not ruined, for they are late in coming up.) ³³So Moses left Pharaoh, went out of the city, and stretched out his hands to the LORD; then the thunder and the hail ceased, and the rain no longer poured down on the earth. ³⁴But when Pharaoh saw that the rain and the hail and the thunder had ceased, he sinned once more and hardened his heart, he and his officials. ³⁵So the heart of Pharaoh was hardened, and he would not let the Israelites go, just as the LORD had spoken through Moses.

The Eighth Plague: Locusts

10 Then the LORD said to Moses, "Go to Pharaoh; for I have hardened his heart and the heart of his officials, in order that I may show these signs of mine among them, ²and that you may tell your children and grandchildren how I have made fools of the Egyptians and what signs I have done among them—so that you may know that I am the LORD."

3 So Moses and Aaron went to Pharaoh, and said to him, "Thus says the LORD, the God of the Hebrews, 'How long will you refuse to humble yourself before me? Let my people go, so that they may worship me. ⁴For if you refuse to let my people go, tomorrow I will bring locusts into your country. ⁵They shall cover the surface of the land, so that no one will be able to see the land. They shall devour the last remnant left you after the hail, and they shall devour every tree of yours that grows in the field. ⁶They shall fill your houses, and the houses of all your officials and of all the Egyptians—something that neither your parents nor your grandparents have seen, from the day they came on earth to this day.'" Then he turned and went out from Pharaoh.

7 Pharaoh's officials said to him, "How long shall this fellow be a snare to us? Let the people go, so that they may worship the LORD their God; do you not yet understand that Egypt is ruined?" ⁸So Moses and Aaron were brought back to Pharaoh, and he said to them, "Go, worship the LORD

your God! But which ones are to go?" [9]Moses said, "We will go with our young and our old; we will go with our sons and daughters and with our flocks and herds, because we have the Lord's festival to celebrate." [10]He said to them, "The Lord indeed will be with you, if ever I let your little ones go with you! Plainly, you have some evil purpose in mind. [11]No, never! Your men may go and worship the Lord, for that is what you are asking." And they were driven out from Pharaoh's presence.

12 Then the Lord said to Moses, "Stretch out your hand over the land of Egypt, so that the locusts may come upon it and eat every plant in the land, all that the hail has left." [13]So Moses stretched out his staff over the land of Egypt, and the Lord brought an east wind upon the land all that day and all that night; when morning came, the east wind had brought the locusts. [14]The locusts came upon all the land of Egypt and settled on the whole country of Egypt, such a dense swarm of locusts as had never been before, nor ever shall be again. [15]They covered the surface of the whole land, so that the land was black; and they ate all the plants in the land and all the fruit of the trees that the hail had left; nothing green was left, no tree, no plant in the field, in all the land of Egypt. [16]Pharaoh hurriedly summoned Moses and Aaron and said, "I have sinned against the Lord your God, and against you. [17]Do forgive my sin just this once, and pray to the Lord your God that at the least he remove this deadly thing from me." [18]So he went out from Pharaoh and prayed to the Lord. [19]The Lord changed the wind into a very strong west wind, which lifted the locusts and drove them into the Red Sea;[a] not a single locust was left in all the country of Egypt. [20]But the Lord hardened Pharaoh's heart, and he would not let the Israelites go.

The Ninth Plague: Darkness

21 Then the Lord said to Moses, "Stretch out your hand toward heaven so that there may be darkness over the land of Egypt, a darkness that can be felt." [22]So Moses stretched out his hand toward heaven, and there was dense darkness in all the land of Egypt for three days. [23]People could not see one another, and for three days they could not move from where they were; but all the Israelites had light where they lived. [24]Then Pharaoh summoned Moses, and said, "Go, worship the Lord. Only your flocks and your herds shall remain behind. Even your children may go with you." [25]But Moses said, "You must also let us have sacrifices and burnt offerings to sacrifice to the Lord our God. [26]Our livestock also must

go with us; not a hoof shall be left behind, for we must choose some of them for the worship of the Lord our God, and we will not know what to use to worship the Lord until we arrive there." [27]But the Lord hardened Pharaoh's heart, and he was unwilling to let them go. [28]Then Pharaoh said to him, "Get away from me! Take care that you do not see my face again, for on the day you see my face you shall die." [29]Moses said, "Just as you say! I will never see your face again."

Warning of the Final Plague

11 The Lord said to Moses, "I will bring one more plague upon Pharaoh and upon Egypt; afterwards he will let you go from here; indeed, when he lets you go, he will drive you away. [2]Tell the people that every man is to ask his neighbor and every woman is to ask her neighbor for objects of silver and gold." [3]The Lord gave the people favor in the sight of the Egyptians. Moreover, Moses himself was a man of great importance in the land of Egypt, in the sight of Pharaoh's officials and in the sight of the people.

4 Moses said, "Thus says the Lord: About midnight I will go out through Egypt. [5]Every firstborn in the land of Egypt shall die, from the firstborn of Pharaoh who sits on his throne to the firstborn of the female slave who is behind the handmill, and all the firstborn of the livestock. [6]Then there will be a loud cry throughout the whole land of Egypt, such as has never been or will ever be again. [7]But not a dog shall growl at any of the Israelites—not at people, not at animals—so that you may know that the Lord makes a distinction between Egypt and Israel. [8]Then all these officials of yours shall come down to me, and bow low to me, saying, 'Leave us, you and all the people who follow you.' After that I will leave." And in hot anger he left Pharaoh.

9 The Lord said to Moses, "Pharaoh will not listen to you, in order that my wonders may be multiplied in the land of Egypt." [10]Moses and Aaron performed all these wonders before Pharaoh; but the Lord hardened Pharaoh's heart, and he did not let the people of Israel go out of his land.

The First Passover Instituted

12 The Lord said to Moses and Aaron in the land of Egypt: [2]This month shall mark for you the beginning of months; it shall be the first month of the year for you. [3]Tell the whole congregation of Israel that on the tenth of this

---

a Or Sea of Reeds

month they are to take a lamb for each family, a lamb for each household. ⁴If a household is too small for a whole lamb, it shall join its closest neighbor in obtaining one; the lamb shall be divided in proportion to the number of people who eat of it. ⁵Your lamb shall be without blemish, a year-old male; you may take it from the sheep or from the goats. ⁶You shall keep it until the fourteenth day of this month; then the whole assembled congregation of Israel shall slaughter it at twilight. ⁷They shall take some of the blood and put it on the two doorposts and the lintel of the houses in which they eat it. ⁸They shall eat the lamb that same night; they shall eat it roasted over the fire with unleavened bread and bitter herbs. ⁹Do not eat any of it raw or boiled in water, but roasted over the fire, with its head, legs, and inner organs. ¹⁰You shall let none of it remain until the morning; anything that remains until the morning you shall burn. ¹¹This is how you shall eat it: your loins girded, your sandals on your feet, and your staff in your hand; and you shall eat it hurriedly. It is the passover of the LORD. ¹²For I will pass through the land of Egypt that night, and I will strike down every firstborn in the land of Egypt, both human beings and animals; on all the gods of Egypt I will execute judgments: I am the LORD. ¹³The blood shall be a sign for you on the houses where you live: when I see the blood, I will pass over you, and no plague shall destroy you when I strike the land of Egypt.

14 This day shall be a day of remembrance for you. You shall celebrate it as a festival to the LORD; throughout your generations you shall observe it as a perpetual ordinance. ¹⁵Seven days you shall eat unleavened bread; on the first day you shall remove leaven from your houses, for whoever eats leavened bread from the first day until the seventh day shall be cut off from Israel. ¹⁶On the first day you shall hold a solemn assembly, and on the seventh day a solemn assembly; no work shall be done on those days; only what everyone must eat, that alone may be prepared by you. ¹⁷You shall observe the festival of unleavened bread, for on this very day I brought your companies out of the land of Egypt: you shall observe this day throughout your generations as a perpetual ordinance. ¹⁸In the first month, from the evening of the fourteenth day until the evening of the twenty-first day, you shall eat unleavened bread. ¹⁹For seven days no leaven shall be found in your houses; for whoever eats what is leavened shall be cut off from the congregation of Israel, whether an alien or a native of the land. ²⁰You shall eat

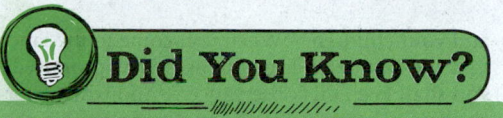

Did You Know?

The Passover

"**W**hy is this night so different from all other nights?" This question, asked by the youngest member of the family, is part of the Jewish celebration of the Passover. Jewish people continue to celebrate the Passover today in fulfillment of Moses' command, "You shall observe this rite as a perpetual ordinance for you and your children" (Ex 12:24).

The Passover is celebrated around a meal including lamb and unleavened bread. The lamb recalls the Passover lamb whose blood was placed on the doorpost to protect the firstborn from the angel of death. The unleavened bread recalls the haste with which the people prepared to depart. Retelling the ancient story, generations of Jews have remembered that "night of nights" when the angel of death passed over the Israelites' houses and struck down the firstborn of the Egyptians. On that night, the people of God were finally released from slavery. Thus, Passover is a celebration of God's gift of freedom—a religious Independence Day, so to speak.

It was during the Passover celebration that Jesus had his farewell dinner (see Lk 22:7–20), placing himself as the Paschal sacrifice. Christians see Jesus as the new Passover; through his death and Resurrection, we are finally liberated from all bondage, including sin and death.

▶ **Ex 12:14–28**

nothing leavened; in all your settlements you shall eat unleavened bread.

21 Then Moses called all the elders of Israel and said to them, "Go, select lambs for your families, and slaughter the passover lamb. Take a bunch of hyssop, dip it in the blood that is in the basin, and touch the lintel and the two doorposts with the blood in the basin. None of you shall go outside the door of your house until morning. ²³For the LORD will pass through to strike down the Egyptians; when he sees the blood on the lintel and on the two doorposts, the LORD will pass over that door and will not allow the destroyer to enter your houses to strike you down. ²⁴You shall observe this rite as a perpetual ordinance for you

and your children. ²⁵When you come to the land that the LORD will give you, as he has promised, you shall keep this observance. ²⁶And when your children ask you, 'What do you mean by this observance?' ²⁷you shall say, 'It is the passover sacrifice to the LORD, for he passed over the houses of the Israelites in Egypt, when he struck down the Egyptians but spared our houses.' " And the people bowed down and worshiped.

28 The Israelites went and did just as the LORD had commanded Moses and Aaron.

The Tenth Plague: Death of the Firstborn

29 At midnight the LORD struck down all the firstborn in the land of Egypt, from the firstborn of Pharaoh who sat on his throne to the firstborn of the prisoner who was in the dungeon, and all the firstborn of the livestock. ³⁰Pharaoh arose in the night, he and all his officials and all the Egyptians; and there was a loud cry in Egypt, for there was not a house without someone dead. ³¹Then he summoned Moses and Aaron in the night, and said, "Rise up, go away from my people, both you and the Israelites! Go, worship the LORD, as you said. ³²Take your flocks and your herds, as you said, and be gone. And bring a blessing on me too!"

The Exodus: From Rameses to Succoth

33 The Egyptians urged the people to hasten their departure from the land, for they said, "We shall all be dead." ³⁴So the people took their dough before it was leavened, with their kneading bowls wrapped up in their cloaks on their shoulders. ³⁵The Israelites had done as Moses told them; they had asked the Egyptians for jewelry of

silver and gold, and for clothing, ³⁶and the LORD had given the people favor in the sight of the Egyptians, so that they let them have what they asked. And so they plundered the Egyptians.

37 The Israelites journeyed from Rameses to Succoth, about six hundred thousand men on foot, besides children. ³⁸A mixed crowd also went up with them, and livestock in great numbers, both flocks and herds. ³⁹They baked unleavened cakes of the dough that they had brought out of Egypt; it was not leavened, because they were driven out of Egypt and could not wait, nor had they prepared any provisions for themselves.

40 The time that the Israelites had lived in Egypt was four hundred thirty years. ⁴¹At the end of four hundred thirty years, on that very day, all the companies of the LORD went out from the land of Egypt. ⁴²That was for the LORD a night of vigil, to bring them out of the land of Egypt. That same night is a vigil to be kept for the LORD by all the Israelites throughout their generations.

Directions for the Passover

43 The LORD said to Moses and Aaron: This is the ordinance for the passover: no foreigner shall eat of it, ⁴⁴but any slave who has been purchased may eat of it after he has been circumcised; ⁴⁵no bound or hired servant may eat of it. ⁴⁶It shall be eaten in one house; you shall not take any of the animal outside the house, and you shall not break any of its bones. ⁴⁷The whole congregation of Israel shall celebrate it. ⁴⁸If an alien who resides with you wants to celebrate the passover to the LORD, all his males shall be circumcised; then he may draw near to celebrate it; he shall be regarded as a native of the land. But no uncircumcised person shall eat of it; ⁴⁹there shall be one law for the native and for the alien who resides among you.

50 All the Israelites did just as the LORD had commanded Moses and Aaron. ⁵¹That very day the LORD brought the Israelites out of the land of Egypt, company by company.

13 The LORD said to Moses: ²Consecrate to me all the firstborn; whatever is the first to open the womb among the Israelites, of human beings and animals, is mine.

The Festival of Unleavened Bread

3 Moses said to the people, "Remember this day on which you came out of Egypt, out of the house of slavery, because the LORD brought you out from there by strength of hand; no leavened bread shall be eaten. ⁴Today, in the month of Abib, you are going out. ⁵When the LORD brings

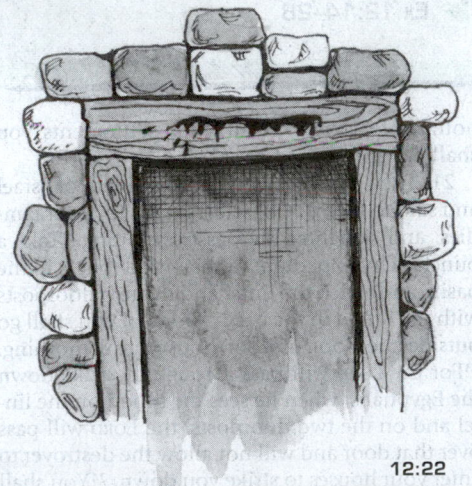

12:22

you into the land of the Canaanites, the Hittites, the Amorites, the Hivites, and the Jebusites, which he swore to your ancestors to give you, a land flowing with milk and honey, you shall keep this observance in this month. ⁶Seven days you shall eat unleavened bread, and on the seventh day there shall be a festival to the Lord. ⁷Unleavened bread shall be eaten for seven days; no leavened bread shall be seen in your possession, and no leaven shall be seen among you in all your territory. ⁸You shall tell your child on that day, 'It is because of what the Lord did for me when I came out of Egypt.' ⁹It shall serve for you as a sign on your hand and as a reminder on your forehead, so that the teaching of the Lord may be on your lips; for with a strong hand the Lord brought you out of Egypt. ¹⁰You shall keep this ordinance at its proper time from year to year.

The Consecration of the Firstborn

11 "When the Lord has brought you into the land of the Canaanites, as he swore to you and your ancestors, and has given it to you, ¹²you shall set apart to the Lord all that first opens the womb. All the firstborn of your livestock that are males shall be the Lord's. ¹³But every firstborn donkey you shall redeem with a sheep; if you do not redeem it, you must break its neck. Every firstborn male among your children you shall redeem. ¹⁴When in the future your child asks you, 'What does this mean?' you shall answer, 'By strength of hand the Lord brought us out of Egypt, from the house of slavery. ¹⁵When Pharaoh stubbornly refused to let us go, the Lord killed all the firstborn in the land of Egypt, from human firstborn to the firstborn of animals. Therefore I sacrifice to the Lord every male that first opens the womb, but every firstborn of my sons I redeem.' ¹⁶It shall serve as a sign on your hand and as an emblem*a* on your forehead that by strength of hand the Lord brought us out of Egypt."

The Pillars of Cloud and Fire

17 When Pharaoh let the people go, God did not lead them by way of the land of the Philistines, although that was nearer; for God thought, "If the people face war, they may change their minds and return to Egypt." ¹⁸So God led the people by the roundabout way of the wilderness toward the Red Sea.*b* The Israelites went up out of the land of Egypt prepared for battle. ¹⁹And Moses took with him the bones of Joseph who had required a solemn oath of the Israelites, saying, "God will surely take notice of you, and then you must carry my bones with you from here."

Live It!

God Liberates Us from Oppression

The crossing of the Red Sea is one of the most famous stories in the Bible. It is ultimately a story that graphically illustrates that God frees us from oppression. The Israelites were free to return once again to the homeland they had left many centuries before. Like so many people before them and since, they became migrants searching for a better place to call home.

Hundreds of thousands of people are migrating at this very moment. Some are fleeing war or political persecution. Many others, like the ancient Israelites when they first went to Egypt, are simply trying to keep their families from starving. Yet, so often, migrants, immigrants, and refugees are treated with disdain. Some people claim that foreigners are "overrunning our country" or "taking our jobs." They forget that the United States, at least, is a nation of immigrants. Their story is very often our own story as well.

● What situations are you aware of where people are being oppressed or exploited because of their immigrant status, their educational level, or their need for food and shelter?
● How can you stand up to unjust situations and welcome the stranger living in your midst?

▶ Ex 14:1–31

²⁰They set out from Succoth, and camped at Etham, on the edge of the wilderness. ²¹The Lord went in front of them in a pillar of cloud by day, to lead them along the way, and in a pillar of fire by night to give them light, so that they might travel by day and by night. ²²Neither the pillar of cloud by day nor the pillar of fire by night left its place in front of the people.

Crossing the Red Sea

14 Then the Lord said to Moses: ²Tell the Israelites to turn back and camp in front of Pi-hahiroth, between Migdol and the sea, in

a Or as a frontlet; meaning of Heb uncertain   *b* Or Sea of Reeds

Cultural Connection

Look to the Hills

An African American theology professor tells a story about two Israelites who, while crossing the Red Sea, kept looking down at their feet. One said: "Look at my feet. They're covered with mud. This is some fine mess that Moses led us into." They crossed the sea without ever looking up. They never saw the sea parted on either side. As they wiped the mud from their feet and garments, they completely missed the sea's closing and the Egyptians' being swallowed up at God's command!

Although it seems like it would have been impossible to miss something so fantastic as the parting of the Red Sea, it is some-times easy to focus so much on the negative that we miss the positive. Some people—especially when life is difficult—keep looking down and miss seeing God's power and their own talents and gifts. Looking down can almost become second nature, poisoning a person's whole attitude. People can waste a lot of time looking down at life's struggles and never looking up.

Brothers and sisters, the resurrected Christ has won victory for all, for people of every race and culture—so look up! Keep your eyes on the high calling of God in Christ Jesus. Remember the hopeful words in Psalm 121:1–2:

I lift up my eyes to the hills—
from where will my help
come?
My help comes from the LORD,
who made heaven and
earth.

● What do you do when self-doubt and negativity tempt you to keep looking down?
● How can you encourage others when it seems that the injustices and struggles of life have beaten them down?

▶ Ex 14:1–31

front of Baal-zephon; you shall camp opposite it, by the sea. ³Pharaoh will say of the Israelites, "They are wandering aimlessly in the land; the wilderness has closed in on them." ⁴I will harden Pharaoh's heart, and he will pursue them, so that I will gain glory for myself over Pharaoh and all his army; and the Egyptians shall know that I am the LORD. And they did so.

5 When the king of Egypt was told that the people had fled, the minds of Pharaoh and his officials were changed toward the people, and they said, "What have we done, letting Israel leave our service?" ⁶So he had his chariot made ready, and took his army with him; ⁷he took six hundred picked chariots and all the other chariots of Egypt with officers over all of them. ⁸The LORD hardened the heart of Pharaoh king of Egypt and he pursued the Israelites, who were going out boldly. ⁹The Egyptians pursued them, all Pharaoh's horses and chariots, his chariot drivers and his army; they overtook them camped by the sea, by Pi-hahiroth, in front of Baal-zephon.

10 As Pharaoh drew near, the Israelites looked back, and there were the Egyptians advancing on them. In great fear the Israelites cried out to the LORD. ¹¹They said to Moses, "Was it because there were no graves in Egypt that you have taken us away to die in the wilderness? What have you done to us, bringing us out of Egypt? ¹²Is this not the very thing we told you in Egypt, 'Let us alone and let us serve the Egyptians'? For it would have been better for us to serve the Egyptians than to die in the wilderness." ¹³But Moses said to the people, "Do not be afraid, stand firm, and see the deliverance that the LORD will accomplish for you today; for the Egyptians whom you see today you shall never see again. ¹⁴The LORD will fight for you, and you have only to keep still."

15 Then the LORD said to Moses, "Why do you cry out to me? Tell the Israelites to go forward. ¹⁶But you lift up your staff, and stretch out your hand over the sea and divide it, that the Israelites may go into the sea on dry ground. ¹⁷Then I will harden the hearts of the Egyptians so that they will go in after them; and so I will gain glory for myself over Pharaoh and all his army, his chariots, and his chariot drivers. ¹⁸And the Egyptians shall know that I am the LORD, when I have gained glory for myself over Pharaoh, his chariots, and his chariot drivers."

19 The angel of God who was going before the Israelite army moved and went behind them; and the pillar of cloud moved from in front of them and took its place behind them. ²⁰It came

between the army of Egypt and the army of Israel. And so the cloud was there with the darkness, and it lit up the night; one did not come near the other all night.

21　Then Moses stretched out his hand over the sea. The LORD drove the sea back by a strong east wind all night, and turned the sea into dry land; and the waters were divided. ²²The Israelites went into the sea on dry ground, the waters forming a wall for them on their right and on their left. ²³The Egyptians pursued, and went into the sea after them, all of Pharaoh's horses, chariots, and chariot drivers. ²⁴At the morning watch the LORD in the pillar of fire and cloud looked down upon the Egyptian army, and threw the Egyptian army into panic. ²⁵He clogged*a* their chariot wheels so that they turned with difficulty. The Egyptians said, "Let us flee from the Israelites, for the LORD is fighting for them against Egypt."

The Pursuers Drowned

26　Then the LORD said to Moses, "Stretch out your hand over the sea, so that the water may come back upon the Egyptians, upon their chariots and chariot drivers." ²⁷So Moses stretched out his hand over the sea, and at dawn the sea returned to its normal depth. As the Egyptians fled before it, the LORD tossed the Egyptians into the sea. ²⁸The waters returned and covered the chariots and the chariot drivers, the entire army of Pharaoh that had followed them into the sea; not one of them remained. ²⁹But the Israelites walked on dry ground through the sea, the waters forming a wall for them on their right and on their left.

30　Thus the LORD saved Israel that day from the Egyptians; and Israel saw the Egyptians dead on the seashore. ³¹Israel saw the great work that the LORD did against the Egyptians. So the people feared the LORD and believed in the LORD and in his servant Moses.

The Song of Moses

15 Then Moses and the Israelites sang this song to the LORD:

"I will sing to the LORD, for he has triumphed
　　gloriously;
　horse and rider he has thrown into the sea.
² The LORD is my strength and my might,*b*
　　and he has become my salvation;
　this is my God, and I will praise him,
　　my father's God, and I will exalt him.
³ The LORD is a warrior;
　　the LORD is his name.

⁴ "Pharaoh's chariots and his army he cast into
　　the sea;

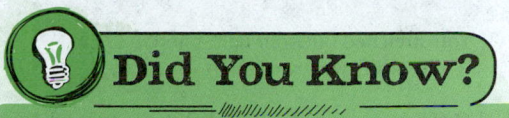

Did You Know?

Song at the Sea

The Song at the Sea in Exodus 15:1–21 is probably the oldest writing in the Bible. It is an example of how the Israelite people put stories of God's mighty deeds into song so that they could be remembered and passed on from generation to generation.

Verses 20–21 tell us that the prophetess Miriam led the prayer—singing and dancing. Miriam was Moses and Aaron's sister. It is most likely Miriam who watched over her younger brother Moses when their mother placed him in the basket amid the reeds (see Ex 2:4,7–8; Num 26:59).

The prophet Micah describes Moses, Aaron, and Miriam as a leadership team sent by God (see Mic 6:4). Many biblical scholars believe that Miriam may be the author of the Song at the Sea. This is one of the few biblical stories that clearly shows a woman serving as a prayer leader.

▶ **Ex 15:1–21**

his picked officers were sunk in the Red Sea.*c*
⁵ The floods covered them;
　　they went down into the depths like a stone.
⁶ Your right hand, O LORD, glorious in power—
　　your right hand, O LORD, shattered the enemy.
⁷ In the greatness of your majesty you overthrew
　　your adversaries;
　you sent out your fury, it consumed them like
　　stubble.
⁸ At the blast of your nostrils the waters piled up,
　　the floods stood up in a heap;
　　the deeps congealed in the heart of the sea.
⁹ The enemy said, 'I will pursue, I will overtake,
　　I will divide the spoil, my desire shall have its
　　　fill of them.
　　I will draw my sword, my hand shall destroy
　　　them.'
¹⁰ You blew with your wind, the sea covered them;
　　they sank like lead in the mighty waters.

¹¹ "Who is like you, O LORD, among the gods?
　　Who is like you, majestic in holiness,
　　awesome in splendor, doing wonders?

---

a Sam Gk Syr: MT removed　b Or song　c Or Sea of Reeds

12 You stretched out your right hand,
     the earth swallowed them.

13 "In your steadfast love you led the people whom
     you redeemed;
     you guided them by your strength to your
     holy abode.

14 The peoples heard, they trembled;
     pangs seized the inhabitants of Philistia.

15 Then the chiefs of Edom were dismayed;
     trembling seized the leaders of Moab;
     all the inhabitants of Canaan melted away.

16 Terror and dread fell upon them;
     by the might of your arm, they became still as
     a stone

until your people, O Lord, passed by,
     until the people whom you acquired
     passed by.

17 You brought them in and planted them on the
     mountain of your own possession,
     the place, O Lord, that you made your abode,
     the sanctuary, O Lord, that your hands have
     established.

18 The Lord will reign forever and ever."

19 When the horses of Pharaoh with his chariots and his chariot drivers went into the sea, the Lord brought back the waters of the sea upon them; but the Israelites walked through the sea on dry ground.

The Song of Miriam

20 Then the prophet Miriam, Aaron's sister, took a tambourine in her hand; and all the women went out after her with tambourines and with dancing. 21 And Miriam sang to them:

"Sing to the Lord, for he has triumphed
     gloriously;
horse and rider he has thrown into the sea."

Bitter Water Made Sweet

22 Then Moses ordered Israel to set out from the Red Sea,ᵃ and they went into the wilderness of Shur. They went three days in the wilderness and found no water. 23 When they came to Marah, they could not drink the water of Marah because it was bitter. That is why it was called Marah.ᵇ 24 And the people complained against Moses, saying, "What shall we drink?" 25 He cried out to the Lord; and the Lord showed him a piece of wood;ᶜ he threw it into the water, and the water became sweet.

There the Lordᵈ made for them a statute and an ordinance and there he put them to the test. 26 He said, "If you will listen carefully to the voice of the Lord your God, and do what is right in his sight, and give heed to his commandments and keep all his statutes, I will not bring upon you any of the diseases that I brought upon the Egyptians; for I am the Lord who heals you."

27 Then they came to Elim, where there were twelve springs of water and seventy palm trees; and they camped there by the water.

Bread from Heaven

16 The whole congregation of the Israelites set out from Elim; and Israel came to the wilderness of Sin, which is between Elim and Sinai, on the fifteenth day of the second month after they had departed from the land of Egypt. 2 The

Introducing...

Moses

Moses is, without doubt, the most important character in the Pentateuch, if not the entire Old Testament. Struggling to find language to describe his greatness, Deuteronomy 34:10 says, "Never since has there arisen a prophet in Israel like Moses, whom the Lord knew face to face." Born to a couple from the tribe of Levi and raised as an Egyptian by the Pharaoh's daughter, Moses was perfectly suited to negotiate Israel's freedom from slavery in Egypt. In event after event, the author of Exodus shows us Moses' wonder-working power, his prophetic skill, and his intimacy with God.

Despite all of Moses' great accomplishments, he never loses his humanness. He lacks confidence in his ability to speak (see Ex 4:10), he is angry and frustrated with his people (see 17:4), and he bargains with God out of love for his people (see 32:11–14). Moses, noble but also knowing sadness, is elegantly portrayed in the passage where he dies within sight of the Promised Land (see Deuteronomy, chapter 34). These qualities paint a picture of someone whose perseverance and trust allow God to work through him.

A prophet is literally God's voice, and Moses was indeed God's voice, which shaped Israel to be a people of the Covenant. All other leaders and figures in the Old Testament are compared with Moses. In the New Testament, even Jesus is compared with Moses.

a Or Sea of Reeds   b That is Bitterness   c Or a tree   d Heb he

whole congregation of the Israelites complained against Moses and Aaron in the wilderness. ³The Israelites said to them, "If only we had died by the hand of the LORD in the land of Egypt, when we sat by the fleshpots and ate our fill of bread; for you have brought us out into this wilderness to kill this whole assembly with hunger."

4 Then the LORD said to Moses, "I am going to rain bread from heaven for you, and each day the people shall go out and gather enough for that day. In that way I will test them, whether they will follow my instruction or not. ⁵On the sixth day, when they prepare what they bring in, it will be twice as much as they gather on other days." ⁶So Moses and Aaron said to all the Israelites, "In the evening you shall know that it was the LORD who brought you out of the land of Egypt, ⁷and in the morning you shall see the glory of the LORD, because he has heard your complaining against the LORD. For what are we, that you complain against us?" ⁸And Moses said, "When the LORD gives you meat to eat in the evening and your fill of bread in the morning, because the LORD has heard the complaining that you utter against him—what are we? Your complaining is not against us but against the LORD."

9 Then Moses said to Aaron, "Say to the whole congregation of the Israelites, 'Draw near to the LORD, for he has heard your complaining.' " ¹⁰And as Aaron spoke to the whole congregation of the Israelites, they looked toward the wilderness, and the glory of the LORD appeared in the cloud. ¹¹The LORD spoke to Moses and said, ¹²"I have heard the complaining of the Israelites; say to them, 'At twilight you shall eat meat, and in the morning you shall have your fill of bread; then you shall know that I am the LORD your God.' "

13 In the evening quails came up and covered the camp; and in the morning there was a layer of dew around the camp. ¹⁴When the layer of dew lifted, there on the surface of the wilderness was a fine flaky substance, as fine as frost on the ground. ¹⁵When the Israelites saw it, they said to one another, "What is it?"ᵃ For they did not know what it was. Moses said to them, "It is the bread that the LORD has given you to eat. ¹⁶This is what the LORD has commanded. 'Gather as much of it as each of you needs, an omer to a person according to the number of persons, all providing for those in their own tents.' " ¹⁷The Israelites did so, some gathering more, some less. ¹⁸But when they measured it with an omer, those who gathered much had nothing over, and those who gathered little had no shortage; they gathered as much as each of them needed. ¹⁹And Moses said to them, "Let no one leave any of it over until

Those Whiny Israelites

It's so easy to complain, isn't it? As soon as things aren't quite the way we would like, we start fussing and whining and grumbling. We have all done it. We are no different from the Israelites who, despite having just been miraculously delivered from slavery, start complaining after a few days in the wilderness. "Why," they ask, "would God lead us through the Red Sea only to let us die of hunger?"

The next time we hear ourselves complaining about something, let's pause and try to see a bigger picture, perhaps the one that God sees. Then we can ask ourselves, Is this really worth complaining about?

▶ Ex 16:1–3

morning." ²⁰But they did not listen to Moses; some left part of it until morning, and it bred worms and became foul. And Moses was angry with them. ²¹Morning by morning they gathered it, as much as each needed; but when the sun grew hot, it melted.

22 On the sixth day they gathered twice as much food, two omers apiece. When all the leaders of the congregation came and told Moses, ²³he said to them, "This is what the LORD has commanded: 'Tomorrow is a day of solemn rest, a holy sabbath to the LORD; bake what you want to bake and boil what you want to boil, and all that is left over put aside to be kept until morning.' " ²⁴So they put it aside until morning, as Moses commanded them; and it did not become foul, and there were no worms in it. ²⁵Moses said, "Eat it today, for today is a sabbath to the LORD; today you will not find it in the field. ²⁶Six days you shall gather it; but on the seventh day, which is a sabbath, there will be none."

27 On the seventh day some of the people went out to gather, and they found none. ²⁸The LORD said to Moses, "How long will you refuse to keep my commandments and instructions? ²⁹See! The LORD has given you the sabbath, therefore on the sixth day he gives you food for

ᵃ Or "It is manna" (Heb man hu, see verse 31)

Cultural Connection

Manna and Rice

Rice is the symbol of our life
We eat rice daily
There are different kinds of rice
But we are one
as the rice-eating community
Rice is the symbol of celebration
We express our joy of harvest with it
There are many sufferings in Asia
but we anticipate the time of cosmic celebration.
> (From Maren C. Tirabassi and
> Kathy Wonson Eddy, editors,
> *Gifts of Many Cultures*, p. 186)

This poem from Japan, by Masao and Fumiko Takenaka, expresses their appreciation for rice, the most basic food of the Japanese. It unites them as a people and reminds them to be joyful. In a similar way, Exodus tells how the gift of manna united the Israelites and gave them a reason for celebration despite their many trials. What foods unite you and your friends? your family? your culture? What connections do you see between manna, rice, and the Eucharist?

▶ Ex 16:1–36

two days; each of you stay where you are; do not leave your place on the seventh day." ³⁰So the people rested on the seventh day.

31 The house of Israel called it manna; it was like coriander seed, white, and the taste of it was like wafers made with honey. ³²Moses said, "This is what the LORD has commanded: 'Let an omer of it be kept throughout your generations, in order that they may see the food with which I fed you in the wilderness, when I brought you out of the land of Egypt.'" ³³And Moses said to Aaron, "Take a jar, and put an omer of manna in it, and place it before the LORD, to be kept throughout your generations." ³⁴As the LORD commanded Moses, so Aaron placed it before the covenant,ᵃ for safekeeping. ³⁵The Israelites ate manna forty years, until they came to a habitable land; they ate manna, until they came to the border of the land of Canaan. ³⁶An omer is a tenth of an ephah.

Water from the Rock

17 From the wilderness of Sin the whole congregation of the Israelites journeyed by stages, as the LORD commanded. They camped at Rephidim, but there was no water for the people to drink. ²The people quarreled with Moses, and said, "Give us water to drink." Moses said to them, "Why do you quarrel with me? Why do you test the LORD?" ³But the people thirsted there for water; and the people complained against Moses and said, "Why did you bring us out of Egypt, to kill us and our children and livestock with thirst?" ⁴So Moses cried out to the LORD, "What shall I do with this people? They are almost ready to stone me." ⁵The LORD said to Moses, "Go on

ahead of the people, and take some of the elders of Israel with you; take in your hand the staff with which you struck the Nile, and go. ⁶I will be standing there in front of you on the rock at Horeb. Strike the rock, and water will come out of it, so that the people may drink." Moses did so, in the sight of the elders of Israel. ⁷He called the place Massahᵇ and Meribah,ᶜ because the Israelites quarreled and tested the LORD, saying, "Is the LORD among us or not?"

Amalek Attacks Israel and Is Defeated

8 Then Amalek came and fought with Israel at Rephidim. ⁹Moses said to Joshua, "Choose some men for us and go out, fight with Amalek. Tomorrow I will stand on the top of the hill with the staff of God in my hand." ¹⁰So Joshua did as Moses told him, and fought with Amalek, while Moses, Aaron, and Hur went up to the top of the hill. ¹¹Whenever Moses held up his hand, Israel prevailed; and whenever he lowered his hand, Amalek prevailed. ¹²But Moses' hands grew weary; so they took a stone and put it under him, and he sat on it. Aaron and Hur held up his hands, one on one side, and the other on the other side; so his hands were steady until the sun set. ¹³And Joshua defeated Amalek and his people with the sword.

14 Then the LORD said to Moses, "Write this as a reminder in a book and recite it in the hearing of Joshua: I will utterly blot out the remembrance of Amalek from under heaven." ¹⁵And Moses built an altar and called it, The LORD is my

---

a Or *treaty* or *testimony*; Heb *eduth*　*b* That is *Test*　*c* That is *Quarrel*

banner. ¹⁶He said, "A hand upon the banner of the Lord!^a The Lord will have war with Amalek from generation to generation."

Jethro's Advice

18 Jethro, the priest of Midian, Moses' father-in-law, heard of all that God had done for Moses and for his people Israel, how the Lord had brought Israel out of Egypt. ²After Moses had sent away his wife Zipporah, his father-in-law Jethro took her back, ³along with her two sons. The name of the one was Gershom (for he said, "I have been an alien^b in a foreign land"), ⁴and the name of the other, Eliezer^c (for he said, "The God of my father was my help, and delivered me from the sword of Pharaoh"). ⁵Jethro, Moses' father-in-law, came into the wilderness where Moses was encamped at the mountain of God, bringing Moses' sons and wife to him. ⁶He sent word to Moses, "I, your father-in-law Jethro, am coming to you, with your wife and her two sons." ⁷Moses went out to meet his father-in-law; he bowed down and kissed him; each asked after the other's welfare, and they went into the tent. ⁸Then Moses told his father-in-law all that the Lord had done to Pharaoh and to the Egyptians for Israel's sake, all the hardship that had beset them on the way, and how the Lord had delivered them. ⁹Jethro rejoiced for all the good that the Lord had done to Israel, in delivering them from the Egyptians.

10 Jethro said, "Blessed be the Lord, who has delivered you from the Egyptians and from Pharaoh. ¹¹Now I know that the Lord is greater than all gods, because he delivered the people from the Egyptians,^d when they dealt arrogantly with them." ¹²And Jethro, Moses' father-in-law, brought a burnt offering and sacrifices to God; and Aaron came with all the elders of Israel to eat bread with Moses' father-in-law in the presence of God.

13 The next day Moses sat as judge for the people, while the people stood around him from morning until evening. ¹⁴When Moses' father-in-law saw all that he was doing for the people, he said, "What is this that you are doing for the people? Why do you sit alone, while all the people stand around you from morning until evening?" ¹⁵Moses said to his father-in-law, "Because the people come to me to inquire of God. ¹⁶When they have a dispute, they come to me and I decide between one person and another, and I make known to them the statutes and instructions of God." ¹⁷Moses' father-in-law said to him, "What you are doing is not good. ¹⁸You will surely wear yourself out, both you and these

Pray It!

Prayer in Support of Others

During the battle against Amalek, Moses' outstretched arms could be understood as a prayer of support for the Israelites. It was an effective prayer too, because as long as he was able to maintain it, the Israelites were winning. When he could not maintain the prayer by himself, Aaron and Hur helped.

Prayer makes a difference. Research has shown that prayer helps people's emotional and physical health and healing, though it cannot explain why. Spiritual energy is a proven, powerful force.

Prayer doesn't even need words. To hold someone in prayer, just think of the person, and quietly take his or her pain or joy into your heart. Who in your life right now needs to be held in prayer? Take a moment to pray for those people.

▶ **Ex 17:8–16**

people with you. For the task is too heavy for you; you cannot do it alone. ¹⁹Now listen to me. I will give you counsel, and God be with you! You should represent the people before God, and you should bring their cases before God; ²⁰teach them the statutes and instructions and make known to them the way they are to go and the things they are to do. ²¹You should also look for able men among all the people, men who fear God, are trustworthy, and hate dishonest gain; set such men over them as officers over thousands, hundreds, fifties, and tens. ²²Let them sit as judges for the people at all times; let them bring every important case to you, but decide every minor case themselves. So it will be easier for you, and they will bear the burden with you. ²³If you do this, and God so commands you, then you will be able to endure, and all these people will go to their home in peace."

24 So Moses listened to his father-in-law and

---

^a Cn: Meaning of Heb uncertain   ^b Heb *ger*   ^c Heb *Eli, my God; ezer, help*   ^d The clause *because . . . Egyptians* has been transposed from verse 10

E X

Live It!

Sharing Responsibility

Was Moses a workaholic (see Ex 18:18)? Maybe he just found himself suddenly overwhelmed by too many responsibilities. Fortunately for Moses, he had a wise father-in-law, Jethro, who offered some advice to help lighten his load. Moses heeded his advice and asked others to help him. In the process, Moses empowered others to take responsibility and was relieved of his burden as well. It was truly a win-win situation.

When leaders share responsibility, they are saying to other people, "I trust you, we're in this together, and you are needed." When you are in a leadership position, remember Jethro's advice to Moses, and don't be a lone ranger; ask others to help!

▶ Ex 18:13–26

did all that he had said. ²⁵Moses chose able men from all Israel and appointed them as heads over the people, as officers over thousands, hundreds, fifties, and tens. ²⁶And they judged the people at all times; hard cases they brought to Moses, but any minor case they decided themselves. ²⁷Then Moses let his father-in-law depart, and he went off to his own country.

The Israelites Reach Mount Sinai

19 On the third new moon after the Israelites had gone out of the land of Egypt, on that very day, they came into the wilderness of Sinai. ²They had journeyed from Rephidim, entered the wilderness of Sinai, and camped in the wilderness; Israel camped there in front of the mountain. ³Then Moses went up to God; the LORD called to him from the mountain, saying, "Thus you shall say to the house of Jacob, and tell the Israelites: ⁴You have seen what I did to the Egyptians, and how I bore you on eagles' wings and brought you to myself. ⁵Now therefore, if you obey my voice and keep my covenant, you shall be my treasured possession out of all the peoples. Indeed, the whole earth is mine, ⁶but you shall be for me a priestly kingdom and a holy

nation. These are the words that you shall speak to the Israelites."

7 So Moses came, summoned the elders of the people, and set before them all these words that the LORD had commanded him. ⁸The people all answered as one: "Everything that the LORD has spoken we will do." Moses reported the words of the people to the LORD. ⁹Then the LORD said to Moses, "I am going to come to you in a dense cloud, in order that the people may hear when I speak with you and so trust you ever after."

The People Consecrated

When Moses had told the words of the people to the LORD, ¹⁰the LORD said to Moses: "Go to the people and consecrate them today and tomorrow. Have them wash their clothes ¹¹and prepare for the third day, because on the third day the LORD will come down upon Mount Sinai in the sight of all the people. ¹²You shall set limits for the people all around, saying, 'Be careful not to go up the mountain or to touch the edge of it. Any who touch the mountain shall be put to death. ¹³No hand shall touch them, but they shall be stoned or shot with arrows;ᵃ whether animal or human being, they shall not live.' When the trumpet sounds a long blast, they may go up on the mountain." ¹⁴So Moses went down from the mountain to the people. He consecrated the people, and they washed their clothes. ¹⁵And he said to the people, "Prepare for the third day; do not go near a woman."

16 On the morning of the third day there was thunder and lightning, as well as a thick cloud on the mountain, and a blast of a trumpet so loud that all the people who were in the camp trembled. ¹⁷Moses brought the people out of the camp to meet God. They took their stand at the foot of the mountain. ¹⁸Now Mount Sinai was wrapped in smoke, because the LORD had descended upon it in fire; the smoke went up like the smoke of a kiln, while the whole mountain shook violently. ¹⁹As the blast of the trumpet grew louder and louder, Moses would speak and God would answer him in thunder. ²⁰When the LORD descended upon Mount Sinai, to the top of the mountain, the LORD summoned Moses to the top of the mountain, and Moses went up. ²¹Then the LORD said to Moses, "Go down and warn the people not to break through to the LORD to look; otherwise many of them will perish. ²²Even the priests who approach the LORD must consecrate themselves or the LORD will break out against them." ²³Moses said to the LORD, "The people are

ᵃ Heb lacks *with arrows*

not permitted to come up to Mount Sinai; for you yourself warned us, saying, 'Set limits around the mountain and keep it holy.'" ²⁴The Lord said to him, "Go down, and come up bringing Aaron with you; but do not let either the priests or the people break through to come up to the Lord; otherwise he will break out against them." ²⁵So Moses went down to the people and told them.

The Ten Commandments

20 Then God spoke all these words:
2 I am the Lord your God, who brought you out of the land of Egypt, out of the house of slavery; ³you shall have no other gods before*ᵃ* me.

4 You shall not make for yourself an idol, whether in the form of anything that is in heaven above, or that is on the earth beneath, or that is in the water under the earth. ⁵You shall not bow down to them or worship them; for I the Lord your God am a jealous God, punishing children for the iniquity of parents, to the third and the fourth generation of those who reject me, ⁶but showing steadfast love to the thousandth generation*ᵇ* of those who love me and keep my commandments.

7 You shall not make wrongful use of the name of the Lord your God, for the Lord will not acquit anyone who misuses his name.

8 Remember the sabbath day, and keep it holy. ⁹Six days you shall labor and do all your work. ¹⁰But the seventh day is a sabbath to the Lord your God; you shall not do any work—you, your son or your daughter, your male or female slave, your livestock, or the alien resident in your towns. ¹¹For in six days the Lord made heaven and earth, the sea, and all that is in them, but rested the seventh day; therefore the Lord blessed the sabbath day and consecrated it.

12 Honor your father and your mother, so

a Or besides   *b* Or to thousands

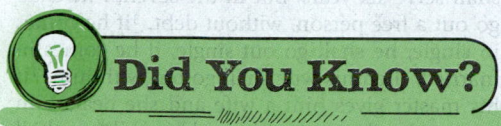

The Ten Commandments

The Covenant God made with the Israelites is often called the Sinai Covenant. The Ten Commandments are a handy summary of the Sinai Covenant—literally handy because they can be counted off on one's fingers. Because the commandments are short (so short that they are sometimes called the Ten Words) and most of them begin with a similar phrase ("You shall not"), they are easily committed to memory. The ancient Israelites believed that everyone had to know and observe these basic rules if God's people were to live together in peace and security. Today, three major world religions—Jewish, Christian, and Islamic—continue to revere the Ten Commandments as basic building blocks of human community.

For the ancient Israelites, the Ten Commandments covered specific behaviors that made them different from the neighboring cultures. Over the centuries, Christians have applied the moral principles of the Ten Commandments to many other moral questions. In fact, the *Catechism of the Catholic Church* presents the Ten Commandments as the structure for teaching about many moral issues. For Jesus' teaching on the commandments, see Matthew 5:1—7:29, 22:34–40; and Mark 12:28–34.

▶ Ex 20:1–17

The Ten Commandments

Listed in the traditional order using the words of Exodus

1. I am the Lord your God . . . you shall have no other gods before me.
2. You shall not make wrongful use of the name of the Lord your God.
3. Remember the sabbath day, and keep it holy.
4. Honor your father and your mother.
5. You shall not murder.
6. You shall not commit adultery.
7. You shall not steal.
8. You shall not bear false witness against your neighbor.
9. & 10. You shall not covet your neighbor's house; you shall not covet your neighbor's wife . . . or anything that belongs to your neighbor.

▶ Ex 20:2–17

Living the Ten Commandments

If there is any part of the Old Testament that most people have heard of, it is probably the Ten Commandments. They are so basic and so familiar to us, primarily because they make so much sense. Disobeying authority, stealing, lying, killing, committing adultery: these actions happen all around us today, just as they did four thousand years ago. The bottom line is that the Ten Commandments still make sense; they are still valid, because human nature hasn't really changed, and God knows that. So, look them over carefully, commit them to memory, and ask God to help you with the ones that are the most challenging.

▶ **Ex 20:1–17**

that your days may be long in the land that the Lord your God is giving you.

13 You shall not murder.[a]

14 You shall not commit adultery.

15 You shall not steal.

16 You shall not bear false witness against your neighbor.

17 You shall not covet your neighbor's house; you shall not covet your neighbor's wife, or male or female slave, or ox, or donkey, or anything that belongs to your neighbor.

18 When all the people witnessed the thunder and lightning, the sound of the trumpet, and the mountain smoking, they were afraid[b] and trembled and stood at a distance, 19and said to Moses, "You speak to us, and we will listen; but do not let God speak to us, or we will die." 20Moses said to the people, "Do not be afraid; for God has come only to test you and to put the fear of him upon you so that you do not sin." 21Then the people stood at a distance, while Moses drew near to the thick darkness where God was.

The Law concerning the Altar

22 The Lord said to Moses: Thus you shall say to the Israelites: "You have seen for yourselves that I spoke with you from heaven. 23You shall not make gods of silver alongside me, nor shall

you make for yourselves gods of gold. 24You need make for me only an altar of earth and sacrifice on it your burnt offerings and your offerings of well-being, your sheep and your oxen; in every place where I cause my name to be remembered I will come to you and bless you. 25But if you make for me an altar of stone, do not build it of hewn stones; for if you use a chisel upon it you profane it. 26You shall not go up by steps to my altar, so that your nakedness may not be exposed on it."

The Law concerning Slaves

21 These are the ordinances that you shall set before them:

2 When you buy a male Hebrew slave, he shall serve six years, but in the seventh he shall go out a free person, without debt. 3If he comes in single, he shall go out single; if he comes in married, then his wife shall go out with him. 4If his master gives him a wife and she bears him sons or daughters, the wife and her children shall be her master's and he shall go out alone. 5But if the slave declares, "I love my master, my wife, and my children; I will not go out a free person," 6then his master shall bring him before God.[c] He shall be brought to the door or the doorpost; and his master shall pierce his ear with an awl; and he shall serve him for life.

7 When a man sells his daughter as a slave, she shall not go out as the male slaves do. 8If she does not please her master, who designated her for himself, then he shall let her be redeemed; he shall have no right to sell her to a foreign people, since he has dealt unfairly with her. 9If he designates her for his son, he shall deal with her as with a daughter. 10If he takes another wife to himself, he shall not diminish the food, clothing, or marital rights of the first wife.[d] 11And if he does not do these three things for her, she shall go out without debt, without payment of money.

The Law concerning Violence

12 Whoever strikes a person mortally shall be put to death. 13If it was not premeditated, but came about by an act of God, then I will appoint for you a place to which the killer may flee. 14But if someone willfully attacks and kills another by treachery, you shall take the killer from my altar for execution.

15 Whoever strikes father or mother shall be put to death.

16 Whoever kidnaps a person, whether that

---

a Or kill   b Sam Gk Syr Vg: MT they saw   c Or to the judges
d Heb of her

person has been sold or is still held in possession, shall be put to death.

17 Whoever curses father or mother shall be put to death.

18 When individuals quarrel and one strikes the other with a stone or fist so that the injured party, though not dead, is confined to bed, 19but recovers and walks around outside with the help of a staff, then the assailant shall be free of liability, except to pay for the loss of time, and to arrange for full recovery.

20 When a slaveowner strikes a male or female slave with a rod and the slave dies immediately, the owner shall be punished. 21But if the slave survives a day or two, there is no punishment; for the slave is the owner's property.

22 When people who are fighting injure a pregnant woman so that there is a miscarriage, and yet no further harm follows, the one responsible shall be fined what the woman's husband demands, paying as much as the judges determine. 23If any harm follows, then you shall give life for life, 24eye for eye, tooth for tooth, hand for hand, foot for foot, 25burn for burn, wound for wound, stripe for stripe.

26 When a slaveowner strikes the eye of a male or female slave, destroying it, the owner shall let the slave go, a free person, to compensate for the eye. 27If the owner knocks out a tooth of a male or female slave, the slave shall be let go, a free person, to compensate for the tooth.

Laws concerning Property

28 When an ox gores a man or a woman to death, the ox shall be stoned, and its flesh shall not be eaten; but the owner of the ox shall not be liable. 29If the ox has been accustomed to gore in the past, and its owner has been warned but has not restrained it, and it kills a man or a woman, the ox shall be stoned, and its owner also shall be put to death. 30If a ransom is imposed on the owner, then the owner shall pay whatever is imposed for the redemption of the victim's life. 31If it gores a boy or a girl, the owner shall be dealt with according to this same rule. 32If the ox gores a male or female slave, the owner shall pay to the slaveowner thirty shekels of silver, and the ox shall be stoned.

33 If someone leaves a pit open, or digs a pit and does not cover it, and an ox or a donkey falls into it, 34the owner of the pit shall make restitution, giving money to its owner, but keeping the dead animal.

35 If someone's ox hurts the ox of another, so that it dies, then they shall sell the live ox and divide the price of it; and the dead animal they shall also divide. 36But if it was known that the ox was accustomed to gore in the past, and its owner has not restrained it, the owner shall restore ox for ox, but keep the dead animal.

Laws of Restitution

22 a When someone steals an ox or a sheep, and slaughters it or sells it, the thief shall pay five oxen for an ox, and four sheep for a sheep.b The thief shall make restitution, but if unable to do so, shall be sold for the theft. 4When the animal, whether ox or donkey or sheep, is found alive in the thief's possession, the thief shall pay double.

2c If a thief is found breaking in, and is beaten to death, no bloodguilt is incurred; 3but if it happens after sunrise, bloodguilt is incurred.

5 When someone causes a field or vineyard to be grazed over, or lets livestock loose to graze in someone else's field, restitution shall be made from the best in the owner's field or vineyard.

6 When fire breaks out and catches in thorns so that the stacked grain or the standing grain or the field is consumed, the one who started the fire shall make full restitution.

7 When someone delivers to a neighbor money or goods for safekeeping, and they are stolen from the neighbor's house, then the thief, if caught, shall pay double. 8If the thief is not caught, the owner of the house shall be brought before God,d to determine whether or not the owner had laid hands on the neighbor's goods.

9 In any case of disputed ownership involving ox, donkey, sheep, clothing, or any other loss, of which one party says, "This is mine," the case of both parties shall come before God;d the one whom God condemnse shall pay double to the other.

10 When someone delivers to another a donkey, ox, sheep, or any other animal for safekeeping, and it dies or is injured or is carried off, without anyone seeing it, 11an oath before the LORD shall decide between the two of them that the one has not laid hands on the property of the other; the owner shall accept the oath, and no restitution shall be made. 12But if it was stolen, restitution shall be made to its owner. 13If it was mangled by beasts, let it be brought as evidence; restitution shall not be made for the mangled remains.

14 When someone borrows an animal from another and it is injured or dies, the owner not being present, full restitution shall be made. 15If

---

a Ch 21.37 in Heb   b Verses 2, 3, and 4 rearranged thus: 3b, 4, 2, 3a   c Ch 22.1 in Heb   d Or before the judges   e Or the judges condemn

Catholic Social Teaching

Caring for the Poor and Vulnerable

"You shall not wrong or oppress a resident alien. . . . You shall not abuse any widow or orphan" (Ex 22:21–22). This section of the Sinai laws reminds the Israelites to take care of the poor and vulnerable in their midst. One of the key principles of Catholic social teaching is the *Option for the Poor and Vulnerable*. This means that as a society we are obliged to always be mindful of how policies and laws affect those who are poorest and most vulnerable. Policies and laws that affect how we develop the land, grow and sell our food, provide health care, price prescription drugs, and make education accessible can either increase or decrease poverty.

The Church tells us that a basic moral test of a society is how it treats its most vulnerable members. So, how do you think we are doing? Does everyone in our society have access to the basic rights of nutrition, housing, education, and health care? If not, what are we doing about it?

▶ **Ex 22:21–27**

Option for the Poor and Vulnerable

---

the owner was present, there shall be no restitution; if it was hired, only the hiring fee is due.

Social and Religious Laws

16 When a man seduces a virgin who is not engaged to be married, and lies with her, he shall give the bride-price for her and make her his wife. ¹⁷But if her father refuses to give her to him, he shall pay an amount equal to the bride-price for virgins.

18 You shall not permit a female sorcerer to live.

19 Whoever lies with an animal shall be put to death.

20 Whoever sacrifices to any god, other than the LORD alone, shall be devoted to destruction.

21 You shall not wrong or oppress a resident alien, for you were aliens in the land of Egypt. ²²You shall not abuse any widow or orphan. ²³If you do abuse them, when they cry out to me, I will surely heed their cry; ²⁴my wrath will burn, and I will kill you with the sword, and your wives shall become widows and your children orphans.

25 If you lend money to my people, to the poor among you, you shall not deal with them as a creditor; you shall not exact interest from them. ²⁶If you take your neighbor's cloak in pawn, you shall restore it before the sun goes down; ²⁷for it may be your neighbor's only clothing to use as cover; in what else shall that person sleep? And if your neighbor cries out to me, I will listen, for I am compassionate.

28 You shall not revile God, or curse a leader of your people.

29 You shall not delay to make offerings from the fullness of your harvest and from the outflow of your presses.ᵃ

The firstborn of your sons you shall give to me. ³⁰You shall do the same with your oxen and with your sheep: seven days it shall remain with its mother; on the eighth day you shall give it to me.

31 You shall be people consecrated to me; therefore you shall not eat any meat that is mangled by beasts in the field; you shall throw it to the dogs.

Justice for All

23 You shall not spread a false report. You shall not join hands with the wicked to act as a malicious witness. ²You shall not follow a majority in wrongdoing; when you bear witness in a lawsuit, you shall not side with the majority so as to pervert justice; ³nor shall you be partial to the poor in a lawsuit.

4 When you come upon your enemy's ox or donkey going astray, you shall bring it back.

5 When you see the donkey of one who hates you lying under its burden and you would hold back from setting it free, you must help to set it free.ᵃ

6 You shall not pervert the justice due to your poor in their lawsuits. ⁷Keep far from a false

---

a Meaning of Heb uncertain

charge, and do not kill the innocent and those in the right, for I will not acquit the guilty. [8]You shall take no bribe, for a bribe blinds the officials, and subverts the cause of those who are in the right.

9 You shall not oppress a resident alien; you know the heart of an alien, for you were aliens in the land of Egypt.

Sabbatical Year and Sabbath

10 For six years you shall sow your land and gather in its yield; [11]but the seventh year you shall let it rest and lie fallow, so that the poor of your people may eat; and what they leave the wild animals may eat. You shall do the same with your vineyard, and with your olive orchard.

12 Six days you shall do your work, but on the seventh day you shall rest, so that your ox and your donkey may have relief, and your homeborn slave and the resident alien may be refreshed. [13]Be attentive to all that I have said to you. Do not invoke the names of other gods; do not let them be heard on your lips.

The Annual Festivals

14 Three times in the year you shall hold a festival for me. [15]You shall observe the festival of unleavened bread; as I commanded you, you shall eat unleavened bread for seven days at the appointed time in the month of Abib, for in it you came out of Egypt.

No one shall appear before me empty-handed.

16 You shall observe the festival of harvest, of the first fruits of your labor, of what you sow in the field. You shall observe the festival of ingathering at the end of the year, when you gather in from the field the fruit of your labor. [17]Three times in the year all your males shall appear before the Lord GOD.

18 You shall not offer the blood of my sacrifice with anything leavened, or let the fat of my festival remain until the morning.

19 The choicest of the first fruits of your ground you shall bring into the house of the LORD your God.

You shall not boil a kid in its mother's milk.

The Conquest of Canaan Promised

20 I am going to send an angel in front of you, to guard you on the way and to bring you to the place that I have prepared. [21]Be attentive to him and listen to his voice; do not rebel against him, for he will not pardon your transgression; for my name is in him.

22 But if you listen attentively to his voice and

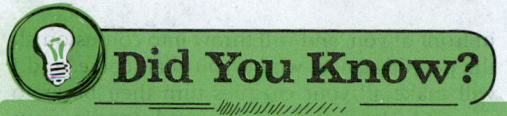

Did You Know?

Sacrifice and the Eucharist

Sacrifice is defined as an offering made to God that becomes holy by being set apart, blessed, and burned or consumed. Just as food and gifts were brought to a king as a form of tribute and worship, so too in Israel animals were brought to God and sacrificed, their blood splattered on the altar, and their meat cooked and eaten as a form of worship that brought communion with God. The blood symbolized God's gift of life, and when the blessed sacrifice was eaten, communion occurred between God and people. In Exodus, chapter 24, when Israel is about to ratify the Covenant with God, Moses smears the blood of the animal on the altar to assert the Israelites' union with God through the observance of the Covenant.

In the New Testament, the language Jesus uses at his Last Supper seems to reflect this sacrificial understanding. Jesus shares bread and wine as his body and blood and speaks about a New Covenant that will be ratified by the giving of his body and the shedding of his blood. Even today, Catholics celebrating the Eucharist in Jesus' memory encounter the real presence of Jesus in the sacred food of bread and wine, recalling the New Covenant of love he established through giving his body and shedding his blood.

▶ Ex 24:1–8

do all that I say, then I will be an enemy to your enemies and a foe to your foes.

23 When my angel goes in front of you, and brings you to the Amorites, the Hittites, the Perizzites, the Canaanites, the Hivites, and the Jebusites, and I blot them out, [24]you shall not bow down to their gods, or worship them, or follow their practices, but you shall utterly demolish them and break their pillars in pieces. [25]You shall worship the LORD your God, and I[a] will bless your bread and your water; and I will take sickness away from among you. [26]No one shall miscarry or be barren in your land; I will fulfill the number of your days. [27]I will send my terror

a Gk Vg: Heb he

in front of you, and will throw into confusion all the people against whom you shall come, and I will make all your enemies turn their backs to you. ²⁸And I will send the pestilence*a* in front of you, which shall drive out the Hivites, the Canaanites, and the Hittites from before you. ²⁹I will not drive them out from before you in one year, or the land would become desolate and the wild animals would multiply against you. ³⁰Little by little I will drive them out from before you, until you have increased and possess the land. ³¹I will set your borders from the Red Sea*b* to the sea of the Philistines, and from the wilderness to the Euphrates; for I will hand over to you the inhabitants of the land, and you shall drive them out before you. ³²You shall make no covenant with them and their gods. ³³They shall not live in your land, or they will make you sin against me; for if you worship their gods, it will surely be a snare to you.

The Blood of the Covenant

24 Then he said to Moses, "Come up to the LORD, you and Aaron, Nadab, and Abihu, and seventy of the elders of Israel, and worship at a distance. ²Moses alone shall come near the LORD; but the others shall not come near, and the people shall not come up with him."

3 Moses came and told the people all the words of the LORD and all the ordinances; and all the people answered with one voice, and said, "All the words that the LORD has spoken we will do." ⁴And Moses wrote down all the words of the LORD. He rose early in the morning, and built an altar at the foot of the mountain, and set up twelve pillars, corresponding to the twelve tribes of Israel. ⁵He sent young men of the people of Israel, who offered burnt offerings and sacrificed oxen as offerings of well-being to the LORD. ⁶Moses took half of the blood and put it in basins, and half of the blood he dashed against the altar. ⁷Then he took the book of the covenant, and read it in the hearing of the people; and they said, "All that the LORD has spoken we will do, and we will be obedient." ⁸Moses took the blood and dashed it on the people, and said, "See the blood of the covenant that the LORD has made with you in accordance with all these words."

On the Mountain with God

9 Then Moses and Aaron, Nadab, and Abihu, and seventy of the elders of Israel went up, ¹⁰and they saw the God of Israel. Under his feet there was something like a pavement of sapphire stone, like the very heaven for clearness. ¹¹God*c* did not lay his hand on the chief men of the people of Israel; also they beheld God, and they ate and drank.

12 The LORD said to Moses, "Come up to me on the mountain, and wait there; and I will give you the tablets of stone, with the law and the commandment, which I have written for their instruction." ¹³So Moses set out with his assistant Joshua, and Moses went up into the mountain of God. ¹⁴To the elders he had said, "Wait here for us, until we come to you again; for Aaron and Hur are with you; whoever has a dispute may go to them."

15 Then Moses went up on the mountain, and the cloud covered the mountain. ¹⁶The glory of the LORD settled on Mount Sinai, and the cloud covered it for six days; on the seventh day he called to Moses out of the cloud. ¹⁷Now the appearance of the glory of the LORD was like a devouring fire on the top of the mountain in the sight of the people of Israel. ¹⁸Moses entered the cloud, and went up on the mountain. Moses was on the mountain for forty days and forty nights.

Offerings for the Tabernacle

25 The LORD said to Moses: ²Tell the Israelites to take for me an offering; from all whose hearts prompt them to give you shall receive the offering for me. ³This is the offering that you shall receive from them: gold, silver, and bronze, ⁴blue, purple, and crimson yarns and fine linen, goats' hair, ⁵tanned rams' skins, fine leather,*d* acacia wood, ⁶oil for the lamps, spices for the anointing oil and for the fragrant incense, ⁷onyx stones and gems to be set in the ephod and for the breastpiece. ⁸And have them make me a sanctuary, so that I may dwell among them. ⁹In accordance with all that I show you concerning the pattern of the tabernacle and of all its furniture, so you shall make it.

a Or *hornets*: Meaning of Heb uncertain   *b* Or *Sea of Reeds*
c Heb *He*   *d* Meaning of Heb uncertain

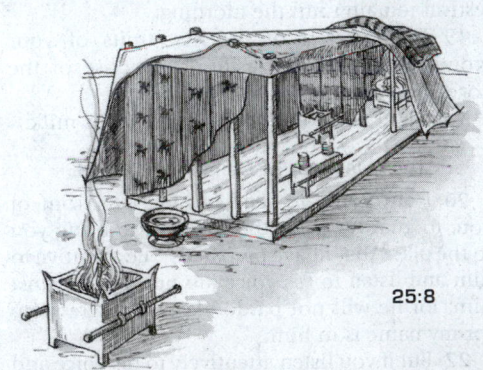

25:8

The Ark of the Covenant

10 They shall make an ark of acacia wood; it shall be two and a half cubits long, a cubit and a half wide, and a cubit and a half high. [11]You shall overlay it with pure gold, inside and outside you shall overlay it, and you shall make a molding of gold upon it all around. [12]You shall cast four rings of gold for it and put them on its four feet, two rings on the one side of it, and two rings on the other side. [13]You shall make poles of acacia wood, and overlay them with gold. [14]And you shall put the poles into the rings on the sides of the ark, by which to carry the ark. [15]The poles shall remain in the rings of the ark; they shall not be taken from it. [16]You shall put into the ark the covenant[a] that I shall give you.

17 Then you shall make a mercy seat[b] of pure gold; two cubits and a half shall be its length, and a cubit and a half its width. [18]You shall make two cherubim of gold; you shall make them of hammered work, at the two ends of the mercy seat.[c] [19]Make one cherub at the one end, and one cherub at the other; of one piece with the mercy seat[c] you shall make the cherubim at its two ends. [20]The cherubim shall spread out their wings above, overshadowing the mercy seat[c] with their wings. They shall face one to another; the faces of the cherubim shall be turned toward the mercy seat.[c] [21]You shall put the mercy seat[c] on the top of the ark; and in the ark you shall put the covenant[a] that I shall give you. [22]There I will meet with you, and from above the mercy seat,[c] from between the two cherubim that are on the ark of the covenant,[a] I will deliver to you all my commands for the Israelites.

The Table for the Bread of the Presence

23 You shall make a table of acacia wood, two cubits long, one cubit wide, and a cubit and a half high. [24]You shall overlay it with pure gold, and make a molding of gold around it. [25]You shall make around it a rim a handbreadth wide, and a molding of gold around the rim. [26]You shall make for it four rings of gold, and fasten the rings to the four corners at its four legs. [27]The rings that hold the poles used for carrying the table shall be close to the rim. [28]You shall make the poles of acacia wood, and overlay them with gold, and the table shall be carried with these. [29]You shall make its plates and dishes for incense, and its flagons and bowls with which to pour drink offerings; you shall make them of pure gold. [30]And you shall set the bread of the Presence on the table before me always.

The Lampstand

31 You shall make a lampstand of pure gold. The base and the shaft of the lampstand shall be made of hammered work; its cups, its calyxes, and its petals shall be of one piece with it; [32]and there shall be six branches going out of its sides, three branches of the lampstand out of one side of it and three branches of the lampstand out of the other side of it; [33]three cups shaped like almond blossoms, each with calyx and petals, on one branch, and three cups shaped like almond blossoms, each with calyx and petals, on the other branch—so for the six branches going out of the lampstand. [34]On the lampstand itself there shall be four cups shaped like almond blossoms, each with its calyxes and petals. [35]There shall be a calyx of one piece with it under the first pair of branches, a calyx of one piece with it under the next pair of branches, and a calyx of one piece with it under the last pair of branches—so for the six branches that go out of the lampstand. [36]Their calyxes and their branches shall be of one piece with it, the whole of it one hammered piece of pure gold. [37]You shall make the seven lamps for it; and the lamps shall be set up so as to give light on the space in front of it. [38]Its snuffers and trays shall be of pure gold. [39]It, and all these utensils, shall be made from a talent of pure gold. [40]And see that you make them according to the pattern for them, which is being shown you on the mountain.

The Tabernacle

26 Moreover you shall make the tabernacle with ten curtains of fine twisted linen, and blue, purple, and crimson yarns; you shall make them with cherubim skillfully worked into them. [2]The length of each curtain shall be twenty-eight cubits, and the width of each curtain four cubits; all the curtains shall be of the same size. [3]Five curtains shall be joined to one another; and the other five curtains shall be joined to one another. [4]You shall make loops of blue on the edge of the outermost curtain in the first set; and likewise you shall make loops on the edge of the outermost curtain in the second set. [5]You shall make fifty loops on the one curtain, and you shall make fifty loops on the edge of the curtain that is in the second set; the loops shall be opposite one another. [6]You shall make fifty clasps of gold, and join the curtains to one another with the clasps, so that the tabernacle may be one whole.

---

a Or *treaty*, or *testimony*; Heb *eduth*   b Or *a cover*   c Or *the cover*

7 You shall also make curtains of goats' hair for a tent over the tabernacle; you shall make eleven curtains. ⁸The length of each curtain shall be thirty cubits, and the width of each curtain four cubits; the eleven curtains shall be of the same size. ⁹You shall join five curtains by themselves, and six curtains by themselves, and the sixth curtain you shall double over at the front of the tent. ¹⁰You shall make fifty loops on the edge of the curtain that is outermost in one set, and fifty loops on the edge of the curtain that is outermost in the second set.

11 You shall make fifty clasps of bronze, and put the clasps into the loops, and join the tent together, so that it may be one whole. ¹²The part that remains of the curtains of the tent, the half curtain that remains, shall hang over the back of the tabernacle. ¹³The cubit on the one side, and the cubit on the other side, of what remains in the length of the curtains of the tent, shall hang over the sides of the tabernacle, on this side and that side, to cover it. ¹⁴You shall make for the tent a covering of tanned rams' skins and an outer covering of fine leather.ᵃ

The Framework

15 You shall make upright frames of acacia wood for the tabernacle. ¹⁶Ten cubits shall be the length of a frame, and a cubit and a half the width of each frame. ¹⁷There shall be two pegs in each frame to fit the frames together; you shall make these for all the frames of the tabernacle. ¹⁸You shall make the frames for the tabernacle: twenty frames for the south side; ¹⁹and you shall make forty bases of silver under the twenty frames, two bases under the first frame for its two pegs, and two bases under the next frame for its two pegs; ²⁰and for the second side of the tabernacle, on the north side twenty frames, ²¹and their forty bases of silver, two bases under the first frame, and two bases under the next frame; ²²and for the rear of the tabernacle westward you shall make six frames. ²³You shall make two frames for corners of the tabernacle in the rear; ²⁴they shall be separate beneath, but joined at the top, at the first ring; it shall be the same with both of them; they shall form the two corners. ²⁵And so there shall be eight frames, with their bases of silver, sixteen bases; two bases under the first frame, and two bases under the next frame.

26 You shall make bars of acacia wood, five for the frames of the one side of the tabernacle, ²⁷and five bars for the frames of the other side of the tabernacle, and five bars for the frames of the side of the tabernacle at the rear westward. ²⁸The middle bar, halfway up the frames, shall pass through from end to end. ²⁹You shall overlay the frames with gold, and shall make their rings of gold to hold the bars; and you shall overlay the bars with gold. ³⁰Then you shall erect the tabernacle according to the plan for it that you were shown on the mountain.

The Curtain

31 You shall make a curtain of blue, purple, and crimson yarns, and of fine twisted linen; it shall be made with cherubim skillfully worked into it. ³²You shall hang it on four pillars of acacia overlaid with gold, which have hooks of gold and rest on four bases of silver. ³³You shall hang the curtain under the clasps, and bring the ark of the covenantᵇ in there, within the curtain; and the curtain shall separate for you the holy place from the most holy. ³⁴You shall put the mercy seatᶜ on the ark of the covenantᵇ in the most holy place. ³⁵You shall set the table outside the curtain, and the lampstand on the south side of the tabernacle opposite the table; and you shall put the table on the north side.

36 You shall make a screen for the entrance of the tent, of blue, purple, and crimson yarns, and of fine twisted linen, embroidered with needlework. ³⁷You shall make for the screen five pillars of acacia, and overlay them with gold; their hooks shall be of gold, and you shall cast five bases of bronze for them.

The Altar of Burnt Offering

27 You shall make the altar of acacia wood, five cubits long and five cubits wide; the altar shall be square, and it shall be three cubits high. ²You shall make horns for it on its four corners; its horns shall be of one piece with it, and you shall overlay it with bronze. ³You shall make pots for it to receive its ashes, and shovels and basins and forks and firepans; you shall make all its utensils of bronze. ⁴You shall also make for it a grating, a network of bronze; and on the net you shall make four bronze rings at its four corners. ⁵You shall set it under the ledge of the altar so that the net shall extend halfway down the altar. ⁶You shall make poles for the altar, poles of acacia wood, and overlay them with bronze; ⁷the poles shall be put through the rings, so that the poles shall be on the two sides of the altar when it is carried. ⁸You shall make it hollow, with boards. They shall be made just as you were shown on the mountain.

---

a Meaning of Heb uncertain   b Or treaty, or testimony; Heb eduth   c Or the cover

The Court and Its Hangings

9 You shall make the court of the tabernacle. On the south side the court shall have hangings of fine twisted linen one hundred cubits long for that side; [10]its twenty pillars and their twenty bases shall be of bronze, but the hooks of the pillars and their bands shall be of silver. [11]Likewise for its length on the north side there shall be hangings one hundred cubits long, their pillars twenty and their bases twenty, of bronze, but the hooks of the pillars and their bands shall be of silver. [12]For the width of the court on the west side there shall be fifty cubits of hangings, with ten pillars and ten bases. [13]The width of the court on the front to the east shall be fifty cubits. [14]There shall be fifteen cubits of hangings on the one side, with three pillars and three bases. [15]There shall be fifteen cubits of hangings on the other side, with three pillars and three bases. [16]For the gate of the court there shall be a screen twenty cubits long, of blue, purple, and crimson yarns, and of fine twisted linen, embroidered with needlework; it shall have four pillars and with them four bases. [17]All the pillars around the court shall be banded with silver; their hooks shall be of silver, and their bases of bronze. [18]The length of the court shall be one hundred cubits, the width fifty, and the height five cubits, with hangings of fine twisted linen and bases of bronze. [19]All the utensils of the tabernacle for every use, and all its pegs and all the pegs of the court, shall be of bronze.

The Oil for the Lamp

20 You shall further command the Israelites to bring you pure oil of beaten olives for the light, so that a lamp may be set up to burn regularly. [21]In the tent of meeting, outside the curtain that is before the covenant,[a] Aaron and his sons shall tend it from evening to morning before the LORD. It shall be a perpetual ordinance to be observed throughout their generations by the Israelites.

Vestments for the Priesthood

28 Then bring near to you your brother Aaron, and his sons with him, from among the Israelites, to serve me as priests—Aaron and Aaron's sons, Nadab and Abihu, Eleazar and Ithamar. [2]You shall make sacred vestments for the glorious adornment of your brother Aaron. [3]And you shall speak to all who have ability, whom I have endowed with skill, that they make Aaron's vestments to consecrate him for my priesthood. [4]These are the vestments that they shall make: a breastpiece, an ephod, a robe, a checkered tunic, a turban, and a sash. When they make these sacred vestments for your brother Aaron and his sons to serve me as priests, [5]they shall use gold, blue, purple, and crimson yarns, and fine linen.

The Ephod

6 They shall make the ephod of gold, of blue, purple, and crimson yarns, and of fine twisted linen, skillfully worked. [7]It shall have two shoulder-pieces attached to its two edges, so that it may be joined together. [8]The decorated band on it shall be of the same workmanship and materials, of gold, of blue, purple, and crimson yarns, and of fine twisted linen. [9]You shall take two onyx stones, and engrave on them the names of the sons of Israel, [10]six of their names on the one stone, and the names of the remaining six on the other stone, in the order of their birth. [11]As a gem-cutter engraves signets, so you shall engrave the two stones with the names of the sons of Israel; you shall mount them in settings of gold filigree. [12]You shall set the two stones on the shoulder-pieces of the ephod, as stones of remembrance for the sons of Israel; and Aaron shall bear their names before the LORD on his two shoulders for remembrance. [13]You shall make settings of gold filigree, [14]and two chains of pure gold, twisted like cords; and you shall attach the corded chains to the settings.

The Breastplate

15 You shall make a breastpiece of judgment, in skilled work; you shall make it in the style of the ephod; of gold, of blue and purple and crimson yarns, and of fine twisted linen you shall make it. [16]It shall be square and doubled, a span in length and a span in width. [17]You shall set in it four rows of stones. A row of carnelian,[b] chrysolite, and emerald shall be the first row; [18]and the second row a turquoise, a sapphire,[c] and a moonstone; [19]and the third row a jacinth, an agate, and an amethyst; [20]and the fourth row a beryl, an onyx, and a jasper; they shall be set in gold filigree. [21]There shall be twelve stones with names corresponding to the names of the sons of Israel; they shall be like signets, each engraved with its name, for the twelve tribes. [22]You shall make for the breastpiece chains of pure gold, twisted like cords; [23]and you shall make for the breastpiece two rings of gold, and put the two rings on the two edges of the breastpiece. [24]You

---

a Or *treaty*, or *testimony*; Heb *eduth*   b The identity of several of these stones is uncertain   c Or *lapis lazuli*

EX

shall put the two cords of gold in the two rings at the edges of the breastpiece; 25the two ends of the two cords you shall attach to the two settings, and so attach it in front to the shoulder-pieces of the ephod. 26You shall make two rings of gold, and put them at the two ends of the breastpiece, on its inside edge next to the ephod. 27You shall make two rings of gold, and attach them in front to the lower part of the two shoulder-pieces of the ephod, at its joining above the decorated band of the ephod. 28The breastpiece shall be bound by its rings to the rings of the ephod with a blue cord, so that it may lie on the decorated band of the ephod, and so that the breastpiece shall not come loose from the ephod. 29So Aaron shall bear the names of the sons of Israel in the breastpiece of judgment on his heart when he goes into the holy place, for a continual remembrance before the Lord. 30In the breastpiece of judgment you shall put the Urim and the Thummim, and they shall be on Aaron's heart when he goes in before the Lord; thus Aaron shall bear the judgment of the Israelites on his heart before the Lord continually.

Other Priestly Vestments

31 You shall make the robe of the ephod all of blue. 32It shall have an opening for the head in the middle of it, with a woven binding around the opening, like the opening in a coat of mail,[a] so that it may not be torn. 33On its lower hem you shall make pomegranates of blue, purple, and crimson yarns, all around the lower hem, with bells of gold between them all around— 34a golden bell and a pomegranate alternating all around the lower hem of the robe. 35Aaron shall wear it when he ministers, and its sound shall be heard when he goes into the holy place before the Lord, and when he comes out, so that he may not die.

36 You shall make a rosette of pure gold, and engrave on it, like the engraving of a signet, "Holy to the Lord." 37You shall fasten it on the turban with a blue cord; it shall be on the front of the turban. 38It shall be on Aaron's forehead, and Aaron shall take on himself any guilt incurred in the holy offering that the Israelites consecrate as their sacred donations; it shall always be on his forehead, in order that they may find favor before the Lord.

39 You shall make the checkered tunic of fine linen, and you shall make a turban of fine linen, and you shall make a sash embroidered with needlework.

40 For Aaron's sons you shall make tunics and sashes and headdresses; you shall make them for their glorious adornment. 41You shall put them on your brother Aaron, and on his sons with him, and shall anoint them and ordain them and consecrate them, so that they may serve me as priests. 42You shall make for them linen undergarments to cover their naked flesh; they shall reach from the hips to the thighs; 43Aaron and his sons shall wear them when they go into the tent of meeting, or when they come near the altar to minister in the holy place; or they will bring guilt on themselves and die. This shall be a perpetual ordinance for him and for his descendants after him.

The Ordination of the Priests

29 Now this is what you shall do to them to consecrate them, so that they may serve me as priests. Take one young bull and two rams without blemish, 2and unleavened bread, unleavened cakes mixed with oil, and unleavened wafers spread with oil. You shall make them of choice wheat flour. 3You shall put them in one basket and bring them in the basket, and bring the bull and the two rams. 4You shall bring Aaron and his sons to the entrance of the tent of meeting, and wash them with water. 5Then you shall take the vestments, and put on Aaron the tunic and the robe of the ephod, and the ephod, and the breastpiece, and gird him with the decorated band of the ephod; 6and you shall set the turban on his head, and put the holy diadem on the turban. 7You shall take the anointing oil, and pour it on his head and anoint him. 8Then you shall bring his sons, and put tunics on them, 9and you shall gird them with sashes[b] and tie headdresses on them; and the priesthood shall be theirs by a perpetual ordinance. You shall then ordain Aaron and his sons.

10 You shall bring the bull in front of the tent of meeting. Aaron and his sons shall lay their hands on the head of the bull, 11and you shall slaughter the bull before the Lord, at the entrance of the tent of meeting, 12and shall take some of the blood of the bull and put it on the horns of the altar with your finger, and all the rest of the blood you shall pour out at the base of the altar. 13You shall take all the fat that covers the entrails, and the appendage of the liver, and the two kidneys with the fat that is on them, and turn them into smoke on the altar. 14But the flesh of the bull, and its skin, and its dung, you shall burn with fire outside the camp; it is a sin offering.

15 Then you shall take one of the rams, and

---

a Meaning of Heb uncertain   b Gk: Heb sashes, Aaron and his sons

Aaron and his sons shall lay their hands on the head of the ram, ¹⁶and you shall slaughter the ram, and shall take its blood and dash it against all sides of the altar. ¹⁷Then you shall cut the ram into its parts, and wash its entrails and its legs, and put them with its parts and its head, ¹⁸and turn the whole ram into smoke on the altar; it is a burnt offering to the Lord; it is a pleasing odor, an offering by fire to the Lord.

19 You shall take the other ram; and Aaron and his sons shall lay their hands on the head of the ram, ²⁰and you shall slaughter the ram, and take some of its blood and put it on the lobe of Aaron's right ear and on the lobes of the right ears of his sons, and on the thumbs of their right hands, and on the big toes of their right feet, and dash the rest of the blood against all sides of the altar. ²¹Then you shall take some of the blood that is on the altar, and some of the anointing oil, and sprinkle it on Aaron and his vestments and on his sons and his sons' vestments with him; then he and his vestments shall be holy, as well as his sons and his sons' vestments.

22 You shall also take the fat of the ram, the fat tail, the fat that covers the entrails, the appendage of the liver, the two kidneys with the fat that is on them, and the right thigh (for it is a ram of ordination), ²³and one loaf of bread, one cake of bread made with oil, and one wafer, out of the basket of unleavened bread that is before the Lord; ²⁴and you shall place all these on the palms of Aaron and on the palms of his sons, and raise them as an elevation offering before the Lord. ²⁵Then you shall take them from their hands, and turn them into smoke on the altar on top of the burnt offering of pleasing odor before the Lord; it is an offering by fire to the Lord.

26 You shall take the breast of the ram of Aaron's ordination and raise it as an elevation offering before the Lord; and it shall be your portion. ²⁷You shall consecrate the breast that was raised as an elevation offering and the thigh that was raised as an elevation offering from the ram of ordination, from that which belonged to Aaron and his sons. ²⁸These things shall be a perpetual ordinance for Aaron and his sons from the Israelites, for this is an offering; and it shall be an offering by the Israelites from their sacrifice of offerings of well-being, their offering to the Lord.

29 The sacred vestments of Aaron shall be passed on to his sons after him; they shall be anointed in them and ordained in them. ³⁰The son who is priest in his place shall wear them seven days, when he comes into the tent of meeting to minister in the holy place.

31 You shall take the ram of ordination, and boil its flesh in a holy place; ³²and Aaron and his sons shall eat the flesh of the ram and the bread that is in the basket, at the entrance of the tent of meeting. ³³They themselves shall eat the food by which atonement is made, to ordain and consecrate them, but no one else shall eat of them, because they are holy. ³⁴If any of the flesh for the ordination, or of the bread, remains until the morning, then you shall burn the remainder with fire; it shall not be eaten, because it is holy.

35 Thus you shall do to Aaron and to his sons, just as I have commanded you; through seven days you shall ordain them. ³⁶Also every day you shall offer a bull as a sin offering for atonement. Also you shall offer a sin offering for the altar, when you make atonement for it, and shall anoint it, to consecrate it. ³⁷Seven days you shall make atonement for the altar, and consecrate it, and the altar shall be most holy; whatever touches the altar shall become holy.

The Daily Offerings

38 Now this is what you shall offer on the altar: two lambs a year old regularly each day. ³⁹One lamb you shall offer in the morning, and the other lamb you shall offer in the evening; ⁴⁰and with the first lamb one-tenth of a measure of choice flour mixed with one-fourth of a hin of beaten oil, and one-fourth of a hin of wine for a drink offering. ⁴¹And the other lamb you shall offer in the evening, and shall offer with it a grain offering and its drink offering, as in the morning, for a pleasing odor, an offering by fire to the Lord. ⁴²It shall be a regular burnt offering throughout your generations at the entrance of the tent of meeting before the Lord, where I will meet with you, to speak to you there. ⁴³I will meet with the Israelites there, and it shall be sanctified by my glory; ⁴⁴I will consecrate the tent of meeting and the altar; Aaron also and his sons I will consecrate, to serve me as priests. ⁴⁵I will dwell among the Israelites, and I will be their God. ⁴⁶And they shall know that I am the Lord their God, who brought them out of the land of Egypt that I might dwell among them; I am the Lord their God.

The Altar of Incense

30 You shall make an altar on which to offer incense; you shall make it of acacia wood. ²It shall be one cubit long, and one cubit wide; it shall be square, and shall be two cubits high; its horns shall be of one piece with it. ³You shall overlay it with pure gold, its top, and its sides all around and its horns; and you shall make for it a molding of gold all around. ⁴And you shall make two golden rings for it; under its molding on two opposite sides of it you shall make them, and they shall hold the poles with which to carry it. ⁵You shall make the poles of acacia wood, and overlay them with gold. ⁶You shall place it in front of the curtain that is above the ark of the covenant,ᵃ in front of the mercy seatᵇ that is over the covenant,ᵃ where I will meet with you. ⁷Aaron shall offer fragrant incense on it; every morning when he dresses the lamps he shall offer it, ⁸and when Aaron sets up the lamps in the evening, he shall offer it, a regular incense offering before the Lord throughout your generations. ⁹You shall not offer unholy incense on it, or a burnt offering, or a grain offering; and you shall not pour a drink offering on it. ¹⁰Once a year Aaron shall perform the rite of atonement on its horns. Throughout your generations he shall perform the atonement for it once a year with the blood of the atoning sin offering. It is most holy to the Lord.

The Half Shekel for the Sanctuary

11 The Lord spoke to Moses: ¹²When you take a census of the Israelites to register them, at registration all of them shall give a ransom for their lives to the Lord, so that no plague may come upon them for being registered. ¹³This is what each one who is registered shall give: half a shekel according to the shekel of the sanctuary (the shekel is twenty gerahs), half a shekel as an offering to the Lord. ¹⁴Each one who is registered, from twenty years old and upward, shall give the Lord's offering. ¹⁵The rich shall not give more, and the poor shall not give less, than the half shekel, when you bring this offering to the Lord to make atonement for your lives. ¹⁶You shall take the atonement money from the Israelites and shall designate it for the service of the tent of meeting; before the Lord it will be a reminder to the Israelites of the ransom given for your lives.

The Bronze Basin

17 The Lord spoke to Moses: ¹⁸You shall make a bronze basin with a bronze stand for washing. You shall put it between the tent of meeting and the altar, and you shall put water in it; ¹⁹with the waterᶜ Aaron and his sons shall wash their hands and their feet. ²⁰When they go into the tent of meeting, or when they come near the altar to minister, to make an offering by fire to the Lord, they shall wash with water, so that they may not die. ²¹They shall wash their hands and their feet, so that they may not die: it shall be

a perpetual ordinance for them, for him and for his descendants throughout their generations.

The Anointing Oil and Incense

22 The Lord spoke to Moses: ²³Take the finest spices: of liquid myrrh five hundred shekels, and of sweet-smelling cinnamon half as much, that is, two hundred fifty, and two hundred fifty of aromatic cane, ²⁴and five hundred of cassia—measured by the sanctuary shekel—and a hin of olive oil; ²⁵and you shall make of these a sacred anointing oil blended as by the perfumer; it shall be a holy anointing oil. ²⁶With it you shall anoint the tent of meeting and the ark of the covenant,ᵃ ²⁷and the table and all its utensils, and the lampstand and its utensils, and the altar of incense, ²⁸and the altar of burnt offering with all its utensils, and the basin with its stand; ²⁹you shall consecrate them, so that they may be most holy; whatever touches them will become holy. ³⁰You shall anoint Aaron and his sons, and consecrate them, in order that they may serve me as priests. ³¹You shall say to the Israelites, "This shall be my holy anointing oil throughout your generations. ³²It shall not be used in any ordinary anointing of the body, and you shall make no other like it in composition; it is holy, and it shall be holy to you. ³³Whoever compounds any like it or whoever puts any of it on an unqualified person shall be cut off from the people."

34 The Lord said to Moses: Take sweet spices, stacte, and onycha, and galbanum, sweet spices with pure frankincense (an equal part of each), ³⁵and make an incense blended as by the perfumer, seasoned with salt, pure and holy; ³⁶and you shall beat some of it into powder, and put part of it before the covenantᵃ in the tent of meeting where I shall meet with you; it shall be for you most holy. ³⁷When you make incense according to this composition, you shall not make it for yourselves; it shall be regarded by you as holy to the Lord. ³⁸Whoever makes any like it to use as perfume shall be cut off from the people.

Bezalel and Oholiab

31 The Lord spoke to Moses: ²See, I have called by name Bezalel son of Uri son of Hur, of the tribe of Judah: ³and I have filled him with divine spirit,ᵈ with ability, intelligence, and knowledge in every kind of craft, ⁴to devise artistic designs, to work in gold, silver, and bronze, ⁵in cutting stones for setting, and in carving wood, in every kind of craft. ⁶Moreover, I have

---

a Or treaty, or testimony; Heb eduth   b Or the cover   c Heb it   d Or with the spirit of God

appointed with him Oholiab son of Ahisamach, of the tribe of Dan; and I have given skill to all the skillful, so that they may make all that I have commanded you: [7]the tent of meeting, and the ark of the covenant,[a] and the mercy seat[b] that is on it, and all the furnishings of the tent, [8]the table and its utensils, and the pure lampstand with all its utensils, and the altar of incense, [9]and the altar of burnt offering with all its utensils, and the basin with its stand, [10]and the finely worked vestments, the holy vestments for the priest Aaron and the vestments of his sons, for their service as priests, [11]and the anointing oil and the fragrant incense for the holy place. They shall do just as I have commanded you.

The Sabbath Law

12 The LORD said to Moses: [13]You yourself are to speak to the Israelites: "You shall keep my sabbaths, for this is a sign between me and you throughout your generations, given in order that you may know that I, the LORD, sanctify you. [14]You shall keep the sabbath, because it is holy for you; everyone who profanes it shall be put to death; whoever does any work on it shall be cut off from among the people. [15]Six days shall work be done, but the seventh day is a sabbath of solemn rest, holy to the LORD; whoever does any work on the sabbath day shall be put to death. [16]Therefore the Israelites shall keep the sabbath, observing the sabbath throughout their generations, as a perpetual covenant. [17]It is a sign forever between me and the people of Israel that in six days the LORD made heaven and earth, and on the seventh day he rested, and was refreshed."

The Two Tablets of the Covenant

18 When God[c] finished speaking with Moses on Mount Sinai, he gave him the two tablets of the covenant,[d] tablets of stone, written with the finger of God.

The Golden Calf

32 When the people saw that Moses delayed to come down from the mountain, the people gathered around Aaron, and said to him, "Come, make gods for us, who shall go before us; as for this Moses, the man who brought us up out of the land of Egypt, we do not know what has become of him." [2]Aaron said to them, "Take off the gold rings that are on the ears of your wives, your sons, and your daughters, and bring them to me." [3]So all the people took off the gold rings from their ears, and brought them to Aaron. [4]He took the gold from them, formed it in a mold,[d] and cast an image of a calf; and

they said, "These are your gods, O Israel, who brought you up out of the land of Egypt!" [5]When Aaron saw this, he built an altar before it; and Aaron made proclamation and said, "Tomorrow

a Or treaty, or testimony; Heb eduth b Or the cover c Heb he d Or fashioned it with a graving tool; Meaning of Heb uncertain

Caught Up in the Moment

Now that I think about it, it was a stupid thing to do. But it is so hard to be objective when you are caught up in the excitement of the moment. We had been waiting a long time for Moses—too long, it seems. We got bored and restless. You know how it is. Someone came up with the idea of the golden calf. It sounded like fun, something to pass the time and remind us of the old gods. And I have to admit, that calf did look pretty good!

I do feel sorry for Aaron. Moses saw what we had done and hurled the stone tablets to the ground in a fit of rage. Aaron tried to explain how it was, but Moses would hear none of it. He was upset. He had a right to be. There is no valid excuse for what we did. Aaron tried to pretend that the calf sort of formed itself, but it was a feeble excuse. We all knew it. And when we learned what was on the stone tablets, we knew we had done wrong. Moses had brought those tablets from the hands of God. This was to have been a solemn moment, followed by a great celebration. But instead, we had to face the wrath of Moses and pick up the shattered pieces of stone.

It is so easy to lose sight of what we are all about. It is so easy to do something stupid when we are bored and tired of waiting. And then we wonder how we could have let ourselves get so far off track. It is too easy, isn't it? We are all too human at times.

No, I don't blame Moses for losing his temper. He had every right. We let him down. We let ourselves down. But most of all, we let God down.

▶ Ex 32:1–35

shall be a festival to the LORD." 6They rose early the next day, and offered burnt offerings and brought sacrifices of well-being; and the people sat down to eat and drink, and rose up to revel.

7 The LORD said to Moses, "Go down at once! Your people, whom you brought up out of the land of Egypt, have acted perversely; 8they have been quick to turn aside from the way that I commanded them; they have cast for themselves an image of a calf, and have worshiped it and sacrificed to it, and said, 'These are your gods, O Israel, who brought you up out of the land of Egypt!' " 9The LORD said to Moses, "I have seen this people, how stiff-necked they are. 10Now let me alone, so that my wrath may burn hot against them and I may consume them; and of you I will make a great nation."

11 But Moses implored the LORD his God, and said, "O LORD, why does your wrath burn hot against your people, whom you brought out of the land of Egypt with great power and with a mighty hand? 12Why should the Egyptians say, 'It was with evil intent that he brought them out to kill them in the mountains, and to consume them from the face of the earth'? Turn from your fierce wrath; change your mind and do not bring disaster on your people. 13Remember Abraham, Isaac, and Israel, your servants, how you swore to them by your own self, saying to them, 'I will multiply your descendants like the stars of heaven, and all this land that I have promised I will give to your descendants, and they shall inherit it forever.' " 14And the LORD changed his mind about the disaster that he planned to bring on his people.

15 Then Moses turned and went down from the mountain, carrying the two tablets of the covenant[a] in his hands, tablets that were written on both sides, written on the front and on the back. 16The tablets were the work of God, and the writing was the writing of God, engraved upon the tablets. 17When Joshua heard the noise of the people as they shouted, he said to Moses, "There is a noise of war in the camp." 18But he said,

"It is not the sound made by victors,
  or the sound made by losers;
it is the sound of revelers that I hear."

19As soon as he came near the camp and saw the calf and the dancing, Moses' anger burned hot, and he threw the tablets from his hands and broke them at the foot of the mountain. 20He took the calf that they had made, burned it with fire, ground it to powder, scattered it on the water, and made the Israelites drink it.

21 Moses said to Aaron, "What did this people do to you that you have brought so great a sin upon them?" 22And Aaron said, "Do not let the anger of my lord burn hot; you know the people, that they are bent on evil. 23They said to me, 'Make us gods, who shall go before us; as for this Moses, the man who brought us up out of the land of Egypt, we do not know what has become of him.' 24So I said to them, 'Whoever has gold, take it off'; so they gave it to me, and I threw it into the fire, and out came this calf!"

25 When Moses saw that the people were running wild (for Aaron had let them run wild, to the derision of their enemies), 26then Moses stood in the gate of the camp, and said, "Who is on the LORD's side? Come to me!" And all the sons of Levi gathered around him. 27He said to them, "Thus says the LORD, the God of Israel, 'Put your sword on your side, each of you! Go back and forth from gate to gate throughout the camp, and each of you kill your brother, your friend, and your neighbor.' " 28The sons of Levi did as Moses commanded, and about three thousand of the people fell on that day. 29Moses said, "Today you have ordained yourselves[b] for the service of the LORD, each one at the cost of a son or a brother, and so have brought a blessing on yourselves this day."

30 On the next day Moses said to the people, "You have sinned a great sin. But now I will go up to the LORD; perhaps I can make atonement for your sin." 31So Moses returned to the LORD and said, "Alas, this people has sinned a great sin; they have made for themselves gods of gold. 32But now, if you will only forgive their sin—but if not, blot me out of the book that you have written." 33But the LORD said to Moses, "Whoever has sinned against me I will blot out of my book. 34But now go, lead the people to the place about which I have spoken to you; see, my angel shall go in front of you. Nevertheless, when the day comes for punishment, I will punish them for their sin."

35 Then the LORD sent a plague on the people, because they made the calf—the one that Aaron made.

The Command to Leave Sinai

33 The LORD said to Moses, "Go, leave this place, you and the people whom you have brought up out of the land of Egypt, and go to the land of which I swore to Abraham, Isaac, and Jacob, saying, 'To your descendants I will give it.' 2I will send an angel before you, and I will drive out the Canaanites, the Amorites, the Hittites, the Perizzites, the Hivites, and the Jebusites. 3Go up

---

a Or treaty, or testimony; Heb eduth   b Gk Vg Compare Tg: Heb Today ordain yourselves

to a land flowing with milk and honey; but I will not go up among you, or I would consume you on the way, for you are a stiff-necked people."

4 When the people heard these harsh words, they mourned, and no one put on ornaments. ⁵For the LORD had said to Moses, "Say to the Israelites, 'You are a stiff-necked people; if for a single moment I should go up among you, I would consume you. So now take off your ornaments, and I will decide what to do to you.' " ⁶Therefore the Israelites stripped themselves of their ornaments, from Mount Horeb onward.

The Tent outside the Camp

7 Now Moses used to take the tent and pitch it outside the camp, far off from the camp; he called it the tent of meeting. And everyone who sought the LORD would go out to the tent of meeting, which was outside the camp. ⁸Whenever Moses went out to the tent, all the people would rise and stand, each of them, at the entrance of their tents and watch Moses until he had gone into the tent. ⁹When Moses entered the tent, the pillar of cloud would descend and stand at the entrance of the tent, and the LORD would speak with Moses. ¹⁰When all the people saw the pillar of cloud standing at the entrance of the tent, all the people would rise and bow down, all of them, at the entrance of their tents. ¹¹Thus the LORD used to speak to Moses face to face, as one speaks to a friend. Then he would return to the camp; but his young assistant, Joshua son of Nun, would not leave the tent.

Moses' Intercession

12 Moses said to the LORD, "See, you have said to me, 'Bring up this people'; but you have not let me know whom you will send with me. Yet you have said, 'I know you by name, and you have also found favor in my sight.' ¹³Now if I have found favor in your sight, show me your ways, so that I may know you and find favor in your sight. Consider too that this nation is your people." ¹⁴He said, "My presence will go with you, and I will give you rest." ¹⁵And he said to him, "If your presence will not go, do not carry us up from here. ¹⁶For how shall it be known that I have found favor in your sight, I and your people, unless you go with us? In this way, we shall be distinct, I and your people, from every people on the face of the earth."

17 The LORD said to Moses, "I will do the very thing that you have asked; for you have found favor in my sight, and I know you by name." ¹⁸Moses said, "Show me your glory, I pray." ¹⁹And he said, "I will make all my goodness pass before

Pray It!

God Passing By

How close can we get to God without actually seeing God's face? If anyone would know, it is Moses. His rather amazing encounter with God is recorded in Exodus 33:17–23.

We too can experience, as many saints and mystics have, a deep intimacy with God. It is significant that God and Moses most often met in nature. If you are lucky, you have a favorite outdoor spot. Perhaps it is a place where you can simply sit and ponder as you gaze at the scenery before you. Perhaps during a sunset on a lovely summer evening or while gazing at the sea or a flowing stream, you somehow connect with God. You may not actually see or feel the hand of God, but somehow you know that God is with you and you are catching a glimpse of God's glory. You feel yourself held in the palm of God's gracious hand. And sometimes, like Moses (see 34:29), you are transformed by the power of God's presence.

Where do you most fully experience the presence of God? Close your eyes and call to mind that place; spend some time in prayer there for awhile.

▶ **Ex 33:17–23**

you, and will proclaim before you the name, 'The LORD';ᵃ and I will be gracious to whom I will be gracious, and will show mercy on whom I will show mercy. ²⁰But," he said, "you cannot see my face; for no one shall see me and live." ²¹And the LORD continued, "See, there is a place by me where you shall stand on the rock; ²²and while my glory passes by I will put you in a cleft of the rock, and I will cover you with my hand until I have passed by; ²³then I will take away my hand, and you shall see my back; but my face shall not be seen."

Moses Makes New Tablets

34 The LORD said to Moses, "Cut two tablets of stone like the former ones, and I will write on the tablets the words that were on the

---

a   Heb *YHWH*; see note at 3.15

former tablets, which you broke. ²Be ready in the morning, and come up in the morning to Mount Sinai and present yourself there to me, on the top of the mountain. ³No one shall come up with you, and do not let anyone be seen throughout all the mountain; and do not let flocks or herds graze in front of that mountain." ⁴So Moses cut two tablets of stone like the former ones; and he rose early in the morning and went up on Mount Sinai, as the LORD had commanded him, and took in his hand the two tablets of stone. ⁵The LORD descended in the cloud and stood with him there, and proclaimed the name, "The LORD."ᵃ ⁶The LORD passed before him, and proclaimed,

"The LORD, the LORD,
a God merciful and gracious,
slow to anger,
and abounding in steadfast love and
    faithfulness,
⁷ keeping steadfast love for the thousandth
    generation,ᵇ
forgiving iniquity and transgression and sin,
yet by no means clearing the guilty,
but visiting the iniquity of the parents
upon the children
and the children's children,
to the third and the fourth generation."

⁸And Moses quickly bowed his head toward the earth, and worshiped. ⁹He said, "If now I have found favor in your sight, O Lord, I pray, let the Lord go with us. Although this is a stiff-necked people, pardon our iniquity and our sin, and take us for your inheritance."

The Covenant Renewed

10 He said: I hereby make a covenant. Before all your people I will perform marvels, such as have not been performed in all the earth or in any nation; and all the people among whom you live shall see the work of the LORD; for it is an awesome thing that I will do with you.

11 Observe what I command you today. See, I will drive out before you the Amorites, the Canaanites, the Hittites, the Perizzites, the Hivites, and the Jebusites. ¹²Take care not to make a covenant with the inhabitants of the land to which you are going, or it will become a snare among you. ¹³You shall tear down their altars, break their pillars, and cut down their sacred polesᶜ ¹⁴(for you shall worship no other god, because the LORD, whose name is Jealous, is a jealous God). ¹⁵You shall not make a covenant with the inhabitants of the land, for when they prostitute themselves to their gods and sacrifice to their gods, someone among them will invite you, and you will eat of the sacrifice. ¹⁶And you will take wives from among their daughters for your sons, and their daughters who prostitute themselves to their gods will make your sons also prostitute themselves to their gods.

17 You shall not make cast idols.

18 You shall keep the festival of unleavened bread. Seven days you shall eat unleavened bread, as I commanded you, at the time appointed in the month of Abib; for in the month of Abib you came out from Egypt.

19 All that first opens the womb is mine, all your maleᵈ livestock, the firstborn of cow and sheep. ²⁰The firstborn of a donkey you shall redeem with a lamb, or if you will not redeem it you shall break its neck. All the firstborn of your sons you shall redeem.

No one shall appear before me empty-handed.

21 Six days you shall work, but on the seventh day you shall rest; even in plowing time and in harvest time you shall rest. ²²You shall observe the festival of weeks, the first fruits of wheat harvest, and the festival of ingathering at the turn of the year. ²³Three times in the year all your males shall appear before the LORD God, the God of Israel. ²⁴For I will cast out nations before you, and enlarge your borders; no one shall covet your land when you go up to appear before the LORD your God three times in the year.

25 You shall not offer the blood of my sacrifice with leaven, and the sacrifice of the festival of the passover shall not be left until the morning.

26 The best of the first fruits of your ground you shall bring to the house of the LORD your God.

You shall not boil a kid in its mother's milk.

27 The LORD said to Moses: Write these words; in accordance with these words I have made a covenant with you and with Israel. ²⁸He was there with the LORD forty days and forty nights; he neither ate bread nor drank water. And he wrote on the tablets the words of the covenant, the ten commandments.ᵉ

The Shining Face of Moses

29 Moses came down from Mount Sinai. As he came down from the mountain with the two tablets of the covenantᶠ in his hand, Moses did not know that the skin of his face shone because he had been talking with God. ³⁰When Aaron and all the Israelites saw Moses, the skin of his face was shining, and they were afraid to come

---

a Heb YHWH; see note at 3.15   b Or for thousands
c Heb Asherim   d Gk Theodotion Vg Tg: Meaning of Heb uncertain   e Heb words   f Or treaty, or testimony; Heb eduth

near him. ³¹But Moses called to them; and Aaron and all the leaders of the congregation returned to him, and Moses spoke with them. ³²Afterward all the Israelites came near, and he gave them in commandment all that the Lord had spoken with him on Mount Sinai. ³³When Moses had finished speaking with them, he put a veil on his face; ³⁴but whenever Moses went in before the Lord to speak with him, he would take the veil off, until he came out; and when he came out, and told the Israelites what he had been commanded, ³⁵the Israelites would see the face of Moses, that the skin of his face was shining; and Moses would put the veil on his face again, until he went in to speak with him.

Sabbath Regulations

35 Moses assembled all the congregation of the Israelites and said to them: These are the things that the Lord has commanded you to do:

2 Six days shall work be done, but on the seventh day you shall have a holy sabbath of solemn rest to the Lord; whoever does any work on it shall be put to death. ³You shall kindle no fire in all your dwellings on the sabbath day.

Preparations for Making the Tabernacle

4 Moses said to all the congregation of the Israelites: This is the thing that the Lord has commanded: ⁵Take from among you an offering to the Lord; let whoever is of a generous heart bring the Lord's offering: gold, silver, and bronze; ⁶blue, purple, and crimson yarns, and fine linen; goats' hair, ⁷tanned rams' skins, and fine leather;ᵃ acacia wood, ⁸oil for the light, spices for the anointing oil and for the fragrant incense, ⁹and onyx stones and gems to be set in the ephod and the breastpiece.

10 All who are skillful among you shall come and make all that the Lord has commanded: the tabernacle, ¹¹its tent and its covering, its clasps and its frames, its bars, its pillars, and its bases; ¹²the ark with its poles, the mercy seat,ᵇ and the curtain for the screen; ¹³the table with its poles and all its utensils, and the bread of the Presence; ¹⁴the lampstand also for the light, with its utensils and its lamps, and the oil for the light, ¹⁵and the altar of incense, with its poles, and the anointing oil and the fragrant incense, and the screen for the entrance, the entrance of the tabernacle; ¹⁶the altar of burnt offering, with its grating of bronze, its poles, and all its utensils, the basin with its stand; ¹⁷the hangings of the court, its pillars and its bases, and the screen for the gate of the court; ¹⁸the pegs of the tabernacle

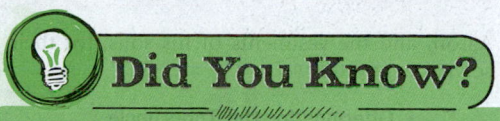

Did You Know?

Major Jewish Feasts

The joyful anticipation we feel before a major holiday seems to be shared by people of all cultures and religious traditions. Certainly, the Israelites had that feeling before the three festivals described in Exodus 34:18–26 (and in 23:14–17). They looked forward to them the way we might look forward to Christmas or Easter.

The *feast of Unleavened Bread*, which began on the day after Passover and lasted a week, marked the beginning of the barley harvest. This feast probably originated in a pre-Passover agricultural holiday. Originally, unleavened bread—bread made without yeast—was eaten during this week to symbolize a fresh start. Later, the feast was connected to the Passover celebration, and the custom of eating unleavened bread came to be seen as a reminder of the haste with which the people had left Egypt—before having time to leaven their bread.

The *feast of Weeks*, or Pentecost, began seven weeks after the barley harvest, to celebrate the start of the wheat harvest. Later, the feast of Weeks took on added significance. Because the Israelites had arrived at Mount Sinai in the third month after their departure from Egypt (see 19:1), this weeklong feast came to be seen as a celebration of God's Covenant with Israel.

The third weeklong festival, the *feast of Booths*, also called the festival of Tabernacles, was celebrated as the produce of the land was gathered. Much like our own Thanksgiving Day, it was a time set aside to thank God for the bounty of the earth. It is the most popular of these feasts. Because booths are tents, this feast reminded the Israelites of the time they spent wandering in the desert. In Exodus it is called the feast at the fruit harvest, and in other places, simply the festival (see 1 Kings 8.2).

▶ Ex 34:18–26

and the pegs of the court, and their cords; ¹⁹the finely worked vestments for ministering in the holy place, the holy vestments for the priest

---

ᵃ Meaning of Heb uncertain   ᵇ Or *the cover*

Aaron, and the vestments of his sons, for their service as priests.

Offerings for the Tabernacle

20 Then all the congregation of the Israelites withdrew from the presence of Moses. 21And they came, everyone whose heart was stirred, and everyone whose spirit was willing, and brought the LORD's offering to be used for the tent of meeting, and for all its service, and for the sacred vestments. 22So they came, both men and women; all who were of a willing heart brought brooches and earrings and signet rings and pendants, all sorts of gold objects, everyone bringing an offering of gold to the LORD. 23And everyone who possessed blue or purple or crimson yarn or fine linen or goats' hair or tanned rams' skins or fine leather,a brought them. 24Everyone who could make an offering of silver or bronze brought it as the LORD's offering; and everyone who possessed acacia wood of any use in the work, brought it. 25All the skillful women spun with their hands, and brought what they had spun in blue and purple and crimson yarns and fine linen; 26all the women whose hearts moved them to use their skill spun the goats' hair. 27And the leaders brought onyx stones and gems to be set in the ephod and the breastpiece, 28and spices and oil for the light, and for the anointing oil, and for the fragrant incense. 29All the Israelite men and women whose hearts made them willing to bring anything for the work that the LORD had commanded by Moses to be done, brought it as a freewill offering to the LORD.

Bezalel and Oholiab

30 Then Moses said to the Israelites: See, the LORD has called by name Bezalel son of Uri son of Hur, of the tribe of Judah; 31he has filled him with divine spirit,b with skill, intelligence, and knowledge in every kind of craft, 32to devise artistic designs, to work in gold, silver, and bronze, 33in cutting stones for setting, and in carving wood, in every kind of craft. 34And he has inspired him to teach, both him and Oholiab son of Ahisamach, of the tribe of Dan. 35He has filled them with skill to do every kind of work done by an artisan or by a designer or by an embroiderer in blue, purple, and crimson yarns, and in fine linen, or by a weaver—by any sort of artisan or skilled designer.

36 Bezalel and Oholiab and every skillful one to whom the LORD has given skill and understanding to know how to do any work in the construction of the sanctuary shall work in accordance with all that the LORD has commanded.

2 Moses then called Bezalel and Oholiab and every skillful one to whom the LORD had given skill, everyone whose heart was stirred to come to do the work; 3and they received from Moses all the freewill offerings that the Israelites had brought for doing the work on the sanctuary. They still kept bringing him freewill offerings every morning, 4so that all the artisans who were doing every sort of task on the sanctuary came, each from the task being performed, 5and said to Moses, "The people are bringing much more than enough for doing the work that the LORD has commanded us to do." 6So Moses gave command, and word was proclaimed throughout the camp: "No man or woman is to make anything else as an offering for the sanctuary." So the people were restrained from bringing; 7for what they had already brought was more than enough to do all the work.

Construction of the Tabernacle

8 All those with skill among the workers made the tabernacle with ten curtains; they were made of fine twisted linen, and blue, purple, and crimson yarns, with cherubim skillfully worked into them. 9The length of each curtain was twenty-eight cubits, and the width of each curtain four cubits; all the curtains were of the same size.

10 He joined five curtains to one another, and the other five curtains he joined to one another. 11He made loops of blue on the edge of the outermost curtain of the first set; likewise he made them on the edge of the outermost curtain of the second set; 12he made fifty loops on the one curtain, and he made fifty loops on the edge of the curtain that was in the second set; the loops were opposite one another. 13And he made fifty clasps of gold, and joined the curtains one to the other with clasps; so the tabernacle was one whole.

14 He also made curtains of goats' hair for a tent over the tabernacle; he made eleven curtains. 15The length of each curtain was thirty cubits, and the width of each curtain four cubits; the eleven curtains were of the same size. 16He joined five curtains by themselves, and six curtains by themselves. 17He made fifty loops on the edge of the outermost curtain of the one set, and fifty loops on the edge of the other connecting curtain. 18He made fifty clasps of bronze to join the tent together so that it might be one whole. 19And he made for the tent a covering of tanned rams' skins and an outer covering of fine leather.a

20 Then he made the upright frames for the

---

a Meaning of Heb uncertain   b Or the spirit of God

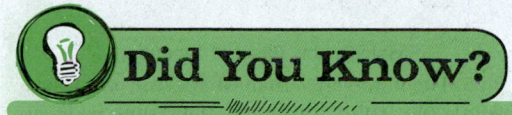

Did You Know?

The Ark of the Covenant

The ark of the Covenant, which Bezalel made in fulfillment of God's command, was a portable box in which the Israelites kept the tablets of the Law (see Deut 10:1–5, 1 Kings 8:9) and possibly other sacred items. The large box was made of gold-plated wood, with four rings attached to its lower corners; through these rings, gold-plated poles were inserted for carrying the ark in procession. On top of the ark sat two golden angels facing each other, their wings touching over their heads.

The ark of the Covenant was a symbol of God's saving presence among the Israelites. It accompanied them during their forty years in the desert (see Num 10:33–36) and was solemnly carried through the Jordan River when they entered the Promised Land (see Josh 3:1–17). Later, the Israelite soldiers took the ark into battle, invoking God's strength against their enemies (see 1 Sam 4:1–11). After the ark was lost in battle to the Philistines, David retrieved it and brought it to Jerusalem (see 2 Sam 6:1–23), where his son Solomon eventually enthroned it in the Temple, in the holy of holies (see 1 Kings 8:1–11). The ark remained there until the destruction of Jerusalem in 587 BC, when it was lost to history.

▶ Ex 37:1–9

the top, at the first ring; he made two of them in this way, for the two corners. ³⁰There were eight frames with their bases of silver: sixteen bases, under every frame two bases.

31 He made bars of acacia wood, five for the frames of the one side of the tabernacle, ³²and five bars for the frames of the other side of the tabernacle, and five bars for the frames of the tabernacle at the rear westward. ³³He made the middle bar to pass through from end to end halfway up the frames. ³⁴And he overlaid the frames with gold, and made rings of gold for them to hold the bars, and overlaid the bars with gold.

35 He made the curtain of blue, purple, and crimson yarns, and fine twisted linen, with cherubim skillfully worked into it. ³⁶For it he made four pillars of acacia, and overlaid them with gold; their hooks were of gold, and he cast for them four bases of silver. ³⁷He also made a screen for the entrance to the tent, of blue, purple, and crimson yarns, and fine twisted linen, embroidered with needlework; ³⁸and its five pillars with their hooks. He overlaid their capitals and their bases with gold, but their five bases were of bronze.

Making the Ark of the Covenant

37 Bezalel made the ark of acacia wood; it was two and a half cubits long, a cubit and a half wide, and a cubit and a half high. ²He overlaid it with pure gold inside and outside, and made a molding of gold around it. ³He cast for it four rings of gold for its four feet, two rings on its one side and two rings on its other side. ⁴He made poles of acacia wood, and overlaid them

tabernacle of acacia wood. ²¹Ten cubits was the length of a frame, and a cubit and a half the width of each frame. ²²Each frame had two pegs for fitting together; he did this for all the frames of the tabernacle. ²³The frames for the tabernacle he made in this way: twenty frames for the south side; ²⁴and he made forty bases of silver under the twenty frames, two bases under the first frame for its two pegs, and two bases under the next frame for its two pegs. ²⁵For the second side of the tabernacle, on the north side, he made twenty frames ²⁶and their forty bases of silver, two bases under the first frame and two bases under the next frame. ²⁷For the rear of the tabernacle westward he made six frames. ²⁸He made two frames for corners of the tabernacle in the rear. ²⁹They were separate beneath, but joined at

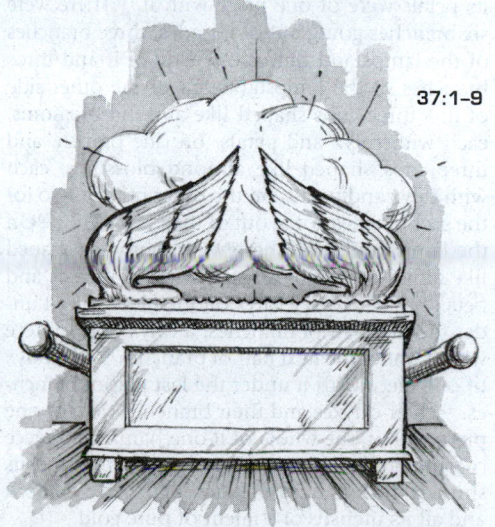

37:1–9

with gold, ⁵and put the poles into the rings on the sides of the ark, to carry the ark. ⁶He made a mercy seat[a] of pure gold; two cubits and a half was its length, and a cubit and a half its width. ⁷He made two cherubim of hammered gold; at the two ends of the mercy seat[b] he made them, ⁸one cherub at the one end, and one cherub at the other end; of one piece with the mercy seat[b] he made the cherubim at its two ends. ⁹The cherubim spread out their wings above, overshadowing the mercy seat[b] with their wings. They faced one another; the faces of the cherubim were turned toward the mercy seat.[b]

Making the Table for the Bread of the Presence

10 He also made the table of acacia wood, two cubits long, one cubit wide, and a cubit and a half high. ¹¹He overlaid it with pure gold, and made a molding of gold around it. ¹²He made around it a rim a handbreadth wide, and made a molding of gold around the rim. ¹³He cast for it four rings of gold, and fastened the rings to the four corners at its four legs. ¹⁴The rings that held the poles used for carrying the table were close to the rim. ¹⁵He made the poles of acacia wood to carry the table, and overlaid them with gold. ¹⁶And he made the vessels of pure gold that were to be on the table, its plates and dishes for incense, and its bowls and flagons with which to pour drink offerings.

Making the Lampstand

17 He also made the lampstand of pure gold. The base and the shaft of the lampstand were made of hammered work; its cups, its calyxes, and its petals were of one piece with it. ¹⁸There were six branches going out of its sides, three branches of the lampstand out of one side of it and three branches of the lampstand out of the other side of it; ¹⁹three cups shaped like almond blossoms, each with calyx and petals, on one branch, and three cups shaped like almond blossoms, each with calyx and petals, on the other branch—so for the six branches going out of the lampstand. ²⁰On the lampstand itself there were four cups shaped like almond blossoms, each with its calyxes and petals. ²¹There was a calyx of one piece with it under the first pair of branches, a calyx of one piece with it under the next pair of branches, and a calyx of one piece with it under the last pair of branches. ²²Their calyxes and their branches were of one piece with it, the whole of it one hammered piece of pure gold. ²³He made its seven lamps and its snuffers and its trays of pure gold. ²⁴He made it and all its utensils of a talent of pure gold.

Making the Altar of Incense

25 He made the altar of incense of acacia wood, one cubit long, and one cubit wide; it was square, and was two cubits high; its horns were of one piece with it. ²⁶He overlaid it with pure gold, its top, and its sides all around, and its horns; and he made for it a molding of gold all around, ²⁷and made two golden rings for it under its molding, on two opposite sides of it, to hold the poles with which to carry it. ²⁸And he made the poles of acacia wood, and overlaid them with gold.

Making the Anointing Oil and the Incense

29 He made the holy anointing oil also, and the pure fragrant incense, blended as by the perfumer.

Making the Altar of Burnt Offering

38 He made the altar of burnt offering also of acacia wood; it was five cubits long, and five cubits wide; it was square, and three cubits high. ²He made horns for it on its four corners; its horns were of one piece with it, and he overlaid it with bronze. ³He made all the utensils of the altar, the pots, the shovels, the basins, the forks, and the firepans: all its utensils he made of bronze. ⁴He made for the altar a grating, a network of bronze, under its ledge, extending halfway down. ⁵He cast four rings on the four corners of the bronze grating to hold the poles; ⁶he made the poles of acacia wood, and overlaid them with bronze. ⁷And he put the poles through the rings on the sides of the altar, to carry it with them; he made it hollow, with boards.

8 He made the basin of bronze with its stand of bronze, from the mirrors of the women who served at the entrance to the tent of meeting.

Making the Court of the Tabernacle

9 He made the court; for the south side the hangings of the court were of fine twisted linen, one hundred cubits long; ¹⁰its twenty pillars and their twenty bases were of bronze, but the hooks of the pillars and their bands were of silver. ¹¹For the north side there were hangings one hundred cubits long; its twenty pillars and their twenty bases were of bronze, but the hooks of the pillars and their bands were of silver. ¹²For the west side there were hangings fifty cubits long, with ten pillars and ten bases; the hooks of the pillars and their bands were of silver. ¹³And for the front to the east, fifty cubits. ¹⁴The hangings for one side

a Or a cover b Or the cover

of the gate were fifteen cubits, with three pillars and three bases. [15]And so for the other side; on each side of the gate of the court were hangings of fifteen cubits, with three pillars and three bases. [16]All the hangings around the court were of fine twisted linen. [17]The bases for the pillars were of bronze, but the hooks of the pillars and their bands were of silver; the overlaying of their capitals was also of silver, and all the pillars of the court were banded with silver. [18]The screen for the entrance to the court was embroidered with needlework in blue, purple, and crimson yarns and fine twisted linen. It was twenty cubits long and, along the width of it, five cubits high, corresponding to the hangings of the court. [19]There were four pillars; their four bases were of bronze, their hooks of silver, and the overlaying of their capitals and their bands of silver. [20]All the pegs for the tabernacle and for the court all around were of bronze.

Materials of the Tabernacle

21 These are the records of the tabernacle, the tabernacle of the covenant,[a] which were drawn up at the commandment of Moses, the work of the Levites being under the direction of Ithamar son of the priest Aaron. [22]Bezalel son of Uri son of Hur, of the tribe of Judah, made all that the LORD commanded Moses; [23]and with him was Oholiab son of Ahisamach, of the tribe of Dan, engraver, designer, and embroiderer in blue, purple, and crimson yarns, and in fine linen.

24 All the gold that was used for the work, in all the construction of the sanctuary, the gold from the offering, was twenty-nine talents and seven hundred thirty shekels, measured by the sanctuary shekel. [25]The silver from those of the congregation who were counted was one hundred talents and one thousand seven hundred seventy-five shekels, measured by the sanctuary shekel; [26]a beka a head (that is, half a shekel, measured by the sanctuary shekel), for everyone who was counted in the census, from twenty years old and upward, for six hundred three thousand, five hundred fifty men. [27]The hundred talents of silver were for casting the bases of the sanctuary, and the bases of the curtain; one hundred bases for the hundred talents, a talent for a base. [28]Of the thousand seven hundred seventy-five shekels he made hooks for the pillars, and overlaid their capitals and made bands for them. [29]The bronze that was contributed was seventy talents, and two thousand four hundred shekels; [30]with it he made the bases for the entrance of the tent of meeting, the bronze altar and the bronze grating for it and all the utensils of the altar, [31]the bases

all around the court, and the bases of the gate of the court, all the pegs of the tabernacle, and all the pegs around the court.

Making the Vestments for the Priesthood

39 Of the blue, purple, and crimson yarns they made finely worked vestments, for ministering in the holy place; they made the sacred vestments for Aaron; as the LORD had commanded Moses.

2 He made the ephod of gold, of blue, purple, and crimson yarns, and of fine twisted linen. [3]Gold leaf was hammered out and cut into threads to work into the blue, purple, and crimson yarns and into the fine twisted linen, in skilled design. [4]They made for the ephod shoulder-pieces, joined to it at its two edges. [5]The decorated band on it was of the same materials and workmanship, of gold, of blue, purple, and crimson yarns, and of fine twisted linen; as the LORD had commanded Moses.

6 The onyx stones were prepared, enclosed in settings of gold filigree and engraved like the engravings of a signet, according to the names of the sons of Israel. [7]He set them on the shoulder-pieces of the ephod, to be stones of remembrance for the sons of Israel; as the LORD had commanded Moses.

8 He made the breastpiece, in skilled work, like the work of the ephod, of gold, of blue, purple, and crimson yarns, and of fine twisted linen. [9]It was square; the breastpiece was made double, a span in length and a span in width when doubled. [10]They set in it four rows of stones. A row of carnelian,[b] chrysolite, and emerald was the first row; [11]and the second row, a turquoise, a sapphire,[c] and a moonstone; [12]and the third row, a jacinth, an agate, and an amethyst; [13]and the fourth row, a beryl, an onyx, and a jasper; they were enclosed in settings of gold filigree. [14]There were twelve stones with names corresponding to the names of the sons of Israel; they were like signets, each engraved with its name, for the twelve tribes. [15]They made on the breastpiece chains of pure gold, twisted like cords; [16]and they made two settings of gold filigree and two gold rings, and put the two rings on the two edges of the breastpiece; [17]and they put the two cords of gold in the two rings at the edges of the breastpiece. [18]Two ends of the two cords they had attached to the two settings of filigree; in this way they attached it in front to the shoulder-pieces of the ephod. [19]Then they made two rings of gold, and

---

a Or treaty, or testimony; Heb eduth   b The identification of several of these stones is uncertain   c Or lapis lazuli

put them at the two ends of the breastpiece, on its inside edge next to the ephod. [20]They made two rings of gold, and attached them in front to the lower part of the two shoulder-pieces of the ephod, at its joining above the decorated band of the ephod. [21]They bound the breastpiece by its rings to the rings of the ephod with a blue cord, so that it should lie on the decorated band of the ephod, and that the breastpiece should not come loose from the ephod; as the Lord had commanded Moses.

22 He also made the robe of the ephod woven all of blue yarn; [23]and the opening of the robe in the middle of it was like the opening in a coat of mail,[a] with a binding around the opening, so that it might not be torn. [24]On the lower hem of the robe they made pomegranates of blue, purple, and crimson yarns, and of fine twisted linen. [25]They also made bells of pure gold, and put the bells between the pomegranates on the lower hem of the robe all around, between the pomegranates; [26]a bell and a pomegranate, a bell and a pomegranate all around on the lower hem of the robe for ministering; as the Lord had commanded Moses.

27 They also made the tunics, woven of fine linen, for Aaron and his sons, [28]and the turban of fine linen, and the headdresses of fine linen, and the linen undergarments of fine twisted linen, [29]and the sash of fine twisted linen, and of blue, purple, and crimson yarns, embroidered with needlework; as the Lord had commanded Moses.

30 They made the rosette of the holy diadem of pure gold, and wrote on it an inscription, like the engraving of a signet, "Holy to the Lord." [31]They tied to it a blue cord, to fasten it on the turban above; as the Lord had commanded Moses.

The Work Completed

32 In this way all the work of the tabernacle of the tent of meeting was finished; the Israelites had done everything just as the Lord had commanded Moses. [33]Then they brought the tabernacle to Moses, the tent and all its utensils, its hooks, its frames, its bars, its pillars, and its bases; [34]the covering of tanned rams' skins and the covering of fine leather,[a] and the curtain for the screen; [35]the ark of the covenant[b] with its poles and the mercy seat;[c] [36]the table with all its utensils, and the bread of the Presence; [37]the pure lampstand with its lamps set on it and all its utensils, and the oil for the light; [38]the golden altar, the anointing oil and the fragrant incense, and the screen for the entrance of the tent; [39]the bronze altar, and its grating of bronze, its poles, and all its utensils; the basin with its stand; [40]the hangings of the court, its pillars, and its bases, and the screen for the gate of the court, its cords, and its pegs; and all the utensils for the service of the tabernacle, for the tent of meeting; [41]the finely worked vestments for ministering in the holy place, the sacred vestments for the priest Aaron, and the vestments of his sons to serve as priests. [42]The Israelites had done all of the work just as the Lord had commanded Moses. [43]When Moses saw that they had done all the work just as the Lord had commanded, he blessed them.

The Tabernacle Erected and Its Equipment Installed

40 The Lord spoke to Moses: [2]On the first day of the first month you shall set up the tabernacle of the tent of meeting. [3]You shall put in it the ark of the covenant,[b] and you shall screen the ark with the curtain. [4]You shall bring in the table, and arrange its setting; and you shall bring in the lampstand, and set up its lamps. [5]You shall put the golden altar for incense before the ark of the covenant,[b] and set up the screen for the entrance of the tabernacle. [6]You shall set the altar of burnt offering before the entrance of the tabernacle of the tent of meeting, [7]and place the basin between the tent of meeting and the altar, and put water in it. [8]You shall set up the court all around, and hang up the screen for the gate of the court. [9]Then you shall take the anointing oil, and anoint the tabernacle and all that is in it, and consecrate it and all its furniture, so that it shall become holy. [10]You shall also anoint the altar of burnt offering and all its utensils, and consecrate the altar, so that the altar shall be most holy. [11]You shall also anoint the basin with its stand, and consecrate it. [12]Then you shall bring Aaron and his sons to the entrance of the tent of meeting, and shall wash them with water, [13]and put on Aaron the sacred vestments, and you shall anoint him and consecrate him, so that he may serve me as priest. [14]You shall bring his sons also and put tunics on them, [15]and anoint them, as you anointed their father, that they may serve me as priests: and their anointing shall admit them to a perpetual priesthood throughout all generations to come.

16 Moses did everything just as the Lord had commanded him. [17]In the first month in the second year, on the first day of the month, the tabernacle was set up. [18]Moses set up the tabernacle; he laid its bases, and set up its frames, and put in

a Meaning of Heb uncertain   b Or *treaty*, or *testimony*; Heb *eduth*   c Or *the cover*

Cultural Connection

Umbrellas, Arks, and Tents

Umbrellas offer protection from the sun or rain. In Asian cultures, servants would hold umbrellas over emperors and kings. Catholics in Indonesia have adapted this custom for their worship. Often an umbrella is set up over the tabernacle. Umbrellas are held over a priest when he carries the Blessed Sacrament or over the statue of Jesus' Sacred Heart when it is carried in a procession. The umbrella has become a sign of reverence for something that symbolizes God's presence.

The ark of the Covenant was built to act like an umbrella, to protect and revere the tablets of the Law (the Commandments). When the ark was not being carried, it rested in the tabernacle in the holy of holies, which was a special tent at the center of the Israelites' camp. The ark and the tent served the same practical purpose as an umbrella and had the same deeper meaning of revering God's presence.

The next time you use an umbrella, remember how umbrellas are used to show respect for that which is holy: the body of Christ, the Ten Commandments, and one of God's greatest creations—*you!*

▶ **Ex 40:1–15**

its poles, and raised up its pillars; ¹⁹and he spread the tent over the tabernacle, and put the covering of the tent over it; as the Lord had commanded Moses. ²⁰He took the covenant[a] and put it into the ark, and put the poles on the ark, and set the mercy seat[b] above the ark; ²¹and he brought the ark into the tabernacle, and set up the curtain for screening, and screened the ark of the covenant;[a] as the Lord had commanded Moses. ²²He put the table in the tent of meeting, on the north side of the tabernacle, outside the curtain, ²³and set the bread in order on it before the Lord; as the Lord had commanded Moses. ²⁴He put the lampstand in the tent of meeting, opposite the table on the south side of the tabernacle, ²⁵and set up the lamps before the Lord; as the Lord had commanded Moses. ²⁶He put the golden altar in the tent of meeting before the curtain, ²⁷and offered fragrant incense on it; as the Lord had commanded Moses. ²⁸He also put in place the screen for the entrance of the tabernacle. ²⁹He set the altar of burnt offering at the entrance of the tabernacle of the tent of meeting, and offered on it the burnt offering and the grain offering as the Lord had commanded Moses. ³⁰He set the basin between the tent of meeting and the altar, and put water in it for washing, ³¹with which Moses and Aaron and his sons washed their hands and their feet. ³²When they went into the tent of meeting, and when they approached the altar, they washed; as the Lord had commanded Moses. ³³He set up the court around the tabernacle and the altar, and put up the screen at the gate of the court. So Moses finished the work.

The Cloud and the Glory

34 Then the cloud covered the tent of meeting, and the glory of the Lord filled the tabernacle. ³⁵Moses was not able to enter the tent of meeting because the cloud settled upon it, and the glory of the Lord filled the tabernacle. ³⁶Whenever the cloud was taken up from the tabernacle, the Israelites would set out on each stage of their journey; ³⁷but if the cloud was not taken up, then they did not set out until the day that it was taken up. ³⁸For the cloud of the Lord was on the tabernacle by day, and fire was in the cloud[c] by night, before the eyes of all the house of Israel at each stage of their journey.

a Or treaty, or testimony; Heb eduth   *b* Or the cover   *c* Heb it

When approaching a stop sign, come to a complete stop before proceeding. No shoes, no shirt, no service. The line forms here. Sometimes it seems that life is just made up of a bunch of rules and laws. But when we really think about it, we realize that rules and laws are designed to help society work smoothly and to make sure we respect one another's rights. The Book of Leviticus has a similar function. It is primarily a list of laws, rules, and instructions to ensure holiness and order in worship and the people's way of life.

At a Glance

- **Chapters 1–7.** laws regulating various sacrifices
- **Chapters 8–10.** the ordination ceremony of Aaron and his sons
- **Chapters 11–16.** purity laws and the celebration of Yom Kippur
- **Chapters 17–26.** holiness laws
- **Chapters 27–34.** the rededication of holy things

Quick Facts

Period Covered: after the Exodus, during the Israelites' encampment at Mount Sinai
Inspired Author: the Priestly writer writing after the Babylonian Exile
Theme:to teach the way of holiness through observance of the Law and religious ritual

The Book of Leviticus

In Depth

Leviticus, the third book of the Pentateuch, or Torah, is named after the tribe of Levi, whose male members were designated priests in Israel. It was their responsibility to conduct appropriate worship of God. For that reason, the book has often been referred to as the Torah (Law) of the Priests.

Most Scripture scholars believe that the laws and regulations in Leviticus developed over hundreds of years after the people entered the Promised Land. The book was compiled at a time when the priests were struggling to unify Israel as it lay in ruins from its Babylonian conquerors. They wished to gather the various traditions and regulations that governed Israel's way of life. The author of Leviticus, referred to as the Priestly writer, writes as if these gathered traditions and regulations were given by God to Moses at Mount Sinai as part of the original Law. The author wishes to show that these laws are an extension of the Sinai Covenant.

If the goal of Israel's existence is to "be holy, for I [the Lord] am holy" (Lev 11:45), then the Book of Leviticus records how holiness becomes part of every aspect of Israel's existence. Chapters 17–26 are described as the Holiness Code. The words on love of neighbor in 19:18 are quoted several times in the New Testament. The purpose of Leviticus is to call Israel to follow the Law, and thus become a holy people and make its land a suitable place for God to dwell.

The customs and rites in Jesus' time are observances of the laws in Leviticus. Many of those customs and rites were left behind as Christianity emerged as a distinct religion.

Leviticus

The Burnt Offering

1 The LORD summoned Moses and spoke to him from the tent of meeting, saying: ²Speak to the people of Israel and say to them: When any of you bring an offering of livestock to the LORD, you shall bring your offering from the herd or from the flock.

3 If the offering is a burnt offering from the herd, you shall offer a male without blemish; you shall bring it to the entrance of the tent of meeting, for acceptance in your behalf before the LORD. ⁴You shall lay your hand on the head of the burnt offering, and it shall be acceptable in your behalf as atonement for you. ⁵The bull shall be slaughtered before the LORD; and Aaron's sons the priests shall offer the blood, dashing the blood against all sides of the altar that is at the entrance of the tent of meeting. ⁶The burnt offering shall be flayed and cut up into its parts. ⁷The sons of the priest Aaron shall put fire on the altar and arrange wood on the fire. ⁸Aaron's sons the priests shall arrange the parts, with the head and the suet, on the wood that is on the fire on the altar; ⁹but its entrails and its legs shall be washed with water. Then the priest shall turn the whole into smoke on the altar as a burnt offering, an offering by fire of pleasing odor to the LORD.

10 If your gift for a burnt offering is from the flock, from the sheep or goats, your offering shall be a male without blemish. ¹¹It shall be slaughtered on the north side of the altar before the LORD, and Aaron's sons the priests shall dash its blood against all sides of the altar. ¹²It shall be cut up into its parts, with its head and its suet, and the priest shall arrange them on the wood that is on the fire on the altar; ¹³but the entrails and the legs shall be washed with water. Then the priest shall offer the whole and turn it into smoke on the altar; it is a burnt offering, an offering by fire of pleasing odor to the LORD.

14 If your offering to the LORD is a burnt offering of birds, you shall choose your offering from turtledoves or pigeons. ¹⁵The priest shall bring it to the altar and wring off its head, and turn it into smoke on the altar; and its blood shall be drained out against the side of the altar. ¹⁶He shall remove its crop with its contents*a* and throw it at the east side of the altar, in the place for ashes. ¹⁷He shall tear it open by its wings without severing it. Then the priest shall turn it into smoke on the altar, on the wood that is on the fire; it is a burnt offering, an offering by fire of pleasing odor to the LORD.

Grain Offerings

2 When anyone presents a grain offering to the LORD, the offering shall be of choice flour; the worshiper shall pour oil on it, and put frankincense on it, ²and bring it to Aaron's sons the priests. After taking from it a handful of the choice flour and oil, with all its frankincense, the priest shall turn this token portion into smoke on the altar, an offering by fire of pleasing odor to

---

a Meaning of Heb uncertain

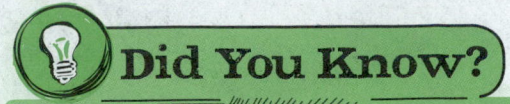

Did You Know?

The Covenant Laws

Even though Christians are not bound by the Jewish religion—see the Letters to the Hebrews and to the Romans—the laws in Leviticus help us understand the meaning of life for the Israelites. These laws developed out of their experience of striving to be faithful to God and were interpreted and taught by the priests of the tribe of Levi.

The purity laws may seem the strangest to us today. They defined who or what was pure—that is, free from contamination—and therefore acceptable to God for the purpose of liturgical worship. They included laws on sickness, especially leprosy, because physical disease was understood as a symptom of sin or spiritual contamination. Purity laws also covered food, animals, bodily discharges, and corpses.

Other laws described proper relationships between people. These laws reflected more the intentions of the heart. Later, the prophets and Jesus would emphasize that impurity comes from the heart, not from something outside the person (see Mk 7:1–23). Other laws regulated priestly ministry, and still others regulated social institutions. Nothing was left to chance. The laws of the Covenant made it clear that God was present in every aspect of the people's lives.

---

the LORD. ³And what is left of the grain offering shall be for Aaron and his sons, a most holy part of the offerings by fire to the LORD.

4 When you present a grain offering baked in the oven, it shall be of choice flour: unleavened cakes mixed with oil, or unleavened wafers spread with oil. ⁵If your offering is grain prepared on a griddle, it shall be of choice flour mixed with oil, unleavened; ⁶break it in pieces, and pour oil on it; it is a grain offering. ⁷If your offering is grain prepared in a pan, it shall be made of choice flour in oil. ⁸You shall bring to the LORD the grain offering that is prepared in any of these ways; and when it is presented to the priest, he shall take it to the altar. ⁹The priest shall remove from the grain offering its token portion and turn this into smoke on the altar, an offering by fire of pleasing odor to the LORD.

¹⁰And what is left of the grain offering shall be for Aaron and his sons; it is a most holy part of the offerings by fire to the LORD.

11 No grain offering that you bring to the LORD shall be made with leaven, for you must not turn any leaven or honey into smoke as an offering by fire to the LORD. ¹²You may bring them to the LORD as an offering of choice products, but they shall not be offered on the altar for a pleasing odor. ¹³You shall not omit from your grain offerings the salt of the covenant with your God; with all your offerings you shall offer salt.

14 If you bring a grain offering of first fruits to the LORD, you shall bring as the grain offering of your first fruits coarse new grain from fresh ears, parched with fire. ¹⁵You shall add oil to it and lay frankincense on it; it is a grain offering. ¹⁶And the priest shall turn a token portion of it into smoke—some of the coarse grain and oil with all its frankincense; it is an offering by fire to the LORD.

Offerings of Well-Being

3 If the offering is a sacrifice of well-being, if you offer an animal of the herd, whether male or female, you shall offer one without blemish before the LORD. ²You shall lay your hand on the head of the offering and slaughter it at the entrance of the tent of meeting; and Aaron's sons the priests shall dash the blood against all sides of the altar. ³You shall offer from the sacrifice of well-being, as an offering by fire to the LORD, the fat that covers the entrails and all the fat that is around the entrails; ⁴the two kidneys with the fat that is on them at the loins, and the appendage of the liver, which he shall remove with the kidneys. ⁵Then Aaron's sons shall turn these into smoke on the altar, with the burnt offering that is on the wood on the fire, as an offering by fire of pleasing odor to the LORD.

6 If your offering for a sacrifice of well-being to the LORD is from the flock, male or female, you shall offer one without blemish. ⁷If you present a sheep as your offering, you shall bring it before the LORD ⁸and lay your hand on the head of the offering. It shall be slaughtered before the tent of meeting, and Aaron's sons shall dash its blood against all sides of the altar. ⁹You shall present its fat from the sacrifice of well-being, as an offering by fire to the LORD: the whole broad tail, which shall be removed close to the backbone, the fat that covers the entrails, and all the fat that is around the entrails; ¹⁰the two kidneys with the fat that is on them at the loins, and the appendage of the liver, which you shall remove with the kidneys. ¹¹Then the priest shall turn these

into smoke on the altar as a food offering by fire to the LORD.

12 If your offering is a goat, you shall bring it before the LORD ¹³and lay your hand on its head; it shall be slaughtered before the tent of meeting; and the sons of Aaron shall dash its blood against all sides of the altar. ¹⁴You shall present as your offering from it, as an offering by fire to the LORD, the fat that covers the entrails, and all the fat that is around the entrails; ¹⁵the two kidneys with the fat that is on them at the loins, and the appendage of the liver, which you shall remove with the kidneys. ¹⁶Then the priest shall turn these into smoke on the altar as a food offering by fire for a pleasing odor.

All fat is the LORD's. ¹⁷It shall be a perpetual statute throughout your generations, in all your settlements: you must not eat any fat or any blood.

Sin Offerings

4 The LORD spoke to Moses, saying, ²Speak to the people of Israel, saying: When anyone sins unintentionally in any of the LORD's commandments about things not to be done, and does any one of them:

3 If it is the anointed priest who sins, thus bringing guilt on the people, he shall offer for the sin that he has committed a bull of the herd without blemish as a sin offering to the LORD. ⁴He shall bring the bull to the entrance of the tent of meeting before the LORD and lay his hand on the head of the bull; the bull shall be slaughtered before the LORD. ⁵The anointed priest shall take some of the blood of the bull and bring it into the tent of meeting. ⁶The priest shall dip his finger in the blood and sprinkle some of the blood seven times before the LORD in front of the curtain of the sanctuary. ⁷The priest shall put some of the blood on the horns of the altar of fragrant incense that is in the tent of meeting before the LORD; and the rest of the blood of the bull he shall pour out at the base of the altar of burnt offering, which is at the entrance of the tent of meeting. ⁸He shall remove all the fat from the bull of sin offering: the fat that covers the entrails and all the fat that is around the entrails; ⁹the two kidneys with the fat that is on them at the loins; and the appendage of the liver which he shall remove with the kidneys, ¹⁰just as these are removed from the ox of the sacrifice of well-being. The priest shall turn them into smoke upon the altar of burnt offering. ¹¹But the skin of the bull and all its flesh, as well as its head, its legs, its entrails, and its dung— ¹²all the rest of the bull—he shall carry out to a clean place outside the camp, to the ash heap, and shall burn it on a wood fire; at the ash heap it shall be burned.

Pray It!

Sin Offering

The sin offering laws probably seem strange to you. The Israelites understood that sin affects not only the sinner but also those whose lives the sinner touches. They understood sin as incurring a debt that must be repaid. The sinner made a guilt offering to atone for the sin. Christians believe that Jesus became the sin offering who took on the debt of the sins of the whole world, once and for all. However, Christians still have an obligation to recognize and confess their sins. For Catholics this occurs formally in the sacrament of Penance and Reconciliation. Catholics admit their sinfulness and receive God's forgiveness by participating in this sacrament.

Take a moment to thank God for the great gift of Jesus and for the forgiveness of our sins.

▶ Lev 4:1—6:7

L
E
V

13 If the whole congregation of Israel errs unintentionally and the matter escapes the notice of the assembly, and they do any one of the things that by the LORD's commandments ought not to be done and incur guilt; ¹⁴when the sin that they have committed becomes known, the assembly shall offer a bull of the herd for a sin offering and bring it before the tent of meeting. ¹⁵The elders of the congregation shall lay their hands on the head of the bull before the LORD, and the bull shall be slaughtered before the LORD. ¹⁶The anointed priest shall bring some of the blood of the bull into the tent of meeting, ¹⁷and the priest shall dip his finger in the blood and sprinkle it seven times before the LORD, in front of the curtain. ¹⁸He shall put some of the blood on the horns of the altar that is before the LORD in the tent of meeting; and the rest of the blood he shall pour out at the base of the altar of burnt offering that is at the entrance of the tent of meeting. ¹⁹He shall remove all its fat and turn it into smoke on the altar. ²⁰He shall do with the bull just as is done with the bull of sin offering; he shall do the same with this. The priest shall make atonement for them, and they shall be forgiven.

21 He shall carry the bull outside the camp, and burn it as he burned the first bull; it is the sin offering for the assembly.

22 When a ruler sins, doing unintentionally any one of all the things that by commandments of the LORD his God ought not to be done and incurs guilt, 23 once the sin that he has committed is made known to him, he shall bring as his offering a male goat without blemish. 24 He shall lay his hand on the head of the goat; it shall be slaughtered at the spot where the burnt offering is slaughtered before the LORD; it is a sin offering. 25 The priest shall take some of the blood of the sin offering with his finger and put it on the horns of the altar of burnt offering, and pour out the rest of its blood at the base of the altar of burnt offering. 26 All its fat he shall turn into smoke on the altar, like the fat of the sacrifice of well-being. Thus the priest shall make atonement on his behalf for his sin, and he shall be forgiven.

27 If anyone of the ordinary people among you sins unintentionally in doing any one of the things that by the LORD's commandments ought not to be done and incurs guilt, 28 when the sin that you have committed is made known to you, you shall bring a female goat without blemish as your offering, for the sin that you have committed. 29 You shall lay your hand on the head of the sin offering; and the sin offering shall be slaughtered at the place of the burnt offering. 30 The priest shall take some of its blood with his finger and put it on the horns of the altar of burnt offering, and he shall pour out the rest of its blood at the base of the altar. 31 He shall remove all its fat, as the fat is removed from the offering of well-being, and the priest shall turn it into smoke on the altar for a pleasing odor to the LORD. Thus the priest shall make atonement on your behalf, and you shall be forgiven.

32 If the offering you bring as a sin offering is a sheep, you shall bring a female without blemish. 33 You shall lay your hand on the head of the sin offering; and it shall be slaughtered as a sin offering at the spot where the burnt offering is slaughtered. 34 The priest shall take some of the blood of the sin offering with his finger and put it on the horns of the altar of burnt offering, and pour out the rest of its blood at the base of the altar. 35 You shall remove all its fat, as the fat of the sheep is removed from the sacrifice of well-being, and the priest shall turn it into smoke on the altar, with the offerings by fire to the LORD. Thus the priest shall make atonement on your behalf for the sin that you have committed, and you shall be forgiven.

5 When any of you sin in that you have heard a public adjuration to testify and—though able to testify as one who has seen or learned of the matter—do not speak up, you are subject to punishment. 2 Or when any of you touch any unclean thing—whether the carcass of an unclean beast or the carcass of unclean livestock or the carcass of an unclean swarming thing—and are unaware of it, you have become unclean, and are guilty. 3 Or when you touch human uncleanness—any uncleanness by which one can become unclean—and are unaware of it, when you come to know it, you shall be guilty. 4 Or when any of you utter aloud a rash oath for a bad or a good purpose, whatever people utter in an oath, and are unaware of it, when you come to know it, you shall in any of these be guilty. 5 When you realize your guilt in any of these, you shall confess the sin that you have committed. 6 And you shall bring to the LORD, as your penalty for the sin that you have committed, a female from the flock, a sheep or a goat, as a sin offering; and the priest shall make atonement on your behalf for your sin.

7 But if you cannot afford a sheep, you shall bring to the LORD, as your penalty for the sin that you have committed, two turtledoves or two pigeons, one for a sin offering and the other for a burnt offering. 8 You shall bring them to the priest, who shall offer first the one for the sin offering, wringing its head at the nape without severing it. 9 He shall sprinkle some of the blood of the sin offering on the side of the altar, while the rest of the blood shall be drained out at the base of the altar; it is a sin offering. 10 And the second he shall offer for a burnt offering according to the regulation. Thus the priest shall make atonement on your behalf for the sin that you have committed, and you shall be forgiven.

11 But if you cannot afford two turtledoves or two pigeons, you shall bring as your offering for the sin that you have committed one-tenth of an ephah of choice flour for a sin offering; you shall not put oil on it or lay frankincense on it, for it is a sin offering. 12 You shall bring it to the priest, and the priest shall scoop up a handful of it as its memorial portion, and turn this into smoke on the altar, with the offerings by fire to the LORD; it is a sin offering. 13 Thus the priest shall make atonement on your behalf for whichever of these sins you have committed, and you shall be forgiven. Like the grain offering, the rest shall be for the priest.

Offerings with Restitution

14 The LORD spoke to Moses, saying: 15 When any of you commit a trespass and sin

unintentionally in any of the holy things of the LORD, you shall bring, as your guilt offering to the LORD, a ram without blemish from the flock, convertible into silver by the sanctuary shekel; it is a guilt offering. ¹⁶And you shall make restitution for the holy thing in which you were remiss, and shall add one-fifth to it and give it to the priest. The priest shall make atonement on your behalf with the ram of the guilt offering, and you shall be forgiven.

17 If any of you sin without knowing it, doing any of the things that by the LORD's commandments ought not to be done, you have incurred guilt, and are subject to punishment. ¹⁸You shall bring to the priest a ram without blemish from the flock, or the equivalent, as a guilt offering; and the priest shall make atonement on your behalf for the error that you committed unintentionally, and you shall be forgiven. ¹⁹It is a guilt offering; you have incurred guilt before the LORD.

6 ᵃ The LORD spoke to Moses, saying: ²When any of you sin and commit a trespass against the LORD by deceiving a neighbor in a matter of a deposit or a pledge, or by robbery, or if you have defrauded a neighbor, ³or have found something lost and lied about it—if you swear falsely regarding any of the various things that one may do and sin thereby— ⁴when you have sinned and realize your guilt, and would restore what you took by robbery or by fraud or the deposit that was committed to you, or the lost thing that you found, ⁵or anything else about which you have sworn falsely, you shall repay the principal amount and shall add one-fifth to it. You shall pay it to its owner when you realize your guilt. ⁶And you shall bring to the priest, as your guilt offering to the LORD, a ram without blemish from the flock, or its equivalent, for a guilt offering. ⁷The priest shall make atonement on your behalf before the LORD, and you shall be forgiven for any of the things that one may do and incur guilt thereby.

Instructions concerning Sacrifices

8ᵇ The LORD spoke to Moses, saying: ⁹Command Aaron and his sons, saying: This is the ritual of the burnt offering. The burnt offering itself shall remain on the hearth upon the altar all night until the morning, while the fire on the altar shall be kept burning. ¹⁰The priest shall put on his linen vestments after putting on his linen undergarments next to his body; and he shall take up the ashes to which the fire has reduced the burnt offering on the altar, and place them beside the altar. ¹¹Then he shall take off his vestments and put on other garments, and carry the ashes out to a clean place outside the camp. ¹²The fire on the altar shall be kept burning; it shall not go out. Every morning the priest shall add wood to it, lay out the burnt offering on it, and turn into smoke the fat pieces of the offerings of well-being. ¹³A perpetual fire shall be kept burning on the altar; it shall not go out.

14 This is the ritual of the grain offering: The sons of Aaron shall offer it before the LORD, in front of the altar. ¹⁵They shall take from it a handful of the choice flour and oil of the grain offering, with all the frankincense that is on the offering, and they shall turn its memorial portion into smoke on the altar as a pleasing odor to the LORD. ¹⁶Aaron and his sons shall eat what is left of it; it shall be eaten as unleavened cakes in a holy place; in the court of the tent of meeting they shall eat it. ¹⁷It shall not be baked with leaven. I have given it as their portion of my offerings by fire; it is most holy, like the sin offering and the guilt offering. ¹⁸Every male among the descendants of Aaron shall eat of it, as their perpetual due throughout your generations, from the LORD's offerings by fire; anything that touches them shall become holy.

19 The LORD spoke to Moses, saying: ²⁰This is the offering that Aaron and his sons shall offer to the LORD on the day when he is anointed: one-tenth of an ephah of choice flour as a regular offering, half of it in the morning and half in the evening. ²¹It shall be made with oil on a griddle; you shall bring it well soaked, as a grain offering of bakedᶜ pieces, and you shall present it as a pleasing odor to the LORD. ²²And so the priest, anointed from among Aaron's descendants as a successor, shall prepare it; it is the LORD's—a perpetual due—to be turned entirely into smoke. ²³Every grain offering of a priest shall be wholly burned; it shall not be eaten.

24 The LORD spoke to Moses, saying: ²⁵Speak to Aaron and his sons, saying: This is the ritual of the sin offering. The sin offering shall be slaughtered before the LORD at the spot where the burnt offering is slaughtered; it is most holy. ²⁶The priest who offers it as a sin offering shall eat of it; it shall be eaten in a holy place, in the court of the tent of meeting. ²⁷Whatever touches its flesh shall become holy; and when any of its blood is spattered on a garment, you shall wash the bespattered part in a holy place. ²⁸An earthen vessel in which it was boiled shall be broken; but if it is boiled in a bronze vessel, that shall be

---

a Ch 5.20 in Heb   *b* Ch 6.1 in Heb   *c* Meaning of Heb uncertain

scoured and rinsed in water. [29]Every male among the priests shall eat of it; it is most holy. [30]But no sin offering shall be eaten from which any blood is brought into the tent of meeting for atonement in the holy place; it shall be burned with fire.

7 This is the ritual of the guilt offering. It is most holy; [2]at the spot where the burnt offering is slaughtered, they shall slaughter the guilt offering, and its blood shall be dashed against all sides of the altar. [3]All its fat shall be offered: the broad tail, the fat that covers the entrails, [4]the two kidneys with the fat that is on them at the loins, and the appendage of the liver, which shall be removed with the kidneys. [5]The priest shall turn them into smoke on the altar as an offering by fire to the LORD; it is a guilt offering. [6]Every male among the priests shall eat of it; it shall be eaten in a holy place; it is most holy.

7 The guilt offering is like the sin offering, there is the same ritual for them; the priest who makes atonement with it shall have it. [8]So, too, the priest who offers anyone's burnt offering shall keep the skin of the burnt offering that he has offered. [9]And every grain offering baked in the oven, and all that is prepared in a pan or on a griddle, shall belong to the priest who offers it. [10]But every other grain offering, mixed with oil or dry, shall belong to all the sons of Aaron equally.

Further Instructions

11 This is the ritual of the sacrifice of the offering of well-being that one may offer to the LORD. [12]If you offer it for thanksgiving, you shall offer with the thank offering unleavened cakes mixed with oil, unleavened wafers spread with oil, and cakes of choice flour well soaked in oil. [13]With your thanksgiving sacrifice of well-being you shall bring your offering with cakes of leavened bread. [14]From this you shall offer one cake from each offering, as a gift to the LORD; it shall belong to the priest who dashes the blood of the offering of well-being. [15]And the flesh of your thanksgiving sacrifice of well-being shall be eaten on the day it is offered; you shall not leave any of it until morning. [16]But if the sacrifice you offer is a votive offering or a freewill offering, it shall be eaten on the day that you offer your sacrifice, and what is left of it shall be eaten the next day; [17]but what is left of the flesh of the sacrifice shall be burned up on the third day. [18]If any of the flesh of your sacrifice of well-being is eaten on the third day, it shall not be acceptable, nor shall it be credited to the one who offers it; it shall be an abomination, and the one who eats of it shall incur guilt.

19 Flesh that touches any unclean thing shall not be eaten; it shall be burned up. As for other flesh, all who are clean may eat such flesh. [20]But those who eat flesh from the LORD's sacrifice of well-being while in a state of uncleanness shall be cut off from their kin. [21]When any one of you touches any unclean thing—human uncleanness or an unclean animal or any unclean creature—and then eats flesh from the LORD's sacrifice of well-being, you shall be cut off from your kin.

22 The LORD spoke to Moses, saying: [23]Speak to the people of Israel, saying: You shall eat no fat of ox or sheep or goat. [24]The fat of an animal that died or was torn by wild animals may be put to any other use, but you must not eat it. [25]If any one of you eats the fat from an animal of which an offering by fire may be made to the LORD, you who eat it shall be cut off from your kin. [26]You must not eat any blood whatever, either of bird or of animal, in any of your settlements. [27]Any one of you who eats any blood shall be cut off from your kin.

28 The LORD spoke to Moses, saying: [29]Speak to the people of Israel, saying: Any one of you who would offer to the LORD your sacrifice of well-being must yourself bring to the LORD your offering from your sacrifice of well-being. [30]Your own hands shall bring the LORD's offering by fire; you shall bring the fat with the breast, so that the breast may be raised as an elevation offering before the LORD. [31]The priest shall turn the fat into smoke on the altar, but the breast shall belong to Aaron and his sons. [32]And the right thigh from your sacrifices of well-being you shall give to the priest as an offering; [33]the one among the sons of Aaron who offers the blood and fat of the offering of well-being shall have the right thigh for a portion. [34]For I have taken the breast of the elevation offering, and the thigh that is offered, from the people of Israel, from their sacrifices of well-being, and have given them to Aaron the priest and to his sons, as a perpetual due from the people of Israel. [35]This is the portion allotted to Aaron and to his sons from the offerings made by fire to the LORD, once they have been brought forward to serve the LORD as priests; [36]these the LORD commanded to be given them, when he anointed them, as a perpetual due from the people of Israel throughout their generations.

37 This is the ritual of the burnt offering, the grain offering, the sin offering, the guilt offering, the offering of ordination, and the sacrifice of well-being, [38]which the LORD commanded Moses on Mount Sinai, when he commanded the people of Israel to bring their offerings to the LORD, in the wilderness of Sinai.

The Rites of Ordination

8 The LORD spoke to Moses, saying: ²Take Aaron and his sons with him, the vestments, the anointing oil, the bull of sin offering, the two rams, and the basket of unleavened bread; ³and assemble the whole congregation at the entrance of the tent of meeting. ⁴And Moses did as the LORD commanded him. When the congregation was assembled at the entrance of the tent of meeting, ⁵Moses said to the congregation, "This is what the LORD has commanded to be done."

6 Then Moses brought Aaron and his sons forward, and washed them with water. ⁷He put the tunic on him, fastened the sash around him, clothed him with the robe, and put the ephod on him. He then put the decorated band of the ephod around him, tying the ephod to him with it. ⁸He placed the breastpiece on him, and in the breastpiece he put the Urim and the Thummim. ⁹And he set the turban on his head, and on the turban, in front, he set the golden ornament, the holy crown, as the LORD commanded Moses.

10 Then Moses took the anointing oil and anointed the tabernacle and all that was in it, and consecrated them. ¹¹He sprinkled some of it on the altar seven times, and anointed the altar and all its utensils, and the basin and its base, to consecrate them. ¹²He poured some of the anointing oil on Aaron's head and anointed him, to consecrate him. ¹³And Moses brought forward Aaron's sons, and clothed them with tunics, and fastened sashes around them, and tied headdresses on them, as the LORD commanded Moses.

14 He led forward the bull of sin offering; and Aaron and his sons laid their hands upon the head of the bull of sin offering, ¹⁵and it was slaughtered. Moses took the blood and with his finger put some on each of the horns of the altar, purifying the altar; then he poured out the blood at the base of the altar. Thus he consecrated it, to make atonement for it. ¹⁶Moses took all the fat that was around the entrails, and the appendage of the liver, and the two kidneys with their fat, and turned them into smoke on the altar. ¹⁷But the bull itself, its skin and flesh and its dung, he burned with fire outside the camp, as the LORD commanded Moses.

18 Then he brought forward the ram of burnt offering. Aaron and his sons laid their hands on the head of the ram, ¹⁹and it was slaughtered. Moses dashed the blood against all sides of the altar. ²⁰The ram was cut into its parts, and Moses turned into smoke the head and the parts and the suet. ²¹And after the entrails and the legs were washed with water, Moses turned into smoke the whole ram on the altar; it was a burnt offering for a pleasing odor, an offering by fire to the LORD, as the LORD commanded Moses.

22 Then he brought forward the second ram, the ram of ordination. Aaron and his sons laid their hands on the head of the ram, ²³and it was slaughtered. Moses took some of its blood and put it on the lobe of Aaron's right ear and on the thumb of his right hand and on the big toe of his right foot. ²⁴After Aaron's sons were brought forward, Moses put some of the blood on the lobes of their right ears and on the thumbs of their right hands and on the big toes of their right feet; and Moses dashed the rest of the blood against all sides of the altar. ²⁵He took the fat—the broad tail, all the fat that was around the entrails, the appendage of the liver, and the two kidneys with their fat—and the right thigh. ²⁶From the basket of unleavened bread that was before the LORD, he took one cake of unleavened bread, one cake of bread with oil, and one wafer, and placed them on the fat and on the right thigh. ²⁷He placed all these on the palms of Aaron and on the palms of

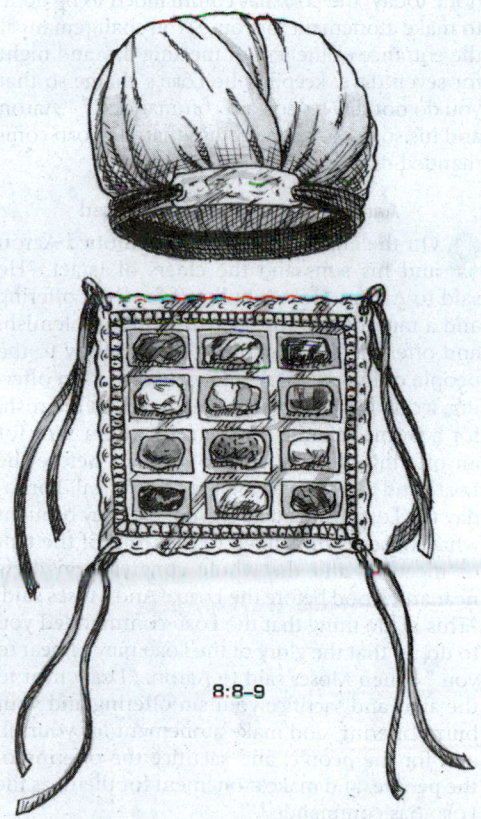

8:8–9

his sons, and raised them as an elevation offering before the LORD. 28Then Moses took them from their hands and turned them into smoke on the altar with the burnt offering. This was an ordination offering for a pleasing odor, an offering by fire to the LORD. 29Moses took the breast and raised it as an elevation offering before the LORD; it was Moses' portion of the ram of ordination, as the LORD commanded Moses.

30 Then Moses took some of the anointing oil and some of the blood that was on the altar and sprinkled them on Aaron and his vestments, and also on his sons and their vestments. Thus he consecrated Aaron and his vestments, and also his sons and their vestments.

31 And Moses said to Aaron and his sons, "Boil the flesh at the entrance of the tent of meeting, and eat it there with the bread that is in the basket of ordination offerings, as I was commanded, 'Aaron and his sons shall eat it'; 32and what remains of the flesh and the bread you shall burn with fire. 33You shall not go outside the entrance of the tent of meeting for seven days, until the day when your period of ordination is completed. For it will take seven days to ordain you; 34as has been done today, the LORD has commanded to be done to make atonement for you. 35You shall remain at the entrance of the tent of meeting day and night for seven days, keeping the LORD's charge so that you do not die; for so I am commanded." 36Aaron and his sons did all the things that the LORD commanded through Moses.

Aaron's Priesthood Inaugurated

9 On the eighth day Moses summoned Aaron and his sons and the elders of Israel. 2He said to Aaron, "Take a bull calf for a sin offering and a ram for a burnt offering, without blemish, and offer them before the LORD. 3And say to the people of Israel, 'Take a male goat for a sin offering; a calf and a lamb, yearlings without blemish, for a burnt offering; 4and an ox and a ram for an offering of well-being to sacrifice before the LORD; and a grain offering mixed with oil. For today the LORD will appear to you.' " 5They brought what Moses commanded to the front of the tent of meeting; and the whole congregation drew near and stood before the LORD. 6And Moses said, "This is the thing that the LORD commanded you to do, so that the glory of the LORD may appear to you." 7Then Moses said to Aaron, "Draw near to the altar and sacrifice your sin offering and your burnt offering, and make atonement for yourself and for the people; and sacrifice the offering of the people, and make atonement for them; as the LORD has commanded."

8 Aaron drew near to the altar, and slaughtered the calf of the sin offering, which was for himself. 9The sons of Aaron presented the blood to him, and he dipped his finger in the blood and put it on the horns of the altar; and the rest of the blood he poured out at the base of the altar. 10But the fat, the kidneys, and the appendage of the liver from the sin offering he turned into smoke on the altar, as the LORD commanded Moses; 11and the flesh and the skin he burned with fire outside the camp.

12 Then he slaughtered the burnt offering. Aaron's sons brought him the blood, and he dashed it against all sides of the altar. 13And they brought him the burnt offering piece by piece, and the head, which he turned into smoke on the altar. 14He washed the entrails and the legs and, with the burnt offering, turned them into smoke on the altar.

15 Next he presented the people's offering. He took the goat of the sin offering that was for the people, and slaughtered it, and presented it as a sin offering like the first one. 16He presented the burnt offering, and sacrificed it according to regulation. 17He presented the grain offering, and, taking a handful of it, he turned it into smoke on the altar, in addition to the burnt offering of the morning.

18 He slaughtered the ox and the ram as a sacrifice of well-being for the people. Aaron's sons brought him the blood, which he dashed against all sides of the altar, 19and the fat of the ox and of the ram—the broad tail, the fat that covers the entrails, the two kidneys and the fat on them,[a] and the appendage of the liver. 20They first laid the fat on the breasts, and the fat was turned into smoke on the altar; 21and the breasts and the right thigh Aaron raised as an elevation offering before the LORD, as Moses had commanded.

22 Aaron lifted his hands toward the people and blessed them; and he came down after sacrificing the sin offering, the burnt offering, and the offering of well-being. 23Moses and Aaron entered the tent of meeting, and then came out and blessed the people; and the glory of the LORD appeared to all the people. 24Fire came out from the LORD and consumed the burnt offering and the fat on the altar; and when all the people saw it, they shouted and fell on their faces.

Nadab and Abihu

10 Now Aaron's sons, Nadab and Abihu, each took his censer, put fire in it, and laid incense on it; and they offered unholy fire before

a Gk: Heb the broad tail, and that which covers, and the kidneys

the Lord, such as he had not commanded them. [2]And fire came out from the presence of the Lord and consumed them, and they died before the Lord. [3]Then Moses said to Aaron, "This is what the Lord meant when he said,

'Through those who are near me
   I will show myself holy,
and before all the people
   I will be glorified.' "
And Aaron was silent.

4 Moses summoned Mishael and Elzaphan, sons of Uzziel the uncle of Aaron, and said to them, "Come forward, and carry your kinsmen away from the front of the sanctuary to a place outside the camp." [5]They came forward and carried them by their tunics out of the camp, as Moses had ordered. [6]And Moses said to Aaron and to his sons Eleazar and Ithamar, "Do not dishevel your hair, and do not tear your vestments, or you will die and wrath will strike all the congregation; but your kindred, the whole house of Israel, may mourn the burning that the Lord has sent. [7]You shall not go outside the entrance of the tent of meeting, or you will die; for the anointing oil of the Lord is on you." And they did as Moses had ordered.

8 And the Lord spoke to Aaron: [9]Drink no wine or strong drink, neither you nor your sons, when you enter the tent of meeting, that you may not die; it is a statute forever throughout your generations. [10]You are to distinguish between the holy and the common, and between the unclean and the clean; [11]and you are to teach the people of Israel all the statutes that the Lord has spoken to them through Moses.

12 Moses spoke to Aaron and to his remaining sons, Eleazar and Ithamar: Take the grain offering that is left from the Lord's offerings by fire, and eat it unleavened beside the altar, for it is most holy; [13]you shall eat it in a holy place, because it is your due and your sons' due, from the offerings by fire to the Lord; for so I am commanded. [14]But the breast that is elevated and the thigh that is raised, you and your sons and daughters as well may eat in any clean place; for they have been assigned to you and your children from the sacrifices of the offerings of well being of the people of Israel. [15]The thigh that is raised and the breast that is elevated they shall bring, together with the offerings by fire of the fat, to raise for an elevation offering before the Lord; they are to be your due and that of your children forever, as the Lord has commanded.

16 Then Moses made inquiry about the goat of the sin offering, and—it had already been burned! He was angry with Eleazar and Ithamar,

Aaron's remaining sons, and said, [17]"Why did you not eat the sin offering in the sacred area? For it is most holy, and God[a] has given it to you that you may remove the guilt of the congregation, to make atonement on their behalf before the Lord. [18]Its blood was not brought into the inner part of the sanctuary. You should certainly have eaten it in the sanctuary, as I commanded." [19]And Aaron spoke to Moses, "See, today they offered their sin offering and their burnt offering before the Lord; and yet such things as these have befallen me! If I had eaten the sin offering today, would it have been agreeable to the Lord?" [20]And when Moses heard that, he agreed.

Clean and Unclean Foods

11 The Lord spoke to Moses and Aaron, saying to them: [2]Speak to the people of Israel, saying:

From among all the land animals, these are the creatures that you may eat. [3]Any animal that has divided hoofs and is cleft-footed and chews the cud—such you may eat. [4]But among those that chew the cud or have divided hoofs, you shall not eat the following: the camel, for even though it chews the cud, it does not have divided hoofs; it is unclean for you. [5]The rock badger, for even though it chews the cud, it does not have divided hoofs; it is unclean for you. [6]The hare, for even though it chews the cud, it does not have divided hoofs; it is unclean for you. [7]The pig, for even though it has divided hoofs and is cleft-footed, it does not chew the cud; it is unclean for you. [8]Of their flesh you shall not eat, and their carcasses you shall not touch; they are unclean for you.

9 These you may eat, of all that are in the waters. Everything in the waters that has fins and scales, whether in the seas or in the streams—such you may eat. [10]But anything in the seas or the streams that does not have fins and scales, of the swarming creatures in the waters and among all the other living creatures that are in the waters—they are detestable to you [11]and detestable they shall remain. Of their flesh you shall not eat, and their carcasses you shall regard as detestable. [12]Everything in the waters that does not have fins and scales is detestable to you.

13 These you shall regard as detestable among the birds. They shall not be eaten; they are an abomination: the eagle, the vulture, the osprey, [14]the buzzard, the kite of any kind; [15]every raven of any kind; [16]the ostrich, the nighthawk, the sea gull, the hawk of any kind; [17]the little owl, the cormorant, the great owl, [18]the water hen, the

---

a Heb *he*

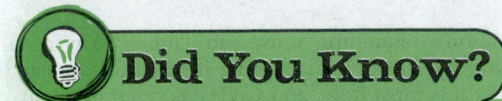

The Israelite Diet

The diet of the ancient Israelites consisted mainly of breads, cereals, fruits, vegetables, and dairy products. Meat was served only on special occasions because it was expensive. A typical family meal was made up of barley or wheat bread, grapes, figs, olive oil, beans, cucumbers, onions, and cheese. On festive occasions, beef or lamb might grace the table.

The laws in Leviticus, chapter 11, contain many restrictions regarding the eating of animals. The reasons for these restrictions are not clear, although many scholars believe one purpose was to keep the Israelites from consuming animals used in pagan worship (for example, the pig offered in Babylonian services). Hygiene was likely another consideration.

The basic "meat laws" were as follows:

- Of the larger animals, those that chewed their cud and had split hooves could be eaten. Therefore, lamb was acceptable, but pork was not.
- Only sea creatures with both fins and scales could be eaten. Thus, catfish and eels were to be avoided.
- Eagles, vultures, buzzards, and many other birds were excluded from the table.
- Rodents, reptiles, and insects (except locusts and grasshoppers) were spurned altogether.
- The blood from all animals had to be drained completely before cooking because blood was seen as the life force and therefore as belonging to God alone.
- It was unlawful to touch or eat any animal found dead; contact with any dead body made one impure.

▶ Lev 11:1–47

---

desert owl,*a* the carrion vulture, [19]the stork, the heron of any kind, the hoopoe, and the bat.*b*

20 All winged insects that walk upon all fours are detestable to you. [21]But among the winged insects that walk on all fours you may eat those that have jointed legs above their feet, with which to leap on the ground. [22]Of them you may eat: the locust according to its kind, the bald locust according to its kind, the cricket according to its kind, and the grasshopper according to its kind. [23]But all other winged insects that have four feet are detestable to you.

Unclean Animals

24 By these you shall become unclean; whoever touches the carcass of any of them shall be unclean until the evening, [25]and whoever carries any part of the carcass of any of them shall wash his clothes and be unclean until the evening. [26]Every animal that has divided hoofs but is not cleft-footed or does not chew the cud is unclean for you; everyone who touches one of them shall be unclean. [27]All that walk on their paws, among the animals that walk on all fours, are unclean for you; whoever touches the carcass of any of them shall be unclean until the evening, [28]and the one who carries the carcass shall wash his clothes and be unclean until the evening; they are unclean for you.

29 These are unclean for you among the creatures that swarm upon the earth: the weasel, the mouse, the great lizard according to its kind, [30]the gecko, the land crocodile, the lizard, the sand lizard, and the chameleon. [31]These are unclean for you among all that swarm; whoever touches one of them when they are dead shall be unclean until the evening. [32]And anything upon which any of them falls when they are dead shall be unclean, whether an article of wood or cloth or skin or sacking, any article that is used for any purpose; it shall be dipped into water, and it shall be unclean until the evening, and then it shall be clean. [33]And if any of them falls into any earthen vessel, all that is in it shall be unclean, and you shall break the vessel. [34]Any food that could be eaten shall be unclean if water from any such vessel comes upon it; and any liquid that could be drunk shall be unclean if it was in any such vessel. [35]Everything on which any part of the carcass falls shall be unclean; whether an oven or stove, it shall be broken in pieces; they are unclean, and shall remain unclean for you. [36]But a spring or a cistern holding water shall be clean, while whatever touches the carcass in it shall be unclean. [37]If any part of their carcass falls upon any seed set aside for sowing, it is clean; [38]but if water is put on the seed and any part of their carcass falls on it, it is unclean for you.

39 If an animal of which you may eat dies, anyone who touches its carcass shall be unclean until the evening. [40]Those who eat of its carcass shall wash their clothes and be unclean until the evening; and those who carry the carcass shall wash their clothes and be unclean until the evening.

---

a Or *pelican* b Identification of several of the birds in verses 13-19 is uncertain

Cultural Connection

A Mother's Prayer at Childbirth

Sun, moon, stars,
you that move in the heavens,
hear this mother!
A new life has come among you.
Make its path smooth that it may reach
the brow of the first hill.

Winds, clouds, rain, mist,
all that move in the air,
hear this mother!
A new life has come among you.
Make its path smooth that it may reach
the brow of the second hill.

Hills, valleys, rivers, lakes, trees, grasses,
all of the earth,
hear this mother!
A new life has come among you.
Make its path smooth that it may reach
the brow of the third hill.

Birds that fly in the air,
animals that dwell in the forest,
insects that creep in the grasses and burrow in
   the ground,
hear this mother!

A new life has come among you.
Make its path smooth that it may reach
the brow of the fourth hill.

All the heavens, air and earth,
hear this mother!
A new life has come among you.
Make its path smooth—then shall it travel beyond
   the four hills!

Like the Israelites, with their purification ritual described in Leviticus, chapter 12, most cultures have rituals and prayers associated with childbirth. In this mother's prayer of the Omaha tribe, the four hills refer to the four parts of human life—childhood, youth, adulthood, and old age. What a wonderful reminder that life is a journey and that all creation is invited to celebrate new life!

▶ Lev 12:1–8

---

41 All creatures that swarm upon the earth are detestable; they shall not be eaten. 42Whatever moves on its belly, and whatever moves on all fours, or whatever has many feet, all the creatures that swarm upon the earth, you shall not eat; for they are detestable. 43You shall not make yourselves detestable with any creature that swarms; you shall not defile yourselves with them, and so become unclean. 44For I am the LORD your God; sanctify yourselves therefore, and be holy, for I am holy. You shall not defile yourselves with any swarming creature that moves on the earth. 45For I am the LORD who brought you up from the land of Egypt, to be your God; you shall be holy, for I am holy.

46 This is the law pertaining to land animal and bird and every living creature that moves through the waters and every creature that swarms upon the earth, 47to make a distinction between the unclean and the clean, and between the living creature that may be eaten and the living creature that may not be eaten.

Purification of Women after Childbirth

12 The LORD spoke to Moses, saying: 2Speak to the people of Israel, saying:

If a woman conceives and bears a male child,

she shall be ceremonially unclean seven days; as at the time of her menstruation, she shall be unclean. 3On the eighth day the flesh of his foreskin shall be circumcised. 4Her time of blood purification shall be thirty-three days; she shall not touch any holy thing, or come into the sanctuary, until the days of her purification are completed. 5If she bears a female child, she shall be unclean two weeks, as in her menstruation; her time of blood purification shall be sixty-six days.

6 When the days of her purification are completed, whether for a son or for a daughter, she shall bring to the priest at the entrance of the tent of meeting a lamb in its first year for a burnt offering, and a pigeon or a turtledove for a sin offering. 7He shall offer it before the LORD, and make atonement on her behalf; then she shall be clean from her flow of blood. This is the law for her who bears a child, male or female. 8If she cannot afford a sheep, she shall take two turtledoves or two pigeons, one for a burnt offering and the other for a sin offering; and the priest shall make atonement on her behalf, and she shall be clean.

Leprosy, Varieties and Symptoms

13 The LORD spoke to Moses and Aaron, saying:

2 When a person has on the skin of his body a swelling or an eruption or a spot, and it turns into a leprous[a] disease on the skin of his body, he shall be brought to Aaron the priest or to one of his sons the priests. ³The priest shall examine the disease on the skin of his body, and if the hair in the diseased area has turned white and the disease appears to be deeper than the skin of his body, it is a leprous[a] disease; after the priest has examined him he shall pronounce him ceremonially unclean. ⁴But if the spot is white in the skin of his body, and appears no deeper than the skin, and the hair in it has not turned white, the priest shall confine the diseased person for seven days. ⁵The priest shall examine him on the seventh day, and if he sees that the disease is checked and the disease has not spread in the skin, then the priest shall confine him seven days more. ⁶The priest shall examine him again on the seventh day, and if the disease has abated and the disease has not spread in the skin, the priest shall pronounce him clean; it is only an eruption; and he shall wash his clothes, and be clean. ⁷But if the eruption spreads in the skin after he has shown himself to the priest for his cleansing, he shall appear again before the priest. ⁸The priest shall make an examination, and if the eruption has spread in the skin, the priest shall pronounce him unclean; it is a leprous[a] disease.

9 When a person contracts a leprous[a] disease, he shall be brought to the priest. ¹⁰The priest shall make an examination, and if there is a white swelling in the skin that has turned the hair white, and there is quick raw flesh in the swelling, ¹¹it is a chronic leprous[a] disease in the skin of his body. The priest shall pronounce him unclean; he shall not confine him, for he is unclean. ¹²But if the disease breaks out in the skin, so that it covers all the skin of the diseased person from head to foot, so far as the priest can see, ¹³then the priest shall make an examination, and if the disease has covered all his body, he shall pronounce him clean of the disease; since it has all turned white, he is clean. ¹⁴But if raw flesh ever appears on him, he shall be unclean; ¹⁵the priest shall examine the raw flesh and pronounce him unclean. Raw flesh is unclean, for it is a leprous[a] disease. ¹⁶But if the raw flesh again turns white, he shall come to the priest; ¹⁷the priest shall examine him, and if the disease has turned white, the priest shall pronounce the diseased person clean. He is clean.

18 When there is on the skin of one's body a boil that has healed, ¹⁹and in the place of the boil there appears a white swelling or a reddish-white spot, it shall be shown to the priest. ²⁰The priest shall make an examination, and if it appears deeper than the skin and its hair has turned white, the priest shall pronounce him unclean; this is a leprous[a] disease, broken out in the boil. ²¹But if the priest examines it and the hair on it is not white, nor is it deeper than the skin but has abated, the priest shall confine him seven days. ²²If it spreads in the skin, the priest shall pronounce him unclean; it is diseased. ²³But if the spot remains in one place and does not spread, it is the scar of the boil; the priest shall pronounce him clean.

24 Or, when the body has a burn on the skin and the raw flesh of the burn becomes a spot, reddish-white or white, ²⁵the priest shall examine it. If the hair in the spot has turned white and it appears deeper than the skin, it is a leprous[a] disease; it has broken out in the burn, and the priest shall pronounce him unclean. This is a leprous[a] disease. ²⁶But if the priest examines it and the hair in the spot is not white, and it is no deeper than the skin but has abated, the priest shall confine him seven days. ²⁷The priest shall examine him the seventh day; if it is spreading in the skin, the priest shall pronounce him unclean. This is a leprous[a] disease. ²⁸But if the spot remains in one place and does not spread in the skin but has abated, it is a swelling from the burn, and the priest shall pronounce him clean; for it is the scar of the burn.

29 When a man or woman has a disease on the head or in the beard, ³⁰the priest shall examine the disease. If it appears deeper than the skin and the hair in it is yellow and thin, the priest shall pronounce him unclean; it is an itch, a leprous[a] disease of the head or the beard. ³¹If the priest examines the itching disease, and it appears no deeper than the skin and there is no black hair in it, the priest shall confine the person with the itching disease for seven days. ³²On the seventh day the priest shall examine the itch; if the itch has not spread, and there is no yellow hair in it, and the itch appears to be no deeper than the skin, ³³he shall shave, but the itch he shall not shave. The priest shall confine the person with the itch for seven days more. ³⁴On the seventh day the priest shall examine the itch; if the itch has not spread in the skin and it appears to be no deeper than the skin, the priest shall pronounce him clean. He shall wash his clothes and be clean. ³⁵But if the itch spreads in the skin after he was pronounced clean, ³⁶the priest shall examine him. If the itch has spread in the skin, the priest need not seek for the yellow hair; he is unclean. ³⁷But if in his eyes the itch is checked, and black hair has grown in it,

---

a A term for several skin diseases; precise meaning uncertain

the itch is healed, he is clean; and the priest shall pronounce him clean.

38 When a man or a woman has spots on the skin of the body, white spots, ³⁹the priest shall make an examination, and if the spots on the skin of the body are of a dull white, it is a rash that has broken out on the skin; he is clean.

40 If anyone loses the hair from his head, he is bald but he is clean. ⁴¹If he loses the hair from his forehead and temples, he has baldness of the forehead but he is clean. ⁴²But if there is on the bald head or the bald forehead a reddish-white diseased spot, it is a leprous[a] disease breaking out on his bald head or his bald forehead. ⁴³The priest shall examine him; if the diseased swelling is reddish-white on his bald head or on his bald forehead, which resembles a leprous[a] disease in the skin of the body, ⁴⁴he is leprous,[a] he is unclean. The priest shall pronounce him unclean; the disease is on his head.

45 The person who has the leprous[a] disease shall wear torn clothes and let the hair of his head be disheveled; and he shall cover his upper lip and cry out, "Unclean, unclean." ⁴⁶He shall remain unclean as long as he has the disease; he is unclean. He shall live alone; his dwelling shall be outside the camp.

47 Concerning clothing: when a leprous[a] disease appears in it, in woolen or linen cloth, ⁴⁸in warp or woof of linen or wool, or in a skin or in anything made of skin, ⁴⁹if the disease shows greenish or reddish in the garment, whether in warp or woof or in skin or in anything made of skin, it is a leprous[a] disease and shall be shown to the priest. ⁵⁰The priest shall examine the disease, and put the diseased article aside for seven days. ⁵¹He shall examine the disease on the seventh day. If the disease has spread in the cloth, in warp or woof, or in the skin, whatever be the use of the skin, this is a spreading leprous[a] disease; it is unclean. ⁵²He shall burn the clothing, whether diseased in warp or woof, woolen or linen, or anything of skin, for it is a spreading leprous[a] disease; it shall be burned in fire.

53 If the priest makes an examination, and the disease has not spread in the clothing, in warp or woof or in anything of skin, ⁵⁴the priest shall command them to wash the article in which the disease appears, and he shall put it aside seven days more. ⁵⁵The priest shall examine the diseased article after it has been washed. If the diseased spot has not changed color, though the disease has not spread, it is unclean; you shall burn it in fire, whether the leprous[a] spot is on the inside or on the outside.

56 If the priest makes an examination, and the disease has abated after it is washed, he shall tear the spot out of the cloth, in warp or woof, or out of skin. ⁵⁷If it appears again in the garment, in warp or woof, or in anything of skin, it is spreading; you shall burn with fire that in which the disease appears. ⁵⁸But the cloth, warp or woof, or anything of skin from which the disease disappears when you have washed it, shall then be washed a second time, and it shall be clean.

59 This is the ritual for a leprous[a] disease in a cloth of wool or linen, either in warp or woof, or in anything of skin, to decide whether it is clean or unclean.

Purification of Lepers and Leprous Houses

14 The Lord spoke to Moses, saying: ²This shall be the ritual for the leprous[a] person at the time of his cleansing:

He shall be brought to the priest; ³the priest shall go out of the camp, and the priest shall make an examination. If the disease is healed in the leprous[a] person, ⁴the priest shall command that two living clean birds and cedarwood and crimson yarn and hyssop be brought for the one who is to be cleansed. ⁵The priest shall command that one of the birds be slaughtered over fresh water in an earthen vessel. ⁶He shall take the living bird with the cedarwood and the crimson yarn and the hyssop, and dip them and the living bird in the blood of the bird that was slaughtered over the fresh water. ⁷He shall sprinkle it seven times upon the one who is to be cleansed of the leprous[a] disease; then he shall pronounce him clean, and he shall let the living bird go into the open field. ⁸The one who is to be cleansed shall wash his clothes, and shave off all his hair, and bathe himself in water, and he shall be clean. After that he shall come into the camp, but shall live outside his tent seven days. ⁹On the seventh day he shall shave all his hair: of head, beard, eyebrows; he shall shave all his hair. Then he shall wash his clothes, and bathe his body in water, and he shall be clean.

10 On the eighth day he shall take two male lambs without blemish, and one ewe lamb in its first year without blemish, and a grain offering of three tenths of an ephah of choice flour mixed with oil, and one log[b] of oil. ¹¹The priest who cleanses shall set the person to be cleansed, along with these things, before the Lord, at the entrance of the tent of meeting. ¹²The priest shall take one of the lambs, and offer it as a guilt offering, along with the log[b] of oil, and raise them as an elevation

---

a A term for several skin diseases; precise meaning uncertain
b A liquid measure

offering before the Lord. ¹³He shall slaughter the lamb in the place where the sin offering and the burnt offering are slaughtered in the holy place; for the guilt offering, like the sin offering, belongs to the priest: it is most holy. ¹⁴The priest shall take some of the blood of the guilt offering and put it on the lobe of the right ear of the one to be cleansed, and on the thumb of the right hand, and on the big toe of the right foot. ¹⁵The priest shall take some of the log^a of oil and pour it into the palm of his own left hand, ¹⁶and dip his right finger in the oil that is in his left hand and sprinkle some oil with his finger seven times before the Lord. ¹⁷Some of the oil that remains in his hand the priest shall put on the lobe of the right ear of the one to be cleansed, and on the thumb of the right hand, and on the big toe of the right foot, on top of the blood of the guilt offering. ¹⁸The rest of the oil that is in the priest's hand he shall put on the head of the one to be cleansed. Then the priest shall make atonement on his behalf before the Lord: ¹⁹the priest shall offer the sin offering, to make atonement for the one to be cleansed from his uncleanness. Afterward he shall slaughter the burnt offering; ²⁰and the priest shall offer the burnt offering and the grain offering on the altar. Thus the priest shall make atonement on his behalf and he shall be clean.

21 But if he is poor and cannot afford so much, he shall take one male lamb for a guilt offering to be elevated, to make atonement on his behalf, and one-tenth of an ephah of choice flour mixed with oil for a grain offering and a log^a of oil; ²²also two turtledoves or two pigeons, such as he can afford, one for a sin offering and the other for a burnt offering. ²³On the eighth day he shall bring them for his cleansing to the priest, to the entrance of the tent of meeting, before the Lord; ²⁴and the priest shall take the lamb of the guilt offering and the log^a of oil, and the priest shall raise them as an elevation offering before the Lord. ²⁵The priest shall slaughter the lamb of the guilt offering and shall take some of the blood of the guilt offering, and put it on the lobe of the right ear of the one to be cleansed, and on the thumb of the right hand, and on the big toe of the right foot. ²⁶The priest shall pour some of the oil into the palm of his own left hand, ²⁷and shall sprinkle with his right finger some of the oil that is in his left hand seven times before the Lord. ²⁸The priest shall put some of the oil that is in his hand on the lobe of the right ear of the one to be cleansed, and on the thumb of the right hand, and the big toe of the right foot, where the blood of the guilt offering was placed. ²⁹The rest of the oil that is in the priest's hand he

shall put on the head of the one to be cleansed, to make atonement on his behalf before the Lord. ³⁰And he shall offer, of the turtledoves or pigeons such as he can afford, ³¹one^b for a sin offering and the other for a burnt offering, along with a grain offering; and the priest shall make atonement before the Lord on behalf of the one being cleansed. ³²This is the ritual for the one who has a leprous^c disease, who cannot afford the offerings for his cleansing.

33 The Lord spoke to Moses and Aaron, saying:

34 When you come into the land of Canaan, which I give you for a possession, and I put a leprous^c disease in a house in the land of your possession, ³⁵the owner of the house shall come and tell the priest, saying, "There seems to me to be some sort of disease in my house." ³⁶The priest shall command that they empty the house before the priest goes to examine the disease, or all that is in the house will become unclean; and afterward the priest shall go in to inspect the house. ³⁷He shall examine the disease; if the disease is in the walls of the house with greenish or reddish spots, and if it appears to be deeper than the surface, ³⁸the priest shall go outside to the door of the house and shut up the house seven days. ³⁹The priest shall come again on the seventh day and make an inspection; if the disease has spread in the walls of the house, ⁴⁰the priest shall command that the stones in which the disease appears be taken out and thrown into an unclean place outside the city. ⁴¹He shall have the inside of the house scraped thoroughly, and the plaster that is scraped off shall be dumped in an unclean place outside the city. ⁴²They shall take other stones and put them in the place of those stones, and take other plaster and plaster the house.

43 If the disease breaks out again in the house, after he has taken out the stones and scraped the house and plastered it, ⁴⁴the priest shall go and make inspection; if the disease has spread in the house, it is a spreading leprous^c disease in the house; it is unclean. ⁴⁵He shall have the house torn down, its stones and timber and all the plaster of the house, and taken outside the city to an unclean place. ⁴⁶All who enter the house while it is shut up shall be unclean until the evening; ⁴⁷and all who sleep in the house shall wash their clothes; and all who eat in the house shall wash their clothes.

48 If the priest comes and makes an inspection, and the disease has not spread in the

---

a A liquid measure   b Gk Syr: Heb afford, ³¹such as he can afford, one   c A term for several skin diseases; precise meaning uncertain house after the house was plastered, the priest shall pronounce the house clean; the disease is healed. ⁴⁹For the cleansing of the house he shall take two birds, with cedarwood and crimson yarn and hyssop, ⁵⁰and shall slaughter one of the birds over fresh water in an earthen vessel, ⁵¹and shall take the cedarwood and the hyssop and the crimson yarn, along with the living bird, and dip them in the blood of the slaughtered bird and the fresh water, and sprinkle the house seven times. ⁵²Thus he shall cleanse the house with the blood of the bird, and with the fresh water, and with the living bird, and with the cedarwood and hyssop and crimson yarn; ⁵³and he shall let the living bird go out of the city into the open field; so he shall make atonement for the house, and it shall be clean.

54 This is the ritual for any leprous*a* disease: for an itch, ⁵⁵for leprous*a* diseases in clothing and houses, ⁵⁶and for a swelling or an eruption or a spot, ⁵⁷to determine when it is unclean and when it is clean. This is the ritual for leprous*a* diseases.

Concerning Bodily Discharges

15 The LORD spoke to Moses and Aaron, saying: ²Speak to the people of Israel and say to them:

When any man has a discharge from his member,*b* his discharge makes him ceremonially unclean. ³The uncleanness of his discharge is this: whether his member*b* flows with his discharge, or his member*b* is stopped from discharging, it is uncleanness for him. ⁴Every bed on which the one with the discharge lies shall be unclean; and everything on which he sits shall be unclean. ⁵Anyone who touches his bed shall wash his clothes, and bathe in water, and be unclean until the evening. ⁶All who sit on anything on which the one with the discharge has sat shall wash their clothes, and bathe in water, and be unclean until the evening. ⁷All who touch the body of the one with the discharge shall wash their clothes, and bathe in water, and be unclean until the evening. ⁸If the one with the discharge spits on persons who are clean, then they shall wash their clothes, and bathe in water, and be unclean until the evening. ⁹Any saddle on which the one with the discharge rides shall be unclean. ¹⁰All who touch anything that was under him shall be unclean until the evening, and all who carry such a thing shall wash their clothes, and bathe in water, and be unclean until the evening. ¹¹All those whom the one with the discharge touches without his having rinsed his hands in water shall wash their clothes, and bathe in water, and be unclean until the evening.

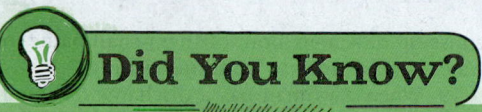

Did You Know?

Monthly Periods

Not every woman suffers pain and swelling as part of her menstrual cycle, but many do. Imagine the life of women in Old Testament days. No sanitary supplies, just strips of cloth. Not much privacy. Not much sympathy from men. No understanding of human biology. Just the monthly flow of blood and the trouble and discomfort of dealing with it.

And on top of the discomfort, women were seen as unclean during their menstrual period. How uncaring this may seem today! How did this unclean concept in Leviticus 15:19–33 develop, anyway? It probably had to do with blood's being a powerful sign of life, implying that a loss of blood meant someone was not healthy and could possibly be a danger to the community.

Thankfully, we do not apply all the Mosaic laws to life today. We have grown in our understanding of human biology and of human dignity. Let's never stop growing.

▶ **Lev 15:19–33**

¹²Any earthen vessel that the one with the discharge touches shall be broken; and every vessel of wood shall be rinsed in water.

13 When the one with a discharge is cleansed of his discharge, he shall count seven days for his cleansing; he shall wash his clothes and bathe his body in fresh water, and he shall be clean. ¹⁴On the eighth day he shall take two turtledoves or two pigeons and come before the LORD to the entrance of the tent of meeting and give them to the priest. ¹⁵The priest shall offer them, one for a sin offering and the other for a burnt offering; and the priest shall make atonement on his behalf before the LORD for his discharge.

16 If a man has an emission of semen, he shall bathe his whole body in water, and be unclean until the evening. ¹⁷Everything made of cloth or of skin on which the semen falls shall be washed with water, and be unclean until the evening. ¹⁸If a man lies with a woman and has an

---

a A term for several skin diseases; precise meaning uncertain
b Heb *flesh*

emission of semen, both of them shall bathe in water, and be unclean until the evening.

19 When a woman has a discharge of blood that is her regular discharge from her body, she shall be in her impurity for seven days, and whoever touches her shall be unclean until the evening. 20Everything upon which she lies during her impurity shall be unclean; everything also upon which she sits shall be unclean. 21Whoever touches her bed shall wash his clothes, and bathe in water, and be unclean until the evening. 22Whoever touches anything upon which she sits shall wash his clothes, and bathe in water, and be unclean until the evening; 23whether it is the bed or anything upon which she sits, when he touches it he shall be unclean until the evening. 24If any man lies with her, and her impurity falls on him, he shall be unclean seven days; and every bed on which he lies shall be unclean.

25 If a woman has a discharge of blood for many days, not at the time of her impurity, or if she has a discharge beyond the time of her impurity, all the days of the discharge she shall continue in uncleanness; as in the days of her impurity, she shall be unclean. 26Every bed on which she lies during all the days of her discharge shall be treated as the bed of her impurity; and everything on which she sits shall be unclean, as in the uncleanness of her impurity. 27Whoever touches these things shall be unclean, and shall wash his clothes, and bathe in water, and be unclean until the evening. 28If she is cleansed of her discharge, she shall count seven days, and after that she shall be clean. 29On the eighth day she shall take two turtledoves or two pigeons and bring them to the priest at the entrance of the tent of meeting. 30The priest shall offer one for a sin offering and the other for a burnt offering; and the priest shall make atonement on her behalf before the Lord for her unclean discharge.

31 Thus you shall keep the people of Israel separate from their uncleanness, so that they do not die in their uncleanness by defiling my tabernacle that is in their midst.

32 This is the ritual for those who have a discharge: for him who has an emission of semen, becoming unclean thereby, 33for her who is in the infirmity of her period, for anyone, male or female, who has a discharge, and for the man who lies with a woman who is unclean.

The Day of Atonement

16 The Lord spoke to Moses after the death of the two sons of Aaron, when they drew near before the Lord and died. 2The Lord said to Moses:

Tell your brother Aaron not to come just at any time into the sanctuary inside the curtain before the mercy seat*a* that is upon the ark, or he will die; for I appear in the cloud upon the mercy seat.*a* 3Thus shall Aaron come into the holy place: with a young bull for a sin offering and a ram for a burnt offering. 4He shall put on the holy linen tunic, and shall have the linen undergarments next to his body, fasten the linen sash, and wear the linen turban; these are the holy vestments. He shall bathe his body in water, and then put them on. 5He shall take from the congregation of the people of Israel two male goats for a sin offering, and one ram for a burnt offering.

6 Aaron shall offer the bull as a sin offering for himself, and shall make atonement for himself and for his house. 7He shall take the two goats and set them before the Lord at the entrance of the tent of meeting; 8and Aaron shall cast lots on the two goats, one lot for the Lord and the other lot for Azazel.*b* 9Aaron shall present the goat on which the lot fell for the Lord, and offer it as a sin offering; 10but the goat on which the lot fell for Azazel*b* shall be presented alive before the Lord to make atonement over it, that it may be sent away into the wilderness to Azazel.*b*

11 Aaron shall present the bull as a sin offering for himself, and shall make atonement for himself and for his house; he shall slaughter the bull as a sin offering for himself. 12He shall take a censer full of coals of fire from the altar before the Lord, and two handfuls of crushed sweet incense, and he shall bring it inside the curtain 13and put the incense on the fire before the Lord, that the cloud of the incense may cover the mercy seat*a* that is upon the covenant,*c* or he will die. 14He shall take some of the blood of the bull, and sprinkle it with his finger on the front of the mercy seat,*a* and before the mercy seat*a* he shall sprinkle the blood with his finger seven times.

15 He shall slaughter the goat of the sin offering that is for the people and bring its blood inside the curtain, and do with its blood as he did with the blood of the bull, sprinkling it upon the mercy seat*a* and before the mercy seat.*a* 16Thus he shall make atonement for the sanctuary, because of the uncleannesses of the people of Israel, and because of their transgressions, all their sins; and so he shall do for the tent of meeting, which remains with them in the midst of their uncleannesses. 17No one shall be in the tent of meeting from the time he enters to make atonement in the

---

a Or the cover　b Traditionally rendered a *scapegoat*
c Or *treaty*, or *testament*; Heb *eduth*

sanctuary until he comes out and has made atonement for himself and for his house and for all the assembly of Israel. ¹⁸Then he shall go out to the altar that is before the Lord and make atonement on its behalf, and shall take some of the blood of the bull and of the blood of the goat, and put it on each of the horns of the altar. ¹⁹He shall sprinkle some of the blood on it with his finger seven times, and cleanse it and hallow it from the uncleannesses of the people of Israel.

20 When he has finished atoning for the holy place and the tent of meeting and the altar, he shall present the live goat. ²¹Then Aaron shall lay both his hands on the head of the live goat, and

The Scapegoat

What an interesting tradition! In the Israelite ritual described in Leviticus 16:20–21, the leader symbolically transfers all the people's sins onto a goat and drives it away. It is a liberating act that allows a fresh start.

But today, the idea of a scapegoat conveys oppression rather than freedom. A person becomes the scapegoat when other people blame him or her for their problems. Here is an example:

Suppose you are on a soccer team that expects this week's game to be easy, so no one works hard at practice. On game day, the score is tied near the end of the game. While your team is consumed in thoughts of going home, the other team scores a goal and wins the game. Everyone gets mad at the goalie for not preventing the goal. The goalie is the scapegoat, but you all should share in the fault for the loss because none of you practiced well or played your best.

- Have you ever been the scapegoat for someone else's problems? If so, how did that feel? What did you do?
- Have you ever scapegoated someone else when you were partly to blame for some situation? What happened? How will you prevent scapegoating in the future?

▶ Lev 16:20–21

confess over it all the iniquities of the people of Israel, and all their transgressions, all their sins, putting them on the head of the goat, and sending it away into the wilderness by means of someone designated for the task.ᵃ ²²The goat shall bear on itself all their iniquities to a barren region; and the goat shall be set free in the wilderness.

23 Then Aaron shall enter the tent of meeting, and shall take off the linen vestments that he put on when he went into the holy place, and shall leave them there. ²⁴He shall bathe his body in water in a holy place, and put on his vestments; then he shall come out and offer his burnt offering and the burnt offering of the people, making atonement for himself and for the people. ²⁵The fat of the sin offering he shall turn into smoke on the altar. ²⁶The one who sets the goat free for Azazelᵇ shall wash his clothes and bathe his body in water, and afterward may come into the camp. ²⁷The bull of the sin offering and the goat of the sin offering, whose blood was brought in to make atonement in the holy place, shall be taken outside the camp; their skin and their flesh and their dung shall be consumed in fire. ²⁸The one who burns them shall wash his clothes and bathe his body in water, and afterward may come into the camp.

a Meaning of Heb uncertain b Traditionally rendered a scapegoat

16:20–22

29 This shall be a statute to you forever: In the seventh month, on the tenth day of the month, you shall deny yourselves,*a* and shall do no work, neither the citizen nor the alien who resides among you. 30For on this day atonement shall be made for you, to cleanse you; from all your sins you shall be clean before the LORD. 31It is a sabbath of complete rest to you, and you shall deny yourselves;*a* it is a statute forever. 32The priest who is anointed and consecrated as priest in his father's place shall make atonement, wearing the linen vestments, the holy vestments. 33He shall make atonement for the sanctuary, and he shall make atonement for the tent of meeting and for the altar, and he shall make atonement for the priests and for all the people of the assembly. 34This shall be an everlasting statute for you, to make atonement for the people of Israel once in the year for all their sins. And Moses did as the LORD had commanded him.

The Slaughtering of Animals

17 The LORD spoke to Moses: 2 Speak to Aaron and his sons and to all the people of Israel and say to them: This is what the LORD has commanded. 3If anyone of the house of Israel slaughters an ox or a lamb or a goat in the camp, or slaughters it outside the camp, 4and does not bring it to the entrance of the tent of meeting, to present it as an offering to the LORD before the tabernacle of the LORD, he shall be held guilty of bloodshed; he has shed blood, and he shall be cut off from the people. 5This is in order that the people of Israel may bring their sacrifices that they offer in the open field, that they may bring them to the LORD, to the priest at the entrance of the tent of meeting, and offer them as sacrifices of well-being to the LORD. 6The priest shall dash the blood against the altar of the LORD at the entrance of the tent of meeting, and turn the fat into smoke as a pleasing odor to the LORD, 7so that they may no longer offer their sacrifices for goat-demons, to whom they prostitute themselves. This shall be a statute forever to them throughout their generations.

8 And say to them further: Anyone of the house of Israel or of the aliens who reside among them who offers a burnt offering or sacrifice, 9and does not bring it to the entrance of the tent of meeting, to sacrifice it to the LORD, shall be cut off from the people.

Eating Blood Prohibited

10 If anyone of the house of Israel or of the aliens who reside among them eats any blood, I will set my face against that person who eats blood, and will cut that person off from the people. 11For the life of the flesh is in the blood; and I have given it to you for making atonement for your lives on the altar; for, as life, it is the blood that makes atonement. 12Therefore I have said to the people of Israel: No person among you shall eat blood, nor shall any alien who resides among you eat blood. 13And anyone of the people of Israel, or of the aliens who reside among them, who hunts down an animal or bird that may be eaten shall pour out its blood and cover it with earth.

14 For the life of every creature—its blood is its life; therefore I have said to the people of Israel: You shall not eat the blood of any creature, for the life of every creature is its blood; whoever eats it shall be cut off. 15All persons, citizens or aliens, who eat what dies of itself or what has been torn by wild animals, shall wash their clothes, and bathe themselves in water, and be unclean until the evening; then they shall be clean. 16But if they do not wash themselves or bathe their body, they shall bear their guilt.

Sexual Relations

18 The LORD spoke to Moses, saying: 2 Speak to the people of Israel and say to them: I am the LORD your God. 3You shall not do as they do in the land of Egypt, where you lived, and you shall not do as they do in the land of Canaan, to which I am bringing you. You shall not follow their statutes. 4My ordinances you shall observe and my statutes you shall keep, following them: I am the LORD your God. 5You shall keep my statutes and my ordinances; by doing so one shall live: I am the LORD.

6 None of you shall approach anyone near of kin to uncover nakedness: I am the LORD. 7You shall not uncover the nakedness of your father, which is the nakedness of your mother; she is your mother, you shall not uncover her nakedness. 8You shall not uncover the nakedness of your father's wife; it is the nakedness of your father. 9You shall not uncover the nakedness of your sister, your father's daughter or your mother's daughter, whether born at home or born abroad. 10You shall not uncover the nakedness of your son's daughter or of your daughter's daughter, for their nakedness is your own nakedness. 11You shall not uncover the nakedness of your father's wife's daughter, begotten by your father, since she is your sister. 12You shall not uncover the nakedness of your father's sister; she is your father's flesh. 13You shall not uncover

---

a Or shall fast

the nakedness of your mother's sister, for she is your mother's flesh. ¹⁴You shall not uncover the nakedness of your father's brother, that is, you shall not approach his wife; she is your aunt. ¹⁵You shall not uncover the nakedness of your daughter-in-law: she is your son's wife; you shall not uncover her nakedness. ¹⁶You shall not uncover the nakedness of your brother's wife; it is your brother's nakedness. ¹⁷You shall not uncover the nakedness of a woman and her daughter, and you shall not take*ᵃ* her son's daughter or her daughter's daughter to uncover her nakedness; they are your*ᵇ* flesh; it is depravity. ¹⁸And you shall not take*ᵃ* a woman as a rival to her sister, uncovering her nakedness while her sister is still alive.

19 You shall not approach a woman to uncover her nakedness while she is in her menstrual uncleanness. ²⁰You shall not have sexual relations with your kinsman's wife, and defile yourself with her. ²¹You shall not give any of your offspring to sacrifice them*ᶜ* to Molech, and so profane the name of your God: I am the Lᴏʀᴅ. ²²You shall not lie with a male as with a woman; it is an abomination. ²³You shall not have sexual relations with any animal and defile yourself with it, nor shall any woman give herself to an animal to have sexual relations with it: it is perversion.

24 Do not defile yourselves in any of these ways, for by all these practices the nations I am casting out before you have defiled themselves. ²⁵Thus the land became defiled; and I punished it for its iniquity, and the land vomited out its inhabitants. ²⁶But you shall keep my statutes and my ordinances and commit none of these abominations, either the citizen or the alien who resides among you ²⁷(for the inhabitants of the land, who were before you, committed all of these abominations, and the land became defiled); ²⁸otherwise the land will vomit you out for defiling it, as it vomited out the nation that was before you. ²⁹For whoever commits any of these abominations shall be cut off from their people. ³⁰So keep my charge not to commit any of these abominations that were done before you, and not to defile yourselves by them: I am the Lᴏʀᴅ your God.

Ritual and Moral Holiness

19 The Lᴏʀᴅ spoke to Moses, saying: 2 Speak to all the congregation of the people of Israel and say to them: You shall be holy, for I the Lᴏʀᴅ your God am holy. ³You shall each revere your mother and father, and you shall keep my sabbaths: I am the Lᴏʀᴅ your

God. ⁴Do not turn to idols or make cast images for yourselves: I am the Lᴏʀᴅ your God.

5 When you offer a sacrifice of well-being to the Lᴏʀᴅ, offer it in such a way that it is acceptable in your behalf. ⁶It shall be eaten on the same

---

a Or *marry*　　*b* Gk: Heb lacks *your*　　*c* Heb *to pass them over*

A Very Special Gift

The laws about sexual relations in Leviticus, chapter 18, are another example of how holiness extended to all aspects of life for the Israelites. The people had experienced the sexual promiscuity of other cultures (see Genesis, chapter 19). To become a great nation, the children of God, they had to abandon unhealthy and unholy sexual practices and follow God's way.

Young people today also receive many confusing cultural messages about when it is okay to have sex. In movies, television, and music, sex happens all the time between unmarried people, with no consequences. But the Church, parents, and teachers are saying to wait until marriage. What is a person to believe?

Think about this: Suppose you are receiving a special gift for Christmas. The gift has been wrapped and hidden, not to come out until Christmas Day. How would you feel if you discovered the present and opened it before Christmas? You probably would initially feel some excitement and pleasure in opening the gift. But the special meaning of opening it on the right day would be lost—for both you and the one presenting it to you.

Sex is a wonderful gift from God, meant for that day when you say, "I do," to someone you are committed to in marriage. Only in marriage can sex unite a couple as God intended. Marriage provides the place where children can be properly raised. That is why the Bible tells us to wait until we are married to have sex—so this gift will be as special as it is meant to be.

▶ **Lev 18:1–30**

You Shall Be Holy

As the Israelites' image of God developed, so did their sense of how they needed to live as God's people. As God's Chosen People, they felt called to behave according to God's plan for them by keeping themselves pure as individuals and as a community. The laws in the Book of Leviticus are examples of how they lived out the call to be holy. For them, holiness was not just for the Sabbath or the Temple but for every day and everything.

Think about the choices you make in your own life. How do your choices help you to be holy in today's world? Ponder these questions for a bit:

● How do you treat your friends?
● How do you spend your money?
● How much time do you spend alone with God?

Being holy has a lot to do with how we live out the moments of our day and how often we remember that we are in God's presence.

▶ **Leviticus, chapters 19–20**

day you offer it, or on the next day; and anything left over until the third day shall be consumed in fire. ⁷If it is eaten at all on the third day, it is an abomination; it will not be acceptable. ⁸All who eat it shall be subject to punishment, because they have profaned what is holy to the LORD; and any such person shall be cut off from the people.

9 When you reap the harvest of your land, you shall not reap to the very edges of your field, or gather the gleanings of your harvest. ¹⁰You shall not strip your vineyard bare, or gather the fallen grapes of your vineyard; you shall leave them for the poor and the alien: I am the LORD your God.

11 You shall not steal; you shall not deal falsely; and you shall not lie to one another. ¹²And you shall not swear falsely by my name, profaning the name of your God: I am the LORD.

13 You shall not defraud your neighbor; you shall not steal; and you shall not keep for yourself the wages of a laborer until morning. ¹⁴You

shall not revile the deaf or put a stumbling block before the blind; you shall fear your God: I am the LORD.

15 You shall not render an unjust judgment; you shall not be partial to the poor or defer to the great: with justice you shall judge your neighbor. ¹⁶You shall not go around as a slanderer*ᵃ* among your people, and you shall not profit by the blood*ᵇ* of your neighbor: I am the LORD.

17 You shall not hate in your heart anyone of your kin; you shall reprove your neighbor, or you will incur guilt yourself. ¹⁸You shall not take vengeance or bear a grudge against any of your people, but you shall love your neighbor as yourself: I am the LORD.

19 You shall keep my statutes. You shall not let your animals breed with a different kind; you shall not sow your field with two kinds of seed; nor shall you put on a garment made of two different materials.

20 If a man has sexual relations with a woman who is a slave, designated for another man but not ransomed or given her freedom, an inquiry shall be held. They shall not be put to death, since she has not been freed; ²¹but he shall bring a guilt offering for himself to the LORD, at the entrance of the tent of meeting, a ram as guilt offering. ²²And the priest shall make atonement for him with the ram of guilt offering before the LORD for his sin that he committed; and the sin he committed shall be forgiven him.

23 When you come into the land and plant all kinds of trees for food, then you shall regard their fruit as forbidden;*ᶜ* three years it shall be forbidden*ᵈ* to you, it must not be eaten. ²⁴In the fourth year all their fruit shall be set apart for rejoicing in the LORD. ²⁵But in the fifth year you may eat of their fruit, that their yield may be increased for you: I am the LORD your God.

26 You shall not eat anything with its blood. You shall not practice augury or witchcraft. ²⁷You shall not round off the hair on your temples or mar the edges of your beard. ²⁸You shall not make any gashes in your flesh for the dead or tattoo any marks upon you: I am the LORD.

29 Do not profane your daughter by making her a prostitute, that the land not become prostituted and full of depravity. ³⁰You shall keep my sabbaths and reverence my sanctuary: I am the LORD.

31 Do not turn to mediums or wizards; do not seek them out, to be defiled by them: I am the LORD your God.

a Meaning of Heb uncertain   b Heb *stand against the blood*
c Heb *as their uncircumcision*   d Heb *uncircumcision*

32 You shall rise before the aged, and defer to the old; and you shall fear your God: I am the LORD.

33 When an alien resides with you in your land, you shall not oppress the alien. 34The alien who resides with you shall be to you as the citizen among you; you shall love the alien as yourself, for you were aliens in the land of Egypt: I am the LORD your God.

35 You shall not cheat in measuring length, weight, or quantity. 36You shall have honest balances, honest weights, an honest ephah, and an honest hin: I am the LORD your God, who brought you out of the land of Egypt. 37You shall keep all my statutes and all my ordinances, and observe them: I am the LORD.

Penalties for Violations of Holiness

20 The LORD spoke to Moses, saying: 2Say further to the people of Israel:

Any of the people of Israel, or of the aliens who reside in Israel, who give any of their offspring to Molech shall be put to death; the people of the land shall stone them to death. 3I myself will set my face against them, and will cut them off from the people, because they have given of their offspring to Molech, defiling my sanctuary and profaning my holy name. 4And if the people of the land should ever close their eyes to them, when they give of their offspring to Molech, and do not put them to death, 5I myself will set my face against them and against their family, and will cut them off from among their people, them and all who follow them in prostituting themselves to Molech.

6 If any turn to mediums and wizards, prostituting themselves to them, I will set my face against them, and will cut them off from the people. 7Consecrate yourselves therefore, and be holy; for I am the LORD your God. 8Keep my statutes, and observe them; I am the LORD; I sanctify you. 9All who curse father or mother shall be put to death; having cursed father or mother, their blood is upon them.

10 If a man commits adultery with the wife ofᵃ his neighbor, both the adulterer and the adulteress shall be put to death. 11The man who lies with his father's wife has uncovered his father's nakedness; both of them shall be put to death; their blood is upon them. 12If a man lies with his daughter-in-law, both of them shall be put to death; they have committed perversion, their blood is upon them. 13If a man lies with a male as with a woman, both of them have committed an abomination; they shall be put to death; their blood is upon them. 14If a man takes a wife and her mother also, it is depravity; they shall be burned to death, both he and they, that there may be no depravity among you. 15If a man has sexual relations with an animal, he shall be put to death; and you shall kill the animal. 16If a woman approaches any animal and has sexual relations with it, you shall kill the woman and the animal; they shall be put to death, their blood is upon them.

17 If a man takes his sister, a daughter of his father or a daughter of his mother, and sees her nakedness, and she sees his nakedness, it is a disgrace, and they shall be cut off in the sight of their people; he has uncovered his sister's nakedness, he shall be subject to punishment. 18If a man lies with a woman having her sickness and uncovers her nakedness, he has laid bare her flow and she has laid bare her flow of blood; both of them shall be cut off from their people. 19You shall not uncover the nakedness of your mother's sister or of your father's sister, for that is to lay bare one's own flesh; they shall be subject to punishment. 20If a man lies with his uncle's wife, he has uncovered his uncle's nakedness; they shall be subject to punishment; they shall die childless. 21If a man takes his brother's wife, it is impurity; he has uncovered his brother's nakedness; they shall be childless.

22 You shall keep all my statutes and all my ordinances, and observe them, so that the land to which I bring you to settle in may not vomit you out. 23You shall not follow the practices of the nation that I am driving out before you. Because they did all these things, I abhorred them. 24But I have said to you: You shall inherit their land, and I will give it to you to possess, a land flowing with milk and honey. I am the LORD your God; I have separated you from the peoples. 25You shall therefore make a distinction between the clean animal and the unclean, and between the unclean bird and the clean; you shall not bring abomination on yourselves by animal or by bird or by anything with which the ground teems, which I have set apart for you to hold unclean. 26You shall be holy to me; for I the LORD am holy, and I have separated you from the other peoples to be mine.

27 A man or a woman who is a medium or a wizard shall be put to death; they shall be stoned to death, their blood is upon them.

The Holiness of Priests

21 The LORD said to Moses: Speak to the priests, the sons of Aaron, and say to them:

a Heb repeats if a man commits adultery with the wife of

No one shall defile himself for a dead person among his relatives, ²except for his nearest kin: his mother, his father, his son, his daughter, his brother; ³likewise, for a virgin sister, close to him because she has had no husband, he may defile himself for her. ⁴But he shall not defile himself as a husband among his people and so profane himself. ⁵They shall not make bald spots upon their heads, or shave off the edges of their beards, or make any gashes in their flesh. ⁶They shall be holy to their God, and not profane the name of their God; for they offer the LORD's offerings by fire, the food of their God; therefore they shall be holy. ⁷They shall not marry a prostitute or a woman who has been defiled; neither shall they marry a woman divorced from her husband. For they are holy to their God, ⁸and you shall treat them as holy, since they offer the food of your God; they shall be holy to you, for I the LORD, I who sanctify you, am holy. ⁹When the daughter of a priest profanes herself through prostitution, she profanes her father; she shall be burned to death.

10 The priest who is exalted above his fellows, on whose head the anointing oil has been poured and who has been consecrated to wear the vestments, shall not dishevel his hair, nor tear his vestments. ¹¹He shall not go where there is a dead body; he shall not defile himself even for his father or mother. ¹²He shall not go outside the sanctuary and thus profane the sanctuary of his God; for the consecration of the anointing oil of his God is upon him: I am the LORD. ¹³He shall marry only a woman who is a virgin. ¹⁴A widow, or a divorced woman, or a woman who has been defiled, a prostitute, these he shall not marry. He shall marry a virgin of his own kin, ¹⁵that he may not profane his offspring among his kin; for I am the LORD; I sanctify him.

16 The LORD spoke to Moses, saying: ¹⁷Speak to Aaron and say: No one of your offspring throughout their generations who has a blemish may approach to offer the food of his God. ¹⁸For no one who has a blemish shall draw near, one who is blind or lame, or one who has a mutilated face or a limb too long, ¹⁹or one who has a broken foot or a broken hand, ²⁰or a hunchback, or a dwarf, or a man with a blemish in his eyes or an itching disease or scabs or crushed testicles. ²¹No descendant of Aaron the priest who has a blemish shall come near to offer the LORD's offerings by fire; since he has a blemish, he shall not come near to offer the food of his God. ²²He may eat the food of his God, of the most holy as well as of the holy. ²³But he shall not come near the curtain or approach the altar, because he has a blemish, that he may not profane my sanctuaries; for I am the LORD; I

sanctify them. ²⁴Thus Moses spoke to Aaron and to his sons and to all the people of Israel.

The Use of Holy Offerings

22 The LORD spoke to Moses, saying: ²Direct Aaron and his sons to deal carefully with the sacred donations of the people of Israel, which they dedicate to me, so that they may not profane my holy name; I am the LORD. ³Say to them: If anyone among all your offspring throughout your generations comes near the sacred donations, which the people of Israel dedicate to the LORD, while he is in a state of uncleanness, that person shall be cut off from my presence: I am the LORD. ⁴No one of Aaron's offspring who has a leprous*ᵃ* disease or suffers a discharge may eat of the sacred donations until he is clean. Whoever touches anything made unclean by a corpse or a man who has had an emission of semen, ⁵and whoever touches any swarming thing by which he may be made unclean or any human being by whom he may be made unclean—whatever his uncleanness may be— ⁶the person who touches any such shall be unclean until evening and shall not eat of the sacred donations unless he has washed his body in water. ⁷When the sun sets he shall be clean; and afterward he may eat of the sacred donations, for they are his food. ⁸That which died or was torn by wild animals he shall not eat, becoming unclean by it: I am the LORD. ⁹They shall keep my charge, so that they may not incur guilt and die in the sanctuary*ᵇ* for having profaned it: I am the LORD; I sanctify them.

10 No lay person shall eat of the sacred donations. No bound or hired servant of the priest shall eat of the sacred donations; ¹¹but if a priest acquires anyone by purchase, the person may eat of them; and those that are born in his house may eat of his food. ¹²If a priest's daughter marries a layman, she shall not eat of the offering of the sacred donations; ¹³but if a priest's daughter is widowed or divorced, without offspring, and returns to her father's house, as in her youth, she may eat of her father's food. No lay person shall eat of it. ¹⁴If a man eats of the sacred donation unintentionally, he shall add one-fifth of its value to it, and give the sacred donation to the priest. ¹⁵No one shall profane the sacred donations of the people of Israel, which they offer to the LORD, ¹⁶causing them to bear guilt requiring a guilt offering, by eating their sacred donations: for I am the LORD; I sanctify them.

ᵃ A term for several skin diseases; precise meaning uncertain
ᵇ Vg: Heb *incur guilt for it and die in it*

Acceptable Offerings

17 The Lord spoke to Moses, saying: [18]Speak to Aaron and his sons and all the people of Israel and say to them: When anyone of the house of Israel or of the aliens residing in Israel presents an offering, whether in payment of a vow or as a freewill offering that is offered to the Lord as a burnt offering, [19]to be acceptable in your behalf it shall be a male without blemish, of the cattle or the sheep or the goats. [20]You shall not offer anything that has a blemish, for it will not be acceptable in your behalf.

21 When anyone offers a sacrifice of well-being to the Lord, in fulfillment of a vow or as a freewill offering, from the herd or from the flock, to be acceptable it must be perfect; there shall be no blemish in it. [22]Anything blind, or injured, or maimed, or having a discharge or an itch or scabs—these you shall not offer to the Lord or put any of them on the altar as offerings by fire to the Lord. [23]An ox or a lamb that has a limb too long or too short you may present for a freewill offering; but it will not be accepted for a vow. [24]Any animal that has its testicles bruised or crushed or torn or cut, you shall not offer to the Lord; such you shall not do within your land, [25]nor shall you accept any such animals from a foreigner to offer as food to your God; since they are mutilated, with a blemish in them, they shall not be accepted in your behalf.

26 The Lord spoke to Moses, saying: [27]When an ox or a sheep or a goat is born, it shall remain seven days with its mother, and from the eighth day on it shall be acceptable as the Lord's offering by fire. [28]But you shall not slaughter, from the herd or the flock, an animal with its young on the same day. [29]When you sacrifice a thanksgiving offering to the Lord, you shall sacrifice it so that it may be acceptable in your behalf. [30]It shall be eaten on the same day; you shall not leave any of it until morning: I am the Lord.

31 Thus you shall keep my commandments and observe them: I am the Lord. [32]You shall not profane my holy name, that I may be sanctified among the people of Israel: I am the Lord; I sanctify you, [33]I who brought you out of the land of Egypt to be your God: I am the Lord.

Appointed Festivals

23 The Lord spoke to Moses, saying: [2]Speak to the people of Israel and say to them: These are the appointed festivals of the Lord that you shall proclaim as holy convocations, my appointed festivals.

The Sabbath, Passover, and Unleavened Bread

3 Six days shall work be done; but the seventh day is a sabbath of complete rest, a holy convocation; you shall do no work: it is a sabbath to the Lord throughout your settlements.

4 These are the appointed festivals of the Lord, the holy convocations, which you shall celebrate at the time appointed for them. [5]In the first month, on the fourteenth day of the month, at twilight,[a] there shall be a passover offering to the Lord, [6]and on the fifteenth day of the same month is the festival of unleavened bread to the Lord; seven days you shall eat unleavened bread. [7]On the first day you shall have a holy convocation; you shall not work at your occupations. [8]For seven days you shall present the Lord's offerings by fire; on the seventh day there shall be a holy convocation: you shall not work at your occupations.

The Offering of First Fruits

9 The Lord spoke to Moses: [10]Speak to the people of Israel and say to them: When you enter the land that I am giving you and you reap its harvest, you shall bring the sheaf of the first fruits of your harvest to the priest. [11]He shall raise the sheaf before the Lord, that you may find acceptance; on the day after the sabbath the priest shall raise it. [12]On the day when you raise the sheaf, you shall offer a lamb a year old, without blemish, as a burnt offering to the Lord. [13]And the grain offering with it shall be two-tenths of an ephah of choice flour mixed with oil, an offering by fire of pleasing odor to the Lord; and the drink offering with it shall be of wine, one-fourth of a hin. [14]You shall eat no bread or parched grain or fresh ears until that very day, until you have brought the offering of your God: it is a statute forever throughout your generations in all your settlements.

The Festival of Weeks

15 And from the day after the sabbath, from the day on which you bring the sheaf of the elevation offering, you shall count off seven weeks; they shall be complete. [16]You shall count until the day after the seventh sabbath, fifty days, then you shall present an offering of new grain to the Lord. [17]You shall bring from your settlements two loaves of bread as an elevation offering, each made of two-tenths of an ephah; they shall be of choice flour, baked with leaven, as first fruits to the Lord. [18]You shall present with the bread seven lambs a year old without blemish, one young bull, and two rams; they shall be a

---

a Heb *between the two evenings*

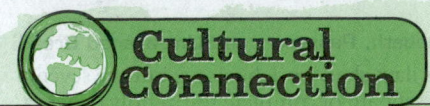

Cultural Connection

Korean Festival Customs

In preparation for the Lunar New Year (in January or February) and for the Moon Festival (a feast of thanksgiving in August), Korean families follow some traditional customs. These customs are similar to those of the Israelite festivals described in Leviticus, chapter 23.

In Korea, the day before each feast is used for purification. People take ceremonial baths, symbolizing the total cleansing of their body, their spirit, and their attitudes. The baths wash away meanness, carelessness, and other faults. The people also wear new clothes and often get a haircut.

Before sunrise on the day of the feast, the people bow before a table holding name cards of their ancestors. They use incense, pour out wine, and pray to their ancestors, asking for their intercession and help. Family members pray silently for all their individual and family needs. During the day, families visit the homes of their extended family. During these visits, the prayer ritual is often repeated.

After a day of visiting, families return home for a feast of the best food and drink possible. The sharing of food is the most significant part of the meal. Neighbors exchange portions of food with one another and bring food to poor families. Families set food on a small table near the door as an offering of thanks to the Creator and sprinkle rice on the ground around their house in gratitude for the crops.

▶ Lev 23:4–44

burnt offering to the LORD, along with their grain offering and their drink offerings, an offering by fire of pleasing odor to the LORD. ¹⁹You shall also offer one male goat for a sin offering, and two male lambs a year old as a sacrifice of well-being. ²⁰The priest shall raise them with the bread of the first fruits as an elevation offering before the LORD, together with the two lambs; they shall be holy to the LORD for the priest. ²¹On that same day you shall make proclamation; you shall hold a holy convocation; you shall not work at your occupations. This is a statute forever in all your settlements throughout your generations.

22 When you reap the harvest of your land, you shall not reap to the very edges of your field, or gather the gleanings of your harvest; you shall leave them for the poor and for the alien: I am the LORD your God.

The Festival of Trumpets

23 The LORD spoke to Moses, saying: ²⁴Speak to the people of Israel, saying: In the seventh month, on the first day of the month, you shall observe a day of complete rest, a holy convocation commemorated with trumpet blasts. ²⁵You shall not work at your occupations; and you shall present the LORD's offering by fire.

The Day of Atonement

26 The LORD spoke to Moses, saying: ²⁷Now, the tenth day of this seventh month is the day of atonement; it shall be a holy convocation for you: you shall deny yourselves[a] and present the LORD's offering by fire; ²⁸and you shall do no work during that entire day; for it is a day of atonement, to make atonement on your behalf before the LORD your God. ²⁹For anyone who does not practice self-denial[b] during that entire day shall be cut off from the people. ³⁰And anyone who does any work during that entire day, such a one I will destroy from the midst of the people. ³¹You shall do no work: it is a statute forever throughout your generations in all your settlements. ³²It shall be to you a sabbath of complete rest, and you shall deny yourselves;[a] on the ninth day of the month at evening, from evening to evening you shall keep your sabbath.

The Festival of Booths

33 The LORD spoke to Moses, saying: ³⁴Speak to the people of Israel, saying: On the fifteenth day of this seventh month, and lasting seven days, there shall be the festival of booths[c] to the LORD. ³⁵The first day shall be a holy convocation; you shall not work at your occupations. ³⁶Seven days you shall present the LORD's offerings by fire; on the eighth day you shall observe a holy

a Or shall fast   b Or does not fast   c Or tabernacles: Heb succoth convocation and present the LORD's offerings by fire; it is a solemn assembly; you shall not work at your occupations.

37 These are the appointed festivals of the LORD, which you shall celebrate as times of holy convocation, for presenting to the LORD offerings by fire—burnt offerings and grain offerings, sacrifices and drink offerings, each on its proper day— [38] apart from the sabbaths of the LORD, and apart from your gifts, and apart from all your votive offerings, and apart from all your freewill offerings, which you give to the LORD.

39 Now, the fifteenth day of the seventh month, when you have gathered in the produce of the land, you shall keep the festival of the LORD, lasting seven days; a complete rest on the first day, and a complete rest on the eighth day. [40] On the first day you shall take the fruit of majestic[a] trees, branches of palm trees, boughs of leafy trees, and willows of the brook; and you shall rejoice before the LORD your God for seven days. [41] You shall keep it as a festival to the LORD seven days in the year; you shall keep it in the seventh month as a statute forever throughout your generations. [42] You shall live in booths for seven days; all that are citizens in Israel shall live in booths, [43] so that your generations may know that I made the people of Israel live in booths when I brought them out of the land of Egypt: I am the LORD your God.

44 Thus Moses declared to the people of Israel the appointed festivals of the LORD.

The Lamp

24 The LORD spoke to Moses, saying: [2] Command the people of Israel to bring you pure oil of beaten olives for the lamp, that a light may be kept burning regularly. [3] Aaron shall set it up in the tent of meeting, outside the curtain of the covenant,[b] to burn from evening to morning before the LORD regularly; it shall be a statute forever throughout your generations. [4] He shall set up the lamps on the lampstand of pure gold[c] before the LORD regularly.

The Bread for the Tabernacle

5 You shall take choice flour, and bake twelve loaves of it; two-tenths of an ephah shall be in each loaf. [6] You shall place them in two rows, six in a row, on the table of pure gold.[d] [7] You shall put pure frankincense with each row, to be a token offering for the bread, as an offering by fire to the LORD. [8] Every sabbath day Aaron shall set them in order before the LORD regularly as a commitment of the people of Israel, as a covenant forever. [9] They shall be for Aaron and his

descendants, who shall eat them in a holy place, for they are most holy portions for him from the offerings by fire to the LORD, a perpetual due.

Blasphemy and Its Punishment

10 A man whose mother was an Israelite and whose father was an Egyptian came out among the people of Israel; and the Israelite woman's son and a certain Israelite began fighting in the camp. [11] The Israelite woman's son blasphemed the Name in a curse. And they brought him to Moses—now his mother's name was Shelomith, daughter of Dibri, of the tribe of Dan— [12] and they put him in custody, until the decision of the LORD should be made clear to them.

13 The LORD said to Moses, saying: [14] Take the blasphemer outside the camp; and let all who were within hearing lay their hands on his head, and let the whole congregation stone him. [15] And speak to the people of Israel, saying: Anyone who curses God shall bear the sin. [16] One who blasphemes the name of the LORD shall be put to death; the whole congregation shall stone the blasphemer. Aliens as well as citizens, when they blaspheme the Name, shall be put to death. [17] Anyone who kills a human being shall be put to death. [18] Anyone who kills an animal shall make restitution for it, life for life. [19] Anyone who maims another shall suffer the same injury in return: [20] fracture for fracture, eye for eye, tooth for tooth; the injury inflicted is the injury to be suffered. [21] One who kills an animal shall make restitution for it; but one who kills a human being shall be put to death. [22] You shall have one law for the alien and for the citizen: for I am the LORD your God. [23] Moses spoke thus to the people of Israel; and they took the blasphemer outside the camp, and stoned him to death. The people of Israel did as the LORD had commanded Moses.

The Sabbatical Year

25 The LORD spoke to Moses on Mount Sinai, saying: [2] Speak to the people of Israel and say to them: When you enter the land that I am giving you, the land shall observe a sabbath for the LORD. [3] Six years you shall sow your field, and six years you shall prune your vineyard, and gather in their yield; [4] but in the seventh year there shall be a sabbath of complete rest for the land, a sabbath for the LORD: you shall not sow your field or prune your vineyard. [5] You shall not reap the aftergrowth of your harvest or gather the

---

a Meaning of Heb uncertain   b Or treaty, or testament; Heb eduth   c Heb pure lampstand   d Heb pure table

💡 Did You Know?

7 x 7 + 1 = Jubilee!

In the Bible, seven is a special number. Just as the seventh day of the week was set aside as a day of rest in ancient Israel, so the seventh year was set aside as a year of rest for the land. Fields were to remain uncultivated during the seventh year; whatever fruits or grains grew on their own were to be left for those who were poor. The "sabbatical year" was a reminder to the people that the land actually belonged to God, not to them.

Seven may be a special number, but seven times seven plus one is very special. The fiftieth year—the year after seven times seven years—was declared the Jubilee year, and God's law demanded some very special things to happen. The people were to take a year of vacation from their normal routine. This meant no planting for a farmer, no lending for a banker, and no big sales for a merchant. Why this break? Because God wanted the Jubilee year to be a time when everyone started over with a clean slate. During the Jubilee, all land was to be returned to its original owners, and all Israelite slaves were to be set free. Debts were to be forgiven and justly settled. The year of Jubilee was like the reset button on a computer, stopping everything and returning it to its original setting. It was a check against the unjust distribution of property and wealth.

The Catholic Church has continued the custom of celebrating the fiftieth year, especially when it marks the end of a century. Faithful to its Jewish roots, the Church sees the Jubilee year as a special time for renewal. In preparation for a Jubilee year, it asks individuals and communities to commit themselves to following Jesus more faithfully.

▶ Leviticus, chapter 25

also, and for the wild animals in your land all its yield shall be for food.

The Year of Jubilee

8 You shall count off seven weeks[a] of years, seven times seven years, so that the period of seven weeks of years gives forty-nine years. 9Then you shall have the trumpet sounded loud; on the tenth day of the seventh month—on the day of atonement—you shall have the trumpet sounded throughout all your land. 10And you shall hallow the fiftieth year and you shall proclaim liberty throughout the land to all its inhabitants. It shall be a jubilee for you: you shall return, every one of you, to your property and every one of you to your family. 11That fiftieth year shall be a jubilee for you: you shall not sow, or reap the aftergrowth, or harvest the unpruned vines. 12For it is a jubilee; it shall be holy to you: you shall eat only what the field itself produces.

13 In this year of jubilee you shall return, every one of you, to your property. 14When you make a sale to your neighbor or buy from your neighbor, you shall not cheat one another. 15When you buy from your neighbor, you shall pay only for the number of years since the jubilee; the seller shall charge you only for the remaining crop years. 16If the years are more, you shall increase the price, and if the years are fewer, you shall diminish the price; for it is a certain number of harvests that are being sold to you. 17You shall not cheat one another, but you shall fear your God; for I am the LORD your God.

18 You shall observe my statutes and faithfully keep my ordinances, so that you may live on the land securely. 19The land will yield its fruit, and you will eat your fill and live on it securely. 20Should you ask, "What shall we eat in the seventh year, if we may not sow or gather in our crop?" 21I will order my blessing for you in the sixth year, so that it will yield a crop for three years. 22When you sow in the eighth year, you will be eating from the old crop; until the ninth year, when its produce comes in, you shall eat the old. 23The land shall not be sold in perpetuity, for the land is mine; with me you are but aliens and tenants. 24Throughout the land that you hold, you shall provide for the redemption of the land.

a Or *sabbaths*

grapes of your unpruned vine: it shall be a year of complete rest for the land. 6You may eat what the land yields during its sabbath—you, your male and female slaves, your hired and your bound laborers who live with you; 7for your livestock

25:9

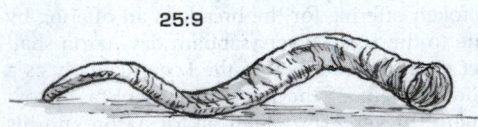

25 If anyone of your kin falls into difficulty and sells a piece of property, then the next of kin shall come and redeem what the relative has sold. 26If the person has no one to redeem it, but then prospers and finds sufficient means to do so, 27the years since its sale shall be computed and the difference shall be refunded to the person to whom it was sold, and the property shall be returned. 28But if there are not sufficient means to recover it, what was sold shall remain with the purchaser until the year of jubilee; in the jubilee it shall be released, and the property shall be returned.

29 If anyone sells a dwelling house in a walled city, it may be redeemed until a year has elapsed since its sale; the right of redemption shall be one year. 30If it is not redeemed before a full year has elapsed, a house that is in a walled city shall pass in perpetuity to the purchaser, throughout the generations; it shall not be released in the jubilee. 31But houses in villages that have no walls around them shall be classed as open country; they may be redeemed, and they shall be released in the jubilee. 32As for the cities of the Levites, the Levites shall forever have the right of redemption of the houses in the cities belonging to them. 33Such property as may be redeemed from the Levites—houses sold in a city belonging to them—shall be released in the jubilee; because the houses in the cities of the Levites are their possession among the people of Israel. 34But the open land around their cities may not be sold; for that is their possession for all time.

35 If any of your kin fall into difficulty and become dependent on you,[a] you shall support them; they shall live with you as though resident aliens. 36Do not take interest in advance or otherwise make a profit from them, but fear your God; let them live with you. 37You shall not lend them your money at interest taken in advance, or provide them food at a profit. 38I am the Lord your God, who brought you out of the land of Egypt, to give you the land of Canaan, to be your God.

39 If any who are dependent on you become so impoverished that they sell themselves to you, you shall not make them serve as slaves. 40They shall remain with you as hired or bound laborers. They shall serve with you until the year of the jubilee. 41Then they and their children with them shall be free from your authority; they shall go back to their own family and return to their ancestral property. 42For they are my servants, whom I brought out of the land of Egypt; they shall not be sold as slaves are sold. 43You shall not rule over them with harshness, but shall fear your God. 44As for the male and female slaves whom you may have, it is from the nations around you that you may acquire male and female slaves. 45You may also acquire them from among the aliens residing with you, and from their families that are with you, who have been born in your land; and they may be your property. 46You may keep them as a possession for your children after you, for them to inherit as property. These you may treat as slaves, but as for your fellow Israelites, no one shall rule over the other with harshness.

47 If resident aliens among you prosper, and if any of your kin fall into difficulty with one of them and sell themselves to an alien, or to a branch of the alien's family, 48after they have sold themselves they shall have the right of redemption; one of their brothers may redeem them, 49or their uncle or their uncle's son may redeem them, or anyone of their family who is of their own flesh may redeem them; or if they prosper they may redeem themselves. 50They shall compute with the purchaser the total from the year when they sold themselves to the alien until the jubilee year; the price of the sale shall be applied to the number of years: the time they were with the owner shall be rated as the time of a hired laborer. 51If many years remain, they shall pay for their redemption in proportion to the purchase price; 52and if few years remain until the jubilee year, they shall compute thus: according to the years involved they shall make payment for their redemption. 53As a laborer hired by the year they shall be under the alien's authority, who shall not, however, rule with harshness over them in your sight. 54And if they have not been redeemed in any of these ways, they and their children with them shall go free in the jubilee year. 55For to me the people of Israel are servants; they are my servants whom I brought out from the land of Egypt: I am the Lord your God.

Rewards for Obedience

26 You shall make for yourselves no idols and erect no carved images or pillars, and you shall not place figured stones in your land, to worship at them; for I am the Lord your God. 2You shall keep my sabbaths and reverence my sanctuary: I am the Lord.

3 If you follow my statutes and keep my commandments and observe them faithfully, 4I will give you your rains in their season, and the land shall yield its produce, and the trees of the field shall yield their fruit. 5Your threshing shall overtake the vintage, and the vintage shall overtake the sowing; you shall eat your bread to the full, and live securely in your land. 6And I will

---

a Meaning of Heb uncertain

grant peace in the land, and you shall lie down, and no one shall make you afraid; I will remove dangerous animals from the land, and no sword shall go through your land. 7You shall give chase to your enemies, and they shall fall before you by the sword. 8Five of you shall give chase to a hundred, and a hundred of you shall give chase to ten thousand; your enemies shall fall before you by the sword. 9I will look with favor upon you and make you fruitful and multiply you; and I will maintain my covenant with you. 10You shall eat old grain long stored, and you shall have to clear out the old to make way for the new. 11I will place my dwelling in your midst, and I shall not abhor you. 12And I will walk among you, and will be your God, and you shall be my people. 13I am the LORD your God who brought you out of the land of Egypt, to be their slaves no more; I have broken the bars of your yoke and made you walk erect.

Penalties for Disobedience

14 But if you will not obey me, and do not observe all these commandments, 15if you spurn my statutes, and abhor my ordinances, so that you will not observe all my commandments, and you break my covenant, 16I in turn will do this to you: I will bring terror on you; consumption and fever that waste the eyes and cause life to pine away. You shall sow your seed in vain, for your enemies shall eat it. 17I will set my face against you, and you shall be struck down by your enemies; your foes shall rule over you, and you shall flee though no one pursues you. 18And if in spite of this you will not obey me, I will continue to punish you sevenfold for your sins. 19I will break your proud glory, and I will make your sky like iron and your earth like copper. 20Your strength shall be spent to no purpose: your land shall not yield its produce, and the trees of the land shall not yield their fruit.

21 If you continue hostile to me, and will not obey me, I will continue to plague you sevenfold for your sins. 22I will let loose wild animals against you, and they shall bereave you of your children and destroy your livestock; they shall make you few in number, and your roads shall be deserted.

23 If in spite of these punishments you have not turned back to me, but continue hostile to me, 24then I too will continue hostile to you: I myself will strike you sevenfold for your sins. 25I will bring the sword against you, executing vengeance for the covenant; and if you withdraw within your cities, I will send pestilence among you, and you shall be delivered into enemy hands. 26When I break your staff of bread, ten women shall bake your bread in a single oven, and they shall dole out your bread by weight; and though you eat, you shall not be satisfied.

27 But if, despite this, you disobey me, and continue hostile to me, 28I will continue hostile to you in fury; I in turn will punish you myself sevenfold for your sins. 29You shall eat the flesh of your sons, and you shall eat the flesh of your daughters. 30I will destroy your high places and cut down your incense altars; I will heap your carcasses on the carcasses of your idols. I will abhor you. 31I will lay your cities waste, will make your sanctuaries desolate, and I will not smell your pleasing odors. 32I will devastate the land, so that your enemies who come to settle in it shall be appalled at it. 33And you I will scatter among the nations, and I will unsheathe the sword against you; your land shall be a desolation, and your cities a waste.

34 Then the land shall enjoy*a* its sabbath years as long as it lies desolate, while you are in the land of your enemies; then the land shall rest, and enjoy*a* its sabbath years. 35As long as it lies desolate, it shall have the rest it did not have on your sabbaths when you were living on it. 36And as for those of you who survive, I will send faintness into their hearts in the lands of their enemies; the sound of a driven leaf shall put them to flight, and they shall flee as one flees from the sword, and they shall fall though no one pursues. 37They shall stumble over one another, as if to escape a sword, though no one pursues; and you shall have no power to stand against your enemies. 38You shall perish among the nations, and the land of your enemies shall devour you. 39And those of you who survive shall languish in the land of your enemies because of their iniquities; also they shall languish because of the iniquities of their ancestors.

40 But if they confess their iniquity and the iniquity of their ancestors, in that they committed treachery against me and, moreover, that they continued hostile to me— 41so that I, in turn, continued hostile to them and brought them into the land of their enemies; if then their uncircumcised heart is humbled and they make amends for their iniquity, 42then will I remember my covenant with Jacob; I will remember also my covenant with Isaac and also my covenant with Abraham, and I will remember the land. 43For the land shall be deserted by them, and enjoy*a* its sabbath years by lying desolate without them, while they shall make amends for their iniquity, because they dared to spurn my

a Or make up for

ordinances, and they abhorred my statutes. ⁴⁴Yet for all that, when they are in the land of their enemies, I will not spurn them, or abhor them so as to destroy them utterly and break my covenant with them; for I am the Lord their God; ⁴⁵but I will remember in their favor the covenant with their ancestors whom I brought out of the land of Egypt in the sight of the nations, to be their God: I am the Lord.

46 These are the statutes and ordinances and laws that the Lord established between himself and the people of Israel on Mount Sinai through Moses.

Votive Offerings

27 The Lord spoke to Moses, saying: ²Speak to the people of Israel and say to them: When a person makes an explicit vow to the Lord concerning the equivalent for a human being, ³the equivalent for a male shall be: from twenty to sixty years of age the equivalent shall be fifty shekels of silver by the sanctuary shekel. ⁴If the person is a female, the equivalent is thirty shekels. ⁵If the age is from five to twenty years of age, the equivalent is twenty shekels for a male and ten shekels for a female. ⁶If the age is from one month to five years, the equivalent for a male is five shekels of silver, and for a female the equivalent is three shekels of silver. ⁷And if the person is sixty years old or over, then the equivalent for a male is fifteen shekels, and for a female ten shekels. ⁸If any cannot afford the equivalent, they shall be brought before the priest and the priest shall assess them; the priest shall assess them according to what each one making a vow can afford.

9 If it concerns an animal that may be brought as an offering to the Lord, any such that may be given to the Lord shall be holy. ¹⁰Another shall not be exchanged or substituted for it, either good for bad or bad for good; and if one animal is substituted for another, both that one and its substitute shall be holy. ¹¹If it concerns any unclean animal that may not be brought as an offering to the Lord, the animal shall be presented before the priest. ¹²The priest shall assess it: whether good or bad, according to the assessment of the priest, so it shall be. ¹³But if it is to be redeemed, one-fifth must be added to the assessment.

14 If a person consecrates a house to the Lord, the priest shall assess it: whether good or bad, as the priest assesses it, so it shall stand. ¹⁵And if the one who consecrates the house wishes to redeem it, one-fifth shall be added to its assessed value, and it shall revert to the original owner.

16 If a person consecrates to the Lord any inherited landholding, its assessment shall be in accordance with its seed requirements: fifty shekels of silver to a homer of barley seed. ¹⁷If the person consecrates the field as of the year of jubilee, that assessment shall stand; ¹⁸but if the field is consecrated after the jubilee, the priest shall compute the price for it according to the years that remain until the year of jubilee, and the assessment shall be reduced. ¹⁹And if the one who consecrates the field wishes to redeem it, then one-fifth shall be added to its assessed value, and it shall revert to the original owner; ²⁰but if the field is not redeemed, or if it has been sold to someone else, it shall no longer be redeemable. ²¹But when the field is released in the jubilee, it shall be holy to the Lord as a devoted field; it becomes the priest's holding. ²²If someone consecrates to the Lord a field that has been purchased, which is not a part of the inherited landholding, ²³the priest shall compute for it the proportionate assessment up to the year of jubilee, and the assessment shall be paid as of that day, a sacred donation to the Lord. ²⁴In the year of jubilee the field shall return to the one from whom it was bought, whose holding the land is. ²⁵All assessments shall be by the sanctuary shekel: twenty gerahs shall make a shekel.

26 A firstling of animals, however, which as a firstling belongs to the Lord, cannot be consecrated by anyone; whether ox or sheep, it is the Lord's. ²⁷If it is an unclean animal, it shall be ransomed at its assessment, with one-fifth added; if it is not redeemed, it shall be sold at its assessment.

28 Nothing that a person owns that has been devoted to destruction for the Lord, be it human or animal, or inherited landholding, may be sold or redeemed; every devoted thing is most holy to the Lord. ²⁹No human beings who have been devoted to destruction can be ransomed; they shall be put to death.

30 All tithes from the land, whether the seed from the ground or the fruit from the tree, are the Lord's; they are holy to the Lord. ³¹If persons wish to redeem any of their tithes, they must add one-fifth to them. ³²All tithes of herd and flock, every tenth one that passes under the shepherd's staff, shall be holy to the Lord. ³³Let no one inquire whether it is good or bad, or make substitution for it; if one makes substitution for it, then both it and the substitute shall be holy and cannot be redeemed.

34 These are the commandments that the Lord gave to Moses for the people of Israel on Mount Sinai.

Sound the trumpet, beat the drum, we are going to war! The call to arms brings out the best and the worst in people—courage and cowardice, love and hate, hope and fear. The Book of Numbers records the varied experiences of the Israelites as they prepare for the armed conquest of the Promised Land. But most important, it tells of God's insistence that they maintain their purity and holiness to be worthy recipients of God's promises.

In Depth

Although the Book of Numbers is named for the two censuses mentioned in it (chapters 1 and 26), the book's original Hebrew name, meaning "in the desert," describes it better. Numbers picks up the story of the Israelites where Exodus leaves off. The first section begins with a census at Mount Sinai to determine who is eligible for military service. As the people prepare to enter the Promised Land, their leaders review the laws and regulations with them.

In the second section, the Israelites begin their journey to the Promised Land. Unfortunately, they have not learned to put their faith in God, and their journey is marked by grumbling, rebellion, and even idolatry. When the first army refuses to enter the Promised Land because of reports that it is inhabited by a race of giants (see Num 13:32–33), God decrees that none of the older generation who left Egypt shall enter the Promised Land. So, the Israelites begin their desert wandering, which lasts thirty-eight years (see map 2, "The Exodus from Egypt").

The third section of Numbers paints a more hopeful picture. The people of the new generation are faithful and obedient as they prepare to enter the Promised Land. They experience victory against the Midianites (see chapter 31) and conquer the land east of the Jordan (see chapter 32). The God who liberated their ancestors from Egypt and sustained and led them through the wilderness with Moses is the same God who now makes ready to fulfill the promise of the Land to Israel.

Numbers was compiled and edited by priestly scribes hundreds of years after these events, after the people had lost the Promised Land to the Babylonians. They fully appreciated the gift of the Land only after they had lost it. For the Israelites in the Babylonian Exile, Numbers portrayed the hopeful, grateful, and faithful hearts required of those whom God blesses.

At a Glance

- 1:1—10:10. preparation at Mount Sinai for conquest of the Promised Land
- 10:11—25:18. the desert journey and the death of the older generation
- Chapters 26–36. the birth of a new generation ready to enter the Promised Land

Quick Facts

Period Covered: the thirty-eight years of wandering in the desert after the Exodus
Inspired Authors: priestly scribes writing during the Babylonian Exile (587–538 BC)
Theme: Faithfulness and gratefulness to God are necessary for Israel to obtain the Promised Land.

The Book of

Numbers

Numbers

The First Census of Israel

1 The LORD spoke to Moses in the wilderness of Sinai, in the tent of meeting, on the first day of the second month, in the second year after they had come out of the land of Egypt, saying: ²Take a census of the whole congregation of Israelites, in their clans, by ancestral houses, according to the number of names, every male individually; ³from twenty years old and upward, everyone in Israel able to go to war. You and Aaron shall enroll them, company by company. ⁴A man from each tribe shall be with you, each man the head of his ancestral house. ⁵These are the names of the men who shall assist you:

From Reuben, Elizur son of Shedeur.
⁶ From Simeon, Shelumiel son of Zurishaddai.
⁷ From Judah, Nahshon son of Amminadab.
⁸ From Issachar, Nethanel son of Zuar.
⁹ From Zebulun, Eliab son of Helon.
¹⁰ From the sons of Joseph:
from Ephraim, Elishama son of Ammihud;
from Manasseh, Gamaliel son of Pedahzur.
¹¹ From Benjamin, Abidan son of Gideoni
¹² From Dan, Ahiezer son of Ammishaddai.
¹³ From Asher, Pagiel son of Ochran.
¹⁴ From Gad, Eliasaph son of Deuel.
¹⁵ From Naphtali, Ahira son of Enan.
¹⁶These were the ones chosen from the congregation, the leaders of their ancestral tribes, the heads of the divisions of Israel.

¹⁷ Moses and Aaron took these men who had been designated by name, ¹⁸and on the first day of the second month they assembled the whole congregation together. They registered themselves in their clans, by their ancestral houses, according to the number of names from twenty years old and upward, individually, ¹⁹as the LORD commanded Moses. So he enrolled them in the wilderness of Sinai.

20 The descendants of Reuben, Israel's firstborn, their lineage, in their clans, by their ancestral houses, according to the number of names, individually, every male from twenty years old and upward, everyone able to go to war: ²¹those enrolled of the tribe of Reuben were forty-six thousand five hundred.

22 The descendants of Simeon, their lineage, in their clans, by their ancestral houses, those of them that were numbered, according to the number of names, individually, every male from twenty years old and upward, everyone able to go to war: ²³those enrolled of the tribe of Simeon were fifty-nine thousand three hundred.

24 The descendants of Gad, their lineage, in their clans, by their ancestral houses, according to the number of the names, from twenty years old and upward, everyone able to go to war: ²⁵those enrolled of the tribe of Gad were forty-five thousand six hundred fifty.

26 The descendants of Judah, their lineage, in their clans, by their ancestral houses, according to the number of names, from twenty years old and upward, everyone able to go to war: ²⁷those enrolled of the tribe of Judah were seventy-four thousand six hundred.

28 The descendants of Issachar, their lineage, in their clans, by their ancestral houses, according to the number of names, from twenty years old and upward, everyone able to go to war: ²⁹those enrolled of the tribe of Issachar were fifty-four thousand four hundred.

30 The descendants of Zebulun, their lineage, in their clans, by their ancestral houses, according to the number of names, from twenty years old and upward, everyone able to go to war: ³¹those enrolled of the tribe of Zebulun were fifty-seven thousand four hundred.

32 The descendants of Joseph, namely, the descendants of Ephraim, their lineage, in their clans, by their ancestral houses, according to the number of names, from twenty years old and upward, everyone able to go to war: ³³those enrolled of the tribe of Ephraim were forty thousand five hundred.

34 The descendants of Manasseh, their lineage, in their clans, by their ancestral houses, according to the number of names, from twenty years old and upward, everyone able to go to war: ³⁵those enrolled of the tribe of Manasseh were thirty-two thousand two hundred.

36 The descendants of Benjamin, their lineage, in their clans, by their ancestral houses, according to the number of names, from twenty years old and upward, everyone able to go to war: ³⁷those enrolled of the tribe of Benjamin were thirty-five thousand four hundred.

38 The descendants of Dan, their lineage, in their clans, by their ancestral houses, according to the number of names, from twenty years old and upward, everyone able to go to war: ³⁹those enrolled of the tribe of Dan were sixty-two thousand seven hundred.

40 The descendants of Asher, their lineage, in their clans, by their ancestral houses, according to the number of names, from twenty years old and upward, everyone able to go to war: ⁴¹those enrolled of the tribe of Asher were forty-one thousand five hundred.

42 The descendants of Naphtali, their lineage, in their clans, by their ancestral houses, according to the number of names, from twenty years old and upward, everyone able to go to war: ⁴³those enrolled of the tribe of Naphtali were fifty-three thousand four hundred.

44 These are those who were enrolled, whom Moses and Aaron enrolled with the help of the leaders of Israel, twelve men, each representing his ancestral house. ⁴⁵So the whole number of the Israelites, by their ancestral houses, from twenty years old and upward, everyone able to go to war in Israel— ⁴⁶their whole number was six hundred three thousand five hundred fifty. ⁴⁷The Levites, however, were not numbered by their ancestral tribe along with them.

48 The Lᴏʀᴅ had said to Moses: ⁴⁹Only the tribe of Levi you shall not enroll, and you shall not take a census of them with the other Israelites. ⁵⁰Rather you shall appoint the Levites over the tabernacle of the covenant,^a and over all its equipment, and over all that belongs to it; they are to carry the tabernacle and all its equipment, and they shall tend it, and shall camp around the tabernacle. ⁵¹When the tabernacle is to set out, the Levites shall take it down; and when the tabernacle is to be pitched, the Levites shall set it up. And any outsider who comes near shall be put to death. ⁵²The other Israelites shall camp in their respective regimental camps, by companies; ⁵³but the Levites shall camp around the tabernacle of the covenant,^a that there may be no wrath on the congregation of the Israelites; and the Levites shall perform the guard duty of the tabernacle of the covenant.^a ⁵⁴The Israelites did so; they did just as the Lᴏʀᴅ commanded Moses.

The Order of Encampment and Marching

2 The Lᴏʀᴅ spoke to Moses and Aaron, saying: ²The Israelites shall camp each in their respective regiments, under ensigns by their ancestral houses; they shall camp facing the tent of meeting on every side. ³Those to camp on the east side toward the sunrise shall be of the regimental encampment of Judah by companies. The leader of the people of Judah shall be Nahshon son of Amminadab, ⁴with a company as enrolled of seventy-four thousand six hundred. ⁵Those to camp next to him shall be the tribe of Issachar. The leader of the Issacharites shall be Nethanel son of Zuar, ⁶with a company as enrolled of fifty-four thousand four hundred. ⁷Then the tribe of Zebulun: The leader of the Zebulunites shall be Eliab son of Helon, ⁸with a company as enrolled of fifty-seven thousand four hundred. ⁹The total enrollment of the camp of Judah, by companies, is one hundred eighty-six thousand four hundred. They shall set out first on the march.

10 On the south side shall be the regimental encampment of Reuben by companies. The leader of the Reubenites shall be Elizur son of Shedeur, ¹¹with a company as enrolled of forty-six thousand five hundred. ¹²And those to camp next to him shall be the tribe of Simeon. The leader of the Simeonites shall be Shelumiel son of Zurishaddai, ¹³with a company as enrolled of fifty-nine thousand three hundred. ¹⁴Then

a Or treaty, or testimony; Heb eduth

the tribe of Gad: The leader of the Gadites shall be Eliasaph son of Reuel, ¹⁵with a company as enrolled of forty-five thousand six hundred fifty. ¹⁶The total enrollment of the camp of Reuben, by companies, is one hundred fifty-one thousand four hundred fifty. They shall set out second.

17 The tent of meeting, with the camp of the Levites, shall set out in the center of the camps; they shall set out just as they camp, each in position, by their regiments.

18 On the west side shall be the regimental encampment of Ephraim by companies. The leader of the people of Ephraim shall be Elishama son of Ammihud, ¹⁹with a company as enrolled of forty thousand five hundred. ²⁰Next to him shall be the tribe of Manasseh. The leader of the people of Manasseh shall be Gamaliel son of Pedahzur, ²¹with a company as enrolled of thirty-two thousand two hundred. ²²Then the tribe of Benjamin: The leader of the Benjaminites shall be Abidan son of Gideoni, ²³with a company as enrolled of thirty-five thousand four hundred. ²⁴The total enrollment of the camp of Ephraim, by companies, is one hundred eight thousand one hundred. They shall set out third on the march.

25 On the north side shall be the regimental encampment of Dan by companies. The leader of the Danites shall be Ahiezer son of Ammishaddai, ²⁶with a company as enrolled of sixty-two thousand seven hundred. ²⁷Those to camp next to him shall be the tribe of Asher. The leader of the Asherites shall be Pagiel son of Ochran, ²⁸with a company as enrolled of forty-one thousand five hundred. ²⁹Then the tribe of Naphtali: The leader of the Naphtalites shall be Ahira son of Enan, ³⁰with a company as enrolled of fifty-three thousand four hundred. ³¹The total enrollment of the camp of Dan is one hundred fifty-seven thousand six hundred. They shall set out last, by companies.ᵃ

32 This was the enrollment of the Israelites by their ancestral houses; the total enrollment in the camps by their companies was six hundred three thousand five hundred fifty. ³³Just as the Lord had commanded Moses, the Levites were not enrolled among the other Israelites.

34 The Israelites did just as the Lord had commanded Moses: They camped by regiments, and they set out the same way, everyone by clans, according to ancestral houses.

The Sons of Aaron

3 This is the lineage of Aaron and Moses at the time when the Lord spoke with Moses on Mount Sinai. ²These are the names of the sons of Aaron: Nadab the firstborn, and Abihu, Eleazar, and Ithamar; ³these are the names of the sons of Aaron, the anointed priests, whom he ordained to minister as priests. ⁴Nadab and Abihu died before the Lord when they offered unholy fire

a Compare verses 9, 16, 24: Heb by their regiments

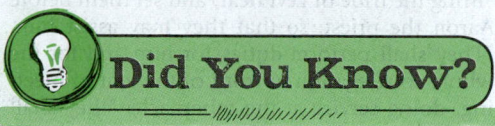

Did You Know?

Holy War

The Book of Numbers begins with a census of "everyone in Israel able to go to war" (1:3). The people of Israel are preparing to take over the land God had promised to them, the Chosen People. This is no ordinary war but a Holy war, a war that they believe is divinely inspired, even a war God commands. In 31:2 God says to Moses, "Avenge the Israelites on the Midianites." The Israelites go on to kill every Midianite except for the young girls who are virgins.

How are we to understand this? Does God really order the killing of innocent people? To answer this, let's first remember that the writers of the Bible were influenced by their own cultural background and understanding of God. Three main things were probably on the mind of the writer of Numbers. First, the early Israelites viewed God as a warrior god fighting for them. Second, they believed the Canaanites were a wicked and idolatrous people who deserved punishment. And finally, they believed the Midianites deserved special punishment because they had led the Israelites into idolatry and sin at Shittim (see 25:1–5).

Holy wars are dangerous. Throughout history people have committed atrocities in the name of God. Christians must interpret the Old Testament in the light of Jesus' teachings in the New Testament. Jesus clearly taught that we are to love our enemies because they too are God's beloved children. Jesus was teaching an insight learned by the Israelites hundreds of years after the conquering of Canaan, an insight understood after the Babylonian Exile and taught in the Book of Jonah. This is one area where the New Testament teaching replaces an earlier Old Testament understanding. Holy wars have no place in the lives of Christians.

NUM

before the LORD in the wilderness of Sinai, and they had no children. Eleazar and Ithamar served as priests in the lifetime of their father Aaron.

The Duties of the Levites

5 Then the LORD spoke to Moses, saying: 6Bring the tribe of Levi near, and set them before Aaron the priest, so that they may assist him. 7They shall perform duties for him and for the whole congregation in front of the tent of meeting, doing service at the tabernacle; 8they shall be in charge of all the furnishings of the tent of meeting, and attend to the duties for the Israelites as they do service at the tabernacle. 9You shall give the Levites to Aaron and his descendants; they are unreservedly given to him from among the Israelites. 10But you shall make a register of Aaron and his descendants; it is they who shall attend to the priesthood, and any outsider who comes near shall be put to death.

11 Then the LORD spoke to Moses, saying: 12I hereby accept the Levites from among the Israelites as substitutes for all the firstborn that open the womb among the Israelites. The Levites shall be mine, 13for all the firstborn are mine; when I killed all the firstborn in the land of Egypt, I consecrated for my own all the firstborn in Israel, both human and animal; they shall be mine. I am the LORD.

A Census of the Levites

14 Then the LORD spoke to Moses in the wilderness of Sinai, saying: 15Enroll the Levites by ancestral houses and by clans. You shall enroll every male from a month old and upward. 16So Moses enrolled them according to the word of the LORD, as he was commanded. 17The following were the sons of Levi, by their names: Gershon, Kohath, and Merari. 18These are the names of the sons of Gershon by their clans: Libni and Shimei. 19The sons of Kohath by their clans: Amram, Izhar, Hebron, and Uzziel. 20The sons of Merari by their clans: Mahli and Mushi. These are the clans of the Levites, by their ancestral houses.

21 To Gershon belonged the clan of the Libnites and the clan of the Shimeites; these were the clans of the Gershonites. 22Their enrollment, counting all the males from a month old and upward, was seven thousand five hundred. 23The clans of the Gershonites were to camp behind the tabernacle on the west, 24with Eliasaph son of Lael as head of the ancestral house of the Gershonites. 25The responsibility of the sons of Gershon in the tent of meeting was to be the tabernacle, the tent with its covering, the screen for the entrance of the tent of meeting, 26the

hangings of the court, the screen for the entrance of the court that is around the tabernacle and the altar, and its cords—all the service pertaining to these.

27 To Kohath belonged the clan of the Amramites, the clan of the Izharites, the clan of the Hebronites, and the clan of the Uzzielites; these are the clans of the Kohathites. 28Counting all the males, from a month old and upward, there were eight thousand six hundred, attending to the duties of the sanctuary. 29The clans of the Kohathites were to camp on the south side of the tabernacle, 30with Elizaphan son of Uzziel as head of the ancestral house of the clans of the Kohathites. 31Their responsibility was to be the ark, the table, the lampstand, the altars, the vessels of the sanctuary with which the priests minister, and the screen—all the service pertaining to these. 32Eleazar son of Aaron the priest was to be chief over the leaders of the Levites, and to have oversight of those who had charge of the sanctuary.

33 To Merari belonged the clan of the Mahlites and the clan of the Mushites: these are the clans of Merari. 34Their enrollment, counting all the males from a month old and upward, was six thousand two hundred. 35The head of the ancestral house of the clans of Merari was Zuriel son of Abihail; they were to camp on the north side of the tabernacle. 36The responsibility assigned to the sons of Merari was to be the frames of the tabernacle, the bars, the pillars, the bases, and all their accessories—all the service pertaining to these; 37also the pillars of the court all around, with their bases and pegs and cords.

38 Those who were to camp in front of the tabernacle on the east—in front of the tent of meeting toward the east—were Moses and Aaron and Aaron's sons, having charge of the rites within the sanctuary, whatever had to be done for the Israelites; and any outsider who came near was to be put to death. 39The total enrollment of the Levites whom Moses and Aaron enrolled at the commandment of the LORD, by their clans, all the males from a month old and upward, was twenty-two thousand.

The Redemption of the Firstborn

40 Then the LORD said to Moses: Enroll all the firstborn males of the Israelites, from a month old and upward, and count their names. 41But you shall accept the Levites for me—I am the LORD—as substitutes for all the firstborn among the Israelites, and the livestock of the Levites as substitutes for all the firstborn among the livestock of the Israelites. 42So Moses enrolled all

the firstborn among the Israelites, as the LORD commanded him. ⁴³The total enrollment, all the firstborn males from a month old and upward, counting the number of names, was twenty-two thousand two hundred seventy-three.

44 Then the LORD spoke to Moses, saying: ⁴⁵Accept the Levites as substitutes for all the firstborn among the Israelites, and the livestock of the Levites as substitutes for their livestock; and the Levites shall be mine. I am the LORD. ⁴⁶As the price of redemption of the two hundred seventy-three of the firstborn of the Israelites, over and above the number of the Levites, ⁴⁷you shall accept five shekels apiece, reckoning by the shekel of the sanctuary, a shekel of twenty gerahs. ⁴⁸Give to Aaron and his sons the money by which the excess number of them is redeemed. ⁴⁹So Moses took the redemption money from those who were over and above those redeemed by the Levites; ⁵⁰from the firstborn of the Israelites he took the money, one thousand three hundred sixty-five shekels, reckoned by the shekel of the sanctuary; ⁵¹and Moses gave the redemption money to Aaron and his sons, according to the word of the LORD, as the LORD had commanded Moses.

The Kohathites

4 The LORD spoke to Moses and Aaron, saying: ²Take a census of the Kohathites separate from the other Levites, by their clans and their ancestral houses, ³from thirty years old up to fifty years old, all who qualify to do work relating to the tent of meeting. ⁴The service of the Kohathites relating to the tent of meeting concerns the most holy things.

5 When the camp is to set out, Aaron and his sons shall go in and take down the screening curtain, and cover the ark of the covenant[a] with it; ⁶then they shall put on it a covering of fine leather,[b] and spread over that a cloth all of blue, and shall put its poles in place. ⁷Over the table of the bread of the Presence they shall spread a blue cloth, and put on it the plates, the dishes for incense, the bowls, and the flagons for the drink offering; the regular bread also shall be on it; ⁸then they shall spread over them a crimson cloth, and cover it with a covering of fine leather,[b] and shall put its poles in place. ⁹They shall take a blue cloth, and cover the lampstand for the light, with its lamps, its snuffers, its trays, and all the vessels for oil with which it is supplied; ¹⁰and they shall put it with all its utensils in a covering of fine leather,[b] and put it on the carrying frame. ¹¹Over the golden altar they shall spread a blue cloth, and cover it with a covering of fine leather,[b]

and shall put its poles in place; ¹²and they shall take all the utensils of the service that are used in the sanctuary, and put them in a blue cloth, and cover them with a covering of fine leather,[b] and put them on the carrying frame. ¹³They shall take away the ashes from the altar, and spread a purple cloth over it; ¹⁴and they shall put on it all the utensils of the altar, which are used for the service there, the firepans, the forks, the shovels, and the basins, all the utensils of the altar; and they shall spread on it a covering of fine leather,[b] and shall put its poles in place. ¹⁵When Aaron and his sons have finished covering the sanctuary and all the furnishings of the sanctuary, as the camp sets out, after that the Kohathites shall come to carry these, but they must not touch the holy things, or they will die. These are the things of the tent of meeting that the Kohathites are to carry.

16 Eleazar son of Aaron the priest shall have charge of the oil for the light, the fragrant incense, the regular grain offering, and the anointing oil, the oversight of all the tabernacle and all that is in it, in the sanctuary and in its utensils.

17 Then the LORD spoke to Moses and Aaron, saying: ¹⁸You must not let the tribe of the clans of the Kohathites be destroyed from among the Levites. ¹⁹This is how you must deal with them in order that they may live and not die when they come near to the most holy things: Aaron and his sons shall go in and assign each to a particular task or burden. ²⁰But the Kohathites[c] must not go in to look on the holy things even for a moment; otherwise they will die.

The Gershonites and Merarites

21 Then the LORD spoke to Moses, saying: ²²Take a census of the Gershonites also, by their ancestral houses and by their clans; ²³from thirty years old up to fifty years old you shall enroll them, all who qualify to do work in the tent of meeting. ²⁴This is the service of the clans of the Gershonites, in serving and bearing burdens: ²⁵They shall carry the curtains of the tabernacle, and the tent of meeting with its covering, and the outer covering of fine leather[b] that is on top of it, and the screen for the entrance of the tent of meeting, ²⁶and the hangings of the court, and the screen for the entrance of the gate of the court that is around the tabernacle and the altar, and their cords, and all the equipment for their service; and they shall do all that needs to be done with regard to them. ²⁷All the service of the

---

a Or treaty, or testimony; Heb eduth   b Meaning of Heb uncertain   c Heb they

Gershonites shall be at the command of Aaron and his sons, in all that they are to carry, and in all that they have to do; and you shall assign to their charge all that they are to carry. 28This is the service of the clans of the Gershonites relating to the tent of meeting, and their responsibilities are to be under the oversight of Ithamar son of Aaron the priest.

29 As for the Merarites, you shall enroll them by their clans and their ancestral houses; 30from thirty years old up to fifty years old you shall enroll them, everyone who qualifies to do the work of the tent of meeting. 31This is what they are charged to carry, as the whole of their service in the tent of meeting: the frames of the tabernacle, with its bars, pillars, and bases, 32and the pillars of the court all around with their bases, pegs, and cords, with all their equipment and all their related service; and you shall assign by name the objects that they are required to carry. 33This is the service of the clans of the Merarites, the whole of their service relating to the tent of meeting, under the hand of Ithamar son of Aaron the priest.

Census of the Levites

34 So Moses and Aaron and the leaders of the congregation enrolled the Kohathites, by their clans and their ancestral houses, 35from thirty years old up to fifty years old, everyone who qualified for work relating to the tent of meeting; 36and their enrollment by clans was two thousand seven hundred fifty. 37This was the enrollment of the clans of the Kohathites, all who served at the tent of meeting, whom Moses and Aaron enrolled according to the commandment of the LORD by Moses.

38 The enrollment of the Gershonites, by their clans and their ancestral houses, 39from thirty years old up to fifty years old, everyone who qualified for work relating to the tent of meeting— 40their enrollment by their clans and their ancestral houses was two thousand six hundred thirty. 41This was the enrollment of the clans of the Gershonites, all who served at the tent of meeting, whom Moses and Aaron enrolled according to the commandment of the LORD.

42 The enrollment of the clans of the Merarites, by their clans and their ancestral houses, 43from thirty years old up to fifty years old, everyone who qualified for work relating to the tent of meeting— 44their enrollment by their clans was three thousand two hundred. 45This is the enrollment of the clans of the Merarites, whom Moses and Aaron enrolled according to the commandment of the LORD by Moses.

46 All those who were enrolled of the Levites, whom Moses and Aaron and the leaders of Israel enrolled, by their clans and their ancestral houses, 47from thirty years old up to fifty years old, everyone who qualified to do the work of service and the work of bearing burdens relating to the tent of meeting, 48their enrollment was eight thousand five hundred eighty. 49According to the commandment of the LORD through Moses they were appointed to their several tasks of serving or carrying; thus they were enrolled by him, as the LORD commanded Moses.

Unclean Persons

5 The LORD spoke to Moses, saying: 2Command the Israelites to put out of the camp everyone who is leprous,*a* or has a discharge, and everyone who is unclean through contact with a corpse; 3you shall put out both male and female, putting them outside the camp; they must not defile their camp, where I dwell among them. 4The Israelites did so, putting them outside the camp; as the LORD had spoken to Moses, so the Israelites did.

Confession and Restitution

5 The LORD spoke to Moses, saying: 6Speak to the Israelites: When a man or a woman wrongs another, breaking faith with the LORD, that person incurs guilt 7and shall confess the sin that has been committed. The person shall make full restitution for the wrong, adding one-fifth to it, and giving it to the one who was wronged. 8If the injured party has no next of kin to whom restitution may be made for the wrong, the restitution for wrong shall go to the LORD for the priest, in addition to the ram of atonement with which atonement is made for the guilty party. 9Among all the sacred donations of the Israelites, every gift that they bring to the priest shall be his. 10The sacred donations of all are their own; whatever anyone gives to the priest shall be his.

Concerning an Unfaithful Wife

11 The LORD spoke to Moses, saying: 12Speak to the Israelites and say to them: If any man's wife goes astray and is unfaithful to him, 13if a man has had intercourse with her but it is hidden from her husband, so that she is undetected though she has defiled herself, and there is no witness against her since she was not caught in the act; 14if a spirit of jealousy comes on him, and he is jealous of his wife who has defiled herself; or if a spirit of jealousy comes on him,

---

a A term for several skin diseases; precise meaning uncertain

and he is jealous of his wife, though she has not defiled herself; [15]then the man shall bring his wife to the priest. And he shall bring the offering required for her, one-tenth of an ephah of barley flour. He shall pour no oil on it and put no frankincense on it, for it is a grain offering of jealousy, a grain offering of remembrance, bringing iniquity to remembrance.

16 Then the priest shall bring her near, and set her before the Lord; [17]the priest shall take holy water in an earthen vessel, and take some of the dust that is on the floor of the tabernacle and put it into the water. [18]The priest shall set the woman before the Lord, dishevel the woman's hair, and place in her hands the grain offering of remembrance, which is the grain offering of jealousy. In his own hand the priest shall have the water of bitterness that brings the curse. [19]Then the priest shall make her take an oath, saying, "If no man has lain with you, if you have not turned aside to uncleanness while under your husband's authority, be immune to this water of bitterness that brings the curse. [20]But if you have gone astray while under your husband's authority, if you have defiled yourself and some man other than your husband has had intercourse with you," [21]—let the priest make the woman take the oath of the curse and say to the woman—"the Lord make you an execration and an oath among your people, when the Lord makes your uterus drop, your womb discharge; [22]now may this water that brings the curse enter your bowels and make your womb discharge, your uterus drop!" And the woman shall say, "Amen. Amen."

23 Then the priest shall put these curses in writing, and wash them off into the water of bitterness. [24]He shall make the woman drink the water of bitterness that brings the curse, and the water that brings the curse shall enter her and cause bitter pain. [25]The priest shall take the grain offering of jealousy out of the woman's hand, and shall elevate the grain offering before the Lord and bring it to the altar; [26]and the priest shall take a handful of the grain offering, as its memorial portion, and turn it into smoke on the altar, and afterward shall make the woman drink the water. [27]When he has made her drink the water, then, if she has defiled herself and has been unfaithful to her husband, the water that brings the curse shall enter into her and cause bitter pain, and her womb shall discharge, her uterus drop, and the woman shall become an execration among her people. [28]But if the woman has not defiled herself and is clean, then she shall be immune and be able to conceive children.

29 This is the law in cases of jealousy, when a wife, while under her husband's authority, goes astray and defiles herself, [30]or when a spirit of jealousy comes on a man and he is jealous of his wife; then he shall set the woman before the Lord, and the priest shall apply this entire law to her. [31]The man shall be free from iniquity, but the woman shall bear her iniquity.

The Nazirites

6 The Lord spoke to Moses, saying: [2]Speak to the Israelites and say to them: When either men or women make a special vow, the vow of a nazirite,[a] to separate themselves to the Lord, [3]they shall separate themselves from wine and strong drink; they shall drink no wine vinegar or other vinegar, and shall not drink any grape juice or eat grapes, fresh or dried. [4]All their days as nazirites[b] they shall eat nothing that is produced by the grapevine, not even the seeds or the skins.

5 All the days of their nazirite vow no razor shall come upon the head; until the time is completed for which they separate themselves to the Lord, they shall be holy; they shall let the locks of the head grow long.

6 All the days that they separate themselves to the Lord they shall not go near a corpse. [7]Even if their father or mother, brother or sister, should die, they may not defile themselves; because their consecration to God is upon the head. [8]All their days as nazirites[b] they are holy to the Lord.

9 If someone dies very suddenly nearby, defiling the consecrated head, then they shall shave the head on the day of their cleansing; on the seventh day they shall shave it. [10]On the eighth day they shall bring two turtledoves or two young pigeons to the priest at the entrance of the tent of meeting, [11]and the priest shall offer one as a sin offering and the other as a burnt offering, and make atonement for them, because they incurred guilt by reason of the corpse. They shall sanctify the head that same day, [12]and separate themselves to the Lord for their days as nazirites,[b] and bring a male lamb a year old as a guilt offering. The former time shall be void, because the consecrated head was defiled.

13 This is the law for the nazirites[b] when the time of their consecration has been completed: they shall be brought to the entrance of the tent of meeting, [14]and they shall offer their gift to the Lord, one male lamb a year old without blemish as a burnt offering, one ewe lamb a year old without blemish as a sin offering, one ram without blemish as an offering of well-being, [15]and a

---

a That is one separated or one consecrated · b That is those separated or those consecrated

Pray It!

God Bless You

A very old blessing in Numbers 6:22–27 (some of which is repeated in Pss 4:6 and 67:1) was not originally a Christian blessing, but its three parts remind us of Christian blessings calling on the Trinity.

This blessing is a good one for special occasions. You could write it on a card for a birthday, Mother's Day or Father's Day, a wedding anniversary, or any other special event. Or you could use it to make a poster or an engraving for a first Communion, a wedding, or a Confirmation.

If this blessing sounds familiar, maybe it's because on New Year's Day (the feast of Mary, mother of God), we hear it as the first reading. It's the perfect way to start the new year.

▶ **Num 6:22–27**

basket of unleavened bread, cakes of choice flour mixed with oil and unleavened wafers spread with oil, with their grain offering and their drink offerings. ¹⁶The priest shall present them before the LORD and offer their sin offering and burnt offering, ¹⁷and shall offer the ram as a sacrifice of well-being to the LORD, with the basket of unleavened bread; the priest also shall make the accompanying grain offering and drink offering. ¹⁸Then the nazirites*ᵃ* shall shave the consecrated head at the entrance of the tent of meeting, and shall take the hair from the consecrated head and put it on the fire under the sacrifice of well-being. ¹⁹The priest shall take the shoulder of the ram, when it is boiled, and one unleavened cake out of the basket, and one unleavened wafer, and shall put them in the palms of the nazirites,*ᵃ* after they have shaved the consecrated head. ²⁰Then the priest shall elevate them as an elevation offering before the LORD; they are a holy portion for the priest, together with the breast that is elevated and the thigh that is offered. After that the nazirites*ᵃ* may drink wine.

21 This is the law for the nazirites*ᵃ* who take a vow. Their offering to the LORD must be in accordance with the nazirite*ᵇ* vow, apart from what else they can afford. In accordance with whatever

vow they take, so they shall do, following the law for their consecration.

The Priestly Benediction

22 The LORD spoke to Moses, saying: ²³Speak to Aaron and his sons, saying, Thus you shall bless the Israelites: You shall say to them,

²⁴ The LORD bless you and keep you;

²⁵ the LORD make his face to shine upon you, and
      be gracious to you;

²⁶ the LORD lift up his countenance upon you, and
      give you peace.

27 So they shall put my name on the Israelites, and I will bless them.

Offerings of the Leaders

7 On the day when Moses had finished setting up the tabernacle, and had anointed and consecrated it with all its furnishings, and had anointed and consecrated the altar with all its utensils, ²the leaders of Israel, heads of their ancestral houses, the leaders of the tribes, who were over those who were enrolled, made offerings. ³They brought their offerings before the LORD, six covered wagons and twelve oxen, a wagon for every two of the leaders, and for each one an ox; they presented them before the tabernacle. ⁴Then the LORD said to Moses: ⁵Accept these from them, that they may be used in doing the service of the tent of meeting, and give them to the Levites, to each according to his service. ⁶So Moses took the wagons and the oxen, and gave them to the Levites. ⁷Two wagons and four oxen he gave to the Gershonites, according to their service; ⁸and four wagons and eight oxen he gave to the Merarites, according to their service, under the direction of Ithamar son of Aaron the priest. ⁹But to the Kohathites he gave none, because they were charged with the care of the holy things that had to be carried on the shoulders.

10 The leaders also presented offerings for the dedication of the altar at the time when it was anointed; the leaders presented their offering before the altar. ¹¹The LORD said to Moses: They shall present their offerings, one leader each day, for the dedication of the altar.

12 The one who presented his offering the first day was Nahshon son of Amminadab, of the tribe of Judah; ¹³his offering was one silver plate weighing one hundred thirty shekels, one silver basin weighing seventy shekels, according to the shekel of the sanctuary, both of them full of choice flour mixed with oil for a grain offering;

---

a That is *those separated* or *those consecrated*   *b* That is *one separated* or *one consecrated*

14one golden dish weighing ten shekels, full of incense; 15one young bull, one ram, one male lamb a year old, for a burnt offering; 16one male goat for a sin offering; 17and for the sacrifice of well-being, two oxen, five rams, five male goats, and five male lambs a year old. This was the offering of Nahshon son of Amminadab.

18 On the second day Nethanel son of Zuar, the leader of Issachar, presented an offering; 19he presented for his offering one silver plate weighing one hundred thirty shekels, one silver basin weighing seventy shekels, according to the shekel of the sanctuary, both of them full of choice flour mixed with oil for a grain offering; 20one golden dish weighing ten shekels, full of incense; 21one young bull, one ram, one male lamb a year old, as a burnt offering; 22one male goat as a sin offering; 23and for the sacrifice of well-being, two oxen, five rams, five male goats, and five male lambs a year old. This was the offering of Nethanel son of Zuar.

24 On the third day Eliab son of Helon, the leader of the Zebulunites: 25his offering was one silver plate weighing one hundred thirty shekels, one silver basin weighing seventy shekels, according to the shekel of the sanctuary, both of them full of choice flour mixed with oil for a grain offering; 26one golden dish weighing ten shekels, full of incense; 27one young bull, one ram, one male lamb a year old, for a burnt offering; 28one male goat for a sin offering; 29and for the sacrifice of well-being, two oxen, five rams, five male goats, and five male lambs a year old. This was the offering of Eliab son of Helon.

30 On the fourth day Elizur son of Shedeur, the leader of the Reubenites: 31his offering was one silver plate weighing one hundred thirty shekels, one silver basin weighing seventy shekels, according to the shekel of the sanctuary, both of them full of choice flour mixed with oil for a grain offering; 32one golden dish weighing ten shekels, full of incense; 33one young bull, one ram, one male lamb a year old, for a burnt offering; 34one male goat for a sin offering; 35and for the sacrifice of well-being, two oxen, five rams, five male goats, and five male lambs a year old. This was the offering of Elizur son of Shedeur.

36 On the fifth day Shelumiel son of Zurishaddai, the leader of the Simeonites: 37his offering was one silver plate weighing one hundred thirty shekels, one silver basin weighing seventy shekels, according to the shekel of the sanctuary, both of them full of choice flour mixed with oil for a grain offering; 38one golden dish weighing ten shekels, full of incense; 39one young bull, one ram, one male lamb a year old, for a burnt offering; 40one male goat for a sin offering; 41and for the sacrifice of well-being, two oxen, five rams, five male goats, and five male lambs a year old. This was the offering of Shelumiel son of Zurishaddai.

42 On the sixth day Eliasaph son of Deuel, the leader of the Gadites: 43his offering was one silver plate weighing one hundred thirty shekels, one silver basin weighing seventy shekels, according to the shekel of the sanctuary, both of them full of choice flour mixed with oil for a grain offering; 44one golden dish weighing ten shekels, full of incense; 45one young bull, one ram, one male lamb a year old, for a burnt offering; 46one male goat for a sin offering; 47and for the sacrifice of well-being, two oxen, five rams, five male goats, and five male lambs a year old. This was the offering of Eliasaph son of Deuel.

48 On the seventh day Elishama son of Ammihud, the leader of the Ephraimites: 49his offering was one silver plate weighing one hundred thirty shekels, one silver basin weighing seventy shekels, according to the shekel of the sanctuary, both of them full of choice flour mixed with oil for a grain offering; 50one golden dish weighing ten shekels, full of incense; 51one young bull, one ram, one male lamb a year old, for a burnt offering; 52one male goat for a sin offering; 53and for the sacrifice of well-being, two oxen, five rams, five male goats, and five male lambs a year old. This was the offering of Elishama son of Ammihud.

54 On the eighth day Gamaliel son of Pedahzur, the leader of the Manassites: 55his offering was one silver plate weighing one hundred thirty shekels, one silver basin weighing seventy shekels, according to the shekel of the sanctuary, both of them full of choice flour mixed with oil for a grain offering; 56one golden dish weighing ten shekels, full of incense; 57one young bull, one ram, one male lamb a year old, for a burnt offering; 58one male goat for a sin offering; 59and for the sacrifice of well-being, two oxen, five rams, five male goats, and five male lambs a year old. This was the offering of Gamaliel son of Pedahzur.

60 On the ninth day Abidan son of Gideoni, the leader of the Benjaminites: 61his offering was one silver plate weighing one hundred thirty shekels, one silver basin weighing seventy shekels, according to the shekel of the sanctuary, both of them full of choice flour mixed with oil for a grain offering; 62one golden dish weighing ten shekels, full of incense; 63one young bull, one ram, one male lamb a year old, for a burnt offering; 64one male goat for a sin offering; 65and for

NUM

the sacrifice of well-being, two oxen, five rams, five male goats, and five male lambs a year old. This was the offering of Abidan son of Gideoni.

66 On the tenth day Ahiezer son of Ammishaddai, the leader of the Danites: [67]his offering was one silver plate weighing one hundred thirty shekels, one silver basin weighing seventy shekels, according to the shekel of the sanctuary, both of them full of choice flour mixed with oil for a grain offering; [68]one golden dish weighing ten shekels, full of incense; [69]one young bull, one ram, one male lamb a year old, for a burnt offering; [70]one male goat for a sin offering; [71]and for the sacrifice of well-being, two oxen, five rams, five male goats, and five male lambs a year old. This was the offering of Ahiezer son of Ammishaddai.

72 On the eleventh day Pagiel son of Ochran, the leader of the Asherites: [73]his offering was one silver plate weighing one hundred thirty shekels, one silver basin weighing seventy shekels, according to the shekel of the sanctuary, both of them full of choice flour mixed with oil for a grain offering; [74]one golden dish weighing ten shekels, full of incense; [75]one young bull, one ram, one male lamb a year old, for a burnt offering; [76]one male goat for a sin offering; [77]and for the sacrifice of well-being, two oxen, five rams, five male goats, and five male lambs a year old. This was the offering of Pagiel son of Ochran.

78 On the twelfth day Ahira son of Enan, the leader of the Naphtalites: [79]his offering was one silver plate weighing one hundred thirty shekels, one silver basin weighing seventy shekels, according to the shekel of the sanctuary, both of them full of choice flour mixed with oil for a grain offering; [80]one golden dish weighing ten shekels, full of incense; [81]one young bull, one ram, one male lamb a year old, for a burnt offering; [82]one male goat for a sin offering; [83]and for the sacrifice of well-being, two oxen, five rams, five male goats, and five male lambs a year old. This was the offering of Ahira son of Enan.

84 This was the dedication offering for the altar, at the time when it was anointed, from the leaders of Israel: twelve silver plates, twelve silver basins, twelve golden dishes, [85]each silver plate weighing one hundred thirty shekels and each basin seventy, all the silver of the vessels two thousand four hundred shekels according to the shekel of the sanctuary, [86]the twelve golden dishes, full of incense, weighing ten shekels apiece according to the shekel of the sanctuary, all the gold of the dishes being one hundred twenty shekels; [87]all the livestock for the burnt offering twelve bulls, twelve rams, twelve male lambs a year old,

with their grain offering; and twelve male goats for a sin offering; [88]and all the livestock for the sacrifice of well-being twenty-four bulls, the rams sixty, the male goats sixty, the male lambs a year old sixty. This was the dedication offering for the altar, after it was anointed.

89 When Moses went into the tent of meeting to speak with the LORD,[a] he would hear the voice speaking to him from above the mercy seat[b] that was on the ark of the covenant[c] from between the two cherubim; thus it spoke to him.

The Seven Lamps

8 The LORD spoke to Moses, saying: [2]Speak to Aaron and say to him: When you set up the lamps, the seven lamps shall give light in front of the lampstand. [3]Aaron did so; he set up its lamps to give light in front of the lampstand, as the LORD had commanded Moses. [4]Now this was how the lampstand was made, out of hammered work of gold. From its base to its flowers, it was hammered work; according to the pattern that the LORD had shown Moses, so he made the lampstand.

Consecration and Service of the Levites

5 The LORD spoke to Moses, saying: [6]Take the Levites from among the Israelites and cleanse them. [7]Thus you shall do to them, to cleanse them: sprinkle the water of purification on them, have them shave their whole body with a razor and wash their clothes, and so cleanse themselves. [8]Then let them take a young bull and its grain offering of choice flour mixed with oil, and you shall take another young bull for a sin offering. [9]You shall bring the Levites before the tent of meeting, and assemble the whole congregation of the Israelites. [10]When you bring the Levites before the LORD, the Israelites shall lay their hands on the Levites, [11]and Aaron shall present the Levites before the LORD as an elevation offering from the Israelites, that they may do the service of the LORD. [12]The Levites shall lay their hands on the heads of the bulls, and he shall offer the one for a sin offering and the other for a burnt offering to the LORD, to make atonement for the Levites. [13]Then you shall have the Levites stand before Aaron and his sons, and you shall present them as an elevation offering to the LORD.

14 Thus you shall separate the Levites from among the other Israelites, and the Levites shall be mine. [15]Thereafter the Levites may go in to do service at the tent of meeting, once you have

---

a Heb *him*   b Or *the cover*   c Or *treaty,* or *testimony;* Heb *eduth*

cleansed them and presented them as an elevation offering. [16]For they are unreservedly given to me from among the Israelites; I have taken them for myself, in place of all that open the womb, the firstborn of all the Israelites. [17]For all the firstborn among the Israelites are mine, both human and animal. On the day that I struck down all the firstborn in the land of Egypt I consecrated them for myself, [18]but I have taken the Levites in place of all the firstborn among the Israelites. [19]Moreover, I have given the Levites as a gift to Aaron and his sons from among the Israelites, to do the service for the Israelites at the tent of meeting, and to make atonement for the Israelites, in order that there may be no plague among the Israelites for coming too close to the sanctuary.

20 Moses and Aaron and the whole congregation of the Israelites did with the Levites accordingly; the Israelites did with the Levites just as the LORD had commanded Moses concerning them. [21]The Levites purified themselves from sin and washed their clothes; then Aaron presented them as an elevation offering before the LORD, and Aaron made atonement for them to cleanse them. [22]Thereafter the Levites went in to do their service in the tent of meeting in attendance on Aaron and his sons. As the LORD had commanded Moses concerning the Levites, so they did with them.

23 The LORD spoke to Moses, saying: [24]This applies to the Levites: from twenty-five years old and upward they shall begin to do duty in the service of the tent of meeting; [25]and from the age of fifty years they shall retire from the duty of the service and serve no more. [26]They may assist their brothers in the tent of meeting in carrying out their duties, but they shall perform no service. Thus you shall do with the Levites in assigning their duties.

The Passover at Sinai

9 The LORD spoke to Moses in the wilderness of Sinai, in the first month of the second year after they had come out of the land of Egypt, saying: [2]Let the Israelites keep the passover at its appointed time. [3]On the fourteenth day of this month, at twilight,[a] you shall keep it at its appointed time; according to all its statutes and all its regulations you shall keep it. [4]So Moses told the Israelites that they should keep the passover. [5]They kept the passover in the first month, on the fourteenth day of the month, at twilight,[a] in the wilderness of Sinai. Just as the LORD had commanded Moses, so the Israelites did. [6]Now there were certain people who were unclean through touching a corpse, so that they could not keep the passover on that day. They came before Moses and Aaron on that day, [7]and said to him, "Although we are unclean through touching a corpse, why must we be kept from presenting the LORD's offering at its appointed time among the Israelites?" [8]Moses spoke to them, "Wait, so that I may hear what the LORD will command concerning you."

9 The LORD spoke to Moses, saying: [10]Speak to the Israelites, saying: Anyone of you or your descendants who is unclean through touching a corpse, or is away on a journey, shall still keep the passover to the LORD. [11]In the second month on the fourteenth day, at twilight,[a] they shall keep it; they shall eat it with unleavened bread and bitter herbs. [12]They shall leave none of it until morning, nor break a bone of it; according to all the statute for the passover they shall keep it. [13]But anyone who is clean and is not on a journey, and yet refrains from keeping the passover, shall be cut off from the people for not presenting the LORD's offering at its appointed time; such a one shall bear the consequences for the sin. [14]Any alien residing among you who wishes to keep the passover to the LORD shall do so according to the statute of the passover and according to its regulation; you shall have one statute for both the resident alien and the native.

The Cloud and the Fire

15 On the day the tabernacle was set up, the cloud covered the tabernacle, the tent of the covenant;[b] and from evening until morning it was over the tabernacle, having the appearance of fire. [16]It was always so: the cloud covered it by day[c] and the appearance of fire by night. [17]Whenever the cloud lifted from over the tent, then the Israelites would set out; and in the place where the cloud settled down, there the Israelites would camp. [18]At the command of the LORD the Israelites would set out, and at the command of the LORD they would camp. As long as the cloud rested over the tabernacle, they would remain in camp. [19]Even when the cloud continued over the tabernacle many days, the Israelites would keep the charge of the LORD, and would not set out. [20]Sometimes the cloud would remain a few days over the tabernacle, and according to the command of the LORD they would remain in camp; then according to the command of the LORD they would set out. [21]Sometimes the cloud would remain from evening until morning; and when the cloud lifted in the morning, they would set

---

a Heb *between the two evenings*   b Or *treaty*, or *testimony*; Heb *eduth*   c Gk Syr Vg: Heb lacks *by day*

out, or if it continued for a day and a night, when the cloud lifted they would set out. ²²Whether it was two days, or a month, or a longer time, that the cloud continued over the tabernacle, resting upon it, the Israelites would remain in camp and would not set out; but when it lifted they would set out. ²³At the command of the LORD they would camp, and at the command of the LORD they would set out. They kept the charge of the LORD, at the command of the LORD by Moses.

The Silver Trumpets

10 The LORD spoke to Moses, saying: ²Make two silver trumpets; you shall make them of hammered work; and you shall use them for summoning the congregation, and for breaking camp. ³When both are blown, the whole congregation shall assemble before you at the entrance of the tent of meeting. ⁴But if only one is blown, then the leaders, the heads of the tribes of Israel, shall assemble before you. ⁵When you blow an alarm, the camps on the east side shall set out; ⁶when you blow a second alarm, the camps on the south side shall set out. An alarm is to be blown whenever they are to set out. ⁷But when the assembly is to be gathered, you shall blow, but you shall not sound an alarm. ⁸The sons of Aaron, the priests, shall blow the trumpets; this shall be a perpetual institution for you throughout your generations. ⁹When you go to war in your land against the adversary who oppresses you, you shall sound an alarm with the trumpets, so that you may be remembered before the LORD your God and be saved from your enemies. ¹⁰Also on your days of rejoicing, at your appointed festivals, and at the beginnings of your months, you shall blow the trumpets over your burnt offerings and over your sacrifices of well-being; they shall serve as a reminder on your behalf before the LORD your God: I am the LORD your God.

Departure from Sinai

11 In the second year, in the second month, on the twentieth day of the month, the cloud lifted from over the tabernacle of the covenant.^a ¹²Then the Israelites set out by stages from the wilderness of Sinai, and the cloud settled down in the wilderness of Paran. ¹³They set out for the first time at the command of the LORD by Moses. ¹⁴The standard of the camp of Judah set out first, company by company, and over the whole company was Nahshon son of Amminadab. ¹⁵Over the company of the tribe of Issachar was Nethanel son of Zuar; ¹⁶and over the company of the tribe of Zebulun was Eliab son of Helon.

17 Then the tabernacle was taken down, and the Gershonites and the Merarites, who carried the tabernacle, set out. ¹⁸Next the standard of the camp of Reuben set out, company by company; and over the whole company was Elizur son of Shedeur. ¹⁹Over the company of the tribe of Simeon was Shelumiel son of Zurishaddai, ²⁰and over the company of the tribe of Gad was Eliasaph son of Deuel.

21 Then the Kohathites, who carried the holy things, set out; and the tabernacle was set up before their arrival. ²²Next the standard of the Ephraimite camp set out, company by company, and over the whole company was Elishama son of Ammihud. ²³Over the company of the tribe of Manasseh was Gamaliel son of Pedahzur, ²⁴and over the company of the tribe of Benjamin was Abidan son of Gideoni.

25 Then the standard of the camp of Dan, acting as the rear guard of all the camps, set out, company by company, and over the whole company was Ahiezer son of Ammishaddai. ²⁶Over the company of the tribe of Asher was Pagiel son of Ochran, ²⁷and over the company of the tribe of Naphtali was Ahira son of Enan. ²⁸This was the order of march of the Israelites, company by company, when they set out.

29 Moses said to Hobab son of Reuel the Midianite, Moses' father-in-law, "We are setting out for the place of which the LORD said, 'I will give it to you'; come with us, and we will treat you well; for the LORD has promised good to Israel." ³⁰But he said to him, "I will not go, but I will go back to my own land and to my kindred." ³¹He said, "Do not leave us, for you know where we should camp in the wilderness, and you will serve as eyes for us. ³²Moreover, if you go with us, whatever good the LORD does for us, the same we will do for you."

33 So they set out from the mount of the LORD three days' journey with the ark of the covenant of the LORD going before them three days' journey, to seek out a resting place for them; ³⁴the cloud of the LORD being over them by day when they set out from the camp.

35 Whenever the ark set out, Moses would say,

"Arise, O LORD, let your enemies be scattered,
    and your foes flee before you."

³⁶And whenever it came to rest, he would say,

"Return, O LORD of the ten thousand thousands
    of Israel."^b

---

a Or *treaty*, or *testimony*; Heb *eduth*   b Meaning of Heb uncertain

Complaining in the Desert

11 Now when the people complained in the hearing of the LORD about their misfortunes, the LORD heard it and his anger was kindled. Then the fire of the LORD burned against them, and consumed some outlying parts of the camp. ²But the people cried out to Moses; and Moses prayed to the LORD, and the fire abated. ³So that place was called Taberah,ᵃ because the fire of the LORD burned against them.

4 The rabble among them had a strong craving; and the Israelites also wept again, and said, "If only we had meat to eat! ⁵We remember the fish we used to eat in Egypt for nothing, the cucumbers, the melons, the leeks, the onions, and the garlic; ⁶but now our strength is dried up, and there is nothing at all but this manna to look at."

7 Now the manna was like coriander seed, and its color was like the color of gum resin. ⁸The people went around and gathered it, ground it in mills or beat it in mortars, then boiled it in pots and made cakes of it; and the taste of it was like the taste of cakes baked with oil. ⁹When the dew fell on the camp in the night, the manna would fall with it.

10 Moses heard the people weeping throughout their families, all at the entrances of their tents. Then the LORD became very angry, and Moses was displeased. ¹¹So Moses said to the LORD, "Why have you treated your servant so badly? Why have I not found favor in your sight, that you lay the burden of all this people on me? ¹²Did I conceive all this people? Did I give birth to them, that you should say to me, 'Carry them in your bosom, as a nurse carries a sucking child, to the land that you promised on oath to their ancestors'? ¹³Where am I to get meat to give to all this people? For they come weeping to me and say, 'Give us meat to eat!' ¹⁴I am not able to carry all this people alone, for they are too heavy for me. ¹⁵If this is the way you are going to treat me, put me to death at once—if I have found favor in your sight—and do not let me see my misery."

The Seventy Elders

16 So the LORD said to Moses, "Gather for me seventy of the elders of Israel, whom you know to be the elders of the people and officers over them; bring them to the tent of meeting, and have them take their place there with you. ¹⁷I will come down and talk with you there; and I will take some of the spirit that is on you and put it on them; and they shall bear the burden of the people along with you so that you will not bear it all by yourself. ¹⁸And say to the people:

Consecrate yourselves for tomorrow, and you shall eat meat; for you have wailed in the hearing of the LORD, saying, 'If only we had meat to eat! Surely it was better for us in Egypt.' Therefore the LORD will give you meat, and you shall eat. ¹⁹You shall eat not only one day, or two days, or five days, or ten days, or twenty days, ²⁰but for a whole month—until it comes out of your nostrils and becomes loathsome to you—because you have rejected the LORD who is among you, and have wailed before him, saying, 'Why did we ever leave Egypt?'" ²¹But Moses said, "The people I am with number six hundred thousand on foot; and you say, 'I will give them meat, that they may eat for a whole month'! ²²Are there enough flocks and herds to slaughter for them? Are there enough fish in the sea to catch for them?" ²³The LORD said to Moses, "Is the LORD's power limited?ᵇ Now you shall see whether my word will come true for you or not."

24 So Moses went out and told the people the words of the LORD; and he gathered seventy elders of the people, and placed them all around the tent. ²⁵Then the LORD came down in the cloud and spoke to him, and took some of the spirit that was on him and put it on the seventy elders; and when the spirit rested upon them, they prophesied. But they did not do so again.

26 Two men remained in the camp, one named Eldad, and the other named Medad, and the spirit rested on them; they were among those registered, but they had not gone out to the tent, and so they prophesied in the camp. ²⁷And a young man ran and told Moses, "Eldad and Medad are prophesying in the camp." ²⁸And Joshua son of Nun, the assistant of Moses, one of his chosen men,ᶜ said, "My lord Moses, stop them!" ²⁹But Moses said to him, "Are you jealous for my sake? Would that all the LORD's people were prophets, and that the LORD would put his spirit on them!" ³⁰And Moses and the elders of Israel returned to the camp.

The Quails

31 Then a wind went out from the LORD, and it brought quails from the sea and let them fall beside the camp, about a day's journey on this side and a day's journey on the other side, all around the camp, about two cubits deep on the ground. ³²So the people worked all that day and night and all the next day, gathering the quails; the least anyone gathered was ten homers; and they spread them out for themselves all around

a That is Burning   b Heb LORD's hand too short?   c Or of Moses from his youth

The Jealousy of Miriam and Aaron

It isn't very hard to identify with the feelings Miriam and Aaron have toward their brother Moses. After all, God speaks directly to Moses, so why can't God speak to them as well? What makes Moses so special?

Jealousy is a sneaky vice that slowly grows and makes itself apparent without us realizing it. Soon we begin to feel a sense of resentment at how someone else seems to be getting all the breaks. We know we've crossed the line when we actually feel glad that something didn't work out for that person or even that something bad happened. Jealousy is like a dangerous cancer, growing until it affects our whole outlook on life (see what happens to Miriam in Num 12:10).

● Think of a time when you felt jealous of another. How did that affect your attitude toward that person?

▶ **Numbers, chapter 12**

NUM

the camp. 33But while the meat was still between their teeth, before it was consumed, the anger of the Lord was kindled against the people, and the Lord struck the people with a very great plague. 34So that place was called Kibroth-hattaavah,*a* because there they buried the people who had the craving. 35From Kibroth-hattaavah the people journeyed to Hazeroth.

Aaron and Miriam Jealous of Moses

12 While they were at Hazeroth, Miriam and Aaron spoke against Moses because of the Cushite woman whom he had married (for he had indeed married a Cushite woman); 2and they said, "Has the Lord spoken only through Moses? Has he not spoken through us also?" And the Lord heard it. 3Now the man Moses was very humble,*b* more so than anyone else on the face of the earth. 4Suddenly the Lord said to Moses, Aaron, and Miriam, "Come out, you three, to the tent of meeting." So the three of them came out. 5Then the Lord came down in a pillar of cloud,

and stood at the entrance of the tent, and called Aaron and Miriam; and they both came forward. 6And he said, "Hear my words:

When there are prophets among you,
  I the Lord make myself known to them in visions;
  I speak to them in dreams.
7 Not so with my servant Moses;
  he is entrusted with all my house.
8 With him I speak face to face— clearly, not in riddles;
  and he beholds the form of the Lord.

Why then were you not afraid to speak against my servant Moses?" 9And the anger of the Lord was kindled against them, and he departed.

10 When the cloud went away from over the tent, Miriam had become leprous,*c* as white as snow. And Aaron turned towards Miriam and saw that she was leprous. 11Then Aaron said to Moses, "Oh, my lord, do not punish us*d* for a sin that we have so foolishly committed. 12Do not let her be like one stillborn, whose flesh is half consumed when it comes out of its mother's womb." 13And Moses cried to the Lord, "O God, please heal her." 14But the Lord said to Moses, "If her father had but spit in her face, would she not bear her shame for seven days? Let her be shut out of the camp for seven days, and after that she may be brought in again." 15So Miriam was shut out of the camp for seven days; and the people did not set out on the march until Miriam had been brought in again. 16After that the people set out from Hazeroth, and camped in the wilderness of Paran.

Spies Sent into Canaan

13 The Lord said to Moses, 2"Send men to spy out the land of Canaan, which I am giving to the Israelites; from each of their ancestral tribes you shall send a man, every one a leader among them." 3So Moses sent them from the wilderness of Paran, according to the command of the Lord, all of them leading men among the Israelites. 4These were their names: From the tribe of Reuben, Shammua son of Zaccur; 5from the tribe of Simeon, Shaphat son of Hori; 6from the tribe of Judah, Caleb son of Jephunneh; 7from the tribe of Issachar, Igal son of Joseph; 8from the tribe of Ephraim, Hoshea son of Nun; 9from the tribe of Benjamin, Palti son of Raphu; 10from the tribe of Zebulun, Gaddiel son of Sodi; 11from the tribe of Joseph (that is, from the tribe of Manasseh),

a That is *Graves of craving*   *b* Or *devout*   *c* A term for several skin diseases; precise meaning uncertain   *d* Heb *do not lay sin upon us*

Gaddi son of Susi; [12]from the tribe of Dan, Ammiel son of Gemalli; [13]from the tribe of Asher, Sethur son of Michael; [14]from the tribe of Naphtali, Nahbi son of Vophsi; [15]from the tribe of Gad, Geuel son of Machi. [16]These were the names of the men whom Moses sent to spy out the land. And Moses changed the name of Hoshea son of Nun to Joshua.

[17] Moses sent them to spy out the land of Canaan, and said to them, "Go up there into the Negeb, and go up into the hill country, [18]and see what the land is like, and whether the people who live in it are strong or weak, whether they are few or many, [19]and whether the land they live in is good or bad, and whether the towns that they live in are unwalled or fortified, [20]and whether the land is rich or poor, and whether there are trees in it or not. Be bold, and bring some of the fruit of the land." Now it was the season of the first ripe grapes.

[21] So they went up and spied out the land from the wilderness of Zin to Rehob, near Lebo-hamath. [22]They went up into the Negeb, and came to Hebron; and Ahiman, Sheshai, and Talmai, the Anakites, were there. (Hebron was built seven years before Zoan in Egypt.) [23]And they came to the Wadi Eshcol, and cut down from there a branch with a single cluster of grapes, and they carried it on a pole between two of them. They also brought some pomegranates and figs. [24]That place was called the Wadi Eshcol,[a] because of the cluster that the Israelites cut down from there.

The Report of the Spies

[25] At the end of forty days they returned from spying out the land. [26]And they came to Moses and Aaron and to all the congregation of the Israelites in the wilderness of Paran, at Kadesh; they brought back word to them and to all the congregation, and showed them the fruit of the land. [27]And they told him, "We came to the land to which you sent us; it flows with milk and honey, and this is its fruit. [28]Yet the people who live in the land are strong, and the towns are fortified and very large; and besides, we saw the descendants of Anak there. [29]The Amalekites live in the land of the Negeb; the Hittites, the Jebusites, and the Amorites live in the hill country; and the Canaanites live by the sea, and along the Jordan."

[30] But Caleb quieted the people before Moses, and said, "Let us go up at once and occupy it, for we are well able to overcome it." [31]Then the men who had gone up with him said, "We are not able to go up against this people, for they are stronger than we." [32]So they brought to the Israelites an unfavorable report of the land that they had spied out, saying, "The land that we have gone through as spies is a land that devours its inhabitants; and all the people that we saw in it are of great size. [33]There we saw the Nephilim (the Anakites come from the Nephilim); and to ourselves we seemed like grasshoppers, and so we seemed to them."

The People Rebel

14 Then all the congregation raised a loud cry, and the people wept that night. [2]And all the Israelites complained against Moses and Aaron; the whole congregation said to them, "Would that we had died in the land of Egypt! Or would that we had died in this wilderness! [3]Why is the LORD bringing us into this land to fall by the sword? Our wives and our little ones will become booty; would it not be better for us to go back to Egypt?" [4]So they said to one another, "Let us choose a captain, and go back to Egypt."

[5] Then Moses and Aaron fell on their faces before all the assembly of the congregation of the Israelites. [6]And Joshua son of Nun and Caleb son of Jephunneh, who were among those who had spied out the land, tore their clothes [7]and said to all the congregation of the Israelites, "The land that we went through as spies is an exceedingly good land. [8]If the LORD is pleased with us, he will bring us into this land and give it to us, a land that flows with milk and honey. [9]Only, do not rebel against the LORD; and do not fear the people of the land, for they are no more than bread for us; their protection is removed from them, and the LORD is with us; do not fear them." [10]But the whole congregation threatened to stone them.

Then the glory of the LORD appeared at the tent of meeting to all the Israelites. [11]And the LORD said to Moses, "How long will this people despise me? And how long will they refuse to believe in me, in spite of all the signs that I have done among them? [12]I will strike them with pestilence and disinherit them, and I will make of you a nation greater and mightier than they."

Moses Intercedes for the People

[13] But Moses said to the LORD, "Then the Egyptians will hear of it, for in your might you brought up this people from among them, [14]and they will tell the inhabitants of this land. They have heard that you, O LORD, are in the midst of this people; for you, O LORD, are seen face to face, and your cloud stands over them and you go in

a That is Cluster

front of them, in a pillar of cloud by day and in a pillar of fire by night. 15Now if you kill this people all at one time, then the nations who have heard about you will say, 16'It is because the LORD was not able to bring this people into the land he swore to give them that he has slaughtered them in the wilderness.' 17And now, therefore, let the power of the LORD be great in the way that you promised when you spoke, saying,

18 'The LORD is slow to anger,
   and abounding in steadfast love,
   forgiving iniquity and transgression,
   but by no means clearing the guilty,
   visiting the iniquity of the parents
   upon the children
   to the third and the fourth generation.'

19Forgive the iniquity of this people according to the greatness of your steadfast love, just as you have pardoned this people, from Egypt even until now."

20 Then the LORD said, "I do forgive, just as you have asked; 21nevertheless—as I live, and as all the earth shall be filled with the glory of the LORD— 22none of the people who have seen my glory and the signs that I did in Egypt and in the wilderness, and yet have tested me these ten times and have not obeyed my voice, 23shall see the land that I swore to give to their ancestors; none of those who despised me shall see it. 24But my servant Caleb, because he has a different spirit and has followed me wholeheartedly, I will bring into the land into which he went, and his descendants shall possess it. 25Now, since the Amalekites and the Canaanites live in the valleys, turn tomorrow and set out for the wilderness by the way to the Red Sea."a

An Attempted Invasion is Repulsed

26 And the LORD spoke to Moses and to Aaron, saying: 27How long shall this wicked congregation complain against me? I have heard the complaints of the Israelites, which they complain against me. 28Say to them, "As I live," says the LORD, "I will do to you the very things I heard you say: 29your dead bodies shall fall in this very wilderness; and of all your number, included in the census, from twenty years old and upward, who have complained against me, 30not one of you shall come into the land in which I swore to settle you, except Caleb son of Jephunneh and Joshua son of Nun. 31But your little ones, who you said would become booty, I will bring in, and they shall know the land that you have despised. 32But as for you, your dead bodies shall fall in this wilderness. 33And your children shall be shepherds in the wilderness for forty years,

and shall suffer for your faithlessness, until the last of your dead bodies lies in the wilderness. 34According to the number of the days in which you spied out the land, forty days, for every day a year, you shall bear your iniquity, forty years, and you shall know my displeasure." 35I the LORD have spoken; surely I will do thus to all this wicked congregation gathered together against me: in this wilderness they shall come to a full end, and there they shall die.

36 And the men whom Moses sent to spy out the land, who returned and made all the congregation complain against him by bringing a bad report about the land— 37the men who brought an unfavorable report about the land died by a plague before the LORD. 38But Joshua son of Nun and Caleb son of Jephunneh alone remained alive, of those men who went to spy out the land.

39 When Moses told these words to all the Israelites, the people mourned greatly. 40They rose early in the morning and went up to the heights of the hill country, saying, "Here we are. We will go up to the place that the LORD has promised, for we have sinned." 41But Moses said, "Why do you continue to transgress the command of the LORD? That will not succeed. 42Do not go up, for the LORD is not with you; do not let yourselves be struck down before your enemies. 43For the Amalekites and the Canaanites will confront you there, and you shall fall by the sword; because you have turned back from following the LORD, the LORD will not be with you." 44But they presumed to go up to the heights of the hill country, even though the ark of the covenant of the LORD, and Moses, had not left the camp. 45Then the Amalekites and the Canaanites who lived in that hill country came down and defeated them, pursuing them as far as Hormah.

Various Offerings

15 The LORD spoke to Moses, saying: 2Speak to the Israelites and say to them: When you come into the land you are to inhabit, which I am giving you, 3and you make an offering by fire to the LORD from the herd or from the flock— whether a burnt offering or a sacrifice, to fulfill a vow or as a freewill offering or at your appointed festivals—to make a pleasing odor for the LORD, 4then whoever presents such an offering to the LORD shall present also a grain offering, one-tenth of an ephah of choice flour, mixed with one-fourth of a hin of oil. 5Moreover, you shall offer one-fourth of a hin of wine as a drink offering

---

a Or Sea of Reeds

with the burnt offering or the sacrifice, for each lamb. [6]For a ram, you shall offer a grain offering, two-tenths of an ephah of choice flour mixed with one-third of a hin of oil; [7]and as a drink offering you shall offer one-third of a hin of wine, a pleasing odor to the LORD. [8]When you offer a bull as a burnt offering or a sacrifice, to fulfill a vow or as an offering of well-being to the LORD, [9]then you shall present with the bull a grain offering, three-tenths of an ephah of choice flour, mixed with half a hin of oil, [10]and you shall present as a drink offering half a hin of wine, as an offering by fire, a pleasing odor to the LORD.

11 Thus it shall be done for each ox or ram, or for each of the male lambs or the kids. [12]According to the number that you offer, so you shall do with each and every one. [13]Every native Israelite shall do these things in this way, in presenting an offering by fire, a pleasing odor to the LORD. [14]An alien who lives with you, or who takes up permanent residence among you, and wishes to offer an offering by fire, a pleasing odor to the LORD, shall do as you do. [15]As for the assembly, there shall be for both you and the resident alien a single statute, a perpetual statute throughout your generations; you and the alien shall be alike before the LORD. [16]You and the alien who resides with you shall have the same law and the same ordinance.

17 The LORD spoke to Moses, saying: [18]Speak to the Israelites and say to them: After you come into the land to which I am bringing you, [19]whenever you eat of the bread of the land, you shall present a donation to the LORD. [20]From your first batch of dough you shall present a loaf as a donation; you shall present it just as you present a donation from the threshing floor. [21]Throughout your generations you shall give to the LORD a donation from the first of your batch of dough.

22 But if you unintentionally fail to observe all these commandments that the LORD has spoken to Moses— [23]everything that the LORD has commanded you by Moses, from the day the LORD gave commandment and thereafter, throughout your generations— [24]then if it was done unintentionally without the knowledge of the congregation, the whole congregation shall offer one young bull for a burnt offering, a pleasing odor to the LORD, together with its grain offering and its drink offering, according to the ordinance, and one male goat for a sin offering. [25]The priest shall make atonement for all the congregation of the Israelites, and they shall be forgiven; it was unintentional, and they have brought their offering, an offering by fire to the

LORD, and their sin offering before the LORD, for their error. [26]All the congregation of the Israelites shall be forgiven, as well as the aliens residing among them, because the whole people was involved in the error.

27 An individual who sins unintentionally shall present a female goat a year old for a sin offering. [28]And the priest shall make atonement before the LORD for the one who commits an error, when it is unintentional, to make atonement for the person, who then shall be forgiven. [29]For both the native among the Israelites and the alien residing among them—you shall have the same law for anyone who acts in error. [30]But whoever acts high-handedly, whether a native or an alien, affronts the LORD, and shall be cut off from among the people. [31]Because of having despised the word of the LORD and broken his commandment, such a person shall be utterly cut off and bear the guilt.

Penalty for Violating the Sabbath

32 When the Israelites were in the wilderness, they found a man gathering sticks on the sabbath day. [33]Those who found him gathering sticks brought him to Moses, Aaron, and to the whole congregation. [34]They put him in custody, because it was not clear what should be done to him. [35]Then the LORD said to Moses, "The man shall be put to death; all the congregation shall stone him outside the camp." [36]The whole congregation brought him outside the camp and stoned him to death, just as the LORD had commanded Moses.

Fringes on Garments

37 The LORD said to Moses: [38]Speak to the Israelites, and tell them to make fringes on the corners of their garments throughout their generations and to put a blue cord on the fringe at each corner. [39]You have the fringe so that, when you see it, you will remember all the commandments of the LORD and do them, and not follow the lust of your own heart and your own eyes. [40]So you shall remember and do all my commandments, and you shall be holy to your God. [41]I am the LORD your God, who brought you out of the land of Egypt, to be your God: I am the LORD your God.

Revolt of Korah, Dathan, and Abiram

16 Now Korah son of Izhar son of Kohath son of Levi, along with Dathan and Abiram sons of Eliab, and On son of Peleth—descendants of Reuben—took [2]two hundred fifty Israelite men, leaders of the congregation, chosen

NUM

from the assembly, well-known men,ᵃ and they confronted Moses. ³They assembled against Moses and against Aaron, and said to them, "You have gone too far! All the congregation are holy, every one of them, and the LORD is among them. So why then do you exalt yourselves above the assembly of the LORD?" ⁴When Moses heard it, he fell on his face. ⁵Then he said to Korah and all his company, "In the morning the LORD will make known who is his, and who is holy, and who will be allowed to approach him; the one whom he will choose he will allow to approach him. ⁶Do this: take censers, Korah and all yourᵇ company, ⁷and tomorrow put fire in them, and lay incense on them before the LORD; and the man whom the LORD chooses shall be the holy one. You Levites have gone too far!" ⁸Then Moses said to Korah, "Hear now, you Levites! ⁹Is it too little for you that the God of Israel has separated you from the congregation of Israel, to allow you to approach him in order to perform the duties of the LORD's tabernacle, and to stand before the congregation and serve them? ¹⁰He has allowed you to approach him, and all your brother Levites with you; yet you seek the priesthood as well! ¹¹Therefore you and all your company have gathered together against the LORD. What is Aaron that you rail against him?"

12 Moses sent for Dathan and Abiram sons of Eliab; but they said, "We will not come! ¹³Is it too little that you have brought us up out of a land flowing with milk and honey to kill us in the wilderness, that you must also lord it over us? ¹⁴It is clear you have not brought us into a land flowing with milk and honey, or given us an inheritance of fields and vineyards. Would you put out the eyes of these men? We will not come!"

15 Moses was very angry and said to the LORD, "Pay no attention to their offering. I have not taken one donkey from them, and I have not harmed any one of them." ¹⁶And Moses said to Korah, "As for you and all your company, be present tomorrow before the LORD, you and they and Aaron; ¹⁷and let each one of you take his censer, and put incense on it, and each one of you present his censer before the LORD, two hundred fifty censers; you also, and Aaron, each his censer." ¹⁸So each man took his censer, and they put fire in the censers and laid incense on them, and they stood at the entrance of the tent of meeting with Moses and Aaron. ¹⁹Then Korah assembled the whole congregation against them at the entrance of the tent of meeting. And the glory of the LORD appeared to the whole congregation.

20 Then the LORD spoke to Moses and to Aaron, saying: ²¹Separate yourselves from this congregation, so that I may consume them in a moment. ²²They fell on their faces, and said, "O God, the God of the spirits of all flesh, shall one person sin and you become angry with the whole congregation?"

23 And the LORD spoke to Moses, saying: ²⁴Say to the congregation: Get away from the dwellings of Korah, Dathan, and Abiram. ²⁵So Moses got up and went to Dathan and Abiram; the elders of Israel followed him. ²⁶He said to the congregation, "Turn away from the tents of these wicked men, and touch nothing of theirs, or you will be swept away for all their sins." ²⁷So they got away from the dwellings of Korah, Dathan, and Abiram; and Dathan and Abiram came out and stood at the entrance of their tents, together with their wives, their children, and their little ones. ²⁸And Moses said, "This is how you shall know that the LORD has sent me to do all these works; it has not been of my own accord: ²⁹If these people die a natural death, or if a natural fate comes on them, then the LORD has not sent me. ³⁰But if the LORD creates something new, and the ground opens its mouth and swallows them up, with all that belongs to them, and they go down alive into Sheol, then you shall know that these men have despised the LORD."

31 As soon as he finished speaking all these words, the ground under them was split apart. ³²The earth opened its mouth and swallowed them up, along with their households—everyone who belonged to Korah and all their goods. ³³So they with all that belonged to them went down alive into Sheol; the earth closed over them, and they perished from the midst of the assembly. ³⁴All Israel around them fled at their outcry, for they said, "The earth will swallow us too!" ³⁵And fire came out from the LORD and consumed the two hundred fifty men offering the incense.

36ᶜ Then the LORD spoke to Moses, saying: ³⁷Tell Eleazar son of Aaron the priest to take the censers out of the blaze; then scatter the fire far and wide. ³⁸For the censers of these sinners have become holy at the cost of their lives. Make them into hammered plates as a covering for the altar, for they presented them before the LORD and they became holy. Thus they shall be a sign to the Israelites. ³⁹So Eleazar the priest took the bronze censers that had been presented by those who were burned; and they were hammered out as a covering for the altar— ⁴⁰a reminder to the Israelites that no outsider, who is not of the descendants of Aaron, shall approach to offer

a Cn: Heb and they confronted Moses, and two hundred fifty men . . . well-known men   b Heb his   c Ch 17.1 in Heb

incense before the LORD, so as not to become like Korah and his company—just as the LORD had said to him through Moses.

41 On the next day, however, the whole congregation of the Israelites rebelled against Moses and against Aaron, saying, "You have killed the people of the LORD." 42And when the congregation had assembled against them, Moses and Aaron turned toward the tent of meeting; the cloud had covered it and the glory of the LORD appeared. 43Then Moses and Aaron came to the front of the tent of meeting, 44and the LORD spoke to Moses, saying, 45"Get away from this congregation, so that I may consume them in a moment." And they fell on their faces. 46Moses said to Aaron, "Take your censer, put fire on it from the altar and lay incense on it, and carry it quickly to the congregation and make atonement for them. For wrath has gone out from the LORD; the plague has begun." 47So Aaron took it as Moses had ordered, and ran into the middle of the assembly, where the plague had already begun among the people. He put on the incense, and made atonement for the people. 48He stood between the dead and the living; and the plague was stopped. 49Those who died by the plague were fourteen thousand seven hundred, besides those who died in the affair of Korah. 50When the plague was stopped, Aaron returned to Moses at the entrance of the tent of meeting.

The Budding of Aaron's Rod

17 [a] The LORD spoke to Moses, saying: 2Speak to the Israelites, and get twelve staffs from them, one for each ancestral house, from all the leaders of their ancestral houses. Write each man's name on his staff, 3and write Aaron's name on the staff of Levi. For there shall be one staff for the head of each ancestral house. 4Place them in the tent of meeting before the covenant,[b] where I meet with you. 5And the staff of the man whom I choose shall sprout; thus I will put a stop to the complaints of the Israelites that they continually make against you. 6Moses spoke to the Israelites; and all their leaders gave him staffs, one for each leader, according to their ancestral houses, twelve staffs; and the staff of Aaron was among theirs. 7So Moses placed the staffs before the LORD in the tent of the covenant.[b]

8 When Moses went into the tent of the covenant[b] on the next day, the staff of Aaron for the house of Levi had sprouted. It put forth buds, produced blossoms, and bore ripe almonds. 9Then Moses brought out all the staffs from before the LORD to all the Israelites; and they looked, and each man took his staff. 10And the LORD said to Moses, "Put back the staff of Aaron before the covenant,[b] to be kept as a warning to rebels, so that you may make an end of their complaints against me, or else they will die." 11Moses did so; just as the LORD commanded him, so he did.

12 The Israelites said to Moses, "We are perishing; we are lost, all of us are lost! 13Everyone who approaches the tabernacle of the LORD will die. Are we all to perish?"

Responsibility of Priests and Levites

18 The LORD said to Aaron: You and your sons and your ancestral house with you shall bear responsibility for offenses connected with the sanctuary, while you and your sons alone shall bear responsibility for offenses connected with the priesthood. 2So bring with you also your brothers of the tribe of Levi, your ancestral tribe, in order that they may be joined to you, and serve you while you and your sons with you are in front of the tent of the covenant.[b] 3They shall perform duties for you and for the whole tent. But they must not approach either the utensils of the sanctuary or the altar, otherwise both they and you will die. 4They are attached to you in order to perform the duties of the tent of meeting, for all the service of the tent; no outsider shall approach you. 5You yourselves shall perform the duties of the sanctuary and the duties of the altar, so that wrath may never again come upon the Israelites. 6It is I who now take your brother Levites from among the Israelites; they are now yours as a gift, dedicated to the LORD, to perform the service of the tent of meeting. 7But you and your sons with you shall diligently perform your priestly duties in all that concerns the altar and the area behind the curtain. I give your priesthood as a gift;[c] any outsider who approaches shall be put to death.

The Priests' Portion

8 The LORD spoke to Aaron: I have given you charge of the offerings made to me, all the holy gifts of the Israelites; I have given them to you and your sons as a priestly portion due you in perpetuity. 9This shall be yours from the most holy things, reserved from the fire: every offering of theirs that they render to me as a most holy thing, whether grain offering, sin offering, or guilt offering, shall belong to you and your sons. 10As a most holy thing you shall eat it; every male may eat it; it shall be holy to you. 11This also is

a Ch 17.16 in Heb   b Or treaty, or testimony; Heb eduth
c Heb as a service of gift

yours: I have given to you, together with your sons and daughters, as a perpetual due, whatever is set aside from the gifts of all the elevation offerings of the Israelites; everyone who is clean in your house may eat them. ¹²All the best of the oil and all the best of the wine and of the grain, the choice produce that they give to the LORD, I have given to you. ¹³The first fruits of all that is in their land, which they bring to the LORD, shall be yours; everyone who is clean in your house may eat of it. ¹⁴Every devoted thing in Israel shall be yours. ¹⁵The first issue of the womb of all creatures, human and animal, which is offered to the LORD, shall be yours; but the firstborn of human beings you shall redeem, and the firstborn of unclean animals you shall redeem. ¹⁶Their redemption price, reckoned from one month of age, you shall fix at five shekels of silver, according to the shekel of the sanctuary (that is, twenty gerahs). ¹⁷But the firstborn of a cow, or the firstborn of a sheep, or the firstborn of a goat, you shall not redeem; they are holy. You shall dash their blood on the altar, and shall turn their fat into smoke as an offering by fire for a pleasing odor to the LORD; ¹⁸but their flesh shall be yours, just as the breast that is elevated and as the right thigh are yours. ¹⁹All the holy offerings that the Israelites present to the LORD I have given to you, together with your sons and daughters, as a perpetual due; it is a covenant of salt forever before the LORD for you and your descendants as well. ²⁰Then the LORD said to Aaron: You shall have no allotment in their land, nor shall you have any share among them; I am your share and your possession among the Israelites.

21 To the Levites I have given every tithe in Israel for a possession in return for the service that they perform, the service in the tent of meeting. ²²From now on the Israelites shall no longer approach the tent of meeting, or else they will incur guilt and die. ²³But the Levites shall perform the service of the tent of meeting, and they shall bear responsibility for their own offenses; it shall be a perpetual statute throughout your generations. But among the Israelites they shall have no allotment, ²⁴because I have given to the Levites as their portion the tithe of the Israelites, which they set apart as an offering to the LORD. Therefore I have said of them that they shall have no allotment among the Israelites.

25 Then the LORD spoke to Moses, saying: ²⁶You shall speak to the Levites, saying: When you receive from the Israelites the tithe that I have given you from them for your portion, you shall set apart an offering from it to the LORD, a tithe of the tithe. ²⁷It shall be reckoned to you as your gift, the same as the grain of the threshing floor and the fullness of the wine press. ²⁸Thus you also shall set apart an offering to the LORD from all the tithes that you receive from the Israelites; and from them you shall give the LORD's offering to the priest Aaron. ²⁹Out of all the gifts to you, you shall set apart every offering due to the LORD; the best of all of them is the part to be consecrated. ³⁰Say also to them: When you have set apart the best of it, then the rest shall be reckoned to the Levites as produce of the threshing floor, and as produce of the wine press. ³¹You may eat it in any place, you and your households; for it is your payment for your service in the tent of meeting. ³²You shall incur no guilt by reason of it, when you have offered the best of it. But you shall not profane the holy gifts of the Israelites, on pain of death.

Ceremony of the Red Heifer

19 The LORD spoke to Moses and Aaron, saying: ²This is a statute of the law that the LORD has commanded: Tell the Israelites to bring you a red heifer without defect, in which there is no blemish and on which no yoke has been laid. ³You shall give it to the priest Eleazar, and it shall be taken outside the camp and slaughtered in his presence. ⁴The priest Eleazar shall take some of its blood with his finger and sprinkle it seven times towards the front of the tent of meeting. ⁵Then the heifer shall be burned in his sight; its skin, its flesh, and its blood, with its dung, shall be burned. ⁶The priest shall take cedarwood, hyssop, and crimson material, and throw them into the fire in which the heifer is burning. ⁷Then the priest shall wash his clothes and bathe his body in water, and afterwards he may come into the camp; but the priest shall remain unclean until evening. ⁸The one who burns the heifer*a* shall wash his clothes in water and bathe his body in water; he shall remain unclean until evening. ⁹Then someone who is clean shall gather up the ashes of the heifer, and deposit them outside the camp in a clean place; and they shall be kept for the congregation of the Israelites for the water for cleansing. It is a purification offering. ¹⁰The one who gathers the ashes of the heifer shall wash his clothes and be unclean until evening.

This shall be a perpetual statute for the Israelites and for the alien residing among them. ¹¹Those who touch the dead body of any human being shall be unclean seven days. ¹²They shall purify themselves with the water on the third day and on the seventh day, and so be clean; but if they

_a_ Heb _it_

do not purify themselves on the third day and on the seventh day, they will not become clean. 13All who touch a corpse, the body of a human being who has died, and do not purify themselves, defile the tabernacle of the LORD; such persons shall be cut off from Israel. Since water for cleansing was not dashed on them, they remain unclean; their uncleanness is still on them.

14 This is the law when someone dies in a tent: everyone who comes into the tent, and everyone who is in the tent, shall be unclean seven days. 15And every open vessel with no cover fastened on it is unclean. 16Whoever in the open field touches one who has been killed by a sword, or who has died naturally,*a* or a human bone, or a grave, shall be unclean seven days. 17For the unclean they shall take some ashes of the burnt purification offering, and running water shall be added in a vessel; 18then a clean person shall take hyssop, dip it in the water, and sprinkle it on the tent, on all the furnishings, on the persons who were there, and on whoever touched the bone, the slain, the corpse, or the grave. 19The clean person shall sprinkle the unclean ones on the third day and on the seventh day, thus purifying them on the seventh day. Then they shall wash their clothes and bathe themselves in water, and at evening they shall be clean. 20Any who are unclean but do not purify themselves, those persons shall be cut off from the assembly, for they have defiled the sanctuary of the LORD. Since the water for cleansing has not been dashed on them, they are unclean.

21 It shall be a perpetual statute for them. The one who sprinkles the water for cleansing shall wash his clothes, and whoever touches the water for cleansing shall be unclean until evening. 22Whatever the unclean person touches shall be unclean, and anyone who touches it shall be unclean until evening.

The Waters of Meribah

20 The Israelites, the whole congregation, came into the wilderness of Zin in the first month, and the people stayed in Kadesh. Miriam died there, and was buried there.

2 Now there was no water for the congregation; so they gathered together against Moses and against Aaron. 3The people quarreled with Moses and said, "Would that we had died when our kindred died before the LORD! 4Why have you brought the assembly of the LORD into this wilderness for us and our livestock to die here? 5Why have you brought us up out of Egypt, to bring us to this wretched place? It is no place for grain, or figs, or vines, or pomegranates; and there is no

water to drink." 6Then Moses and Aaron went away from the assembly to the entrance of the tent of meeting; they fell on their faces, and the glory of the LORD appeared to them. 7The LORD spoke to Moses, saying: 8Take the staff, and assemble the congregation, you and your brother Aaron, and command the rock before their eyes to yield its water. Thus you shall bring water out of the rock for them; thus you shall provide drink for the congregation and their livestock.

9 So Moses took the staff from before the LORD, as he had commanded him. 10Moses and Aaron gathered the assembly together before the rock, and he said to them, "Listen, you rebels, shall we bring water for you out of this rock?" 11Then Moses lifted up his hand and struck the rock twice with his staff; water came out abundantly, and the congregation and their livestock drank. 12But the LORD said to Moses and Aaron, "Because you did not trust in me, to show my holiness before the eyes of the Israelites, therefore you shall not bring this assembly into the land that I have given them." 13These are the waters of Meribah,*b* where the people of Israel quarreled with the LORD, and by which he showed his holiness.

Passage through Edom Refused

14 Moses sent messengers from Kadesh to the king of Edom, "Thus says your brother Israel: You know all the adversity that has befallen us: 15how our ancestors went down to Egypt, and we lived in Egypt a long time; and the Egyptians oppressed us and our ancestors; 16and when we cried to the LORD, he heard our voice, and sent an angel and brought us out of Egypt; and here we are in Kadesh, a town on the edge of your territory. 17Now let us pass through your land. We will not pass through field or vineyard, or drink water from any well; we will go along the King's Highway, not turning aside to the right hand or to the left until we have passed through your territory."

18 But Edom said to him, "You shall not pass through, or we will come out with the sword against you." 19The Israelites said to him, "We will stay on the highway; and if we drink of your water, we and our livestock, then we will pay for it. It is only a small matter; just let us pass through on foot." 20But he said, "You shall not pass through." And Edom came out against them with a large force, heavily armed. 21Thus Edom refused to give Israel passage through their territory; so Israel turned away from them.

---

a Heb lacks *naturally*   *b* That is *Quarrel*

The Death of Aaron

22 They set out from Kadesh, and the Israelites, the whole congregation, came to Mount Hor. [23]Then the LORD said to Moses and Aaron at Mount Hor, on the border of the land of Edom, [24]"Let Aaron be gathered to his people. For he shall not enter the land that I have given to the Israelites, because you rebelled against my command at the waters of Meribah. [25]Take Aaron and his son Eleazar, and bring them up Mount Hor; [26]strip Aaron of his vestments, and put them on his son Eleazar. But Aaron shall be gathered to his people,[a] and shall die there." [27]Moses did as the LORD had commanded; they went up Mount Hor in the sight of the whole congregation. [28]Moses stripped Aaron of his vestments, and put them on his son Eleazar; and Aaron died there on the top of the mountain. Moses and Eleazar came down from the mountain. [29]When all the congregation saw that Aaron had died, all the house of Israel mourned for Aaron thirty days.

The Bronze Serpent

21 When the Canaanite, the king of Arad, who lived in the Negeb, heard that Israel was coming by the way of Atharim, he fought against Israel and took some of them captive. [2]Then Israel made a vow to the LORD and said, "If you will indeed give this people into our hands, then we will utterly destroy their towns." [3]The LORD listened to the voice of Israel, and handed over the Canaanites; and they utterly destroyed them and their towns; so the place was called Hormah.[b]

4 From Mount Hor they set out by the way to the Red Sea,[c] to go around the land of Edom; but the people became impatient on the way. [5]The people spoke against God and against Moses, "Why have you brought us up out of Egypt to die in the wilderness? For there is no food and no water, and we detest this miserable food." [6]Then the LORD sent poisonous[d] serpents among the people, and they bit the people, so that many Israelites died. [7]The people came to Moses and said, "We have sinned by speaking against the LORD and against you; pray to the LORD to take away the serpents from us." So Moses prayed for the people. [8]And the LORD said to Moses, "Make a poisonous[e] serpent, and set it on a pole; and everyone who is bitten shall look at it and live." [9]So Moses made a serpent of bronze, and put it upon a pole; and whenever a serpent bit someone, that person would look at the serpent of bronze and live.

The Journey to Moab

10 The Israelites set out, and camped in Oboth. [11]They set out from Oboth, and camped at Iye-abarim, in the wilderness bordering Moab toward the sunrise. [12]From there they set out, and camped in the Wadi Zered. [13]From there they set out, and camped on the other side of the Arnon, in[f] the wilderness that extends from the boundary of the Amorites; for the Arnon is the boundary of Moab, between Moab and the Amorites. [14]Wherefore it is said in the Book of the Wars of the LORD,

"Waheb in Suphah and the wadis.
The Arnon [15]and the slopes of the wadis
    that extend to the seat of Ar,
    and lie along the border of Moab."[g]

16 From there they continued to Beer;[h] that is the well of which the LORD said to Moses, "Gather the people together, and I will give them water." [17]Then Israel sang this song:

"Spring up, O well!—Sing to it!—
[18] the well that the leaders sank,
    that the nobles of the people dug,
    with the scepter, with the staff."
From the wilderness to Mattanah, [19]from Mattanah to Nahaliel, from Nahaliel to Bamoth, [20]and from Bamoth to the valley lying in the region of Moab by the top of Pisgah that overlooks the wasteland.[i]

King Sihon Defeated

21 Then Israel sent messengers to King Sihon of the Amorites, saying, [22]"Let me pass through your land; we will not turn aside into field or vineyard; we will not drink the water of any well; we will go by the King's Highway until we have passed through your territory." [23]But Sihon would not allow Israel to pass through his territory. Sihon gathered all his people together, and went out against Israel to the wilderness; he came to Jahaz, and fought against Israel. [24]Israel put him to the sword, and took possession of his land from the Arnon to the Jabbok, as far as to the Ammonites; for the boundary of the Ammonites was strong. [25]Israel took all these towns, and Israel settled in all the towns of the Amorites, in Heshbon, and in all its villages. [26]For Heshbon was the city of King Sihon of the Amorites, who had fought against the former king of Moab and captured all his land as far as the Arnon. [27]Therefore the ballad singers say,

---

a Heb lacks *to his people*   b Heb *Destruction*   c Or *Sea of Reeds*   d Or *fiery*; Heb *seraphim*   e Or *fiery*; Heb *seraph*   f Gk: Heb *which is in*   g Meaning of Heb uncertain   h That is *Well*   i Or *Jeshimon*

"Come to Heshbon, let it be built;
　let the city of Sihon be established.
28 For fire came out from Heshbon,
　flame from the city of Sihon.
It devoured Ar of Moab,
　and swallowed up[a] the heights of the Arnon.
29 Woe to you, O Moab!
　You are undone, O people of Chemosh!
He has made his sons fugitives,
　and his daughters captives,
　to an Amorite king, Sihon.
30 So their posterity perished
　from Heshbon[b] to Dibon,
　and we laid waste until fire spread to
　　Medeba."[c]

31 Thus Israel settled in the land of the Amorites. 32Moses sent to spy out Jazer; and they captured its villages, and dispossessed the Amorites who were there.

King Og Defeated

33 Then they turned and went up the road to Bashan; and King Og of Bashan came out against them, he and all his people, to battle at Edrei. 34But the LORD said to Moses, "Do not be afraid of him; for I have given him into your hand, with all his people, and all his land. You shall do to him as you did to King Sihon of the Amorites, who ruled in Heshbon." 35So they killed him, his sons, and all his people, until there was no survivor left; and they took possession of his land.

Balak Summons Balaam to Curse Israel

22 The Israelites set out, and camped in the plains of Moab across the Jordan from Jericho. 2Now Balak son of Zippor saw all that Israel had done to the Amorites. 3Moab was in great dread of the people, because they were so numerous; Moab was overcome with fear of the people of Israel. 4And Moab said to the elders of Midian, "This horde will now lick up all that is around us, as an ox licks up the grass of the field." Now Balak son of Zippor was king of Moab at that time. 5He sent messengers to Balaam son of Beor at Pethor, which is on the Euphrates, in the land of Amaw,[d] to summon him, saying, "A people has come out of Egypt; they have spread over the face of the earth, and they have settled next to me. 6Come now, curse this people for me, since they are stronger than I; perhaps I shall be able to defeat them and drive them from the land; for I know that whomever you bless is blessed, and whomever you curse is cursed."

7 So the elders of Moab and the elders of Midian departed with the fees for divination in their hand; and they came to Balaam, and gave him Balak's message. 8He said to them, "Stay here tonight, and I will bring back word to you, just as the LORD speaks to me"; so the officials of Moab stayed with Balaam. 9God came to Balaam and said, "Who are these men with you?" 10Balaam said to God, "King Balak son of Zippor of Moab, has sent me this message: 11'A people has come out of Egypt and has spread over the face of the earth; now come, curse them for me; perhaps I shall be able to fight against them and drive them out.' " 12God said to Balaam, "You shall not go with them; you shall not curse the people, for they are blessed." 13So Balaam rose in the morning, and said to the officials of Balak, "Go to your own land, for the LORD has refused to let me go with you." 14So the officials of Moab rose and went to Balak, and said, "Balaam refuses to come with us."

15 Once again Balak sent officials, more numerous and more distinguished than these. 16They came to Balaam and said to him, "Thus says Balak son of Zippor: 'Do not let anything hinder you from coming to me; 17for I will surely do you great honor, and whatever you say to me I will do; come, curse this people for me.' " 18But Balaam replied to the servants of Balak, "Although Balak were to give me his house full of silver and gold, I could not go beyond the command of the LORD my God, to do less or more. 19You remain here, as the others did, so that I may learn what more the LORD may say to me." 20That night God came to Balaam and said to him, "If the men have come to summon you, get up and go with them; but do only what I tell you to do." 21So Balaam got up in the morning, saddled his donkey, and went with the officials of Moab.

Balaam, the Donkey, and the Angel

22 God's anger was kindled because he was going, and the angel of the LORD took his stand in the road as his adversary. Now he was riding on the donkey, and his two servants were with him. 23The donkey saw the angel of the LORD standing in the road, with a drawn sword in his hand; so the donkey turned off the road, and went into the field; and Balaam struck the donkey, to turn it back onto the road. 24Then the angel of the LORD stood in a narrow path between the vineyards, with a wall on either side. 25When the donkey saw the angel of the LORD, it scraped against the wall, and scraped Balaam's

N U M

---

a Gk: Heb *and the lords of*　b Gk: Heb *we have shot at them; Heshbon has perished*　c Compare Sam Gk: Meaning of MT uncertain　d Or *land of his kinsfolk*

The Talking Donkey

Balaam is an interesting biblical character. He is not an Israelite and seems to be a sort of prophet for hire. Balak, the king of Moab, hires him to prophesy against Israel. But Balaam, hearing a message from God through his donkey, instead of cursing the Israelites, blesses them four times. Even though the Israelites were unfaithful, God continues to be with them, to bless them.

Balaam is a sign of the universal character of God's call, and the donkey is a symbol of the poor and oppressed. The complaining and whining donkey represents those who usually are not heard but are given a voice through the prophets.

This story gives us two insights into prayer. First, if God can use a donkey to talk to Balaam, God can use anything to talk to us. God speaks to us in many ways—through our experiences, the Scriptures, poetry and music, our relationship with nature, and more. Are we paying attention? Second, God wants us to hear the often unheard voice of those who are poor and oppressed. Do you hear God's voice expressed through them?

▶ **Num 22:22–35**

foot against the wall; so he struck it again. ²⁶Then the angel of the Lord went ahead, and stood in a narrow place, where there was no way to turn either to the right or to the left. ²⁷When the donkey saw the angel of the Lord, it lay down under Balaam; and Balaam's anger was kindled, and he struck the donkey with his staff. ²⁸Then the Lord opened the mouth of the donkey, and it said to Balaam, "What have I done to you, that you have struck me these three times?" ²⁹Balaam said to the donkey, "Because you have made a fool of me! I wish I had a sword in my hand! I would kill you right now!" ³⁰But the donkey said to Balaam, "Am I not your donkey, which you have ridden all your life to this day? Have I been in the habit of treating you this way?" And he said, "No."

31 Then the Lord opened the eyes of Balaam, and he saw the angel of the Lord standing in the road, with his drawn sword in his hand; and he bowed down, falling on his face. ³²The angel of the Lord said to him, "Why have you struck your donkey these three times? I have come out as an adversary, because your way is perverse[a] before me. ³³The donkey saw me, and turned away from me these three times. If it had not turned away from me, surely just now I would have killed you and let it live." ³⁴Then Balaam said to the angel of the Lord, "I have sinned, for I did not know that you were standing in the road to oppose me. Now therefore, if it is displeasing to you, I will return home." ³⁵The angel of the Lord said to Balaam, "Go with the men; but speak only what I tell you to speak." So Balaam went on with the officials of Balak.

36 When Balak heard that Balaam had come, he went out to meet him at Ir-moab, on the boundary formed by the Arnon, at the farthest point of the boundary. ³⁷Balak said to Balaam, "Did I not send to summon you? Why did you not come to me? Am I not able to honor you?" ³⁸Balaam said to Balak, "I have come to you now, but do I have power to say just anything? The word God puts in my mouth, that is what I must say." ³⁹Then Balaam went with Balak, and they came to Kiriath-huzoth. ⁴⁰Balak sacrificed oxen and sheep, and sent them to Balaam and to the officials who were with him.

Balaam's First Oracle

41 On the next day Balak took Balaam and brought him up to Bamoth-baal; and from there he could see part of the people of Israel.[b]

23 ¹Then Balaam said to Balak, "Build me seven altars here, and prepare seven bulls and seven rams for me." ²Balak did as Balaam had said; and Balak and Balaam offered a bull and a ram on each altar. ³Then Balaam said to Balak, "Stay here beside your burnt offerings while I go aside. Perhaps the Lord will come to meet me. Whatever he shows me I will tell you." And he went to a bare height.

4 Then God met Balaam; and Balaam said to him, "I have arranged the seven altars, and have offered a bull and a ram on each altar." ⁵The Lord put a word in Balaam's mouth, and said, "Return to Balak, and this is what you must say." ⁶So he returned to Balak,[c] who was standing beside his burnt offerings with all the officials of Moab. ⁷Then Balaam[d] uttered his oracle, saying:

---

a Meaning of Heb uncertain   b Heb lacks *of Israel*   c Heb *him*
d Heb *he*

NUM

"Balak has brought me from Aram,
  the king of Moab from the eastern mountains:
'Come, curse Jacob for me;
  Come, denounce Israel!'
[8] How can I curse whom God has not cursed?
  How can I denounce those whom the Lord
    has not denounced?
[9] For from the top of the crags I see him,
  from the hills I behold him.
Here is a people living alone,
  and not reckoning itself among the nations!
[10] Who can count the dust of Jacob,
  or number the dust-cloud[a] of Israel?
Let me die the death of the upright,
  and let my end be like his!"

[11] Then Balak said to Balaam, "What have you done to me? I brought you to curse my enemies, but now you have done nothing but bless them." [12] He answered, "Must I not take care to say what the Lord puts into my mouth?"

Balaam's Second Oracle

[13] So Balak said to him, "Come with me to another place from which you may see them; you shall see only part of them, and shall not see them all; then curse them for me from there." [14] So he took him to the field of Zophim, to the top of Pisgah. He built seven altars, and offered a bull and a ram on each altar. [15] Balaam said to Balak, "Stand here beside your burnt offerings, while I meet the Lord over there." [16] The Lord met Balaam, put a word into his mouth, and said, "Return to Balak, and this is what you shall say." [17] When he came to him, he was standing beside his burnt offerings with the officials of Moab. Balak said to him, "What has the Lord said?" [18] Then Balaam uttered his oracle, saying:

"Rise, Balak, and hear;
  listen to me, O son of Zippor:
[19] God is not a human being, that he should lie,
  or a mortal, that he should change his mind.
Has he promised, and will he not do it?
  Has he spoken, and will he not fulfill it?
[20] See, I received a command to bless;
  he has blessed, and I cannot revoke it.
[21] He has not beheld misfortune in Jacob,
  nor has he seen trouble in Israel.
The Lord their God is with them,
  acclaimed as a king among them.
[22] God, who brings them out of Egypt,
  is like the horns of a wild ox for them.
[23] Surely there is no enchantment against Jacob,
  no divination against Israel;
now it shall be said of Jacob and Israel,
  'See what God has done!'
[24] Look, a people rising up like a lioness,
  and rousing itself like a lion!
It does not lie down until it has eaten the prey
  and drunk the blood of the slain."

[25] Then Balak said to Balaam, "Do not curse them at all, and do not bless them at all." [26] But Balaam answered Balak, "Did I not tell you, 'Whatever the Lord says, that is what I must do'?"

[27] So Balak said to Balaam, "Come now, I will take you to another place; perhaps it will please God that you may curse them for me from there." [28] So Balak took Balaam to the top of Peor, which overlooks the wasteland.[b] [29] Balaam said to Balak, "Build me seven altars here, and prepare seven bulls and seven rams for me." [30] So Balak did as Balaam had said, and offered a bull and a ram on each altar.

Balaam's Third Oracle

24 Now Balaam saw that it pleased the Lord to bless Israel, so he did not go, as at other times, to look for omens, but set his face toward the wilderness. [2] Balaam looked up and saw Israel camping tribe by tribe. Then the spirit of God came upon him, [3] and he uttered his oracle, saying:

"The oracle of Balaam son of Beor,
  the oracle of the man whose eye is clear,[c]
[4] the oracle of one who hears the words of God,
  who sees the vision of the Almighty,[d]
  who falls down, but with eyes uncovered:
[5] how fair are your tents, O Jacob,
  your encampments, O Israel!
[6] Like palm groves that stretch far away,
  like gardens beside a river,
like aloes that the Lord has planted,
  like cedar trees beside the waters.
[7] Water shall flow from his buckets,
  and his seed shall have abundant water,
his king shall be higher than Agag,
  and his kingdom shall be exalted.
[8] God who brings him out of Egypt,
  is like the horns of a wild ox for him;
he shall devour the nations that are his foes
  and break their bones.
  He shall strike with his arrows.[e]
[9] He crouched, he lay down like a lion,
  and like a lioness; who will rouse him up?
Blessed is everyone who blesses you,
  and cursed is everyone who curses you."

[10] Then Balak's anger was kindled against Balaam, and he struck his hands together. Balak

NUM

---

a Or fourth part   b Or overlooks Jeshimon   c Or closed or open   d Traditional rendering of Heb Shaddai   e Meaning of Heb uncertain said to Balaam, "I summoned you to curse my enemies, but instead you have blessed them these three times. ¹¹Now be off with you! Go home! I said, 'I will reward you richly,' but the Lord has denied you any reward." ¹²And Balaam said to Balak, "Did I not tell your messengers whom you sent to me, ¹³'If Balak should give me his house full of silver and gold, I would not be able to go beyond the word of the Lord, to do either good or bad of my own will; what the Lord says, that is what I will say'? ¹⁴So now, I am going to my people; let me advise you what this people will do to your people in days to come."

Balaam's Fourth Oracle

15 So he uttered his oracle, saying:

"The oracle of Balaam son of Beor,
   the oracle of the man whose eye is clear,ᵃ
¹⁶ the oracle of one who hears the words of God,
   and knows the knowledge of the Most High,ᵇ
who sees the vision of the Almighty,ᶜ
   who falls down, but with his eyes uncovered:
¹⁷ I see him, but not now;
   I behold him, but not near—
a star shall come out of Jacob,
   and a scepter shall rise out of Israel;
it shall crush the borderlandsᵈ of Moab,
   and the territoryᵉ of all the Shethites.
¹⁸ Edom will become a possession,
   Seir a possession of its enemies,ᶠ
   while Israel does valiantly.
¹⁹ One out of Jacob shall rule,
   and destroy the survivors of Ir."

20 Then he looked on Amalek, and uttered his oracle, saying:

"First among the nations was Amalek,
   but its end is to perish forever."

21 Then he looked on the Kenite, and uttered his oracle, saying:

"Enduring is your dwelling place,
   and your nest is set in the rock;
²² yet Kain is destined for burning.
   How long shall Asshur take you away
      captive?"

23 Again he uttered his oracle, saying:

"Alas, who shall live when God does this?
²⁴   But ships shall come from Kittim
and shall afflict Asshur and Eber;
   and he also shall perish forever."

25 Then Balaam got up and went back to his place, and Balak also went his way.

Worship of Baal of Peor

25 While Israel was staying at Shittim, the people began to have sexual relations with the women of Moab. ²These invited the people to the sacrifices of their gods, and the people ate and bowed down to their gods. ³Thus Israel yoked itself to the Baal of Peor, and the Lord's anger was kindled against Israel. ⁴The Lord said to Moses, "Take all the chiefs of the people, and impale them in the sun before the Lord, in order that the fierce anger of the Lord may turn away from Israel." ⁵And Moses said to the judges of Israel, "Each of you shall kill any of your people who have yoked themselves to the Baal of Peor."

6 Just then one of the Israelites came and brought a Midianite woman into his family, in the sight of Moses and in the sight of the whole congregation of the Israelites, while they were weeping at the entrance of the tent of meeting. ⁷When Phinehas son of Eleazar, son of Aaron the priest, saw it, he got up and left the congregation. Taking a spear in his hand, ⁸he went after the Israelite man into the tent, and pierced the two of them, the Israelite and the woman, through the belly. So the plague was stopped among the people of Israel. ⁹Nevertheless those that died by the plague were twenty-four thousand.

10 The Lord spoke to Moses, saying: ¹¹"Phinehas son of Eleazar, son of Aaron the priest, has turned back my wrath from the Israelites by manifesting such zeal among them on my behalf that in my jealousy I did not consume the Israelites. ¹²Therefore say, 'I hereby grant him my covenant of peace. ¹³It shall be for him and for his descendants after him a covenant of perpetual priesthood, because he was zealous for his God, and made atonement for the Israelites.' "

14 The name of the slain Israelite man, who was killed with the Midianite woman, was Zimri son of Salu, head of an ancestral house belonging to the Simeonites. ¹⁵The name of the Midianite woman who was killed was Cozbi daughter of Zur, who was the head of a clan, an ancestral house in Midian.

16 The Lord said to Moses, ¹⁷"Harass the Midianites, and defeat them; ¹⁸for they have harassed you by the trickery with which they deceived you in the affair of Peor, and in the affair of Cozbi, the daughter of a leader of Midian, their sister; she was killed on the day of the plague that resulted from Peor."

A Census of the New Generation

26 After the plague the Lord said to Moses and to Eleazar son of Aaron the priest,

---

a Or *closed* or *open*   b Or *of Elyon*   c Traditional rendering of Heb *Shaddai*   d Or *forehead*   e Some Mss read *skull*
f Heb *Seir, its enemies, a possession*

2 "Take a census of the whole congregation of the Israelites, from twenty years old and upward, by their ancestral houses, everyone in Israel able to go to war." 3Moses and Eleazar the priest spoke with them in the plains of Moab by the Jordan opposite Jericho, saying, 4"Take a census of the people,ᵃ from twenty years old and upward," as the Lord commanded Moses.

The Israelites, who came out of the land of Egypt, were:

5 Reuben, the firstborn of Israel. The descendants of Reuben: of Hanoch, the clan of the Hanochites; of Pallu, the clan of the Palluites; 6of Hezron, the clan of the Hezronites; of Carmi, the clan of the Carmites. 7These are the clans of the Reubenites; the number of those enrolled was forty-three thousand seven hundred thirty. 8And the descendants of Pallu: Eliab. 9The descendants of Eliab: Nemuel, Dathan, and Abiram. These are the same Dathan and Abiram, chosen from the congregation, who rebelled against Moses and Aaron in the company of Korah, when they rebelled against the Lord, 10and the earth opened its mouth and swallowed them up along with Korah, when that company died, when the fire devoured two hundred fifty men; and they became a warning. 11Notwithstanding, the sons of Korah did not die.

12 The descendants of Simeon by their clans: of Nemuel, the clan of the Nemuelites; of Jamin, the clan of the Jaminites; of Jachin, the clan of the Jachinites; 13of Zerah, the clan of the Zerahites; of Shaul, the clan of the Shaulites.ᵇ 14These are the clans of the Simeonites, twenty-two thousand two hundred.

15 The children of Gad by their clans: of Zephon, the clan of the Zephonites; of Haggi, the clan of the Haggites; of Shuni, the clan of the Shunites; 16of Ozni, the clan of the Oznites; of Eri, the clan of the Erites; 17of Arod, the clan of the Arodites; of Areli, the clan of the Arelites. 18These are the clans of the Gadites: the number of those enrolled was forty thousand five hundred.

19 The sons of Judah: Er and Onan; Er and Onan died in the land of Canaan. 20The descendants of Judah by their clans were: of Shelah, the clan of the Shelanites; of Perez, the clan of the Perezites; of Zerah, the clan of the Zerahites. 21The descendants of Perez were: of Hezron, the clan of the Hezronites; of Hamul, the clan of the Hamulites. 22These are the clans of Judah: the number of those enrolled was seventy-six thousand five hundred.

23 The descendants of Issachar by their clans: of Tola, the clan of the Tolaites; of Puvah, the clan of the Punites; 24of Jashub, the clan of the Jashubites; of Shimron, the clan of the Shimronites. 25These are the clans of Issachar: sixty-four thousand three hundred enrolled.

26 The descendants of Zebulun by their clans: of Sered, the clan of the Seredites; of Elon, the clan of the Elonites; of Jahleel, the clan of the Jahleelites. 27These are the clans of the Zebulunites; the number of those enrolled was sixty thousand five hundred.

28 The sons of Joseph by their clans: Manasseh and Ephraim. 29The descendants of Manasseh: of Machir, the clan of the Machirites; and Machir was the father of Gilead; of Gilead, the clan of the Gileadites. 30These are the descendants of Gilead: of Iezer, the clan of the Iezerites; of Helek, the clan of the Helekites; 31and of Asriel, the clan of the Asrielites; and of Shechem, the clan of the Shechemites; 32and of Shemida, the clan of the Shemidaites; and of Hepher, the clan of the Hepherites. 33Now Zelophehad son of Hepher had no sons, but daughters: and the names of the daughters of Zelophehad were Mahlah, Noah, Hoglah, Milcah, and Tirzah. 34These are the clans of Manasseh; the number of those enrolled was fifty-two thousand seven hundred.

35 These are the descendants of Ephraim according to their clans: of Shuthelah, the clan of the Shuthelahites; of Becher, the clan of the Becherites; of Tahan, the clan of the Tahanites. 36And these are the descendants of Shuthelah: of Eran, the clan of the Eranites. 37These are the clans of the Ephraimites: the number of those enrolled was thirty-two thousand five hundred. These are the descendants of Joseph by their clans.

38 The descendants of Benjamin by their clans: of Bela, the clan of the Belaites; of Ashbel, the clan of the Ashbelites; of Ahiram, the clan of the Ahiramites; 39of Shephupham, the clan of the Shuphamites; of Hupham, the clan of the Huphamites. 40And the sons of Bela were Ard and Naaman: of Ard, the clan of the Ardites; of Naaman, the clan of the Naamites. 41These are the descendants of Benjamin by their clans; the number of those enrolled was forty-five thousand six hundred.

42 These are the descendants of Dan by their clans: of Shuham, the clan of the Shuhamites. These are the clans of Dan by their clans. 43All the clans of the Shuhamites: sixty-four thousand four hundred enrolled.

44 The descendants of Asher by their families: of Imnah, the clan of the Imnites; of Ishvi, the clan of the Ishvites; of Beriah, the clan of

a Heb lacks *take a census of the people*: Compare verse 2
b Or *Saul . . . Saulites*

the Beriites. ⁴⁵Of the descendants of Beriah: of Heber, the clan of the Heberites; of Malchiel, the clan of the Malchielites. ⁴⁶And the name of the daughter of Asher was Serah. ⁴⁷These are the clans of the Asherites: the number of those enrolled was fifty-three thousand four hundred.

48 The descendants of Naphtali by their clans: of Jahzeel, the clan of the Jahzeelites; of Guni, the clan of the Gunites; ⁴⁹of Jezer, the clan of the Jezerites; of Shillem, the clan of the Shillemites. ⁵⁰These are the Naphtalites*a* by their clans: the number of those enrolled was forty-five thousand four hundred.

51 This was the number of the Israelites enrolled: six hundred and one thousand seven hundred thirty.

52 The Lord spoke to Moses, saying: ⁵³To these the land shall be apportioned for inheritance according to the number of names. ⁵⁴To a large tribe you shall give a large inheritance, and to a small tribe you shall give a small inheritance; every tribe shall be given its inheritance according to its enrollment. ⁵⁵But the land shall be apportioned by lot; according to the names of their ancestral tribes they shall inherit. ⁵⁶Their inheritance shall be apportioned according to lot between the larger and the smaller.

57 This is the enrollment of the Levites by their clans: of Gershon, the clan of the Gershonites; of Kohath, the clan of the Kohathites; of Merari, the clan of the Merarites. ⁵⁸These are the clans of Levi: the clan of the Libnites, the clan of the Hebronites, the clan of the Mahlites, the clan of the Mushites, the clan of the Korahites. Now Kohath was the father of Amram. ⁵⁹The name of Amram's wife was Jochebed daughter of Levi, who was born to Levi in Egypt; and she bore to Amram: Aaron, Moses, and their sister Miriam. ⁶⁰To Aaron were born Nadab, Abihu, Eleazar, and Ithamar. ⁶¹But Nadab and Abihu died when they offered unholy fire before the Lord. ⁶²The number of those enrolled was twenty-three thousand, every male one month old and upward; for they were not enrolled among the Israelites because there was no allotment given to them among the Israelites.

63 These were those enrolled by Moses and Eleazar the priest, who enrolled the Israelites in the plains of Moab by the Jordan opposite Jericho. ⁶⁴Among these there was not one of those enrolled by Moses and Aaron the priest, who had enrolled the Israelites in the wilderness of Sinai. ⁶⁵For the Lord had said of them, "They shall die in the wilderness." Not one of them was left, except Caleb son of Jephunneh and Joshua son of Nun.

The Daughters of Zelophehad

27 Then the daughters of Zelophehad came forward. Zelophehad was son of Hepher son of Gilead son of Machir son of Manasseh son of Joseph, a member of the Manassite clans. The names of his daughters were: Mahlah, Noah, Hoglah, Milcah, and Tirzah. ²They stood before Moses, Eleazar the priest, the leaders, and all the congregation, at the entrance of the tent of meeting, and they said, ³"Our father died in the wilderness; he was not among the company of those who gathered themselves together against the Lord in the company of Korah, but died for his own sin; and he had no sons. ⁴Why should the name of our father be taken away from his clan because he had no son? Give to us a possession among our father's brothers."

5 Moses brought their case before the Lord. ⁶And the Lord spoke to Moses, saying: ⁷The daughters of Zelophehad are right in what they are saying; you shall indeed let them possess an inheritance among their father's brothers and pass the inheritance of their father on to them. ⁸You shall also say to the Israelites, "If a man dies, and has no son, then you shall pass his inheritance on to his daughter. ⁹If he has no daughter, then you shall give his inheritance to his brothers. ¹⁰If he has no brothers, then you shall give his inheritance to his father's brothers. ¹¹And if his father has no brothers, then you shall give his inheritance to the nearest kinsman of his clan, and he shall possess it. It shall be for the Israelites a statute and ordinance, as the Lord commanded Moses."

Joshua Appointed Moses' Successor

12 The Lord said to Moses, "Go up this mountain of the Abarim range, and see the land that I have given to the Israelites. ¹³When you have seen it, you also shall be gathered to your people, as your brother Aaron was, ¹⁴because you rebelled against my word in the wilderness of Zin when the congregation quarreled with me.*b* You did not show my holiness before their eyes at the waters." (These are the waters of Meribathkadesh in the wilderness of Zin.) ¹⁵Moses spoke to the Lord, saying, ¹⁶"Let the Lord, the God of the spirits of all flesh, appoint someone over the congregation ¹⁷who shall go out before them and come in before them, who shall lead them out and bring them in, so that the congregation of the Lord may not be like sheep without a shepherd." ¹⁸So the Lord said to Moses, "Take

---

a Heb *clans of Naphtali*   *b* Heb lacks *with me*

Joshua son of Nun, a man in whom is the spirit, and lay your hand upon him; ¹⁹have him stand before Eleazar the priest and all the congregation, and commission him in their sight. ²⁰You shall give him some of your authority, so that all the congregation of the Israelites may obey. ²¹But he shall stand before Eleazar the priest, who shall inquire for him by the decision of the Urim before the LORD; at his word they shall go out, and at his word they shall come in, both he and all the Israelites with him, the whole congregation." ²²So Moses did as the LORD commanded him. He took Joshua and had him stand before Eleazar the priest and the whole congregation; ²³he laid his hands on him and commissioned him—as the LORD had directed through Moses.

Daily Offerings

28 The LORD spoke to Moses, saying: ²Command the Israelites, and say to them: My offering, the food for my offerings by fire, my pleasing odor, you shall take care to offer to me at its appointed time. ³And you shall say to them, This is the offering by fire that you shall offer to the LORD: two male lambs a year old without blemish, daily, as a regular offering. ⁴One lamb you shall offer in the morning, and the other lamb you shall offer at twilight;ᵃ ⁵also one-tenth of an ephah of choice flour for a grain offering, mixed with one-fourth of a hin of beaten oil. ⁶It is a regular burnt offering, ordained at Mount Sinai for a pleasing odor, an offering by fire to the LORD. ⁷Its drink offering shall be one-fourth of a hin for each lamb; in the sanctuary you shall pour out a drink offering of strong drink to the LORD. ⁸The other lamb you shall offer at twilightᵃ with a grain offering and a drink offering like the one in the morning; you shall offer it as an offering by fire, a pleasing odor to the LORD.

Sabbath Offerings

9 On the sabbath day: two male lambs a year old without blemish, and two-tenths of an ephah of choice flour for a grain offering, mixed with oil, and its drink offering— ¹⁰this is the burnt offering for every sabbath, in addition to the regular burnt offering and its drink offering.

Monthly Offerings

11 At the beginnings of your months you shall offer a burnt offering to the LORD: two young bulls, one ram, seven male lambs a year old without blemish; ¹²also three-tenths of an ephah of choice flour for a grain offering, mixed with oil, for each bull; and two-tenths of choice flour for a grain offering, mixed with oil, for the one ram; ¹³and one-tenth of choice flour mixed with oil as a grain offering for every lamb—a burnt offering of pleasing odor, an offering by fire to the LORD. ¹⁴Their drink offerings shall be half a hin of wine for a bull, one-third of a hin for a ram, and one-fourth of a hin for a lamb. This is the burnt offering of every month throughout the months of the year. ¹⁵And there shall be one male goat for a sin offering to the LORD; it shall be offered in addition to the regular burnt offering and its drink offering.

Offerings at Passover

16 On the fourteenth day of the first month there shall be a passover offering to the LORD. ¹⁷And on the fifteenth day of this month is a festival; seven days shall unleavened bread be eaten. ¹⁸On the first day there shall be a holy convocation. You shall not work at your occupations. ¹⁹You shall offer an offering by fire, a burnt offering to the LORD: two young bulls, one ram, and seven male lambs a year old; see that they are without blemish. ²⁰Their grain offering shall be of choice flour mixed with oil: three-tenths of an ephah shall you offer for a bull, and two-tenths for a ram; ²¹one-tenth shall you offer for each of the seven lambs; ²²also one male goat for a sin offering, to make atonement for you. ²³You shall offer these in addition to the burnt offering of the morning, which belongs to the regular burnt offering. ²⁴In the same way you shall offer daily, for seven days, the food of an offering by fire, a pleasing odor to the LORD; it shall be offered in addition to the regular burnt offering and its drink offering. ²⁵And on the seventh day you shall have a holy convocation; you shall not work at your occupations.

Offerings at the Festival of Weeks

26 On the day of the first fruits, when you offer a grain offering of new grain to the LORD at your festival of weeks, you shall have a holy convocation; you shall not work at your occupations. ²⁷You shall offer a burnt offering, a pleasing odor to the LORD: two young bulls, one ram, seven male lambs a year old. ²⁸Their grain offering shall be of choice flour mixed with oil, three-tenths of an ephah for each bull, two-tenths for one ram, ²⁹one-tenth for each of the seven lambs; ³⁰with one male goat, to make atonement for you. ³¹In addition to the regular burnt offering with its grain offering, you shall offer them and their drink offering. They shall be without blemish.

---

a Heb *between the two evenings*

Offerings at the Festival of Trumpets

29 On the first day of the seventh month you shall have a holy convocation; you shall not work at your occupations. It is a day for you to blow the trumpets, ²and you shall offer a burnt offering, a pleasing odor to the LORD: one young bull, one ram, seven male lambs a year old without blemish. ³Their grain offering shall be of choice flour mixed with oil, three-tenths of one ephah for the bull, two-tenths for the ram, ⁴and one-tenth for each of the seven lambs; ⁵with one male goat for a sin offering, to make atonement for you. ⁶These are in addition to the burnt offering of the new moon and its grain offering, and the regular burnt offering and its grain offering, and their drink offerings, according to the ordinance for them, a pleasing odor, an offering by fire to the LORD.

Offerings on the Day of Atonement

7 On the tenth day of this seventh month you shall have a holy convocation, and deny yourselves;ᵃ you shall do no work. ⁸You shall offer a burnt offering to the LORD, a pleasing odor: one young bull, one ram, seven male lambs a year old. They shall be without blemish. ⁹Their grain offering shall be of choice flour mixed with oil,

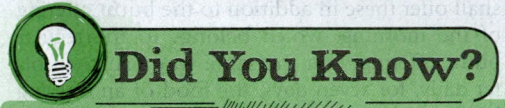

Did You Know?

Other Jewish Feasts

In chapter 29 of Numbers, we find the instructions for two more Jewish festivals. (For other Jewish festivals, see Ex 34:18–26.) The *feast of Trumpets* is a fall celebration prescribed for "the first day of the seventh month" (Num 29:1). This day of rest, marked by trumpet blasts and sacrifices, came to be called Rosh Hashanah (head of the year), the beginning of the Jewish New Year.

On the tenth day of the seventh month, the Israelites celebrated the Day of Atonement (Yom Kippur). On this solemn day of penance and fasting, the high priest laid the sins of the people on a so-called scapegoat (see Lev 16:20–21), then ran the beast into the wilderness, thus symbolically purifying the nation.

▶ **Num 29:1–11**

three-tenths of an ephah for the bull, two-tenths for the one ram, ¹⁰one-tenth for each of the seven lambs; ¹¹with one male goat for a sin offering, in addition to the sin offering of atonement, and the regular burnt offering and its grain offering, and their drink offerings.

Offerings at the Festival of Booths

12 On the fifteenth day of the seventh month you shall have a holy convocation; you shall not work at your occupations. You shall celebrate a festival to the LORD seven days. ¹³You shall offer a burnt offering, an offering by fire, a pleasing odor to the LORD: thirteen young bulls, two rams, fourteen male lambs a year old. They shall be without blemish. ¹⁴Their grain offering shall be of choice flour mixed with oil, three-tenths of an ephah for each of the thirteen bulls, two-tenths for each of the two rams, ¹⁵and one-tenth for each of the fourteen lambs; ¹⁶also one male goat for a sin offering, in addition to the regular burnt offering, its grain offering and its drink offering.

17 On the second day: twelve young bulls, two rams, fourteen male lambs a year old without blemish, ¹⁸with the grain offering and the drink offerings for the bulls, for the rams, and for the lambs, as prescribed in accordance with their number; ¹⁹also one male goat for a sin offering, in addition to the regular burnt offering and its grain offering, and their drink offerings.

20 On the third day: eleven bulls, two rams, fourteen male lambs a year old without blemish, ²¹with the grain offering and the drink offerings for the bulls, for the rams, and for the lambs, as prescribed in accordance with their number; ²²also one male goat for a sin offering, in addition to the regular burnt offering and its grain offering and its drink offering.

23 On the fourth day: ten bulls, two rams, fourteen male lambs a year old without blemish, ²⁴with the grain offering and the drink offerings for the bulls, for the rams, and for the lambs, as prescribed in accordance with their number; ²⁵also one male goat for a sin offering, in addition to the regular burnt offering, its grain offering and its drink offering.

26 On the fifth day: nine bulls, two rams, fourteen male lambs a year old without blemish, ²⁷with the grain offering and the drink offerings for the bulls, for the rams, and for the lambs, as prescribed in accordance with their number; ²⁸also one male goat for a sin offering, in addition to the regular burnt offering and its grain offering and its drink offering.

ᵃ Or *and fast*

29 On the sixth day: eight bulls, two rams, fourteen male lambs a year old without blemish, ³⁰with the grain offering and the drink offerings for the bulls, for the rams, and for the lambs, as prescribed in accordance with their number; ³¹also one male goat for a sin offering, in addition to the regular burnt offering, its grain offering, and its drink offerings.

32 On the seventh day: seven bulls, two rams, fourteen male lambs a year old without blemish, ³³with the grain offering and the drink offerings for the bulls, for the rams, and for the lambs, as prescribed in accordance with their number; ³⁴also one male goat for a sin offering, besides the regular burnt offering, its grain offering, and its drink offering.

35 On the eighth day you shall have a solemn assembly; you shall not work at your occupations. ³⁶You shall offer a burnt offering, an offering by fire, a pleasing odor to the Lord: one bull, one ram, seven male lambs a year old without blemish, ³⁷and the grain offering and the drink offerings for the bull, for the ram, and for the lambs, as prescribed in accordance with their number; ³⁸also one male goat for a sin offering, in addition to the regular burnt offering and its grain offering and its drink offering.

39 These you shall offer to the Lord at your appointed festivals, in addition to your votive offerings and your freewill offerings, as your burnt offerings, your grain offerings, your drink offerings, and your offerings of well-being.

40ᵃ So Moses told the Israelites everything just as the Lord had commanded Moses.

Vows Made by Women

30 Then Moses said to the heads of the tribes of the Israelites: This is what the Lord has commanded. ²When a man makes a vow to the Lord, or swears an oath to bind himself by a pledge, he shall not break his word; he shall do according to all that proceeds out of his mouth.

3 When a woman makes a vow to the Lord, or binds herself by a pledge, while within her father's house, in her youth, ⁴and her father hears of her vow or her pledge by which she has bound herself, and says nothing to her; then all her vows shall stand, and any pledge by which she has bound herself shall stand. ⁵But if her father expresses disapproval to her at the time that he hears of it, no vow of hers, and no pledge by which she has bound herself, shall stand; and the Lord will forgive her, because her father had expressed to her his disapproval.

6 If she marries, while obligated by her vows or any thoughtless utterance of her lips by which

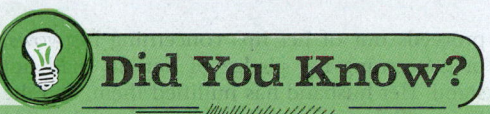

Did You Know?

Making a Vow

Vow. Such a simple word, really. Three letters. One syllable. But its simplicity masks its meaning. If a word's length were directly related to its significance, *vow* would have to become a long word indeed. It is a heavy word, one that we use sparingly. We tend to associate it with marriage or the life commitment of priests and religious sisters and brothers. Vows can be public or private, solemn or simple.

From a faith perspective, a person making a vow is making a deep, binding promise before God. A vow cannot really be captured on paper. A vow must be lived out. It must be internalized. It is the foundation for a life choice. We know, deep in our heart, that God is part of our vows.

The Israelites also took vows seriously. Numbers, chapter 30, is devoted to laws about vows. The laws were sexist by our standards. For example, a father or a husband could veto a woman's vows. Such laws were deemed acceptable in the Israelites' patriarchal society, but they are not in ours.

▶ **Num 30:2–5**

she has bound herself, ⁷and her husband hears of it and says nothing to her at the time that he hears, then her vows shall stand, and her pledges by which she has bound herself shall stand. ⁸But if, at the time that her husband hears of it, he expresses disapproval to her, then he shall nullify the vow by which she was obligated, or the thoughtless utterance of her lips, by which she bound herself; and the Lord will forgive her. ⁹(But every vow of a widow or of a divorced woman, by which she has bound herself, shall be binding upon her.) ¹⁰And if she made a vow in her husband's house, or bound herself by a pledge with an oath, ¹¹and her husband heard it and said nothing to her, and did not express disapproval to her, then all her vows shall stand, and any pledge by which she bound herself shall stand. ¹²But if her husband nullifies them at the time that he hears them, then whatever

a Ch 30.1 in Heb

N U M

proceeds out of her lips concerning her vows, or concerning her pledge of herself, shall not stand. Her husband has nullified them, and the LORD will forgive her. [13]Any vow or any binding oath to deny herself,[a] her husband may allow to stand, or her husband may nullify. [14]But if her husband says nothing to her from day to day,[b] then he validates all her vows, or all her pledges, by which she is obligated; he has validated them, because he said nothing to her at the time that he heard of them. [15]But if he nullifies them some time after he has heard of them, then he shall bear her guilt.

16 These are the statutes that the LORD commanded Moses concerning a husband and his wife, and a father and his daughter while she is still young and in her father's house.

War against Midian

31 The LORD spoke to Moses, saying, [2]"Avenge the Israelites on the Midianites; afterward you shall be gathered to your people." [3]So Moses said to the people, "Arm some of your number for the war, so that they may go against Midian, to execute the LORD's vengeance on Midian. [4]You shall send a thousand from each of the tribes of Israel to the war." [5]So out of the thousands of Israel, a thousand from each tribe were conscripted, twelve thousand armed for battle. [6]Moses sent them to the war, a thousand from each tribe, along with Phinehas son of Eleazar the priest,[c] with the vessels of the sanctuary and the trumpets for sounding the alarm in his hand. [7]They did battle against Midian, as the LORD had commanded Moses, and killed every male. [8]They killed the kings of Midian: Evi, Rekem, Zur, Hur, and Reba, the five kings of Midian, in addition to others who were slain by them; and they also killed Balaam son of Beor with the sword. [9]The Israelites took the women of Midian and their little ones captive; and they took all their cattle, their flocks, and all their goods as booty. [10]All their towns where they had settled, and all their encampments, they burned, [11]but they took all the spoil and all the booty, both people and animals. [12]Then they brought the captives and the booty and the spoil to Moses, to Eleazar the priest, and to the congregation of the Israelites, at the camp on the plains of Moab by the Jordan at Jericho.

Return from the War

13 Moses, Eleazar the priest, and all the leaders of the congregation went to meet them outside the camp. [14]Moses became angry with the officers of the army, the commanders of thousands and the commanders of hundreds, who had come from service in the war. [15]Moses said to them, "Have you allowed all the women to live? [16]These women here, on Balaam's advice, made the Israelites act treacherously against the LORD in the affair of Peor, so that the plague came among the congregation of the LORD. [17]Now therefore, kill every male among the little ones, and kill every woman who has known a man by sleeping with him. [18]But all the young girls who have not known a man by sleeping with him, keep alive for yourselves. [19]Camp outside the camp seven days; whoever of you has killed any person or touched a corpse, purify yourselves and your captives on the third and on the seventh day. [20]You shall purify every garment, every article of skin, everything made of goats' hair, and every article of wood."

21 Eleazar the priest said to the troops who had gone to battle: "This is the statute of the law that the LORD has commanded Moses: [22]gold, silver, bronze, iron, tin, and lead— [23]everything that can withstand fire, shall be passed through fire, and it shall be clean. Nevertheless it shall also be purified with the water for purification; and whatever cannot withstand fire, shall be passed through the water. [24]You must wash your clothes on the seventh day, and you shall be clean; afterward you may come into the camp."

Disposition of Captives and Booty

25 The LORD spoke to Moses, saying, [26]"You and Eleazar the priest and the heads of the ancestral houses of the congregation make an inventory of the booty captured, both human and animal. [27]Divide the booty into two parts, between the warriors who went out to battle and all the congregation. [28]From the share of the warriors who went out to battle, set aside as tribute for the LORD, one item out of every five hundred, whether persons, oxen, donkeys, sheep, or goats. [29]Take it from their half and give it to Eleazar the priest as an offering to the LORD. [30]But from the Israelites' half you shall take one out of every fifty, whether persons, oxen, donkeys, sheep, or goats—all the animals—and give them to the Levites who have charge of the tabernacle of the LORD."

31 Then Moses and Eleazar the priest did as the LORD had commanded Moses:

32 The booty remaining from the spoil that the troops had taken totaled six hundred seventy-five thousand sheep, [33]seventy-two thousand

a Or to fast   b Or from that day to the next   c Gk: Heb adds to the war oxen, [34]sixty-one thousand donkeys, [35]and thirty-two thousand persons in all, women who had not known a man by sleeping with him.

36 The half-share, the portion of those who had gone out to war, was in number three hundred thirty-seven thousand five hundred sheep and goats, [37]and the LORD's tribute of sheep and goats was six hundred seventy-five. [38]The oxen were thirty-six thousand, of which the LORD's tribute was seventy-two. [39]The donkeys were thirty thousand five hundred, of which the LORD's tribute was sixty-one. [40]The persons were sixteen thousand, of which the LORD's tribute was thirty-two persons. [41]Moses gave the tribute, the offering for the LORD, to Eleazar the priest, as the LORD had commanded Moses.

42 As for the Israelites' half, which Moses separated from that of the troops, [43]the congregation's half was three hundred thirty-seven thousand five hundred sheep and goats, [44]thirty-six thousand oxen, [45]thirty thousand five hundred donkeys, [46]and sixteen thousand persons. [47]From the Israelites' half Moses took one of every fifty, both of persons and of animals, and gave them to the Levites who had charge of the tabernacle of the LORD; as the LORD had commanded Moses.

48 Then the officers who were over the thousands of the army, the commanders of thousands and the commanders of hundreds, approached Moses, [49]and said to Moses, "Your servants have counted the warriors who are under our command, and not one of us is missing. [50]And we have brought the LORD's offering, what each of us found, articles of gold, armlets and bracelets, signet rings, earrings, and pendants, to make atonement for ourselves before the LORD." [51]Moses and Eleazar the priest received the gold from them, all in the form of crafted articles. [52]And all the gold of the offering that they offered to the LORD, from the commanders of thousands and the commanders of hundreds, was sixteen thousand seven hundred fifty shekels. [53](The troops had all taken plunder for themselves.) [54]So Moses and Eleazar the priest received the gold from the commanders of thousands and of hundreds, and brought it into the tent of meeting as a memorial for the Israelites before the LORD.

Conquest and Division of Transjordan

32 Now the Reubenites and the Gadites owned a very great number of cattle. When they saw that the land of Jazer and the land of Gilead was a good place for cattle, [2]the Gadites and the Reubenites came and spoke to Moses, to Eleazar the priest, and to the leaders of the congregation, saying, [3]"Ataroth, Dibon, Jazer, Nimrah, Heshbon, Elealeh, Sebam, Nebo, and Beon— [4]the land that the LORD subdued before the congregation of Israel—is a land for cattle; and your servants have cattle." [5]They continued, "If we have found favor in your sight, let this land be given to your servants for a possession; do not make us cross the Jordan."

6 But Moses said to the Gadites and to the Reubenites, "Shall your brothers go to war while you sit here? [7]Why will you discourage the hearts of the Israelites from going over into the land that the LORD has given them? [8]Your fathers did this, when I sent them from Kadesh-barnea to see the land. [9]When they went up to the Wadi Eshcol and saw the land, they discouraged the hearts of the Israelites from going into the land that the LORD had given them. [10]The LORD's anger was kindled on that day and he swore, saying, [11]'Surely none of the people who came up out of Egypt, from twenty years old and upward, shall see the land that I swore to give to Abraham, to Isaac, and to Jacob, because they have not unreservedly followed me— [12]none except Caleb son of Jephunneh the Kenizzite and Joshua son of Nun, for they have unreservedly followed the LORD.' [13]And the LORD's anger was kindled against Israel, and he made them wander in the wilderness for forty years, until all the generation that had done evil in the sight of the LORD had disappeared. [14]And now you, a brood of sinners, have risen in place of your fathers, to increase the LORD's fierce anger against Israel! [15]If you turn away from following him, he will again abandon them in the wilderness; and you will destroy all this people."

16 Then they came up to him and said, "We will build sheepfolds here for our flocks, and towns for our little ones, [17]but we will take up arms as a vanguard[a] before the Israelites, until we have brought them to their place. Meanwhile our little ones will stay in the fortified towns because of the inhabitants of the land. [18]We will not return to our homes until all the Israelites have obtained their inheritance. [19]We will not inherit with them on the other side of the Jordan and beyond, because our inheritance has come to us on this side of the Jordan to the east."

20 So Moses said to them, "If you do this—if you take up arms to go before the LORD for the war, [21]and all those of you who bear arms cross the Jordan before the LORD, until he has driven out his enemies from before him [22]and the land is subdued before the LORD—then after that you may return and be free of obligation to the LORD

---

a Cn: Heb *hurrying*

and to Israel, and this land shall be your possession before the LORD. 23But if you do not do this, you have sinned against the LORD; and be sure your sin will find you out. 24Build towns for your little ones, and folds for your flocks; but do what you have promised."

25 Then the Gadites and the Reubenites said to Moses, "Your servants will do as my lord commands. 26Our little ones, our wives, our flocks, and all our livestock shall remain there in the towns of Gilead; 27but your servants will cross over, everyone armed for war, to do battle for the LORD, just as my lord orders."

28 So Moses gave command concerning them to Eleazar the priest, to Joshua son of Nun, and to the heads of the ancestral houses of the Israelite tribes. 29And Moses said to them, "If the Gadites and the Reubenites, everyone armed for battle before the LORD, will cross over the Jordan with you and the land shall be subdued before you, then you shall give them the land of Gilead for a possession; 30but if they will not cross over with you armed, they shall have possessions among you in the land of Canaan." 31The Gadites and the Reubenites answered, "As the LORD has spoken to your servants, so we will do. 32We will cross over armed before the LORD into the land of Canaan, but the possession of our inheritance shall remain with us on this side ofa the Jordan."

33 Moses gave to them—to the Gadites and to the Reubenites and to the half-tribe of Manasseh son of Joseph—the kingdom of King Sihon of the Amorites and the kingdom of King Og of Bashan, the land and its towns, with the territories of the surrounding towns. 34And the Gadites rebuilt Dibon, Ataroth, Aroer, 35Atroth-shophan, Jazer, Jogbehah, 36Beth-nimrah, and Beth-haran, fortified cities, and folds for sheep. 37And the Reubenites rebuilt Heshbon, Elealeh, Kiriathaim, 38Nebo, and Baal-meon (some names being changed), and Sibmah; and they gave names to the towns that they rebuilt. 39The descendants of Machir son of Manasseh went to Gilead, captured it, and dispossessed the Amorites who were there; 40so Moses gave Gilead to Machir son of Manasseh, and he settled there. 41Jair son of Manasseh went and captured their villages, and renamed them Havvoth-jair,b 42And Nobah went and captured Kenath and its villages, and renamed it Nobah after himself.

The Stages of Israel's Journey from Egypt

33 These are the stages by which the Israelites went out of the land of Egypt in military formation under the leadership of Moses and Aaron. 2Moses wrote down their starting points, stage by stage, by command of the LORD; and these are their stages according to their starting places. 3They set out from Rameses in the first month, on the fifteenth day of the first month; on the day after the passover the Israelites went out boldly in the sight of all the Egyptians, 4while the Egyptians were burying all their firstborn, whom the LORD had struck down among them. The LORD executed judgments even against their gods.

5 So the Israelites set out from Rameses, and camped at Succoth. 6They set out from Succoth, and camped at Etham, which is on the edge of the wilderness. 7They set out from Etham, and turned back to Pi-hahiroth, which faces Baal-zephon; and they camped before Migdol. 8They set out from Pi-hahiroth, passed through the sea into the wilderness, went a three days' journey in the wilderness of Etham, and camped at Marah. 9They set out from Marah and came to Elim; at Elim there were twelve springs of water and seventy palm trees, and they camped there. 10They set out from Elim and camped by the Red Sea.c 11They set out from the Red Seac and camped in the wilderness of Sin. 12They set out from the wilderness of Sin and camped at Dophkah. 13They set out from Dophkah and camped at Alush. 14They set out from Alush and camped at Rephidim, where there was no water for the people to drink. 15They set out from Rephidim and camped in the wilderness of Sinai. 16They set out from the wilderness of Sinai and camped at Kibroth-hattaavah. 17They set out from Kibroth-hattaavah and camped at Hazeroth. 18They set out from Hazeroth and camped at Rithmah. 19They set out from Rithmah and camped at Rimmon-perez. 20They set out from Rimmon-perez and camped at Libnah. 21They set out from Libnah and camped at Rissah. 22They set out from Rissah and camped at Kehelathah. 23They set out from Kehelathah and camped at Mount Shepher. 24They set out from Mount Shepher and camped at Haradah. 25They set out from Haradah and camped at Makheloth. 26They set out from Makheloth and camped at Tahath. 27They set out from Tahath and camped at Terah. 28They set out from Terah and camped at Mithkah. 29They set out from Mithkah and camped at Hashmonah. 30They set out from Hashmonah and camped at Moseroth. 31They set out from Moseroth and camped at Bene-jaakan. 32They set out from Bene-jaakan and camped at Hor-haggidgad. 33They set out from Hor-haggidgad and camped at Jotbathah. 34They set out from Jotbathah and camped at Abronah. 35They set

a Heb beyond　b That is the villages of Jair　c Or Sea of Reeds out from Abronah and camped at Ezion-geber. [36]They set out from Ezion-geber and camped in the wilderness of Zin (that is, Kadesh). [37]They set out from Kadesh and camped at Mount Hor, on the edge of the land of Edom.

38 Aaron the priest went up Mount Hor at the command of the Lord and died there in the fortieth year after the Israelites had come out of the land of Egypt, on the first day of the fifth month. [39]Aaron was one hundred twenty-three years old when he died on Mount Hor.

40 The Canaanite, the king of Arad, who lived in the Negeb in the land of Canaan, heard of the coming of the Israelites.

41 They set out from Mount Hor and camped at Zalmonah. [42]They set out from Zalmonah and camped at Punon. [43]They set out from Punon and camped at Oboth. [44]They set out from Oboth and camped at Iye-abarim, in the territory of Moab. [45]They set out from Iyim and camped at Dibon-gad. [46]They set out from Dibon-gad and camped at Almon-diblathaim. [47]They set out from Almon-diblathaim and camped in the mountains of Abarim, before Nebo. [48]They set out from the mountains of Abarim and camped in the plains of Moab by the Jordan at Jericho; [49]they camped by the Jordan from Beth-jeshimoth as far as Abel-shittim in the plains of Moab.

Directions for the Conquest of Canaan

50 In the plains of Moab by the Jordan at Jericho, the Lord spoke to Moses, saying: [51]Speak to the Israelites, and say to them: When you cross over the Jordan into the land of Canaan, [52]you shall drive out all the inhabitants of the land from before you, destroy all their figured stones, destroy all their cast images, and demolish all their high places. [53]You shall take possession of the land and settle in it, for I have given you the land to possess. [54]You shall apportion the land by lot according to your clans; to a large one you shall give a large inheritance, and to a small one you shall give a small inheritance; the inheritance shall belong to the person on whom the lot falls; according to your ancestral tribes you shall inherit. [55]But if you do not drive out the inhabitants of the land from before you, then those whom you let remain shall be as barbs in your eyes and thorns in your sides; they shall trouble you in the land where you are settling. [56]And I will do to you as I thought to do to them.

The Boundaries of the Land

34 The Lord spoke to Moses, saying: [2]Command the Israelites, and say to them: When you enter the land of Canaan (this is the land that shall fall to you for an inheritance, the land of Canaan, defined by its boundaries), [3]your south sector shall extend from the wilderness of Zin along the side of Edom. Your southern boundary shall begin from the end of the Dead Sea[a] on the east; [4]your boundary shall turn south of the ascent of Akrabbim, and cross to Zin, and its outer limit shall be south of Kadesh-barnea; then it shall go on to Hazar-addar, and cross to Azmon; [5]the boundary shall turn from Azmon to the Wadi of Egypt, and its termination shall be at the Sea.

6 For the western boundary, you shall have the Great Sea and its[b] coast; this shall be your western boundary.

7 This shall be your northern boundary: from the Great Sea you shall mark out your line to Mount Hor; [8]from Mount Hor you shall mark it out to Lebo-hamath, and the outer limit of the boundary shall be at Zedad; [9]then the boundary shall extend to Ziphron, and its end shall be at Hazar-enan; this shall be your northern boundary.

10 You shall mark out your eastern boundary from Hazar-enan to Shepham; [11]and the boundary shall continue down from Shepham to Riblah on the east side of Ain; and the boundary shall go down, and reach the eastern slope of the sea of Chinnereth; [12]and the boundary shall go down to the Jordan, and its end shall be at the Dead Sea.[a] This shall be your land with its boundaries all around.

13 Moses commanded the Israelites, saying: This is the land that you shall inherit by lot, which the Lord has commanded to give to the nine tribes and to the half-tribe; [14]for the tribe of the Reubenites by their ancestral houses and the tribe of the Gadites by their ancestral houses have taken their inheritance, and also the half-tribe of Manasseh; [15]the two tribes and the half-tribe have taken their inheritance beyond the Jordan at Jericho eastward, toward the sunrise.

Tribal Leaders

16 The Lord spoke to Moses, saying: [17]These are the names of the men who shall apportion the land to you for inheritance: the priest Eleazar and Joshua son of Nun. [18]You shall take one leader of every tribe to apportion the land for inheritance. [19]These are the names of the men: Of the tribe of Judah, Caleb son of Jephunneh. [20]Of the tribe of the Simeonites, Shemuel son of Ammihud. [21]Of the tribe of Benjamin, Elidad son of Chislon. [22]Of the tribe of the Danites a

---

a Heb *Salt Sea*   b Syr: Heb lacks *its*

leader, Bukki son of Jogli. ²³Of the Josephites: of the tribe of the Manassites a leader, Hanniel son of Ephod, ²⁴and of the tribe of the Ephraimites a leader, Kemuel son of Shiphtan. ²⁵Of the tribe of the Zebulunites a leader, Eli-zaphan son of Parnach. ²⁶Of the tribe of the Issacharites a leader, Paltiel son of Azzan. ²⁷And of the tribe of the Asherites a leader, Ahihud son of Shelomi. ²⁸Of the tribe of the Naphtalites a leader, Pedahel son of Ammihud. ²⁹These were the ones whom the LORD commanded to apportion the inheritance for the Israelites in the land of Canaan.

Cities for the Levites

35 In the plains of Moab by the Jordan at Jericho, the LORD spoke to Moses, saying: ²Command the Israelites to give, from the inheritance that they possess, towns for the Levites to live in; you shall also give to the Levites pasture lands surrounding the towns. ³The towns shall be theirs to live in, and their pasture lands shall be for their cattle, for their livestock, and for all their animals. ⁴The pasture lands of the towns, which you shall give to the Levites, shall reach from the wall of the town outward a thousand cubits all around. ⁵You shall measure, outside the town, for the east side two thousand cubits, for the south side two thousand cubits, for the west side two thousand cubits, and for the north side two thousand cubits, with the town in the middle; this shall belong to them as pasture land for their towns.

6 The towns that you give to the Levites shall include the six cities of refuge, where you shall permit a slayer to flee, and in addition to them you shall give forty-two towns. ⁷The towns that you give to the Levites shall total forty-eight, with their pasture lands. ⁸And as for the towns that you shall give from the possession of the Israelites, from the larger tribes you shall take many, and from the smaller tribes you shall take few; each, in proportion to the inheritance that it obtains, shall give of its towns to the Levites.

Cities of Refuge

9 The LORD spoke to Moses, saying: ¹⁰Speak to the Israelites, and say to them: When you cross the Jordan into the land of Canaan, ¹¹then you shall select cities to be cities of refuge for you, so that a slayer who kills a person without intent may flee there. ¹²The cities shall be for you a refuge from the avenger, so that the slayer may not die until there is a trial before the congregation.

13 The cities that you designate shall be six cities of refuge for you: ¹⁴you shall designate three cities beyond the Jordan, and three cities in the land of Canaan, to be cities of refuge. ¹⁵These six cities shall serve as refuge for the Israelites, for the resident or transient alien among them, so that anyone who kills a person without intent may flee there.

Concerning Murder and Blood Revenge

16 But anyone who strikes another with an iron object, and death ensues, is a murderer; the murderer shall be put to death. ¹⁷Or anyone who strikes another with a stone in hand that could cause death, and death ensues, is a murderer; the murderer shall be put to death. ¹⁸Or anyone who strikes another with a weapon of wood in hand that could cause death, and death ensues, is a murderer; the murderer shall be put to death. ¹⁹The avenger of blood is the one who shall put the murderer to death; when they meet, the avenger of blood shall execute the sentence. ²⁰Likewise, if someone pushes another from hatred, or hurls something at another, lying in wait, and death ensues, ²¹or in enmity strikes another with the hand, and death ensues, then the one who struck the blow shall be put to death; that person is a murderer; the avenger of blood shall put the murderer to death, when they meet.

22 But if someone pushes another suddenly without enmity, or hurls any object without lying in wait, ²³or, while handling any stone that could cause death, unintentionally*ᵃ* drops it on another and death ensues, though they were not enemies, and no harm was intended, ²⁴then the congregation shall judge between the slayer and the avenger of blood, in accordance with these ordinances; ²⁵and the congregation shall rescue the slayer from the avenger of blood. Then the congregation shall send the slayer back to the original city of refuge. The slayer shall live in it until the death of the high priest who was anointed with the holy oil. ²⁶But if the slayer shall at any time go outside the bounds of the original city of refuge, ²⁷and is found by the avenger of blood outside the bounds of the city of refuge, and is killed by the avenger, no bloodguilt shall be incurred. ²⁸For the slayer must remain in the city of refuge until the death of the high priest; but after the death of the high priest the slayer may return home.

29 These things shall be a statute and ordinance for you throughout your generations wherever you live.

30 If anyone kills another, the murderer shall be put to death on the evidence of witnesses; but no one shall be put to death on the testimony of

_____

a Heb *without seeing*

a single witness. [31]Moreover you shall accept no ransom for the life of a murderer who is subject to the death penalty; a murderer must be put to death. [32]Nor shall you accept ransom for one who has fled to a city of refuge, enabling the fugitive to return to live in the land before the death of the high priest. [33]You shall not pollute the land in which you live; for blood pollutes the land, and no expiation can be made for the land, for the blood that is shed in it, except by the blood of the one who shed it. [34]You shall not defile the land in which you live, in which I also dwell; for I the LORD dwell among the Israelites.

Marriage of Female Heirs

36 The heads of the ancestral houses of the clans of the descendants of Gilead son of Machir son of Manasseh, of the Josephite clans, came forward and spoke in the presence of Moses and the leaders, the heads of the ancestral houses of the Israelites; [2]they said, "The LORD commanded my lord to give the land for inheritance by lot to the Israelites; and my lord was commanded by the LORD to give the inheritance of our brother Zelophehad to his daughters. [3]But if they are married into another Israelite tribe, then their inheritance will be taken from the inheritance of our ancestors and added to the inheritance of the tribe into which they marry; so it will be taken away from the allotted portion of our inheritance. [4]And when the jubilee of the Israelites comes, then their inheritance will be added to the inheritance of the tribe into which they have married; and their inheritance will be taken from the inheritance of our ancestral tribe."

5 Then Moses commanded the Israelites according to the word of the LORD, saying, "The descendants of the tribe of Joseph are right in what they are saying. [6]This is what the LORD commands concerning the daughters of Zelophehad, 'Let them marry whom they think best; only it must be into a clan of their father's tribe that they are married, [7]so that no inheritance of the Israelites shall be transferred from one tribe to another; for all Israelites shall retain the inheritance of their ancestral tribes. [8]Every daughter who possesses an inheritance in any tribe of the Israelites shall marry one from the clan of her father's tribe, so that all Israelites may continue to possess their ancestral inheritance. [9]No inheritance shall be transferred from one tribe to another; for each of the tribes of the Israelites shall retain its own inheritance.' "

10 The daughters of Zelophehad did as the LORD had commanded Moses. [11]Mahlah, Tirzah, Hoglah, Milcah, and Noah, the daughters of Zelophehad, married sons of their father's brothers. [12]They were married into the clans of the descendants of Manasseh son of Joseph, and their inheritance remained in the tribe of their father's clan.

13 These are the commandments and the ordinances that the LORD commanded through Moses to the Israelites in the plains of Moab by the Jordan at Jericho.

N
U
M

Imagine this touching scene: You are standing at the bedside of your aging grandparent with all your cousins and family members. Your grandfather or grandmother begins to speak, sharing stories about the lessons he or she has learned from life. You listen to the familiar stories as if for the first time, and you are awed by the wisdom and love they contain. This is the scene Deuteronomy sets up—Moses is like the wise, aging grandparent, sharing his instructions and encouragement before dying.

At a Glance

- **1:1—4:43. Moses reviews Israel's history.**
- **4:44—11:32. Moses proclaims obedience to the Torah.**
- **Chapters 12–26. Moses adapts the Covenant for settlement in the Land.**
- **Chapters 27–34. Moses gives a farewell address and dies.**

Quick Facts

Period Covered: just before the Israelites enter the Promised Land

Inspired Authors: scribes from the eighth century BC adapting the earlier Covenant Law to Israel's changing situation

Theme: the importance of the Covenant, the total commitment required by God's law

The Book of Deuteronomy

In Depth

The word *Deuteronomy* means "second law" in Greek. The first Law given on Mount Sinai was proposed by God to guide Israel in its wilderness journey. Written at a time when Israel was settled in the Promised Land and in need of religious reformation, Deuteronomy is a "second Law," adapted to the new situation of a people that needs to be reminded of its Covenant with God.

Deuteronomy has four divisions:

In the first section (1:1—4:43), Moses addresses Israel by reviewing its history since Mount Horeb (Deuteronomy's term for Mount Sinai). Moses calls Israel to faithfulness and loyalty.

In the second section (4:44—11:32), Moses reviews the Ten Commandments and the essence of the Law. He reminds the Israelites of the rewards for obeying and the consequences of disobeying the Law.

In the third section (chapters 12–26), the most important section of Deuteronomy, Moses spells out a law to shape and govern the Israelites' new life as they settle in the Land.

Finally, in the fourth section (chapters 27–34), Moses gives his last will and testament, offers a final blessing, and dies. His death is portrayed as the "sealing" of the second Law.

More than anything else, Deuteronomy stresses Israel as one people, with one God, one sanctuary, and now one Land. These elements not only make Israel a unique people but also bind it together in unity and solidarity. The Land of Promise now becomes a symbol of God's blessing and favor, the fulfillment of God's promises in the Covenant.

Deuteronomy

Events at Horeb Recalled

1 These are the words that Moses spoke to all Israel beyond the Jordan—in the wilderness, on the plain opposite Suph, between Paran and Tophel, Laban, Hazeroth, and Di-zahab. ²(By the way of Mount Seir it takes eleven days to reach Kadesh-barnea from Horeb.) ³In the fortieth year, on the first day of the eleventh month, Moses spoke to the Israelites just as the Lord had commanded him to speak to them. ⁴This was after he had defeated King Sihon of the Amorites, who reigned in Heshbon, and King Og of Bashan, who reigned in Ashtaroth and*ᵃ* in Edrei. ⁵Beyond the Jordan in the land of Moab, Moses undertook to expound this law as follows:

6 The Lord our God spoke to us at Horeb, saying, "You have stayed long enough at this mountain. ⁷Resume your journey, and go into the hill country of the Amorites as well as into the neighboring regions—the Arabah, the hill country, the Shephelah, the Negeb, and the seacoast—the land of the Canaanites and the Lebanon, as far as the great river, the river Euphrates. ⁸See, I have set the land before you; go in and take possession of the land that I*ᵇ* swore to your ancestors, to Abraham, to Isaac, and to Jacob, to give to them and to their descendants after them."

Appointment of Tribal Leaders

9 At that time I said to you, "I am unable by myself to bear you. ¹⁰The Lord your God has multiplied you, so that today you are as numerous as the stars of heaven. ¹¹May the Lord, the God of your ancestors, increase you a thousand times more and bless you, as he has promised you! ¹²But how can I bear the heavy burden of your disputes all by myself? ¹³Choose for each of your tribes individuals who are wise, discerning, and reputable to be your leaders." ¹⁴You answered me, "The plan you have proposed is a good one." ¹⁵So I took the leaders of your tribes, wise and reputable individuals, and installed them as leaders over you, commanders of thousands, commanders of hundreds, commanders of fifties, commanders of tens, and officials, throughout your tribes. ¹⁶I charged your judges at that time: "Give the members of your community a fair hearing, and judge rightly between one person and another, whether citizen or resident alien. ¹⁷You must not be partial in judging: hear out the small and the great alike; you shall not be intimidated by anyone, for the judgment is God's. Any case that is too hard for you, bring to me, and I will hear it." ¹⁸So I charged you at that time with all the things that you should do.

Israel's Refusal to Enter the Land

19 Then, just as the Lord our God had ordered us, we set out from Horeb and went through all that great and terrible wilderness that you saw, on the way to the hill country of the Amorites, until we reached Kadesh-barnea. ²⁰I said to you, "You

a Gk Syr Vg Compare Josh 12.4: Heb lacks and   b Sam Gk: MT the Lord

177

have reached the hill country of the Amorites, which the Lord our God is giving us. ²¹See, the Lord your God has given the land to you; go up, take possession, as the Lord, the God of your ancestors, has promised you; do not fear or be dismayed."

22 All of you came to me and said, "Let us send men ahead of us to explore the land for us and bring back a report to us regarding the route by which we should go up and the cities we will come to." ²³The plan seemed good to me, and I selected twelve of you, one from each tribe. ²⁴They set out and went up into the hill country, and when they reached the Valley of Eshcol they spied it out ²⁵and gathered some of the land's produce, which they brought down to us. They brought back a report to us, and said, "It is a good land that the Lord our God is giving us."

26 But you were unwilling to go up. You rebelled against the command of the Lord your God; ²⁷you grumbled in your tents and said, "It is because the Lord hates us that he has brought us out of the land of Egypt, to hand us over to the Amorites to destroy us. ²⁸Where are we headed? Our kindred have made our hearts melt by reporting, 'The people are stronger and taller than we; the cities are large and fortified up to heaven! We actually saw there the offspring of the Anakim!' " ²⁹I said to you, "Have no dread or fear of them. ³⁰The Lord your God, who goes before you, is the one who will fight for you, just as he did for you in Egypt before your very eyes, ³¹and in the wilderness, where you saw how the Lord your God carried you, just as one carries a child, all the way that you traveled until you reached this place. ³²But in spite of this, you have no trust in the Lord your God, ³³who goes before you on the way to seek out a place for you to camp, in fire by night, and in the cloud by day, to show you the route you should take."

The Penalty for Israel's Rebellion

34 When the Lord heard your words, he was wrathful and swore: ³⁵"Not one of these—not one of this evil generation—shall see the good land that I swore to give to your ancestors, ³⁶except Caleb son of Jephunneh. He shall see it, and to him and to his descendants I will give the land on which he set foot, because of his complete fidelity to the Lord." ³⁷Even with me the Lord was angry on your account, saying, "You also shall not enter there. ³⁸Joshua son of Nun, your assistant, shall enter there; encourage him, for he is the one who will secure Israel's possession of it. ³⁹And as for your little ones, who you thought would become booty, your children, who today

do not yet know right from wrong, they shall enter there; to them I will give it, and they shall take possession of it. ⁴⁰But as for you, journey back into the wilderness, in the direction of the Red Sea."ᵃ

41 You answered me, "We have sinned against the Lord! We are ready to go up and fight, just as the Lord our God commanded us." So all of you strapped on your battle gear, and thought it easy to go up into the hill country. ⁴²The Lord said to me, "Say to them, 'Do not go up and do not fight, for I am not in the midst of you; otherwise you will be defeated by your enemies.' " ⁴³Although I told you, you would not listen. You rebelled against the command of the Lord and presumptuously went up into the hill country. ⁴⁴The Amorites who lived in that hill country then came out against you and chased you as bees do. They beat you down in Seir as far as Hormah. ⁴⁵When you returned and wept before the Lord, the Lord would neither heed your voice nor pay you any attention.

The Desert Years

46 After you had stayed at Kadesh as many days as you did, ¹we journeyed back into the wilderness, in the direction of the Red Sea,ᵃ as the Lord had told me and skirted Mount Seir for many days. ²Then the Lord said to me: ³"You have been skirting this hill country long enough. Head north, ⁴and charge the people as follows: You are about to pass through the territory of your kindred, the descendants of Esau, who live in Seir. They will be afraid of you, so, be very careful ⁵not to engage in battle with them, for I will not give you even so much as a foot's length of their land, since I have given Mount Seir to Esau as a possession. ⁶You shall purchase food from them for money, so that you may eat; and you shall also buy water from them for money, so that you may drink. ⁷Surely the Lord your God has blessed you in all your undertakings; he knows your going through this great wilderness. These forty years the Lord your God has been with you; you have lacked nothing." ⁸So we passed by our kin, the descendants of Esau who live in Seir, leaving behind the route of the Arabah, and leaving behind Elath and Ezion-geber.

When we had headed out along the route of the wilderness of Moab, ⁹the Lord said to me: "Do not harass Moab or engage them in battle, for I will not give you any of its land as a possession, since I have given Ar as a possession to the descendants of Lot." ¹⁰(The Emim—a large

---

a Or Sea of Reeds

and numerous people, as tall as the Anakim—had formerly inhabited it. [11]Like the Anakim, they are usually reckoned as Rephaim, though the Moabites call them Emim. [12]Moreover, the Horim had formerly inhabited Seir, but the descendants of Esau dispossessed them, destroying them and settling in their place, as Israel has done in the land that the LORD gave them as a possession.) [13]"Now then, proceed to cross over the Wadi Zered."

So we crossed over the Wadi Zered. [14]And the length of time we had traveled from Kadesh-barnea until we crossed the Wadi Zered was thirty-eight years, until the entire generation of warriors had perished from the camp, as the LORD had sworn concerning them. [15]Indeed, the LORD's own hand was against them, to root them out from the camp, until all had perished.

16 Just as soon as all the warriors had died off from among the people, [17]the LORD spoke to me, saying, [18]"Today you are going to cross the boundary of Moab at Ar. [19]When you approach the frontier of the Ammonites, do not harass them or engage them in battle, for I will not give the land of the Ammonites to you as a possession, because I have given it to the descendants of Lot." [20](It also is usually reckoned as a land of Rephaim. Rephaim formerly inhabited it, though the Ammonites call them Zamzummim, [21]a strong and numerous people, as tall as the Anakim. But the LORD destroyed them from before the Ammonites so that they could dispossess them and settle in their place. [22]He did the same for the descendants of Esau, who live in Seir, by destroying the Horim before them so that they could dispossess them and settle in their place even to this day. [23]As for the Avvim, who had lived in settlements in the vicinity of Gaza, the Caphtorim, who came from Caphtor, destroyed them and settled in their place.) [24]"Proceed on your journey and cross the Wadi Arnon. See, I have handed over to you King Sihon the Amorite of Heshbon, and his land. Begin to take possession by engaging him in battle. [25]This day I will begin to put the dread and fear of you upon the peoples everywhere under heaven; when they hear report of you, they will tremble and be in anguish because of you."

Defeat of King Sihon

26 So I sent messengers from the wilderness of Kedemoth to King Sihon of Heshbon with the following terms of peace: [27]"If you let me pass through your land, I will travel only along the road; I will turn aside neither to the right nor to the left. [28]You shall sell me food for money, so that I may eat, and supply me water for money, so that I may drink. Only allow me to pass through on foot— [29]just as the descendants of Esau who live in Seir have done for me and likewise the Moabites who live in Ar—until I cross the Jordan into the land that the LORD our God is giving us." [30]But King Sihon of Heshbon was not willing to let us pass through, for the LORD your God had hardened his spirit and made his heart defiant in order to hand him over to you, as he has now done.

31 The LORD said to me, "See, I have begun to give Sihon and his land over to you. Begin now to take possession of his land." [32]So when Sihon came out against us, he and all his people for battle at Jahaz, [33]the LORD our God gave him over to us; and we struck him down, along with his offspring and all his people. [34]At that time we captured all his towns, and in each town we utterly destroyed men, women, and children. We left not a single survivor. [35]Only the livestock we kept as spoil for ourselves, as well as the plunder of the towns that we had captured. [36]From Aroer on the edge of the Wadi Arnon (including the town that is in the wadi itself) as far as Gilead, there was no citadel too high for us. The LORD our God gave everything to us. [37]You did not encroach, however, on the land of the Ammonites, avoiding the whole upper region of the Wadi Jabbok as well as the towns of the hill country, just as[a] the LORD our God had charged.

Defeat of King Og

3 When we headed up the road to Bashan, King Og of Bashan came out against us, he and all his people, for battle at Edrei. [2]The LORD said to me, "Do not fear him, for I have handed him over to you, along with his people and his land. Do to him as you did to King Sihon of the Amorites, who reigned in Heshbon." [3]So the LORD our God also handed over to us King Og of Bashan and all his people. We struck him down until not a single survivor was left. [4]At that time we captured all his towns; there was no citadel that we did not take from them—sixty towns, the whole region of Argob, the kingdom of Og in Bashan. [5]All these were fortress towns with high walls, double gates, and bars, besides a great many villages. [6]And we utterly destroyed them, as we had done to King Sihon of Heshbon, in each city utterly destroying men, women, and children. [7]But all the livestock and the plunder of the towns we kept as spoil for ourselves.

8 So at that time we took from the two kings

---

a Gk Tg: Heb *and all*

of the Amorites the land beyond the Jordan, from the Wadi Arnon to Mount Hermon [9](the Sidonians call Hermon Sirion, while the Amorites call it Senir), [10]all the towns of the tableland, the whole of Gilead, and all of Bashan, as far as Salecah and Edrei, towns of Og's kingdom in Bashan. [11](Now only King Og of Bashan was left of the remnant of the Rephaim. In fact his bed, an iron bed, can still be seen in Rabbah of the Ammonites. By the common cubit it is nine cubits long and four cubits wide.) [12]As for the land that we took possession of at that time, I gave to the Reubenites and Gadites the territory north of Aroer,[a] that is on the edge of the Wadi Arnon, as well as half the hill country of Gilead with its towns, [13]and I gave to the half-tribe of Manasseh the rest of Gilead and all of Bashan, Og's kingdom. (The whole region of Argob: all that portion of Bashan used to be called a land of Rephaim; [14]Jair the Manassite acquired the whole region of Argob as far as the border of the Geshurites and the Maacathites, and he named them—that is, Bashan—after himself, Havvoth-jair,[b] as it is to this day.) [15]To Machir I gave Gilead. [16]And to the Reubenites and the Gadites I gave the territory from Gilead as far as the Wadi Arnon, with the middle of the wadi as a boundary, and up to the Jabbok, the wadi being boundary of the Ammonites; [17]the Arabah also, with the Jordan and its banks, from Chinnereth down to the sea of the Arabah, the Dead Sea,[c] with the lower slopes of Pisgah on the east.

18 At that time, I charged you as follows: "Although the Lord your God has given you this land to occupy, all your troops shall cross over armed as the vanguard of your Israelite kin. [19]Only your wives, your children, and your livestock—I know that you have much livestock—shall stay behind in the towns that I have given to you. [20]When the Lord gives rest to your kindred, as to you, and they too have occupied the land that the Lord your God is giving them beyond the Jordan, then each of you may return to the property that I have given to you." [21]And I charged Joshua as well at that time, saying: "Your own eyes have seen everything that the Lord your God has done to these two kings; so the Lord will do to all the kingdoms into which you are about to cross. [22]Do not fear them, for it is the Lord your God who fights for you."

Moses Views Canaan from Pisgah

23 At that time, too, I entreated the Lord, saying: [24]"O Lord God, you have only begun to show your servant your greatness and your might; what god in heaven or on earth can perform deeds and mighty acts like yours! [25]Let me cross over to see the good land beyond the Jordan, that good hill country and the Lebanon." [26]But the Lord was angry with me on your account and would not heed me. The Lord said to me, "Enough from you! Never speak to me of this matter again! [27]Go up to the top of Pisgah and look around you to the west, to the north, to the south, and to the east. Look well, for you shall not cross over this Jordan. [28]But charge Joshua, and encourage and strengthen him, because it is he who shall cross over at the head of this people and who shall secure their possession of the land that you will see." [29]So we remained in the valley opposite Beth-peor.

Moses Commands Obedience

4 So now, Israel, give heed to the statutes and ordinances that I am teaching you to observe, so that you may live to enter and occupy the land that the Lord, the God of your ancestors, is giving you. [2]You must neither add anything to what I command you nor take away anything from it, but keep the commandments of the Lord your God with which I am charging you. [3]You have seen for yourselves what the Lord did with regard to the Baal of Peor—how the Lord your God destroyed from among you everyone who followed the Baal of Peor, [4]while those of you who held fast to the Lord your God are all alive today.

5 See, just as the Lord my God has charged me, I now teach you statutes and ordinances for you to observe in the land that you are about to enter and occupy. [6]You must observe them diligently, for this will show your wisdom and discernment to the peoples, who, when they hear all these statutes, will say, "Surely this great nation is a wise and discerning people!" [7]For what other great nation has a god so near to it as the Lord our God is whenever we call to him? [8]And what other great nation has statutes and ordinances as just as this entire law that I am setting before you today?

9 But take care and watch yourselves closely, so as neither to forget the things that your eyes have seen nor to let them slip from your mind all the days of your life; make them known to your children and your children's children— [10]how you once stood before the Lord your God at Horeb, when the Lord said to me, "Assemble the people for me, and I will let them hear my words, so that they may learn to fear me as long as they live on the earth, and may teach their children

---

a Heb territory from Aroer   b That is Settlement of Jair
c Heb Salt Sea

so"; 11you approached and stood at the foot of the mountain while the mountain was blazing up to the very heavens, shrouded in dark clouds. 12Then the Lord spoke to you out of the fire. You heard the sound of words but saw no form; there was only a voice. 13He declared to you his covenant, which he charged you to observe, that is, the ten commandments;a and he wrote them on two stone tablets. 14And the Lord charged me at that time to teach you statutes and ordinances for you to observe in the land that you are about to cross into and occupy.

15 Since you saw no form when the Lord spoke to you at Horeb out of the fire, take care and watch yourselves closely, 16so that you do not act corruptly by making an idol for yourselves, in the form of any figure—the likeness of male or female, 17the likeness of any animal that is on the earth, the likeness of any winged bird that flies in the air, 18the likeness of anything that creeps on the ground, the likeness of any fish that is in the water under the earth. 19And when you look up to the heavens and see the sun, the moon, and the stars, all the host of heaven, do not be led astray and bow down to them and serve them, things that the Lord your God has allotted to all the peoples everywhere under heaven. 20But the Lord has taken you and brought you out of the iron-smelter, out of Egypt, to become a people of his very own possession, as you are now.

21 The Lord was angry with me because of you, and he vowed that I should not cross the Jordan and that I should not enter the good land that the Lord your God is giving for your possession. 22For I am going to die in this land without crossing over the Jordan, but you are going to cross over to take possession of that good land. 23So be careful not to forget the covenant that the Lord your God made with you, and not to make for yourselves an idol in the form of anything that the Lord your God has forbidden you. 24For the Lord your God is a devouring fire, a jealous God.

25 When you have had children and children's children, and become complacent in the land, if you act corruptly by making an idol in the form of anything, thus doing what is evil in the sight of the Lord your God, and provoking him to anger, 26I call heaven and earth to witness against you today that you will soon utterly perish from the land that you are crossing the Jordan to occupy; you will not live long on it, but will be utterly destroyed. 27The Lord will scatter you among the peoples; only a few of you will be left among the nations where the Lord will lead

you. 28There you will serve other gods made by human hands, objects of wood and stone that neither see, nor hear, nor eat, nor smell. 29From there you will seek the Lord your God, and you will find him if you search after him with all your heart and soul. 30In your distress, when all these things have happened to you in time to come, you will return to the Lord your God and heed him. 31Because the Lord your God is a merciful God, he will neither abandon you nor destroy you; he will not forget the covenant with your ancestors that he swore to them.

32 For ask now about former ages, long before your own, ever since the day that God created human beings on the earth; ask from one end of heaven to the other: has anything so great as this ever happened or has its like ever been heard of? 33Has any people ever heard the voice of a god speaking out of a fire, as you have heard, and lived? 34Or has any god ever attempted to go and take a nation for himself from the midst of another nation, by trials, by signs and wonders, by war, by a mighty hand and an outstretched arm, and by terrifying displays of power, as the Lord your God did for you in Egypt before your very eyes? 35To you it was shown so that you would acknowledge that the Lord is God; there is no other besides him. 36From heaven he made you hear his voice to discipline you. On earth he showed you his great fire, while you heard his words coming out of the fire. 37And because he loved your ancestors, he chose their descendants after them. He brought you out of Egypt with his own presence, by his great power, 38driving out before you nations greater and mightier than yourselves, to bring you in, giving you their land for a possession, as it is still today. 39So acknowledge today and take to heart that the Lord is God in heaven above and on the earth beneath; there is no other. 40Keep his statutes and his commandments, which I am commanding you today for your own well-being and that of your descendants after you, so that you may long remain in the land that the Lord your God is giving you for all time.

Cities of Refuge East of the Jordan

41 Then Moses set apart on the east side of the Jordan three cities 42to which a homicide could flee, someone who unintentionally kills another person, the two not having been at enmity before; the homicide could flee to one of these cities and live: 43Bezer in the wilderness on the tableland belonging to the Reubenites,

---

a Heb *the ten words*

Cultural Connection

The Lakota Code

See how similar these guidelines from a Native American tribal code are to the Ten Commandments (see Deut 5:1–21), not to mention our own civil laws, school policies, and even family rules. What can we learn from them?

- Love one another.
- Pity orphan children. Be kind to them because they are poor; feed them and clothe them.
- Do not kill one another.
- Do not steal anything from anyone, especially from your own people.
- Do not tell lies to anyone, or lie about anyone.
- Respect your brothers and sisters. Do not marry in your own family.
- The ability to make good speech is a great gift from the maker, owner of all things, to the people. This is why you should not talk badly about anyone. Bad talk can hurt one's family or everyday life.
- Never quarrel among one another. Be good to others and always be friendly to whomever you meet, wherever you meet them.
- Do not brag about yourself, or try to hurt another's feelings. The generous person is the one who is respected.

(Ron Zeilinger, *Sacred Ground*, pp. 74–75)

▶ **Deut 5:1–21**

Ramoth in Gilead belonging to the Gadites, and Golan in Bashan belonging to the Manassites.

Transition to the Second Address

44 This is the law that Moses set before the Israelites. ⁴⁵These are the decrees and the statutes and ordinances that Moses spoke to the Israelites when they had come out of Egypt, ⁴⁶beyond the Jordan in the valley opposite Beth-peor, in the land of King Sihon of the Amorites, who reigned at Heshbon, whom Moses and the Israelites defeated when they came out of Egypt. ⁴⁷They occupied his land and the land of King Og of Bashan, the two kings of the Amorites on the eastern side of the Jordan: ⁴⁸from Aroer, which is on the edge of the Wadi Arnon, as far as Mount Sirion*a* (that is, Hermon), ⁴⁹together with all the Arabah on the east side of the Jordan as far as the Sea of the Arabah, under the slopes of Pisgah.

The Ten Commandments

5 Moses convened all Israel, and said to them: Hear, O Israel, the statutes and ordinances that I am addressing to you today; you shall learn them and observe them diligently. ²The LORD our God made a covenant with us at Horeb. ³Not with our ancestors did the LORD make this covenant, but with us, who are all of us here alive today. ⁴The LORD spoke with you face to face at the mountain, out of the fire. ⁵(At that time I was standing between the LORD and you to declare to you the words*b* of the LORD; for you were afraid because of the fire and did not go up the mountain.) And he said:

6 I am the LORD your God, who brought you out of the land of Egypt, out of the house of slavery; ⁷you shall have no other gods before*c* me.

8 You shall not make for yourself an idol, whether in the form of anything that is in heaven above, or that is on the earth beneath, or that is in the water under the earth. ⁹You shall not bow down to them or worship them; for I the LORD your God am a jealous God, punishing children for the iniquity of parents, to the third and fourth generation of those who reject me, ¹⁰but showing steadfast love to the thousandth generation*d* of those who love me and keep my commandments.

11 You shall not make wrongful use of the name of the LORD your God, for the LORD will not acquit anyone who misuses his name.

12 Observe the sabbath day and keep it holy, as the LORD your God commanded you. ¹³Six days you shall labor and do all your work. ¹⁴But the seventh day is a sabbath to the LORD your God; you shall not do any work—you, or your son or your daughter, or your male or female slave, or your ox or your donkey, or any of your livestock, or the resident alien in your towns, so

---

a Syr: Heb *Sion* *b* Q Mss Sam Gk Syr Vg Tg: MT *word*
c Or *besides* *d* Or *to thousands*

Catholic Connection

The Ten Commandments

After a thrilling escape from Egypt and forty long years wandering in the desert, Moses and the Israelites find themselves on the threshold of completing their journey. Unfortunately, Moses has grown old and knows he will not finish the journey with his people. He, therefore, gathers them together and reminds them of their past and their responsibilities. Most importantly, Moses reminds them of the Covenant they made with God on Mount Sinai and of their responsibility to follow the Ten Commandments.

It was through God's offer of love and friendship that the Israelites entered into the Covenant relationship with God. As a natural part of that relationship, God gave the Israelites the Ten Commandments as a path to the new life they were about to begin. These commandments were God's own words and provided a list of moral responsibilities that revealed God's will for each individual and all the Israelites as part of their new relationship with God. As a sign of the commandments' importance, the Israelites built the ark of the Covenant and kept the two stone tablets with them on their journey to the Promised Land. The Ten Commandments showed the Israelites how to live not only free from slavery, but free from the slavery of sin.

Jesus himself lived and taught the importance of the Ten Commandments. He summed them up in his two-fold command to love God and to love our neighbor. Following Jesus' affirmation of the Ten Commandments and their importance throughout the Sacred Scriptures, the Church uses the Ten Commandments as an important part of its moral teachings. The section on morality in the *Catechism of the Catholic Church* even follows the structure of the Ten Commandments as a way to convey Catholic moral teachings.

As followers of Jesus, Christians are obligated to always live by the Ten Commandments. The Ten Commandments can be divided into two groups. The first three commandments focus on our responsibilities toward God, and the remaining seven focus on our responsibilities toward one another. Together the two groups unite our spiritual life and our social life, where one is incomplete without the other. By following the Ten Commandments, we unite ourselves to Christ and to one another.

Try putting a copy of the Ten Commandments up on your mirror. That way each morning you too can be reminded of your responsibilities as a child of God and follower of Jesus. And remember, God never gives us a responsibility without giving us the grace to fulfill it.

▶ **Deut 5:1–21**
Catechism, nos. 2052–2082

that your male and female slave may rest as well as you. [15]Remember that you were a slave in the land of Egypt, and the Lord your God brought you out from there with a mighty hand and an outstretched arm; therefore the Lord your God commanded you to keep the sabbath day.

16 Honor your father and your mother, as the Lord your God commanded you, so that your days may be long and that it may go well with you in the land that the Lord your God is giving you.

17 You shall not murder.[a]

18 Neither shall you commit adultery.

19 Neither shall you steal.

20 Neither shall you bear false witness against your neighbor.

21 Neither shall you covet your neighbor's wife.

Neither shall you desire your neighbor's house, or field, or male or female slave, or ox, or donkey, or anything that belongs to your neighbor.

Moses the Mediator of God's Will

22 These words the Lord spoke with a loud voice to your whole assembly at the mountain, out of the fire, the cloud, and the thick darkness, and he added no more. He wrote them on two stone tablets, and gave them to me. [23]When you heard the voice out of the darkness, while the mountain was burning with fire, you approached me, all the heads of your tribes and your elders; [24]and you said, "Look, the Lord our God has shown us his glory and greatness, and we have heard his voice out of the fire. Today we have seen that God may speak to someone and the person may still live. [25]So now why should we die? For this great fire will consume us; if we hear the voice of the Lord our God any longer, we shall die. [26]For who is there of all flesh that has heard the voice of the living God speaking out of fire, as we have, and remained alive? [27]Go near, you yourself, and hear all that the Lord our God will say. Then tell us everything that the Lord our God tells you, and we will listen and do it."

28 The Lord heard your words when you spoke to me, and the Lord said to me: "I have heard the words of this people, which they have spoken to you; they are right in all that they have spoken. [29]If only they had such a mind as this, to fear me and to keep all my commandments always, so that it might go well with them and with their children forever! [30]Go say to them, 'Return to your tents.' [31]But you, stand here by me, and I will tell you all the commandments, the statutes and the ordinances, that you shall teach them, so that they may do them in the land

that I am giving them to possess." [32]You must therefore be careful to do as the Lord your God has commanded you; you shall not turn to the right or to the left. [33]You must follow exactly the path that the Lord your God has commanded you, so that you may live, and that it may go well with you, and that you may live long in the land that you are to possess.

The Great Commandment

6 Now this is the commandment—the statutes and the ordinances—that the Lord your God charged me to teach you to observe in the land that you are about to cross into and occupy, [2]so that you and your children and your children's children may fear the Lord your God all the days of your life, and keep all his decrees and his commandments that I am commanding you, so that your days may be long. [3]Hear therefore, O Israel, and observe them diligently, so that it may go well with you, and so that you may multiply greatly in a land flowing with milk and honey, as the Lord, the God of your ancestors, has promised you.

4 Hear, O Israel: The Lord is our God, the Lord alone.[b] [5]You shall love the Lord your God with all your heart, and with all your soul, and with all your might. [6]Keep these words that I am commanding you today in your heart. [7]Recite them to your children and talk about them when you are at home and when you are away, when you lie down and when you rise. [8]Bind them as a sign on your hand, fix them as an emblem[c] on your forehead, [9]and write them on the doorposts of your house and on your gates.

Caution against Disobedience

10 When the Lord your God has brought you into the land that he swore to your ancestors, to Abraham, to Isaac, and to Jacob, to give you— a land with fine, large cities that you did not build, [11]houses filled with all sorts of goods that you did not fill, hewn cisterns that you did not hew, vineyards and olive groves that you did not plant—and when you have eaten your fill, [12]take care that you do not forget the Lord, who brought you out of the land of Egypt, out of the house of slavery. [13]The Lord your God you shall fear; him you shall serve, and by his name alone you shall swear. [14]Do not follow other gods, any of the gods of the peoples who are all around you, [15]because the Lord your God, who is present with

a Or kill   b Or The Lord our God is one Lord, or The Lord our God, the Lord is one, or The Lord is our God, the Lord is one
c Or as a frontlet

you, is a jealous God. The anger of the LORD your God would be kindled against you and he would destroy you from the face of the earth.

16 Do not put the LORD your God to the test, as you tested him at Massah. [17]You must diligently keep the commandments of the LORD your God, and his decrees, and his statutes that he has commanded you. [18]Do what is right and good in the sight of the LORD, so that it may go well with you, and so that you may go in and occupy the good land that the LORD swore to your ancestors to give you, [19]thrusting out all your enemies from before you, as the LORD has promised.

20 When your children ask you in time to come, "What is the meaning of the decrees and the statutes and the ordinances that the LORD our God has commanded you?" [21]then you shall say to your children, "We were Pharaoh's slaves in Egypt, but the LORD brought us out of Egypt with a mighty hand. [22]The LORD displayed before our eyes great and awesome signs and wonders against Egypt, against Pharaoh and all his household. [23]He brought us out from there in order to bring us in, to give us the land that he promised on oath to our ancestors. [24]Then the LORD commanded us to observe all these statutes, to fear the LORD our God, for our lasting good, so as to keep us alive, as is now the case. [25]If we diligently observe this entire commandment before the LORD our God, as he has commanded us, we will be in the right."

A Chosen People

7 When the LORD your God brings you into the land that you are about to enter and occupy, and he clears away many nations before you—the Hittites, the Girgashites, the Amorites, the Canaanites, the Perizzites, the Hivites, and the Jebusites, seven nations mightier and more numerous than you— [2]and when the LORD your God gives them over to you and you defeat them, then you must utterly destroy them. Make no covenant with them and show them no mercy. [3]Do not intermarry with them, giving your daughters to their sons or taking their daughters for your sons, [4]for that would turn away your children from following me, to serve other gods. Then the anger of the LORD would be kindled against you, and he would destroy you quickly. [5]But this is how you must deal with them: break down their altars, smash their pillars, hew down their sacred poles,[a] and burn their idols with fire. [6]For you are a people holy to the LORD your God; the LORD your God has chosen you out of all the peoples on earth to be his people, his treasured possession.

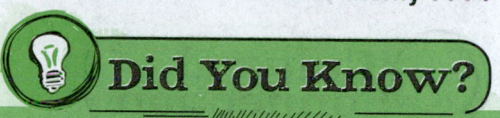

Did You Know?

The Shema: Putting God First

Deuteronomy 6:4 is the most famous declaration of faith in the Old Testament: "Hear, O Israel: The LORD is our God, the LORD alone." This short verse, part of a prayer called the Shema, is uttered daily by faithful Jews. It has been so important that the commands of verses 8–9 often have been interpreted literally. The Pharisees of Jesus' day, for example, wore miniature copies of the prayer on their bodies and attached other copies to their doorposts. Orthodox Jews today continue this tradition. Keeping the law of God is a privilege—something to be "worn" with pride!

The Shema reminds Jewish people to put God first and to love God with all their heart, soul, and might. Think about people who seem to carry God in their heart all the time. Are they lost and frustrated? Do they seem angry and hate filled? Chances are they seem more relaxed and sure of themselves than most people do. Having God in your sights at all times will help in more ways than you could ever imagine!

▶ **Deut 6:4–9**

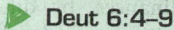

7 It was not because you were more numerous than any other people that the LORD set his heart on you and chose you—for you were the fewest of all peoples. [8]It was because the LORD loved you and kept the oath that he swore to your ancestors, that the LORD has brought you out with a mighty hand, and redeemed you from the house of slavery, from the hand of Pharaoh king of Egypt. [9]Know therefore that the LORD your God is God, the faithful God who maintains covenant loyalty with those who love him and keep his commandments, to a thousand generations, [10]and who repays in their own person those who reject him. He does not delay but repays in their own person those who reject him. [11]Therefore, observe diligently the commandment—the statutes and the ordinances—that I am commanding you today.

a Heb Asherim

DEUT

Cultural Connection

Don't Lose Your Language!

"*Qui perd sa langue, perd sa foi.*" This French Canadian proverb means, "Lose your language, lose your faith."

As Canada was being settled, the French were afraid that the English culture would dominate the land and culture. Most of the French were Catholic, and most of the English were Protestant. The French believed their faith was so tied to their language that the loss of their language would mean a loss to their faith and how they expressed it culturally.

This same fear is present in the Bible. Peter was afraid to eat with the Gentiles—those who were not Jews (see Gal 2:12). The Samaritan woman at the well knew that Jesus, a Jew, should have nothing to do with her because Samaritans were considered "half-Jews" due to intermarriage (see Jn 4:9).

Chapter 7 of Deuteronomy portrays this fear in a frightening way. Israelites were told not just to avoid pagans but to destroy them. Intermarriage would mean losing Jewish language, culture, and faith—and sooner or later would lead to worshiping false gods (see also Ex 23:23–26).

Yet Jesus treated the Samaritan woman with dignity. Paul challenged Peter to eat with the uncircumcised and to let them become Christians without first becoming Jews. We need not be afraid of those who are different from us. We can treat others with dignity and even build friendship without the fear of losing our language or our faith.

▶ **Deut 7:1–5**

Blessings for Obedience

12 If you heed these ordinances, by diligently observing them, the LORD your God will maintain with you the covenant loyalty that he swore to your ancestors; [13]he will love you, bless you, and multiply you; he will bless the fruit of your womb and the fruit of your ground, your grain and your wine and your oil, the increase of your cattle and the issue of your flock, in the land that he swore to your ancestors to give you. [14]You shall be the most blessed of peoples, with neither sterility nor barrenness among you or your livestock. [15]The LORD will turn away from you every illness; all the dread diseases of Egypt that you experienced, he will not inflict on you, but he will lay them on all who hate you. [16]You shall devour all the peoples that the LORD your God is giving over to you, showing them no pity; you shall not serve their gods, for that would be a snare to you.

17 If you say to yourself, "These nations are more numerous than I; how can I dispossess them?" [18]do not be afraid of them. Just remember what the LORD your God did to Pharaoh and to all Egypt, [19]the great trials that your eyes saw, the signs and wonders, the mighty hand and the outstretched arm by which the LORD your God brought you out. The LORD your God will do the same to all the peoples of whom you are afraid. [20]Moreover, the LORD your God will send the pestilence[a] against them, until even the survivors and the fugitives are destroyed. [21]Have no dread of them, for the LORD your God, who is present with you, is a great and awesome God. [22]The LORD your God will clear away these nations before you little by little; you will not be able to make a quick end of them, otherwise the wild animals would become too numerous for you. [23]But the LORD your God will give them over to you, and throw them into great panic, until they are destroyed. [24]He will hand their kings over to you and you shall blot out their name from under heaven; no one will be able to stand against you, until you have destroyed them. [25]The images of their gods you shall burn with fire. Do not covet the silver or the gold that is on them and take it for yourself, because you could be ensnared by it; for it is abhorrent to the LORD your God. [26]Do not bring an abhorrent thing into your house, or you will be set apart for destruction like it. You must utterly detest and abhor it, for it is set apart for destruction.

a Or *hornets*: Meaning of Heb uncertain

Cultural Connection

The Principle of *Ujima*

Decades before the Civil War, the Underground Railroad helped thousands of African slaves find their way to freedom. The Underground Railroad was not a real railroad but a loose network of antislavery northerners—mostly African Americans—who helped escaped slaves reach safety in the free states or Canada. People called conductors guided groups of fugitive slaves through isolated areas at night so that they wouldn't be spotted. Others opened their homes and farms to give them safe places to stay during the day. It was dangerous work because professional slave catchers and local officials were always looking for escaped slaves to return for financial rewards.

The Underground Railroad is just one example of what can be accomplished through the Kwan-zaa principle of *ujima* (see "Kwan-zaa as a Way of Life," near Deut 10:12–22), which is collective work and responsibility. Our African American ancestors in this country worked together bravely for the common good. Many members of the Underground Railroad were former slaves themselves and took responsibility for freeing others as they had been freed. Today, we need young people with the same sense of responsibility and the willingness to work together to free others from poverty, violence, and addiction.

Martin Luther King Jr. did this. In his last speech, he said to you and me: "I've been to the Mountaintop, and I've seen the Promised Land. I may not get there with you, but I want you to know that we as a people will get to the Promised Land." He knew he would not live to see his people freed from prejudice and discrimination. But he spent his whole life working with others toward that goal.

The author of Deuteronomy wrote long after Moses' time. Many of the Chosen People had indeed become wealthy, so he used Moses' authority to remind them of how they had gotten to where they were. Their ancestors—escaped, impoverished slaves—trusted in God and worked together over a long time to bring prosperity to the nation. This is the mentality we too must cultivate to bring success to ourselves and our people.

▶ **Deut 8:11–18**

DEUT

A Warning Not to Forget God in Prosperity

8 This entire commandment that I command you today you must diligently observe, so that you may live and increase, and go in and occupy the land that the Lord promised on oath to your ancestors. ²Remember the long way that the Lord your God has led you these forty years in the wilderness, in order to humble you, testing you to know what was in your heart, whether or not you would keep his commandments. ³He humbled you by letting you hunger, then by feeding you with manna, with which neither you nor your ancestors were acquainted, in order to make you understand that one does not live by bread alone, but by every word that comes from the mouth of the Lord.*ᵃ* ⁴The clothes on your back did not wear out and your feet did not swell these forty years. ⁵Know then in your heart that as a parent disciplines a child so the Lord your God disciplines you. ⁶Therefore keep the commandments of the Lord your God, by walking in his ways and by fearing him. ⁷For the Lord your God is bringing you into a good land, a land with flowing streams, with springs and underground waters welling up in valleys and hills, ⁸a land of wheat and barley, of vines and fig trees and pomegranates, a land of olive trees and honey, ⁹a land where you may eat bread without scarcity, where you will lack nothing, a land whose stones are iron and from whose hills you may mine copper. ¹⁰You shall eat your fill and bless the Lord your God for the good land that he has given you.

11 Take care that you do not forget the Lord your God, by failing to keep his commandments, his ordinances, and his statutes, which I am commanding you today. ¹²When you have eaten your fill and have built fine houses and live in them, ¹³and when your herds and flocks

---

a Or by anything that the Lord decrees

have multiplied, and your silver and gold is multiplied, and all that you have is multiplied, [14]then do not exalt yourself, forgetting the Lord your God, who brought you out of the land of Egypt, out of the house of slavery, [15]who led you through the great and terrible wilderness, an arid wasteland with poisonous[a] snakes and scorpions. He made water flow for you from flint rock, [16]and fed you in the wilderness with manna that your ancestors did not know, to humble you and to test you, and in the end to do you good. [17]Do not say to yourself, "My power and the might of my own hand have gotten me this wealth." [18]But remember the Lord your God, for it is he who gives you power to get wealth, so that he may confirm his covenant that he swore to your ancestors, as he is doing today. [19]If you do forget the Lord your God and follow other gods to serve and worship them, I solemnly warn you today that you shall surely perish. [20]Like the nations that the Lord is destroying before you, so shall you perish, because you would not obey the voice of the Lord your God.

The Consequences of Rebelling against God

9 Hear, O Israel! You are about to cross the Jordan today, to go in and dispossess nations larger and mightier than you, great cities, fortified to the heavens, [2]a strong and tall people, the offspring of the Anakim, whom you know. You have heard it said of them, "Who can stand up to the Anakim?" [3]Know then today that the Lord your God is the one who crosses over before you as a devouring fire; he will defeat them and subdue them before you, so that you may dispossess and destroy them quickly, as the Lord has promised you.

[4]When the Lord your God thrusts them out before you, do not say to yourself, "It is because of my righteousness that the Lord has brought me in to occupy this land"; it is rather because of the wickedness of these nations that the Lord is dispossessing them before you. [5]It is not because of your righteousness or the uprightness of your heart that you are going in to occupy their land; but because of the wickedness of these nations the Lord your God is dispossessing them before you, in order to fulfill the promise that the Lord made on oath to your ancestors, to Abraham, to Isaac, and to Jacob.

[6]Know, then, that the Lord your God is not giving you this good land to occupy because of your righteousness; for you are a stubborn people. [7]Remember and do not forget how you provoked the Lord your God to wrath in the wilderness; you have been rebellious against the Lord from the day you came out of the land of Egypt until you came to this place.

[8]Even at Horeb you provoked the Lord to wrath, and the Lord was so angry with you that he was ready to destroy you. [9]When I went up the mountain to receive the stone tablets, the tablets of the covenant that the Lord made with you, I remained on the mountain forty days and forty nights; I neither ate bread nor drank water. [10]And the Lord gave me the two stone tablets written with the finger of God; on them were all the words that the Lord had spoken to you at the mountain out of the fire on the day of the assembly. [11]At the end of forty days and forty nights the Lord gave me the two stone tablets, the tablets of the covenant. [12]Then the Lord said to me, "Get up, go down quickly from here, for your people whom you have brought from Egypt have acted corruptly. They have been quick to turn from the way that I commanded them; they have cast an image for themselves." [13]Furthermore the Lord said to me, "I have seen that this people is indeed a stubborn people. [14]Let me alone that I may destroy them and blot out their name from under heaven; and I will make of you a nation mightier and more numerous than they."

[15]So I turned and went down from the mountain, while the mountain was ablaze; the two tablets of the covenant were in my two hands. [16]Then I saw that you had indeed sinned against the Lord your God, by casting for yourselves an image of a calf; you had been quick to turn from the way that the Lord had commanded you. [17]So I took hold of the two tablets and flung them from my two hands, smashing them before your eyes. [18]Then I lay prostrate before the Lord as before, forty days and forty nights; I neither ate bread nor drank water, because of all the sin you had committed, provoking the Lord by doing what was evil in his sight. [19]For I was afraid that the anger that the Lord bore against you was so fierce that he would destroy you. But the Lord listened to me that time also. [20]The Lord was so angry with Aaron that he was ready to destroy him, but I interceded also on behalf of Aaron at that same time. [21]Then I took the sinful thing you had made, the calf, and burned it with fire and crushed it, grinding it thoroughly, until it was reduced to dust; and I threw the dust of it into the stream that runs down the mountain.

[22]At Taberah also, and at Massah, and at Kibroth-hattaavah, you provoked the Lord to wrath. [23]And when the Lord sent you from Kadesh-barnea, saying, "Go up and occupy the

a Or *fiery*; Heb *seraph*

land that I have given you," you rebelled against the command of the Lord your God, neither trusting him nor obeying him. 24You have been rebellious against the Lord as long as he has*a* known you.

25 Throughout the forty days and forty nights that I lay prostrate before the Lord when the Lord intended to destroy you, 26I prayed to the Lord and said, "Lord God, do not destroy the people who are your very own possession, whom you redeemed in your greatness, whom you brought out of Egypt with a mighty hand. 27Remember your servants, Abraham, Isaac, and Jacob; pay no attention to the stubbornness of this people, their wickedness and their sin, 28otherwise the land from which you have brought us might say, 'Because the Lord was not able to bring them into the land that he promised them, and because he hated them, he has brought them out to let them die in the wilderness.' 29For they are the people of your very own possession, whom you brought out by your great power and by your outstretched arm."

The Second Pair of Tablets

10 At that time the Lord said to me, "Carve out two tablets of stone like the former ones, and come up to me on the mountain, and make an ark of wood. 2I will write on the tablets the words that were on the former tablets, which you smashed, and you shall put them in the ark." 3So I made an ark of acacia wood, cut two tablets of stone like the former ones, and went up the mountain with the two tablets in my hand. 4Then he wrote on the tablets the same words as before, the ten commandments*b* that the Lord had spoken to you on the mountain out of the fire on the day of the assembly; and the Lord gave them to me. 5So I turned and came down from the mountain, and put the tablets in the ark that I had made; and there they are, as the Lord commanded me.

6 (The Israelites journeyed from Beeroth-bene-jaakan*c* to Moserah. There Aaron died, and there he was buried; his son Eleazar succeeded him as priest. 7From there they journeyed to Gudgodah, and from Gudgodah to Jotbathah, a land with flowing streams. 8At that time the Lord set apart the tribe of Levi to carry the ark of the covenant of the Lord, to stand before the Lord to minister to him, and to bless in his name, to this day. 9Therefore Levi has no allotment or inheritance with his kindred; the Lord is his inheritance, as the Lord your God promised him.)

10 I stayed on the mountain forty days and forty nights, as I had done the first time. And once again the Lord listened to me. The Lord was unwilling to destroy you. 11The Lord said to me, "Get up, go on your journey at the head of the people, that they may go in and occupy the land that I swore to their ancestors to give them."

The Essence of the Law

12 So now, O Israel, what does the Lord your God require of you? Only to fear the Lord your God, to walk in all his ways, to love him, to serve the Lord your God with all your heart and with all your soul, 13and to keep the commandments of the Lord your God*d* and his decrees that I am commanding you today, for your own well-being. 14Although heaven and the heaven of heavens belong to the Lord your God, the earth with all that is in it, 15yet the Lord set his heart in love on your ancestors alone and chose you, their descendants after them, out of all the peoples, as it is today. 16Circumcise, then, the foreskin of your heart, and do not be stubborn any longer. 17For the Lord your God is God of gods and Lord of lords, the great God, mighty and awesome, who is not partial and takes no bribe, 18who executes justice for the orphan and the widow, and who loves the strangers, providing them food and clothing. 19You shall also love the stranger, for you were strangers in the land of Egypt. 20You shall fear the Lord your God; him alone you shall worship; to him you shall hold fast, and by his name you shall swear. 21He is your praise; he is your God, who has done for you these great and awesome things that your own eyes have seen. 22Your ancestors went down to Egypt seventy persons; and now the Lord your God has made you as numerous as the stars in heaven.

Rewards for Obedience

11 You shall love the Lord your God, therefore, and keep his charge, his decrees, his ordinances, and his commandments always. 2Remember today that it was not your children (who have not known or seen the discipline of the Lord your God), but it is you who must acknowledge his greatness, his mighty hand and his outstretched arm, 3his signs and his deeds that he did in Egypt to Pharaoh, the king of Egypt, and to all his land; 4what he did to the Egyptian army, to their horses and chariots, how he made the water of the Red Sea*e* flow over them as they pursued you, so that the Lord has destroyed them to this day; 5what he did to you

a Sam Gk: MT *I have*   *b* Heb *the ten words*   *c* Or *the wells of the Bene-jaakan*   *d* Q Ms Gk Syr: MT lacks *your God*   *e* Or *Sea of Reeds*

Cultural Connection

Kwanzaa as a Way of Life

The heart of the Law is love, our love for God and God's love for us. We express that love through the values we live out. Conflicts occur when the way we rank our values conflicts with the way others rank their values. For example, you may place a value on completing all your schoolwork, studying, and excelling in school. Another person sitting near you in class may not place the same high value on school. The two of you may come into conflict because this person disrupts the class and makes it difficult for you to understand what the teacher is explaining.

This is why a universal value system is important. It is why the Book of Deuteronomy has laws on everything from worship to sanitation. These laws gave the Israelites a common value system.

Kwanzaa is the name of a value system accepted by many African peoples. It was developed by Maulana Karenga after studying many different cultures throughout Africa. In 1965, he codified the unifying aspects of each of these cultures into the seven principles of Kwanzaa (also known as the Nguzo Saba). The seven principles are written in Swahili (an African trade and business language) and speak to the holistic development of the individual, family, community, nation, and race. Kwanzaa is celebrated from December 26 to January 1. It is good that more and more African Americans are celebrating it each year, but these principles must be fully put into practice year-round as a way of life.

Kwanzaa is not a religion or a religious holiday, but it can strengthen the faith that you already practice. Look up the Bible passages listed with the following Kwanzaa principles to learn more about each one:

1. *umoja* (unity): Psalm 133, 1 Cor 12:12–26
2. *kujichagulia* (self-determination): Jdt 8:9–36
3. *ujima* (collective work and responsibility): Deut 8:11–18
4. *ujamaa* (cooperative economics): Mt 16:25
5. *nia* (purpose): Rom 8:28
6. *kuumba* (creativity): Mt 25:14–30
7. *imani* (faith): Gal 6:9

▶ **Deut 10:12–22**

in the wilderness, until you came to this place; [6]and what he did to Dathan and Abiram, sons of Eliab son of Reuben, how in the midst of all Israel the earth opened its mouth and swallowed them up, along with their households, their tents, and every living being in their company; [7]for it is your own eyes that have seen every great deed that the LORD did.

8 Keep, then, this entire commandment that I am commanding you today, so that you may have strength to go in and occupy the land that you are crossing over to occupy, [9]and so that you may live long in the land that the LORD swore to your ancestors to give them and to their descendants, a land flowing with milk and honey. [10]For the land that you are about to enter to occupy is not like the land of Egypt, from which you have come, where you sow your seed and irrigate by foot like a vegetable garden. [11]But the land that you are crossing over to occupy is a land of hills and valleys, watered by rain from the sky, [12]a land that the LORD your God looks after. The eyes of the LORD your God are always on it, from the beginning of the year to the end of the year.

13 If you will only heed his every commandment[a] that I am commanding you today—loving the LORD your God, and serving him with all your heart and with all your soul— [14]then he[b] will give the rain for your land in its season, the early rain and the later rain, and you will gather in your grain, your wine, and your oil; [15]and he[b] will give grass in your fields for your livestock, and you will eat your fill. [16]Take care, or you will be seduced into turning away, serving other gods and worshiping them, [17]for then the anger of the LORD will be kindled against you and he will shut up the heavens, so that there will be no rain and the land will yield no fruit; then you will perish quickly off the good land that the LORD is giving you.

a Compare Gk: Heb *my commandments*   b Sam Gk Vg: MT *I*

18 You shall put these words of mine in your heart and soul, and you shall bind them as a sign on your hand, and fix them as an emblem[a] on your forehead. [19]Teach them to your children, talking about them when you are at home and when you are away, when you lie down and when you rise. [20]Write them on the doorposts of your house and on your gates, [21]so that your days and the days of your children may be multiplied in the land that the LORD swore to your ancestors to give them, as long as the heavens are above the earth.

22 If you will diligently observe this entire commandment that I am commanding you, loving the LORD your God, walking in all his ways, and holding fast to him, [23]then the LORD will drive out all these nations before you, and you will dispossess nations larger and mightier than yourselves. [24]Every place on which you set foot shall be yours; your territory shall extend from the wilderness to the Lebanon and from the River, the river Euphrates, to the Western Sea. [25]No one will be able to stand against you; the LORD your God will put the fear and dread of you on all the land on which you set foot, as he promised you.

26 See, I am setting before you today a blessing and a curse: [27]the blessing, if you obey the commandments of the LORD your God that I am commanding you today; [28]and the curse, if you do not obey the commandments of the LORD your God, but turn from the way that I am commanding you today, to follow other gods that you have not known.

29 When the LORD your God has brought you into the land that you are entering to occupy, you shall set the blessing on Mount Gerizim and the curse on Mount Ebal. [30]As you know, they are beyond the Jordan, some distance to the west, in the land of the Canaanites who live in the Arabah, opposite Gilgal, beside the oak[b] of Moreh. [31] When you cross the Jordan to go in to occupy the land that the LORD your God is giving you, and when you occupy it and live in it, [32]you must diligently observe all the statutes and ordinances that I am setting before you today.

Pagan Shrines to Be Destroyed

12 These are the statutes and ordinances that you must diligently observe in the land that the LORD, the God of your ancestors, has given you to occupy all the days that you live on the earth.

2 You must demolish completely all the places where the nations whom you are about to dispossess served their gods, on the mountain heights, on the hills, and under every leafy tree. [3]Break down their altars, smash their pillars, burn their sacred poles[c] with fire, and hew down the idols of their gods, and thus blot out their name from their places. [4]You shall not worship the LORD your God in such ways. [5]But you shall seek the place that the LORD your God will choose out of all your tribes as his habitation to put his name there. You shall go there, [6]bringing there your burnt offerings and your sacrifices, your tithes and your donations, your votive gifts, your freewill offerings, and the firstlings of your herds and flocks. [7]And you shall eat there in the presence of the LORD your God, you and your households together, rejoicing in all the undertakings in which the LORD your God has blessed you.

8 You shall not act as we are acting here today, all of us according to our own desires, [9]for you have not yet come into the rest and the possession that the LORD your God is giving you. [10]When you cross over the Jordan and live in the land that the LORD your God is allotting to you, and when he gives you rest from your enemies all around so that you live in safety, [11]then you shall bring everything that I command you to the place that the LORD your God will choose as a dwelling for his name: your burnt offerings and your sacrifices, your tithes and your donations, and all your choice votive gifts that you vow to the LORD. [12]And you shall rejoice before the LORD your God, you together with your sons and your daughters, your male and female slaves, and the Levites who reside in your towns (since they have no allotment or inheritance with you).

A Prescribed Place of Worship

13 Take care that you do not offer your burnt offerings at any place you happen to see. [14]But only at the place that the LORD will choose in one of your tribes—there you shall offer your burnt offerings and there you shall do everything I command you.

15 Yet whenever you desire you may slaughter and eat meat within any of your towns, according to the blessing that the LORD your God has given you; the unclean and the clean may eat of it, as they would of gazelle or deer. [16]The blood, however, you must not eat; you shall pour it out on the ground like water. [17]Nor may you eat within your towns the tithe of your grain, your wine, and your oil, the firstlings of your herds and your flocks, any of your votive gifts that you vow, your freewill offerings, or your donations;

a Or as a frontlet   b Gk Syr: Compare Gen 12.6; Heb oaks or terebinths   c Heb Asherim

18these you shall eat in the presence of the LORD your God at the place that the LORD your God will choose, you together with your son and your daughter, your male and female slaves, and the Levites resident in your towns, rejoicing in the presence of the LORD your God in all your undertakings. 19Take care that you do not neglect the Levite as long as you live in your land.

20 When the LORD your God enlarges your territory, as he has promised you, and you say, "I am going to eat some meat," because you wish to eat meat, you may eat meat whenever you have the desire. 21If the place where the LORD your God will choose to put his name is too far from you, and you slaughter as I have commanded you any of your herd or flock that the LORD has given you, then you may eat within your towns whenever you desire. 22Indeed, just as gazelle or deer is eaten, so you may eat it; the unclean and the clean alike may eat it. 23Only be sure that you do not eat the blood; for the blood is the life, and you shall not eat the life with the meat. 24Do not eat it; you shall pour it out on the ground like water. 25Do not eat it, so that all may go well with you and your children after you, because you do what is right in the sight of the LORD. 26But the sacred donations that are due from you, and your votive gifts, you shall bring to the place that the LORD will choose. 27You shall present your burnt offerings, both the meat and the blood, on the altar of the LORD your God; the blood of your other sacrifices shall be poured out beside*a* the altar of the LORD your God, but the meat you may eat.

28 Be careful to obey all these words that I command you today,*b* so that it may go well with you and with your children after you forever, because you will be doing what is good and right in the sight of the LORD your God.

Warning against Idolatry

29 When the LORD your God has cut off before you the nations whom you are about to enter to dispossess them, when you have dispossessed them and live in their land, 30take care that you are not snared into imitating them, after they have been destroyed before you: do not inquire concerning their gods, saying, "How did these nations worship their gods? I also want to do the same." 31You must not do the same for the LORD your God, because every abhorrent thing that the LORD hates they have done for their gods. They would even burn their sons and their daughters in the fire to their gods. 32*c* You must diligently observe everything that I command you; do not add to it or take anything from it.

13 *d* If prophets or those who divine by dreams appear among you and promise you omens or portents, 2and the omens or the portents declared by them take place, and they say, "Let us follow other gods" (whom you have not known) "and let us serve them," 3you must not heed the words of those prophets or those who divine by dreams; for the LORD your God is testing you, to know whether you indeed love the LORD your God with all your heart and soul. 4The LORD your God you shall follow, him alone you shall fear, his commandments you shall keep, his voice you shall obey, him you shall serve, and to him you shall hold fast. 5But those prophets or those who divine by dreams shall be put to death for having spoken treason against the LORD your God—who brought you out of the land of Egypt and redeemed you from the house of slavery—to turn you from the way in which the LORD your God commanded you to walk. So you shall purge the evil from your midst.

6 If anyone secretly entices you—even if it is your brother, your father's son or*e* your mother's son, or your own son or daughter, or the wife you embrace, or your most intimate friend— saying, "Let us go worship other gods," whom neither you nor your ancestors have known, 7any of the gods of the peoples that are around you, whether near you or far away from you, from one end of the earth to the other, 8you must not yield to or heed any such persons. Show them no pity or compassion and do not shield them. 9But you shall surely kill them; your own hand shall be first against them to execute them, and afterwards the hand of all the people. 10Stone them to death for trying to turn you away from the LORD your God, who brought you out of the land of Egypt, out of the house of slavery. 11Then all Israel shall hear and be afraid, and never again do any such wickedness.

12 If you hear it said about one of the towns that the LORD your God is giving you to live in, 13that scoundrels from among you have gone out and led the inhabitants of the town astray, saying, "Let us go and worship other gods," whom you have not known, 14then you shall inquire and make a thorough investigation. If the charge is established that such an abhorrent thing has been done among you, 15you shall put the inhabitants of that town to the sword, utterly destroying it and everything in it—even putting its livestock to the sword. 16All of its spoil you

---

a Or *on*   *b* Gk Sam Syr: MT lacks *today*   *c* Ch 13.1 in Heb   *d* Ch 13.2 in Heb   *e* Sam Gk Compare Tg: MT lacks *your father's son or*

shall gather into its public square; then burn the town and all its spoil with fire, as a whole burnt offering to the Lord your God. It shall remain a perpetual ruin, never to be rebuilt. [17]Do not let anything devoted to destruction stick to your hand, so that the Lord may turn from his fierce anger and show you compassion, and in his compassion multiply you, as he swore to your ancestors, [18]if you obey the voice of the Lord your God by keeping all his commandments that I am commanding you today, doing what is right in the sight of the Lord your God.

Pagan Practices Forbidden

14 You are children of the Lord your God. You must not lacerate yourselves or shave your forelocks for the dead. [2]For you are a people holy to the Lord your God; it is you the Lord has chosen out of all the peoples on earth to be his people, his treasured possession.

Clean and Unclean Foods

3 You shall not eat any abhorrent thing. [4]These are the animals you may eat: the ox, the sheep, the goat, [5]the deer, the gazelle, the roebuck, the wild goat, the ibex, the antelope, and the mountain-sheep. [6]Any animal that divides the hoof and has the hoof cleft in two, and chews the cud, among the animals, you may eat. [7]Yet of those that chew the cud or have the hoof cleft you shall not eat these: the camel, the hare, and the rock badger, because they chew the cud but do not divide the hoof; they are unclean for you. [8]And the pig, because it divides the hoof but does not chew the cud, is unclean for you. You shall not eat their meat, and you shall not touch their carcasses.

9 Of all that live in water you may eat these: whatever has fins and scales you may eat. [10]And whatever does not have fins and scales you shall not eat; it is unclean for you.

11 You may eat any clean birds. [12]But these are the ones that you shall not eat: the eagle, the vulture, the osprey, [13]the buzzard, the kite of any kind; [14]every raven of any kind; [15]the ostrich, the nighthawk, the sea gull, the hawk of any kind; [16]the little owl and the great owl, the water hen [17]and the desert owl,[a] the carrion vulture and the cormorant, [18]the stork, the heron of any kind; the hoopoe and the bat.[b] [19]And all winged insects are unclean for you; they shall not be eaten. [20]You may eat any clean winged creature.

21 You shall not eat anything that dies of itself; you may give it to aliens residing in your towns for them to eat, or you may sell it to a foreigner. For you are a people holy to the Lord your God.

You shall not boil a kid in its mother's milk.

Regulations concerning Tithes

22 Set apart a tithe of all the yield of your seed that is brought in yearly from the field. [23]In the presence of the Lord your God, in the place that he will choose as a dwelling for his name, you shall eat the tithe of your grain, your wine, and your oil, as well as the firstlings of your herd and flock, so that you may learn to fear the Lord your God always. [24]But if, when the Lord your God has blessed you, the distance is so great that you are unable to transport it, because the place where the Lord your God will choose to set his name is too far away from you, [25]then you may turn it into money. With the money secure in hand, go to the place that the Lord your God will choose; [26]spend the money for whatever you wish—oxen, sheep, wine, strong drink, or whatever you desire. And you shall eat there in the presence of the Lord your God, you and your household rejoicing together. [27]As for the Levites resident in your towns, do not neglect them, because they have no allotment or inheritance with you.

28 Every third year you shall bring out the full tithe of your produce for that year, and store it within your towns; [29]the Levites, because they have no allotment or inheritance with you, as well as the resident aliens, the orphans, and the widows in your towns, may come and eat their fill so that the Lord your God may bless you in all the work that you undertake.

Laws concerning the Sabbatical Year

15 Every seventh year you shall grant a remission of debts. [2]And this is the manner of the remission: every creditor shall remit the claim that is held against a neighbor, not exacting it of a neighbor who is a member of the community, because the Lord's remission has been proclaimed. [3]Of a foreigner you may exact it, but you must remit your claim on whatever any member of your community owes you. [4]There will, however, be no one in need among you, because the Lord is sure to bless you in the land that the Lord your God is giving you as a possession to occupy, [5]if only you will obey the Lord your God by diligently observing this entire commandment that I command you today. [6]When the Lord your God has blessed you, as he promised you, you will lend to many nations, but you will not borrow; you will rule over many nations, but they will not rule over you.

---

a Or *pelican*　b Identification of several of the birds in verses 12-18 is uncertain

7 If there is among you anyone in need, a member of your community in any of your towns within the land that the LORD your God is giving you, do not be hard-hearted or tight-fisted toward your needy neighbor. [8]You should rather open your hand, willingly lending enough to meet the need, whatever it may be. [9]Be careful that you do not entertain a mean thought, thinking, "The seventh year, the year of remission, is near," and therefore view your needy neighbor with hostility and give nothing; your neighbor might cry to the LORD against you, and you would incur guilt. [10]Give liberally and be ungrudging when you do so, for on this account the LORD your God will bless you in all your work and in all that you undertake. [11]Since there will never cease to be some in need on the earth, I therefore command you, "Open your hand to the poor and needy neighbor in your land."

12 If a member of your community, whether a Hebrew man or a Hebrew woman, is sold[a] to you and works for you six years, in the seventh year you shall set that person free. [13]And when you send a male slave[b] out from you a free person, you shall not send him out empty-handed. [14]Provide liberally out of your flock, your threshing floor, and your wine press, thus giving to him some of the bounty with which the LORD your God has blessed you. [15]Remember that you were a slave in the land of Egypt, and the LORD your God redeemed you; for this reason I lay this command upon you today. [16]But if he says to you, "I will not go out from you," because he loves you and your household, since he is well off with you, [17]then you shall take an awl and thrust it through his earlobe into the door, and he shall be your slave[c] forever.

You shall do the same with regard to your female slave.[d]

18 Do not consider it a hardship when you send them out from you free persons, because for six years they have given you services worth the wages of hired laborers; and the LORD your God will bless you in all that you do.

The Firstborn of Livestock

19 Every firstling male born of your herd and flock you shall consecrate to the LORD your God; you shall not do work with your firstling ox nor shear the firstling of your flock. [20]You shall eat it, you together with your household, in the presence of the LORD your God year by year at the place that the LORD will choose. [21]But if it has any defect—any serious defect, such as lameness or blindness—you shall not sacrifice it to the LORD your God; [22]within your towns you may eat it,

the unclean and the clean alike, as you would a gazelle or deer. [23]Its blood, however, you must not eat; you shall pour it out on the ground like water.

The Passover Reviewed

16 Observe the month[e] of Abib by keeping the passover to the LORD your God, for in the month of Abib the LORD your God brought you out of Egypt by night. [2]You shall offer the passover sacrifice to the LORD your God, from the flock and the herd, at the place that the LORD will choose as a dwelling for his name. [3]You must not eat with it anything leavened. For seven days you shall eat unleavened bread with it—the bread of affliction—because you came out of the land of Egypt in great haste, so that all the days of your life you may remember the day of your departure from the land of Egypt. [4]No leaven shall be seen with you in all your territory for seven days; and none of the meat of what you slaughter on the evening of the first day shall remain until morning. [5]You are not permitted to offer the passover sacrifice within any of your towns that the LORD your God is giving you. [6]But at the place that the LORD your God will choose as a dwelling for his name, only there shall you offer the passover sacrifice, in the evening at sunset, the time of day when you departed from Egypt. [7]You shall cook it and eat it at the place that the LORD your God will choose; the next morning you may go back to your tents. [8]For six days you shall continue to eat unleavened bread, and on the seventh day there shall be a solemn assembly for the LORD your God, when you shall do no work.

The Festival of Weeks Reviewed

9 You shall count seven weeks; begin to count the seven weeks from the time the sickle is first put to the standing grain. [10]Then you shall keep the festival of weeks to the LORD your God, contributing a freewill offering in proportion to the blessing that you have received from the LORD your God. [11]Rejoice before the LORD your God—you and your sons and your daughters, your male and female slaves, the Levites resident in your towns, as well as the strangers, the orphans, and the widows who are among you—at the place that the LORD your God will choose as a dwelling for his name. [12]Remember that you were a slave in Egypt, and diligently observe these statutes.

a Or sells himself or herself   b Heb him   c Or bondman   d Or bondwoman   e Or new moon

The Festival of Booths Reviewed

13 You shall keep the festival of booths[a] for seven days, when you have gathered in the produce from your threshing floor and your wine press. [14]Rejoice during your festival, you and your sons and your daughters, your male and female slaves, as well as the Levites, the strangers, the orphans, and the widows resident in your towns. [15]Seven days you shall keep the festival to the LORD your God at the place that the LORD will choose; for the LORD your God will bless you in all your produce and in all your undertakings, and you shall surely celebrate.

16 Three times a year all your males shall appear before the LORD your God at the place that he will choose: at the festival of unleavened bread, at the festival of weeks, and at the festival of booths.[a] They shall not appear before the LORD empty-handed; [17]all shall give as they are able, according to the blessing of the LORD your God that he has given you.

Municipal Judges and Officers

18 You shall appoint judges and officials throughout your tribes, in all your towns that the LORD your God is giving you, and they shall render just decisions for the people. [19]You must not distort justice; you must not show partiality; and you must not accept bribes, for a bribe blinds the eyes of the wise and subverts the cause of those who are in the right. [20]Justice, and only justice, you shall pursue, so that you may live and occupy the land that the LORD your God is giving you.

Forbidden Forms of Worship

21 You shall not plant any tree as a sacred pole[b] beside the altar that you make for the LORD your God; [22]nor shall you set up a stone pillar— things that the LORD your God hates.

17 You must not sacrifice to the LORD your God an ox or a sheep that has a defect, anything seriously wrong; for that is abhorrent to the LORD your God.

2 If there is found among you, in one of your towns that the LORD your God is giving you, a man or woman who does what is evil in the sight of the LORD your God, and transgresses his covenant [3]by going to serve other gods and worshiping them—whether the sun or the moon or any of the host of heaven, which I have forbidden— [4]and if it is reported to you or you hear of it, and you make a thorough inquiry, and the charge is proved true that such an abhorrent thing has occurred in Israel, [5]then you shall bring out to your gates that man or that woman who

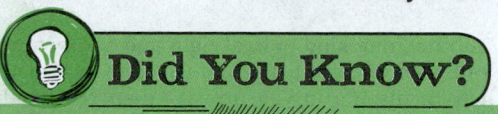

Did You Know?

The Torah

The Hebrew word *Torah* means "instruction" or "teaching," and only over time has come to mean "the Law." Torah refers most fundamentally to the Law that was recorded as given by God to Moses on Mount Sinai. As the people of Israel lived the Torah, it became equated with their very life and existence. It was the key for their organization as a people and gave consistency to their struggle to live their Covenant with God.

Jewish people refer to the first five books of the Bible (the Pentateuch) as the Torah because those books contain the Law and instructions on how to live it. The other books of the Old Testament are also strongly connected to the Torah. The historical books record how the people and their kings kept the Torah or disobeyed it. When they obeyed, they were blessed with happiness, health, and prosperity. When they disobeyed, they were punished with barrenness, destruction, and death. The prophets in the prophetic books call the people to faithfulness to the Law. They condemn idolatry and injustice and call the people to live the spirit of the Torah.

What law are Christians called to live by? For a hint, see the beatitudes (Mt 5:1—7:28), the Letter of Paul to the Galatians, and the Letter of James.

▶ **Deut 17:8–11**

D E U T

has committed this crime and you shall stone the man or woman to death. [6]On the evidence of two or three witnesses the death sentence shall be executed; a person must not be put to death on the evidence of only one witness. [7]The hands of the witnesses shall be the first raised against the person to execute the death penalty, and afterward the hands of all the people. So you shall purge the evil from your midst.

Legal Decisions by Priests and Judges

8 If a judicial decision is too difficult for you to make between one kind of bloodshed and

---

a Or *tabernacles;* Heb *succoth*   b Heb *Asherah*

another, one kind of legal right and another, or one kind of assault and another—any such matters of dispute in your towns—then you shall immediately go up to the place that the LORD your God will choose, ⁹where you shall consult with the levitical priests and the judge who is in office in those days; they shall announce to you the decision in the case. ¹⁰Carry out exactly the decision that they announce to you from the place that the LORD will choose, diligently observing everything they instruct you. ¹¹You must carry out fully the law that they interpret for you or the ruling that they announce to you; do not turn aside from the decision that they announce to you, either to the right or to the left. ¹²As for anyone who presumes to disobey the priest appointed to minister there to the LORD your God, or the judge, that person shall die. So you shall purge the evil from Israel. ¹³All the people will hear and be afraid, and will not act presumptuously again.

Limitations of Royal Authority

14 When you have come into the land that the LORD your God is giving you, and have taken possession of it and settled in it, and you say, "I will set a king over me, like all the nations that are around me," ¹⁵you may indeed set over you a king whom the LORD your God will choose. One of your own community you may set as king over you; you are not permitted to put a foreigner over you, who is not of your own community. ¹⁶Even so, he must not acquire many horses for himself, or return the people to Egypt in order to acquire more horses, since the LORD has said to you, "You must never return that way again." ¹⁷And he must not acquire many wives for himself, or else his heart will turn away; also silver and gold he must not acquire in great quantity for himself. ¹⁸When he has taken the throne of his kingdom, he shall have a copy of this law written for him in the presence of the levitical priests. ¹⁹It shall remain with him and he shall read in it all the days of his life, so that he may learn to fear the LORD his God, diligently observing all the words of this law and these statutes, ²⁰neither exalting himself above other members of the community nor turning aside from the commandment, either to the right or to the left, so that he and his descendants may reign long over his kingdom in Israel.

Privileges of Priests and Levites

18 The levitical priests, the whole tribe of Levi, shall have no allotment or inheritance within Israel. They may eat the sacrifices that are the LORD's portion[a] ²but they shall have no inheritance among the other members of the community; the LORD is their inheritance, as he promised them.

3 This shall be the priests' due from the people, from those offering a sacrifice, whether an ox or a sheep: they shall give to the priest the shoulder, the two jowls, and the stomach. ⁴The first fruits of your grain, your wine, and your oil, as well as the first of the fleece of your sheep, you shall give him. ⁵For the LORD your God has chosen Levi[b] out of all your tribes, to stand and minister in the name of the LORD, him and his sons for all time.

6 If a Levite leaves any of your towns, from wherever he has been residing in Israel, and comes to the place that the LORD will choose (and he may come whenever he wishes), ⁷then he may minister in the name of the LORD his God, like all his fellow-Levites who stand to minister there before the LORD. ⁸They shall have equal portions to eat, even though they have income from the sale of family possessions.[a]

Child-Sacrifice, Divination, and Magic Prohibited

9 When you come into the land that the LORD your God is giving you, you must not learn to imitate the abhorrent practices of those nations. ¹⁰No one shall be found among you who makes a son or daughter pass through fire, or who practices divination, or is a soothsayer, or an augur, or a sorcerer, ¹¹or one who casts spells, or who consults ghosts or spirits, or who seeks oracles from the dead. ¹²For whoever does these things is abhorrent to the LORD; it is because of such abhorrent practices that the LORD your God is driving them out before you. ¹³You must remain completely loyal to the LORD your God. ¹⁴Although these nations that you are about to dispossess do give heed to soothsayers and diviners, as for you, the LORD your God does not permit you to do so.

A New Prophet Like Moses

15 The LORD your God will raise up for you a prophet[c] like me from among your own people; you shall heed such a prophet.[d] ¹⁶This is what you requested of the LORD your God at Horeb on the day of the assembly when you said: "If I hear the voice of the LORD my God any more, or ever again see this great fire, I will die." ¹⁷Then the LORD replied to me: "They are right in what they have said. ¹⁸I will raise up for them a prophet[c]

---

a Meaning of Heb uncertain   b Heb him   c Or prophets
d Or such prophets

like you from among their own people; I will put my words in the mouth of the prophet,[a] who shall speak to them everything that I command. [19]Anyone who does not heed the words that the prophet[b] shall speak in my name, I myself will hold accountable. [20]But any prophet who speaks in the name of other gods, or who presumes to speak in my name a word that I have not commanded the prophet to speak—that prophet shall die." [21]You may say to yourself, "How can we recognize a word that the LORD has not spoken?" [22]If a prophet speaks in the name of the LORD but the thing does not take place or prove true, it is a word that the LORD has not spoken. The prophet has spoken it presumptuously; do not be frightened by it.

Laws concerning the Cities of Refuge

19 When the LORD your God has cut off the nations whose land the LORD your God is giving you, and you have dispossessed them and settled in their towns and in their houses, [2]you shall set apart three cities in the land that the LORD your God is giving you to possess. [3]You shall calculate the distances[c] and divide into three regions the land that the LORD your God gives you as a possession, so that any homicide can flee to one of them.

4 Now this is the case of a homicide who might flee there and live, that is, someone who has killed another person unintentionally when the two had not been at enmity before: [5]Suppose someone goes into the forest with another to cut wood, and when one of them swings the ax to cut down a tree, the head slips from the handle and strikes the other person who then dies; the killer may flee to one of these cities and live. [6]But if the distance is too great, the avenger of blood in hot anger might pursue and overtake and put the killer to death, although a death sentence was not deserved, since the two had not been at enmity before. [7]Therefore I command you: You shall set apart three cities.

8 If the LORD your God enlarges your territory, as he swore to your ancestors—and he will give you all the land that he promised your ancestors to give you, [9]provided you diligently observe this entire commandment that I command you today, by loving the LORD your God and walking always in his ways—then you shall add three more cities to these three, [10]so that the blood of an innocent person may not be shed in the land that the LORD your God is giving you as an inheritance, thereby bringing bloodguilt upon you.

11 But if someone at enmity with another lies in wait and attacks and takes the life of that person, and flees into one of these cities, [12]then the elders of the killer's city shall send to have the culprit taken from there and handed over to the avenger of blood to be put to death. [13]Show no pity; you shall purge the guilt of innocent blood from Israel, so that it may go well with you.

Property Boundaries

14 You must not move your neighbor's boundary marker, set up by former generations, on the property that will be allotted to you in the land that the LORD your God is giving you to possess.

Law concerning Witnesses

15 A single witness shall not suffice to convict a person of any crime or wrongdoing in connection with any offense that may be committed. Only on the evidence of two or three witnesses shall a charge be sustained. [16]If a malicious witness comes forward to accuse someone of wrongdoing, [17]then both parties to the dispute shall appear before the LORD, before the priests and the judges who are in office in those days, [18]and the judges shall make a thorough inquiry. If the witness is a false witness, having testified falsely against another, [19]then you shall do to the false witness just as the false witness had meant to do to the other. So you shall purge the evil from your midst. [20]The rest shall hear and be afraid, and a crime such as this shall never again be committed among you. [21]Show no pity: life for life, eye for eye, tooth for tooth, hand for hand, foot for foot.

Rules of Warfare

20 When you go out to war against your enemies, and see horses and chariots, an army larger than your own, you shall not be afraid of them; for the LORD your God is with you, who brought you up from the land of Egypt. [2]Before you engage in battle, the priest shall come forward and speak to the troops, [3]and shall say to them: "Hear, O Israel! Today you are drawing near to do battle against your enemies. Do not lose heart, or be afraid, or panic, or be in dread of them; [4]for it is the LORD your God who goes with you, to fight for you against your enemies, to give you victory." [5]Then the officials shall address the troops, saying, "Has anyone built a new house but not dedicated it? He should go back to his house, or he might die in the battle and another dedicate it. [6]Has anyone planted a

---

a Or mouths of the prophets   b Heb he   c Or prepare roads to them

DEUT

Facing Life's Battles

What are the wars in your life? Where do you experience conflict and lack of peace? We all hope that we will not face war in armed conflict. But in a sense, war is around us in the conflicts of everyday life.

We have fights with family and friends. We battle the pressures of society and our peers. We are at odds with the future. Deuteronomy 20:1 tells us that we are not to fear times of war because our God is with us and will be our strength.

When we face conflict, our faith will be tested, but we must hold strong and true to what God tells us. If we let our heart be filled with God, the wars we face will become opportunities for God's love to triumph.

What conflicts do you encounter these days? Do you sense that God is with you in these conflicts? If so, how? Pray for peace-filled ways to resolve conflict.

▶ **Deut 20:1**

vineyard but not yet enjoyed its fruit? He should go back to his house, or he might die in the battle and another be first to enjoy its fruit. ⁷Has anyone become engaged to a woman but not yet married her? He should go back to his house, or he might die in the battle and another marry her." ⁸The officials shall continue to address the troops, saying, "Is anyone afraid or disheartened? He should go back to his house, or he might cause the heart of his comrades to melt like his own." ⁹When the officials have finished addressing the troops, then the commanders shall take charge of them.

10 When you draw near to a town to fight against it, offer it terms of peace. ¹¹If it accepts your terms of peace and surrenders to you, then all the people in it shall serve you at forced labor. ¹²If it does not submit to you peacefully, but makes war against you, then you shall besiege it; ¹³and when the LORD your God gives it into your hand, you shall put all its males to the sword. ¹⁴You may, however, take as your booty the women, the children, livestock, and everything else in the town, all its spoil. You may enjoy the spoil of your enemies, which the LORD your God has given you. ¹⁵Thus you shall treat all the towns that are very far from you, which are not towns of the nations here. ¹⁶But as for the towns of these peoples that the LORD your God is giving you as an inheritance, you must not let anything that breathes remain alive. ¹⁷You shall annihilate them—the Hittites and the Amorites, the Canaanites and the Perizzites, the Hivites and the Jebusites—just as the LORD your God has commanded, ¹⁸so that they may not teach you to do all the abhorrent things that they do for their gods, and you thus sin against the LORD your God.

19 If you besiege a town for a long time, making war against it in order to take it, you must not destroy its trees by wielding an ax against them. Although you may take food from them, you must not cut them down. Are trees in the field human beings that they should come under siege from you? ²⁰You may destroy only the trees that you know do not produce food; you may cut them down for use in building siegeworks against the town that makes war with you, until it falls.

Law concerning Murder by Persons Unknown

21 If, in the land that the LORD your God is giving you to possess, a body is found lying in open country, and it is not known who struck the person down, ²then your elders and your judges shall come out to measure the distances to the towns that are near the body. ³The elders of the town nearest the body shall take a heifer that has never been worked, one that has not pulled in the yoke; ⁴the elders of that town shall bring the heifer down to a wadi with running water, which is neither plowed nor sown, and shall break the heifer's neck there in the wadi. ⁵Then the priests, the sons of Levi, shall come forward, for the LORD your God has chosen them to minister to him and to pronounce blessings in the name of the LORD, and by their decision all cases of dispute and assault shall be settled. ⁶All the elders of that town nearest the body shall wash their hands over the heifer whose neck was broken in the wadi, ⁷and they shall declare: "Our hands did not shed this blood, nor were we witnesses to it. ⁸Absolve, O LORD, your people Israel, whom you redeemed; do not let the guilt of innocent blood remain in the midst of your people Israel." Then they will be absolved of bloodguilt. ⁹So you shall purge the guilt of innocent blood from your midst, because you must do what is right in the sight of the LORD.

Female Captives

10 When you go out to war against your enemies, and the LORD your God hands them over to you and you take them captive, [11]suppose you see among the captives a beautiful woman whom you desire and want to marry, [12]and so you bring her home to your house: she shall shave her head, pare her nails, [13]discard her captive's garb, and shall remain in your house a full month, mourning for her father and mother; after that you may go in to her and be her husband, and she shall be your wife. [14]But if you are not satisfied with her, you shall let her go free and not sell her for money. You must not treat her as a slave, since you have dishonored her.

The Right of the Firstborn

15 If a man has two wives, one of them loved and the other disliked, and if both the loved and the disliked have borne him sons, the firstborn being the son of the one who is disliked, [16]then on the day when he wills his possessions to his sons, he is not permitted to treat the son of the loved as the firstborn in preference to the son of the disliked, who is the firstborn. [17]He must acknowledge as firstborn the son of the one who is disliked, giving him a double portion[a] of all that he has; since he is the first issue of his virility, the right of the firstborn is his.

Rebellious Children

18 If someone has a stubborn and rebellious son who will not obey his father and mother, who does not heed them when they discipline him, [19]then his father and his mother shall take hold of him and bring him out to the elders of his town at the gate of that place. [20]They shall say to the elders of his town, "This son of ours is stubborn and rebellious. He will not obey us. He is a glutton and a drunkard." [21]Then all the men of the town shall stone him to death. So you shall purge the evil from your midst; and all Israel will hear, and be afraid.

Miscellaneous Laws

22 When someone is convicted of a crime punishable by death and is executed, and you hang him on a tree, [23]his corpse must not remain all night upon the tree; you shall bury him that same day, for anyone hung on a tree is under God's curse. You must not defile the land that the LORD your God is giving you for possession.

22 You shall not watch your neighbor's ox or sheep straying away and ignore them; you shall take them back to their owner. [2]If the owner does not reside near you or you do not know who the owner is, you shall bring it to your own house, and it shall remain with you until the owner claims it; then you shall return it. [3]You shall do the same with a neighbor's donkey; you shall do the same with a neighbor's garment; and you shall do the same with anything else that your neighbor loses and you find. You may not withhold your help.

4 You shall not see your neighbor's donkey or ox fallen on the road and ignore it; you shall help to lift it up.

5 A woman shall not wear a man's apparel, nor shall a man put on a woman's garment; for whoever does such things is abhorrent to the LORD your God.

6 If you come on a bird's nest, in any tree or on the ground, with fledglings or eggs, with the mother sitting on the fledglings or on the eggs, you shall not take the mother with the young. [7]Let the mother go, taking only the young for yourself, in order that it may go well with you and you may live long.

8 When you build a new house, you shall make a parapet for your roof; otherwise you might have bloodguilt on your house, if anyone should fall from it.

9 You shall not sow your vineyard with a second kind of seed, or the whole yield will have to be forfeited, both the crop that you have sown and the yield of the vineyard itself.

10 You shall not plow with an ox and a donkey yoked together.

11 You shall not wear clothes made of wool and linen woven together.

12 You shall make tassels on the four corners of the cloak with which you cover yourself.

Laws concerning Sexual Relations

13 Suppose a man marries a woman, but after going in to her, he dislikes her [14]and makes up charges against her, slandering her by saying, "I married this woman; but when I lay with her, I did not find evidence of her virginity." [15]The father of the young woman and her mother shall then submit the evidence of the young woman's virginity to the elders of the city at the gate. [16]The father of the young woman shall say to the elders: "I gave my daughter in marriage to this man but he dislikes her; [17]now he has made up charges against her, saying, 'I did not find evidence of your daughter's virginity.' But here is the evidence of my daughter's virginity." Then they shall spread out the cloth before the elders

---

a Heb *two-thirds*

of the town. [18]The elders of that town shall take the man and punish him; [19]they shall fine him one hundred shekels of silver (which they shall give to the young woman's father) because he has slandered a virgin of Israel. She shall remain his wife; he shall not be permitted to divorce her as long as he lives.

20 If, however, this charge is true, that evidence of the young woman's virginity was not found, [21]then they shall bring the young woman out to the entrance of her father's house and the men of her town shall stone her to death, because she committed a disgraceful act in Israel by prostituting herself in her father's house. So you shall purge the evil from your midst.

22 If a man is caught lying with the wife of another man, both of them shall die, the man who lay with the woman as well as the woman. So you shall purge the evil from Israel.

23 If there is a young woman, a virgin already engaged to be married, and a man meets her in the town and lies with her, [24]you shall bring both of them to the gate of that town and stone them to death, the young woman because she did not cry for help in the town and the man because he violated his neighbor's wife. So you shall purge the evil from your midst.

25 But if the man meets the engaged woman in the open country, and the man seizes her and lies with her, then only the man who lay with her shall die. [26]You shall do nothing to the young woman; the young woman has not committed an offense punishable by death, because this case is like that of someone who attacks and murders a neighbor. [27]Since he found her in the open country, the engaged woman may have cried for help, but there was no one to rescue her.

28 If a man meets a virgin who is not engaged, and seizes her and lies with her, and they are caught in the act, [29]the man who lay with her shall give fifty shekels of silver to the young woman's father, and she shall become his wife. Because he violated her he shall not be permitted to divorce her as long as he lives.

30[a] A man shall not marry his father's wife, thereby violating his father's rights.[b]

Those Excluded from the Assembly

23 No one whose testicles are crushed or whose penis is cut off shall be admitted to the assembly of the LORD.

2 Those born of an illicit union shall not be admitted to the assembly of the LORD. Even to the tenth generation, none of their descendants shall be admitted to the assembly of the LORD.

3 No Ammonite or Moabite shall be admitted to the assembly of the LORD. Even to the tenth generation, none of their descendants shall be admitted to the assembly of the LORD, [4]because they did not meet you with food and water on your journey out of Egypt, and because they hired against you Balaam son of Beor, from Pethor of Mesopotamia, to curse you. [5](Yet the LORD your God refused to heed Balaam; the LORD your God turned the curse into a blessing for you, because the LORD your God loved you.) [6]You shall never promote their welfare or their prosperity as long as you live.

7 You shall not abhor any of the Edomites, for they are your kin. You shall not abhor any of the Egyptians, because you were an alien residing in their land. [8]The children of the third generation that are born to them may be admitted to the assembly of the LORD.

Sanitary, Ritual, and Humanitarian Precepts

9 When you are encamped against your enemies you shall guard against any impropriety.

10 If one of you becomes unclean because of a nocturnal emission, then he shall go outside the camp; he must not come within the camp. [11]When evening comes, he shall wash himself with water, and when the sun has set, he may come back into the camp.

12 You shall have a designated area outside the camp to which you shall go. [13]With your utensils you shall have a trowel; when you relieve yourself outside, you shall dig a hole with it and then cover up your excrement. [14]Because the LORD your God travels along with your camp, to save you and to hand over your enemies to you, therefore your camp must be holy, so that he may not see anything indecent among you and turn away from you.

15 Slaves who have escaped to you from their owners shall not be given back to them. [16]They shall reside with you, in your midst, in any place they choose in any one of your towns, wherever they please; you shall not oppress them.

17 None of the daughters of Israel shall be a temple prostitute; none of the sons of Israel shall be a temple prostitute. [18]You shall not bring the fee of a prostitute or the wages of a male prostitute[c] into the house of the LORD your God in payment for any vow, for both of these are abhorrent to the LORD your God.

19 You shall not charge interest on loans to another Israelite, interest on money, interest on

---

a Ch 23.1 in Heb   b Heb *uncovering his father's skirt*   c Heb a dog provisions, interest on anything that is lent. ²⁰On loans to a foreigner you may charge interest, but on loans to another Israelite you may not charge interest, so that the Lord your God may bless you in all your undertakings in the land that you are about to enter and possess.

21 If you make a vow to the Lord your God, do not postpone fulfilling it; for the Lord your God will surely require it of you, and you would incur guilt. ²²But if you refrain from vowing, you will not incur guilt. ²³Whatever your lips utter you must diligently perform, just as you have freely vowed to the Lord your God with your own mouth.

24 If you go into your neighbor's vineyard, you may eat your fill of grapes, as many as you wish, but you shall not put any in a container.

25 If you go into your neighbor's standing grain, you may pluck the ears with your hand, but you shall not put a sickle to your neighbor's standing grain.

Laws concerning Marriage and Divorce

24 Suppose a man enters into marriage with a woman, but she does not please him because he finds something objectionable about her, and so he writes her a certificate of divorce, puts it in her hand, and sends her out of his house; she then leaves his house ²and goes off to become another man's wife. ³Then suppose the second man dislikes her, writes her a bill of divorce, puts it in her hand, and sends her out of his house (or the second man who married her dies); ⁴her first husband, who sent her away, is not permitted to take her again to be his wife after she has been defiled; for that would be abhorrent to the Lord, and you shall not bring guilt on the land that the Lord your God is giving you as a possession.

Miscellaneous Laws

5 When a man is newly married, he shall not go out with the army or be charged with any related duty. He shall be free at home one year, to be happy with the wife whom he has married.

6 No one shall take a mill or an upper millstone in pledge, for that would be taking a life in pledge.

7 If someone is caught kidnaping another Israelite, enslaving or selling the Israelite, then that kidnaper shall die. So you shall purge the evil from your midst.

8 Guard against an outbreak of a leprous[a] skin disease by being very careful; you shall carefully observe whatever the levitical priests instruct you, just as I have commanded them.

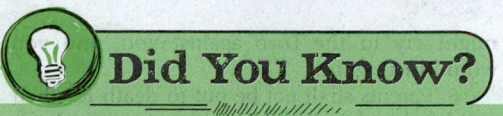

Did You Know?

The Poor, the Strangers, the Widows, and the Orphans

One remarkable aspect of Israel's Covenant was the command to care for the poor, the "aliens" or strangers, the widows, and the orphans. These four groups were the outsiders in ancient Israel because they fell outside Israel's socioeconomic system. Those who were poor often had no means to sustain themselves. Strangers, or aliens, were not part of Israel's tribal organization. Widows depended on the charity of others. Orphans were destitute because they had no family to help them survive.

God provides a reason why Israel must care for the poor and oppressed. Just as the Israelites were enslaved in Egypt—when they were poor, oppressed, orphans in a foreign land—and God responded to their cry for help, so they must care for the poor, oppressed, forgotten, and marginalized in their midst. Can this be any less true for us today?

▶ **Deut 24:10–21**

⁹Remember what the Lord your God did to Miriam on your journey out of Egypt.

10 When you make your neighbor a loan of any kind, you shall not go into the house to take the pledge. ¹¹You shall wait outside, while the person to whom you are making the loan brings the pledge out to you. ¹²If the person is poor, you shall not sleep in the garment given you as[b] the pledge. ¹³You shall give the pledge back by sunset, so that your neighbor may sleep in the cloak and bless you; and it will be to your credit before the Lord your God.

14 You shall not withhold the wages of poor and needy laborers, whether other Israelites or aliens who reside in your land in one of your towns. ¹⁵You shall pay them their wages daily before sunset, because they are poor and their livelihood depends on them; otherwise they

a A term for several skin diseases; precise meaning uncertain
b Heb lacks the garment given you as

might cry to the LORD against you, and you would incur guilt.

16 Parents shall not be put to death for their children, nor shall children be put to death for their parents; only for their own crimes may persons be put to death.

17 You shall not deprive a resident alien or an orphan of justice; you shall not take a widow's garment in pledge. [18]Remember that you were a slave in Egypt and the LORD your God redeemed you from there; therefore I command you to do this.

19 When you reap your harvest in your field and forget a sheaf in the field, you shall not go back to get it; it shall be left for the alien, the orphan, and the widow, so that the LORD your God may bless you in all your undertakings. [20]When you beat your olive trees, do not strip what is left; it shall be for the alien, the orphan, and the widow.

21 When you gather the grapes of your vineyard, do not glean what is left; it shall be for the alien, the orphan, and the widow. [22]Remember that you were a slave in the land of Egypt; therefore I am commanding you to do this.

25 Suppose two persons have a dispute and enter into litigation, and the judges decide between them, declaring one to be in the right and the other to be in the wrong. [2]If the one in the wrong deserves to be flogged, the judge shall make that person lie down and be beaten in his presence with the number of lashes proportionate to the offense. [3]Forty lashes may be given but not more; if more lashes than these are given, your neighbor will be degraded in your sight.

4 You shall not muzzle an ox while it is treading out the grain.

Levirate Marriage

5 When brothers reside together, and one of them dies and has no son, the wife of the deceased shall not be married outside the family to a stranger. Her husband's brother shall go in to her, taking her in marriage, and performing the duty of a husband's brother to her, [6]and the firstborn whom she bears shall succeed to the name of the deceased brother, so that his name may not be blotted out of Israel. [7]But if the man has no desire to marry his brother's widow, then his brother's widow shall go up to the elders at the gate and say, "My husband's brother refuses to perpetuate his brother's name in Israel; he will not perform the duty of a husband's brother to me." [8]Then the elders of his town shall summon him and speak to him. If he persists, saying, "I have no desire to marry her," [9]then his brother's

wife shall go up to him in the presence of the elders, pull his sandal off his foot, spit in his face, and declare, "This is what is done to the man who does not build up his brother's house." [10]Throughout Israel his family shall be known as "the house of him whose sandal was pulled off."

Various Commands

11 If men get into a fight with one another, and the wife of one intervenes to rescue her husband from the grip of his opponent by reaching out and seizing his genitals, [12]you shall cut off her hand; show no pity.

13 You shall not have in your bag two kinds of weights, large and small. [14]You shall not have in your house two kinds of measures, large and small. [15]You shall have only a full and honest weight; you shall have only a full and honest measure, so that your days may be long in the land that the LORD your God is giving you. [16]For all who do such things, all who act dishonestly, are abhorrent to the LORD your God.

17 Remember what Amalek did to you on your journey out of Egypt, [18]how he attacked you on the way, when you were faint and weary, and struck down all who lagged behind you; he did not fear God. [19]Therefore when the LORD your God has given you rest from all your enemies on every hand, in the land that the LORD your God is giving you as an inheritance to possess, you shall blot out the remembrance of Amalek from under heaven; do not forget.

First Fruits and Tithes

26 When you have come into the land that the LORD your God is giving you as an inheritance to possess, and you possess it, and settle in it, [2]you shall take some of the first of all the fruit of the ground, which you harvest from the land that the LORD your God is giving you, and you shall put it in a basket and go to the place that the LORD your God will choose as a dwelling for his name. [3]You shall go to the priest who is in office at that time, and say to him, "Today I declare to the LORD your God that I have come into the land that the LORD swore to our ancestors to give us." [4]When the priest takes the basket from your hand and sets it down before the altar of the LORD your God, [5]you shall make this response before the LORD your God: "A wandering Aramean was my ancestor; he went down into Egypt and lived there as an alien, few in number, and there he became a great nation, mighty and populous. [6]When the Egyptians treated us harshly and afflicted us, by imposing hard labor on us, [7]we cried to the LORD, the God of our ancestors; the LORD heard our voice and saw our affliction, our toil, and our oppression. [8]The LORD brought us out of Egypt with a mighty hand and an outstretched arm, with a terrifying display of power, and with signs and wonders; [9]and he brought us into this place and gave us this land, a land flowing with milk and honey. [10]So now I bring the first of the fruit of the ground that you, O LORD, have given me." You shall set it down before the LORD your God and bow down before the LORD your God. [11]Then you, together with the Levites and the aliens who reside among you, shall celebrate with all the bounty that the LORD your God has given to you and to your house.

12 When you have finished paying all the tithe of your produce in the third year (which is the year of the tithe), giving it to the Levites, the aliens, the orphans, and the widows, so that they may eat their fill within your towns, [13]then you shall say before the LORD your God: "I have removed the sacred portion from the house, and I have given it to the Levites, the resident aliens, the orphans, and the widows, in accordance with your entire commandment that you commanded me; I have neither transgressed nor forgotten any of your commandments: [14]I have not eaten of it while in mourning; I have not removed any of it while I was unclean; and I have not offered any of it to the dead. I have obeyed the LORD my God, doing just as you commanded me. [15]Look down from your holy habitation, from heaven, and bless your people Israel and the ground that you have given us, as you swore to our ancestors—a land flowing with milk and honey."

Concluding Exhortation

16 This very day the LORD your God is commanding you to observe these statutes and ordinances; so observe them diligently with all your heart and with all your soul. [17]Today you have obtained the LORD's agreement: to be your God; and for you to walk in his ways, to keep his statutes, his commandments, and his ordinances, and to obey him. [18]Today the LORD has obtained your agreement: to be his treasured people, as he promised you, and to keep his commandments; [19]for him to set you high above all nations that he has made, in praise and in fame and in honor; and for you to be a people holy to the LORD your God, as he promised.

The Inscribed Stones and Altar on Mount Ebal

27 Then Moses and the elders of Israel charged all the people as follows: Keep the entire commandment that I am commanding you today. [2]On the day that you cross over the Jordan into the land that the LORD your God is giving you, you shall set up large stones and cover them with plaster. [3]You shall write on them all the words of this law when you have crossed over, to enter the land that the LORD your God is giving you, a land flowing with milk and honey, as the LORD, the God of your ancestors, promised you. [4]So when you have crossed over the Jordan, you shall set up these stones, about which I am commanding you today, on Mount Ebal, and you shall cover them with plaster. [5]And you shall build an altar there to the LORD your God, an altar of stones on which you have not used an iron tool. [6]You must build the altar of the LORD your God of unhewn[a] stones. Then offer up burnt offerings on it to the LORD your God, [7]make sacrifices of well-being, and eat them there, rejoicing before the LORD your God. [8]You shall write on the stones all the words of this law very clearly.

9 Then Moses and the levitical priests spoke to all Israel, saying: Keep silence and hear, O Israel! This very day you have become the people of the LORD your God. [10]Therefore obey the LORD your God, observing his commandments and his statutes that I am commanding you today.

Twelve Curses

11 The same day Moses charged the people as follows: [12]When you have crossed over the Jordan, these shall stand on Mount Gerizim for the blessing of the people: Simeon, Levi, Judah, Issachar, Joseph, and Benjamin. [13]And these shall stand on Mount Ebal for the curse: Reuben, Gad, Asher, Zebulun, Dan, and Naphtali. [14]Then the Levites shall declare in a loud voice to all the Israelites:

15 "Cursed be anyone who makes an idol or casts an image, anything abhorrent to the LORD, the work of an artisan, and sets it up in secret." All the people shall respond, saying, "Amen!"

16 "Cursed be anyone who dishonors father or mother." All the people shall say, "Amen!"

17 "Cursed be anyone who moves a neighbor's boundary marker." All the people shall say, "Amen!"

18 "Cursed be anyone who misleads a blind person on the road." All the people shall say, "Amen!"

19 "Cursed be anyone who deprives the alien, the orphan, and the widow of justice." All the people shall say, "Amen!"

DEUT

a Heb whole

20 "Cursed be anyone who lies with his father's wife, because he has violated his father's rights."[a] All the people shall say, "Amen!"

21 "Cursed be anyone who lies with any animal." All the people shall say, "Amen!"

22 "Cursed be anyone who lies with his sister, whether the daughter of his father or the daughter of his mother." All the people shall say, "Amen!"

23 "Cursed be anyone who lies with his mother-in-law." All the people shall say, "Amen!"

24 "Cursed be anyone who strikes down a neighbor in secret." All the people shall say, "Amen!"

25 "Cursed be anyone who takes a bribe to shed innocent blood." All the people shall say, "Amen!"

26 "Cursed be anyone who does not uphold the words of this law by observing them." All the people shall say, "Amen!"

Blessings for Obedience

28 If you will only obey the LORD your God, by diligently observing all his commandments that I am commanding you today, the LORD your God will set you high above all the nations of the earth; 2all these blessings shall come upon you and overtake you, if you obey the LORD your God:

3 Blessed shall you be in the city, and blessed shall you be in the field.

4 Blessed shall be the fruit of your womb, the fruit of your ground, and the fruit of your livestock, both the increase of your cattle and the issue of your flock.

5 Blessed shall be your basket and your kneading bowl.

6 Blessed shall you be when you come in, and blessed shall you be when you go out.

7 The LORD will cause your enemies who rise against you to be defeated before you; they shall come out against you one way, and flee before you seven ways. 8The LORD will command the blessing upon you in your barns, and in all that you undertake; he will bless you in the land that the LORD your God is giving you. 9The LORD will establish you as his holy people, as he has sworn to you, if you keep the commandments of the LORD your God and walk in his ways. 10All the peoples of the earth shall see that you are called by the name of the LORD, and they shall be afraid of you. 11The LORD will make you abound in prosperity, in the fruit of your womb, in the fruit of your livestock, and in the fruit of your ground in the land that the LORD swore to your ancestors to give you. 12The LORD will open for you his rich storehouse, the heavens, to give the rain of your land in its season and to bless all your undertakings. You will lend to many nations, but you will not borrow. 13The LORD will make you the head, and not the tail; you shall be only at the top, and not at the bottom—if you obey the commandments of the LORD your God, which I am commanding you today, by diligently observing them, 14and if you do not turn aside from any of the words that I am commanding you today, either to the right or to the left, following other gods to serve them.

Warnings against Disobedience

15 But if you will not obey the LORD your God by diligently observing all his commandments and decrees, which I am commanding you today, then all these curses shall come upon you and overtake you:

16 Cursed shall you be in the city, and cursed shall you be in the field.

17 Cursed shall be your basket and your kneading bowl.

18 Cursed shall be the fruit of your womb, the fruit of your ground, the increase of your cattle and the issue of your flock.

19 Cursed shall you be when you come in, and cursed shall you be when you go out.

20 The LORD will send upon you disaster, panic, and frustration in everything you attempt to do, until you are destroyed and perish quickly, on account of the evil of your deeds, because you have forsaken me. 21The LORD will make the pestilence cling to you until it has consumed you off the land that you are entering to possess. 22The LORD will afflict you with consumption, fever, inflammation, with fiery heat and drought, and with blight and mildew; they shall pursue you until you perish. 23The sky over your head shall be bronze, and the earth under you iron. 24The LORD will change the rain of your land into powder, and only dust shall come down upon you from the sky until you are destroyed.

25 The LORD will cause you to be defeated before your enemies; you shall go out against them one way and flee before them seven ways. You shall become an object of horror to all the kingdoms of the earth. 26Your corpses shall be food for every bird of the air and animal of the earth, and there shall be no one to frighten them away. 27The LORD will afflict you with the boils of Egypt, with ulcers, scurvy, and itch, of which you cannot be healed. 28The LORD will afflict you with madness, blindness, and confusion

a Heb uncovered his father's skirt

of mind; ²⁹you shall grope about at noon as blind people grope in darkness, but you shall be unable to find your way; and you shall be continually abused and robbed, without anyone to help. ³⁰You shall become engaged to a woman, but another man shall lie with her. You shall build a house, but not live in it. You shall plant a vineyard, but not enjoy its fruit. ³¹Your ox shall be butchered before your eyes, but you shall not eat of it. Your donkey shall be stolen in front of you, and shall not be restored to you. Your sheep shall be given to your enemies, without anyone to help you. ³²Your sons and daughters shall be given to another people, while you look on; you will strain your eyes looking for them all day but be powerless to do anything. ³³A people whom you do not know shall eat up the fruit of your ground and of all your labors; you shall be continually abused and crushed, ³⁴and driven mad by the sight that your eyes shall see. ³⁵The Lord will strike you on the knees and on the legs with grievous boils of which you cannot be healed, from the sole of your foot to the crown of your head. ³⁶The Lord will bring you, and the king whom you set over you, to a nation that neither you nor your ancestors have known, where you shall serve other gods, of wood and stone. ³⁷You shall become an object of horror, a proverb, and a byword among all the peoples where the Lord will lead you.

38 You shall carry much seed into the field but shall gather little in, for the locust shall consume it. ³⁹You shall plant vineyards and dress them, but you shall neither drink the wine nor gather the grapes, for the worm shall eat them. ⁴⁰You shall have olive trees throughout all your territory, but you shall not anoint yourself with the oil, for your olives shall drop off. ⁴¹You shall have sons and daughters, but they shall not remain yours, for they shall go into captivity. ⁴²All your trees and the fruit of your ground the cicada shall take over. ⁴³Aliens residing among you shall ascend above you higher and higher, while you shall descend lower and lower. ⁴⁴They shall lend to you but you shall not lend to them; they shall be the head and you shall be the tail.

45 All these curses shall come upon you, pursuing and overtaking you until you are destroyed, because you did not obey the Lord your God, by observing the commandments and the decrees that he commanded you. ⁴⁶They shall be among you and your descendants as a sign and a portent forever.

47 Because you did not serve the Lord your God joyfully and with gladness of heart for the abundance of everything, ⁴⁸therefore you shall serve your enemies whom the Lord will send against you, in hunger and thirst, in nakedness and lack of everything. He will put an iron yoke on your neck until he has destroyed you. ⁴⁹The Lord will bring a nation from far away, from the end of the earth, to swoop down on you like an eagle, a nation whose language you do not understand, ⁵⁰a grim-faced nation showing no respect to the old or favor to the young. ⁵¹It shall consume the fruit of your livestock and the fruit of your ground until you are destroyed, leaving you neither grain, wine, and oil, nor the increase of your cattle and the issue of your flock, until it has made you perish. ⁵²It shall besiege you in all your towns until your high and fortified walls, in which you trusted, come down throughout your land; it shall besiege you in all your towns throughout the land that the Lord your God has given you. ⁵³In the desperate straits to which the enemy siege reduces you, you will eat the fruit of your womb, the flesh of your own sons and daughters whom the Lord your God has given you. ⁵⁴Even the most refined and gentle of men among you will begrudge food to his own brother, to the wife whom he embraces, and to the last of his remaining children, ⁵⁵giving to none of them any of the flesh of his children whom he is eating, because nothing else remains to him, in the desperate straits to which the enemy siege will reduce you in all your towns. ⁵⁶She who is the most refined and gentle among you, so gentle and refined that she does not venture to set the sole of her foot on the ground, will begrudge food to the husband whom she embraces, to her own son, and to her own daughter, ⁵⁷begrudging even the afterbirth that comes out from between her thighs, and the children that she bears, because she is eating them in secret for lack of anything else, in the desperate straits to which the enemy siege will reduce you in your towns.

58 If you do not diligently observe all the words of this law that are written in this book, fearing this glorious and awesome name, the Lord your God, ⁵⁹then the Lord will overwhelm both you and your offspring with severe and lasting afflictions and grievous and lasting maladies. ⁶⁰He will bring back upon you all the diseases of Egypt, of which you were in dread, and they shall cling to you. ⁶¹Every other malady and affliction, even though not recorded in the book of this law, the Lord will inflict on you until you are destroyed. ⁶²Although once you were as numerous as the stars in heaven, you shall be left few in number, because you did not obey the Lord your God. ⁶³And just as the Lord took delight in making you prosperous and numerous, so the Lord

DEUT

will take delight in bringing you to ruin and destruction; you shall be plucked off the land that you are entering to possess. [64]The LORD will scatter you among all peoples, from one end of the earth to the other; and there you shall serve other gods, of wood and stone, which neither you nor your ancestors have known. [65]Among those nations you shall find no ease, no resting place for the sole of your foot. There the LORD will give you a trembling heart, failing eyes, and a languishing spirit. [66]Your life shall hang in doubt before you; night and day you shall be in dread, with no assurance of your life. [67]In the morning you shall say, "If only it were evening!" and at evening you shall say, "If only it were morning!"—because of the dread that your heart shall feel and the sights that your eyes shall see. [68]The LORD will bring you back in ships to Egypt, by a route that I promised you would never see again; and there you shall offer yourselves for sale to your enemies as male and female slaves, but there will be no buyer.

29 [a] These are the words of the covenant that the LORD commanded Moses to make with the Israelites in the land of Moab, in addition to the covenant that he had made with them at Horeb.

The Covenant Renewed in Moab

2[b] Moses summoned all Israel and said to them: You have seen all that the LORD did before your eyes in the land of Egypt, to Pharaoh and to all his servants and to all his land, [3]the great trials that your eyes saw, the signs, and those great wonders. [4]But to this day the LORD has not given you a mind to understand, or eyes to see, or ears to hear. [5]I have led you forty years in the wilderness. The clothes on your back have not worn out, and the sandals on your feet have not worn out; [6]you have not eaten bread, and you have not drunk wine or strong drink—so that you may know that I am the LORD your God. [7]When you came to this place, King Sihon of Heshbon and King Og of Bashan came out against us for battle, but we defeated them. [8]We took their land and gave it as an inheritance to the Reubenites, the Gadites, and the half-tribe of Manasseh. [9]Therefore diligently observe the words of this covenant, in order that you may succeed[c] in everything that you do.

10 You stand assembled today, all of you, before the LORD your God—the leaders of your tribes,[d] your elders, and your officials, all the men of Israel, [11]your children, your women, and the aliens who are in your camp, both those who cut your wood and those who draw your water— [12]to enter into the covenant of the LORD your God, sworn by an oath, which the LORD your God is making with you today; [13]in order that he may establish you today as his people, and that he may be your God, as he promised you and as he swore to your ancestors, to Abraham, to Isaac, and to Jacob. [14]I am making this covenant, sworn by an oath, not only with you who stand here with us today before the LORD our God, [15]but also with those who are not here with us today. [16]You know how we lived in the land of Egypt, and how we came through the midst of the nations through which you passed. [17]You have seen their detestable things, the filthy idols of wood and stone, of silver and gold, that were among them. [18]It may be that there is among you a man or woman, or a family or tribe, whose heart is already turning away from the LORD our God to serve the gods of those nations. It may be that there is among you a root sprouting poisonous and bitter growth. [19]All who hear the words of this oath and bless themselves, thinking in their hearts, "We are safe even though we go our own stubborn ways" (thus bringing disaster on moist and dry alike)[e]— [20]the LORD will be unwilling to pardon them, for the LORD's anger and passion will smoke against them. All the curses written in this book will descend on them, and the LORD will blot out their names from under heaven. [21]The LORD will single them out from all the tribes of Israel for calamity, in accordance with all the curses of the covenant written in this book of the law. [22]The next generation, your children who rise up after you, as well as the foreigner who comes from a distant country, will see the devastation of that land and the afflictions with which the LORD has afflicted it— [23]all its soil burned out by sulfur and salt, nothing planted, nothing sprouting, unable to support any vegetation, like the destruction of Sodom and Gomorrah, Admah and Zeboiim, which the LORD destroyed in his fierce anger— [24]they and indeed all the nations will wonder, "Why has the LORD done thus to this land? What caused this great display of anger?" [25]They will conclude, "It is because they abandoned the covenant of the LORD, the God of their ancestors, which he made with them when he brought them out of the land of Egypt. [26]They turned and served other gods, worshiping them, gods whom they had not known and whom he had not allotted to them; [27]so the anger of the LORD was kindled against that land, bringing on it every curse written in this book.

---

a Ch 28.69 in Heb   b Ch 29.1 in Heb   c Or *deal wisely*
d Gk Syr: Heb *your leaders, your tribes*   e Meaning of Heb uncertain

28The Lord uprooted them from their land in anger, fury, and great wrath, and cast them into another land, as is now the case." 29The secret things belong to the Lord our God, but the revealed things belong to us and to our children forever, to observe all the words of this law.

God's Fidelity Assured

30 When all these things have happened to you, the blessings and the curses that I have set before you, if you call them to mind among all the nations where the Lord your God has driven you, 2and return to the Lord your God, and you and your children obey him with all your heart and with all your soul, just as I am commanding you today, 3then the Lord your God will restore your fortunes and have compassion on you, gathering you again from all the peoples among whom the Lord your God has scattered you. 4Even if you are exiled to the ends of the world,*a* from there the Lord your God will gather you, and from there he will bring you back. 5The Lord your God will bring you into the land that your ancestors possessed, and you will possess it; he will make you more prosperous and numerous than your ancestors.

6 Moreover, the Lord your God will circumcise your heart and the heart of your descendants, so that you will love the Lord your God with all your heart and with all your soul, in order that you may live. 7The Lord your God will put all these curses on your enemies and on the adversaries who took advantage of you. 8Then you shall again obey the Lord, observing all his commandments that I am commanding you today, 9and the Lord your God will make you abundantly prosperous in all your undertakings, in the fruit of your body, in the fruit of your livestock, and in the fruit of your soil. For the Lord will again take delight in prospering you, just as he delighted in prospering your ancestors, 10when you obey the Lord your God by observing his commandments and decrees that are written in this book of the law, because you turn to the Lord your God with all your heart and with all your soul.

Exhortation to Choose Life

11 Surely, this commandment that I am commanding you today is not too hard for you, nor is it too far away. 12It is not in heaven, that you should say, "Who will go up to heaven for us, and get it for us so that we may hear it and observe it?" 13Neither is it beyond the sea, that you should say, "Who will cross to the other side of the sea for us, and get it for us so that we may hear it and observe it?" 14No, the word is very near to you; it is in your mouth and in your heart for you to observe.

15 See, I have set before you today life and prosperity, death and adversity. 16If you obey the commandments of the Lord your God*b* that I am commanding you today, by loving the Lord your God, walking in his ways, and observing his commandments, decrees, and ordinances, then you shall live and become numerous, and the Lord your God will bless you in the land that you are entering to possess. 17But if your heart turns away and you do not hear, but are led astray to bow down to other gods and serve them, 18I declare to you today that you shall perish; you shall not live long in the land that you are crossing the Jordan to enter and possess. 19I call heaven and earth to witness against you today that I have set before you life and death, blessings and curses. Choose life so that you and your descendants may live, 20loving the Lord your God, obeying him, and holding fast to him; for that means life to you and length of days, so that you may live in the land that the Lord swore to give to your ancestors, to Abraham, to Isaac, and to Jacob.

> **Choose life so that you and your descendants may live.**
> (Deut 30:19)

Joshua Becomes Moses' Successor

31 When Moses had finished speaking all*c* these words to all Israel, 2he said to them: "I am now one hundred twenty years old. I am no longer able to get about, and the Lord has told me, 'You shall not cross over this Jordan.' 3The Lord your God himself will cross over before you. He will destroy these nations before you, and you shall dispossess them. Joshua also will cross over before you, as the Lord promised. 4The Lord will do to them as he did to Sihon and Og, the kings of the Amorites, and to their land, when he destroyed them. 5The Lord will give them over to you and you shall deal with them in full accord with the command that I have given to you. 6Be strong and bold; have no fear or dread of them, because it is the Lord your God who goes with you; he will not fail you or forsake you."

---

a Heb of heaven   *b* Gk: Heb lacks *If you obey the commandments of the Lord your God*   *c* Q Ms Gk: MT *Moses went and spoke*

"Choose life."

This statement is a powerful summons to all of us who are believers. We live in a culture that is constantly filled and refilled with images of violence and death, especially in the media and entertainment. Many people seem to choose options that lead to death rather than life. Temptations to do so are everywhere. Pope John Paul II spoke often of the "culture of death" so prevalent in the world today.

God calls us to choose life—every time. What options before us lead to life rather than death? What choices give life to others?

Life is what we are called to—a full life, lived out in God's presence, a life lived in service to others. Think about the choices you make each day. Your decision to greet someone or smile at someone can make a big difference. That difference can be life giving. Choose life. It is always the right choice!

▶ **Deut 30:19**

7 Then Moses summoned Joshua and said to him in the sight of all Israel: "Be strong and bold, for you are the one who will go with this people into the land that the Lord has sworn to their ancestors to give them; and you will put them in possession of it. ⁸It is the Lord who goes before you. He will be with you; he will not fail you or forsake you. Do not fear or be dismayed."

The Law to Be Read Every Seventh Year

9 Then Moses wrote down this law, and gave it to the priests, the sons of Levi, who carried the ark of the covenant of the Lord, and to all the elders of Israel. ¹⁰Moses commanded them: "Every seventh year, in the scheduled year of remission, during the festival of booths,ᵃ ¹¹when all Israel comes to appear before the Lord your God at the place that he will choose, you shall read this law before all Israel in their hearing. ¹²Assemble the people—men, women, and children, as well as the aliens residing in your towns—so that they may hear and learn to fear the Lord your God

and to observe diligently all the words of this law, ¹³and so that their children, who have not known it, may hear and learn to fear the Lord your God, as long as you live in the land that you are crossing over the Jordan to possess."

Moses and Joshua Receive God's Charge

14 The Lord said to Moses, "Your time to die is near; call Joshua and present yourselves in the tent of meeting, so that I may commission him." So Moses and Joshua went and presented themselves in the tent of meeting, ¹⁵and the Lord appeared at the tent in a pillar of cloud; the pillar of cloud stood at the entrance to the tent.

16 The Lord said to Moses, "Soon you will lie down with your ancestors. Then this people will begin to prostitute themselves to the foreign gods in their midst, the gods of the land into which they are going; they will forsake me, breaking my covenant that I have made with them. ¹⁷My anger will be kindled against them in that day. I will forsake them and hide my face from them; they will become easy prey, and many terrible troubles will come upon them. In that day they will say, 'Have not these troubles come upon us because our God is not in our midst?' ¹⁸On that day I will surely hide my face on account of all the evil they have done by turning to other gods. ¹⁹Now therefore write this song, and teach it to the Israelites; put it in their mouths, in order that this song may be a witness for me against the Israelites. ²⁰For when I have brought them into the land flowing with milk and honey, which I promised on oath to their ancestors, and they have eaten their fill and grown fat, they will turn to other gods and serve them, despising me and breaking my covenant. ²¹And when many terrible troubles come upon them, this song will confront them as a witness, because it will not be lost from the mouths of their descendants. For I know what they are inclined to do even now, before I have brought them into the land that I promised them on oath." ²²That very day Moses wrote this song and taught it to the Israelites.

23 Then the Lord commissioned Joshua son of Nun and said, "Be strong and bold, for you shall bring the Israelites into the land that I promised them; I will be with you."

24 When Moses had finished writing down in a book the words of this law to the very end, ²⁵Moses commanded the Levites who carried the ark of the covenant of the Lord, saying, ²⁶"Take this book of the law and put it beside the ark of the covenant of the Lord your God; let it remain

---

a Or tabernacles; Heb succoth

there as a witness against you. 27For I know well how rebellious and stubborn you are. If you already have been so rebellious toward the Lord while I am still alive among you, how much more after my death! 28Assemble to me all the elders of your tribes and your officials, so that I may recite these words in their hearing and call heaven and earth to witness against them. 29For I know well that after my death you will surely act corruptly, turning aside from the way that I have commanded you. In time to come trouble will befall you, because you will do what is evil in the sight of the Lord, provoking him to anger through the work of your hands."

The Song of Moses

30 Then Moses recited the words of this song, to the very end, in the hearing of the whole assembly of Israel:

32 Give ear, O heavens, and I will speak;
let the earth hear the words of my mouth.
2 May my teaching drop like the rain,
   my speech condense like the dew;
like gentle rain on grass,
   like showers on new growth.
3 For I will proclaim the name of the Lord;
   ascribe greatness to our God!

4 The Rock, his work is perfect,
   and all his ways are just.
A faithful God, without deceit,
   just and upright is he;
5 yet his degenerate children have dealt falsely
      with him,[a]
   a perverse and crooked generation.
6 Do you thus repay the Lord,
   O foolish and senseless people?
Is not he your father, who created you,
   who made you and established you?
7 Remember the days of old,
   consider the years long past;
ask your father, and he will inform you;
   your elders, and they will tell you.
8 When the Most High[b] apportioned the nations,
   when he divided humankind,
he fixed the boundaries of the peoples
   according to the number of the gods;[c]
9 the Lord's own portion was his people,
   Jacob his allotted share.

10 He sustained[d] him in a desert land,
   in a howling wilderness waste;
he shielded him, cared for him,
   guarded him as the apple of his eye.
11 As an eagle stirs up its nest,
   and hovers over its young;

as it spreads its wings, takes them up,
   and bears them aloft on its pinions,
12 the Lord alone guided him;
   no foreign god was with him.
13 He set him atop the heights of the land,
   and fed him with[e] produce of the field;
he nursed him with honey from the crags,
   with oil from flinty rock;
14 curds from the herd, and milk from the flock,
   with fat of lambs and rams;
Bashan bulls and goats,
   together with the choicest wheat—
   you drank fine wine from the blood of grapes.
15 Jacob ate his fill;[f]
Jeshurun grew fat, and kicked.
   You grew fat, bloated, and gorged!
He abandoned God who made him,
   and scoffed at the Rock of his salvation.
16 They made him jealous with strange gods,
   with abhorrent things they provoked him.
17 They sacrificed to demons, not God,
   to deities they had never known,
to new ones recently arrived,
   whom your ancestors had not feared.
18 You were unmindful of the Rock that bore you;[g]
   you forgot the God who gave you birth.

19 The Lord saw it, and was jealous;[h]
   he spurned[i] his sons and daughters.
20 He said: I will hide my face from them,
   I will see what their end will be;
for they are a perverse generation,
   children in whom there is no faithfulness.
21 They made me jealous with what is no god,
   provoked me with their idols.
So I will make them jealous with what is no
      people,
   provoke them with a foolish nation.
22 For a fire is kindled by my anger,
   and burns to the depths of Sheol;
it devours the earth and its increase,
   and sets on fire the foundations of the
      mountains.
23 I will heap disasters upon them,
   spend my arrows against them:
24 wasting hunger,
   burning consumption,
   bitter pestilence.
The teeth of beasts I will send against them,
   with venom of things crawling in the dust.

---

a Meaning of Heb uncertain   b Traditional rendering of Heb Elyon   c Q Ms Compare Gk Tg: MT the Israelites   d Sam Gk Compare Tg: MT found   e Sam Gk Syr Tg: MT he ate   f Q Mss Sam Gk: MT lacks Jacob ate his fill   g Or that begot you   h Q Mss Gk: MT lacks was jealous   i Cn: Heb he spurned because of provocation

Cultural Connection

Hispanics Live the History of Salvation!

As Moses did, Hispanics express their faith in the Lord of history:

Lord, you who are the Lord of all,
we, the Hispanic people of the United States,
conscious of being a people with its own
   identity,
born of common roots,
cultural traditions, language, and faith,
and in diversity united,
direct this prayer to you.

Lord and master of history,
we, a people, as we experience the same
   hungers and hurts,
make a preferential option for the poor,
and we stand in solidarity with this suffering
   humanity.

From your creative womb, we have been born;
we are your family, your believing people.
In this moment of grace, we feel ourselves
   called
to a "prophetic mission";

working together and participating in
   community,
we speak in your name to church and society.
Raised up as a people, intent on being authors
of our own history,
we walk with hope and in a progressive
   process.
Together we contribute to the coming of
the Kingdom of God here and now,
struggling to establish the new society, with an
   economy, relationships, and values based on
   the love and the justice of your Son, Jesus
   Christ.
We ask this in company with Mary,
the mother of all believers. Amen.
(Secretariat for Hispanic Affairs,
Prophetic Voices, p. 23)

DEUT

25 In the street the sword shall bereave,
      and in the chambers terror,
for young man and woman alike,
      nursing child and old gray head.
26 I thought to scatter them[a]
      and blot out the memory of them from
         humankind;
27 but I feared provocation by the enemy,
      for their adversaries might misunderstand
and say, "Our hand is triumphant;
      it was not the LORD who did all this."

28 They are a nation void of sense;
      there is no understanding in them.
29 If they were wise, they would understand this;
      they would discern what the end would be.
30 How could one have routed a thousand,
      and two put a myriad to flight,
unless their Rock had sold them,
      the LORD had given them up?
31 Indeed their rock is not like our Rock;
      our enemies are fools.[a]
32 Their vine comes from the vinestock of Sodom,
      from the vineyards of Gomorrah;
their grapes are grapes of poison,
      their clusters are bitter;
33 their wine is the poison of serpents,
      the cruel venom of asps.

34 Is not this laid up in store with me,
      sealed up in my treasuries?
35 Vengeance is mine, and recompense,
      for the time when their foot shall slip;
because the day of their calamity is at hand,
      their doom comes swiftly.

36 Indeed the LORD will vindicate his people,
      have compassion on his servants,
when he sees that their power is gone,
      neither bond nor free remaining.
37 Then he will say: Where are their gods,
      the rock in which they took refuge,
38 who ate the fat of their sacrifices,
      and drank the wine of their libations?
Let them rise up and help you,
      let them be your protection!

39 See now that I, even I, am he;
      there is no god besides me.
I kill and I make alive;
      I wound and I heal;
      and no one can deliver from my hand.
40 For I lift up my hand to heaven,
      and swear: As I live forever,
41 when I whet my flashing sword,

a Gk: Meaning of Heb uncertain

and my hand takes hold on judgment;
    I will take vengeance on my adversaries,
    and will repay those who hate me.
⁴² I will make my arrows drunk with blood,
    and my sword shall devour flesh—
with the blood of the slain and the captives,
    from the long-haired enemy.

⁴³ Praise, O heavens,ᵃ his people,
    worship him, all you gods!ᵇ
For he will avenge the blood of his children,ᶜ
    and take vengeance on his adversaries;
he will repay those who hate him,ᵇ
    and cleanse the land for his people.ᵈ

44 Moses came and recited all the words of this song in the hearing of the people, he and Joshuaᵉ son of Nun. ⁴⁵When Moses had finished reciting all these words to all Israel, ⁴⁶he said to them: "Take to heart all the words that I am giving in witness against you today; give them as a command to your children, so that they may diligently observe all the words of this law. ⁴⁷This is no trifling matter for you, but rather your very life; through it you may live long in the land that you are crossing over the Jordan to possess."

Moses' Death Foretold

48 On that very day the Lord addressed Moses as follows: ⁴⁹"Ascend this mountain of the Abarim, Mount Nebo, which is in the land of Moab, across from Jericho, and view the land of Canaan, which I am giving to the Israelites for a possession; ⁵⁰you shall die there on the mountain that you ascend and shall be gathered to your kin, as your brother Aaron died on Mount Hor and was gathered to his kin; ⁵¹because both of you broke faith with me among the Israelites at the waters of Meribath-kadesh in the wilderness of Zin, by failing to maintain my holiness among the Israelites. ⁵²Although you may view the land from a distance, you shall not enter it—the land that I am giving to the Israelites."

Moses' Final Blessing on Israel

33 This is the blessing with which Moses, the man of God, blessed the Israelites before his death. ²He said:

The Lord came from Sinai,
    and dawned from Seir upon us;ᶠ
he shone forth from Mount Paran.
With him were myriads of holy ones;ᵍ
    at his right, a host of his own.ʰ
³ Indeed, O favorite amongⁱ peoples,
    all his holy ones were in your charge;
they marched at your heels,
    accepted direction from you.

⁴ Moses charged us with the law,
    as a possession for the assembly of Jacob.
⁵ There arose a king in Jeshurun,
    when the leaders of the people assembled—
    the united tribes of Israel.

⁶ May Reuben live, and not die out,
    even though his numbers are few.

⁷And this he said of Judah:
O Lord, give heed to Judah,
    and bring him to his people;
strengthen his hands for him,ʲ
    and be a help against his adversaries.

⁸And of Levi he said:
Give to Leviᵏ your Thummim,
    and your Urim to your loyal one,
whom you tested at Massah,
    with whom you contended at the waters of
        Meribah;
⁹ who said of his father and mother,
    "I regard them not";
he ignored his kin,
    and did not acknowledge his children.
For they observed your word,
    and kept your covenant.
¹⁰ They teach Jacob your ordinances,
    and Israel your law;
they place incense before you,
    and whole burnt offerings on your altar.
¹¹ Bless, O Lord, his substance,
    and accept the work of his hands;
crush the loins of his adversaries,
    of those that hate him, so that they do not
        rise again.

¹²Of Benjamin he said:
The beloved of the Lord rests in safety—
the High Godˡ surrounds him all day long—
    the belovedᵐ rests between his shoulders.

¹³And of Joseph he said:
Blessed by the Lord be his land,
    with the choice gifts of heaven above,
    and of the deep that lies beneath;
¹⁴ with the choice fruits of the sun,
    and the rich yield of the months;

a Q Ms Gk: MT nations   b Q Ms Gk: MT lacks this line   c Q Ms Gk: MT his servants   d Q Ms Sam Gk Vg: MT his land his people   e Sam Gk Syr Vg: MT Hoshea   f Gk Syr Vg Compare Tg: Heb upon them   g Cn Compare Gk Sam Syr Vg: MT He came from Ribeboth-kadesh,   h Cn Compare Gk: meaning of Heb uncertain   i Or O lover of the   j Cn: Heb with his hands he contended   k Q Ms Gk: MT lacks Give to Levi   l Heb above him   m Heb he

Moses' Death

Why did Moses die on the brink of entering the Promised Land? This question has disturbed many generations of believers. The one who received God's call to lead the Israelites out of slavery, who amazed Pharaoh with wonders and called down plagues on Egypt, who opened the Red Sea and received the tablets of the Law on Mount Sinai—this great leader did not get to enjoy the success of his work Numbers 20:11–12 points to Moses' lack of trust and God's subsequent punishment as the reason for Moses not entering the Promised Land. Deuteronomy 34:1–6 simply tells us that Moses died on Mount Nebo and that his burial place was forgotten. Moses' death at the end of Deuteronomy leaves the Israelites on the banks of the Jordan River, still waiting for God's promise to be fulfilled.

We also experience times when we don't get to enjoy the success of our work or are waiting for a promise to be fulfilled. For example, you may volunteer for some project and never really see the results of your time and effort. But that's not the point, is it? We don't volunteer so that we can take credit for the result. Rather we do it because it is a good and right thing to do. We are helping build the Reign of God. So it was with Moses. He had done what he was called to do—no more, no less. And as the Israelites stood on the verge of entering the Promised Land, we too stand on the verge of our final destination—eternity with God in heaven.

▶ **Deuteronomy, chapter 34**

15 with the finest produce of the ancient
        mountains,
    and the abundance of the everlasting hills;
16 with the choice gifts of the earth and its fullness,
    and the favor of the one who dwells on
        Sinai.*a*
Let these come on the head of Joseph,
    on the brow of the prince among his brothers.
17 A firstborn*b* bull—majesty is his!

His horns are the horns of a wild ox;
with them he gores the peoples,
    driving them to*c* the ends of the earth;
such are the myriads of Ephraim,
    such the thousands of Manasseh.

18 And of Zebulun he said:
Rejoice, Zebulun, in your going out;
    and Issachar, in your tents.
19 They call peoples to the mountain;
    there they offer the right sacrifices;
for they suck the affluence of the seas
    and the hidden treasures of the sand.

20 And of Gad he said:
Blessed be the enlargement of Gad!
    Gad lives like a lion;
    he tears at arm and scalp.
21 He chose the best for himself,
    for there a commander's allotment was
        reserved;
he came at the head of the people,
    he executed the justice of the LORD,
    and his ordinances for Israel.

22 And of Dan he said:
Dan is a lion's whelp
    that leaps forth from Bashan.

23 And of Naphtali he said:
O Naphtali, sated with favor,
    full of the blessing of the LORD,
    possess the west and the south.

24 And of Asher he said:
Most blessed of sons be Asher;
    may he be the favorite of his brothers,
    and may he dip his foot in oil.
25 Your bars are iron and bronze;
    and as your days, so is your strength.

26 There is none like God, O Jeshurun,
    who rides through the heavens to your help,
    majestic through the skies.
27 He subdues the ancient gods,*d*
    shatters*e* the forces of old;*f*
he drove out the enemy before you,
    and said, "Destroy!"
28 So Israel lives in safety,
    untroubled is Jacob's abode*g*
in a land of grain and wine,
    where the heavens drop down dew.

---

a Cn: Heb *in the bush*   b Q Ms Gk Syr Vg: MT *His firstborn*
c Cn: Heb *the peoples, together*   d Or *The eternal God is a dwelling place*   e Cn: Heb *from underneath*   f Or *the everlasting arms*   g Or *fountain*

²⁹ Happy are you, O Israel! Who is like you,
    a people saved by the LORD,
the shield of your help,
    and the sword of your triumph!
Your enemies shall come fawning to you,
    and you shall tread on their backs.

Moses Dies and Is Buried in the Land of Moab

34 Then Moses went up from the plains of Moab to Mount Nebo, to the top of Pisgah, which is opposite Jericho, and the LORD showed him the whole land: Gilead as far as Dan, ²all Naphtali, the land of Ephraim and Manasseh, all the land of Judah as far as the Western Sea, ³the Negeb, and the Plain—that is, the valley of Jericho, the city of palm trees—as far as Zoar. ⁴The LORD said to him, "This is the land of which I swore to Abraham, to Isaac, and to Jacob, saying, 'I will give it to your descendants'; I have let you see it with your eyes, but you shall not cross over there." ⁵Then Moses, the servant of the LORD, died there in the land of Moab, at the LORD's command. ⁶He was buried in a valley in the land of Moab, opposite Beth-peor, but no one knows his burial place to this day. ⁷Moses was one hundred twenty years old when he died; his sight was unimpaired and his vigor had not abated. ⁸The Israelites wept for Moses in the plains of Moab thirty days; then the period of mourning for Moses was ended.

9 Joshua son of Nun was full of the spirit of wisdom, because Moses had laid his hands on him; and the Israelites obeyed him, doing as the LORD had commanded Moses.

10 Never since has there arisen a prophet in Israel like Moses, whom the LORD knew face to face. ¹¹He was unequaled for all the signs and wonders that the LORD sent him to perform in the land of Egypt, against Pharaoh and all his servants and his entire land, ¹²and for all the mighty deeds and all the terrifying displays of power that Moses performed in the sight of all Israel.

Introduction to
the Historical Books

Have you ever noticed that many older people enjoy telling stories about the past? Sometimes it seems that their past experiences are more real to them than present-day events. Those of us who are younger may get tired of hearing about the "good old days." Still, a lot is to be gained from listening carefully to the memories of our elders. The sixteen historical books of the Old Testament, like the voices of respected elders, tell the stories of God at work in ancient Israel. In reading these stories, we can see more clearly how God works in today's world.

In Depth

The historical books recount the period of Israelite history from 1250 to 100 BC. In those books, we read about the following events:

- the Israelites' settlement in the Promised Land and their struggle to protect themselves from their enemies (the Books of Joshua and Judges)

- the rise of a united kingdom under David (1 and 2 Samuel, 1 Kings)

- the division of the kingdom into northern and southern kingdoms, and the various kings and prophets of each, until the fall of Jerusalem in 587 BC (1 and 2 Kings, 1 and 2 Chronicles)

- the return from Exile and the rebuilding of the nation (Ezra and Nehemiah)

- the Jewish resistance to Greek domination in the second century before Christ (1 and 2 Maccabees)

In addition, the books contain three "religious novels" about the human challenge to trust God in difficult times (Tobit, Judith, and Esther).

The historical books of the Old Testament are not like the history books we read in school. Those who write history books today generally try to report the facts with little interpretation. "Let the events speak for themselves," they say. However, those who wrote the historical books of the Old Testament had a different purpose: "Let us tell you what the events *mean in the light of our faith in God.*" Thus, the history contained in these books is often called sacred history because it reveals God's message and God's purpose in history.

Scripture scholars find evidence of two general groups shaping the final form of the historical books. The first group is called the Deuteronomic school of writers because it was responsible for the highly influential Book of Deuteronomy. This group also wrote Joshua, Judges, 1 and 2 Samuel, and 1 and 2 Kings. The Deuteronomists were convinced that God rewarded the good and punished the wicked in this world. Thus, you will find in these books a repeated pattern of (1) God's offer of love, (2) the people's faithlessness and sin, (3) God's just punishment, (4) the people's repentance and cry for help, (5) God's forgiveness and mercy, and (6) the people's repeated sin.

The second group (or person), sometimes called the Chronicler, is responsible for 1 and 2 Chronicles, and probably Ezra and Nehemiah. The Chronicler still emphasized that God rewards the faithful and punishes the unfaithful, but the measurement for what is faithful had changed. Instead of emphasizing faithfulness to the Sinai Covenant, the Chronicler emphasized faithfulness to proper worship, particularly worship at the Temple in Jerusalem. The Chronicler wrote after the return of the exiles to the Holy Land to emphasize the importance of worship in the rebuilt second Temple.

Some of the religious truths you will learn from reading these books are as follows:

God is not removed from the affairs of this world but cares deeply about what is happening in human history.

People are happier when they follow the law of God than when they turn away from the law.

All human beings, from the beginning of history, are joined in a common struggle to find sense and meaning in the ups and downs of life.

As you read these books, remember that the authors' understanding of God is not the same as Jesus' understanding. Although not denying the truths about God taught by these books, reading them in light of Jesus' teaching in the New Testament provides a fuller understanding of God's unconditional love and unlimited mercy. For Christians, both the Old Testament and the New Testament shed light on each other, both are the true word of God.

Other Background

▶ The Book of Ruth was not originally one of the historical books. It was written later than the books it is now sandwiched between.

▶ The Books of 1 and 2 Chronicles review the same historical period as 1 and 2 Samuel and 1 and 2 Kings.

▶ Tobit, Judith, and Esther are inspired folklore that use history only as a backdrop. Their purpose is to encourage fidelity to God's law in hard times.

▶ Tobit, Judith, 1 and 2 Maccabees, and parts of Esther are not found in every translation of the Old Testament and are not contained in many Protestant Bibles. See "The Case of the Missing Books," near Tobit 1:16.

When you were young, did you ask to hear your favorite story over and over again? Often familiar stories appeal to us because of their simple justice—good triumphs over evil. There is something reassuring in knowing that in the end, good wins out and evil is punished, no matter how many times we hear it. That is the basic message of the Book of Joshua. In the conquest of the Promised Land, the author reminds us that those who follow God are rewarded, and those who do not are punished, pure and simple.

At a Glance

- **Chapters 1–12. the conquest of the land of Canaan**
- **Chapters 13–22. the division of the land among the twelve Tribes**
- **Chapters 23–24. Joshua's last words and death**

Quick Facts

Period Covered: after the desert wandering, from about 1250 to 1200 BC

Inspired Author: unknown, from the Deuteronomic tradition the book took its present form in the seventh or sixth century BC

Themes: Israel's conquest of the Promised Land, the triumph of good and the punishment of evil

Of Note: The name Jesus is the Greek form of Joshua, which means "God saves."

In Depth

The Book of Joshua is named after the Israelite hero who succeeds Moses and leads the people in their takeover of the Promised Land. At the beginning of the book, Joshua promises the Israelites they will conquer the land of Canaan and make it their own if they are faithful to the Covenant of Moses. They respond with enthusiasm: "Just as we obeyed Moses in all things, so we will obey you" (1:17). The author describes how by remaining true to the Commandments of God, the various Israelite tribes, under Joshua's leadership, take over the land and settle in it with their families and livestock (see map 2, "The Exodus from Egypt").

Today, biblical scholars doubt that the conquest of the Promised Land by the twelve Tribes of Israel was as complete and easy as it is written in Joshua. Archaeologists have found evidence that Canaanites continued to live in the area after the "conquest." The historical memories preserved in the book were reshaped by subsequent storytellers who lived after the Promised Land had been lost, to emphasize an important lesson of faith: God would preserve the Israelites on their land as long as they obeyed the Commandments.

The belief in the triumph of good and the punishment of evil is at the heart of the Book of Joshua. Like Judges, 1 and 2 Samuel, and 1 and 2 Kings, the Book of Joshua is written from the same point of view as the Book of Deuteronomy, which insists that God rewards the just and punishes the wicked in this world (see Deut 30:15–20). The Book of Joshua challenges us to remember that God is our surest hope in all the ups and downs of history.

The Book of Joshua

Joshua

God's Commission to Joshua

1 After the death of Moses the servant of the LORD, the LORD spoke to Joshua son of Nun, Moses' assistant, saying, ²"My servant Moses is dead. Now proceed to cross the Jordan, you and all this people, into the land that I am giving to them, to the Israelites. ³Every place that the sole of your foot will tread upon I have given to you, as I promised to Moses. ⁴From the wilderness and the Lebanon as far as the great river, the river Euphrates, all the land of the Hittites, to the Great Sea in the west shall be your territory. ⁵No one shall be able to stand against you all the days of your life. As I was with Moses, so I will be with you; I will not fail you or forsake you. ⁶Be strong and courageous; for you shall put this people in possession of the land that I swore to their ancestors to give them. ⁷Only be strong and very courageous, being careful to act in accordance with all the law that my servant Moses commanded you; do not turn from it to the right hand or to the left, so that you may be successful wherever you go. ⁸This book of the law shall not depart out of your mouth; you shall meditate on it day and night, so that you may be careful to act in accordance with all that is written in it. For then you shall make your way prosperous, and then you shall be successful. ⁹I hereby command you: Be strong and courageous; do not be frightened or dismayed, for the LORD your God is with you wherever you go."

Preparations for the Invasion

10 Then Joshua commanded the officers of the people, ¹¹"Pass through the camp, and command the people: 'Prepare your provisions; for in three days you are to cross over the Jordan, to go in to take possession of the land that the LORD your God gives you to possess.'"

12 To the Reubenites, the Gadites, and the half-tribe of Manasseh Joshua said, ¹³"Remember the word that Moses the servant of the LORD commanded you, saying, 'The LORD your God is providing you a place of rest, and will give you this land.' ¹⁴Your wives, your little ones, and your livestock shall remain in the land that Moses gave you beyond the Jordan. But all the warriors among you shall cross over armed before your kindred and shall help them, ¹⁵until the LORD gives rest to your kindred as well as to you, and they too take possession of the land that the LORD your God is giving them. Then you shall return to your own land and take possession of it, the land that Moses the servant of the LORD gave you beyond the Jordan to the east."

16 They answered Joshua: "All that you have commanded us we will do, and wherever you send us we will go. ¹⁷Just as we obeyed Moses in all things, so we will obey you. Only may the LORD your God be with you, as he was with Moses! ¹⁸Whoever rebels against your orders and disobeys your words, whatever you command,

Be Not Afraid

" **B**e strong and courageous; do not be frightened or dismayed, for the LORD your God is with you wherever you go" (Josh 1:9).

Living proof:

Saint Joan of Arc was a humble, uneducated peasant maiden from fifteenth-century France. Inspired by saintly voices, she overcame numerous obstacles to lead the French troops into battle against British invaders.

Saint Thomas More, a distinguished scholar and lawyer, refused to approve King Henry VIII's divorce and remarriage and establishment of the Church of England.

Dorothy Day, twentieth-century American co-founder of the Catholic Worker movement, challenged all Christians to serve poor and homeless people and dedicated her life to nonviolence.

In 1980, Archbishop Oscar Romero of El Salvador was shot while saying Mass, because he dared to speak against the military groups that were terrorizing and killing the poor people of his diocese.

These four people, along with many others, have taken to heart God's words to Joshua. If you are not familiar with their stories, take time to learn more about these Catholic heroes.

▶ **Josh 1:5–9**

shall be put to death. Only be strong and courageous."

Spies Sent to Jericho

2 Then Joshua son of Nun sent two men secretly from Shittim as spies, saying, "Go, view the land, especially Jericho." So they went, and entered the house of a prostitute whose name was Rahab, and spent the night there. ²The king of Jericho was told, "Some Israelites have come here tonight to search out the land." ³Then the king of Jericho sent orders to Rahab, "Bring out the men who have come to you, who entered your house, for they have come only to search out the whole land." ⁴But the woman took the two men and hid them. Then she said, "True,

the men came to me, but I did not know where they came from. ⁵And when it was time to close the gate at dark, the men went out. Where the men went I do not know. Pursue them quickly, for you can overtake them." ⁶She had, however, brought them up to the roof and hidden them with the stalks of flax that she had laid out on the roof. ⁷So the men pursued them on the way to the Jordan as far as the fords. As soon as the pursuers had gone out, the gate was shut.

8 Before they went to sleep, she came up to them on the roof ⁹and said to the men: "I know that the LORD has given you the land, and that dread of you has fallen on us, and that all the inhabitants of the land melt in fear before you. ¹⁰For we have heard how the LORD dried up the water of the Red Sea*a* before you when you came out of Egypt, and what you did to the two kings of the Amorites that were beyond the Jordan, to Sihon and Og, whom you utterly destroyed. ¹¹As soon as we heard it, our hearts melted, and there was no courage left in any of us because of you. The LORD your God is indeed God in heaven above and on earth below. ¹²Now then, since I have dealt kindly with you, swear to me by the LORD that you in turn will deal kindly with my family. Give me a sign of good faith ¹³that you will spare my father and mother, my brothers and sisters, and all who belong to them, and deliver our lives from death." ¹⁴The men said to her, "Our life for yours! If you do not tell this business of ours, then we will deal kindly and faithfully with you when the LORD gives us the land."

15 Then she let them down by a rope through the window, for her house was on the outer side of the city wall and she resided within the wall itself. ¹⁶She said to them, "Go toward the hill country, so that the pursuers may not come upon you. Hide yourselves there three days, until the pursuers have returned; then afterward you may go your way." ¹⁷The men said to her, "We will be released from this oath that you have made us swear to you ¹⁸if we invade the land and you do not tie this crimson cord in the window through which you let us down, and you do not gather into your house your father and mother, your brothers, and all your family. ¹⁹If any of you go out of the doors of your house into the street, they shall be responsible for their own death, and we shall be innocent; but if a hand is laid upon any who are with you in the house, we shall bear the responsibility for their death. ²⁰But if you tell this business of ours, then we shall be released from this oath that you made us swear

---

a Or Sea of Reeds

to you." ²¹She said, "According to your words, so be it." She sent them away and they departed. Then she tied the crimson cord in the window.

22 They departed and went into the hill country and stayed there three days, until the pursuers returned. The pursuers had searched all along the way and found nothing. ²³Then the two men came down again from the hill country. They crossed over, came to Joshua son of Nun, and told him all that had happened to them. ²⁴They said to Joshua, "Truly the LORD has given all the land into our hands; moreover all the inhabitants of the land melt in fear before us."

Israel Crosses the Jordan

3 Early in the morning Joshua rose and set out from Shittim with all the Israelites, and they came to the Jordan. They camped there before crossing over. ²At the end of three days the officers went through the camp ³and commanded the people, "When you see the ark of the covenant of the LORD your God being carried by the levitical priests, then you shall set out from your place. Follow it, ⁴so that you may know the way you should go, for you have not passed this way before. Yet there shall be a space between you and it, a distance of about two thousand cubits; do not come any nearer to it." ⁵Then Joshua said to the people, "Sanctify yourselves; for tomorrow the LORD will do wonders among you." ⁶To the priests Joshua said, "Take up the ark of the covenant, and pass on in front of the people." So they took up the ark of the covenant and went in front of the people.

7 The LORD said to Joshua, "This day I will begin to exalt you in the sight of all Israel, so that they may know that I will be with you as I was with Moses. ⁸You are the one who shall command the priests who bear the ark of the covenant, 'When you come to the edge of the waters of the Jordan, you shall stand still in the Jordan.' " ⁹Joshua then said to the Israelites, "Draw near and hear the words of the LORD your God." ¹⁰Joshua said, "By this you shall know that among you is the living God who without fail will drive out from before you the Canaanites, Hittites, Hivites, Perizzites, Girgashites, Amorites, and Jebusites: ¹¹the ark of the covenant of the Lord of all the earth is going to pass before you into the Jordan. ¹²So now select twelve men from the tribes of Israel, one from each tribe. ¹³When the soles of the feet of the priests who bear the ark of the LORD, the Lord of all the earth, rest in the waters of the Jordan, the waters of the Jordan flowing from above shall be cut off; they shall stand in a single heap."

A Prayer Against Prejudice

Creator of diverse people, the Israelites united themselves with Rahab, someone outside their group, and trusted her. Lead me to be open to befriending those who are different from me so that I may learn to trust them as well.

Forgive my friends and me for every time we have looked at someone different and considered her or him to be of lesser quality. Forgive us for each time we have talked about certain people as if we were superior. Forgive our cliques that look down on others and won't associate with them. Help us to forgive those who have looked down on us. Amen.

▶ **Joshua, chapter 2**

14 When the people set out from their tents to cross over the Jordan, the priests bearing the ark of the covenant were in front of the people. ¹⁵Now the Jordan overflows all its banks throughout the time of harvest. So when those who bore the ark had come to the Jordan, and the feet of the priests bearing the ark were dipped in the edge of the water, ¹⁶the waters flowing from above stood still, rising up in a single heap far off at Adam, the city that is beside Zarethan, while those flowing toward the sea of the Arabah, the Dead Sea,^a were wholly cut off. Then the people crossed over opposite Jericho. ¹⁷While all Israel were crossing over on dry ground, the priests who bore the ark of the covenant of the LORD stood on dry ground in the middle of the Jordan, until the entire nation finished crossing over the Jordan.

Twelve Stones Set Up at Gilgal

4 When the entire nation had finished crossing over the Jordan, the LORD said to Joshua: ²"Select twelve men from the people, one from each tribe, ³and command them, 'Take twelve stones from here out of the middle of the Jordan, from the place where the priests' feet stood, carry them over with you, and lay them down in the place where you camp tonight.' " ⁴Then Joshua

a Heb Salt Sea

summoned the twelve men from the Israelites, whom he had appointed, one from each tribe. [5]Joshua said to them, "Pass on before the ark of the LORD your God into the middle of the Jordan, and each of you take up a stone on his shoulder, one for each of the tribes of the Israelites, [6]so that this may be a sign among you. When your children ask in time to come, 'What do those stones mean to you?' [7]then you shall tell them that the waters of the Jordan were cut off in front of the ark of the covenant of the LORD. When it crossed over the Jordan, the waters of the Jordan were cut off. So these stones shall be to the Israelites a memorial forever."

8 The Israelites did as Joshua commanded. They took up twelve stones out of the middle of the Jordan, according to the number of the tribes of the Israelites, as the LORD told Joshua, carried them over with them to the place where they camped, and laid them down there. [9](Joshua set up twelve stones in the middle of the Jordan, in the place where the feet of the priests bearing the ark of the covenant had stood; and they are there to this day.)

10 The priests who bore the ark remained standing in the middle of the Jordan, until everything was finished that the LORD commanded Joshua to tell the people, according to all that Moses had commanded Joshua. The people crossed over in haste. [11]As soon as all the people had finished crossing over, the ark of the LORD, and the priests, crossed over in front of the people. [12]The Reubenites, the Gadites, and the half-tribe of Manasseh crossed over armed before the Israelites, as Moses had ordered them. [13]About forty thousand armed for war crossed over before the LORD to the plains of Jericho for battle.

14 On that day the LORD exalted Joshua in the sight of all Israel; and they stood in awe of him, as they had stood in awe of Moses, all the days of his life.

15 The LORD said to Joshua, [16]"Command the priests who bear the ark of the covenant,[a] to come up out of the Jordan." [17]Joshua therefore commanded the priests, "Come up out of the Jordan." [18]When the priests bearing the ark of the covenant of the LORD came up from the middle of the Jordan, and the soles of the priests' feet touched dry ground, the waters of the Jordan returned to their place and overflowed all its banks, as before.

19 The people came up out of the Jordan on the tenth day of the first month, and they camped in Gilgal on the east border of Jericho. [20]Those twelve stones, which they had taken out of the Jordan, Joshua set up in Gilgal, [21]saying

to the Israelites, "When your children ask their parents in time to come, 'What do these stones mean?' [22]then you shall let your children know, 'Israel crossed over the Jordan here on dry ground.' [23]For the LORD your God dried up the waters of the Jordan for you until you crossed over, as the LORD your God did to the Red Sea,[b] which he dried up for us until we crossed over, [24]so that all the peoples of the earth may know that the hand of the LORD is mighty, and so that you may fear the LORD your God forever."

The New Generation Circumcised

5 When all the kings of the Amorites beyond the Jordan to the west, and all the kings of the Canaanites by the sea, heard that the LORD had dried up the waters of the Jordan for the Israelites until they had crossed over, their hearts melted, and there was no longer any spirit in them, because of the Israelites.

2 At that time the LORD said to Joshua, "Make flint knives and circumcise the Israelites a second time." [3]So Joshua made flint knives, and circumcised the Israelites at Gibeath-haaraloth.[c] [4]This is the reason why Joshua circumcised them: all the males of the people who came out of Egypt, all the warriors, had died during the journey through the wilderness after they had come out of Egypt. [5]Although all the people who came out had been circumcised, yet all the people born on the journey through the wilderness after they had come out of Egypt had not been circumcised. [6]For the Israelites traveled forty years in the wilderness, until all the nation, the warriors who came out of Egypt, perished, not having listened to the voice of the LORD. To them the LORD swore that he would not let them see the land that he had sworn to their ancestors to give us, a land flowing with milk and honey. [7]So it was their children, whom he raised up in their place, that Joshua circumcised; for they were uncircumcised, because they had not been circumcised on the way.

8 When the circumcising of all the nation was done, they remained in their places in the camp until they were healed. [9]The LORD said to Joshua, "Today I have rolled away from you the disgrace of Egypt." And so that place is called Gilgal[d] to this day.

The Passover at Gilgal

10 While the Israelites were camped in Gilgal they kept the passover in the evening on the fourteenth day of the month in the plains of Jericho.

---

a Or treaty, or testimony; Heb eduth   b Or Sea of Reeds   c That is the Hill of the Foreskins   d Related to Heb galal to roll

[11]On the day after the passover, on that very day, they ate the produce of the land, unleavened cakes and parched grain. [12]The manna ceased on the day they ate the produce of the land, and the Israelites no longer had manna; they ate the crops of the land of Canaan that year.

Joshua's Vision

13 Once when Joshua was by Jericho, he looked up and saw a man standing before him with a drawn sword in his hand. Joshua went to him and said to him, "Are you one of us, or one of our adversaries?" [14]He replied, "Neither; but as commander of the army of the LORD I have now come." And Joshua fell on his face to the earth and worshiped, and he said to him, "What do you command your servant, my lord?" [15]The commander of the army of the LORD said to Joshua, "Remove the sandals from your feet, for the place where you stand is holy." And Joshua did so.

Jericho Taken and Destroyed

6 Now Jericho was shut up inside and out because of the Israelites; no one came out and no one went in. [2]The LORD said to Joshua, "See, I have handed Jericho over to you, along with its king and soldiers. [3]You shall march around the city, all the warriors circling the city once. Thus you shall do for six days, [4]with seven priests bearing seven trumpets of rams' horns before the ark. On the seventh day you shall march around the city seven times, the priests blowing the trumpets. [5]When they make a long blast with the ram's horn, as soon as you hear the sound of the trumpet, then all the people shall shout with a great shout; and the wall of the city will fall down flat, and all the people shall charge straight ahead." [6]So Joshua son of Nun summoned the priests and said to them, "Take up the ark of the covenant, and have seven priests carry seven trumpets of rams' horns in front of the ark of the LORD." [7]To the people he said, "Go forward and march around the city; have the armed men pass on before the ark of the LORD."

8 As Joshua had commanded the people, the seven priests carrying the seven trumpets of rams' horns before the LORD went forward, blowing the trumpets, with the ark of the covenant of the LORD following them. [9]And the armed men went before the priests who blew the trumpets; the rear guard came after the ark, while the trumpets blew continually. [10]To the people Joshua gave this command: "You shall not shout or let your voice be heard, nor shall you utter a word, until the day I tell you to shout. Then you shall shout." [11]So the ark of the LORD went around the city, circling it once; and they came into the camp, and spent the night in the camp.

12 Then Joshua rose early in the morning, and the priests took up the ark of the LORD. [13]The seven priests carrying the seven trumpets of rams' horns before the ark of the LORD passed on, blowing the trumpets continually. The armed men went before them, and the rear guard came after the ark of the LORD, while the trumpets blew continually. [14]On the second day they marched around the city once and then returned to the camp. They did this for six days.

15 On the seventh day they rose early, at dawn, and marched around the city in the same manner seven times. It was only on that day that they marched around the city seven times. [16]And at the seventh time, when the priests had blown the trumpets, Joshua said to the people, "Shout! For the LORD has given you the city. [17]The city and all that is in it shall be devoted to the LORD for destruction. Only Rahab the prostitute and all who are with her in her house shall live because she hid the messengers we sent. [18]As for you, keep away from the things devoted to destruction, so as not to covet[a] and take any of the devoted things and make the camp of Israel an object for destruction, bringing trouble upon it. [19]But all silver and gold, and vessels of bronze and iron, are sacred to the LORD; they shall go into the treasury of the LORD." [20]So the people shouted, and the trumpets were blown. As soon as the people heard the sound of the trumpets, they raised a great shout, and the wall fell down flat; so the people charged straight ahead into the city and captured it. [21]Then they devoted to destruction by the edge of the sword all in the city, both men and women, young and old, oxen, sheep, and donkeys.

22 Joshua said to the two men who had spied out the land, "Go into the prostitute's house, and bring the woman out of it and all who belong to her, as you swore to her." [23]So the young men who had been spies went in and brought Rahab out, along with her father, her mother, her brothers, and all who belonged to her—they brought all her kindred out—and set them outside the camp of Israel. [24]They burned down the city, and everything in it; only the silver and gold, and the vessels of bronze and iron, they put into the treasury of the house of the LORD. [25]But Rahab the prostitute, with her family and all who belonged to her, Joshua spared. Her family[b] has lived in Israel ever since. For she hid the messengers whom Joshua sent to spy out Jericho.

---

a Gk: Heb *devote to destruction* Compare 7.21   b Heb *She*

26 Joshua then pronounced this oath, saying,
"Cursed before the LORD be anyone who tries
    to build this city—this Jericho!
At the cost of his firstborn he shall lay its
    foundation,
    and at the cost of his youngest he shall set up
        its gates!"

27 So the LORD was with Joshua; and his fame
was in all the land.

The Sin of Achan and Its Punishment

7 But the Israelites broke faith in regard to the
devoted things: Achan son of Carmi son of
Zabdi son of Zerah, of the tribe of Judah, took
some of the devoted things; and the anger of the
LORD burned against the Israelites.

2 Joshua sent men from Jericho to Ai, which is
near Beth-aven, east of Bethel, and said to them,
"Go up and spy out the land." And the men
went up and spied out Ai. 3Then they returned to
Joshua and said to him, "Not all the people need
go up; about two or three thousand men should
go up and attack Ai. Since they are so few, do not
make the whole people toil up there." 4So about
three thousand of the people went up there; and
they fled before the men of Ai. 5The men of Ai
killed about thirty-six of them, chasing them
from outside the gate as far as Shebarim and killing them on the slope. The hearts of the people
melted and turned to water.

6 Then Joshua tore his clothes, and fell to the
ground on his face before the ark of the LORD
until the evening, he and the elders of Israel; and
they put dust on their heads. 7Joshua said, "Ah,
Lord GOD! Why have you brought this people
across the Jordan at all, to hand us over to the
Amorites so as to destroy us? Would that we
had been content to settle beyond the Jordan!
8O Lord, what can I say, now that Israel has
turned their backs to their enemies! 9The Canaanites and all the inhabitants of the land will
hear of it, and surround us, and cut off our name
from the earth. Then what will you do for your
great name?"

10 The LORD said to Joshua, "Stand up! Why
have you fallen upon your face? 11Israel has
sinned; they have transgressed my covenant that
I imposed on them. They have taken some of
the devoted things; they have stolen, they have
acted deceitfully, and they have put them among
their own belongings. 12Therefore the Israelites
are unable to stand before their enemies; they
turn their backs to their enemies, because they
have become a thing devoted for destruction
themselves. I will be with you no more, unless
you destroy the devoted things from among you.

13Proceed to sanctify the people, and say, 'Sanctify yourselves for tomorrow; for thus says the
LORD, the God of Israel, "There are devoted things
among you, O Israel; you will be unable to stand
before your enemies until you take away the devoted things from among you." 14In the morning
therefore you shall come forward tribe by tribe.
The tribe that the LORD takes shall come near by
clans, the clan that the LORD takes shall come
near by households, and the household that the
LORD takes shall come near one by one. 15And the
one who is taken as having the devoted things
shall be burned with fire, together with all that
he has, for having transgressed the covenant of
the LORD, and for having done an outrageous
thing in Israel.' "

16 So Joshua rose early in the morning, and
brought Israel near tribe by tribe, and the tribe
of Judah was taken. 17He brought near the clans
of Judah, and the clan of the Zerahites was taken;
and he brought near the clan of the Zerahites,
family by family,a and Zabdi was taken. 18And
he brought near his household one by one, and
Achan son of Carmi son of Zabdi son of Zerah,
of the tribe of Judah, was taken. 19Then Joshua
said to Achan, "My son, give glory to the LORD
God of Israel and make confession to him. Tell
me now what you have done; do not hide it from
me." 20And Achan answered Joshua, "It is true; I
am the one who sinned against the LORD God of
Israel. This is what I did: 21when I saw among
the spoil a beautiful mantle from Shinar, and
two hundred shekels of silver, and a bar of gold
weighing fifty shekels, then I coveted them and
took them. They now lie hidden in the ground
inside my tent, with the silver underneath."

22 So Joshua sent messengers, and they ran
to the tent; and there it was, hidden in his tent
with the silver underneath. 23They took them out
of the tent and brought them to Joshua and all
the Israelites; and they spread them out before the
LORD. 24Then Joshua and all Israel with him took
Achan son of Zerah, with the silver, the mantle,
and the bar of gold, with his sons and daughters,
with his oxen, donkeys, and sheep, and his tent
and all that he had; and they brought them up to
the Valley of Achor. 25Joshua said, "Why did you
bring trouble on us? The LORD is bringing trouble
on you today." And all Israel stoned him to death;
they burned them with fire, cast stones on them,
26and raised over him a great heap of stones that
remains to this day. Then the LORD turned from
his burning anger. Therefore that place to this day
is called the Valley of Achor.b

a Mss Syr: MT *man by man*   b That is *Trouble*

Ai Captured by a Stratagem and Destroyed

8 Then the LORD said to Joshua, "Do not fear or be dismayed; take all the fighting men with you, and go up now to Ai. See, I have handed over to you the king of Ai with his people, his city, and his land. ²You shall do to Ai and its king as you did to Jericho and its king; only its spoil and its livestock you may take as booty for yourselves. Set an ambush against the city, behind it."

3 So Joshua and all the fighting men set out to go up against Ai. Joshua chose thirty thousand warriors and sent them out by night ⁴with the command, "You shall lie in ambush against the city, behind it; do not go very far from the city, but all of you stay alert. ⁵I and all the people who are with me will approach the city. When they come out against us, as before, we shall flee from them. ⁶They will come out after us until we have drawn them away from the city; for they will say, 'They are fleeing from us, as before.' While we flee from them, ⁷you shall rise up from the ambush and seize the city; for the LORD your God will give it into your hand. ⁸And when you have taken the city, you shall set the city on fire, doing as the LORD has ordered; see, I have commanded you." ⁹So Joshua sent them out; and they went to the place of ambush, and lay between Bethel and Ai, to the west of Ai; but Joshua spent that night in the camp.ᵃ

10 In the morning Joshua rose early and mustered the people, and went up, with the elders of Israel, before the people to Ai. ¹¹All the fighting men who were with him went up, and drew near before the city, and camped on the north side of Ai, with a ravine between them and Ai. ¹²Taking about five thousand men, he set them in ambush between Bethel and Ai, to the west of the city. ¹³So they stationed the forces, the main encampment that was north of the city and its rear guard west of the city. But Joshua spent that night in the valley. ¹⁴When the king of Ai saw this, he and all his people, the inhabitants of the city, hurried out early in the morning to the meeting place facing the Arabah to meet Israel in battle; but he did not know that there was an ambush against him behind the city. ¹⁵And Joshua and all Israel made a pretense of being beaten before them, and fled in the direction of the wilderness. ¹⁶So all the people who were in the city were called together to pursue them, and as they pursued Joshua they were drawn away from the city. ¹⁷There was not a man left in Ai or Bethel who did not go out after Israel; they left the city open, and pursued Israel.

18 Then the LORD said to Joshua, "Stretch out the sword that is in your hand toward Ai; for I will give it into your hand." And Joshua stretched out the sword that was in his hand toward the city. ¹⁹As soon as he stretched out his hand, the troops in ambush rose quickly out of their place and rushed forward. They entered the city, took it, and at once set the city on fire. ²⁰So when the men of Ai looked back, the smoke of the city was rising to the sky. They had no power to flee this way or that, for the people who fled to the wilderness turned back against the pursuers. ²¹When Joshua and all Israel saw that the ambush had taken the city and that the smoke of the city was rising, then they turned back and struck down the men of Ai. ²²And the others came out from the city against them; so they were surrounded by Israelites, some on one side, and some on the other; and Israel struck them down until no one was left who survived or escaped. ²³But the king of Ai was taken alive and brought to Joshua.

24 When Israel had finished slaughtering all the inhabitants of Ai in the open wilderness where they pursued them, and when all of them to the very last had fallen by the edge of the sword, all Israel returned to Ai, and attacked it with the edge of the sword. ²⁵The total of those who fell that day, both men and women, was twelve thousand—all the people of Ai. ²⁶For Joshua did not draw back his hand, with which he stretched out the sword, until he had utterly destroyed all the inhabitants of Ai. ²⁷Only the livestock and the spoil of that city Israel took as their booty, according to the word of the LORD that he had issued to Joshua. ²⁸So Joshua burned Ai, and made it forever a heap of ruins, as it is to this day. ²⁹And he hanged the king of Ai on a tree until evening; and at sunset Joshua commanded, and they took his body down from the tree, threw it down at the entrance of the gate of the city, and raised over it a great heap of stones, which stands there to this day.

Joshua Renews the Covenant

30 Then Joshua built on Mount Ebal an altar to the LORD, the God of Israel, ³¹just as Moses the servant of the LORD had commanded the Israelites, as it is written in the book of the law of Moses, "an altar of unhewnᵇ stones, on which no iron tool has been used"; and they offered on it burnt offerings to the LORD, and sacrificed offerings of well-being. ³²And there, in the presence of the Israelites, Joshuaᶜ wrote on the stones a copy of the law of Moses, which he had written. ³³All

---

ᵃ Heb *among the people*   b Heb *whole*   c Heb *he*

✝ Catholic Connection

The Parts of the Mass

Not long after entering the Promised Land, the Israelites followed Moses' command to renew their Covenant with God. They prepared the altar, gathered everyone together, brought out the ark of the Covenant, read from the Law of Moses, and agreed to renew the Covenant. Through these acts, the Israelites reaffirmed their relationship with God and thanked him for all he had done for them.

Just as the altar was a visible sign of God's presence for the Israelites and their need for rededication and renewal as God's people, the altar is a visible sign of Christ's presence for Christians. Catholics gather around the altar to remember and celebrate Jesus' sacrificial death, his Resurrection, and our new Covenant with God. We gather around the altar as the table of the Lord to share a meal. We remember the story of our faith, and we are joined together as a community of faith. These actions form the structure of the Catholic Mass.

The Mass is divided into two main parts: the Liturgy of the Word and the Liturgy of the Eucharist, along with rites that open and close the celebration.

The Mass begins with the **Introductory rites** where those assembled sing, acknowledge Christ's presence, express sorrow for their sins, and pray. Through these rites, all gather together as one in preparation to hear God's word and receive Christ in the Eucharist.

After the opening, the **Liturgy of the Word** begins with readings from the Sacred Scriptures and the assembly singing a Psalm. After the Gospel reading, the priest or deacon gives a homily, which is a short reflection on the readings. Immediately following the homily, the assembly affirms its faith by reciting the Nicene Creed. The Liturgy of the Word concludes with the community offering prayers of intercession.

The **Liturgy of the Eucharist** begins with the preparation of the altar and members of the assembly bringing up the gifts of bread and wine. The priest then prays the Eucharistic prayer, which gives thanks to God and recalls Christ's saving work. Through this prayer, the bread and wine become the Body and Blood of Christ. In response, those assembled agree to unite themselves to Christ's sacrifice in anticipation of the eternal life God promises by saying "Amen." Next everyone prays the Lord's Prayer and offers one another a sign of peace. Then, members receive the Body and Blood of Christ in communion. The Mass ends with the **Concluding rites** when the assembly receives a blessing and is sent forth to live what they have celebrated.

▶ **Josh 8:30–35**
Catechism, nos. 1345–1355

Israel, alien as well as citizen, with their elders and officers and their judges, stood on opposite sides of the ark in front of the levitical priests who carried the ark of the covenant of the LORD, half of them in front of Mount Gerizim and half of them in front of Mount Ebal, as Moses the servant of the LORD had commanded at the first, that they should bless the people of Israel. 34And afterward he read all the words of the law, blessings and curses, according to all that is written in the book of the law. 35There was not a word of all that Moses commanded that Joshua did not read before all the assembly of Israel, and the women, and the little ones, and the aliens who resided among them.

The Gibeonites Save Themselves by Trickery

9 Now when all the kings who were beyond the Jordan in the hill country and in the lowland all along the coast of the Great Sea toward Lebanon—the Hittites, the Amorites, the Canaanites, the Perizzites, the Hivites, and the Jebusites—heard of this, 2they gathered together with one accord to fight Joshua and Israel.

3 But when the inhabitants of Gibeon heard what Joshua had done to Jericho and to Ai, 4they on their part acted with cunning: they went and prepared provisions,a and took worn-out sacks for their donkeys, and wineskins, worn-out and torn and mended, 5with worn-out, patched sandals on their feet, and worn-out clothes; and all their provisions were dry and moldy. 6They went to Joshua in the camp at Gilgal, and said to him and to the Israelites, "We have come from a far country; so now make a treaty with us." 7But the Israelites said to the Hivites, "Perhaps you live among us; then how can we make a treaty with you?" 8They said to Joshua, "We are your servants." And Joshua said to them, "Who are you? And where do you come from?" 9They said to him, "Your servants have come from a very far country, because of the name of the LORD your God; for we have heard a report of him, of all that he did in Egypt, 10and of all that he did to the two kings of the Amorites who were beyond the Jordan, King Sihon of Heshbon, and King Og of Bashan who lived in Ashtaroth. 11So our elders and all the inhabitants of our country said to us, 'Take provisions in your hand for the journey, go to meet them, and say to them, "We are your servants; come now, make a treaty with us."' 12Here is our bread; it was still warm when we took it from our houses as our food for the journey, on the day we set out to come to you, but now, see, it is dry and moldy; 13these wineskins were new when we filled them, and see, they are

burst; and these garments and sandals of ours are worn out from the very long journey." 14So the leadersb partook of their provisions, and did not ask direction from the LORD. 15And Joshua made peace with them, guaranteeing their lives by a treaty; and the leaders of the congregation swore an oath to them.

16 But when three days had passed after they had made a treaty with them, they heard that they were their neighbors and were living among them. 17So the Israelites set out and reached their cities on the third day. Now their cities were Gibeon, Chephirah, Beeroth, and Kiriath-jearim. 18But the Israelites did not attack them, because the leaders of the congregation had sworn to them by the LORD, the God of Israel. Then all the congregation murmured against the leaders. 19But all the leaders said to all the congregation, "We have sworn to them by the LORD, the God of Israel, and now we must not touch them. 20This is what we will do to them: We will let them live, so that wrath may not come upon us, because of the oath that we swore to them." 21The leaders said to them, "Let them live." So they became hewers of wood and drawers of water for all the congregation, as the leaders had decided concerning them.

22 Joshua summoned them, and said to them, "Why did you deceive us, saying, 'We are very far from you,' while in fact you are living among us? 23Now therefore you are cursed, and some of you shall always be slaves, hewers of wood and drawers of water for the house of my God." 24They answered Joshua, "Because it was told to your servants for a certainty that the LORD your God had commanded his servant Moses to give you all the land, and to destroy all the inhabitants of the land before you; so we were in great fear for our lives because of you, and did this thing. 25And now we are in your hand: do as it seems good and right in your sight to do to us." 26This is what he did for them: he saved them from the Israelites; and they did not kill them. 27But on that day Joshua made them hewers of wood and drawers of water for the congregation and for the altar of the LORD, to continue to this day, in the place that he should choose.

The Sun Stands Still

10 When King Adoni-zedek of Jerusalem heard how Joshua had taken Ai, and had utterly destroyed it, doing to Ai and its king as he had done to Jericho and its king, and how the inhabitants of Gibeon had made peace

JOSH

---

a Cn: Meaning of Heb uncertain   b Gk: Heb men

with Israel and were among them, ²he*ª* became greatly frightened, because Gibeon was a large city, like one of the royal cities, and was larger than Ai, and all its men were warriors. ³So King Adoni-zedek of Jerusalem sent a message to King Hoham of Hebron, to King Piram of Jarmuth, to King Japhia of Lachish, and to King Debir of Eglon, saying, ⁴"Come up and help me, and let us attack Gibeon; for it has made peace with Joshua and with the Israelites." ⁵Then the five kings of the Amorites—the king of Jerusalem, the king of Hebron, the king of Jarmuth, the king of Lachish, and the king of Eglon—gathered their forces, and went up with all their armies and camped against Gibeon, and made war against it.

6 And the Gibeonites sent to Joshua at the camp in Gilgal, saying, "Do not abandon your servants; come up to us quickly, and save us, and help us; for all the kings of the Amorites who live in the hill country are gathered against us." ⁷So Joshua went up from Gilgal, he and all the fighting force with him, all the mighty warriors. ⁸The LORD said to Joshua, "Do not fear them, for I have handed them over to you; not one of them shall stand before you." ⁹So Joshua came upon them suddenly, having marched up all night from Gilgal. ¹⁰And the LORD threw them into a panic before Israel, who inflicted a great slaughter on them at Gibeon, chased them by the way of the ascent of Beth-horon, and struck them down as far as Azekah and Makkedah. ¹¹As they fled before Israel, while they were going down the slope of Beth-horon, the LORD threw down huge stones from heaven on them as far as Azekah, and they died; there were more who died because of the hailstones than the Israelites killed with the sword.

12 On the day when the LORD gave the Amorites over to the Israelites, Joshua spoke to the LORD; and he said in the sight of Israel,

"Sun, stand still at Gibeon,
   and Moon, in the valley of Aijalon."
¹³ And the sun stood still, and the moon stopped,
   until the nation took vengeance on their
     enemies.

Is this not written in the Book of Jashar? The sun stopped in midheaven, and did not hurry to set for about a whole day. ¹⁴There has been no day like it before or since, when the LORD heeded a human voice; for the LORD fought for Israel.

15 Then Joshua returned, and all Israel with him, to the camp at Gilgal.

Five Kings Defeated

16 Meanwhile, these five kings fled and hid themselves in the cave at Makkedah. ¹⁷And it was told Joshua, "The five kings have been found, hidden in the cave at Makkedah." ¹⁸Joshua said, "Roll large stones against the mouth of the cave, and set men by it to guard them; ¹⁹but do not stay there yourselves; pursue your enemies, and attack them from the rear. Do not let them enter their towns, for the LORD your God has given them into your hand." ²⁰When Joshua and the Israelites had finished inflicting a very great slaughter on them, until they were wiped out, and when the survivors had entered into the fortified towns, ²¹all the people returned safe to Joshua in the camp at Makkedah; no one dared to speak*ᵇ* against any of the Israelites.

22 Then Joshua said, "Open the mouth of the cave, and bring those five kings out to me from the cave." ²³They did so, and brought the five kings out to him from the cave, the king of Jerusalem, the king of Hebron, the king of Jarmuth, the king of Lachish, and the king of Eglon. ²⁴When they brought the kings out to Joshua, Joshua summoned all the Israelites, and said to the chiefs of the warriors who had gone with him, "Come near, put your feet on the necks of these kings." Then they came near and put their feet on their necks. ²⁵And Joshua said to them, "Do not be afraid or dismayed; be strong and courageous; for thus the LORD will do to all the enemies against whom you fight." ²⁶Afterward Joshua struck them down and put them to death, and he hung them on five trees. And they hung on the trees until evening. ²⁷At sunset Joshua commanded, and they took them down from the trees and threw them into the cave where they had hidden themselves; they set large stones against the mouth of the cave, which remain to this very day.

28 Joshua took Makkedah on that day, and struck it and its king with the edge of the sword; he utterly destroyed every person in it; he left no one remaining. And he did to the king of Makkedah as he had done to the king of Jericho.

29 Then Joshua passed on from Makkedah, and all Israel with him, to Libnah, and fought against Libnah. ³⁰The LORD gave it also and its king into the hand of Israel; and he struck it with the edge of the sword, and every person in it; he left no one remaining in it; and he did to its king as he had done to the king of Jericho.

31 Next Joshua passed on from Libnah, and all Israel with him, to Lachish, and laid siege to it, and assaulted it. ³²The LORD gave Lachish into the hand of Israel, and he took it on the second day, and struck it with the edge of the sword, and every person in it, as he had done to Libnah.

a Heb *they*   *b* Heb *moved his tongue*

33 Then King Horam of Gezer came up to help Lachish; and Joshua struck him and his people, leaving him no survivors.

34 From Lachish Joshua passed on with all Israel to Eglon; and they laid siege to it, and assaulted it; 35and they took it that day, and struck it with the edge of the sword; and every person in it he utterly destroyed that day, as he had done to Lachish.

36 Then Joshua went up with all Israel from Eglon to Hebron; they assaulted it, 37and took it, and struck it with the edge of the sword, and its king and its towns, and every person in it; he left no one remaining, just as he had done to Eglon, and utterly destroyed it with every person in it.

38 Then Joshua, with all Israel, turned back to Debir and assaulted it, 39and he took it with its king and all its towns; they struck them with the edge of the sword, and utterly destroyed every person in it; he left no one remaining; just as he had done to Hebron, and, as he had done to Libnah and its king, so he did to Debir and its king.

40 So Joshua defeated the whole land, the hill country and the Negeb and the lowland and the slopes, and all their kings; he left no one remaining, but utterly destroyed all that breathed, as the LORD God of Israel commanded. 41And Joshua defeated them from Kadesh-barnea to Gaza, and all the country of Goshen, as far as Gibeon. 42Joshua took all these kings and their land at one time, because the LORD God of Israel fought for Israel. 43Then Joshua returned, and all Israel with him, to the camp at Gilgal.

The United Kings of Northern Canaan Defeated

11 When King Jabin of Hazor heard of this, he sent to King Jobab of Madon, to the king of Shimron, to the king of Achshaph, 2and to the kings who were in the northern hill country, and in the Arabah south of Chinneroth, and in the lowland, and in Naphoth-dor on the west, 3to the Canaanites in the east and the west, the Amorites, the Hittites, the Perizzites, and the Jebusites in the hill country, and the Hivites under Hermon in the land of Mizpah. 4They came out, with all their troops, a great army, in number like the sand on the seashore, with very many horses and chariots. 5All these kings joined their forces, and came and camped together at the waters of Merom, to fight with Israel.

6 And the LORD said to Joshua, "Do not be afraid of them, for tomorrow at this time I will hand over all of them, slain, to Israel; you shall hamstring their horses, and burn their chariots with fire." 7So Joshua came suddenly upon them with all his fighting force, by the waters of Merom, and fell upon them. 8And the LORD handed them over to Israel, who attacked them and chased them as far as Great Sidon and Misrephoth-maim, and eastward as far as the valley of Mizpeh. They struck them down, until they had left no one remaining. 9And Joshua did to them as the LORD commanded him; he hamstrung their horses, and burned their chariots with fire.

10 Joshua turned back at that time, and took Hazor, and struck its king down with the sword. Before that time Hazor was the head of all those kingdoms. 11And they put to the sword all who were in it, utterly destroying them; there was no one left who breathed, and he burned Hazor with fire. 12And all the towns of those kings, and all their kings, Joshua took, and struck them with the edge of the sword, utterly destroying them, as Moses the servant of the LORD had commanded. 13But Israel burned none of the towns that stood on mounds except Hazor, which Joshua did burn. 14All the spoil of these towns, and the livestock, the Israelites took for their booty; but all the people they struck down with the edge of the sword, until they had destroyed them, and they did not leave any who breathed. 15As the LORD had commanded his servant Moses, so Moses commanded Joshua, and so Joshua did; he left nothing undone of all that the LORD had commanded Moses.

Summary of Joshua's Conquests

16 So Joshua took all that land: the hill country and all the Negeb and all the land of Goshen and the lowland and the Arabah and the hill country of Israel and its lowland, 17from Mount Halak, which rises toward Seir, as far as Baal-gad in the valley of Lebanon below Mount Hermon. He took all their kings, struck them down, and put them to death. 18Joshua made war a long time with all those kings. 19There was not a town that made peace with the Israelites, except the Hivites, the inhabitants of Gibeon; all were taken in battle. 20For it was the LORD's doing to harden their hearts so that they would come against Israel in battle, in order that they might be utterly destroyed, and might receive no mercy, but be exterminated, just as the LORD had commanded Moses.

21 At that time Joshua came and wiped out the Anakim from the hill country, from Hebron, from Debir, from Anab, and from all the hill country of Judah, and from all the hill country of Israel; Joshua utterly destroyed them with their towns. 22None of the Anakim was left in the land of the Israelites; some remained only in Gaza, in Gath, and in Ashdod. 23So Joshua took the whole

JOSH

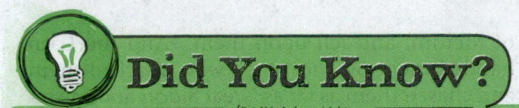

Did You Know?

The Conquest of Canaan

A strong parallel connects the beginning of the story of Joshua—the crossing of the Jordan River, God's direction and protection of the Israelites (symbolized by the ark), and the renewal of the Covenant at Mount Ebal—and the events of the Exodus from Egypt. The parallel reinforces how the conquest of Canaan was part of God's continued liberation of the Chosen People and a key moment in the history of Israel.

As the Israelites moved in on the Promised Land, the Canaanites were one of several groups of people that the Israelites had to deal with. Joshua 12:8 also mentions Hittites, Amorites, Perizzites, Hivites, and Jebusites. But the Canaanites seemed to be the dominant inhabitants. They were primarily an agricultural society and believed that their gods, called baals, controlled the rains, the seasons, and the fertility of the soil. For the Israelites, God was revealed as the only God over all creation and history.

The conquest of the Canaanites through violence might make you wonder what the Israelites believed about God. Basically, they believed that the Canaanite baals were an offense against God. Because the Canaanites would not change, the Israelites felt justified in killing them and taking their land (see "Holy War," near Num 2:1). Later, Christians would not be able to justify such actions because of Jesus' teaching that everyone is loved by God and that we must love even our enemies. But at the time Joshua was written, God and God's plan for humanity had not yet been fully revealed.

▶ Joshua, chapter 12

land, according to all that the LORD had spoken to Moses; and Joshua gave it for an inheritance to Israel according to their tribal allotments. And the land had rest from war.

The Kings Conquered by Moses

12 Now these are the kings of the land, whom the Israelites defeated, whose land they occupied beyond the Jordan toward the east, from the Wadi Arnon to Mount Hermon, with all the Arabah eastward: 2King Sihon of the Amorites who lived at Heshbon, and ruled from Aroer, which is on the edge of the Wadi Arnon, and from the middle of the valley as far as the river Jabbok, the boundary of the Ammonites, that is, half of Gilead, 3and the Arabah to the Sea of Chinneroth eastward, and in the direction of Beth-jeshimoth, to the sea of the Arabah, the Dead Sea,*a* southward to the foot of the slopes of Pisgah; 4and King Og*b* of Bashan, one of the last of the Rephaim, who lived at Ashtaroth and at Edrei 5and ruled over Mount Hermon and Salecah and all Bashan to the boundary of the Geshurites and the Maacathites, and over half of Gilead to the boundary of King Sihon of Heshbon. 6Moses, the servant of the LORD, and the Israelites defeated them; and Moses the servant of the LORD gave their land for a possession to the Reubenites and the Gadites and the half-tribe of Manasseh.

The Kings Conquered by Joshua

7 The following are the kings of the land whom Joshua and the Israelites defeated on the west side of the Jordan, from Baal-gad in the valley of Lebanon to Mount Halak, that rises toward Seir (and Joshua gave their land to the tribes of Israel as a possession according to their allotments, 8in the hill country, in the lowland, in the Arabah, in the slopes, in the wilderness, and in the Negeb, the land of the Hittites, Amorites, Canaanites, Perizzites, Hivites, and Jebusites):

9 the king of Jericho	one
the king of Ai, which is next to Bethel	one
10 the king of Jerusalem	one
the king of Hebron	one
11 the king of Jarmuth	one
the king of Lachish	one
12 the king of Eglon	one
the king of Gezer	one
13 the king of Debir	one
the king of Geder	one
14 the king of Hormah	one
the king of Arad	one
15 the king of Libnah	one
the king of Adullam	one
16 the king of Makkedah	one
the king of Bethel	one
17 the king of Tappuah	one
the king of Hepher	one
18 the king of Aphek	one
the king of Lasharon	one
19 the king of Madon	one
the king of Hazor	one

a Heb *Salt Sea*   *b* Gk: Heb *the boundary of King Og*

20 the king of Shimron-meron one
the king of Achshaph one
21 the king of Taanach one
the king of Megiddo one
22 the king of Kedesh one
the king of Jokneam in Carmel one
23 the king of Dor in Naphath-dor one
the king of Goiim in Galilee,[a] one
24 the king of Tirzah one
thirty-one kings in all.

The Parts of Canaan Still Unconquered

13 Now Joshua was old and advanced in years; and the LORD said to him, "You are old and advanced in years, and very much of the land still remains to be possessed. 2This is the land that still remains: all the regions of the Philistines, and all those of the Geshurites 3(from the Shihor, which is east of Egypt, northward to the boundary of Ekron, it is reckoned as Canaanite; there are five rulers of the Philistines, those of Gaza, Ashdod, Ashkelon, Gath, and Ekron), and those of the Avvim 4in the south; all the land of the Canaanites, and Mearah that belongs to the Sidonians, to Aphek, to the boundary of the Amorites, 5and the land of the Gebalites, and all Lebanon, toward the east, from Baal-gad below Mount Hermon to Lebo-hamath, 6all the inhabitants of the hill country from Lebanon to Misrephoth-maim, even all the Sidonians. I will myself drive them out from before the Israelites; only allot the land to Israel for an inheritance, as I have commanded you. 7Now therefore divide this land for an inheritance to the nine tribes and the half-tribe of Manasseh."

The Territory East of the Jordan

8 With the other half-tribe of Manasseh[b] the Reubenites and the Gadites received their inheritance, which Moses gave them, beyond the Jordan eastward, as Moses the servant of the LORD gave them: 9from Aroer, which is on the edge of the Wadi Arnon, and the town that is in the middle of the valley, and all the tableland from[c] Medeba as far as Dibon; 10and all the cities of King Sihon of the Amorites, who reigned in Heshbon, as far as the boundary of the Ammonites; 11and Gilead, and the region of the Geshurites and Maacathites, and all Mount Hermon, and all Bashan to Salecah; 12all the kingdom of Og in Bashan, who reigned in Ashtaroth and in Edrei (he alone was left of the survivors of the Rephaim); these Moses had defeated and driven out. 13Yet the Israelites did not drive out the Geshurites or the Maacathites; but Geshur and Maacath live within Israel to this day.

14 To the tribe of Levi alone Moses gave no inheritance; the offerings by fire to the LORD God of Israel are their inheritance, as he said to them.

The Territory of Reuben

15 Moses gave an inheritance to the tribe of the Reubenites according to their clans. 16Their territory was from Aroer, which is on the edge of the Wadi Arnon, and the town that is in the middle of the valley, and all the tableland by Medeba; 17with Heshbon, and all its towns that are in the tableland; Dibon, and Bamoth-baal, and Beth-baal-meon, 18and Jahaz, and Kedemoth, and Mephaath, 19and Kiriathaim, and Sibmah, and Zereth-shahar on the hill of the valley, 20and Beth-peor, and the slopes of Pisgah, and Beth-jeshimoth, 21that is, all the towns of the tableland, and all the kingdom of King Sihon of the Amorites, who reigned in Heshbon, whom Moses defeated with the leaders of Midian, Evi and Rekem and Zur and Hur and Reba, as princes of Sihon, who lived in the land. 22Along with the rest of those they put to death, the Israelites also put to the sword Balaam son of Beor, who practiced divination. 23And the border of the Reubenites was the Jordan and its banks. This was the inheritance of the Reubenites according to their families with their towns and villages.

The Territory of Gad

24 Moses gave an inheritance also to the tribe of the Gadites, according to their families. 25Their territory was Jazer, and all the towns of Gilead, and half the land of the Ammonites, to Aroer, which is east of Rabbah, 26and from Heshbon to Ramath-mizpeh and Betonim, and from Mahanaim to the territory of Debir,[d] 27and in the valley Beth-haram, Beth-nimrah, Succoth, and Zaphon, the rest of the kingdom of King Sihon of Heshbon, the Jordan and its banks, as far as the lower end of the Sea of Chinnereth, eastward beyond the Jordan. 28This is the inheritance of the Gadites according to their clans, with their towns and villages.

The Territory of the Half Tribe of Manasseh (East)

29 Moses gave an inheritance to the half-tribe of Manasseh; it was allotted to the half-tribe of the Manassites according to their families. 30Their territory extended from Mahanaim, through all Bashan, the whole kingdom of King Og of

---

a Gk: Heb Gilgal b Cn: Heb With it c Compare Gk: Heb lacks from d Gk Syr Vg: Heb Lidebir

Bashan, and all the settlements of Jair, which are in Bashan, sixty towns, [31]and half of Gilead, and Ashtaroth, and Edrei, the towns of the kingdom of Og in Bashan; these were allotted to the people of Machir son of Manasseh according to their clans—for half the Machirites.

32 These are the inheritances that Moses distributed in the plains of Moab, beyond the Jordan east of Jericho. [33]But to the tribe of Levi Moses gave no inheritance; the LORD God of Israel is their inheritance, as he said to them.

The Distribution of Territory West of the Jordan

14 These are the inheritances that the Israelites received in the land of Canaan, which the priest Eleazar, and Joshua son of Nun, and the heads of the families of the tribes of the Israelites distributed to them. [2]Their inheritance was by lot, as the LORD had commanded Moses for the nine and one-half tribes. [3]For Moses had given an inheritance to the two and one-half tribes beyond the Jordan; but to the Levites he gave no inheritance among them. [4]For the people of Joseph were two tribes, Manasseh and Ephraim; and no portion was given to the Levites in the land, but only towns to live in, with their pasture lands for their flocks and herds. [5]The Israelites did as the LORD commanded Moses; they allotted the land.

Hebron Allotted to Caleb

6 Then the people of Judah came to Joshua at Gilgal; and Caleb son of Jephunneh the Kenizzite said to him, "You know what the LORD said to Moses the man of God in Kadesh-barnea concerning you and me. [7]I was forty years old when Moses the servant of the LORD sent me from Kadesh-barnea to spy out the land; and I brought him an honest report. [8]But my companions who went up with me made the heart of the people melt; yet I wholeheartedly followed the LORD my God. [9]And Moses swore on that day, saying, 'Surely the land on which your foot has trodden shall be an inheritance for you and your children forever, because you have wholeheartedly followed the LORD my God.' [10]And now, as you see, the LORD has kept me alive, as he said, these forty-five years since the time that the LORD spoke this word to Moses, while Israel was journeying through the wilderness; and here I am today, eighty-five years old. [11]I am still as strong today as I was on the day that Moses sent me; my strength now is as my strength was then, for war, and for going and coming. [12]So now give me this hill country of which the LORD spoke on that day;

for you heard on that day how the Anakim were there, with great fortified cities; it may be that the LORD will be with me, and I shall drive them out, as the LORD said."

13 Then Joshua blessed him, and gave Hebron to Caleb son of Jephunneh for an inheritance. [14]So Hebron became the inheritance of Caleb son of Jephunneh the Kenizzite to this day, because he wholeheartedly followed the LORD, the God of Israel. [15]Now the name of Hebron formerly was Kiriath-arba;[a] this Arba was[b] the greatest man among the Anakim. And the land had rest from war.

The Territory of Judah

15 The lot for the tribe of the people of Judah according to their families reached southward to the boundary of Edom, to the wilderness of Zin at the farthest south. [2]And their south boundary ran from the end of the Dead Sea,[c] from the bay that faces southward; [3]it goes out southward of the ascent of Akrabbim, passes along to Zin, and goes up south of Kadesh-barnea, along by Hezron, up to Addar, makes a turn to Karka, [4]passes along to Azmon, goes out by the Wadi of Egypt, and comes to its end at the sea. This shall be your south boundary. [5]And the east boundary is the Dead Sea,[c] to the mouth of the Jordan. And the boundary on the north side runs from the bay of the sea at the mouth of the Jordan; [6]and the boundary goes up to Beth-hoglah, and passes along north of Beth-arabah; and the boundary goes up to the Stone of Bohan, Reuben's son; [7]and the boundary goes up to Debir from the Valley of Achor, and so northward, turning toward Gilgal, which is opposite the ascent of Adummim, which is on the south side of the valley; and the boundary passes along to the waters of En-shemesh, and ends at En-rogel; [8]then the boundary goes up by the valley of the son of Hinnom at the southern slope of the Jebusites (that is, Jerusalem); and the boundary goes up to the top of the mountain that lies over against the valley of Hinnom, on the west, at the northern end of the valley of Rephaim; [9]then the boundary extends from the top of the mountain to the spring of the Waters of Nephtoah, and from there to the towns of Mount Ephron; then the boundary bends around to Baalah (that is, Kiriath-jearim); [10]and the boundary circles west of Baalah to Mount Seir, passes along to the northern slope of Mount Jearim (that is, Chesalon), and goes down to Beth-shemesh, and

---

a That is *the city of Arba*   b Heb lacks *this Arba was*
c Heb *Salt Sea*

passes along by Timnah; [11]the boundary goes out to the slope of the hill north of Ekron, then the boundary bends around to Shikkeron, and passes along to Mount Baalah, and goes out to Jabneel; then the boundary comes to an end at the sea. [12]And the west boundary was the Mediterranean with its coast. This is the boundary surrounding the people of Judah according to their families.

Caleb Occupies His Portion

13 According to the commandment of the LORD to Joshua, he gave to Caleb son of Jephunneh a portion among the people of Judah, Kiriath-arba,[a] that is, Hebron (Arba was the father of Anak). [14]And Caleb drove out from there the three sons of Anak: Sheshai, Ahiman, and Talmai, the descendants of Anak. [15]From there he went up against the inhabitants of Debir; now the name of Debir formerly was Kiriath-sepher. [16]And Caleb said, "Whoever attacks Kiriath-sepher and takes it, to him I will give my daughter Achsah as wife." [17]Othniel son of Kenaz, the brother of Caleb, took it; and he gave him his daughter Achsah as wife. [18]When she came to him, she urged him to ask her father for a field. As she dismounted from her donkey, Caleb said to her, "What do you wish?" [19]She said to him, "Give me a present; since you have set me in the land of the Negeb, give me springs of water as well." So Caleb gave her the upper springs and the lower springs.

The Towns of Judah

20 This is the inheritance of the tribe of the people of Judah according to their families. [21]The towns belonging to the tribe of the people of Judah in the extreme south, toward the boundary of Edom, were Kabzeel, Eder, Jagur, [22]Kinah, Dimonah, Adadah, [23]Kedesh, Hazor, Ithnan, [24]Ziph, Telem, Bealoth, [25]Hazor-hadattah, Kerioth-hezron (that is, Hazor), [26]Amam, Shema, Moladah, [27]Hazar-gaddah, Heshmon, Beth-pelet, [28]Hazar-shual, Beer-sheba, Biziothiah, [29]Baalah, Iim, Ezem, [30]Eltolad, Chesil, Hormah, [31]Ziklag, Madmannah, Sansannah, [32]Lebaoth, Shilhim, Ain, and Rimmon: in all, twenty-nine towns, with their villages.

33 And in the lowland, Eshtaol, Zorah, Ashnah, [34]Zanoah, En-gannim, Tappuah, Enam, [35]Jarmuth, Adullam, Socoh, Azekah, [36]Shaaraim, Adithaim, Gederah, Gederothaim: fourteen towns with their villages.

37 Zenan, Hadashah, Migdal-gad, [38]Dilan, Mizpeh, Jokthe-el, [39]Lachish, Bozkath, Eglon, [40]Cabbon, Lahmam, Chitlish, [41]Gederoth, Beth-dagon, Naamah, and Makkedah: sixteen towns with their villages.

42 Libnah, Ether, Ashan, [43]Iphtah, Ashnah, Nezib, [44]Keilah, Achzib, and Mareshah: nine towns with their villages.

45 Ekron, with its dependencies and its villages; [46]from Ekron to the sea, all that were near Ashdod, with their villages.

47 Ashdod, its towns and its villages; Gaza, its towns and its villages; to the Wadi of Egypt, and the Great Sea with its coast.

48 And in the hill country, Shamir, Jattir, Socoh, [49]Dannah, Kiriath-sannah (that is, Debir), [50]Anab, Eshtemoh, Anim, [51]Goshen, Holon, and Giloh: eleven towns with their villages.

52 Arab, Dumah, Eshan, [53]Janim, Beth-tappuah, Aphekah, [54]Humtah, Kiriath-arba (that is, Hebron), and Zior: nine towns with their villages.

55 Maon, Carmel, Ziph, Juttah, [56]Jezreel, Jokdeam, Zanoah, [57]Kain, Gibeah, and Timnah: ten towns with their villages.

58 Halhul, Beth-zur, Gedor, [59]Maarath, Beth-anoth, and Eltekon: six towns with their villages.

60 Kiriath-baal (that is, Kiriath-jearim) and Rabbah: two towns with their villages.

61 In the wilderness, Beth-arabah, Middin, Secacah, [62]Nibshan, the City of Salt, and En-gedi: six towns with their villages.

63 But the people of Judah could not drive out the Jebusites, the inhabitants of Jerusalem; so the Jebusites live with the people of Judah in Jerusalem to this day.

The Territory of Ephraim

16 The allotment of the Josephites went from the Jordan by Jericho, east of the waters of Jericho, into the wilderness, going up from Jericho into the hill country to Bethel; [2]then going from Bethel to Luz, it passes along to Ataroth, the territory of the Archites; [3]then it goes down westward to the territory of the Japhletites, as far as the territory of Lower Beth-horon, then to Gezer, and it ends at the sea.

4 The Josephites—Manasseh and Ephraim—received their inheritance.

5 The territory of the Ephraimites by their families was as follows: the boundary of their inheritance on the east was Ataroth-addar as far as Upper Beth-horon, [6]and the boundary goes from there to the sea; on the north is Michmethath; then on the east the boundary makes a turn toward Taanath-shiloh, and passes along beyond it

---

a That is *the city of Arba*

on the east to Janoah, [7]then it goes down from Janoah to Ataroth and to Naarah, and touches Jericho, ending at the Jordan. [8]From Tappuah the boundary goes westward to the Wadi Kanah, and ends at the sea. Such is the inheritance of the tribe of the Ephraimites by their families, [9]together with the towns that were set apart for the Ephraimites within the inheritance of the Manassites, all those towns with their villages. [10]They did not, however, drive out the Canaanites who lived in Gezer: so the Canaanites have lived within Ephraim to this day but have been made to do forced labor.

The Other Half-Tribe of Manasseh (West)

17 Then allotment was made to the tribe of Manasseh, for he was the firstborn of Joseph. To Machir the firstborn of Manasseh, the father of Gilead, were allotted Gilead and Bashan, because he was a warrior. [2]And allotments were made to the rest of the tribe of Manasseh, by their families, Abiezer, Helek, Asriel, Shechem, Hepher, and Shemida; these were the male descendants of Manasseh son of Joseph, by their families.

3 Now Zelophehad son of Hepher son of Gilead son of Machir son of Manasseh had no sons, but only daughters; and these are the names of his daughters: Mahlah, Noah, Hoglah, Milcah, and Tirzah. [4]They came before the priest Eleazar and Joshua son of Nun and the leaders, and said, "The Lord commanded Moses to give us an inheritance along with our male kin." So according to the commandment of the Lord he gave them an inheritance among the kinsmen of their father. [5]Thus there fell to Manasseh ten portions, besides the land of Gilead and Bashan, which is on the other side of the Jordan, [6]because the daughters of Manasseh received an inheritance along with his sons. The land of Gilead was allotted to the rest of the Manassites.

7 The territory of Manasseh reached from Asher to Michmethath, which is east of Shechem; then the boundary goes along southward to the inhabitants of En-tappuah. [8]The land of Tappuah belonged to Manasseh, but the town of Tappuah on the boundary of Manasseh belonged to the Ephraimites. [9]Then the boundary went down to the Wadi Kanah. The towns here, to the south of the wadi, among the towns of Manasseh, belong to Ephraim. Then the boundary of Manasseh goes along the north side of the wadi and ends at the sea. [10]The land to the south is Ephraim's and that to the north is Manasseh's, with the sea forming its boundary; on the north Asher is reached, and on the east Issachar. [11]Within

Issachar and Asher, Manasseh had Beth-shean and its villages, Ibleam and its villages, the inhabitants of Dor and its villages, the inhabitants of En-dor and its villages, the inhabitants of Taanach and its villages, and the inhabitants of Megiddo and its villages (the third is Naphath).[a] [12]Yet the Manassites could not take possession of those towns; but the Canaanites continued to live in that land. [13]But when the Israelites grew strong, they put the Canaanites to forced labor, but did not utterly drive them out.

The Tribe of Joseph Protests

14 The tribe of Joseph spoke to Joshua, saying, "Why have you given me but one lot and one portion as an inheritance, since we are a numerous people, whom all along the Lord has blessed?" [15]And Joshua said to them, "If you are a numerous people, go up to the forest, and clear ground there for yourselves in the land of the Perizzites and the Rephaim, since the hill country of Ephraim is too narrow for you." [16]The tribe of Joseph said, "The hill country is not enough for us; yet all the Canaanites who live in the plain have chariots of iron, both those in Beth-shean and its villages and those in the Valley of Jezreel." [17]Then Joshua said to the house of Joseph, to Ephraim and Manasseh, "You are indeed a numerous people, and have great power; you shall not have one lot only, [18]but the hill country shall be yours, for though it is a forest, you shall clear it and possess it to its farthest borders; for you shall drive out the Canaanites, though they have chariots of iron, and though they are strong."

The Territories of the Remaining Tribes

18 Then the whole congregation of the Israelites assembled at Shiloh, and set up the tent of meeting there. The land lay subdued before them.

2 There remained among the Israelites seven tribes whose inheritance had not yet been apportioned. [3]So Joshua said to the Israelites, "How long will you be slack about going in and taking possession of the land that the Lord, the God of your ancestors, has given you? [4]Provide three men from each tribe, and I will send them out that they may begin to go throughout the land, writing a description of it with a view to their inheritances. Then come back to me. [5]They shall divide it into seven portions, Judah continuing in its territory on the south, and the house of Joseph in their territory on the north.

a Meaning of Heb uncertain

[6]You shall describe the land in seven divisions and bring the description here to me; and I will cast lots for you here before the LORD our God. [7]The Levites have no portion among you, for the priesthood of the LORD is their heritage; and Gad and Reuben and the half-tribe of Manasseh have received their inheritance beyond the Jordan eastward, which Moses the servant of the LORD gave them."

8 So the men started on their way; and Joshua charged those who went to write the description of the land, saying, "Go throughout the land and write a description of it, and come back to me; and I will cast lots for you here before the LORD in Shiloh." [9]So the men went and traversed the land and set down in a book a description of it by towns in seven divisions; then they came back to Joshua in the camp at Shiloh, [10]and Joshua cast lots for them in Shiloh before the LORD; and there Joshua apportioned the land to the Israelites, to each a portion.

The Territory of Benjamin

11 The lot of the tribe of Benjamin according to its families came up, and the territory allotted to it fell between the tribe of Judah and the tribe of Joseph. [12]On the north side their boundary began at the Jordan; then the boundary goes up to the slope of Jericho on the north, then up through the hill country westward; and it ends at the wilderness of Beth-aven. [13]From there the boundary passes along southward in the direction of Luz, to the slope of Luz (that is, Bethel), then the boundary goes down to Ataroth-addar, on the mountain that lies south of Lower Beth-horon. [14]Then the boundary goes in another direction, turning on the western side southward from the mountain that lies to the south, opposite Beth-horon, and it ends at Kiriath-baal (that is, Kiriath-jearim), a town belonging to the tribe of Judah. This forms the western side. [15]The southern side begins at the outskirts of Kiriath-jearim; and the boundary goes from there to Ephron,[a] to the spring of the Waters of Neph-toah; [16]then the boundary goes down to the border of the mountain that overlooks the valley of the son of Hinnom, which is at the north end of the valley of Rephaim; and it then goes down the valley of Hinnom, south of the slope of the Jebusites, and downward to En-rogel; [17]then it bends in a northerly direction going on to En-shemesh, and from there goes to Geliloth, which is opposite the ascent of Adummim; then it goes down to the Stone of Bohan, Reuben's son; [18]and passing on to the north of the slope of Beth-arabah[b] it goes down to the Arabah; [19]then

the boundary passes on to the north of the slope of Beth-hoglah; and the boundary ends at the northern bay of the Dead Sea,[c] at the south end of the Jordan: this is the southern border. [20]The Jordan forms its boundary on the eastern side. This is the inheritance of the tribe of Benjamin, according to its families, boundary by boundary all around.

21 Now the towns of the tribe of Benjamin according to their families were Jericho, Beth-hoglah, Emek-keziz, [22]Beth-arabah, Zemaraim, Bethel, [23]Avvim, Parah, Ophrah, [24]Chephar-ammoni, Ophni, and Geba—twelve towns with their villages: [25]Gibeon, Ramah, Beeroth, [26]Mizpeh, Chephirah, Mozah, [27]Rekem, Irpeel, Taralah, [28]Zela, Haeleph, Jebus[d] (that is, Jerusalem), Gibeah[e] and Kiriath-jearim[f]—fourteen towns with their villages. This is the inheritance of the tribe of Benjamin according to its families.

The Territory of Simeon

19 The second lot came out for Simeon, for the tribe of Simeon, according to its families; its inheritance lay within the inheritance of the tribe of Judah. [2]It had for its inheritance Beer-sheba, Sheba, Moladah, [3]Hazar-shual, Balah, Ezem, [4]Eltolad, Bethul, Hormah, [5]Ziklag, Beth-marcaboth, Hazar-susah, [6]Beth-lebaoth, and Sharuhen—thirteen towns with their villages; [7]Ain, Rimmon, Ether, and Ashan—four towns with their villages; [8]together with all the villages all around these towns as far as Baalath-beer, Ramah of the Negeb. This was the inheritance of the tribe of Simeon according to its families. [9]The inheritance of the tribe of Simeon formed part of the territory of Judah; because the portion of the tribe of Judah was too large for them, the tribe of Simeon obtained an inheritance within their inheritance.

The Territory of Zebulun

10 The third lot came up for the tribe of Zebulun, according to its families. The boundary of its inheritance reached as far as Sarid; [11]then its boundary goes up westward, and on to Maralah, and touches Dabbesheth, then the wadi that is east of Jokneam; [12]from Sarid it goes in the other direction eastward toward the sunrise to the boundary of Chisloth-tabor; from there it goes to Daberath, then up to Japhia; [13]from there it passes along on the east toward the sunrise to Gath-hepher, to Eth-kazin, and going on

a Cn See 15.9. Heb *westward*   b Gk: Heb *to the slope over against the Arabah*   c Heb *Salt Sea*   d Gk Syr Vg: Heb *the Jebusite*   e Heb *Gibeath*   f Gk: Heb *Kiriath*

JOSH

to Rimmon it bends toward Neah; ¹⁴then on the north the boundary makes a turn to Hannathon, and it ends at the valley of Iphtah-el; ¹⁵and Kattath, Nahalal, Shimron, Idalah, and Bethlehem—twelve towns with their villages. ¹⁶This is the inheritance of the tribe of Zebulun, according to its families—these towns with their villages.

The Territory of Issachar

17 The fourth lot came out for Issachar, for the tribe of Issachar, according to its families. ¹⁸Its territory included Jezreel, Chesulloth, Shunem, ¹⁹Hapharaim, Shion, Anaharath, ²⁰Rabbith, Kishion, Ebez, ²¹Remeth, En-gannim, En-haddah, Beth-pazzez; ²²the boundary also touches Tabor, Shahazumah, and Beth-shemesh, and its boundary ends at the Jordan—sixteen towns with their villages. ²³This is the inheritance of the tribe of Issachar, according to its families—the towns with their villages.

The Territory of Asher

24 The fifth lot came out for the tribe of Asher according to its families. ²⁵Its boundary included Helkath, Hali, Beten, Achshaph, ²⁶Allammelech, Amad, and Mishal; on the west it touches Carmel and Shihor-libnath, ²⁷then it turns eastward, goes to Beth-dagon, and touches Zebulun and the valley of Iphtah-el northward to Beth-emek and Neiel; then it continues in the north to Cabul, ²⁸Ebron, Rehob, Hammon, Kanah, as far as Great Sidon; ²⁹then the boundary turns to Ramah, reaching to the fortified city of Tyre; then the boundary turns to Hosah, and it ends at the sea; Mahalab,ᵃ Achzib, ³⁰Ummah, Aphek, and Rehob—twenty-two towns with their villages. ³¹This is the inheritance of the tribe of Asher according to its families—these towns with their villages.

The Territory of Naphtali

32 The sixth lot came out for the tribe of Naphtali, for the tribe of Naphtali, according to its families. ³³And its boundary ran from Heleph, from the oak in Zaanannim, and Adami-nekeb, and Jabneel, as far as Lakkum; and it ended at the Jordan; ³⁴then the boundary turns westward to Aznoth-tabor, and goes from there to Hukkok, touching Zebulun at the south, and Asher on the west, and Judah on the east at the Jordan. ³⁵The fortified towns are Ziddim, Zer, Hammath, Rakkath, Chinnereth, ³⁶Adamah, Ramah, Hazor, ³⁷Kedesh, Edrei, En-hazor, ³⁸Iron, Migdal-el, Horem, Beth-anath, and Beth-shemesh—nineteen towns with their villages. ³⁹This is the

inheritance of the tribe of Naphtali according to its families—the towns with their villages.

The Territory of Dan

40 The seventh lot came out for the tribe of Dan, according to its families. ⁴¹The territory of its inheritance included Zorah, Eshtaol, Ir-shemesh, ⁴²Shaalabbin, Aijalon, Ithlah, ⁴³Elon, Timnah, Ekron, ⁴⁴Eltekeh, Gibbethon, Baalath, ⁴⁵Jehud, Bene-berak, Gath-rimmon, ⁴⁶Me-jarkon, and Rakkon at the border opposite Joppa. ⁴⁷When the territory of the Danites was lost to them, the Danites went up and fought against Leshem, and after capturing it and putting it to the sword, they took possession of it and settled in it, calling Leshem, Dan, after their ancestor Dan. ⁴⁸This is the inheritance of the tribe of Dan, according to their families—these towns with their villages.

Joshua's Inheritance

49 When they had finished distributing the several territories of the land as inheritances, the Israelites gave an inheritance among them to Joshua son of Nun. ⁵⁰By command of the LORD they gave him the town that he asked for, Timnath-serah in the hill country of Ephraim; he rebuilt the town, and settled in it.

51 These are the inheritances that the priest Eleazar and Joshua son of Nun and the heads of the families of the tribes of the Israelites distributed by lot at Shiloh before the LORD, at the entrance of the tent of meeting. So they finished dividing the land.

The Cities of Refuge

20 Then the LORD spoke to Joshua, saying, ²"Say to the Israelites, 'Appoint the cities of refuge, of which I spoke to you through Moses, ³so that anyone who kills a person without intent or by mistake may flee there; they shall be for you a refuge from the avenger of blood. ⁴The slayer shall flee to one of these cities and shall stand at the entrance of the gate of the city, and explain the case to the elders of that city; then the fugitive shall be taken into the city, and given a place, and shall remain with them. ⁵And if the avenger of blood is in pursuit, they shall not give up the slayer, because the neighbor was killed by mistake, there having been no enmity between them before. ⁶The slayer shall remain in that city until there is a trial before the congregation, until the death of the one who is high priest at the

---

ᵃ Cn Compare Gk: Heb *Mehebel*

time: then the slayer may return home, to the town in which the deed was done.' "

7 So they set apart Kedesh in Galilee in the hill country of Naphtali, and Shechem in the hill country of Ephraim, and Kiriath-arba (that is, Hebron) in the hill country of Judah. [8]And beyond the Jordan east of Jericho, they appointed Bezer in the wilderness on the tableland, from the tribe of Reuben, and Ramoth in Gilead, from the tribe of Gad, and Golan in Bashan, from the tribe of Manasseh. [9]These were the cities designated for all the Israelites, and for the aliens residing among them, that anyone who killed a person without intent could flee there, so as not to die by the hand of the avenger of blood, until there was a trial before the congregation.

Cities Allotted to the Levites

21 Then the heads of the families of the Levites came to the priest Eleazar and to Joshua son of Nun and to the heads of the families of the tribes of the Israelites; [2]they said to them at Shiloh in the land of Canaan, "The LORD commanded through Moses that we be given towns to live in, along with their pasture lands for our livestock." [3]So by command of the LORD the Israelites gave to the Levites the following towns and pasture lands out of their inheritance.

4 The lot came out for the families of the Kohathites. So those Levites who were descendants of Aaron the priest received by lot thirteen towns from the tribes of Judah, Simeon, and Benjamin.

5 The rest of the Kohathites received by lot ten towns from the families of the tribe of Ephraim, from the tribe of Dan, and the half-tribe of Manasseh.

6 The Gershonites received by lot thirteen towns from the families of the tribe of Issachar, from the tribe of Asher, from the tribe of Naphtali, and from the half-tribe of Manasseh in Bashan.

7 The Merarites according to their families received twelve towns from the tribe of Reuben, the tribe of Gad, and the tribe of Zebulun.

8 These towns and their pasture lands the Israelites gave by lot to the Levites, as the LORD had commanded through Moses.

9 Out of the tribe of Judah and the tribe of Simeon they gave the following towns mentioned by name, [10]which went to the descendants of Aaron, one of the families of the Kohathites who belonged to the Levites, since the lot fell to them first. [11]They gave them Kiriath-arba (Arba being the father of Anak), that is, Hebron, in the hill country of Judah, along with the pasture lands

around it. [12]But the fields of the town and its villages had been given to Caleb son of Jephunneh as his holding.

13 To the descendants of Aaron the priest they gave Hebron, the city of refuge for the slayer, with its pasture lands, Libnah with its pasture lands, [14]Jattir with its pasture lands, Eshtemoa with its pasture lands, [15]Holon with its pasture lands, Debir with its pasture lands, [16]Ain with its pasture lands, Juttah with its pasture lands, and Beth-shemesh with its pasture lands—nine towns out of these two tribes. [17]Out of the tribe of Benjamin: Gibeon with its pasture lands, Geba with its pasture lands, [18]Anathoth with its pasture lands, and Almon with its pasture lands—four towns. [19]The towns of the descendants of Aaron—the priests—were thirteen in all, with their pasture lands.

20 As to the rest of the Kohathites belonging to the Kohathite families of the Levites, the towns allotted to them were out of the tribe of Ephraim. [21]To them were given Shechem, the city of refuge for the slayer, with its pasture lands in the hill country of Ephraim, Gezer with its pasture lands, [22]Kibzaim with its pasture lands, and Beth-horon with its pasture lands—four towns. [23]Out of the tribe of Dan: Elteke with its pasture lands, Gibbethon with its pasture lands, [24]Aijalon with its pasture lands, Gath-rimmon with its pasture lands—four towns. [25]Out of the half-tribe of Manasseh: Taanach with its pasture lands, and Gath-rimmon with its pasture lands—two towns. [26]The towns of the families of the rest of the Kohathites were ten in all, with their pasture lands.

27 To the Gershonites, one of the families of the Levites, were given out of the half-tribe of Manasseh, Golan in Bashan with its pasture lands, the city of refuge for the slayer, and Beeshterah with its pasture lands—two towns. [28]Out of the tribe of Issachar: Kishion with its pasture lands, Daberath with its pasture lands, [29]Jarmuth with its pasture lands, En-gannim with its pasture lands—four towns. [30]Out of the tribe of Asher: Mishal with its pasture lands, Abdon with its pasture lands, [31]Helkath with its pasture lands, and Rehob with its pasture lands—four towns. [32]Out of the tribe of Naphtali: Kedesh in Galilee with its pasture lands, the city of refuge for the slayer, Hammoth-dor with its pasture lands, and Kartan with its pasture lands—three towns. [33]The towns of the several families of the Gershonites were in all thirteen, with their pasture lands.

34 To the rest of the Levites—the Merarite families—were given out of the tribe of Zebulun: Jokneam with its pasture lands, Kartah with its pasture lands, [35]Dimnah with its pasture lands,

J O S H

Nahalal with its pasture lands—four towns. ³⁶Out of the tribe of Reuben: Bezer with its pasture lands, Jahzah with its pasture lands, ³⁷Kedemoth with its pasture lands, and Mephaath with its pasture lands—four towns. ³⁸Out of the tribe of Gad: Ramoth in Gilead with its pasture lands, the city of refuge for the slayer, Mahanaim with its pasture lands, ³⁹Heshbon with its pasture lands, Jazer with its pasture lands—four towns in all. ⁴⁰As for the towns of the several Merarite families, that is, the remainder of the families of the Levites, those allotted to them were twelve in all.

41 The towns of the Levites within the holdings of the Israelites were in all forty-eight towns with their pasture lands. ⁴²Each of these towns had its pasture lands around it; so it was with all these towns.

43 Thus the LORD gave to Israel all the land that he swore to their ancestors that he would give them; and having taken possession of it, they settled there. ⁴⁴And the LORD gave them rest on every side just as he had sworn to their ancestors; not one of all their enemies had withstood them, for the LORD had given all their enemies into their hands. ⁴⁵Not one of all the good promises that the LORD had made to the house of Israel had failed; all came to pass.

The Eastern Tribes Return to Their Territory

22 Then Joshua summoned the Reubenites, the Gadites, and the half-tribe of Manasseh, ²and said to them, "You have observed all that Moses the servant of the LORD commanded you, and have obeyed me in all that I have commanded you; ³you have not forsaken your kindred these many days, down to this day, but have been careful to keep the charge of the LORD your God. ⁴And now the LORD your God has given rest to your kindred, as he promised them; therefore turn and go to your tents in the land where your possession lies, which Moses the servant of the LORD gave you on the other side of the Jordan. ⁵Take good care to observe the commandment and instruction that Moses the servant of the LORD commanded you, to love the LORD your God, to walk in all his ways, to keep his commandments, and to hold fast to him, and to serve him with all your heart and with all your soul." ⁶So Joshua blessed them and sent them away, and they went to their tents.

7 Now to the one half of the tribe of Manasseh Moses had given a possession in Bashan; but to the other half Joshua had given a possession beside their fellow Israelites in the land west of the Jordan. And when Joshua sent them away to their tents and blessed them, ⁸he said to them, "Go

back to your tents with much wealth, and with very much livestock, with silver, gold, bronze, and iron, and with a great quantity of clothing; divide the spoil of your enemies with your kindred." ⁹So the Reubenites and the Gadites and the half-tribe of Manasseh returned home, parting from the Israelites at Shiloh, which is in the land of Canaan, to go to the land of Gilead, their own land of which they had taken possession by command of the LORD through Moses.

A Memorial Altar East of the Jordan

10 When they came to the region*a* near the Jordan that lies in the land of Canaan, the Reubenites and the Gadites and the half-tribe of Manasseh built there an altar by the Jordan, an altar of great size. ¹¹The Israelites heard that the Reubenites and the Gadites and the half-tribe of Manasseh had built an altar at the frontier of the land of Canaan, in the region*b* near the Jordan, on the side that belongs to the Israelites. ¹²And when the people of Israel heard of it, the whole assembly of the Israelites gathered at Shiloh, to make war against them.

13 Then the Israelites sent the priest Phinehas son of Eleazar to the Reubenites and the Gadites and the half-tribe of Manasseh, in the land of Gilead, ¹⁴and with him ten chiefs, one from each of the tribal families of Israel, every one of them the head of a family among the clans of Israel. ¹⁵They came to the Reubenites, the Gadites, and the half-tribe of Manasseh, in the land of Gilead, and they said to them, ¹⁶"Thus says the whole congregation of the LORD, 'What is this treachery that you have committed against the God of Israel in turning away today from following the LORD, by building yourselves an altar today in rebellion against the LORD? ¹⁷Have we not had enough of the sin at Peor from which even yet we have not cleansed ourselves, and for which a plague came upon the congregation of the LORD, ¹⁸that you must turn away today from following the LORD! If you rebel against the LORD today, he will be angry with the whole congregation of Israel tomorrow. ¹⁹But now, if your land is unclean, cross over into the LORD's land where the LORD's tabernacle now stands, and take for yourselves a possession among us; only do not rebel against the LORD, or rebel against us*c* by building yourselves an altar other than the altar of the LORD our God. ²⁰Did not Achan son of Zerah break faith in the matter of the devoted things, and wrath fell upon all the congregation of Israel? And he did not perish alone for his iniquity!' "

a Or to Geliloth   b Or at Geliloth   c Or make rebels of us

21 Then the Reubenites, the Gadites, and the half-tribe of Manasseh said in answer to the heads of the families of Israel, 22"The Lord, God of gods! The Lord, God of gods! He knows; and let Israel itself know! If it was in rebellion or in breach of faith toward the Lord, do not spare us today 23for building an altar to turn away from following the Lord; or if we did so to offer burnt offerings or grain offerings or offerings of well-being on it, may the Lord himself take vengeance. 24No! We did it from fear that in time to come your children might say to our children, 'What have you to do with the Lord, the God of Israel? 25For the Lord has made the Jordan a boundary between us and you, you Reubenites and Gadites; you have no portion in the Lord.' So your children might make our children cease to worship the Lord. 26Therefore we said, 'Let us now build an altar, not for burnt offering, nor for sacrifice, 27but to be a witness between us and you, and between the generations after us, that we do perform the service of the Lord in his presence with our burnt offerings and sacrifices and offerings of well-being; so that your children may never say to our children in time to come, "You have no portion in the Lord."' 28And we thought, If this should be said to us or to our descendants in time to come, we could say, 'Look at this copy of the altar of the Lord, which our ancestors made, not for burnt offerings, nor for sacrifice, but to be a witness between us and you.' 29Far be it from us that we should rebel against the Lord, and turn away this day from following the Lord by building an altar for burnt offering, grain offering, or sacrifice, other than the altar of the Lord our God that stands before his tabernacle!"

30 When the priest Phinehas and the chiefs of the congregation, the heads of the families of Israel who were with him, heard the words that the Reubenites and the Gadites and the Manassites spoke, they were satisfied. 31The priest Phinehas son of Eleazar said to the Reubenites and the Gadites and the Manassites, "Today we know that the Lord is among us, because you have not committed this treachery against the Lord; now you have saved the Israelites from the hand of the Lord." 32 Then the priest Phinehas son of Eleazar and the chiefs returned from the Reubenites and the Gadites in the land of Gilead to the land of Canaan, to the Israelites, and brought back word to them. 33The report pleased the Israelites; and the Israelites blessed God and spoke no more of making war against them, to destroy the land where the Reubenites and the Gadites were settled. 34The Reubenites and the Gadites called the altar Witness;[a] "For," said they, "it is a witness between us that the Lord is God."

Pray It!

A Prayer for Understanding

When the Israelite tribes located east of the Jordan build a large altar to worship God, the Israelite tribes who settled west of the Jordan become concerned. They think that by building more altars, the tribes to the east are compromising their belief in one God. Some are ready to go to war over this issue. But maintaining unity among the tribes is also important. So, the western tribes wisely send Phinehas and others to insist on the importance of one place of worship. Listening to the eastern tribes, Phinehas understands their good intentions, and war is avoided.

Think about times when you have jumped to conclusions about other people's actions. Then say the following prayer:

God of love and wisdom, a misunderstanding almost led to war among the Israelites. Help me to avoid jumping to conclusions about the actions of others. Help me to listen and understand their intentions, as Phinehas did. And let me be gracious in recognizing when I am wrong. Amen.

▶ **Josh 22:13–20**

Joshua Exhorts the People

23 A long time afterward, when the Lord had given rest to Israel from all their enemies all around, and Joshua was old and well advanced in years, 2Joshua summoned all Israel, their elders and heads, their judges and officers, and said to them, "I am now old and well advanced in years; 3and you have seen all that the Lord your God has done to all these nations for your sake, for it is the Lord your God who has fought for you. 4I have allotted to you as an inheritance for your tribes those nations that remain, along with all the nations that I have already cut off, from the Jordan to the Great Sea in the west. 5The Lord your God

a Cn Compare Syr: Heb lacks Witness

JOSH

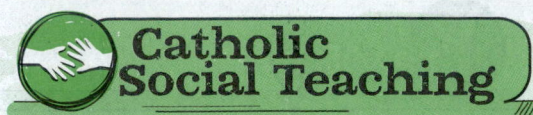

Catholic Social Teaching

Living the Covenant Today

Some people think the Israelites were completely homogenous and without differences, but nothing could be further from the truth. Joshua 24:1 tells how Joshua summoned the leaders of the twelve Tribes of Israel to present themselves before God. In this gathering, they embraced their common faith in God and renewed the Covenant of Sinai, setting aside their differences and political struggles.

One of the major themes of Catholic social teaching is the *Call to Family, Community, and Participation*. What this means is that as humans we are not just spiritual but also social beings. How we organize society directly affects the ability of people to grow in community. Marriage and family must be supported as well as participation in all levels of government. We all need to work together for the common good and to ensure that the needs of everyone are met, especially the most vulnerable. The very word *society* implies people coming together to associate on a variety of levels. Socializing, supporting one another, and actively working to make the world a better place are all ways to live out this important teaching.

● What can you do to foster more unity in your family, school, church, and neighborhood? How can you get more involved in bringing people together?

▶ **Josh 24:1–28**

Call to Family, Community, and Participation

---

will push them back before you, and drive them out of your sight; and you shall possess their land, as the LORD your God promised you. ⁶Therefore be very steadfast to observe and do all that is written in the book of the law of Moses, turning aside from it neither to the right nor to the left, ⁷so that you may not be mixed with these nations left here among you, or make mention of the names of their gods, or swear by them, or serve them, or bow yourselves down to them, ⁸but hold fast to the LORD your God, as you have done to this day. ⁹For the LORD has driven out before you great and strong nations; and as for you, no one has been able to withstand you to this day. ¹⁰One of you puts to flight a thousand, since it is the LORD your God who fights for you, as he promised you. ¹¹Be very careful, therefore, to love the LORD your God. ¹²For if you turn back, and join the survivors of these nations left here among you, and intermarry with them, so that you marry their women and they yours, ¹³know assuredly that the LORD your God will not continue to drive out these nations before you; but they shall be a snare and a trap for you, a scourge on your sides, and thorns in your eyes, until you perish from this good land that the LORD your God has given you.

14 "And now I am about to go the way of all the earth, and you know in your hearts and souls, all of you, that not one thing has failed of all the good things that the LORD your God promised concerning you; all have come to pass for you, not one of them has failed. ¹⁵But just as all the good things that the LORD your God promised concerning you have been fulfilled for you, so the LORD will bring upon you all the bad things, until he has destroyed you from this good land that the LORD your God has given you. ¹⁶If you transgress the covenant of the LORD your God, which he enjoined on you, and go and serve other gods and bow down to them, then the anger of the LORD will be kindled against you, and you shall perish quickly from the good land that he has given to you."

The Tribes Renew the Covenant

24 Then Joshua gathered all the tribes of Israel to Shechem, and summoned the elders, the heads, the judges, and the officers of Israel; and they presented themselves before God. ²And Joshua said to all the people, "Thus says the LORD, the God of Israel: Long ago your ancestors—Terah and his sons Abraham and Nahor—lived beyond the Euphrates and served other gods. ³Then I took your father Abraham from beyond the River and led him through all the land of Canaan and made his offspring many. I gave him Isaac; ⁴and to Isaac I gave Jacob and Esau. I gave Esau the hill country of Seir to possess, but Jacob and his children went down to Egypt. ⁵Then I sent Moses and Aaron, and I

Reading & Studying the Bible

What Is the Bible?

The Bible—which is also called the Sacred Scriptures— tells the story of the loving relationship between God and humankind. Through the sacred writings, God reveals to humankind the truth about God and God's will for us. It is a library of books that is divided into two parts: the Old Testament (before Jesus) and the New Testament (after Jesus' birth). Each part consists of a collection of books that are grouped into these sections:

▓ *The Pentateuch* (five books) tells about God's Chosen People, the Israelites. You'll read about their early stories, their history, and the laws God gave them.

▓ *The historical books* pick up Israelite history from 1250 BC to 100 BC. You will find accounts of the Israelites' settling the Promised Land, the rise and fall of their kings, their dispersion into exile, and their eventual return to the Promised Land.

▓ *The wisdom and poetry books* are a collection of hymns, poems, proverbs, and stories. They use imaginative language to make their points.

▓ *The prophets* are people who speak God's word. In these books, you will find comfort and promise, as well as be challenged to act with justice and mercy.

▓ *The Gospels* (Good News) focus on the person and teachings of Jesus. *The Acts of the Apostles* shows how the Church was formed and how the first Christians spread the Good News. These books cover the time period from 5 BC to the early AD 80s.

▓ The *letters,* or *epistles* (written by Paul, his followers, and other disciples), are actual letters that describe the new Christian faith, give advice, and offer words of hope. *Revelation* is a collection of mystical visions written to encourage the early Christians who were being persecuted.

Core Catholic Teachings on Reason and Revelation

The Catholic Church makes frequent appeal to human reason in teaching about the religious truths God has revealed:

- Revelation is God making himself and his divine plan known to the human race through words and deeds in human history.

- The human person must trust that God has revealed to the Church what God wants it to know for its salvation.

- In listening to the message of Creation and to the voice of conscience, every person can come to certainty about the existence of God.

- Through the natural light of human reason, the one true God can be known from his works—that is, from the world and from the human person. This is one reason the Church teaches that salvation is possible for every person, even those who have never heard of Jesus Christ.

- God has revealed God's self in order to restore the communion that human beings were created to have with God, before the relationship was broken by original sin.

- Revelation is communicated in the Bible's stories of how God made God's self known to the Chosen People by acting throughout their history. But when those attempts met with failure, God took a radical step. God sent God's son, Jesus Christ, into the world as the savior. While remaining fully God, Jesus Christ took on a human nature: he is both true God and true man. Thus Jesus Christ is the full and complete Revelation of who God is, and through Christ, God established the covenant with the human race forever. As the Bible tells us, "[Christ] is the image of the invisible God" (Col 1:15).

  - Everything needed to be known about God; everything needed to be known for eternal union with God has been revealed in Christ. Nothing more needs to be added or taken away.

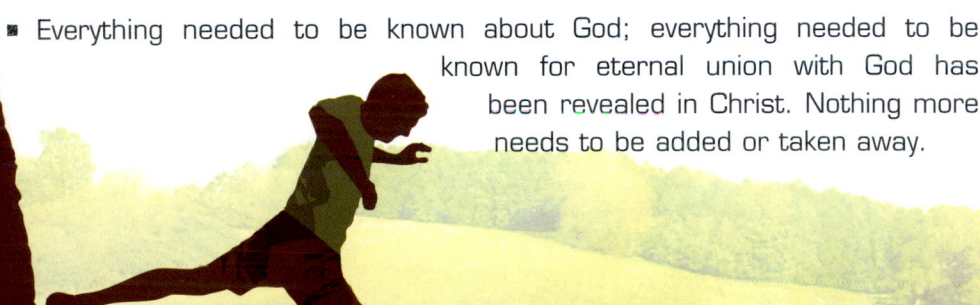

Core Catholic Teachings on the Scriptures and Tradition

The Catholic Church teaches:

- Christ promised to send the Holy Spirit to his closest followers, the Apostles, after he physically left them to ascend into heaven: "When the Spirit of truth comes, he will guide you into all the truth" (Jn 16:13). The Holy Spirit helped the Apostles to remember and understand all that Jesus did and taught. These truths about Jesus and his teachings are therefore called the Apostolic Tradition, or sometimes just the Tradition.

- Under the inspiration of the Holy Spirit, the Apostles handed on everything they knew about Jesus to the first Christians and to the generation of leaders that followed them.

- The Holy Spirit inspired people in the early Church to create written documents explaining what the Apostles had handed down about Jesus.

- The Scriptures and Tradition are two sources of Revelation. They are closely connected and together form a single sacred deposit of truth under the guidance of the Holy Spirit. They can never be in conflict, and each one helps us to understand the other.

- The Church looks to God's Revelation in the Scriptures and Tradition as the only authentic and complete source for knowledge about God and God's will for the whole human race. It is the responsibility of the Church, through her teaching, her worship, and her ministries, to transmit to every new generation all that God has revealed.

- As the successors of the Apostles, it is the particular and exclusive responsibility of the bishops in union with the Pope—the Magisterium—to faithfully teach, interpret, and preserve the Scriptures and Tradition for all believers until Christ returns in glory.

[Christ] is the image of the invisible God.

— Col 1:15

Overview of Salvation History

Primeval History

The Bible starts with some imaginative stories that tell how God made everything, along with the first humans, Adam and Eve. God's Creation was good, but evil crept into the world. After several generations, God decided to flood the world. But God saved Noah, his family, and specimens of land animals on an ark (boat) in order to give humans a chance to start over.

Patriarchs and Matriarchs (1850–1750 BC)

Abraham and Sarah arrived in Canaan, the land God had promised them. They were old, but God gave them a son, Isaac, who had two sons with his wife Rebecca. The younger was Jacob, whom God named Israel. Israel had twelve sons, but his favorite was Joseph. Joseph's jealous brothers sold him as a slave in Egypt, but God helped him to prosper. When Joseph's brothers visited Egypt, Joseph recognized them and told them to come live with him.

Egypt and Exodus (1750–1290 BC)

Israel's descendants (sometimes called Hebrews, Israelites, the Tribes of Israel, or the Children of Israel) became a small nation. But a new Egyptian dynasty came to power and made the Hebrews slaves. Eventually, God told Moses to bring them out of Egypt. To convince Pharaoh to let his cheap labor go, God sent a series of plagues, including the killing of all firstborn sons. The Hebrews were saved by putting the blood of a lamb over their doors. After the Hebrews left, Pharaoh sent his army to bring them back, trapping them at the Red Sea. God made the waters separate so the Hebrew people could escape; then God made the waters fall back, drowning the pursuing army. The Passover meal celebrates this victory.

Settling the Promised Land (1290–1020 BC)

While the Hebrew people were on their way back to Canaan, God made a covenant (an agreement) with them at Mount Sinai. God gave them laws, including the Ten Commandments. God told them to build a tabernacle (worship tent) and the ark of the Covenant (a box symbolizing God's presence). After a generation, the Hebrew people invaded Canaan under the leadership of Joshua. The land was divided into territories, roughly corresponding to the twelve Tribes of Israel. For over two hundred years, the Hebrews fought for the land; there was no central power, so God would occasionally raise up local leaders called judges.

The Kingdom United (1020–922 BC)

God allowed Samuel, the last of the judges, to make Saul the first king. Samuel poured oil on Saul's head, "anointing" him for leadership. The Hebrew word for an "anointed person" is *messiah* (the Greek word is *christ*). The next king was David, the greatest human king the little nation of Israel would ever have. God promised that David's house would be established forever. Next was David's son Solomon the Wise, who built a great palace and the first Temple in Jerusalem. But during Solomon's son's reign, the kingdom divided into two.

The Kingdom Divided (922–587 BC)

The northern kingdom was called Israel, and it went through several dynasties. The southern kingdom was Judah, and the Davidic dynasty stayed in power. Sadly, most of the kings were not faithful to God. So God would send prophets like Elijah to speak the word of God and call the people to faithfulness. When the northern kingdom fell to Assyria, it ceased to exist. Babylon in turn defeated Assyria and then later crushed Judah; Jerusalem and the Temple were utterly destroyed. Many Jews (inhabitants of Judah) were sent into exile in Babylon.

The Exile and the Return (587–5 BC)

Stories about heroes like Daniel kept the faith alive for Jews who were in exile. When Persia defeated Babylon, they let the Jews return home. By 515 BC, the Temple had been rebuilt. Eventually, the Greeks controlled the region and became brutally disrespectful, so Judas Maccabeus led a successful revolt. For a time, Israel was free, until Rome conquered the region in 63 BC. Weary from dark centuries of domination, the Jews began to hope for a new King, a Messiah (Christ), a Son of David, who would restore glory to Israel. In time millions would recognize a baby lying in a manger as the Christ—a light shining in the darkness.

The Life of Jesus, the Christ (5 BC–AD 30)

The angel Gabriel appeared to Mary, a young virgin, and told her she was going to have a baby—Jesus. The child would be conceived by the Holy Spirit and called the Son of God. Jesus was born in Bethlehem, with only a manger for a bed; we celebrate his birth on Christmas. Wise Men guided by a star brought gifts to Jesus; we celebrate this on Epiphany. Jesus grew up in Nazareth in Galilee.

Meanwhile, John the Baptist was baptizing people in the Jordan River when he recognized Jesus as "the Lamb of God." Jesus began teaching, often using stories called parables; he soon had a large following of disciples. Jesus preached the Gospel—Good News—with words that were both challenging and promising: we are to love God and our neighbor; this is God's greatest commandment. Even though we sin, God loves us—unconditionally—and offers us forgiveness; this is God's promise. Jesus performed many miracles, which were signs of the coming of the Reign of God. Some believed, and their faith was strengthened; others rejected Jesus.

The Death and Resurrection of Jesus, the Christ (AD 30)

Many of the Jewish leaders were upset because Jesus talked like he was above Jewish law, claimed to be the Christ, and even claimed to be God. So the authorities planned to kill him. Shortly before he was arrested, Jesus rode into Jerusalem like a king, while crowds honored him with palm branches (Palm Sunday). Later that week (Holy Thursday), Jesus ate a Passover meal with his disciples; this would be their Last Supper (and the first Eucharist). The next day (Good Friday), Jesus was crucified (brutal execution on a cross) under the authority of the Roman governor Pontius Pilate. Early Sunday morning (Easter), some women came to visit his tomb and were told that Jesus had come back to life; several times after his Resurrection, Jesus appeared to his disciples. Forty days later (Ascension Day), Jesus was lifted up into heaven.

The Early Christian Church (AD 30–70)

Fifty days after Jesus' Resurrection on Pentecost (the name of a Jewish feast day), the Holy Spirit came to the disciples and they started preaching in many languages. Thousands believed! Some refer to it as the birth of the Church. Stephen was the first martyr. Paul saw a vision of Jesus and became the first Christian missionary. Peter also had a startling vision—God told him salvation was for the Jews and the Gentiles (non-Jews). Days of persecution were ahead; Rome became increasingly intolerant and destroyed the Temple in AD 70. But Christianity kept spreading and growing. Jesus' mission of spreading the Good News of salvation continues through the Church today.

Understanding God's Revelation

The Bible was written under the inspiration of the Holy Spirit to reveal the truths about God's saving plan for humanity and for all of creation. But like any work of ancient literature, written thousands of years ago in a culture very different from our own, the Bible must be interpreted to be properly understood. If we do not follow good principles of interpretation when reading the Bible, we can arrive at misleading and even erroneous conclusions about what God is trying to say to us.

One way to describe the Church's teaching is to say that there are "lenses" through which we can look at the Bible's books and stories in order to understand what the human authors were trying to communicate to the people of their time. These lenses can also be called "contexts," because they help us put a particular book or story in its proper context or perspective. These are the lenses or contexts:

Historical Context (Conditions of the Time and Culture)

The human authors of the Bible assumed the readers of their time knew basic facts about their world. Two thousand years later, those facts may not be as apparent to us! But the work of biblical scholars has helped us to be more aware of some of the history behind the Bible's books and stories. And the more you know about biblical history, the better you will understand the meaning of certain words and events.

Literary Context (Literary Genres in Use at the Time)

It is important to remember that the Bible is more like a library than a one-volume history book. The authors of the seventy-three books of the Bible used many different literary styles to get across their ideas. Some books are short hero stories; some are religious history; some are collections of the sayings of prophets, collections of short wise sayings, or letters; and some are written in symbolic language. To properly understand the book, we must first understand what kind of literary style, or genre, the book uses. We do this automatically with writing styles we come across every day. In a news story, we expect facts based on real events; in a fairy tale, we expect to learn some truth, but we know the story itself didn't happen in real life. We must apply the same process to the Bible.

Cultural Context (Modes of Feeling, Speaking, and Narrating Then Current)

Every culture has its own cultural practices and traditions. The impact of culture affects almost every facet of life, such as the way we cut our hair; the way we dress; what we eat; how we relate to family, friends, and strangers; the way we do business; even whether we keep pets and, if we do, what kind. Without an understanding of another culture's traditions, many of that culture's practices may seem strange or even repulsive to us.

Unity of the Whole Scripture (Salvation History) Context

In order to understand what the human authors intended, we must consider the books of the Bible as independent documents. This is done to discover each author's purpose when the book was first written. But the Bible is more than just a collection of independent books that have no relationship to one another. When we put them all together, we can see God's bigger plan emerging—a plan the human authors could not fully see or comprehend until the New Testament was written. This overall plan for the salvation of God's people is often called salvation history.

Our interpretation of the Bible does not end after we consider what the human author's intention was in writing a particular book or passage. Next we must ask, "How does this book or passage fit into salvation history?" Many books and resources are available to help us learn about salvation history; being familiar with it is important if we hope to interpret the Bible correctly.

Living Tradition Context

Not all God's revealed truths are contained within the Bible. An oral tradition preceded the writing of the Gospels. Not everything in the oral tradition was written down in the Gospels (see Jn 21:25) or even fully understood at the time the New Testament was written. But guided by the Holy Spirit, all that God revealed through the life and teaching of Christ has been kept alive in the Church. This revelation is passed on through the Bible and through the living Tradition that has been passed on from the Apostles. Together the Scriptures and Tradition form a single deposit of faith. To understand all that God is revealing in the Bible, we must also consider Sacred Tradition.

Harmony Between Elements of Faith Context

This context, also called "the analogy of faith," means that ultimately there can be no contradiction between the truths God has revealed. The truths God reveals for our salvation are in harmony with one another. When, at times, there appear to be contradictions from the human authors' points of view, there are no contradictions in God's revealed truth.

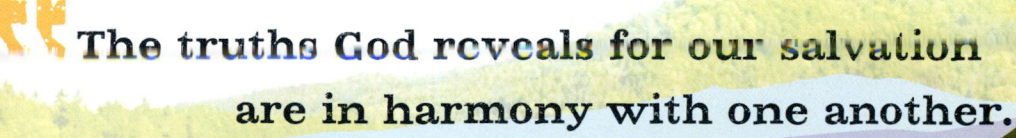

> **The truths God reveals for our salvation are in harmony with one another.**

Core Catholic Understandings on Biblical Inspiration and Interpretation

The way Catholics interpret the Bible has sometimes been a source of conflict between Catholics and other Christians.

- All Christians believe that God is the ultimate author of the Bible because the Holy Spirit inspired the human authors in their writing. But some Christians—sometimes called fundamentalists or literalists—believe that every part of the Bible must be absolutely true in every way: historically true, geographically true, and scientifically true. Thus, for example, they believe God created the world in six twenty-four-hour days.

- The Catholic Church teaches that the Holy Spirit inspired the biblical authors to write what God wanted known for salvation. The Holy Spirit did not take over the biblical authors' humanity when they wrote. Thus the authors were subject to natural human limitations, and they also used their human creativity in their writing. To continue the example above, Catholics believe in the religious truth that God created the world and everything in it, without having to believe that the world was literally created in six twenty-four-hour days.

- Catholics understand that the Bible is without error in communicating what God wants known for salvation without having to be historically and scientifically correct in every detail.

Seven Important Questions for Interpreting the Bible

Based on the six contexts the Church uses for interpreting the Bible, here are seven summary questions you can ask when studying any book or story in the Scriptures:

1. What was the historical situation at the time this book was written? How did the human author(s) address this situation?

2. What is this book or passage's literary genre? What are the rules for understanding it?

3. Is there a cultural practice or attitude reflected in this book or passage that we need to understand to appreciate the human author's intention?

4. How does this book or story fit into the overall story of salvation history?

5. How does Sacred Tradition help us to understand this book or story? How does this book or story help us to better understand God's revealed truths in Sacred Tradition?

6. Is the truth I understand from this book or story consistent with the rest of the Scriptures and Tradition?

7. When I look at everything I learned from these six questions, what spiritual truth is God revealing?

plagued Egypt with what I did in its midst; and afterwards I brought you out. 6When I brought your ancestors out of Egypt, you came to the sea; and the Egyptians pursued your ancestors with chariots and horsemen to the Red Sea.*a* 7When they cried out to the LORD, he put darkness between you and the Egyptians, and made the sea come upon them and cover them; and your eyes saw what I did to Egypt. Afterwards you lived in the wilderness a long time. 8Then I brought you to the land of the Amorites, who lived on the other side of the Jordan; they fought with you, and I handed them over to you, and you took possession of their land, and I destroyed them before you. 9Then King Balak son of Zippor of Moab, set out to fight against Israel. He sent and invited Balaam son of Beor to curse you, 10but I would not listen to Balaam; therefore he blessed you; so I rescued you out of his hand. 11When you went over the Jordan and came to Jericho, the citizens of Jericho fought against you, and also the Amorites, the Perizzites, the Canaanites, the Hittites, the Girgashites, the Hivites, and the Jebusites; and I handed them over to you. 12I sent the hornet*b* ahead of you, which drove out before you the two kings of the Amorites; it was not by your sword or by your bow. 13I gave you a land on which you had not labored, and towns that you had not built, and you live in them; you eat the fruit of vineyards and oliveyards that you did not plant.

14 "Now therefore revere the LORD, and serve him in sincerity and in faithfulness; put away the gods that your ancestors served beyond the River and in Egypt, and serve the LORD. 15Now if you are unwilling to serve the LORD, choose this day whom you will serve, whether the gods your ancestors served in the region beyond the River or the gods of the Amorites in whose land you are living; but as for me and my household, we will serve the LORD."

16 Then the people answered, "Far be it from us that we should forsake the LORD to serve other gods; 17for it is the LORD our God who brought us and our ancestors up from the land of Egypt, out of the house of slavery, and who did those great signs in our sight. He protected us along all the way that we went, and among all the peoples through whom we passed; 18and the LORD drove out before us all the peoples, the Amorites who lived in the land. Therefore we also will serve the LORD, for he is our God."

> **Revere the LORD, and serve him in sincerity and in faithfulness.**
> (Josh 24:14)

19 But Joshua said to the people, "You cannot serve the LORD, for he is a holy God. He is a jealous God; he will not forgive your transgressions or your sins. 20If you forsake the LORD and serve foreign gods, then he will turn and do you harm, and consume you, after having done you good." 21And the people said to Joshua, "No, we will serve the LORD!" 22Then Joshua said to the people, "You are witnesses against yourselves that you have chosen the LORD, to serve him." And they said, "We are witnesses." 23He said, "Then put away the foreign gods that are among you, and incline your hearts to the LORD, the God of Israel." 24The people said to Joshua, "The LORD our God we will serve, and him we will obey." 25So Joshua made a covenant with the people that day, and made statutes and ordinances for them at Shechem. 26Joshua wrote these words in the book of the law of God; and he took a large stone, and set it up there under the oak in the sanctuary of the LORD. 27Joshua said to all the people, "See, this stone shall be a witness against us; for it has heard all the words of the LORD that he spoke to us; therefore it shall be a witness against you, if you deal falsely with your God." 28So Joshua sent the people away to their inheritances.

Death of Joshua and Eleazar

29 After these things Joshua son of Nun, the servant of the LORD, died, being one hundred ten years old. 30They buried him in his own inheritance at Timnath-serah, which is in the hill country of Ephraim, north of Mount Gaash.

31 Israel served the LORD all the days of Joshua, and all the days of the elders who outlived Joshua and had known all the work that the LORD did for Israel.

32 The bones of Joseph, which the Israelites had brought up from Egypt, were buried at Shechem, in the portion of ground that Jacob had bought from the children of Hamor, the father of Shechem, for one hundred pieces of money;*c* it became an inheritance of the descendants of Joseph.

33 Eleazar son of Aaron died; and they buried him at Gibeah, the town of his son Phinehas, which had been given him in the hill country of Ephraim.

---

a Or Sea of Reeds   *b* Meaning of Heb uncertain   *c* Heb one hundred qesitah

Mom and Dad treat me like such a child. I can't get a job without experience, but how can I get experience if I can't get a job? The teenage years often feel like an in-between time, when young people pass from being children to becoming adults who must take responsibility for their own lives. This time of transition holds many challenges. In some ways, the Book of Judges is about Israel's "teenage years." It tells about the difficulties faced by God's People in an in-between time: the two hundred years between the conquest of Canaan under Joshua and the establishment of the kingdom of Israel under Saul.

At a Glance

- 1:1—3:6. historical introduction
- 3:7—16:31. the stories of individual judges
- Chapters 17–21. two appendices

Quick Facts

Period Covered: from 1220 to 1000 BC

Inspired Author: The book was put into final form by an unknown person from the Deuteronomic school, sometime during the Israelite monarchy.

Themes: God raises up mighty heroes to protect the people. God works even through flawed heroes.

In Depth

In the Book of Judges, the twelve Tribes of Israel face two especially difficult challenges: how to live peacefully with one another and how to withstand the attacks of foreign armies. God answers the Israelites' prayers for help by raising up extraordinary men and women to lead the tribes. These famous leaders—Gideon, Deborah, Samson, and nine others—are called judges, but they aren't judges in courtrooms wearing black robes. They are local elders and military heroes who are chosen by God's spirit to lead the Israelites in times of crisis.

The pattern we observe in the Book of Joshua also appears in the Book of Judges: when the people obey God's laws, they thrive; when they are disobedient, they suffer and need to be rescued by a leader raised up by God's Spirit. The stories in Judges probably began as regional tales about local heroes. As they were collected and edited by the author of Judges, they became national stories influenced by the message of Deuteronomy: faithfulness to God is the only road to personal and tribal security.

The Book of Judges reminds us that the challenges of life, especially in the in-between times, are best handled through prayer and reliance on God. We can trust God to lead us through all difficulties, both great and small.

The Book of **Judges**

Judges

Israel's Failure to Complete the Conquest of Canaan

1 After the death of Joshua, the Israelites inquired of the LORD, "Who shall go up first for us against the Canaanites, to fight against them?" ²The LORD said, "Judah shall go up. I hereby give the land into his hand." ³Judah said to his brother Simeon, "Come up with me into the territory allotted to me, that we may fight against the Canaanites; then I too will go with you into the territory allotted to you." So Simeon went with him. ⁴Then Judah went up and the LORD gave the Canaanites and the Perizzites into their hand; and they defeated ten thousand of them at Bezek. ⁵They came upon Adoni-bezek at Bezek, and fought against him, and defeated the Canaanites and the Perizzites. ⁶Adoni-bezek fled; but they pursued him, and caught him, and cut off his thumbs and big toes. ⁷Adoni-bezek said, "Seventy kings with their thumbs and big toes cut off used to pick up scraps under my table; as I have done, so God has paid me back." They brought him to Jerusalem, and he died there.

8 Then the people of Judah fought against Jerusalem and took it. They put it to the sword and set the city on fire. ⁹Afterward the people of Judah went down to fight against the Canaanites who lived in the hill country, in the Negeb, and in the lowland. ¹⁰Judah went against the Canaanites who lived in Hebron (the name of Hebron was formerly Kiriath-arba); and they defeated Sheshai and Ahiman and Talmai.

11 From there they went against the inhabitants of Debir (the name of Debir was formerly Kiriath-sepher). ¹²Then Caleb said, "Whoever attacks Kiriath-sepher and takes it, I will give him my daughter Achsah as wife." ¹³And Othniel son of Kenaz, Caleb's younger brother, took it; and he gave him his daughter Achsah as wife. ¹⁴When she came to him, she urged him to ask her father for a field. As she dismounted from her donkey, Caleb said to her, "What do you wish?" ¹⁵She said to him, "Give me a present; since you have set me in the land of the Negeb, give me also Gulloth-mayim."ᵃ So Caleb gave her Upper Gulloth and Lower Gulloth.

16 The descendants of Hobabᵇ the Kenite, Moses' father-in-law, went up with the people of Judah from the city of palms into the wilderness of Judah, which lies in the Negeb near Arad. Then they went and settled with the Amalekites.ᶜ ¹⁷Judah went with his brother Simeon, and they defeated the Canaanites who inhabited Zephath, and devoted it to destruction. So the city was called Hormah. ¹⁸Judah took Gaza with its territory, Ashkelon with its territory, and Ekron with its territory. ¹⁹The LORD was with Judah, and he took possession of the hill country, but could not drive out the inhabitants of the plain, because they had chariots of iron. ²⁰Hebron was given to Caleb, as Moses had said; and he drove out from it the three sons of Anak. ²¹But the Benjaminites

---

a That is *Basins of Water*   b Gk: Heb lacks *Hobab*   c See 1 Sam 15.6: Heb *people*

Water in the Desert

Caleb's daughter, Achsah, asks for *Gulloth-mayim* (Judg 1:15) as her wedding present. *Gulloth-mayim* means "basins of water," and presumably, she is asking for a place with springs of fresh water. Achsah's new home will be in the desert, and she knows that her family will need water. She's not afraid to ask for what she needs.

Clearly, Achsah's request fits into God's master plan. However, we know that we don't always get what we pray for. When that happens, we need to remind ourselves that God's plan may mean that our prayers are not always answered in a way that we want. That is when we need to trust the wisdom of God in our lives.

In your prayer time, reflect or journal on the following questions:

● Which prayers of yours have not been answered or have been answered differently than you requested?

● Why is "thy will be done" a good way to end your prayer time?

▶ **Judg 1:14–15**

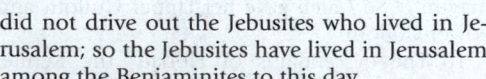

did not drive out the Jebusites who lived in Jerusalem; so the Jebusites have lived in Jerusalem among the Benjaminites to this day.

22 The house of Joseph also went up against Bethel; and the LORD was with them. 23The house of Joseph sent out spies to Bethel (the name of the city was formerly Luz). 24When the spies saw a man coming out of the city, they said to him, "Show us the way into the city, and we will deal kindly with you." 25So he showed them the way into the city; and they put the city to the sword, but they let the man and all his family go. 26So the man went to the land of the Hittites and built a city, and named it Luz; that is its name to this day.

27 Manasseh did not drive out the inhabitants of Beth-shean and its villages, or Taanach and its villages, or the inhabitants of Dor and its villages, or the inhabitants of Ibleam and its villages, or the inhabitants of Megiddo and its villages; but the Canaanites continued to live in

that land. 28When Israel grew strong, they put the Canaanites to forced labor, but did not in fact drive them out.

29 And Ephraim did not drive out the Canaanites who lived in Gezer; but the Canaanites lived among them in Gezer.

30 Zebulun did not drive out the inhabitants of Kitron, or the inhabitants of Nahalol; but the Canaanites lived among them, and became subject to forced labor.

31 Asher did not drive out the inhabitants of Acco, or the inhabitants of Sidon, or of Ahlab, or of Achzib, or of Helbah, or of Aphik, or of Rehob; 32but the Asherites lived among the Canaanites, the inhabitants of the land; for they did not drive them out.

33 Naphtali did not drive out the inhabitants of Beth-shemesh, or the inhabitants of Beth-anath, but lived among the Canaanites, the inhabitants of the land; nevertheless the inhabitants of Beth-shemesh and of Beth-anath became subject to forced labor for them.

34 The Amorites pressed the Danites back into the hill country; they did not allow them to come down to the plain. 35The Amorites continued to live in Har-heres, in Aijalon, and in Shaalbim, but the hand of the house of Joseph rested heavily on them, and they became subject to forced labor. 36The border of the Amorites ran from the ascent of Akrabbim, from Sela and upward.

Israel's Disobedience

2 Now the angel of the LORD went up from Gilgal to Bochim, and said, "I brought you up from Egypt, and brought you into the land that I had promised to your ancestors. I said, 'I will never break my covenant with you. 2For your part, do not make a covenant with the inhabitants of this land; tear down their altars.' But you have not obeyed my command. See what you have done! 3So now I say, I will not drive them out before you; but they shall become adversaries[a] to you, and their gods shall be a snare to you." 4When the angel of the LORD spoke these words to all the Israelites, the people lifted up their voices and wept. 5So they named that place Bochim,[b] and there they sacrificed to the LORD.

Death of Joshua

6 When Joshua dismissed the people, the Israelites all went to their own inheritances to take possession of the land. 7The people worshiped the LORD all the days of Joshua, and all the days of the elders who outlived Joshua, who had seen

a OL Vg Compare Gk: Heb *sides*   *b* That is *Weepers*

JUDG

all the great work that the LORD had done for Israel. [8]Joshua son of Nun, the servant of the LORD, died at the age of one hundred ten years. [9]So they buried him within the bounds of his inheritance in Timnath-heres, in the hill country of Ephraim, north of Mount Gaash. [10]Moreover, that whole generation was gathered to their ancestors, and another generation grew up after them, who did not know the LORD or the work that he had done for Israel.

Israel's Unfaithfulness

11 Then the Israelites did what was evil in the sight of the LORD and worshiped the Baals; [12]and they abandoned the LORD, the God of their ancestors, who had brought them out of the land of Egypt; they followed other gods, from among the gods of the peoples who were all around them, and bowed down to them; and they provoked the LORD to anger. [13]They abandoned the LORD, and worshiped Baal and the Astartes. [14]So the anger of the LORD was kindled against Israel, and he gave them over to plunderers who plundered them, and he sold them into the power of their enemies all around, so that they could no longer withstand their enemies. [15]Whenever they marched out, the hand of the LORD was against them to bring misfortune, as the LORD had warned them and sworn to them; and they were in great distress.

16 Then the LORD raised up judges, who delivered them out of the power of those who plundered them. [17]Yet they did not listen even to their judges; for they lusted after other gods and bowed down to them. They soon turned aside from the way in which their ancestors had walked, who had obeyed the commandments of the LORD; they did not follow their example. [18]Whenever the LORD raised up judges for them, the LORD was with the judge, and he delivered them from the hand of their enemies all the days of the judge; for the LORD would be moved to pity by their groaning because of those who persecuted and oppressed them. [19]But whenever the judge died, they would relapse and behave worse than their ancestors, following other gods, worshiping them and bowing down to them. They would not drop any of their practices or their stubborn ways. [20]So the anger of the LORD was kindled against Israel; and he said, "Because this people have transgressed my covenant that I commanded their ancestors, and have not obeyed my voice, [21]I will no longer drive out before them any of the nations that Joshua left when he died." [22]In order to test Israel, whether or not they would take care to walk in the way

of the LORD as their ancestors did, [23]the LORD had left those nations, not driving them out at once, and had not handed them over to Joshua.

Nations Remaining in the Land

3 Now these are the nations that the LORD left to test all those in Israel who had no experience of any war in Canaan [2](it was only that successive generations of Israelites might know war, to teach those who had no experience of it before): [3]the five lords of the Philistines, and all the Canaanites, and the Sidonians, and the Hivites who lived on Mount Lebanon, from Mount Baal-hermon as far as Lebo-hamath. [4]They were for the testing of Israel, to know whether Israel would obey the commandments of the LORD, which he commanded their ancestors by Moses. [5]So the Israelites lived among the Canaanites, the Hittites,

Obeying Authority

Think of a time when you disobeyed a parent or teacher. What were the consequences? Disobedience to legitimate authority tends to bring about negative consequences. Just read Judges 2:10–15. The people turned from God, and their separation from God led to defeat at the hands of their enemies.

God places parents, teachers, and other authority figures in our lives to protect and support us. Their love and care are an extension of God's love and care. From their vantage point, they often see a bigger picture than we do. When we disobey their reasonable requests, we build walls between them and us, preventing God's love from reaching us. On the other hand, obedience leads to more trust, responsibility, and freedom. Of course, as Jesus himself showed us, no one is obligated to obey requests or directions that are abusive, demeaning, or immoral.

So, the next time you are having a problem with a person in authority, ask yourself, "Might obedience in this situation somehow bring me closer to God?"

▶ Judg 2:10–15

the Amorites, the Perizzites, the Hivites, and the Jebusites; 6and they took their daughters as wives for themselves, and their own daughters they gave to their sons; and they worshiped their gods.

Othniel

7 The Israelites did what was evil in the sight of the LORD, forgetting the LORD their God, and worshiping the Baals and the Asherahs. 8Therefore the anger of the LORD was kindled against Israel, and he sold them into the hand of King Cushan-rishathaim of Aram-naharaim; and the Israelites served Cushan-rishathaim eight years. 9But when the Israelites cried out to the LORD, the LORD raised up a deliverer for the Israelites, who delivered them, Othniel son of Kenaz, Caleb's

The Battle Within

Although the story of Deborah is inspiring, partly because so few women leaders are portrayed in the Bible, it is also a story of war and violence. The Book of Judges records one battle after another. It is wearying to read of so much fighting and of rejoicing over someone's having a tent peg pounded into his head.

We need to keep our perspective here and understand that the way the Israelites viewed life at that time was simple: If they were victorious, God was with them. If they were defeated, God had been offended and had turned away from them.

What can we learn from this story? It teaches that God never turns away from us. The real victories to celebrate are the personal battles we win each day as we strive to become more faithful to God. Jesus calls us to make peace rather than war. Our greatest enemy is often within, as we strive to be the person God wants us to be, whether our name is Deborah or Joshua, Jennifer or Carlos.

● What battle is going on inside you today? What choice in this battle leads to greater faithfulness to God?

▶ Judges, chapter 4

younger brother. 10The spirit of the LORD came upon him, and he judged Israel; he went out to war, and the LORD gave King Cushan-rishathaim of Aram into his hand; and his hand prevailed over Cushan-rishathaim. 11So the land had rest forty years. Then Othniel son of Kenaz died.

Ehud

12 The Israelites again did what was evil in the sight of the LORD; and the LORD strengthened King Eglon of Moab against Israel, because they had done what was evil in the sight of the LORD. 13In alliance with the Ammonites and the Amalekites, he went and defeated Israel; and they took possession of the city of palms. 14So the Israelites served King Eglon of Moab eighteen years.

15 But when the Israelites cried out to the LORD, the LORD raised up for them a deliverer, Ehud son of Gera, the Benjaminite, a left-handed man. The Israelites sent tribute by him to King Eglon of Moab. 16Ehud made for himself a sword with two edges, a cubit in length; and he fastened it on his right thigh under his clothes. 17Then he presented the tribute to King Eglon of Moab. Now Eglon was a very fat man. 18When Ehud had finished presenting the tribute, he sent the people who carried the tribute on their way. 19But he himself turned back at the sculptured stones near Gilgal, and said, "I have a secret message for you, O king." So the king said,a "Silence!" and all his attendants went out from his presence. 20Ehud came to him, while he was sitting alone in his cool roof chamber, and said, "I have a message from God for you." So he rose from his seat. 21Then Ehud reached with his left hand, took the sword from his right thigh, and thrust it into Eglon'sb belly; 22the hilt also went in after the blade, and the fat closed over the blade, for he did not draw the sword out of his belly; and the dirt came out.c 23Then Ehud went out into the vestibule,d and closed the doors of the roof chamber on him, and locked them.

24 After he had gone, the servants came. When they saw that the doors of the roof chamber were locked, they thought, "He must be relieving himselfe in the cool chamber." 25So they waited until they were embarrassed. When he still did not open the doors of the roof chamber, they took the key and opened them. There was their lord lying dead on the floor.

26 Ehud escaped while they delayed, and passed beyond the sculptured stones, and escaped to Seirah. 27When he arrived, he sounded

a Heb he said b Heb his c With Tg Vg: Meaning of Heb uncertain d Meaning of Heb uncertain e Heb covering his feet

the trumpet in the hill country of Ephraim; and the Israelites went down with him from the hill country, having him at their head. ²⁸He said to them, "Follow after me; for the Lord has given your enemies the Moabites into your hand." So they went down after him, and seized the fords of the Jordan against the Moabites, and allowed no one to cross over. ²⁹At that time they killed about ten thousand of the Moabites, all strong, able-bodied men; no one escaped. ³⁰So Moab was subdued that day under the hand of Israel. And the land had rest eighty years.

Shamgar

31 After him came Shamgar son of Anath, who killed six hundred of the Philistines with an oxgoad. He too delivered Israel.

Deborah and Barak

4 The Israelites again did what was evil in the sight of the Lord, after Ehud died. ²So the Lord sold them into the hand of King Jabin of Canaan, who reigned in Hazor; the commander of his army was Sisera, who lived in Harosheth-ha-goiim. ³Then the Israelites cried out to the Lord for help; for he had nine hundred chariots of iron, and had oppressed the Israelites cruelly twenty years.

4 At that time Deborah, a prophetess, wife of Lappidoth, was judging Israel. ⁵She used to sit under the palm of Deborah between Ramah and Bethel in the hill country of Ephraim; and the Israelites came up to her for judgment. ⁶She sent and summoned Barak son of Abinoam from Kedesh in Naphtali, and said to him, "The Lord, the God of Israel, commands you, 'Go, take position at Mount Tabor, bringing ten thousand from the tribe of Naphtali and the tribe of Zebulun. ⁷I will draw out Sisera, the general of Jabin's army, to meet you by the Wadi Kishon with his chariots and his troops; and I will give him into your hand.' " ⁸Barak said to her, "If you will go with me, I will go; but if you will not go with me, I will not go." ⁹And she said, "I will surely go with you; nevertheless, the road on which you are going will not lead to your glory, for the Lord will sell Sisera into the hand of a woman." Then Deborah got up and went with Barak to Kedesh. ¹⁰Barak summoned Zebulun and Naphtali to Kedesh; and ten thousand warriors went up behind him; and Deborah went up with him.

11 Now Heber the Kenite had separated from the other Kenites,ᵃ that is, the descendants of Hobab the father-in-law of Moses, and had encamped as far away as Elon-bezaanannim, which is near Kedesh.

Pray It!

Wartime Women

In Judges, chapter 4, Deborah, a judge and prophet, rallies Barak and the Israelites to war, and Jael, another woman (who is not an Israelite), delivers the final blow to the enemy's commander, Sisera. In chapter 5, Deborah leads the victory celebration with an elaborate prayer-song that is probably one of the oldest texts in the Bible (see also Exodus, chapter 15).

In the Bible, women are often innocent victims of war. Usually, they do not do the fighting but are raped, killed, or widowed. Is Jael's violence the answer to this abuse? Is Jael a hero, or is she still a victim of war, forced to make a violent choice in order to survive in a violent world? The writer of the Book of Judges gives no judgment on her actions.

When we are no longer victims but have become people who abuse others, has the situation really improved, or are we just doing to others what we would never want done to us? In light of Jesus' teachings, these are important questions to ask. Let us pray:

God of love, please deliver us from being both victims of violence and agents of violence. Amen.

▶ **Judges, chapter 4**

12 When Sisera was told that Barak son of Abinoam had gone up to Mount Tabor, ¹³Sisera called out all his chariots, nine hundred chariots of iron, and all the troops who were with him, from Harosheth-ha-goiim to the Wadi Kishon. ¹⁴Then Deborah said to Barak, "Up! For this is the day on which the Lord has given Sisera into your hand. The Lord is indeed going out before you." So Barak went down from Mount Tabor with ten thousand warriors following him. ¹⁵And the Lord threw Sisera and all his chariots and all his army into a panicᵇ before Barak; Sisera got down from his chariot and fled away on foot, ¹⁶while Barak pursued the chariots and the army to Harosheth-ha-goiim. All the army of Sisera fell by the sword; no one was left.

---

a Heb *from the Kain*   b Heb adds *to the sword*; compare verse 16

JUDG

17 Now Sisera had fled away on foot to the tent of Jael wife of Heber the Kenite; for there was peace between King Jabin of Hazor and the clan of Heber the Kenite. [18]Jael came out to meet Sisera, and said to him, "Turn aside, my lord, turn aside to me; have no fear." So he turned aside to her into the tent, and she covered him with a rug. [19]Then he said to her, "Please give me a little water to drink; for I am thirsty." So she opened a skin of milk and gave him a drink and covered him. [20]He said to her, "Stand at the entrance of the tent, and if anybody comes and asks you, 'Is anyone here?' say, 'No.' " [21]But Jael wife of Heber took a tent peg, and took a hammer in her hand, and went softly to him and drove the peg into his temple, until it went down into the ground—he was lying fast asleep from weariness—and he died. [22]Then, as Barak came in pursuit of Sisera, Jael went out to meet him, and said to him, "Come, and I will show you the man whom you are seeking." So he went into her tent; and there was Sisera lying dead, with the tent peg in his temple.

23 So on that day God subdued King Jabin of Canaan before the Israelites. [24]Then the hand of the Israelites bore harder and harder on King Jabin of Canaan, until they destroyed King Jabin of Canaan.

The Song of Deborah

5 Then Deborah and Barak son of Abinoam sang on that day, saying:

2 "When locks are long in Israel,
  when the people offer themselves willingly—
  bless[a] the LORD!

3 "Hear, O kings; give ear, O princes;
  to the LORD I will sing,
  I will make melody to the LORD, the God of
    Israel.

4 "LORD, when you went out from Seir,
  when you marched from the region of Edom,
  the earth trembled,
  and the heavens poured,
  the clouds indeed poured water.

5 The mountains quaked before the LORD, the One
    of Sinai,
  before the LORD, the God of Israel.

6 "In the days of Shamgar son of Anath,
  in the days of Jael, caravans ceased
  and travelers kept to the byways.

7 The peasantry prospered in Israel,
  they grew fat on plunder,
  because you arose, Deborah,
    arose as a mother in Israel.

8 When new gods were chosen,
  then war was in the gates.
  Was shield or spear to be seen
    among forty thousand in Israel?

9 My heart goes out to the commanders of Israel
  who offered themselves willingly among the
    people.
  Bless the LORD.

10 "Tell of it, you who ride on white donkeys,
  you who sit on rich carpets[b]
  and you who walk by the way.

11 To the sound of musicians[b] at the watering
    places,
  there they repeat the triumphs of the LORD,
  the triumphs of his peasantry in Israel.

"Then down to the gates marched the people of
    the LORD.

12 "Awake, awake, Deborah!
  Awake, awake, utter a song!
  Arise, Barak, lead away your captives,
    O son of Abinoam.

13 Then down marched the remnant of the noble;
  the people of the LORD marched down for
    him[c] against the mighty.

14 From Ephraim they set out[d] into the valley,[e]
  following you, Benjamin, with your kin;
  from Machir marched down the commanders,
  and from Zebulun those who bear the
    marshal's staff;

15 the chiefs of Issachar came with Deborah,
  and Issachar faithful to Barak;
  into the valley they rushed out at his heels.
  Among the clans of Reuben
    there were great searchings of heart.

16 Why did you tarry among the sheepfolds,
  to hear the piping for the flocks?
  Among the clans of Reuben
    there were great searchings of heart.

17 Gilead stayed beyond the Jordan;
  and Dan, why did he abide with the ships?
  Asher sat still at the coast of the sea,
  settling down by his landings.

18 Zebulun is a people that scorned death;
  Naphtali too, on the heights of the field.

19 "The kings came, they fought;
  then fought the kings of Canaan,
  at Taanach, by the waters of Megiddo;
  they got no spoils of silver.

---

a Or *You who offer yourselves willingly among the people, bless*
b Meaning of Heb uncertain   c Gk: Heb *me*   d Cn: Heb *From Ephraim their root*   e Gk: Heb *in Amalek*

20 The stars fought from heaven,
    from their courses they fought against Sisera.
21 The torrent Kishon swept them away,
    the onrushing torrent, the torrent Kishon.
    March on, my soul, with might!

22 "Then loud beat the horses' hoofs
    with the galloping, galloping of his steeds.

23 "Curse Meroz, says the angel of the Lord,
    curse bitterly its inhabitants,
because they did not come to the help of the
    Lord,
    to the help of the Lord against the mighty.

24 "Most blessed of women be Jael,
    the wife of Heber the Kenite,
    of tent-dwelling women most blessed.
25 He asked water and she gave him milk,
    she brought him curds in a lordly bowl.
26 She put her hand to the tent peg
    and her right hand to the workmen's mallet;
she struck Sisera a blow,
    she crushed his head,
    she shattered and pierced his temple.
27 He sank, he fell,
    he lay still at her feet;
at her feet he sank, he fell;
    where he sank, there he fell dead.

28 "Out of the window she peered,
    the mother of Sisera gazed*a* through the
        lattice:
'Why is his chariot so long in coming?
    Why tarry the hoofbeats of his chariots?'
29 Her wisest ladies make answer,
    indeed, she answers the question herself:
30 'Are they not finding and dividing the spoil?—
    A girl or two for every man;
spoil of dyed stuffs for Sisera,
    spoil of dyed stuffs embroidered,
    two pieces of dyed work embroidered for my
        neck as spoil?'

31 "So perish all your enemies, O Lord!
    But may your friends be like the sun as it rises
        in its might."

And the land had rest forty years.

The Midianite Oppression

6 The Israelites did what was evil in the sight of the Lord, and the Lord gave them into the hand of Midian seven years. 2The hand of Midian prevailed over Israel; and because of Midian the Israelites provided for themselves hiding places in the mountains, caves and strongholds. 3For whenever the Israelites put in seed, the Midianites and the Amalekites and the people of the east would come up against them. 4They would encamp against them and destroy the produce of the land, as far as the neighborhood of Gaza, and leave no sustenance in Israel, and no sheep or ox or donkey. 5For they and their livestock would come up, and they would even bring their tents, as thick as locusts; neither they nor their camels could be counted; so they wasted the land as they came in. 6Thus Israel was greatly impoverished because of Midian; and the Israelites cried out to the Lord for help.

7 When the Israelites cried to the Lord on account of the Midianites, 8the Lord sent a prophet to the Israelites; and he said to them, "Thus says the Lord, the God of Israel: I led you up from Egypt, and brought you out of the house of slavery; 9and I delivered you from the hand of the Egyptians, and from the hand of all who oppressed you, and drove them out before you, and gave you their land; 10and I said to you, 'I am the Lord your God; you shall not pay reverence to the gods of the Amorites, in whose land you live.' But you have not given heed to my voice."

The Call of Gideon

11 Now the angel of the Lord came and sat under the oak at Ophrah, which belonged to Joash the Abiezrite, as his son Gideon was beating out wheat in the wine press, to hide it from the Midianites. 12The angel of the Lord appeared to him and said to him, "The Lord is with you, you mighty warrior." 13Gideon answered him, "But sir, if the Lord is with us, why then has all this happened to us? And where are all his wonderful deeds that our ancestors recounted to us, saying, 'Did not the Lord bring us up from Egypt?' But now the Lord has cast us off, and given us into the hand of Midian." 14Then the Lord turned to him and said, "Go in this might of yours and deliver Israel from the hand of Midian; I hereby commission you." 15He responded, "But sir, how can I deliver Israel? My clan is the weakest in Manasseh, and I am the least in my family." 16The Lord said to him, "But I will be with you, and you shall strike down the Midianites, every one of them." 17Then he said to him, "If now I have found favor with you, then show me a sign that it is you who speak with me. 18Do not depart from here until I come to you, and bring out my present, and set it before you." And he said, "I will stay until you return."

---

a Gk Compare Tg: Heb exclaimed

Trusting God

The true test of love is loving without testing. Gideon keeps testing God; he cannot
bring himself to believe God's promises. Judges,
chapters 6–8, gives a full picture of this hero
who never quite understands what loving God is
all about. Even after his victory and his words of
devotion to God, he makes a gold idol (see Judg
8:22–28).

Most people are tempted to test God in some
way: "God, I'll know you are there for me if I get
this job." Fortunately, God is big enough to accept our testing. Just do not expect God to answer every request—at least not exactly the way
you would like God to answer it.

How do you test God? Is your prayer more
trusting than Gideon's prayer? The next time you
feel anxious or afraid, use one of these Scripture passages for your prayer: Psalm
25; Psalm 27; John, chapter 14; 1 John
4:7–21. Challenge yourself
to trust God without testing.

▶ **Judg 6:36–40**

19 So Gideon went into his house and prepared a kid, and unleavened cakes from an
ephah of flour; the meat he put in a basket, and
the broth he put in a pot, and brought them to
him under the oak and presented them. ²⁰The
angel of God said to him, "Take the meat and
the unleavened cakes, and put them on this rock,
and pour out the broth." And he did so. ²¹Then
the angel of the LORD reached out the tip of the
staff that was in his hand, and touched the meat
and the unleavened cakes; and fire sprang up
from the rock and consumed the meat and the
unleavened cakes; and the angel of the LORD vanished from his sight. ²²Then Gideon perceived
that it was the angel of the LORD; and Gideon
said, "Help me, Lord GOD! For I have seen the
angel of the LORD face to face." ²³But the LORD
said to him, "Peace be to you; do not fear, you
shall not die." ²⁴Then Gideon built an altar there
to the LORD, and called it, The LORD is peace. To
this day it still stands at Ophrah, which belongs
to the Abiezrites.

25 That night the LORD said to him, "Take
your father's bull, the second bull seven years
old, and pull down the altar of Baal that belongs
to your father, and cut down the sacred pole*ª*
that is beside it; ²⁶and build an altar to the LORD
your God on the top of the stronghold here, in
proper order; then take the second bull, and offer
it as a burnt offering with the wood of the sacred
pole*ª* that you shall cut down." ²⁷So Gideon took
ten of his servants, and did as the LORD had told
him; but because he was too afraid of his family
and the townspeople to do it by day, he did it
by night.

Gideon Destroys the Altar of Baal

28 When the townspeople rose early in the
morning, the altar of Baal was broken down,
and the sacred pole*ª* beside it was cut down, and
the second bull was offered on the altar that had
been built. ²⁹So they said to one another, "Who
has done this?" After searching and inquiring,
they were told, "Gideon son of Joash did it."
³⁰Then the townspeople said to Joash, "Bring out
your son, so that he may die, for he has pulled
down the altar of Baal and cut down the sacred
pole*ª* beside it." ³¹But Joash said to all who were
arrayed against him, "Will you contend for Baal?
Or will you defend his cause? Whoever contends
for him shall be put to death by morning. If he
is a god, let him contend for himself, because
his altar has been pulled down." ³²Therefore on
that day Gideon*ᵇ* was called Jerubbaal, that is to
say, "Let Baal contend against him," because he
pulled down his altar.

33 Then all the Midianites and the Amalekites
and the people of the east came together, and
crossing the Jordan they encamped in the Valley
of Jezreel. ³⁴But the spirit of the LORD took possession of Gideon; and he sounded the trumpet,
and the Abiezrites were called out to follow him.
³⁵He sent messengers throughout all Manasseh,
and they too were called out to follow him. He
also sent messengers to Asher, Zebulun, and
Naphtali, and they went up to meet them.

The Sign of the Fleece

36 Then Gideon said to God, "In order to
see whether you will deliver Israel by my hand,
as you have said, ³⁷I am going to lay a fleece of
wool on the threshing floor; if there is dew on
the fleece alone, and it is dry on all the ground,
then I shall know that you will deliver Israel by
my hand, as you have said." ³⁸And it was so.
When he rose early next morning and squeezed

a Heb *Asherah* *b* Heb *he*

J
U
D
G

the fleece, he wrung enough dew from the fleece to fill a bowl with water. ³⁹Then Gideon said to God, "Do not let your anger burn against me, let me speak one more time; let me, please, make trial with the fleece just once more; let it be dry only on the fleece, and on all the ground let there be dew." ⁴⁰And God did so that night. It was dry on the fleece only, and on all the ground there was dew.

Gideon Surprises and Routs the Midianites

7 Then Jerubbaal (that is, Gideon) and all the troops that were with him rose early and encamped beside the spring of Harod; and the camp of Midian was north of them, below*ᵃ* the hill of Moreh, in the valley.

2 The LORD said to Gideon, "The troops with you are too many for me to give the Midianites into their hand. Israel would only take the credit away from me, saying, 'My own hand has delivered me.' ³Now therefore proclaim this in the hearing of the troops, 'Whoever is fearful and trembling, let him return home.' " Thus Gideon sifted them out;*ᵇ* twenty-two thousand returned, and ten thousand remained.

4 Then the LORD said to Gideon, "The troops are still too many; take them down to the water and I will sift them out for you there. When I say, 'This one shall go with you,' he shall go with you; and when I say, 'This one shall not go with you,' he shall not go." ⁵So he brought the troops down to the water; and the LORD said to Gideon, "All those who lap the water with their tongues, as a dog laps, you shall put to one side; all those who kneel down to drink, putting their hands to their mouths,*ᶜ* you shall put to the other side." ⁶The number of those that lapped was three hundred; but all the rest of the troops knelt down to drink water. ⁷Then the LORD said to Gideon, "With the three hundred that lapped I will deliver you, and give the Midianites into your hand. Let all the others go to their homes." ⁸So he took the jars of the troops from their hands,*ᵈ* and their trumpets; and he sent all the rest of Israel back to their own tents, but retained the three hundred. The camp of Midian was below him in the valley.

9 That same night the LORD said to him, "Get up, attack the camp; for I have given it into your hand. ¹⁰But if you fear to attack, go down to the camp with your servant Purah; ¹¹and you shall hear what they say, and afterward your hands shall be strengthened to attack the camp." Then he went down with his servant Purah to the outposts of the armed men that were in the camp. ¹²The Midianites and the Amalekites and all the people of the east lay along the valley as thick as locusts; and their camels were without number, countless as the sand on the seashore. ¹³When Gideon arrived, there was a man telling a dream to his comrade; and he said, "I had a dream, and in it a cake of barley bread tumbled into the camp of Midian, and came to the tent, and struck it so that it fell; it turned upside down, and the tent collapsed." ¹⁴And his comrade answered, "This is no other than the sword of Gideon son of Joash, a man of Israel; into his hand God has given Midian and all the army."

15 When Gideon heard the telling of the dream and its interpretation, he worshiped; and he returned to the camp of Israel, and said, "Get up; for the LORD has given the army of Midian into your hand." ¹⁶After he divided the three hundred men into three companies, and put trumpets into the hands of all of them, and empty jars, with torches inside the jars, ¹⁷he said to them, "Look at me, and do the same; when I come to the outskirts of the camp, do as I do. ¹⁸When I blow the trumpet, I and all who are with me, then you also blow the trumpets around the whole camp, and shout, 'For the LORD and for Gideon!' "

19 So Gideon and the hundred who were with him came to the outskirts of the camp at the beginning of the middle watch, when they had just set the watch; and they blew the trumpets and smashed the jars that were in their hands. ²⁰So the three companies blew the trumpets and broke the jars, holding in their left hands the torches, and in their right hands the trumpets to blow; and they cried, "A sword for the LORD and for Gideon!" ²¹Every man stood in his place all around the camp, and all the men in camp ran; they cried out and fled. ²²When they blew the three hundred trumpets, the LORD set every man's sword against his fellow and against all the army; and the army fled as far as Beth-shittah toward Zererah,*ᵉ* as far as the border of Abel-meholah, by Tabbath. ²³And the men of Israel were called out from Naphtali and from Asher and from all Manasseh, and they pursued after the Midianites.

24 Then Gideon sent messengers throughout all the hill country of Ephraim, saying, "Come down against the Midianites and seize the waters against them, as far as Beth-barah, and also the Jordan." So all the men of Ephraim were called out, and they seized the waters as far as Beth-barah, and also the Jordan. ²⁵They captured the

---

a Heb *from*   *b* Cn: Heb *home, and depart from Mount Gilead' "*
c Heb places the words *putting their hands to their mouths* after the word *lapped* in verse 6   *d* Cn: Heb *So the people took provisions in their hands*   *e* Another reading is *Zeredah*

two captains of Midian, Oreb and Zeeb; they killed Oreb at the rock of Oreb, and Zeeb they killed at the wine press of Zeeb, as they pursued the Midianites. They brought the heads of Oreb and Zeeb to Gideon beyond the Jordan.

Gideon's Triumph and Vengeance

8 Then the Ephraimites said to him, "What have you done to us, not to call us when you went to fight against the Midianites?" And they upbraided him violently. ²So he said to them, "What have I done now in comparison with you? Is not the gleaning of the grapes of Ephraim better than the vintage of Abiezer? ³God has given into your hands the captains of Midian, Oreb and Zeeb; what have I been able to do in comparison with you?" When he said this, their anger against him subsided.

4 Then Gideon came to the Jordan and crossed over, he and the three hundred who were with him, exhausted and famished.*a* ⁵So he said to the people of Succoth, "Please give some loaves of bread to my followers, for they are exhausted, and I am pursuing Zebah and Zalmunna, the kings of Midian." ⁶But the officials of Succoth said, "Do you already have in your possession the hands of Zebah and Zalmunna, that we should give bread to your army?" ⁷Gideon replied, "Well then, when the Lord has given Zebah and Zalmunna into my hand, I will trample your flesh on the thorns of the wilderness and on briers." ⁸From there he went up to Penuel, and made the same request of them; and the people of Penuel answered him as the people of Succoth had answered. ⁹So he said to the people of Penuel, "When I come back victorious, I will break down this tower."

10 Now Zebah and Zalmunna were in Karkor with their army, about fifteen thousand men, all who were left of all the army of the people of the east; for one hundred twenty thousand men bearing arms had fallen. ¹¹So Gideon went up by the caravan route east of Nobah and Jogbehah, and attacked the army; for the army was off its guard. ¹²Zebah and Zalmunna fled; and he pursued them and took the two kings of Midian, Zebah and Zalmunna, and threw all the army into a panic.

13 When Gideon son of Joash returned from the battle by the ascent of Heres, ¹⁴he caught a young man, one of the people of Succoth, and questioned him; and he listed for him the officials and elders of Succoth, seventy-seven people. ¹⁵Then he came to the people of Succoth, and said, "Here are Zebah and Zalmunna, about whom you taunted me, saying, 'Do you already have in your possession the hands of Zebah and Zalmunna, that we should give bread to your troops who are exhausted?'" ¹⁶So he took the elders of the city and he took thorns of the wilderness and briers and with them he trampled*b* the people of Succoth. ¹⁷He also broke down the tower of Penuel, and killed the men of the city.

18 Then he said to Zebah and Zalmunna, "What about the men whom you killed at Tabor?" They answered, "As you are, so were they, every one of them; they resembled the sons of a king." ¹⁹And he replied, "They were my brothers, the sons of my mother; as the Lord lives, if you had saved them alive, I would not kill you." ²⁰So he said to Jether his firstborn, "Go kill them!" But the boy did not draw his sword, for he was afraid, because he was still a boy. ²¹Then Zebah and Zalmunna said, "You come and kill us; for as the man is, so is his strength." So Gideon proceeded to kill Zebah and Zalmunna; and he took the crescents that were on the necks of their camels.

Gideon's Idolatry

22 Then the Israelites said to Gideon, "Rule over us, you and your son and your grandson also; for you have delivered us out of the hand of Midian." ²³Gideon said to them, "I will not rule over you, and my son will not rule over you; the Lord will rule over you." ²⁴Then Gideon said to them, "Let me make a request of you; each of you give me an earring he has taken as booty." (For the enemy*c* had golden earrings, because they were Ishmaelites.) ²⁵"We will willingly give them," they answered. So they spread a garment, and each threw into it an earring he had taken as booty. ²⁶The weight of the golden earrings that he requested was one thousand seven hundred shekels of gold (apart from the crescents and the pendants and the purple garments worn by the kings of Midian, and the collars that were on the necks of their camels). ²⁷Gideon made an ephod of it and put it in his town, in Ophrah; and all Israel prostituted themselves to it there, and it became a snare to Gideon and to his family. ²⁸So Midian was subdued before the Israelites, and they lifted up their heads no more. So the land had rest forty years in the days of Gideon.

Death of Gideon

29 Jerubbaal son of Joash went to live in his own house. ³⁰Now Gideon had seventy sons, his own offspring, for he had many wives. ³¹His

---

a Gk: Heb *pursuing*   *b* With verse 7, Compare Gk: Heb *he taught*
c Heb *they*

concubine who was in Shechem also bore him a son, and he named him Abimelech. [32] Then Gideon son of Joash died at a good old age, and was buried in the tomb of his father Joash at Ophrah of the Abiezrites.

33 As soon as Gideon died, the Israelites relapsed and prostituted themselves with the Baals, making Baal-berith their god. [34] The Israelites did not remember the Lord their God, who had rescued them from the hand of all their enemies on every side; [35] and they did not exhibit loyalty to the house of Jerubbaal (that is, Gideon) in return for all the good that he had done to Israel.

Abimelech Attempts to Establish a Monarchy

9 Now Abimelech son of Jerubbaal went to Shechem to his mother's kinsfolk and said to them and to the whole clan of his mother's family, [2] "Say in the hearing of all the lords of Shechem, 'Which is better for you, that all seventy of the sons of Jerubbaal rule over you, or that one rule over you?' Remember also that I am your bone and your flesh." [3] So his mother's kinsfolk spoke all these words on his behalf in the hearing of all the lords of Shechem; and their hearts inclined to follow Abimelech, for they said, "He is our brother." [4] They gave him seventy pieces of silver out of the temple of Baal-berith with which Abimelech hired worthless and reckless fellows, who followed him. [5] He went to his father's house at Ophrah, and killed his brothers the sons of Jerubbaal, seventy men, on one stone; but Jotham, the youngest son of Jerubbaal, survived, for he hid himself. [6] Then all the lords of Shechem and all Beth-millo came together, and they went and made Abimelech king, by the oak of the pillar[a] at Shechem.

The Parable of the Trees

7 When it was told to Jotham, he went and stood on the top of Mount Gerizim, and cried aloud and said to them, "Listen to me, you lords of Shechem, so that God may listen to you.
[8] The trees once went out
to anoint a king over themselves.
So they said to the olive tree,
'Reign over us.'
[9] The olive tree answered them,
'Shall I stop producing my rich oil
by which gods and mortals are honored,
and go to sway over the trees?'
[10] Then the trees said to the fig tree,
'You come and reign over us.'
[11] But the fig tree answered them,
'Shall I stop producing my sweetness
and my delicious fruit,

and go to sway over the trees?'
[12] Then the trees said to the vine,
'You come and reign over us.'
[13] But the vine said to them,
'Shall I stop producing my wine
that cheers gods and mortals,
and go to sway over the trees?'
[14] So all the trees said to the bramble,
'You come and reign over us.'
[15] And the bramble said to the trees,
'If in good faith you are anointing me king
over you,
then come and take refuge in my shade;
but if not, let fire come out of the bramble
and devour the cedars of Lebanon.'

16 "Now therefore, if you acted in good faith and honor when you made Abimelech king, and if you have dealt well with Jerubbaal and his house, and have done to him as his actions deserved— [17] for my father fought for you, and risked his life, and rescued you from the hand of Midian; [18] but you have risen up against my father's house this day, and have killed his sons, seventy men on one stone, and have made Abimelech, the son of his slave woman, king over the lords of Shechem, because he is your kinsman— [19] if, I say, you have acted in good faith and honor with Jerubbaal and with his house this day, then rejoice in Abimelech, and let him also rejoice in you; [20] but if not, let fire come out from Abimelech, and devour the lords of Shechem, and Beth-millo; and let fire come out from the lords of Shechem, and from Beth-millo, and devour Abimelech." [21] Then Jotham ran away and fled, going to Beer, where he remained for fear of his brother Abimelech.

The Downfall of Abimelech

22 Abimelech ruled over Israel three years. [23] But God sent an evil spirit between Abimelech and the lords of Shechem; and the lords of Shechem dealt treacherously with Abimelech. [24] This happened so that the violence done to the seventy sons of Jerubbaal might be avenged[b] and their blood be laid on their brother Abimelech who killed them, and on the lords of Shechem, who strengthened his hands to kill his brothers. [25] So, out of hostility to him, the lords of Shechem set ambushes on the mountain tops. They robbed all who passed by them along that way; and it was reported to Abimelech.

26 When Gaal son of Ebed moved into Shechem with his kinsfolk, the lords of Shechem put confidence in him. [27] They went out into the

_____

a Cn: Meaning of Heb uncertain   b Heb *might come*

field and gathered the grapes from their vineyards, trod them, and celebrated. Then they went into the temple of their god, ate and drank, and ridiculed Abimelech. 28Gaal son of Ebed said, "Who is Abimelech, and who are we of Shechem, that we should serve him? Did not the son of Jerubbaal and Zebul his officer serve the men of Hamor father of Shechem? Why then should we serve him? 29If only this people were under my command! Then I would remove Abimelech; I would say*a* to him, 'Increase your army, and come out.' "

30 When Zebul the ruler of the city heard the words of Gaal son of Ebed, his anger was kindled. 31He sent messengers to Abimelech at Arumah,*b* saying, "Look, Gaal son of Ebed and his kinsfolk have come to Shechem, and they are stirring up*c* the city against you. 32Now therefore, go by night, you and the troops that are with you, and lie in wait in the fields. 33Then early in the morning, as soon as the sun rises, get up and rush on the city; and when he and the troops that are with him come out against you, you may deal with them as best you can."

34 So Abimelech and all the troops with him got up by night and lay in wait against Shechem in four companies. 35When Gaal son of Ebed went out and stood in the entrance of the gate of the city, Abimelech and the troops with him rose from the ambush. 36And when Gaal saw them, he said to Zebul, "Look, people are coming down from the mountain tops!" And Zebul said to him, "The shadows on the mountains look like people to you." 37Gaal spoke again and said, "Look, people are coming down from Tabbur-erez, and one company is coming from the direction of Elon-meonenim."*d* 38Then Zebul said to him, "Where is your boast*e* now, you who said, 'Who is Abimelech, that we should serve him?' Are not these the troops you made light of? Go out now and fight with them." 39So Gaal went out at the head of the lords of Shechem, and fought with Abimelech. 40Abimelech chased him, and he fled before him. Many fell wounded, up to the entrance of the gate. 41So Abimelech resided at Arumah; and Zebul drove out Gaal and his kinsfolk, so that they could not live on at Shechem.

42 On the following day the people went out into the fields. When Abimelech was told, 43he took his troops and divided them into three companies, and lay in wait in the fields. When he looked and saw the people coming out of the city, he rose against them and killed them. 44Abimelech and the company that was*f* with him rushed forward and stood at the entrance of the gate of the city, while the two companies rushed on all who were in the fields and killed

them. 45Abimelech fought against the city all that day; he took the city, and killed the people that were in it; and he razed the city and sowed it with salt.

46 When all the lords of the Tower of Shechem heard of it, they entered the stronghold of the temple of El-berith. 47Abimelech was told that all the lords of the Tower of Shechem were gathered together. 48So Abimelech went up to Mount Zalmon, he and all the troops that were with him. Abimelech took an ax in his hand, cut down a bundle of brushwood, and took it up and laid it on his shoulder. Then he said to the troops with him, "What you have seen me do, do quickly, as I have done." 49So every one of the troops cut down a bundle and following Abimelech put it against the stronghold, and they set the stronghold on fire over them, so that all the people of the Tower of Shechem also died, about a thousand men and women.

50 Then Abimelech went to Thebez, and encamped against Thebez, and took it. 51But there was a strong tower within the city, and all the men and women and all the lords of the city fled to it and shut themselves in; and they went to the roof of the tower. 52Abimelech came to the tower, and fought against it, and came near to the entrance of the tower to burn it with fire. 53But a certain woman threw an upper millstone on Abimelech's head, and crushed his skull. 54Immediately he called to the young man who carried his armor and said to him, "Draw your sword and kill me, so people will not say about me, 'A woman killed him.' " So the young man thrust him through, and he died. 55When the Israelites saw that Abimelech was dead, they all went home. 56Thus God repaid Abimelech for the crime he committed against his father in killing his seventy brothers; 57and God also made all the wickedness of the people of Shechem fall back on their heads, and on them came the curse of Jotham son of Jerubbaal.

Tola and Jair

10 After Abimelech, Tola son of Puah son of Dodo, a man of Issachar, who lived at Shamir in the hill country of Ephraim, rose to deliver Israel. 2He judged Israel twenty-three years. Then he died, and was buried at Shamir.

3 After him came Jair the Gileadite, who judged Israel twenty-two years. 4He had thirty sons who rode on thirty donkeys; and they had

---

a Gk: Heb *and he said*   *b* Cn See 9.41. Heb *Tormah*
c Cn: Heb *are besieging*   *d* That is *Diviners' Oak*   *e* Heb *mouth*
f Vg and some Gk Mss: Heb *companies that were*

thirty towns, which are in the land of Gilead, and are called Havvoth-jair to this day. 5Jair died, and was buried in Kamon.

Oppression by the Ammonites

6 The Israelites again did what was evil in the sight of the LORD, worshiping the Baals and the Astartes, the gods of Aram, the gods of Sidon, the gods of Moab, the gods of the Ammonites, and the gods of the Philistines. Thus they abandoned the LORD, and did not worship him. 7So the anger of the LORD was kindled against Israel, and he sold them into the hand of the Philistines and into the hand of the Ammonites, 8and they crushed and oppressed the Israelites that year. For eighteen years they oppressed all the Israelites that were beyond the Jordan in the land of the Amorites, which is in Gilead. 9The Ammonites also crossed the Jordan to fight against Judah and against Benjamin and against the house of Ephraim; so that Israel was greatly distressed.

10 So the Israelites cried to the LORD, saying, "We have sinned against you, because we have abandoned our God and have worshiped the Baals." 11And the LORD said to the Israelites, "Did I not deliver youᵃ from the Egyptians and from the Amorites, from the Ammonites and from the Philistines? 12The Sidonians also, and the Amalekites, and the Maonites, oppressed you; and you cried to me, and I delivered you out of their hand. 13Yet you have abandoned me and worshiped other gods; therefore I will deliver you no more. 14Go and cry to the gods whom you have chosen; let them deliver you in the time of your distress." 15And the Israelites said to the LORD, "We have sinned; do to us whatever seems good to you; but deliver us this day!" 16So they put away the foreign gods from among them and worshiped the LORD; and he could no longer bear to see Israel suffer.

17 Then the Ammonites were called to arms, and they encamped in Gilead; and the Israelites came together, and they encamped at Mizpah. 18The commanders of the people of Gilead said to one another, "Who will begin the fight against the Ammonites? He shall be head over all the inhabitants of Gilead."

Jephthah

11 Now Jephthah the Gileadite, the son of a prostitute, was a mighty warrior. Gilead was the father of Jephthah. 2Gilead's wife also bore him sons; and when his wife's sons grew up, they drove Jephthah away, saying to him, "You shall not inherit anything in our father's house; for you are the son of another woman." 3Then

---

Pray It!

The Effects of Sin

Once again the Israelites lapse into sin and worship other gods (see Judg 10:6). Once again they cry out to God to save them (verse 10). Did they think their sins would have no effect on their lives?

Listen to these words from Pope John Paul II:

There is no sin, not even the most intimate and secret one, the most strictly individual one, that exclusively concerns the person committing it. With greater or lesser violence, with greater or lesser harm, every sin has repercussions on the . . . whole human family.

Have you done anything today that brought harm to you or others? Have you used your gifts and talents as God intended them to be used? Have you neglected an opportunity to share God's love with another person?

Lord, you know all things. Look on me with love, and hear my prayer. Forgive my sins, and give me strength to turn away from the lure of sin. Help me to be more generous in serving you and my neighbor. Help me to be a true follower of your Son, Jesus. Amen.

▶ Judg 10:10–16

Jephthah fled from his brothers and lived in the land of Tob. Outlaws collected around Jephthah and went raiding with him.

4 After a time the Ammonites made war against Israel. 5And when the Ammonites made war against Israel, the elders of Gilead went to bring Jephthah from the land of Tob. 6They said to Jephthah, "Come and be our commander, so that we may fight with the Ammonites." 7But Jephthah said to the elders of Gilead, "Are you not the very ones who rejected me and drove me out of my father's house? So why do you come to me now when you are in trouble?" 8The elders of Gilead said to Jephthah, "Nevertheless, we have now turned back to you, so that you may go with us and fight with the Ammonites, and become head over us, over all the inhabitants of Gilead."

---

a Heb lacks *Did I not deliver you*

9Jephthah said to the elders of Gilead, "If you bring me home again to fight with the Ammonites, and the LORD gives them over to me, I will be your head." 10And the elders of Gilead said to Jephthah, "The LORD will be witness between us; we will surely do as you say." 11So Jephthah went with the elders of Gilead, and the people made him head and commander over them; and Jephthah spoke all his words before the LORD at Mizpah.

12 Then Jephthah sent messengers to the king of the Ammonites and said, "What is there between you and me, that you have come to me to fight against my land?" 13The king of the Ammonites answered the messengers of Jephthah, "Because Israel, on coming from Egypt, took away my land from the Arnon to the Jabbok and to the Jordan; now therefore restore it peaceably." 14Once again Jephthah sent messengers to the king of the Ammonites 15and said to him: "Thus says Jephthah: Israel did not take away the land of Moab or the land of the Ammonites, 16but when they came up from Egypt, Israel went through the wilderness to the Red Sea*a* and came to Kadesh. 17Israel then sent messengers to the king of Edom, saying, 'Let us pass through your land'; but the king of Edom would not listen. They also sent to the king of Moab, but he would not consent. So Israel remained at Kadesh. 18Then they journeyed through the wilderness, went around the land of Edom and the land of Moab, arrived on the east side of the land of Moab, and camped on the other side of the Arnon. They did not enter the territory of Moab, for the Arnon was the boundary of Moab. 19Israel then sent messengers to King Sihon of the Amorites, king of Heshbon; and Israel said to him, 'Let us pass through your land to our country.' 20But Sihon did not trust Israel to pass through his territory; so Sihon gathered all his people together, and encamped at Jahaz, and fought with Israel. 21Then the LORD, the God of Israel, gave Sihon and all his people into the hand of Israel, and they defeated them; so Israel occupied all the land of the Amorites, who inhabited that country. 22They occupied all the territory of the Amorites from the Arnon to the Jabbok and from the wilderness to the Jordan. 23So now the LORD, the God of Israel, has conquered the Amorites for the benefit of his people Israel. Do you intend to take their place? 24Should you not possess what your god Chemosh gives you to possess? And should we not be the ones to possess everything that the LORD our God has conquered for our benefit? 25Now are you any better than King Balak son of Zippor of Moab? Did he ever enter into conflict with Israel, or did he ever go to war with them? 26While Israel lived in Heshbon and its villages, and in Aroer and its villages, and in all the towns that are along the Arnon, three hundred years, why did you not recover them within that time? 27It is not I who have sinned against you, but you are the one who does me wrong by making war on me. Let the LORD, who is judge, decide today for the Israelites or for the Ammonites." 28But the king of the Ammonites did not heed the message that Jephthah sent him.

Jephthah's Vow

29 Then the spirit of the LORD came upon Jephthah, and he passed through Gilead and Manasseh. He passed on to Mizpah of Gilead, and from Mizpah of Gilead he passed on to the Ammonites. 30And Jephthah made a vow to the LORD, and said, "If you will give the Ammonites into my hand, 31then whoever comes out of the doors of my house to meet me, when I return victorious from the Ammonites, shall be the LORD's, to be offered up by me as a burnt offering." 32So Jephthah crossed over to the Ammonites to fight against them; and the LORD gave them into his hand. 33He inflicted a massive defeat on them from Aroer to the neighborhood of Minnith, twenty towns, and as far as Abel-keramim. So the Ammonites were subdued before the people of Israel.

Jephthah's Daughter

34 Then Jephthah came to his home at Mizpah; and there was his daughter coming out to meet him with timbrels and with dancing. She was his only child; he had no son or daughter except her. 35When he saw her, he tore his clothes, and said, "Alas, my daughter! You have brought me very low; you have become the cause of great trouble to me. For I have opened my mouth to the LORD, and I cannot take back my vow." 36She said to him, "My father, if you have opened your mouth to the LORD, do to me according to what has gone out of your mouth, now that the LORD has given you vengeance against your enemies, the Ammonites." 37And she said to her father, "Let this thing be done for me: Grant me two months, so that I may go and wander*b* on the mountains, and bewail my virginity, my companions and I." 38"Go," he said and sent her away for two months. So she departed, she and her companions, and bewailed her virginity on the mountains. 39At the end of two months, she returned to her father, who did with her according to the vow he had made. She had never slept

---

a Or Sea of Reeds   *b* Cn: Heb *go down*

with a man. So there arose an Israelite custom that ⁴⁰for four days every year the daughters of Israel would go out to lament the daughter of Jephthah the Gileadite.

Intertribal Dissension

12 The men of Ephraim were called to arms, and they crossed to Zaphon and said to Jephthah, "Why did you cross over to fight against the Ammonites, and did not call us to go with you? We will burn your house down over you!" ²Jephthah said to them, "My people and I were engaged in conflict with the Ammonites who oppressed us*a* severely. But when I called you, you did not deliver me from their hand. ³When I saw that you would not deliver me, I took my life in my hand, and crossed over against the Ammonites, and the LORD gave them into my hand. Why then have you come up to me this day, to fight against me?" ⁴Then Jephthah gathered all the men of Gilead and fought with Ephraim; and the men of Gilead defeated Ephraim, because they said, "You are fugitives from Ephraim, you Gileadites—in the heart of Ephraim and Manasseh."*b* ⁵Then the Gileadites took the fords of the Jordan against the Ephraimites. Whenever one of the fugitives of Ephraim said, "Let me go over," the men of Gilead would say to him, "Are you an Ephraimite?" When he said, "No," ⁶they said to him, "Then say Shibboleth," and he said, "Sibboleth," for he could not pronounce it right. Then they seized him and killed him at the fords of the Jordan. Forty-two thousand of the Ephraimites fell at that time.

7 Jephthah judged Israel six years. Then Jephthah the Gileadite died, and was buried in his town in Gilead.*c*

Ibzan, Elon, and Abdon

8 After him Ibzan of Bethlehem judged Israel. ⁹He had thirty sons. He gave his thirty daughters in marriage outside his clan and brought in thirty young women from outside for his sons. He judged Israel seven years. ¹⁰Then Ibzan died, and was buried at Bethlehem.

11 After him Elon the Zebulunite judged Israel; and he judged Israel ten years. ¹²Then Elon the Zebulunite died, and was buried at Aijalon in the land of Zebulun.

13 After him Abdon son of Hillel the Pirathonite judged Israel. ¹⁴He had forty sons and thirty grandsons, who rode on seventy donkeys; he judged Israel eight years. ¹⁵Then Abdon son of Hillel the Pirathonite died, and was buried at Pirathon in the land of Ephraim, in the hill country of the Amalekites.

Introducing...

Samson

The story of Samson in Judges, chapters 13–16, is one of the most well known in the Bible. Most of us know Samson for his great feats of strength, such as killing a lion bare-handed and slaying a thousand men with the jawbone of a donkey. But did you also know that Samson's birth was announced by an angel and that the Book of Judges says "the spirit of the LORD rushed on him" (14:6) more often for Samson than for any other judge? Samson was a Nazirite as well as a judge. Nazirites took vows to abstain from alcohol, avoid contact with dead bodies, and refrain from cutting their hair.

Like many of the other judges, Samson was a flawed hero. He broke all his Nazirite vows, was controlled by lust, and used his great strength for personal revenge. Despite these flaws, God chose to use Samson. Samson paid for his sins, but ultimately, his tragic death brought victory over the Philistines. Once again God's purposes were accomplished, even through a flawed and sinful human being.

The Birth of Samson

13 The Israelites again did what was evil in the sight of the LORD, and the LORD gave them into the hand of the Philistines forty years.

2 There was a certain man of Zorah, of the tribe of the Danites, whose name was Manoah. His wife was barren, having borne no children. ³And the angel of the LORD appeared to the woman and said to her, "Although you are barren, having borne no children, you shall conceive and bear a son. ⁴Now be careful not to drink wine or strong drink, or to eat anything unclean, ⁵for you shall conceive and bear a son. No razor is to come on his head, for the boy shall be a nazirite*d* to God from birth. It is he who shall begin to deliver Israel from the hand of the Philistines." ⁶Then the woman came and told her husband, "A man of God came to me, and his appearance was like that of an angel*e* of God,

J
U
D
G

---

a Gk OL, Syr H: Heb lacks *who oppressed us* *b* Meaning of Heb uncertain: Gk omits *because . . . Manasseh* *c* Gk: Heb *in the towns of Gilead* *d* That is *one separated* or *one consecrated* *e* Or *the angel*

most awe-inspiring; I did not ask him where he came from, and he did not tell me his name; [7]but he said to me, 'You shall conceive and bear a son. So then drink no wine or strong drink, and eat nothing unclean, for the boy shall be a nazirite[a] to God from birth to the day of his death.' "

8 Then Manoah entreated the Lord, and said, "O Lord, I pray, let the man of God whom you sent come to us again and teach us what we are to do concerning the boy who will be born." [9]God listened to Manoah, and the angel of God came again to the woman as she sat in the field; but her husband Manoah was not with her. [10]So the woman ran quickly and told her husband, "The man who came to me the other day has appeared to me." [11]Manoah got up and followed his wife, and came to the man and said to him, "Are you the man who spoke to this woman?" And he said, "I am." [12]Then Manoah said, "Now when your words come true, what is to be the boy's rule of life; what is he to do?" [13]The angel of the Lord said to Manoah, "Let the woman give heed to all that I said to her. [14]She may not eat of anything that comes from the vine. She is not to drink wine or strong drink, or eat any unclean thing. She is to observe everything that I commanded her."

15 Manoah said to the angel of the Lord, "Allow us to detain you, and prepare a kid for you." [16]The angel of the Lord said to Manoah, "If you detain me, I will not eat your food; but if you want to prepare a burnt offering, then offer it to the Lord." (For Manoah did not know that he was the angel of the Lord.) [17]Then Manoah said to the angel of the Lord, "What is your name, so that we may honor you when your words come true?" [18]But the angel of the Lord said to him, "Why do you ask my name? It is too wonderful."

19 So Manoah took the kid with the grain offering, and offered it on the rock to the Lord, to him who works[b] wonders.[c] [20]When the flame went up toward heaven from the altar, the angel of the Lord ascended in the flame of the altar while Manoah and his wife looked on; and they fell on their faces to the ground. [21]The angel of the Lord did not appear again to Manoah and his wife. Then Manoah realized that it was the angel of the Lord. [22]And Manoah said to his wife, "We shall surely die, for we have seen God." [23]But his wife said to him, "If the Lord had meant to kill us, he would not have accepted a burnt offering and a grain offering at our hands, or shown us all these things, or now announced to us such things as these."

24 The woman bore a son, and named him Samson. The boy grew, and the Lord blessed him. [25]The spirit of the Lord began to stir him in Mahaneh-dan, between Zorah and Eshtaol.

Samson's Marriage

14 Once Samson went down to Timnah, and at Timnah he saw a Philistine woman. [2]Then he came up, and told his father and mother, "I saw a Philistine woman at Timnah; now get her for me as my wife." [3]But his father and mother said to him, "Is there not a woman among your kin, or among all our[d] people, that you must go to take a wife from the uncircumcised Philistines?" But Samson said to his father, "Get her for me, because she pleases me." [4]His father and mother did not know that this was from the Lord; for he was seeking a pretext to act against the Philistines. At that time the Philistines had dominion over Israel.

5 Then Samson went down with his father and mother to Timnah. When he came to the vineyards of Timnah, suddenly a young lion roared at him. [6]The spirit of the Lord rushed on him, and he tore the lion apart barehanded as one might tear apart a kid. But he did not tell his father or his mother what he had done. [7]Then he went down and talked with the woman, and she pleased Samson. [8]After a while he returned to marry her, and he turned aside to see the carcass of the lion, and there was a swarm of bees in the body of the lion, and honey. [9]He scraped it out into his hands, and went on, eating as he went. When he came to his father and mother, he gave some to them, and they ate it. But he did not tell them that he had taken the honey from the carcass of the lion.

10 His father went down to the woman, and Samson made a feast there as the young men were accustomed to do. [11]When the people saw him, they brought thirty companions to be with him. [12]Samson said to them, "Let me now put a riddle to you. If you can explain it to me within the seven days of the feast, and find it out, then I will give you thirty linen garments and thirty festal garments. [13]But if you cannot explain it to me, then you shall give me thirty linen garments and thirty festal garments." So they said to him, "Ask your riddle; let us hear it." [14]He said to them,

"Out of the eater came something to eat.

Out of the strong came something sweet."
But for three days they could not explain the riddle.

15 On the fourth[e] day they said to Samson's

---

a That is one separated or one consecrated　b Gk Vg: Heb and working　c Heb wonders, while Manoah and his wife looked on　d Cn: Heb my　e Gk Syr: Heb seventh

wife, "Coax your husband to explain the riddle to us, or we will burn you and your father's house with fire. Have you invited us here to impoverish us?" [16]So Samson's wife wept before him, saying, "You hate me; you do not really love me. You have asked a riddle of my people, but you have not explained it to me." He said to her, "Look, I have not told my father or my mother. Why should I tell you?" [17]She wept before him the seven days that their feast lasted; and because she nagged him, on the seventh day he told her. Then she explained the riddle to her people. [18]The men of the town said to him on the seventh day before the sun went down,

"What is sweeter than honey?
What is stronger than a lion?"

And he said to them,

"If you had not plowed with my heifer,
you would not have found out my riddle."

[19]Then the spirit of the LORD rushed on him, and he went down to Ashkelon. He killed thirty men of the town, took their spoil, and gave the festal garments to those who had explained the riddle. In hot anger he went back to his father's house. [20]And Samson's wife was given to his companion, who had been his best man.

Samson Defeats the Philistines

15 After a while, at the time of the wheat harvest, Samson went to visit his wife, bringing along a kid. He said, "I want to go into my wife's room." But her father would not allow him to go in. [2]Her father said, "I was sure that you had rejected her; so I gave her to your companion. Is not her younger sister prettier than she? Why not take her instead?" [3]Samson said to them, "This time, when I do mischief to the Philistines, I will be without blame." [4]So Samson went and caught three hundred foxes, and took some torches; and he turned the foxes[a] tail to tail, and put a torch between each pair of tails. [5]When he had set fire to the torches, he let the foxes go into the standing grain of the Philistines, and burned up the shocks and the standing grain, as well as the vineyards and[b] olive groves. [6]Then the Philistines asked, "Who has done this?" And they said, "Samson, the son-in-law of the Timnite, because he has taken Samson's wife and given her to his companion." So the Philistines came up, and burned her and her father. [7]Samson said to them, "If this is what you do, I swear I will not stop until I have taken revenge on you." [8]He struck them down hip and thigh with great slaughter; and he went down and stayed in the cleft of the rock of Etam.

9 Then the Philistines came up and encamped in Judah, and made a raid on Lehi. [10]The men of Judah said, "Why have you come up against us?" They said, "We have come up to bind Samson, to do to him as he did to us." [11]Then three thousand men of Judah went down to the cleft of the rock of Etam, and they said to Samson, "Do you not know that the Philistines are rulers over us? What then have you done to us?" He replied, "As they did to me, so I have done to them." [12]They said to him, "We have come down to bind you, so that we may give you into the hands of the Philistines." Samson answered them, "Swear to me that you yourselves will not attack me." [13]They said to him, "No, we will only bind you and give you into their hands; we will not kill you." So they bound him with two new ropes, and brought him up from the rock.

14 When he came to Lehi, the Philistines came shouting to meet him; and the spirit of the LORD rushed on him, and the ropes that were on his arms became like flax that has caught fire, and his bonds melted off his hands. [15]Then he found a fresh jawbone of a donkey, reached down and took it, and with it he killed a thousand men. [16]And Samson said,

"With the jawbone of a donkey,
heaps upon heaps,
with the jawbone of a donkey
I have slain a thousand men."

[17]When he had finished speaking, he threw away the jawbone; and that place was called Ramath-lehi.[c]

18 By then he was very thirsty, and he called on the LORD, saying, "You have granted this great victory by the hand of your servant. Am I now to die of thirst, and fall into the hands of the uncircumcised?" [19]So God split open the hollow place that is at Lehi, and water came from it. When he drank, his spirit returned, and he revived. Therefore it was named En-hakkore,[d] which is at Lehi to this day. [20]And he judged Israel in the days of the Philistines twenty years.

Samson and Delilah

16 Once Samson went to Gaza, where he saw a prostitute and went in to her. [2]The Gazites were told,[e] "Samson has come here." So they circled around and lay in wait for him all night at the city gate. They kept quiet all night, thinking, "Let us wait until the light of the morning; then we will kill him." [3]But Samson lay only until midnight. Then at midnight he rose up,

---

a Heb *them*　b Gk Tg Vg: Heb lacks *and*　c That is *The Hill of the Jawbone*　d That is *The Spring of the One who Called*　e Gk: Heb lacks *were told*

Manipulation

You'd think Samson would catch on, wouldn't you? Delilah tries to coax from Samson the secret of his strength. By the third attempt, it seems rather obvious that she wants to betray him to the Philistines. Nonetheless, Samson is finally pestered into revealing his secret, and Delilah uses the information to betray him.

Have you ever been betrayed by a friend? Have you ever trusted someone with a secret only to discover later that your secret is out? It makes it that much harder to trust again, to be open and to share yourself with another. When the person who betrays your confidence is someone you love, the betrayal is even more painful.

We need to do some soul searching here. Ask yourself: Am I the kind of person who can be trusted with someone's secret? Have I ever betrayed a confidence?

It is easier than we like to think to be like Delilah—abusing the trust built up in a relationship and manipulating another person, even someone we care deeply about. We need to resolve to be people of integrity, who would never betray a confidence for personal gain.

▶ Judg 16:4–22

took hold of the doors of the city gate and the two posts, pulled them up, bar and all, put them on his shoulders, and carried them to the top of the hill that is in front of Hebron.

4 After this he fell in love with a woman in the valley of Sorek, whose name was Delilah. ⁵The lords of the Philistines came to her and said to her, "Coax him, and find out what makes his strength so great, and how we may overpower him, so that we may bind him in order to subdue him; and we will each give you eleven hundred pieces of silver." ⁶So Delilah said to Samson, "Please tell me what makes your strength so great, and how you could be bound, so that one could subdue you." ⁷Samson said to her, "If they bind me with seven fresh bowstrings that are not dried out, then I shall become weak, and be like

anyone else." ⁸Then the lords of the Philistines brought her seven fresh bowstrings that had not dried out, and she bound him with them. ⁹While men were lying in wait in an inner chamber, she said to him, "The Philistines are upon you, Samson!" But he snapped the bowstrings, as a strand of fiber snaps when it touches the fire. So the secret of his strength was not known.

10 Then Delilah said to Samson, "You have mocked me and told me lies; please tell me how you could be bound." ¹¹He said to her, "If they bind me with new ropes that have not been used, then I shall become weak, and be like anyone else." ¹²So Delilah took new ropes and bound him with them, and said to him, "The Philistines are upon you, Samson!" (The men lying in wait were in an inner chamber.) But he snapped the ropes off his arms like a thread.

13 Then Delilah said to Samson, "Until now you have mocked me and told me lies; tell me how you could be bound." He said to her, "If you weave the seven locks of my head with the web and make it tight with the pin, then I shall become weak, and be like anyone else." ¹⁴So while he slept, Delilah took the seven locks of his head and wove them into the web,ᵃ and made them tight with the pin. Then she said to him, "The Philistines are upon you, Samson!" But he awoke from his sleep, and pulled away the pin, the loom, and the web.

15 Then she said to him, "How can you say, 'I love you,' when your heart is not with me? You have mocked me three times now and have not told me what makes your strength so great." ¹⁶Finally, after she had nagged him with her words day after day, and pestered him, he was tired to death. ¹⁷So he told her his whole secret, and said to her, "A razor has never come upon my head; for I have been a naziriteᵇ to God from my mother's womb. If my head were shaved, then my strength would leave me; I would become weak, and be like anyone else."

18 When Delilah realized that he had told her his whole secret, she sent and called the lords of the Philistines, saying, "This time come up, for he has told his whole secret to me." Then the lords of the Philistines came up to her, and brought the money in their hands. ¹⁹She let him fall asleep on her lap; and she called a man, and had him shave off the seven locks of his head. He began to weaken,ᶜ and his strength left him. ²⁰Then she said, "The Philistines are upon you,

---

a Compare Gk: in verses 13-14, Heb lacks *and make it tight . . . into the web*   b That is *one separated* or *one consecrated*
c Gk: Heb *She began to torment him*

Samson!" When he awoke from his sleep, he thought, "I will go out as at other times, and shake myself free." But he did not know that the LORD had left him. ²¹So the Philistines seized him and gouged out his eyes. They brought him down to Gaza and bound him with bronze shackles; and he ground at the mill in the prison. ²²But the hair of his head began to grow again after it had been shaved.

Samson's Death

23 Now the lords of the Philistines gathered to offer a great sacrifice to their god Dagon, and to rejoice; for they said, "Our god has given Samson our enemy into our hand." ²⁴When the people saw him, they praised their god; for they said, "Our god has given our enemy into our hand, the ravager of our country, who has killed many of us." ²⁵And when their hearts were merry, they said, "Call Samson, and let him entertain us." So they called Samson out of the prison, and he performed for them. They made him stand between the pillars; ²⁶and Samson said to the attendant who held him by the hand, "Let me feel the pillars on which the house rests, so that I may lean against them." ²⁷Now the house was full of men and women; all the lords of the Philistines were there, and on the roof there were about three thousand men and women, who looked on while Samson performed.

28 Then Samson called to the LORD and said, "Lord GOD, remember me and strengthen me only this once, O God, so that with this one act of revenge I may pay back the Philistines for my two eyes."ᵃ ²⁹And Samson grasped the two middle pillars on which the house rested, and he leaned his weight against them, his right hand on the one and his left hand on the other. ³⁰Then Samson said, "Let me die with the Philistines." He strained with all his might; and the house fell on the lords and all the people who were in it. So those he killed at his death were more than those he had killed during his life. ³¹Then his brothers and all his family came down and took him and brought him up and buried him between Zorah and Eshtaol in the tomb of his father Manoah. He had judged Israel twenty years.

Micah and the Levite

17 There was a man in the hill country of Ephraim whose name was Micah. ²He said to his mother, "The eleven hundred pieces of silver that were taken from you, about which you uttered a curse, and even spoke it in my hearing,—that silver is in my possession; I took it; but now I will return it to you."ᵇ And his

mother said, "May my son be blessed by the LORD!" ³Then he returned the eleven hundred pieces of silver to his mother; and his mother said, "I consecrate the silver to the LORD from my hand for my son, to make an idol of cast metal." ⁴So when he returned the money to his mother, his mother took two hundred pieces of silver, and gave it to the silversmith, who made it into an idol of cast metal; and it was in the house of Micah. ⁵This man Micah had a shrine, and he made an ephod and teraphim, and installed one of his sons, who became his priest. ⁶In those days there was no king in Israel; all the people did what was right in their own eyes.

7 Now there was a young man of Bethlehem in Judah, of the clan of Judah. He was a Levite residing there. ⁸This man left the town of Bethlehem in Judah, to live wherever he could find a place. He came to the house of Micah in the hill country of Ephraim to carry on his work.ᶜ ⁹Micah said to him, "From where do you come?" He replied, "I am a Levite of Bethlehem in Judah, and I am going to live wherever I can find a place." ¹⁰Then Micah said to him, "Stay with me, and be to me a father and a priest, and I will give you ten pieces of silver a year, a set of clothes, and your living."ᵈ ¹¹The Levite agreed to stay with the man; and the young man became to him like one of his sons. ¹²So Micah installed the Levite, and the young man became his priest, and was in the house of Micah. ¹³Then Micah said, "Now I know that the LORD will prosper me, because the Levite has become my priest."

The Migration of Dan

18 In those days there was no king in Israel. And in those days the tribe of the Danites was seeking for itself a territory to live in; for until then no territory among the tribes of Israel had been allotted to them. ²So the Danites sent five valiant men from the whole number of their clan, from Zorah and from Eshtaol, to spy out the land and to explore it; and they said to them, "Go, explore the land." When they came to the hill country of Ephraim, to the house of Micah, they stayed there. ³While they were at Micah's house, they recognized the voice of the young Levite; so they went over and asked him, "Who brought you here? What are you doing in this place? What is your business here?" ⁴He said to them, "Micah did such and such for me, and he hired me, and I have become his priest." ⁵Then

a Or so that I may be avenged upon the Philistines for one of my two eyes   b The words but now I will return it to you are transposed from the end of verse 3 in Heb   c Or Ephraim, continuing his journey   d Heb living, and the Levite went

they said to him, "Inquire of God that we may know whether the mission we are undertaking will succeed." 6The priest replied, "Go in peace. The mission you are on is under the eye of the LORD."

7 The five men went on, and when they came to Laish, they observed the people who were there living securely, after the manner of the Sidonians, quiet and unsuspecting, lacking[a] nothing on earth, and possessing wealth.[b] Furthermore, they were far from the Sidonians and had no dealings with Aram.[c] 8When they came to their kinsfolk at Zorah and Eshtaol, they said to them, "What do you report?" 9They said, "Come, let us go up against them; for we have seen the land, and it is very good. Will you do nothing? Do not be slow to go, but enter in and possess the land. 10When you go, you will come to an unsuspecting people. The land is broad—God has indeed given it into your hands—a place where there is no lack of anything on earth."

11 Six hundred men of the Danite clan, armed with weapons of war, set out from Zorah and Eshtaol, 12and went up and encamped at Kiriath-jearim in Judah. On this account that place is called Mahaneh-dan[d] to this day; it is west of Kiriath-jearim. 13From there they passed on to the hill country of Ephraim, and came to the house of Micah.

14 Then the five men who had gone to spy out the land (that is, Laish) said to their comrades, "Do you know that in these buildings there are an ephod, teraphim, and an idol of cast metal? Now therefore consider what you will do." 15So they turned in that direction and came to the house of the young Levite, at the home of Micah, and greeted him. 16While the six hundred men of the Danites, armed with their weapons of war, stood by the entrance of the gate, 17the five men who had gone to spy out the land proceeded to enter and take the idol of cast metal, the ephod, and the teraphim.[e] The priest was standing by the entrance of the gate with the six hundred men armed with weapons of war. 18When the men went into Micah's house and took the idol of cast metal, the ephod, and the teraphim, the priest said to them, "What are you doing?" 19They said to him, "Keep quiet! Put your hand over your mouth, and come with us, and be to us a father and a priest. Is it better for you to be priest to the house of one person, or to be priest to a tribe and clan in Israel?" 20Then the priest accepted the offer. He took the ephod, the teraphim, and the idol, and went along with the people.

21 So they resumed their journey, putting the little ones, the livestock, and the goods in front of them. 22When they were some distance from the home of Micah, the men who were in the houses near Micah's house were called out, and they overtook the Danites. 23They shouted to the Danites, who turned around and said to Micah, "What is the matter that you come with such a company?" 24He replied, "You take my gods that I made, and the priest, and go away, and what have I left? How then can you ask me, 'What is the matter?' " 25And the Danites said to him, "You had better not let your voice be heard among us or else hot-tempered fellows will attack you, and you will lose your life and the lives of your household." 26Then the Danites went their way. When Micah saw that they were too strong for him, he turned and went back to his home.

The Danites Settle in Laish

27 The Danites, having taken what Micah had made, and the priest who belonged to him, came to Laish, to a people quiet and unsuspecting, put them to the sword, and burned down the city. 28There was no deliverer, because it was far from Sidon and they had no dealings with Aram.[f] It was in the valley that belongs to Beth-rehob. They rebuilt the city, and lived in it. 29They named the city Dan, after their ancestor Dan, who was born to Israel; but the name of the city was formerly Laish. 30Then the Danites set up the idol for themselves. Jonathan son of Gershom, son of Moses,[g] and his sons were priests to the tribe of the Danites until the time the land went into captivity. 31So they maintained as their own Micah's idol that he had made, as long as the house of God was at Shiloh.

The Levite's Concubine

19 In those days, when there was no king in Israel, a certain Levite, residing in the remote parts of the hill country of Ephraim, took to himself a concubine from Bethlehem in Judah. 2But his concubine became angry with[h] him, and she went away from him to her father's house at Bethlehem in Judah, and was there some four months. 3Then her husband set out after her, to speak tenderly to her and bring her back. He had with him his servant and a couple of donkeys. When he reached[i] her father's house, the girl's father saw him and came with joy to meet him.

---

a Cn Compare 18.10: Meaning of Heb uncertain　b Meaning of Heb uncertain　c Symmachus: Heb with anyone　d That is Camp of Dan　e Compare 17.4, 5; 18.14: Heb teraphim and the cast metal　f Cn Compare verse 7: Heb with anyone　g Another reading is son of Manasseh　h Gk OL: Heb prostituted herself against　i Gk: Heb she brought him to

⁴His father-in-law, the girl's father, made him stay, and he remained with him three days; so they ate and drank, and heᵃ stayed there. ⁵On the fourth day they got up early in the morning, and he prepared to go; but the girl's father said to his son-in-law, "Fortify yourself with a bit of food, and after that you may go." ⁶So the two men sat and ate and drank together; and the girl's father said to the man, "Why not spend the night and enjoy yourself?" ⁷When the man got up to go, his father-in-law kept urging him until he spent the night there again. ⁸On the fifth day he got up early in the morning to leave; and the girl's father said, "Fortify yourself." So they lingeredᵇ until the day declined, and the two of them ate and drank.ᶜ ⁹When the man with his concubine and his servant got up to leave, his father-in-law, the girl's father, said to him, "Look, the day has worn on until it is almost evening. Spend the night. See, the day has drawn to a close. Spend the night here and enjoy yourself. Tomorrow you can get up early in the morning for your journey, and go home."

10 But the man would not spend the night; he got up and departed, and arrived opposite Jebus (that is, Jerusalem). He had with him a couple of saddled donkeys, and his concubine was with him. ¹¹When they were near Jebus, the day was far spent, and the servant said to his master, "Come now, let us turn aside to this city of the Jebusites, and spend the night in it." ¹²But his master said to him, "We will not turn aside into a city of foreigners, who do not belong to the people of Israel; but we will continue on to Gibeah." ¹³Then he said to his servant, "Come, let us try to reach one of these places, and spend the night at Gibeah or at Ramah." ¹⁴So they passed on and went their way; and the sun went down on them near Gibeah, which belongs to Benjamin. ¹⁵They turned aside there, to go in and spend the night at Gibeah. He went in and sat down in the open square of the city, but no one took them in to spend the night.

16 Then at evening there was an old man coming from his work in the field. The man was from the hill country of Ephraim, and he was residing in Gibeah. (The people of the place were Benjaminites.) ¹⁷When the old man looked up and saw the wayfarer in the open square of the city, he said, "Where are you going and where do you come from?" ¹⁸He answered him, "We are passing from Bethlehem in Judah to the remote parts of the hill country of Ephraim, from which I come. I went to Bethlehem in Judah; and I am going to my home.ᵈ Nobody has offered to take me in. ¹⁹We your servants have straw and fodder

for our donkeys, with bread and wine for me and the woman and the young man along with us. We need nothing more." ²⁰The old man said, "Peace be to you. I will care for all your wants; only do not spend the night in the square." ²¹So he brought him into his house, and fed the donkeys; they washed their feet, and ate and drank.

Gibeah's Crime

22 While they were enjoying themselves, the men of the city, a perverse lot, surrounded the house, and started pounding on the door. They said to the old man, the master of the house, "Bring out the man who came into your house, so that we may have intercourse with him." ²³And the man, the master of the house, went out to them and said to them, "No, my brothers, do not act so wickedly. Since this man is my guest, do not do this vile thing. ²⁴Here are my virgin daughter and his concubine; let me bring them out now. Ravish them and do whatever you want to them; but against this man do not do such a vile thing." ²⁵But the men would not listen to him. So the man seized his concubine, and put her out to them. They wantonly raped her, and abused her all through the night until the morning. And as the dawn began to break, they let her go. ²⁶As morning appeared, the woman came and fell down at the door of the man's house where her master was, until it was light.

27 In the morning her master got up, opened the doors of the house, and when he went out to go on his way, there was his concubine lying at the door of the house, with her hands on the threshold. ²⁸"Get up," he said to her, "we are going." But there was no answer. Then he put her on the donkey; and the man set out for his home. ²⁹When he had entered his house, he took a knife, and grasping his concubine he cut her into twelve pieces, limb by limb, and sent her throughout all the territory of Israel. ³⁰Then he commanded the men whom he sent, saying, "Thus shall you say to all the Israelites, 'Has such a thing ever happenedᵉ since the day that the Israelites came up from the land of Egypt until this day? Consider it, take counsel, and speak out.'"

The Other Tribes Attack Benjamin

20 Then all the Israelites came out, from Dan to Beer-sheba, including the land of Gilead, and the congregation assembled in one body before the LORD at Mizpah. ²The chiefs

---

a Compare verse 7 and Gk: Heb *they*   b Cn: Heb *Linger*
c Gk: Heb lacks *and drank*   d Gk Compare 19.29. Heb *to the house of the LORD*   e Compare Gk: Heb ³⁰And all who saw it said, "Such a thing has not happened or been seen

of all the people, of all the tribes of Israel, presented themselves in the assembly of the people of God, four hundred thousand foot-soldiers bearing arms. ³(Now the Benjaminites heard that the people of Israel had gone up to Mizpah.) And the Israelites said, "Tell us, how did this criminal act come about?" ⁴The Levite, the husband of the woman who was murdered, answered, "I came to Gibeah that belongs to Benjamin, I and my concubine, to spend the night. ⁵The lords of Gibeah rose up against me, and surrounded the house at night. They intended to kill me, and they raped my concubine until she died. ⁶Then I took my concubine and cut her into pieces, and sent her throughout the whole extent of Israel's territory; for they have committed a vile outrage in Israel. ⁷So now, you Israelites, all of you, give your advice and counsel here."

8 All the people got up as one, saying, "We will not any of us go to our tents, nor will any of us return to our houses. ⁹But now this is what we will do to Gibeah: we will go up*a* against it by lot. ¹⁰We will take ten men of a hundred throughout all the tribes of Israel, and a hundred of a thousand, and a thousand of ten thousand, to bring provisions for the troops, who are going to repay*b* Gibeah of Benjamin for all the disgrace that they have done in Israel." ¹¹So all the men of Israel gathered against the city, united as one.

12 The tribes of Israel sent men through all the tribe of Benjamin, saying, "What crime is this that has been committed among you? ¹³Now then, hand over those scoundrels in Gibeah, so that we may put them to death, and purge the evil from Israel." But the Benjaminites would not listen to their kinsfolk, the Israelites. ¹⁴The Benjaminites came together out of the towns to Gibeah, to go out to battle against the Israelites. ¹⁵On that day the Benjaminites mustered twenty-six thousand armed men from their towns, besides the inhabitants of Gibeah. ¹⁶Of all this force, there were seven hundred picked men who were left-handed; every one could sling a stone at a hair, and not miss. ¹⁷And the Israelites, apart from Benjamin, mustered four hundred thousand armed men, all of them warriors.

18 The Israelites proceeded to go up to Bethel, where they inquired of God, "Which of us shall go up first to battle against the Benjaminites?" And the LORD answered, "Judah shall go up first."

19 Then the Israelites got up in the morning, and encamped against Gibeah. ²⁰The Israelites went out to battle against Benjamin; and the Israelites drew up the battle line against them at Gibeah. ²¹The Benjaminites came out of Gibeah, and struck down on that day twenty-two thousand

of the Israelites. ²³*c* The Israelites went up and wept before the LORD until the evening; and they inquired of the LORD, "Shall we again draw near to battle against our kinsfolk the Benjaminites?" And the LORD said, "Go up against them." ²²The Israelites took courage, and again formed the battle line in the same place where they had formed it on the first day.

24 So the Israelites advanced against the Benjaminites the second day. ²⁵Benjamin moved out against them from Gibeah the second day, and struck down eighteen thousand of the Israelites, all of them armed men. ²⁶Then all the Israelites, the whole army, went back to Bethel and wept, sitting there before the LORD; they fasted that day until evening. Then they offered burnt offerings and sacrifices of well-being before the LORD. ²⁷And the Israelites inquired of the LORD (for the ark of the covenant of God was there in those days, ²⁸and Phinehas son of Eleazar, son of Aaron, ministered before it in those days), saying, "Shall we go out once more to battle against our kinsfolk the Benjaminites, or shall we desist?" The LORD answered, "Go up, for tomorrow I will give them into your hand."

29 So Israel stationed men in ambush around Gibeah. ³⁰Then the Israelites went up against the Benjaminites on the third day, and set themselves in array against Gibeah, as before. ³¹When the Benjaminites went out against the army, they were drawn away from the city. As before they began to inflict casualties on the troops, along the main roads, one of which goes up to Bethel and the other to Gibeah, as well as in the open country, killing about thirty men of Israel. ³²The Benjaminites thought, "They are being routed before us, as previously." But the Israelites said, "Let us retreat and draw them away from the city toward the roads." ³³The main body of the Israelites drew back its battle line to Baal-tamar, while those Israelites who were in ambush rushed out of their place west*d* of Geba. ³⁴There came against Gibeah ten thousand picked men out of all Israel, and the battle was fierce. But the Benjaminites did not realize that disaster was close upon them.

35 The LORD defeated Benjamin before Israel; and the Israelites destroyed twenty-five thousand one hundred men of Benjamin that day, all of them armed.

36 Then the Benjaminites saw that they were defeated.*e*

---

a Gk: Heb lacks *we will go up*   *b* Compare Gk: Meaning of Heb uncertain   *c* Verses 22 and 23 are transposed   *d* Gk Vg: Heb *in the plain*   *e* This sentence is continued by verse 45.

JUDG

The Israelites gave ground to Benjamin, because they trusted to the troops in ambush that they had stationed against Gibeah. 37The troops in ambush rushed quickly upon Gibeah. Then they put the whole city to the sword. 38Now the agreement between the main body of Israel and the men in ambush was that when they sent up a cloud of smoke out of the city 39the main body of Israel should turn in battle. But Benjamin had begun to inflict casualties on the Israelites, killing about thirty of them; so they thought, "Surely they are defeated before us, as in the first battle." 40But when the cloud, a column of smoke, began to rise out of the city, the Benjaminites looked behind them—and there was the whole city going up in smoke toward the sky! 41Then the main body of Israel turned, and the Benjaminites were dismayed, for they saw that disaster was close upon them. 42Therefore they turned away from the Israelites in the direction of the wilderness; but the battle overtook them, and those who came out of the city*a* were slaughtering them in between.*b* 43Cutting down*c* the Benjaminites, they pursued them from Nohah*d* and trod them down as far as a place east of Gibeah. 44Eighteen thousand Benjaminites fell, all of them courageous fighters. 45When they turned and fled toward the wilderness to the rock of Rimmon, five thousand of them were cut down on the main roads, and they were pursued as far as Gidom, and two thousand of them were slain. 46So all who fell that day of Benjamin were twenty-five thousand arms-bearing men, all of them courageous fighters. 47But six hundred turned and fled toward the wilderness to the rock of Rimmon, and remained at the rock of Rimmon for four months. 48Meanwhile, the Israelites turned back against the Benjaminites, and put them to the sword—the city, the people, the animals, and all that remained. Also the remaining towns they set on fire.

The Benjaminites Saved from Extinction

21 Now the Israelites had sworn at Mizpah, "No one of us shall give his daughter in marriage to Benjamin." 2And the people came to Bethel, and sat there until evening before God, and they lifted up their voices and wept bitterly. 3They said, "O Lord, the God of Israel, why has it come to pass that today there should be one tribe lacking in Israel?" 4On the next day, the people got up early, and built an altar there, and offered burnt offerings and sacrifices of well-being. 5Then the Israelites said, "Which of all the tribes of Israel did not come up in the assembly to the Lord?" For a solemn oath had been taken

concerning whoever did not come up to the Lord to Mizpah, saying, "That one shall be put to death." 6But the Israelites had compassion for Benjamin their kin, and said, "One tribe is cut off from Israel this day. 7What shall we do for wives for those who are left, since we have sworn by the Lord that we will not give them any of our daughters as wives?"

8 Then they said, "Is there anyone from the tribes of Israel who did not come up to the Lord to Mizpah?" It turned out that no one from Jabesh-gilead had come to the camp, to the assembly. 9For when the roll was called among the people, not one of the inhabitants of Jabesh-gilead was there. 10So the congregation sent twelve thousand soldiers there and commanded them, "Go, put the inhabitants of Jabesh-gilead to the sword, including the women and the little ones. 11This is what you shall do; every male and every woman that has lain with a male you shall devote to destruction." 12And they found among the inhabitants of Jabesh-gilead four hundred young virgins who had never slept with a man and brought them to the camp at Shiloh, which is in the land of Canaan.

13 Then the whole congregation sent word to the Benjaminites who were at the rock of Rimmon, and proclaimed peace to them. 14Benjamin returned at that time; and they gave them the women whom they had saved alive of the women of Jabesh-gilead; but they did not suffice for them.

15 The people had compassion on Benjamin because the Lord had made a breach in the tribes of Israel. 16So the elders of the congregation said, "What shall we do for wives for those who are left, since there are no women left in Benjamin?" 17And they said, "There must be heirs for the survivors of Benjamin, in order that a tribe may not be blotted out from Israel. 18Yet we cannot give any of our daughters to them as wives." For the Israelites had sworn, "Cursed be anyone who gives a wife to Benjamin." 19So they said, "Look, the yearly festival of the Lord is taking place at Shiloh, which is north of Bethel, on the east of the highway that goes up from Bethel to Shechem, and south of Lebonah." 20And they instructed the Benjaminites, saying, "Go and lie in wait in the vineyards, 21and watch; when the young women of Shiloh come out to dance in the dances, then come out of the vineyards and each of you carry off a wife for himself from the young

---

a Compare Vg and some Gk Mss: Heb *cities*   *b* Compare Syr: Meaning of Heb uncertain   *c* Gk: Heb *Surrounding*   *d* Gk: Heb *pursued them at their resting place*

women of Shiloh, and go to the land of Benjamin. 22Then if their fathers or their brothers come to complain to us, we will say to them, 'Be generous and allow us to have them; because we did not capture in battle a wife for each man. But neither did you incur guilt by giving your daughters to them.' " 23The Benjaminites did so; they took wives for each of them from the dancers whom they abducted. Then they went and returned to their territory, and rebuilt the towns, and lived in them. 24So the Israelites departed from there at that time by tribes and families, and they went out from there to their own territories.

25 In those days there was no king in Israel; all the people did what was right in their own eyes.

Tracing one's family tree has become a popular pastime. People comb through courthouse files, study old tombstones in search of names and dates, and write to churches in foreign countries looking for baptismal and marriage records. In learning about our ancestors, we gain a better sense of our place in history and who we should be in light of that history. Ruth is a beautiful story of love and loyalty about one of Israel's ancestors. The story helps God's People understand who they are and how they should live.

At a Glance

- Chapter 1. Ruth goes with her mother-in-law to Bethlehem.

- Chapters 2–3. Ruth encounters Boaz.

- Chapter 4. the marriage of Ruth and Boaz; Ruth's descendants

Quick Facts

Period Covered: sometime from 1200 to 1000 BC
Inspired Author: unknown; probably took its final form in the sixth century BC
Themes: God's plan includes non-Israelites. God works through ordinary people.

In Depth

The Book of Ruth offers a surprising revelation about the family tree of King David: Ruth, King David's great-grandmother, was a foreigner, born and reared in the land of Moab. The Book of Ruth took its final form long after the death of her famous great-grandson, but it seems to preserve an accurate memory: King David was of mixed ancestry. Many Israelites were probably shocked that God worked through a member of an enemy tribe to advance the divine plan.

The Book of Ruth is sandwiched between the Books of Judges and 1 Samuel because its events take place during the time of the judges. It teaches some extremely important lessons:

Ruth was faithful to Naomi, her mother-in-law, even though she was of a different race and different faith. Ruth challenged the ancient Israelites, who tended to view foreigners with suspicion and to see nothing good in their enemies.

If God's plan included a Moabite woman among David's ancestors, then God's love and favor must extend beyond the boundaries of Israel. After the Exile, when Jewish marriages to foreigners were outlawed, the little Book of Ruth presented a huge challenge!

God works through the faithfulness of ordinary people living ordinary lives. No kings, wars, or dramatic miracles appear in the Book of Ruth.

The Book of Ruth is action packed and full of dialogue. Some of the traditions of ancient Israel may seem strange to us today, but we can still gain a deeper understanding of ourselves and our faith by reading the story of King David's great-grandmother.

Ruth

Elimelech's Family Goes to Moab

1 In the days when the judges ruled, there was a famine in the land, and a certain man of Bethlehem in Judah went to live in the country of Moab, he and his wife and two sons. ²The name of the man was Elimelech and the name of his wife Naomi, and the names of his two sons were Mahlon and Chilion; they were Ephrathites from Bethlehem in Judah. They went into the country of Moab and remained there. ³But Elimelech, the husband of Naomi, died, and she was left with her two sons. ⁴These took Moabite wives; the name of the one was Orpah and the name of the other Ruth. When they had lived there about ten years, ⁵both Mahlon and Chilion also died, so that the woman was left without her two sons and her husband.

Naomi and Her Moabite Daughters-in-Law

6 Then she started to return with her daughters-in-law from the country of Moab, for she had heard in the country of Moab that the LORD had considered his people and given them food. ⁷So she set out from the place where she had been living, she and her two daughters-in-law, and they went on their way to go back to the land of Judah. ⁸But Naomi said to her two daughters-in-law, "Go back each of you to your mother's house. May the LORD deal kindly with you, as you have dealt with the dead and with me. ⁹The LORD grant that you may find security, each of you in the house of your husband." Then she kissed them, and they wept aloud. ¹⁰They said to her, "No, we will return with you to your people." ¹¹But Naomi said, "Turn back, my daughters, why will you go with me? Do I still have sons in my womb that they may become your husbands? ¹²Turn back, my daughters, go your way, for I am too old to have a husband. Even if I thought there was hope for me, even if I should have a husband tonight and bear sons, ¹³would you then wait until they were grown? Would you then refrain from marrying? No, my daughters, it has been far more bitter for me than for you, because the hand of the LORD has turned against me." ¹⁴Then they wept aloud again. Orpah kissed her mother-in-law, but Ruth clung to her.

15 So she said, "See, your sister-in-law has gone back to her people and to her gods; return after your sister-in-law." ¹⁶But Ruth said,

"Do not press me to leave you
    or to turn back from following you!
Where you go, I will go;
    where you lodge, I will lodge;
your people shall be my people,
    and your God my God.
¹⁷ Where you die, I will die—
    there will I be buried.
May the LORD do thus and so to me,
    and more as well,
    if even death parts me from you!"

¹⁸When Naomi saw that she was determined to go with her, she said no more to her.

19 So the two of them went on until they came to Bethlehem. When they came to Bethlehem, the whole town was stirred because of them; and the women said, "Is this Naomi?" 20She said to them,

"Call me no longer Naomi,a
call me Mara,b
for the Almightyc has dealt bitterly with me.
21 I went away full,
but the Lord has brought me back empty;
why call me Naomi
when the Lord has dealt harshly withd me,
and the Almightyc has brought calamity upon me?"

Stand by Me

Loyalty is one of those old-fashioned words, isn't it? How often do we hear it mentioned these days? And what exactly does it mean? The story of Naomi and Ruth gives us an inspiring example of loyalty. After Ruth's husband dies and her mother-in-law decides to return home to Bethlehem, Naomi tells her two widowed daughters-in-law that they should return to their homes and marry again. But Ruth decides to stay with Naomi, which means leaving her own land of Moab and settling in Judea, a foreign land. Ruth's words to Naomi are a powerful statement of what it means to be loyal: "Where you go, I will go; where you lodge, I will lodge; your people shall be my people, and your God my God" [Ruth 1:16]. In other words, "No matter what, I will stand by you."

We are also called to be loyal—especially to our families and friends. In other words, we are to stand by the people we are close to, especially when they are experiencing hard times. Even when it's tough to do so, we are to remain faithful. Loyalty creates trust and deepens relationships.

● To what or whom are you loyal? When have you experienced disloyalty, especially in a friend? How have you proven your loyalty to others? to God?

▶ Ruth 1:1–18

22 So Naomi returned together with Ruth the Moabite, her daughter-in-law, who came back with her from the country of Moab. They came to Bethlehem at the beginning of the barley harvest.

Ruth Meets Boaz

2 Now Naomi had a kinsman on her husband's side, a prominent rich man, of the family of Elimelech, whose name was Boaz. 2And Ruth the Moabite said to Naomi, "Let me go to the field and glean among the ears of grain, behind someone in whose sight I may find favor." She said to her, "Go, my daughter." 3So she went. She came and gleaned in the field behind the reapers. As it happened, she came to the part of the field belonging to Boaz, who was of the family of Elimelech. 4Just then Boaz came from Bethlehem. He said to the reapers, "The Lord be with you." They answered, "The Lord bless you." 5Then Boaz said to his servant who was in charge of the reapers, "To whom does this young woman belong?" 6The servant who was in charge of the reapers answered, "She is the Moabite who came back with Naomi from the country of

a That is *Pleasant* b That is *Bitter* c Traditional rendering of Heb *Shaddai* d Or *has testified against*

Wherever You Go

Ruth is under no obligation to leave her homeland and go to Israel with her mother-in-law, very likely facing a life of poverty. But her loyalty is rewarded, and she finds new life among God's people.

After reading Ruth's story, reflect on these questions:

● What do you find inspiring in Ruth's story?
● To whom are you faithful?
● What would have to be present in a relationship for you to have the kind of loyalty Ruth showed to Naomi?
● Can you make Ruth's words to Naomi your prayer to God?

Where you lead, I will follow; where you direct me, I will live; your people shall be my family. [Adapted from Ruth 1:16]

R
U
T
H

Moab. [7]She said, 'Please, let me glean and gather among the sheaves behind the reapers.' So she came, and she has been on her feet from early this morning until now, without resting even for a moment."[a]

8 Then Boaz said to Ruth, "Now listen, my daughter, do not go to glean in another field or leave this one, but keep close to my young women. [9]Keep your eyes on the field that is being reaped, and follow behind them. I have ordered the young men not to bother you. If you get thirsty, go to the vessels and drink from what the young men have drawn." [10]Then she fell prostrate, with her face to the ground, and said to him, "Why have I found favor in your sight, that you should take notice of me, when I am a foreigner?" [11]But Boaz answered her, "All that you have done for your mother-in-law since the death of your husband has been fully told me, and how you left your father and mother and your native land and came to a people that you did not know before. [12]May the LORD reward you for your deeds, and may you have a full reward from the LORD, the God of Israel, under whose wings you have come for refuge!" [13]Then she said, "May I continue to find favor in your sight, my lord, for you have comforted me and spoken kindly to your servant, even though I am not one of your servants."

14 At mealtime Boaz said to her, "Come here, and eat some of this bread, and dip your morsel in the sour wine." So she sat beside the reapers, and he heaped up for her some parched grain. She ate until she was satisfied, and she had some left over. [15]When she got up to glean, Boaz instructed his young men, "Let her glean even among the standing sheaves, and do not reproach her. [16]You must also pull out some handfuls for her from the bundles, and leave them for her to glean, and do not rebuke her."

17 So she gleaned in the field until evening. Then she beat out what she had gleaned, and it was about an ephah of barley. [18]She picked it up and came into the town, and her mother-in-law saw how much she had gleaned. Then she took out and gave her what was left over after she herself had been satisfied. [19]Her mother-in-law said to her, "Where did you glean today? And where have you worked? Blessed be the man who took notice of you." So she told her mother-in-law with whom she had worked, and said, "The name of the man with whom I worked today is Boaz." [20]Then Naomi said to her daughter-in-law, "Blessed be he by the LORD, whose kindness has not forsaken the living or the dead!" Naomi also said to her, "The man is a relative of ours, one of our nearest kin."[b] [21]Then Ruth the Moabite said, "He even said to me, 'Stay close by my servants, until they have finished all my harvest.'" [22]Naomi said to Ruth, her daughter-in-law, "It is better, my daughter, that you go out with his young women, otherwise you might be bothered in another field." [23]So she stayed close to the young women of Boaz, gleaning until the end of the barley and wheat harvests; and she lived with her mother-in-law.

Ruth and Boaz at the Threshing Floor

3 Naomi her mother-in-law said to her, "My daughter, I need to seek some security for you, so that it may be well with you. [2]Now here is our kinsman Boaz, with whose young women you have been working. See, he is winnowing barley tonight at the threshing floor. [3]Now wash and anoint yourself, and put on your best clothes and go down to the threshing floor; but do not make yourself known to the man until he has finished eating and drinking. [4]When he lies down, observe the place where he lies; then, go and uncover his feet and lie down; and he will tell you what to do." [5]She said to her, "All that you tell me I will do."

6 So she went down to the threshing floor and did just as her mother-in-law had instructed her. [7]When Boaz had eaten and drunk, and he was in a contented mood, he went to lie down at the end of the heap of grain. Then she came stealthily and uncovered his feet, and lay down. [8]At midnight the man was startled, and turned over, and there, lying at his feet, was a woman! [9]He said, "Who are you?" And she answered, "I

Chapters 2–3

---

a Compare Gk Vg: Meaning of Heb uncertain   b Or one with the right to redeem

Catholic Social Teaching

Service to the Poor and the Community

The story of Ruth was a challenge to the Israelites' tendency to distrust foreigners. It is also an example of how service to the poor was an integral part of Israel's society. In the story, Boaz, a wealthy and respected person, both provides for the poor and looks beyond the differences of race and faith to marry Ruth. Boaz's goal is to do God's will. His marriage to Ruth ensures that Naomi's land is redeemed and that she will have descendants

to claim the land. Ruth's faithfulness and Boaz's integrity serve to gradually restore Naomi's hope in God's care.

In the New Testament, it becomes even clearer that God makes no distinctions between people of different races and cultures. And Jesus teaches that caring for the poor is one of the requirements for being God's people. Catholic social teaching reminds us that we are one human family and challenges us to go be-

yond national, racial, ethnic, economic, and ideological boundaries in creating one human family.

- How do you treat people of different races, and how much is service to poor people a part of your life?
- Pray that you can follow Ruth and Boaz's example and be an instrument of faith, hope, and justice for people in need.

▶ **Ruth 4:14–17**
Solidarity

---

am Ruth, your servant; spread your cloak over your servant, for you are next-of-kin."*a* 10He said, "May you be blessed by the LORD, my daughter; this last instance of your loyalty is better than the first; you have not gone after young men, whether poor or rich. 11And now, my daughter, do not be afraid, I will do for you all that you ask, for all the assembly of my people know that you are a worthy woman. 12But now, though it is true that I am a near kinsman, there is another kinsman more closely related than I. 13Remain this night, and in the morning, if he will act as next-of-kin*a* for you, good; let him do it. If he is not willing to act as next-of-kin*a* for you, then, as the LORD lives, I will act as next-of-kin*a* for you. Lie down until the morning."

14 So she lay at his feet until morning, but got up before one person could recognize another; for he said, "It must not be known that the woman came to the threshing floor." 15Then he said, "Bring the cloak you are wearing and hold it out." So she held it, and he measured out six measures of barley, and put it on her back; then he went into the city. 16She came to her mother-in-law, who said, "How did things go with you,*b* my daughter?" Then she told her all that the man had done for her, 17saying, "He gave me these six measures of barley, for he said, 'Do not go back to your mother-in-law empty-handed.' " 18She replied, "Wait, my daughter, until you learn how the matter turns out, for the man will not rest, but will settle the matter today."

The Marriage of Boaz and Ruth

4 No sooner had Boaz gone up to the gate and sat down there than the next-of-kin,*a* of whom Boaz had spoken, came passing by. So Boaz said, "Come over, friend; sit down here." And he went over and sat down. 2Then Boaz took ten men of the elders of the city, and said, "Sit down here"; so they sat down. 3He then said to the next-of-kin,*a* "Naomi, who has come back from the country of Moab, is selling the parcel of land that belonged to our kinsman Elimelech. 4So I thought I would tell you of it, and say: Buy it in the presence of those sitting here, and in the presence of the elders of my people. If you will redeem it, redeem it; but if you will not, tell me, so that I may know; for there is no one prior to you to redeem it, and I come after you." So he said, "I will redeem it." 5Then Boaz said, "The day you acquire the field from the hand of Naomi, you are also acquiring Ruth*c* the Moabite, the widow of the dead man, to maintain the dead man's name on his inheritance." 6At this, the next-of-kin*a* said, "I cannot redeem it for myself without damaging my own inheritance. Take my right of redemption yourself, for I cannot redeem it."

7 Now this was the custom in former times in Israel concerning redeeming and exchanging: to

a Or one with the right to redeem   *b* Or "Who are you,
c OL Vg: Heb from the hand of Naomi and from Ruth

confirm a transaction, the one took off a sandal and gave it to the other; this was the manner of attesting in Israel. [8]So when the next-of-kin[a] said to Boaz, "Acquire it for yourself," he took off his sandal. [9]Then Boaz said to the elders and all the people, "Today you are witnesses that I have acquired from the hand of Naomi all that belonged to Elimelech and all that belonged to Chilion and Mahlon. [10]I have also acquired Ruth the Moabite, the wife of Mahlon, to be my wife, to maintain the dead man's name on his inheritance, in order that the name of the dead may not be cut off from his kindred and from the gate of his native place; today you are witnesses." [11]Then all the people who were at the gate, along with the elders, said, "We are witnesses. May the LORD make the woman who is coming into your house like Rachel and Leah, who together built up the house of Israel. May you produce children in Ephrathah and bestow a name in Bethlehem; [12]and, through the children that the LORD will give you by this young woman, may your house be like the house of Perez, whom Tamar bore to Judah."

The Genealogy of David

13 So Boaz took Ruth and she became his wife. When they came together, the LORD made her conceive, and she bore a son. [14]Then the women said to Naomi, "Blessed be the LORD, who has not left you this day without next-of-kin;[a] and may his name be renowned in Israel! [15]He shall be to you a restorer of life and a nourisher of your old age; for your daughter-in-law who loves you, who is more to you than seven sons, has borne him." [16]Then Naomi took the child and laid him in her bosom, and became his nurse. [17]The women of the neighborhood gave him a name, saying, "A son has been born to Naomi." They named him Obed; he became the father of Jesse, the father of David.

18 Now these are the descendants of Perez: Perez became the father of Hezron, [19]Hezron of Ram, Ram of Amminadab, [20]Amminadab of Nahshon, Nahshon of Salmon, [21]Salmon of Boaz, Boaz of Obed, [22]Obed of Jesse, and Jesse of David.

---

a Or one with the right to redeem

One of the basic ongoing tensions in many countries is the role of government: some believe the government interferes too much in their lives, while others feel the government should do more. Issues like health care and the environment are good examples. The First Book of Samuel reflects a similar tension in Israel as the days of the judges come to an end and the first kings make their appearance. This period of Israelite history is filled with mighty struggles and colorful personalities, including a king who gradually loses his sanity and the shining hero who replaces him.

At a Glance

- Chapters 1–7. stories of Eli and Samuel

- Chapters 8–15. the beginning of Saul's kingship

- Chapters 16–31. stories of King Saul and the young David

Quick Facts

Period Covered: from approximately 1080 to 1040 BC

Inspired Author: unknown; from the Deuteronomic tradition, probably using ancient court records and hero stories

Theme: tension between the need for a king and the people's reliance on God

Of Note: First and Second Samuel, originally one book, were made into two books when they were translated from Hebrew into Greek.

In Depth

This book is named after Samuel, the last of the judges and a reluctant kingmaker. Samuel was a prophet anointed to speak God's Word to the nation. God works through the prophet's words to remind the people of Israel to be faithful to the terms of the Covenant. The people wanted a king, so Samuel anointed Saul to be the first king to rule the whole nation. God works through the king's laws and regulations to ensure that the people of Israel are faithful to the terms of the Covenant. In First Samuel, the rule of the judges gradually gives way to the rule of the kings, with an obvious gain and an obvious loss for the people.

When kings begin to rule Israel in place of judges and prophets, the people gain a more structured way of life and develop a greater national identity. These changes also make them stronger in facing threats from other nations. But at the same time, the people lose a great deal of personal freedom and independence. They are taxed and even forced into labor to support the king's government and building plans. Echoes of the debate between the charismatic style of judges and the structured rule of kings can be found throughout First Samuel (see "Doublets," near 9:1).

Israel's kings were understood as being chosen by God and as being responsible for God's interests. First Samuel clearly emphasizes that the success of kings depends on their obedience to God's Law. First Samuel reminds us that final authority in human affairs rests in no human being but in God alone. Human systems are never perfect; they must constantly be reviewed and renewed.

The First Book of **Samuel**

1 Samuel

Samuel's Birth and Dedication

1 There was a certain man of Ramathaim, a Zuphite[a] from the hill country of Ephraim, whose name was Elkanah son of Jeroham son of Elihu son of Tohu son of Zuph, an Ephraimite. [2]He had two wives; the name of the one was Hannah, and the name of the other Peninnah. Peninnah had children, but Hannah had no children.

3 Now this man used to go up year by year from his town to worship and to sacrifice to the LORD of hosts at Shiloh, where the two sons of Eli, Hophni and Phinehas, were priests of the LORD. [4]On the day when Elkanah sacrificed, he would give portions to his wife Peninnah and to all her sons and daughters; [5]but to Hannah he gave a double portion,[b] because he loved her, though the LORD had closed her womb. [6]Her rival used to provoke her severely, to irritate her, because the LORD had closed her womb. [7]So it went on year by year; as often as she went up to the house of the LORD, she used to provoke her. Therefore Hannah wept and would not eat. [8]Her husband Elkanah said to her, "Hannah, why do you weep? Why do you not eat? Why is your heart sad? Am I not more to you than ten sons?"

9 After they had eaten and drunk at Shiloh, Hannah rose and presented herself before the LORD.[c] Now Eli the priest was sitting on the seat beside the doorpost of the temple of the LORD. [10]She was deeply distressed and prayed to the LORD, and wept bitterly. [11]She made this vow: "O LORD of hosts, if only you will look on the misery of your servant, and remember me, and not forget your servant, but will give to your servant a male child, then I will set him before you as a nazirite[d] until the day of his death. He shall drink neither wine nor intoxicants,[e] and no razor shall touch his head."

12 As she continued praying before the LORD, Eli observed her mouth. [13]Hannah was praying silently; only her lips moved, but her voice was not heard; therefore Eli thought she was drunk. [14]So Eli said to her, "How long will you make a drunken spectacle of yourself? Put away your wine." [15]But Hannah answered, "No, my lord, I am a woman deeply troubled; I have drunk neither wine nor strong drink, but I have been pouring out my soul before the LORD. [16]Do not regard your servant as a worthless woman, for I have been speaking out of my great anxiety and vexation all this time." [17]Then Eli answered, "Go in peace; the God of Israel grant the petition you have made to him." [18]And she said, "Let your servant find favor in your sight." Then the woman went to her quarters,[f] ate and drank with her husband,[g] and her countenance was sad no longer.[h]

19 They rose early in the morning and worshiped before the LORD; then they went back to their house at Ramah. Elkanah knew his wife

---

a Compare Gk and 1 Chr 6.35-36: Heb *Ramathaim-zophim*
b Syr: Meaning of Heb uncertain   c Gk: Heb lacks *and presented herself before the LORD*   d That is *one separated* or *one consecrated*
e Cn Compare Gk Q Ms 1.22: MT *then I will give him to the LORD all the days of his life*   f Gk: Heb *went her way*   g Gk: Heb lacks *and drank with her husband*   h Gk: Meaning of Heb uncertain

Hannah, and the Lord remembered her. 20In due time Hannah conceived and bore a son. She named him Samuel, for she said, "I have asked him of the Lord."

21 The man Elkanah and all his household went up to offer to the Lord the yearly sacrifice, and to pay his vow. 22But Hannah did not go up, for she said to her husband, "As soon as the child is weaned, I will bring him, that he may appear in the presence of the Lord, and remain there forever; I will offer him as a naziritea for all time."b 23Her husband Elkanah said to her, "Do what seems best to you, wait until you have weaned him; only—may the Lord establish his word."c So the woman remained and nursed her son, until she weaned him. 24When she had weaned him, she took him up with her, along with a three-year-old bull,d an ephah of flour, and a skin of wine. She brought him to the house of the Lord at Shiloh; and the child was young. 25Then they slaughtered the bull, and they brought the child to Eli. 26And she said, "Oh, my lord! As you live, my lord, I am the woman who was standing here in your presence, praying to the Lord. 27For this child I prayed; and the Lord has granted me the petition that I made to him. 28Therefore I have lent him to the Lord; as long as he lives, he is given to the Lord."

She left him theree the Lord.

Hannah's Prayer

2 Hannah prayed and said,
　"My heart exults in the Lord;
　　my strength is exalted in my God.f
　My mouth derides my enemies,
　　because I rejoice in myg victory.

2 "There is no Holy One like the Lord,
　no one besides you;
　there is no Rock like our God.
3 Talk no more so very proudly,
　let not arrogance come from your mouth;
　for the Lord is a God of knowledge,
　　and by him actions are weighed.
4 The bows of the mighty are broken,
　but the feeble gird on strength.
5 Those who were full have hired themselves out
　　for bread,
　but those who were hungry are fat with spoil.
　The barren has borne seven,
　but she who has many children is forlorn.
6 The Lord kills and brings to life;
　he brings down to Sheol and raises up.
7 The Lord makes poor and makes rich;
　he brings low, he also exalts.
8 He raises up the poor from the dust;

Pray It!

Prayers of Strong and Holy Women

Compare Hannah's prayer in 1 Samuel 2:1–10 to Mary's prayer in Luke 1:46–55. Notice the joy, the confident faith in God's way, and the understanding that God will raise up those who are hungry, poor, and in need. Notice also how God will deal with the proud, the powerful, and the rich, especially in Mary's prayer. These holy women identify in their lives and in their prayers the bigger picture of what God is all about.

What strong and holy women in your life keep you in their prayers? Take some time now to pray for each of them.

▶ 1 Sam 2:1–10

he lifts the needy from the ash heap,
　to make them sit with princes
　　and inherit a seat of honor.h
For the pillars of the earth are the Lord's,
　and on them he has set the world.

9 "He will guard the feet of his faithful ones,
　but the wicked shall be cut off in darkness;
　for not by might does one prevail.
10 The Lord! His adversaries shall be shattered;
　the Most Highi will thunder in heaven.
The Lord will judge the ends of the earth;
　he will give strength to his king,
　and exalt the power of his anointed."

Eli's Wicked Sons

11 Then Elkanah went home to Ramah, while the boy remained to minister to the Lord, in the presence of the priest Eli.

12 Now the sons of Eli were scoundrels; they had no regard for the Lord 13or for the duties of

---

a That is one separated or one consecrated　b Cn Compare Q Ms: MT lacks I will offer him as a nazirite for all time　c MT: Q Ms Gk Compare Syr that which goes out of your mouth　d Q Ms Gk Syr: MT three bulls　e Gk (Compare Q Ms) and Gk at 2.11: MT And he (that is, Elkanah) worshiped there before　f Gk: Heb the Lord　g Q Ms: MT your　h Gk (Compare Q Ms) adds He grants the vow of the one who vows, and blesses the years of the just　i Cn Heb against him he

the priests to the people. When anyone offered sacrifice, the priest's servant would come, while the meat was boiling, with a three-pronged fork in his hand, 14and he would thrust it into the pan, or kettle, or caldron, or pot; all that the fork brought up the priest would take for himself.[a] This is what they did at Shiloh to all the Israelites who came there. 15Moreover, before the fat was burned, the priest's servant would come and say to the one who was sacrificing, "Give meat for the priest to roast; for he will not accept boiled meat from you, but only raw." 16And if the man said to him, "Let them burn the fat first, and then take whatever you wish," he would say, "No, you must give it now; if not, I will take it by force." 17Thus the sin of the young men was very great in the sight of the LORD; for they treated the offerings of the LORD with contempt.

The Child Samuel at Shiloh

18 Samuel was ministering before the LORD, a boy wearing a linen ephod. 19His mother used to make for him a little robe and take it to him each year, when she went up with her husband to offer the yearly sacrifice. 20Then Eli would bless Elkanah and his wife, and say, "May the LORD repay[b] you with children by this woman for the gift that she made to[c] the LORD"; and then they would return to their home.

21 And[d] the LORD took note of Hannah; she conceived and bore three sons and two daughters. And the boy Samuel grew up in the presence of the LORD.

Prophecy against Eli's Household

22 Now Eli was very old. He heard all that his sons were doing to all Israel, and how they lay with the women who served at the entrance to the tent of meeting. 23He said to them, "Why do you do such things? For I hear of your evil dealings from all these people. 24No, my sons; it is not a good report that I hear the people of the LORD spreading abroad. 25If one person sins against another, someone can intercede for the sinner with the LORD;[e] but if someone sins against the LORD, who can make intercession?" But they would not listen to the voice of their father; for it was the will of the LORD to kill them.

26 Now the boy Samuel continued to grow both in stature and in favor with the LORD and with the people.

27 A man of God came to Eli and said to him, "Thus the LORD has said, 'I revealed[f] myself to the family of your ancestor in Egypt when they were slaves[g] to the house of Pharaoh. 28I chose him out of all the tribes of Israel to be my priest, to go

up to my altar, to offer incense, to wear an ephod before me; and I gave to the family of your ancestor all my offerings by fire from the people of Israel. 29Why then look with greedy eye[h] at my sacrifices and my offerings that I commanded, and honor your sons more than me by fattening yourselves on the choicest parts of every offering of my people Israel?' 30Therefore the LORD the God of Israel declares: 'I promised that your family and the family of your ancestor should go in and out before me forever'; but now the LORD declares: 'Far be it from me; for those who honor me I will honor, and those who despise me shall be treated with contempt. 31See, a time is coming when I will cut off your strength and the strength of your ancestor's family, so that no one in your family will live to old age. 32Then in distress you will look with greedy eye[i] on all the prosperity that shall be bestowed upon Israel; and no one in your family shall ever live to old age. 33The only one of you whom I shall not cut off from my altar shall be spared to weep out his[j] eyes and grieve his[k] heart; all the members of your household shall die by the sword.[l] 34The fate of your two sons, Hophni and Phinehas, shall be the sign to you—both of them shall die on the same day. 35I will raise up for myself a faithful priest, who shall do according to what is in my heart and in my mind. I will build him a sure house, and he shall go in and out before my anointed one forever. 36Everyone who is left in your family shall come to implore him for a piece of silver or a loaf of bread, and shall say, Please put me in one of the priest's places, that I may eat a morsel of bread.' "

Samuel's Calling and Prophetic Activity

3 Now the boy Samuel was ministering to the LORD under Eli. The word of the LORD was rare in those days; visions were not widespread.

2 At that time Eli, whose eyesight had begun to grow dim so that he could not see, was lying down in his room; 3the lamp of God had not yet gone out, and Samuel was lying down in the temple of the LORD, where the ark of God was. 4Then the LORD called, "Samuel! Samuel!"[m] and he said, "Here I am!" 5and ran to Eli, and said, "Here I am, for you called me." But he said, "I did not call; lie down again." So he went and lay down. 6The LORD called again, "Samuel!" Samuel

---

a Gk Syr Vg: Heb *with it*   b Q Ms Gk: MT *give*   c Q Ms Gk: MT *for the petition that she asked of*   d Q Ms Gk: MT *When*   e Gk Compare Q Ms: MT *another, God will mediate for him*   f Gk Tg Syr: Heb *Did I reveal*   g Q Ms Gk: MT lacks *slaves*   h Q Ms Gk: MT *then kick*   i Q Ms Gk: MT *will kick*   j Q Ms Gk: MT *your*   k Q Ms Gk: Heb *your*   l Q Ms See Gk: MT *die like mortals*   m Q Ms Gk See 3.10: MT *the LORD called Samuel*

got up and went to Eli, and said, "Here I am, for you called me." But he said, "I did not call, my son; lie down again." ⁷Now Samuel did not yet know the Lᴏʀᴅ, and the word of the Lᴏʀᴅ had not yet been revealed to him. ⁸The Lᴏʀᴅ called Samuel again, a third time. And he got up and went to Eli, and said, "Here I am, for you called me." Then Eli perceived that the Lᴏʀᴅ was calling the boy. ⁹Therefore Eli said to Samuel, "Go, lie down; and if he calls you, you shall say, 'Speak, Lᴏʀᴅ, for your servant is listening.' " So Samuel went and lay down in his place.

10 Now the Lᴏʀᴅ came and stood there, calling as before, "Samuel! Samuel!" And Samuel said, "Speak, for your servant is listening." ¹¹Then the Lᴏʀᴅ said to Samuel, "See, I am about to do something in Israel that will make both ears of anyone who hears of it tingle. ¹²On that day I will fulfill against Eli all that I have spoken concerning his house, from beginning to end. ¹³For I have told him that I am about to punish his house forever, for the iniquity that he knew, because his sons were blaspheming God,ᵃ and he did not restrain them. ¹⁴Therefore I swear to the house of Eli that the iniquity of Eli's house shall not be expiated by sacrifice or offering forever."

15 Samuel lay there until morning; then he opened the doors of the house of the Lᴏʀᴅ. Samuel was afraid to tell the vision to Eli. ¹⁶But Eli called Samuel and said, "Samuel, my son." He said, "Here I am." ¹⁷Eli said, "What was it that he told you? Do not hide it from me. May God do so to you and more also, if you hide anything from me of all that he told you." ¹⁸So Samuel told him everything and hid nothing from him. Then he said, "It is the Lᴏʀᴅ; let him do what seems good to him."

19 As Samuel grew up, the Lᴏʀᴅ was with him and let none of his words fall to the ground. ²⁰And all Israel from Dan to Beer-sheba knew that Samuel was a trustworthy prophet of the Lᴏʀᴅ. ²¹The Lᴏʀᴅ continued to appear at Shiloh, for the Lᴏʀᴅ revealed himself to Samuel at Shiloh

4 by the word of the Lᴏʀᴅ. ¹And the word of Samuel came to all Israel.

The Ark of God Captured

In those days the Philistines mustered for war against Israel,ᵇ and Israel went out to battle against them;ᶜ they encamped at Ebenezer, and the Philistines encamped at Aphek. ²The Philistines drew up in line against Israel, and when the battle was joined,ᵈ Israel was defeated by the Philistines, who killed about four thousand men on the field of battle. ³When the troops came to the camp, the elders of Israel said, "Why has the

Pray It!

Eli Teaches Samuel How to Pray

Eli taught Samuel to listen to God's voice with a simple sentence: "Speak, Lᴏʀᴅ, for your servant is listening" (1 Sam 3:9). Let's look at that sentence as a prayer:

"Speak, Lᴏʀᴅ . . ." This is an invitation. It shows openness and readiness. It shows your recognition of God: You are the Almighty, and I am ready to hear what you have to say.

". . . for your servant . . ." This shows humility. It is a recognition of yourself: I am your servant. It is my desire to do what you want. My life's purpose is to serve you.

". . . is listening." This demonstrates your response: I am not going to ignore you. I am not going to daydream or just pretend to pay attention. I will take in your message, and it will become part of me.

▶ **1 Sam 3:1–19**

Lᴏʀᴅ put us to rout today before the Philistines? Let us bring the ark of the covenant of the Lᴏʀᴅ here from Shiloh, so that he may come among us and save us from the power of our enemies." ⁴So the people sent to Shiloh, and brought from there the ark of the covenant of the Lᴏʀᴅ of hosts, who is enthroned on the cherubim. The two sons of Eli, Hophni and Phinehas, were there with the ark of the covenant of God.

5 When the ark of the covenant of the Lᴏʀᴅ came into the camp, all Israel gave a mighty shout, so that the earth resounded. ⁶When the Philistines heard the noise of the shouting, they said, "What does this great shouting in the camp of the Hebrews mean?" When they learned that the ark of the Lᴏʀᴅ had come to the camp, ⁷the Philistines were afraid; for they said, "Gods haveᵉ come into the camp." They also said, "Woe to us! For nothing like this has happened before. ⁸Woe to us! Who can deliver us from the power of these mighty gods? These are the gods who struck the Egyptians with every sort of plague

---

ᵃ Another reading is *for themselves*   ᵇ Gk: Heb lacks *In those days the Philistines mustered for war against Israel*   ᶜ Gk: Heb *against the Philistines*   ᵈ Meaning of Heb uncertain   ᵉ Or *A god has*

in the wilderness. [9]Take courage, and be men, O Philistines, in order not to become slaves to the Hebrews as they have been to you; be men and fight."

10 So the Philistines fought; Israel was defeated, and they fled, everyone to his home. There was a very great slaughter, for there fell of Israel thirty thousand foot soldiers. [11]The ark of God was captured; and the two sons of Eli, Hophni and Phinehas, died.

Death of Eli

12 A man of Benjamin ran from the battle line, and came to Shiloh the same day, with his clothes torn and with earth upon his head. [13]When he arrived, Eli was sitting upon his seat by the road watching, for his heart trembled for the ark of God. When the man came into the city and told the news, all the city cried out. [14]When Eli heard the sound of the outcry, he said, "What is this uproar?" Then the man came quickly and told Eli. [15]Now Eli was ninety-eight years old and his eyes were set, so that he could not see. [16]The man said to Eli, "I have just come from the battle; I fled from the battle today." He said, "How did it go, my son?" [17]The messenger replied, "Israel has fled before the Philistines, and there has also been a great slaughter among the troops; your two sons also, Hophni and Phinehas, are dead, and the ark of God has been captured." [18]When he mentioned the ark of God, Eli[a] fell over backward from his seat by the side of the gate; and his neck was broken and he died, for he was an old man, and heavy. He had judged Israel forty years.

19 Now his daughter-in-law, the wife of Phinehas, was pregnant, about to give birth. When she heard the news that the ark of God was captured, and that her father-in-law and her husband were dead, she bowed and gave birth; for her labor pains overwhelmed her. [20]As she was about to die, the women attending her said to her, "Do not be afraid, for you have borne a son." But she did not answer or give heed. [21]She named the child Ichabod, meaning, "The glory has departed from Israel," because the ark of God had been captured and because of her father-in-law and her husband. [22]She said, "The glory has departed from Israel, for the ark of God has been captured."

The Philistines and the Ark

5 When the Philistines captured the ark of God, they brought it from Ebenezer to Ashdod; [2]then the Philistines took the ark of God and brought it into the house of Dagon and placed it beside Dagon. [3]When the people of Ashdod rose early the next day, there was Dagon, fallen on his face to the ground before the ark of the LORD. So they took Dagon and put him back in his place. [4]But when they rose early on the next morning, Dagon had fallen on his face to the ground before the ark of the LORD, and the head of Dagon and both his hands were lying cut off upon the threshold; only the trunk of[b] Dagon was left to him. [5]This is why the priests of Dagon and all who enter the house of Dagon do not step on the threshold of Dagon in Ashdod to this day.

6 The hand of the LORD was heavy upon the people of Ashdod, and he terrified and struck them with tumors, both in Ashdod and in its territory. [7]And when the inhabitants of Ashdod saw how things were, they said, "The ark of the God of Israel must not remain with us; for his hand is heavy on us and on our god Dagon." [8]So they sent and gathered together all the lords of the Philistines, and said, "What shall we do with the ark of the God of Israel?" The inhabitants of Gath replied, "Let the ark of God be moved on to us."[c] So they moved the ark of the God of Israel to Gath.[d] [9]But after they had brought it to Gath,[e] the hand of the LORD was against the city, causing a very great panic; he struck the inhabitants of the city, both young and old, so that tumors broke out on them. [10]So they sent the ark of the God of Israel[f] to Ekron. But when the ark of God came to Ekron, the people of Ekron cried out, "Why[g] have they brought around to us[h] the ark of the God of Israel to kill us[h] and our[i] people?" [11]They sent therefore and gathered together all the lords of the Philistines, and said, "Send away the ark of the God of Israel, and let it return to its own place, that it may not kill us and our people." For there was a deathly panic[j] throughout the whole city. The hand of God was very heavy there; [12]those who did not die were stricken with tumors, and the cry of the city went up to heaven.

The Ark Returned to Israel

6 The ark of the LORD was in the country of the Philistines seven months. [2]Then the Philistines called for the priests and the diviners and said, "What shall we do with the ark of the LORD? Tell us what we should send with it to its place." [3]They said, "If you send away the ark of the God of Israel, do not send it empty, but by all means

a Heb he   b Heb lacks the trunk of   c Gk Compare Q Ms: MT They answered, "Let the ark of the God of Israel be brought around to Gath."   d Gk: Heb lacks to Gath   e Q Ms: MT lacks to Gath   f Q Ms Gk: MT lacks of Israel   g Q Ms Gk: MT lacks Why   h Heb me   i Heb my   j Q Ms reads a panic from the LORD

return him a guilt offering. Then you will be healed and will be ransomed;[a] will not his hand then turn from you?" [4]And they said, "What is the guilt offering that we shall return to him?" They answered, "Five gold tumors and five gold mice, according to the number of the lords of the Philistines; for the same plague was upon all of you and upon your lords. [5]So you must make images of your tumors and images of your mice that ravage the land, and give glory to the God of Israel; perhaps he will lighten his hand on you and your gods and your land. [6]Why should you harden your hearts as the Egyptians and Pharaoh hardened their hearts? After he had made fools of them, did they not let the people go, and they departed? [7]Now then, get ready a new cart and two milch cows that have never borne a yoke, and yoke the cows to the cart, but take their calves home, away from them. [8]Take the ark of the LORD and place it on the cart, and put in a box at its side the figures of gold, which you are returning to him as a guilt offering. Then send it off, and let it go its way. [9]And watch; if it goes up on the way to its own land, to Beth-shemesh, then it is he who has done us this great harm; but if not, then we shall know that it is not his hand that struck us; it happened to us by chance."

10 The men did so; they took two milch cows and yoked them to the cart, and shut up their calves at home. [11]They put the ark of the LORD on the cart, and the box with the gold mice and the images of their tumors. [12]The cows went straight in the direction of Beth-shemesh along one highway, lowing as they went; they turned neither to the right nor to the left, and the lords of the Philistines went after them as far as the border of Beth-shemesh.

13 Now the people of Beth-shemesh were reaping their wheat harvest in the valley. When they looked up and saw the ark, they went with rejoicing to meet it.[b] [14]The cart came into the field of Joshua of Beth-shemesh, and stopped there. A large stone was there; so they split up the wood of the cart and offered the cows as a burnt offering to the LORD. [15]The Levites took down the ark of the LORD and the box that was beside it, in which were the gold objects, and set them upon the large stone. Then the people of Beth-shemesh offered burnt offerings and presented sacrifices on that day to the LORD. [16]When the five lords of the Philistines saw it, they returned that day to Ekron.

17 These are the gold tumors, which the Philistines returned as a guilt offering to the LORD: one for Ashdod, one for Gaza, one for Ashkelon, one for Gath, one for Ekron; [18]also the gold

mice, according to the number of all the cities of the Philistines belonging to the five lords, both fortified cities and unwalled villages. The great stone, beside which they set down the ark of the LORD, is a witness to this day in the field of Joshua of Beth-shemesh.

The Ark at Kiriath-jearim

19 The descendants of Jeconiah did not rejoice with the people of Beth-shemesh when they greeted[c] the ark of the LORD; and he killed seventy men of them.[d] The people mourned because the LORD had made a great slaughter among the people. [20]Then the people of Beth-shemesh said, "Who is able to stand before the LORD, this holy God? To whom shall he go so that we may be rid of him?" [21]So they sent messengers to the inhabitants of Kiriath-jearim, saying, "The Philistines have returned the ark of the LORD. Come down and take it up to you." [1]And the people of Kiriath-jearim came and took up the ark of the LORD, and brought it to the house of Abinadab on the hill. They consecrated his son, Eleazar, to have charge of the ark of the LORD.

2 From the day that the ark was lodged at Kiriath-jearim, a long time passed, some twenty years, and all the house of Israel lamented[e] after the LORD.

Samuel as Judge

3 Then Samuel said to all the house of Israel, "If you are returning to the LORD with all your heart, then put away the foreign gods and the Astartes from among you. Direct your heart to the LORD, and serve him only, and he will deliver you out of the hand of the Philistines." [4]So Israel put away the Baals and the Astartes, and they served the LORD only.

5 Then Samuel said, "Gather all Israel at Mizpah, and I will pray to the LORD for you." [6]So they gathered at Mizpah, and drew water and poured it out before the LORD. They fasted that day, and said, "We have sinned against the LORD." And Samuel judged the people of Israel at Mizpah.

7 When the Philistines heard that the people of Israel had gathered at Mizpah, the lords of the Philistines went up against Israel. And when the people of Israel heard of it they were afraid of the Philistines. [8]The people of Israel said to Samuel, "Do not cease to cry out to the LORD our God for us, and pray that he may save us from the hand of the Philistines." [9]So Samuel took a sucking

a Q Ms Gk: MT and it will be known to you   b Gk: Heb rejoiced to see it   c Gk: Heb And he killed some of the people of Beth-shemesh, because they looked into   d Heb killed seventy men, fifty thousand men   e Meaning of Heb uncertain

1 S A M

lamb and offered it as a whole burnt offering to the LORD; Samuel cried out to the LORD for Israel, and the LORD answered him. ¹⁰As Samuel was offering up the burnt offering, the Philistines drew near to attack Israel; but the LORD thundered with a mighty voice that day against the Philistines and threw them into confusion; and they were routed before Israel. ¹¹And the men of Israel went out of Mizpah and pursued the Philistines, and struck them down as far as beyond Beth-car.

12 Then Samuel took a stone and set it up between Mizpah and Jeshanah,ᵃ and named it Ebenezer;ᵇ for he said, "Thus far the LORD has helped us." ¹³So the Philistines were subdued and did not again enter the territory of Israel; the hand of the LORD was against the Philistines all the days of Samuel. ¹⁴The towns that the Philistines had taken from Israel were restored to Israel, from Ekron to Gath; and Israel recovered their territory from the hand of the Philistines. There was peace also between Israel and the Amorites.

15 Samuel judged Israel all the days of his life. ¹⁶He went on a circuit year by year to Bethel, Gilgal, and Mizpah; and he judged Israel in all these places. ¹⁷Then he would come back to Ramah, for his home was there; he administered justice there to Israel, and built there an altar to the LORD.

Israel Demands a King

8 When Samuel became old, he made his sons judges over Israel. ²The name of his firstborn son was Joel, and the name of his second, Abijah; they were judges in Beer-sheba. ³Yet his sons did not follow in his ways, but turned aside after gain; they took bribes and perverted justice.

4 Then all the elders of Israel gathered together and came to Samuel at Ramah, ⁵and said to him, "You are old and your sons do not follow in your ways; appoint for us, then, a king to govern us, like other nations." ⁶But the thing displeased Samuel when they said, "Give us a king to govern us." Samuel prayed to the LORD, ⁷and the LORD said to Samuel, "Listen to the voice of the people in all that they say to you; for they have not rejected you, but they have rejected me from being king over them. ⁸Just as they have done to me,ᶜ from the day I brought them up out of Egypt to this day, forsaking me and serving other gods, so also they are doing to you. ⁹Now then, listen to their voice; only—you shall solemnly warn them, and show them the ways of the king who shall reign over them."

10 So Samuel reported all the words of the LORD to the people who were asking him for a king. ¹¹He said, "These will be the ways of the king who will reign over you: he will take your sons and appoint them to his chariots and to be his horsemen, and to run before his chariots; ¹²and he will appoint for himself commanders of thousands and commanders of fifties, and some to plow his ground and to reap his harvest, and to make his implements of war and the equipment of his chariots. ¹³He will take your daughters to be perfumers and cooks and bakers. ¹⁴He will take the best of your fields and vineyards and olive orchards and give them to his courtiers. ¹⁵He will take one-tenth of your grain and of your vineyards and give it to his officers and his courtiers. ¹⁶He will take your male and female slaves, and the best of your cattleᵈ and donkeys, and put them to his work. ¹⁷He will take one-tenth of your flocks, and you shall be his slaves. ¹⁸And in that day you will cry out because of your king, whom you have chosen for yourselves; but the LORD will not answer you in that day."

Israel's Request for a King Granted

19 But the people refused to listen to the voice of Samuel; they said, "No! but we are determined to have a king over us, ²⁰so that we also may be like other nations, and that our king may govern us and go out before us and fight our battles." ²¹When Samuel had heard all the words of the people, he repeated them in the ears of the LORD. ²²The LORD said to Samuel, "Listen to their voice and set a king over them." Samuel then said to the people of Israel, "Each of you return home."

Saul Chosen to Be King

9 There was a man of Benjamin whose name was Kish son of Abiel son of Zeror son of Becorath son of Aphiah, a Benjaminite, a man of wealth. ²He had a son whose name was Saul, a handsome young man. There was not a man among the people of Israel more handsome than he; he stood head and shoulders above everyone else.

3 Now the donkeys of Kish, Saul's father, had strayed. So Kish said to his son Saul, "Take one of the boys with you; go and look for the donkeys." ⁴He passed through the hill country of Ephraim and passed through the land of Shalishah, but they did not find them. And they passed through the land of Shaalim, but they were not there. Then he passed through the land of Benjamin, but they did not find them.

---

a Gk Syr: Heb *Shen*   b That is *Stone of Help*   c Gk: Heb lacks *to me*   d Gk: Heb *young men*

5 When they came to the land of Zuph, Saul said to the boy who was with him, "Let us turn back, or my father will stop worrying about the donkeys and worry about us." 6But he said to him, "There is a man of God in this town; he is a man held in honor. Whatever he says always comes true. Let us go there now; perhaps he will tell us about the journey on which we have set out." 7Then Saul replied to the boy, "But if we go, what can we bring the man? For the bread in our sacks is gone, and there is no present to bring to the man of God. What have we?" 8The boy answered Saul again, "Here, I have with me a quarter shekel of silver; I will give it to the man of God, to tell us our way." 9(Formerly in Israel, anyone who went to inquire of God would say, "Come, let us go to the seer"; for the one who is now called a prophet was formerly called a seer.) 10Saul said to the boy, "Good; come, let us go." So they went to the town where the man of God was.

11 As they went up the hill to the town, they met some girls coming out to draw water, and said to them, "Is the seer here?" 12They answered, "Yes, there he is just ahead of you. Hurry; he has come just now to the town, because the people have a sacrifice today at the shrine. 13As soon as you enter the town, you will find him, before he goes up to the shrine to eat. For the people will not eat until he comes, since he must bless the sacrifice; afterward those eat who are invited. Now go up, for you will meet him immediately." 14So they went up to the town. As they were entering the town, they saw Samuel coming out toward them on his way up to the shrine.

15 Now the day before Saul came, the LORD had revealed to Samuel: 16"Tomorrow about this time I will send to you a man from the land of Benjamin, and you shall anoint him to be ruler over my people Israel. He shall save my people from the hand of the Philistines; for I have seen the suffering of[a] my people, because their outcry has come to me." 17When Samuel saw Saul, the LORD told him, "Here is the man of whom I spoke to you. He it is who shall rule over my people." 18Then Saul approached Samuel inside the gate, and said, "Tell me, please, where is the house of the seer?" 19Samuel answered Saul, "I am the seer; go up before me to the shrine, for today you shall eat with me, and in the morning I will let you go and will tell you all that is on your mind. 20As for your donkeys that were lost three days ago, give no further thought to them, for they have been found. And on whom is all Israel's desire fixed, if not on you and on all your ancestral house?" 21Saul answered, "I am only a

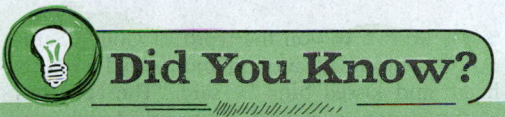

Did You Know?

Doublets

Often more than one version of a story is recorded in the Bible. Genesis has two stories of the Creation (see Gen 1:1—2:4, 2:4–25). The First Book of Samuel has two different attitudes toward the request to have a king in Israel. Compare the anti-king passages of 1 Samuel 8:10–22 and 10:17–19 with the pro-king passages of 9:15–16 and chapter 11. Most likely, the difference of opinion comes from different parts of Israel. The Bible sometimes uses two versions of a story, called doublets, to allow consideration of both sides of an issue.

Benjaminite, from the least of the tribes of Israel, and my family is the humblest of all the families of the tribe of Benjamin. Why then have you spoken to me in this way?"

22 Then Samuel took Saul and his servant-boy and brought them into the hall, and gave them a place at the head of those who had been invited, of whom there were about thirty. 23And Samuel said to the cook, "Bring the portion I gave you, the one I asked you to put aside." 24The cook took up the thigh and what went with it[b] and set them before Saul. Samuel said, "See, what was kept is set before you. Eat; for it is set[c] before you at the appointed time, so that you might eat with the guests."[d]

So Saul ate with Samuel that day. 25When they came down from the shrine into the town, a bed was spread for Saul[e] on the roof, and he lay down to sleep.[f] 26Then at the break of dawn[g] Samuel called to Saul upon the roof, "Get up, so that I may send you on your way." Saul got up, and both he and Samuel went out into the street.

Samuel Anoints Saul

27 As they were going down to the outskirts of the town, Samuel said to Saul, "Tell the boy to go on before us, and when he has passed on, stop here yourself for a while, that I may make

---

a Gk: Heb lacks *the suffering of*   b Meaning of Heb uncertain
c Q Ms Gk: MT *it was kept*   d Cn: Heb *it was kept for you, saying, I have invited the people*   e Gk: Heb *and he spoke with Saul*   f Gk: Heb lacks *and he lay down to sleep*   g Gk: Heb *and they arose early and at break of dawn*

10 known to you the word of God." [1]Samuel took a vial of oil and poured it on his head, and kissed him; he said, "The LORD has anointed you ruler over his people Israel. You shall reign over the people of the LORD and you will save them from the hand of their enemies all around. Now this shall be the sign to you that the LORD has anointed you ruler[a] over his heritage: [2]When you depart from me today you will meet two men by Rachel's tomb in the territory of Benjamin at Zelzah; they will say to you, 'The donkeys that you went to seek are found, and now your father has stopped worrying about them and is worrying about you, saying: What shall I do about my son?' [3]Then you shall go on from there further and come to the oak of Tabor; three men going up to God at Bethel will meet you there, one carrying three kids, another carrying three loaves of bread, and another carrying a skin of wine. [4]They will greet you and give you two loaves of bread, which you shall accept from them. [5]After that you shall come to Gibeath-elohim,[b] at the place where the Philistine garrison is; there, as you come to the town, you will meet a band of prophets coming down from the shrine with harp, tambourine, flute, and lyre playing in front of them; they will be in a prophetic frenzy. [6]Then the spirit of the LORD will possess you, and you will be in a prophetic frenzy along with them and be turned into a different person. [7]Now when these signs meet you, do whatever you see fit to do, for God is with you. [8]And you shall go down to Gilgal ahead of me; then I will come down to you to present burnt offerings and offer sacrifices of well-being. Seven days you shall wait, until I come to you and show you what you shall do."

Saul Prophesies

9 As he turned away to leave Samuel, God gave him another heart; and all these signs were fulfilled that day. [10]When they were going from there[c] to Gibeah,[d] a band of prophets met him; and the spirit of God possessed him, and he fell into a prophetic frenzy along with them. [11]When all who knew him before saw how he prophesied with the prophets, the people said to one another, "What has come over the son of Kish? Is Saul also among the prophets?" [12]A man of the place answered, "And who is their father?" Therefore it became a proverb, "Is Saul also among the prophets?" [13]When his prophetic frenzy had ended, he went home.[e]

14 Saul's uncle said to him and to the boy, "Where did you go?" And he replied, "To seek the donkeys; and when we saw they were not

to be found, we went to Samuel." [15]Saul's uncle said, "Tell me what Samuel said to you." [16]Saul said to his uncle, "He told us that the donkeys had been found." But about the matter of the kingship, of which Samuel had spoken, he did not tell him anything.

Saul Proclaimed King

17 Samuel summoned the people to the LORD at Mizpah [18]and said to them,[f] "Thus says the LORD, the God of Israel, 'I brought up Israel out of Egypt, and I rescued you from the hand of the Egyptians and from the hand of all the kingdoms that were oppressing you.' [19]But today you have rejected your God, who saves you from all your calamities and your distresses; and you have said, 'No! but set a king over us.' Now therefore present yourselves before the LORD by your tribes and by your clans."

20 Then Samuel brought all the tribes of Israel near, and the tribe of Benjamin was taken by lot. [21]He brought the tribe of Benjamin near by its families, and the family of the Matrites was taken by lot. Finally he brought the family of the Matrites near man by man,[g] and Saul the son of Kish was taken by lot. But when they sought him, he could not be found. [22]So they inquired again of the LORD, "Did the man come here?"[h] and the LORD said, "See, he has hidden himself among the baggage." [23]Then they ran and brought him from there. When he took his stand among the people, he was head and shoulders taller than any of them. [24]Samuel said to all the people, "Do you see the one whom the LORD has chosen? There is no one like him among all the people." And all the people shouted, "Long live the king!"

25 Samuel told the people the rights and duties of the kingship; and he wrote them in a book and laid it up before the LORD. Then Samuel sent all the people back to their homes. [26]Saul also went to his home at Gibeah, and with him went warriors whose hearts God had touched. [27]But some worthless fellows said, "How can this man save us?" They despised him and brought him no present. But he held his peace.

Now Nahash, king of the Ammonites, had been grievously oppressing the Gadites and the Reubenites. He would gouge out the right eye of each of them and would not grant Israel a deliverer. No one was left of the Israelites across the Jordan whose right eye Nahash, king of the

---

a Gk: Heb lacks *over his people Israel. You shall . . . anointed you ruler* b Or *the Hill of God* c Gk: Heb *they came there* d Or *the hill* e Cn: Heb *he came to the shrine* f Heb *to the people of Israel* g Gk: Heb lacks *Finally . . . man by man* h Gk: Heb *Is there yet a man to come here?*

Ammonites, had not gouged out. But there were seven thousand men who had escaped from the Ammonites and had entered Jabesh-gilead.[a]

Saul Defeats the Ammonites

11 About a month later,[b] Nahash the Ammonite went up and besieged Jabesh-gilead; and all the men of Jabesh said to Nahash, "Make a treaty with us, and we will serve you." [2]But Nahash the Ammonite said to them, "On this condition I will make a treaty with you, namely that I gouge out everyone's right eye, and thus put disgrace upon all Israel." [3]The elders of Jabesh said to him, "Give us seven days' respite that we may send messengers through all the territory of Israel. Then, if there is no one to save us, we will give ourselves up to you." [4]When the messengers came to Gibeah of Saul, they reported the matter in the hearing of the people; and all the people wept aloud.

[5] Now Saul was coming from the field behind the oxen; and Saul said, "What is the matter with the people, that they are weeping?" So they told him the message from the inhabitants of Jabesh. [6]And the spirit of God came upon Saul in power when he heard these words, and his anger was greatly kindled. [7]He took a yoke of oxen, and cut them in pieces and sent them throughout all the territory of Israel by messengers, saying, "Whoever does not come out after Saul and Samuel, so shall it be done to his oxen!" Then the dread of the LORD fell upon the people, and they came out as one. [8]When he mustered them at Bezek, those from Israel were three hundred thousand, and those from Judah seventy[c] thousand. [9]They said to the messengers who had come, "Thus shall you say to the inhabitants of Jabesh-gilead: 'Tomorrow, by the time the sun is hot, you shall have deliverance.' " When the messengers came and told the inhabitants of Jabesh, they rejoiced. [10]So the inhabitants of Jabesh said, "Tomorrow we will give ourselves up to you, and you may do to us whatever seems good to you." [11]The next day Saul put the people in three companies. At the morning watch they came into the camp and cut down the Ammonites until the heat of the day; and those who survived were scattered, so that no two of them were left together.

[12] The people said to Samuel, "Who is it that said, 'Shall Saul reign over us?' Give them to us so that we may put them to death." [13]But Saul said, "No one shall be put to death this day, for today the LORD has brought deliverance to Israel."

[14] Samuel said to the people, "Come, let us go to Gilgal and there renew the kingship." [15]So all the people went to Gilgal, and there they made Saul king before the LORD in Gilgal. There they sacrificed offerings of well-being before the LORD, and there Saul and all the Israelites rejoiced greatly.

Samuel's Farewell Address

12 Samuel said to all Israel, "I have listened to you in all that you have said to me, and have set a king over you. [2]See, it is the king who leads you now; I am old and gray, but my sons are with you. I have led you from my youth until this day. [3]Here I am; testify against me before the LORD and before his anointed. Whose ox have I taken? Or whose donkey have I taken? Or whom have I defrauded? Whom have I oppressed? Or from whose hand have I taken a bribe to blind my eyes with it? Testify against me[d] and I will restore it to you." [4]They said, "You have not defrauded us or oppressed us or taken anything from the hand of anyone." [5]He said to them, "The LORD is witness against you, and his anointed is witness this day, that you have not found anything in my hand." And they said, "He is witness."

[6] Samuel said to the people, "The LORD is witness, who[e] appointed Moses and Aaron and brought your ancestors up out of the land of Egypt. [7]Now therefore take your stand, so that I may enter into judgment with you before the LORD, and I will declare to you[f] all the saving deeds of the LORD that he performed for you and for your ancestors. [8]When Jacob went into Egypt and the Egyptians oppressed them,[g] then your ancestors cried to the LORD and the LORD sent Moses and Aaron, who brought forth your ancestors out of Egypt, and settled them in this place. [9]But they forgot the LORD their God; and he sold them into the hand of Sisera, commander of the army of King Jabin of[h] Hazor, and into the hand of the Philistines, and into the hand of the king of Moab; and they fought against them. [10]Then they cried to the LORD, and said, 'We have sinned, because we have forsaken the LORD, and have served the Baals and the Astartes; but now rescue us out of the hand of our enemies, and we will serve you.' [11]And the LORD sent Jerubbaal and Barak,[i] and Jephthah, and Samson,[j] and rescued you out of the hand of your enemies on every side; and you lived in safety. [12]But when you

---

a Q Ms Compare Josephus, *Antiquities* VI.v.1 (68-71): MT lacks *Now Nahash . . . entered Jabesh-gilead.*   b Q Ms Gk: MT lacks *About a month later*   c Q Ms Gk: MT *thirty*   d Gk: Heb lacks *Testify against me*   e Gk: Heb lacks *is witness, who* f Gk: Heb lacks *and I will declare to you*   g Gk: Heb lacks *and the Egyptians oppressed them*   h Gk: Heb lacks *King Jabin of* i Gk Syr: Heb *Bedan*   j Gk: Heb *Samuel*

saw that King Nahash of the Ammonites came against you, you said to me, 'No, but a king shall reign over us,' though the LORD your God was your king. [13]See, here is the king whom you have chosen, for whom you have asked; see, the LORD has set a king over you. [14]If you will fear the LORD and serve him and heed his voice and not rebel against the commandment of the LORD, and if both you and the king who reigns over you will follow the LORD your God, it will be well; [15]but if you will not heed the voice of the LORD, but rebel against the commandment of the LORD, then the hand of the LORD will be against you and your king.[a] [16]Now therefore take your stand and see this great thing that the LORD will do before your eyes. [17]Is it not the wheat harvest today? I will call upon the LORD, that he may send thunder and rain; and you shall know and see that the wickedness that you have done in the sight of the LORD is great in demanding a king for yourselves." [18]So Samuel called upon the LORD, and the LORD sent thunder and rain that day; and all the people greatly feared the LORD and Samuel.

19 All the people said to Samuel, "Pray to the LORD your God for your servants, so that we may not die; for we have added to all our sins the evil of demanding a king for ourselves." [20]And Samuel said to the people, "Do not be afraid; you have done all this evil, yet do not turn aside from following the LORD, but serve the LORD with all your heart; [21]and do not turn aside after useless things that cannot profit or save, for they are useless. [22]For the LORD will not cast away his people, for his great name's sake, because it has pleased the LORD to make you a people for himself. [23]Moreover as for me, far be it from me that I should sin against the LORD by ceasing to pray for you; and I will instruct you in the good and the right way. [24]Only fear the LORD, and serve him faithfully with all your heart; for consider what great things he has done for you. [25]But if you still do wickedly, you shall be swept away, both you and your king."

Saul's Unlawful Sacrifice

13 Saul was . . .[b] years old when he began to reign; and he reigned . . . and two[c] years over Israel.

2 Saul chose three thousand out of Israel; two thousand were with Saul in Michmash and the hill country of Bethel, and a thousand were with Jonathan in Gibeah of Benjamin; the rest of the people he sent home to their tents. [3]Jonathan defeated the garrison of the Philistines that was at Geba; and the Philistines heard of it. And Saul blew the trumpet throughout all the land, saying,

"Let the Hebrews hear!" [4]When all Israel heard that Saul had defeated the garrison of the Philistines, and also that Israel had become odious to the Philistines, the people were called out to join Saul at Gilgal.

5 The Philistines mustered to fight with Israel, thirty thousand chariots, and six thousand horsemen, and troops like the sand on the seashore in multitude; they came up and encamped at Michmash, to the east of Beth-aven. [6]When the Israelites saw that they were in distress (for the troops were hard pressed), the people hid themselves in caves and in holes and in rocks and in tombs and in cisterns. [7]Some Hebrews crossed the Jordan to the land of Gad and Gilead. Saul was still at Gilgal, and all the people followed him trembling.

8 He waited seven days, the time appointed by Samuel; but Samuel did not come to Gilgal, and the people began to slip away from Saul.[d] [9]So Saul said, "Bring the burnt offering here to me, and the offerings of well-being." And he offered the burnt offering. [10]As soon as he had finished offering the burnt offering, Samuel arrived; and Saul went out to meet him and salute him. [11]Samuel said, "What have you done?" Saul replied, "When I saw that the people were slipping away from me, and that you did not come within the days appointed, and that the Philistines were mustering at Michmash, [12]I said, 'Now the Philistines will come down upon me at Gilgal, and I have not entreated the favor of the LORD'; so I forced myself, and offered the burnt offering." [13]Samuel said to Saul, "You have done foolishly; you have not kept the commandment of the LORD your God, which he commanded you. The LORD would have established your kingdom over Israel forever, [14]but now your kingdom will not continue; the LORD has sought out a man after his own heart; and the LORD has appointed him to be ruler over his people, because you have not kept what the LORD commanded you." [15]And Samuel left and went on his way from Gilgal.[e] The rest of the people followed Saul to join the army; they went up from Gilgal toward Gibeah of Benjamin.[f]

Preparations for Battle

Saul counted the people who were present with him, about six hundred men. [16]Saul, his son Jonathan, and the people who were present

---

a Gk: Heb and your ancestors   b The number is lacking in the Heb text (the verse is lacking in the Septuagint).   c Two is not the entire number; something has dropped out.   d Heb him   e Gk: Heb went up from Gilgal to Gibeah of Benjamin   f Gk: Heb lacks The rest . . . of Benjamin with them stayed in Geba of Benjamin; but the Philistines encamped at Michmash. [17]And raiders came out of the camp of the Philistines in three companies; one company turned toward Ophrah, to the land of Shual, [18]another company turned toward Beth-horon, and another company turned toward the mountain[a] that looks down upon the valley of Zeboim toward the wilderness.

19 Now there was no smith to be found throughout all the land of Israel; for the Philistines said, "The Hebrews must not make swords or spears for themselves"; [20]so all the Israelites went down to the Philistines to sharpen their plowshares, mattocks, axes, or sickles;[b] [21]The charge was two-thirds of a shekel[c] for the plowshares and for the mattocks, and one-third of a shekel for sharpening the axes and for setting the goads.[d] [22]So on the day of the battle neither sword nor spear was to be found in the possession of any of the people with Saul and Jonathan; but Saul and his son Jonathan had them.

Jonathan Surprises and Routs the Philistines

23 Now a garrison of the Philistines had gone out to the pass of Michmash. [1]One day **14** Jonathan son of Saul said to the young man who carried his armor, "Come, let us go over to the Philistine garrison on the other side." But he did not tell his father. [2]Saul was staying in the outskirts of Gibeah under the pomegranate tree that is at Migron; the troops that were with him were about six hundred men, [3]along with Ahijah son of Ahitub, Ichabod's brother, son of Phinehas son of Eli, the priest of the LORD in Shiloh, carrying an ephod. Now the people did not know that Jonathan had gone. [4]In the pass,[e] by which Jonathan tried to go over to the Philistine garrison, there was a rocky crag on one side and a rocky crag on the other; the name of the one was Bozez, and the name of the other Seneh. [5]One crag rose on the north in front of Michmash, and the other on the south in front of Geba.

6 Jonathan said to the young man who carried his armor, "Come, let us go over to the garrison of these uncircumcised; it may be that the LORD will act for us; for nothing can hinder the LORD from saving by many or by few." [7]His armor-bearer said to him, "Do all that your mind inclines to.[f] I am with you; as your mind is, so is mine."[g] [8]Then Jonathan said, "Now we will cross over to those men and will show ourselves to them. [9]If they say to us, 'Wait until we come to you,' then we will stand still in our place, and we will not go up to them. [10]But if they say, 'Come up to us,' then we will go up; for the LORD has

given them into our hand. That will be the sign for us." [11]So both of them showed themselves to the garrison of the Philistines; and the Philistines said, "Look, Hebrews are coming out of the holes where they have hidden themselves." [12]The men of the garrison hailed Jonathan and his armor-bearer, saying, "Come up to us, and we will show you something." Jonathan said to his armor-bearer, "Come up after me; for the LORD has given them into the hand of Israel." [13]Then Jonathan climbed up on his hands and feet, with his armor-bearer following after him. The Philistines[h] fell before Jonathan, and his armor-bearer, coming after him, killed them. [14]In that first slaughter Jonathan and his armor-bearer killed about twenty men within an area about half a furrow long in an acre[i] of land. [15]There was a panic in the camp, in the field, and among all the people; the garrison and even the raiders trembled; the earth quaked; and it became a very great panic.

16 Saul's lookouts in Gibeah of Benjamin were watching as the multitude was surging back and forth.[j] [17]Then Saul said to the troops that were with him, "Call the roll and see who has gone from us." When they had called the roll, Jonathan and his armor-bearer were not there. [18]Saul said to Ahijah, "Bring the ark[k] of God here." For at that time the ark[k] of God went with the Israelites. [19]While Saul was talking to the priest, the tumult in the camp of the Philistines increased more and more; and Saul said to the priest, "Withdraw your hand." [20]Then Saul and all the people who were with him rallied and went into the battle; and every sword was against the other, so that there was very great confusion. [21]Now the Hebrews who previously had been with the Philistines and had gone up with them into the camp turned and joined the Israelites who were with Saul and Jonathan. [22]Likewise, when all the Israelites who had gone into hiding in the hill country of Ephraim heard that the Philistines were fleeing, they too followed closely after them in the battle. [23]So the LORD gave Israel the victory that day.

The battle passed beyond Beth-aven, and the troops with Saul numbered altogether about ten thousand men. The battle spread out over the hill country of Ephraim.

---

a Cn Compare Gk: Heb *toward the border*　b Gk: Heb *plowshare*　c Heb *was a pim*　d Cn: Meaning of Heb uncertain　e Heb *Between the passes*　f Gk: Heb *Do all that is in your mind. Turn*　g Gk: Heb lacks *so is mine*　h Heb *They*　i Heb *yoke*　j Gk: Heb *they went and there*　k Gk *the ephod*

Saul's Rash Oath

24 Now Saul committed a very rash act on that day.[a] He had laid an oath on the troops, saying, "Cursed be anyone who eats food before it is evening and I have been avenged on my enemies." So none of the troops tasted food. 25All the troops[b] came upon a honeycomb; and there was honey on the ground. 26When the troops came upon the honeycomb, the honey was dripping out; but they did not put their hands to their mouths, for they feared the oath. 27But Jonathan had not heard his father charge the troops with the oath; so he extended the staff that was in his hand, and dipped the tip of it in the honeycomb, and put his hand to his mouth; and his eyes brightened. 28Then one of the soldiers said, "Your father strictly charged the troops with an oath, saying, 'Cursed be anyone who eats food this day.' And so the troops are faint." 29Then Jonathan said, "My father has troubled the land; see how my eyes have brightened because I tasted a little of this honey. 30How much better if today the troops had eaten freely of the spoil taken from their enemies; for now the slaughter among the Philistines has not been great."

31 After they had struck down the Philistines that day from Michmash to Aijalon, the troops were very faint; 32so the troops flew upon the spoil, and took sheep and oxen and calves, and slaughtered them on the ground; and the troops ate them with the blood. 33Then it was reported to Saul, "Look, the troops are sinning against the LORD by eating with the blood." And he said, "You have dealt treacherously; roll a large stone before me here."[c] 34Saul said, "Disperse yourselves among the troops, and say to them, 'Let all bring their oxen or their sheep, and slaughter them here, and eat; and do not sin against the LORD by eating with the blood.' " So all of the troops brought their oxen with them that night, and slaughtered them there. 35And Saul built an altar to the LORD; it was the first altar that he built to the LORD.

Jonathan in Danger of Death

36 Then Saul said, "Let us go down after the Philistines by night and despoil them until the morning light; let us not leave one of them." They said, "Do whatever seems good to you." But the priest said, "Let us draw near to God here." 37So Saul inquired of God, "Shall I go down after the Philistines? Will you give them into the hand of Israel?" But he did not answer him that day. 38Saul said, "Come here, all you leaders of the people; and let us find out how this sin has arisen today. 39For as the LORD lives who saves Israel, even if it is in my son Jonathan, he shall surely die!" But there was no one among all the people who answered him. 40He said to all Israel, "You shall be on one side, and I and my son Jonathan will be on the other side." The people said to Saul, "Do what seems good to you." 41Then Saul said, "O LORD God of Israel, why have you not answered your servant today? If this guilt is in me or in my son Jonathan, O LORD God of Israel, give Urim; but if this guilt is in your people Israel,[d] give Thummim." And Jonathan and Saul were indicated by the lot, but the people were cleared. 42Then Saul said, "Cast the lot between me and my son Jonathan." And Jonathan was taken.

43 Then Saul said to Jonathan, "Tell me what you have done." Jonathan told him, "I tasted a little honey with the tip of the staff that was in my hand; here I am, I will die." 44Saul said, "God do so to me and more also; you shall surely die, Jonathan!" 45Then the people said to Saul, "Shall Jonathan die, who has accomplished this great victory in Israel? Far from it! As the LORD lives, not one hair of his head shall fall to the ground; for he has worked with God today." So the people ransomed Jonathan, and he did not die. 46Then Saul withdrew from pursuing the Philistines; and the Philistines went to their own place.

Saul's Continuing Wars

47 When Saul had taken the kingship over Israel, he fought against all his enemies on every side—against Moab, against the Ammonites, against Edom, against the kings of Zobah, and against the Philistines; wherever he turned he routed them. 48He did valiantly, and struck down the Amalekites, and rescued Israel out of the hands of those who plundered them.

49 Now the sons of Saul were Jonathan, Ishvi, and Malchishua; and the names of his two daughters were these: the name of the firstborn was Merab, and the name of the younger, Michal. 50The name of Saul's wife was Ahinoam daughter of Ahimaaz. And the name of the commander of his army was Abner son of Ner, Saul's uncle; 51Kish was the father of Saul, and Ner the father of Abner was the son of Abiel.

52 There was hard fighting against the Philistines all the days of Saul; and when Saul saw any strong or valiant warrior, he took him into his service.

---

a Gk: Heb *The Israelites were distressed that day*   b Heb *land*
c Gk: Heb *me this day*   d Vg Compare Gk: Heb 41*Saul said to the* LORD, *the God of Israel*

Saul Defeats the Amalekites but Spares Their King

15 Samuel said to Saul, "The LORD sent me to anoint you king over his people Israel; now therefore listen to the words of the LORD. ²Thus says the LORD of hosts, 'I will punish the Amalekites for what they did in opposing the Israelites when they came up out of Egypt. ³Now go and attack Amalek, and utterly destroy all that they have; do not spare them, but kill both man and woman, child and infant, ox and sheep, camel and donkey.'"

4 So Saul summoned the people, and numbered them in Telaim, two hundred thousand foot soldiers, and ten thousand soldiers of Judah. ⁵Saul came to the city of the Amalekites and lay in wait in the valley. ⁶Saul said to the Kenites, "Go! Leave! Withdraw from among the Amalekites, or I will destroy you with them; for you showed kindness to all the people of Israel when they came up out of Egypt." So the Kenites withdrew from the Amalekites. ⁷Saul defeated the Amalekites, from Havilah as far as Shur, which is east of Egypt. ⁸He took King Agag of the Amalekites alive, but utterly destroyed all the people with the edge of the sword. ⁹Saul and the people spared Agag, and the best of the sheep and of the cattle and of the fatlings, and the lambs, and all that was valuable, and would not utterly destroy them; all that was despised and worthless they utterly destroyed.

Saul Rejected as King

10 The word of the LORD came to Samuel: ¹¹"I regret that I made Saul king, for he has turned back from following me, and has not carried out my commands." Samuel was angry; and he cried out to the LORD all night. ¹²Samuel rose early in the morning to meet Saul, and Samuel was told, "Saul went to Carmel, where he set up a monument for himself, and on returning he passed on down to Gilgal." ¹³When Samuel came to Saul, Saul said to him, "May you be blessed by the LORD; I have carried out the command of the LORD." ¹⁴But Samuel said, "What then is this bleating of sheep in my ears, and the lowing of cattle that I hear?" ¹⁵Saul said, "They have brought them from the Amalekites; for the people spared the best of the sheep and the cattle, to sacrifice to the LORD your God; but the rest we have utterly destroyed." ¹⁶Then Samuel said to Saul, "Stop! I will tell you what the LORD said to me last night." He replied, "Speak."

17 Samuel said, "Though you are little in your own eyes, are you not the head of the tribes of

Live It!

Power and Corruption

"**P**ower corrupts." We have often heard that phrase. And in 1 Samuel 15:22–23, we have a vivid example. King Saul once again has decided to take matters in his own hands and goes against the word of the Lord. He seems to assume that his role as king exempts him from obedience to God. But Samuel reminds Saul that he has assumed way too much. No king, no president, no prime minister is above the law, especially when that law comes from God.

● In what ways have you served in a leadership role? How have you been tempted to abuse your privileges?

▶ 1 Sam 15:22–23

Israel? The LORD anointed you king over Israel. ¹⁸And the LORD sent you on a mission, and said, 'Go, utterly destroy the sinners, the Amalekites, and fight against them until they are consumed.' ¹⁹Why then did you not obey the voice of the LORD? Why did you swoop down on the spoil, and do what was evil in the sight of the LORD?" ²⁰Saul said to Samuel, "I have obeyed the voice of the LORD, I have gone on the mission on which the LORD sent me, I have brought Agag the king of Amalek, and I have utterly destroyed the Amalekites. ²¹But from the spoil the people took sheep and cattle, the best of the things devoted to destruction, to sacrifice to the LORD your God in Gilgal." ²²And Samuel said,

"Has the LORD as great delight in burnt offerings and sacrifices,
　　as in obedience to the voice of the LORD?
Surely, to obey is better than sacrifice,
　　and to heed than the fat of rams.
²³ For rebellion is no less a sin than divination,
　　and stubbornness is like iniquity and idolatry.
Because you have rejected the word of the LORD,
　　he has also rejected you from being king."

24 Saul said to Samuel, "I have sinned; for I have transgressed the commandment of the LORD and your words, because I feared the people and obeyed their voice. ²⁵Now therefore, I pray, pardon my sin, and return with me, so that I may

worship the Lord." 26Samuel said to Saul, "I will not return with you; for you have rejected the word of the Lord, and the Lord has rejected you from being king over Israel." 27As Samuel turned to go away, Saul caught hold of the hem of his robe, and it tore. 28And Samuel said to him, "The Lord has torn the kingdom of Israel from you this very day, and has given it to a neighbor of yours, who is better than you. 29Moreover the Glory of Israel will not recant*a* or change his mind; for he is not a mortal, that he should change his mind." 30Then Saul*b* said, "I have sinned; yet honor me now before the elders of my people and before Israel, and return with me, so that I may worship the Lord your God." 31So Samuel turned back after Saul; and Saul worshiped the Lord.

32 Then Samuel said, "Bring Agag king of the Amalekites here to me." And Agag came to him haltingly.*c* Agag said, "Surely this is the bitterness of death."*d* 33But Samuel said,

"As your sword has made women childless,
   so your mother shall be childless among
      women."

And Samuel hewed Agag in pieces before the Lord in Gilgal.

34 Then Samuel went to Ramah; and Saul went up to his house in Gibeah of Saul. 35Samuel did not see Saul again until the day of his death, but Samuel grieved over Saul. And the Lord was sorry that he had made Saul king over Israel.

David Anointed as King

16 The Lord said to Samuel, "How long will you grieve over Saul? I have rejected him from being king over Israel. Fill your horn with oil and set out; I will send you to Jesse the Bethlehemite, for I have provided for myself a king among his sons." 2Samuel said, "How can I go? If Saul hears of it, he will kill me." And the Lord said, "Take a heifer with you, and say, 'I have come to sacrifice to the Lord.' 3Invite Jesse to the sacrifice, and I will show you what you shall do; and you shall anoint for me the one whom I name to you." 4Samuel did what the Lord commanded, and came to Bethlehem. The elders of the city came to meet him trembling, and said, "Do you come peaceably?" 5He said, "Peaceably; I have come to sacrifice to the Lord; sanctify yourselves and come with me to the sacrifice." And he sanctified Jesse and his sons and invited them to the sacrifice.

6 When they came, he looked on Eliab and thought, "Surely the Lord's anointed is now before the Lord."*e* 7But the Lord said to Samuel, "Do not look on his appearance or on the height of his stature, because I have rejected him; for the Lord does not see as mortals see; they look on the outward appearance, but the Lord looks on the heart." 8Then Jesse called Abinadab, and made him pass before Samuel. He said, "Neither has the Lord chosen this one." 9Then Jesse made Shammah pass by. And he said, "Neither has the Lord chosen this one." 10Jesse made seven of his sons pass before Samuel, and Samuel said to Jesse, "The Lord has not chosen any of these." 11Samuel said to Jesse, "Are all your sons here?" And he said, "There remains yet the youngest, but he is keeping the sheep." And Samuel said to Jesse, "Send and bring him; for we will not sit down until he comes here." 12He sent and brought him in. Now he was ruddy, and had beautiful eyes, and was handsome. The Lord said, "Rise and anoint him; for this is the one." 13Then Samuel took the horn of oil, and anointed him in the presence of his brothers; and the spirit of the Lord came mightily upon David from that day forward. Samuel then set out and went to Ramah.

David Plays the Lyre for Saul

14 Now the spirit of the Lord departed from Saul, and an evil spirit from the Lord tormented him. 15And Saul's servants said to him, "See now, an evil spirit from God is tormenting you. 16Let our lord now command the servants who attend you to look for someone who is skillful in playing the lyre; and when the evil spirit from God is upon you, he will play it, and you will feel better." 17So Saul said to his servants, "Provide for me someone who can play well, and bring him to me." 18One of the young men answered, "I have seen a son of Jesse the Bethlehemite who is skillful in playing, a man of valor, a warrior, prudent in speech, and a man of good presence; and the Lord is with him." 19So Saul sent messengers to Jesse, and said, "Send me your son David who is with the sheep." 20Jesse took a donkey loaded with bread, a skin of wine, and

> **The Lord does not see as mortals see; they look on the outward appearance, but the Lord looks on the heart.**
>
> [1 Sam 16:7]

---

a Q Ms Gk: MT *deceive*   *b* Heb *he*   *c* Cn Compare Gk: Meaning of Heb uncertain   *d* Q Ms Gk: MT *Surely the bitterness of death is past*   *e* Heb *him*

a kid, and sent them by his son David to Saul. ²¹And David came to Saul, and entered his service. Saul loved him greatly, and he became his armor-bearer. ²²Saul sent to Jesse, saying, "Let David remain in my service, for he has found favor in my sight." ²³And whenever the evil spirit from God came upon Saul, David took the lyre and played it with his hand, and Saul would be relieved and feel better, and the evil spirit would depart from him.

David and Goliath

17 Now the Philistines gathered their armies for battle; they were gathered at Socoh, which belongs to Judah, and encamped between Socoh and Azekah, in Ephes-dammim. ²Saul and the Israelites gathered and encamped in the valley of Elah, and formed ranks against the Philistines. ³The Philistines stood on the mountain on the one side, and Israel stood on the mountain on the other side, with a valley between them. ⁴And there came out from the camp of the Philistines a champion named Goliath, of Gath, whose height was six*ᵃ* cubits and a span. ⁵He had a helmet of bronze on his head, and he

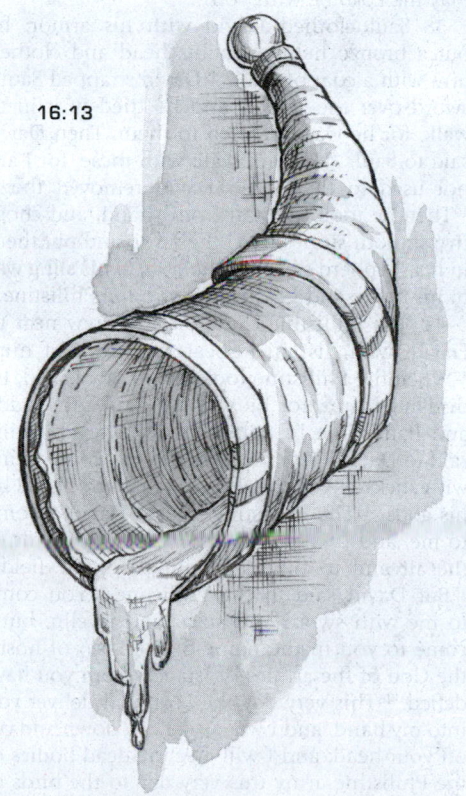

16:13

was armed with a coat of mail; the weight of the coat was five thousand shekels of bronze. ⁶He had greaves of bronze on his legs and a javelin of bronze slung between his shoulders. ⁷The shaft of his spear was like a weaver's beam, and his spear's head weighed six hundred shekels of iron; and his shield-bearer went before him. ⁸He stood and shouted to the ranks of Israel, "Why have you come out to draw up for battle? Am I not a Philistine, and are you not servants of Saul? Choose a man for yourselves, and let him come down to me. ⁹If he is able to fight with me and kill me, then we will be your servants; but if I prevail against him and kill him, then you shall be our servants and serve us." ¹⁰And the Philistine said, "Today I defy the ranks of Israel! Give me a man, that we may fight together." ¹¹When Saul and all Israel heard these words of the Philistine, they were dismayed and greatly afraid.

12 Now David was the son of an Ephrathite of Bethlehem in Judah, named Jesse, who had eight sons. In the days of Saul the man was already old and advanced in years.*ᵇ* ¹³The three eldest sons of Jesse had followed Saul to the battle; the names of his three sons who went to the battle were Eliab the firstborn, and next to him Abinadab, and the third Shammah. ¹⁴David was the youngest; the three eldest followed Saul, ¹⁵but David went back and forth from Saul to feed his father's sheep at Bethlehem. ¹⁶For forty days the Philistine came forward and took his stand, morning and evening.

17 Jesse said to his son David, "Take for your brothers an ephah of this parched grain and these ten loaves, and carry them quickly to the camp to your brothers; ¹⁸also take these ten cheeses to the commander of their thousand. See how your brothers fare, and bring some token from them."

19 Now Saul, and they, and all the men of Israel, were in the valley of Elah, fighting with the Philistines. ²⁰David rose early in the morning, left the sheep with a keeper, took the provisions, and went as Jesse had commanded him. He came to the encampment as the army was going forth to the battle line, shouting the war cry. ²¹Israel and the Philistines drew up for battle, army against army. ²²David left the things in charge of the keeper of the baggage, ran to the ranks, and went and greeted his brothers. ²³As he talked with them, the champion, the Philistine of Gath, Goliath by name, came up out of the ranks of the Philistines, and spoke the same words as before. And David heard him.

ᵃ MT: Q Ms Gk *four* *ᵇ* Gk Syr: Heb *among men*

Live It!

Taking On Goliath

David makes it look so easy. A slingshot, a stone, a skillful aim, and it's all over. Goliath is dead, and the Israelites win the day. It is a story that gives hope to anyone who has ever been bullied or harassed.

A David lives in each of us, and plenty of Goliaths are out there ready to defeat us. The Goliaths we encounter can include peer pressure, an addiction, an abusive situation, or simply self-doubt. We may feel overpowered by these Goliaths, sure that they are too big for us to handle. But they are not! Those of us who believe in God, as David did, know that we are not alone. As followers of Jesus, we rely not on violence but on love and the support of the Christian community to defeat the Goliaths in our lives. We can make David's story our own.

● Identify a Goliath in your life right now, and journal about it. What stepping-stone can you take in defeating it?

▶ 1 Samuel, chapter 17

24 All the Israelites, when they saw the man, fled from him and were very much afraid. 25The Israelites said, "Have you seen this man who has come up? Surely he has come up to defy Israel. The king will greatly enrich the man who kills him, and will give him his daughter and make his family free in Israel." 26David said to the men who stood by him, "What shall be done for the man who kills this Philistine, and takes away the reproach from Israel? For who is this uncircumcised Philistine that he should defy the armies of the living God?" 27The people answered him in the same way, "So shall it be done for the man who kills him."

28 His eldest brother Eliab heard him talking to the men; and Eliab's anger was kindled against David. He said, "Why have you come down? With whom have you left those few sheep in the wilderness? I know your presumption and the evil of your heart; for you have come down

just to see the battle." 29David said, "What have I done now? It was only a question." 30He turned away from him toward another and spoke in the same way; and the people answered him again as before.

31 When the words that David spoke were heard, they repeated them before Saul; and he sent for him. 32David said to Saul, "Let no one's heart fail because of him; your servant will go and fight with this Philistine." 33Saul said to David, "You are not able to go against this Philistine to fight with him; for you are just a boy, and he has been a warrior from his youth." 34But David said to Saul, "Your servant used to keep sheep for his father; and whenever a lion or a bear came, and took a lamb from the flock, 35I went after it and struck it down, rescuing the lamb from its mouth; and if it turned against me, I would catch it by the jaw, strike it down, and kill it. 36Your servant has killed both lions and bears; and this uncircumcised Philistine shall be like one of them, since he has defied the armies of the living God." 37David said, "The LORD, who saved me from the paw of the lion and from the paw of the bear, will save me from the hand of this Philistine." So Saul said to David, "Go, and may the LORD be with you!"

38 Saul clothed David with his armor; he put a bronze helmet on his head and clothed him with a coat of mail. 39David strapped Saul's sword over the armor, and he tried in vain to walk, for he was not used to them. Then David said to Saul, "I cannot walk with these; for I am not used to them." So David removed them. 40Then he took his staff in his hand, and chose five smooth stones from the wadi, and put them in his shepherd's bag, in the pouch; his sling was in his hand, and he drew near to the Philistine.

41 The Philistine came on and drew near to David, with his shield-bearer in front of him. 42When the Philistine looked and saw David, he disdained him, for he was only a youth, ruddy and handsome in appearance. 43The Philistine said to David, "Am I a dog, that you come to me with sticks?" And the Philistine cursed David by his gods. 44The Philistine said to David, "Come to me, and I will give your flesh to the birds of the air and to the wild animals of the field." 45But David said to the Philistine, "You come to me with sword and spear and javelin; but I come to you in the name of the LORD of hosts, the God of the armies of Israel, whom you have defied. 46This very day the LORD will deliver you into my hand, and I will strike you down and cut off your head; and I will give the dead bodies of the Philistine army this very day to the birds of

the air and to the wild animals of the earth, so that all the earth may know that there is a God in Israel, [47]and that all this assembly may know that the LORD does not save by sword and spear; for the battle is the LORD's and he will give you into our hand."

48 When the Philistine drew nearer to meet David, David ran quickly toward the battle line to meet the Philistine. [49]David put his hand in his bag, took out a stone, slung it, and struck the Philistine on his forehead; the stone sank into his forehead, and he fell face down on the ground.

50 So David prevailed over the Philistine with a sling and a stone, striking down the Philistine and killing him; there was no sword in David's hand. [51]Then David ran and stood over the Philistine; he grasped his sword, drew it out of its sheath, and killed him; then he cut off his head with it.

When the Philistines saw that their champion was dead, they fled. [52]The troops of Israel and Judah rose up with a shout and pursued the Philistines as far as Gath[a] and the gates of Ekron, so that the wounded Philistines fell on the way from Shaaraim as far as Gath and Ekron. [53]The Israelites came back from chasing the Philistines, and they plundered their camp. [54]David took the head of the Philistine and brought it to Jerusalem; but he put his armor in his tent.

55 When Saul saw David go out against the Philistine, he said to Abner, the commander of the army, "Abner, whose son is this young man?" Abner said, "As your soul lives, O king, I do not know." [56]The king said, "Inquire whose son the stripling is." [57]On David's return from killing the Philistine, Abner took him and brought him before Saul, with the head of the Philistine in his hand. [58]Saul said to him, "Whose son are you, young man?" And David answered, "I am the son of your servant Jesse the Bethlehemite."

Jonathan's Covenant with David

18 When David[b] had finished speaking to Saul, the soul of Jonathan was bound to the soul of David, and Jonathan loved him as his own soul. [2]Saul took him that day and would not let him return to his father's house. [3]Then Jonathan made a covenant with David, because he loved him as his own soul. [4]Jonathan stripped himself of the robe that he was wearing, and gave it to David, and his armor, and even his sword and his bow and his belt. [5]David went out and was successful wherever Saul sent him; as a result, Saul set him over the army. And all the people, even the servants of Saul, approved.

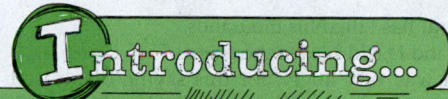

Introducing...

David

Who cannot love David? This shepherd-turned-king is one of the great tragic heroes of the Old Testament. David, whose name means "beloved," was the successor to Saul and the second king (1000–961 BC) of the new nation formed out of the twelve Tribes of Israel. The youngest son of Jesse of the tribe of Judah, David was a member of Saul's court as a young man. Later, when Saul disappointed God, Samuel the prophet anointed David as Saul's successor. After Saul was killed, David established the neutral city of Jerusalem as his capital (see map 4, "The Kingdom Years"). He moved the ark of the Lord there, making this city the new religious center of Israel. Jerusalem is also known as the City of David.

David was a successful warrior, a capable king, and a gifted poet, having written some of the Psalms himself. He was also capable of great sin. His affair with Bathsheba seemed to lead to a string of violence and betrayal affecting his whole family. One of his sons, Absalom, even inspired a revolt against David. But through it all, David was passionately in love with God. God recognized this and promised David that someone from his house would sit upon the throne in Israel.

When Israel was destroyed and its kings taken prisoners, the people developed a hope that another anointed one, a messiah from the house of David, would rise up and lead Israel in God's ways once again. It is this hope for the Davidic messiah that is fulfilled by Jesus in the New Testament.

6 As they were coming home, when David returned from killing the Philistine, the women came out of all the towns of Israel, singing and dancing, to meet King Saul, with tambourines, with songs of joy, and with musical instruments.[c] [7]And the women sang to one another as they made merry,

---

a Gk Syr: Heb Gai   b Heb he   c Or triangles, or three-stringed instruments

"Saul has killed his thousands,
  and David his ten thousands."

8Saul was very angry, for this saying displeased him. He said, "They have ascribed to David ten thousands, and to me they have ascribed thousands; what more can he have but the kingdom?" 9So Saul eyed David from that day on.

Saul Tries to Kill David

10 The next day an evil spirit from God rushed upon Saul, and he raved within his house, while David was playing the lyre, as he did day by day. Saul had his spear in his hand; 11and Saul threw the spear, for he thought, "I will pin David to the wall." But David eluded him twice.

12 Saul was afraid of David, because the LORD was with him but had departed from Saul. 13So Saul removed him from his presence, and made him a commander of a thousand; and David marched out and came in, leading the army. 14David had success in all his undertakings; for the LORD was with him. 15When Saul saw that he had great success, he stood in awe of him. 16But all Israel and Judah loved David; for it was he who marched out and came in leading them.

David Marries Michal

17 Then Saul said to David, "Here is my elder daughter Merab; I will give her to you as a wife; only be valiant for me and fight the LORD's battles." For Saul thought, "I will not raise a hand against him; let the Philistines deal with him." 18David said to Saul, "Who am I and who are my kinsfolk, my father's family in Israel, that I should be son-in-law to the king?" 19But at the time when Saul's daughter Merab should have been given to David, she was given to Adriel the Meholathite as a wife.

20 Now Saul's daughter Michal loved David. Saul was told, and the thing pleased him. 21Saul thought, "Let me give her to him that she may be a snare for him and that the hand of the Philistines may be against him." Therefore Saul said to David a second time,a "You shall now be my son-in-law." 22Saul commanded his servants, "Speak to David in private and say, 'See, the king is delighted with you, and all his servants love you; now then, become the king's son-in-law.' " 23So Saul's servants reported these words to David in private. And David said, "Does it seem to you a little thing to become the king's son-in-law, seeing that I am a poor man and of no repute?" 24The servants of Saul told him, "This is what David said." 25Then Saul said, "Thus shall you say to David, 'The king desires no marriage present except a hundred foreskins of the Philistines,

that he may be avenged on the king's enemies.' " Now Saul planned to make David fall by the hand of the Philistines. 26When his servants told David these words, David was well pleased to be the king's son-in-law. Before the time had expired, 27David rose and went, along with his men, and killed one hundredb of the Philistines; and David brought their foreskins, which were given in full number to the king, that he might become the king's son-in-law. Saul gave him his daughter Michal as a wife. 28But when Saul realized that the LORD was with David, and that Saul's daughter Michal loved him, 29Saul was still more afraid of David. So Saul was David's enemy from that time forward.

30 Then the commanders of the Philistines came out to battle; and as often as they came out, David had more success than all the servants of Saul, so that his fame became very great.

Jonathan Intercedes for David

19 Saul spoke with his son Jonathan and with all his servants about killing David. But Saul's son Jonathan took great delight in David. 2Jonathan told David, "My father Saul is trying to kill you; therefore be on guard tomorrow morning; stay in a secret place and hide yourself. 3I will go out and stand beside my father in the field where you are, and I will speak to my father about you; if I learn anything I will tell you." 4Jonathan spoke well of David to his father Saul, saying to him, "The king should not sin against his servant David, because he has not sinned against you, and because his deeds have been of good service to you; 5for he took his life in his hand when he attacked the Philistine, and the LORD brought about a great victory for all Israel. You saw it, and rejoiced; why then will you sin against an innocent person by killing David without cause?" 6Saul heeded the voice of Jonathan; Saul swore, "As the LORD lives, he shall not be put to death." 7So Jonathan called David and related all these things to him. Jonathan then brought David to Saul, and he was in his presence as before.

Michal Helps David Escape from Saul

8 Again there was war, and David went out to fight the Philistines. He launched a heavy attack on them, so that they fled before him. 9Then an evil spirit from the LORD came upon Saul, as he sat in his house with his spear in his hand, while David was playing music. 10Saul sought to pin David to the wall with the spear; but he eluded

---

a Heb by two   b Gk Compare 2 Sam 3.14: Heb two hundred

Saul, so that he struck the spear into the wall. David fled and escaped that night.

11 Saul sent messengers to David's house to keep watch over him, planning to kill him in the morning. David's wife Michal told him, "If you do not save your life tonight, tomorrow you will be killed." [12]So Michal let David down through the window; he fled away and escaped. [13]Michal took an idol[a] and laid it on the bed; she put a net[b] of goats' hair on its head, and covered it with the clothes. [14]When Saul sent messengers to take David, she said, "He is sick." [15]Then Saul sent the messengers to see David for themselves. He said, "Bring him up to me in the bed, that I may kill him." [16]When the messengers came in, the idol[c] was in the bed, with the covering[b] of goats' hair on its head. [17]Saul said to Michal, "Why have you deceived me like this, and let my enemy go, so that he has escaped?" Michal answered Saul, "He said to me, 'Let me go; why should I kill you?'"

David Joins Samuel in Ramah

18 Now David fled and escaped; he came to Samuel at Ramah, and told him all that Saul had done to him. He and Samuel went and settled at Naioth. [19]Saul was told, "David is at Naioth in Ramah." [20]Then Saul sent messengers to take David. When they saw the company of the prophets in a frenzy, with Samuel standing in charge of[b] them, the spirit of God came upon the messengers of Saul, and they also fell into a prophetic frenzy. [21]When Saul was told, he sent other messengers, and they also fell into a frenzy. Saul sent messengers again the third time, and they also fell into a frenzy. [22]Then he himself went to Ramah. He came to the great well that is in Secu;[d] he asked, "Where are Samuel and David?" And someone said, "They are at Naioth in Ramah." [23]He went there, toward Naioth in Ramah; and the spirit of God came upon him. As he was going, he fell into a prophetic frenzy, until he came to Naioth in Ramah. [24]He too stripped off his clothes, and he too fell into a frenzy before Samuel. He lay naked all that day and all that night. Therefore it is said, "Is Saul also among the prophets?"

The Friendship of David and Jonathan

20 David fled from Naioth in Ramah. He came before Jonathan and said, "What have I done? What is my guilt? And what is my sin against your father that he is trying to take my life?" [2]He said to him, "Far from it! You shall not die. My father does nothing either great or small without disclosing it to me; and why should my

Friends Forever

David and Jonathan have one of the most touching stories of friendship in the Bible. In 1 Samuel 18:1–4, Jonathan makes a special covenant with David. In chapter 20, their deep love leads them to risk their lives for each other. Saul, the king and Jonathan's father, is acting like a madman. He is insanely jealous of David and wants him dead.

Yet, Jonathan and David bring God into their relationship. This gives them the wisdom to see what is right and do it. When they have to part (see 20:41–42), they cry and embrace and remind each other of their vows.

Not many teenagers deal with situations as drastic as this, but tension with parents over your choice of friends can be common. Parents may not understand why you like a person they dislike. It can leave you with a sense of being stuck in the middle.

Your response should be like David and Jonathan's, keeping God part of all your relationships. Each friendship then becomes a living prayer, and God will guide you through conflicts and help you make good decisions.

▶ **1 Samuel, chapter 20**

father hide this from me? Never!" [3]But David also swore, "Your father knows well that you like me; and he thinks, 'Do not let Jonathan know this, or he will be grieved.' But truly, as the LORD lives and as you yourself live, there is but a step between me and death." [4]Then Jonathan said to David, "Whatever you say, I will do for you." [5]David said to Jonathan, "Tomorrow is the new moon, and I should not fail to sit with the king at the meal; but let me go, so that I may hide in the field until the third evening. [6]If your father misses me at all, then say, 'David earnestly asked leave of me to run to Bethlehem his city; for there is a yearly sacrifice there for all the family.' [7]If he says, 'Good!' it will be well with your servant; but if he is angry,

---

a Heb *took the teraphim*   b Meaning of Heb uncertain
c Heb *the teraphim*   d Gk reads *to the well of the threshing floor on the bare height*

then know that evil has been determined by him. [8]Therefore deal kindly with your servant, for you have brought your servant into a sacred covenant[a] with you. But if there is guilt in me, kill me yourself; why should you bring me to your father?" [9]Jonathan said, "Far be it from you! If I knew that it was decided by my father that evil should come upon you, would I not tell you?" [10]Then David said to Jonathan, "Who will tell me if your father answers you harshly?" [11]Jonathan replied to David, "Come, let us go out into the field." So they both went out into the field.

12 Jonathan said to David, "By the LORD, the God of Israel! When I have sounded out my father, about this time tomorrow, or on the third day, if he is well disposed toward David, shall I not then send and disclose it to you? [13]But if my father intends to do you harm, the LORD do so to Jonathan, and more also, if I do not disclose it to you, and send you away, so that you may go in safety. May the LORD be with you, as he has been with my father. [14]If I am still alive, show me the faithful love of the LORD; but if I die,[b] [15]never cut off your faithful love from my house, even if the LORD were to cut off every one of the enemies of David from the face of the earth." [16]Thus Jonathan made a covenant with the house of David, saying, "May the LORD seek out the enemies of David." [17]Jonathan made David swear again by his love for him; for he loved him as he loved his own life.

18 Jonathan said to him, "Tomorrow is the new moon; you will be missed, because your place will be empty. [19]On the day after tomorrow, you shall go a long way down; go to the place where you hid yourself earlier, and remain beside the stone there.[b] [20]I will shoot three arrows to the side of it, as though I shot at a mark. [21]Then I will send the boy, saying, 'Go, find the arrows.' If I say to the boy, 'Look, the arrows are on this side of you, collect them,' then you are to come, for, as the LORD lives, it is safe for you and there is no danger. [22]But if I say to the young man, 'Look, the arrows are beyond you,' then go; for the LORD has sent you away. [23]As for the matter about which you and I have spoken, the LORD is witness[c] between you and me forever."

24 So David hid himself in the field. When the new moon came, the king sat at the feast to eat. [25]The king sat upon his seat, as at other times, upon the seat by the wall. Jonathan stood, while Abner sat by Saul's side; but David's place was empty.

26 Saul did not say anything that day; for he thought, "Something has befallen him; he is not clean, surely he is not clean." [27]But on the second day, the day after the new moon, David's place was empty. And Saul said to his son Jonathan, "Why has the son of Jesse not come to the feast, either yesterday or today?" [28]Jonathan answered Saul, "David earnestly asked leave of me to go to Bethlehem; [29]he said, 'Let me go; for our family is holding a sacrifice in the city, and my brother has commanded me to be there. So now, if I have found favor in your sight, let me get away, and see my brothers.' For this reason he has not come to the king's table."

30 Then Saul's anger was kindled against Jonathan. He said to him, "You son of a perverse, rebellious woman! Do I not know that you have chosen the son of Jesse to your own shame, and to the shame of your mother's nakedness? [31]For as long as the son of Jesse lives upon the earth, neither you nor your kingdom shall be established. Now send and bring him to me, for he shall surely die." [32]Then Jonathan answered his father Saul, "Why should he be put to death? What has he done?" [33]But Saul threw his spear at him to strike him; so Jonathan knew that it was the decision of his father to put David to death. [34]Jonathan rose from the table in fierce anger and ate no food on the second day of the month, for he was grieved for David, and because his father had disgraced him.

35 In the morning Jonathan went out into the field to the appointment with David, and with him was a little boy. [36]He said to the boy, "Run and find the arrows that I shoot." As the boy ran, he shot an arrow beyond him. [37]When the boy came to the place where Jonathan's arrow had fallen, Jonathan called after the boy and said, "Is the arrow not beyond you?" [38]Jonathan called after the boy, "Hurry, be quick, do not linger." So Jonathan's boy gathered up the arrows and came to his master. [39]But the boy knew nothing; only Jonathan and David knew the arrangement. [40]Jonathan gave his weapons to the boy and said to him, "Go and carry them to the city." [41]As soon as the boy had gone, David rose from beside the stone heap[d] and prostrated himself with his face to the ground. He bowed three times, and they kissed each other, and wept with each other; David wept the more.[e] [42]Then Jonathan said to David, "Go in peace, since both of us have sworn in the name of the LORD, saying, 'The LORD shall be between me and you, and between my descendants and your descendants, forever.' " He got up and left; and Jonathan went into the city.[f]

---

a Heb a covenant of the LORD   b Meaning of Heb uncertain
c Gk: Heb lacks witness   d Gk: Heb from beside the south
e Vg: Meaning of Heb uncertain   f This sentence is 21.1 in Heb

David and the Holy Bread

21 [a] David came to Nob to the priest Ahimelech. Ahimelech came trembling to meet David, and said to him, "Why are you alone, and no one with you?" 2 David said to the priest Ahimelech, "The king has charged me with a matter, and said to me, 'No one must know anything of the matter about which I send you, and with which I have charged you.' I have made an appointment[b] with the young men for such and such a place. 3 Now then, what have you at hand? Give me five loaves of bread, or whatever is here." 4 The priest answered David, "I have no ordinary bread at hand, only holy bread—provided that the young men have kept themselves from women." 5 David answered the priest, "Indeed women have been kept from us as always when I go on an expedition; the vessels of the young men are holy even when it is a common journey; how much more today will their vessels be holy?" 6 So the priest gave him the holy bread; for there was no bread there except the bread of the Presence, which is removed from before the Lord, to be replaced by hot bread on the day it is taken away.

7 Now a certain man of the servants of Saul was there that day, detained before the Lord; his name was Doeg the Edomite, the chief of Saul's shepherds.

8 David said to Ahimelech, "Is there no spear or sword here with you? I did not bring my sword or my weapons with me, because the king's business required haste." 9 The priest said, "The sword of Goliath the Philistine, whom you killed in the valley of Elah, is here wrapped in a cloth behind the ephod; if you will take that, take it, for there is none here except that one." David said, "There is none like it; give it to me."

David Flees to Gath

10 David rose and fled that day from Saul; he went to King Achish of Gath. 11 The servants of Achish said to him, "Is this not David the king of the land? Did they not sing to one another of him in dances,

'Saul has killed his thousands,
    and David his ten thousands'?"

12 David took these words to heart and was very much afraid of King Achish of Gath. 13 So he changed his behavior before them; he pretended to be mad when in their presence.[c] He scratched marks on the doors of the gate, and let his spittle run down his beard. 14 Achish said to his servants, "Look, you see the man is mad; why then have you brought him to me? 15 Do I lack madmen, that you have brought this fellow to play the madman in my presence? Shall this fellow come into my house?"

David and His Followers at Adullam

22 David left there and escaped to the cave of Adullam; when his brothers and all his father's house heard of it, they went down there to him. 2 Everyone who was in distress, and everyone who was in debt, and everyone who was discontented gathered to him; and he became captain over them. Those who were with him numbered about four hundred.

3 David went from there to Mizpeh of Moab. He said to the king of Moab, "Please let my father and mother come[d] to you, until I know what God will do for me." 4 He left them with the king of Moab, and they stayed with him all the time that David was in the stronghold. 5 Then the prophet Gad said to David, "Do not remain in the stronghold; leave, and go into the land of Judah." So David left, and went into the forest of Hereth.

Saul Slaughters the Priests at Nob

6 Saul heard that David and those who were with him had been located. Saul was sitting at Gibeah, under the tamarisk tree on the height, with his spear in his hand, and all his servants were standing around him. 7 Saul said to his servants who stood around him, "Hear now, you Benjaminites; will the son of Jesse give every one of you fields and vineyards, will he make you all commanders of thousands and commanders of hundreds? 8 Is that why all of you have conspired against me? No one discloses to me when my son makes a league with the son of Jesse, none of you is sorry for me or discloses to me that my son has stirred up my servant against me, to lie in wait, as he is doing today." 9 Doeg the Edomite, who was in charge of Saul's servants, answered, "I saw the son of Jesse coming to Nob, to Ahimelech son of Ahitub; 10 he inquired of the Lord for him, gave him provisions, and gave him the sword of Goliath the Philistine."

11 The king sent for the priest Ahimelech son of Ahitub and for all his father's house, the priests who were at Nob; and all of them came to the king. 12 Saul said, "Listen now, son of Ahitub." He answered, "Here I am, my lord." 13 Saul said to him, "Why have you conspired against me, you and the son of Jesse, by giving him bread and a sword, and by inquiring of God

---

a Ch 21.2 in Heb   b Q Ms Vg Compare Gk: Meaning of MT uncertain   c Heb in their hands   d Syr Vg: Heb come out

1
S
A
M

for him, so that he has risen against me, to lie in wait, as he is doing today?"

14 Then Ahimelech answered the king, "Who among all your servants is so faithful as David? He is the king's son-in-law, and is quick[a] to do your bidding, and is honored in your house. 15Is today the first time that I have inquired of God for him? By no means! Do not let the king impute anything to his servant or to any member of my father's house; for your servant has known nothing of all this, much or little." 16The king said, "You shall surely die, Ahimelech, you and all your father's house." 17The king said to the guard who stood around him, "Turn and kill the priests of the Lord, because their hand also is with David; they knew that he fled, and did not disclose it to me." But the servants of the king would not raise their hand to attack the priests of the Lord. 18Then the king said to Doeg, "You, Doeg, turn and attack the priests." Doeg the Edomite turned and attacked the priests; on that day he killed eighty-five who wore the linen ephod. 19Nob, the city of the priests, he put to the sword; men and women, children and infants, oxen, donkeys, and sheep, he put to the sword.

20 But one of the sons of Ahimelech son of Ahitub, named Abiathar, escaped and fled after David. 21Abiathar told David that Saul had killed the priests of the Lord. 22David said to Abiathar, "I knew on that day, when Doeg the Edomite was there, that he would surely tell Saul. I am responsible[b] for the lives of all your father's house. 23Stay with me, and do not be afraid; for the one who seeks my life seeks your life; you will be safe with me."

David Saves the City of Keilah

23 Now they told David, "The Philistines are fighting against Keilah, and are robbing the threshing floors." 2David inquired of the Lord, "Shall I go and attack these Philistines?" The Lord said to David, "Go and attack the Philistines and save Keilah." 3But David's men said to him, "Look, we are afraid here in Judah; how much more then if we go to Keilah against the armies of the Philistines?" 4Then David inquired of the Lord again. The Lord answered him, "Yes, go down to Keilah; for I will give the Philistines into your hand." 5So David and his men went to Keilah, fought with the Philistines, brought away their livestock, and dealt them a heavy defeat. Thus David rescued the inhabitants of Keilah.

6 When Abiathar son of Ahimelech fled to David at Keilah, he came down with an ephod in his hand. 7Now it was told Saul that David had come to Keilah. And Saul said, "God has given[c] him into

my hand; for he has shut himself in by entering a town that has gates and bars." 8Saul summoned all the people to war, to go down to Keilah, to besiege David and his men. 9When David learned that Saul was plotting evil against him, he said to the priest Abiathar, "Bring the ephod here." 10David said, "O Lord, the God of Israel, your servant has heard that Saul seeks to come to Keilah, to destroy the city on my account. 11And now, will[d] Saul come down as your servant has heard? O Lord, the God of Israel, I beseech you, tell your servant." The Lord said, "He will come down." 12Then David said, "Will the men of Keilah surrender me and my men into the hand of Saul?" The Lord said, "They will surrender you." 13Then David and his men, who were about six hundred, set out and left Keilah; they wandered wherever they could go. When Saul was told that David had escaped from Keilah, he gave up the expedition. 14David remained in the strongholds in the wilderness, in the hill country of the Wilderness of Ziph. Saul sought him every day, but the Lord[e] did not give him into his hand.

David Eludes Saul in the Wilderness

15 David was in the Wilderness of Ziph at Horesh when he learned that[f] Saul had come out to seek his life. 16Saul's son Jonathan set out and came to David at Horesh; there he strengthened his hand through the Lord.[g] 17He said to him, "Do not be afraid; for the hand of my father Saul shall not find you; you shall be king over Israel, and I shall be second to you; my father Saul also knows that this is so." 18Then the two of them made a covenant before the Lord; David remained at Horesh, and Jonathan went home.

19 Then some Ziphites went up to Saul at Gibeah and said, "David is hiding among us in the strongholds of Horesh, on the hill of Hachilah, which is south of Jeshimon. 20Now, O king, whenever you wish to come down, do so; and our part will be to surrender him into the king's hand." 21Saul said, "May you be blessed by the Lord for showing me compassion! 22Go and make sure once more; find out exactly where he is, and who has seen him there; for I am told that he is very cunning. 23Look around and learn all the hiding places where he lurks, and come back to me with sure information. Then I will go with you; and if he is in the land, I will search him out among all the thousands of Judah." 24So they set out and went to Ziph ahead of Saul.

---

a Heb and turns aside   b Gk Vg: Meaning of Heb uncertain   c Gk Tg: Heb made a stranger of   d Q Ms Compare Gk: MT Will the men of Keilah surrender me into his hand? Will   e Q Ms Gk: MT God   f Or saw that   g Compare Q Ms Gk: MT God

David and his men were in the wilderness of Maon, in the Arabah to the south of Jeshimon. 25Saul and his men went to search for him. When David was told, he went down to the rock and stayed in the wilderness of Maon. When Saul heard that, he pursued David into the wilderness of Maon. 26Saul went on one side of the mountain, and David and his men on the other side of the mountain. David was hurrying to get away from Saul, while Saul and his men were closing in on David and his men to capture them. 27Then a messenger came to Saul, saying, "Hurry and come; for the Philistines have made a raid on the land." 28So Saul stopped pursuing David, and went against the Philistines; therefore that place was called the Rock of Escape.*a* 29*b* David then went up from there, and lived in the strongholds of En-gedi.

David Spares Saul's Life

24 When Saul returned from following the Philistines, he was told, "David is in the wilderness of En-gedi." 2Then Saul took three thousand chosen men out of all Israel, and went to look for David and his men in the direction of the Rocks of the Wild Goats. 3He came to the sheepfolds beside the road, where there was a cave; and Saul went in to relieve himself.*c* Now David and his men were sitting in the innermost parts of the cave. 4The men of David said to him, "Here is the day of which the LORD said to you, 'I will give your enemy into your hand, and you shall do to him as it seems good to you.' " Then David went and stealthily cut off a corner of Saul's cloak. 5Afterward David was stricken to the heart because he had cut off a corner of Saul's cloak. 6He said to his men, "The LORD forbid that I should do this thing to my lord, the LORD's anointed, to raise my hand against him; for he is the LORD's anointed." 7So David scolded his men severely and did not permit them to attack Saul. Then Saul got up and left the cave, and went on his way.

8 Afterwards David also rose up and went out of the cave and called after Saul, "My lord the king!" When Saul looked behind him, David bowed with his face to the ground, and did obeisance. 9David said to Saul, "Why do you listen to the words of those who say, 'David seeks to do you harm'? 10This very day your eyes have seen how the LORD gave you into my hand in the cave; and some urged me to kill you, but I spared*d* you. I said, 'I will not raise my hand against my lord; for he is the LORD's anointed.' 11See, my father, see the corner of your cloak in my hand; for by the fact that I cut off the corner of your cloak,

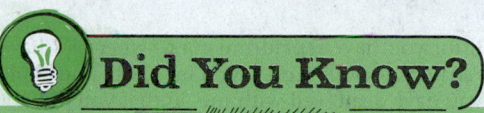

Did You Know?

The Lord's Anointed

Throughout human history, oil has been used as medicine, perfume, and a symbol of blessing. The Israelite kings and prophets were anointed with oil to symbolize the powerful spirit of God present to them as they fulfilled their important role. Often it was olive oil mixed with a small amount of perfume. Oil plays a symbolic role throughout the Bible and has historically played an important role in the life of the Church. In many Old Testament texts, oil was reserved for priests, kings, and people of high importance. Today, we use oil in most of the sacraments of the Church because we are the "priestly people."

The Hebrew word *mashiah*, translated in 1 Samuel 24:6 as "anointed [one]," is the root of the English word *messiah*. Often applied to kings in the Old Testament, this title was attached in the second century BC to the one "like David" who was expected to come (see Dan 9:25). *Mashiah* translated in Greek is *christos*, which became the title given to Jesus by his followers: Jesus, the Christ; Jesus, the anointed one; Jesus, the Messiah.

and did not kill you, you may know for certain that there is no wrong or treason in my hands. I have not sinned against you, though you are hunting me to take my life. 12May the LORD judge between me and you! May the LORD avenge me on you; but my hand shall not be against you. 13As the ancient proverb says, 'Out of the wicked comes forth wickedness'; but my hand shall not be against you. 14Against whom has the king of Israel come out? Whom do you pursue? A dead dog? A single flea? 15May the LORD therefore be judge, and give sentence between me and you. May he see to it, and plead my cause, and vindicate me against you."

16 When David had finished speaking these words to Saul, Saul said, "Is this your voice, my son David?" Saul lifted up his voice and wept. 17He said to David, "You are more righteous than

---

a Or Rock of Division; meaning of Heb uncertain   *b* Ch 24.1 in Heb   *c* Heb *to cover his feet*   *d* Gk Syr Tg Vg: Heb *it* (my eye) spared

I; for you have repaid me good, whereas I have repaid you evil. [18]Today you have explained how you have dealt well with me, in that you did not kill me when the LORD put me into your hands. [19]For who has ever found an enemy, and sent the enemy safely away? So may the LORD reward you with good for what you have done to me this day. [20]Now I know that you shall surely be king, and that the kingdom of Israel shall be established in your hand. [21]Swear to me therefore by the LORD that you will not cut off my descendants after me, and that you will not wipe out my name from my father's house." [22]So David swore this to Saul. Then Saul went home; but David and his men went up to the stronghold.

Death of Samuel

25 Now Samuel died; and all Israel assembled and mourned for him. They buried him at his home in Ramah.

Then David got up and went down to the wilderness of Paran.

David and the Wife of Nabal

2 There was a man in Maon, whose property was in Carmel. The man was very rich; he had three thousand sheep and a thousand goats. He was shearing his sheep in Carmel. [3]Now the name of the man was Nabal, and the name of his wife Abigail. The woman was clever and beautiful, but the man was surly and mean; he was a Calebite. [4]David heard in the wilderness that Nabal was shearing his sheep. [5]So David sent ten young men; and David said to the young men, "Go up to Carmel, and go to Nabal, and greet him in my name. [6]Thus you shall salute him: 'Peace be to you, and peace be to your house, and peace be to all that you have. [7]I hear that you have shearers; now your shepherds have been with us, and we did them no harm, and they missed nothing, all the time they were in Carmel. [8]Ask your young men, and they will tell you. Therefore let my young men find favor in your sight; for we have come on a feast day. Please give whatever you have at hand to your servants and to your son David.' "

9 When David's young men came, they said all this to Nabal in the name of David; and then they waited. [10]But Nabal answered David's servants, "Who is David? Who is the son of Jesse? There are many servants today who are breaking away from their masters. [11]Shall I take my bread and my water and the meat that I have butchered for my shearers, and give it to men who come from I do not know where?" [12]So David's young men turned away, and came back and told him

all this. [13]David said to his men, "Every man strap on his sword!" And every one of them strapped on his sword; David also strapped on his sword; and about four hundred men went up after David, while two hundred remained with the baggage.

14 But one of the young men told Abigail, Nabal's wife, "David sent messengers out of the wilderness to salute our master; and he shouted insults at them. [15]Yet the men were very good to us, and we suffered no harm, and we never missed anything when we were in the fields, as long as we were with them; [16]they were a wall to us both by night and by day, all the while we were with them keeping the sheep. [17]Now therefore know this and consider what you should do; for evil has been decided against our master and against all his house; he is so ill-natured that no one can speak to him."

18 Then Abigail hurried and took two hundred loaves, two skins of wine, five sheep ready dressed, five measures of parched grain, one hundred clusters of raisins, and two hundred cakes of figs. She loaded them on donkeys [19]and said to her young men, "Go on ahead of me; I am coming after you." But she did not tell her husband Nabal. [20]As she rode on the donkey and came down under cover of the mountain, David and his men came down toward her; and she met them. [21]Now David had said, "Surely it was in vain that I protected all that this fellow has in the wilderness, so that nothing was missed of all that belonged to him; but he has returned me evil for good. [22]God do so to David[a] and more also, if by morning I leave so much as one male of all who belong to him."

23 When Abigail saw David, she hurried and alighted from the donkey, and fell before David on her face, bowing to the ground. [24]She fell at his feet and said, "Upon me alone, my lord, be the guilt; please let your servant speak in your ears, and hear the words of your servant. [25]My lord, do not take seriously this ill-natured fellow, Nabal; for as his name is, so is he; Nabal[b] is his name, and folly is with him; but I, your servant, did not see the young men of my lord, whom you sent.

26 "Now then, my lord, as the LORD lives, and as you yourself live, since the LORD has restrained you from bloodguilt and from taking vengeance with your own hand, now let your enemies and those who seek to do evil to my lord be like Nabal. [27]And now let this present that your servant has brought to my lord be given to the young

---

a Gk Compare Syr: Heb *the enemies of David*   b That is *Fool*

men who follow my lord. ²⁸Please forgive the trespass of your servant; for the LORD will certainly make my lord a sure house, because my lord is fighting the battles of the LORD; and evil shall not be found in you so long as you live. ²⁹If anyone should rise up to pursue you and to seek your life, the life of my lord shall be bound in the bundle of the living under the care of the LORD your God; but the lives of your enemies he shall sling out as from the hollow of a sling. ³⁰When the LORD has done to my lord according to all the good that he has spoken concerning you, and has appointed you prince over Israel, ³¹my lord shall have no cause of grief, or pangs of conscience, for having shed blood without cause or for having saved himself. And when the LORD has dealt well with my lord, then remember your servant."

32 David said to Abigail, "Blessed be the LORD, the God of Israel, who sent you to meet me today! ³³Blessed be your good sense, and blessed be you, who have kept me today from bloodguilt and from avenging myself by my own hand! ³⁴For as surely as the LORD the God of Israel lives, who has restrained me from hurting you, unless you had hurried and come to meet me, truly by morning there would not have been left to Nabal so much as one male." ³⁵Then David received from her hand what she had brought him; he said to her, "Go up to your house in peace; see, I have heeded your voice, and I have granted your petition."

36 Abigail came to Nabal; he was holding a feast in his house, like the feast of a king. Nabal's heart was merry within him, for he was very drunk; so she told him nothing at all until the morning light. ³⁷In the morning, when the wine had gone out of Nabal, his wife told him these things, and his heart died within him; he became like a stone. ³⁸About ten days later the LORD struck Nabal, and he died.

39 When David heard that Nabal was dead, he said, "Blessed be the LORD who has judged the case of Nabal's insult to me, and has kept back his servant from evil; the LORD has returned the evildoing of Nabal upon his own head." Then David sent and wooed Abigail to make her his wife. ⁴⁰When David's servants came to Abigail at Carmel, they said to her, "David has sent us to you to take you to him as his wife." ⁴¹She rose and bowed down, with her face to the ground, and said, "Your servant is a slave to wash the feet of the servants of my lord." ⁴²Abigail got up hurriedly and rode away on a donkey; her five maids attended her. She went after the messengers of David and became his wife.

43 David also married Ahinoam of Jezreel; both of them became his wives. ⁴⁴Saul had given his daughter Michal, David's wife, to Palti son of Laish, who was from Gallim.

David Spares Saul's Life a Second Time

26 Then the Ziphites came to Saul at Gibeah, saying, "David is in hiding on the hill of Hachilah, which is opposite Jeshimon."[a] ²So Saul rose and went down to the Wilderness of Ziph, with three thousand chosen men of Israel, to seek David in the Wilderness of Ziph. ³Saul encamped on the hill of Hachilah, which is opposite Jeshimon beside the road. But David remained in the wilderness. When he learned that Saul had come after him into the wilderness, ⁴David sent out spies, and learned that Saul had indeed arrived. ⁵Then David set out and came to the place where Saul had encamped; and David saw the place where Saul lay, with Abner son of Ner, the commander of his army. Saul was lying within the encampment, while the army was encamped around him.

6 Then David said to Ahimelech the Hittite, and to Joab's brother Abishai son of Zeruiah, "Who will go down with me into the camp to Saul?" Abishai said, "I will go down with you." ⁷So David and Abishai went to the army by night; there Saul lay sleeping within the encampment, with his spear stuck in the ground at his head; and Abner and the army lay around him. ⁸Abishai said to David, "God has given your enemy into your hand today; now therefore let me pin him to the ground with one stroke of the spear; I will not strike him twice." ⁹But David said to Abishai, "Do not destroy him; for who can raise his hand against the LORD's anointed, and be guiltless?" ¹⁰David said, "As the LORD lives, the LORD will strike him down; or his day will come to die; or he will go down into battle and perish. ¹¹The LORD forbid that I should raise my hand against the LORD's anointed; but now take the spear that is at his head, and the water jar, and let us go." ¹²So David took the spear that was at Saul's head and the water jar, and they went away. No one saw it, or knew it, nor did anyone awake; for they were all asleep, because a deep sleep from the LORD had fallen upon them.

13 Then David went over to the other side, and stood on top of a hill far away, with a great distance between them. ¹⁴David called to the army and to Abner son of Ner, saying, "Abner! Will you not answer?" Then Abner replied, "Who are you that calls to the king?" ¹⁵David said to

---

a Or *opposite the wasteland*

Abner, "Are you not a man? Who is like you in Israel? Why then have you not kept watch over your lord the king? For one of the people came in to destroy your lord the king. [16]This thing that you have done is not good. As the LORD lives, you deserve to die, because you have not kept watch over your lord, the LORD's anointed. See now, where is the king's spear, or the water jar that was at his head?"

17 Saul recognized David's voice, and said, "Is this your voice, my son David?" David said, "It is my voice, my lord, O king." [18]And he added, "Why does my lord pursue his servant? For what have I done? What guilt is on my hands? [19]Now therefore let my lord the king hear the words of his servant. If it is the LORD who has stirred you up against me, may he accept an offering; but if it is mortals, may they be cursed before the LORD, for they have driven me out today from my share in the heritage of the LORD, saying, 'Go, serve other gods.' [20]Now therefore, do not let my blood fall to the ground, away from the presence of the LORD; for the king of Israel has come out to seek a single flea, like one who hunts a partridge in the mountains."

21 Then Saul said, "I have done wrong; come back, my son David, for I will never harm you again, because my life was precious in your sight today; I have been a fool, and have made a great mistake." [22]David replied, "Here is the spear, O king! Let one of the young men come over and get it. [23]The LORD rewards everyone for his righteousness and his faithfulness; for the LORD gave you into my hand today, but I would not raise my hand against the LORD's anointed. [24]As your life was precious today in my sight, so may my life be precious in the sight of the LORD, and may he rescue me from all tribulation." [25]Then Saul said to David, "Blessed be you, my son David! You will do many things and will succeed in them." So David went his way, and Saul returned to his place.

David Serves King Achish of Gath

27 David said in his heart, "I shall now perish one day by the hand of Saul; there is nothing better for me than to escape to the land of the Philistines; then Saul will despair of seeking me any longer within the borders of Israel, and I shall escape out of his hand." [2]So David set out and went over, he and the six hundred men who were with him, to King Achish son of Maoch of Gath. [3]David stayed with Achish at Gath, he and his troops, every man with his household, and David with his two wives, Ahinoam of Jezreel, and Abigail of Carmel, Nabal's widow.

[4]When Saul was told that David had fled to Gath, he no longer sought for him.

5 Then David said to Achish, "If I have found favor in your sight, let a place be given me in one of the country towns, so that I may live there; for why should your servant live in the royal city with you?" [6]So that day Achish gave him Ziklag; therefore Ziklag has belonged to the kings of Judah to this day. [7]The length of time that David lived in the country of the Philistines was one year and four months.

8 Now David and his men went up and made raids on the Geshurites, the Girzites, and the Amalekites; for these were the landed settlements from Telam[a] on the way to Shur and on to the land of Egypt. [9]David struck the land, leaving neither man nor woman alive, but took away the sheep, the oxen, the donkeys, the camels, and the clothing, and came back to Achish. [10]When Achish asked, "Against whom[b] have you made a raid today?" David would say, "Against the Negeb of Judah," or "Against the Negeb of the Jerahmeelites," or, "Against the Negeb of the Kenites." [11]David left neither man nor woman alive to be brought back to Gath, thinking, "They might tell about us, and say, 'David has done so and so.' " Such was his practice all the time he lived in the country of the Philistines. [12]Achish trusted David, thinking, "He has made himself utterly abhorrent to his people Israel; therefore he shall always be my servant."

28 In those days the Philistines gathered their forces for war, to fight against Israel. Achish said to David, "You know, of course, that you and your men are to go out with me in the army." [2]David said to Achish, "Very well, then you shall know what your servant can do." Achish said to David, "Very well, I will make you my bodyguard for life."

Saul Consults a Medium

3 Now Samuel had died, and all Israel had mourned for him and buried him in Ramah, his own city. Saul had expelled the mediums and the wizards from the land. [4]The Philistines assembled, and came and encamped at Shunem. Saul gathered all Israel, and they encamped at Gilboa. [5]When Saul saw the army of the Philistines, he was afraid, and his heart trembled greatly. [6]When Saul inquired of the LORD, the LORD did not answer him, not by dreams, or by Urim, or by prophets. [7]Then Saul said to his servants, "Seek out for me a woman who is a medium, so that I

---

a Compare Gk 15.4: Heb *from of old*   b Q Ms Gk Vg: MT lacks *whom* may go to her and inquire of her." His servants said to him, "There is a medium at Endor."

8 So Saul disguised himself and put on other clothes and went there, he and two men with him. They came to the woman by night. And he said, "Consult a spirit for me, and bring up for me the one whom I name to you." ⁹The woman said to him, "Surely you know what Saul has done, how he has cut off the mediums and the wizards from the land. Why then are you laying a snare for my life to bring about my death?" ¹⁰But Saul swore to her by the LORD, "As the LORD lives, no punishment shall come upon you for this thing." ¹¹Then the woman said, "Whom shall I bring up for you?" He answered, "Bring up Samuel for me." ¹²When the woman saw Samuel, she cried out with a loud voice; and the woman said to Saul, "Why have you deceived me? You are Saul!" ¹³The king said to her, "Have no fear; what do you see?" The woman said to Saul, "I see a divine being*a* coming up out of the ground." ¹⁴He said to her, "What is his appearance?" She said, "An old man is coming up; he is wrapped in a robe." So Saul knew that it was Samuel, and he bowed with his face to the ground, and did obeisance.

15 Then Samuel said to Saul, "Why have you disturbed me by bringing me up?" Saul answered, "I am in great distress, for the Philistines are warring against me, and God has turned away from me and answers me no more, either by prophets or by dreams; so I have summoned you to tell me what I should do." ¹⁶Samuel said, "Why then do you ask me, since the LORD has turned from you and become your enemy? ¹⁷The LORD has done to you just as he spoke by me; for the LORD has torn the kingdom out of your hand, and given it to your neighbor, David. ¹⁸Because you did not obey the voice of the LORD, and did not carry out his fierce wrath against Amalek, therefore the LORD has done this thing to you today. ¹⁹Moreover the LORD will give Israel along with you into the hands of the Philistines; and tomorrow you and your sons shall be with me; the LORD will also give the army of Israel into the hands of the Philistines."

20 Immediately Saul fell full length on the ground, filled with fear because of the words of Samuel; and there was no strength in him, for he had eaten nothing all day and all night. ²¹The woman came to Saul, and when she saw that he was terrified, she said to him, "Your servant has listened to you; I have taken my life in my hand, and have listened to what you have said to me. ²²Now therefore, you also listen to your servant; let me set a morsel of bread before you.

Eat, that you may have strength when you go on your way." ²³He refused, and said, "I will not eat." But his servants, together with the woman, urged him; and he listened to their words. So he got up from the ground and sat on the bed. ²⁴Now the woman had a fatted calf in the house. She quickly slaughtered it, and she took flour, kneaded it, and baked unleavened cakes. ²⁵She put them before Saul and his servants, and they ate. Then they rose and went away that night.

The Philistines Reject David

29 Now the Philistines gathered all their forces at Aphek, while the Israelites were encamped by the fountain that is in Jezreel. ²As the lords of the Philistines were passing on by hundreds and by thousands, and David and his men were passing on in the rear with Achish, ³the commanders of the Philistines said, "What are these Hebrews doing here?" Achish said to the commanders of the Philistines, "Is this not David, the servant of King Saul of Israel, who has been with me now for days and years? Since he deserted to me I have found no fault in him to this day." ⁴But the commanders of the Philistines were angry with him; and the commanders of the Philistines said to him, "Send the man back, so that he may return to the place that you have assigned to him; he shall not go down with us to battle, or else he may become an adversary to us in the battle. For how could this fellow reconcile himself to his lord? Would it not be with the heads of the men here? ⁵Is this not David, of whom they sing to one another in dances,

'Saul has killed his thousands,
  and David his ten thousands'?"

6 Then Achish called David and said to him, "As the LORD lives, you have been honest, and to me it seems right that you should march out and in with me in the campaign; for I have found nothing wrong in you from the day of your coming to me until today. Nevertheless the lords do not approve of you. ⁷So go back now; and go peaceably; do nothing to displease the lords of the Philistines." ⁸David said to Achish, "But what have I done? What have you found in your servant from the day I entered your service until now, that I should not go and fight against the enemies of my lord the king?" ⁹Achish replied to David, "I know that you are as blameless in my sight as an angel of God; nevertheless, the commanders of the Philistines have said, 'He shall not go up with us to the battle.' ¹⁰Now then rise early in the morning, you and the servants

---

a Or *a god*; or *gods*

of your lord who came with you, and go to the place that I appointed for you. As for the evil report, do not take it to heart, for you have done well before me.[a] Start early in the morning, and leave as soon as you have light." [11]So David set out with his men early in the morning, to return to the land of the Philistines. But the Philistines went up to Jezreel.

David Avenges the Destruction of Ziklag

30 Now when David and his men came to Ziklag on the third day, the Amalekites had made a raid on the Negeb and on Ziklag. They had attacked Ziklag, burned it down, [2]and taken captive the women and all[b] who were in it, both small and great; they killed none of them, but carried them off, and went their way. [3]When David and his men came to the city, they found it burned down, and their wives and sons and daughters taken captive. [4]Then David and the people who were with him raised their voices and wept, until they had no more strength to weep. [5]David's two wives also had been taken captive, Ahinoam of Jezreel, and Abigail the widow of Nabal of Carmel. [6]David was in great danger; for the people spoke of stoning him, because all the people were bitter in spirit for their sons and daughters. But David strengthened himself in the LORD his God.

[7] David said to the priest Abiathar son of Ahimelech, "Bring me the ephod." So Abiathar brought the ephod to David. [8]David inquired of the LORD, "Shall I pursue this band? Shall I overtake them?" He answered him, "Pursue; for you shall surely overtake and shall surely rescue." [9]So David set out, he and the six hundred men who were with him. They came to the Wadi Besor, where those stayed who were left behind. [10]But David went on with the pursuit, he and four hundred men; two hundred stayed behind, too exhausted to cross the Wadi Besor.

[11] In the open country they found an Egyptian, and brought him to David. They gave him bread and he ate; they gave him water to drink; [12]they also gave him a piece of fig cake and two clusters of raisins. When he had eaten, his spirit revived; for he had not eaten bread or drunk water for three days and three nights. [13]Then David said to him, "To whom do you belong? Where are you from?" He said, "I am a young man of Egypt, servant to an Amalekite. My master left me behind because I fell sick three days ago. [14]We had made a raid on the Negeb of the Cherethites and on that which belongs to Judah and on the Negeb of Caleb; and we burned Ziklag down." [15]David said to him, "Will you take me down to this raiding party?" He said, "Swear to me by God that you will not kill me, or hand me over to my master, and I will take you down to them."

[16] When he had taken him down, they were spread out all over the ground, eating and drinking and dancing, because of the great amount of spoil they had taken from the land of the Philistines and from the land of Judah. [17]David attacked them from twilight until the evening of the next day. Not one of them escaped, except four hundred young men, who mounted camels and fled. [18]David recovered all that the Amalekites had taken; and David rescued his two wives. [19]Nothing was missing, whether small or great, sons or daughters, spoil or anything that had been taken; David brought back everything. [20]David also captured all the flocks and herds, which were driven ahead of the other cattle; people said, "This is David's spoil."

[21] Then David came to the two hundred men who had been too exhausted to follow David, and who had been left at the Wadi Besor. They went out to meet David and to meet the people who were with him. When David drew near to the people he saluted them. [22]Then all the corrupt and worthless fellows among the men who had gone with David said, "Because they did not go with us, we will not give them any of the spoil that we have recovered, except that each man may take his wife and children, and leave." [23]But David said, "You shall not do so, my brothers, with what the LORD has given us; he has preserved us and handed over to us the raiding party that attacked us. [24]Who would listen to you in this matter? For the share of the one who goes down into the battle shall be the same as the share of the one who stays by the baggage; they shall share alike." [25]From that day forward he made it a statute and an ordinance for Israel; it continues to the present day.

[26] When David came to Ziklag, he sent part of the spoil to his friends, the elders of Judah, saying, "Here is a present for you from the spoil of the enemies of the LORD"; [27]it was for those in Bethel, in Ramoth of the Negeb, in Jattir, [28]in Aroer, in Siphmoth, in Eshtemoa, [29]in Racal, in the towns of the Jerahmeelites, in the towns of the Kenites, [30]in Hormah, in Bor-ashan, in Athach, [31]in Hebron, all the places where David and his men had roamed.

1 SAM

---

a Gk: Heb lacks and go to the place . . . done well before me
b Gk: Heb lacks and all

The Death of Saul and His Sons

31 Now the Philistines fought against Israel; and the men of Israel fled before the Philistines, and many fell[a] on Mount Gilboa. ²The Philistines overtook Saul and his sons; and the Philistines killed Jonathan and Abinadab and Malchishua, the sons of Saul. ³The battle pressed hard upon Saul; the archers found him, and he was badly wounded by them. ⁴Then Saul said to his armor-bearer, "Draw your sword and thrust me through with it, so that these uncircumcised may not come and thrust me through, and make sport of me." But his armor-bearer was unwilling; for he was terrified. So Saul took his own sword and fell upon it. ⁵When his armor-bearer saw that Saul was dead, he also fell upon his sword and died with him. ⁶So Saul and his three sons and his armor-bearer and all his men died together on the same day. ⁷When the men of Israel who were on the other side of the valley and those beyond the Jordan saw that the men of Israel had fled and that Saul and his sons were dead, they forsook their towns and fled; and the Philistines came and occupied them.

8 The next day, when the Philistines came to strip the dead, they found Saul and his three sons fallen on Mount Gilboa. ⁹They cut off his head, stripped off his armor, and sent messengers throughout the land of the Philistines to carry the good news to the houses of their idols and to the people. ¹⁰They put his armor in the temple of Astarte;[b] and they fastened his body to the wall of Beth-shan. ¹¹But when the inhabitants of Jabesh-gilead heard what the Philistines had done to Saul, ¹²all the valiant men set out, traveled all night long, and took the body of Saul and the bodies of his sons from the wall of Beth-shan. They came to Jabesh and burned them there. ¹³Then they took their bones and buried them under the tamarisk tree in Jabesh, and fasted seven days.

---

a Heb *and they fell slain*   *b* Heb plural

Live It!

Suicide Is Not an Answer

In 1 Samuel 31:4, Saul commits suicide out of fear of what his enemies would do to him. His death leaves a gap for the Israelites, and David, Saul's enemy, deeply mourns his death in 2 Samuel, chapter 1.

A popular newspaper advice columnist printed a letter from someone who was writing to share a thought on suicide. He had decided that his life was not worth living anymore and planned to kill himself. The moment before he was about to do it, he thought about who would find him, and then he stopped. He realized that he couldn't put someone through the pain and suffering of finding him dead from suicide. Because he thought of another, he no longer looked at his life as hopeless.

No life is worthless! No pain is invincible! No matter how overwhelming your struggles and challenges seem, there are people who can help you, and people who could not bear to lose you. Seek God for help, seek others for help—suicide is never a solution!

For more on suicide, see "Judas's Suicide," near Matthew 27:3–10.

▶ 1 Sam 31:1–6

"**P**olitician Guilty of Taking Bribes!" "Military Officer Charged with Sexual Misconduct!" "Pro Athlete Convicted of Using Drugs!" Sometimes it seems as if the news is filled with one scandal after another. "What's happening in the world today?" we may ask in despair. "Are there no honest, decent people left?" After reading Second Samuel, you will realize that scandals involving the rich and powerful are nothing new. But more important, God's will rises above human sin and weakness to accomplish good.

In Depth

The main character in Second Samuel is King David, whom we already met in First Samuel. The youngest of Jesse's sons, David is secretly anointed to succeed King Saul; he kills Goliath, plays music in Saul's court, and is befriended by the king's son Jonathan. At the beginning of Second Samuel, when David takes the throne and quickly extends Israel's boundaries in every direction, everything looks hopeful for the nation.

As Second Samuel continues, however, we discover that this hero is far from perfect: he sleeps with Bathsheba, the wife of one of his soldiers, and then tries to deceive the man when Bathsheba reports that she is pregnant. Later, he has the soldier killed and takes Bathsheba as his own. Soon, several tragedies befall his family, and further bad decisions hurt his reign, leaving us with a mixed picture of the second king of Israel. Was David a great saint or a great sinner?

At a Glance

- **Chapter 1.** David mourns Saul's death.
- **Chapters 2–20.** the reign of David
- **Chapters 21–24.** miscellaneous texts, including David's last words

Quick Facts

Period Covered: from 1000 to 961 BC

Inspired Author: same as for First Samuel

Theme: David's rise to power and his fall into sin

Of Note: Samuel does not appear in this book, even though it carries his name.

It was during David's reign that the people's understanding of their covenant relationship with God began to center less on the Exodus experience and more on the ideas of king and kingdom (see 7:1–17). This fact is underlined in a memorable way when David, after completing his own magnificent palace, declares that he will build a house for God. But God does not want a temple; God wishes to maintain a covenantal relationship with the people of Israel through all history: "Your throne shall be established forever" (verse 16).

Although a talented military leader and a powerful ruler, King David shared our broken human nature. The author of Second Samuel reminds us that even the great and the mighty stand in need of God's help and mercy; even they must keep God's Covenant. Because of David's reliance on God, he became a symbol of the ideal king and of the future messiah. David's greatness—and our own—comes from a willing reliance on God.

The Second Book of **Samuel**

2 Samuel

David Mourns for Saul and Jonathan

1 After the death of Saul, when David had returned from defeating the Amalekites, David remained two days in Ziklag. ²On the third day, a man came from Saul's camp, with his clothes torn and dirt on his head. When he came to David, he fell to the ground and did obeisance. ³David said to him, "Where have you come from?" He said to him, "I have escaped from the camp of Israel." ⁴David said to him, "How did things go? Tell me!" He answered, "The army fled from the battle, but also many of the army fell and died; and Saul and his son Jonathan also died." ⁵Then David asked the young man who was reporting to him, "How do you know that Saul and his son Jonathan died?" ⁶The young man reporting to him said, "I happened to be on Mount Gilboa; and there was Saul leaning on his spear, while the chariots and the horsemen drew close to him. ⁷When he looked behind him, he saw me, and called to me. I answered, 'Here sir.' ⁸And he said to me, 'Who are you?' I answered him, 'I am an Amalekite.' ⁹He said to me, 'Come, stand over me and kill me; for convulsions have seized me, and yet my life still lingers.' ¹⁰So I stood over him, and killed him, for I knew that he could not live after he had fallen. I took the crown that was on his head and the armlet that was on his arm, and I have brought them here to my lord."

11 Then David took hold of his clothes and tore them; and all the men who were with him did the same. ¹²They mourned and wept, and fasted until evening for Saul and for his son Jonathan, and for the army of the LORD and for the house of Israel, because they had fallen by the sword. ¹³David said to the young man who had reported to him, "Where do you come from?" He answered, "I am the son of a resident alien, an Amalekite." ¹⁴David said to him, "Were you not afraid to lift your hand to destroy the LORD's anointed?" ¹⁵Then David called one of the young men and said, "Come here and strike him down." So he struck him down and he died. ¹⁶David said to him, "Your blood be on your head; for your own mouth has testified against you, saying, 'I have killed the LORD's anointed.' "

17 David intoned this lamentation over Saul and his son Jonathan. ¹⁸(He ordered that The Song of the Bow[a] be taught to the people of Judah; it is written in the Book of Jashar.) He said:

¹⁹ Your glory, O Israel, lies slain upon your high
    places!
  How the mighty have fallen!
²⁰ Tell it not in Gath,
    proclaim it not in the streets of Ashkelon;
  or the daughters of the Philistines will rejoice,
    the daughters of the uncircumcised will exult.

²¹ You mountains of Gilboa,
    let there be no dew or rain upon you,
    nor bounteous fields![b]
  For there the shield of the mighty was defiled,
    the shield of Saul, anointed with oil no more.

---

a Heb *that The Bow* b Meaning of Heb uncertain

David the Musician

Most of us know that music can be a powerful force. Most of us listen to music every day. It helps us get through hard times. It is also an essential part of most celebrations. What would a wedding be like without music? What would a party be like without music? No doubt each of us has a favorite song or musician we turn to often, especially when we need a lift. And no doubt God works through music to touch our hearts.

David also knew the power of music. His song of mourning for Saul and Jonathan is an emotional tribute to both men, but especially to his close friend, Jonathan. If you are a musician, you know that God also works through you to touch the hearts of others and speak to them. Let David be your inspiration. He played the lyre (harp), sang, and wrote beautiful songs, which we call psalms. He prayed through music. There is a saying that goes, "Those who sing pray twice." David seemed to live that out in his life.

● What are the songs and music that help you to pray and to recall God's presence? If you are a musician, when have you felt God's presence while making music?

▶ **2 Sam 1:17–27**

22 From the blood of the slain,
   from the fat of the mighty,
the bow of Jonathan did not turn back,
   nor the sword of Saul return empty.

23 Saul and Jonathan, beloved and lovely!
   In life and in death they were not divided;
they were swifter than eagles,
   they were stronger than lions.

24 O daughters of Israel, weep over Saul,
   who clothed you with crimson, in luxury,
   who put ornaments of gold on your apparel.

25 How the mighty have fallen
   in the midst of the battle!

Jonathan lies slain upon your high places.
26   I am distressed for you, my brother Jonathan;
greatly beloved were you to me;
      your love to me was wonderful,
      passing the love of women.

27 How the mighty have fallen,
   and the weapons of war perished!

David Anointed King of Judah

2 After this David inquired of the LORD, "Shall I go up into any of the cities of Judah?" The LORD said to him, "Go up." David said, "To which shall I go up?" He said, "To Hebron." ²So David went up there, along with his two wives, Ahinoam of Jezreel, and Abigail the widow of Nabal of Carmel. ³David brought up the men who were with him, every one with his household; and they settled in the towns of Hebron. ⁴Then the people of Judah came, and there they anointed David king over the house of Judah.

When they told David, "It was the people of Jabesh-gilead who buried Saul," ⁵David sent messengers to the people of Jabesh-gilead, and said to them, "May you be blessed by the LORD, because you showed this loyalty to Saul your lord, and buried him! ⁶Now may the LORD show steadfast love and faithfulness to you! And I too will reward you because you have done this thing. ⁷Therefore let your hands be strong, and be valiant; for Saul your lord is dead, and the house of Judah has anointed me king over them."

Ishbaal King of Israel

8 But Abner son of Ner, commander of Saul's army, had taken Ishbaal*a* son of Saul, and brought him over to Mahanaim. ⁹He made him king over Gilead, the Ashurites, Jezreel, Ephraim, Benjamin, and over all Israel. ¹⁰Ishbaal,*a* Saul's son, was forty years old when he began to reign over Israel, and he reigned two years. But the house of Judah followed David. ¹¹The time that David was king in Hebron over the house of Judah was seven years and six months.

The Battle of Gibeon

12 Abner son of Ner, and the servants of Ishbaal*a* son of Saul, went out from Mahanaim to Gibeon. ¹³Joab son of Zeruiah, and the servants of David, went out and met them at the pool of Gibeon. One group sat on one side of the pool, while the other sat on the other side of the pool. ¹⁴Abner said to Joab, "Let the young men come forward and have a contest before us." Joab said,

a Gk Compare 1 Chr 8.33; 9.39: Heb *Ish-bosheth*, "man of shame"

"Let them come forward." [15]So they came forward and were counted as they passed by, twelve for Benjamin and Ishbaal[a] son of Saul, and twelve of the servants of David. [16]Each grasped his opponent by the head, and thrust his sword in his opponent's side; so they fell down together. Therefore that place was called Helkath-hazzurim,[b] which is at Gibeon. [17]The battle was very fierce that day; and Abner and the men of Israel were beaten by the servants of David.

18 The three sons of Zeruiah were there, Joab, Abishai, and Asahel. Now Asahel was as swift of foot as a wild gazelle. [19]Asahel pursued Abner, turning neither to the right nor to the left as he followed him. [20]Then Abner looked back and said, "Is it you, Asahel?" He answered, "Yes, it is." [21]Abner said to him, "Turn to your right or to your left, and seize one of the young men, and take his spoil." But Asahel would not turn away from following him. [22]Abner said again to Asahel, "Turn away from following me; why should I strike you to the ground? How then could I show my face to your brother Joab?" [23]But he refused to turn away. So Abner struck him in the stomach with the butt of his spear, so that the spear came out at his back. He fell there, and died where he lay. And all those who came to the place where Asahel had fallen and died, stood still.

24 But Joab and Abishai pursued Abner. As the sun was going down they came to the hill of Ammah, which lies before Giah on the way to the wilderness of Gibeon. [25]The Benjaminites rallied around Abner and formed a single band; they took their stand on the top of a hill. [26]Then Abner called to Joab, "Is the sword to keep devouring forever? Do you not know that the end will be bitter? How long will it be before you order your people to turn from the pursuit of their kinsmen?" [27]Joab said, "As God lives, if you had not spoken, the people would have continued to pursue their kinsmen, not stopping until morning." [28]Joab sounded the trumpet and all the people stopped; they no longer pursued Israel or engaged in battle any further.

29 Abner and his men traveled all that night through the Arabah; they crossed the Jordan, and, marching the whole forenoon,[c] they came to Mahanaim. [30]Joab returned from the pursuit of Abner; and when he had gathered all the people together, there were missing of David's servants nineteen men besides Asahel. [31]But the servants of David had killed of Benjamin three hundred sixty of Abner's men. [32]They took up Asahel and buried him in the tomb of his father, which was at Bethlehem. Joab and his men marched all night, and the day broke upon them at Hebron.

Abner Defects to David

3 There was a long war between the house of Saul and the house of David; David grew stronger and stronger, while the house of Saul became weaker and weaker.

2 Sons were born to David at Hebron: his firstborn was Amnon, of Ahinoam of Jezreel; [3]his second, Chileab, of Abigail the widow of Nabal of Carmel; the third, Absalom son of Maacah, daughter of King Talmai of Geshur; [4]the fourth, Adonijah son of Haggith; the fifth, Shephatiah son of Abital; [5]and the sixth, Ithream, of David's wife Eglah. These were born to David in Hebron.

6 While there was war between the house of Saul and the house of David, Abner was making himself strong in the house of Saul. [7]Now Saul had a concubine whose name was Rizpah daughter of Aiah. And Ishbaal[d] said to Abner, "Why have you gone in to my father's concubine?" [8]The words of Ishbaal[d] made Abner very angry; he said, "Am I a dog's head for Judah? Today I keep showing loyalty to the house of your father Saul, to his brothers, and to his friends, and have not given you into the hand of David; and yet you charge me now with a crime concerning this woman. [9]So may God do to Abner and so may he add to it! For just what the LORD has sworn to David, that will I accomplish for him, [10]to transfer the kingdom from the house of Saul, and set up the throne of David over Israel and over Judah, from Dan to Beer-sheba." [11]And Ishbaal[d] could not answer Abner another word, because he feared him.

12 Abner sent messengers to David at Hebron,[e] saying, "To whom does the land belong? Make your covenant with me, and I will give you my support to bring all Israel over to you." [13]He said, "Good; I will make a covenant with you. But one thing I require of you: you shall never appear in my presence unless you bring Saul's daughter Michal when you come to see me." [14]Then David sent messengers to Saul's son Ishbaal,[f] saying, "Give me my wife Michal, to whom I became engaged at the price of one hundred foreskins of the Philistines." [15]Ishbaal[f] sent and took her from her husband Paltiel the son of Laish. [16]But her husband went with her, weeping as he walked behind her all the way to Bahurim.

---

a Gk Compare 1 Chr 8.33; 9.39: Heb Ish-bosheth, "man of shame"
b That is Field of Sword-edges   c Meaning of Heb uncertain
d Heb And he   e Gk: Heb where he was   f Heb Ish-bosheth

Then Abner said to him, "Go back home!" So he went back.

17 Abner sent word to the elders of Israel, saying, "For some time past you have been seeking David as king over you. 18Now then bring it about; for the LORD has promised David: Through my servant David I will save my people Israel from the hand of the Philistines, and from all their enemies." 19Abner also spoke directly to the Benjaminites; then Abner went to tell David at Hebron all that Israel and the whole house of Benjamin were ready to do.

20 When Abner came with twenty men to David at Hebron, David made a feast for Abner and the men who were with him. 21Abner said to David, "Let me go and rally all Israel to my lord the king, in order that they may make a covenant with you, and that you may reign over all that your heart desires." So David dismissed Abner, and he went away in peace.

Abner Is Killed by Joab

22 Just then the servants of David arrived with Joab from a raid, bringing much spoil with them. But Abner was not with David at Hebron, for David*a* had dismissed him, and he had gone away in peace. 23When Joab and all the army that was with him came, it was told Joab, "Abner son of Ner came to the king, and he has dismissed him, and he has gone away in peace." 24Then Joab went to the king and said, "What have you done? Abner came to you; why did you dismiss him, so that he got away? 25You know that Abner son of Ner came to deceive you, and to learn your comings and goings and to learn all that you are doing."

26 When Joab came out from David's presence, he sent messengers after Abner, and they brought him back from the cistern of Sirah; but David did not know about it. 27When Abner returned to Hebron, Joab took him aside in the gateway to speak with him privately, and there he stabbed him in the stomach. So he died for shedding*b* the blood of Asahel, Joab's*c* brother. 28Afterward, when David heard of it, he said, "I and my kingdom are forever guiltless before the LORD for the blood of Abner son of Ner. 29May the guilt*d* fall on the head of Joab, and on all his father's house; and may the house of Joab never be without one who has a discharge, or who is leprous,*e* or who holds a spindle, or who falls by the sword, or who lacks food!" 30So Joab and his brother Abishai murdered Abner because he had killed their brother Asahel in the battle at Gibeon.

31 Then David said to Joab and to all the people who were with him, "Tear your clothes, and put on sackcloth, and mourn over Abner." And King David followed the bier. 32They buried Abner at Hebron. The king lifted up his voice and wept at the grave of Abner, and all the people wept. 33The king lamented for Abner, saying,

"Should Abner die as a fool dies?
34 Your hands were not bound,
    your feet were not fettered;
as one falls before the wicked
    you have fallen."

And all the people wept over him again. 35Then all the people came to persuade David to eat something while it was still day; but David swore, saying, "So may God do to me, and more, if I taste bread or anything else before the sun goes down!" 36All the people took notice of it, and it pleased them; just as everything the king did pleased all the people. 37So all the people and all Israel understood that day that the king had no part in the killing of Abner son of Ner. 38And the king said to his servants, "Do you not know that a prince and a great man has fallen this day in Israel? 39Today I am powerless, even though anointed king; these men, the sons of Zeruiah, are too violent for me. The LORD pay back the one who does wickedly in accordance with his wickedness!"

Ishbaal Assassinated

4 When Saul's son Ishbaal*f* heard that Abner had died at Hebron, his courage failed, and all Israel was dismayed. 2Saul's son had two captains of raiding bands; the name of the one was Baanah, and the name of the other Rechab. They were sons of Rimmon a Benjaminite from Beeroth—for Beeroth is considered to belong to Benjamin. 3(Now the people of Beeroth had fled to Gittaim and are there as resident aliens to this day).

4 Saul's son Jonathan had a son who was crippled in his feet. He was five years old when the news about Saul and Jonathan came from Jezreel. His nurse picked him up and fled; and, in her haste to flee, it happened that he fell and became lame. His name was Mephibosheth.*g*

5 Now the sons of Rimmon the Beerothite, Rechab and Baanah, set out, and about the heat of the day they came to the house of Ishbaal,*h* while he was taking his noonday rest. 6They came inside the house as though to take wheat, and they struck him in the stomach; then Rechab and his brother Baanah escaped.*i* 7Now they had

a Heb *he*   *b* Heb lacks *shedding*   *c* Heb *his*   *d* Heb *May it*
e A term for several skin diseases; precise meaning uncertain
f Heb lacks *Ishbaal*   *g* In 1 Chr 8.34 and 9.40, *Merib-baal*
h Heb *Ish-bosheth*   *i* Meaning of Heb of verse 6 uncertain

come into the house while he was lying on his couch in his bedchamber; they attacked him, killed him, and beheaded him. Then they took his head and traveled by way of the Arabah all night long. [8]They brought the head of Ishbaal[a] to David at Hebron and said to the king, "Here is the head of Ishbaal,[a] son of Saul, your enemy, who sought your life; the LORD has avenged my lord the king this day on Saul and on his offspring."

9 David answered Rechab and his brother Baanah, the sons of Rimmon the Beerothite, "As the LORD lives, who has redeemed my life out of every adversity, [10]when the one who told me, 'See, Saul is dead,' thought he was bringing good news, I seized him and killed him at Ziklag—this was the reward I gave him for his news. [11]How much more then, when wicked men have killed a righteous man on his bed in his own house! And now shall I not require his blood at your hand, and destroy you from the earth?" [12]So David commanded the young men, and they killed them; they cut off their hands and feet, and hung their bodies beside the pool at Hebron. But the head of Ishbaal[a] they took and buried in the tomb of Abner at Hebron.

David Anointed King of All Israel

5 Then all the tribes of Israel came to David at Hebron, and said, "Look, we are your bone and flesh. [2]For some time, while Saul was king over us, it was you who led out Israel and brought it in. The LORD said to you: It is you who shall be shepherd of my people Israel, you who shall be ruler over Israel." [3]So all the elders of Israel came to the king at Hebron; and King David made a covenant with them at Hebron before the LORD, and they anointed David king over Israel. [4]David was thirty years old when he began to reign, and he reigned forty years. [5]At Hebron he reigned over Judah seven years and six months; and at Jerusalem he reigned over all Israel and Judah thirty-three years.

Jerusalem Made Capital of the United Kingdom

6 The king and his men marched to Jerusalem against the Jebusites, the inhabitants of the land, who said to David, "You will not come in here, even the blind and the lame will turn you back"—thinking, "David cannot come in here." [7]Nevertheless David took the stronghold of Zion, which is now the city of David. [8]David had said on that day, "Whoever would strike down the Jebusites, let him get up the water shaft to attack the lame and the blind, those whom David hates."[b] Therefore it is said, "The blind and the lame shall

not come into the house." [9]David occupied the stronghold, and named it the city of David. David built the city all around from the Millo inward. [10]And David became greater and greater, for the LORD, the God of hosts, was with him.

11 King Hiram of Tyre sent messengers to David, along with cedar trees, and carpenters and masons who built David a house. [12]David then perceived that the LORD had established him king over Israel, and that he had exalted his kingdom for the sake of his people Israel.

13 In Jerusalem, after he came from Hebron, David took more concubines and wives; and more sons and daughters were born to David. [14]These are the names of those who were born to him in Jerusalem: Shammua, Shobab, Nathan, Solomon, [15]Ibhar, Elishua, Nepheg, Japhia, [16]Elishama, Eliada, and Eliphelet.

Philistine Attack Repulsed

17 When the Philistines heard that David had been anointed king over Israel, all the Philistines went up in search of David; but David heard about it and went down to the stronghold. [18]Now the Philistines had come and spread out in the valley of Rephaim. [19]David inquired of the LORD, "Shall I go up against the Philistines? Will you give them into my hand?" The LORD said to David, "Go up; for I will certainly give the Philistines into your hand." [20]So David came to Baal-perazim, and David defeated them there. He said, "The LORD has burst forth against[c] my enemies before me, like a bursting flood." Therefore that place is called Baal-perazim.[d] [21]The Philistines abandoned their idols there, and David and his men carried them away.

22 Once again the Philistines came up, and were spread out in the valley of Rephaim. [23]When David inquired of the LORD, he said, "You shall not go up; go around to their rear, and come upon them opposite the balsam trees. [24]When you hear the sound of marching in the tops of the balsam trees, then be on the alert; for then the LORD has gone out before you to strike down the army of the Philistines." [25]David did just as the LORD had commanded him; and he struck down the Philistines from Geba all the way to Gezer.

David Brings the Ark to Jerusalem

6 David again gathered all the chosen men of Israel, thirty thousand. [2]David and all the people with him set out and went from Baale-judah,

---

a Heb *Ish-bosheth*   b Another reading is *those who hate David*
c Heb *paraz*   d That is *Lord of Bursting Forth*

2 SAM

The Dance of Life

It's a party! How else could we describe the festivities surrounding the triumphant bringing of the ark of the Lord into Jerusalem? And King David is leading the way, dancing before the Lord "with all his might" (2 Sam 6:14). What a scene that must have been! What a wonderfully uninhibited way for David to express his great joy at escorting the ark into the city he has made his own.

So often we attend religious rituals as mere observers, much like Michal, David's wife, being critical and uninvolved. David shows us the true way to celebrate—with singing and dancing and eating. We need to celebrate together the presence of the Lord in our lives! Here David is our role model. Let us sing the song in our heart and dance to the music God has planted within us.

● How can we do a better job of celebrating the Lord in our lives? Are we observers or participants in the dance of life?

▶ 2 Sam 6:11–19

to bring up from there the ark of God, which is called by the name of the Lord of hosts who is enthroned on the cherubim. ³They carried the ark of God on a new cart, and brought it out of the house of Abinadab, which was on the hill. Uzzah and Ahio,ᵃ the sons of Abinadab, were driving the new cart ⁴with the ark of God;ᵇ and Ahioᵃ went in front of the ark. ⁵David and all the house of Israel were dancing before the Lord with all their might, with songsᶜ and lyres and harps and tambourines and castanets and cymbals.

6 When they came to the threshing floor of Nacon, Uzzah reached out his hand to the ark of God and took hold of it, for the oxen shook it. ⁷The anger of the Lord was kindled against Uzzah; and God struck him there because he reached out his hand to the ark;ᵈ and he died there beside the ark of God. ⁸David was angry because the Lord had burst forth with an outburst upon Uzzah; so that place is called Perez-

uzzah,ᵉ to this day. ⁹David was afraid of the Lord that day; he said, "How can the ark of the Lord come into my care?" ¹⁰So David was unwilling to take the ark of the Lord into his care in the city of David; instead David took it to the house of Obed-edom the Gittite. ¹¹The ark of the Lord remained in the house of Obed-edom the Gittite three months; and the Lord blessed Obed-edom and all his household.

12 It was told King David, "The Lord has blessed the household of Obed-edom and all that belongs to him, because of the ark of God." So David went and brought up the ark of God from the house of Obed-edom to the city of David with rejoicing; ¹³and when those who bore the ark of the Lord had gone six paces, he sacrificed an ox and a fatling. ¹⁴David danced before the Lord with all his might; David was girded with a linen ephod. ¹⁵So David and all the house of Israel brought up the ark of the Lord with shouting, and with the sound of the trumpet.

16 As the ark of the Lord came into the city of David, Michal daughter of Saul looked out of the window, and saw King David leaping and dancing before the Lord; and she despised him in her heart.

17 They brought in the ark of the Lord, and set it in its place, inside the tent that David had pitched for it; and David offered burnt offerings and offerings of well-being before the Lord. ¹⁸When David had finished offering the burnt offerings and the offerings of well-being, he blessed the people in the name of the Lord of hosts, ¹⁹and distributed food among all the people, the whole multitude of Israel, both men and women, to each a cake of bread, a portion of meat,ᶠ and a cake of raisins. Then all the people went back to their homes.

20 David returned to bless his household. But Michal the daughter of Saul came out to meet David, and said, "How the king of Israel honored himself today, uncovering himself today before the eyes of his servants' maids, as any vulgar fellow might shamelessly uncover himself!" ²¹David said to Michal, "It was before the Lord, who chose me in place of your father and all his household, to appoint me as prince over Israel, the people of the Lord, that I have danced before the Lord. ²²I will make myself yet more contemptible than this, and I will be abased in my own eyes; but by the maids of whom you

a Or and his brother   b Compare Gk: Heb and brought it out of the house of Abinadab, which was on the hill with the ark of God   c Q Ms Gk 1 Chr 13.8: Heb fir trees   d 1 Chr 13.10 Compare Q Ms: Meaning of Heb uncertain   e That is Bursting Out Against Uzzah   f Vg: Meaning of Heb uncertain

have spoken, by them I shall be held in honor." ²³And Michal the daughter of Saul had no child to the day of her death.

God's Covenant with David

7 Now when the king was settled in his house, and the Lord had given him rest from all his enemies around him, ²the king said to the prophet Nathan, "See now, I am living in a house of cedar, but the ark of God stays in a tent." ³Nathan said to the king, "Go, do all that you have in mind; for the Lord is with you."

⁴ But that same night the word of the Lord came to Nathan: ⁵Go and tell my servant David: Thus says the Lord: Are you the one to build me a house to live in? ⁶I have not lived in a house since the day I brought up the people of Israel from Egypt to this day, but I have been moving about in a tent and a tabernacle. ⁷Wherever I have moved about among all the people of Israel, did I ever speak a word with any of the tribal leaders*ᵃ* of Israel, whom I commanded to shepherd my people Israel, saying, "Why have you not built me a house of cedar?" ⁸Now therefore thus you shall say to my servant David: Thus says the Lord of hosts: I took you from the pasture, from following the sheep to be prince over my people Israel; ⁹and I have been with you wherever you went, and have cut off all your enemies from before you; and I will make for you a great name, like the name of the great ones of the earth. ¹⁰And I will appoint a place for my people Israel and will plant them, so that they may live in their own place, and be disturbed no more; and evildoers shall afflict them no more, as formerly, ¹¹from the time that I appointed judges over my people Israel; and I will give you rest from all your enemies. Moreover the Lord declares to you that the Lord will make you a house. ¹²When your days are fulfilled and you lie down with your ancestors, I will raise up your offspring after you, who shall come forth from your body, and I will establish his kingdom. ¹³He shall build a house for my name, and I will establish the throne of his kingdom forever. ¹⁴I will be a father to him, and he shall be a son to me. When he commits iniquity, I will punish him with a rod such as mortals use, with blows inflicted by human beings. ¹⁵But I will not take*ᵇ* my steadfast love from him, as I took it from Saul, whom I put away from before you. ¹⁶Your house and your kingdom shall be made sure forever before me;*ᶜ* your throne shall be established forever. ¹⁷In accordance with all these words and with all this vision, Nathan spoke to David.

David's Prayer

18 Then King David went in and sat before the Lord, and said, "Who am I, O Lord God, and what is my house, that you have brought me thus far? ¹⁹And yet this was a small thing in your eyes, O Lord God; you have spoken also of your servant's house for a great while to come. May this be instruction for the people,*ᵈ* O Lord God! ²⁰And what more can David say to you? For you know your servant, O Lord God! ²¹Because of your promise, and according to your own heart, you have wrought all this greatness, so that your servant may know it. ²²Therefore you are great, O Lord God; for there is no one like you, and there is no God besides you, according to all that we have heard with our ears. ²³Who is like your people, like Israel? Is there another*ᵉ* nation on earth whose God went to redeem it

---

a Or any of the tribes   b Gk Syr Vg 1 Chr 17.13: Heb shall not depart   c Gk Heb Mss: MT before you; Compare 2 Sam 7.26, 29   d Meaning of Heb uncertain   e Gk Heb one

David Praises God

Then King David went in and sat before the Lord, and said, "Who am I, O Lord God, and what is my house, that you have brought me thus far?" [2 Sam 7:18]. When was the last time you brought yourself before God, like King David, simply to offer praise for all God has done for you?

It is easy for us to feel too busy to take time for God. Then we complain and get frustrated because God does not seem to be around to give our lives direction. Taking quiet moments to place ourselves in humility before our God and to praise God for the good we experience is important.

Find a quiet place. Take just fifteen minutes. No radio, no television, no book. Think of all the positive and happy things in your life, and in your own words, say, "Thank you, God, for caring for me and the people I love!"

▶ **2 Sam 7:18–29**

as a people, and to make a name for himself, doing great and awesome things for them,[a] by driving out[b] before his people nations and their gods?[c] 24And you established your people Israel for yourself to be your people forever; and you, O LORD, became their God. 25And now, O LORD God, as for the word that you have spoken concerning your servant and concerning his house, confirm it forever; do as you have promised. 26Thus your name will be magnified forever in the saying, 'The LORD of hosts is God over Israel'; and the house of your servant David will be established before you. 27For you, O LORD of hosts, the God of Israel, have made this revelation to your servant, saying, 'I will build you a house'; therefore your servant has found courage to pray this prayer to you. 28And now, O Lord GOD, you are God, and your words are true, and you have promised this good thing to your servant; 29now therefore may it please you to bless the house of your servant, so that it may continue forever before you; for you, O Lord GOD, have spoken, and with your blessing shall the house of your servant be blessed forever."

David's Wars

8 Some time afterward, David attacked the Philistines and subdued them; David took Metheg-ammah out of the hand of the Philistines.

2 He also defeated the Moabites and, making them lie down on the ground, measured them off with a cord; he measured two lengths of cord for those who were to be put to death, and one length[d] for those who were to be spared. And the Moabites became servants to David and brought tribute.

3 David also struck down King Hadadezer son of Rehob of Zobah, as he went to restore his monument[e] at the river Euphrates. 4David took from him one thousand seven hundred horsemen, and twenty thousand foot soldiers. David hamstrung all the chariot horses, but left enough for a hundred chariots. 5When the Arameans of Damascus came to help King Hadadezer of Zobah, David killed twenty-two thousand men of the Arameans. 6Then David put garrisons among the Arameans of Damascus; and the Arameans became servants to David and brought tribute. The LORD gave victory to David wherever he went. 7David took the gold shields that were carried by the servants of Hadadezer, and brought them to Jerusalem. 8From Betah and from Berothai, towns of Hadadezer, King David took a great amount of bronze.

9 When King Toi of Hamath heard that David had defeated the whole army of Hadadezer,

10Toi sent his son Joram to King David, to greet him and to congratulate him because he had fought against Hadadezer and defeated him. Now Hadadezer had often been at war with Toi. Joram brought with him articles of silver, gold, and bronze; 11these also King David dedicated to the LORD, together with the silver and gold that he dedicated from all the nations he subdued, 12from Edom, Moab, the Ammonites, the Philistines, Amalek, and from the spoil of King Hadadezer son of Rehob of Zobah.

13 David won a name for himself. When he returned, he killed eighteen thousand Edomites[f] in the Valley of Salt. 14He put garrisons in Edom; throughout all Edom he put garrisons, and all the Edomites became David's servants. And the LORD gave victory to David wherever he went.

David's Officers

15 So David reigned over all Israel; and David administered justice and equity to all his people. 16Joab son of Zeruiah was over the army; Jehoshaphat son of Ahilud was recorder; 17Zadok son of Ahitub and Ahimelech son of Abiathar were priests; Seraiah was secretary; 18Benaiah son of Jehoiada was over[g] the Cherethites and the Pelethites; and David's sons were priests.

David's Kindness to Mephibosheth

9 David asked, "Is there still anyone left of the house of Saul to whom I may show kindness for Jonathan's sake?" 2Now there was a servant of the house of Saul whose name was Ziba, and he was summoned to David. The king said to him, "Are you Ziba?" And he said, "At your service!" 3The king said, "Is there anyone remaining of the house of Saul to whom I may show the kindness of God?" Ziba said to the king, "There remains a son of Jonathan; he is crippled in his feet." 4The king said to him, "Where is he?" Ziba said to the king, "He is in the house of Machir son of Ammiel, at Lo-debar." 5Then King David sent and brought him from the house of Machir son of Ammiel, at Lo-debar. 6Mephibosheth[h] son of Jonathan son of Saul came to David, and fell on his face and did obeisance. David said, "Mephibosheth!"[h] He answered, "I am your servant." 7David said to him, "Do not be afraid, for I will show you kindness for the sake of your father Jonathan; I will restore to you all the land

---

a Heb you   b Gk 1 Chr 17.21: Heb for your land   c Cn: Heb before your people, whom you redeemed for yourself from Egypt, nations and its gods   d Heb one full length   e Compare 1 Sam 15.12 and 2 Sam 18.18   f Gk: Heb returned from striking down eighteen thousand Arameans   g Syr Tg Vg 20.23; 1 Chr 18.17: Heb lacks was over   h Or Merib-baal : See 4.4 note

of your grandfather Saul, and you yourself shall eat at my table always." [8]He did obeisance and said, "What is your servant, that you should look upon a dead dog such as I?"

9 Then the king summoned Saul's servant Ziba, and said to him, "All that belonged to Saul and to all his house I have given to your master's grandson. [10]You and your sons and your servants shall till the land for him, and shall bring in the produce, so that your master's grandson may have food to eat; but your master's grandson Mephibosheth[a] shall always eat at my table." Now Ziba had fifteen sons and twenty servants. [11]Then Ziba said to the king, "According to all that my lord the king commands his servant, so your servant will do." Mephibosheth[a] ate at David's[b] table, like one of the king's sons. [12]Mephibosheth[a] had a young son whose name was Mica. And all who lived in Ziba's house became Mephibosheth's[c] servants. [13]Mephibosheth[a] lived in Jerusalem, for he always ate at the king's table. Now he was lame in both his feet.

The Ammonites and Arameans Are Defeated

10 Some time afterward, the king of the Ammonites died, and his son Hanun succeeded him. [2]David said, "I will deal loyally with Hanun son of Nahash, just as his father dealt loyally with me." So David sent envoys to console him concerning his father. When David's envoys came into the land of the Ammonites, [3]the princes of the Ammonites said to their lord Hanun, "Do you really think that David is honoring your father just because he has sent messengers with condolences to you? Has not David sent his envoys to you to search the city, to spy it out, and to overthrow it?" [4]So Hanun seized David's envoys, shaved off half the beard of each, cut off their garments in the middle at their hips, and sent them away. [5]When David was told, he sent to meet them, for the men were greatly ashamed. The king said, "Remain at Jericho until your beards have grown, and then return."

6 When the Ammonites saw that they had become odious to David, the Ammonites sent and hired the Arameans of Beth-rehob and the Arameans of Zobah, twenty thousand foot soldiers, as well as the king of Maacah, one thousand men, and the men of Tob, twelve thousand men. [7]When David heard of it, he sent Joab and all the army with the warriors. [8]The Ammonites came out and drew up in battle array at the entrance of the gate; but the Arameans of Zobah and of Rehob, and the men of Tob and Maacah, were by themselves in the open country. 9 When Joab saw that the battle was set against

him both in front and in the rear, he chose some of the picked men of Israel, and arrayed them against the Arameans; [10]the rest of his men he put in the charge of his brother Abishai, and he arrayed them against the Ammonites. [11]He said, "If the Arameans are too strong for me, then you shall help me; but if the Ammonites are too strong for you, then I will come and help you. [12]Be strong, and let us be courageous for the sake of our people, and for the cities of our God; and may the LORD do what seems good to him." [13]So Joab and the people who were with him moved forward into battle against the Arameans; and they fled before him. [14]When the Ammonites saw that the Arameans fled, they likewise fled before Abishai, and entered the city. Then Joab returned from fighting against the Ammonites, and came to Jerusalem.

15 But when the Arameans saw that they had been defeated by Israel, they gathered themselves together. [16]Hadadezer sent and brought out the Arameans who were beyond the Euphrates; and they came to Helam, with Shobach the commander of the army of Hadadezer at their head. [17]When it was told David, he gathered all Israel together, and crossed the Jordan, and came to Helam. The Arameans arrayed themselves against David and fought with him. [18]The Arameans fled before Israel; and David killed of the Arameans seven hundred chariot teams, and forty thousand horsemen,[d] and wounded Shobach the commander of their army, so that he died there. [19]When all the kings who were servants of Hadadezer saw that they had been defeated by Israel, they made peace with Israel, and became subject to them. So the Arameans were afraid to help the Ammonites any more.

David Commits Adultery with Bathsheba

11 In the spring of the year, the time when kings go out to battle, David sent Joab with his officers and all Israel with him; they ravaged the Ammonites, and besieged Rabbah. But David remained at Jerusalem.

2 It happened, late one afternoon, when David rose from his couch and was walking about on the roof of the king's house, that he saw from the roof a woman bathing; the woman was very beautiful. [3]David sent someone to inquire about the woman. It was reported, "This is Bathsheba daughter of Eliam, the wife of Uriah the Hittite." [4]So David sent messengers to get her, and she

---

a Or Merib-baal : See 4.4 note   *b* Gk: Heb *my*   *c* Or Merib-baal's : See 4.4 note   *d* 1 Chr 19.18 and some Gk Mss read *foot soldiers*

Lust and Its Consequences

What the king wants, the king gets. That seems to be the message of 2 Samuel 11:1–5. We are spared many of the details about the encounter between David and Bathsheba, but we do know this: Bathsheba is married to Uriah, so David has coveted another man's wife and committed adultery. When Bathsheba becomes pregnant, David attempts to deceive Uriah into thinking the baby is Uriah's, by bringing him home to have sex with Bathsheba. But Uriah refuses to do so because he and his comrades are in the midst of a war. Finally, David arranges for Uriah to be murdered in battle. In one brief episode, David has broken four commandments. He has given in to lust, and it has led him into a situation that will affect his family, his kingship, and the whole nation of Israel. It is so easy to give in to temptation, especially lust, because it can be so alluring, and because we generally fail to think beyond the moment. A dangerous thing.

▶ **2 Sam 11:1–5**

came to him, and he lay with her. (Now she was purifying herself after her period.) Then she returned to her house. [5]The woman conceived; and she sent and told David, "I am pregnant."

6 So David sent word to Joab, "Send me Uriah the Hittite." And Joab sent Uriah to David. [7]When Uriah came to him, David asked how Joab and the people fared, and how the war was going. [8]Then David said to Uriah, "Go down to your house, and wash your feet." Uriah went out of the king's house, and there followed him a present from the king. [9]But Uriah slept at the entrance of the king's house with all the servants of his lord, and did not go down to his house. [10]When they told David, "Uriah did not go down to his house," David said to Uriah, "You have just come from a journey. Why did you not go down to your house?" [11]Uriah said to David, "The ark and Israel and Judah remain in booths;[a] and my lord Joab and the servants of my lord are camping in the open field; shall I then go to my house, to eat and to drink, and to lie with my wife? As you live, and as your soul lives, I will not do such a thing." [12]Then David said to Uriah, "Remain here today also, and tomorrow I will send you back." So Uriah remained in Jerusalem that day. On the next day, [13]David invited him to eat and drink in his presence and made him drunk; and in the evening he went out to lie on his couch with the servants of his lord, but he did not go down to his house.

David Has Uriah Killed

14 In the morning David wrote a letter to Joab, and sent it by the hand of Uriah. [15]In the letter he wrote, "Set Uriah in the forefront of the hardest fighting, and then draw back from him, so that he may be struck down and die." [16]As Joab was besieging the city, he assigned Uriah to the place where he knew there were valiant warriors. [17]The men of the city came out and fought with Joab; and some of the servants of David among the people fell. Uriah the Hittite was killed as well. [18]Then Joab sent and told David all the news about the fighting; [19]and he instructed the messenger, "When you have finished telling the king all the news about the fighting, [20]then, if the king's anger rises, and if he says to you, 'Why did you go so near the city to fight? Did you not know that they would shoot from the wall? [21]Who killed Abimelech son of Jerubbaal?[b] Did not a woman throw an upper millstone on him from the wall, so that he died at Thebez? Why did you go so near the wall?' then you shall say, 'Your servant Uriah the Hittite is dead too.' "

22 So the messenger went, and came and told David all that Joab had sent him to tell. [23]The messenger said to David, "The men gained an advantage over us, and came out against us in the field; but we drove them back to the entrance of the gate. [24]Then the archers shot at your servants from the wall; some of the king's servants are dead; and your servant Uriah the Hittite is dead also." [25]David said to the messenger, "Thus you shall say to Joab, 'Do not let this matter trouble you, for the sword devours now one and now another; press your attack on the city, and overthrow it.' And encourage him."

26 When the wife of Uriah heard that her husband was dead, she made lamentation for him. [27]When the mourning was over, David sent and brought her to his house, and she became his wife, and bore him a son.

---

a Or at Succoth   b Gk Syr Judg 7.1: Heb Jerubbesheth

Nathan Condemns David

12 But the thing that David had done displeased the Lord, [1]and the Lord sent Nathan to David. He came to him, and said to him, "There were two men in a certain city, the one rich and the other poor. [2]The rich man had very many flocks and herds; [3]but the poor man had nothing but one little ewe lamb, which he had bought. He brought it up, and it grew up with him and with his children; it used to eat of his meager fare, and drink from his cup, and lie in his bosom, and it was like a daughter to him. [4]Now there came a traveler to the rich man, and he was loath to take one of his own flock or herd to prepare for the wayfarer who had come to him, but he took the poor man's lamb, and prepared that for the guest who had come to him." [5]Then David's anger was greatly kindled against the man. He said to Nathan, "As the Lord lives, the man who has done this deserves to die; [6]he shall restore the lamb fourfold, because he did this thing, and because he had no pity."

[7] Nathan said to David, "You are the man! Thus says the Lord, the God of Israel: I anointed you king over Israel, and I rescued you from the hand of Saul; [8]I gave you your master's house, and your master's wives into your bosom, and gave you the house of Israel and of Judah; and if that had been too little, I would have added as much more. [9]Why have you despised the word of the Lord, to do what is evil in his sight? You have struck down Uriah the Hittite with the sword, and have taken his wife to be your wife, and have killed him with the sword of the Ammonites. [10]Now therefore the sword shall never depart from your house, for you have despised me, and have taken the wife of Uriah the Hittite to be your wife. [11]Thus says the Lord: I will raise up trouble against you from within your own house; and I will take your wives before your eyes, and give them to your neighbor, and he shall lie with your wives in the sight of this very sun. [12]For you did it secretly; but I will do this thing before all Israel, and before the sun." [13]David said to Nathan, "I have sinned against the Lord." Nathan said to David, "Now the Lord has put away your sin; you shall not die. [14]Nevertheless, because by this deed you have utterly scorned the Lord,[a] the child that is born to you shall die." [15]Then Nathan went to his house.

Bathsheba's Child Dies

The Lord struck the child that Uriah's wife bore to David, and it became very ill. [16]David therefore pleaded with God for the child; David fasted, and went in and lay all night on the ground. [17]The elders of his house stood beside him, urging him to rise from the ground; but he would not, nor did he eat food with them. [18]On the seventh day the child died. And the servants of David were afraid to tell him that the child was dead; for they said, "While the child was still alive, we spoke to him, and he did not listen to us; how then can we tell him the child is dead? He may do himself some harm." [19]But when David saw that his servants were whispering together, he perceived that the child was dead; and David said to his servants, "Is the child dead?" They said, "He is dead."

20 Then David rose from the ground, washed, anointed himself, and changed his clothes. He went into the house of the Lord, and worshiped;

---

a Ancient scribal tradition: Compare 1 Sam 25.22 note: Heb *scorned the enemies of the Lord*

The Power of a Good Story

Stories can be powerful. Jesus knew the power of stories, so he often responded to questions by telling a story.

The prophet Nathan also knew the power of stories. His challenge was to force David to come to grips with what he had done with Bathsheba and Uriah. In Second Samuel, Nathan cleverly creates a story in which David is to assume his familiar role as judge. David hears the case and is furious at the actions of the rich man in it, declaring that he should die for what he has done. Then, with four words, Nathan turns David's world upside down: "You are the man!" (12:7).

What can David say? He just condemned himself, and he knows it. Nathan has cleverly forced him into a moment of truth. You may want to read Psalm 51, which poetically records David's confession.

Yes, a story can be a powerful thing. Just ask Nathan. Or David. Or Jesus.

▶ 2 Sam 12:1–12

he then went to his own house; and when he asked, they set food before him and he ate. ²¹Then his servants said to him, "What is this thing that you have done? You fasted and wept for the child while it was alive; but when the child died, you rose and ate food." ²²He said, "While the child was still alive, I fasted and wept; for I said, 'Who knows? The LORD may be gracious to me, and the child may live.' ²³But now he is dead; why should I fast? Can I bring him back again? I shall go to him, but he will not return to me."

Solomon Is Born

24 Then David consoled his wife Bathsheba, and went to her, and lay with her; and she bore a son, and he named him Solomon. The LORD loved him, ²⁵and sent a message by the prophet Nathan; so he named him Jedidiah,ᵃ because of the LORD.

The Ammonites Crushed

26 Now Joab fought against Rabbah of the Ammonites, and took the royal city. ²⁷Joab sent messengers to David, and said, "I have fought against Rabbah; moreover, I have taken the water city. ²⁸Now, then, gather the rest of the people together, and encamp against the city, and take it; or I myself will take the city, and it will be called by my name." ²⁹So David gathered all the people together and went to Rabbah, and fought against it and took it. ³⁰He took the crown of Milcomᵇ from his head; the weight of it was a talent of gold, and in it was a precious stone; and it was placed on David's head. He also brought forth the spoil of the city, a very great amount. ³¹He brought out the people who were in it, and set them to work with saws and iron picks and iron axes, or sent them to the brickworks. Thus he did to all the cities of the Ammonites. Then David and all the people returned to Jerusalem.

Amnon and Tamar

13 Some time passed. David's son Absalom had a beautiful sister whose name was Tamar; and David's son Amnon fell in love with her. ²Amnon was so tormented that he made himself ill because of his sister Tamar, for she was a virgin and it seemed impossible to Amnon to do anything to her. ³But Amnon had a friend whose name was Jonadab, the son of David's brother Shimeah; and Jonadab was a very crafty man. ⁴He said to him, "O son of the king, why are you so haggard morning after morning? Will you not tell me?" Amnon said to him, "I love Tamar, my brother Absalom's sister." ⁵Jonadab

said to him, "Lie down on your bed, and pretend to be ill; and when your father comes to see you, say to him, 'Let my sister Tamar come and give me something to eat, and prepare the food in my sight, so that I may see it and eat it from her hand.' " ⁶So Amnon lay down, and pretended to be ill; and when the king came to see him, Amnon said to the king, "Please let my sister Tamar come and make a couple of cakes in my sight, so that I may eat from her hand."

7 Then David sent home to Tamar, saying, "Go to your brother Amnon's house, and prepare food for him." ⁸So Tamar went to her brother Amnon's house, where he was lying down. She took dough, kneaded it, made cakes in his sight, and baked the cakes. ⁹Then she took the pan and set themᶜ out before him, but he refused to eat. Amnon said, "Send out everyone from me." So everyone went out from him. ¹⁰Then Amnon said to Tamar, "Bring the food into the chamber, so that I may eat from your hand." So Tamar took the cakes she had made, and brought them into the chamber to Amnon her brother. ¹¹But when she brought them near him to eat, he took hold of her, and said to her, "Come, lie with me, my sister." ¹²She answered him, "No, my brother, do not force me; for such a thing is not done in Israel; do not do anything so vile! ¹³As for me, where could I carry my shame? And as for you, you would be as one of the scoundrels in Israel. Now therefore, I beg you, speak to the king; for he will not withhold me from you." ¹⁴But he would not listen to her; and being stronger than she, he forced her and lay with her.

15 Then Amnon was seized with a very great loathing for her; indeed, his loathing was even greater than the lust he had felt for her. Amnon said to her, "Get out!" ¹⁶But she said to him, "No, my brother;ᵈ for this wrong in sending me away is greater than the other that you did to me." But he would not listen to her. ¹⁷He called the young man who served him and said, "Put this woman out of my presence, and bolt the door after her." ¹⁸(Now she was wearing a long robe with sleeves; for this is how the virgin daughters of the king were clothed in earlier times.ᵉ) So his servant put her out, and bolted the door after her. ¹⁹But Tamar put ashes on her head, and tore the long robe that she was wearing; she put her hand on her head, and went away, crying aloud as she went.

20 Her brother Absalom said to her, "Has

ᵃ That is *Beloved of the LORD*   ᵇ Gk See 1 Kings 11.5, 33: Heb *their kings*   ᶜ Heb *and poured*   ᵈ Cn Compare Gk Vg: Meaning of Heb uncertain   ᵉ Cn: Heb *were clothed in robes*

Amnon your brother been with you? Be quiet for now, my sister; he is your brother; do not take this to heart." So Tamar remained, a desolate woman, in her brother Absalom's house. ²¹When King David heard of all these things, he became very angry, but he would not punish his son Amnon, because he loved him, for he was his firstborn.ᵃ ²²But Absalom spoke to Amnon neither good nor bad; for Absalom hated Amnon, because he had raped his sister Tamar.

Absalom Avenges the Violation of His Sister

23 After two full years Absalom had sheep-shearers at Baal-hazor, which is near Ephraim, and Absalom invited all the king's sons. ²⁴Absalom came to the king, and said, "Your servant has sheepshearers; will the king and his servants please go with your servant?" ²⁵But the king said to Absalom, "No, my son, let us not all go, or else we will be burdensome to you." He pressed him, but he would not go but gave him his blessing. ²⁶Then Absalom said, "If not, please let my brother Amnon go with us." The king said to him, "Why should he go with you?" ²⁷But Absalom pressed him until he let Amnon and all the king's sons go with him. Absalom made a feast like a king's feast.ᵇ ²⁸Then Absalom commanded his servants, "Watch when Amnon's heart is merry with wine, and when I say to you, 'Strike Amnon,' then kill him. Do not be afraid; have I not myself commanded you? Be courageous and valiant." ²⁹So the servants of Absalom did to Amnon as Absalom had commanded. Then all the king's sons rose, and each mounted his mule and fled.

30 While they were on the way, the report came to David that Absalom had killed all the king's sons, and not one of them was left. ³¹The king rose, tore his garments, and lay on the ground; and all his servants who were standing by tore their garments. ³²But Jonadab, the son of David's brother Shimeah, said, "Let not my lord suppose that they have killed all the young men the king's sons; Amnon alone is dead. This has been determined by Absalom from the day Amnonᶜ raped his sister Tamar. ³³Now therefore, do not let my lord the king take it to heart, as if all the king's sons were dead; for Amnon alone is dead."

34 But Absalom fled. When the young man who kept watch looked up, he saw many people coming from the Horonaim roadᵈ by the side of the mountain. ³⁵Jonadab said to the king, "See, the king's sons have come; as your servant said, so it has come about." ³⁶As soon as he had finished speaking, the king's sons arrived, and

Family Violence

How should we react to the story of the rape of Tamar by her half-brother, Amnon, and the subsequent murder of Amnon by Absalom to avenge his sister's disgrace? This story of lust, cruelty, and revenge has all the makings of a TV movie or a bestselling paperback. So, what is it doing in the Bible?

We have to remind ourselves that these are all David's children. We also have to remind ourselves that after Nathan confronts David about his affair with Bathsheba and his arrangement of Uriah's death, he tells David that "the sword shall never depart from your house" (2 Sam 12:10).

This brutal chain of events unfolds within one family. We are all aware of families in which members do not get along. More serious is the fact that families are often caught up in domestic violence, which can pass from one generation to the next. So how do we stop the "sword of violence" within families?

Each of us needs to make sure we are doing what we can to build bridges in our own families rather than putting up walls. And we need to seek help for individuals who are affected by domestic violence. There are many resources available for people so affected.

● What can you do to help someone affected by family violence? Where can you go for help?

▶ **2 Samuel, chapter 13**

raised their voices and wept; and the king and all his servants also wept very bitterly.

37 But Absalom fled, and went to Talmai son of Ammihud, king of Geshur. David mourned for his son day after day. ³⁸Absalom, having fled to Geshur, stayed there three years. ³⁹And the heart ofᵉ the king went out, yearning for Absalom;

ᵃ Q Ms Gk: MT lacks *but he would not punish . . . firstborn*
ᵇ Gk Compare Q Ms: MT lacks *Absalom made a feast like a king's feast*   ᶜ Heb *he*   ᵈ Cn Compare Gk: Heb *the road behind him*
ᵉ Q Ms Gk: MT *And David*

for he was now consoled over the death of Amnon.

Absalom Returns to Jerusalem

14 Now Joab son of Zeruiah perceived that the king's mind was on Absalom. ²Joab sent to Tekoa and brought from there a wise woman. He said to her, "Pretend to be a mourner; put on mourning garments, do not anoint yourself with oil, but behave like a woman who has been mourning many days for the dead. ³Go to the king and speak to him as follows." And Joab put the words into her mouth.

4 When the woman of Tekoa came to the king, she fell on her face to the ground and did obeisance, and said, "Help, O king!" ⁵The king asked her, "What is your trouble?" She answered, "Alas, I am a widow; my husband is dead. ⁶Your servant had two sons, and they fought with one another in the field; there was no one to part them, and one struck the other and killed him. ⁷Now the whole family has risen against your servant. They say, 'Give up the man who struck his brother, so that we may kill him for the life of his brother whom he murdered, even if we destroy the heir as well.' Thus they would quench my one remaining ember, and leave to my husband neither name nor remnant on the face of the earth."

8 Then the king said to the woman, "Go to your house, and I will give orders concerning you." ⁹The woman of Tekoa said to the king, "On me be the guilt, my lord the king, and on my father's house; let the king and his throne be guiltless." ¹⁰The king said, "If anyone says anything to you, bring him to me, and he shall never touch you again." ¹¹Then she said, "Please, may the king keep the LORD your God in mind, so that the avenger of blood may kill no more, and my son not be destroyed." He said, "As the LORD lives, not one hair of your son shall fall to the ground."

12 Then the woman said, "Please let your servant speak a word to my lord the king." He said, "Speak." ¹³The woman said, "Why then have you planned such a thing against the people of God? For in giving this decision the king convicts himself, inasmuch as the king does not bring his banished one home again. ¹⁴We must all die; we are like water spilled on the ground, which cannot be gathered up. But God will not take away a life; he will devise plans so as not to keep an outcast banished forever from his presence.ᵃ ¹⁵Now I have come to say this to my lord the king because the people have made me afraid; your servant thought, 'I will speak to the king; it may be that the king will perform the request of his servant. ¹⁶For the king will hear, and deliver his servant from the hand of the man who would cut both me and my son off from the heritage of God.' ¹⁷Your servant thought, 'The word of my lord the king will set me at rest'; for my lord the king is like the angel of God, discerning good and evil. The LORD your God be with you!"

18 Then the king answered the woman, "Do not withhold from me anything I ask you." The woman said, "Let my lord the king speak." ¹⁹The king said, "Is the hand of Joab with you in all this?" The woman answered and said, "As surely as you live, my lord the king, one cannot turn right or left from anything that my lord the king has said. For it was your servant Joab who commanded me; it was he who put all these words into the mouth of your servant. ²⁰In order to change the course of affairs your servant Joab did this. But my lord has wisdom like the wisdom of the angel of God to know all things that are on the earth."

21 Then the king said to Joab, "Very well, I grant this; go, bring back the young man Absalom." ²²Joab prostrated himself with his face to the ground and did obeisance, and blessed the king; and Joab said, "Today your servant knows that I have found favor in your sight, my lord the king, in that the king has granted the request of his servant." ²³So Joab set off, went to Geshur, and brought Absalom to Jerusalem. ²⁴The king said, "Let him go to his own house; he is not to come into my presence." So Absalom went to his own house, and did not come into the king's presence.

David Forgives Absalom

25 Now in all Israel there was no one to be praised so much for his beauty as Absalom; from the sole of his foot to the crown of his head there was no blemish in him. ²⁶When he cut the hair of his head (for at the end of every year he used to cut it; when it was heavy on him, he cut it), he weighed the hair of his head, two hundred shekels by the king's weight. ²⁷There were born to Absalom three sons, and one daughter whose name was Tamar; she was a beautiful woman.

28 So Absalom lived two full years in Jerusalem, without coming into the king's presence. ²⁹Then Absalom sent for Joab to send him to the king; but Joab would not come to him. He sent a second time, but Joab would not come. ³⁰Then he said to his servants, "Look, Joab's field is next to mine, and he has barley there; go and set it on fire." So Absalom's servants set the field on

---

a Meaning of Heb uncertain

fire. ³¹Then Joab rose and went to Absalom at his house, and said to him, "Why have your servants set my field on fire?" ³²Absalom answered Joab, "Look, I sent word to you: Come here, that I may send you to the king with the question, 'Why have I come from Geshur? It would be better for me to be there still.' Now let me go into the king's presence; if there is guilt in me, let him kill me!" ³³Then Joab went to the king and told him; and he summoned Absalom. So he came to the king and prostrated himself with his face to the ground before the king; and the king kissed Absalom.

Absalom Usurps the Throne

15 After this Absalom got himself a chariot and horses, and fifty men to run ahead of him. ²Absalom used to rise early and stand beside the road into the gate; and when anyone brought a suit before the king for judgment, Absalom would call out and say, "From what city are you?" When the person said, "Your servant is of such and such a tribe in Israel," ³Absalom would say, "See, your claims are good and right; but there is no one deputed by the king to hear you." ⁴Absalom said moreover, "If only I were judge in the land! Then all who had a suit or cause might come to me, and I would give them justice." ⁵Whenever people came near to do obeisance to him, he would put out his hand and take hold of them, and kiss them. ⁶Thus Absalom did to every Israelite who came to the king for judgment; so Absalom stole the hearts of the people of Israel.

7 At the end of four*ᵃ* years Absalom said to the king, "Please let me go to Hebron and pay the vow that I have made to the LORD. ⁸For your servant made a vow while I lived at Geshur in Aram: If the LORD will indeed bring me back to Jerusalem, then I will worship the LORD in Hebron."*ᵇ* ⁹The king said to him, "Go in peace." So he got up, and went to Hebron. ¹⁰But Absalom sent secret messengers throughout all the tribes of Israel, saying, "As soon as you hear the sound of the trumpet, then shout: Absalom has become king at Hebron!" ¹¹Two hundred men from Jerusalem went with Absalom; they were invited guests, and they went in their innocence, knowing nothing of the matter. ¹²While Absalom was offering the sacrifices, he sent for*ᶜ* Ahithophel the Gilonite, David's counselor, from his city Giloh. The conspiracy grew in strength, and the people with Absalom kept increasing.

David Flees from Jerusalem

13 A messenger came to David, saying, "The hearts of the Israelites have gone after Absalom."

¹⁴Then David said to all his officials who were with him at Jerusalem, "Get up! Let us flee, or there will be no escape for us from Absalom. Hurry, or he will soon overtake us, and bring disaster down upon us, and attack the city with the edge of the sword." ¹⁵The king's officials said to the king, "Your servants are ready to do whatever our lord the king decides." ¹⁶So the king left, followed by all his household, except ten concubines whom he left behind to look after the house. ¹⁷The king left, followed by all the people; and they stopped at the last house. ¹⁸All his officials passed by him; and all the Cherethites, and all the Pelethites, and all the six hundred Gittites who had followed him from Gath, passed on before the king.

19 Then the king said to Ittai the Gittite, "Why are you also coming with us? Go back, and stay with the king; for you are a foreigner, and also an exile from your home. ²⁰You came only yesterday, and shall I today make you wander about with us, while I go wherever I can? Go back, and take your kinsfolk with you; and may the LORD show*ᵈ* steadfast love and faithfulness to you." ²¹But Ittai answered the king, "As the LORD lives, and as my lord the king lives, wherever my lord the king may be, whether for death or for life, there also your servant will be." ²²David said to Ittai, "Go then, march on." So Ittai the Gittite marched on, with all his men and all the little ones who were with him. ²³The whole country wept aloud as all the people passed by; the king crossed the Wadi Kidron, and all the people moved on toward the wilderness.

24 Abiathar came up, and Zadok also, with all the Levites, carrying the ark of the covenant of God. They set down the ark of God, until the people had all passed out of the city. ²⁵Then the king said to Zadok, "Carry the ark of God back into the city. If I find favor in the eyes of the LORD, he will bring me back and let me see both it and the place where it stays. ²⁶But if he says, 'I take no pleasure in you,' here I am, let him do to me what seems good to him." ²⁷The king also said to the priest Zadok, "Look,*ᵉ* go back to the city in peace, you and Abiathar,*ᶠ* with your two sons, Ahimaaz your son, and Jonathan son of Abiathar. ²⁸See, I will wait at the fords of the wilderness until word comes from you to inform me." ²⁹So Zadok and Abiathar carried the ark of God back to Jerusalem, and they remained there.

---

a Gk Syr: Heb *forty*   *b* Gk Mss: Heb lacks *in Hebron*   *c* Or *he sent*   *d* Gk Compare 2.6: Heb lacks *may the LORD show*   *e* Gk: Heb *Are you a seer* or *Do you see?*   *f* Cn: Heb lacks *and Abiathar*

30 But David went up the ascent of the Mount of Olives, weeping as he went, with his head covered and walking barefoot; and all the people who were with him covered their heads and went up, weeping as they went. ³¹David was told that Ahithophel was among the conspirators with Absalom. And David said, "O Lord, I pray you, turn the counsel of Ahithophel into foolishness."

Hushai Becomes David's Spy

32 When David came to the summit, where God was worshiped, Hushai the Archite came to meet him with his coat torn and earth on his head. ³³David said to him, "If you go on with me, you will be a burden to me. ³⁴But if you return to the city and say to Absalom, 'I will be your servant, O king; as I have been your father's servant in time past, so now I will be your servant,' then you will defeat for me the counsel of Ahithophel. ³⁵The priests Zadok and Abiathar will be with you there. So whatever you hear from the king's house, tell it to the priests Zadok and Abiathar. ³⁶Their two sons are with them there, Zadok's son Ahimaaz and Abiathar's son Jonathan; and by them you shall report to me everything you hear." ³⁷So Hushai, David's friend, came into the city, just as Absalom was entering Jerusalem.

David's Adversaries

16 When David had passed a little beyond the summit, Ziba the servant of Mephibosheth[a] met him, with a couple of donkeys saddled, carrying two hundred loaves of bread, one hundred bunches of raisins, one hundred of summer fruits, and one skin of wine. ²The king said to Ziba, "Why have you brought these?" Ziba answered, "The donkeys are for the king's household to ride, the bread and summer fruit for the young men to eat, and the wine is for those to drink who faint in the wilderness." ³The king said, "And where is your master's son?" Ziba said to the king, "He remains in Jerusalem; for he said, 'Today the house of Israel will give me back my grandfather's kingdom.' " ⁴Then the king said to Ziba, "All that belonged to Mephibosheth[a] is now yours." Ziba said, "I do obeisance; let me find favor in your sight, my lord the king."

Shimei Curses David

5 When King David came to Bahurim, a man of the family of the house of Saul came out whose name was Shimei son of Gera; he came out cursing. ⁶He threw stones at David and at all the servants of King David; now all the people and all the warriors were on his right and on his left. ⁷Shimei shouted while he cursed,

"Out! Out! Murderer! Scoundrel! ⁸The Lord has avenged on all of you the blood of the house of Saul, in whose place you have reigned; and the Lord has given the kingdom into the hand of your son Absalom. See, disaster has overtaken you; for you are a man of blood."

9 Then Abishai son of Zeruiah said to the king, "Why should this dead dog curse my lord the king? Let me go over and take off his head." ¹⁰But the king said, "What have I to do with you, you sons of Zeruiah? If he is cursing because the Lord has said to him, 'Curse David,' who then shall say, 'Why have you done so?' " ¹¹David said to Abishai and to all his servants, "My own son seeks my life; how much more now may this Benjaminite! Let him alone, and let him curse; for the Lord has bidden him. ¹²It may be that the Lord will look on my distress,[b] and the Lord will repay me with good for this cursing of me today." ¹³So David and his men went on the road, while Shimei went along on the hillside opposite him and cursed as he went, throwing stones and flinging dust at him. ¹⁴The king and all the people who were with him arrived weary at the Jordan;[c] and there he refreshed himself.

The Counsel of Ahithophel

15 Now Absalom and all the Israelites[d] came to Jerusalem; Ahithophel was with him. ¹⁶When Hushai the Archite, David's friend, came to Absalom, Hushai said to Absalom, "Long live the king! Long live the king!" ¹⁷Absalom said to Hushai, "Is this your loyalty to your friend? Why did you not go with your friend?" ¹⁸Hushai said to Absalom, "No; but the one whom the Lord and this people and all the Israelites have chosen, his I will be, and with him I will remain. ¹⁹Moreover, whom should I serve? Should it not be his son? Just as I have served your father, so I will serve you."

20 Then Absalom said to Ahithophel, "Give us your counsel; what shall we do?" ²¹Ahithophel said to Absalom, "Go in to your father's concubines, the ones he has left to look after the house; and all Israel will hear that you have made yourself odious to your father, and the hands of all who are with you will be strengthened." ²²So they pitched a tent for Absalom upon the roof; and Absalom went in to his father's concubines in the sight of all Israel. ²³Now in those days the counsel that Ahithophel gave was as if one consulted the oracle[e] of God; so all the counsel of Ahithophel was esteemed, both by David and by Absalom.

---

a Or Merib-baal: See 4.4 note   b Gk Vg: Heb iniquity
c Gk: Heb lacks at the Jordan   d Gk: Heb all the people, the men
of Israel   e Heb word

17 Moreover Ahithophel said to Absalom, "Let me choose twelve thousand men, and I will set out and pursue David tonight. [2] I will come upon him while he is weary and discouraged, and throw him into a panic; and all the people who are with him will flee. I will strike down only the king, [3] and I will bring all the people back to you as a bride comes home to her husband. You seek the life of only one man,[a] and all the people will be at peace." [4] The advice pleased Absalom and all the elders of Israel.

The Counsel of Hushai

5 Then Absalom said, "Call Hushai the Archite also, and let us hear too what he has to say." [6] When Hushai came to Absalom, Absalom said to him, "This is what Ahithophel has said; shall we do as he advises? If not, you tell us." [7] Then Hushai said to Absalom, "This time the counsel that Ahithophel has given is not good." [8] Hushai continued, "You know that your father and his men are warriors, and that they are enraged, like a bear robbed of her cubs in the field. Besides, your father is expert in war; he will not spend the night with the troops. [9] Even now he has hidden himself in one of the pits, or in some other place. And when some of our troops[b] fall at the first attack, whoever hears it will say, 'There has been a slaughter among the troops who follow Absalom.' [10] Then even the valiant warrior, whose heart is like the heart of a lion, will utterly melt with fear; for all Israel knows that your father is a warrior, and that those who are with him are valiant warriors. [11] But my counsel is that all Israel be gathered to you, from Dan to Beer-sheba, like the sand by the sea for multitude, and that you go to battle in person. [12] So we shall come upon him in whatever place he may be found, and we shall light on him as the dew falls on the ground; and he will not survive, nor will any of those with him. [13] If he withdraws into a city, then all Israel will bring ropes to that city, and we shall drag it into the valley, until not even a pebble is to be found there." [14] Absalom and all the men of Israel said, "The counsel of Hushai the Archite is better than the counsel of Ahithophel." For the LORD had ordained to defeat the good counsel of Ahithophel, so that the LORD might bring ruin on Absalom.

Hushai Warns David to Escape

15 Then Hushai said to the priests Zadok and Abiathar, "Thus and so did Ahithophel counsel Absalom and the elders of Israel; and thus and so I have counseled. [16] Therefore send quickly and tell David, 'Do not lodge tonight at the fords of the wilderness, but by all means cross over; otherwise the king and all the people who are with him will be swallowed up.' " [17] Jonathan and Ahimaaz were waiting at En-rogel; a servant-girl used to go and tell them, and they would go and tell King David; for they could not risk being seen entering the city. [18] But a boy saw them, and told Absalom; so both of them went away quickly, and came to the house of a man at Bahurim, who had a well in his courtyard; and they went down into it. [19] The man's wife took a covering, stretched it over the well's mouth, and spread out grain on it; and nothing was known of it. [20] When Absalom's servants came to the woman at the house, they said, "Where are Ahimaaz and Jonathan?" The woman said to them, "They have crossed over the brook[c] of water." And when they had searched and could not find them, they returned to Jerusalem.

21 After they had gone, the men came up out of the well, and went and told King David. They said to David, "Go and cross the water quickly; for thus and so has Ahithophel counseled against you." [22] So David and all the people who were with him set out and crossed the Jordan; by daybreak not one was left who had not crossed the Jordan.

23 When Ahithophel saw that his counsel was not followed, he saddled his donkey and went off home to his own city. He set his house in order, and hanged himself; he died and was buried in the tomb of his father.

24 Then David came to Mahanaim, while Absalom crossed the Jordan with all the men of Israel. [25] Now Absalom had set Amasa over the army in the place of Joab. Amasa was the son of a man named Ithra the Ishmaelite,[d] who had married Abigal daughter of Nahash, sister of Zeruiah, Joab's mother. [26] The Israelites and Absalom encamped in the land of Gilead.

27 When David came to Mahanaim, Shobi son of Nahash from Rabbah of the Ammonites, and Machir son of Ammiel from Lo-debar, and Barzillai the Gileadite from Rogelim, [28] brought beds, basins, and earthen vessels, wheat, barley, meal, parched grain, beans and lentils,[e] [29] honey and curds, sheep, and cheese from the herd, for David and the people with him to eat; for they said, "The troops are hungry and weary and thirsty in the wilderness."

---

a Gk: Heb *like the return of the whole (is) the man whom you seek*
b Gk Mss: Heb *some of them*   c Meaning of Heb uncertain
d 1 Chr 2.17: Heb *Israelite*   e Heb *and lentils and parched grain*

The Defeat and Death of Absalom

18 Then David mustered the men who were with him, and set over them commanders of thousands and commanders of hundreds. [2]And David divided the army into three groups:[a] one third under the command of Joab, one third under the command of Abishai son of Zeruiah, Joab's brother, and one third under the command of Ittai the Gittite. The king said to the men, "I myself will also go out with you." [3]But the men said, "You shall not go out. For if we flee, they will not care about us. If half of us die, they will not care about us. But you are worth ten thousand of us;[b] therefore it is better that you send us help from the city." [4]The king said to them, "Whatever seems best to you I will do." So the king stood at the side of the gate, while all the army marched out by hundreds and by thousands. [5]The king ordered Joab and Abishai and Ittai, saying, "Deal gently for my sake with the young man Absalom." And all the people heard when the king gave orders to all the commanders concerning Absalom.

6 So the army went out into the field against Israel; and the battle was fought in the forest of Ephraim. [7]The men of Israel were defeated there by the servants of David, and the slaughter there was great on that day, twenty thousand men. [8]The battle spread over the face of all the country; and the forest claimed more victims that day than the sword.

9 Absalom happened to meet the servants of David. Absalom was riding on his mule, and the mule went under the thick branches of a great oak. His head caught fast in the oak, and he was left hanging[c] between heaven and earth, while the mule that was under him went on. [10]A man saw it, and told Joab, "I saw Absalom hanging in an oak." [11]Joab said to the man who told him, "What, you saw him! Why then did you not strike him there to the ground? I would have been glad to give you ten pieces of silver and a belt." [12]But the man said to Joab, "Even if I felt in my hand the weight of a thousand pieces of silver, I would not raise my hand against the king's son; for in our hearing the king commanded you and Abishai and Ittai, saying: For my sake protect the young man Absalom! [13]On the other hand, if I had dealt treacherously against his life[d] (and there is nothing hidden from the king), then you yourself would have stood aloof." [14]Joab said, "I will not waste time like this with you." He took three spears in his hand, and thrust them into the heart of Absalom, while he was still alive in the oak. [15]And ten young men, Joab's armor-bearers, surrounded Absalom and struck him, and killed him.

16 Then Joab sounded the trumpet, and the troops came back from pursuing Israel, for Joab restrained the troops. [17]They took Absalom, threw him into a great pit in the forest, and raised over him a very great heap of stones. Meanwhile all the Israelites fled to their homes. [18]Now Absalom in his lifetime had taken and set up for himself a pillar that is in the King's Valley, for he said, "I have no son to keep my name in remembrance"; he called the pillar by his own name. It is called Absalom's Monument to this day.

David Hears of Absalom's Death

19 Then Ahimaaz son of Zadok said, "Let me run, and carry tidings to the king that the LORD has delivered him from the power of his enemies." [20]Joab said to him, "You are not to carry tidings today; you may carry tidings another day, but today you shall not do so, because the king's son is dead." [21]Then Joab said to a Cushite, "Go, tell the king what you have seen." The Cushite bowed before Joab, and ran. [22]Then Ahimaaz son of Zadok said again to Joab, "Come what may, let me also run after the Cushite." And Joab said, "Why will you run, my son, seeing that you have no reward[e] for the tidings?" [23]"Come what may," he said, "I will run." So he said to him, "Run." Then Ahimaaz ran by the way of the Plain, and outran the Cushite.

24 Now David was sitting between the two gates. The sentinel went up to the roof of the gate by the wall, and when he looked up, he saw a man running alone. [25]The sentinel shouted and told the king. The king said, "If he is alone, there are tidings in his mouth." He kept coming, and drew near. [26]Then the sentinel saw another man running; and the sentinel called to the gatekeeper and said, "See, another man running alone!" The king said, "He also is bringing tidings." [27]The sentinel said, "I think the running of the first one is like the running of Ahimaaz son of Zadok." The king said, "He is a good man, and comes with good tidings."

28 Then Ahimaaz cried out to the king, "All is well!" He prostrated himself before the king with his face to the ground, and said, "Blessed be the LORD your God, who has delivered up the men who raised their hand against my lord the king." [29]The king said, "Is it well with the young

---

a Gk: Heb sent forth the army   b Gk Vg Symmachus: Heb for now there are ten thousand such as we   c Gk Syr Tg: Heb was put   d Another reading is at the risk of my life   e Meaning of Heb uncertain

man Absalom?" Ahimaaz answered, "When Joab sent your servant,[a] I saw a great tumult, but I do not know what it was." [30]The king said, "Turn aside, and stand here." So he turned aside, and stood still.

31 Then the Cushite came; and the Cushite said, "Good tidings for my lord the king! For the LORD has vindicated you this day, delivering you from the power of all who rose up against you." [32]The king said to the Cushite, "Is it well with the young man Absalom?" The Cushite answered, "May the enemies of my lord the king, and all who rise up to do you harm, be like that young man."

David Mourns for Absalom

[33][b] The king was deeply moved, and went up to the chamber over the gate, and wept; and as he went, he said, "O my son Absalom, my son, my son Absalom! Would I had died instead of you, O Absalom, my son, my son!"

19 It was told Joab, "The king is weeping and mourning for Absalom." [2]So the victory that day was turned into mourning for all the troops; for the troops heard that day, "The king is grieving for his son." [3]The troops stole into the city that day as soldiers steal in who are ashamed when they flee in battle. [4]The king covered his face, and the king cried with a loud voice, "O my son Absalom, O Absalom, my son, my son!" [5]Then Joab came into the house to the king, and said, "Today you have covered with shame the faces of all your officers who have saved your life today, and the lives of your sons and your daughters, and the lives of your wives and your concubines, [6]for love of those who hate you and for hatred of those who love you. You have made it clear today that commanders and officers are nothing to you; for I perceive that if Absalom were alive and all of us were dead today, then you would be pleased. [7]So go out at once and speak kindly to your servants; for I swear by the LORD, if you do not go, not a man will stay with you this night; and this will be worse for you than any disaster that has come upon you from your youth until now." [8]Then the king got up and took his seat in the gate. The troops were all told, "See, the king is sitting in the gate"; and all the troops came before the king.

David Recalled to Jerusalem

Meanwhile, all the Israelites had fled to their homes. [9]All the people were disputing throughout all the tribes of Israel, saying, "The king delivered us from the hand of our enemies, and saved us from the hand of the Philistines; and now he has fled out of the land because of Absalom. [10]But Absalom, whom we anointed over us, is dead in battle. Now therefore why do you say nothing about bringing the king back?"

11 King David sent this message to the priests Zadok and Abiathar, "Say to the elders of Judah, 'Why should you be the last to bring the king back to his house? The talk of all Israel has come to the king.[c] [12]You are my kin, you are my bone and my flesh; why then should you be the last to bring back the king?' [13]And say to Amasa, 'Are you not my bone and my flesh? So may God do to me, and more, if you are not the commander of my army from now on, in place of Joab.'"

Surviving Grief

It is a cold winter day when the state trooper comes to the door with the news that James Washington has just lost his son in an automobile accident. James falls to the ground in utter pain. Michael was just sixteen years old. James weeps as the trooper helps him up; the young officer begins to cry as he thinks of his own son, just three years old.

There is no greater loss for parents than the death of a child. In 2 Samuel 18:33, King David is devastated by the death of his son Absalom, despite Absalom's betrayal. There is no easy answer or explanation when someone we love dies. How could God allow this? It is too hard to understand. What helps is to allow ourselves to mourn like David and to place ourselves in God's healing hands.

Life continues. Joab challenges David not to forget the people who have served him faithfully and count on his leadership (verses 6–8). In our grief, we must not forget the family and friends who grieve with us. We need them, and they need us to heal the pain of loss.

▶ 2 Sam 19:1–9

¹⁴Amasa^a swayed the hearts of all the people of Judah as one, and they sent word to the king, "Return, both you and all your servants." ¹⁵So the king came back to the Jordan; and Judah came to Gilgal to meet the king and to bring him over the Jordan.

16 Shimei son of Gera, the Benjaminite, from Bahurim, hurried to come down with the people of Judah to meet King David; ¹⁷with him were a thousand people from Benjamin. And Ziba, the servant of the house of Saul, with his fifteen sons and his twenty servants, rushed down to the Jordan ahead of the king, ¹⁸while the crossing was taking place,^b to bring over the king's household, and to do his pleasure.

David's Mercy to Shimei

Shimei son of Gera fell down before the king, as he was about to cross the Jordan, ¹⁹and said to the king, "May my lord not hold me guilty or remember how your servant did wrong on the day my lord the king left Jerusalem; may the king not bear it in mind. ²⁰For your servant knows that I have sinned; therefore, see, I have come this day, the first of all the house of Joseph to come down to meet my lord the king." ²¹Abishai son of Zeruiah answered, "Shall not Shimei be put to death for this, because he cursed the Lord's anointed?" ²²But David said, "What have I to do with you, you sons of Zeruiah, that you should today become an adversary to me? Shall anyone be put to death in Israel this day? For do I not know that I am this day king over Israel?" ²³The king said to Shimei, "You shall not die." And the king gave him his oath.

David and Mephibosheth Meet

24 Mephibosheth^c grandson of Saul came down to meet the king; he had not taken care of his feet, or trimmed his beard, or washed his clothes, from the day the king left until the day he came back in safety. ²⁵When he came from Jerusalem to meet the king, the king said to him, "Why did you not go with me, Mephibosheth?"^c ²⁶He answered, "My lord, O king, my servant deceived me; for your servant said to him, 'Saddle a donkey for me,^d so that I may ride on it and go with the king.' For your servant is lame. ²⁷He has slandered your servant to my lord the king. But my lord the king is like the angel of God; do therefore what seems good to you. ²⁸For all my father's house were doomed to death before my lord the king; but you set your servant among those who eat at your table. What further right have I, then, to appeal to the king?" ²⁹The king said to him, "Why speak any more of your affairs? I have decided: you and Ziba shall divide the land." ³⁰Mephibosheth^c said to the king, "Let him take it all, since my lord the king has arrived home safely."

David's Kindness to Barzillai

31 Now Barzillai the Gileadite had come down from Rogelim; he went on with the king to the Jordan, to escort him over the Jordan. ³²Barzillai was a very aged man, eighty years old. He had provided the king with food while he stayed at Mahanaim, for he was a very wealthy man. ³³The king said to Barzillai, "Come over with me, and I will provide for you in Jerusalem at my side." ³⁴But Barzillai said to the king, "How many years have I still to live, that I should go up with the king to Jerusalem? ³⁵Today I am eighty years old; can I discern what is pleasant and what is not? Can your servant taste what he eats or what he drinks? Can I still listen to the voice of singing men and singing women? Why then should your servant be an added burden to my lord the king? ³⁶Your servant will go a little way over the Jordan with the king. Why should the king recompense me with such a reward? ³⁷Please let your servant return, so that I may die in my own town, near the graves of my father and my mother. But here is your servant Chimham; let him go over with my lord the king; and do for him whatever seems good to you." ³⁸The king answered, "Chimham shall go over with me, and I will do for him whatever seems good to you; and all that you desire of me I will do for you." ³⁹Then all the people crossed over the Jordan, and the king crossed over; the king kissed Barzillai and blessed him, and he returned to his own home. ⁴⁰The king went on to Gilgal, and Chimham went on with him; all the people of Judah, and also half the people of Israel, brought the king on his way.

41 Then all the people of Israel came to the king, and said to him, "Why have our kindred the people of Judah stolen you away, and brought the king and his household over the Jordan, and all David's men with him?" ⁴²All the people of Judah answered the people of Israel, "Because the king is near of kin to us. Why then are you angry over this matter? Have we eaten at all at the king's expense? Or has he given us any gift?" ⁴³But the people of Israel answered the people of Judah, "We have ten shares in the king, and in David also we have more than you.

---

a Heb *He*   b Cn: Heb *the ford crossed*   c Or *Merib-baal* : See 4.4 note   d Gk Syr Vg: Heb *said, 'I will saddle a donkey for myself*

Why then did you despise us? Were we not the first to speak of bringing back our king?" But the words of the people of Judah were fiercer than the words of the people of Israel.

The Rebellion of Sheba

20 Now a scoundrel named Sheba son of Bichri, a Benjaminite, happened to be there. He sounded the trumpet and cried out,

"We have no portion in David,
no share in the son of Jesse!
Everyone to your tents, O Israel!"

2 So all the people of Israel withdrew from David and followed Sheba son of Bichri; but the people of Judah followed their king steadfastly from the Jordan to Jerusalem.

3 David came to his house at Jerusalem; and the king took the ten concubines whom he had left to look after the house, and put them in a house under guard, and provided for them, but did not go in to them. So they were shut up until the day of their death, living as if in widowhood.

4 Then the king said to Amasa, "Call the men of Judah together to me within three days, and be here yourself." 5 So Amasa went to summon Judah; but he delayed beyond the set time that had been appointed him. 6 David said to Abishai, "Now Sheba son of Bichri will do us more harm than Absalom; take your lord's servants and pursue him, or he will find fortified cities for himself, and escape from us." 7 Joab's men went out after him, along with the Cherethites, the Pelethites, and all the warriors; they went out from Jerusalem to pursue Sheba son of Bichri. 8 When they were at the large stone that is in Gibeon, Amasa came to meet them. Now Joab was wearing a soldier's garment and over it was a belt with a sword in its sheath fastened at his waist; as he went forward it fell out. 9 Joab said to Amasa, "Is it well with you, my brother?" And Joab took Amasa by the beard with his right hand to kiss him. 10 But Amasa did not notice the sword in Joab's hand; Joab struck him in the belly so that his entrails poured out on the ground, and he died. He did not strike a second blow.

Then Joab and his brother Abishai pursued Sheba son of Bichri. 11 And one of Joab's men took his stand by Amasa, and said, "Whoever favors Joab, and whoever is for David, let him follow Joab." 12 Amasa lay wallowing in his blood on the highway, and the man saw that all the people were stopping. Since he saw that all who came by him were stopping, he carried Amasa from the highway into a field, and threw a garment over him. 13 Once he was removed from the highway, all the people went on after Joab to pursue Sheba son of Bichri.

14 Sheba[a] passed through all the tribes of Israel to Abel of Beth-maacah;[b] and all the Bichrites[c] assembled, and followed him inside. 15 Joab's forces[d] came and besieged him in Abel of Beth-maacah; they threw up a siege ramp against the city, and it stood against the rampart. Joab's forces were battering the wall to break it down. 16 Then a wise woman called from the city, "Listen! Listen! Tell Joab, 'Come here, I want to speak to you.' " 17 He came near her; and the woman said, "Are you Joab?" He answered, "I am." Then she said to him, "Listen to the words of your servant." He answered, "I am listening." 18 Then she said, "They used to say in the old days, 'Let them inquire at Abel'; and so they would settle a matter. 19 I am one of those who are peaceable and faithful in Israel; you seek to destroy a city that is a mother in Israel; why will you swallow up the heritage of the LORD?" 20 Joab answered, "Far be it from me, far be it, that I should swallow up or destroy! 21 That is not the case! But a man of the hill country of Ephraim, called Sheba son of Bichri, has lifted up his hand against King David; give him up alone, and I will withdraw from the city." The woman said to Joab, "His head shall be thrown over the wall to you." 22 Then the woman went to all the people with her wise plan. And they cut off the head of Sheba son of Bichri, and threw it out to Joab. So he blew the trumpet, and they dispersed from the city, and all went to their homes, while Joab returned to Jerusalem to the king.

23 Now Joab was in command of all the army of Israel;[e] Benaiah son of Jehoiada was in command of the Cherethites and the Pelethites; 24 Adoram was in charge of the forced labor; Jehoshaphat son of Ahilud was the recorder; 25 Sheva was secretary; Zadok and Abiathar were priests; 26 and Ira the Jairite was also David's priest.

David Avenges the Gibeonites

21 Now there was a famine in the days of David for three years, year after year; and David inquired of the LORD. The LORD said, "There is bloodguilt on Saul and on his house, because he put the Gibeonites to death." 2 So the king called the Gibeonites and spoke to them. (Now the Gibeonites were not of the people of Israel, but of the remnant of the Amorites; although the people of Israel had sworn to spare them, Saul

a Heb He   b Compare 20.15: Heb and Beth-maacah
c Compare Gk Vg: Heb Berites   d Heb They   e Cn: Heb Joab to all the army, Israel

had tried to wipe them out in his zeal for the people of Israel and Judah.) [3]David said to the Gibeonites, "What shall I do for you? How shall I make expiation, that you may bless the heritage of the LORD?" [4]The Gibeonites said to him, "It is not a matter of silver or gold between us and Saul or his house; neither is it for us to put anyone to death in Israel." He said, "What do you say that I should do for you?" [5]They said to the king, "The man who consumed us and planned to destroy us, so that we should have no place in all the territory of Israel— [6]let seven of his sons be handed over to us, and we will impale them before the LORD at Gibeon on the mountain of the LORD."[a] The king said, "I will hand them over."

[7] But the king spared Mephibosheth,[b] the son of Saul's son Jonathan, because of the oath of the LORD that was between them, between David and Jonathan son of Saul. [8]The king took the two sons of Rizpah daughter of Aiah, whom she bore to Saul, Armoni and Mephibosheth;[b] and the five sons of Merab[c] daughter of Saul, whom she bore to Adriel son of Barzillai the Meholathite; [9]he gave them into the hands of the Gibeonites, and they impaled them on the mountain before the LORD. The seven of them perished together. They were put to death in the first days of harvest, at the beginning of barley harvest.

[10] Then Rizpah the daughter of Aiah took sackcloth, and spread it on a rock for herself, from the beginning of harvest until rain fell on them from the heavens; she did not allow the birds of the air to come on the bodies[d] by day, or the wild animals by night. [11]When David was told what Rizpah daughter of Aiah, the concubine of Saul, had done, [12]David went and took the bones of Saul and the bones of his son Jonathan from the people of Jabesh-gilead, who had stolen them from the public square of Beth-shan, where the Philistines had hung them up, on the day the Philistines killed Saul on Gilboa. [13]He brought up from there the bones of Saul and the bones of his son Jonathan; and they gathered the bones of those who had been impaled. [14]They buried the bones of Saul and of his son Jonathan in the land of Benjamin in Zela, in the tomb of his father Kish; they did all that the king commanded. After that, God heeded supplications for the land.

Exploits of David's Men

[15] The Philistines went to war again with Israel, and David went down together with his servants. They fought against the Philistines, and David grew weary. [16]Ishbi-benob, one of the descendants of the giants, whose spear weighed three hundred shekels of bronze, and who was fitted out with new weapons,[e] said he would kill David. [17]But Abishai son of Zeruiah came to his aid, and attacked the Philistine and killed him. Then David's men swore to him, "You shall not go out with us to battle any longer, so that you do not quench the lamp of Israel."

[18] After this a battle took place with the Philistines, at Gob; then Sibbecai the Hushathite killed Saph, who was one of the descendants of the giants. [19]Then there was another battle with the Philistines at Gob; and Elhanan son of Jaare-oregim, the Bethlehemite, killed Goliath the Gittite, the shaft of whose spear was like a weaver's beam. [20]There was again war at Gath, where there was a man of great size, who had six fingers on each hand, and six toes on each foot, twenty-four in number; he too was descended from the giants. [21]When he taunted Israel, Jonathan son of David's brother Shimei, killed him. [22]These four were descended from the giants in Gath; they fell by the hands of David and his servants.

David's Song of Thanksgiving

22 David spoke to the LORD the words of this song on the day when the LORD delivered him from the hand of all his enemies, and from the hand of Saul. [2]He said:
The LORD is my rock, my fortress, and my
    deliverer,
[3] my God, my rock, in whom I take refuge,
my shield and the horn of my salvation,
    my stronghold and my refuge,
    my savior; you save me from violence.
[4] I call upon the LORD, who is worthy to be praised,
    and I am saved from my enemies.

[5] For the waves of death encompassed me,
    the torrents of perdition assailed me;
[6] the cords of Sheol entangled me,
    the snares of death confronted me.

[7] In my distress I called upon the LORD;
    to my God I called.
From his temple he heard my voice,
    and my cry came to his ears.

[8] Then the earth reeled and rocked;
    the foundations of the heavens trembled
    and quaked, because he was angry.
[9] Smoke went up from his nostrils,
    and devouring fire from his mouth;

---

a Cn Compare Gk and 21.9: Heb at *Gibeah of Saul, the chosen of the LORD*   b Or *Merib-baal*: See 4.4 note   c Two Heb Mss Syr Compare Gk: MT *Michal*   d Heb *them*   e Heb *was belted anew*

glowing coals flamed forth from him.

10 He bowed the heavens, and came down;
   thick darkness was under his feet.

11 He rode on a cherub, and flew;
   he was seen upon the wings of the wind.

12 He made darkness around him a canopy,
   thick clouds, a gathering of water.

13 Out of the brightness before him
   coals of fire flamed forth.

14 The LORD thundered from heaven;
   the Most High uttered his voice.

15 He sent out arrows, and scattered them
   —lightning, and routed them.

16 Then the channels of the sea were seen,
   the foundations of the world were laid bare
   at the rebuke of the LORD,
   at the blast of the breath of his nostrils.

17 He reached from on high, he took me,
   he drew me out of mighty waters.

18 He delivered me from my strong enemy,
   from those who hated me;
   for they were too mighty for me.

19 They came upon me in the day of my calamity,
   but the LORD was my stay.

20 He brought me out into a broad place;
   he delivered me, because he delighted in me.

21 The LORD rewarded me according to my
      righteousness;
   according to the cleanness of my hands he
      recompensed me.

22 For I have kept the ways of the LORD,
   and have not wickedly departed from my God.

23 For all his ordinances were before me,
   and from his statutes I did not turn aside.

24 I was blameless before him,
   and I kept myself from guilt.

25 Therefore the LORD has recompensed me
      according to my righteousness,
   according to my cleanness in his sight.

26 With the loyal you show yourself loyal;
   with the blameless you show yourself
      blameless;

27 with the pure you show yourself pure,
   and with the crooked you show yourself
      perverse.

28 You deliver a humble people,
   but your eyes are upon the haughty to bring
      them down.

29 Indeed, you are my lamp, O LORD,
   the LORD lightens my darkness.

30 By you I can crush a troop,
   and by my God I can leap over a wall.

31 This God—his way is perfect;

Live It!

The Lord Is My Rock

Build on the rock! What exactly does that mean? Have you ever watched a house being built? One of the first things a contractor does is level the ground and put in a foundation. Upon the foundation, the structure begins to grow. A solid foundation will enable that house to stand for many years.

The same goes for our lives, both personally and communally. What is the foundation—the rock—that your life is built on? In 2 Samuel 22:2, King David says to the Lord, "[You are] my rock, my fortress, and my deliverer." David built his life on the rock and foundation of the Lord. As a result, he found refuge in times of fear. It was this rock that saved David and the people of Israel from the hands of their enemies. Because of David's reliance on God, his kingdom is seen by later generations of Jews as the ideal kingdom for Israel.

You too can find this same refuge, this same saving grace. Starting today, build your life with the Lord as your foundation (see Mt 7:24–27). The next time you face a battle, be it drugs or envy or anger or lust, stand on the rock!

▶ 2 Sam 22:1–4

the promise of the LORD proves true;
   he is a shield for all who take refuge in him.

32 For who is God, but the LORD?
   And who is a rock, except our God?

33 The God who has girded me with strength[a]
   has opened wide my path.[b]

34 He made my[c] feet like the feet of deer,
   and set me secure on the heights.

35 He trains my hands for war,
   so that my arms can bend a bow of bronze.

36 You have given me the shield of your salvation,
   and your help[d] has made me great.

---

a Q Ms Gk Syr Vg Compare Ps 18.32: MT *God is my strong refuge*
b Meaning of Heb uncertain   c Another reading is *his*   d Q Ms:
MT *your answering*

37 You have made me stride freely,
and my feet do not slip;
38 I pursued my enemies and destroyed them,
and did not turn back until they were
consumed.
39 I consumed them; I struck them down, so that
they did not rise;
they fell under my feet.
40 For you girded me with strength for the battle;
you made my assailants sink under me.
41 You made my enemies turn their backs to me,
those who hated me, and I destroyed them.
42 They looked, but there was no one to save them;
they cried to the LORD, but he did not answer
them.
43 I beat them fine like the dust of the earth,
I crushed them and stamped them down like
the mire of the streets.

44 You delivered me from strife with the peoples;[a]
you kept me as the head of the nations;
people whom I had not known served me.
45 Foreigners came cringing to me;
as soon as they heard of me, they obeyed me.
46 Foreigners lost heart,
and came trembling out of their strongholds.

47 The LORD lives! Blessed be my rock,
and exalted be my God, the rock of my
salvation,
48 the God who gave me vengeance
and brought down peoples under me,
49 who brought me out from my enemies;
you exalted me above my adversaries,
you delivered me from the violent.

50 For this I will extol you, O LORD, among the
nations,
and sing praises to your name.
51 He is a tower of salvation for his king,
and shows steadfast love to his anointed,
to David and his descendants forever.

The Last Words of David

23 Now these are the last words of David:
The oracle of David, son of Jesse,
the oracle of the man whom God exalted,[b]
the anointed of the God of Jacob,
the favorite of the Strong One of Israel:

2 The spirit of the LORD speaks through me,
his word is upon my tongue.
3 The God of Israel has spoken,
the Rock of Israel has said to me:
One who rules over people justly,
ruling in the fear of God,

4 is like the light of morning,
like the sun rising on a cloudless morning,
gleaming from the rain on the grassy land.

5 Is not my house like this with God?
For he has made with me an everlasting
covenant,
ordered in all things and secure.
Will he not cause to prosper
all my help and my desire?
6 But the godless are[c] all like thorns that are
thrown away;
for they cannot be picked up with the hand;
7 to touch them one uses an iron bar
or the shaft of a spear.
And they are entirely consumed in fire on the
spot.[d]

David's Mighty Men

8 These are the names of the warriors whom
David had: Josheb-basshebeth a Tahchemonite;
he was chief of the Three;[e] he wielded his spear[f]
against eight hundred whom he killed at one
time.

9 Next to him among the three warriors was
Eleazar son of Dodo son of Ahohi. He was with
David when they defied the Philistines who were
gathered there for battle. The Israelites withdrew,
10but he stood his ground. He struck down the
Philistines until his arm grew weary, though
his hand clung to the sword. The LORD brought
about a great victory that day. Then the people
came back to him—but only to strip the dead.

11 Next to him was Shammah son of Agee,
the Hararite. The Philistines gathered together
at Lehi, where there was a plot of ground full of
lentils; and the army fled from the Philistines.
12But he took his stand in the middle of the plot,
defended it, and killed the Philistines; and the
LORD brought about a great victory.

13 Towards the beginning of harvest three
of the thirty[g] chiefs went down to join David at
the cave of Adullam, while a band of Philistines
was encamped in the valley of Rephaim. 14David
was then in the stronghold; and the garrison of
the Philistines was then at Bethlehem. 15David
said longingly, "O that someone would give me
water to drink from the well of Bethlehem that
is by the gate!" 16Then the three warriors broke
through the camp of the Philistines, drew water
from the well of Bethlehem that was by the gate,
and brought it to David. But he would not drink

---

a Gk: Heb from strife with my people   b Q Ms: MT who was
raised on high   c Heb But worthlessness   d Heb in sitting
e Gk Vg Compare 1 Chr 11.11: Meaning of Heb uncertain
f 1 Chr 11.11: Meaning of Heb uncertain   g Heb adds head

2
S
AM

of it; he poured it out to the LORD, [17]for he said, "The LORD forbid that I should do this. Can I drink the blood of the men who went at the risk of their lives?" Therefore he would not drink it. The three warriors did these things.

18 Now Abishai son of Zeruiah, the brother of Joab, was chief of the Thirty.[a] With his spear he fought against three hundred men and killed them, and won a name beside the Three. [19]He was the most renowned of the Thirty,[b] and became their commander; but he did not attain to the Three.

20 Benaiah son of Jehoiada was a valiant warrior[c] from Kabzeel, a doer of great deeds; he struck down two sons of Ariel[d] of Moab. He also went down and killed a lion in a pit on a day when snow had fallen. [21]And he killed an Egyptian, a handsome man. The Egyptian had a spear in his hand; but Benaiah went against him with a staff, snatched the spear out of the Egyptian's hand, and killed him with his own spear. [22]Such were the things Benaiah son of Jehoiada did, and won a name beside the three warriors. [23]He was renowned among the Thirty, but he did not attain to the Three. And David put him in charge of his bodyguard.

24 Among the Thirty were Asahel brother of Joab; Elhanan son of Dodo of Bethlehem; [25]Shammah of Harod; Elika of Harod; [26]Helez the Paltite; Ira son of Ikkesh of Tekoa; [27]Abiezer of Anathoth; Mebunnai the Hushathite; [28]Zalmon the Ahohite; Maharai of Netophah; [29]Heleb son of Baanah of Netophah; Ittai son of Ribai of Gibeah of the Benjaminites; [30]Benaiah of Pirathon; Hiddai of the torrents of Gaash; [31]Abi-albon the Arbathite; Azmaveth of Bahurim; [32]Eliahba of Shaalbon; the sons of Jashen: Jonathan [33]son of[e] Shammah the Hararite; Ahiam son of Sharar the Hararite; [34]Eliphelet son of Ahasbai of Maacah; Eliam son of Ahithophel the Gilonite; [35]Hezro[f] of Carmel; Paarai the Arbite; [36]Igal son of Nathan of Zobah; Bani the Gadite; [37]Zelek the Ammonite; Naharai of Beeroth, the armor-bearer of Joab son of Zeruiah; [38]Ira the Ithrite; Gareb the Ithrite; [39]Uriah the Hittite—thirty-seven in all.

David's Census of Israel and Judah

24 Again the anger of the LORD was kindled against Israel, and he incited David against them, saying, "Go, count the people of Israel and Judah." [2]So the king said to Joab and the commanders of the army,[g] who were with him, "Go through all the tribes of Israel, from Dan to Beer-sheba, and take a census of the people, so that I may know how many there are." [3]But Joab said to the king, "May the LORD your God increase the number of the people a hundredfold, while the eyes of my lord the king can still see it! But why does my lord the king want to do this?" [4]But the king's word prevailed against Joab and the commanders of the army. So Joab and the commanders of the army went out from the presence of the king to take a census of the people of Israel. [5]They crossed the Jordan, and began from[h] Aroer and from the city that is in the middle of the valley, toward Gad and on to Jazer. [6]Then they came to Gilead, and to Kadesh in the land of the Hittites;[i] and they came to Dan, and from Dan[j] they went around to Sidon, [7]and came to the fortress of Tyre and to all the cities of the Hivites and Canaanites; and they went out to the Negeb of Judah at Beer-sheba. [8]So when they had gone through all the land, they came back to Jerusalem at the end of nine months and twenty days. [9]Joab reported to the king the number of those who had been recorded: in Israel there were eight hundred thousand soldiers able to draw the sword, and those of Judah were five hundred thousand.

Judgment on David's Sin

10 But afterward, David was stricken to the heart because he had numbered the people. David said to the LORD, "I have sinned greatly in what I have done. But now, O LORD, I pray you, take away the guilt of your servant; for I have done very foolishly." [11]When David rose in the morning, the word of the LORD came to the prophet Gad, David's seer, saying, [12]"Go and say to David: Thus says the LORD: Three things I offer[k] you; choose one of them, and I will do it to you." [13]So Gad came to David and told him; he asked him, "Shall three[l] years of famine come to you on your land? Or will you flee three months before your foes while they pursue you? Or shall there be three days' pestilence in your land? Now consider, and decide what answer I shall return to the one who sent me." [14]Then David said to Gad, "I am in great distress; let us fall into the hand of the LORD, for his mercy is great; but let me not fall into human hands."

15 So the LORD sent a pestilence on Israel from that morning until the appointed time; and seventy thousand of the people died, from Dan to Beer-sheba. [16]But when the angel stretched

---

a Two Heb Mss Syr: MT *Three*   b Syr Compare 1 Chr 11.25: Heb *Was he the most renowned of the Three?*   c Another reading is *the son of Ish-hai*   d Gk: Heb lacks *sons of*   e Gk: Heb lacks *son of*   f Another reading is *Hezrai*   g 1 Chr 21.2 Gk: Heb *to Joab the commander of the army*   h Gk Mss: Heb *encamped in Aroer south of*   i Gk: Heb *to the land of Tahtim-hodshi*   j Cn Compare Gk: Heb *they came to Dan-jaan and*   k Or *hold over*   l 1 Chr 21.12 Gk: Heb *seven*

out his hand toward Jerusalem to destroy it, the LORD relented concerning the evil, and said to the angel who was bringing destruction among the people, "It is enough; now stay your hand." The angel of the LORD was then by the threshing floor of Araunah the Jebusite. [17]When David saw the angel who was destroying the people, he said to the LORD, "I alone have sinned, and I alone have done wickedly; but these sheep, what have they done? Let your hand, I pray, be against me and against my father's house."

David's Altar on the Threshing Floor

[18] That day Gad came to David and said to him, "Go up and erect an altar to the LORD on the threshing floor of Araunah the Jebusite." [19]Following Gad's instructions, David went up, as the LORD had commanded. [20]When Araunah looked down, he saw the king and his servants coming toward him; and Araunah went out and prostrated himself before the king with his face to the ground. [21]Araunah said, "Why has my lord the king come to his servant?" David said, "To buy the threshing floor from you in order to build an altar to the LORD, so that the plague may be averted from the people." [22]Then Araunah said to David, "Let my lord the king take and offer up what seems good to him; here are the oxen for the burnt offering, and the threshing sledges and the yokes of the oxen for the wood. [23]All this, O king, Araunah gives to the king." And Araunah said to the king, "May the LORD your God respond favorably to you."

[24] But the king said to Araunah, "No, but I will buy them from you for a price; I will not offer burnt offerings to the LORD my God that cost me nothing." So David bought the threshing floor and the oxen for fifty shekels of silver. [25]David built there an altar to the LORD, and offered burnt offerings and offerings of well-being. So the LORD answered his supplication for the land, and the plague was averted from Israel.

The ancient Egyptians had an advanced civilization, yet today the remains of their handiwork lie buried under centuries of sand. The great Roman Empire spanned the Western world at the time of Jesus, yet today, only scattered ruins testify to its existence. The same is true of the glorious but short-lived Israelite kingdom. The Books of First and Second Kings trace its tragic collapse from the glories of Solomon's Temple to the Babylonian Exile.

In Depth

If the kingships of Saul and David could be described as the spring and summer of the Israelite kingdom, the Books of First and Second Kings describe its fall and winter. The beginning of First Kings covers the glorious late summer under King Solomon. Solomon accumulated great riches, constructed a beautiful Temple, and built Jerusalem into a city rivaling any other center of power. But the summer was quickly over at Solomon's death, when the kingdom was split in two (see map 4, "The Kingdom Years"). The northern kingdom, called Israel, and the southern kingdom, called Judah, were ruled by a succession of kings, most of whom proved to be weak and sinful leaders. Their incompetence had disastrous consequences: the two kingdoms fell to foreign powers. Israel fell to the Assyrians in 721 BC, and Judah to the Babylonians in 587 BC.

The sorrow we hear in First and Second Kings is accompanied by a clear explanation: the people have fallen because of their wickedness and the wickedness of their leaders. Not surprisingly, the author of First and Second Kings fashions the history of God's People into a kind of morality tale, emphasizing the importance of faithfulness to the Covenant and the Law.

Of special interest in these books is the appearance of the classical prophet. Unlike the prophets of other lands, who were mere tools in the ruler's hand, the great prophets of Israel and Judah, like Elijah and Elisha, often directly opposed royal decisions and actions. Their job was not to pamper the ruler's pride but to speak God's word clearly and boldly.

As we read about the terrible crises that the kingdoms of Judah and Israel faced, we can reflect on one of the basic truths of human history: Apart from God, there is no hope. Only one thing remains as history passes: God's promise.

At a Glance

- 1 Kings, chapters 1–11, the reign of King Solomon
- 1 Kings, chapter 12, to 2 Kings, chapter 17, the various kings of Israel and Judah
- 2 Kings, chapters 18–30, the kingdom of Judah until its fall in 587 BC

Quick Facts

Period Covered: from 961 to 587 BC

Inspired Author: unknown; from the Deuteronomic tradition, writing after the fall of Jerusalem

Theme: the history of Israel's and Judah's kings from Solomon until the fall of Jerusalem, the faithfulness, or lack of faithfulness, of the rulers and people of Israel and Judah to God

Of Note: The two Books of Kings were originally one book.

1 Kings

The Struggle for the Succession

1 King David was old and advanced in years; and although they covered him with clothes, he could not get warm. ²So his servants said to him, "Let a young virgin be sought for my lord the king, and let her wait on the king, and be his attendant; let her lie in your bosom, so that my lord the king may be warm." ³So they searched for a beautiful girl throughout all the territory of Israel, and found Abishag the Shunammite, and brought her to the king. ⁴The girl was very beautiful. She became the king's attendant and served him, but the king did not know her sexually.

5 Now Adonijah son of Haggith exalted himself, saying, "I will be king"; he prepared for himself chariots and horsemen, and fifty men to run before him. ⁶His father had never at any time displeased him by asking, "Why have you done thus and so?" He was also a very handsome man, and he was born next after Absalom. ⁷He conferred with Joab son of Zeruiah and with the priest Abiathar, and they supported Adonijah. ⁸But the priest Zadok, and Benaiah son of Jehoiada, and the prophet Nathan, and Shimei, and Rei, and David's own warriors did not side with Adonijah.

9 Adonijah sacrificed sheep, oxen, and fatted cattle by the stone Zoheleth, which is beside En-rogel, and he invited all his brothers, the king's sons, and all the royal officials of Judah, ¹⁰but he did not invite the prophet Nathan or Benaiah or the warriors or his brother Solomon.

11 Then Nathan said to Bathsheba, Solomon's mother, "Have you not heard that Adonijah son of Haggith has become king and our lord David does not know it? ¹²Now therefore come, let me give you advice, so that you may save your own life and the life of your son Solomon. ¹³Go in at once to King David, and say to him, 'Did you not, my lord the king, swear to your servant, saying: Your son Solomon shall succeed me as king, and he shall sit on my throne? Why then is Adonijah king?' ¹⁴Then while you are still there speaking with the king, I will come in after you and confirm your words."

15 So Bathsheba went to the king in his room. The king was very old; Abishag the Shunammite was attending the king. ¹⁶Bathsheba bowed and did obeisance to the king, and the king said, "What do you wish?" ¹⁷She said to him, "My lord, you swore to your servant by the LORD your God, saying: Your son Solomon shall succeed me as king, and he shall sit on my throne. ¹⁸But now suddenly Adonijah has become king, though you, my lord the king, do not know it. ¹⁹He has sacrificed oxen, fatted cattle, and sheep in abundance, and has invited all the children of the king, the priest Abiathar, and Joab the commander of the army; but your servant Solomon he has not invited. ²⁰But you, my lord the king—the eyes of all Israel are on you to tell them who shall sit on the throne of my lord the king after him. ²¹Otherwise it will come to pass, when my lord the king sleeps with his ancestors, that my son Solomon and I will be counted offenders."

22 While she was still speaking with the king, the prophet Nathan came in. 23The king was told, "Here is the prophet Nathan." When he came in before the king, he did obeisance to the king, with his face to the ground. 24Nathan said, "My lord the king, have you said, 'Adonijah shall succeed me as king, and he shall sit on my throne'? 25For today he has gone down and has sacrificed oxen, fatted cattle, and sheep in abundance, and has invited all the king's children, Joab the commander[a] of the army, and the priest Abiathar, who are now eating and drinking before him, and saying, 'Long live King Adonijah!' 26But he did not invite me, your servant, and the priest Zadok, and Benaiah son of Jehoiada, and your servant Solomon. 27Has this thing been brought about by my lord the king and you have not let your servants know who should sit on the throne of my lord the king after him?"

The Accession of Solomon

28 King David answered, "Summon Bathsheba to me." So she came into the king's presence, and stood before the king. 29The king swore, saying, "As the LORD lives, who has saved my life from every adversity, 30as I swore to you by the LORD, the God of Israel, 'Your son Solomon shall succeed me as king, and he shall sit on my throne in my place,' so will I do this day." 31Then Bathsheba bowed with her face to the ground, and did obeisance to the king, and said, "May my lord King David live forever!"

32 King David said, "Summon to me the priest Zadok, the prophet Nathan, and Benaiah son of Jehoiada." When they came before the king, 33the king said to them, "Take with you the servants of your lord, and have my son Solomon ride on my own mule, and bring him down to Gihon. 34There let the priest Zadok and the prophet Nathan anoint him king over Israel; then blow the trumpet, and say, 'Long live King Solomon!' 35You shall go up following him. Let him enter and sit on my throne; he shall be king in my place; for I have appointed him to be ruler over Israel and over Judah." 36Benaiah son of Jehoiada answered the king, "Amen! May the LORD, the God of my lord the king, so ordain. 37As the LORD has been with my lord the king, so may he be with Solomon, and make his throne greater than the throne of my lord King David."

38 So the priest Zadok, the prophet Nathan, and Benaiah son of Jehoiada, and the Cherethites and the Pelethites, went down and had Solomon ride on King David's mule, and led him to Gihon. 39There the priest Zadok took the horn of oil from the tent and anointed Solomon. Then they blew the trumpet, and all the people said, "Long live King Solomon!" 40And all the people went up following him, playing on pipes and rejoicing with great joy, so that the earth quaked at their noise.

41 Adonijah and all the guests who were with him heard it as they finished feasting. When Joab heard the sound of the trumpet, he said, "Why is the city in an uproar?" 42While he was still speaking, Jonathan son of the priest Abiathar arrived. Adonijah said, "Come in, for you are a worthy man and surely you bring good news." 43Jonathan answered Adonijah, "No, for our lord King David has made Solomon king; 44the king has sent with him the priest Zadok, the prophet Nathan, and Benaiah son of Jehoiada, and the Cherethites and the Pelethites; and they had him ride on the king's mule; 45the priest Zadok and the prophet Nathan have anointed him king at Gihon; and they have gone up from there rejoicing, so that the city is in an uproar. This is the noise that you heard. 46Solomon now sits on the royal throne. 47Moreover the king's servants came to congratulate our lord King David, saying, 'May God make the name of Solomon more famous than yours, and make his throne greater than your throne.' The king bowed in worship on the bed 48and went on to pray thus, 'Blessed be the LORD, the God of Israel, who today has granted one of my offspring[b] to sit on my throne and permitted me to witness it.' "

49 Then all the guests of Adonijah got up trembling and went their own ways. 50Adonijah, fearing Solomon, got up and went to grasp the horns of the altar. 51Solomon was informed, "Adonijah is afraid of King Solomon; see, he has laid hold of the horns of the altar, saying, 'Let King Solomon swear to me first that he will not kill his servant with the sword.' " 52So Solomon responded, "If he proves to be a worthy man, not one of his hairs shall fall to the ground; but if wickedness is found in him, he shall die." 53Then King Solomon sent to have him brought down from the altar. He came to do obeisance to King Solomon; and Solomon said to him, "Go home."

David's Instruction to Solomon

2 When David's time to die drew near, he charged his son Solomon, saying: 2"I am about to go the way of all the earth. Be strong, be courageous, 3and keep the charge of the LORD your God, walking in his ways and keeping his statutes, his commandments, his ordinances,

---

a Gk: Heb the commanders   b Gk: Heb one

Introducing...

Solomon

Solomon was one of the sons of David and Bathsheba. He ruled for forty years after King David died, and he was the third and last king to rule over the united kingdom of Israel.

There is an old saying that often our personal strengths are our greatest weaknesses. This is true of Solomon. He was a tremendous organizer, an able ruler, a clever politician, and a great builder—it was during his reign that the first Temple was built in Jerusalem. To fulfill these great accomplishments, however, Solomon taxed his people heavily, married foreign women to seal political alliances with other nations, and used forced labor to complete his building projects. These things offended God and made Solomon unpopular with the people of Israel.

When Solomon died, ten of the original twelve Tribes from the northern part of Israel left the kingdom and set up their own kingdom. Israel never again existed as a united kingdom ruled by an Israelite king. The author of Kings attributes this more to Solomon's acceptance of other gods near the end of his life than to his political mistakes.

and his testimonies, as it is written in the law of Moses, so that you may prosper in all that you do and wherever you turn. ⁴Then the LORD will establish his word that he spoke concerning me: 'If your heirs take heed to their way, to walk before me in faithfulness with all their heart and with all their soul, there shall not fail you a successor on the throne of Israel.'

5 "Moreover you know also what Joab son of Zeruiah did to me, how he dealt with the two commanders of the armies of Israel, Abner son of Ner, and Amasa son of Jether, whom he murdered, retaliating in time of peace for blood that had been shed in war, and putting the blood of war on the belt around his waist, and on the sandals on his feet. ⁶Act therefore according to your wisdom, but do not let his gray head go down to Sheol in peace. ⁷Deal loyally, however, with the sons of Barzillai the Gileadite, and let them be among those who eat at your table; for with such loyalty they met me when I fled from your

brother Absalom. ⁸There is also with you Shimei son of Gera, the Benjaminite from Bahurim, who cursed me with a terrible curse on the day when I went to Mahanaim; but when he came down to meet me at the Jordan, I swore to him by the LORD, 'I will not put you to death with the sword.' ⁹Therefore do not hold him guiltless, for you are a wise man; you will know what you ought to do to him, and you must bring his gray head down with blood to Sheol."

Death of David

10 Then David slept with his ancestors, and was buried in the city of David. ¹¹The time that David reigned over Israel was forty years; he reigned seven years in Hebron, and thirty-three years in Jerusalem. ¹²So Solomon sat on the throne of his father David; and his kingdom was firmly established.

Solomon Consolidates His Reign

13 Then Adonijah son of Haggith came to Bathsheba, Solomon's mother. She asked, "Do you come peaceably?" He said, "Peaceably." ¹⁴Then he said, "May I have a word with you?" She said, "Go on." ¹⁵He said, "You know that the kingdom was mine, and that all Israel expected me to reign; however, the kingdom has turned about and become my brother's, for it was his from the LORD. ¹⁶And now I have one request to make of you; do not refuse me." She said to him, "Go on." ¹⁷He said, "Please ask King Solomon—he will not refuse you—to give me Abishag the Shunammite as my wife." ¹⁸Bathsheba said, "Very well; I will speak to the king on your behalf."

19 So Bathsheba went to King Solomon, to speak to him on behalf of Adonijah. The king rose to meet her, and bowed down to her; then he sat on his throne, and had a throne brought for the king's mother, and she sat on his right. ²⁰Then she said, "I have one small request to make of you; do not refuse me." And the king said to her, "Make your request, my mother; for I will not refuse you." ²¹She said, "Let Abishag the Shunammite be given to your brother Adonijah as his wife." ²²King Solomon answered his mother, "And why do you ask Abishag the Shunammite for Adonijah? Ask for him the kingdom as well! For he is my elder brother; ask not only for him but also for the priest Abiathar and for Joab son of Zeruiah!" ²³Then King Solomon swore by the LORD, "So may God do to me, and more also, for Adonijah has devised this scheme at the risk of his life! ²⁴Now therefore as the LORD lives, who has established me and placed me on the throne of my father David, and who has made

me a house as he promised, today Adonijah shall be put to death." ²⁵So King Solomon sent Benaiah son of Jehoiada; he struck him down, and he died.

26 The king said to the priest Abiathar, "Go to Anathoth, to your estate; for you deserve death. But I will not at this time put you to death, because you carried the ark of the Lord GOD before my father David, and because you shared in all the hardships my father endured." ²⁷So Solomon banished Abiathar from being priest to the LORD, thus fulfilling the word of the LORD that he had spoken concerning the house of Eli in Shiloh.

28 When the news came to Joab—for Joab had supported Adonijah though he had not supported Absalom—Joab fled to the tent of the LORD and grasped the horns of the altar. ²⁹When it was told King Solomon, "Joab has fled to the tent of the LORD and now is beside the altar," Solomon sent Benaiah son of Jehoiada, saying, "Go, strike him down." ³⁰So Benaiah came to the tent of the LORD and said to him, "The king commands, 'Come out.'" But he said, "No, I will die here." Then Benaiah brought the king word again, saying, "Thus said Joab, and thus he answered me." ³¹The king replied to him, "Do as he has said, strike him down and bury him; and thus take away from me and from my father's house the guilt for the blood that Joab shed without cause. ³²The LORD will bring back his bloody deeds on his own head, because, without the knowledge of my father David, he attacked and killed with the sword two men more righteous and better than himself, Abner son of Ner, commander of the army of Israel, and Amasa son of Jether, commander of the army of Judah. ³³So shall their blood come back on the head of Joab and on the head of his descendants forever; but to David, and to his descendants, and to his house, and to his throne, there shall be peace from the LORD forevermore." ³⁴Then Benaiah son of Jehoiada went up and struck him down and killed him; and he was buried at his own house near the wilderness. ³⁵The king put Benaiah son of Jehoiada over the army in his place, and the king put the priest Zadok in the place of Abiathar.

36 Then the king sent and summoned Shimei, and said to him, "Build yourself a house in Jerusalem, and live there, and do not go out from there to any place whatever. ³⁷For on the day you go out, and cross the Wadi Kidron, know for certain that you shall die; your blood shall be on your own head." ³⁸And Shimei said to the king, "The sentence is fair; as my lord the king has said, so will your servant do." So Shimei lived in Jerusalem many days.

39 But it happened at the end of three years that two of Shimei's slaves ran away to King Achish son of Maacah of Gath. When it was told Shimei, "Your slaves are in Gath," ⁴⁰Shimei arose and saddled a donkey, and went to Achish in Gath, to search for his slaves; Shimei went and brought his slaves from Gath. ⁴¹When Solomon was told that Shimei had gone from Jerusalem to Gath and returned, ⁴²the king sent and summoned Shimei, and said to him, "Did I not make you swear by the LORD, and solemnly adjure you, saying, 'Know for certain that on the day you go out and go to any place whatever, you shall die'? And you said to me, 'The sentence is fair; I accept.' ⁴³Why then have you not kept your oath to the LORD and the commandment with which I charged you?" ⁴⁴The king also said to Shimei, "You know in your own heart all the evil that you did to my father David; so the LORD will bring back your evil on your own head. ⁴⁵But King Solomon shall be blessed, and the throne of David shall be established before the LORD forever." ⁴⁶Then the king commanded Benaiah son of Jehoiada; and he went out and struck him down, and he died.

So the kingdom was established in the hand of Solomon.

Solomon's Prayer for Wisdom

3 Solomon made a marriage alliance with Pharaoh king of Egypt; he took Pharaoh's daughter and brought her into the city of David, until he had finished building his own house and the house of the LORD and the wall around Jerusalem. ²The people were sacrificing at the high places, however, because no house had yet been built for the name of the LORD.

3 Solomon loved the LORD, walking in the statutes of his father David; only, he sacrificed and offered incense at the high places. ⁴The king went to Gibeon to sacrifice there, for that was the principal high place; Solomon used to offer a thousand burnt offerings on that altar. ⁵At Gibeon the LORD appeared to Solomon in a dream by night; and God said, "Ask what I should give you." ⁶And Solomon said, "You have shown great and steadfast love to your servant my father David, because he walked before you in faithfulness, in righteousness, and in uprightness of heart toward you; and you have kept for him this great and steadfast love, and have given him a son to sit on his throne today. ⁷And now, O LORD my God, you have made your servant king in place of my father David, although I am only a little child; I do not know how to go out or come in. ⁸And your servant is in the midst

of the people whom you have chosen, a great people, so numerous they cannot be numbered or counted. ⁹Give your servant therefore an understanding mind to govern your people, able to discern between good and evil; for who can govern this your great people?"

10 It pleased the Lord that Solomon had asked this. ¹¹God said to him, "Because you have asked this, and have not asked for yourself long life or riches, or for the life of your enemies, but have asked for yourself understanding to discern what is right, ¹²I now do according to your word. Indeed I give you a wise and discerning mind; no one like you has been before you and no one like you shall arise after you. ¹³I give you also what you have not asked, both riches and honor all your life; no other king shall compare with you. ¹⁴If you will walk in my ways, keeping my statutes and my commandments, as your father David walked, then I will lengthen your life."

15 Then Solomon awoke; it had been a dream. He came to Jerusalem where he stood before the ark of the covenant of the LORD. He offered up burnt offerings and offerings of well-being, and provided a feast for all his servants.

God, Give Me Wisdom!

Isn't it interesting that of all the things Solomon could have asked God for, he chose wisdom? Actually, he asked for an understanding heart. That really is a wonderful thing to ask God for. And indeed Solomon was noted for his wisdom, far and wide.

We generally associate wisdom with old age. There is some truth in that connection. As we grow through life and gain experience, we tend to grow wiser. That growth is a sign of maturity. We know there are some people who never seem to learn from their mistakes, and we know there are also foolish old people. But generally, as we mature, we become wiser.

● Why not make Solomon's prayer for an understanding heart your own? In what ways have you become more mature?

▶ 1 Kings 3:4–15

Solomon's Wisdom in Judgment

16 Later, two women who were prostitutes came to the king and stood before him. ¹⁷The one woman said, "Please, my lord, this woman and I live in the same house; and I gave birth while she was in the house. ¹⁸Then on the third day after I gave birth, this woman also gave birth. We were together; there was no one else with us in the house, only the two of us were in the house. ¹⁹Then this woman's son died in the night, because she lay on him. ²⁰She got up in the middle of the night and took my son from beside me while your servant slept. She laid him at her breast, and laid her dead son at my breast. ²¹When I rose in the morning to nurse my son, I saw that he was dead; but when I looked at him closely in the morning, clearly it was not the son I had borne." ²²But the other woman said, "No, the living son is mine, and the dead son is yours." The first said, "No, the dead son is yours, and the living son is mine." So they argued before the king.

23 Then the king said, "The one says, 'This is my son that is alive, and your son is dead'; while the other says, 'Not so! Your son is dead, and my son is the living one.' " ²⁴So the king said, "Bring me a sword," and they brought a sword before the king. ²⁵The king said, "Divide the living boy in two; then give half to the one, and half to the other." ²⁶But the woman whose son was alive said to the king—because compassion for her son burned within her—"Please, my lord, give her the living boy; certainly do not kill him!" The other said, "It shall be neither mine nor yours; divide it." ²⁷Then the king responded: "Give the first woman the living boy; do not kill him. She is his mother." ²⁸All Israel heard of the judgment that the king had rendered; and they stood in awe of the king, because they perceived that the wisdom of God was in him, to execute justice.

Solomon's Administrative Officers

4 King Solomon was king over all Israel, ²and these were his high officials: Azariah son of Zadok was the priest; ³Elihoreph and Ahijah sons of Shisha were secretaries; Jehoshaphat son of Ahilud was recorder; ⁴Benaiah son of Jehoiada was in command of the army; Zadok and Abiathar were priests; ⁵Azariah son of Nathan was over the officials; Zabud son of Nathan was priest and king's friend; ⁶Ahishar was in charge of the palace; and Adoniram son of Abda was in charge of the forced labor.

7 Solomon had twelve officials over all Israel, who provided food for the king and his household;

each one had to make provision for one month in the year. ⁸These were their names: Ben-hur, in the hill country of Ephraim; ⁹Ben-deker, in Makaz, Shaalbim, Beth-shemesh, and Elon-beth-hanan; ¹⁰Ben-hesed, in Arubboth (to him belonged Socoh and all the land of Hepher); ¹¹Ben-abinadab, in all Naphath-dor (he had Taphath, Solomon's daughter, as his wife); ¹²Baana son of Ahilud, in Taanach, Megiddo, and all Beth-shean, which is beside Zarethan below Jezreel, and from Beth-shean to Abel-meholah, as far as the other side of Jokmeam; ¹³Ben-geber, in Ramoth-gilead (he had the villages of Jair son of Manasseh, which are in Gilead, and he had the region of Argob, which is in Bashan, sixty great cities with walls and bronze bars); ¹⁴Ahinadab son of Iddo, in Mahanaim; ¹⁵Ahimaaz, in Naphtali (he had taken Basemath, Solomon's daughter, as his wife); ¹⁶Baana son of Hushai, in Asher and Bealoth; ¹⁷Jehoshaphat son of Paruah, in Issachar; ¹⁸Shimei son of Ela, in Benjamin; ¹⁹Geber son of Uri, in the land of Gilead, the country of King Sihon of the Amorites and of King Og of Bashan. And there was one official in the land of Judah.

Magnificence of Solomon's Rule

20 Judah and Israel were as numerous as the sand by the sea; they ate and drank and were happy. ²¹ᵃ Solomon was sovereign over all the kingdoms from the Euphrates to the land of the Philistines, even to the border of Egypt; they brought tribute and served Solomon all the days of his life.

22 Solomon's provision for one day was thirty cors of choice flour, and sixty cors of meal, ²³ten fat oxen, and twenty pasture-fed cattle, one hundred sheep, besides deer, gazelles, roebucks, and fatted fowl. ²⁴For he had dominion over all the region west of the Euphrates from Tiphsah to Gaza, over all the kings west of the Euphrates; and he had peace on all sides. ²⁵During Solomon's lifetime Judah and Israel lived in safety, from Dan even to Beer-sheba, all of them under their vines and fig trees. ²⁶Solomon also had forty thousand stalls of horses for his chariots, and twelve thousand horsemen. ²⁷Those officials supplied provisions for King Solomon and for all who came to King Solomon's table, each one in his month; they let nothing be lacking. ²⁸They also brought to the required place barley and straw for the horses and swift steeds, each according to his charge.

Fame of Solomon's Wisdom

29 God gave Solomon very great wisdom, discernment, and breadth of understanding as vast

Pray It!

A Wise Heart

A famous prayer, often called the "Peace Prayer," by Saint Francis of Assisi (AD 1181–1226), contains the line "Lord, grant that I may not so much seek to be . . . understood, as to understand."

It is almost as if Saint Francis is echoing the prayer of King Solomon, who lived two thousand years before him. The request is the same. Both men ask God to give them the gift of a wise heart—the ability to see things as God sees things.

What a difference wisdom can make in our lives. What a wonderful thing to pray for. What a blessing to increase the amount of wisdom in our world. What inspiring examples we have in the prayers of Solomon a millennium before Jesus, and of Francis a millennium after.

Let us ask God daily for a wise heart.

▶ **1 Kings 3:9**

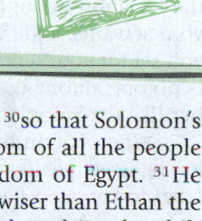

as the sand on the seashore, ³⁰so that Solomon's wisdom surpassed the wisdom of all the people of the east, and all the wisdom of Egypt. ³¹He was wiser than anyone else, wiser than Ethan the Ezrahite, and Heman, Calcol, and Darda, children of Mahol; his fame spread throughout all the surrounding nations. ³²He composed three thousand proverbs, and his songs numbered a thousand and five. ³³He would speak of trees, from the cedar that is in the Lebanon to the hyssop that grows in the wall; he would speak of animals, and birds, and reptiles, and fish. ³⁴People came from all the nations to hear the wisdom of Solomon; they came from all the kings of the earth who had heard of his wisdom.

Preparations and Materials for the Temple

5 ᵇ Now King Hiram of Tyre sent his servants to Solomon, when he heard that they had anointed him king in place of his father; for Hiram had always been a friend to David. ²Solomon sent word to Hiram, saying, ³"You know

a Ch 5.1 in Heb   *b* Ch 5.15 in Heb

Cultural Connection

The First Book of Kings says, "Solomon's wisdom surpassed the wisdom of all the people of the east, and all the wisdom of Egypt" (4:30).

This should be a source of pride for young African Americans. The people of Egypt and of the East are dark-skinned people. Ancient southern Egypt included the country of modern Ethiopia. The people in these countries must have been well known for their wisdom in order for the biblical author to use them in a comparison with Solomon. African Americans can praise God for their African ancestors: the wise, black people from Egypt and the East.

▶ **1 Kings 4:30**

---

that my father David could not build a house for the name of the LORD his God because of the warfare with which his enemies surrounded him, until the LORD put them under the soles of his feet.[a] [4]But now the LORD my God has given me rest on every side; there is neither adversary nor misfortune. [5]So I intend to build a house for the name of the LORD my God, as the LORD said to my father David, 'Your son, whom I will set on your throne in your place, shall build the house for my name.' [6]Therefore command that cedars from the Lebanon be cut for me. My servants will join your servants, and I will give you whatever wages you set for your servants; for you know that there is no one among us who knows how to cut timber like the Sidonians."

[7] When Hiram heard the words of Solomon, he rejoiced greatly, and said, "Blessed be the LORD today, who has given to David a wise son to be over this great people." [8]Hiram sent word to Solomon, "I have heard the message that you have sent to me; I will fulfill all your needs in the matter of cedar and cypress timber. [9]My servants shall bring it down to the sea from the Lebanon; I will make it into rafts to go by sea to the place you indicate. I will have them broken up there for you to take away. And you shall meet my needs by providing food for my household." [10]So Hiram supplied Solomon's every need for timber of cedar and cypress. [11]Solomon in turn gave Hiram twenty thousand cors of wheat as food for his household, and twenty cors of fine oil. Solomon gave this to Hiram year by year. [12]So the LORD gave Solomon wisdom, as he promised him. There was peace between Hiram and Solomon; and the two of them made a treaty.

13 King Solomon conscripted forced labor out of all Israel; the levy numbered thirty thousand men. [14]He sent them to the Lebanon, ten thousand a month in shifts; they would be a month in the Lebanon and two months at home; Adoniram was in charge of the forced labor. [15]Solomon also had seventy thousand laborers and eighty thousand stonecutters in the hill country, [16]besides Solomon's three thousand three hundred supervisors who were over the work, having charge of the people who did the work. [17]At the king's command, they quarried out great, costly stones in order to lay the foundation of the house with dressed stones. [18]So Solomon's builders and Hiram's builders and the Gebalites did the stonecutting and prepared the timber and the stone to build the house.

Solomon Builds the Temple

6 In the four hundred eightieth year after the Israelites came out of the land of Egypt, in the fourth year of Solomon's reign over Israel, in the month of Ziv, which is the second month, he

5:8–10

---

a Gk Tg Vg: Heb *my feet* or *his feet*

began to build the house of the Lord. [2]The house that King Solomon built for the Lord was sixty cubits long, twenty cubits wide, and thirty cubits high. [3]The vestibule in front of the nave of the house was twenty cubits wide, across the width of the house. Its depth was ten cubits in front of the house. [4]For the house he made windows with recessed frames.[a] [5]He also built a structure against the wall of the house, running around the walls of the house, both the nave and the inner sanctuary; and he made side chambers all around. [6]The lowest story[b] was five cubits wide, the middle one was six cubits wide, and the third was seven cubits wide; for around the outside of the house he made offsets on the wall in order that the supporting beams should not be inserted into the walls of the house.

7 The house was built with stone finished at the quarry, so that neither hammer nor ax nor any tool of iron was heard in the temple while it was being built.

8 The entrance for the middle story was on the south side of the house: one went up by winding stairs to the middle story, and from the middle story to the third. [9]So he built the house, and finished it; he roofed the house with beams and planks of cedar. [10]He built the structure against the whole house, each story[c] five cubits high, and it was joined to the house with timbers of cedar.

11 Now the word of the Lord came to Solomon, [12]"Concerning this house that you are building, if you will walk in my statutes, obey my ordinances, and keep all my commandments by walking in them, then I will establish my promise with you, which I made to your father David. [13]I will dwell among the children of Israel, and will not forsake my people Israel."

14 So Solomon built the house, and finished it. [15]He lined the walls of the house on the inside with boards of cedar; from the floor of the house to the rafters of the ceiling, he covered them on the inside with wood; and he covered the floor of the house with boards of cypress. [16]He built twenty cubits of the rear of the house with boards of cedar from the floor to the rafters, and he built this within as an inner sanctuary, as the most holy place. [17]The house, that is, the nave in front of the inner sanctuary, was forty cubits long. [18]The cedar within the house had carvings of gourds and open flowers; all was cedar, no stone was seen. [19]The inner sanctuary he prepared in the innermost part of the house, to set there the ark of the covenant of the Lord. [20]The interior of the inner sanctuary was twenty cubits long, twenty cubits wide, and twenty cubits high; he overlaid it with pure gold. He also overlaid the altar with cedar.[d] [21]Solomon overlaid the inside of the house with pure gold, then he drew chains of gold across, in front of the inner sanctuary, and overlaid it with gold. [22]Next he overlaid the whole house with gold, in order that the whole house might be perfect; even the whole altar that belonged to the inner sanctuary he overlaid with gold.

The Furnishings of the Temple

23 In the inner sanctuary he made two cherubim of olivewood, each ten cubits high. [24]Five cubits was the length of one wing of the cherub, and five cubits the length of the other wing of the cherub; it was ten cubits from the tip of one wing to the tip of the other. [25]The other cherub also measured ten cubits; both cherubim had the same measure and the same form. [26]The height of one cherub was ten cubits, and so was that of the other cherub. [27]He put the cherubim in the innermost part of the house; the wings of the cherubim were spread out so that a wing of one was touching the one wall, and a wing of the other cherub was touching the other wall; their other wings toward the center of the house were touching wing to wing. [28]He also overlaid the cherubim with gold.

29 He carved the walls of the house all around about with carved engravings of cherubim, palm trees, and open flowers, in the inner and outer rooms. [30]The floor of the house he overlaid with gold, in the inner and outer rooms.

31 For the entrance to the inner sanctuary he made doors of olivewood; the lintel and the doorposts were five-sided.[d] [32]He covered the two doors of olivewood with carvings of cherubim, palm trees, and open flowers; he overlaid them with gold, and spread gold on the cherubim and on the palm trees.

33 So also he made for the entrance to the nave doorposts of olivewood, four-sided each, [34]and two doors of cypress wood; the two leaves of the one door were folding, and the two leaves of the other door were folding. [35]He carved cherubim, palm trees, and open flowers, overlaying them with gold evenly applied upon the carved work. [36]He built the inner court with three courses of dressed stone to one course of cedar beams.

37 In the fourth year the foundation of the house of the Lord was laid, in the month of Ziv. [38]In the eleventh year, in the month of Bul, which

---

a Gk: Meaning of Heb uncertain   b Gk: Heb structure
c Heb lacks each story   d Meaning of Heb uncertain

is the eighth month, the house was finished in all its parts, and according to all its specifications. He was seven years in building it.

Solomon's Palace and Other Buildings

7 Solomon was building his own house thirteen years, and he finished his entire house.

2 He built the House of the Forest of the Lebanon one hundred cubits long, fifty cubits wide, and thirty cubits high, built on four rows of cedar pillars, with cedar beams on the pillars. ³It was roofed with cedar on the forty-five rafters, fifteen in each row, which were on the pillars. ⁴There were window frames in the three rows, facing each other in the three rows. ⁵All the doorways and doorposts had four-sided frames, opposite, facing each other in the three rows.

6 He made the Hall of Pillars fifty cubits long and thirty cubits wide. There was a porch in front with pillars, and a canopy in front of them.

7 He made the Hall of the Throne where he was to pronounce judgment, the Hall of Justice, covered with cedar from floor to floor.

8 His own house where he would reside, in the other court back of the hall, was of the same construction. Solomon also made a house like this hall for Pharaoh's daughter, whom he had taken in marriage.

9 All these were made of costly stones, cut according to measure, sawed with saws, back and front, from the foundation to the coping, and from outside to the great court. ¹⁰The foundation was of costly stones, huge stones, stones of eight and ten cubits. ¹¹There were costly stones above, cut to measure, and cedarwood. ¹²The great court had three courses of dressed stone to one layer of cedar beams all around; so had the inner court of the house of the Lord, and the vestibule of the house.

Products of Hiram the Bronzeworker

13 Now King Solomon invited and received Hiram from Tyre. ¹⁴He was the son of a widow of the tribe of Naphtali, whose father, a man of Tyre, had been an artisan in bronze; he was full of skill, intelligence, and knowledge in working bronze. He came to King Solomon, and did all his work.

15 He cast two pillars of bronze. Eighteen cubits was the height of the one, and a cord of twelve cubits would encircle it; the second pillar was the same.[a] ¹⁶He also made two capitals of molten bronze, to set on the tops of the pillars; the height of the one capital was five cubits, and the height of the other capital was five cubits. ¹⁷There were nets of checker work with wreaths

of chain work for the capitals on the tops of the pillars; seven[b] for the one capital, and seven[b] for the other capital. ¹⁸He made the columns with two rows around each latticework to cover the capitals that were above the pomegranates; he did the same with the other capital. ¹⁹Now the capitals that were on the tops of the pillars in the vestibule were of lily-work, four cubits high. ²⁰The capitals were on the two pillars and also above the rounded projection that was beside the latticework; there were two hundred pomegranates in rows all around; and so with the other capital. ²¹He set up the pillars at the vestibule of the temple; he set up the pillar on the south and called it Jachin; and he set up the pillar on the north and called it Boaz. ²²On the tops of the pillars was lily-work. Thus the work of the pillars was finished.

23 Then he made the molten sea; it was round, ten cubits from brim to brim, and five cubits high. A line of thirty cubits would encircle it completely. ²⁴Under its brim were panels all around it, each of ten cubits, surrounding the sea; there were two rows of panels, cast when it was cast. ²⁵It stood on twelve oxen, three facing north, three facing west, three facing south, and three facing east; the sea was set on them. The hindquarters of each were toward the inside. ²⁶Its thickness was a handbreadth; its brim was made like the brim of a cup, like the flower of a lily; it held two thousand baths.[c]

27 He also made the ten stands of bronze; each stand was four cubits long, four cubits wide, and three cubits high. ²⁸This was the construction of the stands: they had borders; the borders were within the frames; ²⁹on the borders that were set in the frames were lions, oxen, and cherubim. On the frames, both above and below the lions and oxen, there were wreaths of beveled work. ³⁰Each stand had four bronze wheels and axles of bronze; at the four corners were supports for a basin. The supports were cast with wreaths at the side of each. ³¹Its opening was within the crown whose height was one cubit; its opening was round, as a pedestal is made; it was a cubit and a half wide. At its opening there were carvings; its borders were four-sided, not round. ³²The four wheels were underneath the borders; the axles of the wheels were in the stands; and the height of a wheel was a cubit and a half. ³³The wheels were made like a chariot wheel; their axles, their rims, their spokes, and their hubs were all cast.

---

a Cn: Heb *and a cord of twelve cubits encircled the second pillar*; Compare Jer 52.21   b Heb: Gk *a net*   c A Heb measure of volume

34There were four supports at the four corners of each stand; the supports were of one piece with the stands. 35On the top of the stand there was a round band half a cubit high; on the top of the stand, its stays and its borders were of one piece with it. 36On the surfaces of its stays and on its borders he carved cherubim, lions, and palm trees, where each had space, with wreaths all around. 37In this way he made the ten stands; all of them were cast alike, with the same size and the same form.

38 He made ten basins of bronze; each basin held forty baths,*a* each basin measured four cubits; there was a basin for each of the ten stands. 39He set five of the stands on the south side of the house, and five on the north side of the house; he set the sea on the southeast corner of the house.

40 Hiram also made the pots, the shovels, and the basins. So Hiram finished all the work that he did for King Solomon on the house of the Lord: 41the two pillars, the two bowls of the capitals that were on the tops of the pillars, the two latticeworks to cover the two bowls of the capitals that were on the tops of the pillars; 42the four hundred pomegranates for the two latticeworks, two rows of pomegranates for each latticework, to cover the two bowls of the capitals that were on the pillars; 43the ten stands, the ten basins on the stands; 44the one sea, and the twelve oxen underneath the sea.

45 The pots, the shovels, and the basins, all these vessels that Hiram made for King Solomon for the house of the Lord were of burnished bronze. 46In the plain of the Jordan the king cast them, in the clay ground between Succoth and Zarethan. 47Solomon left all the vessels unweighed, because there were so many of them; the weight of the bronze was not determined.

48 So Solomon made all the vessels that were in the house of the Lord: the golden altar, the golden table for the bread of the Presence, 49the lampstands of pure gold, five on the south side and five on the north, in front of the inner sanctuary; the flowers, the lamps, and the tongs, of gold; 50the cups, snuffers, basins, dishes for incense, and firepans, of pure gold; the sockets for the doors of the innermost part of the house, the most holy place, and for the doors of the nave of the temple, of gold.

51 Thus all the work that King Solomon did on the house of the Lord was finished. Solomon brought in the things that his father David had dedicated, the silver, the gold, and the vessels, and stored them in the treasuries of the house of the Lord.

Dedication of the Temple

8 Then Solomon assembled the elders of Israel and all the heads of the tribes, the leaders of the ancestral houses of the Israelites, before King Solomon in Jerusalem, to bring up the ark of the covenant of the Lord out of the city of David, which is Zion. 2All the people of Israel assembled to King Solomon at the festival in the month Ethanim, which is the seventh month. 3And all the elders of Israel came, and the priests carried the ark. 4So they brought up the ark of the Lord, the tent of meeting, and all the holy vessels that were in the tent; the priests and the Levites brought them up. 5King Solomon and all the congregation of Israel, who had assembled before him, were with him before the ark, sacrificing so many sheep and oxen that they could not be counted or numbered. 6Then the priests brought the ark of the covenant of the Lord to its place, in the inner sanctuary of the house, in the most holy place, underneath the wings of the cherubim. 7For the cherubim spread out their wings over the place of the ark, so that the cherubim made a covering above the ark and its poles. 8The poles were so long that the ends of the poles were seen from the holy place in front of the inner sanctuary; but they could not be seen from outside; they are there to this day. 9There was nothing in the ark except the two tablets of stone that Moses had placed there at Horeb, where the Lord made a covenant with the Israelites, when they came out of the land of Egypt. 10And when the priests came out of the holy place, a cloud filled the house of the Lord, 11so that the priests could not stand to minister because of the cloud; for the glory of the Lord filled the house of the Lord.

12 Then Solomon said,

"The Lord has said that he would dwell in thick
 darkness.
13 I have built you an exalted house,
 a place for you to dwell in forever."

Solomon's Speech

14 Then the king turned around and blessed all the assembly of Israel, while all the assembly of Israel stood. 15He said, "Blessed be the Lord, the God of Israel, who with his hand has fulfilled what he promised with his mouth to my father David, saying, 16'Since the day that I brought my people Israel out of Egypt, I have not chosen a city from any of the tribes of Israel in which to build a house, that my name might be there; but

---

a A Heb measure of volume

Holy Places

Solomon knows that the Temple will not hold God. Holy places are not cages to keep God contained. People need holy places more than God does. We gather together in public holy places to experience God's presence as a community. But we can also meet God one-on-one in private holy places, special to us alone.

Try creating a holy space in your bedroom. Clear out a corner, and place there a small table and a chair or rug to sit on. On the table, put your Bible and an object or two to help you focus on God. You might use a candle, a special picture or statue, or something from a retreat or a special place. Try to spend a little time each day in your holy space with God.

▶ **1 Kings 8:27–30**

I chose David to be over my people Israel.' ¹⁷My father David had it in mind to build a house for the name of the LORD, the God of Israel. ¹⁸But the LORD said to my father David, 'You did well to consider building a house for my name; ¹⁹nevertheless you shall not build the house, but your son who shall be born to you shall build the house for my name.' ²⁰Now the LORD has upheld the promise that he made; for I have risen in the place of my father David; I sit on the throne of Israel, as the LORD promised, and have built the house for the name of the LORD, the God of Israel. ²¹There I have provided a place for the ark, in which is the covenant of the LORD that he made with our ancestors when he brought them out of the land of Egypt."

Solomon's Prayer of Dedication

22 Then Solomon stood before the altar of the LORD in the presence of all the assembly of Israel, and spread out his hands to heaven. ²³He said, "O LORD, God of Israel, there is no God like you in heaven above or on earth beneath, keeping covenant and steadfast love for your servants who walk before you with all their heart, ²⁴the covenant that you kept for your servant my father David as you declared to him; you promised

with your mouth and have this day fulfilled with your hand. ²⁵Therefore, O LORD, God of Israel, keep for your servant my father David that which you promised him, saying, 'There shall never fail you a successor before me to sit on the throne of Israel, if only your children look to their way, to walk before me as you have walked before me.' ²⁶Therefore, O God of Israel, let your word be confirmed, which you promised to your servant my father David.

27 "But will God indeed dwell on the earth? Even heaven and the highest heaven cannot contain you, much less this house that I have built! ²⁸Regard your servant's prayer and his plea, O LORD my God, heeding the cry and the prayer that your servant prays to you today; ²⁹that your eyes may be open night and day toward this house, the place of which you said, 'My name shall be there,' that you may heed the prayer that your servant prays toward this place. ³⁰Hear the plea of your servant and of your people Israel when they pray toward this place; O hear in heaven your dwelling place; heed and forgive.

31 "If someone sins against a neighbor and is given an oath to swear, and comes and swears before your altar in this house, ³²then hear in heaven, and act, and judge your servants, condemning the guilty by bringing their conduct on their own head, and vindicating the righteous by rewarding them according to their righteousness.

33 "When your people Israel, having sinned against you, are defeated before an enemy but turn again to you, confess your name, pray and plead with you in this house, ³⁴then hear in heaven, forgive the sin of your people Israel, and bring them again to the land that you gave to their ancestors.

35 "When heaven is shut up and there is no rain because they have sinned against you, and then they pray toward this place, confess your name, and turn from their sin, because you punish[a] them, ³⁶then hear in heaven, and forgive the sin of your servants, your people Israel, when you teach them the good way in which they should walk; and grant rain on your land, which you have given to your people as an inheritance.

37 "If there is famine in the land, if there is plague, blight, mildew, locust, or caterpillar; if their enemy besieges them in any[b] of their cities; whatever plague, whatever sickness there is; ³⁸whatever prayer, whatever plea there is from any individual or from all your people Israel, all knowing the afflictions of their own hearts

a Or *when you answer*   *b* Gk Syr: Heb *in the land*

so that they stretch out their hands toward this house; [39]then hear in heaven your dwelling place, forgive, act, and render to all whose hearts you know—according to all their ways, for only you know what is in every human heart— [40]so that they may fear you all the days that they live in the land that you gave to our ancestors.

41 "Likewise when a foreigner, who is not of your people Israel, comes from a distant land because of your name [42]—for they shall hear of your great name, your mighty hand, and your outstretched arm—when a foreigner comes and prays toward this house, [43]then hear in heaven your dwelling place, and do according to all that the foreigner calls to you, so that all the peoples of the earth may know your name and fear you, as do your people Israel, and so that they may know that your name has been invoked on this house that I have built.

44 "If your people go out to battle against their enemy, by whatever way you shall send them, and they pray to the LORD toward the city that you have chosen and the house that I have built for your name, [45]then hear in heaven their prayer and their plea, and maintain their cause.

46 "If they sin against you—for there is no one who does not sin—and you are angry with them and give them to an enemy, so that they are carried away captive to the land of the enemy, far off or near; [47]yet if they come to their senses in the land to which they have been taken captive, and repent, and plead with you in the land of their captors, saying, 'We have sinned, and have done wrong; we have acted wickedly'; [48]if they repent with all their heart and soul in the land of their enemies, who took them captive, and pray to you toward their land, which you gave to their ancestors, the city that you have chosen, and the house that I have built for your name; [49]then hear in heaven your dwelling place their prayer and their plea, maintain their cause [50]and forgive your people who have sinned against you, and all their transgressions that they have committed against you; and grant them compassion in the sight of their captors, so that they may have compassion on them [51](for they are your people and heritage, which you brought out of Egypt, from the midst of the iron-smelter). [52]Let your eyes be open to the plea of your servant, and to the plea of your people Israel, listening to them whenever they call to you. [53]For you have separated them from among all the peoples of the earth, to be your heritage, just as you promised through Moses, your servant, when you brought our ancestors out of Egypt, O Lord GOD."

Solomon Blesses the Assembly

54 Now when Solomon finished offering all this prayer and this plea to the LORD, he arose from facing the altar of the LORD, where he had knelt with hands outstretched toward heaven; [55]he stood and blessed all the assembly of Israel with a loud voice:

56 "Blessed be the LORD, who has given rest to his people Israel according to all that he promised; not one word has failed of all his good promise, which he spoke through his servant Moses. [57]The LORD our God be with us, as he was with our ancestors; may he not leave us or abandon us, [58]but incline our hearts to him, to walk in all his ways, and to keep his commandments, his statutes, and his ordinances, which he commanded our ancestors. [59]Let these words of mine, with which I pleaded before the LORD, be near to the LORD our God day and night, and may he maintain the cause of his servant and the cause of his people Israel, as each day requires; [60]so that all the peoples of the earth may know that the LORD is God; there is no other. [61]Therefore devote yourselves completely to the LORD our God, walking in his statutes and keeping his commandments, as at this day."

Solomon Offers Sacrifices

62 Then the king, and all Israel with him, offered sacrifice before the LORD. [63]Solomon offered as sacrifices of well-being to the LORD twenty-two thousand oxen and one hundred twenty thousand sheep. So the king and all the people of Israel dedicated the house of the LORD. [64]The same day the king consecrated the middle of the court that was in front of the house of the LORD; for there he offered the burnt offerings and the grain offerings and the fat pieces of the sacrifices of well-being, because the bronze altar that was before the LORD was too small to receive the burnt offerings and the grain offerings and the fat pieces of the sacrifices of well-being.

65 So Solomon held the festival at that time, and all Israel with him—a great assembly, people from Lebo-hamath to the Wadi of Egypt—before the LORD our God, seven days.[a] [66]On the eighth day he sent the people away; and they blessed the king, and went to their tents, joyful and in good spirits because of all the goodness that the LORD had shown to his servant David and to his people Israel.

a Compare Gk: Heb seven days and seven days, fourteen days

God Appears Again to Solomon

9 When Solomon had finished building the house of the LORD and the king's house and all that Solomon desired to build, [2]the LORD appeared to Solomon a second time, as he had appeared to him at Gibeon. [3]The LORD said to him, "I have heard your prayer and your plea, which you made before me; I have consecrated this house that you have built, and put my name there forever; my eyes and my heart will be there for all time. [4]As for you, if you will walk before me, as David your father walked, with integrity of heart and uprightness, doing according to all that I have commanded you, and keeping my statutes and my ordinances, [5]then I will establish your royal throne over Israel forever, as I promised your father David, saying, 'There shall not fail you a successor on the throne of Israel.'

6 "If you turn aside from following me, you or your children, and do not keep my commandments and my statutes that I have set before you, but go and serve other gods and worship them, [7]then I will cut Israel off from the land that I have given them; and the house that I have consecrated for my name I will cast out of my sight; and Israel will become a proverb and a taunt among all peoples. [8]This house will become a heap of ruins;[a] everyone passing by it will be astonished, and will hiss; and they will say, 'Why has the LORD done such a thing to this land and to this house?' [9]Then they will say, 'Because they have forsaken the LORD their God, who brought their ancestors out of the land of Egypt, and embraced other gods, worshiping them and serving them; therefore the LORD has brought this disaster upon them.' "

10 At the end of twenty years, in which Solomon had built the two houses, the house of the LORD and the king's house, [11]King Hiram of Tyre having supplied Solomon with cedar and cypress timber and gold, as much as he desired, King Solomon gave to Hiram twenty cities in the land of Galilee. [12]But when Hiram came from Tyre to see the cities that Solomon had given him, they did not please him. [13]Therefore he said, "What kind of cities are these that you have given me, my brother?" So they are called the land of Cabul[b] to this day. [14]But Hiram had sent to the king one hundred twenty talents of gold.

Other Acts of Solomon

15 This is the account of the forced labor that King Solomon conscripted to build the house of the LORD and his own house, the Millo and the wall of Jerusalem, Hazor, Megiddo, Gezer [16](Pharaoh king of Egypt had gone up and captured Gezer and burned it down, had killed the Canaanites who lived in the city, and had given it as dowry to his daughter, Solomon's wife; [17]so Solomon rebuilt Gezer), Lower Beth-horon, [18]Baalath, Tamar in the wilderness, within the land, [19]as well as all of Solomon's storage cities, the cities for his chariots, the cities for his cavalry, and whatever Solomon desired to build, in Jerusalem, in Lebanon, and in all the land of his dominion. [20]All the people who were left of the Amorites, the Hittites, the Perizzites, the Hivites, and the Jebusites, who were not of the people of Israel— [21]their descendants who were still left in the land, whom the Israelites were unable to destroy completely—these Solomon conscripted for slave labor, and so they are to this day. [22]But of the Israelites Solomon made no slaves; they were the soldiers, they were his officials, his commanders, his captains, and the commanders of his chariotry and cavalry.

23 These were the chief officers who were over Solomon's work: five hundred fifty, who had charge of the people who carried on the work.

24 But Pharaoh's daughter went up from the city of David to her own house that Solomon had built for her; then he built the Millo.

25 Three times a year Solomon used to offer up burnt offerings and sacrifices of well-being on the altar that he built for the LORD, offering incense[c] before the LORD. So he completed the house.

Solomon's Commercial Activity

26 King Solomon built a fleet of ships at Ezion-geber, which is near Eloth on the shore of the Red Sea,[d] in the land of Edom. [27]Hiram sent his servants with the fleet, sailors who were familiar with the sea, together with the servants of Solomon. [28]They went to Ophir, and imported from there four hundred twenty talents of gold, which they delivered to King Solomon.

Visit of the Queen of Sheba

10 When the queen of Sheba heard of the fame of Solomon (fame due to[e] the name of the LORD), she came to test him with hard questions. [2]She came to Jerusalem with a very great retinue, with camels bearing spices, and very much gold, and precious stones; and when she came to Solomon, she told him all that was on her mind. [3]Solomon answered all her questions;

---

a Syr Old Latin: Heb *will become high*   b Perhaps meaning *a land good for nothing*   c Gk: Heb *offering incense with it that was*   d Or *Sea of Reeds*   e Meaning of Heb uncertain

there was nothing hidden from the king that he could not explain to her. ⁴When the queen of Sheba had observed all the wisdom of Solomon, the house that he had built, ⁵the food of his table, the seating of his officials, and the attendance of his servants, their clothing, his valets, and his burnt offerings that he offered at the house of the Lord, there was no more spirit in her.

6 So she said to the king, "The report was true that I heard in my own land of your accomplishments and of your wisdom, ⁷but I did not believe the reports until I came and my own eyes had seen it. Not even half had been told me; your wisdom and prosperity far surpass the report that I had heard. ⁸Happy are your wives!ᵃ Happy are these your servants, who continually attend you and hear your wisdom! ⁹Blessed be the Lord your God, who has delighted in you and set you on the throne of Israel! Because the Lord loved Israel forever, he has made you king to execute justice and righteousness." ¹⁰Then she gave the king one hundred twenty talents of gold, a great quantity of spices, and precious stones; never again did spices come in such quantity as that which the queen of Sheba gave to King Solomon.

11 Moreover, the fleet of Hiram, which carried gold from Ophir, brought from Ophir a great quantity of almug wood and precious stones. ¹²From the almug wood the king made supports for the house of the Lord, and for the king's house, lyres also and harps for the singers; no such almug wood has come or been seen to this day.

13 Meanwhile King Solomon gave to the queen of Sheba every desire that she expressed, as well as what he gave her out of Solomon's royal bounty. Then she returned to her own land, with her servants.

14 The weight of gold that came to Solomon in one year was six hundred sixty-six talents of gold, ¹⁵besides that which came from the traders and from the business of the merchants, and from all the kings of Arabia and the governors of the land. ¹⁶King Solomon made two hundred large shields of beaten gold; six hundred shekels of gold went into each large shield. ¹⁷He made three hundred shields of beaten gold; three minas of gold went into each shield; and the king put them in the House of the Forest of Lebanon. ¹⁸The king also made a great ivory throne, and overlaid it with the finest gold. ¹⁹The throne had six steps. The top of the throne was rounded in the back, and on each side of the seat were arm rests and two lions standing beside the arm rests, ²⁰while twelve lions were standing, one on each end of a step on the six steps. Nothing like it was ever made in any kingdom. ²¹All King Solomon's

drinking vessels were of gold, and all the vessels of the House of the Forest of Lebanon were of pure gold; none were of silver—it was not considered as anything in the days of Solomon. ²²For the king had a fleet of ships of Tarshish at sea with the fleet of Hiram. Once every three years the fleet of ships of Tarshish used to come bringing gold, silver, ivory, apes, and peacocks.ᵇ

23 Thus King Solomon excelled all the kings of the earth in riches and in wisdom. ²⁴The whole earth sought the presence of Solomon to hear his wisdom, which God had put into his mind. ²⁵Every one of them brought a present, objects of silver and gold, garments, weaponry, spices, horses, and mules, so much year by year.

26 Solomon gathered together chariots and horses; he had fourteen hundred chariots and twelve thousand horses, which he stationed in the chariot cities and with the king in Jerusalem. ²⁷The king made silver as common in Jerusalem as stones, and he made cedars as numerous as the sycamores of the Shephelah. ²⁸Solomon's import of horses was from Egypt and Kue, and the king's traders received them from Kue at a price. ²⁹A chariot could be imported from Egypt for six hundred shekels of silver, and a horse for one hundred fifty; so through the king's traders they were exported to all the kings of the Hittites and the kings of Aram.

Solomon's Errors

11 King Solomon loved many foreign women along with the daughter of Pharaoh: Moabite, Ammonite, Edomite, Sidonian, and Hittite women, ²from the nations concerning which the Lord had said to the Israelites, "You shall not enter into marriage with them, neither shall they with you; for they will surely incline your heart to follow their gods"; Solomon clung to these in love. ³Among his wives were seven hundred princesses and three hundred concubines; and his wives turned away his heart. ⁴For when Solomon was old, his wives turned away his heart after other gods; and his heart was not true to the Lord his God, as was the heart of his father David. ⁵For Solomon followed Astarte the goddess of the Sidonians, and Milcom the abomination of the Ammonites. ⁶So Solomon did what was evil in the sight of the Lord, and did not completely follow the Lord, as his father David had done. ⁷Then Solomon built a high place for Chemosh the abomination of Moab, and for Molech the abomination of the Ammonites, on the mountain east of Jerusalem. ⁸He did the same

ᵃ Gk Syr: Heb men   ᵇ Or baboons

Pray It!

Solomon's Sin

Sometimes when we think we are strongest, we are actually weakest. Solomon replaces his poverty of spirit with pride (see 1 Kings 3:4–14). He seems to believe that he is strong enough to go against God's command not to take foreign wives and that he can withstand the influence of their foreign gods. But Solomon falls into the sin of idolatry (worshiping other gods), breaking the Covenant.

Have you ever considered doing something you knew was wrong? Did you tell yourself that it wouldn't hurt to do it just this once? Maybe that is what Solomon said when he took his first foreign wife.

In your prayer time, reflect or journal on the following questions:

- Think of a time when you deliberately gave in to temptation. What excuses did you use to do so?
- What takes your attention away from God?
- Have you ever tried asking God to give you strength to avoid doing something wrong?
- Pray Psalm 86:11 to end your prayer.

▶ **1 Kings 11:1–8**

for all his foreign wives, who offered incense and sacrificed to their gods.

9 Then the LORD was angry with Solomon, because his heart had turned away from the LORD, the God of Israel, who had appeared to him twice, 10and had commanded him concerning this matter, that he should not follow other gods; but he did not observe what the LORD commanded. 11Therefore the LORD said to Solomon, "Since this has been your mind and you have not kept my covenant and my statutes that I have commanded you, I will surely tear the kingdom from you and give it to your servant. 12Yet for the sake of your father David I will not do it in your lifetime; I will tear it out of the hand of your son. 13I will not, however, tear away the entire kingdom; I will give one tribe to your son, for the sake of my servant David and for the sake of Jerusalem, which I have chosen."

Adversaries of Solomon

14 Then the LORD raised up an adversary against Solomon, Hadad the Edomite; he was of the royal house in Edom. 15For when David was in Edom, and Joab the commander of the army went up to bury the dead, he killed every male in Edom 16(for Joab and all Israel remained there six months, until he had eliminated every male in Edom); 17but Hadad fled to Egypt with some Edomites who were servants of his father. He was a young boy at that time. 18They set out from Midian and came to Paran; they took people with them from Paran and came to Egypt, to Pharaoh king of Egypt, who gave him a house, assigned him an allowance of food, and gave him land. 19Hadad found great favor in the sight of Pharaoh, so that he gave him his sister-in-law for a wife, the sister of Queen Tahpenes. 20The sister of Tahpenes gave birth by him to his son Genubath, whom Tahpenes weaned in Pharaoh's house; Genubath was in Pharaoh's house among the children of Pharaoh. 21When Hadad heard in Egypt that David slept with his ancestors and that Joab the commander of the army was dead, Hadad said to Pharaoh, "Let me depart, that I may go to my own country." 22But Pharaoh said to him, "What do you lack with me that you now seek to go to your own country?" And he said, "No, do let me go."

23 God raised up another adversary against Solomon,*a* Rezon son of Eliada, who had fled from his master, King Hadadezer of Zobah. 24He gathered followers around him and became leader of a marauding band, after the slaughter by David; they went to Damascus, settled there, and made him king in Damascus. 25He was an adversary of Israel all the days of Solomon, making trouble as Hadad did; he despised Israel and reigned over Aram.

Jeroboam's Rebellion

26 Jeroboam son of Nebat, an Ephraimite of Zeredah, a servant of Solomon, whose mother's name was Zeruah, a widow, rebelled against the king. 27The following was the reason he rebelled against the king. Solomon built the Millo, and closed up the gap in the wall*b* of the city of his father David. 28The man Jeroboam was very able, and when Solomon saw that the young man was industrious he gave him charge over all the forced labor of the house of Joseph. 29About that time, when Jeroboam was leaving Jerusalem, the prophet Ahijah the

a Heb *him*   b Heb lacks *in the wall*

Shilonite found him on the road. Ahijah had clothed himself with a new garment. The two of them were alone in the open country ³⁰when Ahijah laid hold of the new garment he was wearing and tore it into twelve pieces. ³¹He then said to Jeroboam: Take for yourself ten pieces; for thus says the LORD, the God of Israel, "See, I am about to tear the kingdom from the hand of Solomon, and will give you ten tribes. ³²One tribe will remain his, for the sake of my servant David and for the sake of Jerusalem, the city that I have chosen out of all the tribes of Israel. ³³This is because he hasᵃ forsaken me, worshiped Astarte the goddess of the Sidonians, Chemosh the god of Moab, and Milcom the god of the Ammonites, and hasᵃ not walked in my ways, doing what is right in my sight and keeping my statutes and my ordinances, as his father David did. ³⁴Nevertheless I will not take the whole kingdom away from him but will make him ruler all the days of his life, for the sake of my servant David whom I chose and who did keep my commandments and my statutes; ³⁵but I will take the kingdom away from his son and give it to you—that is, the ten tribes. ³⁶Yet to his son I will give one tribe, so that my servant David may always have a lamp before me in Jerusalem, the city where I have chosen to put my name. ³⁷I will take you, and you shall reign over all that your soul desires; you shall be king over Israel. ³⁸If you will listen to all that I command you, walk in my ways, and do what is right in my sight by keeping my statutes and my commandments, as David my servant did, I will be with you, and will build you an enduring house, as I built for David, and I will give Israel to you. ³⁹For this reason I will punish the descendants of David, but not forever." ⁴⁰Solomon sought therefore to kill Jeroboam; but Jeroboam promptly fled to Egypt, to King Shishak of Egypt, and remained in Egypt until the death of Solomon.

Death of Solomon

41 Now the rest of the acts of Solomon, all that he did as well as his wisdom, are they not written in the Book of the Acts of Solomon? ⁴²The time that Solomon reigned in Jerusalem over all Israel was forty years. ⁴³Solomon slept with his ancestors and was buried in the city of his father David; and his son Rehoboam succeeded him.

The Northern Tribes Secede

12 Rehoboam went to Shechem, for all Israel had come to Shechem to make him king.

²When Jeroboam son of Nebat heard of it (for he was still in Egypt, where he had fled from King Solomon), then Jeroboam returned fromᵇ Egypt. ³And they sent and called him; and Jeroboam and all the assembly of Israel came and said to Rehoboam, ⁴"Your father made our yoke heavy. Now therefore lighten the hard service of your father and his heavy yoke that he placed on us, and we will serve you." ⁵He said to them, "Go away for three days, then come again to me." So the people went away.

6 Then King Rehoboam took counsel with the older men who had attended his father Solomon while he was still alive, saying, "How do you advise me to answer this people?" ⁷They answered him, "If you will be a servant to this people today and serve them, and speak good words to them when you answer them, then they will be your servants forever." ⁸But he disregarded the advice that the older men gave him, and consulted with the young men who had grown up with him and now attended him. ⁹He said to them, "What do you advise that we answer this people who have said to me, 'Lighten the yoke that your father put on us'?" ¹⁰The young men who had grown up with him said to him, "Thus you should say to this people who spoke to you, 'Your father made our yoke heavy, but you must lighten it for us'; thus you should say to them, 'My little finger is thicker than my father's loins. ¹¹Now, whereas my father laid on you a heavy yoke, I will add to your yoke. My father disciplined you with whips, but I will discipline you with scorpions.' "

12 So Jeroboam and all the people came to Rehoboam the third day, as the king had said, "Come to me again the third day." ¹³The king answered the people harshly. He disregarded the advice that the older men had given him ¹⁴and spoke to them according to the advice of the young men, "My father made your yoke heavy, but I will add to your yoke; my father disciplined you with whips, but I will discipline you with scorpions." ¹⁵So the king did not listen to the people, because it was a turn of affairs brought about by the LORD that he might fulfill his word, which the LORD had spoken by Ahijah the Shilonite to Jeroboam son of Nebat.

16 When all Israel saw that the king would not listen to them, the people answered the king,

"What share do we have in David?
  We have no inheritance in the son of Jesse.
To your tents, O Israel!
  Look now to your own house, O David."

ᵃ Gk Syr Vg: Heb *they have*   ᵇ Gk Vg Compare 2 Chr 10.2: Heb *lived in*

1
K
I
N
G
S

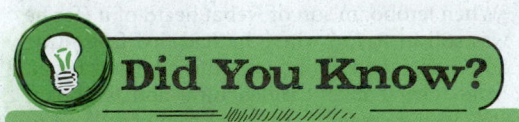

The Kingdom of Israel Splits

When the people of Israel first came to settle in Canaan, they organized into twelve Tribes, ruled by chieftains, that supported and protected one another. As Israel grew in size, it was necessary to have one central ruler who would unite the tribes into one nation. Saul was the first king of this united Israel. David followed Saul and expanded the kingdom's territory. David's son Solomon continued ruling over the expanded kingdom and engaged in expensive building projects.

At Solomon's death, many Israelites wanted a less demanding king. They had suffered under the burden of heavy taxes and forced labor. When Solomon's son Rehoboam refused to make any changes (see 1 Kings 12:11), ten of the northern tribes pulled away and placed their own king, Jeroboam, on the throne. The northern kingdom was called Israel. The southern kingdom, composed of two tribes, was called Judah (see map 4, "The Kingdom Years"). The kingdom was now split in two, and it was never again reunited.

Saul (1020 BC)
|
David (1000 BC)
|
Solomon (961 BC)

Kingdom splits
(931 BC)

JUDAH (south)	ISRAEL (north)
Capital: Jerusalem	Capital: Samaria
Twenty kings	Twenty kings
Falls to Babylonians (587 BC)	Falls to Assyrians (721 BC)
Exile to Babylon	Exile to Assyria

▶ 1 Kings 12:1–19

So Israel went away to their tents. [17]But Rehoboam reigned over the Israelites who were living in the towns of Judah. [18]When King Rehoboam sent Adoram, who was taskmaster over the forced labor, all Israel stoned him to death. King Rehoboam then hurriedly mounted his chariot to flee to Jerusalem. [19]So Israel has been in rebellion against the house of David to this day.

First Dynasty: Jeroboam Reigns over Israel

20 When all Israel heard that Jeroboam had returned, they sent and called him to the assembly and made him king over all Israel. There was no one who followed the house of David, except the tribe of Judah alone.

21 When Rehoboam came to Jerusalem, he assembled all the house of Judah and the tribe of Benjamin, one hundred eighty thousand chosen troops to fight against the house of Israel, to restore the kingdom to Rehoboam son of Solomon. [22]But the word of God came to Shemaiah the man of God: [23]Say to King Rehoboam of Judah, son of Solomon, and to all the house of Judah and Benjamin, and to the rest of the people, [24]"Thus says the LORD, You shall not go up or fight against your kindred the people of Israel. Let everyone go home, for this thing is from me." So they heeded the word of the LORD and went home again, according to the word of the LORD.

Jeroboam's Golden Calves

25 Then Jeroboam built Shechem in the hill country of Ephraim, and resided there; he went out from there and built Penuel. [26]Then Jeroboam said to himself, "Now the kingdom may well revert to the house of David. [27]If this people continues to go up to offer sacrifices in the house of the LORD at Jerusalem, the heart of this people will turn again to their master, King Rehoboam of Judah; they will kill me and return to King Rehoboam of Judah." [28]So the king took counsel, and made two calves of gold. He said to the people,[a] "You have gone up to Jerusalem long enough. Here are your gods, O Israel, who brought you up out of the land of Egypt." [29]He set one in Bethel, and the other he put in Dan. [30]And this thing became a sin, for the people went to worship before the one at Bethel and before the other as far as Dan.[b] [31]He also made houses[c] on high places, and appointed priests from among all the people, who were not Levites. [32]Jeroboam appointed a festival on the fifteenth day of the eighth month like the festival

---

a Gk: Heb *to them*   b Compare Gk: Heb *went to the one as far as Dan*   c Gk Vg Compare 13.32: Heb *a house*

that was in Judah, and he offered sacrifices on the altar; so he did in Bethel, sacrificing to the calves that he had made. And he placed in Bethel the priests of the high places that he had made. [33]He went up to the altar that he had made in Bethel on the fifteenth day in the eighth month, in the month that he alone had devised; he appointed a festival for the people of Israel, and he went up to the altar to offer incense.

A Man of God from Judah

13 While Jeroboam was standing by the altar to offer incense, a man of God came out of Judah by the word of the LORD to Bethel [2]and proclaimed against the altar by the word of the LORD, and said, "O altar, altar, thus says the LORD: 'A son shall be born to the house of David, Josiah by name; and he shall sacrifice on you the priests of the high places who offer incense on you, and human bones shall be burned on you.' " [3]He gave a sign the same day, saying, "This is the sign that the LORD has spoken: 'The altar shall be torn down, and the ashes that are on it shall be poured out.' " [4]When the king heard what the man of God cried out against the altar at Bethel, Jeroboam stretched out his hand from the altar, saying, "Seize him!" But the hand that he stretched out against him withered so that he could not draw it back to himself. [5]The altar also was torn down, and the ashes poured out from the altar, according to the sign that the man of God had given by the word of the LORD. [6]The king said to the man of God, "Entreat now the favor of the LORD your God, and pray for me, so that my hand may be restored to me." So the man of God entreated the LORD; and the king's hand was restored to him, and became as it was before. [7]Then the king said to the man of God, "Come home with me and dine, and I will give you a gift." [8]But the man of God said to the king, "If you give me half your kingdom, I will not go in with you; nor will I eat food or drink water in this place. [9]For thus I was commanded by the word of the LORD: You shall not eat food, or drink water, or return by the way that you came." [10]So he went another way, and did not return by the way that he had come to Bethel.

[11] Now there lived an old prophet in Bethel. One of his sons came and told him all that the man of God had done that day in Bethel; the words also that he had spoken to the king, they told to their father. [12]Their father said to them, "Which way did he go?" And his sons showed him the way that the man of God who came from Judah had gone. [13]Then he said to his sons, "Saddle a donkey for me." So they saddled a donkey for him, and he mounted it. [14]He went after the man of God, and found him sitting under an oak tree. He said to him, "Are you the man of God who came from Judah?" He answered, "I am." [15]Then he said to him, "Come home with me and eat some food." [16]But he said, "I cannot return with you, or go in with you; nor will I eat food or drink water with you in this place; [17]for it was said to me by the word of the LORD: You shall not eat food or drink water there, or return by the way that you came." [18]Then the other[a] said to him, "I also am a prophet as you are, and an angel spoke to me by the word of the LORD: Bring him back with you into your house so that he may eat food and drink water." But he was deceiving him. [19]Then the man of God[a] went back with him, and ate food and drank water in his house.

[20] As they were sitting at the table, the word of the LORD came to the prophet who had brought him back; [21]and he proclaimed to the man of God who came from Judah, "Thus says the LORD: Because you have disobeyed the word of the LORD, and have not kept the commandment that the LORD your God commanded you, [22]but have come back and have eaten food and drunk water in the place of which he said to you, 'Eat no food, and drink no water,' your body shall not come to your ancestral tomb." [23]After the man of God[a] had eaten food and had drunk, they saddled for him a donkey belonging to the prophet who had brought him back. [24]Then as he went away, a lion met him on the road and killed him. His body was thrown in the road, and the donkey stood beside it; the lion also stood beside the body. [25]People passed by and saw the body thrown in the road, with the lion standing by the body. And they came and told it in the town where the old prophet lived.

[26] When the prophet who had brought him back from the way heard of it, he said, "It is the man of God who disobeyed the word of the LORD; therefore the LORD has given him to the lion, which has torn him and killed him according to the word that the LORD spoke to him " [27]Then he said to his sons, "Saddle a donkey for me." So they saddled one, [28]and he went and found the body thrown in the road, with the donkey and the lion standing beside the body. The lion had not eaten the body or attacked the donkey. [29]The prophet took up the body of the man of God, laid it on the donkey, and brought it back to the city,[b] to mourn and to bury him. [30]He laid the body in his own grave; and they mourned over him, saying,

---

a Heb he   b Gk: Heb he came to the town of the old prophet

"Alas, my brother!" [31]After he had buried him, he said to his sons, "When I die, bury me in the grave in which the man of God is buried; lay my bones beside his bones. [32]For the saying that he proclaimed by the word of the LORD against the altar in Bethel, and against all the houses of the high places that are in the cities of Samaria, shall surely come to pass."

33 Even after this event Jeroboam did not turn from his evil way, but made priests for the high places again from among all the people; any who wanted to be priests he consecrated for the high places. [34]This matter became sin to the house of Jeroboam, so as to cut it off and to destroy it from the face of the earth.

Judgment on the House of Jeroboam

14 At that time Abijah son of Jeroboam fell sick. [2]Jeroboam said to his wife, "Go, disguise yourself, so that it will not be known that you are the wife of Jeroboam, and go to Shiloh; for the prophet Ahijah is there, who said of me that I should be king over this people. [3]Take with you ten loaves, some cakes, and a jar of honey, and go to him; he will tell you what shall happen to the child."

4 Jeroboam's wife did so; she set out and went to Shiloh, and came to the house of Ahijah. Now Ahijah could not see, for his eyes were dim because of his age. [5]But the LORD said to Ahijah, "The wife of Jeroboam is coming to inquire of you concerning her son; for he is sick. Thus and thus you shall say to her."

When she came, she pretended to be another woman. [6]But when Ahijah heard the sound of her feet, as she came in at the door, he said, "Come in, wife of Jeroboam; why do you pretend to be another? For I am charged with heavy tidings for you. [7]Go, tell Jeroboam, 'Thus says the LORD, the God of Israel: Because I exalted you from among the people, made you leader over my people Israel, [8]and tore the kingdom away from the house of David to give it to you; yet you have not been like my servant David, who kept my commandments and followed me with all his heart, doing only that which was right in my sight, [9]but you have done evil above all those who were before you and have gone and made for yourself other gods, and cast images, provoking me to anger, and have thrust me behind your back; [10]therefore, I will bring evil upon the house of Jeroboam. I will cut off from Jeroboam every male, both bond and free in Israel, and will consume the house of Jeroboam, just as one burns up dung until it is all gone. [11]Anyone belonging to Jeroboam who dies in the city, the dogs shall eat; and anyone who dies in the open country, the birds of the air shall eat; for the LORD has spoken.' [12]Therefore set out, go to your house. When your feet enter the city, the child shall die. [13]All Israel shall mourn for him and bury him; for he alone of Jeroboam's family shall come to the grave, because in him there is found something pleasing to the LORD, the God of Israel, in the house of Jeroboam. [14]Moreover the LORD will raise up for himself a king over Israel, who shall cut off the house of Jeroboam today, even right now![a]

15 "The LORD will strike Israel, as a reed is shaken in the water; he will root up Israel out of this good land that he gave to their ancestors, and scatter them beyond the Euphrates, because they have made their sacred poles,[b] provoking the LORD to anger. [16]He will give Israel up because of the sins of Jeroboam, which he sinned and which he caused Israel to commit."

17 Then Jeroboam's wife got up and went away, and she came to Tirzah. As she came to the threshold of the house, the child died. [18]All Israel buried him and mourned for him, according to the word of the LORD, which he spoke by his servant the prophet Ahijah.

Death of Jeroboam

19 Now the rest of the acts of Jeroboam, how he warred and how he reigned, are written in the Book of the Annals of the Kings of Israel. [20]The time that Jeroboam reigned was twenty-two years; then he slept with his ancestors, and his son Nadab succeeded him.

Rehoboam Reigns over Judah

21 Now Rehoboam son of Solomon reigned in Judah. Rehoboam was forty-one years old when he began to reign, and he reigned seventeen years in Jerusalem, the city that the LORD had chosen out of all the tribes of Israel, to put his name there. His mother's name was Naamah the Ammonite. [22]Judah did what was evil in the sight of the LORD; they provoked him to jealousy with their sins that they committed, more than all that their ancestors had done. [23]For they also built for themselves high places, pillars, and sacred poles[b] on every high hill and under every green tree; [24]there were also male temple prostitutes in the land. They committed all the abominations of the nations that the LORD drove out before the people of Israel.

25 In the fifth year of King Rehoboam, King

a Meaning of Heb uncertain   b Heb Asherim

Shishak of Egypt came up against Jerusalem; [26]he took away the treasures of the house of the LORD and the treasures of the king's house; he took everything. He also took away all the shields of gold that Solomon had made; [27]so King Rehoboam made shields of bronze instead, and committed them to the hands of the officers of the guard, who kept the door of the king's house. [28]As often as the king went into the house of the LORD, the guard carried them and brought them back to the guardroom.

29 Now the rest of the acts of Rehoboam, and all that he did, are they not written in the Book of the Annals of the Kings of Judah? [30]There was war between Rehoboam and Jeroboam continually. [31]Rehoboam slept with his ancestors and was buried with his ancestors in the city of David. His mother's name was Naamah the Ammonite. His son Abijam succeeded him.

Abijam Reigns over Judah: Idolatry and War

15 Now in the eighteenth year of King Jeroboam son of Nebat, Abijam began to reign over Judah. [2]He reigned for three years in Jerusalem. His mother's name was Maacah daughter of Abishalom. [3]He committed all the sins that his father did before him; his heart was not true to the LORD his God, like the heart of his father David. [4]Nevertheless for David's sake the LORD his God gave him a lamp in Jerusalem, setting up his son after him, and establishing Jerusalem; [5]because David did what was right in the sight of the LORD, and did not turn aside from anything that he commanded him all the days of his life, except in the matter of Uriah the Hittite. [6]The war begun between Rehoboam and Jeroboam continued all the days of his life. [7]The rest of the acts of Abijam, and all that he did, are they not written in the Book of the Annals of the Kings of Judah? There was war between Abijam and Jeroboam. [8]Abijam slept with his ancestors, and they buried him in the city of David. Then his son Asa succeeded him.

Asa Reigns over Judah

9 In the twentieth year of King Jeroboam of Israel, Asa began to reign over Judah; [10]he reigned forty-one years in Jerusalem. His mother's name was Maacah daughter of Abishalom. [11]Asa did what was right in the sight of the LORD, as his father David had done. [12]He put away the male temple prostitutes out of the land, and removed all the idols that his ancestors had made. [13]He also removed his mother Maacah from being queen mother, because she had made an abominable image for Asherah; Asa cut down her image and burned it at the Wadi Kidron. [14]But the high places were not taken away. Nevertheless the heart of Asa was true to the LORD all his days. [15]He brought into the house of the LORD the votive gifts of his father and his own votive gifts—silver, gold, and utensils.

Alliance with Aram against Israel

16 There was war between Asa and King Baasha of Israel all their days. [17]King Baasha of Israel went up against Judah, and built Ramah, to prevent anyone from going out or coming in to King Asa of Judah. [18]Then Asa took all the silver and the gold that were left in the treasures of the house of the LORD and the treasures of the king's house, and gave them into the hands of his servants. King Asa sent them to King Ben-hadad son of Tabrimmon son of Hezion of Aram, who resided in Damascus, saying, [19]"Let there be an alliance between me and you, like that between my father and your father: I am sending you a present of silver and gold; go, break your alliance with King Baasha of Israel, so that he may withdraw from me." [20]Ben-hadad listened to King Asa, and sent the commanders of his armies against the cities of Israel. He conquered Ijon, Dan, Abel-beth-maacah, and all Chinneroth, with all the land of Naphtali. [21]When Baasha heard of it, he stopped building Ramah and lived in Tirzah. [22]Then King Asa made a proclamation to all Judah, none was exempt: they carried away the stones of Ramah and its timber, with which Baasha had been building; with them King Asa built Geba of Benjamin and Mizpah. [23]Now the rest of all the acts of Asa, all his power, all that he did, and the cities that he built, are they not written in the Book of the Annals of the Kings of Judah? But in his old age he was diseased in his feet. [24]Then Asa slept with his ancestors, and was buried with his ancestors in the city of his father David; his son Jehoshaphat succeeded him.

Nadab Reigns over Israel

25 Nadab son of Jeroboam began to reign over Israel in the second year of King Asa of Judah; he reigned over Israel two years. [26]He did what was evil in the sight of the LORD, walking in the way of his ancestor and in the sin that he caused Israel to commit.

27 Baasha son of Ahijah, of the house of Issachar, conspired against him; and Baasha struck him down at Gibbethon, which belonged to the Philistines; for Nadab and all Israel were laying siege to Gibbethon. [28]So Baasha killed Nadab[a]

a Heb him

in the third year of King Asa of Judah, and succeeded him. ²⁹As soon as he was king, he killed all the house of Jeroboam; he left to the house of Jeroboam not one that breathed, until he had destroyed it, according to the word of the Lord that he spoke by his servant Ahijah the Shilonite— ³⁰because of the sins of Jeroboam that he committed and that he caused Israel to commit, and because of the anger to which he provoked the Lord, the God of Israel.

31 Now the rest of the acts of Nadab, and all that he did, are they not written in the Book of the Annals of the Kings of Israel? ³²There was war between Asa and King Baasha of Israel all their days.

Second Dynasty: Baasha Reigns over Israel

33 In the third year of King Asa of Judah, Baasha son of Ahijah began to reign over all Israel at Tirzah; he reigned twenty-four years. ³⁴He did what was evil in the sight of the Lord, walking in the way of Jeroboam and in the sin that he caused Israel to commit.

16 The word of the Lord came to Jehu son of Hanani against Baasha, saying, ²"Since I exalted you out of the dust and made you leader over my people Israel, and you have walked in the way of Jeroboam, and have caused my people Israel to sin, provoking me to anger with their sins, ³therefore, I will consume Baasha and his house, and I will make your house like the house of Jeroboam son of Nebat. ⁴Anyone belonging to Baasha who dies in the city the dogs shall eat; and anyone of his who dies in the field the birds of the air shall eat."

5 Now the rest of the acts of Baasha, what he did, and his power, are they not written in the Book of the Annals of the Kings of Israel? ⁶Baasha slept with his ancestors, and was buried at Tirzah; and his son Elah succeeded him. ⁷Moreover the word of the Lord came by the prophet Jehu son of Hanani against Baasha and his house, both because of all the evil that he did in the sight of the Lord, provoking him to anger with the work of his hands, in being like the house of Jeroboam, and also because he destroyed it.

Elah Reigns over Israel

8 In the twenty-sixth year of King Asa of Judah, Elah son of Baasha began to reign over Israel in Tirzah; he reigned two years. ⁹But his servant Zimri, commander of half his chariots, conspired against him. When he was at Tirzah, drinking himself drunk in the house of Arza, who was in charge of the palace at Tirzah,

¹⁰Zimri came in and struck him down and killed him, in the twenty-seventh year of King Asa of Judah, and succeeded him.

11 When he began to reign, as soon as he had seated himself on his throne, he killed all the house of Baasha; he did not leave him a single male of his kindred or his friends. ¹²Thus Zimri destroyed all the house of Baasha, according to the word of the Lord, which he spoke against Baasha by the prophet Jehu— ¹³because of all the sins of Baasha and the sins of his son Elah that they committed, and that they caused Israel to commit, provoking the Lord God of Israel to anger with their idols. ¹⁴Now the rest of the acts of Elah, and all that he did, are they not written in the Book of the Annals of the Kings of Israel?

Third Dynasty: Zimri Reigns over Israel

15 In the twenty-seventh year of King Asa of Judah, Zimri reigned seven days in Tirzah. Now the troops were encamped against Gibbethon, which belonged to the Philistines, ¹⁶and the troops who were encamped heard it said, "Zimri has conspired, and he has killed the king"; therefore all Israel made Omri, the commander of the army, king over Israel that day in the camp. ¹⁷So Omri went up from Gibbethon, and all Israel with him, and they besieged Tirzah. ¹⁸When Zimri saw that the city was taken, he went into the citadel of the king's house; he burned down the king's house over himself with fire, and died— ¹⁹because of the sins that he committed, doing evil in the sight of the Lord, walking in the way of Jeroboam, and for the sin that he committed, causing Israel to sin. ²⁰Now the rest of the acts of Zimri, and the conspiracy that he made, are they not written in the Book of the Annals of the Kings of Israel?

Fourth Dynasty: Omri Reigns over Israel

21 Then the people of Israel were divided into two parts; half of the people followed Tibni son of Ginath, to make him king, and half followed Omri. ²²But the people who followed Omri overcame the people who followed Tibni son of Ginath; so Tibni died, and Omri became king. ²³In the thirty-first year of King Asa of Judah, Omri began to reign over Israel; he reigned for twelve years, six of them in Tirzah.

Samaria the New Capital

24 He bought the hill of Samaria from Shemer for two talents of silver; he fortified the hill, and called the city that he built, Samaria, after the name of Shemer, the owner of the hill.

25 Omri did what was evil in the sight of the

LORD; he did more evil than all who were before him. 26For he walked in all the way of Jeroboam son of Nebat, and in the sins that he caused Israel to commit, provoking the LORD, the God of Israel, to anger by their idols. 27Now the rest of the acts of Omri that he did, and the power that he showed, are they not written in the Book of the Annals of the Kings of Israel? 28Omri slept with his ancestors, and was buried in Samaria; his son Ahab succeeded him.

Ahab Reigns over Israel

29 In the thirty-eighth year of King Asa of Judah, Ahab son of Omri began to reign over Israel; Ahab son of Omri reigned over Israel in Samaria twenty-two years. 30Ahab son of Omri did evil in the sight of the LORD more than all who were before him.

Ahab Marries Jezebel and Worships Baal

31 And as if it had been a light thing for him to walk in the sins of Jeroboam son of Nebat, he took as his wife Jezebel daughter of King Ethbaal of the Sidonians, and went and served Baal, and worshiped him. 32He erected an altar for Baal in the house of Baal, which he built in Samaria. 33Ahab also made a sacred pole.*a* Ahab did more to provoke the anger of the LORD, the God of Israel, than had all the kings of Israel who were before him. 34In his days Hiel of Bethel built Jericho; he laid its foundation at the cost of Abiram his firstborn, and set up its gates at the cost of his youngest son Segub, according to the word of the LORD, which he spoke by Joshua son of Nun.

Elijah Predicts a Drought

17 Now Elijah the Tishbite, of Tishbe*b* in Gilead, said to Ahab, "As the LORD the God of Israel lives, before whom I stand, there shall be neither dew nor rain these years, except by my word." 2The word of the LORD came to him, saying, 3"Go from here and turn eastward, and hide yourself by the Wadi Cherith, which is east of the Jordan. 4You shall drink from the wadi, and I have commanded the ravens to feed you there." 5So he went and did according to the word of the LORD; he went and lived by the Wadi Cherith, which is east of the Jordan. 6The ravens brought him bread and meat in the morning, and bread and meat in the evening; and he drank from the wadi. 7But after a while the wadi dried up, because there was no rain in the land.

The Widow of Zarephath

8 Then the word of the LORD came to him, saying, 9"Go now to Zarephath, which belongs to Sidon, and live there; for I have commanded a widow there to feed you." 10So he set out and went to Zarephath. When he came to the gate of the town, a widow was there gathering sticks; he called to her and said, "Bring me a little water in a vessel, so that I may drink." 11As she was going to bring it, he called to her and said, "Bring me a morsel of bread in your hand." 12But she said, "As the LORD your God lives, I have nothing baked, only a handful of meal in a jar, and a little oil in a jug; I am now gathering a couple of sticks, so that I may go home and prepare it for myself and my son, that we may eat it, and die." 13Elijah said to her, "Do not be afraid; go and do as you have said; but first make me a little cake of it and bring it to me, and afterwards make something for yourself and your son. 14For thus says the LORD the God of Israel: The jar of meal will not be emptied and the jug of oil will not fail until the day that the LORD sends rain on the earth." 15She went and did as Elijah said, so that she as well as he and her household ate for many days. 16The jar of meal was not emptied, neither did the jug of oil fail, according to the word of the LORD that he spoke by Elijah.

Elijah Revives the Widow's Son

17 After this the son of the woman, the mistress of the house, became ill; his illness was so severe that there was no breath left in him. 18She then said to Elijah, "What have you against me, O man of God? You have come to me to bring my sin to remembrance, and to cause the death of my son!" 19But he said to her, "Give me your son." He took him from her bosom, carried him up into the upper chamber where he was lodging, and laid him on his own bed. 20He cried out to the LORD, "O LORD my God, have you brought calamity even upon the widow with whom I am staying, by killing her son?" 21Then he stretched himself upon the child three times, and cried out to the LORD, "O LORD my God, let this child's life come into him again." 22The LORD listened to the voice of Elijah; the life of the child came into him again, and he revived. 23Elijah took the child, brought him down from the upper chamber into the house, and gave him to his mother; then Elijah said, "See, your son is alive." 24So the woman said to Elijah, "Now I know that you are a man of God, and that the word of the LORD in your mouth is truth."

---

a Heb *Asherah*   *b* Gk: Heb *of the settlers*

1 KINGS

Elijah's Message to Ahab

18 After many days the word of the Lord came to Elijah, in the third year of the drought,[a] saying, "Go, present yourself to Ahab; I will send rain on the earth." ²So Elijah went to present himself to Ahab. The famine was severe in Samaria. ³Ahab summoned Obadiah, who was in charge of the palace. (Now Obadiah revered the Lord greatly; ⁴when Jezebel was killing off the prophets of the Lord, Obadiah took a hundred prophets, hid them fifty to a cave, and provided them with bread and water.) ⁵Then Ahab said to Obadiah, "Go through the land to all the springs of water and to all the wadis; perhaps we may find grass to keep the horses and mules alive, and not lose some of the animals." ⁶So they divided the land between them to pass through it; Ahab went in one direction by himself, and Obadiah went in another direction by himself.

7 As Obadiah was on the way, Elijah met him; Obadiah recognized him, fell on his face, and said, "Is it you, my lord Elijah?" ⁸He answered him, "It is I. Go, tell your lord that Elijah is here." ⁹And he said, "How have I sinned, that you would hand your servant over to Ahab, to kill me? ¹⁰As the Lord your God lives, there is no nation or kingdom to which my lord has not sent to seek you; and when they would say, 'He is not here,' he would require an oath of the kingdom or nation, that they had not found you. ¹¹But now you say, 'Go, tell your lord that Elijah is here.' ¹²As soon as I have gone from you, the spirit of the Lord will carry you I know not where; so, when I come and tell Ahab and he cannot find you, he will kill me, although I your servant have revered the Lord from my youth. ¹³Has it not been told my lord what I did when Jezebel killed the prophets of the Lord, how I hid a hundred of the Lord's prophets fifty to a cave, and provided them with bread and water? ¹⁴Yet now you say, 'Go, tell your lord that Elijah is here'; he will surely kill me." ¹⁵Elijah said, "As the Lord of hosts lives, before whom I stand, I will surely show myself to him today." ¹⁶So Obadiah went to meet Ahab, and told him; and Ahab went to meet Elijah.

17 When Ahab saw Elijah, Ahab said to him, "Is it you, you troubler of Israel?" ¹⁸He answered, "I have not troubled Israel; but you have, and your father's house, because you have forsaken the commandments of the Lord and followed the Baals. ¹⁹Now therefore have all Israel assemble for me at Mount Carmel, with the four hundred fifty prophets of Baal and the four hundred prophets of Asherah, who eat at Jezebel's table."

Elijah's Triumph over the Priests of Baal

20 So Ahab sent to all the Israelites, and assembled the prophets at Mount Carmel. ²¹Elijah then came near to all the people, and said, "How long will you go limping with two different opinions? If the Lord is God, follow him; but if Baal, then follow him." The people did not answer him a word. ²²Then Elijah said to the people, "I, even I only, am left a prophet of the Lord; but Baal's prophets number four hundred fifty. ²³Let two bulls be given to us; let them choose one bull for themselves, cut it in pieces, and lay it on the wood, but put no fire to it; I will prepare the other bull and lay it on the wood, but put no fire to it. ²⁴Then you call on the name of your god and I will call on the name of the Lord; the god who answers by fire is indeed God." All the people answered, "Well spoken!" ²⁵Then Elijah said to the prophets of Baal, "Choose for yourselves one bull and prepare it first, for you are many; then call on the name of your god, but put no fire to it." ²⁶So they took the bull that was given them, prepared it, and called on the name of Baal from morning until noon, crying, "O Baal, answer us!" But there was no voice, and no answer. They limped about the altar that they had made. ²⁷At noon Elijah mocked them, saying, "Cry aloud! Surely he is a god; either he is meditating, or he has wandered away, or he is on a journey, or perhaps he is asleep and must be awakened." ²⁸Then they cried aloud and, as was their custom, they cut themselves with swords and lances until the blood gushed out over them. ²⁹As midday passed, they raved on until the time of the offering of the oblation, but there was no voice, no answer, and no response.

30 Then Elijah said to all the people, "Come closer to me"; and all the people came closer to him. First he repaired the altar of the Lord that had been thrown down; ³¹Elijah took twelve stones, according to the number of the tribes of the sons of Jacob, to whom the word of the Lord came, saying, "Israel shall be your name"; ³²with the stones he built an altar in the name of the Lord. Then he made a trench around the altar, large enough to contain two measures of seed. ³³Next he put the wood in order, cut the bull in pieces, and laid it on the wood. He said, "Fill four jars with water and pour it on the burnt offering and on the wood." ³⁴Then he said, "Do it a second time"; and they did it a second time. Again he said, "Do it a third time";

---

a Heb lacks *of the drought*

and they did it a third time, ³⁵so that the water ran all around the altar, and filled the trench also with water.

36 At the time of the offering of the oblation, the prophet Elijah came near and said, "O Lord, God of Abraham, Isaac, and Israel, let it be known this day that you are God in Israel, that I am your servant, and that I have done all these things at your bidding. ³⁷Answer me, O Lord, answer me, so that this people may know that you, O Lord, are God, and that you have turned their hearts back." ³⁸Then the fire of the Lord fell and consumed the burnt offering, the wood, the stones, and the dust, and even licked up the water that was in the trench. ³⁹When all the people saw it, they fell on their faces and said, "The Lord indeed is God; the Lord indeed is God." ⁴⁰Elijah said to them, "Seize the prophets of Baal; do not let one of them escape." Then they seized them; and Elijah brought them down to the Wadi Kishon, and killed them there.

The Drought Ends

41 Elijah said to Ahab, "Go up, eat and drink; for there is a sound of rushing rain." ⁴²So Ahab went up to eat and to drink. Elijah went up to the top of Carmel; there he bowed himself down upon the earth and put his face between his knees. ⁴³He said to his servant, "Go up now, look toward the sea." He went up and looked, and said, "There is nothing." Then he said, "Go again seven times." ⁴⁴At the seventh time he said, "Look, a little cloud no bigger than a person's hand is rising out of the sea." Then he said, "Go say to Ahab, 'Harness your chariot and go down before the rain stops you.' " ⁴⁵In a little while the heavens grew black with clouds and wind; there was a heavy rain. Ahab rode off and went to Jezreel. ⁴⁶But the hand of the Lord was on Elijah; he girded up his loins and ran in front of Ahab to the entrance of Jezreel.

Elijah Flees from Jezebel

19 Ahab told Jezebel all that Elijah had done, and how he had killed all the prophets with the sword. ²Then Jezebel sent a messenger to Elijah, saying, "So may the gods do to me, and more also, if I do not make your life like the life of one of them by this time tomorrow." ³Then he was afraid; he got up and fled for his life, and came to Beer-sheba, which belongs to Judah; he left his servant there.

4 But he himself went a day's journey into the wilderness, and came and sat down under a solitary broom tree. He asked that he might die: "It is enough; now, O Lord, take away my life, for I am

Pray It!

Looking for God

Elijah was told to meet God on the mountain. God's presence could have been in fire, in an earthquake, or in a great wind, but God was in none of these. God was in the tiny whispering sound.

Let's face it. Our lives tend to be pretty noisy and cluttered. How will we ever hear God in that tiny whispering sound? In order to hear God's voice, we need to take time away from the noise and clutter to just be quiet in God's presence. We also know that God often "whispers" to us through our friends, our family, and often through teachers and counselors. Like Elijah we have to be open to God's voice speaking through others as well as through the events in our lives.

God is always with us, in the quiet depths of our heart and in the people and situations God has placed in our lives. We need to be like Elijah—tuning out things that are not God and tuning in to God's presence. Taking quiet time to think and pray is a great start.

▶ **1 Kings 19:9–13**

no better than my ancestors." ⁵Then he lay down under the broom tree and fell asleep. Suddenly an angel touched him and said to him, "Get up and eat." ⁶He looked, and there at his head was a cake baked on hot stones, and a jar of water. He ate and drank, and lay down again. ⁷The angel of the Lord came a second time, touched him, and said, "Get up and eat, otherwise the journey will be too much for you." ⁸He got up, and ate and drank; then he went in the strength of that food forty days and forty nights to Horeb the mount of God. ⁹At that place he came to a cave, and spent the night there.

Then the word of the Lord came to him, saying, "What are you doing here, Elijah?" ¹⁰He answered, "I have been very zealous for the Lord, the God of hosts; for the Israelites have forsaken your covenant, thrown down your altars, and killed your prophets with the sword. I alone am left, and they are seeking my life, to take it away."

1 KINGS

Elijah Meets God at Horeb

11 He said, "Go out and stand on the mountain before the Lord, for the Lord is about to pass by." Now there was a great wind, so strong that it was splitting mountains and breaking rocks in pieces before the Lord, but the Lord was not in the wind; and after the wind an earthquake, but the Lord was not in the earthquake; 12and

Introducing...

Elijah and Elisha

You don't want to mess with Elijah and Elisha. They are take-no-prisoners kinds of prophets. According to First Kings, Elijah has 450 prophets of Baal killed after publicly humiliating them (see 18:40). And when a bunch of boys call Elisha "baldhead," they are attacked by bears (see 2 Kings 2:23–24).

Elijah, whose name means "Yahweh is my God," shows up in the second half of First Kings, reminding the Israelites that God is their God alone and that keeping God's Covenant means not worshiping the Canaanite baals (gods). In a dramatic story, he shows the idol-worshiping King Ahab and Queen Jezebel that God is superior to their false gods (see 1 Kings 18:21–40).

Elijah was recorded as being carried to heaven in a fiery chariot (see 2 Kings 2:11) as a sign of his greatness, and he was expected to reappear before the "day of the Lord" arrived (see Mal 4:5). By New Testament times, Elijah had come to represent the prophets as Moses had come to represent the Law. Referring to Moses and Elijah was a way of summarizing everything God had revealed before Christ.

Elisha was Elijah's disciple and successor. He plays an important role in the first half of Second Kings. Elisha's name means "God is salvation." He was a man of wisdom and a miracle worker.

These "tough guys" also had tender hearts. Both miraculously multiplied food for widows (see 1 Kings 17:16, 2 Kings 4:5), and both brought a dead child back to life (see 1 Kings 17:22, 2 Kings 4:34). Elijah and Elisha are revered both for their uncompromising faith and for their compassion for the "little ones."

after the earthquake a fire, but the Lord was not in the fire; and after the fire a sound of sheer silence. 13When Elijah heard it, he wrapped his face in his mantle and went out and stood at the entrance of the cave. Then there came a voice to him that said, "What are you doing here, Elijah?" 14He answered, "I have been very zealous for the Lord, the God of hosts; for the Israelites have forsaken your covenant, thrown down your altars, and killed your prophets with the sword. I alone am left, and they are seeking my life, to take it away." 15Then the Lord said to him, "Go, return on your way to the wilderness of Damascus; when you arrive, you shall anoint Hazael as king over Aram. 16Also you shall anoint Jehu son of Nimshi as king over Israel; and you shall anoint Elisha son of Shaphat of Abel-meholah as prophet in your place. 17Whoever escapes from the sword of Hazael, Jehu shall kill; and whoever escapes from the sword of Jehu, Elisha shall kill. 18Yet I will leave seven thousand in Israel, all the knees that have not bowed to Baal, and every mouth that has not kissed him."

Elisha Becomes Elijah's Disciple

19 So he set out from there, and found Elisha son of Shaphat, who was plowing. There were twelve yoke of oxen ahead of him, and he was with the twelfth. Elijah passed by him and threw his mantle over him. 20He left the oxen, ran after Elijah, and said, "Let me kiss my father and my mother, and then I will follow you." Then Elijah*a* said to him, "Go back again; for what have I done to you?" 21He returned from following him, took the yoke of oxen, and slaughtered them; using the equipment from the oxen, he boiled their flesh, and gave it to the people, and they ate. Then he set out and followed Elijah, and became his servant.

Ahab's Wars with the Arameans

20 King Ben-hadad of Aram gathered all his army together; thirty-two kings were with him, along with horses and chariots. He marched against Samaria, laid siege to it, and attacked it. 2Then he sent messengers into the city to King Ahab of Israel, and said to him: "Thus says Ben-hadad: 3Your silver and gold are mine; your fairest wives and children also are mine." 4The king of Israel answered, "As you say, my lord, O king, I am yours, and all that I have." 5The messengers came again and said: "Thus says Ben-hadad: I sent to you, saying, 'Deliver to me your silver and gold, your wives and children'; 6nevertheless

a Heb he

I will send my servants to you tomorrow about this time, and they shall search your house and the houses of your servants, and lay hands on whatever pleases them,[a] and take it away."

7 Then the king of Israel called all the elders of the land, and said, "Look now! See how this man is seeking trouble; for he sent to me for my wives, my children, my silver, and my gold; and I did not refuse him." [8]Then all the elders and all the people said to him, "Do not listen or consent." [9]So he said to the messengers of Ben-hadad, "Tell my lord the king: All that you first demanded of your servant I will do; but this thing I cannot do." The messengers left and brought him word again. [10]Ben-hadad sent to him and said, "The gods do so to me, and more also, if the dust of Samaria will provide a handful for each of the people who follow me." [11]The king of Israel answered, "Tell him: One who puts on armor should not brag like one who takes it off." [12]When Ben-hadad heard this message—now he had been drinking with the kings in the booths—he said to his men, "Take your positions!" And they took their positions against the city.

Prophetic Opposition to Ahab

13 Then a certain prophet came up to King Ahab of Israel and said, "Thus says the LORD, Have you seen all this great multitude? Look, I will give it into your hand today; and you shall know that I am the LORD." [14]Ahab said, "By whom?" He said, "Thus says the LORD, By the young men who serve the district governors." Then he said, "Who shall begin the battle?" He answered, "You." [15]Then he mustered the young men who served the district governors, two hundred thirty-two; after them he mustered all the people of Israel, seven thousand.

16 They went out at noon, while Ben-hadad was drinking himself drunk in the booths, he and the thirty-two kings allied with him. [17]The young men who served the district governors went out first. Ben-hadad had sent out scouts,[b] and they reported to him, "Men have come out from Samaria." [18]He said, "If they have come out for peace, take them alive, if they have come out for war, take them alive."

19 But these had already come out of the city: the young men who served the district governors, and the army that followed them. [20]Each killed his man; the Arameans fled and Israel pursued them, but King Ben-hadad of Aram escaped on a horse with the cavalry. [21]The king of Israel went out, attacked the horses and chariots, and defeated the Arameans with a great slaughter.

22 Then the prophet approached the king of Israel and said to him, "Come, strengthen yourself, and consider well what you have to do; for in the spring the king of Aram will come up against you."

The Arameans Are Defeated

23 The servants of the king of Aram said to him, "Their gods are gods of the hills, and so they were stronger than we; but let us fight against them in the plain, and surely we shall be stronger than they. [24]Also do this: remove the kings, each from his post, and put commanders in place of them; [25]and muster an army like the army that you have lost, horse for horse, and chariot for chariot; then we will fight against them in the plain, and surely we shall be stronger than they." He heeded their voice, and did so.

26 In the spring Ben-hadad mustered the Arameans and went up to Aphek to fight against Israel. [27]After the Israelites had been mustered and provisioned, they went out to engage them; the people of Israel encamped opposite them like two little flocks of goats, while the Arameans filled the country. [28]A man of God approached and said to the king of Israel, "Thus says the LORD: Because the Arameans have said, 'The LORD is a god of the hills but he is not a god of the valleys,' therefore I will give all this great multitude into your hand, and you shall know that I am the LORD." [29]They encamped opposite one another seven days. Then on the seventh day the battle began; the Israelites killed one hundred thousand Aramean foot soldiers in one day. [30]The rest fled into the city of Aphek; and the wall fell on twenty-seven thousand men that were left.

Ben-hadad also fled, and entered the city to hide. [31]His servants said to him, "Look, we have heard that the kings of the house of Israel are merciful kings; let us put sackcloth around our waists and ropes on our heads, and go out to the king of Israel; perhaps he will spare your life." [32]So they tied sackcloth around their waists, put ropes on their heads, went to the king of Israel, and said, "Your servant Ben-hadad says, 'Please let me live.' " And he said, "Is he still alive? He is my brother." [33]Now the men were watching for an omen; they quickly took it up from him and said, "Yes, Ben-hadad is your brother." Then he said, "Go and bring him." So Ben-hadad came out to him; and he had him come up into the chariot. [34]Ben-hadad[c] said to him, "I will restore the towns that my father took from your father; and you may establish bazaars for yourself in

---

a Gk Syr Vg: Heb *you*   b Heb lacks *scouts*   c Heb *He*

Damascus, as my father did in Samaria." The king of Israel responded,[a] "I will let you go on those terms." So he made a treaty with him and let him go.

A Prophet Condemns Ahab

35 At the command of the LORD a certain member of a company of prophets[b] said to another, "Strike me!" But the man refused to strike him. ³⁶Then he said to him, "Because you have not obeyed the voice of the LORD, as soon as you have left me, a lion will kill you." And when he had left him, a lion met him and killed him. ³⁷Then he found another man and said, "Strike me!" So the man hit him, striking and wounding him. ³⁸Then the prophet departed, and waited for the king along the road, disguising himself with a bandage over his eyes. ³⁹As the king passed by, he cried to the king and said, "Your servant went out into the thick of the battle; then a soldier turned and brought a man to me, and said, 'Guard this man; if he is missing, your life shall be given for his life, or else you shall pay a talent of silver.' ⁴⁰While your servant was busy here and there, he was gone." The king of Israel said to him, "So shall your judgment be; you yourself have decided it." ⁴¹Then he quickly took the bandage away from his eyes. The king of Israel recognized him as one of the prophets. ⁴²Then he said to him, "Thus says the LORD, 'Because you have let the man go whom I had devoted to destruction, therefore your life shall be for his life, and your people for his people.' " ⁴³The king of Israel set out toward home, resentful and sullen, and came to Samaria.

Naboth's Vineyard

21 Later the following events took place: Naboth the Jezreelite had a vineyard in Jezreel, beside the palace of King Ahab of Samaria. ²And Ahab said to Naboth, "Give me your vineyard, so that I may have it for a vegetable garden, because it is near my house; I will give you a better vineyard for it; or, if it seems good to you, I will give you its value in money." ³But Naboth said to Ahab, "The LORD forbid that I should give you my ancestral inheritance." ⁴Ahab went home resentful and sullen because of what Naboth the Jezreelite had said to him; for he had said, "I will not give you my ancestral inheritance." He lay down on his bed, turned away his face, and would not eat.

5 His wife Jezebel came to him and said, "Why are you so depressed that you will not eat?" ⁶He said to her, "Because I spoke to Naboth the Jezreelite and said to him, 'Give me your vineyard

for money; or else, if you prefer, I will give you another vineyard for it'; but he answered, 'I will not give you my vineyard.' " ⁷His wife Jezebel said to him, "Do you now govern Israel? Get up, eat some food, and be cheerful; I will give you the vineyard of Naboth the Jezreelite."

8 So she wrote letters in Ahab's name and sealed them with his seal; she sent the letters to the elders and the nobles who lived with Naboth in his city. ⁹She wrote in the letters, "Proclaim a fast, and seat Naboth at the head of the assembly; ¹⁰seat two scoundrels opposite him, and have them bring a charge against him, saying, 'You have cursed God and the king.' Then take him out, and stone him to death." ¹¹The men of his city, the elders and the nobles who lived in his city, did as Jezebel had sent word to them. Just as it was written in the letters that she had sent to them, ¹²they proclaimed a fast and seated Naboth at the head of the assembly. ¹³The two scoundrels came in and sat opposite him; and the scoundrels brought a charge against Naboth, in the presence of the people, saying, "Naboth cursed God and the king." So they took him outside the city, and stoned him to death. ¹⁴Then they sent to Jezebel, saying, "Naboth has been stoned; he is dead."

15 As soon as Jezebel heard that Naboth had been stoned and was dead, Jezebel said to Ahab, "Go, take possession of the vineyard of Naboth the Jezreelite, which he refused to give you for money; for Naboth is not alive, but dead." ¹⁶As soon as Ahab heard that Naboth was dead, Ahab set out to go down to the vineyard of Naboth the Jezreelite, to take possession of it.

Elijah Pronounces God's Sentence

17 Then the word of the LORD came to Elijah the Tishbite, saying: ¹⁸Go down to meet King Ahab of Israel, who rules[c] in Samaria; he is now in the vineyard of Naboth, where he has gone to take possession. ¹⁹You shall say to him, "Thus says the LORD: Have you killed, and also taken possession?" You shall say to him, "Thus says the LORD: In the place where dogs licked up the blood of Naboth, dogs will also lick up your blood."

20 Ahab said to Elijah, "Have you found me, O my enemy?" He answered, "I have found you. Because you have sold yourself to do what is evil in the sight of the LORD, ²¹I will bring disaster on you; I will consume you, and will cut off from Ahab every male, bond or free, in Israel; ²²and I

---

a Heb lacks *The king of Israel responded*   b Heb of the sons of the prophets   c Heb *who is*

will make your house like the house of Jeroboam son of Nebat, and like the house of Baasha son of Ahijah, because you have provoked me to anger and have caused Israel to sin. 23Also concerning Jezebel the LORD said, 'The dogs shall eat Jezebel within the bounds of Jezreel.' 24Anyone belonging to Ahab who dies in the city the dogs shall eat; and anyone of his who dies in the open country the birds of the air shall eat."

25 (Indeed, there was no one like Ahab, who sold himself to do what was evil in the sight of the LORD, urged on by his wife Jezebel. 26He acted most abominably in going after idols, as the Amorites had done, whom the LORD drove out before the Israelites.)

27 When Ahab heard those words, he tore his clothes and put sackcloth over his bare flesh; he fasted, lay in the sackcloth, and went about dejectedly. 28Then the word of the LORD came to Elijah the Tishbite: 29"Have you seen how Ahab has humbled himself before me? Because he has humbled himself before me, I will not bring the disaster in his days; but in his son's days I will bring the disaster on his house."

Joint Campaign with Judah against Aram

22 For three years Aram and Israel continued without war. 2But in the third year King Jehoshaphat of Judah came down to the king of Israel. 3The king of Israel said to his servants, "Do you know that Ramoth-gilead belongs to us, yet we are doing nothing to take it out of the hand of the king of Aram?" 4He said to Jehoshaphat, "Will you go with me to battle at Ramoth-gilead?" Jehoshaphat replied to the king of Israel, "I am as you are; my people are your people, my horses are your horses."

5 But Jehoshaphat also said to the king of Israel, "Inquire first for the word of the LORD." 6Then the king of Israel gathered the prophets together, about four hundred of them, and said to them, "Shall I go to battle against Ramoth-gilead, or shall I refrain?" They said, "Go up; for the LORD will give it into the hand of the king." 7But Jehoshaphat said, "Is there no other prophet of the LORD here of whom we may inquire?" 8The king of Israel said to Jehoshaphat, "There is still one other by whom we may inquire of the LORD, Micaiah son of Imlah; but I hate him, for he never prophesies anything favorable about me, but only disaster." Jehoshaphat said, "Let the king not say such a thing." 9Then the king of Israel summoned an officer and said, "Bring quickly Micaiah son of Imlah." 10Now the king of Israel and King Jehoshaphat of Judah were sitting on their thrones, arrayed in their robes,

at the threshing floor at the entrance of the gate of Samaria; and all the prophets were prophesying before them. 11Zedekiah son of Chenaanah made for himself horns of iron, and he said, "Thus says the LORD: With these you shall gore the Arameans until they are destroyed." 12All the prophets were prophesying the same and saying, "Go up to Ramoth-gilead and triumph; the LORD will give it into the hand of the king."

Micaiah Predicts Failure

13 The messenger who had gone to summon Micaiah said to him, "Look, the words of the prophets with one accord are favorable to the king; let your word be like the word of one of them, and speak favorably." 14But Micaiah said, "As the LORD lives, whatever the LORD says to me, that I will speak."

15 When he had come to the king, the king said to him, "Micaiah, shall we go to Ramoth-gilead to battle, or shall we refrain?" He answered him, "Go up and triumph; the LORD will give it into the hand of the king." 16But the king said to him, "How many times must I make you swear to tell me nothing but the truth in the name of the LORD?" 17Then Micaiah[a] said, "I saw all Israel scattered on the mountains, like sheep that have no shepherd; and the LORD said, 'These have no master; let each one go home in peace.' " 18The king of Israel said to Jehoshaphat, "Did I not tell you that he would not prophesy anything favorable about me, but only disaster?"

19 Then Micaiah[a] said, "Therefore hear the word of the LORD: I saw the LORD sitting on his throne, with all the host of heaven standing beside him to the right and to the left of him. 20And the LORD said, 'Who will entice Ahab, so that he may go up and fall at Ramoth-gilead?' Then one said one thing, and another said another, 21until a spirit came forward and stood before the LORD, saying, 'I will entice him.' 22'How?' the LORD asked him. He replied, 'I will go out and be a lying spirit in the mouth of all his prophets.' Then the LORD[a] said, 'You are to entice him, and you shall succeed; go out and do it.' 23So you see, the LORD has put a lying spirit in the mouth of all these your prophets; the LORD has decreed disaster for you."

24 Then Zedekiah son of Chenaanah came up to Micaiah, slapped him on the cheek, and said, "Which way did the spirit of the LORD pass from me to speak to you?" 25Micaiah replied, "You will find out on that day when you go in to hide in an inner chamber." 26The king of Israel

a Heb he

then ordered, "Take Micaiah, and return him to Amon the governor of the city and to Joash the king's son, 27and say, 'Thus says the king: Put this fellow in prison, and feed him on reduced rations of bread and water until I come in peace.' " 28Micaiah said, "If you return in peace, the LORD has not spoken by me." And he said, "Hear, you peoples, all of you!"

Defeat and Death of Ahab

29 So the king of Israel and King Jehoshaphat of Judah went up to Ramoth-gilead. 30The king of Israel said to Jehoshaphat, "I will disguise myself and go into battle, but you wear your robes." So the king of Israel disguised himself and went into battle. 31Now the king of Aram had commanded the thirty-two captains of his chariots, "Fight with no one small or great, but only with the king of Israel." 32When the captains of the chariots saw Jehoshaphat, they said, "It is surely the king of Israel." So they turned to fight against him; and Jehoshaphat cried out. 33When the captains of the chariots saw that it was not the king of Israel, they turned back from pursuing him. 34But a certain man drew his bow and unknowingly struck the king of Israel between the scale armor and the breastplate; so he said to the driver of his chariot, "Turn around, and carry me out of the battle, for I am wounded." 35The battle grew hot that day, and the king was propped up in his chariot facing the Arameans, until at evening he died; the blood from the wound had flowed into the bottom of the chariot. 36Then about sunset a shout went through the army, "Every man to his city, and every man to his country!"

37 So the king died, and was brought to Samaria; they buried the king in Samaria. 38They washed the chariot by the pool of Samaria; the dogs licked up his blood, and the prostitutes washed themselves in it,*a* according to the word of the LORD that he had spoken. 39Now the rest of the acts of Ahab, and all that he did, and the ivory house that he built, and all the cities that he built, are they not written in the Book of the Annals of the Kings of Israel? 40So Ahab slept with his ancestors; and his son Ahaziah succeeded him.

Jehoshaphat Reigns over Judah

41 Jehoshaphat son of Asa began to reign over Judah in the fourth year of King Ahab of Israel. 42Jehoshaphat was thirty-five years old when he began to reign, and he reigned twenty-five years in Jerusalem. His mother's name was Azubah daughter of Shilhi. 43He walked in all the way of his father Asa; he did not turn aside from it, doing what was right in the sight of the LORD; yet the high places were not taken away, and the people still sacrificed and offered incense on the high places. 44Jehoshaphat also made peace with the king of Israel.

45 Now the rest of the acts of Jehoshaphat, and his power that he showed, and how he waged war, are they not written in the Book of the Annals of the Kings of Judah? 46The remnant of the male temple prostitutes who were still in the land in the days of his father Asa, he exterminated.

47 There was no king in Edom; a deputy was king. 48Jehoshaphat made ships of the Tarshish type to go to Ophir for gold; but they did not go, for the ships were wrecked at Ezion-geber. 49Then Ahaziah son of Ahab said to Jehoshaphat, "Let my servants go with your servants in the ships," but Jehoshaphat was not willing. 50Jehoshaphat slept with his ancestors and was buried with his ancestors in the city of his father David; his son Jehoram succeeded him.

Ahaziah Reigns over Israel

51 Ahaziah son of Ahab began to reign over Israel in Samaria in the seventeenth year of King Jehoshaphat of Judah; he reigned two years over Israel. 52He did what was evil in the sight of the LORD, and walked in the way of his father and mother, and in the way of Jeroboam son of Nebat, who caused Israel to sin. 53He served Baal and worshiped him; he provoked the LORD, the God of Israel, to anger, just as his father had done.

---

a Heb lacks *in it*

For background on this book, see the introduction to 1 and 2 Kings before 1 Kings.

2 Kings

Elijah Denounces Ahaziah

1 After the death of Ahab, Moab rebelled against Israel.

2 Ahaziah had fallen through the lattice in his upper chamber in Samaria, and lay injured; so he sent messengers, telling them, "Go, inquire of Baal-zebub, the god of Ekron, whether I shall recover from this injury." ³But the angel of the LORD said to Elijah the Tishbite, "Get up, go to meet the messengers of the king of Samaria, and say to them, 'Is it because there is no God in Israel that you are going to inquire of Baal-zebub, the god of Ekron?' ⁴Now therefore thus says the LORD, 'You shall not leave the bed to which you have gone, but you shall surely die.' " So Elijah went.

5 The messengers returned to the king, who said to them, "Why have you returned?" ⁶They answered him, "There came a man to meet us, who said to us, 'Go back to the king who sent you, and say to him: Thus says the LORD: Is it because there is no God in Israel that you are sending to inquire of Baal-zebub, the god of Ekron? Therefore you shall not leave the bed to which you have gone, but shall surely die.' " ⁷He said to them, "What sort of man was he who came to meet you and told you these things?" ⁸They answered him, "A hairy man, with a leather belt around his waist." He said, "It is Elijah the Tishbite."

9 Then the king sent to him a captain of fifty with his fifty men. He went up to Elijah, who was sitting on the top of a hill, and said to him, "O man of God, the king says, 'Come down.' "

¹⁰But Elijah answered the captain of fifty, "If I am a man of God, let fire come down from heaven and consume you and your fifty." Then fire came down from heaven, and consumed him and his fifty.

11 Again the king sent to him another captain of fifty with his fifty. He went up*ᵃ* and said to him, "O man of God, this is the king's order: Come down quickly!" ¹²But Elijah answered them, "If I am a man of God, let fire come down from heaven and consume you and your fifty." Then the fire of God came down from heaven and consumed him and his fifty.

13 Again the king sent the captain of a third fifty with his fifty. So the third captain of fifty went up, and came and fell on his knees before Elijah, and entreated him, "O man of God, please let my life, and the life of these fifty servants of yours, be precious in your sight. ¹⁴Look, fire came down from heaven and consumed the two former captains of fifty men with their fifties; but now let my life be precious in your sight." ¹⁵Then the angel of the LORD said to Elijah, "Go down with him, do not be afraid of him." So he set out and went down with him to the king, ¹⁶and said to him, "Thus says the LORD: Because you have sent messengers to inquire of Baal-zebub, the god of Ekron,—is it because there is no God in Israel to inquire of his word?—therefore you shall not leave the bed to which you have gone, but you shall surely die."

---

a Gk Compare verses 9, 13: Heb *He answered*

2 KINGS

Death of Ahaziah

17 So he died according to the word of the LORD that Elijah had spoken. His brother,[a] Jehoram succeeded him as king in the second year of King Jehoram son of Jehoshaphat of Judah, because Ahaziah had no son. [18]Now the rest of the acts of Ahaziah that he did, are they not written in the Book of the Annals of the Kings of Israel?

Elijah Ascends to Heaven

2 Now when the LORD was about to take Elijah up to heaven by a whirlwind, Elijah and Elisha were on their way from Gilgal. [2]Elijah said to Elisha, "Stay here; for the LORD has sent me as far as Bethel." But Elisha said, "As the LORD lives, and as you yourself live, I will not leave you."

Elijah, Prophet of God in Solidarity with the People

Elijah was a passionate prophet who read the history of the monarchy (Israel's kings) from the perspective of God. He saw division in the people of Israel. On the one hand were the kings, the noblemen, and the leaders of the army; on the other hand were the peasants, the widows, and the persecuted prophets. The Covenant had been broken. Elijah denounced the unfaithfulness of Queen Jezebel and Kings Ahab and Ahaziah. They had introduced idolatry in the form of the false god Baal, who favored the powerful and allowed injustices.

Elijah's faithfulness to the Covenant and his solidarity with the poor led him to speak against kings and queens, to fight false prophets, and to intervene in national affairs. The powerful rulers wanted to kill him and silence his voice. After his dramatic departure (see 2 Kings 2:11), the people never forgot him; they always expected his return.

● Who do you see as a contemporary Elijah in our world today? In what ways and in what situations are you called to be a prophet?

▶ 2 Kings 2:11

So they went down to Bethel. [3]The company of prophets[b] who were in Bethel came out to Elisha, and said to him, "Do you know that today the LORD will take your master away from you?" And he said, "Yes, I know; keep silent."

4 Elijah said to him, "Elisha, stay here; for the LORD has sent me to Jericho." But he said, "As the LORD lives, and as you yourself live, I will not leave you." So they came to Jericho. [5]The company of prophets[b] who were at Jericho drew near to Elisha, and said to him, "Do you know that today the LORD will take your master away from you?" And he answered, "Yes, I know; be silent."

6 Then Elijah said to him, "Stay here; for the LORD has sent me to the Jordan." But he said, "As the LORD lives, and as you yourself live, I will not leave you." So the two of them went on. [7]Fifty men of the company of prophets[b] also went, and stood at some distance from them, as they both were standing by the Jordan. [8]Then Elijah took his mantle and rolled it up, and struck the water; the water was parted to the one side and to the other, until the two of them crossed on dry ground.

9 When they had crossed, Elijah said to Elisha, "Tell me what I may do for you, before I am taken from you." Elisha said, "Please let me inherit a double share of your spirit." [10]He responded, "You have asked a hard thing; yet, if you see me as I am being taken from you, it will be granted you; if not, it will not." [11]As they continued walking and talking, a chariot of fire and horses of fire separated the two of them, and Elijah ascended in a whirlwind into heaven. [12]Elisha kept watching and crying out, "Father, father! The chariots of Israel and its horsemen!" But when he could no longer see him, he grasped his own clothes and tore them in two pieces.

Elisha Succeeds Elijah

13 He picked up the mantle of Elijah that had fallen from him, and went back and stood on the bank of the Jordan. [14]He took the mantle of Elijah that had fallen from him, and struck the water, saying, "Where is the LORD, the God of Elijah?" When he had struck the water, the water was parted to the one side and to the other, and Elisha went over.

15 When the company of prophets[b] who were at Jericho saw him at a distance, they declared, "The spirit of Elijah rests on Elisha." They came to meet him and bowed to the ground before him. [16]They said to him, "See now, we have fifty

---

a Gk Syr: Heb lacks *His brother*　b Heb *sons of the prophets* strong men among your servants; please let them go and seek your master; it may be that the spirit of the LORD has caught him up and thrown him down on some mountain or into some valley." He responded, "No, do not send them." ¹⁷But when they urged him until he was ashamed, he said, "Send them." So they sent fifty men who searched for three days but did not find him. ¹⁸When they came back to him (he had remained at Jericho), he said to them, "Did I not say to you, Do not go?"

Elisha Performs Miracles

19 Now the people of the city said to Elisha, "The location of this city is good, as my lord sees; but the water is bad, and the land is unfruitful." ²⁰He said, "Bring me a new bowl, and put salt in it." So they brought it to him. ²¹Then he went to the spring of water and threw the salt into it, and said, "Thus says the LORD, I have made this water wholesome; from now on neither death nor miscarriage shall come from it." ²²So the water has been wholesome to this day, according to the word that Elisha spoke.

23 He went up from there to Bethel; and while he was going up on the way, some small boys came out of the city and jeered at him, saying, "Go away, baldhead! Go away, baldhead!" ²⁴When he turned around and saw them, he cursed them in the name of the LORD. Then two she-bears came out of the woods and mauled forty-two of the boys. ²⁵From there he went on to Mount Carmel, and then returned to Samaria.

Jehoram Reigns over Israel

3 In the eighteenth year of King Jehoshaphat of Judah, Jehoram son of Ahab became king over Israel in Samaria; he reigned twelve years. ²He did what was evil in the sight of the LORD, though not like his father and mother, for he removed the pillar of Baal that his father had made. ³Nevertheless he clung to the sin of Jeroboam son of Nebat, which he caused Israel to commit; he did not depart from it.

War with Moab

4 Now King Mesha of Moab was a sheep breeder, who used to deliver to the king of Israel one hundred thousand lambs, and the wool of one hundred thousand rams. ⁵But when Ahab died, the king of Moab rebelled against the king of Israel. ⁶So King Jehoram marched out of Samaria at that time and mustered all Israel. ⁷As he went he sent word to King Jehoshaphat of Judah, "The king of Moab has rebelled against me; will you go with me to battle against Moab?"

He answered, "I will; I am with you, my people are your people, my horses are your horses." ⁸Then he asked, "By which way shall we march?" Jehoram answered, "By the way of the wilderness of Edom."

9 So the king of Israel, the king of Judah, and the king of Edom set out; and when they had made a roundabout march of seven days, there was no water for the army or for the animals that were with them. ¹⁰Then the king of Israel said, "Alas! The LORD has summoned us, three kings, only to be handed over to Moab." ¹¹But Jehoshaphat said, "Is there no prophet of the LORD here, through whom we may inquire of the LORD?" Then one of the servants of the king of Israel answered, "Elisha son of Shaphat, who used to pour water on the hands of Elijah, is here." ¹²Jehoshaphat said, "The word of the LORD is with him." So the king of Israel and Jehoshaphat and the king of Edom went down to him.

13 Elisha said to the king of Israel, "What have I to do with you? Go to your father's prophets or to your mother's." But the king of Israel said to him, "No; it is the LORD who has summoned us, three kings, only to be handed over to Moab." ¹⁴Elisha said, "As the LORD of hosts lives, whom I serve, were it not that I have regard for King Jehoshaphat of Judah, I would give you neither a look nor a glance. ¹⁵But get me a musician." And then, while the musician was playing, the power of the LORD came on him. ¹⁶And he said, "Thus says the LORD, 'I will make this wadi full of pools.' ¹⁷For thus says the LORD, 'You shall see neither wind nor rain, but the wadi shall be filled with water, so that you shall drink, you, your cattle, and your animals.' ¹⁸This is only a trifle in the sight of the LORD, for he will also hand Moab over to you. ¹⁹You shall conquer every fortified city and every choice city; every good tree you shall fell, all springs of water you shall stop up, and every good piece of land you shall ruin with stones." ²⁰The next day, about the time of the morning offering, suddenly water began to flow from the direction of Edom, until the country was filled with water.

21 When all the Moabites heard that the kings had come up to fight against them, all who were able to put on armor, from the youngest to the oldest, were called out and were drawn up at the frontier. ²²When they rose early in the morning, and the sun shone upon the water, the Moabites saw the water opposite them as red as blood. ²³They said, "This is blood; the kings must have fought together, and killed one another. Now then, Moab, to the spoil!" ²⁴But when they came to the camp of Israel, the Israelites rose up and

attacked the Moabites, who fled before them; as they entered Moab they continued the attack.ᵃ ²⁵The cities they overturned, and on every good piece of land everyone threw a stone, until it was covered; every spring of water they stopped up, and every good tree they felled. Only at Kir-hare-seth did the stone walls remain, until the slingers surrounded and attacked it. ²⁶When the king of Moab saw that the battle was going against him, he took with him seven hundred swordsmen to break through, opposite the king of Edom; but they could not. ²⁷Then he took his firstborn son who was to succeed him, and offered him as a burnt offering on the wall. And great wrath came upon Israel, so they withdrew from him and returned to their own land.

Elisha and the Widow's Oil

4 Now the wife of a member of the company of prophetsᵇ cried to Elisha, "Your servant my husband is dead; and you know that your servant feared the LORD, but a creditor has come to take my two children as slaves." ²Elisha said to her, "What shall I do for you? Tell me, what do you have in the house?" She answered, "Your servant has nothing in the house, except a jar of oil." ³He said, "Go outside, borrow vessels from all your neighbors, empty vessels and not just a few. ⁴Then go in, and shut the door behind you and your children, and start pouring into all these vessels; when each is full, set it aside." ⁵So she left him and shut the door behind her and her children; they kept bringing vessels to her, and she kept pouring. ⁶When the vessels were full, she said to her son, "Bring me another vessel." But he said to her, "There are no more." Then the oil stopped flowing. ⁷She came and told the man of God, and he said, "Go sell the oil and pay your debts, and you and your children can live on the rest."

Elisha Raises the Shunammite's Son

8 One day Elisha was passing through Shunem, where a wealthy woman lived, who urged him to have a meal. So whenever he passed that way, he would stop there for a meal. ⁹She said to her husband, "Look, I am sure that this man who regularly passes our way is a holy man of God. ¹⁰Let us make a small roof chamber with walls, and put there for him a bed, a table, a chair, and a lamp, so that he can stay there whenever he comes to us."

11 One day when he came there, he went up to the chamber and lay down there. ¹²He said to his servant Gehazi, "Call the Shunammite woman." When he had called her, she stood before him. ¹³He said to him, "Say to her, Since you have taken all this trouble for us, what may be done for you? Would you have a word spoken on your behalf to the king or to the commander of the army?" She answered, "I live among my own people." ¹⁴He said, "What then may be done for her?" Gehazi answered, "Well, she has no son, and her husband is old." ¹⁵He said, "Call her." When he had called her, she stood at the door. ¹⁶He said, "At this season, in due time, you shall embrace a son." She replied, "No, my lord, O man of God; do not deceive your servant."

17 The woman conceived and bore a son at that season, in due time, as Elisha had declared to her.

18 When the child was older, he went out one day to his father among the reapers. ¹⁹He complained to his father, "Oh, my head, my head!" The father said to his servant, "Carry him to his mother." ²⁰He carried him and brought him to his mother; the child sat on her lap until noon, and he died. ²¹She went up and laid him on the bed of the man of God, closed the door on him, and left. ²²Then she called to her husband, and said, "Send me one of the servants and one of the donkeys, so that I may quickly go to the man of God and come back again." ²³He said, "Why

Did You Know?

New Testament Parallels

The story in 2 Kings 4:42–44 reminds us of a famous story about Jesus feeding a crowd of people with a tiny amount of food. This story is famous because it is the only one told six times in the Gospels. Jesus feeds a crowd of five thousand in all four Gospels (see Mt 14:13–21, Mk 6:34–44, Lk 9:10–17, Jn 6:1–14) and a crowd of four thousand in two Gospels (see Mt 15:32–39, Mk 8:1–9).

Several events in the Old Testament have close parallels in the New Testament. For Christians these Old Testament parallels have even richer meaning in the light of Jesus' life and ministry.

▶ 2 Kings 4:42–44

ᵃ Compare Gk Syr: Meaning of Heb uncertain   ᵇ Heb the sons of the prophets

go to him today? It is neither new moon nor sabbath." She said, "It will be all right." [24]Then she saddled the donkey and said to her servant, "Urge the animal on; do not hold back for me unless I tell you." [25]So she set out, and came to the man of God at Mount Carmel.

When the man of God saw her coming, he said to Gehazi his servant, "Look, there is the Shunammite woman; [26]run at once to meet her, and say to her, Are you all right? Is your husband all right? Is the child all right?" She answered, "It is all right." [27]When she came to the man of God at the mountain, she caught hold of his feet. Gehazi approached to push her away. But the man of God said, "Let her alone, for she is in bitter distress; the LORD has hidden it from me and has not told me." [28]Then she said, "Did I ask my lord for a son? Did I not say, Do not mislead me?" [29]He said to Gehazi, "Gird up your loins, and take my staff in your hand, and go. If you meet anyone, give no greeting, and if anyone greets you, do not answer; and lay my staff on the face of the child." [30]Then the mother of the child said, "As the LORD lives, and as you yourself live, I will not leave without you." So he rose up and followed her. [31]Gehazi went on ahead and laid the staff on the face of the child, but there was no sound or sign of life. He came back to meet him and told him, "The child has not awakened."

32 When Elisha came into the house, he saw the child lying dead on his bed. [33]So he went in and closed the door on the two of them, and prayed to the LORD. [34]Then he got up on the bed[a] and lay upon the child, putting his mouth upon his mouth, his eyes upon his eyes, and his hands upon his hands; and while he lay bent over him, the flesh of the child became warm. [35]He got down, walked once to and fro in the room, then got up again and bent over him; the child sneezed seven times, and the child opened his eyes. [36]Elisha[b] summoned Gehazi and said, "Call the Shunammite woman." So he called her. When she came to him, he said, "Take your son." [37]She came and fell at his feet, bowing to the ground; then she took her son and left.

Elisha Purifies the Pot of Stew

38 When Elisha returned to Gilgal, there was a famine in the land. As the company of prophets was[c] sitting before him, he said to his servant, "Put the large pot on, and make some stew for the company of prophets."[d] [39]One of them went out into the field to gather herbs; he found a wild vine and gathered from it a lapful of wild gourds, and came and cut them up into the pot of stew, not knowing what they were. [40]They served some

Feed Your Soul

Elisha's miracle in 2 Kings 4:44 fed the body, but it is just as important to feed the appetite of the soul, such as the need for hope, for affirmation, and for being loved. It's easy to go to the nearest fast-food restaurant to satisfy your physical appetite, but when it comes to feeding your soul, where do you go?

God gives us plenty of opportunities to feed our soul. We just need to take advantage of them. Go to church. Participate in your youth program. Start a Bible study. Go on a retreat or to a youth conference. Talk to friends about your faith and theirs. Take a walk and pray. You'll find that feeding your faith can be fun, and it often costs less than a value meal at your local fast-food restaurant.

▶ 2 Kings 4:42–44

for the men to eat. But while they were eating the stew, they cried out, "O man of God, there is death in the pot!" They could not eat it. [41]He said, "Then bring some flour." He threw it into the pot, and said, "Serve the people and let them eat." And there was nothing harmful in the pot.

Elisha Feeds One Hundred Men

42 A man came from Baal-shalishah, bringing food from the first fruits to the man of God: twenty loaves of barley and fresh ears of grain in his sack. Elisha said, "Give it to the people and let them eat." [43]But his servant said, "How can I set this before a hundred people?" So he repeated, "Give it to the people and let them eat, for thus says the LORD, 'They shall eat and have some left.'" [44]He set it before them, they ate, and had some left, according to the word of the LORD.

The Healing of Naaman

5 Naaman, commander of the army of the king of Aram, was a great man and in high favor with his master, because by him the LORD had

a Heb lacks *on the bed* b Heb *he* c Heb *sons of the prophets were* d Heb *sons of the prophets*

given victory to Aram. The man, though a mighty warrior, suffered from leprosy.[a] 2Now the Arameans on one of their raids had taken a young girl captive from the land of Israel, and she served Naaman's wife. 3She said to her mistress, "If only my lord were with the prophet who is in Samaria! He would cure him of his leprosy."[a] 4So Naaman[b] went in and told his lord just what the girl from the land of Israel had said. 5And the king of Aram said, "Go then, and I will send along a letter to the king of Israel."

He went, taking with him ten talents of silver, six thousand shekels of gold, and ten sets of garments. 6He brought the letter to the king of Israel, which read, "When this letter reaches you, know that I have sent to you my servant Naaman, that you may cure him of his leprosy."[a] 7When the king of Israel read the letter, he tore his clothes and said, "Am I God, to give death or life, that this man sends word to me to cure a man of his leprosy?[a] Just look and see how he is trying to pick a quarrel with me."

8 But when Elisha the man of God heard that the king of Israel had torn his clothes, he sent a message to the king, "Why have you torn your clothes? Let him come to me, that he may learn that there is a prophet in Israel." 9So Naaman came with his horses and chariots, and halted at the entrance of Elisha's house. 10Elisha sent a messenger to him, saying, "Go, wash in the Jordan seven times, and your flesh shall be restored and you shall be clean." 11But Naaman became angry and went away, saying, "I thought that for me he would surely come out, and stand and call on the name of the LORD his God, and would wave his hand over the spot, and cure the leprosy![a] 12Are not Abana[c] and Pharpar, the rivers of Damascus, better than all the waters of Israel? Could I not wash in them, and be clean?" He turned and went away in a rage. 13But his servants approached and said to him, "Father, if the prophet had commanded you to do something difficult, would you not have done it? How much more, when all he said to you was, 'Wash, and be clean'?" 14So he went down and immersed himself seven times in the Jordan, according to the word of the man of God; his flesh was restored like the flesh of a young boy, and he was clean.

15 Then he returned to the man of God, he and all his company; he came and stood before him and said, "Now I know that there is no God in all the earth except in Israel; please accept a present from your servant." 16But he said, "As the LORD lives, whom I serve, I will accept nothing!" He urged him to accept, but he refused. 17Then Naaman said, "If not, please let two mule-loads of earth be given to your servant; for your servant will no longer offer burnt offering or sacrifice to any god except the LORD. 18But may the LORD pardon your servant on one count: when my master goes into the house of Rimmon to worship there, leaning on my arm, and I bow down in the house of Rimmon, when I do bow down in the house of Rimmon, may the LORD pardon your servant on this one count." 19He said to him, "Go in peace."

Gehazi's Greed

But when Naaman had gone from him a short distance, 20Gehazi, the servant of Elisha the man of God, thought, "My master has let that Aramean Naaman off too lightly by not accepting from him what he offered. As the LORD lives, I will run after him and get something out of him." 21So Gehazi went after Naaman. When Naaman saw someone running after him, he jumped down from the chariot to meet him and said, "Is everything all right?" 22He replied, "Yes, but my master has sent me to say, 'Two members of a company of prophets[d] have just come to me from the hill country of Ephraim; please give them a talent of silver and two changes of clothing.'" 23Naaman said, "Please accept two talents." He urged him, and tied up two talents of silver in two bags, with two changes of clothing, and gave them to two of his servants, who carried them in front of Gehazi.[e] 24When he came to the citadel, he took the bags[f] from them, and stored them inside; he dismissed the men, and they left.

25 He went in and stood before his master; and Elisha said to him, "Where have you been, Gehazi?" He answered, "Your servant has not gone anywhere at all." 26But he said to him, "Did I not go with you in spirit when someone left his chariot to meet you? Is this a time to accept money and to accept clothing, olive orchards and vineyards, sheep and oxen, and male and female slaves? 27Therefore the leprosy[a] of Naaman shall cling to you, and to your descendants forever." So he left his presence leprous,[a] as white as snow.

The Miracle of the Ax Head

6 Now the company of prophets[d] said to Elisha, "As you see, the place where we live under your charge is too small for us. 2Let us go to the Jordan, and let us collect logs there, one

---

a A term for several skin diseases; precise meaning uncertain
b Heb he   c Another reading is Amana   d Heb sons of the prophets   e Heb him   f Heb lacks the bags

for each of us, and build a place there for us to live." He answered, "Do so." ³Then one of them said, "Please come with your servants." And he answered, "I will." ⁴So he went with them. When they came to the Jordan, they cut down trees. ⁵But as one was felling a log, his ax head fell into the water; he cried out, "Alas, master! It was borrowed." ⁶Then the man of God said, "Where did it fall?" When he showed him the place, he cut off a stick, and threw it in there, and made the iron float. ⁷He said, "Pick it up." So he reached out his hand and took it.

The Aramean Attack Is Thwarted

8 Once when the king of Aram was at war with Israel, he took counsel with his officers. He said, "At such and such a place shall be my camp." ⁹But the man of God sent word to the king of Israel, "Take care not to pass this place, because the Arameans are going down there." ¹⁰The king of Israel sent word to the place of which the man of God spoke. More than once or twice he warned such a place*a* so that it was on the alert.

11 The mind of the king of Aram was greatly perturbed because of this; he called his officers and said to them, "Now tell me who among us sides with the king of Israel?" ¹²Then one of his officers said, "No one, my lord king. It is Elisha, the prophet in Israel, who tells the king of Israel the words that you speak in your bedchamber." ¹³He said, "Go and find where he is; I will send and seize him." He was told, "He is in Dothan." ¹⁴So he sent horses and chariots there and a great army; they came by night, and surrounded the city.

15 When an attendant of the man of God rose early in the morning and went out, an army with horses and chariots was all around the city. His servant said, "Alas, master! What shall we do?" ¹⁶He replied, "Do not be afraid, for there are more with us than there are with them." ¹⁷Then Elisha prayed: "O LORD, please open his eyes that he may see." So the LORD opened the eyes of the servant, and he saw; the mountain was full of horses and chariots of fire all around Elisha. ¹⁸When the Arameans*h* came down against him, Elisha prayed to the LORD, and said, "Strike this people, please, with blindness." So he struck them with blindness as Elisha had asked. ¹⁹Elisha said to them, "This is not the way, and this is not the city; follow me, and I will bring you to the man whom you seek." And he led them to Samaria.

20 As soon as they entered Samaria, Elisha said, "O LORD, open the eyes of these men so that

they may see." The LORD opened their eyes, and they saw that they were inside Samaria. ²¹When the king of Israel saw them he said to Elisha, "Father, shall I kill them? Shall I kill them?" ²²He answered, "No! Did you capture with your sword and your bow those whom you want to kill? Set food and water before them so that they may eat and drink; and let them go to their master." ²³So he prepared for them a great feast; after they ate and drank, he sent them on their way, and they went to their master. And the Arameans no longer came raiding into the land of Israel.

Ben-hadad's Siege of Samaria

24 Some time later King Ben-hadad of Aram mustered his entire army; he marched against Samaria and laid siege to it. ²⁵As the siege continued, famine in Samaria became so great that a donkey's head was sold for eighty shekels of silver, and one-fourth of a kab of dove's dung for five shekels of silver. ²⁶Now as the king of Israel was walking on the city wall, a woman cried out to him, "Help, my lord king!" ²⁷He said, "No! Let the LORD help you. How can I help you? From the threshing floor or from the wine press?" ²⁸But then the king asked her, "What is your complaint?" She answered, "This woman said to me, 'Give up your son; we will eat him today, and we will eat my son tomorrow.' ²⁹So we cooked my son and ate him. The next day I said to her, 'Give up your son and we will eat him.' But she has hidden her son." ³⁰When the king heard the words of the woman he tore his clothes—now since he was walking on the city wall, the people could see that he had sackcloth on his body underneath— ³¹and he said, "So may God do to me, and more, if the head of Elisha son of Shaphat stays on his shoulders today." ³²So he dispatched a man from his presence.

Now Elisha was sitting in his house, and the elders were sitting with him. Before the messenger arrived, Elisha said to the elders, "Are you aware that this murderer has sent someone to take off my head? When the messenger comes, see that you shut the door and hold it closed against him. Is not the sound of his master's feet behind him?" ³³While he was still speaking with them, the king*c* came down to him and said, "This trouble is from the LORD! Why should I hope in the LORD any longer?" ¹But Elisha said, "Hear the word of the LORD: thus says the LORD, Tomorrow about this time a measure of choice meal shall be sold for a shekel, and two measures of barley for a shekel, at the gate

a Heb warned it   b Heb they   c See 7.2: Heb messenger

of Samaria." ²Then the captain on whose hand the king leaned said to the man of God, "Even if the LORD were to make windows in the sky, could such a thing happen?" But he said, "You shall see it with your own eyes, but you shall not eat from it."

The Arameans Flee

3 Now there were four leprousᵃ men outside the city gate, who said to one another, "Why should we sit here until we die? ⁴If we say, 'Let us enter the city,' the famine is in the city, and we shall die there; but if we sit here, we shall also die. Therefore, let us desert to the Aramean camp; if they spare our lives, we shall live; and if they kill us, we shall but die." ⁵So they arose at twilight to go to the Aramean camp; but when they came to the edge of the Aramean camp, there was no one there at all. ⁶For the Lord had caused the Aramean army to hear the sound of chariots, and of horses, the sound of a great army, so that they said to one another, "The king of Israel has hired the kings of the Hittites and the kings of Egypt to fight against us." ⁷So they fled away in the twilight and abandoned their tents, their horses, and their donkeys leaving the camp just as it was, and fled for their lives. ⁸When these leprousᵃ men had come to the edge of the camp, they went into a tent, ate and drank, carried off silver, gold, and clothing, and went and hid them. Then they came back, entered another tent, carried off things from it, and went and hid them.

9 Then they said to one another, "What we are doing is wrong. This is a day of good news; if we are silent and wait until the morning light, we will be found guilty; therefore let us go and tell the king's household." ¹⁰So they came and called to the gatekeepers of the city, and told them, "We went to the Aramean camp, but there was no one to be seen or heard there, nothing but the horses tied, the donkeys tied, and the tents as they were." ¹¹Then the gatekeepers called out and proclaimed it to the king's household. ¹²The king got up in the night, and said to his servants, "I will tell you what the Arameans have prepared against us. They know that we are starving; so they have left the camp to hide themselves in the open country, thinking, 'When they come out of the city, we shall take them alive and get into the city.' " ¹³One of his servants said, "Let some men take five of the remaining horses, since those left here will suffer the fate of the whole multitude of Israel that have perished already;ᵇ let us send and find out." ¹⁴So they took two mounted men, and the king sent them after the Aramean army, saying, "Go and find out." ¹⁵So they went after

them as far as the Jordan; the whole way was littered with garments and equipment that the Arameans had thrown away in their haste. So the messengers returned, and told the king.

16 Then the people went out, and plundered the camp of the Arameans. So a measure of choice meal was sold for a shekel, and two measures of barley for a shekel, according to the word of the LORD. ¹⁷Now the king had appointed the captain on whose hand he leaned to have charge of the gate; the people trampled him to death in the gate, just as the man of God had said when the king came down to him. ¹⁸For when the man of God had said to the king, "Two measures of barley shall be sold for a shekel, and a measure of choice meal for a shekel, about this time tomorrow in the gate of Samaria," ¹⁹the captain had answered the man of God, "Even if the LORD were to make windows in the sky, could such a thing happen?" And he had answered, "You shall see it with your own eyes, but you shall not eat from it." ²⁰It did indeed happen to him; the people trampled him to death in the gate.

The Shunammite Woman's Land Restored

8 Now Elisha had said to the woman whose son he had restored to life, "Get up and go with your household, and settle wherever you can; for the LORD has called for a famine, and it will come on the land for seven years." ²So the woman got up and did according to the word of the man of God; she went with her household and settled in the land of the Philistines seven years. ³At the end of the seven years, when the woman returned from the land of the Philistines, she set out to appeal to the king for her house and her land. ⁴Now the king was talking with Gehazi the servant of the man of God, saying, "Tell me all the great things that Elisha has done." ⁵While he was telling the king how Elisha had restored a dead person to life, the woman whose son he had restored to life appealed to the king for her house and her land. Gehazi said, "My lord king, here is the woman, and here is her son whom Elisha restored to life." ⁶When the king questioned the woman, she told him. So the king appointed an official for her, saying, "Restore all that was hers, together with all the revenue of the fields from the day that she left the land until now."

Death of Ben-hadad

7 Elisha went to Damascus while King Ben-hadad of Aram was ill. When it was told him,

---

ᵃ A term for several skin diseases; precise meaning uncertain
ᵇ Compare Gk Syr Vg: Meaning of Heb uncertain

"The man of God has come here," 8the king said to Hazael, "Take a present with you and go to meet the man of God. Inquire of the LORD through him, whether I shall recover from this illness." 9So Hazael went to meet him, taking a present with him, all kinds of goods of Damascus, forty camel loads. When he entered and stood before him, he said, "Your son King Benhadad of Aram has sent me to you, saying, 'Shall I recover from this illness?' " 10Elisha said to him, "Go, say to him, 'You shall certainly recover'; but the LORD has shown me that he shall certainly die." 11He fixed his gaze and stared at him, until he was ashamed. Then the man of God wept. 12Hazael asked, "Why does my lord weep?" He answered, "Because I know the evil that you will do to the people of Israel; you will set their fortresses on fire, you will kill their young men with the sword, dash in pieces their little ones, and rip up their pregnant women." 13Hazael said, "What is your servant, who is a mere dog, that he should do this great thing?" Elisha answered, "The LORD has shown me that you are to be king over Aram." 14Then he left Elisha, and went to his master Ben-hadad,*a* who said to him, "What did Elisha say to you?" And he answered, "He told me that you would certainly recover." 15But the next day he took the bed-cover and dipped it in water and spread it over the king's face, until he died. And Hazael succeeded him.

Jehoram Reigns over Judah

16 In the fifth year of King Joram son of Ahab of Israel,*b* Jehoram son of King Jehoshaphat of Judah began to reign. 17He was thirty-two years old when he became king, and he reigned eight years in Jerusalem. 18He walked in the way of the kings of Israel, as the house of Ahab had done, for the daughter of Ahab was his wife. He did what was evil in the sight of the LORD. 19Yet the LORD would not destroy Judah, for the sake of his servant David, since he had promised to give a lamp to him and to his descendants forever.

20 In his days Edom revolted against the rule of Judah, and set up a king of their own. 21Then Joram crossed over to Zair with all his chariots. He set out by night and attacked the Edomites and their chariot commanders who had surrounded him;*c* but his army fled home. 22So Edom has been in revolt against the rule of Judah to this day. Libnah also revolted at the same time. 23Now the rest of the acts of Joram, and all that he did, are they not written in the Book of the Annals of the Kings of Judah? 24So Joram slept with his ancestors, and was buried with them in the city of David; his son Ahaziah succeeded him.

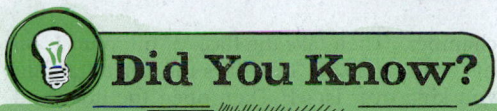

Did You Know?

Grading Kings

As you read the remaining chapters of Second Kings, notice that the author gives a kind of report card for each of the rulers of Israel and Judah. Jehoram, for example, receives an F: "He did what was evil in the sight of the LORD" (8:18). Josiah receives an A: "He did what was right in the sight of the LORD" (22:2). The author, who wrote after the fall of both kingdoms, provides a theological reason for Israel's and Judah's failure. Because most of the rulers continually violated God's law, they were largely responsible for the fall of the kingdoms.

Ahaziah Reigns over Judah

25 In the twelfth year of King Joram son of Ahab of Israel, Ahaziah son of King Jehoram of Judah began to reign. 26Ahaziah was twenty-two years old when he began to reign; he reigned one year in Jerusalem. His mother's name was Athaliah, a granddaughter of King Omri of Israel. 27He also walked in the way of the house of Ahab, doing what was evil in the sight of the LORD, as the house of Ahab had done, for he was son-in-law to the house of Ahab.

28 He went with Joram son of Ahab to wage war against King Hazael of Aram at Ramothgilead, where the Arameans wounded Joram. 29King Joram returned to be healed in Jezreel of the wounds that the Arameans had inflicted on him at Ramah, when he fought against King Hazael of Aram. King Ahaziah son of Jehoram of Judah went down to see Joram son of Ahab in Jezreel, because he was wounded.

Anointing of Jehu

9 Then the prophet Elisha called a member of the company of prophets*d* and said to him, "Gird up your loins; take this flask of oil in your hand, and go to Ramoth-gilead. 2When you arrive, look there for Jehu son of Jehoshaphat, son of Nimshi; go in and get him to leave his companions, and take him into an inner

---

a Heb lacks *Ben-hadad*   *b* Gk Syr: Heb adds *Jehoshaphat being king of Judah,*   *c* Meaning of Heb uncertain   *d* Heb *sons of the prophets*

chamber. ³Then take the flask of oil, pour it on his head, and say, 'Thus says the Lord: I anoint you king over Israel.' Then open the door and flee; do not linger."

4 So the young man, the young prophet, went to Ramoth-gilead. ⁵He arrived while the commanders of the army were in council, and he announced, "I have a message for you, commander." "For which one of us?" asked Jehu. "For you, commander." ⁶So Jehu*a* got up and went inside; the young man poured the oil on his head, saying to him, "Thus says the Lord the God of Israel: I anoint you king over the people of the Lord, over Israel. ⁷You shall strike down the house of your master Ahab, so that I may avenge on Jezebel the blood of my servants the prophets, and the blood of all the servants of the Lord. ⁸For the whole house of Ahab shall perish; I will cut off from Ahab every male, bond or free, in Israel. ⁹I will make the house of Ahab like the house of Jeroboam son of Nebat, and like the house of Baasha son of Ahijah. ¹⁰The dogs shall eat Jezebel in the territory of Jezreel, and no one shall bury her." Then he opened the door and fled.

11 When Jehu came back to his master's officers, they said to him, "Is everything all right? Why did that madman come to you?" He answered them, "You know the sort and how they babble." ¹²They said, "Liar! Come on, tell us!" So he said, "This is just what he said to me: 'Thus says the Lord, I anoint you king over Israel.'" ¹³Then hurriedly they all took their cloaks and spread them for him on the bare*b* steps; and they blew the trumpet, and proclaimed, "Jehu is king."

Joram of Israel Killed

14 Thus Jehu son of Jehoshaphat son of Nimshi conspired against Joram. Joram with all Israel had been on guard at Ramoth-gilead against King Hazael of Aram; ¹⁵but King Joram had returned to be healed in Jezreel of the wounds that the Arameans had inflicted on him, when he fought against King Hazael of Aram. So Jehu said, "If this is your wish, then let no one slip out of the city to go and tell the news in Jezreel." ¹⁶Then Jehu mounted his chariot and went to Jezreel, where Joram was lying ill. King Ahaziah of Judah had come down to visit Joram.

17 In Jezreel, the sentinel standing on the tower spied the company of Jehu arriving, and said, "I see a company." Joram said, "Take a horseman; send him to meet them, and let him say, 'Is it peace?'" ¹⁸So the horseman went to meet him; he said, "Thus says the king, 'Is it peace?'" Jehu responded, "What have you to

do with peace? Fall in behind me." The sentinel reported, saying, "The messenger reached them, but he is not coming back." ¹⁹Then he sent out a second horseman, who came to them and said, "Thus says the king, 'Is it peace?'" Jehu answered, "What have you to do with peace? Fall in behind me." ²⁰Again the sentinel reported, "He reached them, but he is not coming back. It looks like the driving of Jehu son of Nimshi; for he drives like a maniac."

21 Joram said, "Get ready." And they got his chariot ready. Then King Joram of Israel and King Ahaziah of Judah set out, each in his chariot, and went to meet Jehu; they met him at the property of Naboth the Jezreelite. ²²When Joram saw Jehu, he said, "Is it peace, Jehu?" He answered, "What peace can there be, so long as the many whoredoms and sorceries of your mother Jezebel continue?" ²³Then Joram reined about and fled, saying to Ahaziah, "Treason, Ahaziah!" ²⁴Jehu drew his bow with all his strength, and shot Joram between the shoulders, so that the arrow pierced his heart; and he sank in his chariot. ²⁵Jehu said to his aide Bidkar, "Lift him out, and throw him on the plot of ground belonging to Naboth the Jezreelite; for remember, when you and I rode side by side behind his father Ahab how the Lord uttered this oracle against him: ²⁶'For the blood of Naboth and for the blood of his children that I saw yesterday, says the Lord, I swear I will repay you on this very plot of ground.' Now therefore lift him out and throw him on the plot of ground, in accordance with the word of the Lord."

Ahaziah of Judah Killed

27 When King Ahaziah of Judah saw this, he fled in the direction of Beth-haggan. Jehu pursued him, saying, "Shoot him also!" And they shot him*c* in the chariot at the ascent to Gur, which is by Ibleam. Then he fled to Megiddo, and died there. ²⁸His officers carried him in a chariot to Jerusalem, and buried him in his tomb with his ancestors in the city of David.

29 In the eleventh year of Joram son of Ahab, Ahaziah began to reign over Judah.

Jezebel's Violent Death

30 When Jehu came to Jezreel, Jezebel heard of it; she painted her eyes, and adorned her head, and looked out of the window. ³¹As Jehu entered the gate, she said, "Is it peace, Zimri, murderer of your master?" ³²He looked up to the window and

a Heb *he*   *b* Meaning of Heb uncertain   *c* Syr Vg Compare Gk: Heb lacks *and they shot him*

said, "Who is on my side? Who?" Two or three eunuchs looked out at him. ³³He said, "Throw her down." So they threw her down; some of her blood spattered on the wall and on the horses, which trampled on her. ³⁴Then he went in and ate and drank; he said, "See to that cursed woman and bury her; for she is a king's daughter." ³⁵But when they went to bury her, they found no more of her than the skull and the feet and the palms of her hands. ³⁶When they came back and told him, he said, "This is the word of the Lord, which he spoke by his servant Elijah the Tishbite, 'In the territory of Jezreel the dogs shall eat the flesh of Jezebel; ³⁷the corpse of Jezebel shall be like dung on the field in the territory of Jezreel, so that no one can say, This is Jezebel.'"

Massacre of Ahab's Descendants

10 Now Ahab had seventy sons in Samaria. So Jehu wrote letters and sent them to Samaria, to the rulers of Jezreel,ᵃ to the elders, and to the guardians of the sons ofᵇ Ahab, saying, ²"Since your master's sons are with you and you have at your disposal chariots and horses, a fortified city, and weapons, ³select the son of your master who is the best qualified, set him on his father's throne, and fight for your master's house." ⁴But they were utterly terrified and said, "Look, two kings could not withstand him; how then can we stand?" ⁵So the steward of the palace, and the governor of the city, along with the elders and the guardians, sent word to Jehu: "We are your servants; we will do anything you say. We will not make anyone king; do whatever you think right." ⁶Then he wrote them a second letter, saying, "If you are on my side, and if you are ready to obey me, take the heads of your master's sons and come to me at Jezreel tomorrow at this time." Now the king's sons, seventy persons, were with the leaders of the city, who were charged with their upbringing. ⁷When the letter reached them, they took the king's sons and killed them, seventy persons; they put their heads in baskets and sent them to him at Jezreel. ⁸When the messenger came and told him, "They have brought the heads of the king's sons," he said, "Lay them in two heaps at the entrance of the gate until the morning." ⁹Then in the morning when he went out, he stood and said to all the people, "You are innocent. It was I who conspired against my master and killed him; but who struck down all these? ¹⁰Know then that there shall fall to the earth nothing of the word of the Lord, which the Lord spoke concerning the house of Ahab; for the Lord has done what he said through his servant Elijah." ¹¹So Jehu

killed all who were left of the house of Ahab in Jezreel, all his leaders, close friends, and priests, until he left him no survivor.

12 Then he set out and went to Samaria. On the way, when he was at Beth-eked of the Shepherds, ¹³Jehu met relatives of King Ahaziah of Judah and said, "Who are you?" They answered, "We are kin of Ahaziah; we have come down to visit the royal princes and the sons of the queen mother." ¹⁴He said, "Take them alive." They took them alive, and slaughtered them at the pit of Beth-eked, forty-two in all; he spared none of them.

15 When he left there, he met Jehonadab son of Rechab coming to meet him; he greeted him, and said to him, "Is your heart as true to mine as mine is to yours?"ᶜ Jehonadab answered, "It is." Jehu said,ᵈ "If it is, give me your hand." So he gave him his hand. Jehu took him up with him into the chariot. ¹⁶He said, "Come with me, and see my zeal for the Lord." So heᵉ had him ride in his chariot. ¹⁷When he came to Samaria, he killed all who were left to Ahab in Samaria, until he had wiped them out, according to the word of the Lord that he spoke to Elijah.

Slaughter of Worshipers of Baal

18 Then Jehu assembled all the people and said to them, "Ahab offered Baal small service; but Jehu will offer much more. ¹⁹Now therefore summon to me all the prophets of Baal, all his worshipers, and all his priests; let none be missing, for I have a great sacrifice to offer to Baal; whoever is missing shall not live." But Jehu was acting with cunning in order to destroy the worshipers of Baal. ²⁰Jehu decreed, "Sanctify a solemn assembly for Baal." So they proclaimed it. ²¹Jehu sent word throughout all Israel; all the worshipers of Baal came, so that there was no one left who did not come. They entered the temple of Baal, until the temple of Baal was filled from wall to wall. ²²He said to the keeper of the wardrobe, "Bring out the vestments for all the worshipers of Baal." So he brought out the vestments for them. ²³Then Jehu entered the temple of Baal with Jehonadab son of Rechab; he said to the worshipers of Baal, "Search and see that there is no worshiper of the Lord here among you, but only worshipers of Baal." ²⁴Then they proceeded to offer sacrifices and burnt offerings.

Now Jehu had stationed eighty men outside, saying, "Whoever allows any of those to escape

---

ᵃ Or of the city; Vg Compare Gk   ᵇ Gk: Heb lacks of the sons of   ᶜ Gk: Heb Is it right with your heart, as my heart is with your heart?   ᵈ Gk: Heb lacks Jehu said   ᵉ Gk Syr Tg: Heb they

whom I deliver into your hands shall forfeit his life." 25As soon as he had finished presenting the burnt offering, Jehu said to the guards and to the officers, "Come in and kill them; let no one escape." So they put them to the sword. The guards and the officers threw them out, and then went into the citadel of the temple of Baal. 26They brought out the pillar*a* that was in the temple of Baal, and burned it. 27Then they demolished the pillar of Baal, and destroyed the temple of Baal, and made it a latrine to this day.

28 Thus Jehu wiped out Baal from Israel. 29But Jehu did not turn aside from the sins of Jeroboam son of Nebat, which he caused Israel to commit—the golden calves that were in Bethel and in Dan. 30The Lord said to Jehu, "Because you have done well in carrying out what I consider right, and in accordance with all that was in my heart have dealt with the house of Ahab, your sons of the fourth generation shall sit on the throne of Israel." 31But Jehu was not careful to follow the law of the Lord the God of Israel with all his heart; he did not turn from the sins of Jeroboam, which he caused Israel to commit.

Death of Jehu

32 In those days the Lord began to trim off parts of Israel. Hazael defeated them throughout the territory of Israel: 33from the Jordan eastward, all the land of Gilead, the Gadites, the Reubenites, and the Manassites, from Aroer, which is by the Wadi Arnon, that is, Gilead and Bashan. 34Now the rest of the acts of Jehu, all that he did, and all his power, are they not written in the Book of the Annals of the Kings of Israel? 35So Jehu slept with his ancestors, and they buried him in Samaria. His son Jehoahaz succeeded him. 36The time that Jehu reigned over Israel in Samaria was twenty-eight years.

Athaliah Reigns over Judah

11 Now when Athaliah, Ahaziah's mother, saw that her son was dead, she set about to destroy all the royal family. 2But Jehosheba, King Joram's daughter, Ahaziah's sister, took Joash son of Ahaziah, and stole him away from among the king's children who were about to be killed; she put*b* him and his nurse in a bedroom. Thus she*c* hid him from Athaliah, so that he was not killed; 3he remained with her six years, hidden in the house of the Lord, while Athaliah reigned over the land.

Jehoiada Anoints the Child Joash

4 But in the seventh year Jehoiada summoned the captains of the Carites and of the guards and had them come to him in the house of the Lord. He made a covenant with them and put them under oath in the house of the Lord; then he showed them the king's son. 5He commanded them, "This is what you are to do: one-third of you, those who go off duty on the sabbath and guard the king's house 6(another third being at the gate Sur and a third at the gate behind the guards), shall guard the palace; 7and your two divisions that come on duty in force on the sabbath and guard the house of the Lord*d* 8shall surround the king, each with weapons in hand; and whoever approaches the ranks is to be killed. Be with the king in his comings and goings."

9 The captains did according to all that the priest Jehoiada commanded; each brought his men who were to go off duty on the sabbath, with those who were to come on duty on the sabbath, and came to the priest Jehoiada. 10The priest delivered to the captains the spears and shields that had been King David's, which were in the house of the Lord; 11the guards stood, every man with his weapons in his hand, from the south side of the house to the north side of the house, around the altar and the house, to guard the king on every side. 12Then he brought out the king's son, put the crown on him, and gave him the covenant;*e* they proclaimed him king, and anointed him; they clapped their hands and shouted, "Long live the king!"

Death of Athaliah

13 When Athaliah heard the noise of the guard and of the people, she went into the house of the Lord to the people; 14when she looked, there was the king standing by the pillar, according to custom, with the captains and the trumpeters beside the king, and all the people of the land rejoicing and blowing trumpets. Athaliah tore her clothes and cried, "Treason! Treason!" 15Then the priest Jehoiada commanded the captains who were set over the army, "Bring her out between the ranks, and kill with the sword anyone who follows her." For the priest said, "Let her not be killed in the house of the Lord." 16So they laid hands on her; she went through the horses' entrance to the king's house, and there she was put to death.

17 Jehoiada made a covenant between the Lord and the king and people, that they should be the Lord's people; also between the king and the people. 18Then all the people of the land went to the house of Baal, and tore it down; his

---

a Gk Vg Syr Tg: Heb *pillars*　*b* With 2 Chr 22.11: Heb lacks *she put*　*c* Gk Syr Vg Compare 2 Chr 22.11: Heb *they*　*d* Heb *the Lord to the king*　*e* Or *treaty* or *testimony*; Heb *eduth*

altars and his images they broke in pieces, and they killed Mattan, the priest of Baal, before the altars. The priest posted guards over the house of the LORD. ¹⁹He took the captains, the Carites, the guards, and all the people of the land; then they brought the king down from the house of the LORD, marching through the gate of the guards to the king's house. He took his seat on the throne of the kings. ²⁰So all the people of the land rejoiced; and the city was quiet after Athaliah had been killed with the sword at the king's house.

²¹ᵃ Jehoashᵇ was seven years old when he began to reign.

The Temple Repaired

12 In the seventh year of Jehu, Jehoash began to reign; he reigned forty years in Jerusalem. His mother's name was Zibiah of Beersheba. ²Jehoash did what was right in the sight of the LORD all his days, because the priest Jehoiada instructed him. ³Nevertheless the high places were not taken away; the people continued to sacrifice and make offerings on the high places.

4 Jehoash said to the priests, "All the money offered as sacred donations that is brought into the house of the LORD, the money for which each person is assessed—the money from the assessment of persons—and the money from the voluntary offerings brought into the house of the LORD, ⁵let the priests receive from each of the donors; and let them repair the house wherever any need of repairs is discovered." ⁶But by the twenty-third year of King Jehoash the priests had made no repairs on the house. ⁷Therefore King Jehoash summoned the priest Jehoiada with the other priests and said to them, "Why are you not repairing the house? Now therefore do not accept any more money from your donors but hand it over for the repair of the house." ⁸So the priests agreed that they would neither accept more money from the people nor repair the house.

9 Then the priest Jehoiada took a chest, made a hole in its lid, and set it beside the altar on the right side as one entered the house of the LORD; the priests who guarded the threshold put in it all the money that was brought into the house of the LORD. ¹⁰Whenever they saw that there was a great deal of money in the chest, the king's secretary and the high priest went up, counted the money that was found in the house of the LORD, and tied it up in bags. ¹¹They would give the money that was weighed out into the hands of the workers who had the oversight of the house of the LORD; then they paid it out to the carpenters and the builders who worked on

the house of the LORD, ¹²to the masons and the stonecutters, as well as to buy timber and quarried stone for making repairs on the house of the LORD, as well as for any outlay for repairs of the house. ¹³But for the house of the LORD no basins of silver, snuffers, bowls, trumpets, or any vessels of gold, or of silver, were made from the money that was brought into the house of the LORD, ¹⁴for that was given to the workers who were repairing the house of the LORD with it. ¹⁵They did not ask an accounting from those into whose hand they delivered the money to pay out to the workers, for they dealt honestly. ¹⁶The money from the guilt offerings and the money from the sin offerings was not brought into the house of the LORD; it belonged to the priests.

Hazael Threatens Jerusalem

17 At that time King Hazael of Aram went up, fought against Gath, and took it. But when Hazael set his face to go up against Jerusalem, ¹⁸King Jehoash of Judah took all the votive gifts that Jehoshaphat, Jehoram, and Ahaziah, his ancestors, the kings of Judah, had dedicated, as well as his own votive gifts, all the gold that was found in the treasuries of the house of the LORD and of the king's house, and sent these to King Hazael of Aram. Then Hazael withdrew from Jerusalem.

Death of Joash

19 Now the rest of the acts of Joash, and all that he did, are they not written in the Book of the Annals of the Kings of Judah? ²⁰His servants arose, devised a conspiracy, and killed Joash in the house of Millo, on the way that goes down to Silla. ²¹It was Jozacar son of Shimeath and Jehozabad son of Shomer, his servants, who struck him down, so that he died. He was buried with his ancestors in the city of David; then his son Amaziah succeeded him.

Jehoahaz Reigns over Israel

13 In the twenty-third year of King Joash son of Ahaziah of Judah, Jehoahaz son of Jehu began to reign over Israel in Samaria; he reigned seventeen years. ²He did what was evil in the sight of the LORD, and followed the sins of Jeroboam son of Nebat, which he caused Israel to sin; he did not depart from them. ³The anger of the LORD was kindled against Israel, so that he gave them repeatedly into the hand of King Hazael of Aram, then into the hand of Benhadad son of Hazael. ⁴But Jehoahaz entreated the LORD, and the LORD heeded him; for he saw

---

a Ch 12.1 in Heb   b Another spelling is *Joash*; see verse 19

the oppression of Israel, how the king of Aram oppressed them. [5]Therefore the LORD gave Israel a savior, so that they escaped from the hand of the Arameans; and the people of Israel lived in their homes as formerly. [6]Nevertheless they did not depart from the sins of the house of Jeroboam, which he caused Israel to sin, but walked[a] in them; the sacred pole[b] also remained in Samaria. [7]So Jehoahaz was left with an army of not more than fifty horsemen, ten chariots and ten thousand footmen; for the king of Aram had destroyed them and made them like the dust at threshing. [8]Now the rest of the acts of Jehoahaz and all that he did, including his might, are they not written in the Book of the Annals of the Kings of Israel? [9]So Jehoahaz slept with his ancestors, and they buried him in Samaria; then his son Joash succeeded him.

Jehoash Reigns over Israel

10 In the thirty-seventh year of King Joash of Judah, Jehoash son of Jehoahaz began to reign over Israel in Samaria; he reigned sixteen years. [11]He also did what was evil in the sight of the LORD; he did not depart from all the sins of Jeroboam son of Nebat, which he caused Israel to sin, but he walked in them. [12]Now the rest of the acts of Joash, and all that he did, as well as the might with which he fought against King Amaziah of Judah, are they not written in the Book of the Annals of the Kings of Israel? [13]So Joash slept with his ancestors, and Jeroboam sat upon his throne; Joash was buried in Samaria with the kings of Israel.

Death of Elisha

14 Now when Elisha had fallen sick with the illness of which he was to die, King Joash of Israel went down to him, and wept before him, crying, "My father, my father! The chariots of Israel and its horsemen!" [15]Elisha said to him, "Take a bow and arrows"; so he took a bow and arrows. [16]Then he said to the king of Israel, "Draw the bow"; and he drew it. Elisha laid his hands on the king's hands. [17]Then he said, "Open the window eastward"; and he opened it. Elisha said, "Shoot"; and he shot. Then he said, "The LORD's arrow of victory, the arrow of victory over Aram! For you shall fight the Arameans in Aphek until you have made an end of them." [18]He continued, "Take the arrows"; and he took them. He said to the king of Israel, "Strike the ground with them"; he struck three times, and stopped. [19]Then the man of God was angry with him, and said, "You should have struck five or six times; then you would have struck down Aram until you had made an end of it, but now you will strike down Aram only three times."

20 So Elisha died, and they buried him. Now bands of Moabites used to invade the land in the spring of the year. [21]As a man was being buried, a marauding band was seen and the man was thrown into the grave of Elisha; as soon as the man touched the bones of Elisha, he came to life and stood on his feet.

Israel Recaptures Cities from Aram

22 Now King Hazael of Aram oppressed Israel all the days of Jehoahaz. [23]But the LORD was gracious to them and had compassion on them; he turned toward them, because of his covenant with Abraham, Isaac, and Jacob, and would not destroy them; nor has he banished them from his presence until now.

24 When King Hazael of Aram died, his son Ben-hadad succeeded him. [25]Then Jehoash son of Jehoahaz took again from Ben-hadad son of Hazael the towns that he had taken from his father Jehoahaz in war. Three times Joash defeated him and recovered the towns of Israel.

Amaziah Reigns over Judah

14 In the second year of King Joash son of Jo-ahaz of Israel, King Amaziah son of Joash of Judah, began to reign. [2]He was twenty-five years old when he began to reign, and he reigned twenty-nine years in Jerusalem. His mother's name was Jehoaddin of Jerusalem. [3]He did what was right in the sight of the LORD, yet not like his ancestor David; in all things he did as his father Joash had done. [4]But the high places were not removed; the people still sacrificed and made offerings on the high places. [5]As soon as the royal power was firmly in his hand he killed his servants who had murdered his father the king. [6]But he did not put to death the children of the murderers; according to what is written in the book of the law of Moses, where the LORD commanded, "The parents shall not be put to death for the children, or the children be put to death for the parents; but all shall be put to death for their own sins."

7 He killed ten thousand Edomites in the Valley of Salt and took Sela by storm; he called it Jokthe-el, which is its name to this day.

8 Then Amaziah sent messengers to King Jehoash son of Jehoahaz, son of Jehu, of Israel, saying, "Come, let us look one another in the face." [9]King Jehoash of Israel sent word to King Amaziah of Judah, "A thornbush on Lebanon

---

a Gk Syr Tg Vg: Heb *he walked*　　b Heb *Asherah*

sent to a cedar on Lebanon, saying, 'Give your daughter to my son for a wife'; but a wild animal of Lebanon passed by and trampled down the thornbush. ¹⁰You have indeed defeated Edom, and your heart has lifted you up. Be content with your glory, and stay at home; for why should you provoke trouble so that you fall, you and Judah with you?"

11 But Amaziah would not listen. So King Jehoash of Israel went up; he and King Amaziah of Judah faced one another in battle at Beth-shemesh, which belongs to Judah. ¹²Judah was defeated by Israel; everyone fled home. ¹³King Jehoash of Israel captured King Amaziah of Judah son of Jehoash, son of Ahaziah, at Beth-shemesh; he came to Jerusalem, and broke down the wall of Jerusalem from the Ephraim Gate to the Corner Gate, a distance of four hundred cubits. ¹⁴He seized all the gold and silver, and all the vessels that were found in the house of the LORD and in the treasuries of the king's house, as well as hostages; then he returned to Samaria.

15 Now the rest of the acts that Jehoash did, his might, and how he fought with King Amaziah of Judah, are they not written in the Book of the Annals of the Kings of Israel? ¹⁶Jehoash slept with his ancestors, and was buried in Samaria with the kings of Israel; then his son Jeroboam succeeded him.

17 King Amaziah son of Joash of Judah lived fifteen years after the death of King Jehoash son of Jehoahaz of Israel. ¹⁸Now the rest of the deeds of Amaziah, are they not written in the Book of the Annals of the Kings of Judah? ¹⁹They made a conspiracy against him in Jerusalem, and he fled to Lachish. But they sent after him to Lachish, and killed him there. ²⁰They brought him on horses; he was buried in Jerusalem with his ancestors in the city of David. ²¹All the people of Judah took Azariah, who was sixteen years old, and made him king to succeed his father Amaziah. ²²He rebuilt Elath and restored it to Judah, after King Amaziah*ᵈ* slept with his ancestors.

Jeroboam II Reigns over Israel

23 In the fifteenth year of King Amaziah son of Joash of Judah, King Jeroboam son of Joash of Israel began to reign in Samaria; he reigned forty-one years. ²⁴He did what was evil in the sight of the LORD; he did not depart from all the sins of Jeroboam son of Nebat, which he caused Israel to sin. ²⁵He restored the border of Israel from Lebo-hamath as far as the Sea of the Arabah, according to the word of the LORD, the God of Israel, which he spoke by his servant Jonah son of Amittai, the prophet, who was from Gath-

hepher. ²⁶For the LORD saw that the distress of Israel was very bitter; there was no one left, bond or free, and no one to help Israel. ²⁷But the LORD had not said that he would blot out the name of Israel from under heaven, so he saved them by the hand of Jeroboam son of Joash.

28 Now the rest of the acts of Jeroboam, and all that he did, and his might, how he fought, and how he recovered for Israel Damascus and Hamath, which had belonged to Judah, are they not written in the Book of the Annals of the Kings of Israel? ²⁹Jeroboam slept with his ancestors, the kings of Israel; his son Zechariah succeeded him.

Azariah Reigns over Judah

15 In the twenty-seventh year of King Jeroboam of Israel King Azariah son of Amaziah of Judah began to reign. ²He was sixteen years old when he began to reign, and he reigned fifty-two years in Jerusalem. His mother's name was Jecoliah of Jerusalem. ³He did what was right in the sight of the LORD, just as his father Amaziah had done. ⁴Nevertheless the high places were not taken away; the people still sacrificed and made offerings on the high places. ⁵The LORD struck the king, so that he was leprous*ᵇ* to the day of his death, and lived in a separate house. Jotham the king's son was in charge of the palace, governing the people of the land. ⁶Now the rest of the acts of Azariah, and all that he did, are they not written in the Book of the Annals of the Kings of Judah? ⁷Azariah slept with his ancestors; they buried him with his ancestors in the city of David; his son Jotham succeeded him.

---

a Heb *the king*   *b* A term for several skin diseases; precise meaning uncertain

14:4

Zechariah Reigns over Israel

8 In the thirty-eighth year of King Azariah of Judah, Zechariah son of Jeroboam reigned over Israel in Samaria six months. 9He did what was evil in the sight of the LORD, as his ancestors had done. He did not depart from the sins of Jeroboam son of Nebat, which he caused Israel to sin. 10Shallum son of Jabesh conspired against him, and struck him down in public and killed him, and reigned in place of him. 11Now the rest of the deeds of Zechariah are written in the Book of the Annals of the Kings of Israel. 12This was the promise of the LORD that he gave to Jehu, "Your sons shall sit on the throne of Israel to the fourth generation." And so it happened.

Shallum Reigns over Israel

13 Shallum son of Jabesh began to reign in the thirty-ninth year of King Uzziah of Judah; he reigned one month in Samaria. 14Then Menahem son of Gadi came up from Tirzah and came to Samaria; he struck down Shallum son of Jabesh in Samaria and killed him; he reigned in place of him. 15Now the rest of the deeds of Shallum, including the conspiracy that he made, are written in the Book of the Annals of the Kings of Israel. 16At that time Menahem sacked Tiphsah, all who were in it and its territory from Tirzah on; because they did not open it to him, he sacked it. He ripped open all the pregnant women in it.

Menahem Reigns over Israel

17 In the thirty-ninth year of King Azariah of Judah, Menahem son of Gadi began to reign over Israel; he reigned ten years in Samaria. 18He did what was evil in the sight of the LORD; he did not depart all his days from any of the sins of Jeroboam son of Nebat, which he caused Israel to sin. 19King Pul of Assyria came against the land; Menahem gave Pul a thousand talents of silver, so that he might help him confirm his hold on the royal power. 20Menahem exacted the money from Israel, that is, from all the wealthy, fifty shekels of silver from each one, to give to the king of Assyria. So the king of Assyria turned back, and did not stay there in the land. 21Now the rest of the deeds of Menahem, and all that he did, are they not written in the Book of the Annals of the Kings of Israel? 22Menahem slept with his ancestors, and his son Pekahiah succeeded him.

Pekahiah Reigns over Israel

23 In the fiftieth year of King Azariah of Judah, Pekahiah son of Menahem began to reign over Israel in Samaria; he reigned two years. 24He did what was evil in the sight of the LORD; he did not turn away from the sins of Jeroboam son of Nebat, which he caused Israel to sin. 25Pekah son of Remaliah, his captain, conspired against him with fifty of the Gileadites, and attacked him in Samaria, in the citadel of the palace along with Argob and Arieh; he killed him, and reigned in place of him. 26Now the rest of the deeds of Pekahiah, and all that he did, are written in the Book of the Annals of the Kings of Israel.

Pekah Reigns over Israel

27 In the fifty-second year of King Azariah of Judah, Pekah son of Remaliah began to reign over Israel in Samaria; he reigned twenty years. 28He did what was evil in the sight of the LORD; he did not depart from the sins of Jeroboam son of Nebat, which he caused Israel to sin.

29 In the days of King Pekah of Israel, King Tiglath-pileser of Assyria came and captured Ijon, Abel-beth-maacah, Janoah, Kedesh, Hazor, Gilead, and Galilee, all the land of Naphtali; and he carried the people captive to Assyria. 30Then Hoshea son of Elah made a conspiracy against Pekah son of Remaliah, attacked him, and killed him; he reigned in place of him, in the twentieth year of Jotham son of Uzziah. 31Now the rest of the acts of Pekah, and all that he did, are written in the Book of the Annals of the Kings of Israel.

Jotham Reigns over Judah

32 In the second year of King Pekah son of Remaliah of Israel, King Jotham son of Uzziah of Judah began to reign. 33He was twenty-five years old when he began to reign and reigned sixteen years in Jerusalem. His mother's name was Jerusha daughter of Zadok. 34He did what was right in the sight of the LORD, just as his father Uzziah had done. 35Nevertheless the high places were not removed; the people still sacrificed and made offerings on the high places. He built the upper gate of the house of the LORD. 36Now the rest of the acts of Jotham, and all that he did, are they not written in the Book of the Annals of the Kings of Judah? 37In those days the LORD began to send King Rezin of Aram and Pekah son of Remaliah against Judah. 38Jotham slept with his ancestors, and was buried with his ancestors in the city of David, his ancestor; his son Ahaz succeeded him.

Ahaz Reigns over Judah

16 In the seventeenth year of Pekah son of Remaliah, King Ahaz son of Jotham of Judah began to reign. 2Ahaz was twenty years old

when he began to reign; he reigned sixteen years in Jerusalem. He did not do what was right in the sight of the LORD his God, as his ancestor David had done, 3but he walked in the way of the kings of Israel. He even made his son pass through fire, according to the abominable practices of the nations whom the LORD drove out before the people of Israel. 4He sacrificed and made offerings on the high places, on the hills, and under every green tree.

5 Then King Rezin of Aram and King Pekah son of Remaliah of Israel came up to wage war on Jerusalem; they besieged Ahaz but could not conquer him. 6At that time the king of Edom*a* recovered Elath for Edom,*b* and drove the Judeans from Elath; and the Edomites came to Elath, where they live to this day. 7Ahaz sent messengers to King Tiglath-pileser of Assyria, saying, "I am your servant and your son. Come up, and rescue me from the hand of the king of Aram and from the hand of the king of Israel, who are attacking me." 8Ahaz also took the silver and gold found in the house of the LORD and in the treasures of the king's house, and sent a present to the king of Assyria. 9The king of Assyria listened to him; the king of Assyria marched up against Damascus, and took it, carrying its people captive to Kir; then he killed Rezin.

10 When King Ahaz went to Damascus to meet King Tiglath-pileser of Assyria, he saw the altar that was at Damascus. King Ahaz sent to the priest Uriah a model of the altar, and its pattern, exact in all its details. 11The priest Uriah built the altar; in accordance with all that King Ahaz had sent from Damascus, just so did the priest Uriah build it, before King Ahaz arrived from Damascus. 12When the king came from Damascus, the king viewed the altar. Then the king drew near to the altar, went up on it, 13and offered his burnt offering and his grain offering, poured his drink offering, and dashed the blood of his offerings of well-being against the altar. 14The bronze altar that was before the LORD he removed from the front of the house, from the place between his altar and the house of the LORD, and put it on the north side of his altar. 15King Ahaz commanded the priest Uriah, saying, "Upon the great altar offer the morning burnt offering, and the evening grain offering, and the king's burnt offering, and his grain offering, with the burnt offering of all the people of the land, their grain offering, and their drink offering; then dash against it all the blood of the burnt offering, and all the blood of the sacrifice; but the bronze altar shall be for me to inquire by." 16The priest Uriah did everything that King Ahaz commanded.

17 Then King Ahaz cut off the frames of the stands, and removed the laver from them; he removed the sea from the bronze oxen that were under it, and put it on a pediment of stone. 18The covered portal for use on the sabbath that had been built inside the palace, and the outer entrance for the king he removed from*c* the house of the LORD. He did this because of the king of Assyria. 19Now the rest of the acts of Ahaz that he did, are they not written in the Book of the Annals of the Kings of Judah? 20Ahaz slept with his ancestors, and was buried with his ancestors in the city of David; his son Hezekiah succeeded him.

Hoshea Reigns over Israel

17 In the twelfth year of King Ahaz of Judah, Hoshea son of Elah began to reign in Samaria over Israel; he reigned nine years. 2He did what was evil in the sight of the LORD, yet not like the kings of Israel who were before him. 3King Shalmaneser of Assyria came up against him; Hoshea became his vassal, and paid him tribute. 4But the king of Assyria found treachery in Hoshea; for he had sent messengers to King So of Egypt, and offered no tribute to the king of Assyria, as he had done year by year; therefore the king of Assyria confined him and imprisoned him.

Israel Carried Captive to Assyria

5 Then the king of Assyria invaded all the land and came to Samaria; for three years he besieged it. 6In the ninth year of Hoshea the king of Assyria captured Samaria; he carried the Israelites away to Assyria. He placed them in Halah, on the Habor, the river of Gozan, and in the cities of the Medes.

7 This occurred because the people of Israel had sinned against the LORD their God, who had brought them up out of the land of Egypt from under the hand of Pharaoh king of Egypt. They had worshiped other gods 8and walked in the customs of the nations whom the LORD drove out before the people of Israel, and in the customs that the kings of Israel had introduced.*d* 9The people of Israel secretly did things that were not right against the LORD their God. They built for themselves high places at all their towns, from watchtower to fortified city; 10they set up for themselves pillars and sacred poles*e* on every high hill and under every green tree; 11there they made offerings on all the high places, as the nations did whom the LORD carried away before

---

a Cn: Heb *King Rezin of Aram*   *b* Cn: Heb *Aram*   *c* Cn: Heb lacks *from*   *d* Meaning of Heb uncertain   *e* Heb *Asherim*

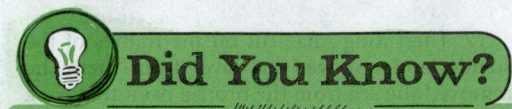

Did You Know?

The First Captivity

The Second Book of Kings describes two captivities and exiles. The first one is the Assyrian conquest of the northern kingdom, Israel, which occurred in 721 BC (see map 5, "The Assyrian Empire"). According to the author of Second Kings, Israel fell first because its kings and people were even less faithful to God than the kings and people of Judah, the southern kingdom. Notice that the Assyrian conquest is described in the briefest detail (see 17:5–6), but the reasons for it are described in great detail (see verses 7–18).

▶ 2 Kings 17:5–18

them. They did wicked things, provoking the LORD to anger; ¹²they served idols, of which the LORD had said to them, "You shall not do this." ¹³Yet the LORD warned Israel and Judah by every prophet and every seer, saying, "Turn from your evil ways and keep my commandments and my statutes, in accordance with all the law that I commanded your ancestors and that I sent to you by my servants the prophets." ¹⁴They would not listen but were stubborn, as their ancestors had been, who did not believe in the LORD their God. ¹⁵They despised his statutes, and his covenant that he made with their ancestors, and the warnings that he gave them. They went after false idols and became false; they followed the nations that were around them, concerning whom the LORD had commanded them that they should not do as they did. ¹⁶They rejected all the commandments of the LORD their God and made for themselves cast images of two calves; they made a sacred pole,ᵃ worshiped all the host of heaven, and served Baal. ¹⁷They made their sons and their daughters pass through fire; they used divination and augury; and they sold themselves to do evil in the sight of the LORD, provoking him to anger. ¹⁸Therefore the LORD was very angry with Israel and removed them out of his sight; none was left but the tribe of Judah alone.

19 Judah also did not keep the commandments of the LORD their God but walked in the customs that Israel had introduced. ²⁰The LORD rejected all the descendants of Israel; he

punished them and gave them into the hand of plunderers, until he had banished them from his presence.

21 When he had torn Israel from the house of David, they made Jeroboam son of Nebat king. Jeroboam drove Israel from following the LORD and made them commit great sin. ²²The people of Israel continued in all the sins that Jeroboam committed; they did not depart from them ²³until the LORD removed Israel out of his sight, as he had foretold through all his servants the prophets. So Israel was exiled from their own land to Assyria until this day.

Assyria Resettles Samaria

24 The king of Assyria brought people from Babylon, Cuthah, Avva, Hamath, and Sepharvaim, and placed them in the cities of Samaria in place of the people of Israel; they took possession of Samaria, and settled in its cities. ²⁵When they first settled there, they did not worship the LORD; therefore the LORD sent lions among them, which killed some of them. ²⁶So the king of Assyria was told, "The nations that you have carried away and placed in the cities of Samaria do not know the law of the god of the land; therefore he has sent lions among them; they are killing them, because they do not know the law of the god of the land." ²⁷Then the king of Assyria commanded, "Send there one of the priests whom you carried away from there; let himᵇ go and live there, and teach them the law of the god of the land." ²⁸So one of the priests whom they had carried away from Samaria came and lived in Bethel; he taught them how they should worship the LORD.

29 But every nation still made gods of its own and put them in the shrines of the high places that the people of Samaria had made, every nation in the cities in which they lived; ³⁰the people of Babylon made Succoth-benoth, the people of Cuth made Nergal, the people of Hamath made Ashima; ³¹the Avvites made Nibhaz and Tartak; the Sepharvites burned their children in the fire to Adrammelech and Anammelech, the gods of Sepharvaim. ³²They also worshiped the LORD and appointed from among themselves all sorts of people as priests of the high places, who sacrificed for them in the shrines of the high places. ³³So they worshiped the LORD but also served their own gods, after the manner of the nations from among whom they had been carried away. ³⁴To this day they continue to practice their former customs.

They do not worship the LORD and they do not

a Heb Asherah   b Syr Vg: Heb them

follow the statutes or the ordinances or the law or the commandment that the LORD commanded the children of Jacob, whom he named Israel. 35The LORD had made a covenant with them and commanded them, "You shall not worship other gods or bow yourselves to them or serve them or sacrifice to them, 36but you shall worship the LORD, who brought you out of the land of Egypt with great power and with an outstretched arm; you shall bow yourselves to him, and to him you shall sacrifice. 37The statutes and the ordinances and the law and the commandment that he wrote for you, you shall always be careful to observe. You shall not worship other gods; 38you shall not forget the covenant that I have made with you. You shall not worship other gods, 39but you shall worship the LORD your God; he will deliver you out of the hand of all your enemies." 40They would not listen, however, but they continued to practice their former custom.

41 So these nations worshiped the LORD, but also served their carved images; to this day their children and their children's children continue to do as their ancestors did.

Hezekiah's Reign over Judah

18 In the third year of King Hoshea son of Elah of Israel, Hezekiah son of King Ahaz of Judah began to reign. 2He was twenty-five years old when he began to reign; he reigned twenty-nine years in Jerusalem. His mother's name was Abi daughter of Zechariah. 3He did what was right in the sight of the LORD just as his ancestor David had done. 4He removed the high places, broke down the pillars, and cut down the sacred pole.*a* He broke in pieces the bronze serpent that Moses had made, for until those days the people of Israel had made offerings to it; it was called Nehushtan. 5He trusted in the LORD the God of Israel; so that there was no one like him among all the kings of Judah after him, or among those who were before him. 6For he held fast to the LORD; he did not depart from following him but kept the commandments that the LORD commanded Moses. The LORD was with him; wherever he went, he prospered. He rebelled against the king of Assyria and would not serve him. 8He attacked the Philistines as far as Gaza and its territory, from watchtower to fortified city.

9 In the fourth year of King Hezekiah, which was the seventh year of King Hoshea son of Elah of Israel, King Shalmaneser of Assyria came up against Samaria, besieged it, 10and at the end of three years, took it. In the sixth year of Hezekiah, which was the ninth year of King Hoshea of

Israel, Samaria was taken. 11The king of Assyria carried the Israelites away to Assyria, settled them in Halah, on the Habor, the river of Gozan, and in the cities of the Medes, 12because they did not obey the voice of the LORD their God but transgressed his covenant—all that Moses the servant of the LORD had commanded; they neither listened nor obeyed.

Sennacherib Invades Judah

13 In the fourteenth year of King Hezekiah, King Sennacherib of Assyria came up against all the fortified cities of Judah and captured them. 14King Hezekiah of Judah sent to the king of Assyria at Lachish, saying, "I have done wrong; withdraw from me; whatever you impose on me I will bear." The king of Assyria demanded of King Hezekiah of Judah three hundred talents of silver and thirty talents of gold. 15Hezekiah gave him all the silver that was found in the house of the LORD and in the treasuries of the king's house. 16At that time Hezekiah stripped the gold from the doors of the temple of the LORD, and from the doorposts that King Hezekiah of Judah had overlaid and gave it to the king of Assyria. 17The king of Assyria sent the Tartan, the Rabsaris, and the Rabshakeh with a great army from Lachish to King Hezekiah at Jerusalem. They went up and came to Jerusalem. When they arrived, they came and stood by the conduit of the upper pool, which is on the highway to the Fuller's Field. 18When they called for the king, there came out to them Eliakim son of Hilkiah, who was in charge of the palace, and Shebnah the secretary, and Joah son of Asaph, the recorder.

19 The Rabshakeh said to them, "Say to Hezekiah: Thus says the great king, the king of Assyria: On what do you base this confidence of yours? 20Do you think that mere words are strategy and power for war? On whom do you now rely, that you have rebelled against me? 21See, you are relying now on Egypt, that broken reed of a staff, which will pierce the hand of anyone who leans on it. Such is Pharaoh king of Egypt to all who rely on him. 22But if you say to me, 'We rely on the LORD our God,' is it not he whose high places and altars Hezekiah has removed, saying to Judah and to Jerusalem, 'You shall worship before this altar in Jerusalem'? 23Come now, make a wager with my master the king of Assyria: I will give you two thousand horses, if you are able on your part to set riders on them. 24How then can you repulse a single captain among the least of my master's servants, when you rely on Egypt

a Heb *Asherah*

for chariots and for horsemen? 25Moreover, is it without the LORD that I have come up against this place to destroy it? The LORD said to me, Go up against this land, and destroy it."

26 Then Eliakim son of Hilkiah, and Shebnah, and Joah said to the Rabshakeh, "Please speak to your servants in the Aramaic language, for we understand it; do not speak to us in the language of Judah within the hearing of the people who are on the wall." 27But the Rabshakeh said to them, "Has my master sent me to speak these words to your master and to you, and not to the people sitting on the wall, who are doomed with you to eat their own dung and to drink their own urine?"

28 Then the Rabshakeh stood and called out in a loud voice in the language of Judah, "Hear the word of the great king, the king of Assyria! 29Thus says the king: 'Do not let Hezekiah deceive you, for he will not be able to deliver you out of my hand. 30Do not let Hezekiah make you rely on the LORD by saying, The LORD will surely deliver us, and this city will not be given into the hand of the king of Assyria.' 31Do not listen to Hezekiah; for thus says the king of Assyria: 'Make your peace with me and come out to me; then every one of you will eat from your own vine and your own fig tree, and drink water from your own cistern, 32until I come and take you away to a land like your own land, a land of grain and wine, a land of bread and vineyards, a land of olive oil and honey, that you may live and not die. Do not listen to Hezekiah when he misleads you by saying, The LORD will deliver us. 33Has any of the gods of the nations ever delivered its land out of the hand of the king of Assyria? 34Where are the gods of Hamath and Arpad? Where are the gods of Sepharvaim, Hena, and Ivvah? Have they delivered Samaria out of my hand? 35Who among all the gods of the countries have delivered their countries out of my hand, that the LORD should deliver Jerusalem out of my hand?' "

36 But the people were silent and answered him not a word, for the king's command was, "Do not answer him." 37Then Eliakim son of Hilkiah, who was in charge of the palace, and Shebna the secretary, and Joah son of Asaph, the recorder, came to Hezekiah with their clothes torn and told him the words of the Rabshakeh.

Hezekiah Consults Isaiah

19 When King Hezekiah heard it, he tore his clothes, covered himself with sackcloth, and went into the house of the LORD. 2And he sent Eliakim, who was in charge of the palace,

and Shebna the secretary, and the senior priests, covered with sackcloth, to the prophet Isaiah son of Amoz. 3They said to him, "Thus says Hezekiah, This day is a day of distress, of rebuke, and of disgrace; children have come to the birth, and there is no strength to bring them forth. 4It may be that the LORD your God heard all the words of the Rabshakeh, whom his master the king of Assyria has sent to mock the living God, and will rebuke the words that the LORD your God has heard; therefore lift up your prayer for the remnant that is left." 5When the servants of King Hezekiah came to Isaiah, 6Isaiah said to them, "Say to your master, 'Thus says the LORD: Do not be afraid because of the words that you have heard, with which the servants of the king of Assyria have reviled me. 7I myself will put a spirit in him, so that he shall hear a rumor and return to his own land; I will cause him to fall by the sword in his own land.' "

Sennacherib's Threat

8 The Rabshakeh returned, and found the king of Assyria fighting against Libnah; for he had heard that the king had left Lachish. 9When the king*a* heard concerning King Tirhakah of Ethiopia,*b* "See, he has set out to fight against you," he sent messengers again to Hezekiah, saying, 10"Thus shall you speak to King Hezekiah of Judah: Do not let your God on whom you rely deceive you by promising that Jerusalem will not be given into the hand of the king of Assyria. 11See, you have heard what the kings of Assyria have done to all lands, destroying them utterly. Shall you be delivered? 12Have the gods of the nations delivered them, the nations that my predecessors destroyed, Gozan, Haran, Rezeph, and the people of Eden who were in Telassar? 13Where is the king of Hamath, the king of Arpad, the king of the city of Sepharvaim, the king of Hena, or the king of Ivvah?"

Hezekiah's Prayer

14 Hezekiah received the letter from the hand of the messengers and read it; then Hezekiah went up to the house of the LORD and spread it before the LORD. 15And Hezekiah prayed before the LORD, and said: "O LORD the God of Israel, who are enthroned above the cherubim, you are God, you alone, of all the kingdoms of the earth; you have made heaven and earth. 16Incline your ear, O LORD, and hear; open your eyes, O LORD, and see; hear the words of Sennacherib, which has sent to mock the living God. 17Truly, O LORD,

---

a Heb *he*   b Or Nubia; Heb *Cush*

the kings of Assyria have laid waste the nations and their lands, 18and have hurled their gods into the fire, though they were no gods but the work of human hands—wood and stone—and so they were destroyed. 19So now, O LORD our God, save us, I pray you, from his hand, so that all the kingdoms of the earth may know that you, O LORD, are God alone."

20 Then Isaiah son of Amoz sent to Hezekiah, saying, "Thus says the LORD, the God of Israel: I have heard your prayer to me about King Sennacherib of Assyria. 21This is the word that the LORD has spoken concerning him:

She despises you, she scorns you—
   virgin daughter Zion;
she tosses her head—behind your back,
   daughter Jerusalem.

22 "Whom have you mocked and reviled?
   Against whom have you raised your voice
and haughtily lifted your eyes?
   Against the Holy One of Israel!
23 By your messengers you have mocked the
      Lord,
   and you have said, 'With my many
      chariots
I have gone up the heights of the mountains,
   to the far recesses of Lebanon;
I felled its tallest cedars,
   its choicest cypresses;
I entered its farthest retreat,
   its densest forest.
24 I dug wells
   and drank foreign waters,
I dried up with the sole of my foot
   all the streams of Egypt.'

25 "Have you not heard
   that I determined it long ago?
I planned from days of old
   what now I bring to pass,
that you should make fortified cities
   crash into heaps of ruins,
26 while their inhabitants, shorn of strength,
   are dismayed and confounded,
they have become like plants of the field
   and like tender grass,
like grass on the housetops,
   blighted before it is grown.

27 "But I know your rising[a] and your sitting,
   your going out and coming in,
   and your raging against me.
28 Because you have raged against me
   and your arrogance has come to my ears,
I will put my hook in your nose

and my bit in your mouth;
I will turn you back on the way
   by which you came.

29 "And this shall be the sign for you: This year you shall eat what grows of itself, and in the second year what springs from that; then in the third year sow, reap, plant vineyards, and eat their fruit. 30The surviving remnant of the house of Judah shall again take root downward, and bear fruit upward; 31for from Jerusalem a remnant shall go out, and from Mount Zion a band of survivors. The zeal of the LORD of hosts will do this.

32 "Therefore thus says the LORD concerning the king of Assyria: He shall not come into this city, shoot an arrow there, come before it with a shield, or cast up a siege ramp against it. 33By the way that he came, by the same he shall return; he shall not come into this city, says the LORD. 34For I will defend this city to save it, for my own sake and for the sake of my servant David."

Sennacherib's Defeat and Death

35 That very night the angel of the LORD set out and struck down one hundred eighty-five thousand in the camp of the Assyrians; when morning dawned, they were all dead bodies. 36Then King Sennacherib of Assyria left, went home, and lived at Nineveh. 37As he was worshiping in the house of his god Nisroch, his sons Adrammelech and Sharezer killed him with the sword, and they escaped into the land of Ararat. His son Esar-haddon succeeded him.

Hezekiah's Illness

20 In those days Hezekiah became sick and was at the point of death. The prophet Isaiah son of Amoz came to him, and said to him, "Thus says the LORD: Set your house in order, for you shall die; you shall not recover." 2Then Hezekiah turned his face to the wall and prayed to the LORD: 3"Remember now, O LORD, I implore you, how I have walked before you in faithfulness with a whole heart, and have done what is good in your sight." Hezekiah wept bitterly. 4Before Isaiah had gone out of the middle court, the word of the LORD came to him: 5"Turn back, and say to Hezekiah prince of my people, Thus says the LORD, the God of your ancestor David: I have heard your prayer, I have seen your tears; indeed, I will heal you; on the third day you shall go up to the house of the LORD. 6I will add fifteen years to your life. I will deliver you

a Gk Compare Isa 37.27 Q Ms: MT lacks *rising*

and this city out of the hand of the king of Assyria; I will defend this city for my own sake and for my servant David's sake." 7Then Isaiah said, "Bring a lump of figs. Let them take it and apply it to the boil, so that he may recover."

8 Hezekiah said to Isaiah, "What shall be the sign that the LORD will heal me, and that I shall go up to the house of the LORD on the third day?" 9Isaiah said, "This is the sign to you from the LORD, that the LORD will do the thing that he has promised: the shadow has now advanced ten intervals; shall it retreat ten intervals?" 10Hezekiah answered, "It is normal for the shadow to lengthen ten intervals; rather let the shadow retreat ten intervals." 11The prophet Isaiah cried to the LORD; and he brought the shadow back the ten intervals, by which the suna had declined on the dial of Ahaz.

Envoys from Babylon

12 At that time King Merodach-baladan son of Baladan of Babylon sent envoys with letters and a present to Hezekiah, for he had heard that Hezekiah had been sick. 13Hezekiah welcomed them;b he showed them all his treasure house, the silver, the gold, the spices, the precious oil, his armory, all that was found in his storehouses; there was nothing in his house or in all his realm that Hezekiah did not show them. 14Then the prophet Isaiah came to King Hezekiah, and said to him, "What did these men say? From where did they come to you?" Hezekiah answered, "They have come from a far country, from Babylon." 15He said, "What have they seen in your house?" Hezekiah answered, "They have seen all that is in my house; there is nothing in my storehouses that I did not show them."

16 Then Isaiah said to Hezekiah, "Hear the word of the LORD: 17Days are coming when all that is in your house, and that which your ancestors have stored up until this day, shall be carried to Babylon; nothing shall be left, says the LORD. 18Some of your own sons who are born to you shall be taken away; they shall be eunuchs in the palace of the king of Babylon." 19Then Hezekiah said to Isaiah, "The word of the LORD that you have spoken is good." For he thought, "Why not, if there will be peace and security in my days?"

Death of Hezekiah

20 The rest of the deeds of Hezekiah, all his power, how he made the pool and the conduit and brought water into the city, are they not written in the Book of the Annals of the Kings of Judah? 21Hezekiah slept with his ancestors; and his son Manasseh succeeded him.

Manasseh Reigns over Judah

21 Manasseh was twelve years old when he began to reign; he reigned fifty-five years in Jerusalem. His mother's name was Hephzibah. 2He did what was evil in the sight of the LORD, following the abominable practices of the nations that the LORD drove out before the people of Israel. 3For he rebuilt the high places that his father Hezekiah had destroyed; he erected altars for Baal, made a sacred pole,c as King Ahab of Israel had done, worshiped all the host of heaven, and served them. 4He built altars in the house of the LORD, of which the LORD had said, "In Jerusalem I will put my name." 5He built altars for all the host of heaven in the two courts of the house of the LORD. 6He made his son pass through fire; he practiced soothsaying and augury, and dealt with mediums and with wizards. He did much evil in the sight of the LORD, provoking him to anger. 7The carved image of Asherah that he had made he set in the house of which the LORD said to David and to his son Solomon, "In this house, and in Jerusalem, which I have chosen out of all the tribes of Israel, I will put my name forever; 8I will not cause the feet of Israel to wander any more out of the land that I gave to their ancestors, if only they will be careful to do according to all that I have commanded them, and according to all the law that my servant Moses commanded them." 9But they did not listen; Manasseh misled them to do more evil than the nations had done that the LORD destroyed before the people of Israel.

10 The LORD said by his servants the prophets, 11"Because King Manasseh of Judah has committed these abominations, has done things more wicked than all that the Amorites did, who were before him, and has caused Judah also to sin with his idols; 12therefore thus says the LORD, the God of Israel, I am bringing upon Jerusalem and Judah such evil that the ears of everyone who hears of it will tingle. 13I will stretch over Jerusalem the measuring line for Samaria, and the plummet for the house of Ahab; I will wipe Jerusalem as one wipes a dish, wiping it and turning it upside down. 14I will cast off the remnant of my heritage, and give them into the hand of their enemies; they shall become a prey and a spoil to all their enemies, 15because they have done what is evil in my sight and have provoked me to anger, since the day their ancestors came out of Egypt, even to this day."

a Syr See Isa 38.8 and Tg: Heb it　b Gk Vg Syr: Heb When Hezekiah heard about them　c Heb Asherah

16 Moreover Manasseh shed very much innocent blood, until he had filled Jerusalem from one end to another, besides the sin that he caused Judah to sin so that they did what was evil in the sight of the LORD.

17 Now the rest of the acts of Manasseh, all that he did, and the sin that he committed, are they not written in the Book of the Annals of the Kings of Judah? ¹⁸Manasseh slept with his ancestors, and was buried in the garden of his house, in the garden of Uzza. His son Amon succeeded him.

Amon Reigns over Judah

19 Amon was twenty-two years old when he began to reign; he reigned two years in Jerusalem. His mother's name was Meshullemeth daughter of Haruz of Jotbah. ²⁰He did what was evil in the sight of the LORD, as his father Manasseh had done. ²¹He walked in all the way in which his father walked, served the idols that his father served, and worshiped them; ²²he abandoned the LORD, the God of his ancestors, and did not walk in the way of the LORD. ²³The servants of Amon conspired against him, and killed the king in his house. ²⁴But the people of the land killed all those who had conspired against King Amon, and the people of the land made his son Josiah king in place of him. ²⁵Now the rest of the acts of Amon that he did, are they not written in the Book of the Annals of the Kings of Judah? ²⁶He was buried in his tomb in the garden of Uzza; then his son Josiah succeeded him.

Josiah Reigns over Judah

22 Josiah was eight years old when he began to reign; he reigned thirty-one years in Jerusalem. His mother's name was Jedidah daughter of Adaiah of Bozkath. ²He did what was right in the sight of the LORD, and walked in all the way of his father David; he did not turn aside to the right or to the left.

Hilkiah Finds the Book of the Law

3 In the eighteenth year of King Josiah, the king sent Shaphan son of Azaliah, son of Meshullam, the secretary, to the house of the LORD, saying, ⁴"Go up to the high priest Hilkiah, and have him count the entire sum of the money that has been brought into the house of the LORD, which the keepers of the threshold have collected from the people; ⁵let it be given into the hand of the workers who have the oversight of the house of the LORD; let them give it to the workers who are at the house of the LORD, repairing the house, ⁶that is, to the carpenters, to the builders,

Josiah Brings Back the Ways of God

What happened to the Covenant? What happened to the Israelites' true traditions and prayer rituals? After worshiping false gods for so long, it seems as if people just forgot about the Covenant! Then in 2 Kings 22:8, Hilkiah discovers an old book, King Josiah reads it, and a religious reform is started. Josiah's reform is an effort to know and obey God's law and to restore worship to the one, true God. The holy days and holy ways of God are back—at least for a while (see also 2 Chronicles, chapters 34–35).

Reading can be powerful. Christians have a tremendous tradition of spiritual writings that inspire and renew faith. Spiritual autobiographies like *The Confessions of Saint Augustine; The Story of a Soul*, by Saint Thérèse of Lisieux; and *The Seven Storey Mountain*, by Thomas Merton, are classics. You might try starting with entertaining fictional books that have a strong spiritual message, like the seven volumes of The Chronicles of Narnia, by C. S. Lewis, or the Joshua books, by Joseph F. Girzone. For other suggestions of spiritual writings you might enjoy, ask a parent, youth minister, teacher, or pastor.

▶ **2 Kings, chapters 22–23**

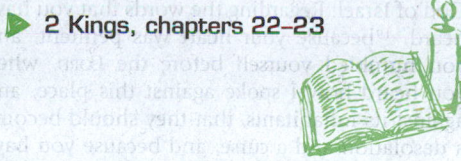

to the masons; and let them use it to buy timber and quarried stone to repair the house. ⁷But no accounting shall be asked from them for the money that is delivered into their hand, for they deal honestly."

8 The high priest Hilkiah said to Shaphan the secretary, "I have found the book of the law in the house of the LORD." When Hilkiah gave the book to Shaphan, he read it. ⁹Then Shaphan the secretary came to the king, and reported to the king, "Your servants have emptied out the money that was found in the house, and have delivered it into the hand of the workers

who have oversight of the house of the Lord." [10]Shaphan the secretary informed the king, "The priest Hilkiah has given me a book." Shaphan then read it aloud to the king.

11 When the king heard the words of the book of the law, he tore his clothes. [12]Then the king commanded the priest Hilkiah, Ahikam son of Shaphan, Achbor son of Micaiah, Shaphan the secretary, and the king's servant Asaiah, saying, [13]"Go, inquire of the Lord for me, for the people, and for all Judah, concerning the words of this book that has been found; for great is the wrath of the Lord that is kindled against us, because our ancestors did not obey the words of this book, to do according to all that is written concerning us."

14 So the priest Hilkiah, Ahikam, Achbor, Shaphan, and Asaiah went to the prophetess Huldah the wife of Shallum son of Tikvah, son of Harhas, keeper of the wardrobe; she resided in Jerusalem in the Second Quarter, where they consulted her. [15]She declared to them, "Thus says the Lord, the God of Israel: Tell the man who sent you to me, [16]Thus says the Lord, I will indeed bring disaster on this place and on its inhabitants—all the words of the book that the king of Judah has read. [17]Because they have abandoned me and have made offerings to other gods, so that they have provoked me to anger with all the work of their hands, therefore my wrath will be kindled against this place, and it will not be quenched. [18]But as to the king of Judah, who sent you to inquire of the Lord, thus shall you say to him, Thus says the Lord, the God of Israel: Regarding the words that you have heard, [19]because your heart was penitent, and you humbled yourself before the Lord, when you heard how I spoke against this place, and against its inhabitants, that they should become a desolation and a curse, and because you have torn your clothes and wept before me, I also have heard you, says the Lord. [20]Therefore, I will gather you to your ancestors, and you shall be gathered to your grave in peace; your eyes shall not see all the disaster that I will bring on this place." They took the message back to the king.

Josiah's Reformation

23 Then the king directed that all the elders of Judah and Jerusalem should be gathered to him. [2]The king went up to the house of the Lord, and with him went all the people of Judah, all the inhabitants of Jerusalem, the priests, the prophets, and all the people, both small and great; he read in their hearing all the words of the book of the covenant that had been found in the house of the Lord. [3]The king stood by the pillar and made a covenant before the Lord, to follow the Lord, keeping his commandments, his decrees, and his statutes, with all his heart and all his soul, to perform the words of this covenant that were written in this book. All the people joined in the covenant.

4 The king commanded the high priest Hilkiah, the priests of the second order, and the guardians of the threshold, to bring out of the temple of the Lord all the vessels made for Baal, for Asherah, and for all the host of heaven; he burned them outside Jerusalem in the fields of the Kidron, and carried their ashes to Bethel. [5]He deposed the idolatrous priests whom the kings of Judah had ordained to make offerings in the high places at the cities of Judah and around Jerusalem; those also who made offerings to Baal, to the sun, the moon, the constellations, and all the host of the heavens. [6]He brought out the image of[a] Asherah from the house of the Lord, outside Jerusalem, to the Wadi Kidron, burned it at the Wadi Kidron, beat it to dust and threw the dust of it upon the graves of the common people. [7]He broke down the houses of the male temple prostitutes that were in the house of the Lord, where the women did weaving for Asherah. [8]He brought all the priests out of the towns of Judah, and defiled the high places where the priests had made offerings, from Geba to Beer-sheba; he broke down the high places of the gates that were at the entrance of the gate of Joshua the governor of the city, which were on the left at the gate of the city. [9]The priests of the high places, however, did not come up to the altar of the Lord in Jerusalem, but ate unleavened bread among their kindred. [10]He defiled Topheth, which is in the valley of Ben-hinnom, so that no one would make a son or a daughter pass through fire as an offering to Molech. [11]He removed the horses that the kings of Judah had dedicated to the sun, at the entrance to the house of the Lord, by the chamber of the eunuch Nathan-melech, which was in the precincts;[b] then he burned the chariots of the sun with fire. [12]The altars on the roof of the upper chamber of Ahaz, which the kings of Judah had made, and the altars that Manasseh had made in the two courts of the house of the Lord, he pulled down from there and broke in pieces, and threw the rubble into the Wadi Kidron. [13]The king defiled the high places that were east of Jerusalem, to the south of the Mount of Destruction, which King Solomon of Israel had built for Astarte the abomination of the Sidonians, for Chemosh

---

a Heb lacks *image of*   b Meaning of Heb uncertain

the abomination of Moab, and for Milcom the abomination of the Ammonites. [14]He broke the pillars in pieces, cut down the sacred poles,[a] and covered the sites with human bones.

15 Moreover, the altar at Bethel, the high place erected by Jeroboam son of Nebat, who caused Israel to sin—he pulled down that altar along with the high place. He burned the high place, crushing it to dust; he also burned the sacred pole.[b] [16]As Josiah turned, he saw the tombs there on the mount; and he sent and took the bones out of the tombs, and burned them on the altar, and defiled it, according to the word of the Lord that the man of God proclaimed,[c] when Jeroboam stood by the altar at the festival; he turned and looked up at the tomb of the man of God who had predicted these things. [17]Then he said, "What is that monument that I see?" The people of the city told him, "It is the tomb of the man of God who came from Judah and predicted these things that you have done against the altar at Bethel." [18]He said, "Let him rest; let no one move his bones." So they let his bones alone, with the bones of the prophet who came out of Samaria. [19]Moreover, Josiah removed all the shrines of the high places that were in the towns of Samaria, which kings of Israel had made, provoking the Lord to anger; he did to them just as he had done at Bethel. [20]He slaughtered on the altars all the priests of the high places who were there, and burned human bones on them. Then he returned to Jerusalem.

The Passover Celebrated

21 The king commanded all the people, "Keep the passover to the Lord your God as prescribed in this book of the covenant." [22]No such passover had been kept since the days of the judges who judged Israel, even during all the days of the kings of Israel and of the kings of Judah; [23]but in the eighteenth year of King Josiah this passover was kept to the Lord in Jerusalem.

24 Moreover Josiah put away the mediums, wizards, teraphim,[d] idols, and all the abominations that were seen in the land of Judah and in Jerusalem, so that he established the words of the law that were written in the book that the priest Hilkiah had found in the house of the Lord. [25]Before him there was no king like him, who turned to the Lord with all his heart, with all his soul, and with all his might, according to all the law of Moses; nor did any like him arise after him.

26 Still the Lord did not turn from the fierceness of his great wrath, by which his anger was kindled against Judah, because of all the provocations with which Manasseh had provoked him. [27]The Lord said, "I will remove Judah also out of my sight, as I have removed Israel; and I will reject this city that I have chosen, Jerusalem, and the house of which I said, My name shall be there."

Josiah Dies in Battle

28 Now the rest of the acts of Josiah, and all that he did, are they not written in the Book of the Annals of the Kings of Judah? [29]In his days Pharaoh Neco king of Egypt went up to the king of Assyria to the river Euphrates. King Josiah went to meet him; but when Pharaoh Neco met him at Megiddo, he killed him. [30]His servants carried him dead in a chariot from Megiddo, brought him to Jerusalem, and buried him in his own tomb. The people of the land took Jehoahaz son of Josiah, anointed him, and made him king in place of his father.

Reign and Captivity of Jehoahaz

31 Jehoahaz was twenty-three years old when he began to reign; he reigned three months in Jerusalem. His mother's name was Hamutal daughter of Jeremiah of Libnah. [32]He did what was evil in the sight of the Lord, just as his ancestors had done. [33]Pharaoh Neco confined him at Riblah in the land of Hamath, so that he might not reign in Jerusalem, and imposed tribute on the land of one hundred talents of silver and a talent of gold. [34]Pharaoh Neco made Eliakim son of Josiah king in place of his father Josiah, and changed his name to Jehoiakim. But he took Jehoahaz away; he came to Egypt, and died there. [35]Jehoiakim gave the silver and the gold to Pharaoh, but he taxed the land in order to meet Pharaoh's demand for money. He exacted the silver and the gold from the people of the land, from all according to their assessment, to give it to Pharaoh Neco.

Jehoiakim Reigns over Judah

36 Jehoiakim was twenty-five years old when he began to reign; he reigned eleven years in Jerusalem. His mother's name was Zebidah daughter of Pedaiah of Rumah. [37]He did what was evil in the sight of the Lord, just as all his ancestors had done.

Judah Overrun by Enemies

24 In his days King Nebuchadnezzar of Babylon came up; Jehoiakim became his servant for three years; then he turned and rebelled

---

a Heb *Asherim* b Heb *Asherah* c Gk: *He proclaimed, who had predicted these things* d Or *household gods*

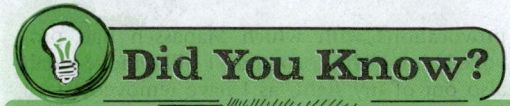

Did You Know?

The Fall of Jerusalem

The second conquest and exile described in Second Kings (see "The First Captivity," near 2 Kings 17:5–18, for the first) involves the southern kingdom, Judah. Judah was conquered by the Babylonians in 587 BC, which is why that event is often referred to as the Babylonian Exile (see map 6, "The Babylonian Empire"). The author of Kings implies that the kingdom of Judah lasted longer than the kingdom of Israel because it had faithful reformer kings like Hezekiah and Josiah. The fall of Judah was particularly devastating because both Jerusalem, David's city, and the Temple, the central place of worship, were destroyed. The whole Book of Lamentations is an expression of the sorrow and grief the people experienced as a result.

▶ 2 Kings 25:1–21

against him. ²The LORD sent against him bands of the Chaldeans, bands of the Arameans, bands of the Moabites, and bands of the Ammonites; he sent them against Judah to destroy it, according to the word of the LORD that he spoke by his servants the prophets. ³Surely this came upon Judah at the command of the LORD, to remove them out of his sight, for the sins of Manasseh, for all that he had committed, ⁴and also for the innocent blood that he had shed; for he filled Jerusalem with innocent blood, and the LORD was not willing to pardon. ⁵Now the rest of the deeds of Jehoiakim, and all that he did, are they not written in the Book of the Annals of the Kings of Judah? ⁶So Jehoiakim slept with his ancestors; then his son Jehoiachin succeeded him. ⁷The king of Egypt did not come again out of his land, for the king of Babylon had taken over all that belonged to the king of Egypt from the Wadi of Egypt to the River Euphrates.

Reign and Captivity of Jehoiachin

8 Jehoiachin was eighteen years old when he began to reign; he reigned three months in Jerusalem. His mother's name was Nehushta daughter of Elnathan of Jerusalem. ⁹He did what was evil in the sight of the LORD, just as his father had done.

10 At that time the servants of King Nebuchadnezzar of Babylon came up to Jerusalem, and the city was besieged. ¹¹King Nebuchadnezzar of Babylon came to the city, while his servants were besieging it; ¹²King Jehoiachin of Judah gave himself up to the king of Babylon, himself, his mother, his servants, his officers, and his palace officials. The king of Babylon took him prisoner in the eighth year of his reign.

Capture of Jerusalem

13 He carried off all the treasures of the house of the LORD, and the treasures of the king's house; he cut in pieces all the vessels of gold in the temple of the LORD, which King Solomon of Israel had made, all this as the LORD had foretold. ¹⁴He carried away all Jerusalem, all the officials, all the warriors, ten thousand captives, all the artisans and the smiths; no one remained, except the poorest people of the land. ¹⁵He carried away Jehoiachin to Babylon; the king's mother, the king's wives, his officials, and the elite of the land, he took into captivity from Jerusalem to Babylon. ¹⁶The king of Babylon brought captive to Babylon all the men of valor, seven thousand, the artisans and the smiths, one thousand, all of them strong and fit for war. ¹⁷The king of Babylon made Mattaniah, Jehoiachin's uncle, king in his place, and changed his name to Zedekiah.

Zedekiah Reigns over Judah

18 Zedekiah was twenty-one years old when he began to reign; he reigned eleven years in Jerusalem. His mother's name was Hamutal daughter of Jeremiah of Libnah. ¹⁹He did what was evil in the sight of the LORD, just as Jehoiakim had done. ²⁰Indeed, Jerusalem and Judah so angered the LORD that he expelled them from his presence.

The Fall and Captivity of Judah

25 Zedekiah rebelled against the king of Babylon. ¹And in the ninth year of his reign, in the tenth month, on the tenth day of the month, King Nebuchadnezzar of Babylon came with all his army against Jerusalem, and laid siege to it; they built siegeworks against it all around. ²So the city was besieged until the eleventh year of King Zedekiah. ³On the ninth day of the fourth month the famine became so severe in the city that there was no food for the people of the land. ⁴Then a breach was made in the city wall;ᵃ the king with all the soldiers fledᵇ by night by the way of the gate between the two walls, by

---

a Heb lacks *wall*   b Gk Compare Jer 39.4; 52.7: Heb lacks *the king* and lacks *fled*

the king's garden, though the Chaldeans were all around the city. They went in the direction of the Arabah. ⁵But the army of the Chaldeans pursued the king, and overtook him in the plains of Jericho; all his army was scattered, deserting him. ⁶Then they captured the king and brought him up to the king of Babylon at Riblah, who passed sentence on him. ⁷They slaughtered the sons of Zedekiah before his eyes, then put out the eyes of Zedekiah; they bound him in fetters and took him to Babylon.

8 In the fifth month, on the seventh day of the month—which was the nineteenth year of King Nebuchadnezzar, king of Babylon—Nebuzaradan, the captain of the bodyguard, a servant of the king of Babylon, came to Jerusalem. ⁹He burned the house of the LORD, the king's house, and all the houses of Jerusalem; every great house he burned down. ¹⁰All the army of the Chaldeans who were with the captain of the guard broke down the walls around Jerusalem. ¹¹Nebuzaradan the captain of the guard carried into exile the rest of the people who were left in the city and the deserters who had defected to the king of Babylon—all the rest of the population. ¹²But the captain of the guard left some of the poorest people of the land to be vinedressers and tillers of the soil.

13 The bronze pillars that were in the house of the LORD, as well as the stands and the bronze sea that were in the house of the LORD, the Chaldeans broke in pieces, and carried the bronze to Babylon. ¹⁴They took away the pots, the shovels, the snuffers, the dishes for incense, and all the bronze vessels used in the temple service, ¹⁵as well as the firepans and the basins. What was made of gold the captain of the guard took away for the gold, and what was made of silver, for the silver. ¹⁶As for the two pillars, the one sea, and the stands, which Solomon had made for the house of the LORD, the bronze of all these vessels was beyond weighing. ¹⁷The height of the one pillar was eighteen cubits, and on it was a bronze capital; the height of the capital was three cubits; latticework and pomegranates, all of bronze, were on the capital all around. The second pillar had the same, with the latticework.

18 The captain of the guard took the chief priest Seraiah, the second priest Zephaniah, and the three guardians of the threshold; ¹⁹from the city he took an officer who had been in command of the soldiers, and five men of the king's

council who were found in the city; the secretary who was the commander of the army who mustered the people of the land; and sixty men of the people of the land who were found in the city. ²⁰Nebuzaradan the captain of the guard took them, and brought them to the king of Babylon at Riblah. ²¹The king of Babylon struck them down and put them to death at Riblah in the land of Hamath. So Judah went into exile out of its land.

Gedaliah Made Governor of Judah

22 He appointed Gedaliah son of Ahikam son of Shaphan as governor over the people who remained in the land of Judah, whom King Nebuchadnezzar of Babylon had left. ²³Now when all the captains of the forces and their men heard that the king of Babylon had appointed Gedaliah as governor, they came with their men to Gedaliah at Mizpah, namely, Ishmael son of Nethaniah, Johanan son of Kareah, Seraiah son of Tanhumeth the Netophathite, and Jaazaniah son of the Maacathite. ²⁴Gedaliah swore to them and their men, saying, "Do not be afraid because of the Chaldean officials; live in the land, serve the king of Babylon, and it shall be well with you." ²⁵But in the seventh month, Ishmael son of Nethaniah son of Elishama, of the royal family, came with ten men; they struck down Gedaliah so that he died, along with the Judeans and Chaldeans who were with him at Mizpah. ²⁶Then all the people, high and low,ᵃ and the captains of the forces set out and went to Egypt; for they were afraid of the Chaldeans.

Jehoiachin Released from Prison

27 In the thirty-seventh year of the exile of King Jehoiachin of Judah, in the twelfth month, on the twenty-seventh day of the month, King Evil-merodach of Babylon, in the year that he began to reign, released King Jehoiachin of Judah from prison; ²⁸he spoke kindly to him, and gave him a seat above the other seats of the kings who were with him in Babylon. ²⁹So Jehoiachin put aside his prison clothes. Every day of his life he dined regularly in the king's presence. ³⁰For his allowance, a regular allowance was given him by the king, a portion every day, as long as he lived.

_____

a Or young and old

Wait! That's not the way I saw it! Doesn't it seem that there is always more than one version of an event? This often happens with accidents. Two individuals can witness the same accident with very different points of view. The First and Second Books of Chronicles provide a second interpretation, or version, of the history of the people of Israel, presenting that history from another point of view. In contrast to the previous account, the account in these books tends to downplay the Covenant and emphasizes the importance of institutional ritual and worship of God.

In Depth

The Chronicler is the name given to the unknown author (or authors) of First and Second Chronicles. The Chronicler, writing after the Israelites' return from the Exile in Babylon, has a unique perspective, so unique that he almost never mentions the Sinai Covenant or Moses (central themes throughout other parts of the Old Testament). Because the Israelites still hope to have their own king, the Chronicler emphasizes that fidelity to Temple worship is necessary for God's promises regarding land and kingship to be fulfilled.

At a Glance

- **1 Chronicles, chapters 1–9. genealogies of Israel**
- **1 Chronicles, chapters 10–29. David's kingship**
- **2 Chronicles, chapters 1–9. Solomon's kingship**
- **2 Chronicles, chapters 10–36. the kings of Judah after Solomon's death**

Quick Facts

Period Covered: Creation to the end of the Babylonian captivity
Inspired Author: a Levite cantor and scribe writing after the return to Jerusalem around 400 BC
Theme: Israel can secure its future by continuing its worship in the pattern established by David, by being united as one people worshiping the one true God at the Temple in Jerusalem.

The Chronicler uses two types of material—genealogies and legends edited to emphasize the Chroniclers' point—to summarize Israel's history from the Creation to around 525 BC. But he focuses primarily on kings David and Solomon. They are praised extensively because of their role in centralizing worship in Jerusalem and building the Temple. Many of the negative stories about David from Second Samuel—such as his affair with Bathsheba—are not even mentioned. The Chronicler wants nothing to tarnish the people's memory of an ideal kingdom that might one day be restored.

Second Chronicles also focuses on the southern kingdom of Judah and ignores the northern kingdom of Israel after Solomon's death. This may well be due to a bias of the priestly class in Jerusalem against the religious practice of the northern tribes. This bias lasted into Jesus' time.

The goal of First and Second Chronicles was to give the Israelites hope for the future after returning from the Exile. The Chronicler reminds them that if they maintain their religious practices and worship of God, they will continue to be God's People.

1 Chronicles

Chapter 15

From Adam to Abraham

1 Adam, Seth, Enosh; ²Kenan, Mahalalel, Jared; ³Enoch, Methuselah, Lamech; ⁴Noah, Shem, Ham, and Japheth.

5 The descendants of Japheth: Gomer, Magog, Madai, Javan, Tubal, Meshech, and Tiras. ⁶The descendants of Gomer: Ashkenaz, Diphath,ᵃ and Togarmah. ⁷The descendants of Javan: Elishah, Tarshish, Kittim, and Rodanim.ᵇ

8 The descendants of Ham: Cush, Egypt, Put, and Canaan. ⁹The descendants of Cush: Seba, Havilah, Sabta, Raama, and Sabteca. The descendants of Raamah: Sheba and Dedan. ¹⁰Cush became the father of Nimrod; he was the first to be a mighty one on the earth.

11 Egypt became the father of Ludim, Anamim, Lehabim, Naphtuhim, ¹²Pathrusim, Casluhim, and Caphtorim, from whom the Philistines come.ᶜ

13 Canaan became the father of Sidon his firstborn, and Heth, ¹⁴and the Jebusites, the Amorites, the Girgashites, ¹⁵the Hivites, the Arkites, the Sinites, ¹⁶the Arvadites, the Zemarites, and the Hamathites.

17 The descendants of Shem: Elam, Asshur, Arpachshad, Lud, Aram, Uz, Hul, Gether, and Meshech.ᵈ ¹⁸Arpachshad became the father of Shelah; and Shelah became the father of Eber. ¹⁹To Eber were born two sons: the name of the one was Peleg (for in his days the earth was divided), and the name of his brother Joktan. ²⁰Joktan became the father of Almodad, Sheleph, Hazarmaveth, Jerah, ²¹Hadoram, Uzal, Diklah, ²²Ebal, Abimael, Sheba, ²³Ophir, Havilah, and Jobab; all these were the descendants of Joktan.

24 Shem, Arpachshad, Shelah; ²⁵Eber, Peleg, Reu; ²⁶Serug, Nahor, Terah; ²⁷Abram, that is, Abraham.

From Abraham to Jacob

28 The sons of Abraham: Isaac and Ishmael. ²⁹These are their genealogies: the firstborn of Ishmael, Nebaioth; and Kedar, Adbeel, Mibsam, ³⁰Mishma, Dumah, Massa, Hadad, Tema, ³¹Jetur, Naphish, and Kedemah. These are the sons of Ishmael. ³²The sons of Keturah, Abraham's concubine: she bore Zimran, Jokshan, Medan, Midian, Ishbak, and Shuah. The sons of Jokshan: Sheba and Dedan. ³³The sons of Midian: Ephah, Epher, Hanoch, Abida, and Eldaah. All these were the descendants of Keturah.

34 Abraham became the father of Isaac. The sons of Isaac: Esau and Israel. ³⁵The sons of Esau: Eliphaz, Reuel, Jeush, Jalam, and Korah. ³⁶The sons of Eliphaz: Teman, Omar, Zephi, Gatam, Kenaz, Timna, and Amalek. ³⁷The sons of Reuel: Nahath, Zerah, Shammah, and Mizzah.

38 The sons of Seir: Lotan, Shobal, Zibeon, Anah, Dishon, Ezer, and Dishan. ³⁹The sons of Lotan: Hori and Homam; and Lotan's sister was Timna. ⁴⁰The sons of Shobal: Alian, Manahath,

---

a Gen 10.3 *Ripath*; See Gk Vg   *b* Gen 10.4 *Dodanim*; See Syr Vg
c Heb *Casluhim, from which the Philistines come, Caphtorim*; See Am 9.7, Jer 47.4   *d* *Mash* in Gen 10.23

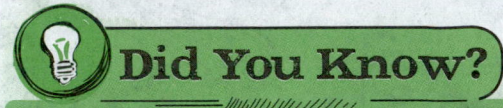

Did You Know?

Genealogies

Look at all these names! Our present-day interest in family trees obviously has ancient roots. The first nine chapters of First Chronicles consist entirely of family trees—or genealogies—tracing the history of Israel from Adam to Saul. In a culture where not only money and identity but also the offices of priest and king passed from one generation to another, it was essential to be able to trace one's tribal roots.

The many genealogies of the Old Testament answer important questions: How were the various tribes related to one another? Who were a particular tribe's ancestors? What right did a certain group or person have to the office of priest or king? The Chronicler lists the genealogies of David and Levi in considerable detail. The kingship and the priesthood were clearly of special interest to him.

▶ 1 Chronicles, chapters 1–9

Ebal, Shephi, and Onam. The sons of Zibeon: Aiah and Anah. ⁴¹The sons of Anah: Dishon. The sons of Dishon: Hamran, Eshban, Ithran, and Cheran. ⁴²The sons of Ezer: Bilhan, Zaavan, and Jaakan.ᵃ The sons of Dishan:ᵇ Uz and Aran.

43 These are the kings who reigned in the land of Edom before any king reigned over the Israelites: Bela son of Beor, whose city was called Dinhabah. ⁴⁴When Bela died, Jobab son of Zerah of Bozrah succeeded him. ⁴⁵When Jobab died, Husham of the land of the Temanites succeeded him. ⁴⁶When Husham died, Hadad son of Bedad, who defeated Midian in the country of Moab, succeeded him; and the name of his city was Avith. ⁴⁷When Hadad died, Samlah of Masrekah succeeded him. ⁴⁸When Samlah died, Shaulᶜ of Rehoboth on the Euphrates succeeded him. ⁴⁹When Shaulᶜ died, Baal-hanan son of Achbor succeeded him. ⁵⁰When Baal-hanan died, Hadad succeeded him; the name of his city was Pai, and his wife's name Mehetabel daughter of Matred, daughter of Me-zahab. ⁵¹And Hadad died.

The clansᵈ of Edom were: clansᵈ Timna, Aliah,ᵉ Jetheth, ⁵²Oholibamah, Elah, Pinon, ⁵³Kenaz, Teman, Mibzar, ⁵⁴Magdiel, and Iram; these are the clansᵈ of Edom.

The Sons of Israel and the Descendants of Judah

2 These are the sons of Israel: Reuben, Simeon, Levi, Judah, Issachar, Zebulun, ²Dan, Joseph, Benjamin, Naphtali, Gad, and Asher. ³The sons of Judah: Er, Onan, and Shelah; these three the Canaanite woman Bath-shua bore to him. Now Er, Judah's firstborn, was wicked in the sight of the LORD, and he put him to death. ⁴His daughter-in-law Tamar also bore him Perez and Zerah. Judah had five sons in all.

5 The sons of Perez: Hezron and Hamul. ⁶The sons of Zerah: Zimri, Ethan, Heman, Calcol, and Dara,ᶠ five in all. ⁷The sons of Carmi: Achar, the troubler of Israel, who transgressed in the matter of the devoted thing; ⁸and Ethan's son was Azariah.

9 The sons of Hezron, who were born to him: Jerahmeel, Ram, and Chelubai. ¹⁰Ram became the father of Amminadab, and Amminadab became the father of Nahshon, prince of the sons of Judah. ¹¹Nahshon became the father of Salma, Salma of Boaz, ¹²Boaz of Obed, Obed of Jesse. ¹³Jesse became the father of Eliab his firstborn, Abinadab the second, Shimea the third, ¹⁴Nethanel the fourth, Raddai the fifth, ¹⁵Ozem the sixth, David the seventh; ¹⁶and their sisters were Zeruiah and Abigail. The sons of Zeruiah: Abishai, Joab, and Asahel, three. ¹⁷Abigail bore Amasa, and the father of Amasa was Jether the Ishmaelite.

18 Caleb son of Hezron had children by his wife Azubah, and by Jerioth; these were her sons: Jesher, Shobab, and Ardon. ¹⁹When Azubah died, Caleb married Ephrath, who bore him Hur. ²⁰Hur became the father of Uri, and Uri became the father of Bezalel.

21 Afterward Hezron went in to the daughter of Machir father of Gilead, whom he married when he was sixty years old; and she bore him Segub; ²²and Segub became the father of Jair, who had twenty-three towns in the land of Gilead. ²³But Geshur and Aram took from them Havvoth-jair, Kenath and its villages, sixty towns. All these were descendants of Machir, father of Gilead. ²⁴After the death of Hezron, in Caleb-ephrathah, Abijah wife of Hezron bore him Ashhur, father of Tekoa.

25 The sons of Jerahmeel, the firstborn of Hezron: Ram his firstborn, Bunah, Oren, Ozem, and Ahijah. ²⁶Jerahmeel also had another wife,

---

ᵃ Or *and Akan*; See Gen 36.27   ᵇ See 1.38: Heb *Dishon*
ᶜ Or *Saul*   ᵈ Or *chiefs*   ᵉ Or *Alvah*; See Gen 36.40
ᶠ Or *Darda*; Compare Syr Tg some Gk Mss; See 1 Kings 4.31

whose name was Atarah; she was the mother of Onam. 27The sons of Ram, the firstborn of Jerahmeel: Maaz, Jamin, and Eker. 28The sons of Onam: Shammai and Jada. The sons of Shammai: Nadab and Abishur. 29The name of Abishur's wife was Abihail, and she bore him Ahban and Molid. 30The sons of Nadab: Seled and Appaim; and Seled died childless. 31The son*a* of Appaim: Ishi. The son*a* of Ishi: Sheshan. The son*a* of Sheshan: Ahlai. 32The sons of Jada, Shammai's brother: Jether and Jonathan; and Jether died childless. 33The sons of Jonathan: Peleth and Zaza. These were the descendants of Jerahmeel. 34Now Sheshan had no sons, only daughters; but Sheshan had an Egyptian slave, whose name was Jarha. 35So Sheshan gave his daughter in marriage to his slave Jarha; and she bore him Attai. 36Attai became the father of Nathan, and Nathan of Zabad. 37Zabad became the father of Ephlal, and Ephlal of Obed. 38Obed became the father of Jehu, and Jehu of Azariah. 39Azariah became the father of Helez, and Helez of Eleasah. 40Eleasah became the father of Sismai, and Sismai of Shallum. 41Shallum became the father of Jekamiah, and Jekamiah of Elishama.

42 The sons of Caleb brother of Jerahmeel: Mesha*b* his firstborn, who was father of Ziph. The sons of Mareshah father of Hebron. 43The sons of Hebron: Korah, Tappuah, Rekem, and Shema. 44Shema became father of Raham, father of Jorkeam; and Rekem became the father of Shammai. 45The son of Shammai: Maon; and Maon was the father of Beth-zur. 46Ephah also, Caleb's concubine, bore Haran, Moza, and Gazez; and Haran became the father of Gazez. 47The sons of Jahdai: Regem, Jotham, Geshan, Pelet, Ephah, and Shaaph. 48Maacah, Caleb's concubine, bore Sheber and Tirhanah. 49She also bore Shaaph father of Madmannah, Sheva father of Machbenah and father of Gibea; and the daughter of Caleb was Achsah. 50These were the descendants of Caleb.

The sons*c* of Hur the firstborn of Ephrathah: Shobal father of Kiriath-jearim, 51Salma father of Bethlehem, and Hareph father of Beth-gader. 52Shobal father of Kiriath-jearim had other sons: Haroeh, half of the Menuhoth. 53And the families of Kiriath-jearim: the Ithrites, the Puthites, the Shumathites, and the Mishraites; from these came the Zorathites and the Eshtaolites. 54The sons of Salma: Bethlehem, the Netophathites, Atroth-beth-joab, and half of the Manahathites, the Zorites. 55The families also of the scribes that lived at Jabez: the Tirathites, the Shimeathites, and the Sucathites. These are the Kenites who came from Hammath, father of the house of Rechab.

Descendants of David and Solomon

3 These are the sons of David who were born to him in Hebron: the firstborn Amnon, by Ahinoam the Jezreelite; the second Daniel, by Abigail the Carmelite; 2the third Absalom, son of Maacah, daughter of King Talmai of Geshur; the fourth Adonijah, son of Haggith; 3the fifth Shephatiah, by Abital; the sixth Ithream, by his wife Eglah; 4six were born to him in Hebron, where he reigned for seven years and six months. And he reigned thirty-three years in Jerusalem. 5These were born to him in Jerusalem: Shimea, Shobab, Nathan, and Solomon, four by Bathshua, daughter of Ammiel; 6then Ibhar, Elishama, Eliphelet, 7Nogah, Nepheg, Japhia, 8Elishama, Eliada, and Eliphelet, nine. 9All these were David's sons, besides the sons of the concubines; and Tamar was their sister.

10 The descendants of Solomon: Rehoboam, Abijah his son, Asa his son, Jehoshaphat his son, 11Joram his son, Ahaziah his son, Joash his son, 12Amaziah his son, Azariah his son, Jotham his son, 13Ahaz his son, Hezekiah his son, Manasseh his son, 14Amon his son, Josiah his son. 15The sons of Josiah: Johanan the firstborn, the second Jehoiakim, the third Zedekiah, the fourth Shallum. 16The descendants of Jehoiakim: Jeconiah his son, Zedekiah his son; 17and the sons of Jeconiah, the captive: Shealtiel his son, 18Malchiram, Pedaiah, Shenazzar, Jekamiah, Hoshama, and Nedabiah; 19The sons of Pedaiah: Zerubbabel and Shimei; and the sons of Zerubbabel: Meshullam and Hananiah, and Shelomith was their sister; 20and Hashubah, Ohel, Berechiah, Hasadiah, and Jushab-hesed, five. 21The sons of Hananiah: Pelatiah and Jeshaiah, his son*d* Rephaiah, his son*d* Arnan, his son*d* Obadiah, his son*d* Shecaniah. 22The son*a* of Shecaniah: Shemaiah. And the sons of Shemaiah: Hattush, Igal, Bariah, Neariah, and Shaphat, six. 23The sons of Neariah: Elioenai, Hizkiah, and Azrikam, three. 24The sons of Elioenai: Hodaviah, Eliashib, Pelaiah, Akkub, Johanan, Delaiah, and Anani, seven.

Descendants of Judah

4 The sons of Judah: Perez, Hezron, Carmi, Hur, and Shobal. 2Reaiah son of Shobal became the father of Jahath, and Jahath became the father of Ahumai and Lahad. These were the families of the Zorathites. 3These were the

---

a Heb *sons*   *b* Gk reads *Mareshah*   *c* Gk Vg: Heb *son*
d Gk Compare Syr Vg: Heb *sons of*

sons[f] of Etam: Jezreel, Ishma, and Idbash; and the name of their sister was Hazzelelponi, [4]and Penuel was the father of Gedor, and Ezer the father of Hushah. These were the sons of Hur, the firstborn of Ephrathah, the father of Bethlehem. [5]Ashhur father of Tekoa had two wives, Helah and Naarah; [6]Naarah bore him Ahuzzam, Hepher, Temeni, and Haahashtari.[b] These were the sons of Naarah. [7]The sons of Helah: Zereth, Izhar,[c] and Ethnan. [8]Koz became the father of Anub, Zobebah, and the families of Aharhel son of Harum. [9]Jabez was honored more than his brothers; and his mother named him Jabez, saying, "Because I bore him in pain." [10]Jabez called on the God of Israel, saying, "Oh that you would bless me and enlarge my border, and that your hand might be with me, and that you would keep me from hurt and harm!" And God granted what he asked. [11]Chelub the brother of Shuhah became the father of Mehir, who was the father of Eshton. [12]Eshton became the father of Beth-rapha, Paseah, and Tehinnah the father of Ir-nahash. These are the men of Recah. [13]The sons of Kenaz: Othniel and Seraiah; and the sons of Othniel: Hathath and Meonothai.[d] [14]Meonothai became the father of Ophrah; and Seraiah became the father of Joab father of Geharashim,[e] so-called because they were artisans. [15]The sons of Caleb son of Jephunneh: Iru, Elah, and Naam; and the son[f] of Elah: Kenaz. [16]The sons of Jehallelel: Ziph, Ziphah, Tiria, and Asarel. [17]The sons of Ezrah: Jether, Mered, Epher, and Jalon. These are the sons of Bithiah, daughter of Pharaoh, whom Mered married;[g] and she conceived and bore[h] Miriam, Shammai, and Ishbah father of Eshtemoa. [18]And his Judean wife bore Jered father of Gedor, Heber father of Soco, and Jekuthiel father of Zanoah. [19]The sons of the wife of Hodiah, the sister of Naham, were the fathers of Keilah the Garmite and Eshtemoa the Maacathite. [20]The sons of Shimon: Amnon, Rinnah, Ben-hanan, and Tilon. The sons of Ishi: Zoheth and Ben-zoheth. [21]The sons of Shelah son of Judah: Er father of Lecah, Laadah father of Mareshah, and the families of the guild of linen workers at Beth-ashbea; [22]and Jokim, and the men of Cozeba, and Joash, and Saraph, who married into Moab but returned to Lehem[i] (now the records[j] are ancient). [23]These were the potters and inhabitants of Netaim and Gederah; they lived there with the king in his service.

Descendants of Simeon

24 The sons of Simeon: Nemuel, Jamin, Jarib, Zerah, Shaul;[k] [25]Shallum was his son, Mibsam his son, Mishma his son. [26]The sons of Mishma: Hammuel his son, Zaccur his son, Shimei his son. [27]Shimei had sixteen sons and six daughters; but his brothers did not have many children, nor did all their family multiply like the Judeans. [28]They lived in Beer-sheba, Moladah, Hazar-shual, [29]Bilhah, Ezem, Tolad, [30]Bethuel, Hormah, Ziklag, [31]Beth-marcaboth, Hazar-susim, Beth-biri, and Shaaraim. These were their towns until David became king. [32]And their villages were Etam, Ain, Rimmon, Tochen, and Ashan, five towns, [33]along with all their villages that were around these towns as far as Baal. These were their settlements. And they kept a genealogical record.

34 Meshobab, Jamlech, Joshah son of Amaziah, [35]Joel, Jehu son of Joshibiah son of Seraiah son of Asiel, [36]Elioenai, Jaakobah, Jeshohaiah, Asaiah, Adiel, Jesimiel, Benaiah, [37]Ziza son of Shiphi son of Allon son of Jedaiah son of Shimri son of Shemaiah— [38]these mentioned by name were leaders in their families, and their clans increased greatly. [39]They journeyed to the entrance of Gedor, to the east side of the valley, to seek pasture for their flocks, [40]where they found rich, good pasture, and the land was very broad, quiet, and peaceful; for the former inhabitants there belonged to Ham. [41]These, registered by name, came in the days of King Hezekiah of Judah, and attacked their tents and the Meunim who were found there, and exterminated them to this day, and settled in their place, because there was pasture there for their flocks. [42]And some of them, five hundred men of the Simeonites, went to Mount Seir, having as their leaders Pelatiah, Neariah, Rephaiah, and Uzziel, sons of Ishi; [43]they destroyed the remnant of the Amalekites that had escaped, and they have lived there to this day.

Descendants of Reuben

5 The sons of Reuben the firstborn of Israel. (He was the firstborn, but because he defiled his father's bed his birthright was given to the sons of Joseph son of Israel, so that he is not enrolled in the genealogy according to the birthright; [2]though Judah became prominent among his brothers and a ruler came from him, yet the birthright belonged to Joseph.) [3]The sons of Reuben, the firstborn of Israel: Hanoch, Pallu, Hezron, and Carmi. [4]The sons of Joel: Shemaiah his son, Gog his son, Shimei his son, [5]Micah his son, Reaiah his son, Baal his son,

---

a Gk Compare Vg: Heb *the father*   b Or *Ahashtari*   c Another reading is *Zohar*   d Gk Vg: Heb lacks *and Meonothai*   e That is *Valley of artisans*   f Heb *sons*   g The clause: *These are . . . married* is transposed from verse 18   h Heb lacks *and bore*   i Vg Compare Gk: Heb *and Jashubi-lahem*   j Or *matters*   k Or *Saul*

⁶Beerah his son, whom King Tilgath-pilneser of Assyria carried away into exile; he was a chieftain of the Reubenites. ⁷And his kindred by their families, when the genealogy of their generations was reckoned: the chief, Jeiel, and Zechariah, ⁸and Bela son of Azaz, son of Shema, son of Joel, who lived in Aroer, as far as Nebo and Baal-meon. ⁹He also lived to the east as far as the beginning of the desert this side of the Euphrates, because their cattle had multiplied in the land of Gilead. ¹⁰And in the days of Saul they made war on the Hagrites, who fell by their hand; and they lived in their tents throughout all the region east of Gilead.

Descendants of Gad

11 The sons of Gad lived beside them in the land of Bashan as far as Salecah: ¹²Joel the chief, Shapham the second, Janai, and Shaphat in Bashan. ¹³And their kindred according to their clans: Michael, Meshullam, Sheba, Jorai, Jacan, Zia, and Eber, seven. ¹⁴These were the sons of Abihail son of Huri, son of Jaroah, son of Gilead, son of Michael, son of Jeshishai, son of Jahdo, son of Buz; ¹⁵Ahi son of Abdiel, son of Guni, was chief in their clan; ¹⁶and they lived in Gilead, in Bashan and in its towns, and in all the pasture lands of Sharon to their limits. ¹⁷All of these were enrolled by genealogies in the days of King Jotham of Judah, and in the days of King Jeroboam of Israel.

18 The Reubenites, the Gadites, and the half-tribe of Manasseh had valiant warriors, who carried shield and sword, and drew the bow, expert in war, forty-four thousand seven hundred sixty, ready for service. ¹⁹They made war on the Hagrites, Jetur, Naphish, and Nodab; ²⁰and when they received help against them, the Hagrites and all who were with them were given into their hands, for they cried to God in the battle, and he granted their entreaty because they trusted in him. ²¹They captured their livestock: fifty thousand of their camels, two hundred fifty thousand sheep, two thousand donkeys, and one hundred thousand captives. ²²Many fell slain, because the war was of God. And they lived in their territory until the exile.

The Half-Tribe of Manasseh

23 The members of the half-tribe of Manasseh lived in the land; they were very numerous from Bashan to Baal-hermon, Senir, and Mount Hermon. ²⁴These were the heads of their clans: Epher,ᵃ Ishi, Eliel, Azriel, Jeremiah, Hodaviah, and Jahdiel, mighty warriors, famous men, heads of their clans. ²⁵But they transgressed

against the God of their ancestors, and prostituted themselves to the gods of the peoples of the land, whom God had destroyed before them. ²⁶So the God of Israel stirred up the spirit of King Pul of Assyria, the spirit of King Tilgath-pilneser of Assyria, and he carried them away, namely, the Reubenites, the Gadites, and the half-tribe of Manasseh, and brought them to Halah, Habor, Hara, and the river Gozan, to this day.

Descendants of Levi

6 ᵇ The sons of Levi: Gershom,ᶜ Kohath, and Merari. ²The sons of Kohath: Amram, Izhar, Hebron, and Uzziel. ³The children of Amram: Aaron, Moses, and Miriam. The sons of Aaron: Nadab, Abihu, Eleazar, and Ithamar. ⁴Eleazar became the father of Phinehas, Phinehas of Abishua, ⁵Abishua of Bukki, Bukki of Uzzi, ⁶Uzzi of Zerahiah, Zerahiah of Meraioth, ⁷Meraioth of Amariah, Amariah of Ahitub, ⁸Ahitub of Zadok, Zadok of Ahimaaz, ⁹Ahimaaz of Azariah, Azariah of Johanan, ¹⁰and Johanan of Azariah (it was he who served as priest in the house that Solomon built in Jerusalem). ¹¹Azariah became the father of Amariah, Amariah of Ahitub, ¹²Ahitub of Zadok, Zadok of Shallum, ¹³Shallum of Hilkiah, Hilkiah of Azariah, ¹⁴Azariah of Seraiah, Seraiah of Jehozadak; ¹⁵and Jehozadak went into exile when the LORD sent Judah and Jerusalem into exile by the hand of Nebuchadnezzar.

16ᵈ The sons of Levi: Gershom, Kohath, and Merari. ¹⁷These are the names of the sons of Gershom: Libni and Shimei. ¹⁸The sons of Kohath: Amram, Izhar, Hebron, and Uzziel. ¹⁹The sons of Merari: Mahli and Mushi. These are the clans of the Levites according to their ancestry. ²⁰Of Gershom: Libni his son, Jahath his son, Zimmah his son, ²¹Joah his son, Iddo his son, Zerah his son, Jeatherai his son. ²²The sons of Kohath: Amminadab his son, Korah his son, Assir his son, ²³Elkanah his son, Ebiasaph his son, Assir his son, ²⁴Tahath his son, Uriel his son, Uzziah his son, and Shaul his son. ²⁵The sons of Elkanah: Amasai and Ahimoth, ²⁶Elkanah his son, Zophai his son, Nahath his son, ²⁷Eliab his son, Jeroham his son, Elkanah his son. ²⁸The sons of Samuel: Joelᵉ his firstborn, the second Abijah.ᶠ ²⁹The sons of Merari: Mahli, Libni his son, Shimei his son, Uzzah his son, ³⁰Shimea his son, Haggiah his son, and Asaiah his son.

a Gk Vg: Heb and Epher   b Ch 5.27 in Heb   c Heb Gershon, variant of Gershom; See 6.16   d Ch 6.1 in Heb   e Gk Syr Compare verse 33 and 1 Sam 8.2: Heb lacks Joel   f Heb reads Vashni, and Abijah for the second Abijah, taking the second as a proper name

Musicians Appointed by David

31 These are the men whom David put in charge of the service of song in the house of the LORD, after the ark came to rest there. ³²They ministered with song before the tabernacle of the tent of meeting, until Solomon had built the house of the LORD in Jerusalem; and they performed their service in due order. ³³These are the men who served; and their sons were: Of the Kohathites: Heman, the singer, son of Joel, son of Samuel, ³⁴son of Elkanah, son of Jeroham, son of Eliel, son of Toah, ³⁵son of Zuph, son of Elkanah, son of Mahath, son of Amasai, ³⁶son of Elkanah, son of Joel, son of Azariah, son of Zephaniah, ³⁷son of Tahath, son of Assir, son of Ebiasaph, son of Korah, ³⁸son of Izhar, son of Kohath, son of Levi, son of Israel; ³⁹and his brother Asaph, who stood on his right, namely, Asaph son of Berechiah, son of Shimea, ⁴⁰son of Michael, son of Baaseiah, son of Malchijah, ⁴¹son of Ethni, son of Zerah, son of Adaiah, ⁴²son of Ethan, son of Zimmah, son of Shimei, ⁴³son of Jahath, son of Gershom, son of Levi. ⁴⁴On the left were their kindred the sons of Merari: Ethan son of Kishi, son of Abdi, son of Malluch, ⁴⁵son of Hashabiah, son of Amaziah, son of Hilkiah, ⁴⁶son of Amzi, son of Bani, son of Shemer, ⁴⁷son of Mahli, son of Mushi, son of Merari, son of Levi; ⁴⁸and their kindred the Levites were appointed for all the service of the tabernacle of the house of God.

49 But Aaron and his sons made offerings on the altar of burnt offering and on the altar of incense, doing all the work of the most holy place, to make atonement for Israel, according to all that Moses the servant of God had commanded. ⁵⁰These are the sons of Aaron: Eleazar his son, Phinehas his son, Abishua his son, ⁵¹Bukki his son, Uzzi his son, Zerahiah his son, ⁵²Meraioth his son, Amariah his son, Ahitub his son, ⁵³Zadok his son, Ahimaaz his son.

Settlements of the Levites

54 These are their dwelling places according to their settlements within their borders: to the sons of Aaron of the families of Kohathites—for the lot fell to them first— ⁵⁵to them they gave Hebron in the land of Judah and its surrounding pasture lands, ⁵⁶but the fields of the city and its villages they gave to Caleb son of Jephunneh. ⁵⁷To the sons of Aaron they gave the cities of refuge: Hebron, Libnah with its pasture lands, Jattir, Eshtemoa with its pasture lands, ⁵⁸Hilen*a* with its pasture lands, Debir with its pasture lands, ⁵⁹Ashan with its pasture lands, and Beth-shemesh with its pasture lands. ⁶⁰From the tribe of Benjamin, Geba with its pasture lands, Alemeth with its pasture lands, and Anathoth with its pasture lands. All their towns throughout their families were thirteen.

61 To the rest of the Kohathites were given by lot out of the family of the tribe, out of the half-tribe, the half of Manasseh, ten towns. ⁶²To the Gershomites according to their families were allotted thirteen towns out of the tribes of Issachar, Asher, Naphtali, and Manasseh in Bashan. ⁶³To the Merarites according to their families were allotted twelve towns out of the tribes of Reuben, Gad, and Zebulun. ⁶⁴So the people of Israel gave the Levites the towns with their pasture lands. ⁶⁵They also gave them by lot out of the tribes of Judah, Simeon, and Benjamin these towns that are mentioned by name.

66 And some of the families of the sons of Kohath had towns of their territory out of the tribe of Ephraim. ⁶⁷They were given the cities of refuge: Shechem with its pasture lands in the hill country of Ephraim, Gezer with its pasture lands, ⁶⁸Jokmeam with its pasture lands, Beth-horon with its pasture lands, ⁶⁹Aijalon with its pasture lands, Gath-rimmon with its pasture lands; ⁷⁰and out of the half-tribe of Manasseh, Aner with its pasture lands, and Bileam with its pasture lands, for the rest of the families of the Kohathites.

71 To the Gershomites: out of the half-tribe of Manasseh: Golan in Bashan with its pasture lands and Ashtaroth with its pasture lands; ⁷²and out of the tribe of Issachar: Kedesh with its pasture lands, Daberath*b* with its pasture lands, ⁷³Ramoth with its pasture lands, and Anem with its pasture lands; ⁷⁴out of the tribe of Asher: Mashal with its pasture lands, Abdon with its pasture lands, ⁷⁵Hukok with its pasture lands, and Rehob with its pasture lands; ⁷⁶and out of the tribe of Naphtali: Kedesh in Galilee with its pasture lands, Hammon with its pasture lands, and Kiriathaim with its pasture lands. ⁷⁷To the rest of the Merarites out of the tribe of Zebulun: Rimmono with its pasture lands, Tabor with its pasture lands, ⁷⁸and across the Jordan from Jericho, on the east side of the Jordan, out of the tribe of Reuben: Bezer in the steppe with its pasture lands, Jahzah with its pasture lands, ⁷⁹Kedemoth with its pasture lands, and Mephaath with its pasture lands; ⁸⁰and out of the tribe of Gad: Ramoth in Gilead with its pasture lands, Mahanaim with its pasture lands, ⁸¹Heshbon with its pasture lands, and Jazer with its pasture lands.

a Other readings *Hilez, Holon;* See Josh 21.15   b Or *Dobrath*

Descendants of Issachar

7 The sons[a] of Issachar: Tola, Puah, Jashub, and Shimron, four. [2]The sons of Tola: Uzzi, Rephaiah, Jeriel, Jahmai, Ibsam, and Shemuel, heads of their ancestral houses, namely of Tola, mighty warriors of their generations, their number in the days of David being twenty-two thousand six hundred. [3]The son[b] of Uzzi: Izrahiah. And the sons of Izrahiah: Michael, Obadiah, Joel, and Isshiah, five, all of them chiefs; [4]and along with them, by their generations, according to their ancestral houses, were units of the fighting force, thirty-six thousand, for they had many wives and sons. [5]Their kindred belonging to all the families of Issachar were in all eighty-seven thousand mighty warriors, enrolled by genealogy.

Descendants of Benjamin

6 The sons of Benjamin: Bela, Becher, and Jediael, three. [7]The sons of Bela: Ezbon, Uzzi, Uzziel, Jerimoth, and Iri, five, heads of ancestral houses, mighty warriors; and their enrollment by genealogies was twenty-two thousand thirty-four. [8]The sons of Becher: Zemirah, Joash, Eliezer, Elioenai, Omri, Jeremoth, Abijah, Anathoth, and Alemeth. All these were the sons of Becher; [9]and their enrollment by genealogies, according to their generations, as heads of their ancestral houses, mighty warriors, was twenty thousand two hundred. [10]The sons of Jediael: Bilhan. And the sons of Bilhan: Jeush, Benjamin, Ehud, Chenaanah, Zethan, Tarshish, and Ahishahar. [11]All these were the sons of Jediael according to the heads of their ancestral houses, mighty warriors, seventeen thousand two hundred, ready for service in war. [12]And Shuppim and Huppim were the sons of Ir, Hushim the son[b] of Aher.

Descendants of Naphtali

13 The descendants of Naphtali: Jahziel, Guni, Jezer, and Shallum, the descendants of Bilhah.

Descendants of Manasseh

14 The sons of Manasseh: Asriel, whom his Aramean concubine bore; she bore Machir the father of Gilead. [15]And Machir took a wife for Huppim and for Shuppim. The name of his sister was Maacah. And the name of the second was Zelophehad; and Zelophehad had daughters. [16]Maacah the wife of Machir bore a son, and she named him Peresh; the name of his brother was Sheresh; and his sons were Ulam and Rekem. [17]The son[b] of Ulam: Bedan. These were the sons of Gilead son of Machir, son of Manasseh. [18]And his sister Hammolecheth bore Ishhod, Abiezer, and Mahlah. [19]The sons of Shemida were Ahian, Shechem, Likhi, and Aniam.

Descendants of Ephraim

20 The sons of Ephraim: Shuthelah, and Bered his son, Tahath his son, Eleadah his son, Tahath his son, [21]Zabad his son, Shuthelah his son, and Ezer and Elead. Now the people of Gath, who were born in the land, killed them, because they came down to raid their cattle. [22]And their father Ephraim mourned many days, and his brothers came to comfort him. [23]Ephraim[c] went in to his wife, and she conceived and bore a son; and he named him Beriah, because disaster[d] had befallen his house. [24]His daughter was Sheerah, who built both Lower and Upper Beth-horon, and Uzzen-sheerah. [25]Rephah was his son, Resheph his son, Telah his son, Tahan his son, [26]Ladan his son, Ammihud his son, Elishama his son, [27]Nun[e] his son, Joshua his son. [28]Their possessions and settlements were Bethel and its towns, and eastward Naaran, and westward Gezer and its towns, Shechem and its towns, as far as Ayyah and its towns; [29]also along the borders of the Manassites, Beth-shean and its towns, Taanach and its towns, Megiddo and its towns, Dor and its towns. In these lived the sons of Joseph son of Israel.

Descendants of Asher

30 The sons of Asher: Imnah, Ishvah, Ishvi, Beriah, and their sister Serah. [31]The sons of Beriah: Heber and Malchiel, who was the father of Birzaith. [32]Heber became the father of Japhlet, Shomer, Hotham, and their sister Shua. [33]The sons of Japhlet: Pasach, Bimhal, and Ashvath. These are the sons of Japhlet. [34]The sons of Shemer: Ahi, Rohgah, Hubbah, and Aram. [35]The sons of Helem[f] his brother: Zophah, Imna, Shelesh, and Amal. [36]The sons of Zophah: Suah, Harnepher, Shual, Beri, Imrah, [37]Bezer, Hod, Shamma, Shilshah, Ithran, and Beera. [38]The sons of Jether: Jephunneh, Pispa, and Ara. [39]The sons of Ulla: Arah, Hanniel, and Rizia. [40]All of these were men of Asher, heads of ancestral houses, select mighty warriors, chief of the princes. Their number enrolled by genealogies, for service in war, was twenty-six thousand men.

Descendants of Benjamin

8 Benjamin became the father of Bela his first-born, Ashbel the second, Aharah the third, [2]Nohah the fourth, and Rapha the fifth. [3]And

---

a Syr Compare Vg: Heb *And to the sons*   b Heb *sons*
c Heb *He*   d Heb *beraah*   e Here spelled *Non*; see Ex 33.11
f. Or *Hotham*; see 7.32

Bela had sons: Addar, Gera, Abihud,[a] [4]Abishua, Naaman, Ahoah, [5]Gera, Shephuphan, and Huram. [6]These are the sons of Ehud (they were heads of ancestral houses of the inhabitants of Geba, and they were carried into exile to Manahath): [7]Naaman,[b] Ahijah, and Gera, that is, Heglam,[c] who became the father of Uzza and Ahihud. [8]And Shaharaim had sons in the country of Moab after he had sent away his wives Hushim and Baara. [9]He had sons by his wife Hodesh: Jobab, Zibia, Mesha, Malcam, [10]Jeuz, Sachia, and Mirmah. These were his sons, heads of ancestral houses. [11]He also had sons by Hushim: Abitub and Elpaal. [12]The sons of Elpaal: Eber, Misham, and Shemed, who built Ono and Lod with its towns, [13]and Beriah and Shema (they were heads of ancestral houses of the inhabitants of Aijalon, who put to flight the inhabitants of Gath); [14]and Ahio, Shashak, and Jeremoth. [15]Zebadiah, Arad, Eder, [16]Michael, Ishpah, and Joha were sons of Beriah. [17]Zebadiah, Meshullam, Hizki, Heber, [18]Ishmerai, Izliah, and Jobab were the sons of Elpaal. [19]Jakim, Zichri, Zabdi, [20]Elienai, Zillethai, Eliel, [21]Adaiah, Beraiah, and Shimrath were the sons of Shimei. [22]Ishpan, Eber, Eliel, [23]Abdon, Zichri, Hanan, [24]Hananiah, Elam, Anthothijah, [25]Iphdeiah, and Penuel were the sons of Shashak. [26]Shamsherai, Shehariah, Athaliah, [27]Jaareshiah, Elijah, and Zichri were the sons of Jeroham. [28]These were the heads of ancestral houses, according to their generations, chiefs. These lived in Jerusalem.

[29] Jeiel[d] the father of Gibeon lived in Gibeon, and the name of his wife was Maacah. [30]His firstborn son: Abdon, then Zur, Kish, Baal,[e] Nadab, [31]Gedor, Ahio, Zecher, [32]and Mikloth, who became the father of Shimeah. Now these also lived opposite their kindred in Jerusalem, with their kindred. [33]Ner became the father of Kish, Kish of Saul,[f] Saul[f] of Jonathan, Malchishua, Abinadab, and Esh-baal; [34]and the son of Jonathan was Merib-baal; and Merib-baal became the father of Micah. [35]The sons of Micah: Pithon, Melech, Tarea, and Ahaz. [36]Ahaz became the father of Jehoaddah; and Jehoaddah became the father of Alemeth, Azmaveth, and Zimri; Zimri became the father of Moza. [37]Moza became the father of Binea; Raphah was his son, Eleasah his son, Azel his son. [38]Azel had six sons, and these are their names: Azrikam, Bocheru, Ishmael, Sheariah, Obadiah, and Hanan; all these were the sons of Azel. [39]The sons of his brother Eshek: Ulam his firstborn, Jeush the second, and Eliphelet the third. [40]The sons of Ulam were mighty warriors, archers, having many children and grandchildren, one hundred fifty. All these were Benjaminites.

[9] So all Israel was enrolled by genealogies; and these are written in the Book of the Kings of Israel. And Judah was taken into exile in Babylon because of their unfaithfulness. [2]Now the first to live again in their possessions in their towns were Israelites, priests, Levites, and temple servants.

Inhabitants of Jerusalem after the Exile

[3] And some of the people of Judah, Benjamin, Ephraim, and Manasseh lived in Jerusalem: [4]Uthai son of Ammihud, son of Omri, son of Imri, son of Bani, from the sons of Perez son of Judah. [5]And of the Shilonites: Asaiah the firstborn, and his sons. [6]Of the sons of Zerah: Jeuel and their kin, six hundred ninety. [7]Of the Benjaminites: Sallu son of Meshullam, son of Hodaviah, son of Hassenuah, [8]Ibneiah son of Jeroham, Elah son of Uzzi, son of Michri, and Meshullam son of Shephatiah, son of Reuel, son of Ibnijah; [9]and their kindred according to their generations, nine hundred fifty-six. All these were heads of families according to their ancestral houses.

Priestly Families

[10] Of the priests: Jedaiah, Jehoiarib, Jachin, [11]and Azariah son of Hilkiah, son of Meshullam, son of Zadok, son of Meraioth, son of Ahitub, the chief officer of the house of God; [12]and Adaiah son of Jeroham, son of Pashhur, son of Malchijah, and Maasai son of Adiel, son of Jahzerah, son of Meshullam, son of Meshillemith, son of Immer; [13]besides their kindred, heads of their ancestral houses, one thousand seven hundred sixty, qualified for the work of the service of the house of God.

Levitical Families

[14] Of the Levites: Shemaiah son of Hasshub, son of Azrikam, son of Hashabiah, of the sons of Merari; [15]and Bakbakkar, Heresh, Galal, and Mattaniah son of Mica, son of Zichri, son of Asaph; [16]and Obadiah son of Shemaiah, son of Galal, son of Jeduthun, and Berechiah son of Asa, son of Elkanah, who lived in the villages of the Netophathites.

[17] The gatekeepers were: Shallum, Akkub, Talmon, Ahiman; and their kindred Shallum was the chief, [18]stationed previously in the king's gate on the east side. These were the gatekeepers of the camp of the Levites. [19]Shallum son of Kore, son of Ebiasaph, son of Korah, and his kindred of his ancestral house, the Korahites, were in charge of

---

a Or father of Ehud; see 8.6   b Heb and Naaman   c Or he carried them into exile   d Compare 9.35: Heb lacks Jeiel   e Gk Ms adds Ner; Compare 8.33 and 9.36   f Or Shaul

the work of the service, guardians of the thresholds of the tent, as their ancestors had been in charge of the camp of the Lord, guardians of the entrance. ²⁰And Phinehas son of Eleazar was chief over them in former times; the Lord was with him. ²¹Zechariah son of Meshelemiah was gatekeeper at the entrance of the tent of meeting. ²²All these, who were chosen as gatekeepers at the thresholds, were two hundred twelve. They were enrolled by genealogies in their villages. David and the seer Samuel established them in their office of trust. ²³So they and their descendants were in charge of the gates of the house of the Lord, that is, the house of the tent, as guards. ²⁴The gatekeepers were on the four sides, east, west, north, and south; ²⁵and their kindred who were in their villages were obliged to come in every seven days, in turn, to be with them; ²⁶for the four chief gatekeepers, who were Levites, were in charge of the chambers and the treasures of the house of God. ²⁷And they would spend the night near the house of God; for on them lay the duty of watching, and they had charge of opening it every morning.

28 Some of them had charge of the utensils of service, for they were required to count them when they were brought in and taken out. ²⁹Others of them were appointed over the furniture, and over all the holy utensils, also over the choice flour, the wine, the oil, the incense, and the spices. ³⁰Others, of the sons of the priests, prepared the mixing of the spices, ³¹and Mattithiah, one of the Levites, the firstborn of Shallum the Korahite, was in charge of making the flat cakes. ³²Also some of their kindred of the Kohathites had charge of the rows of bread, to prepare them for each sabbath.

33 Now these are the singers, the heads of ancestral houses of the Levites, living in the chambers of the temple free from other service, for they were on duty day and night. ³⁴These were heads of ancestral houses of the Levites, according to their generations; these leaders lived in Jerusalem.

The Family of King Saul

35 In Gibeon lived the father of Gibeon, Jeiel, and the name of his wife was Maacah. ³⁶His firstborn son was Abdon, then Zur, Kish, Baal, Ner, Nadab, ³⁷Gedor, Ahio, Zechariah, and Mikloth; ³⁸and Mikloth became the father of Shimeam; and these also lived opposite their kindred in Jerusalem, with their kindred. ³⁹Ner became the father of Kish, Kish of Saul, Saul of Jonathan, Malchishua, Abinadab, and Esh-baal; ⁴⁰and the son of Jonathan was Merib-baal; and Merib-baal became the father of Micah. ⁴¹The sons of Micah: Pithon, Melech, Tahrea, and Ahaz;ᵃ ⁴²and Ahaz became the father of Jarah, and Jarah of Alemeth, Azmaveth, and Zimri; and Zimri became the father of Moza. ⁴³Moza became the father of Binea; and Rephaiah was his son, Eleasah his son, Azel his son. ⁴⁴Azel had six sons, and these are their names: Azrikam, Bocheru, Ishmael, Sheariah, Obadiah, and Hanan; these were the sons of Azel.

Death of Saul and His Sons

10 Now the Philistines fought against Israel; and the men of Israel fled before the Philistines, and fell slain on Mount Gilboa. ²The Philistines overtook Saul and his sons; and the Philistines killed Jonathan and Abinadab and Malchishua, sons of Saul. ³The battle pressed hard on Saul; and the archers found him, and he was wounded by the archers. ⁴Then Saul said to his armor-bearer, "Draw your sword, and thrust me through with it, so that these uncircumcised may not come and make sport of me." But his armor-bearer was unwilling, for he was terrified. So Saul took his own sword and fell on it. ⁵When his armor-bearer saw that Saul was dead, he also fell on his sword and died. ⁶Thus Saul died; he and his three sons and all his house died together. ⁷When all the men of Israel who were in the valley saw that the armyᵇ had fled and that Saul and his sons were dead, they abandoned their towns and fled; and the Philistines came and occupied them.

8 The next day when the Philistines came to strip the dead, they found Saul and his sons fallen on Mount Gilboa. ⁹They stripped him and took his head and his armor, and sent messengers throughout the land of the Philistines to carry the good news to their idols and to the people. ¹⁰They put his armor in the temple of their gods, and fastened his head in the temple of Dagon. ¹¹But when all Jabesh-gilead heard everything that the Philistines had done to Saul, ¹²all the valiant warriors got up and took away the body of Saul and the bodies of his sons, and brought them to Jabesh. Then they buried their bones under the oak in Jabesh, and fasted seven days.

13 So Saul died for his unfaithfulness; he was unfaithful to the Lord in that he did not keep the command of the Lord; moreover, he had consulted a medium, seeking guidance, ¹⁴and did not seek guidance from the Lord. Therefore the Lordᶜ put him to death and turned the kingdom over to David son of Jesse.

---

a Compare 8.35: Heb lacks *and Ahaz*   *b* Heb *they*   *c* Heb *he*

David Anointed King of All Israel

11 Then all Israel gathered together to David at Hebron and said, "See, we are your bone and flesh. ²For some time now, even while Saul was king, it was you who commanded the army of Israel. The LORD your God said to you: It is you who shall be shepherd of my people Israel, you who shall be ruler over my people Israel." ³So all the elders of Israel came to the king at Hebron, and David made a covenant with them at Hebron before the LORD. And they anointed David king over Israel, according to the word of the LORD by Samuel.

Jerusalem Captured

4 David and all Israel marched to Jerusalem, that is Jebus, where the Jebusites were, the inhabitants of the land. ⁵The inhabitants of Jebus said to David, "You will not come in here." Nevertheless David took the stronghold of Zion, now the city of David. ⁶David had said, "Whoever attacks the Jebusites first shall be chief and commander." And Joab son of Zeruiah went up first, so he became chief. ⁷David resided in the stronghold; therefore it was called the city of David. ⁸He built the city all around, from the Millo in complete circuit; and Joab repaired the rest of the city. ⁹And David became greater and greater, for the LORD of hosts was with him.

David's Mighty Men and Their Exploits

10 Now these are the chiefs of David's warriors, who gave him strong support in his kingdom, together with all Israel, to make him king, according to the word of the LORD concerning Israel. ¹¹This is an account of David's mighty warriors: Jashobeam, son of Hachmoni,ᵃ was chief of the Three;ᵇ he wielded his spear against three hundred whom he killed at one time.

12 And next to him among the three warriors was Eleazar son of Dodo, the Ahohite. ¹³He was with David at Pas-dammim when the Philistines were gathered there for battle. There was a plot of ground full of barley. Now the people had fled from the Philistines, ¹⁴but he and David took their stand in the middle of the plot, defended it, and killed the Philistines; and the LORD saved them by a great victory.

15 Three of the thirty chiefs went down to the rock to David at the cave of Adullam, while the army of Philistines was encamped in the valley of Rephaim. ¹⁶David was then in the stronghold; and the garrison of the Philistines was then at Bethlehem. ¹⁷David said longingly, "O that someone would give me water to drink from the well of Bethlehem that is by the gate!" ¹⁸Then the Three broke through the camp of the Philistines, and drew water from the well of Bethlehem that was by the gate, and they brought it to David. But David would not drink of it; he poured it out to the LORD, ¹⁹and said, "My God forbid that I should do this. Can I drink the blood of these men? For at the risk of their lives they brought it." Therefore he would not drink it. The three warriors did these things.

20 Now Abishai,ᶜ the brother of Joab, was chief of the Thirty.ᵈ With his spear he fought against three hundred and killed them, and won a name beside the Three. ²¹He was the most renownedᵉ of the Thirty,ᵈ and became their commander; but he did not attain to the Three.

22 Benaiah son of Jehoiada was a valiant manᶠ of Kabzeel, a doer of great deeds; he struck down two sons ofᵍ Ariel of Moab. He also went down and killed a lion in a pit on a day when snow had fallen. ²³And he killed an Egyptian, a man of great stature, five cubits tall. The Egyptian had in his hand a spear like a weaver's beam; but Benaiah went against him with a staff, snatched the spear out of the Egyptian's hand, and killed him with his own spear. ²⁴Such were the things Benaiah son of Jehoiada did, and he won a name beside the three warriors. ²⁵He was renowned among the Thirty, but he did not attain to the Three. And David put him in charge of his bodyguard.

26 The warriors of the armies were Asahel brother of Joab, Elhanan son of Dodo of Bethlehem, ²⁷Shammoth of Harod,ʰ Helez the Pelonite, ²⁸Ira son of Ikkesh of Tekoa, Abiezer of Anathoth, ²⁹Sibbecai the Hushathite, Ilai the Ahohite, ³⁰Maharai of Netophah, Heled son of Baanah of Netophah, ³¹Ithai son of Ribai of Gibeah of the Benjaminites, Benaiah of Pirathon, ³²Hurai of the wadis of Gaash, Abiel the Arbathite, ³³Azmaveth of Baharum, Eliahba of Shaalbon, ³⁴Hashemⁱ the Gizonite, Jonathan son of Shagee the Hararite, ³⁵Ahiam son of Sachar the Hararite, Eliphal son of Ur, ³⁶Hepher the Mecherathite, Ahijah the Pelonite, ³⁷Hezro of Carmel, Naarai son of Ezbai, ³⁸Joel the brother of Nathan, Mibhar son of Hagri, ³⁹Zelek the Ammonite, Naharai of Beeroth, the armor-bearer of Joab son of Zeruiah, ⁴⁰Ira the Ithrite, Gareb the Ithrite, ⁴¹Uriah the Hittite, Zabad son of

---

a Or a Hachmonite   b Compare 2 Sam 23.8: Heb *Thirty* or *captains*   c Gk Vg Tg Compare 2 Sam 23.18: Heb *Abishai*   d Syr: Heb *Three*   e Compare 2 Sam 23.19: Heb *more renowned among the two*   f Syr: Heb *the son of a valiant man*   g See 2 Sam 23.20: Heb lacks *sons of*   h Compare 2 Sam 23.25: Heb *the Harorite*   i Compare Gk and 2 Sam 23.32: Heb *the sons of Hashem*

Ahlai, ⁴²Adina son of Shiza the Reubenite, a leader of the Reubenites, and thirty with him, ⁴³Hanan son of Maacah, and Joshaphat the Mithnite, ⁴⁴Uzzia the Ashterathite, Shama and Jeiel sons of Hotham the Aroerite, ⁴⁵Jediael son of Shimri, and his brother Joha the Tizite, ⁴⁶Eliel the Mahavite, and Jeribai and Joshaviah sons of Elnaam, and Ithmah the Moabite, ⁴⁷Eliel, and Obed, and Jaasiel the Mezobaite.

David's Followers in the Wilderness

12 The following are those who came to David at Ziklag, while he could not move about freely because of Saul son of Kish; they were among the mighty warriors who helped him in war. ²They were archers, and could shoot arrows and sling stones with either the right hand or the left; they were Benjaminites, Saul's kindred. ³The chief was Ahiezer, then Joash, both sons of Shemaah of Gibeah; also Jeziel and Pelet sons of Azmaveth; Beracah, Jehu of Anathoth, ⁴Ishmaiah of Gibeon, a warrior among the Thirty and a leader over the Thirty; Jeremiah,^a Jahaziel, Johanan, Jozabad of Gederah, ⁵Eluzai,^b Jerimoth, Bealiah, Shemariah, Shephatiah the Haruphite; ⁶Elkanah, Isshiah, Azarel, Joezer, and Jashobeam, the Korahites; ⁷and Joelah and Zebadiah, sons of Jeroham of Gedor.

8 From the Gadites there went over to David at the stronghold in the wilderness mighty and experienced warriors, expert with shield and spear, whose faces were like the faces of lions, and who were swift as gazelles on the mountains: ⁹Ezer the chief, Obadiah second, Eliab third, ¹⁰Mishmannah fourth, Jeremiah fifth, ¹¹Attai sixth, Eliel seventh, ¹²Johanan eighth, Elzabad ninth, ¹³Jeremiah tenth, Machbannai eleventh. ¹⁴These Gadites were officers of the army, the least equal to a hundred and the greatest to a thousand. ¹⁵These are the men who crossed the Jordan in the first month, when it was overflowing all its banks, and put to flight all those in the valleys, to the east and to the west.

16 Some Benjaminites and Judahites came to the stronghold to David. ¹⁷David went out to meet them and said to them, "If you have come to me in friendship, to help me, then my heart will be knit to you; but if you have come to betray me to my adversaries, though my hands have done no wrong, then may the God of our ancestors see and give judgment." ¹⁸Then the spirit came upon Amasai, chief of the Thirty, and he said,

"We are yours, O David;
and with you, O son of Jesse!

Peace, peace to you,
and peace to the one who helps you!
For your God is the one who helps you."

Then David received them, and made them officers of his troops.

19 Some of the Manassites deserted to David when he came with the Philistines for the battle against Saul. (Yet he did not help them, for the rulers of the Philistines took counsel and sent him away, saying, "He will desert to his master Saul at the cost of our heads.") ²⁰As he went to Ziklag these Manassites deserted to him: Adnah, Jozabad, Jediael, Michael, Jozabad, Elihu, and Zillethai, chiefs of the thousands in Manasseh. ²¹They helped David against the band of raiders,^c for they were all warriors and commanders in the army. ²²Indeed from day to day people kept coming to David to help him, until there was a great army, like an army of God.

David's Army at Hebron

23 These are the numbers of the divisions of the armed troops who came to David in Hebron to turn the kingdom of Saul over to him, according to the word of the LORD. ²⁴The people of Judah bearing shield and spear numbered six thousand eight hundred armed troops. ²⁵Of the Simeonites, mighty warriors, seven thousand one hundred. ²⁶Of the Levites four thousand six hundred. ²⁷Jehoiada, leader of the house of Aaron, and with him three thousand seven hundred. ²⁸Zadok, a young warrior, and twenty-two commanders from his own ancestral house. ²⁹Of the Benjaminites, the kindred of Saul, three thousand, of whom the majority had continued to keep their allegiance to the house of Saul. ³⁰Of the Ephraimites, twenty thousand eight hundred, mighty warriors, notables in their ancestral houses. ³¹Of the half-tribe of Manasseh, eighteen thousand, who were expressly named to come and make David king. ³²Of Issachar, those who had understanding of the times, to know what Israel ought to do, two hundred chiefs, and all their kindred under their command. ³³Of Zebulun, fifty thousand seasoned troops, equipped for battle with all the weapons of war, to help David^d with singleness of purpose. ³⁴Of Naphtali, a thousand commanders, with whom there were thirty-seven thousand armed with shield and spear. ³⁵Of the Danites, twenty-eight thousand six hundred equipped for battle. ³⁶Of Asher, forty thousand seasoned troops ready for battle. ³⁷Of the Reubenites and Gadites and

a Heb verse 5   b Heb verse 6   c Or as officers of his troops
d Gk: Heb lacks David

the half-tribe of Manasseh from beyond the Jordan, one hundred twenty thousand armed with all the weapons of war.

38 All these, warriors arrayed in battle order, came to Hebron with full intent to make David king over all Israel; likewise all the rest of Israel were of a single mind to make David king. ³⁹They were there with David for three days, eating and drinking, for their kindred had provided for them. ⁴⁰And also their neighbors, from as far away as Issachar and Zebulun and Naphtali, came bringing food on donkeys, camels, mules, and oxen—abundant provisions of meal, cakes of figs, clusters of raisins, wine, oil, oxen, and sheep, for there was joy in Israel.

The Ark Brought from Kiriath-jearim

13 David consulted with the commanders of the thousands and of the hundreds, with every leader. ²David said to the whole assembly

Chapters 14–15

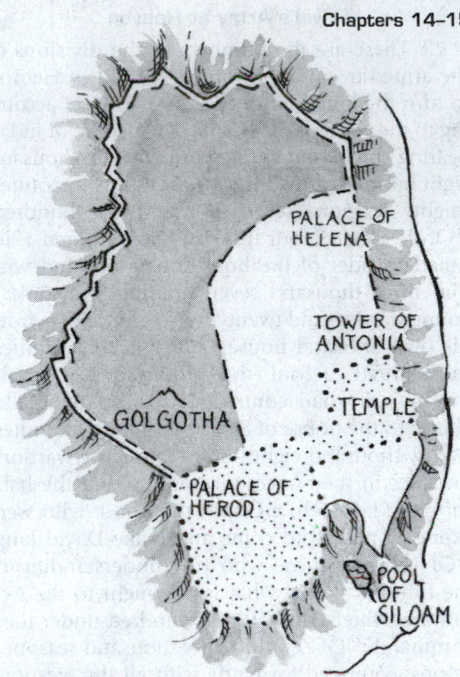

····· FIRST WALL, CITY OF DAVID AND SOLOMON

─ ─ ─ SECOND WALL BUILT BY JOTHAM HEZEKIAH AND MANASSEH

═══ THIRD WALL BUILT BY HEROD AGRIPPA

of Israel, "If it seems good to you, and if it is the will of the LORD our God, let us send abroad to our kindred who remain in all the land of Israel, including the priests and Levites in the cities that have pasture lands, that they may come together to us. ³Then let us bring again the ark of our God to us; for we did not turn to it in the days of Saul." ⁴The whole assembly agreed to do so, for the thing pleased all the people.

5 So David assembled all Israel from the Shihor of Egypt to Lebo-hamath, to bring the ark of God from Kiriath-jearim. ⁶And David and all Israel went up to Baalah, that is, to Kiriath-jearim, which belongs to Judah, to bring up from there the ark of God, the LORD, who is enthroned on the cherubim, which is called by his^a name. ⁷They carried the ark of God on a new cart, from the house of Abinadab, and Uzzah and Ahio^b were driving the cart. ⁸David and all Israel were dancing before God with all their might, with song and lyres and harps and tambourines and cymbals and trumpets.

9 When they came to the threshing floor of Chidon, Uzzah put out his hand to hold the ark, for the oxen shook it. ¹⁰The anger of the LORD was kindled against Uzzah; he struck him down because he put out his hand to the ark; and he died there before God. ¹¹David was angry because the LORD had burst out against Uzzah; so that place is called Perez-uzzah^c to this day. ¹²David was afraid of God that day; he said, "How can I bring the ark of God into my care?" ¹³So David did not take the ark into his care into the city of David; he took it instead to the house of Obed-edom the Gittite. ¹⁴The ark of God remained with the household of Obed-edom in his house three months, and the LORD blessed the household of Obed-edom and all that he had.

David Established at Jerusalem

14 King Hiram of Tyre sent messengers to David, along with cedar logs, and masons and carpenters to build a house for him. ²David then perceived that the LORD had established him as king over Israel, and that his kingdom was highly exalted for the sake of his people Israel.

3 David took more wives in Jerusalem, and David became the father of more sons and daughters. ⁴These are the names of the children whom he had in Jerusalem: Shammua, Shobab, and Nathan; Solomon, ⁵Ibhar, Elishua, and Elpelet; ⁶Nogah, Nepheg, and Japhia; ⁷Elishama, Beeliada, and Eliphelet.

---

a Heb lacks *his*   b Or *and his brother*   c That is *Bursting Out Against Uzzah*

Defeat of the Philistines

8 When the Philistines heard that David had been anointed king over all Israel, all the Philistines went up in search of David; and David heard of it and went out against them. 9Now the Philistines had come and made a raid in the valley of Rephaim. 10David inquired of God, "Shall I go up against the Philistines? Will you give them into my hand?" The LORD said to him, "Go up, and I will give them into your hand." 11So he went up to Baal-perazim, and David defeated them there. David said, "God has burst out*a* against my enemies by my hand, like a bursting flood." Therefore that place is called Baal-perazim.*b* 12They abandoned their gods there, and at David's command they were burned.

13 Once again the Philistines made a raid in the valley. 14When David again inquired of God, God said to him, "You shall not go up after them; go around and come on them opposite the balsam trees. 15When you hear the sound of marching in the tops of the balsam trees, then go out to battle; for God has gone out before you to strike down the army of the Philistines." 16David did as God had commanded him, and they struck down the Philistine army from Gibeon to Gezer. 17The fame of David went out into all lands, and the LORD brought the fear of him on all nations.

The Ark Brought to Jerusalem

15 David*c* built houses for himself in the city of David, and he prepared a place for the ark of God and pitched a tent for it. 2Then David commanded that no one but the Levites were to carry the ark of God, for the LORD had chosen them to carry the ark of the LORD and to minister to him forever. 3David assembled all Israel in Jerusalem to bring up the ark of the LORD to its place, which he had prepared for it. 4Then David gathered together the descendants of Aaron and the Levites: 5of the sons of Kohath, Uriel the chief, with one hundred twenty of his kindred; 6of the sons of Merari, Asaiah the chief, with two hundred twenty of his kindred; 7of the sons of Gershom, Joel the chief, with one hundred thirty of his kindred; 8of the sons of Elizaphan, Shemaiah the chief, with two hundred of his kindred; 9of the sons of Hebron, Eliel the chief, with eighty of his kindred; 10of the sons of Uzziel, Amminadab the chief, with one hundred twelve of his kindred.

11 David summoned the priests Zadok and Abiathar, and the Levites Uriel, Asaiah, Joel, Shemaiah, Eliel, and Amminadab. 12He said to them, "You are the heads of families of the Levites; sanctify yourselves, you and your kindred, so that you may bring up the ark of the LORD, the God of Israel, to the place that I have prepared for it. 13Because you did not carry it the first time,*d* the LORD our God burst out against us, because we did not give it proper care." 14So the priests and the Levites sanctified themselves to bring up the ark of the LORD, the God of Israel. 15And the Levites carried the ark of God on their shoulders with the poles, as Moses had commanded according to the word of the LORD.

16 David also commanded the chiefs of the Levites to appoint their kindred as the singers to play on musical instruments, on harps and lyres and cymbals, to raise loud sounds of joy. 17So the Levites appointed Heman son of Joel; and of his kindred Asaph son of Berechiah; and of the sons of Merari, their kindred, Ethan son of Kushaiah; 18and with them their kindred of the second order, Zechariah, Jaaziel, Shemiramoth, Jehiel, Unni, Eliab, Benaiah, Maaseiah, Mattithiah, Eliphelehu, and Mikneiah, and the gatekeepers Obed-edom and Jeiel. 19The singers Heman, Asaph, and Ethan were to sound bronze cymbals; 20Zechariah, Aziel, Shemiramoth, Jehiel, Unni, Eliab, Maaseiah, and Benaiah were to play harps according to Alamoth; 21but Mattithiah, Eliphelehu, Mikneiah, Obed-edom, Jeiel, and Azaziah were to lead with lyres according to the Sheminith. 22Chenaniah, leader of the Levites in music, was to direct the music, for he understood it. 23Berechiah and Elkanah were to be gatekeepers for the ark. 24Shebaniah, Joshaphat, Nethanel, Amasai, Zechariah, Benaiah, and Eliezer, the priests, were to blow the trumpets before the ark of God. Obed-edom and Jehiah also were to be gatekeepers for the ark.

25 So David and the elders of Israel, and the commanders of the thousands, went to bring up the ark of the covenant of the LORD from the house of Obed-edom with rejoicing. 26And because God helped the Levites who were carrying the ark of the covenant of the LORD, they sacrificed seven bulls and seven rams. 27David was clothed with a robe of fine linen, as also were all the Levites who were carrying the ark, and the singers, and Chenaniah the leader of the music of the singers; and David wore a linen ephod. 28So all Israel brought up the ark of the covenant of the LORD with shouting, to the sound of the horn, trumpets, and cymbals, and made loud music on harps and lyres.

---

a Heb *paraz*   *b* That is *Lord of Bursting Out*   *c* Heb *He*
d Meaning of Heb uncertain

1 CHR

29 As the ark of the covenant of the LORD came to the city of David, Michal daughter of Saul looked out of the window, and saw King David leaping and dancing; and she despised him in her heart.

The Ark Placed in the Tent

16 They brought in the ark of God, and set it inside the tent that David had pitched for it; and they offered burnt offerings and offerings of well-being before God. ²When David had finished offering the burnt offerings and the offerings of well-being, he blessed the people in the name of the LORD; ³and he distributed to every person in Israel—man and woman alike—to each a loaf of bread, a portion of meat,ᵃ and a cake of raisins.

4 He appointed certain of the Levites as ministers before the ark of the LORD, to invoke, to thank, and to praise the LORD, the God of Israel. ⁵Asaph was the chief, and second to him Zechariah, Jeiel, Shemiramoth, Jehiel, Mattithiah, Eliab, Benaiah, Obed-edom, and Jeiel, with harps and lyres; Asaph was to sound the cymbals, ⁶and the priests Benaiah and Jahaziel were to blow trumpets regularly, before the ark of the covenant of God.

David's Psalm of Thanksgiving

7 Then on that day David first appointed the singing of praises to the LORD by Asaph and his kindred.

8 O give thanks to the LORD, call on his name,
   make known his deeds among the peoples.
9 Sing to him, sing praises to him,
   tell of all his wonderful works.
10 Glory in his holy name;
   let the hearts of those who seek the LORD
      rejoice.
11 Seek the LORD and his strength,
   seek his presence continually.
12 Remember the wonderful works he has done,
   his miracles, and the judgments he uttered,
13 O offspring of his servant Israel,ᵇ
   children of Jacob, his chosen ones.

14 He is the LORD our God;
   his judgments are in all the earth.
15 Remember his covenant forever,
   the word that he commanded, for a thousand
      generations,
16 the covenant that he made with Abraham,

his sworn promise to Isaac,
17 which he confirmed to Jacob as a statute,
   to Israel as an everlasting covenant,
18 saying, "To you I will give the land of Canaan
   as your portion for an inheritance."
19 When they were few in number,
   of little account, and strangers in the land,ᶜ
20 wandering from nation to nation,
   from one kingdom to another people,
21 he allowed no one to oppress them;
   he rebuked kings on their account,
22 saying, "Do not touch my anointed ones;
   do my prophets no harm."

23 Sing to the LORD, all the
      earth.
   Tell of his salvation from
      day to day.
24 Declare his glory among the
      nations,
   his marvelous works
      among all the peoples.
25 For great is the LORD, and
      greatly to be praised;
he is to be revered above all gods.
26 For all the gods of the peoples are idols,
   but the LORD made the heavens.
27 Honor and majesty are before him;
   strength and joy are in his place.

28 Ascribe to the LORD, O families of the peoples,
   ascribe to the LORD glory and strength.
29 Ascribe to the LORD the glory due his name;
   bring an offering, and come before him.
   Worship the LORD in holy splendor;
30   tremble before him, all the earth.
   The world is firmly established; it shall never
      be moved.
31 Let the heavens be glad, and let the earth
      rejoice,
   and let them say among the nations, "The
      LORD is king!"
32 Let the sea roar, and all that fills it;
   let the field exult, and everything in it.
33 Then shall the trees of the forest sing for joy
   before the LORD, for he comes to judge the
      earth.
34 O give thanks to the LORD, for he is good;
   for his steadfast love endures forever.

35 Say also:
   "Save us, O God of our salvation,

> Give thanks to the LORD,
> call on his name,
> make known his deeds
> among the peoples.
>
> (1 Chr 16:8)

---

a Compare Gk Syr Vg: Meaning of Heb uncertain   b Another reading is *Abraham* (compare Ps 105.6)   c Heb *in it*

✝ Catholic Connection

Types of Prayer

Think of all the time you spend during the week e-mailing, texting, or talking on the phone with your friends. What would happen to your friendship if one of you consistently failed to respond to the other? The relationship most likely would not last long. In order to maintain relationships, both parties need to communicate with one another. Our relationship with God also relies on good communication. In 1 Chronicles 16:37–42, we read how King David wanted to help the Israelites stay close to God, so he established regular times and forms of prayer to remind the Israelites of God's presence and their identity as God's people.

Our need to be close to God through prayer is just as important today as it was for King David. For when we pray, we open our heart and enter into conversation with God. You can use the events of your day as a guide to help you open those lines of communication. Here are some suggestions:

- Feeling blessed? Offer prayers of **blessings and adoration** in response to all the ways you have been blessed by God's immeasurable goodness and greatness.
- Have a need? Offer a **prayer of petition** by simply asking God for whatever is needed, acknowledging your dependency on God and trusting in God's goodness.

- Have a friend in need? Offer a **prayer of intercession** asking God for help on his or her behalf.
- Feeling thankful? Offer a **prayer of thanksgiving** for God's mercy and love. Join in the ultimate prayer of thanksgiving by participating in the Church's celebration of the Eucharist.
- Feeling in awe of God? Offer a **prayer of praise** and acknowledge God, not for what God has done for you, but for simply being God.

No matter what form of prayer we use, there are different ways we can express it. We can put the desires of our heart into words, whether spoken aloud or interiorly, in **vocal prayer**. We can reflect on the Scriptures, or other spiritual writings, and listen to what God is saying to us through them in **meditative prayer**. Finally, we can pray deep in our heart by focusing on Jesus in **contemplative prayer**, which enables us to simply be present with Christ whom we love and who loves us.

Setting aside a regular time for prayer each day is essential if you hope to maintain your relationship with God. It will help you remember that God is always present and that you are a disciple of Christ.

▶ **1 Chr 16:37–42**

Catechism, nos. 2623–2649, 2697–2758

and gather and rescue us from among the
  nations,
that we may give thanks to your holy name,
  and glory in your praise.
36 Blessed be the LORD, the God of Israel,
  from everlasting to everlasting."
Then all the people said "Amen!" and praised
the LORD.

Regular Worship Maintained

37 David left Asaph and his kinsfolk there
before the ark of the covenant of the LORD to
minister regularly before the ark as each day
required, 38and also Obed-edom and his*a* sixty-
eight kinsfolk; while Obed-edom son of Jeduthun and Hosah were to be gatekeepers. 39And

1
CHR

Where Do We Place God?

How the world loves boxes and containers
and compartments! Remember the old
saying, "A place for everything and everything
in its place"? There is something comforting in
knowing that everything is where it should be.

Don't we often try to put God away in a special place? Isn't it more convenient to think of
God as residing "up there" in the tabernacle or
sanctuary? Perhaps that is why, in 1 Chronicles
17:4–6, God seems less than enthusiastic about
David's desire to build a temple. The danger is
clear: identify God with a building, however grand
and beautiful, and in people's minds, God *stays*
there.

When we enter a chapel or a church, we become reverent, sensing that we are in the presence of God. And, indeed, we are. But we need
to remember that we do not leave God behind
when we step out of that structure. Simply put,
God cannot and will not be confined, despite our
best efforts.

Our God walks with us. God's place is everywhere.
● How can you practice living in the constant
  presence of God?

▶ 1 Chr 17:1–15

he left the priest Zadok and his kindred the
priests before the tabernacle of the LORD in the
high place that was at Gibeon, 40to offer burnt
offerings to the LORD on the altar of burnt offering regularly, morning and evening, according
to all that is written in the law of the LORD that
he commanded Israel. 41With them were Heman
and Jeduthun, and the rest of those chosen and
expressly named to render thanks to the LORD,
for his steadfast love endures forever. 42Heman
and Jeduthun had with them trumpets and cymbals for the music, and instruments for sacred
song. The sons of Jeduthun were appointed to
the gate.

43 Then all the people departed to their
homes, and David went home to bless his household.

God's Covenant with David

17 Now when David settled in his house,
David said to the prophet Nathan, "I am
living in a house of cedar, but the ark of the covenant of the LORD is under a tent." 2Nathan said
to David, "Do all that you have in mind, for God
is with you."

3 But that same night the word of the LORD
came to Nathan, saying: 4Go and tell my servant
David: Thus says the LORD: You shall not build me
a house to live in. 5For I have not lived in a house
since the day I brought out Israel to this very
day, but I have lived in a tent and a tabernacle.*b*
6Wherever I have moved about among all Israel,
did I ever speak a word with any of the judges of
Israel, whom I commanded to shepherd my people, saying, Why have you not built me a house
of cedar? 7Now therefore thus you shall say to
my servant David: Thus says the LORD of hosts:
I took you from the pasture, from following the
sheep, to be ruler over my people Israel; 8and I
have been with you wherever you went, and have
cut off all your enemies before you; and I will
make for you a name, like the name of the great
ones of the earth. 9I will appoint a place for my
people Israel, and will plant them, so that they
may live in their own place, and be disturbed no
more; and evildoers shall wear them down no
more, as they did formerly, 10from the time that
I appointed judges over my people Israel; and I
will subdue all your enemies.

Moreover I declare to you that the LORD will
build you a house. 11When your days are fulfilled
to go to be with your ancestors, I will raise up your
offspring after you, one of your own sons, and I

a Gk Syr Vg: Heb *their*   b Gk 2 Sam 7.6: Heb *but I have been
from tent to tent and from tabernacle*

will establish his kingdom. [12]He shall build a house for me, and I will establish his throne forever. [13]I will be a father to him, and he shall be a son to me. I will not take my steadfast love from him, as I took it from him who was before you, [14]but I will confirm him in my house and in my kingdom forever, and his throne shall be established forever. [15]In accordance with all these words and all this vision, Nathan spoke to David.

David's Prayer

16 Then King David went in and sat before the Lord, and said, "Who am I, O Lord God, and what is my house, that you have brought me thus far? [17]And even this was a small thing in your sight, O God; you have also spoken of your servant's house for a great while to come. You regard me as someone of high rank,[a] O Lord God! [18]And what more can David say to you for honoring your servant? You know your servant. [19]For your servant's sake, O Lord, and according to your own heart, you have done all these great deeds, making known all these great things. [20]There is no one like you, O Lord, and there is no God besides you, according to all that we have heard with our ears. [21]Who is like your people Israel, one nation on the earth whom God went to redeem to be his people, making for yourself a name for great and terrible things, in driving out nations before your people whom you redeemed from Egypt? [22]And you made your people Israel to be your people forever; and you, O Lord, became their God.

23 "And now, O Lord, as for the word that you have spoken concerning your servant and concerning his house, let it be established forever, and do as you have promised. [24]Thus your name will be established and magnified forever in the saying, 'The Lord of hosts, the God of Israel, is Israel's God'; and the house of your servant David will be established in your presence. [25]For you, my God, have revealed to your servant that you will build a house for him; therefore your servant has found it possible to pray before you. [26]And now, O Lord, you are God, and you have promised this good thing to your servant; [27]therefore may it please you to bless the house of your servant, that it may continue forever before you. For you, O Lord, have blessed and are blessed[b] forever."

David's Kingdom Established and Extended

18 Some time afterward, David attacked the Philistines and subdued them; he took Gath and its villages from the Philistines.

2 He defeated Moab, and the Moabites became subject to David and brought tribute.

3 David also struck down King Hadadezer of Zobah, toward Hamath,[a] as he went to set up a monument at the river Euphrates. [4]David took from him one thousand chariots, seven thousand cavalry, and twenty thousand foot soldiers. David hamstrung all the chariot horses, but left one hundred of them. [5]When the Arameans of Damascus came to help King Hadadezer of Zobah, David killed twenty-two thousand Arameans. [6]Then David put garrisons[c] in Aram of Damascus; and the Arameans became subject to David, and brought tribute. The Lord gave victory to David wherever he went. [7]David took the gold shields that were carried by the servants of Hadadezer, and brought them to Jerusalem. [8]From Tibhath and from Cun, cities of Hadadezer, David took a vast quantity of bronze; with it Solomon made the bronze sea and the pillars and the vessels of bronze.

9 When King Tou of Hamath heard that David had defeated the whole army of King Hadadezer of Zobah, [10]he sent his son Hadoram to King David, to greet him and to congratulate him, because he had fought against Hadadezer and defeated him. Now Hadadezer had often been at war with Tou. He sent all sorts of articles of gold, of silver, and of bronze; [11]these also King David dedicated to the Lord, together with the silver and gold that he had carried off from all the nations, from Edom, Moab, the Ammonites, the Philistines, and Amalek.

12 Abishai son of Zeruiah killed eighteen thousand Edomites in the Valley of Salt. [13]He put garrisons in Edom; and all the Edomites became subject to David. And the Lord gave victory to David wherever he went.

David's Administration

14 So David reigned over all Israel; and he administered justice and equity to all his people. [15]Joab son of Zeruiah was over the army; Jehoshaphat son of Ahilud was recorder; [16]Zadok son of Ahitub and Ahimelech son of Abiathar were priests; Shavsha was secretary; [17]Benaiah son of Jehoiada was over the Cherethites and the Pelethites; and David's sons were the chief officials in the service of the king.

Defeat of the Ammonites and Arameans

19 Some time afterward, King Nahash of the Ammonites died, and his son succeeded him. [2]David said, "I will deal loyally with Hanun son of Nahash, for his father dealt loyally with me." So David sent messengers to console him concerning his father. When David's servants came to Hanun in the land of the Ammonites, to console him, ³the officials of the Ammonites said to Hanun, "Do you think, because David has sent consolers to you, that he is honoring your father? Have not his servants come to you to search and to overthrow and to spy out the land?" ⁴So Hanun seized David's servants, shaved them, cut off their garments in the middle at their hips, and sent them away; ⁵and they departed. When David was told about the men, he sent messengers to them, for they felt greatly humiliated. The king said, "Remain at Jericho until your beards have grown, and then return."

6 When the Ammonites saw that they had made themselves odious to David, Hanun and the Ammonites sent a thousand talents of silver to hire chariots and cavalry from Mesopotamia, from Aram-maacah and from Zobah. ⁷They hired thirty-two thousand chariots and the king of Maacah with his army, who came and camped before Medeba. And the Ammonites were mustered from their cities and came to battle. ⁸When David heard of it, he sent Joab and all the army of the warriors. ⁹The Ammonites came out and drew up in battle array at the entrance of the city, and the kings who had come were by themselves in the open country.

10 When Joab saw that the line of battle was set against him both in front and in the rear, he chose some of the picked men of Israel and arrayed them against the Arameans; ¹¹the rest of his troops he put in the charge of his brother Abishai, and they were arrayed against the Ammonites. ¹²He said, "If the Arameans are too strong for me, then you shall help me; but if the Ammonites are too strong for you, then I will help you. ¹³Be strong, and let us be courageous for our people and for the cities of our God; and may the LORD do what seems good to him." ¹⁴So Joab and the troops who were with him advanced toward the Arameans for battle; and they fled before him. ¹⁵When the Ammonites saw that the Arameans fled, they likewise fled before Abishai, Joab's brother, and entered the city. Then Joab came to Jerusalem.

16 But when the Arameans saw that they had been defeated by Israel, they sent messengers and brought out the Arameans who were beyond the Euphrates, with Shophach the commander of the army of Hadadezer at their head. ¹⁷When David was informed, he gathered all Israel together, crossed the Jordan, came to them, and drew up his forces against them. When David set the battle in array against the Arameans, they fought with him. ¹⁸The Arameans fled before Israel; and David killed seven thousand Aramean charioteers and forty thousand foot soldiers, and also killed Shophach the commander of their army. ¹⁹When the servants of Hadadezer saw that they had been defeated by Israel, they made peace with David, and became subject to him. So the Arameans were not willing to help the Ammonites any more.

Siege and Capture of Rabbah

20 In the spring of the year, the time when kings go out to battle, Joab led out the army, ravaged the country of the Ammonites, and came and besieged Rabbah. But David remained at Jerusalem. Joab attacked Rabbah, and overthrew it. ²David took the crown of Milcomᵃ from his head; he found that it weighed a talent of gold, and in it was a precious stone; and it was placed on David's head. He also brought out the booty of the city, a very great amount. ³He brought out the people who were in it, and set them to workᵇ with saws and iron picks and axes.ᶜ Thus David did to all the cities of the Ammonites. Then David and all the people returned to Jerusalem.

Exploits against the Philistines

4 After this, war broke out with the Philistines at Gezer; then Sibbecai the Hushathite killed Sippai, who was one of the descendants of the giants; and the Philistines were subdued. ⁵Again there was war with the Philistines; and Elhanan son of Jair killed Lahmi the brother of Goliath the Gittite, the shaft of whose spear was like a weaver's beam. ⁶Again there was war at Gath, where there was a man of great size, who had six fingers on each hand, and six toes on each foot, twenty-four in number; he also was descended from the giants. ⁷When he taunted Israel, Jonathan son of Shimea, David's brother, killed him. ⁸These were descended from the giants in Gath; they fell by the hand of David and his servants.

The Census and Plague

21 Satan stood up against Israel, and incited David to count the people of Israel. ²So David said to Joab and the commanders of the army, "Go, number Israel, from Beer-sheba to Dan, and bring me a report, so that I may know their number." ³But Joab said, "May the LORD increase the number of his people a hundredfold!

---

a Gk Vg See 1 Kings 11.5, 33: MT *of their king*   b Compare 2 Sam 12.31: Heb *and he sawed*   c Compare 2 Sam 12.31: Heb *saws*

Are they not, my lord the king, all of them my lord's servants? Why then should my lord require this? Why should he bring guilt on Israel?" [4]But the king's word prevailed against Joab. So Joab departed and went throughout all Israel, and came back to Jerusalem. [5]Joab gave the total count of the people to David. In all Israel there were one million one hundred thousand men who drew the sword, and in Judah four hundred seventy thousand who drew the sword. [6]But he did not include Levi and Benjamin in the numbering, for the king's command was abhorrent to Joab.

7 But God was displeased with this thing, and he struck Israel. [8]David said to God, "I have sinned greatly in that I have done this thing. But now, I pray you, take away the guilt of your servant; for I have done very foolishly." [9]The LORD spoke to Gad, David's seer, saying, [10]"Go and say to David, 'Thus says the LORD: Three things I offer you; choose one of them, so that I may do it to you.' " [11]So Gad came to David and said to him, "Thus says the LORD, 'Take your choice: [12]either three years of famine; or three months of devastation by your foes, while the sword of your enemies overtakes you; or three days of the sword of the LORD, pestilence on the land, and the angel of the LORD destroying throughout all the territory of Israel.' Now decide what answer I shall return to the one who sent me." [13]Then David said to Gad, "I am in great distress; let me fall into the hand of the LORD, for his mercy is very great; but let me not fall into human hands."

14 So the LORD sent a pestilence on Israel; and seventy thousand persons fell in Israel. [15]And God sent an angel to Jerusalem to destroy it; but when he was about to destroy it, the LORD took note and relented concerning the calamity; he said to the destroying angel, "Enough! Stay your hand." The angel of the LORD was then standing by the threshing floor of Ornan the Jebusite. [16]David looked up and saw the angel of the LORD standing between earth and heaven, and in his hand a drawn sword stretched out over Jerusalem. Then David and the elders, clothed in sackcloth, fell on their faces. [17]And David said to God, "Was it not I who gave the command to count the people? It is I who have sinned and done very wickedly. But these sheep, what have they done? Let your hand, I pray, O LORD my God, be against me and against my father's house; but do not let your people be plagued!"

David's Altar and Sacrifice

18 Then the angel of the LORD commanded Gad to tell David that he should go up and erect

Live It!

True Repentance

Think of a time when you said you were sorry, just because you felt you had to. Now think of a time when you were truly sorry for causing harm to another by doing something God had commanded you not to do. There is a big difference between going through the motions of repentance and being truly repentant before another and before God. For example, David sinned by ordering a census to count his people (see 1 Chr 21:2). He accepted a consequence that he hoped would be the easiest (see verse 13). But when he saw the harm he had caused, he became truly repentant and asked God's mercy upon the Israelites (see verse 17).

Repentance requires true sorrow and asking God to change our heart. It leads to an active response to make amends with God and with the Church. Such repentance is called reconciliation, and Catholics celebrate it in the sacrament of Penance and Reconciliation.

▶ 1 Chr 21:1–17

an altar to the LORD on the threshing floor of Ornan the Jebusite. [19]So David went up following Gad's instructions, which he had spoken in the name of the LORD. [20]Ornan turned and saw the angel; and while his four sons who were with him hid themselves, Ornan continued to thresh wheat. [21]As David came to Ornan, Ornan looked and saw David; he went out from the threshing floor, and did obeisance to David with his face to the ground. [22]David said to Ornan, "Give me the site of the threshing floor that I may build on it an altar to the LORD—give it to me at its full price—so that the plague may be averted from the people." [23]Then Ornan said to David, "Take it; and let my lord the king do what seems good to him; see, I present the oxen for burnt offerings, and the threshing sledges for the wood, and the wheat for a grain offering. I give it all." [24]But King David said to Ornan, "No; I will buy them for the full price. I will not take for the LORD what is yours, nor offer burnt offerings that cost me

1

C
H
R

nothing." ²⁵So David paid Ornan six hundred shekels of gold by weight for the site. ²⁶David built there an altar to the Lord and presented burnt offerings and offerings of well-being. He called upon the Lord, and he answered him with fire from heaven on the altar of burnt offering. ²⁷Then the Lord commanded the angel, and he put his sword back into its sheath.

The Place Chosen for the Temple

28 At that time, when David saw that the Lord had answered him at the threshing floor of Ornan the Jebusite, he made his sacrifices there. ²⁹For the tabernacle of the Lord, which Moses had made in the wilderness, and the altar of burnt offering were at that time in the high place at Gibeon; ³⁰but David could not go before it to inquire of God, for he was afraid of the sword of **22** the angel of the Lord. ¹Then David said, "Here shall be the house of the Lord God and here the altar of burnt offering for Israel."

David Prepares to Build the Temple

2 David gave orders to gather together the aliens who were residing in the land of Israel, and he set stonecutters to prepare dressed stones for building the house of God. ³David also provided great stores of iron for nails for the doors of the gates and for clamps, as well as bronze in quantities beyond weighing, ⁴and cedar logs without number—for the Sidonians and Tyrians brought great quantities of cedar to David. ⁵For David said, "My son Solomon is young and inexperienced, and the house that is to be built for the Lord must be exceedingly magnificent, famous and glorified throughout all lands; I will therefore make preparation for it." So David provided materials in great quantity before his death.

David's Charge to Solomon and the Leaders

6 Then he called for his son Solomon and charged him to build a house for the Lord, the God of Israel. ⁷David said to Solomon, "My son, I had planned to build a house to the name of the Lord my God. ⁸But the word of the Lord came to me, saying, 'You have shed much blood and have waged great wars; you shall not build a house to my name, because you have shed so much blood in my sight on the earth. ⁹See, a son shall be born to you; he shall be a man of peace. I will give him peace from all his enemies on every side; for his name shall be Solomon,ᵃ and I will give peaceᵇ and quiet to Israel in his days. ¹⁰He shall build a house for my name. He shall be a son to me, and I will be a father to him, and I will establish his royal throne in Israel forever.' ¹¹Now, my son, the Lord be with you, so that you may succeed in building the house of the Lord your God, as he has spoken concerning you. ¹²Only, may the Lord grant you discretion and understanding, so that when he gives you charge over Israel you may keep the law of the Lord your God. ¹³Then you will prosper if you are careful to observe the statutes and the ordinances that the Lord commanded Moses for Israel. Be strong and of good courage. Do not be afraid or dismayed. ¹⁴With great pains I have provided for the house of the Lord one hundred thousand talents of gold, one million talents of silver, and bronze and iron beyond weighing, for there is so much of it; timber and stone too I have provided. To these you must add more. ¹⁵You have an abundance of workers: stonecutters, masons, carpenters, and all kinds of artisans without number, skilled in working ¹⁶gold, silver, bronze, and iron. Now begin the work, and the Lord be with you."

17 David also commanded all the leaders of Israel to help his son Solomon, saying, ¹⁸"Is not the Lord your God with you? Has he not given you peace on every side? For he has delivered the inhabitants of the land into my hand; and the land is subdued before the Lord and his people. ¹⁹Now set your mind and heart to seek the Lord your God. Go and build the sanctuary of the Lord God so that the ark of the covenant of the Lord and the holy vessels of God may be brought into a house built for the name of the Lord."

Families of the Levites and Their Functions

23 When David was old and full of days, he made his son Solomon king over Israel.

2 David assembled all the leaders of Israel and the priests and the Levites. ³The Levites, thirty years old and upward, were counted, and the total was thirty-eight thousand. ⁴"Twenty-four thousand of these," David said, "shall have charge of the work in the house of the Lord, six thousand shall be officers and judges, ⁵four thousand gatekeepers, and four thousand shall offer praises to the Lord with the instruments that I have made for praise." ⁶And David organized them in divisions corresponding to the sons of Levi: Gershon,ᶜ Kohath, and Merari.

7 The sons of Gershonᵈ were Ladan and Shimei. ⁸The sons of Ladan: Jehiel the chief, Zetham, and Joel, three. ⁹The sons of Shimei: Shelomoth, Haziel, and Haran, three. These were the heads of families of Ladan. ¹⁰And the sons of

---

ᵃ Heb *Shelomoh*   ᵇ Heb *shalom*   ᶜ Or *Gershom*; See 1 Chr 6.1, note, and 23.15   ᵈ Vg Compare Gk Syr: Heb *to the Gershonite*

Shimei: Jahath, Zina, Jeush, and Beriah. These four were the sons of Shimei. ¹¹Jahath was the chief, and Zizah the second; but Jeush and Beriah did not have many sons, so they were enrolled as a single family.

12 The sons of Kohath: Amram, Izhar, Hebron, and Uzziel, four. ¹³The sons of Amram: Aaron and Moses. Aaron was set apart to consecrate the most holy things, so that he and his sons forever should make offerings before the LORD, and minister to him and pronounce blessings in his name forever; ¹⁴but as for Moses the man of God, his sons were to be reckoned among the tribe of Levi. ¹⁵The sons of Moses: Gershom and Eliezer. ¹⁶The sons of Gershom: Shebuel the chief. ¹⁷The sons of Eliezer: Rehabiah the chief; Eliezer had no other sons, but the sons of Rehabiah were very numerous. ¹⁸The sons of Izhar: Shelomith the chief. ¹⁹The sons of Hebron: Jeriah the chief, Amariah the second, Jahaziel the third, and Jekameam the fourth. ²⁰The sons of Uzziel: Micah the chief and Isshiah the second.

21 The sons of Merari: Mahli and Mushi. The sons of Mahli: Eleazar and Kish. ²²Eleazar died having no sons, but only daughters; their kindred, the sons of Kish, married them. ²³The sons of Mushi: Mahli, Eder, and Jeremoth, three.

24 These were the sons of Levi by their ancestral houses, the heads of families as they were enrolled according to the number of the names of the individuals from twenty years old and upward who were to do the work for the service of the house of the LORD. ²⁵For David said, "The LORD, the God of Israel, has given rest to his people; and he resides in Jerusalem forever. ²⁶And so the Levites no longer need to carry the tabernacle or any of the things for its service"— ²⁷for according to the last words of David these were the number of the Levites from twenty years old and upward— ²⁸"but their duty shall be to assist the descendants of Aaron for the service of the house of the LORD, having the care of the courts and the chambers, the cleansing of all that is holy, and any work for the service of the house of God; ²⁹to assist also with the rows of bread, the choice flour for the grain offering, the wafers of unleavened bread, the baked offering, the offering mixed with oil, and all measures of quantity or size. ³⁰And they shall stand every morning, thanking and praising the LORD, and likewise at evening, ³¹and whenever burnt offerings are offered to the LORD on sabbaths, new moons, and appointed festivals, according to the number required of them, regularly before the LORD. ³²Thus they shall keep charge of the tent of meeting and the sanctuary, and shall attend the descendants of Aaron, their kindred, for the service of the house of the LORD."

Divisions of the Priests

24 The divisions of the descendants of Aaron were these. The sons of Aaron: Nadab, Abihu, Eleazar, and Ithamar. ²But Nadab and Abihu died before their father, and had no sons; so Eleazar and Ithamar became the priests. ³Along with Zadok of the sons of Eleazar, and Ahimelech of the sons of Ithamar, David organized them according to the appointed duties in their service. ⁴Since more chief men were found among the sons of Eleazar than among the sons of Ithamar, they organized them under sixteen heads of ancestral houses of the sons of Eleazar, and eight of the sons of Ithamar. ⁵They organized them by lot, all alike, for there were officers of the sanctuary and officers of God among both the sons of Eleazar and the sons of Ithamar. ⁶The scribe Shemaiah son of Nethanel, a Levite, recorded them in the presence of the king, and the officers, and Zadok the priest, and Ahimelech son of Abiathar, and the heads of ancestral houses of the priests and of the Levites; one ancestral house being chosen for Eleazar and one chosen for Ithamar.

7 The first lot fell to Jehoiarib, the second to Jedaiah, ⁸the third to Harim, the fourth to Seorim, ⁹the fifth to Malchijah, the sixth to Mijamin, ¹⁰the seventh to Hakkoz, the eighth to Abijah, ¹¹the ninth to Jeshua, the tenth to Shecaniah, ¹²the eleventh to Eliashib, the twelfth to Jakim, ¹³the thirteenth to Huppah, the fourteenth to Jeshebeab, ¹⁴the fifteenth to Bilgah, the sixteenth to Immer, ¹⁵the seventeenth to Hezir, the eighteenth to Happizzez, ¹⁶the nineteenth to Pethahiah, the twentieth to Jehezkel, ¹⁷the twenty-first to Jachin, the twenty-second to Gamul, ¹⁸the twenty-third to Delaiah, the twenty-fourth to Maaziah. ¹⁹These had as their appointed duty in their service to enter the house of the LORD according to the procedure established for them by their ancestor Aaron, as the LORD God of Israel had commanded him.

Other Levites

20 And of the rest of the sons of Levi: of the sons of Amram, Shubael; of the sons of Shubael, Jehdeiah. ²¹Of Rehabiah: of the sons of Rehabiah, Isshiah the chief. ²²Of the Izharites, Shelomoth; of the sons of Shelomoth, Jahath. ²³The sons of Hebron:ᵃ Jeriah the chief,ᵇ Amariah the second, Jahaziel the third, Jekameam the fourth. ²⁴The

---

a See 23.19: Heb lacks *Hebron*   b See 23.19: Heb lacks *the chief*

sons of Uzziel, Micah; of the sons of Micah, Shamir. 25The brother of Micah, Isshiah; of the sons of Isshiah, Zechariah. 26The sons of Merari: Mahli and Mushi. The sons of Jaaziah: Beno.*ᵃ 27The sons of Merari: of Jaaziah, Beno,ᵃ Shoham, Zaccur, and Ibri. 28Of Mahli: Eleazar, who had no sons. 29Of Kish, the sons of Kish: Jerahmeel. 30The sons of Mushi: Mahli, Eder, and Jerimoth. These were the sons of the Levites according to their ancestral houses. 31These also cast lots corresponding to their kindred, the descendants of Aaron, in the presence of King David, Zadok, Ahimelech, and the heads of ancestral houses of the priests and of the Levites, the chief as well as the youngest brother.

The Temple Musicians

25 David and the officers of the army also set apart for the service the sons of Asaph, and of Heman, and of Jeduthun, who should prophesy with lyres, harps, and cymbals. The list of those who did the work and of their duties was: 2Of the sons of Asaph: Zaccur, Joseph, Nethaniah, and Asarelah, sons of Asaph, under the direction of Asaph, who prophesied under the direction of the king. 3Of Jeduthun, the sons of Jeduthun: Gedaliah, Zeri, Jeshaiah, Shimei,ᵇ Hashabiah, and Mattithiah, six, under the direction of their father Jeduthun, who prophesied with the lyre in thanksgiving and praise to the Lord. 4Of Heman, the sons of Heman: Bukkiah, Mattaniah, Uzziel, Shebuel, and Jerimoth, Hananiah, Hanani, Eliathah, Giddalti, and Romamti-ezer, Joshbekashah, Mallothi, Hothir, Mahazioth. 5All these were the sons of Heman the king's seer, according to the promise of God to exalt him; for God had given Heman fourteen sons and three daughters. 6They were all under the direction of their father for the music in the house of the Lord with cymbals, harps, and lyres for the service of the house of God. Asaph, Jeduthun, and Heman were under the order of the king. 7They and their kindred, who were trained in singing to the Lord, all of whom were skillful, numbered two hundred eighty-eight. 8And they cast lots for their duties, small and great, teacher and pupil alike.

9 The first lot fell for Asaph to Joseph; the second to Gedaliah, to him and his brothers and his sons, twelve; 10the third to Zaccur, his sons and his brothers, twelve; 11the fourth to Izri, his sons and his brothers, twelve; 12the fifth to Nethaniah, his sons and his brothers, twelve; 13the sixth to Bukkiah, his sons and his brothers, twelve; 14the seventh to Jesarelah,ᶜ his sons and his brothers, twelve; 15the eighth to Jeshaiah, his sons and his brothers, twelve; 16the ninth to Mattaniah, his sons and his brothers, twelve; 17the tenth to Shimei, his sons and his brothers, twelve; 18the eleventh to Azarel, his sons and his brothers, twelve; 19the twelfth to Hashabiah, his sons and his brothers, twelve; 20to the thirteenth, Shubael, his sons and his brothers, twelve; 21to the fourteenth, Mattithiah, his sons and his brothers, twelve; 22to the fifteenth, to Jeremoth, his sons and his brothers, twelve; 23to the sixteenth, to Hananiah, his sons and his brothers, twelve; 24to the seventeenth, to Joshbekashah, his sons and his brothers, twelve; 25to the eighteenth, to Hanani, his sons and his brothers, twelve; 26to the nineteenth, to Mallothi, his sons and his brothers, twelve; 27to the twentieth, to Eliathah, his sons and his brothers, twelve; 28to the twenty-first, to Hothir, his sons and his brothers, twelve; 29to the twenty-second, to Giddalti, his sons and his brothers, twelve; 30to the twenty-third, to Mahazioth, his sons and his brothers, twelve; 31to the twenty-fourth, to Romamti-ezer, his sons and his brothers, twelve.

The Gatekeepers

26 As for the divisions of the gatekeepers: of the Korahites, Meshelemiah son of Kore, of the sons of Asaph. 2Meshelemiah had sons: Zechariah the firstborn, Jediael the second, Zebadiah the third, Jathniel the fourth, 3Elam the fifth, Jehohanan the sixth, Eliehoenai the seventh. 4Obed-edom had sons: Shemaiah the firstborn, Jehozabad the second, Joah the third, Sachar the fourth, Nethanel the fifth, 5Ammiel the sixth, Issachar the seventh, Peullethai the eighth; for God blessed him. 6Also to his son Shemaiah sons were born who exercised authority in their ancestral houses, for they were men of great ability. 7The sons of Shemaiah: Othni, Rephael, Obed, and Elzabad, whose brothers were able men, Elihu and Semachiah. 8All these, sons of Obed-edom with their sons and brothers, were able men qualified for the service; sixty-two of Obed-edom. 9Meshelemiah had sons and brothers, able men, eighteen. 10Hosah, of the sons of Merari, had sons: Shimri the chief (for though he was not the firstborn, his father made him chief), 11Hilkiah the second, Tebaliah the third, Zechariah the fourth: all the sons and brothers of Hosah totaled thirteen.

12 These divisions of the gatekeepers, corresponding to their leaders, had duties, just as their kindred did, ministering in the house of

---

ᵃ Or his son: Meaning of Heb uncertain   ᵇ One Ms: Gk: MT lacks Shimei   ᶜ Or Asarelah; see 25.2

the LORD; [13]and they cast lots by ancestral houses, small and great alike, for their gates. [14]The lot for the east fell to Shelemiah. They cast lots also for his son Zechariah, a prudent counselor, and his lot came out for the north. [15]Obededom's came out for the south, and to his sons was allotted the storehouse. [16]For Shuppim and Hosah it came out for the west, at the gate of Shallecheth on the ascending road. Guard corresponded to guard. [17]On the east there were six Levites each day,[a] on the north four each day, on the south four each day, as well as two and two at the storehouse; [18]and for the colonnade[b] on the west there were four at the road and two at the colonnade.[b] [19]These were the divisions of the gatekeepers among the Korahites and the sons of Merari.

The Treasurers, Officers, and Judges

20 And of the Levites, Ahijah had charge of the treasuries of the house of God and the treasuries of the dedicated gifts. [21]The sons of Ladan, the sons of the Gershonites belonging to Ladan, the heads of families belonging to Ladan the Gershonite: Jehieli.[c]

22 The sons of Jehieli, Zetham and his brother Joel, were in charge of the treasuries of the house of the LORD. [23]Of the Amramites, the Izharites, the Hebronites, and the Uzzielites: [24]Shebuel son of Gershom, son of Moses, was chief officer in charge of the treasuries. [25]His brothers: from Eliezer were his son Rehabiah, his son Jeshaiah, his son Joram, his son Zichri, and his son Shelomoth. [26]This Shelomoth and his brothers were in charge of all the treasuries of the dedicated gifts that King David, and the heads of families, and the officers of the thousands and the hundreds, and the commanders of the army, had dedicated. [27]From booty won in battles they dedicated gifts for the maintenance of the house of the LORD. [28]Also all that Samuel the seer, and Saul son of Kish, and Abner son of Ner, and Joab son of Zeruiah had dedicated—all dedicated gifts were in the care of Shelomoth[d] and his brothers.

[29]Of the Izharites, Chenaniah and his sons were appointed to outside duties for Israel, as officers and judges. [30]Of the Hebronites, Hashabiah and his brothers, one thousand seven hundred men of ability, had the oversight of Israel west of the Jordan for all the work of the LORD and for the service of the king. [31]Of the Hebronites, Jerijah was chief of the Hebronites. (In the fortieth year of David's reign search was made, of whatever genealogy or family, and men of great ability among them were found at Jazer in Gilead.) [32]King David appointed him and his brothers, two thousand seven hundred men of ability, heads of families, to have the oversight of the Reubenites, the Gadites, and the half-tribe of the Manassites for everything pertaining to God and for the affairs of the king.

The Military Divisions

27 This is the list of the people of Israel, the heads of families, the commanders of the thousands and the hundreds, and their officers who served the king in all matters concerning the divisions that came and went, month after month throughout the year, each division numbering twenty-four thousand:

2 Jashobeam son of Zabdiel was in charge of the first division in the first month; in his division were twenty-four thousand. [3]He was a descendant of Perez, and was chief of all the commanders of the army for the first month. [4]Dodai the Ahohite was in charge of the division of the second month; Mikloth was the chief officer of his division. In his division were twenty-four thousand. [5]The third commander, for the third month, was Benaiah son of the priest Jehoiada, as chief; in his division were twenty-four thousand. [6]This is the Benaiah who was a mighty man of the Thirty and in command of the Thirty; his son Ammizabad was in charge of his division.[e] [7]Asahel brother of Joab was fourth, for the fourth month, and his son Zebadiah after him; in his division were twenty-four thousand. [8]The fifth commander, for the fifth month, was Shamhuth, the Izrahite; in his division were twenty-four thousand. [9]Sixth, for the sixth month, was Ira son of Ikkesh the Tekoite; in his division were twenty-four thousand. [10]Seventh, for the seventh month, was Helez the Pelonite, of the Ephraimites; in his division were twenty-four thousand. [11]Eighth, for the eighth month, was Sibbecai the Hushathite, of the Zerahites; in his division were twenty-four thousand. [12]Ninth, for the ninth month, was Abiezer of Anathoth, a Benjaminite; in his division were twenty-four thousand. [13]Tenth, for the tenth month, was Maharai of Netophah, of the Zerahites; in his division were twenty-four thousand. [14]Eleventh, for the eleventh month, was Benaiah of Pirathon, of the Ephraimites; in his division were twenty-four thousand. [15]Twelfth, for the twelfth month, was Heldai the Netophathite, of Othniel; in his division were twenty-four thousand.

---

a Gk: Heb lacks each day   b Heb parbar: meaning uncertain
c The Hebrew text of verse 21 is confused   d Gk Compare 26:28:
Heb Shelomith   e Gk Vg: Heb Ammizabad was his division

Leaders of Tribes

16 Over the tribes of Israel, for the Reuben-ites, Eliezer son of Zichri was chief officer; for the Simeonites, Shephatiah son of Maacah; 17for Levi, Hashabiah son of Kemuel; for Aaron, Za-dok; 18for Judah, Elihu, one of David's brothers; for Issachar, Omri son of Michael; 19for Zebulun, Ishmaiah son of Obadiah; for Naphtali, Jerimoth son of Azriel; 20for the Ephraimites, Hoshea son of Azaziah; for the half-tribe of Manasseh, Joel son of Pedaiah; 21for the half-tribe of Manasseh in Gilead, Iddo son of Zechariah; for Benjamin, Jaasiel son of Abner; 22for Dan, Azarel son of Jeroham. These were the leaders of the tribes of Israel. 23David did not count those below twenty years of age, for the LORD had promised to make Israel as numerous as the stars of heaven. 24Joab son of Zeruiah began to count them, but did not finish; yet wrath came upon Israel for this, and the number was not entered into the account of the Annals of King David.

Other Civic Officials

25 Over the king's treasuries was Azmaveth son of Adiel. Over the treasuries in the country, in the cities, in the villages and in the towers, was Jonathan son of Uzziah. 26Over those who did the work of the field, tilling the soil, was Ezri son of Chelub. 27Over the vineyards was Shimei the Ramathite. Over the produce of the vineyards for the wine cellars was Zabdi the Shiphmite. 28Over the olive and sycamore trees in the Shephelah was Baal-hanan the Gederite. Over the stores of oil was Joash. 29Over the herds that pastured in Sharon was Shitrai the Sharonite. Over the herds in the valleys was Shaphat son of Adlai. 30Over the camels was Obil the Ishmaelite. Over the donkeys was Jehdeiah the Meronothite. Over the flocks was Jaziz the Hagrite. 31All these were stewards of King David's property.

32 Jonathan, David's uncle, was a counselor, being a man of understanding and a scribe; Jehiel son of Hachmoni attended the king's sons. 33Ahithophel was the king's counselor, and Hushai the Archite was the king's friend. 34After Ahithophel came Jehoiada son of Benaiah, and Abiathar. Joab was commander of the king's army.

Solomon Instructed to Build the Temple

28 David assembled at Jerusalem all the of-ficials of Israel, the officials of the tribes, the officers of the divisions that served the king, the commanders of the thousands, the com-manders of the hundreds, the stewards of all the property and cattle of the king and his sons, to-gether with the palace officials, the mighty war-riors, and all the warriors. 2Then King David rose to his feet and said: "Hear me, my brothers and my people. I had planned to build a house of rest for the ark of the covenant of the LORD, for the footstool of our God; and I made preparations for building. 3But God said to me, 'You shall not build a house for my name, for you are a warrior and have shed blood.' 4Yet the LORD God of Israel chose me from all my ancestral house to be king over Israel forever; for he chose Judah as leader, and in the house of Judah my father's house, and among my father's sons he took delight in making me king over all Israel. 5And of all my sons, for the LORD has given me many, he has chosen my son Solomon to sit upon the throne of the kingdom of the LORD over Israel. 6He said to me, 'It is your son Solomon who shall build my house and my courts, for I have chosen him to be a son to me, and I will be a father to him. 7I will establish his kingdom forever if he continues resolute in keeping my commandments and my ordinances, as he is today.' 8Now therefore in the sight of all Israel, the assembly of the LORD, and in the hearing of our God, observe and search out all the commandments of the LORD your God; that you may possess this good land, and leave it for an inheritance to your children after you forever.

9 "And you, my son Solomon, know the God of your father, and serve him with single mind and willing heart; for the LORD searches every mind, and understands every plan and thought. If you seek him, he will be found by you; but if you forsake him, he will abandon you forever. 10Take heed now, for the LORD has chosen you to build a house as the sanctuary; be strong, and act."

11 Then David gave his son Solomon the plan of the vestibule of the temple, and of its houses, its treasuries, its upper rooms, and its inner chambers, and of the room for the mercy seat;a 12and the plan of all that he had in mind: for the courts of the house of the LORD, all the surround-ing chambers, the treasuries of the house of God, and the treasuries for dedicated gifts; 13for the divisions of the priests and of the Levites, and all the work of the service in the house of the LORD; for all the vessels for the service in the house of the LORD, 14the weight of gold for all golden vessels for each service, the weight of silver ves-sels for each service, 15the weight of the golden lampstands and their lamps, the weight of gold for each lampstand and its lamps, the weight of

a Or the cover

Cultural Connection

God's Name

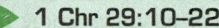

As David neared the end of his life and reign, he blessed God's name in the midst of the people. The Israelites, who believed in one God, were surrounded by other cultures who believed in many different gods, both good and evil. The name of the Israelites' one God was sacred and precious to them, and they often associated God's name with power, glory, majesty, and victory over all creation.

In Hmong, the name of God is *Huab Tais Ntuj*, which can be translated as Highest One or Emperor Spirit or Overriding Spirit. The Hmong culture developed as a subculture within the Central Highlands of China. The Hmong believed in different spirits, both good and evil, angelic and demonic. So, in naming God Highest Emperor, overriding all other spirits, they clearly also developed a belief in one God with power over all creation.

▶ **1 Chr 29:10–22**

silver for a lampstand and its lamps, according to the use of each in the service, ¹⁶the weight of gold for each table for the rows of bread, the silver for the silver tables, ¹⁷and pure gold for the forks, the basins, and the cups; for the golden bowls and the weight of each; for the silver bowls and the weight of each; ¹⁸for the altar of incense made of refined gold, and its weight; also his plan for the golden chariot of the cherubim that spread their wings and covered the ark of the covenant of the Lord.

19 "All this, in writing at the Lord's direction, he made clear to me—the plan of all the works."

20 David said further to his son Solomon, "Be strong and of good courage, and act. Do not be afraid or dismayed; for the Lord God, my God, is with you. He will not fail you or forsake you, until all the work for the service of the house of the Lord is finished. ²¹Here are the divisions of the priests and the Levites for all the service of the house of God; and with you in all the work will be every volunteer who has skill for any kind of service; also the officers and all the people will be wholly at your command."

Offerings for Building the Temple

29 King David said to the whole assembly, "My son Solomon, whom alone God has chosen, is young and inexperienced, and the work is great; for the temple*ᵃ* will not be for mortals but for the Lord God. ²So I have provided for the house of my God, so far as I was able, the gold for the things of gold, the silver for the things of silver, and the bronze for the things of bronze, the iron for the things of iron, and wood for the things of wood, besides great quantities of onyx and stones for setting, antimony, colored stones, all sorts of precious stones, and marble in abundance. ³Moreover, in addition to all that I have provided for the holy house, I have a treasure of my own of gold and silver, and because of my devotion to the house of my God I give it to the house of my God: ⁴three thousand talents of gold, of the gold of Ophir, and seven thousand talents of refined silver, for overlaying the walls of the house, ⁵and for all the work to be done by artisans, gold for the things of gold and silver for the things of silver. Who then will offer willingly, consecrating themselves today to the Lord?"

6 Then the leaders of ancestral houses made their freewill offerings, as did also the leaders of the tribes, the commanders of the thousands and of the hundreds, and the officers over the king's work. ⁷They gave for the service of the house of God five thousand talents and ten thousand darics of gold, ten thousand talents of silver, eighteen thousand talents of bronze, and one hundred thousand talents of iron. ⁸Whoever had precious stones gave them to the treasury of the house of the Lord, into the care of Jehiel the Gershonite. ⁹Then the people rejoiced because these had given willingly, for with single mind they had offered freely to the Lord; King David also rejoiced greatly.

David's Praise to God

10 Then David blessed the Lord in the presence of all the assembly; David said: "Blessed are you, O Lord, the God of our ancestor Israel,

1
C
H
R

forever and ever. [11]Yours, O LORD, are the greatness, the power, the glory, the victory, and the majesty; for all that is in the heavens and on the earth is yours; yours is the kingdom, O LORD, and you are exalted as head above all. [12]Riches and honor come from you, and you rule over all. In your hand are power and might; and it is in your hand to make great and to give strength to all. [13]And now, our God, we give thanks to you and praise your glorious name.

14 "But who am I, and what is my people, that we should be able to make this freewill offering? For all things come from you, and of your own have we given you. [15]For we are aliens and transients before you, as were all our ancestors; our days on the earth are like a shadow, and there is no hope. [16]O LORD our God, all this abundance that we have provided for building you a house for your holy name comes from your hand and is all your own. [17]I know, my God, that you search the heart, and take pleasure in uprightness; in the uprightness of my heart I have freely offered all these things, and now I have seen your people, who are present here, offering freely and joyously to you. [18]O LORD, the God of Abraham, Isaac, and Israel, our ancestors, keep forever such purposes and thoughts in the hearts of your people, and direct their hearts toward you. [19]Grant to my son Solomon that with single mind he may keep your commandments, your decrees, and your statutes, performing all of them, and that he may build the temple[a] for which I have made provision."

20 Then David said to the whole assembly, "Bless the LORD your God." And all the assembly blessed the LORD, the God of their ancestors, and bowed their heads and prostrated themselves before the LORD and the king. [21]On the next day they offered sacrifices and burnt offerings to the LORD, a thousand bulls, a thousand rams, and a thousand lambs, with their libations, and sacrifices in abundance for all Israel; [22]and they ate and drank before the LORD on that day with great joy.

Solomon Anointed King

They made David's son Solomon king a second time; they anointed him as the LORD's prince, and Zadok as priest. [23]Then Solomon sat on the throne of the LORD, succeeding his father David as king; he prospered, and all Israel obeyed him. [24]All the leaders and the mighty warriors, and also all the sons of King David, pledged their allegiance to King Solomon. [25]The LORD highly exalted Solomon in the sight of all Israel, and bestowed upon him such royal majesty as had not been on any king before him in Israel.

Summary of David's Reign

26 Thus David son of Jesse reigned over all Israel. [27]The period that he reigned over Israel was forty years; he reigned seven years in Hebron, and thirty-three years in Jerusalem. [28]He died in a good old age, full of days, riches, and honor; and his son Solomon succeeded him. [29]Now the acts of King David, from first to last, are written in the records of the seer Samuel, and in the records of the prophet Nathan, and in the records of the seer Gad, [30]with accounts of all his rule and his might and of the events that befell him and Israel and all the kingdoms of the earth.

---

a Heb fortress

For background on this book, see the introduction to 1 and 2 Chronicles before 1 Chronicles.

2 Chronicles

Chapter 3

Solomon Requests Wisdom

1 Solomon son of David established himself in his kingdom; the Lord his God was with him and made him exceedingly great.

2 Solomon summoned all Israel, the commanders of the thousands and of the hundreds, the judges, and all the leaders of all Israel, the heads of families. ³Then Solomon, and the whole assembly with him, went to the high place that was at Gibeon; for God's tent of meeting, which Moses the servant of the Lord had made in the wilderness, was there. ⁴(But David had brought the ark of God up from Kiriath-jearim to the place that David had prepared for it; for he had pitched a tent for it in Jerusalem.) ⁵Moreover the bronze altar that Bezalel son of Uri, son of Hur, had made, was there in front of the tabernacle of the Lord. And Solomon and the assembly inquired at it. ⁶Solomon went up there to the bronze altar before the Lord, which was at the tent of meeting, and offered a thousand burnt offerings on it.

7 That night God appeared to Solomon, and said to him, "Ask what I should give you." ⁸Solomon said to God, "You have shown great and steadfast love to my father David, and have made me succeed him as king. ⁹O Lord God, let your promise to my father David now be fulfilled, for you have made me king over a people as numerous as the dust of the earth. ¹⁰Give me now wisdom and knowledge to go out and come in before this people, for who can rule this great people of yours?" ¹¹God answered Solomon, "Because this was in your heart, and you have not asked for possessions, wealth, honor, or the life of those who hate you, and have not even asked for long life, but have asked for wisdom and knowledge for yourself that you may rule my people over whom I have made you king, ¹²wisdom and knowledge are granted to you. I will also give you riches, possessions, and honor, such as none of the kings had who were before you, and none after you shall have the like." ¹³So Solomon came from*ᵃ the high place at Gibeon, from the tent of meeting, to Jerusalem. And he reigned over Israel.

Solomon's Military and Commercial Activity

14 Solomon gathered together chariots and horses; he had fourteen hundred chariots and twelve thousand horses, which he stationed in the chariot cities and with the king in Jerusalem. ¹⁵The king made silver and gold as common in Jerusalem as stone, and he made cedar as plentiful as the sycamore of the Shephelah. ¹⁶Solomon's horses were imported from Egypt and Kue; the king's traders received them from Kue at the prevailing price. ¹⁷They imported from Egypt, and then exported, a chariot for six hundred shekels of silver, and a horse for one hundred fifty; so through them these were exported to all the kings of the Hittites and the kings of Aram.

a Gk Vg: Heb *to*

413

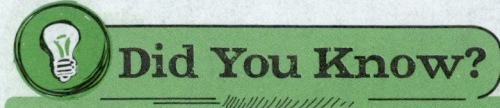

Did You Know?

Wisdom and the Torah

What a deal for Solomon! God tells him to ask for anything and Solomon will have it (see 2 Chr 1:7). Solomon prays to be wise (see verse 10), which pleases God because it indicates Solomon's desire to rule God's people according to God's will. But what is wisdom? For the Chronicler, wisdom is ultimately living one's life in conformity with God's instruction, or the Torah (see Deut 17:8–11). Wisdom is evident in the person who worships God correctly and lives a moral life in keeping with the Law, and in the king who governs justly. To learn more about the Israelites' view of wisdom, take a look at the wisdom books in the next section of the Old Testament. For a New Testament perspective, see Luke 2:41–52 and 1 Corinthians 1:18–31.

▶ 2 Chr 1:7–12

Preparations for Building the Temple

2 *a* Solomon decided to build a temple for the name of the LORD, and a royal palace for himself. 2*b* Solomon conscripted seventy thousand laborers and eighty thousand stonecutters in the hill country, with three thousand six hundred to oversee them.

Alliance with Huram of Tyre

3 Solomon sent word to King Huram of Tyre: "Once you dealt with my father David and sent him cedar to build himself a house to live in. 4I am now about to build a house for the name of the LORD my God and dedicate it to him for offering fragrant incense before him, and for the regular offering of the rows of bread, and for burnt offerings morning and evening, on the sabbaths and the new moons and the appointed festivals of the LORD our God, as ordained forever for Israel. 5The house that I am about to build will be great, for our God is greater than other gods. 6But who is able to build him a house, since heaven, even highest heaven, cannot contain him? Who am I to build a house for him, except as a place to make offerings before him? 7So now send me an artisan skilled to work in gold, silver, bronze, and iron, and in purple, crimson, and blue fabrics, trained also in engraving, to join the skilled workers who are with me in Judah and Jerusalem, whom my father David provided. 8Send me also cedar, cypress, and algum timber from Lebanon, for I know that your servants are skilled in cutting Lebanon timber. My servants will work with your servants 9to prepare timber for me in abundance, for the house I am about to build will be great and wonderful. 10I will provide for your servants, those who cut the timber, twenty thousand cors of crushed wheat, twenty thousand cors of barley, twenty thousand baths*c* of wine, and twenty thousand baths of oil."

11 Then King Huram of Tyre answered in a letter that he sent to Solomon, "Because the LORD loves his people he has made you king over them." 12Huram also said, "Blessed be the LORD God of Israel, who made heaven and earth, who has given King David a wise son, endowed with discretion and understanding, who will build a temple for the LORD, and a royal palace for himself.

13 "I have dispatched Huram-abi, a skilled artisan, endowed with understanding, 14the son of one of the Danite women, his father a Tyrian. He is trained to work in gold, silver, bronze, iron, stone, and wood, and in purple, blue, and crimson fabrics and fine linen, and to do all sorts of engraving and execute any design that may be assigned him, with your artisans, the artisans of my lord, your father David. 15Now, as for the wheat, barley, oil, and wine, of which my lord has spoken, let him send them to his servants. 16We will cut whatever timber you need from Lebanon, and bring it to you as rafts by sea to Joppa; you will take it up to Jerusalem."

17 Then Solomon took a census of all the aliens who were residing in the land of Israel, after the census that his father David had taken; and there were found to be one hundred fifty-three thousand six hundred. 18Seventy thousand of them he assigned as laborers, eighty thousand as stonecutters in the hill country, and three thousand six hundred as overseers to make the people work.

Solomon Builds the Temple

3 Solomon began to build the house of the LORD in Jerusalem on Mount Moriah, where the LORD had appeared to his father David, at the place that David had designated, on the threshing floor of Ornan the Jebusite. 2He began to build on the second day of the second month

---

a Ch 1.18 in Heb   *b* Ch 2.1 in Heb   *c* A Hebrew measure of volume

of the fourth year of his reign. ³These are Solomon's measurements*ᵃ* for building the house of God: the length, in cubits of the old standard, was sixty cubits, and the width twenty cubits. ⁴The vestibule in front of the nave of the house was twenty cubits long, across the width of the house;*ᵇ* and its height was one hundred twenty cubits. He overlaid it on the inside with pure gold. ⁵The nave he lined with cypress, covered it with fine gold, and made palms and chains on it. ⁶He adorned the house with settings of precious stones. The gold was gold from Parvaim. ⁷So he lined the house with gold—its beams, its thresholds, its walls, and its doors; and he carved cherubim on the walls.

8 He made the most holy place; its length, corresponding to the width of the house, was twenty cubits, and its width was twenty cubits; he overlaid it with six hundred talents of fine gold. ⁹The weight of the nails was fifty shekels of gold. He overlaid the upper chambers with gold.

10 In the most holy place he made two carved cherubim and overlaid*ᶜ* them with gold. ¹¹The wings of the cherubim together extended twenty cubits: one wing of the one, five cubits long, touched the wall of the house, and its other wing, five cubits long, touched the wing of the other cherub; ¹²and of this cherub, one wing, five cubits long, touched the wall of the house, and the other wing, also five cubits long, was joined to the wing of the first cherub. ¹³The wings of these cherubim extended twenty cubits; the cherubim*ᵈ* stood on their feet, facing the nave. ¹⁴And Solomon*ᵉ* made the curtain of blue and purple and crimson fabrics and fine linen, and worked cherubim into it.

15 In front of the house he made two pillars thirty-five cubits high, with a capital of five cubits on the top of each. ¹⁶He made encircling*ᶠ* chains and put them on the tops of the pillars; and he made one hundred pomegranates, and put them on the chains. ¹⁷He set up the pillars in front of the temple, one on the right, the other on the left; the one on the right he called Jachin, and the one on the left, Boaz.

Furnishings of the Temple

4 He made an altar of bronze, twenty cubits long, twenty cubits wide, and ten cubits high. ²Then he made the molten sea; it was round, ten cubits from rim to rim, and five cubits high. A line of thirty cubits would encircle it completely. ³Under it were panels all around, each of ten cubits, surrounding the sea; there were two rows of panels, cast when it was cast. ⁴It stood on twelve oxen, three facing north, three facing

west, three facing south, and three facing east; the sea was set on them. The hindquarters of each were toward the inside. ⁵Its thickness was a handbreadth; its rim was made like the rim of a cup, like the flower of a lily; it held three thousand baths.*ᵍ* ⁶He also made ten basins in which to wash, and set five on the right side, and five on the left. In these they were to rinse what was used for the burnt offering. The sea was for the priests to wash in.

7 He made ten golden lampstands as prescribed, and set them in the temple, five on the south side and five on the north. ⁸He also made ten tables and placed them in the temple, five on the right side and five on the left. And he made one hundred basins of gold. ⁹He made the court of the priests, and the great court, and doors for the court; he overlaid their doors with bronze. ¹⁰He set the sea at the southeast corner of the house.

11 And Huram made the pots, the shovels, and the basins. Thus Huram finished the work that he did for King Solomon on the house of God: ¹²the two pillars, the bowls, and the two capitals on the top of the pillars; and the two latticeworks to cover the two bowls of the capitals that were on the top of the pillars; ¹³the four hundred pomegranates for the two latticeworks,

---

a Syr: Heb *foundations*   *b* Compare 1 Kings 6.3: Meaning of Heb uncertain   *c* Heb *they overlaid*   *d* Heb *they*   *e* Heb *he* *f* Cn: Heb *in the inner sanctuary*   *g* A Hebrew measure of volume

Chapter 4

two rows of pomegranates for each latticework, to cover the two bowls of the capitals that were on the pillars. 14He made the stands, the basins on the stands, 15the one sea, and the twelve oxen underneath it. 16The pots, the shovels, the forks, and all the equipment for these Huram-abi made of burnished bronze for King Solomon for the house of the LORD. 17In the plain of the Jordan the king cast them, in the clay ground between Succoth and Zeredah. 18Solomon made all these things in great quantities, so that the weight of the bronze was not determined.

19 So Solomon made all the things that were in the house of God: the golden altar, the tables for the bread of the Presence, 20the lampstands and their lamps of pure gold to burn before the inner sanctuary, as prescribed; 21the flowers, the lamps, and the tongs, of purest gold; 22the snuffers, basins, ladles, and firepans, of pure gold. As for the entrance to the temple: the inner doors to the most holy place and the doors of the nave of the temple were of gold.

5 Thus all the work that Solomon did for the house of the LORD was finished. Solomon brought in the things that his father David had dedicated, and stored the silver, the gold, and all the vessels in the treasuries of the house of God.

The Ark Brought into the Temple

2 Then Solomon assembled the elders of Israel and all the heads of the tribes, the leaders of the ancestral houses of the people of Israel, in Jerusalem, to bring up the ark of the covenant of the LORD out of the city of David, which is Zion. 3And all the Israelites assembled before the king at the festival that is in the seventh month. 4And all the elders of Israel came, and the Levites carried the ark. 5So they brought up the ark, the tent of meeting, and all the holy vessels that were in the tent; the priests and the Levites brought them up. 6King Solomon and all the congregation of Israel, who had assembled before him, were before the ark, sacrificing so many sheep and oxen that they could not be numbered or counted. 7Then the priests brought the ark of the covenant of the LORD to its place, in the inner sanctuary of the house, in the most holy place, underneath the wings of the cherubim. 8For the cherubim spread out their wings over the place of the ark, so that the cherubim made a covering above the ark and its poles. 9The poles were so long that the ends of the poles were seen from the holy place in front of the inner sanctuary; but they could not be seen from outside; they are there to this day. 10There was nothing in the ark except the two tablets that Moses put there at Horeb, where the LORD made a covenanta with the people of Israel after they came out of Egypt.

11 Now when the priests came out of the holy place (for all the priests who were present had sanctified themselves, without regard to their divisions), 12all the levitical singers, Asaph, Heman, and Jeduthun, their sons and kindred, arrayed in fine linen, with cymbals, harps, and lyres, stood east of the altar with one hundred twenty priests who were trumpeters. 13It was the duty of the trumpeters and singers to make themselves heard in unison in praise and thanksgiving to the LORD, and when the song was raised, with trumpets and cymbals and other musical instruments, in praise to the LORD,

"For he is good,
    for his steadfast love endures forever,"

the house, the house of the LORD, was filled with a cloud, 14so that the priests could not stand to minister because of the cloud; for the glory of the LORD filled the house of God.

Dedication of the Temple

6 Then Solomon said, "The LORD has said that he would reside in thick darkness. 2I have built you an exalted house, a place for you to reside in forever."

3 Then the king turned around and blessed all the assembly of Israel, while all the assembly of Israel stood. 4And he said, "Blessed be the LORD, the God of Israel, who with his hand has fulfilled what he promised with his mouth to my father David, saying, 5'Since the day that I brought my people out of the land of Egypt, I have not chosen a city from any of the tribes of Israel in which to build a house, so that my name might be there, and I chose no one as ruler over my people Israel; 6but I have chosen Jerusalem in order that my name may be there, and I have chosen David to be over my people Israel.' 7My father David had it in mind to build a house for the name of the LORD, the God of Israel. 8But the LORD said to my father David, 'You did well to consider building a house for my name; 9nevertheless you shall not build the house, but your son who shall be born to you shall build the house for my name.' 10Now the LORD has fulfilled his promise that he made; for I have succeeded my father David, and sit on the throne of Israel, as the LORD promised, and have built the house for the name of the LORD, the God of Israel. 11There I have set the ark, in which is the covenant of the LORD that he made with the people of Israel."

a Heb lacks a covenant

Solomon's Prayer of Dedication

12 Then Solomon[a] stood before the altar of the Lord in the presence of the whole assembly of Israel, and spread out his hands. 13Solomon had made a bronze platform five cubits long, five cubits wide, and three cubits high, and had set it in the court; and he stood on it. Then he knelt on his knees in the presence of the whole assembly of Israel, and spread out his hands toward heaven. 14He said, "O Lord, God of Israel, there is no God like you, in heaven or on earth, keeping covenant in steadfast love with your servants who walk before you with all their heart— 15you who have kept for your servant, my father David, what you promised to him. Indeed, you promised with your mouth and this day have fulfilled with your hand. 16Therefore, O Lord, God of Israel, keep for your servant, my father David, that which you promised him, saying, 'There shall never fail you a successor before me to sit on the throne of Israel, if only your children keep to their way, to walk in my law as you have walked before me.' 17Therefore, O Lord, God of Israel, let your word be confirmed, which you promised to your servant David.

18 "But will God indeed reside with mortals on earth? Even heaven and the highest heaven cannot contain you, how much less this house that I have built! 19Regard your servant's prayer and his plea, O Lord my God, heeding the cry and the prayer that your servant prays to you. 20May your eyes be open day and night toward this house, the place where you promised to set your name, and may you heed the prayer that your servant prays toward this place. 21And hear the plea of your servant and of your people Israel, when they pray toward this place; may you hear from heaven your dwelling place; hear and forgive.

22 "If someone sins against another and is required to take an oath and comes and swears before your altar in this house, 23may you hear from heaven, and act, and judge your servants, repaying the guilty by bringing their conduct on their own head, and vindicating those who are in the right by rewarding them in accordance with their righteousness.

24 "When your people Israel, having sinned against you, are defeated before an enemy but turn again to you, confess your name, pray and plead with you in this house, 25may you hear from heaven, and forgive the sin of your people Israel, and bring them again to the land that you gave to them and to their ancestors.

26 "When heaven is shut up and there is no rain because they have sinned against you, and then they pray toward this place, confess your name, and turn from their sin, because you punish them, 27may you hear in heaven, forgive the sin of your servants, your people Israel, when you teach them the good way in which they should walk; and send down rain upon your land, which you have given to your people as an inheritance.

28 "If there is famine in the land, if there is plague, blight, mildew, locust, or caterpillar; if their enemies besiege them in any of the settlements of the lands; whatever suffering, whatever sickness there is; 29whatever prayer, whatever plea from any individual or from all your people Israel, all knowing their own suffering and their own sorrows so that they stretch out their hands toward this house; 30may you hear from heaven, your dwelling place, forgive, and render to all whose heart you know, according to all their ways, for only you know the human heart. 31Thus may they fear you and walk in your ways all the days that they live in the land that you gave to our ancestors.

32 "Likewise when foreigners, who are not of your people Israel, come from a distant land because of your great name, and your mighty hand, and your outstretched arm, when they come and pray toward this house, 33may you hear from heaven your dwelling place, and do whatever the foreigners ask of you, in order that all the peoples of the earth may know your name and fear you, as do your people Israel, and that they may know that your name has been invoked on this house that I have built.

34 "If your people go out to battle against their enemies, by whatever way you shall send them, and they pray to you toward this city that you have chosen and the house that I have built for your name, 35then hear from heaven their prayer and their plea, and maintain their cause.

36 "If they sin against you—for there is no one who does not sin—and you are angry with them and give them to an enemy, so that they are carried away captive to a land far or near; 37then if they come to their senses in the land to which they have been taken captive, and repent, and plead with you in the land of their captivity, saying, 'We have sinned, and have done wrong; we have acted wickedly'; 38if they repent with all their heart and soul in the land of their captivity, to which they were taken captive, and pray toward their land, which you gave to their ancestors, the city that you have chosen, and the house

---

a Heb he

that I have built for your name, [39] then hear from heaven your dwelling place their prayer and their pleas, maintain their cause and forgive your people who have sinned against you. [40] Now, O my God, let your eyes be open and your ears attentive to prayer from this place.

[41] "Now rise up, O Lord God, and go to your
    resting place,
  you and the ark of your might.
Let your priests, O Lord God, be clothed with
    salvation,
  and let your faithful rejoice in your goodness.
[42] O Lord God, do not reject your anointed one.
  Remember your steadfast love for your
    servant David."

Solomon Dedicates the Temple

7 When Solomon had ended his prayer, fire came down from heaven and consumed the burnt offering and the sacrifices; and the glory of the Lord filled the temple. [2] The priests could not enter the house of the Lord, because the glory of the Lord filled the Lord's house. [3] When all the people of Israel saw the fire come down and the glory of the Lord on the temple, they bowed down on the pavement with their faces to the ground, and worshiped and gave thanks to the Lord, saying,

  "For he is good,
    for his steadfast love endures forever."

[4] Then the king and all the people offered sacrifice before the Lord. [5] King Solomon offered as a sacrifice twenty-two thousand oxen and one hundred twenty thousand sheep. So the king and all the people dedicated the house of God. [6] The priests stood at their posts; the Levites also, with the instruments for music to the Lord that King David had made for giving thanks to the Lord—for his steadfast love endures forever—whenever David offered praises by their ministry. Opposite them the priests sounded trumpets; and all Israel stood.

[7] Solomon consecrated the middle of the court that was in front of the house of the Lord; for there he offered the burnt offerings and the fat of the offerings of well-being because the bronze altar Solomon had made could not hold the burnt offering and the grain offering and the fat parts.

[8] At that time Solomon held the festival for seven days, and all Israel with him, a very great congregation, from Lebo-hamath to the Wadi of Egypt. [9] On the eighth day they held a solemn assembly; for they had observed the dedication of the altar seven days and the festival seven days. [10] On the twenty-third day of the seventh month

he sent the people away to their homes, joyful and in good spirits because of the goodness that the Lord had shown to David and to Solomon and to his people Israel.

[11] Thus Solomon finished the house of the Lord and the king's house; all that Solomon had planned to do in the house of the Lord and in his own house he successfully accomplished.

God's Second Appearance to Solomon

[12] Then the Lord appeared to Solomon in the night and said to him: "I have heard your prayer, and have chosen this place for myself as a house of sacrifice. [13] When I shut up the heavens so that there is no rain, or command the locust to devour the land, or send pestilence among my people, [14] if my people who are called by my name humble themselves, pray, seek my face, and turn from their wicked ways, then I will hear from heaven, and will forgive their sin and heal their land. [15] Now my eyes will be open and my ears attentive to the prayer that is made in this place. [16] For now I have chosen and consecrated this house so that my name may be there forever; my eyes and my heart will be there for all time. [17] As for you, if you walk before me, as your father David walked, doing according to all that I have commanded you and keeping my statutes and my ordinances, [18] then I will establish your royal throne, as I made covenant with your father David saying, 'You shall never lack a successor to rule over Israel.'

[19] "But if you[a] turn aside and forsake my statutes and my commandments that I have set before you, and go and serve other gods and worship them, [20] then I will pluck you[b] up from the land that I have given you;[b] and this house, which I have consecrated for my name, I will cast out of my sight, and will make it a proverb and a byword among all peoples. [21] And regarding this house, now exalted, everyone passing by will be astonished, and say, 'Why has the Lord done such a thing to this land and to this house?' [22] Then they will say, 'Because they abandoned the Lord the God of their ancestors who brought them out of the land of Egypt, and they adopted other gods, and worshiped them and served them; therefore he has brought all this calamity upon them.' "

Various Activities of Solomon

8 At the end of twenty years, during which Solomon had built the house of the Lord and his own house, [2] Solomon rebuilt the cities that

---

a The word *you* in this verse is plural   *b* Heb *them*

Huram had given to him, and settled the people of Israel in them.

3 Solomon went to Hamath-zobah, and captured it. [4]He built Tadmor in the wilderness and all the storage towns that he built in Hamath. [5]He also built Upper Beth-horon and Lower Beth-horon, fortified cities, with walls, gates, and bars, [6]and Baalath, as well as all Solomon's storage towns, and all the towns for his chariots, the towns for his cavalry, and whatever Solomon desired to build, in Jerusalem, in Lebanon, and in all the land of his dominion. [7]All the people who were left of the Hittites, the Amorites, the Perizzites, the Hivites, and the Jebusites, who were not of Israel, [8]from their descendants who were still left in the land, whom the people of Israel had not destroyed—these Solomon conscripted for forced labor, as is still the case today. [9]But of the people of Israel Solomon made no slaves for his work; they were soldiers, and his officers, the commanders of his chariotry and cavalry. [10]These were the chief officers of King Solomon, two hundred fifty of them, who exercised authority over the people.

11 Solomon brought Pharaoh's daughter from the city of David to the house that he had built for her, for he said, "My wife shall not live in the house of King David of Israel, for the places to which the ark of the Lord has come are holy."

12 Then Solomon offered up burnt offerings to the Lord on the altar of the Lord that he had built in front of the vestibule, [13]as the duty of each day required, offering according to the commandment of Moses for the sabbaths, the new moons, and the three annual festivals—the festival of unleavened bread, the festival of weeks, and the festival of booths. [14]According to the ordinance of his father David, he appointed the divisions of the priests for their service, and the Levites for their offices of praise and ministry alongside the priests as the duty of each day required, and the gatekeepers in their divisions for the several gates; for so David the man of God had commanded. [15]They did not turn away from what the king had commanded the priests and Levites regarding anything at all, or regarding the treasuries.

16 Thus all the work of Solomon was accomplished from[a] the day the foundation of the house of the Lord was laid until the house of the Lord was finished completely.

17 Then Solomon went to Ezion-geber and Eloth on the shore of the sea, in the land of Edom. [18]Huram sent him, in the care of his servants, ships and servants familiar with the sea. They went to Ophir, together with the servants of Solomon, and imported from there four hundred fifty talents of gold and brought it to King Solomon.

Visit of the Queen of Sheba

9 When the queen of Sheba heard of the fame of Solomon, she came to Jerusalem to test him with hard questions, having a very great retinue and camels bearing spices and very much gold and precious stones. When she came to Solomon, she discussed with him all that was on her mind. [2]Solomon answered all her questions; there was nothing hidden from Solomon that he could not explain to her. [3]When the queen of Sheba had observed the wisdom of Solomon, the house that he had built, [4]the food of his table, the seating of his officials, and the attendance of his servants, and their clothing, his valets, and their clothing, and his burnt offerings[b] that he offered at the house of the Lord, there was no more spirit left in her.

5 So she said to the king, "The report was true that I heard in my own land of your accomplishments and of your wisdom, [6]but I did not believe the[c] reports until I came and my own eyes saw it. Not even half of the greatness of your wisdom had been told to me; you far surpass the report that I had heard. [7]Happy are your people! Happy are these your servants, who continually attend you and hear your wisdom! [8]Blessed be the Lord your God, who has delighted in you and set you on his throne as king for the Lord your God. Because your God loved Israel and would establish them forever, he has made you king over them, that you may execute justice and righteousness." [9]Then she gave the king one hundred twenty talents of gold, a very great quantity of spices, and precious stones: there were no spices such as those that the queen of Sheba gave to King Solomon.

10 Moreover the servants of Huram and the servants of Solomon who brought gold from Ophir brought algum wood and precious stones. [11]From the algum wood, the king made steps[d] for the house of the Lord and for the king's house, lyres also and harps for the singers; there never was seen the like of them before in the land of Judah.

12 Meanwhile King Solomon granted the queen of Sheba every desire that she expressed, well beyond what she had brought to the king. Then she returned to her own land, with her servants.

---

a Gk Syr Vg: Heb to   b Gk Syr Vg 1 Kings 10.5: Heb ascent
c Heb their   d Gk Vg: Meaning of Heb uncertain

Solomon's Great Wealth

13 The weight of gold that came to Solomon in one year was six hundred sixty-six talents of gold, ¹⁴besides that which the traders and merchants brought; and all the kings of Arabia and the governors of the land brought gold and silver to Solomon. ¹⁵King Solomon made two hundred large shields of beaten gold; six hundred shekels of beaten gold went into each large shield. ¹⁶He made three hundred shields of beaten gold; three hundred shekels of gold went into each shield; and the king put them in the House of the Forest of Lebanon. ¹⁷The king also made a great ivory throne, and overlaid it with pure gold. ¹⁸The throne had six steps and a footstool of gold, which were attached to the throne, and on each side of the seat were arm rests and two lions standing beside the arm rests, ¹⁹while twelve lions were standing, one on each end of a step on the six steps. The like of it was never made in any kingdom. ²⁰All King Solomon's drinking vessels were of gold, and all the vessels of the House of the Forest of Lebanon were of pure gold; silver was not considered as anything in the days of Solomon. ²¹For the king's ships went to Tarshish with the servants of Huram; once every three years the ships of Tarshish used to come bringing gold, silver, ivory, apes, and peacocks.ᵃ

22 Thus King Solomon excelled all the kings of the earth in riches and in wisdom. ²³All the kings of the earth sought the presence of Solomon to hear his wisdom, which God had put into his mind. ²⁴Every one of them brought a present, objects of silver and gold, garments, weaponry, spices, horses, and mules, so much year by year. ²⁵Solomon had four thousand stalls for horses and chariots, and twelve thousand horses, which he stationed in the chariot cities and with the king in Jerusalem. ²⁶He ruled over all the kings from the Euphrates to the land of the Philistines, and to the border of Egypt. ²⁷The king made silver as common in Jerusalem as stone, and cedar as plentiful as the sycamore of the Shephelah. ²⁸Horses were imported for Solomon from Egypt and from all lands.

Death of Solomon

29 Now the rest of the acts of Solomon, from first to last, are they not written in the history of the prophet Nathan, and in the prophecy of Ahijah the Shilonite, and in the visions of the seer Iddo concerning Jeroboam son of Nebat? ³⁰Solomon reigned in Jerusalem over all Israel forty years. ³¹Solomon slept with his ancestors and was buried in the city of his father David; and his son Rehoboam succeeded him.

The Revolt against Rehoboam

10 Rehoboam went to Shechem, for all Israel had come to Shechem to make him king. ²When Jeroboam son of Nebat heard of it (for he was in Egypt, where he had fled from King Solomon), then Jeroboam returned from Egypt. ³They sent and called him; and Jeroboam and all Israel came and said to Rehoboam, ⁴"Your father made our yoke heavy. Now therefore lighten the hard service of your father and his heavy yoke that he placed on us, and we will serve you." ⁵He said to them, "Come to me again in three days." So the people went away.

6 Then King Rehoboam took counsel with

Money Talks

"**Y**ou can't take it with you." How often have we heard this statement? We know it's true. Yet we are so easily impressed with wealth and riches. King Solomon, whose wealth is described in 2 Chronicles 9:13–28, would be right at home in our world, which seems so taken with the rich and the famous.

A common saying of those promoting sustainable living is "Live simply, so others may simply live." This is a powerful summons to us who live in a society obsessed with shopping and buying and always getting the latest and the best. In the meantime, so much of the world has to go without even the basic necessities of life.

- Think about the clothes you have, for instance. Do you wear all of them?
- What do you spend your money on? Are you generous or pretty tight-fisted? What values are expressed in how you spend your money? Is there a way that you can spend your money so the lives of others could improve?
- What is one thing you can do today to live more simply?

▶ 2 Chr 9:13–28

the older men who had attended his father Solomon while he was still alive, saying, "How do you advise me to answer this people?" [7]They answered him, "If you will be kind to this people and please them, and speak good words to them, then they will be your servants forever." [8]But he rejected the advice that the older men gave him, and consulted the young men who had grown up with him and now attended him. [9]He said to them, "What do you advise that we answer this people who have said to me, 'Lighten the yoke that your father put on us'?" [10]The young men who had grown up with him said to him, "Thus should you speak to the people who said to you, 'Your father made our yoke heavy, but you must lighten it for us'; tell them, 'My little finger is thicker than my father's loins. [11]Now, whereas my father laid on you a heavy yoke, I will add to your yoke. My father disciplined you with whips, but I will discipline you with scorpions.' "

12 So Jeroboam and all the people came to Rehoboam the third day, as the king had said, "Come to me again the third day." [13]The king answered them harshly. King Rehoboam rejected the advice of the older men; [14]he spoke to them in accordance with the advice of the young men, "My father made your yoke heavy, but I will add to it; my father disciplined you with whips, but I will discipline you with scorpions." [15]So the king did not listen to the people, because it was a turn of affairs brought about by God so that the LORD might fulfill his word, which he had spoken by Ahijah the Shilonite to Jeroboam son of Nebat.

16 When all Israel saw that the king would not listen to them, the people answered the king,

"What share do we have in David?
    We have no inheritance in the son of Jesse.
Each of you to your tents, O Israel!
    Look now to your own house, O David."

So all Israel departed to their tents. [17]But Rehoboam reigned over the people of Israel who were living in the cities of Judah. [18]When King Rehoboam sent Hadoram, who was taskmaster over the forced labor, the people of Israel stoned him to death. King Rehoboam hurriedly mounted his chariot to flee to Jerusalem. [19]So Israel has been in rebellion against the house of David to this day.

Judah and Benjamin Fortified

11 When Rehoboam came to Jerusalem, he assembled one hundred eighty thousand chosen troops of the house of Judah and Benjamin to fight against Israel, to restore the kingdom to Rehoboam. [2]But the word of the LORD came to Shemaiah the man of God: [3]Say to King Rehoboam of Judah, son of Solomon, and to all Israel in Judah and Benjamin, [4]"Thus says the LORD: You shall not go up or fight against your kindred. Let everyone return home, for this thing is from me." So they heeded the word of the LORD and turned back from the expedition against Jeroboam.

5 Rehoboam resided in Jerusalem, and he built cities for defense in Judah. [6]He built up Bethlehem, Etam, Tekoa, [7]Beth-zur, Soco, Adullam, [8]Gath, Mareshah, Ziph, [9]Adoraim, Lachish, Azekah, [10]Zorah, Aijalon, and Hebron, fortified cities that are in Judah and in Benjamin. [11]He made the fortresses strong, and put commanders in them, and stores of food, oil, and wine. [12]He also put large shields and spears in all the cities, and made them very strong. So he held Judah and Benjamin.

Priests and Levites Support Rehoboam

13 The priests and the Levites who were in all Israel presented themselves to him from all their territories. [14]The Levites had left their common lands and their holdings and had come to Judah and Jerusalem, because Jeroboam and his sons had prevented them from serving as priests of the LORD, [15]and had appointed his own priests for the high places, and for the goat-demons, and for the calves that he had made. [16]Those who had set their hearts to seek the LORD God of Israel came after them from all the tribes of Israel to Jerusalem to sacrifice to the LORD, the God of their ancestors. [17]They strengthened the kingdom of Judah, and for three years they made Rehoboam son of Solomon secure, for they walked for three years in the way of David and Solomon.

Rehoboam's Marriages

18 Rehoboam took as his wife Mahalath daughter of Jerimoth son of David, and of Abihail daughter of Eliab son of Jesse. [19]She bore him sons: Jeush, Shemariah, and Zaham. [20]After her he took Maacah daughter of Absalom, who bore him Abijah, Attai, Ziza, and Shelomith. [21]Rehoboam loved Maacah daughter of Absalom more than all his other wives and concubines (he took eighteen wives and sixty concubines, and became the father of twenty-eight sons and sixty daughters). [22]Rehoboam appointed Abijah son of Maacah as chief prince among his brothers, for he intended to make him king. [23]He dealt wisely, and distributed some of his sons through all the districts of Judah and Benjamin, in all the fortified cities; he gave them abundant provisions, and found many wives for them.

Live It!

Selling Out

King Rehoboam, son of Solomon, sold out and abandoned the law of the Lord after he thought his rule was secure (see 2 Chr 12:1). The Chronicler tells us that the Lord abandoned Rehoboam to the Egyptians because of this. Fortunately, Rehoboam and his officers repented, and the Lord showed mercy on them.

Popularity has its price. It sometimes can seem so important to hang out with the "right" people, but what do you have to give up to do that? Is it worth the price? What happens to you when you compromise your values to gain the approval of others, or when you see someone you are close to do something just to be accepted?

It is so easy to fall into the trap of "selling out." But what happens to our soul when that happens?

▶ 2 Chr 12:1–12

Egypt Attacks Judah

12 When the rule of Rehoboam was established and he grew strong, he abandoned the law of the LORD, he and all Israel with him. ²In the fifth year of King Rehoboam, because they had been unfaithful to the LORD, King Shishak of Egypt came up against Jerusalem ³with twelve hundred chariots and sixty thousand cavalry. A countless army came with him from Egypt—Libyans, Sukkiim, and Ethiopians.ᵃ ⁴He took the fortified cities of Judah and came as far as Jerusalem. ⁵Then the prophet Shemaiah came to Rehoboam and to the officers of Judah, who had gathered at Jerusalem because of Shishak, and said to them, "Thus says the LORD: You abandoned me, so I have abandoned you to the hand of Shishak." ⁶Then the officers of Israel and the king humbled themselves and said, "The LORD is in the right." ⁷When the LORD saw that they humbled themselves, the word of the LORD came to Shemaiah, saying: "They have humbled themselves; I will not destroy them, but I will grant them some deliverance, and my wrath shall not be poured out on Jerusalem by

the hand of Shishak. ⁸Nevertheless they shall be his servants, so that they may know the difference between serving me and serving the kingdoms of other lands."

9 So King Shishak of Egypt came up against Jerusalem; he took away the treasures of the house of the LORD and the treasures of the king's house; he took everything. He also took away the shields of gold that Solomon had made; ¹⁰but King Rehoboam made in place of them shields of bronze, and committed them to the hands of the officers of the guard, who kept the door of the king's house. ¹¹Whenever the king went into the house of the LORD, the guard would come along bearing them, and would then bring them back to the guardroom. ¹²Because he humbled himself the wrath of the LORD turned from him, so as not to destroy them completely; moreover, conditions were good in Judah.

Death of Rehoboam

13 So King Rehoboam established himself in Jerusalem and reigned. Rehoboam was forty-one years old when he began to reign; he reigned seventeen years in Jerusalem, the city that the LORD had chosen out of all the tribes of Israel to put his name there. His mother's name was Naamah the Ammonite. ¹⁴He did evil, for he did not set his heart to seek the LORD.

15 Now the acts of Rehoboam, from first to last, are they not written in the records of the prophet Shemaiah and of the seer Iddo, recorded by genealogy? There were continual wars between Rehoboam and Jeroboam. ¹⁶Rehoboam slept with his ancestors and was buried in the city of David; and his son Abijah succeeded him.

Abijah Reigns over Judah

13 In the eighteenth year of King Jeroboam, Abijah began to reign over Judah. ²He reigned for three years in Jerusalem. His mother's name was Micaiah daughter of Uriel of Gibeah.

Now there was war between Abijah and Jeroboam. ³Abijah engaged in battle, having an army of valiant warriors, four hundred thousand picked men; and Jeroboam drew up his line of battle against him with eight hundred thousand picked mighty warriors. ⁴Then Abijah stood on the slope of Mount Zemaraim that is in the hill country of Ephraim, and said, "Listen to me, Jeroboam and all Israel! ⁵Do you not know that the LORD God of Israel gave the kingship over Israel forever to David and his sons by a covenant of salt? ⁶Yet

---

a Or *Nubians*; Heb *Cushites*

Jeroboam son of Nebat, a servant of Solomon son of David, rose up and rebelled against his lord; [7]and certain worthless scoundrels gathered around him and defied Rehoboam son of Solomon, when Rehoboam was young and irresolute and could not withstand them.

8 "And now you think that you can withstand the kingdom of the Lord in the hand of the sons of David, because you are a great multitude and have with you the golden calves that Jeroboam made as gods for you. [9]Have you not driven out the priests of the Lord, the descendants of Aaron, and the Levites, and made priests for yourselves like the peoples of other lands? Whoever comes to be consecrated with a young bull or seven rams becomes a priest of what are no gods. [10]But as for us, the Lord is our God, and we have not abandoned him. We have priests ministering to the Lord who are descendants of Aaron, and Levites for their service. [11]They offer to the Lord every morning and every evening burnt offerings and fragrant incense, set out the rows of bread on the table of pure gold, and care for the golden lampstand so that its lamps may burn every evening; for we keep the charge of the Lord our God, but you have abandoned him. [12]See, God is with us at our head, and his priests have their battle trumpets to sound the call to battle against you. O Israelites, do not fight against the Lord, the God of your ancestors; for you cannot succeed."

13 Jeroboam had sent an ambush around to come on them from behind; thus his troops[a] were in front of Judah, and the ambush was behind them. [14]When Judah turned, the battle was in front of them and behind them. They cried out to the Lord, and the priests blew the trumpets. [15]Then the people of Judah raised the battle shout. And when the people of Judah shouted, God defeated Jeroboam and all Israel before Abijah and Judah. [16]The Israelites fled before Judah, and God gave them into their hands. [17]Abijah and his army defeated them with great slaughter; five hundred thousand picked men of Israel fell slain. [18]Thus the Israelites were subdued at that time, and the people of Judah prevailed, because they relied on the Lord, the God of their ancestors. [19]Abijah pursued Jeroboam, and took cities from him: Bethel with its villages and Jeshanah with its villages and Ephron[b] with its villages. [20]Jeroboam did not recover his power in the days of Abijah; the Lord struck him down, and he died. [21]But Abijah grew strong. He took fourteen wives, and became the father of twenty-two sons and sixteen daughters. [22]The rest of the acts of Abijah, his behavior and his deeds, are written in the story of the prophet Iddo.

Asa Reigns

14[c] So Abijah slept with his ancestors, and they buried him in the city of David. His son Asa succeeded him. In his days the land had rest for ten years. [2d] Asa did what was good and right in the sight of the Lord his God. [3]He took away the foreign altars and the high places, broke down the pillars, hewed down the sacred poles,[e] [4]and commanded Judah to seek the Lord, the God of their ancestors, and to keep the law and the commandment. [5]He also removed from all the cities of Judah the high places and the incense altars. And the kingdom had rest under him. [6]He built fortified cities in Judah while the land had rest. He had no war in those years, for the Lord gave him peace. [7]He said to Judah, "Let us build these cities, and surround them with walls and towers, gates and bars; the land is still ours because we have sought the Lord our God; we have sought him, and he has given us peace on every side." So they built and prospered. [8]Asa had an army of three hundred thousand from Judah, armed with large shields and spears, and two hundred eighty thousand troops from Benjamin who carried shields and drew bows; all these were mighty warriors.

Ethiopian Invasion Repulsed

9 Zerah the Ethiopian[f] came out against them with an army of a million men and three hundred chariots, and came as far as Mareshah. [10]Asa went out to meet him, and they drew up their lines of battle in the valley of Zephathah at Mareshah. [11]Asa cried to the Lord his God, "O Lord, there is no difference for you between helping the mighty and the weak. Help us, O Lord our God, for we rely on you, and in your name we have come against this multitude. O Lord, you are our God; let no mortal prevail against you." [12]So the Lord defeated the Ethiopians[g] before Asa and before Judah, and the Ethiopians[g] fled. [13]Asa and the army with him pursued them as far as Gerar, and the Ethiopians[g] fell until no one remained alive; for they were broken before the Lord and his army. The people of Judah[h] carried away a great quantity of booty. [14]They defeated all the cities around Gerar, for the fear of the Lord was on them. They plundered all the cities; for there was much plunder in them. [15]They also attacked the tents of those who had livestock,[i] and carried

---

a Heb *they*   b Another reading is *Ephrain*   c Ch 13.23 in Heb
d Ch 14.1 in Heb   e Heb *Asherim*   f Or Nubian; Heb *Cushite*
g Or Nubians; Heb *Cushites*   h Heb *They*   i Meaning of Heb
uncertain

away sheep and goats in abundance, and camels. Then they returned to Jerusalem.

15 The spirit of God came upon Azariah son of Oded. ²He went out to meet Asa and said to him, "Hear me, Asa, and all Judah and Benjamin: The LORD is with you, while you are with him. If you seek him, he will be found by you, but if you abandon him, he will abandon you. ³For a long time Israel was without the true God, and without a teaching priest, and without law; ⁴but when in their distress they turned to the LORD, the God of Israel, and sought him, he was found by them. ⁵In those times it was not safe for anyone to go or come, for great disturbances afflicted all the inhabitants of the lands. ⁶They were broken in pieces, nation against nation and city against city, for God troubled them with every sort of distress. ⁷But you, take courage! Do not let your hands be weak, for your work shall be rewarded."

8 When Asa heard these words, the prophecy of Azariah son of Oded,ᵃ he took courage, and put away the abominable idols from all the land of Judah and Benjamin and from the towns that he had taken in the hill country of Ephraim. He repaired the altar of the LORD that was in front of the vestibule of the house of the LORD.ᵇ ⁹He gathered all Judah and Benjamin, and those from Ephraim, Manasseh, and Simeon who were residing as aliens with them, for great numbers had deserted to him from Israel when they saw that the LORD his God was with him. ¹⁰They were gathered at Jerusalem in the third month of the fifteenth year of the reign of Asa. ¹¹They sacrificed to the LORD on that day, from the booty that they had brought, seven hundred oxen and seven thousand sheep. ¹²They entered into a covenant to seek the LORD, the God of their ancestors, with all their heart and with all their soul. ¹³Whoever would not seek the LORD, the God of Israel, should be put to death, whether young or old, man or woman. ¹⁴They took an oath to the LORD with a loud voice, and with shouting, and with trumpets, and with horns. ¹⁵All Judah rejoiced over the oath; for they had sworn with all their heart, and had sought him with their whole desire, and he was found by them, and the LORD gave them rest all around.

16 King Asa even removed his mother Maacah from being queen mother because she had made an abominable image for Asherah. Asa cut down her image, crushed it, and burned it at the Wadi Kidron. ¹⁷But the high places were not taken out of Israel. Nevertheless the heart of Asa was true all his days. ¹⁸He brought into the house of God the votive gifts of his father and his own votive gifts—silver, gold, and utensils. ¹⁹And there was no more war until the thirty-fifth year of the reign of Asa.

Alliance with Aram Condemned

16 In the thirty-sixth year of the reign of Asa, King Baasha of Israel went up against Judah, and built Ramah, to prevent anyone from going out or coming into the territory ofᶜ King Asa of Judah. ²Then Asa took silver and gold from the treasures of the house of the LORD and the king's house, and sent them to King Ben-hadad of Aram, who resided in Damascus, saying, ³"Let there be an alliance between me and you, like that between my father and your father; I am

Keep On Turning

Conversion. This is an important word for Christians. Its Latin root means "to turn around." We turn from sin and toward God, as individuals and as a people. In 2 Chronicles 15:8–15, we read about King Asa and his people hearing the words of the prophet Azariah and then turning away from idols and turning back to God.

Conversion is not a one-time event. It is a process all of us go through again and again as our faith and understanding grow. We are reminded of that especially during the season of Lent. On Ash Wednesday, as individuals and as a community, we hear, "Repent, and believe the Gospel" (*Roman Missal*). The Israelites went through the same thing. Again and again, they were called to turn back to God.

If we are committed to following Jesus, conversion is a lifelong process of deepening our faith.

● Where are you most in need of conversion? Where is our nation most in need of conversion?

▶ 2 Chr 15:8–15

ᵃ Compare Syr Vg: Heb *the prophecy, the prophet Obed*
ᵇ Heb *the vestibule of the LORD*   ᶜ Heb lacks *the territory of*

sending to you silver and gold; go, break your alliance with King Baasha of Israel, so that he may withdraw from me." [4]Ben-hadad listened to King Asa, and sent the commanders of his armies against the cities of Israel. They conquered Ijon, Dan, Abel-maim, and all the store-cities of Naphtali. [5]When Baasha heard of it, he stopped building Ramah, and let his work cease. [6]Then King Asa brought all Judah, and they carried away the stones of Ramah and its timber, with which Baasha had been building, and with them he built up Geba and Mizpah.

[7] At that time the seer Hanani came to King Asa of Judah, and said to him, "Because you relied on the king of Aram, and did not rely on the LORD your God, the army of the king of Aram has escaped you. [8]Were not the Ethiopians[a] and the Libyans a huge army with exceedingly many chariots and cavalry? Yet because you relied on the LORD, he gave them into your hand. [9]For the eyes of the LORD range throughout the entire earth, to strengthen those whose heart is true to him. You have done foolishly in this; for from now on you will have wars." [10]Then Asa was angry with the seer, and put him in the stocks, in prison, for he was in a rage with him because of this. And Asa inflicted cruelties on some of the people at the same time.

Asa's Disease and Death

[11] The acts of Asa, from first to last, are written in the Book of the Kings of Judah and Israel. [12]In the thirty-ninth year of his reign Asa was diseased in his feet, and his disease became severe; yet even in his disease he did not seek the LORD, but sought help from physicians. [13]Then Asa slept with his ancestors, dying in the forty-first year of his reign. [14]They buried him in the tomb that he had hewn out for himself in the city of David. They laid him on a bier that had been filled with various kinds of spices prepared by the perfumer's art; and they made a very great fire in his honor.

Jehoshaphat's Reign

17 His son Jehoshaphat succeeded him, and strengthened himself against Israel. [2]He placed forces in all the fortified cities of Judah, and set garrisons in the land of Judah, and in the cities of Ephraim that his father Asa had taken. [3]The LORD was with Jehoshaphat, because he walked in the earlier ways of his father;[b] he did not seek the Baals, [4]but sought the God of his father and walked in his commandments, and not according to the ways of Israel. [5]Therefore the LORD established the kingdom in his hand.

All Judah brought tribute to Jehoshaphat, and he had great riches and honor. [6]His heart was courageous in the ways of the LORD; and furthermore he removed the high places and the sacred poles[c] from Judah.

[7] In the third year of his reign he sent his officials, Ben-hail, Obadiah, Zechariah, Nethanel, and Micaiah, to teach in the cities of Judah. [8]With them were the Levites, Shemaiah, Nethaniah, Zebadiah, Asahel, Shemiramoth, Jehonathan, Adonijah, Tobijah, and Tob-adonijah; and with these Levites, the priests Elishama and Jehoram. [9]They taught in Judah, having the book of the law of the LORD with them; they went around through all the cities of Judah and taught among the people.

[10] The fear of the LORD fell on all the kingdoms of the lands around Judah, and they did not make war against Jehoshaphat. [11]Some of the Philistines brought Jehoshaphat presents, and silver for tribute; and the Arabs also brought him seven thousand seven hundred rams and seven thousand seven hundred male goats. [12]Jehoshaphat grew steadily greater. He built fortresses and storage cities in Judah. [13]He carried out great works in the cities of Judah. He had soldiers, mighty warriors, in Jerusalem. [14]This was the muster of them by ancestral houses: Of Judah, the commanders of the thousands: Adnah the commander, with three hundred thousand mighty warriors, [15]and next to him Jehohanan the commander, with two hundred eighty thousand, [16]and next to him Amasiah son of Zichri, a volunteer for the service of the LORD, with two hundred thousand mighty warriors. [17]Of Benjamin: Eliada, a mighty warrior, with two hundred thousand armed with bow and shield, [18]and next to him Jehozabad with one hundred eighty thousand armed for war. [19]These were in the service of the king, besides those whom the king had placed in the fortified cities throughout all Judah.

Micaiah Predicts Failure

18 Now Jehoshaphat had great riches and honor; and he made a marriage alliance with Ahab. [2]After some years he went down to Ahab in Samaria. Ahab slaughtered an abundance of sheep and oxen for him and for the people who were with him, and induced him to go up against Ramoth-gilead. [3]King Ahab of Israel said to King Jehoshaphat of Judah, "Will you go with me to Ramoth-gilead?" He answered

---

a Or Nubians; Heb Cushites   b Another reading is *his father David*   c Heb *Asherim*

him, "I am with you, my people are your people. We will be with you in the war."

4 But Jehoshaphat also said to the king of Israel, "Inquire first for the word of the LORD." 5Then the king of Israel gathered the prophets together, four hundred of them, and said to them, "Shall we go to battle against Ramoth-gilead, or shall I refrain?" They said, "Go up; for God will give it into the hand of the king." 6But Jehoshaphat said, "Is there no other prophet of the LORD here of whom we may inquire?" 7The king of Israel said to Jehoshaphat, "There is still one other by whom we may inquire of the LORD, Micaiah son of Imlah; but I hate him, for he never prophesies anything favorable about me, but only disaster." Jehoshaphat said, "Let the king not say such a thing." 8Then the king of Israel summoned an officer and said, "Bring quickly Micaiah son of Imlah." 9Now the king of Israel and King Jehoshaphat of Judah were sitting on their thrones, arrayed in their robes; and they were sitting at the threshing floor at the entrance of the gate of Samaria; and all the prophets were prophesying before them. 10Zedekiah son of Chenaanah made for himself horns of iron, and he said, "Thus says the LORD: With these you shall gore the Arameans until they are destroyed." 11All the prophets were prophesying the same and saying, "Go up to Ramoth-gilead and triumph; the LORD will give it into the hand of the king."

12 The messenger who had gone to summon Micaiah said to him, "Look, the words of the prophets with one accord are favorable to the king; let your word be like the word of one of them, and speak favorably." 13But Micaiah said, "As the LORD lives, whatever my God says, that I will speak."

14 When he had come to the king, the king said to him, "Micaiah, shall we go to Ramoth-gilead to battle, or shall I refrain?" He answered, "Go up and triumph; they will be given into your hand." 15But the king said to him, "How many times must I make you swear to tell me nothing but the truth in the name of the LORD?" 16Then Micaiah[a] said, "I saw all Israel scattered on the mountains, like sheep without a shepherd; and the LORD said, 'These have no master; let each one go home in peace.' " 17The king of Israel said to Jehoshaphat, "Did I not tell you that he would not prophesy anything favorable about me, but only disaster?"

18 Then Micaiah[a] said, "Therefore hear the word of the LORD: I saw the LORD sitting on his throne, with all the host of heaven standing to the right and to the left of him. 19And the LORD said, 'Who will entice King Ahab of Israel, so that

he may go up and fall at Ramoth-gilead?' Then one said one thing, and another said another, 20until a spirit came forward and stood before the LORD, saying, 'I will entice him.' The LORD asked him, 'How?' 21He replied, 'I will go out and be a lying spirit in the mouth of all his prophets.' Then the LORD[a] said, 'You are to entice him, and you shall succeed; go out and do it.' 22So you see, the LORD has put a lying spirit in the mouth of these your prophets; the LORD has decreed disaster for you."

23 Then Zedekiah son of Chenaanah came up to Micaiah, slapped him on the cheek, and said, "Which way did the spirit of the LORD pass from me to speak to you?" 24Micaiah replied, "You will find out on that day when you go in to hide in an inner chamber." 25The king of Israel then ordered, "Take Micaiah, and return him to Amon the governor of the city and to Joash the king's son; 26and say, 'Thus says the king: Put this fellow in prison, and feed him on reduced rations of bread and water until I return in peace.' " 27Micaiah said, "If you return in peace, the LORD has not spoken by me." And he said, "Hear, you peoples, all of you!"

Defeat and Death of Ahab

28 So the king of Israel and King Jehoshaphat of Judah went up to Ramoth-gilead. 29The king of Israel said to Jehoshaphat, "I will disguise myself and go into battle, but you wear your robes." So the king of Israel disguised himself, and they went into battle. 30Now the king of Aram had commanded the captains of his chariots, "Fight with no one small or great, but only with the king of Israel." 31When the captains of the chariots saw Jehoshaphat, they said, "It is the king of Israel." So they turned to fight against him; and Jehoshaphat cried out, and the LORD helped him. God drew them away from him, 32for when the captains of the chariots saw that it was not the king of Israel, they turned back from pursuing him. 33But a certain man drew his bow and unknowingly struck the king of Israel between the scale armor and the breastplate; so he said to the driver of his chariot, "Turn around, and carry me out of the battle, for I am wounded." 34The battle grew hot that day, and the king of Israel propped himself up in his chariot facing the Arameans until evening; then at sunset he died.

19 King Jehoshaphat of Judah returned in safety to his house in Jerusalem. 2Jehu son of Hanani the seer went out to meet him and said to King Jehoshaphat, "Should you help the wicked

a Heb he

and love those who hate the LORD? Because of this, wrath has gone out against you from the LORD. ³Nevertheless, some good is found in you, for you destroyed the sacred poles*a* out of the land, and have set your heart to seek God."

The Reforms of Jehoshaphat

4 Jehoshaphat resided at Jerusalem; then he went out again among the people, from Beer-sheba to the hill country of Ephraim, and brought them back to the LORD, the God of their ancestors. ⁵He appointed judges in the land in all the fortified cities of Judah, city by city, ⁶and said to the judges, "Consider what you are doing, for you judge not on behalf of human beings but on the LORD's behalf; he is with you in giving judgment. ⁷Now, let the fear of the LORD be upon you; take care what you do, for there is no perversion of justice with the LORD our God, or partiality, or taking of bribes."

8 Moreover in Jerusalem Jehoshaphat appointed certain Levites and priests and heads of families of Israel, to give judgment for the LORD and to decide disputed cases. They had their seat at Jerusalem. ⁹He charged them: "This is how you shall act: in the fear of the LORD, in faithfulness, and with your whole heart; ¹⁰whenever a case comes to you from your kindred who live in their cities, concerning bloodshed, law or commandment, statutes or ordinances, then you shall instruct them, so that they may not incur guilt before the LORD and wrath may not come on you and your kindred. Do so, and you will not incur guilt. ¹¹See, Amariah the chief priest is over you in all matters of the LORD; and Zebadiah son of Ishmael, the governor of the house of Judah, in all the king's matters; and the Levites will serve you as officers. Deal courageously, and may the LORD be with the good!"

Invasion from the East

20 After this the Moabites and Ammonites, and with them some of the Meunites,*b* came against Jehoshaphat for battle. ²Messengers*c* came and told Jehoshaphat, "A great multitude is coming against you from Edom,*d* from beyond the sea; already they are at Hazazon-tamar" (that is, En-gedi). ³Jehoshaphat was afraid; he set himself to seek the LORD, and proclaimed a fast throughout all Judah. ⁴Judah assembled to seek help from the LORD; from all the towns of Judah they came to seek the LORD.

Jehoshaphat's Prayer and Victory

5 Jehoshaphat stood in the assembly of Judah and Jerusalem, in the house of the LORD, before the new court, ⁶and said, "O LORD, God of our ancestors, are you not God in heaven? Do you not rule over all the kingdoms of the nations? In your hand are power and might, so that no one is able to withstand you. ⁷Did you not, O our God, drive out the inhabitants of this land before your people Israel, and give it forever to the descendants of your friend Abraham? ⁸They have lived in it, and in it have built you a sanctuary for your name, saying, ⁹'If disaster comes upon us, the sword, judgment,*e* or pestilence, or famine, we will stand before this house, and before you, for your name is in this house, and cry to you in our distress, and you will hear and save.' ¹⁰See now, the people of Ammon, Moab, and Mount Seir, whom you would not let Israel invade when they came from the land of Egypt, and whom they avoided and did not destroy— ¹¹they reward us by coming to drive us out of your possession that you have given us to inherit. ¹²O our God, will you not execute judgment upon them? For we are powerless against this great multitude that is coming against us. We do not know what to do, but our eyes are on you."

13 Meanwhile all Judah stood before the LORD, with their little ones, their wives, and their children. ¹⁴Then the spirit of the LORD came upon Jahaziel son of Zechariah, son of Benaiah, son of Jeiel, son of Mattaniah, a Levite of the sons of Asaph, in the middle of the assembly. ¹⁵He said, "Listen, all Judah and inhabitants of Jerusalem, and King Jehoshaphat: Thus says the LORD to you: 'Do not fear or be dismayed at this great multitude; for the battle is not yours but God's. ¹⁶Tomorrow go down against them; they will come up by the ascent of Ziz; you will find them at the end of the valley, before the wilderness of Jeruel. ¹⁷This battle is not for you to fight; take your position, stand still, and see the victory of the LORD on your behalf, O Judah and Jerusalem.' Do not fear or be dismayed; tomorrow go out against them, and the LORD will be with you."

18 Then Jehoshaphat bowed down with his face to the ground, and all Judah and the inhabitants of Jerusalem fell down before the LORD, worshiping the LORD. ¹⁹And the Levites, of the Kohathites and the Korahites, stood up to praise the LORD, the God of Israel, with a very loud voice.

20 They rose early in the morning and went out into the wilderness of Tekoa; and as they went out, Jehoshaphat stood and said, "Listen to me, O Judah and inhabitants of Jerusalem!

a Heb *Asheroth*   b Compare 26.7: Heb *Ammonites*
c Heb *They*   d One Ms: MT *Aram*   e Or *the sword of judgment*

2 CHR

Believe in the LORD your God and you will be established; believe his prophets." ²¹When he had taken counsel with the people, he appointed those who were to sing to the LORD and praise him in holy splendor, as they went before the army, saying,

"Give thanks to the LORD,

for his steadfast love endures forever."

²²As they began to sing and praise, the LORD set an ambush against the Ammonites, Moab, and Mount Seir, who had come against Judah, so that they were routed. ²³For the Ammonites and Moab attacked the inhabitants of Mount Seir, destroying them utterly; and when they had made an end of the inhabitants of Seir, they all helped to destroy one another.

24 When Judah came to the watchtower of the wilderness, they looked toward the multitude; they were corpses lying on the ground; no one had escaped. ²⁵When Jehoshaphat and his people came to take the booty from them, they found livestock*a* in great numbers, goods, clothing, and precious things, which they took for themselves until they could carry no more. They spent three days taking the booty, because of its abundance. ²⁶On the fourth day they assembled in the Valley of Beracah, for there they blessed the LORD; therefore that place has been called the Valley of Beracah*b* to this day. ²⁷Then all the people of Judah and Jerusalem, with Jehoshaphat at their head, returned to Jerusalem with joy, for the LORD had enabled them to rejoice over their enemies. ²⁸They came to Jerusalem, with harps and lyres and trumpets, to the house of the LORD. ²⁹The fear of God came on all the kingdoms of the countries when they heard that the LORD had fought against the enemies of Israel. ³⁰And the realm of Jehoshaphat was quiet, for his God gave him rest all around.

The End of Jehoshaphat's Reign

31 So Jehoshaphat reigned over Judah. He was thirty-five years old when he began to reign; he reigned twenty-five years in Jerusalem. His mother's name was Azubah daughter of Shilhi. ³²He walked in the way of his father Asa and did not turn aside from it, doing what was right in the sight of the LORD. ³³Yet the high places were not removed; the people had not yet set their hearts upon the God of their ancestors.

34 Now the rest of the acts of Jehoshaphat, from first to last, are written in the Annals of Jehu son of Hanani, which are recorded in the Book of the Kings of Israel.

35 After this King Jehoshaphat of Judah joined with King Ahaziah of Israel, who did wickedly.

³⁶He joined him in building ships to go to Tarshish; they built the ships in Ezion-geber. ³⁷Then Eliezer son of Dodavahu of Mareshah prophesied against Jehoshaphat, saying, "Because you have joined with Ahaziah, the LORD will destroy what you have made." And the ships were wrecked and were not able to go to Tarshish.

Jehoram's Reign

21 Jehoshaphat slept with his ancestors and was buried with his ancestors in the city of David; his son Jehoram succeeded him. ²He had brothers, the sons of Jehoshaphat: Azariah, Jehiel, Zechariah, Azariah, Michael, and Shephatiah; all these were the sons of King Jehoshaphat of Judah.*c* ³Their father gave them many gifts, of silver, gold, and valuable possessions, together with fortified cities in Judah; but he gave the kingdom to Jehoram, because he was the firstborn. ⁴When Jehoram had ascended the throne of his father and was established, he put all his brothers to the sword, and also some of the officials of Israel. ⁵Jehoram was thirty-two years old when he began to reign; he reigned eight years in Jerusalem. ⁶He walked in the way of the kings of Israel, as the house of Ahab had done; for the daughter of Ahab was his wife. He did what was evil in the sight of the LORD. ⁷Yet the LORD would not destroy the house of David because of the covenant that he had made with David, and since he had promised to give a lamp to him and to his descendants forever.

Revolt of Edom

8 In his days Edom revolted against the rule of Judah and set up a king of their own. ⁹Then Jehoram crossed over with his commanders and all his chariots. He set out by night and attacked the Edomites, who had surrounded him and his chariot commanders. ¹⁰So Edom has been in revolt against the rule of Judah to this day. At that time Libnah also revolted against his rule, because he had forsaken the LORD, the God of his ancestors.

Elijah's Letter

11 Moreover he made high places in the hill country of Judah, and led the inhabitants of Jerusalem into unfaithfulness, and made Judah go astray. ¹²A letter came to him from the prophet Elijah, saying: "Thus says the LORD, the God of your father David: Because you have not walked in the ways of your father Jehoshaphat or in the ways of King Asa of Judah, ¹³but have walked

---

a Gk: Heb *among them*   *b* That is *Blessing*   *c* Gk Syr: Heb *Israel*

in the way of the kings of Israel, and have led Judah and the inhabitants of Jerusalem into unfaithfulness, as the house of Ahab led Israel into unfaithfulness, and because you also have killed your brothers, members of your father's house, who were better than yourself, [14]see, the LORD will bring a great plague on your people, your children, your wives, and all your possessions, [15]and you yourself will have a severe sickness with a disease of your bowels, until your bowels come out, day after day, because of the disease."

16 The LORD aroused against Jehoram the anger of the Philistines and of the Arabs who are near the Ethiopians.[a] [17]They came up against Judah, invaded it, and carried away all the possessions they found that belonged to the king's house, along with his sons and his wives, so that no son was left to him except Jehoahaz, his youngest son.

Disease and Death of Jehoram

18 After all this the LORD struck him in his bowels with an incurable disease. [19]In course of time, at the end of two years, his bowels came out because of the disease, and he died in great agony. His people made no fire in his honor, like the fires made for his ancestors. [20]He was thirty-two years old when he began to reign; he reigned eight years in Jerusalem. He departed with no one's regret. They buried him in the city of David, but not in the tombs of the kings.

Ahaziah's Reign

22 The inhabitants of Jerusalem made his youngest son Ahaziah king as his successor; for the troops who came with the Arabs to the camp had killed all the older sons. So Ahaziah son of Jehoram reigned as king of Judah. [2]Ahaziah was forty-two years old when he began to reign; he reigned one year in Jerusalem. His mother's name was Athaliah, a granddaughter of Omri. [3]He also walked in the ways of the house of Ahab, for his mother was his counselor in doing wickedly. [4]He did what was evil in the sight of the LORD, as the house of Ahab had done; for after the death of his father they were his counselors, to his ruin. [5]He even followed their advice, and went with Jehoram son of King Ahab of Israel to make war against King Hazael of Aram at Ramoth-gilead. The Arameans wounded Joram, [6]and he returned to be healed in Jezreel of the wounds that he had received at Ramah, when he fought King Hazael of Aram. And Ahaziah son of King Jehoram of Judah went down to see Joram son of Ahab in Jezreel, because he was sick.

7 But it was ordained by God that the downfall

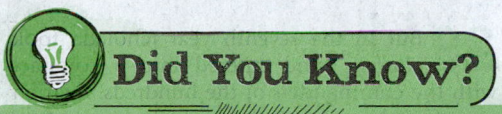

Did You Know?

The Role of the Prophet

The letter from Elijah to King Jehoram discussed in 2 Chronicles 21:12–15 underscores the principal role of the Hebrew prophet: to be God's voice, the one who speaks for God. Although many early figures are called prophets, including Moses and Deborah, the classical prophet—*nabi'* in Hebrew—appeared later in Israelite history. The primary function of the prophet was not to foretell the future but to announce God's judgment, to confront those who violated God's law, and to console those who suffered. In short, the prophets were the conscience of the Israelite nation.

▶ 2 Chr 21:12–15

of Ahaziah should come about through his going to visit Joram. For when he came there he went out with Jehoram to meet Jehu son of Nimshi, whom the LORD had anointed to destroy the house of Ahab. [8]When Jehu was executing judgment on the house of Ahab, he met the officials of Judah and the sons of Ahaziah's brothers, who attended Ahaziah, and he killed them. [9]He searched for Ahaziah, who was captured while hiding in Samaria and was brought to Jehu, and put to death. They buried him, for they said, "He is the grandson of Jehoshaphat, who sought the LORD with all his heart." And the house of Ahaziah had no one able to rule the kingdom.

Athaliah Seizes the Throne

10 Now when Athaliah, Ahaziah's mother, saw that her son was dead, she set about to destroy all the royal family of the house of Judah. [11]But Jehoshabeath, the king's daughter, took Joash son of Ahaziah, and stole him away from among the king's children who were about to be killed; she put him and his nurse in a bedroom. Thus Jehoshabeath, daughter of King Jehoram and wife of the priest Jehoiada—because she was a sister of Ahaziah—hid him from Athaliah, so that she did not kill him; [12]he remained with them six years, hidden in the house of God, while Athaliah reigned over the land.

a Or *Nubians*; Heb *Cushites*

2 CHR

23

But in the seventh year Jehoiada took courage, and entered into a compact with the commanders of the hundreds, Azariah son of Jeroham, Ishmael son of Jehohanan, Azariah son of Obed, Maaseiah son of Adaiah, and Elishaphat son of Zichri. ²They went around through Judah and gathered the Levites from all the towns of Judah, and the heads of families of Israel, and they came to Jerusalem. ³Then the whole assembly made a covenant with the king in the house of God. Jehoiada*a* said to them, "Here is the king's son! Let him reign, as the LORD promised concerning the sons of David. ⁴This is what you are to do: one-third of you, priests and Levites, who come on duty on the sabbath, shall be gatekeepers, ⁵one-third shall be at the king's house, and one-third at the Gate of the Foundation; and all the people shall be in the courts of the house of the LORD. ⁶Do not let anyone enter the house of the LORD except the priests and ministering Levites; they may enter, for they are holy, but all the other*b* people shall observe the instructions of the LORD. ⁷The Levites shall surround the king, each with his weapons in his hand; and whoever enters the house shall be killed. Stay with the king in his comings and goings."

Joash Crowned King

8 The Levites and all Judah did according to all that the priest Jehoiada commanded; each brought his men, who were to come on duty on the sabbath, with those who were to go off duty on the sabbath; for the priest Jehoiada did not dismiss the divisions. ⁹The priest Jehoiada delivered to the captains the spears and the large and small shields that had been King David's, which were in the house of God; ¹⁰and he set all the people as a guard for the king, everyone with weapon in hand, from the south side of the house to the north side of the house, around the altar and the house. ¹¹Then he brought out the king's son, put the crown on him, and gave him the covenant;*c* they proclaimed him king, and Jehoiada and his sons anointed him; and they shouted, "Long live the king!"

Athaliah Murdered

12 When Athaliah heard the noise of the people running and praising the king, she went into the house of the LORD to the people; ¹³and when she looked, there was the king standing by his pillar at the entrance, and the captains and the trumpeters beside the king, and all the people of the land rejoicing and blowing trumpets, and the singers with their musical instruments leading in the celebration. Athaliah tore her clothes, and cried, "Treason! Treason!" ¹⁴Then the priest Jehoiada brought out the captains who were set over the army, saying to them, "Bring her out between the ranks; anyone who follows her is to be put to the sword." For the priest said, "Do not put her to death in the house of the LORD." ¹⁵So they laid hands on her; she went into the entrance of the Horse Gate of the king's house, and there they put her to death.

16 Jehoiada made a covenant between himself and all the people and the king that they should be the LORD's people. ¹⁷Then all the people went to the house of Baal, and tore it down; his altars and his images they broke in pieces, and they killed Mattan, the priest of Baal, in front of the altars. ¹⁸Jehoiada assigned the care of the house of the LORD to the levitical priests whom David had organized to be in charge of the house of the LORD, to offer burnt offerings to the LORD, as it is written in the law of Moses, with rejoicing and with singing, according to the order of David. ¹⁹He stationed the gatekeepers at the gates of the house of the LORD so that no one should enter who was in any way unclean. ²⁰And he took the captains, the nobles, the governors of the people, and all the people of the land, and they brought the king down from the house of the LORD, marching through the upper gate to the king's house. They set the king on the royal throne. ²¹So all the people of the land rejoiced, and the city was quiet after Athaliah had been killed with the sword.

Joash Repairs the Temple

24

Joash was seven years old when he began to reign; he reigned forty years in Jerusalem; his mother's name was Zibiah of Beer-sheba. ²Joash did what was right in the sight of the LORD all the days of the priest Jehoiada. ³Jehoiada got two wives for him, and he became the father of sons and daughters.

4 Some time afterward Joash decided to restore the house of the LORD. ⁵He assembled the priests and the Levites and said to them, "Go out to the cities of Judah and gather money from all Israel to repair the house of your God, year by year; and see that you act quickly." But the Levites did not act quickly. ⁶So the king summoned Jehoiada the chief, and said to him, "Why have you not required the Levites to bring in from Judah and Jerusalem the tax levied by Moses, the servant of the LORD, on*d* the congregation

---

a Heb *He*   *b* Heb lacks *other*   *c* Or *treaty,* or *testimony;* Heb *eduth*   *d* Compare Vg: Heb *and*

of Israel for the tent of the covenant?"*a* 7For the children of Athaliah, that wicked woman, had broken into the house of God, and had even used all the dedicated things of the house of the Lord for the Baals.

8 So the king gave command, and they made a chest, and set it outside the gate of the house of the Lord. 9A proclamation was made throughout Judah and Jerusalem to bring in for the Lord the tax that Moses the servant of God laid on Israel in the wilderness. 10All the leaders and all the people rejoiced and brought their tax and dropped it into the chest until it was full. 11Whenever the chest was brought to the king's officers by the Levites, when they saw that there was a large amount of money in it, the king's secretary and the officer of the chief priest would come and empty the chest and take it and return it to its place. So they did day after day, and collected money in abundance. 12The king and Jehoiada gave it to those who had charge of the work of the house of the Lord, and they hired masons and carpenters to restore the house of the Lord, and also workers in iron and bronze to repair the house of the Lord. 13So those who were engaged in the work labored, and the repairing went forward at their hands, and they restored the house of God to its proper condition and strengthened it. 14When they had finished, they brought the rest of the money to the king and Jehoiada, and with it were made utensils for the house of the Lord, utensils for the service and for the burnt offerings, and ladles, and vessels of gold and silver. They offered burnt offerings in the house of the Lord regularly all the days of Jehoiada.

Apostasy of Joash

15 But Jehoiada grew old and full of days, and died; he was one hundred thirty years old at his death. 16And they buried him in the city of David among the kings, because he had done good in Israel, and for God and his house.

17 Now after the death of Jehoiada the officials of Judah came and did obeisance to the king; then the king listened to them. 18They abandoned the house of the Lord, the God of their ancestors, and served the sacred poles*b* and the idols. And wrath came upon Judah and Jerusalem for this guilt of theirs. 19Yet he sent prophets among them to bring them back to the Lord; they testified against them, but they would not listen.

20 Then the spirit of God took possession of*c* Zechariah son of the priest Jehoiada; he stood above the people and said to them, "Thus says

God: Why do you transgress the commandments of the Lord, so that you cannot prosper? Because you have forsaken the Lord, he has also forsaken you." 21But they conspired against him, and by command of the king they stoned him to death in the court of the house of the Lord. 22King Joash did not remember the kindness that Jehoiada, Zechariah's father, had shown him, but killed his son. As he was dying, he said, "May the Lord see and avenge!"

Death of Joash

23 At the end of the year the army of Aram came up against Joash. They came to Judah and Jerusalem, and destroyed all the officials of the people from among them, and sent all the booty they took to the king of Damascus. 24Although the army of Aram had come with few men, the Lord delivered into their hand a very great army, because they had abandoned the Lord, the God of their ancestors. Thus they executed judgment on Joash.

25 When they had withdrawn, leaving him severely wounded, his servants conspired against him because of the blood of the son*d* of the priest Jehoiada, and they killed him on his bed. So he died; and they buried him in the city of David, but they did not bury him in the tombs of the kings. 26Those who conspired against him were Zabad son of Shimeath the Ammonite, and Jehozabad son of Shimrith the Moabite. 27Accounts of his sons, and of the many oracles against him, and of the rebuilding*e* of the house of God are written in the Commentary on the Book of the Kings. And his son Amaziah succeeded him.

Reign of Amaziah

25 Amaziah was twenty-five years old when he began to reign, and he reigned twenty-nine years in Jerusalem. His mother's name was Jehoaddan of Jerusalem. 2He did what was right in the sight of the Lord, yet not with a true heart. 3As soon as the royal power was firmly in his hand he killed his servants who had murdered his father the king. 4But he did not put their children to death, according to what is written in the law, in the book of Moses, where the Lord commanded, "The parents shall not be put to death for the children, or the children be put to death for the parents; but all shall be put to death for their own sins."

---

a Or treaty, or testimony; Heb eduth *b* Heb Asherim *c* Heb clothed itself with *d* Gk Vg: Heb sons *e* Heb founding

Slaughter of the Edomites

5 Amaziah assembled the people of Judah, and set them by ancestral houses under commanders of the thousands and of the hundreds for all Judah and Benjamin. He mustered those twenty years old and upward, and found that they were three hundred thousand picked troops fit for war, able to handle spear and shield. [6]He also hired one hundred thousand mighty warriors from Israel for one hundred talents of silver. [7]But a man of God came to him and said, "O king, do not let the army of Israel go with you, for the LORD is not with Israel—all these Ephraimites. [8]Rather, go by yourself and act; be strong in battle, or God will fling you down before the enemy; for God has power to help or to overthrow." [9]Amaziah said to the man of God, "But what shall we do about the hundred talents that I have given to the army of Israel?" The man of God answered, "The LORD is able to give you much more than this." [10]Then Amaziah discharged the army that had come to him from Ephraim, letting them go home again. But they became very angry with Judah, and returned home in fierce anger.

11 Amaziah took courage, and led out his people; he went to the Valley of Salt, and struck down ten thousand men of Seir. [12]The people of Judah captured another ten thousand alive, took them to the top of Sela, and threw them down from the top of Sela, so that all of them were dashed to pieces. [13]But the men of the army whom Amaziah sent back, not letting them go with him to battle, fell on the cities of Judah from Samaria to Beth-horon; they killed three thousand people in them, and took much booty.

14 Now after Amaziah came from the slaughter of the Edomites, he brought the gods of the people of Seir, set them up as his gods, and worshiped them, making offerings to them. [15]The LORD was angry with Amaziah and sent to him a prophet, who said to him, "Why have you resorted to a people's gods who could not deliver their own people from your hand?" [16]But as he was speaking the king[a] said to him, "Have we made you a royal counselor? Stop! Why should you be put to death?" So the prophet stopped, but said, "I know that God has determined to destroy you, because you have done this and have not listened to my advice."

Israel Defeats Judah

17 Then King Amaziah of Judah took counsel and sent to King Joash son of Jehoahaz son of Jehu of Israel, saying, "Come, let us look one another in the face." [18]King Joash of Israel sent word to King Amaziah of Judah, "A thornbush on Lebanon sent to a cedar on Lebanon, saying, 'Give your daughter to my son for a wife'; but a wild animal of Lebanon passed by and trampled down the thornbush. [19]You say, 'See, I have defeated Edom,' and your heart has lifted you up in boastfulness. Now stay at home; why should you provoke trouble so that you fall, you and Judah with you?"

20 But Amaziah would not listen—it was God's doing, in order to hand them over, because they had sought the gods of Edom. [21]So King Joash of Israel went up; he and King Amaziah of Judah faced one another in battle at Beth-shemesh, which belongs to Judah. [22]Judah was defeated by Israel; everyone fled home. [23]King Joash of Israel captured King Amaziah of Judah, son of Joash, son of Ahaziah, at Beth-shemesh; he brought him to Jerusalem, and broke down the wall of Jerusalem from the Ephraim Gate to the Corner Gate, a distance of four hundred cubits. [24]He seized all the gold and silver, and all the vessels that were found in the house of God, and Obed-edom with them; he seized also the treasuries of the king's house, also hostages; then he returned to Samaria.

Death of Amaziah

25 King Amaziah son of Joash of Judah, lived fifteen years after the death of King Joash son of Jehoahaz of Israel. [26]Now the rest of the deeds of Amaziah, from first to last, are they not written in the Book of the Kings of Judah and Israel? [27]From the time that Amaziah turned away from the LORD they made a conspiracy against him in Jerusalem, and he fled to Lachish. But they sent after him to Lachish, and killed him there. [28]They brought him back on horses; he was buried with his ancestors in the city of David.

Reign of Uzziah

26 Then all the people of Judah took Uzziah, who was sixteen years old, and made him king to succeed his father Amaziah. [2]He rebuilt Eloth and restored it to Judah, after the king slept with his ancestors. [3]Uzziah was sixteen years old when he began to reign, and he reigned fifty-two years in Jerusalem. His mother's name was Jecoliah of Jerusalem. [4]He did what was right in the sight of the LORD, just as his father Amaziah had done. [5]He set himself to seek God in the days of Zechariah, who instructed him in the

a Heb he

fear of God; and as long as he sought the LORD, God made him prosper.

6 He went out and made war against the Philistines, and broke down the wall of Gath and the wall of Jabneh and the wall of Ashdod; he built cities in the territory of Ashdod and elsewhere among the Philistines. 7 God helped him against the Philistines, against the Arabs who lived in Gur-baal, and against the Meunites. 8 The Ammonites paid tribute to Uzziah, and his fame spread even to the border of Egypt, for he became very strong. 9 Moreover Uzziah built towers in Jerusalem at the Corner Gate, at the Valley Gate, and at the Angle, and fortified them. 10 He built towers in the wilderness and hewed out many cisterns, for he had large herds, both in the Shephelah and in the plain, and he had farmers and vinedressers in the hills and in the fertile lands, for he loved the soil. 11 Moreover Uzziah had an army of soldiers, fit for war, in divisions according to the numbers in the muster made by the secretary Jeiel and the officer Maaseiah, under the direction of Hananiah, one of the king's commanders. 12 The whole number of the heads of ancestral houses of mighty warriors was two thousand six hundred. 13 Under their command was an army of three hundred seven thousand five hundred, who could make war with mighty power, to help the king against the enemy. 14 Uzziah provided for all the army the shields, spears, helmets, coats of mail, bows, and stones for slinging. 15 In Jerusalem he set up machines, invented by skilled workers, on the towers and the corners for shooting arrows and large stones. And his fame spread far, for he was marvelously helped until he became strong.

Pride and Apostasy

16 But when he had become strong he grew proud, to his destruction. For he was false to the LORD his God, and entered the temple of the LORD to make offering on the altar of incense. 17 But the priest Azariah went in after him, with eighty priests of the LORD who were men of valor; 18 they withstood King Uzziah, and said to him, "It is not for you, Uzziah, to make offering to the LORD, but for the priests the descendants of Aaron, who are consecrated to make offering. Go out of the sanctuary; for you have done wrong, and it will bring you no honor from the LORD God." 19 Then Uzziah was angry. Now he had a censer in his hand to make offering, and when he became angry with the priests a leprous*a* disease broke out on his forehead, in the presence of the priests in the house of the LORD, by the altar of incense. 20 When the chief priest Azariah, and all

the priests, looked at him, he was leprous*a* in his forehead. They hurried him out, and he himself hurried to get out, because the LORD had struck him. 21 King Uzziah was leprous*a* to the day of his death, and being leprous*a* lived in a separate house, for he was excluded from the house of the LORD. His son Jotham was in charge of the palace of the king, governing the people of the land.

22 Now the rest of the acts of Uzziah, from first to last, the prophet Isaiah son of Amoz wrote. 23 Uzziah slept with his ancestors; they buried him near his ancestors in the burial field that belonged to the kings, for they said, "He is leprous."*a* His son Jotham succeeded him.

Reign of Jotham

27 Jotham was twenty-five years old when he began to reign; he reigned sixteen years in Jerusalem. His mother's name was Jerushah daughter of Zadok. 2 He did what was right in the sight of the LORD just as his father Uzziah had done—only he did not invade the temple of the LORD. But the people still followed corrupt practices. 3 He built the upper gate of the house of the LORD, and did extensive building on the wall of Ophel. 4 Moreover he built cities in the hill country of Judah, and forts and towers on the wooded hills. 5 He fought with the king of the Ammonites and prevailed against them. The Ammonites gave him that year one hundred talents of silver, ten thousand cors of wheat and ten thousand of barley. The Ammonites paid him the same amount in the second and the third years. 6 So Jotham became strong because he ordered his ways before the LORD his God. 7 Now the rest of the acts of Jotham, and all his wars and his ways, are written in the Book of the Kings of Israel and Judah. 8 He was twenty-five years old when he began to reign; he reigned sixteen years in Jerusalem. 9 Jotham slept with his ancestors, and they buried him in the city of David; and his son Ahaz succeeded him.

Reign of Ahaz

28 Ahaz was twenty years old when he began to reign; he reigned sixteen years in Jerusalem. He did not do what was right in the sight of the LORD, as his ancestor David had done, 2 but he walked in the ways of the kings of Israel. He even made cast images for the Baals; 3 and he made offerings in the valley of the son of Hinnom, and made his sons pass through fire, according to the abominable practices of the nations whom the LORD drove out before the

a A term for several skin diseases; precise meaning uncertain

people of Israel. ⁴He sacrificed and made offerings on the high places, on the hills, and under every green tree.

Aram and Israel Defeat Judah

5 Therefore the LORD his God gave him into the hand of the king of Aram, who defeated him and took captive a great number of his people and brought them to Damascus. He was also given into the hand of the king of Israel, who defeated him with great slaughter. ⁶Pekah son of Remaliah killed one hundred twenty thousand in Judah in one day, all of them valiant warriors, because they had abandoned the LORD, the God of their ancestors. ⁷And Zichri, a mighty warrior of Ephraim, killed the king's son Maaseiah, Azrikam the commander of the palace, and Elkanah the next in authority to the king.

Intervention of Oded

8 The people of Israel took captive two hundred thousand of their kin, women, sons, and daughters; they also took much booty from them and brought the booty to Samaria. ⁹But a prophet of the LORD was there, whose name was Oded; he went out to meet the army that came to Samaria, and said to them, "Because the LORD, the God of your ancestors, was angry with Judah, he gave them into your hand, but you have killed them in a rage that has reached up to heaven. ¹⁰Now you intend to subjugate the people of Judah and Jerusalem, male and female, as your slaves. But what have you except sins against the LORD your God? ¹¹Now hear me, and send back the captives whom you have taken from your kindred, for the fierce wrath of the LORD is upon you." ¹²Moreover, certain chiefs of the Ephraimites, Azariah son of Johanan, Berechiah son of Meshillemoth, Jehizkiah son of Shallum, and Amasa son of Hadlai, stood up against those who were coming from the war, ¹³and said to them, "You shall not bring the captives in here, for you propose to bring on us guilt against the LORD in addition to our present sins and guilt. For our guilt is already great, and there is fierce wrath against Israel." ¹⁴So the warriors left the captives and the booty before the officials and all the assembly. ¹⁵Then those who were mentioned by name got up and took the captives, and with the booty they clothed all that were naked among them; they clothed them, gave them sandals, provided them with food and drink, and anointed them; and carrying all the feeble among them on donkeys, they brought them to their kindred at Jericho, the city of palm trees. Then they returned to Samaria.

Assyria Refuses to Help Judah

16 At that time King Ahaz sent to the king*ᵃ* of Assyria for help. ¹⁷For the Edomites had again invaded and defeated Judah, and carried away captives. ¹⁸And the Philistines had made raids on the cities in the Shephelah and the Negeb of Judah, and had taken Beth-shemesh, Aijalon, Gederoth, Soco with its villages, Timnah with its villages, and Gimzo with its villages; and they settled there. ¹⁹For the LORD brought Judah low because of King Ahaz of Israel, for he had behaved without restraint in Judah and had been faithless to the LORD. ²⁰So King Tilgath-pilneser of Assyria came against him, and oppressed him instead of strengthening him. ²¹For Ahaz plundered the house of the LORD and the houses of the king and of the officials, and gave tribute to the king of Assyria; but it did not help him.

Apostasy and Death of Ahaz

22 In the time of his distress he became yet more faithless to the LORD—this same King Ahaz. ²³For he sacrificed to the gods of Damascus, which had defeated him, and said, "Because the gods of the kings of Aram helped them, I will sacrifice to them so that they may help me." But they were the ruin of him, and of all Israel. ²⁴Ahaz gathered together the utensils of the house of God, and cut in pieces the utensils of the house of God. He shut up the doors of the house of the LORD and made himself altars in every corner of Jerusalem. ²⁵In every city of Judah he made high places to make offerings to other gods, provoking to anger the LORD, the God of his ancestors. ²⁶Now the rest of his acts and all his ways, from first to last, are written in the Book of the Kings of Judah and Israel. ²⁷Ahaz slept with his ancestors, and they buried him in the city, in Jerusalem; but they did not bring him into the tombs of the kings of Israel. His son Hezekiah succeeded him.

Reign of Hezekiah

29 Hezekiah began to reign when he was twenty-five years old; he reigned twenty-nine years in Jerusalem. His mother's name was Abijah daughter of Zechariah. ²He did what was right in the sight of the LORD, just as his ancestor David had done.

The Temple Cleansed

3 In the first year of his reign, in the first month, he opened the doors of the house of

---

a Gk Syr Vg Compare 2 Kings 16.7: Heb *kings*

the Lord and repaired them. ⁴He brought in the priests and the Levites and assembled them in the square on the east. ⁵He said to them, "Listen to me, Levites! Sanctify yourselves, and sanctify the house of the Lord, the God of your ancestors, and carry out the filth from the holy place. ⁶For our ancestors have been unfaithful and have done what was evil in the sight of the Lord our God; they have forsaken him, and have turned away their faces from the dwelling of the Lord, and turned their backs. ⁷They also shut the doors of the vestibule and put out the lamps, and have not offered incense or made burnt offerings in the holy place to the God of Israel. ⁸Therefore the wrath of the Lord came upon Judah and Jerusalem, and he has made them an object of horror, of astonishment, and of hissing, as you see with your own eyes. ⁹Our fathers have fallen by the sword and our sons and our daughters and our wives are in captivity for this. ¹⁰Now it is in my heart to make a covenant with the Lord, the God of Israel, so that his fierce anger may turn away from us. ¹¹My sons, do not now be negligent, for the Lord has chosen you to stand in his presence to minister to him, and to be his ministers and make offerings to him."

12 Then the Levites arose, Mahath son of Amasai, and Joel son of Azariah, of the sons of the Kohathites; and of the sons of Merari, Kish son of Abdi, and Azariah son of Jehallelel; and of the Gershonites, Joah son of Zimmah, and Eden son of Joah; ¹³and of the sons of Elizaphan, Shimri and Jeuel; and of the sons of Asaph, Zechariah and Mattaniah; ¹⁴and of the sons of Heman, Jehuel and Shimei; and of the sons of Jeduthun, Shemaiah and Uzziel. ¹⁵They gathered their brothers, sanctified themselves, and went in as the king had commanded, by the words of the Lord, to cleanse the house of the Lord. ¹⁶The priests went into the inner part of the house of the Lord to cleanse it, and they brought out all the unclean things that they found in the temple of the Lord into the court of the house of the Lord; and the Levites took them and carried them out to the Wadi Kidron. ¹⁷They began to sanctify on the first day of the first month, and on the eighth day of the month they came to the vestibule of the Lord; then for eight days they sanctified the house of the Lord, and on the sixteenth day of the first month they finished. ¹⁸Then they went inside to King Hezekiah and said, "We have cleansed all the house of the Lord, the altar of burnt offering and all its utensils, and the table for the rows of bread and all its utensils. ¹⁹All the utensils that King Ahaz repudiated during his reign when he was faithless, we

Pray It!

Renewing Your Prayer Life

Hezekiah was one of Judah's reformer kings. Before he became king, the people had neglected the Temple in Jerusalem for a long time. At the beginning of Hezekiah's reign, the Temple needed some intense effort to get it back in order.

Sometimes our prayer lives suffer from neglect too. We get busy and do not take enough time to pray, or we forget to pray altogether. When we decide to commit ourselves to regular prayer, it may take some intense effort to get rid of our bad habits.

Imagine your prayer life as being like the Temple. How does it look? Is it in need of a little dusting? full of cobwebs? ready for major renovation? What steps can you take to make sure you do not neglect your prayer life?

It is also easy to fall into a rut when we pray. One way to energize your prayer life is to try different ways to pray. You could begin your prayer with a line from a psalm that you like or by picturing Jesus beside you. Other alternatives would be to start prayer with a song that means a lot to you or to simply place yourself in the Holy Presence of God.

▶ **2 Chr 29:1–11**

have made ready and sanctified; see, they are in front of the altar of the Lord."

Temple Worship Restored

20 Then King Hezekiah rose early, assembled the officials of the city, and went up to the house of the Lord. ²¹They brought seven bulls, seven rams, seven lambs, and seven male goats for a sin offering for the kingdom and for the sanctuary and for Judah. He commanded the priests the descendants of Aaron to offer them on the altar of the Lord. ²²So they slaughtered the bulls, and the priests received the blood and dashed it against the altar; they slaughtered the rams and their blood was dashed against the altar; they also slaughtered the lambs and their blood was dashed against the altar. ²³Then the

male goats for the sin offering were brought to the king and the assembly; they laid their hands on them, ²⁴and the priests slaughtered them and made a sin offering with their blood at the altar, to make atonement for all Israel. For the king commanded that the burnt offering and the sin offering should be made for all Israel.

25 He stationed the Levites in the house of the LORD with cymbals, harps, and lyres, according to the commandment of David and of Gad the king's seer and of the prophet Nathan, for the commandment was from the LORD through his prophets. ²⁶The Levites stood with the instruments of David, and the priests with the trumpets. ²⁷Then Hezekiah commanded that the burnt offering be offered on the altar. When the burnt offering began, the song to the LORD began also, and the trumpets, accompanied by the instruments of King David of Israel. ²⁸The whole assembly worshiped, the singers sang, and the trumpeters sounded; all this continued until the burnt offering was finished. ²⁹When the offering was finished, the king and all who were present with him bowed down and worshiped. ³⁰King Hezekiah and the officials commanded the Levites to sing praises to the LORD with the words of David and of the seer Asaph. They sang praises with gladness, and they bowed down and worshiped.

31 Then Hezekiah said, "You have now consecrated yourselves to the LORD; come near, bring sacrifices and thank offerings to the house of the LORD." The assembly brought sacrifices and thank offerings; and all who were of a willing heart brought burnt offerings. ³²The number of the burnt offerings that the assembly brought was seventy bulls, one hundred rams, and two hundred lambs; all these were for a burnt offering to the LORD. ³³The consecrated offerings were six hundred bulls and three thousand sheep. ³⁴But the priests were too few and could not skin all the burnt offerings, so, until other priests had sanctified themselves, their kindred, the Levites, helped them until the work was finished—for the Levites were more conscientious[a] than the priests in sanctifying themselves. ³⁵Besides the great number of burnt offerings there was the fat of the offerings of well-being, and there were the drink offerings for the burnt offerings. Thus the service of the house of the LORD was restored. ³⁶And Hezekiah and all the people rejoiced because of what God had done for the people; for the thing had come about suddenly.

The Great Passover

30 Hezekiah sent word to all Israel and Judah, and wrote letters also to Ephraim and Manasseh, that they should come to the house of the LORD at Jerusalem, to keep the passover to the LORD the God of Israel. ²For the king and his officials and all the assembly in Jerusalem had taken counsel to keep the passover in the second month ³(for they could not keep it at its proper time because the priests had not sanctified themselves in sufficient number, nor had the people assembled in Jerusalem). ⁴The plan seemed right to the king and all the assembly. ⁵So they decreed to make a proclamation throughout all Israel, from Beer-sheba to Dan, that the people should come and keep the passover to the LORD the God of Israel, at Jerusalem; for they had not kept it in great numbers as prescribed. ⁶So couriers went throughout all Israel and Judah with letters from the king and his officials, as the king had commanded, saying, "O people of Israel, return to the LORD, the God of Abraham, Isaac, and Israel, so that he may turn again to the remnant of you who have escaped from the hand of the kings of Assyria. ⁷Do not be like your ancestors and your kindred, who were faithless to the LORD God of their ancestors, so that he made them a desolation, as you see. ⁸Do not now be stiff-necked as your ancestors were, but yield yourselves to the LORD and come to his sanctuary, which he has sanctified forever, and serve the LORD your God, so that his fierce anger may turn away from you. ⁹For as you return to the LORD, your kindred and your children will find compassion with their captors, and return to this land. For the LORD your God is gracious and merciful, and will not turn away his face from you, if you return to him."

10 So the couriers went from city to city through the country of Ephraim and Manasseh, and as far as Zebulun; but they laughed them to scorn, and mocked them. ¹¹Only a few from Asher, Manasseh, and Zebulun humbled themselves and came to Jerusalem. ¹²The hand of God was also on Judah to give them one heart to do what the king and the officials commanded by the word of the LORD.

13 Many people came together in Jerusalem to keep the festival of unleavened bread in the second month, a very large assembly. ¹⁴They set to work and removed the altars that were in Jerusalem, and all the altars for offering incense they took away and threw into the Wadi Kidron. ¹⁵They slaughtered the passover lamb on the fourteenth day of the second month. The priests and the Levites were ashamed, and they sanctified themselves and brought burnt

a Heb upright in heart

offerings into the house of the LORD. ¹⁶They took their accustomed posts according to the law of Moses the man of God; the priests dashed the blood that they received[a] from the hands of the Levites. ¹⁷For there were many in the assembly who had not sanctified themselves; therefore the Levites had to slaughter the passover lamb for everyone who was not clean, to make it holy to the LORD. ¹⁸For a multitude of the people, many of them from Ephraim, Manasseh, Issachar, and Zebulun, had not cleansed themselves, yet they ate the passover otherwise than as prescribed. But Hezekiah prayed for them, saying, "The good LORD pardon all ¹⁹who set their hearts to seek God, the LORD the God of their ancestors, even though not in accordance with the sanctuary's rules of cleanness." ²⁰The LORD heard Hezekiah, and healed the people. ²¹The people of Israel who were present at Jerusalem kept the festival of unleavened bread seven days with great gladness; and the Levites and the priests praised the LORD day by day, accompanied by loud instruments for the LORD. ²²Hezekiah spoke encouragingly to all the Levites who showed good skill in the service of the LORD. So the people ate the food of the festival for seven days, sacrificing offerings of well-being and giving thanks to the LORD the God of their ancestors.

23 Then the whole assembly agreed together to keep the festival for another seven days; so they kept it for another seven days with gladness. ²⁴For King Hezekiah of Judah gave the assembly a thousand bulls and seven thousand sheep for offerings, and the officials gave the assembly a thousand bulls and ten thousand sheep. The priests sanctified themselves in great numbers. ²⁵The whole assembly of Judah, the priests and the Levites, and the whole assembly that came out of Israel, and the resident aliens who came out of the land of Israel, and the resident aliens who lived in Judah, rejoiced. ²⁶There was great joy in Jerusalem, for since the time of Solomon son of King David of Israel there had been nothing like this in Jerusalem. ²⁷Then the priests and the Levites stood up and blessed the people, and their voice was heard; their prayer came to his holy dwelling in heaven.

Pagan Shrines Destroyed

31 Now when all this was finished, all Israel who were present went out to the cities of Judah and broke down the pillars, hewed down the sacred poles,[b] and pulled down the high places and the altars throughout all Judah and Benjamin, and in Ephraim and Manasseh, until they had destroyed them all. Then all the people

Giving the Best of the Best

In 2 Chronicles 31:5, we read about how the people "gave in abundance the first fruits of grain, wine, oil, honey, and of all the produce of the field." They gave the best of the best, in gratitude for the gifts from God. That is what being generous is all about. True generosity springs from the heart and motivates us to give the best of what we have, not just what we do not want or need anymore.

The word *tithe* appears in this verse. For the Israelites, to tithe meant to give 10 percent of one's earnings as a tax for the upkeep of the Temple. Some Christians continue the spirit of tithing by giving 10 percent of all they earn to their church and other charities. They are offering God their best, the firstfruits of their labor (see Lk 21:1–4 and Acts 4:32–37).

We all need to search our heart and continue this tradition of offering our best back to God—not because it makes us look good and gives us "extra points" with God, but because it comes from our gratitude for the gifts we have received.

▶ **2 Chr 31:2–10**

of Israel returned to their cities, all to their individual properties.

2 Hezekiah appointed the divisions of the priests and of the Levites, division by division, everyone according to his service, the priests and the Levites, for burnt offerings and offerings of well-being, to minister in the gates of the camp of the LORD and to give thanks and praise. ³The contribution of the king from his own possessions was for the burnt offerings: the burnt offerings of morning and evening, and the burnt offerings for the sabbaths, the new moons, and the appointed festivals, as it is written in the law of the LORD. ⁴He commanded the people who lived in Jerusalem to give the portion due to the priests and the Levites, so that they might devote

a Heb lacks *that they received*   *b* Heb *Asherim*

2 CHR

themselves to the law of the LORD. ⁵As soon as the word spread, the people of Israel gave in abundance the first fruits of grain, wine, oil, honey, and of all the produce of the field; and they brought in abundantly the tithe of everything. ⁶The people of Israel and Judah who lived in the cities of Judah also brought in the tithe of cattle and sheep, and the tithe of the dedicated things that had been consecrated to the LORD their God, and laid them in heaps. ⁷In the third month they began to pile up the heaps, and finished them in the seventh month. ⁸When Hezekiah and the officials came and saw the heaps, they blessed the LORD and his people Israel. ⁹Hezekiah questioned the priests and the Levites about the heaps. ¹⁰The chief priest Azariah, who was of the house of Zadok, answered him, "Since they began to bring the contributions into the house of the LORD, we have had enough to eat and have plenty to spare; for the LORD has blessed his people, so that we have this great supply left over."

Reorganization of Priests and Levites

11 Then Hezekiah commanded them to prepare store-chambers in the house of the LORD; and they prepared them. ¹²Faithfully they brought in the contributions, the tithes and the dedicated things. The chief officer in charge of them was Conaniah the Levite, with his brother Shimei as second; ¹³while Jehiel, Azaziah, Nahath, Asahel, Jerimoth, Jozabad, Eliel, Ismachiah, Mahath, and Benaiah were overseers assisting Conaniah and his brother Shimei, by the appointment of King Hezekiah and of Azariah the chief officer of the house of God. ¹⁴Kore son of Imnah the Levite, keeper of the east gate, was in charge of the freewill offerings to God, to apportion the contribution reserved for the LORD and the most holy offerings. ¹⁵Eden, Miniamin, Jeshua, Shemaiah, Amariah, and Shecaniah were faithfully assisting him in the cities of the priests, to distribute the portions to their kindred, old and young alike, by divisions, ¹⁶except those enrolled by genealogy, males from three years old and upwards, all who entered the house of the LORD as the duty of each day required, for their service according to their offices, by their divisions. ¹⁷The enrollment of the priests was according to their ancestral houses; that of the Levites from twenty years old and upwards was according to their offices, by their divisions. ¹⁸The priests were enrolled with all their little children, their wives, their sons, and their daughters, the whole multitude; for they were faithful in keeping themselves holy. ¹⁹And for the descendants of Aaron, the priests, who were in the fields of common land

belonging to their towns, town by town, the people designated by name were to distribute portions to every male among the priests and to everyone among the Levites who was enrolled.

20 Hezekiah did this throughout all Judah; he did what was good and right and faithful before the LORD his God. ²¹And every work that he undertook in the service of the house of God, and in accordance with the law and the commandments, to seek his God, he did with all his heart; and he prospered.

Sennacherib's Invasion

32 After these things and these acts of faithfulness, King Sennacherib of Assyria came and invaded Judah and encamped against the fortified cities, thinking to win them for himself. ²When Hezekiah saw that Sennacherib had come and intended to fight against Jerusalem, ³he planned with his officers and his warriors to stop the flow of the springs that were outside the city; and they helped him. ⁴A great many people were gathered, and they stopped all the springs and the wadi that flowed through the land, saying, "Why should the Assyrian kings come and find water in abundance?" ⁵Hezekiah[a] set to work resolutely and built up the entire wall that was broken down, and raised towers on it,[b] and outside it he built another wall; he also strengthened the Millo in the city of David, and made weapons and shields in abundance. ⁶He appointed combat commanders over the people, and gathered them together to him in the square at the gate of the city and spoke encouragingly to them, saying, ⁷"Be strong and of good courage. Do not be afraid or dismayed before the king of Assyria and all the horde that is with him; for there is one greater with us than with him. ⁸With him is an arm of flesh; but with us is the LORD our God, to help us and to fight our battles." The people were encouraged by the words of King Hezekiah of Judah.

9 After this, while King Sennacherib of Assyria was at Lachish with all his forces, he sent his servants to Jerusalem to King Hezekiah of Judah and to all the people of Judah that were in Jerusalem, saying, ¹⁰"Thus says King Sennacherib of Assyria: On what are you relying, that you undergo the siege of Jerusalem? ¹¹Is not Hezekiah misleading you, handing you over to die by famine and by thirst, when he tells you, 'The LORD our God will save us from the hand of the king of Assyria'? ¹²Was it not this same Hezekiah who took away his high places and

---

a Heb He   b Vg: Heb and raised on the towers

his altars and commanded Judah and Jerusalem, saying, 'Before one altar you shall worship, and upon it you shall make your offerings'? [13]Do you not know what I and my ancestors have done to all the peoples of other lands? Were the gods of the nations of those lands at all able to save their lands out of my hand? [14]Who among all the gods of those nations that my ancestors utterly destroyed was able to save his people from my hand, that your God should be able to save you from my hand? [15]Now therefore do not let Hezekiah deceive you or mislead you in this fashion, and do not believe him, for no god of any nation or kingdom has been able to save his people from my hand or from the hand of my ancestors. How much less will your God save you out of my hand!"

16 His servants said still more against the Lord God and against his servant Hezekiah. [17]He also wrote letters to throw contempt on the Lord the God of Israel and to speak against him, saying, "Just as the gods of the nations in other lands did not rescue their people from my hands, so the God of Hezekiah will not rescue his people from my hand." [18]They shouted it with a loud voice in the language of Judah to the people of Jerusalem who were on the wall, to frighten and terrify them, in order that they might take the city. [19]They spoke of the God of Jerusalem as if he were like the gods of the peoples of the earth, which are the work of human hands.

Sennacherib's Defeat and Death

20 Then King Hezekiah and the prophet Isaiah son of Amoz prayed because of this and cried to heaven. [21]And the Lord sent an angel who cut off all the mighty warriors and commanders and officers in the camp of the king of Assyria. So he returned in disgrace to his own land. When he came into the house of his god, some of his own sons struck him down there with the sword. [22]So the Lord saved Hezekiah and the inhabitants of Jerusalem from the hand of King Sennacherib of Assyria and from the hand of all his enemies; he gave them rest[a] on every side. [23]Many brought gifts to the Lord in Jerusalem and precious things to King Hezekiah of Judah, so that he was exalted in the sight of all nations from that time onward.

Hezekiah's Sickness

24 In those days Hezekiah became sick and was at the point of death. He prayed to the Lord, and he answered him and gave him a sign. [25]But Hezekiah did not respond according to the benefit done to him, for his heart was proud.

Therefore wrath came upon him and upon Judah and Jerusalem. [26]Then Hezekiah humbled himself for the pride of his heart, both he and the inhabitants of Jerusalem, so that the wrath of the Lord did not come upon them in the days of Hezekiah.

Hezekiah's Prosperity and Achievements

27 Hezekiah had very great riches and honor; and he made for himself treasuries for silver, for gold, for precious stones, for spices, for shields, and for all kinds of costly objects; [28]storehouses also for the yield of grain, wine, and oil; and stalls for all kinds of cattle, and sheepfolds.[b] [29]He likewise provided cities for himself, and flocks and herds in abundance; for God had given him very

---

a Gk Vg: Heb *guided them*   b Gk Vg: Heb *flocks for folds*

Perseverance

King Hezekiah persevered and prospered. He had many riches and provided for the people in his kingdom. One great accomplishment was a tunnel he had dug under the City of David (see 2 Chr 32:30). The tunnel allowed the springs of Gihon to flow into the city so that the people had easier access to water.

That tunnel, more than seventeen hundred feet long, was carved through stone. Today, it would not take much to complete such a task, but in Hezekiah's time, it was done little by little with simple tools.

Perseverance is a valuable skill that everyone can benefit from, especially when great obstacles stand in the way. People can get discouraged and lose heart when faced with difficult tasks. Those who refuse to be discouraged or to give up can serve as a source of encouragement and vision for others.

● When you've been faced with an obstacle or difficult situation, what or who motivated you to persevere? Have you ever gotten discouraged and given up? Why did you?

▶ 2 Chr 32:27–33

great possessions. ³⁰This same Hezekiah closed the upper outlet of the waters of Gihon and directed them down to the west side of the city of David. Hezekiah prospered in all his works. ³¹So also in the matter of the envoys of the officials of Babylon, who had been sent to him to inquire about the sign that had been done in the land, God left him to himself, in order to test him and to know all that was in his heart.

32 Now the rest of the acts of Hezekiah, and his good deeds, are written in the vision of the prophet Isaiah son of Amoz in the Book of the Kings of Judah and Israel. ³³Hezekiah slept with his ancestors, and they buried him on the ascent to the tombs of the descendants of David; and all Judah and the inhabitants of Jerusalem did him honor at his death. His son Manasseh succeeded him.

Reign of Manasseh

33 Manasseh was twelve years old when he began to reign; he reigned fifty-five years in Jerusalem. ²He did what was evil in the sight of the LORD, according to the abominable practices of the nations whom the LORD drove out before the people of Israel. ³For he rebuilt the high places that his father Hezekiah had pulled down, and erected altars to the Baals, made sacred poles,ᵃ worshiped all the host of heaven, and served them. ⁴He built altars in the house of the LORD, of which the LORD had said, "In Jerusalem shall my name be forever." ⁵He built altars for all the host of heaven in the two courts of the house of the LORD. ⁶He made his son pass through fire in the valley of the son of Hinnom, practiced soothsaying and augury and sorcery, and dealt with mediums and with wizards. He did much evil in the sight of the LORD, provoking him to anger. ⁷The carved image of the idol that he had made he set in the house of God, of which God said to David and to his son Solomon, "In this house, and in Jerusalem, which I have chosen out of all the tribes of Israel, I will put my name forever; ⁸I will never again remove the feet of Israel from the land that I appointed for your ancestors, if only they will be careful to do all that I have commanded them, all the law, the statutes, and the ordinances given through Moses." ⁹Manasseh misled Judah and the inhabitants of Jerusalem, so that they did more evil than the nations whom the LORD had destroyed before the people of Israel.

Manasseh Restored after Repentance

10 The LORD spoke to Manasseh and to his people, but they gave no heed. ¹¹Therefore the LORD brought against them the commanders of the army of the king of Assyria, who took Manasseh captive in manacles, bound him with fetters, and brought him to Babylon. ¹²While he was in distress he entreated the favor of the LORD his God and humbled himself greatly before the God of his ancestors. ¹³He prayed to him, and God received his entreaty, heard his plea, and restored him again to Jerusalem and to his kingdom. Then Manasseh knew that the LORD indeed was God.

14 Afterward he built an outer wall for the city of David west of Gihon, in the valley, reaching the entrance at the Fish Gate; he carried it around Ophel, and raised it to a very great height. He also put commanders of the army in all the fortified cities in Judah. ¹⁵He took away the foreign gods and the idol from the house of the LORD, and all the altars that he had built on the mountain of the house of the LORD and in Jerusalem, and he threw them out of the city. ¹⁶He also restored the altar of the LORD and offered on it sacrifices of well-being and of thanksgiving; and he commanded Judah to serve the LORD the God of Israel. ¹⁷The people, however, still sacrificed at the high places, but only to the LORD their God.

Death of Manasseh

18 Now the rest of the acts of Manasseh, his prayer to his God, and the words of the seers who spoke to him in the name of the LORD God of Israel, these are in the Annals of the Kings of Israel. ¹⁹His prayer, and how God received his entreaty, all his sin and his faithlessness, the sites on which he built high places and set up the sacred polesᵇ and the images, before he humbled himself, these are written in the records of the seers.ᶜ ²⁰So Manasseh slept with his ancestors, and they buried him in his house. His son Amon succeeded him.

Amon's Reign and Death

21 Amon was twenty-two years old when he began to reign; he reigned two years in Jerusalem. ²²He did what was evil in the sight of the LORD, as his father Manasseh had done. Amon sacrificed to all the images that his father Manasseh had made, and served them. ²³He did not humble himself before the LORD, as his father Manasseh had humbled himself, but this Amon incurred more and more guilt. ²⁴His servants conspired against him and killed him in his house. ²⁵But the people of the land killed all those who had

---

a Heb *Asheroth*   b Heb *Asherim*   c One Ms Gk: MT *of Hozai*

conspired against King Amon; and the people of the land made his son Josiah king to succeed him.

Reign of Josiah

34 Josiah was eight years old when he began to reign; he reigned thirty-one years in Jerusalem. [2] He did what was right in the sight of the LORD, and walked in the ways of his ancestor David; he did not turn aside to the right or to the left. [3] For in the eighth year of his reign, while he was still a boy, he began to seek the God of his ancestor David, and in the twelfth year he began to purge Judah and Jerusalem of the high places, the sacred poles,[a] and the carved and the cast images. [4] In his presence they pulled down the altars of the Baals; he demolished the incense altars that stood above them. He broke down the sacred poles[a] and the carved and the cast images; he made dust of them and scattered it over the graves of those who had sacrificed to them. [5] He also burned the bones of the priests on their altars, and purged Judah and Jerusalem. [6] In the towns of Manasseh, Ephraim, and Simeon, and as far as Naphtali, in their ruins[b] all around, [7] he broke down the altars, beat the sacred poles[a] and the images into powder, and demolished all the incense altars throughout all the land of Israel. Then he returned to Jerusalem.

Discovery of the Book of the Law

8 In the eighteenth year of his reign, when he had purged the land and the house, he sent Shaphan son of Azaliah, Maaseiah the governor of the city, and Joah son of Joahaz, the recorder, to repair the house of the LORD his God. [9] They came to the high priest Hilkiah and delivered the money that had been brought into the house of God, which the Levites, the keepers of the threshold, had collected from Manasseh and Ephraim and from all the remnant of Israel and from all Judah and Benjamin and from the inhabitants of Jerusalem. [10] They delivered it to the workers who had the oversight of the house of the LORD, and the workers who were working in the house of the LORD gave it for repairing and restoring the house. [11] They gave it to the carpenters and the builders to buy quarried stone, and timber for binders, and beams for the buildings that the kings of Judah had let go to ruin. [12] The people did the work faithfully. Over them were appointed the Levites Jahath and Obadiah, of the sons of Merari, along with Zechariah and Meshullam, of the sons of the Kohathites, to have oversight. Other Levites, all skillful with instruments of music, [13] were over the burden bearers

and directed all who did work in every kind of service; and some of the Levites were scribes, and officials, and gatekeepers.

14 While they were bringing out the money that had been brought into the house of the LORD, the priest Hilkiah found the book of the law of the LORD given through Moses. [15] Hilkiah said to the secretary Shaphan, "I have found the book of the law in the house of the LORD"; and Hilkiah gave the book to Shaphan. [16] Shaphan brought the book to the king, and further reported to the king, "All that was committed to your servants they are doing. [17] They have emptied out the money that was found in the house of the LORD and have delivered it into the hand of the overseers and the workers." [18] The secretary Shaphan informed the king, "The priest Hilkiah has given me a book." Shaphan then read it aloud to the king.

19 When the king heard the words of the law he tore his clothes. [20] Then the king commanded Hilkiah, Ahikam son of Shaphan, Abdon son of Micah, the secretary Shaphan, and the king's servant Asaiah: [21] "Go, inquire of the LORD for me and for those who are left in Israel and in Judah, concerning the words of the book that has been found; for the wrath of the LORD that is poured out on us is great, because our ancestors did not keep the word of the LORD, to act in accordance with all that is written in this book."

The Prophet Huldah Consulted

22 So Hilkiah and those whom the king had sent went to the prophet Huldah, the wife of Shallum son of Tokhath son of Hasrah, keeper of the wardrobe (who lived in Jerusalem in the Second Quarter) and spoke to her to that effect. [23] She declared to them, "Thus says the LORD, the God of Israel: Tell the man who sent you to me, [24] Thus says the LORD: I will indeed bring disaster upon this place and upon its inhabitants, all the curses that are written in the book that was read before the king of Judah. [25] Because they have forsaken me and have made offerings to other gods, so that they have provoked me to anger with all the works of their hands, my wrath will be poured out on this place and will not be quenched. [26] But as to the king of Judah, who sent you to inquire of the LORD, thus shall you say to him: Thus says the LORD, the God of Israel: Regarding the words that you have heard, [27] because your heart was penitent and you humbled yourself before God when you heard his words against this place and its inhabitants, and you have humbled yourself

a Heb Asherim   b Meaning of Heb uncertain

before me, and have torn your clothes and wept before me, I also have heard you, says the Lord. [28]I will gather you to your ancestors and you shall be gathered to your grave in peace; your eyes shall not see all the disaster that I will bring on this place and its inhabitants." They took the message back to the king.

The Covenant Renewed

29 Then the king sent word and gathered together all the elders of Judah and Jerusalem. [30]The king went up to the house of the Lord, with all the people of Judah, the inhabitants of Jerusalem, the priests and the Levites, all the people both great and small; he read in their hearing all the words of the book of the covenant that had been found in the house of the Lord. [31]The king stood in his place and made a covenant before the Lord, to follow the Lord, keeping his commandments, his decrees, and his statutes, with all his heart and all his soul, to perform the words of the covenant that were written in this book. [32]Then he made all who were present in Jerusalem and in Benjamin pledge themselves to it. And the inhabitants of Jerusalem acted according to the covenant of God, the God of their ancestors. [33]Josiah took away all the abominations from all the territory that belonged to the people of Israel, and made all who were in Israel worship the Lord their God. All his days they did not turn away from following the Lord the God of their ancestors.

Celebration of the Passover

35 Josiah kept a passover to the Lord in Jerusalem; they slaughtered the passover lamb on the fourteenth day of the first month. [2]He appointed the priests to their offices and encouraged them in the service of the house of the Lord. [3]He said to the Levites who taught all Israel and who were holy to the Lord, "Put the holy ark in the house that Solomon son of David, king of Israel, built; you need no longer carry it on your shoulders. Now serve the Lord your God and his people Israel. [4]Make preparations by your ancestral houses by your divisions, following the written directions of King David of Israel and the written directions of his son Solomon. [5]Take position in the holy place according to the groupings of the ancestral houses of your kindred the people, and let there be Levites for each division of an ancestral house.[a] [6]Slaughter the passover lamb, sanctify yourselves, and on behalf of your kindred make preparations, acting according to the word of the Lord by Moses."

7 Then Josiah contributed to the people,

as passover offerings for all that were present, lambs and kids from the flock to the number of thirty thousand, and three thousand bulls; these were from the king's possessions. [8]His officials contributed willingly to the people, to the priests, and to the Levites. Hilkiah, Zechariah, and Jehiel, the chief officers of the house of God, gave to the priests for the passover offerings two thousand six hundred lambs and kids and three hundred bulls. [9]Conaniah also, and his brothers Shemaiah and Nethanel, and Hashabiah and Jeiel and Jozabad, the chiefs of the Levites, gave to the Levites for the passover offerings five thousand lambs and kids and five hundred bulls.

10 When the service had been prepared for, the priests stood in their place, and the Levites in their divisions according to the king's command. [11]They slaughtered the passover lamb, and the priests dashed the blood that they received[b] from them, while the Levites did the skinning. [12]They set aside the burnt offerings so that they might distribute them according to the groupings of the ancestral houses of the people, to offer to the Lord, as it is written in the book of Moses. And they did the same with the bulls. [13]They roasted the passover lamb with fire according to the ordinance; and they boiled the holy offerings in pots, in caldrons, and in pans, and carried them quickly to all the people. [14]Afterward they made preparations for themselves and for the priests, because the priests the descendants of Aaron were occupied in offering the burnt offerings and the fat parts until night; so the Levites made preparations for themselves and for the priests, the descendants of Aaron. [15]The singers, the descendants of Asaph, were in their place according to the command of David, and Asaph, and Heman, and the king's seer Jeduthun. The gatekeepers were at each gate; they did not need to interrupt their service, for their kindred the Levites made preparations for them.

16 So all the service of the Lord was prepared that day, to keep the passover and to offer burnt offerings on the altar of the Lord, according to the command of King Josiah. [17]The people of Israel who were present kept the passover at that time, and the festival of unleavened bread seven days. [18]No passover like it had been kept in Israel since the days of the prophet Samuel; none of the kings of Israel had kept such a passover as was kept by Josiah, by the priests and the Levites, by all Judah and Israel who were present, and by the inhabitants of Jerusalem. [19]In the eighteenth year of the reign of Josiah this passover was kept.

---

a Meaning of Heb uncertain   b Heb lacks *that they received*

Defeat by Pharaoh Neco and Death of Josiah

20 After all this, when Josiah had set the temple in order, King Neco of Egypt went up to fight at Carchemish on the Euphrates, and Josiah went out against him. ²¹But Neco*ᵃ* sent envoys to him, saying, "What have I to do with you, king of Judah? I am not coming against you today, but against the house with which I am at war; and God has commanded me to hurry. Cease opposing God, who is with me, so that he will not destroy you." ²²But Josiah would not turn away from him, but disguised himself in order to fight with him. He did not listen to the words of Neco from the mouth of God, but joined battle in the plain of Megiddo. ²³The archers shot King Josiah; and the king said to his servants, "Take me away, for I am badly wounded." ²⁴So his servants took him out of the chariot and carried him in his second chariot*ᵇ* and brought him to Jerusalem. There he died, and was buried in the tombs of his ancestors. All Judah and Jerusalem mourned for Josiah. ²⁵Jeremiah also uttered a lament for Josiah, and all the singing men and singing women have spoken of Josiah in their laments to this day. They made these a custom in Israel; they are recorded in the Laments. ²⁶Now the rest of the acts of Josiah and his faithful deeds in accordance with what is written in the law of the Lord, ²⁷and his acts, first and last, are written in the Book of the Kings of Israel and Judah.

Reign of Jehoahaz

36 The people of the land took Jehoahaz son of Josiah and made him king to succeed his father in Jerusalem. ²Jehoahaz was twenty-three years old when he began to reign; he reigned three months in Jerusalem. ³Then the king of Egypt deposed him in Jerusalem and laid on the land a tribute of one hundred talents of silver and one talent of gold. ⁴The king of Egypt made his brother Eliakim king over Judah and Jerusalem, and changed his name to Jehoiakim; but Neco took his brother Jehoahaz and carried him to Egypt.

Reign and Captivity of Jehoiakim

5 Jehoiakim was twenty-five years old when he began to reign; he reigned eleven years in Jerusalem. He did what was evil in the sight of the Lord his God. ⁶Against him King Nebuchadnezzar of Babylon came up, and bound him with fetters to take him to Babylon. ⁷Nebuchadnezzar also carried some of the vessels of the house of the Lord to Babylon and put them in his palace in Babylon. ⁸Now the rest of the acts of

Live It!

Stiff Neck

It happened so quickly. I was waiting at a stoplight when the car behind me slammed into my car and my neck snapped back. Whiplash! It hurt, but it didn't seem very serious. I was much more upset at the damage that had been done to my car. But by the next morning, I was in agony. I could barely move my head, and my neck was stiff and sore. By the end of the day, my neck was in a brace, and I was taking pain medication.

Now I understand a little better why the Bible so often uses the metaphor of stiff-necked people (see 2 Chr 36:13). To be unable or unwilling to turn their heads deprives people of the ability to look toward God. They just keep looking straight ahead as if it were not possible to look in any other direction. You miss out on a lot if you don't or can't look from side to side, believe me!

● How often have you refused to turn toward God or to gain a new perspective on life?

▶ 2 Chr 36:11–14

Jehoiakim, and the abominations that he did, and what was found against him, are written in the Book of the Kings of Israel and Judah; and his son Jehoiachin succeeded him.

Reign and Captivity of Jehoiachin

9 Jehoiachin was eight years old when he began to reign; he reigned three months and ten days in Jerusalem. He did what was evil in the sight of the Lord. ¹⁰In the spring of the year King Nebuchadnezzar sent and brought him to Babylon, along with the precious vessels of the house of the Lord, and made his brother Zedekiah king over Judah and Jerusalem.

Reign of Zedekiah

11 Zedekiah was twenty-one years old when he began to reign; he reigned eleven years in Jerusalem. ¹²He did what was evil in the sight of

a Heb *he*   *b* Or *the chariot of his deputy*

the LORD his God. He did not humble himself before the prophet Jeremiah who spoke from the mouth of the LORD. [13]He also rebelled against King Nebuchadnezzar, who had made him swear by God; he stiffened his neck and hardened his heart against turning to the LORD, the God of Israel. [14]All the leading priests and the people also were exceedingly unfaithful, following all the abominations of the nations; and they polluted the house of the LORD that he had consecrated in Jerusalem.

The Fall of Jerusalem

15 The LORD, the God of their ancestors, sent persistently to them by his messengers, because he had compassion on his people and on his dwelling place; [16]but they kept mocking the messengers of God, despising his words, and scoffing at his prophets, until the wrath of the LORD against his people became so great that there was no remedy.

17 Therefore he brought up against them the king of the Chaldeans, who killed their youths with the sword in the house of their sanctuary, and had no compassion on young man or young woman, the aged or the feeble; he gave them all into his hand. [18]All the vessels of the house of God, large and small, and the treasures of the house of the LORD, and the treasures of the king and of his officials, all these he brought to Babylon. [19]They burned the house of God, broke down the wall of Jerusalem, burned all its palaces with fire, and destroyed all its precious vessels. [20]He took into exile in Babylon those who had escaped from the sword, and they became servants to him and to his sons until the establishment of the kingdom of Persia, [21]to fulfill the word of the LORD by the mouth of Jeremiah, until the land had made up for its sabbaths. All the days that it lay desolate it kept sabbath, to fulfill seventy years.

Cyrus Proclaims Liberty for the Exiles

22 In the first year of King Cyrus of Persia, in fulfillment of the word of the LORD spoken by Jeremiah, the LORD stirred up the spirit of King Cyrus of Persia so that he sent a herald throughout all his kingdom and also declared in a written edict: [23]"Thus says King Cyrus of Persia: The LORD, the God of heaven, has given me all the kingdoms of the earth, and he has charged me to build him a house at Jerusalem, which is in Judah. Whoever is among you of all his people, may the LORD his God be with him! Let him go up."

Imagine the worst vacation ever. The car breaks down twice, you are sick almost the whole time, and the weather is awful. You can't wait to get home—but when you walk in the front door, you see that the house is trashed. Now imagine how the Israelites felt. They didn't just have a bad vacation; they spent fifty years as captives in a foreign land. When they finally returned home, they faced the overwhelming task of rebuilding Jerusalem and starting their new life. Fortunately, they had Ezra and Nehemiah to help lead and encourage them.

At a Glance

- Ezra, chapters 1–6. Israel's return to Judah
- Ezra, chapters 7–10. Ezra's coming and works
- Neh 1:1—7:72. Nehemiah's appointment as governor
- Neh 7:73—9:38. Ezra's proclaiming of the Torah
- Nehemiah, chapters 10–13. the various reforms of Nehemiah

Quick Facts

Period Covered: from the Exiles' return to Jerusalem through Nehemiah's tenure as governor of Judah, from 538 to about 400 BC

Inspired Author: a scribe (the Chronicler) drawing on Ezra's and Nehemiah's memoirs and other sources

Themes: The return of the Israelites from captivity, the rebuilding of Jerusalem and the Temple

In Depth

In 587 BC, the land of Judah and the city of Jerusalem were conquered by the Babylonians, and many Israelites were exiled to Babylon. The Books of Ezra and Nehemiah pick up the story with the return of some Israelites from Babylon to Judah in 538 BC. The two books were originally a single work, perhaps written in their final form by the same person (or persons) who wrote First and Second Chronicles.

Ezra, a descendant of Israelite priests, was born in Babylonian captivity and became a priest. Because priests couldn't exercise their religious functions during the Exile, they dedicated themselves to studying the Scriptures. Eventually, Ezra was sent to Judah by the Persian emperor Artaxerxes to restore Israel's faithfulness to God. Ezra appointed scribes and judges to establish civil and moral order in the new community returned from Exile.

Nehemiah was a Jewish cupbearer for Emperor Artaxerxes (a cupbearer tastes the contents of whatever the emperor drinks to assure it is not poisoned). When Nehemiah heard reports of Jerusalem's poverty and ruin, he persuaded the emperor to appoint him governor of Judah to help rebuild the city. Nehemiah turned out to be a gifted governor. Under Nehemiah's direction, Jerusalem's walls were rebuilt, and economic and social reforms helped restore order and hope to the community.

Ezra and Nehemiah's leadership was extremely important to Israel as the people returned and began the difficult task of rebuilding Jerusalem. The need to save the faith and customs of the Israelites led to a strict observance of the Law and the beginnings of modern Judaism.

The Books of **Ezra and Nehemiah**

Ezra

End of the Babylonian Captivity

1 In the first year of King Cyrus of Persia, in order that the word of the LORD by the mouth of Jeremiah might be accomplished, the LORD stirred up the spirit of King Cyrus of Persia so that he sent a herald throughout all his kingdom, and also in a written edict declared:

2 "Thus says King Cyrus of Persia: The LORD, the God of heaven, has given me all the kingdoms of the earth, and he has charged me to build him a house at Jerusalem in Judah. ³Any of those among you who are of his people—may their God be with them!—are now permitted to go up to Jerusalem in Judah, and rebuild the house of the LORD, the God of Israel—he is the God who is in Jerusalem; ⁴and let all survivors, in whatever place they reside, be assisted by the people of their place with silver and gold, with goods and with animals, besides freewill offerings for the house of God in Jerusalem."

5 The heads of the families of Judah and Benjamin, and the priests and the Levites—everyone whose spirit God had stirred—got ready to go up and rebuild the house of the LORD in Jerusalem. ⁶All their neighbors aided them with silver vessels, with gold, with goods, with animals, and with valuable gifts, besides all that was freely offered. ⁷King Cyrus himself brought out the vessels of the house of the LORD that Nebuchadnezzar had carried away from Jerusalem and placed in the house of his gods. ⁸King Cyrus of Persia had them released into the charge of Mithredath the treasurer, who counted them out to Sheshbazzar the prince of Judah. ⁹And this was the inventory: gold basins, thirty; silver basins, one thousand; knives,ᵃ twenty-nine; ¹⁰gold bowls, thirty; other silver bowls, four hundred ten; other vessels, one thousand; ¹¹the total of the gold and silver vessels was five thousand four hundred. All these Sheshbazzar brought up, when the exiles were brought up from Babylonia to Jerusalem.

List of the Returned Exiles

2 Now these were the people of the province who came from those captive exiles whom King Nebuchadnezzar of Babylon had carried captive to Babylonia; they returned to Jerusalem and Judah, all to their own towns. ²They came with Zerubbabel, Jeshua, Nehemiah, Seraiah, Reelaiah, Mordecai, Bilshan, Mispar, Bigvai, Rehum, and Baanah.

The number of the Israelite people: ³the descendants of Parosh, two thousand one hundred seventy-two. ⁴Of Shephatiah, three hundred seventy-two. ⁵Of Arah, seven hundred seventy-five. ⁶Of Pahath-moab, namely the descendants of Jeshua and Joab, two thousand eight hundred twelve. ⁷Of Elam, one thousand two hundred fifty-four. ⁸Of Zattu, nine hundred forty-five. ⁹Of Zaccai, seven hundred sixty. ¹⁰Of Bani, six hundred forty-two. ¹¹Of Bebai, six hundred twenty-three. ¹²Of Azgad, one thousand two hundred twenty-two. ¹³Of Adonikam, six hundred sixty-six. ¹⁴Of

---

ᵃ Vg: Meaning of Heb uncertain

446

Bigvai, two thousand fifty-six. ¹⁵Of Adin, four hundred fifty-four. ¹⁶Of Ater, namely of Hezekiah, ninety-eight. ¹⁷Of Bezai, three hundred twenty-three. ¹⁸Of Jorah, one hundred twelve. ¹⁹Of Hashum, two hundred twenty-three. ²⁰Of Gibbar, ninety-five. ²¹Of Bethlehem, one hundred twenty-three. ²²The people of Netophah, fifty-six. ²³Of Anathoth, one hundred twenty-eight. ²⁴The descendants of Azmaveth, forty-two. ²⁵Of Kiriatharim, Chephirah, and Beeroth, seven hundred forty-three. ²⁶Of Ramah and Geba, six hundred twenty-one. ²⁷The people of Michmas, one hundred twenty-two. ²⁸Of Bethel and Ai, two hundred twenty-three. ²⁹The descendants of Nebo, fifty-two. ³⁰Of Magbish, one hundred fifty-six. ³¹Of the other Elam, one thousand two hundred fifty-four. ³²Of Harim, three hundred twenty. ³³Of Lod, Hadid, and Ono, seven hundred twenty-five. ³⁴Of Jericho, three hundred forty-five. ³⁵Of Senaah, three thousand six hundred thirty.

36 The priests: the descendants of Jedaiah, of the house of Jeshua, nine hundred seventy-three. ³⁷Of Immer, one thousand fifty-two. ³⁸Of Pashhur, one thousand two hundred forty-seven. ³⁹Of Harim, one thousand seventeen.

40 The Levites: the descendants of Jeshua and Kadmiel, of the descendants of Hodaviah, seventy-four. ⁴¹The singers: the descendants of Asaph, one hundred twenty-eight. ⁴²The descendants of the gatekeepers: of Shallum, of Ater, of Talmon, of Akkub, of Hatita, and of Shobai, in all one hundred thirty-nine.

43 The temple servants: the descendants of Ziha, Hasupha, Tabbaoth, ⁴⁴Keros, Siaha, Padon, ⁴⁵Lebanah, Hagabah, Akkub, ⁴⁶Hagab, Shamlai, Hanan, ⁴⁷Giddel, Gahar, Reaiah, ⁴⁸Rezin, Nekoda, Gazzam, ⁴⁹Uzza, Paseah, Besai, ⁵⁰Asnah, Meunim, Nephisim, ⁵¹Bakbuk, Hakupha, Harhur, ⁵²Bazluth, Mehida, Harsha, ⁵³Barkos, Sisera, Temah, ⁵⁴Neziah, and Hatipha.

55 The descendants of Solomon's servants: Sotai, Hassophereth, Peruda, ⁵⁶Jaalah, Darkon, Giddel, ⁵⁷Shephatiah, Hattil, Pochereth-hazzebaim, and Ami.

58 All the temple servants and the descendants of Solomon's servants were three hundred ninety-two.

59 The following were those who came up from Tel-melah, Tel-harsha, Cherub, Addan, and Immer, though they could not prove their families or their descent, whether they belonged to Israel: ⁶⁰the descendants of Delaiah, Tobiah, and Nekoda, six hundred fifty-two. ⁶¹Also, of the descendants of the priests: the descendants of Habaiah, Hakkoz, and Barzillai (who had married one of the daughters of Barzillai the Gileadite, and was called by their name). ⁶²These looked for their entries in the genealogical records, but they were not found there, and so they were excluded from the priesthood as unclean; ⁶³the governor told them that they were not to partake of the most holy food, until there should be a priest to consult Urim and Thummim.

64 The whole assembly together was forty-two thousand three hundred sixty, ⁶⁵besides their male and female servants, of whom there were seven thousand three hundred thirty-seven; and they had two hundred male and female singers.

The Spirit of Giving

Nine eleven. Whenever we hear those two words, we are reminded of a horrible day in the history of the United States. The image of the twin towers of the World Trade Center burning and collapsing will stay with us forever. That event affected all of us, but it especially affected the citizens of New York City. Many stories of heroism surround that awful time. The people of New York City and the entire nation came together to grieve and especially to rebuild. Countless people volunteered untold hours to help with rescue efforts and clean-up. Countless more donated money to the families of those directly affected by the tragedy. Despite the horror of the attack, the aftermath of September 11, 2001, brought millions of people together to help rebuild a broken city. It was perhaps one of our finest hours as a nation.

For the Jews returning to Jerusalem, the task of rebuilding their ruined city must have seemed just as overwhelming, if not more so. (Their whole city was destroyed.) King Cyrus understood this and asked that family, friends, and neighbors help by giving whatever they could to the rebuilding effort.

● Who has been there to help you when you have felt completely overwhelmed? How do you offer help to others in their times of tragedy and crisis?

▶ Ezra 1:6–11

⁶⁶They had seven hundred thirty-six horses, two hundred forty-five mules, ⁶⁷four hundred thirty-five camels, and six thousand seven hundred twenty donkeys.

68 As soon as they came to the house of the LORD in Jerusalem, some of the heads of families made freewill offerings for the house of God, to erect it on its site. ⁶⁹According to their resources they gave to the building fund sixty-one thousand darics of gold, five thousand minas of silver, and one hundred priestly robes.

70 The priests, the Levites, and some of the people lived in Jerusalem and its vicinity;ᵃ and the singers, the gatekeepers, and the temple servants lived in their towns, and all Israel in their towns.

Worship Restored at Jerusalem

3 When the seventh month came, and the Israelites were in the towns, the people gathered together in Jerusalem. ²Then Jeshua son of

Holy Tears

Ezra 3:12 tells us that many of the older Israelites who remembered the first Temple wept at the grand celebration that marked its rebirth. Were they shedding tears of joy that the Temple was being built again? Or were they shedding tears of sorrow over what they had lost and never regained? Most likely, they were doing both.

Weeping can be a holy and healing part of life. Unfortunately, some people believe that strong men and women never cry. But tears are appropriate on many occasions: the loss of a dear friend or family member, reconciliation with someone after a long separation, and the moment we recognize we have sinned and hurt someone deeply, to name a few. Recall that moving scene in the Gospel where the sinful woman washed Jesus' feet with her tears (see Lk 7:36–50). We should bring our tears to God in prayer. They will turn into holy tears as God's healing love enters our lives.

▶ **Ezra 3:10–13**

Jozadak, with his fellow priests, and Zerubbabel son of Shealtiel with his kin set out to build the altar of the God of Israel, to offer burnt offerings on it, as prescribed in the law of Moses the man of God. ³They set up the altar on its foundation, because they were in dread of the neighboring peoples, and they offered burnt offerings upon it to the LORD, morning and evening. ⁴And they kept the festival of booths,ᵇ as prescribed, and offered the daily burnt offerings by number according to the ordinance, as required for each day, ⁵and after that the regular burnt offerings, the offerings at the new moon and at all the sacred festivals of the LORD, and the offerings of everyone who made a freewill offering to the LORD. ⁶From the first day of the seventh month they began to offer burnt offerings to the LORD. But the foundation of the temple of the LORD was not yet laid. ⁷So they gave money to the masons and the carpenters, and food, drink, and oil to the Sidonians and the Tyrians to bring cedar trees from Lebanon to the sea, to Joppa, according to the grant that they had from King Cyrus of Persia.

Foundation Laid for the Temple

8 In the second year after their arrival at the house of God at Jerusalem, in the second month, Zerubbabel son of Shealtiel and Jeshua son of Jozadak made a beginning, together with the rest of their people, the priests and the Levites and all who had come to Jerusalem from the captivity. They appointed the Levites, from twenty years old and upward, to have the oversight of the work on the house of the LORD. ⁹And Jeshua with his sons and his kin, and Kadmiel and his sons, Binnui and Hodaviahᶜ along with the sons of Henadad, the Levites, their sons and kin, together took charge of the workers in the house of God.

10 When the builders laid the foundation of the temple of the LORD, the priests in their vestments were stationed to praise the LORD with trumpets, and the Levites, the sons of Asaph, with cymbals, according to the directions of King David of Israel; ¹¹and they sang responsively, praising and giving thanks to the LORD,

"For he is good,
for his steadfast love endures forever toward
Israel."

And all the people responded with a great shout when they praised the LORD, because the

---

ᵃ 1 Esdras 5.46: Heb lacks *lived in Jerusalem and its vicinity*
ᵇ Or *tabernacles*; Heb *succoth*   ᶜ Compare 2.40; Neh 7.43;
1 Esdras 5.58: Heb *sons of Judah*

foundation of the house of the Lord was laid. ¹²But many of the priests and Levites and heads of families, old people who had seen the first house on its foundations, wept with a loud voice when they saw this house, though many shouted aloud for joy, ¹³so that the people could not distinguish the sound of the joyful shout from the sound of the people's weeping, for the people shouted so loudly that the sound was heard far away.

Resistance to Rebuilding the Temple

4 When the adversaries of Judah and Benjamin heard that the returned exiles were building a temple to the Lord, the God of Israel, ²they approached Zerubbabel and the heads of families and said to them, "Let us build with you, for we worship your God as you do, and we have been sacrificing to him ever since the days of King Esar-haddon of Assyria who brought us here." ³But Zerubbabel, Jeshua, and the rest of the heads of families in Israel said to them, "You shall have no part with us in building a house to our God; but we alone will build to the Lord, the God of Israel, as King Cyrus of Persia has commanded us."

4 Then the people of the land discouraged the people of Judah, and made them afraid to build, ⁵and they bribed officials to frustrate their plan throughout the reign of King Cyrus of Persia and until the reign of King Darius of Persia.

Rebuilding of Jerusalem Opposed

6 In the reign of Ahasuerus, in his accession year, they wrote an accusation against the inhabitants of Judah and Jerusalem.

7 And in the days of Artaxerxes, Bishlam and Mithredath and Tabeel and the rest of their associates wrote to King Artaxerxes of Persia; the letter was written in Aramaic and translated.*^a ⁸Rehum the royal deputy and Shimshai the scribe wrote a letter against Jerusalem to King Artaxerxes as follows ⁹(then Rehum the royal deputy, Shimshai the scribe, and the rest of their associates, the judges, the envoys, the officials, the Persians, the people of Erech, the Babylonians, the people of Susa, that is, the Elamites, ¹⁰and the rest of the nations whom the great and noble Osnappar deported and settled in the cities of Samaria and in the rest of the province Beyond the River wrote—and now ¹¹this is a copy of the letter that they sent).

"To King Artaxerxes: Your servants, the people of the province Beyond the River, send greeting. And now ¹²may it be known to the king that the Jews who came up from you to us have gone to

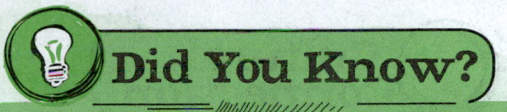

Did You Know?

The Second Temple

The first Temple, built during Solomon's reign, was destroyed in 587 BC when the southern kingdom of Judah was conquered by the Babylonians. The Persian king, Cyrus II, conquered Babylon in 539 BC and a year later liberated the Jewish exiles in Babylon. He also decreed that the Temple in Jerusalem be rebuilt (see Ezra 6:3). Between the years 520 and 515, the second Temple was rebuilt in Jerusalem. The second Temple was an essential aspect of the Israelites' rebuilding of their life, culture, and religion after the Babylonian Exile. This Temple, rather than a king, became the central focus of Jewish identity.

Jerusalem. They are rebuilding that rebellious and wicked city; they are finishing the walls and repairing the foundations. ¹³Now may it be known to the king that, if this city is rebuilt and the walls finished, they will not pay tribute, custom, or toll, and the royal revenue will be reduced. ¹⁴Now because we share the salt of the palace and it is not fitting for us to witness the king's dishonor, therefore we send and inform the king, ¹⁵so that a search may be made in the annals of your ancestors. You will discover in the annals that this is a rebellious city, hurtful to kings and provinces, and that sedition was stirred up in it from long ago. On that account this city was laid waste. ¹⁶We make known to the king that, if this city is rebuilt and its walls finished, you will then have no possession in the province Beyond the River."

17 The king sent an answer: "To Rehum the royal deputy and Shimshai the scribe and the rest of their associates who live in Samaria and in the rest of the province Beyond the River, greeting. And now ¹⁸the letter that you sent to us has been read in translation before me. ¹⁹So I made a decree, and someone searched and discovered that this city has risen against kings from long ago, and that rebellion and sedition have been made in it. ²⁰Jerusalem has had mighty kings who ruled over the whole province Beyond the River,

---

a Heb adds *in Aramaic,* indicating that 4.8-6.18 is in Aramaic. Another interpretation is *The letter was written in the Aramaic script and set forth in the Aramaic language*

Cultural Connection

The Rebirth of a Nation

Among the first things oppressive governments often do, historically speaking, is destroy or shut down religious establishments and make religious gatherings illegal. This is what happened to the Israelites taken into exile. But when oppressive governments can no longer hold the people down, when oppressive methods lose their grip, one of the first things the people do is bring back religious establishments and religious gatherings. This is what the Israelites did upon return to their land.

The reopening of the Catholic Cathedral in Moscow, Russia, in December 1999, marked the symbolic end of Roman Catholic religious persecution in Russia. For over eighty years, radical socialist, Marxist, and communist political leaders persecuted almost all religious communities in Russia, especially Roman Catholics. Faith and religion were seen as not just unimportant but as unnecessary and unwanted, to say the least.

Russia now struggles to rise above those years of oppression, and not just the religious oppression but the social and economic oppression as well. Many see the reopening of the Catholic Cathedral as an important step toward rebuilding the wounded country and leading it out of its past misery.

Have you ever felt uncomfortable speaking about your beliefs in a group of people? What kinds of statements did people make that caused you to feel uncomfortable sharing your beliefs? How can you help to eliminate intolerance of this kind?

▶ **Ezra, chapter 5**

to whom tribute, custom, and toll were paid. ²¹Therefore issue an order that these people be made to cease, and that this city not be rebuilt, until I make a decree. ²²Moreover, take care not to be slack in this matter; why should damage grow to the hurt of the king?"

23 Then when the copy of King Artaxerxes' letter was read before Rehum and the scribe Shimshai and their associates, they hurried to the Jews in Jerusalem and by force and power made them cease. ²⁴At that time the work on the house of God in Jerusalem stopped and was discontinued until the second year of the reign of King Darius of Persia.

Restoration of the Temple Resumed

5 Now the prophets, Haggai[a] and Zechariah son of Iddo, prophesied to the Jews who were in Judah and Jerusalem, in the name of the God of Israel who was over them. ²Then Zerubbabel son of Shealtiel and Jeshua son of Jozadak set out to rebuild the house of God in Jerusalem; and with them were the prophets of God, helping them.

3 At the same time Tattenai the governor of the province Beyond the River and Shethar-bozenai and their associates came to them and spoke to them thus, "Who gave you a decree to build this house and to finish this structure?" ⁴They[b]

also asked them this, "What are the names of the men who are building this building?" ⁵But the eye of their God was upon the elders of the Jews, and they did not stop them until a report reached Darius and then answer was returned by letter in reply to it.

6 The copy of the letter that Tattenai the governor of the province Beyond the River and Shethar-bozenai and his associates the envoys who were in the province Beyond the River sent to King Darius; ⁷they sent him a report, in which was written as follows: "To Darius the king, all peace! ⁸May it be known to the king that we went to the province of Judah, to the house of the great God. It is being built of hewn stone, and timber is laid in the walls; this work is being done diligently and prospers in their hands. ⁹Then we spoke to those elders and asked them, 'Who gave you a decree to build this house and to finish this structure?' ¹⁰We also asked them their names, for your information, so that we might write down the names of the men at their head. ¹¹This was their reply to us: 'We are the servants of the God of heaven and earth, and we are rebuilding the house that was built many years ago, which a great king of Israel built and finished. ¹²But because our ancestors had angered

a Aram adds *the prophet*   b Gk Syr: Aram *We*

the God of heaven, he gave them into the hand of King Nebuchadnezzar of Babylon, the Chaldean, who destroyed this house and carried away the people to Babylonia. ¹³However, King Cyrus of Babylon, in the first year of his reign, made a decree that this house of God should be rebuilt. ¹⁴Moreover, the gold and silver vessels of the house of God, which Nebuchadnezzar had taken out of the temple in Jerusalem and had brought into the temple of Babylon, these King Cyrus took out of the temple of Babylon, and they were delivered to a man named Sheshbazzar, whom he had made governor. ¹⁵He said to him, "Take these vessels; go and put them in the temple in Jerusalem, and let the house of God be rebuilt on its site." ¹⁶Then this Sheshbazzar came and laid the foundations of the house of God in Jerusalem; and from that time until now it has been under construction, and it is not yet finished.' ¹⁷And now, if it seems good to the king, have a search made in the royal archives there in Babylon, to see whether a decree was issued by King Cyrus for the rebuilding of this house of God in Jerusalem. Let the king send us his pleasure in this matter."

The Decree of Darius

6 Then King Darius made a decree, and they searched the archives where the documents were stored in Babylon. ²But it was in Ecbatana, the capital in the province of Media, that a scroll was found on which this was written: "A record. ³In the first year of his reign, King Cyrus issued a decree: Concerning the house of God at Jerusalem, let the house be rebuilt, the place where sacrifices are offered and burnt offerings are brought;ᵃ its height shall be sixty cubits and its width sixty cubits, ⁴with three courses of hewn stones and one course of timber; let the cost be paid from the royal treasury. ⁵Moreover, let the gold and silver vessels of the house of God, which Nebuchadnezzar took out of the temple in Jerusalem and brought to Babylon, be restored and brought back to the temple in Jerusalem, each to its place; you shall put them in the house of God."

⁶ "Now you, Tattenai, governor of the province Beyond the River, Shethar-bozenai, and you, their associates, the envoys in the province Beyond the River, keep away; ⁷let the work on this house of God alone; let the governor of the Jews and the elders of the Jews rebuild this house of God on its site. ⁸Moreover I make a decree regarding what you shall do for these elders of the Jews for the rebuilding of this house of God: the cost is to be paid to these people, in full and

without delay, from the royal revenue, the tribute of the province Beyond the River. ⁹Whatever is needed—young bulls, rams, or sheep for burnt offerings to the God of heaven, wheat, salt, wine, or oil, as the priests in Jerusalem require—let that be given to them day by day without fail, ¹⁰so that they may offer pleasing sacrifices to the God of heaven, and pray for the life of the king and his children. ¹¹Furthermore I decree that if anyone alters this edict, a beam shall be pulled out of the house of the perpetrator, who then shall be impaled on it. The house shall be made a dunghill. ¹²May the God who has established his name there overthrow any king or people that shall put forth a hand to alter this, or to destroy this house of God in Jerusalem. I, Darius, make a decree; let it be done with all diligence."

Completion and Dedication of the Temple

13 Then, according to the word sent by King Darius, Tattenai, the governor of the province Beyond the River, Shethar-bozenai, and their associates did with all diligence what King Darius had ordered. ¹⁴So the elders of the Jews built and prospered, through the prophesying of the prophet Haggai and Zechariah son of Iddo. They finished their building by command of the God

---

a Meaning of Aram uncertain

5:8

of Israel and by decree of Cyrus, Darius, and King Artaxerxes of Persia; [15]and this house was finished on the third day of the month of Adar, in the sixth year of the reign of King Darius.

16 The people of Israel, the priests and the Levites, and the rest of the returned exiles, celebrated the dedication of this house of God with joy. [17]They offered at the dedication of this house of God one hundred bulls, two hundred rams, four hundred lambs, and as a sin offering for all Israel, twelve male goats, according to the number of the tribes of Israel. [18]Then they set the priests in their divisions and the Levites in their courses for the service of God at Jerusalem, as it is written in the book of Moses.

The Passover Celebrated

19 On the fourteenth day of the first month the returned exiles kept the passover. [20]For both the priests and the Levites had purified themselves; all of them were clean. So they killed the passover lamb for all the returned exiles, for their fellow priests, and for themselves. [21]It was eaten by the people of Israel who had returned from exile, and also by all who had joined them and separated themselves from the pollutions of the nations of the land to worship the LORD, the God of Israel. [22]With joy they celebrated the festival of unleavened bread seven days; for the LORD had made them joyful, and had turned the heart of the king of Assyria to them, so that he aided them in the work on the house of God, the God of Israel.

The Coming and Work of Ezra

7 After this, in the reign of King Artaxerxes of Persia, Ezra son of Seraiah, son of Azariah, son of Hilkiah, [2]son of Shallum, son of Zadok, son of Ahitub, [3]son of Amariah, son of Azariah, son of Meraioth, [4]son of Zerahiah, son of Uzzi, son of Bukki, [5]son of Abishua, son of Phinehas, son of Eleazar, son of the chief priest Aaron— [6]this Ezra went up from Babylonia. He was a scribe skilled in the law of Moses that the LORD the God of Israel had given; and the king granted him all that he asked, for the hand of the LORD his God was upon him.

7 Some of the people of Israel, and some of the priests and Levites, the singers and gatekeepers, and the temple servants also went up to Jerusalem, in the seventh year of King Artaxerxes. [8]They came to Jerusalem in the fifth month, which was in the seventh year of the king. [9]On the first day of the first month the journey up from Babylon was begun, and on the first day of the fifth month he came to Jerusalem, for the

gracious hand of his God was upon him. [10]For Ezra had set his heart to study the law of the LORD, and to do it, and to teach the statutes and ordinances in Israel.

The Letter of Artaxerxes to Ezra

11 This is a copy of the letter that King Artaxerxes gave to the priest Ezra, the scribe, a scholar of the text of the commandments of the LORD and his statutes for Israel: [12]"Artaxerxes, king of kings, to the priest Ezra, the scribe of the law of the God of heaven: Peace.[a] And now [13]I decree that any of the people of Israel or their priests or Levites in my kingdom who freely offers to go to Jerusalem may go with you. [14]For you are sent by the king and his seven counselors to make inquiries about Judah and Jerusalem according to the law of your God, which is in your hand, [15]and also to convey the silver and gold that the king and his counselors have freely offered to the God of Israel, whose dwelling is in Jerusalem, [16]with all the silver and gold that you shall find in the whole province of Babylonia, and with the freewill offerings of the people and the priests, given willingly for the house of their God in Jerusalem. [17]With this money, then, you shall with all diligence buy bulls, rams, and lambs, and their grain offerings and their drink offerings, and you shall offer them on the altar of the house of your God in Jerusalem. [18]Whatever seems good to you and your colleagues to do with the rest of the silver and gold, you may do, according to the will of your God. [19]The vessels that have been given you for the service of the house of your God, you shall deliver before the God of Jerusalem. [20]And whatever else is required for the house of your God, which you are responsible for providing, you may provide out of the king's treasury.

21 "I, King Artaxerxes, decree to all the treasurers in the province Beyond the River: Whatever the priest Ezra, the scribe of the law of the God of heaven, requires of you, let it be done with all diligence, [22]up to one hundred talents of silver, one hundred cors of wheat, one hundred baths[b] of wine, one hundred baths[b] of oil, and unlimited salt. [23]Whatever is commanded by the God of heaven, let it be done with zeal for the house of the God of heaven, or wrath will come upon the realm of the king and his heirs. [24]We also notify you that it shall not be lawful to impose tribute, custom, or toll on any of the priests, the Levites, the singers, the doorkeepers, the temple servants, or other servants of this house of God.

25 "And you, Ezra, according to the God-

---

a Syr Vg 1 Esdras 8.9: Aram *Perfect*   b A Heb measure of volume given wisdom you possess, appoint magistrates and judges who may judge all the people in the province Beyond the River who know the laws of your God; and you shall teach those who do not know them. ²⁶All who will not obey the law of your God and the law of the king, let judgment be strictly executed on them, whether for death or for banishment or for confiscation of their goods or for imprisonment."

27 Blessed be the LORD, the God of our ancestors, who put such a thing as this into the heart of the king to glorify the house of the LORD in Jerusalem, ²⁸and who extended to me steadfast love before the king and his counselors, and before all the king's mighty officers. I took courage, for the hand of the LORD my God was upon me, and I gathered leaders from Israel to go up with me.

Heads of Families Who Returned with Ezra

8 These are their family heads, and this is the genealogy of those who went up with me from Babylonia, in the reign of King Artaxerxes: ²Of the descendants of Phinehas, Gershom. Of Ithamar, Daniel. Of David, Hattush, ³of the descendants of Shecaniah. Of Parosh, Zechariah, with whom were registered one hundred fifty males. ⁴Of the descendants of Pahath-moab, Eliehoenai son of Zerahiah, and with him two hundred males. ⁵Of the descendants of Zattu,^a Shecaniah son of Jahaziel, and with him three hundred males. ⁶Of the descendants of Adin, Ebed son of Jonathan, and with him fifty males. ⁷Of the descendants of Elam, Jeshaiah son of Athaliah, and with him seventy males. ⁸Of the descendants of Shephatiah, Zebadiah son of Michael, and with him eighty males. ⁹Of the descendants of Joab, Obadiah son of Jehiel, and with him two hundred eighteen males. ¹⁰Of the descendants of Bani,^b Shelomith son of Josiphiah, and with him one hundred sixty males. ¹¹Of the descendants of Bebai, Zechariah son of Bebai, and with him twenty-eight males. ¹²Of the descendants of Azgad, Johanan son of Hakkatan, and with him one hundred ten males. ¹³Of the descendants of Adonikam, those who came later, their names being Eliphelet, Jeuel, and Shemaiah, and with them sixty males. ¹⁴Of the descendants of Bigvai, Uthai and Zaccur, and with them seventy males.

Servants for the Temple

15 I gathered them by the river that runs to Ahava, and there we camped three days. As I reviewed the people and the priests, I found there none of the descendants of Levi. ¹⁶Then I sent for Eliezer, Ariel, Shemaiah, Elnathan, Jarib, Elnathan, Nathan, Zechariah, and Meshullam, who were leaders, and for Joiarib and Elnathan, who were wise, ¹⁷and sent them to Iddo, the leader at the place called Casiphia, telling them what to say to Iddo and his colleagues the temple servants at Casiphia, namely, to send us ministers for the house of our God. ¹⁸Since the gracious hand of our God was upon us, they brought us a man of discretion, of the descendants of Mahli son of Levi son of Israel, namely Sherebiah, with his sons and kin, eighteen; ¹⁹also Hashabiah and with him Jeshaiah of the descendants of Merari, with his kin and their sons, twenty; ²⁰besides two hundred twenty of the temple servants, whom David and his officials had set apart to attend the Levites. These were all mentioned by name.

Fasting and Prayer for Protection

21 Then I proclaimed a fast there, at the river Ahava, that we might deny ourselves^c before our God, to seek from him a safe journey for ourselves, our children, and all our possessions. ²²For I was ashamed to ask the king for a band of soldiers and cavalry to protect us against the enemy on our way, since we had told the king that the hand of our God is gracious to all who seek him, but his power and his wrath are against all who forsake him. ²³So we fasted and petitioned our God for this, and he listened to our entreaty.

Gifts for the Temple

24 Then I set apart twelve of the leading priests: Sherebiah, Hashabiah, and ten of their kin with them. ²⁵And I weighed out to them the silver and the gold and the vessels, the offering for the house of our God that the king, his counselors, his lords, and all Israel there present had offered; ²⁶I weighed out into their hand six hundred fifty talents of silver, and one hundred silver vessels worth . . . talents,^d and one hundred talents of gold, ²⁷twenty gold bowls worth a thousand darics, and two vessels of fine polished bronze as precious as gold. ²⁸And I said to them, "You are holy to the LORD, and the vessels are holy; and the silver and the gold are a freewill offering to the LORD, the God of your ancestors. ²⁹Guard them and keep them until you weigh them before the chief priests and the Levites and the heads of families in Israel at Jerusalem, within the chambers of the house of the LORD." ³⁰So the priests and the Levites took over

a Gk 1 Esdras 8.32: Heb lacks *of Zattu*   b Gk 1 Esdras 8.36: Heb lacks *Bani*   c Or *might fast*   d The number of talents is lacking

the silver, the gold, and the vessels as they were weighed out, to bring them to Jerusalem, to the house of our God.

The Return to Jerusalem

31 Then we left the river Ahava on the twelfth day of the first month, to go to Jerusalem; the hand of our God was upon us, and he delivered us from the hand of the enemy and from ambushes along the way. 32We came to Jerusalem and remained there three days. 33On the fourth day, within the house of our God, the silver, the gold, and the vessels were weighed into the hands of the priest Meremoth son of Uriah, and with him was Eleazar son of Phinehas, and with them were the Levites, Jozabad son of Jeshua and Noadiah son of Binnui. 34The total was counted and weighed, and the weight of everything was recorded.

35 At that time those who had come from captivity, the returned exiles, offered burnt offerings to the God of Israel, twelve bulls for all Israel, ninety-six rams, seventy-seven lambs, and as a sin offering twelve male goats; all this was a burnt offering to the LORD. 36They also delivered the king's commissions to the king's satraps and to the governors of the province Beyond the River; and they supported the people and the house of God.

Denunciation of Mixed Marriages

9 After these things had been done, the officials approached me and said, "The people of Israel, the priests, and the Levites have not separated themselves from the peoples of the lands with their abominations, from the Canaanites, the Hittites, the Perizzites, the Jebusites, the Ammonites, the Moabites, the Egyptians, and the Amorites. 2For they have taken some of their daughters as wives for themselves and for their sons. Thus the holy seed has mixed itself with the peoples of the lands, and in this faithlessness the officials and leaders have led the way." 3When I heard this, I tore my garment and my mantle, and pulled hair from my head and beard, and sat appalled. 4Then all who trembled at the words of the God of Israel, because of the faithlessness of the returned exiles, gathered around me while I sat appalled until the evening sacrifice.

Ezra's Prayer

5 At the evening sacrifice I got up from my fasting, with my garments and my mantle torn, and fell on my knees, spread out my hands to the LORD my God, 6and said,

"O my God, I am too ashamed and embarrassed to lift my face to you, my God, for our iniquities have risen higher than our heads, and our guilt has mounted up to the heavens. 7From the days of our ancestors to this day we have been deep in guilt, and for our iniquities we, our kings, and our priests have been handed over to the kings of the lands, to the sword, to captivity, to plundering, and to utter shame, as is now the case. 8But now for a brief moment favor has been shown by the LORD our God, who has left us a remnant, and given us a stake in his holy place, in order that he*a* may brighten our eyes and grant us a little sustenance in our slavery. 9For we are slaves; yet our God has not forsaken us in our slavery, but has extended to us his steadfast love before the kings of Persia, to give us new life to set up the house of our God, to repair its ruins, and to give us a wall in Judea and Jerusalem.

10 "And now, our God, what shall we say after this? For we have forsaken your commandments, 11which you commanded by your servants the prophets, saying, 'The land that you are entering to possess is a land unclean with the pollutions of the peoples of the lands, with their abominations. They have filled it from end to end with their uncleanness. 12Therefore do not give your daughters to their sons, neither take their daughters for your sons, and never seek their peace or prosperity, so that you may be strong and eat the good of the land and leave it for an inheritance to your children forever.' 13After all that has come upon us for our evil deeds and for our great guilt, seeing that you, our God, have punished us less than our iniquities deserved and have given us such a remnant as this, 14shall we break your commandments again and intermarry with the peoples who practice these abominations? Would you not be angry with us until you destroy us without remnant or survivor? 15O LORD, God of Israel, you are just, but we have escaped as a remnant, as is now the case. Here we are before you in our guilt, though no one can face you because of this."

The People's Response

10 While Ezra prayed and made confession, weeping and throwing himself down before the house of God, a very great assembly of men, women, and children gathered to him out of Israel; the people also wept bitterly. 2Shecaniah son of Jehiel, of the descendants of Elam, addressed Ezra, saying, "We have broken faith with our God and have married foreign women from the peoples of the land, but even

a Heb our God

now there is hope for Israel in spite of this. ³So now let us make a covenant with our God to send away all these wives and their children, according to the counsel of my lord and of those who tremble at the commandment of our God; and let it be done according to the law. ⁴Take action, for it is your duty, and we are with you; be strong, and do it." ⁵Then Ezra stood up and made the leading priests, the Levites, and all Israel swear that they would do as had been said. So they swore.

Foreign Wives and Their Children Rejected

6 Then Ezra withdrew from before the house of God, and went to the chamber of Jehohanan son of Eliashib, where he spent the night.ᵃ He did not eat bread or drink water, for he was mourning over the faithlessness of the exiles. ⁷They made a proclamation throughout Judah and Jerusalem to all the returned exiles that they should assemble at Jerusalem, ⁸and that if any did not come within three days, by order of the officials and the elders all their property should be forfeited, and they themselves banned from the congregation of the exiles.

9 Then all the people of Judah and Benjamin assembled at Jerusalem within the three days; it was the ninth month, on the twentieth day of the month. All the people sat in the open square before the house of God, trembling because of this matter and because of the heavy rain. ¹⁰Then Ezra the priest stood up and said to them, "You have trespassed and married foreign women, and so increased the guilt of Israel. ¹¹Now make confession to the Lᴏʀᴅ the God of your ancestors, and do his will; separate yourselves from the peoples of the land and from the foreign wives." ¹²Then all the assembly answered with a loud voice, "It is so; we must do as you have said. ¹³But the people are many, and it is a time of heavy rain; we cannot stand in the open. Nor is this a task for one day or for two, for many of us have transgressed in this matter. ¹⁴Let our officials represent the whole assembly, and let all in our towns who have taken foreign wives come at appointed times, and with them the elders and judges of every town, until the fierce wrath of our God on this account is averted from us." ¹⁵Only Jonathan son of Asahel and Jahzeiah son of Tikvah opposed this, and Meshullam and Shabbethai the Levites supported them.

16 Then the returned exiles did so. Ezra the priest selected men,ᵇ heads of families, according to their families, each of them designated by name. On the first day of the tenth month they sat down to examine the matter. ¹⁷By the first day

Live It!

Who Belongs, and Who Does Not?

In Ezra, chapters 9–10, Ezra tells the people to reject their foreign wives and children. Nehemiah does the same in Nehemiah 13:23–27. This probably strikes us as harsh, but we can try to understand the Israelites' situation. Only a remnant of the Israelites was left to re-establish Israel's identity. History had taught the Israelites that intermarriage led to a watering down of their faith and of the people's loyalty to their religious practices. Back then, the only way to survive as a people was to separate from outsiders.

This separation led to an even greater animosity between the Jews from Judah and their cousins in faith, the Samaritans. We see some of this prejudice in the Gospels (see Jn 4:1–42 and "Discrimination in Jesus' Time," near Lk 10:25–37). Christians have had similar separations throughout our history. Today, the Church teaches us to be faithful to our beliefs but also to be open to others who believe differently and discover together what we have in common.

● Why is it often so hard for people to be open to those from other faith traditions?

▶ Ezra, chapters 9–10

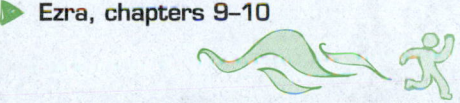

of the first month they had come to the end of all the men who had married foreign women.

18 There were found of the descendants of the priests who had married foreign women, of the descendants of Jeshua son of Jozadak and his brothers: Maaseiah, Eliezer, Jarib, and Gedaliah. ¹⁹They pledged themselves to send away their wives, and their guilt offering was a ram of the flock for their guilt. ²⁰Of the descendants of Immer: Hanani and Zebadiah. ²¹Of the descendants of Harim: Maaseiah, Elijah, Shemaiah, Jehiel, and Uzziah. ²²Of the descendants of Pashhur: Elioenai, Maaseiah, Ishmael, Nethanel, Jozabad, and Elasah.

ᵃ 1 Esdras 9.2: Heb *where he went*   ᵇ 1 Esdras 9.16: Syr: Heb *And there were selected Ezra,*

23 Of the Levites: Jozabad, Shimei, Kelaiah (that is, Kelita), Pethahiah, Judah, and Eliezer. 24Of the singers: Eliashib. Of the gatekeepers: Shallum, Telem, and Uri.

25 And of Israel: of the descendants of Parosh: Ramiah, Izziah, Malchijah, Mijamin, Eleazar, Hashabiah,*a* and Benaiah. 26Of the descendants of Elam: Mattaniah, Zechariah, Jehiel, Abdi, Jeremoth, and Elijah. 27Of the descendants of Zattu: Elioenai, Eliashib, Mattaniah, Jeremoth, Zabad, and Aziza. 28Of the descendants of Bebai: Jehohanan, Hananiah, Zabbai, and Athlai. 29Of the descendants of Bani: Meshullam, Malluch, Adaiah, Jashub, Sheal, and Jeremoth. 30Of the descendants of Pahath-moab: Adna, Chelal, Benaiah, Maaseiah, Mattaniah, Bezalel, Binnui, and Manasseh. 31Of the descendants of Harim: Eliezer, Isshijah,

Malchijah, Shemaiah, Shimeon, 32Benjamin, Malluch, and Shemariah. 33Of the descendants of Hashum: Mattenai, Mattattah, Zabad, Eliphelet, Jeremai, Manasseh, and Shimei. 34Of the descendants of Bani: Maadai, Amram, Uel, 35Benaiah, Bedeiah, Cheluhi, 36Vaniah, Meremoth, Eliashib, 37Mattaniah, Mattenai, and Jaasu. 38Of the descendants of Binnui:*b* Shimei, 39Shelemiah, Nathan, Adaiah, 40Machnadebai, Shashai, Sharai, 41Azarel, Shelemiah, Shemariah, 42Shallum, Amariah, and Joseph. 43Of the descendants of Nebo: Jeiel, Mattithiah, Zabad, Zebina, Jaddai, Joel, and Benaiah. 44All these had married foreign women, and they sent them away with their children.*c*

---

a 1 Esdras 9.26 Gk: Heb *Malchijah* b Gk: Heb *Bani, Binnui*
c 1 Esdras 9.36; meaning of Heb uncertain

For background on this book,
see the introduction to Ezra
and Nehemiah before Ezra.

Nehemiah

Nehemiah Prays for His People

1 The words of Nehemiah son of Hacaliah. In the month of Chislev, in the twentieth year, while I was in Susa the capital, ²one of my brothers, Hanani, came with certain men from Judah; and I asked them about the Jews that survived, those who had escaped the captivity, and about Jerusalem. ³They replied, "The survivors there in the province who escaped captivity are in great trouble and shame; the wall of Jerusalem is broken down, and its gates have been destroyed by fire."

4 When I heard these words I sat down and wept, and mourned for days, fasting and praying before the God of heaven. ⁵I said, "O LORD God of heaven, the great and awesome God who keeps covenant and steadfast love with those who love him and keep his commandments; ⁶let your ear be attentive and your eyes open to hear the prayer of your servant that I now pray before you day and night for your servants, the people of Israel, confessing the sins of the people of Israel, which we have sinned against you. Both I and my family have sinned. ⁷We have offended you deeply, failing to keep the commandments, the statutes, and the ordinances that you commanded your servant Moses. ⁸Remember the word that you commanded your servant Moses, 'If you are unfaithful, I will scatter you among the peoples; ⁹but if you return to me and keep my commandments and do them, though your outcasts are under the farthest skies, I will gather them from there and bring them to the place at which I have chosen to establish my name.' ¹⁰They are your servants and your people, whom you redeemed by your great power and your strong hand. ¹¹O Lord, let your ear be attentive to the prayer of your servant, and to the prayer of your servants who delight in revering your name. Give success to your servant today, and grant him mercy in the sight of this man!"

At the time, I was cupbearer to the king.

Nehemiah Sent to Judah

2 In the month of Nisan, in the twentieth year of King Artaxerxes, when wine was served him, I carried the wine and gave it to the king. Now, I had never been sad in his presence before. ²So the king said to me, "Why is your face sad, since you are not sick? This can only be sadness of the heart." Then I was very much afraid. ³I said to the king, "May the king live forever! Why should my face not be sad, when the city, the place of my ancestors' graves, lies waste, and its gates have been destroyed by fire?" ⁴Then the king said to me, "What do you request?" So I prayed to the God of heaven. ⁵Then I said to the king, "If it pleases the king, and if your servant has found favor with you, I ask that you send me to Judah, to the city of my ancestors' graves, so that I may rebuild it." ⁶The king said to me (the queen also was sitting beside him), "How long will you be gone, and when will you return?" So it pleased the king to send me, and I set him a date. ⁷Then I said to the king, "If it pleases the king, let letters be given me to the governors of the province Beyond the River, that they may grant me passage

457

Nehemiah Prepares for Action

Do you ever watch the news and think, Why bother trying to make the world a better place? Christians are called to social action—action for justice, action to make the world a better place. But social sin can scare Christians away from social action. Social sin—such as poverty, racism, violence, materialism, and indifference—seems too big for any individual to do much about. In the overwhelming face of social sin, it is easy to say, "I give up."

But then we have Nehemiah's example. When Nehemiah heard of the results of Israel's collective sin, he could have said, "I give up." Instead, he turned to God in fasting and prayer. In your prayer time, reflect or journal on the following questions:

● What social issue are you most concerned about?

● What can you do to learn more about this issue?

● How can you get more involved in acting on this issue?

● What do you need to bring to God in prayer about this issue?

▶ **Nehemiah, chapter 1**

---

until I arrive in Judah; [8]and a letter to Asaph, the keeper of the king's forest, directing him to give me timber to make beams for the gates of the temple fortress, and for the wall of the city, and for the house that I shall occupy." And the king granted me what I asked, for the gracious hand of my God was upon me.

9 Then I came to the governors of the province Beyond the River, and gave them the king's letters. Now the king had sent officers of the army and cavalry with me. [10]When Sanballat the Horonite and Tobiah the Ammonite official heard this, it displeased them greatly that someone had come to seek the welfare of the people of Israel.

Nehemiah's Inspection of the Walls

11 So I came to Jerusalem and was there for three days. [12]Then I got up during the night, I and a few men with me; I told no one what my God had put into my heart to do for Jerusalem. The only animal I took was the animal I rode. [13]I went out by night by the Valley Gate past the Dragon's Spring and to the Dung Gate, and I inspected the walls of Jerusalem that had been broken down and its gates that had been destroyed by fire. [14]Then I went on to the Fountain Gate and to the King's Pool; but there was no place for the animal I was riding to continue. [15]So I went up by way of the valley by night and inspected the wall. Then I turned back and entered by the Valley Gate, and so returned. [16]The officials did not know where I had gone or what I was doing; I had not yet told the Jews, the priests, the nobles, the officials, and the rest that were to do the work.

Decision to Restore the Walls

17 Then I said to them, "You see the trouble we are in, how Jerusalem lies in ruins with its gates burned. Come, let us rebuild the wall of Jerusalem, so that we may no longer suffer disgrace." [18]I told them that the hand of my God had been gracious upon me, and also the words that the king had spoken to me. Then they said, "Let us start building!" So they committed themselves to the common good. [19]But when Sanballat the Horonite and Tobiah the Ammonite official, and Geshem the Arab heard of it, they mocked and ridiculed us, saying, "What is this that you are doing? Are you rebelling against the king?" [20]Then I replied to them, "The God of heaven is the one who will give us success, and we his servants are going to start building; but you have no share or claim or historic right in Jerusalem."

Organization of the Work

3 Then the high priest Eliashib set to work with his fellow priests and rebuilt the Sheep Gate. They consecrated it and set up its doors; they consecrated it as far as the Tower of the Hundred and as far as the Tower of Hananel. [2]And the men of Jericho built next to him. And next to them[a] Zaccur son of Imri built.

3 The sons of Hassenaah built the Fish Gate; they laid its beams and set up its doors, its bolts, and its bars. [4]Next to them Meremoth son of Uriah son of Hakkoz made repairs. Next to them Meshullam son of Berechiah son of Meshezabel made repairs. Next to them Zadok son of Baana made repairs. [5]Next to them the Tekoites made repairs; but their nobles would not put their shoulders to the work of their Lord.[b]

---

a Heb *him*   *b* Or *lords*

6 Joiada son of Paseah and Meshullam son of Besodeiah repaired the Old Gate; they laid its beams and set up its doors, its bolts, and its bars. [7]Next to them repairs were made by Melatiah the Gibeonite and Jadon the Meronothite—the men of Gibeon and of Mizpah—who were under the jurisdiction of[a] the governor of the province Beyond the River. [8]Next to them Uzziel son of Harhaiah, one of the goldsmiths, made repairs. Next to him Hananiah, one of the perfumers, made repairs; and they restored Jerusalem as far as the Broad Wall. [9]Next to them Rephaiah son of Hur, ruler of half the district of[b] Jerusalem, made repairs. [10]Next to them Jedaiah son of Harumaph made repairs opposite his house; and next to him Hattush son of Hashabneiah made repairs. [11]Malchijah son of Harim and Hasshub son of Pahath-moab repaired another section and the Tower of the Ovens. [12]Next to him Shallum son of Hallohesh, ruler of half the district of[b] Jerusalem, made repairs, he and his daughters.

13 Hanun and the inhabitants of Zanoah repaired the Valley Gate; they rebuilt it and set up its doors, its bolts, and its bars, and repaired a thousand cubits of the wall, as far as the Dung Gate.

14 Malchijah son of Rechab, ruler of the district of[c] Beth-haccherem, repaired the Dung Gate; he rebuilt it and set up its doors, its bolts, and its bars.

15 And Shallum son of Col-hozeh, ruler of the district of[c] Mizpah, repaired the Fountain Gate; he rebuilt it and covered it and set up its doors, its bolts, and its bars; and he built the wall of the Pool of Shelah of the king's garden, as far as the stairs that go down from the City of David. [16]After him Nehemiah son of Azbuk, ruler of half the district of[b] Beth-zur, repaired from a point opposite the graves of David, as far as the artificial pool and the house of the warriors. [17]After him the Levites made repairs: Rehum son of Bani; next to him Hashabiah, ruler of half the district of[b] Keilah, made repairs for his district. [18]After him their kin made repairs: Binnui,[d] son of Henadad, ruler of half the district of[b] Keilah; [19]next to him Ezer son of Jeshua, ruler[e] of Mizpah, repaired another section opposite the ascent to the armory at the Angle. [20]After him Baruch son of Zabbai repaired another section from the Angle to the door of the house of the high priest Eliashib. [21]After him Meremoth son of Uriah son of Hakkoz repaired another section from the door of the house of Eliashib to the end of the house of Eliashib. [22]After him the priests, the men of the surrounding area, made repairs. [23]After them Benjamin and Hasshub made repairs

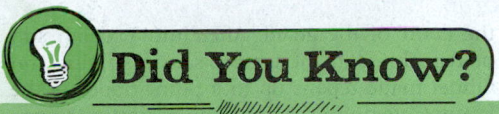

Did You Know?

Rebuilding Hiroshima and Nagasaki

Nehemiah faced the difficult task of rebuilding a city completely destroyed by war. Unfortunately, this type of destruction has happened too many times in human history. We all remember how the twin towers of the destroyed World Trade Center were virtual cities that were utterly destroyed in a terrorist attack. But the most dramatic destruction of entire cities in modern times was the atomic bombing of Hiroshima and Nagasaki, Japan, on August 6 and August 9, 1945. The bombings flattened those cities and melted and destroyed objects and people within 1.5 miles of its epicenter. The Catholic Church condemns all such indiscriminate destruction—whether by atomic, biological, or chemical weapons.

Although the effects of these bombings were catastrophic, they did not wipe out the human spirit. Since that day, citizens of Hiroshima and Nagasaki have been recovering and rebuilding, first by burying the dead, then by rebuilding homes, stores, churches, and temples. Today, Hiroshima and Nagasaki are thriving cities. The destruction and rebuilding of these cities are probably best summarized in this haiku, written by Yasuhiko Shigemoto, who was a teenager when the bomb hit Hiroshima:

How freely
butterflies are flying about
in the A-bomb Dome!
　　　　　　　　("My Haiku of Hiroshima")

▶ Neh 2:17–18

opposite their house. After them Azariah son of Maaseiah son of Ananiah made repairs beside his own house. [24]After him Binnui son of Henadad repaired another section, from the house of Azariah to the Angle and to the corner. [25]Palal son of Uzai repaired opposite the Angle and the tower projecting from the upper house of the king at

a Meaning of Heb uncertain　b Or supervisor of half the portion assigned to　c Or supervisor of the portion assigned to　d Gk Syr Compare verse 24, 10.9: Heb Bavvai　e Or supervisor

the court of the guard. After him Pedaiah son of Parosh ²⁶and the temple servants living*ᵃ* on Ophel made repairs up to a point opposite the Water Gate on the east and the projecting tower. ²⁷After him the Tekoites repaired another section opposite the great projecting tower as far as the wall of Ophel.

28 Above the Horse Gate the priests made repairs, each one opposite his own house. ²⁹After them Zadok son of Immer made repairs opposite his own house. After him Shemaiah son of Shecaniah, the keeper of the East Gate, made repairs. ³⁰After him Hananiah son of Shelemiah and Hanun sixth son of Zalaph repaired another section. After him Meshullam son of Berechiah made

Nehemiah's Strength

Many young people have traumatic experiences, such as the divorce of their parents, domestic and community violence, the death of a parent or sibling, prejudice, and poverty. Some young people come through these experiences as victims, unable to take any control in their lives. Others take the attitude "if you can't beat them, join them," and become cynical, violent, or antisocial. But some rise above their hurt to live happy and healthy lives. What can account for the difference in people's reactions?

Perhaps Nehemiah provides a clue. He was confronted by cynical people (see Neh 4:2–3) and violent people (see 4:7–9). But he trusted in something bigger than himself. "The God of heaven is the one who will give us success" (2:20), he proclaimed to those with negative attitudes.

Prayer and faith in God gave Nehemiah strength to take action in difficult times. They can work for us too. Don't let life's traumas make you powerless. Don't let them make you cynical and part of the problem. Pray and have faith, and you too will have the strength to meet your problems with action.

▶ **Nehemiah, chapter 4**

repairs opposite his living quarters. ³¹After him Malchijah, one of the goldsmiths, made repairs as far as the house of the temple servants and of the merchants, opposite the Muster Gate,*ᵇ* and to the upper room of the corner. ³²And between the upper room of the corner and the Sheep Gate the goldsmiths and the merchants made repairs.

Hostile Plots Thwarted

4 *ᶜ*Now when Sanballat heard that we were building the wall, he was angry and greatly enraged, and he mocked the Jews. ²He said in the presence of his associates and of the army of Samaria, "What are these feeble Jews doing? Will they restore things? Will they sacrifice? Will they finish it in a day? Will they revive the stones out of the heaps of rubbish—and burned ones at that?" ³Tobiah the Ammonite was beside him, and he said, "That stone wall they are building— any fox going up on it would break it down!" ⁴Hear, O our God, for we are despised; turn their taunt back on their own heads, and give them over as plunder in a land of captivity. ⁵Do not cover their guilt, and do not let their sin be blotted out from your sight; for they have hurled insults in the face of the builders.

6 So we rebuilt the wall, and all the wall was joined together to half its height; for the people had a mind to work.

7*ᵈ* But when Sanballat and Tobiah and the Arabs and the Ammonites and the Ashdodites heard that the repairing of the walls of Jerusalem was going forward and the gaps were beginning to be closed, they were very angry, ⁸and all plotted together to come and fight against Jerusalem and to cause confusion in it. ⁹So we prayed to our God, and set a guard as a protection against them day and night.

10 But Judah said, "The strength of the burden bearers is failing, and there is too much rubbish so that we are unable to work on the wall." ¹¹And our enemies said, "They will not know or see anything before we come upon them and kill them and stop the work." ¹²When the Jews who lived near them came, they said to us ten times, "From all the places where they live*ᵉ* they will come up against us."*ᶠ* ¹³So in the lowest parts of the space behind the wall, in open places, I stationed the people according to their families,*ᵍ* with their swords, their spears, and their bows. ¹⁴After I looked these things over, I stood up and said to the nobles and the officials and the

---

a Cn: Heb *were living*   *b* Or *Hammiphkad Gate*   *c* Ch 3.33 in Heb   *d* Ch 4.1 in Heb   *e* Cn: Heb *you return*   *f* Compare Gk Syr: Meaning of Heb uncertain   *g* Meaning of Heb uncertain

Catholic Social Teaching

Hunger Pains

When Nehemiah's people were hungry, he saw the problem right away. The problem was not a lack of food. It was that some people were using their wealth and influence to control who got the food (see Neh 5:7–8). Nehemiah took the radical step of demanding that the powerful and wealthy stop taking advantage of those less well off. He demanded that the wealthy restore the money and property they had taken from others through unjust charging of interest (see verses 10–11).

Experts tell us that much the same is true today. People are starving not because food is scarce but because political and economic conditions prevent them from getting the food. Catholic social teaching asserts that human dignity can be respected and nurtured only if basic rights and responsibilities are met. Those basics include food, shelter, and clothing. Christians have an obligation to make sure people have access to food. Nehemiah acted, and so must we.

What can you do to make sure this is happening?

▶ **Nehemiah, chapter 5**

Rights and Responsibilities

---

rest of the people, "Do not be afraid of them. Remember the LORD, who is great and awesome, and fight for your kin, your sons, your daughters, your wives, and your homes."

15 When our enemies heard that their plot was known to us, and that God had frustrated it, we all returned to the wall, each to his work. [16]From that day on, half of my servants worked on construction, and half held the spears, shields, bows, and body-armor; and the leaders posted themselves behind the whole house of Judah, [17]who were building the wall. The burden bearers carried their loads in such a way that each labored on the work with one hand and with the other held a weapon. [18]And each of the builders had his sword strapped at his side while he built. The man who sounded the trumpet was beside me. [19]And I said to the nobles, the officials, and the rest of the people, "The work is great and widely spread out, and we are separated far from one another on the wall. [20]Rally to us wherever you hear the sound of the trumpet. Our God will fight for us."

21 So we labored at the work, and half of them held the spears from break of dawn until the stars came out. [22]I also said to the people at that time, "Let every man and his servant pass the night inside Jerusalem, so that they may be a guard for us by night and may labor by day." [23]So neither I nor my brothers nor my servants nor the men of the guard who followed me ever took off our clothes; each kept his weapon in his right hand.[a]

Nehemiah Deals with Oppression

5 Now there was a great outcry of the people and of their wives against their Jewish kin. [2]For there were those who said, "With our sons and our daughters, we are many; we must get grain, so that we may eat and stay alive." [3]There were also those who said, "We are having to pledge our fields, our vineyards, and our houses in order to get grain during the famine." [4]And there were those who said, "We are having to borrow money on our fields and vineyards to pay the king's tax. [5]Now our flesh is the same as that of our kindred; our children are the same as their children; and yet we are forcing our sons and daughters to be slaves, and some of our daughters have been ravished; we are powerless, and our fields and vineyards now belong to others."

6 I was very angry when I heard their outcry and these complaints. [7]After thinking it over, I brought charges against the nobles and the officials; I said to them, "You are all taking interest from your own people." And I called a great assembly to deal with them, [8]and said to them, "As far as we were able, we have bought back our Jewish kindred who had been sold to other nations; but now you are selling your own kin, who must then be bought back by us!" They were silent, and could not find a word to say. [9]So I said, "The thing that you are doing is not good.

---

a Cn: Heb *each his weapon the water*

NEH

Should you not walk in the fear of our God, to prevent the taunts of the nations our enemies? [10]Moreover I and my brothers and my servants are lending them money and grain. Let us stop this taking of interest. [11]Restore to them, this very day, their fields, their vineyards, their olive orchards, and their houses, and the interest on money, grain, wine, and oil that you have been exacting from them." [12]Then they said, "We will restore everything and demand nothing more from them. We will do as you say." And I called the priests, and made them take an oath to do as they had promised. [13]I also shook out the fold of my garment and said, "So may God shake out everyone from house and from property who does not perform this promise. Thus may they be shaken out and emptied." And all the assembly said, "Amen," and praised the LORD. And the people did as they had promised.

The Generosity of Nehemiah

14 Moreover from the time that I was appointed to be their governor in the land of Judah, from the twentieth year to the thirty-second year of King Artaxerxes, twelve years, neither I nor my brothers ate the food allowance of the governor. [15]The former governors who were before me laid heavy burdens on the people, and took food and wine from them, besides forty shekels of silver. Even their servants lorded it over the people. But I did not do so, because of the fear of God. [16]Indeed, I devoted myself to the work on this wall, and acquired no land; and all my servants were gathered there for the work. [17]Moreover there were at my table one hundred fifty people, Jews and officials, besides those who came to us from the nations around us. [18]Now that which was prepared for one day was one ox and six choice sheep; also fowls were prepared for me, and every ten days skins of wine in abundance; yet with all this I did not demand the food allowance of the governor, because of the heavy burden of labor on the people. [19]Remember for my good, O my God, all that I have done for this people.

Intrigues of Enemies Foiled

6 Now when it was reported to Sanballat and Tobiah and to Geshem the Arab and to the rest of our enemies that I had built the wall and that there was no gap left in it (though up to that time I had not set up the doors in the gates), [2]Sanballat and Geshem sent to me, saying, "Come and let us meet together in one of the villages in the plain of Ono." But they intended to do me harm. [3]So I sent messengers to them, saying, "I am doing a great work and I cannot come down. Why should the work stop while I leave it to come down to you?" [4]They sent to me four times in this way, and I answered them in the same manner. [5]In the same way Sanballat for the fifth time sent his servant to me with an open letter in his hand. [6]In it was written, "It is reported among the nations—and Geshem[a] also says it—that you and the Jews intend to rebel; that is why you are building the wall; and according to this report you wish to become their king. [7]You have also set up prophets to proclaim in Jerusalem concerning you, 'There is a king in Judah!' And now it will be reported to the king according to these words. So come, therefore, and let us confer together." [8]Then I sent to him, saying, "No such things as you say have been done; you are inventing them out of your own mind" [9]—for they all wanted to frighten us, thinking, "Their hands will drop from the work, and it will not be done." But now, O God, strengthen my hands.

10 One day when I went into the house of Shemaiah son of Delaiah son of Mehetabel, who was confined to his house, he said, "Let us meet together in the house of God, within the temple, and let us close the doors of the temple, for they are coming to kill you; indeed, tonight they are coming to kill you." [11]But I said, "Should a man like me run away? Would a man like me go into the temple to save his life? I will not go in!" [12]Then I perceived and saw that God had not sent him at all, but he had pronounced the prophecy against me because Tobiah and Sanballat had hired him. [13]He was hired for this purpose, to intimidate me and make me sin by acting in this way, and so they could give me a bad name, in order to taunt me. [14]Remember Tobiah and Sanballat, O my God, according to these things that they did, and also the prophetess Noadiah and the rest of the prophets who wanted to make me afraid.

The Wall Completed

15 So the wall was finished on the twenty-fifth day of the month Elul, in fifty-two days. [16]And when all our enemies heard of it, all the nations around us were afraid[b] and fell greatly in their own esteem; for they perceived that this work had been accomplished with the help of our God. [17]Moreover in those days the nobles of Judah sent many letters to Tobiah, and Tobiah's letters came to them. [18]For many in Judah were bound by oath to him, because he was the son-in-law of Shecaniah son of Arah: and his son Jehohanan had married the daughter of

---

a Heb *Gashmu*   *b* Another reading is *saw*

Meshullam son of Berechiah. [19]Also they spoke of his good deeds in my presence, and reported my words to him. And Tobiah sent letters to intimidate me.

7 Now when the wall had been built and I had set up the doors, and the gatekeepers, the singers, and the Levites had been appointed, [2]I gave my brother Hanani charge over Jerusalem, along with Hananiah the commander of the citadel—for he was a faithful man and feared God more than many. [3]And I said to them, "The gates of Jerusalem are not to be opened until the sun is hot; while the gatekeepers[a] are still standing guard, let them shut and bar the doors. Appoint guards from among the inhabitants of Jerusalem, some at their watch posts, and others before their own houses." [4]The city was wide and large, but the people within it were few and no houses had been built.

Lists of the Returned Exiles

5 Then my God put it into my mind to assemble the nobles and the officials and the people to be enrolled by genealogy. And I found the book of the genealogy of those who were the first to come back, and I found the following written in it:

6 These are the people of the province who came up out of the captivity of those exiles whom King Nebuchadnezzar of Babylon had carried into exile; they returned to Jerusalem and Judah, each to his town. [7]They came with Zerubbabel, Jeshua, Nehemiah, Azariah, Raamiah, Nahamani, Mordecai, Bilshan, Mispereth, Bigvai, Nehum, Baanah.

The number of the Israelite people: [8]the descendants of Parosh, two thousand one hundred seventy-two. [9]Of Shephatiah, three hundred seventy-two. [10]Of Arah, six hundred fifty-two. [11]Of Pahath-moab, namely the descendants of Jeshua and Joab, two thousand eight hundred eighteen. [12]Of Elam, one thousand two hundred fifty-four. [13]Of Zattu, eight hundred forty-five. [14]Of Zaccai, seven hundred sixty. [15]Of Binnui, six hundred forty-eight. [16]Of Bebai, six hundred twenty-eight. [17]Of Azgad, two thousand three hundred twenty-two. [18]Of Adonikam, six hundred sixty-seven. [19]Of Bigvai, two thousand sixty-seven. [20]Of Adin, six hundred fifty-five. [21]Of Ater, namely of Hezekiah, ninety-eight. [22]Of Hashum, three hundred twenty-eight. [23]Of Bezai, three hundred twenty-four. [24]Of Hariph, one hundred twelve. [25]Of Gibeon, ninety-five. [26]The people of Bethlehem and Netophah, one hundred eighty-eight. [27]Of Anathoth, one hundred twenty-eight. [28]Of Beth-azmaveth, forty-two.

[29]Of Kiriath-jearim, Chephirah, and Beeroth, seven hundred forty-three. [30]Of Ramah and Geba, six hundred twenty-one. [31]Of Michmas, one hundred twenty-two. [32]Of Bethel and Ai, one hundred twenty-three. [33]Of the other Nebo, fifty-two. [34]The descendants of the other Elam, one thousand two hundred fifty-four. [35]Of Harim, three hundred twenty. [36]Of Jericho, three hundred forty-five. [37]Of Lod, Hadid, and Ono, seven hundred twenty-one. [38]Of Senaah, three thousand nine hundred thirty.

39 The priests: the descendants of Jedaiah, namely the house of Jeshua, nine hundred seventy-three. [40]Of Immer, one thousand fifty-two. [41]Of Pashhur, one thousand two hundred forty-seven. [42]Of Harim, one thousand seventeen.

43 The Levites: the descendants of Jeshua, namely of Kadmiel of the descendants of Hodevah, seventy-four. [44]The singers: the descendants of Asaph, one hundred forty-eight. [45]The gatekeepers: the descendants of Shallum, of Ater, of Talmon, of Akkub, of Hatita, of Shobai, one hundred thirty-eight.

46 The temple servants: the descendants of Ziha, of Hasupha, of Tabbaoth, [47]of Keros, of Sia, of Padon, [48]of Lebana, of Hagaba, of Shalmai, [49]of Hanan, of Giddel, of Gahar, [50]of Reaiah, of Rezin, of Nekoda, [51]of Gazzam, of Uzza, of Paseah, [52]of Besai, of Meunim, of Nephushesim, [53]of Bakbuk, of Hakupha, of Harhur, [54]of Bazlith, of Mehida, of Harsha, [55]of Barkos, of Sisera, of Temah, [56]of Neziah, of Hatipha.

57 The descendants of Solomon's servants: of Sotai, of Sophereth, of Perida, [58]of Jaala, of Darkon, of Giddel, [59]of Shephatiah, of Hattil, of Pochereth-hazzebaim, of Amon.

60 All the temple servants and the descendants of Solomon's servants were three hundred ninety-two.

61 The following were those who came up from Tel-melah, Tel-harsha, Cherub, Addon, and Immer, but they could not prove their ancestral houses or their descent, whether they belonged to Israel: [62]the descendants of Delaiah, of Tobiah, of Nekoda, six hundred forty-two. [63]Also, of the priests: the descendants of Hobaiah, of Hakkoz, of Barzillai (who had married one of the daughters of Barzillai the Gileadite and was called by their name). [64]These sought their registration among those enrolled in the genealogies, but it was not found there, so they were excluded from the priesthood as unclean; [65]the governor told them that they were not to partake of the

most holy food, until a priest with Urim and Thummim should come.

66 The whole assembly together was forty-two thousand three hundred sixty, [67]besides their male and female slaves, of whom there were seven thousand three hundred thirty-seven; and they had two hundred forty-five singers, male and female. [68]They had seven hundred thirty-six horses, two hundred forty-five mules,[a] [69]four hundred thirty-five camels, and six thousand seven hundred twenty donkeys.

70 Now some of the heads of ancestral houses contributed to the work. The governor gave to the treasury one thousand darics of gold, fifty basins, and five hundred thirty priestly robes. [71]And some of the heads of ancestral houses gave into the building fund twenty thousand darics of gold and two thousand two hundred minas of silver. [72]And what the rest of the people gave was twenty thousand darics of gold, two thousand minas of silver, and sixty-seven priestly robes.

73 So the priests, the Levites, the gatekeepers, the singers, some of the people, the temple servants, and all Israel settled in their towns.

Ezra Summons the People to Obey the Law

8 When the seventh month came—the people of Israel being settled in their towns— [1]all the people gathered together into the square before the Water Gate. They told the scribe Ezra to bring the book of the law of Moses, which the LORD had given to Israel. [2]Accordingly, the priest Ezra brought the law before the assembly, both men and women and all who could hear with understanding. This was on the first day of the seventh month. [3]He read from it facing the square before the Water Gate from early morning until midday, in the presence of the men and the women and those who could understand; and the ears of all the people were attentive to the book of the law. [4]The scribe Ezra stood on a wooden platform that had been made for the purpose; and beside him stood Mattithiah, Shema, Anaiah, Uriah, Hilkiah, and Maaseiah on his right hand; and Pedaiah, Mishael, Malchijah, Hashum, Hash-baddanah, Zechariah, and Meshullam on his left hand. [5]And Ezra opened the book in the sight of all the people, for he was standing above all the people; and when he opened it, all the people stood up. [6]Then Ezra blessed the LORD, the great God, and all the people answered, "Amen, Amen," lifting up their hands. Then they bowed their heads and worshiped the LORD with their faces to the ground. [7]Also Jeshua, Bani, Sherebiah, Jamin, Akkub, Shabbethai, Hodiah, Maaseiah, Kelita, Azariah,

Jozabad, Hanan, Pelaiah, the Levites,[b] helped the people to understand the law, while the people remained in their places. [8]So they read from the book, from the law of God, with interpretation. They gave the sense, so that the people understood the reading.

9 And Nehemiah, who was the governor, and Ezra the priest and scribe, and the Levites who taught the people said to all the people, "This day is holy to the LORD your God; do not mourn or weep." For all the people wept when they heard the words of the law. [10]Then he said to them, "Go your way, eat the fat and drink sweet wine and send portions of them to those for whom nothing is prepared, for this day is holy to our LORD; and do not be grieved, for the joy of the LORD is your strength." [11]So the Levites stilled all the people, saying, "Be quiet, for this day is holy; do not be grieved." [12]And all the people went their way to eat and drink and to send portions and to make great rejoicing, because they had understood the words that were declared to them.

The Festival of Booths Celebrated

13 On the second day the heads of ancestral houses of all the people, with the priests and the Levites, came together to the scribe Ezra in order to study the words of the law. [14]And they found it written in the law, which the LORD had commanded by Moses, that the people of Israel should live in booths[c] during the festival of the seventh month, [15]and that they should publish and proclaim in all their towns and in Jerusalem as follows, "Go out to the hills and bring branches of olive, wild olive, myrtle, palm, and other leafy trees to make booths,[c] as it is written." [16]So the people went out and brought them, and made booths[c] for themselves, each on the roofs of their houses, and in their courts and in the courts of the house of God, and in the square at the Water Gate and in the square at the Gate of Ephraim. [17]And all the assembly of those who had returned from the captivity made booths[c] and lived in them; for from the days of Jeshua son of Nun to that day the people of Israel had not done so. And there was very great rejoicing. [18]And day by day, from the first day to the last day, he read from the book of the law of God. They kept the festival seven days; and on the eighth day there was a solemn assembly, according to the ordinance.

---

a Ezra 2.66 and the margins of some Hebrew Mss: MT lacks *They had . . . forty-five mules*   b 1 Esdras 9.48 Vg: Heb *and the Levites*   c Or *tabernacles*; Heb *succoth*

National Confession

9 Now on the twenty-fourth day of this month the people of Israel were assembled with fasting and in sackcloth, and with earth on their heads.[a] [2]Then those of Israelite descent separated themselves from all foreigners, and stood and confessed their sins and the iniquities of their ancestors. [3]They stood up in their place and read from the book of the law of the Lord their God for a fourth part of the day, and for another fourth they made confession and worshiped the Lord their God. [4]Then Jeshua, Bani, Kadmiel, Shebaniah, Bunni, Sherebiah, Bani, and Chenani stood on the stairs of the Levites and cried out with a loud voice to the Lord their God. [5]Then the Levites, Jeshua, Kadmiel, Bani, Hashabneiah, Sherebiah, Hodiah, Shebaniah, and Pethahiah, said, "Stand up and bless the Lord your God from everlasting to everlasting. Blessed be your glorious name, which is exalted above all blessing and praise."

6 And Ezra said:[b] "You are the Lord, you alone; you have made heaven, the heaven of heavens, with all their host, the earth and all that is on it, the seas and all that is in them. To all of them you give life, and the host of heaven worships you. [7]You are the Lord, the God who chose Abram and brought him out of Ur of the Chaldeans and gave him the name Abraham; [8]and you found his heart faithful before you, and made with him a covenant to give to his descendants the land of the Canaanite, the Hittite, the Amorite, the Perizzite, the Jebusite, and the Girgashite; and you have fulfilled your promise, for you are righteous.

9 "And you saw the distress of our ancestors in Egypt and heard their cry at the Red Sea.[c] [10]You performed signs and wonders against Pharaoh and all his servants and all the people of his land, for you knew that they acted insolently against our ancestors. You made a name for yourself, which remains to this day. [11]And you divided the sea before them, so that they passed through the sea on dry land, but you threw their pursuers into the depths, like a stone into mighty waters. [12]Moreover, you led them by day with a pillar of cloud, and by night with a pillar of fire, to give them light on the way in which they should go. [13]You came down also upon Mount Sinai, and spoke with them from heaven, and gave them right ordinances and true laws, good statutes and commandments, [14]and you made

known your holy sabbath to them and gave them commandments and statutes and a law through your servant Moses. [15]For their hunger you gave them bread from heaven, and for their thirst you brought water for them out of the rock, and you told them to go in to possess the land that you swore to give them.

16 "But they and our ancestors acted presumptuously and stiffened their necks and did not obey your commandments; [17]they refused to obey, and were not mindful of the wonders that you performed among them; but they stiffened their necks and determined to return to their slavery in Egypt. But you are a God ready to forgive, gracious and merciful, slow to anger and abounding in steadfast love, and you did not forsake them. [18]Even when they had cast an image of a calf for themselves and said, 'This is your God who brought you up out of Egypt,' and had committed great blasphemies, [19]you in your great mercies did not forsake them in the wilderness; the pillar of cloud that led them in the way did not leave them by day, nor the pillar of fire by night that gave them light on the way by which they should go. [20]You gave your good spirit to instruct them, and did not withhold your manna from their mouths, and gave them water for their thirst. [21]Forty years you sustained them in the wilderness so that they lacked nothing; their clothes did not wear out and their feet did not swell. [22]And you gave them kingdoms and peoples, and allotted to them every corner,[d] so they took possession of the land of King Sihon of Heshbon and the land of King Og of Bashan. [23]You multiplied their descendants like the stars of heaven, and brought them into the land that you had told their ancestors to enter and possess. [24]So the descendants went in and possessed the land, and you subdued before them the inhabitants of the land, the Canaanites, and gave them into their hands, with their kings and the peoples of the land, to do with them as they pleased. [25]And they captured fortress cities and a rich land, and took possession of houses filled with all sorts of goods, hewn cisterns, vineyards, olive orchards, and fruit trees in abundance; so they ate, and were filled and became fat, and delighted themselves in your great goodness.

> Stand up and bless the Lord your God from everlasting to everlasting.
> (Neh 9:5)

---

a Heb *on them*   b Gk: Heb lacks *And Ezra said*   c Or *Sea of Reeds*   d Meaning of Heb uncertain

26 "Nevertheless they were disobedient and rebelled against you and cast your law behind their backs and killed your prophets, who had warned them in order to turn them back to you, and they committed great blasphemies. 27Therefore you gave them into the hands of their enemies, who made them suffer. Then in the time of their suffering they cried out to you and you heard them from heaven, and according to your great mercies you gave them saviors who saved them from the hands of their enemies. 28But after they had rest, they again did evil before you, and you abandoned them to the hands of their enemies, so that they had dominion over them; yet when they turned and cried to you, you heard from heaven, and many times you rescued them according to your mercies. 29And you warned them in order to turn them back to your law. Yet they acted presumptuously and did not obey your commandments, but sinned against your ordinances, by the observance of which a person shall live. They turned a stubborn shoulder and stiffened their neck and would not obey. 30Many years you were patient with them, and warned them by your spirit through your prophets; yet they would not listen. Therefore you handed them over to the peoples of the lands. 31Nevertheless, in your great mercies you did not make an end of them or forsake them, for you are a gracious and merciful God.

32 "Now therefore, our God—the great and mighty and awesome God, keeping covenant and steadfast love—do not treat lightly all the hardship that has come upon us, upon our kings, our officials, our priests, our prophets, our ancestors, and all your people, since the time of the kings of Assyria until today. 33You have been just in all that has come upon us, for you have dealt faithfully and we have acted wickedly; 34our kings, our officials, our priests, and our ancestors have not kept your law or heeded the commandments and the warnings that you gave them. 35Even in their own kingdom, and in the great goodness you bestowed on them, and in the large and rich land that you set before them, they did not serve you and did not turn from their wicked works. 36Here we are, slaves to this day—slaves in the land that you gave to our ancestors to enjoy its fruit and its good gifts. 37Its rich yield goes to the kings whom you have set over us because of our sins; they have power also over our bodies and over our livestock at their pleasure, and we are in great distress."

Those Who Signed the Covenant

38ᵃ Because of all this we make a firm agreement in writing, and on that sealed document are inscribed the names of our officials, our Levites, and our priests.

10 ᵇ Upon the sealed document are the names of Nehemiah the governor, son of Hacaliah, and Zedekiah; 2Seraiah, Azariah, Jeremiah, 3Pashhur, Amariah, Malchijah, 4Hattush, Shebaniah, Malluch, 5Harim, Meremoth, Obadiah, 6Daniel, Ginnethon, Baruch, 7Meshullam, Abijah, Mijamin, 8Maaziah, Bilgai, Shemaiah; these are the priests. 9And the Levites: Jeshua son of Azaniah, Binnui of the sons of Henadad, Kadmiel; 10and their associates, Shebaniah, Hodiah, Kelita, Pelaiah, Hanan, 11Mica, Rehob, Hashabiah, 12Zaccur, Sherebiah, Shebaniah, 13Hodiah, Bani, Beninu. 14The leaders of the people: Parosh, Pahath-moab, Elam, Zattu, Bani, 15Bunni, Azgad, Bebai, 16Adonijah, Bigvai, Adin, 17Ater, Hezekiah, Azzur, 18Hodiah, Hashum, Bezai, 19Hariph, Anathoth, Nebai, 20Magpiash, Meshullam, Hezir, 21Meshezabel, Zadok, Jaddua, 22Pelatiah, Hanan, Anaiah, 23Hoshea, Hananiah, Hasshub, 24Hallohesh, Pilha, Shobek, 25Rehum, Hashabnah, Maaseiah, 26Ahiah, Hanan, Anan, 27Malluch, Harim, and Baanah.

Summary of the Covenant

28 The rest of the people, the priests, the Levites, the gatekeepers, the singers, the temple servants, and all who have separated themselves from the peoples of the lands to adhere to the law of God, their wives, their sons, their daughters, all who have knowledge and understanding, 29join with their kin, their nobles, and enter into a curse and an oath to walk in God's law, which was given by Moses the servant of God, and to observe and do all the commandments of the LORD our Lord and his ordinances and his statutes. 30We will not give our daughters to the peoples of the land or take their daughters for our sons; 31and if the peoples of the land bring in merchandise or any grain on the sabbath day to sell, we will not buy it from them on the sabbath or on a holy day; and we will forego the crops of the seventh year and the exaction of every debt.

32 We also lay on ourselves the obligation to charge ourselves yearly one-third of a shekel for the service of the house of our God: 33for the rows of bread, the regular grain offering, the regular burnt offering, the sabbaths, the new moons, the appointed festivals, the sacred donations, and the sin offerings to make atonement for Israel, and for all the work of the house of our God. 34We have also cast lots among the priests, the Levites, and the people, for the wood offering, to

NEH

bring it into the house of our God, by ancestral houses, at appointed times, year by year, to burn on the altar of the LORD our God, as it is written in the law. [35]We obligate ourselves to bring the first fruits of our soil and the first fruits of all fruit of every tree, year by year, to the house of the LORD; [36]also to bring to the house of our God, to the priests who minister in the house of our God, the firstborn of our sons and of our livestock, as it is written in the law, and the firstlings of our herds and of our flocks; [37]and to bring the first of our dough, and our contributions, the fruit of every tree, the wine and the oil, to the priests, to the chambers of the house of our God; and to bring to the Levites the tithes from our soil, for it is the Levites who collect the tithes in all our rural towns. [38]And the priest, the descendant of Aaron, shall be with the Levites when the Levites receive the tithes; and the Levites shall bring up a tithe of the tithes to the house of our God, to the chambers of the storehouse. [39]For the people of Israel and the sons of Levi shall bring the contribution of grain, wine, and oil to the storerooms where the vessels of the sanctuary are, and where the priests that minister, and the gatekeepers and the singers are. We will not neglect the house of our God.

Population of the City Increased

11 Now the leaders of the people lived in Jerusalem; and the rest of the people cast lots to bring one out of ten to live in the holy city Jerusalem, while nine-tenths remained in the other towns. [2]And the people blessed all those who willingly offered to live in Jerusalem.

3 These are the leaders of the province who lived in Jerusalem; but in the towns of Judah all lived on their property in their towns: Israel, the priests, the Levites, the temple servants, and the descendants of Solomon's servants. [4]And in Jerusalem lived some of the Judahites and of the Benjaminites. Of the Judahites: Athaiah son of Uzziah son of Zechariah son of Amariah son of Shephatiah son of Mahalalel, of the descendants of Perez; [5]and Maaseiah son of Baruch son of Col-hozeh son of Hazaiah son of Adaiah son of Joiarib son of Zechariah son of the Shilonite. [6]All the descendants of Perez who lived in Jerusalem were four hundred sixty-eight valiant warriors.

7 And these are the Benjaminites: Sallu son of Meshullam son of Joed son of Pedaiah son of Kolaiah son of Maaseiah son of Ithiel son of Jeshaiah. [8]And his brothers[a] Gabbai, Sallai: nine hundred twenty-eight. [9]Joel son of Zichri was their overseer; and Judah son of Hassenuah was second in charge of the city.

10 Of the priests: Jedaiah son of Joiarib, Jachin, [11]Seraiah son of Hilkiah son of Meshullam son of Zadok son of Meraioth son of Ahitub, officer of the house of God, [12]and their associates who did the work of the house, eight hundred twenty-two; and Adaiah son of Jeroham son of Pelaliah son of Amzi son of Zechariah son of Pashhur son of Malchijah, [13]and his associates, heads of ancestral houses, two hundred forty-two; and Amashsai son of Azarel son of Ahzai son of Meshillemoth son of Immer, [14]and their associates, valiant warriors, one hundred twenty-eight; their overseer was Zabdiel son of Haggedolim.

15 And of the Levites: Shemaiah son of Hasshub son of Azrikam son of Hashabiah son of Bunni; [16]and Shabbethai and Jozabad, of the leaders of the Levites, who were over the outside work of the house of God; [17]and Mattaniah son of Mica son of Zabdi son of Asaph, who was the leader to begin the thanksgiving in prayer, and Bakbukiah, the second among his associates; and Abda son of Shammua son of Galal son of Jeduthun. [18]All the Levites in the holy city were two hundred eighty-four.

19 The gatekeepers, Akkub, Talmon and their associates, who kept watch at the gates, were one hundred seventy-two. [20]And the rest of Israel, and of the priests and the Levites, were in all the towns of Judah, all of them in their inheritance. [21]But the temple servants lived on Ophel; and Ziha and Gishpa were over the temple servants.

22 The overseer of the Levites in Jerusalem was Uzzi son of Bani son of Hashabiah son of Mattaniah son of Mica, of the descendants of Asaph, the singers, in charge of the work of the house of God. [23]For there was a command from the king concerning them, and a settled provision for the singers, as was required every day. [24]And Pethahiah son of Meshezabel, of the descendants of Zerah son of Judah, was at the king's hand in all matters concerning the people.

Villages outside Jerusalem

25 And as for the villages, with their fields, some of the people of Judah lived in Kiriath-arba and its villages, and in Dibon and its villages, and in Jekabzeel and its villages, [26]and in Jeshua and in Moladah and Beth-pelet, [27]in Hazar-shual, in Beer-sheba and its villages, [28]in Ziklag, in Meconah and its villages, [29]in En-rimmon, in Zorah, in Jarmuth, [30]Zanoah, Adullam, and their villages, Lachish and its fields, and Azekah and its villages. So they camped from Beer-sheba to

---

a Gk Mss: Heb *And after him*

the valley of Hinnom. [31]The people of Benjamin also lived from Geba onward, at Michmash, Aija, Bethel and its villages, [32]Anathoth, Nob, Ananiah, [33]Hazor, Ramah, Gittaim, [34]Hadid, Zeboim, Neballat, [35]Lod, and Ono, the valley of artisans. [36]And certain divisions of the Levites in Judah were joined to Benjamin.

A List of Priests and Levites

12 These are the priests and the Levites who came up with Zerubbabel son of Shealtiel, and Jeshua: Seraiah, Jeremiah, Ezra, [2]Amariah, Malluch, Hattush, [3]Shecaniah, Rehum, Meremoth, [4]Iddo, Ginnethoi, Abijah, [5]Mijamin, Maadiah, Bilgah, [6]Shemaiah, Joiarib, Jedaiah, [7]Sallu, Amok, Hilkiah, Jedaiah. These were the leaders of the priests and of their associates in the days of Jeshua.

8 And the Levites: Jeshua, Binnui, Kadmiel, Sherebiah, Judah, and Mattaniah, who with his associates was in charge of the songs of thanksgiving. [9]And Bakbukiah and Unno their associates stood opposite them in the service. [10]Jeshua was the father of Joiakim, Joiakim the father of Eliashib, Eliashib the father of Joiada, [11]Joiada the father of Jonathan, and Jonathan the father of Jaddua.

12 In the days of Joiakim the priests, heads of ancestral houses, were: of Seraiah, Meraiah; of Jeremiah, Hananiah; [13]of Ezra, Meshullam; of Amariah, Jehohanan; [14]of Malluchi, Jonathan; of Shebaniah, Joseph; [15]of Harim, Adna; of Meraioth, Helkai; [16]of Iddo, Zechariah; of Ginnethon, Meshullam; [17]of Abijah, Zichri; of Miniamin, of Moadiah, Piltai; [18]of Bilgah, Shammua; of Shemaiah, Jehonathan; [19]of Joiarib, Mattenai; of Jedaiah, Uzzi; [20]of Sallai, Kallai; of Amok, Eber; [21]of Hilkiah, Hashabiah; of Jedaiah, Nethanel.

22 As for the Levites, in the days of Eliashib, Joiada, Johanan, and Jaddua, there were recorded the heads of ancestral houses; also the priests until the reign of Darius the Persian. [23]The Levites, heads of ancestral houses, were recorded in the Book of the Annals until the days of Johanan son of Eliashib. [24]And the leaders of the Levites: Hashabiah, Sherebiah, and Jeshua son of Kadmiel, with their associates over against them, to praise and to give thanks, according to the commandment of David the man of God, section opposite to section. [25]Mattaniah, Bakbukiah, Obadiah, Meshullam, Talmon, and Akkub were gatekeepers standing guard at the storehouses of the gates. [26]These were in the days of Joiakim son of Jeshua son of Jozadak, and in the days of the governor Nehemiah and of the priest Ezra, the scribe.

Dedication of the City Wall

27 Now at the dedication of the wall of Jerusalem they sought out the Levites in all their places, to bring them to Jerusalem to celebrate the dedication with rejoicing, with thanksgivings and with singing, with cymbals, harps, and lyres. [28]The companies of the singers gathered together from the circuit around Jerusalem and from the villages of the Netophathites; [29]also from Beth-gilgal and from the region of Geba and Azmaveth; for the singers had built for themselves villages around Jerusalem. [30]And the priests and the Levites purified themselves; and they purified the people and the gates and the wall.

31 Then I brought the leaders of Judah up onto the wall, and appointed two great companies that gave thanks and went in procession. One went to the right on the wall to the Dung Gate; [32]and after them went Hoshaiah and half the officials of Judah, [33]and Azariah, Ezra, Meshullam, [34]Judah, Benjamin, Shemaiah, and Jeremiah, [35]and some of the young priests with trumpets: Zechariah son of Jonathan son of Shemaiah son of Mattaniah son of Micaiah son of Zaccur son of Asaph; [36]and his kindred, Shemaiah, Azarel, Milalai, Gilalai, Maai, Nethanel, Judah, and Hanani, with the musical instruments of David the man of God; and the scribe Ezra went in front of them. [37]At the Fountain Gate, in front of them, they went straight up by the stairs of the city of David, at the ascent of the wall, above the house of David, to the Water Gate on the east.

38 The other company of those who gave thanks went to the left,[a] and I followed them with half of the people on the wall, above the Tower of the Ovens, to the Broad Wall, [39]and above the Gate of Ephraim, and by the Old Gate, and by the Fish Gate and the Tower of Hananel and the Tower of the Hundred, to the Sheep Gate; and they came to a halt at the Gate of the Guard. [40]So both companies of those who gave thanks stood in the house of God, and I and half of the officials with me; [41]and the priests Eliakim, Maaseiah, Miniamin, Micaiah, Elioenai, Zechariah, and Hananiah, with trumpets; [42]and Maaseiah, Shemaiah, Eleazar, Uzzi, Jehohanan, Malchijah, Elam, and Ezer. And the singers sang with Jezrahiah as their leader. [43]They offered great sacrifices that day and rejoiced, for God had made them rejoice with great joy; the women and children also rejoiced. The joy of Jerusalem was heard far away.

a Cn: Heb opposite

Temple Responsibilities

44 On that day men were appointed over the chambers for the stores, the contributions, the first fruits, and the tithes, to gather into them the portions required by the law for the priests and for the Levites from the fields belonging to the towns; for Judah rejoiced over the priests and the Levites who ministered. 45They performed the service of their God and the service of purification, as did the singers and the gatekeepers, according to the command of David and his son Solomon. 46For in the days of David and Asaph long ago there was a leader of the singers, and there were songs of praise and thanksgiving to God. 47In the days of Zerubbabel and in the days of Nehemiah all Israel gave the daily portions for the singers and the gatekeepers. They set apart that which was for the Levites; and the Levites set apart that which was for the descendants of Aaron.

Foreigners Separated from Israel

13 On that day they read from the book of Moses in the hearing of the people; and in it was found written that no Ammonite or Moabite should ever enter the assembly of God, 2because they did not meet the Israelites with bread and water, but hired Balaam against them to curse them—yet our God turned the curse into a blessing. 3When the people heard the law, they separated from Israel all those of foreign descent.

The Reforms of Nehemiah

4 Now before this, the priest Eliashib, who was appointed over the chambers of the house of our God, and who was related to Tobiah, 5prepared for Tobiah a large room where they had previously put the grain offering, the frankincense, the vessels, and the tithes of grain, wine, and oil, which were given by commandment to the Levites, singers, and gatekeepers, and the contributions for the priests. 6While this was taking place I was not in Jerusalem, for in the thirty-second year of King Artaxerxes of Babylon I went to the king. After some time I asked leave of the king 7and returned to Jerusalem. I then discovered the wrong that Eliashib had done on behalf of Tobiah, preparing a room for him in the courts of the house of God. 8And I was very angry, and I threw all the household furniture of Tobiah out of the room. 9Then I gave orders and they cleansed the chambers, and I brought back the vessels of the house of God, with the grain offering and the frankincense.

10 I also found out that the portions of the Levites had not been given to them; so that the Levites and the singers, who had conducted the service, had gone back to their fields. 11So I remonstrated with the officials and said, "Why is the house of God forsaken?" And I gathered them together and set them in their stations. 12Then all Judah brought the tithe of the grain, wine, and oil into the storehouses. 13And I appointed as treasurers over the storehouses the priest Shelemiah, the scribe Zadok, and Pedaiah of the Levites, and as their assistant Hanan son of Zaccur son of Mattaniah, for they were considered faithful; and their duty was to distribute to their associates. 14Remember me, O my God, concerning this, and do not wipe out my good deeds that I have done for the house of my God and for his service.

Sabbath Reforms Begun

15 In those days I saw in Judah people treading wine presses on the sabbath, and bringing in heaps of grain and loading them on donkeys; and also wine, grapes, figs, and all kinds of burdens, which they brought into Jerusalem on the sabbath day; and I warned them at that time against selling food. 16Tyrians also, who lived in the city, brought in fish and all kinds of merchandise and sold them on the sabbath to the people of Judah, and in Jerusalem. 17Then I remonstrated with the nobles of Judah and said to them, "What is this evil thing that you are doing, profaning the sabbath day? 18Did not your ancestors act in this way, and did not our God bring all this disaster on us and on this city? Yet you bring more wrath on Israel by profaning the sabbath."

19 When it began to be dark at the gates of Jerusalem before the sabbath, I commanded that the doors should be shut and gave orders that they should not be opened until after the sabbath. And I set some of my servants over the gates, to prevent any burden from being brought in on the sabbath day. 20Then the merchants and sellers of all kinds of merchandise spent the night outside Jerusalem once or twice. 21But I warned them and said to them, "Why do you spend the night in front of the wall? If you do so again, I will lay hands on you." From that time on they did not come on the sabbath. 22And I commanded the Levites that they should purify themselves and come and guard the gates, to keep the sabbath day holy. Remember this also in my favor, O my God, and spare me according to the greatness of your steadfast love.

Mixed Marriages Condemned

23 In those days also I saw Jews who had married women of Ashdod, Ammon, and Moab; [24]and half of their children spoke the language of Ashdod, and they could not speak the language of Judah, but spoke the language of various peoples. [25]And I contended with them and cursed them and beat some of them and pulled out their hair; and I made them take an oath in the name of God, saying, "You shall not give your daughters to their sons, or take their daughters for your sons or for yourselves. [26]Did not King Solomon of Israel sin on account of such women? Among the many nations there was no king like him, and he was beloved by his God, and God made him king over all Israel; nevertheless, foreign women made even him to sin. [27]Shall we then listen to you and do all this great evil and act treacherously against our God by marrying foreign women?"

28 And one of the sons of Jehoiada, son of the high priest Eliashib, was the son-in-law of Sanballat the Horonite; I chased him away from me. [29]Remember them, O my God, because they have defiled the priesthood, the covenant of the priests and the Levites.

30 Thus I cleansed them from everything foreign, and I established the duties of the priests and Levites, each in his work; [31]and I provided for the wood offering, at appointed times, and for the first fruits. Remember me, O my God, for good.

There's nothing quite like a good story. Such a story often involves good people struggling, a young hero, and love overcoming challenges. Throw in an undercover angel and a miraculous cure, and these are the elements that make up the Book of Tobit. Part fairy tale, part love story, and part religious adventure, this short story will bring a smile to your face and maybe even a tear to your eye. Enjoy!

At a Glance

- Chapters 1–3. the sufferings of Tobit and Sarah
- Chapters 4–10. the journey of Tobias and his marriage to Sarah
- Chapters 11–12. Tobias's homecoming and Tobit's cure
- Chapters 13–14. Tobit's prayer of thanksgiving, and death

Quick Facts

Setting: although fictional, the book reflects the historical situation of the Israelites deported from Israel to Nineveh in 721 BC.

Inspired Author: unknown, writing sometime in the second century BC

Theme: In time, God will aid the faithful who suffer. God always rewards the faithful, even if it takes awhile.

Of Note: Raphael is one of only three angels named in the Bible; the others are Michael and Gabriel.

In Depth

For the author of the Book of Tobit, understanding God's will was not difficult. The conviction that God rewards good people, especially those who have experienced great suffering, is evident on every page. In the story, the faithful Tobit, who is blinded after doing a good deed, and the virtuous Sarah, who is ridiculed because she has had seven husbands die on their wedding night, pray for death because of their suffering and humiliation. In answer to their prayers, God sends the angel Raphael to lead Tobit's son Tobias on a journey to Sarah's town. The story ends happily—but you will have to read it yourself to find out exactly how.

The Book of Tobit is inspired folklore that teaches a moral lesson. The author was writing at a time when the Jews were governed by oppressive Greek rulers, and the people needed the reassurance of this happy tale. They had not forgotten the fall of Jerusalem or the Exile in Babylon, and Israel's suffering weighed heavily on them. What was the advantage of following God's Law if all they had to look forward to was more suffering? (Belief in an afterlife had not yet developed among the Jewish people.) The book assured the faithful that God would eventually reward them: it was just a matter of time.

Although the book's miraculous answers may seem too simple to modern-day readers, its insistence on God's presence in human life and God's concern for those who suffer remains as important as ever. All people—even Christians who believe in life after death—need encouragement to face the challenges of this world with faith and hope.

The Book of **Tobit**

Tobit

1 This book tells the story of Tobit son of Tobiel son of Hananiel son of Aduel son of Gabael son of Raphael son of Raguel of the descendants[a] of Asiel, of the tribe of Naphtali, [2]who in the days of King Shalmaneser[b] of the Assyrians was taken into captivity from Thisbe, which is to the south of Kedesh Naphtali in Upper Galilee, above Asher toward the west, and north of Phogor.

Tobit's Youth and Virtuous Life

3 I, Tobit, walked in the ways of truth and righteousness all the days of my life. I performed many acts of charity for my kindred and my people who had gone with me in exile to Nineveh in the land of the Assyrians. [4]When I was in my own country, in the land of Israel, while I was still a young man, the whole tribe of my ancestor Naphtali deserted the house of David and Jerusalem. This city had been chosen from among all the tribes of Israel, where all the tribes of Israel should offer sacrifice and where the temple, the dwelling of God, had been consecrated and established for all generations forever.

5 All my kindred and our ancestral house of Naphtali sacrificed to the calf[c] that King Jeroboam of Israel had erected in Dan and on all the mountains of Galilee. [6]But I alone went often to Jerusalem for the festivals, as it is prescribed for all Israel by an everlasting decree. I would hurry off to Jerusalem with the first fruits of the crops and the firstlings of the flock, the tithes of the cattle, and the first shearings of the sheep. [7]I would give these to the priests, the sons of Aaron, at the altar;

likewise the tenth of the grain, wine, olive oil, pomegranates, figs, and the rest of the fruits to the sons of Levi who ministered at Jerusalem. Also for six years I would save up a second tenth in money and go and distribute it in Jerusalem. [8]A third tenth[d] I would give to the orphans and widows and to the converts who had attached themselves to Israel. I would bring it and give it to them in the third year, and we would eat it according to the ordinance decreed concerning it in the law of Moses and according to the instructions of Deborah, the mother of my father Tobiel,[e] for my father had died and left me an orphan. [9]When I became a man I married a woman,[f] a member of our own family, and by her I became the father of a son whom I named Tobias.

Taken Captive to Nineveh

10 After I was carried away captive to Assyria and came as a captive to Nineveh, everyone of my kindred and my people ate the food of the Gentiles, [11]but I kept myself from eating the food of the Gentiles. [12]Because I was mindful of God with all my heart, [13]the Most High gave me favor and good standing with Shalmaneser,[b] and I used to buy everything he needed. [14]Until his death I used to go into Media, and buy for him there. While in the country of Media I left bags of silver worth ten talents in trust with Gabael, the brother

---

a Other ancient authorities lack *of Raphael son of Raguel of the descendants*   b Gk *Enemessaros*   c Other ancient authorities read *heifer*   d *A third tenth* added from other ancient authorities   e Lat: Gk *Hananiel*   f Other ancient authorities add *Anna*

of Gabri. [15]But when Shalmaneser[a] died, and his son Sennacherib reigned in his place, the highways into Media became unsafe and I could no longer go there.

Courage in Burying the Dead

16 In the days of Shalmaneser[a] I performed many acts of charity to my kindred, those of my tribe. [17]I would give my food to the hungry and my clothing to the naked; and if I saw the dead body of any of my people thrown out behind the wall of Nineveh, I would bury it. [18]I also buried any whom King Sennacherib put to death when he came fleeing from Judea in those days of judgment that the king of heaven executed upon him because of his blasphemies. For in his anger he put to death many Israelites; but I would secretly remove the bodies and bury them. So when Sennacherib looked for them he could not find them. [19]Then one of the Ninevites went and informed the king about me, that I was burying them; so I hid myself. But when I realized that the king knew about me and that I was being searched for to be put to death, I was afraid and ran away. [20]Then all my property was confiscated; nothing was left to me that was not taken into the royal treasury except my wife Anna and my son Tobias.

21 But not forty[b] days passed before two of Sennacherib's[c] sons killed him, and they fled to the mountains of Ararat, and his son Esar-haddon[d] reigned after him. He appointed Ahikar, the son of my brother Hanael[e] over all the accounts of his kingdom, and he had authority over the entire administration. [22]Ahikar interceded for me, and I returned to Nineveh. Now Ahikar was chief cupbearer, keeper of the signet, and in charge of administration of the accounts under King Sennacherib of Assyria; so Esar-haddon[d] reappointed him. He was my nephew and so a close relative.

2 Then during the reign of Esar-haddon[d] I returned home, and my wife Anna and my son Tobias were restored to me. At our festival of Pentecost, which is the sacred festival of weeks, a good dinner was prepared for me and I reclined to eat. [2]When the table was set for me and an abundance of food placed before me, I said to my son Tobias, "Go, my child, and bring whatever poor person you may find of our people among the exiles in Nineveh, who is wholeheartedly mindful of God,[f] and he shall eat together with me. I will wait for you, until you come back." [3]So Tobias went to look for some poor person of our people. When he had returned he said, "Father!" And I replied, "Here I am, my child." Then he went on to say, "Look, father,

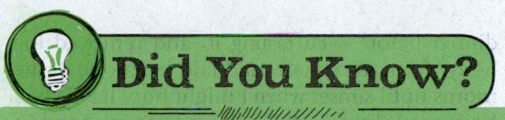

Did You Know?

The Case of the Missing Books

The Book of Tobit is treated differently in some versions of the Bible. Some put it in a section of books separated from the rest of the Old Testament. Some do not include it at all. We can find an explanation to this puzzle if we look back in time.

Sometime in the second or third century BC, Jewish scholars translated the Scriptures from Hebrew and Aramaic into Greek. Many Jews living throughout the Mediterranean world spoke Greek, which had become a common language in that area at the time. For Greek-speaking Jews, this translation, called the Septuagint, was the Bible they used. Because most of the early Christians spoke Greek, including Jews such as Paul, the Septuagint was adopted by the Church as its Bible (Old Testament).

After the destruction of the Jerusalem Temple by the Romans in AD 70, leading rabbis strove to reorganize Jewish worship, which could no longer center on the Temple in Jerusalem. They reviewed the existing editions of the Bible and developed an official list of thirty-nine holy books. They rejected certain books contained in the Greek Septuagint for which there was no existing original Hebrew or Aramaic text, such as Tobit, Judith, First and Second Maccabees, Wisdom, Sirach, Baruch, and additions to the Books of Esther and Daniel.

Many centuries later, the Christian reformer Martin Luther used the Jewish canon of the Old Testament in his translation of the Bible. He placed the additional books in a separate section, entitling them the Apocrypha (from the Greek for "hidden"). The Catholic Church and the Orthodox churches continue to use the fuller Greek canon, preferring the term deuterocanonical (from the Greek for "second canon") for the disputed books.

one of our own people has been murdered and thrown into the market place, and now he lies there strangled." [4]Then I sprang up, left the

---

a Gk Enemessaros   b Other ancient authorities read either forty-five or fifty   c Gk his   d Gk Sacherdonos   e Other authorities read Hananael   f Lat: Gk wholeheartedly mindful

dinner before even tasting it, and removed the body[a] from the square[b] and laid it[a] in one of the rooms until sunset when I might bury it.[a] [5]When I returned, I washed myself and ate my food in sorrow. [6]Then I remembered the prophecy of Amos, how he said against Bethel,[c]

"Your festivals shall be turned into mourning, and all your songs into lamentation."

And I wept.

Tobit Becomes Blind

7 When the sun had set, I went and dug a grave and buried him. [8]And my neighbors laughed and said, "Is he still not afraid? He has already been hunted down to be put to death for doing this, and he ran away; yet here he is again burying the dead!" [9]That same night I washed myself and went into my courtyard and slept by the wall of the courtyard; and my face was uncovered because of the heat. [10]I did not know that there were sparrows on the wall; their fresh droppings fell into my eyes and produced white films. I went to physicians to be healed, but the more they treated me with ointments the more my vision was obscured by the white films, until I became completely blind. For four years I remained unable to see. All my kindred were sorry for me, and Ahikar took care of me for two years before he went to Elymais.

Tobit's Wife Earns Their Livelihood

11 At that time, also, my wife Anna earned money at women's work. [12]She used to send what she made to the owners and they would pay wages to her. One day, the seventh of Dystrus, when she cut off a piece she had woven and sent it to the owners, they paid her full wages and also gave her a young goat for a meal. [13]When she returned to me, the goat began to bleat. So I called her and said, "Where did you get this goat? It is surely not stolen, is it? Return it to the owners; for we have no right to eat anything stolen." [14]But she said to me, "It was given to me as a gift in addition to my wages." But I did not believe her, and told her to return it to the owners. I became flushed with anger against her over this. Then she replied to me, "Where are your acts of charity? Where are your righteous deeds? These things are known about you!"[d]

Tobit's Prayer

3 Then with much grief and anguish of heart I wept, and with groaning began to pray:

[2] "You are righteous, O Lord,
    and all your deeds are just;
all your ways are mercy and truth;

you judge the world.[e]

[3] And now, O Lord, remember me
    and look favorably upon me.
Do not punish me for my sins
    and for my unwitting offenses
    and those that my ancestors committed
        before you.
They sinned against you,
[4]   and disobeyed your commandments.
So you gave us over to plunder, exile, and death,
    to become the talk, the byword, and an object
        of reproach
    among all the nations among whom you have
        dispersed us.
[5] And now your many judgments are true
    in exacting penalty from me for my sins.
For we have not kept your commandments
    and have not walked in accordance with truth
        before you.
[6] So now deal with me as you will;
    command my spirit to be taken from me,
    so that I may be released from the face of the
        earth and become dust.
For it is better for me to die than to live,
    because I have had to listen to undeserved
        insults,
    and great is the sorrow within me.
Command, O Lord, that I be released from this
        distress;
    release me to go to the eternal home,
    and do not, O Lord, turn your face away
        from me.
For it is better for me to die
    than to see so much distress in my life
    and to listen to insults."

Sarah Falsely Accused

7 On the same day, at Ecbatana in Media, it also happened that Sarah, the daughter of Raguel, was reproached by one of her father's maids. [8]For she had been married to seven husbands, and the wicked demon Asmodeus had killed each of them before they had been with her as is customary for wives. So the maid said to her, "You are the one who kills[f] your husbands! See, you have already been married to seven husbands and have not borne the name of[g] a single one of them. [9]Why do you beat us? Because your husbands are dead? Go with them! May we never see a son or daughter of yours!"

---

a Gk *him*   b Other ancient authorities lack *from the square*
c Other ancient authorities read *against Bethlehem*   d Or *to you;*
Gk *with you*   e Other ancient authorities read *you render true and righteous judgment forever*   f Other ancient authorities read *strangles*   g Other ancient authorities read *have had no benefit from*

Sarah's Prayer for Death

10 On that day she was grieved in spirit and wept. When she had gone up to her father's upper room, she intended to hang herself. But she thought it over and said, "Never shall they reproach my father, saying to him, 'You had only one beloved daughter but she hanged herself because of her distress.' And I shall bring my father in his old age down in sorrow to Hades. It is better for me not to hang myself, but to pray the Lord that I may die and not listen to these reproaches anymore." ¹¹At that same time, with hands outstretched toward the window, she prayed and said,

"Blessed are you, merciful God!
    Blessed is your name forever;
    let all your works praise you forever.
¹² And now, Lord,ᵃ I turn my face to you,
    and raise my eyes toward you.
¹³ Command that I be released from the earth
    and not listen to such reproaches any more.
¹⁴ You know, O Master, that I am innocent
    of any defilement with a man,
¹⁵ and that I have not disgraced my name
        or the name of my father in the land of my
            exile.
    I am my father's only child;
        he has no other child to be his heir;
    and he has no close relative or other kindred
        for whom I should keep myself as wife.
    Already seven husbands of mine have died.
        Why should I still live?
    But if it is not pleasing to you, O Lord, to take
        my life,
        hear me in my disgrace."

An Answer to Prayer

16 At that very moment, the prayers of both of them were heard in the glorious presence of God. ¹⁷So Raphael was sent to heal both of them: Tobit, by removing the white films from his eyes, so that he might see God's light with his eyes; and Sarah, daughter of Raguel, by giving her in marriage to Tobias son of Tobit, and by setting her free from the wicked demon Asmodeus. For Tobias was entitled to have her before all others who had desired to marry her. At the same time that Tobit returned from the courtyard into his house, Sarah daughter of Raguel came down from her upper room.

Tobit Gives Instructions to His Son

4 That same day Tobit remembered the money that he had left in trust with Gabael at Rages in Media, ²and he said to himself, "Now I have

asked for death. Why do I not call my son Tobias and explain to him about the money before I die?" ³Then he called his son Tobias, and when he came to him he said, "My son, when I die,ᵇ give me a proper burial. Honor your mother and do not abandon her all the days of her life. Do whatever pleases her, and do not grieve her in anything. ⁴Remember her, my son, because she faced many dangers for you while you were in her womb. And when she dies, bury her beside me in the same grave.

5 "Revere the Lord all your days, my son, and refuse to sin or to transgress his commandments. Live uprightly all the days of your life, and do not walk in the ways of wrongdoing; ⁶for those

---

ᵃ Other ancient authorities lack *Lord*   ᵇ Lat

Praying for Death

Tobit and Sarah are at the end of their rope. They have experienced such suffering and disgrace that life no longer has any meaning for them. They know suicide is wrong, so they each pray that God will send death to end their suffering and humiliation (see Tob 3:6,10).

It is not uncommon for people who are very sick or in great pain or very old to pray for death, like Tobit. Unfortunately, young people who have experienced great loss or trauma often wish for death too, like Sarah. No one can completely explain the mystery of why we—both young and old—suffer. But we know that God is with us through our suffering, and God's grace can help us endure whatever comes our way. At those times, however, it is often hard to see God. That is why we need to be there for one another. We can act as God's hands and presence. Through our loving actions and prayers, we can support one another in our suffering.

What people do you know who are suffering to the point of despair? Take a few moments to remember these people in prayer, and call or write to let them know you are thinking of them.

▶ Tobit, chapter 3

T O B

Cultural Connection

Give Food to the Hungry

In China, whenever you see a friend, it is customary to ask whether he or she has eaten a meal yet. If your friend responds, "No, I haven't eaten yet," it may mean that his or her last meal was yesterday or even the day before that. Then you invite your friend to your home and share whatever food you have. This custom goes back to the great famine of China (1958–1959), when people were dying of starvation and even eating tree bark.

Tobit gives his son good advice when he instructs him to share his food with the hungry and his clothing with the poor (see Tob 4:16).

Read Matthew 25:31–46 to hear how seriously Jesus wants us to follow this advice.

▶ **Tob 4:16**

who act in accordance with truth will prosper in all their activities. To all those who practice righteousness[a] 7give alms from your possessions, and do not let your eye begrudge the gift when you make it. Do not turn your face away from anyone who is poor, and the face of God will not be turned away from you. 8If you have many possessions, make your gift from them in proportion; if few, do not be afraid to give according to the little you have. 9So you will be laying up a good treasure for yourself against the day of necessity. 10For almsgiving delivers from death and keeps you from going into the Darkness. 11Indeed, almsgiving, for all who practice it, is an excellent offering in the presence of the Most High.

12 "Beware, my son, of every kind of fornication. First of all, marry a woman from among the descendants of your ancestors; do not marry a foreign woman, who is not of your father's tribe; for we are the descendants of the prophets. Remember, my son, that Noah, Abraham, Isaac, and Jacob, our ancestors of old, all took wives from among their kindred. They were blessed in their children, and their posterity will inherit the land. 13So now, my son, love your kindred, and in your heart do not disdain your kindred, the sons and daughters of your people, by refusing to take a wife for yourself from among them. For in pride there is ruin and great confusion. And in idleness there is loss and dire poverty, because idleness is the mother of famine.

14 "Do not keep over until the next day the wages of those who work for you, but pay them at once. If you serve God you will receive payment. Watch yourself, my son, in everything you do, and discipline yourself in all your conduct. 15And what you hate, do not do to anyone. Do not drink wine to excess or let drunkenness go

with you on your way. 16Give some of your food to the hungry, and some of your clothing to the naked. Give all your surplus as alms, and do not let your eye begrudge your giving of alms. 17Place your bread on the grave of the righteous, but give none to sinners. 18Seek advice from every wise person and do not despise any useful counsel. 19At all times bless the Lord God, and ask him that your ways may be made straight and that all your paths and plans may prosper. For none of the nations has understanding, but the Lord himself will give them good counsel; but if he chooses otherwise, he casts down to deepest Hades. So now, my child, remember these commandments, and do not let them be erased from your heart.

Money Left in Trust with Gabael

20 "And now, my son, let me explain to you that I left ten talents of silver in trust with Gabael son of Gabrias, at Rages in Media. 21Do not be afraid, my son, because we have become poor. You have great wealth if you fear God and flee from every sin and do what is good in the sight of the Lord your God."

The Angel Raphael

5 Then Tobias answered his father Tobit, "I will do everything that you have commanded me, father; 2but how can I obtain the money[b] from him, since he does not know me and I do not know him? What evidence[c] am I to give him so that he will recognize and trust me, and give me the money? Also, I do not know the roads

---

a The text of codex Sinaiticus goes directly from verse 6 to verse 19, reading *To those who practice righteousness* 19*the Lord will give good counsel.* In order to fill the lacuna verses 7 to 18 are derived from other ancient authorities   b Gk *it*   c Gk *sign*

TOB

to Media, or how to get there." ³Then Tobit answered his son Tobias, "He gave me his bond and I gave him my bond. I*a* divided his in two; we each took one part, and I put one with the money. And now twenty years have passed since I left this money in trust. So now, my son, find yourself a trustworthy man to go with you, and we will pay him wages until you return. But get back the money from Gabael."*b*

4 So Tobias went out to look for a man to go with him to Media, someone who was acquainted with the way. He went out and found the angel Raphael standing in front of him; but he did not perceive that he was an angel of God. ⁵Tobias*c* said to him, "Where do you come from, young man?" "From your kindred, the Israelites," he replied, "and I have come here to work." Then Tobias*d* said to him, "Do you know the way to go to Media?" ⁶"Yes," he replied, "I have been there many times; I am acquainted with it and know all the roads. I have often traveled to Media, and would stay with our kinsman Gabael who lives in Rages of Media. It is a journey of two days from Ecbatana to Rages; for it lies in a mountainous area, while Ecbatana is in the middle of the plain." ⁷Then Tobias said to him, "Wait for me, young man, until I go in and tell my father; for I do need you to travel with me, and I will pay you your wages." ⁸He replied, "All right, I will wait; but do not take too long."

9 So Tobias*d* went in to tell his father Tobit and said to him, "I have just found a man who is one of our own Israelite kindred!" He replied, "Call the man in, my son, so that I may learn about his family and to what tribe he belongs, and whether he is trustworthy enough to go with you."

10 Then Tobias went out and called him, and said, "Young man, my father is calling for you." So he went in to him, and Tobit greeted him first. He replied, "Joyous greetings to you!" But Tobit retorted, "What joy is left for me any more? I am a man without eyesight; I cannot see the light of heaven, but I lie in darkness like the dead who no longer see the light. Although still alive, I am among the dead. I hear people but I cannot see them." But the young man*d* said, "Take courage, the time is near for God to heal you; take courage." Then Tobit said to him, "My son Tobias wishes to go to Media. Can you accompany him and guide him? I will pay your wages, brother." He answered, "I can go with him and I know all the roads, for I have often gone to Media and have crossed all its plains, and I am familiar with its mountains and all of its roads."

11 Then Tobit*d* said to him, "Brother, of what family are you and from what tribe? Tell me,

brother." ¹²He replied, "Why do you need to know my tribe?" But Tobit*d* said, "I want to be sure, brother, whose son you are and what your name is." ¹³He replied, "I am Azariah, the son of the great Hananiah, one of your relatives." ¹⁴Then Tobit said to him, "Welcome! God save you, brother. Do not feel bitter toward me, brother, because I wanted to be sure about your ancestry. It turns out that you are a kinsman, and of good and noble lineage. For I knew Hananiah and Nathan,*e* the two sons of Shemeliah,*f* and they used to go with me to Jerusalem and worshiped with me there, and were not led astray. Your kindred are good people; you come of good stock. Hearty welcome!"

15 Then he added, "I will pay you a drachma a day as wages, as well as expenses for yourself and my son. So go with my son, ¹⁶and*g* I will add something to your wages." Raphael*c* answered, "I will go with him; so do not fear. We shall leave in good health and return to you in good health, because the way is safe." ¹⁷So Tobit*d* said to him, "Blessings be upon you, brother."

Then he called his son and said to him, "Son, prepare supplies for the journey and set out with your brother. May God in heaven bring you safely there and return you in good health to me; and may his angel, my son, accompany you both for your safety."

Before he went out to start his journey, he kissed his father and mother. Tobit then said to him, "Have a safe journey."

18 But his mother*h* began to weep, and said to Tobit, "Why is it that you have sent my child away? Is he not the staff of our hand as he goes in and out before us? ¹⁹Do not heap money upon money, but let it be a ransom for our child. ²⁰For the life that is given to us by the Lord is enough for us." ²¹Tobit*c* said to her, "Do not worry; our child will leave in good health and return to us in good health. Your eyes will see him on the day when he returns to you in good health. Say no more! Do not fear for them, my sister. ²²For a good angel will accompany him; his journey

6 will be successful, and he will come back in good health." ¹So she stopped weeping.

Journey to Rages

The young man went out and the angel went with him; ²and the dog came out with him and went along with them. So they both journeyed

---

a Other authorities read *He*   b Gk *from him*   c Gk *He*
d Gk *he*   e Other ancient authorities read *Jathan* or *Nathaniah*
f Other ancient authorities read *Shemaiah*   g Other ancient
authorities add *when you return safely*   h Other ancient
authorities add *Anna*

along, and when the first night overtook them they camped by the Tigris river. ³Then the young man went down to wash his feet in the Tigris river. Suddenly a large fish leaped up from the water and tried to swallow the young man's foot, and he cried out. ⁴But the angel said to the young man, "Catch hold of the fish and hang on to it!" So the young man grasped the fish and drew it up on the land. ⁵Then the angel said to him, "Cut open the fish and take out its gall, heart, and liver. Keep them with you, but throw away the intestines. For its gall, heart, and liver are useful as medicine." ⁶So after cutting open the fish the young man gathered together the gall, heart, and liver; then he roasted and ate some of the fish, and kept some to be salted.

Angels Among Us

Many older Catholics were taught as children that they were to leave a bit of space on their chair for their guardian angel. We smile at that story, partly because it was a creative way to make angels real in the lives of children, and partly because it points to a truth about God's presence in our lives.

In the fictional story of Tobit, we meet the angel Raphael. In other parts of the Bible, angels serve primarily as God's messengers. But Raphael is much more than a messenger. He disguises himself as a kindly but unknown relative who guides Tobias to the secrets he needs to know to relieve both Tobit's and Sarah's suffering.

The truth is that many angels are around us. Most of us have heard stories about kind strangers who appear seemingly out of nowhere to help and then disappear. Our seat may not have a lot of room for an angel, but our world certainly does. Angels remind us that God is with us, protecting us and guiding us.

● Have you, or has someone you know, been touched by an angel? In return, look for opportunities to be someone else's "angel."

The two continued on their way together until they were near Media.ᵃ ⁷Then the young man questioned the angel and said to him, "Brother Azariah, what medicinal value is there in the fish's heart and liver, and in the gall?" ⁸He replied, "As for the fish's heart and liver, you must burn them to make a smoke in the presence of a man or woman afflicted by a demon or evil spirit, and every affliction will flee away and never remain with that person any longer. ⁹And as for the gall, anoint a person's eyes where white films have appeared on them; blow upon them, upon the white films, and the eyesᵇ will be healed."

Raphael's Instructions

10 When he entered Media and already was approaching Ecbatana,ᶜ ¹¹Raphael said to the young man, "Brother Tobias." "Here I am," he answered. Then Raphaelᵈ said to him, "We must stay this night in the home of Raguel. He is your relative, and he has a daughter named Sarah. ¹²He has no male heir and no daughter except Sarah only, and you, as next of kin to her, have before all other men a hereditary claim on her. Also it is right for you to inherit her father's possessions. Moreover, the girl is sensible, brave, and very beautiful, and her father is a good man." ¹³He continued, "You have every right to take her in marriage. So listen to me, brother; tonight I will speak to her father about the girl, so that we may take her to be your bride. When we return from Rages we will celebrate her marriage. For I know that Raguel can by no means keep her from you or promise her to another man without incurring the penalty of death according to the decree of the book of Moses. Indeed he knows that you, rather than any other man, are entitled to marry his daughter. So now listen to me, brother, and tonight we shall speak concerning the girl and arrange her engagement to you. And when we return from Rages we will take her and bring her back with us to your house."

14 Then Tobias said in answer to Raphael, "Brother Azariah, I have heard that she already has been married to seven husbands and that they died in the bridal chamber. On the night when they went in to her, they would die. I have heard people saying that it was a demon that killed them. ¹⁵It does not harm her, but it kills anyone who desires to approach her. So now, since I am the only son my father has, I

a Other ancient authorities read *Ecbatana*   b Gk *they*   c Other ancient authorities read *Rages*   d Gk *he*

TOB

am afraid that I may die and bring my father's and mother's life down to their grave, grieving for me—and they have no other son to bury them."

16 But Raphael[a] said to him, "Do you not remember your father's orders when he commanded you to take a wife from your father's house? Now listen to me, brother, and say no more about this demon. Take her. I know that this very night she will be given to you in marriage. [17]When you enter the bridal chamber, take some of the fish's liver and heart, and put them on the embers of the incense. An odor will be given off; [18]the demon will smell it and flee, and will never be seen near her any more. Now when you are about to go to bed with her, both of you must first stand up and pray, imploring the Lord of heaven that mercy and safety may be granted to you. Do not be afraid, for she was set apart for you before the world was made. You will save her, and she will go with you. I presume that you will have children by her, and they will be as brothers to you. Now say no more!" When Tobias heard the words of Raphael and learned that she was his kinswoman,[b] related through his father's lineage, he loved her very much, and his heart was drawn to her.

Arrival at Home of Raguel

7 Now when they[c] entered Ecbatana, Tobias[a] said to him, "Brother Azariah, take me straight to our brother Raguel." So he took him to Raguel's house, where they found him sitting beside the courtyard door. They greeted him first, and he replied, "Joyous greetings, brothers; welcome and good health!" Then he brought them into his house. [2]He said to his wife Edna, "How much the young man resembles my kinsman Tobit!" [3]Then Edna questioned them, saying, "Where are you from, brothers?" They answered, "We belong to the descendants of Naphtali who are exiles in Nineveh." [4]She said to them, "Do you know our kinsman Tobit?" And they replied, "Yes, we know him." Then she asked them, "Is he[d] in good health?" [5]They replied, "He is alive and in good health." And Tobias added, "He is my father!" [6]At that Raguel jumped up and kissed him and wept. [7]He also spoke to him as follows, "Blessings on you, my child, son of a good and noble father![e] O most miserable of calamities that such an upright and beneficent man has become blind!" He then embraced his kinsman Tobias and wept. [8]His wife Edna also wept for him, and their daughter Sarah likewise wept. [9]Then Raguel[a] slaughtered a ram from the flock and received them very warmly.

Marriage of Tobias and Sarah

When they had bathed and washed themselves and had reclined to dine, Tobias said to Raphael, "Brother Azariah, ask Raguel to give me my kinswoman[b] Sarah." [10]But Raguel overheard it and said to the lad, "Eat and drink, and be merry tonight. For no one except you, brother, has the right to marry my daughter Sarah. Likewise I am not at liberty to give her to any other man than yourself, because you are my nearest relative. But let me explain to you the true situation more fully, my child. [11]I have given her to seven men of our kinsmen, and all died on the night when they went in to her. But now, my child, eat and drink, and the Lord will act on behalf of you both." But Tobias said, "I will neither eat nor drink anything until you settle the things that pertain to me." So Raguel said, "I will do so. She is given to you in accordance with the decree in the book of Moses, and it has been decreed from heaven that she be given to you. Take your kinswoman;[b] from now on you are her brother and she is your sister. She is given to you from today and forever. May the Lord of heaven, my child, guide and prosper you both this night and grant you mercy and peace." [12]Then Raguel summoned his daughter Sarah. When she came to him he took her by the hand and gave her to Tobias,[f] saying, "Take her to be your wife in accordance with the law and decree written in the book of Moses. Take her and bring her safely to your father. And may the God of heaven prosper your journey with his peace." [13]Then he called her mother and told her to bring writing material; and he wrote out a copy of a marriage contract, to the effect that he gave her to him as wife according to the decree of the law of Moses. [14]Then they began to eat and drink.

15 Raguel called his wife Edna and said to her, "Sister, get the other room ready, and take her there." [16]So she went and made the bed in the room as he had told her, and brought Sarah[g] there. She wept for her daughter.[g] Then, wiping away the tears,[h] she said to her, "Take courage, my daughter; the Lord of heaven grant you joy[i] in place of your sorrow. Take courage, my daughter." Then she went out.

---

a Gk *he*   b Gk *sister*   c Other ancient authorities read *he*   d Other ancient authorities add *alive and*   e Other ancient authorities add *When he heard that Tobit had lost his sight, he was stricken with grief and wept. Then he said,*   f Gk *him*   g Gk *her*   h Other ancient authorities read *the tears of her daughter*   i Other ancient authorities read *favor*

Tobias Routs the Demon

8 When they had finished eating and drinking they wanted to retire; so they took the young man and brought him into the bedroom. [2]Then Tobias remembered the words of Raphael, and he took the fish's liver and heart out of the bag where he had them and put them on the embers of the incense. [3]The odor of the fish so repelled the demon that he fled to the remotest parts[a] of Egypt. But Raphael followed him, and at once bound him there hand and foot.

4 When the parents[b] had gone out and shut the door of the room, Tobias got out of bed and said to Sarah,[c] "Sister, get up, and let us pray and implore our Lord that he grant us mercy and safety." [5]So she got up, and they began to pray and implore that they might be kept safe. Tobias[d] began by saying,

"Blessed are you, O God of our ancestors,
   and blessed is your name in all generations
     forever.
Let the heavens and the whole creation bless
     you forever.
[6] You made Adam, and for him you made his
     wife Eve
   as a helper and support.
From the two of them the human race has
     sprung.
You said, 'It is not good that the man should be
     alone;
   let us make a helper for him like himself.'
[7] I now am taking this kinswoman of mine,
   not because of lust,
   but with sincerity.
Grant that she and I may find mercy
   and that we may grow old together."

[8]And they both said, "Amen, Amen." [9]Then they went to sleep for the night.

But Raguel arose and called his servants to him, and they went and dug a grave, [10]for he said, "It is possible that he will die and we will become an object of ridicule and derision." [11]When they had finished digging the grave, Raguel went into his house and called his wife, [12]saying, "Send one of the maids and have her go in to see if he is alive. But if he is dead, let us bury him without anyone knowing it." [13]So they sent the maid, lit a lamp, and opened the door; and she went in and found them sound asleep together. [14]Then the maid came out and informed them that he was alive and that nothing was wrong. [15]So they blessed the God of heaven, and Raguel[b] said,

"Blessed are you, O God, with every pure
     blessing;
let all your chosen ones bless you.[e]

Let them bless you forever.
[16] Blessed are you because you have made me glad.
   It has not turned out as I expected,
   but you have dealt with us according to your
     great mercy.
[17] Blessed are you because you had compassion
     on two only children.
Be merciful to them, O Master, and keep them
     safe;
   bring their lives to fulfillment
   in happiness and mercy."
[18]Then he ordered his servants to fill in the grave before daybreak.

Wedding Feast

19 After this he asked his wife to bake many loaves of bread; and he went out to the herd and brought two steers and four rams and ordered them to be slaughtered. So they began to make preparations. [20]Then he called for Tobias and swore on oath to him in these words:[f] "You shall not leave here for fourteen days, but shall stay here eating and drinking with me; and you shall cheer up my daughter, who has been depressed. [21]Take at once half of what I own and return in safety to your father; the other half will be yours when my wife and I die. Take courage, my child. I am your father and Edna is your mother, and we belong to you as well as to your wife[g] now and forever. Take courage, my child."

The Money Recovered

9 Then Tobias called Raphael and said to him, [2]"Brother Azariah, take four servants and two camels with you and travel to Rages. Go to the home of Gabael, give him the bond, get the money, and then bring him with you to the wedding celebration. [4]For you know that my father must be counting the days, and if I delay even one day I will upset him very much. [3]You are witness to the oath Raguel has sworn, and I cannot violate his oath."[h] [5]So Raphael with the four servants and two camels went to Rages in Media and stayed with Gabael. Raphael[d] gave him the bond and informed him that Tobit's son Tobias had married and was inviting him to the wedding celebration. So Gabael[i] got up and counted out to him the money bags, with their seals intact; then they loaded them on the camels.[j] [6]In the morning they both got up early and went to the wedding celebration. When they came into

T
O
B

Raguel's house they found Tobias reclining at table. He sprang up and greeted Gabael,[a] who wept and blessed him with the words, "Good and noble son of a father good and noble, upright and generous! May the Lord grant the blessing of heaven to you and your wife, and to your wife's father and mother. Blessed be God, for I see in Tobias the very image of my cousin Tobit."

Anxiety of the Parents

10 Now, day by day, Tobit kept counting how many days Tobias[b] would need for going and for returning. And when the days had passed and his son did not appear, [2]he said, "Is it possible that he has been detained? Or that Gabael has died, and there is no one to give him the money?" [3]And he began to worry. [4]His wife Anna said, "My child has perished and is no longer among the living." And she began to weep and mourn for her son, saying, [5]"Woe to me, my child, the light of my eyes, that I let you make the journey." [6]But Tobit kept saying to her, "Be quiet and stop worrying, my dear;[c] he is all right. Probably something unexpected has happened there. The man who went with him is trustworthy and is one of our own kin. Do not grieve for him, my dear;[c] he will soon be here." [7]She answered him, "Be quiet yourself! Stop trying to deceive me! My child has perished." She would rush out every day and watch the road her son had taken, and would heed no one.[d] When the sun had set she would go in and mourn and weep all night long, getting no sleep at all.

Tobias and Sarah Start for Home

Now when the fourteen days of the wedding celebration had ended that Raguel had sworn to observe for his daughter, Tobias came to him and said, "Send me back, for I know that my father and mother do not believe that they will see me again. So I beg of you, father, to let me go so that I may return to my own father. I have already explained to you how I left him." [8]But Raguel said to Tobias, "Stay, my child, stay with me; I will send messengers to your father Tobit and they will inform him about you." [9]But he said, "No! I beg you to send me back to my father." [10]So Raguel promptly gave Tobias his wife Sarah, as well as half of all his property: male and female slaves, oxen and sheep, donkeys and camels, clothing, money, and household goods. [11]Then he saw them safely off; he embraced Tobias[a] and said, "Farewell, my child; have a safe journey. The Lord of heaven prosper you and your wife Sarah, and may I see children of yours before I die." [12]Then he kissed his daughter Sarah and

said to her, "My daughter, honor your father-in-law and your mother-in-law,[e] since from now on they are as much your parents as those who gave you birth. Go in peace, daughter, and may I hear a good report about you as long as I live." Then he bade them farewell and let them go. Then Edna said to Tobias, "My child and dear brother, the Lord of heaven bring you back safely, and may I live long enough to see children of you and of my daughter Sarah before I die. In the sight of the Lord I entrust my daughter to you; do nothing to grieve her all the days of your life. Go in peace, my child. From now on I am your mother and Sarah is your beloved wife.[c] May we all prosper together all the days of our lives." Then she kissed them both and saw them safely off. [13]Tobias parted from Raguel with happiness and joy, praising the Lord of heaven and earth, King over all, because he had made his journey a success. Finally, he blessed Raguel and his wife Edna, and said, "I have been commanded by the Lord to honor you all the days of my life."[f]

Homeward Journey

11 When they came near to Kaserin, which is opposite Nineveh, Raphael said, [2]"You are aware of how we left your father. [3]Let us run ahead of your wife and prepare the house while they are still on the way." [4]As they went on together Raphael[b] said to him, "Have the gall ready." And the dog[g] went along behind them.

[5] Meanwhile Anna sat looking intently down the road by which her son would come. [6]When she caught sight of him coming, she said to his father, "Look, your son is coming, and the man who went with him!"

Tobit's Sight Restored

[7] Raphael said to Tobias, before he had approached his father, "I know that his eyes will be opened. [8]Smear the gall of the fish on his eyes; the medicine will make the white films shrink and peel off from his eyes, and your father will regain his sight and see the light."

[9] Then Anna ran up to her son and threw her arms around him, saying, "Now that I have seen you, my child, I am ready to die." And she wept. [10]Then Tobit got up and came stumbling out through the courtyard door. Tobias went up to him, [11]with the gall of the fish in his hand, and holding him firmly, he blew into his eyes, saying, "Take courage, father." With this he applied the

---

a Gk him   b Gk he   c Gk sister   d Other ancient authorities read and she would eat nothing   e Other ancient authorities lack parts of Then . . . mother-in-law   f Lat: Meaning of Gk uncertain   g Codex Sinaiticus reads And the Lord

medicine on his eyes, [12]and it made them smart.[a] [13]Next, with both his hands he peeled off the white films from the corners of his eyes. Then Tobit[b] saw his son and[c] threw his arms around him, [14]and he wept and said to him, "I see you, my son, the light of my eyes!" Then he said,

"Blessed be God,
　　and blessed be his great name,
　　and blessed be all his holy angels.
May his holy name be blessed[d]
　　throughout all the ages.
[15] Though he afflicted me,
　　he has had mercy upon me.[e]
　　Now I see my son Tobias!"

So Tobit went in rejoicing and praising God at the top of his voice. Tobias reported to his father that his journey had been successful, that he had brought the money, that he had married Raguel's daughter Sarah, and that she was, indeed, on her way there, very near to the gate of Nineveh.

16 Then Tobit, rejoicing and praising God, went out to meet his daughter-in-law at the gate of Nineveh. When the people of Nineveh saw him coming, walking along in full vigor and with no one leading him, they were amazed. [17]Before them all, Tobit acknowledged that God had been merciful to him and had restored his sight. When Tobit met Sarah the wife of his son Tobias, he blessed her saying, "Come in, my daughter, and welcome. Blessed be your God who has brought you to us, my daughter. Blessed be your father and your mother, blessed be my son Tobias, and blessed be you, my daughter. Come in now to your home, and welcome, with blessing and joy. Come in, my daughter." So on that day there was rejoicing among all the Jews who were in Nineveh. [18]Ahikar and his nephew Nadab were also present to share Tobit's joy. With merriment they celebrated Tobias's wedding feast for seven days, and many gifts were given to him.[f]

Raphael's Wages

12 When the wedding celebration was ended, Tobit called his son Tobias and said to him, "My child, see to paying the wages of the man who went with you, and give him a bonus as well." [2]He replied, "Father, how much shall I pay him? It would do no harm to give him half of the possessions brought back with me. [3]For he has led me back to you safely, he cured my wife, he brought the money back with me, and he healed you. How much extra shall I give him as a bonus?" [4]Tobit said, "He deserves, my child, to receive half of all that he brought back." [5]So Tobias[b] called him and said, "Take for your wages half of all that you brought back, and farewell."

Raphael's Exhortation

6 Then Raphael[b] called the two of them privately and said to them, "Bless God and acknowledge him in the presence of all the living for the good things he has done for you. Bless and sing praise to his name. With fitting honor declare to all people the deeds[g] of God. Do not be slow to acknowledge him. [7]It is good to conceal the secret of a king, but to acknowledge and reveal the works of God, and with fitting honor to acknowledge him. Do good and evil will not overtake you. [8]Prayer with fasting[h] is good, but better than both is almsgiving with righteousness. A little with righteousness is better than wealth with wrongdoing.[i] It is better to give alms than to lay up gold. [9]For almsgiving saves from death and purges away every sin. Those who give alms will enjoy a full life, [10]but those who commit sin and do wrong are their own worst enemies.

Raphael Discloses His Identity

11 "I will now declare the whole truth to you and will conceal nothing from you. Already I have declared it to you when I said, 'It is good to conceal the secret of a king, but to reveal with due honor the works of God.' [12]So now when you and Sarah prayed, it was I who brought and read[j] the record of your prayer before the glory of the Lord, and likewise whenever you would bury the dead. [13]And that time when you did not hesitate to get up and leave your dinner to go and bury the dead, [14]I was sent to you to test you. And at the same time God sent me to heal you and Sarah your daughter-in-law. [15]I am Raphael, one of the seven angels who stand ready and enter before the glory of the Lord."

16 The two of them were shaken; they fell face down, for they were afraid. [17]But he said to them, "Do not be afraid; peace be with you. Bless God forevermore. [18]As for me, when I was with you, I was not acting on my own will, but by the will of God. Bless him each and every day; sing his praises. [19]Although you were watching me, I really did not eat or drink anything—but what you saw was a vision. [20]So now get up from the ground,[k] and acknowledge God. See, I am ascending to him who sent me. Write down

---

a Lat: Meaning of Gk uncertain　b Gk he　c Other ancient authorities lack saw his son and　d Codex Sinaiticus reads May his great name be upon us and blessed be all the angels　e Lat: Gk lacks this line　f Other ancient authorities lack parts of this sentence　g Gk words; other ancient authorities read words of the deeds　h Codex Sinaiticus with sincerity　i Lat　j Lat: Gk lacks and read　k Other ancient authorities read now bless the Lord on earth

all these things that have happened to you." And he ascended. ²¹Then they stood up, and could see him no more. ²²They kept blessing God and singing his praises, and they acknowledged God for these marvelous deeds of his, when an angel of God had appeared to them.

Tobit's Thanksgiving to God

13 Then Tobit[a] said:
"Blessed be God who lives forever,
because his kingdom[b] lasts throughout all ages.
² For he afflicts, and he shows mercy;
he leads down to Hades in the lowest regions of the earth,
and he brings up from the great abyss,[c]
and there is nothing that can escape his hand.
³ Acknowledge him before the nations, O children of Israel;
for he has scattered you among them.
⁴ He has shown you his greatness even there.
Exalt him in the presence of every living being,
because he is our Lord and he is our God;
he is our Father and he is God forever.
⁵ He will afflict[d] you for your iniquities,
but he will again show mercy on all of you.
He will gather you from all the nations among whom you have been scattered.
⁶ If you turn to him with all your heart and with all your soul,
to do what is true before him,
then he will turn to you
and will no longer hide his face from you.
So now see what he has done for you;
acknowledge him at the top of your voice.
Bless the Lord of righteousness,
and exalt the King of the ages.[e]
In the land of my exile I acknowledge him,
and show his power and majesty to a nation of sinners:
'Turn back, you sinners, and do what is right before him;
perhaps he may look with favor upon you and show you mercy.'
⁷ As for me, I exalt my God,
and my soul rejoices in the King of heaven.
⁸ Let all people speak of his majesty,
and acknowledge him in Jerusalem.
⁹ O Jerusalem, the holy city,
he afflicted[f] you for the deeds of your hands,[g]
but will again have mercy on the children of the righteous.
¹⁰ Acknowledge the Lord, for he is good,[h]
and bless the King of the ages,
so that his tent[i] may be rebuilt in you in joy.

Hope for the Faithful

When the Jews lived under the influence of Greek culture, there was a great need for hope. The story of Tobit and Tobias, whose names mean "goodness" and "God is good," was written to give hope to those who continue to be faithful to God, even in difficult times.

Tobit is the model of the good Israelite at all times and places. God's saving actions for him and his family symbolize God's actions toward Israel. In this spirit, before his death, Tobit sings a beautiful hymn in thanksgiving for God's goodness and with hope in the triumph of Jerusalem over its oppressors.

- Recognize the goodness of God in your life and the ways in which you fail God.
- Take a moment to pray in Tobit's style. Praise God for the blessings in your life; ask forgiveness for the times you have failed God; give thanks for the times God has answered your prayers in a wiser way than what you had asked for. Pray not only for yourself but for all people, with hope for the triumph of God's love and peace over the self-centeredness, hatred, and violence so common today.

▶ **Tobit, chapter 13**

May he cheer all those within you who are captives,
and love all those within you who are distressed,
to all generations forever.
¹¹ A bright light will shine to all the ends of the earth;
many nations will come to you from far away,
the inhabitants of the remotest parts of the earth to your holy name,
bearing gifts in their hands for the King of heaven.

a Gk he   b Other ancient authorities read *forever, and his kingdom*   c Gk *from destruction*   d Other ancient authorities read *He afflicted*   e The lacuna in codex Sinaiticus, verses 6b to 10a, is filled in from other ancient authorities   f Other ancient authorities read *will afflict*   g Other ancient authorities read *your children*   h Other ancient authorities read *Lord worthily*   i Or *tabernacle*

Generation after generation will give joyful
>   praise in you;
> the name of the chosen city will endure
>   forever.

12 Cursed are all who speak a harsh word against
>   you;
> cursed are all who conquer you
> and pull down your walls,
> all who overthrow your towers
> and set your homes on fire.
> But blessed forever will be all who revere
>   you.[a]

13 Go, then, and rejoice over the children of the
>   righteous,
> for they will be gathered together
> and will praise the Lord of the ages.

14 Happy are those who love you,
> and happy are those who rejoice in your
>   prosperity.
> Happy also are all people who grieve with you
> because of your afflictions;
> for they will rejoice with you
> and witness all your glory forever.

15 My soul blesses[b] the Lord, the great King!

16   For Jerusalem will be built[c] as his house for
>   all ages.
> How happy I will be if a remnant of my
>   descendants should survive
> to see your glory and acknowledge the King of
>   heaven.
> The gates of Jerusalem will be built with
>   sapphire and emerald,
> and all your walls with precious stones.
> The towers of Jerusalem will be built with gold,
> and their battlements with pure gold.
> The streets of Jerusalem will be paved
> with ruby and with stones of Ophir.

17 The gates of Jerusalem will sing hymns of joy,
> and all her houses will cry, 'Hallelujah!
> Blessed be the God of Israel!'
> and the blessed will bless the holy name
> forever and ever."

Tobit's Final Counsel

14 So ended Tobit's words of praise.
2 Tobit[d] died in peace when he was one
hundred twelve years old, and was buried with
great honor in Nineveh. He was sixty-two[e] years
old when he lost his eyesight, and after regain-
ing it he lived in prosperity, giving alms and
continually blessing God and acknowledging
God's majesty.

3 When he was about to die, he called his son
Tobias and the seven sons of Tobias[f] and gave
this command: "My son, take your children 4and
hurry off to Media, for I believe the word of God

that Nahum spoke about Nineveh, that all these
things will take place and overtake Assyria and
Nineveh. Indeed, everything that was spoken by
the prophets of Israel, whom God sent, will occur. None of all their words will fail, but all will
come true at their appointed times. So it will be
safer in Media than in Assyria and Babylon. For I
know and believe that whatever God has said will
be fulfilled and will come true; not a single word
of the prophecies will fail. All of our kindred,
inhabitants of the land of Israel, will be scattered
and taken as captives from the good land; and
the whole land of Israel will be desolate, even
Samaria and Jerusalem will be desolate. And the
temple of God in it will be burned to the ground,
and it will be desolate for a while.[g]

5 "But God will again have mercy on them,
and God will bring them back into the land of Israel; and they will rebuild the temple of God, but
not like the first one until the period when the
times of fulfillment shall come. After this they
all will return from their exile and will rebuild
Jerusalem in splendor; and in it the temple of
God will be rebuilt, just as the prophets of Israel
have said concerning it. 6Then the nations in the
whole world will all be converted and worship
God in truth. They will all abandon their idols,
which deceitfully have led them into their error;
7and in righteousness they will praise the eternal
God. All the Israelites who are saved in those
days and are truly mindful of God will be gathered together; they will go to Jerusalem and live
in safety forever in the land of Abraham, and it
will be given over to them. Those who sincerely
love God will rejoice, but those who commit sin
and injustice will vanish from all the earth. 8,9So
now, my children, I command you, serve God
faithfully and do what is pleasing in his sight.
Your children are also to be commanded to do
what is right and to give alms, and to be mindful
of God and to bless his name at all times with
sincerity and with all their strength. So now,
my son, leave Nineveh; do not remain here.
10On whatever day you bury your mother beside
me, do not stay overnight within the confines
of the city. For I see that there is much wickedness within it, and that much deceit is practiced
within it, while the people are without shame.
See, my son, what Nadab did to Ahikar who had
reared him. Was he not, while still alive, brought
down into the earth? For God repaid him to his

---

a Other ancient authorities read *who build you up*   b Or *O my
soul, bless*   c Other ancient authorities add *for a city*   d Gk *He*
e Other ancient authorities read *fifty-eight*   f Lat: Gk lacks *and
the seven sons of Tobias*   g Lat: Other ancient authorities read *of
God will be in distress and will be burned for a while*

face for this shameful treatment. Ahikar came out into the light, but Nadab went into the eternal darkness, because he tried to kill Ahikar. Because he gave alms, Ahikar[a] escaped the fatal trap that Nadab had set for him, but Nadab fell into it himself, and was destroyed. [11]So now, my children, see what almsgiving accomplishes, and what injustice does—it brings death! But now my breath fails me."

Death of Tobit and Anna

Then they laid him on his bed, and he died; and he received an honorable funeral. [12]When Tobias's mother died, he buried her beside his father. Then he and his wife and children[b] returned to Media and settled in Ecbatana with Raguel his father-in-law. [13]He treated his parents-in-law[c] with great respect in their old age, and buried them in Ecbatana of Media. He inherited both the property of Raguel and that of his father Tobit. [14]He died highly respected at the age of one hundred seventeen[d] years. [15]Before he died he heard[e] of the destruction of Nineveh, and he saw its prisoners being led into Media, those whom King Cyaxares[f] of Media had taken captive. Tobias[g] praised God for all he had done to the people of Nineveh and Assyria; before he died he rejoiced over Nineveh, and he blessed the Lord God forever and ever. Amen.[h]

---

a Gk *he*; other ancient authorities read *Manasses*   b Codex Sinaiticus lacks *and children*   c Gk *them*   d Other authorities read other numbers   e Codex Sinaiticus reads *saw and heard*   f Cn: Codex Sinaiticus *Ahikar*; other ancient authorities read *Nebuchadnezzar and Ahasuerus*   g Gk *He*   h Other ancient authorities lack *Amen*

Do you like to cheer for the underdog? If so, you are like most people. Whether in a court of law, on a football field, or in politics, we get a thrill from seeing the high and mighty toppled by a courageous and determined underdog. This theme is evident in some of the most popular stories of the Old Testament: a group of Hebrew slaves escapes from Pharaoh's army, the teenage David topples the giant Goliath, the prophet Daniel escapes injury in the lions' den. Judith's story is another in which the little people—against all odds—somehow come out on top.

At a Glance

- **Chapters 1–7. the Jews in danger**
- **Chapters 8–16. Judith to the rescue**

Quick Facts

Setting: a wisdom story without a clear historical setting
Inspired Author: unknown, writing at the end of the second or the beginning of the first century BC
Themes: a woman of faith and courage, God's saving power

In Depth

As the Book of Judith opens, the mighty Assyrian army is on the march against Jerusalem. To block the advance, the citizens of the small town of Bethulia are asked by the high priest to resist the army's movement. With little hope of success but a great deal of courage, the Bethulians accept the challenge. When they are at the point of surrender, a childless widow named Judith steps forward. Putting all her trust in the "God of the lowly, helper of the oppressed, upholder of the weak, protector of the forsaken, savior of those without hope" (9:11), she bravely delivers her nation from certain defeat.

The story of Judith must have presented a challenge to the male-dominated world of the Israelites. As a childless widow, Judith would have had little social standing. Yet she succeeds where the king, the priests, and the leaders of the city fail. It is interesting that the name Judith is probably not even a proper name. It simply means "Jewish woman." In a sense, Judith stands for all the Jewish women of the past who have served God through their faith, courage, and decisive action.

Because of its many historical errors, the Book of Judith is clearly not a historical document. With remarkable storytelling flair, the author underlines one of the major elements of Hebrew faith: "O Lord, you are great and glorious, / wonderful in strength, invincible" (16:13). This was the kind of faith the underdog People of God needed as they faced the growing might of the Roman Empire.

Judith

Arphaxad Fortifies Ecbatana

1 It was the twelfth year of the reign of Nebuchadnezzar, who ruled over the Assyrians in the great city of Nineveh. In those days Arphaxad ruled over the Medes in Ecbatana. ²He built walls around Ecbatana with hewn stones three cubits thick and six cubits long; he made the walls seventy cubits high and fifty cubits wide. ³At its gates he raised towers one hundred cubits high and sixty cubits wide at the foundations. ⁴He made its gates seventy cubits high and forty cubits wide to allow his armies to march out in force and his infantry to form their ranks. ⁵Then King Nebuchadnezzar made war against King Arphaxad in the great plain that is on the borders of Ragau. ⁶There rallied to him all the people of the hill country and all those who lived along the Euphrates, the Tigris, and the Hydaspes, and, on the plain, Arioch, king of the Elymeans. Thus, many nations joined the forces of the Chaldeans.ª

Nebuchadnezzar Issues Ultimatum

7 Then Nebuchadnezzar, king of the Assyrians, sent messengers to all who lived in Persia and to all who lived in the west, those who lived in Cilicia and Damascus, Lebanon and Antilebanon, and all who lived along the seacoast, ⁸and those among the nations of Carmel and Gilead, and Upper Galilee and the great plain of Esdraelon, ⁹and all who were in Samaria and its towns, and beyond the Jordan as far as Jerusalem and Bethany and Chelous and Kadesh and the river of Egypt, and Tahpanhes and Raamses and the whole land of Goshen, ¹⁰even beyond Tanis and Memphis, and all who lived in Egypt as far as the borders of Ethiopia. ¹¹But all who lived in the whole region disregarded the summons of Nebuchadnezzar, king of the Assyrians, and refused to join him in the war; for they were not afraid of him, but regarded him as only one man.ᵇ So they sent back his messengers empty-handed and in disgrace.

12 Then Nebuchadnezzar became very angry with this whole region, and swore by his throne and kingdom that he would take revenge on the whole territory of Cilicia and Damascus and Syria, that he would kill with his sword also all the inhabitants of the land of Moab, and the people of Ammon, and all Judea, and every one in Egypt, as far as the coasts of the two seas.

Arphaxad Is Defeated

13 In the seventeenth year he led his forces against King Arphaxad and defeated him in battle, overthrowing the whole army of Arphaxad and all his cavalry and all his chariots. ¹⁴Thus he took possession of his towns and came to Ecbatana, captured its towers, plundered its markets, and turned its glory into disgrace. ¹⁵He captured Arphaxad in the mountains of Ragau and struck him down with his spears, thus destroying him once and for all. ¹⁶Then he returned to Nineveh, he and all his combined forces, a vast body of troops; and

---

a Syr: Gk *Cheleoudites*   b Or *a man*

487

there he and his forces rested and feasted for one hundred twenty days.

The Expedition against the West

2 In the eighteenth year, on the twenty-second day of the first month, there was talk in the palace of Nebuchadnezzar, king of the Assyrians, about carrying out his revenge on the whole region, just as he had said. ²He summoned all his ministers and all his nobles and set before them his secret plan and recounted fully, with his own lips, all the wickedness of the region.[a] ³They decided that every one who had not obeyed his command should be destroyed.

4 When he had completed his plan, Nebuchadnezzar, king of the Assyrians, called Holofernes, the chief general of his army, second only to himself, and said to him, ⁵"Thus says the Great King, the lord of the whole earth: Leave my presence and take with you men confident in their strength, one hundred twenty thousand foot soldiers and twelve thousand cavalry. ⁶March out against all the land to the west, because they disobeyed my orders. ⁷Tell them to prepare earth and water, for I am coming against them in my anger, and will cover the whole face of the earth with the feet of my troops, to whom I will hand them over to be plundered. ⁸Their wounded shall fill their ravines and gullies, and the swelling river shall be filled with their dead. ⁹I will lead them away captive to the ends of the whole earth. ¹⁰You shall go and seize all their territory for me in advance. They must yield themselves to you, and you shall hold them for me until the day of their punishment. ¹¹But to those who resist show no mercy, but hand them over to slaughter and plunder throughout your whole region. ¹²For as I live, and by the power of my kingdom, what I have spoken I will accomplish by my own hand. ¹³And you—take care not to transgress any of your lord's commands, but carry them out exactly as I have ordered you; do it without delay."

Campaign of Holofernes

14 So Holofernes left the presence of his lord, and summoned all the commanders, generals, and officers of the Assyrian army. ¹⁵He mustered the picked troops by divisions as his lord had ordered him to do, one hundred twenty thousand of them, together with twelve thousand archers on horseback, ¹⁶and he organized them as a great army is marshaled for a campaign. ¹⁷He took along a vast number of camels and donkeys and mules for transport, and innumerable sheep and oxen and goats for food; ¹⁸also ample rations for everyone, and a huge amount of gold and silver from the royal palace.

19 Then he set out with his whole army, to go ahead of King Nebuchadnezzar and to cover the whole face of the earth to the west with their chariots and cavalry and picked foot soldiers. ²⁰Along with them went a mixed crowd like a swarm of locusts, like the dust[b] of the earth—a multitude that could not be counted.

21 They marched for three days from Nineveh to the plain of Bectileth, and camped opposite Bectileth near the mountain that is to the north of Upper Cilicia. ²²From there Holofernes[c] took his whole army, the infantry, cavalry, and chariots, and went up into the hill country. ²³He ravaged Put and Lud, and plundered all the Rassisites and the Ishmaelites on the border of the desert, south of the country of the Chelleans. ²⁴Then he followed[d] the Euphrates and passed through Mesopotamia and destroyed all the fortified towns along the brook Abron, as far as the sea. ²⁵He also seized the territory of Cilicia, and killed everyone who resisted him. Then he came to the southern borders of Japheth, facing Arabia. ²⁶He surrounded all the Midianites, and burned their tents and plundered their sheepfolds. ²⁷Then he went down into the plain of Damascus during the wheat harvest, and burned all their fields and destroyed their flocks and herds and sacked their towns and ravaged their lands and put all their young men to the sword.

28 So fear and dread of him fell upon all the people who lived along the seacoast, at Sidon and Tyre, and those who lived in Sur and Ocina and all who lived in Jamnia. Those who lived in Azotus and Ascalon feared him greatly.

Entreaties for Peace

3 They therefore sent messengers to him to sue for peace in these words: ²"We, the servants of Nebuchadnezzar, the Great King, lie prostrate before you. Do with us whatever you will. ³See, our buildings and all our land and all our wheat fields and our flocks and herds and all our encampments[e] lie before you; do with them as you please. ⁴Our towns and their inhabitants are also your slaves; come and deal with them as you see fit."

5 The men came to Holofernes and told him all this. ⁶Then he went down to the seacoast with his army and stationed garrisons in the fortified towns and took picked men from them as auxiliaries. ⁷These people and all in the

---

a Meaning of Gk uncertain   b Gk sand   c Gk he
d Or crossed   e Gk all the sheepfolds of our tents

countryside welcomed him with garlands and dances and tambourines. [8]Yet he demolished all their shrines[a] and cut down their sacred groves; for he had been commissioned to destroy all the gods of the land, so that all nations should worship Nebuchadnezzar alone, and that all their dialects and tribes should call upon him as a god.

9 Then he came toward Esdraelon, near Dothan, facing the great ridge of Judea; [10]he camped between Geba and Scythopolis, and remained for a whole month in order to collect all the supplies for his army.

Judea on the Alert

4 When the Israelites living in Judea heard of everything that Holofernes, the general of Nebuchadnezzar, the king of the Assyrians, had done to the nations, and how he had plundered and destroyed all their temples, [2]they were therefore greatly terrified at his approach; they were alarmed both for Jerusalem and for the temple of the Lord their God. [3]For they had only recently returned from exile, and all the people of Judea had just now gathered together, and the sacred vessels and the altar and the temple had been consecrated after their profanation. [4]So they sent word to every district of Samaria, and to Kona, Beth-horon, Belmain, and Jericho, and to Choba and Aesora, and the valley of Salem. [5]They immediately seized all the high hilltops and fortified the villages on them and stored up food in preparation for war—since their fields had recently been harvested.

6 The high priest, Joakim, who was in Jerusalem at the time, wrote to the people of Bethulia and Betomesthaim, which faces Esdraelon opposite the plain near Dothan, [7]ordering them to seize the mountain passes, since by them Judea could be invaded; and it would be easy to stop any who tried to enter, for the approach was narrow, wide enough for only two at a time to pass.

Prayer and Penance

8 So the Israelites did as they had been ordered by the high priest Joakim and the senate of the whole people of Israel, in session at Jerusalem. [9]And every man of Israel cried out to God with great fervor, and they humbled themselves with much fasting. [10]They and their wives and their children and their cattle and every resident alien and hired laborer and purchased slave— they all put sackcloth around their waists. [11]And all the Israelite men, women, and children living at Jerusalem prostrated themselves before the temple and put ashes on their heads and spread out their sackcloth before the Lord. [12]They even draped the altar with sackcloth and cried out in unison, praying fervently to the God of Israel not to allow their infants to be carried off and their wives to be taken as booty, and the towns they had inherited to be destroyed, and the sanctuary to be profaned and desecrated to the malicious joy of the Gentiles.

13 The Lord heard their prayers and had regard for their distress; for the people fasted many days throughout Judea and in Jerusalem before the sanctuary of the Lord Almighty. [14]The high priest Joakim and all the priests who stood before the Lord and ministered to the Lord, with sackcloth around their loins, offered the daily burnt offerings, the votive offerings, and freewill offerings of the people. [15]With ashes on their turbans, they cried out to the Lord with all their might to look with favor on the whole house of Israel.

Council against the Israelites

5 It was reported to Holofernes, the general of the Assyrian army, that the people of Israel had prepared for war and had closed the mountain passes and fortified all the high hilltops and set up barricades in the plains. [2]In great anger he called together all the princes of Moab and the commanders of Ammon and all the governors of the coastland, [3]and said to them, "Tell me, you Canaanites, what people is this that lives in the hill country? What towns do they inhabit? How large is their army, and in what does their power and strength consist? Who rules over them as king and leads their army? [4]And why have they alone, of all who live in the west, refused to come out and meet me?"

Achior's Report

5 Then Achior, the leader of all the Ammonites, said to him, "May my lord please listen to a report from the mouth of your servant, and I will tell you the truth about this people that lives in the mountain district near you. No falsehood shall come from your servant's mouth. [6]These people are descended from the Chaldeans. [7]At one time they lived in Mesopotamia, because they did not wish to follow the gods of their ancestors who were in Chaldea. [8]Since they had abandoned the ways of their ancestors, and worshiped the God of heaven, the God they had come to know, their ancestors[b] drove them out from the presence of their gods. So they fled to

---

a Syr: Gk borders b Gk they

Mesopotamia, and lived there for a long time. [9]Then their God commanded them to leave the place where they were living and go to the land of Canaan. There they settled, and grew very prosperous in gold and silver and very much livestock. [10]When a famine spread over the land of Canaan they went down to Egypt and lived there as long as they had food. There they became so great a multitude that their race could not be counted. [11]So the king of Egypt became hostile to them; he exploited them and forced them to make bricks. [12]They cried out to their God, and he afflicted the whole land of Egypt with incurable plagues. So the Egyptians drove them out of their sight. [13]Then God dried up the Red Sea before them, [14]and he led them by the way of Sinai and Kadesh-barnea. They drove out all the people of the desert, [15]and took up residence in the land of the Amorites, and by their might destroyed all the inhabitants of Heshbon; and crossing over the Jordan they took possession of all the hill country. [16]They drove out before them the Canaanites, the Perizzites, the Jebusites, the Shechemites, and all the Gergesites, and lived there a long time.

[17] "As long as they did not sin against their God they prospered, for the God who hates iniquity is with them. [18]But when they departed from the way he had prescribed for them, they were utterly defeated in many battles and were led away captive to a foreign land. The temple of their God was razed to the ground, and their towns were occupied by their enemies. [19]But now they have returned to their God, and have come back from the places where they were scattered, and have occupied Jerusalem, where their sanctuary is, and have settled in the hill country, because it was uninhabited.

[20] "So now, my master and lord, if there is any oversight in this people and they sin against their God and we find out their offense, then we can go up and defeat them. [21]But if they are not a guilty nation, then let my lord pass them by; for their Lord and God will defend them, and we shall become the laughingstock of the whole world."

[22] When Achior had finished saying these things, all the people standing around the tent began to complain; Holofernes' officers and all the inhabitants of the seacoast and Moab insisted that he should be cut to pieces. [23]They said, "We are not afraid of the Israelites; they are a people with no strength or power for making war. [24]Therefore let us go ahead, Lord Holofernes, and your vast army will swallow them up."

Achior Handed over to the Israelites

6 When the disturbance made by the people outside the council had died down, Holofernes, the commander of the Assyrian army, said to Achior[a] in the presence of all the foreign contingents:

2 "Who are you, Achior and you mercenaries of Ephraim, to prophesy among us as you have done today and tell us not to make war against the people of Israel because their God will defend them? What god is there except Nebuchadnezzar? He will send his forces and destroy them from the face of the earth. Their God will not save them; [3]we the king's[b] servants will destroy them as one man. They cannot resist the might of our cavalry. [4]We will overwhelm them;[c] their mountains will be drunk with their blood, and their fields will be full of their dead. Not even their footprints will survive our attack; they will utterly perish. So says King Nebuchadnezzar, lord of the whole earth. For he has spoken; none of his words shall be in vain.

5 "As for you, Achior, you Ammonite mercenary, you have said these words in a moment of perversity; you shall not see my face again from this day until I take revenge on this race that came out of Egypt. [6]Then at my return the sword of my army and the spear[d] of my servants shall pierce your sides, and you shall fall among their wounded. [7]Now my slaves are going to take you back into the hill country and put you in one of the towns beside the passes. [8]You will not die until you perish along with them. [9]If you really hope in your heart that they will not be taken, then do not look downcast! I have spoken, and none of my words shall fail to come true."

10 Then Holofernes ordered his slaves, who waited on him in his tent, to seize Achior and take him away to Bethulia and hand him over to the Israelites. [11]So the slaves took him and led him out of the camp into the plain, and from the plain they went up into the hill country and came to the springs below Bethulia. [12]When the men of the town saw them,[e] they seized their weapons and ran out of the town to the top of the hill, and all the slingers kept them from coming up by throwing stones at them. [13]So having taken shelter below the hill, they bound Achior and left him lying at the foot of the hill, and returned to their master.

14 Then the Israelites came down from their

---

a Other ancient authorities add *and to all the Moabites* b Gk *his*
c Other ancient authorities add *with it* d Lat Syr: Gk *people*
e Other ancient authorities add *on the top of the hill*

town and found him; they untied him and brought him into Bethulia and placed him before the magistrates of their town, [15]who in those days were Uzziah son of Micah, of the tribe of Simeon, and Chabris son of Gothoniel, and Charmis son of Melchiel. [16]They called together all the elders of the town, and all their young men and women ran to the assembly. They set Achior in the midst of all their people, and Uzziah questioned him about what had happened. [17]He answered and told them what had taken place at the council of Holofernes, and all that he had said in the presence of the Assyrian leaders, and all that Holofernes had boasted he would do against the house of Israel. [18]Then the people fell down and worshiped God, and cried out:

19 "O Lord God of heaven, see their arrogance, and have pity on our people in their humiliation, and look kindly today on the faces of those who are consecrated to you."

20 Then they reassured Achior, and praised him highly. [21]Uzziah took him from the assembly to his own house and gave a banquet for the elders; and all that night they called on the God of Israel for help.

The Campaign against Bethulia

7 The next day Holofernes ordered his whole army, and all the allies who had joined him, to break camp and move against Bethulia, and to seize the passes up into the hill country and make war on the Israelites. [2]So all their warriors marched off that day; their fighting forces numbered one hundred seventy thousand infantry and twelve thousand cavalry, not counting the baggage and the foot soldiers handling it, a very great multitude. [3]They encamped in the valley near Bethulia, beside the spring, and they spread out in breadth over Dothan as far as Balbaim and in length from Bethulia to Cyamon, which faces Esdraelon.

4 When the Israelites saw their vast numbers, they were greatly terrified and said to one another, "They will now strip clean the whole land; neither the high mountains nor the valleys nor the hills will bear their weight." [5]Yet they all seized their weapons, and when they had kindled fires on their towers, they remained on guard all that night.

6 On the second day Holofernes led out all his cavalry in full view of the Israelites in Bethulia. [7]He reconnoitered the approaches to their town, and visited the springs that supplied their water; he seized them and set guards of soldiers over them, and then returned to his army.

8 Then all the chieftains of the Edomites and all the leaders of the Moabites and the commanders of the coastland came to him and said, [9]"Listen to what we have to say, my lord, and your army will suffer no losses. [10]This people, the Israelites, do not rely on their spears but on the height of the mountains where they live, for it is not easy to reach the tops of their mountains. [11]Therefore, my lord, do not fight against them in regular formation, and not a man of your army will fall. [12]Remain in your camp, and keep all the men in your forces with you; let your servants take possession of the spring of water that flows from the foot of the mountain, [13]for this is where all the people of Bethulia get their water. So thirst will destroy them, and they will surrender their town. Meanwhile, we and our people will go up to the tops of the nearby mountains and camp there to keep watch to see that no one gets out of the town. [14]They and their wives and children will waste away with famine, and before the sword reaches them they will be strewn about in the streets where they live. [15]Thus you will pay them back with evil, because they rebelled and did not receive you peaceably."

16 These words pleased Holofernes and all his attendants, and he gave orders to do as they had said. [17]So the army of the Ammonites moved forward, together with five thousand Assyrians, and they encamped in the valley and seized the water supply and the springs of the Israelites. [18]And the Edomites and Ammonites went up and encamped in the hill country opposite Dothan; and they sent some of their men toward the south and the east, toward Egrebeh, which is near Chusi beside the Wadi Mochmur. The rest of the Assyrian army encamped in the plain, and covered the whole face of the land. Their tents and supply trains spread out in great number, and they formed a vast multitude.

The Distress of the Israelites

19 The Israelites then cried out to the Lord their God, for their courage failed, because all their enemies had surrounded them, and there was no way of escape from them. [20]The whole Assyrian army, their infantry, chariots, and cavalry, surrounded them for thirty-four days, until all the water containers of every inhabitant of Bethulia were empty; [21]their cisterns were going dry, and on no day did they have enough water to drink, for their drinking water was rationed. [22]Their children were listless, and the women and young men fainted from thirst and were collapsing in the streets of the town and in the gateways; they no longer had any strength.

23 Then all the people, the young men, the

women, and the children, gathered around Uzziah and the rulers of the town and cried out with a loud voice, and said before all the elders, 24"Let God judge between you and us! You have done us a great injury in not making peace with the Assyrians. 25For now we have no one to help us; God has sold us into their hands, to be strewn before them in thirst and exhaustion. 26Now summon them and surrender the whole town as booty to the army of Holofernes and to all his forces. 27For it would be better for us to be captured by them.a We shall indeed become slaves, but our lives will be spared, and we shall not witness our little ones dying before our eyes, and our wives and children drawing their last breath. 28We call to witness against you heaven and earth and our God, the Lord of our ancestors, who punishes us for our sins and the sins of our ancestors; do today the things that we have described!"

29 Then great and general lamentation arose throughout the assembly, and they cried out to the Lord God with a loud voice. 30But Uzziah said to them, "Courage, my brothers and sisters!b Let us hold out for five days more; by that time the Lord our God will turn his mercy to us again, for he will not forsake us utterly. 31But if these days pass by, and no help comes for us, I will do as you say."

32 Then he dismissed the people to their various posts, and they went up on the walls and towers of their town. The women and children he sent home. In the town they were in great misery.

The Character of Judith

8 Now in those days Judith heard about these things: she was the daughter of Merari son of Ox son of Joseph son of Oziel son of Elkiah son of Ananias son of Gideon son of Raphain son of Ahitub son of Elijah son of Hilkiah son of Eliab son of Nathanael son of Salamiel son of Sarasadai son of Israel. 2Her husband Manasseh, who belonged to her tribe and family, had died during the barley harvest. 3For as he stood overseeing those who were binding sheaves in the field, he was overcome by the burning heat, and took to his bed and died in his town Bethulia. So they buried him with his ancestors in the field between Dothan and Balamon. 4Judith remained as a widow for three years and four months 5at home where she set up a tent for herself on the roof of her house. She put sackcloth around her waist and dressed in widow's clothing. 6She fasted all the days of her widowhood, except the day before the sabbath and the sabbath itself,

the day before the new moon and the day of the new moon, and the festivals and days of rejoicing of the house of Israel. 7She was beautiful in appearance, and was very lovely to behold. Her husband Manasseh had left her gold and silver, men and women slaves, livestock, and fields; and she maintained this estate. 8No one spoke ill of her, for she feared God with great devotion.

Judith and the Elders

9 When Judith heard the harsh words spoken by the people against the ruler, because they were faint for lack of water, and when she heard all that Uzziah said to them, and how he promised them under oath to surrender the town to the Assyrians after five days, 10she sent her maid, who was in charge of all she possessed, to summon Uzziah andc Chabris and Charmis, the elders of her town. 11They came to her, and she said to them:

"Listen to me, rulers of the people of Bethulia! What you have said to the people today is not right; you have even sworn and pronounced this oath between God and you, promising to surrender the town to our enemies unless the Lord turns and helps us within so many days. 12Who are you to put God to the test today, and to set yourselves up in the place ofd God in human affairs? 13You are putting the Lord Almighty to the test, but you will never learn anything! 14You cannot plumb the depths of the human heart or understand the workings of the human mind; how do you expect to search out God, who made all these things, and find out his mind or comprehend his thought? No, my brothers, do not anger the Lord our God. 15For if he does not choose to help us within these five days, he has power to protect us within any time he pleases, or even to destroy us in the presence of our enemies. 16Do not try to bind the purposes of the Lord our God; for God is not like a human being, to be threatened, or like a mere mortal, to be won over by pleading. 17Therefore, while we wait for his deliverance, let us call upon him to help us, and he will hear our voice, if it pleases him.

18 "For never in our generation, nor in these present days, has there been any tribe or family or people or town of ours that worships gods made with hands, as was done in days gone by. 19That was why our ancestors were handed over to the sword and to pillage, and so they suffered a great catastrophe before our enemies. 20But we know

---

a Other ancient authorities add *than to die of thirst*
b Gk *Courage, brothers*   c Other ancient authorities lack *Uzziah and* (see verses 28 and 35)   d Or *above*

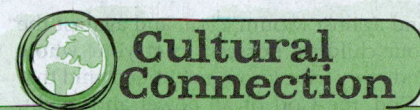

Cultural Connection

The Principle of *Kujichagulia*

That man over there says that women need to be helped into carriages, and lifted over ditches, and to have the best place everywhere. Nobody ever helps me into carriages, or over mud puddles, or gives me any best place! And ain't I a woman? (Sojourner Truth, 1851)

When people who are abused cower quietly in corners, injustice lives on. Bent heads, muffled voices, and terrified spirits invite wrongs to continue.

Judith was a biblical heroine who refused to let her role be determined by others. As a woman and a widow, she had little social standing in ancient Israel. Yet, she did not let this keep her from speaking out and challenging the community leaders to action.

Sojourner Truth was a modern hero who refused to keep quiet despite being mistreated and devalued. Her womanhood was slighted, and her personhood was trampled, yet she traveled America to tell all who would listen about the evils of slavery.

The Kwanzaa principle of *kujichagulia* (see "Kwanzaa as a Way of Life," near Deut 10:12–22), or self-determination, sometimes requires us to stand up and speak out. Silence can be compliance. Thank God for the gift of boldness of speech! It gives us the power to speak the truth even in the most oppressive situations.

Dear God, give me the boldness of Judith and Sojourner Truth to address the wrongs of this world. Amen.

▶ Jdt 8:9–36

no other god but him, and so we hope that he will not disdain us or any of our nation. [21]For if we are captured, all Judea will be captured and our sanctuary will be plundered; and he will make us pay for its desecration with our blood. [22]The slaughter of our kindred and the captivity of the land and the desolation of our inheritance—all this he will bring on our heads among the Gentiles, wherever we serve as slaves; and we shall be an offense and a disgrace in the eyes of those who acquire us. [23]For our slavery will not bring us into favor, but the Lord our God will turn it to dishonor.

24 "Therefore, my brothers, let us set an example for our kindred, for their lives depend upon us, and the sanctuary—both the temple and the altar—rests upon us. [25]In spite of everything let us give thanks to the Lord our God, who is putting us to the test as he did our ancestors. [26]Remember what he did with Abraham, and how he tested Isaac, and what happened to Jacob in Syrian Mesopotamia, while he was tending the sheep of Laban, his mother's brother. [27]For he has not tried us with fire, as he did them, to search their hearts, nor has he taken vengeance on us; but the Lord scourges those who are close to him in order to admonish them."

28 Then Uzziah said to her, "All that you have said was spoken out of a true heart, and there is no one who can deny your words. [29]Today is not the first time your wisdom has been shown, but from the beginning of your life all the people have recognized your understanding, for your heart's disposition is right. [30]But the people were so thirsty that they compelled us to do for them what we have promised, and made us take an oath that we cannot break. [31]Now since you are a God-fearing woman, pray for us, so that the Lord may send us rain to fill our cisterns. Then we will no longer feel faint from thirst."

32 Then Judith said to them, "Listen to me. I am about to do something that will go down through all generations of our descendants. [33]Stand at the town gate tonight so that I may go out with my maid; and within the days after which you have promised to surrender the town to our enemies, the Lord will deliver Israel by my hand. [34]Only, do not try to find out what I am doing, for I will not tell you until I have finished what I am about to do."

35 Uzziah and the rulers said to her, "Go in peace, and may the Lord God go before you, to take vengeance on our enemies." [36]So they returned from the tent and went to their posts.

The Prayer of Judith

9 Then Judith prostrated herself, put ashes on her head, and uncovered the sackcloth she was wearing. At the very time when the evening

JDT

incense was being offered in the house of God in Jerusalem, Judith cried out to the Lord with a loud voice, and said,

2 "O Lord God of my ancestor Simeon, to whom you gave a sword to take revenge on those strangers who had torn off a virgin's clothing[a] to defile her, and exposed her thighs to put her to shame, and polluted her womb to disgrace her; for you said, 'It shall not be done'—yet they did it; [3]so you gave up their rulers to be killed, and their bed, which was ashamed of the deceit they had practiced, was stained with blood, and you struck down slaves along with princes, and princes on their thrones. [4]You gave up their wives for booty and their daughters to captivity, and all their booty to be divided among your beloved children who burned with zeal for you and abhorred the pollution of their blood and called on you for help. O God, my God, hear me also, a widow.

5 "For you have done these things and those that went before and those that followed. You have designed the things that are now, and those that are to come. What you had in mind has happened; [6]the things you decided on presented themselves and said, 'Here we are!' For all your ways are prepared in advance, and your judgment is with foreknowledge.

7 "Here now are the Assyrians, a greatly increased force, priding themselves in their horses and riders, boasting in the strength of their foot soldiers, and trusting in shield and spear, in bow and sling. They do not know that you are the Lord who crushes wars; the Lord is your name. [8]Break their strength by your might, and bring down their power in your anger; for they intend to defile your sanctuary, and to pollute the tabernacle where your glorious name resides, and to break off the horns[b] of your altar with the sword. [9]Look at their pride, and send your wrath upon their heads. Give to me, a widow, the strong hand to do what I plan. [10]By the deceit of my lips strike down the slave with the prince and the prince with his servant; crush their arrogance by the hand of a woman.

11 "For your strength does not depend on numbers, nor your might on the powerful. But you are the God of the lowly, helper of the oppressed, upholder of the weak, protector of the forsaken, savior of those without hope. [12]Please, please, God of my father, God of the heritage of Israel, Lord of heaven and earth, Creator of the waters, King of all your creation, hear my prayer! [13]Make my deceitful words bring wound and bruise on those who have planned cruel things against your covenant, and against your sacred house, and against Mount Zion, and against the house your children possess. [14]Let your whole nation and every tribe know and understand that you are God, the God of all power and might, and that there is no other who protects the people of Israel but you alone!"

Judith Prepares to Go to Holofernes

10 When Judith[c] had stopped crying out to the God of Israel, and had ended all these words, [2]she rose from where she lay prostrate. She called her maid and went down into the house where she lived on sabbaths and on her festal days. [3]She removed the sackcloth she had been wearing, took off her widow's garments, bathed her body with water, and anointed herself with precious ointment. She combed her hair, put on a tiara, and dressed herself in the festive attire that she used to wear while her husband Manasseh was living. [4]She put sandals on her feet, and put on her anklets, bracelets, rings, earrings, and all her other jewelry. Thus she made herself very beautiful, to entice the eyes of all the men who might see her. [5]She gave her maid a skin of wine and a flask of oil, and filled a bag with roasted grain, dried fig cakes, and fine bread;[d] then she wrapped up all her dishes and gave them to her to carry.

6 Then they went out to the town gate of Bethulia and found Uzziah standing there with the elders of the town, Chabris and Charmis. [7]When they saw her transformed in appearance and dressed differently, they were very greatly astounded at her beauty and said to her, [8]"May the God of our ancestors grant you favor and fulfill your plans, so that the people of Israel may glory and Jerusalem may be exalted." She bowed down to God.

9 Then she said to them, "Order the gate of the town to be opened for me so that I may go out and accomplish the things you have just said to me." So they ordered the young men to open the gate for her, as she requested. [10]When they had done this, Judith went out, accompanied by her maid. The men of the town watched her until she had gone down the mountain and passed through the valley, where they lost sight of her.

Judith Is Captured

11 As the women[e] were going straight on through the valley, an Assyrian patrol met her [12]and took her into custody. They asked her, "To what people do you belong, and where are you

---

a Cn: Gk *loosed her womb*   b Syr: Gk *horn*   c Gk *she*
d Other ancient authorities add *and cheese*   e Gk *they*

coming from, and where are you going?" She replied, "I am a daughter of the Hebrews, but I am fleeing from them, for they are about to be handed over to you to be devoured. [13]I am on my way to see Holofernes the commander of your army, to give him a true report; I will show him a way by which he can go and capture all the hill country without losing one of his men, captured or slain."

14 When the men heard her words, and observed her face—she was in their eyes marvelously beautiful—they said to her, [15]"You have saved your life by hurrying down to see our lord. Go at once to his tent; some of us will escort you and hand you over to him. [16]When you stand before him, have no fear in your heart, but tell him what you have just said, and he will treat you well."

17 They chose from their number a hundred men to accompany her and her maid, and they brought them to the tent of Holofernes. [18]There was great excitement in the whole camp, for her arrival was reported from tent to tent. They came and gathered around her as she stood outside the tent of Holofernes, waiting until they told him about her. [19]They marveled at her beauty and admired the Israelites, judging them by her. They said to one another, "Who can despise these people, who have women like this among them? It is not wise to leave one of their men alive, for if we let them go they will be able to beguile the whole world!"

Judith Is Brought before Holofernes

20 Then the guards of Holofernes and all his servants came out and led her into the tent. [21]Holofernes was resting on his bed under a canopy that was woven with purple and gold, emeralds and other precious stones. [22]When they told him of her, he came to the front of the tent, with silver lamps carried before him. [23]When Judith came into the presence of Holofernes[a] and his servants, they all marveled at the beauty of her face. She prostrated herself and did obeisance to him, but his slaves raised her up.

11 Then Holofernes said to her, "Take courage, woman, and do not be afraid in your heart, for I have never hurt anyone who chose to serve Nebuchadnezzar, king of all the earth. [2]Even now, if your people who live in the hill country had not slighted me, I would never have lifted my spear against them. They have brought this on themselves. [3]But now tell me why you have fled from them and have come over to us. In any event, you have come to safety. Take courage! You will live tonight and ever after. [4]No one will hurt you. Rather, all will treat you well, as they do the servants of my lord King Nebuchadnezzar."

Judith Explains Her Presence

5 Judith answered him, "Accept the words of your slave, and let your servant speak in your presence. I will say nothing false to my lord this night. [6]If you follow out the words of your servant, God will accomplish something through you, and my lord will not fail to achieve his purposes. [7]By the life of Nebuchadnezzar, king of the whole earth, and by the power of him who has sent you to direct every living being! Not only do human beings serve him because of you, but also the animals of the field and the cattle and the birds of the air will live, because of your power, under Nebuchadnezzar and all his house. [8]For we have heard of your wisdom and skill, and it is reported throughout the whole world that you alone are the best in the whole kingdom, the most informed and the most astounding in military strategy.

9 "Now as for Achior's speech in your council, we have heard his words, for the people of Bethulia spared him and he told them all he had said to you. [10]Therefore, lord and master, do not disregard what he said, but keep it in your mind, for it is true. Indeed our nation cannot be punished, nor can the sword prevail against them, unless they sin against their God.

11 "But now, in order that my lord may not be defeated and his purpose frustrated, death will fall upon them, for a sin has overtaken them by which they are about to provoke their God to anger when they do what is wrong. [12]Since their food supply is exhausted and their water has almost given out, they have planned to kill their livestock and have determined to use all that God by his laws has forbidden them to eat. [13]They have decided to consume the first fruits of the grain and the tithes of the wine and oil, which they had consecrated and set aside for the priests who minister in the presence of our God in Jerusalem—things it is not lawful for any of the people even to touch with their hands. [14]Since even the people in Jerusalem have been doing this, they have sent messengers there in order to bring back permission from the council of the elders. [15]When the response reaches them and they act upon it, on that very day they will be handed over to you to be destroyed.

16 "So when I, your slave, learned all this, I fled from them. God has sent me to accomplish

---

a Gk him

with you things that will astonish the whole world wherever people shall hear about them. [17] Your servant is indeed God-fearing and serves the God of heaven night and day. So, my lord, I will remain with you; but every night your servant will go out into the valley and pray to God. He will tell me when they have committed their sins. [18] Then I will come and tell you, so that you may go out with your whole army, and not one of them will be able to withstand you. [19] Then I will lead you through Judea, until you come to Jerusalem; there I will set your throne.[a] You will drive them like sheep that have no shepherd, and no dog will so much as growl at you. For this was told me to give me foreknowledge; it was announced to me, and I was sent to tell you."

20 Her words pleased Holofernes and all his servants. They marveled at her wisdom and said, [21] "No other woman from one end of the earth to the other looks so beautiful or speaks so wisely!" [22] Then Holofernes said to her, "God has done well to send you ahead of the people, to strengthen our hands and bring destruction on those who have despised my lord. [23] You are not only beautiful in appearance, but wise in speech. If you do as you have said, your God shall be

Dead Drunk!

Getting drunk is a pretty common way for people to have a good time—young and old. It seems like harmless fun, but we all know that it can lead to some dire consequences. It is very easy to be taken advantage of when you are drunk or passed out. Every year we learn of college students who have died from too much alcohol. And drinking and driving can be deadly.

In the Book of Judith, chapter 13, Judith takes advantage of Holofernes' drunkenness to kill him. She gives the term *dead drunk* a whole new meaning. If you do not believe that getting drunk can destroy your life, think again. It doesn't take a widow with a sword to help drunkenness destroy your life.

▶ **Jdt 12:15—13:10**

my God, and you shall live in the palace of King Nebuchadnezzar and be renowned throughout the whole world."

Judith as a Guest of Holofernes

12 Then he commanded them to bring her in where his silver dinnerware was kept, and ordered them to set a table for her with some of his own delicacies, and with some of his own wine to drink. [2] But Judith said, "I cannot partake of them, or it will be an offense; but I will have enough with the things I brought with me." [3] Holofernes said to her, "If your supply runs out, where can we get you more of the same? For none of your people are here with us." [4] Judith replied, "As surely as you live, my lord, your servant will not use up the supplies I have with me before the Lord carries out by my hand what he has determined."

[5] Then the servants of Holofernes brought her into the tent, and she slept until midnight. Toward the morning watch she got up [6] and sent this message to Holofernes: "Let my lord now give orders to allow your servant to go out and pray." [7] So Holofernes commanded his guards not to hinder her. She remained in the camp three days. She went out each night to the valley of Bethulia, and bathed at the spring in the camp.[b] [8] After bathing, she prayed the Lord God of Israel to direct her way for the triumph of his[c] people. [9] Then she returned purified and stayed in the tent until she ate her food toward evening.

Judith Attends Holofernes' Banquet

[10] On the fourth day Holofernes held a banquet for his personal attendants only, and did not invite any of his officers. [11] He said to Bagoas, the eunuch who had charge of his personal affairs, "Go and persuade the Hebrew woman who is in your care to join us and to eat and drink with us. [12] For it would be a disgrace if we let such a woman go without having intercourse with her. If we do not seduce her, she will laugh at us."

13 So Bagoas left the presence of Holofernes, and approached her and said, "Let this pretty girl not hesitate to come to my lord to be honored in his presence, and to enjoy drinking wine with us, and to become today like one of the Assyrian women who serve in the palace of Nebuchadnezzar." [14] Judith replied, "Who am I to refuse my lord? Whatever pleases him I will do at once, and it will be a joy to me until the day of my

---

a Or *chariot*   b Other ancient authorities lack *in the camp*
c Other ancient authorities read *her*

death." 15So she proceeded to dress herself in all her woman's finery. Her maid went ahead and spread for her on the ground before Holofernes the lambskins she had received from Bagoas for her daily use in reclining.

16 Then Judith came in and lay down. Holofernes' heart was ravished with her and his passion was aroused, for he had been waiting for an opportunity to seduce her from the day he first saw her. 17So Holofernes said to her, "Have a drink and be merry with us!" 18Judith said, "I will gladly drink, my lord, because today is the greatest day in my whole life." 19Then she took what her maid had prepared and ate and drank before him. 20Holofernes was greatly pleased with her, and drank a great quantity of wine, much more than he had ever drunk in any one day since he was born.

Judith Beheads Holofernes

13 When evening came, his slaves quickly withdrew. Bagoas closed the tent from outside and shut out the attendants from his master's presence. They went to bed, for they all were weary because the banquet had lasted so long. 2But Judith was left alone in the tent, with Holofernes stretched out on his bed, for he was dead drunk.

3 Now Judith had told her maid to stand outside the bedchamber and to wait for her to come out, as she did on the other days; for she said she would be going out for her prayers. She had said the same thing to Bagoas. 4So everyone went out, and no one, either small or great, was left in the bedchamber. Then Judith, standing beside his bed, said in her heart, "O Lord God of all might, look in this hour on the work of my hands for the exaltation of Jerusalem. 5Now indeed is the time to help your heritage and to carry out my design to destroy the enemies who have risen up against us."

6 She went up to the bedpost near Holofernes' head, and took down his sword that hung there. 7She came close to his bed, took hold of the hair of his head, and said, "Give me strength today, O Lord God of Israel!" 8Then she struck his neck twice with all her might, and cut off his head. 9Next she rolled his body off the bed and pulled down the canopy from the posts. Soon afterward she went out and gave Holofernes' head to her maid, 10who placed it in her food bag.

Judith Returns to Bethulia

Then the two of them went out together, as they were accustomed to do for prayer. They passed through the camp, circled around the

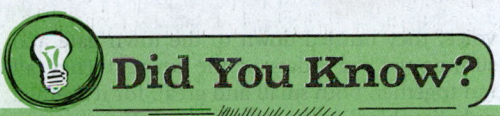

Did You Know?

Is God a Fan of Violence?

Is it hard to believe that God strengthened Judith to cut off Holofernes' head (see Jdt 13:7–8)? or that God was angry at Saul for not destroying Agag and his possessions (see 1 Sam 15:18–19)? or that Jephthah had to sacrifice his daughter because of a vow he had made (see Judg 11:29–40)? The violence portrayed in the Old Testament is often horrifying, especially when the Old Testament authors view it as part of God's will.

In the ancient world, tribes and nations viewed their gods as the leaders of their armies. The Hebrews were no exception. One of God's oldest titles is "LORD God of hosts" (Ps 89:8, Isa 6:3); the image is of an almighty warrior who fought on Israel's side (see Ex 15:3, 1 Sam 14:23). The enemies of Israel were seen as God's enemies, and their destruction as God's will. The military victories of Joshua, Saul, and David were understood as proof of heaven's blessing on the nation.

Later in history, as the Israelites experienced one agonizing defeat after another and the prophets challenged them to consider God's love for all nations, a new understanding of God's will began to develop in certain Jewish circles. Later prophets spoke of beating "swords into plowshares" (Isa 2:4), of making "a covenant of peace" (Ezek 37:26), of seeking "to do justice, and to love kindness, / and to walk humbly with your God" (Mic 6:8). From their own painful history, the Chosen People started to see that war and violence always meant unspeakable suffering for many, and they began to question whether holy war was part of God's will.

▶ **Jdt 13:1–10**

valley, and went up the mountain to Bethulia, and came to its gates. 11From a distance Judith called out to the sentries at the gates, "Open, open the gate! God, our God, is with us, still showing his power in Israel and his strength against our enemies, as he has done today!"

12 When the people of her town heard her

voice, they hurried down to the town gate and summoned the elders of the town. 13They all ran together, both small and great, for it seemed unbelievable that she had returned. They opened the gate and welcomed them. Then they lit a fire to give light, and gathered around them. 14Then she said to them with a loud voice, "Praise God, O praise him! Praise God, who has not withdrawn his mercy from the house of Israel, but has destroyed our enemies by my hand this very night!"

15 Then she pulled the head out of the bag and showed it to them, and said, "See here, the head of Holofernes, the commander of the Assyrian army, and here is the canopy beneath which he lay in his drunken stupor. The Lord has struck him down by the hand of a woman. 16As the Lord lives, who has protected me in the way I went, I swear that it was my face that seduced him to his destruction, and that he committed no sin with me, to defile and shame me."

17 All the people were greatly astonished. They bowed down and worshiped God, and said with one accord, "Blessed are you our God, who have this day humiliated the enemies of your people."

18 Then Uzziah said to her, "O daughter, you are blessed by the Most High God above all other women on earth; and blessed be the Lord God, who created the heavens and the earth, who has guided you to cut off the head of the leader of our enemies. 19Your praise*a* will never depart from the hearts of those who remember the power of God. 20May God grant this to be a perpetual honor to you, and may he reward you with blessings, because you risked your own life when our nation was brought low, and you averted our ruin, walking in the straight path before our God." And all the people said, "Amen. Amen."

Judith's Counsel

14 Then Judith said to them, "Listen to me, my friends. Take this head and hang it upon the parapet of your wall. 2As soon as day breaks and the sun rises on the earth, each of you take up your weapons, and let every able-bodied man go out of the town; set a captain over them, as if you were going down to the plain against the Assyrian outpost; only do not go down. 3Then they will seize their arms and go into the camp and rouse the officers of the Assyrian army. They will rush into the tent of Holofernes and will not find him. Then panic will come over them, and they will flee before you. 4Then you and all who live within the borders of Israel will

pursue them and cut them down in their tracks. 5But before you do all this, bring Achior the Ammonite to me so that he may see and recognize the man who despised the house of Israel and sent him to us as if to his death."

6 So they summoned Achior from the house of Uzziah. When he came and saw the head of Holofernes in the hand of one of the men in the assembly of the people, he fell down on his face in a faint. 7When they raised him up he threw himself at Judith's feet, and did obeisance to her, and said, "Blessed are you in every tent of Judah! In every nation those who hear your name will be alarmed. 8Now tell me what you have done during these days."

So Judith told him in the presence of the people all that she had done, from the day she left until the moment she began speaking to them. 9When she had finished, the people raised a great shout and made a joyful noise in their town. 10When Achior saw all that the God of Israel had done, he believed firmly in God. So he was circumcised, and joined the house of Israel, remaining so to this day.

Holofernes' Death Is Discovered

11 As soon as it was dawn they hung the head of Holofernes on the wall. Then they all took their weapons, and they went out in companies to the mountain passes. 12When the Assyrians saw them they sent word to their commanders, who then went to the generals and the captains and to all their other officers. 13They came to Holofernes' tent and said to the steward in charge of all his personal affairs, "Wake up our lord, for the slaves have been so bold as to come down against us to give battle, to their utter destruction."

14 So Bagoas went in and knocked at the entry of the tent, for he supposed that he was sleeping with Judith. 15But when no one answered, he opened it and went into the bedchamber and found him sprawled on the floor dead, with his head missing. 16He cried out with a loud voice and wept and groaned and shouted, and tore his clothes. 17Then he went to the tent where Judith had stayed, and when he did not find her, he rushed out to the people and shouted, 18"The slaves have tricked us! One Hebrew woman has brought disgrace on the house of King Nebuchadnezzar. Look, Holofernes is lying on the ground, and his head is missing!"

19 When the leaders of the Assyrian army heard this, they tore their tunics and were greatly

---

a Other ancient authorities read *hope*

dismayed, and their loud cries and shouts rose up throughout the camp.

The Assyrians Flee in Panic

15 When the men in the tents heard it, they were amazed at what had happened. ²Overcome with fear and trembling, they did not wait for one another, but with one impulse all rushed out and fled by every path across the plain and through the hill country. ³Those who had camped in the hills around Bethulia also took to flight. Then the Israelites, everyone that was a soldier, rushed out upon them. ⁴Uzziah sent men to Betomasthaim*a* and Choba and Kola, and to all the frontiers of Israel, to tell what had taken place and to urge all to rush out upon the enemy to destroy them. ⁵When the Israelites heard it, with one accord they fell upon the enemy,*b* and cut them down as far as Choba. Those in Jerusalem and all the hill country also came, for they were told what had happened in the camp of the enemy. The men in Gilead and in Galilee outflanked them with great slaughter, even beyond Damascus and its borders. ⁶The rest of the people of Bethulia fell upon the Assyrian camp and plundered it, acquiring great riches. ⁷And the Israelites, when they returned from the slaughter, took possession of what remained. Even the villages and towns in the hill country and in the plain got a great amount of booty, since there was a vast quantity of it.

The Israelites Celebrate Their Victory

8 Then the high priest Joakim and the elders of the Israelites who lived in Jerusalem came to witness the good things that the Lord had done for Israel, and to see Judith and to wish her well. ⁹When they met her, they all blessed her with one accord and said to her, "You are the glory of Jerusalem, you are the great boast of Israel, you are the great pride of our nation! ¹⁰You have done all this with your own hand; you have done great good to Israel, and God is well pleased with it. May the Almighty Lord bless you forever!" And all the people said, "Amen."

11 All the people plundered the camp for thirty days. They gave Judith the tent of Holofernes and all his silver dinnerware, his beds, his bowls, and all his furniture. She took them and loaded her mules and hitched up her carts and piled the things on them.

12 All the women of Israel gathered to see her, and blessed her, and some of them performed a dance in her honor. She took ivy-wreathed wands in her hands and distributed them to the women who were with her; ¹³and she and those who were with her crowned themselves with olive wreaths. She went before all the people in the dance, leading all the women, while all the men of Israel followed, bearing their arms and wearing garlands and singing hymns.

Judith Offers Her Hymn of Praise

14 Judith began this thanksgiving before all Israel, and all the people loudly sang this song **16** of praise. ¹And Judith said,

Begin a song to my God with tambourines,
    sing to my Lord with cymbals.
Raise to him a new psalm;*c*
    exalt him, and call upon his name.
² For the Lord is a God who crushes wars;
    he sets up his camp among his people;
    he delivered me from the hands of my
        pursuers.
³ The Assyrian came down from the mountains of
        the north;
    he came with myriads of his warriors;
  their numbers blocked up the wadis,
    and their cavalry covered the hills.
⁴ He boasted that he would burn up my
        territory,
    and kill my young men with the sword,
  and dash my infants to the ground,
    and seize my children as booty,
    and take my virgins as spoil.

---

a Other ancient authorities add *and Bebai* *b* Gk *them* *c* Other ancient authorities read *a psalm and praise*

Judith Leads the Prayer-Song

In the Book of Judith, chapter 16, Judith sings praises to God and leads the people in a holy celebration after victory over the enemy.

Notice the similarity to Miriam's song (see Exodus, chapter 15), Deborah's song (see Judges, chapter 5), and even Tobit's song (see Tobit, chapter 13).

Singing, dancing, and retelling special stories go hand in hand with praising God. Try singing a favorite religious or spiritual song as your prayer today.

▶ Jdt 16:1–20

5 But the Lord Almighty has foiled them
   by the hand of a woman.ᵃ
6 For their mighty one did not fall by the hands of
   the young men,
      nor did the sons of the Titans strike him
      down,
      nor did tall giants set upon him;
   but Judith daughter of Merari
      with the beauty of her countenance undid
      him.

7 For she put away her widow's clothing
   to exalt the oppressed in Israel.
   She anointed her face with perfume;
8   she fastened her hair with a tiara
      and put on a linen gown to beguile him.
9 Her sandal ravished his eyes,
      her beauty captivated his mind,
      and the sword severed his neck!
10 The Persians trembled at her boldness,
      the Medes were daunted at her daring.

11 Then my oppressed people shouted;
      my weak people cried out,ᵇ and the enemyᶜ
      trembled;
      they lifted up their voices, and the enemyᶜ
      were turned back.
12 Sons of slave-girls pierced them through
      and wounded them like the children of
      fugitives;
      they perished before the army of my Lord.

13 I will sing to my God a new song:
   O Lord, you are great and glorious,
      wonderful in strength, invincible.
14 Let all your creatures serve you,
      for you spoke, and they were made.
   You sent forth your spirit,ᵈ and it formed them;ᵉ
      there is none that can resist your voice.
15 For the mountains shall be shaken to their
      foundations with the waters;
      before your glance the rocks shall melt like
      wax.
   But to those who fear you
      you show mercy.
16 For every sacrifice as a fragrant offering is a
      small thing,

and the fat of all whole burnt offerings to you
      is a very little thing;
   but whoever fears the Lord is great forever.

17 Woe to the nations that rise up against my
      people!
   The Lord Almighty will take vengeance on
      them in the day of judgment;
   he will send fire and worms into their flesh;
      they shall weep in pain forever.

18 When they arrived at Jerusalem, they worshiped God. As soon as the people were purified, they offered their burnt offerings, their freewill offerings, and their gifts. 19Judith also dedicated to God all the possessions of Holofernes, which the people had given her; and the canopy that she had taken for herself from his bedchamber she gave as a votive offering. 20For three months the people continued feasting in Jerusalem before the sanctuary, and Judith remained with them.

The Renown and Death of Judith

21 After this they all returned home to their own inheritances. Judith went to Bethulia, and remained on her estate. For the rest of her life she was honored throughout the whole country. 22Many desired to marry her, but she gave herself to no man all the days of her life after her husband Manasseh died and was gathered to his people. 23She became more and more famous, and grew old in her husband's house, reaching the age of one hundred five. She set her maid free. She died in Bethulia, and they buried her in the cave of her husband Manasseh; 24and the house of Israel mourned her for seven days. Before she died she distributed her property to all those who were next of kin to her husband Manasseh, and to her own nearest kindred. 25No one ever again spread terror among the Israelites during the lifetime of Judith, or for a long time after her death.

---

a Other ancient authorities add he has confounded them
b Other ancient authorities read feared   c Gk they   d Or breath
e Other ancient authorities read they were created

Most of us cannot understand what would possess a group of people to plot the complete destruction of another group of people. Yet, in our own time, ethnic groups have been targeted for extinction through wars, concentration camps, and death squads. The Book of Esther is the story of a genocidal plot against a Jewish population and how Mordecai and his courageous cousin Esther prevented the plot from being carried out.

At a Glance

- Addition A. prologue
- Chapters 1–2. the choice of Esther as queen
- Chapters 3–5,13–15. the plot against the Jews
- 6:1—10:3, chapter 16. the rescue of the Jews
- 10:4–13. epilogue

Quick Facts

Setting: Persia after the Babylonian Exile

Inspired Authors: *Hebrew version.* unknown, probably writing in the late fourth century BC

Greek version. unknown, writing about two centuries later

Themes: God's love for the little ones, the origin of the feast of Purim

Of Note: Catholic Bibles include the Greek version of Esther, inserted as additions A to F.

In Depth

In the five centuries before Jesus, many of the Jewish people who were uprooted from their homeland had to be on the lookout for their safety. Several of the late Old Testament books—Sirach, Tobit, and Daniel—reflect the challenges these emigrant Jews had to face. The story of Queen Esther belongs to this group. Like Joseph in Egypt, Esther rose to a position of power in a foreign government. When a plot was hatched to destroy the Jews, she used her influence with the king of Persia to save her people. Each year, Esther's victory is celebrated in the Jewish feast of Purim (9:18–32)—the feast of little people who have triumphed over larger forces.

Like the Book of Daniel, the Book of Esther has come down to us in two versions: the Hebrew and the Greek. The difference in style between these two versions is obvious:

The shorter Hebrew text is clearly not a historical document and does not even mention God's name. The Greek text, a later reworking of the Hebrew, adds sections to bring out the religious dimension of the story and to make the book appear more historical.

The Hebrew version emphasizes the human actors; the Greek version, the divine Actor. The two versions stress different aspects of the same truth: God is the Savior of the Chosen People (Greek) but works through human beings to achieve that goal (Hebrew).

Despite the confusing numbering, the book reads as a unified story; it's full of action and has a happy ending. What is more, it challenges us to recognize in our hatred of others the seeds of unthinkable destruction.

The Book of Esther

Esther

NOTE: The deuterocanonical portions of the Book of Esther are translated from the Greek version (Septuagint) and comprise one hundred and seven additional verses that have been inserted at the appropriate places in the translation of the Hebrew form of the book. The disordered chapter numbers come from the displacement of the additions to the end of the Hebrew form of the Book of Esther by St. Jerome in his Latin Vulgate translation and from the subsequent division of the Bible into chapters by Stephen Langton, who numbered the additions consecutively as though they formed a direct continuation of the Hebrew text. The deuterocanonical portions are given in the order found in the Greek text so that they may be read in their proper context, but the chapter and verse numbers conform to those of the King James or Authorized Version. Proper names are given according to their Hebrew rather than their Greek form; for example, Ahasuerus and Mordecai instead of Artaxerxes and Mardocheus. The additions, conveniently indicated by the letters A–F, are located as follows: A, before 1.1; B, after 3.13; C and D, after 4.17; E, after 8.12; F, after 10.3.

ADDITION A

Mordecai's Dream

11 *a* [2]In the second year of the reign of Ahasuerus the Great, on the first day of Nisan, Mordecai son of Jair son of Shimei*b* son of Kish, of the tribe of Benjamin, had a dream. [3]He was a Jew living in the city of Susa, a great man, serving in the court of the king. [4]He was one of the captives whom King Nebuchadnezzar of Babylon had brought from Jerusalem with King Jeconiah of Judah. And this was his dream: [5]Noises*c* and confusion, thunders and earthquake, tumult on the earth! [6]Then two great dragons came forward, both ready to fight, and they roared terribly. [7]At their roaring every nation prepared for war, to fight against the righteous nation. [8]It was a day of darkness and gloom, of tribulation and distress, affliction and great tumult on the earth! [9]And the whole righteous nation was troubled; they feared the evils that threatened them,*d* and were ready to perish. [10]Then they cried out to God; and at their outcry, as though from a tiny spring, there came a great river, with abundant water; [11]light came, and the sun rose, and the lowly were exalted and devoured those held in honor.

12 Mordecai saw in this dream what God had determined to do, and after he awoke he had it on his mind, seeking all day to understand it in every detail.

A Plot against the King

12 Now Mordecai took his rest in the courtyard with Bigthan and Teresh, the two

---

a Chapters 11.2–12.6 correspond to chapter A 1-17 in some translations. *b* Gk *Semeios* *c* Or *Voices* *d* Gk *their own evils*

eunuchs of the king who kept watch in the courtyard. ²He overheard their conversation and inquired into their purposes, and learned that they were preparing to lay hands on King Ahasuerus; and he informed the king concerning them. ³Then the king examined the two eunuchs, and after they had confessed it, they were led away to execution. ⁴The king made a permanent record of these things, and Mordecai wrote an account of them. ⁵And the king ordered Mordecai to serve in the court, and rewarded him for these things. ⁶But Haman son of Hammedatha, the Agagite, who was in great honor with the king, determined to injure Mordecai and his people because of the two eunuchs of the king.

END OF ADDITION A

King Ahasuerus Deposes Queen Vashti

1 This happened in the days of Ahasuerus, the same Ahasuerus who ruled over one hundred twenty-seven provinces from India to Ethiopia.ᵃ ²In those days when King Ahasuerus sat on his royal throne in the citadel of Susa, ³in the third year of his reign, he gave a banquet for all his officials and ministers. The army of Persia and Media and the nobles and governors of the provinces were present, ⁴while he displayed the great wealth of his kingdom and the splendor and pomp of his majesty for many days, one hundred eighty days in all.

5 When these days were completed, the king gave for all the people present in the citadel of Susa, both great and small, a banquet lasting for seven days, in the court of the garden of the king's palace. ⁶There were white cotton curtains and blue hangings tied with cords of fine linen and purple to silver ringsᵇ and marble pillars. There were couches of gold and silver on a mosaic pavement of porphyry, marble, mother-of-pearl, and colored stones. ⁷Drinks were served in golden goblets, goblets of different kinds, and the royal wine was lavished according to the bounty of the king. ⁸Drinking was by flagons, without restraint; for the king had given orders to all the officials of his palace to do as each one desired. ⁹Furthermore, Queen Vashti gave a banquet for the women in the palace of King Ahasuerus.

10 On the seventh day, when the king was merry with wine, he commanded Mehuman, Biztha, Harbona, Bigtha and Abagtha, Zethar and Carkas, the seven eunuchs who attended him, ¹¹to bring Queen Vashti before the king, wearing the royal crown, in order to show the peoples

and the officials her beauty; for she was fair to behold. ¹²But Queen Vashti refused to come at the king's command conveyed by the eunuchs. At this the king was enraged, and his anger burned within him.

13 Then the king consulted the sages who knew the lawsᶜ (for this was the king's procedure toward all who were versed in law and custom, ¹⁴and those next to him were Carshena, Shethar, Admatha, Tarshish, Meres, Marsena, and Memucan, the seven officials of Persia and Media, who had access to the king, and sat first in the kingdom): ¹⁵"According to the law, what is to be done to Queen Vashti because she has not performed the command of King Ahasuerus conveyed by the eunuchs?" ¹⁶Then Memucan said in the presence of the king and the officials, "Not only has Queen Vashti done wrong to the king, but also to all the officials and all the peoples who are in all the provinces of King Ahasuerus. ¹⁷For this deed of the queen will be made known to all women, causing them to look with contempt on their husbands, since they will say, 'King Ahasuerus commanded Queen Vashti to be brought before him, and she did not come.' ¹⁸This very day the noble ladies of Persia and Media who have heard of the queen's behavior will rebel againstᵈ the king's officials, and there will be no end of contempt and wrath! ¹⁹If it pleases the king, let a royal order go out from him, and let it be written among the laws of the Persians and the Medes so that it may not be altered, that Vashti is never again to come before King Ahasuerus; and let the king give her royal position to another who is better than she. ²⁰So when the decree made by the king is proclaimed throughout all his kingdom, vast as it is, all women will give honor to their husbands, high and low alike."

21 This advice pleased the king and the officials, and the king did as Memucan proposed; ²²he sent letters to all the royal provinces, to every province in its own script and to every people in its own language, declaring that every man should be master in his own house.ᵉ

Esther Becomes Queen

2 After these things, when the anger of King Ahasuerus had abated, he remembered Vashti and what she had done and what had been decreed against her. ²Then the king's servants who attended him said, "Let beautiful young virgins be sought out for the king. ³And

---

a Or Nubia; Heb Cush   b Or rods   c Cn: Heb times
d Cn: Heb will tell   e Heb adds and speak according to the language of his people

let the king appoint commissioners in all the provinces of his kingdom to gather all the beautiful young virgins to the harem in the citadel of Susa under custody of Hegai, the king's eunuch, who is in charge of the women; let their cosmetic treatments be given them. 4And let the girl who pleases the king be queen instead of Vashti." This pleased the king, and he did so.

5 Now there was a Jew in the citadel of Susa whose name was Mordecai son of Jair son of Shimei son of Kish, a Benjaminite. 6Kish*a* had been carried away from Jerusalem among the captives carried away with King Jeconiah of Judah, whom King Nebuchadnezzar of Babylon had carried away. 7Mordecai*b* had brought up Hadassah, that is Esther, his cousin, for she had neither father nor mother; the girl was fair and beautiful, and when her father and her mother died, Mordecai adopted her as his own daughter. 8So when the king's order and his edict were proclaimed, and when many young women were gathered in the citadel of Susa in custody of Hegai, Esther also was taken into the king's palace and put in custody of Hegai, who had charge of the women. 9The girl pleased him and won his favor, and he quickly provided her with her cosmetic treatments and her portion of food, and with seven chosen maids from the king's palace, and advanced her and her maids to the best place in the harem. 10Esther did not reveal her people or kindred, for Mordecai had charged her not to

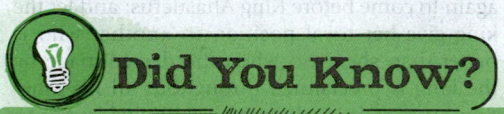

Did You Know?

Diaspora Jews

The story of Esther implies that Mordecai and Esther were members of the Diaspora. The Greek word *diaspora* means "scattered abroad." It refers to the Jews who lived outside of Palestine. When the Babylonians destroyed Jerusalem (587 BC), many of the Jews who were forced to leave the land of Israel decided to settle in various Greco-Roman cities and not return home. They maintained their Jewish identity by adapting the language and customs of their new home into their Jewish traditions. The Diaspora Jews were responsible for the translation of the Hebrew Bible into Greek, a translation called the Septuagint.

tell. 11Every day Mordecai would walk around in front of the court of the harem, to learn how Esther was and how she fared.

12 The turn came for each girl to go in to King Ahasuerus, after being twelve months under the regulations for the women, since this was the regular period of their cosmetic treatment, six months with oil of myrrh and six months with perfumes and cosmetics for women. 13When the girl went in to the king she was given whatever she asked for to take with her from the harem to the king's palace. 14In the evening she went in; then in the morning she came back to the second harem in custody of Shaashgaz, the king's eunuch, who was in charge of the concubines; she did not go in to the king again, unless the king delighted in her and she was summoned by name.

15 When the turn came for Esther daughter of Abihail the uncle of Mordecai, who had adopted her as his own daughter, to go in to the king, she asked for nothing except what Hegai the king's eunuch, who had charge of the women, advised. Now Esther was admired by all who saw her. 16When Esther was taken to King Ahasuerus in his royal palace in the tenth month, which is the month of Tebeth, in the seventh year of his reign, 17the king loved Esther more than all the other women; of all the virgins she won his favor and devotion, so that he set the royal crown on her head and made her queen instead of Vashti. 18Then the king gave a great banquet to all his officials and ministers—"Esther's banquet." He also granted a holiday*c* to the provinces, and gave gifts with royal liberality.

Mordecai Discovers a Plot

19 When the virgins were being gathered together,*d* Mordecai was sitting at the king's gate. 20Now Esther had not revealed her kindred or her people, as Mordecai had charged her; for Esther obeyed Mordecai just as when she was brought up by him. 21In those days, while Mordecai was sitting at the king's gate, Bigthan and Teresh, two of the king's eunuchs, who guarded the threshold, became angry and conspired to assassinate*e* King Ahasuerus. 22But the matter came to the knowledge of Mordecai, and he told it to Queen Esther, and Esther told the king in the name of Mordecai. 23When the affair was investigated and found to be so, both the men were hanged on the gallows. It was recorded in the book of the annals in the presence of the king.

---

a Heb *a Benjaminite* 6*who*   *b* Heb *He*   *c* Or *an amnesty*
d Heb adds *a second time*   *e* Heb *to lay hands on*

Catholic Social Teaching

Body Count

Genocide. Such a frightening word. The complete destruction of a people. This is what Haman plots in the Book of Esther: to destroy all the Jews in the kingdom. Fortunately, he does not succeed.

In our time, we know only too well that the past two centuries have been marked by many attempts to exterminate whole groups of people. The most systematic and ambitious of these attempts was that of Adolf Hitler and the Third Reich. Six million Jews were put to death in Nazi concentration camps, along with four million other "undesirables." Every decade seems to bring new stories of genocide and "ethnic cleansing" somewhere on our planet.

Catholic social teaching calls us to solidarity. That means we cannot avoid the fact that as followers of Christ, we are brothers and sisters with everyone in the world. We are one human family, despite our cultural and ethnic differences. And we must strive to promote peace in a world that often seems dedicated to violence. We need to work for justice, which will lead to a lasting peace. We must always think globally, for we are part of a very large family!

What can you do to promote solidarity in your school, parish, or community?

▶ **Esth 3:1–7**

Solidarity

Haman Undertakes to Destroy the Jews

3 After these things King Ahasuerus promoted Haman son of Hammedatha the Agagite, and advanced him and set his seat above all the officials who were with him. ²And all the king's servants who were at the king's gate bowed down and did obeisance to Haman; for the king had so commanded concerning him. But Mordecai did not bow down or do obeisance. ³Then the king's servants who were at the king's gate said to Mordecai, "Why do you disobey the king's command?" ⁴When they spoke to him day after day and he would not listen to them, they told Haman, in order to see whether Mordecai's words would avail; for he had told them that he was a Jew. ⁵When Haman saw that Mordecai did not bow down or do obeisance to him, Haman was infuriated. ⁶But he thought it beneath him to lay hands on Mordecai alone. So, having been told who Mordecai's people were, Haman plotted to destroy all the Jews, the people of Mordecai, throughout the whole kingdom of Ahasuerus.

7 In the first month, which is the month of Nisan, in the twelfth year of King Ahasuerus, they cast Pur—which means "the lot"—before Haman for the day and for the month, and the lot fell on the thirteenth day*ᵃ* of the twelfth month, which is the month of Adar. ⁸Then Haman said to King Ahasuerus, "There is a certain people scattered and separated among the peoples in all the provinces of your kingdom; their laws are different from those of every other people, and they do not keep the king's laws, so that it is not appropriate for the king to tolerate them. ⁹If it pleases the king, let a decree be issued for their destruction, and I will pay ten thousand talents of silver into the hands of those who have charge of the king's business, so that they may put it into the king's treasuries." ¹⁰So the king took his signet ring from his hand and gave it to Haman son of Hammedatha the Agagite, the enemy of the Jews. ¹¹The king said to Haman, "The money is given to you, and the people as well, to do with them as it seems good to you."

12 Then the king's secretaries were summoned on the thirteenth day of the first month, and an edict, according to all that Haman commanded, was written to the king's satraps and to the governors over all the provinces and to the officials of all the peoples, to every province in its own script and every people in its own language; it was written in the name of King Ahasuerus and sealed with the king's ring. ¹³Letters were sent by couriers to all the king's provinces, giving orders to destroy, to kill, and to annihilate all Jews, young and old, women and children, in one day, the thirteenth day of the twelfth month, which is the month of Adar, and to plunder their goods.

---

a Cn Compare Gk and verse 13 below: Heb *the twelfth month*

ADDITION B

The King's Letter

13 [a] This is a copy of the letter: "The Great King, Ahasuerus, writes the following to the governors of the hundred twenty-seven provinces from India to Ethiopia and to the officials under them:

2 "Having become ruler of many nations and master of the whole world (not elated with presumption of authority but always acting reasonably and with kindness), I have determined to settle the lives of my subjects in lasting tranquility and, in order to make my kingdom peaceable and open to travel throughout all its extent, to restore the peace desired by all people.

3 "When I asked my counselors how this might be accomplished, Haman—who excels among us in sound judgment, and is distinguished for his unchanging goodwill and steadfast fidelity, and has attained the second place in the kingdom— [4]pointed out to us that among all the nations in the world there is scattered a certain hostile people, who have laws contrary to those of every nation and continually disregard the ordinances of kings, so that the unifying of the kingdom that we honorably intend cannot be brought about. [5]We understand that this people, and it alone, stands constantly in opposition to every nation, perversely following a strange manner of life and laws, and is ill-disposed to our government, doing all the harm they can so that our kingdom may not attain stability.

6 "Therefore we have decreed that those indicated to you in the letters written by Haman, who is in charge of affairs and is our second father, shall all—wives and children included—be utterly destroyed by the swords of their enemies, without pity or restraint, on the fourteenth day of the twelfth month, Adar, of this present year, [7]so that those who have long been hostile and remain so may in a single day go down in violence to Hades, and leave our government completely secure and untroubled hereafter."

END OF ADDITION B

3 [14]A copy of the document was to be issued as a decree in every province by proclamation, calling on all the peoples to be ready for that day. [15]The couriers went quickly by order of the king, and the decree was issued in the citadel of Susa. The king and Haman sat down to drink; but the city of Susa was thrown into confusion.

Esther Agrees to Help the Jews

4 When Mordecai learned all that had been done, Mordecai tore his clothes and put on sackcloth and ashes, and went through the city, wailing with a loud and bitter cry; [2]he went up to the entrance of the king's gate, for no one might enter the king's gate clothed with sackcloth. [3]In every province, wherever the king's command and his decree came, there was great mourning among the Jews, with fasting and weeping and lamenting, and most of them lay in sackcloth and ashes.

4 When Esther's maids and her eunuchs came and told her, the queen was deeply distressed; she sent garments to clothe Mordecai, so that he might take off his sackcloth; but he would not accept them. [5]Then Esther called for Hathach, one of the king's eunuchs, who had been appointed to attend her, and ordered him to go to Mordecai to learn what was happening and why. [6]Hathach went out to Mordecai in the open square of the city in front of the king's gate, [7]and Mordecai told him all that had happened to him, and the exact sum of money that Haman had promised to pay into the king's treasuries for the destruction of the Jews. [8]Mordecai also gave him a copy of the written decree issued in Susa for their destruction, that he might show it to Esther, explain it to her, and charge her to go to the king to make supplication to him and entreat him for her people.

9 Hathach went and told Esther what Mordecai had said. [10]Then Esther spoke to Hathach and gave him a message for Mordecai, saying, [11]"All the king's servants and the people of the king's provinces know that if any man or woman goes to the king inside the inner court without being called, there is but one law—all alike are to be put to death. Only if the king holds out the golden scepter to someone, may that person live. I myself have not been called to come in to the king for thirty days." [12]When they told Mordecai what Esther had said, [13]Mordecai told them to reply to Esther, "Do not think that in the king's palace you will escape any more than all the other Jews. [14]For if you keep silence at such a time as this, relief and deliverance will rise for the Jews from another quarter, but you and your father's family will perish. Who knows? Perhaps you have come to royal dignity for just such a time as this." [15]Then Esther said in reply to Mordecai, [16]"Go, gather all the Jews to be found in

---

a Chapter 13.1-7 corresponds to chapter B 1-7 in some translations.

Susa, and hold a fast on my behalf, and neither eat nor drink for three days, night or day. I and my maids will also fast as you do. After that I will go to the king, though it is against the law; and if I perish, I perish." [17]Mordecai then went away and did everything as Esther had ordered him.

ADDITION C

Mordecai's Prayer

13 [8a] Then Mordecai[b] prayed to the Lord, calling to remembrance all the works of the Lord.

9 He said, "O Lord, Lord, you rule as King over all things, for the universe is in your power and there is no one who can oppose you when it is your will to save Israel, [10]for you have made heaven and earth and every wonderful thing under heaven. [11]You are Lord of all, and there is no one who can resist you, the Lord. [12]You know all things; you know, O Lord, that it was not in insolence or pride or for any love of glory that I did this, and refused to bow down to this proud Haman; [13]for I would have been willing to kiss the soles of his feet to save Israel! [14]But I did this so that I might not set human glory above the glory of God, and I will not bow down to anyone but you, who are my Lord; and I will not do these things in pride. [15]And now, O Lord God and King, God of Abraham, spare your people; for the eyes of our foes are upon us[c] to annihilate us, and they desire to destroy the inheritance that has been yours from the beginning. [16]Do not neglect your portion, which you redeemed for yourself out of the land of Egypt. [17]Hear my prayer, and have mercy upon your inheritance; turn our mourning into feasting that we may live and sing praise to your name, O Lord; do not destroy the lips[d] of those who praise you."

18 And all Israel cried out mightily, for their death was before their eyes.

Esther's Prayer

14 Then Queen Esther, seized with deadly anxiety, fled to the Lord. [2]She took off her splendid apparel and put on the garments of distress and mourning, and instead of costly perfumes she covered her head with ashes and dung, and she utterly humbled her body; every part that she loved to adorn she covered with her tangled hair. [3]She prayed to the Lord God of Israel, and said: "O my Lord, you only are our king; help me, who am alone and have no helper but you, [4]for my danger is in my hand.

Did You Know?

The Silent Women of the Bible

"**M**ordecai then went away and did everything as Esther had ordered him" (Esth 4:17). What a surprise: to hear of a man in the ancient world taking orders from a woman! As a fictional character, Esther, like Judith, has an exceptional role in the Old Testament. However, many women who appear in stories that have an historical core are not even named: Jephthah's daughter and Samson's mother, for instance. Even the Hebrew women whose names have become famous—Sarah, Rebekah, Rachel, Miriam, Bathsheba—played second fiddle to their more famous husbands or brothers. They depended on indirect influence or trickery to get what they wanted.

In the biblical world, a woman was defined by her relationships with men. Before marriage she belonged to her father's household and had no status outside of it. Once married, a woman left her father's family and joined the family of her husband. If her husband died, she remained in the new family, rearing children for her deceased spouse or, if childless, marrying a brother-in-law. Although many women undoubtedly lived happily under this system, many others just as surely suffered abuse or felt oppressed. The stories of Lot's daughters (see Gen 19:8) and the woman of Gibeah (see Judg 19:24–30) testify to this horrifying truth.

A system of scriptural interpretation that was developed during recent decades attempts to give voice to the many silent, forgotten, abused women of the Bible. More and more biblical scholars reread the familiar stories, searching for quiet messages that have long been overlooked. All of us—males and females alike—can benefit from this effort to listen to the voices of these women who have been silenced for so many centuries.

▶ Esth 4:15–17

---

a Chapters 13.8–15.16 correspond to chapters C 1-30 and D 1-16 in some translations.   b Gk he   c Gk for they are eying us   d Gk mouth

5 Ever since I was born I have heard in the tribe of my family that you, O Lord, took Israel out of all the nations, and our ancestors from among all their forebears, for an everlasting inheritance, and that you did for them all that you promised. 6 And now we have sinned before you, and you have handed us over to our enemies 7 because we glorified their gods. You are righteous, O Lord! 8 And now they are not satisfied that we are in bitter slavery, but they have covenanted with their idols 9 to abolish what your mouth has ordained, and to destroy your inheritance, to stop the mouths of those who praise you and to quench your altar and the glory of your house, 10 to open the mouths of the nations for the praise of vain idols, and to magnify forever a mortal king.

11 "O Lord, do not surrender your scepter to what has no being; and do not let them laugh at our downfall; but turn their plan against them, and make an example of him who began this against us. 12 Remember, O Lord; make yourself known in this time of our affliction, and give me courage, O King of the gods and Master of all dominion! 13 Put eloquent speech in my mouth before the lion, and turn his heart to hate the man who is fighting against us, so that there may be an end of him and those who agree with him. 14 But save us by your hand, and help me, who am alone and have no helper but you, O Lord. 15 You have knowledge of all things, and you know that I hate the splendor of the wicked and abhor the bed of the uncircumcised and of any alien. 16 You know my necessity—that I abhor the sign of my proud position, which is upon my head on days when I appear in public. I abhor it like a filthy rag, and I do not wear it on the days when I am at leisure. 17 And your servant has not eaten at Haman's table, and I have not honored the king's feast or drunk the wine of libations. 18 Your servant has had no joy since the day that I was brought here until now, except in you, O Lord God of Abraham. 19 O God, whose might is over all, hear the voice of the despairing, and save us from the hands of evildoers. And save me from my fear!"

END OF ADDITION C

ADDITION D

Esther Is Received by the King

15 On the third day, when she ended her prayer, she took off the garments in which she had worshiped, and arrayed herself in splendid attire. 2 Then, majestically adorned, after invoking the aid of the all-seeing God and Savior, she took two maids with her; 3 on one she leaned gently for support, 4 while the other followed, carrying her train. 5 She was radiant with perfect beauty, and she looked happy, as if beloved, but her heart was frozen with fear. 6 When she had gone through all the doors, she stood before the king. He was seated on his royal throne, clothed in the full array of his majesty, all covered with gold and precious stones. He was most terrifying.

7 Lifting his face, flushed with splendor, he looked at her in fierce anger. The queen faltered, and turned pale and faint, and collapsed on the head of the maid who went in front of her. 8 Then God changed the spirit of the king to gentleness, and in alarm he sprang from his throne and took her in his arms until she came to herself. He comforted her with soothing words, and said to her, 9 "What is it, Esther? I am your husband.[a] Take courage; 10 You shall not die, for our law applies only to our subjects.[b] Come near."

11 Then he raised the golden scepter and touched her neck with it; 12 he embraced her, and said, "Speak to me." 13 She said to him, "I saw you, my lord, like an angel of God, and my heart was shaken with fear at your glory. 14 For you are wonderful, my lord, and your countenance is full of grace." 15 And while she was speaking, she fainted and fell. 16 Then the king was agitated, and all his servants tried to comfort her.

END OF ADDITION D

Esther's Banquet

5[c] 3 The king said to her, "What is it, Queen Esther? What is your request? It shall be given you, even to the half of my kingdom." 4 Then Esther said, "If it pleases the king, let the king and Haman come today to a banquet that I have prepared for the king." 5 Then the king said, "Bring Haman quickly, so that we may do as Esther desires." So the king and Haman came to the banquet that Esther had prepared. 6 While they were drinking wine, the king said to Esther, "What is your petition? It shall be granted you. And what is your request? Even to the half of my kingdom, it shall be fulfilled." 7 Then Esther said, "This is my petition and request: 8 If I have won the king's favor, and if it pleases the king to grant my petition and fulfill my request, let the king and Haman come tomorrow to the banquet that I will prepare for them, and then I will do as the king has said."

a Gk brother   b Meaning of Gk uncertain   c In Greek, Chapter D replaces verses 1 and 2 in Hebrew.

Haman Plans to Have Mordecai Hanged

9 Haman went out that day happy and in good spirits. But when Haman saw Mordecai in the king's gate, and observed that he neither rose nor trembled before him, he was infuriated with Mordecai; [10]nevertheless Haman restrained himself and went home. Then he sent and called for his friends and his wife Zeresh, [11]and Haman recounted to them the splendor of his riches, the number of his sons, all the promotions with which the king had honored him, and how he had advanced him above the officials and the ministers of the king. [12]Haman added, "Even Queen Esther let no one but myself come with the king to the banquet that she prepared. Tomorrow also I am invited by her, together with the king. [13]Yet all this does me no good so long as I see the Jew Mordecai sitting at the king's gate." [14]Then his wife Zeresh and all his friends said to him, "Let a gallows fifty cubits high be made, and in the morning tell the king to have Mordecai hanged on it; then go with the king to the banquet in good spirits." This advice pleased Haman, and he had the gallows made.

The King Honors Mordecai

6 On that night the king could not sleep, and he gave orders to bring the book of records, the annals, and they were read to the king. [2]It was found written how Mordecai had told about Bigthana and Teresh, two of the king's eunuchs, who guarded the threshold, and who had conspired to assassinate[a] King Ahasuerus. [3]Then the king said, "What honor or distinction has been bestowed on Mordecai for this?" The king's servants who attended him said, "Nothing has been done for him." [4]The king said, "Who is in the court?" Now Haman had just entered the outer court of the king's palace to speak to the king about having Mordecai hanged on the gallows that he had prepared for him. [5]So the king's servants told him, "Haman is there, standing in the court." The king said, "Let him come in." [6]So Haman came in, and the king said to him, "What shall be done for the man whom the king wishes to honor?" Haman said to himself, "Whom would the king wish to honor more than me?" [7]So Haman said to the king, "For the man whom the king wishes to honor, [8]let royal robes be brought, which the king has worn, and a horse that the king has ridden, with a royal crown on its head. [9]Let the robes and the horse be handed over to one of the king's most noble officials; let him[b] robe the man whom the king wishes to honor, and let him[b] conduct the man on

horseback through the open square of the city, proclaiming before him: 'Thus shall it be done for the man whom the king wishes to honor.' " [10]Then the king said to Haman, "Quickly, take the robes and the horse, as you have said, and do so to the Jew Mordecai who sits at the king's gate. Leave out nothing that you have mentioned." [11]So Haman took the robes and the horse and robed Mordecai and led him riding through the open square of the city, proclaiming, "Thus shall it be done for the man whom the king wishes to honor."

12 Then Mordecai returned to the king's gate, but Haman hurried to his house, mourning and with his head covered. [13]When Haman told his wife Zeresh and all his friends everything that had happened to him, his advisers and his wife Zeresh said to him, "If Mordecai, before whom your downfall has begun, is of the Jewish people, you will not prevail against him, but will surely fall before him."

Haman's Downfall and Mordecai's Advancement

14 While they were still talking with him, the king's eunuchs arrived and hurried Haman off to

7 the banquet that Esther had prepared. [1]So the king and Haman went in to feast with Queen Esther. [2]On the second day, as they were drinking wine, the king again said to Esther, "What is your petition, Queen Esther? It shall be granted you. And what is your request? Even to the half of my kingdom, it shall be fulfilled." [3]Then Queen Esther answered, "If I have won your favor, O king, and if it pleases the king, let my life be given me—that is my petition—and the lives of my people—that is my request. [4]For we have been sold, I and my people, to be destroyed, to be killed, and to be annihilated. If we had been sold merely as slaves, men and women, I would have held my peace; but no enemy can compensate for this damage to the king."[c] [5]Then King Ahasuerus said to Queen Esther, "Who is he, and where is he, who has presumed to do this?" [6]Esther said, "A foe and enemy, this wicked Haman!" Then Haman was terrified before the king and the queen. [7]The king rose from the feast in wrath and went into the palace garden, but Haman stayed to beg his life from Queen Esther, for he saw that the king had determined to destroy him. [8]When the king returned from the palace garden to the banquet hall, Haman had thrown himself on the couch where Esther

a Heb to lay hands on   b Heb them   c Meaning of Heb uncertain

ESTH

was reclining; and the king said, "Will he even assault the queen in my presence, in my own house?" As the words left the mouth of the king, they covered Haman's face. [9]Then Harbona, one of the eunuchs in attendance on the king, said, "Look, the very gallows that Haman has prepared for Mordecai, whose word saved the king, stands at Haman's house, fifty cubits high." And the king said, "Hang him on that." [10]So they hanged Haman on the gallows that he had prepared for Mordecai. Then the anger of the king abated.

Esther Saves the Jews

8 On that day King Ahasuerus gave to Queen Esther the house of Haman, the enemy of the Jews; and Mordecai came before the king, for Esther had told what he was to her. [2]Then the king took off his signet ring, which he had taken from Haman, and gave it to Mordecai. So Esther set Mordecai over the house of Haman.

3 Then Esther spoke again to the king; she fell at his feet, weeping and pleading with him to avert the evil design of Haman the Agagite and the plot that he had devised against the Jews. [4]The king held out the golden scepter to Esther, [5]and Esther rose and stood before the king. She said, "If it pleases the king, and if I have won his favor, and if the thing seems right before the king, and I have his approval, let an order be written to revoke the letters devised by Haman son of Hammedatha the Agagite, which he wrote giving orders to destroy the Jews who are in all the provinces of the king. [6]For how can I bear to see the calamity that is coming on my people? Or how can I bear to see the destruction of my kindred?" [7]Then King Ahasuerus said to Queen Esther and to the Jew Mordecai, "See, I have given Esther the house of Haman, and they have hanged him on the gallows, because he plotted to lay hands on the Jews. [8]You may write as you please with regard to the Jews, in the name of the king, and seal it with the king's ring; for an edict written in the name of the king and sealed with the king's ring cannot be revoked."

9 The king's secretaries were summoned at that time, in the third month, which is the month of Sivan, on the twenty-third day; and an edict was written, according to all that Mordecai commanded, to the Jews and to the satraps and the governors and the officials of the provinces from India to Ethiopia,[a] one hundred twenty-seven provinces, to every province in its own script and to every people in its own language, and also to the Jews in their script and their language. [10]He wrote letters in the name of King Ahasuerus, sealed them with the king's ring, and sent them by mounted couriers riding on fast steeds bred from the royal herd.[b] [11]By these letters the king allowed the Jews who were in every city to assemble and defend their lives, to destroy, to kill, and to annihilate any armed force of any people or province that might attack them, with their children and women, and to plunder their goods [12]on a single day throughout all the provinces of King Ahasuerus, on the thirteenth day of the twelfth month, which is the month of Adar.

ADDITION E

The Decree of Ahasuerus

16 [c]The following is a copy of this letter:
"The Great King, Ahasuerus, to the governors of the provinces from India to Ethiopia, one hundred twenty-seven provinces, and to those who are loyal to our government, greetings.

2 "Many people, the more they are honored with the most generous kindness of their benefactors, the more proud do they become, [3]and not only seek to injure our subjects, but in their inability to stand prosperity, they even undertake to scheme against their own benefactors. [4]They not only take away thankfulness from others, but, carried away by the boasts of those who know nothing of goodness, they even assume that they will escape the evil-hating justice of God, who always sees everything. [5]And often many of those who are set in places of authority have been made in part responsible for the shedding of innocent blood, and have been involved in irremediable calamities, by the persuasion of friends who have been entrusted with the administration of public affairs, [6]when these persons by the false trickery of their evil natures beguile the sincere goodwill of their sovereigns.

7 "What has been wickedly accomplished through the pestilent behavior of those who exercise authority unworthily can be seen, not so much from the more ancient records that we hand on, as from investigation of matters close at hand.[d] [8]In the future we will take care to render our kingdom quiet and peaceable for all, [9]by changing our methods and always judging what comes before our eyes with more equitable consideration. [10]For Haman son of Hammedatha, a Macedonian (really an alien to the Persian blood, and quite devoid of our kindliness), having

---

a Or Nubia; Heb Cush   b Meaning of Heb uncertain   c Chapter 16.1-24 corresponds to chapter E 1-24 in some translations.
d Gk matters beside (your) feet

become our guest, ¹¹enjoyed so fully the goodwill that we have for every nation that he was called our father and was continually bowed down to by all as the person second to the royal throne. ¹²But, unable to restrain his arrogance, he undertook to deprive us of our kingdom and our life,ᵃ ¹³and with intricate craft and deceit asked for the destruction of Mordecai, our savior and perpetual benefactor, and of Esther, the blameless partner of our kingdom, together with their whole nation. ¹⁴He thought that by these methods he would catch us undefended and would transfer the kingdom of the Persians to the Macedonians.

15 "But we find that the Jews, who were consigned to annihilation by this thrice-accursed man, are not evildoers, but are governed by most righteous laws ¹⁶and are children of the living God, most high, most mighty,ᵇ who has directed the kingdom both for us and for our ancestors in the most excellent order.

17 "You will therefore do well not to put in execution the letters sent by Haman son of Hammedatha, ¹⁸since he, the one who did these things, has been hanged at the gate of Susa with all his household—for God, who rules over all things, has speedily inflicted on him the punishment that he deserved.

19 "Therefore post a copy of this letter publicly in every place, and permit the Jews to live under their own laws. ²⁰And give them reinforcements, so that on the thirteenth day of the twelfth month, Adar, on that very day, they may defend themselves against those who attack them at the time of oppression. ²¹For God, who rules over all things, has made this day to be a joy for his chosen people instead of a day of destruction for them.

22 "Therefore you shall observe this with all good cheer as a notable day among your commemorative festivals, ²³so that both now and hereafter it may represent deliverance for youᶜ and the loyal Persians, but that it may be a reminder of destruction for those who plot against us.

24 "Every city and country, without exception, that does not act accordingly shall be destroyed in wrath with spear and fire. It shall be made not only impassable for human beings, but also most hateful to wild animals and birds for all time.

END OF ADDITION E

---

8 ¹³A copy of the writ was to be issued as a decree in every province and published to all peoples, and the Jews were to be ready on that

day to take revenge on their enemies. ¹⁴So the couriers, mounted on their swift royal steeds, hurried out, urged by the king's command. The decree was issued in the citadel of Susa.

15 Then Mordecai went out from the presence of the king, wearing royal robes of blue and white, with a great golden crown and a mantle of fine linen and purple, while the city of Susa shouted and rejoiced. ¹⁶For the Jews there was light and gladness, joy and honor. ¹⁷In every province and in every city, wherever the king's command and his edict came, there was gladness and joy among the Jews, a festival and a holiday. Furthermore, many of the peoples of the country professed to be Jews, because the fear of the Jews had fallen upon them.

Destruction of the Enemies of the Jews

9 Now in the twelfth month, which is the month of Adar, on the thirteenth day, when the king's command and edict were about to be executed, on the very day when the enemies of the Jews hoped to gain power over them, but which had been changed to a day when the Jews would gain power over their foes, ²the Jews gathered in their cities throughout all the provinces of King Ahasuerus to lay hands on those who had sought their ruin; and no one could withstand them, because the fear of them had fallen upon all peoples. ³All the officials of the provinces, the satraps and the governors, and the royal officials were supporting the Jews, because the fear of Mordecai had fallen upon them. ⁴For Mordecai was powerful in the king's house, and his fame spread throughout all the provinces as the man Mordecai grew more and more powerful. ⁵So the Jews struck down all their enemies with the sword, slaughtering, and destroying them, and did as they pleased to those who hated them. ⁶In the citadel of Susa the Jews killed and destroyed five hundred people. ⁷They killed Parshandatha, Dalphon, Aspatha, ⁸Poratha, Adalia, Aridatha, ⁹Parmashta, Arisai, Aridai, Vaizatha, ¹⁰the ten sons of Haman son of Hammedatha, the enemy of the Jews; but they did not touch the plunder.

11 That very day the number of those killed in the citadel of Susa was reported to the king. ¹²The king said to Queen Esther, "In the citadel of Susa the Jews have killed five hundred people and also the ten sons of Haman. What have they done in the rest of the king's provinces? Now what is your petition? It shall be granted you. And what further is your request? It shall be

---

ᵃ Gk *our spirit*   ᵇ Gk *greatest*   ᶜ Other ancient authorities read *for us*

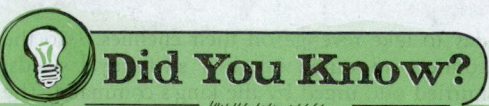

Did You Know?

Purim

The feast of Purim ("lots" in Hebrew) is a minor festival in the Jewish calendar. Purim is celebrated in late winter and is marked by the retelling of the legendary victory of Queen Esther and Mordecai, the exchange of gifts, and the sharing of meals.

▶ **Esth 9:20–32**

fulfilled." ¹³Esther said, "If it pleases the king, let the Jews who are in Susa be allowed tomorrow also to do according to this day's edict, and let the ten sons of Haman be hanged on the gallows." ¹⁴So the king commanded this to be done; a decree was issued in Susa, and the ten sons of Haman were hanged. ¹⁵The Jews who were in Susa gathered also on the fourteenth day of the month of Adar and they killed three hundred persons in Susa; but they did not touch the plunder.

16 Now the other Jews who were in the king's provinces also gathered to defend their lives, and gained relief from their enemies, and killed seventy-five thousand of those who hated them; but they laid no hands on the plunder. ¹⁷This was on the thirteenth day of the month of Adar, and on the fourteenth day they rested and made that a day of feasting and gladness.

The Feast of Purim Inaugurated

18 But the Jews who were in Susa gathered on the thirteenth day and on the fourteenth, and rested on the fifteenth day, making that a day of feasting and gladness. ¹⁹Therefore the Jews of the villages, who live in the open towns, hold the fourteenth day of the month of Adar as a day for gladness and feasting, a holiday on which they send gifts of food to one another.

20 Mordecai recorded these things, and sent letters to all the Jews who were in all the provinces of King Ahasuerus, both near and far, ²¹enjoining them that they should keep the fourteenth day of the month Adar and also the fifteenth day of the same month, year by year, ²²as the days on which the Jews gained relief from their enemies, and as the month that had been turned for them from sorrow into gladness

and from mourning into a holiday; that they should make them days of feasting and gladness, days for sending gifts of food to one another and presents to the poor. ²³So the Jews adopted as a custom what they had begun to do, as Mordecai had written to them.

24 Haman son of Hammedatha the Agagite, the enemy of all the Jews, had plotted against the Jews to destroy them, and had cast Pur—that is "the lot"—to crush and destroy them; ²⁵but when Esther came before the king, he gave orders in writing that the wicked plot that he had devised against the Jews should come upon his own head, and that he and his sons should be hanged on the gallows. ²⁶Therefore these days are called Purim, from the word Pur. Thus because of all that was written in this letter, and of what they had faced in this matter, and of what had happened to them, ²⁷the Jews established and accepted as a custom for themselves and their descendants and all who joined them, that without fail they would continue to observe these two days every year, as it was written and at the time appointed. ²⁸These days should be remembered and kept throughout every generation, in every family, province, and city; and these days of Purim should never fall into disuse among the Jews, nor should the commemoration of these days cease among their descendants.

29 Queen Esther daughter of Abihail, along with the Jew Mordecai, gave full written authority, confirming this second letter about Purim. ³⁰Letters were sent wishing peace and security to all the Jews, to the one hundred twenty-seven provinces of the kingdom of Ahasuerus, ³¹and giving orders that these days of Purim should be observed at their appointed seasons, as the Jew Mordecai and Queen Esther enjoined on the Jews, just as they had laid down for themselves and for their descendants regulations concerning their fasts and their lamentations. ³²The command of Queen Esther fixed these practices of Purim, and it was recorded in writing.

10 King Ahasuerus laid tribute on the land and on the islands of the sea. ²All the acts of his power and might, and the full account of the high honor of Mordecai, to which the king advanced him, are they not written in the annals of the kings of Media and Persia? ³For Mordecai the Jew was next in rank to King Ahasuerus, and he was powerful among the Jews and popular with his many kindred, for he sought the good of his people and interceded for the welfare of all his descendants.

Mordecai's Dream Fulfilled

4[a] And Mordecai said, "These things have come from God; [5]for I remember the dream that I had concerning these matters, and none of them has failed to be fulfilled. [6]There was the little spring that became a river, and there was light and sun and abundant water—the river is Esther, whom the king married and made queen. [7]The two dragons are Haman and myself. [8]The nations are those that gathered to destroy the name of the Jews. [9]And my nation, this is Israel, who cried out to God and was saved. The Lord has saved his people; the Lord has rescued us from all these evils; God has done great signs and wonders, wonders that have never happened among the nations. [10]For this purpose he made two lots, one for the people of God and one for all the nations, [11]and these two lots came to the hour and moment and day of decision before God and among all the nations. [12]And God remembered his people and vindicated his inheritance. [13]So they will observe these days in the month of Adar, on the fourteenth and fifteenth[b] of that month, with an assembly and joy and gladness before God, from generation to generation forever among his people Israel."

Postscript

11 [1]In the fourth year of the reign of Ptolemy and Cleopatra, Dositheus, who said that he was a priest and a Levite,[c] and his son Ptolemy brought to Egypt[d] the preceding Letter about Purim, which they said was authentic and had been translated by Lysimachus son of Ptolemy, one of the residents of Jerusalem.

a Chapter 10.4-13 and 11.1 correspond to chapter F 1-11 in some translations.　b Other ancient authorities lack *and fifteenth*　c Or *priest, and Levitas*　d Cn: Gk *brought in*

Have you ever listened as two fighting siblings tell their parents about a conflict? Usually, each child blames the other one and protests his or her complete innocence. Sometimes you have to wonder if they are even talking about the same fight. In a similar way, the author of First Maccabees, reporting on the Jewish resistance to the persecution of their pagan rulers, tells one version of the story. This book defends the violent resistance of one family, while Second Maccabees has a broader perspective in telling of other forms of Jewish resistance.

At a Glance

- Chapters 1–2. the revolt of the Jews
- 3:1—9:22. the leadership of Judas Maccabeus
- 9:23—16:24. the leadership of Judas's brothers Jonathan and Simon

Quick Facts

Period Covered: from 175 to 134 BC
Inspired Author: unknown, writing around 100 BC
Theme: God brings Israel to freedom through the family of Mattathias.
Of Note: First Maccabees is not found in some Protestant Bibles (see "The Case of the Missing Books," near Tob 1:16).

In Depth

The writer of First Maccabees has a clear purpose in mind: to defend the family of Mattathias, whose sons—the Maccabees—held positions of authority in the Jewish community. The most famous of them, Judas Maccabeus, led the Jews in a successful revolt (167–164 BC) against the Greek persecution—an incredible feat given the military might of the Greeks. After Judas's death, his brothers and nephews held positions of power, and Israel remained free from foreign domination for the next hundred years.

For traditional Jews, the power of the Maccabees posed a problem: Because Mattathias's bloodline could be traced to neither King David nor Aaron the priest, by what right had his descendants assumed kingly and priestly authority? Against such criticism, the author of First Maccabees tries to prove that God's plan was accomplished through Mattathias's family.

The interpretation of Jewish history contained in First Maccabees invites us to believe in God's choice of Mattathias's sons as saviors of the nation. Even more important, it invites us to believe in the utter reliability of God: "And so observe, from generation to generation, that none of those who put their trust in him will lack strength" (2:61).

1 Maccabees

Alexander the Great

1 After Alexander son of Philip, the Macedonian, who came from the land of Kittim, had defeated[a] King Darius of the Persians and the Medes, he succeeded him as king. (He had previously become king of Greece.) ²He fought many battles, conquered strongholds, and put to death the kings of the earth. ³He advanced to the ends of the earth, and plundered many nations. When the earth became quiet before him, he was exalted, and his heart was lifted up. ⁴He gathered a very strong army and ruled over countries, nations, and princes, and they became tributary to him.

5 After this he fell sick and perceived that he was dying. ⁶So he summoned his most honored officers, who had been brought up with him from youth, and divided his kingdom among them while he was still alive. ⁷And after Alexander had reigned twelve years, he died.

8 Then his officers began to rule, each in his own place. ⁹They all put on crowns after his death, and so did their descendants after them for many years, and they caused many evils on the earth.

Antiochus Epiphanes and Renegade Jews

10 From them came forth a sinful root, Antiochus Epiphanes, son of King Antiochus; he had been a hostage in Rome. He began to reign in the one hundred thirty-seventh year of the kingdom of the Greeks.[b]

11 In those days certain renegades came out from Israel and misled many, saying, "Let us go and make a covenant with the Gentiles around us, for since we separated from them many disasters have come upon us." ¹²This proposal pleased them, ¹³and some of the people eagerly went to the king, who authorized them to observe the ordinances of the Gentiles. ¹⁴So they built a gymnasium in Jerusalem, according to Gentile custom, ¹⁵and removed the marks of circumcision, and abandoned the holy covenant. They joined with the Gentiles and sold themselves to do evil.

Antiochus in Egypt

16 When Antiochus saw that his kingdom was established, he determined to become king of the land of Egypt, in order that he might reign over both kingdoms. ¹⁷So he invaded Egypt with a strong force, with chariots and elephants and cavalry and with a large fleet. ¹⁸He engaged King Ptolemy of Egypt in battle, and Ptolemy turned and fled before him, and many were wounded and fell. ¹⁹They captured the fortified cities in the land of Egypt, and he plundered the land of Egypt.

Persecution of the Jews

20 After subduing Egypt, Antiochus returned in the one hundred forty-third year.[c] He went up against Israel and came to Jerusalem with a strong force. ²¹He arrogantly entered the sanctuary and took the golden altar, the lampstand for

---

a Gk adds *and he defeated*   b 175 B.C.   c 169 B.C.

the light, and all its utensils. 22He took also the table for the bread of the Presence, the cups for drink offerings, the bowls, the golden censers, the curtain, the crowns, and the gold decoration on the front of the temple; he stripped it all off. 23He took the silver and the gold, and the costly vessels; he took also the hidden treasures that he found. 24Taking them all, he went into his own land.

He shed much blood,
   and spoke with great arrogance.
25 Israel mourned deeply in every community,
26   rulers and elders groaned,
   young women and young men became faint,
      the beauty of the women faded.
27 Every bridegroom took up the lament;
   she who sat in the bridal chamber was
      mourning.
28 Even the land trembled for its inhabitants,
   and all the house of Jacob was clothed with
      shame.

The Occupation of Jerusalem

29 Two years later the king sent to the cities of Judah a chief collector of tribute, and he came to Jerusalem with a large force. 30Deceitfully he spoke peaceable words to them, and they believed him; but he suddenly fell upon the city, dealt it a severe blow, and destroyed many people of Israel. 31He plundered the city, burned it with fire, and tore down its houses and its surrounding walls. 32They took captive the women and children, and seized the livestock. 33Then they fortified the city of David with a great strong wall and strong towers, and it became their citadel. 34They stationed there a sinful people, men who were renegades. These strengthened their position; 35they stored up arms and food, and collecting the spoils of Jerusalem they stored them there, and became a great menace,
36 for the citadel[a] became an ambush against the
      sanctuary,
   an evil adversary of Israel at all times.
37 On every side of the sanctuary they shed
      innocent blood;
   they even defiled the sanctuary.
38 Because of them the residents of Jerusalem fled;
   she became a dwelling of strangers;
she became strange to her offspring,
   and her children forsook her.
39 Her sanctuary became desolate like a desert;
   her feasts were turned into mourning,
her sabbaths into a reproach,
   her honor into contempt.
40 Her dishonor now grew as great as her glory;
   her exaltation was turned into mourning.

Installation of Gentile Cults

41 Then the king wrote to his whole kingdom that all should be one people, 42and that all should give up their particular customs. 43All the Gentiles accepted the command of the king. Many even from Israel gladly adopted his religion; they sacrificed to idols and profaned the sabbath. 44And the king sent letters by messengers to Jerusalem and the towns of Judah; he directed them to follow customs strange to the land, 45to forbid burnt offerings and sacrifices and drink offerings in the sanctuary, to profane sabbaths and festivals, 46to defile the sanctuary and the priests, 47to build altars and sacred precincts and shrines for idols, to sacrifice swine and other unclean animals, 48and to leave their sons uncircumcised. They were to make themselves abominable by everything unclean and profane, 49so that they would forget the law and change all the ordinances. 50He added,[b] "And whoever does not obey the command of the king shall die."

51 In such words he wrote to his whole kingdom. He appointed inspectors over all the people and commanded the towns of Judah to offer sacrifice, town by town. 52Many of the people, everyone who forsook the law, joined them, and they did evil in the land; 53they drove Israel into hiding in every place of refuge they had.

54 Now on the fifteenth day of Chislev, in the one hundred forty-fifth year,[c] they erected a desolating sacrilege on the altar of burnt offering. They also built altars in the surrounding towns of Judah, 55and offered incense at the doors of the houses and in the streets. 56The books of the law that they found they tore to pieces and burned with fire. 57Anyone found possessing the book of the covenant, or anyone who adhered to the law, was condemned to death by decree of the king. 58They kept using violence against Israel, against those who were found month after month in the towns. 59On the twenty-fifth day of the month they offered sacrifice on the altar that was on top of the altar of burnt offering. 60According to the decree, they put to death the women who had their children circumcised, 61and their families and those who circumcised them; and they hung the infants from their mothers' necks.

62 But many in Israel stood firm and were resolved in their hearts not to eat unclean food. 63They chose to die rather than to be defiled by food or to profane the holy covenant; and they did die. 64Very great wrath came upon Israel.

---

a Gk it   b Gk lacks He added   c 167 B.C.

Mattathias and His Sons

2 In those days Mattathias son of John son of Simeon, a priest of the family of Joarib, moved from Jerusalem and settled in Modein. [2]He had five sons, John surnamed Gaddi, [3]Simon called Thassi, [4]Judas called Maccabeus, [5]Eleazar called Avaran, and Jonathan called Apphus. [6]He saw the blasphemies being committed in Judah and Jerusalem, [7]and said,

"Alas! Why was I born to see this,
the ruin of my people, the ruin of the holy city,
and to live there when it was given over to the enemy,
the sanctuary given over to aliens?
[8] Her temple has become like a person without honor;[a]
[9] her glorious vessels have been carried into exile.
Her infants have been killed in her streets,
her youths by the sword of the foe.
[10] What nation has not inherited her palaces[b]
and has not seized her spoils?
[11] All her adornment has been taken away;
no longer free, she has become a slave.
[12] And see, our holy place, our beauty,
and our glory have been laid waste;
the Gentiles have profaned them.
[13] Why should we live any longer?"

14 Then Mattathias and his sons tore their clothes, put on sackcloth, and mourned greatly.

Pagan Worship Refused

15 The king's officers who were enforcing the apostasy came to the town of Modein to make them offer sacrifice. [16]Many from Israel came to them; and Mattathias and his sons were assembled. [17]Then the king's officers spoke to Mattathias as follows: "You are a leader, honored and great in this town, and supported by sons and brothers. [18]Now be the first to come and do what the king commands, as all the Gentiles and the people of Judah and those that are left in Jerusalem have done. Then you and your sons will be numbered among the Friends of the king, and you and your sons will be honored with silver and gold and many gifts."

19 But Mattathias answered and said in a loud voice: "Even if all the nations that live under the rule of the king obey him, and have chosen to obey his commandments, every one of them abandoning the religion of their ancestors, [20]I and my sons and my brothers will continue to live by the covenant of our ancestors. [21]Far be it from us to desert the law and the ordinances.

Religious Persecution

The Jews were facing a societal attack on their faith. But Mattathias and his sons chose to fight the official and cultural pressure to turn away from their faith.

● Are there times when you feel persecuted because of your belief in God?
● In what subtle ways does contemporary society ridicule people with religious beliefs?
● If you were to be judged or questioned because of your religion, how would you respond?

▶ 1 Macc 2:19–22

[22]We will not obey the king's words by turning aside from our religion to the right hand or to the left."

23 When he had finished speaking these words, a Jew came forward in the sight of all to offer sacrifice on the altar in Modein, according to the king's command. [24]When Mattathias saw it, he burned with zeal and his heart was stirred. He gave vent to righteous anger; he ran and killed him on the altar. [25]At the same time he killed the king's officer who was forcing them to sacrifice, and he tore down the altar. [26]Thus he burned with zeal for the law, just as Phinehas did against Zimri son of Salu.

27 Then Mattathias cried out in the town with a loud voice, saying: "Let every one who is zealous for the law and supports the covenant come out with me!" [28]Then he and his sons fled to the hills and left all that they had in the town.

29 At that time many who were seeking righteousness and justice went down to the wilderness to live there, [30]they, their sons, their wives, and their livestock, because troubles pressed heavily upon them. [31]And it was reported to the king's officers, and to the troops in Jerusalem the city of David, that those who had rejected the king's command had gone down to the hiding places in the wilderness. [32]Many pursued them, and overtook them; they encamped opposite them and prepared for battle against them on the

a Meaning of Gk uncertain   b Other ancient authorities read has not had a part in her kingdom

sabbath day. ³³They said to them, "Enough of this! Come out and do what the king commands, and you will live." ³⁴But they said, "We will not come out, nor will we do what the king commands and so profane the sabbath day." ³⁵Then the enemy[a] quickly attacked them. ³⁶But they did not answer them or hurl a stone at them or block up their hiding places, ³⁷for they said, "Let us all die in our innocence; heaven and earth testify for us that you are killing us unjustly." ³⁸So they attacked them on the sabbath, and they died, with their wives and children and livestock, to the number of a thousand persons.

39 When Mattathias and his friends learned of it, they mourned for them deeply. ⁴⁰And all said to their neighbors: "If we all do as our kindred have done and refuse to fight with the Gentiles for our lives and for our ordinances, they will quickly destroy us from the earth." ⁴¹So they made this decision that day: "Let us fight against anyone who comes to attack us on the sabbath day; let us not all die as our kindred died in their hiding places."

Counter-Attack

42 Then there united with them a company of Hasideans, mighty warriors of Israel, all who offered themselves willingly for the law. ⁴³And all who became fugitives to escape their troubles joined them and reinforced them. ⁴⁴They organized an army, and struck down sinners in their anger and renegades in their wrath; the survivors fled to the Gentiles for safety. ⁴⁵And Mattathias and his friends went around and tore down the altars; ⁴⁶they forcibly circumcised all the uncircumcised boys that they found within the borders of Israel. ⁴⁷They hunted down the arrogant, and the work prospered in their hands. ⁴⁸They rescued the law out of the hands of the Gentiles and kings, and they never let the sinner gain the upper hand.

The Last Words of Mattathias

49 Now the days drew near for Mattathias to die, and he said to his sons: "Arrogance and scorn have now become strong; it is a time of ruin and furious anger. ⁵⁰Now, my children, show zeal for the law, and give your lives for the covenant of our ancestors.

51 "Remember the deeds of the ancestors, which they did in their generations; and you will receive great honor and an everlasting name. ⁵²Was not Abraham found faithful when tested, and it was reckoned to him as righteousness? ⁵³Joseph in the time of his distress kept the commandment, and became lord of Egypt.

⁵⁴Phinehas our ancestor, because he was deeply zealous, received the covenant of everlasting priesthood. ⁵⁵Joshua, because he fulfilled the command, became a judge in Israel. ⁵⁶Caleb, because he testified in the assembly, received an inheritance in the land. ⁵⁷David, because he was merciful, inherited the throne of the kingdom forever. ⁵⁸Elijah, because of great zeal for the law, was taken up into heaven. ⁵⁹Hananiah, Azariah, and Mishael believed and were saved from the flame. ⁶⁰Daniel, because of his innocence, was delivered from the mouth of the lions.

61 "And so observe, from generation to generation, that none of those who put their trust in him will lack strength. ⁶²Do not fear the words of sinners, for their splendor will turn into dung and worms. ⁶³Today they will be exalted, but tomorrow they will not be found, because they will have returned to the dust, and their plans will have perished. ⁶⁴My children, be courageous and grow strong in the law, for by it you will gain honor.

65 "Here is your brother Simeon who, I know, is wise in counsel; always listen to him; he shall be your father. ⁶⁶Judas Maccabeus has been a mighty warrior from his youth; he shall command the army for you and fight the battle against the peoples.[b] ⁶⁷You shall rally around you all who observe the law, and avenge the wrong done to your people. ⁶⁸Pay back the Gentiles in full, and obey the commands of the law."

69 Then he blessed them, and was gathered to his ancestors. ⁷⁰He died in the one hundred forty-sixth year[c] and was buried in the tomb of his ancestors at Modein. And all Israel mourned for him with great lamentation.

The Early Victories of Judas

3 Then his son Judas, who was called Maccabeus, took command in his place. ²All his brothers and all who had joined his father helped him; they gladly fought for Israel.

³ He extended the glory of his people.
    Like a giant he put on his breastplate;
he bound on his armor of war and waged
        battles,
    protecting the camp by his sword.
⁴ He was like a lion in his deeds,
    like a lion's cub roaring for prey.
⁵ He searched out and pursued those who broke
        the law;
    he burned those who troubled his people.

---

a Gk they   *b* Or of the people   *c* 166 B.C.

6 Lawbreakers shrank back for fear of him;
   all the evildoers were confounded;
   and deliverance prospered by his hand.
7 He embittered many kings,
   but he made Jacob glad by his deeds,
   and his memory is blessed forever.
8 He went through the cities of Judah;
   he destroyed the ungodly out of the land;[a]
   thus he turned away wrath from Israel.
9 He was renowned to the ends of the earth;
   he gathered in those who were perishing.

10 Apollonius now gathered together Gentiles and a large force from Samaria to fight against Israel. [11]When Judas learned of it, he went out to meet him, and he defeated and killed him. Many were wounded and fell, and the rest fled. [12]Then they seized their spoils; and Judas took the sword of Apollonius, and used it in battle the rest of his life.

13 When Seron, the commander of the Syrian army, heard that Judas had gathered a large company, including a body of faithful soldiers who stayed with him and went out to battle, [14]he said, "I will make a name for myself and win honor in the kingdom. I will make war on Judas and his companions, who scorn the king's command." [15]Once again a strong army of godless men went up with him to help him, to take vengeance on the Israelites.

16 When he approached the ascent of Beth-horon, Judas went out to meet him with a small company. [17]But when they saw the army coming to meet them, they said to Judas, "How can we, few as we are, fight against so great and so strong a multitude? And we are faint, for we have eaten nothing today." [18]Judas replied, "It is easy for many to be hemmed in by few, for in the sight of Heaven there is no difference between saving by many or by few. [19]It is not on the size of the army that victory in battle depends, but strength comes from Heaven. [20]They come against us in great insolence and lawlessness to destroy us and our wives and our children, and to despoil us; [21]but we fight for our lives and our laws. [22]He himself will crush them before us; as for you, do not be afraid of them."

23 When he finished speaking, he rushed suddenly against Seron and his army, and they were crushed before him. [24]They pursued them[b] down the descent of Beth-horon to the plain; eight hundred of them fell, and the rest fled into the land of the Philistines. [25]Then Judas and his brothers began to be feared, and terror fell on the Gentiles all around them. [26]His fame reached the king, and the Gentiles talked of the battles of Judas.

The Policy of Antiochus

27 When King Antiochus heard these reports, he was greatly angered; and he sent and gathered all the forces of his kingdom, a very strong army. [28]He opened his coffers and gave a year's pay to his forces, and ordered them to be ready for any need. [29]Then he saw that the money in the treasury was exhausted, and that the revenues from the country were small because of the dissension and disaster that he had caused in the land by abolishing the laws that had existed from the earliest days. [30]He feared that he might not have such funds as he had before for his expenses and for the gifts that he used to give more lavishly than preceding kings. [31]He was greatly perplexed in mind; then he determined to go to Persia and collect the revenues from those regions and raise a large fund.

32 He left Lysias, a distinguished man of royal lineage, in charge of the king's affairs from the river Euphrates to the borders of Egypt. [33]Lysias was also to take care of his son Antiochus until he returned. [34]And he turned over to Lysias[c] half of his forces and the elephants, and gave him orders about all that he wanted done. As for the residents of Judea and Jerusalem, [35]Lysias was to send a force against them to wipe out and destroy the strength of Israel and the remnant of Jerusalem; he was to banish the memory of them from the place, [36]settle aliens in all their territory, and distribute their land by lot. [37]Then the king took the remaining half of his forces and left Antioch his capital in the one hundred and forty-seventh year.[d] He crossed the Euphrates river and went through the upper provinces.

Preparations for Battle

38 Lysias chose Ptolemy son of Dorymenes, and Nicanor and Gorgias, able men among the Friends of the king, [39]and sent with them forty thousand infantry and seven thousand cavalry to go into the land of Judah and destroy it, as the king had commanded. [40]So they set out with their entire force, and when they arrived they encamped near Emmaus in the plain. [41]When the traders of the region heard what was said to them, they took silver and gold in immense amounts, and fetters,[e] and went to the camp to get the Israelites for slaves. And forces from Syria and the land of the Philistines joined with them.

42 Now Judas and his brothers saw that misfortunes had increased and that the forces were encamped in their territory. They also learned

---

a Gk it   b Other ancient authorities read him   c Gk him
d 165 B.C.   e Syr: Gk Mss, Vg slaves

what the king had commanded to do to the people to cause their final destruction. ⁴³But they said to one another, "Let us restore the ruins of our people, and fight for our people and the sanctuary." ⁴⁴So the congregation assembled to be ready for battle, and to pray and ask for mercy and compassion.

⁴⁵ Jerusalem was uninhabited like a wilderness;
   not one of her children went in or out.
The sanctuary was trampled down,
   and aliens held the citadel;
   it was a lodging place for the Gentiles.
Joy was taken from Jacob;
   the flute and the harp ceased to play.

46 Then they gathered together and went to Mizpah, opposite Jerusalem, because Israel formerly had a place of prayer in Mizpah. ⁴⁷They fasted that day, put on sackcloth and sprinkled ashes on their heads, and tore their clothes. ⁴⁸And they opened the book of the law to inquire into those matters about which the Gentiles consulted the likenesses of their gods. ⁴⁹They also brought the vestments of the priesthood and the first fruits and the tithes, and they stirred up the nazirites^a who had completed their days; ⁵⁰and they cried aloud to Heaven, saying,

"What shall we do with these?
   Where shall we take them?
⁵¹ Your sanctuary is trampled down and profaned,
   and your priests mourn in humiliation.
⁵² Here the Gentiles are assembled against us to
     destroy us;
   you know what they plot against us.
⁵³ How will we be able to withstand them,
   if you do not help us?"

54 Then they sounded the trumpets and gave a loud shout. ⁵⁵After this Judas appointed leaders of the people, in charge of thousands and hundreds and fifties and tens. ⁵⁶Those who were building houses, or were about to be married, or were planting a vineyard, or were fainthearted, he told to go home again, according to the law. ⁵⁷Then the army marched out and encamped to the south of Emmaus.

58 And Judas said, "Arm yourselves and be courageous. Be ready early in the morning to fight with these Gentiles who have assembled against us to destroy us and our sanctuary. ⁵⁹It is better for us to die in battle than to see the misfortunes of our nation and of the sanctuary. ⁶⁰But as his will in heaven may be, so shall he do."

The Battle at Emmaus

4 Now Gorgias took five thousand infantry and one thousand picked cavalry, and this division moved out by night ²to fall upon the camp of the Jews and attack them suddenly. Men from the citadel were his guides. ³But Judas heard of it, and he and his warriors moved out to attack the king's force in Emmaus ⁴while the division was still absent from the camp. ⁵When Gorgias entered the camp of Judas by night, he found no one there, so he looked for them in the hills, because he said, "These men are running away from us."

6 At daybreak Judas appeared in the plain with three thousand men, but they did not have armor and swords such as they desired. ⁷And they saw the camp of the Gentiles, strong and fortified, with cavalry all around it; and these men were trained in war. ⁸But Judas said to those who were with him, "Do not fear their numbers or be afraid when they charge. ⁹Remember how our ancestors were saved at the Red Sea, when Pharaoh with his forces pursued them. ¹⁰And now, let us cry to Heaven, to see whether he will favor us and remember his covenant with our ancestors and crush this army before us today. ¹¹Then all the Gentiles will know that there is one who redeems and saves Israel."

12 When the foreigners looked up and saw them coming against them, ¹³they went out from their camp to battle. Then the men with Judas blew their trumpets ¹⁴and engaged in battle. The Gentiles were crushed, and fled into the plain, ¹⁵and all those in the rear fell by the sword. They pursued them to Gazara, and to the plains of Idumea, and to Azotus and Jamnia; and three thousand of them fell. ¹⁶Then Judas and his force turned back from pursuing them, ¹⁷and he said to the people, "Do not be greedy for plunder, for there is a battle before us; ¹⁸Gorgias and his force are near us in the hills. But stand now against our enemies and fight them, and afterward seize the plunder boldly."

19 Just as Judas was finishing this speech, a detachment appeared, coming out of the hills. ²⁰They saw that their army^b had been put to flight, and that the Jews^b were burning the camp, for the smoke that was seen showed what had happened. ²¹When they perceived this, they were greatly frightened, and when they also saw the army of Judas drawn up in the plain for battle, ²²they all fled into the land of the Philistines. ²³Then Judas returned to plunder the camp, and they seized a great amount of gold and silver, and cloth dyed blue and sea purple, and great riches. ²⁴On their return they sang hymns and praises to Heaven—"For he is good, for his mercy endures forever." ²⁵Thus Israel had a great deliverance that day.

---

a That is *those separated* or *those consecrated*   b Gk *they*

First Campaign of Lysias

26 Those of the foreigners who escaped went and reported to Lysias all that had happened. ²⁷When he heard it, he was perplexed and discouraged, for things had not happened to Israel as he had intended, nor had they turned out as the king had ordered. ²⁸But the next year he mustered sixty thousand picked infantry and five thousand cavalry to subdue them. ²⁹They came into Idumea and encamped at Beth-zur, and Judas met them with ten thousand men.

30 When he saw that their army was strong, he prayed, saying, "Blessed are you, O Savior of Israel, who crushed the attack of the mighty warrior by the hand of your servant David, and gave the camp of the Philistines into the hands of Jonathan son of Saul, and of the man who carried his armor. ³¹Hem in this army by the hand of your people Israel, and let them be ashamed of their troops and their cavalry. ³²Fill them with cowardice; melt the boldness of their strength; let them tremble in their destruction. ³³Strike them down with the sword of those who love you, and let all who know your name praise you with hymns."

34 Then both sides attacked, and there fell of the army of Lysias five thousand men; they fell in action.ᵃ ³⁵When Lysias saw the rout of his troops and observed the boldness that inspired those of Judas, and how ready they were either to live or to die nobly, he withdrew to Antioch and enlisted mercenaries in order to invade Judea again with an even larger army.

Cleansing and Dedication of the Temple

36 Then Judas and his brothers said, "See, our enemies are crushed; let us go up to cleanse the sanctuary and dedicate it." ³⁷So all the army assembled and went up to Mount Zion. ³⁸There they saw the sanctuary desolate, the altar profaned, and the gates burned. In the courts they saw bushes sprung up as in a thicket, or as on one of the mountains. They saw also the chambers of the priests in ruins. ³⁹Then they tore their clothes and mourned with great lamentation; they sprinkled themselves with ashes ⁴⁰and fell face down on the ground. And when the signal was given with the trumpets, they cried out to Heaven.

41 Then Judas detailed men to fight against those in the citadel until he had cleansed the sanctuary. ⁴²He chose blameless priests devoted to the law, ⁴³and they cleansed the sanctuary and removed the defiled stones to an unclean place. ⁴⁴They deliberated what to do about the altar of burnt offering, which had been profaned. ⁴⁵And they thought it best to tear it down, so that it would not be a lasting shame to them that the Gentiles had defiled it. So they tore down the altar, ⁴⁶and stored the stones in a convenient place on the temple hill until a prophet should come to tell what to do with them. ⁴⁷Then they took unhewnᵇ stones, as the law directs, and built a new altar like the former one. ⁴⁸They also rebuilt the sanctuary and the interior of the temple, and consecrated the courts. ⁴⁹They made new holy vessels, and brought the lampstand, the altar of incense, and the table into the temple. ⁵⁰Then they offered incense on the altar and lit the lamps on the lampstand, and these gave light in the temple. ⁵¹They placed the bread on the table and hung up the curtains. Thus they finished all the work they had undertaken.

52 Early in the morning on the twenty-fifth day of the ninth month, which is the month of Chislev, in the one hundred forty-eighth year,ᶜ ⁵³they rose and offered sacrifice, as the law directs, on the new altar of burnt offering that they had built. ⁵⁴At the very season and on the very day that the Gentiles had profaned it, it was dedicated with songs and harps and lutes and cymbals. ⁵⁵All the people fell on their faces and worshiped and blessed Heaven, who had prospered them. ⁵⁶So they celebrated the dedication of the altar for eight days, and joyfully offered burnt offerings; they offered a sacrifice

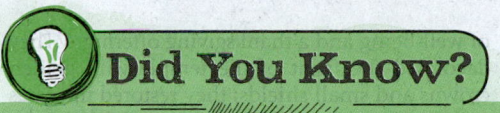

Did You Know?

Hanukkah

Hanukkah, or the feast of Dedication, is a joyful eight-day celebration in the month of Chislev (December). On each night of the festival, a candle is lit in joyful remembrance of the Maccabees' rededication of the Temple in Jerusalem after it was robbed and desecrated by Antiochus IV Epiphanes (see 1 Macc 4:56). Even more deeply, the candlelight symbolizes the gratitude of the Jewish people for the survival, often against great odds, of their age-old faith.

▶ 1 Macc 4:52–59

ᵃ Or and some fell on the opposite side   ᵇ Gk whole
ᶜ 164 B.C.

of well-being and a thanksgiving offering. [57]They decorated the front of the temple with golden crowns and small shields; they restored the gates and the chambers for the priests, and fitted them with doors. [58]There was very great joy among the people, and the disgrace brought by the Gentiles was removed.

59 Then Judas and his brothers and all the assembly of Israel determined that every year at that season the days of dedication of the altar should be observed with joy and gladness for eight days, beginning with the twenty-fifth day of the month of Chislev.

60 At that time they fortified Mount Zion with high walls and strong towers all around, to keep the Gentiles from coming and trampling them down as they had done before. [61]Judas[a] stationed a garrison there to guard it; he also fortified Beth-zur to guard it, so that the people might have a stronghold that faced Idumea.

Wars with Neighboring Peoples

5 When the Gentiles all around heard that the altar had been rebuilt and the sanctuary dedicated as it was before, they became very angry, [2]and they determined to destroy the descendants of Jacob who lived among them. So they began to kill and destroy among the people. [3]But Judas made war on the descendants of Esau in Idumea, at Akrabattene, because they kept lying in wait for Israel. He dealt them a heavy blow and humbled them and despoiled them. [4]He also remembered the wickedness of the sons of Baean, who were a trap and a snare to the people and ambushed them on the highways. [5]They were shut up by him in their[b] towers; and he encamped against them, vowed their complete destruction, and burned with fire their towers and all who were in them. [6]Then he crossed over to attack the Ammonites, where he found a strong band and many people, with Timothy as their leader. [7]He engaged in many battles with them, and they were crushed before him; he struck them down. [8]He also took Jazer and its villages; then he returned to Judea.

Liberation of Galilean Jews

9 Now the Gentiles in Gilead gathered together against the Israelites who lived in their territory, and planned to destroy them. But they fled to the stronghold of Dathema, [10]and sent to Judas and his brothers a letter that said, "The Gentiles around us have gathered together to destroy us. [11]They are preparing to come and capture the stronghold to which we have fled, and Timothy is leading their forces. [12]Now then,

come and rescue us from their hands, for many of us have fallen, [13]and all our kindred who were in the land of Tob have been killed; the enemy[c] have captured their wives and children and goods, and have destroyed about a thousand persons there."

14 While the letter was still being read, other messengers, with their garments torn, came from Galilee and made a similar report; [15]they said that the people of Ptolemais and Tyre and Sidon, and all Galilee of the Gentiles,[d] had gathered together against them "to annihilate us." [16]When Judas and the people heard these messages, a great assembly was called to determine what they should do for their kindred who were in distress and were being attacked by enemies.[e] [17]Then Judas said to his brother Simon, "Choose your men and go and rescue your kindred in Galilee; Jonathan my brother and I will go to Gilead." [18]But he left Joseph, son of Zechariah, and Azariah, a leader of the people, with the rest of the forces, in Judea to guard it; [19]and he gave them this command, "Take charge of this people, but do not engage in battle with the Gentiles until we return." [20]Then three thousand men were assigned to Simon to go to Galilee, and eight thousand to Judas for Gilead.

21 So Simon went to Galilee and fought many battles against the Gentiles, and the Gentiles were crushed before him. [22]He pursued them to the gate of Ptolemais; as many as three thousand of the Gentiles fell, and he despoiled them. [23]Then he took the Jews[f] of Galilee and Arbatta, with their wives and children, and all they possessed, and led them to Judea with great rejoicing.

Judas and Jonathan in Gilead

24 Judas Maccabeus and his brother Jonathan crossed the Jordan and made three days' journey into the wilderness. [25]They encountered the Nabateans, who met them peaceably and told them all that had happened to their kindred in Gilead: [26]"Many of them have been shut up in Bozrah and Bosor, in Alema and Chaspho, Maked and Carnaim"—all these towns were strong and large— [27]"and some have been shut up in the other towns of Gilead; the enemy[c] are getting ready to attack the strongholds tomorrow and capture and destroy all these people in a single day."

28 Then Judas and his army quickly turned back by the wilderness road to Bozrah; and he

---

a Gk He   b Gk her   c Gk they   d Gk aliens   e Gk them
f Gk those

took the town, and killed every male by the edge of the sword; then he seized all its spoils and burned it with fire. [29]He left the place at night, and they went all the way to the stronghold of Dathema.[a] [30]At dawn they looked out and saw a large company, which could not be counted, carrying ladders and engines of war to capture the stronghold, and attacking the Jews within.[b] [31]So Judas saw that the battle had begun and that the cry of the town went up to Heaven, with trumpets and loud shouts, [32]and he said to the men of his forces, "Fight today for your kindred!" [33]Then he came up behind them in three companies, who sounded their trumpets and cried aloud in prayer. [34]And when the army of Timothy realized that it was Maccabeus, they fled before him, and he dealt them a heavy blow. As many as eight thousand of them fell that day.

35 Next he turned aside to Maapha,[c] and fought against it and took it; and he killed every male in it, plundered it, and burned it with fire. [36]From there he marched on and took Chaspho, Maked, and Bosor, and the other towns of Gilead.

37 After these things Timothy gathered another army and encamped opposite Raphon, on the other side of the stream. [38]Judas sent men to spy out the camp, and they reported to him, "All the Gentiles around us have gathered to him; it is a very large force. [39]They also have hired Arabs to help them, and they are encamped across the stream, ready to come and fight against you." And Judas went to meet them.

40 Now as Judas and his army drew near to the stream of water, Timothy said to the officers of his forces, "If he crosses over to us first, we will not be able to resist him, for he will surely defeat us. [41]But if he shows fear and camps on the other side of the river, we will cross over to him and defeat him." [42]When Judas approached the stream of water, he stationed the officers[d] of the army at the stream and gave them this command, "Permit no one to encamp, but make them all enter the battle." [43]Then he crossed over against them first, and the whole army followed him. All the Gentiles were defeated before him, and they threw away their arms and fled into the sacred precincts at Carnaim. [44]But he took the town and burned the sacred precincts with fire, together with all who were in them. Thus Carnaim was conquered; they could stand before Judas no longer.

The Return to Jerusalem

45 Then Judas gathered together all the Israelites in Gilead, the small and the great, with their wives and children and goods, a very large company, to go to the land of Judah. [46]So they came to Ephron. This was a large and very strong town on the road, and they could not go around it to the right or to the left; they had to go through it. [47]But the people of the town shut them out and blocked up the gates with stones.

48 Judas sent them this friendly message, "Let us pass through your land to get to our land. No one will do you harm; we will simply pass by on foot." But they refused to open to him. [49]Then Judas ordered proclamation to be made to the army that all should encamp where they were. [50]So the men of the forces encamped, and he fought against the town all that day and all the night, and the town was delivered into his hands. [51]He destroyed every male by the edge of the sword, and razed and plundered the town. Then he passed through the town over the bodies of the dead.

52 Then they crossed the Jordan into the large plain before Beth-shan. [53]Judas kept rallying the laggards and encouraging the people all the way until he came to the land of Judah. [54]So they went up to Mount Zion with joy and gladness, and offered burnt offerings, because they had returned in safety; not one of them had fallen.

Joseph and Azariah Defeated

55 Now while Judas and Jonathan were in Gilead and their[e] brother Simon was in Galilee before Ptolemais, [56]Joseph son of Zechariah, and Azariah, the commanders of the forces, heard of their brave deeds and of the heroic war they had fought. [57]So they said, "Let us also make a name for ourselves; let us go and make war on the Gentiles around us." [58]So they issued orders to the men of the forces that were with them and marched against Jamnia. [59]Gorgias and his men came out of the town to meet them in battle. [60]Then Joseph and Azariah were routed, and were pursued to the borders of Judea; as many as two thousand of the people of Israel fell that day. [61]Thus the people suffered a great rout because, thinking to do a brave deed, they did not listen to Judas and his brothers. [62]But they did not belong to the family of those men through whom deliverance was given to Israel.

63 The man Judas and his brothers were greatly honored in all Israel and among all the Gentiles, wherever their name was heard. [64]People gathered to them and praised them.

---

a Gk lacks *of Dathema.* See verse 9   b Gk *and they were attacking them*   c Other ancient authorities read *Alema*   d Or *scribes*   e Gk *his*

Success at Hebron and Philistia

65 Then Judas and his brothers went out and fought the descendants of Esau in the land to the south. He struck Hebron and its villages and tore down its strongholds and burned its towers on all sides. 66 Then he marched off to go into the land of the Philistines, and passed through Marisa.ᵃ 67 On that day some priests, who wished to do a brave deed, fell in battle, for they went out to battle unwisely. 68 But Judas turned aside to Azotus in the land of the Philistines; he tore down their altars, and the carved images of their gods he burned with fire; he plundered the towns and returned to the land of Judah.

The Last Days of Antiochus Epiphanes

6 King Antiochus was going through the upper provinces when he heard that Elymais in Persia was a city famed for its wealth in silver and gold. 2 Its temple was very rich, containing golden shields, breastplates, and weapons left there by Alexander son of Philip, the Macedonian king who first reigned over the Greeks. 3 So he came and tried to take the city and plunder it, but he could not because his plan had become known to the citizens 4 and they withstood him in battle. So he fled and in great disappointment left there to return to Babylon.

5 Then someone came to him in Persia and reported that the armies that had gone into the land of Judah had been routed; 6 that Lysias had gone first with a strong force, but had turned and fled before the Jews;ᵇ that the Jewsᶜ had grown strong from the arms, supplies, and abundant spoils that they had taken from the armies they had cut down; 7 that they had torn down the abomination that he had erected on the altar in Jerusalem; and that they had surrounded the sanctuary with high walls as before, and also Beth-zur, his town.

8 When the king heard this news, he was astounded and badly shaken. He took to his bed and became sick from disappointment, because things had not turned out for him as he had planned. 9 He lay there for many days, because deep disappointment continually gripped him, and he realized that he was dying. 10 So he called all his Friends and said to them, "Sleep has departed from my eyes and I am downhearted with worry. 11 I said to myself, 'To what distress I have come! And into what a great flood I now am plunged! For I was kind and beloved in my power.' 12 But now I remember the wrong I did in Jerusalem. I seized all its vessels of silver and gold, and I sent to destroy the inhabitants of Judah without good reason. 13 I know that it is because of this that these misfortunes have come upon me; here I am, perishing of bitter disappointment in a strange land."

14 Then he called for Philip, one of his Friends, and made him ruler over all his kingdom. 15 He gave him the crown and his robe and the signet, so that he might guide his son Antiochus and bring him up to be king. 16 Thus King Antiochus died there in the one hundred forty-ninth year.ᵈ 17 When Lysias learned that the king was dead, he set up Antiochus the king'sᵉ son to reign. Lysiasᶠ had brought him up from boyhood; he named him Eupator.

Renewed Attacks from Syria

18 Meanwhile the garrison in the citadel kept hemming Israel in around the sanctuary. They were trying in every way to harm them and strengthen the Gentiles. 19 Judas therefore resolved to destroy them, and assembled all the people to besiege them. 20 They gathered together and besieged the citadelᵍ in the one hundred fiftieth year;ʰ and he built siege towers and other engines of war. 21 But some of the garrison escaped from the siege and some of the ungodly Israelites joined them. 22 They went to the king and said, "How long will you fail to do justice and to avenge our kindred? 23 We were happy to serve your father, to live by what he said, and to follow his commands. 24 For this reason the sons of our people besieged the citadelⁱ and became hostile to us; moreover, they have put to death as many of us as they have caught, and they have seized our inheritances. 25 It is not against us alone that they have stretched out their hands; they have also attacked all the lands on their borders. 26 And see, today they have encamped against the citadel in Jerusalem to take it; they have fortified both the sanctuary and Beth-zur; 27 unless you quickly prevent them, they will do still greater things, and you will not be able to stop them."

28 The king was enraged when he heard this. He assembled all his Friends, the commanders of his forces and those in authority.ʲ 29 Mercenary forces also came to him from other kingdoms and from islands of the seas. 30 The number of his forces was one hundred thousand foot soldiers, twenty thousand horsemen, and thirty-two elephants accustomed to war. 31 They came through Idumea and encamped against Beth-zur, and for

---

a Other ancient authorities read *Samaria*   b Gk *them*   c Gk *they*   d 163 B.C.   e Gk *his*   f Gk *He*   g Gk *it*   h 162 B.C.   i Meaning of Gk uncertain   j Gk *those over the reins*

many days they fought and built engines of war; but the Jews[a] sallied out and burned these with fire, and fought courageously.

The Battle at Beth-zechariah

32 Then Judas marched away from the citadel and encamped at Beth-zechariah, opposite the camp of the king. [33]Early in the morning the king set out and took his army by a forced march along the road to Beth-zechariah, and his troops made ready for battle and sounded their trumpets. [34]They offered the elephants the juice of grapes and mulberries, to arouse them for battle. [35]They distributed the animals among the phalanxes; with each elephant they stationed a thousand men armed with coats of mail, and with brass helmets on their heads; and five hundred picked horsemen were assigned to each beast. [36]These took their position beforehand wherever the animal was; wherever it went, they went with it, and they never left it. [37]On the elephants[b] were wooden towers, strong and covered; they were fastened on each animal by special harness, and on each were four[c] armed men who fought from there, and also its Indian driver. [38]The rest of the cavalry were stationed on either side, on the two flanks of the army, to harass the enemy while being themselves protected by the phalanxes. [39]When the sun shone on the shields of gold and brass, the hills were ablaze with them and gleamed like flaming torches.

40 Now a part of the king's army was spread out on the high hills, and some troops were on the plain, and they advanced steadily and in good order. [41]All who heard the noise made by their multitude, by the marching of the multitude and the clanking of their arms, trembled, for the army was very large and strong. [42]But Judas and his army advanced to the battle, and six hundred of the king's army fell. [43]Now Eleazar, called Avaran, saw that one of the animals was equipped with royal armor. It was taller than all the others, and he supposed that the king was on it. [44]So he gave his life to save his people and to win for himself an everlasting name. [45]He courageously ran into the midst of the phalanx to reach it; he killed men right and left, and they parted before him on both sides. [46]He got under the elephant, stabbed it from beneath, and killed it; but it fell to the ground upon him and he died. [47]When the Jews[a] saw the royal might and the fierce attack of the forces, they turned away in flight.

The Siege of the Temple

48 The soldiers of the king's army went up to Jerusalem against them, and the king encamped

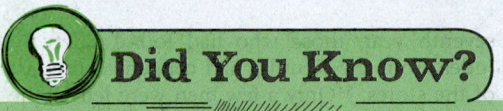

Did You Know?

A Just War

Have you ever believed in something so strongly that you could justify a war to protect it? The Maccabees did, and they led a violent resistance against terrible religious persecution.

The Catholic Church teaches that "all citizens and all governments are obliged to work for the avoidance of war" (*Catechism*, no. 2308). But it also teaches that there can be occasions for legitimate defense by military force (no. 2309), or what is sometimes called a just war. The criteria for a just war are as follows:

- All other means to avoid war must be exhausted.
- The damage done by the aggressor must be grave and certain.
- There must be serious prospects of success.
- The use of arms must not produce evils that are greater than the evil to be eliminated.

No one should be required to participate in any war that does not meet all these criteria.

War is not the answer; peace is. But at times in history, some Christians have felt that the only response to a grave injustice was violent resistance. However, no Christian is obligated to fight in a war if doing so goes against his or her conscience—although he or she may be required to serve the community in some other way—and nonviolent resistance is always an option (see "Nonviolent Resistance," near 2 Macc 7:42).

in Judea and at Mount Zion. [49]He made peace with the people of Beth-zur, and they evacuated the town because they had no provisions there to withstand a siege, since it was a sabbatical year for the land. [50]So the king took Beth-zur and stationed a guard there to hold it. [51]Then he encamped before the sanctuary for many days. He set up siege towers, engines of war to throw fire and stones, machines to shoot arrows, and catapults. [52]The Jews[a] also made engines of war to match theirs, and fought for many days. [53]But they had no food in storage,[d] because it was the seventh year; those who had found safety in Judea from the Gentiles had consumed the last of the stores. [54]Only a few men were left in the sanctuary; the rest scattered to their own homes, for the famine proved too much for them.

Syria Offers Terms

55 Then Lysias heard that Philip, whom King Antiochus while still living had appointed to bring up his son Antiochus to be king, [56]had returned from Persia and Media with the forces that had gone with the king, and that he was trying to seize control of the government. [57]So he quickly gave orders to withdraw, and said to the king, to the commanders of the forces, and to the troops, "Daily we grow weaker, our food supply is scant, the place against which we are fighting is strong, and the affairs of the kingdom press urgently on us. [58]Now then let us come to terms with these people, and make peace with them and with all their nation. [59]Let us agree to let them live by their laws as they did before; for it was on account of their laws that we abolished that they became angry and did all these things."

60 The speech pleased the king and the commanders, and he sent to the Jews[a] an offer of peace, and they accepted it. [61]So the king and the commanders gave them their oath. On these conditions the Jews[b] evacuated the stronghold. [62]But when the king entered Mount Zion and saw what a strong fortress the place was, he broke the oath he had sworn and gave orders to tear down the wall all around. [63]Then he set off in haste and returned to Antioch. He found Philip in control of the city, but he fought against him, and took the city by force.

Expedition of Bacchides and Alcimus

7 In the one hundred fifty-first year[c] Demetrius son of Seleucus set out from Rome, sailed with a few men to a town by the sea, and there began to reign. [2]As he was entering the royal palace of his ancestors, the army seized Antiochus and Lysias to bring them to him. [3]But when this act became known to him, he said, "Do not let me see their faces!" [4]So the army killed them, and Demetrius took his seat on the throne of his kingdom.

5 Then there came to him all the renegade and godless men of Israel; they were led by Alcimus, who wanted to be high priest. [6]They brought to the king this accusation against the people: "Judas and his brothers have destroyed all your Friends, and have driven us out of our land. [7]Now then send a man whom you trust; let him go and see all the ruin that Judas[d] has brought on us and on the land of the king, and let him punish them and all who help them."

8 So the king chose Bacchides, one of the king's Friends, governor of the province Beyond the River; he was a great man in the kingdom and was faithful to the king. [9]He sent him, and with him he sent the ungodly Alcimus, whom he made high priest; and he commanded him to take vengeance on the Israelites. [10]So they marched away and came with a large force into the land of Judah; and he sent messengers to Judas and his brothers with peaceable but treacherous words. [11]But they paid no attention to their words, for they saw that they had come with a large force.

12 Then a group of scribes appeared in a body before Alcimus and Bacchides to ask for just terms. [13]The Hasideans were first among the Israelites to seek peace from them, [14]for they said, "A priest of the line of Aaron has come with the army, and he will not harm us." [15]Alcimus[e] spoke peaceable words to them and swore this oath to them, "We will not seek to injure you or your friends." [16]So they trusted him; but he seized sixty of them and killed them in one day, in accordance with the word that was written,

[17] "The flesh of your faithful ones and their blood
   they poured out all around Jerusalem,
 and there was no one to bury them."

[18]Then the fear and dread of them fell on all the people, for they said, "There is no truth or justice in them, for they have violated the agreement and the oath that they swore."

19 Then Bacchides withdrew from Jerusalem and encamped in Beth-zaith. And he sent and seized many of the men who had deserted to him,[f] and some of the people, and killed them and threw them into a great pit. [20]He placed Alcimus in charge of the country and left with him a force to help him; then Bacchides went back to the king.

21 Alcimus struggled to maintain his high priesthood, [22]and all who were troubling their people joined him. They gained control of the land of Judah and did great damage in Israel. [23]And Judas saw all the wrongs that Alcimus and those with him had done among the Israelites; it was more than the Gentiles had done. [24]So Judas[d] went out into all the surrounding parts of Judea, taking vengeance on those who had deserted and preventing those in the city[g] from going out into the country. [25]When Alcimus saw

a Gk them   b Gk they   c 161 B.C.   d Gk he   e Gk He
f Or many of his men who had deserted   g Gk and they were prevented

that Judas and those with him had grown strong, and realized that he could not withstand them, he returned to the king and brought malicious charges against them.

Nicanor in Judea

26 Then the king sent Nicanor, one of his honored princes, who hated and detested Israel, and he commanded him to destroy the people. [27]So Nicanor came to Jerusalem with a large force, and treacherously sent to Judas and his brothers this peaceable message, [28]"Let there be no fighting between you and me; I shall come with a few men to see you face to face in peace."

29 So he came to Judas, and they greeted one another peaceably; but the enemy were preparing to kidnap Judas. [30]It became known to Judas that Nicanor[a] had come to him with treacherous intent, and he was afraid of him and would not meet him again. [31]When Nicanor learned that his plan had been disclosed, he went out to meet Judas in battle near Caphar-salama. [32]About five hundred of the army of Nicanor fell, and the rest[b] fled into the city of David.

Nicanor Threatens the Temple

33 After these events Nicanor went up to Mount Zion. Some of the priests from the sanctuary and some of the elders of the people came out to greet him peaceably and to show him the burnt offering that was being offered for the king. [34]But he mocked them and derided them and defiled them and spoke arrogantly, [35]and in anger he swore this oath, "Unless Judas and his army are delivered into my hands this time, then if I return safely I will burn up this house." And he went out in great anger. [36]At this the priests went in and stood before the altar and the temple; they wept and said,

[37] "You chose this house to be called by your
    name,
  and to be for your people a house of prayer
    and supplication.
[38] Take vengeance on this man and on his army,
  and let them fall by the sword;
  remember their blasphemies,
  and let them live no longer."

The Death of Nicanor

39 Now Nicanor went out from Jerusalem and encamped in Beth-horon, and the Syrian army joined him. [40]Judas encamped in Adasa with three thousand men. Then Judas prayed and said, [41]"When the messengers from the king spoke blasphemy, your angel went out and struck down one hundred eighty-five thousand

of the Assyrians.[c] [42]So also crush this army before us today; let the rest learn that Nicanor[a] has spoken wickedly against the sanctuary, and judge him according to this wickedness."

43 So the armies met in battle on the thirteenth day of the month of Adar. The army of Nicanor was crushed, and he himself was the first to fall in the battle. [44]When his army saw that Nicanor had fallen, they threw down their arms and fled. [45]The Jews[b] pursued them a day's journey, from Adasa as far as Gazara, and as they followed they kept sounding the battle call on the trumpets. [46]People came out of all the surrounding villages of Judea, and they outflanked the enemy[d] and drove them back to their pursuers,[e] so that they all fell by the sword; not even one of them was left. [47]Then the Jews[b] seized the spoils and the plunder; they cut off Nicanor's head and the right hand that he had so arrogantly stretched out, and brought them and displayed them just outside Jerusalem. [48]The people rejoiced greatly and celebrated that day as a day of great gladness. [49]They decreed that this day should be celebrated each year on the thirteenth day of Adar. [50]So the land of Judah had rest for a few days.

A Eulogy of the Romans

8 Now Judas heard of the fame of the Romans, that they were very strong and were well-disposed toward all who made an alliance with them, that they pledged friendship to those who came to them, [2]and that they were very strong. He had been told of their wars and of the brave deeds that they were doing among the Gauls, how they had defeated them and forced them to pay tribute, [3]and what they had done in the land of Spain to get control of the silver and gold mines there, [4]and how they had gained control of the whole region by their planning and patience, even though the place was far distant from them. They also subdued the kings who came against them from the ends of the earth, until they crushed them and inflicted great disaster on them; the rest paid them tribute every year. [5]They had crushed in battle and conquered Philip, and King Perseus of the Macedonians,[f] and the others who rose up against them. [6]They also had defeated Antiochus the Great, king of Asia, who went to fight against them with one hundred twenty elephants and with cavalry and chariots and a very large army. He was crushed by them; [7]they took him alive and decreed that he and those who would reign after him should

---

a Gk he   b Gk they   c Gk of them   d Gk them   e Gk these
f Or Kittim

pay a heavy tribute and give hostages and surrender some of their best provinces, 8the countries
of India, Media, and Lydia. These they took from
him and gave to King Eumenes. 9The Greeks
planned to come and destroy them, 10but this
became known to them, and they sent a general
against the Greeks*a* and attacked them. Many of
them were wounded and fell, and the Romans*b*
took captive their wives and children; they plundered them, conquered the land, tore down
their strongholds, and enslaved them to this
day. 11The remaining kingdoms and islands, as
many as ever opposed them, they destroyed and
enslaved; 12but with their friends and those who
rely on them they have kept friendship. They
have subdued kings far and near, and as many
as have heard of their fame have feared them.
13Those whom they wish to help and to make
kings, they make kings, and those whom they
wish depose; and they have been greatly exalted. 14Yet for all this not one of them has put
on a crown or worn purple as a mark of pride,
15but they have built for themselves a senate
chamber, and every day three hundred twenty
senators constantly deliberate concerning the
people, to govern them well. 16They trust one
man each year to rule over them and to control
all their land; they all heed the one man, and
there is no envy or jealousy among them.

An Alliance with Rome

17 So Judas chose Eupolemus son of John
son of Accos, and Jason son of Eleazar, and sent
them to Rome to establish friendship and alliance, 18and to free themselves from the yoke;
for they saw that the kingdom of the Greeks
was enslaving Israel completely. 19They went to
Rome, a very long journey; and they entered the
senate chamber and spoke as follows: 20"Judas,
who is also called Maccabeus, and his brothers
and the people of the Jews have sent us to you to
establish alliance and peace with you, so that we
may be enrolled as your allies and friends." 21The
proposal pleased them, 22and this is a copy of the
letter that they wrote in reply, on bronze tablets,
and sent to Jerusalem to remain with them there
as a memorial of peace and alliance:

23 "May all go well with the Romans and with
the nation of the Jews at sea and on land forever,
and may sword and enemy be far from them. 24If
war comes first to Rome or to any of their allies
in all their dominion, 25the nation of the Jews
shall act as their allies wholeheartedly, as the occasion may indicate to them. 26To the enemy that
makes war they shall not give or supply grain,
arms, money, or ships, just as Rome has decided;

and they shall keep their obligations without
receiving any return. 27In the same way, if war
comes first to the nation of the Jews, the Romans
shall willingly act as their allies, as the occasion
may indicate to them. 28And to their enemies
there shall not be given grain, arms, money, or
ships, just as Rome has decided; and they shall
keep these obligations and do so without deceit.
29Thus on these terms the Romans make a treaty
with the Jewish people. 30If after these terms are
in effect both parties shall determine to add or
delete anything, they shall do so at their discretion, and any addition or deletion that they may
make shall be valid.

31 "Concerning the wrongs that King Demetrius is doing to them, we have written to him as
follows, 'Why have you made your yoke heavy
on our friends and allies the Jews? 32If now they
appeal again for help against you, we will defend
their rights and fight you on sea and on land.' "

Bacchides Returns to Judea

9 When Demetrius heard that Nicanor and his
army had fallen in battle, he sent Bacchides
and Alcimus into the land of Judah a second
time, and with them the right wing of the army.
2They went by the road that leads to Gilgal and
encamped against Mesaloth in Arbela, and they
took it and killed many people. 3In the first
month of the one hundred fifty-second year*c*
they encamped against Jerusalem; 4then they
marched off and went to Berea with twenty thousand foot soldiers and two thousand cavalry.

5 Now Judas was encamped in Elasa, and
with him were three thousand picked men.
6When they saw the huge number of the enemy
forces, they were greatly frightened, and many
slipped away from the camp, until no more than
eight hundred of them were left.

7 When Judas saw that his army had slipped
away and the battle was imminent, he was
crushed in spirit, for he had no time to assemble
them. 8He became faint, but he said to those
who were left, "Let us get up and go against
our enemies. We may have the strength to fight
them." 9But they tried to dissuade him, saying,
"We do not have the strength. Let us rather save
our own lives now, and let us come back with
our kindred and fight them; we are too few."
10But Judas said, "Far be it from us to do such a
thing as to flee from them. If our time has come,
let us die bravely for our kindred, and leave no
cause to question our honor."

---

a Gk them   *b* Gk they   *c* 160 B.C.

The Last Battle of Judas

11 Then the army of Bacchides[a] marched out from the camp and took its stand for the encounter. The cavalry was divided into two companies, and the slingers and the archers went ahead of the army, as did all the chief warriors. [12]Bacchides was on the right wing. Flanked by the two companies, the phalanx advanced to the sound of the trumpets; and the men with Judas also blew their trumpets. [13]The earth was shaken by the noise of the armies, and the battle raged from morning until evening.

14 Judas saw that Bacchides and the strength of his army were on the right; then all the stouthearted men went with him, [15]and they crushed the right wing, and he pursued them as far as Mount Azotus. [16]When those on the left wing saw that the right wing was crushed, they turned and followed close behind Judas and his men. [17]The battle became desperate, and many on both sides were wounded and fell. [18]Judas also fell, and the rest fled.

19 Then Jonathan and Simon took their brother Judas and buried him in the tomb of their ancestors at Modein, [20]and wept for him. All Israel made great lamentation for him; they mourned many days and said,

21 "How is the mighty fallen,
    the savior of Israel!"

[22]Now the rest of the acts of Judas, and his wars and the brave deeds that he did, and his greatness, have not been recorded, but they were very many.

Jonathan Succeeds Judas

23 After the death of Judas, the renegades emerged in all parts of Israel; all the wrongdoers reappeared. [24]In those days a very great famine occurred, and the country went over to their side. [25]Bacchides chose the godless and put them in charge of the country. [26]They made inquiry and searched for the friends of Judas, and brought them to Bacchides, who took vengeance on them and made sport of them. [27]So there was great distress in Israel, such as had not been since the time that prophets ceased to appear among them.

28 Then all the friends of Judas assembled and said to Jonathan, [29]"Since the death of your brother Judas there has been no one like him to go against our enemies and Bacchides, and to deal with those of our nation who hate us. [30]Now therefore we have chosen you today to take his place as our ruler and leader, to fight our battle." [31]So Jonathan accepted the leadership at that time in place of his brother Judas.

Live It!

What Makes a Hero?

History is full of heroes, those bigger-than-life men and women like Judas Maccabeus who have made a difference because of their courageous acts and their willingness to take risks that frighten other people. What makes someone a hero? Is each of us capable of heroism?

Someone we have grown up with, who now seems ordinary, could one day be a hero. None of us knows when we could be called on to do something heroic. We need an openness to God's call and a willingness to take a risk—to let go of our fears and to reach deep within ourselves for courage and strength. You may amaze yourself at what you can accomplish in extraordinary situations. The stuff of heroes, of great and brave persons such as Judas Maccabeus, is already within us. We need only to believe in ourselves and believe that God is with us.

You may not end up in a history book or be memorialized in a statue, but you can make a difference in the lives of one or perhaps many people. What really counts is to be a hero in the eyes of God.

▶ 1 Macc 9:19–22

The Campaigns of Jonathan

32 When Bacchides learned of this, he tried to kill him. [33]But Jonathan and his brother Simon and all who were with him heard of it, and they fled into the wilderness of Tekoa and camped by the water of the pool of Asphar. [34]Bacchides found this out on the sabbath day, and he with all his army crossed the Jordan.

35 So Jonathan[b] sent his brother as leader of the multitude and begged the Nabateans, who were his friends, for permission to store with them the great amount of baggage that they had. [36]But the family of Jambri from Medeba came out and seized John and all that he had, and left with it.

---

37 After these things it was reported to Jonathan and his brother Simon, "The family of Jambri are celebrating a great wedding, and are conducting the bride, a daughter of one of the great nobles of Canaan, from Nadabath with a large escort." 38Remembering how their brother John had been killed, they went up and hid under cover of the mountain. 39They looked out and saw a tumultuous procession with a great amount of baggage; and the bridegroom came out with his friends and his brothers to meet them with tambourines and musicians and many weapons. 40Then they rushed on them from the ambush and began killing them. Many were wounded and fell, and the rest fled to the mountain; and the Jews*a* took all their goods. 41So the wedding was turned into mourning and the voice of their musicians into a funeral dirge. 42After they had fully avenged the blood of their brother, they returned to the marshes of the Jordan.

43 When Bacchides heard of this, he came with a large force on the sabbath day to the banks of the Jordan. 44And Jonathan said to those with him, "Let us get up now and fight for our lives, for today things are not as they were before. 45For look! the battle is in front of us and behind us; the water of the Jordan is on this side and on that, with marsh and thicket; there is no place to turn. 46Cry out now to Heaven that you may be delivered from the hands of our enemies." 47So the battle began, and Jonathan stretched out his hand to strike Bacchides, but he eluded him and went to the rear. 48Then Jonathan and the men with him leaped into the Jordan and swam across to the other side, and the enemy*a* did not cross the Jordan to attack them. 49And about one thousand of Bacchides' men fell that day.

Bacchides Builds Fortifications

50 Then Bacchides*b* returned to Jerusalem and built strong cities in Judea: the fortress in Jericho, and Emmaus, and Beth-horon, and Bethel, and Timnath, and*c* Pharathon, and Tephon, with high walls and gates and bars. 51And he placed garrisons in them to harass Israel. 52He also fortified the town of Beth-zur, and Gazara, and the citadel, and in them he put troops and stores of food. 53And he took the sons of the leading men of the land as hostages and put them under guard in the citadel at Jerusalem.

54 In the one hundred and fifty-third year,*d* in the second month, Alcimus gave orders to tear down the wall of the inner court of the sanctuary. He tore down the work of the prophets! 55But he only began to tear it down, for at that time Alcimus was stricken and his work was hindered; his mouth was stopped and he was paralyzed, so that he could no longer say a word or give commands concerning his house. 56And Alcimus died at that time in great agony. 57When Bacchides saw that Alcimus was dead, he returned to the king, and the land of Judah had rest for two years.

The End of the War

58 Then all the lawless plotted and said, "See! Jonathan and his men are living in quiet and confidence. So now let us bring Bacchides back, and he will capture them all in one night." 59And they went and consulted with him. 60He started to come with a large force, and secretly sent letters to all his allies in Judea, telling them to seize Jonathan and his men; but they were unable to do it, because their plan became known. 61And Jonathan's men*a* seized about fifty of the men of the country who were leaders in this treachery, and killed them.

62 Then Jonathan with his men, and Simon, withdrew to Bethbasi in the wilderness; he rebuilt the parts of it that had been demolished, and they fortified it. 63When Bacchides learned of this, he assembled all his forces, and sent orders to the men of Judea. 64Then he came and encamped against Bethbasi; he fought against it for many days and made machines of war.

65 But Jonathan left his brother Simon in the town, while he went out into the country; and he went with only a few men. 66He struck down Odomera and his kindred and the people of Phasiron in their tents. 67Then he*e* began to attack and went into battle with his forces; and Simon and his men sallied out from the town and set fire to the machines of war. 68They fought with Bacchides, and he was crushed by them. They pressed him very hard, for his plan and his expedition had been in vain. 69So he was very angry at the renegades who had counseled him to come into the country, and he killed many of them. Then he decided to go back to his own land.

70 When Jonathan learned of this, he sent ambassadors to him to make peace with him and obtain release of the captives. 71He agreed, and did as he said; and he swore to Jonathan*f* that he would not try to harm him as long as he lived. 72He restored to him the captives whom he had taken previously from the land of Judah; then he turned and went back to his own land, and did not come again into their territory. 73Thus

---

a Gk *they*   *b* Gk *he*   *c* Some authorities omit *and*   *d* 159 B.C.
e Other ancient authorities read *they*   *f* Gk *him*

the sword ceased from Israel. Jonathan settled in Michmash and began to judge the people; and he destroyed the godless out of Israel.

Revolt of Alexander Epiphanes

10 In the one hundred sixtieth year[a] Alexander Epiphanes, son of Antiochus, landed and occupied Ptolemais. They welcomed him, and there he began to reign. [2]When King Demetrius heard of it, he assembled a very large army and marched out to meet him in battle. [3]Demetrius sent Jonathan a letter in peaceable words to honor him; [4]for he said to himself, "Let us act first to make peace with him[b] before he makes peace with Alexander against us, [5]for he will remember all the wrongs that we did to him and to his brothers and his nation." [6]So Demetrius[c] gave him authority to recruit troops, to equip them with arms, and to become his ally; and he commanded that the hostages in the citadel should be released to him.

7 Then Jonathan came to Jerusalem and read the letter in the hearing of all the people and of those in the citadel. [8]They were greatly alarmed when they heard that the king had given him authority to recruit troops. [9]But those in the citadel released the hostages to Jonathan, and he returned them to their parents.

10 And Jonathan took up residence in Jerusalem and began to rebuild and restore the city. [11]He directed those who were doing the work to build the walls and encircle Mount Zion with squared stones, for better fortification; and they did so.

12 Then the foreigners who were in the strongholds that Bacchides had built fled; [13]all of them left their places and went back to their own lands. [14]Only in Beth-zur did some remain who had forsaken the law and the commandments, for it served as a place of refuge.

15 Now King Alexander heard of all the promises that Demetrius had sent to Jonathan, and he heard of the battles that Jonathan[c] and his brothers had fought, of the brave deeds that they had done, and of the troubles that they had endured. [16]So he said, "Shall we find another such man? Come now, we will make him our friend and ally." [17]And he wrote a letter and sent it to him, in the following words:

Jonathan Becomes High Priest

18 "King Alexander to his brother Jonathan, greetings. [19]We have heard about you, that you are a mighty warrior and worthy to be our friend. [20]And so we have appointed you today to be the high priest of your nation; you are to be called the king's Friend and you are to take our side and keep friendship with us." He also sent him a purple robe and a golden crown.

21 So Jonathan put on the sacred vestments in the seventh month of the one hundred sixtieth year,[d] at the festival of booths,[e] and he recruited troops and equipped them with arms in abundance. [22]When Demetrius heard of these things he was distressed and said, [23]"What is this that we have done? Alexander has gotten ahead of us in forming a friendship with the Jews to strengthen himself. [24]I also will write them words of encouragement and promise them honor and gifts, so that I may have their help." [25]So he sent a message to them in the following words:

A Letter from Demetrius to Jonathan

"King Demetrius to the nation of the Jews, greetings. [26]Since you have kept your agreement with us and have continued your friendship with us, and have not sided with our enemies, we have heard of it and rejoiced. [27]Now continue still to keep faith with us, and we will repay you with good for what you do for us. [28]We will grant you many immunities and give you gifts.

29 "I now free you and exempt all the Jews from payment of tribute and salt tax and crown levies, [30]and instead of collecting the third of the grain and the half of the fruit of the trees that I should receive, I release them from this day and henceforth. I will not collect them from the land of Judah or from the three districts added to it from Samaria and Galilee, from this day and for all time. [31]Jerusalem and its environs, its tithes and its revenues, shall be holy and free from tax. [32]I release also my control of the citadel in Jerusalem and give it to the high priest, so that he may station in it men of his own choice to guard it. [33]And everyone of the Jews taken as a captive from the land of Judah into any part of my kingdom, I set free without payment; and let all officials cancel also the taxes on their livestock.

34 "All the festivals and sabbaths and new moons and appointed days, and the three days before a festival and the three after a festival—let them all be days of immunity and release for all the Jews who are in my kingdom. [35]No one shall have authority to exact anything from them or annoy any of them about any matter.

36 "Let Jews be enrolled in the king's forces to the number of thirty thousand men, and let the maintenance be given them that is due to all the forces of the king. [37]Let some of them be

---

a 152 B.C.   b Gk them   c Gk he   d 152 B.C.
e Or tabernacles

stationed in the great strongholds of the king, and let some of them be put in positions of trust in the kingdom. Let their officers and leaders be of their own number, and let them live by their own laws, just as the king has commanded in the land of Judah.

38 "As for the three districts that have been added to Judea from the country of Samaria, let them be annexed to Judea so that they may be considered to be under one ruler and obey no other authority than the high priest. ³⁹Ptolemais and the land adjoining it I have given as a gift to the sanctuary in Jerusalem, to meet the necessary expenses of the sanctuary. ⁴⁰I also grant fifteen thousand shekels of silver yearly out of the king's revenues from appropriate places. ⁴¹And all the additional funds that the government officials have not paid as they did in the first years,ᵃ they shall give from now on for the service of the temple.ᵇ ⁴²Moreover, the five thousand shekels of silver that my officialsᶜ have received every year from the income of the services of the temple, this too is canceled, because it belongs to the priests who minister there. ⁴³And all who take refuge at the temple in Jerusalem, or in any of its precincts, because they owe money to the king or are in debt, let them be released and receive back all their property in my kingdom.

44 "Let the cost of rebuilding and restoring the structures of the sanctuary be paid from the revenues of the king. ⁴⁵And let the cost of rebuilding the walls of Jerusalem and fortifying it all around, and the cost of rebuilding the walls in Judea, also be paid from the revenues of the king."

Death of Demetrius

46 When Jonathan and the people heard these words, they did not believe or accept them, because they remembered the great wrongs that Demetriusᵈ had done in Israel and how much he had oppressed them. ⁴⁷They favored Alexander, because he had been the first to speak peaceable words to them, and they remained his allies all his days.

48 Now King Alexander assembled large forces and encamped opposite Demetrius. ⁴⁹The two kings met in battle, and the army of Demetrius fled, and Alexanderᵉ pursued him and defeated them. ⁵⁰He pressed the battle strongly until the sun set, and on that day Demetrius fell.

Treaty of Ptolemy and Alexander

51 Then Alexander sent ambassadors to Ptolemy king of Egypt with the following message: ⁵²"Since I have returned to my kingdom and have taken my seat on the throne of my ancestors, and

established my rule—for I crushed Demetrius and gained control of our country; ⁵³I met him in battle, and he and his army were crushed by us, and we have taken our seat on the throne of his kingdom— ⁵⁴now therefore let us establish friendship with one another; give me now your daughter as my wife, and I will become your son-in-law, and will make gifts to you and to her in keeping with your position."

55 Ptolemy the king replied and said, "Happy was the day on which you returned to the land of your ancestors and took your seat on the throne of their kingdom. ⁵⁶And now I will do for you as you wrote, but meet me at Ptolemais, so that we may see one another, and I will become your father-in-law, as you have said."

57 So Ptolemy set out from Egypt, he and his daughter Cleopatra, and came to Ptolemais in the one hundred sixty-second year.ᶠ ⁵⁸King Alexander met him, and Ptolemyᵈ gave him his daughter Cleopatra in marriage, and celebrated her wedding at Ptolemais with great pomp, as kings do.

59 Then King Alexander wrote to Jonathan to come and meet him. ⁶⁰So he went with pomp to Ptolemais and met the two kings; he gave them and their Friends silver and gold and many gifts, and found favor with them. ⁶¹A group of malcontents from Israel, renegades, gathered together against him to accuse him; but the king paid no attention to them. ⁶²The king gave orders to take off Jonathan's garments and to clothe him in purple, and they did so. ⁶³The king also seated him at his side; and he said to his officers, "Go out with him into the middle of the city and proclaim that no one is to bring charges against him about any matter, and let no one annoy him for any reason." ⁶⁴When his accusers saw the honor that was paid him, in accord with the proclamation, and saw him clothed in purple, they all fled. ⁶⁵Thus the king honored him and enrolled him among his chiefᵍ Friends, and made him general and governor of the province. ⁶⁶And Jonathan returned to Jerusalem in peace and gladness.

Apollonius Is Defeated by Jonathan

67 In the one hundred sixty-fifth yearʰ Demetrius son of Demetrius came from Crete to the land of his ancestors. ⁶⁸When King Alexander heard of it, he was greatly distressed and returned to Antioch. ⁶⁹And Demetrius appointed

---

a Meaning of Gk uncertain   b Gk *house*   c Gk *they*   d Gk *he*
e Other ancient authorities read *Alexander fled, and Demetrius*
f 150 B.C.   g Gk *first*   h 147 B.C.

Apollonius the governor of Coelesyria, and he assembled a large force and encamped against Jamnia. Then he sent the following message to the high priest Jonathan:

70 "You are the only one to rise up against us, and I have fallen into ridicule and disgrace because of you. Why do you assume authority against us in the hill country? 71If you now have confidence in your forces, come down to the plain to meet us, and let us match strength with each other there, for I have with me the power of the cities. 72Ask and learn who I am and who the others are that are helping us. People will tell you that you cannot stand before us, for your ancestors were twice put to flight in their own land. 73And now you will not be able to withstand my cavalry and such an army in the plain, where there is no stone or pebble, or place to flee."

74 When Jonathan heard the words of Apollonius, his spirit was aroused. He chose ten thousand men and set out from Jerusalem, and his brother Simon met him to help him. 75He encamped before Joppa, but the people of the city closed its gates, for Apollonius had a garrison in Joppa. 76So they fought against it, and the people of the city became afraid and opened the gates, and Jonathan gained possession of Joppa.

77 When Apollonius heard of it, he mustered three thousand cavalry and a large army, and went to Azotus as though he were going farther. At the same time he advanced into the plain, for he had a large troop of cavalry and put confidence in it. 78Jonathan[a] pursued him to Azotus, and the armies engaged in battle. 79Now Apollonius had secretly left a thousand cavalry behind them. 80Jonathan learned that there was an ambush behind him, for they surrounded his army and shot arrows at his men from early morning until late afternoon. 81But his men stood fast, as Jonathan had commanded, and the enemy's[b] horses grew tired.

82 Then Simon brought forward his force and engaged the phalanx in battle (for the cavalry was exhausted); they were overwhelmed by him and fled, 83and the cavalry was dispersed in the plain. They fled to Azotus and entered Bethdagon, the temple of their idol, for safety. 84But Jonathan burned Azotus and the surrounding towns and plundered them; and the temple of Dagon, and those who had taken refuge in it, he burned with fire. 85The number of those who fell by the sword, with those burned alive, came to eight thousand.

86 Then Jonathan left there and encamped against Askalon, and the people of the city came out to meet him with great pomp.

87 He and those with him then returned to Jerusalem with a large amount of booty. 88When King Alexander heard of these things, he honored Jonathan still more; 89and he sent to him a golden buckle, such as it is the custom to give to the King's Kinsmen. He also gave him Ekron and all its environs as his possession.

Ptolemy Invades Syria

11 Then the king of Egypt gathered great forces, like the sand by the seashore, and many ships; and he tried to get possession of Alexander's kingdom by trickery and add it to his own kingdom. 2He set out for Syria with peaceable words, and the people of the towns opened their gates to him and went to meet him, for King Alexander had commanded them to meet him, since he was Alexander's[c] father-in-law. 3But when Ptolemy entered the towns he stationed forces as a garrison in each town.

4 When he[d] approached Azotus, they showed him the burnt-out temple of Dagon, and Azotus and its suburbs destroyed, and the corpses lying about, and the charred bodies of those whom Jonathan[d] had burned in the war, for they had piled them in heaps along his route. 5They also told the king what Jonathan had done, to throw blame on him; but the king kept silent. 6Jonathan met the king at Joppa with pomp, and they greeted one another and spent the night there. 7And Jonathan went with the king as far as the river called Eleutherus; then he returned to Jerusalem.

8 So King Ptolemy gained control of the coastal cities as far as Seleucia by the sea, and he kept devising wicked designs against Alexander. 9He sent envoys to King Demetrius, saying, "Come, let us make a covenant with each other, and I will give you in marriage my daughter who was Alexander's wife, and you shall reign over your father's kingdom. 10I now regret that I gave him my daughter, for he has tried to kill me." 11He threw blame on Alexander[e] because he coveted his kingdom. 12So he took his daughter away from him and gave her to Demetrius. He was estranged from Alexander, and their enmity became manifest.

13 Then Ptolemy entered Antioch and put on the crown of Asia. Thus he put two crowns on his head, the crown of Egypt and that of Asia. 14Now King Alexander was in Cilicia at that time, because the people of that region were in revolt. 15When Alexander heard of it, he came against

him in battle. Ptolemy marched out and met him with a strong force, and put him to flight. ¹⁶So Alexander fled into Arabia to find protection there, and King Ptolemy was triumphant. ¹⁷Zabdiel the Arab cut off the head of Alexander and sent it to Ptolemy. ¹⁸But King Ptolemy died three days later, and his troops in the strongholds were killed by the inhabitants of the strongholds. ¹⁹So Demetrius became king in the one hundred sixty-seventh year.ᵃ

Jonathan's Diplomacy

20 In those days Jonathan assembled the Judeans to attack the citadel in Jerusalem, and he built many engines of war to use against it. ²¹But certain renegades who hated their nation went to the king and reported to him that Jonathan was besieging the citadel. ²²When he heard this he was angry, and as soon as he heard it he set out and came to Ptolemais; and he wrote Jonathan not to continue the siege, but to meet him for a conference at Ptolemais as quickly as possible.

23 When Jonathan heard this, he gave orders to continue the siege. He chose some of the elders of Israel and some of the priests, and put himself in danger, ²⁴for he went to the king at Ptolemais, taking silver and gold and clothing and numerous other gifts. And he won his favor. ²⁵Although certain renegades of his nation kept making complaints against him, ²⁶the king treated him as his predecessors had treated him; he exalted him in the presence of all his Friends. ²⁷He confirmed him in the high priesthood and in as many other honors as he had formerly had, and caused him to be reckoned among his chiefᵇ Friends. ²⁸Then Jonathan asked the king to free Judea and the three districts of Samariaᶜ from tribute, and promised him three hundred talents. ²⁹The king consented, and wrote a letter to Jonathan about all these things; its contents were as follows:

30 "King Demetrius to his brother Jonathan and to the nation of the Jews, greetings. ³¹This copy of the letter that we wrote concerning you to our kinsman Lasthenes we have written to you also, so that you may know what it says. ³²'King Demetrius to his father Lasthenes, greetings. ³³We have determined to do good to the nation of the Jews, who are our friends and fulfill their obligations to us, because of the goodwill they show toward us. ³⁴We have confirmed as their possession both the territory of Judea and the three districts of Aphairema and Lydda and Rathamin; the latter, with all the region bordering them, were added to Judea from Samaria. To all those who offer sacrifice in Jerusalem we have granted release fromᵈ the royal taxes that the king formerly received from them each year, from the crops of the land and the fruit of the trees. ³⁵And the other payments henceforth due to us of the tithes, and the taxes due to us, and the salt pits and the crown taxes due to us—from all these we shall grant them release. ³⁶And not one of these grants shall be canceled from this time on forever. ³⁷Now therefore take care to make a copy of this, and let it be given to Jonathan and put up in a conspicuous place on the holy mountain.' "

The Intrigue of Trypho

38 When King Demetrius saw that the land was quiet before him and that there was no opposition to him, he dismissed all his troops, all of them to their own homes, except the foreign troops that he had recruited from the islands of the nations. So all the troops who had served under his predecessors hated him. ³⁹A certain Trypho had formerly been one of Alexander's supporters; he saw that all the troops were grumbling against Demetrius. So he went to Imalkue the Arab, who was bringing up Antiochus, the young son of Alexander, ⁴⁰and insistently urged him to hand Antiochusᵉ over to him, to become king in place of his father. He also reported to Imalkueᵉ what Demetrius had done and told of the hatred that the troops of Demetriusᶠ had for him; and he stayed there many days.

41 Now Jonathan sent to King Demetrius the request that he remove the troops of the citadel from Jerusalem, and the troops in the strongholds; for they kept fighting against Israel. ⁴²And Demetrius sent this message back to Jonathan: "Not only will I do these things for you and your nation, but I will confer great honor on you and your nation, if I find an opportunity. ⁴³Now then you will do well to send me men who will help me, for all my troops have revolted." ⁴⁴So Jonathan sent three thousand stalwart men to him at Antioch, and when they came to the king, the king rejoiced at their arrival.

45 Then the people of the city assembled within the city, to the number of a hundred and twenty thousand, and they wanted to kill the king. ⁴⁶But the king fled into the palace. Then the people of the city seized the main streets of the city and began to fight. ⁴⁷So the king called the Jews to his aid, and they all rallied around him and then spread out through the city; and they killed on that day about one hundred

---

a 145 B.C.   b Gk first   c Cn: Gk the three districts and Samaria   d Or Samaria, for all those who offer sacrifice in Jerusalem, in place of   e Gk him   f Gk his troops

thousand. [48]They set fire to the city and seized a large amount of spoil on that day, and saved the king. [49]When the people of the city saw that the Jews had gained control of the city as they pleased, their courage failed and they cried out to the king with this entreaty: [50]"Grant us peace, and make the Jews stop fighting against us and our city." [51]And they threw down their arms and made peace. So the Jews gained glory in the sight of the king and of all the people in his kingdom, and they returned to Jerusalem with a large amount of spoil.

52 So King Demetrius sat on the throne of his kingdom, and the land was quiet before him. [53]But he broke his word about all that he had promised; he became estranged from Jonathan and did not repay the favors that Jonathan[a] had done him, but treated him very harshly.

Trypho Seizes Power

54 After this Trypho returned, and with him the young boy Antiochus who began to reign and put on the crown. [55]All the troops that Demetrius had discharged gathered around him; they fought against Demetrius,[b] and he fled and was routed. [56]Trypho captured the elephants[c] and gained control of Antioch. [57]Then the young Antiochus wrote to Jonathan, saying, "I confirm you in the high priesthood and set you over the four districts and make you one of the king's Friends." [58]He also sent him gold plates and a table service, and granted him the right to drink from gold cups and dress in purple and wear a gold buckle. [59]He appointed Jonathan's[d] brother Simon governor from the Ladder of Tyre to the borders of Egypt.

Campaigns of Jonathan and Simon

60 Then Jonathan set out and traveled beyond the river and among the towns, and all the army of Syria gathered to him as allies. When he came to Askalon, the people of the city met him and paid him honor. [61]From there he went to Gaza, but the people of Gaza shut him out. So he besieged it and burned its suburbs with fire and plundered them. [62]Then the people of Gaza pleaded with Jonathan, and he made peace with them, and took the sons of their rulers as hostages and sent them to Jerusalem. And he passed through the country as far as Damascus.

63 Then Jonathan heard that the officers of Demetrius had come to Kadesh in Galilee with a large army, intending to remove him from office. [64]He went to meet them, but left his brother Simon in the country. [65]Simon encamped before Beth-zur and fought against it for many days and hemmed it in. [66]Then they asked him to grant them terms of peace, and he did so. He removed them from there, took possession of the town, and set a garrison over it.

67 Jonathan and his army encamped by the waters of Gennesaret. Early in the morning they marched to the plain of Hazor, [68]and there in the plain the army of the foreigners met him; they had set an ambush against him in the mountains, but they themselves met him face to face. [69]Then the men in ambush emerged from their places and joined battle. [70]All the men with Jonathan fled; not one of them was left except Mattathias son of Absalom and Judas son of Chalphi, commanders of the forces of the army. [71]Jonathan tore his clothes, put dust on his head, and prayed. [72]Then he turned back to the battle against the enemy[e] and routed them, and they fled. [73]When his men who were fleeing saw this, they returned to him and joined him in the pursuit as far as Kadesh, to their camp, and there they encamped. [74]As many as three thousand of the foreigners fell that day. And Jonathan returned to Jerusalem.

Alliances with Rome and Sparta

12 Now when Jonathan saw that the time was favorable for him, he chose men and sent them to Rome to confirm and renew the friendship with them. [2]He also sent letters to the same effect to the Spartans and to other places. [3]So they went to Rome and entered the senate chamber and said, "The high priest Jonathan and the Jewish nation have sent us to renew the former friendship and alliance with them." [4]And the Romans[f] gave them letters to the people in every place, asking them to provide for the envoys[e] safe conduct to the land of Judah.

5 This is a copy of the letter that Jonathan wrote to the Spartans: [6]"The high priest Jonathan, the senate of the nation, the priests, and the rest of the Jewish people to their brothers the Spartans, greetings. [7]Already in time past a letter was sent to the high priest Onias from Arius[g] who was king among you, stating that you are our brothers, as the appended copy shows. [8]Onias welcomed the envoy with honor, and received the letter, which contained a clear declaration of alliance and friendship. [9]Therefore, though we have no need of these things, since we have as encouragement the holy books that are in our hands, [10]we have undertaken to send to renew our family ties and friendship with

---

a Gk he   b Gk him   c Gk animals   d Gk his   e Gk them
f Gk they   g Vg Compare verse 20: Gk Darius

you, so that we may not become estranged from you, for considerable time has passed since you sent your letter to us. [11]We therefore remember you constantly on every occasion, both at our festivals and on other appropriate days, at the sacrifices that we offer and in our prayers, as it is right and proper to remember brothers. [12]And we rejoice in your glory. [13]But as for ourselves, many trials and many wars have encircled us; the kings around us have waged war against us. [14]We were unwilling to annoy you and our other allies and friends with these wars, [15]for we have the help that comes from Heaven for our aid, and so we were delivered from our enemies, and our enemies were humbled. [16]We therefore have chosen Numenius son of Antiochus and Antipater son of Jason, and have sent them to Rome to renew our former friendship and alliance with them. [17]We have commanded them to go also to you and greet you and deliver to you this letter from us concerning the renewal of our family ties. [18]And now please send us a reply to this."

[19] This is a copy of the letter that they sent to Onias: [20]"King Arius of the Spartans, to the high priest Onias, greetings. [21]It has been found in writing concerning the Spartans and the Jews that they are brothers and are of the family of Abraham. [22]And now that we have learned this, please write us concerning your welfare; [23]we on our part write to you that your livestock and your property belong to us, and ours belong to you. We therefore command that our envoys[a] report to you accordingly."

Further Campaigns of Jonathan and Simon

[24] Now Jonathan heard that the commanders of Demetrius had returned, with a larger force than before, to wage war against him. [25]So he marched away from Jerusalem and met them in the region of Hamath, for he gave them no opportunity to invade his own country. [26]He sent spies to their camp, and they returned and reported to him that the enemy[a] were being drawn up in formation to attack the Jews[b] by night. [27]So when the sun had set, Jonathan commanded his troops to be alert and to keep their arms at hand so as to be ready all night for battle, and he stationed outposts around the camp. [28]When the enemy heard that Jonathan and his troops were prepared for battle, they were afraid and were terrified at heart; so they kindled fires in their camp and withdrew.[c] [29]But Jonathan and his troops did not know it until morning, for they saw the fires burning. [30]Then Jonathan pursued them, but he did not overtake them, for they had crossed the Eleutherus river. [31]So Jonathan

turned aside against the Arabs who are called Zabadeans, and he crushed them and plundered them. [32]Then he broke camp and went to Damascus, and marched through all that region.

[33] Simon also went out and marched through the country as far as Askalon and the neighboring strongholds. He turned aside to Joppa and took it by surprise, [34]for he had heard that they were ready to hand over the stronghold to those whom Demetrius had sent. And he stationed a garrison there to guard it.

[35] When Jonathan returned he convened the elders of the people and planned with them to build strongholds in Judea, [36]to build the walls of Jerusalem still higher, and to erect a high barrier between the citadel and the city to separate it from the city, in order to isolate it so that its garrison[a] could neither buy nor sell. [37]So they gathered together to rebuild the city; part of the wall on the valley to the east had fallen, and he repaired the section called Chaphenatha. [38]Simon also built Adida in the Shephelah; he fortified it and installed gates with bolts.

Trypho Captures Jonathan

[39] Then Trypho attempted to become king in Asia and put on the crown, and to raise his hand against King Antiochus. [40]He feared that Jonathan might not permit him to do so, but might make war on him, so he kept seeking to seize and kill him, and he marched out and came to Beth-shan. [41]Jonathan went out to meet him with forty thousand picked warriors, and he came to Beth-shan. [42]When Trypho saw that he had come with a large army, he was afraid to raise his hand against him. [43]So he received him with honor and commended him to all his Friends, and he gave him gifts and commanded his Friends and his troops to obey him as they would himself. [44]Then he said to Jonathan, "Why have you put all these people to so much trouble when we are not at war? [45]Dismiss them now to their homes and choose for yourself a few men to stay with you, and come with me to Ptolemais. I will hand it over to you as well as the other strongholds and the remaining troops and all the officials, and will turn around and go home. For that is why I am here."

[46] Jonathan[d] trusted him and did as he said; he sent away the troops, and they returned to the land of Judah. [47]He kept with himself three thousand men, two thousand of whom he left in Galilee, while one thousand accompanied him.

---

a Gk they   b Gk them   c Other ancient authorities omit and withdrew   d Gk he

48But when Jonathan entered Ptolemais, the people of Ptolemais closed the gates and seized him, and they killed with the sword all who had entered with him.

49 Then Trypho sent troops and cavalry into Galilee and the Great Plain to destroy all Jonathan's soldiers. 50But they realized that Jonathan had been seized and had perished along with his men, and they encouraged one another and kept marching in close formation, ready for battle. 51When their pursuers saw that they would fight for their lives, they turned back. 52So they all reached the land of Judah safely, and they mourned for Jonathan and his companions and were in great fear; and all Israel mourned deeply. 53All the nations around them tried to destroy them, for they said, "They have no leader or helper. Now therefore let us make war on them and blot out the memory of them from humankind."

Simon Takes Command

13 Simon heard that Trypho had assembled a large army to invade the land of Judah and destroy it, 2and he saw that the people were trembling with fear. So he went up to Jerusalem, and gathering the people together 3he encouraged them, saying to them, "You yourselves know what great things my brothers and I and the house of my father have done for the laws and the sanctuary; you know also the wars and the difficulties that my brothers and I have seen. 4By reason of this all my brothers have perished for the sake of Israel, and I alone am left. 5And now, far be it from me to spare my life in any time of distress, for I am not better than my brothers. 6But I will avenge my nation and the sanctuary and your wives and children, for all the nations have gathered together out of hatred to destroy us."

7 The spirit of the people was rekindled when they heard these words, 8and they answered in a loud voice, "You are our leader in place of Judas and your brother Jonathan. 9Fight our battles, and all that you say to us we will do." 10So he assembled all the warriors and hurried to complete the walls of Jerusalem, and he fortified it on every side. 11He sent Jonathan son of Absalom to Joppa, and with him a considerable army; he drove out its occupants and remained there.

Deceit and Treachery of Trypho

12 Then Trypho left Ptolemais with a large army to invade the land of Judah, and Jonathan was with him under guard. 13Simon encamped in Adida, facing the plain. 14Trypho learned that Simon had risen up in place of his brother Jonathan, and that he was about to join battle with him, so he sent envoys to him and said, 15"It is for the money that your brother Jonathan owed the royal treasury, in connection with the offices he held, that we are detaining him. 16Send now one hundred talents of silver and two of his sons as hostages, so that when released he will not revolt against us, and we will release him."

17 Simon knew that they were speaking deceitfully to him, but he sent to get the money and the sons, so that he would not arouse great hostility among the people, who might say, 18"It was because Simon*a* did not send him the money and the sons, that Jonathan*b* perished." 19So he sent the sons and the hundred talents, but Trypho*b* broke his word and did not release Jonathan.

20 After this Trypho came to invade the country and destroy it, and he circled around by the way to Adora. But Simon and his army kept marching along opposite him to every place he went. 21Now the men in the citadel kept sending envoys to Trypho urging him to come to them by way of the wilderness and to send them food. 22So Trypho got all his cavalry ready to go, but that night a very heavy snow fell, and he did not go because of the snow. He marched off and went into the land of Gilead. 23When he approached Baskama, he killed Jonathan, and he was buried there. 24Then Trypho turned and went back to his own land.

Jonathan's Tomb

25 Simon sent and took the bones of his brother Jonathan, and buried him in Modein, the city of his ancestors. 26All Israel bewailed him with great lamentation, and mourned for him many days. 27And Simon built a monument over the tomb of his father and his brothers; he made it high so that it might be seen, with polished stone at the front and back. 28He also erected seven pyramids, opposite one another, for his father and mother and four brothers. 29For the pyramids*c* he devised an elaborate setting, erecting about them great columns, and on the columns he put suits of armor for a permanent memorial, and beside the suits of armor he carved ships, so that they could be seen by all who sail the sea. 30This is the tomb that he built in Modein; it remains to this day.

Judea Gains Independence

31 Trypho dealt treacherously with the young King Antiochus; he killed him 32and became king

---

a Gk *I*   *b* Gk *he*   *c* Gk *For these*

in his place, putting on the crown of Asia; and he brought great calamity on the land. [33]But Simon built up the strongholds of Judea and walled them all around, with high towers and great walls and gates and bolts, and he stored food in the strongholds. [34]Simon also chose emissaries and sent them to King Demetrius with a request to grant relief to the country, for all that Trypho did was to plunder. [35]King Demetrius sent him a favorable reply to this request, and wrote him a letter as follows, [36]"King Demetrius to Simon, the high priest and friend of kings, and to the elders and nation of the Jews, greetings. [37]We have received the gold crown and the palm branch that you[a] sent, and we are ready to make a general peace with you and to write to our officials to grant you release from tribute. [38]All the grants that we have made to you remain valid, and let the strongholds that you have built be your possession. [39]We pardon any errors and offenses committed to this day, and cancel the crown tax that you owe; and whatever other tax has been collected in Jerusalem shall be collected no longer. [40]And if any of you are qualified to be enrolled in our bodyguard,[b] let them be enrolled, and let there be peace between us."

41 In the one hundred seventieth year[c] the yoke of the Gentiles was removed from Israel, [42]and the people began to write in their documents and contracts, "In the first year of Simon the great high priest and commander and leader of the Jews."

The Capture of Gazara by Simon

43 In those days Simon[d] encamped against Gazara[e] and surrounded it with troops. He made a siege engine, brought it up to the city, and battered and captured one tower. [44]The men in the siege engine leaped out into the city, and a great tumult arose in the city. [45]The men in the city, with their wives and children, went up on the wall with their clothes torn, and they cried out with a loud voice, asking Simon to make peace with them; [46]they said, "Do not treat us according to our wicked acts but according to your mercy." [47]So Simon reached an agreement with them and stopped fighting against them. But he expelled them from the city and cleansed the houses in which the idols were located, and then entered it with hymns and praise. [48]He removed all uncleanness from it, and settled in it those who observed the law. He also strengthened its fortifications and built in it a house for himself.

Simon Regains the Citadel at Jerusalem

49 Those who were in the citadel at Jerusalem were prevented from going in and out to buy and sell in the country. So they were very hungry, and many of them perished from famine. [50]Then they cried to Simon to make peace with them, and he did so. But he expelled them from there and cleansed the citadel from its pollutions. [51]On the twenty-third day of the second month, in the one hundred seventy-first year,[f] the Jews[g] entered it with praise and palm branches, and with harps and cymbals and stringed instruments, and with hymns and songs, because a great enemy had been crushed and removed from Israel. [52]Simon[h] decreed that every year they should celebrate this day with rejoicing. He strengthened the fortifications of the temple hill alongside the citadel, and he and his men lived there. [53]Simon saw that his son John had reached manhood, and so he made him commander of all the forces; and he lived at Gazara.

Capture of Demetrius

14 In the one hundred seventy-second year[i] King Demetrius assembled his forces and marched into Media to obtain help, so that he could make war against Trypho. [2]When King Arsaces of Persia and Media heard that Demetrius had invaded his territory, he sent one of his generals to take him alive. [3]The general[h] went and defeated the army of Demetrius, and seized him and took him to Arsaces, who put him under guard.

Eulogy of Simon

4 The land[j] had rest all the days of Simon.
  He sought the good of his nation;
his rule was pleasing to them,
  as was the honor shown him, all his days.
5 To crown all his honors he took Joppa for a
  harbor,
  and opened a way to the isles of the sea.
6 He extended the borders of his nation,
  and gained full control of the country.
7 He gathered a host of captives;
  he ruled over Gazara and Beth-zur and the
  citadel,
  and he removed its uncleanness from it;
  and there was none to oppose him.
8 They tilled their land in peace;
  the ground gave its increase,
  and the trees of the plains their fruit.
9 Old men sat in the streets;
  they all talked together of good things,
  and the youths put on splendid military attire.

---

a The word you in verses 37–40 is plural   b Or court   c 142 B.C.
d Gk he   e Cn: Gk Gaza   f 141 B.C.   g Gk they   h Gk He
i 140 B.C.   j Other ancient authorities add of Judah

¹⁰ He supplied the towns with food,
  and furnished them with the means of defense,
  until his renown spread to the ends of the earth.
¹¹ He established peace in the land,
  and Israel rejoiced with great joy.
¹² All the people sat under their own vines and fig trees,
  and there was none to make them afraid.
¹³ No one was left in the land to fight them,
  and the kings were crushed in those days.
¹⁴ He gave help to all the humble among his people;
  he sought out the law,
  and did away with all the renegades and outlaws.
¹⁵ He made the sanctuary glorious,
  and added to the vessels of the sanctuary.

Diplomacy with Rome and Sparta

16 It was heard in Rome, and as far away as Sparta, that Jonathan had died, and they were deeply grieved. ¹⁷When they heard that his brother Simon had become high priest in his stead, and that he was ruling over the country and the towns in it, ¹⁸they wrote to him on bronze tablets to renew with him the friendship and alliance that they had established with his brothers Judas and Jonathan. ¹⁹And these were read before the assembly in Jerusalem.

20 This is a copy of the letter that the Spartans sent:

"The rulers and the city of the Spartans to the high priest Simon and to the elders and the priests and the rest of the Jewish people, our brothers, greetings. ²¹The envoys who were sent to our people have told us about your glory and honor, and we rejoiced at their coming. ²²We have recorded what they said in our public decrees, as follows, 'Numenius son of Antiochus and Antipater son of Jason, envoys of the Jews, have come to us to renew their friendship with us. ²³It has pleased our people to receive these men with honor and to put a copy of their words in the public archives, so that the people of the Spartans may have a record of them. And they have sent a copy of this to the high priest Simon.'"

24 After this Simon sent Numenius to Rome with a large gold shield weighing one thousand minas, to confirm the alliance with the Romans.^a

Official Honors for Simon

25 When the people heard these things they said, "How shall we thank Simon and his sons?

²⁶For he and his brothers and the house of his father have stood firm; they have fought and repulsed Israel's enemies and established its freedom." ²⁷So they made a record on bronze tablets and put it on pillars on Mount Zion.

This is a copy of what they wrote: "On the eighteenth day of Elul, in the one hundred seventy-second year,^b which is the third year of the great high priest Simon, ²⁸in Asaramel,^c in the great assembly of the priests and the people and the rulers of the nation and the elders of the country, the following was proclaimed to us:

29 "Since wars often occurred in the country, Simon son of Mattathias, a priest of the sons^d of Joarib, and his brothers, exposed themselves to danger and resisted the enemies of their nation, in order that their sanctuary and the law might be preserved; and they brought great glory to their nation. ³⁰Jonathan rallied the^e nation, became their high priest, and was gathered to his people. ³¹When their enemies decided to invade their country and lay hands on their sanctuary, ³²then Simon rose up and fought for his nation. He spent great sums of his own money; he armed the soldiers of his nation and paid them wages. ³³He fortified the towns of Judea, and Beth-zur on the borders of Judea, where formerly the arms of the enemy had been stored, and he placed there a garrison of Jews. ³⁴He also fortified Joppa, which is by the sea, and Gazara, which is on the borders of Azotus, where the enemy formerly lived. He settled Jews there, and provided in those towns^a whatever was necessary for their restoration.

35 "The people saw Simon's faithfulness^f and the glory that he had resolved to win for his nation, and they made him their leader and high priest, because he had done all these things and because of the justice and loyalty that he had maintained toward his nation. He sought in every way to exalt his people. ³⁶In his days things prospered in his hands, so that the Gentiles were put out of the^e country, as were also those in the city of David in Jerusalem, who had built themselves a citadel from which they used to sally forth and defile the environs of the sanctuary, doing great damage to its purity. ³⁷He settled Jews in it and fortified it for the safety of the country and of the city, and built the walls of Jerusalem higher.

38 "In view of these things King Demetrius confirmed him in the high priesthood, ³⁹made him one of his Friends, and paid him high

a Gk them b 140 B.C. c This word resembles the Hebrew words for the court of the people of God or the prince of the people of God d Meaning of Gk uncertain e Gk their f Other ancient authorities read conduct

honors. [40]For he had heard that the Jews were addressed by the Romans as friends and allies and brothers, and that the Romans[a] had received the envoys of Simon with honor.

[41] "The Jews and their priests have resolved that Simon should be their leader and high priest forever, until a trustworthy prophet should arise, [42]and that he should be governor over them and that he should take charge of the sanctuary and appoint officials over its tasks and over the country and the weapons and the strongholds, and that he should take charge of the sanctuary, [43]and that he should be obeyed by all, and that all contracts in the country should be written in his name, and that he should be clothed in purple and wear gold.

[44] "None of the people or priests shall be permitted to nullify any of these decisions or to oppose what he says, or to convene an assembly in the country without his permission, or to be clothed in purple or put on a gold buckle. [45]Whoever acts contrary to these decisions or rejects any of them shall be liable to punishment."

[46] All the people agreed to grant Simon the right to act in accordance with these decisions. [47]So Simon accepted and agreed to be high priest, to be commander and ethnarch of the Jews and priests, and to be protector of them all.[b] [48]And they gave orders to inscribe this decree on bronze tablets, to put them up in a conspicuous place in the precincts of the sanctuary, [49]and to deposit copies of them in the treasury, so that Simon and his sons might have them.

Letter of Antiochus VII

15 Antiochus, son of King Demetrius, sent a letter from the islands of the sea to Simon, the priest and ethnarch of the Jews, and to all the nation; [2]its contents were as follows: "King Antiochus to Simon the high priest and ethnarch and to the nation of the Jews, greetings. [3]Whereas certain scoundrels have gained control of the kingdom of our ancestors, and I intend to lay claim to the kingdom so that I may restore it as it formerly was, and have recruited a host of mercenary troops and have equipped warships, [4]and intend to make a landing in the country so that I may proceed against those who have destroyed our country and those who have devastated many cities in my kingdom, [5]now therefore I confirm to you all the tax remissions that the kings before me have granted you, and a release from all the other payments from which they have released you. [6]I permit you to mint your own coinage as money for your country, [7]and I grant freedom to Jerusalem and the sanctuary.

All the weapons that you have prepared and the strongholds that you have built and now hold shall remain yours. [8]Every debt you owe to the royal treasury and any such future debts shall be canceled for you from henceforth and for all time. [9]When we gain control of our kingdom, we will bestow great honor on you and your nation and the temple, so that your glory will become manifest in all the earth."

[10] In the one hundred seventy-fourth year[c] Antiochus set out and invaded the land of his ancestors. All the troops rallied to him, so that there were only a few with Trypho. [11]Antiochus pursued him, and Trypho[d] came in his flight to Dor, which is by the sea; [12]for he knew that troubles had converged on him, and his troops had deserted him. [13]So Antiochus encamped against Dor, and with him were one hundred twenty thousand warriors and eight thousand cavalry. [14]He surrounded the town, and the ships joined battle from the sea; he pressed the town hard from land and sea, and permitted no one to leave or enter it.

Rome Supports the Jews

[15] Then Numenius and his companions arrived from Rome, with letters to the kings and countries, in which the following was written: [16]"Lucius, consul of the Romans, to King Ptolemy, greetings. [17]The envoys of the Jews have come to us as our friends and allies to renew our ancient friendship and alliance. They had been sent by the high priest Simon and by the Jewish people [18]and have brought a gold shield weighing one thousand minas. [19]We therefore have decided to write to the kings and countries that they should not seek their harm or make war against them and their cities and their country, or make alliance with those who war against them. [20]And it has seemed good to us to accept the shield from them. [21]Therefore if any scoundrels have fled to you from their country, hand them over to the high priest Simon, so that he may punish them according to their law."

[22] The consul[e] wrote the same thing to King Demetrius and to Attalus and Ariarathes and Arsaces, [23]and to all the countries, and to Sampsames,[f] and to the Spartans, and to Delos, and to Myndos, and to Sicyon, and to Caria, and to Samos, and to Pamphylia, and to Lycia, and to Halicarnassus, and to Rhodes, and to Phaselis, and to Cos, and to Side, and to Aradus and Gortyna and Cnidus and Cyprus and Cyrene. [24]They

---

a Gk they   b Or to preside over them all   c 138 B.C.   d Gk he
e Gk He   f The name is uncertain

also sent a copy of these things to the high priest Simon.

Antiochus VII Threatens Simon

25 King Antiochus besieged Dor for the second time, continually throwing his forces against it and making engines of war; and he shut Trypho up and kept him from going out or in. 26And Simon sent to Antiochus[a] two thousand picked troops, to fight for him, and silver and gold and a large amount of military equipment. 27But he refused to receive them, and broke all the agreements he formerly had made with Simon, and became estranged from him. 28He sent to him Athenobius, one of his Friends, to confer with him, saying, "You hold control of Joppa and Gazara and the citadel in Jerusalem; they are cities of my kingdom. 29You have devastated their territory, you have done great damage in the land, and you have taken possession of many places in my kingdom. 30Now then, hand over the cities that you have seized and the tribute money of the places that you have conquered outside the borders of Judea; 31or else pay me five hundred talents of silver for the destruction that you have caused and five hundred talents more for the tribute money of the cities. Otherwise we will come and make war on you."

32 So Athenobius, the king's Friend, came to Jerusalem, and when he saw the splendor of Simon, and the sideboard with its gold and silver plate, and his great magnificence, he was amazed. When he reported to him the king's message, 33Simon said to him in reply: "We have neither taken foreign land nor seized foreign property, but only the inheritance of our ancestors, which at one time had been unjustly taken by our enemies. 34Now that we have the opportunity, we are firmly holding the inheritance of our ancestors. 35As for Joppa and Gazara, which you demand, they were causing great damage among the people and to our land; for them we will give you one hundred talents."

Athenobius[b] did not answer him a word, 36but returned in wrath to the king and reported to him these words, and also the splendor of Simon and all that he had seen. And the king was very angry.

Victory over Cendebeus

37 Meanwhile Trypho embarked on a ship and escaped to Orthosia. 38Then the king made Cendebeus commander-in-chief of the coastal country, and gave him troops of infantry and cavalry. 39He commanded him to encamp against Judea, to build up Kedron and fortify its

gates, and to make war on the people; but the king pursued Trypho. 40So Cendebeus came to Jamnia and began to provoke the people and invade Judea and take the people captive and kill them. 41He built up Kedron and stationed horsemen and troops there, so that they might go out and make raids along the highways of Judea, as the king had ordered him.

16 John went up from Gazara and reported to his father Simon what Cendebeus had done. 2And Simon called in his two eldest sons Judas and John, and said to them: "My brothers and I and my father's house have fought the wars of Israel from our youth until this day, and things have prospered in our hands so that we have delivered Israel many times. 3But now I have grown old, and you by Heaven's[c] mercy are mature in years. Take my place and my brother's, and go out and fight for our nation, and may the help that comes from Heaven be with you."

4 So John[d] chose out of the country twenty thousand warriors and cavalry, and they marched against Cendebeus and camped for the night in Modein. 5Early in the morning they started out and marched into the plain, where a large force of infantry and cavalry was coming to meet them; and a stream lay between them. 6Then he and his army lined up against them. He saw that the soldiers were afraid to cross the stream, so he crossed over first; and when his troops saw him, they crossed over after him. 7Then he divided the army and placed the cavalry in the center of the infantry, for the cavalry of the enemy were very numerous. 8They sounded the trumpets, and Cendebeus and his army were put to flight; many of them fell wounded and the rest fled into the stronghold. 9At that time Judas the brother of John was wounded, but John pursued them until Cendebeus[e] reached Kedron, which he had built. 10They also fled into the towers that were in the fields of Azotus, and John[e] burned it with fire, and about two thousand of them fell. He then returned to Judea safely.

Murder of Simon and His Sons

11 Now Ptolemy son of Abubus had been appointed governor over the plain of Jericho; he had a large store of silver and gold, 12for he was son-in-law of the high priest. 13His heart was lifted up; he determined to get control of the country, and made treacherous plans against Simon and his sons, to do away with them. 14Now Simon was visiting the towns of the country and

---

a Gk him　b Gk He　c Gk his　d Other ancient authorities read he　e Gk he

attending to their needs, and he went down to Jericho with his sons Mattathias and Judas, in the one hundred seventy-seventh year,[a] in the eleventh month, which is the month of Shebat. [15]The son of Abubus received them treacherously in the little stronghold called Dok, which he had built; he gave them a great banquet, and hid men there. [16]When Simon and his sons were drunk, Ptolemy and his men rose up, took their weapons, rushed in against Simon in the banquet hall and killed him and his two sons, as well as some of his servants. [17]So he committed an act of great treachery and returned evil for good.

John Succeeds Simon

18 Then Ptolemy wrote a report about these things and sent it to the king, asking him to send troops to aid him and to turn over to him the towns and the country. [19]He sent other troops to Gazara to do away with John; he sent letters to the captains asking them to come to him so that he might give them silver and gold and gifts; [20]and he sent other troops to take possession of Jerusalem and the temple hill. [21]But someone ran ahead and reported to John at Gazara that his father and brothers had perished, and that "he has sent men to kill you also." [22]When he heard this, he was greatly shocked; he seized the men who came to destroy him and killed them, for he had found out that they were seeking to destroy him.

23 The rest of the acts of John and his wars and the brave deeds that he did, and the building of the walls that he completed, and his achievements, [24]are written in the annals of his high priesthood, from the time that he became high priest after his father.

---

a 134 B.C.

When you are suffering, what is your first response? to escape? to look for relief? to cry out in pain? These are normal and healthy responses: no well-adjusted person chooses to suffer willingly. Sometimes, though, people inflict unspeakable suffering on one another, especially through violence such as rape and torture. What meaning could there be in such suffering? In response, Second Maccabees insists that God will vindicate all those who suffer innocently at the hands of the unjust.

At a Glance

- **Chapters 1–2.** two letters to the Jews in Egypt, the author's preface
- **Chapters 3–7.** the persecution of the Jews
- **8:1—10:9.** the victory of Judas
- **10:10—15:39.** the renewal of persecution

Quick Facts

Period Covered: from 180 to 161 BC

Inspired Author: someone around 100 BC, summarizing a lost work by Jason of Cyrene

Themes: differing responses to persecution, the just and suffering, the glorification of God's holy martyrs

Of Note: Second Maccabees is not found in every version of the Old Testament (see "The Case of the Missing Books," near Tob 1:16).

In Depth

In 167 BC, the Jewish people faced a new persecution under the Seleucid (Greek) king Antiochus IV Epiphanes. In an effort to unify the many different peoples under his rule, Antiochus imposed his own language, customs, and religion on all of them, including the Jews. Second Maccabees covers some of the same history as First Maccabees but with different purposes: to show the variety of ways the Jews resisted persecution and to give hope to persecuted Jews in the author's time.

The Book of Job had already struggled with the mystery of human suffering and concluded that only God could understand it. Not content with this answer, the author of Second Maccabees presses forward with new insights:

■ In the famous story of the martyrdom of a Jewish mother and her seven sons (7:1–42), Second Maccabees talks about the resurrection of the dead.

■ In chapter 12, the value of praying for the dead is commended.

■ In chapter 15, the book speaks confidently of the prayers of the saints in Heaven for those on earth.

Second Maccabees is less concerned with the facts of history than with the meaning of history. It insists that whenever God's faithful people suffer, they can be assured of receiving justice—if not in this life, then in the resurrection. The book shows how the Jewish faith continued to develop as it faced the sometimes painful events of history.

The Second Book of Maccabees

2 Maccabees

Chapter 8

A Letter to the Jews in Egypt

1 The Jews in Jerusalem and those in the land of Judea,

To their Jewish kindred in Egypt,

Greetings and true peace.

2 May God do good to you, and may he remember his covenant with Abraham and Isaac and Jacob, his faithful servants. 3May he give you all a heart to worship him and to do his will with a strong heart and a willing spirit. 4May he open your heart to his law and his commandments, and may he bring peace. 5May he hear your prayers and be reconciled to you, and may he not forsake you in time of evil. 6We are now praying for you here.

7 In the reign of Demetrius, in the one hundred sixty-ninth year,*a* we Jews wrote to you, in the critical distress that came upon us in those years after Jason and his company revolted from the holy land and the kingdom 8and burned the gate and shed innocent blood. We prayed to the Lord and were heard, and we offered sacrifice and grain offering, and we lit the lamps and set out the loaves. 9And now see that you keep the festival of booths in the month of Chislev, in the one hundred eighty-eighth year.*b*

A Letter to Aristobulus

10 The people of Jerusalem and of Judea and the senate and Judas,

To Aristobulus, who is of the family of the anointed priests, teacher of King Ptolemy, and to the Jews in Egypt,

Greetings and good health.

11 Having been saved by God out of grave dangers we thank him greatly for taking our side against the king,*c* 12for he drove out those who fought against the holy city. 13When the leader reached Persia with a force that seemed irresistible, they were cut to pieces in the temple of Nanea by a deception employed by the priests of the goddess*d* Nanea. 14On the pretext of intending to marry her, Antiochus came to the place together with his Friends, to secure most of its treasures as a dowry. 15When the priests of the temple of Nanea had set out the treasures and Antiochus had come with a few men inside the wall of the sacred precinct, they closed the temple as soon as he entered it. 16Opening a secret door in the ceiling, they threw stones and struck down the leader and his men; they dismembered them and cut off their heads and threw them to the people outside. 17Blessed in every way be our God, who has brought judgment on those who have behaved impiously.

Fire Consumes Nehemiah's Sacrifice

18 Since on the twenty-fifth day of Chislev we shall celebrate the purification of the temple, we thought it necessary to notify you, in order that you also may celebrate the festival of booths and the festival of the fire given when Nehemiah, who built the temple and the altar, offered sacrifices.

---

a 143 B.C. *b* 124 B.C. *c* Cn: Gk as those who array themselves against a king *d* Gk lacks the goddess

19 For when our ancestors were being led captive to Persia, the pious priests of that time took some of the fire of the altar and secretly hid it in the hollow of a dry cistern, where they took such precautions that the place was unknown to anyone. 20But after many years had passed, when it pleased God, Nehemiah, having been commissioned by the king of Persia, sent the descendants of the priests who had hidden the fire to get it. And when they reported to us that they had not found fire but only a thick liquid, he ordered them to dip it out and bring it. 21When the materials for the sacrifices were presented, Nehemiah ordered the priests to sprinkle the liquid on the wood and on the things laid upon it. 22When this had been done and some time had passed, and when the sun, which had been clouded over, shone out, a great fire blazed up, so that all marveled. 23And while the sacrifice was being consumed, the priests offered prayer— the priests and everyone. Jonathan led, and the rest responded, as did Nehemiah. 24The prayer was to this effect:

"O Lord, Lord God, Creator of all things, you are awe-inspiring and strong and just and merciful, you alone are king and are kind, 25you alone are bountiful, you alone are just and almighty and eternal. You rescue Israel from every evil; you chose the ancestors and consecrated them. 26Accept this sacrifice on behalf of all your people Israel and preserve your portion and make it holy. 27Gather together our scattered people, set free those who are slaves among the Gentiles, look on those who are rejected and despised, and let the Gentiles know that you are our God. 28Punish those who oppress and are insolent with pride. 29Plant your people in your holy place, as Moses promised."

30 Then the priests sang the hymns. 31After the materials of the sacrifice had been consumed, Nehemiah ordered that the liquid that was left should be poured on large stones. 32When this was done, a flame blazed up; but when the light from the altar shone back, it went out. 33When this matter became known, and it was reported to the king of the Persians that, in the place where the exiled priests had hidden the fire, the liquid had appeared with which Nehemiah and his associates had burned the materials of the sacrifice, 34the king investigated the matter, and enclosed the place and made it sacred. 35And with those persons whom the king favored he exchanged many excellent gifts. 36Nehemiah and his associates called this "nephthar," which means purification, but by most people it is called naphtha.a

Jeremiah Hides the Tent, Ark, and Altar

2 One finds in the records that the prophet Jeremiah ordered those who were being deported to take some of the fire, as has been mentioned, 2and that the prophet, after giving them the law, instructed those who were being deported not to forget the commandments of the Lord, or to be led astray in their thoughts on seeing the gold and silver statues and their adornment. 3And with other similar words he exhorted them that the law should not depart from their hearts.

4 It was also in the same document that the prophet, having received an oracle, ordered that the tent and the ark should follow with him, and that he went out to the mountain where Moses had gone up and had seen the inheritance of God. 5Jeremiah came and found a cave-dwelling, and he brought there the tent and the ark and the altar of incense; then he sealed up the entrance. 6Some of those who followed him came up intending to mark the way, but could not find it. 7When Jeremiah learned of it, he rebuked them and declared: "The place shall remain unknown until God gathers his people together again and shows his mercy. 8Then the Lord will disclose these things, and the glory of the Lord and the cloud will appear, as they were shown in the case of Moses, and as Solomon asked that the place should be specially consecrated."

9 It was also made clear that being possessed of wisdom Solomonb offered sacrifice for the dedication and completion of the temple. 10Just as Moses prayed to the Lord, and fire came down from heaven and consumed the sacrifices, so also Solomon prayed, and the fire came down and consumed the whole burnt offerings. 11And Moses said, "They were consumed because the sin offering had not been eaten." 12Likewise Solomon also kept the eight days.

13 The same things are reported in the records and in the memoirs of Nehemiah, and also that he founded a library and collected the books about the kings and prophets, and the writings of David, and letters of kings about votive offerings. 14In the same way Judas also collected all the books that had been lost on account of the war that had come upon us, and they are in our possession. 15So if you have need of them, send people to get them for you.

16 Since, therefore, we are about to celebrate the purification, we write to you. Will you therefore please keep the days? 17It is God who has

a Gk nephthai   b Gk he

saved all his people, and has returned the inheritance to all, and the kingship and the priesthood and the consecration, [18]as he promised through the law. We have hope in God that he will soon have mercy on us and will gather us from everywhere under heaven into his holy place, for he has rescued us from great evils and has purified the place.

The Compiler's Preface

[19] The story of Judas Maccabeus and his brothers, and the purification of the great temple, and the dedication of the altar, [20]and further the wars against Antiochus Epiphanes and his son Eupator, [21]and the appearances that came from heaven to those who fought bravely for Judaism, so that though few in number they seized the whole land and pursued the barbarian hordes, [22]and regained possession of the temple famous throughout the world, and liberated the city, and re-established the laws that were about to be abolished, while the Lord with great kindness became gracious to them— [23]all this, which has been set forth by Jason of Cyrene in five volumes, we shall attempt to condense into a single book. [24]For considering the flood of statistics involved and the difficulty there is for those who wish to enter upon the narratives of history because of the mass of material, [25]we have aimed to please those who wish to read, to make it easy for those who are inclined to memorize, and to profit all readers. [26]For us who have undertaken the toil of abbreviating, it is no light matter but calls for sweat and loss of sleep, [27]just as it is not easy for one who prepares a banquet and seeks the benefit of others. Nevertheless, to secure the gratitude of many we will gladly endure the uncomfortable toil, [28]leaving the responsibility for exact details to the compiler, while devoting our effort to arriving at the outlines of the condensation. [29]For as the master builder of a new house must be concerned with the whole construction, while the one who undertakes its painting and decoration has to consider only what is suitable for its adornment, such in my judgment is the case with us. [30]It is the duty of the original historian to occupy the ground, to discuss matters from every side, and to take trouble with details, [31]but the one who recasts the narrative should be allowed to strive for brevity of expression and to forego exhaustive treatment. [32]At this point therefore let us begin our narrative, without adding any more to what has already been said; for it would be foolish to lengthen the preface while cutting short the history itself.

Arrival of Heliodorus in Jerusalem

3 While the holy city was inhabited in unbroken peace and the laws were strictly observed because of the piety of the high priest Onias and his hatred of wickedness, [2]it came about that the kings themselves honored the place and glorified the temple with the finest presents, [3]even to the extent that King Seleucus of Asia defrayed from his own revenues all the expenses connected with the service of the sacrifices.

[4] But a man named Simon, of the tribe of Benjamin, who had been made captain of the temple, had a disagreement with the high priest about the administration of the city market. [5]Since he could not prevail over Onias, he went to Apollonius of Tarsus,[a] who at that time was governor of Coelesyria and Phoenicia, [6]and reported to him that the treasury in Jerusalem was full of untold sums of money, so that the amount of the funds could not be reckoned, and that they did not belong to the account of the sacrifices, but that it was possible for them to fall under the control of the king. [7]When Apollonius met the king, he told him of the money about which he had been informed. The king[b] chose Heliodorus, who was in charge of his affairs, and sent him with commands to effect the removal of the reported wealth. [8]Heliodorus at once set out on his journey, ostensibly to make a tour of inspection of the cities of Coelesyria and Phoenicia, but in fact to carry out the king's purpose.

[9] When he had arrived at Jerusalem and had been kindly welcomed by the high priest of[c] the city, he told about the disclosure that had been made and stated why he had come, and he inquired whether this really was the situation. [10]The high priest explained that there were some deposits belonging to widows and orphans, [11]and also some money of Hyrcanus son of Tobias, a man of very prominent position, and that it totaled in all four hundred talents of silver and two hundred of gold. To such an extent the impious Simon had misrepresented the facts. [12]And he said that it was utterly impossible that wrong should be done to those people who had trusted in the holiness of the place and in the sanctity and inviolability of the temple that is honored throughout the whole world.

Heliodorus Plans to Rob the Temple

[13] But Heliodorus, because of the orders he had from the king, said that this money must in

---

a Gk *Apollonius son of Tharseas*   b Gk *He*   c Other ancient authorities read *and* any case be confiscated for the king's treasury. ¹⁴So he set a day and went in to direct the inspection of these funds.

There was no little distress throughout the whole city. ¹⁵The priests prostrated themselves before the altar in their priestly vestments and called toward heaven upon him who had given the law about deposits, that he should keep them safe for those who had deposited them. ¹⁶To see the appearance of the high priest was to be wounded at heart, for his face and the change in his color disclosed the anguish of his soul. ¹⁷For terror and bodily trembling had come over the man, which plainly showed to those who looked at him the pain lodged in his heart. ¹⁸People also hurried out of their houses in crowds to make a general supplication because the holy place was about to be brought into dishonor. ¹⁹Women, girded with sackcloth under their breasts, thronged the streets. Some of the young women who were kept indoors ran together to the gates, and some to the walls, while others peered out of the windows. ²⁰And holding up their hands to heaven, they all made supplication. ²¹There was something pitiable in the prostration of the whole populace and the anxiety of the high priest in his great anguish.

The Lord Protects His Temple

22 While they were calling upon the Almighty Lord that he would keep what had been entrusted safe and secure for those who had entrusted it, ²³Heliodorus went on with what had been decided. ²⁴But when he arrived at the treasury with his bodyguard, then and there the Sovereign of spirits and of all authority caused so great a manifestation that all who had been so bold as to accompany him were astounded by the power of God, and became faint with terror. ²⁵For there appeared to them a magnificently caparisoned horse, with a rider of frightening mien; it rushed furiously at Heliodorus and struck at him with its front hoofs. Its rider was seen to have armor and weapons of gold. ²⁶Two young men also appeared to him, remarkably strong, gloriously beautiful and splendidly dressed, who stood on either side of him and flogged him continuously, inflicting many blows on him. ²⁷When he suddenly fell to the ground and deep darkness came over him, his men took him up, put him on a stretcher, ²⁸and carried him away—this man who had just entered the aforesaid treasury with a great retinue and all his bodyguard but was now unable to help himself. They recognized clearly the sovereign power of God.

Pray It!

Arrogance

Arrogance seems to run in the family of Simon. First, Simon seeks to embarrass the high priest, Onias, because of a minor disagreement (see 2 Macc 3:1–14). When that fails, he falsely accuses Onias of a crime (see 4:1–6). Several years later, Simon's brother bribes his way into power (see verses 23–29).

We have all encountered arrogant people who think they can do no wrong, and when they do err, cover it up by attacking others. Many of us are intimidated by such people and resent that we felt talked down to or easily dismissed as unimportant. So, how should we respond to arrogant people? The most obvious solution is to ignore them. If that is not possible, then we need to react to them calmly and confidently. Finally, we should keep them in our prayers. Their arrogance can be masking an insecurity or a hurt that needs God's healing touch.

In your prayer time, reflect or journal on the following questions:

- Who intimidates you by her or his arrogant behavior?
- How could you respond in a loving and just way?
- What do you need to bring to God in prayer?

▶ **2 Macc 3:1—4:29**

Onias Prays for Heliodorus

29 While he lay prostrate, speechless because of the divine intervention and deprived of any hope of recovery, ³⁰they praised the Lord who had acted marvelously for his own place. And the temple, which a little while before was full of fear and disturbance, was filled with joy and gladness, now that the Almighty Lord had appeared. 31 Some of Heliodorus's friends quickly begged Onias to call upon the Most High to grant life to one who was lying quite at his last breath. ³²So the high priest, fearing that the king might get the notion that some foul play had been perpetrated by the Jews with regard to Heliodorus, offered sacrifice for the man's recovery. ³³While the high priest was making

an atonement, the same young men appeared again to Heliodorus dressed in the same clothing, and they stood and said, "Be very grateful to the high priest Onias, since for his sake the Lord has granted you your life. 34And see that you, who have been flogged by heaven, report to all people the majestic power of God." Having said this they vanished.

The Conversion of Heliodorus

35 Then Heliodorus offered sacrifice to the Lord and made very great vows to the Savior of his life, and having bidden Onias farewell, he marched off with his forces to the king. 36He bore testimony to all concerning the deeds of the supreme God, which he had seen with his own eyes. 37When the king asked Heliodorus what sort of person would be suitable to send on another mission to Jerusalem, he replied, 38"If you have any enemy or plotter against your government, send him there, for you will get him back thoroughly flogged, if he survives at all; for there is certainly some power of God about the place. 39For he who has his dwelling in heaven watches over that place himself and brings it aid, and he strikes and destroys those who come to do it injury." 40This was the outcome of the episode of Heliodorus and the protection of the treasury.

Simon Accuses Onias

4 The previously mentioned Simon, who had informed about the money against[a] his own country, slandered Onias, saying that it was he who had incited Heliodorus and had been the real cause of the misfortune. 2He dared to designate as a plotter against the government the man who was the benefactor of the city, the protector of his compatriots, and a zealot for the laws. 3When his hatred progressed to such a degree that even murders were committed by one of Simon's approved agents, 4Onias recognized that the rivalry was serious and that Apollonius son of Menestheus,[b] and governor of Coelesyria and Phoenicia, was intensifying the malice of Simon. 5So he appealed to the king, not accusing his compatriots but having in view the welfare, both public and private, of all the people. 6For he saw that without the king's attention public affairs could not again reach a peaceful settlement, and that Simon would not stop his folly.

Jason's Reforms

7 When Seleucus died and Antiochus, who was called Epiphanes, succeeded to the kingdom, Jason the brother of Onias obtained the high priesthood by corruption, 8promising the king at an interview[c] three hundred sixty talents of silver, and from another source of revenue eighty talents. 9In addition to this he promised to pay one hundred fifty more if permission were given to establish by his authority a gymnasium and a body of youth for it, and to enroll the people of Jerusalem as citizens of Antioch. 10When the king assented and Jason[d] came to office, he at once shifted his compatriots over to the Greek way of life.

11 He set aside the existing royal concessions to the Jews, secured through John the father of Eupolemus, who went on the mission to establish friendship and alliance with the Romans; and he destroyed the lawful ways of living and introduced new customs contrary to the law. 12He took delight in establishing a gymnasium right under the citadel, and he induced the noblest of the young men to wear the Greek hat. 13There was such an extreme of Hellenization and increase in the adoption of foreign ways because of the surpassing wickedness of Jason, who was ungodly and no true[e] high priest, 14that the priests were no longer intent upon their service at the altar. Despising the sanctuary and neglecting the sacrifices, they hurried to take part in the unlawful proceedings in the wrestling arena after the signal for the discus-throwing, 15disdaining the honors prized by their ancestors and putting the highest value upon Greek forms of prestige. 16For this reason heavy disaster overtook them, and those whose ways of living they admired and wished to imitate completely became their enemies and punished them. 17It is no light thing to show irreverence to the divine laws—a fact that later events will make clear.

Jason Introduces Greek Customs

18 When the quadrennial games were being held at Tyre and the king was present, 19the vile Jason sent envoys, chosen as being Antiochian citizens from Jerusalem, to carry three hundred silver drachmas for the sacrifice to Hercules. Those who carried the money, however, thought best not to use it for sacrifice, because that was inappropriate, but to expend it for another purpose. 20So this money was intended by the sender for the sacrifice to Hercules, but by the decision of its carriers it was applied to the construction of triremes.

21 When Apollonius son of Menestheus was sent to Egypt for the coronation[f] of Philometor as king, Antiochus learned that Philometor[d] had

a Gk and   b Vg Compare verse 21: Meaning of Gk uncertain
c Or by a petition   d Gk he   e Gk lacks true   f Meaning of
Gk uncertain

become hostile to his government, and he took measures for his own security. Therefore upon arriving at Joppa he proceeded to Jerusalem. ²²He was welcomed magnificently by Jason and the city, and ushered in with a blaze of torches and with shouts. Then he marched his army into Phoenicia.

Menelaus Becomes High Priest

23 After a period of three years Jason sent Menelaus, the brother of the previously mentioned Simon, to carry the money to the king and to complete the records of essential business. ²⁴But he, when presented to the king, extolled him with an air of authority, and secured the high priesthood for himself, outbidding Jason by three hundred talents of silver. ²⁵After receiving the king's orders he returned, possessing no qualification for the high priesthood, but having the hot temper of a cruel tyrant and the rage of a savage wild beast. ²⁶So Jason, who after supplanting his own brother was supplanted by another man, was driven as a fugitive into the land of Ammon. ²⁷Although Menelaus continued to hold the office, he did not pay regularly any of the money promised to the king. ²⁸When Sostratus the captain of the citadel kept requesting payment—for the collection of the revenue was his responsibility—the two of them were summoned by the king on account of this issue. ²⁹Menelaus left his own brother Lysimachus as deputy in the high priesthood, while Sostratus left Crates, the commander of the Cyprian troops.

The Murder of Onias

30 While such was the state of affairs, it happened that the people of Tarsus and of Mallus revolted because their cities had been given as a present to Antiochis, the king's concubine. ³¹So the king went hurriedly to settle the trouble, leaving Andronicus, a man of high rank, to act as his deputy. ³²But Menelaus, thinking he had obtained a suitable opportunity, stole some of the gold vessels of the temple and gave them to Andronicus; other vessels, as it happened, he had sold to Tyre and the neighboring cities. ³³When Onias became fully aware of these acts, he publicly exposed them, having first withdrawn to a place of sanctuary at Daphne near Antioch. ³⁴Therefore Menelaus, taking Andronicus aside, urged him to kill Onias. Andronicus^a came to Onias, and resorting to treachery, offered him sworn pledges and gave him his right hand; he persuaded him, though still suspicious, to come out from the place of sanctuary; then, with no regard for justice, he immediately put him out of the way.

Andronicus Is Punished

35 For this reason not only Jews, but many also of other nations, were grieved and displeased at the unjust murder of the man. ³⁶When the king returned from the region of Cilicia, the Jews in the city^b appealed to him with regard to the unreasonable murder of Onias, and the Greeks shared their hatred of the crime. ³⁷Therefore Antiochus was grieved at heart and filled with pity, and wept because of the moderation and good conduct of the deceased. ³⁸Inflamed with anger, he immediately stripped off the purple robe from Andronicus, tore off his clothes, and led him around the whole city to that very place where he had committed the outrage against Onias, and there he dispatched the bloodthirsty fellow. The Lord thus repaid him with the punishment he deserved.

Unpopularity of Lysimachus and Menelaus

39 When many acts of sacrilege had been committed in the city by Lysimachus with the connivance of Menelaus, and when report of them had spread abroad, the populace gathered against Lysimachus, because many of the gold vessels had already been stolen. ⁴⁰Since the crowds were becoming aroused and filled with anger, Lysimachus armed about three thousand men and launched an unjust attack, under the leadership of a certain Auranus, a man advanced in years and no less advanced in folly. ⁴¹But when the Jews^c became aware that Lysimachus was attacking them, some picked up stones, some blocks of wood, and others took handfuls of the ashes that were lying around, and threw them in wild confusion at Lysimachus and his men. ⁴²As a result, they wounded many of them, and killed some, and put all the rest to flight; the temple robber himself they killed close by the treasury.

43 Charges were brought against Menelaus about this incident. ⁴⁴When the king came to Tyre, three men sent by the senate presented the case before him. ⁴⁵But Menelaus, already as good as beaten, promised a substantial bribe to Ptolemy son of Dorymenes to win over the king. ⁴⁶Therefore Ptolemy, taking the king aside into a colonnade as if for refreshment, induced the king to change his mind. ⁴⁷Menelaus, the cause of all the trouble, he acquitted of the charges against him, while he sentenced to death those unfortunate men, who would have been freed uncondemned if they had pleaded even before

a Gk He   *b* Or in each city   *c* Gk they

Scythians. [48]And so those who had spoken for the city and the villages[a] and the holy vessels quickly suffered the unjust penalty. [49]Therefore even the Tyrians, showing their hatred of the crime, provided magnificently for their funeral. [50]But Menelaus, because of the greed of those in power, remained in office, growing in wickedness, having become the chief plotter against his compatriots.

Jason Tries to Regain Control

5 About this time Antiochus made his second invasion of Egypt. [2]And it happened that, for almost forty days, there appeared over all the city golden-clad cavalry charging through the air, in companies fully armed with lances and drawn swords— [3]troops of cavalry drawn up, attacks and counterattacks made on this side and on that, brandishing of shields, massing of spears, hurling of missiles, the flash of golden trappings, and armor of all kinds. [4]Therefore everyone prayed that the apparition might prove to have been a good omen.

[5] When a false rumor arose that Antiochus was dead, Jason took no fewer than a thousand men and suddenly made an assault on the city. When the troops on the wall had been forced back and at last the city was being taken, Menelaus took refuge in the citadel. [6]But Jason kept relentlessly slaughtering his compatriots, not realizing that success at the cost of one's kindred is the greatest misfortune, but imagining that he was setting up trophies of victory over enemies and not over compatriots. [7]He did not, however, gain control of the government; in the end he got only disgrace from his conspiracy, and fled again into the country of the Ammonites. [8]Finally he met a miserable end. Accused[b] before Aretas the ruler of the Arabs, fleeing from city to city, pursued by everyone, hated as a rebel against the laws, and abhorred as the executioner of his country and his compatriots, he was cast ashore in Egypt. [9]There he who had driven many from their own country into exile died in exile, having embarked to go to the Lacedaemonians in hope of finding protection because of their kinship. [10]He who had cast out many to lie unburied had no one to mourn for him; he had no funeral of any sort and no place in the tomb of his ancestors.

[11] When news of what had happened reached the king, he took it to mean that Judea was in revolt. So, raging inwardly, he left Egypt and took the city by storm. [12]He commanded his soldiers to cut down relentlessly everyone they met and to kill those who went into their houses. [13]Then there was massacre of young and old, destruction of boys, women, and children, and slaughter of young girls and infants. [14]Within the total of three days eighty thousand were destroyed, forty thousand in hand-to-hand fighting, and as many were sold into slavery as were killed.

Pillage of the Temple

[15] Not content with this, Antiochus[c] dared to enter the most holy temple in all the world, guided by Menelaus, who had become a traitor both to the laws and to his country. [16]He took the holy vessels with his polluted hands, and swept away with profane hands the votive offerings that other kings had made to enhance the glory and honor of the place. [17]Antiochus was elated in spirit, and did not perceive that the Lord was angered for a little while because of the sins of those who lived in the city, and that this was the reason he was disregarding the holy place. [18]But if it had not happened that they were involved in many sins, this man would have been flogged and turned back from his rash act as soon as he came forward, just as Heliodorus had been, whom King Seleucus sent to inspect the treasury. [19]But the Lord did not choose the nation for the sake of the holy place, but the place for the sake of the nation. [20]Therefore the place itself shared in the misfortunes that befell the nation and afterward participated in its benefits; and what was forsaken in the wrath of the Almighty was restored again in all its glory when the great Lord became reconciled.

[21] So Antiochus carried off eighteen hundred talents from the temple, and hurried away to Antioch, thinking in his arrogance that he could sail on the land and walk on the sea, because his mind was elated. [22]He left governors to oppress the people: at Jerusalem, Philip, by birth a Phrygian and in character more barbarous than the man who appointed him; [23]and at Gerizim, Andronicus; and besides these Menelaus, who lorded it over his compatriots worse than the others did. In his malice toward the Jewish citizens,[d] [24]Antiochus[c] sent Apollonius, the captain of the Mysians, with an army of twenty-two thousand, and commanded him to kill all the grown men and to sell the women and boys as slaves. [25]When this man arrived in Jerusalem, he pretended to be peaceably disposed and waited until the holy sabbath day; then, finding the Jews

---

a Other ancient authorities read *the people*   b Cn: Gk *Imprisoned*   c Gk *he*   d Or *worse than the others did in his malice toward the Jewish citizens*

not at work, he ordered his troops to parade under arms. [26]He put to the sword all those who came out to see them, then rushed into the city with his armed warriors and killed great numbers of people.

27 But Judas Maccabeus, with about nine others, got away to the wilderness, and kept himself and his companions alive in the mountains as wild animals do; they continued to live on what grew wild, so that they might not share in the defilement.

The Suppression of Judaism

6 Not long after this, the king sent an Athenian[a] senator[b] to compel the Jews to forsake the laws of their ancestors and no longer to live by the laws of God; [2]also to pollute the temple in Jerusalem and to call it the temple of Olympian Zeus, and to call the one in Gerizim the temple of Zeus-the-Friend-of-Strangers, as did the people who lived in that place.

3 Harsh and utterly grievous was the onslaught of evil. [4]For the temple was filled with debauchery and reveling by the Gentiles, who dallied with prostitutes and had intercourse with women within the sacred precincts, and besides brought in things for sacrifice that were unfit. [5]The altar was covered with abominable offerings that were forbidden by the laws. [6]People could neither keep the sabbath, nor observe the festivals of their ancestors, nor so much as confess themselves to be Jews.

7 On the monthly celebration of the king's birthday, the Jews[c] were taken, under bitter constraint, to partake of the sacrifices; and when a festival of Dionysus was celebrated, they were compelled to wear wreaths of ivy and to walk in the procession in honor of Dionysus. [8]At the suggestion of the people of Ptolemais[d] a decree was issued to the neighboring Greek cities that they should adopt the same policy toward the Jews and make them partake of the sacrifices, [9]and should kill those who did not choose to change over to Greek customs. One could see, therefore, the misery that had come upon them. [10]For example, two women were brought in for having circumcised their children. They publicly paraded them around the city, with their babies hanging at their breasts, and then hurled them down headlong from the wall. [11]Others who had assembled in the caves nearby, in order to observe the seventh day secretly, were betrayed to Philip and were all burned together, because their piety kept them from defending themselves, in view of their regard for that most holy day.

Providential Significance of the Persecution

12 Now I urge those who read this book not to be depressed by such calamities, but to recognize that these punishments were designed not to destroy but to discipline our people. [13]In fact, it is a sign of great kindness not to let the impious alone for long, but to punish them immediately. [14]For in the case of the other nations the Lord waits patiently to punish them until they have reached the full measure of their sins; but he does not deal in this way with us, [15]in order that he may not take vengeance on us afterward when our sins have reached their height. [16]Therefore he never withdraws his mercy from us. Although he disciplines us with calamities, he does not forsake his own people. [17]Let what we have said serve as a reminder; we must go on briefly with the story.

The Martyrdom of Eleazar

18 Eleazar, one of the scribes in high position, a man now advanced in age and of noble presence, was being forced to open his mouth to eat swine's flesh. [19]But he, welcoming death with honor rather than life with pollution, went up to the rack of his own accord, spitting out the flesh, [20]as all ought to go who have the courage to refuse things that it is not right to taste, even for the natural love of life.

21 Those who were in charge of that unlawful sacrifice took the man aside because of their long acquaintance with him, and privately urged him to bring meat of his own providing, proper for him to use, and to pretend that he was eating the flesh of the sacrificial meal that had been commanded by the king, [22]so that by doing this he might be saved from death, and be treated kindly on account of his old friendship with them. [23]But making a high resolve, worthy of his years and the dignity of his old age and the gray hairs that he had reached with distinction and his excellent life even from childhood, and moreover according to the holy God-given law, he declared himself quickly, telling them to send him to Hades.

24 "Such pretense is not worthy of our time of life," he said, "for many of the young might suppose that Eleazar in his ninetieth year had gone over to an alien religion, [25]and through my pretense, for the sake of living a brief moment longer, they would be led astray because of me,

---

a Other ancient authorities read *Antiochian*   b Or *Geron an Athenian*   c Gk *they*   d Cn: Gk *suggestion of the Ptolemies* (or *of Ptolemy*)

while I defile and disgrace my old age. [26]Even if for the present I would avoid the punishment of mortals, yet whether I live or die I will not escape the hands of the Almighty. [27]Therefore, by bravely giving up my life now, I will show myself worthy of my old age [28]and leave to the young a noble example of how to die a good death willingly and nobly for the revered and holy laws."

When he had said this, he went[a] at once to the rack. [29]Those who a little before had acted toward him with goodwill now changed to ill will, because the words he had uttered were in their opinion sheer madness.[b] [30]When he was about to die under the blows, he groaned aloud and said: "It is clear to the Lord in his holy knowledge that, though I might have been saved from death, I am enduring terrible sufferings in my body under this beating, but in my soul I am glad to suffer these things because I fear him."

Teaching by Example

Second Maccabees tells the story of Eleazar, a dignified, elderly scribe who has followed God his whole life. Rather than compromise his principles, Eleazar courageously accepts death by torture. He knows his example will influence younger people (see 6:28). His example gives others courage (see verse 31).

Young people watch and learn. An old television commercial shows a father and son driving along in a car. The son has a toy steering wheel in front of him and imitates his father's driving. When the father turns the wheel, so does the son. When the father switches the turn signal, so does the son. Then the father pulls a cigarette from a pack. He lights it and begins smoking. The next scene shows the son going for the pack of cigarettes.

The next time you find yourself struggling to make the right choice, think about the example you might be giving to someone younger than you.

▶ 2 Macc 6:18–31

[31] So in this way he died, leaving in his death an example of nobility and a memorial of courage, not only to the young but to the great body of his nation.

The Martyrdom of Seven Brothers

7 It happened also that seven brothers and their mother were arrested and were being compelled by the king, under torture with whips and thongs, to partake of unlawful swine's flesh. [2]One of them, acting as their spokesman, said, "What do you intend to ask and learn from us? For we are ready to die rather than transgress the laws of our ancestors."

3 The king fell into a rage, and gave orders to have pans and caldrons heated. [4]These were heated immediately, and he commanded that the tongue of their spokesman be cut out and that they scalp him and cut off his hands and feet, while the rest of the brothers and the mother looked on. [5]When he was utterly helpless, the king[c] ordered them to take him to the fire, still breathing, and to fry him in a pan. The smoke from the pan spread widely, but the brothers[d] and their mother encouraged one another to die nobly, saying, [6]"The Lord God is watching over us and in truth has compassion on us, as Moses declared in his song that bore witness against the people to their faces, when he said, 'And he will have compassion on his servants.' "[e]

7 After the first brother had died in this way, they brought forward the second for their sport. They tore off the skin of his head with the hair, and asked him, "Will you eat rather than have your body punished limb by limb?" [8]He replied in the language of his ancestors and said to them, "No." Therefore he in turn underwent tortures as the first brother had done. [9]And when he was at his last breath, he said, "You accursed wretch, you dismiss us from this present life, but the King of the universe will raise us up to an everlasting renewal of life, because we have died for his laws."

10 After him, the third was the victim of their sport. When it was demanded, he quickly put out his tongue and courageously stretched forth his hands, [11]and said nobly, "I got these from Heaven, and because of his laws I disdain them, and from him I hope to get them back again." [12]As a result the king himself and those with him were astonished at the young man's spirit, for he regarded his sufferings as nothing.

13 After he too had died, they maltreated and

---

[a] Other ancient authorities read *was dragged*   [b] Meaning of Gk uncertain   [c] Gk *he*   [d] Gk *they*   [e] Gk *slaves*

Cultural Connection

I Will Sacrifice Myself

If I were a bird
and able to fly afar,
I would like to be a white dove
to guide the people to freedom.
If I were the cloud in the sky,
I would shelter and bring rains
to the rice field.
If I were a grain of sand
I would throw myself down
to make a path for the people.
I will sacrifice my life
for the suffering people.
I would sacrifice myself
no matter how many times
I would have to die.

     ("For the People," by Nid, Thailand,
         in *Your Will Be Done*)

This song was written by a twenty-two-year-old Thai student. He was later shot and killed by police officers at a demonstration against the return of a corrupt leader. His love for Thailand echoes the love of the mother and her seven sons for God and their Jewish faith in chapter 7 of Second Maccabees.

▶ **2 Maccabees, chapter 7**

---

tortured the fourth in the same way. [14]When he was near death, he said, "One cannot but choose to die at the hands of mortals and to cherish the hope God gives of being raised again by him. But for you there will be no resurrection to life!"

15 Next they brought forward the fifth and maltreated him. [16]But he looked at the king,[a] and said, "Because you have authority among mortals, though you also are mortal, you do what you please. But do not think that God has forsaken our people. [17]Keep on, and see how his mighty power will torture you and your descendants!"

18 After him they brought forward the sixth. And when he was about to die, he said, "Do not deceive yourself in vain. For we are suffering these things on our own account, because of our sins against our own God. Therefore[b] astounding things have happened. [19]But do not think that you will go unpunished for having tried to fight against God!"

20 The mother was especially admirable and worthy of honorable memory. Although she saw her seven sons perish within a single day, she bore it with good courage because of her hope in the Lord. [21]She encouraged each of them in the language of their ancestors. Filled with a noble spirit, she reinforced her woman's reasoning with a man's courage, and said to them, [22]"I do not know how you came into being in my womb. It was not I who gave you life and breath,

nor I who set in order the elements within each of you. [23]Therefore the Creator of the world, who shaped the beginning of humankind and devised the origin of all things, will in his mercy give life and breath back to you again, since you now forget yourselves for the sake of his laws."

24 Antiochus felt that he was being treated with contempt, and he was suspicious of her reproachful tone. The youngest brother being still alive, Antiochus[c] not only appealed to him in words, but promised with oaths that he would make him rich and enviable if he would turn from the ways of his ancestors, and that he would take him for his Friend and entrust him with public affairs. [25]Since the young man would not listen to him at all, the king called the mother to him and urged her to advise the youth to save himself. [26]After much urging on his part, she undertook to persuade her son. [27]But, leaning close to him, she spoke in their native language as follows, deriding the cruel tyrant. "My son, have pity on me. I carried you nine months in my womb, and nursed you for three years, and have reared you and brought you up to this point in your life, and have taken care of you.[d] [28]I beg you, my child, to look at the heaven and the earth and see everything that is in them, and recognize that God did not make them out

---

a Gk *at him*   *b* Lat: Other ancient authorities lack *Therefore*
c Gk *he*   *d* Or *have borne the burden of your education*

of things that existed.*a* And in the same way the human race came into being. ²⁹Do not fear this butcher, but prove worthy of your brothers. Accept death, so that in God's mercy I may get you back again along with your brothers."

30 While she was still speaking, the young man said, "What are you*b* waiting for? I will not obey the king's command, but I obey the command of the law that was given to our ancestors through Moses. ³¹But you,*c* who have contrived all sorts of evil against the Hebrews, will certainly not escape the hands of God. ³²For we are suffering because of our own sins. ³³And if our living Lord is angry for a little while, to rebuke and discipline us, he will again be reconciled with his own servants.*d* ³⁴But you, unholy wretch, you most defiled of all mortals, do not be elated in vain and puffed up by uncertain hopes, when you raise your hand against the children of heaven. ³⁵You have not yet escaped the judgment of the almighty, all-seeing God. ³⁶For our brothers after enduring a brief suffering have drunk*e* of ever-flowing life, under God's covenant; but you, by the judgment of God, will receive just punishment for your arrogance. ³⁷I, like my brothers, give up body and life for the laws of our ancestors, appealing to God to show mercy soon to our nation and by trials and plagues to make you confess that he alone is God, ³⁸and through me and my brothers to bring to an end the wrath of the Almighty that has justly fallen on our whole nation."

39 The king fell into a rage, and handled him worse than the others, being exasperated at his scorn. ⁴⁰So he died in his integrity, putting his whole trust in the Lord.

41 Last of all, the mother died, after her sons.

42 Let this be enough, then, about the eating of sacrifices and the extreme tortures.

The Revolt of Judas Maccabeus

8 Meanwhile Judas, who was also called Maccabeus, and his companions secretly entered the villages and summoned their kindred and enlisted those who had continued in the Jewish faith, and so they gathered about six thousand. ²They implored the Lord to look upon the people who were oppressed by all; and to have pity on the temple that had been profaned by the godless; ³to have mercy on the city that was being destroyed and about to be leveled to the ground; to hearken to the blood that cried out to him; ⁴to remember also the lawless destruction of the innocent babies and the blasphemies committed against his name; and to show his hatred of evil.

5 As soon as Maccabeus got his army organized, the Gentiles could not withstand him, for

Did You Know?

Nonviolent Resistance

The article "A Just War," near 1 Maccabees 6:32, discusses just war as a response to the Seleucid persecution of the Jews. Second Maccabees, chapters 6–7, hints at another response—nonviolent resistance. Despite being ordered to forsake their faith and to adopt Greek customs, Jews resisted. We read of women continuing to have their baby boys circumcised (see 6:10), of secret gatherings to celebrate the Sabbath (see 6:11), and of martyrs refusing to eat unlawful meat (see 6:19, 7:1). Although the stories focus on the violent responses and tortures inflicted by the Greeks, they indicate that at least part of the population neither gave up its religious practices nor took up arms in violent conflict.

Christians have continued to develop the concept of nonviolent resistance—sometimes called pacifism. Nonviolent resistance is rooted in Jesus' teachings to turn the other cheek (see Mt 5:39) and "love your enemies" (5:44). Nonviolent resistance is not passive. It confronts evil and refuses to cooperate with it without resorting to violence. Those who practice nonviolent resistance accept the suffering that results because they know God can bring good out of the suffering of the just. The Catholic Church teaches that nonviolent resistance gives witness to God's redeeming love and that no person who objects to committing violence should be forced into military service.

Christian nonviolence is a challenge for everyone. How do you practice it in your relationships with others? In what situations, if any, do you think it is necessary to respond with violence? In what situations would you refuse to participate in military service?

the wrath of the Lord had turned to mercy. [6]Coming without warning, he would set fire to towns and villages. He captured strategic positions and put to flight not a few of the enemy. [7]He found the nights most advantageous for such attacks. And talk of his valor spread everywhere.

8 When Philip saw that the man was gaining ground little by little, and that he was pushing ahead with more frequent successes, he wrote to Ptolemy, the governor of Coelesyria and Phoenicia, to come to the aid of the king's government. [9]Then Ptolemy[a] promptly appointed Nicanor son of Patroclus, one of the king's chief[b] Friends, and sent him, in command of no fewer than twenty thousand Gentiles of all nations, to wipe out the whole race of Judea. He associated with him Gorgias, a general and a man of experience in military service. [10]Nicanor determined to make up for the king the tribute due to the Romans, two thousand talents, by selling the captured Jews into slavery. [11]So he immediately sent to the towns on the seacoast, inviting them to buy Jewish slaves and promising to hand over ninety slaves for a talent, not expecting the judgment from the Almighty that was about to overtake him.

Preparation for Battle

12 Word came to Judas concerning Nicanor's invasion; and when he told his companions of the arrival of the army, [13]those who were cowardly and distrustful of God's justice ran off and got away. [14]Others sold all their remaining property, and at the same time implored the Lord to rescue those who had been sold by the ungodly Nicanor before he ever met them, [15]if not for their own sake, then for the sake of the covenants made with their ancestors, and because he had called them by his holy and glorious name. [16]But Maccabeus gathered his forces together, to the number six thousand, and exhorted them not to be frightened by the enemy and not to fear the great multitude of Gentiles who were wickedly coming against them, but to fight nobly, [17]keeping before their eyes the lawless outrage that the Gentiles[c] had committed against the holy place, and the torture of the derided city, and besides, the overthrow of their ancestral way of life. [18]"For they trust to arms and acts of daring," he said, "but we trust in the Almighty God, who is able with a single nod to strike down those who are coming against us, and even, if necessary, the whole world."

19 Moreover, he told them of the occasions when help came to their ancestors; how, in the time of Sennacherib, when one hundred eighty-

five thousand perished, [20]and the time of the battle against the Galatians that took place in Babylonia, when eight thousand Jews[d] fought along with four thousand Macedonians; yet when the Macedonians were hard pressed, the eight thousand, by the help that came to them from heaven, destroyed one hundred twenty thousand Galatians[e] and took a great amount of booty.

Judas Defeats Nicanor

21 With these words he filled them with courage and made them ready to die for their laws and their country; then he divided his army into four parts. [22]He appointed his brothers also, Simon and Joseph and Jonathan, each to command a division, putting fifteen hundred men under each. [23]Besides, he appointed Eleazar to read aloud[f] from the holy book, and gave the watchword, "The help of God"; then, leading the first division himself, he joined battle with Nicanor.

24 With the Almighty as their ally, they killed more than nine thousand of the enemy, and wounded and disabled most of Nicanor's army, and forced them all to flee. [25]They captured the money of those who had come to buy them as slaves. After pursuing them for some distance, they were obliged to return because the hour was late. [26]It was the day before the sabbath, and for that reason they did not continue their pursuit. [27]When they had collected the arms of the enemy and stripped them of their spoils, they kept the sabbath, giving great praise and thanks to the Lord, who had preserved them for that day and allotted it to them as the beginning of mercy. [28]After the sabbath they gave some of the spoils to those who had been tortured and to the widows and orphans, and distributed the rest among themselves and their children. [29]When they had done this, they made common supplication and implored the merciful Lord to be wholly reconciled with his servants.[g]

Judas Defeats Timothy and Bacchides

30 In encounters with the forces of Timothy and Bacchides they killed more than twenty thousand of them and got possession of some exceedingly high strongholds, and they divided a very large amount of plunder, giving to those who had been tortured and to the orphans and widows, and also to the aged, shares equal to their own. [31]They collected the arms of the

a Gk he   b Gk one of the first   c Gk they   d Gk lacks Jews
e Gk lacks Galatians   f Meaning of Gk uncertain   g Gk slaves

enemy,[a] and carefully stored all of them in strategic places; the rest of the spoils they carried to Jerusalem. [32]They killed the commander of Timothy's forces, a most wicked man, and one who had greatly troubled the Jews. [33]While they were celebrating the victory in the city of their ancestors, they burned those who had set fire to the sacred gates, Callisthenes and some others, who had fled into one little house; so these received the proper reward for their impiety.[b]

34 The thrice-accursed Nicanor, who had brought the thousand merchants to buy the Jews, [35]having been humbled with the help of the Lord by opponents whom he regarded as of the least account, took off his splendid uniform and made his way alone like a runaway slave across the country until he reached Antioch, having succeeded chiefly in the destruction of his own army! [36]So he who had undertaken to secure tribute for the Romans by the capture of the people of Jerusalem proclaimed that the Jews had a Defender, and that therefore the Jews were invulnerable, because they followed the laws ordained by him.

The Last Campaign of Antiochus Epiphanes

9 About that time, as it happened, Antiochus had retreated in disorder from the region of Persia. [2]He had entered the city called Persepolis and attempted to rob the temples and control the city. Therefore the people rushed to the rescue with arms, and Antiochus and his army were defeated,[c] with the result that Antiochus was put to flight by the inhabitants and beat a shameful retreat. [3]While he was in Ecbatana, news came to him of what had happened to Nicanor and the forces of Timothy. [4]Transported with rage, he conceived the idea of turning upon the Jews the injury done by those who had put him to flight; so he ordered his charioteer to drive without stopping until he completed the journey. But the judgment of heaven rode with him! For in his arrogance he said, "When I get there I will make Jerusalem a cemetery of Jews."

5 But the all-seeing Lord, the God of Israel, struck him with an incurable and invisible blow. As soon as he stopped speaking he was seized with a pain in his bowels, for which there was no relief, and with sharp internal tortures— [6]and that very justly, for he had tortured the bowels of others with many and strange inflictions. [7]Yet he did not in any way stop his insolence, but was even more filled with arrogance, breathing fire in his rage against the Jews, and giving orders to drive even faster. And so it came about that he fell out of his chariot as it was rushing along,

and the fall was so hard as to torture every limb of his body. [8]Thus he who only a little while before had thought in his superhuman arrogance that he could command the waves of the sea, and had imagined that he could weigh the high mountains in a balance, was brought down to earth and carried in a litter, making the power of God manifest to all. [9]And so the ungodly man's body swarmed with worms, and while he was still living in anguish and pain, his flesh rotted away, and because of the stench the whole army felt revulsion at his decay. [10]Because of his intolerable stench no one was able to carry the man who a little while before had thought that he could touch the stars of heaven. [11]Then it was that, broken in spirit, he began to lose much of his arrogance and to come to his senses under the scourge of God, for he was tortured with pain every moment. [12]And when he could not endure his own stench, he uttered these words, "It is right to be subject to God; mortals should not think that they are equal to God."[d]

Antiochus Makes a Promise to God

13 Then the abominable fellow made a vow to the Lord, who would no longer have mercy on him, stating [14]that the holy city, which he was hurrying to level to the ground and to make a cemetery, he was now declaring to be free; [15]and the Jews, whom he had not considered worth burying but had planned to throw out with their children for the wild animals and for the birds to eat, he would make, all of them, equal to citizens of Athens; [16]and the holy sanctuary, which he had formerly plundered, he would adorn with the finest offerings; and all the holy vessels he would give back, many times over; and the expenses incurred for the sacrifices he would provide from his own revenues; [17]and in addition to all this he also would become a Jew and would visit every inhabited place to proclaim the power of God. [18]But when his sufferings did not in any way abate, for the judgment of God had justly come upon him, he gave up all hope for himself and wrote to the Jews the following letter, in the form of a supplication. This was its content:

Antiochus's Letter and Death

19 "To his worthy Jewish citizens, Antiochus their king and general sends hearty greetings and good wishes for their health and prosperity. [20]If you and your children are well and your affairs are as you wish, I am glad. As my hope is in

---

a Gk their arms   b Meaning of Gk uncertain   c Gk they were defeated   d Or not think thoughts proper only to God

heaven, [21]I remember with affection your esteem and goodwill. On my way back from the region of Persia I suffered an annoying illness, and I have deemed it necessary to take thought for the general security of all. [22]I do not despair of my condition, for I have good hope of recovering from my illness, [23]but I observed that my father, on the occasions when he made expeditions into the upper country, appointed his successor, [24]so that, if anything unexpected happened or any unwelcome news came, the people throughout the realm would not be troubled, for they would know to whom the government was left. [25]Moreover, I understand how the princes along the borders and the neighbors of my kingdom keep watching for opportunities and waiting to see what will happen. So I have appointed my son Antiochus to be king, whom I have often entrusted and commended to most of you when I hurried off to the upper provinces; and I have written to him what is written here. [26]I therefore urge and beg you to remember the public and private services rendered to you and to maintain your present goodwill, each of you, toward me and my son. [27]For I am sure that he will follow my policy and will treat you with moderation and kindness."

28 So the murderer and blasphemer, having endured the more intense suffering, such as he had inflicted on others, came to the end of his life by a most pitiable fate, among the mountains in a strange land. [29]And Philip, one of his courtiers, took his body home; then, fearing the son of Antiochus, he withdrew to Ptolemy Philometor in Egypt.

Purification of the Temple

10 Now Maccabeus and his followers, the Lord leading them on, recovered the temple and the city; [2]they tore down the altars that had been built in the public square by the foreigners, and also destroyed the sacred precincts. [3]They purified the sanctuary, and made another altar of sacrifice; then, striking fire out of flint, they offered sacrifices, after a lapse of two years, and they offered incense and lighted lamps and set out the bread of the Presence. [4]When they had done this, they fell prostrate and implored the Lord that they might never again fall into such misfortunes, but that, if they should ever sin, they might be disciplined by him with forbearance and not be handed over to blasphemous and barbarous nations. [5]It happened that on the same day on which the sanctuary had been profaned by the foreigners, the purification of the sanctuary took place, that is, on the twenty-fifth day of the same month, which was Chislev. [6]They celebrated it for eight days with rejoicing, in the manner of the festival of booths, remembering how not long before, during the festival of booths, they had been wandering in the mountains and caves like wild animals. [7]Therefore, carrying ivy-wreathed wands and beautiful branches and also fronds of palm, they offered hymns of thanksgiving to him who had given success to the purifying of his own holy place. [8]They decreed by public edict, ratified by vote, that the whole nation of the Jews should observe these days every year.

9 Such then was the end of Antiochus, who was called Epiphanes.

Accession of Antiochus Eupator

10 Now we will tell what took place under Antiochus Eupator, who was the son of that ungodly man, and will give a brief summary of the principal calamities of the wars. [11]This man, when he succeeded to the kingdom, appointed one Lysias to have charge of the government and to be chief governor of Coelesyria and Phoenicia. [12]Ptolemy, who was called Macron, took the lead in showing justice to the Jews because of the wrong that had been done to them, and attempted to maintain peaceful relations with

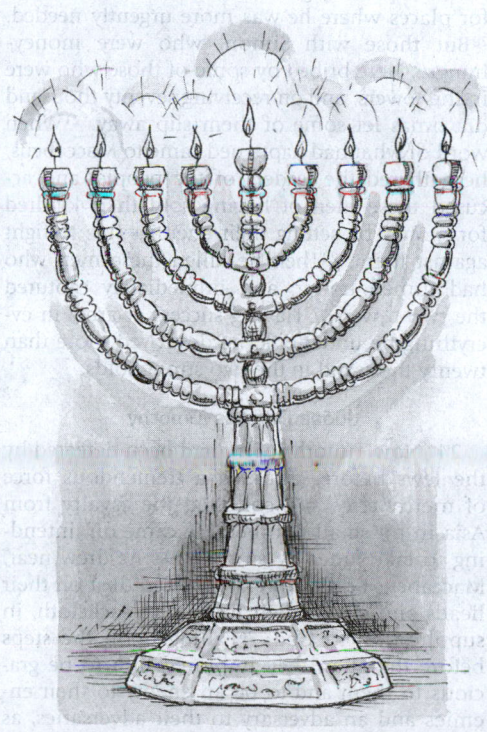

them. [13]As a result he was accused before Eupator by the king's Friends. He heard himself called a traitor at every turn, because he had abandoned Cyprus, which Philometor had entrusted to him, and had gone over to Antiochus Epiphanes. Unable to command the respect due his office,[a] he took poison and ended his life.

Campaign in Idumea

14 When Gorgias became governor of the region, he maintained a force of mercenaries, and at every turn kept attacking the Jews. [15]Besides this, the Idumeans, who had control of important strongholds, were harassing the Jews; they received those who were banished from Jerusalem, and endeavored to keep up the war. [16]But Maccabeus and his forces, after making solemn supplication and imploring God to fight on their side, rushed to the strongholds of the Idumeans. [17]Attacking them vigorously, they gained possession of the places, and beat off all who fought upon the wall, and slaughtered those whom they encountered, killing no fewer than twenty thousand.

18 When at least nine thousand took refuge in two very strong towers well equipped to withstand a siege, [19]Maccabeus left Simon and Joseph, and also Zacchaeus and his troops, a force sufficient to besiege them; and he himself set off for places where he was more urgently needed. [20]But those with Simon, who were money-hungry, were bribed by some of those who were in the towers, and on receiving seventy thousand drachmas let some of them slip away. [21]When word of what had happened came to Maccabeus, he gathered the leaders of the people, and accused these men of having sold their kindred for money by setting their enemies free to fight against them. [22]Then he killed these men who had turned traitor, and immediately captured the two towers. [23]Having success at arms in everything he undertook, he destroyed more than twenty thousand in the two strongholds.

Judas Defeats Timothy

24 Now Timothy, who had been defeated by the Jews before, gathered a tremendous force of mercenaries and collected the cavalry from Asia in no small number. He came on, intending to take Judea by storm. [25]As he drew near, Maccabeus and his men sprinkled dust on their heads and girded their loins with sackcloth, in supplication to God. [26]Falling upon the steps before the altar, they implored him to be gracious to them and to be an enemy to their enemies and an adversary to their adversaries, as

the law declares. [27]And rising from their prayer they took up their arms and advanced a considerable distance from the city; and when they came near the enemy they halted. [28]Just as dawn was breaking, the two armies joined battle, the one having as pledge of success and victory not only their valor but also their reliance on the Lord, while the other made rage their leader in the fight.

29 When the battle became fierce, there appeared to the enemy from heaven five resplendent men on horses with golden bridles, and they were leading the Jews. [30]Two of them took Maccabeus between them, and shielding him with their own armor and weapons, they kept him from being wounded. They showered arrows and thunderbolts on the enemy, so that, confused and blinded, they were thrown into disorder and cut to pieces. [31]Twenty thousand five hundred were slaughtered, besides six hundred cavalry.

32 Timothy himself fled to a stronghold called Gazara, especially well garrisoned, where Chaereas was commander. [33]Then Maccabeus and his men were glad, and they besieged the fort for four days. [34]The men within, relying on the strength of the place, kept blaspheming terribly and uttering wicked words. [35]But at dawn of the fifth day, twenty young men in the army of Maccabeus, fired with anger because of the blasphemies, bravely stormed the wall and with savage fury cut down everyone they met. [36]Others who came up in the same way wheeled around against the defenders and set fire to the towers; they kindled fires and burned the blasphemers alive. Others broke open the gates and let in the rest of the force, and they occupied the city. [37]They killed Timothy, who was hiding in a cistern, and his brother Chaereas, and Apollophanes. [38]When they had accomplished these things, with hymns and thanksgivings they blessed the Lord who shows great kindness to Israel and gives them the victory.

Lysias Besieges Beth-zur

11 Very soon after this, Lysias, the king's guardian and kinsman, who was in charge of the government, being vexed at what had happened, [2]gathered about eighty thousand infantry and all his cavalry and came against the Jews. He intended to make the city a home for Greeks, [3]and to levy tribute on the temple as he did on the sacred places of the other

---

a Cn: Meaning of Gk uncertain

Praying with the Bible

"My dear young friends, I urge you to become familiar with the Bible, and to have it at hand so that it can be your compass pointing out the road to follow."

(Message of the Holy Father Benedict XVI to the Youth of the World on the Occasion of the 21st World Youth Day)

The Bible is one of the greatest sources of inspiration we can tap into. When we pray with the Bible, God can deeply touch and change our lives. The more we are willing to pray with the Scriptures, the more we can enter into the profound mystery of God's relationship with all of humanity. God's word is the compass that leads us more deeply into the immense heart of God. This is why the Church proclaims the Scriptures every time we worship together and why all are encouraged to use the Bible in our private prayer.

The pages of this insert teach specific techniques for praying with the Bible. Look these over and think about which suggestions might work for you.

By praying with the Scriptures, we discover that God's story is our story. God's life is intimately connected with our lives. The unfinished part of the story is our response to God's love for us. Each of us has a part in the great story of God's salvation of all humanity.

Tips for Praying with the Bible

For our spiritual journey, our earthly pilgrimage, God has provided us with a guide who knows of the human experience from the inside out. God the Father has given us Jesus the Son as the Way, the way to the New Jerusalem—one of the biblical descriptions of heaven.

Jesus shows us the importance of prayer for our journey. Through prayer Jesus clearly understood the will of his Father. Through prayer Jesus gained and maintained his burning desire to do the will of God. We know from the Gospels that the Hebrew Scriptures were an important part of Jesus' prayer life. The Bible was a compass that helped point Jesus to his Father. God wishes the Bible to be the same for us. So here are some tips for using the Bible in your prayer:

Tip 1: Be Creative in Making Time for Prayer

Your life is busy. Sometimes finding even fifteen minutes for prayer seems impossible, but it can be done. Allow your daily routine to call you to prayer. Mark a favorite psalm in your Bible and pray it when you get up in the morning. When you head off for school, say a short verse like "Prosper the work of our hands" (Ps 90:17, see "Memorizing Bible Passages" section). Before going to bed, spend a few minutes using lectio divina (see next section) to listen to God before going to sleep.

Tip 2: Engage Your Imagination

When praying with the Bible, use your imagination to let the Bible stories come alive in a personal way. Put yourself in the Bible story, and ask, "What do I see? What do I smell? What do I hear?" Pretend you are one of the people in the story, and ask, "How do I feel about what is happening or what is being said?"

Tip 3: Listen

Saint Ambrose once said, "We speak to [God] when we pray; we listen to him when we read the [Scriptures]." Prayer is a dialogue with God, and Scripture is one of the primary ways God speaks to us. So when you read the Bible, it is always a good idea to take a quiet moment to "listen." What might God be saying to you through these sacred words?

What might God be saying to YOU through these sacred words?

Lectio Divina

Lectio divina is a very ancient art for praying with the Bible. It is a prayer technique for reading the Bible slowly and contemplatively, allowing God's word to shed insights on your life. It cultivates the ability to listen deeply, to hear the word of God with the ear of your heart. Lectio divina was practiced in the early Christian monasteries of the third and fourth centuries. In the sixth century, it was written into the Rule of Saint Benedict as a requirement for the spiritual life of monks.

The Movements of Lectio Divina

In traditional lectio divina, there are five movements. These movements lead you from hearing the word of God to applying God's word to your everyday life.

Step 1: Lectio (lex–ee–oh). This step is the reading of and listening to the word of God. This is a reverential listening, listening in a spirit of silence and awe because it is the sacred word of God. In this step, listen for a word or phrase from the Scripture passage that is God's word for you today.

Step 2: Meditatio (med–it–tots–ee–oh). This step is meditation on the Scripture passage. Allow the word of God to interact with your thoughts, your hopes, your memories, and your desires. Allow the Scriptures to touch you and affect you at your deepest level of being.

Step 3: Oratio (or–ot–see–oh). This step is responding to God with conscious prayer. It is both a dialogue with God and an offering of a part of yourself to God. In this prayer, open your real self to be touched and changed by the word of God.

Step 4: Contemplatio (con–tem–plot–see–oh). This step is contemplation. In silence, rest in the unconditional love of God.

Step 5: Actio (ax–ee–oh) (also known as operatio). In this step, ask yourself:
- What does the word of God invite me to do?
- What does this passage of Scripture call me to do or undo, or to be?

Praying with the Psalms

The Psalms are Israel's religious poetry and song. They express the people's very real and concrete experiences of God. The Psalms are filled with the same wide range of feelings and moods that we experience in our lives today. The people who wrote the Psalms poured out their hearts to God in words of joy and sorrow, regret and celebration, earnest pleading and praise. These are the prayers of people who struggled to live righteous lives.

There are many different kinds of psalms. There are psalms of lament, which express the anguish and sorrow experienced in illness, death, and personal loss. There are psalms of thanksgiving and rejoicing, which recognize God's hand when the people are rescued from evil or wickedness. There are psalms of praise to a majestic God, witnessed in all of creation.

The Book of Psalms serves as a common book of prayer for Jews and Christians. As Catholics we use psalms at Mass, the Liturgy of the Hours, and many other times when we gather for prayer. Because they address feelings and experiences common to all, they speak to us today just as strongly as they did to the people who first used them thousands of years ago.

Saint Athanasius advised us to hear the Psalms as being addressed to us, as believers in the present. So read Psalms slowly and reverently, savoring each word as if God is saying it for the first time. You will gain deeper insights if you read the Psalms in this way.

When you read the Psalms, look for their rhythm and repetition. Just as modern music and poetry use rhythm and repetition to emphasize certain things, so the Psalms use rhythm and repetition to emphasize their authors' keen insights into our relationship with God. Perhaps you will share the experience of Saint Ambrose, who once said, "When I am reading divine Scripture God walks again in the earthly Paradise."

> **When I am reading divine Scripture God walks again in the earthly Paradise.**

Psalm Theme Index

The Psalms are a wonderful place to turn when you are seeking ways to express your feelings in prayer. This index covers a range of emotions and moods to help you pray the Psalms in all of life's situations.

Ambiguity: Psalm 97:7–12

Anger: Psalms 9:1–6, 25:19–22, 35:1–10, 37:8–17

Anxiety: Psalms 69:1–8, 88:1–7, 94:16–23, 102:3–11

Betrayal: Psalms 41:4–13, 55:13–23

Bullying: Psalm 70

Compassion of God: Psalms 102:12–17, 113, 145:13–21, 146:5–10

Confession of sin: Psalms 38:12–22, 51:3–6, 119:65–72, 143:1–6

Death: Psalms 6:1–10; 18:1–6; 39:1–6; 49:10–20; 88:13–18; 102:23–28; 116:1–4,12–19; 118:10–17

Despair: Psalms 6:1–5; 22:1–5,14–21; 38:1–11; 40:11–17; 55:1–11; 119:25–32; 130:1–4

Envy: Psalm 73:1–3

Face of God: Psalms 27:7–14, 80:1–7, 119:129–136

Faith: Psalms 25:1–5, 116:1–10, 146:1–7

Fear of God: Psalm 76:7–12

Folly: Psalms 14, 53:1–3, 94:11

Forgiveness: Psalms 25:1–18, 32:1–5, 51:7–9, 85:1–3, 103:6–13

Generosity: Psalm 112:6–10

Gossip: Psalms 7:6–17, 50:16–23, 141:1–4

Guilt: Psalms 4:1–3, 25:11–18, 51:1–2, 79:8–10

Holiness: Psalm 77:11–15; 93; 99:1–5

Hope: Psalms 9:13–20, 33:14–22, 39:7–8, 43:1–5, 62:1–8, 65:1–8, 71:3–14, 91:1–12, 119:41–45, 146:1–7

Hypocrisy: Psalm 36:1–6

Joy: Psalms 16:1–11, 35:27–28, 43:1–5, 67:1–7, 71:20–24, 98:1–9, 126:1–6, 149:1–5

Judgment: Psalms 50:1–6, 73:1–20, 111:6–10

Justice: Psalms 9:7–10, 18:31–42, 33:1–5, 37:18–28

Law: Psalms 19:7–10, 37:28–34, 119:89–96

Light: Psalms 36:7–12, 43, 119:105

Love: Psalms 17:6–9, 18:1–3, 25:6–10, 26:1–3, 36:5–10, 63:1–4, 98:1–6, 108:1–6, 136:1–26

Nationalism and religion: Psalms 72:1–11, 132:11–18

Poverty: Psalms 9:11–20, 22:21–26, 34:1–10, 72:12–14, 107:39–43, 146:5–10, 147:1–6

(Psalm Theme Index continued)

Pride: Psalms 20:6–9; 52; 94:1–11; 119:97–104,161–168

Resurrection: Psalms 16:9–11, 27:13–14, 88:8–12

Righteousness: Psalms 5:8–12, 7:6–17, 11:1–5, 15, 31:1–8, 119:137–144

Self–pity: Psalms 69:22–29, 119:25–32

Sickness: Psalms 6:6–10, 38:1–11, 39:7–10, 107:17–22

Sin: Psalms 32:1–5, 38:12–22, 51:1–6, 85:1–3, 130:1–8

Steadfast love of God: Psalms 17:1–7, 86:14–17, 103:14–22, 117, 136:23–26

Success: Psalm 18:43–50

Thanksgiving: Psalms 30:4–12, 75:1–3, 92:1–9, 100:1–5, 107:1–9, 118:19–29, 147:1–11

Truth: Psalms 43, 86:8–13

Values: Psalms 85:10–13, 101

Waiting: Psalms 13, 37:28–34, 39:7–10, 119:122–128, 130:5–8

Wisdom of God: Psalms 51:6, 104:24

"God's word is the compass that leads us more deeply into the immense heart of God."

nations, and to put up the high priesthood for sale every year. [4]He took no account whatever of the power of God, but was elated with his ten thousands of infantry, and his thousands of cavalry, and his eighty elephants. [5]Invading Judea, he approached Beth-zur, which was a fortified place about five stadia[a] from Jerusalem, and pressed it hard.

[6] When Maccabeus and his men got word that Lysias[b] was besieging the strongholds, they and all the people, with lamentations and tears, prayed the Lord to send a good angel to save Israel. [7]Maccabeus himself was the first to take up arms, and he urged the others to risk their lives with him to aid their kindred. Then they eagerly rushed off together. [8]And there, while they were still near Jerusalem, a horseman appeared at their head, clothed in white and brandishing weapons of gold. [9]And together they all praised the merciful God, and were strengthened in heart, ready to assail not only humans but the wildest animals or walls of iron. [10]They advanced in battle order, having their heavenly ally, for the Lord had mercy on them. [11]They hurled themselves like lions against the enemy, and laid low eleven thousand of them and sixteen hundred cavalry, and forced all the rest to flee. [12]Most of them got away stripped and wounded, and Lysias himself escaped by disgraceful flight.

Lysias Makes Peace with the Jews

[13] As he was not without intelligence, he pondered over the defeat that had befallen him, and realized that the Hebrews were invincible because the mighty God fought on their side. So he sent to them [14]and persuaded them to settle everything on just terms, promising that he would persuade the king, constraining him to be their friend.[a] [15]Maccabeus, having regard for the common good, agreed to all that Lysias urged. For the king granted every request in behalf of the Jews which Maccabeus delivered to Lysias in writing.

[16] The letter written to the Jews by Lysias was to this effect:

"Lysias to the people of the Jews, greetings. [17]John and Absalom, who were sent by you, have delivered your signed communication and have asked about the matters indicated in it. [18]I have informed the king of everything that needed to be brought before him, and he has agreed to what was possible. [19]If you will maintain your goodwill toward the government, I will endeavor in the future to help promote your welfare. [20]And concerning such matters and their details, I have ordered these men and my representatives to confer with you. [21]Farewell. The one hundred forty-eighth year,[c] Dioscorinthius twenty-fourth."

[22] The king's letter ran thus:

"King Antiochus to his brother Lysias, greetings. [23]Now that our father has gone on to the gods, we desire that the subjects of the kingdom be undisturbed in caring for their own affairs. [24]We have heard that the Jews do not consent to our father's change to Greek customs, but prefer their own way of living and ask that their own customs be allowed them. [25]Accordingly, since we choose that this nation also should be free from disturbance, our decision is that their temple be restored to them and that they shall live according to the customs of their ancestors. [26]You will do well, therefore, to send word to them and give them pledges of friendship, so that they may know our policy and be of good cheer and go on happily in the conduct of their own affairs."

[27] To the nation the king's letter was as follows:

"King Antiochus to the senate of the Jews and to the other Jews, greetings. [28]If you are well, it is as we desire. We also are in good health. [29]Menelaus has informed us that you wish to return home and look after your own affairs. [30]Therefore those who go home by the thirtieth of Xanthicus will have our pledge of friendship and full permission [31]for the Jews to enjoy their own food and laws, just as formerly, and none of them shall be molested in any way for what may have been done in ignorance. [32]And I have also sent Menelaus to encourage you. [33]Farewell. The one hundred forty-eighth year,[c] Xanthicus fifteenth."

[34] The Romans also sent them a letter, which read thus:

"Quintus Memmius and Titus Manius, envoys of the Romans, to the people of the Jews, greetings. [35]With regard to what Lysias the kinsman of the king has granted you, we also give consent. [36]But as to the matters that he decided are to be referred to the king, as soon as you have considered them, send some one promptly so that we may make proposals appropriate for you. For we are on our way to Antioch. [37]Therefore make haste and send messengers so that we may have your judgment. [38]Farewell. The one hundred forty-eighth year,[c] Xanthicus fifteenth."

---

a Meaning of Gk uncertain   b Gk he   c 164 B.C.

Incidents at Joppa and Jamnia

12 When this agreement had been reached, Lysias returned to the king, and the Jews went about their farming.

2 But some of the governors in various places, Timothy and Apollonius son of Gennaeus, as well as Hieronymus and Demophon, and in addition to these Nicanor the governor of Cyprus, would not let them live quietly and in peace. 3And the people of Joppa did so ungodly a deed as this: they invited the Jews who lived among them to embark, with their wives and children, on boats that they had provided, as though there were no ill will to the Jews;*a* 4and this was done by public vote of the city. When they accepted, because they wished to live peaceably and suspected nothing, the people of Joppa*b* took them out to sea and drowned them, at least two hundred. 5When Judas heard of the cruelty visited on his compatriots, he gave orders to his men 6and, calling upon God, the righteous judge, attacked the murderers of his kindred. He set fire to the harbor by night, burned the boats, and massacred those who had taken refuge there. 7Then, because the city's gates were closed, he withdrew, intending to come again and root out the whole community of Joppa. 8But learning that the people in Jamnia meant in the same way to wipe out the Jews who were living among them, 9he attacked the Jamnites by night and set fire to the harbor and the fleet, so that the glow of the light was seen in Jerusalem, thirty miles*c* distant.

The Campaign in Gilead

10 When they had gone more than a mile*d* from there, on their march against Timothy, at least five thousand Arabs with five hundred cavalry attacked them. 11After a hard fight, Judas and his companions, with God's help, were victorious. The defeated nomads begged Judas to grant them pledges of friendship, promising to give him livestock and to help his people*e* in all other ways. 12Judas, realizing that they might indeed be useful in many ways, agreed to make peace with them; and after receiving his pledges they went back to their tents.

13 He also attacked a certain town that was strongly fortified with earthworks*f* and walls, and inhabited by all sorts of Gentiles. Its name was Caspin. 14Those who were within, relying on the strength of the walls and on their supply of provisions, behaved most insolently toward Judas and his men, railing at them and even blaspheming and saying unholy things. 15But Judas and his men, calling upon the great Sovereign of the world, who without battering rams or engines of war overthrew Jericho in the days of Joshua, rushed furiously upon the walls. 16They took the town by the will of God, and slaughtered untold numbers, so that the adjoining lake, a quarter of a mile*g* wide, appeared to be running over with blood.

Judas Defeats Timothy's Army

17 When they had gone ninety-five miles*h* from there, they came to Charax, to the Jews who are called Toubiani. 18They did not find Timothy in that region, for he had by then left there without accomplishing anything, though in one place he had left a very strong garrison. 19Dositheus and Sosipater, who were captains under Maccabeus, marched out and destroyed those whom Timothy had left in the stronghold, more than ten thousand men. 20But Maccabeus arranged his army in divisions, set men*e* in command of the divisions, and hurried after Timothy, who had with him one hundred twenty thousand infantry and two thousand five hundred cavalry. 21When Timothy learned of the approach of Judas, he sent off the women and the children and also the baggage to a place called Carnaim; for that place was hard to besiege and difficult of access because of the narrowness of all the approaches. 22But when Judas's first division appeared, terror and fear came over the enemy at the manifestation to them of him who sees all things. In their flight they rushed headlong in every direction, so that often they were injured by their own men and pierced by the points of their own swords. 23Judas pressed the pursuit with the utmost vigor, putting the sinners to the sword, and destroyed as many as thirty thousand.

24 Timothy himself fell into the hands of Dositheus and Sosipater and their men. With great guile he begged them to let him go in safety, because he held the parents of most of them, and the brothers of some, to whom no consideration would be shown. 25And when with many words he had confirmed his solemn promise to restore them unharmed, they let him go, for the sake of saving their kindred.

Judas Wins Other Victories

26 Then Judas*i* marched against Carnaim and the temple of Atargatis, and slaughtered

---

a Gk to them *b* Gk they *c* Gk two hundred forty stadia
d Gk nine stadia *e* Gk them *f* Meaning of Gk uncertain
g Gk two stadia *h* Gk seven hundred fifty stadia *i* Gk he

twenty-five thousand people. [27]After the rout and destruction of these, he marched also against Ephron, a fortified town where Lysias lived with multitudes of people of all nationalities.[a] Stalwart young men took their stand before the walls and made a vigorous defense; and great stores of war engines and missiles were there. [28]But the Jews[b] called upon the Sovereign who with power shatters the might of his enemies, and they got the town into their hands, and killed as many as twenty-five thousand of those who were in it.

29 Setting out from there, they hastened to Scythopolis, which is seventy-five miles[c] from Jerusalem. [30]But when the Jews who lived there bore witness to the goodwill that the people of Scythopolis had shown them and their kind treatment of them in times of misfortune, [31]they thanked them and exhorted them to be well disposed to their race in the future also. Then they went up to Jerusalem, as the festival of weeks was close at hand.

Judas Defeats Gorgias

32 After the festival called Pentecost, they hurried against Gorgias, the governor of Idumea, [33]who came out with three thousand infantry and four hundred cavalry. [34]When they joined battle, it happened that a few of the Jews fell. [35]But a certain Dositheus, one of Bacenor's men, who was on horseback and was a strong man, caught hold of Gorgias, and grasping his cloak was dragging him off by main strength, wishing to take the accursed man alive, when one of the Thracian cavalry bore down on him and cut off his arm; so Gorgias escaped and reached Marisa.

36 As Esdris and his men had been fighting for a long time and were weary, Judas called upon the Lord to show himself their ally and leader in the battle. [37]In the language of their ancestors he raised the battle cry, with hymns; then he charged against Gorgias's troops when they were not expecting it, and put them to flight.

Prayers for Those Killed in Battle

38 Then Judas assembled his army and went to the city of Adullam. As the seventh day was coming on, they purified themselves according to the custom, and kept the sabbath there.

39 On the next day, as had now become necessary, Judas and his men went to take up the bodies of the fallen and to bring them back to lie with their kindred in the sepulchres of their ancestors. [40]Then under the tunic of each one of the dead they found sacred tokens of the idols of Jamnia, which the law forbids the Jews to wear. And it became clear to all that this was the reason these men had fallen. [41]So they all blessed the ways of the Lord, the righteous judge, who reveals the things that are hidden; [42]and they turned to supplication, praying that the sin that had been committed might be wholly blotted out. The noble Judas exhorted the people to keep themselves free from sin, for they had seen with their own eyes what had happened as the result of the sin of those who had fallen. [43]He also took up a collection, man by man, to the amount of two thousand drachmas of silver, and sent it to Jerusalem to provide for a sin offering. In doing this he acted very well and honorably, taking account of the resurrection. [44]For if he were not expecting that those who had fallen would rise again, it would have been superfluous and foolish to pray for the dead. [45]But if he was looking to the splendid reward that is laid up for those who fall asleep in godliness, it was a holy and pious thought. Therefore he made atonement for the dead, so that they might be delivered from their sin.

Menelaus Is Put to Death

13 In the one hundred forty-ninth year[d] word came to Judas and his men that Antiochus Eupator was coming with a great army against Judea, [2]and with him Lysias, his guardian, who had charge of the government. Each of them had a Greek force of one hundred ten thousand infantry, five thousand three hundred cavalry, twenty-two elephants, and three hundred chariots armed with scythes.

3 Menelaus also joined them and with utter hypocrisy urged Antiochus on, not for the sake of his country's welfare, but because he thought that he would be established in office. [4]But the King of kings aroused the anger of Antiochus against the scoundrel; and when Lysias informed him that this man was to blame for all the trouble, he ordered them to take him to Beroea and to put him to death by the method that is customary in that place. [5]For there is a tower there, fifty cubits high, full of ashes, and it has a rim running around it that on all sides inclines precipitously into the ashes. [6]There they all push to destruction anyone guilty of sacrilege or notorious for other crimes. [7]By such a fate it came about that Menelaus the lawbreaker died, without even burial in the earth. [8]And this was

---

a Meaning of Gk uncertain   b Gk they   c Gk six hundred stadia
d 163 B.C.

✝ Catholic Connection

Final Judgment

When a loved one dies, we often turn our attention to life after death and our deepest hopes. Take for example the passage about Judas Maccabeus and his fallen warriors. During battle the warriors had broken the First Commandment by wearing charms that contained symbols worshiping a false god. While burying the dead, Judas discovers their sin and immediately calls for his followers to pray for the fallen. Judas's call to pray for the dead is born out of hope in God's mercy, hope in the ability to influence God's mercy on behalf of those who have died, and a belief that there is something more after death.

The hopes and beliefs shown by Judas Maccabeus are still embraced by the Catholic Church today. The Church believes there is something more after death—much more! The Church teaches that when we die, our souls will receive what is called a "particular judgment," where Christ will judge our soul and determine whether we enter heaven or hell. Heaven is eternal happiness, where we know God face to face and live in perfect peace with God and one another. Hell is total separation from God, resulting from one's own choice to reject God's love and mercy. There also are those who die in God's friendship but who still need to be purified of their sins and, therefore, are unable to enter heaven. According to Church teaching, these individuals undergo a purification called Purgatory. The Church calls us to pray for those who have died and may need to be purified of their sins, just as Judas prayed for his fallen comrades, so that they too will enjoy eternal salvation.

At the end of time, there will be a Final Judgment. This judgment will be preceded by the resurrection of the body, where the graves will open and every soul will be united with her or his body. At this judgment, everyone will stand before Christ and receive her or his final reward or punishment, heaven or hell. Then those who are found worthy of the eternal reward will live forever in perfect peace, happiness, and love in God's everlasting Kingdom.

▶ **2 Macc 12:38–45**
Catechism, nos. 1020–1060

eminently just; because he had committed many sins against the altar whose fire and ashes were holy, he met his death in ashes.

A Battle Near the City of Modein

9 The king with barbarous arrogance was coming to show the Jews things far worse than those that had been done[a] in his father's time. [10]But when Judas heard of this, he ordered the people to call upon the Lord day and night, now if ever to help those who were on the point of being deprived of the law and their country and the holy temple, [11]and not to let the people who had just begun to revive fall into the hands of the blasphemous Gentiles. [12]When they had all joined in the same petition and had implored the merciful Lord with weeping and fasting and lying prostrate for three days without ceasing, Judas exhorted them and ordered them to stand ready.

13 After consulting privately with the elders, he determined to march out and decide the matter by the help of God before the king's army could enter Judea and get possession of the city. [14]So, committing the decision to the Creator of the world and exhorting his troops to fight bravely to the death for the laws, temple, city, country, and commonwealth, he pitched his camp near Modein. [15]He gave his troops the watchword, "God's victory," and with a picked force of the bravest young men, he attacked the king's pavilion at night and killed as many as two thousand men in the camp. He stabbed[b] the leading elephant and its rider. [16]In the end they filled the camp with terror and confusion and withdrew in triumph. [17]This happened, just as day was dawning, because the Lord's help protected him.

Antiochus Makes a Treaty with the Jews

18 The king, having had a taste of the daring of the Jews, tried strategy in attacking their positions. [19]He advanced against Beth-zur, a strong fortress of the Jews, was turned back, attacked again,[c] and was defeated. [20]Judas sent in to the garrison whatever was necessary. [21]But Rhodocus, a man from the ranks of the Jews, gave secret information to the enemy; he was sought for, caught, and put in prison. [22]The king negotiated a second time with the people in Beth-zur, gave pledges, received theirs, withdrew, attacked Judas and his men, was defeated; [23]he got word that Philip, who had been left in charge of the government, had revolted in Antioch; he was dismayed, called in the Jews,

yielded and swore to observe all their rights, settled with them and offered sacrifice, honored the sanctuary and showed generosity to the holy place. [24]He received Maccabeus, left Hegemonides as governor from Ptolemais to Gerar, [25]and went to Ptolemais. The people of Ptolemais were indignant over the treaty; in fact they were so angry that they wanted to annul its terms.[b] [26]Lysias took the public platform, made the best possible defense, convinced them, appeased them, gained their goodwill, and set out for Antioch. This is how the king's attack and withdrawal turned out.

Alcimus Speaks against Judas

14 Three years later, word came to Judas and his men that Demetrius son of Seleucus had sailed into the harbor of Tripolis with a strong army and a fleet, [2]and had taken possession of the country, having made away with Antiochus and his guardian Lysias.

3 Now a certain Alcimus, who had formerly been high priest but had willfully defiled himself in the times of separation,[d] realized that there was no way for him to be safe or to have access again to the holy altar, [4]and went to King Demetrius in about the one hundred fifty-first year,[e] presenting to him a crown of gold and a palm, and besides these some of the customary olive branches from the temple. During that day he kept quiet. [5]But he found an opportunity that furthered his mad purpose when he was invited by Demetrius to a meeting of the council and was asked about the attitude and intentions of the Jews. He answered:

6 "Those of the Jews who are called Hasideans, whose leader is Judas Maccabeus, are keeping up war and stirring up sedition, and will not let the kingdom attain tranquility. [7]Therefore I have laid aside my ancestral glory—I mean the high priesthood—and have now come here, [8]first because I am genuinely concerned for the interests of the king, and second because I have regard also for my compatriots. For through the folly of those whom I have mentioned our whole nation is now in no small misfortune. [9]Since you are acquainted, O king, with the details of this matter, may it please you to take thought for our country and our hard-pressed nation with the gracious kindness that you show to all. [10]For as long as Judas lives, it is

---

a Or *the worst of the things that had been done*   b Meaning of Gk uncertain   c Or *faltered*   d Other ancient authorities read *of mixing*   e 161 B.C.

Introducing...

Jewish Sects

In the last two centuries before Christ, a diversity of ways of being Jewish emerged. Different groups arose emphasizing different ways of remaining faithful to their Jewish heritage. These groups, or factions, within a religion are sometimes called sects. Primarily three sects emerged within Judaism.

Pharisees. The Pharisees were descendants of the Hasidim, Jews devoted to a strict observance of the Law who opposed King Antiochus IV Epiphanes' attempts to destroy the Jewish religion. *Pharisee* means "separated" and probably reflects the Pharisees' rigorous observance of the Law. They were often greatly respected. In the New Testament, Jesus argues with some Pharisees but is also a guest of others. Saint Paul was a Pharisee. Not surprisingly, some of the Pharisees' teachings were similar to those of the early Christians.

Sadducees. The Sadducees were a conservative Jewish sect that emerged in the first century BC and lasted only to around AD 70. The Sadducees were wealthy and politically influential landowners, and some of them had important roles in the Temple. They emphasized the necessity of worshiping at the Temple in Jerusalem. Unlike the Pharisees, they did not believe in the resurrection of the body.

Essenes. The Essenes, like the Pharisees, seem to have descended from the Hasidim. They existed in the first century BC and disappeared after AD 70. *Essene* can mean "healer" or "pious." The Essenes did not believe in the necessity of Temple sacrifice and often lived together in isolated communities where they practiced a simple lifestyle. Some of them were connected with the desert monastery at Qumran and were responsible for writing the Dead Sea Scrolls. John the Baptist's preaching and some of Jesus' teaching in the Gospels closely reflected the writings and teachings of the Essenes.

impossible for the government to find peace." [11]When he had said this, the rest of the king's Friends,[a] who were hostile to Judas, quickly inflamed Demetrius still more. [12]He immediately chose Nicanor, who had been in command of the elephants, appointed him governor of Judea, and sent him off [13]with orders to kill Judas and scatter his troops, and to install Alcimus as high priest of the great[b] temple. [14]And the Gentiles throughout Judea, who had fled before[c] Judas, flocked to join Nicanor, thinking that the misfortunes and calamities of the Jews would mean prosperity for themselves.

Nicanor Makes Friends with Judas

15 When the Jews[d] heard of Nicanor's coming and the gathering of the Gentiles, they sprinkled dust on their heads and prayed to him who established his own people forever and always upholds his own heritage by manifesting himself. [16]At the command of the leader, they[e] set out from there immediately and engaged them in battle at a village called Dessau.[c] [17]Simon, the brother of Judas, had encountered Nicanor, but had been temporarily[f] checked because of the sudden consternation created by the enemy.

18 Nevertheless Nicanor, hearing of the valor of Judas and his troops and their courage in battle for their country, shrank from deciding the issue by bloodshed. [19]Therefore he sent Posidonius, Theodotus, and Mattathias to give and receive pledges of friendship. [20]When the terms had been fully considered, and the leader had informed the people, and it had appeared that they were of one mind, they agreed to the covenant. [21]The leaders[g] set a day on which to meet by themselves. A chariot came forward from each army; seats of honor were set in place; [22]Judas posted armed men in readiness at key places to prevent sudden treachery on the part of the enemy; so they duly held the consultation.

23 Nicanor stayed on in Jerusalem and did nothing out of the way, but dismissed the flocks of people that had gathered. [24]And he kept Judas always in his presence; he was warmly attached to the man. [25]He urged him to marry and have children; so Judas[e] married, settled down, and shared the common life.

---

a Gk *of the Friends*   b Gk *greatest*   c Meaning of Gk uncertain
d Gk *they*   e Gk *he*   f Other ancient authorities read *slowly*
g Gk *They*

Nicanor Turns against Judas

26 But when Alcimus noticed their goodwill for one another, he took the covenant that had been made and went to Demetrius. He told him that Nicanor was disloyal to the government, since he had appointed that conspirator against the kingdom, Judas, to be his successor. 27The king became excited and, provoked by the false accusations of that depraved man, wrote to Nicanor, stating that he was displeased with the covenant and commanding him to send Maccabeus to Antioch as a prisoner without delay.

28 When this message came to Nicanor, he was troubled and grieved that he had to annul their agreement when the man had done no wrong. 29Since it was not possible to oppose the king, he watched for an opportunity to accomplish this by a stratagem. 30But Maccabeus, noticing that Nicanor was more austere in his dealings with him and was meeting him more rudely than had been his custom, concluded that this austerity did not spring from the best motives. So he gathered not a few of his men, and went into hiding from Nicanor. 31When the latter became aware that he had been cleverly outwitted by the man, he went to the great[a] and holy temple while the priests were offering the customary sacrifices, and commanded them to hand the man over. 32When they declared on oath that they did not know where the man was whom he wanted, 33he stretched out his right hand toward the sanctuary, and swore this oath: "If you do not hand Judas over to me as a prisoner, I will level this shrine of God to the ground and tear down the altar, and build here a splendid temple to Dionysus."

34 Having said this, he went away. Then the priests stretched out their hands toward heaven and called upon the constant Defender of our nation, in these words: 35"O Lord of all, though you have need of nothing, you were pleased that there should be a temple for your habitation among us; 36so now, O holy One, Lord of all holiness, keep undefiled forever this house that has been so recently purified."

Razis Dies for His Country

37 A certain Razis, one of the elders of Jerusalem, was denounced to Nicanor as a man who loved his compatriots and was very well thought of and for his goodwill was called father of the Jews. 38In former times, when there was no mingling with the Gentiles, he had been accused of Judaism, and he had most zealously risked body and life for Judaism. 39Nicanor,

wishing to exhibit the enmity that he had for the Jews, sent more than five hundred soldiers to arrest him; 40for he thought that by arresting[b] him he would do them an injury. 41When the troops were about to capture the tower and were forcing the door of the courtyard, they ordered that fire be brought and the doors burned. Being surrounded, Razis[c] fell upon his own sword, 42preferring to die nobly rather than to fall into the hands of sinners and suffer outrages unworthy of his noble birth. 43But in the heat of the struggle he did not hit exactly, and the crowd was now rushing in through the doors. He courageously ran up on the wall, and bravely threw himself down into the crowd. 44But as they quickly drew back, a space opened and he fell in the middle of the empty space. 45Still alive and aflame with anger, he rose, and though his blood gushed forth and his wounds were severe he ran through the crowd; and standing upon a steep rock, 46with his blood now completely drained from him, he tore out his entrails, took them in both hands and hurled them at the crowd, calling upon the Lord of life and spirit to give them back to him again. This was the manner of his death.

Nicanor's Arrogance

15 When Nicanor heard that Judas and his troops were in the region of Samaria, he made plans to attack them with complete safety on the day of rest. 2When the Jews who were compelled to follow him said, "Do not destroy so savagely and barbarously, but show respect for the day that he who sees all things has honored and hallowed above other days," 3the thrice-accursed wretch asked if there were a sovereign in heaven who had commanded the keeping of the sabbath day. 4When they declared, "It is the living Lord himself, the Sovereign in heaven, who ordered us to observe the seventh day," 5he replied, "But I am a sovereign also, on earth, and I command you to take up arms and finish the king's business." Nevertheless, he did not succeed in carrying out his abominable design.

Judas Prepares the Jews for Battle

6 This Nicanor in his utter boastfulness and arrogance had determined to erect a public monument of victory over Judas and his forces. 7But Maccabeus did not cease to trust with all confidence that he would get help from the

Lord. ⁸He exhorted his troops not to fear the attack of the Gentiles, but to keep in mind the former times when help had come to them from heaven, and so to look for the victory that the Almighty would give them. ⁹Encouraging them from the law and the prophets, and reminding them also of the struggles they had won, he made them the more eager. ¹⁰When he had aroused their courage, he issued his orders, at the same time pointing out the perfidy of the Gentiles and their violation of oaths. ¹¹He armed each of them not so much with confidence in shields and spears as with the inspiration of brave words, and he cheered them all by relating a dream, a sort of vision,ᵃ which was worthy of belief.

12 What he saw was this: Onias, who had been high priest, a noble and good man, of modest bearing and gentle manner, one who spoke fittingly and had been trained from childhood in all that belongs to excellence, was praying with outstretched hands for the whole body of the Jews. ¹³Then in the same fashion another appeared, distinguished by his gray hair and dignity, and of marvelous majesty and authority. ¹⁴And Onias spoke, saying, "This is a man who loves the family of Israel and prays much for the people and the holy city—Jeremiah, the prophet of God." ¹⁵Jeremiah stretched out his right hand and gave to Judas a golden sword, and as he gave it he addressed him thus: ¹⁶"Take this holy sword, a gift from God, with which you will strike down your adversaries."

17 Encouraged by the words of Judas, so noble and so effective in arousing valor and awaking courage in the souls of the young, they determined not to carry on a campaignᵇ but to attack bravely, and to decide the matter by fighting hand to hand with all courage, because the city and the sanctuary and the temple were in danger. ¹⁸Their concern for wives and children, and also for brothers and sistersᶜ and relatives, lay upon them less heavily; their greatest and first fear was for the consecrated sanctuary. ¹⁹And those who had to remain in the city were in no little distress, being anxious over the encounter in the open country.

The Defeat and Death of Nicanor

20 When all were now looking forward to the coming issue, and the enemy was already close at hand with their army drawn up for battle, the elephantsᵈ strategically stationed and the cavalry deployed on the flanks, ²¹Maccabeus, observing the masses that were in front of him and the varied supply of arms and the savagery of the elephants, stretched out his hands toward heaven and called upon the Lord who works wonders; for he knew that it is not by arms, but as the Lordᵉ decides, that he gains the victory for those who deserve it. ²²He called upon him in these words: "O Lord, you sent your angel in the time of King Hezekiah of Judea, and he killed fully one hundred eighty-five thousand in the camp of Sennacherib. ²³So now, O Sovereign of the heavens, send a good angel to spread terror and trembling before us. ²⁴By the might of your arm may these blasphemers who come against your holy people be struck down." With these words he ended his prayer.

25 Nicanor and his troops advanced with trumpets and battle songs, ²⁶but Judas and his troops met the enemy in battle with invocations to God and prayers. ²⁷So, fighting with their hands and praying to God in their hearts, they laid low at least thirty-five thousand, and were greatly gladdened by God's manifestation.

28 When the action was over and they were returning with joy, they recognized Nicanor, lying dead, in full armor. ²⁹Then there was shouting and tumult, and they blessed the Sovereign Lord in the language of their ancestors. ³⁰Then the man who was ever in body and soul the defender of his people, the man who maintained his youthful goodwill toward his compatriots, ordered them to cut off Nicanor's head and arm and carry them to Jerusalem. ³¹When he arrived there and had called his compatriots together and stationed the priests before the altar, he sent for those who were in the citadel. ³²He showed them the vile Nicanor's head and that profane man's arm, which had been boastfully stretched out against the holy house of the Almighty. ³³He cut out the tongue of the ungodly Nicanor and said that he would feed it piecemeal to the birds and would hang up these rewards of his folly opposite the sanctuary. ³⁴And they all, looking to heaven, blessed the Lord who had manifested himself, saying, "Blessed is he who has kept his own place undefiled!" ³⁵Judasᶠ hung Nicanor's head from the citadel, a clear and conspicuous sign to everyone of the help of the Lord. ³⁶And they all decreed by public vote never to let this day go unobserved, but to celebrate the thirteenth day of the twelfth month—which is called Adar in the Aramaic language—the day before Mordecai's day.

37 This, then, is how matters turned out with

ᵃ Meaning of Gk uncertain   ᵇ Or to remain in camp   ᶜ Gk for brothers   ᵈ Gk animals   ᵉ Gk he   ᶠ Gk He

Nicanor, and from that time the city has been in the possession of the Hebrews. So I will here end my story.

The Compiler's Epilogue

38 If it is well told and to the point, that is what I myself desired; if it is poorly done and mediocre, that was the best I could do. 39 For just as it is harmful to drink wine alone, or, again, to drink water alone, while wine mixed with water is sweet and delicious and enhances one's enjoyment, so also the style of the story delights the ears of those who read the work. And here will be the end.

Introduction to the
Wisdom and Poetry Books

The LORD is my shepherd, I shall not want.

(Ps 23:1)

A soft answer turns away wrath,
   but a harsh word stirs up anger.

(Prov 15:1)

For everything there is a season, and a time for every matter under heaven.
(Eccl 3:1)

The books these words are taken from, the wisdom and poetry books of the Old Testament, are among the most quoted books of the Bible. The distilled wisdom they contain and the beauty of the language they use have universal appeal. Across cultures and across time, these books touch thoughtful minds and inquiring hearts.

In Depth

This section of the Bible contains a variety of books. The Book of Psalms consists of religious hymns, many written for use in Jewish worship. The Song of Solomon is a love poem. The Book of Job is a debate on why innocent people suffer. The Wisdom of Solomon, Proverbs, and Sirach give advice on moral and virtuous living. And Ecclesiastes is a sort of journal on the purpose of human life. The most obvious common element among these books is the use of poetic language to convey their message. These are not the only books of the Old Testament that use poetry, but they make such extensive application of it that a little background on the nature of Hebrew poetry is helpful for reading them.

The most important feature of Hebrew poetry is parallelism. Parallelism involves the repetition of words or ideas in successive lines of a verse. Sometimes, the second line contrasts with the first:

The LORD watches over the way of the righteous,
   but the way of the wicked will perish.

(Ps 1:6)

Other times, the second line completes the thought of the first:

The LORD looks down from heaven on humankind
   to see if there are any who are wise,
   who seek after God.

(14:2)

Still other times, the second line seems to restate the first line more forcefully:

For I know my transgressions,
   and my sin is ever before me.

(51:3)

In its many forms, parallelism—not a rhythmic pattern or rhyming words—is the organizing principle of Hebrew poetry.

Hebrew poetry also uses symbolic language that is characteristic of poetry in any language. This includes metaphors ("My God, my rock in whom I take refuge" [18:2]) and similes ("As a deer longs for flowing streams, / so my soul longs for you, O God" [42:1]). To appreciate the beauty of Old Testament poetry and feel its impact, one must be willing to wrestle with symbolic ways of interpreting words and phrases.

Whereas the other books of the Old Testament emphasize ancient Israel's distinctive religious values, the wisdom and poetry books focus on its unique view of wisdom. Wisdom literature is something the ancient Israelites shared with neighboring cultures. The Egyptians, Sumerians, and Babylonians all had literature that offered practical, time-tested advice for people seeking trustworthy guidance. For the Israelites, however, true wisdom was more than mere common sense: it was a gift from God given to those who sought it. Some passages of the wisdom literature even describe wisdom personified as divine, beautiful, eternal, holy, and with feminine characteristics (see Wis 7:22—8:8 and Sirach, chapter 1).

In general, the wisdom writings have these characteristics:

- few references to the law or the covenant
- a minimal interest in Israel's history
- a search for harmony and the meaning of life
- a willingness to explore the difficult mysteries of life, such as suffering and death
- a commitment to discovering the moral lessons of everyday experiences
- a fundamental belief that good and wise living is rewarded, whereas evil and foolish ways lead to ruin.

The poetry and wisdom books of the Old Testament had an enormous influence on the writers of the New Testament and continue to be popular. Their poetic structure, which often makes them difficult to comprehend, also gives them a richness and depth that centuries of reading and rereading have not exhausted. Each time you read from these books, you will discover new treasures to enrich your life.

Other Background

▶ The Book of Psalms is quoted more often in the New Testament than is any other Old Testament book. Also, it is used extensively in the Church's liturgy.

▶ Job and Ecclesiastes posed serious challenges to the traditional understanding of Israelite faith. For help in understanding why, see the introductions to these books.

▶ Solomon's reputation for wisdom was so great that he was indicated as the author of four books actually written by others: Proverbs, Ecclesiastes, Song of Solomon, and Wisdom of Solomon.

▶ The Books of Wisdom of Solomon and Sirach are not found in all translations of the Old Testament (see "The Case of the Missing Books," near Tob 1:16).

Suffering is an abundant reality in our world. You've seen the images—a mother holding her poor, dead child, against the background of a country ravaged by drought; the innocent victims of war and violence; the devastation resulting from natural disasters like hurricanes and earthquakes. Or perhaps you have watched someone close to you suffer from a debilitating illness, or the grief that comes with losing a loved one. Inevitably, the questions arise: Why do innocent people suffer? How can God allow this to happen? These are the basic questions struggled with in the Book of Job.

In Depth

At the time Job was written, most Israelites believed that if they obeyed God's Commandments, God would bless them and protect them in this life. The Israelites also believed that if people were suffering or poor, God was punishing them for some sin they or their parents had committed, even if they did not know what that sin was. The Israelites' thinking was extremely logical—because God is all-powerful and completely just, God will not allow people or communities to suffer unless they have sinned in some way.

At a Glance

- Chapters 1–2. God and an adversary (Satan) agree to test Job.

- Chapters 3–37. Job and his friends debate the cause of his suffering.

- 38:1—42:6. God responds to Job.

- 42:7–17. The story has a happy ending.

Quick Facts

Inspired Author: unknown, written during the sixth or fifth centuries BC

Themes: Why do good people suffer? God's power, presence, and wisdom are beyond human understanding.

Of Note: Job is a story within a story: chapters 1–2 and 42:7–17 constitute a folktale; set within that tale, in 3:1—42:6, is a poetic debate about the cause of suffering.

The Book of Job challenges that way of thinking. Job is a good man who has received great wealth and a wonderful family from God. In fact, Job's final defense in chapter 31 is one of the finest summaries of the Old Testament vision of a righteous person. The Book of Job begins with God's allowing Job's wealth and children and health to be taken from him. Three friends come to mourn with Job. In a series of lengthy debates, they point out that his misfortunes must be the result of some sin or wrong he has committed. Job maintains his innocence, sometimes forcefully, and demands another explanation from God. Finally, God appears to Job and overwhelms him with questions about the nature of the universe. Job realizes that God is beyond human knowledge and that some mysteries—including suffering—can never be completely understood; they can only be accepted.

The Book of Job does not give the final answer about why bad things happen to good people. But it does make it clear that good people do suffer and that their suffering is not a punishment sent by God. And Job is a reminder to the Israelites and to us that God's purposes are too far beyond human understanding for anyone to claim to know everything there is to know about God.

The Book of Job

Job

Job and His Family

1 There was once a man in the land of Uz whose name was Job. That man was blameless and upright, one who feared God and turned away from evil. ²There were born to him seven sons and three daughters. ³He had seven thousand sheep, three thousand camels, five hundred yoke of oxen, five hundred donkeys, and very many servants; so that this man was the greatest of all the people of the east. ⁴His sons used to go and hold feasts in one another's houses in turn; and they would send and invite their three sisters to eat and drink with them. ⁵And when the feast days had run their course, Job would send and sanctify them, and he would rise early in the morning and offer burnt offerings according to the number of them all; for Job said, "It may be that my children have sinned, and cursed God in their hearts." This is what Job always did.

Attack on Job's Character

6 One day the heavenly beings*ᵃ* came to present themselves before the LORD, and Satan*ᵇ* also came among them. ⁷The LORD said to Satan,*ᵇ* "Where have you come from?" Satan*ᵇ* answered the LORD, "From going to and fro on the earth, and from walking up and down on it." ⁸The LORD said to Satan,*ᵇ* "Have you considered my servant Job? There is no one like him on the earth, a blameless and upright man who fears God and turns away from evil." ⁹Then Satan*ᵇ* answered the LORD, "Does Job fear God for nothing? ¹⁰Have you not put a fence around him and his house and all that he has, on every side? You have blessed the work of his hands, and his possessions have increased in the land. ¹¹But stretch out your hand now, and touch all that he has, and he will curse you to your face." ¹²The LORD said to Satan,*ᵇ* "Very well, all that he has is in your power; only do not stretch out your hand against him!" So Satan*ᵇ* went out from the presence of the LORD.

Job Loses Property and Children

13 One day when his sons and daughters were eating and drinking wine in the eldest brother's house, ¹⁴a messenger came to Job and said, "The oxen were plowing and the donkeys were feeding beside them, ¹⁵and the Sabeans fell on them and carried them off, and killed the servants with the edge of the sword; I alone have escaped to tell you." ¹⁶While he was still speaking, another came and said, "The fire of God fell from heaven and burned up the sheep and the servants, and consumed them; I alone have escaped to tell you." ¹⁷While he was still speaking, another came and said, "The Chaldeans formed three columns, made a raid on the camels and carried them off, and killed the servants with the edge of the sword; I alone have escaped to tell you." ¹⁸While he was still speaking, another came and said, "Your sons and daughters were eating and drinking wine in

---

a Heb *sons of God*   *b* Or *the Accuser;* Heb *ha-satan*

In Good Times and Bad

Have you ever felt so angry at the loss of something that you cursed and swore at God? Have you ever felt like just giving up on God because of your loss? In Job 1:13–19, a man named Job experiences an unimaginable loss. His children, his home, and his property are all destroyed at the same time. Job responds with great anger and great pain, but instead of cursing or blaming God, he blesses (praises) God (see verse 21).

Job never loses his faith in God, even when he loses so much else. Through most of the rest of this book, he struggles to understand why this has happened to him. Job is an important model for us. When faced with great suffering, he does not lose his belief in the goodness of God, nor does he let his friends talk him into false confessions of sinfulness. Like Job, we must not fall into the trap of thinking that when bad things happen, God is punishing us.

Furthermore, when we try to explain suffering by saying things like, "God has a reason for everything," we risk making God out to be detached and uncaring, someone who wills evil into the world and upon his people. This is not the God of our faith. Instead of trying to explain suffering, we must reach out to God, the good and compassionate healer who offers us comfort in our times of distress.

▶ Job 1:13–21

their eldest brother's house, ¹⁹and suddenly a great wind came across the desert, struck the four corners of the house, and it fell on the young people, and they are dead; I alone have escaped to tell you."

20 Then Job arose, tore his robe, shaved his head, and fell on the ground and worshiped. ²¹He said, "Naked I came from my mother's womb, and naked shall I return there; the LORD gave, and the LORD has taken away; blessed be the name of the LORD."

22 In all this Job did not sin or charge God with wrongdoing.

Attack on Job's Health

2 One day the heavenly beings^a came to present themselves before the LORD, and Satan^b also came among them to present himself before the LORD. ²The LORD said to Satan,^{b} "Where have you come from?" Satan^c answered the LORD, "From going to and fro on the earth, and from walking up and down on it." ³The LORD said to Satan,^{b} "Have you considered my servant Job? There is no one like him on the earth, a blameless and upright man who fears God and turns away from evil. He still persists in his integrity, although you incited me against him, to destroy him for no reason." ⁴Then Satan^b answered the LORD, "Skin for skin! All that people have they will give to save their lives.^{d} ⁵But stretch out your hand now and touch his bone and his flesh, and he will curse you to your face." ⁶The LORD said to Satan,^{b} "Very well, he is in your power; only spare his life."

7 So Satan^b went out from the presence of the LORD, and inflicted loathsome sores on Job from the sole of his foot to the crown of his head. ⁸Job^e took a potsherd with which to scrape himself, and sat among the ashes.

9 Then his wife said to him, "Do you still persist in your integrity? Curse^f God, and die." ¹⁰But he said to her, "You speak as any foolish woman would speak. Shall we receive the good at the hand of God, and not receive the bad?" In all this Job did not sin with his lips.

Job's Three Friends

11 Now when Job's three friends heard of all these troubles that had come upon him, each of them set out from his home—Eliphaz the Temanite, Bildad the Shuhite, and Zophar the Naamathite. They met together to go and console and comfort him. ¹²When they saw him from a distance, they did not recognize him, and they raised their voices and wept aloud; they tore their robes and threw dust in the air upon their heads. ¹³They sat with him on the ground seven days and seven nights, and no one spoke a word to him, for they saw that his suffering was very great.

Job Curses the Day He Was Born

3 After this Job opened his mouth and cursed the day of his birth. ²Job said:

³ "Let the day perish in which I was born,
   and the night that said,

---

^{a} Heb sons of God ^{b} Or the Accuser; Heb ha-satan ^{c} Or The Accuser; Heb ha-satan ^{d} Or All that the man has he will give for his life ^{e} Heb He ^{f} Heb Bless

J
O
B

'A man-child is conceived.'

4 Let that day be darkness!
  May God above not seek it,
    or light shine on it.

5 Let gloom and deep darkness claim it.
  Let clouds settle upon it;
    let the blackness of the day terrify it.

6 That night—let thick darkness seize it!
    let it not rejoice among the days of the year;
    let it not come into the number of the
      months.

7 Yes, let that night be barren;
    let no joyful cry be heard*a* in it.

8 Let those curse it who curse the Sea,*b*
    those who are skilled to rouse up Leviathan.

9 Let the stars of its dawn be dark;
    let it hope for light, but have none;
    may it not see the eyelids of the morning—

10 because it did not shut the doors of my mother's
    womb,
    and hide trouble from my eyes.

11 "Why did I not die at birth,
    come forth from the womb and expire?

12 Why were there knees to receive me,
    or breasts for me to suck?

13 Now I would be lying down and quiet;
    I would be asleep; then I would be at rest

---

a Heb *come*   *b* Cn: Heb *day*

Introducing...

Satan

Does the word *Satan* conjure for you an image of a demon with horns and a tail, torturing people in the fires of hell? or perhaps an evil presence wandering the world looking for souls to corrupt? Does it surprise you that Job 1:6 and Zechariah 3:1 present Satan as actually working for God? In fact, the word *Satan* is more of a job description than a name; it means "adversary." In the Old Testament, Satan is depicted as a member of God's court whose responsibility it is to accuse or test humans before God (although, contrary to popular belief, the snake in the Garden of Eden is never identified as Satan in the Bible!).

It is only much later that Satan is seen as the enemy of God and the controller of the forces of evil. The notion of Satan as an evildoer seems to have been borrowed from a similar figure in Persian religion and developed in Israel as time passed. By the New Testament period, Satan is identified as a powerful agent of evil fighting against God (see 1 Thess 2:18), is instrumental in Jesus' death (see Lk 22:3), tempts people to sin (see 1 Cor 7:5), and is called the devil (see Rev 12:9). The good news is that in the death and Resurrection of Jesus, God overcomes the evil associated with Satan, both now and forever.

▶ **Job 1:6—2:10**

Live It!

Being There

What is the best way to respond to the suffering of another? Many of us shy away from funerals and hospitals because we just don't know what to say or how to act.

In Job 2:11–13, Job was visited by three friends. They did not recognize him at first because of his great suffering; then they cried. And then something remarkable happened: "They sat with him on the ground seven days and seven nights, and no one spoke a word to him, for they saw that his suffering was very great" (verse 13).

We must give Job's friends credit for being there, for spending time with him, and for letting him know they cared, especially when they first arrived. That is all we have to do for a friend who is hurting—offer a hug and a simple "I'm sorry," and then just stay around. Though this sounds easy, it can be very hard; we can feel so helpless. We need to keep in mind that what matters most is that we are there. That is what will be remembered.

If you know people are suffering or grieving, don't avoid them. Go up to them, let them know how you feel, and just be there for them. That is all. And that is a lot.

▶ **Job 2:11–13**

14 with kings and counselors of the earth
　　who rebuild ruins for themselves,
15 or with princes who have gold,
　　who fill their houses with silver.
16 Or why was I not buried like a stillborn child,
　　like an infant that never sees the light?
17 There the wicked cease from troubling,
　　and there the weary are at rest.
18 There the prisoners are at ease together;
　　they do not hear the voice of the taskmaster.
19 The small and the great are there,
　　and the slaves are free from their masters.

20 "Why is light given to one in misery,
　　and life to the bitter in soul,
21 who long for death, but it does not come,
　　and dig for it more than for hidden
　　　treasures;
22 who rejoice exceedingly,
　　and are glad when they find the grave?
23 Why is light given to one who cannot see the
　　way,
　　whom God has fenced in?
24 For my sighing comes like*a* my bread,
　　and my groanings are poured out like water.
25 Truly the thing that I fear comes upon me,
　　and what I dread befalls me.
26 I am not at ease, nor am I quiet;
　　I have no rest; but trouble comes."

Eliphaz Speaks: Job Has Sinned

4 Then Eliphaz the Temanite answered:
2 "If one ventures a word with you, will you be
　　offended?
　　But who can keep from speaking?
3 See, you have instructed many;
　　you have strengthened the weak hands.
4 Your words have supported those who were
　　stumbling,
　　and you have made firm the feeble knees.
5 But now it has come to you, and you are
　　impatient;
　　it touches you, and you are dismayed.
6 Is not your fear of God your confidence,
　　and the integrity of your ways your hope?

7 "Think now, who that was innocent ever
　　perished?
　　Or where were the upright cut off?
8 As I have seen, those who plow iniquity
　　and sow trouble reap the same.
9 By the breath of God they perish,
　　and by the blast of his anger they are
　　　consumed.
10 The roar of the lion, the voice of the fierce lion,
　　and the teeth of the young lions are broken.

11 The strong lion perishes for lack of prey,
　　and the whelps of the lioness are scattered.

12 "Now a word came stealing to me,
　　my ear received the whisper of it.
13 Amid thoughts from visions of the night,
　　when deep sleep falls on mortals,
14 dread came upon me, and trembling,
　　which made all my bones shake.
15 A spirit glided past my face;
　　the hair of my flesh bristled.
16 It stood still,
　　but I could not discern its appearance.
　A form was before my eyes;
　　there was silence, then I heard a voice:
17 'Can mortals be righteous before*b* God?
　　Can human beings be pure before*b* their
　　　Maker?
18 Even in his servants he puts no trust,
　　and his angels he charges with error;
19 how much more those who live in houses of
　　clay,
　　whose foundation is in the dust,
　　who are crushed like a moth.
20 Between morning and evening they are
　　destroyed;
　　they perish forever without any regarding it.
21 Their tent-cord is plucked up within them,
　　and they die devoid of wisdom.'

Job Is Corrected by God

5 "Call now; is there anyone who will answer
　　you?
　To which of the holy ones will you turn?
2 Surely vexation kills the fool,
　　and jealousy slays the simple.
3 I have seen fools taking root,
　　but suddenly I cursed their dwelling.
4 Their children are far from safety,
　　they are crushed in the gate,
　　and there is no one to deliver them.
5 The hungry eat their harvest,
　　and they take it even out of the thorns;*c*
　　and the thirsty*d* pant after their wealth.
6 For misery does not come from the earth,
　　nor does trouble sprout from the ground;
7 but human beings are born to trouble
　　just as sparks*e* fly upward.

8 "As for me, I would seek God,
　　and to God I would commit my cause.
9 He does great things and unsearchable,

---

a Heb *before*　b Or *more than*　c Meaning of Heb uncertain
d Aquila Symmachus Syr Vg: Heb *snare*　e Or *birds*; Heb *sons
of Resheph*

marvelous things without number.

10 He gives rain on the earth
  and sends waters on the fields;

11 he sets on high those who are lowly,
  and those who mourn are lifted to safety.

12 He frustrates the devices of the crafty,
  so that their hands achieve no success.

13 He takes the wise in their own craftiness;
  and the schemes of the wily are brought to a
    quick end.

14 They meet with darkness in the daytime,
  and grope at noonday as in the night.

15 But he saves the needy from the sword of their
    mouth,
  from the hand of the mighty.

16 So the poor have hope,
  and injustice shuts its mouth.

17 "How happy is the one whom God reproves;
  therefore do not despise the discipline of the
    Almighty.*a*

18 For he wounds, but he binds up;
  he strikes, but his hands heal.

19 He will deliver you from six troubles;
  in seven no harm shall touch you.

20 In famine he will redeem you from death,
  and in war from the power of the sword.

21 You shall be hidden from the scourge of the
    tongue,
  and shall not fear destruction when it comes.

22 At destruction and famine you shall laugh,
  and shall not fear the wild animals of the
    earth.

23 For you shall be in league with the stones of the
    field,
  and the wild animals shall be at peace with
    you.

24 You shall know that your tent is safe,
  you shall inspect your fold and miss nothing.

25 You shall know that your descendants will be
    many,
  and your offspring like the grass of the earth.

26 You shall come to your grave in ripe old age,
  as a shock of grain comes up to the threshing
    floor in its season.

27 See, we have searched this out, it is true.
  Hear, and know it for yourself."

Job Replies: My Complaint Is Just

6 Then Job answered:
2 "O that my vexation were weighed,
  and all my calamity laid in the balances!

3 For then it would be heavier than the sand of
    the sea;
  therefore my words have been rash.

4 For the arrows of the Almighty*a* are in me;

my spirit drinks their poison;
  the terrors of God are arrayed against me.

5 Does the wild ass bray over its grass,
  or the ox low over its fodder?

6 Can that which is tasteless be eaten without salt,
  or is there any flavor in the juice of mallows?*b*

7 My appetite refuses to touch them;
  they are like food that is loathsome to me.*b*

8 "O that I might have my request,
  and that God would grant my desire;

9 that it would please God to crush me,
  that he would let loose his hand and cut me
    off!

10 This would be my consolation;
  I would even exult*b* in unrelenting pain;
  for I have not denied the words of the Holy
    One.

11 What is my strength, that I should wait?
  And what is my end, that I should be patient?

12 Is my strength the strength of stones,
  or is my flesh bronze?

13 In truth I have no help in me,
  and any resource is driven from me.

14 "Those who withhold*c* kindness from a friend
  forsake the fear of the Almighty.*a*

15 My companions are treacherous like a torrent-
    bed,
  like freshets that pass away,

16 that run dark with ice,
  turbid with melting snow.

17 In time of heat they disappear;
  when it is hot, they vanish from their place.

18 The caravans turn aside from their course;
  they go up into the waste, and perish.

19 The caravans of Tema look,
  the travelers of Sheba hope.

20 They are disappointed because they were
    confident;
  they come there and are confounded.

21 Such you have now become to me;*d*
  you see my calamity, and are afraid.

22 Have I said, 'Make me a gift'?
  Or, 'From your wealth offer a bribe for me'?

23 Or, 'Save me from an opponent's hand'?
  Or, 'Ransom me from the hand of
    oppressors'?

24 "Teach me, and I will be silent;
  make me understand how I have gone wrong.

25 How forceful are honest words!

---

a Traditional rendering of Heb *Shaddai*   *b* Meaning of Heb
uncertain   *c* Syr Vg Compare Tg: Meaning of Heb uncertain
d Cn Compare Gk Syr: Meaning of Heb uncertain

J
O
B

But your reproof, what does it reprove?

²⁶ Do you think that you can reprove words,
   as if the speech of the desperate were wind?

²⁷ You would even cast lots over the orphan,
   and bargain over your friend.

²⁸ "But now, be pleased to look at me;
   for I will not lie to your face.

²⁹ Turn, I pray, let no wrong be done.
   Turn now, my vindication is at stake.

³⁰ Is there any wrong on my tongue?
   Cannot my taste discern calamity?

Job: My Suffering Is without End

7 "Do not human beings have a hard service on
   earth,
   and are not their days like the days of a
   laborer?

Suffering

Job's words in Job, chapter 7, are almost a prayer describing his suffering and asking, Why me? Job isn't worried about being polite; he says it like it is. What can you learn from Job about prayer during suffering?

First, you need to be honest with God and yourself. If you are hurt or in pain, don't play games with God. Tell God what you are feeling, in your own words. Write it down in a journal if you want to. And be honest. Because if you aren't honest with God, you probably aren't being honest with yourself.

Second, let all your feelings out, just like Job did—including your anger. God is big enough to handle it. When you suppress your negative feelings, they may come out in unhealthy ways. So, let God help you deal with them.

Finally, let your prayer lead you to take some action. Job debated with his friends. That's probably how people did counseling back then! Your prayer to God for help might lead you to a counselor, a minister, or a support group. God works in many ways.

▶ **Job 7:1–21**

² Like a slave who longs for the shadow,
   and like laborers who look for their wages,

³ so I am allotted months of emptiness,
   and nights of misery are apportioned to me.

⁴ When I lie down I say, 'When shall I rise?'
   But the night is long,
   and I am full of tossing until dawn.

⁵ My flesh is clothed with worms and dirt;
   my skin hardens, then breaks out again.

⁶ My days are swifter than a weaver's shuttle,
   and come to their end without hope.ᵃ

⁷ "Remember that my life is a breath;
   my eye will never again see good.

⁸ The eye that beholds me will see me no more;
   while your eyes are upon me, I shall be gone.

⁹ As the cloud fades and vanishes,
   so those who go down to Sheol do not
      come up;

¹⁰ they return no more to their houses,
   nor do their places know them any more.

¹¹ "Therefore I will not restrain my mouth;
   I will speak in the anguish of my spirit;
   I will complain in the bitterness of my soul.

¹² Am I the Sea, or the Dragon,
   that you set a guard over me?

¹³ When I say, 'My bed will comfort me,
   my couch will ease my complaint,'

¹⁴ then you scare me with dreams
   and terrify me with visions,

¹⁵ so that I would choose strangling
   and death rather than this body.

¹⁶ I loathe my life; I would not live forever.
   Let me alone, for my days are a breath.

¹⁷ What are human beings, that you make so much
      of them,
   that you set your mind on them,

¹⁸ visit them every morning,
   test them every moment?

¹⁹ Will you not look away from me for a while,
   let me alone until I swallow my spittle?

²⁰ If I sin, what do I do to you, you watcher of
      humanity?
   Why have you made me your target?
   Why have I become a burden to you?

²¹ Why do you not pardon my transgression
   and take away my iniquity?
   For now I shall lie in the earth;
   you will seek me, but I shall not be."

Bildad Speaks: Job Should Repent

8 Then Bildad the Shuhite answered:
   ² "How long will you say these things,

ᵃ Or *as the thread runs out*

and the words of your mouth be a great wind?

3 Does God pervert justice?
　Or does the Almighty[a] pervert the right?

4 If your children sinned against him,
　he delivered them into the power of their
　　transgression.

5 If you will seek God
　and make supplication to the Almighty,[a]

6 if you are pure and upright,
　surely then he will rouse himself for you
　and restore to you your rightful place.

7 Though your beginning was small,
　your latter days will be very great.

8 "For inquire now of bygone generations,
　and consider what their ancestors have found;

9 for we are but of yesterday, and we know
　　nothing,
　for our days on earth are but a shadow.

10 Will they not teach you and tell you
　and utter words out of their understanding?

11 "Can papyrus grow where there is no marsh?
　Can reeds flourish where there is no water?

12 While yet in flower and not cut down,
　they wither before any other plant.

13 Such are the paths of all who forget God;
　the hope of the godless shall perish.

14 Their confidence is gossamer,
　a spider's house their trust.

15 If one leans against its house, it will not stand;
　if one lays hold of it, it will not endure.

16 The wicked thrive[b] before the sun,
　and their shoots spread over the garden.

17 Their roots twine around the stoneheap;
　they live among the rocks.[c]

18 If they are destroyed from their place,
　then it will deny them, saying, 'I have never
　　seen you.'

19 See, these are their happy ways,[d]
　and out of the earth still others will spring.

20 "See, God will not reject a blameless person,
　nor take the hand of evildoers.

21 He will yet fill your mouth with laughter,
　and your lips with shouts of joy.

22 Those who hate you will be clothed with shame,
　and the tent of the wicked will be no more."

Job Replies: There Is No Mediator

9 Then Job answered:
2 "Indeed I know that this is so;
　but how can a mortal be just before God?

3 If one wished to contend with him,
　one could not answer him once in a
　　thousand.

4 He is wise in heart, and mighty in strength
　—who has resisted him, and succeeded?—

5 he who removes mountains, and they do not
　　know it,
　when he overturns them in his anger;

6 who shakes the earth out of its place,
　and its pillars tremble;

7 who commands the sun, and it does not rise;
　who seals up the stars;

8 who alone stretched out the heavens
　and trampled the waves of the Sea;[e]

9 who made the Bear and Orion,
　the Pleiades and the chambers of the south;

10 who does great things beyond understanding,
　and marvelous things without number.

11 Look, he passes by me, and I do not see him;
　he moves on, but I do not perceive him.

12 He snatches away; who can stop him?
　Who will say to him, 'What are you doing?'

13 "God will not turn back his anger;
　the helpers of Rahab bowed beneath him.

14 How then can I answer him,
　choosing my words with him?

15 Though I am innocent, I cannot answer him;
　I must appeal for mercy to my accuser.[f]

16 If I summoned him and he answered me,
　I do not believe that he would listen to my
　　voice.

17 For he crushes me with a tempest,
　and multiplies my wounds without cause;

18 he will not let me get my breath,
　but fills me with bitterness.

19 If it is a contest of strength, he is the strong one!
　If it is a matter of justice, who can summon
　　him?[g]

20 Though I am innocent, my own mouth would
　　condemn me;
　though I am blameless, he would prove me
　　perverse.

21 I am blameless; I do not know myself;
　I loathe my life.

22 It is all one; therefore I say,
　he destroys both the blameless and the wicked.

23 When disaster brings sudden death,
　he mocks at the calamity[d] of the innocent.

24 The earth is given into the hand of the wicked;
　he covers the eyes of its judges—
　if it is not he, who then is it?

25 "My days are swifter than a runner;
　they flee away, they see no good.

---

a Traditional rendering of Heb *Shaddai*　　b Heb *He thrives*
c Gk Vg: Meaning of Heb uncertain　　d Meaning of Heb
uncertain　　e Or *trampled the back of the sea dragon*　　f Or *for
my right*　　g Compare Gk: Heb *me*

JOB

26 They go by like skiffs of reed,
   like an eagle swooping on the prey.
27 If I say, 'I will forget my complaint;
   I will put off my sad countenance and be of
      good cheer,'
28 I become afraid of all my suffering,
   for I know you will not hold me innocent.
29 I shall be condemned;
   why then do I labor in vain?
30 If I wash myself with soap
   and cleanse my hands with lye,
31 yet you will plunge me into filth,
   and my own clothes will abhor me.
32 For he is not a mortal, as I am, that I might
      answer him,
   that we should come to trial together.
33 There is no umpire*a* between us,
   who might lay his hand on us both.
34 If he would take his rod away from me,
   and not let dread of him terrify me,
35 then I would speak without fear of him,
   for I know I am not what I am thought to be.*b*

Job: I Loathe My Life

10 "I loathe my life;
   I will give free utterance to my complaint;
   I will speak in the bitterness of my soul.
2 I will say to God, Do not condemn me;
   let me know why you contend against me.
3 Does it seem good to you to oppress,
   to despise the work of your hands
   and favor the schemes of the wicked?
4 Do you have eyes of flesh?
   Do you see as humans see?
5 Are your days like the days of mortals,
   or your years like human years,
6 that you seek out my iniquity
   and search for my sin,
7 although you know that I am not guilty,
   and there is no one to deliver out of your
      hand?
8 Your hands fashioned and made me;
   and now you turn and destroy me.*c*
9 Remember that you fashioned me like clay;
   and will you turn me to dust again?
10 Did you not pour me out like milk
   and curdle me like cheese?
11 You clothed me with skin and flesh,
   and knit me together with bones and sinews.
12 You have granted me life and steadfast love,
   and your care has preserved my spirit.
13 Yet these things you hid in your heart;
   I know that this was your purpose.
14 If I sin, you watch me,
   and do not acquit me of my iniquity.
15 If I am wicked, woe to me!

If I am righteous, I cannot lift up my head,
   for I am filled with disgrace
   and look upon my affliction.
16 Bold as a lion you hunt me;
   you repeat your exploits against me.
17 You renew your witnesses against me,
   and increase your vexation toward me;
   you bring fresh troops against me.*d*

18 "Why did you bring me forth from the womb?
   Would that I had died before any eye had
      seen me,
19 and were as though I had not been,
   carried from the womb to the grave.
20 Are not the days of my life few?*e*
   Let me alone, that I may find a little comfort*f*
21 before I go, never to return,
   to the land of gloom and deep darkness,
22 the land of gloom*g* and chaos,
   where light is like darkness."

Zophar Speaks: Job's Guilt Deserves Punishment

11 Then Zophar the Naamathite answered:
2 "Should a multitude of words go
      unanswered,
   and should one full of talk be vindicated?
3 Should your babble put others to silence,
   and when you mock, shall no one shame you?
4 For you say, 'My conduct*h* is pure,
   and I am clean in God's*i* sight.'
5 But O that God would speak,
   and open his lips to you,
6 and that he would tell you the secrets of
      wisdom!
   For wisdom is many-sided.*j*
Know then that God exacts of you less than your
      guilt deserves.

7 "Can you find out the deep things of God?
   Can you find out the limit of the Almighty?*k*
8 It is higher than heaven*l*—what can you do?
   Deeper than Sheol—what can you know?
9 Its measure is longer than the earth,
   and broader than the sea.
10 If he passes through, and imprisons,
   and assembles for judgment, who can hinder
      him?

---

a Another reading is *Would that there were an umpire*
b Cn: Heb *for I am not so in myself* c Cn Compare Gk
Syr: Heb *made me together all around, and you destroy me*
d Cn Compare Gk: Heb *toward me; changes and a troop are
with me* e Cn Compare Gk Syr: Heb *Are not my days few? Let
him cease!* f Heb *that I may brighten up a little* g Heb *gloom
as darkness, deep darkness* h Gk: Heb *teaching* i Heb *your*
j Meaning of Heb uncertain k Traditional rendering of Heb
Shaddai l Heb *The heights of heaven*

¹¹ For he knows those who are worthless;
    when he sees iniquity, will he not consider it?
¹² But a stupid person will get understanding,
    when a wild ass is born human.[a]

¹³ "If you direct your heart rightly,
    you will stretch out your hands toward him.
¹⁴ If iniquity is in your hand, put it far away,
    and do not let wickedness reside in your
      tents.
¹⁵ Surely then you will lift up your face without
      blemish;
    you will be secure, and will not fear.
¹⁶ You will forget your misery;
    you will remember it as waters that have
      passed away.
¹⁷ And your life will be brighter than the noonday;
    its darkness will be like the morning.
¹⁸ And you will have confidence, because there is
      hope;
    you will be protected[b] and take your rest in
      safety.
¹⁹ You will lie down, and no one will make you
      afraid;
    many will entreat your favor.
²⁰ But the eyes of the wicked will fail;
    all way of escape will be lost to them,
    and their hope is to breathe their last."

Job Replies: I Am a Laughingstock

12 Then Job answered:
² "No doubt you are the people,
    and wisdom will die with you.
³ But I have understanding as well as you;
    I am not inferior to you.
    Who does not know such things as these?
⁴ I am a laughingstock to my friends;
    I, who called upon God and he answered me,
    a just and blameless man, I am a
      laughingstock.
⁵ Those at ease have contempt for misfortune,[a]
    but it is ready for those whose feet are
      unstable.
⁶ The tents of robbers are at peace,
    and those who provoke God are secure,
    who bring their god in their hands.[c]

⁷ "But ask the animals, and they will teach you;
    the birds of the air, and they will tell you;
⁸ ask the plants of the earth,[d] and they will teach
      you;
    and the fish of the sea will declare to you.
⁹ Who among all these does not know
    that the hand of the LORD has done this?
¹⁰ In his hand is the life of every living thing
    and the breath of every human being.

¹¹ Does not the ear test words
    as the palate tastes food?
¹² Is wisdom with the aged,
    and understanding in length of days?

¹³ "With God[e] are wisdom and strength;
    he has counsel and understanding.
¹⁴ If he tears down, no one can rebuild;
    if he shuts someone in, no one can open up.
¹⁵ If he withholds the waters, they dry up;
    if he sends them out, they overwhelm the
      land.
¹⁶ With him are strength and wisdom;
    the deceived and the deceiver are his.
¹⁷ He leads counselors away stripped,
    and makes fools of judges.
¹⁸ He looses the sash of kings,
    and binds a waistcloth on their loins.
¹⁹ He leads priests away stripped,
    and overthrows the mighty.
²⁰ He deprives of speech those who are trusted,
    and takes away the discernment of the elders.
²¹ He pours contempt on princes,
    and looses the belt of the strong.
²² He uncovers the deeps out of darkness,
    and brings deep darkness to light.
²³ He makes nations great, then destroys them;
    he enlarges nations, then leads them away.
²⁴ He strips understanding from the leaders[f] of the
      earth,
    and makes them wander in a pathless waste.
²⁵ They grope in the dark without light;
    he makes them stagger like a drunkard.

13 "Look, my eye has seen all this,
    my ear has heard and understood it.
² What you know, I also know;
    I am not inferior to you.
³ But I would speak to the Almighty,[g]
    and I desire to argue my case with God.
⁴ As for you, you whitewash with lies;
    all of you are worthless physicians.
⁵ If you would only keep silent,
    that would be your wisdom!
⁶ Hear now my reasoning,
    and listen to the pleadings of my lips.
⁷ Will you speak falsely for God,
    and speak deceitfully for him?
⁸ Will you show partiality toward him,
    will you plead the case for God?
⁹ Will it be well with you when he searches you
      out?

---

a Meaning of Heb uncertain   b Or *you will look around*
c Or *whom God brought forth by his hand*; Meaning of Heb
uncertain   d Or *speak to the earth*   e Heb *him*   f Heb adds *of
the people*   g Traditional rendering of Heb *Shaddai*

Or can you deceive him, as one person
    deceives another?
10 He will surely rebuke you
    if in secret you show partiality.
11 Will not his majesty terrify you,
    and the dread of him fall upon you?
12 Your maxims are proverbs of ashes,
    your defenses are defenses of clay.

13 "Let me have silence, and I will speak,
    and let come on me what may.
14 I will take my flesh in my teeth,
    and put my life in my hand.[a]
15 See, he will kill me; I have no hope;[b]
    but I will defend my ways to his face.
16 This will be my salvation,
    that the godless shall not come before him.
17 Listen carefully to my words,
    and let my declaration be in your ears.
18 I have indeed prepared my case;
    I know that I shall be vindicated.
19 Who is there that will contend with me?
    For then I would be silent and die.

Job's Despondent Prayer

20 Only grant two things to me,
    then I will not hide myself from your face:
21 withdraw your hand far from me,
    and do not let dread of you terrify me.
22 Then call, and I will answer;
    or let me speak, and you reply to me.
23 How many are my iniquities and my sins?
    Make me know my transgression and my
        sin.
24 Why do you hide your face,
    and count me as your enemy?
25 Will you frighten a windblown leaf
    and pursue dry chaff?
26 For you write bitter things against me,
    and make me reap[c] the iniquities of my
        youth.
27 You put my feet in the stocks,
    and watch all my paths;
    you set a bound to the soles of my feet.
28 One wastes away like a rotten thing,
    like a garment that is moth-eaten.

14 "A mortal, born of woman, few of days and
        full of trouble,
2   comes up like a flower and withers,
    flees like a shadow and does not last.
3 Do you fix your eyes on such a one?
    Do you bring me into judgment with you?
4 Who can bring a clean thing out of an
        unclean?
    No one can.

5 Since their days are determined,
    and the number of their months is known to
        you,
    and you have appointed the bounds that they
        cannot pass,
6 look away from them, and desist,[d]
    that they may enjoy, like laborers, their days.

7 "For there is hope for a tree,
    if it is cut down, that it will sprout again,
    and that its shoots will not cease.
8 Though its root grows old in the earth,
    and its stump dies in the ground,
9 yet at the scent of water it will bud
    and put forth branches like a young plant.
10 But mortals die, and are laid low;
    humans expire, and where are they?
11 As waters fail from a lake,
    and a river wastes away and dries up,
12 so mortals lie down and do not rise again;
    until the heavens are no more, they will not
        awake
    or be roused out of their sleep.
13 O that you would hide me in Sheol,
    that you would conceal me until your wrath
        is past,
    that you would appoint me a set time, and
        remember me!
14 If mortals die, will they live again?
    All the days of my service I would wait
    until my release should come.
15 You would call, and I would answer you;
    you would long for the work of your hands.
16 For then you would not[e] number my steps,
    you would not keep watch over my sin;
17 my transgression would be sealed up in a bag,
    and you would cover over my iniquity.

18 "But the mountain falls and crumbles away,
    and the rock is removed from its place;
19 the waters wear away the stones;
    the torrents wash away the soil of the earth;
    so you destroy the hope of mortals.
20 You prevail forever against them, and they pass
        away;
    you change their countenance, and send them
        away.
21 Their children come to honor, and they do not
        know it;
    they are brought low, and it goes unnoticed.
22 They feel only the pain of their own bodies,
    and mourn only for themselves."

---

a Gk: Heb *Why should I take . . . in my hand?*   b Or *Though he
kill me, yet I will trust in him*   c Heb *inherit*   d Cn: Heb *that they
may desist*   e Syr: Heb lacks *not*

Eliphaz Speaks: Job Undermines Religion

15 Then Eliphaz the Temanite answered:
2 "Should the wise answer with windy
  knowledge,
  and fill themselves with the east wind?
3 Should they argue in unprofitable talk,
  or in words with which they can do no good?
4 But you are doing away with the fear of God,
  and hindering meditation before God.
5 For your iniquity teaches your mouth,
  and you choose the tongue of the crafty.
6 Your own mouth condemns you, and not I;
  your own lips testify against you.

7 "Are you the firstborn of the human race?
  Were you brought forth before the hills?
8 Have you listened in the council of God?
  And do you limit wisdom to yourself?
9 What do you know that we do not know?
  What do you understand that is not clear to us?
10 The gray-haired and the aged are on our side,
  those older than your father.
11 Are the consolations of God too small for you,
  or the word that deals gently with you?
12 Why does your heart carry you away,
  and why do your eyes flash,[a]
13 so that you turn your spirit against God,
  and let such words go out of your mouth?
14 What are mortals, that they can be clean?
  Or those born of woman, that they can be
  righteous?
15 God puts no trust even in his holy ones,
  and the heavens are not clean in his sight;
16 how much less one who is abominable and
  corrupt,
  one who drinks iniquity like water!

17 "I will show you; listen to me;
  what I have seen I will declare—
18 what sages have told,
  and their ancestors have not hidden,
19 to whom alone the land was given,
  and no stranger passed among them.
20 The wicked writhe in pain all their days,
  through all the years that are laid up for the
  ruthless.
21 Terrifying sounds are in their ears;
  in prosperity the destroyer will come upon
  them.
22 They despair of returning from darkness,
  and they are destined for the sword.
23 They wander abroad for bread, saying, 'Where is
  it?'
  They know that a day of darkness is ready at
  hand;

24 distress and anguish terrify them;
  they prevail against them, like a king prepared
  for battle.
25 Because they stretched out their hands against
  God,
  and bid defiance to the Almighty,[b]
26 running stubbornly against him
  with a thick-bossed shield;
27 because they have covered their faces with their
  fat,
  and gathered fat upon their loins,
28 they will live in desolate cities,
  in houses that no one should inhabit,
  houses destined to become heaps of ruins;
29 they will not be rich, and their wealth will not
  endure,
  nor will they strike root in the earth;[c]
30 they will not escape from darkness;
  the flame will dry up their shoots,
  and their blossom[d] will be swept away[e] by the
  wind.
31 Let them not trust in emptiness, deceiving
  themselves;
  for emptiness will be their recompense.
32 It will be paid in full before their time,
  and their branch will not be green.
33 They will shake off their unripe grape, like the
  vine,
  and cast off their blossoms, like the olive tree.
34 For the company of the godless is barren,
  and fire consumes the tents of bribery.
35 They conceive mischief and bring forth evil
  and their heart prepares deceit."

Job Reaffirms His Innocence

16 Then Job answered:
2 "I have heard many such things;
  miserable comforters are you all.
3 Have windy words no limit?
  Or what provokes you that you keep on
  talking?
4 I also could talk as you do,
  if you were in my place;
  I could join words together against you,
  and shake my head at you.
5 I could encourage you with my mouth,
  and the solace of my lips would assuage your
  pain.

6 "If I speak, my pain is not assuaged,
  and if I forbear, how much of it leaves me?
7 Surely now God has worn me out;

---

a Meaning of Heb uncertain   b Traditional rendering of Heb
Shaddai   c Vg: Meaning of Heb uncertain   d Gk: Heb mouth
e Cn: Heb will depart

he has[a] made desolate all my company.

8 And he has[a] shriveled me up,
which is a witness against me;
my leanness has risen up against me,
and it testifies to my face.

9 He has torn me in his wrath, and hated me;
he has gnashed his teeth at me;
my adversary sharpens his eyes against me.

10 They have gaped at me with their mouths;
they have struck me insolently on the cheek;
they mass themselves together against me.

11 God gives me up to the ungodly,
and casts me into the hands of the wicked.

12 I was at ease, and he broke me in two;
he seized me by the neck and dashed me to
pieces;
he set me up as his target;

13   his archers surround me.
He slashes open my kidneys, and shows no
mercy;
he pours out my gall on the ground.

14 He bursts upon me again and again;
he rushes at me like a warrior.

15 I have sewed sackcloth upon my skin,
and have laid my strength in the dust.

16 My face is red with weeping,
and deep darkness is on my eyelids,

17 though there is no violence in my hands,
and my prayer is pure.

18 "O earth, do not cover my blood;
let my outcry find no resting place.

19 Even now, in fact, my witness is in heaven,
and he that vouches for me is on high.

20 My friends scorn me;
my eye pours out tears to God,

21 that he would maintain the right of a mortal
with God,
as[b] one does for a neighbor.

22 For when a few years have come,
I shall go the way from which I shall not
return.

Job Prays for Relief

17 My spirit is broken, my days are extinct,
the grave is ready for me.

2 Surely there are mockers around me,
and my eye dwells on their provocation.

3 "Lay down a pledge for me with yourself;
who is there that will give surety for me?

4 Since you have closed their minds to
understanding,
therefore you will not let them triumph.

5 Those who denounce friends for reward—
the eyes of their children will fail.

6 "He has made me a byword of the peoples,
and I am one before whom people spit.

7 My eye has grown dim from grief,
and all my members are like a shadow.

8 The upright are appalled at this,
and the innocent stir themselves up against
the godless.

9 Yet the righteous hold to their way,
and they that have clean hands grow stronger
and stronger.

10 But you, come back now, all of you,
and I shall not find a sensible person among
you.

11 My days are past, my plans are broken off,
the desires of my heart.

12 They make night into day;
'The light,' they say, 'is near to the
darkness.'[c]

13 If I look for Sheol as my house,
if I spread my couch in darkness,

14 if I say to the Pit, 'You are my father,'
and to the worm, 'My mother,' or 'My sister,'

15 where then is my hope?
Who will see my hope?

16 Will it go down to the bars of Sheol?
Shall we descend together into the dust?"

Bildad Speaks: God Punishes the Wicked

18 Then Bildad the Shuhite answered:
2 "How long will you hunt for words?
Consider, and then we shall speak.

3 Why are we counted as cattle?
Why are we stupid in your sight?

4 You who tear yourself in your anger—
shall the earth be forsaken because of you,
or the rock be removed out of its place?

5 "Surely the light of the wicked is put out,
and the flame of their fire does not shine.

6 The light is dark in their tent,
and the lamp above them is put out.

7 Their strong steps are shortened,
and their own schemes throw them down.

8 For they are thrust into a net by their own feet,
and they walk into a pitfall.

9 A trap seizes them by the heel;
a snare lays hold of them.

10 A rope is hid for them in the ground,
a trap for them in the path.

11 Terrors frighten them on every side,
and chase them at their heels.

12 Their strength is consumed by hunger,[d]
and calamity is ready for their stumbling.

---

a Heb *you have*   b Syr Vg Tg: Heb *and*   c Meaning of Heb
uncertain   d Or *Disaster is hungry for them*

13 By disease their skin is consumed,[a]
        the firstborn of Death consumes their limbs.
14 They are torn from the tent in which they
        trusted,
        and are brought to the king of terrors.
15 In their tents nothing remains;
        sulfur is scattered upon their habitations.
16 Their roots dry up beneath,
        and their branches wither above.
17 Their memory perishes from the earth,
        and they have no name in the street.
18 They are thrust from light into darkness,
        and driven out of the world.
19 They have no offspring or descendant among
        their people,
        and no survivor where they used to live.
20 They of the west are appalled at their fate,
        and horror seizes those of the east.
21 Surely such are the dwellings of the ungodly,
        such is the place of those who do not know
        God."

Job Replies: I Know That My Redeemer Lives

19 Then Job answered:
    2 "How long will you torment me,
        and break me in pieces with words?
3 These ten times you have cast reproach
        upon me;
        are you not ashamed to wrong me?
4 And even if it is true that I have erred,
        my error remains with me.
5 If indeed you magnify yourselves against me,
        and make my humiliation an argument
        against me,
6 know then that God has put me in the wrong,
        and closed his net around me.
7 Even when I cry out, 'Violence!' I am not
        answered;
        I call aloud, but there is no justice.
8 He has walled up my way so that I cannot
        pass,
        and he has set darkness upon my paths.
9 He has stripped my glory from me,
        and taken the crown from my head.
10 He breaks me down on every side, and I am
        gone,
        he has uprooted my hope like a tree.
11 He has kindled his wrath against me,
        and counts me as his adversary.
12 His troops come on together;
        they have thrown up siegeworks[b] against me,
        and encamp around my tent.

13 "He has put my family far from me,
        and my acquaintances are wholly estranged
        from me.

14 My relatives and my close friends have
        failed me;
15   the guests in my house have forgotten me;
        my serving girls count me as a stranger;
        I have become an alien in their eyes.
16 I call to my servant, but he gives me no answer;
        I must myself plead with him.
17 My breath is repulsive to my wife;
        I am loathsome to my own family.
18 Even young children despise me;
        when I rise, they talk against me.
19 All my intimate friends abhor me,
        and those whom I loved have turned
        against me.
20 My bones cling to my skin and to my flesh,
        and I have escaped by the skin of my teeth.
21 Have pity on me, have pity on me, O you my
        friends,
        for the hand of God has touched me!
22 Why do you, like God, pursue me,
        never satisfied with my flesh?

23 "O that my words were written down!
        O that they were inscribed in a book!
24 O that with an iron pen and with lead
        they were engraved on a rock forever!
25 For I know that my Redeemer[c] lives,
        and that at the last he[d] will stand upon the
        earth;[e]
26 and after my skin has been thus destroyed,
        then in[f] my flesh I shall see God,[g]
27 whom I shall see on my side,[h]
        and my eyes shall behold, and not another.
        My heart faints within me!
28 If you say, 'How we will persecute him!'
        and, 'The root of the matter is found in him';
29 be afraid of the sword,
        for wrath brings the punishment of the sword,
        so that you may know there is a judgment."

Zophar Speaks: Wickedness Receives Just
    Retribution

20 Then Zophar the Naamathite answered:
    2 "Pay attention! My thoughts urge me to
        answer,
        because of the agitation within me.
3 I hear censure that insults me,
        and a spirit beyond my understanding
        answers me.
4 Do you not know this from of old,
        ever since mortals were placed on earth,
5 that the exulting of the wicked is short,

---

a Cn: Heb *It consumes the limbs of his skin*   b Cn: Heb *their
way*   c Or *Vindicator*   d Or *that he the Last*   e Heb *dust*
f Or *without*   g Meaning of Heb of this verse uncertain
h Or *for myself*

and the joy of the godless is but for a
        moment?
6 Even though they mount up high as the
        heavens,
    and their head reaches to the clouds,
7 they will perish forever like their own dung;
    those who have seen them will say, 'Where
        are they?'
8 They will fly away like a dream, and not be
        found;
    they will be chased away like a vision of the
        night.
9 The eye that saw them will see them no more,
    nor will their place behold them any longer.
10 Their children will seek the favor of the poor,
    and their hands will give back their wealth.
11 Their bodies, once full of youth,
    will lie down in the dust with them.

12 "Though wickedness is sweet in their mouth,
    though they hide it under their tongues,
13 though they are loath to let it go,
    and hold it in their mouths;
14 yet their food is turned in their stomachs;
    it is the venom of asps within them.
15 They swallow down riches and vomit them up
        again;
    God casts them out of their bellies.
16 They will suck the poison of asps;
    the tongue of a viper will kill them.
17 They will not look on the rivers,
    the streams flowing with honey and curds.
18 They will give back the fruit of their toil,
    and will not swallow it down;
  from the profit of their trading
    they will get no enjoyment.
19 For they have crushed and abandoned the
        poor,
    they have seized a house that they did not
        build.

20 "They knew no quiet in their bellies;
    in their greed they let nothing escape.
21 There was nothing left after they had eaten;
    therefore their prosperity will not endure.
22 In full sufficiency they will be in distress;
    all the force of misery will come upon them.
23 To fill their belly to the full
    God^a will send his fierce anger into them,
    and rain it upon them as their food.^{b}
24 They will flee from an iron weapon;
    a bronze arrow will strike them through.
25 It is drawn forth and comes out of their body,
    and the glittering point comes out of their
        gall;
    terrors come upon them.

26 Utter darkness is laid up for their treasures;
    a fire fanned by no one will devour them;
    what is left in their tent will be consumed.
27 The heavens will reveal their iniquity,
    and the earth will rise up against them.
28 The possessions of their house will be carried
        away,
    dragged off in the day of God's^c wrath.
29 This is the portion of the wicked from God,
    the heritage decreed for them by God."

Job Replies: The Wicked Often Go Unpunished

21 Then Job answered:
2 "Listen carefully to my words,
    and let this be your consolation.
3 Bear with me, and I will speak;
    then after I have spoken, mock on.
4 As for me, is my complaint addressed to
        mortals?
    Why should I not be impatient?
5 Look at me, and be appalled,
    and lay your hand upon your mouth.
6 When I think of it I am dismayed,
    and shuddering seizes my flesh.
7 Why do the wicked live on,
    reach old age, and grow mighty in power?
8 Their children are established in their presence,
    and their offspring before their eyes.
9 Their houses are safe from fear,
    and no rod of God is upon them.
10 Their bull breeds without fail;
    their cow calves and never miscarries.
11 They send out their little ones like a flock,
    and their children dance around.
12 They sing to the tambourine and the lyre,
    and rejoice to the sound of the pipe.
13 They spend their days in prosperity,
    and in peace they go down to Sheol.
14 They say to God, 'Leave us alone!
    We do not desire to know your ways.
15 What is the Almighty,^{d} that we should serve
        him?
    And what profit do we get if we pray to him?'
16 Is not their prosperity indeed their own
        achievement?^{e}
    The plans of the wicked are repugnant to me.

17 "How often is the lamp of the wicked put out?
    How often does calamity come upon them?
    How often does God^a distribute pains in his
        anger?
18 How often are they like straw before the wind,
    and like chaff that the storm carries away?

---

a Heb *he* b Cn: Meaning of Heb uncertain c Heb *his*
d Traditional rendering of Heb *Shaddai* e Heb *in their hand*

¹⁹ You say, 'God stores up their iniquity for their
    children.'
    Let it be paid back to them, so that they may
        know it.
²⁰ Let their own eyes see their destruction,
    and let them drink of the wrath of the
        Almighty.^a
²¹ For what do they care for their household after
        them,
    when the number of their months is cut off?
²² Will any teach God knowledge,
    seeing that he judges those that are on high?
²³ One dies in full prosperity,
    being wholly at ease and secure,
²⁴ his loins full of milk
    and the marrow of his bones moist.
²⁵ Another dies in bitterness of soul,
    never having tasted of good.
²⁶ They lie down alike in the dust,
    and the worms cover them.

²⁷ "Oh, I know your thoughts,
    and your schemes to wrong me.
²⁸ For you say, 'Where is the house of the prince?
    Where is the tent in which the wicked lived?'
²⁹ Have you not asked those who travel the roads,
    and do you not accept their testimony,
³⁰ that the wicked are spared in the day of calamity,
    and are rescued in the day of wrath?
³¹ Who declares their way to their face,
    and who repays them for what they have
        done?
³² When they are carried to the grave,
    a watch is kept over their tomb.
³³ The clods of the valley are sweet to them;
    everyone will follow after,
    and those who went before are innumerable.
³⁴ How then will you comfort me with empty
        nothings?
    There is nothing left of your answers but
        falsehood."

Eliphaz Speaks: Job's Wickedness Is Great

22 Then Eliphaz the Temanite answered:
² "Can a mortal be of use to God?
    Can even the wisest be of service to him?
³ Is it any pleasure to the Almighty^a if you are
        righteous,
    or is it gain to him if you make your ways
        blameless?
⁴ Is it for your piety that he reproves you,
    and enters into judgment with you?
⁵ Is not your wickedness great?
    There is no end to your iniquities.
⁶ For you have exacted pledges from your family
        for no reason,

    and stripped the naked of their clothing.
⁷ You have given no water to the weary to drink,
    and you have withheld bread from the
        hungry.
⁸ The powerful possess the land,
    and the favored live in it.
⁹ You have sent widows away empty-handed,
    and the arms of the orphans you have
        crushed.^b
¹⁰ Therefore snares are around you,
    and sudden terror overwhelms you,
¹¹ or darkness so that you cannot see;
    a flood of water covers you.

¹² "Is not God high in the heavens?
    See the highest stars, how lofty they are!
¹³ Therefore you say, 'What does God know?
    Can he judge through the deep darkness?
¹⁴ Thick clouds enwrap him, so that he does not
        see,
    and he walks on the dome of heaven.'
¹⁵ Will you keep to the old way
    that the wicked have trod?
¹⁶ They were snatched away before their time;
    their foundation was washed away by a
        flood.
¹⁷ They said to God, 'Leave us alone,'
    and 'What can the Almighty^a do to us?'^c
¹⁸ Yet he filled their houses with good things—
    but the plans of the wicked are repugnant
        to me.
¹⁹ The righteous see it and are glad;
    the innocent laugh them to scorn,
²⁰ saying, 'Surely our adversaries are cut off,
    and what they left, the fire has consumed.'

²¹ "Agree with God,^d and be at peace;
    in this way good will come to you.
²² Receive instruction from his mouth,
    and lay up his words in your heart.
²³ If you return to the Almighty,^a you will be
        restored,
    if you remove unrighteousness from your
        tents,
²⁴ if you treat gold like dust,
    and gold of Ophir like the stones of the
        torrent bed,
²⁵ and if the Almighty^a is your gold
    and your precious silver,
²⁶ then you will delight yourself in the Almighty,^a
    and lift up your face to God.
²⁷ You will pray to him, and he will hear you,
    and you will pay your vows.

---

a Traditional rendering of Heb *Shaddai*   b Gk Syr Tg Vg: Heb
were crushed   c Gk Syr: Heb *them*   d Heb *him*

28 You will decide on a matter, and it will be
　　established for you,
　　and light will shine on your ways.
29 When others are humiliated, you say it is pride;
　　for he saves the humble.
30 He will deliver even those who are guilty;
　　they will escape because of the cleanness of
　　your hands."[a]

Job Replies: My Complaint Is Bitter

23 Then Job answered:
　2 "Today also my complaint is bitter;[b]
　　his[c] hand is heavy despite my groaning.
3 Oh, that I knew where I might find him,
　　that I might come even to his dwelling!
4 I would lay my case before him,
　　and fill my mouth with arguments.
5 I would learn what he would answer me,
　　and understand what he would say to me.
6 Would he contend with me in the greatness of
　　his power?
　　No; but he would give heed to me.
7 There an upright person could reason with him,
　　and I should be acquitted forever by my
　　judge.

8 "If I go forward, he is not there;
　　or backward, I cannot perceive him;
9 on the left he hides, and I cannot behold him;
　　I turn[d] to the right, but I cannot see him.
10 But he knows the way that I take;
　　when he has tested me, I shall come out like
　　gold.
11 My foot has held fast to his steps;
　　I have kept his way and have not turned
　　aside.
12 I have not departed from the commandment of
　　his lips;
　　I have treasured in[e] my bosom the words of
　　his mouth.
13 But he stands alone and who can dissuade him?
　　What he desires, that he does.
14 For he will complete what he appoints for me;
　　and many such things are in his mind.
15 Therefore I am terrified at his presence;
　　when I consider, I am in dread of him.
16 God has made my heart faint;
　　the Almighty[f] has terrified me;
17 If only I could vanish in darkness,
　　and thick darkness would cover my face![g]

Job Complains of Violence on the Earth

24 "Why are times not kept by the Almighty,[f]
　　and why do those who know him never
　　see his days?
2 The wicked[h] remove landmarks;

　　they seize flocks and pasture them.
3 They drive away the donkey of the orphan;
　　they take the widow's ox for a pledge.
4 They thrust the needy off the road;
　　the poor of the earth all hide themselves.
5 Like wild asses in the desert
　　they go out to their toil,
　scavenging in the wasteland
　food for their young.
6 They reap in a field not their own
　　and they glean in the vineyard of the wicked.
7 They lie all night naked, without clothing,
　　and have no covering in the cold.
8 They are wet with the rain of the mountains,
　　and cling to the rock for want of shelter.

9 "There are those who snatch the orphan child
　　　from the breast,
　　and take as a pledge the infant of the poor.
10 They go about naked, without clothing;
　　though hungry, they carry the sheaves;
11 between their terraces[a] they press out oil;
　　they tread the wine presses, but suffer thirst.
12 From the city the dying groan,
　　and the throat of the wounded cries for help;
　　yet God pays no attention to their prayer.

13 "There are those who rebel against the light,
　　who are not acquainted with its ways,
　　and do not stay in its paths.
14 The murderer rises at dusk
　　to kill the poor and needy,
　　and in the night is like a thief.
15 The eye of the adulterer also waits for the
　　　twilight,
　　saying, 'No eye will see me';
　　and he disguises his face.
16 In the dark they dig through houses;
　　by day they shut themselves up;
　　they do not know the light.
17 For deep darkness is morning to all of them;
　　for they are friends with the terrors of deep
　　　darkness.

18 "Swift are they on the face of the waters;
　　their portion in the land is cursed;
　　no treader turns toward their vineyards.
19 Drought and heat snatch away the snow waters;
　　so does Sheol those who have sinned.
20 The womb forgets them;
　　the worm finds them sweet;

---

a Meaning of Heb uncertain　b Syr Vg Tg: Heb *rebellious*
c Gk Syr: Heb *my*　d Syr Vg: Heb *he turns*　e Gk Vg: Heb
from　f Traditional rendering of Heb *Shaddai*　g Or *But I am not
destroyed by the darkness; he has concealed the thick darkness
from me*　h Gk: Heb *they*

they are no longer remembered;
  so wickedness is broken like a tree.

21 "They harm*a* the childless woman,
    and do no good to the widow.
22 Yet God*b* prolongs the life of the mighty by his
      power;
    they rise up when they despair of life.
23 He gives them security, and they are supported;
    his eyes are upon their ways.
24 They are exalted a little while, and then are
      gone;
    they wither and fade like the mallow;*c*
    they are cut off like the heads of grain.
25 If it is not so, who will prove me a liar,
    and show that there is nothing in what I say?"

Bildad Speaks: How Can a Mortal Be Righteous Before God?

25 Then Bildad the Shuhite answered:
  2 "Dominion and fear are with God;*d*
    he makes peace in his high heaven.
3 Is there any number to his armies?
    Upon whom does his light not arise?
4 How then can a mortal be righteous before
      God?
    How can one born of woman be pure?
5 If even the moon is not bright
    and the stars are not pure in his sight,
6 how much less a mortal, who is a maggot,
    and a human being, who is a worm!"

Job Replies: God's Majesty Is Unsearchable

26 Then Job answered:
  2 "How you have helped one who has no
      power!
    How you have assisted the arm that has no
      strength!
3 How you have counseled one who has no
      wisdom,
    and given much good advice!
4 With whose help have you uttered words,
    and whose spirit has come forth from you?
5 The shades below tremble,
    the waters and their inhabitants.
6 Sheol is naked before God,
    and Abaddon has no covering.
7 He stretches out Zaphon*e* over the void,
    and hangs the earth upon nothing.
8 He binds up the waters in his thick clouds,
    and the cloud is not torn open by them.
9 He covers the face of the full moon,
    and spreads over it his cloud.
10 He has described a circle on the face of the
      waters,
    at the boundary between light and darkness.

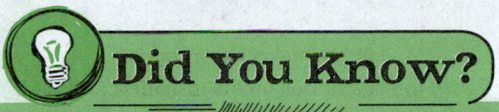

Did You Know?

A Long Debate

Why are Job's friends so insistent that sin and suffering are connected? Why do they go on, chapter after chapter, telling Job that his suffering is a punishment for his sins? The author of the Book of Job uses the debate of Job and his friends to contrast two positions. The position of Job's friends is that God rewards people who are good and punishes those who are wicked: if Job is suffering terribly, then Job must have sinned terribly. Job's repeated denial of sin reveals the second position, which is that sometimes innocent people suffer. This second position is harder to argue because it leaves a huge question: Why?

Because Job has too much integrity to repent for sins he never committed (see Job 27:1–6), he keeps searching for another answer. Finally, Job makes an oath of innocence. Such an oath has God as its witness, and if it is false, it requires that God strike down the person who made it. But God appears to Job in an awesome show of power (see chapters 38–41) and reminds Job that human intelligence is too limited to comprehend the deeper mysteries of creation. God alone knows why innocent people suffer; Job must trust God's plan.

Read chapters 20–24 to get a sense of the long debate in Job about human suffering. This debate reflects the long history of the Israelites wrestling with this complex question.

11 The pillars of heaven tremble,
    and are astounded at his rebuke.
12 By his power he stilled the Sea;
    by his understanding he struck down
      Rahab.
13 By his wind the heavens were made fair;
    his hand pierced the fleeing serpent.
14 These are indeed but the outskirts of his ways;
    and how small a whisper do we hear of
      him!
    But the thunder of his power who can
      understand?"

a Gk Tg: Heb *feed on or associate with*   *b* Heb *he*   *c* Gk: Heb
like all others   *d* Heb *him*   *e* Or *the North*

JOB

Job Maintains His Integrity

27 Job again took up his discourse and said:

2 "As God lives, who has taken away my
   right,
  and the Almighty,[a] who has made my soul
   bitter,
3 as long as my breath is in me
  and the spirit of God is in my nostrils,
4 my lips will not speak falsehood,
  and my tongue will not utter deceit.
5 Far be it from me to say that you are right;
  until I die I will not put away my integrity
   from me.
6 I hold fast my righteousness, and will not let
   it go;
  my heart does not reproach me for any of my
   days.

7 "May my enemy be like the wicked,
  and may my opponent be like the
   unrighteous.
8 For what is the hope of the godless when God
   cuts them off,
  when God takes away their lives?
9 Will God hear their cry
  when trouble comes upon them?
10 Will they take delight in the Almighty?[a]
  Will they call upon God at all times?
11 I will teach you concerning the hand of God;
  that which is with the Almighty[a] I will not
   conceal.
12 All of you have seen it yourselves;
  why then have you become altogether vain?

13 "This is the portion of the wicked with God,
  and the heritage that oppressors receive from
   the Almighty:[a]
14 If their children are multiplied, it is for the
   sword;
  and their offspring have not enough to eat.
15 Those who survive them the pestilence buries,
  and their widows make no lamentation.
16 Though they heap up silver like dust,
  and pile up clothing like clay—
17 they may pile it up, but the just will wear it,
  and the innocent will divide the silver.
18 They build their houses like nests,
  like booths made by sentinels of the vineyard.
19 They go to bed with wealth, but will do so no
   more;
  they open their eyes, and it is gone.
20 Terrors overtake them like a flood;
  in the night a whirlwind carries them off.
21 The east wind lifts them up and they are gone;
  it sweeps them out of their place.

22 It[b] hurls at them without pity;
  they flee from its[c] power in headlong flight.
23 It[b] claps its[c] hands at them,
  and hisses at them from its[c] place.

Interlude: Where Wisdom Is Found

28 "Surely there is a mine for silver,
  and a place for gold to be refined.
2 Iron is taken out of the earth,
  and copper is smelted from ore.
3 Miners put[d] an end to darkness,
  and search out to the farthest bound
  the ore in gloom and deep darkness.
4 They open shafts in a valley away from human
   habitation;
  they are forgotten by travelers,
  they sway suspended, remote from people.
5 As for the earth, out of it comes bread;
  but underneath it is turned up as by fire.
6 Its stones are the place of sapphires,[e]
  and its dust contains gold.

7 "That path no bird of prey knows,
  and the falcon's eye has not seen it.
8 The proud wild animals have not trodden it;
  the lion has not passed over it.

9 "They put their hand to the flinty rock,
  and overturn mountains by the roots.
10 They cut out channels in the rocks,
  and their eyes see every precious thing.
11 The sources of the rivers they probe;[f]
  hidden things they bring to light.

12 "But where shall wisdom be found?
  And where is the place of understanding?
13 Mortals do not know the way to it,[g]
  and it is not found in the land of the living.
14 The deep says, 'It is not in me,'
  and the sea says, 'It is not with me.'
15 It cannot be gotten for gold,
  and silver cannot be weighed out as its price.
16 It cannot be valued in the gold of Ophir,
  in precious onyx or sapphire.[e]
17 Gold and glass cannot equal it,
  nor can it be exchanged for jewels of fine
   gold.
18 No mention shall be made of coral or of crystal;
  the price of wisdom is above pearls.
19 The chrysolite of Ethiopia[h] cannot compare
   with it,
  nor can it be valued in pure gold.

---

a Traditional rendering of Heb *Shaddai*   b Or *He* (that is God)
c Or *his*   d Heb *He puts*   e Or *lapis lazuli*   f Gk Vg: Heb *bind*
g Gk: Heb *its price*   h Or *Nubia;* Heb *Cush*

20 "Where then does wisdom come from?
  And where is the place of understanding?
21 It is hidden from the eyes of all living,
  and concealed from the birds of the air.
22 Abaddon and Death say,
  'We have heard a rumor of it with our ears.'

23 "God understands the way to it,
  and he knows its place.
24 For he looks to the ends of the earth,
  and sees everything under the heavens.
25 When he gave to the wind its weight,
  and apportioned out the waters by measure;
26 when he made a decree for the rain,
  and a way for the thunderbolt;
27 then he saw it and declared it;
  he established it, and searched it out.
28 And he said to humankind,
  'Truly, the fear of the Lord, that is wisdom;
  and to depart from evil is understanding.' "

Job Finishes His Defense

29 Job again took up his discourse and said:
2 "O that I were as in the months of old,
  as in the days when God watched over me;
3 when his lamp shone over my head,
  and by his light I walked through darkness;
4 when I was in my prime,
  when the friendship of God was upon my tent;
5 when the Almighty[a] was still with me,
  when my children were around me;
6 when my steps were washed with milk,
  and the rock poured out for me streams of oil!
7 When I went out to the gate of the city,
  when I took my seat in the square,
8 the young men saw me and withdrew,
  and the aged rose up and stood;
9 the nobles refrained from talking,
  and laid their hands on their mouths;
10 the voices of princes were hushed,
  and their tongues stuck to the roof of their mouths.
11 When the ear heard, it commended me,
  and when the eye saw, it approved;
12 because I delivered the poor who cried,
  and the orphan who had no helper.
13 The blessing of the wretched came upon me,
  and I caused the widow's heart to sing for joy.
14 I put on righteousness, and it clothed me;
  my justice was like a robe and a turban.
15 I was eyes to the blind,
  and feet to the lame.
16 I was a father to the needy,

and I championed the cause of the stranger.
17 I broke the fangs of the unrighteous,
  and made them drop their prey from their teeth.
18 Then I thought, 'I shall die in my nest,
  and I shall multiply my days like the phoenix;[b]
19 my roots spread out to the waters,
  with the dew all night on my branches;
20 my glory was fresh with me,
  and my bow ever new in my hand.'

21 "They listened to me, and waited,
  and kept silence for my counsel.
22 After I spoke they did not speak again,
  and my word dropped upon them like dew.[c]
23 They waited for me as for the rain;
  they opened their mouths as for the spring rain.
24 I smiled on them when they had no confidence;
  and the light of my countenance they did not extinguish.[d]
25 I chose their way, and sat as chief,
  and I lived like a king among his troops,
  like one who comforts mourners.

30 "But now they make sport of me,
  those who are younger than I,
  whose fathers I would have disdained
  to set with the dogs of my flock.
2 What could I gain from the strength of their hands?
  All their vigor is gone.
3 Through want and hard hunger
  they gnaw the dry and desolate ground,
4 they pick mallow and the leaves of bushes,
  and to warm themselves the roots of broom.
5 They are driven out from society;
  people shout after them as after a thief.
6 In the gullies of wadis they must live,
  in holes in the ground, and in the rocks.
7 Among the bushes they bray;
  under the nettles they huddle together.
8 A senseless, disreputable brood,
  they have been whipped out of the land.

9 "And now they mock me in song;
  I am a byword to them.
10 They abhor me, they keep aloof from me;
  they do not hesitate to spit at the sight of me.
11 Because God has loosed my bowstring and humbled me,
  they have cast off restraint in my presence.

---

a Traditional rendering of Heb *Shaddai*   b Or *like sand*
c Heb lacks *like dew*   d Meaning of Heb uncertain

Hey, God! Did You Hear Me?

How do we know that God hears and answers our prayers? The books of Job and the Psalms describe many instances of both cries for help and God's responses to those cries. In our day-to-day reality, however, we can't always tell when God is answering our prayers. It isn't like we walk by trees that burn and speak to us, or hear whispers in the wind that call our name, or see and hear angels who give us God's answer. But God does hear and answer our prayers. One way to determine how God is answering our prayers is through discernment.

In the discernment process, an adult mentor or spiritual director can help you try to figure out what God is saying to you. If you don't already know of someone who can help you in this way (like a priest, religion teacher, campus or youth minister, or parent), you can ask at your parish or school for help in finding an adult mentor.

Even after engaging in the discernment process, the answers still aren't going to appear to most of us in dramatic and miraculous ways. In order to discover how God is speaking to us, we must simply pay attention to the common, ordinary experiences and relationships of our everyday lives—experiences and relationships in which God is abundantly present, helping us to understand more about ourselves and our place in this world.

▶ **Job 30:20**

12 On my right hand the rabble rise up;
    they send me sprawling,
    and build roads for my ruin.
13 They break up my path,
    they promote my calamity;
    no one restrains*a* them.
14 As through a wide breach they come;
    amid the crash they roll on.
15 Terrors are turned upon me;
    my honor is pursued as by the wind,
    and my prosperity has passed away like a
        cloud.

16 "And now my soul is poured out within me;
    days of affliction have taken hold of me.
17 The night racks my bones,
    and the pain that gnaws me takes no rest.
18 With violence he seizes my garment;*b*
    he grasps me by*c* the collar of my tunic.
19 He has cast me into the mire,
    and I have become like dust and ashes.
20 I cry to you and you do not answer me;
    I stand, and you merely look at me.
21 You have turned cruel to me;
    with the might of your hand you
        persecute me.
22 You lift me up on the wind, you make me ride
        on it,
    and you toss me about in the roar of the
        storm.
23 I know that you will bring me to death,
    and to the house appointed for all living.

24 "Surely one does not turn against the needy,*d*
    when in disaster they cry for help.*e*
25 Did I not weep for those whose day was hard?
    Was not my soul grieved for the poor?
26 But when I looked for good, evil came;
    and when I waited for light, darkness came.
27 My inward parts are in turmoil, and are never
        still;
    days of affliction come to meet me.
28 I go about in sunless gloom;
    I stand up in the assembly and cry for help.
29 I am a brother of jackals,
    and a companion of ostriches.
30 My skin turns black and falls from me,
    and my bones burn with heat.
31 My lyre is turned to mourning,
    and my pipe to the voice of those who weep.

31 "I have made a covenant with my eyes;
    how then could I look upon a virgin?
2 What would be my portion from God above,
    and my heritage from the Almighty*f* on
        high?
3 Does not calamity befall the unrighteous,
    and disaster the workers of iniquity?
4 Does he not see my ways,
    and number all my steps?

5 "If I have walked with falsehood,
    and my foot has hurried to deceit—
6 let me be weighed in a just balance,
    and let God know my integrity!—

---

a Cn: Heb *helps*   b Gk: Heb *my garment is disfigured*
c Heb *like*   d Heb *ruin*   e Cn: Meaning of Heb uncertain
f Traditional rendering of Heb *Shaddai*

7 if my step has turned aside from the way,
   and my heart has followed my eyes,
   and if any spot has clung to my hands;
8 then let me sow, and another eat;
   and let what grows for me be rooted out.

9 "If my heart has been enticed by a woman,
   and I have lain in wait at my neighbor's door;
10 then let my wife grind for another,
   and let other men kneel over her.
11 For that would be a heinous crime;
   that would be a criminal offense;
12 for that would be a fire consuming down to
   Abaddon,
   and it would burn to the root all my harvest.

13 "If I have rejected the cause of my male or
   female slaves,
   when they brought a complaint against me;
14 what then shall I do when God rises up?
   When he makes inquiry, what shall I answer
   him?
15 Did not he who made me in the womb make
   them?
   And did not one fashion us in the womb?

16 "If I have withheld anything that the poor
   desired,
   or have caused the eyes of the widow to fail,
17 or have eaten my morsel alone,
   and the orphan has not eaten from it—
18 for from my youth I reared the orphan[a] like a
   father,
   and from my mother's womb I guided the
   widow[b]—
19 if I have seen anyone perish for lack of clothing,
   or a poor person without covering,
20 whose loins have not blessed me,
   and who was not warmed with the fleece of
   my sheep;
21 if I have raised my hand against the orphan,
   because I saw I had supporters at the gate;
22 then let my shoulder blade fall from my
   shoulder,
   and let my arm be broken from its socket.
23 For I was in terror of calamity from God,
   and I could not have faced his majesty.

24 "If I have made gold my trust,
   or called fine gold my confidence;
25 if I have rejoiced because my wealth was great,
   or because my hand had gotten much;
26 if I have looked at the sun[c] when it shone,
   or the moon moving in splendor,
27 and my heart has been secretly enticed,
   and my mouth has kissed my hand;

28 this also would be an iniquity to be punished by
   the judges,
   for I should have been false to God above.

29 "If I have rejoiced at the ruin of those who
   hated me,
   or exulted when evil overtook them—
30 I have not let my mouth sin
   by asking for their lives with a curse—
31 if those of my tent ever said,
   'O that we might be sated with his flesh!'[d]—
32 the stranger has not lodged in the street;
   I have opened my doors to the traveler—
33 if I have concealed my transgressions as others
   do,[e]
   by hiding my iniquity in my bosom,
34 because I stood in great fear of the multitude,
   and the contempt of families terrified me,
   so that I kept silence, and did not go out of
   doors—
35 O that I had one to hear me!
   (Here is my signature! Let the Almighty[f]
   answer me!)
   O that I had the indictment written by my
   adversary!
36 Surely I would carry it on my shoulder;
   I would bind it on me like a crown;
37 I would give him an account of all my steps;
   like a prince I would approach him.

38 "If my land has cried out against me,
   and its furrows have wept together;
39 if I have eaten its yield without payment,
   and caused the death of its owners;
40 let thorns grow instead of wheat,
   and foul weeds instead of barley."

The words of Job are ended.

Elihu Rebukes Job's Friends

32 So these three men ceased to answer Job, because he was righteous in his own eyes. 2Then Elihu son of Barachel the Buzite, of the family of Ram, became angry. He was angry at Job because he justified himself rather than God; 3he was angry also at Job's three friends because they had found no answer, though they had declared Job to be in the wrong.[g] 4Now Elihu had waited to speak to Job, because they were older than he. 5But when Elihu saw that there was no answer in the mouths of these three men, he became angry.

---

a Heb *him*   b Heb *her*   c Heb *the light*   d Meaning of Heb uncertain   e Or *as Adam did*   f Traditional rendering of Heb *Shaddai*   g Another ancient tradition reads *answer, and had put God in the wrong*

6 Elihu son of Barachel the Buzite answered:
"I am young in years,
and you are aged;
therefore I was timid and afraid
to declare my opinion to you.
7 I said, 'Let days speak,
and many years teach wisdom.'
8 But truly it is the spirit in a mortal,
the breath of the Almighty,*a* that makes for
understanding.

> **Truly it is the spirit in a mortal,**
> **the breath of the Almighty, that makes for understanding.**
>
> (Job 32:8)

9 It is not the old*b* that are wise,
nor the aged that understand what is right.
10 Therefore I say, 'Listen to me;
let me also declare my opinion.'

11 "See, I waited for your words,
I listened for your wise sayings,
while you searched out what to say.
12 I gave you my attention,
but there was in fact no one that confuted
Job,
no one among you that answered his words.
13 Yet do not say, 'We have found wisdom;
God may vanquish him, not a human.'
14 He has not directed his words against me,
and I will not answer him with your speeches.

15 "They are dismayed, they answer no more;
they have not a word to say.
16 And am I to wait, because they do not speak,
because they stand there, and answer no
more?
17 I also will give my answer;
I also will declare my opinion.
18 For I am full of words;
the spirit within me constrains me.
19 My heart is indeed like wine that has no vent;
like new wineskins, it is ready to burst.
20 I must speak, so that I may find relief;
I must open my lips and answer.
21 I will not show partiality to any person
or use flattery toward anyone.
22 For I do not know how to flatter—
or my Maker would soon put an end to me!

Elihu Rebukes Job

33 "But now, hear my speech, O Job,
and listen to all my words.
2 See, I open my mouth;
the tongue in my mouth speaks.
3 My words declare the uprightness of my heart,
and what my lips know they speak sincerely.
4 The spirit of God has made me,
and the breath of the Almighty*a* gives me life.
5 Answer me, if you can;
set your words in order before me; take your
stand.
6 See, before God I am as you are;
I too was formed from a piece of clay.
7 No fear of me need terrify you;
my pressure will not be heavy on you.

8 "Surely, you have spoken in my hearing,
and I have heard the sound of your words.
9 You say, 'I am clean, without transgression;
I am pure, and there is no iniquity in me.
10 Look, he finds occasions against me,
he counts me as his enemy;
11 he puts my feet in the stocks,
and watches all my paths.'

12 "But in this you are not right. I will answer you:
God is greater than any mortal.
13 Why do you contend against him,
saying, 'He will answer none of my*c* words'?
14 For God speaks in one way,
and in two, though people do not perceive it.
15 In a dream, in a vision of the night,
when deep sleep falls on mortals,
while they slumber on their beds,
16 then he opens their ears,
and terrifies them with warnings,
17 that he may turn them aside from their deeds,
and keep them from pride,
18 to spare their souls from the Pit,
their lives from traversing the River.
19 They are also chastened with pain upon their
beds,
and with continual strife in their bones,
20 so that their lives loathe bread,
and their appetites dainty food.
21 Their flesh is so wasted away that it cannot be
seen;
and their bones, once invisible, now stick out.
22 Their souls draw near the Pit,
and their lives to those who bring death.
23 Then, if there should be for one of them an angel,

---

a Traditional rendering of Heb *Shaddai*   *b* Gk Syr Vg: Heb *many*
c Compare Gk: Heb *his*

a mediator, one of a thousand,
  one who declares a person upright,
24 and he is gracious to that person, and says,
  'Deliver him from going down into the Pit;
  I have found a ransom;
25 let his flesh become fresh with youth;
  let him return to the days of his youthful vigor';
26 then he prays to God, and is accepted by him,
  he comes into his presence with joy,
and God*a* repays him for his righteousness.
27   That person sings to others and says,
  'I sinned, and perverted what was right,
  and it was not paid back to me.
28 He has redeemed my soul from going down to
    the Pit,
  and my life shall see the light.'

29 "God indeed does all these things,
  twice, three times, with mortals,
30 to bring back their souls from the Pit,
  so that they may see the light of life.*b*
31 Pay heed, Job, listen to me;
  be silent, and I will speak.
32 If you have anything to say, answer me;
  speak, for I desire to justify you.
33 If not, listen to me;
  be silent, and I will teach you wisdom."

Elihu Proclaims God's Justice

34 Then Elihu continued and said:
2 "Hear my words, you wise men,
  and give ear to me, you who know;
3 for the ear tests words
  as the palate tastes food.
4 Let us choose what is right;
  let us determine among ourselves what is good.
5 For Job has said, 'I am innocent,
  and God has taken away my right;
6 in spite of being right I am counted a liar;
  my wound is incurable, though I am without
    transgression.'
7 Who is there like Job,
  who drinks up scoffing like water,
8 who goes in company with evildoers
  and walks with the wicked?
9 For he has said, 'It profits one nothing
  to take delight in God.'

10 "Therefore, hear me, you who have sense,
  far be it from God that he should do
    wickedness,
  and from the Almighty*c* that he should do
    wrong.
11 For according to their deeds he will repay them,
  and according to their ways he will make it
    befall them.

12 Of a truth, God will not do wickedly,
  and the Almighty*c* will not pervert justice.
13 Who gave him charge over the earth
  and who laid on him*d* the whole world?
14 If he should take back his spirit*e* to himself,
  and gather to himself his breath,
15 all flesh would perish together,
  and all mortals return to dust.

16 "If you have understanding, hear this;
  listen to what I say.
17 Shall one who hates justice govern?
  Will you condemn one who is righteous and
    mighty,
18 who says to a king, 'You scoundrel!'
  and to princes, 'You wicked men!';
19 who shows no partiality to nobles,
  nor regards the rich more than the poor,
  for they are all the work of his hands?
20 In a moment they die;
  at midnight the people are shaken and pass
    away,
  and the mighty are taken away by no human
    hand.

21 "For his eyes are upon the ways of mortals,
  and he sees all their steps.
22 There is no gloom or deep darkness
  where evildoers may hide themselves.
23 For he has not appointed a time*f* for anyone
  to go before God in judgment.
24 He shatters the mighty without investigation,
  and sets others in their place.
25 Thus, knowing their works,
  he overturns them in the night, and they are
    crushed.
26 He strikes them for their wickedness
  while others look on,
27 because they turned aside from following him,
  and had no regard for any of his ways,
28 so that they caused the cry of the poor to come
    to him,
  and he heard the cry of the afflicted—
29 When he is quiet, who can condemn?
  When he hides his face, who can behold him,
  whether it be a nation or an individual?—
30 so that the godless should not reign,
  or those who ensnare the people.

31 "For has anyone said to God,
  'I have endured punishment; I will not offend
    any more;

---

a Heb he   b Syr: Heb to be lighted with the light of life
c Traditional rendering of Heb *Shaddai*   d Heb lacks *on him*
e Heb *his heart his spirit*   f Cn: Heb *yet*

32 teach me what I do not see;
    if I have done iniquity, I will do it no more'?
33 Will he then pay back to suit you,
    because you reject it?
  For you must choose, and not I;
    therefore declare what you know.[a]
34 Those who have sense will say to me,
    and the wise who hear me will say,
35 'Job speaks without knowledge,
    his words are without insight.'
36 Would that Job were tried to the limit,
    because his answers are those of the wicked.
37 For he adds rebellion to his sin;
    he claps his hands among us,
    and multiplies his words against God."

Elihu Condemns Self-Righteousness

35 Elihu continued and said:
2 "Do you think this to be just?
    You say, 'I am in the right before God.'
3 If you ask, 'What advantage have I?
    How am I better off than if I had sinned?'
4 I will answer you
    and your friends with you.
5 Look at the heavens and see;
    observe the clouds, which are higher than you.
6 If you have sinned, what do you accomplish
        against him?
    And if your transgressions are multiplied,
        what do you do to him?
7 If you are righteous, what do you give to him;
    or what does he receive from your hand?
8 Your wickedness affects others like you,
    and your righteousness, other human beings.

9 "Because of the multitude of oppressions people
        cry out;
    they call for help because of the arm of the
        mighty.
10 But no one says, 'Where is God my Maker,
    who gives strength in the night,
11 who teaches us more than the animals of the
        earth,
    and makes us wiser than the birds of the air?'
12 There they cry out, but he does not answer,
    because of the pride of evildoers.
13 Surely God does not hear an empty cry,
    nor does the Almighty[b] regard it.
14 How much less when you say that you do not
        see him,
    that the case is before him, and you are
        waiting for him!
15 And now, because his anger does not punish,
    and he does not greatly heed transgression,[c]
16 Job opens his mouth in empty talk,
    he multiplies words without knowledge."

Elihu Exalts God's Goodness

36 Elihu continued and said:
2 "Bear with me a little, and I will show
        you,
    for I have yet something to say on God's
        behalf.
3 I will bring my knowledge from far away,
    and ascribe righteousness to my Maker.
4 For truly my words are not false;
    one who is perfect in knowledge is with you.

5 "Surely God is mighty and does not despise any;
    he is mighty in strength of understanding.
6 He does not keep the wicked alive,
    but gives the afflicted their right.
7 He does not withdraw his eyes from the
        righteous,
    but with kings on the throne
    he sets them forever, and they are exalted.
8 And if they are bound in fetters
    and caught in the cords of affliction,
9 then he declares to them their work
    and their transgressions, that they are
        behaving arrogantly.
10 He opens their ears to instruction,
    and commands that they return from iniquity.
11 If they listen, and serve him,
    they complete their days in prosperity,
    and their years in pleasantness.
12 But if they do not listen, they shall perish by the
        sword,
    and die without knowledge.

13 "The godless in heart cherish anger;
    they do not cry for help when he binds them.
14 They die in their youth,
    and their life ends in shame.[d]
15 He delivers the afflicted by their affliction,
    and opens their ear by adversity.
16 He also allured you out of distress
    into a broad place where there was no
        constraint,
    and what was set on your table was full of
        fatness.

17 "But you are obsessed with the case of the wicked;
    judgment and justice seize you.
18 Beware that wrath does not entice you into
        scoffing,
    and do not let the greatness of the ransom
        turn you aside.

---

a Meaning of Heb of verses 29-33 uncertain   b Traditional
rendering of Heb *Shaddai*   c Theodotion Symmachus Compare
Vg: Meaning of Heb uncertain   d Heb *ends among the temple
prostitutes*

¹⁹ Will your cry avail to keep you from distress,
　　or will all the force of your strength?
²⁰ Do not long for the night,
　　when peoples are cut off in their place.
²¹ Beware! Do not turn to iniquity;
　　because of that you have been tried by
　　　affliction.
²² See, God is exalted in his power;
　　who is a teacher like him?
²³ Who has prescribed for him his way,
　　or who can say, 'You have done wrong'?

Elihu Proclaims God's Majesty

²⁴ "Remember to extol his work,
　　of which mortals have sung.
²⁵ All people have looked on it;
　　everyone watches it from far away.
²⁶ Surely God is great, and we do not know him;
　　the number of his years is unsearchable.
²⁷ For he draws up the drops of water;
　　he distills*a* his mist in rain,
²⁸ which the skies pour down
　　and drop upon mortals abundantly.
²⁹ Can anyone understand the spreading of the
　　　clouds,
　　the thunderings of his pavilion?
³⁰ See, he scatters his lightning around him
　　and covers the roots of the sea.
³¹ For by these he governs peoples;
　　he gives food in abundance.
³² He covers his hands with the lightning,
　　and commands it to strike the mark.
³³ Its crashing*b* tells about him;
　　he is jealous*b* with anger against iniquity.

37 "At this also my heart trembles,
　　and leaps out of its place.
² Listen, listen to the thunder of his voice
　　and the rumbling that comes from his mouth.
³ Under the whole heaven he lets it loose,
　　and his lightning to the corners of the earth.
⁴ After it his voice roars;
　　he thunders with his majestic voice
　　and he does not restrain the lightnings*c* when
　　　his voice is heard.
⁵ God thunders wondrously with his voice;
　　he does great things that we cannot
　　　comprehend.
⁶ For to the snow he says, 'Fall on the earth';
　　and the shower of rain, his heavy shower of
　　　rain,
⁷ serves as a sign on everyone's hand,
　　so that all whom he has made may know it.*d*
⁸ Then the animals go into their lairs
　　and remain in their dens.
⁹ From its chamber comes the whirlwind,

and cold from the scattering winds.
¹⁰ By the breath of God ice is given,
　　and the broad waters are frozen fast.
¹¹ He loads the thick cloud with moisture;
　　the clouds scatter his lightning.
¹² They turn round and round by his guidance,
　　to accomplish all that he commands them
　　on the face of the habitable world.
¹³ Whether for correction, or for his land,
　　or for love, he causes it to happen.

¹⁴ "Hear this, O Job;
　　stop and consider the wondrous works of
　　　God.
¹⁵ Do you know how God lays his command upon
　　　them,
　　and causes the lightning of his cloud to
　　　shine?
¹⁶ Do you know the balancings of the clouds,
　　the wondrous works of the one whose
　　　knowledge is perfect,
¹⁷ you whose garments are hot
　　when the earth is still because of the south
　　　wind?
¹⁸ Can you, like him, spread out the skies,
　　hard as a molten mirror?
¹⁹ Teach us what we shall say to him;
　　we cannot draw up our case because of
　　　darkness.
²⁰ Should he be told that I want to speak?
　　Did anyone ever wish to be swallowed up?
²¹ Now, no one can look on the light
　　when it is bright in the skies,
　　when the wind has passed and cleared them.
²² Out of the north comes golden splendor;
　　around God is awesome majesty.
²³ The Almighty*e*—we cannot find him;
　　he is great in power and justice,
　　and abundant righteousness he will not
　　　violate.
²⁴ Therefore mortals fear him;
　　he does not regard any who are wise in their
　　　own conceit."

The Lord Answers Job

38 Then the Lord answered Job out of the
　　whirlwind:
² "Who is this that darkens counsel by words
　　without knowledge?
³ Gird up your loins like a man,
　　I will question you, and you shall declare
　　to me.

---

a Cn: Heb *they distill*　　*b* Meaning of Heb uncertain
c Heb *them*　　*d* Meaning of Heb of verse 7 uncertain
e Traditional rendering of Heb *Shaddai*

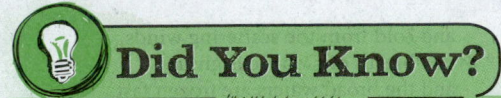

Did You Know?

Heaven and Earth

The questions God asks Job about the formation of the cosmos (see Job 38:4–38) give us a clue about how the ancient Israelites thought the universe was put together. They believed God had created it in three levels: the heavens, which were contained in a giant vault above the earth; the earth itself, which was a disk that rested on the waters of the abyss; and the abyss, which was the underworld. Over time the heavens and the earth developed symbolic meanings. The heavens became known as the place where God dwells and the earth as the place that humans inhabit. Even later, the abyss became known as the place of the dead.

▶ Job 38:4–38

4 "Where were you when I laid the foundation of the earth?
Tell me, if you have understanding.
5 Who determined its measurements—surely you know!
Or who stretched the line upon it?
6 On what were its bases sunk,
or who laid its cornerstone
7 when the morning stars sang together
and all the heavenly beings[a] shouted for joy?

8 "Or who shut in the sea with doors
when it burst out from the womb?—
9 when I made the clouds its garment,
and thick darkness its swaddling band,
10 and prescribed bounds for it,
and set bars and doors,
11 and said, 'Thus far shall you come, and no farther,
and here shall your proud waves be stopped'?

12 "Have you commanded the morning since your days began,
and caused the dawn to know its place,
13 so that it might take hold of the skirts of the earth,
and the wicked be shaken out of it?
14 It is changed like clay under the seal,
and it is dyed[b] like a garment.

15 Light is withheld from the wicked,
and their uplifted arm is broken.

16 "Have you entered into the springs of the sea,
or walked in the recesses of the deep?
17 Have the gates of death been revealed to you,
or have you seen the gates of deep darkness?
18 Have you comprehended the expanse of the earth?
Declare, if you know all this.

19 "Where is the way to the dwelling of light,
and where is the place of darkness,
20 that you may take it to its territory
and that you may discern the paths to its home?
21 Surely you know, for you were born then,
and the number of your days is great!

22 "Have you entered the storehouses of the snow,
or have you seen the storehouses of the hail,
23 which I have reserved for the time of trouble,
for the day of battle and war?
24 What is the way to the place where the light is distributed,
or where the east wind is scattered upon the earth?

25 "Who has cut a channel for the torrents of rain,
and a way for the thunderbolt,
26 to bring rain on a land where no one lives,
on the desert, which is empty of human life,
27 to satisfy the waste and desolate land,
and to make the ground put forth grass?

28 "Has the rain a father,
or who has begotten the drops of dew?
29 From whose womb did the ice come forth,
and who has given birth to the hoarfrost of heaven?
30 The waters become hard like stone,
and the face of the deep is frozen.

31 "Can you bind the chains of the Pleiades,
or loose the cords of Orion?
32 Can you lead forth the Mazzaroth in their season,
or can you guide the Bear with its children?
33 Do you know the ordinances of the heavens?
Can you establish their rule on the earth?

34 "Can you lift up your voice to the clouds,
so that a flood of waters may cover you?

_a_ Heb _sons of God_   _b_ Cn: Heb _and they stand forth_

JOB

35 Can you send forth lightnings, so that they
     may go
     and say to you, 'Here we are'?
36 Who has put wisdom in the inward parts,[a]
     or given understanding to the mind?[a]
37 Who has the wisdom to number the clouds?
     Or who can tilt the waterskins of the heavens,
38 when the dust runs into a mass
     and the clods cling together?

39 "Can you hunt the prey for the lion,
     or satisfy the appetite of the young lions,
40 when they crouch in their dens,
     or lie in wait in their covert?
41 Who provides for the raven its prey,
     when its young ones cry to God,
     and wander about for lack of food?

39 "Do you know when the mountain goats
     give birth?
     Do you observe the calving of the deer?
2 Can you number the months that they fulfill,
     and do you know the time when they give
     birth,
3 when they crouch to give birth to their
     offspring,
     and are delivered of their young?
4 Their young ones become strong, they grow up
     in the open;
     they go forth, and do not return to them.

5 "Who has let the wild ass go free?
     Who has loosed the bonds of the swift ass,
6 to which I have given the steppe for its home,
     the salt land for its dwelling place?
7 It scorns the tumult of the city;
     it does not hear the shouts of the driver.
8 It ranges the mountains as its pasture,
     and it searches after every green thing.

9 "Is the wild ox willing to serve you?
     Will it spend the night at your crib?
10 Can you tie it in the furrow with ropes,
     or will it harrow the valleys after you?
11 Will you depend on it because its strength is
     great,
     and will you hand over your labor to it?
12 Do you have faith in it that it will return,
     and bring your grain to your threshing floor?[b]

13 "The ostrich's wings flap wildly,
     though its pinions lack plumage.[a]
14 For it leaves its eggs to the earth,
     and lets them be warmed on the ground,
15 forgetting that a foot may crush them,
     and that a wild animal may trample them.

16 It deals cruelly with its young, as if they were
     not its own;
     though its labor should be in vain, yet it has
     no fear;
17 because God has made it forget wisdom,
     and given it no share in understanding.
18 When it spreads its plumes aloft,[a]
     it laughs at the horse and its rider.

19 "Do you give the horse its might?
     Do you clothe its neck with mane?
20 Do you make it leap like the locust?
     Its majestic snorting is terrible.
21 It paws[c] violently, exults mightily;
     it goes out to meet the weapons.
22 It laughs at fear, and is not dismayed;
     it does not turn back from the sword.
23 Upon it rattle the quiver,

a Meaning of Heb uncertain   b Heb your grain and your
threshing floor   c Gk Syr Vg: Heb they dig

Pray It!

Too Big to Understand

When God asks Job a series of questions about creation and good and evil, he's trying to make one simple point: You can never understand me. I am too big. You are too small.

The author of Job seems to be saying to readers, If you think you've got God all figured out—like Job's friends thought they had, or like even Job wanted to have—you're wrong. The author is reminding readers that God is a mystery—powerful and awesome beyond our imagination and control.

In your prayer time, reflect or journal on the following questions:

- In what ways has God been too big for you to understand?
- Do you expect God to provide you with happiness? peace? friends?
- What happens if God doesn't meet your expectations in the way you want them to be met?
- Can you let go of your expectations and trust in God's love? Why or why not?

▶ **Job, chapters 38–41**

the flashing spear, and the javelin.
24 With fierceness and rage it swallows the ground;
  it cannot stand still at the sound of the
    trumpet.
25 When the trumpet sounds, it says 'Aha!'
  From a distance it smells the battle,
    the thunder of the captains, and the shouting.

26 "Is it by your wisdom that the hawk soars,
  and spreads its wings toward the south?
27 Is it at your command that the eagle mounts up
  and makes its nest on high?
28 It lives on the rock and makes its home
  in the fastness of the rocky crag.
29 From there it spies the prey;
  its eyes see it from far away.
30 Its young ones suck up blood;
  and where the slain are, there it is."

40
And the LORD said to Job:
2 "Shall a faultfinder contend with the
  Almighty?[a]
  Anyone who argues with God must respond."

Job's Response to God

3 Then Job answered the LORD:
4 "See, I am of small account; what shall I answer
  you?
  I lay my hand on my mouth.
5 I have spoken once, and I will not answer;
  twice, but will proceed no further."

God's Challenge to Job

6 Then the LORD answered Job out of the
whirlwind:
7 "Gird up your loins like a man;
  I will question you, and you declare to me.
8 Will you even put me in the wrong?
  Will you condemn me that you may be
    justified?
9 Have you an arm like God,
  and can you thunder with a voice like his?

10 "Deck yourself with majesty and dignity;
  clothe yourself with glory and splendor.
11 Pour out the overflowings of your anger,
  and look on all who are proud, and abase
    them.
12 Look on all who are proud, and bring them
    low;
  tread down the wicked where they stand.
13 Hide them all in the dust together;
  bind their faces in the world below.[b]
14 Then I will also acknowledge to you
  that your own right hand can give you
    victory.

15 "Look at Behemoth,
  which I made just as I made you;
  it eats grass like an ox.
16 Its strength is in its loins,
  and its power in the muscles of its belly.
17 It makes its tail stiff like a cedar;
  the sinews of its thighs are knit together.
18 Its bones are tubes of bronze,
  its limbs like bars of iron.

19 "It is the first of the great acts of God—
  only its Maker can approach it with the sword.
20 For the mountains yield food for it
  where all the wild animals play.
21 Under the lotus plants it lies,
  in the covert of the reeds and in the marsh.
22 The lotus trees cover it for shade;
  the willows of the wadi surround it.
23 Even if the river is turbulent, it is not frightened;
  it is confident though Jordan rushes against
    its mouth.
24 Can one take it with hooks[c]
  or pierce its nose with a snare?

41
[d] "Can you draw out Leviathan[e] with a
  fishhook,
  or press down its tongue with a cord?
2 Can you put a rope in its nose,
  or pierce its jaw with a hook?
3 Will it make many supplications to you?
  Will it speak soft words to you?
4 Will it make a covenant with you
  to be taken as your servant forever?
5 Will you play with it as with a bird,
  or will you put it on leash for your girls?
6 Will traders bargain over it?
  Will they divide it up among the merchants?
7 Can you fill its skin with harpoons,
  or its head with fishing spears?
8 Lay hands on it;
  think of the battle; you will not do it again!
9[f] Any hope of capturing it[g] will be disappointed;
  were not even the gods[h] overwhelmed at the
    sight of it?
10 No one is so fierce as to dare to stir it up.
  Who can stand before it?[i]
11 Who can confront it[i] and be safe?[j]
  —under the whole heaven, who?[k]

12 "I will not keep silence concerning its limbs,
  or its mighty strength, or its splendid frame.

a Traditional rendering of Heb *Shaddai*   b Heb *the hidden place*
c Cn: Heb *in his eyes*   d Ch 40.25 in Heb   e Or *the crocodile*
f Ch 41.1 in Heb   g Heb *of it*   h Cn Compare Symmachus
Syr: Heb *one is*   i Heb *me*   j Gk: Heb *that I shall repay*
k Heb *to me*

¹³ Who can strip off its outer garment?
    Who can penetrate its double coat of mail?ᵃ

¹⁴ Who can open the doors of its face?
    There is terror all around its teeth.

¹⁵ Its backᵇ is made of shields in rows,
    shut up closely as with a seal.

¹⁶ One is so near to another
    that no air can come between them.

¹⁷ They are joined one to another;
    they clasp each other and cannot be separated.

¹⁸ Its sneezes flash forth light,
    and its eyes are like the eyelids of the dawn.

¹⁹ From its mouth go flaming torches;
    sparks of fire leap out.

²⁰ Out of its nostrils comes smoke,
    as from a boiling pot and burning rushes.

²¹ Its breath kindles coals,
    and a flame comes out of its mouth.

²² In its neck abides strength,
    and terror dances before it.

²³ The folds of its flesh cling together;
    it is firmly cast and immovable.

²⁴ Its heart is as hard as stone,
    as hard as the lower millstone.

²⁵ When it raises itself up the gods are afraid;
    at the crashing they are beside themselves.

²⁶ Though the sword reaches it, it does not avail,
    nor does the spear, the dart, or the javelin.

²⁷ It counts iron as straw,
    and bronze as rotten wood.

²⁸ The arrow cannot make it flee;
    slingstones, for it, are turned to chaff.

²⁹ Clubs are counted as chaff;
    it laughs at the rattle of javelins.

³⁰ Its underparts are like sharp potsherds;
    it spreads itself like a threshing sledge on the
    mire.

³¹ It makes the deep boil like a pot;
    it makes the sea like a pot of ointment.

³² It leaves a shining wake behind it;
    one would think the deep to be white-haired.

³³ On earth it has no equal,
    a creature without fear.

³⁴ It surveys everything that is lofty;
    it is king over all that are proud."

Job Is Humbled and Satisfied

42 Then Job answered the LORD:
² "I know that you can do all things,
    and that no purpose of yours can be thwarted.

³ 'Who is this that hides counsel without
    knowledge?'
Therefore I have uttered what I did not
    understand,
    things too wonderful for me, which I did not
    know.

⁴ 'Hear, and I will speak;
    I will question you, and you declare to me.'

⁵ I had heard of you by the hearing of the ear,
    but now my eye sees you;

---

a Gk: Heb *bridle*   b Cn Compare Gk Vg: Heb *pride*

Live It!

Why?

So, that's it? God just shows up, overwhelms Job with a bunch of questions he can't answer, and then gives Job back double everything he lost? God doesn't even answer Job's question about why he had to suffer!

And what about *our* questions? Why do innocent children die? Why is someone we love taken from us? Why do people die from hunger in a world that has so much? Why did that plane crash? Why did our friend die?

Why was Job satisfied with God's response? Perhaps Job's mind and heart struggled with God's answer, and his heart won. Maybe his heart told him to trust in God's love even when his mind couldn't understand the mystery of his suffering.

With Job the Israelite people began to see the suffering of innocent people as mystery and not as punishment. In the New Testament, this suffering would continue to be seen as mystery but also as something more. The death of Jesus—the ultimate innocent suffering person—and his Resurrection led to the understanding that God ultimately brings good out of the suffering of faithful people (see Jn 12:24–25 and the introduction to First Peter).

Thankfully, the story of our faith does not end with Jesus' suffering on the cross, but with the glory of Jesus' Resurrection. For Christians, death, sin, and suffering hold no power. If we believe in the truth of the Resurrection. We may not be able to explain why bad things happen, but we are empowered by a faith that shows us that suffering and evil never have the final word.

▶ **Job 38:1—42:6**

6 therefore I despise myself,
  and repent in dust and ashes."

Job's Friends Are Humiliated

7 After the Lord had spoken these words to Job, the Lord said to Eliphaz the Temanite: "My wrath is kindled against you and against your two friends; for you have not spoken of me what is right, as my servant Job has. 8 Now therefore take seven bulls and seven rams, and go to my servant Job, and offer up for yourselves a burnt offering; and my servant Job shall pray for you, for I will accept his prayer not to deal with you according to your folly; for you have not spoken of me what is right, as my servant Job has done." 9 So Eliphaz the Temanite and Bildad the Shuhite and Zophar the Naamathite went and did what the Lord had told them; and the Lord accepted Job's prayer.

Job's Fortunes Are Restored Twofold

10 And the Lord restored the fortunes of Job when he had prayed for his friends; and the Lord gave Job twice as much as he had before. 11 Then there came to him all his brothers and sisters and all who had known him before, and they ate bread with him in his house; they showed him sympathy and comforted him for all the evil that the Lord had brought upon him; and each of them gave him a piece of money[a] and a gold ring. 12 The Lord blessed the latter days of Job more than his beginning; and he had fourteen thousand sheep, six thousand camels, a thousand yoke of oxen, and a thousand donkeys. 13 He also had seven sons and three daughters. 14 He named the first Jemimah, the second Keziah, and the third Keren-happuch. 15 In all the land there were no women so beautiful as Job's daughters; and their father gave them an inheritance along with their brothers. 16 After this Job lived one hundred and forty years, and saw his children, and his children's children, four generations. 17 And Job died, old and full of days.

---

a Heb a qesitah

JOB

Rock! Pop! Salsa! Rhythm and blues! Hip-hop! Rap! Jazz! Country! Alternative! We each have our own favorite music that somehow resonates with our being, and maybe even expresses our attitude and philosophy toward life. So much so that we often refer to it as *our* music, even though it was written by someone else. In the same way, we can say that the Psalms are Israel's music. They are the hymns or songs that Israel used in its Temple worship. They give voice to the souls of the Israelites and tell about the ups and downs of the Israelites' relationship with God.

At a Glance

Psalms is divided into five books without any particular organizing theme:

- Psalms 1–41. Book I
- Psalms 42–72. Book II
- Psalms 73–89. Book III
- Psalms 90–106. Book IV
- Psalms 107–150. Book V

Quick Facts

Inspired Authors: many, sometimes called psalmists
Themes: a variety
Of Note: The psalms are used by Catholic Christians regularly at Mass and in the Church's official prayer, the Liturgy of the Hours.

In Depth

The Hebrew version of Psalms is titled *Tehillim*, or Praises, because its hymns praise God. The Greek translation calls them *Psalmoi*, or Psalms, which means "religious songs performed to music." The 150 Psalms can be grouped into one or more of five general categories:

The *hymns of praise and thanksgiving* sing of God's majesty, power, and wisdom (for example, Psalms 8, 24, 47, 93, 95–99, 113–118, 136, and 150).

The *hymns of lament or petition* include both individual and communal cries to God for help in some need (for example, Psalms 38, 51, 55, 58, 59, 74, 78, 105, and 106).

The *hymns of wisdom* sing of Israel's insights into how to live according to God's law and what brings true happiness (for example, Psalms 1, 34, 37, 49, 73, 112, and 128).

The *liturgical or worship psalms* are used for entrance hymns at liturgies or during worship services at the Temple (for example, Psalms 15, 24, and 134).

The *historical psalms* sing of the great wonders God has worked throughout the history of Israel (for example, Psalms 78, 105, 106, 135, and 136).

Because of King David's reputation for writing and performing music, he is named as the author of many of the Psalms. Actually, though, many of them were written long after his death. It is more accurate to understand the Psalms as a collection of songs that reflect different times and experiences throughout Israel's existence. Just as your favorite music might tell others what you value as a person, the Psalms tell us about Israel and its wondrous relationship with God.

BOOK I
(Psalms 1-41)

PSALM 1

The Two Ways

1 Happy are those
  who do not follow the advice of the wicked,
or take the path that sinners tread,
  or sit in the seat of scoffers;
2 but their delight is in the law of the LORD,
  and on his law they meditate day and night.
3 They are like trees
  planted by streams of water,
which yield their fruit in its season,
  and their leaves do not wither.
In all that they do, they prosper.

4 The wicked are not so,
  but are like chaff that the wind drives away.
5 Therefore the wicked will not stand in the
    judgment,
  nor sinners in the congregation of the righteous;
6 for the LORD watches over the way of the righteous,
  but the way of the wicked will perish.

PSALM 2

God's Promise to His Anointed

1 Why do the nations conspire,
  and the peoples plot in vain?

2 The kings of the earth set themselves,
  and the rulers take counsel together,
  against the LORD and his anointed, saying,
3 "Let us burst their bonds asunder,
  and cast their cords from us."

4 He who sits in the heavens laughs;
  the LORD has them in derision.
5 Then he will speak to them in his wrath,
  and terrify them in his fury, saying,
6 "I have set my king on Zion, my holy hill."

7 I will tell of the decree of the LORD:
He said to me, "You are my son;
  today I have begotten you.
8 Ask of me, and I will make the nations your
    heritage,
  and the ends of the earth your possession.
9 You shall break them with a rod of iron,
  and dash them in pieces like a potter's vessel."

10 Now therefore, O kings, be wise;
  be warned, O rulers of the earth.
11 Serve the LORD with fear,
  with trembling 12kiss his feet,*a*
or he will be angry, and you will perish in the
    way;
  for his wrath is quickly kindled.

Happy are all who take refuge in him.

---

a Cn: Meaning of Heb of verses 11b and 12a is uncertain

PSALM 3

Trust in God under Adversity

A Psalm of David, when he fled from his son
Absalom.

1 O Lord, how many are my foes!
   Many are rising against me;
2 many are saying to me,
   "There is no help for you[a] in God."   *Selah*

3 But you, O Lord, are a shield around me,
   my glory, and the one who lifts up my head.
4 I cry aloud to the Lord,
   and he answers me from his holy hill.   *Selah*

5 I lie down and sleep;
   I wake again, for the Lord sustains me.
6 I am not afraid of ten thousands of people
   who have set themselves against me all
       around.

7 Rise up, O Lord!
   Deliver me, O my God!
For you strike all my enemies on the cheek;
   you break the teeth of the wicked.

8 Deliverance belongs to the Lord;
   may your blessing be on your people!   *Selah*

PSALM 4

Confident Plea for Deliverance from Enemies

To the leader: with stringed instruments. A Psalm
of David.

1 Answer me when I call, O God of my right!
   You gave me room when I was in distress.
   Be gracious to me, and hear my prayer.

2 How long, you people, shall my honor suffer
       shame?
   How long will you love vain words, and seek
       after lies?   *Selah*
3 But know that the Lord has set apart the faithful
       for himself;
   the Lord hears when I call to him.

4 When you are disturbed,[b] do not sin;
   ponder it on your beds, and be silent.   *Selah*
5 Offer right sacrifices,
   and put your trust in the Lord.

6 There are many who say, "O that we might see
       some good!
   Let the light of your face shine on us,
       O Lord!"

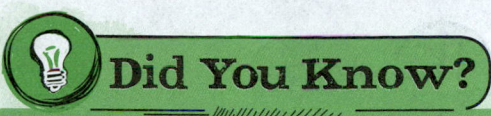

Did You Know?

Understanding the Psalms

"**P**raise God!" "Why am I suffering?" "Save
us from oppression and injustice." "God,
give me rest." These phrases illustrate types of
prayer: praise, lament, and petition. The Book
of Psalms includes these and many other kinds
of prayer, made by individuals, small groups, or
the whole Jewish nation. Yet, throughout the
Psalms, there is one constant: human experience is viewed through the eyes of faith. For example, Psalm 3 reflects the human experience
of being attacked by others (see verses 1–2). The
writer of this psalm, rather than losing all hope,
calls God to the rescue (see verse 7). In a similar
way, all the Psalms teach us that every human
experience can also be a faith experience.

7 You have put gladness in my heart
   more than when their grain and wine
       abound.

8 I will both lie down and sleep in peace;
   for you alone, O Lord, make me lie down in
       safety.

PSALM 5

Trust in God for Deliverance from Enemies

To the leader: for the flutes. A Psalm of David.

1 Give ear to my words, O Lord;
   give heed to my sighing.
2 Listen to the sound of my cry,
   my King and my God,
   for to you I pray.
3 O Lord, in the morning you hear my voice;
   in the morning I plead my case to you, and
       watch.

4 For you are not a God who delights in
       wickedness;
   evil will not sojourn with you.
5 The boastful will not stand before your eyes;
   you hate all evildoers.
6 You destroy those who speak lies;
   the Lord abhors the bloodthirsty and deceitful.

---

a Syr: Heb *him*   b Or *are angry*

P
S

Live It!

Our Cross to Bear

In Psalm 6, the psalmist is praying for deliverance from physical and mental suffering. Christians often refer to the suffering or sacrifice that comes as part of life as their cross to bear, because they see it as connected to Jesus' own suffering on the cross. Indeed, we all have crosses to bear. Some crosses are heavier than others, and like the psalmist, we ask God to deliver us from them. But unlike the psalmist, Christians also pray that God will transform their suffering and use it in some way for the good of others.

● What are some of the crosses you have had to bear? How were you saved from your suffering? How has someone else's suffering or sacrifice helped or inspired you?

▶ Psalm 6

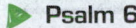

7 But I, through the abundance of your steadfast
        love,
    will enter your house,
I will bow down toward your holy temple
    in awe of you.
8 Lead me, O Lord, in your righteousness
        because of my enemies;
    make your way straight before me.

9 For there is no truth in their mouths;
        their hearts are destruction;
    their throats are open graves;
        they flatter with their tongues.
10 Make them bear their guilt, O God;
        let them fall by their own counsels;
    because of their many transgressions cast them
        out,
        for they have rebelled against you.

11 But let all who take refuge in you rejoice;
        let them ever sing for joy.
    Spread your protection over them,
        so that those who love your name may exult
        in you.
12 For you bless the righteous, O Lord;
        you cover them with favor as with a shield.

PSALM 6

Prayer for Recovery from Grave Illness

*To the leader: with stringed instruments; according
to The Sheminith. A Psalm of David.*

1 O Lord, do not rebuke me in your anger,
    or discipline me in your wrath.
2 Be gracious to me, O Lord, for I am languishing;
    O Lord, heal me, for my bones are shaking
        with terror.
3 My soul also is struck with terror,
    while you, O Lord—how long?

4 Turn, O Lord, save my life;
    deliver me for the sake of your steadfast love.
5 For in death there is no remembrance of you;
    in Sheol who can give you praise?

6 I am weary with my moaning;
    every night I flood my bed with tears;
    I drench my couch with my weeping.
7 My eyes waste away because of grief;
    they grow weak because of all my foes.

8 Depart from me, all you workers of evil,
    for the Lord has heard the sound of my
        weeping.
9 The Lord has heard my supplication;
    the Lord accepts my prayer.
10 All my enemies shall be ashamed and struck
        with terror;
    they shall turn back, and in a moment be put
        to shame.

PSALM 7

Plea for Help against Persecutors

*A Shiggaion of David, which he sang to the Lord
concerning Cush, a Benjaminite.*

1 O Lord my God, in you I take refuge;
    save me from all my pursuers, and deliver me,
2 or like a lion they will tear me apart;
    they will drag me away, with no one to rescue.

3 O Lord my God, if I have done this,
    if there is wrong in my hands,
4 if I have repaid my ally with harm
    or plundered my foe without cause,
5 then let the enemy pursue and overtake me,
    trample my life to the ground,
    and lay my soul in the dust.   *Selah*

6 Rise up, O Lord, in your anger;
    lift yourself up against the fury of my
        enemies;

awake, O my God;[a] you have appointed a
    judgment.

7 Let the assembly of the peoples be gathered
    around you,
    and over it take your seat[b] on high.

8 The LORD judges the peoples;
    judge me, O LORD, according to my
        righteousness
    and according to the integrity that is in me.

9 O let the evil of the wicked come to an end,
    but establish the righteous,
you who test the minds and hearts,
    O righteous God.

10 God is my shield,
    who saves the upright in heart.

11 God is a righteous judge,
    and a God who has indignation every day.

12 If one does not repent, God[c] will whet his sword;
    he has bent and strung his bow;

13 he has prepared his deadly weapons,
    making his arrows fiery shafts.

14 See how they conceive evil,
    and are pregnant with mischief,
    and bring forth lies.

15 They make a pit, digging it out,
    and fall into the hole that they have made.

16 Their mischief returns upon their own heads,
    and on their own heads their violence
        descends.

17 I will give to the LORD the thanks due to his
        righteousness,
    and sing praise to the name of the LORD, the
        Most High.

PSALM 8

Divine Majesty and Human Dignity

To the leader: according to The Gittith. A Psalm
of David.

1 O LORD, our Sovereign,
    how majestic is your name in all the earth!

You have set your glory above the heavens.

2   Out of the mouths of babes and infants
you have founded a bulwark because of your
        foes,
    to silence the enemy and the avenger.

3 When I look at your heavens, the work of your
        fingers,
    the moon and the stars that you have
        established;

4 what are human beings that you are mindful of
        them,
    mortals[d] that you care for them?

5 Yet you have made them a little lower than God,[e]
    and crowned them with glory and honor.

6 You have given them dominion over the works
        of your hands;
    you have put all things under their feet,

7 all sheep and oxen,
    and also the beasts of the field,

8 the birds of the air, and the fish of the sea,
    whatever passes along the paths of the seas.

9 O LORD, our Sovereign,
    how majestic is your name in all the earth!

PSALM 9

God's Power and Justice

To the leader: according to Muth-labben. A Psalm
of David.

1 I will give thanks to the LORD with my whole
        heart;
    I will tell of all your wonderful deeds.

2 I will be glad and exult in you;
    I will sing praise to your name, O Most High.

3 When my enemies turned back,
    they stumbled and perished before you.

4 For you have maintained my just cause;
    you have sat on the throne giving righteous
        judgment.

5 You have rebuked the nations, you have
        destroyed the wicked;
    you have blotted out their name forever and
        ever.

6 The enemies have vanished in everlasting ruins;
    their cities you have rooted out;
    the very memory of them has perished.

7 But the LORD sits enthroned forever,
    he has established his throne for judgment.

8 He judges the world with righteousness;
    he judges the peoples with equity.

9 The LORD is a stronghold for the oppressed,
    a stronghold in times of trouble.

10 And those who know your name put their trust
        in you,

---

a Or awake for me   b Cn: Heb return   c Heb he   d Heb ben
adam, lit. son of man   e Or than the divine beings or angels: Heb
elohim

for you, O LORD, have not forsaken those who
     seek you.

11 Sing praises to the LORD, who dwells in Zion.
     Declare his deeds among the peoples.
12 For he who avenges blood is mindful of them;
     he does not forget the cry of the afflicted.

13 Be gracious to me, O LORD.
     See what I suffer from those who hate me;
     you are the one who lifts me up from the
        gates of death,
14 so that I may recount all your praises,
     and, in the gates of daughter Zion,
     rejoice in your deliverance.

15 The nations have sunk in the pit that they made;
     in the net that they hid has their own foot
        been caught.
16 The LORD has made himself known, he has
        executed judgment;
     the wicked are snared in the work of their
        own hands.   *Higgaion. Selah*

17 The wicked shall depart to Sheol,
     all the nations that forget God.

18 For the needy shall not always be forgotten,
     nor the hope of the poor perish forever.

19 Rise up, O LORD! Do not let mortals prevail;
     let the nations be judged before you.
20 Put them in fear, O LORD;
     let the nations know that they are only
        human.   *Selah*

PSALM 10

Prayer for Deliverance from Enemies

1 Why, O LORD, do you stand far off?
     Why do you hide yourself in times of trouble?
2 In arrogance the wicked persecute the poor—
     let them be caught in the schemes they have
        devised.

3 For the wicked boast of the desires of their heart,
     those greedy for gain curse and renounce the
        LORD.
4 In the pride of their countenance the wicked say,
     "God will not seek it out";
     all their thoughts are, "There is no God."

5 Their ways prosper at all times;
     your judgments are on high, out of their sight;
     as for their foes, they scoff at them.

6 They think in their heart, "We shall not be
        moved;
     throughout all generations we shall not meet
        adversity."

7 Their mouths are filled with cursing and deceit
        and oppression;
     under their tongues are mischief and iniquity.
8 They sit in ambush in the villages;
     in hiding places they murder the innocent.

   Their eyes stealthily watch for the helpless;
9   they lurk in secret like a lion in its covert;
   they lurk that they may seize the poor;
     they seize the poor and drag them off in their
        net.

10 They stoop, they crouch,
     and the helpless fall by their might.
11 They think in their heart, "God has forgotten,
     he has hidden his face, he will never see it."

12 Rise up, O LORD; O God, lift up your hand;
     do not forget the oppressed.
13 Why do the wicked renounce God,
     and say in their hearts, "You will not call us
        to account"?

14 But you do see! Indeed you note trouble and
        grief,
     that you may take it into your hands;
   the helpless commit themselves to you;
     you have been the helper of the orphan.

15 Break the arm of the wicked and evildoers;
     seek out their wickedness until you find none.
16 The LORD is king forever and ever;
     the nations shall perish from his land.

17 O LORD, you will hear the desire of the meek;
     you will strengthen their heart, you will
        incline your ear
18 to do justice for the orphan and the oppressed,
     so that those from earth may strike terror no
        more.[a]

PSALM 11

Song of Trust in God

To the leader. Of David.

1 In the LORD I take refuge; how can you say to me,
     "Flee like a bird to the mountains;[b]

a Meaning of Heb uncertain   b Gk Syr Jerome Tg: Heb *flee to
your mountain, O bird*

2 for look, the wicked bend the bow,
  they have fitted their arrow to the string,
  to shoot in the dark at the upright in
    heart.
3 If the foundations are destroyed,
  what can the righteous do?"

4 The LORD is in his holy temple;
  the LORD's throne is in heaven.
  His eyes behold, his gaze examines
    humankind.
5 The LORD tests the righteous and the wicked,
  and his soul hates the lover of violence.
6 On the wicked he will rain coals of fire and
    sulfur;
  a scorching wind shall be the portion of their
    cup.
7 For the LORD is righteous;
  he loves righteous deeds;
  the upright shall behold his face.

PSALM 12

Plea for Help in Evil Times

*To the leader: according to The Sheminith.
A Psalm of David.*

1 Help, O LORD, for there is no longer anyone who
    is godly;
  the faithful have disappeared from
    humankind.
2 They utter lies to each other;
  with flattering lips and a double heart they
    speak.

3 May the LORD cut off all flattering lips,
  the tongue that makes great boasts,
4 those who say, "With our tongues we will
    prevail;
  our lips are our own—who is our master?"

5 "Because the poor are despoiled, because the
    needy groan,
  I will now rise up," says the LORD;
  "I will place them in the safety for which they
    long."
6 The promises of the LORD are promises that are
    pure,
  silver refined in a furnace on the ground,
  purified seven times.

7 You, O LORD, will protect us;
  you will guard us from this generation
    forever.
8 On every side the wicked prowl,
  as vileness is exalted among humankind.

PSALM 13

Prayer for Deliverance from Enemies

To the leader. A Psalm of David.

1 How long, O LORD? Will you forget me forever?
  How long will you hide your face from me?
2 How long must I bear pain[a] in my soul,
  and have sorrow in my heart all day long?
  How long shall my enemy be exalted over me?

3 Consider and answer me, O LORD my God!
  Give light to my eyes, or I will sleep the sleep
    of death,
4 and my enemy will say, "I have prevailed";
  my foes will rejoice because I am shaken.

5 But I trusted in your steadfast love;
  my heart shall rejoice in your salvation.
6 I will sing to the LORD,
  because he has dealt bountifully with me.

PSALM 14

Denunciation of Godlessness

To the leader. Of David.

1 Fools say in their hearts, "There is no God."
  They are corrupt, they do abominable deeds;
  there is no one who does good.

2 The LORD looks down from heaven on
    humankind
  to see if there are any who are wise,
  who seek after God.

3 They have all gone astray, they are all alike
    perverse;
  there is no one who does good,
  no, not one.

4 Have they no knowledge, all the evildoers
  who eat up my people as they eat bread,
  and do not call upon the LORD?

5 There they shall be in great terror,
  for God is with the company of the righteous.
6 You would confound the plans of the poor,
  but the LORD is their refuge.

7 O that deliverance for Israel would come from
    Zion!
  When the LORD restores the fortunes of his
    people,
  Jacob will rejoice; Israel will be glad.

---

a Syr: Heb *hold counsels*

PSALM 15

Who Shall Abide in God's Sanctuary?

A Psalm of David.

1 O LORD, who may abide in your tent?
   Who may dwell on your holy hill?

2 Those who walk blamelessly, and do what is
      right,
   and speak the truth from their heart;
3 who do not slander with their tongue,
   and do no evil to their friends,
      nor take up a reproach against their
      neighbors;
4 in whose eyes the wicked are despised,
   but who honor those who fear the LORD;
who stand by their oath even to their hurt;
5 who do not lend money at interest,
   and do not take a bribe against the
      innocent.

Those who do these things shall never be
   moved.

Believing

Although it was written thousands of years
ago, Psalm 14 could have been written
about today's world. The earth is still filled with
those who freely say there is no God. Our faith
may tell us that such beliefs are foolish, but
all people have the freedom to believe as they
choose. One cannot be forced to believe in God.

How do we get through to those who refuse to
believe? Perhaps the most powerful way we can
show others that God exists is through our own
actions. God's presence in our world is most
clearly revealed when we love one another. We
must also trust that God is already at work in the
lives of those who do not believe, and hope that
one day their eyes will be opened to the presence of God in their lives.

▶ Psalm 14

PSALM 16

Song of Trust and Security in God

A Miktam of David.

1 Protect me, O God, for in you I take refuge.
2 I say to the LORD, "You are my Lord;
   I have no good apart from you."[a]

3 As for the holy ones in the land, they are the
      noble,
   in whom is all my delight.

4 Those who choose another god multiply their
      sorrows;[b]
   their drink offerings of blood I will not
      pour out
   or take their names upon my lips.

5 The LORD is my chosen portion and my cup;
   you hold my lot.
6 The boundary lines have fallen for me in
      pleasant places;
   I have a goodly heritage.

7 I bless the LORD who gives me counsel;
   in the night also my heart instructs me.
8 I keep the LORD always before me;
   because he is at my right hand, I shall not be
      moved.

9 Therefore my heart is glad, and my soul rejoices;
   my body also rests secure.
10 For you do not give me up to Sheol,
   or let your faithful one see the Pit.

11 You show me the path of life.
   In your presence there is fullness of joy;
   in your right hand are pleasures forevermore.

PSALM 17

Prayer for Deliverance from Persecutors

A Prayer of David.

1 Hear a just cause, O LORD; attend to my cry;
   give ear to my prayer from lips free of deceit.
2 From you let my vindication come;
   let your eyes see the right.

3 If you try my heart, if you visit me by night,
   if you test me, you will find no wickedness
      in me;
   my mouth does not transgress.

---

a Jerome Tg: Meaning of Heb uncertain   b Cn: Meaning of Heb
uncertain

Cultural Connection

Living in Your Tent, on Your Holy Hill

Native Americans can appreciate the imagery of Psalm 15. Both tents and hills have a sacred meaning for them. The Lakota have the phrase *mit-a-ku-ye O-ya-sin*, which means "all my relatives." This phrase is often used at the end of a prayer, much like "amen." It expresses the deep belief that all human beings are our brothers and sisters, and we all belong in the Holy Tent of the Great Spirit. All creatures—the two-legged and the four-legged, those that crawl and those that fly—are our relatives. In fact, we are related to all of creation—the sea, the rocks, the caves, the sky, the trees, the holy hills. Native Americans understand human beings as connected to all creation, and they believe that any harm we do to creation we do to ourselves.

▶ **Psalm 15**

4 As for what others do, by the word of your lips
  I have avoided the ways of the violent.
5 My steps have held fast to your paths;
  my feet have not slipped.

6 I call upon you, for you will answer me, O God;
  incline your ear to me, hear my words.
7 Wondrously show your steadfast love,
  O savior of those who seek refuge
  from their adversaries at your right hand.

8 Guard me as the apple of the eye;
  hide me in the shadow of your wings,
9 from the wicked who despoil me,
  my deadly enemies who surround me.
10 They close their hearts to pity;
  with their mouths they speak arrogantly.
11 They track me down;[a] now they surround me;
  they set their eyes to cast me to the ground.
12 They are like a lion eager to tear,
  like a young lion lurking in ambush.

13 Rise up, O LORD, confront them, overthrow them!
  By your sword deliver my life from the
    wicked,
14 from mortals—by your hand, O LORD—
  from mortals whose portion in life is in this
    world.
  May their bellies be filled with what you have
    stored up for them;
  may their children have more than enough;
  may they leave something over to their little
    ones.

15 As for me, I shall behold your face in
  righteousness;

when I awake I shall be satisfied, beholding
  your likeness.

PSALM 18

Royal Thanksgiving for Victory

To the leader. A Psalm of David the servant of the LORD, who addressed the words of this song to the LORD on the day when the LORD delivered him from the hand of all his enemies, and from the hand of Saul. He said:

1 I love you, O LORD, my strength.
2 The LORD is my rock, my fortress, and my
    deliverer,
  my God, my rock in whom I take refuge,
  my shield, and the horn of my salvation, my
    stronghold.
3 I call upon the LORD, who is worthy to be praised,
  so I shall be saved from my enemies.

4 The cords of death encompassed me;
  the torrents of perdition assailed me;
5 the cords of Sheol entangled me;
  the snares of death confronted me.

6 In my distress I called upon the LORD;
  to my God I cried for help.
  From his temple he heard my voice,
  and my cry to him reached his ears.

7 Then the earth reeled and rocked;
  the foundations also of the mountains
    trembled

---

a One Ms Compare Syr: MT *Our steps*

and quaked, because he was angry.
8 Smoke went up from his nostrils,
  and devouring fire from his mouth;
  glowing coals flamed forth from him.
9 He bowed the heavens, and came down;
  thick darkness was under his feet.
10 He rode on a cherub, and flew;
  he came swiftly upon the wings of the wind.
11 He made darkness his covering around him,
  his canopy thick clouds dark with water.
12 Out of the brightness before him
  there broke through his clouds
  hailstones and coals of fire.
13 The LORD also thundered in the heavens,
  and the Most High uttered his voice.*a*
14 And he sent out his arrows, and scattered them;
  he flashed forth lightnings, and routed them.
15 Then the channels of the sea were seen,
  and the foundations of the world were laid
    bare
  at your rebuke, O LORD,
  at the blast of the breath of your nostrils.

16 He reached down from on high, he took me;
  he drew me out of mighty waters.
17 He delivered me from my strong enemy,
  and from those who hated me;
  for they were too mighty for me.
18 They confronted me in the day of my calamity;
  but the LORD was my support.
19 He brought me out into a broad place;
  he delivered me, because he delighted in me.

20 The LORD rewarded me according to my
    righteousness;
  according to the cleanness of my hands he
    recompensed me.
21 For I have kept the ways of the LORD,
  and have not wickedly departed from my
    God.
22 For all his ordinances were before me,
  and his statutes I did not put away from me.
23 I was blameless before him,
  and I kept myself from guilt.
24 Therefore the LORD has recompensed me
    according to my righteousness,
  according to the cleanness of my hands in his
    sight.

25 With the loyal you show yourself loyal;
  with the blameless you show yourself
    blameless;
26 with the pure you show yourself pure;
  and with the crooked you show yourself
    perverse.
27 For you deliver a humble people,

  but the haughty eyes you bring down.
28 It is you who light my lamp;
  the LORD, my God, lights up my darkness.
29 By you I can crush a troop,
  and by my God I can leap over a wall.
30 This God—his way is perfect;
  the promise of the LORD proves true;
  he is a shield for all who take refuge in him.

31 For who is God except the LORD?
  And who is a rock besides our God?—
32 the God who girded me with strength,
  and made my way safe.
33 He made my feet like the feet of a deer,
  and set me secure on the heights.
34 He trains my hands for war,
  so that my arms can bend a bow of bronze.
35 You have given me the shield of your
    salvation,
  and your right hand has supported me;
  your help*b* has made me great.
36 You gave me a wide place for my steps
    under me,
  and my feet did not slip.
37 I pursued my enemies and overtook them;
  and did not turn back until they were
    consumed.
38 I struck them down, so that they were not able
    to rise;
  they fell under my feet.
39 For you girded me with strength for the battle;
  you made my assailants sink under me.
40 You made my enemies turn their backs to me,
  and those who hated me I destroyed.
41 They cried for help, but there was no one to save
    them;
  they cried to the LORD, but he did not answer
    them.
42 I beat them fine, like dust before the wind;
  I cast them out like the mire of the streets.

43 You delivered me from strife with the peoples;*c*
  you made me head of the nations;
  people whom I had not known served me.
44 As soon as they heard of me they obeyed me;
  foreigners came cringing to me.
45 Foreigners lost heart,
  and came trembling out of their strongholds.

46 The LORD lives! Blessed be my rock,
  and exalted be the God of my salvation,
47 the God who gave me vengeance
  and subdued peoples under me;

a Gk See 2 Sam 22.14: Heb adds *hailstones and coals of fire*
b Or *gentleness*   *c* Gk Tg: Heb *people*

⁴⁸ who delivered me from my enemies;
    indeed, you exalted me above my adversaries;
    you delivered me from the violent.

⁴⁹ For this I will extol you, O LORD, among the
        nations,
    and sing praises to your name.
⁵⁰ Great triumphs he gives to his king,
    and shows steadfast love to his anointed,
    to David and his descendants forever.

PSALM 19

God's Glory in Creation and the Law

To the leader. A Psalm of David.

¹ The heavens are telling the glory of God;
    and the firmament*ᵃ* proclaims his handiwork.
² Day to day pours forth speech,
    and night to night declares knowledge.
³ There is no speech, nor are there words;
    their voice is not heard;
⁴ yet their voice*ᵇ* goes out through all the earth,
    and their words to the end of the world.

In the heavens*ᶜ* he has set a tent for the sun,
⁵ which comes out like a bridegroom from his
        wedding canopy,
    and like a strong man runs its course with
        joy.
⁶ Its rising is from the end of the heavens,
    and its circuit to the end of them;
    and nothing is hid from its heat.

⁷ The law of the LORD is perfect,
    reviving the soul;
the decrees of the LORD are sure,
    making wise the simple;
⁸ the precepts of the LORD are right,
    rejoicing the heart;
the commandment of the LORD is clear,
    enlightening the eyes;
⁹ the fear of the LORD is pure,
    enduring forever;
the ordinances of the LORD are true
    and righteous altogether.
¹⁰ More to be desired are they than gold,
    even much fine gold;
sweeter also than honey,
    and drippings of the honeycomb.

¹¹ Moreover by them is your servant warned;
    in keeping them there is great reward.
¹² But who can detect their errors?
    Clear me from hidden faults.
¹³ Keep back your servant also from the insolent;*ᵈ*

do not let them have dominion over me.
Then I shall be blameless,
    and innocent of great transgression.

¹⁴ Let the words of my mouth and the meditation
        of my heart
    be acceptable to you,
    O LORD, my rock and my redeemer.

PSALM 20

Prayer for Victory

To the leader. A Psalm of David.

¹ The LORD answer you in the day of trouble!
    The name of the God of Jacob protect you!
² May he send you help from the sanctuary,
    and give you support from Zion.

---

a Or *dome*   *b* Gk Jerome Compare Syr: Heb *line*   *c* Heb *In them*   *d* Or *from proud thoughts*

"The Heavens Are Telling the Glory of God"

Does that opening line of Psalm 19 sound familiar? Perhaps you've seen it on a poster or sung it at Mass. The sky constantly tells us how glorious and magnificent God is!

Have you ever watched the awesome show of a thunder and lightning storm? been delighted by a rainbow? marveled at the power behind a tornado or a hurricane? been tickled by a gentle spring breeze? caught snowflakes on your tongue? had leaves dance around you in a brisk autumn wind? lost yourself looking up into a star-filled night? felt breathless watching a magnificent sunset?

As amazing as the sky is, it only hints at how amazing God is! And in the second half of Psalm 19, the psalmist reminds us that God's law is equally wonderful. Read Psalm 19 as your own prayer of praise to God for the many ways God communicates to us.

▶ Psalm 19

3 May he remember all your offerings,
  and regard with favor your burnt sacrifices.
                                          Selah

4 May he grant you your heart's desire,
  and fulfill all your plans.
5 May we shout for joy over your victory,
  and in the name of our God set up our
    banners.
  May the Lord fulfill all your petitions.

6 Now I know that the Lord will help his
    anointed;
  he will answer him from his holy heaven
  with mighty victories by his right hand.
7 Some take pride in chariots, and some in horses,
  but our pride is in the name of the Lord our
    God.
8 They will collapse and fall,
  but we shall rise and stand upright.

9 Give victory to the king, O Lord;
  answer us when we call.*a*

PSALM 21

Thanksgiving for Victory

To the leader. A Psalm of David.

1 In your strength the king rejoices, O Lord,
  and in your help how greatly he exults!
2 You have given him his heart's desire,
  and have not withheld the request of his lips.
                                          Selah

3 For you meet him with rich blessings;
  you set a crown of fine gold on his head.
4 He asked you for life; you gave it to him—
  length of days forever and ever.
5 His glory is great through your help;
  splendor and majesty you bestow on him.
6 You bestow on him blessings forever;
  you make him glad with the joy of your
    presence.
7 For the king trusts in the Lord,
  and through the steadfast love of the Most
    High he shall not be moved.

8 Your hand will find out all your enemies;
  your right hand will find out those who hate
    you.
9 You will make them like a fiery furnace
  when you appear.
  The Lord will swallow them up in his wrath,
  and fire will consume them.
10 You will destroy their offspring from the earth,
  and their children from among humankind.

11 If they plan evil against you,
  if they devise mischief, they will not succeed.
12 For you will put them to flight;
  you will aim at their faces with your bows.

13 Be exalted, O Lord, in your strength!
  We will sing and praise your power.

PSALM 22

Plea for Deliverance from Suffering
and Hostility

To the leader: according to The Deer of the Dawn.
A Psalm of David.

1 My God, my God, why have you forsaken me?
  Why are you so far from helping me, from the
    words of my groaning?
2 O my God, I cry by day, but you do not answer;
  and by night, but find no rest.

3 Yet you are holy,
  enthroned on the praises of Israel.
4 In you our ancestors trusted;
  they trusted, and you delivered them.
5 To you they cried, and were saved;
  in you they trusted, and were not put to
    shame.

6 But I am a worm, and not human;
  scorned by others, and despised by the
    people.
7 All who see me mock at me;
  they make mouths at me, they shake their
    heads;
8 "Commit your cause to the Lord; let him
    deliver—
  let him rescue the one in whom he
    delights!"

9 Yet it was you who took me from the womb;
  you kept me safe on my mother's breast.
10 On you I was cast from my birth,
  and since my mother bore me you have been
    my God.
11 Do not be far from me,
  for trouble is near
  and there is no one to help.

12 Many bulls encircle me,
  strong bulls of Bashan surround me;
13 they open wide their mouths at me,
  like a ravening and roaring lion.

---

a Gk: Heb *give victory, O Lord; let the King answer us when we
call*

¹⁴ I am poured out like water,
and all my bones are out of joint;
my heart is like wax;
it is melted within my breast;

¹⁵ my mouth*a* is dried up like a potsherd,
and my tongue sticks to my jaws;
you lay me in the dust of death.

¹⁶ For dogs are all around me;
a company of evildoers encircles me.
My hands and feet have shriveled;*b*

¹⁷ I can count all my bones.
They stare and gloat over me;

¹⁸ they divide my clothes among themselves,
and for my clothing they cast lots.

¹⁹ But you, O Lord, do not be far away!
O my help, come quickly to my aid!

²⁰ Deliver my soul from the sword,
my life*c* from the power of the dog!

²¹ Save me from the mouth of the lion!

From the horns of the wild oxen you have
rescued*d* me.

²² I will tell of your name to my brothers and
sisters;*e*
in the midst of the congregation I will praise
you:

²³ You who fear the Lord, praise him!
All you offspring of Jacob, glorify him;
stand in awe of him, all you offspring of
Israel!

²⁴ For he did not despise or abhor
the affliction of the afflicted;
he did not hide his face from me,*f*
but heard when I*g* cried to him.

²⁵ From you comes my praise in the great
congregation;
my vows I will pay before those who fear
him.

²⁶ The poor*h* shall eat and be satisfied;
those who seek him shall praise the Lord.
May your hearts live forever!

²⁷ All the ends of the earth shall remember
and turn to the Lord;
and all the families of the nations
shall worship before him.*i*

²⁸ For dominion belongs to the Lord,
and he rules over the nations.

²⁹ To him,*j* indeed, shall all who sleep in*k* the earth
bow down;
before him shall bow all who go down to the
dust,

and I shall live for him.*l*

³⁰ Posterity will serve him;
future generations will be told about the Lord,

³¹ and*m* proclaim his deliverance to a people yet
unborn,
saying that he has done it.

PSALM 23

The Divine Shepherd

A Psalm of David.

¹ The Lord is my shepherd, I shall not want.
² He makes me lie down in green pastures;
he leads me beside still waters;*n*
³ he restores my soul.*o*
He leads me in right paths*p*
for his name's sake.

⁴ Even though I walk through the darkest valley,*q*
I fear no evil;

---

a Cn: Heb *strength*   *b* Meaning of Heb uncertain   *c* Heb *my
only one*   *d* Heb *answered*   *e* Or *kindred*   *f* Heb *him*
g Heb *he*   *h* Or *afflicted*   *i* Gk Syr Jerome: Heb *you*   *j* Cn: Heb
They have eaten and   *k* Cn: Heb *all the fat ones*   *l* Compare Gk
Syr Vg: Heb *and he who cannot keep himself alive*   *m* Compare
Gk: Heb *it will be told about the Lord to the generation,* ³¹*they
will come and*   *n* Heb *waters of rest*   *o* Or *life*   *p* Or *paths of
righteousness*   *q* Or *the valley of the shadow of death*

Write Your Own Psalm

As you may know, there are many types of
psalms (see the introduction to the Book
of Psalms). You may also know that more than
one person wrote the Psalms. Even today there
are psalmists, people who write songs or poems
similar in tone and style to the psalms in the
Bible. Would you like to write your own psalm?
Try it in your journal:

● Choose the type of psalm you want to write.
● Use poetic language and symbolism.
● Illustrate your psalm.
● Set it to music (like the original ones).
● Or, choose an existing Psalm and rewrite it to
reflect a current issue.

Cultural Connection

The Good Shepherd Looks After Us

The famous Psalm 23 offers two images of God: the Good Shepherd and a generous host. Both images speak of God's closeness and gentle care for us. In the New Testament, Jesus appears as the Good Shepherd who gives his life for the life of his sheep (see Jn 10:1–29). He also appears several times as a host, particularly in the stories about the multiplication of the loaves and the Last Supper.

Similar images repeat time and again in Hispanic homes. The following traditional sayings are just some examples of the caring and generous attitudes among Hispanic families: My home is your home *(Mi casa es su casa)*; God help you! What can I do for you? *(¡Dios te ampare! ¿Cómo puedo ayudarte?)*; Where two eat, three eat; where six eat, seven eat *(Donde comen dos comen tres; donde comen seis comen siete)*; Welcome! We just add water to the beans *(¡Bienvenidos! Le echamos más agua a los frijoles)*; and Stay with us! From wall to wall, all is mattress *(¡Quédense con nosotros! De pared a pared todo es colchón!)*.

As a Christian, you should pray Psalm 23, feeling the closeness of Jesus, the Good Shepherd, and asking his help to be a good shepherd for people in need:

- Pray the psalm slowly, letting God fill you with peace and security.
- Pray the psalm again, this time thinking of friends who might be feeling like sheep without a shepherd. How can you lead them to Jesus? How can you care more for them?

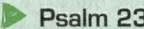 Psalm 23

PS

for you are with me;
   your rod and your staff—
   they comfort me.

5 You prepare a table before me
   in the presence of my enemies;
you anoint my head with oil;
   my cup overflows.
6 Surely[a] goodness and mercy[b] shall follow me
   all the days of my life,
and I shall dwell in the house of the LORD
   my whole life long.[c]

PSALM 24

Entrance into the Temple

Of David. A Psalm.

1 The earth is the LORD's and all that is in it,
   the world, and those who live in it;
2 for he has founded it on the seas,
   and established it on the rivers.

3 Who shall ascend the hill of the LORD?
   And who shall stand in his holy place?
4 Those who have clean hands and pure hearts,
who do not lift up their souls to what is false,
   and do not swear deceitfully.
5 They will receive blessing from the LORD,
   and vindication from the God of their salvation.
6 Such is the company of those who seek him,
   who seek the face of the God of Jacob.[d]
                                   Selah

7 Lift up your heads, O gates!
   and be lifted up, O ancient doors!
   that the King of glory may come in.
8 Who is the King of glory?
   The LORD, strong and mighty,
   the LORD, mighty in battle.
9 Lift up your heads, O gates!
   and be lifted up, O ancient doors!
   that the King of glory may come in.
10 Who is this King of glory?
   The LORD of hosts,
   he is the King of glory.   *Selah*

---

a Or *Only*   b Or *kindness*   c Heb *for length of days*   d Gk Syr: Heb *your face, O Jacob*

PSALM 25
Prayer for Guidance and for Deliverance
Of David.

1 To you, O Lord, I lift up my soul.
2 O my God, in you I trust;
    do not let me be put to shame;
    do not let my enemies exult over me.
3 Do not let those who wait for you be put to
        shame;
    let them be ashamed who are wantonly
        treacherous.

4 Make me to know your ways, O Lord;
    teach me your paths.
5 Lead me in your truth, and teach me,
    for you are the God of my salvation;
    for you I wait all day long.

6 Be mindful of your mercy, O Lord, and of your
        steadfast love,
    for they have been from of old.
7 Do not remember the sins of my youth or my
        transgressions;
    according to your steadfast love remember me,
    for your goodness' sake, O Lord!

8 Good and upright is the Lord;
    therefore he instructs sinners in the way.
9 He leads the humble in what is right,
    and teaches the humble his way.
10 All the paths of the Lord are steadfast love and
        faithfulness,
    for those who keep his covenant and his
        decrees.

11 For your name's sake, O Lord,
    pardon my guilt, for it is great.
12 Who are they that fear the Lord?
    He will teach them the way that they should
        choose.

13 They will abide in prosperity,
    and their children shall possess the land.
14 The friendship of the Lord is for those who fear
        him,
    and he makes his covenant known to them.
15 My eyes are ever toward the Lord,
    for he will pluck my feet out of the net.

16 Turn to me and be gracious to me,
    for I am lonely and afflicted.
17 Relieve the troubles of my heart,
    and bring me*a* out of my distress.
18 Consider my affliction and my trouble,
    and forgive all my sins.

19 Consider how many are my foes,
    and with what violent hatred they hate me.
20 O guard my life, and deliver me;
    do not let me be put to shame, for I take
        refuge in you.
21 May integrity and uprightness preserve me,
    for I wait for you.

22 Redeem Israel, O God,
    out of all its troubles.

---

a Or *The troubles of my heart are enlarged; bring me*

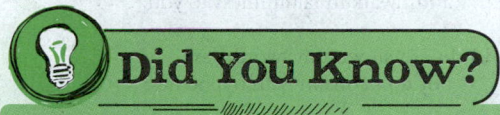

Did You Know?

Temple Worship

When Israel was ruled by kings (1000–587 BC), worship in the Temple at Jerusalem was an important part of the people's religious life. Many of the psalms, like Psalm 24, refer to going up to the Temple (the "holy place" in verse 3). Although the first Temple was destroyed in 587 BC, it was later rebuilt. Temple worship started again and continued into Jesus' time. This is what the priests did during some of the Temple ceremonies:

Daily Temple worship
- every morning, presented a burnt offering (a year-old male lamb), grain, drink, and an incense offering
- every evening, presented a second burnt offering and a cereal offering

Sabbath (weekly) Temple worship
- gave two additional burnt offerings
- replaced the twelve loaves of bread, called the bread of Presence (see 1 Kings 7:48, Mt 12:4, Heb 9:2), recalling the manna with which God fed Israel in the desert
- made an incense offering

Monthly and festival Temple worship
- blew the trumpet
- presented additional burnt offerings and a sin offering (a male goat)
- on the Day of Atonement, laid their hands on a living goat while confessing the people's sins and then sent the goat away into the wilderness

P
S

PSALM 26

Plea for Justice and Declaration of Righteousness

Of David.

1 Vindicate me, O LORD,
    for I have walked in my integrity,
    and I have trusted in the LORD without
        wavering.
2 Prove me, O LORD, and try me;
    test my heart and mind.
3 For your steadfast love is before my eyes,
    and I walk in faithfulness to you.[a]

4 I do not sit with the worthless,
    nor do I consort with hypocrites;

5 I hate the company of evildoers,
    and will not sit with the wicked.

6 I wash my hands in innocence,
    and go around your altar, O LORD,
7 singing aloud a song of thanksgiving,
    and telling all your wondrous deeds.

8 O LORD, I love the house in which you dwell,
    and the place where your glory abides.
9 Do not sweep me away with sinners,
    nor my life with the bloodthirsty,
10 those in whose hands are evil devices,
    and whose right hands are full of bribes.

11 But as for me, I walk in my integrity;
    redeem me, and be gracious to me.
12 My foot stands on level ground;
    in the great congregation I will bless the LORD.

Pray It!

Integrity and Values

People with integrity have a fundamental set of core values—values that have been instilled in them by parents, teachers, mentors, and role models. When they act, they consistently make sure all their actions and decisions accurately reflect these core principles. There is no disconnect between what they say they believe and what they actually do.

It is impossible for us to have integrity if we follow one set of values in one situation and another set of values in a different situation. The integrity of the writer of Psalm 26 comes from following God in everything (see Ps 26:1). The psalmist even wants to be tested by God (see verse 2) to be sure of complete faithfulness! To have the kind of integrity that the psalmist writes about, we have to let God be the only ruler of our lives. Being able to do that takes a lifetime of growth and conversion.

- What values are you committed to consistently?
- Can you think of times when your actions did not reflect your values or beliefs?

Pray that God will give you strength to do what is right, even when it is most difficult.

▶ **Psalm 26**

PSALM 27

Triumphant Song of Confidence

Of David.

1 The LORD is my light and my salvation;
    whom shall I fear?
The LORD is the stronghold[b] of my life;
    of whom shall I be afraid?

2 When evildoers assail me
    to devour my flesh—
my adversaries and foes—
    they shall stumble and fall.

3 Though an army encamp against me,
    my heart shall not fear;
though war rise up against me,
    yet I will be confident.

4 One thing I asked of the LORD,
    that will I seek after:
to live in the house of the LORD
    all the days of my life,
to behold the beauty of the LORD,
    and to inquire in his temple.

5 For he will hide me in his shelter
    in the day of trouble;
he will conceal me under the cover of his tent;
    he will set me high on a rock.

6 Now my head is lifted up
    above my enemies all around me,

a Or *in your faithfulness*   b Or *refuge*

and I will offer in his tent
    sacrifices with shouts of joy;
I will sing and make melody to the LORD.

7 Hear, O LORD, when I cry aloud,
    be gracious to me and answer me!
8 "Come," my heart says, "seek his face!"
    Your face, LORD, do I seek.
9   Do not hide your face from me.

Do not turn your servant away in anger,
    you who have been my help.
Do not cast me off, do not forsake me,
    O God of my salvation!
10 If my father and mother forsake me,
    the LORD will take me up.

11 Teach me your way, O LORD,
    and lead me on a level path
    because of my enemies.
12 Do not give me up to the will of my adversaries,
    for false witnesses have risen against me,
    and they are breathing out violence.

13 I believe that I shall see the goodness of the LORD
    in the land of the living.
14 Wait for the LORD;
    be strong, and let your heart take courage;
    wait for the LORD!

PSALM 28

Prayer for Help and Thanksgiving for It
Of David.

1 To you, O LORD, I call;
    my rock, do not refuse to hear me,
for if you are silent to me,
    I shall be like those who go down to the Pit.
2 Hear the voice of my supplication,
    as I cry to you for help,
as I lift up my hands
    toward your most holy sanctuary.[a]

3 Do not drag me away with the wicked,
    with those who are workers of evil,
who speak peace with their neighbors,
    while mischief is in their hearts.
4 Repay them according to their work,
    and according to the evil of their deeds;
repay them according to the work of their
    hands;
    render them their due reward.
5 Because they do not regard the works of the
    LORD,
    or the work of his hands,

The Eye of the Storm

Thunderstorms can be frightening. They often come up quickly and without warning. The winds and lightning that accompany them can be destructive. Children and animals (okay, lots of adults too) are often afraid at the sheer force of it all.

It would be difficult to read Psalm 29 aloud and not be expressive. Statements like "the God of glory thunders" (verse 3), "the voice of the LORD breaks the cedars" (verse 5), and "the voice of the LORD flashes forth flames of fire" (verse 7) evoke a divine splendor that we do not often hear about. The psalmist speaks with admiration about the power and majesty of God.

When have you experienced the awesome power of God?

▶ Psalm 29

he will break them down and build them up
    no more.

6 Blessed be the LORD,
    for he has heard the sound of my pleadings.
7 The LORD is my strength and my shield;
    in him my heart trusts;
so I am helped, and my heart exults,
    and with my song I give thanks to him.

8 The LORD is the strength of his people;
    he is the saving refuge of his anointed.
9 O save your people, and bless your heritage;
    be their shepherd, and carry them forever.

PSALM 29

The Voice of God in a Great Storm
A Psalm of David.

1 Ascribe to the LORD, O heavenly beings,[b]
    ascribe to the LORD glory and strength.

---

a Heb *your innermost sanctuary*   b Heb *sons of gods*

P
S

2 Ascribe to the Lord the glory of his name;
    worship the Lord in holy splendor.

3 The voice of the Lord is over the waters;
    the God of glory thunders,
    the Lord, over mighty waters.
4 The voice of the Lord is powerful;
    the voice of the Lord is full of majesty.

5 The voice of the Lord breaks the cedars;
    the Lord breaks the cedars of Lebanon.
6 He makes Lebanon skip like a calf,
    and Sirion like a young wild ox.

7 The voice of the Lord flashes forth flames of
    fire.
8 The voice of the Lord shakes the wilderness;
    the Lord shakes the wilderness of Kadesh.

9 The voice of the Lord causes the oaks to whirl,[a]
    and strips the forest bare;
    and in his temple all say, "Glory!"

10 The Lord sits enthroned over the flood;
    the Lord sits enthroned as king forever.
11 May the Lord give strength to his people!
    May the Lord bless his people with peace!

PSALM 30

Thanksgiving for Recovery from Grave Illness

A Psalm. A Song at the dedication of the temple.
Of David.

1 I will extol you, O Lord, for you have drawn
    me up,
    and did not let my foes rejoice over me.
2 O Lord my God, I cried to you for help,
    and you have healed me.
3 O Lord, you brought up my soul from Sheol,
    restored me to life from among those gone
    down to the Pit.[b]

4 Sing praises to the Lord, O you his faithful ones,
    and give thanks to his holy name.
5 For his anger is but for a moment;
    his favor is for a lifetime.
Weeping may linger for the night,
    but joy comes with the morning.

6 As for me, I said in my prosperity,
    "I shall never be moved."
7 By your favor, O Lord,
    you had established me as a strong mountain;
you hid your face;
    I was dismayed.

8 To you, O Lord, I cried,
    and to the Lord I made supplication:
9 "What profit is there in my death,
    if I go down to the Pit?
Will the dust praise you?
    Will it tell of your faithfulness?
10 Hear, O Lord, and be gracious to me!
    O Lord, be my helper!"

11 You have turned my mourning into dancing;
    you have taken off my sackcloth
    and clothed me with joy,
12 so that my soul[c] may praise you and not be
    silent.
    O Lord my God, I will give thanks to you
    forever.

PSALM 31

Prayer and Praise for Deliverance
from Enemies

To the leader. A Psalm of David.

1 In you, O Lord, I seek refuge;
    do not let me ever be put to shame;
    in your righteousness deliver me.
2 Incline your ear to me;
    rescue me speedily.
Be a rock of refuge for me,
    a strong fortress to save me.

3 You are indeed my rock and my fortress;
    for your name's sake lead me and guide me,
4 take me out of the net that is hidden for me,
    for you are my refuge.
5 Into your hand I commit my spirit;
    you have redeemed me, O Lord, faithful God.

6 You hate[d] those who pay regard to worthless
    idols,
    but I trust in the Lord.
7 I will exult and rejoice in your steadfast love,
    because you have seen my affliction;
    you have taken heed of my adversities,
8 and have not delivered me into the hand of the
    enemy;
    you have set my feet in a broad place.

9 Be gracious to me, O Lord, for I am in distress;
    my eye wastes away from grief,
    my soul and body also.
10 For my life is spent with sorrow,

---

a Or causes the deer to calve   b Or that I should not go down
to the Pit   c Heb that glory   d One Heb Ms Gk Syr Jerome: MT
I hate

Cultural Connection

Courage

Psalm 31 ends "Be strong, and let your heart take courage, / all you who wait for the LORD" (verse 24). Courage is an important value for many Native American peoples. For the Lakota tribe, it is one of four primary values. The Lakota word for courage is *woo-hit-i-ka*.

Leaders particularly have to be brave. It takes courage to make unpopular decisions and to go against peer pressure. It takes courage to do the right thing when the wrong thing might be easier or more enjoyable. It takes courage to protect others and to care for their needs. Because these kinds of actions take courage, practicing them will earn you honor.

What is the most courageous thing you have done for the sake of someone else?

To explore the other primary Lakota virtues, see the "Cultural Connections" articles for Psalms 73, 89, and 112.

▶ **Psalm 31**

and my years with sighing;
my strength fails because of my misery,[a]
and my bones waste away.

11 I am the scorn of all my adversaries,
a horror[b] to my neighbors,
an object of dread to my acquaintances;
those who see me in the street flee from me.
12 I have passed out of mind like one who is dead;
I have become like a broken vessel.
13 For I hear the whispering of many—
terror all around!—
as they scheme together against me,
as they plot to take my life.

14 But I trust in you, O LORD;
I say, "You are my God."
15 My times are in your hand;
deliver me from the hand of my enemies and
persecutors.
16 Let your face shine upon your servant;
save me in your steadfast love.
17 Do not let me be put to shame, O LORD,
for I call on you;
let the wicked be put to shame;
let them go dumbfounded to Sheol.
18 Let the lying lips be stilled
that speak insolently against the righteous
with pride and contempt.

19 O how abundant is your goodness
that you have laid up for those who fear you,
and accomplished for those who take refuge in
you,
in the sight of everyone!

20 In the shelter of your presence you hide them
from human plots;
you hold them safe under your shelter
from contentious tongues.

21 Blessed be the LORD,
for he has wondrously shown his steadfast
love to me
when I was beset as a city under siege.
22 I had said in my alarm,
"I am driven far[c] from your sight."
But you heard my supplications
when I cried out to you for help.

23 Love the LORD, all you his saints.
The LORD preserves the faithful,
but abundantly repays the one who acts
haughtily.
24 Be strong, and let your heart take courage,
all you who wait for the LORD.

PSALM 32

The Joy of Forgiveness

Of David. A Maskil.

1 Happy are those whose transgression is
forgiven,
whose sin is covered.
2 Happy are those to whom the LORD imputes no
iniquity,
and in whose spirit there is no deceit.

---

a Gk Syr: Heb *my iniquity*   b Cn: Heb *exceedingly*   c Another reading is *cut off*

3 While I kept silence, my body wasted away
    through my groaning all day long.
4 For day and night your hand was heavy upon me;
    my strength was dried up*a* as by the heat of
       summer.   *Selah*

5 Then I acknowledged my sin to you,
    and I did not hide my iniquity;
I said, "I will confess my transgressions to the
    Lord,"
    and you forgave the guilt of my sin.   *Selah*

6 Therefore let all who are faithful
    offer prayer to you;
at a time of distress,*b* the rush of mighty waters
    shall not reach them.
7 You are a hiding place for me;
    you preserve me from trouble;
    you surround me with glad cries of
       deliverance.   *Selah*

8 I will instruct you and teach you the way you
       should go;
I will counsel you with my eye upon you.
9 Do not be like a horse or a mule, without
       understanding,
    whose temper must be curbed with bit and
       bridle,
    else it will not stay near you.

10 Many are the torments of the wicked,
    but steadfast love surrounds those who trust
       in the Lord.
11 Be glad in the Lord and rejoice, O righteous,
    and shout for joy, all you upright in heart.

PSALM 33

The Greatness and Goodness of God

1 Rejoice in the Lord, O you righteous.
    Praise befits the upright.
2 Praise the Lord with the lyre;
    make melody to him with the harp of ten
       strings.
3 Sing to him a new song;
    play skillfully on the strings, with loud shouts.

4 For the word of the Lord is upright,
    and all his work is done in faithfulness.
5 He loves righteousness and justice;
    the earth is full of the steadfast love of the
       Lord.

6 By the word of the Lord the heavens were made,
    and all their host by the breath of his mouth.

7 He gathered the waters of the sea as in a bottle;
    he put the deeps in storehouses.

8 Let all the earth fear the Lord;
    let all the inhabitants of the world stand in
       awe of him.
9 For he spoke, and it came to be;
    he commanded, and it stood firm.

10 The Lord brings the counsel of the nations to
       nothing;
    he frustrates the plans of the peoples.
11 The counsel of the Lord stands forever,
    the thoughts of his heart to all generations.
12 Happy is the nation whose God is the Lord,
    the people whom he has chosen as his
       heritage.

13 The Lord looks down from heaven;
    he sees all humankind.
14 From where he sits enthroned he watches
    all the inhabitants of the earth—
15 he who fashions the hearts of them all,
    and observes all their deeds.
16 A king is not saved by his great army;
    a warrior is not delivered by his great strength.
17 The war horse is a vain hope for victory,
    and by its great might it cannot save.

18 Truly the eye of the Lord is on those who fear
       him,
    on those who hope in his steadfast love,
19 to deliver their soul from death,
    and to keep them alive in famine.

20 Our soul waits for the Lord;
    he is our help and shield.
21 Our heart is glad in him,
    because we trust in his holy name.
22 Let your steadfast love, O Lord, be upon us,
    even as we hope in you.

PSALM 34

Praise for Deliverance from Trouble

Of David, when he feigned madness before Abimelech,
    so that he drove him out, and he went away.

1 I will bless the Lord at all times;
    his praise shall continually be in my mouth.
2 My soul makes its boast in the Lord;
    let the humble hear and be glad.
3 O magnify the Lord with me,
    and let us exalt his name together.

---

a Meaning of Heb uncertain   *b* Cn: Heb *at a time of finding only*

4 I sought the Lord, and he answered me,
and delivered me from all my fears.
5 Look to him, and be radiant;
so your[a] faces shall never be ashamed.
6 This poor soul cried, and was heard by the Lord,
and was saved from every trouble.
7 The angel of the Lord encamps
around those who fear him, and delivers them.
8 O taste and see that the Lord is good;
happy are those who take refuge in him.
9 O fear the Lord, you his holy ones,
for those who fear him have no want.
10 The young lions suffer want and hunger,
but those who seek the Lord lack no good
thing.

11 Come, O children, listen to me;
I will teach you the fear of the Lord.
12 Which of you desires life,
and covets many days to enjoy good?
13 Keep your tongue from evil,
and your lips from speaking deceit.
14 Depart from evil, and do good;
seek peace, and pursue it.

15 The eyes of the Lord are on the righteous,
and his ears are open to their cry.
16 The face of the Lord is against evildoers,
to cut off the remembrance of them from the
earth.
17 When the righteous cry for help, the Lord hears,
and rescues them from all their troubles.
18 The Lord is near to the brokenhearted,
and saves the crushed in spirit.

19 Many are the afflictions of the righteous,
but the Lord rescues them from them all.
20 He keeps all their bones;
not one of them will be broken.
21 Evil brings death to the wicked,
and those who hate the righteous will be
condemned.
22 The Lord redeems the life of his servants;
none of those who take refuge in him will be
condemned.

PSALM 35

Prayer for Deliverance from Enemies

Of David.

1 Contend, O Lord, with those who contend
with me;
fight against those who fight against me!
2 Take hold of shield and buckler,
and rise up to help me!

3 Draw the spear and javelin
against my pursuers;
say to my soul,
"I am your salvation."

4 Let them be put to shame and dishonor
who seek after my life.
Let them be turned back and confounded
who devise evil against me.
5 Let them be like chaff before the wind,
with the angel of the Lord driving them on.
6 Let their way be dark and slippery,
with the angel of the Lord pursuing them.

7 For without cause they hid their net[b] for me;
without cause they dug a pit[c] for my life.
8 Let ruin come on them unawares.
And let the net that they hid ensnare them;
let them fall in it—to their ruin.

9 Then my soul shall rejoice in the Lord,
exulting in his deliverance.
10 All my bones shall say,
"O Lord, who is like you?
You deliver the weak
from those too strong for them,
the weak and needy from those who despoil
them."

11 Malicious witnesses rise up;
they ask me about things I do not know.
12 They repay me evil for good;
my soul is forlorn.
13 But as for me, when they were sick,
I wore sackcloth;
I afflicted myself with fasting.
I prayed with head bowed[d] on my bosom,
14 as though I grieved for a friend or a brother;
I went about as one who laments for a
mother,
bowed down and in mourning.

15 But at my stumbling they gathered in glee,
they gathered together against me;
ruffians whom I did not know
tore at me without ceasing;
16 they impiously mocked more and more,[e]
gnashing at me with their teeth.

17 How long, O Lord, will you look on?
Rescue me from their ravages,
my life from the lions!

PS

a Gk Syr Jerome: Heb *their* b Heb *a pit, their net* c The word *pit* is transposed from the preceding line d Or *My prayer turned back* e Cn Compare Gk: Heb *like the profanest of mockers of a cake*

18 Then I will thank you in the great congregation;
   in the mighty throng I will praise you.

19 Do not let my treacherous enemies rejoice
     over me,
   or those who hate me without cause wink the
     eye.
20 For they do not speak peace,
   but they conceive deceitful words
   against those who are quiet in the land.
21 They open wide their mouths against me;
   they say, "Aha, Aha,
   our eyes have seen it."

22 You have seen, O Lord; do not be silent!
   O Lord, do not be far from me!
23 Wake up! Bestir yourself for my defense,
   for my cause, my God and my Lord!
24 Vindicate me, O Lord, my God,
   according to your righteousness,
   and do not let them rejoice over me.
25 Do not let them say to themselves,
   "Aha, we have our heart's desire."
   Do not let them say, "We have swallowed
     you[a] up."

26 Let all those who rejoice at my calamity
     be put to shame and confusion;
   let those who exalt themselves against me
     be clothed with shame and dishonor.

27 Let those who desire my vindication
     shout for joy and be glad,
   and say evermore,
   "Great is the Lord,
   who delights in the welfare of his servant."
28 Then my tongue shall tell of your
     righteousness
   and of your praise all day long.

PSALM 36

Human Wickedness and Divine Goodness

To the leader. Of David, the servant of the Lord.

1 Transgression speaks to the wicked
   deep in their hearts;
   there is no fear of God
   before their eyes.
2 For they flatter themselves in their own eyes
   that their iniquity cannot be found out and
     hated.
3 The words of their mouths are mischief and
     deceit;
   they have ceased to act wisely and do good.
4 They plot mischief while on their beds;

they are set on a way that is not good;
   they do not reject evil.

5 Your steadfast love, O Lord, extends to the
     heavens,
   your faithfulness to the clouds.
6 Your righteousness is like the mighty mountains,
   your judgments are like the great deep;
   you save humans and animals alike, O Lord.

7 How precious is your steadfast love, O God!
   All people may take refuge in the shadow of
     your wings.
8 They feast on the abundance of your house,
   and you give them drink from the river of
     your delights.
9 For with you is the fountain of life;
   in your light we see light.

10 O continue your steadfast love to those who
     know you,
   and your salvation to the upright of heart!
11 Do not let the foot of the arrogant tread on me,
   or the hand of the wicked drive me away.
12 There the evildoers lie prostrate;
   they are thrust down, unable to rise.

PSALM 37

Exhortation to Patience and Trust

Of David.

1 Do not fret because of the wicked;
   do not be envious of wrongdoers,
2 for they will soon fade like the grass,
   and wither like the green herb.

3 Trust in the Lord, and do good;
   so you will live in the land, and enjoy security.
4 Take delight in the Lord,
   and he will give you the desires of your heart.

5 Commit your way to the Lord;
   trust in him, and he will act.
6 He will make your vindication shine like the
     light,
   and the justice of your cause like the
     noonday.

7 Be still before the Lord, and wait patiently for
     him;
   do not fret over those who prosper in their
     way,
   over those who carry out evil devices.

---

a Heb *him*

8 Refrain from anger, and forsake wrath.
   Do not fret—it leads only to evil.
9 For the wicked shall be cut off,
   but those who wait for the LORD shall inherit
       the land.

10 Yet a little while, and the wicked will be no more;
   though you look diligently for their place,
       they will not be there.
11 But the meek shall inherit the land,
   and delight themselves in abundant
       prosperity.

12 The wicked plot against the righteous,
   and gnash their teeth at them;
13 but the LORD laughs at the wicked,
   for he sees that their day is coming.

14 The wicked draw the sword and bend their bows
   to bring down the poor and needy,
   to kill those who walk uprightly;
15 their sword shall enter their own heart,
   and their bows shall be broken.

16 Better is a little that the righteous person has
   than the abundance of many wicked.
17 For the arms of the wicked shall be broken,
   but the LORD upholds the righteous.

18 The LORD knows the days of the blameless,
   and their heritage will abide forever;
19 they are not put to shame in evil times,
   in the days of famine they have abundance.

20 But the wicked perish,
   and the enemies of the LORD are like the glory
       of the pastures;
   they vanish—like smoke they vanish away.

21 The wicked borrow, and do not pay back,
   but the righteous are generous and keep
       giving;
22 for those blessed by the LORD shall inherit the
       land,
   but those cursed by him shall be cut off.

23 Our steps*a* are made firm by the LORD,
   when he delights in our*b* way;
24 though we stumble,*c* we*d* shall not fall headlong,
   for the LORD holds us*e* by the hand.

25 I have been young, and now am old,
   yet I have not seen the righteous forsaken
       or their children begging bread.
26 They are ever giving liberally and lending,
   and their children become a blessing.

27 Depart from evil, and do good;
   so you shall abide forever.
28 For the LORD loves justice;
   he will not forsake his faithful ones.

The righteous shall be kept safe forever,
   but the children of the wicked shall be cut off.
29 The righteous shall inherit the land,
   and live in it forever.

30 The mouths of the righteous utter wisdom,
   and their tongues speak justice.
31 The law of their God is in their hearts;
   their steps do not slip.

32 The wicked watch for the righteous,
   and seek to kill them.
33 The LORD will not abandon them to their
       power,
   or let them be condemned when they are
       brought to trial.

34 Wait for the LORD, and keep to his way,
   and he will exalt you to inherit the land;
   you will look on the destruction of the
       wicked.

35 I have seen the wicked oppressing,
   and towering like a cedar of Lebanon.*f*
36 Again I*g* passed by, and they were no more;
   though I sought them, they could not be
       found.

37 Mark the blameless, and behold the upright,
   for there is posterity for the peaceable.
38 But transgressors shall be altogether destroyed;
   the posterity of the wicked shall be cut off.

39 The salvation of the righteous is from the LORD;
   he is their refuge in the time of trouble.
40 The LORD helps them and rescues them;
   he rescues them from the wicked, and saves
       them,
   because they take refuge in him.

PSALM 38

A Penitent Sufferer's Plea for Healing

A Psalm of David, for the memorial offering.

1 O LORD, do not rebuke me in your anger,
   or discipline me in your wrath.

---

a Heb *A man's steps*   b Heb *his*   c Heb *he stumbles*
d Heb *he*   e Heb *him*   f Gk: Meaning of Heb uncertain
g Gk Syr Jerome: Heb *he*

2 For your arrows have sunk into me,
　　and your hand has come down on me.

3 There is no soundness in my flesh
　　because of your indignation;
there is no health in my bones
　　because of my sin.
4 For my iniquities have gone over my head;
　　they weigh like a burden too heavy for me.

5 My wounds grow foul and fester
　　because of my foolishness;
6 I am utterly bowed down and prostrate;
　　all day long I go around mourning.
7 For my loins are filled with burning,
　　and there is no soundness in my flesh.
8 I am utterly spent and crushed;
　　I groan because of the tumult of my heart.

9 O Lord, all my longing is known to you;
　　my sighing is not hidden from you.
10 My heart throbs, my strength fails me;
　　as for the light of my eyes—it also has gone
　　　from me.
11 My friends and companions stand aloof from
　　　my affliction,
　　and my neighbors stand far off.

12 Those who seek my life lay their snares;
　　those who seek to hurt me speak of ruin,
　　and meditate treachery all day long.

13 But I am like the deaf, I do not hear;
　　like the mute, who cannot speak.
14 Truly, I am like one who does not hear,
　　and in whose mouth is no retort.

15 But it is for you, O Lord, that I wait;
　　it is you, O Lord my God, who will
　　　answer.
16 For I pray, "Only do not let them rejoice
　　　over me,
　　those who boast against me when my foot
　　　slips."

17 For I am ready to fall,
　　and my pain is ever with me.
18 I confess my iniquity;
　　I am sorry for my sin.
19 Those who are my foes without cause[a] are
　　　mighty,
　　and many are those who hate me
　　　wrongfully.
20 Those who render me evil for good
　　are my adversaries because I follow after
　　　good.

21 Do not forsake me, O Lord;
　　O my God, do not be far from me;
22 make haste to help me,
　　O Lord, my salvation.

PSALM 39

Prayer for Wisdom and Forgiveness

To the leader: to Jeduthun. A Psalm of David.

1 I said, "I will guard my ways
　　that I may not sin with my tongue;
I will keep a muzzle on my mouth
　　as long as the wicked are in my presence."
2 I was silent and still;
　　I held my peace to no avail;
my distress grew worse,
3 　　my heart became hot within me.
While I mused, the fire burned;
　　then I spoke with my tongue:

4 "Lord, let me know my end,
　　and what is the measure of my days;
　　let me know how fleeting my life is.
5 You have made my days a few handbreadths,
　　and my lifetime is as nothing in your sight.
Surely everyone stands as a mere breath.　　Selah
6 　　Surely everyone goes about like a shadow.
Surely for nothing they are in turmoil;
　　they heap up, and do not know who will
　　　gather.

7 "And now, O Lord, what do I wait for?
　　My hope is in you.
8 Deliver me from all my transgressions.
　　Do not make me the scorn of the fool.
9 I am silent; I do not open my mouth,
　　for it is you who have done it.
10 Remove your stroke from me;
　　I am worn down by the blows[b] of your hand.

11 "You chastise mortals
　　in punishment for sin,
consuming like a moth what is dear to them;
　　surely everyone is a mere breath.　　Selah

12 "Hear my prayer, O Lord,
　　and give ear to my cry;
　　do not hold your peace at my tears.
For I am your passing guest,
　　an alien, like all my forebears.
13 Turn your gaze away from me, that I may smile
　　　again,
　　before I depart and am no more."

---

a Q Ms: MT my living foes　b Heb hostility

PSALM 40

Thanksgiving for Deliverance and Prayer for Help

To the leader. Of David. A Psalm.

1 I waited patiently for the Lord;
  he inclined to me and heard my cry.
2 He drew me up from the desolate pit,[a]
  out of the miry bog,
and set my feet upon a rock,
  making my steps secure.
3 He put a new song in my mouth,
  a song of praise to our God.
Many will see and fear,
  and put their trust in the Lord.

4 Happy are those who make
  the Lord their trust,
who do not turn to the proud,
  to those who go astray after false gods.
5 You have multiplied, O Lord my God,
  your wondrous deeds and your thoughts
    toward us;
  none can compare with you.
Were I to proclaim and tell of them,
  they would be more than can be counted.

6 Sacrifice and offering you do not desire,
  but you have given me an open ear.[b]
Burnt offering and sin offering
  you have not required.
7 Then I said, "Here I am;
  in the scroll of the book it is written of me.[c]
8 I delight to do your will, O my God;
  your law is within my heart."

9 I have told the glad news of deliverance
  in the great congregation;
see, I have not restrained my lips,
  as you know, O Lord.
10 I have not hidden your saving help within my
    heart,
  I have spoken of your faithfulness and your
    salvation;
I have not concealed your steadfast love and
  your faithfulness
    from the great congregation.

11 Do not, O Lord, withhold
  your mercy from me;
let your steadfast love and your faithfulness
  keep me safe forever.
12 For evils have encompassed me
  without number;
my iniquities have overtaken me,
  until I cannot see;

they are more than the hairs of my head,
  and my heart fails me.

13 Be pleased, O Lord, to deliver me;
  O Lord, make haste to help me.
14 Let all those be put to shame and confusion
  who seek to snatch away my life;
let those be turned back and brought to dishonor
  who desire my hurt.
15 Let those be appalled because of their shame
  who say to me, "Aha, Aha!"

16 But may all who seek you
  rejoice and be glad in you;
may those who love your salvation
  say continually, "Great is the Lord!"
17 As for me, I am poor and needy,
  but the Lord takes thought for me.
You are my help and my deliverer;
  do not delay, O my God.

PSALM 41

Assurance of God's Help and a Plea for Healing

To the leader. A Psalm of David.

1 Happy are those who consider the poor;[d]
  the Lord delivers them in the day of trouble.
2 The Lord protects them and keeps them alive;
  they are called happy in the land.
  You do not give them up to the will of their
    enemies.
3 The Lord sustains them on their sickbed;
  in their illness you heal all their infirmities.[e]

4 As for me, I said, "O Lord, be gracious to me;
  heal me, for I have sinned against you."
5 My enemies wonder in malice
  when I will die, and my name perish.
6 And when they come to see me, they utter
    empty words,
  while their hearts gather mischief;
  when they go out, they tell it abroad.
7 All who hate me whisper together about me;
  they imagine the worst for me.

8 They think that a deadly thing has fastened
    on me,
  that I will not rise again from where I lie.
9 Even my bosom friend in whom I trusted,
  who ate of my bread, has lifted the heel
    against me.

---

a Cn: Heb *pit of tumult*   b Heb *ears you have dug for me*
c Meaning of Heb uncertain   d Or *weak*   e Heb *you change
all his bed*

¹⁰ But you, O Lᴏʀᴅ, be gracious to me,
and raise me up, that I may repay them.

¹¹ By this I know that you are pleased with me;
because my enemy has not triumphed
over me.
¹² But you have upheld me because of my integrity,
and set me in your presence forever.

¹³ Blessed be the Lᴏʀᴅ, the God of Israel,
from everlasting to everlasting.
Amen and Amen.

BOOK II
(Psalms 42–72)

PSALM 42

Longing for God and His Help in Distress

To the leader. A Maskil of the Korahites.

¹ As a deer longs for flowing streams,
so my soul longs for you, O God.
² My soul thirsts for God,
for the living God.
When shall I come and behold
the face of God?
³ My tears have been my food
day and night,
while people say to me continually,
"Where is your God?"

42:1

⁴ These things I remember,
as I pour out my soul:
how I went with the throng,[a]
and led them in procession to the house of
God,
with glad shouts and songs of thanksgiving,
a multitude keeping festival.
⁵ Why are you cast down, O my soul,
and why are you disquieted within me?
Hope in God; for I shall again praise him,
my help ⁶and my God.

My soul is cast down within me;
therefore I remember you
from the land of Jordan and of Hermon,
from Mount Mizar.
⁷ Deep calls to deep
at the thunder of your cataracts;
all your waves and your billows
have gone over me.
⁸ By day the Lᴏʀᴅ commands his steadfast love,
and at night his song is with me,
a prayer to the God of my life.

⁹ I say to God, my rock,
"Why have you forgotten me?
Why must I walk about mournfully
because the enemy oppresses me?"
¹⁰ As with a deadly wound in my body,
my adversaries taunt me,
while they say to me continually,
"Where is your God?"

¹¹ Why are you cast down, O my soul,
and why are you disquieted within me?
Hope in God; for I shall again praise him,
my help and my God.

PSALM 43

Prayer to God in Time of Trouble

¹ Vindicate me, O God, and defend my cause
against an ungodly people;
from those who are deceitful and unjust
deliver me!
² For you are the God in whom I take refuge;
why have you cast me off?
Why must I walk about mournfully
because of the oppression of the enemy?

³ O send out your light and your truth;
let them lead me;
let them bring me to your holy hill

a Meaning of Heb uncertain

and to your dwelling.
4 Then I will go to the altar of God,
    to God my exceeding joy;
and I will praise you with the harp,
    O God, my God.

5 Why are you cast down, O my soul,
    and why are you disquieted within me?
Hope in God; for I shall again praise him,
    my help and my God.

PSALM 44

National Lament and Prayer for Help

To the leader. Of the Korahites. A Maskil.

1 We have heard with our ears, O God,
    our ancestors have told us,
what deeds you performed in their days,
    in the days of old:
2 you with your own hand drove out the nations,
    but them you planted;
you afflicted the peoples,
    but them you set free;
3 for not by their own sword did they win the land,
    nor did their own arm give them victory;
but your right hand, and your arm,
    and the light of your countenance,
    for you delighted in them.

4 You are my King and my God;
    you command[a] victories for Jacob.
5 Through you we push down our foes;
    through your name we tread down our
        assailants.
6 For not in my bow do I trust,
    nor can my sword save me.
7 But you have saved us from our foes,
    and have put to confusion those who hate us.
8 In God we have boasted continually,
    and we will give thanks to your name forever.
                                    Selah

9 Yet you have rejected us and abased us,
    and have not gone out with our armies.
10 You made us turn back from the foe,
    and our enemies have gotten spoil.
11 You have made us like sheep for slaughter,
    and have scattered us among the nations.
12 You have sold your people for a trifle,
    demanding no high price for them.

13 You have made us the taunt of our neighbors,
    the derision and scorn of those around us.
14 You have made us a byword among the nations,
    a laughingstock[b] among the peoples.

Pray It!

Randy's First Day of School

Randy and his family have just moved to a new town. Randy is hopeful about this move because he didn't like his old neighborhood and school. There he was often made fun of for his size. So he figures this will be a new start for him, and just maybe the kids here will give him a chance.

Randy is nervous but can't wait to meet some new people. As the principal walks him down to his new homeroom, he has hopeful visions of how great it will be. When they walk into the classroom, all that changes. As the principal introduces him, someone yells from the back of the room, "Hey, hey, hey, it's Fat Albert!" Everyone laughs. Randy smiles, only to hide the pain and anger he feels inside.

Have you ever experienced painful moments like the one Randy went through? Psalm 42 is a good prayer to turn to during moments like these. Verses 5–6 say, "Hope in God; for I shall again praise him, / my help and my God." If you follow this advice, the situation may not change, but your heart may find peace rather than anger.

▶ **Psalm 42**

15 All day long my disgrace is before me,
    and shame has covered my face
16 at the words of the taunters and revilers,
    at the sight of the enemy and the avenger.

17 All this has come upon us,
    yet we have not forgotten you,
    or been false to your covenant.
18 Our heart has not turned back,
    nor have our steps departed from your way,
19 yet you have broken us in the haunt of jackals,
    and covered us with deep darkness.

20 If we had forgotten the name of our God,
    or spread out our hands to a strange god,

---

a Gk Syr: Heb *You are my King, O God; command*   b Heb a *shaking of the head*

P
S

21 would not God discover this?
  For he knows the secrets of the heart.
22 Because of you we are being killed all day long,
  and accounted as sheep for the slaughter.

23 Rouse yourself! Why do you sleep, O Lord?
  Awake, do not cast us off forever!
24 Why do you hide your face?
  Why do you forget our affliction and
    oppression?
25 For we sink down to the dust;
  our bodies cling to the ground.
26 Rise up, come to our help.
  Redeem us for the sake of your steadfast love.

PSALM 45

Ode for a Royal Wedding

To the leader: according to Lilies. Of the Korahites.
A Maskil. A love song.

1 My heart overflows with a goodly theme;
  I address my verses to the king;
  my tongue is like the pen of a ready scribe.

2 You are the most handsome of men;
  grace is poured upon your lips;
  therefore God has blessed you forever.
3 Gird your sword on your thigh, O mighty one,
  in your glory and majesty.

4 In your majesty ride on victoriously
  for the cause of truth and to defend*a* the right;
  let your right hand teach you dread deeds.
5 Your arrows are sharp
  in the heart of the king's enemies;
  the peoples fall under you.

6 Your throne, O God,*b* endures forever and ever.
  Your royal scepter is a scepter of equity;
7   you love righteousness and hate wickedness.
  Therefore God, your God, has anointed you
    with the oil of gladness beyond your
      companions;
8   your robes are all fragrant with myrrh and
      aloes and cassia.
  From ivory palaces stringed instruments make
    you glad;
9   daughters of kings are among your ladies of
      honor;
  at your right hand stands the queen in gold of
    Ophir.

10 Hear, O daughter, consider and incline your ear;
  forget your people and your father's house,
11   and the king will desire your beauty.

Since he is your lord, bow to him;
12   the people*c* of Tyre will seek your favor with
      gifts,
  the richest of the people 13with all kinds of
    wealth.

The princess is decked in her chamber with
    gold-woven robes;*d*
14   in many-colored robes she is led to the king;
  behind her the virgins, her companions,
    follow.
15 With joy and gladness they are led along
  as they enter the palace of the king.

16 In the place of ancestors you, O king,*e* shall have
      sons;
  you will make them princes in all the earth.
17 I will cause your name to be celebrated in all
      generations;
  therefore the peoples will praise you forever
    and ever.

PSALM 46

God's Defense of His City and People

To the leader. Of the Korahites. According to
    Alamoth. A Song.

1 God is our refuge and strength,
  a very present*f* help in trouble.
2 Therefore we will not fear, though the earth
      should change,
  though the mountains shake in the heart of
    the sea;
3 though its waters roar and foam,
  though the mountains tremble with its
    tumult.   *Selah*

4 There is a river whose streams make glad the city
      of God,
  the holy habitation of the Most High.
5 God is in the midst of the city;*g* it shall not be
      moved;
  God will help it when the morning dawns.
6 The nations are in an uproar, the kingdoms totter;
  he utters his voice, the earth melts.
7 The LORD of hosts is with us;
  the God of Jacob is our refuge.*h*   *Selah*

8 Come, behold the works of the LORD;
  see what desolations he has brought on the
    earth.

---

a Cn: Heb *and the meekness of*   *b* Or *Your throne is a throne
of God, it*   *c* Heb *daughter*   *d* Or *people.* 13*All glorious is the
princess within, gold embroidery is her clothing*   *e* Heb lacks
O king*   *f* Or *well proved*   *g* Heb *of it*   *h* Or *fortress*

9 He makes wars cease to the end of the earth;
  he breaks the bow, and shatters the spear;
  he burns the shields with fire.
10 "Be still, and know that I am God!
  I am exalted among the nations,
  I am exalted in the earth."
11 The Lord of hosts is with us;
  the God of Jacob is our refuge.[a]   *Selah*

PSALM 47

God's Rule over the Nations

To the leader. Of the Korahites. A Psalm.

1 Clap your hands, all you peoples;
  shout to God with loud songs of joy.
2 For the Lord, the Most High, is awesome,
  a great king over all the earth.
3 He subdued peoples under us,
  and nations under our feet.
4 He chose our heritage for us,
  the pride of Jacob whom he loves.   *Selah*

5 God has gone up with a shout,
  the Lord with the sound of a trumpet.
6 Sing praises to God, sing praises;
  sing praises to our King, sing praises.
7 For God is the king of all the earth;
  sing praises with a psalm.[b]

8 God is king over the nations;
  God sits on his holy throne.
9 The princes of the peoples gather
  as the people of the God of Abraham.
  For the shields of the earth belong to God;
  he is highly exalted.

PSALM 48

The Glory and Strength of Zion

A Song. A Psalm of the Korahites.

1 Great is the Lord and greatly to be praised
  in the city of our God.
  His holy mountain, 2beautiful in elevation,
  is the joy of all the earth,
  Mount Zion, in the far north,
  the city of the great King.
3 Within its citadels God
  has shown himself a sure defense.

4 Then the kings assembled,
  they came on together.
5 As soon as they saw it, they were astounded;
  they were in panic, they took to flight;
6 trembling took hold of them there,

  pains as of a woman in labor,
7 as when an east wind shatters
  the ships of Tarshish.
8 As we have heard, so have we seen
  in the city of the Lord of hosts,
  in the city of our God,
  which God establishes forever.   *Selah*

9 We ponder your steadfast love, O God,
  in the midst of your temple.
10 Your name, O God, like your praise,
  reaches to the ends of the earth.
  Your right hand is filled with victory.
11   Let Mount Zion be glad,
  let the towns[c] of Judah rejoice
  because of your judgments.

12 Walk about Zion, go all around it,
  count its towers,
13 consider well its ramparts;
  go through its citadels,
  that you may tell the next generation
14   that this is God,
  our God forever and ever.
  He will be our guide forever.

PSALM 49

The Folly of Trust in Riches

To the leader. Of the Korahites. A Psalm.

1 Hear this, all you peoples;
  give ear, all inhabitants of the world,
2 both low and high,
  rich and poor together.
3 My mouth shall speak wisdom;
  the meditation of my heart shall be
  understanding.
4 I will incline my ear to a proverb;
  I will solve my riddle to the music of the
  harp.

5 Why should I fear in times of trouble,
  when the iniquity of my persecutors
  surrounds me,
6 those who trust in their wealth
  and boast of the abundance of their riches?
7 Truly, no ransom avails for one's life,[d]
  there is no price one can give to God for it.
8 For the ransom of life is costly,
  and can never suffice,
9 that one should live on forever
  and never see the grave.[e]

---

a Or *fortress*   b Heb *Maskil*   c Heb *daughters*   d Another
reading is *no one can ransom a brother*   e Heb *the pit*

P
S

10 When we look at the wise, they die;
    fool and dolt perish together
    and leave their wealth to others.
11 Their graves[a] are their homes forever,
    their dwelling places to all generations,
    though they named lands their own.
12 Mortals cannot abide in their pomp;
    they are like the animals that perish.

13 Such is the fate of the foolhardy,
    the end of those[b] who are pleased with their
        lot.   Selah
14 Like sheep they are appointed for Sheol;
    Death shall be their shepherd;
    straight to the grave they descend,[c]
    and their form shall waste away;
    Sheol shall be their home.[d]
15 But God will ransom my soul from the power of
        Sheol,
    for he will receive me.   Selah

16 Do not be afraid when some become rich,
    when the wealth of their houses increases.
17 For when they die they will carry nothing away;
    their wealth will not go down after them.
18 Though in their lifetime they count themselves
        happy
    —for you are praised when you do well for
        yourself—
19 they[e] will go to the company of their
        ancestors,
    who will never again see the light.
20 Mortals cannot abide in their pomp;
    they are like the animals that perish.

PSALM 50

The Acceptable Sacrifice

A Psalm of Asaph.

1 The mighty one, God the LORD,
    speaks and summons the earth
    from the rising of the sun to its setting.
2 Out of Zion, the perfection of beauty,
    God shines forth.

3 Our God comes and does not keep silence,
    before him is a devouring fire,
    and a mighty tempest all around him.
4 He calls to the heavens above
    and to the earth, that he may judge his
        people:
5 "Gather to me my faithful ones,
    who made a covenant with me by sacrifice!"
6 The heavens declare his righteousness,
    for God himself is judge.   Selah

7 "Hear, O my people, and I will speak,
    O Israel, I will testify against you.
    I am God, your God.
8 Not for your sacrifices do I rebuke you;
    your burnt offerings are continually
        before me.
9 I will not accept a bull from your house,
    or goats from your folds.
10 For every wild animal of the forest is mine,
    the cattle on a thousand hills.
11 I know all the birds of the air,[f]
    and all that moves in the field is mine.

12 "If I were hungry, I would not tell you,
    for the world and all that is in it is mine.
13 Do I eat the flesh of bulls,
    or drink the blood of goats?
14 Offer to God a sacrifice of thanksgiving,[g]
    and pay your vows to the Most High.
15 Call on me in the day of trouble;
    I will deliver you, and you shall
        glorify me."

16 But to the wicked God says:
    "What right have you to recite my statutes,
    or take my covenant on your lips?
17 For you hate discipline,
    and you cast my words behind you.
18 You make friends with a thief when you see
        one,
    and you keep company with adulterers.

19 "You give your mouth free rein for evil,
    and your tongue frames deceit.
20 You sit and speak against your kin;
    you slander your own mother's child.
21 These things you have done and I have been
        silent;
    you thought that I was one just like
        yourself.
    But now I rebuke you, and lay the charge
        before you.

22 "Mark this, then, you who forget God,
    or I will tear you apart, and there will be no
        one to deliver.
23 Those who bring thanksgiving as their sacrifice
        honor me;
    to those who go the right way[h]
    I will show the salvation of God."

---

a Gk Syr Compare Tg: Heb *their inward* (thought)   b Tg: Heb
after them   c Cn: Heb *the upright shall have dominion over
them in the morning*   d Meaning of Heb uncertain   e Cn: Heb
you   f Gk Syr Tg: Heb *mountains*   g Or *make thanksgiving your
sacrifice to God*   h Heb *who set a way*

PSALM 51

Prayer for Cleansing and Pardon

To the leader. A Psalm of David, when the prophet
Nathan came to him, after he had gone
in to Bathsheba.

1 Have mercy on me, O God,
according to your steadfast love;
according to your abundant mercy
blot out my transgressions.
2 Wash me thoroughly from my iniquity,
and cleanse me from my sin.

3 For I know my transgressions,
and my sin is ever before me.
4 Against you, you alone, have I sinned,
and done what is evil in your sight,
so that you are justified in your sentence
and blameless when you pass judgment.
5 Indeed, I was born guilty,
a sinner when my mother conceived me.

6 You desire truth in the inward being;[a]
therefore teach me wisdom in my secret
heart.
7 Purge me with hyssop, and I shall be clean;
wash me, and I shall be whiter than snow.
8 Let me hear joy and gladness;
let the bones that you have crushed
rejoice.
9 Hide your face from my sins,
and blot out all my iniquities.

10 Create in me a clean heart, O God,
and put a new and right[b] spirit within me.
11 Do not cast me away from your presence,
and do not take your holy spirit from me.
12 Restore to me the joy of your salvation,
and sustain in me a willing[c] spirit.

13 Then I will teach transgressors your ways,
and sinners will return to you.
14 Deliver me from bloodshed, O God,
O God of my salvation,
and my tongue will sing aloud of your
deliverance.

15 O Lord, open my lips,
and my mouth will declare your praise.
16 For you have no delight in sacrifice;
if I were to give a burnt offering, you would
not be pleased.
17 The sacrifice acceptable to God[d] is a broken
spirit;
a broken and contrite heart, O God, you will
not despise.

18 Do good to Zion in your good pleasure;
rebuild the walls of Jerusalem,
19 then you will delight in right sacrifices,
in burnt offerings and whole burnt
offerings;
then bulls will be offered on your altar.

---

a Meaning of Heb uncertain   b Or steadfast   c Or generous
d Or My sacrifice, O God,

A Fresh Start

Psalm 51 is a beautiful prayer of sorrow and remorse. It is attributed to King David, who would have written it seeking forgiveness and a fresh start after committing adultery with Bathsheba. Take a few minutes to read this psalm prayerfully and reflect on the marvelous way it asks for God's help in starting over.

In our time too, people can fall into a sinful pattern of having sex outside of marriage. Many people experience a deep regret and sadness in losing their virginity in a short-term and un-committed relationship. Thinking they can never regain their moral virtue, they then pursue one loveless relationship after another. The promise of Psalm 51 is that they can start fresh at any point in this cycle! Some people call this new be-ginning a secondary virginity—not, of course, a physical virginity, but a virginity of the heart and soul. It means a commitment not to have sex again, except with the person they marry.

So whenever you are feeling the weight of sin, whether it is premarital sex or some other sin, pray Psalm 51. Let it mark your commitment to start fresh with God's help. Ask God to show you what situations to avoid and what people you need to ask to support you. Remember, God is always ready to forgive you, and all of heaven rejoices each time you make a fresh start!

▶ **Psalm 51**

P
S

PSALM 52

Judgment on the Deceitful

To the leader. A Maskil of David, when Doeg the
Edomite came to Saul and said to him, "David has
come to the house of Ahimelech."

1 Why do you boast, O mighty one,
    of mischief done against the godly?*a*
  All day long 2you are plotting destruction.
Your tongue is like a sharp razor,
    you worker of treachery.
3 You love evil more than good,
    and lying more than speaking the
      truth.   *Selah*
4 You love all words that devour,
    O deceitful tongue.

5 But God will break you down forever;
    he will snatch and tear you from your tent;
    he will uproot you from the land of the
      living.   *Selah*
6 The righteous will see, and fear,
    and will laugh at the evildoer,*b* saying,
7 "See the one who would not take
    refuge in God,
  but trusted in abundant riches,
    and sought refuge in wealth!"*c*

8 But I am like a green olive tree
    in the house of God.
I trust in the steadfast love of God
    forever and ever.
9 I will thank you forever,
    because of what you have done.
In the presence of the faithful
    I will proclaim*d* your name, for it is good.

PSALM 53

Denunciation of Godlessness

To the leader: according to Mahalath. A Maskil
of David.

1 Fools say in their hearts, "There is no God."
    They are corrupt, they commit abominable
      acts;
  there is no one who does good.

2 God looks down from heaven on humankind
    to see if there are any who are wise,
  who seek after God.

3 They have all fallen away, they are all alike
    perverse;
  there is no one who does good,
    no, not one.

4 Have they no knowledge, those evildoers,
    who eat up my people as they eat bread,
    and do not call upon God?

5 There they shall be in great terror,
    in terror such as has not been.
For God will scatter the bones of the ungodly;*e*
    they will be put to shame,*f* for God has
      rejected them.

6 O that deliverance for Israel would come from
    Zion!
When God restores the fortunes of his people,
    Jacob will rejoice; Israel will be glad.

PSALM 54

Prayer for Vindication

To the leader: with stringed instruments. A Maskil
of David, when the Ziphites went and told Saul,
"David is in hiding among us."

1 Save me, O God, by your name,
    and vindicate me by your might.
2 Hear my prayer, O God;
    give ear to the words of my mouth.

3 For the insolent have risen against me,
    the ruthless seek my life;
    they do not set God before them.   *Selah*

4 But surely, God is my helper;
    the Lord is the upholder of*g* my life.
5 He will repay my enemies for their evil.
    In your faithfulness, put an end to them.

6 With a freewill offering I will sacrifice to you;
    I will give thanks to your name, O LORD, for it
      is good.
7 For he has delivered me from every trouble,
    and my eye has looked in triumph on my
      enemies.

PSALM 55

Complaint about a Friend's Treachery

To the leader: with stringed instruments. A Maskil
of David.

1 Give ear to my prayer, O God;
    do not hide yourself from my supplication.

---

a Cn Compare Syr: Heb *the kindness of God*   b Heb *him*   c Syr
Tg: Heb *in his destruction*   d Cn: Heb *wait for*   e Cn Compare
Gk Syr: Heb *him who encamps against you*   f Gk: Heb *you have
put (them) to shame*   g Gk Syr Jerome: Heb *is of those who
uphold* or *is with those who uphold*

2 Attend to me, and answer me;
   I am troubled in my complaint.
I am distraught 3by the noise of the
      enemy,
   because of the clamor of the wicked.
For they bring[a] trouble upon me,
   and in anger they cherish enmity
      against me.

4 My heart is in anguish within me,
   the terrors of death have fallen upon me.
5 Fear and trembling come upon me,
   and horror overwhelms me.
6 And I say, "O that I had wings like a dove!
   I would fly away and be at rest;
7 truly, I would flee far away;
   I would lodge in the wilderness;   *Selah*
8 I would hurry to find a shelter for myself
   from the raging wind and tempest."

9 Confuse, O Lord, confound their speech;
   for I see violence and strife in the city.
10 Day and night they go around it
   on its walls,
and iniquity and trouble are within it;
11   ruin is in its midst;
oppression and fraud
   do not depart from its marketplace.

12 It is not enemies who taunt me—
   I could bear that;
it is not adversaries who deal insolently
      with me—
   I could hide from them.
13 But it is you, my equal,
   my companion, my familiar friend,
14 with whom I kept pleasant company;
   we walked in the house of God with the
      throng.
15 Let death come upon them;
   let them go down alive to Sheol;
   for evil is in their homes and in their
      hearts.

16 But I call upon God,
   and the LORD will save me.
17 Evening and morning and at noon
   I utter my complaint and moan,
   and he will hear my voice.
18 He will redeem me unharmed
   from the battle that I wage,
   for many are arrayed against me.
19 God, who is enthroned from of old,   *Selah*
   will hear, and will humble them—
because they do not change,
   and do not fear God.

20 My companion laid hands on a friend
   and violated a covenant with me[b]
21 with speech smoother than butter,
   but with a heart set on war;
with words that were softer than oil,
   but in fact were drawn swords.

22 Cast your burden[c] on the LORD,
   and he will sustain you;
he will never permit
   the righteous to be moved.

23 But you, O God, will cast them down
   into the lowest pit;
the bloodthirsty and treacherous
   shall not live out half their days.
But I will trust in you.

---

a Cn Compare Gk: Heb *they cause to totter*   b Heb lacks *with me*   c Or *Cast what he has given you*

Betrayed!

Maybe you don't have enemies quite as bad as the enemies described in Psalm 55, but you may be able to sympathize with the psalmist when he writes this: "My companion laid hands on a friend / and violated a covenant with me" (verse 20).

When you feel betrayed by others like the psalmist does—maybe betrayed by a friend who didn't keep a promise or by a parent who seemed to treat you unfairly or by anyone else for whatever reason—call on God, and say a prayer like this:

I trust you, God; I want to believe you are with me. When others choose to abandon or betray me, help me to know you are here and that I am never alone. May I always honor my covenant with you. Amen.

▶ **Psalm 55**

PSALM 56

Trust in God under Persecution

*To the leader: according to The Dove on Far-off
Terebinths. Of David. A Miktam, when the
Philistines seized him in Gath.*

1 Be gracious to me, O God, for people trample
    on me;
  all day long foes oppress me;
2 my enemies trample on me all day long,
    for many fight against me.
  O Most High, 3when I am afraid,
    I put my trust in you.
4 In God, whose word I praise,
    in God I trust; I am not afraid;
  what can flesh do to me?

5 All day long they seek to injure my cause;
    all their thoughts are against me for evil.
6 They stir up strife, they lurk,
    they watch my steps.
  As they hoped to have my life,
7   so repay*a* them for their crime;
    in wrath cast down the peoples, O God!

8 You have kept count of my tossings;
    put my tears in your bottle.
  Are they not in your record?
9 Then my enemies will retreat
    in the day when I call.
  This I know, that*b* God is for me.
10 In God, whose word I praise,
    in the LORD, whose word I praise,
11 in God I trust; I am not afraid.
    What can a mere mortal do to me?

12 My vows to you I must perform, O God;
    I will render thank offerings to you.
13 For you have delivered my soul from death,
    and my feet from falling,
  so that I may walk before God
    in the light of life.

PSALM 57

Praise and Assurance under Persecution

*To the leader: Do Not Destroy. Of David.
A Miktam, when he fled from Saul, in the cave.*

1 Be merciful to me, O God, be merciful to me,
    for in you my soul takes refuge;
  in the shadow of your wings I will take refuge,
    until the destroying storms pass by.
2 I cry to God Most High,
    to God who fulfills his purpose for me.
3 He will send from heaven and save me,

he will put to shame those who trample
    on me. *Selah*
God will send forth his steadfast love and his
    faithfulness.

4 I lie down among lions
    that greedily devour*c* human prey;
  their teeth are spears and arrows,
    their tongues sharp swords.

5 Be exalted, O God, above the heavens.
    Let your glory be over all the earth.

6 They set a net for my steps;
    my soul was bowed down.
  They dug a pit in my path,
    but they have fallen into it themselves. *Selah*
7 My heart is steadfast, O God,
    my heart is steadfast.
  I will sing and make melody.
8   Awake, my soul!
  Awake, O harp and lyre!
    I will awake the dawn.
9 I will give thanks to you, O Lord, among the
    peoples;
  I will sing praises to you among the nations.
10 For your steadfast love is as high as the heavens;
    your faithfulness extends to the clouds.

11 Be exalted, O God, above the heavens.
    Let your glory be over all the earth.

PSALM 58

Prayer for Vengeance

*To the leader: Do Not Destroy. Of David.
A Miktam.*

1 Do you indeed decree what is right, you gods?*d*
    Do you judge people fairly?
2 No, in your hearts you devise wrongs;
    your hands deal out violence on earth.

3 The wicked go astray from the womb;
    they err from their birth, speaking lies.
4 They have venom like the venom of a serpent,
    like the deaf adder that stops its ear,
5 so that it does not hear the voice of charmers
    or of the cunning enchanter.

6 O God, break the teeth in their mouths;
    tear out the fangs of the young lions, O LORD!
7 Let them vanish like water that runs away;

*a Cn: Heb rescue   b Or because   c Cn: Heb are aflame for
d Or mighty lords*

like grass let them be trodden down[a] and
    wither.
8 Let them be like the snail that dissolves into
    slime;
    like the untimely birth that never sees the sun.
9 Sooner than your pots can feel the heat of
    thorns,
    whether green or ablaze, may he sweep them
    away!

10 The righteous will rejoice when they see
    vengeance done;
    they will bathe their feet in the blood of the
    wicked.
11 People will say, "Surely there is a reward for the
    righteous;
    surely there is a God who judges on earth."

PSALM 59

Prayer for Deliverance from Enemies

*To the leader: Do Not Destroy. Of David.
A Miktam, when Saul ordered his house to be
watched in order to kill him.*

1 Deliver me from my enemies, O my God;
    protect me from those who rise up against me.
2 Deliver me from those who work evil;
    from the bloodthirsty save me.

3 Even now they lie in wait for my life;
    the mighty stir up strife against me.
For no transgression or sin of mine, O Lord,
4   for no fault of mine, they run and make
    ready.

Rouse yourself, come to my help and see!
5   You, Lord God of hosts, are God of Israel.
Awake to punish all the nations;
    spare none of those who treacherously plot
    evil.   *Selah*

6 Each evening they come back,
    howling like dogs
    and prowling about the city.
7 There they are, bellowing with their mouths,
    with sharp words[b] on their lips—
    for "Who," they think,[c] "will hear us?"

8 But you laugh at them, O Lord;
    you hold all the nations in derision.
9 O my strength, I will watch for you;
    for you, O God, are my fortress.
10 My God in his steadfast love will meet me;
    my God will let me look in triumph on my
    enemies.

11 Do not kill them, or my people may forget;
    make them totter by your power, and bring
    them down,
    O Lord, our shield.
12 For the sin of their mouths, the words of their
    lips,
    let them be trapped in their pride.
For the cursing and lies that they utter,
13   consume them in wrath;
    consume them until they are no more.
Then it will be known to the ends of the earth
    that God rules over Jacob.   *Selah*

14 Each evening they come back,
    howling like dogs
    and prowling about the city.
15 They roam about for food,
    and growl if they do not get their fill.

16 But I will sing of your might;
    I will sing aloud of your steadfast love in the
    morning.
For you have been a fortress for me
    and a refuge in the day of my distress.
17 O my strength, I will sing praises to you,
    for you, O God, are my fortress,
    the God who shows me steadfast love.

PSALM 60

Prayer for National Victory after Defeat

*To the leader: according to the Lily of the
Covenant. A Miktam of David; for instruction;
when he struggled with Aram-naharaim and with
Aram-zobah, and when Joab on his return killed
twelve thousand Edomites in the Valley of Salt.*

1 O God, you have rejected us, broken our defenses;
    you have been angry; now restore us!
2 You have caused the land to quake; you have
    torn it open;
    repair the cracks in it, for it is tottering.
3 You have made your people suffer hard things;
    you have given us wine to drink that made us
    reel.

4 You have set up a banner for those who fear you,
    to rally to it out of bowshot.[d]   *Selah*
5 Give victory with your right hand, and answer us,[e]
    so that those whom you love may be rescued.

6 God has promised in his sanctuary:[f]
    "With exultation I will divide up Shechem,

---

a Cn: Meaning of Heb uncertain   b Heb *with swords*
c Heb lacks *they think*   d Gk Syr Jerome: Heb *because of the
truth*   e Another reading is *me*   f Or *by his holiness*

The Agony of Defeat

The person who has never lost something or someone important to him or her does not exist. Nor does the athletic team that has never experienced the awful feeling that comes with losing. As a matter of fact, losing is what often inspires athletic teams to get stronger or faster or score more points.

The psalmist who sang Psalm 60 knew how it felt to lose. Although this psalm was written after defeat in battle, its spirit has echoed through the ages by athletic teams and all others who have been defeated in some way. The next time you experience loss, read verses 1–5, and think about how the psalmist calls on God as a helper. Strengthened and inspired by God, there is much that can be gained from defeat.

▶ Ps 60:1–5

and portion out the Vale of Succoth.
⁷ Gilead is mine, and Manasseh is mine;
   Ephraim is my helmet;
   Judah is my scepter.
⁸ Moab is my washbasin;
   on Edom I hurl my shoe;
   over Philistia I shout in triumph."

⁹ Who will bring me to the fortified city?
   Who will lead me to Edom?
¹⁰ Have you not rejected us, O God?
   You do not go out, O God, with our armies.
¹¹ O grant us help against the foe,
   for human help is worthless.
¹² With God we shall do valiantly;
   it is he who will tread down our foes.

PSALM 61

Assurance of God's Protection

To the leader: with stringed instruments.
Of David.

¹ Hear my cry, O God;
   listen to my prayer.

² From the end of the earth I call to you,
   when my heart is faint.

Lead me to the rock
   that is higher than I;
³ for you are my refuge,
   a strong tower against the enemy.

⁴ Let me abide in your tent forever,
   find refuge under the shelter of your wings. *Selah*

⁵ For you, O God, have heard my vows;
   you have given me the heritage of those who
      fear your name.

⁶ Prolong the life of the king;
   may his years endure to all generations!
⁷ May he be enthroned forever before God;
   appoint steadfast love and faithfulness to
      watch over him!

⁸ So I will always sing praises to your name,
   as I pay my vows day after day.

PSALM 62

Song of Trust in God Alone

To the leader: according to Jeduthun. A Psalm
of David.

¹ For God alone my soul waits in silence;
   from him comes my salvation.
² He alone is my rock and my salvation,
   my fortress; I shall never be shaken.

³ How long will you assail a person,
   will you batter your victim, all of you,
   as you would a leaning wall, a tottering
      fence?
⁴ Their only plan is to bring down a person of
      prominence.
   They take pleasure in falsehood;
they bless with their mouths,
   but inwardly they curse. *Selah*

⁵ For God alone my soul waits in silence,
   for my hope is from him.
⁶ He alone is my rock and my salvation,
   my fortress; I shall not be shaken.
⁷ On God rests my deliverance and my
      honor;
   my mighty rock, my refuge is in God.

⁸ Trust in him at all times, O people;
   pour out your heart before him;
   God is a refuge for us. *Selah*

9 Those of low estate are but a breath,
    those of high estate are a delusion;
in the balances they go up;
    they are together lighter than a breath.
10 Put no confidence in extortion,
    and set no vain hopes on robbery;
    if riches increase, do not set your heart on
       them.

11 Once God has spoken;
    twice have I heard this:
that power belongs to God,
12   and steadfast love belongs to you,
       O Lord.
For you repay to all
    according to their work.

PSALM 63

Comfort and Assurance in God's Presence

A Psalm of David, when he was in the Wilderness
of Judah.

1 O God, you are my God, I seek you,
    my soul thirsts for you;
my flesh faints for you,
    as in a dry and weary land where there is no
       water.
2 So I have looked upon you in the sanctuary,
    beholding your power and glory.
3 Because your steadfast love is better than life,
    my lips will praise you.
4 So I will bless you as long as I live;
    I will lift up my hands and call on your
       name.

5 My soul is satisfied as with a rich feast,[a]
    and my mouth praises you with joyful lips
6 when I think of you on my bed,
    and meditate on you in the watches of the
       night;
7 for you have been my help,
    and in the shadow of your wings I sing for
       joy.
8 My soul clings to you;
    your right hand upholds me.

9 But those who seek to destroy my life
    shall go down into the depths of the
       earth;
10 they shall be given over to the power of the
       sword,
    they shall be prey for jackals.
11 But the king shall rejoice in God;
    all who swear by him shall exult,
    for the mouths of liars will be stopped.

PSALM 64

Prayer for Protection from Enemies

To the leader. A Psalm of David.

1 Hear my voice, O God, in my complaint;
    preserve my life from the dread enemy.
2 Hide me from the secret plots of the wicked,
    from the scheming of evildoers,
3 who whet their tongues like swords,
    who aim bitter words like arrows,
4 shooting from ambush at the blameless;
    they shoot suddenly and without fear.
5 They hold fast to their evil purpose;
    they talk of laying snares secretly,
thinking, "Who can see us?[b]
6   Who can search out our crimes?[c]
We have thought out a cunningly conceived
       plot."
    For the human heart and mind are deep.

7 But God will shoot his arrow at them;
    they will be wounded suddenly.
8 Because of their tongue he will bring them to
       ruin;[d]
    all who see them will shake with horror.
9 Then everyone will fear;
    they will tell what God has brought about,
    and ponder what he has done.

---

a Heb with fat and fatness   b Syr: Heb them   c Cn: Heb They
search out crimes   d Cn: Heb They will bring him to ruin, their
tongue being against them

Decide!

Whom are you going to trust? Where will
you find your power? in the right people? in the right clothes? in money? in the right
job? or can you trust God to be your rock and
your salvation (see Ps 62:2)? Will you let God be
your refuge (see 61:4, 62:7) in times of hardship? Why is it so hard sometimes to let your
soul wait for God in silence (see 62:1)?

*God, I am weak. Help me every day to put
my trust in you. Help me to believe that
you and I can do anything
together.*

▶ **Psalm 62**

10 Let the righteous rejoice in the LORD
    and take refuge in him.
Let all the upright in heart glory.

PSALM 65

Thanksgiving for Earth's Bounty

To the leader. A Psalm of David. A Song.

1 Praise is due to you,
    O God, in Zion;
and to you shall vows be performed,
2   O you who answer prayer!
To you all flesh shall come.
3 When deeds of iniquity overwhelm us,
    you forgive our transgressions.
4 Happy are those whom you choose and bring
        near
    to live in your courts.
We shall be satisfied with the goodness of your
        house,
    your holy temple.

5 By awesome deeds you answer us with
        deliverance,
    O God of our salvation;
you are the hope of all the ends of the earth
    and of the farthest seas.
6 By your[a] strength you established the
        mountains;
    you are girded with might.
7 You silence the roaring of the seas,
    the roaring of their waves,
    the tumult of the peoples.
8 Those who live at earth's farthest bounds are
        awed by your signs;
you make the gateways of the morning and the
        evening shout for joy.

9 You visit the earth and water it,
    you greatly enrich it;
the river of God is full of water;
    you provide the people with grain,
    for so you have prepared it.
10 You water its furrows abundantly,
    settling its ridges,
softening it with showers,
    and blessing its growth.
11 You crown the year with your bounty;
    your wagon tracks overflow with
        richness.
12 The pastures of the wilderness overflow,
    the hills gird themselves with joy,
13 the meadows clothe themselves with flocks,
    the valleys deck themselves with grain,
    they shout and sing together for joy.

PSALM 66

Praise for God's Goodness to Israel

To the leader. A Song. A Psalm.

1 Make a joyful noise to God, all the earth;
2   sing the glory of his name;
    give to him glorious praise.
3 Say to God, "How awesome are your deeds!
    Because of your great power, your enemies
        cringe before you.
4 All the earth worships you;
    they sing praises to you,
    sing praises to your name."   Selah

5 Come and see what God has done:
    he is awesome in his deeds among mortals.
6 He turned the sea into dry land;
    they passed through the river on foot.
There we rejoiced in him,
7   who rules by his might forever,
    whose eyes keep watch on the nations—
    let the rebellious not exalt themselves.   Selah

8 Bless our God, O peoples,
    let the sound of his praise be heard,
9 who has kept us among the living,
    and has not let our feet slip.
10 For you, O God, have tested us;
    you have tried us as silver is tried.
11 You brought us into the net;
    you laid burdens on our backs;
12 you let people ride over our heads;
    we went through fire and through water;
yet you have brought us out to a spacious place.[b]

13 I will come into your house with burnt
        offerings;
    I will pay you my vows,
14 those that my lips uttered
    and my mouth promised when I was in
        trouble.
15 I will offer to you burnt offerings of fatlings,
    with the smoke of the sacrifice of rams;
I will make an offering of bulls and goats.   Selah

16 Come and hear, all you who fear God,
    and I will tell what he has done for me.
17 I cried aloud to him,
    and he was extolled with my tongue.
18 If I had cherished iniquity in my heart,
    the Lord would not have listened.
19 But truly God has listened;
    he has given heed to the words of my prayer.

---

a Gk Jerome: Heb his   b Cn Compare Gk Syr Jerome Tg: Heb to
a saturation

²⁰ Blessed be God,
     because he has not rejected my prayer
     or removed his steadfast love from me.

PSALM 67

The Nations Called to Praise God

To the leader: with stringed instruments. A Psalm.
A Song.

¹ May God be gracious to us and bless us
     and make his face to shine upon us,   Selah
² that your way may be known upon earth,
     your saving power among all nations.
³ Let the peoples praise you, O God;
     let all the peoples praise you.

⁴ Let the nations be glad and sing for joy,
     for you judge the peoples with equity
     and guide the nations upon earth.   Selah
⁵ Let the peoples praise you, O God;
     let all the peoples praise you.

⁶ The earth has yielded its increase;
     God, our God, has blessed us.
⁷ May God continue to bless us;
     let all the ends of the earth revere him.

PSALM 68

Praise and Thanksgiving

To the leader. Of David. A Psalm. A Song.

¹ Let God rise up, let his enemies be scattered;
     let those who hate him flee before him.
² As smoke is driven away, so drive them away;
     as wax melts before the fire,
     let the wicked perish before God.
³ But let the righteous be joyful;
     let them exult before God;
     let them be jubilant with joy.

⁴ Sing to God, sing praises to his name;
     lift up a song to him who rides upon the
         cloudsᵃ—
     his name is the Lord,
     be exultant before him.

⁵ Father of orphans and protector of widows
     is God in his holy habitation.
⁶ God gives the desolate a home to live in;
     he leads out the prisoners to prosperity,
     but the rebellious live in a parched land.

⁷ O God, when you went out before your
     people,

when you marched through the wilderness,
                                         Selah
⁸ the earth quaked, the heavens poured down rain
     at the presence of God, the God of Sinai,
     at the presence of God, the God of Israel.
⁹ Rain in abundance, O God, you showered
         abroad;
     you restored your heritage when it
         languished;
¹⁰ your flock found a dwelling in it;
     in your goodness, O God, you provided for
         the needy.

¹¹ The Lord gives the command;
     great is the company of thoseᵇ who bore the
         tidings:
¹²   "The kings of the armies, they flee, they flee!"
     The women at home divide the spoil,
¹³   though they stay among the sheepfolds—
     the wings of a dove covered with silver,
     its pinions with green gold.
¹⁴ When the Almightyᶜ scattered kings there,
     snow fell on Zalmon.

¹⁵ O mighty mountain, mountain of Bashan;
     O many-peaked mountain, mountain of
         Bashan!
¹⁶ Why do you look with envy, O many-peaked
         mountain,
     at the mount that God desired for his abode,
     where the Lord will reside forever?

¹⁷ With mighty chariotry, twice ten thousand,
     thousands upon thousands,
     the Lord came from Sinai into the holy place.ᵈ
¹⁸ You ascended the high mount,
     leading captives in your train
     and receiving gifts from people,
     even from those who rebel against the Lord
         God's abiding there.
¹⁹ Blessed be the Lord,
     who daily bears us up;
     God is our salvation.   Selah
²⁰ Our God is a God of salvation,
     and to God, the Lord, belongs escape from
         death.

²¹ But God will shatter the heads of his enemies,
     the hairy crown of those who walk in their
         guilty ways.
²² The Lord said,
     "I will bring them back from Bashan,

---

a Or cast up a highway for him who rides through the deserts
b Or company of the women   c Traditional rendering of Heb
Shaddai   d Cn: Heb The Lord among them Sinai in the holy
(place)

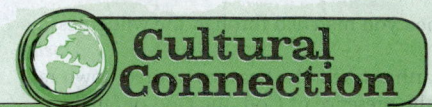

Cultural Connection

Black People Praise the Lord

Psalm 68 commands us to sing praises to the Lord. We are told to praise the Lord because God is the "Father of orphans and protector of widows" (verse 5), "gives the desolate a home to live in" and "leads out the prisoners to prosperity" (verse 6), "daily bears us up" (verse 19), and "will shatter the heads of his enemies" (verse 21).

Near the end of all this praise, the psalmist says, "Let bronze be brought from Egypt; / let Ethiopia hasten to stretch out its hands to God" (verse 31). The psalmist's call to Egypt and Ethiopia is significant for African Americans because the Egyptians and the Ethiopians were North African black people.

Nevertheless, the message of Psalm 68 is for all people, whether they are black, brown, red, yellow, or white. All people ought to submit to the Lord, all people ought to praise the Lord, and all people ought to render their whole self and their whole substance to the Lord. It matters not who we are or where we come from; the Lord is God and worthy of all praise!

▶ **Psalm 68**

I will bring them back from the depths of the sea,

23 so that you may bathe^a your feet in blood,
    so that the tongues of your dogs may have
      their share from the foe."

24 Your solemn processions are seen,^b O God,
    the processions of my God, my King, into the
      sanctuary—

25 the singers in front, the musicians last,
    between them girls playing tambourines:

26 "Bless God in the great congregation,
    the LORD, O you who are of Israel's fountain!"

27 There is Benjamin, the least of them, in the lead,
    the princes of Judah in a body,
    the princes of Zebulun, the princes of Naphtali.

28 Summon your might, O God;
    show your strength, O God, as you have done
      for us before.

29 Because of your temple at Jerusalem
    kings bear gifts to you.

30 Rebuke the wild animals that live among the
      reeds,
    the herd of bulls with the calves of the
      peoples.
Trample^c under foot those who lust after tribute;
    scatter the peoples who delight in war.^d

31 Let bronze be brought from Egypt;
    let Ethiopia^e hasten to stretch out its hands to
      God.

32 Sing to God, O kingdoms of the earth;
    sing praises to the Lord,   *Selah*

33 O rider in the heavens, the ancient heavens;
    listen, he sends out his voice, his mighty voice.

34 Ascribe power to God,
    whose majesty is over Israel;
    and whose power is in the skies.

35 Awesome is God in his^f sanctuary,
    the God of Israel;
    he gives power and strength to his people.

Blessed be God!

PSALM 69

Prayer for Deliverance from Persecution

To the leader: according to Lilies. Of David.

1 Save me, O God,
    for the waters have come up to my neck.

2 I sink in deep mire,
    where there is no foothold;
I have come into deep waters,
    and the flood sweeps over me.

3 I am weary with my crying;
    my throat is parched.
My eyes grow dim
    with waiting for my God.

4 More in number than the hairs of my head
    are those who hate me without cause;

---

^a Gk Syr Tg: Heb *shatter*   ^b Or *have been seen*   ^c Cn: Heb *Trampling*   ^d Meaning of Heb of verse 30 is uncertain   ^e Or *Nubia*; Heb *Cush*   ^f Gk: Heb *from your*

many are those who would destroy me,
　　my enemies who accuse me falsely.
What I did not steal
　　must I now restore?
5 O God, you know my folly;
　　the wrongs I have done are not hidden from
　　　you.

6 Do not let those who hope in you be put to
　　　shame because of me,
　　O Lord GOD of hosts;
do not let those who seek you be dishonored
　　　because of me,
　　O God of Israel.
7 It is for your sake that I have borne reproach,
　　that shame has covered my face.
8 I have become a stranger to my kindred,
　　an alien to my mother's children.

9 It is zeal for your house that has consumed me;
　　the insults of those who insult you have fallen
　　　on me.
10 When I humbled my soul with fasting,[a]
　　they insulted me for doing so.
11 When I made sackcloth my clothing,
　　I became a byword to them.
12 I am the subject of gossip for those who sit in
　　　the gate,
　　and the drunkards make songs about me.

13 But as for me, my prayer is to you, O LORD.
　　At an acceptable time, O God,
　　in the abundance of your steadfast love,
　　　answer me.
With your faithful help 14rescue me
　　from sinking in the mire;
let me be delivered from my enemies
　　and from the deep waters.
15 Do not let the flood sweep over me,
　　or the deep swallow me up,
　　or the Pit close its mouth over me.

16 Answer me, O LORD, for your steadfast love is
　　　good;
　　according to your abundant mercy, turn to me.
17 Do not hide your face from your servant,
　　for I am in distress—make haste to answer
　　　me.
18 Draw near to me, redeem me,
　　set me free because of my enemies.

19 You know the insults I receive,
　　and my shame and dishonor;
　　my foes are all known to you.
20 Insults have broken my heart,
　　so that I am in despair.

I looked for pity, but there was none;
　　and for comforters, but I found none.
21 They gave me poison for food,
　　and for my thirst they gave me vinegar to
　　　drink.

22 Let their table be a trap for them,
　　a snare for their allies.
23 Let their eyes be darkened so that they cannot
　　　see,
　　and make their loins tremble continually.
24 Pour out your indignation upon them,
　　and let your burning anger overtake them.
25 May their camp be a desolation;
　　let no one live in their tents.
26 For they persecute those whom you have struck
　　　down,
　　and those whom you have wounded, they
　　　attack still more.[b]
27 Add guilt to their guilt;
　　may they have no acquittal from you.
28 Let them be blotted out of the book of the living;
　　let them not be enrolled among the righteous.
29 But I am lowly and in pain;
　　let your salvation, O God, protect me.

30 I will praise the name of God with a song;
　　I will magnify him with thanksgiving.
31 This will please the LORD more than an ox
　　or a bull with horns and hoofs.
32 Let the oppressed see it and be glad;
　　you who seek God, let your hearts revive.
33 For the LORD hears the needy,
　　and does not despise his own that are in
　　　bonds.

34 Let heaven and earth praise him,
　　the seas and everything that moves in them.
35 For God will save Zion
　　and rebuild the cities of Judah;
and his servants shall live[c] there and possess it;
36　　the children of his servants shall inherit it,
　　and those who love his name shall live in it.

PSALM 70

Prayer for Deliverance from Enemies

To the leader. Of David, for the memorial offering.

1 Be pleased, O God, to deliver me.
　　O LORD, make haste to help me!
2 Let those be put to shame and confusion

---

a Gk Syr: Heb *I wept, with fasting my soul,* or *I made my
soul mourn with fasting*　　b Gk Syr: Heb *recount the pain of*
c Syr: Heb *and they shall live*

who seek my life.
Let those be turned back and brought to
   dishonor
   who desire to hurt me.
3 Let those who say, "Aha, Aha!"
   turn back because of their shame.

4 Let all who seek you
   rejoice and be glad in you.
Let those who love your salvation
   say evermore, "God is great!"
5 But I am poor and needy;
   hasten to me, O God!
You are my help and my deliverer;
   O LORD, do not delay!

PSALM 71

Prayer for Lifelong Protection and Help

1 In you, O LORD, I take refuge;
   let me never be put to shame.
2 In your righteousness deliver me and rescue me;
   incline your ear to me and save me.
3 Be to me a rock of refuge,
   a strong fortress,[a] to save me,
   for you are my rock and my fortress.

4 Rescue me, O my God, from the hand of the
   wicked,
   from the grasp of the unjust and cruel.
5 For you, O Lord, are my hope,
   my trust, O LORD, from my youth.
6 Upon you I have leaned from my birth;
   it was you who took me from my mother's
   womb.
   My praise is continually of you.

7 I have been like a portent to many,
   but you are my strong refuge.
8 My mouth is filled with your praise,
   and with your glory all day long.
9 Do not cast me off in the time of old age;
   do not forsake me when my strength is spent.
10 For my enemies speak concerning me,
   and those who watch for my life consult
   together.
11 They say, "Pursue and seize that person
   whom God has forsaken,
   for there is no one to deliver."

12 O God, do not be far from me;
   O my God, make haste to help me!
13 Let my accusers be put to shame and consumed;
   let those who seek to hurt me
   be covered with scorn and disgrace.

14 But I will hope continually,
   and will praise you yet more and more.
15 My mouth will tell of your righteous acts,
   of your deeds of salvation all day long,
   though their number is past my knowledge.
16 I will come praising the mighty deeds of the
   Lord GOD,
   I will praise your righteousness, yours alone.

17 O God, from my youth you have taught me,
   and I still proclaim your wondrous deeds.
18 So even to old age and gray hairs,
   O God, do not forsake me,
   until I proclaim your might
   to all the generations to come.[b]
   Your power 19and your righteousness, O God,
   reach the high heavens.

You who have done great things,
   O God, who is like you?
20 You who have made me see many troubles and
   calamities
   will revive me again;
   from the depths of the earth
   you will bring me up again.
21 You will increase my honor,
   and comfort me once again.

22 I will also praise you with the harp
   for your faithfulness, O my God;
I will sing praises to you with the lyre,
   O Holy One of Israel.
23 My lips will shout for joy
   when I sing praises to you;
   my soul also, which you have rescued.
24 All day long my tongue will talk of your
   righteous help,
   for those who tried to do me harm
   have been put to shame, and disgraced.

PSALM 72

Prayer for Guidance and Support for the King

Of Solomon.

1 Give the king your justice, O God,
   and your righteousness to a king's son.
2 May he judge your people with righteousness,
   and your poor with justice.
3 May the mountains yield prosperity for the
   people,
   and the hills, in righteousness.

---

a Gk Compare 31.3: Heb *to come continually you have
commanded*   b Gk Compare Syr: Heb *to a generation, to all that
come*

Cultural Connection

Open Up Your Treasure

African Americans and other ethnic groups have often been relegated to the background and their contributions ignored. But as Ecclesiastes 3:1 says, "For everything there is a season, and a time for every matter under heaven." And from Psalm 72, we see there is a timing for God's call to us.

Psalm 72:10 says the kings of Sheba and Seba shall come to pay tribute to the King of Israel. Sheba, or Seba, was an ancient kingdom, located near Ethiopia, that included black-skinned people.

In Matthew's story of Jesus' birth, God sends a message in the heavens to inform the dark-skinned wise men from the East when it is time to come and open up their treasures to the King.

God is sending a star to us now. God is talking loudly to us. "Get yourself ready, and be prepared to bring your gifts to me," God says. God has opened the door for us to come, but we must be willing to fall down and worship God and open up our treasures. If we do that, we too will be wise people who acknowledge the One who is born King. Are you ready to acknowledge our real King?

▶ **Ps 72:10–11**

4 May he defend the cause of the poor of the
        people,
    give deliverance to the needy,
    and crush the oppressor.

5 May he live*a* while the sun endures,
    and as long as the moon, throughout all
        generations.
6 May he be like rain that falls on the mown
        grass,
    like showers that water the earth.
7 In his days may righteousness flourish
    and peace abound, until the moon is no
        more.

8 May he have dominion from sea to sea,
    and from the River to the ends of the earth.
9 May his foes*b* bow down before him,
    and his enemies lick the dust.
10 May the kings of Tarshish and of the isles
        render him tribute,
    may the kings of Sheba and Seba
        bring gifts.
11 May all kings fall down before him,
    all nations give him service.

12 For he delivers the needy when they call,
    the poor and those who have no helper.
13 He has pity on the weak and the needy,
    and saves the lives of the needy.

14 From oppression and violence he redeems their
        life;
    and precious is their blood in his sight.

15 Long may he live!
    May gold of Sheba be given to him.
May prayer be made for him continually,
    and blessings invoked for him all day long.
16 May there be abundance of grain in the land;
    may it wave on the tops of the mountains;
    may its fruit be like Lebanon;
and may people blossom in the cities
    like the grass of the field.
17 May his name endure forever,
    his fame continue as long as the sun.
May all nations be blessed in him;*c*
    may they pronounce him happy.

18 Blessed be the LORD, the God of Israel,
    who alone does wondrous things.
19 Blessed be his glorious name forever;
    may his glory fill the whole earth.
        Amen and Amen.

20 The prayers of David son of Jesse are ended.

---

a Gk: Heb *may they fear you*   b Cn: Heb *those who live in the wilderness*   c Or *bless themselves by him*

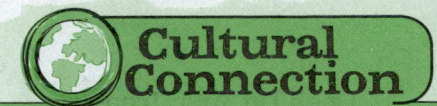

Cultural Connection

Wisdom

Psalm 73 explores the common wisdom question of why the wicked prosper (verse 3). The psalmist finally sees clearly that the wicked eventually fall to ruin (verse 17). The gift of wisdom is also an important value for many Native American peoples. For the Lakota tribe, it is one of four primary values. The Lakota word for wisdom is *wok-sa-pe*.

Wisdom is the ability to see clearly and not be taken in by illusions or outer appearances. The wise person knows that what is inside someone is more important than what is outside. The wise person also knows that we are nothing without the power of *Wakan-Tanka*, the Great Spirit. Because the sun helps us see things the way they really are,

many Native Americans face the rising sun each day to pray to God for wisdom.

To explore the other primary Lakota virtues, see the "Cultural Connections" articles for Psalms 31, 89, and 112.

▶ **Psalm 73**

BOOK III
(Psalms 73-89)

PSALM 73

Plea for Relief from Oppressors
A Psalm of Asaph.

1 Truly God is good to the upright,*a*
   to those who are pure in heart.
2 But as for me, my feet had almost stumbled;
   my steps had nearly slipped.
3 For I was envious of the arrogant;
   I saw the prosperity of the wicked.

4 For they have no pain;
   their bodies are sound and sleek.
5 They are not in trouble as others are;
   they are not plagued like other people.
6 Therefore pride is their necklace;
   violence covers them like a garment.
7 Their eyes swell out with fatness;
   their hearts overflow with follies.
8 They scoff and speak with malice;
   loftily they threaten oppression.
9 They set their mouths against heaven,
   and their tongues range over the earth.

10 Therefore the people turn and praise them,*b*
   and find no fault in them.*c*
11 And they say, "How can God know?
   Is there knowledge in the Most High?"
12 Such are the wicked;
   always at ease, they increase in riches.
13 All in vain I have kept my heart clean
   and washed my hands in innocence.

14 For all day long I have been plagued,
   and am punished every morning.

15 If I had said, "I will talk on in this way,"
   I would have been untrue to the circle of your
      children.
16 But when I thought how to understand this,
   it seemed to me a wearisome task,
17 until I went into the sanctuary of God;
   then I perceived their end.
18 Truly you set them in slippery places;
   you make them fall to ruin.
19 How they are destroyed in a moment,
   swept away utterly by terrors!
20 They are*d* like a dream when one awakes;
   on awaking you despise their phantoms.

21 When my soul was embittered,
   when I was pricked in heart,
22 I was stupid and ignorant;
   I was like a brute beast toward you.
23 Nevertheless I am continually with you;
   you hold my right hand.
24 You guide me with your counsel,
   and afterward you will receive me with honor.*e*
25 Whom have I in heaven but you?
   And there is nothing on earth that I desire
      other than you.
26 My flesh and my heart may fail,
   but God is the strength*f* of my heart and my
      portion forever.

---

a Or *good to Israel*   *b* Cn: Heb *his people return here*
c Cn: Heb *abundant waters are drained by them*   *d* Cn: Heb *Lord*
e Or *to glory*   *f* Heb *rock*

²⁷ Indeed, those who are far from you will perish;
    you put an end to those who are false to you.
²⁸ But for me it is good to be near God;
    I have made the Lord God my refuge,
    to tell of all your works.

PSALM 74

Plea for Help in Time of National Humiliation

A Maskil of Asaph.

¹ O God, why do you cast us off forever?
    Why does your anger smoke against the sheep
    of your pasture?
² Remember your congregation, which you
    acquired long ago,
    which you redeemed to be the tribe of your
    heritage.
    Remember Mount Zion, where you came to
    dwell.
³ Direct your steps to the perpetual ruins;
    the enemy has destroyed everything in the
    sanctuary.

⁴ Your foes have roared within your holy place;
    they set up their emblems there.
⁵ At the upper entrance they hacked
    the wooden trellis with axes.[a]
⁶ And then, with hatchets and hammers,
    they smashed all its carved work.
⁷ They set your sanctuary on fire;
    they desecrated the dwelling place of your
    name,
    bringing it to the ground.
⁸ They said to themselves, "We will utterly subdue
    them";
    they burned all the meeting places of God in
    the land.

⁹ We do not see our emblems;
    there is no longer any prophet,
    and there is no one among us who knows
    how long.
¹⁰ How long, O God, is the foe to scoff?
    Is the enemy to revile your name forever?
¹¹ Why do you hold back your hand;
    why do you keep your hand in[b] your bosom?

¹² Yet God my King is from of old,
    working salvation in the earth.
¹³ You divided the sea by your might;
    you broke the heads of the dragons in the
    waters.
¹⁴ You crushed the heads of Leviathan;
    you gave him as food[c] for the creatures of the
    wilderness.

¹⁵ You cut openings for springs and torrents;
    you dried up ever-flowing streams.
¹⁶ Yours is the day, yours also the night;
    you established the luminaries[d] and the sun.
¹⁷ You have fixed all the bounds of the earth;
    you made summer and winter.

¹⁸ Remember this, O Lord, how the enemy scoffs,
    and an impious people reviles your name.
¹⁹ Do not deliver the soul of your dove to the wild
    animals;
    do not forget the life of your poor forever.

²⁰ Have regard for your[e] covenant,
    for the dark places of the land are full of the
    haunts of violence.
²¹ Do not let the downtrodden be put to shame;
    let the poor and needy praise your name.
²² Rise up, O God, plead your cause;
    remember how the impious scoff at you all
    day long.
²³ Do not forget the clamor of your foes,
    the uproar of your adversaries that goes up
    continually.

PSALM 75

Thanksgiving for God's Wondrous Deeds

To the leader: Do Not Destroy. A Psalm of Asaph.
A Song.

¹ We give thanks to you, O God;
    we give thanks; your name is near.
People tell of your wondrous deeds.

² At the set time that I appoint
    I will judge with equity.
³ When the earth totters, with all its inhabitants,
    it is I who keep its pillars steady.   *Selah*
⁴ I say to the boastful, "Do not boast,"
    and to the wicked, "Do not lift up your horn;
⁵ do not lift up your horn on high,
    or speak with insolent neck."

⁶ For not from the east or from the west
    and not from the wilderness comes lifting up;
⁷ but it is God who executes judgment,
    putting down one and lifting up another.
⁸ For in the hand of the Lord there is a cup
    with foaming wine, well mixed;
he will pour a draught from it,
    and all the wicked of the earth

---

a Cn Compare Gk Syr: Meaning of Heb uncertain   *b* Cn: Heb *do
you consume your right hand from*   *c* Heb *food for the people*
d Or *moon*; Heb *light*   *e* Gk Syr: Heb *the*

P
S

shall drain it down to the dregs.
9 But I will rejoice[a] forever;
   I will sing praises to the God of Jacob.

10 All the horns of the wicked I will cut off,
   but the horns of the righteous shall be exalted.

PSALM 76

Israel's God—Judge of All the Earth

To the leader: with stringed instruments. A Psalm
of Asaph. A Song.

1 In Judah God is known,
   his name is great in Israel.
2 His abode has been established in Salem,
   his dwelling place in Zion.
3 There he broke the flashing arrows,
   the shield, the sword, and the weapons of
      war.   *Selah*

4 Glorious are you, more majestic
   than the everlasting mountains.[b]
5 The stouthearted were stripped of their spoil;
   they sank into sleep;
none of the troops
   was able to lift a hand.
6 At your rebuke, O God of Jacob,
   both rider and horse lay stunned.

7 But you indeed are awesome!
   Who can stand before you
   when once your anger is roused?
8 From the heavens you uttered judgment;
   the earth feared and was still
9 when God rose up to establish judgment,
   to save all the oppressed of the earth.   *Selah*

10 Human wrath serves only to praise you,
   when you bind the last bit of your[c] wrath
      around you.
11 Make vows to the LORD your God, and perform
      them;
   let all who are around him bring gifts
   to the one who is awesome,
12 who cuts off the spirit of princes,
   who inspires fear in the kings of the earth.

PSALM 77

God's Mighty Deeds Recalled

To the leader: according to Jeduthun. Of Asaph.
A Psalm.

1 I cry aloud to God,
   aloud to God, that he may hear me.

2 In the day of my trouble I seek the Lord;
   in the night my hand is stretched out without
      wearying;
   my soul refuses to be comforted.
3 I think of God, and I moan;
   I meditate, and my spirit faints.   *Selah*

4 You keep my eyelids from closing;
   I am so troubled that I cannot speak.
5 I consider the days of old,
   and remember the years of long ago.
6 I commune[d] with my heart in the night;
   I meditate and search my spirit:[e]
7 "Will the Lord spurn forever,
   and never again be favorable?
8 Has his steadfast love ceased forever?
   Are his promises at an end for all time?
9 Has God forgotten to be gracious?
   Has he in anger shut up his compassion?"
                              Selah
10 And I say, "It is my grief
   that the right hand of the Most High has
      changed."

11 I will call to mind the deeds of the LORD;
   I will remember your wonders of old.
12 I will meditate on all your work,
   and muse on your mighty deeds.
13 Your way, O God, is holy.
   What god is so great as our God?
14 You are the God who works wonders;
   you have displayed your might among the
      peoples.
15 With your strong arm you redeemed your
      people,
   the descendants of Jacob and Joseph.   *Selah*

16 When the waters saw you, O God,
   when the waters saw you, they were afraid;
   the very deep trembled.
17 The clouds poured out water;
   the skies thundered;
   your arrows flashed on every side.
18 The crash of your thunder was in the
      whirlwind;
   your lightnings lit up the world;
   the earth trembled and shook.
19 Your way was through the sea,
   your path, through the mighty waters;
   yet your footprints were unseen.
20 You led your people like a flock
   by the hand of Moses and Aaron.

---

a Gk: Heb *declare*   *b* Gk: Heb *the mountains of prey*
c Heb lacks *your*   *d* Gk Syr: Heb *My music*   *e* Syr Jerome: Heb
my spirit searches

PSALM 78

God's Goodness and Israel's Ingratitude

A Maskil of Asaph.

1 Give ear, O my people, to my teaching;
    incline your ears to the words of my mouth.
2 I will open my mouth in a parable;
    I will utter dark sayings from of old,
3 things that we have heard and known,
    that our ancestors have told us.
4 We will not hide them from their children;
    we will tell to the coming generation
the glorious deeds of the LORD, and his might,
    and the wonders that he has done.

5 He established a decree in Jacob,
    and appointed a law in Israel,
which he commanded our ancestors
    to teach to their children;
6 that the next generation might know them,
    the children yet unborn,
and rise up and tell them to their children,
7   so that they should set their hope in God,
and not forget the works of God,
    but keep his commandments;
8 and that they should not be like their ancestors,
    a stubborn and rebellious generation,
a generation whose heart was not steadfast,
    whose spirit was not faithful to God.

9 The Ephraimites, armed with^a the bow,
    turned back on the day of battle.
10 They did not keep God's covenant,
    but refused to walk according to his law.
11 They forgot what he had done,
    and the miracles that he had shown them.
12 In the sight of their ancestors he worked marvels
    in the land of Egypt, in the fields of Zoan.
13 He divided the sea and let them pass through it,
    and made the waters stand like a heap.
14 In the daytime he led them with a cloud,
    and all night long with a fiery light.
15 He split rocks open in the wilderness,
    and gave them drink abundantly as from the deep.
16 He made streams come out of the rock,
    and caused waters to flow down like rivers.

17 Yet they sinned still more against him,
    rebelling against the Most High in the desert.
18 They tested God in their heart
    by demanding the food they craved.
19 They spoke against God, saying,
    "Can God spread a table in the wilderness?
20 Even though he struck the rock so that water
    gushed out
and torrents overflowed,
can he also give bread,
    or provide meat for his people?"

21 Therefore, when the LORD heard, he was full of
    rage;
    a fire was kindled against Jacob,
    his anger mounted against Israel,
22 because they had no faith in God,
    and did not trust his saving power.

---

a Heb *armed with shooting*

The Big Picture

Perspective is a valuable thing. It is easy for us to get caught up in the moment, overwhelmed by the urgency of school assignments, sports, and time with family and friends. As difficult as it is, we need to step back for a moment or two and try to grasp the big picture.

When we look back at our lives and see where we have come from, the path often makes sense. The twists and turns that were so frustrating and confusing can now be recognized as temporary diversions on our journey. Everything we experienced—the good and the bad—contains lessons for us. The question is, How good a student are we?

The key to wisdom is reflection. Psalm 77 keeps saying this in different ways: "I meditate" (verses 3, 6, 12), "I consider" (verse 5), and "I will call to mind" (verse 11). How do you take the time to remember where you have been and to meditate on where you hope to go? Do you learn from the great teacher, life experience? Do you see the whole forest or only the trees right in front of you?

If you don't already spend some time at the end of each day reflecting on the events of that day, begin doing so. Keep a journal on how you felt or what you learned. Over time you will see the big picture emerge and even have a greater sense of God's presence in your life.

▶ Psalm 77

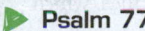

23 Yet he commanded the skies above,
and opened the doors of heaven;
24 he rained down on them manna to eat,
and gave them the grain of heaven.
25 Mortals ate of the bread of angels;
he sent them food in abundance.
26 He caused the east wind to blow in the heavens,
and by his power he led out the south wind;
27 he rained flesh upon them like dust,
winged birds like the sand of the seas;
28 he let them fall within their camp,
all around their dwellings.
29 And they ate and were well filled,
for he gave them what they craved.
30 But before they had satisfied their craving,
while the food was still in their mouths,
31 the anger of God rose against them
and he killed the strongest of them,
and laid low the flower of Israel.

32 In spite of all this they still sinned;
they did not believe in his wonders.
33 So he made their days vanish like a breath,
and their years in terror.
34 When he killed them, they sought for him;
they repented and sought God earnestly.
35 They remembered that God was their rock,
the Most High God their redeemer.
36 But they flattered him with their mouths;
they lied to him with their tongues.
37 Their heart was not steadfast toward him;
they were not true to his covenant.
38 Yet he, being compassionate,
forgave their iniquity,
and did not destroy them;
often he restrained his anger,
and did not stir up all his wrath.
39 He remembered that they were but flesh,
a wind that passes and does not come again.
40 How often they rebelled against him in the
wilderness
and grieved him in the desert!
41 They tested God again and again,
and provoked the Holy One of Israel.
42 They did not keep in mind his power,
or the day when he redeemed them from the
foe;
43 when he displayed his signs in Egypt,
and his miracles in the fields of Zoan.
44 He turned their rivers to blood,
so that they could not drink of their streams.
45 He sent among them swarms of flies, which
devoured them,
and frogs, which destroyed them.
46 He gave their crops to the caterpillar,
and the fruit of their labor to the locust.

47 He destroyed their vines with hail,
and their sycamores with frost.
48 He gave over their cattle to the hail,
and their flocks to thunderbolts.
49 He let loose on them his fierce anger,
wrath, indignation, and distress,
a company of destroying angels.
50 He made a path for his anger;
he did not spare them from death,
but gave their lives over to the plague.
51 He struck all the firstborn in Egypt,
the first issue of their strength in the tents of
Ham.
52 Then he led out his people like sheep,
and guided them in the wilderness like a
flock.
53 He led them in safety, so that they were not
afraid;
but the sea overwhelmed their enemies.
54 And he brought them to his holy hill,
to the mountain that his right hand had won.
55 He drove out nations before them;
he apportioned them for a possession
and settled the tribes of Israel in their tents.

56 Yet they tested the Most High God,
and rebelled against him.
They did not observe his decrees,
57 but turned away and were faithless like their
ancestors;
they twisted like a treacherous bow.
58 For they provoked him to anger with their high
places;
they moved him to jealousy with their idols.
59 When God heard, he was full of wrath,
and he utterly rejected Israel.
60 He abandoned his dwelling at Shiloh,
the tent where he dwelt among mortals,
61 and delivered his power to captivity,
his glory to the hand of the foe.
62 He gave his people to the sword,
and vented his wrath on his heritage.
63 Fire devoured their young men,
and their girls had no marriage song.
64 Their priests fell by the sword,
and their widows made no lamentation.
65 Then the Lord awoke as from sleep,
like a warrior shouting because of wine.
66 He put his adversaries to rout;
he put them to everlasting disgrace.

67 He rejected the tent of Joseph,
he did not choose the tribe of Ephraim;
68 but he chose the tribe of Judah,
Mount Zion, which he loves.
69 He built his sanctuary like the high heavens,

like the earth, which he has founded forever.
70 He chose his servant David,
    and took him from the sheepfolds;
71 from tending the nursing ewes he brought him
    to be the shepherd of his people Jacob,
    of Israel, his inheritance.
72 With upright heart he tended them,
    and guided them with skillful hand.

PSALM 79

Plea for Mercy for Jerusalem

A Psalm of Asaph.

1 O God, the nations have come into your
    inheritance;
    they have defiled your holy temple;
    they have laid Jerusalem in ruins.
2 They have given the bodies of your servants
    to the birds of the air for food,
    the flesh of your faithful to the wild animals
        of the earth.
3 They have poured out their blood like water
    all around Jerusalem,
    and there was no one to bury them.
4 We have become a taunt to our neighbors,
    mocked and derided by those around us.

5 How long, O LORD? Will you be angry forever?
    Will your jealous wrath burn like fire?
6 Pour out your anger on the nations
    that do not know you,
    and on the kingdoms
    that do not call on your name.
7 For they have devoured Jacob
    and laid waste his habitation.

8 Do not remember against us the iniquities of
        our ancestors;
    let your compassion come speedily to meet us,
    for we are brought very low.
9 Help us, O God of our salvation,
    for the glory of your name;
    deliver us, and forgive our sins,
    for your name's sake.
10 Why should the nations say,
    "Where is their God?"
    Let the avenging of the outpoured blood of your
        servants
    be known among the nations before our eyes.

11 Let the groans of the prisoners come before you;
    according to your great power preserve those
        doomed to die.
12 Return sevenfold into the bosom of our
    neighbors

the taunts with which they taunted you,
    O Lord!
13 Then we your people, the flock of your pasture,
    will give thanks to you forever;
    from generation to generation we will recount
    your praise.

PSALM 80

Prayer for Israel's Restoration

To the leader: on Lilies, a Covenant. Of Asaph.
A Psalm.

1 Give ear, O Shepherd of Israel,
    you who lead Joseph like a flock!
    You who are enthroned upon the cherubim,
        shine forth
2   before Ephraim and Benjamin and Manasseh.
    Stir up your might,
    and come to save us!

3 Restore us, O God;
    let your face shine, that we may be saved.

4 O LORD God of hosts,
    how long will you be angry with your
        people's prayers?
5 You have fed them with the bread of tears,
    and given them tears to drink in full measure.
6 You make us the scorn[a] of our neighbors;
    our enemies laugh among themselves.

7 Restore us, O God of hosts;
    let your face shine, that we may be saved.

8 You brought a vine out of Egypt;
    you drove out the nations and planted it.
9 You cleared the ground for it;
    it took deep root and filled the land.
10 The mountains were covered with its shade,
    the mighty cedars with its branches;
11 it sent out its branches to the sea,
    and its shoots to the River.
12 Why then have you broken down its walls,
    so that all who pass along the way pluck its
        fruit?
13 The boar from the forest ravages it,
    and all that move in the field feed on it.

14 Turn again, O God of hosts;
    look down from heaven, and see;
    have regard for this vine,
15   the stock that your right hand planted.[b]

___

a Syr: Heb strife   b Heb adds from verse 17 and upon the one
whom you made strong for yourself

Catholic Social Teaching   AIDS—a Matter of Compassion

After a local man died of complications due to the AIDS virus, a newspaper carried an article about his life. The writer said: "His worst fears were not realized. His church did not reject him in the end. It surrounded him with love." What an awesome example of love and justice. His parish did not condemn him; it showed compassion for his life.

Even though our faith calls us to show compassion towards those who suffer, we are sometimes tempted to blame those who are suffering for the situation they are in and to excuse ourselves from any need to help. We say that people who are poor are too lazy to work, that those who are hungry should get a job, that people dying of AIDS deserve it because of their choices. These attitudes portray a cold justice without mercy. They are not from the mind of God. For God mercy and justice go hand in hand.

Psalm 82 is a plea for God's justice, a cry to "maintain the right of the lowly" (verse 3). Catholic social teaching echoes this theme, reminding us that every person's life has a God-given sense of dignity that must always be upheld. This is especially true regarding the weak, needy, orphaned, and destitute. We must never condemn or judge those in dire situations, even if they have made seemingly poor life decisions. Instead, our words and actions must be directed towards lifting up the lowly, surrounding them, as the man's local church did, with great love in their time of need.

▶ **Psalm 82**

Life and Dignity of the Human Person

PS

16 They have burned it with fire, they have cut it
  down;[a]
  may they perish at the rebuke of your
  countenance.
17 But let your hand be upon the one at your right
  hand,
  the one whom you made strong for yourself.
18 Then we will never turn back from you;
  give us life, and we will call on your name.

19 Restore us, O Lord God of hosts;
  let your face shine, that we may be saved.

PSALM 81

God's Appeal to Stubborn Israel

To the leader: according to The Gittith. Of Asaph.

1 Sing aloud to God our strength;
  shout for joy to the God of Jacob.
2 Raise a song, sound the tambourine,
  the sweet lyre with the harp.
3 Blow the trumpet at the new moon,
  at the full moon, on our festal day.
4 For it is a statute for Israel,
  an ordinance of the God of Jacob.
5 He made it a decree in Joseph,
  when he went out over[b] the land of Egypt.

I hear a voice I had not known:
6 "I relieved your[c] shoulder of the burden;
  your[c] hands were freed from the basket.
7 In distress you called, and I rescued you;
  I answered you in the secret place of thunder;
  I tested you at the waters of Meribah.   *Selah*
8 Hear, O my people, while I admonish you;
  O Israel, if you would but listen to me!
9 There shall be no strange god among you;
  you shall not bow down to a foreign god.
10 I am the Lord your God,
  who brought you up out of the land of
  Egypt.
  Open your mouth wide and I will fill it.

11 "But my people did not listen to my voice;
  Israel would not submit to me.
12 So I gave them over to their stubborn hearts,
  to follow their own counsels.
13 O that my people would listen to me,
  that Israel would walk in my ways!
14 Then I would quickly subdue their enemies,
  and turn my hand against their foes.
15 Those who hate the Lord would cringe before
  him,
  and their doom would last forever.

a Cn: Heb *it is cut down*   *b* Or *against*   *c* Heb *his*

16 I would feed you[a] with the finest of the wheat,
  and with honey from the rock I would satisfy
    you."

PSALM 82

A Plea for Justice

A Psalm of Asaph.

1 God has taken his place in the divine council;
  in the midst of the gods he holds judgment:
2 "How long will you judge unjustly
  and show partiality to the wicked?   *Selah*
3 Give justice to the weak and the orphan;
  maintain the right of the lowly and the
    destitute.
4 Rescue the weak and the needy;
  deliver them from the hand of the wicked."

5 They have neither knowledge nor understanding,
  they walk around in darkness;
  all the foundations of the earth are shaken.

6 I say, "You are gods,
  children of the Most High, all of you;
7 nevertheless, you shall die like mortals,
  and fall like any prince."[b]

8 Rise up, O God, judge the earth;
  for all the nations belong to you!

PSALM 83

Prayer for Judgment on Israel's Foes

A Song. A Psalm of Asaph.

1 O God, do not keep silence;
  do not hold your peace or be still, O God!
2 Even now your enemies are in tumult;
  those who hate you have raised their heads.
3 They lay crafty plans against your people;
  they consult together against those you
    protect.
4 They say, "Come, let us wipe them out as a
    nation;
  let the name of Israel be remembered no
    more."
5 They conspire with one accord;
  against you they make a covenant—
6 the tents of Edom and the Ishmaelites,
  Moab and the Hagrites,
7 Gebal and Ammon and Amalek,
  Philistia with the inhabitants of Tyre;
8 Assyria also has joined them;
  they are the strong arm of the children
    of Lot.   *Selah*

9 Do to them as you did to Midian,
  as to Sisera and Jabin at the Wadi Kishon,
10 who were destroyed at En-dor,
  who became dung for the ground.
11 Make their nobles like Oreb and Zeeb,
  all their princes like Zebah and Zalmunna,
12 who said, "Let us take the pastures of God
  for our own possession."

13 O my God, make them like whirling dust,[c]
  like chaff before the wind.
14 As fire consumes the forest,
  as the flame sets the mountains ablaze,
15 so pursue them with your tempest
  and terrify them with your hurricane.
16 Fill their faces with shame,
  so that they may seek your name, O LORD.
17 Let them be put to shame and dismayed
    forever;
  let them perish in disgrace.
18 Let them know that you alone,
  whose name is the LORD,
  are the Most High over all the earth.

PSALM 84

The Joy of Worship in the Temple

To the leader: according to The Gittith.
Of the Korahites. A Psalm.

1 How lovely is your dwelling place,
  O LORD of hosts!
2 My soul longs, indeed it faints
  for the courts of the LORD;
my heart and my flesh sing for joy
  to the living God.

3 Even the sparrow finds a home,
  and the swallow a nest for herself,
  where she may lay her young,
at your altars, O LORD of hosts,
  my King and my God.
4 Happy are those who live in your house,
  ever singing your praise.   *Selah*

5 Happy are those whose strength is in you,
  in whose heart are the highways to Zion.[d]
6 As they go through the valley of Baca
  they make it a place of springs;
  the early rain also covers it with pools.
7 They go from strength to strength;
  the God of gods will be seen in Zion.

P
S

---

a Cn Compare verse 16b: Heb *he would feed him*   b Or *fall as
one man, O princes*   c Or *a tumbleweed*   d Heb lacks *to Zion*

8 O Lord God of hosts, hear my prayer;
    give ear, O God of Jacob!   *Selah*
9 Behold our shield, O God;
    look on the face of your anointed.

10 For a day in your courts is better
    than a thousand elsewhere.
  I would rather be a doorkeeper in the house of
      my God
    than live in the tents of wickedness.
11 For the Lord God is a sun and shield;
    he bestows favor and honor.
  No good thing does the Lord withhold
    from those who walk uprightly.
12 O Lord of hosts,
    happy is everyone who trusts in you.

PSALM 85

Prayer for the Restoration of God's Favor

To the leader. Of the Korahites. A Psalm.

1 Lord, you were favorable to your land;
    you restored the fortunes of Jacob.
2 You forgave the iniquity of your people;
    you pardoned all their sin.   *Selah*
3 You withdrew all your wrath;
    you turned from your hot anger.

4 Restore us again, O God of our salvation,
    and put away your indignation toward us.
5 Will you be angry with us forever?
    Will you prolong your anger to all
      generations?
6 Will you not revive us again,
    so that your people may rejoice in you?
7 Show us your steadfast love, O Lord,
    and grant us your salvation.

8 Let me hear what God the Lord will speak,
    for he will speak peace to his people,
    to his faithful, to those who turn to him in
      their hearts.[a]
9 Surely his salvation is at hand for those who fear
      him,
    that his glory may dwell in our land.

10 Steadfast love and faithfulness will meet;
    righteousness and peace will kiss each other.
11 Faithfulness will spring up from the ground,
    and righteousness will look down from the
      sky.
12 The Lord will give what is good,
    and our land will yield its increase.
13 Righteousness will go before him,
    and will make a path for his steps.

PSALM 86

Supplication for Help against Enemies

A Prayer of David.

1 Incline your ear, O Lord, and answer me,
    for I am poor and needy.
2 Preserve my life, for I am devoted to you;
    save your servant who trusts in you.
  You are my God; 3be gracious to me, O Lord,
    for to you do I cry all day long.
4 Gladden the soul of your servant,
    for to you, O Lord, I lift up my soul.
5 For you, O Lord, are good and forgiving,
    abounding in steadfast love to all who call on
      you.
6 Give ear, O Lord, to my prayer;
    listen to my cry of supplication.
7 In the day of my trouble I call on you,
    for you will answer me.

8 There is none like you among the gods, O Lord,
    nor are there any works like yours.
9 All the nations you have made shall come
    and bow down before you, O Lord,
    and shall glorify your name.
10 For you are great and do wondrous things;
    you alone are God.
11 Teach me your way, O Lord,
    that I may walk in your truth;
    give me an undivided heart to revere your
      name.
12 I give thanks to you, O Lord my God, with my
      whole heart,
    and I will glorify your name forever.
13 For great is your steadfast love toward me;
    you have delivered my soul from the depths
      of Sheol.

14 O God, the insolent rise up against me;
    a band of ruffians seeks my life,
    and they do not set you before them.
15 But you, O Lord, are a God merciful and
      gracious,
    slow to anger and abounding in steadfast love
      and faithfulness.
16 Turn to me and be gracious to me;
    give your strength to your servant;
    save the child of your serving girl.
17 Show me a sign of your favor,
    so that those who hate me may see it and be
      put to shame,
    because you, Lord, have helped me and
      comforted me.

a Gk: Heb *but let them not turn back to folly*

PSALM 87

The Joy of Living in Zion

Of the Korahites. A Psalm. A Song.

1 On the holy mount stands the city he founded;
2   the LORD loves the gates of Zion
    more than all the dwellings of Jacob.
3 Glorious things are spoken of you,
    O city of God.   *Selah*

4 Among those who know me I mention Rahab
        and Babylon;
    Philistia too, and Tyre, with Ethiopia*a*—
    "This one was born there," they say.

5 And of Zion it shall be said,
    "This one and that one were born in it";
    for the Most High himself will establish it.
6 The LORD records, as he registers the peoples,
    "This one was born there."   *Selah*

7 Singers and dancers alike say,
    "All my springs are in you."

PSALM 88

Prayer for Help in Despondency

A Song. A Psalm of the Korahites. To the leader:
according to Mahalath Leannoth. A Maskil
of Heman the Ezrahite.

1 O LORD, God of my salvation,
    when, at night, I cry out in your presence,
2 let my prayer come before you;
    incline your ear to my cry.

3 For my soul is full of troubles,
    and my life draws near to Sheol.
4 I am counted among those who go down to the
        Pit;
    I am like those who have no help,
5 like those forsaken among the dead,
    like the slain that lie in the grave,
    like those whom you remember no more,
    for they are cut off from your hand.
6 You have put me in the depths of the Pit,
    in the regions dark and deep.
7 Your wrath lies heavy upon me,
    and you overwhelm me with all your waves. *Selah*

8 You have caused my companions to shun me;
    you have made me a thing of horror to them.
    I am shut in so that I cannot escape;
9   my eye grows dim through sorrow.
    Every day I call on you, O LORD;

    I spread out my hands to you.
10 Do you work wonders for the dead?
    Do the shades rise up to praise you?   *Selah*
11 Is your steadfast love declared in the grave,
    or your faithfulness in Abaddon?
12 Are your wonders known in the darkness,
    or your saving help in the land of
        forgetfulness?

13 But I, O LORD, cry out to you;
    in the morning my prayer comes before you.
14 O LORD, why do you cast me off?
    Why do you hide your face from me?
15 Wretched and close to death from my youth up,
    I suffer your terrors; I am desperate.*b*
16 Your wrath has swept over me;
    your dread assaults destroy me.
17 They surround me like a flood all day long;
    from all sides they close in on me.
18 You have caused friend and neighbor to shun me;
    my companions are in darkness.

PSALM 89

God's Covenant with David

A Maskil of Ethan the Ezrahite.

1 I will sing of your steadfast love, O LORD,*c*
        forever;
    with my mouth I will proclaim your
        faithfulness to all generations.
2 I declare that your steadfast love is established
        forever;
    your faithfulness is as firm as the heavens.

3 You said, "I have made a covenant with my
        chosen one,
    I have sworn to my servant David:
4 'I will establish your descendants forever,
    and build your throne for all generations.' "
                                            Selah

5 Let the heavens praise your wonders, O LORD,
    your faithfulness in the assembly of the holy
        ones.
6 For who in the skies can be compared to the
        LORD?
    Who among the heavenly beings is like the
        LORD,
7 a God feared in the council of the holy ones,
    great and awesome*d* above all that are around
        him?

---

a Or Nubia; Heb Cush   *b* Meaning of Heb uncertain
c Gk: Heb the steadfast love of the LORD   *d* Gk Syr: Heb greatly
awesome

Cultural Connection

Respect

Respect is an important value for many Native American peoples. For the Lakota tribe, it is one of four primary values. The Lakota word for respect is *wo-wac-in-tan-ka.*

Psalm 89:6–9 speaks to the Lakota people of the power and the awesomeness of the Great Spirit. We owe reverence and re-spect not only to our God but also to all our God has created—the earth, the animals, and one an-other. The young respect the el-ders because the elders are peo-ple of history and experience. The old respect the young because they are the future of the world. When everyone lives in respect, the earth is at peace.

To explore the other primary Lakota virtues, see the "Cultural Connections" articles for Psalms 31, 73, and 112.

▶ **Psalm 89**

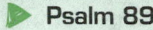

8 O Lord God of hosts,
  who is as mighty as you, O Lord?
  Your faithfulness surrounds you.
9 You rule the raging of the sea;
  when its waves rise, you still them.
10 You crushed Rahab like a carcass;
  you scattered your enemies with your mighty arm.
11 The heavens are yours, the earth also is yours;
  the world and all that is in it—you have founded them.
12 The north and the south*a*—you created them;
  Tabor and Hermon joyously praise your name.
13 You have a mighty arm;
  strong is your hand, high your right hand.
14 Righteousness and justice are the foundation of your throne;
  steadfast love and faithfulness go before you.
15 Happy are the people who know the festal shout,
  who walk, O Lord, in the light of your countenance;
16 they exult in your name all day long,
  and extol*b* your righteousness.
17 For you are the glory of their strength;
  by your favor our horn is exalted.
18 For our shield belongs to the Lord,
  our king to the Holy One of Israel.

19 Then you spoke in a vision to your faithful one, and said:
  "I have set the crown*c* on one who is mighty,
  I have exalted one chosen from the people.
20 I have found my servant David;
  with my holy oil I have anointed him;
21 my hand shall always remain with him;

  my arm also shall strengthen him.
22 The enemy shall not outwit him,
  the wicked shall not humble him.
23 I will crush his foes before him
  and strike down those who hate him.
24 My faithfulness and steadfast love shall be with him;
  and in my name his horn shall be exalted.
25 I will set his hand on the sea
  and his right hand on the rivers.
26 He shall cry to me, 'You are my Father,
  my God, and the Rock of my salvation!'
27 I will make him the firstborn,
  the highest of the kings of the earth.
28 Forever I will keep my steadfast love for him,
  and my covenant with him will stand firm.
29 I will establish his line forever,
  and his throne as long as the heavens endure.
30 If his children forsake my law
  and do not walk according to my ordinances,
31 if they violate my statutes
  and do not keep my commandments,
32 then I will punish their transgression with the rod
  and their iniquity with scourges;
33 but I will not remove from him my steadfast love,
  or be false to my faithfulness.
34 I will not violate my covenant,
  or alter the word that went forth from my lips.
35 Once and for all I have sworn by my holiness;
  I will not lie to David.
36 His line shall continue forever,
  and his throne endure before me like the sun.

a Or Zaphon and Yamin   b Cn: Heb are exalted in   c Cn: Heb help

37 It shall be established forever like the moon,
   an enduring witness in the skies." Selah

38 But now you have spurned and rejected him;
   you are full of wrath against your anointed.
39 You have renounced the covenant with your
       servant;
   you have defiled his crown in the dust.
40 You have broken through all his walls;
   you have laid his strongholds in ruins.
41 All who pass by plunder him;
   he has become the scorn of his neighbors.
42 You have exalted the right hand of his foes;
   you have made all his enemies rejoice.
43 Moreover, you have turned back the edge of his
       sword,
   and you have not supported him in battle.
44 You have removed the scepter from his hand,[a]
   and hurled his throne to the ground.
45 You have cut short the days of his youth;
   you have covered him with shame. Selah

46 How long, O Lord? Will you hide yourself
       forever?
   How long will your wrath burn like fire?
47 Remember how short my time is—[b]
   for what vanity you have created all mortals!
48 Who can live and never see death?
   Who can escape the power of Sheol? Selah

49 Lord, where is your steadfast love of old,
   which by your faithfulness you swore to David?
50 Remember, O Lord, how your servant is taunted;
   how I bear in my bosom the insults of the
       peoples,[c]
51 with which your enemies taunt, O Lord,
   with which they taunted the footsteps of your
       anointed.

52 Blessed be the Lord forever.
   Amen and Amen.

BOOK IV
(Psalms 90–106)

PSALM 90

God's Eternity and Human Frailty

A Prayer of Moses, the man of God.

1 Lord, you have been our dwelling place[d]
   in all generations.
2 Before the mountains were brought forth,
   or ever you had formed the earth and the
       world,
   from everlasting to everlasting you are God.

3 You turn us[e] back to dust,
   and say, "Turn back, you mortals."
4 For a thousand years in your sight
   are like yesterday when it is past,
   or like a watch in the night.

5 You sweep them away; they are like a dream,
   like grass that is renewed in the morning;
6 in the morning it flourishes and is renewed;
   in the evening it fades and withers.

7 For we are consumed by your anger;
   by your wrath we are overwhelmed.
8 You have set our iniquities before you,
   our secret sins in the light of your
       countenance.

9 For all our days pass away under your wrath;
   our years come to an end[f] like a sigh.
10 The days of our life are seventy years,
   or perhaps eighty, if we are strong;
   even then their span[g] is only toil and trouble;
   they are soon gone, and we fly away.

11 Who considers the power of your anger?
   Your wrath is as great as the fear that is due
       you.
12 So teach us to count our days
   that we may gain a wise heart.

13 Turn, O Lord! How long?
   Have compassion on your servants!
14 Satisfy us in the morning with your steadfast
       love,
   so that we may rejoice and be glad all our
       days.
15 Make us glad as many days as you have
       afflicted us,
   and as many years as we have seen evil.
16 Let your work be manifest to your servants,
   and your glorious power to their children.
17 Let the favor of the Lord our God be upon us,
   and prosper for us the work of our hands—
   O prosper the work of our hands!

PSALM 91

Assurance of God's Protection

1 You who live in the shelter of the Most High,
   who abide in the shadow of the Almighty,[h]

---

a Cn: Heb *removed his cleanness*   b Meaning of Heb uncertain
c Cn: Heb *bosom all of many peoples*   d Another reading is *our
refuge*   e Heb *humankind*   f Syr: Heb *we bring our years to an
end*   g Cn Compare Gk Syr Jerome Tg: Heb *pride*   h Traditional
rendering of Heb *Shaddai*

P
S

2 will say to the LORD, "My refuge and my fortress;
　　my God, in whom I trust."
3 For he will deliver you from the snare of the
　　fowler
　　and from the deadly pestilence;
4 he will cover you with his pinions,
　　and under his wings you will find refuge;
　　his faithfulness is a shield and buckler.
5 You will not fear the terror of the night,
　　or the arrow that flies by day,
6 or the pestilence that stalks in darkness,
　　or the destruction that wastes at noonday.

7 A thousand may fall at your side,
　　ten thousand at your right hand,
　　but it will not come near you.
8 You will only look with your eyes
　　and see the punishment of the wicked.

9 Because you have made the LORD your refuge,*a*
　　the Most High your dwelling place,
10 no evil shall befall you,
　　no scourge come near your tent.

11 For he will command his angels concerning you
　　to guard you in all your ways.

Have You Sung This Before?

Psalm 91 might sound familiar! Have you
ever sung "On Eagle's Wings" or "Blest Be
the Lord"? Both are based on this psalm. Both
express confidence that God will protect us, no
matter what. This idea was sung long before
Jesus lived, and we still sing it today.

　And He will raise you up on eagle's wings,
　bear you on the breath of dawn,
　make you to shine like the sun,
　and hold you in the palm of His hand.
　　(Jan Michael Joncas, "On Eagle's Wings")

　Blest be the Lord; blest be the Lord,
　the God of mercy, the God who saves.
　I shall not fear the dark of night,
　nor the arrow that flies by day.
　　(Dan Schutte,
　　"Blest Be the Lord")

▶ **Psalm 91**

12 On their hands they will bear you up,
　　so that you will not dash your foot against a
　　　stone.
13 You will tread on the lion and the adder,
　　the young lion and the serpent you will
　　　trample under foot.

14 Those who love me, I will deliver;
　　I will protect those who know my name.
15 When they call to me, I will answer them;
　　I will be with them in trouble,
　　I will rescue them and honor them.
16 With long life I will satisfy them,
　　and show them my salvation.

PSALM 92

Thanksgiving for Vindication

A Psalm. A Song for the Sabbath Day.

1 It is good to give thanks to the LORD,
　　to sing praises to your name, O Most High;
2 to declare your steadfast love in the morning,
　　and your faithfulness by night,
3 to the music of the lute and the harp,
　　to the melody of the lyre.
4 For you, O LORD, have made me glad by your
　　　work;
　　at the works of your hands I sing for joy.

5 How great are your works, O LORD!
　　Your thoughts are very deep!
6 The dullard cannot know,
　　the stupid cannot understand this:
7 though the wicked sprout like grass
　　and all evildoers flourish,
　they are doomed to destruction forever,
8 　but you, O LORD, are on high forever.
9 For your enemies, O LORD,
　　for your enemies shall perish;
　　all evildoers shall be scattered.

10 But you have exalted my horn like that of the
　　　wild ox;
　　you have poured over me*b* fresh oil.
11 My eyes have seen the downfall of my enemies;
　　my ears have heard the doom of my evil
　　　assailants.

12 The righteous flourish like the palm tree,
　　and grow like a cedar in Lebanon.
13 They are planted in the house of the LORD;
　　they flourish in the courts of our God.

---

a Cn: Heb *Because you,* LORD, *are my refuge; you have made*
b Syr: Meaning of Heb uncertain

¹⁴ In old age they still produce fruit;
    they are always green and full of sap,
¹⁵ showing that the LORD is upright;
    he is my rock, and there is no unrighteousness
      in him.

PSALM 93

The Majesty of God's Rule

¹ The LORD is king, he is robed in majesty;
    the LORD is robed, he is girded with strength.
  He has established the world; it shall never be
      moved;
²   your throne is established from of old;
    you are from everlasting.

³ The floods have lifted up, O LORD,
    the floods have lifted up their voice;
    the floods lift up their roaring.
⁴ More majestic than the thunders of mighty
      waters,
    more majestic than the waves[a] of the sea,
    majestic on high is the LORD!

⁵ Your decrees are very sure;
    holiness befits your house,
    O LORD, forevermore.

PSALM 94

God the Avenger of the Righteous

¹ O LORD, you God of vengeance,
    you God of vengeance, shine forth!
² Rise up, O judge of the earth;
    give to the proud what they deserve!
³ O LORD, how long shall the wicked,
    how long shall the wicked exult?

⁴ They pour out their arrogant words;
    all the evildoers boast.
⁵ They crush your people, O LORD,
    and afflict your heritage.
⁶ They kill the widow and the stranger,
    they murder the orphan,
⁷ and they say, "The LORD does not see;
    the God of Jacob does not perceive."

⁸ Understand, O dullest of the people;
    fools, when will you be wise?
⁹ He who planted the ear, does he not hear?
  He who formed the eye, does he not see?
¹⁰ He who disciplines the nations,
  he who teaches knowledge to humankind,
    does he not chastise?

¹¹ The LORD knows our thoughts,[b]
    that they are but an empty breath.

¹² Happy are those whom you discipline, O LORD,
    and whom you teach out of your law,
¹³ giving them respite from days of trouble,
    until a pit is dug for the wicked.
¹⁴ For the LORD will not forsake his people;
    he will not abandon his heritage;
¹⁵ for justice will return to the righteous,
    and all the upright in heart will follow it.

¹⁶ Who rises up for me against the wicked?
    Who stands up for me against evildoers?
¹⁷ If the LORD had not been my help,
    my soul would soon have lived in the land of
      silence.
¹⁸ When I thought, "My foot is slipping,"
    your steadfast love, O LORD, held me up.
¹⁹ When the cares of my heart are many,
    your consolations cheer my soul.
²⁰ Can wicked rulers be allied with you,
    those who contrive mischief by statute?
²¹ They band together against the life of the
      righteous,
    and condemn the innocent to death.
²² But the LORD has become my stronghold,
    and my God the rock of my refuge.
²³ He will repay them for their iniquity
    and wipe them out for their wickedness;
    the LORD our God will wipe them out.

PSALM 95

A Call to Worship and Obedience

¹ O come, let us sing to the LORD;
    let us make a joyful noise to the rock of our
      salvation!
² Let us come into his presence with thanksgiving;
    let us make a joyful noise to him with songs
      of praise!
³ For the LORD is a great God,
    and a great King above all gods.
⁴ In his hand are the depths of the earth,
    the heights of the mountains are his also.
⁵ The sea is his, for he made it,
    and the dry land, which his hands have
      formed.

⁶ O come, let us worship and bow down,
    let us kneel before the LORD, our Maker!
⁷ For he is our God,

---

a Cn: Heb *majestic are the waves*   b Heb *the thoughts of*
humankind

Cultural Connection

Lebanese Catholics

Catholics are a celebratory people. By holding feasts, we celebrate our great God and the wondrous ways God has shown love for us. We also hold feasts in remembrance of the saints who have gone before us. The saints are shining examples of individuals leading lives in unity with the will of God.

In some parts of the Middle East, like Lebanon, Catholic feast days are extravagant events. Each town has a patron saint, and on the eve of his or her feast day, nearly everyone in the community comes to the church. The townspeople pray, eat, and dance in the church all night long, and some even sleep there. Feast days in Lebanon are celebrations that include great processions, festive liturgies, and the participation of the whole community.

In parts of the United States where there are congregations of Middle Eastern Catholics, similar events take place. Some occur on a large scale with overnight festivities, and some occur on a smaller scale, but all have common characteristics: great processions, festive liturgies, good food, and the participation of the whole parish community.

Consider trying to get your youth group or campus ministry team to begin a similar tradition on the feast day of your parish or school.

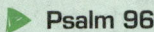

▶ **Psalm 96**

P
S

and we are the people of his pasture,
and the sheep of his hand.

O that today you would listen to his voice!
8 Do not harden your hearts, as at Meribah,
as on the day at Massah in the wilderness,
9 when your ancestors tested me,
and put me to the proof, though they had
seen my work.
10 For forty years I loathed that generation
and said, "They are a people whose hearts go
astray,
and they do not regard my ways."
11 Therefore in my anger I swore,
"They shall not enter my rest."

PSALM 96

Praise to God Who Comes in Judgment

1 O sing to the LORD a new song;
sing to the LORD, all the earth.
2 Sing to the LORD, bless his name;
tell of his salvation from day to day.
3 Declare his glory among the nations,
his marvelous works among all the peoples.
4 For great is the LORD, and greatly to be praised;
he is to be revered above all gods.
5 For all the gods of the peoples are idols,
but the LORD made the heavens.

6 Honor and majesty are before him;
strength and beauty are in his sanctuary.

7 Ascribe to the LORD, O families of the peoples,
ascribe to the LORD glory and strength.
8 Ascribe to the LORD the glory due his name;
bring an offering, and come into his courts.
9 Worship the LORD in holy splendor;
tremble before him, all the earth.

10 Say among the nations, "The LORD is king!
The world is firmly established; it shall never
be moved.
He will judge the peoples with equity."
11 Let the heavens be glad, and let the earth rejoice;
let the sea roar, and all that fills it;
12   let the field exult, and everything in it.
Then shall all the trees of the forest sing for joy
13   before the LORD; for he is coming,
for he is coming to judge the earth.
He will judge the world with righteousness,
and the peoples with his truth.

PSALM 97

The Glory of God's Reign

1 The LORD is king! Let the earth rejoice;
let the many coastlands be glad!
2 Clouds and thick darkness are all around him;

righteousness and justice are the foundation
of his throne.
³ Fire goes before him,
and consumes his adversaries on every side.
⁴ His lightnings light up the world;
the earth sees and trembles.
⁵ The mountains melt like wax before the LORD,
before the Lord of all the earth.

> O sing to the LORD
> a new song;
> sing to the LORD,
> all the earth.
> Sing to the LORD,
> bless his name;
> tell of his salvation
> from day to day.
>
> (Ps 96:1–2)

⁶ The heavens proclaim his righteousness;
and all the peoples behold his glory.
⁷ All worshipers of images are put to shame,
those who make their boast in worthless idols;
all gods bow down before him.
⁸ Zion hears and is glad,
and the towns*ᵃ* of Judah rejoice,
because of your judgments, O God.
⁹ For you, O LORD, are most high over all the earth;
you are exalted far above all gods.

¹⁰ The LORD loves those who hate*ᵇ* evil;
he guards the lives of his faithful;
he rescues them from the hand of the wicked.
¹¹ Light dawns*ᶜ* for the righteous,
and joy for the upright in heart.
¹² Rejoice in the LORD, O you righteous,
and give thanks to his holy name!

PSALM 98

Praise the Judge of the World

A Psalm.

¹ O sing to the LORD a new song,
for he has done marvelous things.
His right hand and his holy arm
have gotten him victory.
² The LORD has made known his victory;
he has revealed his vindication in the sight of
the nations.

³ He has remembered his steadfast love and
faithfulness
to the house of Israel.
All the ends of the earth have seen
the victory of our God.

⁴ Make a joyful noise to the LORD, all the earth;
break forth into joyous song and sing praises.
⁵ Sing praises to the LORD with the lyre,
with the lyre and the sound of melody.
⁶ With trumpets and the sound of the horn
make a joyful noise before the King, the LORD.

⁷ Let the sea roar, and all that fills it;
the world and those who live in it.
⁸ Let the floods clap their hands;
let the hills sing together for joy
⁹ at the presence of the LORD, for he is coming
to judge the earth.
He will judge the world with righteousness,
and the peoples with equity.

PSALM 99

Praise to God for His Holiness

¹ The LORD is king; let the peoples tremble!
He sits enthroned upon the cherubim; let the
earth quake!
² The LORD is great in Zion;
he is exalted over all the peoples.
³ Let them praise your great and awesome name.
Holy is he!
⁴ Mighty King,*ᵈ* lover of justice,
you have established equity;
you have executed justice
and righteousness in Jacob.
⁵ Extol the LORD our God;
worship at his footstool.
Holy is he!

⁶ Moses and Aaron were among his priests,
Samuel also was among those who called on
his name.
They cried to the LORD, and he answered them.
⁷ He spoke to them in the pillar of cloud;
they kept his decrees,
and the statutes that he gave them.

⁸ O LORD our God, you answered them;
you were a forgiving God to them,
but an avenger of their wrongdoings.
⁹ Extol the LORD our God,

PS

a Heb *daughters* b Cn: Heb *You who love the LORD hate*
c Gk Syr Jerome: Heb *is sown* d Cn: Heb *And a king's strength*

and worship at his holy mountain;
for the Lord our God is holy.

PSALM 100

All Lands Summoned to Praise God

A Psalm of thanksgiving.

1 Make a joyful noise to the Lord, all the earth.
2   Worship the Lord with gladness;
    come into his presence with singing.

3 Know that the Lord is God.
    It is he that made us, and we are his;[a]
    we are his people, and the sheep of his pasture.

4 Enter his gates with thanksgiving,
    and his courts with praise.
    Give thanks to him, bless his name.

5 For the Lord is good;
    his steadfast love endures forever,
    and his faithfulness to all generations.

PSALM 101

A Sovereign's Pledge of Integrity and Justice

Of David. A Psalm.

1 I will sing of loyalty and of justice;
    to you, O Lord, I will sing.
2 I will study the way that is blameless.
    When shall I attain it?

    I will walk with integrity of heart
    within my house;
3 I will not set before my eyes
    anything that is base.

    I hate the work of those who fall away;
    it shall not cling to me.
4 Perverseness of heart shall be far from me;
    I will know nothing of evil.

5 One who secretly slanders a neighbor
    I will destroy.
    A haughty look and an arrogant heart
    I will not tolerate.

6 I will look with favor on the faithful in the land,
    so that they may live with me;
whoever walks in the way that is blameless
    shall minister to me.

7 No one who practices deceit
    shall remain in my house;

no one who utters lies
    shall continue in my presence.

8 Morning by morning I will destroy
    all the wicked in the land,
cutting off all evildoers
    from the city of the Lord.

PSALM 102

Prayer to the Eternal King for Help

*A prayer of one afflicted, when faint and pleading
before the Lord.*

1 Hear my prayer, O Lord;
    let my cry come to you.
2 Do not hide your face from me
    in the day of my distress.
Incline your ear to me;
    answer me speedily in the day when I call.

3 For my days pass away like smoke,
    and my bones burn like a furnace.
4 My heart is stricken and withered like grass;
    I am too wasted to eat my bread.
5 Because of my loud groaning
    my bones cling to my skin.
6 I am like an owl of the wilderness,
    like a little owl of the waste places.
7 I lie awake;
    I am like a lonely bird on the housetop.
8 All day long my enemies taunt me;
    those who deride me use my name for a curse.
9 For I eat ashes like bread,
    and mingle tears with my drink,
10 because of your indignation and anger;
    for you have lifted me up and thrown me
        aside.
11 My days are like an evening shadow;
    I wither away like grass.

12 But you, O Lord, are enthroned forever;
    your name endures to all generations.
13 You will rise up and have compassion on Zion,
    for it is time to favor it;
    the appointed time has come.
14 For your servants hold its stones dear,
    and have pity on its dust.
15 The nations will fear the name of the Lord,
    and all the kings of the earth your glory.
16 For the Lord will build up Zion;
    he will appear in his glory.
17 He will regard the prayer of the destitute,
    and will not despise their prayer.

a Another reading is *and not we ourselves*

18 Let this be recorded for a generation to come,
  so that a people yet unborn may praise the
  LORD:
19 that he looked down from his holy height,
  from heaven the LORD looked at the earth,
20 to hear the groans of the prisoners,
  to set free those who were doomed to die;
21 so that the name of the LORD may be declared in
  Zion,
  and his praise in Jerusalem,
22 when peoples gather together,
  and kingdoms, to worship the LORD.

23 He has broken my strength in midcourse;
  he has shortened my days.
24 "O my God," I say, "do not take me away
  at the midpoint of my life,
  you whose years endure
  throughout all generations."

25 Long ago you laid the foundation of the earth,
  and the heavens are the work of your hands.
26 They will perish, but you endure;
  they will all wear out like a garment.
  You change them like clothing, and they pass
  away;
27 but you are the same, and your years have no
  end.
28 The children of your servants shall live secure;
  their offspring shall be established in your
  presence.

PSALM 103

Thanksgiving for God's Goodness
Of David.

1 Bless the LORD, O my soul,
  and all that is within me,
  bless his holy name.
2 Bless the LORD, O my soul,
  and do not forget all his benefits—
3 who forgives all your iniquity,
  who heals all your diseases,
4 who redeems your life from the Pit,
  who crowns you with steadfast love and mercy,
5 who satisfies you with good as long as you live[a]
  so that your youth is renewed like the eagle's.

6 The LORD works vindication
  and justice for all who are oppressed.
7 He made known his ways to Moses,
  his acts to the people of Israel.
8 The LORD is merciful and gracious,
  slow to anger and abounding in steadfast
  love.

9 He will not always accuse,
  nor will he keep his anger forever.
10 He does not deal with us according to our sins,
  nor repay us according to our iniquities.
11 For as the heavens are high above the earth,
  so great is his steadfast love toward those who
  fear him;
12 as far as the east is from the west,
  so far he removes our transgressions from us.
13 As a father has compassion for his children,
  so the LORD has compassion for those who
  fear him.
14 For he knows how we were made;
  he remembers that we are dust.

———
a Meaning of Heb uncertain

Letting Go of Anger

Psalm 103 is a beautiful prayer praising God's love and compassion. Verse 9 reminds us that God will not stay angry forever. What better lesson could we learn from our God? Anger is a natural human emotion—but in imitation of God, we should not hold on to it. When we let go of our anger, we build better relationships, because hidden anger puts other people on the defensive and destroys trust.

How do you let go of anger? Here are some suggestions:
- Express your feelings in a letter or a journal.
- Tell the person you are angry with how you feel and that you would like to reconcile.
- Go for a fast walk or run, or use another form of exercise to "vent" your anger.
- Relax with some quiet, reflective music.
- Try to identify why you feel angry. Often anger is a symptom of another feeling, such as hurt, disappointment, or even tiredness.
- Express your anger in prayer to God, and ask for help in forgiveness.

God's way and God's goodness can be yours if you desire them. Make an effort; God does!

▶ Psalm 103

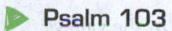

15 As for mortals, their days are like grass;
   they flourish like a flower of the field;
16 for the wind passes over it, and it is gone,
   and its place knows it no more.
17 But the steadfast love of the Lord is from
        everlasting to everlasting
   on those who fear him,
   and his righteousness to children's children,
18 to those who keep his covenant
   and remember to do his commandments.

19 The Lord has established his throne in the
        heavens,
   and his kingdom rules over all.
20 Bless the Lord, O you his angels,
   you mighty ones who do his bidding,
   obedient to his spoken word.
21 Bless the Lord, all his hosts,
   his ministers that do his will.
22 Bless the Lord, all his works,
   in all places of his dominion.
   Bless the Lord, O my soul.

PSALM 104

God the Creator and Provider

1 Bless the Lord, O my soul.
   O Lord my God, you are very great.
   You are clothed with honor and majesty,
2   wrapped in light as with a garment.
   You stretch out the heavens like a tent,
3   you set the beams of your[a] chambers on the
        waters,
   you make the clouds your[a] chariot,
   you ride on the wings of the wind,
4 you make the winds your[a] messengers,
   fire and flame your[a] ministers.

5 You set the earth on its foundations,
   so that it shall never be shaken.
6 You cover it with the deep as with a garment;
   the waters stood above the mountains.
7 At your rebuke they flee;
   at the sound of your thunder they take to
        flight.
8 They rose up to the mountains, ran down to the
        valleys
   to the place that you appointed for them.
9 You set a boundary that they may not pass,
   so that they might not again cover the earth.

10 You make springs gush forth in the valleys;
   they flow between the hills,
11 giving drink to every wild animal;
   the wild asses quench their thirst.

12 By the streams[b] the birds of the air have their
        habitation;
   they sing among the branches.
13 From your lofty abode you water the mountains;
   the earth is satisfied with the fruit of your work.

14 You cause the grass to grow for the cattle,
   and plants for people to use,[c]
   to bring forth food from the earth,
15   and wine to gladden the human heart,
   oil to make the face shine,
   and bread to strengthen the human heart.
16 The trees of the Lord are watered abundantly,
   the cedars of Lebanon that he planted.
17 In them the birds build their nests;
   the stork has its home in the fir trees.
18 The high mountains are for the wild goats;
   the rocks are a refuge for the coneys.
19 You have made the moon to mark the seasons;
   the sun knows its time for setting.
20 You make darkness, and it is night,
   when all the animals of the forest come
        creeping out.
21 The young lions roar for their prey,
   seeking their food from God.
22 When the sun rises, they withdraw
   and lie down in their dens.
23 People go out to their work
   and to their labor until the evening.

24 O Lord, how manifold are your works!
   In wisdom you have made them all;
   the earth is full of your creatures.
25 Yonder is the sea, great and wide,
   creeping things innumerable are there,
   living things both small and great.
26 There go the ships,
   and Leviathan that you formed to sport in it.

27 These all look to you
   to give them their food in due season;
28 when you give to them, they gather it up;
   when you open your hand, they are filled
        with good things.
29 When you hide your face, they are dismayed;
   when you take away their breath, they die
   and return to their dust.
30 When you send forth your spirit,[d] they are
        created;
   and you renew the face of the ground.

31 May the glory of the Lord endure forever;
   may the Lord rejoice in his works—

---

a Heb *his*   b Heb *By them*   c Or *to cultivate*   d Or *your breath*

Catholic Social Teaching

The Urgent Need to Care for Our Planet

Psalm 104 describes the beauty of creation as God is shown actively involved in the unfolding of the natural world. The writer describes the intimate and dependent relationship all living things have with their creator. We are called to revere God's creation and to care for it in a way that reflects God's boundless and ongoing care.

The Church's social teaching underscores the urgency of caring for creation. In a statement on global warming, the United States bishops speak about the threat of climate change and its implications for the most vulnerable of our world. They urge us to recognize the interdependence that exists between all creation and that any action we take must consider the common good. The destruction of a rain forest in one part of the world or a country that uses a disproportionate amount of the earth's resources in another part of the world can have significant impact on the entire planet. Often it is those with the least amount of power to affect political policies who suffer the most; and things will continue to worsen if steps are not taken to reverse this trend.

Caring for creation must be directed by God's plan and not by our own self-interests. When we contribute to the destruction of our environment, we dishonor God and all creation. Let us reflect on how our individual actions impact the global community and pray for the wisdom to understand our role in restoring order to the natural world, because our very survival depends upon it.

● How does my use of energy affect the environment and others? What can I do to reduce my energy use?
● How dependent am I upon having material things? What are some ways I can live more simply so others can simply live?

▶ **Psalm 104**

Care for God's Creation

P
S

---

³² who looks on the earth and it trembles,
    who touches the mountains and they smoke.
³³ I will sing to the LORD as long as I live;
    I will sing praise to my God while I have
        being.
³⁴ May my meditation be pleasing to him,
    for I rejoice in the LORD.
³⁵ Let sinners be consumed from the earth,
    and let the wicked be no more.
    Bless the LORD, O my soul.
    Praise the LORD!

PSALM 105

God's Faithfulness to Israel

¹ O give thanks to the LORD, call on his name,
    make known his deeds among the peoples.
² Sing to him, sing praises to him;
    tell of all his wonderful works.
³ Glory in his holy name;
    let the hearts of those who seek the LORD
        rejoice.
⁴ Seek the LORD and his strength;
    seek his presence continually.

⁵ Remember the wonderful works he has done,
    his miracles, and the judgments he has
        uttered,
⁶ O offspring of his servant Abraham,ᵃ
    children of Jacob, his chosen ones.

⁷ He is the LORD our God;
    his judgments are in all the earth.
⁸ He is mindful of his covenant forever,
    of the word that he commanded, for a
        thousand generations,
⁹ the covenant that he made with Abraham,
    his sworn promise to Isaac,
¹⁰ which he confirmed to Jacob as a statute,
    to Israel as an everlasting covenant,
¹¹ saying, "To you I will give the land of Canaan
    as your portion for an inheritance."

¹² When they were few in number,
    of little account, and strangers in it,
¹³ wandering from nation to nation,
    from one kingdom to another people,
¹⁴ he allowed no one to oppress them;

---

a Another reading is *Israel* (compare 1 Chr 16.13)

he rebuked kings on their account,
15 saying, "Do not touch my anointed ones;
    do my prophets no harm."

16 When he summoned famine against the land,
    and broke every staff of bread,
17 he had sent a man ahead of them,
    Joseph, who was sold as a slave.
18 His feet were hurt with fetters,
    his neck was put in a collar of iron;
19 until what he had said came to pass,
    the word of the Lord kept testing him.
20 The king sent and released him;
    the ruler of the peoples set him free.
21 He made him lord of his house,
    and ruler of all his possessions,
22 to instruct[a] his officials at his pleasure,
    and to teach his elders wisdom.

23 Then Israel came to Egypt;
    Jacob lived as an alien in the land of Ham.
24 And the Lord made his people very fruitful,
    and made them stronger than their foes,
25 whose hearts he then turned to hate his people,
    to deal craftily with his servants.

26 He sent his servant Moses,
    and Aaron whom he had chosen.
27 They performed his signs among them,
    and miracles in the land of Ham.
28 He sent darkness, and made the land dark;
    they rebelled[b] against his words.
29 He turned their waters into blood,
    and caused their fish to die.
30 Their land swarmed with frogs,
    even in the chambers of their kings.
31 He spoke, and there came swarms of flies,
    and gnats throughout their country.
32 He gave them hail for rain,
    and lightning that flashed through their land.
33 He struck their vines and fig trees,
    and shattered the trees of their country.
34 He spoke, and the locusts came,
    and young locusts without number;
35 they devoured all the vegetation in their land,
    and ate up the fruit of their ground.
36 He struck down all the firstborn in their land,
    the first issue of all their strength.

37 Then he brought Israel[c] out with silver and gold,
    and there was no one among their tribes who
      stumbled.
38 Egypt was glad when they departed,
    for dread of them had fallen upon it.
39 He spread a cloud for a covering,
    and fire to give light by night.

40 They asked, and he brought quails,
    and gave them food from heaven in
      abundance.
41 He opened the rock, and water gushed out;
    it flowed through the desert like a river.
42 For he remembered his holy promise,
    and Abraham, his servant.

43 So he brought his people out with joy,
    his chosen ones with singing.
44 He gave them the lands of the nations,
    and they took possession of the wealth of the
      peoples,
45 that they might keep his statutes
    and observe his laws.
    Praise the Lord!

PSALM 106

A Confession of Israel's Sins

1 Praise the Lord!
    O give thanks to the Lord, for he is good;
    for his steadfast love endures forever.
2 Who can utter the mighty doings of the Lord,
    or declare all his praise?
3 Happy are those who observe justice,
    who do righteousness at all times.

4 Remember me, O Lord, when you show favor to
      your people;
    help me when you deliver them;
5 that I may see the prosperity of your chosen ones,
    that I may rejoice in the gladness of your
      nation,
    that I may glory in your heritage.

6 Both we and our ancestors have sinned;
    we have committed iniquity, have done
      wickedly.
7 Our ancestors, when they were in Egypt,
    did not consider your wonderful works;
    they did not remember the abundance of your
      steadfast love,
    but rebelled against the Most High[d] at the Red
      Sea.[e]
8 Yet he saved them for his name's sake,
    so that he might make known his mighty
      power.
9 He rebuked the Red Sea,[e] and it became dry;
    he led them through the deep as through a
      desert.

---

a Gk Syr Jerome: Heb *to bind*   b Cn Compare Gk Syr: Heb *they did not rebel*   c Heb *them*   d Cn Compare 78.17, 56: Heb *rebelled at the sea*   e Or *Sea of Reeds*

10 So he saved them from the hand of the foe,
   and delivered them from the hand of the
      enemy.
11 The waters covered their adversaries;
   not one of them was left.
12 Then they believed his words;
   they sang his praise.

13 But they soon forgot his works;
   they did not wait for his counsel.
14 But they had a wanton craving in the
      wilderness,
   and put God to the test in the desert;
15 he gave them what they asked,
   but sent a wasting disease among them.

16 They were jealous of Moses in the camp,
   and of Aaron, the holy one of the LORD.
17 The earth opened and swallowed up Dathan,
   and covered the faction of Abiram.
18 Fire also broke out in their company;
   the flame burned up the wicked.

19 They made a calf at Horeb
   and worshiped a cast image.
20 They exchanged the glory of God[a]
   for the image of an ox that eats grass.
21 They forgot God, their Savior,
   who had done great things in Egypt,
22 wondrous works in the land of Ham,
   and awesome deeds by the Red Sea.[b]
23 Therefore he said he would destroy them—
   had not Moses, his chosen one,
   stood in the breach before him,
   to turn away his wrath from destroying them.

24 Then they despised the pleasant land,
   having no faith in his promise.
25 They grumbled in their tents,
   and did not obey the voice of the LORD.
26 Therefore he raised his hand and swore to
      them
   that he would make them fall in the
      wilderness,
27 and would disperse[c] their descendants among
      the nations,
   scattering them over the lands.

28 Then they attached themselves to the Baal of
      Peor,
   and ate sacrifices offered to the dead;
29 they provoked the LORD to anger with their
      deeds,
   and a plague broke out among them.
30 Then Phinehas stood up and interceded,
   and the plague was stopped.

31 And that has been reckoned to him as
      righteousness
   from generation to generation forever.

32 They angered the LORD[d] at the waters of Meribah,
   and it went ill with Moses on their account;
33 for they made his spirit bitter,
   and he spoke words that were rash.

34 They did not destroy the peoples,
   as the LORD commanded them,
35 but they mingled with the nations
   and learned to do as they did.
36 They served their idols,
   which became a snare to them.
37 They sacrificed their sons
   and their daughters to the demons;
38 they poured out innocent blood,
   the blood of their sons and daughters,
   whom they sacrificed to the idols of Canaan;
   and the land was polluted with blood.
39 Thus they became unclean by their acts,
   and prostituted themselves in their doings.

40 Then the anger of the LORD was kindled against
      his people,
   and he abhorred his heritage;
41 he gave them into the hand of the nations,
   so that those who hated them ruled over
      them.
42 Their enemies oppressed them,
   and they were brought into subjection under
      their power.
43 Many times he delivered them,
   but they were rebellious in their purposes,
   and were brought low through their iniquity.
44 Nevertheless he regarded their distress
   when he heard their cry.
45 For their sake he remembered his covenant,
   and showed compassion according to the
      abundance of his steadfast love.
46 He caused them to be pitied
   by all who held them captive.

47 Save us, O LORD our God,
   and gather us from among the nations,
   that we may give thanks to your holy name
   and glory in your praise.

48 Blessed be the LORD, the God of Israel,
   from everlasting to everlasting.
   And let all the people say, "Amen."
   Praise the LORD!

---

a Compare Gk Mss: Heb *exchanged their glory*   b Or *Sea of Reeds*   c Syr Compare Ezek 20.23: Heb *cause to fall*   d Heb *him*

P
S

Cultural Connection

Thankfulness

It's good and natural for people to express thankfulness for their blessings. Psalm 107 is an extended thanksgiving for God's love and saving power. Indonesians have a custom for offering thanks on certain special occasions, such as after a new house is built, during the seventh month of pregnancy, and thirty-five days after the birth of a child.

During a thanksgiving for a new house, the family gathers in the house and offers prayers for the people who will live, eat, work, and die there. Similar prayers are said for a mother during pregnancy and for a child after birth—in thanksgiving for their health, well-being, and happiness. After the prayers, those who are gathered share a simple traditional meal of rice, vegetables, fish or chicken, and fruit.

▶ **Psalm 107**

BOOK V
(Psalms 107-150)

PSALM 107

Thanksgiving for Deliverance from Many Troubles

1 O give thanks to the Lord, for he is good;
　　for his steadfast love endures forever.
2 Let the redeemed of the Lord say so,
　　those he redeemed from trouble
3 and gathered in from the lands,
　　from the east and from the west,
　　from the north and from the south.*a*

4 Some wandered in desert wastes,
　　finding no way to an inhabited town;
5 hungry and thirsty,
　　their soul fainted within them.
6 Then they cried to the Lord in their trouble,
　　and he delivered them from their distress;
7 he led them by a straight way,
　　until they reached an inhabited town.
8 Let them thank the Lord for his steadfast love,
　　for his wonderful works to humankind.
9 For he satisfies the thirsty,
　　and the hungry he fills with good things.

10 Some sat in darkness and in gloom,
　　prisoners in misery and in irons,
11 for they had rebelled against the words of God,
　　and spurned the counsel of the Most High.
12 Their hearts were bowed down with hard labor;
　　they fell down, with no one to help.
13 Then they cried to the Lord in their trouble,

and he saved them from their distress;
14 he brought them out of darkness and gloom,
　　and broke their bonds asunder.
15 Let them thank the Lord for his steadfast love,
　　for his wonderful works to humankind.
16 For he shatters the doors of bronze,
　　and cuts in two the bars of iron.

17 Some were sick*b* through their sinful ways,
　　and because of their iniquities endured
　　　affliction;
18 they loathed any kind of food,
　　and they drew near to the gates of death.
19 Then they cried to the Lord in their trouble,
　　and he saved them from their distress;
20 he sent out his word and healed them,
　　and delivered them from destruction.
21 Let them thank the Lord for his steadfast love,
　　for his wonderful works to humankind.
22 And let them offer thanksgiving sacrifices,
　　and tell of his deeds with songs of joy.

23 Some went down to the sea in ships,
　　doing business on the mighty waters;
24 they saw the deeds of the Lord,
　　his wondrous works in the deep.
25 For he commanded and raised the stormy wind,
　　which lifted up the waves of the sea.
26 They mounted up to heaven, they went down to
　　　the depths;
　　their courage melted away in their calamity;
27 they reeled and staggered like drunkards,
　　and were at their wits' end.

---

a Cn: Heb *sea*   *b* Cn: Heb *fools*

28 Then they cried to the LORD in their trouble,
  and he brought them out from their distress;
29 he made the storm be still,
  and the waves of the sea were hushed.
30 Then they were glad because they had quiet,
  and he brought them to their desired haven.
31 Let them thank the LORD for his steadfast love,
  for his wonderful works to humankind.
32 Let them extol him in the congregation of the
    people,
  and praise him in the assembly of the elders.

33 He turns rivers into a desert,
  springs of water into thirsty ground,
34 a fruitful land into a salty waste,
  because of the wickedness of its inhabitants.
35 He turns a desert into pools of water,
  a parched land into springs of water.
36 And there he lets the hungry live,
  and they establish a town to live in;
37 they sow fields, and plant vineyards,
  and get a fruitful yield.
38 By his blessing they multiply greatly,
  and he does not let their cattle decrease.

39 When they are diminished and brought low
  through oppression, trouble, and sorrow,
40 he pours contempt on princes
  and makes them wander in trackless wastes;
41 but he raises up the needy out of distress,
  and makes their families like flocks.
42 The upright see it and are glad;
  and all wickedness stops its mouth.
43 Let those who are wise give heed to these things,
  and consider the steadfast love of the LORD.

PSALM 108

Praise and Prayer for Victory

A Song. A Psalm of David.

1 My heart is steadfast, O God, my heart is
    steadfast;[a]
  I will sing and make melody.
  Awake, my soul![b]
2 Awake, O harp and lyre!
  I will awake the dawn.
3 I will give thanks to you, O LORD, among the
    peoples,
  and I will sing praises to you among the
    nations.
4 For your steadfast love is higher than the heavens,
  and your faithfulness reaches to the clouds.

5 Be exalted, O God, above the heavens,
  and let your glory be over all the earth.

6 Give victory with your right hand, and answer
    me,
  so that those whom you love may be rescued.

7 God has promised in his sanctuary:[c]
  "With exultation I will divide up Shechem,
  and portion out the Vale of Succoth.
8 Gilead is mine; Manasseh is mine;
  Ephraim is my helmet;
  Judah is my scepter.
9 Moab is my washbasin;
  on Edom I hurl my shoe;
  over Philistia I shout in triumph."

10 Who will bring me to the fortified city?
  Who will lead me to Edom?
11 Have you not rejected us, O God?
  You do not go out, O God, with our armies.
12 O grant us help against the foe,
  for human help is worthless.
13 With God we shall do valiantly;
  it is he who will tread down our foes.

PSALM 109

Prayer for Vindication and Vengeance

To the leader. Of David. A Psalm.

1 Do not be silent, O God of my praise.
2 For wicked and deceitful mouths are opened
    against me,
  speaking against me with lying tongues.
3 They beset me with words of hate,
  and attack me without cause.
4 In return for my love they accuse me,
  even while I make prayer for them.[d]
5 So they reward me evil for good,
  and hatred for my love.

6 They say,[e] "Appoint a wicked man against him;
  let an accuser stand on his right.
7 When he is tried, let him be found guilty;
  let his prayer be counted as sin.
8 May his days be few;
  may another seize his position.
9 May his children be orphans,
  and his wife a widow.
10 May his children wander about and beg;
  may they be driven out of[f] the ruins they
    inhabit.
11 May the creditor seize all that he has;
  may strangers plunder the fruits of his toil.

a Heb Mss Gk Syr: MT lacks *my heart is steadfast*   b Compare
57.8: Heb *also my soul*   c Or *by his holiness*   d Syr: Heb
I prayer   e Heb lacks *They say*   f Gk: Heb *and seek*

¹² May there be no one to do him a kindness,
  nor anyone to pity his orphaned children.
¹³ May his posterity be cut off;
  may his name be blotted out in the second
    generation.
¹⁴ May the iniquity of his father*a* be remembered
    before the LORD,
  and do not let the sin of his mother be
    blotted out.
¹⁵ Let them be before the LORD continually,
  and may his*b* memory be cut off from the
    earth.
¹⁶ For he did not remember to show kindness,
  but pursued the poor and needy
  and the brokenhearted to their death.
¹⁷ He loved to curse; let curses come on him.
  He did not like blessing; may it be far from
    him.
¹⁸ He clothed himself with cursing as his coat,
  may it soak into his body like water,
  like oil into his bones.
¹⁹ May it be like a garment that he wraps around
    himself,
  like a belt that he wears every day."

²⁰ May that be the reward of my accusers from the
    LORD,
  of those who speak evil against my life.
²¹ But you, O LORD my Lord,
  act on my behalf for your name's sake;
  because your steadfast love is good, deliver me.
²² For I am poor and needy,
  and my heart is pierced within me.
²³ I am gone like a shadow at evening;
  I am shaken off like a locust.
²⁴ My knees are weak through fasting;
  my body has become gaunt.
²⁵ I am an object of scorn to my accusers;
  when they see me, they shake their heads.

²⁶ Help me, O LORD my God!
  Save me according to your steadfast love.
²⁷ Let them know that this is your hand;
  you, O LORD, have done it.
²⁸ Let them curse, but you will bless.
  Let my assailants be put to shame;*c* may your
    servant be glad.
²⁹ May my accusers be clothed with dishonor;
  may they be wrapped in their own shame as
    in a mantle.
³⁰ With my mouth I will give great thanks to the
    LORD;
  I will praise him in the midst of the throng.
³¹ For he stands at the right hand of the needy,
  to save them from those who would condemn
    them to death.

PSALM 110

Assurance of Victory for God's Priest-King

Of David. A Psalm.

¹ The LORD says to my lord,
  "Sit at my right hand
  until I make your enemies your footstool."

² The LORD sends out from Zion
  your mighty scepter.
  Rule in the midst of your foes.
³ Your people will offer themselves willingly
  on the day you lead your forces
  on the holy mountains.*d*
From the womb of the morning,
  like dew, your youth*e* will come to you.
⁴ The LORD has sworn and will not change his
    mind,
  "You are a priest forever according to the
    order of Melchizedek."*f*

⁵ The Lord is at your right hand;
  he will shatter kings on the day of his wrath.
⁶ He will execute judgment among the nations,
    filling them with corpses;
  he will shatter heads
    over the wide earth.
⁷ He will drink from the stream by the path;
  therefore he will lift up his head.

PSALM 111

Praise for God's Wonderful Works

¹ Praise the LORD!
I will give thanks to the LORD with my whole
    heart,
  in the company of the upright, in the
    congregation.
² Great are the works of the LORD,
  studied by all who delight in them.
³ Full of honor and majesty is his work,
  and his righteousness endures forever.
⁴ He has gained renown by his wonderful deeds;
  the LORD is gracious and merciful.
⁵ He provides food for those who fear him;
  he is ever mindful of his covenant.
⁶ He has shown his people the power of his
    works,
  in giving them the heritage of the nations.
⁷ The works of his hands are faithful and just;
  all his precepts are trustworthy.

a Cn: Heb *fathers*   b Gk: Heb *their*   c Gk: Heb *They have risen
up and have been put to shame*   d Another reading is *in holy
splendor*   e Cn: Heb *the dew of your youth*   f Or *forever, a
rightful king by my edict*

Cultural Connection

Generosity

"It is well with those who deal generously and lend, / who conduct their affairs with justice" (Ps 112:5). Generosity is an important value for many Native American peoples. For the Lakota tribe, it is one of four primary values. The Lakota word for generosity is *wa-can-tog-na-ka*.

In this Native American culture, it is a great insult to be called selfish, and a high compliment to be called generous. You are not able to raise your social status by showing off the things that you own. You can do it only by giving things away. In fact, there is a special ceremony called the *otuhan*, or the "giveaway," in which people give away many of their possessions to honor one another. For example, young people may have a giveaway when they graduate from high school, as a way of honoring all who have helped them along the way.

To explore the other primary Lakota virtues, see the "Cultural Connections" articles for Psalms 31, 73, and 89.

▶ **Psalm 112**

---

8 They are established forever and ever,
　　to be performed with faithfulness and
　　　uprightness.
9 He sent redemption to his people;
　　he has commanded his covenant forever.
　　Holy and awesome is his name.
10 The fear of the LORD is the beginning of wisdom;
　　all those who practice it[a] have a good
　　　understanding.
　　His praise endures forever.

PSALM 112

Blessings of the Righteous

1 Praise the LORD!
　　Happy are those who fear the LORD,
　　who greatly delight in his commandments.
2 Their descendants will be mighty in the land;
　　the generation of the upright will be blessed.
3 Wealth and riches are in their houses,
　　and their righteousness endures forever.
4 They rise in the darkness as a light for the
　　　upright;
　　they are gracious, merciful, and righteous.
5 It is well with those who deal generously and
　　　lend,
　　who conduct their affairs with justice.
6 For the righteous will never be moved;
　　they will be remembered forever.
7 They are not afraid of evil tidings;
　　their hearts are firm, secure in the LORD.
8 Their hearts are steady, they will not be afraid;

in the end they will look in triumph on their
　　foes.
9 They have distributed freely, they have given to
　　the poor;
　　their righteousness endures forever;
　　their horn is exalted in honor.
10 The wicked see it and are angry;
　　they gnash their teeth and melt away;
　　the desire of the wicked comes to nothing.

PSALM 113

God the Helper of the Needy

1 Praise the LORD!
Praise, O servants of the LORD;
　　praise the name of the LORD.

2 Blessed be the name of the LORD
　　from this time on and forevermore.
3 From the rising of the sun to its setting
　　the name of the LORD is to be praised.
4 The LORD is high above all nations,
　　and his glory above the heavens.

5 Who is like the LORD our God,
　　who is seated on high,
6 who looks far down
　　on the heavens and the earth?
7 He raises the poor from the dust,
　　and lifts the needy from the ash heap,

a Gk Syr: Heb *them*

What Lasts?

Will a car last forever? a house? the sun? Does anything other than God truly have no end? No matter how much you look, you won't find such a thing. So, why do we spend much of our time with what won't last, rather than what *will* last?

Psalm 115 proclaims the greatness of God and the foolishness of idols. In the end, the things that matter most won't be how many awards you were given, how much money you made, or how many possessions you had, but rather how much you loved others, how much you served, and how much you loved God!

Find a mission trip, outreach, or a way in which you can serve others.

▶ Psalm 115

8 to make them sit with princes,
    with the princes of his people.
9 He gives the barren woman a home,
    making her the joyous mother of children.
Praise the LORD!

PSALM 114

God's Wonders at the Exodus

1 When Israel went out from Egypt,
    the house of Jacob from a people of strange
        language,
2 Judah became God's[a] sanctuary,
    Israel his dominion.

3 The sea looked and fled;
    Jordan turned back.
4 The mountains skipped like rams,
    the hills like lambs.

5 Why is it, O sea, that you flee?
    O Jordan, that you turn back?
6 O mountains, that you skip like rams?
    O hills, like lambs?

7 Tremble, O earth, at the presence of the LORD,
    at the presence of the God of Jacob,

8 who turns the rock into a pool of water,
    the flint into a spring of water.

PSALM 115

The Impotence of Idols and the Greatness of God

1 Not to us, O LORD, not to us, but to your name
        give glory,
    for the sake of your steadfast love and your
        faithfulness.
2 Why should the nations say,
    "Where is their God?"

3 Our God is in the heavens;
    he does whatever he pleases.
4 Their idols are silver and gold,
    the work of human hands.
5 They have mouths, but do not speak;
    eyes, but do not see.
6 They have ears, but do not hear;
    noses, but do not smell.
7 They have hands, but do not feel;
    feet, but do not walk;
    they make no sound in their throats.
8 Those who make them are like them;
    so are all who trust in them.

9 O Israel, trust in the LORD!
    He is their help and their shield.
10 O house of Aaron, trust in the LORD!
    He is their help and their shield.
11 You who fear the LORD, trust in the LORD!
    He is their help and their shield.

12 The LORD has been mindful of us; he will bless us;
    he will bless the house of Israel;
    he will bless the house of Aaron;
13 he will bless those who fear the LORD,
    both small and great.

14 May the LORD give you increase,
    both you and your children.
15 May you be blessed by the LORD,
    who made heaven and earth.

16 The heavens are the LORD's heavens,
    but the earth he has given to human beings.
17 The dead do not praise the LORD,
    nor do any that go down into silence.
18 But we will bless the LORD
    from this time on and forevermore.
    Praise the LORD!

a Heb *his*

PSALM 116

Thanksgiving for Recovery from Illness

1 I love the LORD, because he has heard
     my voice and my supplications.
2 Because he inclined his ear to me,
     therefore I will call on him as long as I live.
3 The snares of death encompassed me;
     the pangs of Sheol laid hold on me;
     I suffered distress and anguish.
4 Then I called on the name of the LORD:
     "O LORD, I pray, save my life!"

5 Gracious is the LORD, and righteous;
     our God is merciful.
6 The LORD protects the simple;
     when I was brought low, he saved me.
7 Return, O my soul, to your rest,
     for the LORD has dealt bountifully with you.

8 For you have delivered my soul from death,
     my eyes from tears,
     my feet from stumbling.
9 I walk before the LORD
     in the land of the living.
10 I kept my faith, even when I said,
     "I am greatly afflicted";
11 I said in my consternation,
     "Everyone is a liar."

12 What shall I return to the LORD
     for all his bounty to me?
13 I will lift up the cup of salvation
     and call on the name of the LORD,
14 I will pay my vows to the LORD
     in the presence of all his people.
15 Precious in the sight of the LORD
     is the death of his faithful ones.
16 O LORD, I am your servant;
     I am your servant, the child of your serving
        girl.
     You have loosed my bonds.
17 I will offer to you a thanksgiving sacrifice
     and call on the name of the LORD.
18 I will pay my vows to the LORD
     in the presence of all his people,
19 in the courts of the house of the LORD,
     in your midst, O Jerusalem.
     Praise the LORD!

PSALM 117

Universal Call to Worship

1 Praise the LORD, all you nations!
     Extol him, all you peoples!

2 For great is his steadfast love toward us,
     and the faithfulness of the LORD endures
        forever.
     Praise the LORD!

PSALM 118

A Song of Victory

1 O give thanks to the LORD, for he is good;
     his steadfast love endures forever!

2 Let Israel say,
     "His steadfast love endures forever."
3 Let the house of Aaron say,
     "His steadfast love endures forever."
4 Let those who fear the LORD say,
     "His steadfast love endures forever."

5 Out of my distress I called on the LORD;
     the LORD answered me and set me in a broad
        place.
6 With the LORD on my side I do not fear.
     What can mortals do to me?
7 The LORD is on my side to help me;
     I shall look in triumph on those who hate me.
8 It is better to take refuge in the LORD
     than to put confidence in mortals.

Gratitude

Thank God! Have you ever uttered these words in response to something finally going your way? or perhaps in response to a personal situation that turned out just as you had hoped it would? Psalm 116 is all about this feeling—a feeling of true gratitude towards God for making our lives better.

In our prayers, we may get so caught up in asking God for help that we forget to thank God for the various ways he has already blessed our lives. Psalm 116 reminds us to be grateful at all times, thanking and praising God for the many gifts we have received, especially those we have asked for so diligently.

▶ **Psalm 116**

Pray It!

The Longest Psalm

Psalm 119 is the longest psalm. Also, it has an interesting structure that you cannot appreciate in the English translation: it consists of twenty-two sections, and all the lines of a particular section begin with the same letter of the Hebrew alphabet. All the lines of the first section begin with *Aleph*, the Hebrew equivalent of the letter *A*. All the lines of the second section begin with *Beth*, the Hebrew equivalent of the letter *B*. And so on through the whole Hebrew alphabet!

This type of structure is called an acrostic. An acrostic is a poem in which the beginning letters of each line form a word or a phrase or a logical sequence. You may have written a poem like this in grade school using the word *mother* or *father*.

Write your own acrostic prayer, beginning the lines of the prayer with the letters of your name or of the name of someone or something you would like to pray for.

▶ **Psalm 119**

---

9 It is better to take refuge in the LORD
　　than to put confidence in princes.

10 All nations surrounded me;
　　in the name of the LORD I cut them off!
11 They surrounded me, surrounded me on every
　　side;
　　in the name of the LORD I cut them off!
12 They surrounded me like bees;
　　they blazed*a* like a fire of thorns;
　　in the name of the LORD I cut them off!
13 I was pushed hard,*b* so that I was falling,
　　but the LORD helped me.
14 The LORD is my strength and my might;
　　he has become my salvation.
15 There are glad songs of victory in the tents of the
　　righteous:
　　"The right hand of the LORD does valiantly;
16 　　the right hand of the LORD is exalted;
　　the right hand of the LORD does valiantly."
17 I shall not die, but I shall live,
　　and recount the deeds of the LORD.

18 The LORD has punished me severely,
　　but he did not give me over to death.

19 Open to me the gates of righteousness,
　　that I may enter through them
　　and give thanks to the LORD.
20 This is the gate of the LORD;
　　the righteous shall enter through it.

21 I thank you that you have answered me
　　and have become my salvation.
22 The stone that the builders rejected
　　has become the chief cornerstone.
23 This is the LORD's doing;
　　it is marvelous in our eyes.
24 This is the day that the LORD has made;
　　let us rejoice and be glad in it.*c*
25 Save us, we beseech you, O LORD!
　　O LORD, we beseech you, give us success!

26 Blessed is the one who comes in the name of
　　the LORD.*d*
　　We bless you from the house of the LORD.
27 The LORD is God,
　　and he has given us light.
　　Bind the festal procession with branches,
　　up to the horns of the altar.*e*

28 You are my God, and I will give thanks to you;
　　you are my God, I will extol you.

29 O give thanks to the LORD, for he is good,
　　for his steadfast love endures forever.

PSALM 119

The Glories of God's Law

1 Happy are those whose way is blameless,
　　who walk in the law of the LORD.
2 Happy are those who keep his decrees,
　　who seek him with their whole heart,
3 who also do no wrong,
　　but walk in his ways.
4 You have commanded your precepts
　　to be kept diligently.
5 O that my ways may be steadfast
　　in keeping your statutes!
6 Then I shall not be put to shame,
　　having my eyes fixed on all your
　　commandments.

---

a Gk: Heb *were extinguished*　　*b* Gk Syr Jerome: Heb *You pushed
me hard*　　*c* Or *in him*　　*d* Or *Blessed in the name of the* LORD *is
the one who comes*　　*e* Meaning of Heb uncertain

7 I will praise you with an upright heart,
    when I learn your righteous ordinances.
8 I will observe your statutes;
    do not utterly forsake me.

9 How can young people keep their way pure?
    By guarding it according to your word.
10 With my whole heart I seek you;
    do not let me stray from your
      commandments.
11 I treasure your word in my heart,
    so that I may not sin against you.
12 Blessed are you, O Lord;
    teach me your statutes.
13 With my lips I declare
    all the ordinances of your mouth.
14 I delight in the way of your decrees
    as much as in all riches.
15 I will meditate on your precepts,
    and fix my eyes on your ways.
16 I will delight in your statutes;
    I will not forget your word.

17 Deal bountifully with your servant,
    so that I may live and observe your word.
18 Open my eyes, so that I may behold
    wondrous things out of your law.
19 I live as an alien in the land;
    do not hide your commandments from me.
20 My soul is consumed with longing
    for your ordinances at all times.
21 You rebuke the insolent, accursed ones,
    who wander from your commandments;
22 take away from me their scorn and contempt,
    for I have kept your decrees.
23 Even though princes sit plotting against me,
    your servant will meditate on your statutes.
24 Your decrees are my delight,
    they are my counselors.

25 My soul clings to the dust;
    revive me according to your word.
26 When I told of my ways, you answered me;
    teach me your statutes.
27 Make me understand the way of your precepts,
    and I will meditate on your wondrous works.
28 My soul melts away for sorrow;
    strengthen me according to your word.
29 Put false ways far from me;
    and graciously teach me your law.
30 I have chosen the way of faithfulness;
    I set your ordinances before me.
31 I cling to your decrees, O Lord;
    let me not be put to shame.
32 I run the way of your commandments,
    for you enlarge my understanding.

33 Teach me, O Lord, the way of your statutes,
    and I will observe it to the end.
34 Give me understanding, that I may keep your
      law
    and observe it with my whole heart.
35 Lead me in the path of your commandments,
    for I delight in it.
36 Turn my heart to your decrees,
    and not to selfish gain.
37 Turn my eyes from looking at vanities;
    give me life in your ways.
38 Confirm to your servant your promise,
    which is for those who fear you.
39 Turn away the disgrace that I dread,
    for your ordinances are good.
40 See, I have longed for your precepts;
    in your righteousness give me life.

41 Let your steadfast love come to me, O Lord,
    your salvation according to your promise.
42 Then I shall have an answer for those who
      taunt me,
    for I trust in your word.
43 Do not take the word of truth utterly out of my
      mouth,
    for my hope is in your ordinances.
44 I will keep your law continually,
    forever and ever.
45 I shall walk at liberty,
    for I have sought your precepts.
46 I will also speak of your decrees before kings,
    and shall not be put to shame;
47 I find my delight in your commandments,
    because I love them.
48 I revere your commandments, which I love,
    and I will meditate on your statutes.

49 Remember your word to your servant,
    in which you have made me hope.
50 This is my comfort in my distress,
    that your promise gives me life.
51 The arrogant utterly deride me,
    but I do not turn away from your law.
52 When I think of your ordinances from of old,
    I take comfort, O Lord.
53 Hot indignation seizes me because of the wicked,
    those who forsake your law.
54 Your statutes have been my songs
    wherever I make my home.
55 I remember your name in the night, O Lord,
    and keep your law.
56 This blessing has fallen to me,
    for I have kept your precepts.

57 The Lord is my portion;
    I promise to keep your words.

P
S

58 I implore your favor with all my heart;
     be gracious to me according to your promise.
59 When I think of your ways,
     I turn my feet to your decrees;
60 I hurry and do not delay
     to keep your commandments.
61 Though the cords of the wicked ensnare me,
     I do not forget your law.
62 At midnight I rise to praise you,
     because of your righteous ordinances.
63 I am a companion of all who fear you,
     of those who keep your precepts.
64 The earth, O Lord, is full of your steadfast love;
     teach me your statutes.

65 You have dealt well with your servant,
     O Lord, according to your word.
66 Teach me good judgment and knowledge,
     for I believe in your commandments.
67 Before I was humbled I went astray,
     but now I keep your word.
68 You are good and do good;
     teach me your statutes.
69 The arrogant smear me with lies,
     but with my whole heart I keep your precepts.
70 Their hearts are fat and gross,
     but I delight in your law.
71 It is good for me that I was humbled,
     so that I might learn your statutes.
72 The law of your mouth is better to me
     than thousands of gold and silver pieces.

73 Your hands have made and fashioned me;
     give me understanding that I may learn your
        commandments.
74 Those who fear you shall see me and rejoice,
     because I have hoped in your word.
75 I know, O Lord, that your judgments are right,
     and that in faithfulness you have humbled
        me.
76 Let your steadfast love become my comfort
     according to your promise to your servant.
77 Let your mercy come to me, that I may live;
     for your law is my delight.
78 Let the arrogant be put to shame,
     because they have subverted me with guile;
     as for me, I will meditate on your precepts.
79 Let those who fear you turn to me,
     so that they may know your decrees.
80 May my heart be blameless in your statutes,
     so that I may not be put to shame.

81 My soul languishes for your salvation;
     I hope in your word.
82 My eyes fail with watching for your promise;
     I ask, "When will you comfort me?"

83 For I have become like a wineskin in the smoke,
     yet I have not forgotten your statutes.
84 How long must your servant endure?
     When will you judge those who persecute
        me?
85 The arrogant have dug pitfalls for me;
     they flout your law.
86 All your commandments are enduring;
     I am persecuted without cause; help me!
87 They have almost made an end of me on earth;
     but I have not forsaken your precepts.
88 In your steadfast love spare my life,
     so that I may keep the decrees of your mouth.

89 The Lord exists forever;
     your word is firmly fixed in heaven.
90 Your faithfulness endures to all generations;
     you have established the earth, and it stands
        fast.
91 By your appointment they stand today,
     for all things are your servants.
92 If your law had not been my delight,
     I would have perished in my misery.
93 I will never forget your precepts,
     for by them you have given me life.
94 I am yours; save me,
     for I have sought your precepts.
95 The wicked lie in wait to destroy me,
     but I consider your decrees.
96 I have seen a limit to all perfection,
     but your commandment is exceedingly broad.

97 Oh, how I love your law!
     It is my meditation all day long.
98 Your commandment makes me wiser than my
        enemies,
     for it is always with me.
99 I have more understanding than all my
        teachers,
     for your decrees are my meditation.
100 I understand more than the aged,
     for I keep your precepts.
101 I hold back my feet from every evil way,
     in order to keep your word.
102 I do not turn away from your ordinances,
     for you have taught me.
103 How sweet are your words to my taste,
     sweeter than honey to my mouth!
104 Through your precepts I get understanding;
     therefore I hate every false way.

105 Your word is a lamp to my feet
     and a light to my path.
106 I have sworn an oath and confirmed it,
     to observe your righteous ordinances.
107 I am severely afflicted;

PS

give me life, O LORD, according to your word.

108 Accept my offerings of praise, O LORD,
and teach me your ordinances.

109 I hold my life in my hand continually,
but I do not forget your law.

110 The wicked have laid a snare for me,
but I do not stray from your precepts.

111 Your decrees are my heritage forever;
they are the joy of my heart.

112 I incline my heart to perform your statutes
forever, to the end.

113 I hate the double-minded,
but I love your law.

114 You are my hiding place and my shield;
I hope in your word.

115 Go away from me, you evildoers,
that I may keep the commandments of my
God.

116 Uphold me according to your promise, that I
may live,
and let me not be put to shame in my hope.

117 Hold me up, that I may be safe
and have regard for your statutes continually.

118 You spurn all who go astray from your statutes;
for their cunning is in vain.

119 All the wicked of the earth you count as dross;
therefore I love your decrees.

120 My flesh trembles for fear of you,
and I am afraid of your judgments.

121 I have done what is just and right;
do not leave me to my oppressors.

122 Guarantee your servant's well-being;
do not let the godless oppress me.

123 My eyes fail from watching for your salvation,
and for the fulfillment of your righteous
promise.

124 Deal with your servant according to your
steadfast love,
and teach me your statutes.

125 I am your servant; give me understanding,
so that I may know your decrees.

126 It is time for the LORD to act,
for your law has been broken.

127 Truly I love your commandments
more than gold, more than fine gold.

128 Truly I direct my steps by all your precepts;[a]
I hate every false way.

129 Your decrees are wonderful;
therefore my soul keeps them.

130 The unfolding of your words gives light;
it imparts understanding to the simple.

131 With open mouth I pant,
because I long for your commandments.

132 Turn to me and be gracious to me,
as is your custom toward those who love your
name.

133 Keep my steps steady according to your
promise,
and never let iniquity have dominion over me.

134 Redeem me from human oppression,
that I may keep your precepts.

---

a   Gk Jerome: Meaning of Heb uncertain

Connected to God

God's word can indeed light our way as we journey through life. Traditionally, we have heard or read God's word at worship or in the Bible. However, today with the remarkable advances in communication technology, God's word and spiritual messages can be sent through the Internet. There are countless Web sites devoted to spirituality, faith, and religion. Online prayers and meditations are available daily.

As followers of Christ, we are told to be bearers of the Good News. Now more than ever, that Good News can be shared through technology. Like anything else, Internet access can lead us to sites that are destructive to our faith, but we have the option to choose sites that will enhance our faith and actually draw us closer to God. The worldwide availability of the Internet can also connect people across the globe in prayer and inspiration. It is hard for us to imagine a world without books, and yet in biblical times, they did not exist. It is perhaps equally hard for us to imagine our lives without the ability to access information quickly and to be so connected with so many.

The challenge is how to make sure technology truly can serve to light our way to God. How can we better use this powerful force to share both prayer and blessings with others and also to deepen our understanding of the mysteries of our faith?

▶ **Ps 119:105**

135 Make your face shine upon your servant,
   and teach me your statutes.
136 My eyes shed streams of tears
   because your law is not kept.

137 You are righteous, O LORD,
   and your judgments are right.
138 You have appointed your decrees in
      righteousness
   and in all faithfulness.
139 My zeal consumes me
   because my foes forget your words.
140 Your promise is well tried,
   and your servant loves it.
141 I am small and despised,
   yet I do not forget your precepts.
142 Your righteousness is an everlasting
      righteousness,
   and your law is the truth.
143 Trouble and anguish have come upon me,
   but your commandments are my delight.
144 Your decrees are righteous forever;
   give me understanding that I may live.

145 With my whole heart I cry; answer me, O LORD.
   I will keep your statutes.
146 I cry to you; save me,
   that I may observe your decrees.
147 I rise before dawn and cry for help;
   I put my hope in your words.
148 My eyes are awake before each watch of the
      night,
   that I may meditate on your promise.
149 In your steadfast love hear my voice;
   O LORD, in your justice preserve my life.
150 Those who persecute me with evil purpose
      draw near;
   they are far from your law.
151 Yet you are near, O LORD,
   and all your commandments are true.
152 Long ago I learned from your decrees
   that you have established them forever.

153 Look on my misery and rescue me,
   for I do not forget your law.
154 Plead my cause and redeem me;
   give me life according to your promise.
155 Salvation is far from the wicked,
   for they do not seek your statutes.
156 Great is your mercy, O LORD;
   give me life according to your justice.
157 Many are my persecutors and my adversaries,
   yet I do not swerve from your decrees.
158 I look at the faithless with disgust,
   because they do not keep your commands.
159 Consider how I love your precepts;

preserve my life according to your steadfast
      love.
160 The sum of your word is truth;
   and every one of your righteous ordinances
      endures forever.

161 Princes persecute me without cause,
   but my heart stands in awe of your words.
162 I rejoice at your word
   like one who finds great spoil.
163 I hate and abhor falsehood,
   but I love your law.
164 Seven times a day I praise you
   for your righteous ordinances.
165 Great peace have those who love your law;
   nothing can make them stumble.
166 I hope for your salvation, O LORD,
   and I fulfill your commandments.
167 My soul keeps your decrees;
   I love them exceedingly.
168 I keep your precepts and decrees,
   for all my ways are before you.

169 Let my cry come before you, O LORD;
   give me understanding according to your
      word.
170 Let my supplication come before you;
   deliver me according to your promise.
171 My lips will pour forth praise,
   because you teach me your statutes.
172 My tongue will sing of your promise,
   for all your commandments are right.
173 Let your hand be ready to help me,
   for I have chosen your precepts.
174 I long for your salvation, O LORD,
   and your law is my delight.
175 Let me live that I may praise you,
   and let your ordinances help me.
176 I have gone astray like a lost sheep; seek out
      your servant,
   for I do not forget your commandments.

PSALM 120

Prayer for Deliverance from Slanderers

A Song of Ascents.

1 In my distress I cry to the LORD,
   that he may answer me:
2 "Deliver me, O LORD,
   from lying lips,
   from a deceitful tongue."

3 What shall be given to you?
   And what more shall be done to you,
   you deceitful tongue?

⁴ A warrior's sharp arrows,
  with glowing coals of the broom tree!

⁵ Woe is me, that I am an alien in Meshech,
  that I must live among the tents of Kedar.
⁶ Too long have I had my dwelling
  among those who hate peace.
⁷ I am for peace;
  but when I speak,
  they are for war.

PSALM 121

Assurance of God's Protection

A Song of Ascents.

¹ I lift up my eyes to the hills—
  from where will my help come?
² My help comes from the LORD,
  who made heaven and earth.

³ He will not let your foot be moved;
  he who keeps you will not slumber.
⁴ He who keeps Israel
  will neither slumber nor sleep.

⁵ The LORD is your keeper;
  the LORD is your shade at your right hand.
⁶ The sun shall not strike you by day,
  nor the moon by night.

⁷ The LORD will keep you from all evil;
  he will keep your life.
⁸ The LORD will keep
  your going out and your coming in
  from this time on and forevermore.

PSALM 122

Song of Praise and Prayer for Jerusalem

A Song of Ascents. Of David.

¹ I was glad when they said to me,
  "Let us go to the house of the LORD!"
² Our feet are standing
  within your gates, O Jerusalem.

³ Jerusalem—built as a city
  that is bound firmly together.
⁴ To it the tribes go up,
  the tribes of the LORD,
  as was decreed for Israel,
  to give thanks to the name of the LORD.
⁵ For there the thrones for judgment were
      set up,
  the thrones of the house of David.

⁶ Pray for the peace of Jerusalem:
  "May they prosper who love you.
⁷ Peace be within your walls,
  and security within your towers."
⁸ For the sake of my relatives and friends
  I will say, "Peace be within you."
⁹ For the sake of the house of the LORD our God,
  I will seek your good.

PSALM 123

Supplication for Mercy

A Song of Ascents.

¹ To you I lift up my eyes,
  O you who are enthroned in the heavens!
² As the eyes of servants
  look to the hand of their master,
  as the eyes of a maid
  to the hand of her mistress,
  so our eyes look to the LORD our God,
  until he has mercy upon us.

³ Have mercy upon us, O LORD, have mercy
      upon us,
  for we have had more than enough of
      contempt.
⁴ Our soul has had more than its fill
  of the scorn of those who are at ease,
  of the contempt of the proud.

PSALM 124

Thanksgiving for Israel's Deliverance

A Song of Ascents. Of David.

¹ If it had not been the LORD who was on our
      side
  —let Israel now say—
² if it had not been the LORD who was on our
      side,
  when our enemies attacked us,
³ then they would have swallowed us up alive,
  when their anger was kindled against us;
⁴ then the flood would have swept us away,
  the torrent would have gone over us;
⁵ then over us would have gone
  the raging waters.

⁶ Blessed be the LORD,
  who has not given us
  as prey to their teeth.
⁷ We have escaped like a bird
  from the snare of the fowlers;
  the snare is broken,
  and we have escaped.

PS

Live It!

The Lord Was on Our Side

You often hear a team or group that has just played well or completed a great task say, "God was with us." The writer of Psalm 124 expresses the same sentiment in verses 1–2. What a gift it is to recognize God's help in our lives. It is God who carries us when we are down, who rescues us when we are in trouble, and who gives us the talent we have. If we reach out in relationship to God and do the things necessary to grow in that relationship, God will most assuredly be with us.

If you have ever been afraid or felt lost, read Psalm 124 and be assured that others have felt the same way. Whether you are unsure about school, a job, a relationship, or your future, just remember, "Our help is in the name of the Lord, / who made heaven and earth" (verse 8).

▶ **Psalm 124**

8 Our help is in the name of the Lord,
 who made heaven and earth.

PSALM 125

The Security of God's People

A Song of Ascents.

1 Those who trust in the Lord are like Mount Zion,
 which cannot be moved, but abides forever.
2 As the mountains surround Jerusalem,
 so the Lord surrounds his people,
 from this time on and forevermore.
3 For the scepter of wickedness shall not rest
 on the land allotted to the righteous,
 so that the righteous might not stretch out
 their hands to do wrong.
4 Do good, O Lord, to those who are good,
 and to those who are upright in their hearts.
5 But those who turn aside to their own crooked ways
 the Lord will lead away with evildoers.
 Peace be upon Israel!

PSALM 126

A Harvest of Joy

A Song of Ascents.

1 When the Lord restored the fortunes of Zion,[a]
 we were like those who dream.
2 Then our mouth was filled with laughter,
 and our tongue with shouts of joy;
 then it was said among the nations,
 "The Lord has done great things for them."
3 The Lord has done great things for us,
 and we rejoiced.

4 Restore our fortunes, O Lord,
 like the watercourses in the Negeb.
5 May those who sow in tears
 reap with shouts of joy.
6 Those who go out weeping,
 bearing the seed for sowing,
shall come home with shouts of joy,
 carrying their sheaves.

PSALM 127

God's Blessings in the Home

A Song of Ascents. Of Solomon.

1 Unless the Lord builds the house,
 those who build it labor in vain.
Unless the Lord guards the city,
 the guard keeps watch in vain.
2 It is in vain that you rise up early
 and go late to rest,
eating the bread of anxious toil;
 for he gives sleep to his beloved.[b]

3 Sons are indeed a heritage from the Lord,
 the fruit of the womb a reward.
4 Like arrows in the hand of a warrior
 are the sons of one's youth.
5 Happy is the man who has
 his quiver full of them.
He shall not be put to shame
 when he speaks with his enemies in the gate.

PSALM 128

The Happy Home of the Faithful

A Song of Ascents.

1 Happy is everyone who fears the Lord,
 who walks in his ways.
2 You shall eat the fruit of the labor of your hands;

---

a Or *brought back those who returned to Zion* b Or *for he provides for his beloved during sleep*

you shall be happy, and it shall go well with
you.

3 Your wife will be like a fruitful vine
within your house;
your children will be like olive shoots
around your table.
4 Thus shall the man be blessed
who fears the LORD.

5 The LORD bless you from Zion.
May you see the prosperity of Jerusalem
all the days of your life.
6 May you see your children's children.
Peace be upon Israel!

PSALM 129

Prayer for the Downfall of Israel's Enemies

A Song of Ascents.

1 "Often have they attacked me from my youth"
—let Israel now say—
2 "often have they attacked me from my youth,
yet they have not prevailed against me.
3 The plowers plowed on my back;
they made their furrows long."
4 The LORD is righteous;
he has cut the cords of the wicked.
5 May all who hate Zion
be put to shame and turned backward.
6 Let them be like the grass on the housetops
that withers before it grows up,
7 with which reapers do not fill their hands
or binders of sheaves their arms,
8 while those who pass by do not say,
"The blessing of the LORD be upon you!
We bless you in the name of the LORD!"

PSALM 130

Waiting for Divine Redemption

A Song of Ascents.

1 Out of the depths I cry to you, O LORD.
2 Lord, hear my voice!
Let your ears be attentive
to the voice of my supplications!

3 If you, O LORD, should mark iniquities,
Lord, who could stand?
4 But there is forgiveness with you,
so that you may be revered.

5 I wait for the LORD, my soul waits,
and in his word I hope;

6 my soul waits for the Lord
more than those who watch for the morning,
more than those who watch for the morning.

7 O Israel, hope in the LORD!
For with the LORD there is steadfast love,
and with him is great power to redeem.
8 It is he who will redeem Israel
from all its iniquities.

PSALM 131

Song of Quiet Trust

A Song of Ascents. Of David.

1 O LORD, my heart is not lifted up,
my eyes are not raised too high;
I do not occupy myself with things
too great and too marvelous for me.
2 But I have calmed and quieted my soul,
like a weaned child with its mother;
my soul is like the weaned child that is
with me.[a]

3 O Israel, hope in the LORD
from this time on and forevermore.

a Or my soul within me is like a weaned child

Hold Me, Nurturing God

Psalm 131 is a humble prayer of childlike trust. It gives the wonderful image of God holding us like a child in a mother's lap. Like a mother, God hugs us close and keeps us safe and warm and protected. We don't need to solve problems or be concerned about our performance. We are loved just because we are us. God created us; God loves us and cradles us.

Do you remember sitting quietly in your mother's or grandmother's lap when you were a small child? If so, do you recall her telling you stories or singing you lullabies? How is God's love like that? In your prayer time, imagine being held by God, as a child is held by a mother. You might be surprised at how safe and secure you feel!

▶ **Psalm 131**

✝ Catholic Connection

Prayer

What do you do when you are sad and overwhelmed by sin? You might begin by crying out to God in prayer! That's just what the psalmist did when faced with the weight of personal sins and the sins of the Israelites. The cry to God for help arose from the very depths of the psalmist's own heart and confidently proclaimed trust in God's mercy and faithfulness. Through this passage, the psalmist gives us insight into the nature of prayer.

Prayer is a turning away from sin toward God. We enter into prayer through faith and the grace of the Holy Spirit, who fills our hearts with hope in God's merciful love. When we pray, we respond to God's ceaseless offer of love and friendship by focusing our heart and mind on God and entering into dialogue with God. This dialogue takes place in the "depths" of our heart where we encounter God and discover our own true self. It serves as a way to develop a loving and personal relationship with God. In order to foster a life of prayer, we must, like the disciples, ask Jesus to teach us how to pray, call on the guidance of the Holy Spirit, and make prayer an integral part of our daily routine. (See "The Lord's Prayer," near Lk 11:1–4, for more on how Jesus teaches us to pray.)

There are many ways we can encounter God in prayer. One way is to pray with the Sacred Scriptures, which open our heart to hear and respond to the living word of God. This type of prayer is often called *lectio divina*. Another way is through the liturgy of the Church, particularly the Mass, where our prayers are united in a special way with Christ and the community. We can also meet God in prayer by recognizing God's presence in each moment of our day. (See "Types of Prayer," near 1 Chr 16:37–42, to learn about additional forms of prayer.)

Praying is not always easy. Sometimes distractions in our lives make it difficult to focus on God. Yet, that is when we need to offer up any distractions to God in prayer so that God may purify our hearts and help us to focus on God's will for us. Other times, we may feel God is not there or that our prayers are not being answered. It is at those times that we are called to simply trust in God's faithfulness, recognizing that God is always present and wants what is best for us.

▶ **Ps 130:1–8**

Catechism, nos. 2558–2567, 2650–2662

PSALM 132

The Eternal Dwelling of God in Zion

A Song of Ascents.

¹ O Lord, remember in David's favor
    all the hardships he endured;
² how he swore to the Lord
    and vowed to the Mighty One of Jacob,
³ "I will not enter my house
    or get into my bed;
⁴ I will not give sleep to my eyes
    or slumber to my eyelids,
⁵ until I find a place for the Lord,
    a dwelling place for the Mighty One of Jacob."

⁶ We heard of it in Ephrathah;
    we found it in the fields of Jaar.
⁷ "Let us go to his dwelling place;
    let us worship at his footstool."

⁸ Rise up, O Lord, and go to your resting place,
    you and the ark of your might.
⁹ Let your priests be clothed with righteousness,
    and let your faithful shout for joy.
¹⁰ For your servant David's sake
    do not turn away the face of your anointed one.

¹¹ The Lord swore to David a sure oath
    from which he will not turn back:
"One of the sons of your body
    I will set on your throne.
¹² If your sons keep my covenant
    and my decrees that I shall teach them,
their sons also, forevermore,
    shall sit on your throne."

¹³ For the Lord has chosen Zion;
    he has desired it for his habitation:
¹⁴ "This is my resting place forever;
    here I will reside, for I have desired it.
¹⁵ I will abundantly bless its provisions;
    I will satisfy its poor with bread.
¹⁶ Its priests I will clothe with salvation,
    and its faithful will shout for joy.
¹⁷ There I will cause a horn to sprout up for David;
    I have prepared a lamp for my anointed one.
¹⁸ His enemies I will clothe with disgrace,
    but on him, his crown will gleam."

PSALM 133

The Blessedness of Unity

A Song of Ascents.

¹ How very good and pleasant it is
    when kindred live together in unity!

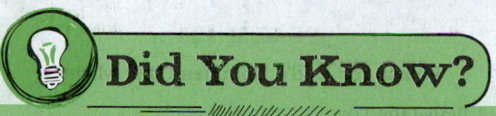

Did You Know?

Jerusalem, Zion, City of David

Jerusalem, Zion, City of David—you have probably noticed that these three names keep popping up throughout the Psalms. They all refer to the heart of Israel, the city of Jerusalem. When David became king of the united Tribes of Israel, he needed a neutral place between the northern and southern tribes. He conquered Jerusalem and elevated it as the political and religious center—thus, Jerusalem was also known as the City of David. Mount Zion, located within Jerusalem, was the site of the Temple—the sacred place where God dwelt. So, Zion became another way to refer to Jerusalem.

At that time, the Israelites felt that Jerusalem was invincible because it was God's dwelling place. But eventually, Jerusalem and the Temple were destroyed. Afterward, a hope arose that one day, a messiah from David's line would renew Jerusalem and true worship of God on Zion. The New Testament portrays Jesus as the fulfillment of this hope.

▶ **Psalm 132**

² It is like the precious oil on the head,
    running down upon the beard,
on the beard of Aaron,
    running down over the collar of his robes.
³ It is like the dew of Hermon,
    which falls on the mountains of Zion.
For there the Lord ordained his blessing,
    life forevermore.

PSALM 134

Praise in the Night

A Song of Ascents.

¹ Come, bless the Lord, all you servants of the
    Lord,
    who stand by night in the house of the Lord!
² Lift up your hands to the holy place,
    and bless the Lord.
³ May the Lord, maker of heaven and earth,
    bless you from Zion.

PSALM 135

Praise for God's Goodness and Might

1 Praise the LORD!
  Praise the name of the LORD;
  give praise, O servants of the LORD,
2 you that stand in the house of the LORD,
  in the courts of the house of our God.
3 Praise the LORD, for the LORD is good;
  sing to his name, for he is gracious.
4 For the LORD has chosen Jacob for himself,
  Israel as his own possession.

5 For I know that the LORD is great;
  our Lord is above all gods.
6 Whatever the LORD pleases he does,
  in heaven and on earth,
  in the seas and all deeps.
7 He it is who makes the clouds rise at the end of
      the earth;
  he makes lightnings for the rain
  and brings out the wind from his storehouses.

8 He it was who struck down the firstborn of
      Egypt,
  both human beings and animals;
9 he sent signs and wonders
  into your midst, O Egypt,
  against Pharaoh and all his servants.
10 He struck down many nations
  and killed mighty kings—
11 Sihon, king of the Amorites,
  and Og, king of Bashan,
  and all the kingdoms of Canaan—
12 and gave their land as a heritage,
  a heritage to his people Israel.

13 Your name, O LORD, endures forever,
  your renown, O LORD, throughout all ages.
14 For the LORD will vindicate his people,
  and have compassion on his servants.

15 The idols of the nations are silver and gold,
  the work of human hands.
16 They have mouths, but they do not speak;
  they have eyes, but they do not see;
17 they have ears, but they do not hear,
  and there is no breath in their mouths.
18 Those who make them
  and all who trust them
  shall become like them.

19 O house of Israel, bless the LORD!
  O house of Aaron, bless the LORD!
20 O house of Levi, bless the LORD!
  You that fear the LORD, bless the LORD!

21 Blessed be the LORD from Zion,
  he who resides in Jerusalem.
Praise the LORD!

PSALM 136

God's Work in Creation and in History

1 O give thanks to the LORD, for he is good,
  for his steadfast love endures forever.
2 O give thanks to the God of gods,
  for his steadfast love endures forever.
3 O give thanks to the Lord of lords,
  for his steadfast love endures forever;

4 who alone does great wonders,
  for his steadfast love endures forever;
5 who by understanding made the heavens,
  for his steadfast love endures forever;
6 who spread out the earth on the waters,
  for his steadfast love endures forever;
7 who made the great lights,
  for his steadfast love endures forever;
8 the sun to rule over the day,
  for his steadfast love endures forever;
9 the moon and stars to rule over the night,
  for his steadfast love endures forever;

10 who struck Egypt through their firstborn,
  for his steadfast love endures forever;
11 and brought Israel out from among them,
  for his steadfast love endures forever;
12 with a strong hand and an outstretched arm,
  for his steadfast love endures forever;
13 who divided the Red Sea[a] in two,
  for his steadfast love endures forever;
14 and made Israel pass through the midst of it,
  for his steadfast love endures forever;
15 but overthrew Pharaoh and his army in the Red
      Sea,[a]
  for his steadfast love endures forever;
16 who led his people through the wilderness,
  for his steadfast love endures forever;
17 who struck down great kings,
  for his steadfast love endures forever;
18 and killed famous kings,
  for his steadfast love endures forever;
19 Sihon, king of the Amorites,
  for his steadfast love endures forever;
20 and Og, king of Bashan,
  for his steadfast love endures forever;
21 and gave their land as a heritage,
  for his steadfast love endures forever;

a *Or Sea of Reeds*

22 a heritage to his servant Israel,
　　for his steadfast love endures forever.

23 It is he who remembered us in our low estate,
　　for his steadfast love endures forever;
24 and rescued us from our foes,
　　for his steadfast love endures forever;
25 who gives food to all flesh,
　　for his steadfast love endures forever.

26 O give thanks to the God of heaven,
　　for his steadfast love endures forever.

PSALM 137

Lament over the Destruction of Jerusalem

1 By the rivers of Babylon—
　　there we sat down and there we wept
　　when we remembered Zion.
2 On the willows*a* there
　　we hung up our harps.
3 For there our captors
　　asked us for songs,
and our tormentors asked for mirth, saying,
　　"Sing us one of the songs of Zion!"

4 How could we sing the Lord's song
　　in a foreign land?
5 If I forget you, O Jerusalem,
　　let my right hand wither!
6 Let my tongue cling to the roof of my mouth,
　　if I do not remember you,
if I do not set Jerusalem
　　above my highest joy.

7 Remember, O Lord, against the Edomites
　　the day of Jerusalem's fall,
how they said, "Tear it down! Tear it down!
　　Down to its foundations!"
8 O daughter Babylon, you devastator!*b*
　　Happy shall they be who pay you back
　　what you have done to us!
9 Happy shall they be who take your little ones
　　and dash them against the rock!

PSALM 138

Thanksgiving and Praise

Of David.

1 I give you thanks, O Lord, with my whole heart;
　　before the gods I sing your praise;
2 I bow down toward your holy temple
　　and give thanks to your name for your
　　　steadfast love and your faithfulness;

for you have exalted your name and your word
　　above everything.*c*
3 On the day I called, you answered me,
　　you increased my strength of soul.*d*

4 All the kings of the earth shall praise you,
　　　O Lord,
　　for they have heard the words of your mouth.
5 They shall sing of the ways of the Lord,
　　for great is the glory of the Lord.
6 For though the Lord is high, he regards the lowly;
　　but the haughty he perceives from far away.

7 Though I walk in the midst of trouble,
　　you preserve me against the wrath of my
　　　enemies;
you stretch out your hand,
　　and your right hand delivers me.
8 The Lord will fulfill his purpose for me;
　　your steadfast love, O Lord, endures forever.
　　Do not forsake the work of your hands.

PSALM 139

The Inescapable God

To the leader. Of David. A Psalm.

1 O Lord, you have searched me and known me.
2 You know when I sit down and when I rise up;
　　you discern my thoughts from far away.
3 You search out my path and my lying down,
　　and are acquainted with all my ways.
4 Even before a word is on my tongue,
　　O Lord, you know it completely.
5 You hem me in, behind and before,
　　and lay your hand upon me.
6 Such knowledge is too wonderful for me;
　　it is so high that I cannot attain it.

7 Where can I go from your spirit?
　　Or where can I flee from your presence?
8 If I ascend to heaven, you are there;
　　if I make my bed in Sheol, you are there.
9 If I take the wings of the morning
　　and settle at the farthest limits of the sea,
10 even there your hand shall lead me,
　　and your right hand shall hold me fast.
11 If I say, "Surely the darkness shall cover me,
　　and the light around me become night,"
12 even the darkness is not dark to you;
　　the night is as bright as the day,
　　for darkness is as light to you.

---

a Or *poplars*　　*b* Or *you who are devastated*　　*c* Cn: Heb *you have exalted your word above all your name*　　*d* Syr Compare Gk Tg: Heb *you made me arrogant in my soul with strength*

Cultural Connection

Celtic Traditions

Many people of the British Isles, especially the Irish, have for hundreds of years celebrated their Celtic traditions. Over the years, their Celtic traditions have become fused with their expressions of their Catholic faith. One of the central Celtic Christian themes is the presence and protection of God. Like the psalmist who wrote Psalm 139, the author of "Saint Patrick's Breastplate" illustrates how the Celts call God into their life and world:

> Christ be with me, Christ within me
> Christ behind me, Christ before me,
> Christ beside me, Christ to win me,
> Christ to comfort and restore me,

Christ beneath me, Christ above me,
> Christ in quiet, Christ in danger,
Christ in the hearts of all that love me,
> Christ in mouth of friend or stranger.

The next time you want to pray for the presence of God, try praying in the Celtic tradition so beautifully expressed in "Saint Patrick's Breastplate."

▶ **Psalm 139**

13 For it was you who formed my inward parts;
   you knit me together in my mother's womb.
14 I praise you, for I am fearfully and wonderfully
      made.
   Wonderful are your works;
that I know very well.
15   My frame was not hidden from you,
when I was being made in secret,
   intricately woven in the depths of the earth.
16 Your eyes beheld my unformed substance.
In your book were written
   all the days that were formed for me,
   when none of them as yet existed.
17 How weighty to me are your thoughts, O God!
   How vast is the sum of them!
18 I try to count them—they are more than the
      sand;
   I come to the end[a]—I am still with you.

19 O that you would kill the wicked, O God,
   and that the bloodthirsty would depart from
      me—
20 those who speak of you maliciously,
   and lift themselves up against you for evil![b]
21 Do I not hate those who hate you, O Lord?
   And do I not loathe those who rise up against
      you?
22 I hate them with perfect hatred;
   I count them my enemies.
23 Search me, O God, and know my heart;
   test me and know my thoughts.
24 See if there is any wicked[c] way in me,
   and lead me in the way everlasting.[d]

PSALM 140

Prayer for Deliverance from Enemies

To the leader. A Psalm of David.

1 Deliver me, O Lord, from evildoers;
   protect me from those who are violent,
2 who plan evil things in their minds
   and stir up wars continually.
3 They make their tongue sharp as a snake's,
   and under their lips is the venom of vipers.
                                          Selah

4 Guard me, O Lord, from the hands of the
      wicked;
   protect me from the violent
   who have planned my downfall.
5 The arrogant have hidden a trap for me,
   and with cords they have spread a net,[e]
   along the road they have set snares for me.
                                          Selah

6 I say to the Lord, "You are my God;
   give ear, O Lord, to the voice of my
      supplications."
7 O Lord, my Lord, my strong deliverer,
   you have covered my head in the day of
      battle.
8 Do not grant, O Lord, the desires of the wicked;
   do not further their evil plot.[f]   *Selah*

---

a Or *I awake*   b Cn: Meaning of Heb uncertain   c Heb *hurtful*
d Or *the ancient way.* Compare Jer 6.16   e Or *they have spread
cords as a net*   f Heb adds *they are exalted*

PS

9 Those who surround me lift up their heads;[a]
> let the mischief of their lips overwhelm
> them!
10 Let burning coals fall on them!
> Let them be flung into pits, no more to rise!
11 Do not let the slanderer be established in the
> land;
> let evil speedily hunt down the violent!

12 I know that the LORD maintains the cause of the
> needy,
> and executes justice for the poor.
13 Surely the righteous shall give thanks to your
> name;
> the upright shall live in your presence.

---

a Cn Compare Gk: Heb *those who surround me are uplifted in head*; Heb divides verses 8 and 9 differently

The Sacredness of Life

"For it was you who formed my inward parts; / you knit me together in my mother's womb" (Ps 139:13).

Psalm 139 speaks poetically of God's intimate care for each of us, long before we were even formed. It is perhaps the most powerful argument against abortion in the entire Bible. Who can deny that God gave us life long before we actually saw the light of day? How can we deny that every unborn child is fashioned by the hand of God?

It is easy to get caught up in arguments about individual rights and scientific terminology. But this is not about science or government or even when life begins. It is about poetry and love and the faith God has knit together within each of us in our mother's womb. God has great plans for each of us, whether we have been born, are in the womb, or have not yet even been thought of. God knows and loves us, and has through all eternity.

▶ **Psalm 139**

God Cares for Those Who Suffer Persecution

Many of us like to think that persecution rarely occurs. Unfortunately, this is not true. All too frequently, people are persecuted because of their color, their ethnic origin, their political beliefs, or even their faith. Harassment can be as subtle as a rude comment or a patronizing attitude, or as aggressive as a beating or killing. Young people know the feeling of persecution. They may experience it because of their origin, the way they look or talk, or what they believe.

Psalm 140 is one of several psalms (see also Psalms 35, 86) and prayers seeking God's help in times of persecution. These typically have two parts. The first part asks for God's protection against persecutors, and the second part praises God's love, justice, and mercy. This illustrates the continual tension for all believers: feeling the need for God's action while at the same time being certain that God cares for them in the midst of their persecution.

For Christians, Jesus is the perfect model of the persecuted person. He was persecuted without reason (see Lk 23:4), and he felt God's absence (see Mk 15:34), but he still put his entire faith and trust in God's will (see Mt 26:39). Following Jesus' example, Christians throughout history have bravely endured persecution, and even death, for their faith.

Have you or your family experienced some kind of persecution? If so, how and why? If you have ever participated in some kind of persecution of someone else, pray for forgiveness, and if possible make amends.

Thank God for the blessings you have, and ask God for the strength to endure whatever persecutions come your way. Pray for those who are suffering persecution, regardless of the motive.

▶ **Psalm 140**

P
S

PSALM 141

Prayer for Preservation from Evil

A Psalm of David.

1 I call upon you, O Lord; come quickly to me;
    give ear to my voice when I call to you.
2 Let my prayer be counted as incense before you,
    and the lifting up of my hands as an evening
        sacrifice.

3 Set a guard over my mouth, O Lord;
    keep watch over the door of my lips.
4 Do not turn my heart to any evil,
    to busy myself with wicked deeds
in company with those who work iniquity;
    do not let me eat of their delicacies.

5 Let the righteous strike me;
    let the faithful correct me.
Never let the oil of the wicked anoint my head,*a*
    for my prayer is continually*b* against their
        wicked deeds.
6 When they are given over to those who shall
        condemn them,
    then they shall learn that my words were
        pleasant.
7 Like a rock that one breaks apart and shatters on
        the land,
    so shall their bones be strewn at the mouth of
        Sheol.*c*

8 But my eyes are turned toward you, O God, my
        Lord;
    in you I seek refuge; do not leave me
        defenseless.
9 Keep me from the trap that they have laid for me,
    and from the snares of evildoers.
10 Let the wicked fall into their own nets,
    while I alone escape.

PSALM 142

Prayer for Deliverance from Persecutors

A Maskil of David. When he was in the cave.
A Prayer.

1 With my voice I cry to the Lord;
    with my voice I make supplication to the
        Lord.
2 I pour out my complaint before him;
    I tell my trouble before him.
3 When my spirit is faint,
    you know my way.

In the path where I walk
    they have hidden a trap for me.

4 Look on my right hand and see—
    there is no one who takes notice of me;
no refuge remains to me;
    no one cares for me.

5 I cry to you, O Lord;
    I say, "You are my refuge,
    my portion in the land of the living."
6 Give heed to my cry,
    for I am brought very low.

Save me from my persecutors,
    for they are too strong for me.
7 Bring me out of prison,
    so that I may give thanks to your name.
The righteous will surround me,
    for you will deal bountifully with me.

PSALM 143

Prayer for Deliverance from Enemies

A Psalm of David.

1 Hear my prayer, O Lord;
    give ear to my supplications in your
        faithfulness;
    answer me in your righteousness.
2 Do not enter into judgment with your servant,
    for no one living is righteous before you.

3 For the enemy has pursued me,
    crushing my life to the ground,
    making me sit in darkness like those long
        dead.
4 Therefore my spirit faints within me;
    my heart within me is appalled.

5 I remember the days of old,
    I think about all your deeds,
    I meditate on the works of your hands.
6 I stretch out my hands to you;
    my soul thirsts for you like a parched land.

Selah

7 Answer me quickly, O Lord;
    my spirit fails.
Do not hide your face from me,
    or I shall be like those who go down to the
        Pit.
8 Let me hear of your steadfast love in the morning,
    for in you I put my trust.
Teach me the way I should go,
    for to you I lift up my soul.

---

a Gk: Meaning of Heb uncertain   *b* Cn: Heb *for continually and
my prayer*   *c* Meaning of Heb of verses 5-7 is uncertain

9 Save me, O Lord, from my enemies;
    I have fled to you for refuge.[a]
10 Teach me to do your will,
    for you are my God.
  Let your good spirit lead me
    on a level path.

11 For your name's sake, O Lord, preserve my life.
    In your righteousness bring me out of trouble.
12 In your steadfast love cut off my enemies,
    and destroy all my adversaries,
    for I am your servant.

PSALM 144

Prayer for National Deliverance and Security

Of David.

1 Blessed be the Lord, my rock,
    who trains my hands for war, and my fingers
      for battle;
2 my rock[b] and my fortress,
    my stronghold and my deliverer,
  my shield, in whom I take refuge,
    who subdues the peoples[c] under me.

3 O Lord, what are human beings that you regard
      them,
    or mortals that you think of them?
4 They are like a breath;
    their days are like a passing shadow.

5 Bow your heavens, O Lord, and come down;
    touch the mountains so that they smoke.
6 Make the lightning flash and scatter them;
    send out your arrows and rout them.
7 Stretch out your hand from on high;
    set me free and rescue me from the mighty
      waters,
    from the hand of aliens,
8 whose mouths speak lies,
    and whose right hands are false.

9 I will sing a new song to you, O God;
    upon a ten-stringed harp I will play to you,
10 the one who gives victory to kings,
    who rescues his servant David.
11 Rescue me from the cruel sword,
    and deliver me from the hand of aliens,
  whose mouths speak lies,
    and whose right hands are false.

12 May our sons in their youth
    be like plants full grown,
  our daughters like corner pillars,
    cut for the building of a palace.

Pray It!

A Prayer for the Young

We praise you, God, for all our nation's
    blessings!
We thank you for our young people, our sons
    and daughters who come forward to serve
    the people of God.
We ask you to make them strong, to call them
    into a trusting relationship with you, and to
    help them live faithful lives and to be
    leaders and examples for others.
Happy the people whose
    God is the Lord!

▶ Psalm 144

13 May our barns be filled,
    with produce of every kind;
  may our sheep increase by thousands,
    by tens of thousands in our fields,
14   and may our cattle be heavy with young.
  May there be no breach in the walls,[d] no exile,
    and no cry of distress in our streets.

15 Happy are the people to whom such blessings
      fall;
    happy are the people whose God is the Lord.

PSALM 145

The Greatness and the Goodness of God

Praise. Of David.

1 I will extol you, my God and King,
    and bless your name forever and ever.
2 Every day I will bless you,
    and praise your name forever and ever.
3 Great is the Lord, and greatly to be praised;
    his greatness is unsearchable.

4 One generation shall laud your works to
      another,
    and shall declare your mighty acts.
5 On the glorious splendor of your majesty,
    and on your wondrous works, I will meditate.

a One Heb Ms Gk: MT to you I have hidden   b With 18.2
and 2 Sam 22.2: Heb my steadfast love   c Heb Mss Syr Aquila
Jerome: MT my people   d Heb lacks in the walls

P
S

6 The might of your awesome deeds shall be
        proclaimed,
    and I will declare your greatness.
7 They shall celebrate the fame of your abundant
        goodness,
    and shall sing aloud of your righteousness.

8 The LORD is gracious and merciful,
    slow to anger and abounding in steadfast love.
9 The LORD is good to all,
    and his compassion is over all that he has
        made.

10 All your works shall give thanks to you, O LORD,
    and all your faithful shall bless you.
11 They shall speak of the glory of your kingdom,
    and tell of your power,
12 to make known to all people your[a] mighty
        deeds,
    and the glorious splendor of your[b] kingdom.
13 Your kingdom is an everlasting kingdom,
    and your dominion endures throughout all
        generations.

The LORD is faithful in all his words,
    and gracious in all his deeds.[c]
14 The LORD upholds all who are falling,
    and raises up all who are bowed down.
15 The eyes of all look to you,
    and you give them their food in due season.
16 You open your hand,
    satisfying the desire of every living thing.
17 The LORD is just in all his ways,
    and kind in all his doings.
18 The LORD is near to all who call on him,
    to all who call on him in truth.
19 He fulfills the desire of all who fear him;
    he also hears their cry, and saves them.
20 The LORD watches over all who love him,
    but all the wicked he will destroy.

21 My mouth will speak the praise of the LORD,
    and all flesh will bless his holy name forever
        and ever.

PSALM 146

Praise for God's Help

1 Praise the LORD!
Praise the LORD, O my soul!
2 I will praise the LORD as long as I live;
    I will sing praises to my God all my life long.

3 Do not put your trust in princes,
    in mortals, in whom there is no help.

4 When their breath departs, they return to the
        earth;
    on that very day their plans perish.

5 Happy are those whose help is the God of
        Jacob,
    whose hope is in the LORD their God,
6 who made heaven and earth,
    the sea, and all that is in them;
who keeps faith forever;
7   who executes justice for the oppressed;
    who gives food to the hungry.

The LORD sets the prisoners free;
8   the LORD opens the eyes of the blind.
The LORD lifts up those who are bowed down;
    the LORD loves the righteous.
9 The LORD watches over the strangers;
    he upholds the orphan and the widow,
    but the way of the wicked he brings to ruin.

10 The LORD will reign forever,
    your God, O Zion, for all generations.
Praise the LORD!

PSALM 147

Praise for God's Care for Jerusalem

1 Praise the LORD!
How good it is to sing praises to our God;
    for he is gracious, and a song of praise is
        fitting.
2 The LORD builds up Jerusalem;
    he gathers the outcasts of Israel.
3 He heals the brokenhearted,
    and binds up their wounds.
4 He determines the number of the stars;
    he gives to all of them their names.
5 Great is our Lord, and abundant in power;
    his understanding is beyond measure.
6 The LORD lifts up the downtrodden;
    he casts the wicked to the ground.

7 Sing to the LORD with thanksgiving;
    make melody to our God on the lyre.
8 He covers the heavens with clouds,
    prepares rain for the earth,
    makes grass grow on the hills.
9 He gives to the animals their food,
    and to the young ravens when they cry.
10 His delight is not in the strength of the horse,
    nor his pleasure in the speed of a runner;[d]

a Gk Jerome Syr: Heb his   b Heb his   c These two lines
supplied by Q Ms Gk Syr   d Heb legs of a person

Catholic Social Teaching

Care for God's Creation

Psalm 148 calls on all of creation to praise God. As one of the seven themes of Catholic social teaching, caring for God's creation is one way we can respond to God and the needs of others. Working to keep water clean for safe drinking and for the protection of sea life, educating ourselves and others about the effects of pollution on animal habitats and nesting sites, protecting endangered species, and reducing carbon emissions are some of the ways we can fulfill our call to care for God's creation.

Psalm 148 asks us to complete a cycle—God creates, and we are called to be "co-creators" with God, continuing the work of creation by acting as caretakers for the goods of the earth. Our work as co-creators is often referred to as stewardship. Stewardship is centered around the notion that we are on this earth for a short time only and thus we have a moral responsibility to take care of the earth for future generations. Indeed, God demands that we be

good stewards of all that he has blessed us with, so that all people can share in the overwhelming goodness of God's creation.

How can you be a better steward of God's creation?

▶ **Psalm 148**

Care for God's Creation

---

¹¹ but the Lord takes pleasure in those who fear him,
    in those who hope in his steadfast love.

¹² Praise the Lord, O Jerusalem!
    Praise your God, O Zion!
¹³ For he strengthens the bars of your gates;
    he blesses your children within you.
¹⁴ He grants peace*a* within your borders;
    he fills you with the finest of wheat.
¹⁵ He sends out his command to the earth;
    his word runs swiftly.
¹⁶ He gives snow like wool;
    he scatters frost like ashes.
¹⁷ He hurls down hail like crumbs—
    who can stand before his cold?
¹⁸ He sends out his word, and melts them;
    he makes his wind blow, and the waters flow.
¹⁹ He declares his word to Jacob,
    his statutes and ordinances to Israel.
²⁰ He has not dealt thus with any other nation;
    they do not know his ordinances.
    Praise the Lord!

PSALM 148

Praise for God's Universal Glory

¹ Praise the Lord!
Praise the Lord from the heavens;
    praise him in the heights!

² Praise him, all his angels;
    praise him, all his host!

³ Praise him, sun and moon;
    praise him, all you shining stars!
⁴ Praise him, you highest heavens,
    and you waters above the heavens!

⁵ Let them praise the name of the Lord,
    for he commanded and they were created.
⁶ He established them forever and ever;
    he fixed their bounds, which cannot be
        passed.*b*

⁷ Praise the Lord from the earth,
    you sea monsters and all deeps,
⁸ fire and hail, snow and frost,
    stormy wind fulfilling his command!

⁹ Mountains and all hills,
    fruit trees and all cedars!
¹⁰ Wild animals and all cattle,
    creeping things and flying birds!

¹¹ Kings of the earth and all peoples,
    princes and all rulers of the earth!
¹² Young men and women alike,
    old and young together!

---

a Or *prosperity*   *b* Or *he set a law that cannot pass away*

P
S

Psalm 150, Part 2

Praise God with clarinet and saxophone;
  praise God with flute and oboe!
Praise God with French horn and tuba;
  praise God with marimba and xylophone!
Praise God with guitar and fiddle;
  praise God with banjo and ukulele!
Praise God with bagpipe and accordion;
  praise God with piano and calliope!
Praise God with steel drum and harmonica;
  praise God with bongo and maracas!
Praise God with soaring classical music;
  praise God with mellow blues and tango!
Praise God with reggae and rap;
  praise God with jazz and rock!
Praise God with square dancing and line
    dancing;
  praise God with polka and waltz!
Let everyone who has breath and hands and
    feet and voices—
  sopranos, altos, tenors, and basses—
  praise the Lord!

▶ **Psalm 150**

13 Let them praise the name of the Lord,
    for his name alone is exalted;
    his glory is above earth and heaven.
14 He has raised up a horn for his people,
    praise for all his faithful,
    for the people of Israel who are close to him.
  Praise the Lord!

PSALM 149

Praise for God's Goodness to Israel

1 Praise the Lord!
  Sing to the Lord a new song,
    his praise in the assembly of the faithful.
2 Let Israel be glad in its Maker;
    let the children of Zion rejoice in their King.
3 Let them praise his name with dancing,
    making melody to him with tambourine and
      lyre.
4 For the Lord takes pleasure in his people;
    he adorns the humble with victory.
5 Let the faithful exult in glory;
    let them sing for joy on their couches.
6 Let the high praises of God be in their throats
    and two-edged swords in their hands,
7 to execute vengeance on the nations
    and punishment on the peoples,
8 to bind their kings with fetters
    and their nobles with chains of iron,
9 to execute on them the judgment decreed.
    This is glory for all his faithful ones.
  Praise the Lord!

PSALM 150

Praise for God's Surpassing Greatness

1 Praise the Lord!
  Praise God in his sanctuary;
    praise him in his mighty firmament![a]
2 Praise him for his mighty deeds;
    praise him according to his surpassing
      greatness!

3 Praise him with trumpet sound;
    praise him with lute and harp!
4 Praise him with tambourine and dance;
    praise him with strings and pipe!
5 Praise him with clanging cymbals;
    praise him with loud clashing cymbals!
6 Let everything that breathes praise the Lord!
  Praise the Lord!

---

a Or *dome*

When we pick up the daily newspaper, many of us turn first to the advice columns. "My mom just doesn't understand me," we read. "Why won't she let me make my own decisions?" Or "I think my boyfriend is cheating on me. Should I show him the door?" Or "All my friends take drugs. How do I resist the pressure?" The Book of Proverbs is the advice column of the Old Testament. It covers everything from raising children to choosing friends.

At a Glance

- Chapters 1–9. introduction and instructions for young people
- 10:1–31:9. assorted collections of proverbs
- 31:10–31. a reflection on being a good wife

Quick Facts

Inspired Authors: King Solomon is introduced as the author, probably because of his legendary wisdom. However, the actual authors are unknown, writing from the reign of King Solomon (970–931 BC) to sometime after the Babylonian Exile (587–538 BC).

Of Note: The book is made up of several collections of proverbs.

In Depth

Proverbs teaches that the wise person listens to the "voices" of history: experience, intelligence, and common sense. The ancient Israelites had a long tradition of reflecting on the challenges of life. Over the centuries, a whole body of writings developed to record their reflections. These writings gave advice on common problems and questions people faced, and directions for wise living.

Proverbs is the best-known example of this type of literature in the Old Testament. It contains two basic kinds of writings: longer instructions addressed to young people and short sayings addressed to all. With advice on matters ranging from laziness (see 6:6–11), cheating (see 11:1), pride (see 16:18), and the training of children (see 22:6), to laughter (see 14:13), eyewinks (see 16:30), visiting neighbors (see 25:17), and being a good wife (see 31:10–31), Proverbs is a treasure chest of advice from the ancient world. Although some of the sayings may seem outdated or funny to us today, the overall lesson is something Jesus insists on in the Gospels: faith is not just a matter of right believing; it is also a matter of right living.

The poetic devices used in Proverbs—found in most wisdom literature—reveal another basic insight of our ancestors in faith: how something is said is as important as what is said. In addition, parallelism makes the generally short sayings in this book easy to memorize. We would do well to consult Proverbs regularly for good advice, and to remember what we read. To all who care to hear, this book tells of the rewards of virtue and the dangers of vice.

The Book of Proverbs

Happy the man who finds wisdom.

Proverbs

1 The proverbs of Solomon son of David, king of Israel:

Prologue

2 For learning about wisdom and instruction,
   for understanding words of insight,
3 for gaining instruction in wise dealing,
   righteousness, justice, and equity;
4 to teach shrewdness to the simple,
   knowledge and prudence to the young—
5 let the wise also hear and gain in learning,
   and the discerning acquire skill,
6 to understand a proverb and a figure,
   the words of the wise and their riddles.

7 The fear of the LORD is the beginning of
      knowledge;
   fools despise wisdom and instruction.

Warnings against Evil Companions

8 Hear, my child, your father's instruction,
   and do not reject your mother's teaching;
9 for they are a fair garland for your head,
   and pendants for your neck.
10 My child, if sinners entice you,
   do not consent.
11 If they say, "Come with us, let us lie in wait for
      blood;
   let us wantonly ambush the innocent;
12 like Sheol let us swallow them alive
   and whole, like those who go down to the Pit.
13 We shall find all kinds of costly things;
   we shall fill our houses with booty.

14 Throw in your lot among us;
   we will all have one purse"—
15 my child, do not walk in their way,
   keep your foot from their paths;
16 for their feet run to evil,
   and they hurry to shed blood.
17 For in vain is the net baited
   while the bird is looking on;
18 yet they lie in wait—to kill themselves!
   and set an ambush—for their own lives!
19 Such is the end*a* of all who are greedy for gain;
   it takes away the life of its possessors.

The Call of Wisdom

20 Wisdom cries out in the street;
   in the squares she raises her voice.
21 At the busiest corner she cries out;
   at the entrance of the city gates she speaks:
22 "How long, O simple ones, will you love being
      simple?
How long will scoffers delight in their scoffing
   and fools hate knowledge?
23 Give heed to my reproof;
   I will pour out my thoughts to you;
   I will make my words known to you.
24 Because I have called and you refused,
   have stretched out my hand and no one
      heeded,
25 and because you have ignored all my counsel
   and would have none of my reproof,
26 I also will laugh at your calamity;

a Gk: Heb *are the ways*

692

I will mock when panic strikes you,
27 when panic strikes you like a storm,
   and your calamity comes like a whirlwind,
   when distress and anguish come upon you.
28 Then they will call upon me, but I will not
   answer;
   they will seek me diligently, but will not find
   me.
29 Because they hated knowledge
   and did not choose the fear of the Lord,
30 would have none of my counsel,
   and despised all my reproof,
31 therefore they shall eat the fruit of their way
   and be sated with their own devices.
32 For waywardness kills the simple,
   and the complacency of fools destroys
   them;
33 but those who listen to me will be secure
   and will live at ease, without dread of
   disaster."

The Value of Wisdom

2 My child, if you accept my words
  and treasure up my commandments within
  you,
2 making your ear attentive to wisdom
  and inclining your heart to understanding;
3 if you indeed cry out for insight,
  and raise your voice for understanding;
4 if you seek it like silver,
  and search for it as for hidden treasures—
5 then you will understand the fear of the Lord
  and find the knowledge of God.
6 For the Lord gives wisdom;
  from his mouth come knowledge and
  understanding;
7 he stores up sound wisdom for the upright;
  he is a shield to those who walk blamelessly,
8 guarding the paths of justice
  and preserving the way of his faithful ones.
9 Then you will understand righteousness and
  justice
  and equity, every good path;
10 for wisdom will come into your heart,
  and knowledge will be pleasant to your
  soul;
11 prudence will watch over you;
  and understanding will guard you.
12 It will save you from the way of evil,
  from those who speak perversely,
13 who forsake the paths of uprightness
  to walk in the ways of darkness,
14 who rejoice in doing evil
  and delight in the perverseness of evil;
15 those whose paths are crooked,
  and who are devious in their ways.

Media Literacy

Our society today has a powerful, persuasive tool: the media. We are influenced in many ways by what we read, watch, and hear in the many forms of modern media.

We might buy things because something we read says it's the best. We might look the other way when someone is being robbed because we see so much violence at the movies that it doesn't seem to bother us. We might dance to the beat of a song and not even realize that the words are suggesting an immoral behavior.

Certainly not all the messages in the media are bad. But to resist the influence of the media's negative messages, we must educate ourselves to watch for them. In Proverbs 1:10, we read "My child, if sinners entice you, / do not consent." Take time to really think about a message in the media before you choose to follow it. Verse 7 says it best: Only a fool despises wisdom!

▶ **Prov 1:10**

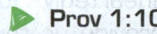

16 You will be saved from the loose[a] woman,
   from the adulteress with her smooth words,
17 who forsakes the partner of her youth
   and forgets her sacred covenant;
18 for her way[b] leads down to death,
   and her paths to the shades;
19 those who go to her never come back,
   nor do they regain the paths of life.

20 Therefore walk in the way of the good,
   and keep to the paths of the just.
21 For the upright will abide in the land,
   and the innocent will remain in it;
22 but the wicked will be cut off from the land,
   and the treacherous will be rooted out of it.

Admonition to Trust and Honor God

3 My child, do not forget my teaching,
  but let your heart keep my commandments;
2 for length of days and years of life
  and abundant welfare they will give you.

a Heb strange   b Cn: Heb house

P R O V

✝ Catholic Connection

Sources of Moral Truth

We often hear people say that morality is all relative, that it is solely up to each individual to determine what is right and what is wrong. But the Scriptures teach that there is a moral law with moral truths that never change and we must seek to know them. To guide us, Proverbs speaks of one's need to wholeheartedly seek "wisdom," "understanding," and "insight." One must "cry out," be "attentive," and treat this knowledge as a highly treasured prize.

The Catholic Church teaches that there are different expressions of the moral law that each one of us is called to seek wholeheartedly. Together these sources provide us the understanding and insight we need to obey God and work toward the common good.

One expression of the moral law is the natural law. The natural law is the God-given ability to use reason to tell right from wrong. This ability can be found in all people throughout history, regardless of their religion, and leads us to do good and avoid evil. It sounds simple, but sometimes we forget that we each must use reason when confronted with a moral dilemma.

Another expression of the moral law is from the Old Testament. In the Old Testament, we find the "Old Law," which is the law given to Moses and summed up in the Ten Commandments. This law provides us with moral truths regarding ways we are to love God and our neighbor. Knowing and applying the Ten Commandments is essential to making a moral decision.

A third expression is the "New Law" or "Law of the Gospel" given to us by Jesus. The New Law together with the Old Law are essential parts of the moral law that God has revealed to the world. The New Law fulfills and gives us a deeper understanding of the Old Law; it not only shows us how to love God and others, but also, through the power of the Holy Spirit, gives us the grace and strength necessary to follow the law. The Holy Spirit also empowers the Church to serve as a guide to moral truth and to instruct the faithful about faith and morals without error.

Through much prayer and study, we all can wholeheartedly seek moral truth as Proverbs calls us to do. How is God calling you to grow in wisdom, understanding, and insight into moral truth?

▶ **Prov 2:1–22**
Catechism, nos. 1949–1986

3 Do not let loyalty and faithfulness forsake you;
    bind them around your neck,
    write them on the tablet of your heart.
4 So you will find favor and good repute
    in the sight of God and of people.

5 Trust in the Lord with all your heart,
    and do not rely on your own insight.
6 In all your ways acknowledge him,
    and he will make straight your paths.
7 Do not be wise in your own eyes;
    fear the Lord, and turn away from evil.
8 It will be a healing for your flesh
    and a refreshment for your body.

9 Honor the Lord with your substance
    and with the first fruits of all your produce;
10 then your barns will be filled with plenty,
    and your vats will be bursting with wine.

11 My child, do not despise the Lord's discipline
    or be weary of his reproof,
12 for the Lord reproves the one he loves,
    as a father the son in whom he delights.

The True Wealth

13 Happy are those who find wisdom,
    and those who get understanding,
14 for her income is better than silver,
    and her revenue better than gold.
15 She is more precious than jewels,
    and nothing you desire can compare with her.
16 Long life is in her right hand;
    in her left hand are riches and honor.
17 Her ways are ways of pleasantness,
    and all her paths are peace.
18 She is a tree of life to those who lay hold of her;
    those who hold her fast are called happy.

God's Wisdom in Creation

19 The Lord by wisdom founded the earth;
    by understanding he established the heavens;
20 by his knowledge the deeps broke open,
    and the clouds drop down the dew.

The True Security

21 My child, do not let these escape from your
    sight:
    keep sound wisdom and prudence,
22 and they will be life for your soul
    and adornment for your neck.
23 Then you will walk on your way securely
    and your foot will not stumble.
24 If you sit down,[a] you will not be afraid;
    when you lie down, your sleep will be sweet.
25 Do not be afraid of sudden panic,

Pray It!

Your Future

Read Proverbs 3:5–8 and think about your plans for the future. How does God play a part in them? Do they include discernment of (prayerful listening to) God's plans for you? Here are some clues for discerning where God is calling you:

- Pray about your future, and ask for God's direction.
- Look at your talents and interests. These are gifts from God to be used for the good of others as well as yourself.
- Imagine yourself doing whatever you are considering. What feelings surface? Peace and joy are usually signs of God's presence. Excessive anxiety, fear, and shame are usually signs of God's absence.
- Talk with a trusted adult about your options. If this person is wise, she or he will not give you a direct answer but will help you sort out where God is leading.

▶ **Prov 3:5–8**

    or of the storm that strikes the wicked;
26 for the Lord will be your confidence
    and will keep your foot from being caught.

27 Do not withhold good from those to whom it is
    due,[b]
    when it is in your power to do it.
28 Do not say to your neighbor, "Go, and come
    again,
    tomorrow I will give it"—when you have it
    with you.
29 Do not plan harm against your neighbor
    who lives trustingly beside you.
30 Do not quarrel with anyone without cause,
    when no harm has been done to you.
31 Do not envy the violent
    and do not choose any of their ways;
32 for the perverse are an abomination to the Lord,
    but the upright are in his confidence.
33 The Lord's curse is on the house of the wicked,
    but he blesses the abode of the righteous.
34 Toward the scorners he is scornful,

a Gk: Heb lie down   b Heb from its owners

True Security

We often hear, "When the going gets tough, the tough get going." But how do we know how to get going? Where do we get going to? Our faith gives us good advice and wise counsel (see Prov 3:21). Prayer keeps us close to God (see verse 26). And knowing we have made the right decision is true security.

When the going gets tough, first the tough get faithful and prayerful and thoughtful. Then they get going.

▶ **Prov 3:21–26**

but to the humble he shows favor.
35 The wise will inherit honor,
   but stubborn fools, disgrace.

Parental Advice

4 Listen, children, to a father's instruction,
   and be attentive, that you may gain[a] insight;
2 for I give you good precepts:
   do not forsake my teaching.
3 When I was a son with my father,
   tender, and my mother's favorite,
4 he taught me, and said to me,
   "Let your heart hold fast my words;
   keep my commandments, and live.
5 Get wisdom; get insight: do not forget, nor turn away
   from the words of my mouth.
6 Do not forsake her, and she will keep you;
   love her, and she will guard you.
7 The beginning of wisdom is this: Get wisdom,
   and whatever else you get, get insight.
8 Prize her highly, and she will exalt you;
   she will honor you if you embrace her.
9 She will place on your head a fair garland;
   she will bestow on you a beautiful crown."

Admonition to Keep to the Right Path

10 Hear, my child, and accept my words,
   that the years of your life may be many.
11 I have taught you the way of wisdom;
   I have led you in the paths of uprightness.
12 When you walk, your step will not be hampered;
   and if you run, you will not stumble.

13 Keep hold of instruction; do not let go;
   guard her, for she is your life.
14 Do not enter the path of the wicked,
   and do not walk in the way of evildoers.
15 Avoid it; do not go on it;
   turn away from it and pass on.
16 For they cannot sleep unless they have done wrong;
   they are robbed of sleep unless they have made someone stumble.
17 For they eat the bread of wickedness
   and drink the wine of violence.
18 But the path of the righteous is like the light of dawn,
   which shines brighter and brighter until full day.
19 The way of the wicked is like deep darkness;
   they do not know what they stumble over.
20 My child, be attentive to my words;
   incline your ear to my sayings.
21 Do not let them escape from your sight;
   keep them within your heart.
22 For they are life to those who find them,
   and healing to all their flesh.
23 Keep your heart with all vigilance,
   for from it flow the springs of life.
24 Put away from you crooked speech,
   and put devious talk far from you.
25 Let your eyes look directly forward,
   and your gaze be straight before you.
26 Keep straight the path of your feet,
   and all your ways will be sure.
27 Do not swerve to the right or to the left;
   turn your foot away from evil.

Warning against Impurity and Infidelity

5 My child, be attentive to my wisdom;
   incline your ear to my understanding,
2 so that you may hold on to prudence,
   and your lips may guard knowledge.
3 For the lips of a loose[b] woman drip honey,
   and her speech is smoother than oil;
4 but in the end she is bitter as wormwood,
   sharp as a two-edged sword.
5 Her feet go down to death;
   her steps follow the path to Sheol.
6 She does not keep straight to the path of life;
   her ways wander, and she does not know it.

7 And now, my child,[c] listen to me,
   and do not depart from the words of my mouth.
8 Keep your way far from her,
   and do not go near the door of her house;

_a_ Heb _know_   _b_ Heb _strange_   _c_ Gk Vg: Heb _children_

PROV

9 or you will give your honor to others,
  and your years to the merciless,

10 and strangers will take their fill of your wealth,
   and your labors will go to the house of an
      alien;

11 and at the end of your life you will groan,
   when your flesh and body are consumed,

12 and you say, "Oh, how I hated discipline,
   and my heart despised reproof!

13 I did not listen to the voice of my teachers
   or incline my ear to my instructors.

14 Now I am at the point of utter ruin
   in the public assembly."

15 Drink water from your own cistern,
   flowing water from your own well.

16 Should your springs be scattered abroad,
   streams of water in the streets?

17 Let them be for yourself alone,
   and not for sharing with strangers.

18 Let your fountain be blessed,
   and rejoice in the wife of your youth,

19   a lovely deer, a graceful doe.
   May her breasts satisfy you at all times;
   may you be intoxicated always by her love.

20 Why should you be intoxicated, my son, by
      another woman
   and embrace the bosom of an adulteress?

21 For human ways are under the eyes of the LORD,
   and he examines all their paths.

22 The iniquities of the wicked ensnare them,
   and they are caught in the toils of their sin.

23 They die for lack of discipline,
   and because of their great folly they are lost.

Practical Admonitions

6 My child, if you have given your pledge to
      your neighbor,
   if you have bound yourself to another,[a]

2 you are snared by the utterance of your lips,[b]
   caught by the words of your mouth.

3 So do this, my child, and save yourself,
   for you have come into your neighbor's
      power:
   go, hurry,[c] and plead with your neighbor.

4 Give your eyes no sleep
   and your eyelids no slumber;

5 save yourself like a gazelle from the hunter,[d]
   like a bird from the hand of the fowler.

6 Go to the ant, you lazybones;
   consider its ways, and be wise.

7 Without having any chief
   or officer or ruler,

8 it prepares its food in summer,
   and gathers its sustenance in harvest.

9 How long will you lie there, O lazybones?
   When will you rise from your sleep?

10 A little sleep, a little slumber,
   a little folding of the hands to rest,

11 and poverty will come upon you like a robber,
   and want, like an armed warrior.

12 A scoundrel and a villain
   goes around with crooked speech,

13 winking the eyes, shuffling the feet,
   pointing the fingers,

14 with perverted mind devising evil,
   continually sowing discord;

15 on such a one calamity will descend suddenly;
   in a moment, damage beyond repair.

---

a Or *a stranger*   *b* Cn Compare Gk Syr: Heb *the words of your*
mouth   *c* Or *humble yourself*   *d* Cn: Heb *from the hand*

All the Days of My Life

The phrase "all the days of my life" has been repeated by countless couples on their wedding day, and for some of those couples, it is prophetic. The husband and wife will be together till death separates them, and then they will be reunited in heaven. Though we live in a society where divorce is frequent, many couples make it through all the trials and difficulties and are together to celebrate their twenty-fifth and fiftieth anniversaries.

The writer of Proverbs 5:15–23 is warning men, in particular, against adultery, which remains, even today, a primary reason marriages break up. But one does not have to be a man, or even married, to be challenged by the words of this proverb. We are all called to exhibit the virtue of chastity—sexual self-control—in our relationships. This means we must never abuse the gift of sexuality by using it for self-serving purposes or immediate gratification, remembering that our "human ways are under the eyes of the LORD" (verse 21).

▶ **Prov 5:15–23**

P
R
O
V

Leaders with Character

Look at the list of the things the Lord hates in Proverbs 6:17–19. It looks like a popular description of a corrupt politician or business-person! Now take the list and put it in the positive: humble eyes, a truthful tongue, hands that protect the innocent, a heart that plans good, feet that hurry to help, a truthful witness, and someone who brings harmony to families. That's the kind of leader everyone wants! Perhaps you know of a leader in your school, family, church, or local community who exhibits many of these positive qualities. These sorts of leaders have a unique ability to inspire others to follow, providing great insight and direction when one is faced with difficult situations or decisions.

The author of Proverbs is constantly reminding us to be of good character. When you are called to be a leader—and we all will be at some time in our lives—keep the advice of Proverbs in mind. Be a leader of character and integrity by doing the things the Lord loves, not the things the Lord hates.

▶ **Prov 6:16–19**

16 There are six things that the Lord hates,
    seven that are an abomination to him:
17 haughty eyes, a lying tongue,
    and hands that shed innocent blood,
18 a heart that devises wicked plans,
    feet that hurry to run to evil,
19 a lying witness who testifies falsely,
    and one who sows discord in a family.

20 My child, keep your father's commandment,
    and do not forsake your mother's teaching.
21 Bind them upon your heart always;
    tie them around your neck.
22 When you walk, they[a] will lead you;
    when you lie down, they[a] will watch over you;
    and when you awake, they[a] will talk with you.
23 For the commandment is a lamp and the
    teaching a light,
    and the reproofs of discipline are the way of
    life,

24 to preserve you from the wife of another,[b]
    from the smooth tongue of the adulteress.
25 Do not desire her beauty in your heart,
    and do not let her capture you with her
      eyelashes;
26 for a prostitute's fee is only a loaf of bread,[c]
    but the wife of another stalks a man's very
      life.
27 Can fire be carried in the bosom
    without burning one's clothes?
28 Or can one walk on hot coals
    without scorching the feet?
29 So is he who sleeps with his neighbor's wife;
    no one who touches her will go unpunished.
30 Thieves are not despised who steal only
    to satisfy their appetite when they are hungry.
31 Yet if they are caught, they will pay sevenfold;
    they will forfeit all the goods of their house.
32 But he who commits adultery has no sense;
    he who does it destroys himself.
33 He will get wounds and dishonor,
    and his disgrace will not be wiped away.
34 For jealousy arouses a husband's fury,
    and he shows no restraint when he takes
      revenge.
35 He will accept no compensation,
    and refuses a bribe no matter how great.

The False Attractions of Adultery

7 My child, keep my words
    and store up my commandments with you;
2 keep my commandments and live,
    keep my teachings as the apple of your eye;
3 bind them on your fingers,
    write them on the tablet of your heart.
4 Say to wisdom, "You are my sister,"
    and call insight your intimate friend,
5 that they may keep you from the loose[d] woman,
    from the adulteress with her smooth words.

6 For at the window of my house
    I looked out through my lattice,
7 and I saw among the simple ones,
    I observed among the youths,
    a young man without sense,
8 passing along the street near her corner,
    taking the road to her house
9 in the twilight, in the evening,
    at the time of night and darkness.

10 Then a woman comes toward him,
    decked out like a prostitute, wily of heart.[e]

---

a Heb it   b Gk: MT *the evil woman*   c Cn Compare Gk Syr Vg
Tg: Heb *for because of a harlot to a piece of bread*   d Heb *strange*
e Meaning of Heb uncertain

PROV

¹¹ She is loud and wayward;
   her feet do not stay at home;
¹² now in the street, now in the squares,
   and at every corner she lies in wait.
¹³ She seizes him and kisses him,
   and with impudent face she says to him:
¹⁴ "I had to offer sacrifices,
   and today I have paid my vows;
¹⁵ so now I have come out to meet you,
   to seek you eagerly, and I have found you!
¹⁶ I have decked my couch with coverings,
   colored spreads of Egyptian linen;
¹⁷ I have perfumed my bed with myrrh,
   aloes, and cinnamon.
¹⁸ Come, let us take our fill of love until morning;
   let us delight ourselves with love.
¹⁹ For my husband is not at home;
   he has gone on a long journey.
²⁰ He took a bag of money with him;
   he will not come home until full moon."

²¹ With much seductive speech she persuades him;
   with her smooth talk she compels him.
²² Right away he follows her,
   and goes like an ox to the slaughter,
   or bounds like a stag toward the trap[a]
²³   until an arrow pierces its entrails.
   He is like a bird rushing into a snare,
   not knowing that it will cost him his life.

²⁴ And now, my children, listen to me,
   and be attentive to the words of my mouth.
²⁵ Do not let your hearts turn aside to her ways;
   do not stray into her paths.
²⁶ For many are those she has laid low,
   and numerous are her victims.
²⁷ Her house is the way to Sheol,
   going down to the chambers of death.

The Gifts of Wisdom

8 Does not wisdom call,
   and does not understanding raise her voice?
² On the heights, beside the way,
   at the crossroads she takes her stand;
³ beside the gates in front of the town,
   at the entrance of the portals she cries out:
⁴ "To you, O people, I call,
   and my cry is to all that live.
⁵ O simple ones, learn prudence;
   acquire intelligence, you who lack it.
⁶ Hear, for I will speak noble things,
   and from my lips will come what is right;
⁷ for my mouth will utter truth;
   wickedness is an abomination to my lips.
⁸ All the words of my mouth are righteous;
   there is nothing twisted or crooked in them.

⁹ They are all straight to one who understands
   and right to those who find knowledge.
¹⁰ Take my instruction instead of silver,
   and knowledge rather than choice gold;
¹¹ for wisdom is better than jewels,
   and all that you may desire cannot compare
      with her.
¹² I, wisdom, live with prudence,[b]
   and I attain knowledge and discretion.
¹³ The fear of the Lᴏʀᴅ is hatred of evil.
   Pride and arrogance and the way of evil
   and perverted speech I hate.
¹⁴ I have good advice and sound wisdom;
   I have insight, I have strength.
¹⁵ By me kings reign,
   and rulers decree what is just;
¹⁶ by me rulers rule,
   and nobles, all who govern rightly.
¹⁷ I love those who love me,
   and those who seek me diligently find me.
¹⁸ Riches and honor are with me,
   enduring wealth and prosperity.
¹⁹ My fruit is better than gold, even fine gold,
   and my yield than choice silver.
²⁰ I walk in the way of righteousness,

---

a Cn Compare Gk: Meaning of Heb uncertain   b Meaning of Heb uncertain

Lady Wisdom

As you read the description of wisdom in Proverbs 8:1—9:6, you might get the impression that you are reading about a goddess. But that's not the case. The wisdom writers borrowed from neighboring cultures the idea of describing wisdom as a beautiful and eternal aspect of God. They exquisitely embodied the idea of wisdom in the figure of Lady Wisdom. Lady Wisdom comes from God. She was present at the Creation of the world, and she has a special understanding of the world and its workings. For the wisdom writers, Lady Wisdom was an aspect of God that wise people would want to pursue because she reveals the right ways to live and behave.

▶ **Prov 8:1—9:6**

The Gifts of Wisdom

To gain wisdom, you have to hunger for it, really want it, and actively seek it out. You will not find it by yourself: wisdom is found where other people are—"beside the gates" where people meet (Prov 8:3).

Wisdom's gifts described in Proverbs, chapter 8, include prudence, insight, truth, knowledge, instruction or understanding, strength, and justice. Which of these gifts do you have? Which would you like to develop? Who could help you? Write a prayer to the Holy Spirit, asking for the strength and courage to seek out these gifts.

▶ **Prov 8:1–21**

along the paths of justice,
21 endowing with wealth those who love me,
     and filling their treasuries.

Wisdom's Part in Creation

22 The Lord created me at the beginning[a] of his work,[b]
     the first of his acts of long ago.
23 Ages ago I was set up,
     at the first, before the beginning of the earth.
24 When there were no depths I was brought forth,
     when there were no springs abounding with water.
25 Before the mountains had been shaped,
     before the hills, I was brought forth—
26 when he had not yet made earth and fields,[c]
     or the world's first bits of soil.
27 When he established the heavens, I was there,
     when he drew a circle on the face of the deep,
28 when he made firm the skies above,
     when he established the fountains of the deep,
29 when he assigned to the sea its limit,
     so that the waters might not transgress his command,
     when he marked out the foundations of the earth,
30   then I was beside him, like a master worker;[d]
and I was daily his[e] delight,
     rejoicing before him always,

31 rejoicing in his inhabited world
     and delighting in the human race.
32 "And now, my children, listen to me:
     happy are those who keep my ways.
33 Hear instruction and be wise,
     and do not neglect it.
34 Happy is the one who listens to me,
     watching daily at my gates,
     waiting beside my doors.
35 For whoever finds me finds life
     and obtains favor from the Lord;
36 but those who miss me injure themselves;
     all who hate me love death."

Wisdom's Feast

9 Wisdom has built her house,
     she has hewn her seven pillars.
2 She has slaughtered her animals, she has mixed her wine,
     she has also set her table.
3 She has sent out her servant-girls, she calls
     from the highest places in the town,
4 "You that are simple, turn in here!"
     To those without sense she says,
5 "Come, eat of my bread
     and drink of the wine I have mixed.
6 Lay aside immaturity,[f] and live,
     and walk in the way of insight."

General Maxims

7 Whoever corrects a scoffer wins abuse;
     whoever rebukes the wicked gets hurt.
8 A scoffer who is rebuked will only hate you;
     the wise, when rebuked, will love you.
9 Give instruction[g] to the wise, and they will become wiser still;
     teach the righteous and they will gain in learning.
10 The fear of the Lord is the beginning of wisdom,
     and the knowledge of the Holy One is insight.
11 For by me your days will be multiplied,
     and years will be added to your life.
12 If you are wise, you are wise for yourself;
     if you scoff, you alone will bear it.

Folly's Invitation and Promise

13 The foolish woman is loud;
     she is ignorant and knows nothing.
14 She sits at the door of her house,
     on a seat at the high places of the town,
15 calling to those who pass by,
     who are going straight on their way,

---

a Or *me as the beginning*   b Heb *way*   c Meaning of Heb uncertain   d Another reading is *little child*   e Gk: Heb lacks *his*   f Or *simpleness*   g Heb lacks *instruction*

PROV

16 "You who are simple, turn in here!"
      And to those without sense she says,
17 "Stolen water is sweet,
      and bread eaten in secret is pleasant."
18 But they do not know that the dead[a] are there,
      that her guests are in the depths of Sheol.

> "The fear of the LORD is the
> beginning of wisdom,
> and the knowledge of the
> Holy One is insight."
>
> (Prov 9:10)

Wise Sayings of Solomon

10 The proverbs of Solomon.

A wise child makes a glad father,
   but a foolish child is a mother's grief.
2 Treasures gained by wickedness do not profit,
   but righteousness delivers from death.
3 The LORD does not let the righteous go hungry,
   but he thwarts the craving of the wicked.
4 A slack hand causes poverty,
   but the hand of the diligent makes rich.
5 A child who gathers in summer is prudent,
   but a child who sleeps in harvest brings
      shame.
6 Blessings are on the head of the righteous,
   but the mouth of the wicked conceals
      violence.
7 The memory of the righteous is a blessing,
   but the name of the wicked will rot.
8 The wise of heart will heed commandments,
   but a babbling fool will come to ruin.
9 Whoever walks in integrity walks securely,
   but whoever follows perverse ways will be
      found out.
10 Whoever winks the eye causes trouble,
   but the one who rebukes boldly makes peace.[b]
11 The mouth of the righteous is a fountain of life,
   but the mouth of the wicked conceals violence.
12 Hatred stirs up strife,
   but love covers all offenses.
13 On the lips of one who has understanding
      wisdom is found,
   but a rod is for the back of one who lacks
      sense.
14 The wise lay up knowledge,
   but the babbling of a fool brings ruin near.
15 The wealth of the rich is their fortress;
   the poverty of the poor is their ruin.

16 The wage of the righteous leads to life,
   the gain of the wicked to sin.
17 Whoever heeds instruction is on the path to life,
   but one who rejects a rebuke goes astray.
18 Lying lips conceal hatred,
   and whoever utters slander is a fool.
19 When words are many, transgression is not
      lacking,
   but the prudent are restrained in speech.
20 The tongue of the righteous is choice silver;
   the mind of the wicked is of little worth.
21 The lips of the righteous feed many,
   but fools die for lack of sense.
22 The blessing of the LORD makes rich,
   and he adds no sorrow with it.[c]
23 Doing wrong is like sport to a fool,
   but wise conduct is pleasure to a person of
      understanding.
24 What the wicked dread will come upon them,
   but the desire of the righteous will be granted.
25 When the tempest passes, the wicked are no
      more,
   but the righteous are established forever.
26 Like vinegar to the teeth, and smoke to the eyes,
   so are the lazy to their employers.
27 The fear of the LORD prolongs life,
   but the years of the wicked will be short.

---

a Heb *shades*   b Gk: Heb *but a babbling fool will come to ruin*
c Or *and toil adds nothing to it*

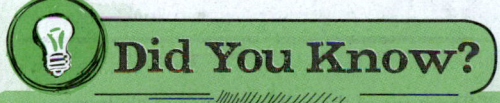

Did You Know?

Live Justly

In Proverbs, chapter 10, we are given a list of the benefits of being a just person. In this chapter, a just person is one who is fair, right, moral, honest, and truthful. We read that a just person not only receives blessings, life, wisdom, and joy; he or she, by acting justly, also fulfills God's will.

Throughout the New Testament, Jesus tells his followers that his way is the just way. The parables of the good Samaritan (see Lk 10:29-37) and the unforgiving servant (see Mt 18:21-35) are reminders of this. Living as a just person may not be easy, but it is what Christ asks of his followers.

 Proverbs, chapter 10

Nothing But the Truth

Do you swear to tell the truth, the whole truth, and nothing but the truth, so help you God? We have all heard these words. They are asked of every witness about to testify in a courtroom. In addition to responding positively to this crucial question, witnesses are called to place a hand on the Bible. All of this is to try to ensure that they will be honest. But despite this oath, some witnesses lie. We call that crime perjury, and it carries a severe penalty because someone's innocence or guilt may be hanging on the sworn testimony.

Proverbs 10:18 tells us, "Lying lips conceal hatred." Just as dishonesty is an act of hatred, so is honesty an act of love. Ultimately, our lies end up hurting others and damaging our integrity. Whether in the courtroom or in everyday life, we must always strive to tell "the truth, the whole truth, and nothing but the truth."

▶ **Prov 10:18–21**

28 The hope of the righteous ends in gladness,
   but the expectation of the wicked comes to
      nothing.
29 The way of the Lord is a stronghold for the
      upright,
   but destruction for evildoers.
30 The righteous will never be removed,
   but the wicked will not remain in the land.
31 The mouth of the righteous brings forth
      wisdom,
   but the perverse tongue will be cut off.
32 The lips of the righteous know what is
      acceptable,
   but the mouth of the wicked what is perverse.

11 A false balance is an abomination to the
         Lord,
   but an accurate weight is his delight.
2 When pride comes, then comes disgrace;
   but wisdom is with the humble.
3 The integrity of the upright guides them,
   but the crookedness of the treacherous
      destroys them.

4 Riches do not profit in the day of wrath,
   but righteousness delivers from death.
5 The righteousness of the blameless keeps their
      ways straight,
   but the wicked fall by their own wickedness.
6 The righteousness of the upright saves them,
   but the treacherous are taken captive by their
      schemes.
7 When the wicked die, their hope perishes,
   and the expectation of the godless comes to
      nothing.
8 The righteous are delivered from trouble,
   and the wicked get into it instead.
9 With their mouths the godless would destroy
      their neighbors,
   but by knowledge the righteous are delivered.
10 When it goes well with the righteous, the city
      rejoices;
   and when the wicked perish, there is
      jubilation.
11 By the blessing of the upright a city is exalted,
   but it is overthrown by the mouth of the
      wicked.
12 Whoever belittles another lacks sense,
   but an intelligent person remains silent.
13 A gossip goes about telling secrets,
   but one who is trustworthy in spirit keeps a
      confidence.
14 Where there is no guidance, a nation[a] falls,
   but in an abundance of counselors there is
      safety.
15 To guarantee loans for a stranger brings trouble,
   but there is safety in refusing to do so.
16 A gracious woman gets honor,
   but she who hates virtue is covered with
      shame.[b]
   The timid become destitute,[c]
   but the aggressive gain riches.
17 Those who are kind reward themselves,
   but the cruel do themselves harm.
18 The wicked earn no real gain,
   but those who sow righteousness get a true
      reward.
19 Whoever is steadfast in righteousness will live,
   but whoever pursues evil will die.
20 Crooked minds are an abomination to the Lord,
   but those of blameless ways are his delight.
21 Be assured, the wicked will not go unpunished,
   but those who are righteous will escape.
22 Like a gold ring in a pig's snout
   is a beautiful woman without good sense.
23 The desire of the righteous ends only in good;
   the expectation of the wicked in wrath.

---

a Or *an army*   b Compare Gk Syr: Heb lacks *but she . . . shame*
c Gk: Heb lacks *The timid . . . destitute*

24 Some give freely, yet grow all the richer;
  others withhold what is due, and only suffer
  want.
25 A generous person will be enriched,
  and one who gives water will get water.
26 The people curse those who hold back grain,
  but a blessing is on the head of those who
  sell it.
27 Whoever diligently seeks good seeks favor,
  but evil comes to the one who searches for it.
28 Those who trust in their riches will wither,[a]
  but the righteous will flourish like green
  leaves.
29 Those who trouble their households will inherit
  wind,
  and the fool will be servant to the wise.
30 The fruit of the righteous is a tree of life,
  but violence[b] takes lives away.
31 If the righteous are repaid on earth,
  how much more the wicked and the sinner!

12 Whoever loves discipline loves knowledge,
  but those who hate to be rebuked are
  stupid.
2 The good obtain favor from the LORD,
  but those who devise evil he condemns.
3 No one finds security by wickedness,
  but the root of the righteous will never be
  moved.
4 A good wife is the crown of her husband,
  but she who brings shame is like rottenness in
  his bones.
5 The thoughts of the righteous are just;
  the advice of the wicked is treacherous.
6 The words of the wicked are a deadly ambush,
  but the speech of the upright delivers them.
7 The wicked are overthrown and are no more,
  but the house of the righteous will stand.
8 One is commended for good sense,
  but a perverse mind is despised.
9 Better to be despised and have a servant,
  than to be self-important and lack food.
10 The righteous know the needs of their animals,
  but the mercy of the wicked is cruel.
11 Those who till their land will have plenty of
  food,
  but those who follow worthless pursuits have
  no sense.
12 The wicked covet the proceeds of wickedness,[c]
  but the root of the righteous bears fruit.
13 The evil are ensnared by the transgression of
  their lips,
  but the righteous escape from trouble.
14 From the fruit of the mouth one is filled with
  good things,
  and manual labor has its reward.
15 Fools think their own way is right,

but the wise listen to advice.
16 Fools show their anger at once,
  but the prudent ignore an insult.
17 Whoever speaks the truth gives honest evidence,
  but a false witness speaks deceitfully.
18 Rash words are like sword thrusts,
  but the tongue of the wise brings healing.
19 Truthful lips endure forever,
  but a lying tongue lasts only a moment.
20 Deceit is in the mind of those who plan evil,
  but those who counsel peace have joy.
21 No harm happens to the righteous,
  but the wicked are filled with trouble.
22 Lying lips are an abomination to the LORD,
  but those who act faithfully are his delight.
23 One who is clever conceals knowledge,
  but the mind of a fool[d] broadcasts folly.
24 The hand of the diligent will rule,
  while the lazy will be put to forced labor.
25 Anxiety weighs down the human heart,
  but a good word cheers it up.
26 The righteous gives good advice to friends,[e]
  but the way of the wicked leads astray.

a Cn: Heb *fall*   b Cn Compare Gk Syr: Heb *a wise man*
c Or *covet the catch of the wicked*   d Heb *the heart of fools*
e Syr: Meaning of Heb uncertain

Gossip

Oh, God, forgive me!
  I gossiped about someone's family today.
I don't even know if what I said was true.
But it made me feel important to tell it to my
  friends.
Help me keep my mouth shut!
When someone tells me a secret, seal it into
  my heart,
and keep it away from my lips!
Gossip can seem like fun, but it hurts people.
I can't stop thinking about how the target of my
  gossip would feel
if she or he knew what I said about the
  family.
Oh, God, teach me to be trustworthy!
Amen.

▶ **Prov 11:13**

P
R
O
V

27 The lazy do not roast*a* their game,
    but the diligent obtain precious wealth.*a*
28 In the path of righteousness there is life,
    in walking its path there is no death.

13 A wise child loves discipline,*b*
    but a scoffer does not listen to rebuke.
2 From the fruit of their words good persons eat
    good things,
    but the desire of the treacherous is for
    wrongdoing.
3 Those who guard their mouths preserve their
    lives;

Break the Cycle of Hopelessness

The story is all too frequent in many urban areas today. . . . A young man joins a gang, thinking that he has finally found a place to belong and that his new "family" will do anything for him. The gang offers many things he doesn't find at home or in school. He spends a great deal of time with his new friends, and before long, they encourage him to do things he doesn't feel comfortable doing. His fellow gang members are able to sell what he has stolen, the money is good, and the gang enjoys freely spending it. The young man, however, ends up in prison, serving time for armed robbery.

Proverbs 13:11 tells us that quick wealth doesn't last. Verse 20 goes further, saying that the companion of fools will not do well in life. For many youth in detention centers or prisons, this story sounds familiar. This proverb offers wisdom that they and many others—maybe we too—need to hear.

In the absence of caring adults, healthy role models, and detention center ministers, the cycle of hopelessness is free to continue and often results in stories like this one. Find out how your parish or youth group can help at-risk youth, young people in prison, or anyone suffering from a lack of real hope. Help them break the cycle of hopelessness.

▶ **Prov 13:11–20**

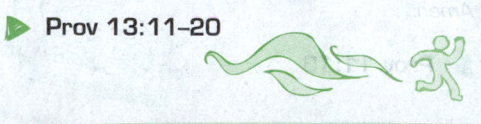

those who open wide their lips come to ruin.
4 The appetite of the lazy craves, and gets nothing,
    while the appetite of the diligent is richly
      supplied.
5 The righteous hate falsehood,
    but the wicked act shamefully and disgracefully.
6 Righteousness guards one whose way is upright,
    but sin overthrows the wicked.
7 Some pretend to be rich, yet have nothing;
    others pretend to be poor, yet have great
      wealth.
8 Wealth is a ransom for a person's life,
    but the poor get no threats.
9 The light of the righteous rejoices,
    but the lamp of the wicked goes out.
10 By insolence the heedless make strife,
    but wisdom is with those who take advice.
11 Wealth hastily gotten*c* will dwindle,
    but those who gather little by little will
      increase it.
12 Hope deferred makes the heart sick,
    but a desire fulfilled is a tree of life.
13 Those who despise the word bring destruction
      on themselves,
    but those who respect the commandment will
      be rewarded.
14 The teaching of the wise is a fountain of life,
    so that one may avoid the snares of death.
15 Good sense wins favor,
    but the way of the faithless is their ruin.*d*
16 The clever do all things intelligently,
    but the fool displays folly.
17 A bad messenger brings trouble,
    but a faithful envoy, healing.
18 Poverty and disgrace are for the one who ignores
      instruction,
    but one who heeds reproof is honored.
19 A desire realized is sweet to the soul,
    but to turn away from evil is an abomination
      to fools.
20 Whoever walks with the wise becomes wise,
    but the companion of fools suffers harm.
21 Misfortune pursues sinners,
    but prosperity rewards the righteous.
22 The good leave an inheritance to their children's
      children,
    but the sinner's wealth is laid up for the
      righteous.
23 The field of the poor may yield much food,
    but it is swept away through injustice.
24 Those who spare the rod hate their children,

---

a Meaning of Heb uncertain *b* Cn: Heb *A wise child the discipline of his father* *c* Gk Vg: Heb *from vanity*
d Cn Compare Gk Syr Vg Tg: Heb *is enduring*

but those who love them are diligent to
discipline them.
25 The righteous have enough to satisfy their
appetite,
but the belly of the wicked is empty.

14 The wise woman*a* builds her house,
but the foolish tears it down with her own
hands.
2 Those who walk uprightly fear the LORD,
but one who is devious in conduct despises
him.
3 The talk of fools is a rod for their backs,*b*
but the lips of the wise preserve them.
4 Where there are no oxen, there is no grain;
abundant crops come by the strength of
the ox.
5 A faithful witness does not lie,
but a false witness breathes out lies.
6 A scoffer seeks wisdom in vain,
but knowledge is easy for one who
understands.
7 Leave the presence of a fool,
for there you do not find words of knowledge.
8 It is the wisdom of the clever to understand
where they go,
but the folly of fools misleads.
9 Fools mock at the guilt offering,*c*
but the upright enjoy God's favor.
10 The heart knows its own bitterness,
and no stranger shares its joy.
11 The house of the wicked is destroyed,
but the tent of the upright flourishes.
12 There is a way that seems right to a person,
but its end is the way to death.*d*
13 Even in laughter the heart is sad,
and the end of joy is grief.
14 The perverse get what their ways deserve,
and the good, what their deeds deserve.*e*
15 The simple believe everything,
but the clever consider their steps.
16 The wise are cautious and turn away from evil,
but the fool throws off restraint and is careless.
17 One who is quick-tempered acts foolishly,
and the schemer is hated.
18 The simple are adorned with*f* folly,
but the clever are crowned with knowledge.
19 The evil bow down before the good,
the wicked at the gates of the righteous.
20 The poor are disliked even by their neighbors,
but the rich have many friends.
21 Those who despise their neighbors are sinners,
but happy are those who are kind to the poor.
22 Do they not err that plan evil?
Those who plan good find loyalty and
faithfulness.
23 In all toil there is profit,

but mere talk leads only to poverty.
24 The crown of the wise is their wisdom,*g*
but folly is the garland*h* of fools.
25 A truthful witness saves lives,
but one who utters lies is a betrayer.
26 In the fear of the LORD one has strong
confidence,
and one's children will have a refuge.
27 The fear of the LORD is a fountain of life,
so that one may avoid the snares of death.
28 The glory of a king is a multitude of people;
without people a prince is ruined.
29 Whoever is slow to anger has great
understanding,
but one who has a hasty temper exalts folly.
30 A tranquil mind gives life to the flesh,
but passion makes the bones rot.
31 Those who oppress the poor insult their Maker,
but those who are kind to the needy honor
him.
32 The wicked are overthrown by their evildoing,
but the righteous find a refuge in their
integrity.*i*
33 Wisdom is at home in the mind of one who has
understanding,
but it is not*j* known in the heart of fools.
34 Righteousness exalts a nation,
but sin is a reproach to any people.
35 A servant who deals wisely has the king's favor,
but his wrath falls on one who acts
shamefully.

15 A soft answer turns away wrath,
but a harsh word stirs up anger.
2 The tongue of the wise dispenses knowledge,*k*
but the mouths of fools pour out folly.
3 The eyes of the LORD are in every place,
keeping watch on the evil and the good.
4 A gentle tongue is a tree of life,
but perverseness in it breaks the spirit.
5 A fool despises a parent's instruction,
but the one who heeds admonition is
prudent.
6 In the house of the righteous there is much
treasure,
but trouble befalls the income of the wicked.
7 The lips of the wise spread knowledge;
not so the minds of fools.
8 The sacrifice of the wicked is an abomination to
the LORD,
but the prayer of the upright is his delight.

---

a Heb *Wisdom of women*   *b* Cn: Heb *a rod of pride*
c Meaning of Heb uncertain   *d* Heb *ways of death*   *e* Cn: Heb
from upon him   *f* Or *inherit*   *g* Cn Compare Gk: Heb *riches*
h Cn: Heb *is the folly*   *i* Gk Syr: Heb *in their death*   *j* Gk Syr:
Heb lacks *not*   *k* Cn: Heb *makes knowledge good*

9 The way of the wicked is an abomination to the
  LORD,
    but he loves the one who pursues
      righteousness.
10 There is severe discipline for one who forsakes
   the way,
    but one who hates a rebuke will die.
11 Sheol and Abaddon lie open before the LORD,
    how much more human hearts!
12 Scoffers do not like to be rebuked;
    they will not go to the wise.
13 A glad heart makes a cheerful countenance,
    but by sorrow of heart the spirit is broken.
14 The mind of one who has understanding seeks
   knowledge,
    but the mouths of fools feed on folly.
15 All the days of the poor are hard,
    but a cheerful heart has a continual feast.
16 Better is a little with the fear of the LORD
    than great treasure and trouble with it.
17 Better is a dinner of vegetables where love is
    than a fatted ox and hatred with it.
18 Those who are hot-tempered stir up strife,
    but those who are slow to anger calm
      contention.
19 The way of the lazy is overgrown with thorns,
    but the path of the upright is a level highway.
20 A wise child makes a glad father,
    but the foolish despise their mothers.
21 Folly is a joy to one who has no sense,
    but a person of understanding walks straight
      ahead.
22 Without counsel, plans go wrong,
    but with many advisers they succeed.
23 To make an apt answer is a joy to anyone,
    and a word in season, how good it is!
24 For the wise the path of life leads upward,

in order to avoid Sheol below.
25 The LORD tears down the house of the proud,
    but maintains the widow's boundaries.
26 Evil plans are an abomination to the LORD,
    but gracious words are pure.
27 Those who are greedy for unjust gain make
    trouble for their households,
    but those who hate bribes will live.
28 The mind of the righteous ponders how to
    answer,
    but the mouth of the wicked pours out evil.
29 The LORD is far from the wicked,
    but he hears the prayer of the righteous.
30 The light of the eyes rejoices the heart,
    and good news refreshes the body.
31 The ear that heeds wholesome admonition
    will lodge among the wise.
32 Those who ignore instruction despise
    themselves,
    but those who heed admonition gain
      understanding.
33 The fear of the LORD is instruction in wisdom,
    and humility goes before honor.

16 The plans of the mind belong to mortals,
    but the answer of the tongue is from the
      LORD.
2 All one's ways may be pure in one's own eyes,
    but the LORD weighs the spirit.
3 Commit your work to the LORD,
    and your plans will be established.
4 The LORD has made everything for its purpose,
    even the wicked for the day of trouble.
5 All those who are arrogant are an abomination
    to the LORD;
    be assured, they will not go unpunished.
6 By loyalty and faithfulness iniquity is atoned for,
    and by the fear of the LORD one avoids evil.
7 When the ways of people please the LORD,
    he causes even their enemies to be at peace
      with them.
8 Better is a little with righteousness
    than large income with injustice.
9 The human mind plans the way,
    but the LORD directs the steps.
10 Inspired decisions are on the lips of a king;
    his mouth does not sin in judgment.
11 Honest balances and scales are the LORD's;
    all the weights in the bag are his work.
12 It is an abomination to kings to do evil,
    for the throne is established by righteousness.
13 Righteous lips are the delight of a king,
    and he loves those who speak what is right.
14 A king's wrath is a messenger of death,
    and whoever is wise will appease it.
15 In the light of a king's face there is life,

Offering Your Day to God

Follow the advice of Proverbs 16:3 by starting each day with a prayer like this one:

*Dearest Lord, today I offer you all my
thoughts, deeds, and words. Let everything I do reflect your love
and goodness. Amen.*

▶ **Prov 16:3**

and his favor is like the clouds that bring the
  spring rain.

16 How much better to get wisdom than gold!
  To get understanding is to be chosen rather
    than silver.

17 The highway of the upright avoids evil;
  those who guard their way preserve their lives.

18 Pride goes before destruction,
  and a haughty spirit before a fall.

19 It is better to be of a lowly spirit among the
    poor
  than to divide the spoil with the proud.

20 Those who are attentive to a matter will prosper,
  and happy are those who trust in the LORD.

21 The wise of heart is called perceptive,
  and pleasant speech increases persuasiveness.

22 Wisdom is a fountain of life to one who has it,
  but folly is the punishment of fools.

23 The mind of the wise makes their speech
    judicious,
  and adds persuasiveness to their lips.

24 Pleasant words are like a honeycomb,
  sweetness to the soul and health to the body.

25 Sometimes there is a way that seems to be right,
  but in the end it is the way to death.

26 The appetite of workers works for them;
  their hunger urges them on.

27 Scoundrels concoct evil,
  and their speech is like a scorching fire.

28 A perverse person spreads strife,
  and a whisperer separates close friends.

29 The violent entice their neighbors,
  and lead them in a way that is not good.

30 One who winks the eyes plans[a] perverse things;
  one who compresses the lips brings evil to
    pass.

31 Gray hair is a crown of glory;
  it is gained in a righteous life.

32 One who is slow to anger is better than the
    mighty,
  and one whose temper is controlled than one
    who captures a city.

33 The lot is cast into the lap,
  but the decision is the LORD's alone.

17 Better is a dry morsel with quiet
  than a house full of feasting with strife.

2 A slave who deals wisely will rule over a child
    who acts shamefully,
  and will share the inheritance as one of the
    family.

3 The crucible is for silver, and the furnace is for
    gold,
  but the LORD tests the heart.

4 An evildoer listens to wicked lips;
  and a liar gives heed to a mischievous tongue.

5 Those who mock the poor insult their Maker;

those who are glad at calamity will not go
    unpunished.

6 Grandchildren are the crown of the aged,
  and the glory of children is their parents.

7 Fine speech is not becoming to a fool;
  still less is false speech to a ruler.[b]

8 A bribe is like a magic stone in the eyes of those
    who give it;
  wherever they turn they prosper.

9 One who forgives an affront fosters friendship,
  but one who dwells on disputes will alienate
    a friend.

10 A rebuke strikes deeper into a discerning person
  than a hundred blows into a fool.

11 Evil people seek only rebellion,
  but a cruel messenger will be sent against
    them.

12 Better to meet a she-bear robbed of its cubs
  than to confront a fool immersed in folly.

13 Evil will not depart from the house
  of one who returns evil for good.

14 The beginning of strife is like letting out water;
  so stop before the quarrel breaks out.

15 One who justifies the wicked and one who
    condemns the righteous
  are both alike an abomination to the LORD.

16 Why should fools have a price in hand
  to buy wisdom, when they have no mind to
    learn?

17 A friend loves at all times,
  and kinsfolk are born to share adversity.

18 It is senseless to give a pledge,
  to become surety for a neighbor.

19 One who loves transgression loves strife;
  one who builds a high threshold invites
    broken bones.

20 The crooked of mind do not prosper,
  and the perverse of tongue fall into calamity.

21 The one who begets a fool gets trouble;
  the parent of a fool has no joy.

22 A cheerful heart is a good medicine,
  but a downcast spirit dries up the bones.

23 The wicked accept a concealed bribe
  to pervert the ways of justice.

24 The discerning person looks to wisdom,
  but the eyes of a fool to the ends of the
    earth.

25 Foolish children are a grief to their father
  and bitterness to her who bore them.

26 To impose a fine on the innocent is not right,
  or to flog the noble for their integrity.

27 One who spares words is knowledgeable;
  one who is cool in spirit has understanding.

_a_ Gk Syr Vg Tg: Heb _to plan_   _b_ Or _a noble person_

Be Proactive

"The beginning of strife is like letting out water; / so stop before the quarrel breaks out" (Prov 17:14). Have you ever noticed how people quickly congregate when a fight breaks out, especially at school? Many of the spectators seem to be in entertainment mode and are generally on one side or the other. Others want the fight to stop but lack the courage or confidence to break it up. Typically, everyone ends up waiting until someone in authority comes along to intervene or until one of the contenders is hurt and the fight stops.

A fight can begin so quickly—a word, a taunting phrase, a sudden turn and a punch. Some of us have a shorter fuse than others, a temper that flares easily, or an ego that won't allow us to walk away when provoked. To paraphrase the image used in Proverbs 17:14, once the water breaks through the dam, it is very hard to stop. If this sounds like you, then it's important to figure out ways to better control your responses and reactions. If we are always quick to react when provoked, then situations will soon escalate beyond our control. If we are proactive, however, and take time to think and reflect before making decisions, then we are much more likely to respond in ways that reflect the positive values that are at our core.

- How do you react when you see an argument or a fight? Are you reluctant to get involved?
- If you have a quick temper, what can you do to control it? How can you be more proactive?

▶ Prov 17:14

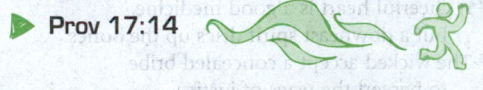

28 Even fools who keep silent are considered wise;
   when they close their lips, they are deemed intelligent.

18 The one who lives alone is self-indulgent,
   showing contempt for all who have sound judgment.[a]
2 A fool takes no pleasure in understanding,
   but only in expressing personal opinion.
3 When wickedness comes, contempt comes also;
   and with dishonor comes disgrace.

4 The words of the mouth are deep waters;
   the fountain of wisdom is a gushing stream.
5 It is not right to be partial to the guilty,
   or to subvert the innocent in judgment.
6 A fool's lips bring strife,
   and a fool's mouth invites a flogging.
7 The mouths of fools are their ruin,
   and their lips a snare to themselves.
8 The words of a whisperer are like delicious morsels;
   they go down into the inner parts of the body.
9 One who is slack in work
   is close kin to a vandal.
10 The name of the LORD is a strong tower;
   the righteous run into it and are safe.
11 The wealth of the rich is their strong city;
   in their imagination it is like a high wall.
12 Before destruction one's heart is haughty,
   but humility goes before honor.
13 If one gives answer before hearing,
   it is folly and shame.
14 The human spirit will endure sickness;
   but a broken spirit—who can bear?
15 An intelligent mind acquires knowledge,
   and the ear of the wise seeks knowledge.
16 A gift opens doors;
   it gives access to the great.
17 The one who first states a case seems right,
   until the other comes and cross-examines.
18 Casting the lot puts an end to disputes
   and decides between powerful contenders.
19 An ally offended is stronger than a city;[b]
   such quarreling is like the bars of a castle.
20 From the fruit of the mouth one's stomach is satisfied;
   the yield of the lips brings satisfaction.
21 Death and life are in the power of the tongue,
   and those who love it will eat its fruits.
22 He who finds a wife finds a good thing,
   and obtains favor from the LORD.
23 The poor use entreaties,
   but the rich answer roughly.
24 Some[c] friends play at friendship[d]
   but a true friend sticks closer than one's nearest kin.

19 Better the poor walking in integrity
   than one perverse of speech who is a fool.
2 Desire without knowledge is not good,
   and one who moves too hurriedly misses the way.
3 One's own folly leads to ruin,
   yet the heart rages against the LORD.

a Meaning of Heb uncertain   b Gk Syr Vg Tg: Meaning of Heb uncertain   c Syr Tg: Heb A man of   d Cn Compare Syr Vg Tg: Meaning of Heb uncertain

⁴ Wealth brings many friends,
   but the poor are left friendless.
⁵ A false witness will not go unpunished,
   and a liar will not escape.
⁶ Many seek the favor of the generous,
   and everyone is a friend to a giver of gifts.
⁷ If the poor are hated even by their kin,
   how much more are they shunned by their
      friends!
   When they call after them, they are not there.ᵃ
⁸ To get wisdom is to love oneself;
   to keep understanding is to prosper.
⁹ A false witness will not go unpunished,
   and the liar will perish.
¹⁰ It is not fitting for a fool to live in luxury,
   much less for a slave to rule over princes.
¹¹ Those with good sense are slow to anger,
   and it is their glory to overlook an offense.
¹² A king's anger is like the growling of a lion,
   but his favor is like dew on the grass.
¹³ A stupid child is ruin to a father,
   and a wife's quarreling is a continual dripping
      of rain.
¹⁴ House and wealth are inherited from parents,
   but a prudent wife is from the LORD.
¹⁵ Laziness brings on deep sleep;
   an idle person will suffer hunger.
¹⁶ Those who keep the commandment will live;
   those who are heedless of their ways will die.
¹⁷ Whoever is kind to the poor lends to the LORD,
   and will be repaid in full.
¹⁸ Discipline your children while there is hope;
   do not set your heart on their destruction.
¹⁹ A violent tempered person will pay the penalty;
   if you effect a rescue, you will only have to do
      it again.ᵃ
²⁰ Listen to advice and accept instruction,
   that you may gain wisdom for the future.
²¹ The human mind may devise many plans,
   but it is the purpose of the LORD that will be
      established.
²² What is desirable in a person is loyalty,
   and it is better to be poor than a liar.
²³ The fear of the LORD is life indeed;
   filled with it one rests secure
   and suffers no harm.
²⁴ The lazy person buries a hand in the dish,
   and will not even bring it back to the mouth.
²⁵ Strike a scoffer, and the simple will learn
      prudence;
   reprove the intelligent, and they will gain
      knowledge.
²⁶ Those who do violence to their father and chase
      away their mother
   are children who cause shame and bring
      reproach.

²⁷ Cease straying, my child, from the words of
      knowledge,
   in order that you may hear instruction.
²⁸ A worthless witness mocks at justice,
   and the mouth of the wicked devours
      iniquity.
²⁹ Condemnation is ready for scoffers,
   and flogging for the backs of fools.

20 Wine is a mocker, strong drink a brawler,
   and whoever is led astray by it is not wise.
² The dread anger of a king is like the growling of
      a lion;
   anyone who provokes him to anger forfeits
      life itself.
³ It is honorable to refrain from strife,
   but every fool is quick to quarrel.
⁴ The lazy person does not plow in season;
   harvest comes, and there is nothing to be
      found.
⁵ The purposes in the human mind are like deep
      water,
   but the intelligent will draw them out.
⁶ Many proclaim themselves loyal,
   but who can find one worthy of trust?
⁷ The righteous walk in integrity—
   happy are the children who follow them!
⁸ A king who sits on the throne of judgment

a Meaning of Heb uncertain

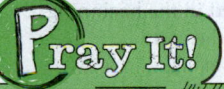

Fear of the Lord

The phrase "fear of the LORD" is used fourteen times in Proverbs (see, for example,
19:23). You might ask why the author of Proverbs keeps telling us to be afraid of God. But in
the Bible, fear of the Lord has less to do with
terror and fright than with awe, reverence, and
respect. It's a reminder that God is far from ordinary. To fear the Lord is to take God very seriously.

   Take some time to reflect or journal on this
question: What does it mean to fear the
Lord? Describe a time when you were
awed by something about God. Explain
how you give God respect.

▶ **Prov 19:23**

PROV

winnows all evil with his eyes.

9 Who can say, "I have made my heart clean;
    I am pure from my sin"?

10 Diverse weights and diverse measures
    are both alike an abomination to the LORD.

11 Even children make themselves known by their
    acts,
    by whether what they do is pure and right.

12 The hearing ear and the seeing eye—
    the LORD has made them both.

13 Do not love sleep, or else you will come to
    poverty;
    open your eyes, and you will have plenty of
    bread.

14 "Bad, bad," says the buyer,
    then goes away and boasts.

15 There is gold, and abundance of costly stones;
    but the lips informed by knowledge are a
    precious jewel.

16 Take the garment of one who has given surety
    for a stranger;
    seize the pledge given as surety for foreigners.

17 Bread gained by deceit is sweet,
    but afterward the mouth will be full of gravel.

18 Plans are established by taking advice;
    wage war by following wise guidance.

19 A gossip reveals secrets;
    therefore do not associate with a babbler.

20 If you curse father or mother,
    your lamp will go out in utter darkness.

21 An estate quickly acquired in the beginning
    will not be blessed in the end.

22 Do not say, "I will repay evil";
    wait for the LORD, and he will help you.

23 Differing weights are an abomination to the
    LORD,
    and false scales are not good.

24 All our steps are ordered by the LORD;
    how then can we understand our own ways?

25 It is a snare for one to say rashly, "It is holy,"
    and begin to reflect only after making a vow.

26 A wise king winnows the wicked,
    and drives the wheel over them.

27 The human spirit is the lamp of the LORD,
    searching every inmost part.

28 Loyalty and faithfulness preserve the king,
    and his throne is upheld by righteousness.*a*

29 The glory of youths is their strength,
    but the beauty of the aged is their gray hair.

30 Blows that wound cleanse away evil;
    beatings make clean the innermost parts.

21 The king's heart is a stream of water in the
    hand of the LORD;
    he turns it wherever he will.

2 All deeds are right in the sight of the doer,
    but the LORD weighs the heart.

3 To do righteousness and justice
    is more acceptable to the LORD than sacrifice.

4 Haughty eyes and a proud heart—
    the lamp of the wicked—are sin.

5 The plans of the diligent lead surely to
    abundance,
    but everyone who is hasty comes only to want.

6 The getting of treasures by a lying tongue
    is a fleeting vapor and a snare*b* of death.

7 The violence of the wicked will sweep them away,
    because they refuse to do what is just.

8 The way of the guilty is crooked,
    but the conduct of the pure is right.

9 It is better to live in a corner of the housetop
    than in a house shared with a contentious
    wife.

10 The souls of the wicked desire evil;
    their neighbors find no mercy in their eyes.

11 When a scoffer is punished, the simple become
    wiser;
    when the wise are instructed, they increase in
    knowledge.

12 The Righteous One observes the house of the
    wicked;
    he casts the wicked down to ruin.

13 If you close your ear to the cry of the poor,
    you will cry out and not be heard.

14 A gift in secret averts anger;
    and a concealed bribe in the bosom, strong
    wrath.

15 When justice is done, it is a joy to the righteous,
    but dismay to evildoers.

16 Whoever wanders from the way of
    understanding
    will rest in the assembly of the dead.

17 Whoever loves pleasure will suffer want;
    whoever loves wine and oil will not be rich.

18 The wicked is a ransom for the righteous,
    and the faithless for the upright.

19 It is better to live in a desert land
    than with a contentious and fretful wife.

20 Precious treasure remains*c* in the house of the
    wise,
    but the fool devours it.

21 Whoever pursues righteousness and kindness
    will find life*d* and honor.

22 One wise person went up against a city of
    warriors
    and brought down the stronghold in which
    they trusted.

23 To watch over mouth and tongue
    is to keep out of trouble.

24 The proud, haughty person, named "Scoffer,"

---

a Gk: Heb *loyalty*   b Gk: Heb *seekers*   c Gk: Heb *and oil*
d Gk: Heb *life and righteousness*

acts with arrogant pride.
25 The craving of the lazy person is fatal,
for lazy hands refuse to labor.
26 All day long the wicked covet,*a*
but the righteous give and do not hold back.
27 The sacrifice of the wicked is an abomination;
how much more when brought with evil intent.
28 A false witness will perish,
but a good listener will testify successfully.
29 The wicked put on a bold face,
but the upright give thought to*b* their ways.
30 No wisdom, no understanding, no counsel,
can avail against the LORD.
31 The horse is made ready for the day of battle,
but the victory belongs to the LORD.

22
A good name is to be chosen rather than great riches,
and favor is better than silver or gold.
2 The rich and the poor have this in common:
the LORD is the maker of them all.
3 The clever see danger and hide;
but the simple go on, and suffer for it.
4 The reward for humility and fear of the LORD
is riches and honor and life.
5 Thorns and snares are in the way of the perverse;
the cautious will keep far from them.
6 Train children in the right way,
and when old, they will not stray.
7 The rich rule over the poor,
and the borrower is the slave of the lender.
8 Whoever sows injustice will reap calamity,
and the rod of anger will fail.
9 Those who are generous are blessed,
for they share their bread with the poor.
10 Drive out a scoffer, and strife goes out;
quarreling and abuse will cease.
11 Those who love a pure heart and are gracious in speech
will have the king as a friend.
12 The eyes of the LORD keep watch over knowledge,
but he overthrows the words of the faithless.
13 The lazy person says, "There is a lion outside!
I shall be killed in the streets!"
14 The mouth of a loose*c* woman is a deep pit;
he with whom the LORD is angry falls into it.
15 Folly is bound up in the heart of a boy,
but the rod of discipline drives it far away.
16 Oppressing the poor in order to enrich oneself,
and giving to the rich, will lead only to loss.

Sayings of the Wise

17 The words of the wise:

Incline your ear and hear my words,*d*
and apply your mind to my teaching;

18 for it will be pleasant if you keep them within you,
if all of them are ready on your lips.
19 So that your trust may be in the LORD,
I have made them known to you today—yes, to you.
20 Have I not written for you thirty sayings
of admonition and knowledge,
21 to show you what is right and true,
so that you may give a true answer to those who sent you?

22 Do not rob the poor because they are poor,
or crush the afflicted at the gate;
23 for the LORD pleads their cause
and despoils of life those who despoil them.
24 Make no friends with those given to anger,
and do not associate with hotheads,
25 or you may learn their ways
and entangle yourself in a snare.
26 Do not be one of those who give pledges,
who become surety for debts.
27 If you have nothing with which to pay,
why should your bed be taken from under you?
28 Do not remove the ancient landmark
that your ancestors set up.
29 Do you see those who are skillful in their work?
They will serve kings;
they will not serve common people.

23
When you sit down to eat with a ruler,
observe carefully what*e* is before you,
2 and put a knife to your throat
if you have a big appetite.
3 Do not desire the ruler's*f* delicacies,
for they are deceptive food.
4 Do not wear yourself out to get rich;
be wise enough to desist.
5 When your eyes light upon it, it is gone;
for suddenly it takes wings to itself,
flying like an eagle toward heaven.
6 Do not eat the bread of the stingy;
do not desire their delicacies;
7 for like a hair in the throat, so are they;*g*
"Eat and drink!" they say to you;
but they do not mean it.
8 You will vomit up the little you have eaten,
and you will waste your pleasant words.
9 Do not speak in the hearing of a fool,
who will only despise the wisdom of your words.

PROV

---

a Gk: Heb *all day long one covets covetously*   *b* Another reading is *establish*   *c* Heb *strange*   *d* Cn Compare Gk: Heb *Incline your ear, and hear the words of the wise*   *e* Or *who*   *f* Heb *his*   *g* Meaning of Heb uncertain

10 Do not remove an ancient landmark
   or encroach on the fields of orphans,
11 for their redeemer is strong;
   he will plead their cause against you.
12 Apply your mind to instruction
   and your ear to words of knowledge.
13 Do not withhold discipline from your children;
   if you beat them with a rod, they will not die.
14 If you beat them with the rod,
   you will save their lives from Sheol.
15 My child, if your heart is wise,
   my heart too will be glad.
16 My soul will rejoice
   when your lips speak what is right.
17 Do not let your heart envy sinners,
   but always continue in the fear of the Lord.
18 Surely there is a future,
   and your hope will not be cut off.

19 Hear, my child, and be wise,
   and direct your mind in the way.
20 Do not be among winebibbers,
   or among gluttonous eaters of meat;
21 for the drunkard and the glutton will come to
     poverty,
   and drowsiness will clothe them with rags.

22 Listen to your father who begot you,
   and do not despise your mother when she is
     old.
23 Buy truth, and do not sell it;
   buy wisdom, instruction, and understanding.
24 The father of the righteous will greatly rejoice;
   he who begets a wise son will be glad in him.
25 Let your father and mother be glad;
   let her who bore you rejoice.

26 My child, give me your heart,
   and let your eyes observe[a] my ways.
27 For a prostitute is a deep pit;
   an adulteress[b] is a narrow well.
28 She lies in wait like a robber
   and increases the number of the faithless.

29 Who has woe? Who has sorrow?
   Who has strife? Who has complaining?
   Who has wounds without cause?
   Who has redness of eyes?
30 Those who linger late over wine,
   those who keep trying mixed wines.
31 Do not look at wine when it is red,
   when it sparkles in the cup
   and goes down smoothly.
32 At the last it bites like a serpent,
   and stings like an adder.
33 Your eyes will see strange things,

   and your mind utter perverse things.
34 You will be like one who lies down in the midst
     of the sea,
   like one who lies on the top of a mast.[c]
35 "They struck me," you will say,[d] "but I was not
     hurt;
   they beat me, but I did not feel it.
   When shall I awake?
   I will seek another drink."

24 Do not envy the wicked,
   nor desire to be with them;
2 for their minds devise violence,
   and their lips talk of mischief.

3 By wisdom a house is built,
   and by understanding it is established;
4 by knowledge the rooms are filled
   with all precious and pleasant riches.
5 Wise warriors are mightier than strong ones,[e]
   and those who have knowledge than those
     who have strength;
6 for by wise guidance you can wage your war,
   and in abundance of counselors there is victory.
7 Wisdom is too high for fools;
   in the gate they do not open their mouths.

8 Whoever plans to do evil
   will be called a mischief-maker.
9 The devising of folly is sin,
   and the scoffer is an abomination to all.

10 If you faint in the day of adversity,
   your strength being small;
11 if you hold back from rescuing those taken away
     to death,
   those who go staggering to the slaughter;
12 if you say, "Look, we did not know this"—
   does not he who weighs the heart perceive it?
   Does not he who keeps watch over your soul
     know it?
   And will he not repay all according to their
     deeds?

13 My child, eat honey, for it is good,
   and the drippings of the honeycomb are
     sweet to your taste.
14 Know that wisdom is such to your soul;
   if you find it, you will find a future,
   and your hope will not be cut off.

15 Do not lie in wait like an outlaw against the
     home of the righteous;

---

a Another reading is *delight in*   b Heb *an alien woman*
c Meaning of Heb uncertain   d Gk Syr Vg Tg: Heb lacks *you will*
say   e Gk Compare Syr Tg: Heb *A wise man is strength*

Cultural Connection

Wisdom and the Elders

"By wisdom a house is built . . . / by knowledge the rooms are filled" [Prov 24:3–4]. Becoming wise is like building and furnishing a house. It doesn't happen all at once; it takes time, experience, and work. Native American cultures understand this. Wisdom is an important value for them.

In many Native American cultures, the elders have the highest place of honor because of their wisdom. Native Americans understand that it takes an entire life to grow wise. The elders have lived through much, and their advice is always worth seeking. They are relied on to settle disagreements because they have learned to judge people by their heart and their integrity, not by their money or possessions. The others in the tribe know that by listening to the elders, they too, over time, will grow wise.

▶ **Prov 24:3–4**

do no violence to the place where the
    righteous live;
16 for though they fall seven times, they will rise
    again;
    but the wicked are overthrown by calamity.

17 Do not rejoice when your enemies fall,
    and do not let your heart be glad when they
        stumble,
18 or else the LORD will see it and be displeased,
    and turn away his anger from them.

19 Do not fret because of evildoers.
    Do not envy the wicked;
20 for the evil have no future;
    the lamp of the wicked will go out.

21 My child, fear the LORD and the king,
    and do not disobey either of them;[a]
22 for disaster comes from them suddenly,
    and who knows the ruin that both can
        bring?

Further Sayings of the Wise

23   These also are sayings of the wise:

    Partiality in judging is not good.
24 Whoever says to the wicked, "You are
        innocent,"
    will be cursed by peoples, abhorred by
        nations;
25 but those who rebuke the wicked will have
        delight,
    and a good blessing will come upon them.
26 One who gives an honest answer
    gives a kiss on the lips.

27 Prepare your work outside,
    get everything ready for you in the field;
    and after that build your house.

28 Do not be a witness against your neighbor
        without cause,
    and do not deceive with your lips.
29 Do not say, "I will do to others as they have
        done to me;
    I will pay them back for what they have
        done."

30 I passed by the field of one who was lazy,
    by the vineyard of a stupid person;
31 and see, it was all overgrown with thorns;
    the ground was covered with nettles,
    and its stone wall was broken down.
32 Then I saw and considered it;
    I looked and received instruction.
33 A little sleep, a little slumber,
    a little folding of the hands to rest,
34 and poverty will come upon you like a robber,
    and want, like an armed warrior.

Further Wise Sayings of Solomon

25 These are other proverbs of Solomon that
    the officials of King Hezekiah of Judah
copied.

2 It is the glory of God to conceal things,
    but the glory of kings to search things out.
3 Like the heavens for height, like the earth for
        depth,
    so the mind of kings is unsearchable.

---

a Gk: Heb *do not associate with those who change*

PROV

4 Take away the dross from the silver,
　and the smith has material for a vessel;
5 take away the wicked from the presence of the
　　king,
　and his throne will be established in
　　righteousness.
6 Do not put yourself forward in the king's
　　presence
　or stand in the place of the great;
7 for it is better to be told, "Come up here,"
　than to be put lower in the presence of a
　　noble.

What your eyes have seen
8 　do not hastily bring into court;
for[a] what will you do in the end,
　when your neighbor puts you to shame?
9 Argue your case with your neighbor directly,
　and do not disclose another's secret;
10 or else someone who hears you will bring
　　shame upon you,
　and your ill repute will have no end.

11 A word fitly spoken
　is like apples of gold in a setting of silver.
12 Like a gold ring or an ornament of gold
　is a wise rebuke to a listening ear.
13 Like the cold of snow in the time of harvest
　are faithful messengers to those who send
　　them;
　they refresh the spirit of their masters.
14 Like clouds and wind without rain
　is one who boasts of a gift never given.
15 With patience a ruler may be persuaded,
　and a soft tongue can break bones.
16 If you have found honey, eat only enough for
　　you,
　or else, having too much, you will vomit it.
17 Let your foot be seldom in your neighbor's
　　house,
　otherwise the neighbor will become weary of
　　you and hate you.
18 Like a war club, a sword, or a sharp arrow
　is one who bears false witness against a
　　neighbor.
19 Like a bad tooth or a lame foot
　is trust in a faithless person in time of trouble.
20 Like vinegar on a wound[b]
　is one who sings songs to a heavy heart.
　Like a moth in clothing or a worm in wood,
　　sorrow gnaws at the human heart.[c]
21 If your enemies are hungry, give them bread to
　　eat;
　and if they are thirsty, give them water to
　　drink;
22 for you will heap coals of fire on their heads,

and the Lord will reward you.
23 The north wind produces rain,
　and a backbiting tongue, angry looks.
24 It is better to live in a corner of the housetop
　than in a house shared with a contentious
　　wife.
25 Like cold water to a thirsty soul,
　so is good news from a far country.
26 Like a muddied spring or a polluted fountain
　are the righteous who give way before the
　　wicked.
27 It is not good to eat much honey,
　or to seek honor on top of honor.
28 Like a city breached, without walls,
　is one who lacks self-control.

26 Like snow in summer or rain in harvest,
　so honor is not fitting for a fool.
2 Like a sparrow in its flitting, like a swallow in its
　　flying,
　an undeserved curse goes nowhere.
3 A whip for the horse, a bridle for the donkey,
　and a rod for the back of fools.
4 Do not answer fools according to their folly,
　or you will be a fool yourself.
5 Answer fools according to their folly,
　or they will be wise in their own eyes.
6 It is like cutting off one's foot and drinking
　　down violence,
　to send a message by a fool.
7 The legs of a disabled person hang limp;
　so does a proverb in the mouth of a fool.
8 It is like binding a stone in a sling
　to give honor to a fool.
9 Like a thornbush brandished by the hand of a
　　drunkard
　is a proverb in the mouth of a fool.
10 Like an archer who wounds everybody
　is one who hires a passing fool or drunkard.[d]
11 Like a dog that returns to its vomit
　is a fool who reverts to his folly.
12 Do you see persons wise in their own eyes?
　There is more hope for fools than for them.
13 The lazy person says, "There is a lion in the
　　road!
　There is a lion in the streets!"
14 As a door turns on its hinges,
　so does a lazy person in bed.
15 The lazy person buries a hand in the dish,
　and is too tired to bring it back to the
　　mouth.
16 The lazy person is wiser in self-esteem
　than seven who can answer discreetly.

---

a Cn: Heb or else　b Gk: Heb Like one who takes off a garment
on a cold day, like vinegar on lye　c Gk Syr Tg: Heb lacks Like a
moth . . . human heart　d Meaning of Heb uncertain

17 Like somebody who takes a passing dog by the
     ears
   is one who meddles in the quarrel of another.
18 Like a maniac who shoots deadly firebrands and
     arrows,
19 so is one who deceives a neighbor
   and says, "I am only joking!"
20 For lack of wood the fire goes out,
   and where there is no whisperer, quarreling
     ceases.
21 As charcoal is to hot embers and wood to fire,
   so is a quarrelsome person for kindling strife.
22 The words of a whisperer are like delicious
     morsels;
   they go down into the inner parts of the body.
23 Like the glaze[a] covering an earthen vessel
   are smooth[b] lips with an evil heart.
24 An enemy dissembles in speaking
   while harboring deceit within;
25 when an enemy speaks graciously, do not
     believe it,
   for there are seven abominations concealed
     within;
26 though hatred is covered with guile,
   the enemy's wickedness will be exposed in the
     assembly.
27 Whoever digs a pit will fall into it,
   and a stone will come back on the one who
     starts it rolling.
28 A lying tongue hates its victims,
   and a flattering mouth works ruin.

27 Do not boast about tomorrow,
     for you do not know what a day may bring.
2 Let another praise you, and not your own
     mouth—
   a stranger, and not your own lips.
3 A stone is heavy, and sand is weighty,
   but a fool's provocation is heavier than both.
4 Wrath is cruel, anger is overwhelming,
   but who is able to stand before jealousy?
5 Better is open rebuke
   than hidden love.
6 Well meant are the wounds a friend inflicts,
   but profuse are the kisses of an enemy.
7 The sated appetite spurns honey,
   but to a ravenous appetite even the bitter is
     sweet.
8 Like a bird that strays from its nest
   is one who strays from home.
9 Perfume and incense make the heart glad,
   but the soul is torn by trouble.[c]
10 Do not forsake your friend or the friend of your
     parent;
   do not go to the house of your kindred in the
     day of your calamity.
   Better is a neighbor who is nearby

than kindred who are far away.
11 Be wise, my child, and make my heart glad,
   so that I may answer whoever reproaches me.
12 The clever see danger and hide;
   but the simple go on, and suffer for it.
13 Take the garment of one who has given surety
     for a stranger;
   seize the pledge given as surety for foreigners.[d]
14 Whoever blesses a neighbor with a loud voice,
   rising early in the morning,
   will be counted as cursing.

> "Do not boast about
> tomorrow,
> for you do not know what a
> day may bring."
> (Prov 27:1)

15 A continual dripping on a rainy day
   and a contentious wife are alike;
16 to restrain her is to restrain the wind
   or to grasp oil in the right hand.[e]
17 Iron sharpens iron,
   and one person sharpens the wits[f] of another.
18 Anyone who tends a fig tree will eat its fruit,
   and anyone who takes care of a master will be
     honored.
19 Just as water reflects the face,
   so one human heart reflects another.
20 Sheol and Abaddon are never satisfied,
   and human eyes are never satisfied.
21 The crucible is for silver, and the furnace is for
     gold,
   so a person is tested[g] by being praised.
22 Crush a fool in a mortar with a pestle
   along with crushed grain,
   but the folly will not be driven out.

23 Know well the condition of your flocks,
   and give attention to your herds;
24 for riches do not last forever,
   nor a crown for all generations.
25 When the grass is gone, and new growth appears,
   and the herbage of the mountains is gathered,
26 the lambs will provide your clothing,
   and the goats the price of a field;
27 there will be enough goats' milk for your food,
   for the food of your household
   and nourishment for your servant-girls.

a Cn: Heb silver of dross   b Gk: Heb burning   c Gk: Heb the
sweetness of a friend is better than one's own counsel   d Vg and
20.16: Heb for a foreign woman   e Meaning of Heb uncertain
f Heb face   g Heb lacks is tested

28 The wicked flee when no one pursues,
but the righteous are as bold as a lion.
2 When a land rebels
it has many rulers;
but with an intelligent ruler
there is lasting order.[a]
3 A ruler[b] who oppresses the poor
is a beating rain that leaves no food.
4 Those who forsake the law praise the wicked,
but those who keep the law struggle against
them.
5 The evil do not understand justice,
but those who seek the LORD understand it
completely.
6 Better to be poor and walk in integrity
than to be crooked in one's ways even though
rich.
7 Those who keep the law are wise children,
but companions of gluttons shame their
parents.
8 One who augments wealth by exorbitant interest
gathers it for another who is kind to the poor.
9 When one will not listen to the law,
even one's prayers are an abomination.
10 Those who mislead the upright into evil ways
will fall into pits of their own making,
but the blameless will have a goodly
inheritance.

Integrity

A person with integrity does the right thing,
even if it doesn't lead to fame or riches. A
person with integrity won't lie, steal, or cheat;
won't gossip, betray, or insult—not even when
everyone else seems to be doing it. A person
with integrity is trustworthy, dependable, and reliable. Such a person admits making mistakes
and apologizes. Such a person forgives freely
and doesn't hold grudges.

*Lord, I'm far from perfect. But with every word
I speak, every action I take, every choice I
make, may I become more aware of how
I am growing into a person of
integrity.*

▶ **Prov 28:6**

11 The rich is wise in self-esteem,
but an intelligent poor person sees through
the pose.
12 When the righteous triumph, there is great glory,
but when the wicked prevail, people go into
hiding.
13 No one who conceals transgressions will
prosper,
but one who confesses and forsakes them will
obtain mercy.
14 Happy is the one who is never without fear,
but one who is hard-hearted will fall into
calamity.
15 Like a roaring lion or a charging bear
is a wicked ruler over a poor people.
16 A ruler who lacks understanding is a cruel
oppressor;
but one who hates unjust gain will enjoy a
long life.
17 If someone is burdened with the blood of
another,
let that killer be a fugitive until death;
let no one offer assistance.
18 One who walks in integrity will be safe,
but whoever follows crooked ways will fall
into the Pit.[c]
19 Anyone who tills the land will have plenty of
bread,
but one who follows worthless pursuits will
have plenty of poverty.
20 The faithful will abound with blessings,
but one who is in a hurry to be rich will not
go unpunished.
21 To show partiality is not good—
yet for a piece of bread a person may do
wrong.
22 The miser is in a hurry to get rich
and does not know that loss is sure to come.
23 Whoever rebukes a person will afterward find
more favor
than one who flatters with the tongue.
24 Anyone who robs father or mother
and says, "That is no crime,"
is partner to a thug.
25 The greedy person stirs up strife,
but whoever trusts in the LORD will be
enriched.
26 Those who trust in their own wits are fools;
but those who walk in wisdom come through
safely.
27 Whoever gives to the poor will lack nothing,
but one who turns a blind eye will get many a
curse.

a Meaning of Heb uncertain   b Cn: Heb *A poor person*
c Syr: Heb *fall all at once*

28 When the wicked prevail, people go into hiding;
    but when they perish, the righteous increase.

29

One who is often reproved, yet remains
    stubborn,
will suddenly be broken beyond healing.

2 When the righteous are in authority, the people
    rejoice;
    but when the wicked rule, the people groan.

3 A child who loves wisdom makes a parent glad,
    but to keep company with prostitutes is to
    squander one's substance.

4 By justice a king gives stability to the land,
    but one who makes heavy exactions ruins it.

5 Whoever flatters a neighbor
    is spreading a net for the neighbor's feet.

6 In the transgression of the evil there is a snare,
    but the righteous sing and rejoice.

7 The righteous know the rights of the poor;
    the wicked have no such understanding.

8 Scoffers set a city aflame,
    but the wise turn away wrath.

9 If the wise go to law with fools,
    there is ranting and ridicule without relief.

10 The bloodthirsty hate the blameless,
    and they seek the life of the upright.

11 A fool gives full vent to anger,
    but the wise quietly holds it back.

12 If a ruler listens to falsehood,
    all his officials will be wicked.

13 The poor and the oppressor have this in common:
    the Lord gives light to the eyes of both.

14 If a king judges the poor with equity,
    his throne will be established forever.

15 The rod and reproof give wisdom,
    but a mother is disgraced by a neglected
    child.

16 When the wicked are in authority, transgression
    increases,
    but the righteous will look upon their
    downfall.

17 Discipline your children, and they will give you
    rest;
    they will give delight to your heart.

18 Where there is no prophecy, the people cast off
    restraint,
    but happy are those who keep the law.

19 By mere words servants are not disciplined,
    for though they understand, they will not give
    heed.

20 Do you see someone who is hasty in speech?
    There is more hope for a fool than for anyone
    like that.

21 A slave pampered from childhood
    will come to a bad end.[a]

22 One given to anger stirs up strife,
    and the hothead causes much transgression.

23 A person's pride will bring humiliation,
    but one who is lowly in spirit will obtain
    honor.

24 To be a partner of a thief is to hate one's own life;
    one hears the victim's curse, but discloses
    nothing.[b]

25 The fear of others[c] lays a snare,
    but one who trusts in the Lord is secure.

26 Many seek the favor of a ruler,
    but it is from the Lord that one gets justice.

27 The unjust are an abomination to the righteous,
    but the upright are an abomination to the
    wicked.

Sayings of Agur

30

The words of Agur son of Jakeh. An oracle.

Thus says the man: I am weary, O God,
    I am weary, O God. How can I prevail?[d]

2 Surely I am too stupid to be human;
    I do not have human understanding.

3 I have not learned wisdom,
    nor have I knowledge of the holy ones.[e]

4 Who has ascended to heaven and come down?
    Who has gathered the wind in the hollow of
    the hand?
Who has wrapped up the waters in a garment?
    Who has established all the ends of the earth?
What is the person's name?
    And what is the name of the person's child?
    Surely you know!

5 Every word of God proves true;
    he is a shield to those who take refuge in him.

6 Do not add to his words,
    or else he will rebuke you, and you will be
    found a liar.

7 Two things I ask of you;
    do not deny them to me before I die:

8 Remove far from me falsehood and lying;
    give me neither poverty nor riches;
    feed me with the food that I need,

9 or I shall be full, and deny you,
    and say, "Who is the Lord?"
    or I shall be poor, and steal,
    and profane the name of my God.

10 Do not slander a servant to a master,
    or the servant will curse you, and you will be
    held guilty.

---

a Vg: Meaning of Heb uncertain   b Meaning of Heb uncertain
c Or human fear   d Or I am spent. Meaning of Heb uncertain
e Or Holy One

PROV

Birds of Prey

The eye that mocks a father
and scorns to obey a mother
will be pecked out by the ravens of the valley
and eaten by the vultures.

(Prov 30:17)

If this passage reflected reality, most of us would already have been eaten by those birds of prey hovering overhead. For who among us has not at one time mocked our parents, if not to their face, then perhaps to our friends? And is there anyone who has not disobeyed a parent?

We live in a time when families have many different forms. You might live with biological parents, stepparents, adopted parents, or foster parents. Whatever kind and number of parents you have, they need your respect, despite their weaknesses and flaws (although you must not accept verbal, physical, sexual, or other abuse).

The vast majority of us are loved by our parents. In most cases, they are trying their hardest to do what is best for us, even though it doesn't always seem that way. If we can accept this, it might be easier to forgive them their faults and overlook some of the things they do that irritate us.

Let's keep the birds of prey far away!

● What can you do to let your parents know you love them?
● What can you do today to show them more respect?

▶ **Prov 30:17**

11 There are those who curse their fathers
and do not bless their mothers.
12 There are those who are pure in their own
eyes
yet are not cleansed of their filthiness.
13 There are those—how lofty are their eyes,
how high their eyelids lift!—
14 there are those whose teeth are swords,
whose teeth are knives,
to devour the poor from off the earth,
the needy from among mortals.

15 The leech[a] has two daughters;
"Give, give," they cry.
Three things are never satisfied;
four never say, "Enough":
16 Sheol, the barren womb,
the earth ever thirsty for water,
and the fire that never says, "Enough."[a]

17 The eye that mocks a father
and scorns to obey a mother
will be pecked out by the ravens of the valley
and eaten by the vultures.

18 Three things are too wonderful for me;
four I do not understand:
19 the way of an eagle in the sky,
the way of a snake on a rock,
the way of a ship on the high seas,
and the way of a man with a girl.

20 This is the way of an adulteress:
she eats, and wipes her mouth,
and says, "I have done no wrong."

21 Under three things the earth trembles;
under four it cannot bear up:
22 a slave when he becomes king,
and a fool when glutted with food;
23 an unloved woman when she gets a husband,
and a maid when she succeeds her mistress.

24 Four things on earth are small,
yet they are exceedingly wise:
25 the ants are a people without strength,
yet they provide their food in the summer;
26 the badgers are a people without power,
yet they make their homes in the rocks;
27 the locusts have no king,
yet all of them march in rank;
28 the lizard[b] can be grasped in the hand,
yet it is found in kings' palaces.

29 Three things are stately in their stride;
four are stately in their gait:
30 the lion, which is mightiest among wild
animals
and does not turn back before any;
31 the strutting rooster,[c] the he-goat,
and a king striding before[a] his people.

32 If you have been foolish, exalting yourself,
or if you have been devising evil,

---

a Meaning of Heb uncertain   b Or *spider*   c Gk Syr Tg
Compare Vg: Meaning of Heb uncertain

put your hand on your mouth.
33 For as pressing milk produces curds,
    and pressing the nose produces blood,
    so pressing anger produces strife.

The Teaching of King Lemuel's Mother

31 The words of King Lemuel. An oracle that
his mother taught him:

2 No, my son! No, son of my womb!
    No, son of my vows!
3 Do not give your strength to women,
    your ways to those who destroy kings.
4 It is not for kings, O Lemuel,
    it is not for kings to drink wine,
    or for rulers to desire*ᵃ* strong drink;
5 or else they will drink and forget what has been
        decreed,
    and will pervert the rights of all the afflicted.
6 Give strong drink to one who is perishing,
    and wine to those in bitter distress;
7 let them drink and forget their poverty,
    and remember their misery no more.
8 Speak out for those who cannot speak,
    for the rights of all the destitute.*ᵇ*
9 Speak out, judge righteously,
    defend the rights of the poor and needy.

Ode to a Capable Wife

10 A capable wife who can find?
    She is far more precious than jewels.
11 The heart of her husband trusts in her,
    and he will have no lack of gain.
12 She does him good, and not harm,
    all the days of her life.
13 She seeks wool and flax,
    and works with willing hands.
14 She is like the ships of the merchant,
    she brings her food from far away.
15 She rises while it is still night
    and provides food for her household
    and tasks for her servant-girls.
16 She considers a field and buys it;
    with the fruit of her hands she plants a
        vineyard.
17 She girds herself with strength,
    and makes her arms strong.
18 She perceives that her merchandise is profitable.
    Her lamp does not go out at night.
19 She puts her hands to the distaff,
    and her hands hold the spindle.
20 She opens her hand to the poor,
    and reaches out her hands to the needy.
21 She is not afraid for her household when it snows,
    for all her household are clothed in crimson.
22 She makes herself coverings;

her clothing is fine linen and purple.
23 Her husband is known in the city gates,
    taking his seat among the elders of the land.
24 She makes linen garments and sells them;
    she supplies the merchant with sashes.
25 Strength and dignity are her clothing,
    and she laughs at the time to come.
26 She opens her mouth with wisdom,
    and the teaching of kindness is on her tongue.
27 She looks well to the ways of her household,
    and does not eat the bread of idleness.
28 Her children rise up and call her happy;
    her husband too, and he praises her:
29 "Many women have done excellently,
    but you surpass them all."
30 Charm is deceitful, and beauty is vain,
    but a woman who fears the Lord is to be
        praised.
31 Give her a share in the fruit of her hands,
    and let her works praise her in the city gates.

---

a Cn: Heb *where*   b Heb *all children of passing away*

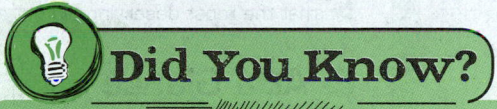

Did You Know?

A Woman's Place

You've probably noticed that women had a much different role in biblical times than they do now. Then it was common, and expected, for women to be in the home—either their father's or their husband's—doing household chores.

Today, the Catholic Church teaches that women and men share equality and that both deserve respect and mutual appreciation. It is not appropriate or just, therefore, to say that a woman's place is in the home. Women now choose where they spend their time!

Thousands of women today hold leadership positions at parish, diocesan, archdiocesan, and national levels. The Church celebrates the inclusion of women in leadership positions and continues to strive for and support a more even distribution of men and women in these positions. If you are a young woman or young man interested in working for the Church, ask for more information at your parish or school.

▶ **Prov 31:10–31**

PROV

"**T**here is nothing new under the sun." "For in much wisdom is much vexation / and those who increase knowledge increase sorrow." "No one can anticipate the time of disaster." If you were to see these comments on the Internet, what would you think? That you had just found the Web site of the National Association of Pessimists? Would you be surprised to learn that all these lines come from the Bible? The author of Ecclesiastes, who was called the Teacher (Eccl 1:1), wrote all of them. Yet, the book is hardly a defense of pessimism. The Teacher was pointing out to the Israelites the need for a new understanding of God and life.

In Depth

After a long life of careful observation, the author of Ecclesiastes was disturbed by many things:

- that wise people perished just like fools (see 2:12–17)
- that those who worked hard for a living had to leave their possessions behind in death (see 5:13–17)
- that sometimes bad people lived longer than good people (see 7:15)
- that the most deserving did not always get what they had earned (see 9:11–12)

At a Glance

- **1:1—6:9.** thoughts on life's difficulties, along with the Teacher's advice
- **6:10—12:8.** thoughts on the future
- **12:9-14.** the final editor's addition, affirming the Teacher's insights

Quick Facts

Inspired Author: the Teacher, writing in the fourth or third century BC

Themes: Life is not always fair. There are no easy answers. Only in faith in God is true wisdom found.

Of Note: The Book of Ecclesiastes is often attributed to King Solomon, although he did not write it.

Observing these puzzling things, the Teacher asked the obvious question: "Why should we work so hard to be wise and good?" For centuries, believers had struggled to be honest, law-abiding people in the hope of being rewarded by God. And what had they gotten? Sickness, suffering, and death—like everyone else! "Something's wrong!" the Teacher insisted. "Something's terribly wrong!"

After raising the question, the author of Ecclesiastes did not provide an answer—nor is a convincing one to be found in the writings of others in the Old Testament. However, later generations of Jews, pondering the possibility of life after death—a concept that developed late in Jewish religion—began to see things in a different light. Does God possibly reward the faithful in a life beyond the grave? For Christians, the New Testament answers that question with a resounding yes.

The Book of Ecclesiastes stands as a reminder to believers that all things change, even our understanding of God. The Teacher was not a pessimist, but a realist with a mission—to stretch the traditional understanding of faith in order to embrace the difficult questions of life.

The Book of Ecclesiastes

Ecclesiastes

Reflections of a Royal Philosopher

1 The words of the Teacher,[a] the son of David, king in Jerusalem.

2 Vanity of vanities, says the Teacher,[a]
  vanity of vanities! All is vanity.
3 What do people gain from all the toil
  at which they toil under the sun?
4 A generation goes, and a generation comes,
  but the earth remains forever.
5 The sun rises and the sun goes down,
  and hurries to the place where it rises.
6 The wind blows to the south,
  and goes around to the north;
round and round goes the wind,
  and on its circuits the wind returns.
7 All streams run to the sea,
  but the sea is not full;
to the place where the streams flow,
  there they continue to flow.
8 All things[b] are wearisome;
  more than one can express;
the eye is not satisfied with seeing,
  or the ear filled with hearing.
9 What has been is what will be,
  and what has been done is what will be done;
  there is nothing new under the sun.
10 Is there a thing of which it is said,
  "See, this is new"?
It has already been,
  in the ages before us.
11 The people of long ago are not remembered,
  nor will there be any remembrance

of people yet to come
  by those who come after them.

The Futility of Seeking Wisdom

12 I, the Teacher,[a] when king over Israel in Jerusalem, 13applied my mind to seek and to search out by wisdom all that is done under heaven; it is an unhappy business that God has given to human beings to be busy with. 14I saw all the deeds that are done under the sun; and see, all is vanity and a chasing after wind.[c]
15 What is crooked cannot be made straight,
  and what is lacking cannot be counted.

16 I said to myself, "I have acquired great wisdom, surpassing all who were over Jerusalem before me; and my mind has had great experience of wisdom and knowledge." 17And I applied my mind to know wisdom and to know madness and folly. I perceived that this also is but a chasing after wind.[c]
18 For in much wisdom is much vexation,
  and those who increase knowledge increase
    sorrow.

The Futility of Self-Indulgence

2 I said to myself, "Come now, I will make a test of pleasure; enjoy yourself." But again, this also was vanity. 2I said of laughter, "It is mad," and of pleasure, "What use is it?" 3I searched with my mind how to cheer my body with wine—my mind still guiding me with wisdom—and how to lay

---

a Heb *Qoheleth*, traditionally rendered *Preacher*   b Or *words*
c Or *a feeding on wind*. See Hos 12.1

hold on folly, until I might see what was good for mortals to do under heaven during the few days of their life. [4]I made great works; I built houses and planted vineyards for myself; [5]I made myself gardens and parks, and planted in them all kinds of fruit trees. [6]I made myself pools from which to water the forest of growing trees. [7]I bought male and female slaves, and had slaves who were born in my house; I also had great possessions of herds and flocks, more than any who had been before me in Jerusalem. [8]I also gathered for myself silver and gold and the treasure of kings and of the provinces; I got singers, both men and women, and delights of the flesh, and many concubines.[a]

9 So I became great and surpassed all who were before me in Jerusalem; also my wisdom remained with me. [10]Whatever my eyes desired I did not keep from them; I kept my heart from no pleasure, for my heart found pleasure in all my toil, and this was my reward for all my toil. [11]Then I considered all that my hands had done and the toil I had spent in doing it, and again, all was vanity and a chasing after wind,[b] and there was nothing to be gained under the sun.

Wisdom and Joy Given to One Who Pleases God

12 So I turned to consider wisdom and madness and folly; for what can the one do who comes after the king? Only what has already been done. [13]Then I saw that wisdom excels folly as light excels darkness.

[14] The wise have eyes in their head,
   but fools walk in darkness.

Yet I perceived that the same fate befalls all of them. [15]Then I said to myself, "What happens to the fool will happen to me also; why then have I been so very wise?" And I said to myself that this also is vanity. [16]For there is no enduring remembrance of the wise or of fools, seeing that in the days to come all will have been long forgotten. How can the wise die just like fools? [17]So I hated life, because what is done under the sun was grievous to me; for all is vanity and a chasing after wind.[b]

18 I hated all my toil in which I had toiled under the sun, seeing that I must leave it to those who come after me [19]—and who knows whether they will be wise or foolish? Yet they will be master of all for which I toiled and used my wisdom under the sun. This also is vanity. [20]So I turned and gave my heart up to despair concerning all the toil of my labors under the sun, [21]because sometimes one who has toiled with wisdom and knowledge and skill must leave all to be enjoyed by another who did not toil for it. This also is vanity and a great evil. [22]What do mortals get from all the toil and strain with which they toil under the sun? [23]For all their days are full of pain, and their work is a vexation; even at night their minds do not rest. This also is vanity.

24 There is nothing better for mortals than to eat and drink, and find enjoyment in their toil. This also, I saw, is from the hand of God; [25]for apart from him[c] who can eat or who can have enjoyment? [26]For to the one who pleases him God gives wisdom and knowledge and joy; but to the sinner he gives the work of gathering and heaping, only to give to one who pleases God. This also is vanity and a chasing after wind.[b]

New and Improved!

NEW! IMPROVED! These two words are basic to many ad campaigns. No matter how good a product is, sooner or later, it will be "new and improved." The reason is simple: the advertisers want us to think the product is even better.

The writer of Ecclesiastes would not be very impressed with the claims of advertisers today. The author sounds skeptical in 1:9: "There is nothing new under the sun." The Teacher is not going to be taken in by claims that something is new and improved. This person has seen it all before.

Advertising can get us thinking that our lives aren't good enough, that we have to have more things and new things in order to be happy. In fact, we need to have a little bit of the attitude of the Teacher if we want to find contentment. Throughout the Book of Ecclesiastes, this writer invites us to enjoy what we have now.

- Have you ever gotten something because of its advertising, only to be disappointed afterward?
- Are you content and happy with the things you have—home, food, clothes, and so on?

▶ Eccl 1:1–11

---

a Meaning of Heb uncertain   b Or a feeding on wind. See Hos 12.1   c Gk Syr: Heb apart from me

Everything Has Its Time

3 For everything there is a season, and a time for every matter under heaven:

2 a time to be born, and a time to die;
   a time to plant, and a time to pluck up what is planted;
3 a time to kill, and a time to heal;
   a time to break down, and a time to build up;
4 a time to weep, and a time to laugh;
   a time to mourn, and a time to dance;
5 a time to throw away stones, and a time to gather stones together;
   a time to embrace, and a time to refrain from embracing;
6 a time to seek, and a time to lose;
   a time to keep, and a time to throw away;
7 a time to tear, and a time to sew;
   a time to keep silence, and a time to speak;
8 a time to love, and a time to hate;
   a time for war, and a time for peace.

The God-Given Task

9 What gain have the workers from their toil? 10 I have seen the business that God has given to everyone to be busy with. 11 He has made everything suitable for its time; moreover he has put a sense of past and future into their minds, yet they cannot find out what God has done from the beginning to the end. 12 I know that there is nothing better for them than to be happy and enjoy themselves as long as they live; 13 moreover, it is God's gift that all should eat and drink and take pleasure in all their toil. 14 I know that whatever God does endures forever; nothing can be added to it, nor anything taken from it; God has done this, so that all should stand in awe before him. 15 That which is, already has been; that which is to be, already is; and God seeks out what has gone by.*a*

Judgment and the Future Belong to God

16 Moreover I saw under the sun that in the place of justice, wickedness was there, and in the place of righteousness, wickedness was there as well. 17 I said in my heart, God will judge the righteous and the wicked, for he has appointed a time for every matter, and for every work. 18 I said in my heart with regard to human beings that God is testing them to show that they are but animals. 19 For the fate of humans and the fate of animals is the same; as one dies, so dies the other. They all have the same breath, and humans have no advantage over the animals; for all is vanity. 20 All go to one place; all are from the dust, and all turn to dust again. 21 Who

Pray It!

The Balance of Life

God of all seasons,
Help me to remember the sun when rain is falling.
Help me to remember the rain when the sun is shining.
Teach me to respect the seniors when I am a sophomore.
Teach me to respect the sophomores when I am a senior.
When I win on the field, let me remember the times I lost.
When I lose on the field, let me remember the times I won.
Guide me to appreciate studying when I'm taking a hard test.
Guide me to appreciate hard tests when I'm studying.
During times with friends, remind me of times alone.
During times alone, remind me of times with friends.
Help me to live all moments and remember there is a balance to life.
Amen.

▶ Eccl 3:1–8

knows whether the human spirit goes upward and the spirit of animals goes downward to the earth? 22 So I saw that there is nothing better than that all should enjoy their work, for that is their lot; who can bring them to see what will be after them?

4 Again I saw all the oppressions that are practiced under the sun. Look, the tears of the oppressed—with no one to comfort them! On the side of their oppressors there was power—with no one to comfort them. 2 And I thought the dead, who have already died, more fortunate than the living, who are still alive; 3 but better than both is the one who has not yet been, and has not seen the evil deeds that are done under the sun.

4 Then I saw that all toil and all skill in work

---

a Heb *what is pursued*

E C C L

Cultural Connection

A Time for Connections

The *Tao te Ching* (pronounced "Dow deh JING") is the ancient Chinese Book of the Way. This piece of Chinese wisdom literature was written by Lao-tzu, who probably lived about 500 BC, close to the time of the author of Ecclesiastes. See how similar the following passage from the *Tao te Ching* is to Ecclesiastes 3:1–8:

There is a time for being ahead,
a time for being behind;
a time for being in motion,
a time for being at rest;
a time for being vigorous,
a time for being exhausted;
a time for being safe,
a time for being in danger.
(Stephen Mitchell, translator, *Tao te Ching*, no. 29)

▶ **Eccl 3:1–8**

---

come from one person's envy of another. This also is vanity and a chasing after wind.[a]

5 Fools fold their hands
    and consume their own flesh.

6 Better is a handful with quiet
    than two handfuls with toil,
    and a chasing after wind.[a]

7 Again, I saw vanity under the sun: [8]the case of solitary individuals, without sons or brothers; yet there is no end to all their toil, and their eyes are never satisfied with riches. "For whom am I toiling," they ask, "and depriving myself of pleasure?" This also is vanity and an unhappy business.

The Value of a Friend

9 Two are better than one, because they have a good reward for their toil. [10]For if they fall, one will lift up the other; but woe to one who is alone and falls and does not have another to help. [11]Again, if two lie together, they keep warm; but how can one keep warm alone? [12]And though one might prevail against another, two will withstand one. A threefold cord is not quickly broken.

13 Better is a poor but wise youth than an old but foolish king, who will no longer take advice. [14]One can indeed come out of prison to reign, even though born poor in the kingdom. [15]I saw all the living who, moving about under the sun, follow that[b] youth who replaced the king;[c] [16]there was no end to all those people whom he led. Yet those who come later will not rejoice in him. Surely this also is vanity and a chasing after wind.[a]

Reverence, Humility, and Contentment

5[d] Guard your steps when you go to the house of God; to draw near to listen is better than the sacrifice offered by fools; for they do not know how to keep from doing evil.[e] [2f]Never be rash with your mouth, nor let your heart be quick to utter a word before God, for God is in heaven, and you upon earth; therefore let your words be few.

3 For dreams come with many cares, and a fool's voice with many words.

4 When you make a vow to God, do not delay fulfilling it; for he has no pleasure in fools. Fulfill what you vow. [5]It is better that you should not vow than that you should vow and not fulfill it. [6]Do not let your mouth lead you into sin, and do not say before the messenger that it was a mistake; why should God be angry at your words, and destroy the work of your hands?

7 With many dreams come vanities and a multitude of words;[g] but fear God.

8 If you see in a province the oppression of the poor and the violation of justice and right, do not be amazed at the matter; for the high official is watched by a higher, and there are yet higher ones over them. [9]But all things considered, this is an advantage for a land: a king for a plowed field.[g]

10 The lover of money will not be satisfied with money; nor the lover of wealth, with gain. This also is vanity.

11 When goods increase, those who eat them increase; and what gain has their owner but to see them with his eyes?

12 Sweet is the sleep of laborers, whether they eat little or much; but the surfeit of the rich will not let them sleep.

13 There is a grievous ill that I have seen

---

a Or *a feeding on wind.* See Hos 12.1   b Heb *the second*
c Heb *him*   d Ch 4.17 in Heb   e Cn: Heb *they do not know how to do evil*   f Ch 5.1 in Heb   g Meaning of Heb uncertain

under the sun: riches were kept by their owners to their hurt, [14]and those riches were lost in a bad venture; though they are parents of children, they have nothing in their hands. [15]As they came from their mother's womb, so they shall go again, naked as they came; they shall take nothing for their toil, which they may carry away with their hands. [16]This also is a grievous ill: just as they came, so shall they go; and what gain do they have from toiling for the wind? [17]Besides, all their days they eat in darkness, in much vexation and sickness and resentment.

18 This is what I have seen to be good: it is fitting to eat and drink and find enjoyment in all the toil with which one toils under the sun the few days of the life God gives us; for this is our lot. [19]Likewise all to whom God gives wealth and possessions and whom he enables to enjoy them, and to accept their lot and find enjoyment in their toil—this is the gift of God. [20]For they will scarcely brood over the days of their lives, because God keeps them occupied with the joy of their hearts.

The Frustration of Desires

6 There is an evil that I have seen under the sun, and it lies heavy upon humankind: [2]those to whom God gives wealth, possessions, and honor, so that they lack nothing of all that they desire, yet God does not enable them to enjoy these things, but a stranger enjoys them. This is vanity; it is a grievous ill. [3]A man may beget a hundred children, and live many years; but however many are the days of his years, if he does not enjoy life's good things, or has no burial, I say that a stillborn child is better off than he. [4]For it comes into vanity and goes into darkness, and in darkness its name is covered; [5]moreover it has not seen the sun or known anything; yet it finds rest rather than he. [6]Even though he should live a thousand years twice over, yet enjoy no good— do not all go to one place?

7 All human toil is for the mouth, yet the appetite is not satisfied. [8]For what advantage have the wise over fools? And what do the poor have who know how to conduct themselves before the living? [9]Better is the sight of the eyes than the wandering of desire; this also is vanity and a chasing after wind.[a]

10 Whatever has come to be has already been named, and it is known what human beings are, and that they are not able to dispute with those who are stronger. [11]The more words, the more vanity, so how is one the better? [12]For who knows what is good for mortals while they live the few days of their vain life, which they pass like a shadow? For who can tell them what will be after them under the sun?

A Disillusioned View of Life

7 A good name is better than precious ointment,
and the day of death, than the day of birth.
[2] It is better to go to the house of mourning
than to go to the house of feasting;
for this is the end of everyone,
and the living will lay it to heart.
[3] Sorrow is better than laughter,
for by sadness of countenance the heart is
made glad.
[4] The heart of the wise is in the house of
mourning;
but the heart of fools is in the house of mirth.
[5] It is better to hear the rebuke of the wise
than to hear the song of fools.
[6] For like the crackling of thorns under a pot,
so is the laughter of fools;
this also is vanity.

a Or a feeding on wind. See Hos 12.1

How Much Is Enough?

How much wealth does one need? In surveys, most young people reply they want just enough money to be happy. It's an interesting answer because they are implying they don't want to be greedy, but it takes money to be happy!

According to the Teacher, in Ecclesiastes 5:10, those who love money will always want more. What is God trying to tell us here? Maybe that real happiness is not found in material wealth. The more we want, the less satisfied we are. Money can be an evil when it is all we want and think about.

For a week, try to do things with your family and friends that do not cost anything. Play board games, go for walks or hikes, even volunteer some time at a community organization. Consider taking the money you save and donating it to a worthy cause.

▶ Eccl 5:10

ECCL

7 Surely oppression makes the wise foolish,
   and a bribe corrupts the heart.
8 Better is the end of a thing than its beginning;
   the patient in spirit are better than the proud
      in spirit.
9 Do not be quick to anger,
   for anger lodges in the bosom of fools.
10 Do not say, "Why were the former days better
      than these?"
   For it is not from wisdom that you ask this.
11 Wisdom is as good as an inheritance,
   an advantage to those who see the sun.
12 For the protection of wisdom is like the
      protection of money,
   and the advantage of knowledge is that
      wisdom gives life to the one who
      possesses it.
13 Consider the work of God;
   who can make straight what he has made
      crooked?

14 In the day of prosperity be joyful, and in the day of adversity consider; God has made the one as well as the other, so that mortals may not find out anything that will come after them.

The Riddles of Life

15 In my vain life I have seen everything; there are righteous people who perish in their righteousness, and there are wicked people who prolong their life in their evildoing. 16Do not be too righteous, and do not act too wise; why should you destroy yourself? 17Do not be too wicked, and do not be a fool; why should you die before your time? 18It is good that you should take hold of the one, without letting go of the other; for the one who fears God shall succeed with both.

19 Wisdom gives strength to the wise more than ten rulers that are in a city.

20 Surely there is no one on earth so righteous as to do good without ever sinning.

21 Do not give heed to everything that people say, or you may hear your servant cursing you; 22your heart knows that many times you have yourself cursed others.

23 All this I have tested by wisdom; I said, "I will be wise," but it was far from me. 24That which is, is far off, and deep, very deep; who can find it out? 25I turned my mind to know and to search out and to seek wisdom and the sum of things, and to know that wickedness is folly and that foolishness is madness. 26I found more bitter than death the woman who is a trap, whose heart is snares and nets, whose hands are fetters; one who pleases God escapes her, but the sinner is taken by her. 27See, this is what I found, says

the Teacher,[a] adding one thing to another to find the sum, 28which my mind has sought repeatedly, but I have not found. One man among a thousand I found, but a woman among all these I have not found. 29See, this alone I found, that God made human beings straightforward, but they have devised many schemes.

Obey the King and Enjoy Yourself

8 Who is like the wise man?
   And who knows the interpretation of a thing?
Wisdom makes one's face shine,
   and the hardness of one's countenance is
      changed.

2 Keep[b] the king's command because of your sacred oath. 3Do not be terrified; go from his presence, do not delay when the matter is unpleasant, for he does whatever he pleases. 4For the word of the king is powerful, and who can say to him, "What are you doing?" 5Whoever obeys a command will meet no harm, and the wise mind will know the time and way. 6For every matter has its time and way, although the troubles of mortals lie heavy upon them. 7Indeed, they do not know what is to be, for who can tell them how it will be? 8No one has power over the wind[c] to restrain the wind,[c] or power over the day of death; there is no discharge from the battle, nor does wickedness deliver those who practice it. 9All this I observed, applying my mind to all that is done under the sun, while one person exercises authority over another to the other's hurt.

God's Ways Are Inscrutable

10 Then I saw the wicked buried; they used to go in and out of the holy place, and were praised in the city where they had done such things.[d] This also is vanity. 11Because sentence against an evil deed is not executed speedily, the human heart is fully set to do evil. 12Though sinners do evil a hundred times and prolong their lives, yet I know that it will be well with those who fear God, because they stand in fear before him, 13but it will not be well with the wicked, neither will they prolong their days like a shadow, because they do not stand in fear before God.

14 There is a vanity that takes place on earth, that there are righteous people who are treated according to the conduct of the wicked, and there are wicked people who are treated according to the conduct of the righteous. I said that this also is vanity. 15So I commend enjoyment, for there is nothing better for people under the sun than to

---

a Qoheleth, traditionally rendered Preacher   b Heb I keep
c Or breath   d Meaning of Heb uncertain

eat, and drink, and enjoy themselves, for this will go with them in their toil through the days of life that God gives them under the sun.

16 When I applied my mind to know wisdom, and to see the business that is done on earth, how one's eyes see sleep neither day nor night, [17]then I saw all the work of God, that no one can find out what is happening under the sun. However much they may toil in seeking, they will not find it out; even though those who are wise claim to know, they cannot find it out.

Take Life as It Comes

9 All this I laid to heart, examining it all, how the righteous and the wise and their deeds are in the hand of God; whether it is love or hate one does not know. Everything that confronts them [2]is vanity,[a] since the same fate comes to all, to the righteous and the wicked, to the good and the evil,[b] to the clean and the unclean, to those who sacrifice and those who do not sacrifice. As are the good, so are the sinners; those who swear are like those who shun an oath. [3]This is an evil in all that happens under the sun, that the same fate comes to everyone. Moreover, the hearts of all are full of evil; madness is in their hearts while they live, and after that they go to the dead. [4]But whoever is joined with all the living has hope, for a living dog is better than a dead lion. [5]The living know that they will die, but the dead know nothing; they have no more reward, and even the memory of them is lost. [6]Their love and their hate and their envy have already perished; never again will they have any share in all that happens under the sun.

7 Go, eat your bread with enjoyment, and drink your wine with a merry heart; for God has long ago approved what you do. [8]Let your garments always be white; do not let oil be lacking on your head. [9]Enjoy life with the wife whom you love, all the days of your vain life that are given you under the sun, because that is your portion in life and in your toil at which you toil under the sun. [10]Whatever your hand finds to do, do with your might; for there is no work or thought or knowledge or wisdom in Sheol, to which you are going.

11 Again I saw that under the sun the race is not to the swift, nor the battle to the strong, nor bread to the wise, nor riches to the intelligent, nor favor to the skillful; but time and chance happen to them all. [12]For no one can anticipate the time of disaster. Like fish taken in a cruel net, and like birds caught in a snare, so mortals are snared at a time of calamity, when it suddenly falls upon them.

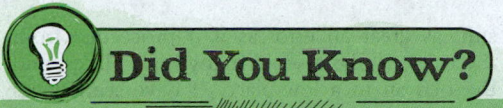

Did You Know?

Imagine There Is No Heaven

Some people assume that the ancient Israelites believed in an afterlife as we do today. However, Ecclesiastes speaks of the end of earthly life without any hint of eternal life: "The dead know nothing; they have no more reward, and even the memory of them is lost" (9:5). The book reflects the author's belief that all life ends with death. It was not until the last two centuries before Jesus that the idea of life after death began to take root among the Jewish people.

▶ Eccl 9:5

Wisdom Superior to Folly

13 I have also seen this example of wisdom under the sun, and it seemed great to me. [14]There was a little city with few people in it. A great king came against it and besieged it, building great siegeworks against it. [15]Now there was found in it a poor wise man, and he by his wisdom delivered the city. Yet no one remembered that poor man. [16]So I said, "Wisdom is better than might; yet the poor man's wisdom is despised, and his words are not heeded."

17 The quiet words of the wise are more to be heeded
    than the shouting of a ruler among fools.
18 Wisdom is better than weapons of war,
    but one bungler destroys much good.

Miscellaneous Observations

10 Dead flies make the perfumer's ointment
    give off a foul odor;
so a little folly outweighs wisdom and honor.
2 The heart of the wise inclines to the right,
    but the heart of a fool to the left.
3 Even when fools walk on the road, they lack sense,
    and show to everyone that they are fools.
4 If the anger of the ruler rises against you, do not leave your post,
    for calmness will undo great offenses.
5 There is an evil that I have seen under the

ECCL

---

a Syr Compare Gk: Heb *Everything that confronts them* [2]is *everything*   b Gk Syr Vg: Heb lacks *and the evil*

sun, as great an error as if it proceeded from the ruler: ⁶folly is set in many high places, and the rich sit in a low place. ⁷I have seen slaves on horseback, and princes walking on foot like slaves.

⁸ Whoever digs a pit will fall into it;
  and whoever breaks through a wall will be
    bitten by a snake.
⁹ Whoever quarries stones will be hurt by them;
  and whoever splits logs will be endangered by
    them.
¹⁰ If the iron is blunt, and one does not whet the
    edge,
  then more strength must be exerted;
  but wisdom helps one to succeed.
¹¹ If the snake bites before it is charmed,
  there is no advantage in a charmer.

¹² Words spoken by the wise bring them favor,
  but the lips of fools consume them.
¹³ The words of their mouths begin in foolishness,
  and their talk ends in wicked madness;

Carpe Diem—"Seize the Day"!

"**Y**outh is wasted on the young." Perhaps you have heard that statement uttered by not-so-young adults struggling with growing older. There is some truth in it: many young people do not reflect on life and do not pause to appreciate being young.

The Teacher says some beautiful and profound things about youthfulness. He advises young people to "follow the inclination of your heart" (Eccl 11:9) and to "banish anxiety from your mind" (verse 10). Someone like the Teacher might say today: "Follow your heart, and do not spend so much time worrying. It is a blessing to be young, to have so much energy and so many dreams. There are many pressures and stresses on young people today, but do not let them dominate your life. Enjoy this special time of growth and discovery."

It is good to be young. Seize the day!

▶ Eccl 11:7–10

¹⁴ yet fools talk on and on.
  No one knows what is to happen,
    and who can tell anyone what the future
      holds?
¹⁵ The toil of fools wears them out,
  for they do not even know the way to town.

¹⁶ Alas for you, O land, when your king is a
    servant,ᵃ
  and your princes feast in the morning!
¹⁷ Happy are you, O land, when your king is a
    nobleman,
  and your princes feast at the proper time—
  for strength, and not for drunkenness!
¹⁸ Through sloth the roof sinks in,
  and through indolence the house leaks.
¹⁹ Feasts are made for laughter;
  wine gladdens life,
  and money meets every need.
²⁰ Do not curse the king, even in your thoughts,
  or curse the rich, even in your bedroom;
  for a bird of the air may carry your voice,
  or some winged creature tell the matter.

The Value of Diligence

11 Send out your bread upon the waters,
  for after many days you will get it back.
² Divide your means seven ways, or even eight,
  for you do not know what disaster may
    happen on earth.
³ When clouds are full,
  they empty rain on the earth;
  whether a tree falls to the south or to the north,
  in the place where the tree falls, there it will lie.
⁴ Whoever observes the wind will not sow;
  and whoever regards the clouds will not reap.

5 Just as you do not know how the breath comes to the bones in the mother's womb, so you do not know the work of God, who makes everything.

6 In the morning sow your seed, and at evening do not let your hands be idle; for you do not know which will prosper, this or that, or whether both alike will be good.

Youth and Old Age

7 Light is sweet, and it is pleasant for the eyes to see the sun.

8 Even those who live many years should rejoice in them all; yet let them remember that the days of darkness will be many. All that comes is vanity.

9 Rejoice, young man, while you are young, and let your heart cheer you in the days of your

ECCL

youth. Follow the inclination of your heart and the desire of your eyes, but know that for all these things God will bring you into judgment.

10 Banish anxiety from your mind, and put away pain from your body; for youth and the dawn of life are vanity.

12 Remember your creator in the days of your youth, before the days of trouble come, and the years draw near when you will say, "I have no pleasure in them"; [2]before the sun and the light and the moon and the stars are darkened and the clouds return with[a] the rain; [3]in the day when the guards of the house tremble, and the strong men are bent, and the women who grind cease working because they are few, and those who look through the windows see dimly; [4]when the doors on the street are shut, and the sound of the grinding is low, and one rises up at the sound of a bird, and all the daughters of song are brought low; [5]when one is afraid of heights, and terrors are in the road; the almond tree blossoms, the grasshopper drags itself along[b] and desire fails; because all must go to their eternal home, and the mourners will go about the streets; [6]before the silver cord is snapped,[c] and the golden bowl is broken, and the pitcher is broken at the fountain, and the wheel broken at the cistern, [7]and the dust returns to the earth as it was, and the breath[d] returns to God who gave it. [8]Vanity of vanities, says the Teacher;[e] all is vanity.

Epilogue

9 Besides being wise, the Teacher[e] also taught the people knowledge, weighing and studying and arranging many proverbs. [10]The Teacher[e] sought to find pleasing words, and he wrote words of truth plainly.

11 The sayings of the wise are like goads, and like nails firmly fixed are the collected sayings that are given by one shepherd.[f] [12]Of anything beyond these, my child, beware. Of making many books there is no end, and much study is a weariness of the flesh.

Live It!

Remember the Elderly

Ecclesiastes 12:1–8 is a bittersweet poem about the difficulties of the aging process. To understand it, you need to be aware of the metaphors used, like these:

- Guards of the house = arms and hands
- Strong men = legs
- Women who grind = teeth
- Windows = eyes
- Doors = ears or lips
- Silver cord, golden bowl = life itself

Aging is a natural part of life, but it is a struggle for many people. No one enjoys its accompanying loss of mobility, loss of strength, and problems with seeing and hearing. The struggle is even greater if one is alone. If you have aging grandparents, family friends, or neighbors, keep in mind how much they need to be noticed by you. Stay in touch with them so you can learn from their wisdom and so they can be strengthened by your youth!

▶ **Eccl 12:1–8**

13 The end of the matter; all has been heard. Fear God, and keep his commandments; for that is the whole duty of everyone. [14]For God will bring every deed into judgment, including[g] every secret thing, whether good or evil.

---

a Or after; Heb 'ahar   b Or is a burden   c Syr Vg Compare Gk: Heb is removed   d Or the spirit   e Qoheleth, traditionally rendered Preacher   f Meaning of Heb uncertain   g Or into the judgment on

Sex sells. When we see an ad with a beautiful woman slipping out of a sports car or a bare-chested man grabbing an ice-cold soda, we sit up and take notice. Advertisers love to take advantage of our fascination with sex. Once they have our attention, they can sell us something we might not even be interested in! The Song of Solomon—a collection of ancient love poems—reminds us that this powerful force is ultimately a gift from God.

In Depth

From an advertiser's point of view, the Song of Solomon is a well-kept secret. How many people are aware of its explicit sexual images? Consider these verses:

- "Let him kiss me with the kisses of his mouth!" (1:2).
- "Your lips distill nectar, my bride; / honey and milk are under your tongue" (4:11).
- "May your breasts be like clusters of the vine, / and the scent of your breath like apples" (7:8).

Some people find some of these images in this book so surprising that they wonder why the Song of Solomon is found in the Bible at all.

Scholars believe that the naming of King Solomon in the Song's first verse is the main reason that this book was preserved and eventually included with the Jewish holy books. Although written long after Solomon's death, this book—like Proverbs and Ecclesiastes—was attributed to him to give it authority.

At a Glance

- 1:1–6. introduction
- 1:7—2:7. opening dialogue between the lovers
- 2:8—8:4. various reflections and other dialogues
- 8:5–14. final thoughts

Quick Facts

Inspired Author: unknown, probably writing after the Jews' return from the Babylonian Exile in 538 BC
Theme: poetry that expresses the goodness and passion of human love and God's love for his people
Of Note: In other translations, this book is called the Song of Songs or the Canticle of Canticles.

Through the centuries, some people have not been able to accept the Song of Solomon as simply love poetry and have hunted for a deeper meaning. One of the most complex books of the Old Testament, it can be interpreted from many perspectives, i.e., allegorical, cultic, dramatic, and literal. Many people believe that the lover and the beloved in this book stand for Israel and God, or for Jesus and the church. Modern-day scholars, however, begin their interpretation of the Song of Solomon at the literal level, that is, as a collection of love poems. The book's inclusion among the other holy books, they insist, is an affirmation of the goodness of human sexuality: human love is holy because it is a gift from God. Catholic scholars generally interpret this book as allegorical of God and Israel, but do not eliminate the possibility of interpreting it literally as an inspired portrayal of human love. The passion and beauty of human sexual attraction is a reflection of the passion and beauty of God's love for us!

The **Song of Solomon**

Song of Solomon

1 The Song of Songs, which is Solomon's.

Colloquy of Bride and Friends

2 Let him kiss me with the kisses of his mouth!
For your love is better than wine,
3   your anointing oils are fragrant,
your name is perfume poured out;
    therefore the maidens love you.
4 Draw me after you, let us make haste.
    The king has brought me into his chambers.
We will exult and rejoice in you;
    we will extol your love more than wine;
    rightly do they love you.

5 I am black and beautiful,
    O daughters of Jerusalem,
like the tents of Kedar,
    like the curtains of Solomon.
6 Do not gaze at me because I am dark,
    because the sun has gazed on me.
My mother's sons were angry with me;
    they made me keeper of the vineyards,
    but my own vineyard I have not kept!
7 Tell me, you whom my soul loves,
    where you pasture your flock,
    where you make it lie down at noon;
for why should I be like one who is veiled
    beside the flocks of your companions?

8 If you do not know,
    O fairest among women,
follow the tracks of the flock,
and pasture your kids
    beside the shepherds' tents.

Colloquy of Bridegroom, Friends, and Bride

9 I compare you, my love,
    to a mare among Pharaoh's chariots.
10 Your cheeks are comely with ornaments,
    your neck with strings of jewels.
11 We will make you ornaments of gold,
    studded with silver.

12 While the king was on his couch,
    my nard gave forth its fragrance.
13 My beloved is to me a bag of myrrh
    that lies between my breasts.
14 My beloved is to me a cluster of henna blossoms
    in the vineyards of En-gedi.

15 Ah, you are beautiful, my love;
    ah, you are beautiful;
    your eyes are doves.
16 Ah, you are beautiful, my beloved,
    truly lovely.
Our couch is green;
17   the beams of our house are cedar,
    our rafters*a* are pine.

2 I am a rose*b* of Sharon,
    a lily of the valleys.

---

a Meaning of Heb uncertain   *b* Heb *crocus*

Cultural Connection

Black and Beautiful

I am black and beautiful,
  O daughters of Jerusalem,
like the tents of Kedar,
  like the curtains of Solomon.
      (Song 1:5)

Who is speaking to us in this Scripture text? Who is so boldly and confidently proclaiming to us that she is black and beautiful? Some traditions say this is the bride of Solomon, the son of David and the third king of Israel.

Many of the people in the Old Testament world were black Africans or Afro-Asiatics (Asians of black African heritage). They had various shades of dark skin. In Song of Solomon 1:5, the bride describes herself as black like the tents of Kedar; in 5:10, she describes her lover as ruddy (reddish) in color.

Some African Americans are ruddy; others are darker. Together, all African Americans are a rainbow of blackness. Whatever shade they are, it is good. And if you are one of them, you are black and beautiful!

▶ **Song 1:5**

2 As a lily among brambles,
  so is my love among maidens.

3 As an apple tree among the trees of the wood,
  so is my beloved among young men.
With great delight I sat in his shadow,
  and his fruit was sweet to my taste.
4 He brought me to the banqueting house,
  and his intention toward me was love.
5 Sustain me with raisins,
  refresh me with apples;
  for I am faint with love.
6 O that his left hand were under my head,
  and that his right hand embraced me!
7 I adjure you, O daughters of Jerusalem,
  by the gazelles or the wild does:
do not stir up or awaken love
  until it is ready!

Springtime Rhapsody

8 The voice of my beloved!
  Look, he comes,
leaping upon the mountains,
  bounding over the hills.
9 My beloved is like a gazelle
  or a young stag.
Look, there he stands
  behind our wall,
gazing in at the windows,
  looking through the lattice.
10 My beloved speaks and says to me:
"Arise, my love, my fair one,
  and come away;
11 for now the winter is past,

the rain is over and gone.
12 The flowers appear on the earth;
  the time of singing has come,
and the voice of the turtledove
  is heard in our land.
13 The fig tree puts forth its figs,
  and the vines are in blossom;
  they give forth fragrance.
Arise, my love, my fair one,
  and come away.
14 O my dove, in the clefts of the rock,
  in the covert of the cliff,
let me see your face,
  let me hear your voice;
for your voice is sweet,
  and your face is lovely.
15 Catch us the foxes,
  the little foxes,
that ruin the vineyards—
  for our vineyards are in blossom."

16 My beloved is mine and I am his;
  he pastures his flock among the lilies.
17 Until the day breathes
  and the shadows flee,
turn, my beloved, be like a gazelle
  or a young stag on the cleft mountains.[a]

Love's Dream

3 Upon my bed at night
  I sought him whom my soul loves;

---

a Or *on the mountains of Bether*; meaning of Heb uncertain

SONG

Cultural Connection

Romantic Love

God loves us passionately and seeks us with the enthusiasm of a lover who memorizes every detail and cherishes every moment (see Song 1:9–17). Romantic, playful love was created by God for us to enjoy. The way we express such love can bring joy and delight; it also can devastate and destroy if it is abused and not respected. Be careful with love. God gave us our sexuality as a gift, not as a weapon.

Hear the tender respect of this love poem from the Cherokee tradition:

You are part of me now
    You touched me.
With your kindness and love
    So enchanted.

Your soft lips are kind.
    Your eyes glow with life.
I'm glad you touched me.
    You're part of me now.
    (Lloyd Carl Owle, "You Are
                    Part of Me")

 **Song 1:9–17**

I sought him, but found him not;
    I called him, but he gave no answer.[a]
2 "I will rise now and go about the city,
    in the streets and in the squares;
I will seek him whom my soul loves."
    I sought him, but found him not.
3 The sentinels found me,
    as they went about in the city.
"Have you seen him whom my soul loves?"
4 Scarcely had I passed them,
    when I found him whom my soul loves.
I held him, and would not let him go
    until I brought him into my mother's house,
    and into the chamber of her that
        conceived me.
5 I adjure you, O daughters of Jerusalem,
    by the gazelles or the wild does:
do not stir up or awaken love
    until it is ready!

The Groom and His Party Approach

6 What is that coming up from the wilderness,
    like a column of smoke,
perfumed with myrrh and frankincense,
    with all the fragrant powders of the merchant?
7 Look, it is the litter of Solomon!
    Around it are sixty mighty men
    of the mighty men of Israel,
8 all equipped with swords
    and expert in war,
each with his sword at his thigh
    because of alarms by night.
9 King Solomon made himself a palanquin
    from the wood of Lebanon.
10 He made its posts of silver,
    its back of gold, its seat of purple;

its interior was inlaid with love.[b]
    Daughters of Jerusalem,
11 come out.
Look, O daughters of Zion,
    at King Solomon,
at the crown with which his mother crowned
        him
    on the day of his wedding,
    on the day of the gladness of his heart.

The Bride's Beauty Extolled

4 How beautiful you are, my love,
    how very beautiful!
Your eyes are doves
    behind your veil.
Your hair is like a flock of goats,
    moving down the slopes of Gilead.
2 Your teeth are like a flock of shorn ewes
    that have come up from the washing,

---

a Gk: Heb lacks this line   b Meaning of Heb uncertain

3:7

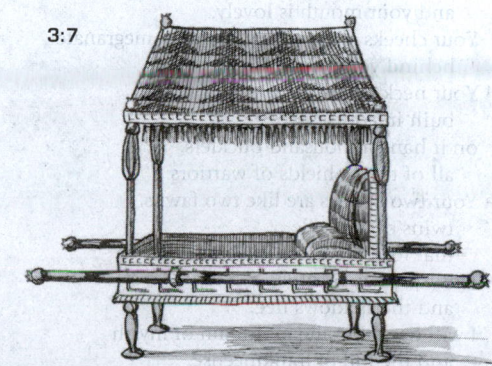

The Illusion of Pornography

Everywhere you look, it seems, you can find ads for phone sex, pornographic magazines and videos, and Internet porn sites. People are lured into the immoral world of false love through an industry that preys on those who are weak and lost, those unfortunate souls searching for love in all the wrong places.

One interpretation proposes that the Song of Solomon is about passion and sexual longing between a bride and a bridegroom. Their love is committed: "My beloved is mine and I am his" (Song 2:16). Their love is at once both urgent ("Draw me after you, let us make haste" [1:4]) and patient ("Do not stir up or awaken love / until it is ready" [2:7]). This is not the kind of love offered to us in pornography, which has nothing at all to do with real love.

If you find yourself drawn to pornography, ask yourself: Is this God's purpose for human sexuality? Is this enriching to human love, or degrading? Pray for the strength to avoid the temptation and illusion of pornography. Find an adult or someone you can trust to talk to if this is a problem for you.

▶ **Song 2:1–17**

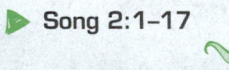

all of which bear twins,
    and not one among them is bereaved.
3 Your lips are like a crimson thread,
    and your mouth is lovely.
Your cheeks are like halves of a pomegranate
    behind your veil.
4 Your neck is like the tower of David,
    built in courses;
on it hang a thousand bucklers,
    all of them shields of warriors.
5 Your two breasts are like two fawns,
    twins of a gazelle,
    that feed among the lilies.
6 Until the day breathes
    and the shadows flee,
I will hasten to the mountain of myrrh
    and the hill of frankincense.

7 You are altogether beautiful, my love;
    there is no flaw in you.
8 Come with me from Lebanon, my bride;
    come with me from Lebanon.
Depart[a] from the peak of Amana,
    from the peak of Senir and Hermon,
from the dens of lions,
    from the mountains of leopards.

> **"You have ravished my heart, my sister, my bride, you have ravished my heart with a glance of your eyes."**
>
> (Song 4:9)

9 You have ravished my heart, my sister, my bride,
    you have ravished my heart with a glance of
        your eyes,
    with one jewel of your necklace.
10 How sweet is your love, my sister, my bride!
    how much better is your love than wine,
    and the fragrance of your oils than any spice!
11 Your lips distill nectar, my bride;
    honey and milk are under your tongue;
    the scent of your garments is like the scent of
        Lebanon.
12 A garden locked is my sister, my bride,
    a garden locked, a fountain sealed.
13 Your channel[b] is an orchard of pomegranates
    with all choicest fruits,
    henna with nard,
14 nard and saffron, calamus and cinnamon,
    with all trees of frankincense,
myrrh and aloes,
    with all chief spices—
15 a garden fountain, a well of living water,
    and flowing streams from Lebanon.

16 Awake, O north wind,
    and come, O south wind!
Blow upon my garden
    that its fragrance may be wafted abroad.
Let my beloved come to his garden,
    and eat its choicest fruits.

5 I come to my garden, my sister, my bride;
    I gather my myrrh with my spice,
    I eat my honeycomb with my honey,
    I drink my wine with my milk.

---

a Or *Look*   b Meaning of Heb uncertain

Eat, friends, drink,
    and be drunk with love.

Another Dream

2 I slept, but my heart was awake.
    Listen! my beloved is knocking.
    "Open to me, my sister, my love,
      my dove, my perfect one;
    for my head is wet with dew,
      my locks with the drops of the night."
3 I had put off my garment;
    how could I put it on again?
    I had bathed my feet;
    how could I soil them?
4 My beloved thrust his hand into the opening,
    and my inmost being yearned for him.
5 I arose to open to my beloved,
    and my hands dripped with myrrh,
    my fingers with liquid myrrh,
      upon the handles of the bolt.
6 I opened to my beloved,
    but my beloved had turned and was gone.
    My soul failed me when he spoke.
    I sought him, but did not find him;
    I called him, but he gave no answer.
7 Making their rounds in the city
    the sentinels found me;
    they beat me, they wounded me,
    they took away my mantle,
    those sentinels of the walls.
8 I adjure you, O daughters of Jerusalem,
    if you find my beloved,
    tell him this:
    I am faint with love.

Colloquy of Friends and Bride

9 What is your beloved more than another
    beloved,
    O fairest among women?
    What is your beloved more than another
    beloved,
    that you thus adjure us?

10 My beloved is all radiant and ruddy,
    distinguished among ten thousand.
11 His head is the finest gold;
    his locks are wavy,
    black as a raven.
12 His eyes are like doves
    beside springs of water,
    bathed in milk,
    fitly set.*a*
13 His cheeks are like beds of spices,
    yielding fragrance.
    His lips are lilies,
    distilling liquid myrrh.

14 His arms are rounded gold,
    set with jewels.
    His body is ivory work,*a*
    encrusted with sapphires.*b*
15 His legs are alabaster columns,
    set upon bases of gold.

---

a Meaning of Heb uncertain   *b* Heb *lapis lazuli*

Sexuality and Dialogue

A number of the love songs included in the Song of Solomon are addressed to the bridegroom and the beloved. It is as if a romantic dialogue has been recorded as lovers express the depth of feeling and desire they have for each other.

Dialogue is an essential aspect in any relationship. Open and honest communication provides the basis for maintaining and deepening the bonds of respect, friendship, and love.

Here is a time-honored test for any deep relationship: Is it possible for the two of you to speak honestly with each other about anything—especially problems and difficulties? Are you willing and able to discuss all dimensions of your love—including sexual feelings and desires?

Young couples often avoid such sensitive conversations. They fall victim to embarrassment and confusion and often leave important things unsaid. Such failure to communicate can result in hurt feelings, misunderstandings, and even behaviors that can lead to manipulation, selfishness, and sin.

Don't be afraid to discuss sexual issues. Always be ready to examine the nature of your relationships, especially when the power and passion of sexuality are present. True sexual love is rooted in dialogue, honest communication, and commitment. It finds its fullest expression in the context of marriage.

▶ **Song of Solomon, chapters 2–7**

SONG

The Song of Solomon

If you looked at human love as a reflection of divine love, then parts of this love poem, called the Song of Solomon, could be understood as prayer. Try reading parts of it as your words to God, and other parts as God's words to you. Look at these sections:

- 2:2–6. a prayer describing your passion for God
- 5:6–8. a prayer to God when God seems absent
- 8:6–7. God's words of love to you

The words may seem strange in this context, but if we are passionate about pursuing a human relationship, why can't we be passionate about pursuing our relationship with God? Some of the greatest saints expressed their love of God as a passionate, romantic love. You can do the same in your prayer with God!

His appearance is like Lebanon,
  choice as the cedars.
16 His speech is most sweet,
  and he is altogether desirable.
This is my beloved and this is my friend,
  O daughters of Jerusalem.

6 Where has your beloved gone,
  O fairest among women?
Which way has your beloved turned,
  that we may seek him with you?

2 My beloved has gone down to his garden,
  to the beds of spices,
to pasture his flock in the gardens,
  and to gather lilies.
3 I am my beloved's and my beloved is mine;
  he pastures his flock among the lilies.

The Bride's Matchless Beauty

4 You are beautiful as Tirzah, my love,
  comely as Jerusalem,
  terrible as an army with banners.
5 Turn away your eyes from me,
  for they overwhelm me!

Your hair is like a flock of goats,
  moving down the slopes of Gilead.
6 Your teeth are like a flock of ewes,
  that have come up from the washing;
all of them bear twins,
  and not one among them is bereaved.
7 Your cheeks are like halves of a pomegranate
  behind your veil.
8 There are sixty queens and eighty concubines,
  and maidens without number.
9 My dove, my perfect one, is the only one,
  the darling of her mother,
  flawless to her that bore her.
The maidens saw her and called her happy;
  the queens and concubines also, and they
  praised her.
10 "Who is this that looks forth like the dawn,
  fair as the moon, bright as the sun,
  terrible as an army with banners?"

11 I went down to the nut orchard,
  to look at the blossoms of the valley,
to see whether the vines had budded,
  whether the pomegranates were in bloom.
12 Before I was aware, my fancy set me
  in a chariot beside my prince.[a]

13b Return, return, O Shulammite!
  Return, return, that we may look upon you.

Why should you look upon the Shulammite,
  as upon a dance before two armies?[c]

Expressions of Praise

7 How graceful are your feet in sandals,
  O queenly maiden!
Your rounded thighs are like jewels,
  the work of a master hand.
2 Your navel is a rounded bowl
  that never lacks mixed wine.
Your belly is a heap of wheat,
  encircled with lilies.
3 Your two breasts are like two fawns,
  twins of a gazelle.
4 Your neck is like an ivory tower.
Your eyes are pools in Heshbon,
  by the gate of Bath-rabbim.
Your nose is like a tower of Lebanon,
  overlooking Damascus.
5 Your head crowns you like Carmel,
  and your flowing locks are like purple;
  a king is held captive in the tresses.[d]

---

a Cn: Meaning of Heb uncertain   b Ch 7.1 in Heb   c Or dance
of Mahanaim   d Meaning of Heb uncertain

6 How fair and pleasant you are,
      O loved one, delectable maiden![a]
7 You are stately[b] as a palm tree,
      and your breasts are like its clusters.
8 I say I will climb the palm tree
      and lay hold of its branches.
   O may your breasts be like clusters of the vine,
      and the scent of your breath like apples,
9 and your kisses[c] like the best wine
      that goes down[d] smoothly,
      gliding over lips and teeth.[e]

10 I am my beloved's,
      and his desire is for me.
11 Come, my beloved,
      let us go forth into the fields,
      and lodge in the villages;
12 let us go out early to the vineyards,
      and see whether the vines have budded,
   whether the grape blossoms have opened
      and the pomegranates are in bloom.
   There I will give you my love.
13 The mandrakes give forth fragrance,
      and over our doors are all choice fruits,
   new as well as old,
      which I have laid up for you, O my beloved.

8 O that you were like a brother to me,
      who nursed at my mother's breast!
   If I met you outside, I would kiss you,
      and no one would despise me.
2 I would lead you and bring you
      into the house of my mother,
      and into the chamber of the one who
         bore me.[f]
   I would give you spiced wine to drink,
      the juice of my pomegranates.
3 O that his left hand were under my head,
      and that his right hand embraced me!
4 I adjure you, O daughters of Jerusalem,
      do not stir up or awaken love
      until it is ready!

Homecoming

5 Who is that coming up from the wilderness,
      leaning upon her beloved?

Under the apple tree I awakened you.
There your mother was in labor with you;
      there she who bore you was in labor.

6 Set me as a seal upon your heart,
      as a seal upon your arm;
   for love is strong as death,
      passion fierce as the grave.
   Its flashes are flashes of fire,
      a raging flame.

7 Many waters cannot quench love,
      neither can floods drown it.
   If one offered for love
      all the wealth of one's house,
      it would be utterly scorned.

a Syr: Heb *in delights*   b Heb *This your stature is*   c Heb *palate*
d Heb *down for my lover*   e Gk Syr Vg: Heb *lips of sleepers*
f Gk Syr: Heb *my mother; she* (or *you*) *will teach me*

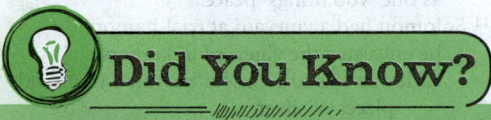

Did You Know?

Sex in the Old Testament

Through its surprisingly graphic sexual content (see, for example, 7:1–9), the Song of Solomon has surprised many generations of readers. It reminds us that one of the richest images of the Old Testament is a sexual one: God as the faithful lover of Israel. In Exodus 20:5, we hear of God's jealous love of the Chosen People. By the time of the early prophets, the image of God as lover was fully developed: "On that day, says the LORD, you will call me, 'My husband'" (Hos 2:16).

Because of ancient Israel's conviction that human love reflects divine love—and vice versa—there was a high regard for human sexuality. This regard was reflected in Israel's sexual morality. Free-for-all sex stood in clear contradiction to the holiness of God, whose faithful love was the model for all human love. The Ten Commandments prohibit not only having sex with someone else's spouse but also desiring someone else's spouse.

Despite these high standards, some Bible stories do not comment on the morality of behavior that would be unacceptable in Christian morality. They make no comment on the many patriarchs and kings who have more than one wife, and take for granted an inferior status of women in marriage. Because moral insights have developed over the centuries, we must remember to read biblical passages in light of the *whole* Bible and the Christian tradition. In the Old Testament, we find the seeds of Christian sexual morality, not its full flower.

8 We have a little sister,
  and she has no breasts.
What shall we do for our sister,
  on the day when she is spoken for?
9 If she is a wall,
  we will build upon her a battlement of silver;
but if she is a door,
  we will enclose her with boards of cedar.
10 I was a wall,
  and my breasts were like towers;
then I was in his eyes
  as one who brings[a] peace.
11 Solomon had a vineyard at Baal-hamon;
  he entrusted the vineyard to keepers;
  each one was to bring for its fruit a thousand
    pieces of silver.

12 My vineyard, my very own, is for myself;
  you, O Solomon, may have the thousand,
  and the keepers of the fruit two hundred!

13 O you who dwell in the gardens,
  my companions are listening for your voice;
  let me hear it.

14 Make haste, my beloved,
  and be like a gazelle
or a young stag
  upon the mountains of spices!

---

a Or finds

Do you know what life was like for your great-grandparents? Were they, or other members of your family, immigrants to the United States? How much of their history do you know? Time and distance have a way of fading the memories that keep our roots alive. The same was true for the ancient Jewish people after they had settled in different countries. The Book of Wisdom of Solomon was written to remind them of their roots and the wisdom of their traditions.

At a Glance

- **1:1—6:21.** the destinies of the wicked and the righteous
- **6:22—11:1.** in praise of wisdom
- **11:2—19:22.** wisdom's role in the Exodus

Quick Facts

Inspired Author: unknown, writing around 50 BC, making this the latest of all Old Testament books

Theme: the reward of the righteous, the praise of wisdom, the importance of trust in God

Of Note: The book is not found in every version of the Old Testament (see "The Case of the Missing Books," near Tob 1:16).

In Depth

The Jewish people living in Alexandria, Egypt, in the first century BC had long forgotten the difficult transition their ancestors had experienced in moving from Judea. In fact, they had come to feel so much at home in Alexandria that certain leaders began to fear that the Jewish faith and way of life might be lost (see "Diaspora Jews," near Esth 2:5). One of those leaders wrote the Book of Wisdom of Solomon to encourage the "displaced" Jews to remain faithful to their heritage. Although incorporating new ideas into traditional arguments, the author insists that true wisdom is, in fact, very old. Its course can be traced "from the beginning" (Wis 6:22).

The Book of Wisdom of Solomon grapples with another problem—good versus evil—in a refreshing way. The author is convinced that there will be a final judgment, in which good people will confront their oppressors "with great confidence," and their oppressors will "be shaken with dreadful fear" (5:1–2). What is more, the just will "live forever" (5:15), whereas the evil will "be left utterly dry and barren" (4:19). Like Second Maccabees, the Book of Wisdom of Solomon sees life after death as the answer to the troubling question, Why do innocent people suffer although God is good and just?

The Book of Wisdom of Solomon claims King Solomon as its honorary author, even though it was written long after his death. In this quiet way, it reminds the Jewish faithful that they must never forget their roots in their ancient faith, even though they feel at home in their new land. The book shows how people of faith take the best of their history and tradition to find new answers in new situations.

The **Wisdom of Solomon**

Wisdom

Exhortation to Uprightness

1 Love righteousness, you rulers of the earth,
 think of the Lord in goodness
and seek him with sincerity of heart;
² because he is found by those who do not put
  him to the test,
and manifests himself to those who do not
  distrust him.
³ For perverse thoughts separate people from God,
and when his power is tested, it exposes the
  foolish;
⁴ because wisdom will not enter a deceitful soul,
or dwell in a body enslaved to sin.
⁵ For a holy and disciplined spirit will flee from
  deceit,
and will leave foolish thoughts behind,
and will be ashamed at the approach of
  unrighteousness.

⁶ For wisdom is a kindly spirit,
but will not free blasphemers from the guilt of
  their words;
because God is witness of their inmost feelings,
and a true observer of their hearts, and a hearer
  of their tongues.
⁷ Because the spirit of the Lord has filled the world,
and that which holds all things together knows
  what is said,
⁸ therefore those who utter unrighteous things will
  not escape notice,
and justice, when it punishes, will not pass
  them by.

⁹ For inquiry will be made into the counsels of the
  ungodly,
and a report of their words will come to the Lord,
to convict them of their lawless deeds;
¹⁰ because a jealous ear hears all things,
and the sound of grumbling does not go
  unheard.
¹¹ Beware then of useless grumbling,
and keep your tongue from slander;
because no secret word is without result,ᵃ
and a lying mouth destroys the soul.
¹² Do not invite death by the error of your life,
or bring on destruction by the works of your
  hands;
¹³ because God did not make death,
and he does not delight in the death of the living.
¹⁴ For he created all things so that they might exist;
the generative forcesᵇ of the world are
  wholesome,
and there is no destructive poison in them,
and the dominionᶜ of Hades is not on earth.
¹⁵ For righteousness is immortal.

Life as the Ungodly See It

¹⁶ But the ungodly by their words and deeds
  summoned death;ᵈ
considering him a friend, they pined away
and made a covenant with him,
because they are fit to belong to his company.

---

a Or *will go unpunished*   b Or *the creatures*   c Or *palace*
d Gk *him*

2 For they reasoned unsoundly, saying to
     themselves,
"Short and sorrowful is our life,
and there is no remedy when a life comes to its
     end,
and no one has been known to return from
     Hades.
2 For we were born by mere chance,
and hereafter we shall be as though we had
     never been,
for the breath in our nostrils is smoke,
and reason is a spark kindled by the beating of
     our hearts;
3 when it is extinguished, the body will turn to
     ashes,
and the spirit will dissolve like empty air.
4 Our name will be forgotten in time,
and no one will remember our works;
our life will pass away like the traces of a cloud,
and be scattered like mist
that is chased by the rays of the sun
and overcome by its heat.
5 For our allotted time is the passing of a shadow,
and there is no return from our death,
because it is sealed up and no one turns back.

6 "Come, therefore, let us enjoy the good things
     that exist,
and make use of the creation to the full as in
     youth.
7 Let us take our fill of costly wine and perfumes,
and let no flower of spring pass us by.
8 Let us crown ourselves with rosebuds before
     they wither.
9 Let none of us fail to share in our revelry;
everywhere let us leave signs of enjoyment,
because this is our portion, and this our lot.
10 Let us oppress the righteous poor man;
let us not spare the widow
or regard the gray hairs of the aged.
11 But let our might be our law of right,
for what is weak proves itself to be useless.

12 "Let us lie in wait for the righteous man,
because he is inconvenient to us and opposes
     our actions;
he reproaches us for sins against the law,
and accuses us of sins against our training.
13 He professes to have knowledge of God,
and calls himself a child*a* of the Lord.
14 He became to us a reproof of our thoughts;
15 the very sight of him is a burden to us,
because his manner of life is unlike that of
     others,
and his ways are strange.
16 We are considered by him as something base,

Pray It!

God Knows Our Heart

*God, you know my heart (see Wis 1:6) even
better than I do. This could scare me, or
it could give me peace—the peace of knowing
that despite my weakness and sin, you still love
me. I choose to feel peace! And knowing that
you see into my heart and still love me, I choose
to do good. Give me the courage to do the right
thing. Help me never to say a word to
injure another person. Give me too the
wisdom of loving justice, so that my heart
might be a reflection of your
own. Amen.*

▶ **Wis 1:6–15**

and he avoids our ways as unclean;
he calls the last end of the righteous happy,
and boasts that God is his father.
17 Let us see if his words are true,
and let us test what will happen at the end of
     his life;
18 for if the righteous man is God's child, he will
     help him,
and will deliver him from the hand of his
     adversaries.
19 Let us test him with insult and torture,
so that we may find out how gentle he is,
and make trial of his forbearance.
20 Let us condemn him to a shameful death,
for, according to what he says, he will be
     protected."

Error of the Wicked

21 Thus they reasoned, but they were led astray,
for their wickedness blinded them,
22 and they did not know the secret purposes of
     God,
nor hoped for the wages of holiness,
nor discerned the prize for blameless souls;
23 for God created us for incorruption,
and made us in the image of his own eternity,*b*
24 but through the devil's envy death entered the
     world,
and those who belong to his company
     experience it.

---

a Or *servant*   *b* Other ancient authorities read *nature*

WIS

The Destiny of the Righteous

3 But the souls of the righteous are in the hand
    of God,
and no torment will ever touch them.
2 In the eyes of the foolish they seemed to have
    died,
and their departure was thought to be a disaster,
3 and their going from us to be their destruction;
but they are at peace.
4 For though in the sight of others they were
    punished,
their hope is full of immortality.
5 Having been disciplined a little, they will receive
    great good,
because God tested them and found them
    worthy of himself;
6 like gold in the furnace he tried them,
and like a sacrificial burnt offering he accepted
    them.
7 In the time of their visitation they will shine
    forth,
and will run like sparks through the stubble.
8 They will govern nations and rule over peoples,
and the Lord will reign over them forever.
9 Those who trust in him will understand truth,
and the faithful will abide with him in love,
because grace and mercy are upon his holy ones,
and he watches over his elect.*a*

> **"The souls of the righteous
> are in the hand of God,
> and no torment will ever
> touch them."**
> (Wis 3:1)

The Destiny of the Ungodly

10 But the ungodly will be punished as their
    reasoning deserves,
those who disregarded the righteous*b*
and rebelled against the Lord;
11 for those who despise wisdom and instruction
    are miserable.
Their hope is vain, their labors are unprofitable,
and their works are useless.
12 Their wives are foolish, and their children evil;
13 their offspring are accursed.

On Childlessness

For blessed is the barren woman who is
    undefiled,
who has not entered into a sinful union;
she will have fruit when God examines souls.
14 Blessed also is the eunuch whose hands have
    done no lawless deed,
and who has not devised wicked things against
    the Lord;
for special favor will be shown him for his
    faithfulness,
and a place of great delight in the temple of the
    Lord.
15 For the fruit of good labors is renowned,
and the root of understanding does not fail.
16 But children of adulterers will not come to
    maturity,
and the offspring of an unlawful union will
    perish.
17 Even if they live long they will be held of no
    account,
and finally their old age will be without honor.
18 If they die young, they will have no hope
and no consolation on the day of judgment.
19 For the end of an unrighteous generation is
    grievous.

4 Better than this is childlessness with virtue,
    for in the memory of virtue*c* is immortality,
because it is known both by God and by
    mortals.
2 When it is present, people imitate*d* it,
and they long for it when it has gone;
throughout all time it marches, crowned in
    triumph,
victor in the contest for prizes that are undefiled.
3 But the prolific brood of the ungodly will be of
    no use,
and none of their illegitimate seedlings will
    strike a deep root
or take a firm hold.
4 For even if they put forth boughs for a while,
standing insecurely they will be shaken by the
    wind,
and by the violence of the winds they will be
    uprooted.
5 The branches will be broken off before they
    come to maturity,
and their fruit will be useless,
not ripe enough to eat, and good for nothing.
6 For children born of unlawful unions
are witnesses of evil against their parents when
    God examines them.*e*
7 But the righteous, though they die early, will be
    at rest.

*a Text of this line uncertain; omitted by some ancient authorities.
Compare 4.15   b Or what is right   c Gk it   d Other ancient
authorities read honor   e Gk at their examination*

⁸ For old age is not honored for length of time,
or measured by number of years;
⁹ but understanding is gray hair for anyone,
and a blameless life is ripe old age.

¹⁰ There were some who pleased God and were
loved by him,
and while living among sinners were taken up.
¹¹ They were caught up so that evil might not
change their understanding
or guile deceive their souls.
¹² For the fascination of wickedness obscures what
is good,
and roving desire perverts the innocent mind.
¹³ Being perfected in a short time, they fulfilled
long years;
¹⁴ for their souls were pleasing to the Lord,
therefore he took them quickly from the midst
of wickedness.
¹⁵ Yet the peoples saw and did not understand,
or take such a thing to heart,
that God's grace and mercy are with his elect,
and that he watches over his holy ones.

The Triumph of the Righteous

¹⁶ The righteous who have died will condemn the
ungodly who are living,
and youth that is quickly perfected[a] will
condemn the prolonged old age of the
unrighteous.
¹⁷ For they will see the end of the wise,
and will not understand what the Lord purposed
for them,
and for what he kept them safe.
¹⁸ The unrighteous[b] will see, and will have
contempt for them,
but the Lord will laugh them to scorn.
After this they will become dishonored corpses,
and an outrage among the dead forever;
¹⁹ because he will dash them speechless to the
ground,
and shake them from the foundations;
they will be left utterly dry and barren,
and they will suffer anguish,
and the memory of them will perish.

The Final Judgment

²⁰ They will come with dread when their sins are
reckoned up,
and their lawless deeds will convict them to
their face.
5 Then the righteous will stand with great
confidence
in the presence of those who have oppressed
them
and those who make light of their labors.

² When the unrighteous[c] see them, they will be
shaken with dreadful fear,
and they will be amazed at the unexpected
salvation of the righteous.
³ They will speak to one another in repentance,
and in anguish of spirit they will groan, and say,
⁴ "These are persons whom we once held in
derision
and made a byword of reproach—fools that we
were!
We thought that their lives were madness
and that their end was without honor.
⁵ Why have they been numbered among the
children of God?
And why is their lot among the saints?
⁶ So it was we who strayed from the way of truth,
and the light of righteousness did not shine
on us,
and the sun did not rise upon us.
⁷ We took our fill of the paths of lawlessness and
destruction,
and we journeyed through trackless deserts,
but the way of the Lord we have not known.
⁸ What has our arrogance profited us?
And what good has our boasted wealth
brought us?

⁹ "All those things have vanished like a shadow,
and like a rumor that passes by;
¹⁰ like a ship that sails through the billowy water,
and when it has passed no trace can be found,
no track of its keel in the waves;
¹¹ or as, when a bird flies through the air,
no evidence of its passage is found;
the light air, lashed by the beat of its pinions
and pierced by the force of its rushing flight,
is traversed by the movement of its wings,
and afterward no sign of its coming is found
there;
¹² or as, when an arrow is shot at a target,
the air, thus divided, comes together at once,
so that no one knows its pathway.
¹³ So we also, as soon as we were born, ceased
to be,
and we had no sign of virtue to show,
but were consumed in our wickedness."
¹⁴ Because the hope of the ungodly is like
thistledown[d] carried by the wind,
and like a light frost[e] driven away by a storm;
it is dispersed like smoke before the wind,
and it passes like the remembrance of a guest
who stays but a day.

WIS

---

a Or ended b Gk They c Gk they d Other ancient
authorities read *dust* e Other ancient authorities read *spider's
web*

The Reward of the Righteous

15 But the righteous live forever,
and their reward is with the Lord;
the Most High takes care of them.

16 Therefore they will receive a glorious crown
and a beautiful diadem from the hand of the
Lord,
because with his right hand he will cover them,
and with his arm he will shield them.

17 The Lord[a] will take his zeal as his whole
armor,
and will arm all creation to repel[b] his enemies;

18 he will put on righteousness as a breastplate,
and wear impartial justice as a helmet;

19 he will take holiness as an invincible shield,

20 and sharpen stern wrath for a sword,
and creation will join with him to fight against
his frenzied foes.

21 Shafts of lightning will fly with true aim,
and will leap from the clouds to the target, as
from a well-drawn bow,

22 and hailstones full of wrath will be hurled as
from a catapult;
the water of the sea will rage against them,
and rivers will relentlessly overwhelm them;

23 a mighty wind will rise against them,
and like a tempest it will winnow them away.
Lawlessness will lay waste the whole earth,
and evildoing will overturn the thrones of rulers.

Kings Should Seek Wisdom

6 Listen therefore, O kings, and understand;
learn, O judges of the ends of the earth.

2 Give ear, you that rule over multitudes,
and boast of many nations.

3 For your dominion was given you from the
Lord,
and your sovereignty from the Most High;
he will search out your works and inquire into
your plans.

4 Because as servants of his kingdom you did not
rule rightly,
or keep the law,
or walk according to the purpose of God,

5 he will come upon you terribly and swiftly,
because severe judgment falls on those in high
places.

6 For the lowliest may be pardoned in mercy,
but the mighty will be mightily tested.

7 For the Lord of all will not stand in awe of
anyone,
or show deference to greatness;
because he himself made both small and great,
and he takes thought for all alike.

8 But a strict inquiry is in store for the mighty.

9 To you then, O monarchs, my words are
directed,
so that you may learn wisdom and not
transgress.

10 For they will be made holy who observe holy
things in holiness,
and those who have been taught them will find
a defense.

11 Therefore set your desire on my words;
long for them, and you will be instructed.

Description of Wisdom

12 Wisdom is radiant and unfading,
and she is easily discerned by those who love
her,
and is found by those who seek her.

13 She hastens to make herself known to those
who desire her.

14 One who rises early to seek her will have no
difficulty,
for she will be found sitting at the gate.

15 To fix one's thought on her is perfect
understanding,
and one who is vigilant on her account will
soon be free from care,

16 because she goes about seeking those worthy of
her,
and she graciously appears to them in their
paths,
and meets them in every thought.

17 The beginning of wisdom[c] is the most sincere
desire for instruction,
and concern for instruction is love of her,

18 and love of her is the keeping of her laws,
and giving heed to her laws is assurance of
immortality,

19 and immortality brings one near to God;

20 so the desire for wisdom leads to a kingdom.

21 Therefore if you delight in thrones and scepters,
O monarchs over the peoples,
honor wisdom, so that you may reign forever.

22 I will tell you what wisdom is and how she
came to be,
and I will hide no secrets from you,
but I will trace her course from the beginning of
creation,
and make knowledge of her clear,
and I will not pass by the truth;

23 nor will I travel in the company of sickly envy,
for envy[d] does not associate with wisdom.

24 The multitude of the wise is the salvation of the
world,

---

a Gk He   b Or punish   c Gk Her beginning   d Gk this

Cultural Connection

The Source of Wisdom

Solomon valued wisdom above riches, authority, health, and beauty (see Wis 7:7–10). Native American spirituality values wisdom in a similar way. The elders are seen as the people's connection to history and experience; they are a source of wisdom and sound advice. In fact, all of God's creation is seen as a potential source of wisdom. Notice how this is reflected in the following prayer from the Sioux tradition:

*Oh Great Spirit, whose voice I
    hear in the winds
And whose breath gives life
    to everyone,
Hear me.*

*I come to you as one of your
    many children;
I am weak . . . I am small
    . . . I need your wisdom
    and your strength.
Let me walk in beauty,
    and make my eyes ever
    behold the red and purple
    sunsets.
Make my hands respect the
    things you have made, and
    make my ears sharp so I
    may hear your voice.
Make me wise, so that I may
    understand what you have
    taught my people and
The lessons you have hidden
    in each leaf and each rock.
I ask for wisdom and
    strength,*

*Not to be superior to my
    brothers, but to be able to
    fight my greatest enemy,
    myself.
Make me ever ready to come
    before you with clean
    hands and a straight eye,
So as life fades away as a
    fading sunset,
My spirit may come to you
    without shame.*
                (Author unknown,
                  "Sioux Prayer")

▶ **Wis 7:7–14**

and a sensible king is the stability of any
    people.
25 Therefore be instructed by my words, and you
    will profit.

Solomon Like Other Mortals

7 I also am mortal, like everyone else,
    a descendant of the first-formed child of earth;
and in the womb of a mother I was molded into
    flesh,
2 within the period of ten months, compacted
    with blood,
from the seed of a man and the pleasure of
    marriage.
3 And when I was born, I began to breathe the
    common air,
and fell upon the kindred earth;
my first sound was a cry, as is true of all.
4 I was nursed with care in swaddling cloths.
5 For no king has had a different beginning of
    existence;
6 there is for all one entrance into life, and one
    way out.

Solomon's Respect for Wisdom

7 Therefore I prayed, and understanding was
    given me;
I called on God, and the spirit of wisdom came
    to me.

8 I preferred her to scepters and thrones,
    and I accounted wealth as nothing in
        comparison with her.
9 Neither did I liken to her any priceless gem,
    because all gold is but a little sand in her
        sight,
and silver will be accounted as clay before her.
10 I loved her more than health and beauty,
    and I chose to have her rather than light,
because her radiance never ceases.
11 All good things came to me along with her,
    and in her hands uncounted wealth.
12 I rejoiced in them all, because wisdom leads
        them;
but I did not know that she was their mother.
13 I learned without guile and I impart without
        grudging;
I do not hide her wealth,
14 for it is an unfailing treasure for mortals;
those who get it obtain friendship with God,
commended for the gifts that come from
    instruction.

Solomon Prays for Wisdom

15 May God grant me to speak with judgment,
    and to have thoughts worthy of what I have
        received;
for he is the guide even of wisdom
and the corrector of the wise.

16 For both we and our words are in his hand,
　　as are all understanding and skill in crafts.
17 For it is he who gave me unerring knowledge of
　　　　what exists,
　　to know the structure of the world and the
　　　　activity of the elements;
18 the beginning and end and middle of times,
　　the alternations of the solstices and the changes
　　　　of the seasons,
19 the cycles of the year and the constellations of
　　　　the stars,
20 the natures of animals and the tempers of wild
　　　　animals,
　　the powers of spirits*a* and the thoughts of
　　　　human beings,
　　the varieties of plants and the virtues of roots;
21 I learned both what is secret and what is
　　　　manifest,
22 for wisdom, the fashioner of all things, taught me.

How Do You Image God?

Old Testament writers sometimes used attributes of God, such as spirit, word, and justice, as titles for God. Wisdom is another of these titles. Each title gives us some insight into God's nature, although not one of them, or even all of them together, can give us the whole picture. The author of the Book of Wisdom of Solomon describes God's wisdom as a woman, which gives us insight into God's feminine dimension.

Read the qualities of wisdom given in Wisdom of Solomon 7:22—8:1. This passage summarizes the author's understanding of God's nature. It was probably familiar to New Testament authors. Aspects of it show up in the Letter to the Hebrews (1:1–4) and in the Gospel of John (1:1–14).

Explore your images of God. Choose an attribute of God that is significant for you. It might be love, faithfulness, truth, or some other quality. Write a poem, like the one in Wisdom of Solomon 8:2–8, that describes this quality as a person.

▶ **Wis 7:22—8:8**

The Nature of Wisdom

There is in her a spirit that is intelligent, holy,
　　unique, manifold, subtle,
mobile, clear, unpolluted,
distinct, invulnerable, loving the good, keen,
irresistible, 23beneficent, humane,
steadfast, sure, free from anxiety,
all-powerful, overseeing all,
and penetrating through all spirits
that are intelligent, pure, and altogether subtle.
24 For wisdom is more mobile than any motion;
　　because of her pureness she pervades and
　　　　penetrates all things.
25 For she is a breath of the power of God,
　　and a pure emanation of the glory of the
　　　　Almighty;
　　therefore nothing defiled gains entrance into
　　　　her.
26 For she is a reflection of eternal light,
　　a spotless mirror of the working of God,
　　and an image of his goodness.
27 Although she is but one, she can do all things,
　　and while remaining in herself, she renews all
　　　　things;
　　in every generation she passes into holy souls
　　and makes them friends of God, and prophets;
28 for God loves nothing so much as the person
　　　　who lives with wisdom.
29 She is more beautiful than the sun,
　　and excels every constellation of the stars.
　　Compared with the light she is found to be
　　　　superior,
30 for it is succeeded by the night,
　　but against wisdom evil does not prevail.
8 She reaches mightily from one end of the earth
　　　　to the other,
　　and she orders all things well.

Solomon's Love for Wisdom

2 I loved her and sought her from my youth;
　　I desired to take her for my bride,
　　and became enamored of her beauty.
3 She glorifies her noble birth by living with God,
　　and the Lord of all loves her.
4 For she is an initiate in the knowledge of God,
　　and an associate in his works.
5 If riches are a desirable possession in life,
　　what is richer than wisdom, the active cause of
　　　　all things?
6 And if understanding is effective,
　　who more than she is fashioner of what exists?
7 And if anyone loves righteousness,
　　her labors are virtues;

---

a Or *winds*

✝ Catholic Connection

The Cardinal Virtues

The Scriptures refer to seeking wisdom and learning from her. In return, wisdom teaches us virtues—the cardinal virtues of prudence, justice, fortitude, and temperance. Simply put: "Nothing in life is more profitable for mortals than these!" (Wis 8:7).

Prudence. Of the four virtues, prudence sets the course for all other virtues. Prudence enables one to look at a situation and determine the right thing to do and how to go about doing it. It points our conscience in the right direction and helps us to accurately apply moral principles to any situation.

Justice. Justice is ultimately about relationships, our relationship with God, with one another, and with the world around us. This virtue helps us recognize and acknowledge God's limitless power and love. It also helps us treat one another and all of God's creation with love and respect.

Fortitude. Doing the right thing can be scary; fortitude helps us overcome that fear. This virtue helps us withstand persecution, even to the point of sacrificing our own lives for what is right. It also strengthens us when we resolve to avoid temptation and sin.

Temperance. Self-control or temperance helps us keep our lives in proper balance. Our natural attraction to pleasures, whether physical or material, can overwhelm us and lead us astray. This virtue helps us master our desires and keep the attractions within proper limits.

Because virtues are attitudes or habits that guide our heart and mind, we must consciously work to develop them. So take time to learn about your faith, read the Scriptures, and purposely do things that build up these habits. However, if you fail, do not be discouraged; keep trying. And most important, seek God's grace in all that you do.

Try focusing on one cardinal virtue each week during your prayer time and daily activities. At the end of four weeks, look back and see how you have grown in virtue and closeness to God!

▶ **Wis 8:7**
Catechism, nos. 1803–1811

for she teaches self-control and prudence,
justice and courage;
nothing in life is more profitable for mortals
    than these.
8 And if anyone longs for wide experience,
she knows the things of old, and infers the
    things to come;
she understands turns of speech and the
    solutions of riddles;
she has foreknowledge of signs and wonders
and of the outcome of seasons and times.

Wisdom Indispensible to Rulers

9 Therefore I determined to take her to live
    with me,
knowing that she would give me good counsel
and encouragement in cares and grief.
10 Because of her I shall have glory among the
    multitudes
and honor in the presence of the elders, though
    I am young.
11 I shall be found keen in judgment,
and in the sight of rulers I shall be admired.
12 When I am silent they will wait for me,
and when I speak they will give heed;
if I speak at greater length,
they will put their hands on their mouths.
13 Because of her I shall have immortality,
and leave an everlasting remembrance to those
    who come after me.
14 I shall govern peoples,
and nations will be subject to me;
15 dread monarchs will be afraid of me when they
    hear of me;
among the people I shall show myself capable,
and courageous in war.
16 When I enter my house, I shall find rest with
    her;
for companionship with her has no bitterness,
and life with her has no pain, but gladness and
    joy.
17 When I considered these things inwardly,
and pondered in my heart
that in kinship with wisdom there is
    immortality,
18 and in friendship with her, pure delight,
and in the labors of her hands, unfailing
    wealth,
and in the experience of her company,
    understanding,
and renown in sharing her words,
I went about seeking how to get her for myself.
19 As a child I was naturally gifted,
and a good soul fell to my lot;
20 or rather, being good, I entered an undefiled
    body.

21 But I perceived that I would not possess wisdom
    unless God gave her to me—
and it was a mark of insight to know whose gift
    she was—
so I appealed to the Lord and implored him,
and with my whole heart I said:

Solomon's Prayer for Wisdom

9 "O God of my ancestors and Lord of mercy,
   who have made all things by your word,
2 and by your wisdom have formed humankind
to have dominion over the creatures you have
    made,
3 and rule the world in holiness and
    righteousness,
and pronounce judgment in uprightness of soul,
4 give me the wisdom that sits by your throne,
and do not reject me from among your servants.
5 For I am your servant[a] the son of your serving
    girl,
a man who is weak and short-lived,
with little understanding of judgment and laws;
6 for even one who is perfect among human beings
will be regarded as nothing without the wisdom
    that comes from you.
7 You have chosen me to be king of your people
and to be judge over your sons and daughters.
8 You have given command to build a temple on
    your holy mountain,
and an altar in the city of your habitation,
a copy of the holy tent that you prepared from
    the beginning.
9 With you is wisdom, she who knows your works
and was present when you made the world;
she understands what is pleasing in your sight
and what is right according to your
    commandments.
10 Send her forth from the holy heavens,
and from the throne of your glory send her,
that she may labor at my side,
and that I may learn what is pleasing to you.
11 For she knows and understands all things,
and she will guide me wisely in my actions
and guard me with her glory.
12 Then my works will be acceptable,
and I shall judge your people justly,
and shall be worthy of the throne[b] of my father.
13 For who can learn the counsel of God?
Or who can discern what the Lord wills?
14 For the reasoning of mortals is worthless,
and our designs are likely to fail;
15 for a perishable body weighs down the soul,
and this earthy tent burdens the thoughtful[c]
    mind.

---

a Gk slave   b Gk thrones   c Or anxious

WIS

Cultural Connection

Words from a Father to His Son

The following translation of a text originally written in Nahuatl is the wisdom of a native father in sixteenth-century Mexico. This spirit of wisdom still exists in many Mexican families.

My son, . . . my precious feather, you have come to life, been born, been blessed to come into the world in the land of our Lord. The One for whom we live forged your life, gave you shape. We, your mother and father, have watched over you; your aunts and uncles, all your family, have watched over you, have cried for you, have suffered for you that you might be born. (P. 49)

Love and serve others in holiness; respect and obey your mother and father, and do their hearts' desire. Your gift of service, obedience, and respect will be the recompense they deserve. (p. 53)

Push away from you all that is not good: that which is wrong, all the things that dishonor you. . . . Do no damage to the community, or the peace. Because if you do bad things, you will not come away unscathed: you must eventually suffer for such actions. (P. 79)

With these words, I encourage and strengthen you; through them, I console you. Throw away nothing I have told you, nothing you have heard. May all this be your inspiration, helping you always to remember the Lord, our God. (P. 86)

(Miguel Léon-Portilla and Librado Silva Galeana, *Huehuehtlahtolli*, as translated by Richard Wood)

16 We can hardly guess at what is on earth,
  and what is at hand we find with labor;
  but who has traced out what is in the heavens?
17 Who has learned your counsel,
  unless you have given wisdom
  and sent your holy spirit from on high?
18 And thus the paths of those on earth were set right,
  and people were taught what pleases you,
  and were saved by wisdom."

The Work of Wisdom from Adam to Moses

10 Wisdom[a] protected the first-formed father of the world, when he alone had been created;
she delivered him from his transgression,
2 and gave him strength to rule all things.
3 But when an unrighteous man departed from her in his anger,
he perished because in rage he killed his brother.
4 When the earth was flooded because of him,
  wisdom again saved it,
steering the righteous man by a paltry piece of wood.

5 Wisdom[a] also, when the nations in wicked agreement had been put to confusion,
recognized the righteous man and preserved him blameless before God,
and kept him strong in the face of his compassion for his child.

6 Wisdom[a] rescued a righteous man when the ungodly were perishing;
he escaped the fire that descended on the Five Cities.[b]
7 Evidence of their wickedness still remains:
a continually smoking wasteland,
plants bearing fruit that does not ripen,
and a pillar of salt standing as a monument to an unbelieving soul.
8 For because they passed wisdom by,
they not only were hindered from recognizing the good,
but also left for humankind a reminder of their folly,
so that their failures could never go unnoticed.
9 Wisdom rescued from troubles those who served her.
10 When a righteous man fled from his brother's wrath,
  she guided him on straight paths;
  she showed him the kingdom of God,
  and gave him knowledge of holy things;
  she prospered him in his labors,
  and increased the fruit of his toil.
11 When his oppressors were covetous,
  she stood by him and made him rich.
12 She protected him from his enemies,

a Gk She *b* Or on Pentapolis

WIS

Catholic Social Teaching

Workers' Rights

"**W**isdom rescued from troubles those who served her" (Wis 10:9). In this passage from the Wisdom of Solomon, workers are rewarded for their labor and taken care of during times of strife. If only this were true for all workers throughout the world! Unfortunately, the reality for many workers is that their labor, which is often performed under unjust conditions, comes with little reward. When unexpected difficulties arise in the workplace due to injury or illness, many workers, instead of being rescued from their troubles, simply lose their jobs, with no safety net to fall back upon.

Catholic social teaching reminds us that there are numerous basic rights that all workers deserve. Included among these are just wages, safe working conditions, reasonable hours, equal pay for equal work, adequate benefits, and the right to unionize. Workers should also be able to maintain their job status when medical or personal difficulties make continuing work temporarily impossible. They should not have to worry about losing their jobs because they get sick or injured, or become pregnant. And yet, this is the reality that many workers—particularly low-wage workers—face in our world, as some employers find it easier to replace workers than to show compassion toward them. In these cases, the dignity of the human person and the dignity of work are both diminished.

In turn, workers also have responsibilities to their employers—namely, to faithfully carry out the work they are entrusted with providing, while treating their employers with the same sort of dignity and respect that they want to be treated with.

- In what ways can you uphold the dignity of work by being a responsible worker?
- How can you advocate for those who are being treated unfairly or discriminated against in the workplace?

▶ **Wis 10:9–14**

The Dignity of Work and the Rights of Workers

---

and kept him safe from those who lay in wait
     for him;
in his arduous contest she gave him the victory,
so that he might learn that godliness is more
     powerful than anything else.

13 When a righteous man was sold, wisdom[a] did
     not desert him,
but delivered him from sin.
She descended with him into the dungeon,
14 and when he was in prison she did not leave him,
until she brought him the scepter of a kingdom
and authority over his masters.
Those who accused him she showed to be false,
and she gave him everlasting honor.

Wisdom Led the Israelites out of Egypt

15 A holy people and blameless race
wisdom delivered from a nation of oppressors.
16 She entered the soul of a servant of the Lord,
and withstood dread kings with wonders and
     signs.
17 She gave to holy people the reward of their
     labors;

she guided them along a marvelous way,
and became a shelter to them by day,
and a starry flame through the night.
18 She brought them over the Red Sea,
and led them through deep waters;
19 but she drowned their enemies,
and cast them up from the depth of the sea.
20 Therefore the righteous plundered the ungodly;
they sang hymns, O Lord, to your holy name,
and praised with one accord your defending
     hand;
21 for wisdom opened the mouths of those who
     were mute,
and made the tongues of infants speak clearly.

Wisdom Led the Israelites through the Desert

11 Wisdom[b] prospered their works by the hand
     of a holy prophet.
2 They journeyed through an uninhabited
     wilderness,
and pitched their tents in untrodden places.

---

a Gk *she*   *b* Gk *She*

W
I
S

³ They withstood their enemies and fought off
     their foes.
⁴ When they were thirsty, they called upon you,
     and water was given them out of flinty rock,
     and from hard stone a remedy for their thirst.
⁵ For through the very things by which their
          enemies were punished,
     they themselves received benefit in their need.
⁶ Instead of the fountain of an ever-flowing river,
     stirred up and defiled with blood
⁷ in rebuke for the decree to kill the infants,
     you gave them abundant water unexpectedly,
⁸ showing by their thirst at that time
     how you punished their enemies.
⁹ For when they were tried, though they were
          being disciplined in mercy,
     they learned how the ungodly were tormented
          when judged in wrath.
¹⁰ For you tested them as a parentᵃ does in warning,
     but you examined the ungodlyᵇ as a stern king
          does in condemnation.
¹¹ Whether absent or present, they were equally
          distressed,
¹² for a twofold grief possessed them,
     and a groaning at the memory of what had
          occurred.
¹³ For when they heard that through their own
          punishments
     the righteousᶜ had received benefit, they
          perceived it was the Lord's doing.
¹⁴ For though they had mockingly rejected him
          who long before had been cast out and
          exposed,
     at the end of the events they marveled at him,
     when they felt thirst in a different way from the
          righteous.

Punishment of the Wicked

¹⁵ In return for their foolish and wicked thoughts,
     which led them astray to worship irrational
          serpents and worthless animals,
     you sent upon them a multitude of irrational
          creatures to punish them,
¹⁶ so that they might learn that one is punished by
          the very things by which one sins.
¹⁷ For your all-powerful hand,
     which created the world out of formless matter,
     did not lack the means to send upon them a
          multitude of bears, or bold lions,
¹⁸ or newly-created unknown beasts full of rage,
     or such as breathe out fiery breath,
     or belch forth a thick pall of smoke,
     or flash terrible sparks from their eyes;
¹⁹ not only could the harm they did destroy
          people,ᵈ
     but the mere sight of them could kill by fright.

²⁰ Even apart from these, peopleᶜ could fall at a
          single breath
     when pursued by justice
     and scattered by the breath of your power.
     But you have arranged all things by measure and
          number and weight.

God Is Powerful and Merciful

²¹ For it is always in your power to show great
          strength,
     and who can withstand the might of your arm?
²² Because the whole world before you is like a
          speck that tips the scales,
     and like a drop of morning dew that falls on the
          ground.
²³ But you are merciful to all, for you can do all
          things,
     and you overlook people's sins, so that they may
          repent.

---

a Gk a father   b Gk those   c Gk they   d Gk them

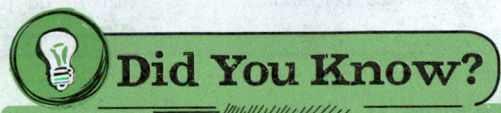

Did You Know?

The Exodus Pattern

The Exodus refers to all the events surrounding God's leading the formerly enslaved Israelites out of Egypt as recorded in the books of Exodus, Leviticus, Numbers, and Deuteronomy. Because the Exodus was an important experience in the Israelites' religious history, later biblical writers began to see in it a pattern in which God rescued the just and punished the wicked.

The author of the Wisdom of Solomon applies the Exodus pattern to explain how the righteous will be rewarded and sinners will be punished in the author's time. Throughout chapters 11–19, the writer refers to the journey through the desert, the Egyptians, the plagues, the manna in the desert, the pillars of fire, and the Red Sea. The author even takes the liberty of adding details that were not recorded in the original books! In doing so, the writer reminds the people of that time that the pattern of the Exodus is being repeated in their lives now, so they should not lose hope that God will be with them always.

▶ **Wis 11:1—19:22**

W
I
S

Cultural Connection — Words from a Mother to Her Daughter

The following translation of a text originally written in Nahuatl is the wisdom of a native mother in sixteenth-century Mexico. This spirit of wisdom still exists in many Mexican families.

Now, my daughter, my turtledove, little woman: you have life, you are born. You have entered the world, emerged from my womb, nourished at my breast. Our Lord forged your life, shaped you, made you within me. . . . Our Lord makes each of us earn our reputation, our honor, our warmth, our passion, our sweetness, our savor. . . .

Sing well, speak well, converse deeply, respond to all, pray deeply; words are not to be bought and sold. Never allow the world to make you stupid, or silly. . . . In this way, you will live among the people, and you will be worthy of all you need . . . you will please our Lord and be worthy of our Lord's kindness and mercy. (Pp. 91–92)

Be not a friend to liars, to thieves, to evil women, to meddlers, to those who are lazy. . . .

And if you have belongings or property, do not waste them; do not display them when you go out to the market. . . . Then you will leave what is yours to your children and grandchildren after you.

If you live in this way, as I have taught you, then in truth, you will live well among your own people, favored by all. (Pp. 95–97)

(Miguel Léon-Portilla and Librado Silva Galeana, *Huehuehtlahtolli*, as translated by Richard Wood)

24 For you love all things that exist,
   and detest none of the things that you have made,
   for you would not have made anything if you had hated it.
25 How would anything have endured if you had not willed it?
   Or how would anything not called forth by you have been preserved?
26 You spare all things, for they are yours, O Lord,
   you who love the living.

12 For your immortal spirit is in all things.
  2 Therefore you correct little by little those who trespass,
   and you remind and warn them of the things through which they sin,
   so that they may be freed from wickedness and put their trust in you, O Lord.

The Sins of the Canaanites

3 Those who lived long ago in your holy land
4 you hated for their detestable practices,
   their works of sorcery and unholy rites,
5 their merciless slaughter[a] of children,
   and their sacrificial feasting on human flesh and blood.
   These initiates from the midst of a heathen cult,[b]
6 these parents who murder helpless lives,
   you willed to destroy by the hands of our ancestors,

7 so that the land most precious of all to you might receive a worthy colony of the servants[c] of God.
8 But even these you spared, since they were but mortals,
   and sent wasps[d] as forerunners of your army to destroy them little by little,
9 though you were not unable to give the ungodly into the hands of the righteous in battle,
   or to destroy them at one blow by dread wild animals or your stern word.
10 But judging them little by little you gave them an opportunity to repent,
   though you were not unaware that their origin[e] was evil
   and their wickedness inborn,
   and that their way of thinking would never change.
11 For they were an accursed race from the beginning,
   and it was not through fear of anyone that you left them unpunished for their sins.

God Is Sovereign

12 For who will say, "What have you done?"
   or will resist your judgment?

---

a Gk *slaughterers*   b Meaning of Gk uncertain   c Or *children*
d Or *hornets*   e Or *nature*

WIS

Who will accuse you for the destruction of
    nations that you made?
Or who will come before you to plead as an
    advocate for the unrighteous?
13 For neither is there any god besides you, whose
    care is for all people,[a]
to whom you should prove that you have not
    judged unjustly;
14 nor can any king or monarch confront you
    about those whom you have punished.
15 You are righteous and you rule all things
    righteously,
deeming it alien to your power
to condemn anyone who does not deserve to be
    punished.
16 For your strength is the source of righteousness,
and your sovereignty over all causes you to spare
    all.
17 For you show your strength when people doubt
    the completeness of your power,
and you rebuke any insolence among those who
    know it.[b]
18 Although you are sovereign in strength, you
    judge with mildness,
and with great forbearance you govern us;
for you have power to act whenever you choose.

God's Lessons for Israel

19 Through such works you have taught your people
that the righteous must be kind,
and you have filled your children with good hope,
because you give repentance for sins.
20 For if you punished with such great care and
    indulgence[c]
the enemies of your servants[d] and those
    deserving of death,
granting them time and opportunity to give up
    their wickedness,
21 with what strictness you have judged your
    children,
to whose ancestors you gave oaths and
    covenants full of good promises!
22 So while chastening us you scourge our enemies
    ten thousand times more,
so that, when we judge, we may meditate upon
    your goodness,
and when we are judged, we may expect mercy.

The Punishment of the Egyptians

23 Therefore those who lived unrighteously, in a
    life of folly,
you tormented through their own abominations.
24 For they went far astray on the paths of error,
accepting as gods those animals that even their
    enemies[e] despised;
they were deceived like foolish infants.

25 Therefore, as though to children who cannot
    reason,
you sent your judgment to mock them.
26 But those who have not heeded the warning of
    mild rebukes
will experience the deserved judgment of God.
27 For when in their suffering they became incensed
at those creatures that they had thought to be
    gods, being punished by means of them,
they saw and recognized as the true God the one
    whom they had before refused to know.
Therefore the utmost condemnation came upon
    them.

The Foolishness of Nature Worship

13 For all people who were ignorant of God
    were foolish by nature;
and they were unable from the good things that
    are seen to know the one who exists,
nor did they recognize the artisan while paying
    heed to his works;
2 but they supposed that either fire or wind or
    swift air,
or the circle of the stars, or turbulent water,
or the luminaries of heaven were the gods that
    rule the world.
3 If through delight in the beauty of these things
    people assumed them to be gods,
let them know how much better than these is
    their Lord,
for the author of beauty created them.
4 And if people[e] were amazed at their power and
    working,
let them perceive from them
how much more powerful is the one who
    formed them.
5 For from the greatness and beauty of created
    things
comes a corresponding perception of their
    Creator.
6 Yet these people are little to be blamed,
for perhaps they go astray
while seeking God and desiring to find him.
7 For while they live among his works, they keep
    searching,
and they trust in what they see, because the
    things that are seen are beautiful.
8 Yet again, not even they are to be excused;
9 for if they had the power to know so much
that they could investigate the world,
how did they fail to find sooner the Lord of
    these things?

---

a Or *all things*   *b* Meaning of Gk uncertain   *c* Other ancient
authorities lack *and indulgence*; others read *and entreaty*
d Or *children*   *e* Gk *they*

The Foolishness of Idolatry

10 But miserable, with their hopes set on dead
things, are those
who give the name "gods" to the works of
human hands,
gold and silver fashioned with skill,
and likenesses of animals,
or a useless stone, the work of an ancient hand.

11 A skilled woodcutter may saw down a tree easy
to handle
and skillfully strip off all its bark,
and then with pleasing workmanship
make a useful vessel that serves life's needs,

12 and burn the cast-off pieces of his work
to prepare his food, and eat his fill.

13 But a cast-off piece from among them, useful for
nothing,
a stick crooked and full of knots,
he takes and carves with care in his leisure,
and shapes it with skill gained in idleness;*a*
he forms it in the likeness of a human being,

14 or makes it like some worthless animal,
giving it a coat of red paint and coloring its
surface red
and covering every blemish in it with paint;

15 then he makes a suitable niche for it,

God Is My Copilot

Have you ever seen the bumper sticker that says, "God is my copilot"? This seems to be the message in Wisdom of Solomon 14:3. The author seems to be saying, "Don't put your trust in a little idol made of wood; it is the one true God who helps you, who guides you, who sets your course!"

Your life has many challenges. One way to face those challenges is to take God along on the journey. When you feel like you can't go on, call on God. When you fail and stumble, call on God. When you succeed, call on God and celebrate. God is here to be your copilot, to help you navigate through life—so call on God, talk to God. God will answer!

▶ **Wis 14:1–7**

and sets it in the wall, and fastens it there with
iron.

16 He takes thought for it, so that it may not fall,
because he knows that it cannot help itself,
for it is only an image and has need of help.

17 When he prays about possessions and his
marriage and children,
he is not ashamed to address a lifeless thing.

18 For health he appeals to a thing that is weak;
for life he prays to a thing that is dead;
for aid he entreats a thing that is utterly
inexperienced;
for a prosperous journey, a thing that cannot
take a step;

19 for money-making and work and success with
his hands
he asks strength of a thing whose hands have no
strength.

Folly of a Navigator Praying to an Idol

14 Again, one preparing to sail and about to
voyage over raging waves
calls upon a piece of wood more fragile than the
ship that carries him.

2 For it was desire for gain that planned that
vessel,
and wisdom was the artisan who built it;

3 but it is your providence, O Father, that steers its
course,
because you have given it a path in the sea,
and a safe way through the waves,

4 showing that you can save from every danger,
so that even a person who lacks skill may put to
sea.

5 It is your will that works of your wisdom should
not be without effect;
therefore people trust their lives even to the
smallest piece of wood,
and passing through the billows on a raft they
come safely to land.

6 For even in the beginning, when arrogant giants
were perishing,
the hope of the world took refuge on a raft,
and guided by your hand left to the world the
seed of a new generation.

7 For blessed is the wood by which righteousness
comes.

8 But the idol made with hands is accursed, and
so is the one who made it—
he for having made it, and the perishable thing
because it was named a god.

9 For equally hateful to God are the ungodly and
their ungodliness;

---

a Other ancient authorities read with intelligent skill

10 for what was done will be punished together
  with the one who did it.
11 Therefore there will be a visitation also upon the
  heathen idols,
  because, though part of what God created, they
    became an abomination,
  snares for human souls
  and a trap for the feet of the foolish.

The Origin and Evils of Idolatry

12 For the idea of making idols was the beginning
    of fornication,
  and the invention of them was the corruption of
    life;
13 for they did not exist from the beginning,
  nor will they last forever.
14 For through human vanity they entered the
    world,
  and therefore their speedy end has been
    planned.

15 For a father, consumed with grief at an untimely
    bereavement,
  made an image of his child, who had been
    suddenly taken from him;
  he now honored as a god what was once a dead
    human being,
  and handed on to his dependents secret rites
    and initiations.
16 Then the ungodly custom, grown strong with
    time, was kept as a law,
  and at the command of monarchs carved images
    were worshiped.
17 When people could not honor monarchs[a] in
    their presence, since they lived at a
    distance,
  they imagined their appearance far away,
  and made a visible image of the king whom
    they honored,
  so that by their zeal they might flatter the absent
    one as though present.
18 Then the ambition of the artisan impelled
  even those who did not know the king to
    intensify their worship.
19 For he, perhaps wishing to please his ruler,
  skillfully forced the likeness to take more
    beautiful form,
20 and the multitude, attracted by the charm of his
    work,
  now regarded as an object of worship the one
    whom shortly before they had honored
    as a human being.
21 And this became a hidden trap for humankind,
  because people, in bondage to misfortune or to
    royal authority,

bestowed on objects of stone or wood the name
    that ought not to be shared.

22 Then it was not enough for them to err about
    the knowledge of God,
  but though living in great strife due to
    ignorance,
  they call such great evils peace.
23 For whether they kill children in their
    initiations, or celebrate secret mysteries,
  or hold frenzied revels with strange customs,
24 they no longer keep either their lives or their
    marriages pure,
  but they either treacherously kill one another, or
    grieve one another by adultery,
25 and all is a raging riot of blood and
    murder, theft and deceit, corruption,
    faithlessness, tumult, perjury,
26 confusion over what is good, forgetfulness of
    favors,
  defiling of souls, sexual perversion,
  disorder in marriages, adultery, and debauchery.
27 For the worship of idols not to be named
  is the beginning and cause and end of every
    evil.
28 For their worshipers[b] either rave in exultation,
  or prophesy lies, or live unrighteously, or readily
    commit perjury;
29 for because they trust in lifeless idols
  they swear wicked oaths and expect to suffer no
    harm.
30 But just penalties will overtake them on two
    counts:
  because they thought wrongly about God in
    devoting themselves to idols,
  and because in deceit they swore unrighteously
    through contempt for holiness.
31 For it is not the power of the things by which
    people swear,[c]
  but the just penalty for those who sin,
  that always pursues the transgression of the
    unrighteous.

Benefits of Worshiping the True God

15 But you, our God, are kind and true,
  patient, and ruling all things[d] in mercy.
2 For even if we sin we are yours, knowing your
    power;
  but we will not sin, because we know that you
    acknowledge us as yours.
3 For to know you is complete righteousness,
  and to know your power is the root of
    immortality.

---

a Gk them   b Gk they   c Or of the oaths people swear
d Or ruling the universe

WIS

4 For neither has the evil intent of human art
    misled us,
nor the fruitless toil of painters,
a figure stained with varied colors,
5 whose appearance arouses yearning in fools,
so that they desire[a] the lifeless form of a dead
    image.
6 Lovers of evil things and fit for such objects of
    hope[b]
are those who either make or desire or worship
    them.

The Foolishness of Worshiping Clay Idols

7 A potter kneads the soft earth
and laboriously molds each vessel for our
    service,
fashioning out of the same clay
both the vessels that serve clean uses
and those for contrary uses, making all alike;
but which shall be the use of each of them
the worker in clay decides.
8 With misspent toil, these workers form a futile
    god from the same clay—
these mortals who were made of earth a short
    time before
and after a little while go to the earth from
    which all mortals are taken,
when the time comes to return the souls that
    were borrowed.
9 But the workers are not concerned that mortals
    are destined to die
or that their life is brief,
but they compete with workers in gold and
    silver,
and imitate workers in copper;
and they count it a glorious thing to mold
    counterfeit gods.
10 Their heart is ashes, their hope is cheaper than
    dirt,
and their lives are of less worth than clay,
11 because they failed to know the one who
    formed them
and inspired them with active souls
and breathed a living spirit into them.
12 But they considered our existence an idle game,
and life a festival held for profit,
for they say one must get money however one
    can, even by base means.
13 For these persons, more than all others, know
    that they sin
when they make from earthy matter fragile
    vessels and carved images.

14 But most foolish, and more miserable than an
    infant,
are all the enemies who oppressed your people.

15 For they thought that all their heathen idols
    were gods,
though these have neither the use of their eyes
    to see with,
nor nostrils with which to draw breath,
nor ears with which to hear,
nor fingers to feel with,
and their feet are of no use for walking.
16 For a human being made them,
and one whose spirit is borrowed formed them;
for none can form gods that are like themselves.
17 People are mortal, and what they make with
    lawless hands is dead;
for they are better than the objects they worship,
since[c] they have life, but the idols[d] never had.

Serpents in the Desert

18 Moreover, they worship even the most hateful
    animals,
which are worse than all others when judged by
    their lack of intelligence;
19 and even as animals they are not so beautiful in
    appearance that one would desire them,
but they have escaped both the praise of God
    and his blessing.

16 Therefore those people[e] were deservedly
    punished through such creatures,
and were tormented by a multitude of animals.
2 Instead of this punishment you showed
    kindness to your people,
and you prepared quails to eat,
a delicacy to satisfy the desire of appetite;
3 in order that those people, when they desired
    food,
might lose the least remnant of appetite[f]
because of the odious creatures sent to them,
while your people,[e] after suffering want a short
    time,
might partake of delicacies.
4 For it was necessary that upon those oppressors
    inescapable want should come,
while to these others it was merely shown how
    their enemies were being tormented.

5 For when the terrible rage of wild animals came
    upon your people[g]
and they were being destroyed by the bites of
    writhing serpents,
your wrath did not continue to the end;
6 they were troubled for a little while as a warning,
and received a symbol of deliverance to remind
    them of your law's command.

---

a Gk and he desires   b Gk such hopes   c Other ancient
authorities read of which   d Gk but they   e Gk they
f Gk loathed the necessary appetite   g Gk them

7 For the one who turned toward it was saved, not
        by the thing that was beheld,
    but by you, the Savior of all.
8 And by this also you convinced our enemies
    that it is you who deliver from every evil.
9 For they were killed by the bites of locusts and
        flies,
    and no healing was found for them,
    because they deserved to be punished by such
        things.
10 But your children were not conquered even by
        the fangs of venomous serpents,
    for your mercy came to their help and healed
        them.
11 To remind them of your oracles they were
        bitten,
    and then were quickly delivered,
    so that they would not fall into deep
        forgetfulness
    and become unresponsive[a] to your kindness.
12 For neither herb nor poultice cured them,
    but it was your word, O Lord, that heals all
        people.
13 For you have power over life and death;
    you lead mortals down to the gates of Hades
        and back again.
14 A person in wickedness kills another,
    but cannot bring back the departed spirit,
    or set free the imprisoned soul.

Disastrous Storms Strike Egypt

15 To escape from your hand is impossible;
16 for the ungodly, refusing to know you,
    were flogged by the strength of your arm,
    pursued by unusual rains and hail and relentless
        storms,
    and utterly consumed by fire.
17 For—most incredible of all—in water, which
        quenches all things,
    the fire had still greater effect,
    for the universe defends the righteous.
18 At one time the flame was restrained,
    so that it might not consume the creatures sent
        against the ungodly,
    but that seeing this they might know
    that they were being pursued by the judgment of
        God;
19 and at another time even in the midst of water it
        burned more intensely than fire,
    to destroy the crops of the unrighteous land.

The Israelites Receive Manna

20 Instead of these things you gave your people
        food of angels,
    and without their toil you supplied them from
        heaven with bread ready to eat,

Live It!

Wisdom Speaks

My name is Wisdom. In Greek, I am called Sophia. The Bible speaks of me as an aspect, or image, of God. I am sought after by many. I reveal myself to few. I appear many times in the Scriptures, yet I am elusive. What is it about me that is so attractive, so appealing? Solomon prayed for understanding, and I came to him. Indeed, wisdom is often associated with his name.

Those who seek me must desire deep in their heart to know me. That desire is the first step to finding me. The next is patience. Nothing of true and lasting importance comes quickly. I am not "fast food." In fact, you must experience a deep hunger before you can taste me. Quiet time is essential. You must be willing to simply be present, with no agenda. Imagine a "radiant and unfading" flame (Wis 6:12). Let that be your focus.

Soon, I will come to you. I will seek you out. I will meet you in your thoughts, and we will become friends. We will dance together, you and I. You will be changed, transformed. You will grow deeper, quieter, and peace will begin to fill your soul.

My name is Wisdom. I want to be your friend. I wait for you.

providing every pleasure and suited to every
        taste.
21 For your sustenance manifested your sweetness
        toward your children;
    and the bread, ministering[b] to the desire of the
        one who took it,
    was changed to suit everyone's liking.
22 Snow and ice withstood fire without melting,
    so that they might know that the crops of their
        enemies
    were being destroyed by the fire that blazed in
        the hail
    and flashed in the showers of rain;

---

a Meaning of Gk uncertain   b Gk and it, ministering

WIS

23 whereas the fire,[a] in order that the righteous
might be fed,
even forgot its native power.

24 For creation, serving you who made it,
exerts itself to punish the unrighteous,
and in kindness relaxes on behalf of those who
trust in you.

25 Therefore at that time also, changed into all
forms,
it served your all-nourishing bounty,
according to the desire of those who had need,[b]

26 so that your children, whom you loved, O Lord,
might learn
that it is not the production of crops that feeds
humankind
but that your word sustains those who trust in
you.

27 For what was not destroyed by fire
was melted when simply warmed by a fleeting
ray of the sun,

28 to make it known that one must rise before the
sun to give you thanks,
and must pray to you at the dawning of the
light;

29 for the hope of an ungrateful person will melt
like wintry frost,
and flow away like waste water.

Terror Strikes the Egyptians at Night

17 Great are your judgments and hard to
describe;
therefore uninstructed souls have gone astray.

2 For when lawless people supposed that they
held the holy nation in their power,
they themselves lay as captives of darkness and
prisoners of long night,
shut in under their roofs, exiles from eternal
providence.

3 For thinking that in their secret sins they were
unobserved
behind a dark curtain of forgetfulness,
they were scattered, terribly[c] alarmed,
and appalled by specters.

4 For not even the inner chamber that held them
protected them from fear,
but terrifying sounds rang out around them,
and dismal phantoms with gloomy faces
appeared.

5 And no power of fire was able to give light,
nor did the brilliant flames of the stars
avail to illumine that hateful night.

6 Nothing was shining through to them
except a dreadful, self-kindled fire,
and in terror they deemed the things that
they saw

to be worse than that unseen appearance.

7 The delusions of their magic art lay humbled,
and their boasted wisdom was scornfully
rebuked.

8 For those who promised to drive off the fears
and disorders of a sick soul
were sick themselves with ridiculous fear.

9 For even if nothing disturbing frightened them,
yet, scared by the passing of wild animals and
the hissing of snakes

10 they perished in trembling fear,
refusing to look even at the air, though it
nowhere could be avoided.

11 For wickedness is a cowardly thing, condemned
by its own testimony;[d]
distressed by conscience, it has always
exaggerated[e] the difficulties.

12 For fear is nothing but a giving up of the helps
that come from reason;

13 and hope, defeated by this inward weakness,
prefers ignorance of what causes the torment.

14 But throughout the night, which was really
powerless
and which came upon them from the recesses of
powerless Hades,
they all slept the same sleep,

15 and now were driven by monstrous specters,
and now were paralyzed by their souls' surrender;
for sudden and unexpected fear overwhelmed
them.

16 And whoever was there fell down,
and thus was kept shut up in a prison not made
of iron;

17 for whether they were farmers or shepherds
or workers who toiled in the wilderness,
they were seized, and endured the inescapable
fate;
for with one chain of darkness they all were
bound.

18 Whether there came a whistling wind,
or a melodious sound of birds in wide-spreading
branches,
or the rhythm of violently rushing water,

19 or the harsh crash of rocks hurled down,
or the unseen running of leaping animals,
or the sound of the most savage roaring beasts,
or an echo thrown back from a hollow of the
mountains,
it paralyzed them with terror.

20 For the whole world was illumined with
brilliant light,
and went about its work unhindered,

---

a Gk *this*   b Or *who made supplication*   c Other ancient
authorities read *unobserved, they were darkened behind a dark
curtain of forgetfulness, terribly*   d Meaning of Gk uncertain
e Other ancient authorities read *anticipated*

21 while over those people alone heavy night was
spread,
an image of the darkness that was destined to
receive them;
but still heavier than darkness were they to
themselves.

Light Shines on the Israelites

18 But for your holy ones there was very great
light.
Their enemies[a] heard their voices but did not see
their forms,
and counted them happy for not having
suffered,
2 and were thankful that your holy ones,[b] though
previously wronged, were doing them no
injury;
and they begged their pardon for having been at
variance with them.[b]
3 Therefore you provided a flaming pillar of fire
as a guide for your people's[c] unknown journey,
and a harmless sun for their glorious wandering.
4 For their enemies[d] deserved to be deprived of
light and imprisoned in darkness,
those who had kept your children imprisoned,
through whom the imperishable light of the law
was to be given to the world.

The Death of the Egyptian Firstborn

5 When they had resolved to kill the infants of
your holy ones,
and one child had been abandoned and rescued,
you in punishment took away a multitude of
their children;
and you destroyed them all together by a mighty
flood.
6 That night was made known beforehand to our
ancestors,
so that they might rejoice in sure knowledge of
the oaths in which they trusted.
7 The deliverance of the righteous and the
destruction of their enemies
were expected by your people.
8 For by the same means by which you punished
our enemies
you called us to yourself and glorified us.
9 For in secret the holy children of good people
offered sacrifices,
and with one accord agreed to the divine law,
so that the saints would share alike the same
things,
both blessings and dangers;
and already they were singing the praises of the
ancestors.[e]
10 But the discordant cry of their enemies echoed
back,

and their piteous lament for their children was
spread abroad.
11 The slave was punished with the same penalty as
the master,
and the commoner suffered the same loss as the
king;
12 and they all together, by the one form[f] of death,
had corpses too many to count.
For the living were not sufficient even to bury
them,
since in one instant their most valued children
had been destroyed.
13 For though they had disbelieved everything
because of their magic arts,
yet, when their firstborn were destroyed, they
acknowledged your people to be God's
child.
14 For while gentle silence enveloped all things,
and night in its swift course was now half gone,
15 your all-powerful word leaped from heaven,
from the royal throne,
into the midst of the land that was doomed,
a stern warrior
16 carrying the sharp sword of your authentic
command,
and stood and filled all things with death,
and touched heaven while standing on the
earth.
17 Then at once apparitions in dreadful dreams
greatly troubled them,
and unexpected fears assailed them;
18 and one here and another there, hurled down
half dead,
made known why they were dying;
19 for the dreams that disturbed them forewarned
them of this,
so that they might not perish without knowing
why they suffered.

Threat of Annihilation in the Desert

20 The experience of death touched also the
righteous,
and a plague came upon the multitude in the
desert,
but the wrath did not long continue.
21 For a blameless man was quick to act as their
champion;
he brought forward the shield of his ministry,
prayer and propitiation by incense;
he withstood the anger and put an end to the
disaster,
showing that he was your servant.

W
I
S

---

a Gk *They*   b Meaning of Gk uncertain   c Gk *their*
d Gk *those persons*   e Other ancient authorities read *dangers, the
ancestors already leading the songs of praise*   f Gk *name*

22 He conquered the wrath[a] not by strength of body,
   not by force of arms,
   but by his word he subdued the avenger,
   appealing to the oaths and covenants given to
      our ancestors.
23 For when the dead had already fallen on one
      another in heaps,
   he intervened and held back the wrath,
   and cut off its way to the living.
24 For on his long robe the whole world was
      depicted,
   and the glories of the ancestors were engraved
      on the four rows of stones,
   and your majesty was on the diadem upon his
      head.

Supernatural Resources

The Book of Wisdom of Solomon ends with an inspiring statement of faith: "For in everything, O Lord, you have exalted and glorified your people, / and you have not neglected to help them at all times and in all places" (19:22).

Could you say these words? Do you have the kind of faith that is able to see the hand of God at work through everything that happens?

So many times, we pray for God's help, especially if we are struggling or someone we love is suffering. Later, when that particular crisis is over, we quickly forget how God helped us through. The Bible's message is that God is at work through all the times in our lives, even in ways we do not realize at the moment. The Church's word for God's help is *grace*. Unlike most of our natural resources, the supernatural resource of grace is never in danger of being used up. In fact, the more we use it, the more of it there is!

Find a way of keeping track of how God has helped you through life. Perhaps you can maintain a journal of the difficult times you've made it through and the people who have supported you. You might be surprised by this record of how God's grace has been active!

▶ Wis 19:22

25 To these the destroyer yielded, these he[b] feared;
   for merely to test the wrath was enough.

The Red Sea

19 But the ungodly were assailed to the end by
      pitiless anger,
   for God[c] knew in advance even their future
      actions:
2 how, though they themselves had permitted[d]
      your people to depart
   and hastily sent them out,
   they would change their minds and pursue
      them.
3 For while they were still engaged in mourning,
   and were lamenting at the graves of their dead,
   they reached another foolish decision,
   and pursued as fugitives those whom they had
      begged and compelled to leave.
4 For the fate they deserved drew them on to this
      end,
   and made them forget what had happened,
   in order that they might fill up the punishment
      that their torments still lacked,
5 and that your people might experience[e] an
      incredible journey,
   but they themselves might meet a strange death.

God Guides and Protects His People

6 For the whole creation in its nature was
      fashioned anew,
   complying with your commands,
   so that your children[f] might be kept unharmed.
7 The cloud was seen overshadowing the camp,
   and dry land emerging where water had stood
      before,
   an unhindered way out of the Red Sea,
   and a grassy plain out of the raging waves,
8 where those protected by your hand passed
      through as one nation,
   after gazing on marvelous wonders.
9 For they ranged like horses,
   and leaped like lambs,
   praising you, O Lord, who delivered them.
10 For they still recalled the events of their sojourn,
   how instead of producing animals the earth
      brought forth gnats,
   and instead of fish the river spewed out vast
      numbers of frogs.
11 Afterward they saw also a new kind[g] of birds,
   when desire led them to ask for luxurious food;
12 for, to give them relief, quails came up from the
      sea.

a Cn: Gk *multitude*   b Other ancient authorities read *they*
c Gk *he*   d Other ancient authorities read *had changed their minds to permit*   e Other ancient authorities read *accomplish*
f Or *servants*   g Or *production*

The Punishment of the Egyptians

13 The punishments did not come upon the
  sinners
without prior signs in the violence of
  thunder,
for they justly suffered because of their wicked
  acts;
for they practiced a more bitter hatred of
  strangers.
14 Others had refused to receive strangers when
  they came to them,
but these made slaves of guests who were their
  benefactors.
15 And not only so—but, while punishment of
  some sort will come upon the former
for having received strangers with hostility,
16 the latter, having first received them with festal
  celebrations,
afterward afflicted with terrible sufferings
those who had already shared the same
  rights.
17 They were stricken also with loss of sight—
just as were those at the door of the righteous
  man—
when, surrounded by yawning darkness,
all of them tried to find the way through their
  own doors.

A New Harmony in Nature

18 For the elements changed[a] places with one
  another,
as on a harp the notes vary the nature of the
  rhythm,
while each note remains the same.[b]
This may be clearly inferred from the sight of
  what took place.
19 For land animals were transformed into water
  creatures,
and creatures that swim moved over to the land.
20 Fire even in water retained its normal power,
and water forgot its fire-quenching nature.
21 Flames, on the contrary, failed to consume
the flesh of perishable creatures that walked
  among them,
nor did they melt[c] the crystalline, quick-melting
  kind of heavenly food.

Conclusion

22 For in everything, O Lord, you have exalted and
  glorified your people,
and you have not neglected to help them at all
  times and in all places.

---

a Gk *changing*   b Meaning of Gk uncertain   c Cn: Gk *nor
could be melted*

Imagine that many years ago, your grandfather—a learned and wise man—wrote a book summarizing all his wisdom. Recently, you read the book and discovered it has answers to many of the problems you and your friends are struggling with. But the book is written in your grandfather's native language, which your friends don't understand. So, what do you do? You translate the book! This is exactly what the grandson of Jesus Ben Sira did. He translated into Greek the book his grandfather had written in Hebrew.

The Book of Sirach (Ecclesiasticus)

In Depth

The Book of Sirach is unique in the Old Testament because it clearly identifies its author: Jesus Ben Sira, a wise teacher who lived early in the second century BC. Living in Jerusalem during a time of great change, he saw many of his people—especially those who were rich—deserting traditional Jewish beliefs in favor of more fashionable ideas coming from Greece. A book underlining the superiority of Jewish wisdom was needed, Ben Sira thought. So, he collected his class notes into a single volume and offered it to those who desired to learn the ways of living well. Though full of many different kinds of writing—sayings, hymns, prayers, and lists—the book is unified in its overall conviction: "All wisdom is from the Lord, / and with him it remains forever" (1:1).

◉ At a Glance

- Chapters 1–43. praise of wisdom and general moral teaching
- 44:1—50:24. praise of the heroes of Israel
- 50:25—51:30. a concluding prayer and poem

★ Quick Facts

Inspired Author: Jesus Ben Sira, writing around 180 BC
Theme: the superiority of Jewish wisdom over Greek wisdom
Of Note: Sirach is not found in every version of the Old Testament (see "The Case of the Missing Books," near Tob 1:16).

The Book of Sirach holds fast to the long-standing belief that in this life, good is rewarded and evil is punished. Unlike Second Maccabees and Daniel—also written in the second century BC—Sirach never mentions the possibility of life after death. But like other wisdom books, it celebrates the glories of wisdom (see chapter 1) and recalls the heroes of Jewish faith (see chapters 44–50). Its view of women is harsher than that of most of the Old Testament, though. In interpreting Sirach, you must take special care not to conclude that women are the source of most of men's troubles!

Sometimes called Ecclesiasticus or Ben Sira (which is the short form for "son of Sirach"), the Book of Sirach was well known among the ancient Jews. It was popular in the early Christian church as well. Its influence can be found in the New Testament, especially in the Letter of James. Long after his death, Ben Sira continues to share the wisdom of the past and offers us trustworthy guidance for the present.

Sirach

Chapter 3

THE PROLOGUE

Many great teachings have been given to us through the Law and the Prophets and the others[a] that followed them, and for these we should praise Israel for instruction and wisdom. Now, those who read the scriptures must not only themselves understand them, but must also as lovers of learning be able through the spoken and written word to help the outsiders. So my grandfather Jesus, who had devoted himself especially to the reading of the Law and the Prophets and the other books of our ancestors, and had acquired considerable proficiency in them, was himself also led to write something pertaining to instruction and wisdom, so that by becoming familiar also with his book[b] those who love learning might make even greater progress in living according to the law.

You are invited therefore to read it with good-will and attention, and to be indulgent in cases where, despite our diligent labor in translating, we may seem to have rendered some phrases imperfectly. For what was originally expressed in Hebrew does not have exactly the same sense when translated into another language. Not only this book, but even the Law itself, the Prophecies, and the rest of the books differ not a little when read in the original.

When I came to Egypt in the thirty-eighth year of the reign of Euergetes and stayed for some time, I found opportunity for no little instruction.[c] It seemed highly necessary that I should myself devote some diligence and labor to the translation of this book. During that time I have applied my skill day and night to complete and publish the book for those living abroad who wished to gain learning and are disposed to live according to the law.

In Praise of Wisdom

1 All wisdom is from the Lord,
    and with him it remains forever.
2 The sand of the sea, the drops of rain,
    and the days of eternity—who can count
      them?
3 The height of heaven, the breadth of the earth,
    the abyss, and wisdom[d]—who can search them
      out?
4 Wisdom was created before all other things,
    and prudent understanding from eternity.[e]
6 The root of wisdom—to whom has it been
      revealed?
    Her subtleties—who knows them?[f]
8 There is but one who is wise, greatly to be
      feared,
    seated upon his throne—the Lord.
9 It is he who created her,
    he saw her and took her measure;
    he poured her out upon all his works,

---

a Or other books   b Gk with these things   c Other ancient authorities read I found a copy affording no little instruction   d Other ancient authorities read the depth of the abyss   e Other ancient authorities add as verse 5, The source of wisdom is God's word in the highest heaven, and her ways are the eternal commandments.   f Other ancient authorities add as verse 7, The knowledge of wisdom—to whom was it manifested? And her abundant experience—who has understood it?

[10] upon all the living according to his gift;
  he lavished her upon those who love him.[a]

Fear of the Lord Is True Wisdom

[11] The fear of the Lord is glory and exultation,
  and gladness and a crown of rejoicing.
[12] The fear of the Lord delights the heart,
  and gives gladness and joy and long life.[b]
[13] Those who fear the Lord will have a happy end;
  on the day of their death they will be blessed.

[14] To fear the Lord is the beginning of wisdom;
  she is created with the faithful in the womb.
[15] She made[c] among human beings an eternal
    foundation,
  and among their descendants she will abide
    faithfully.
[16] To fear the Lord is fullness of wisdom;
  she inebriates mortals with her fruits;
[17] she fills their[d] whole house with desirable goods,
  and their[d] storehouses with her produce.
[18] The fear of the Lord is the crown of wisdom,
  making peace and perfect health to flourish.[e]
[19] She rained down knowledge and discerning
    comprehension,
  and she heightened the glory of those who
    held her fast.
[20] To fear the Lord is the root of wisdom,
  and her branches are long life.[f]

[22] Unjust anger cannot be justified,
  for anger tips the scale to one's ruin.
[23] Those who are patient stay calm until the right
    moment,
  and then cheerfulness comes back to them.
[24] They hold back their words until the right
    moment;
  then the lips of many tell of their good sense.

[25] In the treasuries of wisdom are wise sayings,
  but godliness is an abomination to a sinner.
[26] If you desire wisdom, keep the commandments,
  and the Lord will lavish her upon you.
[27] For the fear of the Lord is wisdom and
    discipline,
  fidelity and humility are his delight.

[28] Do not disobey the fear of the Lord;
  do not approach him with a divided mind.
[29] Do not be a hypocrite before others,
  and keep watch over your lips.
[30] Do not exalt yourself, or you may fall
  and bring dishonor upon yourself.
  The Lord will reveal your secrets
  and overthrow you before the whole
    congregation,

because you did not come in the fear of the
    Lord,
  and your heart was full of deceit.

Duties toward God

2 My child, when you come to serve the Lord,
  prepare yourself for testing.[g]
[2] Set your heart right and be steadfast,
  and do not be impetuous in time of calamity.
[3] Cling to him and do not depart,
  so that your last days may be prosperous.
[4] Accept whatever befalls you,
  and in times of humiliation be patient.
[5] For gold is tested in the fire,
  and those found acceptable, in the furnace of
    humiliation.[h]
[6] Trust in him, and he will help you;
  make your ways straight, and hope in him.

[7] You who fear the Lord, wait for his mercy;
  do not stray, or else you may fall.
[8] You who fear the Lord, trust in him,
  and your reward will not be lost.
[9] You who fear the Lord, hope for good things,
  for lasting joy and mercy.[i]
[10] Consider the generations of old and see:
  has anyone trusted in the Lord and been
    disappointed?
  Or has anyone persevered in the fear of the
    Lord[j] and been forsaken?
  Or has anyone called upon him and been
    neglected?
[11] For the Lord is compassionate and merciful;
  he forgives sins and saves in time of distress.

[12] Woe to timid hearts and to slack hands,
  and to the sinner who walks a double path!
[13] Woe to the fainthearted who have no trust!
  Therefore they will have no shelter.
[14] Woe to you who have lost your nerve!
  What will you do when the Lord's reckoning
    comes?

[15] Those who fear the Lord do not disobey his
    words,
  and those who love him keep his ways.

---

a Other ancient authorities add *Love of the Lord is glorious
wisdom; to those to whom he appears he apportions her, that
they may see him.*   b Other ancient authorities add *The fear of
the Lord is a gift from the Lord; also for love he makes firm paths.*
c Gk *made as a nest*   d Other ancient authorities read *her*
e Other ancient authorities add *Both are gifts of God for peace;
glory opens out for those who love him. He saw her and took her
measure.*   f Other ancient authorities add as verse 21, *The fear of
the Lord drives away sins; and where it abides, it will turn away all
anger.*   g Or *trials*   h Other ancient authorities add *in sickness
and poverty put your trust in him*   i Other ancient authorities add
For his reward is an everlasting gift with joy.   j Gk *of him*

Cultural Connection

Honoring Our Parents in God's Way

You hear Sirach 3:1–7 every year on Holy Family Sunday, the weekend after Christmas. This reading calls us to honor our parents, because this is the way God established children's responsibilities toward parents. To honor our parents is to revere them (see verse 6), to be kind to them (see verse 14), to not dishonor them in order to feel superior (see verse 10), and to take care of them and be considerate of them as they age (see verses 12–13). According to Ben Sira, God assures many blessings to those who honor their parents, including safety, happiness, forgiveness of sins, the hearing of their prayers, and a long life.

Hispanics have a long tradition of being parented not only by birth parents but by the extended family, including grandparents, godparents, aunts, and uncles. Today, many young people are also parented by foster parents, stepparents, and adoptive parents.

● Take a moment to think of the adults who have parented you. In what specific ways do you honor and show your love to them? In what ways might you have failed to do so?

● Thank God, our heavenly parent, for the love and sacrifices of all the people who have parented you. Ask God to give you love, understanding, strength, and patience to honor them in word and deed.

▶ Sir 3:1–16

---

16 Those who fear the Lord seek to please him,
   and those who love him are filled with his law.
17 Those who fear the Lord prepare their hearts,
   and humble themselves before him.
18 Let us fall into the hands of the Lord,
   but not into the hands of mortals;
   for equal to his majesty is his mercy,
   and equal to his name are his works.[a]

Duties toward Parents

3 Listen to me your father, O children;
   act accordingly, that you may be kept in safety.
2 For the Lord honors a father above his children,
   and he confirms a mother's right over her children.
3 Those who honor their father atone for sins,
4   and those who respect their mother are like those who lay up treasure.
5 Those who honor their father will have joy in their own children,
   and when they pray they will be heard.
6 Those who respect their father will have long life,
   and those who honor[b] their mother obey the Lord;
7   they will serve their parents as their masters.[c]
8 Honor your father by word and deed,
   that his blessing may come upon you.
9 For a father's blessing strengthens the houses of the children,

but a mother's curse uproots their foundations.
10 Do not glorify yourself by dishonoring your father,
   for your father's dishonor is no glory to you.
11 The glory of one's father is one's own glory,
   and it is a disgrace for children not to respect their mother.
12 My child, help your father in his old age,
   and do not grieve him as long as he lives;
13 even if his mind fails, be patient with him;
   because you have all your faculties do not despise him.
14 For kindness to a father will not be forgotten,
   and will be credited to you against your sins;
15 in the day of your distress it will be remembered in your favor;
   like frost in fair weather, your sins will melt away.
16 Whoever forsakes a father is like a blasphemer,
   and whoever angers a mother is cursed by the Lord.

Humility

17 My child, perform your tasks with humility;[d]
   then you will be loved by those whom God accepts.

---

a Syr: Gk lacks this line   b Heb: Other ancient authorities read comfort   c In other ancient authorities this line is preceded by Those who fear the Lord honor their father,   d Heb: Gk meekness

Cultural Connection

Celebrating Families

Ben Sira holds family relationships in high esteem. In chapter 3, he emphasizes the importance of honor and respect among family members. Many cultures have special days honoring parents and children. In the United States, we celebrate Mother's Day, Father's Day, and Grandparent's Day.

Japan also has special days honoring family members. Girls' Festival (*Hinamatsuri*) is celebrated on March 3 with doll displays and peach blossoms. Boys' Festival (*Kodomo No Hi*) is celebrated on May 5 with streamers. Respect for the Aged Day (*Keiro No Hi*) is celebrated on September 15. On January 15, the Coming of Age Festival (*Seigin No Hi*) takes place. This day celebrates all young people who have turned twenty during the previous year—the age when young adults are permitted to vote, drink, and smoke.

If you have Japanese friends or acquaintances, consider marking these holidays on your calendar and sending a card or note with a prayer on the appropriate day.

▶ Sir 3:1–16

18 The greater you are, the more you must humble
    yourself;
    so you will find favor in the sight of the Lord.*a*
20 For great is the might of the Lord;
    but by the humble he is glorified.
21 Neither seek what is too difficult for you,
    nor investigate what is beyond your power.
22 Reflect upon what you have been commanded,
    for what is hidden is not your concern.
23 Do not meddle in matters that are beyond you,
    for more than you can understand has been
    shown you.
24 For their conceit has led many astray,
    and wrong opinion has impaired their
    judgment.

25 Without eyes there is no light;
    without knowledge there is no wisdom.*b*
26 A stubborn mind will fare badly at the end,
    and whoever loves danger will perish in it.
27 A stubborn mind will be burdened by troubles,
    and the sinner adds sin to sins.
28 When calamity befalls the proud, there is no
    healing,
    for an evil plant has taken root in him.
29 The mind of the intelligent appreciates proverbs,
    and an attentive ear is the desire of the wise.

Alms for the Poor

30 As water extinguishes a blazing fire,
    so almsgiving atones for sin.
31 Those who repay favors give thought to the
    future;
    when they fall they will find support.

Duties toward the Poor and the Oppressed

4 My child, do not cheat the poor of their living,
    and do not keep needy eyes waiting.
2 Do not grieve the hungry,
    or anger one in need.
3 Do not add to the troubles of the desperate,
    or delay giving to the needy.
4 Do not reject a suppliant in distress,
    or turn your face away from the poor.
5 Do not avert your eye from the needy,
    and give no one reason to curse you;
6 for if in bitterness of soul some should curse you,
    their Creator will hear their prayer.

7 Endear yourself to the congregation;
    bow your head low to the great.
8 Give a hearing to the poor,
    and return their greeting politely.
9 Rescue the oppressed from the oppressor;
    and do not be hesitant in giving a verdict.
10 Be a father to orphans,
    and be like a husband to their mother;
    you will then be like a son of the Most High,
    and he will love you more than does your
    mother.

The Rewards of Wisdom

11 Wisdom teaches*c* her children
    and gives help to those who seek her.

---

a Other ancient authorities add as verse 19, *Many are lofty and renowned, but to the humble he reveals his secrets.*   *b* Heb: Other ancient authorities lack verse 25   *c* Heb Syr: Gk *exalts*

12 Whoever loves her loves life,
   and those who seek her from early morning
      are filled with joy.
13 Whoever holds her fast inherits glory,
   and the Lord blesses the place she*a* enters.
14 Those who serve her minister to the Holy One;
   the Lord loves those who love her.
15 Those who obey her will judge the nations,
   and all who listen to her will live secure.
16 If they remain faithful, they will inherit her;
   their descendants will also obtain her.
17 For at first she will walk with them on tortuous
      paths;
   she will bring fear and dread upon them,
and will torment them by her discipline
   until she trusts them,*b*
and she will test them with her ordinances.
18 Then she will come straight back to them again
      and gladden them,
   and will reveal her secrets to them.
19 If they go astray she will forsake them,
   and hand them over to their ruin.

20 Watch for the opportune time, and beware of
      evil,
   and do not be ashamed to be yourself.
21 For there is a shame that leads to sin,
   and there is a shame that is glory and favor.
22 Do not show partiality, to your own harm,
   or deference, to your downfall.
23 Do not refrain from speaking at the proper
      moment,*c*
   and do not hide your wisdom.*d*
24 For wisdom becomes known through speech,
   and education through the words of the
      tongue.
25 Never speak against the truth,
   but be ashamed of your ignorance.
26 Do not be ashamed to confess your sins,
   and do not try to stop the current of a river.
27 Do not subject yourself to a fool,
   or show partiality to a ruler.
28 Fight to the death for truth,
   and the Lord God will fight for you.

29 Do not be reckless in your speech,
   or sluggish and remiss in your deeds.
30 Do not be like a lion in your home,
   or suspicious of your servants.
31 Do not let your hand be stretched out to receive
   and closed when it is time to give.

Precepts for Everyday Living

5 Do not rely on your wealth,
   or say, "I have enough."
2 Do not follow your inclination and strength

in pursuing the desires of your heart.
3 Do not say, "Who can have power over me?"
   for the Lord will surely punish you.

4 Do not say, "I sinned, yet what has happened to
      me?"
   for the Lord is slow to anger.
5 Do not be so confident of forgiveness*e*
   that you add sin to sin.
6 Do not say, "His mercy is great,
   he will forgive*f* the multitude of my sins,"
for both mercy and wrath are with him,
   and his anger will rest on sinners.
7 Do not delay to turn back to the Lord,
   and do not postpone it from day to day;
for suddenly the wrath of the Lord will come
      upon you,
   and at the time of punishment you will perish.
8 Do not depend on dishonest wealth,
   for it will not benefit you on the day of
      calamity.

9 Do not winnow in every wind,
   or follow every path.*g*
10 Stand firm for what you know,
   and let your speech be consistent.
11 Be quick to hear,
   but deliberate in answering.
12 If you know what to say, answer your neighbor;
   but if not, put your hand over your mouth.

13 Honor and dishonor come from speaking,
   and the tongue of mortals may be their
      downfall.
14 Do not be called double-tongued*h*
   and do not lay traps with your tongue;
for shame comes to the thief,
   and severe condemnation to the double-
      tongued.
15 In great and small matters cause no harm,*i*

6 1and do not become an enemy instead of a
      friend;
   for a bad name incurs shame and reproach;
   so it is with the double-tongued sinner.

2 Do not fall into the grip of passion,*j*
   or you may be torn apart as by a bull.*k*
3 Your leaves will be devoured and your fruit
      destroyed,
   and you will be left like a withered tree.

a Or *he*   *b* Or *until they remain faithful in their heart*   *c* Heb:
Gk *at a time of salvation*   *d* So some Gk Mss and Heb Syr Lat:
Other Gk Mss lack *and do not hide your wisdom*   *e* Heb: Gk
atonement   *f* Heb: Gk *he* (or *it*) *will atone for*   *g* Gk adds *so it is
with the double-tongued sinner* (see 6.1)   *h* Heb: Gk *a slanderer*
i Heb Syr: Gk *be ignorant*   *j* Heb: Meaning of Gk uncertain
k Meaning of Gk uncertain

4 Evil passion destroys those who have it,
  and makes them the laughingstock of their
  enemies.

Friendship, False and True

5 Pleasant speech multiplies friends,
  and a gracious tongue multiplies courtesies.
6 Let those who are friendly with you be many,
  but let your advisers be one in a thousand.
7 When you gain friends, gain them through
  testing,
  and do not trust them hastily.
8 For there are friends who are such when it suits
  them,
  but they will not stand by you in time of
  trouble.
9 And there are friends who change into
  enemies,
  and tell of the quarrel to your disgrace.
10 And there are friends who sit at your table,
  but they will not stand by you in time of
  trouble.
11 When you are prosperous, they become your
  second self,
  and lord it over your servants;
12 but if you are brought low, they turn against
  you,
  and hide themselves from you.
13 Keep away from your enemies,
  and be on guard with your friends.

Friends

God of friendship,
Thank you for my friends, especially for
those who give me wise advice.
Thank you for my closest friends whom I see
every day, who motivate me to grow and
serve.
Thank you for all the good friends whom I used
to see more often but don't see as much
anymore.
Lord, continue to give me good friends
throughout my life, and
help me be a better friend
to all. Amen.

▶ Sir 6:5–17

14 Faithful friends are a sturdy shelter:
  whoever finds one has found a treasure.
15 Faithful friends are beyond price;
  no amount can balance their worth.
16 Faithful friends are life-saving medicine;
  and those who fear the Lord will find them.
17 Those who fear the Lord direct their friendship
  aright,
  for as they are, so are their neighbors also.

Blessings of Wisdom

18 My child, from your youth choose discipline,
  and when you have gray hair you will still
  find wisdom.
19 Come to her like one who plows and sows,
  and wait for her good harvest.
  For when you cultivate her you will toil but little,
  and soon you will eat of her produce.
20 She seems very harsh to the undisciplined;
  fools cannot remain with her.
21 She will be like a heavy stone to test them,
  and they will not delay in casting her aside.
22 For wisdom is like her name;
  she is not readily perceived by many.

23 Listen, my child, and accept my judgment;
  do not reject my counsel.
24 Put your feet into her fetters,
  and your neck into her collar.
25 Bend your shoulders and carry her,
  and do not fret under her bonds.
26 Come to her with all your soul,
  and keep her ways with all your might.
27 Search out and seek, and she will become
  known to you;
  and when you get hold of her, do not let her
  go.
28 For at last you will find the rest she gives,
  and she will be changed into joy for you.
29 Then her fetters will become for you a strong
  defense,
  and her collar a glorious robe.
30 Her yoke[a] is a golden ornament,
  and her bonds a purple cord.
31 You will wear her like a glorious robe,
  and put her on like a splendid crown.[b]

32 If you are willing, my child, you can be
  disciplined,
  and if you apply yourself you will become
  clever.
33 If you love to listen you will gain knowledge,
  and if you pay attention you will become
  wise.

a Heb: Gk Upon her   b Heb: Gk crown of gladness

34 Stand in the company of the elders.
   Who is wise? Attach yourself to such a one.
35 Be ready to listen to every godly discourse,
   and let no wise proverbs escape you.
36 If you see an intelligent person, rise early to visit
   him;
   let your foot wear out his doorstep.
37 Reflect on the statutes of the Lord,
   and meditate at all times on his
   commandments.
   It is he who will give insight to[a] your mind,
   and your desire for wisdom will be granted.

Miscellaneous Advice

7 Do no evil, and evil will never overtake you.
   2 Stay away from wrong, and it will turn away
      from you.
3 Do[b] not sow in the furrows of injustice,
   and you will not reap a sevenfold crop.

4 Do not seek from the Lord high office,
   or the seat of honor from the king.
5 Do not assert your righteousness before the Lord,
   or display your wisdom before the king.
6 Do not seek to become a judge,
   or you may be unable to root out injustice;
   you may be partial to the powerful,
   and so mar your integrity.
7 Commit no offense against the public,
   and do not disgrace yourself among the
   people.
8 Do not commit a sin twice;
   not even for one will you go unpunished.
9 Do not say, "He will consider the great number
   of my gifts,
   and when I make an offering to the Most
   High God, he will accept it."
10 Do not grow weary when you pray;
   do not neglect to give alms.
11 Do not ridicule a person who is embittered in
   spirit,
   for there is One who humbles and exalts.
12 Do not devise[c] a lie against your brother,
   or do the same to a friend.
13 Refuse to utter any lie,
   for it is a habit that results in no good.
14 Do not babble in the assembly of the elders,
   and do not repeat yourself when you pray.

15 Do not hate hard labor
   or farm work, which was created by the Most
   High.
16 Do not enroll in the ranks of sinners;
   remember that retribution does not delay.
17 Humble yourself to the utmost,

for the punishment of the ungodly is fire and
worms.[d]

Relations with Others

18 Do not exchange a friend for money,
   or a real brother for the gold of Ophir.
19 Do not dismiss[e] a wise and good wife,
   for her charm is worth more than gold.
20 Do not abuse slaves who work faithfully,
   or hired laborers who devote themselves to
   their task.
21 Let your soul love intelligent slaves;[f]
   do not withhold from them their freedom.

22 Do you have cattle? Look after them;
   if they are profitable to you, keep them.
23 Do you have children? Discipline them,
   and make them obedient[g] from their youth.
24 Do you have daughters? Be concerned for their
   chastity,[h]
   and do not show yourself too indulgent with
   them.
25 Give a daughter in marriage, and you complete a
   great task;
   but give her to a sensible man.
26 Do you have a wife who pleases you?[i] Do not
   divorce her;
   but do not trust yourself to one whom you
   detest.

27 With all your heart honor your father,
   and do not forget the birth pangs of your
   mother.
28 Remember that it was of your parents[j] you were
   born;
   how can you repay what they have given to
   you?
29 With all your soul fear the Lord,
   and revere his priests.
30 With all your might love your Maker,
   and do not neglect his ministers.
31 Fear the Lord and honor the priest,
   and give him his portion, as you have been
   commanded:
   the first fruits, the guilt offering, the gift of the
   shoulders,
   the sacrifice of sanctification, and the first
   fruits of the holy things.

32 Stretch out your hand to the poor,
   so that your blessing may be complete.

---

a Heb: Gk *will confirm*   b Gk *My child, do*   c Heb: Gk *plow*
d Heb *for the expectation of mortals is worms*   e Heb: Gk *deprive
yourself of*   f Heb *Love a wise slave as yourself*   g Gk *bend their
necks*   h Gk *body*   i Heb Syr *lack who pleases you*   j Gk *them*

33 Give graciously to all the living;
   do not withhold kindness even from the
    dead.
34 Do not avoid those who weep,
   but mourn with those who mourn.
35 Do not hesitate to visit the sick,
   because for such deeds you will be loved.
36 In all you do, remember the end of your life,
   and then you will never sin.

Prudence and Common Sense

8 Do not contend with the powerful,
   or you may fall into their hands.
2 Do not quarrel with the rich,
   in case their resources outweigh yours;
for gold has ruined many,
   and has perverted the minds of kings.
3 Do not argue with the loud of mouth,
   and do not heap wood on their fire.

4 Do not make fun of one who is ill-bred,
   or your ancestors may be insulted.
5 Do not reproach one who is turning away from
    sin;
   remember that we all deserve punishment.
6 Do not disdain one who is old,
   for some of us are also growing old.
7 Do not rejoice over anyone's death;
   remember that we must all die.

8 Do not slight the discourse of the sages,
   but busy yourself with their maxims;
because from them you will learn discipline
   and how to serve princes.
9 Do not ignore the discourse of the aged,
   for they themselves learned from their
    parents;[a]
from them you learn how to understand
   and to give an answer when the need arises.

10 Do not kindle the coals of sinners,
   or you may be burned in their flaming fire.
11 Do not let the insolent bring you to your feet,
   or they may lie in ambush against your
    words.
12 Do not lend to one who is stronger than you;
   but if you do lend anything, count it as a loss.
13 Do not give surety beyond your means;
   but if you give surety, be prepared to pay.

14 Do not go to law against a judge,
   for the decision will favor him because of his
    standing.
15 Do not go traveling with the reckless,
   or they will be burdensome to you;
for they will act as they please,

and through their folly you will perish with
   them.
16 Do not pick a fight with the quick-tempered,
   and do not journey with them through lonely
    country,
because bloodshed means nothing to them,
   and where no help is at hand, they will strike
    you down.
17 Do not consult with fools,
   for they cannot keep a secret.
18 In the presence of strangers do nothing that is to
    be kept secret,
   for you do not know what they will divulge.[b]
19 Do not reveal your thoughts to anyone,
   or you may drive away your happiness.[c]

Advice concerning Women

9 Do not be jealous of the wife of your bosom,
   or you will teach her an evil lesson to your
    own hurt.
2 Do not give yourself to a woman
   and let her trample down your strength.
3 Do not go near a loose woman,
   or you will fall into her snares.
4 Do not dally with a singing girl,
   or you will be caught by her tricks.
5 Do not look intently at a virgin,
   or you may stumble and incur penalties for her.
6 Do not give yourself to prostitutes,
   or you may lose your inheritance.
7 Do not look around in the streets of a city,
   or wander about in its deserted sections.
8 Turn away your eyes from a shapely woman,
   and do not gaze at beauty belonging to
    another;
many have been seduced by a woman's beauty,
   and by it passion is kindled like a fire.
9 Never dine with another man's wife,
   or revel with her at wine;
or your heart may turn aside to her,
   and in blood[d] you may be plunged into
    destruction.

Choice of Friends

10 Do not abandon old friends,
   for new ones cannot equal them.
A new friend is like new wine;
   when it has aged, you can drink it with
    pleasure.

11 Do not envy the success of sinners,
   for you do not know what their end will be
    like.

---

a Or *ancestors*   b Or *it will bring forth*   c Heb: Gk *and let him
not return a favor to you*   d Heb: Gk *by your spirit*

¹² Do not delight in what pleases the ungodly;
        remember that they will not be held guiltless
            all their lives.

¹³ Keep far from those who have power to kill,
        and you will not be haunted by the fear of
            death.
    But if you approach them, make no misstep,
        or they may rob you of your life.
    Know that you are stepping among snares,
        and that you are walking on the city
            battlements.

¹⁴ As much as you can, aim to know your
        neighbors,
        and consult with the wise.
¹⁵ Let your conversation be with intelligent people,
        and let all your discussion be about the law of
            the Most High.
¹⁶ Let the righteous be your dinner companions,
        and let your glory be in the fear of the Lord.

Concerning Rulers

¹⁷ A work is praised for the skill of the artisan;
        so a people's leader is proved wise by his
            words.
¹⁸ The loud of mouth are feared in their city,
        and the one who is reckless in speech is hated.

10 A wise magistrate educates his people,
        and the rule of an intelligent person is well
            ordered.
² As the people's judge is, so are his officials;
        as the ruler of the city is, so are all its
            inhabitants.
³ An undisciplined king ruins his people,
        but a city becomes fit to live in through the
            understanding of its rulers.
⁴ The government of the earth is in the hand of
        the Lord,
        and over it he will raise up the right leader for
            the time.
⁵ Human success is in the hand of the Lord,
        and it is he who confers honor upon the
            lawgiver.ᵃ

The Sin of Pride

⁶ Do not get angry with your neighbor for every
        injury,
        and do not resort to acts of insolence.
⁷ Arrogance is hateful to the Lord and to mortals,
        and injustice is outrageous to both.
⁸ Sovereignty passes from nation to nation
        on account of injustice and insolence and
            wealth.ᵇ
⁹ How can dust and ashes be proud?
        Even in life the human body decays.ᶜ

Friends, Old and New

Out there, somewhere, is a special person
you have not yet met, someone who will
eventually become a key person in your life. In
fact, a lot of such people are out there, somewhere—including future classmates, coworkers,
roommates, and friends. The challenge is in finding the particular people who will become close
to you and share with you the experiences of
your life.

Ben Sira reminds us in Sirach 9:10 that in
the excitement that accompanies making new
friends, we should not forget the pleasure and
comfort that an old friend brings us. A friend we
have known for a long time is someone to trust,
someone who knows and accepts us, in spite of
our shortcomings. And when the circumstances
of life cause separation from old friends, there
is value in reconnecting occasionally, to share
where life has taken us or even to seek direction and support if life has become confusing or
hard. We need to treasure our tried-and-true
friendships, as well as welcome new ones.

Spend some time reflecting on your friends,
old and new, and their value in your life.

▶ Sir 9:10

¹⁰ A long illness baffles the physician;ᵈ
        the king of today will die tomorrow.
¹¹ For when one is dead
        he inherits maggots and verminᵉ and worms.
¹² The beginning of human pride is to forsake the
        Lord;
        the heart has withdrawn from its Maker.
¹³ For the beginning of pride is sin,
        and the one who clings to it pours out
            abominations.
    Therefore the Lord brings upon them unheard-
        of calamities,
        and destroys them completely.

a Heb: Gk *scribe*   b Other ancient authorities add here or after
verse 9a, *Nothing is more wicked than one who loves money, for
such a person puts his own soul up for sale.*   c Heb: Meaning of
Gk uncertain   d Heb Lat: Meaning of Gk uncertain   e Heb: Gk
wild animals

14 The Lord overthrows the thrones of rulers,
   and enthrones the lowly in their place.
15 The Lord plucks up the roots of the nations,ᵃ
   and plants the humble in their place.
16 The Lord lays waste the lands of the nations,
   and destroys them to the foundations of the
      earth.
17 He removes some of them and destroys them,
   and erases the memory of them from the
      earth.
18 Pride was not created for human beings,
   or violent anger for those born of women.

Persons Deserving Honor

19 Whose offspring are worthy of honor?
   Human offspring.
   Whose offspring are worthy of honor?
   Those who fear the Lord.
   Whose offspring are unworthy of honor?
   Human offspring.
   Whose offspring are unworthy of honor?
   Those who break the commandments.
20 Among family members their leader is worthy of
      honor,
   but those who fear the Lord are worthy of
      honor in his eyes.ᵇ
22 The rich, and the eminent, and the poor—
   their glory is the fear of the Lord.
23 It is not right to despise one who is intelligent
      but poor,
   and it is not proper to honor one who is
      sinful.
24 The prince and the judge and the ruler are
      honored,
   but none of them is greater than the one who
      fears the Lord.
25 Free citizens will serve a wise servant,
   and an intelligent person will not complain.

Concerning Humility

26 Do not make a display of your wisdom when
      you do your work,
   and do not boast when you are in need.
27 Better is the worker who has goods in plenty
   than the boaster who lacks bread.

28 My child, honor yourself with humility,
   and give yourself the esteem you deserve.
29 Who will acquit those who condemnᶜ
      themselves?
   And who will honor those who dishonor
      themselves?ᵈ
30 The poor are honored for their knowledge,
   while the rich are honored for their wealth.
31 One who is honored in poverty, how much
      more in wealth!

And one dishonored in wealth, how much
   more in poverty!

The Deceptiveness of Appearances

11 The wisdom of the humble lifts their heads
      high,
   and seats them among the great.
2 Do not praise individuals for their good looks,
   or loathe anyone because of appearance
      alone.
3 The bee is small among flying creatures,
   but what it produces is the best of sweet
      things.
4 Do not boast about wearing fine clothes,
   and do not exalt yourself when you are
      honored;
   for the works of the Lord are wonderful,
   and his works are concealed from
      humankind.
5 Many kings have had to sit on the ground,
   but one who was never thought of has worn a
      crown.
6 Many rulers have been utterly disgraced,
   and the honored have been handed over to
      others.

Deliberation and Caution

7 Do not find fault before you investigate;
   examine first, and then criticize.
8 Do not answer before you listen,
   and do not interrupt when another is
      speaking.
9 Do not argue about a matter that does not
      concern you,
   and do not sit with sinners when they judge a
      case.

10 My child, do not busy yourself with many
      matters;
   if you multiply activities, you will not be held
      blameless.
   If you pursue, you will not overtake,
   and by fleeing you will not escape.
11 There are those who work and struggle and
      hurry,
   but are so much the more in want.
12 There are others who are slow and need help,
   who lack strength and abound in poverty;
   but the eyes of the Lord look kindly upon them;
   he lifts them out of their lowly condition
13 and raises up their heads
   to the amazement of the many.

---

a Other ancient authorities read *proud nations* b Other ancient
authorities add as verse 21, *The fear of the Lord is the beginning
of acceptance; obduracy and pride are the beginning of rejection.*
c Heb: Gk *sin against* d Heb Lat: Gk *their own life*

14 Good things and bad, life and death,
poverty and wealth, come from the Lord.ᵃ
17 The Lord's gift remains with the devout,
and his favor brings lasting success.
18 One becomes rich through diligence and self-
denial,
and the reward allotted to him is this:
19 when he says, "I have found rest,
and now I shall feast on my goods!"
he does not know how long it will be
until he leaves them to others and dies.
20 Stand by your agreement and attend to it,
and grow old in your work.
21 Do not wonder at the works of a sinner,
but trust in the Lord and keep at your job;
for it is easy in the sight of the Lord
to make the poor rich suddenly, in an
instant.
22 The blessing of the Lord isᵇ the reward of the
pious,
and quickly God causes his blessing to
flourish.
23 Do not say, "What do I need,
and what further benefit can be mine?"
24 Do not say, "I have enough,
and what harm can come to me now?"
25 In the day of prosperity, adversity is forgotten,
and in the day of adversity, prosperity is not
remembered.
26 For it is easy for the Lord on the day of death
to reward individuals according to their
conduct.
27 An hour's misery makes one forget past
delights,
and at the close of one's life one's deeds are
revealed.
28 Call no one happy before his death;
by how he ends, a person becomes known.ᶜ

Care in Choosing Friends

29 Do not invite everyone into your home,
for many are the tricks of the crafty.
30 Like a decoy partridge in a cage, so is the mind
of the proud,
and like spies they observe your weakness;ᵈ
31 for they lie in wait, turning good into evil,
and to worthy actions they attach blame.
32 From a spark many coals are kindled,
and a sinner lies in wait to shed blood.
33 Beware of scoundrels, for they devise evil,
and they may ruin your reputation forever.
34 Receive strangers into your home and they will
stir up trouble for you,
and will make you a stranger to your own
family.

12 If you do good, know to whom you do it,
and you will be thanked for your good
deeds.
2 Do good to the devout, and you will be repaid—
if not by them, certainly by the Most High.
3 No good comes to one who persists in evil
or to one who does not give alms.
4 Give to the devout, but do not help the sinner.
5 Do good to the humble, but do not give to
the ungodly;
hold back their bread, and do not give it to
them,
for by means of it they might subdue you;
then you will receive twice as much evil
for all the good you have done to them.
6 For the Most High also hates sinners
and will inflict punishment on the ungodly.ᵉ
7 Give to the one who is good, but do not help
the sinner.
8 A friend is not knownᶠ in prosperity,
nor is an enemy hidden in adversity.
9 One's enemies are friendlyᵍ when one prospers,
but in adversity even one's friend disappears.
10 Never trust your enemy,
for like corrosion in copper, so is his
wickedness.
11 Even if he humbles himself and walks bowed
down,
take care to be on your guard against him.
Be to him like one who polishes a mirror,
to be sure it does not become completely
tarnished.
12 Do not put him next to you,
or he may overthrow you and take your place.
Do not let him sit at your right hand,
or else he may try to take your own seat,
and at last you will realize the truth of my
words,
and be stung by what I have said.

13 Who pities a snake charmer when he is bitten,
or all those who go near wild animals?
14 So no one pities a person who associates with a
sinner
and becomes involved in the other's sins.
15 He stands by you for a while,
but if you falter, he will not be there.
16 An enemy speaks sweetly with his lips,

---

a Other ancient authorities add as verses 15 and 16, ¹⁵*Wisdom,
understanding, and knowledge of the law come from the Lord;
affection and the ways of good works come from him.* ¹⁶*Error and
darkness were created with sinners; evil grows old with those who
take pride in malice.*   b Heb: Gk *is in*   c Heb: Gk *and through
his children a person becomes known*   d Heb: Gk *downfall*
e Other ancient authorities add *and he is keeping them for the day
of their punishment*   f Other ancient authorities read *punished*
g Heb: Gk *grieved*

but in his heart he plans to throw you into a
pit;
an enemy may have tears in his eyes,
but if he finds an opportunity he will never
have enough of your blood.
¹⁷ If evil comes upon you, you will find him there
ahead of you;
pretending to help, he will trip you up.
¹⁸ Then he will shake his head, and clap his hands,
and whisper much, and show his true face.

Caution Regarding Associates

13 Whoever touches pitch gets dirty,
and whoever associates with a proud person
becomes like him.
² Do not lift a weight too heavy for you,
or associate with one mightier and richer than
you.
How can the clay pot associate with the iron
kettle?
The pot will strike against it and be smashed.
³ A rich person does wrong, and even adds insults;
a poor person suffers wrong, and must add
apologies.
⁴ A rich person^a will exploit you if you can be of
use to him,
but if you are in need he will abandon you.
⁵ If you own something, he will live with you;
he will drain your resources without a qualm.
⁶ When he needs you he will deceive you,
and will smile at you and encourage you;
he will speak to you kindly and say, "What do
you need?"
⁷ He will embarrass you with his delicacies,
until he has drained you two or three times,
and finally he will laugh at you.
Should he see you afterwards, he will pass
you by
and shake his head at you.

⁸ Take care not to be led astray
and humiliated when you are enjoying
yourself.^b
⁹ When an influential person invites you, be
reserved,
and he will invite you more insistently.
¹⁰ Do not be forward, or you may be rebuffed;
do not stand aloof, or you will be forgotten.
¹¹ Do not try to treat him as an equal,
or trust his lengthy conversations;
for he will test you by prolonged talk,
and while he smiles he will be examining
you.
¹² Cruel are those who do not keep your secrets;
they will not spare you harm or
imprisonment.

¹³ Be on your guard and very careful,
for you are walking about with your own
downfall.^c

¹⁵ Every creature loves its like,
and every person the neighbor.
¹⁶ All living beings associate with their own kind,
and people stick close to those like
themselves.
¹⁷ What does a wolf have in common with a lamb?
No more has a sinner with the devout.
¹⁸ What peace is there between a hyena and a dog?
And what peace between the rich and the
poor?
¹⁹ Wild asses in the wilderness are the prey of
lions;
likewise the poor are feeding grounds for the
rich.
²⁰ Humility is an abomination to the proud;
likewise the poor are an abomination to the
rich.

²¹ When the rich person totters, he is supported by
friends,
but when the humble^d falls, he is pushed
away even by friends.
²² If the rich person slips, many come to the rescue;
he speaks unseemly words, but they justify
him.
If the humble person slips, they even criticize
him;
he talks sense, but is not given a hearing.
²³ The rich person speaks and all are silent;
they extol to the clouds what he says.
The poor person speaks and they say, "Who is
this fellow?"
And should he stumble, they even push him
down.
²⁴ Riches are good if they are free from sin;
poverty is evil only in the opinion of the
ungodly.

²⁵ The heart changes the countenance,
either for good or for evil.^e
²⁶ The sign of a happy heart is a cheerful face,
but to devise proverbs requires painful
thinking.

14 Happy are those who do not blunder with
their lips,
and need not suffer remorse for sin.

---

a Gk *He*   *b* Other ancient authorities read *in your folly*   *c* Other
ancient authorities add as verse 14, *When you hear these things
in your sleep, wake up! During all your life love the Lord, and call
on him for your salvation.*   *d* Other ancient authorities read *poor*
e Other ancient authorities add *and a glad heart makes a cheerful
countenance*

2 Happy are those whose hearts do not condemn
them,
  and who have not given up their hope.

Responsible Use of Wealth

3 Riches are inappropriate for a small-minded
person;
  and of what use is wealth to a miser?
4 What he denies himself he collects for others;
  and others will live in luxury on his goods.
5 If one is mean to himself, to whom will he be
generous?
  He will not enjoy his own riches.
6 No one is worse than one who is grudging to
himself;
  this is the punishment for his meanness.
7 If ever he does good, it is by mistake;
  and in the end he reveals his meanness.
8 The miser is an evil person;
  he turns away and disregards people.
9 The eye of the greedy person is not satisfied with
his share;
  greedy injustice withers the soul.
10 A miser begrudges bread,
  and it is lacking at his table.

11 My child, treat yourself well, according to your
means,
  and present worthy offerings to the Lord.
12 Remember that death does not tarry,
  and the decree[a] of Hades has not been shown
to you.
13 Do good to friends before you die,
  and reach out and give to them as much as
you can.
14 Do not deprive yourself of a day's enjoyment;
  do not let your share of desired good pass by
you.
15 Will you not leave the fruit of your labors to
another,
  and what you acquired by toil to be divided
by lot?
16 Give, and take, and indulge yourself,
  because in Hades one cannot look for luxury.
17 All living beings become old like a garment,
  for the decree[b] from of old is, "You must die!"
18 Like abundant leaves on a spreading tree
  that sheds some and puts forth others,
so are the generations of flesh and blood:
  one dies and another is born.
19 Every work decays and ceases to exist,
  and the one who made it will pass away with it.

The Happiness of Seeking Wisdom

20 Happy is the person who meditates on[c] wisdom
  and reasons intelligently,

21 who[d] reflects in his heart on her ways
  and ponders her secrets,
22 pursuing her like a hunter,
  and lying in wait on her paths;
23 who peers through her windows
  and listens at her doors;
24 who camps near her house
  and fastens his tent peg to her walls;
25 who pitches his tent near her,
  and so occupies an excellent lodging place;
26 who places his children under her shelter,
  and lodges under her boughs;
27 who is sheltered by her from the heat,
  and dwells in the midst of her glory.

15 Whoever fears the Lord will do this,
  and whoever holds to the law will obtain
wisdom.[e]
2 She will come to meet him like a mother,
  and like a young bride she will welcome him.
3 She will feed him with the bread of learning,
  and give him the water of wisdom to drink.
4 He will lean on her and not fall,
  and he will rely on her and not be put to
shame.
5 She will exalt him above his neighbors,
  and will open his mouth in the midst of the
assembly.
6 He will find gladness and a crown of rejoicing,
  and will inherit an everlasting name.
7 The foolish will not obtain her,
  and sinners will not see her.
8 She is far from arrogance,
  and liars will never think of her.
9 Praise is unseemly on the lips of a sinner,
  for it has not been sent from the Lord.
10 For in wisdom must praise be uttered,
  and the Lord will make it prosper.

Freedom of Choice

11 Do not say, "It was the Lord's doing that I fell
away";
  for he does not do[f] what he hates.
12 Do not say, "It was he who led me astray";
  for he has no need of the sinful.
13 The Lord hates all abominations;
  such things are not loved by those who fear
him.
14 It was he who created humankind in the
beginning,
  and he left them in the power of their own
free choice.

a Heb Syr: Gk covenant   b Heb: Gk covenant   c Other ancient
authorities read dies in   d The structure adopted in verses 21–27
follows the Heb   e Gk her   f Heb: Gk you ought not to do

S
I
R

Taking Responsibility

"**I**t isn't my fault; she made me do it." "He started it!" "They pressured me into doing it!" We have lots of ways of blaming others when bad things happen. Sirach 15:11 tells of one way people in Ben Sira's time tried to put the blame on someone else: "It was the Lord's doing." Evidently, some people blamed God when they fell into sin. Ben Sira tells us it isn't God's will when bad things happen as a result of human choice (see verses 14–17)—which is why we need to stop the blame game and take responsibility for our own actions.

In your prayer, take some time to reflect or journal on the following questions:

- Do you tend to blame others when bad things happen?
- Have there been hurtful situations in which you would not accept your part of the responsibility? If so, describe one and explain how you could have owned up to your responsibility.

▶ Sir 15:11–20

15 If you choose, you can keep the
   commandments,
      and to act faithfully is a matter of your own
         choice.
16 He has placed before you fire and water;
      stretch out your hand for whichever you
         choose.
17 Before each person are life and death,
      and whichever one chooses will be given.
18 For great is the wisdom of the Lord;
      he is mighty in power and sees everything;
19 his eyes are on those who fear him,
      and he knows every human action.
20 He has not commanded anyone to be wicked,
      and he has not given anyone permission to
         sin.

God's Punishment of Sinners

16 Do not desire a multitude of worthless[a]
   children,
      and do not rejoice in ungodly offspring.
2 If they multiply, do not rejoice in them,

unless the fear of the Lord is in them.
3 Do not trust in their survival,
      or rely on their numbers;[b]
   for one can be better than a thousand,
      and to die childless is better than to have
         ungodly children.
4 For through one intelligent person a city can be
      filled with people,
      but through a clan of outlaws it becomes
         desolate.
5 Many such things my eye has seen,
      and my ear has heard things more striking
         than these.
6 In an assembly of sinners a fire is kindled,
      and in a disobedient nation wrath blazes up.
7 He did not forgive the ancient giants
      who revolted in their might.
8 He did not spare the neighbors of Lot,
      whom he loathed on account of their
         arrogance.
9 He showed no pity on the doomed nation,
      on those dispossessed because of their sins;[c]
10 or on the six hundred thousand foot soldiers
      who assembled in their stubbornness.[d]
11 Even if there were only one stiff-necked person,
      it would be a wonder if he remained
         unpunished.
   For mercy and wrath are with the Lord;[e]
      he is mighty to forgive—but he also pours out
         wrath.
12 Great as is his mercy, so also is his
      chastisement;
      he judges a person according to his or her
         deeds.
13 The sinner will not escape with plunder,
      and the patience of the godly will not be
         frustrated.
14 He makes room for every act of mercy;
      everyone receives in accordance with his or
         her deeds.[f]

17 Do not say, "I am hidden from the Lord,
      and who from on high has me in mind?
   Among so many people I am unknown,
      for what am I in a boundless creation?
18 Lo, heaven and the highest heaven,

a Heb: Gk unprofitable   b Other ancient authorities add For you will groan in untimely mourning, and will know of their sudden end.   c Other ancient authorities add All these things he did to the hard-hearted nations, and by the multitude of his holy ones he was not appeased.   d Other ancient authorities add Chastising, showing mercy, striking, healing, the Lord persisted in mercy and discipline.   e Gk him   f Other ancient authorities add 15The Lord hardened Pharaoh so that he did not recognize him, in order that his works might be known under heaven. 16His mercy is manifest to the whole of creation, and he divided his light and darkness with a plumb line.

the abyss and the earth, tremble at his
     visitation!*a*
19 The very mountains and the foundations of the
     earth
     quiver and quake when he looks upon them.
20 But no human mind can grasp this,
     and who can comprehend his ways?
21 Like a tempest that no one can see,
     so most of his works are concealed.*b*
22 Who is to announce his acts of justice?
     Or who can await them? For his decree*c* is far
     off."*d*
23 Such are the thoughts of one devoid of
     understanding;
     a senseless and misguided person thinks
     foolishly.

God's Wisdom Seen in Creation

24 Listen to me, my child, and acquire knowledge,
     and pay close attention to my words.
25 I will impart discipline precisely*e*
     and declare knowledge accurately.

26 When the Lord created*f* his works from the
     beginning,
     and, in making them, determined their
     boundaries,
27 he arranged his works in an eternal order,
     and their dominion*g* for all generations.
     They neither hunger nor grow weary,
     and they do not abandon their tasks.
28 They do not crowd one another,
     and they never disobey his word.
29 Then the Lord looked upon the earth,
     and filled it with his good things.
30 With all kinds of living beings he covered its
     surface,
     and into it they must return.

17 The Lord created human beings out of earth,
     and makes them return to it again.
2 He gave them a fixed number of days,
     but granted them authority over everything
     on the earth.*h*
3 He endowed them with strength like his own,*i*
     and made them in his own image.
4 He put the fear of them*j* in all living beings,
     and gave them dominion over beasts and
     birds.*k*
6 Discretion and tongue and eyes,
     ears and a mind for thinking he gave them.
7 He filled them with knowledge and
     understanding,
     and showed them good and evil.
8 He put the fear of him into*l* their hearts
     to show them the majesty of his works.*m*

10 And they will praise his holy name,
9   to proclaim the grandeur of his works.
11 He bestowed knowledge upon them,
     and allotted to them the law of life.*n*
12 He established with them an eternal covenant,
     and revealed to them his decrees.
13 Their eyes saw his glorious majesty,
     and their ears heard the glory of his voice.
14 He said to them, "Beware of all evil."
     And he gave commandment to each of them
     concerning the neighbor.
15 Their ways are always known to him;
     they will not be hid from his eyes.*o*
17 He appointed a ruler for every nation,
     but Israel is the Lord's own portion.*p*
19 All their works are as clear as the sun before him,
     and his eyes are ever upon their ways.
20 Their iniquities are not hidden from him,
     and all their sins are before the Lord.*q*
22 One's almsgiving is like a signet ring with the
     Lord,*r*
     and he will keep a person's kindness like the
     apple of his eye.*s*
23 Afterward he will rise up and repay them,
     and he will bring their recompense on their
     heads.
24 Yet to those who repent he grants a return,
     and he encourages those who are losing hope.

A Call to Repentance

25 Turn back to the Lord and forsake your sins;
     pray in his presence and lessen your offense.
26 Return to the Most High and turn away from
     iniquity,*t*
     and hate intensely what he abhors.
27 Who will sing praises to the Most High in Hades
     in place of the living who give thanks?

---

a Other ancient authorities add *The whole world past and present
is in his will.*   *b* Meaning of Gk uncertain: Heb Syr *If I sin, no
eye can see me, and if I am disloyal all in secret, who is to know?*
c Heb *the decree:* Gk *the covenant*   *d* Other ancient authorities
add *and a scrutiny for all comes at the end*   *e* Gk *by weight*
f Heb: Gk *judged*   *g* Or *elements*   *h* Lat: Gk *it*   *i* Lat: Gk
proper to them   *j* Syr: Gk *him*   *k* Other ancient authorities add
as verse 5, *They obtained the use of the five faculties of the Lord; as
sixth he distributed to them the gift of mind, and as seventh, reason,
the interpreter of one's faculties.*   *l* Other ancient authorities
read *He set his eye upon*   *m* Other ancient authorities add *and
he gave them to boast of his marvels forever*   *n* Other ancient
authorities add *so that they may know that they who are alive now
are mortal*   *o* Other ancient authorities add *16Their ways from
youth tend toward evil, and they are unable to make for themselves
hearts of flesh in place of their stony hearts.*   *17For in the division
of the nations of the whole earth, he appointed*   *p* Other ancient
authorities add as verse 18, *whom, being his firstborn, he brings up
with discipline, and allotting to him the light of his love, he does not
neglect him.*   *q* Other ancient authorities add as verse 21, *But the
Lord, who is gracious and knows how they are formed, has neither
left them nor abandoned them, but has spared them.*   *r* Gk *him*
s Other ancient authorities add *apportioning repentance to his sons
and daughters*   *t* Other ancient authorities add *for he will lead
you out of darkness to the light of health.*

28 From the dead, as from one who does not exist,
     thanksgiving has ceased;
     those who are alive and well sing the Lord's
       praises.
29 How great is the mercy of the Lord,
     and his forgiveness for those who return to
       him!
30 For not everything is within human capability,
     since human beings are not immortal.
31 What is brighter than the sun? Yet it can be
     eclipsed.
     So flesh and blood devise evil.
32 He marshals the host of the height of heaven;
     but all human beings are dust and ashes.

The Majesty of God

18 He who lives forever created the whole
     universe;
2   the Lord alone is just.*a*
4 To none has he given power to proclaim his
     works;
     and who can search out his mighty deeds?
5 Who can measure his majestic power?
     And who can fully recount his mercies?
6 It is not possible to diminish or increase them,
     nor is it possible to fathom the wonders of
       the Lord.
7 When human beings have finished, they are just
     beginning,
     and when they stop, they are still perplexed.
8 What are human beings, and of what use are they?
     What is good in them, and what is evil?
9 The number of days in their life is great if they
     reach one hundred years.*b*
10 Like a drop of water from the sea and a grain of
     sand,
     so are a few years among the days of eternity.
11 That is why the Lord is patient with them
     and pours out his mercy upon them.
12 He sees and recognizes that their end is miserable;
     therefore he grants them forgiveness all the
       more.
13 The compassion of human beings is for their
     neighbors,
     but the compassion of the Lord is for every
       living thing.
     He rebukes and trains and teaches them,
     and turns them back, as a shepherd his flock.
14 He has compassion on those who accept his
     discipline
     and who are eager for his precepts.

The Right Spirit in Giving Alms

15 My child, do not mix reproach with your good
     deeds,
     or spoil your gift by harsh words.

16 Does not the dew give relief from the scorching
     heat?
     So a word is better than a gift.
17 Indeed, does not a word surpass a good gift?
     Both are to be found in a gracious person.
18 A fool is ungracious and abusive,
     and the gift of a grudging giver makes the eyes
       dim.

The Need of Reflection and Self-control

19 Before you speak, learn;
     and before you fall ill, take care of your
       health.
20 Before judgment comes, examine yourself;
     and at the time of scrutiny you will find
       forgiveness.
21 Before falling ill, humble yourself;
     and when you have sinned, repent.
22 Let nothing hinder you from paying a vow
     promptly,
     and do not wait until death to be released
       from it.
23 Before making a vow, prepare yourself;
     do not be like one who puts the Lord to the
       test.
24 Think of his wrath on the day of death,
     and of the moment of vengeance when he
       turns away his face.
25 In the time of plenty think of the time of hunger;
     in days of wealth think of poverty and need.
26 From morning to evening conditions change;
     all things move swiftly before the Lord.

27 One who is wise is cautious in everything;
     when sin is all around, one guards against
       wrongdoing.
28 Every intelligent person knows wisdom,
     and praises the one who finds her.
29 Those who are skilled in words become wise
     themselves,
     and pour forth apt proverbs.*c*

SELF-CONTROL*d*

30 Do not follow your base desires,
     but restrain your appetites.
31 If you allow your soul to take pleasure in base
     desire,
     it will make you the laughingstock of your
       enemies.

---

a Other ancient authorities add *and there is no other beside him;*
*3he steers the world with the span of his hand, and all things
obey his will; for he is king of all things by his power, separating
among them the holy things from the profane.* b Other ancient
authorities add *but the death of each one is beyond the calculation
of all* c Other ancient authorities add *Better is confidence in the
one Lord than clinging with a dead heart to a dead one.* d This
heading is included in the Gk text.

³² Do not revel in great luxury,
  or you may become impoverished by its
    expense.
³³ Do not become a beggar by feasting with
  borrowed money,
  when you have nothing in your purse.ᵃ

19 The one who does thisᵇ will not become
  rich;
  one who despises small things will fail little
    by little.
² Wine and women lead intelligent men astray,
  and the man who consorts with prostitutes is
    reckless.
³ Decay and worms will take possession of him,
  and the reckless person will be snatched away.

Against Loose Talk

⁴ One who trusts others too quickly has a shallow
    mind,
  and one who sins does wrong to himself.
⁵ One who rejoices in wickednessᶜ will be
    condemned,ᵈ
⁶   but one who hates gossip has less evil.
⁷ Never repeat a conversation,
  and you will lose nothing at all.
⁸ With friend or foe do not report it,
  and unless it would be a sin for you, do not
    reveal it;
⁹ for someone may have heard you and watched
    you,
  and in time will hate you.
¹⁰ Have you heard something? Let it die with you.
  Be brave, it will not make you burst!
¹¹ Having heard something, the fool suffers birth
    pangs
  like a woman in labor with a child.
¹² Like an arrow stuck in a person's thigh,
  so is gossip inside a fool.

¹³ Question a friend; perhaps he did not do it;
  or if he did, so that he may not do it again.
¹⁴ Question a neighbor; perhaps he did not say it;
  or if he said it, so that he may not repeat it.
¹⁵ Question a friend, for often it is slander;
  so do not believe everything you hear.
¹⁶ A person may make a slip without intending it.
  Who has not sinned with his tongue?
¹⁷ Question your neighbor before you threaten him;
  and let the law of the Most High take its
    course.ᵉ

True and False Wisdom

²⁰ The whole of wisdom is fear of the Lord,
  and in all wisdom there is the fulfillment of
    the law.ᶠ
²² The knowledge of wickedness is not wisdom,

Live It!

Don't Get Burned

It is easy to give in to temptation. Every day, we face decisions that can hurt our relationship with God. Ben Sira soundly advises us not to give in to our base desires (Sir 18:30). These are attitudes and practices that include laziness, drunkenness, and lust, which might bring some immediate pleasure but also lead to long-term problems. Self-control is the strength to resist the lusts that lead to lifelong problems.

An old saying—If you play with matches, you might get burned—is often used by people recovering from addictions. It reminds them that risky behaviors often end up hurting them. It helps them stay focused on their long-term goal of leading a healthy and happy life. If they follow Ben Sira's advice—practice self-control—they won't end up getting burned!
● What base desires tempt you the most?
● What do you need to do to avoid getting burned by them?

▶ Sir 18:30—19:3

nor is there prudence in the counsel of sinners.
²³ There is a cleverness that is detestable,
  and there is a fool who merely lacks wisdom.
²⁴ Better are the God-fearing who lack
    understanding
  than the highly intelligent who transgress the
    law.
²⁵ There is a cleverness that is exact but unjust,
  and there are people who abuse favors to gain
  a verdict.

---

a Other ancient authorities add *for you will be plotting against your own life*   b Heb: Gk *A worker who is a drunkard*   c Other ancient authorities read *heart*   d Other ancient authorities add *but one who withstands pleasures crowns his life.* ⁶*One who controls the tongue will live without strife.*   e Other ancient authorities add *and do not be angry.* ¹⁸*The fear of the Lord is the beginning of acceptance, and wisdom obtains his love.* ¹⁹*The knowledge of the Lord's commandments is life-giving discipline; and those who do what is pleasing to him enjoy the fruit of the tree of immortality.*   f Other ancient authorities add *and the knowledge of his omnipotence.* ²¹*When a slave says to his master, "I will not act as you wish," even if later he does it, he angers the one who supports him.*

SIR

26 There is the villain bowed down in mourning,
    but inwardly he is full of deceit.
27 He hides his face and pretends not to hear,
    but when no one notices, he will take
        advantage of you.
28 Even if lack of strength keeps him from sinning,
    he will nevertheless do evil when he finds the
        opportunity.
29 A person is known by his appearance,
    and a sensible person is known when first
        met, face to face.
30 A person's attire and hearty laughter,
    and the way he walks, show what he is.

Silence and Speech

20 There is a rebuke that is untimely,
    and there is the person who is wise
        enough to keep silent.
2 How much better it is to rebuke than to fume!

Examine Your Conscience

An examination of conscience is a moral
inventory of one's life. When we examine
our conscience, we can recognize those we have
hurt, make amends where possible, and turn our
lives around before a pattern of sin becomes a
major obstacle in our relationships with God and
with others. We can also recognize the positive
moral choices we have made. Chapters 19–22
of Sirach list some of the sins from Ben Sira's
time. Use them as a guide for making your own
examination of conscience, as follows:

● Have you gossiped (see 19:5–12)?
● Have you offended others with your language
  (see 20:18–19)?
● Have you lied (see 20:24–26)?
● Have you stolen from others (see 21:8)?
● Have you been lazy in your use of time (see
  22:1–2)?
● Have you disobeyed your parents (see
  22:3–5)?

When you have finished this examination, read 22:27—23:6 as your own
prayer for God's help against
sinning.

▶ Sir 19:5—23:6

---

3 And the one who admits his fault will be kept
    from failure.
4 Like a eunuch lusting to violate a girl
    is the person who does right under
        compulsion.
5 Some people keep silent and are thought to be
        wise,
    while others are detested for being talkative.
6 Some people keep silent because they have
        nothing to say,
    while others keep silent because they know
        when to speak.
7 The wise remain silent until the right moment,
    but a boasting fool misses the right moment.
8 Whoever talks too much is detested,
    and whoever pretends to authority is hated.ᵃ

Paradoxes

9 There may be good fortune for a person in
        adversity,
    and a windfall may result in a loss.
10 There is the gift that profits you nothing,
    and the gift to be paid back double.
11 There are losses for the sake of glory,
    and there are some who have raised their
        heads from humble circumstances.
12 Some buy much for little,
    but pay for it seven times over.
13 The wise make themselves beloved by only few
        words,ᵇ
    but the courtesies of fools are wasted.
14 A fool's gift will profit you nothing,ᶜ
    for he looks for recompense sevenfold.ᵈ
15 He gives little and upbraids much;
    he opens his mouth like a town crier.
    Today he lends and tomorrow he asks it back;
    such a one is hateful to God and humans.ᵉ
16 The fool says, "I have no friends,
    and I get no thanks for my good deeds.
    Those who eat my bread are evil-tongued."
17 How many will ridicule him, and how often!ᶠ

Inappropriate Speech

18 A slip on the pavement is better than a slip of
        the tongue;
    the downfall of the wicked will occur just as
        speedily.
19 A coarse person is like an inappropriate story,
    continually on the lips of the ignorant.

ᵃ Other ancient authorities add *How good it is to show repentance
when you are reproved, for so you will escape deliberate sin!*
ᵇ Heb: Gk *by words*   ᶜ Other ancient authorities add *so it is with
the envious who give under compulsion*   ᵈ Syr: Gk *he has many
eyes instead of one*   ᵉ Other ancient authorities lack *to God and
humans*   ᶠ Other ancient authorities add *for he has not honestly
received what he has, and what he does not have is unimportant
to him*

20 A proverb from a fool's lips will be rejected,
     for he does not tell it at the proper time.

21 One may be prevented from sinning by poverty;
     so when he rests he feels no remorse.
22 One may lose his life through shame,
     or lose it because of human respect.[a]
23 Another out of shame makes promises to a
     friend,
     and so makes an enemy for nothing.

Lying

24 A lie is an ugly blot on a person;
     it is continually on the lips of the ignorant.
25 A thief is preferable to a habitual liar,
     but the lot of both is ruin.
26 A liar's way leads to disgrace,
     and his shame is ever with him.

Proverbial Sayings[b]

27 The wise person advances himself by his words,
     and one who is sensible pleases the great.
28 Those who cultivate the soil heap up their
     harvest,
     and those who please the great atone for
     injustice.
29 Favors and gifts blind the eyes of the wise;
     like a muzzle on the mouth they stop
     reproofs.
30 Hidden wisdom and unseen treasure,
     of what value is either?
31 Better are those who hide their folly
     than those who hide their wisdom.[c]

Various Sins

21 Have you sinned, my child? Do so no more,
     but ask forgiveness for your past sins.
2 Flee from sin as from a snake;
     for if you approach sin, it will bite you.
     Its teeth are lion's teeth,
     and can destroy human lives.
3 All lawlessness is like a two-edged sword;
     there is no healing for the wound it inflicts.

4 Panic and insolence will waste away riches;
     thus the house of the proud will be laid
     waste.[d]
5 The prayer of the poor goes from their lips to
     the ears of God,[e]
     and his judgment comes speedily.
6 Those who hate reproof walk in the sinner's
     steps,
     but those who fear the Lord repent in their
     heart.
7 The mighty in speech are widely known;
     when they slip, the sensible person knows it.

8 Whoever builds his house with other people's
     money
     is like one who gathers stones for his burial
     mound.[f]
9 An assembly of the wicked is like a bundle of
     tow,
     and their end is a blazing fire.
10 The way of sinners is paved with smooth stones,
     but at its end is the pit of Hades.

Wisdom and Foolishness

11 Whoever keeps the law controls his thoughts,
     and the fulfillment of the fear of the Lord is
     wisdom.
12 The one who is not clever cannot be taught,
     but there is a cleverness that increases
     bitterness.
13 The knowledge of the wise will increase like a
     flood,
     and their counsel like a life-giving spring.
14 The mind[g] of a fool is like a broken jar;
     it can hold no knowledge.

15 When an intelligent person hears a wise saying,
     he praises it and adds to it;
     when a fool[h] hears it, he laughs at[i] it
     and throws it behind his back.
16 A fool's chatter is like a burden on a journey,
     but delight is found in the speech of the
     intelligent.
17 The utterance of a sensible person is sought in
     the assembly,
     and they ponder his words in their minds.

18 Like a house in ruins is wisdom to a fool,
     and to the ignorant, knowledge is talk that
     has no meaning.
19 To a senseless person education is fetters on his
     feet,
     and like manacles on his right hand.
20 A fool raises his voice when he laughs,
     but the wise[j] smile quietly.
21 To the sensible person education is like a golden
     ornament,
     and like a bracelet on the right arm.

22 The foot of a fool rushes into a house,
     but an experienced person waits respectfully
     outside.
23 A boor peers into the house from the door,

---

a Other ancient authorities read *his foolish look*   b This
heading is included in the Gk text.   c Other ancient authorities
add *32Unwearied endurance in seeking the Lord is better than
a masterless charioteer of one's own life*.   d Other ancient
authorities read *uprooted*   e Gk *his ears*   f Other ancient
authorities read *for the winter*   g Syr Lat: Gk *entrails*   h Syr: Gk
reveler   i Syr: Gk *dislikes*   j Syr Lat: Gk *clever*

but a cultivated person remains outside.

24 It is ill-mannered for a person to listen at a
door;
the discreet would be grieved by the
disgrace.

25 The lips of babblers speak of what is not their
concern,[a]
but the words of the prudent are weighed in
the balance.

26 The mind of fools is in their mouth,
but the mouth of the wise is in[b] their mind.

27 When an ungodly person curses an adversary,[c]
he curses himself.

28 A whisperer degrades himself
and is hated in his neighborhood.

The Idler

22 The idler is like a filthy stone,
and every one hisses at his disgrace.

2 The idler is like the filth of dunghills;
anyone that picks it up will shake it off his
hand.

Degenerate Children

3 It is a disgrace to be the father of an
undisciplined son,
and the birth of a daughter is a loss.

4 A sensible daughter obtains a husband of her
own,
but one who acts shamefully is a grief to her
father.

5 An impudent daughter disgraces father and
husband,
and is despised by both.

6 Like music in time of mourning is ill-timed
conversation,
but a thrashing and discipline are at all times
wisdom.[d]

Wisdom and Folly

9 Whoever teaches a fool is like one who glues
potsherds together,
or who rouses a sleeper from deep slumber.

10 Whoever tells a story to a fool tells it to a
drowsy man;
and at the end he will say, "What is it?"

11 Weep for the dead, for he has left the light
behind;
and weep for the fool, for he has left
intelligence behind.
Weep less bitterly for the dead, for he is at rest;
but the life of the fool is worse than death.

12 Mourning for the dead lasts seven days,
but for the foolish or the ungodly it lasts all
the days of their lives.

13 Do not talk much with a senseless person
or visit an unintelligent person.[e]
Stay clear of him, or you may have trouble,
and be spattered when he shakes himself off.
Avoid him and you will find rest,
and you will never be wearied by his lack of
sense.

14 What is heavier than lead?
And what is its name except "Fool"?

15 Sand, salt, and a piece of iron
are easier to bear than a stupid person.

16 A wooden beam firmly bonded into a building
is not loosened by an earthquake;
so the mind firmly resolved after due reflection
will not be afraid in a crisis.

17 A mind settled on an intelligent thought
is like stucco decoration that makes a wall
smooth.

18 Fences[f] set on a high place
will not stand firm against the wind;
so a timid mind with a fool's resolve
will not stand firm against any fear.

The Preservation of Friendship

19 One who pricks the eye brings tears,
and one who pricks the heart makes clear its
feelings.

20 One who throws a stone at birds scares them
away,
and one who reviles a friend destroys a
friendship.

21 Even if you draw your sword against a friend,
do not despair, for there is a way back.

22 If you open your mouth against your friend,
do not worry, for reconciliation is possible.
But as for reviling, arrogance, disclosure of
secrets, or a treacherous blow—
in these cases any friend will take to flight.

23 Gain the trust of your neighbor in his poverty,
so that you may rejoice with him in his
prosperity.
Stand by him in time of distress,
so that you may share with him in his
inheritance.[g]

24 The vapor and smoke of the furnace precede the
fire;

---

a Other ancient authorities read *of strangers speak of these
things*   b Other ancient authorities omit *in*   c Or *curses Satan*
d Other ancient authorities add *⁷Children who are brought up in
a good life, conceal the lowly birth of their parents. ⁸Children who
are disdainfully and boorishly haughty stain the nobility of their
kindred.*   e Other ancient authorities add *For being without sense
he will despise everything about you*   f Other ancient authorities
read *Pebbles*   g Other ancient authorities add *For one should not
always despise restricted circumstances, or admire a rich person
who is stupid.*

so insults precede bloodshed.

²⁵ I am not ashamed to shelter a friend,
  and I will not hide from him.
²⁶ But if harm should come to me because of him,
  whoever hears of it will beware of him.

A Prayer for Help against Sinning

²⁷ Who will set a guard over my mouth,
  and an effective seal upon my lips,
  so that I may not fall because of them,
  and my tongue may not destroy me?

23 O Lord, Father and Master of my life,
  do not abandon me to their designs,
  and do not let me fall because of them!
² Who will set whips over my thoughts,
  and the discipline of wisdom over my mind,
  so as not to spare me in my errors,
  and not overlook my*ᵃ* sins?
³ Otherwise my mistakes may be multiplied,
  and my sins may abound,
  and I may fall before my adversaries,
  and my enemy may rejoice over me.*ᵇ*
⁴ O Lord, Father and God of my life,
  do not give me haughty eyes,
⁵   and remove evil desire from me.
⁶ Let neither gluttony nor lust overcome me,
  and do not give me over to shameless passion.

DISCIPLINE OF THE TONGUE*ᶜ*

⁷ Listen, my children, to instruction concerning
    the mouth;
  the one who observes it will never be caught.
⁸ Sinners are overtaken through their lips;
  by them the reviler and the arrogant are
    tripped up.
⁹ Do not accustom your mouth to oaths,
  nor habitually utter the name of the Holy One;
¹⁰ for as a servant who is constantly under scrutiny
  will not lack bruises,
  so also the person who always swears and utters
    the Name
  will never be cleansed*ᵈ* from sin.
¹¹ The one who swears many oaths is full of iniquity,
  and the scourge will not leave his house.
  If he swears in error, his sin remains on him,
  and if he disregards it, he sins doubly;
  if he swears a false oath, he will not be justified,
  for his house will be filled with calamities.

Foul Language

¹² There is a manner of speaking comparable to
    death;*ᵉ*
  may it never be found in the inheritance of
    Jacob!
  Such conduct will be far from the godly,
  and they will not wallow in sins.

Live It!

Four-Letter Words

Four-letter words. You've heard them plenty. You have undoubtedly used them yourself. They roll off the tongue so easily. They get attention. They help you fit in with some groups of people.

You might wonder, So, what's the problem with foul language? Why does Ben Sira call it "sinful speech" (Sir 23:13)? Well, part of the problem is that using it easily becomes a habit. You become less aware of when you are using it. You can get yourself into trouble. Ben Sira warns that you may "behave like a fool through bad habit" (verse 14).

Maybe the worst part of the problem is that frequent use of foul language shows a lack of respect and reverence for others and certainly for God's name. Ben Sira reminds us, "Such conduct will be far from the godly" (verse 12).

Certainly, in a language with over 600,000 words, there are more creative ways to express emotion or frustration than relying on those all-too-familiar four-letter words. If you've developed the habit of using them, ask God and your friends to help you stop.

▶ Sir 23:12–15

¹³ Do not accustom your mouth to coarse, foul
    language,
  for it involves sinful speech.
¹⁴ Remember your father and mother
  when you sit among the great,
  or you may forget yourself in their presence,
  and behave like a fool through bad habit;
  then you will wish that you had never been
    born,
  and you will curse the day of your birth.
¹⁵ Those who are accustomed to using abusive
    language
  will never become disciplined as long as they
    live.

---

a Gk *their*   *b* Other ancient authorities add *From them the hope of your mercy is remote*   *c* This heading is included in the Gk text.   *d* Syr *be free*   *e* Other ancient authorities read *clothed about with death*

✝ Catholic Connection

Sin and Moral Decision Making

Have you ever intentionally said or done something mean and later wished you could take it back? In the Book of Sirach (Ecclesiasticus), Ben Sira offers a wonderful and rather dramatic prayer for help to avoid sinning. Ben Sira uses words like *guard* and *discipline* to describe how diligently his thoughts and words should be monitored. The strong language helps emphasize the importance of avoiding sin and the need to be vigilant in the process.

We too must be vigilant and seek God's help in avoiding sin, for sin is an offense against God that breaks God's law of love. The Church teaches that sin occurs when one goes against the truth and right reason, and one's conscience. It is when a person consciously chooses through thoughts, words, or deeds not to love God, neighbor, or self. Sin harms not only a person's relationship with God but also his or her relationships with other people and one's self.

One way to avoid sin is to always try to make good moral decisions. Whenever we are faced with a decision, we must ask ourselves three questions: First, is the act I am considering doing morally good, like loving my neighbor, or morally evil, like murder? Second, what are my intentions for doing this act? For example, am I helping my neighbor out of love or in the hopes of getting something in return? Third,

what are the circumstances surrounding the action? The circumstances cannot change an evil act into a good act, but they may diminish your level of responsibility for committing the act. For example, if you are acting out of fear for your own life when you harm someone else, although the act is still morally evil, your personal responsibility may be diminished. Together all three questions help us determine the moral quality of our actions by examining what we are doing, why we are doing it, and the circumstances surrounding the act.

The Church does make distinctions between two types of sin based on the gravity of the act committed. Some sins, called mortal sins, are so serious they break our relationship with God entirely. These sins are committed when a person goes against his or her conscience and willfully commits a seriously immoral act, like murder. Venial sins entail a less serious immoral act, or a lack of full knowledge or willingness, and only weaken our relationship with God. And rest assured, no matter what, we can always seek God's forgiveness and restore our relationship with him through the sacrament of Penance and Reconciliation.

▶ **Sir 22:27—23:6**
Catechism, nos. 1749–1761, 1846–1864

Concerning Sexual Sins

16 Two kinds of individuals multiply sins,
   and a third incurs wrath.
Hot passion that blazes like a fire
   will not be quenched until it burns itself out;
one who commits fornication with his near
      of kin
   will never cease until the fire burns him up.
17 To a fornicator all bread is sweet;
   he will never weary until he dies.
18 The one who sins against his marriage bed
   says to himself, "Who can see me?
Darkness surrounds me, the walls hide me,
   and no one sees me. Why should I worry?
The Most High will not remember sins."
19 His fear is confined to human eyes
   and he does not realize that the eyes of the
      Lord
   are ten thousand times brighter than the sun;
they look upon every aspect of human behavior
   and see into hidden corners.
20 Before the universe was created, it was known to
      him,
   and so it is since its completion.
21 This man will be punished in the streets of the
      city,
   and where he least suspects it, he will be
      seized.

22 So it is with a woman who leaves her husband
   and presents him with an heir by another
      man.
23 For first of all, she has disobeyed the law of the
      Most High;
   second, she has committed an offense against
      her husband;
and third, through her fornication she has
      committed adultery
   and brought forth children by another man.
24 She herself will be brought before the assembly,
   and her punishment will extend to her
      children.
25 Her children will not take root,
   and her branches will not bear fruit.
26 She will leave behind an accursed memory
   and her disgrace will never be blotted out.
27 Those who survive her will recognize
   that nothing is better than the fear of the Lord,
and nothing sweeter than to heed the
   commandments of the Lord.[a]

The Praise of Wisdom[b]

24 Wisdom praises herself,
   and tells of her glory in the midst of her
      people.
2 In the assembly of the Most High she opens her
      mouth,
   and in the presence of his hosts she tells of
      her glory:
3 "I came forth from the mouth of the Most High,
   and covered the earth like a mist.
4 I dwelt in the highest heavens,
   and my throne was in a pillar of cloud.
5 Alone I compassed the vault of heaven
   and traversed the depths of the abyss.
6 Over waves of the sea, over all the earth,
   and over every people and nation I have held
      sway.[c]
7 Among all these I sought a resting place;
   in whose territory should I abide?
8 "Then the Creator of all things gave me a
      command,
   and my Creator chose the place for my tent.
He said, 'Make your dwelling in Jacob,
   and in Israel receive your inheritance.'
9 Before the ages, in the beginning, he created
      me,
   and for all the ages I shall not cease to be.
10 In the holy tent I ministered before him,
   and so I was established in Zion.
11 Thus in the beloved city he gave me a resting
      place,
   and in Jerusalem was my domain.
12 I took root in an honored people,
   in the portion of the Lord, his heritage.
13 "I grew tall like a cedar in Lebanon,
   and like a cypress on the heights of Hermon.
14 I grew tall like a palm tree in En-gedi,[d]
   and like rosebushes in Jericho;
like a fair olive tree in the field,
   and like a plane tree beside water[e] I grew tall.
15 Like cassia and camel's thorn I gave forth
      perfume,
   and like choice myrrh I spread my fragrance,
like galbanum, onycha, and stacte,
   and like the odor of incense in the tent.
16 Like a terebinth I spread out my branches,
   and my branches are glorious and graceful.
17 Like the vine I bud forth delights,
   and my blossoms become glorious and
      abundant fruit.[f]

---

a Other ancient authorities add as verse 28, *It is a great honor to follow God, and to be received by him is long life.*   b This heading is included in the Gk text.   c Other ancient authorities read *I have acquired a possession*   d Other ancient authorities read *on the beaches*   e Other ancient authorities omit *beside water*   f Other ancient authorities add as verse 18, *I am the mother of beautiful love, of fear, of knowledge, and of holy hope; being eternal, I am given to all my children, to those who are named by him.*

19 "Come to me, you who desire me,
   and eat your fill of my fruits.
20 For the memory of me is sweeter than honey,
   and the possession of me sweeter than the
      honeycomb.
21 Those who eat of me will hunger for more,
   and those who drink of me will thirst for
      more.
22 Whoever obeys me will not be put to shame,
   and those who work with me will not sin."

Wisdom and the Law

23 All this is the book of the covenant of the Most
      High God,
   the law that Moses commanded us
   as an inheritance for the congregations of
      Jacob.*a*
25 It overflows, like the Pishon, with wisdom,
   and like the Tigris at the time of the first
      fruits.
26 It runs over, like the Euphrates, with
      understanding,
   and like the Jordan at harvest time.
27 It pours forth instruction like the Nile,*b*
   like the Gihon at the time of vintage.
28 The first man did not know wisdom*c* fully,
   nor will the last one fathom her.
29 For her thoughts are more abundant than the
      sea,
   and her counsel deeper than the great abyss.

30 As for me, I was like a canal from a river,
   like a water channel into a garden.
31 I said, "I will water my garden
   and drench my flower-beds."
   And lo, my canal became a river,
   and my river a sea.
32 I will again make instruction shine forth like the
      dawn,
   and I will make it clear from far away.
33 I will again pour out teaching like prophecy,
   and leave it to all future generations.
34 Observe that I have not labored for myself
      alone,
   but for all who seek wisdom.*c*

Those Who Are Worthy of Praise

25
I take pleasure in three things,
   and they are beautiful in the sight of God
      and of mortals:*d*
   agreement among brothers and sisters,
      friendship among neighbors,
   and a wife and a husband who live in
      harmony.
2 I hate three kinds of people,
   and I loathe their manner of life:

a pauper who boasts, a rich person who lies,
   and an old fool who commits adultery.

3 If you gathered nothing in your youth,
   how can you find anything in your old age?
4 How attractive is sound judgment in the gray-
      haired,
   and for the aged to possess good counsel!
5 How attractive is wisdom in the aged,
   and understanding and counsel in the
      venerable!
6 Rich experience is the crown of the aged,
   and their boast is the fear of the Lord.

7 I can think of nine whom I would call blessed,
   and a tenth my tongue proclaims:
   a man who can rejoice in his children;
   a man who lives to see the downfall of his
      foes.
8 Happy the man who lives with a sensible wife,
   and the one who does not plow with ox and
      ass together.*e*
Happy is the one who does not sin with the
      tongue,
   and the one who has not served an inferior.
9 Happy is the one who finds a friend,*f*
   and the one who speaks to attentive listeners.
10 How great is the one who finds wisdom!
   But none is superior to the one who fears the
      Lord.
11 Fear of the Lord surpasses everything;
   to whom can we compare the one who has it?*g*

Some Extreme Forms of Evil

13 Any wound, but not a wound of the heart!
   Any wickedness, but not the wickedness of a
      woman!
14 Any suffering, but not suffering from those who
      hate!
   And any vengeance, but not the vengeance of
      enemies!
15 There is no venom*h* worse than a snake's venom,*h*
   and no anger worse than a woman's*i* wrath.

The Evil of a Wicked Woman

16 I would rather live with a lion and a dragon
   than live with an evil woman.

---

a Other ancient authorities add as verse 24, "Do not cease to be
strong in the Lord, cling to him so that he may strengthen you; the
Lord Almighty alone is God, and besides him there is no savior."
b Syr: Gk It makes instruction shine forth like light   c Gk her
d Syr Lat: Gk In three things I was beautiful and I stood in beauty
before the Lord and mortals.   e Heb Syr: Gk lacks and the one
who does not plow with ox and ass together   f Lat Syr: Gk good
sense   g Other ancient authorities add as verse 12, The fear of
the Lord is the beginning of love for him, and faith is the beginning
of clinging to him.   h Syr: Gk head   i Other ancient authorities
read an enemy's

17 A woman's wickedness changes her appearance,
  and darkens her face like that of a bear.
18 Her husband sits[a] among the neighbors,
  and he cannot help sighing[b] bitterly.
19 Any iniquity is small compared to a woman's
  iniquity;
  may a sinner's lot befall her!
20 A sandy ascent for the feet of the aged—
  such is a garrulous wife to a quiet husband.
21 Do not be ensnared by a woman's beauty,
  and do not desire a woman for her
  possessions.[c]
22 There is wrath and impudence and great disgrace
  when a wife supports her husband.
23 Dejected mind, gloomy face,
  and wounded heart come from an evil wife.
  Drooping hands and weak knees
  come from the wife who does not make her
  husband happy.
24 From a woman sin had its beginning,
  and because of her we all die.
25 Allow no outlet to water,
  and no boldness of speech to an evil wife.
26 If she does not go as you direct,
  separate her from yourself.

The Joy of a Good Wife

26 Happy is the husband of a good wife;
  the number of his days will be doubled.
2 A loyal wife brings joy to her husband,
  and he will complete his years in peace.
3 A good wife is a great blessing;
  she will be granted among the blessings of the
  man who fears the Lord.
4 Whether rich or poor, his heart is content,
  and at all times his face is cheerful.

The Worst of Evils: A Wicked Wife

5 Of three things my heart is frightened,
  and of a fourth I am in great fear:[d]
  Slander in the city, the gathering of a mob,
  and false accusation—all these are worse than
  death.
6 But it is heartache and sorrow when a wife is
  jealous of a rival,
  and a tongue-lashing makes it known to all.
7 A bad wife is a chafing yoke;
  taking hold of her is like grasping a scorpion.
8 A drunken wife arouses great anger;
  she cannot hide her shame.
9 The haughty stare betrays an unchaste wife;
  her eyelids give her away.
10 Keep strict watch over a headstrong daughter,
  or else, when she finds liberty, she will make
  use of it.

11 Be on guard against her impudent eye,
  and do not be surprised if she sins against you.
12 As a thirsty traveler opens his mouth
  and drinks from any water near him,
  so she will sit in front of every tent peg
  and open her quiver to the arrow.

The Blessing of a Good Wife

13 A wife's charm delights her husband,
  and her skill puts flesh on his bones.
14 A silent wife is a gift from the Lord,
  and nothing is so precious as her self-
  discipline.
15 A modest wife adds charm to charm,
  and no scales can weigh the value of her
  chastity.
16 Like the sun rising in the heights of the Lord,
  so is the beauty of a good wife in her well-
  ordered home.
17 Like the shining lamp on the holy lampstand,
  so is a beautiful face on a stately figure.
18 Like golden pillars on silver bases,
  so are shapely legs and steadfast feet.

_____

Other ancient authorities add verses 19-27:

19 *My child, keep sound the bloom of your youth,*
  and do not give your strength to strangers.
20 *Seek a fertile field within the whole plain,*
  and sow it with your own seed, trusting in your
  fine stock.
21 *So your offspring will prosper,*
  and, having confidence in their good descent, will
  grow great.
22 *A prostitute is regarded as spittle,*
  and a married woman as a tower of death to her
  lovers.
23 *A godless wife is given as a portion to a lawless man,*
  but a pious wife is given to the man who fears the
  Lord.
24 *A shameless woman constantly acts disgracefully,*
  but a modest daughter will even be embarrassed
  before her husband.
25 *A headstrong wife is regarded as a dog,*
  but one who has a sense of shame will fear the
  Lord.
26 *A wife honoring her husband will seem wise to all,*
  but if she dishonors him in her pride she will be
  known to all as ungodly.
  Happy is the husband of a good wife;
  for the number of his years will be doubled.

_____

a Heb Syr: Gk *loses heart*   b Other ancient authorities read *and*
listening he sighs   c Heb Syr: Other Gk authorities read *for her*
beauty   d Syr: Meaning of Gk uncertain

27 A loud-voiced and garrulous wife is like a trumpet
    sounding the charge,
  and every person like this lives in the anarchy of
    war.

Three Depressing Things

28 At two things my heart is grieved,
    and because of a third anger comes over me:
  a warrior in want through poverty,
    intelligent men who are treated
      contemptuously,
  and a man who turns back from righteousness
    to sin—
    the Lord will prepare him for the sword!

The Temptations of Commerce

29 A merchant can hardly keep from wrongdoing,
    nor is a tradesman innocent of sin.

27 Many have committed sin for gain,[a]
    and those who seek to get rich will avert
      their eyes.
2 As a stake is driven firmly into a fissure between
    stones,
  so sin is wedged in between selling and
    buying.
3 If a person is not steadfast in the fear of the Lord,
    his house will be quickly overthrown.

Tests in Life

4 When a sieve is shaken, the refuse appears;
    so do a person's faults when he speaks.
5 The kiln tests the potter's vessels;
    so the test of a person is in his conversation.
6 Its fruit discloses the cultivation of a tree;
    so a person's speech discloses the cultivation
      of his mind.
7 Do not praise anyone before he speaks,
    for this is the way people are tested.

Reward and Retribution

8 If you pursue justice, you will attain it
    and wear it like a glorious robe.
9 Birds roost with their own kind,
    so honesty comes home to those who
      practice it.
10 A lion lies in wait for prey;
    so does sin for evildoers.

Varieties of Speech

11 The conversation of the godly is always wise,
    but the fool changes like the moon.
12 Among stupid people limit your time,
    but among thoughtful people linger on.
13 The talk of fools is offensive,
    and their laughter is wantonly sinful.

14 Their cursing and swearing make one's hair
    stand on end,
  and their quarrels make others stop their ears.
15 The strife of the proud leads to bloodshed,
    and their abuse is grievous to hear.

Betraying Secrets

16 Whoever betrays secrets destroys confidence,
    and will never find a congenial friend.
17 Love your friend and keep faith with him;
    but if you betray his secrets, do not follow
      after him.
18 For as a person destroys his enemy,
    so you have destroyed the friendship of your
      neighbor.
19 And as you allow a bird to escape from your
    hand,
  so you have let your neighbor go, and will
    not catch him again.
20 Do not go after him, for he is too far off,
    and has escaped like a gazelle from a snare.
21 For a wound may be bandaged,
    and there is reconciliation after abuse,
  but whoever has betrayed secrets is without
    hope.

Hypocrisy and Retribution

22 Whoever winks the eye plots mischief,
    and those who know him will keep their
      distance.
23 In your presence his mouth is all sweetness,
    and he admires your words;
  but later he will twist his speech
    and with your own words he will trip you up.
24 I have hated many things, but him above all;
    even the Lord hates him.
25 Whoever throws a stone straight up throws it on
    his own head,
  and a treacherous blow opens up many
    wounds.
26 Whoever digs a pit will fall into it,
    and whoever sets a snare will be caught in it.
27 If a person does evil, it will roll back upon him,
    and he will not know where it came from.
28 Mockery and abuse issue from the proud,
    but vengeance lies in wait for them like a lion.
29 Those who rejoice in the fall of the godly will be
    caught in a snare,
  and pain will consume them before their
    death.

Anger and Vengeance

30 Anger and wrath, these also are abominations,
    yet a sinner holds on to them.

---

a Other ancient authorities read a trifle

28 The vengeful will face the Lord's vengeance,
for he keeps a strict account of[a] their sins.

2 Forgive your neighbor the wrong he has done,
and then your sins will be pardoned when you pray.

3 Does anyone harbor anger against another,
and expect healing from the Lord?

4 If one has no mercy toward another like himself,
can he then seek pardon for his own sins?

5 If a mere mortal harbors wrath,
who will make an atoning sacrifice for his sins?

6 Remember the end of your life, and set enmity aside;
remember corruption and death, and be true to the commandments.

7 Remember the commandments, and do not be angry with your neighbor;
remember the covenant of the Most High,
and overlook faults.

8 Refrain from strife, and your sins will be fewer;
for the hot-tempered kindle strife,

9 and the sinner disrupts friendships
and sows discord among those who are at peace.

10 In proportion to the fuel, so will the fire burn,
and in proportion to the obstinacy, so will strife increase;[b]
in proportion to a person's strength will be his anger,
and in proportion to his wealth he will increase his wrath.

11 A hasty quarrel kindles a fire,
and a hasty dispute sheds blood.

The Evil Tongue

12 If you blow on a spark, it will glow;
if you spit on it, it will be put out;
yet both come out of your mouth.

13 Curse the gossips and the double-tongued,
for they destroy the peace of many.

14 Slander[c] has shaken many,
and scattered them from nation to nation;
it has destroyed strong cities,
and overturned the houses of the great.

15 Slander[c] has driven virtuous women from their homes,
and deprived them of the fruit of their toil.

16 Those who pay heed to slander[d] will not find rest,
nor will they settle down in peace.

Live It!

Just Walk Away

"Hey, did you hear the latest about Valerie?"

"No, what?"

"Well, last Friday night, she and Maria were at Jason's party, and . . . ."

"Wait a minute, here comes Maria. Tell me later."

"Curse the gossips and the double-tongued, / for they destroy the peace of many" (Sir 28:13).

"Guess what I heard!"

"What?"

"Well, Teresa, who is usually so stuck-up—"

"I know. I can't stand her. She thinks she's so cool."

"Well, anyway, she went to this party and . . ."

"Those who pay heed to slander will not find rest, / nor will they settle down in peace" (verse 16).

"I can't believe what I just heard!"

"What? Tell me!"

"I heard that Juan and Sunyub went out last night, got totally trashed, and spent the night together."

"Are you kidding? Sunyub, little miss honor student? And Juan, athlete of the year? Are you sure?"

"I know. I can't believe it either, but I heard it from two different people. . . ."

"Many have fallen by the edge of the sword, / but not as many as have fallen because of the tongue" (verse 18).

"If you blow on a spark, it will glow; / if you spit on it, it will be put out; / yet both come out of your mouth" (verse 12).

The next time you hear a piece of gossip or a rumor, don't blow on it—spit on it and walk away. Someone's reputation is at stake. One of these times, it could be yours. Check out the third chapter of James in the New Testament for another version of the hazards of gossip and slander.

▶ Sir 28:12–18

S
I
R

---

a Other ancient authorities read *for he firmly establishes*   b Other ancient authorities read *burn*   c Gk *A third tongue*   d Gk *it*

S I R

17 The blow of a whip raises a welt,
　　but a blow of the tongue crushes the bones.
18 Many have fallen by the edge of the sword,
　　but not as many as have fallen because of the
　　　tongue.
19 Happy is the one who is protected from it,
　　who has not been exposed to its anger,
　who has not borne its yoke,
　　and has not been bound with its fetters.
20 For its yoke is a yoke of iron,
　　and its fetters are fetters of bronze;
21 its death is an evil death,
　　and Hades is preferable to it.
22 It has no power over the godly;
　　they will not be burned in its flame.
23 Those who forsake the Lord will fall into its
　　　power;
　　it will burn among them and will not be put
　　　out.
　It will be sent out against them like a lion;
　　like a leopard it will mangle them.
24a As you fence in your property with thorns,
25b 　so make a door and a bolt for your mouth.
24b As you lock up your silver and gold,
25a 　so make balances and scales for your words.
26 Take care not to err with your tongue,*a*
　　and fall victim to one lying in wait.

On Lending and Borrowing

29 The merciful lend to their neighbors;
　　by holding out a helping hand they keep
　　the commandments.
2 Lend to your neighbor in his time of need;
　　repay your neighbor when a loan falls due.
3 Keep your promise and be honest with him,
　　and on every occasion you will find what you
　　　need.
4 Many regard a loan as a windfall,
　　and cause trouble to those who help them.
5 One kisses another's hands until he gets a loan,
　　and is deferential in speaking of his
　　　neighbor's money;
　but at the time for repayment he delays,
　　and pays back with empty promises,
　　and finds fault with the time.
6 If he can pay, his creditor*b* will hardly get back
　　　half,
　　and will regard that as a windfall.
　If he cannot pay, the borrower*b* has robbed the
　　　other of his money,
　　and he has needlessly made him an enemy;
　he will repay him with curses and reproaches,
　　and instead of glory will repay him with
　　　dishonor.
7 Many refuse to lend, not because of meanness,
　　but from fear*c* of being defrauded needlessly.

8 Nevertheless, be patient with someone in
　　　humble circumstances,
　　and do not keep him waiting for your alms.
9 Help the poor for the commandment's sake,
　　and in their need do not send them away
　　　empty-handed.
10 Lose your silver for the sake of a brother or a
　　　friend,
　　and do not let it rust under a stone and be
　　　lost.
11 Lay up your treasure according to the
　　　commandments of the Most High,
　　and it will profit you more than gold.
12 Store up almsgiving in your treasury,
　　and it will rescue you from every disaster;
13 better than a stout shield and a sturdy spear,
　　it will fight for you against the enemy.

On Guaranteeing Debts

14 A good person will be surety for his neighbor,
　　but the one who has lost all sense of shame
　　　will fail him.
15 Do not forget the kindness of your guarantor,
　　for he has given his life for you.
16 A sinner wastes the property of his guarantor,
17 　and the ungrateful person abandons his
　　　rescuer.
18 Being surety has ruined many who were
　　　prosperous,
　　and has tossed them about like waves of the
　　　sea;
　it has driven the influential into exile,
　　and they have wandered among foreign
　　　nations.
19 The sinner comes to grief through surety;
　　his pursuit of gain involves him in lawsuits.
20 Assist your neighbor to the best of your ability,
　　but be careful not to fall yourself.

Home and Hospitality

21 The necessities of life are water, bread, and
　　　clothing,
　　and also a house to assure privacy.
22 Better is the life of the poor under their own
　　　crude roof
　　than sumptuous food in the house of others.
23 Be content with little or much,
　　and you will hear no reproach for being a
　　　guest.*d*
24 It is a miserable life to go from house to house;
　　as a guest you should not open your mouth;

---

a Gk *with it*　*b* Gk *he*　*c* Other ancient authorities read *many refuse to lend, therefore, because of such meanness; they are afraid* *d* Lat: Gk *reproach from your family*; other ancient authorities lack this line

S
I
R

²⁵ you will play the host and provide drink
  without being thanked,
  and besides this you will hear rude words like
    these:
²⁶ "Come here, stranger, prepare the table;
  let me eat what you have there."
²⁷ "Be off, stranger, for an honored guest is here;
  my brother has come for a visit, and I need
    the guest-room."
²⁸ It is hard for a sensible person to bear
  scolding about lodging*a* and the insults of the
    moneylender.

Concerning Children*b*

30 He who loves his son will whip him often,
  so that he may rejoice at the way he turns
    out.
² He who disciplines his son will profit by him,
  and will boast of him among acquaintances.
³ He who teaches his son will make his enemies
    envious,
  and will glory in him among his friends.
⁴ When the father dies he will not seem to be
    dead,
  for he has left behind him one like himself,
⁵ whom in his life he looked upon with joy
  and at death, without grief.
⁶ He has left behind him an avenger against his
    enemies,
  and one to repay the kindness of his friends.

⁷ Whoever spoils his son will bind up his wounds,
  and will suffer heartache at every cry.
⁸ An unbroken horse turns out stubborn,
  and an unchecked son turns out headstrong.
⁹ Pamper a child, and he will terrorize you;
  play with him, and he will grieve you.
¹⁰ Do not laugh with him, or you will have sorrow
    with him,
  and in the end you will gnash your teeth.
¹¹ Give him no freedom in his youth,
  and do not ignore his errors.
¹² Bow down his neck in his youth,*c*
  and beat his sides while he is young,
  or else he will become stubborn and disobey
    you,
  and you will have sorrow of soul from him.*d*
¹³ Discipline your son and make his yoke heavy,*e*
  so that you may not be offended by his
    shamelessness.

¹⁴ Better off poor, healthy, and fit
  than rich and afflicted in body.
¹⁵ Health and fitness are better than any gold,
  and a robust body than countless riches.
¹⁶ There is no wealth better than health of body,

and no gladness above joy of heart.
¹⁷ Death is better than a life of misery,
  and eternal sleep*f* than chronic sickness.

Concerning Foods*g*

¹⁸ Good things poured out upon a mouth that is
    closed
  are like offerings of food placed upon a grave.
¹⁹ Of what use to an idol is a sacrifice?
  For it can neither eat nor smell.
  So is the one punished by the Lord;
²⁰ he sees with his eyes and groans
  as a eunuch groans when embracing a girl.*h*

²¹ Do not give yourself over to sorrow,
  and do not distress yourself deliberately.
²² A joyful heart is life itself,
  and rejoicing lengthens one's life span.
²³ Indulge yourself*i* and take comfort,
  and remove sorrow far from you,
  for sorrow has destroyed many,
  and no advantage ever comes from it.
²⁴ Jealousy and anger shorten life,
  and anxiety brings on premature old age.
²⁵ Those who are cheerful and merry at table
  will benefit from their food.

Right Attitude toward Riches

31 Wakefulness over wealth wastes away one's
    flesh,
  and anxiety about it drives away sleep.
² Wakeful anxiety prevents slumber,
  and a severe illness carries off sleep.*j*
³ The rich person toils to amass a fortune,
  and when he rests he fills himself with his
    dainties.
⁴ The poor person toils to make a meager living,
  and if ever he rests he becomes needy.

⁵ One who loves gold will not be justified;
  one who pursues money will be led astray*k*
    by it.
⁶ Many have come to ruin because of gold,
  and their destruction has met them face to
    face.
⁷ It is a stumbling block to those who are avid
    for it,
  and every fool will be taken captive by it.

a Or *scolding from the household*   *b* This heading is included
in the Gk text.   *c* Other ancient authorities lack this line and the
preceding line   *d* Other ancient authorities lack this line   *e* Heb:
Gk *take pains with him*   *f* Other ancient authorities lack *eternal
sleep*   *g* This heading is included in the Gk text; other ancient
authorities place the heading before verse 16   *h* Other ancient
authorities add *So is the person who does right under compulsion*
i Other ancient authorities read *Beguile yourself*   *j* Other ancient
authorities read *sleep carries off a severe illness*   *k* Heb Syr: Gk
pursues destruction will be filled

S
I
R

8 Blessed is the rich person who is found
       blameless,
   and who does not go after gold.
9 Who is he, that we may praise him?
   For he has done wonders among his
       people.
10 Who has been tested by it and been found
       perfect?
   Let it be for him a ground for boasting.
   Who has had the power to transgress and did
       not transgress,
   and to do evil and did not do it?
11 His prosperity will be established,*a*
   and the assembly will proclaim his acts of
       charity.

A Tragic Tale

"**D**runkenness increases the anger of a
fool to his own hurt" (Sir 31:30).

This is the true story of a young man we'll call
Kevin. Kevin had a drinking problem. It all began when he had his first beer at age thirteen.
It tasted horrible, but all his friends told him to
keep drinking, and he would grow to love the feeling it gave him. He did keep drinking, and the
alcohol made him feel more outgoing and more
funny. This didn't seem all that bad.

Unfortunately, Kevin became an alcoholic.
Weekend drinking turned into weekday drinking,
and before long, he was drinking on his way to
school. Kevin drank so much that he blacked out
almost every other day.

One day, Kevin had drunk nearly a fifth of vod-
ka. He was at home and was supposed to be
watching his six-year-old sister, Veronica. Kevin
got angry at her and slammed her across the
side of the head. She fell to the ground and lay
there without moving. Kevin tried calling 911 but
couldn't see the numbers well enough to dial.

Veronica died as a result of Kevin's blow. Now
Kevin has to live with the horror of killing his own
sister. He wishes he could tell every thirteen-
year-old in the world not to try that first beer.

▶ Sir 31:25–31

Table Etiquette

12 Are you seated at the table of the great?*b*
   Do not be greedy at it,
   and do not say, "How much food there is
       here!"
13 Remember that a greedy eye is a bad thing.
   What has been created more greedy than the
       eye?
   Therefore it sheds tears for any reason.
14 Do not reach out your hand for everything you
       see,
   and do not crowd your neighbor*c* at the dish.
15 Judge your neighbor's feelings by your own,
   and in every matter be thoughtful.
16 Eat what is set before you like a well brought-up
       person,*d*
   and do not chew greedily, or you will give
       offense.
17 Be the first to stop, as befits good manners,
   and do not be insatiable, or you will give
       offense.
18 If you are seated among many persons,
   do not help yourself*e* before they do.

19 How ample a little is for a well-disciplined
       person!
   He does not breathe heavily when in bed.
20 Healthy sleep depends on moderate eating;
   he rises early, and feels fit.
   The distress of sleeplessness and of nausea
   and colic are with the glutton.
21 If you are overstuffed with food,
   get up to vomit, and you will have relief.
22 Listen to me, my child, and do not disregard me,
   and in the end you will appreciate my words.
   In everything you do be moderate,*f*
   and no sickness will overtake you.
23 People bless the one who is liberal with food,
   and their testimony to his generosity is
       trustworthy.
24 The city complains of the one who is stingy with
       food,
   and their testimony to his stinginess is
       accurate.

Temperance in Drinking Wine

25 Do not try to prove your strength by wine-
       drinking,
   for wine has destroyed many.
26 As the furnace tests the work of the smith,*g*
   so wine tests hearts when the insolent quarrel.

---

a Other ancient authorities add *because of this*   *b* Heb Syr:
Gk *at a great table*   *c* Gk *him*   *d* Heb: Gk *like a human being*
e Gk *reach out your hand*   *f* Heb Syr: Gk *industrious*   *g* Heb:
Gk *tests the hardening of steel by dipping*

27 Wine is very life to human beings
     if taken in moderation.
   What is life to one who is without wine?
     It has been created to make people happy.
28 Wine drunk at the proper time and in
     moderation
     is rejoicing of heart and gladness of soul.
29 Wine drunk to excess leads to bitterness of spirit,
     to quarrels and stumbling.
30 Drunkenness increases the anger of a fool to his
     own hurt,
     reducing his strength and adding wounds.
31 Do not reprove your neighbor at a banquet of
     wine,
   and do not despise him in his merrymaking;
   speak no word of reproach to him,
   and do not distress him by making demands
     of him.

Etiquette at a Banquet

32 If they make you master of the feast, do
       not exalt yourself;
   be among them as one of their number.
   Take care of them first and then sit down;
2   when you have fulfilled all your duties, take
     your place,
   so that you may be merry along with them
     and receive a wreath for your excellent
     leadership.

3 Speak, you who are older, for it is your right,
   but with accurate knowledge, and do not
     interrupt the music.
4 Where there is entertainment, do not pour out
     talk;
   do not display your cleverness at the wrong
     time.
5 A ruby seal in a setting of gold
   is a concert of music at a banquet of wine.
6 A seal of emerald in a rich setting of gold
   is the melody of music with good wine.

7 Speak, you who are young, if you are obliged to,
   but no more than twice, and only if asked.
8 Be brief; say much in few words;
   be as one who knows and can still hold his
     tongue.
9 Among the great do not act as their equal;
   and when another is speaking, do not babble.

10 Lightning travels ahead of the thunder,
   and approval goes before one who is modest.
11 Leave in good time and do not be the last;
   go home quickly and do not linger.
12 Amuse yourself there to your heart's content,
   but do not sin through proud speech.

13 But above all bless your Maker,
   who fills you with his good gifts.

The Providence of God

14 The one who seeks God[a] will accept his
     discipline,
   and those who rise early to seek him[b] will
     find favor.
15 The one who seeks the law will be filled with it,
   but the hypocrite will stumble at it.
16 Those who fear the Lord will form true
     judgments,
   and they will kindle righteous deeds like a
     light.
17 The sinner will shun reproof,
   and will find a decision according to his
     liking.

18 A sensible person will not overlook a thoughtful
     suggestion;
   an insolent[c] and proud person will not be
     deterred by fear.[d]
19 Do nothing without deliberation,
   but when you have acted, do not regret it.
20 Do not go on a path full of hazards,
   and do not stumble at an obstacle twice.[e]
21 Do not be overconfident on a smooth[f] road,
22   and give good heed to your paths.[g]
23 Guard[h] yourself in every act,
   for this is the keeping of the commandments.

24 The one who keeps the law preserves himself,[i]
   and the one who trusts the Lord will not
     suffer loss.

33 No evil will befall the one who fears the
       Lord,
   but in trials such a one will be rescued again
     and again.
2 The wise will not hate the law,
   but the one who is hypocritical about it is like
     a boat in a storm.
3 The sensible person will trust in the law;
   for such a one the law is as dependable as a
     divine oracle.

4 Prepare what to say, and then you will be
     listened to;
   draw upon your training, and give your
     answer.
5 The heart of a fool is like a cart wheel,

---

a Heb: Gk *who fears the Lord*   b Other ancient authorities lack
to seek him   c Heb: Gk *alien*   d Meaning of Gk uncertain.
Other ancient authorities add *and after acting, with him, without
deliberation*   e Heb: Gk *stumble on stony ground*   f Or *an
unexplored*   g Heb Syr: Gk *and beware of your children*
h Heb Syr: Gk *Trust*   i Heb: Gk *who believes the law heeds the
commandments*

and his thoughts like a turning axle.

6 A mocking friend is like a stallion
   that neighs no matter who the rider is.

Differences in Nature and in Humankind

7 Why is one day more important than another,
   when all the daylight in the year is from the
      sun?

8 By the Lord's wisdom they were distinguished,
   and he appointed the different seasons and
      festivals.

9 Some days he exalted and hallowed,
   and some he made ordinary days.

10 All human beings come from the ground,
   and humankind*a* was created out of the dust.

11 In the fullness of his knowledge the Lord
      distinguished them
   and appointed their different ways.

12 Some he blessed and exalted,
   and some he made holy and brought near to
      himself;
   but some he cursed and brought low,
   and turned them out of their place.

13 Like clay in the hand of the potter,
   to be molded as he pleases,
   so all are in the hand of their Maker,
   to be given whatever he decides.

14 Good is the opposite of evil,
   and life the opposite of death;
   so the sinner is the opposite of the godly.

15 Look at all the works of the Most High;
   they come in pairs, one the opposite of the
      other.

16 Now I was the last to keep vigil;
   I was like a gleaner following the grape-
      pickers;

17 by the blessing of the Lord I arrived first,
   and like a grape-picker I filled my wine press.

18 Consider that I have not labored for myself
      alone,
   but for all who seek instruction.

19 Hear me, you who are great among the people,
   and you leaders of the congregation, pay
      heed!

The Advantage of Independence

20 To son or wife, to brother or friend,
   do not give power over yourself, as long as
      you live;
   and do not give your property to another,
   in case you change your mind and must ask
      for it.

21 While you are still alive and have breath in you,
   do not let anyone take your place.

22 For it is better that your children should ask
      from you
   than that you should look to the hand of
      your children.

23 Excel in all that you do;
   bring no stain upon your honor.

24 At the time when you end the days of your life,
   in the hour of death, distribute your
      inheritance.

The Treatment of Slaves

25 Fodder and a stick and burdens for a donkey;
   bread and discipline and work for a slave.

26 Set your slave to work, and you will find rest;
   leave his hands idle, and he will seek liberty.

27 Yoke and thong will bow the neck,
   and for a wicked slave there are racks and
      tortures.

28 Put him to work, in order that he may not be
      idle,

29   for idleness teaches much evil.

30 Set him to work, as is fitting for him,
   and if he does not obey, make his fetters heavy.
   Do not be overbearing toward anyone,
   and do nothing unjust.

31 If you have but one slave, treat him like yourself,
   because you have bought him with blood.
   If you have but one slave, treat him like a
      brother,
   for you will need him as you need your life.

32 If you ill-treat him, and he leaves you and runs
      away,

33   which way will you go to seek him?

Dreams Mean Nothing

34 The senseless have vain and false hopes,
   and dreams give wings to fools.

2 As one who catches at a shadow and pursues the
      wind,
   so is anyone who believes in*b* dreams.

3 What is seen in dreams is but a reflection,
   the likeness of a face looking at itself.

4 From an unclean thing what can be clean?
   And from something false what can be true?

5 Divinations and omens and dreams are unreal,
   and like a woman in labor, the mind has
      fantasies.

6 Unless they are sent by intervention from the
      Most High,
   pay no attention to them.

7 For dreams have deceived many,
   and those who put their hope in them have
      perished.

---

a Heb: Gk *Adam*   b Syr: Gk *pays heed to*

8 Without such deceptions the law will be fulfilled,
   and wisdom is complete in the mouth of the
   faithful.

Experience as a Teacher

9 An educated[a] person knows many things,
   and one with much experience knows what
   he is talking about.
10 An inexperienced person knows few things,
11   but he that has traveled acquires much
     cleverness.
12 I have seen many things in my travels,
   and I understand more than I can express.
13 I have often been in danger of death,
   but have escaped because of these
   experiences.

Fear the Lord

14 The spirit of those who fear the Lord will live,
15   for their hope is in him who saves them.
16 Those who fear the Lord will not be timid,
   or play the coward, for he is their hope.
17 Happy is the soul that fears the Lord!
18   To whom does he look? And who is his
     support?
19 The eyes of the Lord are on those who love him,
   a mighty shield and strong support,
   a shelter from scorching wind and a shade from
     noonday sun,
   a guard against stumbling and a help against
     falling.
20 He lifts up the soul and makes the eyes sparkle;
   he gives health and life and blessing.

Offering Sacrifices

21 If one sacrifices ill-gotten goods, the offering is
   blemished;[b]
22   the gifts[c] of the lawless are not acceptable.
23 The Most High is not pleased with the offerings
   of the ungodly,
   nor for a multitude of sacrifices does he
     forgive sins.
24 Like one who kills a son before his father's eyes
   is the person who offers a sacrifice from the
   property of the poor.
25 The bread of the needy is the life of the poor;
   whoever deprives them of it is a murderer.
26 To take away a neighbor's living is to commit
   murder;
27   to deprive an employee of wages is to shed
     blood.

28 When one builds and another tears down,
   what do they gain but hard work?
29 When one prays and another curses,
   to whose voice will the Lord listen?

30 If one washes after touching a corpse, and
     touches it again,
   what has been gained by washing?
31 So if one fasts for his sins,
   and goes again and does the same things,
   who will listen to his prayer?
   And what has he gained by humbling himself?

The Law and Sacrifices

35 The one who keeps the law makes many
   offerings;
2   one who heeds the commandments makes an
     offering of well-being.
3 The one who returns a kindness offers choice
   flour,
4   and one who gives alms sacrifices a thank
     offering.
5 To keep from wickedness is pleasing to the Lord,
   and to forsake unrighteousness is an
     atonement.
6 Do not appear before the Lord empty-handed,
7   for all that you offer is in fulfillment of the
     commandment.
8 The offering of the righteous enriches the altar,
   and its pleasing odor rises before the Most
     High.
9 The sacrifice of the righteous is acceptable,
   and it will never be forgotten.
10 Be generous when you worship the Lord,
   and do not stint the first fruits of your hands.
11 With every gift show a cheerful face,
   and dedicate your tithe with gladness.

> "Give to the Most High as
> he has given to you,
> and as generously as you
> can afford."
> (Sir 35:12)

12 Give to the Most High as he has given to you,
   and as generously as you can afford.
13 For the Lord is the one who repays,
   and he will repay you sevenfold.

Divine Justice

14 Do not offer him a bribe, for he will not accept it;
15   and do not rely on a dishonest sacrifice;
   for the Lord is the judge,
   and with him there is no partiality.

---

a Other ancient authorities read A traveled   b Other ancient
authorities read is made in mockery   c Other ancient authorities
read mockeries

16 He will not show partiality to the poor;
  but he will listen to the prayer of one who is
    wronged.

17 He will not ignore the supplication of the
    orphan,
  or the widow when she pours out her
    complaint.

18 Do not the tears of the widow run down her
    cheek

19   as she cries out against the one who causes
    them to fall?

20 The one whose service is pleasing to the Lord
    will be accepted,
  and his prayer will reach to the clouds.

21 The prayer of the humble pierces the clouds,
  and it will not rest until it reaches its goal;
  it will not desist until the Most High responds

22   and does justice for the righteous, and
    executes judgment.
  Indeed, the Lord will not delay,
  and like a warrior[a] will not be patient
  until he crushes the loins of the unmerciful

23   and repays vengeance on the nations;
  until he destroys the multitude of the insolent,
  and breaks the scepters of the unrighteous;

24 until he repays mortals according to their deeds,
  and the works of all according to their
    thoughts;

25 until he judges the case of his people
  and makes them rejoice in his mercy.

26 His mercy is as welcome in time of distress
  as clouds of rain in time of drought.

A Prayer for God's People

36 Have mercy upon us, O God[b] of all,
  2 and put all the nations in fear of you.

3 Lift up your hand against foreign nations
  and let them see your might.

4 As you have used us to show your holiness to
    them,
  so use them to show your glory to us.

5 Then they will know,[c] as we have known,
  that there is no God but you, O Lord.

6 Give new signs, and work other wonders;

7   make your hand and right arm glorious.

8 Rouse your anger and pour out your wrath;

9   destroy the adversary and wipe out the
    enemy.

10 Hasten the day, and remember the appointed
    time,[d]
  and let people recount your mighty deeds.

11 Let survivors be consumed in the fiery wrath,
  and may those who harm your people meet
    destruction.

12 Crush the heads of hostile rulers
  who say, "There is no one but ourselves."

13 Gather all the tribes of Jacob,[e]

16   and give them their inheritance, as at the
    beginning.

17 Have mercy, O Lord, on the people called by
    your name,
  on Israel, whom you have named[f] your
    firstborn,

18 Have pity on the city of your sanctuary,[g]
  Jerusalem, the place of your dwelling.[h]

19 Fill Zion with your majesty,[i]
  and your temple[j] with your glory.

20 Bear witness to those whom you created in the
    beginning,
  and fulfill the prophecies spoken in your
    name.

21 Reward those who wait for you
  and let your prophets be found trustworthy.

22 Hear, O Lord, the prayer of your servants,
  according to your goodwill toward[k] your
    people,
  and all who are on the earth will know
  that you are the Lord, the God of the ages.

Concerning Discrimination

23 The stomach will take any food,
  yet one food is better than another.

24 As the palate tastes the kinds of game,
  so an intelligent mind detects false words.

25 A perverse mind will cause grief,
  but a person with experience will pay him
    back.

26 A woman will accept any man as a husband,
  but one girl is preferable to another.

27 A woman's beauty lights up a man's face,
  and there is nothing he desires more.

28 If kindness and humility mark her speech,
  her husband is more fortunate than other men.

29 He who acquires a wife gets his best possession,[l]
  a helper fit for him and a pillar of support.[m]

30 Where there is no fence, the property will be
    plundered;
  and where there is no wife, a man will
    become a fugitive and a wanderer.[n]

31 For who will trust a nimble robber
  that skips from city to city?
  So who will trust a man that has no nest,
  but lodges wherever night overtakes him?

---

a Heb: Gk and with them   b Heb: Gk O Master, the God
c Heb: Gk And let them know you   d Other ancient authorities
read remember your oath   e Owing to a dislocation in the Greek
Mss of Sirach, the verse numbers 14 and 15 are not used in chapter
36, though no text is missing.   f Other ancient authorities read
you have likened to   g Or on your holy city   h Heb: Gk your
rest   i Heb Syr: Gk the celebration of your wondrous deeds
j Heb Syr: Gk Lat people   k Heb and two Gk witnesses: Lat and
most Gk witnesses read according to the blessing of Aaron for
l Heb: Gk enters upon a possession   m Heb: Gk rest   n Heb:
Gk wander about and sigh

False Friends

37 Every friend says, "I too am a friend";
but some friends are friends only in name.
2 Is it not a sorrow like that for death itself
when a dear friend turns into an enemy?
3 O inclination to evil, why were you formed
to cover the land with deceit?
4 Some companions rejoice in the happiness of a
friend,
but in time of trouble they are against him.
5 Some companions help a friend for their
stomachs' sake,
yet in battle they will carry his shield.
6 Do not forget a friend during the battle,[a]
and do not be unmindful of him when you
distribute your spoils.[b]

Caution in Taking Advice

7 All counselors praise the counsel they give,
but some give counsel in their own interest.
8 Be wary of a counselor,
and learn first what is his interest,
for he will take thought for himself.
He may cast the lot against you
9 and tell you, "Your way is good,"
and then stand aside to see what happens to
you.
10 Do not consult the one who regards you with
suspicion;
hide your intentions from those who are
jealous of you.
11 Do not consult with a woman about her rival
or with a coward about war,
with a merchant about business
or with a buyer about selling,
with a miser about generosity[c]
or with the merciless about kindness,
with an idler about any work
or with a seasonal laborer about completing
his work,
with a lazy servant about a big task—
pay no attention to any advice they give.
12 But associate with a godly person
whom you know to be a keeper of the
commandments,
who is like-minded with yourself,
and who will grieve with you if you fail.
13 And heed[d] the counsel of your own heart,
for no one is more faithful to you than it is.
14 For our own mind sometimes keeps us better
informed
than seven sentinels sitting high on a
watchtower.
15 But above all pray to the Most High
that he may direct your way in truth.

True and False Wisdom

16 Discussion is the beginning of every work,
and counsel precedes every undertaking.
17 The mind is the root of all conduct;
18 it sprouts four branches,[e]
good and evil, life and death;
and it is the tongue that continually rules
them.
19 Some people may be clever enough to teach
many,
and yet be useless to themselves.
20 A skillful speaker may be hated;
he will be destitute of all food,
21 for the Lord has withheld the gift of charm,
since he is lacking in all wisdom.
22 If a person is wise to his own advantage,
the fruits of his good sense will be
praiseworthy.[f]
23 A wise person instructs his own people,
and the fruits of his good sense will endure.
24 A wise person will have praise heaped upon him,
and all who see him will call him happy.
25 The days of a person's life are numbered,
but the days of Israel are without number.
26 One who is wise among his people will inherit
honor,[g]
and his name will live forever.

Concerning Moderation

27 My child, test yourself while you live;
see what is bad for you and do not give in
to it.
28 For not everything is good for everyone,
and no one enjoys everything.
29 Do not be greedy for every delicacy,
and do not eat without restraint;
30 for overeating brings sickness,
and gluttony leads to nausea.
31 Many have died of gluttony,
but the one who guards against it prolongs
his life.

Concerning Physicians and Health

38 Honor physicians for their services,
for the Lord created them;
2 for their gift of healing comes from the Most
High,
and they are rewarded by the king.
3 The skill of physicians makes them
distinguished,

---

a Heb: Gk *in your heart*   *b* Heb: Gk *him in your wealth*   *c* Heb:
Gk *gratitude*   *d* Heb: Gk *establish*   *e* Heb: Gk *As a clue to
changes of heart four kinds of destiny appear*   *f* Other ancient
witnesses read *trustworthy*   *g* Other ancient authorities read
confidence

S
I
R

Healthcare Providers

When was the last time you went to the doctor? How often do you take medicine? Have you ever spent a night in a hospital? It's humbling to realize that the basic health care we take for granted is not available to millions of people in this country and throughout the world.

God gives the skill to heal to doctors, nurses, dentists, pharmacists, therapists, and medical technicians of every kind (see Sir 38:2). Their jobs often demand huge amounts of time and energy. Take a moment to remember in prayer the healthcare providers you know personally, and ask yourself if you have a vocation in the medical profession.

 Sir 38:1–15

and in the presence of the great they are
   admired.
4 The Lord created medicines out of the earth,
   and the sensible will not despise them.
5 Was not water made sweet with a tree
   in order that its*ᵃ* power might be known?
6 And he gave skill to human beings
   that he*ᵇ* might be glorified in his marvelous
   works.
7 By them the physician*ᶜ* heals and takes away
   pain;
8   the pharmacist makes a mixture from them.
   God's*ᵈ* works will never be finished;
   and from him health*ᵉ* spreads over all the
   earth.

9 My child, when you are ill, do not delay,
   but pray to the Lord, and he will heal you.
10 Give up your faults and direct your hands
   rightly,
   and cleanse your heart from all sin.
11 Offer a sweet-smelling sacrifice, and a memorial
   portion of choice flour,
   and pour oil on your offering, as much as you
   can afford.*ᶠ*
12 Then give the physician his place, for the Lord
   created him;
   do not let him leave you, for you need him.

13 There may come a time when recovery lies in
   the hands of physicians,*ᵍ*
14   for they too pray to the Lord
   that he grant them success in diagnosis*ʰ*
   and in healing, for the sake of preserving life.
15 He who sins against his Maker,
   will be defiant toward the physician.*ⁱ*

On Mourning for the Dead

16 My child, let your tears fall for the dead,
   and as one in great pain begin the lament.
   Lay out the body with due ceremony,
   and do not neglect the burial.
17 Let your weeping be bitter and your wailing
   fervent;
   make your mourning worthy of the departed,
   for one day, or two, to avoid criticism;
   then be comforted for your grief.
18 For grief may result in death,
   and a sorrowful heart saps one's strength.
19 When a person is taken away, sorrow is over;
   but the life of the poor weighs down the
   heart.
20 Do not give your heart to grief;
   drive it away, and remember your own end.
21 Do not forget, there is no coming back;
   you do the dead*ʲ* no good, and you injure
   yourself.
22 Remember his*ᵏ* fate, for yours is like it;
   yesterday it was his,*ˡ* and today it is yours.
23 When the dead is at rest, let his remembrance
   rest too,
   and be comforted for him when his spirit has
   departed.

Trades and Crafts

24 The wisdom of the scribe depends on the
   opportunity of leisure;
   only the one who has little business can
   become wise.
25 How can one become wise who handles the
   plow,
   and who glories in the shaft of a goad,
   who drives oxen and is occupied with their
   work,
   and whose talk is about bulls?
26 He sets his heart on plowing furrows,
   and he is careful about fodder for the heifers.
27 So it is with every artisan and master artisan
   who labors by night as well as by day;
   those who cut the signets of seals,

---

a Or his   b Or they   c Heb: Gk he   d Gk His   e Or peace
f Heb: Lat lacks as much as you can afford; Meaning of Gk
uncertain   g Gk in their hands   h Heb: Gk rest   i Heb: Gk may
he fall into the hands of the physician   j Gk him   k Heb: Gk my
l Heb: Gk mine

each is diligent in making a great variety;
 they set their heart on painting a lifelike image,
 and they are careful to finish their work.
²⁸ So it is with the smith, sitting by the anvil,
 intent on his iron-work;
 the breath of the fire melts his flesh,
 and he struggles with the heat of the furnace;
 the sound of the hammer deafens his ears,ᵃ
 and his eyes are on the pattern of the object.
 He sets his heart on finishing his handiwork,
 and he is careful to complete its decoration.
²⁹ So it is with the potter sitting at his work
 and turning the wheel with his feet;
 he is always deeply concerned over his products,
 and he produces them in quantity.
³⁰ He molds the clay with his arm
 and makes it pliable with his feet;
 he sets his heart to finish the glazing,
 and he takes care in firingᵇ the kiln.

³¹ All these rely on their hands,
 and all are skillful in their own work.
³² Without them no city can be inhabited,
 and wherever they live, they will not go
 hungry.ᶜ
 Yet they are not sought out for the council of the
 people,ᵈ
³³ nor do they attain eminence in the public
 assembly.
 They do not sit in the judge's seat,
 nor do they understand the decisions of the
 courts;
 they cannot expound discipline or judgment,
 and they are not found among the rulers.ᵉ
³⁴ But they maintain the fabric of the world,
 and their concern is forᶠ the exercise of their
 trade.

The Activity of the Scribe

How different the one who devotes himself
 to the study of the law of the Most High!

39 He seeks out the wisdom of all the
 ancients,
 and is concerned with prophecies;
² he preserves the sayings of the famous
 and penetrates the subtleties of parables;
³ he seeks out the hidden meanings of proverbs
 and is at home with the obscurities of
 parables.
⁴ He serves among the great
 and appears before rulers;
 he travels in foreign lands
 and learns what is good and evil in the
 human lot.
⁵ He sets his heart to rise early
 to seek the Lord who made him,

and to petition the Most High;
 he opens his mouth in prayer
 and asks pardon for his sins.

⁶ If the great Lord is willing,
 he will be filled with the spirit of
 understanding;
 he will pour forth words of wisdom of his own
 and give thanks to the Lord in prayer.
⁷ The Lordᵍ will direct his counsel and knowledge,
 as he meditates on his mysteries.
⁸ He will show the wisdom of what he has
 learned,
 and will glory in the law of the Lord's
 covenant.
⁹ Many will praise his understanding;
 it will never be blotted out.
 His memory will not disappear,
 and his name will live through all
 generations.
¹⁰ Nations will speak of his wisdom,
 and the congregation will proclaim his praise.
¹¹ If he lives long, he will leave a name greater
 than a thousand,
 and if he goes to rest, it is enoughʰ for him.

A Hymn of Praise to God

¹² I have more on my mind to express;
 I am full like the full moon.
¹³ Listen to me, my faithful children, and blossom
 like a rose growing by a stream of water.

---

a Cn: Gk *renews his ear* b Cn: Gk *cleaning* c Syr: Gk *and
people can neither live nor walk there* d Most ancient authorities
lack this line e Cn: Gk *among parables* f Syr: Gk *prayer is in*
g Gk *He himself* h Cn: Meaning of Gk uncertain

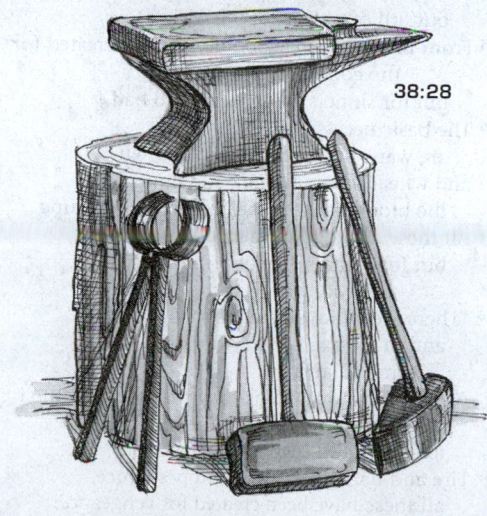

38:28

14 Send out fragrance like incense,
   and put forth blossoms like a lily.
Scatter the fragrance, and sing a hymn of praise;
   bless the Lord for all his works.
15 Ascribe majesty to his name
   and give thanks to him with praise,
with songs on your lips, and with harps;
   this is what you shall say in thanksgiving:

16 "All the works of the Lord are very good,
   and whatever he commands will be done at
      the appointed time.
17 No one can say, 'What is this?' or 'Why is
      that?'—
   for at the appointed time all such questions
      will be answered.
At his word the waters stood in a heap,
   and the reservoirs of water at the word of his
      mouth.
18 When he commands, his every purpose is
      fulfilled,
   and none can limit his saving power.
19 The works of all are before him,
   and nothing can be hidden from his eyes.
20 From the beginning to the end of time he can
      see everything,
   and nothing is too marvelous for him.
21 No one can say, 'What is this?' or 'Why is
      that?'—
   for everything has been created for its own
      purpose.

22 "His blessing covers the dry land like a river,
   and drenches it like a flood.
23 But his wrath drives out the nations,
   as when he turned a watered land into salt.
24 To the faithful his ways are straight,
   but full of pitfalls for the wicked.
25 From the beginning good things were created for
      the good,
   but for sinners good things and bad.ᵃ
26 The basic necessities of human life
   are water and fire and iron and salt
and wheat flour and milk and honey,
   the blood of the grape and oil and clothing.
27 All these are good for the godly,
   but for sinners they turn into evils.

28 "There are winds created for vengeance,
   and in their anger they can dislodge
      mountains;ᵇ
on the day of reckoning they will pour out their
      strength
   and calm the anger of their Maker.
29 Fire and hail and famine and pestilence,
   all these have been created for vengeance;

30 the fangs of wild animals and scorpions and
      vipers,
   and the sword that punishes the ungodly with
      destruction.
31 They take delight in doing his bidding,
   always ready for his service on earth;
   and when their time comes they never
      disobey his command."

32 So from the beginning I have been convinced of
      all this
   and have thought it out and left it in writing:
33 All the works of the Lord are good,
   and he will supply every need in its time.
34 No one can say, "This is not as good as that,"
   for everything proves good in its appointed
      time.
35 So now sing praise with all your heart and voice,
   and bless the name of the Lord.

Human Wretchedness

40 Hard work was created for everyone,
   and a heavy yoke is laid on the children
      of Adam,
from the day they come forth from their
      mother's womb
   until the day they return toᶜ the mother of all
      the living.ᵈ
2 Perplexities and fear of heart are theirs,
   and anxious thought of the day of their death.
3 From the one who sits on a splendid throne
   to the one who grovels in dust and ashes,
4 from the one who wears purple and a crown
   to the one who is clothed in burlap,
5 there is anger and envy and trouble and unrest,
   and fear of death, and fury and strife.
And when one rests upon his bed,
   his sleep at night confuses his mind.
6 He gets little or no rest;
   he struggles in his sleep as he did by day.ᵉ
He is troubled by the visions of his mind
   like one who has escaped from the battlefield.
7 At the moment he reaches safety he wakes up,
   astonished that his fears were groundless.
8 To all creatures, human and animal,
   but to sinners seven times more,
9 come death and bloodshed and strife and sword,
   calamities and famine and ruin and plague.
10 All these were created for the wicked,
   and on their account the flood came.
11 All that is of earth returns to earth,
   and what is from above returns above.ᶠ

---

a Heb Lat: Gk *sinners bad things*   b Heb Syr: Gk *can scourge
mightily*   c Other Gk and Lat authorities read *are buried in*
d Heb: Gk *of all*   e Arm: Meaning of Gk uncertain   f Heb Syr:
Gk Lat *from the waters returns to the sea*

Injustice Will Not Prosper

¹² All bribery and injustice will be blotted out,
　　but good faith will last forever.

¹³ The wealth of the unjust will dry up like a river,
　　and crash like a loud clap of thunder in a
　　　storm.

¹⁴ As a generous person has cause to rejoice,
　　so lawbreakers will utterly fail.

¹⁵ The children of the ungodly put out few
　　branches;
　　they are unhealthy roots on sheer rock.

¹⁶ The reeds by any water or river bank
　　are plucked up before any grass;

¹⁷ but kindness is like a garden of blessings,
　　and almsgiving endures forever.

The Joys of Life

¹⁸ Wealth and wages make life sweet,ᵃ
　　but better than either is finding a treasure.

¹⁹ Children and the building of a city establish
　　one's name,
　　but better than either is the one who finds
　　wisdom.
　Cattle and orchards make one prosperous;ᵇ
　　but a blameless wife is accounted better than
　　either.

²⁰ Wine and music gladden the heart,
　　but the love of friendsᶜ is better than either.

²¹ The flute and the harp make sweet melody,
　　but a pleasant voice is better than either.

²² The eye desires grace and beauty,
　　but the green shoots of grain more than either.

²³ A friend or companion is always welcome,
　　but a sensible wifeᵈ is better than either.

²⁴ Kindred and helpers are for a time of trouble,
　　but almsgiving rescues better than either.

²⁵ Gold and silver make one stand firm,
　　but good counsel is esteemed more than
　　either.

²⁶ Riches and strength build up confidence,
　　but the fear of the Lord is better than either.
　There is no want in the fear of the Lord,
　　and with it there is no need to seek for help.

²⁷ The fear of the Lord is like a garden of blessing,
　　and covers a person better than any glory.

The Disgrace of Begging

²⁸ My child, do not lead the life of a beggar;
　　it is better to die than to beg.

²⁹ When one looks to the table of another,
　　one's way of life cannot be considered a life.
　One loses self-respect with another person's
　　food,
　　but one who is intelligent and well instructed
　　guards against that.

³⁰ In the mouth of the shameless begging is sweet,
　　but it kindles a fire inside him.

Concerning Death

41 O death, how bitter is the thought of you
　　to the one at peace among possessions,
　who has nothing to worry about and is
　　prosperous in everything,
　and still is vigorous enough to enjoy food!

² O death, how welcome is your sentence
　　to one who is needy and failing in strength,
　worn down by age and anxious about
　　everything;
　to one who is contrary, and has lost all
　　patience!

³ Do not fear death's decree for you;
　　remember those who went before you and
　　those who will come after.

⁴ This is the Lord's decree for all flesh;
　　why then should you reject the will of the
　　Most High?
　Whether life lasts for ten years or a hundred or a
　　thousand,
　　there are no questions asked in Hades.

The Fate of the Wicked

⁵ The children of sinners are abominable children,
　　and they frequent the haunts of the ungodly.

⁶ The inheritance of the children of sinners will
　　perish,
　　and on their offspring will be a perpetual
　　disgrace.

⁷ Children will blame an ungodly father,
　　for they suffer disgrace because of him.

⁸ Woe to you, the ungodly,
　　who have forsaken the law of the Most High
　　God!

⁹ If you have children, calamity will be theirs;
　　you will beget them only for groaning.
　When you stumble, there is lasting joy;ᵉ
　　and when you die, a curse is your lot.

¹⁰ Whatever comes from earth returns to earth;
　　so the ungodly go from curse to destruction.

¹¹ The human body is a fleeting thing,
　　but a virtuous name will never be blotted out.ᶠ

¹² Have regard for your name, since it will outlive
　　you
　　longer than a thousand hoards of gold.

¹³ The days of a good life are numbered,
　　but a good name lasts forever.

---

a Heb: Gk *Life is sweet for the self-reliant worker*　b Heb Syr:
Gk lacks *but better . . . prosperous*　c Heb: Gk *wisdom*
d Heb Compare Syr: Gk *wife with her husband*　e Heb: Meaning
of Gk uncertain　f Heb: Gk *People grieve over the death of the
body, but the bad name of sinners will be blotted out*

14 My children, be true to your training and be at
  peace;
  hidden wisdom and unseen treasure—
  of what value is either?

A Series of Contrasts

15 Better are those who hide their folly
  than those who hide their wisdom.
16 Therefore show respect for my words;

Shame on You!

"You ought to be ashamed of yourself!"
  How many times do we hear that while
growing up? Or the simpler, more direct version:
"Shame on you!" We've probably heard these
and similar expressions often, but what exactly
is the point of shame?

Although it is true that sometimes false sham-
ing can be harmful to our growth and development, there are other times when we really
should be ashamed of ourselves. We did something that we should not have done. Perhaps
we hurt another person or broke a promise or
brought dishonor to our family. These are all
valid reasons for feeling ashamed, and it is often
someone else who brings us to this realization.
Upon realizing our mistakes, though, we should
never let this sense of shame, or guilt, weigh us
down. Rather, we must learn from our missteps,
develop a more informed conscience, and make
better decisions when faced with similar situations in the future.

The author of Sirach knew human nature well
and gave advice about true and false shame.
Think about times when you have felt ashamed of
something. What caused you to feel ashamed?
What role does your conscience play in feeling
a sense of shame? What do you do with that
sense of shame? Think about the role shame
plays in the story of Adam and Eve (see Genesis,
chapters 2–3) and the story of David and Bathsheba (see 2 Samuel, chapters 11–12).

▶ Sir 41:14—42:8

for it is not good to feel shame in every
    circumstance,
  nor is every kind of abashment to be
    approved.[a]

17 Be ashamed of sexual immorality, before your
    father or mother;
  and of a lie, before a prince or a ruler;
18 of a crime, before a judge or magistrate;
  and of a breach of the law, before the
    congregation and the people;
  of unjust dealing, before your partner or your
    friend;
19 and of theft, in the place where you live.
  Be ashamed of breaking an oath or
    agreement,[b]
  and of leaning on your elbow at meals;
  of surliness in receiving or giving,
20 and of silence, before those who greet you;
  of looking at a prostitute,
21 and of rejecting the appeal of a relative;
  of taking away someone's portion or gift,
  and of gazing at another man's wife;
22 of meddling with his servant-girl—
    and do not approach her bed;
  of abusive words, before friends—
    and do not be insulting after making a gift.

42 Be ashamed of repeating what you hear,
  and of betraying secrets.
Then you will show proper shame,
  and will find favor with everyone.

Of the following things do not be ashamed,
  and do not sin to save face:
2 Do not be ashamed of the law of the Most High
    and his covenant,
  and of rendering judgment to acquit the
    ungodly;
3 of keeping accounts with a partner or with
    traveling companions,
  and of dividing the inheritance of friends;
4 of accuracy with scales and weights,
  and of acquiring much or little;
5 of profit from dealing with merchants,
  and of frequent disciplining of children,
  and of drawing blood from the back of a
    wicked slave.
6 Where there is an untrustworthy wife, a seal is a
    good thing;
  and where there are many hands, lock things
    up.
7 When you make a deposit, be sure it is counted
    and weighed,

---

a Heb: Gk *and not everything is confidently esteemed by everyone*
b Heb: Gk *before the truth of God and the covenant*

and when you give or receive, put it all in
   writing.
⁸ Do not be ashamed to correct the stupid or
   foolish
   or the aged who are guilty of sexual
   immorality.
Then you will show your sound training,
   and will be approved by all.

Daughters and Fathers

⁹ A daughter is a secret anxiety to her father,
   and worry over her robs him of sleep;
when she is young, for fear she may not marry,
   or if married, for fear she may be disliked;
¹⁰ while a virgin, for fear she may be seduced
   and become pregnant in her father's house;
or having a husband, for fear she may go astray,
   or, though married, for fear she may be
   barren.
¹¹ Keep strict watch over a headstrong daughter,
   or she may make you a laughingstock to your
   enemies,
a byword in the city and the assembly of*ᵃ the
   people,
and put you to shame in public gatherings.ᵇ
See that there is no lattice in her room,
   no spot that overlooks the approaches to the
   house.ᶜ
¹² Do not let her parade her beauty before any
   man,
   or spend her time among married women;ᵈ
¹³ for from garments comes the moth,
   and from a woman comes woman's
   wickedness.
¹⁴ Better is the wickedness of a man than a woman
   who does good;
   it is woman who brings shame and disgrace.

The Works of God in Nature

¹⁵ I will now call to mind the works of the Lord,
   and will declare what I have seen.
By the word of the Lord his works are made;
   and all his creatures do his will.ᵈ
¹⁶ The sun looks down on everything with its light,
   and the work of the Lord is full of his glory.
¹⁷ The Lord has not empowered even his holy ones
   to recount all his marvelous works,
which the Lord the Almighty has established
   so that the universe may stand firm in his
   glory.
¹⁸ He searches out the abyss and the human heart;
   he understands their innermost secrets.
For the Most High knows all that may be
   known;
   he sees from of old the things that are to
   come.ᵉ

Live It!

The Sexism of Sirach

Let's just get this right out in the open: Ben
Sira was sexist by today's standards. As you
read Sirach 42:9–14, you probably think it's a
curse to have a daughter! Verse 14 says, "Better is the wickedness of a man than a woman
who does good; / it is woman who brings shame
and disgrace." Wow, with an attitude like that,
Ben Sira wouldn't be welcomed by many modern
people.

Once again, we have to remember that the
Bible was written by human beings and reflects
their cultural standards. Ben Sira's attitude was
commonly accepted in his culture. But the cultural standards in the Bible don't always reflect
God's truth. That's why we need the help of the
larger Church community to properly interpret
the Bible. Today, the Church teaches that women
and men are to be treated with equal dignity and
respect. Let's work together to continue making
that vision a reality.

▶ Sir 42:9–14

¹⁹ He discloses what has been and what is to be,
   and he reveals the traces of hidden things.
²⁰ No thought escapes him,
   and nothing is hidden from him.
²¹ He has set in order the splendors of his wisdom;
   he is from all eternity one and the same.
Nothing can be added or taken away,
   and he needs no one to be his counselor.
²² How desirable are all his works,
   and how sparkling they are to see!ᶠ
²³ All these things live and remain forever;
   each creature is preserved to meet a particular
   need.ᵍ
²⁴ All things come in pairs, one opposite the other,
   and he has made nothing incomplete.
²⁵ Each supplements the virtues of the other.
   Who could ever tire of seeing his glory?

---

a Heb: Meaning of Gk uncertain   b Heb: Gk to shame before the
great multitude   c Heb: Gk lacks See . . . house   d Syr Compare
Heb: most Gk witnesses lack and all . . . will   e Heb: Gk he sees
the sign(s) of the age   f Meaning of Gk uncertain   g Heb: Gk
forever for every need, and all are obedient

The Splendor of the Sun

43 The pride of the higher realms is the clear vault of the sky,
  as glorious to behold as the sight of the heavens.

2 The sun, when it appears, proclaims as it rises
  what a marvelous instrument it is, the work of the Most High.

3 At noon it parches the land,
  and who can withstand its burning heat?

4 A man tending[a] a furnace works in burning heat,
  but three times as hot is the sun scorching the mountains;
it breathes out fiery vapors,
  and its bright rays blind the eyes.

5 Great is the Lord who made it;
  at his orders it hurries on its course.

The Splendor of the Moon

6 It is the moon that marks the changing seasons,[b]
governing the times, their everlasting sign.

7 From the moon comes the sign for festal days,
  a light that wanes when it completes its course.

8 The new moon, as its name suggests, renews itself;[c]
how marvelous it is in this change,
a beacon to the hosts on high,
  shining in the vault of the heavens!

The Glory of the Stars and the Rainbow

9 The glory of the stars is the beauty of heaven,
  a glittering array in the heights of the Lord.

10 On the orders of the Holy One they stand in their appointed places;
they never relax in their watches.

11 Look at the rainbow, and praise him who made it;
it is exceedingly beautiful in its brightness.

12 It encircles the sky with its glorious arc;
  the hands of the Most High have stretched it out.

The Marvels of Nature

13 By his command he sends the driving snow
  and speeds the lightnings of his judgment.

14 Therefore the storehouses are opened,
  and the clouds fly out like birds.

15 In his majesty he gives the clouds their strength,
  and the hailstones are broken in pieces.

17a The voice of his thunder rebukes the earth;

16   when he appears, the mountains shake.
At his will the south wind blows;

17b   so do the storm from the north and the whirlwind.
He scatters the snow like birds flying down,
  and its descent is like locusts alighting.

18 The eye is dazzled by the beauty of its whiteness,
  and the mind is amazed as it falls.

19 He pours frost over the earth like salt,
  and icicles form like pointed thorns.

20 The cold north wind blows,
  and ice freezes on the water;
it settles on every pool of water,
  and the water puts it on like a breastplate.

21 He consumes the mountains and burns up the wilderness,
  and withers the tender grass like fire.

22 A mist quickly heals all things;
  the falling dew gives refreshment from the heat.

23 By his plan he stilled the deep
  and planted islands in it.

24 Those who sail the sea tell of its dangers,
  and we marvel at what we hear.

25 In it are strange and marvelous creatures,
  all kinds of living things, and huge sea-monsters.

26 Because of him each of his messengers succeeds,
  and by his word all things hold together.

27 We could say more but could never say enough;
  let the final word be: "He is the all."

28 Where can we find the strength to praise him?
  For he is greater than all his works.

29 Awesome is the Lord and very great,
  and marvelous is his power.

30 Glorify the Lord and exalt him as much as you can,
  for he surpasses even that.
When you exalt him, summon all your strength,
  and do not grow weary, for you cannot praise him enough.

31 Who has seen him and can describe him?
  Or who can extol him as he is?

32 Many things greater than these lie hidden,
  for I[d] have seen but few of his works.

33 For the Lord has made all things,
  and to the godly he has given wisdom.

HYMN IN HONOR OF OUR ANCESTORS[e]

44 Let us now sing the praises of famous men,
  our ancestors in their generations.

2 The Lord apportioned to them[f] great glory,
  his majesty from the beginning.

---

a Other ancient authorities read *blowing upon*   b Heb: Meaning of Gk uncertain   c Heb: Gk *The month is named after the moon*   d Heb: Gk *we*   e This title is included in the Gk text.   f Heb: Gk *created*

3 There were those who ruled in their kingdoms,
    and made a name for themselves by their
        valor;
those who gave counsel because they were
    intelligent;
those who spoke in prophetic oracles;
4 those who led the people by their counsels
    and by their knowledge of the people's lore;
    they were wise in their words of instruction;
5 those who composed musical tunes,
    or put verses in writing;
6 rich men endowed with resources,
    living peacefully in their homes—
7 all these were honored in their generations,
    and were the pride of their times.
8 Some of them have left behind a name,
    so that others declare their praise.
9 But of others there is no memory;
    they have perished as though they had never
        existed;
    they have become as though they had never
        been born,
    they and their children after them.
10 But these also were godly men,
    whose righteous deeds have not been
        forgotten;
11 their wealth will remain with their descendants,
    and their inheritance with their children's
        children.[a]
12 Their descendants stand by the covenants;
    their children also, for their sake.
13 Their offspring will continue forever,
    and their glory will never be blotted out.
14 Their bodies are buried in peace,
    but their name lives on generation after
        generation.
15 The assembly declares[b] their wisdom,
    and the congregation proclaims their praise.

Enoch

16 Enoch pleased the Lord and was taken up,
    an example of repentance to all generations.

Noah

17 Noah was found perfect and righteous;
    in the time of wrath he kept the race alive;[c]
therefore a remnant was left on the earth
    when the flood came.
18 Everlasting covenants were made with him
    that all flesh should never again be blotted
        out by a flood.

Abraham

19 Abraham was the great father of a multitude of
    nations,
    and no one has been found like him in glory.

20 He kept the law of the Most High,
    and entered into a covenant with him;
he certified the covenant in his flesh,
    and when he was tested he proved faithful.
21 Therefore the Lord[d] assured him with an oath
    that the nations would be blessed through his
        offspring;
that he would make him as numerous as the
    dust of the earth,
    and exalt his offspring like the stars,
and give them an inheritance from sea to sea
    and from the Euphrates[e] to the ends of the
        earth.

Isaac and Jacob

22 To Isaac also he gave the same assurance
    for the sake of his father Abraham.
The blessing of all people and the covenant
23   he made to rest on the head of Jacob;
he acknowledged him with his blessings,
    and gave him his inheritance;
he divided his portions,
    and distributed them among twelve tribes.

Moses

From his descendants the Lord[d] brought forth a
    godly man,
who found favor in the sight of all

45 ¹and was beloved by God and people,
    Moses, whose memory is blessed.
2 He made him equal in glory to the holy ones,
    and made him great, to the terror of his
        enemies.
3 By his words he performed swift miracles;[f]
    the Lord[d] glorified him in the presence of
        kings.
He gave him commandments for his people,
    and revealed to him his glory.
4 For his faithfulness and meekness he
    consecrated him,
    choosing him out of all humankind.
5 He allowed him to hear his voice,
    and led him into the dark cloud,
and gave him the commandments face to face,
    the law of life and knowledge,
so that he might teach Jacob the covenant,
    and Israel his decrees

Aaron

6 He exalted Aaron, a holy man like Moses[g]
    who was his brother, of the tribe of Levi.
7 He made an everlasting covenant with him,

---

a Heb Compare Lat Syr: Meaning of Gk uncertain   b Heb: Gk
Peoples declare   c Heb: Gk was taken in exchange   d Gk he
e Syr: Heb Gk River   f Heb: Gk caused signs to cease
g Gk him

Live It!

Heroes

Who are your heroes? Maybe they include a teacher, a coach, a friend, or a parent. What sets them apart and makes them people you look up to? Their accomplishments? a cause they represent? or a personal trait that only someone who knows them personally would be aware of?

The kind of people we look to as heroes says a lot about us. If our heroes are kind and generous, then maybe we value kindness and generosity. If our heroes are wealthy, perhaps we desire wealth.

Read the last section of Sirach, starting with chapter 44, which honors many Old Testament heroes. Ben Sira considered them heroes because their hearts were fixed on the Lord (see 49:3). What an awesome way to describe heroes!

- Whom do you know who has his or her heart fixed on the Lord?
- What does your choice of heroes say about your dreams and values?

▶ **Sirach, chapters 44–49**

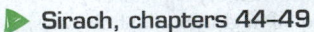

and gave him the priesthood of the people.
He blessed him with stateliness,
and put a glorious robe on him.
8 He clothed him in perfect splendor,
and strengthened him with the symbols of authority,
the linen undergarments, the long robe, and the ephod.
9 And he encircled him with pomegranates,
with many golden bells all around,
to send forth a sound as he walked,
to make their ringing heard in the temple
as a reminder to his people;
10 with the sacred vestment, of gold and violet
and purple, the work of an embroiderer;
with the oracle of judgment, Urim and Thummim;
11   with twisted crimson, the work of an artisan;
with precious stones engraved like seals,

in a setting of gold, the work of a jeweler,
to commemorate in engraved letters
each of the tribes of Israel;
12 with a gold crown upon his turban,
inscribed like a seal with "Holiness,"
a distinction to be prized, the work of an expert,
a delight to the eyes, richly adorned.
13 Before him such beautiful things did not exist.
No outsider ever put them on,
but only his sons
and his descendants in perpetuity.
14 His sacrifices shall be wholly burned
twice every day continually.
15 Moses ordained him,
and anointed him with holy oil;
it was an everlasting covenant for him
and for his descendants as long as the heavens endure,
to minister to the Lord[a] and serve as priest
and bless his people in his name.
16 He chose him out of all the living
to offer sacrifice to the Lord,
incense and a pleasing odor as a memorial portion,
to make atonement for the[b] people.
17 In his commandments he gave him
authority and statutes and[c] judgments,
to teach Jacob the testimonies,
and to enlighten Israel with his law.
18 Outsiders conspired against him,
and envied him in the wilderness,
Dathan and Abiram and their followers
and the company of Korah, in wrath and anger.
19 The Lord saw it and was not pleased,
and in the heat of his anger they were destroyed;
he performed wonders against them
to consume them in flaming fire.
20 He added glory to Aaron
and gave him a heritage;
he allotted to him the best of the first fruits,
and prepared bread of first fruits in abundance;
21 for they eat the sacrifices of the Lord,
which he gave to him and his descendants.
22 But in the land of the people he has no inheritance,
and he has no portion among the people;
for the Lord[d] himself is his[e] portion and inheritance.

---

a Gk *him*   b Other ancient authorities read *his* or *your*   c Heb:
Gk *authority in covenants of*   d Gk *he*   e Other ancient
authorities read *your*

Phinehas

23 Phinehas son of Eleazar ranks third in glory
for being zealous in the fear of the Lord,
and standing firm, when the people turned
away,
in the noble courage of his soul;
and he made atonement for Israel.
24 Therefore a covenant of friendship was
established with him,
that he should be leader of the sanctuary and
of his people,
that he and his descendants should have
the dignity of the priesthood forever.
25 Just as a covenant was established with David
son of Jesse of the tribe of Judah,
that the king's heritage passes only from son to
son,
so the heritage of Aaron is for his descendants
alone.

26 And now bless the Lord
who has crowned you with glory.[a]
May the Lord[b] grant you wisdom of mind
to judge his people with justice,
so that their prosperity may not vanish,
and that their glory may endure through all
their generations.

Joshua and Caleb

46 Joshua son of Nun was mighty in war,
and was the successor of Moses in the
prophetic office.
He became, as his name implies,
a great savior of God's[c] elect,
to take vengeance on the enemies that rose
against them,
so that he might give Israel its inheritance.
2 How glorious he was when he lifted his hands
and brandished his sword against the cities!
3 Who before him ever stood so firm?
For he waged the wars of the Lord.
4 Was it not through him that the sun stood still
and one day became as long as two?
5 He called upon the Most High, the Mighty
One,
when enemies pressed him on every side,
and the great Lord answered him
with hailstones of mighty power.
6 He overwhelmed that nation in battle,
and on the slope he destroyed his
opponents,
so that the nations might know his armament,
that he was fighting in the sight of the Lord;
for he was a devoted follower of the Mighty
One.

7 And in the days of Moses he proved his
loyalty,
he and Caleb son of Jephunneh:
they opposed the congregation,[d]
restrained the people from sin,
and stilled their wicked grumbling.
8 And these two alone were spared
out of six hundred thousand infantry,
to lead the people[e] into their inheritance,
the land flowing with milk and honey.
9 The Lord gave Caleb strength,
which remained with him in his old age,
so that he went up to the hill country,
and his children obtained it for an
inheritance,
10 so that all the Israelites might see
how good it is to follow the Lord.

The Judges

11 The judges also, with their respective names,
whose hearts did not fall into idolatry
and who did not turn away from the Lord—
may their memory be blessed!
12 May their bones send forth new life from where
they lie,
and may the names of those who have been
honored
live again in their children!

13 Samuel was beloved by his Lord;
a prophet of the Lord, he established the
kingdom
and anointed rulers over his people.
14 By the law of the Lord he judged the
congregation,
and the Lord watched over Jacob.
15 By his faithfulness he was proved to be a
prophet,
and by his words he became known as a
trustworthy seer.
16 He called upon the Lord, the Mighty One,
when his enemies pressed him on every
side,
and he offered in sacrifice a suckling lamb.
17 Then the Lord thundered from heaven,
and made his voice heard with a mighty
sound;
18 he subdued the leaders of the enemy[f]
and all the rulers of the Philistines.
19 Before the time of his eternal sleep,
Samuel[b] bore witness before the Lord and his
anointed:

---

a Heb: Gk lacks And . . . glory   b Gk he   c Gk his   d Other
ancient authorities read the enemy   e Gk them   f Heb: Gk
leaders of the people of Tyre

"No property, not so much as a pair of shoes,
   have I taken from anyone!"
And no one accused him.
20 Even after he had fallen asleep, he
      prophesied
   and made known to the king his death,
and lifted up his voice from the ground
   in prophecy, to blot out the wickedness of the
      people.

Nathan

47
After him Nathan rose up
   to prophesy in the days of David.

David

2 As the fat is set apart from the offering of well-
      being,
   so David was set apart from the Israelites.
3 He played with lions as though they were young
      goats,
   and with bears as though they were lambs of
      the flock.
4 In his youth did he not kill a giant,
   and take away the people's disgrace,
when he whirled the stone in the sling
   and struck down the boasting Goliath?
5 For he called on the Lord, the Most High,
   and he gave strength to his right arm
to strike down a mighty warrior,
   and to exalt the power*a* of his people.
6 So they glorified him for the tens of thousands
      he conquered,
   and praised him for the blessings bestowed by
      the Lord,
when the glorious diadem was given to him.
7 For he wiped out his enemies on every side,
   and annihilated his adversaries the
      Philistines;
he crushed their power*a* to our own day.
8 In all that he did he gave thanks
   to the Holy One, the Most High, proclaiming
      his glory;
he sang praise with all his heart,
   and he loved his Maker.
9 He placed singers before the altar,
   to make sweet melody with their voices.*b*
10 He gave beauty to the festivals,
   and arranged their times throughout the
      year,*c*
while they praised God's*d* holy name,
   and the sanctuary resounded from early
      morning.
11 The Lord took away his sins,
   and exalted his power*a* forever;
he gave him a covenant of kingship
   and a glorious throne in Israel.

Solomon

12 After him a wise son rose up
   who because of him lived in security;*e*
13 Solomon reigned in an age of peace,
   because God made all his borders tranquil,
so that he might build a house in his name
   and provide a sanctuary to stand forever.
14 How wise you were when you were young!
   You overflowed like the Nile*f* with
      understanding.
15 Your influence spread throughout the earth,
   and you filled it with proverbs having deep
      meaning.
16 Your fame reached to far-off islands,
   and you were loved for your peaceful reign.
17 Your songs, proverbs, and parables,
   and the answers you gave astounded the
      nations.
18 In the name of the Lord God,
   who is called the God of Israel,
you gathered gold like tin
   and amassed silver like lead.
19 But you brought in women to lie at your side,
   and through your body you were brought into
      subjection.
20 You stained your honor,
   and defiled your family line,
so that you brought wrath upon your children,
   and they were grieved*g* at your folly,
21 because the sovereignty was divided
   and a rebel kingdom arose out of Ephraim.
22 But the Lord will never give up his mercy,
   or cause any of his works to perish;
he will never blot out the descendants of his
      chosen one,
   or destroy the family line of him who loved
      him.
So he gave a remnant to Jacob,
   and to David a root from his own family.

Rehoboam and Jeroboam

23 Solomon rested with his ancestors,
   and left behind him one of his sons,
broad in*h* folly and lacking in sense,
   Rehoboam, whose policy drove the people to
      revolt.
Then Jeroboam son of Nebat led Israel into
      sin
   and started Ephraim on its sinful ways.

---

a Gk *horn*   *b* Other ancient authorities add *and daily they sing
his praises*   *c* Gk *to completion*   *d* Gk *his*   *e* Heb: Gk *in a
broad place*   *f* Heb: Gk *a river*   *g* Other ancient authorities read
I was grieved*   *h* Heb (with a play on the name Rehoboam) Syr:
Gk *the people's*

24 Their sins increased more and more,
  until they were exiled from their land.
25 For they sought out every kind of wickedness,
  until vengeance came upon them.

Elijah

48 Then Elijah arose, a prophet like fire,
  and his word burned like a torch.
2 He brought a famine upon them,
  and by his zeal he made them few in
    number.
3 By the word of the Lord he shut up the
    heavens,
  and also three times brought down fire.
4 How glorious you were, Elijah, in your
    wondrous deeds!
  Whose glory is equal to yours?
5 You raised a corpse from death
  and from Hades, by the word of the Most
    High.
6 You sent kings down to destruction,
  and famous men, from their sickbeds.
7 You heard rebuke at Sinai
  and judgments of vengeance at Horeb.
8 You anointed kings to inflict retribution,
  and prophets to succeed you.a
9 You were taken up by a whirlwind of fire,
  in a chariot with horses of fire.
10 At the appointed time, it is written, you are
    destinedb
  to calm the wrath of God before it breaks out
    in fury,
  to turn the hearts of parents to their children,
  and to restore the tribes of Jacob.
11 Happy are those who saw you
  and were adornedc with your love!
  For we also shall surely live.d

Elisha

12 When Elijah was enveloped in the whirlwind,
  Elisha was filled with his spirit.
  He performed twice as many signs,
  and marvels with every utterance of his
    mouth.e
  Never in his lifetime did he tremble before any
    ruler,
  nor could anyone intimidate him at all.
13 Nothing was too hard for him,
  and when he was dead, his body prophesied.
14 In his life he did wonders,
  and in death his deeds were marvelous.

15 Despite all this the people did not repent,
  nor did they forsake their sins,
  until they were carried off as plunder from their
    land,

  and were scattered over all the earth.
  The people were left very few in number,
  but with a ruler from the house of David.
16 Some of them did what was right,
  but others sinned more and more.

Hezekiah

17 Hezekiah fortified his city,
  and brought water into its midst;
  he tunneled the rock with iron tools,
  and built cisterns for the water.
18 In his days Sennacherib invaded the country;
  he sent his commanderf and departed;
  he shook his fist against Zion,
  and made great boasts in his arrogance.
19 Then their hearts were shaken and their hands
    trembled,
  and they were in anguish, like women in
    labor.
20 But they called upon the Lord who is merciful,
  spreading out their hands toward him.
  The Holy One quickly heard them from
    heaven,
  and delivered them through Isaiah.
21 The Lordg struck down the camp of the
    Assyrians,
  and his angel wiped them out.
22 For Hezekiah did what was pleasing to the
    Lord,
  and he kept firmly to the ways of his ancestor
    David,
  as he was commanded by the prophet Isaiah,
  who was great and trustworthy in his
    visions.

Isaiah

23 In Isaiah'sh days the sun went backward,
  and he prolonged the life of the king.
24 By his dauntless spirit he saw the future,
  and comforted the mourners in Zion.
25 He revealed what was to occur to the end of
    time,
  and the hidden things before they happened.

Josiah and Other Worthies

49 The name of Josiah is like blended
  incense
  prepared by the skill of the perfumer;
  his memoryi is as sweet as honey to every
    mouth,

---

a Heb: Gk *him*   b Heb: Gk *are for reproofs*   c Other ancient
authorities read *and have died*   d Text and meaning of Gk
uncertain   e Heb: Gk lacks *He performed . . . mouth*   f Other
ancient authorities add *from Lachish*   g Gk *He*   h Gk *his*
i Heb: Gk *memory*   j Heb: Gk *it*

and like music at a banquet of wine.
2 He did what was right by reforming the people,
   and removing the wicked abominations.
3 He kept his heart fixed on the Lord;
   in lawless times he made godliness prevail.

4 Except for David and Hezekiah and Josiah,
   all of them were great sinners,
for they abandoned the law of the Most High;
   the kings of Judah came to an end.
5 They[a] gave their power to others,
   and their glory to a foreign nation,
6 who set fire to the chosen city of the sanctuary,
   and made its streets desolate,
   as Jeremiah had foretold.[b]
7 For they had mistreated him,
   who even in the womb had been consecrated
      a prophet,
to pluck up and ruin and destroy,
   and likewise to build and to plant.

8 It was Ezekiel who saw the vision of glory,
   which God[c] showed him above the chariot of
      the cherubim.
9 For God[d] also mentioned Job
   who held fast to all the ways of justice.[e]
10 May the bones of the Twelve Prophets
   send forth new life from where they lie,
for they comforted the people of Jacob
   and delivered them with confident hope.

11 How shall we magnify Zerubbabel?
   He was like a signet ring on the right hand,
12   and so was Jeshua son of Jozadak;
in their days they built the house
   and raised a temple[f] holy to the Lord,
   destined for everlasting glory.
13 The memory of Nehemiah also is lasting;
   he raised our fallen walls,
and set up gates and bars,
   and rebuilt our ruined houses.

Retrospect

14 Few have[g] ever been created on earth like
      Enoch,
   for he was taken up from the earth.
15 Nor was anyone ever born like Joseph;[h]
   even his bones were cared for.
16 Shem and Seth and Enosh were honored,[i]
   but above every other created living being was
      Adam.

Simon Son of Onias

50 The leader of his brothers and the pride of
   his people[j]
was the high priest, Simon son of Onias,

who in his life repaired the house,
   and in his time fortified the temple.
2 He laid the foundations for the high double
      walls,
   the high retaining walls for the temple
      enclosure.
3 In his days a water cistern was dug,[k]
   a reservoir like the sea in circumference.
4 He considered how to save his people from
      ruin,
   and fortified the city against siege.
5 How glorious he was, surrounded by the
      people,
   as he came out of the house of the curtain.
6 Like the morning star among the clouds,
   like the full moon at the festal season;[k]
7 like the sun shining on the temple of the Most
      High,
   like the rainbow gleaming in splendid
      clouds;
8 like roses in the days of first fruits,
   like lilies by a spring of water,
   like a green shoot on Lebanon on a summer
      day;
9 like fire and incense in the censer,
   like a vessel of hammered gold
   studded with all kinds of precious stones;
10 like an olive tree laden with fruit,
   and like a cypress towering in the clouds.
11 When he put on his glorious robe
   and clothed himself in perfect splendor,
when he went up to the holy altar,
   he made the court of the sanctuary glorious.

12 When he received the portions from the hands
      of the priests,
   as he stood by the hearth of the altar
with a garland of brothers around him,
   he was like a young cedar on Lebanon
   surrounded by the trunks of palm trees.
13 All the sons of Aaron in their splendor
   held the Lord's offering in their hands
   before the whole congregation of Israel.
14 Finishing the service at the altars,[l]
   and arranging the offering to the Most High,
      the Almighty,
15 he held out his hand for the cup
   and poured a drink offering of the blood of
      the grape;

---

a Heb *He*   b Gk *by the hand of Jeremiah*   c Gk *He*   d Gk *he*
e Heb Compare Syr: Meaning of Gk uncertain   f Other ancient
authorities read *people*   g Heb Syr: Gk *No one has*   h Heb Syr:
Gk adds *the leader of his brothers, the support of the people*
i Heb: Gk *Shem and Seth were honored by people*   j Heb Syr:
Gk lacks this line. Compare 49.15   k Heb: Meaning of Gk
uncertain   l Other ancient authorities read *altar*

he poured it out at the foot of the altar,
　　a pleasing odor to the Most High, the king of
　　　all.

16 Then the sons of Aaron shouted;
　　they blew their trumpets of hammered
　　　metal;
　　they sounded a mighty fanfare
　　as a reminder before the Most High.

17 Then all the people together quickly
　　fell to the ground on their faces
　　to worship their Lord,
　　the Almighty, God Most High.

18 Then the singers praised him with their voices
　　in sweet and full-toned melody.ᵃ

19 And the people of the Lord Most High offered
　　their prayers before the Merciful One,
　　until the order of worship of the Lord was
　　　ended,
　　and they completed his ritual.

20 Then Simonᵇ came down and raised his hands
　　over the whole congregation of Israelites,
　　to pronounce the blessing of the Lord with his
　　　lips,
　　and to glory in his name;

21 and they bowed down in worship a second
　　time,
　　to receive the blessing from the Most High.

A Benediction

22 And now bless the God of all,
　　who everywhere works great wonders,
　　who fosters our growth from birth,
　　and deals with us according to his mercy.

23 May he give usᶜ gladness of heart,
　　and may there be peace in ourᵈ days
　　in Israel, as in the days of old.

24 May he entrust to us his mercy,
　　and may he deliver us in ourᵉ days!

Epilogue

25 Two nations my soul detests,
　　and the third is not even a people:

26 Those who live in Seir,ᶠ and the Philistines,
　　and the foolish people that live in
　　　Shechem.

27 Instruction in understanding and knowledge
　　I have written in this book,
　　Jesus son of Eleazar son of Sirachᵍ of
　　　Jerusalem,
　　whose mind poured forth wisdom.

28 Happy are those who concern themselves with
　　these things,
　　and those who lay them to heart will become
　　wise.

29 For if they put them into practice, they will be
　　equal to anything,
　　for the fearʰ of the Lord is their path.

PRAYER OF JESUS SON OF SIRACHⁱ

51 I give you thanks, O Lord and King,
　　and praise you, O God my Savior.
　I give thanks to your name,

2　for you have been my protector and helper
　and have delivered me from destruction
　　and from the trap laid by a slanderous
　　　tongue,
　　from lips that fabricate lies.
　In the face of my adversaries
　　you have been my helper ³and delivered
　　　me,
　　in the greatness of your mercy and of your
　　　name,
　from grinding teeth about to devour me,
　　from the hand of those seeking my life,
　　from the many troubles I endured,

4 from choking fire on every side,
　　and from the midst of fire that I had not
　　　kindled,

5 from the deep belly of Hades,
　　from an unclean tongue and lying words—

6　the slander of an unrighteous tongue to the
　　　king.
　My soul drew near to death,
　　and my life was on the brink of Hades
　　　below.

7 They surrounded me on every side,
　　and there was no one to help me;
　I looked for human assistance,
　　and there was none.

8 Then I remembered your mercy, O Lord,
　　and your kindnessʲ from of old,
　for you rescue those who wait for you
　　and save them from the hand of their
　　　enemies.

9 And I sent up my prayer from the earth,
　　and begged for rescue from death.

10 I cried out, "Lord, you are my Father;ᵏ
　　do not forsake me in the days of trouble,
　　when there is no help against the proud.

11 I will praise your name continually,
　　and will sing hymns of thanksgiving."
　My prayer was heard,

12　for you saved me from destruction
　　and rescued me in time of trouble.

ᵃ Other ancient authorities read *in sweet melody throughout the house*   ᵇ Gk *he*   ᶜ Other ancient authorities read *you*   ᵈ Other ancient authorities read *your*   ᵉ Other ancient authorities read *his*   ᶠ Heb Compare Lat: Gk *on the mountain of Samaria*   ᵍ Heb: Meaning of Gk uncertain   ʰ Heb: Other ancient authorities read *light*   ⁱ This title is included in the Gk text.   ʲ Other ancient authorities read *work*   ᵏ Heb: Gk *the Father of my lord*

For this reason I thank you and praise you,
    and I bless the name of the Lord.

———————————

Heb adds:

Give thanks to the LORD, for he is good,
    for his steadfast love endures forever;

Give thanks to the God of praises,
    for his steadfast love endures forever;

Give thanks to the guardian of Israel,
    for his steadfast love endures forever;

Give thanks to him who formed all things,
    for his steadfast love endures forever;

Give thanks to the redeemer of Israel,
    for his steadfast love endures forever;

Give thanks to him who gathers the dispersed of
    Israel,
    for his steadfast love endures forever;

Give thanks to him who rebuilt his city and his
    sanctuary,
    for his steadfast love endures forever;

Give thanks to him who makes a horn to sprout for
    the house of David,
    for his steadfast love endures forever;

Give thanks to him who has chosen the sons of
    Zadok to be priests,
    for his steadfast love endures forever;

Give thanks to the shield of Abraham,
    for his steadfast love endures forever;

Give thanks to the rock of Isaac,
    for his steadfast love endures forever;

Give thanks to the mighty one of Jacob,
    for his steadfast love endures forever;

Give thanks to him who has chosen Zion,
    for his steadfast love endures forever;

Give thanks to the King of the kings of kings,
    for his steadfast love endures forever;

He has raised up a horn for his people,
    praise for all his loyal ones.

For the children of Israel, the people close to him.
    Praise the LORD!

Autobiographical Poem on Wisdom

13 While I was still young, before I went on my
        travels,
    I sought wisdom openly in my prayer.
14 Before the temple I asked for her,
    and I will search for her until the end.

15 From the first blossom to the ripening grape
    my heart delighted in her;
    my foot walked on the straight path;
    from my youth I followed her steps.

16 I inclined my ear a little and received her,
    and I found for myself much instruction.
17 I made progress in her;
    to him who gives wisdom I will give glory.

18 For I resolved to live according to wisdom,[a]
    and I was zealous for the good,
    and I shall never be disappointed.
19 My soul grappled with wisdom,[a]
    and in my conduct I was strict;[b]

I spread out my hands to the heavens,
    and lamented my ignorance of her.
20 I directed my soul to her,
    and in purity I found her.

With her I gained understanding from the first;
    therefore I will never be forsaken.
21 My heart was stirred to seek her;
    therefore I have gained a prize possession.
22 The Lord gave me my tongue as a reward,
    and I will praise him with it.

23 Draw near to me, you who are uneducated,
    and lodge in the house of instruction.
24 Why do you say you are lacking in these
        things,[c]
    and why do you endure such great thirst?
25 I opened my mouth and said,
    Acquire wisdom[d] for yourselves without
        money.

26 Put your neck under her[e] yoke,
    and let your souls receive instruction;
    it is to be found close by.

27 See with your own eyes that I have labored but
        little
    and found for myself much serenity.

———————————

a Gk *her*   b Meaning of Gk uncertain   c Cn Compare Heb Syr:
Meaning of Gk uncertain   d Heb: Gk lacks *wisdom*   e Heb:
other ancient authorities read *the*

[28] Hear but a little of my instruction,
   and through me you will acquire silver and
   gold.[a]

[29] May your soul rejoice in God's[b] mercy,
   and may you never be ashamed to praise him.

[30] Do your work in good time,
   and in his own time God[c] will give you your
   reward.

---

a Syr Compare Heb: Gk *Get instruction with a large sum of silver, and you will gain by it much gold.*   b Gk *his*   c Gk *he*

Introduction to
the Prophets

Have you ever met someone who inspired you to make some needed changes in your life and gave you hope for the future? Someone who was unafraid to speak the truth or to challenge you to live a more just life? If so, you've encountered a modern-day prophet—a person who names what God wants to say to us. In this section of books, you will meet the prophets of the Bible—unique and courageous people who did these things for ancient Israel.

In Depth

What is a prophet? First and foremost, a prophet is a person—or sometimes a group—who speaks for God. The prophet's words spoken in God's name—usually called prophecies or oracles—are God's words. Some people think prophets can predict the future, but this is not their role in the Bible. The biblical prophets were called by God during times of crisis to offer God's People challenge or comfort, depending on their circumstances. So, to properly understand biblical prophecies, we must try to understand the historical situation God was addressing through the prophets.

Through the prophets' inspired messages, God reminded the Israelites of the covenant God had made with them (see "Introduction to the Pentateuch"). If the people or their leaders were not keeping their side of the covenant, the prophets challenged them to do so. If the people were in despair that God was not keeping God's side of the covenant, the prophets promised that God would. Here are some common covenant themes the prophets emphasized:

▣ *Warnings against idolatry.* The Israelites were constantly tempted to worship the gods of other nations and cultures. The prophets had to keep reminding the kings and people of the first law of the Ten Commandments: "I am the LORD your God, who brought you out of the land of Egypt, out of the house of slavery; you shall have no other gods before me" (Ex 20:2–3).

▣ *Warnings to act justly and to treat the poor fairly.* In their greed and struggle for power, the wealthy and the ruling class often cheated and oppressed other people. Operating as Israel's conscience, the prophets were unanimous in challenging Israel to act justly and to care for the poor and marginalized. This did not always make the prophets popular with the kings and the ruling class—they were often ridiculed and even threatened with violence.

▣ *Attempts to deepen the understanding of God's love and mercy.* Some Israelites felt God would not forgive them after Israel (the northern kingdom) and Judah (the southern kingdom) were conquered by foreign nations. The prophets assured them they would receive God's forgiveness if they turned to God and kept the covenant. In addition, some of the prophets began to teach that God was Lord over—and cared for—all nations, not just Israel.

Promises of hope for the future. During these troubled and often violent times, it must have seemed to many Israelites that their world was coming to an end. The prophets responded to the people's despair with hope-filled promises that ultimately God's love and justice would prevail. These hopeful prophecies took different forms: the coming of the Ideal Ruler, the restoration of Jerusalem and the Temple, a time of judgment when good is rewarded and evil punished, and so on.

The stories of the earliest prophets—Samuel, Nathan, Elijah, and Elisha—are in the Bible's historical Books of 1 and 2 Samuel and 1 and 2 Kings. God's revelation through the later prophets is recorded in the books of this section of the Bible. The introduction to each book in this section gives background about the historical situation the prophet faced. The timeline in the back of this Bible identifies the time period for each prophet.

As you read these books, keep this in mind: the role of prophets has not died, only changed. In every age, there are people who challenge us to be faithful to God and remind us about God's faithful love for us. In fact, Christians believe that through their Baptism, God calls them to be priest, prophet, and king. You can fulfill your prophetic calling by challenging others to live justly and reminding them of God's love. It's exciting and humbling to be called into such a proud tradition.

Other Background

▶ Isaiah, Jeremiah, and Ezekiel are sometimes called the major prophets because their books are long and because of the role they played in Israelite history.

▶ Hosea, Amos, Jeremiah, First Isaiah, Obadiah, Micah, Nahum, Habakkuk, and Zephaniah prophesied before the Babylonian Exile.

▶ Ezekiel, Second Isaiah, and Lamentations are set during the Exile.

▶ Joel, Haggai, Zechariah, Malachi, Third Isaiah, and Baruch prophesied after the Exile.

▶ Jonah wasn't a historical prophet, but a fictional, reluctant prophet.

▶ Seven of the prophets talk about "the day of the LORD"—a final time of God's judgment when evil will be punished.

Once in a while, Hollywood releases a new movie that is a remake of an older film. The new movie has a new director and new actors and actresses. It keeps the same basic plot as the original but is adapted to appeal to a modern audience. This is what happened with the prophet Isaiah. The original Isaiah was such a hit that, years after he died, a second and even a third person or group adapted his ideas to their situation. The stories of the original Isaiah and his two "remakes" were collected into the single Book of Isaiah we have today.

In Depth

Prophets from three different periods in Israel's history contributed to the Book of Isaiah. Chapters 1–39 reflect the prophecies of the original Isaiah, called First Isaiah. His career began with his call in the Temple during the reign of Uzziah around 742 BC (see the timeline at the back of this Bible). First Isaiah advised the kings of Judah about the dangers of alliances with foreign nations and cautioned them to trust only in God. He cried out against the social injustices of the rich ruling class against the poor and taught that God had a plan in which all, rich and poor, powerful and oppressed, would have a part. First Isaiah is responsible for the messianic prophecies, which tell of the coming of a perfect king.

Years later, when Israel was exiled in Babylon (587–538 BC), another prophet, Second Isaiah, reworked First Isaiah's prophecies to address his own people (chapters 40–55). Second Isaiah's people were struggling to understand why God allowed them to be captives in a strange land. The prophet comforted them with a hopeful message: They had been taken captive so that they would turn away from their sinful practices; now that they had learned their lesson, God would return them to rebuild Israel. Contained in this prophet's writings are the famous servant songs (see "The Servant Songs," near 42:1–7).

After the Israelites returned from exile and resettled in Judah (537–500 BC), they once again fell into patterns of social injustice and religious apathy. Third Isaiah responded by demanding that they practice justice toward one another, and even toward the Gentiles, non-Jews (chapters 56–66). Realizing that Israel would never be a perfect community, he spoke of "new heavens / and a new earth" (65:17), where people would live according to God's plan.

🟢 At a Glance

- **Chapters 1–39. First Isaiah (before the Babylonian Exile)**
- **Chapters 40–55. Second Isaiah (during the Exile)**
- **Chapters 56–66. Third Isaiah (after the Exile)**

⭐ Quick Facts

Period Covered: from 742 to 500 BC

Inspired Authors: the three Isaiahs or their followers

Themes: faithfulness to God, justice for the poor, hope for the future, messianic prophecies, God as lord over all nations

The Book of **Isaiah**

Isaiah

1 The vision of Isaiah son of Amoz, which he saw concerning Judah and Jerusalem in the days of Uzziah, Jotham, Ahaz, and Hezekiah, kings of Judah.

The Wickedness of Judah

2 Hear, O heavens, and listen, O earth;
  for the LORD has spoken:
I reared children and brought them up,
  but they have rebelled against me.
3 The ox knows its owner,
  and the donkey its master's crib;
but Israel does not know,
  my people do not understand.

4 Ah, sinful nation,
  people laden with iniquity,
offspring who do evil,
  children who deal corruptly,
who have forsaken the LORD,
  who have despised the Holy One of Israel,
  who are utterly estranged!

5 Why do you seek further beatings?
  Why do you continue to rebel?
The whole head is sick,
  and the whole heart faint.
6 From the sole of the foot even to the head,
  there is no soundness in it,
but bruises and sores
  and bleeding wounds;
they have not been drained, or bound up,
  or softened with oil.

7 Your country lies desolate,
  your cities are burned with fire;
in your very presence
  aliens devour your land;
  it is desolate, as overthrown by foreigners.
8 And daughter Zion is left
  like a booth in a vineyard,
like a shelter in a cucumber field,
  like a besieged city.
9 If the LORD of hosts
  had not left us a few survivors,
we would have been like Sodom,
  and become like Gomorrah.

10 Hear the word of the LORD,
  you rulers of Sodom!
Listen to the teaching of our God,
  you people of Gomorrah!
11 What to me is the multitude of your sacrifices?
  says the LORD;
I have had enough of burnt offerings of rams
  and the fat of fed beasts;
I do not delight in the blood of bulls,
  or of lambs, or of goats.

12 When you come to appear before me,[a]
  who asked this from your hand?
  Trample my courts no more;
13 bringing offerings is futile;
  incense is an abomination to me.

---

a Or see my face

New moon and sabbath and calling of
convocation—
I cannot endure solemn assemblies with
iniquity.
14 Your new moons and your appointed festivals
my soul hates;
they have become a burden to me,
I am weary of bearing them.
15 When you stretch out your hands,
I will hide my eyes from you;
even though you make many prayers,
I will not listen;
your hands are full of blood.
16 Wash yourselves; make yourselves clean;
remove the evil of your doings
from before my eyes;
cease to do evil,
17 learn to do good;
seek justice,
rescue the oppressed,
defend the orphan,
plead for the widow.

God Wants Justice, Not Empty Rites

First Isaiah denounces the hypocrisy of practicing empty religious rituals that are not grounded in justice, sincerity, and good deeds. Speaking for God, he calls the people to do good, seek justice, rescue the oppressed, and defend the orphans and the widows.

How can we do this today? By volunteering our time to serve those in need; by speaking out against those who persecute, demean, or ridicule; by educating ourselves about the plight of those who suffer; and by praying vigilantly for the impoverished, oppressed, orphaned, and widowed in our world.

● How do you actively seek justice and take care of people in need?

● In your prayer, ask God's forgiveness for when you have not responded to God's call to practice justice or help people in need.

▶ Isa 1:10–20

18 Come now, let us argue it out,
says the LORD:
though your sins are like scarlet,
they shall be like snow;
though they are red like crimson,
they shall become like wool.
19 If you are willing and obedient,
you shall eat the good of the land;
20 but if you refuse and rebel,
you shall be devoured by the sword;
for the mouth of the LORD has spoken.

The Degenerate City

21 How the faithful city
has become a whore!
She that was full of justice,
righteousness lodged in her—
but now murderers!
22 Your silver has become dross,
your wine is mixed with water.
23 Your princes are rebels
and companions of thieves.
Everyone loves a bribe
and runs after gifts.
They do not defend the orphan,
and the widow's cause does not come before
them.

24 Therefore says the Sovereign, the LORD of hosts,
the Mighty One of Israel:
Ah, I will pour out my wrath on my enemies,
and avenge myself on my foes!
25 I will turn my hand against you;
I will smelt away your dross as with lye
and remove all your alloy.
26 And I will restore your judges as at the first,
and your counselors as at the beginning.
Afterward you shall be called the city of
righteousness,
the faithful city.

27 Zion shall be redeemed by justice,
and those in her who repent, by
righteousness.
28 But rebels and sinners shall be destroyed
together,
and those who forsake the LORD shall be
consumed.
29 For you shall be ashamed of the oaks
in which you delighted;
and you shall blush for the gardens
that you have chosen.
30 For you shall be like an oak
whose leaf withers,
and like a garden without water.
31 The strong shall become like tinder,

and their work[a] like a spark;
they and their work shall burn together,
    with no one to quench them.

The Future House of God

2 The word that Isaiah son of Amoz saw concerning Judah and Jerusalem.

² In days to come
    the mountain of the LORD's house
shall be established as the highest of the
        mountains,
    and shall be raised above the hills;
all the nations shall stream to it.
³   Many peoples shall come and say,
"Come, let us go up to the mountain of the
    LORD,
    to the house of the God of Jacob;
that he may teach us his ways
    and that we may walk in his paths."
For out of Zion shall go forth instruction,
    and the word of the LORD from Jerusalem.
⁴ He shall judge between the nations,
    and shall arbitrate for many peoples;
they shall beat their swords into plowshares,
    and their spears into pruning hooks;
nation shall not lift up sword against nation,
    neither shall they learn war any more.

Judgment Pronounced on Arrogance

⁵ O house of Jacob,
    come, let us walk
    in the light of the LORD!
⁶ For you have forsaken the ways of[b] your people,
    O house of Jacob.
Indeed they are full of diviners[c] from the east
    and of soothsayers like the Philistines,
    and they clasp hands with foreigners.
⁷ Their land is filled with silver and gold,
    and there is no end to their treasures;
their land is filled with horses,
    and there is no end to their chariots.
⁸ Their land is filled with idols;
    they bow down to the work of their hands,
    to what their own fingers have made.
⁹ And so people are humbled,
    and everyone is brought low—
    do not forgive them!
¹⁰ Enter into the rock,
    and hide in the dust
from the terror of the LORD,
    and from the glory of his majesty.
¹¹ The haughty eyes of people shall be brought
        low,
    and the pride of everyone shall be humbled;
and the LORD alone will be exalted on that day.

Pray It!

From Violence to Love

We hear Isaiah 2:1–5 every three years in church on the first Sunday of Advent. Its "swords into plowshares" theme is all about moving from violence to nonviolence and ultimately to love in our responses to conflict (see also Joel 3:10 and Mic 4:3).

But what exactly is a plowshare? A plowshare is a tool that helps a farmer harvest the fields. The message is that instead of tools of violence (swords), a world of peace needs only tools to feed and nourish its people (plowshares). God's Reign is present when swords are turned into plowshares.

Our society often glorifies violence, weapons, battle, and war. Take a few minutes to pray, reflect, or journal on the following questions:

● Why does our society glorify violence?
● As a member of society, do you support violence or nonviolence? How?
● What nonviolent actions can you take when you find yourself in conflict situations? (For example, walking away from the situation, remaining calm, and counting to ten before responding.)
● How can we be people of love in a world that is all too often hateful?

▶ **Isa 2:1–5**

¹² For the LORD of hosts has a day
    against all that is proud and lofty,
    against all that is lifted up and high;[d]
¹³ against all the cedars of Lebanon,
    lofty and lifted up;
    and against all the oaks of Bashan;
¹⁴ against all the high mountains,
    and against all the lofty hills;
¹⁵ against every high tower,
    and against every fortified wall;
¹⁶ against all the ships of Tarshish,
    and against all the beautiful craft.[e]
¹⁷ The haughtiness of people shall be humbled,

a Or its makers   b Heb lacks the ways of   c Cn: Heb lacks of
diviners   d Cn Compare Gk: Heb low   e Compare Gk: Meaning
of Heb uncertain

I
S
A

and the pride of everyone shall be brought low;
and the Lord alone will be exalted on that day.
18 The idols shall utterly pass away.
19 Enter the caves of the rocks
and the holes of the ground,
from the terror of the Lord,
and from the glory of his majesty,
when he rises to terrify the earth.
20 On that day people will throw away
to the moles and to the bats
their idols of silver and their idols of gold,
which they made for themselves to worship,
21 to enter the caverns of the rocks
and the clefts in the crags,
from the terror of the Lord,
and from the glory of his majesty,
when he rises to terrify the earth.
22 Turn away from mortals,
who have only breath in their nostrils,
for of what account are they?

3 For now the Sovereign, the Lord of hosts,
is taking away from Jerusalem and from Judah
support and staff—
all support of bread,
and all support of water—
2 warrior and soldier,
judge and prophet,
diviner and elder,
3 captain of fifty
and dignitary,
counselor and skillful magician
and expert enchanter.
4 And I will make boys their princes,
and babes shall rule over them.
5 The people will be oppressed,
everyone by another
and everyone by a neighbor;
the youth will be insolent to the elder,
and the base to the honorable.

6 Someone will even seize a relative,
a member of the clan, saying,
"You have a cloak;
you shall be our leader,
and this heap of ruins
shall be under your rule."
7 But the other will cry out on that day, saying,
"I will not be a healer;
in my house there is neither bread nor cloak;
you shall not make me
leader of the people."
8 For Jerusalem has stumbled
and Judah has fallen,
because their speech and their deeds are against
the Lord,
defying his glorious presence.

9 The look on their faces bears witness against
them;
they proclaim their sin like Sodom,
they do not hide it.
Woe to them!
For they have brought evil on themselves.
10 Tell the innocent how fortunate they are,
for they shall eat the fruit of their labors.
11 Woe to the guilty! How unfortunate they are,
for what their hands have done shall be done
to them.
12 My people—children are their oppressors,
and women rule over them.
O my people, your leaders mislead you,
and confuse the course of your paths.

13 The Lord rises to argue his case;
he stands to judge the peoples.
14 The Lord enters into judgment
with the elders and princes of his people:
It is you who have devoured the vineyard;
the spoil of the poor is in your houses.
15 What do you mean by crushing my people,
by grinding the face of the poor? says the
Lord God of hosts.

16 The Lord said:
Because the daughters of Zion are haughty
and walk with outstretched necks,
glancing wantonly with their eyes,
mincing along as they go,
tinkling with their feet;
17 the Lord will afflict with scabs
the heads of the daughters of Zion,
and the Lord will lay bare their secret parts.

18 In that day the Lord will take away the finery
of the anklets, the headbands, and the crescents;
19 the pendants, the bracelets, and the scarfs; 20 the
headdresses, the armlets, the sashes, the perfume
boxes, and the amulets; 21 the signet rings and nose
rings; 22 the festal robes, the mantles, the cloaks,
and the handbags; 23 the garments of gauze, the
linen garments, the turbans, and the veils.
24 Instead of perfume there will be a stench;
and instead of a sash, a rope;
and instead of well-set hair, baldness;
and instead of a rich robe, a binding of
sackcloth;
instead of beauty, shame.[a]
25 Your men shall fall by the sword
and your warriors in battle.
26 And her gates shall lament and mourn;
ravaged, she shall sit upon the ground.

a Q Ms: MT lacks shame

4 Seven women shall take hold of one man in that day, saying,
"We will eat our own bread and wear our own clothes;
just let us be called by your name;
take away our disgrace."

The Future Glory of the Survivors in Zion

2 On that day the branch of the LORD shall be beautiful and glorious, and the fruit of the land shall be the pride and glory of the survivors of Israel. ³Whoever is left in Zion and remains in Jerusalem will be called holy, everyone who has been recorded for life in Jerusalem, ⁴once the Lord has washed away the filth of the daughters of Zion and cleansed the bloodstains of Jerusalem from its midst by a spirit of judgment and by a spirit of burning. ⁵Then the LORD will create over the whole site of Mount Zion and over its places of assembly a cloud by day and smoke and the shining of a flaming fire by night. Indeed over all the glory there will be a canopy. ⁶It will serve as a pavilion, a shade by day from the heat, and a refuge and a shelter from the storm and rain.

The Song of the Unfruitful Vineyard

5 Let me sing for my beloved
my love-song concerning his vineyard:
My beloved had a vineyard
on a very fertile hill.
² He dug it and cleared it of stones,
and planted it with choice vines;
he built a watchtower in the midst of it,
and hewed out a wine vat in it;
he expected it to yield grapes,
but it yielded wild grapes.

³ And now, inhabitants of Jerusalem
and people of Judah,
judge between me
and my vineyard.
⁴ What more was there to do for my vineyard
that I have not done in it?
When I expected it to yield grapes,
why did it yield wild grapes?

⁵ And now I will tell you
what I will do to my vineyard.
I will remove its hedge,
and it shall be devoured;
I will break down its wall,
and it shall be trampled down.
⁶ I will make it a waste;
it shall not be pruned or hoed,

and it shall be overgrown with briers and thorns;
I will also command the clouds
that they rain no rain upon it.

⁷ For the vineyard of the LORD of hosts
is the house of Israel,
and the people of Judah
are his pleasant planting;
he expected justice,
but saw bloodshed;
righteousness,
but heard a cry!

Social Injustice Denounced

⁸ Ah, you who join house to house,
who add field to field,
until there is room for no one but you,
and you are left to live alone
in the midst of the land!
⁹ The LORD of hosts has sworn in my hearing:
Surely many houses shall be desolate,
large and beautiful houses, without inhabitant.
¹⁰ For ten acres of vineyard shall yield but one bath,
and a homer of seed shall yield a mere ephah.ᵃ

¹¹ Ah, you who rise early in the morning
in pursuit of strong drink,
who linger in the evening
to be inflamed by wine,
¹² whose feasts consist of lyre and harp,
tambourine and flute and wine,
but who do not regard the deeds of the LORD,
or see the work of his hands!
¹³ Therefore my people go into exile without knowledge;
their nobles are dying of hunger,
and their multitude is parched with thirst.

¹⁴ Therefore Sheol has enlarged its appetite
and opened its mouth beyond measure;
the nobility of Jerusalemᵇ and her multitude go down,
her throng and all who exult in her.
¹⁵ People are bowed down, everyone is brought low,
and the eyes of the haughty are humbled.
¹⁶ But the LORD of hosts is exalted by justice,
and the Holy God shows himself holy by righteousness.

---

a The Heb bath, homer, and ephah are measures of quantity
b Heb her nobility

17 Then the lambs shall graze as in their pasture,
  fatlings and kids[a] shall feed among the ruins.

18 Ah, you who drag iniquity along with cords of
    falsehood,
  who drag sin along as with cart ropes,
19 who say, "Let him make haste,
    let him speed his work
  that we may see it;
  let the plan of the Holy One of Israel hasten to
    fulfillment,
  that we may know it!"
20 Ah, you who call evil good
    and good evil,
  who put darkness for light
    and light for darkness,
  who put bitter for sweet
    and sweet for bitter!
21 Ah, you who are wise in your own eyes,
  and shrewd in your own sight!
22 Ah, you who are heroes in drinking wine
  and valiant at mixing drink,
23 who acquit the guilty for a bribe,
  and deprive the innocent of their rights!

Foreign Invasion Predicted

24 Therefore, as the tongue of fire devours the
    stubble,
  and as dry grass sinks down in the flame,
  so their root will become rotten,
    and their blossom go up like dust;
  for they have rejected the instruction of the LORD
    of hosts,
  and have despised the word of the Holy One
    of Israel.

25 Therefore the anger of the LORD was kindled
    against his people,
  and he stretched out his hand against them
    and struck them;
  the mountains quaked,
  and their corpses were like refuse
    in the streets.
  For all this his anger has not turned away,
    and his hand is stretched out still.

26 He will raise a signal for a nation far away,
    and whistle for a people at the ends of the
      earth;
  Here they come, swiftly, speedily!
27 None of them is weary, none stumbles,
    none slumbers or sleeps,
  not a loincloth is loose,
    not a sandal-thong broken;
28 their arrows are sharp,
    all their bows bent,

their horses' hoofs seem like flint,
  and their wheels like the whirlwind.
29 Their roaring is like a lion,
    like young lions they roar;
  they growl and seize their prey,
    they carry it off, and no one can rescue.
30 They will roar over it on that day,
    like the roaring of the sea.
  And if one look to the land—
    only darkness and distress;
  and the light grows dark with clouds.

A Vision of God in the Temple

6 In the year that King Uzziah died, I saw the Lord sitting on a throne, high and lofty; and the hem of his robe filled the temple. 2Seraphs were in attendance above him; each had six wings: with two they covered their faces, and with two they covered their feet, and with two they flew. 3And one called to another and said:
  "Holy, holy, holy is the LORD of hosts;
    the whole earth is full of his glory."
4The pivots[b] on the thresholds shook at the voices of those who called, and the house filled with smoke. 5And I said: "Woe is me! I am lost, for I am a man of unclean lips, and I live among a people of unclean lips; yet my eyes have seen the King, the LORD of hosts!"

6 Then one of the seraphs flew to me, holding a live coal that had been taken from the altar with a pair of tongs. 7The seraph[c] touched my mouth with it and said: "Now that this has touched your lips, your guilt has departed and your sin is blotted out." 8Then I heard the voice of the Lord saying, "Whom shall I send, and who will go for us?" And I said, "Here am I; send me!" 9And he said, "Go and say to this people:
  'Keep listening, but do not comprehend;
    keep looking, but do not understand.'
10 Make the mind of this people dull,
    and stop their ears,
    and shut their eyes,
  so that they may not look with their eyes,
    and listen with their ears,
  and comprehend with their minds,
    and turn and be healed."
11 Then I said, "How long, O Lord?" And he said:
  "Until cities lie waste
    without inhabitant,
  and houses without people,
    and the land is utterly desolate;
12 until the LORD sends everyone far away,

---

a Cn Compare Gk: Heb *aliens*   b Meaning of Heb uncertain
c Heb *He*

and vast is the emptiness in the midst of the
land.
[13] Even if a tenth part remain in it,
it will be burned again,
like a terebinth or an oak
whose stump remains standing
when it is felled."[a]
The holy seed is its stump.

Isaiah Reassures King Ahaz

7 In the days of Ahaz son of Jotham son of Uzziah, king of Judah, King Rezin of Aram and King Pekah son of Remaliah of Israel went up to attack Jerusalem, but could not mount an attack against it. [2]When the house of David heard that Aram had allied itself with Ephraim, the heart of Ahaz[b] and the heart of his people shook as the trees of the forest shake before the wind.

[3] Then the Lord said to Isaiah, Go out to meet Ahaz, you and your son Shear-jashub,[c] at the end of the conduit of the upper pool on the highway to the Fuller's Field, [4]and say to him, Take heed, be quiet, do not fear, and do not let your heart be faint because of these two smoldering stumps of firebrands, because of the fierce anger of Rezin and Aram and the son of Remaliah. [5]Because Aram—with Ephraim and the son of Remaliah—has plotted evil against you, saying, [6]Let us go up against Judah and cut off Jerusalem[d] and conquer it for ourselves and make the son of Tabeel king in it; [7]therefore thus says the Lord God:

It shall not stand,
and it shall not come to pass.
[8] For the head of Aram is Damascus,
and the head of Damascus is Rezin.
(Within sixty-five years Ephraim will be shattered, no longer a people.)
[9] The head of Ephraim is Samaria,
and the head of Samaria is the son of
Remaliah.
If you do not stand firm in faith,
you shall not stand at all.

Isaiah Gives Ahaz the Sign of Immanuel

[10] Again the Lord spoke to Ahaz, saying, [11]Ask a sign of the Lord your God, let it be deep as Sheol or high as heaven. [12]But Ahaz said, I will not ask, and I will not put the Lord to the test. [13]Then Isaiah[e] said: "Hear then, O house of David! Is it too little for you to weary mortals, that you weary my God also? [14]Therefore the Lord himself will give you a sign. Look, the young woman[f] is with child and shall bear a son, and shall name him Immanuel.[g] [15]He shall eat curds and honey by the time he knows how to refuse the evil and choose the good. [16]For before the

Live It!

Here I Am, Lord!

Phrases from the sixth chapter of Isaiah may be familiar from the song "Here I Am, Lord." This chapter tells of First Isaiah's call, which follows a biblical pattern:

1. *The person has some experience of God.* Isaiah has a dramatic vision of God in the Temple.
2. *God gives the person a mission.* God sends Isaiah to speak to the people.
3. *The person may deny being worthy.* Isaiah knows he has unclean (or sinful) lips.
4. *God addresses the denial and reassures the person.* God purifies Isaiah with fire and words of forgiveness.

You can see the same pattern for Moses' call in Exodus 3:1–12, Samuel's call in 1 Samuel 3:1–14, Jeremiah's call in Jeremiah 1:4–10, and Mary's call in Luke 1:26–38.

Christians are called by God to participate in Jesus' saving mission. They believe everyone needs to discover the way God wants them to live out that call.

● Do you believe that God has a mission for your life?
● How can you use your talents to create a more loving and just world?

▶ Isa 6:1–13

child knows how to refuse the evil and choose the good, the land before whose two kings you are in dread will be deserted. [17]The Lord will bring on you and on your people and on your ancestral house such days as have not come since the day that Ephraim departed from Judah—the king of Assyria."

[18] On that day the Lord will whistle for the fly that is at the sources of the streams of Egypt, and for the bee that is in the land of Assyria. [19]And they will all come and settle in the steep

a Meaning of Heb uncertain b Heb *his heart* c That is *A remnant shall return* d Heb *cut it off* e Heb *he* f Gk *the virgin* g That is *God is with us*

Catholic Connection

Mary

Have you ever wondered what Mary, the mother of Jesus, was like as a young girl? Do you think Mary realized when she heard the reading from Isaiah 7:14 that the prophecy would be fulfilled through her? Imagine what it would be like to discover that you are destined to play such an important role in the salvation of the world!

We know little of Mary's childhood, but the Gospel writers give us insight into how Mary, through faith and the Holy Spirit, helped fulfill Isaiah's prophecy by becoming the Mother of God. Out of faith, Mary, while still a young virgin, willingly responded yes to the angel Gabriel when told that through the power of the Holy Spirit she would give birth to God's only son, Jesus (see Lk 1:26–38). Mary had to have faith that God's Spirit was at work in Jesus' life as he grew from a child into a man (see Lk 2:41–52). It was Mary's faith in God's plan and the power of the Holy Spirit that prompted her to encourage Jesus to begin his public ministry at the wedding at Cana (see Jn 2:1–12) and sustained her as she stood at the foot of the cross during her own son's Crucifixion (see Jn 19:17–30). After Jesus' Resurrection, it was faith in Christ's promises that motivated Mary to stay with the disciples and pray for the coming of the Holy Spirit who would guide them and give them the courage to spread the Gospel message (see Acts 1:12–14).

The Church recognizes Mary as not only the Mother of God but also the Mother of the Church because of the role she has had and continues to have in bringing others to salvation in Christ. Mary is the first to receive what has been promised to all of us—freedom from sin and everlasting life. According to Church teaching, Mary was free from all sin, including original sin, from the moment of her conception. This belief, called the Immaculate Conception, is rooted in the angel Gabriel's words to Mary, which describe her as "favored" or "full of grace." Because Mary was without original sin, which leads to death, the Church also teaches that Mary was taken, body and soul, into heaven without suffering death. This belief is called the Assumption.

Mary's willingness to say yes to God's plan and allow God's Spirit to work in her life has made her a model of faith for all believers. Her rescue from sin and death foreshadows God's promise to those who remain faithful. Ask Mary to pray that God's Spirit will fill your life, so that you too will have the faith needed to say yes to God's plan and bring his message of salvation to the world.

▶ **Isa 7:14**
Catechism, nos. 484–511, 721–726, 963–975

Cultural Connection

God-with-Us!

Many Bibles refer to Isaiah, chapters 7–12, as the Book of Immanuel. In these chapters, First Isaiah announces that Israel's salvation will come from a child from the family of Jesse, the father of King David. This child will be named Immanuel (also spelled Emmanuel), which means "God-with-us." With this message, Isaiah emphasizes that God is with the little ones who trust in God's saving power.

Biblical scholars agree that the child Isaiah is referring to is the son of King Ahaz—the future king Hezekiah. But the Gospel writers later see in this passage a reference to Jesus (see Mt 1:23), the Son of God, who is truly Immanuel, God-with-us.

For Hispanic people, Immanuel is a constant reality. Hispanics give witness of the nearness of God in daily affairs through the following expressions, which you may hear more than a dozen times a day in their communities: "God help you" (*Dios te ayude*), "Go with God" (*Ve con Dios*), "If God wants it" (*Si Dios quiere*), "With God's permission" (*Si Dios lo permite*), "Through the power of God" (*Dios mediante*), "Thanks to God" (*Gracias a Dios*), "For the love of God" (*Por el amor de Dios*), "God give you a good day" (*Buen día te dé Dios*), and "God bless you" (*Dios te bendiga*).

- If you come from a family or community tradition where these faith expressions are common, feel the presence of God each time they are voiced, and use them boldly yourself.
- Think about what happened to you today. How many of these expressions could you have applied to different situations and felt God-with-you? Choose the expression that best fits the yearnings of your heart at this time, and pray with it, repeating it several times.

▶ **Isaiah, chapters 7–12**

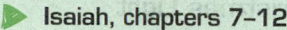

---

ravines, and in the clefts of the rocks, and on all the thornbushes, and on all the pastures.

20 On that day the Lord will shave with a razor hired beyond the River—with the king of Assyria—the head and the hair of the feet, and it will take off the beard as well.

21 On that day one will keep alive a young cow and two sheep, ²²and will eat curds because of the abundance of milk that they give; for everyone that is left in the land shall eat curds and honey.

23 On that day every place where there used to be a thousand vines, worth a thousand shekels of silver, will become briers and thorns. ²⁴With bow and arrows one will go there, for all the land will be briers and thorns; ²⁵and as for all the hills that used to be hoed with a hoe, you will not go there for fear of briers and thorns; but they will become a place where cattle are let loose and where sheep tread.

Isaiah's Son a Sign of the Assyrian Invasion

8 Then the Lord said to me, Take a large tablet and write on it in common characters, "Belonging to Maher-shalal-hash-baz,"*a* ²and have it attested*b* for me by reliable witnesses, the priest Uriah and Zechariah son of Jeberechiah. ³And I went to the prophetess, and she conceived and bore a son. Then the Lord said to me, Name him Maher-shalal-hash-baz; ⁴for before the child knows how to call "My father" or "My mother," the wealth of Damascus and the spoil of Samaria will be carried away by the king of Assyria.

5 The Lord spoke to me again: ⁶Because this people has refused the waters of Shiloah that flow gently, and melt in fear before*c* Rezin and the son of Remaliah; ⁷therefore, the Lord is bringing up against it the mighty flood waters of the River, the king of Assyria and all his glory; it will rise above all its channels and overflow all its banks; ⁸it will sweep on into Judah as a flood, and, pouring over, it will reach up to the neck; and its outspread wings will fill the breadth of your land, O Immanuel.

⁹ Band together, you peoples, and be dismayed;
   listen, all you far countries;
gird yourselves and be dismayed;
   gird yourselves and be dismayed!

---

a That is *The spoil speeds, the prey hastens*   *b* Q Ms Gk Syr: MT *and I caused to be attested*   *c* Cn: Meaning of Heb uncertain

10 Take counsel together, but it shall be brought to
naught;
speak a word, but it will not stand,
for God is with us.*a*

11 For the LORD spoke thus to me while his
hand was strong upon me, and warned me not to
walk in the way of this people, saying: 12 Do not
call conspiracy all that this people calls conspiracy, and do not fear what it fears, or be in dread.
13 But the LORD of hosts, him you shall regard as
holy; let him be your fear, and let him be your
dread. 14 He will become a sanctuary, a stone one
strikes against; for both houses of Israel he will
become a rock one stumbles over—a trap and
a snare for the inhabitants of Jerusalem. 15 And

Christmas Light

Isaiah 9:2–7 describes Immanuel as a wise,
brave, courageous, virtuous, and righteous
king. Here, First Isaiah may be referring to
King Hezekiah, the reformer king of Judah (see
2 Chronicles, chapters 29–33). However, after
Hezekiah's death, the passage came to be understood as predicting the coming of a future
savior or messiah. That's why the passage is
called a messianic prophecy.

Christians see in these words a perfect description of Jesus. In fact, Catholics read these
verses at Christmas during midnight Mass. On
one of the longest nights of the year, they imagine Jesus' presence in the world as a light dispel-
ling the darkness of sin.

This is the opening prayer for the Christmas
Mass at midnight:

O God, who have made this most sacred
*   night*
radiant with the splendor of the true light,
grant, we pray, that we, who have known
*   the mysteries of his light on earth,*
may also delight in his gladness in heaven.
Who lives and reigns with you in the unity of
*   the Holy Spirit,*
one God, for ever and ever.
*   (Roman Missal)*

▶ Isa 9:2–7

many among them shall stumble; they shall fall
and be broken; they shall be snared and taken.

Disciples of Isaiah

16 Bind up the testimony, seal the teaching
among my disciples. 17 I will wait for the LORD,
who is hiding his face from the house of Jacob,
and I will hope in him. 18 See, I and the children whom the LORD has given me are signs and
portents in Israel from the LORD of hosts, who
dwells on Mount Zion. 19 Now if people say to
you, "Consult the ghosts and the familiar spirits
that chirp and mutter; should not a people consult their gods, the dead on behalf of the living,
20 for teaching and for instruction?" surely, those
who speak like this will have no dawn! 21 They
will pass through the land,*b* greatly distressed
and hungry; when they are hungry, they will be
enraged and will curse*c* their king and their gods.
They will turn their faces upward, 22 or they will
look to the earth, but will see only distress and
darkness, the gloom of anguish; and they will be
thrust into thick darkness.*d*

The Righteous Reign of the Coming King

9*e* But there will be no gloom for those who
were in anguish. In the former time he
brought into contempt the land of Zebulun and
the land of Naphtali, but in the latter time he
will make glorious the way of the sea, the land
beyond the Jordan, Galilee of the nations.
2 *f* The people who walked in darkness
    have seen a great light;
those who lived in a land of deep darkness—
    on them light has shined.
3 You have multiplied the nation,
    you have increased its joy;
they rejoice before you
    as with joy at the harvest,
    as people exult when dividing plunder.
4 For the yoke of their burden,
    and the bar across their shoulders,
    the rod of their oppressor,
    you have broken as on the day of Midian.
5 For all the boots of the tramping warriors
    and all the garments rolled in blood
    shall be burned as fuel for the fire.
6 For a child has been born for us,
    a son given to us;
authority rests upon his shoulders;
    and he is named
Wonderful Counselor, Mighty God,
    Everlasting Father, Prince of Peace.

a Heb *immanu el*   *b* Heb *it*   *c* Or *curse by*   *d* Meaning of Heb
uncertain   *e* Ch 8.23 in Heb   *f* Ch 9.1 in Heb

7 His authority shall grow continually,
  and there shall be endless peace
for the throne of David and his kingdom.
  He will establish and uphold it
with justice and with righteousness
  from this time onward and forevermore.
The zeal of the Lord of hosts will do this.

Judgment on Arrogance and Oppression

8 The Lord sent a word against Jacob,
  and it fell on Israel;
9 and all the people knew it—
  Ephraim and the inhabitants of Samaria—
  but in pride and arrogance of heart they said:
10 "The bricks have fallen,
  but we will build with dressed stones;
the sycamores have been cut down,
  but we will put cedars in their place."
11 So the Lord raised adversaries[a] against them,
  and stirred up their enemies,
12 the Arameans on the east and the Philistines on
    the west,
  and they devoured Israel with open mouth.
For all this his anger has not turned away;
  his hand is stretched out still.

13 The people did not turn to him who struck them,
  or seek the Lord of hosts.
14 So the Lord cut off from Israel head and tail,
  palm branch and reed in one day—
15 elders and dignitaries are the head,
  and prophets who teach lies are the tail;
16 for those who led this people led them astray,
  and those who were led by them were left in
    confusion.
17 That is why the Lord did not have pity on[b] their
    young people,
  or compassion on their orphans and widows;
for everyone was godless and an evildoer,
  and every mouth spoke folly.
For all this his anger has not turned away;
  his hand is stretched out still.

18 For wickedness burned like a fire,
  consuming briers and thorns;
it kindled the thickets of the forest,
  and they swirled upward in a column of
    smoke.
19 Through the wrath of the Lord of hosts
  the land was burned,
and the people became like fuel for the fire;
  no one spared another.
20 They gorged on the right, but still were hungry,
  and they devoured on the left, but were not
    satisfied;
they devoured the flesh of their own kindred;[c]

21 Manasseh devoured Ephraim, and Ephraim
    Manasseh,
  and together they were against Judah.
For all this his anger has not turned away;
  his hand is stretched out still.

10 Ah, you who make iniquitous decrees,
  who write oppressive statutes,
2 to turn aside the needy from justice
  and to rob the poor of my people of their
    right,
that widows may be your spoil,
  and that you may make the orphans your
    prey!
3 What will you do on the day of punishment,
  in the calamity that will come from far away?
To whom will you flee for help,
  and where will you leave your wealth,
4 so as not to crouch among the prisoners
  or fall among the slain?
For all this his anger has not turned away;
  his hand is stretched out still.

Arrogant Assyria Also Judged

5 Ah, Assyria, the rod of my anger—
  the club in their hands is my fury!
6 Against a godless nation I send him,
  and against the people of my wrath I
    command him,
to take spoil and seize plunder,
  and to tread them down like the mire of the
    streets.
7 But this is not what he intends,
  nor does he have this in mind;
but it is in his heart to destroy,
  and to cut off nations not a few.
8 For he says:
"Are not my commanders all kings?
9 Is not Calno like Carchemish?
  Is not Hamath like Arpad?
  Is not Samaria like Damascus?
10 As my hand has reached to the kingdoms of the
    idols
  whose images were greater than those of
    Jerusalem and Samaria,
11 shall I not do to Jerusalem and her idols
  what I have done to Samaria and her
    images?"

12 When the Lord has finished all his work on Mount Zion and on Jerusalem, he[d] will punish the arrogant boasting of the king of Assyria and his haughty pride. 13 For he says:

---

a Cn: Heb *the adversaries of Rezin*   b Q Ms: MT *rejoice over*
c Or *arm*   d Heb *I*

"By the strength of my hand I have done it,
  and by my wisdom, for I have understanding;
I have removed the boundaries of peoples,
  and have plundered their treasures;
  like a bull I have brought down those who sat
    on thrones.
14 My hand has found, like a nest,
  the wealth of the peoples;
and as one gathers eggs that have been forsaken,
  so I have gathered all the earth;
and there was none that moved a wing,
  or opened its mouth, or chirped."

15 Shall the ax vaunt itself over the one who
    wields it,
  or the saw magnify itself against the one who
    handles it?
As if a rod should raise the one who lifts it up,
  or as if a staff should lift the one who is not
    wood!
16 Therefore the Sovereign, the Lord of hosts,
  will send wasting sickness among his stout
    warriors,
and under his glory a burning will be kindled,
  like the burning of fire.
17 The light of Israel will become a fire,
  and his Holy One a flame;
and it will burn and devour
  his thorns and briers in one day.
18 The glory of his forest and his fruitful land
  the Lord will destroy, both soul and body,
and it will be as when an invalid wastes away.
19 The remnant of the trees of his forest will be
    so few
  that a child can write them down.

The Repentant Remnant of Israel

20 On that day the remnant of Israel and the survivors of the house of Jacob will no more lean on the one who struck them, but will lean on the Lord, the Holy One of Israel, in truth. 21A remnant will return, the remnant of Jacob, to the mighty God. 22For though your people Israel were like the sand of the sea, only a remnant of them will return. Destruction is decreed, overflowing with righteousness. 23For the Lord God of hosts will make a full end, as decreed, in all the earth.ᵃ

24 Therefore thus says the Lord God of hosts: O my people, who live in Zion, do not be afraid of the Assyrians when they beat you with a rod and lift up their staff against you as the Egyptians did. 25For in a very little while my indignation will come to an end, and my anger will be directed to their destruction. 26The Lord of hosts will wield a whip against them, as when he struck Midian at the rock of Oreb; his staff will be over the sea, and he will lift it as he did in Egypt. 27On that day his burden will be removed from your shoulder, and his yoke will be destroyed from your neck.

He has gone up from Rimmon,ᵇ
28   he has come to Aiath;
he has passed through Migron,
  at Michmash he stores his baggage;
29 they have crossed over the pass,
  at Geba they lodge for the night;
Ramah trembles,
  Gibeah of Saul has fled.
30 Cry aloud, O daughter Gallim!
  Listen, O Laishah!
  Answer her, O Anathoth!
31 Madmenah is in flight,
  the inhabitants of Gebim flee for safety.
32 This very day he will halt at Nob,
  he will shake his fist
    at the mount of daughter Zion,
  the hill of Jerusalem.

33 Look, the Sovereign, the Lord of hosts,
  will lop the boughs with terrifying power;
the tallest trees will be cut down,
  and the lofty will be brought low.
34 He will hack down the thickets of the forest with
    an ax,
  and Lebanon with its majestic treesᶜ will fall.

The Peaceful Kingdom

11 A shoot shall come out from the stump of
    Jesse,
  and a branch shall grow out of his roots.
2 The spirit of the Lord shall rest on him,
  the spirit of wisdom and understanding,
  the spirit of counsel and might,
  the spirit of knowledge and the fear of the
    Lord.
3 His delight shall be in the fear of the Lord.

He shall not judge by what his eyes see,
  or decide by what his ears hear;
4 but with righteousness he shall judge the poor,
  and decide with equity for the meek of the
    earth;
he shall strike the earth with the rod of his
    mouth,
  and with the breath of his lips he shall kill
    the wicked.

---

a Or land   b Cn: Heb and his yoke from your neck, and a yoke will be destroyed because of fatness   c Cn Compare Gk Vg: Heb with a majestic one

✝ Catholic Connection

The Gifts of the Holy Spirit

Have you ever wanted to make the world a better place but did not know where to begin? Isaiah, too, wanted to see the world become a better place. Isaiah prophesied about a world marked by justice and peace and led by the ideal king. This ideal king would embody the following gifts, known as the gifts of the Holy Spirit: wisdom, understanding, counsel, fortitude, knowledge, piety, and fear of the Lord.

Nearly eight hundred years later, Isaiah's ideal king arrived; he was Jesus of Nazareth, the Son of God. Jesus' life, death, and Resurrection reveal that Jesus truly is the ideal king. The Church teaches that the gifts of the Holy Spirit prophesied by Isaiah so many years before are fully present in Jesus Christ.

The same gifts embodied in Christ are handed on to Jesus' followers through the grace of Baptism and increased through the sacrament of Confirmation. The gifts shape our heart and character so that we may humbly and willingly follow the guidance offered by the Holy Spirit and by doing so begin to make the world a better place.

Here are some suggestions for using the gifts of the Holy Spirit in your daily life:

- Pray for **wisdom** when life gets complicated and you have lost sight of the big picture.
- Pray for **understanding** when you have a problem and need to figure out what is at the heart of it.
- Pray for **counsel (right judgment)** when a friend asks you for advice.
- Pray for **fortitude (courage)** when you know the right thing to do but are afraid to do it.
- Pray for **knowledge** when you need to separate the truth from lies.
- Pray for **piety** when you are struggling to trust God.
- Pray for **fear of the Lord (awe in God's presence)** every day so that you may know in your heart how very awesome God is.

If each one of us works to develop the gifts of the Holy Spirit in our own lives, then we will all be working together to make the world a better place!

▶ **Isa 11:1–2**

Catechism, nos. 1830–1832

ISA

⁵ Righteousness shall be the belt around his
      waist,
  and faithfulness the belt around his loins.

⁶ The wolf shall live with the lamb,
    the leopard shall lie down with the kid,
  the calf and the lion and the fatling together,
    and a little child shall lead them.
⁷ The cow and the bear shall graze,
    their young shall lie down together;
    and the lion shall eat straw like the ox.
⁸ The nursing child shall play over the hole of
      the asp,
    and the weaned child shall put its hand on
      the adder's den.
⁹ They will not hurt or destroy
    on all my holy mountain;
  for the earth will be full of the knowledge of the
    Lord
    as the waters cover the sea.

Lions and Lambs

There are so many troubled spots in the world. It seems that almost every week, violence and ethnic clashes occur somewhere. How easily we forget that we are all members of the human family.

Yet, we are drawn to the image of the peaceable kingdom in Isaiah 11:6–9. To imagine natural predators such as wolves and lions living together in harmony with lambs and calves, their natural prey, gives us an insight into the Reign of God. Harmony. Peace. Gentleness. No wonder this scene has been the inspiration for numerous artists.

It is a vision we must all aim for, while also doing our best to resist all the things that pull us apart as a human family. We are all in this together. We need to work to make the peaceable Reign of God a reality. It is God's work we do.

It is inspiring that First Isaiah also uses the image of youth to express his vision of peace. What can you as a young person do to help bring about the peaceable kingdom?

▶ **Isa 11:6–9**

Return of the Remnant of Israel and Judah

10 On that day the root of Jesse shall stand as a signal to the peoples; the nations shall inquire of him, and his dwelling shall be glorious.

11 On that day the Lord will extend his hand yet a second time to recover the remnant that is left of his people, from Assyria, from Egypt, from Pathros, from Ethiopia,ᵃ from Elam, from Shinar, from Hamath, and from the coastlands of the sea.

¹² He will raise a signal for the nations,
    and will assemble the outcasts of Israel,
  and gather the dispersed of Judah
    from the four corners of the earth.
¹³ The jealousy of Ephraim shall depart,
    the hostility of Judah shall be cut off;
  Ephraim shall not be jealous of Judah,
    and Judah shall not be hostile towards
      Ephraim.
¹⁴ But they shall swoop down on the backs of the
      Philistines in the west,
    together they shall plunder the people of the
      east.
  They shall put forth their hand against Edom
      and Moab,
    and the Ammonites shall obey them.
¹⁵ And the Lord will utterly destroy
    the tongue of the sea of Egypt;
  and will wave his hand over the River
    with his scorching wind;
  and will split it into seven channels,
    and make a way to cross on foot;
¹⁶ so there shall be a highway from Assyria
    for the remnant that is left of his people,
  as there was for Israel
    when they came up from the land of Egypt.

Thanksgiving and Praise

12 You will say in that day:
    I will give thanks to you, O Lord,
      for though you were angry with me,
    your anger turned away,
      and you comforted me.

² Surely God is my salvation;
    I will trust, and will not be afraid,
  for the Lord Godᵇ is my strength and my might;
    he has become my salvation.

3 With joy you will draw water from the wells of salvation. ⁴And you will say in that day:
    Give thanks to the Lord,
      call on his name;

---

a Or *Nubia;* Heb *Cush*   b Heb *for Yah, the* Lord

make known his deeds among the nations;
  proclaim that his name is exalted.

5 Sing praises to the Lord, for he has done
      gloriously;
  let this be known[a] in all the earth.
6 Shout aloud and sing for joy, O royal[b] Zion,
  for great in your midst is the Holy One of
      Israel.

Proclamation against Babylon

13 The oracle concerning Babylon that Isaiah
    son of Amoz saw.

2 On a bare hill raise a signal,
    cry aloud to them;
  wave the hand for them to enter
    the gates of the nobles.
3 I myself have commanded my consecrated ones,
    have summoned my warriors, my proudly
        exulting ones,
    to execute my anger.

4 Listen, a tumult on the mountains
    as of a great multitude!
  Listen, an uproar of kingdoms,
    of nations gathering together!
  The Lord of hosts is mustering
    an army for battle.
5 They come from a distant land,
    from the end of the heavens,
  the Lord and the weapons of his indignation,
    to destroy the whole earth.

6 Wail, for the day of the Lord is near;
    it will come like destruction from the
        Almighty![c]
7 Therefore all hands will be feeble,
    and every human heart will melt,
8   and they will be dismayed.
  Pangs and agony will seize them;
    they will be in anguish like a woman in labor.
  They will look aghast at one another;
    their faces will be aflame.
9 See, the day of the Lord comes,
    cruel, with wrath and fierce anger,
  to make the earth a desolation,
    and to destroy its sinners from it.
10 For the stars of the heavens and their
        constellations
    will not give their light;
  the sun will be dark at its rising,
    and the moon will not shed its light.
11 I will punish the world for its evil,
    and the wicked for their iniquity;
  I will put an end to the pride of the arrogant,

and lay low the insolence of tyrants.
12 I will make mortals more rare than fine gold,
    and humans than the gold of Ophir.
13 Therefore I will make the heavens tremble,
    and the earth will be shaken out of its place,
  at the wrath of the Lord of hosts
    in the day of his fierce anger.
14 Like a hunted gazelle,
    or like sheep with no one to gather them,
  all will turn to their own people,
    and all will flee to their own lands.
15 Whoever is found will be thrust through,
    and whoever is caught will fall by the sword.
16 Their infants will be dashed to pieces
    before their eyes;
  their houses will be plundered,
    and their wives ravished.
17 See, I am stirring up the Medes against them,
    who have no regard for silver
    and do not delight in gold.
18 Their bows will slaughter the young men;
    they will have no mercy on the fruit of the
        womb;
    their eyes will not pity children.

---

a Or this is made known   b Or O inhabitant of   c Traditional
rendering of Heb Shaddai

Live It!

In God We Trust

In God we trust. Every piece of U.S. currency bears this statement, yet many of us never notice it. First Isaiah proclaims this same message: "Surely God is my salvation; / I will trust, and will not be afraid, / for the Lord God is my strength and my might" (Isa 12:2).

How often does fear keep us from trusting? How often does it keep us from being and doing what God is calling us to be and do? We need to reach out to God and to others in our lives and trust that God is with us. Jesus came to tell us that love is more powerful than fear, and his life and death testified to his deep trust in his Father. Many times, he told his disciples, "Do not be afraid."

Let us truly live the words "In God we trust."

▶ Isa 12:1–6

I
S
A

19 And Babylon, the glory of kingdoms,
  the splendor and pride of the Chaldeans,
will be like Sodom and Gomorrah
  when God overthrew them.
20 It will never be inhabited
  or lived in for all generations;
Arabs will not pitch their tents there,
  shepherds will not make their flocks lie down
    there.
21 But wild animals will lie down there,
  and its houses will be full of howling
    creatures;
there ostriches will live,
  and there goat-demons will dance.
22 Hyenas will cry in its towers,
  and jackals in the pleasant palaces;
its time is close at hand,
  and its days will not be prolonged.

Restoration of Judah

14 But the LORD will have compassion on Jacob and will again choose Israel, and will set them in their own land; and aliens will join them and attach themselves to the house of Jacob. 2And the nations will take them and bring them to their place, and the house of Israel will possess the nations*a* as male and female slaves in the LORD's land; they will take captive those who were their captors, and rule over those who oppressed them.

Downfall of the King of Babylon

3 When the LORD has given you rest from your pain and turmoil and the hard service with which you were made to serve, 4you will take up this taunt against the king of Babylon:
How the oppressor has ceased!
  How his insolence*b* has ceased!
5 The LORD has broken the staff of the wicked,
  the scepter of rulers,
6 that struck down the peoples in wrath
  with unceasing blows,
that ruled the nations in anger
  with unrelenting persecution.
7 The whole earth is at rest and quiet;
  they break forth into singing.
8 The cypresses exult over you,
  the cedars of Lebanon, saying,
"Since you were laid low,
  no one comes to cut us down."
9 Sheol beneath is stirred up
  to meet you when you come;
it rouses the shades to greet you,
  all who were leaders of the earth;
it raises from their thrones
  all who were kings of the nations.

10 All of them will speak
  and say to you:
"You too have become as weak as we!
  You have become like us!"
11 Your pomp is brought down to Sheol,
  and the sound of your harps;
maggots are the bed beneath you,
  and worms are your covering.
12 How you are fallen from heaven,
  O Day Star, son of Dawn!
How you are cut down to the ground,
  you who laid the nations low!
13 You said in your heart,
  "I will ascend to heaven;
I will raise my throne
  above the stars of God;
I will sit on the mount of assembly
  on the heights of Zaphon;*c*
14 I will ascend to the tops of the clouds,
  I will make myself like the Most High."
15 But you are brought down to Sheol,
  to the depths of the Pit.
16 Those who see you will stare at you,
  and ponder over you:
"Is this the man who made the earth tremble,
  who shook kingdoms,
17 who made the world like a desert
  and overthrew its cities,
  who would not let his prisoners go home?"
18 All the kings of the nations lie in glory,
  each in his own tomb;
19 but you are cast out, away from your grave,
  like loathsome carrion,*d*
clothed with the dead, those pierced by the
    sword,
  who go down to the stones of the Pit,
  like a corpse trampled underfoot.
20 You will not be joined with them in burial,
  because you have destroyed your land,
  you have killed your people.

May the descendants of evildoers
  nevermore be named!
21 Prepare slaughter for his sons
  because of the guilt of their father.*e*
Let them never rise to possess the earth
  or cover the face of the world with cities.

22 I will rise up against them, says the LORD of hosts, and will cut off from Babylon name and remnant, offspring and posterity, says the LORD.

---

a Heb *them*   b Q Ms Compare Gk Syr Vg: Meaning of MT uncertain   c Or *assembly in the far north*   d Cn Compare Gk: Heb *like a loathed branch*   e Syr Compare Gk: Heb *fathers*

23And I will make it a possession of the hedgehog, and pools of water, and I will sweep it with the broom of destruction, says the LORD of hosts.

An Oracle concerning Assyria

24 The LORD of hosts has sworn:
As I have designed,
  so shall it be;
and as I have planned,
  so shall it come to pass:
25 I will break the Assyrian in my land,
  and on my mountains trample him under foot;
his yoke shall be removed from them,
  and his burden from their shoulders.
26 This is the plan that is planned
  concerning the whole earth;
and this is the hand that is stretched out
  over all the nations.
27 For the LORD of hosts has planned,
  and who will annul it?
His hand is stretched out,
  and who will turn it back?

An Oracle concerning Philistia

28 In the year that King Ahaz died this oracle came:

29 Do not rejoice, all you Philistines,
  that the rod that struck you is broken,
for from the root of the snake will come forth
    an adder,
  and its fruit will be a flying fiery serpent.
30 The firstborn of the poor will graze,
  and the needy lie down in safety;
but I will make your root die of famine,
  and your remnant Ia will kill.
31 Wail, O gate; cry, O city;
  melt in fear, O Philistia, all of you!
For smoke comes out of the north,
  and there is no straggler in its ranks.

32 What will one answer the messengers of the
    nation?
"The LORD has founded Zion,
  and the needy among his people
will find refuge in her."

An Oracle concerning Moab

15 An oracle concerning Moab.

Because Ar is laid waste in a night,
  Moab is undone;
because Kir is laid waste in a night,
  Moab is undone.
2 Dibonb has gone up to the temple,
  to the high places to weep;

over Nebo and over Medeba
  Moab wails.
On every head is baldness,
  every beard is shorn;
3 in the streets they bind on sackcloth;
  on the housetops and in the squares
  everyone wails and melts in tears.
4 Heshbon and Elealeh cry out,
  their voices are heard as far as Jahaz;
therefore the loins of Moab quiver;c
  his soul trembles.
5 My heart cries out for Moab;
  his fugitives flee to Zoar,
  to Eglath-shelishiyah.
For at the ascent of Luhith
  they go up weeping;
on the road to Horonaim
  they raise a cry of destruction;
6 the waters of Nimrim
  are a desolation;
the grass is withered, the new growth fails,
  the verdure is no more.
7 Therefore the abundance they have gained
  and what they have laid up
they carry away
  over the Wadi of the Willows.
8 For a cry has gone
  around the land of Moab;
the wailing reaches to Eglaim,
  the wailing reaches to Beer-elim.
9 For the waters of Dibond are full of blood;
  yet I will bring upon Dibond even more—
a lion for those of Moab who escape,
  for the remnant of the land.

16 Send lambs
  to the ruler of the land,
from Sela, by way of the desert,
  to the mount of daughter Zion.
2 Like fluttering birds,
  like scattered nestlings,
so are the daughters of Moab
  at the fords of the Arnon.
3 "Give counsel,
  grant justice;
make your shade like night
  at the height of noon;
hide the outcasts,
  do not betray the fugitive;
4 let the outcasts of Moab
  settle among you;
be a refuge to them
  from the destroyer."

---

a Q Ms Vg: MT he   b Cn: Heb the house and Dibon
c Cn Compare Gk Syr: Heb the armed men of Moab cry aloud
d Q Ms Vg Compare Syr: MT Dimon

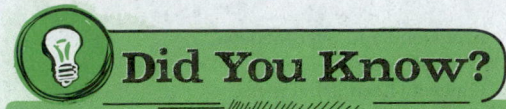

Did You Know?

Oracles

In the ancient world, an oracle was understood as a communication of the gods. By means of oracles, First Isaiah presents God's judgment on Israel's enemies, including Egypt, Babylon, Assyria, Philistia, Moab, and Edom (see Isaiah, chapters 13–23). When we read these oracles today, we can understand their angry and vengeful spirit if we recall the terrible suffering that these nations inflicted on Israel. Still, we should also keep in mind the New Testament commandment to avoid revenge in all its forms (see Mt 5:38–48). Jesus calls us to be peacemakers in spite of our suffering.

▶ Isaiah, chapters 13–23

When the oppressor is no more,
   and destruction has ceased,
and marauders have vanished from the land,
5 then a throne shall be established in steadfast
         love
   in the tent of David,
   and on it shall sit in faithfulness
a ruler who seeks justice
   and is swift to do what is right.

6 We have heard of the pride of Moab
   —how proud he is!—
of his arrogance, his pride, and his insolence;
   his boasts are false.
7 Therefore let Moab wail,
   let everyone wail for Moab.
Mourn, utterly stricken,
   for the raisin cakes of Kir-hareseth.

8 For the fields of Heshbon languish,
   and the vines of Sibmah,
whose clusters once made drunk
   the lords of the nations,
reached to Jazer
   and strayed to the desert;
their shoots once spread abroad
   and crossed over the sea.
9 Therefore I weep with the weeping of Jazer
   for the vines of Sibmah;
I drench you with my tears,
   O Heshbon and Elealeh;

for the shout over your fruit harvest
   and your grain harvest has ceased.
10 Joy and gladness are taken away
   from the fruitful field;
and in the vineyards no songs are sung,
   no shouts are raised;
no treader treads out wine in the presses;
   the vintage-shout is hushed.[a]
11 Therefore my heart throbs like a harp for Moab,
   and my very soul for Kir-heres.

12 When Moab presents himself, when he wearies himself upon the high place, when he comes to his sanctuary to pray, he will not prevail.

13 This was the word that the LORD spoke concerning Moab in the past. 14But now the LORD says, In three years, like the years of a hired worker, the glory of Moab will be brought into contempt, in spite of all its great multitude; and those who survive will be very few and feeble.

An Oracle concerning Damascus

17 An oracle concerning Damascus.

See, Damascus will cease to be a city,
   and will become a heap of ruins.
2 Her towns will be deserted forever;[b]
   they will be places for flocks,
   which will lie down, and no one will make
         them afraid.
3 The fortress will disappear from Ephraim,
   and the kingdom from Damascus;
and the remnant of Aram will be
   like the glory of the children of Israel,
                    says the LORD of hosts.

4 On that day
   the glory of Jacob will be brought low,
   and the fat of his flesh will grow lean.
5 And it shall be as when reapers gather standing
         grain
   and their arms harvest the ears,
and as when one gleans the ears of grain
   in the Valley of Rephaim.
6 Gleanings will be left in it,
   as when an olive tree is beaten—
two or three berries
   in the top of the highest bough,
four or five
   on the branches of a fruit tree,
                    says the LORD God of Israel.

7 On that day people will regard their Maker, and their eyes will look to the Holy One of Israel;

---

a Gk: Heb I have hushed   b Cn Compare Gk: Heb the cities of Aroer are deserted

8 they will not have regard for the altars, the work of their hands, and they will not look to what their own fingers have made, either the sacred poles[a] or the altars of incense.

9 On that day their strong cities will be like the deserted places of the Hivites and the Amorites,[b] which they deserted because of the children of Israel, and there will be desolation.

10 For you have forgotten the God of your
    salvation,
    and have not remembered the Rock of your
      refuge;
therefore, though you plant pleasant plants
    and set out slips of an alien god,
11 though you make them grow on the day that
    you plant them,
    and make them blossom in the morning that
      you sow;
yet the harvest will flee away
    in a day of grief and incurable pain.

12 Ah, the thunder of many peoples,
    they thunder like the thundering of the sea!
Ah, the roar of nations,
    they roar like the roaring of mighty waters!
13 The nations roar like the roaring of many waters,
    but he will rebuke them, and they will flee far
      away,
chased like chaff on the mountains before the
      wind
    and whirling dust before the storm.
14 At evening time, lo, terror!
    Before morning, they are no more.
This is the fate of those who despoil us,
    and the lot of those who plunder us.

An Oracle concerning Ethiopia

18 Ah, land of whirring wings
    beyond the rivers of Ethiopia,[c]
2 sending ambassadors by the Nile
    in vessels of papyrus on the waters!
Go, you swift messengers,
    to a nation tall and smooth,
to a people feared near and far,
    a nation mighty and conquering,
    whose land the rivers divide.

3 All you inhabitants of the world,
    you who live on the earth,
when a signal is raised on the mountains, look!
    When a trumpet is blown, listen!
4 For thus the Lord said to me:
I will quietly look from my dwelling
    like clear heat in sunshine,
    like a cloud of dew in the heat of harvest.

5 For before the harvest, when the blossom is over
    and the flower becomes a ripening grape,
he will cut off the shoots with pruning hooks,
    and the spreading branches he will hew away.
6 They shall all be left
    to the birds of prey of the mountains
    and to the animals of the earth.
And the birds of prey will summer on them,
    and all the animals of the earth will winter on
      them.

7 At that time gifts will be brought to the Lord of hosts from[d] a people tall and smooth, from a people feared near and far, a nation mighty and conquering, whose land the rivers divide, to Mount Zion, the place of the name of the Lord of hosts.

An Oracle concerning Egypt

19 An oracle concerning Egypt.

See, the Lord is riding on a swift cloud
    and comes to Egypt;
the idols of Egypt will tremble at his presence,
    and the heart of the Egyptians will melt
      within them.
2 I will stir up Egyptians against Egyptians,
    and they will fight, one against the other,
    neighbor against neighbor,
    city against city, kingdom against kingdom;
3 the spirit of the Egyptians within them will be
    emptied out,
    and I will confound their plans;
they will consult the idols and the spirits of the
    dead
    and the ghosts and the familiar spirits;
4 I will deliver the Egyptians
    into the hand of a hard master;
a fierce king will rule over them,
    says the Sovereign, the Lord of hosts.

5 The waters of the Nile will be dried up,
    and the river will be parched and dry;
6 its canals will become foul,
    and the branches of Egypt's Nile will diminish
      and dry up,
    reeds and rushes will rot away
7 There will be bare places by the Nile,
    on the brink of the Nile;
and all that is sown by the Nile will dry up,
    be driven away, and be no more.
8 Those who fish will mourn;

---

a Heb Asherim   b Cn Compare Gk: Heb places of the wood and the highest bough   c Or Nubia; Heb Cush   d Q Ms Gk Vg: MT of

all who cast hooks in the Nile will lament,
and those who spread nets on the water will
    languish.
⁹ The workers in flax will be in despair,
    and the carders and those at the loom will
      grow pale.
¹⁰ Its weavers will be dismayed,
    and all who work for wages will be grieved.

¹¹ The princes of Zoan are utterly foolish;
    the wise counselors of Pharaoh give stupid
      counsel.
How can you say to Pharaoh,
    "I am one of the sages,
    a descendant of ancient kings"?
¹² Where now are your sages?
    Let them tell you and make known
    what the Lord of hosts has planned against
      Egypt.
¹³ The princes of Zoan have become fools,
    and the princes of Memphis are deluded;
those who are the cornerstones of its tribes
    have led Egypt astray.
¹⁴ The Lord has poured into them*ᵃ*
    a spirit of confusion;
and they have made Egypt stagger in all its
      doings
as a drunkard staggers around in vomit.
¹⁵ Neither head nor tail, palm branch or reed,
    will be able to do anything for Egypt.

16 On that day the Egyptians will be like
women, and tremble with fear before the hand
that the Lord of hosts raises against them. ¹⁷And
the land of Judah will become a terror to the
Egyptians; everyone to whom it is mentioned
will fear because of the plan that the Lord of
hosts is planning against them.

Egypt, Assyria, and Israel Blessed

18 On that day there will be five cities in the
land of Egypt that speak the language of Canaan
and swear allegiance to the Lord of hosts. One of
these will be called the City of the Sun.

19 On that day there will be an altar to the
Lord in the center of the land of Egypt, and a
pillar to the Lord at its border. ²⁰It will be a sign
and a witness to the Lord of hosts in the land
of Egypt; when they cry to the Lord because of
oppressors, he will send them a savior, and will
defend and deliver them. ²¹The Lord will make
himself known to the Egyptians; and the Egyptians will know the Lord on that day, and will
worship with sacrifice and burnt offering, and
they will make vows to the Lord and perform
them. ²²The Lord will strike Egypt, striking and

healing; they will return to the Lord, and he will
listen to their supplications and heal them.

23 On that day there will be a highway from
Egypt to Assyria, and the Assyrian will come into
Egypt, and the Egyptian into Assyria, and the
Egyptians will worship with the Assyrians.

24 On that day Israel will be the third with
Egypt and Assyria, a blessing in the midst of the
earth, ²⁵whom the Lord of hosts has blessed, saying, "Blessed be Egypt my people, and Assyria the
work of my hands, and Israel my heritage."

Isaiah Dramatizes the Conquest of Egypt and Ethiopia

20 In the year that the commander-in-chief,
who was sent by King Sargon of Assyria,
came to Ashdod and fought against it and took
it— ²at that time the Lord had spoken to Isaiah
son of Amoz, saying, "Go, and loose the sackcloth from your loins and take your sandals off
your feet," and he had done so, walking naked
and barefoot. ³Then the Lord said, "Just as my
servant Isaiah has walked naked and barefoot for
three years as a sign and a portent against Egypt
and Ethiopia,ᵇ ⁴so shall the king of Assyria lead
away the Egyptians as captives and the Ethiopi-
ansᶜ as exiles, both the young and the old, naked
and barefoot, with buttocks uncovered, to the
shame of Egypt. ⁵And they shall be dismayed and
confounded because of Ethiopiaᵇ their hope and
of Egypt their boast. ⁶In that day the inhabitants
of this coastland will say, 'See, this is what has
happened to those in whom we hoped and to
whom we fled for help and deliverance from the
king of Assyria! And we, how shall we escape?' "

Oracles concerning Babylon, Edom, and Arabia

21 The oracle concerning the wilderness of
the sea.

As whirlwinds in the Negeb sweep on,
    it comes from the desert,
    from a terrible land.
² A stern vision is told to me;
    the betrayer betrays,
    and the destroyer destroys.
Go up, O Elam,
    lay siege, O Media;
all the sighing she has caused
    I bring to an end.
³ Therefore my loins are filled with anguish;
    pangs have seized me,
    like the pangs of a woman in labor;

a Gk Compare Tg: Heb *it*   *b* Or Nubia; Heb *Cush*
c Or *Nubians*; Heb *Cushites*

I am bowed down so that I cannot hear,
     I am dismayed so that I cannot see.
[4] My mind reels, horror has appalled me;
     the twilight I longed for
     has been turned for me into trembling.
[5] They prepare the table,
     they spread the rugs,
     they eat, they drink.
Rise up, commanders,
     oil the shield!
[6] For thus the Lord said to me:
"Go, post a lookout,
     let him announce what he sees.
[7] When he sees riders, horsemen in pairs,
     riders on donkeys, riders on camels,
let him listen diligently,
     very diligently."
[8] Then the watcher[a] called out:
"Upon a watchtower I stand, O Lord,
     continually by day,
and at my post I am stationed
     throughout the night.
[9] Look, there they come, riders,
     horsemen in pairs!"
Then he responded,
     "Fallen, fallen is Babylon;
and all the images of her gods
     lie shattered on the ground."
[10] O my threshed and winnowed one,
     what I have heard from the LORD of hosts,
     the God of Israel, I announce to you.

11 The oracle concerning Dumah.

One is calling to me from Seir,
     "Sentinel, what of the night?
     Sentinel, what of the night?"
[12] The sentinel says:
"Morning comes, and also the night.
     If you will inquire, inquire;
     come back again."

13 The oracle concerning the desert plain.

In the scrub of the desert plain you will lodge,
     O caravans of Dedanites.
[14] Bring water to the thirsty,
     meet the fugitive with bread,
     O inhabitants of the land of Tema.
[15] For they have fled from the swords,
     from the drawn sword,
from the bent bow,
     and from the stress of battle.

16 For thus the Lord said to me: Within a year, according to the years of a hired worker, all the glory of Kedar will come to an end; [17]and the

remaining bows of Kedar's warriors will be few; for the LORD, the God of Israel, has spoken.

A Warning of Destruction of Jerusalem

22 The oracle concerning the valley of vision.

What do you mean that you have gone up,
     all of you, to the housetops,
[2] you that are full of shoutings,
     tumultuous city, exultant town?
Your slain are not slain by the sword,
     nor are they dead in battle.
[3] Your rulers have all fled together;
     they were captured without the use of a bow.[b]
All of you who were found were captured,
     though they had fled far away.[c]
[4] Therefore I said:
Look away from me,
     let me weep bitter tears;
do not try to comfort me
     for the destruction of my beloved people.

[5] For the Lord GOD of hosts has a day
     of tumult and trampling and confusion
     in the valley of vision,
a battering down of walls
     and a cry for help to the mountains.
[6] Elam bore the quiver
     with chariots and cavalry,[d]
     and Kir uncovered the shield.
[7] Your choicest valleys were full of chariots,
     and the cavalry took their stand at the gates.
[8] He has taken away the covering of Judah.

On that day you looked to the weapons of the House of the Forest, [9]and you saw that there were many breaches in the city of David, and you collected the waters of the lower pool. [10]You counted the houses of Jerusalem, and you broke down the houses to fortify the wall. [11]You made a reservoir between the two walls for the water of the old pool. But you did not look to him who did it, or have regard for him who planned it long ago.

[12] In that day the Lord GOD of hosts
     called to weeping and mourning,
     to baldness and putting on sackcloth;
[13] but instead there was joy and festivity,
     killing oxen and slaughtering sheep,
     eating meat and drinking wine.
"Let us eat and drink,

---

a Q Ms: MT *a lion*   b Or *without their bows*   c Gk Syr Vg: Heb *fled from far away*   d Meaning of Heb uncertain

Catholic Social Teaching

Faith and Politics

Every group we belong to has a leader. Some leaders are committed to serving others; other leaders are corrupt. Like First Isaiah, we have a right to demand integrity from our leaders as well as a responsibility to practice it ourselves.

In Isaiah 22:15–25, the prophet denounces the steward Shebna for his self-seeking ways. Evidently, Shebna is using his position of leadership to prepare an expensive tomb for himself (see verse 16) and to acquire ornate chariots (see verse 18). Isaiah prefers Eliakim to take over his position. The prophet's interest in local politics points out a biblical truth: Our faith applies to our daily lives, including our political choices.

When choosing our school, community, and government leaders, we must seek out people who are committed to protecting basic human rights and enhancing the dignity of the human person. They must be people of integrity—people whose actions and decisions accurately reflect their core values and beliefs. Good leaders are also willing to speak up for the voiceless and advocate for those who are suffering, ensuring that every human being has the opportunity to live life abundantly.

Catholic social teaching reminds us that even if we are not in a position of leadership, as citizens of society, we too have been entrusted with the task of promoting the common good and protecting human dignity.

- What can you do to learn more about the social issues that impact the dignity of people in our world today?
- How can you use your time and talents to provide direct service to those in need?

▶ **Isa 22:15–25**
Rights and Responsibilities

---

for tomorrow we die."
14 The Lord of hosts has revealed himself in my
     ears:
  Surely this iniquity will not be forgiven you
     until you die,
  says the Lord God of hosts.

Denunciation of Self-Seeking Officials

15 Thus says the Lord God of hosts: Come, go to this steward, to Shebna, who is master of the household, and say to him: 16What right do you have here? Who are your relatives here, that you have cut out a tomb here for yourself, cutting a tomb on the height, and carving a habitation for yourself in the rock? 17The Lord is about to hurl you away violently, my fellow. He will seize firm hold on you, 18whirl you round and round, and throw you like a ball into a wide land; there you shall die, and there your splendid chariots shall lie, O you disgrace to your master's house! 19I will thrust you from your office, and you will be pulled down from your post.

20 On that day I will call my servant Eliakim son of Hilkiah, 21and will clothe him with your robe and bind your sash on him. I will commit your authority to his hand, and he shall be a father to the inhabitants of Jerusalem and to the house of Judah. 22I will place on his shoulder the key of the house of David; he shall open, and no one shall shut; he shall shut, and no one shall open. 23I will fasten him like a peg in a secure place, and he will become a throne of honor to his ancestral house. 24And they will hang on him the whole weight of his ancestral house, the offspring and issue, every small vessel, from the cups to all the flagons. 25On that day, says the Lord of hosts, the peg that was fastened in a secure place will give way; it will be cut down and fall, and the load that was on it will perish, for the Lord has spoken.

An Oracle concerning Tyre

23 The oracle concerning Tyre.

  Wail, O ships of Tarshish,
     for your fortress is destroyed.*a*
  When they came in from Cyprus
     they learned of it.
2 Be still, O inhabitants of the coast,
     O merchants of Sidon,
  your messengers crossed over the sea*b*

---

a Cn Compare verse 14: Heb *for it is destroyed, without houses*
b Q Ms: MT *crossing over the sea, they replenished you*

³ and were on the mighty waters;
  your revenue was the grain of Shihor,
      the harvest of the Nile;
  you were the merchant of the nations.
⁴ Be ashamed, O Sidon, for the sea has spoken,
      the fortress of the sea, saying:
  "I have neither labored nor given birth,
      I have neither reared young men
      nor brought up young women."
⁵ When the report comes to Egypt,
      they will be in anguish over the report about
          Tyre.
⁶ Cross over to Tarshish—
      wail, O inhabitants of the coast!
⁷ Is this your exultant city
      whose origin is from days of old,
  whose feet carried her
      to settle far away?
⁸ Who has planned this
      against Tyre, the bestower of crowns,
  whose merchants were princes,
      whose traders were the honored of the earth?
⁹ The Lord of hosts has planned it—
      to defile the pride of all glory,
      to shame all the honored of the earth.
¹⁰ Cross over to your own land,
      O ships of*ᵃ* Tarshish;
      this is a harborᵇ no more.
¹¹ He has stretched out his hand over the sea,
      he has shaken the kingdoms;
  the Lord has given command concerning
          Canaan
      to destroy its fortresses.
¹² He said:
  You will exult no longer,
      O oppressed virgin daughter Sidon;
  rise, cross over to Cyprus—
      even there you will have no rest.

13 Look at the land of the Chaldeans! This is the people; it was not Assyria. They destined Tyre for wild animals. They erected their siege towers, they tore down her palaces, they made her a ruin.ᶜ
¹⁴ Wail, O ships of Tarshish,
      for your fortress is destroyed.
¹⁵ From that day Tyre will be forgotten for seventy years, the lifetime of one king. At the end of seventy years, it will happen to Tyre as in the song about the prostitute:
¹⁶ Take a harp,
      go about the city,
      you forgotten prostitute!
  Make sweet melody,
      sing many songs,
      that you may be remembered.

¹⁷ At the end of seventy years, the Lord will visit Tyre, and she will return to her trade, and will prostitute herself with all the kingdoms of the world on the face of the earth. ¹⁸ Her merchandise and her wages will be dedicated to the Lord; her profitsᵈ will not be stored or hoarded, but her merchandise will supply abundant food and fine clothing for those who live in the presence of the Lord.

Impending Judgment on the Earth

24 Now the Lord is about to lay waste the
      earth and make it desolate,
  and he will twist its surface and scatter its
      inhabitants.
² And it shall be, as with the people, so with the
          priest;
  as with the slave, so with his master;
  as with the maid, so with her mistress;
  as with the buyer, so with the seller;
  as with the lender, so with the borrower;
  as with the creditor, so with the debtor.
³ The earth shall be utterly laid waste and utterly
          despoiled;
  for the Lord has spoken this word.

⁴ The earth dries up and withers,
      the world languishes and withers;
      the heavens languish together with the earth.
⁵ The earth lies polluted
      under its inhabitants;
  for they have transgressed laws,
      violated the statutes,
      broken the everlasting covenant.
⁶ Therefore a curse devours the earth,
      and its inhabitants suffer for their guilt;
  therefore the inhabitants of the earth dwindled,
      and few people are left.
⁷ The wine dries up,
      the vine languishes,
      all the merry-hearted sigh.
⁸ The mirth of the timbrels is stilled,
      the noise of the jubilant has ceased,
      the mirth of the lyre is stilled.
⁹ No longer do they drink wine with singing;
      strong drink is bitter to those who drink it.
¹⁰ The city of chaos is broken down,
      every house is shut up so that no one can
          enter.
¹¹ There is an outcry in the streets for lack of wine;
      all joy has reached its eventide;
      the gladness of the earth is banished.
¹² Desolation is left in the city,

ᵃ Cn Compare Gk: Heb *like the Nile, daughter*   ᵇ Cn: Heb *restraint*   ᶜ Meaning of Heb uncertain   ᵈ Heb *it*

ISA

the gates are battered into ruins.
13 For thus it shall be on the earth
and among the nations,
as when an olive tree is beaten,
as at the gleaning when the grape harvest is
ended.

14 They lift up their voices, they sing for joy;
they shout from the west over the majesty of
the LORD.
15 Therefore in the east give glory to the LORD;
in the coastlands of the sea glorify the name
of the LORD, the God of Israel.
16 From the ends of the earth we hear songs of praise,
of glory to the Righteous One.
But I say, I pine away,
I pine away. Woe is me!
For the treacherous deal treacherously,
the treacherous deal very treacherously.

17 Terror, and the pit, and the snare
are upon you, O inhabitant of the earth!
18 Whoever flees at the sound of the terror
shall fall into the pit;
and whoever climbs out of the pit
shall be caught in the snare.
For the windows of heaven are opened,
and the foundations of the earth tremble.
19 The earth is utterly broken,
the earth is torn asunder,
the earth is violently shaken.
20 The earth staggers like a drunkard,
it sways like a hut;
its transgression lies heavy upon it,
and it falls, and will not rise again.

21 On that day the LORD will punish
the host of heaven in heaven,
and on earth the kings of the earth.
22 They will be gathered together
like prisoners in a pit;
they will be shut up in a prison,
and after many days they will be punished.
23 Then the moon will be abashed,
and the sun ashamed;
for the LORD of hosts will reign
on Mount Zion and in Jerusalem,
and before his elders he will manifest his glory.

Praise for Deliverance from Oppression

25 O LORD, you are my God;
I will exalt you, I will praise your name;
for you have done wonderful things,
plans formed of old, faithful and sure.
2 For you have made the city a heap,
the fortified city a ruin;

the palace of aliens is a city no more,
it will never be rebuilt.
3 Therefore strong peoples will glorify you;
cities of ruthless nations will fear you.
4 For you have been a refuge to the poor,
a refuge to the needy in their distress,
a shelter from the rainstorm and a shade from
the heat.
When the blast of the ruthless was like a winter
rainstorm,
5 the noise of aliens like heat in a dry place,
you subdued the heat with the shade of clouds;
the song of the ruthless was stilled.

6 On this mountain the LORD of hosts will make
for all peoples
a feast of rich food, a feast of well-aged wines,
of rich food filled with marrow, of well-aged
wines strained clear.
7 And he will destroy on this mountain
the shroud that is cast over all peoples,
the sheet that is spread over all nations;
8 he will swallow up death forever.
Then the Lord GOD will wipe away the tears
from all faces,
and the disgrace of his people he will take
away from all the earth,
for the LORD has spoken.
9 It will be said on that day,
Lo, this is our God; we have waited for him,
so that he might save us.
This is the LORD for whom we have waited;
let us be glad and rejoice in his salvation.
10 For the hand of the LORD will rest on this
mountain.

The Moabites shall be trodden down in their
place
as straw is trodden down in a dung-pit.
11 Though they spread out their hands in the midst
of it,
as swimmers spread out their hands to swim,
their pride will be laid low despite the
struggle*a* of their hands.
12 The high fortifications of his walls will be
brought down,
laid low, cast to the ground, even to the dust.

Judah's Song of Victory

26 On that day this song will be sung in the
land of Judah:
We have a strong city;
he sets up victory
like walls and bulwarks.

---

a Meaning of Heb uncertain

2 Open the gates,
    so that the righteous nation that keeps faith
    may enter in.
3 Those of steadfast mind you keep in peace—
    in peace because they trust in you.
4 Trust in the LORD forever,
    for in the LORD GOD[a]
    you have an everlasting rock.
5 For he has brought low
    the inhabitants of the height;
    the lofty city he lays low.
He lays it low to the ground,
    casts it to the dust.
6 The foot tramples it,
    the feet of the poor,
    the steps of the needy.

7 The way of the righteous is level;
    O Just One, you make smooth the path of the
    righteous.
8 In the path of your judgments,
    O LORD, we wait for you;
    your name and your renown
    are the soul's desire.
9 My soul yearns for you in the night,
    my spirit within me earnestly seeks you.
For when your judgments are in the earth,
    the inhabitants of the world learn
    righteousness.
10 If favor is shown to the wicked,
    they do not learn righteousness;
in the land of uprightness they deal perversely
    and do not see the majesty of the LORD.
11 O LORD, your hand is lifted up,
    but they do not see it.
Let them see your zeal for your people, and be
    ashamed.
    Let the fire for your adversaries consume them.
12 O LORD, you will ordain peace for us,
    for indeed, all that we have done, you have
    done for us.
13 O LORD our God,
    other lords besides you have ruled over us,
    but we acknowledge your name alone.
14 The dead do not live;
    shades do not rise—
because you have punished and destroyed them,
    and wiped out all memory of them.
15 But you have increased the nation, O LORD,
    you have increased the nation; you are glorified;
    you have enlarged all the borders of the land.

16 O LORD, in distress they sought you,
    they poured out a prayer[b]
    when your chastening was on them.
17 Like a woman with child,

Introducing...

First Isaiah

The name Isaiah means "God is salvation" in Hebrew, and First Isaiah's preaching certainly reflects that message. Born in Jerusalem, he prophesied there during the reigns of Kings Uzziah, Jotham, Ahaz, and Hezekiah, between 742 and 701 BC (see 2 Kings, chapters 15–20, and 2 Chronicles, chapters 26–32). He was married to a prophetess, and they had two sons whose names played a symbolic role in his prophecy: Shear-jashub, meaning "a remnant shall return," and Maher-shalal-hash-baz, meaning "the spoil speeds, the prey hastes." In his preaching, he emphasized the role of Jerusalem (Zion) as God's dwelling place and home to King David's dynasty. For this reason, he is also called Isaiah of Jerusalem.

First Isaiah had ready access to Judah's kings and was probably a member of an aristocratic family. His education shows in his use of language—he is responsible for some of the loftiest and most beautiful poetry in the Old Testament.

who writhes and cries out in her pangs
    when she is near her time,
so were we because of you, O LORD;
18   we were with child, we writhed,
    but we gave birth only to wind.
We have won no victories on earth,
    and no one is born to inhabit the world.
19 Your dead shall live, their corpses[c] shall rise.
    O dwellers in the dust, awake and sing for joy!
For your dew is a radiant dew,
    and the earth will give birth to those long
    dead.[d]

20 Come, my people, enter your chambers,
    and shut your doors behind you;
hide yourselves for a little while
    until the wrath is past.
21 For the LORD comes out from his place
    to punish the inhabitants of the earth for
    their iniquity;
the earth will disclose the blood shed on it,
    and will no longer cover its slain.

---

a Heb in Yah, the LORD   b Meaning of Heb uncertain
c Cn Compare Syr Tg: Heb my corpse   d Heb to the shades

Israel's Redemption

27 On that day the LORD with his cruel and great and strong sword will punish Leviathan the fleeing serpent, Leviathan the twisting serpent, and he will kill the dragon that is in the sea.

2 On that day:
A pleasant vineyard, sing about it!
3 I, the LORD, am its keeper;
every moment I water it.
I guard it night and day
so that no one can harm it;
4 I have no wrath.
If it gives me thorns and briers,
I will march to battle against it.
I will burn it up.
5 Or else let it cling to me for protection,
let it make peace with me,
let it make peace with me.

6 In days to come[a] Jacob shall take root,
Israel shall blossom and put forth shoots,
and fill the whole world with fruit.

7 Has he struck them down as he struck down
those who struck them?
Or have they been killed as their killers were
killed?
8 By expulsion,[b] by exile you struggled against
them;
with his fierce blast he removed them in the
day of the east wind.
9 Therefore by this the guilt of Jacob will be
expiated,
and this will be the full fruit of the removal of
his sin:
when he makes all the stones of the altars
like chalkstones crushed to pieces,
no sacred poles[c] or incense altars will remain
standing.
10 For the fortified city is solitary,
a habitation deserted and forsaken, like the
wilderness;
the calves graze there,
there they lie down, and strip its branches.
11 When its boughs are dry, they are broken;
women come and make a fire of them.
For this is a people without understanding;
therefore he that made them will not have
compassion on them,
he that formed them will show them no favor.

12 On that day the LORD will thresh from the channel of the Euphrates to the Wadi of Egypt,

and you will be gathered one by one, O people of Israel. 13And on that day a great trumpet will be blown, and those who were lost in the land of Assyria and those who were driven out to the land of Egypt will come and worship the LORD on the holy mountain at Jerusalem.

Judgment on Corrupt Rulers, Priests, and Prophets

28 Ah, the proud garland of the drunkards of
Ephraim,
and the fading flower of its glorious beauty,
which is on the head of those bloated with
rich food, of those overcome with
wine!
2 See, the Lord has one who is mighty and strong;
like a storm of hail, a destroying tempest,
like a storm of mighty, overflowing waters;
with his hand he will hurl them down to the
earth.
3 Trampled under foot will be
the proud garland of the drunkards of
Ephraim.
4 And the fading flower of its glorious beauty,
which is on the head of those bloated with
rich food,
will be like a first-ripe fig before the summer;
whoever sees it, eats it up
as soon as it comes to hand.

5 In that day the LORD of hosts will be a garland of
glory,
and a diadem of beauty, to the remnant of his
people;
6 and a spirit of justice to the one who sits in
judgment,
and strength to those who turn back the battle
at the gate.

7 These also reel with wine
and stagger with strong drink;
the priest and the prophet reel with strong
drink,
they are confused with wine,
they stagger with strong drink;
they err in vision,
they stumble in giving judgment.
8 All tables are covered with filthy vomit;
no place is clean.

9 "Whom will he teach knowledge,
and to whom will he explain the message?
Those who are weaned from milk,

---

a Heb *Those to come*   b Meaning of Heb uncertain
c Heb *Asherim*

those taken from the breast?

10 For it is precept upon precept, precept upon
precept,
line upon line, line upon line,
here a little, there a little."[a]

11 Truly, with stammering lip
and with alien tongue
he will speak to this people,
12   to whom he has said,
"This is rest;
give rest to the weary;
and this is repose";
yet they would not hear.

13 Therefore the word of the LORD will be to them,
"Precept upon precept, precept upon precept,
line upon line, line upon line,
here a little, there a little;"[a]
in order that they may go, and fall backward,
and be broken, and snared, and taken.

14 Therefore hear the word of the LORD, you
scoffers
who rule this people in Jerusalem.

15 Because you have said, "We have made a
covenant with death,
and with Sheol we have an agreement;
when the overwhelming scourge passes through
it will not come to us;
for we have made lies our refuge,
and in falsehood we have taken shelter";

16 therefore thus says the Lord GOD,
See, I am laying in Zion a foundation stone,
a tested stone,
a precious cornerstone, a sure foundation:
"One who trusts will not panic."

17 And I will make justice the line,
and righteousness the plummet;
hail will sweep away the refuge of lies,
and waters will overwhelm the shelter.

18 Then your covenant with death will be annulled,
and your agreement with Sheol will not
stand;
when the overwhelming scourge passes through
you will be beaten down by it.

19 As often as it passes through, it will take you;
for morning by morning it will pass through,
by day and by night;
and it will be sheer terror to understand the
message.

20 For the bed is too short to stretch oneself on it,
and the covering too narrow to wrap oneself
in it.

21 For the LORD will rise up as on Mount Perazim,
he will rage as in the valley of Gibeon
to do his deed—strange is his deed!—

and to work his work—alien is his work!

22 Now therefore do not scoff,
or your bonds will be made stronger;
for I have heard a decree of destruction
from the Lord GOD of hosts upon the whole
land.

23 Listen, and hear my voice;
Pay attention, and hear my speech.
24 Do those who plow for sowing plow
continually?
Do they continually open and harrow their
ground?
25 When they have leveled its surface,
do they not scatter dill, sow cummin,
and plant wheat in rows
and barley in its proper place,
and spelt as the border?
26 For they are well instructed;
their God teaches them.

27 Dill is not threshed with a threshing sledge,
nor is a cart wheel rolled over cummin;
but dill is beaten out with a stick,
and cummin with a rod.
28 Grain is crushed for bread,
but one does not thresh it forever;
one drives the cart wheel and horses over it,
but does not pulverize it.
29 This also comes from the LORD of hosts;
he is wonderful in counsel,
and excellent in wisdom.

The Siege of Jerusalem

29 Ah, Ariel, Ariel,
the city where David encamped!
Add year to year;
let the festivals run their round.
2 Yet I will distress Ariel,
and there shall be moaning and lamentation,
and Jerusalem[b] shall be to me like an Ariel.[c]
3 And like David[d] I will encamp against you;
I will besiege you with towers
and raise siegeworks against you.
4 Then deep from the earth you shall speak,
from low in the dust your words shall come,
your voice shall come from the ground like the
voice of a ghost,
and your speech shall whisper out of the dust.

5 But the multitude of your foes[e] shall be like
small dust,

a Meaning of Heb of this verse uncertain   b Heb she
c Probable meaning, altar hearth; compare Ezek 43.15
d Gk: Meaning of Heb uncertain   e Cn: Heb strangers

Preference for the Poor

Isaiah 29:17–21 proclaims that God's power will transform society: the deaf will hear, the blind will see, the lowly will know joy and the poor will rejoice. First Isaiah's words are reflected in Jesus' words in the Beatitudes (see Lk 6:20–26). Both Jesus and Isaiah say that in God's Reign, the rights and needs of the lowliest and the weakest come first (see Isaiah, chapters 58, 61).

The Catholic Church refers to this principle as preferential love for the poor. People who are poor and helpless have a right to a just society where they get what they need to live with dignity and where they have a voice in the structures that govern their lives. One can tell how near a society is to the Reign of God by seeing how it treats the most vulnerable members of the human family. Those who are poor should never be ignored when others have the resources to share.

Write your own prayer describing God's vision for those who are poor. Use Isaiah's words and the Beatitudes for ideas. Share your prayer with your family or youth group.

▶ Isa 29:17–21

and the multitude of tyrants like flying chaff.
And in an instant, suddenly,
6   you will be visited by the Lord of hosts
with thunder and earthquake and great noise,
    with whirlwind and tempest, and the flame of
        a devouring fire.
7 And the multitude of all the nations that fight
        against Ariel,
    all that fight against her and her stronghold,
        and who distress her,
    shall be like a dream, a vision of the night.
8 Just as when a hungry person dreams of eating
    and wakes up still hungry,
or a thirsty person dreams of drinking
    and wakes up faint, still thirsty,
so shall the multitude of all the nations be
    that fight against Mount Zion.

9 Stupefy yourselves and be in a stupor,
    blind yourselves and be blind!
Be drunk, but not from wine;
    stagger, but not from strong drink!
10 For the Lord has poured out upon you
    a spirit of deep sleep;
he has closed your eyes, you prophets,
    and covered your heads, you seers.

11 The vision of all this has become for you like the words of a sealed document. If it is given to those who can read, with the command, "Read this," they say, "We cannot, for it is sealed." 12 And if it is given to those who cannot read, saying, "Read this," they say, "We cannot read."

13 The Lord said:
Because these people draw near with their
        mouths
    and honor me with their lips,
    while their hearts are far from me,
and their worship of me is a human
        commandment learned by rote;
14 so I will again do
    amazing things with this people,
    shocking and amazing.
The wisdom of their wise shall perish,
    and the discernment of the discerning shall be
        hidden.

15 Ha! You who hide a plan too deep for the Lord,
    whose deeds are in the dark,
    and who say, "Who sees us? Who knows us?"
16 You turn things upside down!
    Shall the potter be regarded as the clay?
Shall the thing made say of its maker,
    "He did not make me";
or the thing formed say of the one who
        formed it,
    "He has no understanding"?

Hope for the Future

17 Shall not Lebanon in a very little while
    become a fruitful field,
    and the fruitful field be regarded as a forest?
18 On that day the deaf shall hear
    the words of a scroll,
    and out of their gloom and darkness
    the eyes of the blind shall see.
19 The meek shall obtain fresh joy in the Lord,
    and the neediest people shall exult in the
        Holy One of Israel.
20 For the tyrant shall be no more,
    and the scoffer shall cease to be;
    all those alert to do evil shall be cut off—
21 those who cause a person to lose a lawsuit,

who set a trap for the arbiter in the gate,
   and without grounds deny justice to the one
      in the right.

22 Therefore thus says the LORD, who redeemed Abraham, concerning the house of Jacob:
   No longer shall Jacob be ashamed,
      no longer shall his face grow pale.
23 For when he sees his children,
   the work of my hands, in his midst,
      they will sanctify my name;
   they will sanctify the Holy One of Jacob,
      and will stand in awe of the God of Israel.
24 And those who err in spirit will come to
      understanding,
   and those who grumble will accept
      instruction.

The Futility of Reliance on Egypt

30 Oh, rebellious children, says the LORD,
      who carry out a plan, but not mine;
   who make an alliance, but against my will,
      adding sin to sin;
2 who set out to go down to Egypt
      without asking for my counsel,
   to take refuge in the protection of Pharaoh,
      and to seek shelter in the shadow of Egypt;
3 Therefore the protection of Pharaoh shall
         become your shame,
   and the shelter in the shadow of Egypt your
      humiliation.
4 For though his officials are at Zoan
      and his envoys reach Hanes,
5 everyone comes to shame
   through a people that cannot profit them,
      that brings neither help nor profit,
   but shame and disgrace.

6 An oracle concerning the animals of the
Negeb.
   Through a land of trouble and distress,
      of lioness and roaring[a] lion,
      of viper and flying serpent,
   they carry their riches on the backs of donkeys,
      and their treasures on the humps of camels,
   to a people that cannot profit them.
7 For Egypt's help is worthless and empty,
      therefore I have called her,
   "Rahab who sits still."[b]

A Rebellious People

8 Go now, write it before them on a tablet,
      and inscribe it in a book,
   so that it may be for the time to come
      as a witness forever.

9 For they are a rebellious people,
      faithless children,
   children who will not hear
      the instruction of the LORD;
10 who say to the seers, "Do not see";
   and to the prophets, "Do not prophesy to us
      what is right;
   speak to us smooth things,
      prophesy illusions,
11 leave the way, turn aside from the path,
      let us hear no more about the Holy One of
         Israel."
12 Therefore thus says the Holy One of Israel:
   Because you reject this word,
      and put your trust in oppression and deceit,
      and rely on them;
13 therefore this iniquity shall become for you
   like a break in a high wall, bulging out, and
         about to collapse,
   whose crash comes suddenly, in an instant;
14 its breaking is like that of a potter's vessel
      that is smashed so ruthlessly
   that among its fragments not a sherd is found
      for taking fire from the hearth,
      or dipping water out of the cistern.

15 For thus said the Lord GOD, the Holy One of Israel:
   In returning and rest you shall be saved;
      in quietness and in trust shall be your
         strength.
   But you refused 16and said,
      "No! We will flee upon horses"—
         therefore you shall flee!
   and, "We will ride upon swift steeds"—
      therefore your pursuers shall be swift!
17 A thousand shall flee at the threat of one,
      at the threat of five you shall flee,
   until you are left
      like a flagstaff on the top of a mountain,
      like a signal on a hill.

God's Promise to Zion

18 Therefore the LORD waits to be gracious to you;
      therefore he will rise up to show mercy to you.
   For the LORD is a God of justice;
      blessed are all those who wait for him.

19 Truly, O people in Zion, inhabitants of Jerusalem, you shall weep no more. He will surely
be gracious to you at the sound of your cry;
when he hears it, he will answer you. 20Though
the Lord may give you the bread of adversity and
the water of affliction, yet your Teacher will not
hide himself any more, but your eyes shall see
your Teacher. 21And when you turn to the right

---

a Cn: Heb from them   b Meaning of Heb uncertain

or when you turn to the left, your ears shall hear a word behind you, saying, "This is the way; walk in it." 22Then you will defile your silver-covered idols and your gold-plated images. You will scatter them like filthy rags; you will say to them, "Away with you!"

23 He will give rain for the seed with which you sow the ground, and grain, the produce of the ground, which will be rich and plenteous. On that day your cattle will graze in broad pastures; 24and the oxen and donkeys that till the ground will eat silage, which has been winnowed with shovel and fork. 25On every lofty mountain and every high hill there will be brooks running with water—on a day of the great slaughter, when the towers fall. 26Moreover the light of the moon will be like the light of the sun, and the light of the sun will be sevenfold, like the light of seven days, on the day when the LORD binds up the injuries of his people, and heals the wounds inflicted by his blow.

Judgment on Assyria

27 See, the name of the LORD comes from far away,
    burning with his anger, and in thick rising
        smoke;[a]
    his lips are full of indignation,
        and his tongue is like a devouring fire;
28 his breath is like an overflowing stream
        that reaches up to the neck—
    to sift the nations with the sieve of destruction,
        and to place on the jaws of the peoples a
            bridle that leads them astray.

29 You shall have a song as in the night when a holy festival is kept; and gladness of heart, as when one sets out to the sound of the flute to go to the mountain of the LORD, to the Rock of Israel. 30And the LORD will cause his majestic voice to be heard and the descending blow of his arm to be seen, in furious anger and a flame of devouring fire, with a cloudburst and tempest and hailstones. 31The Assyrian will be terror-stricken at the voice of the LORD, when he strikes with his rod. 32And every stroke of the staff of punishment that the LORD lays upon him will be to the sound of timbrels and lyres; battling with brandished arm he will fight with him. 33For his burning place[b] has long been prepared; truly it is made ready for the king,[c] its pyre made deep and wide, with fire and wood in abundance; the breath of the LORD, like a stream of sulfur, kindles it.

Alliance with Egypt Is Futile

31 Alas for those who go down to Egypt for
        help
    and who rely on horses,

who trust in chariots because they are many
    and in horsemen because they are very strong,
but do not look to the Holy One of Israel
    or consult the LORD!
2 Yet he too is wise and brings disaster;
    he does not call back his words,
but will rise against the house of the evildoers,
    and against the helpers of those who work
        iniquity.
3 The Egyptians are human, and not God;
    their horses are flesh, and not spirit.
When the LORD stretches out his hand,
    the helper will stumble, and the one helped
        will fall,
    and they will all perish together.

4 For thus the LORD said to me,
As a lion or a young lion growls over its prey,
    and—when a band of shepherds is called out
        against it—
is not terrified by their shouting
    or daunted at their noise,
so the LORD of hosts will come down
    to fight upon Mount Zion and upon its hill.
5 Like birds hovering overhead, so the LORD of
        hosts
    will protect Jerusalem;
he will protect and deliver it,
    he will spare and rescue it.

6 Turn back to him whom you[d] have deeply betrayed, O people of Israel. 7For on that day all of you shall throw away your idols of silver and idols of gold, which your hands have sinfully made for you.
8 "Then the Assyrian shall fall by a sword, not of
        mortals;
    and a sword, not of humans, shall devour
        him;
he shall flee from the sword,
    and his young men shall be put to forced
        labor.
9 His rock shall pass away in terror,
    and his officers desert the standard in panic,"
says the LORD, whose fire is in Zion,
    and whose furnace is in Jerusalem.

Government with Justice Predicted

32 See, a king will reign in righteousness,
    and princes will rule with justice.
2 Each will be like a hiding place from the wind,
    a covert from the tempest,
    like streams of water in a dry place,

---

a Meaning of Heb uncertain   b Or Topheth   c Or Molech
d Heb they

like the shade of a great rock in a weary land.
3 Then the eyes of those who have sight will not
      be closed,
  and the ears of those who have hearing will
      listen.
4 The minds of the rash will have good judgment,
  and the tongues of stammerers will speak
      readily and distinctly.
5 A fool will no longer be called noble,
  nor a villain said to be honorable.
6 For fools speak folly,
  and their minds plot iniquity:
to practice ungodliness,
  to utter error concerning the LORD,
to leave the craving of the hungry unsatisfied,
  and to deprive the thirsty of drink.
7 The villainies of villains are evil;
  they devise wicked devices
to ruin the poor with lying words,
  even when the plea of the needy is right.
8 But those who are noble plan noble things,
  and by noble things they stand.

Complacent Women Warned of Disaster

9 Rise up, you women who are at ease, hear my
     voice;
  you complacent daughters, listen to my
     speech.
10 In little more than a year
  you will shudder, you complacent ones;
for the vintage will fail,
  the fruit harvest will not come.
11 Tremble, you women who are at ease,
  shudder, you complacent ones;
strip, and make yourselves bare,
  and put sackcloth on your loins.
12 Beat your breasts for the pleasant fields,
  for the fruitful vine,
13 for the soil of my people
  growing up in thorns and briers;
yes, for all the joyous houses
  in the jubilant city.
14 For the palace will be forsaken,
  the populous city deserted;
the hill and the watchtower
  will become dens forever,
the joy of wild asses,
  a pasture for flocks;
15 until a spirit from on high is poured out on us,
  and the wilderness becomes a fruitful field,
  and the fruitful field is deemed a forest.

The Peace of God's Reign

16 Then justice will dwell in the wilderness,
  and righteousness abide in the fruitful field.
17 The effect of righteousness will be peace,

Live It!

Shalom

In Israel, people greet one another by saying "Shalom." In the Bible, *shalom* means "peace" in its fullest sense (see Isa 32:16–20). Shalom is not just the absence of war and violence but also the presence of justice, righteousness, happiness, and fullness of life. What better way to greet your neighbors or friends than to wish them shalom.

In your own life, seek peace. Begin each day by praying for peace of mind and heart, and to act with justice in all that you do. The very prayer you speak will become the way you live. Peace can become a reality only when we become a shalom people. It begins with us. Pray for shalom today.

▶ Isa 32:16–20

  and the result of righteousness, quietness and
     trust forever.
18 My people will abide in a peaceful habitation,
  in secure dwellings, and in quiet resting
     places.
19 The forest will disappear completely,[a]
  and the city will be utterly laid low.
20 Happy will you be who sow beside every stream,
  who let the ox and the donkey range freely.

A Prophecy of Deliverance from Foes

33 Ah, you destroyer,
  who yourself have not been destroyed;
you treacherous one,
  with whom no one has dealt treacherously!
When you have ceased to destroy,
  you will be destroyed;
and when you have stopped dealing
     treacherously,
  you will be dealt with treacherously.

2 O LORD, be gracious to us; we wait for you.
  Be our arm every morning,
  our salvation in the time of trouble.
3 At the sound of tumult, peoples fled;

a Cn: Heb *And it will hail when the forest comes down*

before your majesty, nations scattered.
4 Spoil was gathered as the caterpillar gathers;
  as locusts leap, they leaped[a] upon it.
5 The LORD is exalted, he dwells on high;
  he filled Zion with justice and righteousness;
6 he will be the stability of your times,
  abundance of salvation, wisdom, and
    knowledge;
  the fear of the LORD is Zion's treasure.[b]

7 Listen! the valiant[a] cry in the streets;
  the envoys of peace weep bitterly.
8 The highways are deserted,
  travelers have quit the road.
The treaty is broken,
  its oaths[c] are despised,
  its obligation[d] is disregarded.
9 The land mourns and languishes;
  Lebanon is confounded and withers away;
Sharon is like a desert;
  and Bashan and Carmel shake off their leaves.

10 "Now I will arise," says the LORD,
  "now I will lift myself up;
  now I will be exalted.
11 You conceive chaff, you bring forth stubble;
  your breath is a fire that will consume you.
12 And the peoples will be as if burned to lime,
  like thorns cut down, that are burned in the
    fire."

13 Hear, you who are far away, what I have done;
  and you who are near, acknowledge my
    might.
14 The sinners in Zion are afraid;
  trembling has seized the godless:
"Who among us can live with the devouring
    fire?
Who among us can live with everlasting
    flames?"
15 Those who walk righteously and speak
    uprightly,
who despise the gain of oppression,
who wave away a bribe instead of accepting it,
who stop their ears from hearing of
    bloodshed
and shut their eyes from looking on evil,
16 they will live on the heights;
  their refuge will be the fortresses of rocks;
  their food will be supplied, their water
    assured.

The Land of the Majestic King

17 Your eyes will see the king in his beauty;
  they will behold a land that stretches far
    away.

18 Your mind will muse on the terror:
  "Where is the one who counted?
  Where is the one who weighed the tribute?
  Where is the one who counted the towers?"
19 No longer will you see the insolent people,
  the people of an obscure speech that you
    cannot comprehend,
  stammering in a language that you cannot
    understand.
20 Look on Zion, the city of our appointed
    festivals!
  Your eyes will see Jerusalem,
  a quiet habitation, an immovable tent,
whose stakes will never be pulled up,
  and none of whose ropes will be broken.
21 But there the LORD in majesty will be for us
  a place of broad rivers and streams,
where no galley with oars can go,
  nor stately ship can pass.
22 For the LORD is our judge, the LORD is our ruler,
  the LORD is our king; he will save us.

23 Your rigging hangs loose;
  it cannot hold the mast firm in its place,
  or keep the sail spread out.

Then prey and spoil in abundance will be
    divided;
  even the lame will fall to plundering.
24 And no inhabitant will say, "I am sick";
  the people who live there will be forgiven
    their iniquity.

Judgment on the Nations

34 Draw near, O nations, to hear;
  O peoples, give heed!
Let the earth hear, and all that fills it;
  the world, and all that comes from it.
2 For the LORD is enraged against all the nations,
  and furious against all their hordes;
  he has doomed them, has given them over for
    slaughter.
3 Their slain shall be cast out,
  and the stench of their corpses shall rise;
  the mountains shall flow with their blood.
4 All the host of heaven shall rot away,
  and the skies roll up like a scroll.
All their host shall wither
  like a leaf withering on a vine,
  or fruit withering on a fig tree.

5 When my sword has drunk its fill in the
    heavens,

---

a Meaning of Heb uncertain   b Heb *his treasure*; meaning of Heb uncertain   c Q Ms: MT *cities*   d Or *everyone*

lo, it will descend upon Edom,
  upon the people I have doomed to judgment.
6 The LORD has a sword; it is sated with blood,
  it is gorged with fat,
with the blood of lambs and goats,
  with the fat of the kidneys of rams.
For the LORD has a sacrifice in Bozrah,
  a great slaughter in the land of Edom.
7 Wild oxen shall fall with them,
  and young steers with the mighty bulls.
Their land shall be soaked with blood,
  and their soil made rich with fat.

8 For the LORD has a day of vengeance,
  a year of vindication by Zion's cause.[a]
9 And the streams of Edom[b] shall be turned into
    pitch,
  and her soil into sulfur;
  her land shall become burning pitch.
10 Night and day it shall not be quenched;
  its smoke shall go up forever.
From generation to generation it shall lie waste;
  no one shall pass through it forever and ever.
11 But the hawk[c] and the hedgehog[c] shall possess it;
  the owl[c] and the raven shall live in it.
He shall stretch the line of confusion over it,
  and the plummet of chaos over[d] its nobles.
12 They shall name it No Kingdom There,
  and all its princes shall be nothing.
13 Thorns shall grow over its strongholds,
  nettles and thistles in its fortresses.
It shall be the haunt of jackals,
  an abode for ostriches.
14 Wildcats shall meet with hyenas,
  goat-demons shall call to each other;
there too Lilith shall repose,
  and find a place to rest.
15 There shall the owl nest
  and lay and hatch and brood in its shadow;
there too the buzzards shall gather,
  each one with its mate.
16 Seek and read from the book of the LORD:
  Not one of these shall be missing;
  none shall be without its mate.
For the mouth of the LORD has commanded,
  and his spirit has gathered them.
17 He has cast the lot for them,
  his hand has portioned it out to them with
    the line;
they shall possess it forever,
  from generation to generation they shall live
    in it.

The Return of the Redeemed to Zion

35 The wilderness and the dry land shall be
  glad,

the desert shall rejoice and blossom;
like the crocus 2it shall blossom abundantly,
  and rejoice with joy and singing.
The glory of Lebanon shall be given to it,
  the majesty of Carmel and Sharon.
They shall see the glory of the LORD,
  the majesty of our God.

3 Strengthen the weak hands,
  and make firm the feeble knees.
4 Say to those who are of a fearful heart,
  "Be strong, do not fear!
Here is your God.
  He will come with vengeance,
with terrible recompense.
  He will come and save you."

5 Then the eyes of the blind shall be opened,
  and the ears of the deaf unstopped;
6 then the lame shall leap like a deer,
  and the tongue of the speechless sing for joy.
For waters shall break forth in the wilderness,
  and streams in the desert;
7 the burning sand shall become a pool,
  and the thirsty ground springs of water;
the haunt of jackals shall become a swamp,[e]
  the grass shall become reeds and rushes.

8 A highway shall be there,
  and it shall be called the Holy Way;
the unclean shall not travel on it,[f]
  but it shall be for God's people;[g]
  no traveler, not even fools, shall go astray.
9 No lion shall be there,
  nor shall any ravenous beast come up on it;
they shall not be found there,
  but the redeemed shall walk there.
10 And the ransomed of the LORD shall return,
  and come to Zion with singing;
everlasting joy shall be upon their heads;
  they shall obtain joy and gladness,
  and sorrow and sighing shall flee away.

Sennacherib Threatens Jerusalem

36 In the fourteenth year of King Hezekiah, King Sennacherib of Assyria came up against all the fortified cities of Judah and captured them. 2The king of Assyria sent the Rabshakeh from Lachish to King Hezekiah at Jerusalem, with a great army. He stood by the conduit of the upper pool on the highway to the Fuller's Field. 3And there came out to him

---

a Or of recompense by Zion's defender   b Heb her streams
c Identification uncertain   d Heb lacks over   e Cn: Heb in the haunt of jackals is her resting place   f Or pass it by   g Cn: Heb for them

✝ Catholic Connection

The Liturgical Year

What is your favorite time of year? Perhaps you like the warmth of summer or the changing leaves of fall. Each season brings its own unique joys. The Church year, called the liturgical year, has seasons too, and each one brings its own joys and message. For example, Isaiah's prophecy in Isaiah 35:1–10 is shared with the Church when it is read at Mass during the Advent Season, as God's people joyfully prepare to celebrate the Messiah's birth and his glorious return.

The Advent Season is the first of six time periods that make up the liturgical year. The others are Christmas, Lent, the Easter Triduum, Easter, and Ordinary Time. Each period focuses on some aspect of Christ's saving work; this is done most particularly in the readings and prayers that are shared during Mass. The Sunday readings follow a three-year cycle (A, B, and C). Each Sunday's readings contain a reading from the Old Testament, one of the Epistles (Letters), and one of the four Gospels (Matthew, Mark, Luke, or John).

The liturgical year begins with the four Sundays prior to Christmas. This season is called **Advent** and is marked by God's people preparing for the celebration of Christ's birth as well as his Second Coming.

The **Christmas Season** begins with the celebration of Jesus' birth on Christmas and continues through the Feast of the Baptism of the Lord. During this time, we celebrate the birth of the Messiah as well as special feasts honoring the Holy Family and Mary.

The forty days of **Lent** begin on Ash Wednesday and continue through to Holy Thursday. This season is marked by repentance and preparations for the celebration of Easter.

The **Easter Triduum** begins on Holy Thursday and ends with Easter Sunday. These three days are the high point during the liturgical year when we focus on Jesus' Passion, death, and Resurrection.

The **Easter Season** spans fifty days from Easter to Pentecost. During this season, we celebrate Christ's Resurrection, the descent of the Holy Spirit, and the birth of the Church.

The remaining weeks during the year that do not fall into one of the other seasons fall into **Ordinary Time**. During Ordinary Time, the Church focuses on living the Gospel message.

▶ **Isa 35:1–10**
Catechism, nos. 1163–1173

Eliakim son of Hilkiah, who was in charge of the palace, and Shebna the secretary, and Joah son of Asaph, the recorder.

4 The Rabshakeh said to them, "Say to Hezekiah: Thus says the great king, the king of Assyria: On what do you base this confidence of yours? ⁵Do you think that mere words are strategy and power for war? On whom do you now rely, that you have rebelled against me? ⁶See, you are relying on Egypt, that broken reed of a staff, which will pierce the hand of anyone who leans on it. Such is Pharaoh king of Egypt to all who rely on him. ⁷But if you say to me, 'We rely on the LORD our God,' is it not he whose high places and altars Hezekiah has removed, saying to Judah and to Jerusalem, 'You shall worship before this altar'? ⁸Come now, make a wager with my master the king of Assyria: I will give you two thousand horses, if you are able on your part to set riders on them. ⁹How then can you repulse a single captain among the least of my master's servants, when you rely on Egypt for chariots and for horsemen? ¹⁰Moreover, is it without the LORD that I have come up against this land to destroy it? The LORD said to me, Go up against this land, and destroy it."

11 Then Eliakim, Shebna, and Joah said to the Rabshakeh, "Please speak to your servants in Aramaic, for we understand it; do not speak to us in the language of Judah within the hearing of the people who are on the wall." ¹²But the Rabshakeh said, "Has my master sent me to speak these words to your master and to you, and not to the people sitting on the wall, who are doomed with you to eat their own dung and drink their own urine?"

13 Then the Rabshakeh stood and called out in a loud voice in the language of Judah, "Hear the words of the great king, the king of Assyria! ¹⁴Thus says the king: 'Do not let Hezekiah deceive you, for he will not be able to deliver you. ¹⁵Do not let Hezekiah make you rely on the LORD by saying, The LORD will surely deliver us; this city will not be given into the hand of the king of Assyria.' ¹⁶Do not listen to Hezekiah, for thus says the king of Assyria: 'Make your peace with me and come out to me; then every one of you will eat from your own vine and your own fig tree and drink water from your own cistern, ¹⁷until I come and take you away to a land like your own land, a land of grain and wine, a land of bread and vineyards. ¹⁸Do not let Hezekiah mislead you by saying, The LORD will save us. Has any of the gods of the nations saved their land out of the hand of the king of Assyria? ¹⁹Where are the gods of Hamath and Arpad? Where are the gods of Sepharvaim? Have they delivered Samaria out of my hand? ²⁰Who among all the gods of these countries have saved their countries out of my hand, that the LORD should save Jerusalem out of my hand?' "

21 But they were silent and answered him not a word, for the king's command was, "Do not answer him." ²²Then Eliakim son of Hilkiah, who was in charge of the palace, and Shebna the secretary, and Joah son of Asaph, the recorder, came to Hezekiah with their clothes torn, and told him the words of the Rabshakeh.

Hezekiah Consults Isaiah

37 When King Hezekiah heard it, he tore his clothes, covered himself with sackcloth, and went into the house of the LORD. ²And he sent Eliakim, who was in charge of the palace, and Shebna the secretary, and the senior priests, covered with sackcloth, to the prophet Isaiah son of Amoz. ³They said to him, "Thus says Hezekiah, This day is a day of distress, of rebuke, and of disgrace; children have come to the birth, and there is no strength to bring them forth. ⁴It may be that the LORD your God heard the words of the Rabshakeh, whom his master the king of Assyria has sent to mock the living God, and will rebuke the words that the LORD your God has heard; therefore lift up your prayer for the remnant that is left."

5 When the servants of King Hezekiah came to Isaiah, ⁶Isaiah said to them, "Say to your master, 'Thus says the LORD: Do not be afraid because of the words that you have heard, with which the servants of the king of Assyria have reviled me. ⁷I myself will put a spirit in him, so that he shall hear a rumor, and return to his own land; I will cause him to fall by the sword in his own land.' "

8 The Rabshakeh returned, and found the king of Assyria fighting against Libnah; for he had heard that the king had left Lachish. ⁹Now the king[a] heard concerning King Tirhakah of Ethiopia,[b] "He has set out to fight against you." When he heard it, he sent messengers to Hezekiah, saying ¹⁰"Thus shall you speak to King Hezekiah of Judah: Do not let your God on whom you rely deceive you by promising that Jerusalem will not be given into the hand of the king of Assyria. ¹¹See, you have heard what the kings of Assyria have done to all lands, destroying them utterly. Shall you be delivered? ¹²Have the gods of the nations delivered them, the nations that my predecessors destroyed, Gozan, Haran, Rezeph, and the people of Eden who

---

a Heb he　b Or Nubia; Heb Cush

were in Telassar? ¹³Where is the king of Hamath, the king of Arpad, the king of the city of Sepharvaim, the king of Hena, or the king of Ivvah?"

Hezekiah's Prayer

14 Hezekiah received the letter from the hand of the messengers and read it; then Hezekiah went up to the house of the LORD and spread it before the LORD. ¹⁵And Hezekiah prayed to the LORD, saying: ¹⁶"O LORD of hosts, God of Israel, who are enthroned above the cherubim, you are God, you alone, of all the kingdoms of the earth; you have made heaven and earth. ¹⁷Incline your ear, O LORD, and hear; open your eyes, O LORD, and see; hear all the words of Sennacherib, which he has sent to mock the living God. ¹⁸Truly, O LORD, the kings of Assyria have laid waste all the nations and their lands, ¹⁹and have hurled their gods into the fire, though they were no gods, but the work of human hands—wood and stone—and so they were destroyed. ²⁰So now, O LORD our God, save us from his hand, so that all the kingdoms of the earth may know that you alone are the LORD."

21 Then Isaiah son of Amoz sent to Hezekiah, saying: "Thus says the LORD, the God of Israel: Because you have prayed to me concerning King Sennacherib of Assyria, ²²this is the word that the LORD has spoken concerning him:

She despises you, she scorns you—
  virgin daughter Zion;
she tosses her head—behind your back,
  daughter Jerusalem.

²³ "Whom have you mocked and reviled?
  Against whom have you raised your voice
and haughtily lifted your eyes?
  Against the Holy One of Israel!
²⁴ By your servants you have mocked the Lord,
  and you have said, 'With my many chariots
I have gone up the heights of the mountains,
  to the far recesses of Lebanon;
I felled its tallest cedars,
  its choicest cypresses;
I came to its remotest height,
  its densest forest.
²⁵ I dug wells
  and drank waters,
I dried up with the sole of my foot
  all the streams of Egypt.'
²⁶ "Have you not heard
  that I determined it long ago?
I planned from days of old
  what now I bring to pass,
that you should make fortified cities

crash into heaps of ruins,
²⁷ while their inhabitants, shorn of strength,
  are dismayed and confounded;
they have become like plants of the field
  and like tender grass,
like grass on the housetops,
  blighted*a* before it is grown.
²⁸ "I know your rising up*b* and your sitting down,
  your going out and coming in,
  and your raging against me.
²⁹ Because you have raged against me
  and your arrogance has come to my ears,
I will put my hook in your nose
  and my bit in your mouth;
I will turn you back on the way
  by which you came.

30 "And this shall be the sign for you: This year eat what grows of itself, and in the second year what springs from that; then in the third year sow, reap, plant vineyards, and eat their fruit. ³¹The surviving remnant of the house of Judah shall again take root downward, and bear fruit upward; ³²for from Jerusalem a remnant shall go out, and from Mount Zion a band of survivors. The zeal of the LORD of hosts will do this.

33 "Therefore thus says the LORD concerning the king of Assyria: He shall not come into this city, shoot an arrow there, come before it with a shield, or cast up a siege ramp against it. ³⁴By the way that he came, by the same he shall return; he shall not come into this city, says the LORD. ³⁵For I will defend this city to save it, for my own sake and for the sake of my servant David."

Sennacherib's Defeat and Death

36 Then the angel of the LORD set out and struck down one hundred eighty-five thousand in the camp of the Assyrians; when morning dawned, they were all dead bodies. ³⁷Then King Sennacherib of Assyria left, went home, and lived at Nineveh. ³⁸As he was worshiping in the house of his god Nisroch, his sons Adrammelech and Sharezer killed him with the sword, and they escaped into the land of Ararat. His son Esarhaddon succeeded him.

Hezekiah's Illness

38 In those days Hezekiah became sick and was at the point of death. The prophet Isaiah son of Amoz came to him, and said to him, "Thus says the LORD: Set your house in

---

a With 2 Kings 19.26: Heb *field*   *b* Q Ms Gk: MT lacks *your rising up*

order, for you shall die; you shall not recover." ²Then Hezekiah turned his face to the wall, and prayed to the LORD: ³"Remember now, O LORD, I implore you, how I have walked before you in faithfulness with a whole heart, and have done what is good in your sight." And Hezekiah wept bitterly.

4 Then the word of the LORD came to Isaiah: ⁵"Go and say to Hezekiah, Thus says the LORD, the God of your ancestor David: I have heard your prayer, I have seen your tears; I will add fifteen years to your life. ⁶I will deliver you and this city out of the hand of the king of Assyria, and defend this city.

7 "This is the sign to you from the LORD, that the LORD will do this thing that he has promised: ⁸See, I will make the shadow cast by the declining sun on the dial of Ahaz turn back ten steps." So the sun turned back on the dial the ten steps by which it had declined.ᵃ

9 A writing of King Hezekiah of Judah, after he had been sick and had recovered from his sickness:

¹⁰ I said: In the noontide of my days
 I must depart;
I am consigned to the gates of Sheol
 for the rest of my years.
¹¹ I said, I shall not see the LORD
 in the land of the living;
I shall look upon mortals no more
 among the inhabitants of the world.
¹² My dwelling is plucked up and removed from me
 like a shepherd's tent;
like a weaver I have rolled up my life;
 he cuts me off from the loom;
from day to night you bring me to an end;ᵃ
¹³   I cry for helpᵇ until morning;
like a lion he breaks all my bones;
 from day to night you bring me to an end.ᵃ

¹⁴ Like a swallow or a craneᵃ I clamor,
 I moan like a dove.
My eyes are weary with looking upward.
 O Lord, I am oppressed; be my security!
¹⁵ But what can I say? For he has spoken to me,
 and he himself has done it.
All my sleep has fledᶜ
 because of the bitterness of my soul.

¹⁶ O Lord, by these things people live,
 and in all these is the life of my spirit.ᵃ
 Oh, restore me to health and make me live!
¹⁷ Surely it was for my welfare
 that I had great bitterness;
but you have held backᵈ my life

from the pit of destruction,
 for you have cast all my sins
 behind your back.
¹⁸ For Sheol cannot thank you,
 death cannot praise you;
those who go down to the Pit cannot hope
 for your faithfulness.
¹⁹ The living, the living, they thank you,
 as I do this day;
fathers make known to children
 your faithfulness.

²⁰ The LORD will save me,
 and we will sing to stringed instrumentsᵉ
all the days of our lives,
 at the house of the LORD.

21 Now Isaiah had said, "Let them take a lump of figs, and apply it to the boil, so that he may recover." ²²Hezekiah also had said, "What is the sign that I shall go up to the house of the LORD?"

Envoys from Babylon Welcomed

39 At that time King Merodach-baladan son of Baladan of Babylon sent envoys with letters and a present to Hezekiah, for he heard that he had been sick and had recovered. ²Hezekiah welcomed them; he showed them his treasure house, the silver, the gold, the spices, the precious oil, his whole armory, all that was found in his storehouses. There was nothing in his house or in all his realm that Hezekiah did not show them. ³Then the prophet Isaiah came to King Hezekiah and said to him, "What did these men say? From where did they come to you?" Hezekiah answered, "They have come to me from a far country, from Babylon." ⁴He said, "What have they seen in your house?" Hezekiah answered, "They have seen all that is in my house; there is nothing in my storehouses that I did not show them."

5 Then Isaiah said to Hezekiah, "Hear the word of the LORD of hosts: ⁶Days are coming when all that is in your house, and that which your ancestors have stored up until this day, shall be carried to Babylon; nothing shall be left, says the LORD. ⁷Some of your own sons who are born to you shall be taken away; they shall be eunuchs in the palace of the king of Babylon." ⁸Then Hezekiah said to Isaiah, "The word of the LORD that you have spoken is good." For he thought, "There will be peace and security in my days."

ᵃ Meaning of Heb uncertain   ᵇ Cn: Meaning of Heb uncertain   ᶜ Cn Compare Syr: Heb I will walk slowly all my years   ᵈ Cn Compare Gk Vg: Heb loved   ᵉ Heb my stringed instruments

Pray It!

The Hope of Second Isaiah

Second Isaiah prophesies to the Israelites living in exile in Babylon with words full of love and hope: "Comfort, O comfort my people, / says your God" (Isa 40:1). Isaiah promises these Israelites a new liberation and the eventual restoration of Jerusalem and the Temple (see 44:26–28).

The author of the Gospel of Luke uses Isaiah 40:3–5 to describe the ministry of John the Baptist in announcing Jesus' arrival (see Lk 3:4–6). This writer wants to make it clear that Isaiah's promises are answered by the coming of Jesus.

In your prayer, reflect or journal on the following questions:

- Is there hope for our society?
- What are some things that you are hopeful for?
- Imagine God is speaking words of hope to you. What is God saying?

▶ Isa 40:1–5

God's People Are Comforted

40 Comfort, O comfort my people,
        says your God.
2 Speak tenderly to Jerusalem,
    and cry to her
that she has served her term,
    that her penalty is paid,
that she has received from the Lord's hand
    double for all her sins.

3 A voice cries out:
"In the wilderness prepare the way of the Lord,
    make straight in the desert a highway for our
        God.
4 Every valley shall be lifted up,
    and every mountain and hill be made low;
the uneven ground shall become level,
    and the rough places a plain.
5 Then the glory of the Lord shall be revealed,
    and all people shall see it together,
    for the mouth of the Lord has spoken."

6 A voice says, "Cry out!"
    And I said, "What shall I cry?"
All people are grass,
    their constancy is like the flower of the field.
7 The grass withers, the flower fades,
    when the breath of the Lord blows upon it;
    surely the people are grass.
8 The grass withers, the flower fades;
    but the word of our God will stand forever.
9 Get you up to a high mountain,
    O Zion, herald of good tidings;*a*
lift up your voice with strength,
    O Jerusalem, herald of good tidings,*b*
    lift it up, do not fear;
say to the cities of Judah,
    "Here is your God!"
10 See, the Lord God comes with might,
    and his arm rules for him;
his reward is with him,
    and his recompense before him.
11 He will feed his flock like a shepherd;
    he will gather the lambs in his arms,
and carry them in his bosom,
    and gently lead the mother sheep.

12 Who has measured the waters in the hollow of
        his hand
    and marked off the heavens with a span,
enclosed the dust of the earth in a measure,
    and weighed the mountains in scales
    and the hills in a balance?
13 Who has directed the spirit of the Lord,
    or as his counselor has instructed him?
14 Whom did he consult for his enlightenment,
    and who taught him the path of justice?

> **"Prepare the way of the Lord,**
> **make straight in the desert**
> **a highway for our God."**
>
> (Isa 40:3)

Who taught him knowledge,
    and showed him the way of understanding?
15 Even the nations are like a drop from a
        bucket,
    and are accounted as dust on the scales;
    see, he takes up the isles like fine dust.

---

a Or *O herald of good tidings to Zion*   *b* Or *O herald of good tidings to Jerusalem*

¹⁶ Lebanon would not provide fuel enough,
    nor are its animals enough for a burnt
       offering.
¹⁷ All the nations are as nothing before him;
    they are accounted by him as less than
       nothing and emptiness.

¹⁸ To whom then will you liken God,
    or what likeness compare with him?
¹⁹ An idol? —A workman casts it,
    and a goldsmith overlays it with gold,
    and casts for it silver chains.
²⁰ As a gift one chooses mulberry wood*ᵃ*
    —wood that will not rot—
    then seeks out a skilled artisan
       to set up an image that will not topple.

²¹ Have you not known? Have you not heard?
    Has it not been told you from the
       beginning?
    Have you not understood from the
       foundations of the earth?
²² It is he who sits above the circle of the earth,
    and its inhabitants are like grasshoppers;
    who stretches out the heavens like a curtain,
    and spreads them like a tent to live in;
²³ who brings princes to naught,
    and makes the rulers of the earth as nothing.

²⁴ Scarcely are they planted, scarcely sown,
    scarcely has their stem taken root in the
       earth,
    when he blows upon them, and they wither,
    and the tempest carries them off like stubble.

²⁵ To whom then will you compare me,
    or who is my equal? says the Holy One.
²⁶ Lift up your eyes on high and see:
    Who created these?
    He who brings out their host and numbers
       them,
    calling them all by name;
    because he is great in strength,
    mighty in power,
    not one is missing.

²⁷ Why do you say, O Jacob,
    and speak, O Israel,
    "My way is hidden from the LORD,
    and my right is disregarded by my God"?
²⁸ Have you not known? Have you not heard?
    The LORD is the everlasting God,
    the Creator of the ends of the earth.
    He does not faint or grow weary;
    his understanding is unsearchable.
²⁹ He gives power to the faint,

    and strengthens the powerless.
³⁰ Even youths will faint and be weary,
    and the young will fall exhausted;

---

a Meaning of Heb uncertain

Between a Rock and a Soft Place

Joe. Is God a rock or a pillow?

Valerie. A rock, I guess. God is strong and reliable. When I think of a rock, I think of something I can brace myself against when things are changing all around me.

Joe. For me, God is a pillow. God is someone I can come home to and be comfortable with. I can sit back and relax, leaning against God and feeling at ease.

Valerie. But a pillow is so ordinary and doesn't have any character. A rock is distinctive and doesn't change.

Joe. But a rock is so hard and unyielding. What kind of compassion can you get from a rock?

Valerie. What kind of strength can you draw from a pillow?

Joe. The strength that comes from relaxing and resting and being comforted. The strength that comes from being energized to go forward again.

Valerie. I'm sorry, but a pillow seems too soft to be like God.

Joe. And a rock seems much too hard.

Valerie. Isn't God both a pillow and a rock? In chapter 40 of Isaiah, it seems that the pillow image wins out. The picture of a comforting God gathering the lambs conveys a softness that is sometimes hard to find in the Old Testament.

Joe. That's true. There are times when we need a pillow to get comfortable. It is good to know that God is there waiting for us, helping us to feel at home.

Valerie. And it is also good to know that God the rock is there for the times when we need something to hold on to (see Ps 18:2).

▶ Isa 40:1–11

Cultural Connection

The Tent and the Circle

Isaiah 40:22-23 has significance in Native American spirituality for several reasons. First, the circle (see verse 22) is a symbol of unity and healing. In silhouette, the sun, the moon, and the earth are all circles. The poles of a teepee are arranged in a circle, and the teepees of a village are placed in a circle. The people of a nation are called the hoop or the circle, and sit in a circle for the sweat lodge ceremony (see "You Will Be Cleansed," near Ezek 36:25-26) and to smoke from the sacred pipe.

Second, the tent (see verse 22) is a symbol of home and family for a people that traditionally dwelled in tents.

Third, the Great Spirit is well described as the one "who sits above the circle" (verse 22).

Last, the insight that God, the Great Spirit, cares very little about the status of princes and rulers (see verse 23) is powerful to a people that is oppressed, treated violently, scattered, and despised in its homeland. Native Americans have been subjected to such treatment by the explor-

ers, then the colonists, then the pioneers, and now many citizens of the United States.

● Pray for the circle of humanity—that we learn to celebrate the diversity of our cultures and cease oppression of any form.

▶ Isa 40:22-23

31 but those who wait for the LORD shall renew
    their strength,
  they shall mount up with wings like eagles,
they shall run and not be weary,
    they shall walk and not faint.

Israel Assured of God's Help

41 Listen to me in silence, O coastlands;
    let the peoples renew their strength;
let them approach, then let them speak;
    let us together draw near for judgment.

2 Who has roused a victor from the east,
    summoned him to his service?
He delivers up nations to him,
    and tramples kings under foot;
he makes them like dust with his sword,
    like driven stubble with his bow.
3 He pursues them and passes on safely,
    scarcely touching the path with his feet.
4 Who has performed and done this,
    calling the generations from the
      beginning?
I, the LORD, am first,
    and will be with the last.
5 The coastlands have seen and are afraid,
    the ends of the earth tremble;
    they have drawn near and come.
6 Each one helps the other,
    saying to one another, "Take courage!"
7 The artisan encourages the goldsmith,

and the one who smooths with the hammer
    encourages the one who strikes the
      anvil,
saying of the soldering, "It is good";
    and they fasten it with nails so that it cannot
      be moved.
8 But you, Israel, my servant,
    Jacob, whom I have chosen,
    the offspring of Abraham, my friend;
9 you whom I took from the ends of the earth,
    and called from its farthest corners,
saying to you, "You are my servant,
    I have chosen you and not cast you off";
10 do not fear, for I am with you,
    do not be afraid, for I am your God;
I will strengthen you, I will help you,
    I will uphold you with my victorious right
      hand.

11 Yes, all who are incensed against you
    shall be ashamed and disgraced;
those who strive against you
    shall be as nothing and shall perish.
12 You shall seek those who contend with you,
    but you shall not find them;
those who war against you
    shall be as nothing at all.
13 For I, the LORD your God,
    hold your right hand;
it is I who say to you, "Do not fear,
    I will help you."

¹⁴ Do not fear, you worm Jacob,
  you insect[a] Israel!
I will help you, says the LORD;
  your Redeemer is the Holy One of Israel.
¹⁵ Now, I will make of you a threshing sledge,
  sharp, new, and having teeth;
you shall thresh the mountains and crush
      them,
  and you shall make the hills like chaff.
¹⁶ You shall winnow them and the wind shall carry
      them away,
  and the tempest shall scatter them.
Then you shall rejoice in the LORD;
  in the Holy One of Israel you shall glory.

¹⁷ When the poor and needy seek water,
  and there is none,
  and their tongue is parched with thirst,
I the LORD will answer them,
  I the God of Israel will not forsake them.
¹⁸ I will open rivers on the bare heights,[b]
  and fountains in the midst of the valleys;
I will make the wilderness a pool of water,
  and the dry land springs of water.
¹⁹ I will put in the wilderness the cedar,
  the acacia, the myrtle, and the olive;
I will set in the desert the cypress,
  the plane and the pine together,
²⁰ so that all may see and know,
  all may consider and understand,
that the hand of the LORD has done this,
  the Holy One of Israel has created it.

The Futility of Idols

²¹ Set forth your case, says the LORD;
  bring your proofs, says the King of Jacob.
²² Let them bring them, and tell us
  what is to happen.
Tell us the former things, what they are,
  so that we may consider them,
and that we may know their outcome;
  or declare to us the things to come.
²³ Tell us what is to come hereafter,
  that we may know that you are gods;
do good, or do harm,
  that we may be afraid and terrified.
²⁴ You, indeed, are nothing
  and your work is nothing at all;
  whoever chooses you is an abomination.

²⁵ I stirred up one from the north, and he has
      come,
  from the rising of the sun he was summoned
      by name.[c]
He shall trample[d] on rulers as on mortar,
  as the potter treads clay.

²⁶ Who declared it from the beginning, so that we
      might know,
  and beforehand, so that we might say, "He is
      right"?
There was no one who declared it, none who
      proclaimed,
  none who heard your words.
²⁷ I first have declared it to Zion,[e]
  and I give to Jerusalem a herald of good
      tidings.
²⁸ But when I look there is no one;
  among these there is no counselor
  who, when I ask, gives an answer.
²⁹ No, they are all a delusion;
  their works are nothing;
  their images are empty wind.

The Servant, a Light to the Nations

42 Here is my servant, whom I uphold,
  my chosen, in whom my soul delights;
I have put my spirit upon him;
  he will bring forth justice to the nations.
² He will not cry or lift up his voice,
  or make it heard in the street;
³ a bruised reed he will not break,
  and a dimly burning wick he will not
      quench;
  he will faithfully bring forth justice.
⁴ He will not grow faint or be crushed
  until he has established justice in the
      earth;
  and the coastlands wait for his teaching.

---

a Syr: Heb *men of*   b Or *trails*   c Cn Compare Q Ms Gk: MT
and he shall call on my name   d Cn: Heb *come*   e Cn: Heb *First
to Zion—Behold, behold them*

The Servant's Mission

Read Isaiah 42:1–7 and then reflect or journal on the following questions:
● What is the servant's mission from God?
● How does Jesus fulfill this mission (compare Isa 42:6–7 with Lk 4:18–19)?
● How do you participate in
  this mission?

▶ Isa 42:1–7

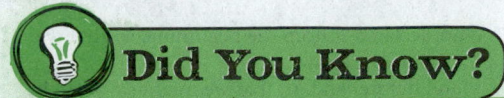

Did You Know?

The Servant Songs

Second Isaiah's four songs of the servant (see Isa 42:1–7, 49:1–6, 50:4–9, 52:13—53:12) have had an important place in Christian theology and worship. They portray the qualities of the ideal servant leader. Through these songs, the prophet speaks of hope: the faithful Israelites, though in exile, are still God's servants (see 42:1), chosen from the womb (see 49:1). Through their courageous suffering (see 50:7–8), Israel will be restored to bring salvation to all nations (see 53:5).

It is not surprising that the early Christians saw in the servant songs a remarkable similarity to Jesus' words and actions. The fourth song in particular—which talks of a suffering servant—helped the followers of Jesus understand his suffering and humiliating death on the cross. Because of this, these passages have become part of the Catholic Church's formal worship during Holy Week (the week before Easter): Isaiah 42:1–7 on Monday, 49:1–6 on Tuesday, 50:4–9 on Wednesday, and 52:13—53:12 on Friday.

▶ **Isa 42:1–7**

5 Thus says God, the LORD,
    who created the heavens and stretched them out,
    who spread out the earth and what comes from it,
who gives breath to the people upon it
    and spirit to those who walk in it:
6 I am the LORD, I have called you in righteousness,
    I have taken you by the hand and kept you;
I have given you as a covenant to the people,[a]
    a light to the nations,
7   to open the eyes that are blind,
to bring out the prisoners from the dungeon,
    from the prison those who sit in darkness.
8 I am the LORD, that is my name;
    my glory I give to no other,
    nor my praise to idols.
9 See, the former things have come to pass,
    and new things I now declare;
before they spring forth,
    I tell you of them.

A Hymn of Praise

10 Sing to the LORD a new song,
    his praise from the end of the earth!
Let the sea roar[b] and all that fills it,
    the coastlands and their inhabitants.
11 Let the desert and its towns lift up their voice,
    the villages that Kedar inhabits;
let the inhabitants of Sela sing for joy,
    let them shout from the tops of the mountains.
12 Let them give glory to the LORD,
    and declare his praise in the coastlands.
13 The LORD goes forth like a soldier,
    like a warrior he stirs up his fury;
he cries out, he shouts aloud,
    he shows himself mighty against his foes.

14 For a long time I have held my peace,
    I have kept still and restrained myself;
now I will cry out like a woman in labor,
    I will gasp and pant.
15 I will lay waste mountains and hills,
    and dry up all their herbage;
I will turn the rivers into islands,
    and dry up the pools.
16 I will lead the blind
    by a road they do not know,
by paths they have not known
    I will guide them.
I will turn the darkness before them into light,
    the rough places into level ground.
These are the things I will do,
    and I will not forsake them.
17 They shall be turned back and utterly put to shame—
    those who trust in carved images,
who say to cast images,
    "You are our gods."

18 Listen, you that are deaf;
    and you that are blind, look up and see!
19 Who is blind but my servant,
    or deaf like my messenger whom I send?
Who is blind like my dedicated one,
    or blind like the servant of the LORD?
20 He sees many things, but does[c] not observe them;
    his ears are open, but he does not hear.

Israel's Disobedience

21 The LORD was pleased, for the sake of his righteousness,

---

a Meaning of Heb uncertain   b Cn Compare Ps 96.11; 98.7: Heb Those who go down to the sea   c Heb You see many things but do

to magnify his teaching and make it glorious.
²² But this is a people robbed and plundered,
 all of them are trapped in holes
 and hidden in prisons;
they have become a prey with no one to rescue,
 a spoil with no one to say, "Restore!"
²³ Who among you will give heed to this,
 who will attend and listen for the time to
  come?
²⁴ Who gave up Jacob to the spoiler,
 and Israel to the robbers?
Was it not the LORD, against whom we have
  sinned,
 in whose ways they would not walk,
 and whose law they would not obey?
²⁵ So he poured upon him the heat of his anger
 and the fury of war;
it set him on fire all around, but he did not
  understand;
it burned him, but he did not take it to heart.

Restoration and Protection Promised

43 But now thus says the LORD,
 he who created you, O Jacob,
he who formed you, O Israel:
Do not fear, for I have redeemed you;
 I have called you by name, you are mine.
² When you pass through the waters, I will be
  with you;
 and through the rivers, they shall not
  overwhelm you;
when you walk through fire you shall not be
  burned,
 and the flame shall not consume you.
³ For I am the LORD your God,
 the Holy One of Israel, your Savior.
I give Egypt as your ransom,
 Ethiopia*ᵃ* and Seba in exchange for you.
⁴ Because you are precious in my sight,
 and honored, and I love you,
I give people in return for you,
 nations in exchange for your life.
⁵ Do not fear, for I am with you;
 I will bring your offspring from the east,
 and from the west I will gather you;
⁶ I will say to the north, "Give them up,"
 and to the south, "Do not withhold;
bring my sons from far away
 and my daughters from the end of the earth—
⁷ everyone who is called by my name,
 whom I created for my glory,
 whom I formed and made."

⁸ Bring forth the people who are blind, yet have
  eyes,
who are deaf, yet have ears!

⁹ Let all the nations gather together,
 and let the peoples assemble.
Who among them declared this,
 and foretold to us the former things?
Let them bring their witnesses to justify them,
 and let them hear and say, "It is true."
¹⁰ You are my witnesses, says the LORD,
 and my servant whom I have chosen,
so that you may know and believe me
 and understand that I am he.
Before me no god was formed,
 nor shall there be any after me.
¹¹ I, I am the LORD,
 and besides me there is no savior.
¹² I declared and saved and proclaimed,
 when there was no strange god among you;
 and you are my witnesses, says the LORD.
¹³ I am God, and also henceforth I am He;
 there is no one who can deliver from my
  hand;
 I work and who can hinder it?

¹⁴ Thus says the LORD,
 your Redeemer, the Holy One of Israel:
For your sake I will send to Babylon
 and break down all the bars,
 and the shouting of the Chaldeans will be
  turned to lamentation.*ᵇ*
¹⁵ I am the LORD, your Holy One,

---

a Or *Nubia;* Heb *Cush* *b* Meaning of Heb uncertain

Be Not Afraid

The words of Isaiah 43:1–5 might sound
familiar to you. Most of the song "Be Not
Afraid" is based on these verses.
 God calls us to be disciples and leaders. God
calls us from within our faith community to serve
others. How easy is it for you to go forth and do
God's work? How easy is it to be not afraid?

 Be not afraid.
 I go before you always.
 Come follow me,
 and I will give you rest.
  (From Bob Dufford,
   "Be Not Afraid")

 Isa 43:1–5

the Creator of Israel, your King.
16 Thus says the LORD,
   who makes a way in the sea,
   a path in the mighty waters,
17 who brings out chariot and horse,
   army and warrior;
   they lie down, they cannot rise,
   they are extinguished, quenched like a wick:
18 Do not remember the former things,
   or consider the things of old.
19 I am about to do a new thing;
   now it springs forth, do you not perceive it?
   I will make a way in the wilderness
   and rivers in the desert.
20 The wild animals will honor me,
   the jackals and the ostriches;
   for I give water in the wilderness,
   rivers in the desert,
   to give drink to my chosen people,
21   the people whom I formed for myself
   so that they might declare my praise.

22 Yet you did not call upon me, O Jacob;
   but you have been weary of me, O Israel!
23 You have not brought me your sheep for burnt
      offerings,
   or honored me with your sacrifices.
   I have not burdened you with offerings,
   or wearied you with frankincense.
24 You have not bought me sweet cane with
      money,
   or satisfied me with the fat of your sacrifices.
   But you have burdened me with your sins;
   you have wearied me with your iniquities.

25 I, I am He
   who blots out your transgressions for my own
      sake,
   and I will not remember your sins.
26 Accuse me, let us go to trial;
   set forth your case, so that you may be proved
      right.
27 Your first ancestor sinned,
   and your interpreters transgressed against me.
28 Therefore I profaned the princes of the
      sanctuary,
   I delivered Jacob to utter destruction,
   and Israel to reviling.

God's Blessing on Israel

44 But now hear, O Jacob my servant,
   Israel whom I have chosen!
2 Thus says the LORD who made you,
   who formed you in the womb and will help
      you:
   Do not fear, O Jacob my servant,

Jeshurun whom I have chosen.
3 For I will pour water on the thirsty land,
   and streams on the dry ground;
   I will pour my spirit upon your descendants,
   and my blessing on your offspring.
4 They shall spring up like a green tamarisk,
   like willows by flowing streams.
5 This one will say, "I am the LORD's,"
   another will be called by the name of Jacob,
   yet another will write on the hand, "The LORD's,"
   and adopt the name of Israel.

6 Thus says the LORD, the King of Israel,
   and his Redeemer, the LORD of hosts:
   I am the first and I am the last;
   besides me there is no god.
7 Who is like me? Let them proclaim it,
   let them declare and set it forth before me.
   Who has announced from of old the things to
      come?[a]
   Let them tell us[b] what is yet to be.
8 Do not fear, or be afraid;
   have I not told you from of old and
      declared it?
   You are my witnesses!
   Is there any god besides me?
   There is no other rock; I know not one.

The Absurdity of Idol Worship

9 All who make idols are nothing, and the things they delight in do not profit; their witnesses neither see nor know. And so they will be put to shame. 10Who would fashion a god or cast an image that can do no good? 11Look, all its devotees shall be put to shame; the artisans too are merely human. Let them all assemble, let them stand up; they shall be terrified, they shall all be put to shame.

12 The ironsmith fashions it[c] and works it over the coals, shaping it with hammers, and forging it with his strong arm; he becomes hungry and his strength fails, he drinks no water and is faint. 13The carpenter stretches a line, marks it out with a stylus, fashions it with planes, and marks it with a compass; he makes it in human form, with human beauty, to be set up in a shrine. 14He cuts down cedars or chooses a holm tree or an oak and lets it grow strong among the trees of the forest. He plants a cedar and the rain nourishes it. 15Then it can be used as fuel. Part of it he takes and warms himself; he kindles a fire and bakes bread. Then he makes a god and worships it, makes it a carved image and bows down

---

a Cn: Heb *from my placing an eternal people and things to come*
b Tg: Heb *them*   c Cn: Heb *an ax*

before it. [16]Half of it he burns in the fire; over this half he roasts meat, eats it and is satisfied. He also warms himself and says, "Ah, I am warm, I can feel the fire!" [17]The rest of it he makes into a god, his idol, bows down to it and worships it; he prays to it and says, "Save me, for you are my god!"

18 They do not know, nor do they comprehend; for their eyes are shut, so that they cannot see, and their minds as well, so that they cannot understand. [19]No one considers, nor is there knowledge or discernment to say, "Half of it I burned in the fire; I also baked bread on its coals, I roasted meat and have eaten. Now shall I make the rest of it an abomination? Shall I fall down before a block of wood?" [20]He feeds on ashes; a deluded mind has led him astray, and he cannot save himself or say, "Is not this thing in my right hand a fraud?"

Israel Is Not Forgotten

[21] Remember these things, O Jacob,
    and Israel, for you are my servant;
I formed you, you are my servant;
    O Israel, you will not be forgotten by me.
[22] I have swept away your transgressions like a
        cloud,
    and your sins like mist;
return to me, for I have redeemed you.

[23] Sing, O heavens, for the LORD has done it;
    shout, O depths of the earth;
break forth into singing, O mountains,
    O forest, and every tree in it!
For the LORD has redeemed Jacob,
    and will be glorified in Israel.

[24] Thus says the LORD, your Redeemer,
    who formed you in the womb:
I am the LORD, who made all things,
    who alone stretched out the heavens,
    who by myself spread out the earth;
[25] who frustrates the omens of liars,
    and makes fools of diviners;
who turns back the wise,
    and makes their knowledge foolish;
[26] who confirms the word of his servant,
    and fulfills the prediction of his messengers;
who says of Jerusalem, "It shall be inhabited,"
    and of the cities of Judah, "They shall be
        rebuilt,
    and I will raise up their ruins";
[27] who says to the deep, "Be dry—
    I will dry up your rivers";
[28] who says of Cyrus, "He is my shepherd,
    and he shall carry out all my purpose";

and who says of Jerusalem, "It shall be rebuilt,"
    and of the temple, "Your foundation shall be
        laid."

Cyrus, God's Instrument

45 Thus says the LORD to his anointed, to
        Cyrus,
    whose right hand I have grasped
to subdue nations before him
    and strip kings of their robes,
to open doors before him—
    and the gates shall not be closed:
[2] I will go before you
    and level the mountains,[a]
I will break in pieces the doors of bronze
    and cut through the bars of iron,
[3] I will give you the treasures of darkness
    and riches hidden in secret places,
so that you may know that it is I, the LORD,
    the God of Israel, who call you by your name.
[4] For the sake of my servant Jacob,
    and Israel my chosen,
I call you by your name,
    I surname you, though you do not know me.
[5] I am the LORD, and there is no other;
    besides me there is no god.
    I arm you, though you do not know me,
[6] so that they may know, from the rising of
        the sun
    and from the west, that there is no one
        besides me;
    I am the LORD, and there is no other.
[7] I form light and create darkness,
    I make weal and create woe;
    I the LORD do all these things.

[8] Shower, O heavens, from above,
    and let the skies rain down righteousness;
let the earth open, that salvation may spring up,[b]
    and let it cause righteousness to sprout up
        also;
    I the LORD have created it.

[9] Woe to you who strive with your Maker,
    earthen vessels with the potter![c]
Does the clay say to the one who fashions it,
    "What are you making"?
    or "Your work has no handles"?
[10] Woe to anyone who says to a father, "What are
        you begetting?"
    or to a woman, "With what are you in labor?"
[11] Thus says the LORD,
    the Holy One of Israel, and its Maker:

---

a Q Ms Gk: MT *the swellings*   b Q Ms: MT *that they may bring forth salvation*   c Cn: Heb *with the potsherds*, or *with the potters*

Will you question me*a* about my children,
  or command me concerning the work of my
    hands?
12 I made the earth,
  and created humankind upon it;
it was my hands that stretched out the heavens,
  and I commanded all their host.
13 I have aroused Cyrus*b* in righteousness,
  and I will make all his paths straight;
he shall build my city
  and set my exiles free,
not for price or reward,
  says the LORD of hosts.
14 Thus says the LORD:
The wealth of Egypt and the merchandise of
    Ethiopia,*c*
  and the Sabeans, tall of stature,
shall come over to you and be yours,
  they shall follow you;
  they shall come over in chains and bow down
    to you.
They will make supplication to you, saying,
  "God is with you alone, and there is no other;
  there is no god besides him."
15 Truly, you are a God who hides himself,
  O God of Israel, the Savior.
16 All of them are put to shame and confounded,
  the makers of idols go in confusion together.
17 But Israel is saved by the LORD
  with everlasting salvation;
you shall not be put to shame or confounded
  to all eternity.

18 For thus says the LORD,
who created the heavens
  (he is God!),
who formed the earth and made it
  (he established it;
he did not create it a chaos,
  he formed it to be inhabited!):
I am the LORD, and there is no other.
19 I did not speak in secret,
  in a land of darkness;
I did not say to the offspring of Jacob,
  "Seek me in chaos."
I the LORD speak the truth,
  I declare what is right.

Idols Cannot Save Babylon

20 Assemble yourselves and come together,
  draw near, you survivors of the nations!
They have no knowledge—
  those who carry about their wooden idols,
and keep on praying to a god
  that cannot save.
21 Declare and present your case;

let them take counsel together!
Who told this long ago?
  Who declared it of old?
Was it not I, the LORD?
  There is no other god besides me,
a righteous God and a Savior;
  there is no one besides me.

22 Turn to me and be saved,
  all the ends of the earth!
For I am God, and there is no other.
23 By myself I have sworn,
  from my mouth has gone forth in
    righteousness
  a word that shall not return:
"To me every knee shall bow,
  every tongue shall swear."

24 Only in the LORD, it shall be said of me,
  are righteousness and strength;
all who were incensed against him
  shall come to him and be ashamed.
25 In the LORD all the offspring of Israel
  shall triumph and glory.

46 Bel bows down, Nebo stoops,
  their idols are on beasts and cattle;
these things you carry are loaded
  as burdens on weary animals.
2 They stoop, they bow down together;
  they cannot save the burden,
  but themselves go into captivity.

3 Listen to me, O house of Jacob,
  all the remnant of the house of Israel,
who have been borne by me from your birth,
  carried from the womb;
4 even to your old age I am he,
  even when you turn gray I will carry you.
I have made, and I will bear;
  I will carry and will save.

5 To whom will you liken me and make me equal,
  and compare me, as though we were alike?
6 Those who lavish gold from the purse,
  and weigh out silver in the scales—
they hire a goldsmith, who makes it into a god;
  then they fall down and worship!
7 They lift it to their shoulders, they carry it,
  they set it in its place, and it stands there;
  it cannot move from its place.
If one cries out to it, it does not answer
  or save anyone from trouble.

---

a Cn: Heb *Ask me of things to come*   b Heb *him*   c Or Nubia;
Heb *Cush*

8 Remember this and consider,[a]
   recall it to mind, you transgressors,
9   remember the former things of old;
for I am God, and there is no other;
   I am God, and there is no one like me,
10 declaring the end from the beginning
   and from ancient times things not yet done,
saying, "My purpose shall stand,
   and I will fulfill my intention,"
11 calling a bird of prey from the east,
   the man for my purpose from a far country.
I have spoken, and I will bring it to pass;
   I have planned, and I will do it.

12 Listen to me, you stubborn of heart,
   you who are far from deliverance:
13 I bring near my deliverance, it is not far off,
   and my salvation will not tarry;
I will put salvation in Zion,
   for Israel my glory.

The Humiliation of Babylon

47 Come down and sit in the dust,
   virgin daughter Babylon!
Sit on the ground without a throne,
   daughter Chaldea!
For you shall no more be called
   tender and delicate.
2 Take the millstones and grind meal,
   remove your veil,
strip off your robe, uncover your legs,
   pass through the rivers.
3 Your nakedness shall be uncovered,
   and your shame shall be seen.
I will take vengeance,
   and I will spare no one.
4 Our Redeemer—the LORD of hosts is his name—
   is the Holy One of Israel.

5 Sit in silence, and go into darkness,
   daughter Chaldea!
For you shall no more be called
   the mistress of kingdoms.
6 I was angry with my people,
   I profaned my heritage;
I gave them into your hand,
   you showed them no mercy;
on the aged you made your yoke
   exceedingly heavy.
7 You said, "I shall be mistress forever,"
   so that you did not lay these things to heart
   or remember their end.

8 Now therefore hear this, you lover of pleasures,
   who sit securely,
who say in your heart,

"I am, and there is no one besides me;
I shall not sit as a widow
   or know the loss of children"—
9 both these things shall come upon you
   in a moment, in one day:
the loss of children and widowhood
   shall come upon you in full measure,
in spite of your many sorceries
   and the great power of your enchantments.

10 You felt secure in your wickedness;
   you said, "No one sees me."
Your wisdom and your knowledge
   led you astray,
and you said in your heart,
   "I am, and there is no one besides me."
11 But evil shall come upon you,
   which you cannot charm away;
disaster shall fall upon you,
   which you will not be able to ward off;
and ruin shall come on you suddenly,
   of which you know nothing.

12 Stand fast in your enchantments
   and your many sorceries,
   with which you have labored from your
      youth;
perhaps you may be able to succeed,
   perhaps you may inspire terror.
13 You are wearied with your many consultations;
   let those who study[a] the heavens
stand up and save you,
   those who gaze at the stars,
and at each new moon predict
   what[b] shall befall you.

14 See, they are like stubble,
   the fire consumes them;
they cannot deliver themselves
   from the power of the flame.
No coal for warming oneself is this,
   no fire to sit before!
15 Such to you are those with whom you have
      labored,
   who have trafficked with you from your
      youth;
they all wander about in their own paths;
   there is no one to save you.

God the Creator and Redeemer

48 Hear this, O house of Jacob,
   who are called by the name of Israel,
   and who came forth from the loins[c] of Judah;

---

a Meaning of Heb uncertain   b Gk Syr Compare Vg: Heb *from what*   c Cn: Heb *waters*

who swear by the name of the LORD,
and invoke the God of Israel,
but not in truth or right.
2 For they call themselves after the holy city,
and lean on the God of Israel;
the LORD of hosts is his name.

3 The former things I declared long ago,
they went out from my mouth and I made
them known;
then suddenly I did them and they came to
pass.
4 Because I know that you are obstinate,
and your neck is an iron sinew
and your forehead brass,
5 I declared them to you from long ago,
before they came to pass I announced them
to you,
so that you would not say, "My idol did them,
my carved image and my cast image
commanded them."

6 You have heard; now see all this;
and will you not declare it?
From this time forward I make you hear new
things,
hidden things that you have not known.
7 They are created now, not long ago;
before today you have never heard of them,
so that you could not say, "I already knew
them."
8 You have never heard, you have never known,
from of old your ear has not been opened.
For I knew that you would deal very
treacherously,
and that from birth you were called a rebel.

9 For my name's sake I defer my anger,
for the sake of my praise I restrain it for
you,
so that I may not cut you off.
10 See, I have refined you, but not like[b] silver;
I have tested you in the furnace of
adversity.
11 For my own sake, for my own sake, I do it,
for why should my name[c] be profaned?
My glory I will not give to another.

12 Listen to me, O Jacob,
and Israel, whom I called:
I am He; I am the first,
and I am the last.
13 My hand laid the foundation of the earth,
and my right hand spread out the heavens;
when I summon them,
they stand at attention.

14 Assemble, all of you, and hear!
Who among them has declared these things?
The LORD loves him;
he shall perform his purpose on Babylon,
and his arm shall be against the Chaldeans.
15 I, even I, have spoken and called him,
I have brought him, and he will prosper in his
way.
16 Draw near to me, hear this!
From the beginning I have not spoken in
secret,
from the time it came to be I have been there.
And now the Lord GOD has sent me and his
spirit.

17 Thus says the LORD,
your Redeemer, the Holy One of Israel:
I am the LORD your God,
who teaches you for your own good,
who leads you in the way you should go.
18 O that you had paid attention to my
commandments!
Then your prosperity would have been like a
river,
and your success like the waves of the sea;
19 your offspring would have been like the sand,
and your descendants like its grains;
their name would never be cut off
or destroyed from before me.

20 Go out from Babylon, flee from Chaldea,
declare this with a shout of joy, proclaim it,
send it forth to the end of the earth;
say, "The LORD has redeemed his servant
Jacob!"
21 They did not thirst when he led them through
the deserts;
he made water flow for them from the rock;
he split open the rock and the water gushed
out.

22 "There is no peace," says the LORD, "for the
wicked."

The Servant's Mission

49 Listen to me, O coastlands,
pay attention, you peoples from far away!
The LORD called me before I was born,
while I was in my mother's womb he named
me.
2 He made my mouth like a sharp sword,
in the shadow of his hand he hid me;
he made me a polished arrow,
in his quiver he hid me away.

b Cn: Heb with   c Gk Old Latin: Heb for why should it

³ And he said to me, "You are my servant,
Israel, in whom I will be glorified."
⁴ But I said, "I have labored in vain,
I have spent my strength for nothing and
vanity;
yet surely my cause is with the LORD,
and my reward with my God."

⁵ And now the LORD says,
who formed me in the womb to be his servant,
to bring Jacob back to him,
and that Israel might be gathered to him,
for I am honored in the sight of the LORD,
and my God has become my strength—
⁶ he says,
"It is too light a thing that you should be my
servant
to raise up the tribes of Jacob
and to restore the survivors of Israel;
I will give you as a light to the nations,
that my salvation may reach to the end of the
earth."

⁷ Thus says the LORD,
the Redeemer of Israel and his Holy One,
to one deeply despised, abhorred by the nations,
the slave of rulers,
"Kings shall see and stand up,
princes, and they shall prostrate themselves,
because of the LORD, who is faithful,
the Holy One of Israel, who has chosen you."

Zion's Children to Be Brought Home

⁸ Thus says the LORD:
In a time of favor I have answered you,
on a day of salvation I have helped you;
I have kept you and given you
as a covenant to the people,ᵃ
to establish the land,
to apportion the desolate heritages;
⁹ saying to the prisoners, "Come out,"
to those who are in darkness, "Show
yourselves."
They shall feed along the ways,
on all the bare heightsᵇ shall be their pasture;
¹⁰ they shall not hunger or thirst,
neither scorching wind nor sun shall strike
them down,
for he who has pity on them will lead them,
and by springs of water will guide them.
¹¹ And I will turn all my mountains into a road,
and my highways shall be raised up.
¹² Lo, these shall come from far away,
and lo, these from the north and from the
west,
and these from the land of Syene.ᶜ

Pray It!

The Servant's Success

Isaiah 49:1–6 is the second of the four servant songs (see "The Servant Songs," near Isa 42:1–7). In this passage, the servant expresses a feeling of failure (see 49:4). But God responds that the servant will be a success, a "light to the nations" (verse 6). In your prayer, reflect or journal on a time when you felt you failed, but something good happened anyway. How do you now see God's hand at work in the situation?

▶ Isa 49:1–6

¹³ Sing for joy, O heavens, and exult, O earth;
break forth, O mountains, into singing!
For the LORD has comforted his people,
and will have compassion on his suffering
ones.

¹⁴ But Zion said, "The LORD has forsaken me,
my Lord has forgotten me."
¹⁵ Can a woman forget her nursing child,
or show no compassion for the child of her
womb?
Even these may forget,
yet I will not forget you.
¹⁶ See, I have inscribed you on the palms of my
hands;
your walls are continually before me.
¹⁷ Your builders outdo your destroyers,ᵈ
and those who laid you waste go away from
you.
¹⁸ Lift up your eyes all around and see;
they all gather, they come to you.
As I live, says the LORD,
you shall put all of them on like an ornament,
and like a bride you shall bind them on.

¹⁹ Surely your waste and your desolate places
and your devastated land—
surely now you will be too crowded for your
inhabitants,
and those who swallowed you up will be far
away.

ᵃ Meaning of Heb uncertain   ᵇ Or the trails   ᶜ Q Ms: MT *Sinim*
ᵈ Or *Your children come swiftly; your destroyers*

ISA

20 The children born in the time of your
          bereavement
      will yet say in your hearing:
   "The place is too crowded for me;
      make room for me to settle."
21 Then you will say in your heart,
   "Who has borne me these?
   I was bereaved and barren,
      exiled and put away—
   so who has reared these?
   I was left all alone—
      where then have these come from?"

22 Thus says the Lord GOD:
   I will soon lift up my hand to the nations,
      and raise my signal to the peoples;
   and they shall bring your sons in their bosom,
      and your daughters shall be carried on their
          shoulders.
23 Kings shall be your foster fathers,
      and their queens your nursing mothers.
   With their faces to the ground they shall bow
          down to you,
      and lick the dust of your feet.

I Will Never Forget You, My People

In chapter 49, Isaiah introduces us to one of the feminine images of God—God as mother. Although we most often use masculine words to describe God, it's easy to imagine God as a loving mother—forgiving us when we make mistakes, embracing us when we need comfort, nurturing us through difficult times, and acting gently toward us at all times. The Hebrew root of the word *compassion* actually means "womb." Thus, a God of compassion and love, a God who will never forget the suffering of God's people, is by definition a God of the womb, a God of motherly tenderness.

   Picture the mother figures in your life: perhaps your birth mother, grandmother, adoptive mother, stepmother, or godmother. How do you see God's love reflected in her love?

▶ **Isa 49:13–16**

Then you will know that I am the LORD;
      those who wait for me shall not be put to
          shame.

24 Can the prey be taken from the mighty,
      or the captives of a tyrant[a] be rescued?
25 But thus says the LORD:
   Even the captives of the mighty shall be taken,
      and the prey of the tyrant be rescued;
   for I will contend with those who contend with
          you,
      and I will save your children.
26 I will make your oppressors eat their own flesh,
      and they shall be drunk with their own blood
          as with wine.
   Then all flesh shall know
      that I am the LORD your Savior,
      and your Redeemer, the Mighty One of
          Jacob.

50 Thus says the LORD:
   Where is your mother's bill of divorce
      with which I put her away?
   Or which of my creditors is it
      to whom I have sold you?
   No, because of your sins you were sold,
      and for your transgressions your mother was
          put away.
2 Why was no one there when I came?
      Why did no one answer when I called?
   Is my hand shortened, that it cannot redeem?
      Or have I no power to deliver?
   By my rebuke I dry up the sea,
      I make the rivers a desert;
   their fish stink for lack of water,
      and die of thirst.[b]
3 I clothe the heavens with blackness,
      and make sackcloth their covering.

The Servant's Humiliation and Vindication

4 The Lord GOD has given me
      the tongue of a teacher,[c]
   that I may know how to sustain
      the weary with a word.
   Morning by morning he wakens—
      wakens my ear
      to listen as those who are taught.
5 The Lord GOD has opened my ear,
      and I was not rebellious,
      I did not turn backward.
6 I gave my back to those who struck me,
      and my cheeks to those who pulled out the
          beard;

---

a Q Ms Syr Vg: MT *of a righteous person*   b Or *die on the thirsty ground*   c Cn: Heb *of those who are taught*

I did not hide my face
    from insult and spitting.

7 The Lord GOD helps me;
    therefore I have not been disgraced;
therefore I have set my face like flint,
    and I know that I shall not be put to shame;
8   he who vindicates me is near.
Who will contend with me?
    Let us stand up together.
Who are my adversaries?
    Let them confront me.
9 It is the Lord GOD who helps me;
    who will declare me guilty?
All of them will wear out like a garment;
    the moth will eat them up.

10 Who among you fears the LORD
    and obeys the voice of his servant,
who walks in darkness
    and has no light,
yet trusts in the name of the LORD
    and relies upon his God?
11 But all of you are kindlers of fire,
    lighters of firebrands.[a]
Walk in the flame of your fire,
    and among the brands that you have kindled!
This is what you shall have from my hand:
    you shall lie down in torment.

Blessings in Store for God's People

51 Listen to me, you that pursue righteousness,
    you that seek the LORD.
Look to the rock from which you were hewn,
    and to the quarry from which you were dug.
2 Look to Abraham your father
    and to Sarah who bore you;
for he was but one when I called him,
    but I blessed him and made him many.
3 For the LORD will comfort Zion;
    he will comfort all her waste places,
and will make her wilderness like Eden,
    her desert like the garden of the LORD;
joy and gladness will be found in her,
    thanksgiving and the voice of song.

4 Listen to me, my people,
    and give heed to me, my nation;
for a teaching will go out from me,
    and my justice for a light to the peoples.
5 I will bring near my deliverance swiftly,
    my salvation has gone out
    and my arms will rule the peoples;
the coastlands wait for me,
    and for my arm they hope.
6 Lift up your eyes to the heavens,

Pray It!

The Servant's Strength

Isaiah 50:4–9 is the third of the four servant songs (see "The Servant Songs," near Isa 42:1–7). Read the song twice. The first time, think of how it reflects Jesus' relationship with his heavenly Father. The second time, meditate on the verses that inspire you and give you strength to be a prophet to other young people.

▶ Isa 50:4–9

ISA

    and look at the earth beneath;
for the heavens will vanish like smoke,
    the earth will wear out like a garment,
    and those who live on it will die like gnats;[b]
but my salvation will be forever,
    and my deliverance will never be ended.

7 Listen to me, you who know righteousness,
    you people who have my teaching in your
        hearts;
do not fear the reproach of others,
    and do not be dismayed when they revile
        you.
8 For the moth will eat them up like a garment,
    and the worm will eat them like wool;
but my deliverance will be forever,
    and my salvation to all generations.

9 Awake, awake, put on strength,
    O arm of the LORD!
Awake, as in days of old,
    the generations of long ago!
Was it not you who cut Rahab in pieces,
    who pierced the dragon?
10 Was it not you who dried up the sea,
    the waters of the great deep;
who made the depths of the sea a way
    for the redeemed to cross over?
11 So the ransomed of the LORD shall return,
    and come to Zion with singing;
everlasting joy shall be upon their heads;
    they shall obtain joy and gladness,
    and sorrow and sighing shall flee away.

---

a Syr: Heb *you gird yourselves with firebrands*   b Or *in like manner*

12 I, I am he who comforts you;
    why then are you afraid of a mere mortal who
        must die,
    a human being who fades like grass?
13 You have forgotten the LORD, your Maker,
    who stretched out the heavens
    and laid the foundations of the earth.
You fear continually all day long
    because of the fury of the oppressor,
who is bent on destruction.
    But where is the fury of the oppressor?
14 The oppressed shall speedily be released;
    they shall not die and go down to the Pit,
    nor shall they lack bread.
15 For I am the LORD your God,
    who stirs up the sea so that its waves roar—
    the LORD of hosts is his name.
16 I have put my words in your mouth,
    and hidden you in the shadow of my hand,
stretching out*a* the heavens
    and laying the foundations of the earth,
    and saying to Zion, "You are my people."

17 Rouse yourself, rouse yourself!
    Stand up, O Jerusalem,
you who have drunk at the hand of the LORD
    the cup of his wrath,
who have drunk to the dregs
    the bowl of staggering.
18 There is no one to guide her
    among all the children she has borne;
there is no one to take her by the hand
    among all the children she has brought up.
19 These two things have befallen you
    —who will grieve with you?—
devastation and destruction, famine and
        sword—
    who will comfort you?*b*
20 Your children have fainted,
    they lie at the head of every street
    like an antelope in a net;
they are full of the wrath of the LORD,
    the rebuke of your God.

21 Therefore hear this, you who are wounded,*c*
    who are drunk, but not with wine:
22 Thus says your Sovereign, the LORD,
    your God who pleads the cause of his people:
See, I have taken from your hand the cup of
        staggering;
you shall drink no more
    from the bowl of my wrath.
23 And I will put it into the hand of your
        tormentors,
    who have said to you,
    "Bow down, that we may walk on you";

and you have made your back like the ground
    and like the street for them to walk on.

Let Zion Rejoice

52 Awake, awake,
        put on your strength, O Zion!
Put on your beautiful garments,
    O Jerusalem, the holy city;
for the uncircumcised and the unclean
    shall enter you no more.
2 Shake yourself from the dust, rise up,
    O captive*d* Jerusalem;
loose the bonds from your neck,
    O captive daughter Zion!

3 For thus says the LORD: You were sold for
nothing, and you shall be redeemed without
money. 4For thus says the Lord GOD: Long ago,
my people went down into Egypt to reside there
as aliens; the Assyrian, too, has oppressed them
without cause. 5Now therefore what am I doing
here, says the LORD, seeing that my people are
taken away without cause? Their rulers howl,
says the LORD, and continually, all day long, my
name is despised. 6Therefore my people shall
know my name; therefore in that day they shall
know that it is I who speak; here am I.

7 How beautiful upon the mountains
    are the feet of the messenger who announces
        peace,
who brings good news,
    who announces salvation,
    who says to Zion, "Your God reigns."
8 Listen! Your sentinels lift up their voices,
    together they sing for joy;
for in plain sight they see
    the return of the LORD to Zion.
9 Break forth together into singing,
    you ruins of Jerusalem;
for the LORD has comforted his people,
    he has redeemed Jerusalem.
10 The LORD has bared his holy arm
    before the eyes of all the nations;
and all the ends of the earth shall see
    the salvation of our God.

11 Depart, depart, go out from there!
    Touch no unclean thing;
go out from the midst of it, purify yourselves,
    you who carry the vessels of the LORD.
12 For you shall not go out in haste,
    and you shall not go in flight;

---

a Syr: Heb *planting*   b Q Ms Gk Syr Vg: MT *how may I comfort
you?*   c Or *humbled*   d Cn: Heb *rise up, sit*

for the Lord will go before you,
    and the God of Israel will be your rear guard.

The Suffering Servant

13 See, my servant shall prosper;
    he shall be exalted and lifted up,
    and shall be very high.
14 Just as there were many who were astonished at
    him[a]
      —so marred was his appearance, beyond
      human semblance,
    and his form beyond that of mortals—
15 so he shall startle[b] many nations;
    kings shut their mouths because of him;
for that which had not been told them they
    shall see,
    and that which they had not heard they shall
    contemplate.

53

Who has believed what we have heard?
    And to whom has the arm of the Lord been
    revealed?
2 For he grew up before him like a young plant,
    and like a root out of dry ground;
he had no form or majesty that we should look
    at him,
    nothing in his appearance that we should
    desire him.
3 He was despised and rejected by others;
    a man of suffering[c] and acquainted with
    infirmity;
and as one from whom others hide their faces[d]
    he was despised, and we held him of no
    account.

4 Surely he has borne our infirmities
    and carried our diseases;
yet we accounted him stricken,
    struck down by God, and afflicted.
5 But he was wounded for our transgressions,
    crushed for our iniquities;
upon him was the punishment that made us
    whole,
    and by his bruises we are healed.
6 All we like sheep have gone astray;
    we have all turned to our own way,
and the Lord has laid on him
    the iniquity of us all.

7 He was oppressed, and he was afflicted,
    yet he did not open his mouth;
like a lamb that is led to the slaughter,
    and like a sheep that before its shearers is
    silent,
    so he did not open his mouth.
8 By a perversion of justice he was taken away.
    Who could have imagined his future?

For he was cut off from the land of the living,
    stricken for the transgression of my people.
9 They made his grave with the wicked
    and his tomb[e] with the rich,[f]
although he had done no violence,
    and there was no deceit in his mouth.

10 Yet it was the will of the Lord to crush him with
    pain.[g]
When you make his life an offering for sin,[b]
    he shall see his offspring, and shall prolong
    his days;
through him the will of the Lord shall prosper.
11   Out of his anguish he shall see light;[h]
    he shall find satisfaction through his knowledge.
    The righteous one,[i] my servant, shall make
    many righteous,
    and he shall bear their iniquities.
12 Therefore I will allot him a portion with the
    great,
    and he shall divide the spoil with the strong;
because he poured out himself to death,
    and was numbered with the transgressors;
yet he bore the sin of many,
    and made intercession for the transgressors.

The Eternal Covenant of Peace

54

Sing, O barren one who did not bear;
    burst into song and shout,
    you who have not been in labor!
For the children of the desolate woman will be
    more
    than the children of her that is married, says
    the Lord.
2 Enlarge the site of your tent,
    and let the curtains of your habitations be
    stretched out;
do not hold back; lengthen your cords
    and strengthen your stakes.
3 For you will spread out to the right and to the
    left,
    and your descendants will possess the nations
    and will settle the desolate towns.

4 Do not fear, for you will not be ashamed;
    do not be discouraged, for you will not suffer
    disgrace;
for you will forget the shame of your youth,
    and the disgrace of your widowhood you will
    remember no more.
5 For your Maker is your husband,

---

a Syr Tg: Heb *you*   b Meaning of Heb uncertain   c Or *a man of sorrows*   d Or *as one who hides his face from us*   e Q Ms: MT *and in his death*   f Cn: Heb *with a rich person*   g Or *by disease; meaning of Heb uncertain*   h Q Mss: MT lacks *light*   i Or *and he shall find satisfaction. Through his knowledge, the righteous one*

the LORD of hosts is his name;
the Holy One of Israel is your Redeemer,
the God of the whole earth he is called.
⁶ For the LORD has called you
like a wife forsaken and grieved in spirit,
like the wife of a man's youth when she is cast
off,
says your God.
⁷ For a brief moment I abandoned you,
but with great compassion I will gather you.
⁸ In overflowing wrath for a moment
I hid my face from you,
but with everlasting love I will have compassion
on you,
says the LORD, your Redeemer.

⁹ This is like the days of Noah to me:
Just as I swore that the waters of Noah
would never again go over the earth,
so I have sworn that I will not be angry with you
and will not rebuke you.
¹⁰ For the mountains may depart
and the hills be removed,
but my steadfast love shall not depart from you,
and my covenant of peace shall not be
removed,
says the LORD, who has compassion on you.

¹¹ O afflicted one, storm-tossed, and not
comforted,
I am about to set your stones in antimony,
and lay your foundations with sapphires.ᵃ
¹² I will make your pinnacles of rubies,
your gates of jewels,
and all your wall of precious stones.
¹³ All your children shall be taught by the LORD,
and great shall be the prosperity of your
children.
¹⁴ In righteousness you shall be established;
you shall be far from oppression, for you
shall not fear;
and from terror, for it shall not come near you.
¹⁵ If anyone stirs up strife,
it is not from me;
whoever stirs up strife with you
shall fall because of you.
¹⁶ See it is I who have created the smith
who blows the fire of coals,
and produces a weapon fit for its purpose;
I have also created the ravager to destroy.
¹⁷   No weapon that is fashioned against you shall
prosper,
and you shall confute every tongue that rises
against you in judgment.
This is the heritage of the servants of the LORD
and their vindication from me, says the LORD.

An Invitation to Abundant Life

55 Ho, everyone who thirsts,
come to the waters;
and you that have no money,
come, buy and eat!
Come, buy wine and milk
without money and without price.
² Why do you spend your money for that which is
not bread,
and your labor for that which does not
satisfy?
Listen carefully to me, and eat what is good,
and delight yourselves in rich food.
³ Incline your ear, and come to me;
listen, so that you may live.
I will make with you an everlasting covenant,
my steadfast, sure love for David.
⁴ See, I made him a witness to the peoples,
a leader and commander for the peoples.
⁵ See, you shall call nations that you do not
know,
and nations that do not know you shall run
to you,
because of the LORD your God, the Holy One of
Israel,
for he has glorified you.

⁶ Seek the LORD while he may be found,
call upon him while he is near;
⁷ let the wicked forsake their way,
and the unrighteous their thoughts;
let them return to the LORD, that he may have
mercy on them,
and to our God, for he will abundantly
pardon.
⁸ For my thoughts are not your thoughts,
nor are your ways my ways, says the LORD.
⁹ For as the heavens are higher than the earth,
so are my ways higher than your ways
and my thoughts than your thoughts.
¹⁰ For as the rain and the snow come down from
heaven,
and do not return there until they have
watered the earth,
making it bring forth and sprout,
giving seed to the sower and bread to the
eater,
¹¹ so shall my word be that goes out from my
mouth;
it shall not return to me empty,
but it shall accomplish that which I purpose,
and succeed in the thing for which I sent it.

ᵃ Or lapis lazuli

12 For you shall go out in joy,
    and be led back in peace;
the mountains and the hills before you
    shall burst into song,
    and all the trees of the field shall clap their
        hands.
13 Instead of the thorn shall come up the cypress;
    instead of the brier shall come up the myrtle;
and it shall be to the LORD for a memorial,
    for an everlasting sign that shall not be cut
        off.

The Covenant Extended to All Who Obey

56 Thus says the LORD:
Maintain justice, and do what is right,
for soon my salvation will come,
    and my deliverance be revealed.

2 Happy is the mortal who does this,
    the one who holds it fast,
who keeps the sabbath, not profaning it,
    and refrains from doing any evil.

3 Do not let the foreigner joined to the LORD say,
    "The LORD will surely separate me from his
        people";
and do not let the eunuch say,
    "I am just a dry tree."
4 For thus says the LORD:
To the eunuchs who keep my sabbaths,
    who choose the things that please me
    and hold fast my covenant,
5 I will give, in my house and within my walls,
    a monument and a name
    better than sons and daughters;
I will give them an everlasting name
    that shall not be cut off.

6 And the foreigners who join themselves to the
        LORD,
    to minister to him, to love the name of the
        LORD,
    and to be his servants,
all who keep the sabbath, and do not
    profane it,
    and hold fast my covenant—
7 these I will bring to my holy mountain,
    and make them joyful in my house of prayer;
their burnt offerings and their sacrifices
    will be accepted on my altar;
for my house shall be called a house of prayer
    for all peoples.
8 Thus says the Lord GOD,
    who gathers the outcasts of Israel,
I will gather others to them
    besides those already gathered.[a]

The Optimism of Third Isaiah

The last eleven chapters of Isaiah contain the messages of several prophets known collectively as Third Isaiah. The common element of these prophecies is optimism. They proclaim the hopeful message that God's Covenant will be extended to all nations and that Jerusalem will become God's holy city, the throne of the Eternal King.

Third Isaiah, in contrast to many of the other biblical prophets, proclaims joy as a sign of God's presence. Joy is absent in the lives of many people today, as it was in the time of Isaiah. Let us remember all the wonderful things God has done for us, and we too will find cause for rejoicing!

● When have you experienced true joy in your life?
● Where have you seen the presence of God in your life? in our world?
● How can you help others to experience joy?

▶ Isa 56:1—66:24

The Corruption of Israel's Rulers

9 All you wild animals,
    all you wild animals in the forest, come to
        devour!
10 Israel's[b] sentinels are blind,
    they are all without knowledge;
they are all silent dogs
    that cannot bark;
dreaming, lying down,
    loving to slumber.
11 The dogs have a mighty appetite;
    they never have enough.
The shepherds also have no understanding;
    they have all turned to their own way,
    to their own gain, one and all.
12 "Come," they say, "let us[c] get wine;
    let us fill ourselves with strong drink.
And tomorrow will be like today,
    great beyond measure."

a Heb besides his gathered ones   b Heb His   c Q Ms Syr Vg
Tg: MT me

Israel's Futile Idolatry

57 The righteous perish,
    and no one takes it to heart;
the devout are taken away,
    while no one understands.
For the righteous are taken away from calamity,
2   and they enter into peace;
those who walk uprightly
    will rest on their couches.
3 But as for you, come here,
    you children of a sorceress,
    you offspring of an adulterer and a whore.[a]
4 Whom are you mocking?
    Against whom do you open your mouth wide
    and stick out your tongue?
Are you not children of transgression,
    the offspring of deceit—
5 you that burn with lust among the oaks,
    under every green tree;
you that slaughter your children in the valleys,
    under the clefts of the rocks?
6 Among the smooth stones of the valley is your
        portion;
    they, they, are your lot;
to them you have poured out a drink offering,
    you have brought a grain offering.
    Shall I be appeased for these things?
7 Upon a high and lofty mountain
    you have set your bed,
    and there you went up to offer sacrifice.
8 Behind the door and the doorpost
    you have set up your symbol;
for, in deserting me,[b] you have uncovered your
        bed,
    you have gone up to it,
    you have made it wide;
and you have made a bargain for yourself with
        them,
    you have loved their bed,
    you have gazed on their nakedness.[c]
9 You journeyed to Molech[d] with oil,
    and multiplied your perfumes;
you sent your envoys far away,
    and sent down even to Sheol.
10 You grew weary from your many wanderings,
    but you did not say, "It is useless."
You found your desire rekindled,
    and so you did not weaken.

11 Whom did you dread and fear
    so that you lied,
and did not remember me
    or give me a thought?
Have I not kept silent and closed my eyes,[e]
    and so you do not fear me?

12 I will concede your righteousness and your
        works,
    but they will not help you.
13 When you cry out, let your collection of idols
        deliver you!
    The wind will carry them off,
    a breath will take them away.
But whoever takes refuge in me shall possess the
        land
    and inherit my holy mountain.

A Promise of Help and Healing

14 It shall be said,
"Build up, build up, prepare the way,
    remove every obstruction from my people's
        way."
15 For thus says the high and lofty one
    who inhabits eternity, whose name is Holy:
I dwell in the high and holy place,
    and also with those who are contrite and
        humble in spirit,
to revive the spirit of the humble,
    and to revive the heart of the contrite.
16 For I will not continually accuse,
    nor will I always be angry;
for then the spirits would grow faint before me,
    even the souls that I have made.
17 Because of their wicked covetousness I was
        angry;
    I struck them, I hid and was angry;
    but they kept turning back to their own ways.
18 I have seen their ways, but I will heal them;
    I will lead them and repay them with comfort,
    creating for their mourners the fruit of the
        lips.[b]
19 Peace, peace, to the far and the near, says the
        Lord;
    and I will heal them.
20 But the wicked are like the tossing sea
    that cannot keep still;
    its waters toss up mire and mud.
21 There is no peace, says my God, for the wicked.

False and True Worship

58 Shout out, do not hold back!
    Lift up your voice like a trumpet!
Announce to my people their rebellion,
    to the house of Jacob their sins.
2 Yet day after day they seek me
    and delight to know my ways,
as if they were a nation that practiced
        righteousness

---

a Heb *an adulterer and she plays the whore*   b Meaning of Heb
uncertain   c Or *their phallus;* Heb *the hand*   d Or *the king*
e Gk Vg: Heb *silent even for a long time*

Catholic Connection

The Corporal and Spiritual Works of Mercy

Have you ever done something just to get others to notice you? The Israelites were apparently performing pious acts to get God's attention and complained when God did not notice when they fasted or humbled themselves. In response, God points out that when they fast, they do it for self-serving reasons and commit numerous sins in the process. God then explains what true fasting, or worship, looks like. True worship involves not serving yourself, but serving others. Only then will one's prayers and deeds be answered and blessed by God.

The acts of serving others mentioned in Isaiah form the basis for what the Church calls the corporal and spiritual works of mercy. These works of mercy are founded on God's call for justice and self sacrifice. They are best exemplified in Jesus' command to love one's neighbor and most vividly portrayed in his description of the Final Judgment (see Mt 25:31–46).

The corporal works of mercy focus on addressing the physical needs of others. The word *corporal* actually comes from the Latin word *corpus,* which means *body.* These works include helping the injured, freeing the oppressed, feeding the hungry, clothing the naked, and giving shelter to the homeless. Through all of these acts, we honor God by showing respect for every human being that God created.

The spiritual works of mercy focus on addressing the spiritual needs of others. These works include teaching others about the faith, giving advice, forgiving others, and comforting those who are mourning. Through all these acts, we honor God by being an example of God's love to someone else during an important time in her or his life.

The corporal and spiritual works of mercy will not only help others, but they can also build us up as individuals. Try reading this passage from Isaiah every morning for a week and look for ways that you can live out various works of mercy each day. By focusing on the needs of others, we can learn about Christ's sacrificial love and also find notice and favor with God.

▶ **Isa 58:1–9**
Catechism, nos. 2443–2449

Cultural Connection

"If You Want Peace, Work for Justice"

"If you want peace, work for justice" is a famous quote of Pope Paul VI. We hear a similar message in Isaiah 56:1, and 58:6–14 gives us clear examples of works that create justice and peace.

At the core of justice is the understanding that life—all life—is precious. All people are to be honored, protected, and celebrated. Ensuring that this happens is our responsibility, even when it seems to be a burden. The following prayer by a worker of Peace Market in Korea reflects this passion:

*Make us keep the sputtering lantern burning
and not to break a wounded reed.
Make us understand
the secret of eternal life
from the pulse of blood in our veins
and realise the worth of a life
from the movement of a warm heart.
Make us not discriminate
the rich and the poor,
the high and the low,
the learned and the ignorant
those we know well and those we do not know.
Oh!*

*A human life can't be exchanged for the whole world
this supreme task of keeping the lives
of the sons and daughters of God.
Let us realise how lovely it is
to feel the burdens of responsibility.*

("Our Prayer,"
Your Will Be Done)

 **Isa 58:6–14**

---

and did not forsake the ordinance of their
        God;
they ask of me righteous judgments,
        they delight to draw near to God.
³ "Why do we fast, but you do not see?
        Why humble ourselves, but you do not
                notice?"
Look, you serve your own interest on your fast
        day,
        and oppress all your workers.
⁴ Look, you fast only to quarrel and to fight
        and to strike with a wicked fist.
Such fasting as you do today
        will not make your voice heard on high.
⁵ Is such the fast that I choose,
        a day to humble oneself?
Is it to bow down the head like a bulrush,
        and to lie in sackcloth and ashes?
Will you call this a fast,
        a day acceptable to the Lord?
⁶ Is not this the fast that I choose:
        to loose the bonds of injustice,
        to undo the thongs of the yoke,
to let the oppressed go free,
        and to break every yoke?
⁷ Is it not to share your bread with the hungry,
        and bring the homeless poor into your house;
when you see the naked, to cover them,
        and not to hide yourself from your own kin?
⁸ Then your light shall break forth like the dawn,
        and your healing shall spring up quickly;

your vindicator[a] shall go before you,
        the glory of the Lord shall be your rear guard.
⁹ Then you shall call, and the Lord will answer;
        you shall cry for help, and he will say,
                Here I am.

If you remove the yoke from among you,
        the pointing of the finger, the speaking of
                evil,
¹⁰ if you offer your food to the hungry
        and satisfy the needs of the afflicted,
then your light shall rise in the darkness
        and your gloom be like the noonday.
¹¹ The Lord will guide you continually,
        and satisfy your needs in parched places,
        and make your bones strong;
and you shall be like a watered garden,
        like a spring of water,
        whose waters never fail.
¹² Your ancient ruins shall be rebuilt;
        you shall raise up the foundations of many
                generations;
you shall be called the repairer of the breach,
        the restorer of streets to live in.

¹³ If you refrain from trampling the sabbath,
        from pursuing your own interests on my holy
                day;
        if you call the sabbath a delight

---

a Or vindication

and the holy day of the Lord honorable;
if you honor it, not going your own ways,
     serving your own interests, or pursuing your
     own affairs;[a]
14 then you shall take delight in the Lord,
     and I will make you ride upon the heights of
     the earth;
I will feed you with the heritage of your ancestor
     Jacob,
     for the mouth of the Lord has spoken.

Injustice and Oppression to Be Punished

59 See, the Lord's hand is not too short to
     save,
     nor his ear too dull to hear.
2 Rather, your iniquities have been barriers
     between you and your God,
and your sins have hidden his face from you
     so that he does not hear.
3 For your hands are defiled with blood,
     and your fingers with iniquity;
your lips have spoken lies,
     your tongue mutters wickedness.
4 No one brings suit justly,
     no one goes to law honestly;
they rely on empty pleas, they speak lies,
     conceiving mischief and begetting iniquity.
5 They hatch adders' eggs,
     and weave the spider's web;
whoever eats their eggs dies,
     and the crushed egg hatches out a viper.
6 Their webs cannot serve as clothing;
     they cannot cover themselves with what they
     make.
Their works are works of iniquity,
     and deeds of violence are in their hands.
7 Their feet run to evil,
     and they rush to shed innocent blood;
their thoughts are thoughts of iniquity,
     desolation and destruction are in their
     highways.
8 The way of peace they do not know,
     and there is no justice in their paths.
Their roads they have made crooked;
     no one who walks in them knows peace.

9 Therefore justice is far from us,
     and righteousness does not reach us;
we wait for light, and lo! there is darkness;
     and for brightness, but we walk in gloom.
10 We grope like the blind along a wall,
     groping like those who have no eyes;
we stumble at noon as in the twilight,
     among the vigorous[b] as though we were dead.
11 We all growl like bears;
     like doves we moan mournfully.

We wait for justice, but there is none;
     for salvation, but it is far from us.
12 For our transgressions before you are many,
     and our sins testify against us.
Our transgressions indeed are with us,
     and we know our iniquities:
13 transgressing, and denying the Lord,
     and turning away from following our God,
talking oppression and revolt,
     conceiving lying words and uttering them
     from the heart.
14 Justice is turned back,
     and righteousness stands at a distance;
for truth stumbles in the public square,
     and uprightness cannot enter.
15 Truth is lacking,
     and whoever turns from evil is despoiled.

The Lord saw it, and it displeased him
     that there was no justice.
16 He saw that there was no one,
     and was appalled that there was no one to
          intervene;
so his own arm brought him victory,
     and his righteousness upheld him.
17 He put on righteousness like a breastplate,
     and a helmet of salvation on his head;
he put on garments of vengeance for clothing,
     and wrapped himself in fury as in a mantle.
18 According to their deeds, so will he repay;
     wrath to his adversaries, requital to his enemies;
     to the coastlands he will render requital.
19 So those in the west shall fear the name of the
     Lord,
     and those in the east, his glory;
for he will come like a pent-up stream
     that the wind of the Lord drives on.

20 And he will come to Zion as Redeemer,
     to those in Jacob who turn from
          transgression, says the Lord.
21 And as for me, this is my covenant with them,
says the Lord: my spirit that is upon you, and my
words that I have put in your mouth, shall not
depart out of your mouth, or out of the mouths
of your children, or out of the mouths of your
children's children, says the Lord, from now on
and forever.

The Ingathering of the Dispersed

60 Arise, shine; for your light has come,
     and the glory of the Lord has risen upon
     you.

---

a Heb *or speaking words*   b Meaning of Heb uncertain

2 For darkness shall cover the earth,
  and thick darkness the peoples;
but the LORD will arise upon you,
  and his glory will appear over you.
3 Nations shall come to your light,
  and kings to the brightness of your dawn.

4 Lift up your eyes and look around;
  they all gather together, they come to you;
your sons shall come from far away,
  and your daughters shall be carried on their
    nurses' arms.
5 Then you shall see and be radiant;
  your heart shall thrill and rejoice,[a]
because the abundance of the sea shall be
    brought to you,
  the wealth of the nations shall come to you.
6 A multitude of camels shall cover you,
  the young camels of Midian and Ephah;
all those from Sheba shall come.
They shall bring gold and frankincense,
  and shall proclaim the praise of the LORD.
7 All the flocks of Kedar shall be gathered to you,
  the rams of Nebaioth shall minister to you;
they shall be acceptable on my altar,
  and I will glorify my glorious house.

8 Who are these that fly like a cloud,
  and like doves to their windows?
9 For the coastlands shall wait for me,
  the ships of Tarshish first,
to bring your children from far away,
  their silver and gold with them,
for the name of the LORD your God,
  and for the Holy One of Israel,
  because he has glorified you.

10 Foreigners shall build up your walls,
  and their kings shall minister to you;
for in my wrath I struck you down,
  but in my favor I have had mercy on you.
11 Your gates shall always be open;
  day and night they shall not be shut,
so that nations shall bring you their wealth,
  with their kings led in procession.
12 For the nation and kingdom
  that will not serve you shall perish;
  those nations shall be utterly laid waste.
13 The glory of Lebanon shall come to you,
  the cypress, the plane, and the pine,
to beautify the place of my sanctuary;
  and I will glorify where my feet rest.
14 The descendants of those who oppressed you
  shall come bending low to you,
and all who despised you
  shall bow down at your feet;
they shall call you the City of the LORD,

the Zion of the Holy One of Israel.
15 Whereas you have been forsaken and hated,
  with no one passing through,
I will make you majestic forever,
  a joy from age to age.
16 You shall suck the milk of nations,
  you shall suck the breasts of kings;
and you shall know that I, the LORD, am your
    Savior
  and your Redeemer, the Mighty One of Jacob.

17 Instead of bronze I will bring gold,
  instead of iron I will bring silver;
instead of wood, bronze,
  instead of stones, iron.
I will appoint Peace as your overseer
  and Righteousness as your taskmaster.
18 Violence shall no more be heard in your land,
  devastation or destruction within your
    borders;
you shall call your walls Salvation,
  and your gates Praise.

God the Glory of Zion

19 The sun shall no longer be
  your light by day,
nor for brightness shall the moon
  give light to you by night;[b]
but the LORD will be your everlasting light,
  and your God will be your glory.
20 Your sun shall no more go down,
  or your moon withdraw itself;
for the LORD will be your everlasting light,
  and your days of mourning shall be ended.
21 Your people shall all be righteous;
  they shall possess the land forever.
They are the shoot that I planted, the work of
    my hands,
  so that I might be glorified.
22 The least of them shall become a clan,
  and the smallest one a mighty nation;
I am the LORD;
  in its time I will accomplish it quickly.

The Good News of Deliverance

61 The spirit of the Lord GOD is upon me,
  because the LORD has anointed me;
he has sent me to bring good news to the
    oppressed,
  to bind up the brokenhearted,
to proclaim liberty to the captives,
  and release to the prisoners;
2 to proclaim the year of the LORD's favor,
  and the day of vengeance of our God;

---

a Heb *be enlarged*   b Q Ms Gk Old Latin Tg: MT lacks *by night*

to comfort all who mourn;
³ to provide for those who mourn in Zion—
to give them a garland instead of ashes,
the oil of gladness instead of mourning,
the mantle of praise instead of a faint spirit.
They will be called oaks of righteousness,
the planting of the LORD, to display his glory.
⁴ They shall build up the ancient ruins,
they shall raise up the former devastations;
they shall repair the ruined cities,
the devastations of many generations.

⁵ Strangers shall stand and feed your flocks,
foreigners shall till your land and dress your
vines;
⁶ but you shall be called priests of the LORD,
you shall be named ministers of our God;
you shall enjoy the wealth of the nations,
and in their riches you shall glory.
⁷ Because their*a* shame was double,
and dishonor was proclaimed as their lot,
therefore they shall possess a double portion;
everlasting joy shall be theirs.

⁸ For I the LORD love justice,
I hate robbery and wrongdoing;*b*
I will faithfully give them their recompense,
and I will make an everlasting covenant with
them.
⁹ Their descendants shall be known among the
nations,
and their offspring among the peoples;
all who see them shall acknowledge
that they are a people whom the LORD has
blessed.
¹⁰ I will greatly rejoice in the LORD,
my whole being shall exult in my God;
for he has clothed me with the garments of
salvation,
he has covered me with the robe of
righteousness,
as a bridegroom decks himself with a garland,
and as a bride adorns herself with her jewels.
¹¹ For as the earth brings forth its shoots,
and as a garden causes what is sown in it to
spring up,
so the Lord GOD will cause righteousness and
praise
to spring up before all the nations.

The Vindication and Salvation of Zion

62 For Zion's sake I will not keep silent,
and for Jerusalem's sake I will not rest,
until her vindication shines out like the dawn,
and her salvation like a burning torch.
² The nations shall see your vindication,

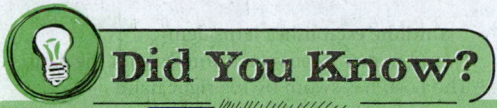

Did You Know?

Bride and Bridegroom

In ancient Israel, the bride and bridegroom gradually became a metaphor, or symbol, for the relation between Israel and God as pictured in Isaiah 61:10 and 62:5. In these passages, Israel is the bride, and God is the faithful bridegroom, who loves her, lavishes her with blessings, and continues to be faithful to her. When Israel strays from the covenant or goes after foreign gods, she is compared to an unfaithful lover, even a prostitute who pursues other partners (for a graphic example, see Ezek 16:1–43). The prophet Hosea even marries a prostitute as a living example of God's faithfulness (see Hos 1:2)! The wonder of God's love is that through all of Israel's infidelity (and ours), God always remains willing to take her (and us) back.

▶ **Isa 61:10**

and all the kings your glory;
and you shall be called by a new name
that the mouth of the LORD will give.
³ You shall be a crown of beauty in the hand of
the LORD,
and a royal diadem in the hand of your God.
⁴ You shall no more be termed Forsaken,*c*
and your land shall no more be termed
Desolate;*d*
but you shall be called My Delight Is in Her,*e*
and your land Married;*f*
for the LORD delights in you,
and your land shall be married.
⁵ For as a young man marries a young woman,
so shall your builder*g* marry you,
and as the bridegroom rejoices over the bride,
so shall your God rejoice over you.
⁶ Upon your walls, O Jerusalem,
I have posted sentinels;
all day and all night
they shall never be silent.
You who remind the LORD,
take no rest,
⁷ and give him no rest

a Heb *your*   b Or *robbery with a burnt offering*   c Heb *Azubah*
d Heb *Shemamah*   e Heb *Hephzibah*   f Heb *Beulah*
g Cn: Heb *your sons*

until he establishes Jerusalem
  and makes it renowned throughout the earth.
8 The Lord has sworn by his right hand
  and by his mighty arm:
I will not again give your grain
  to be food for your enemies,
and foreigners shall not drink the wine
  for which you have labored;
9 but those who garner it shall eat it
  and praise the Lord,
and those who gather it shall drink it
  in my holy courts.

10 Go through, go through the gates,
  prepare the way for the people;
build up, build up the highway,
  clear it of stones,
  lift up an ensign over the peoples.
11 The Lord has proclaimed
  to the end of the earth:
Say to daughter Zion,
  "See, your salvation comes;
his reward is with him,
  and his recompense before him."
12 They shall be called, "The Holy People,
  The Redeemed of the Lord";
and you shall be called, "Sought Out,
  A City Not Forsaken."

Vengeance on Edom

63 "Who is this that comes from Edom,
  from Bozrah in garments stained crimson?
Who is this so splendidly robed,
  marching in his great might?"

  "It is I, announcing vindication,
    mighty to save."

2 "Why are your robes red,
  and your garments like theirs who tread the
    wine press?"

3 "I have trodden the wine press alone,
  and from the peoples no one was with me;
I trod them in my anger
  and trampled them in my wrath;
their juice spattered on my garments,
  and stained all my robes.
4 For the day of vengeance was in my heart,
  and the year for my redeeming work had
    come.
5 I looked, but there was no helper;
  I stared, but there was no one to sustain me;
so my own arm brought me victory,
  and my wrath sustained me.
6 I trampled down peoples in my anger,

I crushed them in my wrath,
  and I poured out their lifeblood on the
    earth."

God's Mercy Remembered

7 I will recount the gracious deeds of the Lord,
  the praiseworthy acts of the Lord,
because of all that the Lord has done for us,
  and the great favor to the house of Israel
that he has shown them according to his mercy,
  according to the abundance of his steadfast
    love.
8 For he said, "Surely they are my people,
  children who will not deal falsely";
and he became their savior
9   in all their distress.
It was no messenger[a] or angel
  but his presence that saved them;[b]
in his love and in his pity he redeemed them;
  he lifted them up and carried them all the
    days of old.

10 But they rebelled
  and grieved his holy spirit;
therefore he became their enemy;
  he himself fought against them.
11 Then they[c] remembered the days of old,
  of Moses his servant.[d]
Where is the one who brought them up out of
    the sea
  with the shepherds of his flock?
Where is the one who put within them
  his holy spirit,
12 who caused his glorious arm
  to march at the right hand of Moses,
who divided the waters before them
  to make for himself an everlasting name,
13   who led them through the depths?
Like a horse in the desert,
  they did not stumble.
14 Like cattle that go down into the valley,
  the spirit of the Lord gave them rest.
Thus you led your people,
  to make for yourself a glorious name.

A Prayer of Penitence

15 Look down from heaven and see,
  from your holy and glorious habitation.
Where are your zeal and your might?
  The yearning of your heart and your
    compassion?
  They are withheld from me.

a Gk: Heb anguish   b Or savior. 9In all their distress he was distressed; the angel of his presence saved them;   c Heb he
d Cn: Heb his people

Living Biblical Principles

"Today too there is a need for disciples of Christ who give unstintingly of their time and energy to serve the Gospel. There is a need for young people who will allow God's love to burn within them and who will respond generously to his urgent call, just as many young blesseds and saints did in the past and also in more recent times."

Pope Benedict XVI, Message for WYD, 2008

How does one follow the road of discipleship today? What special principles and values must a follower of Jesus Christ take on in order to have God's love burn within them so brightly that others will actually see the light? The best answer of course is found in the Scriptures, mainly in the Gospels, specifically through the words and deeds of Jesus himself. This is where the saints of yesterday and today began and it's where all young disciples should also start. And while there are many admirable qualities, principles, and attributes that can be gleaned from the Gospels, here are six that will serve as a solid foundation for would-be followers of Jesus to begin to build their lives around:

- See God in Everything
- Trust in God Always
- Stand Up for the Poor and Vulnerable
- Be Courageous
- Serve Humbly
- Share the Faith

Stand Up for the Poor and Vulnerable

Who are the poor and vulnerable? They are all around us, not just the poverty-stricken or worn-torn faces staring back at us from the flat-screen TV. They are the marginalized, those who live on the edge of society—including the homeless, the poor, the ill, and the isolated. They include the outcast, the weak, those who are put down, and those forced to the lower rungs of the social ladder. They are the vulnerable, the ones we are taught to hurry past and look away from. But in the dictionary of discipleship "they" also are our brothers and sisters, our family, and we are required by faith to reach out to them—not with a meaningless hand out, but with a comforting and empowering hand up so they can live a life marked by respect, dignity, and hope.

© 2010 Saint Mary's Press/Illustration by Vicki Shuck

Climbing Down the Ladder of Success

Elizabeth Ann Seton (1774–1821) began life in luxury and wealth, and then gained more wealth through marriage. But the money and status did not fulfill her. After her husband's death, Elizabeth was drawn to the Catholic Church, especially the Eucharist, and converted to Catholicism, which caused Elizabeth's society friends and family to turn their backs on her. In order to support herself and her family, Elizabeth opened up a school for boys. Eventually, this led to the establishment of the Sisters of Charity of Saint Joseph whose mission was to educate children, especially poor girls who did not have schools to attend. Elizabeth is the patron saint of Catholic schools and the first American-born saint.

> Truly I tell you, just as you did it to one of the least of these who are members of my family, you did it to me.
>
> — Mt 25:40

Be Courageous

Young people are often excellent risk takers, and taking risks requires courage. Though some of these risky actions are seen in a negative light, there are other risks that often serve to bring light to others. Befriending an isolated student, speaking out against unjust practices, confronting discrimination, or standing up to those who abuse the environment are not always the easiest things for someone to do. Yet, young people are often found leading the way. Catholic tradition celebrates risk takers—people who have given up their comfort, their lifestyle, and sometimes their very lives to proclaim their faith. These courageous risk takers are called saints, and their lives challenge and inspire others to live out that same courageous faith.

The Seven-Million-Dollar Decision

© 2010 Saint Mary's Press/Illustration by Vicki Shuck

When Katharine Drexel (1858–1955), the daughter of a wealthy Philadelphia banker, decided to heed Pope Leo XIII's challenge to become a missionary to the Native Americans and African Americans in 1889, the newspaper headlines declared that she "[Gave] Up Seven Million!" The headline illustrates just how much Katherine was willing to risk to answer that challenge. Katharine's risky and courageous decision helped to provide education, needed services, and ultimately dignity to people experiencing the most discrimination in America. Katharine helped to create over a hundred schools and missions to serve these disadvantaged groups, and her courageous and loving vision of service continues to this day through the Sisters of the Blessed Sacrament, the religious order she founded.

> Stand firm in the your faith,
>   be courageous, be strong.
>   Let all that you do be done in love.
>
> — 1 Cor 16:13–14

Serve Humbly

Think of the most faith-filled person you know. Chances are, she or he is one of the most humble individuals you can name. It's no mistake that humility and faith go hand in hand. Humble people proclaim through their actions and words, "It's not about me!" Indeed, living our faith as disciples of Jesus Christ requires that we place God first, so that our deeds point to God and not to ourselves. Living our faith humbly does not mean we must be quiet about what we believe; it simply means that we let the light of God's love and grace shine through us to others, choosing to be a window to God's presence, not a wall to oneself.

© 2010 Saint Mary's Press/Illustration by Vicki Shuck

Falling into Grace

Imagine the person from school who was voted "Most Popular" or "Most Likely to Party" shaving his or her head and wearing simple used clothing while wandering the streets and hanging out with the outcasts, the sick, and the isolated. Many people would be saddened and shocked by such a loss of power, influence, wealth, and fame—a societal "fall from grace." But to Francis of Assisi, this was a fall into grace. Francis literally turned his back on the sought-after life he had known in order to fully embrace the message of the gospel. His turn toward humility proved to be an attractive beacon of light, and others sought him out, wanting to know for themselves the inner light and faith that reflected from within him.

"So if I, your Lord and Teacher, have washed your feet, you also ought to wash one another's feet. For I have set you an example, that you also should do as I have done to you."

— Jn 13:14–15

Share the Faith

It is one thing to know the faith, another to live the faith, and yet another to share the faith. Disciples of Jesus Christ are called to do all three. A faith that is alive, that echoes the reason for its being, is one that is meant to be passed along so others may be transformed by the God who is at the center of it all. But a faith that is challenging and demands much is not a faith that is easily shared. Today, people want a nice, convenient faith, something that allows them to live their lives undisturbed and unencumbered. So to share this total, radical, and world-changing faith that Jesus lived, died, and rose for is not the easiest of assignments; it is one that requires much resolve, integrity, and commitment.

Spreading the Good News

Blessed Junipero Serra (1713–1784) was a Franciscan priest who was a creative and convincing evangelizer. Junipero shared his faith so effectively through both word and deed that he baptized nearly six thousand people whose hearts were touched by his message. Many of these he met while establishing missions throughout Mexico and California as he promoted the gospel message as well as the dignity of the people he came to serve. Today, the Serra Club, a Catholic organization dedicated to promoting vocations to the priesthood, bears his name.

© 2010 Saint Mary's Press/Illustration by Vicki Shuck

"Proclaim the message; be persistent whether the time is favorable or unfavorable; convince, rebuke, and encourage with the utmost patience in teaching. For the time is coming when people will not put up with sound doctrine, but having itching ears, they will accumulate for themselves teachers to suit their own desires, and will turn away from listening to the truth and wander away to myths. As for you, always be sober, endure suffering, do the work of an evangelist, carry out your ministry fully."

— 2 Tim 4:2–5

Seven Significant Themes of Catholic Social Teaching

Living out the six biblical principles requires that we do so while respecting the dignity and worth of all people. The Catholic faith has much to say about being people of justice and peace. Here are seven significant themes that summarize much of Catholic social teaching, which is rooted in the Scriptures and Tradition and should be woven into the biblical principles that every disciple lives by:

Life and Dignity of the Human Person
At the root of justice is the belief in the dignity and worth of all people. Every person, every life, is precious. People are more important than things. (See articles on pages 12, 650,1108,1195.)

Call to Family, Community, and Participation
The family is sacred and must be supported and strengthened. Much of this strength comes from being an active part of one's community where we can work together for the common good and well-being of all, especially those who are poor and vulnerable. (See articles on pages 238, 1224, 1281, 1402.)

Rights and Responsibilities
Each person has a responsibility to help protect for all people the basic rights required for human decency, including the right to life. (See articles on pages 461, 838, 1068, 1146.)

Option for the Poor and Vulnerable
The Gospel call of Jesus Christ challenges us to place the needs of the poor and vulnerable first, even above our own comforts and wants. (See articles on pages 88,1053, 1113, 1449.)

The Dignity of Work and the Rights of Workers
Every person has a right to work and earn a living. By honoring fair wages, we assist people in being active participants in God's ongoing work of creation through honest and meaningful employment. (See articles on pages 68, 750,1137,1165.)

Solidarity
As members of a global family, we are all connected by an intricate web of life, whatever our national, racial, ethnic, economic, and ideological differences. This interconnectedness requires us to live together, united as brothers and sisters, in relationships that are marked by peace, love, and reconciliation instead of war, hatred, and mistrust. (See articles on pages 269, 505, 1207, 1380.)

Care for God's Creation
Care for the earth is a requirement of our faith. We are called to live our faith in relationship with all of God's creation, protecting both people and planet. (See articles on pages 7, 663,689,1057.)

16 For you are our father,
   though Abraham does not know us
   and Israel does not acknowledge us;
you, O Lᴏʀᴅ, are our father;
   our Redeemer from of old is your name.
17 Why, O Lᴏʀᴅ, do you make us stray from your
      ways
   and harden our heart, so that we do not fear
      you?
Turn back for the sake of your servants,
   for the sake of the tribes that are your
      heritage.
18 Your holy people took possession for a little
      while;
   but now our adversaries have trampled down
      your sanctuary.
19 We have long been like those whom you do not
      rule,
   like those not called by your name.

64 O that you would tear open the heavens
      and come down,
   so that the mountains would quake at your
      presence—
2 ᵃ as when fire kindles brushwood
   and the fire causes water to boil—
to make your name known to your adversaries,
   so that the nations might tremble at your
      presence!
3 When you did awesome deeds that we did not
      expect,
   you came down, the mountains quaked at
      your presence.
4 From ages past no one has heard,
   no ear has perceived,
no eye has seen any God besides you,
   who works for those who wait for him.
5 You meet those who gladly do right,
   those who remember you in your ways.
But you were angry, and we sinned;
   because you hid yourself we transgressed.ᵇ
6 We have all become like one who is unclean,
   and all our righteous deeds are like a filthy
      cloth.
We all fade like a leaf,
   and our iniquities, like the wind, take us
      away.
7 There is no one who calls on your name,
   or attempts to take hold of you;
for you have hidden your face from us,
   and have deliveredᶜ us into the hand of our
      iniquity.
8 Yet, O Lᴏʀᴅ, you are our Father;
   we are the clay, and you are our potter;
   we are all the work of your hand.
9 Do not be exceedingly angry, O Lᴏʀᴅ,

Pray It!

The Master Potter

Have you ever seen a potter at work? Perhaps you have even made pottery yourself. Pottery-making is still practiced today much as it was at the time of Third Isaiah: The potter takes a lump of moist clay and begins to shape it by hand, with an image in mind of what the finished product will look like. The artisan then puts the piece of clay on a potter's wheel and spins the wheel, continuing to form the pot with his or her hands. Because it is designed by hand, rather than mass-produced by machine, each work of the potter is original; there is no other just like it.

The image of God as a potter and each of us as a clay pot reminds us of the second Creation story, where God scoops up clay from the earth and forms the first human being and breathes life into the being (see Gen 2:7). It also reminds us of the description in Psalm 139 of our being knit together in our mother's womb.

The idea of God's hands shaping us like clay is intimate and comforting. No one but the potter knows how much time and love went into the fashioning of a particular pot. The potter gives each pot its own special design and markings. The potter also knows its flaws. The potter and the pot share a bond that seems much like the one between each of us and God. Isaiah 64:8 indeed gives us a vivid and beautiful image for God's relationship with each of us (see also Jer 18:1–6).

In your prayer, reflect or journal on the following questions:
● How has God molded you as a unique person?
● What are your special features and markings (gifts), and what are your flaws (weaknesses)?
● How is God still molding you?

▶ Isa 64:8

ᵃ Ch 64.1 in Heb   ᵇ Meaning of Heb uncertain   ᶜ Gk Syr Old
Latin Tg: Heb *melted*

ISA

and do not remember iniquity forever.
Now consider, we are all your people.

10 Your holy cities have become a wilderness,
Zion has become a wilderness,
Jerusalem a desolation.
11 Our holy and beautiful house,
where our ancestors praised you,
has been burned by fire,
and all our pleasant places have become
ruins.
12 After all this, will you restrain yourself, O Lord?
Will you keep silent, and punish us so
severely?

The Righteousness of God's Judgment

65 I was ready to be sought out by those who
did not ask,
to be found by those who did not seek me.
I said, "Here I am, here I am,"
to a nation that did not call on my name.
2 I held out my hands all day long
to a rebellious people,
who walk in a way that is not good,
following their own devices;
3 a people who provoke me
to my face continually,
sacrificing in gardens
and offering incense on bricks;
4 who sit inside tombs,
and spend the night in secret places;
who eat swine's flesh,
with broth of abominable things in their
vessels;
5 who say, "Keep to yourself,
do not come near me, for I am too holy for
you."
These are a smoke in my nostrils,
a fire that burns all day long.
6 See, it is written before me:
I will not keep silent, but I will repay;
I will indeed repay into their laps
7 their*a* iniquities and their*a* ancestors' iniquities
together,
says the Lord;
because they offered incense on the mountains
and reviled me on the hills,
I will measure into their laps
full payment for their actions.
8 Thus says the Lord:
As the wine is found in the cluster,
and they say, "Do not destroy it,
for there is a blessing in it,"
so I will do for my servants' sake,
and not destroy them all.
9 I will bring forth descendants*b* from Jacob,
and from Judah inheritors*c* of my mountains;

my chosen shall inherit it,
and my servants shall settle there.
10 Sharon shall become a pasture for flocks,
and the Valley of Achor a place for herds to
lie down,
for my people who have sought me.
11 But you who forsake the Lord,
who forget my holy mountain,
who set a table for Fortune
and fill cups of mixed wine for Destiny;
12 I will destine you to the sword,
and all of you shall bow down to the
slaughter;
because, when I called, you did not answer,
when I spoke, you did not listen,
but you did what was evil in my sight,
and chose what I did not delight in.
13 Therefore thus says the Lord God:
My servants shall eat,
but you shall be hungry;
my servants shall drink,
but you shall be thirsty;
my servants shall rejoice,
but you shall be put to shame;
14 my servants shall sing for gladness of heart,
but you shall cry out for pain of heart,
and shall wail for anguish of spirit.
15 You shall leave your name to my chosen to use
as a curse,
and the Lord God will put you to death;
but to his servants he will give a different
name.
16 Then whoever invokes a blessing in the land
shall bless by the God of faithfulness,
and whoever takes an oath in the land
shall swear by the God of faithfulness;
because the former troubles are forgotten
and are hidden from my sight.

The Glorious New Creation

17 For I am about to create new heavens
and a new earth;
the former things shall not be remembered
or come to mind.
18 But be glad and rejoice forever
in what I am creating;
for I am about to create Jerusalem as a joy,
and its people as a delight.
19 I will rejoice in Jerusalem,
and delight in my people;
no more shall the sound of weeping be heard
in it,
or the cry of distress.
20 No more shall there be in it

---

a Gk Syr: Heb *your*   *b* Or *a descendant*   *c* Or *an inheritor*

an infant that lives but a few days,
  or an old person who does not live out a
    lifetime;
for one who dies at a hundred years will be
  considered a youth,
  and one who falls short of a hundred will be
    considered accursed.
21 They shall build houses and inhabit them;
  they shall plant vineyards and eat their fruit.
22 They shall not build and another inhabit;
  they shall not plant and another eat;
for like the days of a tree shall the days of my
  people be,
  and my chosen shall long enjoy the work of
    their hands.
23 They shall not labor in vain,
  or bear children for calamity;[a]
for they shall be offspring blessed by the LORD—
  and their descendants as well.
24 Before they call I will answer,
  while they are yet speaking I will hear.
25 The wolf and the lamb shall feed together,
  the lion shall eat straw like the ox;
  but the serpent—its food shall be dust!
They shall not hurt or destroy
  on all my holy mountain,
                says the LORD.

The Worship God Demands

66 Thus says the LORD:
  Heaven is my throne
  and the earth is my footstool;
what is the house that you would build for me,
  and what is my resting place?
2 All these things my hand has made,
  and so all these things are mine,[b]
                says the LORD.
But this is the one to whom I will look,
  to the humble and contrite in spirit,
  who trembles at my word.

3 Whoever slaughters an ox is like one who kills a
  human being;
  whoever sacrifices a lamb, like one who
    breaks a dog's neck;
whoever presents a grain offering, like one who
  offers swine's blood;[c]
  whoever makes a memorial offering of
  frankincense, like one who blesses an
  idol.
These have chosen their own ways,
  and in their abominations they take delight;
4 I also will choose to mock[d] them,
  and bring upon them what they fear;
because, when I called, no one answered,
  when I spoke, they did not listen;

but they did what was evil in my sight,
  and chose what did not please me.

The LORD Vindicates Zion

5 Hear the word of the LORD,
  you who tremble at his word:
Your own people who hate you
  and reject you for my name's sake
have said, "Let the LORD be glorified,
  so that we may see your joy";
  but it is they who shall be put to shame.

6 Listen, an uproar from the city!
  A voice from the temple!
The voice of the LORD,
  dealing retribution to his enemies!

7 Before she was in labor
  she gave birth;
before her pain came upon her
  she delivered a son.
8 Who has heard of such a thing?
  Who has seen such things?
Shall a land be born in one day?
  Shall a nation be delivered in one moment?
Yet as soon as Zion was in labor
  she delivered her children.

---

a Or *sudden terror* b Gk Syr: Heb *these things came to be*
c Meaning of Heb uncertain d Or *to punish*

66:1

9 Shall I open the womb and not deliver?
   says the LORD;
shall I, the one who delivers, shut the womb?
   says your God.

10 Rejoice with Jerusalem, and be glad for her,
    all you who love her;
rejoice with her in joy,
    all you who mourn over her—
11 that you may nurse and be satisfied
    from her consoling breast;
that you may drink deeply with delight
    from her glorious bosom.

12 For thus says the LORD:
I will extend prosperity to her like a river,
    and the wealth of the nations like an
        overflowing stream;
and you shall nurse and be carried on her arm,
    and dandled on her knees.
13 As a mother comforts her child,
    so I will comfort you;
    you shall be comforted in Jerusalem.

The Reign and Indignation of God

14 You shall see, and your heart shall rejoice;
    your bodies[a] shall flourish like the grass;
and it shall be known that the hand of the LORD
    is with his servants,
    and his indignation is against his enemies.
15 For the LORD will come in fire,
    and his chariots like the whirlwind,
to pay back his anger in fury,
    and his rebuke in flames of fire.
16 For by fire will the LORD execute judgment,
    and by his sword, on all flesh;
    and those slain by the LORD shall be many.

17 Those who sanctify and purify themselves
to go into the gardens, following the one in the
center, eating the flesh of pigs, vermin, and rodents, shall come to an end together, says the
LORD.

18 For I know[b] their works and their thoughts,
and I am[c] coming to gather all nations and
tongues; and they shall come and shall see my
glory, 19and I will set a sign among them. From
them I will send survivors to the nations, to Tarshish, Put,[d] and Lud—which draw the bow—to
Tubal and Javan, to the coastlands far away that
have not heard of my fame or seen my glory; and
they shall declare my glory among the nations.
20They shall bring all your kindred from all the
nations as an offering to the LORD, on horses,
and in chariots, and in litters, and on mules, and
on dromedaries, to my holy mountain Jerusalem, says the LORD, just as the Israelites bring a
grain offering in a clean vessel to the house of
the LORD. 21And I will also take some of them as
priests and as Levites, says the LORD.

22 For as the new heavens and the new earth,
    which I will make,
shall remain before me, says the LORD;
    so shall your descendants and your name
        remain.
23 From new moon to new moon,
    and from sabbath to sabbath,
all flesh shall come to worship before me,
says the LORD.

24 And they shall go out and look at the dead
bodies of the people who have rebelled against
me; for their worm shall not die, their fire shall
not be quenched, and they shall be an abhor-
rence to all flesh.

a Heb bones   b Gk Syr: Heb lacks *know*   c Gk Syr Vg Tg: Heb
it is   d Gk: Heb *Pul*

Imagine you're watching a movie. One of the leading characters imposes severe hardships on others and then goes off to dine in luxury. Immediately, you know the character is a villain. Another leading character calls for others to endure sacrifice and lives under the same conditions as they do. You know this is a hero, because heroes practice what they preach. Jeremiah the prophet was such a hero; he not only preached a hard message but accepted the trials that came with it.

In Depth

At the beginning of Jeremiah's prophetic ministry, King Josiah ruled the southern kingdom of Judah (see 2 Chronicles, chapters 34–35). He was a good king who expanded Judah's territory and started a religious reform. Jeremiah approved of Josiah and Josiah's reforms, but he was afraid they were too little, too late. Chapters 2–5 of his book contain his prophecies during Josiah's rule. In them, he speaks out against Israel's sin and corruption but hopes things will improve if the people turn to God (see 4:1–2). Unfortunately, King Josiah was suddenly killed in battle, and things went from bad to worse.

Kings Jehoiakim and Zedekiah were the main rulers who followed Josiah, and they were Josiah's complete opposite (see 2 Chr 36:5–14). Both were ruthless, power hungry, and corrupt. During Jehoiakim's reign, Jeremiah had to go into hiding out of fear for his life. Chapters 7–20 of Jeremiah's book contain his prophecies during this time, when his preaching against the sins of Israel became stronger. Chapters 21–29 and 34–45 record his life and preaching during Zedekiah's reign—the last few years before the Babylonian Exile. While Zedekiah ruled, Jeremiah was imprisoned, beaten, and thrown into a well to die.

Jeremiah survived his experience in the well to see Jerusalem and the Temple destroyed by the Babylonians. To give the people hope that God was still on their side, he prophesied the destruction of all Israel's enemies, especially Babylon (see chapters 46–51).

Ultimately, Jeremiah realized that even a new king like David would not be enough to correct what was wrong. The people were unable to fulfill God's Commandments because they had hearts of stone. In chapters 30–33, the Book of Consolation, Jeremiah said the Lord would make a new Covenant with Israel in the future, and this time, the Law would be written on the people's hearts (see 31:31–34).

At a Glance

- Chapter 1. Jeremiah's call
- Chapters 2–25. prophecies against Judah and Jerusalem
- Chapters 26–45. biographical material and a discussion of the restoration of Israel
- Chapters 46–52. prophecies against other nations

Quick Facts

Period Covered: from 626 to 583 BC
Inspired Authors: Jeremiah and his disciples, including Baruch
Themes: Israel's need for repentance, Jeremiah's struggles, the New Covenant

The Book of Jeremiah

Jeremiah

1 The words of Jeremiah son of Hilkiah, of the priests who were in Anathoth in the land of Benjamin, ²to whom the word of the LORD came in the days of King Josiah son of Amon of Judah, in the thirteenth year of his reign. ³It came also in the days of King Jehoiakim son of Josiah of Judah, and until the end of the eleventh year of King Zedekiah son of Josiah of Judah, until the captivity of Jerusalem in the fifth month.

Jeremiah's Call and Commission

4 Now the word of the LORD came to me saying,

⁵ "Before I formed you in the womb I knew you,
  and before you were born I consecrated you;
  I appointed you a prophet to the nations."
⁶Then I said, "Ah, Lord GOD! Truly I do not know how to speak, for I am only a boy." ⁷But the LORD said to me,

  "Do not say, 'I am only a boy';
  for you shall go to all to whom I send you,
  and you shall speak whatever I command you.
⁸ Do not be afraid of them,
  for I am with you to deliver you,

                                    says the LORD."
⁹Then the LORD put out his hand and touched my mouth; and the LORD said to me,

  "Now I have put my words in your mouth.
¹⁰ See, today I appoint you over nations and over
      kingdoms,
  to pluck up and to pull down,
  to destroy and to overthrow,
  to build and to plant."

11 The word of the LORD came to me, saying, "Jeremiah, what do you see?" And I said, "I see a branch of an almond tree."*ᵃ* ¹²Then the LORD said to me, "You have seen well, for I am watching*ᵇ* over my word to perform it." ¹³The word of the LORD came to me a second time, saying, "What do you see?" And I said, "I see a boiling pot, tilted away from the north."

14 Then the LORD said to me: Out of the north disaster shall break out on all the inhabitants of the land. ¹⁵For now I am calling all the tribes of the kingdoms of the north, says the LORD; and they shall come and all of them shall set their thrones at the entrance of the gates of Jerusalem, against all its surrounding walls and against all the cities of Judah. ¹⁶And I will utter my judgments against them, for all their wickedness in forsaking me; they have made offerings to other gods, and worshiped the works of their own hands. ¹⁷But you, gird up your loins; stand up and tell them everything that I command you. Do not break down before them, or I will break you before them. ¹⁸And I for my part have made you today a fortified city, an iron pillar, and a bronze wall, against the whole land—against the kings of Judah, its princes, its priests, and the people of the land. ¹⁹They will fight against you; but they shall not prevail against you, for I am with you, says the LORD, to deliver you.

---

a Heb *shaqed*   b Heb *shoqed*

God Pleads with Israel to Repent

2 The word of the LORD came to me, saying: ²Go and proclaim in the hearing of Jerusalem, Thus says the LORD:

I remember the devotion of your youth,
  your love as a bride,
how you followed me in the wilderness,
  in a land not sown.
³ Israel was holy to the LORD,
  the first fruits of his harvest.
All who ate of it were held guilty;
  disaster came upon them,
                    says the LORD.

4 Hear the word of the LORD, O house of Jacob, and all the families of the house of Israel. ⁵Thus says the LORD:

What wrong did your ancestors find in me
  that they went far from me,
and went after worthless things, and became
      worthless themselves?
⁶ They did not say, "Where is the LORD
  who brought us up from the land of Egypt,
who led us in the wilderness,
  in a land of deserts and pits,
in a land of drought and deep darkness,
in a land that no one passes through,
  where no one lives?"
⁷ I brought you into a plentiful land
  to eat its fruits and its good things.
But when you entered you defiled my land,
  and made my heritage an abomination.
⁸ The priests did not say, "Where is the LORD?"
  Those who handle the law did not know me;
the rulers*a* transgressed against me;
  the prophets prophesied by Baal,
  and went after things that do not profit.

⁹ Therefore once more I accuse you,
                    says the LORD,
and I accuse your children's children.
¹⁰ Cross to the coasts of Cyprus and look,
  send to Kedar and examine with care;
  see if there has ever been such a thing.
¹¹ Has a nation changed its gods,
  even though they are no gods?
But my people have changed their glory
  for something that does not profit.
¹² Be appalled, O heavens, at this,
  be shocked, be utterly desolate,
                    says the LORD,
¹³ for my people have committed two evils:
  they have forsaken me,
the fountain of living water,
  and dug out cisterns for themselves,

cracked cisterns
  that can hold no water.

¹⁴ Is Israel a slave? Is he a homeborn servant?
  Why then has he become plunder?
¹⁵ The lions have roared against him,
  they have roared loudly.
They have made his land a waste;
  his cities are in ruins, without inhabitant.
¹⁶ Moreover, the people of Memphis and
      Tahpanhes
  have broken the crown of your head.
¹⁷ Have you not brought this upon yourself
  by forsaking the LORD your God,
  while he led you in the way?
¹⁸ What then do you gain by going to Egypt,
  to drink the waters of the Nile?
Or what do you gain by going to Assyria,
  to drink the waters of the Euphrates?
¹⁹ Your wickedness will punish you,
  and your apostasies will convict you.
Know and see that it is evil and bitter
  for you to forsake the LORD your God;
  the fear of me is not in you,
                    says the Lord GOD of hosts.

²⁰ For long ago you broke your yoke
  and burst your bonds,

___
a Heb shepherds

You Are Not Too Young!

Jeremiah was a young man when God tapped him on the shoulder. In response to God, Jeremiah said, "Truly I do not know how to speak, for I am only a boy" (verse 6). But God gave Jeremiah the words and the ability to become a hero.

When you need to do something difficult for the good of others, remember God's response to Jeremiah: "Do not say, 'I am only a boy'" (verse 7). God wants you to know that you too are capable of bringing about positive change in the world. God knows what you are able to do and say and be. Listen to God.

▶ Jer 1:4–10

J
E
R

and you said, "I will not serve!"
On every high hill
  and under every green tree
    you sprawled and played the whore.
21 Yet I planted you as a choice vine,
  from the purest stock.
How then did you turn degenerate
  and become a wild vine?
22 Though you wash yourself with lye
  and use much soap,
    the stain of your guilt is still before me,
          says the Lord God.

Introducing...

Jeremiah

Have you ever felt ridiculed for defending your values or doing a good deed? If so, then you can probably relate to Jeremiah, who once told God:

O Lord, you have enticed me,
  and I was enticed;
. . . .
I have become a laughingstock all day long;
  everyone mocks me.

(Jer 20:7)

Jeremiah knew what it was like to be rejected for delivering God's message.

Jeremiah was born in 645 BC of a priestly family from a northern Israelite tribe. He was very young when he began his prophetic career. Like Isaiah, Jeremiah was a prophet for all seasons. He was both optimistic (see chapter 31) and condemning (see 22:18–23). He was courageous (see chapter 37), enduring beatings, imprisonment, and even being thrown into a well to die (see 38:1–6) for the sake of delivering God's message. He loved his people so much that he was sometimes called the weeping prophet because of his bitter tears for them and their fast-approaching doom (see 9:1; 13:7).

The Book of Jeremiah gives us a fascinating inside look at the prophet's relationship with God. Several passages, called the Confessions of Jeremiah, are personal accounts of his struggles with God (see 12:1–6, 15:10–21, 17:12–18, 18:18–23, 20:7–18). If you take the time to read these passages, you may find that your own doubts and struggles aren't all that different.

23 How can you say, "I am not defiled,
  I have not gone after the Baals"?
Look at your way in the valley;
  know what you have done—
a restive young camel interlacing her tracks,
24   a wild ass at home in the wilderness,
in her heat sniffing the wind!
  Who can restrain her lust?
None who seek her need weary themselves;
  in her month they will find her.
25 Keep your feet from going unshod
  and your throat from thirst.
But you said, "It is hopeless,
  for I have loved strangers,
  and after them I will go."

26 As a thief is shamed when caught,
  so the house of Israel shall be shamed—
they, their kings, their officials,
  their priests, and their prophets,
27 who say to a tree, "You are my father,"
  and to a stone, "You gave me birth."
For they have turned their backs to me,
  and not their faces.
But in the time of their trouble they say,
  "Come and save us!"
28 But where are your gods
  that you made for yourself?
Let them come, if they can save you,
  in your time of trouble;
for you have as many gods
  as you have towns, O Judah.

29 Why do you complain against me?
  You have all rebelled against me,
          says the Lord.
30 In vain I have struck down your children;
  they accepted no correction.
Your own sword devoured your prophets
  like a ravening lion.
31 And you, O generation, behold the word of the
  Lord![a]
Have I been a wilderness to Israel,
  or a land of thick darkness?
Why then do my people say, "We are free,
  we will come to you no more"?
32 Can a girl forget her ornaments,
  or a bride her attire?
Yet my people have forgotten me,
  days without number.

33 How well you direct your course
  to seek lovers!
So that even to wicked women

---

a Meaning of Heb uncertain

Cultural Connection · Hispanics Assume Their Mission as Prophets

Jeremiah and many of the other Old Testament prophets call for solidarity with the poor and oppressed. During the Third Encuentro Nacional Hispano de Pastoral, in 1985, Hispanics assumed their mission as prophets in contemporary society. They expressed their solidarity with the social groups in need of liberation and their desire to live and promote justice. The following statements are from the Encuentro:

- We, as Hispanic people, make a preferential option for and in solidarity with the poor and marginalized.
- We, as Hispanic people, make a preferential option for Hispanic youth so that they will participate at all levels of pastoral ministry.
- We, as Hispanic people, want to follow the line of a Church that promotes and exemplifies justice.
- We, as Hispanic people, wish to follow an approach of valuing and promoting women, recognizing their equality and dignity and their role in the Church, the family, and society.

[Secretariat for Hispanic Affairs, *Prophetic Voices*, p. 6]

you have taught your ways.
³⁴ Also on your skirts is found
   the lifeblood of the innocent poor,
though you did not catch them breaking in.
   Yet in spite of all these things*a*
³⁵ you say, "I am innocent;
   surely his anger has turned from me."
Now I am bringing you to judgment
   for saying, "I have not sinned."
³⁶ How lightly you gad about,
   changing your ways!
You shall be put to shame by Egypt
   as you were put to shame by Assyria.
³⁷ From there also you will come away
   with your hands on your head;
for the LORD has rejected those in whom you
      trust,
   and you will not prosper through them.

Unfaithful Israel

3 If*b* a man divorces his wife
   and she goes from him
and becomes another man's wife,
   will he return to her?
Would not such a land be greatly polluted?
You have played the whore with many lovers;
   and would you return to me?
                                        says the LORD.

² Look up to the bare heights,*c* and see!
   Where have you not been lain with?
By the waysides you have sat waiting for lovers,
   like a nomad in the wilderness.
You have polluted the land
   with your whoring and wickedness.

³ Therefore the showers have been withheld,
   and the spring rain has not come;
yet you have the forehead of a whore,
   you refuse to be ashamed.
⁴ Have you not just now called to me,
   "My Father, you are the friend of my youth—
⁵ will he be angry forever,
   will he be indignant to the end?"
This is how you have spoken,
   but you have done all the evil that you could.

A Call to Repentance

6 The LORD said to me in the days of King Josiah: Have you seen what she did, that faithless one, Israel, how she went up on every high hill and under every green tree, and played the whore there? ⁷And I thought, "After she has done all this she will return to me"; but she did not return, and her false sister Judah saw it. ⁸She*d* saw that for all the adulteries of that faithless one, Israel, I had sent her away with a decree of divorce; yet her false sister Judah did not fear, but she too went and played the whore. ⁹Because she took her whoredom so lightly, she polluted the land, committing adultery with stone and tree. ¹⁰Yet for all this her false sister Judah did not return to me with her whole heart, but only in pretense, says the LORD.

11 Then the LORD said to me: Faithless Israel has shown herself less guilty than false Judah. ¹²Go, and proclaim these words toward the north, and say:

---

a Meaning of Heb uncertain   b Q Ms Gk Syr: MT *Saying, If*
c Or *the trails*   d Q Ms Gk Mss Syr: MT *I*

Return, faithless Israel,

says the LORD.
I will not look on you in anger,
for I am merciful,

says the LORD;
I will not be angry forever.
13 Only acknowledge your guilt,
that you have rebelled against the LORD your
God,
and scattered your favors among strangers under
every green tree,
and have not obeyed my voice,

says the LORD.
14 Return, O faithless children,

says the LORD,
for I am your master;
I will take you, one from a city and two from a
family,
and I will bring you to Zion.

15 I will give you shepherds after my own heart, who will feed you with knowledge and understanding. 16And when you have multiplied and increased in the land, in those days, says the LORD, they shall no longer say, "The ark of the covenant of the LORD." It shall not come to mind, or be remembered, or missed; nor shall another one be made. 17At that time Jerusalem shall be called the throne of the LORD, and all nations shall gather to it, to the presence of the LORD in Jerusalem, and they shall no longer stubbornly follow their own evil will. 18In those days the house of Judah shall join the house of Israel, and together they shall come from the land of the north to the land that I gave your ancestors for a heritage.

19 I thought
how I would set you among my children,
and give you a pleasant land,
the most beautiful heritage of all the nations.
And I thought you would call me, My Father,
and would not turn from following me.
20 Instead, as a faithless wife leaves her husband,
so you have been faithless to me, O house of
Israel,

says the LORD.

21 A voice on the bare heights*a* is heard,
the plaintive weeping of Israel's children,
because they have perverted their way,
they have forgotten the LORD their God:
22 Return, O faithless children,
I will heal your faithlessness.

"Here we come to you;
for you are the LORD our God.

23 Truly the hills are*b* a delusion,
the orgies on the mountains.
Truly in the LORD our God
is the salvation of Israel.
24 "But from our youth the shameful thing has devoured all for which our ancestors had labored, their flocks and their herds, their sons and their daughters. 25Let us lie down in our shame, and let our dishonor cover us; for we have sinned against the LORD our God, we and our ancestors, from our youth even to this day; and we have not obeyed the voice of the LORD our God."

4 If you return, O Israel,

says the LORD,
if you return to me,
if you remove your abominations from my
presence,
and do not waver,
2 and if you swear, "As the LORD lives!"
in truth, in justice, and in uprightness,
then nations shall be blessed*c* by him,
and by him they shall boast.
3 For thus says the LORD to the people of Judah and to the inhabitants of Jerusalem:
Break up your fallow ground,
and do not sow among thorns.
4 Circumcise yourselves to the LORD,
remove the foreskin of your hearts,
O people of Judah and inhabitants of
Jerusalem,
or else my wrath will go forth like fire,
and burn with no one to quench it,
because of the evil of your doings.

Invasion and Desolation of Judah Threatened

5 Declare in Judah, and proclaim in Jerusalem, and say:
Blow the trumpet through the land;
shout aloud*d* and say,
"Gather together, and let us go
into the fortified cities!"
6 Raise a standard toward Zion,
flee for safety, do not delay,
for I am bringing evil from the north,
and a great destruction.
7 A lion has gone up from its thicket,
a destroyer of nations has set out;
he has gone out from his place
to make your land a waste;
your cities will be ruins
without inhabitant.

---

a Or *the trails*   *b* Gk Syr Vg: Heb *Truly from the hills is*
c Or *shall bless themselves*   *d* Or *shout, take your weapons*: Heb
shout, fill (your hand)

8 Because of this put on sackcloth,
       lament and wail:
  "The fierce anger of the LORD
       has not turned away from us."

9 On that day, says the LORD, courage shall fail the king and the officials; the priests shall be appalled and the prophets astounded. 10Then I said, "Ah, Lord GOD, how utterly you have deceived this people and Jerusalem, saying, 'It shall be well with you,' even while the sword is at the throat!"

11 At that time it will be said to this people and to Jerusalem: A hot wind comes from me out of the bare heights*a* in the desert toward my poor people, not to winnow or cleanse— 12a wind too strong for that. Now it is I who speak in judgment against them.
13 Look! He comes up like clouds,
       his chariots like the whirlwind;
  his horses are swifter than eagles—
       woe to us, for we are ruined!
14 O Jerusalem, wash your heart clean of
              wickedness
       so that you may be saved.
  How long shall your evil schemes
       lodge within you?
15 For a voice declares from Dan
       and proclaims disaster from Mount Ephraim.
16 Tell the nations, "Here they are!"
       Proclaim against Jerusalem,
  "Besiegers come from a distant land;
       they shout against the cities of Judah."
17 They have closed in around her like watchers of
              a field,
       because she has rebelled against me,
                                 says the LORD.
18 Your ways and your doings
       have brought this upon you.
  This is your doom; how bitter it is!
       It has reached your very heart."

Sorrow for a Doomed Nation

19 My anguish, my anguish! I writhe in pain!
       Oh, the walls of my heart!
  My heart is beating wildly;
       I cannot keep silent;
  for I*b* hear the sound of the trumpet,
       the alarm of war.
20 Disaster overtakes disaster,
       the whole land is laid waste.
  Suddenly my tents are destroyed,
       my curtains in a moment.
21 How long must I see the standard,
       and hear the sound of the trumpet?

22 "For my people are foolish,
       they do not know me;
  they are stupid children,
       they have no understanding.
  They are skilled in doing evil,
       but do not know how to do good."

23 I looked on the earth, and lo, it was waste and
              void;
       and to the heavens, and they had no light.
24 I looked on the mountains, and lo, they were
              quaking,
       and all the hills moved to and fro.
25 I looked, and lo, there was no one at all,
       and all the birds of the air had fled.
26 I looked, and lo, the fruitful land was a desert,
       and all its cities were laid in ruins
       before the LORD, before his fierce anger.

27 For thus says the LORD: The whole land shall be a desolation; yet I will not make a full end.
28 Because of this the earth shall mourn,
       and the heavens above grow black;
  for I have spoken, I have purposed;
       I have not relented nor will I turn back.

29 At the noise of horseman and archer
       every town takes to flight;
  they enter thickets; they climb among rocks;
       all the towns are forsaken,
       and no one lives in them.
30 And you, O desolate one,
  what do you mean that you dress in crimson,
       that you deck yourself with ornaments of
              gold,
       that you enlarge your eyes with paint?
  In vain you beautify yourself.
       Your lovers despise you;
       they seek your life.
31 For I heard a cry as of a woman in labor,
       anguish as of one bringing forth her first
              child,
  the cry of daughter Zion gasping for breath,
       stretching out her hands,
  "Woe is me! I am fainting before killers!"

The Utter Corruption of God's People

5 Run to and fro through the streets of
       Jerusalem,
  look around and take note!
  Search its squares and see
       if you can find one person
  who acts justly
       and seeks truth—

---

a Or *the trails*   *b* Another reading is *for you, O my soul,* so that I may pardon Jerusalem.*a*

2 Although they say, "As the Lord lives,"
  yet they swear falsely.
3 O Lord, do your eyes not look for truth?
  You have struck them,
    but they felt no anguish;
  you have consumed them,
    but they refused to take correction.
  They have made their faces harder than rock;
    they have refused to turn back.

4 Then I said, "These are only the poor,
    they have no sense;
  for they do not know the way of the Lord,
    the law of their God.
5 Let me go to the rich*b*
    and speak to them;
  surely they know the way of the Lord,
    the law of their God."
  But they all alike had broken the yoke,
    they had burst the bonds.

6 Therefore a lion from the forest shall kill them,
    a wolf from the desert shall destroy them.
  A leopard is watching against their cities;
    everyone who goes out of them shall be torn
      in pieces—
  because their transgressions are many,
    their apostasies are great.

7 How can I pardon you?
    Your children have forsaken me,
    and have sworn by those who are no gods.
  When I fed them to the full,
    they committed adultery
    and trooped to the houses of prostitutes.
8 They were well-fed lusty stallions,
    each neighing for his neighbor's wife.
9 Shall I not punish them for these things?
                              says the Lord;
  and shall I not bring retribution
    on a nation such as this?

10 Go up through her vine-rows and destroy,
    but do not make a full end;
  strip away her branches,
    for they are not the Lord's.
11 For the house of Israel and the house of Judah
    have been utterly faithless to me,
                              says the Lord.
12 They have spoken falsely of the Lord,
    and have said, "He will do nothing.
  No evil will come upon us,
    and we shall not see sword or famine."
13 The prophets are nothing but wind,
    for the word is not in them.

Thus shall it be done to them!

14 Therefore thus says the Lord, the God of hosts:
  Because they*c* have spoken this word,
  I am now making my words in your mouth a
      fire,
    and this people wood, and the fire shall
      devour them.
15 I am going to bring upon you
    a nation from far away, O house of Israel,
                              says the Lord.
  It is an enduring nation,
    it is an ancient nation,
  a nation whose language you do not know,
    nor can you understand what they say.
16 Their quiver is like an open tomb;
    all of them are mighty warriors.
17 They shall eat up your harvest and your food;
    they shall eat up your sons and your
      daughters;
  they shall eat up your flocks and your herds;
    they shall eat up your vines and your fig trees;
  they shall destroy with the sword
    your fortified cities in which you trust.

18 But even in those days, says the Lord, I will
not make a full end of you. 19And when your
people say, "Why has the Lord our God done all
these things to us?" you shall say to them, "As
you have forsaken me and served foreign gods in
your land, so you shall serve strangers in a land
that is not yours."

20 Declare this in the house of Jacob,
    proclaim it in Judah:
21 Hear this, O foolish and senseless people,
    who have eyes, but do not see,
    who have ears, but do not hear.
22 Do you not fear me? says the Lord;
    Do you not tremble before me?
  I placed the sand as a boundary for the sea,
    a perpetual barrier that it cannot pass;
  though the waves toss, they cannot prevail,
    though they roar, they cannot pass over it.
23 But this people has a stubborn and rebellious
      heart;
    they have turned aside and gone away.
24 They do not say in their hearts,
    "Let us fear the Lord our God,
  who gives the rain in its season,
    the autumn rain and the spring rain,
  and keeps for us
    the weeks appointed for the harvest."
25 Your iniquities have turned these away,

---

a Heb *it*   b Or *the great*   c Heb *you*

and your sins have deprived you of good.
26 For scoundrels are found among my people;
    they take over the goods of others.
Like fowlers they set a trap;[a]
    they catch human beings.
27 Like a cage full of birds,
    their houses are full of treachery;
therefore they have become great and rich,
28   they have grown fat and sleek.
They know no limits in deeds of wickedness;
    they do not judge with justice
the cause of the orphan, to make it prosper,
    and they do not defend the rights of the
      needy.
29 Shall I not punish them for these things?
                    says the LORD,
    and shall I not bring retribution
    on a nation such as this?

30 An appalling and horrible thing
    has happened in the land:
31 the prophets prophesy falsely,
    and the priests rule as the prophets direct;[b]
my people love to have it so,
    but what will you do when the end comes?

The Imminence and Horror of the Invasion

6 Flee for safety, O children of Benjamin,
    from the midst of Jerusalem!
Blow the trumpet in Tekoa,
    and raise a signal on Beth-haccherem;
for evil looms out of the north,
    and great destruction.
2 I have likened daughter Zion
    to the loveliest pasture.[c]
3 Shepherds with their flocks shall come against
    her.
    They shall pitch their tents around her;
    they shall pasture, all in their places.
4 "Prepare war against her;
    up, and let us attack at noon!"
"Woe to us, for the day declines,
    the shadows of evening lengthen!"
5 "Up, and let us attack by night,
    and destroy her palaces!"
6 For thus says the LORD of hosts:
Cut down her trees;
    cast up a siege ramp against Jerusalem.
This is the city that must be punished;[d]
    there is nothing but oppression within her.
7 As a well keeps its water fresh,
    so she keeps fresh her wickedness;
violence and destruction are heard within her;
    sickness and wounds are ever before me.
8 Take warning, O Jerusalem,
    or I shall turn from you in disgust,

and make you a desolation,
    an uninhabited land.

9 Thus says the LORD of hosts:
Glean[e] thoroughly as a vine
    the remnant of Israel;
like a grape-gatherer, pass your hand again
    over its branches.

10 To whom shall I speak and give warning,
    that they may hear?
See, their ears are closed,[f]
    they cannot listen.
The word of the LORD is to them an object of
      scorn;
    they take no pleasure in it.
11 But I am full of the wrath of the LORD;
    I am weary of holding it in.

Pour it out on the children in the street,
    and on the gatherings of young men as well;
both husband and wife shall be taken,
    the old folk and the very aged.
12 Their houses shall be turned over to others,
    their fields and wives together;
for I will stretch out my hand
    against the inhabitants of the land,
                    says the LORD.

13 For from the least to the greatest of them,
    everyone is greedy for unjust gain;
and from prophet to priest,
    everyone deals falsely.
14 They have treated the wound of my people
      carelessly,
    saying, "Peace, peace,"
    when there is no peace.
15 They acted shamefully, they committed
      abomination;
    yet they were not ashamed,
    they did not know how to blush.
Therefore they shall fall among those who fall;
    at the time that I punish them, they shall be
      overthrown,
                    says the LORD.

16 Thus says the LORD:
Stand at the crossroads, and look,
    and ask for the ancient paths,
    where the good way lies, and walk in it,
    and find rest for your souls.
But they said, "We will not walk in it."
17 Also I raised up sentinels for you:

---

a Meaning of Heb uncertain   b Or rule by their own authority
c Or I will destroy daughter Zion, the loveliest pasture   d Or the
city of license   e Cn: Heb They shall glean   f Heb are
uncircumcised

"Give heed to the sound of the trumpet!"
But they said, "We will not give heed."

18 Therefore hear, O nations,
　and know, O congregation, what will happen
　　to them.
19 Hear, O earth; I am going to bring disaster on
　　this people,
　the fruit of their schemes,
because they have not given heed to my words;
　and as for my teaching, they have rejected it.
20 Of what use to me is frankincense that comes
　　from Sheba,
　or sweet cane from a distant land?
Your burnt offerings are not acceptable,
　nor are your sacrifices pleasing to me.
21 Therefore thus says the LORD:
See, I am laying before this people
　stumbling blocks against which they shall
　　stumble;
parents and children together,
　neighbor and friend shall perish.

22 Thus says the LORD:
See, a people is coming from the land of the
　　north,
　a great nation is stirring from the farthest
　　parts of the earth.
23 They grasp the bow and the javelin,
　they are cruel and have no mercy,
　their sound is like the roaring sea;
they ride on horses,
　equipped like a warrior for battle,
　against you, O daughter Zion!

24 "We have heard news of them,
　our hands fall helpless;
anguish has taken hold of us,
　pain as of a woman in labor.
25 Do not go out into the field,
　or walk on the road;
for the enemy has a sword,
　terror is on every side."

26 O my poor people, put on sackcloth,
　and roll in ashes;
make mourning as for an only child,
　most bitter lamentation:
for suddenly the destroyer
　will come upon us.

27 I have made you a tester and a refiner[a] among
　　my people
so that you may know and test their ways.
28 They are all stubbornly rebellious,
　going about with slanders;
they are bronze and iron,
　all of them act corruptly.
29 The bellows blow fiercely,
　the lead is consumed by the fire;
in vain the refining goes on,
　for the wicked are not removed.
30 They are called "rejected silver,"
　for the LORD has rejected them.

Jeremiah Proclaims God's Judgment
on the Nation

7 The word that came to Jeremiah from the LORD: ²Stand in the gate of the LORD's house, and proclaim there this word, and say, Hear the word of the LORD, all you people of Judah, you that enter these gates to worship the LORD. ³Thus says the LORD of hosts, the God of Israel: Amend your ways and your doings, and let me dwell with you[b] in this place. ⁴Do not trust in these deceptive words: "This is[c] the temple of the LORD, the temple of the LORD, the temple of the LORD."

5 For if you truly amend your ways and your doings, if you truly act justly one with another, ⁶if you do not oppress the alien, the orphan, and the widow, or shed innocent blood in this place, and if you do not go after other gods to your own hurt, ⁷then I will dwell with you in this place, in the land that I gave of old to your ancestors forever and ever.

8 Here you are, trusting in deceptive words to no avail. ⁹Will you steal, murder, commit adultery, swear falsely, make offerings to Baal, and go after other gods that you have not known, ¹⁰and then come and stand before me in this house, which is called by my name, and say, "We are safe!"—only to go on doing all these abominations? ¹¹Has this house, which is called by my name, become a den of robbers in your sight? You know, I too am watching, says the LORD. ¹²Go now to my place that was in Shiloh, where I made my name dwell at first, and see what I did to it for the wickedness of my people Israel. ¹³And now, because you have done all these things, says the LORD, and when I spoke to you persistently, you did not listen, and when I called you, you did not answer, ¹⁴therefore I will do to the house that is called by my name, in which you trust, and to the place that I gave to you and to your ancestors, just what I did to Shiloh. ¹⁵And I will cast you out of my sight, just as I cast out all your kinsfolk, all the offspring of Ephraim.

The People's Disobedience

16 As for you, do not pray for this people, do not raise a cry or prayer on their behalf, and do

---

a Or a fortress　b Or and I will let you dwell　c Heb They are not intercede with me, for I will not hear you. ¹⁷Do you not see what they are doing in the towns of Judah and in the streets of Jerusalem? ¹⁸The children gather wood, the fathers kindle fire, and the women knead dough, to make cakes for the queen of heaven; and they pour out drink offerings to other gods, to provoke me to anger. ¹⁹Is it I whom they provoke? says the Lord. Is it not themselves, to their own hurt? ²⁰Therefore thus says the Lord God: My anger and my wrath shall be poured out on this place, on human beings and animals, on the trees of the field and the fruit of the ground; it will burn and not be quenched.

21 Thus says the Lord of hosts, the God of Israel: Add your burnt offerings to your sacrifices, and eat the flesh. ²²For in the day that I brought your ancestors out of the land of Egypt, I did not speak to them or command them concerning burnt offerings and sacrifices. ²³But this command I gave them, "Obey my voice, and I will be your God, and you shall be my people; and walk only in the way that I command you, so that it may be well with you." ²⁴Yet they did not obey or incline their ear, but, in the stubbornness of their evil will, they walked in their own counsels, and looked backward rather than forward. ²⁵From the day that your ancestors came out of the land of Egypt until this day, I have persistently sent all my servants the prophets to them, day after day; ²⁶yet they did not listen to me, or pay attention, but they stiffened their necks. They did worse than their ancestors did.

27 So you shall speak all these words to them, but they will not listen to you. You shall call to them, but they will not answer you. ²⁸You shall say to them: This is the nation that did not obey the voice of the Lord their God, and did not accept discipline; truth has perished; it is cut off from their lips.

²⁹ Cut off your hair and throw it away;
   raise a lamentation on the bare heights,ᵃ
for the Lord has rejected and forsaken
  the generation that provoked his wrath.

30 For the people of Judah have done evil in my sight, says the Lord; they have set their abominations in the house that is called by my name, defiling it. ³¹And they go on building the high placeᵇ of Topheth, which is in the valley of the son of Hinnom, to burn their sons and their daughters in the fire—which I did not command, nor did it come into my mind. ³²Therefore, the days are surely coming, says the Lord, when it will no more be called Topheth, or the valley of the son of Hinnom, but the valley of Slaughter: for they will bury in Topheth until there is no

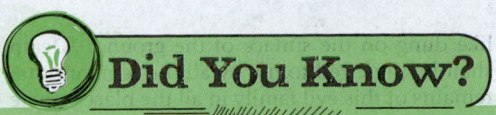

Did You Know?

The Prophet and the Temple

In ancient Israel, the Temple was considered the dwelling place of God. Most Israelites felt that as long as the Temple stood, God was keeping the covenant promise to stay with Israel. They believed this because Jerusalem and Judea had been spared when the northern kingdom fell to Assyria (721 BC). The Israelites failed to remember that God's covenant with them was a mutual one—that they in turn had to keep their commitment to worship God alone.

Speaking for God at the gates of the Temple, Jeremiah told the people the Temple would be destroyed if Israel continued to disobey the commandments of the covenant (see how the sins he accused them of in Jeremiah 7:8–9 reflect the Ten Commandments). The destruction of the Temple would be a visible sign that the covenant had been broken—not by God, but by the people.

The Temple was destroyed, and then rebuilt. Centuries later, Jesus preached to a new generation who thought the Temple was a guarantee of God's presence and favor. He predicted the Temple would be destroyed again (see Mt 24:1–2).

▶ Jer 7:1–14

more room. ³³The corpses of this people will be food for the birds of the air, and for the animals of the earth; and no one will frighten them away. ³⁴And I will bring to an end the sound of mirth and gladness, the voice of the bride and bridegroom in the cities of Judah and in the streets of Jerusalem; for the land shall become a waste.

8 At that time, says the Lord, the bones of the kings of Judah, the bones of its officials, the bones of the priests, the bones of the prophets, and the bones of the inhabitants of Jerusalem shall be brought out of their tombs; ²and they shall be spread before the sun and the moon and all the host of heaven, which they have loved and served, which they have followed, and which they have inquired of and worshiped; and they shall not be gathered or buried; they shall be

---

ᵃ Or the trails ᵇ Gk Tg: Heb high places

J
E
R

like dung on the surface of the ground. ³Death shall be preferred to life by all the remnant that remains of this evil family in all the places where I have driven them, says the LORD of hosts.

The Blind Perversity of the Whole Nation

⁴ You shall say to them, Thus says the LORD:
When people fall, do they not get up again?
    If they go astray, do they not turn back?
⁵ Why then has this people[a] turned away
    in perpetual backsliding?
They have held fast to deceit,
    they have refused to return.
⁶ I have given heed and listened,
    but they do not speak honestly;
no one repents of wickedness,
    saying, "What have I done!"
All of them turn to their own course,
    like a horse plunging headlong into battle.
⁷ Even the stork in the heavens
    knows its times;
and the turtledove, swallow, and crane[b]
    observe the time of their coming;
but my people do not know
    the ordinance of the LORD.

⁸ How can you say, "We are wise,
    and the law of the LORD is with us,"
when, in fact, the false pen of the scribes
    has made it into a lie?
⁹ The wise shall be put to shame,
    they shall be dismayed and taken;
since they have rejected the word of the LORD,
    what wisdom is in them?
¹⁰ Therefore I will give their wives to others
    and their fields to conquerors,
because from the least to the greatest
    everyone is greedy for unjust gain;
from prophet to priest
    everyone deals falsely.
¹¹ They have treated the wound of my people
    carelessly,
    saying, "Peace, peace,"
    when there is no peace.
¹² They acted shamefully, they committed
    abomination;
    yet they were not at all ashamed,
    they did not know how to blush.
Therefore they shall fall among those who fall;
    at the time when I punish them, they shall be
    overthrown,
                                    says the LORD.
¹³ When I wanted to gather them, says the LORD,
    there are[c] no grapes on the vine,
    nor figs on the fig tree;
even the leaves are withered,

and what I gave them has passed away from
    them.[b]

¹⁴ Why do we sit still?
Gather together, let us go into the fortified cities
    and perish there;
for the LORD our God has doomed us to perish,
    and has given us poisoned water to drink,
    because we have sinned against the LORD.
¹⁵ We look for peace, but find no good,
    for a time of healing, but there is terror
        instead.

¹⁶ The snorting of their horses is heard from Dan;
    at the sound of the neighing of their stallions
    the whole land quakes.
They come and devour the land and all that
        fills it,
    the city and those who live in it.
¹⁷ See, I am letting snakes loose among you,
    adders that cannot be charmed,
    and they shall bite you,
                                    says the LORD.

The Prophet Mourns for the People

¹⁸ My joy is gone, grief is upon me,
    my heart is sick.
¹⁹ Hark, the cry of my poor people
    from far and wide in the land:
"Is the LORD not in Zion?
    Is her King not in her?"
("Why have they provoked me to anger with
        their images,
    with their foreign idols?")
²⁰ "The harvest is past, the summer is ended,
    and we are not saved."
²¹ For the hurt of my poor people I am hurt,
    I mourn, and dismay has taken hold of me.

²² Is there no balm in Gilead?
    Is there no physician there?
Why then has the health of my poor people
    not been restored?

9[d] O that my head were a spring of water,
    and my eyes a fountain of tears,
so that I might weep day and night
    for the slain of my poor people!
² [e] O that I had in the desert
    a traveler's lodging place,
that I might leave my people
    and go away from them!
For they are all adulterers,

---

a One Ms Gk: MT *this people, Jerusalem,*   b Meaning of Heb uncertain   c Or *I will make an end of them, says the LORD. There are*   d Ch 8.23 in Heb   e Ch 9.1 in Heb

a band of traitors.
3 They bend their tongues like bows;
   they have grown strong in the land for
         falsehood, and not for truth;
for they proceed from evil to evil,
   and they do not know me, says the LORD.

4 Beware of your neighbors,
   and put no trust in any of your kin;[a]
for all your kin[b] are supplanters,
   and every neighbor goes around like a
         slanderer.
5 They all deceive their neighbors,
   and no one speaks the truth;
they have taught their tongues to speak lies;
   they commit iniquity and are too weary to
         repent.[c]
6 Oppression upon oppression, deceit[d] upon
         deceit!
   They refuse to know me, says the LORD.

7 Therefore thus says the LORD of hosts:
   I will now refine and test them,
      for what else can I do with my sinful people?[e]
8 Their tongue is a deadly arrow;
   it speaks deceit through the mouth.
They all speak friendly words to their neighbors,
   but inwardly are planning to lay an ambush.
9 Shall I not punish them for these things? says
         the LORD;
   and shall I not bring retribution
   on a nation such as this?

10 Take up[f] weeping and wailing for the
         mountains,
   and a lamentation for the pastures of the
         wilderness,
because they are laid waste so that no one passes
         through,
   and the lowing of cattle is not heard;
both the birds of the air and the animals
   have fled and are gone.
11 I will make Jerusalem a heap of ruins,
   a lair of jackals;
and I will make the towns of Judah a desolation,
   without inhabitant.

12 Who is wise enough to understand this?
To whom has the mouth of the LORD spoken, so
that they may declare it? Why is the land ruined
and laid waste like a wilderness, so that no one
passes through? 13And the LORD says: Because
they have forsaken my law that I set before them,
and have not obeyed my voice, or walked in accordance with it, 14but have stubbornly followed
their own hearts and have gone after the Baals,

as their ancestors taught them. 15Therefore thus
says the LORD of hosts, the God of Israel: I am
feeding this people with wormwood, and giving
them poisonous water to drink. 16I will scatter
them among nations that neither they nor their
ancestors have known; and I will send the sword
after them, until I have consumed them.

The People Mourn in Judgment

17 Thus says the LORD of hosts:
   Consider, and call for the mourning women to
         come;
   send for the skilled women to come;
18 let them quickly raise a dirge over us,
   so that our eyes may run down with tears,
   and our eyelids flow with water.
19 For a sound of wailing is heard from Zion:
   "How we are ruined!
   We are utterly shamed,
because we have left the land,
   because they have cast down our dwellings."

20 Hear, O women, the word of the LORD,
   and let your ears receive the word of his
         mouth;
   teach to your daughters a dirge,
   and each to her neighbor a lament.
21 "Death has come up into our windows,
   it has entered our palaces,
to cut off the children from the streets
   and the young men from the squares."
22 Speak! Thus says the LORD:
   "Human corpses shall fall
   like dung upon the open field,
like sheaves behind the reaper,
   and no one shall gather them."

23 Thus says the LORD: Do not let the wise
boast in their wisdom, do not let the mighty
boast in their might, do not let the wealthy boast
in their wealth; 24but let those who boast boast
in this, that they understand and know me, that
I am the LORD; I act with steadfast love, justice,
and righteousness in the earth, for in these things
I delight, says the LORD.

25 The days are surely coming, says the LORD,
when I will attend to all those who are circumcised only in the foreskin; 26Egypt, Judah, Edom,
the Ammonites, Moab, and all those with shaven
temples who live in the desert. For all these nations are uncircumcised, and all the house of
Israel is uncircumcised in heart.

---

a Heb in a brother   b Heb for every brother   c Cn Compare
Gk: Heb they weary themselves with iniquity. 6Your dwelling
d Cn: Heb Your dwelling in the midst of deceit   e Or my poor
people   f Gk Syr: Heb I will take up

Idolatry Has Brought Ruin on Israel

10 Hear the word that the Lord speaks to you,
O house of Israel. ²Thus says the Lord:
Do not learn the way of the nations,
  or be dismayed at the signs of the heavens;
  for the nations are dismayed at them.
³ For the customs of the peoples are false:
a tree from the forest is cut down,
  and worked with an ax by the hands of an
  artisan;
⁴ people deck it with silver and gold;
  they fasten it with hammer and nails
  so that it cannot move.
⁵ Their idols[a] are like scarecrows in a cucumber
  field,
  and they cannot speak;
they have to be carried,
  for they cannot walk.
Do not be afraid of them,
  for they cannot do evil,
  nor is it in them to do good.

⁶ There is none like you, O Lord;
  you are great, and your name is great in
  might.
⁷ Who would not fear you, O King of the nations?
  For that is your due;
among all the wise ones of the nations
  and in all their kingdoms
  there is no one like you.
⁸ They are both stupid and foolish;
  the instruction given by idols
  is no better than wood![b]
⁹ Beaten silver is brought from Tarshish,
  and gold from Uphaz.
They are the work of the artisan and of the
  hands of the goldsmith;
  their clothing is blue and purple;
  they are all the product of skilled workers.
¹⁰ But the Lord is the true God;
  he is the living God and the everlasting King.
At his wrath the earth quakes,
  and the nations cannot endure his
  indignation.

11 Thus shall you say to them: The gods who
did not make the heavens and the earth shall perish from the earth and from under the heavens.[c]

¹² It is he who made the earth by his power,
  who established the world by his wisdom,
  and by his understanding stretched out the
  heavens.
¹³ When he utters his voice, there is a tumult of
  waters in the heavens,

and he makes the mist rise from the ends of
  the earth.
He makes lightnings for the rain,
  and he brings out the wind from his
  storehouses.
¹⁴ Everyone is stupid and without knowledge;
  goldsmiths are all put to shame by their idols;
  for their images are false,
  and there is no breath in them.
¹⁵ They are worthless, a work of delusion;
  at the time of their punishment they shall
  perish.
¹⁶ Not like these is the Lord,[d] the portion of Jacob,
  for he is the one who formed all things,
and Israel is the tribe of his inheritance;
  the Lord of hosts is his name.

The Coming Exile

¹⁷ Gather up your bundle from the ground,
  O you who live under siege!
¹⁸ For thus says the Lord:
I am going to sling out the inhabitants of the land
  at this time,
and I will bring distress on them,
  so that they shall feel it.

¹⁹ Woe is me because of my hurt!
  My wound is severe.
But I said, "Truly this is my punishment,
  and I must bear it."
²⁰ My tent is destroyed,
  and all my cords are broken;
my children have gone from me,
  and they are no more;
there is no one to spread my tent again,
  and to set up my curtains.
²¹ For the shepherds are stupid,
  and do not inquire of the Lord;
therefore they have not prospered,
  and all their flock is scattered.

²² Hear, a noise! Listen, it is coming—
  a great commotion from the land of the north
to make the cities of Judah a desolation,
  a lair of jackals.

²³ I know, O Lord, that the way of human beings is
  not in their control,
  that mortals as they walk cannot direct their
  steps.
²⁴ Correct me, O Lord, but in just measure;
  not in your anger, or you will bring me to
  nothing.

a Heb *They*   b Meaning of Heb uncertain   c This verse is in
Aramaic   d Heb lacks *the Lord*

25 Pour out your wrath on the nations that do not
    know you,
  and on the peoples that do not call on your
    name;
  for they have devoured Jacob;
    they have devoured him and consumed him,
    and have laid waste his habitation.

Israel and Judah Have Broken the Covenant

11 The word that came to Jeremiah from the
LORD: ²Hear the words of this covenant, and
speak to the people of Judah and the inhabitants
of Jerusalem. ³You shall say to them, Thus says
the LORD, the God of Israel: Cursed be anyone
who does not heed the words of this covenant,
⁴which I commanded your ancestors when I
brought them out of the land of Egypt, from the
iron-smelter, saying, Listen to my voice, and do
all that I command you. So shall you be my people, and I will be your God, ⁵that I may perform
the oath that I swore to your ancestors, to give
them a land flowing with milk and honey, as at
this day. Then I answered, "So be it, LORD."

6 And the LORD said to me: Proclaim all these
words in the cities of Judah, and in the streets of
Jerusalem: Hear the words of this covenant and
do them. ⁷For I solemnly warned your ancestors when I brought them up out of the land of
Egypt, warning them persistently, even to this
day, saying, Obey my voice. ⁸Yet they did not
obey or incline their ear, but everyone walked
in the stubbornness of an evil will. So I brought
upon them all the words of this covenant, which
I commanded them to do, but they did not.

9 And the LORD said to me: Conspiracy exists
among the people of Judah and the inhabitants
of Jerusalem. ¹⁰They have turned back to the iniquities of their ancestors of old, who refused to
heed my words; they have gone after other gods
to serve them; the house of Israel and the house
of Judah have broken the covenant that I made
with their ancestors. ¹¹Therefore, thus says the
LORD, assuredly I am going to bring disaster upon
them that they cannot escape; though they cry
out to me, I will not listen to them. ¹²Then the cities of Judah and the inhabitants of Jerusalem will
go and cry out to the gods to whom they make offerings, but they will never save them in the time
of their trouble. ¹³For your gods have become as
many as your towns, O Judah; and as many as the
streets of Jerusalem are the altars to shame you
have set up, altars to make offerings to Baal.

14 As for you, do not pray for this people, or
lift up a cry or prayer on their behalf, for I will
not listen when they call to me in the time of
their trouble. ¹⁵What right has my beloved in my

house, when she has done vile deeds? Can vows[a]
and sacrificial flesh avert your doom? Can you
then exult? ¹⁶The LORD once called you, "A green
olive tree, fair with goodly fruit"; but with the
roar of a great tempest he will set fire to it, and its
branches will be consumed. ¹⁷The LORD of hosts,
who planted you, has pronounced evil against
you, because of the evil that the house of Israel
and the house of Judah have done, provoking me
to anger by making offerings to Baal.

Jeremiah's Life Threatened

18 It was the LORD who made it known to me, and I
    knew;
  then you showed me their evil deeds.
19 But I was like a gentle lamb
    led to the slaughter.
  And I did not know it was against me
    that they devised schemes, saying,
  "Let us destroy the tree with its fruit,
    let us cut him off from the land of the living,
    so that his name will no longer be
      remembered!"
20 But you, O LORD of hosts, who judge righteously,
    who try the heart and the mind,
  let me see your retribution upon them,
    for to you I have committed my cause.

21 Therefore thus says the LORD concerning
the people of Anathoth, who seek your life, and
say, "You shall not prophesy in the name of the
LORD, or you will die by our hand"— ²²therefore
thus says the LORD of hosts: I am going to punish them; the young men shall die by the sword;
their sons and their daughters shall die by famine; ²³and not even a remnant shall be left of
them. For I will bring disaster upon the people of
Anathoth, the year of their punishment.

Jeremiah Complains to God

12 You will be in the right, O LORD,
      when I lay charges against you;
    but let me put my case to you.
  Why does the way of the guilty prosper?
    Why do all who are treacherous thrive?
2 You plant them, and they take root;
    they grow and bring forth fruit;
  you are near in their mouths
    yet far from their hearts.
3 But you, O LORD, know me;
    You see me and test me—my heart is with
      you.
  Pull them out like sheep for the slaughter,
    and set them apart for the day of slaughter.
4 How long will the land mourn,

---

a Gk: Heb Can many

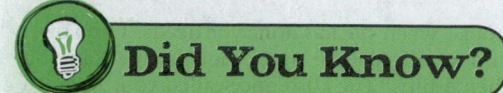

Did You Know?

The Confessions of Jeremiah

Jeremiah 12:1–6 is the first of five passages that are sometimes called the Confessions of Jeremiah (see 12:1–6, 15:10–21, 17:12–18, 18:18–23, 20:7–18). In the confessions, Jeremiah speaks to God in a very personal, very direct way. He complains to God about the people's stubbornness, he complains about his treatment, and he accuses God of deceiving him. Some scholars believe the confessions are a private journal kept by Jeremiah that he never intended to be made public.

In 12:1–4, Jeremiah asks God why God lets evil people prosper—why doesn't God just slaughter them like sheep? God's reply in verses 5–6 is that things are going to get worse before they get better and that even Jeremiah's own family will turn against him. God never answers Jeremiah directly in any of the confessions—although in 15:19–21, God does promise to support Jeremiah.

If this famous prophet shared his anger, doubts, and fears with God honestly, so can we. Jeremiah's confessions are a good reminder that God wants to share everything with us—not just our happy thoughts.

▶ **Jer 12:1–6**

and the grass of every field wither?
For the wickedness of those who live in it
   the animals and the birds are swept away,
   and because people said, "He is blind to our
      ways."*a*

God Replies to Jeremiah

5 If you have raced with foot-runners and they
      have wearied you,
   how will you compete with horses?
And if in a safe land you fall down,
   how will you fare in the thickets of the
      Jordan?
6 For even your kinsfolk and your own family,
   even they have dealt treacherously with you;
   they are in full cry after you;
do not believe them,
   though they speak friendly words to you.

7 I have forsaken my house,
   I have abandoned my heritage;
   I have given the beloved of my heart
      into the hands of her enemies.
8 My heritage has become to me
   like a lion in the forest;
   she has lifted up her voice against me—
      therefore I hate her.
9 Is the hyena greedy*b* for my heritage at my
      command?
   Are the birds of prey all around her?
Go, assemble all the wild animals;
   bring them to devour her.
10 Many shepherds have destroyed my vineyard,
   they have trampled down my portion,
   they have made my pleasant portion
      a desolate wilderness.
11 They have made it a desolation;
   desolate, it mourns to me.
The whole land is made desolate,
   but no one lays it to heart.
12 Upon all the bare heights*c* in the desert
      spoilers have come;
   for the sword of the Lord devours
      from one end of the land to the other;
      no one shall be safe.
13 They have sown wheat and have reaped thorns,
   they have tired themselves out but profit
      nothing.
They shall be ashamed of their*d* harvests
   because of the fierce anger of the Lord.

14 Thus says the Lord concerning all my evil neighbors who touch the heritage that I have given my people Israel to inherit: I am about to pluck them up from their land, and I will pluck up the house of Judah from among them. 15 And after I have plucked them up, I will again have compassion on them, and I will bring them again to their heritage and to their land, every one of them. 16 And then, if they will diligently learn the ways of my people, to swear by my name, "As the Lord lives," as they taught my people to swear by Baal, then they shall be built up in the midst of my people. 17 But if any nation will not listen, then I will completely uproot it and destroy it, says the Lord.

The Linen Loincloth

13 Thus said the Lord to me, "Go and buy yourself a linen loincloth, and put it on your loins, but do not dip it in water." 2 So I bought a loincloth according to the word of the

*a Gk: Heb to our future   b Cn: Heb Is the hyena, the bird of prey
c Or the trails   d Heb your*

Lord, and put it on my loins. ³And the word of the Lord came to me a second time, saying, ⁴"Take the loincloth that you bought and are wearing, and go now to the Euphrates,ᵃ and hide it there in a cleft of the rock." ⁵So I went, and hid it by the Euphrates,ᵇ as the Lord commanded me. ⁶And after many days the Lord said to me, "Go now to the Euphrates,ᵃ and take from there the loincloth that I commanded you to hide there." ⁷Then I went to the Euphrates,ᵃ and dug, and I took the loincloth from the place where I had hidden it. But now the loincloth was ruined; it was good for nothing.

8 Then the word of the Lord came to me: ⁹Thus says the Lord: Just so I will ruin the pride of Judah and the great pride of Jerusalem. ¹⁰This evil people, who refuse to hear my words, who stubbornly follow their own will and have gone after other gods to serve them and worship them, shall be like this loincloth, which is good for nothing. ¹¹For as the loincloth clings to one's loins, so I made the whole house of Israel and the whole house of Judah cling to me, says the Lord, in order that they might be for me a people, a name, a praise, and a glory. But they would not listen.

Symbol of the Wine-Jars

12 You shall speak to them this word: Thus says the Lord, the God of Israel: Every wine-jar should be filled with wine. And they will say to you, "Do you think we do not know that every wine-jar should be filled with wine?" ¹³Then you shall say to them: Thus says the Lord: I am about to fill all the inhabitants of this land—the kings who sit on David's throne, the priests, the prophets, and all the inhabitants of Jerusalem—with drunkenness. ¹⁴And I will dash them one against another, parents and children together, says the Lord. I will not pity or spare or have compassion when I destroy them.

Exile Threatened

¹⁵ Hear and give ear; do not be haughty,
    for the Lord has spoken.
¹⁶ Give glory to the Lord your God
    before he brings darkness,
and before your feet stumble
    on the mountains at twilight;
while you look for light,
    he turns it into gloom
    and makes it deep darkness.
¹⁷ But if you will not listen,
    my soul will weep in secret for your pride;
my eyes will weep bitterly and run down with
        tears,
    because the Lord's flock has been taken captive.

¹⁸ Say to the king and the queen mother:
    "Take a lowly seat,
for your beautiful crown
    has come down from your head."ᶜ
¹⁹ The towns of the Negeb are shut up
    with no one to open them;
all Judah is taken into exile,
    wholly taken into exile.

²⁰ Lift up your eyes and see
    those who come from the north.
Where is the flock that was given you,
    your beautiful flock?
²¹ What will you say when they set as head over you
    those whom you have trained
    to be your allies?
Will not pangs take hold of you,
    like those of a woman in labor?
²² And if you say in your heart,
    "Why have these things come upon me?"
it is for the greatness of your iniquity
    that your skirts are lifted up,
    and you are violated.
²³ Can Ethiopiansᵈ change their skin
    or leopards their spots?
Then also you can do good
    who are accustomed to do evil.
²⁴ I will scatter youᵉ like chaff
    driven by the wind from the desert.
²⁵ This is your lot,
    the portion I have measured out to you, says
        the Lord,
because you have forgotten me
    and trusted in lies.
²⁶ I myself will lift up your skirts over your face,
    and your shame will be seen.
²⁷ I have seen your abominations,
    your adulteries and neighings, your shameless
        prostitutions
    on the hills of the countryside.
Woe to you, O Jerusalem!
    How long will it be
    before you are made clean?

The Great Drought

14 The word of the Lord that came to Jeremiah concerning the drought:

² Judah mourns
    and her gates languish;
they lie in gloom on the ground,
    and the cry of Jerusalem goes up.
³ Her nobles send their servants for water;

ᵃ Or to Parah; Heb perath   ᵇ Or by Parah; Heb perath
ᶜ Gk Syr Vg: Meaning of Heb uncertain   ᵈ Or Nubians; Heb
Cushites   ᵉ Heb them

they come to the cisterns,
they find no water,
  they return with their vessels empty.
They are ashamed and dismayed
  and cover their heads,
⁴ because the ground is cracked.
  Because there has been no rain on the land
the farmers are dismayed;
  they cover their heads.
⁵ Even the doe in the field forsakes her newborn
      fawn
  because there is no grass.
⁶ The wild asses stand on the bare heights,^a
  they pant for air like jackals;
their eyes fail
  because there is no herbage.

⁷ Although our iniquities testify against us,
    act, O Lord, for your name's sake;
our apostasies indeed are many,
    and we have sinned against you.
⁸ O hope of Israel,
    its savior in time of trouble,
why should you be like a stranger in the land,

The Empty Promises of False Prophets

In Jeremiah 14:13–16, Jeremiah attacks prophets who preach what the people want to hear. The people want peace and plenty, so that is what the false prophets preach. They offer false and dangerous security.

People deceive themselves when they listen to only what they want to hear. Sometimes, God tells us things that are hard to hear or asks us to do things that are hard to do.

In your prayer, reflect or journal on the following questions:

- When have you tried to ignore God's message for you?
- When have you heard and responded to God even if God's message was difficult?
- What are the hardest things for you to hear or do?

▶ Jer 14:13–16

like a traveler turning aside for the night?
⁹ Why should you be like someone confused,
  like a mighty warrior who cannot give help?
Yet you, O Lord, are in the midst of us,
  and we are called by your name;
  do not forsake us!

¹⁰ Thus says the Lord concerning this people:
  Truly they have loved to wander,
  they have not restrained their feet;
therefore the Lord does not accept them,
  now he will remember their iniquity
  and punish their sins.

11 The Lord said to me: Do not pray for the welfare of this people. ¹²Although they fast, I do not hear their cry, and although they offer burnt offering and grain offering, I do not accept them; but by the sword, by famine, and by pestilence I consume them.

Denunciation of Lying Prophets

13 Then I said: "Ah, Lord God! Here are the prophets saying to them, 'You shall not see the sword, nor shall you have famine, but I will give you true peace in this place.' " ¹⁴And the Lord said to me: The prophets are prophesying lies in my name; I did not send them, nor did I command them or speak to them. They are prophesying to you a lying vision, worthless divination, and the deceit of their own minds. ¹⁵Therefore thus says the Lord concerning the prophets who prophesy in my name though I did not send them, and who say, "Sword and famine shall not come on this land": By sword and famine those prophets shall be consumed. ¹⁶And the people to whom they prophesy shall be thrown out into the streets of Jerusalem, victims of famine and sword. There shall be no one to bury them—themselves, their wives, their sons, and their daughters. For I will pour out their wickedness upon them.

¹⁷ You shall say to them this word:
  Let my eyes run down with tears night and day,
    and let them not cease,
  for the virgin daughter—my people—is struck
      down with a crushing blow,
    with a very grievous wound.
¹⁸ If I go out into the field,
    look—those killed by the sword!
  And if I enter the city,
    look—those sick with^b famine!

---

^a Or the trails   ^b Heb look—the sicknesses of

For both prophet and priest ply their trade
    throughout the land,
and have no knowledge.

The People Plead for Mercy

19 Have you completely rejected Judah?
    Does your heart loathe Zion?
Why have you struck us down
    so that there is no healing for us?
We look for peace, but find no good;
    for a time of healing, but there is terror instead.
20 We acknowledge our wickedness, O Lord,
    the iniquity of our ancestors,
    for we have sinned against you.
21 Do not spurn us, for your name's sake;
    do not dishonor your glorious throne;
    remember and do not break your covenant
      with us.
22 Can any idols of the nations bring rain?
    Or can the heavens give showers?
Is it not you, O Lord our God?
    We set our hope on you,
    for it is you who do all this.

Punishment Is Inevitable

15 Then the Lord said to me: Though Moses and Samuel stood before me, yet my heart would not turn toward this people. Send them out of my sight, and let them go! 2And when they say to you, "Where shall we go?" you shall say to them: Thus says the Lord:
Those destined for pestilence, to pestilence,
    and those destined for the sword, to the sword;
those destined for famine, to famine,
    and those destined for captivity, to captivity.

3And I will appoint over them four kinds of destroyers, says the Lord: the sword to kill, the dogs to drag away, and the birds of the air and the wild animals of the earth to devour and destroy. 4I will make them a horror to all the kingdoms of the earth because of what King Manasseh son of Hezekiah of Judah did in Jerusalem.

5 Who will have pity on you, O Jerusalem,
    or who will bemoan you?
Who will turn aside
    to ask about your welfare?
6 You have rejected me, says the Lord,
    you are going backward;
so I have stretched out my hand against you and
    destroyed you—
    I am weary of relenting.
7 I have winnowed them with a winnowing fork
    in the gates of the land;
I have bereaved them, I have destroyed my
    people;

they did not turn from their ways.
8 Their widows became more numerous
    than the sand of the seas;
I have brought against the mothers of youths
    a destroyer at noonday;
I have made anguish and terror
    fall upon her suddenly.
9 She who bore seven has languished;
    she has swooned away;
her sun went down while it was yet day;
    she has been shamed and disgraced.
And the rest of them I will give to the sword
    before their enemies,
               says the Lord.

Jeremiah Complains Again and Is Reassured

10 Woe is me, my mother, that you ever bore me, a man of strife and contention to the whole land! I have not lent, nor have I borrowed, yet all of them curse me. 11The Lord said: Surely I have intervened in your life[a] for good, surely I have imposed enemies on you in a time of trouble and in a time of distress.[b] 12Can iron and bronze break iron from the north?

13 Your wealth and your treasures I will give as plunder, without price, for all your sins, throughout all your territory. 14I will make you serve your enemies in a land that you do not know, for in my anger a fire is kindled that shall burn forever.

15 O Lord, you know;
    remember me and visit me,
    and bring down retribution for me on my
      persecutors.
In your forbearance do not take me away;
    know that on your account I suffer insult.
16 Your words were found, and I ate them,
    and your words became to me a joy
    and the delight of my heart;
for I am called by your name,
    O Lord, God of hosts.
17 I did not sit in the company of merrymakers,
    nor did I rejoice;
under the weight of your hand I sat alone,
    for you had filled me with indignation.
18 Why is my pain unceasing,
    my wound incurable,
    refusing to be healed?
Truly, you are to me like a deceitful brook,
    like waters that fail.

19 Therefore thus says the Lord:
If you turn back, I will take you back,
    and you shall stand before me.

---

a Heb *intervened with you*   b Meaning of Heb uncertain

If you utter what is precious, and not what is
     worthless,
  you shall serve as my mouth.
It is they who will turn to you,
  not you who will turn to them.
20 And I will make you to this people
  a fortified wall of bronze;
they will fight against you,
  but they shall not prevail over you,
for I am with you
  to save you and deliver you,
                              says the LORD.
21 I will deliver you out of the hand of the wicked,
  and redeem you from the grasp of the
     ruthless.

Jeremiah's Celibacy and Message

16 The word of the LORD came to me: ²You
shall not take a wife, nor shall you have
sons or daughters in this place. ³For thus says
the LORD concerning the sons and daughters
who are born in this place, and concerning the
mothers who bear them and the fathers who
beget them in this land: ⁴They shall die of deadly
diseases. They shall not be lamented, nor shall
they be buried; they shall become like dung on
the surface of the ground. They shall perish by
the sword and by famine, and their dead bodies
shall become food for the birds of the air and for
the wild animals of the earth.

5 For thus says the LORD: Do not enter the
house of mourning, or go to lament, or bemoan
them; for I have taken away my peace from this
people, says the LORD, my steadfast love and
mercy. ⁶Both great and small shall die in this
land; they shall not be buried, and no one shall
lament for them; there shall be no gashing, no
shaving of the head for them. ⁷No one shall
break bread*a* for the mourner, to offer comfort
for the dead; nor shall anyone give them the cup
of consolation to drink for their fathers or their
mothers. ⁸You shall not go into the house of
feasting to sit with them, to eat and drink. ⁹For
thus says the LORD of hosts, the God of Israel: I
am going to banish from this place, in your days
and before your eyes, the voice of mirth and the
voice of gladness, the voice of the bridegroom
and the voice of the bride.

10 And when you tell this people all these
words, and they say to you, "Why has the LORD
pronounced all this great evil against us? What is
our iniquity? What is the sin that we have committed against the LORD our God?" ¹¹then you
shall say to them: It is because your ancestors
have forsaken me, says the LORD, and have gone
after other gods and have served and worshiped

them, and have forsaken me and have not kept
my law; ¹²and because you have behaved worse
than your ancestors, for here you are, every one
of you, following your stubborn evil will, refusing to listen to me. ¹³Therefore I will hurl you
out of this land into a land that neither you nor
your ancestors have known, and there you shall
serve other gods day and night, for I will show
you no favor.

God Will Restore Israel

14 Therefore, the days are surely coming, says
the LORD, when it shall no longer be said, "As the
LORD lives who brought the people of Israel up
out of the land of Egypt," ¹⁵but "As the LORD lives
who brought the people of Israel up out of the
land of the north and out of all the lands where
he had driven them." For I will bring them back
to their own land that I gave to their ancestors.

16 I am now sending for many fishermen, says
the LORD, and they shall catch them; and afterward
I will send for many hunters, and they shall hunt
them from every mountain and every hill, and out
of the clefts of the rocks. ¹⁷For my eyes are on all
their ways; they are not hidden from my presence,
nor is their iniquity concealed from my sight.
¹⁸And*b* I will doubly repay their iniquity and their
sin, because they have polluted my land with the
carcasses of their detestable idols, and have filled
my inheritance with their abominations.

19 O LORD, my strength and my stronghold,
  my refuge in the day of trouble,
to you shall the nations come
  from the ends of the earth and say:
Our ancestors have inherited nothing but lies,
  worthless things in which there is no profit.
20 Can mortals make for themselves gods?
  Such are no gods!

21 "Therefore I am surely going to teach
them, this time I am going to teach them my
power and my might, and they shall know that
my name is the LORD."

Judah's Sin and Punishment

17 The sin of Judah is written with an iron
pen; with a diamond point it is engraved
on the tablet of their hearts, and on the horns of
their altars, ²while their children remember their
altars and their sacred poles,*c* beside every green
tree, and on the high hills, ³on the mountains
in the open country. Your wealth and all your

---

a Two Mss Gk: MT *break for them*   b Gk: Heb *And first*
c Heb *Asherim*

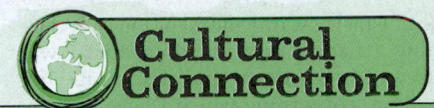

Cultural Connection

Children and Green Trees

The land is very important in Native American spirituality; trees, grass, and flowers are treated with respect, love, and awe, similar to that afforded people, because all are connected. It is the greatest wish of the elders that the children learn this lesson and carry it on to their own children. Native Americans would view the loss and destruction of the land described in Jeremiah 17:1–3 as a horrible punishment. See how their value for the land is reflected in this prayer from the Mohawk tradition:

Oh Great Spirit, Creator of all
  things;
Human Beings, trees, grass,
  berries.
Help us, be kind to us.
Let us be happy on earth.
Let us lead our children
To a good life and old age.
These our people; give them
  good minds
To love one another.
Oh Great Spirit,
Be kind to us.
Give these people the favour

To see green trees,
Green grass, flowers, and
  berries
This next spring;
So we all meet again.
Oh Great Spirit,
We ask of you.
      [Author unknown,
      "Mohawk Indian Prayer"]

▶ **Jer 17:1–3**

J
E
R

---

treasures I will give for spoil as the price of your sin[a] throughout all your territory. ⁴By your own act you shall lose the heritage that I gave you, and I will make you serve your enemies in a land that you do not know, for in my anger a fire is kindled[b] that shall burn forever.

⁵ Thus says the LORD:
　Cursed are those who trust in mere mortals
　　and make mere flesh their strength,
　　whose hearts turn away from the LORD.
⁶ They shall be like a shrub in the desert,
　　and shall not see when relief comes.
　They shall live in the parched places of the
　　wilderness,
　　in an uninhabited salt land.

⁷ Blessed are those who trust in the LORD,
　　whose trust is the LORD.
⁸ They shall be like a tree planted by water,
　　sending out its roots by the stream.
　It shall not fear when heat comes,
　　and its leaves shall stay green;
　in the year of drought it is not anxious,
　　and it does not cease to bear fruit.

⁹ The heart is devious above all else;
　　it is perverse—
　　who can understand it?
¹⁰ I the LORD test the mind
　　and search the heart,
　to give to all according to their ways,
　　according to the fruit of their doings.

¹¹ Like the partridge hatching what it did not lay,
　　so are all who amass wealth unjustly;
　in mid-life it will leave them,
　　and at their end they will prove to be fools.

¹² O glorious throne, exalted from the beginning,
　　shrine of our sanctuary!
¹³ O hope of Israel! O LORD!
　　All who forsake you shall be put to shame;
　those who turn away from you[c] shall be
　　recorded in the underworld,[d]
　for they have forsaken the fountain of living
　　water, the LORD.

Jeremiah Prays for Vindication

¹⁴ Heal me, O LORD, and I shall be healed;
　　save me, and I shall be saved;
　　for you are my praise.
¹⁵ See how they say to me,
　　"Where is the word of the LORD?
　　Let it come!"
¹⁶ But I have not run away from being a shepherd[e]
　　in your service,
　　nor have I desired the fatal day.
　You know what came from my lips;
　　it was before your face.
¹⁷ Do not become a terror to me;
　　you are my refuge in the day of disaster;
¹⁸ Let my persecutors be shamed,

---

a Cn: Heb *spoil your high places for sin*   b Two Mss Theodotion: *you kindled*   c Heb *me*   d Or *in the earth*   e Meaning of Heb uncertain

but do not let me be shamed;
 let them be dismayed,
  but do not let me be dismayed;
bring on them the day of disaster;
 destroy them with double destruction!

Hallow the Sabbath Day

19 Thus said the Lord to me: Go and stand in the People's Gate, by which the kings of Judah enter and by which they go out, and in all the gates of Jerusalem, 20and say to them: Hear the word of the Lord, you kings of Judah, and all Judah, and all the inhabitants of Jerusalem, who enter by these gates. 21Thus says the Lord: For the sake of your lives, take care that you do not bear a burden on the sabbath day or bring it in by the gates of Jerusalem. 22And do not carry a burden out of your houses on the sabbath or do any work, but keep the sabbath day holy, as I commanded your ancestors. 23Yet they did not listen or incline their ear; they stiffened their necks and would not hear or receive instruction.

24 But if you listen to me, says the Lord, and bring in no burden by the gates of this city on the sabbath day, but keep the sabbath day holy and do no work on it, 25then there shall enter by the gates of this city kings*a* who sit on the throne of David, riding in chariots and on horses, they and their officials, the people of Judah and the inhabitants of Jerusalem; and this city shall be inhabited forever. 26And people shall come from the towns of Judah and the places around Jerusalem, from the land of Benjamin, from the Shephelah, from the hill country, and from the Negeb, bringing burnt offerings and sacrifices, grain offerings and frankincense, and bringing thank offerings to the house of the Lord. 27But if you do not listen to me, to keep the sabbath day holy, and to carry in no burden through the gates of Jerusalem on the sabbath day, then I will kindle a fire in its gates; it shall devour the palaces of Jerusalem and shall not be quenched.

The Potter and the Clay

18 The word that came to Jeremiah from the Lord: 2"Come, go down to the potter's house, and there I will let you hear my words." 3So I went down to the potter's house, and there he was working at his wheel. 4The vessel he was making of clay was spoiled in the potter's hand, and he reworked it into another vessel, as seemed good to him.

5 Then the word of the Lord came to me: 6Can I not do with you, O house of Israel, just as this potter has done? says the Lord. Just like the clay in the potter's hand, so are you in my hand,

O house of Israel. 7At one moment I may declare concerning a nation or a kingdom, that I will pluck up and break down and destroy it, 8but if that nation, concerning which I have spoken, turns from its evil, I will change my mind about the disaster that I intended to bring on it. 9And at another moment I may declare concerning a nation or a kingdom that I will build and plant it, 10but if it does evil in my sight, not listening to my voice, then I will change my mind about the good that I had intended to do to it. 11Now, therefore, say to the people of Judah and the inhabitants of Jerusalem: Thus says the Lord: Look, I am a potter shaping evil against you and devising a plan against you. Turn now, all of you from your evil way, and amend your ways and your doings.

Israel's Stubborn Idolatry

12 But they say, "It is no use! We will follow our own plans, and each of us will act according to the stubbornness of our evil will."

13 Therefore thus says the Lord:
 Ask among the nations:
  Who has heard the like of this?
 The virgin Israel has done
  a most horrible thing.
14 Does the snow of Lebanon leave
  the crags of Sirion?*b*
 Do the mountain*c* waters run dry,*d*
  the cold flowing streams?
15 But my people have forgotten me,
  they burn offerings to a delusion;
 they have stumbled*e* in their ways,
  in the ancient roads,
 and have gone into bypaths,
  not the highway,
16 making their land a horror,
  a thing to be hissed at forever.
 All who pass by it are horrified
  and shake their heads.
17 Like the wind from the east,
  I will scatter them before the enemy.
 I will show them my back, not my face,
  in the day of their calamity.

A Plot against Jeremiah

18 Then they said, "Come, let us make plots against Jeremiah—for instruction shall not perish from the priest, nor counsel from the wise, nor the word from the prophet. Come, let us

---

a Cn: Heb *kings and officials* *b* Cn: Heb *of the field* *c* Cn: Heb *foreign* *d* Cn: Heb *Are . . . plucked up?* *e* Gk Syr Vg: Heb *they made them stumble*

bring charges against him,*a* and let us not heed any of his words."

¹⁹ Give heed to me, O Lord,
　　and listen to what my adversaries say!
²⁰ Is evil a recompense for good?
　　Yet they have dug a pit for my life.
　Remember how I stood before you
　　to speak good for them,
　　to turn away your wrath from them.
²¹ Therefore give their children over to famine;
　　hurl them out to the power of the sword,
　let their wives become childless and widowed.
　　May their men meet death by pestilence,
　　their youths be slain by the sword in battle.
²² May a cry be heard from their houses,
　　when you bring the marauder suddenly upon
　　　them!
　For they have dug a pit to catch me,
　　and laid snares for my feet.
²³ Yet you, O Lord, know
　　all their plotting to kill me.
　Do not forgive their iniquity,
　　do not blot out their sin from your sight.
　Let them be tripped up before you;
　　deal with them while you are angry.

The Broken Earthenware Jug

19 Thus said the Lord: Go and buy a potter's earthenware jug. Take with you*b* some of the elders of the people and some of the senior priests, ²and go out to the valley of the son of Hinnom at the entry of the Potsherd Gate, and proclaim there the words that I tell you. ³You shall say: Hear the word of the Lord, O kings of Judah and inhabitants of Jerusalem. Thus says the Lord of hosts, the God of Israel: I am going to bring such disaster upon this place that the ears of everyone who hears of it will tingle. ⁴Because the people have forsaken me, and have profaned this place by making offerings in it to other gods whom neither they nor their ancestors nor the kings of Judah have known, and because they have filled this place with the blood of the innocent, ⁵and gone on building the high places of Baal to burn their children in the fire as burnt offerings to Baal, which I did not command or decree, nor did it enter my mind; ⁶therefore the days are surely coming, says the Lord, when this place shall no more be called Topheth, or the valley of the son of Hinnom, but the valley of Slaughter. ⁷And in this place I will make void the plans of Judah and Jerusalem, and will make them fall by the sword before their enemies, and by the hand of those who seek their life. I will give their dead bodies for food to the birds of the

air and to the wild animals of the earth. ⁸And I will make this city a horror, a thing to be hissed at; everyone who passes by it will be horrified and will hiss because of all its disasters. ⁹And I will make them eat the flesh of their sons and the flesh of their daughters, and all shall eat the flesh of their neighbors in the siege, and in the distress with which their enemies and those who seek their life afflict them.

¹⁰ Then you shall break the jug in the sight of those who go with you, ¹¹and shall say to them: Thus says the Lord of hosts: So will I break this people and this city, as one breaks a potter's vessel, so that it can never be mended. In Topheth they shall bury until there is no more room to bury. ¹²Thus will I do to this place, says the Lord, and to its inhabitants, making this city like Topheth. ¹³And the houses of Jerusalem and the houses of the kings of Judah shall be defiled like the place of Topheth—all the houses upon whose roofs offerings have been made to the whole host of heaven, and libations have been poured out to other gods.

¹⁴ When Jeremiah came from Topheth, where the Lord had sent him to prophesy, he stood in the court of the Lord's house and said to all the people: ¹⁵Thus says the Lord of hosts, the God of Israel: I am now bringing upon this city and upon all its towns all the disaster that I have pronounced against it, because they have stiffened their necks, refusing to hear my words.

Jeremiah Persecuted by Pashhur

20 Now the priest Pashhur son of Immer, who was chief officer in the house of the Lord, heard Jeremiah prophesying these things. ²Then Pashhur struck the prophet Jeremiah, and put him in the stocks that were in the upper Benjamin Gate of the house of the Lord. ³The next morning when Pashhur released Jeremiah from the stocks, Jeremiah said to him, The Lord has named you not Pashhur but "Terror-all-around." ⁴For thus says the Lord: I am making you a terror to yourself and to all your friends; and they shall fall by the sword of their enemies while you look on. And I will give all Judah into the hand of the king of Babylon; he shall carry them captive to Babylon, and shall kill them with the sword. ⁵I will give all the wealth of this city, all its gains, all its prized belongings, and all the treasures of the kings of Judah into the hand of their enemies, who shall plunder them, and seize them, and carry them to Babylon.

---

a Heb *strike him with the tongue*　　*b* Syr Tg Compare Gk: Heb lacks *take with you*

⁶And you, Pashhur, and all who live in your house, shall go into captivity, and to Babylon you shall go; there you shall die, and there you shall be buried, you and all your friends, to whom you have prophesied falsely.

Jeremiah Denounces His Persecutors

⁷ O Lᴏʀᴅ, you have enticed me,
  and I was enticed;
you have overpowered me,
  and you have prevailed.
I have become a laughingstock all day long;
  everyone mocks me.
⁸ For whenever I speak, I must cry out,
  I must shout, "Violence and destruction!"
For the word of the Lᴏʀᴅ has become for me
  a reproach and derision all day long.
⁹ If I say, "I will not mention him,
  or speak any more in his name,"
then within me there is something like a
    burning fire
  shut up in my bones;
I am weary with holding it in,
  and I cannot.
¹⁰ For I hear many whispering:
  "Terror is all around!
Denounce him! Let us denounce him!"
  All my close friends
  are watching for me to stumble.
"Perhaps he can be enticed,
  and we can prevail against him,
  and take our revenge on him."
¹¹ But the Lᴏʀᴅ is with me like a dread warrior;
  therefore my persecutors will stumble,
  and they will not prevail.
They will be greatly shamed,
  for they will not succeed.
Their eternal dishonor
  will never be forgotten.
¹² O Lᴏʀᴅ of hosts, you test the righteous,
  you see the heart and the mind;
let me see your retribution upon them,
  for to you I have committed my cause.

¹³ Sing to the Lᴏʀᴅ;
  praise the Lᴏʀᴅ!
For he has delivered the life of the needy
  from the hands of evildoers.

¹⁴ Cursed be the day
  on which I was born!
The day when my mother bore me,
  let it not be blessed!
¹⁵ Cursed be the man
  who brought the news to my father,
    saying,

"A child is born to you, a son,"
  making him very glad.
¹⁶ Let that man be like the cities
  that the Lᴏʀᴅ overthrew without pity;
let him hear a cry in the morning
  and an alarm at noon,
¹⁷ because he did not kill me in the womb;
  so my mother would have been my grave,
  and her womb forever great.
¹⁸ Why did I come forth from the womb
  to see toil and sorrow,
  and spend my days in shame?

Jerusalem Will Fall to Nebuchadrezzar

21 This is the word that came to Jeremiah from the Lᴏʀᴅ, when King Zedekiah sent to him Pashhur son of Malchiah and the priest Zephaniah son of Maaseiah, saying, ²"Please inquire of the Lᴏʀᴅ on our behalf, for King Nebuchadrezzar of Babylon is making war against us; perhaps the Lᴏʀᴅ will perform a wonderful deed for us, as he has often done, and will make him withdraw from us."

3 Then Jeremiah said to them: ⁴Thus you shall say to Zedekiah: Thus says the Lᴏʀᴅ, the God of Israel: I am going to turn back the weapons of war that are in your hands and with which you are fighting against the king of Babylon and against the Chaldeans who are besieging you outside the walls; and I will bring them together into the center of this city. ⁵I myself will fight against you with outstretched hand and mighty arm, in anger, in fury, and in great wrath. ⁶And I will strike down the inhabitants of this city, both human beings and animals; they shall die of a great pestilence. ⁷Afterward, says the Lᴏʀᴅ, I will give King Zedekiah of Judah, and his servants, and the people in this city—those who survive the pestilence, sword, and famine—into the hands of King Nebuchadrezzar of Babylon, into the hands of their enemies, into the hands of those who seek their lives. He shall strike them down with the edge of the sword; he shall not pity them, or spare them, or have compassion.

8 And to this people you shall say: Thus says the Lᴏʀᴅ: See, I am setting before you the way of life and the way of death. ⁹Those who stay in this city shall die by the sword, by famine, and by pestilence; but those who go out and surrender to the Chaldeans who are besieging you shall live and shall have their lives as a prize of war. ¹⁰For I have set my face against this city for evil and not for good, says the Lᴏʀᴅ: it shall be given into the hands of the king of Babylon, and he shall burn it with fire.

Message to the House of David

11 To the house of the king of Judah say: Hear the word of the LORD, 12O house of David! Thus says the LORD:

Execute justice in the morning,
  and deliver from the hand of the oppressor
  anyone who has been robbed,
or else my wrath will go forth like fire,
  and burn, with no one to quench it,
  because of your evil doings.

13 See, I am against you, O inhabitant of the valley,
  O rock of the plain,
                              says the LORD;
you who say, "Who can come down against us,
  or who can enter our places of refuge?"
14 I will punish you according to the fruit of your
    doings,
                              says the LORD;
I will kindle a fire in its forest,
  and it shall devour all that is around it.

Exhortation to Repent

22 Thus says the LORD: Go down to the house of the king of Judah, and speak there this word, 2and say: Hear the word of the LORD, O King of Judah sitting on the throne of David—you, and your servants, and your people who enter these gates. 3Thus says the LORD: Act with justice and righteousness, and deliver from the hand of the oppressor anyone who has been robbed. And do no wrong or violence to the alien, the orphan, and the widow, or shed innocent blood in this place. 4For if you will indeed obey this word, then through the gates of this house shall enter kings who sit on the throne of David, riding in chariots and on horses, they, and their servants, and their people. 5But if you will not heed these words, I swear by myself, says the LORD, that this house shall become a desolation. 6For thus says the LORD concerning the house of the king of Judah:

You are like Gilead to me,
  like the summit of Lebanon;
but I swear that I will make you a desert,
  an uninhabited city.a
7 I will prepare destroyers against you,
  all with their weapons;
they shall cut down your choicest cedars
  and cast them into the fire.

8 And many nations will pass by this city, and all of them will say one to another, "Why has the LORD dealt in this way with that great city?" 9And they will answer, "Because they abandoned the covenant of the LORD their God, and worshiped other gods and served them."

10 Do not weep for him who is dead,
  nor bemoan him;
weep rather for him who goes away,
  for he shall return no more
  to see his native land.

Message to the Sons of Josiah

11 For thus says the LORD concerning Shallum son of King Josiah of Judah, who succeeded his father Josiah, and who went away from this place: He shall return here no more, 12but in the place where they have carried him captive he shall die, and he shall never see this land again.

13 Woe to him who builds his house by
      unrighteousness,
  and his upper rooms by injustice;
who makes his neighbors work for nothing,
  and does not give them their wages;
14 who says, "I will build myself a spacious house
    with large upper rooms,"
and who cuts out windows for it,
    paneling it with cedar,
    and painting it with vermilion.
15 Are you a king
    because you compete in cedar?
Did not your father eat and drink
    and do justice and righteousness?
    Then it was well with him.
16 He judged the cause of the poor and needy;
    then it was well.
  Is not this to know me?
    says the LORD.
17 But your eyes and heart
    are only on your dishonest gain,
  for shedding innocent blood,
    and for practicing oppression and violence.

18 Therefore thus says the LORD concerning King Jehoiakim son of Josiah of Judah:

They shall not lament for him, saying,
    "Alas, my brother!" or "Alas, sister!"
They shall not lament for him, saying,
    "Alas, lord!" or "Alas, his majesty!"
19 With the burial of a donkey he shall be buried—
    dragged off and thrown out beyond the gates
        of Jerusalem.

20 Go up to Lebanon, and cry out,
    and lift up your voice in Bashan;
  cry out from Abarim,
    for all your lovers are crushed.
21 I spoke to you in your prosperity,
    but you said, "I will not listen."
  This has been your way from your youth,

---

a Cn: Heb *uninhabited cities*

Admit It!

Jeremiah's words against King Jehoiakim in Jeremiah 22:21–23 are harsh. Jehoiakim is guilty of some serious sin and is leading the nation to destruction. But he doesn't want to hear about it. In fact, when Jehoiakim is presented with a scroll of Jeremiah's prophecies, he burns it (see 36:23)!

Forgiving God,
Help us to hear the prophets in today's world
    who call us to own our sin.
The prophets who call us to end
    discrimination,
who call us to care for the needy,
who call us to care for the earth,
who call us to end violence,
who call us to healthy relationships,
who call us to be people of integrity,
    avoiding sin in all its forms.
May we be humble enough to admit our
    faults
and courageous enough to do
    something about
    them.

▶ **Jer 22:18–23**

for you have not obeyed my voice.
²² The wind shall shepherd all your shepherds,
    and your lovers shall go into captivity;
then you will be ashamed and dismayed
    because of all your wickedness.
²³ O inhabitant of Lebanon,
    nested among the cedars,
how you will groan*ᵃ* when pangs come upon you,
    pain as of a woman in labor!

Judgment on Coniah (Jehoiachin)

24 As I live, says the LORD, even if King Coniah son of Jehoiakim of Judah were the signet ring on my right hand, even from there I would tear you off ²⁵and give you into the hands of those who seek your life, into the hands of those of whom you are afraid, even into the hands of King Nebuchadrezzar of Babylon and into the hands of the Chaldeans. ²⁶I will hurl you and the mother who bore you into another country,

where you were not born, and there you shall die. ²⁷But they shall not return to the land to which they long to return.
²⁸ Is this man Coniah a despised broken pot,
    a vessel no one wants?
Why are he and his offspring hurled out
    and cast away in a land that they do not know?
²⁹ O land, land, land,
    hear the word of the LORD!
³⁰ Thus says the LORD:
Record this man as childless,
    a man who shall not succeed in his days;
for none of his offspring shall succeed
    in sitting on the throne of David,
    and ruling again in Judah.

Restoration after Exile

23 Woe to the shepherds who destroy and scatter the sheep of my pasture! says the LORD. ²Therefore thus says the LORD, the God of Israel, concerning the shepherds who shepherd my people: It is you who have scattered my flock, and have driven them away, and you have not attended to them. So I will attend to you for your evil doings, says the LORD. ³Then I myself will gather the remnant of my flock out of all the lands where I have driven them, and I will bring them back to their fold, and they shall be fruitful and multiply. ⁴I will raise up shepherds over them who will shepherd them, and they shall not fear any longer, or be dismayed, nor shall any be missing, says the LORD.

The Righteous Branch of David

5 The days are surely coming, says the LORD, when I will raise up for David a righteous Branch, and he shall reign as king and deal wisely, and shall execute justice and righteousness in the land. ⁶In his days Judah will be saved and Israel will live in safety. And this is the name by which he will be called: "The LORD is our righteousness."

7 Therefore, the days are surely coming, says the LORD, when it shall no longer be said, "As the LORD lives who brought the people of Israel up out of the land of Egypt," ⁸but "As the LORD lives who brought out and led the offspring of the house of Israel out of the land of the north and out of all the lands where he*ᵇ* had driven them." Then they shall live in their own land.

False Prophets of Hope Denounced

9 Concerning the prophets:
My heart is crushed within me,

a Gk Vg Syr: Heb *will be pitied*   *b* Gk: Heb *I*

all my bones shake;
I have become like a drunkard,
    like one overcome by wine,
because of the LORD
    and because of his holy words.
10 For the land is full of adulterers;
    because of the curse the land mourns,
    and the pastures of the wilderness are
        dried up.
Their course has been evil,
    and their might is not right.
11 Both prophet and priest are ungodly;
    even in my house I have found their
        wickedness,
                    says the LORD.
12 Therefore their way shall be to them
    like slippery paths in the darkness,
    into which they shall be driven and fall;
for I will bring disaster upon them
    in the year of their punishment,
                    says the LORD.
13 In the prophets of Samaria
    I saw a disgusting thing:
they prophesied by Baal
    and led my people Israel astray.
14 But in the prophets of Jerusalem
    I have seen a more shocking thing:
they commit adultery and walk in lies;
    they strengthen the hands of evildoers,
    so that no one turns from wickedness;
all of them have become like Sodom to me,
    and its inhabitants like Gomorrah.
15 Therefore thus says the LORD of hosts concerning
        the prophets:
"I am going to make them eat wormwood,
    and give them poisoned water to drink;
for from the prophets of Jerusalem
    ungodliness has spread throughout the land."

16 Thus says the LORD of hosts: Do not listen to the words of the prophets who prophesy to you; they are deluding you. They speak visions of their own minds, not from the mouth of the LORD. 17They keep saying to those who despise the word of the LORD, "It shall be well with you"; and to all who stubbornly follow their own stubborn hearts, they say, "No calamity shall come upon you."

18 For who has stood in the council of the LORD
    so as to see and to hear his word?
    Who has given heed to his word so as to
        proclaim it?
19 Look, the storm of the LORD!
    Wrath has gone forth,
a whirling tempest;

it will burst upon the head of the wicked.
20 The anger of the LORD will not turn back
    until he has executed and accomplished
    the intents of his mind.
In the latter days you will understand it clearly.

21 I did not send the prophets,
    yet they ran;
I did not speak to them,
    yet they prophesied.
22 But if they had stood in my council,
    then they would have proclaimed my words
        to my people,
and they would have turned them from their
        evil way,
    and from the evil of their doings.

23 Am I a God near by, says the LORD, and not a God far off? 24Who can hide in secret places so that I cannot see them? says the LORD. Do I not fill heaven and earth? says the LORD. 25I have heard what the prophets have said who prophesy lies in my name, saying, "I have dreamed, I have dreamed!" 26How long? Will the hearts of the prophets ever turn back—those who prophesy lies, and who prophesy the deceit of their own heart? 27They plan to make my people forget my name by their dreams that they tell one another, just as their ancestors forgot my name for Baal. 28Let the prophet who has a dream tell the dream, but let the one who has my word speak my word faithfully. What has straw in common with wheat? says the LORD. 29Is not my word like fire, says the LORD, and like a hammer that breaks a rock in pieces? 30See, therefore, I am against the prophets, says the LORD, who steal my words from one another. 31See, I am against the prophets, says the LORD, who use their own tongues and say, "Says the LORD." 32See, I am against those who prophesy lying dreams, says the LORD, and who tell them, and who lead my people astray by their lies and their recklessness, when I did not send them or appoint them; so they do not profit this people at all, says the LORD.

33 When this people, or a prophet, or a priest asks you, "What is the burden of the LORD?" you shall say to them, "You are the burden,a and I will cast you off, says the LORD." 34And as for the prophet, priest, or the people who say, "The burden of the LORD," I will punish them and their households. 35Thus shall you say to one another, among yourselves, "What has the LORD answered?" or "What has the LORD spoken?" 36But "the burden of the LORD" you shall mention no

---

a Gk Vg: Heb *What burden*

more, for the burden is everyone's own word, and so you pervert the words of the living God, the LORD of hosts, our God. ³⁷Thus you shall ask the prophet, "What has the LORD answered you?" or "What has the LORD spoken?" ³⁸But if you say, "the burden of the LORD," thus says the LORD: Because you have said these words, "the burden of the LORD," when I sent to you, saying, You shall not say, "the burden of the LORD," ³⁹therefore, I will surely lift you up[a] and cast you away from my presence, you and the city that I gave to you and your ancestors. ⁴⁰And I will bring upon you everlasting disgrace and perpetual shame, which shall not be forgotten.

The Good and the Bad Figs

24 The LORD showed me two baskets of figs placed before the temple of the LORD. This was after King Nebuchadrezzar of Babylon had taken into exile from Jerusalem King Jeconiah son of Jehoiakim of Judah, together with the officials of Judah, the artisans, and the smiths, and had brought them to Babylon. ²One basket had very good figs, like first-ripe figs, but the other basket had very bad figs, so bad that they could not be eaten. ³And the LORD said to me, "What do you see, Jeremiah?" I said, "Figs, the good figs very good, and the bad figs very bad, so bad that they cannot be eaten."

4 Then the word of the LORD came to me: ⁵Thus says the LORD, the God of Israel: Like these good figs, so I will regard as good the exiles from Judah, whom I have sent away from this place

to the land of the Chaldeans. ⁶I will set my eyes upon them for good, and I will bring them back to this land. I will build them up, and not tear them down; I will plant them, and not pluck them up. ⁷I will give them a heart to know that I am the LORD; and they shall be my people and I will be their God, for they shall return to me with their whole heart.

8 But thus says the LORD: Like the bad figs that are so bad they cannot be eaten, so will I treat King Zedekiah of Judah, his officials, the remnant of Jerusalem who remain in this land, and those who live in the land of Egypt. ⁹I will make them a horror, an evil thing, to all the kingdoms of the earth—a disgrace, a byword, a taunt, and a curse in all the places where I shall drive them. ¹⁰And I will send sword, famine, and pestilence upon them, until they are utterly destroyed from the land that I gave to them and their ancestors.

The Babylonian Captivity Foretold

25 The word that came to Jeremiah concerning all the people of Judah, in the fourth year of King Jehoiakim son of Josiah of Judah (that was the first year of King Nebuchadrezzar of Babylon), ²which the prophet Jeremiah spoke to all the people of Judah and all the inhabitants of Jerusalem: ³For twenty-three years, from the thirteenth year of King Josiah son of Amon of Judah, to this day, the word of the LORD has come to me, and I have spoken persistently to you, but you have not listened. ⁴And though the LORD persistently sent you all his servants the prophets, you have neither listened nor inclined your ears to hear ⁵when they said, "Turn now, every one of you, from your evil way and wicked doings, and you will remain upon the land that the LORD has given to you and your ancestors from of old and forever; ⁶do not go after other gods to serve and worship them, and do not provoke me to anger with the work of your hands. Then I will do you no harm." ⁷Yet you did not listen to me, says the LORD, and so you have provoked me to anger with the work of your hands to your own harm.

8 Therefore thus says the LORD of hosts: Because you have not obeyed my words, ⁹I am going to send for all the tribes of the north, says the LORD, even for King Nebuchadrezzar of Babylon, my servant, and I will bring them against this land and its inhabitants, and against all these nations around; I will utterly destroy them, and make them an object of horror and of hissing, and an everlasting disgrace.[b] ¹⁰And I will banish

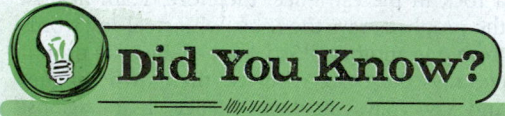

Did You Know?

Fig Trees

The fig tree was widely cultivated in the ancient Near East. Its sweet fruit was a delight to taste, and its broad leaves offered welcome shade from the scorching summer sun. In Jeremiah 24:5–7, ripe figs are presented as an image of the faithful exiles in Babylon. In 1 Kings 4:25, fig leaves symbolize protection and safety. Jesus tells a parable about a fig tree in Luke 13:6–9. Think about it the next time you eat a Fig Newton!

▶ Jeremiah, chapter 24

---

a Heb Mss Gk Vg: MT *forget you*   b Gk Compare Syr: Heb *and everlasting desolations*

from them the sound of mirth and the sound of gladness, the voice of the bridegroom and the voice of the bride, the sound of the millstones and the light of the lamp. [11]This whole land shall become a ruin and a waste, and these nations shall serve the king of Babylon seventy years. [12]Then after seventy years are completed, I will punish the king of Babylon and that nation, the land of the Chaldeans, for their iniquity, says the LORD, making the land an everlasting waste. [13]I will bring upon that land all the words that I have uttered against it, everything written in this book, which Jeremiah prophesied against all the nations. [14]For many nations and great kings shall make slaves of them also; and I will repay them according to their deeds and the work of their hands.

The Cup of God's Wrath

15 For thus the LORD, the God of Israel, said to me: Take from my hand this cup of the wine of wrath, and make all the nations to whom I send you drink it. [16]They shall drink and stagger and go out of their minds because of the sword that I am sending among them.

17 So I took the cup from the LORD's hand, and made all the nations to whom the LORD sent me drink it: [18]Jerusalem and the towns of Judah, its kings and officials, to make them a desolation and a waste, an object of hissing and of cursing, as they are today; [19]Pharaoh king of Egypt, his servants, his officials, and all his people; [20]all the mixed people;[a] all the kings of the land of Uz; all the kings of the land of the Philistines—Ashkelon, Gaza, Ekron, and the remnant of Ashdod; [21]Edom, Moab, and the Ammonites; [22]all the kings of Tyre, all the kings of Sidon, and the kings of the coastland across the sea; [23]Dedan, Tema, Buz, and all who have shaven temples; [24]all the kings of Arabia and all the kings of the mixed peoples[a] that live in the desert; [25]all the kings of Zimri, all the kings of Elam, and all the kings of Media; [26]all the kings of the north, far and near, one after another, and all the kingdoms of the world that are on the face of the earth. And after them the king of Sheshach[b] shall drink.

27 Then you shall say to them, Thus says the LORD of hosts, the God of Israel: Drink, get drunk and vomit, fall and rise no more, because of the sword that I am sending among you.

28 And if they refuse to accept the cup from your hand to drink, then you shall say to them: Thus says the LORD of hosts: You must drink! [29]See, I am beginning to bring disaster on the city that is called by my name, and how can you possibly avoid punishment? You shall not go unpunished, for I am summoning a sword against all the inhabitants of the earth, says the LORD of hosts.

30 You, therefore, shall prophesy against them all these words, and say to them: .
The LORD will roar from on high,
    and from his holy habitation utter his voice;
he will roar mightily against his fold,
    and shout, like those who tread grapes,
    against all the inhabitants of the earth.
[31] The clamor will resound to the ends of the earth,
    for the LORD has an indictment against the nations;
he is entering into judgment with all flesh,
    and the guilty he will put to the sword,
                    says the LORD.

[32] Thus says the LORD of hosts:
See, disaster is spreading
    from nation to nation,
and a great tempest is stirring
    from the farthest parts of the earth!

33 Those slain by the LORD on that day shall extend from one end of the earth to the other. They shall not be lamented, or gathered, or buried; they shall become dung on the surface of the ground.

[34] Wail, you shepherds, and cry out;
    roll in ashes, you lords of the flock,
for the days of your slaughter have come—and
        your dispersions,[a]
    and you shall fall like a choice vessel.
[35] Flight shall fail the shepherds,
    and there shall be no escape for the lords of
        the flock.
[36] Hark! the cry of the shepherds,
    and the wail of the lords of the flock!
For the LORD is despoiling their pasture,
[37]   and the peaceful folds are devastated,
    because of the fierce anger of the LORD.
[38] Like a lion he has left his covert;
    for their land has become a waste
because of the cruel sword,
    and because of his fierce anger.

Jeremiah's Prophecies in the Temple

26 At the beginning of the reign of King Jehoiakim son of Josiah of Judah, this word came from the LORD: [2]Thus says the LORD: Stand in the court of the LORD's house, and speak to all the cities of Judah that come to worship in the

---

a Meaning of Heb uncertain   b Sheshach is a cryptogram for Babel, Babylon

house of the LORD; speak to them all the words that I command you; do not hold back a word. ³It may be that they will listen, all of them, and will turn from their evil way, that I may change my mind about the disaster that I intend to bring on them because of their evil doings. ⁴You shall say to them: Thus says the LORD: If you will not listen to me, to walk in my law that I have set before you, ⁵and to heed the words of my servants the prophets whom I send to you urgently— though you have not heeded— ⁶then I will make this house like Shiloh, and I will make this city a curse for all the nations of the earth.

7 The priests and the prophets and all the people heard Jeremiah speaking these words in the house of the LORD. ⁸And when Jeremiah had finished speaking all that the LORD had commanded him to speak to all the people, then the priests and the prophets and all the people laid hold of him, saying, "You shall die! ⁹Why have you prophesied in the name of the LORD, saying, 'This house shall be like Shiloh, and this city shall be desolate, without inhabitant'?" And all the people gathered around Jeremiah in the house of the LORD.

10 When the officials of Judah heard these things, they came up from the king's house to the house of the LORD and took their seat in the entry of the New Gate of the house of the LORD. ¹¹Then the priests and the prophets said to the officials and to all the people, "This man deserves the sentence of death because he has prophesied against this city, as you have heard with your own ears."

12 Then Jeremiah spoke to all the officials and all the people, saying, "It is the LORD who sent me to prophesy against this house and this city all the words you have heard. ¹³Now therefore amend your ways and your doings, and obey the voice of the LORD your God, and the LORD will change his mind about the disaster that he has pronounced against you. ¹⁴But as for me, here I am in your hands. Do with me as seems good and right to you. ¹⁵Only know for certain that if you put me to death, you will be bringing innocent blood upon yourselves and upon this city and its inhabitants, for in truth the LORD sent me to you to speak all these words in your ears."

16 Then the officials and all the people said to the priests and the prophets, "This man does not deserve the sentence of death, for he has spoken to us in the name of the LORD our God." ¹⁷And some of the elders of the land arose and said to all the assembled people, ¹⁸"Micah of Moresheth, who prophesied during the days of King Hezekiah of Judah, said to all the people of Judah: Thus says the LORD of hosts,

> Zion shall be plowed as a field;
> Jerusalem shall become a heap of ruins,
>   and the mountain of the house a wooded
>   height.'

¹⁹Did King Hezekiah of Judah and all Judah actually put him to death? Did he not fear the LORD and entreat the favor of the LORD, and did not the LORD change his mind about the disaster that he had pronounced against them? But we are about to bring great disaster on ourselves!"

20 There was another man prophesying in the name of the LORD, Uriah son of Shemaiah from Kiriath-jearim. He prophesied against this city and against this land in words exactly like those of Jeremiah. ²¹And when King Jehoiakim, with all his warriors and all the officials, heard his words, the king sought to put him to death; but when Uriah heard of it, he was afraid and fled and escaped to Egypt. ²²Then King Jehoiakim sentᵃ Elnathan son of Achbor and men with him to Egypt, ²³and they took Uriah from Egypt and brought him to King Jehoiakim, who struck him down with the sword and threw his dead body into the burial place of the common people.

24 But the hand of Ahikam son of Shaphan was with Jeremiah so that he was not given over into the hands of the people to be put to death.

The Sign of the Yoke

27 In the beginning of the reign of King Zedekiahᵇ son of Josiah of Judah, this word came to Jeremiah from the LORD. ²Thus the LORD said to me: Make yourself a yoke of straps and bars, and put them on your neck. ³Send wordᶜ to the king of Edom, the king of Moab, the king of the Ammonites, the king of Tyre, and the king of Sidon by the hand of the envoys who have come to Jerusalem to King Zedekiah of Judah. ⁴Give them this charge for their masters: Thus says the LORD of hosts, the God of Israel: This is what you shall say to your masters: ⁵It is I who by my great power and my outstretched arm have made the earth, with the people and animals that are on the earth, and I give it to whomever I please. ⁶Now I have given all these lands into the hand of King Nebuchadnezzar of Babylon, my servant, and I have given him even the wild animals of the field to serve him. ⁷All the nations shall serve him and his son and his grandson, until the time of his own land comes; then many nations and great kings shall make him their slave.

8 But if any nation or kingdom will not serve this king, Nebuchadnezzar of Babylon, and put

---

a Heb adds *men* to *Egypt*   b Another reading is *Jehoiakim*
c Cn: Heb *send them*

its neck under the yoke of the king of Babylon, then I will punish that nation with the sword, with famine, and with pestilence, says the Lord, until I have completed its[a] destruction by his hand. 9You, therefore, must not listen to your prophets, your diviners, your dreamers,[b] your soothsayers, or your sorcerers, who are saying to you, "You shall not serve the king of Babylon." 10For they are prophesying a lie to you, with the result that you will be removed far from your land; I will drive you out, and you will perish. 11But any nation that will bring its neck under the yoke of the king of Babylon and serve him, I will leave on its own land, says the Lord, to till it and live there.

12 I spoke to King Zedekiah of Judah in the same way: Bring your necks under the yoke of the king of Babylon, and serve him and his people, and live. 13Why should you and your people die by the sword, by famine, and by pestilence, as the Lord has spoken concerning any nation that will not serve the king of Babylon? 14Do not listen to the words of the prophets who are telling you not to serve the king of Babylon, for they are prophesying a lie to you. 15I have not sent them, says the Lord, but they are prophesying falsely in my name, with the result that I will drive you out and you will perish, you and the prophets who are prophesying to you.

16 Then I spoke to the priests and to all this people, saying, Thus says the Lord: Do not listen to the words of your prophets who are prophesying to you, saying, "The vessels of the Lord's house will soon be brought back from Babylon," for they are prophesying a lie to you. 17Do not listen to them; serve the king of Babylon and live. Why should this city become a desolation? 18If indeed they are prophets, and if the word of the Lord is with them, then let them intercede with the Lord of hosts, that the vessels left in the house of the Lord, in the house of the king of Judah, and in Jerusalem may not go to Babylon. 19For thus says the Lord of hosts concerning the pillars, the sea, the stands, and the rest of the vessels that are left in this city, 20which King Nebuchadnezzar of Babylon did not take away when he took into exile from Jerusalem to Babylon King Jeconiah son of Jehoiakim of Judah, and all the nobles of Judah and Jerusalem— 21thus says the Lord of hosts, the God of Israel, concerning the vessels left in the house of the Lord, in the house of the king of Judah, and in Jerusalem: 22They shall be carried to Babylon, and there they shall stay, until the day when I give attention to them, says the Lord. Then I will bring them up and restore them to this place.

Hananiah Opposes Jeremiah and Dies

28 In that same year, at the beginning of the reign of King Zedekiah of Judah, in the fifth month of the fourth year, the prophet Hananiah son of Azzur, from Gibeon, spoke to me in the house of the Lord, in the presence of the priests and all the people, saying, 2"Thus says the Lord of hosts, the God of Israel: I have broken the yoke of the king of Babylon. 3Within two years I will bring back to this place all the vessels of the Lord's house, which King Nebuchadnezzar of Babylon took away from this place and carried to Babylon. 4I will also bring back to this place King Jeconiah son of Jehoiakim of Judah, and all the exiles from Judah who went to Babylon, says the Lord, for I will break the yoke of the king of Babylon."

5 Then the prophet Jeremiah spoke to the prophet Hananiah in the presence of the priests and all the people who were standing in the house of the Lord; 6and the prophet Jeremiah said, "Amen! May the Lord do so; may the Lord fulfill the words that you have prophesied, and bring back to this place from Babylon the vessels of the house of the Lord, and all the exiles. 7But listen now to this word that I speak in your hearing and in the hearing of all the people. 8The prophets who preceded you and me from ancient times prophesied war, famine, and pestilence against many countries and great kingdoms. 9As for the prophet who prophesies peace, when the word of that prophet comes true, then it will be known that the Lord has truly sent the prophet."

a Heb *their*   b Gk Syr Vg: Heb *dreams*

27:8

10 Then the prophet Hananiah took the yoke from the neck of the prophet Jeremiah, and broke it. [11]And Hananiah spoke in the presence of all the people, saying, "Thus says the LORD: This is how I will break the yoke of King Nebuchadnezzar of Babylon from the neck of all the nations within two years." At this, the prophet Jeremiah went his way.

12 Sometime after the prophet Hananiah had broken the yoke from the neck of the prophet Jeremiah, the word of the LORD came to Jeremiah: [13]Go, tell Hananiah, Thus says the LORD: You have broken wooden bars only to forge iron bars in place of them! [14]For thus says the LORD of hosts, the God of Israel: I have put an iron yoke on the neck of all these nations so that they may serve King Nebuchadnezzar of Babylon, and they shall indeed serve him; I have even given him the wild animals. [15]And the prophet Jeremiah said to the prophet Hananiah, "Listen, Hananiah, the LORD has not sent you, and you made this people trust in a lie. [16]Therefore thus says the LORD: I am going to send you off the face of the earth. Within this year you will be dead, because you have spoken rebellion against the LORD."

17 In that same year, in the seventh month, the prophet Hananiah died.

Jeremiah's Letter to the Exiles in Babylon

29 These are the words of the letter that the prophet Jeremiah sent from Jerusalem to the remaining elders among the exiles, and to the priests, the prophets, and all the people, whom Nebuchadnezzar had taken into exile from Jerusalem to Babylon. [2]This was after King Jeconiah, and the queen mother, the court officials, the leaders of Judah and Jerusalem, the artisans, and the smiths had departed from Jerusalem. [3]The letter was sent by the hand of Elasah son of Shaphan and Gemariah son of Hilkiah, whom King Zedekiah of Judah sent to Babylon to King Nebuchadnezzar of Babylon. It said: [4]Thus says the LORD of hosts, the God of Israel, to all the exiles whom I have sent into exile from Jerusalem to Babylon: [5]Build houses and live in them; plant gardens and eat what they produce. [6]Take wives and have sons and daughters; take wives for your sons, and give your daughters in marriage, that they may bear sons and daughters; multiply there, and do not decrease. [7]But seek the welfare of the city where I have sent you into exile, and pray to the LORD on its behalf, for in its welfare you will find your welfare. [8]For thus says the LORD of hosts, the God of Israel: Do not let the prophets and the diviners who are among you deceive you, and do not listen to the dreams that they dream,[a] [9]for it is a lie that they are prophesying to you in my name; I did not send them, says the LORD.

10 For thus says the LORD: Only when Babylon's seventy years are completed will I visit you, and I will fulfill to you my promise and bring you back to this place. [11]For surely I know the plans I have for you, says the LORD, plans for your welfare and not for harm, to give you a future with hope. [12]Then when you call upon me and come and pray to me, I will hear you. [13]When you search for me, you will find me; if you seek me with all your heart, [14]I will let you find me, says the LORD, and I will restore your fortunes and gather you from all the nations and all the places where I have driven you, says the LORD, and I will bring you back to the place from which I sent you into exile.

15 Because you have said, "The LORD has raised up prophets for us in Babylon,"— [16]Thus says the LORD concerning the king who sits on the throne of David, and concerning all the people who live in this city, your kinsfolk who did not go out with you into exile: [17]Thus says the LORD of hosts, I am going to let loose on them sword, famine, and pestilence, and I will make them like rotten figs that are so bad they cannot be eaten. [18]I will pursue them with the sword, with famine, and with pestilence, and will make them a horror to all the kingdoms of the earth, to be an object of cursing, and horror, and hissing, and a derision among all the nations where I have driven them, [19]because they did not heed my words, says the LORD, when I persistently sent to you my servants the prophets, but they[b] would not listen, says the LORD. [20]But now, all you exiles whom I sent away from Jerusalem to Babylon, hear the word of the LORD: [21]Thus says the LORD of hosts, the God of Israel, concerning Ahab son of Kolaiah and Zedekiah son of Maaseiah, who are prophesying a lie to you in my name: I am going to deliver them into the hand of King Nebuchadrezzar of Babylon, and he shall kill them before your eyes. [22]And on account of them this curse shall be used by all the exiles from Judah in Babylon: "The LORD make you like Zedekiah and Ahab, whom the king of Babylon roasted in the fire," [23]because they have perpetrated outrage in Israel and have committed adultery with their neighbors' wives, and have spoken in my name lying words that I did not command them; I am the one who knows and bears witness, says the LORD.

---

a Cn: Heb *your dreams that you cause to dream*   b Syr: Heb *you*

The Letter of Shemaiah

24 To Shemaiah of Nehelam you shall say: [25]Thus says the LORD of hosts, the God of Israel: In your own name you sent a letter to all the people who are in Jerusalem, and to the priest Zephaniah son of Maaseiah, and to all the priests, saying, [26]The LORD himself has made you priest instead of the priest Jehoiada, so that there may be officers in the house of the LORD to control any madman who plays the prophet, to put him in the stocks and the collar. [27]So now why have you not rebuked Jeremiah of Anathoth who plays the prophet for you? [28]For he has actually sent to us in Babylon, saying, "It will be a long time; build houses and live in them, and plant gardens and eat what they produce."

29 The priest Zephaniah read this letter in the hearing of the prophet Jeremiah. [30]Then the word of the LORD came to Jeremiah: [31]Send to all the exiles, saying, Thus says the LORD concerning Shemaiah of Nehelam: Because Shemaiah has prophesied to you, though I did not send him, and has led you to trust in a lie, [32]therefore thus says the LORD: I am going to punish Shemaiah of Nehelam and his descendants; he shall not have anyone living among this people to see[a] the good that I am going to do to my people, says the LORD, for he has spoken rebellion against the LORD.

Restoration Promised for Israel and Judah

30 The word that came to Jeremiah from the LORD: [2]Thus says the LORD, the God of Israel: Write in a book all the words that I have spoken to you. [3]For the days are surely coming, says the LORD, when I will restore the fortunes of my people, Israel and Judah, says the LORD, and I will bring them back to the land that I gave to their ancestors and they shall take possession of it.

4 These are the words that the LORD spoke concerning Israel and Judah:

[5] Thus says the LORD:
We have heard a cry of panic,
   of terror, and no peace.
[6] Ask now, and see,
   can a man bear a child?
Why then do I see every man
   with his hands on his loins like a woman in
     labor?
Why has every face turned pale?
[7] Alas! that day is so great
   there is none like it;
it is a time of distress for Jacob;
   yet he shall be rescued from it.

8 On that day, says the LORD of hosts, I will break the yoke from off his[b] neck, and I will burst his[b] bonds, and strangers shall no more make a servant of him. [9]But they shall serve the LORD their God and David their king, whom I will raise up for them.

[10] But as for you, have no fear, my servant Jacob,
    says the LORD,
   and do not be dismayed, O Israel;
for I am going to save you from far away,
   and your offspring from the land of their
     captivity.
Jacob shall return and have quiet and ease,
   and no one shall make him afraid.
[11] For I am with you, says the LORD, to save you;
I will make an end of all the nations
   among which I scattered you,
   but of you I will not make an end.
I will chastise you in just measure,
   and I will by no means leave you unpunished.

[12] For thus says the LORD:
Your hurt is incurable,
   your wound is grievous.
[13] There is no one to uphold your cause,
   no medicine for your wound,
   no healing for you.
[14] All your lovers have forgotten you;
   they care nothing for you;
for I have dealt you the blow of an enemy,
   the punishment of a merciless foe,
because your guilt is great,
   because your sins are so numerous.
[15] Why do you cry out over your hurt?
   Your pain is incurable.
Because your guilt is great,
   because your sins are so numerous,
I have done these things to you.
[16] Therefore all who devour you shall be devoured,
   and all your foes, every one of them, shall go
    into captivity;
those who plunder you shall be plundered,
   and all who prey on you I will make a prey.
[17] For I will restore health to you,
   and your wounds I will heal,
              says the LORD,
because they have called you an outcast:
   "It is Zion; no one cares for her!"

[18] Thus says the LORD:
I am going to restore the fortunes of the tents of
    Jacob,
   and have compassion on his dwellings;

---

a Gk: Heb *and he shall not see*   b Cn: Heb *your*

the city shall be rebuilt upon its mound,
and the citadel set on its rightful site.
¹⁹ Out of them shall come thanksgiving,
and the sound of merrymakers.
I will make them many, and they shall not be
few;
I will make them honored, and they shall not
be disdained.
²⁰ Their children shall be as of old,
their congregation shall be established
before me;
and I will punish all who oppress them.
²¹ Their prince shall be one of their own,
their ruler shall come from their midst;
I will bring him near, and he shall approach me,
for who would otherwise dare to approach me?
says the Lord.
²² And you shall be my people,
and I will be your God.

²³ Look, the storm of the Lord!
Wrath has gone forth,
a whirling*a* tempest;
it will burst upon the head of the wicked.
²⁴ The fierce anger of the Lord will not turn back
until he has executed and accomplished
the intents of his mind.
In the latter days you will understand this.

The Joyful Return of the Exiles

31 At that time, says the Lord, I will be the
God of all the families of Israel, and they
shall be my people.
² Thus says the Lord:
The people who survived the sword
found grace in the wilderness;
when Israel sought for rest,
³   the Lord appeared to him*b* from far away.*c*
I have loved you with an everlasting love;
therefore I have continued my faithfulness to
you.
⁴ Again I will build you, and you shall be built,
O virgin Israel!
Again you shall take*d* your tambourines,
and go forth in the dance of the merrymakers.
⁵ Again you shall plant vineyards
on the mountains of Samaria;
the planters shall plant,
and shall enjoy the fruit.
⁶ For there shall be a day when sentinels will call
in the hill country of Ephraim:
"Come, let us go up to Zion,
to the Lord our God."

⁷ For thus says the Lord:
Sing aloud with gladness for Jacob,

and raise shouts for the chief of the nations;
proclaim, give praise, and say,
"Save, O Lord, your people,
the remnant of Israel."
⁸ See, I am going to bring them from the land of
the north,
and gather them from the farthest parts of the
earth,
among them the blind and the lame,
those with child and those in labor,
together;
a great company, they shall return here.
⁹ With weeping they shall come,
and with consolations*e* I will lead them back,
I will let them walk by brooks of water,
in a straight path in which they shall not
stumble;
for I have become a father to Israel,
and Ephraim is my firstborn.

¹⁰ Hear the word of the Lord, O nations,
and declare it in the coastlands far away;
say, "He who scattered Israel will gather him,
and will keep him as a shepherd a flock."
¹¹ For the Lord has ransomed Jacob,
and has redeemed him from hands too strong
for him.
¹² They shall come and sing aloud on the height of
Zion,
and they shall be radiant over the goodness of
the Lord,
over the grain, the wine, and the oil,
and over the young of the flock and the herd;
their life shall become like a watered garden,
and they shall never languish again.
¹³ Then shall the young women rejoice in the
dance,
and the young men and the old shall be
merry.
I will turn their mourning into joy,
I will comfort them, and give them gladness
for sorrow.
¹⁴ I will give the priests their fill of fatness,
and my people shall be satisfied with my
bounty,
says the Lord.

¹⁵ Thus says the Lord:
A voice is heard in Ramah,
lamentation and bitter weeping.
Rachel is weeping for her children;
she refuses to be comforted for her children,

---

a One Ms: Meaning of MT uncertain   *b* Gk: Heb *me*   *c* Or *to
him long ago*   *d* Or *adorn yourself with*   *e* Gk Compare Vg Tg:
Heb *supplications*

because they are no more.
¹⁶ Thus says the LORD:

Keep your voice from weeping,
and your eyes from tears;
for there is a reward for your work,

says the LORD:

they shall come back from the land of the
enemy;
¹⁷ there is hope for your future,

says the LORD:

your children shall come back to their own
country.

¹⁸ Indeed I heard Ephraim pleading:
"You disciplined me, and I took the
discipline;
I was like a calf untrained.
Bring me back, let me come back,
for you are the LORD my God.
¹⁹ For after I had turned away I repented;
and after I was discovered, I struck my thigh;
I was ashamed, and I was dismayed
because I bore the disgrace of my youth."
²⁰ Is Ephraim my dear son?
Is he the child I delight in?
As often as I speak against him,
I still remember him.
Therefore I am deeply moved for him;
I will surely have mercy on him,

says the LORD.

²¹ Set up road markers for yourself,
make yourself signposts;
consider well the highway,
the road by which you went.
Return, O virgin Israel,
return to these your cities.
²² How long will you waver,
O faithless daughter?
For the LORD has created a new thing on the
earth:
a woman encompasses*ᵃ* a man.

²³ Thus says the LORD of hosts, the God of
Israel: Once more they shall use these words in
the land of Judah and in its towns when I restore
their fortunes:

"The LORD bless you, O abode of righteousness,
O holy hill!"
²⁴And Judah and all its towns shall live there together, and the farmers and those who wander*ᵇ*
with their flocks.
²⁵ I will satisfy the weary,
and all who are faint I will replenish.

²⁶ Thereupon I awoke and looked, and my
sleep was pleasant to me.

Pray It!

Rachel Weeps

Rachel was the "mother of Israel," the favored wife of Jacob (see Gen 29:28–30)—the patriarch whose twelve sons formed the twelve Tribes of Israel. In Jeremiah 31:15–17, she is symbolically weeping over the death and captivity of her children—the Israelites—after the Babylonian invasion.

Rachel's weeping has become an image of trauma and unrelenting grief over violence, death, and slaughter, especially when children are involved. For example, Matthew 2:16–18 quotes Jeremiah 31:15–17 in a story about the massacre of infants in Bethlehem. Project Rachel is an organized ministry for women who have had abortions. And Rachel Weeps is a Holocaust exhibition recalling the murder of millions of Jewish men, women, and children.

Jeremiah goes on in verses 16–17 with words of hope. God promises that the scattered children will be brought back. We can trust that God is with the victims of senseless violence and those who grieve for them. Let us pray for Rachel's grief to end.

▶ Jer 31:15–17

Individual Retribution

27 The days are surely coming, says the LORD, when I will sow the house of Israel and the house of Judah with the seed of humans and the seed of animals. ²⁸And just as I have watched over them to pluck up and break down, to overthrow, destroy, and bring evil, so I will watch over them to build and to plant, says the LORD. ²⁹In those days they shall no longer say:

"The parents have eaten sour grapes,
and the children's teeth are set on edge."
³⁰But all shall die for their own sins; the teeth of everyone who eats sour grapes shall be set on edge.

---

a Meaning of Heb uncertain   *b* Cn Compare Syr Vg Tg: Heb *and they shall wander*

A New Covenant

31 The days are surely coming, says the LORD, when I will make a new covenant with the house of Israel and the house of Judah. ³²It will not be like the covenant that I made with their ancestors when I took them by the hand to bring them out of the land of Egypt—a covenant that they broke, though I was their husband,ᵃ says the LORD. ³³But this is the covenant that I will make with the house of Israel after those days, says the LORD: I will put my law within them, and I will write it on their hearts; and I will be their God, and they shall be my people. ³⁴No longer shall they teach one another, or say to each other, "Know the LORD," for they shall all know me, from the least of them to the greatest, says the LORD; for I will forgive their iniquity, and remember their sin no more.

³⁵ Thus says the LORD,
who gives the sun for light by day
and the fixed order of the moon and the stars
for light by night,
who stirs up the sea so that its waves roar—

the LORD of hosts is his name:
³⁶ If this fixed order were ever to cease
from my presence, says the LORD,
then also the offspring of Israel would cease
to be a nation before me forever.

³⁷ Thus says the LORD:
If the heavens above can be measured,
and the foundations of the earth below can be explored,
then I will reject all the offspring of Israel
because of all they have done,

says the LORD.

Jerusalem to Be Enlarged

38 The days are surely coming, says the LORD, when the city shall be rebuilt for the LORD from the tower of Hananel to the Corner Gate. ³⁹And the measuring line shall go out farther, straight to the hill Gareb, and shall then turn to Goah. ⁴⁰The whole valley of the dead bodies and the ashes, and all the fields as far as the Wadi Kidron, to the corner of the Horse Gate toward the east, shall be sacred to the LORD. It shall never again be uprooted or overthrown.

Jeremiah Buys a Field During the Siege

32 The word that came to Jeremiah from the LORD in the tenth year of King Zedekiah of Judah, which was the eighteenth year of Nebuchadrezzar. ²At that time the army of the king of Babylon was besieging Jerusalem, and the prophet Jeremiah was confined in the court of the guard that was in the palace of the king of Judah, ³where King Zedekiah of Judah had confined him. Zedekiah had said, "Why do you prophesy and say: Thus says the LORD: I am going to give this city into the hand of the king of Babylon, and he shall take it; ⁴King Zedekiah of Judah shall not escape out of the hands of the Chaldeans, but shall surely be given into the hands of the king of Babylon, and shall speak with him face to face and see him eye to eye; ⁵and he shall take Zedekiah to Babylon, and there he shall remain until I attend to him, says the LORD; though you fight against the Chaldeans, you shall not succeed?"

6 Jeremiah said, The word of the LORD came to me: ⁷Hanamel son of your uncle Shallum is going to come to you and say, "Buy my field that is at Anathoth, for the right of redemption by purchase is yours." ⁸Then my cousin Hanamel came to me in the court of the guard, in accordance with the word of the LORD, and said to me, "Buy

The Heart of the Matter

The Ten Commandments. The stone tablets on which they were written are the most famous stone tablets in the world, and yet no one knows where they are. The ark of the Covenant, in which they were once kept, was taken during a raid on the Temple (see Jer 52:17–23). What a find they would be today! Imagine all the people flocking to see the original Ten Commandments.

But perhaps their absence makes Jeremiah's beautiful words about the New Covenant in Jeremiah 31:31–34 even more fitting. What was etched in stone on those tablets needs to be etched in our heart. We keep in our heart what is most valuable to us. If we keep God's law there, we have no need for it written in stone.

When you look into your heart, what do you find written there?

▶ Jer 31:31–34

ᵃ Or master

my field that is at Anathoth in the land of Benjamin, for the right of possession and redemption is yours; buy it for yourself." Then I knew that this was the word of the LORD.

9 And I bought the field at Anathoth from my cousin Hanamel, and weighed out the money to him, seventeen shekels of silver. 10I signed the deed, sealed it, got witnesses, and weighed the money on scales. 11Then I took the sealed deed of purchase, containing the terms and conditions, and the open copy; 12and I gave the deed of purchase to Baruch son of Neriah son of Mahseiah, in the presence of my cousin Hanamel, in the presence of the witnesses who signed the deed of purchase, and in the presence of all the Judeans who were sitting in the court of the guard. 13In their presence I charged Baruch, saying, 14Thus says the LORD of hosts, the God of Israel: Take these deeds, both this sealed deed of purchase and this open deed, and put them in an earthenware jar, in order that they may last for a long time. 15For thus says the LORD of hosts, the God of Israel: Houses and fields and vineyards shall again be bought in this land.

Jeremiah Prays for Understanding

16 After I had given the deed of purchase to Baruch son of Neriah, I prayed to the LORD, saying: 17Ah Lord GOD! It is you who made the heavens and the earth by your great power and by your outstretched arm! Nothing is too hard for you. 18You show steadfast love to the thousandth generation,[a] but repay the guilt of parents into the laps of their children after them, O great and mighty God whose name is the LORD of hosts, 19great in counsel and mighty in deed; whose eyes are open to all the ways of mortals, rewarding all according to their ways and according to the fruit of their doings. 20You showed signs and wonders in the land of Egypt, and to this day in Israel and among all humankind, and have made yourself a name that continues to this very day. 21You brought your people Israel out of the land of Egypt with signs and wonders, with a strong hand and outstretched arm, and with great terror; 22and you gave them this land, which you swore to their ancestors to give them, a land flowing with milk and honey; 23and they entered and took possession of it. But they did not obey your voice or follow your law; of all you commanded them to do, they did nothing. Therefore you have made all these disasters come upon them. 24See, the siege ramps have been cast up against the city to take it, and the city, faced with sword, famine, and pestilence, has been given into the hands of the Chaldeans who are fighting

against it. What you spoke has happened, as you yourself can see. 25Yet you, O Lord GOD, have said to me, "Buy the field for money and get witnesses"—though the city has been given into the hands of the Chaldeans.

God's Assurance of the People's Return

26 The word of the LORD came to Jeremiah: 27See, I am the LORD, the God of all flesh; is anything too hard for me? 28Therefore, thus says the LORD: I am going to give this city into the hands of the Chaldeans and into the hand of King Nebuchadrezzar of Babylon, and he shall take it. 29The Chaldeans who are fighting against this city shall come, set it on fire, and burn it, with the houses on whose roofs offerings have been made to Baal and libations have been poured out to other gods, to provoke me to anger. 30For the people of Israel and the people of Judah have done nothing but evil in my sight from their youth; the people of Israel have done nothing but provoke me to anger by the work of their hands, says the LORD. 31This city has aroused my anger and wrath, from the day it was built until this day, so that I will remove it from my sight 32because of all the evil of the people of Israel and the people of Judah that they did to provoke me to anger—they, their kings and their officials, their priests and their prophets, the citizens of Judah and the inhabitants of Jerusalem. 33They have turned their backs to me, not their faces; though I have taught them persistently, they would not listen and accept correction. 34They set up their abominations in the house that bears my name, and defiled it. 35They built the high places of Baal in the valley of the son of Hinnom, to offer up their sons and daughters to Molech, though I did not command them, nor did it enter my mind that they should do this abomination, causing Judah to sin.

36 Now therefore thus says the LORD, the God of Israel, concerning this city of which you say, "It is being given into the hand of the king of Babylon by the sword, by famine, and by pestilence": 37See, I am going to gather them from all the lands to which I drove them in my anger and my wrath and in great indignation; I will bring them back to this place, and I will settle them in safety. 38They shall be my people, and I will be their God. 39I will give them one heart and one way, that they may fear me for all time, for their own good and the good of their children after them. 40I will make an everlasting covenant with them, never to draw back from doing good to them; and I will put the fear of me in their

---

a Or to thousands

hearts, so that they may not turn from me. [41]I will rejoice in doing good to them, and I will plant them in this land in faithfulness, with all my heart and all my soul.

42 For thus says the LORD: Just as I have brought all this great disaster upon this people, so I will bring upon them all the good fortune that I now promise them. [43]Fields shall be bought in this land of which you are saying, It is a desolation, without human beings or animals; it has been given into the hands of the Chaldeans. [44]Fields shall be bought for money, and deeds shall be signed and sealed and witnessed, in the land of Benjamin, in the places around Jerusalem, and in the cities of Judah, of the hill country, of the Shephelah, and of the Negeb; for I will restore their fortunes, says the LORD.

Healing after Punishment

33 The word of the LORD came to Jeremiah a second time, while he was still confined in the court of the guard: [2]Thus says the LORD who made the earth,[a] the LORD who formed it to establish it—the LORD is his name: [3]Call to me and I will answer you, and will tell you great and hidden things that you have not known. [4]For thus says the LORD, the God of Israel, concerning the houses of this city and the houses of the kings of Judah that were torn down to make a defense against the siege ramps and before the sword:[b] [5]The Chaldeans are coming in to fight[c] and to fill them with the dead bodies of those whom I shall strike down in my anger and my wrath, for I have hidden my face from this city because of all their wickedness. [6]I am going to bring it recovery and healing; I will heal them and reveal to them abundance[b] of prosperity and security. [7]I will restore the fortunes of Judah and the fortunes of Israel, and rebuild them as they were at first. [8]I will cleanse them from all the guilt of their sin against me, and I will forgive all the guilt of their sin and rebellion against me. [9]And this city[d] shall be to me a name of joy, a praise and a glory before all the nations of the earth who shall hear of all the good that I do for them; they shall fear and tremble because of all the good and all the prosperity I provide for it.

10 Thus says the LORD: In this place of which you say, "It is a waste without human beings or animals," in the towns of Judah and the streets of Jerusalem that are desolate, without inhabitants, human or animal, there shall once more be heard [11]the voice of mirth and the voice of gladness, the voice of the bridegroom and the voice of the bride, the voices of those who sing, as they bring thank offerings to the house of the LORD:

"Give thanks to the LORD of hosts,
  for the LORD is good,
  for his steadfast love endures forever!"
For I will restore the fortunes of the land as at first, says the LORD.

12 Thus says the LORD of hosts: In this place that is waste, without human beings or animals, and in all its towns there shall again be pasture for shepherds resting their flocks. [13]In the towns of the hill country, of the Shephelah, and of the Negeb, in the land of Benjamin, the places around Jerusalem, and in the towns of Judah, flocks shall again pass under the hands of the one who counts them, says the LORD.

The Righteous Branch and the Covenant with David

14 The days are surely coming, says the LORD, when I will fulfill the promise I made to the house of Israel and the house of Judah. [15]In those days and at that time I will cause a righteous Branch to spring up for David; and he shall execute justice and righteousness in the land. [16]In those days Judah will be saved and Jerusalem will live in safety. And this is the name by which it will be called: "The LORD is our righteousness."

17 For thus says the LORD: David shall never lack a man to sit on the throne of the house of Israel, [18]and the levitical priests shall never lack a man in my presence to offer burnt offerings, to make grain offerings, and to make sacrifices for all time.

19 The word of the LORD came to Jeremiah: [20]Thus says the LORD: If any of you could break my covenant with the day and my covenant with the night, so that day and night would not come at their appointed time, [21]only then could my covenant with my servant David be broken, so that he would not have a son to reign on his throne, and my covenant with my ministers the Levites. [22]Just as the host of heaven cannot be numbered and the sands of the sea cannot be measured, so I will increase the offspring of my servant David, and the Levites who minister to me.

23 The word of the LORD came to Jeremiah: [24]Have you not observed how these people say, "The two families that the LORD chose have been rejected by him," and how they hold my people in such contempt that they no longer regard them as a nation? [25]Thus says the LORD: Only if I had not established my covenant with day and night and the ordinances of heaven and earth, [26]would I reject the offspring of Jacob and of my

---

a Gk: Heb it   b Meaning of Heb uncertain   c Cn: Heb They are coming in to fight against the Chaldeans   d Heb And it

servant David and not choose any of his descendants as rulers over the offspring of Abraham, Isaac, and Jacob. For I will restore their fortunes, and will have mercy upon them.

Death in Captivity Predicted for Zedekiah

34 The word that came to Jeremiah from the LORD, when King Nebuchadrezzar of Babylon and all his army and all the kingdoms of the earth and all the peoples under his dominion were fighting against Jerusalem and all its cities: ²Thus says the LORD, the God of Israel: Go and speak to King Zedekiah of Judah and say to him: Thus says the LORD: I am going to give this city into the hand of the king of Babylon, and he shall burn it with fire. ³And you yourself shall not escape from his hand, but shall surely be captured and handed over to him; you shall see the king of Babylon eye to eye and speak with him face to face; and you shall go to Babylon. ⁴Yet hear the word of the LORD, O King Zedekiah of Judah! Thus says the LORD concerning you: You shall not die by the sword; ⁵you shall die in peace. And as spices were burned*ᵃ* for your ancestors, the earlier kings who preceded you, so they shall burn spices*ᵇ* for you and lament for you, saying, "Alas, lord!" For I have spoken the word, says the LORD.

6 Then the prophet Jeremiah spoke all these words to Zedekiah king of Judah, in Jerusalem, ⁷when the army of the king of Babylon was fighting against Jerusalem and against all the cities of Judah that were left, Lachish and Azekah; for these were the only fortified cities of Judah that remained.

Treacherous Treatment of Slaves

8 The word that came to Jeremiah from the LORD, after King Zedekiah had made a covenant with all the people in Jerusalem to make a proclamation of liberty to them— ⁹that all should set free their Hebrew slaves, male and female, so that no one should hold another Judean in slavery. ¹⁰And they obeyed, all the officials and all the people who had entered into the covenant that all would set free their slaves, male or female, so that they would not be enslaved again; they obeyed and set them free. ¹¹But afterward they turned around and took back the male and female slaves they had set free, and brought them again into subjection as slaves. ¹²The word of the LORD came to Jeremiah from the LORD: ¹³Thus says the LORD, the God of Israel: I myself made a covenant with your ancestors when I brought them out of the land of Egypt, out of the house of slavery, saying, ¹⁴"Every seventh year each of you must set free any Hebrews who have been sold to you and have served you six years; you must set them free from your service." But your ancestors did not listen to me or incline their ears to me. ¹⁵You yourselves recently repented and did what was right in my sight by proclaiming liberty to one another, and you made a covenant before me in the house that is called by my name; ¹⁶but then you turned around and profaned my name when each of you took back your male and female slaves, whom you had set free according to their desire, and you brought them again into subjection to be your slaves. ¹⁷Therefore, thus says the LORD: You have not obeyed me by granting a release to your neighbors and friends; I am going to grant a release to you, says the LORD—a release to the sword, to pestilence, and to famine. I will make you a horror to all the kingdoms of the earth. ¹⁸And those who transgressed my covenant and did not keep the terms of the covenant that they made before me, I will make like*ᶜ* the calf when they cut it in two and passed between its parts: ¹⁹the officials of Judah, the officials of Jerusalem, the eunuchs, the priests, and all the people of the land who passed between the parts of the calf ²⁰shall be handed over to their enemies and to those who seek their lives. Their corpses shall become food for the birds of the air and the wild animals of the earth. ²¹And as for King Zedekiah of Judah and his officials, I will hand them over to their enemies and to those who seek their lives, to the army of the king of Babylon, which has withdrawn from you. ²²I am going to command, says the LORD, and will bring them back to this city; and they will fight against it, and take it, and burn it with fire. The towns of Judah I will make a desolation without inhabitant.

The Rechabites Commended

35 The word that came to Jeremiah from the LORD in the days of King Jehoiakim son of Josiah of Judah: ²Go to the house of the Rechabites, and speak with them, and bring them to the house of the LORD, into one of the chambers; then offer them wine to drink. ³So I took Jaazaniah son of Jeremiah son of Habazziniah, and his brothers, and all his sons, and the whole house of the Rechabites. ⁴I brought them to the house of the LORD into the chamber of the sons of Hanan son of Igdaliah, the man of God, which was near the chamber of the officials, above the chamber of Maaseiah son of

---

a Heb *as there was burning* *b* Heb *shall burn* *c* Cn: Heb lacks *like*

Shallum, keeper of the threshold. [5]Then I set before the Rechabites pitchers full of wine, and cups; and I said to them, "Have some wine." [6]But they answered, "We will drink no wine, for our ancestor Jonadab son of Rechab commanded us, 'You shall never drink wine, neither you nor your children; [7]nor shall you ever build a house, or sow seed; nor shall you plant a vineyard, or even own one; but you shall live in tents all your days, that you may live many days in the land where you reside.' [8]We have obeyed the charge of our ancestor Jonadab son of Rechab in all that he commanded us, to drink no wine all our days, ourselves, our wives, our sons, or our daughters, [9]and not to build houses to live in. We have no vineyard or field or seed; [10]but we have lived in tents, and have obeyed and done all that our ancestor Jonadab commanded us. [11]But when King Nebuchadrezzar of Babylon came up against the land, we said, 'Come, and let us go to Jerusalem for fear of the army of the Chaldeans and the army of the Arameans.' That is why we are living in Jerusalem."

12 Then the word of the Lord came to Jeremiah: [13]Thus says the Lord of hosts, the God of Israel: Go and say to the people of Judah and the inhabitants of Jerusalem, Can you not learn a lesson and obey my words? says the Lord. [14]The command has been carried out that Jonadab son of Rechab gave to his descendants to drink no wine; and they drink none to this day, for they have obeyed their ancestor's command. But I myself have spoken to you persistently, and you have not obeyed me. [15]I have sent to you all my servants the prophets, sending them persistently, saying, "Turn now every one of you from your evil way, and amend your doings, and do not go after other gods to serve them, and then you shall live in the land that I gave to you and your ancestors." But you did not incline your ear or obey me. [16]The descendants of Jonadab son of Rechab have carried out the command that their ancestor gave them, but this people has not obeyed me. [17]Therefore, thus says the Lord, the God of hosts, the God of Israel: I am going to bring on Judah and on all the inhabitants of Jerusalem every disaster that I have pronounced against them; because I have spoken to them and they have not listened, I have called to them and they have not answered.

18 But to the house of the Rechabites Jeremiah said: Thus says the Lord of hosts, the God of Israel: Because you have obeyed the command of your ancestor Jonadab, and kept all his precepts, and done all that he commanded you, [19]therefore thus says the Lord of hosts, the God of Israel: Jonadab son of Rechab shall not lack a descendant to stand before me for all time.

The Scroll Read in the Temple

36 In the fourth year of King Jehoiakim son of Josiah of Judah, this word came to Jeremiah from the Lord: [2]Take a scroll and write on it all the words that I have spoken to you against Israel and Judah and all the nations, from the day I spoke to you, from the days of Josiah until today. [3]It may be that when the house of Judah hears of all the disasters that I intend to do to them, all of them may turn from their evil ways, so that I may forgive their iniquity and their sin.

4 Then Jeremiah called Baruch son of Neriah, and Baruch wrote on a scroll at Jeremiah's dictation all the words of the Lord that he had spoken to him. [5]And Jeremiah ordered Baruch, saying, "I am prevented from entering the house of the Lord; [6]so you go yourself, and on a fast day in the hearing of the people in the Lord's house you shall read the words of the Lord from the scroll that you have written at my dictation. You shall read them also in the hearing of all the people of Judah who come up from their towns. [7]It may be that their plea will come before the Lord, and that all of them will turn from their evil ways, for great is the anger and wrath that the Lord has pronounced against this people." [8]And Baruch son of Neriah did all that the prophet Jeremiah ordered him about reading from the scroll the words of the Lord in the Lord's house.

9 In the fifth year of King Jehoiakim son of Josiah of Judah, in the ninth month, all the people in Jerusalem and all the people who came from the towns of Judah to Jerusalem proclaimed a fast before the Lord. [10]Then, in the hearing of all the people, Baruch read the words of Jeremiah from the scroll, in the house of the Lord, in the chamber of Gemariah son of Shaphan the secretary, which was in the upper court, at the entry of the New Gate of the Lord's house.

The Scroll Read in the Palace

11 When Micaiah son of Gemariah son of Shaphan heard all the words of the Lord from the scroll, [12]he went down to the king's house, into the secretary's chamber; and all the officials were sitting there: Elishama the secretary, Delaiah son of Shemaiah, Elnathan son of Achbor, Gemariah son of Shaphan, Zedekiah son of Hananiah, and all the officials. [13]And Micaiah told them all the words that he had heard, when Baruch read the scroll in the hearing of the people. [14]Then all the officials sent Jehudi son of Nethaniah son of Shelemiah son of Cushi to say

to Baruch, "Bring the scroll that you read in the hearing of the people, and come." So Baruch son of Neriah took the scroll in his hand and came to them. ¹⁵And they said to him, "Sit down and read it to us." So Baruch read it to them. ¹⁶When they heard all the words, they turned to one another in alarm, and said to Baruch, "We certainly must report all these words to the king." ¹⁷Then they questioned Baruch, "Tell us now, how did you write all these words? Was it at his dictation?" ¹⁸Baruch answered them, "He dictated all these words to me, and I wrote them with ink on the scroll." ¹⁹Then the officials said to Baruch, "Go and hide, you and Jeremiah, and let no one know where you are."

Jehoiakim Burns the Scroll

20 Leaving the scroll in the chamber of Elishama the secretary, they went to the court of the king; and they reported all the words to the king. ²¹Then the king sent Jehudi to get the scroll, and he took it from the chamber of Elishama the secretary; and Jehudi read it to the king and all the officials who stood beside the king. ²²Now the king was sitting in his winter apartment (it was the ninth month), and there was a fire burning in the brazier before him. ²³As Jehudi read three or four columns, the king*a* would cut them off with a penknife and throw them into the fire in the brazier, until the entire scroll was consumed in the fire that was in the brazier. ²⁴Yet neither the king, nor any of his servants who heard all these words, was alarmed, nor did they tear their garments. ²⁵Even when Elnathan and Delaiah and Gemariah urged the king not to burn the scroll, he would not listen to them. ²⁶And the king commanded Jerahmeel the king's son and Seraiah son of Azriel and Shelemiah son of Abdeel to arrest the secretary Baruch and the prophet Jeremiah. But the LORD hid them.

Jeremiah Dictates Another

27 Now, after the king had burned the scroll with the words that Baruch wrote at Jeremiah's dictation, the word of the LORD came to Jeremiah: ²⁸Take another scroll and write on it all the former words that were in the first scroll, which King Jehoiakim of Judah has burned. ²⁹And concerning King Jehoiakim of Judah you shall say: Thus says the LORD, You have dared to burn this scroll, saying, Why have you written in it that the king of Babylon will certainly come and destroy this land, and will cut off from it human beings and animals? ³⁰Therefore thus says the LORD concerning King Jehoiakim of Judah: He shall have no one to sit upon the throne of David, and his dead body shall be cast out to the heat by day and the frost by night. ³¹And I will punish him and his offspring and his servants for their iniquity; I will bring on them, and on the inhabitants of Jerusalem, and on the people of Judah, all the disasters with which I have threatened them— but they would not listen.

32 Then Jeremiah took another scroll and gave it to the secretary Baruch son of Neriah, who wrote on it at Jeremiah's dictation all the words of the scroll that King Jehoiakim of Judah had burned in the fire; and many similar words were added to them.

Zedekiah's Vain Hope

37 Zedekiah son of Josiah, whom King Nebuchadrezzar of Babylon made king in the land of Judah, succeeded Coniah son of Jehoiakim. ²But neither he nor his servants nor the people of the land listened to the words of the LORD that he spoke through the prophet Jeremiah.

3 King Zedekiah sent Jehucal son of Shelemiah and the priest Zephaniah son of Maaseiah to the prophet Jeremiah saying, "Please pray for us to the LORD our God." ⁴Now Jeremiah was still going in and out among the people, for he had not yet been put in prison. ⁵Meanwhile, the army of Pharaoh had come out of Egypt; and when the Chaldeans who were besieging Jerusalem heard news of them, they withdrew from Jerusalem.

6 Then the word of the LORD came to the prophet Jeremiah: ⁷Thus says the LORD, God of Israel: This is what the two of you shall say to the king of Judah, who sent you to me to inquire of me: Pharaoh's army, which set out to help you, is going to return to its own land, to Egypt. ⁸And the Chaldeans shall return and fight against this city; they shall take it and burn it with fire. ⁹Thus says the LORD: Do not deceive yourselves, saying, "The Chaldeans will surely go away from us," for they will not go away. ¹⁰Even if you defeated the whole army of Chaldeans who are fighting against you, and there remained of them only wounded men in their tents, they would rise up and burn this city with fire.

Jeremiah Is Imprisoned

11 Now when the Chaldean army had withdrawn from Jerusalem at the approach of Pharaoh's army, ¹²Jeremiah set out from Jerusalem to go to the land of Benjamin to receive his share of property*b* among the people there. ¹³When he reached the Benjamin Gate, a sentinel there named Irijah son of Shelemiah son of Hananiah

---

a Heb *he*   b Meaning of Heb uncertain

arrested the prophet Jeremiah saying, "You are deserting to the Chaldeans." 14And Jeremiah said, "That is a lie; I am not deserting to the Chaldeans." But Irijah would not listen to him, and arrested Jeremiah and brought him to the officials. 15The officials were enraged at Jeremiah, and they beat him and imprisoned him in the house of the secretary Jonathan, for it had been made a prison. 16Thus Jeremiah was put in the cistern house, in the cells, and remained there many days.

17 Then King Zedekiah sent for him, and received him. The king questioned him secretly in his house, and said, "Is there any word from the LORD?" Jeremiah said, "There is!" Then he said, "You shall be handed over to the king of

Facing Fear

You can bet Jeremiah felt fear at times. For example, in Jeremiah 37:17, King Zedekiah asks the prophet if he has had any word from God. Jeremiah has just been beaten and imprisoned (see verse 15). Surely, he has some fear for what will happen to him if he delivers a message that angers the king. But Jeremiah courageously tells Zedekiah that he, Zedekiah, will be handed over to the king of Babylon (see verse 17).

Throughout our lives, when trying to do God's will, we will face situations that cause us to fear for our safety, for our reputation, or even that our friends will abandon us. This isn't the same fear we feel when watching a horror film or riding a roller coaster. It is an anxiety that can cause us to shut down and quit trying. We need to offer up that fear to God and ask the Lord to calm our heart.

Quiet your mind and pray:

Lord, give me the courage I need to be faithful to you. Let my love for you and for other people be so great that my fears will never be able to keep me from doing what is right. Amen!

▶ **Jer 37:11–21**

Babylon." 18Jeremiah also said to King Zedekiah, "What wrong have I done to you or your servants or this people, that you have put me in prison? 19Where are your prophets who prophesied to you, saying, 'The king of Babylon will not come against you and against this land'? 20Now please hear me, my lord king: be good enough to listen to my plea, and do not send me back to the house of the secretary Jonathan to die there." 21So King Zedekiah gave orders, and they committed Jeremiah to the court of the guard; and a loaf of bread was given him daily from the bakers' street, until all the bread of the city was gone. So Jeremiah remained in the court of the guard.

Jeremiah in the Cistern

38 Now Shephatiah son of Mattan, Gedaliah son of Pashhur, Jucal son of Shelemiah, and Pashhur son of Malchiah heard the words that Jeremiah was saying to all the people, 2Thus says the LORD, Those who stay in this city shall die by the sword, by famine, and by pestilence; but those who go out to the Chaldeans shall live; they shall have their lives as a prize of war, and live. 3Thus says the LORD, This city shall surely be handed over to the army of the king of Babylon and be taken. 4Then the officials said to the king, "This man ought to be put to death, because he is discouraging the soldiers who are left in this city, and all the people, by speaking such words to them. For this man is not seeking the welfare of this people, but their harm." 5King Zedekiah said, "Here he is; he is in your hands; for the king is powerless against you." 6So they took Jeremiah and threw him into the cistern of Malchiah, the king's son, which was in the court of the guard, letting Jeremiah down by ropes. Now there was no water in the cistern, but only mud, and Jeremiah sank in the mud.

Jeremiah Is Rescued by Ebed-melech

7 Ebed-melech the Ethiopian,*a* a eunuch in the king's house, heard that they had put Jeremiah into the cistern. The king happened to be sitting at the Benjamin Gate, 8So Ebed-melech left the king's house and spoke to the king, 9"My lord king, these men have acted wickedly in all they did to the prophet Jeremiah by throwing him into the cistern to die there of hunger, for there is no bread left in the city." 10Then the king commanded Ebed-melech the Ethiopian,*a* "Take three men with you from here, and pull the prophet Jeremiah up from the cistern before he dies." 11So Ebed-melech took the men with

him and went to the house of the king, to a wardrobe of[a] the storehouse, and took from there old rags and worn-out clothes, which he let down to Jeremiah in the cistern by ropes. [12]Then Ebed-melech the Ethiopian[b] said to Jeremiah, "Just put the rags and clothes between your armpits and the ropes." Jeremiah did so. [13]Then they drew Jeremiah up by the ropes and pulled him out of the cistern. And Jeremiah remained in the court of the guard.

Zedekiah Consults Jeremiah Again

14 King Zedekiah sent for the prophet Jeremiah and received him at the third entrance of the temple of the LORD. The king said to Jeremiah, "I have something to ask you; do not hide anything from me." [15]Jeremiah said to Zedekiah, "If I tell you, you will put me to death, will you not? And if I give you advice, you will not listen to me." [16]So King Zedekiah swore an oath in secret to Jeremiah, "As the LORD lives, who gave us our lives, I will not put you to death or hand you over to these men who seek your life."

17 Then Jeremiah said to Zedekiah, "Thus says the LORD, the God of hosts, the God of Israel, If you will only surrender to the officials of the king of Babylon, then your life shall be spared, and this city shall not be burned with fire, and you and your house shall live. [18]But if you do not surrender to the officials of the king of Babylon, then this city shall be handed over to the Chaldeans, and they shall burn it with fire, and you yourself shall not escape from their hand." [19]King Zedekiah said to Jeremiah, "I am afraid of the Judeans who have deserted to the Chaldeans, for I might be handed over to them and they would abuse me." [20]Jeremiah said, "That will not happen. Just obey the voice of the LORD in what I say to you, and it shall go well with you, and your life shall be spared. [21]But if you are determined not to surrender, this is what the LORD has shown me— [22]a vision of all the women remaining in the house of the king of Judah being led out to the officials of the king of Babylon and saying,

'Your trusted friends have seduced you
    and have overcome you;
Now that your feet are stuck in the mud,
    they desert you.'

[23]All your wives and your children shall be led out to the Chaldeans, and you yourself shall not escape from their hand, but shall be seized by the king of Babylon; and this city shall be burned with fire."

24 Then Zedekiah said to Jeremiah, "Do not let anyone else know of this conversation, or you

Pray It!

Prayer from the Cistern (Well)

Savior God, like Jeremiah, I often find myself at the bottom. Sometimes, I just fall there; other times, I am thrown there. It's cold, dark, and lonely there.

Bless me with friends, like Ebed-melech, who will care for me and lift me up when I am down or in trouble. And make me the kind of friend who is loyal enough to advocate for those in need and willing to do what is necessary to lift others up.
Amen.

▶ Jer 38:1–13

will die. [25]If the officials should hear that I have spoken with you, and they should come and say to you, 'Just tell us what you said to the king; do not conceal it from us, or we will put you to death. What did the king say to you?' [26]then you shall say to them, 'I was presenting my plea to the king not to send me back to the house of Jonathan to die there.' " [27]All the officials did come to Jeremiah and questioned him; and he answered them in the very words the king had commanded. So they stopped questioning him, for the conversation had not been overheard. [28]And Jeremiah remained in the court of the guard until the day that Jerusalem was taken.

The Fall of Jerusalem

39 In the ninth year of King Zedekiah of Judah, in the tenth month, King Nebuchadrezzar of Babylon and all his army came against Jerusalem and besieged it; [2]in the eleventh year of Zedekiah, in the fourth month, on the ninth day of the month, a breach was made in the city. [3]When Jerusalem was taken,[c] all the officials of the king of Babylon came and sat in the middle gate: Nergal-sharezer, Samgar-nebo, Sarsechim the Rabsaris, Nergal-sharezer the Rabmag, with all the rest of the officials of the king of Babylon. [4]When King Zedekiah of Judah and all the soldiers saw them, they fled, going out of the city at night by way of the king's garden through

---

a Cn: Heb to under   b Or Nubian; Heb Cushite   c This clause has been transposed from 38.28

Cultural Connection

Risky Business

Ebed-melech is a biblical character we do not hear too much about. But he played a significant role in Jeremiah's life, and he has special meaning for African Americans because he was black. The Bible refers to him as the Ethiopian.

Ebed-melech is important because he was available to God and he was willing to risk his neck. Although Ebed-melech had the king's permission to rescue Jeremiah, he would have lost his life if his plan to do so had been discovered by the king's generals and counselors (see Jer 38:7–13). Ebed-melech shows us that being a servant of God is risky business. We cannot do God's will without taking risks. There is just no such thing as playing it safe and doing what God wants us to do.

Ebed-melech is also important because he was willing to help his "brother." Jeremiah was a Jew, and Ebed-melech was an Ethiopian, but still they were brothers in the Lord. Ebed-melech knew that he had to act when he saw his brother in trouble. When destruction finally came upon Jerusalem, God rewarded Ebed-melech by keeping him safe (see 39:18) because he had trusted in God enough to help his brother Jeremiah.

Lord, grant me a large portion of trust in you, that I might step out at your bidding and not be afraid of the outcome. Amen.

▶ **Jer 39:15–18**

---

the gate between the two walls; and they went toward the Arabah. [5]But the army of the Chaldeans pursued them, and overtook Zedekiah in the plains of Jericho; and when they had taken him, they brought him up to King Nebuchadrezzar of Babylon, at Riblah, in the land of Hamath; and he passed sentence on him. [6]The king of Babylon slaughtered the sons of Zedekiah at Riblah before his eyes; also the king of Babylon slaughtered all the nobles of Judah. [7]He put out the eyes of Zedekiah, and bound him in fetters to take him to Babylon. [8]The Chaldeans burned the king's house and the houses of the people, and broke down the walls of Jerusalem. [9]Then Nebuzaradan the captain of the guard exiled to Babylon the rest of the people who were left in the city, those who had deserted to him, and the people who remained. [10]Nebuzaradan the captain of the guard left in the land of Judah some of the poor people who owned nothing, and gave them vineyards and fields at the same time.

Jeremiah, Set Free, Remembers Ebed-melech

11 King Nebuchadrezzar of Babylon gave command concerning Jeremiah through Nebuzaradan, the captain of the guard, saying, [12]"Take him, look after him well and do him no harm, but deal with him as he may ask you." [13]So Nebuzaradan the captain of the guard, Nebushazban the Rabsaris, Nergal-sharezer the Rabmag, and all the chief officers of the king of Babylon sent

[14]and took Jeremiah from the court of the guard. They entrusted him to Gedaliah son of Ahikam son of Shaphan to be brought home. So he stayed with his own people.

15 The word of the LORD came to Jeremiah while he was confined in the court of the guard: [16]Go and say to Ebed-melech the Ethiopian:[a] Thus says the LORD of hosts, the God of Israel: I am going to fulfill my words against this city for evil and not for good, and they shall be accomplished in your presence on that day. [17]But I will save you on that day, says the LORD, and you shall not be handed over to those whom you dread. [18]For I will surely save you, and you shall not fall by the sword; but you shall have your life as a prize of war, because you have trusted in me, says the LORD.

Jeremiah with Gedaliah the Governor

40 The word that came to Jeremiah from the LORD after Nebuzaradan the captain of the guard had let him go from Ramah, when he took him bound in fetters along with all the captives of Jerusalem and Judah who were being exiled to Babylon. [2]The captain of the guard took Jeremiah and said to him, "The LORD your God threatened this place with this disaster; [3]and now the LORD has brought it about, and has done as he said, because all of you sinned against the

---

a Or *Nubian*; Heb *Cushite*

LORD and did not obey his voice. Therefore this thing has come upon you. ⁴Now look, I have just released you today from the fetters on your hands. If you wish to come with me to Babylon, come, and I will take good care of you; but if you do not wish to come with me to Babylon, you need not come. See, the whole land is before you; go wherever you think it good and right to go. ⁵If you remain,ᵃ then return to Gedaliah son of Ahikam son of Shaphan, whom the king of Babylon appointed governor of the towns of Judah, and stay with him among the people; or go wherever you think it right to go." So the captain of the guard gave him an allowance of food and a present, and let him go. ⁶Then Jeremiah went to Gedaliah son of Ahikam at Mizpah, and stayed with him among the people who were left in the land.

7 When all the leaders of the forces in the open country and their troops heard that the king of Babylon had appointed Gedaliah son of Ahikam governor in the land, and had committed to him men, women, and children, those of the poorest of the land who had not been taken into exile to Babylon, ⁸they went to Gedaliah at Mizpah—Ishmael son of Nethaniah, Johanan son of Kareah, Seraiah son of Tanhumeth, the sons of Ephai the Netophathite, Jezaniah son of the Maacathite, they and their troops. ⁹Gedaliah son of Ahikam son of Shaphan swore to them and their troops, saying, "Do not be afraid to serve the Chaldeans. Stay in the land and serve the king of Babylon, and it shall go well with you. ¹⁰As for me, I am staying at Mizpah to represent you before the Chaldeans who come to us; but as for you, gather wine and summer fruits and oil, and store them in your vessels, and live in the towns that you have taken over." ¹¹Likewise, when all the Judeans who were in Moab and among the Ammonites and in Edom and in other lands heard that the king of Babylon had left a remnant in Judah and had appointed Gedaliah son of Ahikam son of Shaphan as governor over them, ¹²then all the Judeans returned from all the places to which they had been scattered and came to the land of Judah, to Gedaliah at Mizpah; and they gathered wine and summer fruits in great abundance.

13 Now Johanan son of Kareah and all the leaders of the forces in the open country came to Gedaliah at Mizpah ¹⁴and said to him, "Are you at all aware that Baalis king of the Ammonites has sent Ishmael son of Nethaniah to take your life?" But Gedaliah son of Ahikam would not believe them. ¹⁵Then Johanan son of Kareah spoke secretly to Gedaliah at Mizpah, "Please let me go

and kill Ishmael son of Nethaniah, and no one else will know. Why should he take your life, so that all the Judeans who are gathered around you would be scattered, and the remnant of Judah would perish?" ¹⁶But Gedaliah son of Ahikam said to Johanan son of Kareah, "Do not do such a thing, for you are telling a lie about Ishmael."

Insurrection against Gedaliah

41 In the seventh month, Ishmael son of Nethaniah son of Elishama, of the royal family, one of the chief officers of the king, came with ten men to Gedaliah son of Ahikam, at Mizpah. As they ate bread together there at Mizpah, ²Ishmael son of Nethaniah and the ten men with him got up and struck down Gedaliah son of Ahikam son of Shaphan with the sword and killed him, because the king of Babylon had appointed him governor in the land. ³Ishmael also killed all the Judeans who were with Gedaliah at Mizpah, and the Chaldean soldiers who happened to be there.

4 On the day after the murder of Gedaliah, before anyone knew of it, ⁵eighty men arrived from Shechem and Shiloh and Samaria, with their beards shaved and their clothes torn, and their bodies gashed, bringing grain offerings and incense to present at the temple of the LORD. ⁶And Ishmael son of Nethaniah came out from Mizpah to meet them, weeping as he came. As he met them, he said to them, "Come to Gedaliah son of Ahikam." ⁷When they reached the middle of the city, Ishmael son of Nethaniah and the men with him slaughtered them, and threw themᵇ into a cistern. ⁸But there were ten men among them who said to Ishmael, "Do not kill us, for we have stores of wheat, barley, oil, and honey hidden in the fields." So he refrained, and did not kill them along with their companions.

9 Now the cistern into which Ishmael had thrown all the bodies of the men whom he had struck down was the large cisternᶜ that King Asa had made for defense against King Baasha of Israel; Ishmael son of Nethaniah filled that cistern with those whom he had killed. ¹⁰Then Ishmael took captive all the rest of the people who were in Mizpah, the king's daughters and all the people who were left at Mizpah, whom Nebuzaradan, the captain of the guard, had committed to Gedaliah son of Ahikam. Ishmael son of Nethaniah took them captive and set out to cross over to the Ammonites.

---

a Syr: Meaning of Heb uncertain   b Syr: Heb lacks *and threw them*; compare verse 9   c Gk: Heb *whom he had killed by the hand of Gedaliah*

11 But when Johanan son of Kareah and all the leaders of the forces with him heard of all the crimes that Ishmael son of Nethaniah had done, [12]they took all their men and went to fight against Ishmael son of Nethaniah. They came upon him at the great pool that is in Gibeon. [13]And when all the people who were with Ishmael saw Johanan son of Kareah and all the leaders of the forces with him, they were glad. [14]So all the people whom Ishmael had carried away captive from Mizpah turned around and came back, and went to Johanan son of Kareah. [15]But Ishmael son of Nethaniah escaped from Johanan with eight men, and went to the Ammonites. [16]Then Johanan son of Kareah and all the leaders of the forces with him took all the rest of the people whom Ishmael son of Nethaniah had carried away captive[a] from Mizpah after he had slain Gedaliah son of Ahikam—soldiers, women, children, and eunuchs, whom Johanan brought back from Gibeon.[b] [17]And they set out, and stopped at Geruth Chimham near Bethlehem, intending to go to Egypt [18]because of the Chaldeans; for they were afraid of them, because Ishmael son of Nethaniah had killed Gedaliah son of Ahikam, whom the king of Babylon had made governor over the land.

Jeremiah Advises Survivors Not to Migrate

42 Then all the commanders of the forces, and Johanan son of Kareah and Azariah[c] son of Hoshaiah, and all the people from the least to the greatest, approached [2]the prophet Jeremiah and said, "Be good enough to listen to our plea, and pray to the Lord your God for us—for all this remnant. For there are only a few of us left out of many, as your eyes can see. [3]Let the Lord your God show us where we should go and what we should do." [4]The prophet Jeremiah said to them, "Very well: I am going to pray to the Lord your God as you request, and whatever the Lord answers you I will tell you; I will keep nothing back from you." [5]They in their turn said to Jeremiah, "May the Lord be a true and faithful witness against us if we do not act according to everything that the Lord your God sends us through you. [6]Whether it is good or bad, we will obey the voice of the Lord our God to whom we are sending you, in order that it may go well with us when we obey the voice of the Lord our God."

7 At the end of ten days the word of the Lord came to Jeremiah. [8]Then he summoned Johanan son of Kareah and all the commanders of the forces who were with him, and all the people from the least to the greatest, [9]and said to them,

"Thus says the Lord, the God of Israel, to whom you sent me to present your plea before him: [10]If you will only remain in this land, then I will build you up and not pull you down; I will plant you, and not pluck you up; for I am sorry for the disaster that I have brought upon you. [11]Do not be afraid of the king of Babylon, as you have been; do not be afraid of him, says the Lord, for I am with you, to save you and to rescue you from his hand. [12]I will grant you mercy, and he will have mercy on you and restore you to your native soil. [13]But if you continue to say, 'We will not stay in this land,' thus disobeying the voice of the Lord your God [14]and saying, 'No, we will go to the land of Egypt, where we shall not see war, or hear the sound of the trumpet, or be hungry for bread, and there we will stay,' [15]then hear the word of the Lord, O remnant of Judah. Thus says the Lord of hosts, the God of Israel: If you are determined to enter Egypt and go to settle there, [16]then the sword that you fear shall overtake you there, in the land of Egypt; and the famine that you dread shall follow close after you into Egypt; and there you shall die. [17]All the people who have determined to go to Egypt to settle there shall die by the sword, by famine, and by pestilence; they shall have no remnant or survivor from the disaster that I am bringing upon them.

18 "For thus says the Lord of hosts, the God of Israel: Just as my anger and my wrath were poured out on the inhabitants of Jerusalem, so my wrath will be poured out on you when you go to Egypt. You shall become an object of execration and horror, of cursing and ridicule. You shall see this place no more. [19]The Lord has said to you, O remnant of Judah, Do not go to Egypt. Be well aware that I have warned you today [20]that you have made a fatal mistake. For you yourselves sent me to the Lord your God, saying, 'Pray for us to the Lord our God, and whatever the Lord our God says, tell us and we will do it.' [21]So I have told you today, but you have not obeyed the voice of the Lord your God in anything that he sent me to tell you. [22]Be well aware, then, that you shall die by the sword, by famine, and by pestilence in the place where you desire to go and settle."

Taken to Egypt, Jeremiah Warns of Judgment

43 When Jeremiah finished speaking to all the people all these words of the Lord their God, with which the Lord their God had

---

a Cn: Heb *whom he recovered from Ishmael son of Nethaniah*
b Meaning of Heb uncertain   c Gk: Heb *Jezaniah*

sent him to them, [2]Azariah son of Hoshaiah and Johanan son of Kareah and all the other insolent men said to Jeremiah, "You are telling a lie. The LORD our God did not send you to say, 'Do not go to Egypt to settle there'; [3]but Baruch son of Neriah is inciting you against us, to hand us over to the Chaldeans, in order that they may kill us or take us into exile in Babylon." [4]So Johanan son of Kareah and all the commanders of the forces and all the people did not obey the voice of the LORD, to stay in the land of Judah. [5]But Johanan son of Kareah and all the commanders of the forces took all the remnant of Judah who had returned to settle in the land of Judah from all the nations to which they had been driven— [6]the men, the women, the children, the princesses, and everyone whom Nebuzaradan the captain of the guard had left with Gedaliah son of Ahikam son of Shaphan; also the prophet Jeremiah and Baruch son of Neriah. [7]And they came into the land of Egypt, for they did not obey the voice of the LORD. And they arrived at Tahpanhes.

8 Then the word of the LORD came to Jeremiah in Tahpanhes: [9]Take some large stones in your hands, and bury them in the clay pavement[a] that is at the entrance to Pharaoh's palace in Tahpanhes. Let the Judeans see you do it, [10]and say to them, Thus says the LORD of hosts, the God of Israel: I am going to send and take my servant King Nebuchadrezzar of Babylon, and he[b] will set his throne above these stones that I have buried, and he will spread his royal canopy over them. [11]He shall come and ravage the land of Egypt, giving

> those who are destined for pestilence, to pestilence,
> and those who are destined for captivity, to captivity,
> and those who are destined for the sword, to the sword.

[12]He[c] shall kindle a fire in the temples of the gods of Egypt; and he shall burn them and carry them away captive; and he shall pick clean the land of Egypt, as a shepherd picks his cloak clean of vermin; and he shall depart from there safely. [13]He shall break the obelisks of Heliopolis, which is in the land of Egypt; and the temples of the gods of Egypt he shall burn with fire.

Denunciation of Persistent Idolatry

44 The word that came to Jeremiah for all the Judeans living in the land of Egypt, at Migdol, at Tahpanhes, at Memphis, and in the land of Pathros, [2]Thus says the LORD of hosts, the God of Israel: You yourselves have seen all the disaster that I have brought on Jerusalem and on all the towns of Judah. Look at them; today

they are a desolation, without an inhabitant in them, [3]because of the wickedness that they committed, provoking me to anger, in that they went to make offerings and serve other gods that they had not known, neither they, nor you, nor your ancestors. [4]Yet I persistently sent to you all my servants the prophets, saying, "I beg you not to do this abominable thing that I hate!" [5]But they did not listen or incline their ear, to turn from their wickedness and make no offerings to other gods. [6]So my wrath and my anger were poured out and kindled in the towns of Judah and in the streets of Jerusalem; and they became a waste and a desolation, as they still are today. [7]And now thus says the LORD God of hosts, the God of Israel: Why are you doing such great harm to yourselves, to cut off man and woman, child and infant, from the midst of Judah, leaving yourselves without a remnant? [8]Why do you provoke me to anger with the works of your hands, making offerings to other gods in the land of Egypt where you have come to settle? Will you be cut off and become an object of cursing and ridicule among all the nations of the earth? [9]Have you forgotten the crimes of your ancestors, of the kings of Judah, of their[d] wives, your own crimes and those of your wives, which they committed in the land of Judah and in the streets of Jerusalem? [10]They have shown no contrition or fear to this day, nor have they walked in my law and my statutes that I set before you and before your ancestors.

11 Therefore thus says the LORD of hosts, the God of Israel: I am determined to bring disaster on you, to bring all Judah to an end. [12]I will take the remnant of Judah who are determined to come to the land of Egypt to settle, and they shall perish, everyone; in the land of Egypt they shall fall; by the sword and by famine they shall perish; from the least to the greatest, they shall die by the sword and by famine; and they shall become an object of execration and horror, of cursing and ridicule. [13]I will punish those who live in the land of Egypt, as I have punished Jerusalem, with the sword, with famine, and with pestilence, [14]so that none of the remnant of Judah who have come to settle in the land of Egypt shall escape or survive or return to the land of Judah. Although they long to go back to live there, they shall not go back, except some fugitives.

15 Then all the men who were aware that their wives had been making offerings to other gods, and all the women who stood by, a great

---

a Meaning of Heb uncertain   b Gk Syr: Heb I   c Gk Syr Vg: Heb I   d Heb his

assembly, all the people who lived in Pathros in the land of Egypt, answered Jeremiah: 16 "As for the word that you have spoken to us in the name of the LORD, we are not going to listen to you. 17 Instead, we will do everything that we have vowed, make offerings to the queen of heaven and pour out libations to her, just as we and our ancestors, our kings and our officials, used to do in the towns of Judah and in the streets of Jerusalem. We used to have plenty of food, and prospered, and saw no misfortune. 18 But from the time we stopped making offerings to the queen of heaven and pouring out libations to her, we have lacked everything and have perished by the sword and by famine." 19 And the women said,[a] "Indeed we will go on making offerings to the queen of heaven and pouring out libations to her; do you think that we made cakes for her, marked with her image, and poured out libations to her without our husbands' being involved?"

20 Then Jeremiah said to all the people, men and women, all the people who were giving him this answer: 21 "As for the offerings that you made in the towns of Judah and in the streets of Jerusalem, you and your ancestors, your kings and your officials, and the people of the land, did not the LORD remember them? Did it not come into his mind? 22 The LORD could no longer bear the sight of your evil doings, the abominations that you committed; therefore your land became a desolation and a waste and a curse, without inhabitant, as it is to this day. 23 It is because you burned offerings, and because you sinned against the LORD and did not obey the voice of the LORD or walk in his law and in his statutes and in his decrees, that this disaster has befallen you, as is still evident today."

24 Jeremiah said to all the people and all the women, "Hear the word of the LORD, all you Judeans who are in the land of Egypt, 25 Thus says the LORD of hosts, the God of Israel: You and your wives have accomplished in deeds what you declared in words, saying, 'We are determined to perform the vows that we have made, to make offerings to the queen of heaven and to pour out libations to her.' By all means, keep your vows and make your libations! 26 Therefore hear the word of the LORD, all you Judeans who live in the land of Egypt: Lo, I swear by my great name, says the LORD, that my name shall no longer be pronounced on the lips of any of the people of Judah in all the land of Egypt, saying, 'As the Lord GOD lives.' 27 I am going to watch over them for harm and not for good; all the people of Judah who are in the land of Egypt shall perish by the sword and by

famine, until not one is left. 28 And those who escape the sword shall return from the land of Egypt to the land of Judah, few in number; and all the remnant of Judah, who have come to the land of Egypt to settle, shall know whose words will stand, mine or theirs! 29 This shall be the sign to you, says the LORD, that I am going to punish you in this place, in order that you may know that my words against you will surely be carried out: 30 Thus says the LORD, I am going to give Pharaoh Hophra, king of Egypt, into the hands of his enemies, those who seek his life, just as I gave King Zedekiah of Judah into the hand of King Nebuchadrezzar of Babylon, his enemy who sought his life."

A Word of Comfort to Baruch

45 The word that the prophet Jeremiah spoke to Baruch son of Neriah, when he wrote these words in a scroll at the dictation of Jeremiah, in the fourth year of King Jehoiakim son of Josiah of Judah: 2 Thus says the LORD, the God of Israel, to you, O Baruch: 3 You said, "Woe is me! The LORD has added sorrow to my pain; I am weary with my groaning, and I find no rest." 4 Thus you shall say to him, "Thus says the LORD: I am going to break down what I have built, and pluck up what I have planted—that is, the whole land. 5 And you, do you seek great things for yourself? Do not seek them; for I am going to bring disaster upon all flesh, says the LORD; but I will give you your life as a prize of war in every place to which you may go."

Judgment on Egypt

46 The word of the LORD that came to the prophet Jeremiah concerning the nations.

2 Concerning Egypt, about the army of Pharaoh Neco, king of Egypt, which was by the river Euphrates at Carchemish and which King Nebuchadrezzar of Babylon defeated in the fourth year of King Jehoiakim son of Josiah of Judah:

3 Prepare buckler and shield,
    and advance for battle!
4 Harness the horses;
    mount the steeds!
Take your stations with your helmets,
    whet your lances,
    put on your coats of mail!
5 Why do I see them terrified?
    They have fallen back;
their warriors are beaten down,
    and have fled in haste.

---

a Compare Syr: Heb lacks And the women said

They do not look back—
  terror is all around!

                                              says the LORD.

6 The swift cannot flee away,
  nor can the warrior escape;
in the north by the river Euphrates
  they have stumbled and fallen.

7 Who is this, rising like the Nile,
  like rivers whose waters surge?
8 Egypt rises like the Nile,
  like rivers whose waters surge.
It said, Let me rise, let me cover the earth,
  let me destroy cities and their inhabitants.
9 Advance, O horses,
  and dash madly, O chariots!
Let the warriors go forth:
  Ethiopia*a* and Put who carry the shield,
  the Ludim, who draw*b* the bow.
10 That day is the day of the Lord GOD of hosts,
  a day of retribution,
  to gain vindication from his foes.
The sword shall devour and be sated,
  and drink its fill of their blood.
For the Lord GOD of hosts holds a sacrifice
  in the land of the north by the river
    Euphrates.
11 Go up to Gilead, and take balm,
  O virgin daughter Egypt!
In vain you have used many medicines;
  there is no healing for you.
12 The nations have heard of your shame,
  and the earth is full of your cry;
for warrior has stumbled against warrior;
  both have fallen together.

Babylonia Will Strike Egypt

13 The word that the LORD spoke to the prophet Jeremiah about the coming of King Nebuchadrezzar of Babylon to attack the land of Egypt:

14 Declare in Egypt, and proclaim in Migdol;
  proclaim in Memphis and Tahpanhes;
Say, "Take your stations and be ready,
  for the sword shall devour those around
    you."
15 Why has Apis fled?*c*
  Why did your bull not stand?
  —because the LORD thrust him down.
16 Your multitude stumbled*d* and fell,
  and one said to another,*e*
"Come, let us go back to our own people
  and to the land of our birth,
  because of the destroying sword."
17 Give Pharaoh, king of Egypt, the name
  "Braggart who missed his chance."

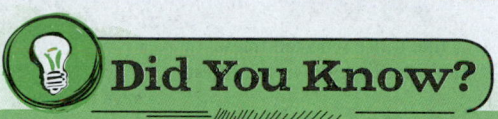

Did You Know?

Oracles Against the Nations

The Oracles Against the Nations, in Jeremiah, chapters 46–51, resemble the oracles in chapters 13–23 of Isaiah. In both, God's threats to destroy the enemies of Israel, as proclaimed by a prophet, reflect the bitterness that has welled up in the nation's heart during its long history of suffering.

Is God really as vengeful as the prophecies from Jeremiah suggest? We must balance our understanding of God's vengeance with Jesus' teachings—for example, Jesus' claim that God makes the "sun rise on the evil and on the good" (Mt 5:45). The God whom Jesus called Abba is the parent of all nations, who wants enemies to be reconciled with one another. The Oracles Against the Nations challenge Christians to be the first to offer the handshake of forgiveness and break the cycle of violence.

 Jeremiah, chapters 46–51

18 As I live, says the King,
  whose name is the LORD of hosts,
one is coming
  like Tabor among the mountains,
  and like Carmel by the sea.
19 Pack your bags for exile,
  sheltered daughter Egypt!
For Memphis shall become a waste,
  a ruin, without inhabitant.

20 A beautiful heifer is Egypt—
  a gadfly from the north lights upon her.
21 Even her mercenaries in her midst
  are like fatted calves;
they too have turned and fled together,
  they did not stand;
for the day of their calamity has come upon them,
  the time of their punishment.

22 She makes a sound like a snake gliding away;
  for her enemies march in force,
  and come against her with axes,

---

a Or *Nubia*; Heb *Cush*   b Cn: Heb *who grasp, who draw*
c Gk: Heb *Why was it swept away*   d Gk: Meaning of Heb uncertain   e Gk: Heb *and fell one to another and they said*

J
E
R

like those who fell trees.

23 They shall cut down her forest,

says the Lord,

though it is impenetrable,
because they are more numerous
than locusts;
they are without number.

24 Daughter Egypt shall be put to shame;
she shall be handed over to a people from the
north.

25 The Lord of hosts, the God of Israel, said: See, I am bringing punishment upon Amon of Thebes, and Pharaoh, and Egypt and her gods and her kings, upon Pharaoh and those who trust in him. 26I will hand them over to those who seek their life, to King Nebuchadrezzar of Babylon and his officers. Afterward Egypt shall be inhabited as in the days of old, says the Lord.

God Will Save Israel

27 But as for you, have no fear, my servant Jacob,
and do not be dismayed, O Israel;
for I am going to save you from far away,
and your offspring from the land of their
captivity.
Jacob shall return and have quiet and ease,
and no one shall make him afraid.

28 As for you, have no fear, my servant Jacob,

says the Lord,

for I am with you.
I will make an end of all the nations
among which I have banished you,
but I will not make an end of you!
I will chastise you in just measure,
and I will by no means leave you unpunished.

Judgment on the Philistines

47 The word of the Lord that came to the prophet Jeremiah concerning the Philistines, before Pharaoh attacked Gaza:

2 Thus says the Lord:
See, waters are rising out of the north
and shall become an overflowing torrent;
they shall overflow the land and all that fills it,
the city and those who live in it.
People shall cry out,
and all the inhabitants of the land shall wail.

3 At the noise of the stamping of the hoofs of his
stallions,
at the clatter of his chariots, at the rumbling
of their wheels,
parents do not turn back for children,
so feeble are their hands,

4 because of the day that is coming

to destroy all the Philistines,
to cut off from Tyre and Sidon
every helper that remains.
For the Lord is destroying the Philistines,
the remnant of the coastland of Caphtor.

5 Baldness has come upon Gaza,
Ashkelon is silenced.
O remnant of their power!ᵃ
How long will you gash yourselves?

6 Ah, sword of the Lord!
How long until you are quiet?
Put yourself into your scabbard,
rest and be still!

7 How can itᵇ be quiet,
when the Lord has given it an order?
Against Ashkelon and against the seashore—
there he has appointed it.

Judgment on Moab

48 Concerning Moab.

Thus says the Lord of hosts, the God of Israel:
Alas for Nebo, it is laid waste!
Kiriathaim is put to shame, it is taken;
the fortress is put to shame and broken down;

2 the renown of Moab is no more.
In Heshbon they planned evil against her:
"Come, let us cut her off from being a
nation!"
You also, O Madmen, shall be brought to
silence;ᶜ
the sword shall pursue you.

3 Hark! a cry from Horonaim,
"Desolation and great destruction!"

4 "Moab is destroyed!"
her little ones cry out.

5 For at the ascent of Luhith
they goᵈ up weeping bitterly;
for at the descent of Horonaim
they have heard the distressing cry of anguish.

6 Flee! Save yourselves!
Be like a wild assᵉ in the desert!

7 Surely, because you trusted in your strongholdsᶠ
and your treasures,
you also shall be taken;
Chemosh shall go out into exile,
with his priests and his attendants.

8 The destroyer shall come upon every town,
and no town shall escape;
the valley shall perish,

---

a Gk: Heb *their valley*   b Gk Vg: Heb *you*   c The place-name *Madmen* sounds like the Hebrew verb *to be silent*   d Cn: Heb *he goes*   e Gk Aquila: Heb *like Aroer*   f Gk: Heb *works*

and the plain shall be destroyed,
as the Lord has spoken.

9 Set aside salt for Moab,
for she will surely fall;
her towns shall become a desolation,
with no inhabitant in them.

10 Accursed is the one who is slack in doing
the work of the Lord; and accursed is the one
who keeps back the sword from bloodshed.

11 Moab has been at ease from his youth,
settled like wine[a] on its dregs;
he has not been emptied from vessel to vessel,
nor has he gone into exile;
therefore his flavor has remained
and his aroma is unspoiled.

12 Therefore, the time is surely coming, says
the Lord, when I shall send to him decanters to
decant him, and empty his vessels, and break his[b]
jars in pieces. 13Then Moab shall be ashamed of
Chemosh, as the house of Israel was ashamed of
Bethel, their confidence.

14 How can you say, "We are heroes
and mighty warriors"?
15 The destroyer of Moab and his towns has
come up,
and the choicest of his young men have gone
down to slaughter,
says the King, whose name is the Lord of hosts.
16 The calamity of Moab is near at hand
and his doom approaches swiftly.
17 Mourn over him, all you his neighbors,
and all who know his name;
say, "How the mighty scepter is broken,
the glorious staff!"

18 Come down from glory,
and sit on the parched ground,
enthroned daughter Dibon!
For the destroyer of Moab has come up against
you;
he has destroyed your strongholds.
19 Stand by the road and watch,
you inhabitant of Aroer!
Ask the man fleeing and the woman escaping;
say, "What has happened?"
20 Moab is put to shame, for it is broken down;
wail and cry!
Tell it by the Arnon,
that Moab is laid waste.

21 Judgment has come upon the tableland,
upon Holon, and Jahzah, and Mephaath, 22and

Dibon, and Nebo, and Beth-diblathaim, 23and
Kiriathaim, and Beth-gamul, and Beth-meon,
24and Kerioth, and Bozrah, and all the towns
of the land of Moab, far and near. 25The horn
of Moab is cut off, and his arm is broken, says
the Lord.

26 Make him drunk, because he magnified
himself against the Lord; let Moab wallow in
his vomit; he too shall become a laughingstock.
27Israel was a laughingstock for you, though he
was not caught among thieves; but whenever you
spoke of him you shook your head!

28 Leave the towns, and live on the rock,
O inhabitants of Moab!
Be like the dove that nests
on the sides of the mouth of a gorge.
29 We have heard of the pride of Moab—
he is very proud—
of his loftiness, his pride, and his arrogance,
and the haughtiness of his heart.
30 I myself know his insolence, says the Lord;
his boasts are false,
his deeds are false.
31 Therefore I wail for Moab;
I cry out for all Moab;
for the people of Kir-heres I mourn.
32 More than for Jazer I weep for you,
O vine of Sibmah!
Your branches crossed over the sea,
reached as far as Jazer;[c]
upon your summer fruits and your vintage
the destroyer has fallen.
33 Gladness and joy have been taken away
from the fruitful land of Moab;
I have stopped the wine from the wine presses;
no one treads them with shouts of joy;
the shouting is not the shout of joy.

34 Heshbon and Elealeh cry out;[d] as far as
Jahaz they utter their voice, from Zoar to Horonaim and Eglath-shelishiyah. For even the waters
of Nimrim have become desolate. 35And I will
bring to an end in Moab, says the Lord, those
who offer sacrifice at a high place and make offerings to their gods. 36Therefore my heart moans
for Moab like a flute, and my heart moans like
a flute for the people of Kir-heres; for the riches
they gained have perished.

37 For every head is shaved and every beard
cut off; on all the hands there are gashes, and
on the loins sackcloth. 38On all the housetops

---

a Heb lacks *like wine*   b Gk Aquila: Heb *their*   c Two Mss and
Isa 16.8: MT *the sea of Jazer*   d Cn: Heb *From the cry of Heshbon
to Elealeh*

Cultural Connection

The Eagle

Jeremiah 48:40 portrays the punisher of Moab as an eagle. In the Bible, that is not an unusual description for this majestic bird (see also Job 39:27, Isa 40:31, Ezek 17:3, Dan 7:4). Native American cultures admire the eagle as the strongest and bravest of all birds, and therefore view eagle feathers as a symbol of what is high and holy.

So, in some Native American tribes, when someone is honored for being brave, strong, and holy, an eagle feather is given to her or him. Native Americans also use eagle feathers for blessings. They hold or wave the feathers over a person's head as a prayer for peace and happiness. (*Note:* Native Americans are able to acquire feathers for use in their rituals. But keep in mind that it is generally illegal to hunt eagles or even to take a feather you find!)

The next time you see an eagle or a picture of an eagle, remember what its feathers symbolize, and pray about those ideals of honor, peace, protection, strength, courage, and holiness.

▶ **Jer 48:40**

---

of Moab and in the squares there is nothing but lamentation; for I have broken Moab like a vessel that no one wants, says the LORD. ³⁹ How it is broken! How they wail! How Moab has turned his back in shame! So Moab has become a derision and a horror to all his neighbors.

⁴⁰ For thus says the LORD:

Look, he shall swoop down like an eagle,
    and spread his wings against Moab;
⁴¹ the towns*ᵃ* shall be taken
    and the strongholds seized.
The hearts of the warriors of Moab, on that day,
    shall be like the heart of a woman in labor.
⁴² Moab shall be destroyed as a people,
    because he magnified himself against the
        LORD.
⁴³ Terror, pit, and trap
    are before you, O inhabitants of Moab!
                    says the LORD.
⁴⁴ Everyone who flees from the terror
    shall fall into the pit,
and everyone who climbs out of the pit
    shall be caught in the trap.
For I will bring these things*ᵇ* upon Moab
    in the year of their punishment,
                    says the LORD.

⁴⁵ In the shadow of Heshbon
    fugitives stop exhausted;
for a fire has gone out from Heshbon,
    a flame from the house of Sihon;
it has destroyed the forehead of Moab,
    the scalp of the people of tumult.*ᶜ*
⁴⁶ Woe to you, O Moab!

The people of Chemosh have perished,
for your sons have been taken captive,
    and your daughters into captivity.
⁴⁷ Yet I will restore the fortunes of Moab
    in the latter days, says the LORD.
Thus far is the judgment on Moab.

Judgment on the Ammonites

49 Concerning the Ammonites.

Thus says the LORD:
    Has Israel no sons?
        Has he no heir?
    Why then has Milcom dispossessed Gad,
        and his people settled in its towns?
² Therefore, the time is surely coming,
        says the LORD,
    when I will sound the battle alarm
        against Rabbah of the Ammonites;
    it shall become a desolate mound,
        and its villages shall be burned with fire;
    then Israel shall dispossess those who
            dispossessed him,
        says the LORD.

³ Wail, O Heshbon, for Ai is laid waste!
        Cry out, O daughters*ᵈ* of Rabbah!
    Put on sackcloth,
        lament, and slash yourselves with whips!*ᵉ*
    For Milcom shall go into exile,
        with his priests and his attendants.

---

a Or *Kerioth*   *b* Gk Syr: Heb *bring upon it*   *c* Or *of Shaon*
d Or *villages*   *e* Cn: Meaning of Heb uncertain

4 Why do you boast in your strength?
   Your strength is ebbing,
O faithless daughter.
   You trusted in your treasures, saying,
   "Who will attack me?"
5 I am going to bring terror upon you,
   says the Lord GOD of hosts,
   from all your neighbors,
and you will be scattered, each headlong,
   with no one to gather the fugitives.
6 But afterward I will restore the fortunes of
the Ammonites, says the LORD.

Judgment on Edom

7 Concerning Edom.

Thus says the LORD of hosts:
   Is there no longer wisdom in Teman?
      Has counsel perished from the prudent?
      Has their wisdom vanished?
8 Flee, turn back, get down low,
      inhabitants of Dedan!
   For I will bring the calamity of Esau upon
      him,
      the time when I punish him.
9 If grape-gatherers came to you,
      would they not leave gleanings?
   If thieves came by night,
      even they would pillage only what they
         wanted.
10 But as for me, I have stripped Esau bare,
   I have uncovered his hiding places,
   and he is not able to conceal himself.
His offspring are destroyed, his kinsfolk
   and his neighbors; and he is no more.
11 Leave your orphans, I will keep them alive;
   and let your widows trust in me.

12 For thus says the LORD: If those who do
not deserve to drink the cup still have to drink it,
shall you be the one to go unpunished? You shall
not go unpunished; you must drink it. 13For by
myself I have sworn, says the LORD, that Bozrah
shall become an object of horror and ridicule, a
waste, and an object of cursing; and all her towns
shall be perpetual wastes.
14 I have heard tidings from the LORD,
   and a messenger has been sent among the
      nations:
   "Gather yourselves together and come against
      her,
   and rise up for battle!"
15 For I will make you least among the nations,
   despised by humankind.
16 The terror you inspire
   and the pride of your heart have deceived
      you,

you who live in the clefts of the rock,[a]
   who hold the height of the hill.
Although you make your nest as high as the
      eagle's,
   from there I will bring you down,
                              says the LORD.
17 Edom shall become an object of horror;
everyone who passes by it will be horrified and
will hiss because of all its disasters. 18As when
Sodom and Gomorrah and their neighbors were
overthrown, says the LORD, no one shall live
there, nor shall anyone settle in it. 19Like a
lion coming up from the thickets of the Jordan
against a perennial pasture, I will suddenly chase
Edom[b] away from it; and I will appoint over it
whomever I choose.[c] For who is like me? Who
can summon me? Who is the shepherd who can
stand before me? 20Therefore hear the plan that
the LORD has made against Edom and the purposes that he has formed against the inhabitants
of Teman: Surely the little ones of the flock shall
be dragged away; surely their fold shall be appalled at their fate. 21At the sound of their fall the
earth shall tremble; the sound of their cry shall
be heard at the Red Sea.[d] 22Look, he shall mount
up and swoop down like an eagle, and spread his
wings against Bozrah, and the heart of the warriors of Edom in that day shall be like the heart
of a woman in labor.

Judgment on Damascus

23 Concerning Damascus.

Hamath and Arpad are confounded,
   for they have heard bad news;
they melt in fear, they are troubled like the sea[e]
   that cannot be quiet.
24 Damascus has become feeble, she turned to
      flee,
   and panic seized her;
anguish and sorrows have taken hold of her,
   as of a woman in labor.
25 How the famous city is forsaken,[f]
   the joyful town![g]
26 Therefore her young men shall fall in her
      squares,
   and all her soldiers shall be destroyed in that
      day,
                           says the LORD of hosts.
27 And I will kindle a fire at the wall of Damascus,
   and it shall devour the strongholds of
      Ben-hadad.

a Or of Sela   b Heb him   c Or and I will single out the choicest
of his rams: Meaning of Heb uncertain   d Or Sea of Reeds
e Cn: Heb there is trouble in the sea   f Vg: Heb is not forsaken
g Syr Vg Tg: Heb the town of my joy

Judgment on Kedar and Hazor

28 Concerning Kedar and the kingdoms of Hazor that King Nebuchadrezzar of Babylon defeated.

Thus says the LORD:
Rise up, advance against Kedar!
   Destroy the people of the east!
29 Take their tents and their flocks,
   their curtains and all their goods;
carry off their camels for yourselves,
   and a cry shall go up: "Terror is all around!"
30 Flee, wander far away, hide in deep places,
   O inhabitants of Hazor!
          says the LORD.
For King Nebuchadrezzar of Babylon
   has made a plan against you
   and formed a purpose against you.

31 Rise up, advance against a nation at ease,
   that lives secure,
          says the LORD,
that has no gates or bars,
   that lives alone.
32 Their camels shall become booty,
   their herds of cattle a spoil.
I will scatter to every wind
   those who have shaven temples,
and I will bring calamity
   against them from every side,
          says the LORD.
33 Hazor shall become a lair of jackals,
   an everlasting waste;
no one shall live there,
   nor shall anyone settle in it.

Judgment on Elam

34 The word of the LORD that came to the prophet Jeremiah concerning Elam, at the beginning of the reign of King Zedekiah of Judah.

35 Thus says the LORD of hosts: I am going to break the bow of Elam, the mainstay of their might; 36and I will bring upon Elam the four winds from the four quarters of heaven; and I will scatter them to all these winds, and there shall be no nation to which the exiles from Elam shall not come. 37I will terrify Elam before their enemies, and before those who seek their life; I will bring disaster upon them, my fierce anger, says the LORD. I will send the sword after them, until I have consumed them; 38and I will set my throne in Elam, and destroy their king and officials, says the LORD.

39 But in the latter days I will restore the fortunes of Elam, says the LORD.

Judgment on Babylon

50 The word that the LORD spoke concerning Babylon, concerning the land of the Chaldeans, by the prophet Jeremiah:

2 Declare among the nations and proclaim,
   set up a banner and proclaim,
   do not conceal it, say:
Babylon is taken,
   Bel is put to shame,
   Merodach is dismayed.
Her images are put to shame,
   her idols are dismayed.

3 For out of the north a nation has come up against her; it shall make her land a desolation, and no one shall live in it; both human beings and animals shall flee away.

4 In those days and in that time, says the LORD, the people of Israel shall come, they and the people of Judah together; they shall come weeping as they seek the LORD their God. 5They shall ask the way to Zion, with faces turned toward it, and they shall come and join[a] themselves to the LORD by an everlasting covenant that will never be forgotten.

6 My people have been lost sheep; their shepherds have led them astray, turning them away on the mountains; from mountain to hill they have gone, they have forgotten their fold. 7All who found them have devoured them, and their enemies have said, "We are not guilty, because they have sinned against the LORD, the true pasture, the LORD, the hope of their ancestors."

8 Flee from Babylon, and go out of the land of the Chaldeans, and be like male goats leading the flock. 9For I am going to stir up and bring against Babylon a company of great nations from the land of the north; and they shall array themselves against her; from there she shall be taken. Their arrows are like the arrows of a skilled warrior who does not return empty-handed. 10Chaldea shall be plundered; all who plunder her shall be sated, says the LORD.

11 Though you rejoice, though you exult,
   O plunderers of my heritage,
   though you frisk about like a heifer on the grass,
      and neigh like stallions,
12 your mother shall be utterly shamed,
   and she who bore you shall be disgraced.
Lo, she shall be the last of the nations,

---

a Gk: Heb *toward it. Come! They shall join*

a wilderness, dry land, and a desert.

13 Because of the wrath of the LORD she shall not
       be inhabited,
   but shall be an utter desolation;
everyone who passes by Babylon shall be
       appalled
   and hiss because of all her wounds.
14 Take up your positions around Babylon,
   all you that bend the bow;
shoot at her, spare no arrows,
   for she has sinned against the LORD.
15 Raise a shout against her from all sides,
   "She has surrendered;
her bulwarks have fallen,
   her walls are thrown down."
For this is the vengeance of the LORD:
   take vengeance on her,
   do to her as she has done.
16 Cut off from Babylon the sower,
   and the wielder of the sickle in time of
       harvest;
because of the destroying sword
   all of them shall return to their own people,
   and all of them shall flee to their own land.

17 Israel is a hunted sheep driven away by
lions. First the king of Assyria devoured it, and
now at the end King Nebuchadrezzar of Babylon
has gnawed its bones. 18Therefore, thus says the
LORD of hosts, the God of Israel: I am going to
punish the king of Babylon and his land, as I
punished the king of Assyria. 19I will restore
Israel to its pasture, and it shall feed on Carmel
and in Bashan, and on the hills of Ephraim and
in Gilead its hunger shall be satisfied. 20In those
days and at that time, says the LORD, the iniquity of Israel shall be sought, and there shall be
none; and the sins of Judah, and none shall be
found; for I will pardon the remnant that I have
spared.

21 Go up to the land of Merathaim;a
   go up against her,
and attack the inhabitants of Pekodb
   and utterly destroy the last of them,c
                         says the LORD;
   do all that I have commanded you.
22 The noise of battle is in the land,
   and great destruction!
23 How the hammer of the whole earth
   is cut down and broken!
How Babylon has become
   a horror among the nations!
24 You set a snare for yourself and you were
       caught, O Babylon,
   but you did not know it;

you were discovered and seized,
   because you challenged the LORD.
25 The LORD has opened his armory,
   and brought out the weapons of his wrath,
for the Lord GOD of hosts has a task to do
   in the land of the Chaldeans.
26 Come against her from every quarter;
   open her granaries;
pile her up like heaps of grain, and destroy her
       utterly;
   let nothing be left of her.
27 Kill all her bulls,
   let them go down to the slaughter.
Alas for them, their day has come,
   the time of their punishment!

28 Listen! Fugitives and refugees from the
land of Babylon are coming to declare in Zion
the vengeance of the LORD our God, vengeance
for his temple.

29 Summon archers against Babylon, all who
bend the bow. Encamp all around her; let no one
escape. Repay her according to her deeds; just as
she has done, do to her—for she has arrogantly
defied the LORD, the Holy One of Israel. 30There-
fore her young men shall fall in her squares, and
all her soldiers shall be destroyed on that day,
says the LORD.

31 I am against you, O arrogant one,
   says the Lord GOD of hosts;
for your day has come,
   the time when I will punish you.
32 The arrogant one shall stumble and fall,
   with no one to raise him up,
and I will kindle a fire in his cities,
   and it will devour everything around him.

33 Thus says the LORD of hosts: The people of
Israel are oppressed, and so too are the people of
Judah; all their captors have held them fast and
refuse to let them go. 34Their Redeemer is strong;
the LORD of hosts is his name. He will surely
plead their cause, that he may give rest to the
earth, but unrest to the inhabitants of Babylon.

35 A sword against the Chaldeans, says the LORD,
   and against the inhabitants of Babylon,
   and against her officials and her sages!
36 A sword against the diviners,
   so that they may become fools!
A sword against her warriors,

a Or of Double Rebellion   b Or of Punishment   c Tg: Heb
destroy after them

so that they may be destroyed!

37 A sword against her[a] horses and against her[a] chariots,
　and against all the foreign troops in her midst,
　so that they may become women!
A sword against all her treasures,
　that they may be plundered!
38 A drought[b] against her waters,
　that they may be dried up!
For it is a land of images,
　and they go mad over idols.

39 Therefore wild animals shall live with hyenas in Babylon,[c] and ostriches shall inhabit her; she shall never again be peopled, or inhabited for all generations. 40As when God overthrew Sodom and Gomorrah and their neighbors, says the LORD, so no one shall live there, nor shall anyone settle in her.

41 Look, a people is coming from the north;
　a mighty nation and many kings
　are stirring from the farthest parts of the earth.
42 They wield bow and spear,
　they are cruel and have no mercy.
The sound of them is like the roaring sea;
　they ride upon horses,
set in array as a warrior for battle,
　against you, O daughter Babylon!

43 The king of Babylon heard news of them,
　and his hands fell helpless;
anguish seized him,
　pain like that of a woman in labor.

44 Like a lion coming up from the thickets of the Jordan against a perennial pasture, I will suddenly chase them away from her; and I will appoint over her whomever I choose.[d] For who is like me? Who can summon me? Who is the shepherd who can stand before me? 45Therefore hear the plan that the LORD has made against Babylon, and the purposes that he has formed against the land of the Chaldeans: Surely the little ones of the flock shall be dragged away; surely their[e] fold shall be appalled at their fate. 46At the sound of the capture of Babylon the earth shall tremble, and her cry shall be heard among the nations.

51 Thus says the LORD:
I am going to stir up a destructive wind[f]
　against Babylon
　and against the inhabitants of Leb-qamai;[g]
2 and I will send winnowers to Babylon,
　and they shall winnow her.
They shall empty her land

when they come against her from every side
　on the day of trouble.
3 Let not the archer bend his bow,
　and let him not array himself in his coat of mail.
Do not spare her young men;
　utterly destroy her entire army.
4 They shall fall down slain in the land of the Chaldeans,
　and wounded in her streets.
5 Israel and Judah have not been forsaken
　by their God, the LORD of hosts,
though their land is full of guilt
　before the Holy One of Israel.

6 Flee from the midst of Babylon,
　save your lives, each of you!
Do not perish because of her guilt,
　for this is the time of the LORD's vengeance;
　he is repaying her what is due.
7 Babylon was a golden cup in the LORD's hand,
　making all the earth drunken;
the nations drank of her wine,
　and so the nations went mad.
8 Suddenly Babylon has fallen and is shattered;
　wail for her!
Bring balm for her wound;
　perhaps she may be healed.
9 We tried to heal Babylon,
　but she could not be healed.
Forsake her, and let each of us go
　to our own country;
for her judgment has reached up to heaven
　and has been lifted up even to the skies.
10 The LORD has brought forth our vindication;
　come, let us declare in Zion
　the work of the LORD our God.

11 Sharpen the arrows!
　Fill the quivers!
The LORD has stirred up the spirit of the kings of the Medes, because his purpose concerning Babylon is to destroy it, for that is the vengeance of the LORD, vengeance for his temple.
12 Raise a standard against the walls of Babylon;
　make the watch strong;
post sentinels;
　prepare the ambushes;
for the LORD has both planned and done
　what he spoke concerning the inhabitants of Babylon.

---

a Cn: Heb *his*　b Another reading is *A sword in Babylon*　c Heb lacks *in Babylon*　d Or *and I will single out the choicest of her rams*: Meaning of Heb uncertain　e Syr Gk Tg Compare 49.20: Heb lacks *their*　f Or *stir up the spirit of a destroyer*　g *Leb-qamai* is a cryptogram for *Kasdim*, Chaldea

¹³ You who live by mighty waters,
  rich in treasures,
your end has come,
  the thread of your life is cut.
¹⁴ The LORD of hosts has sworn by himself:
Surely I will fill you with troops like a swarm of
    locusts,
  and they shall raise a shout of victory over you.

¹⁵ It is he who made the earth by his power,
  who established the world by his wisdom,
and by his understanding stretched out the
    heavens.
¹⁶ When he utters his voice there is a tumult of
    waters in the heavens,
  and he makes the mist rise from the ends of
    the earth.
He makes lightnings for the rain,
  and he brings out the wind from his
    storehouses.
¹⁷ Everyone is stupid and without knowledge;
  goldsmiths are all put to shame by their idols;
for their images are false,
  and there is no breath in them.
¹⁸ They are worthless, a work of delusion;
  at the time of their punishment they shall
    perish.
¹⁹ Not like these is the LORD,ᵃ the portion of Jacob,
  for he is the one who formed all things,
and Israel is the tribe of his inheritance;
  the LORD of hosts is his name.

Israel the Creator's Instrument

²⁰ You are my war club, my weapon of battle:
with you I smash nations;
  with you I destroy kingdoms;
²¹ with you I smash the horse and its rider;
  with you I smash the chariot and the
    charioteer;
²² with you I smash man and woman;
  with you I smash the old man and the boy;
with you I smash the young man and the girl;
²³   with you I smash shepherds and their flocks;
with you I smash farmers and their teams;
  with you I smash governors and deputies.

The Doom of Babylon

24 I will repay Babylon and all the inhabitants of Chaldea before your very eyes for all
the wrong that they have done in Zion, says the
LORD.

²⁵ I am against you, O destroying mountain,
                         says the LORD,
  that destroys the whole earth;
I will stretch out my hand against you,

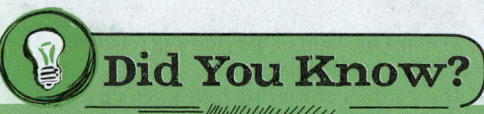

Did You Know?

Whatever Happened to Babylon?

In his time, Jeremiah prophesied about the destruction of Babylon, the powerful empire with the most glamorous and glittering capital in the Middle East (see Jeremiah, chapters 50–51). Not long afterward, in 587 BC, King Nebuchadrezzar (also called Nebuchadnezzar) of Babylon destroyed Jerusalem, blinded the king of Judah, and led the leaders of Judah off to exile. This seemed to be the end of Jerusalem and perhaps even the Israelites. However, the captives were eventually released when Persia defeated Babylon. Today, Jerusalem is a thriving city, and Judaism—as it emerged after the Exile—is a great religion. Babylon is long gone, and no one worships its chief god, Marduk.

Jeremiah saw past the immediate destruction of Jerusalem to the eventual doom of Babylon. He had a much broader vision of the future. Great cities come and go, but God is forever, and the people of God live on through all the ebbs and flows of history.

▶ **Jeremiah, chapter 51**

and roll you down from the crags,
  and make you a burned-out mountain.
²⁶ No stone shall be taken from you for a corner
  and no stone for a foundation,
but you shall be a perpetual waste,
  says the LORD.

²⁷ Raise a standard in the land,
  blow the trumpet among the nations;
prepare the nations for war against her,
  summon against her the kingdoms,
  Ararat, Minni, and Ashkenaz;
appoint a marshal against her,
  bring up horses like bristling locusts.
²⁸ Prepare the nations for war against her,
  the kings of the Medes, with their governors
    and deputies,
  and every land under their dominion.
²⁹ The land trembles and writhes,
  for the LORD's purposes against Babylon stand,

ᵃ Heb lacks *the* LORD

to make the land of Babylon a desolation,
  without inhabitant.
30 The warriors of Babylon have given up
      fighting,
  they remain in their strongholds;
their strength has failed,
  they have become women;
her buildings are set on fire,
  her bars are broken.
31 One runner runs to meet another,
  and one messenger to meet another,
to tell the king of Babylon
  that his city is taken from end to end:
32 the fords have been seized,
  the marshes have been burned with fire,
  and the soldiers are in panic.
33 For thus says the LORD of hosts, the God of
      Israel:
Daughter Babylon is like a threshing floor
  at the time when it is trodden;
yet a little while
  and the time of her harvest will come.

34 "King Nebuchadrezzar of Babylon has
      devoured me,
  he has crushed me;
he has made me an empty vessel,
  he has swallowed me like a monster;
he has filled his belly with my delicacies,
  he has spewed me out.
35 May my torn flesh be avenged on Babylon,"
  the inhabitants of Zion shall say.
"May my blood be avenged on the inhabitants
      of Chaldea,"
  Jerusalem shall say.
36 Therefore thus says the LORD:
I am going to defend your cause
  and take vengeance for you.
I will dry up her sea
  and make her fountain dry;
37 and Babylon shall become a heap of ruins,
  a den of jackals,
an object of horror and of hissing,
  without inhabitant.

38 Like lions they shall roar together;
  they shall growl like lions' whelps.
39 When they are inflamed, I will set out their
      drink
  and make them drunk, until they become
      merry
and then sleep a perpetual sleep
  and never wake, says the LORD.
40 I will bring them down like lambs to the
      slaughter,
  like rams and goats.

41 How Sheshach[a] is taken,
  the pride of the whole earth seized!
How Babylon has become
  an object of horror among the nations!
42 The sea has risen over Babylon;
  she has been covered by its tumultuous
      waves.
43 Her cities have become an object of horror,
  a land of drought and a desert,
a land in which no one lives,
  and through which no mortal passes.
44 I will punish Bel in Babylon,
  and make him disgorge what he has
      swallowed.
The nations shall no longer stream to him;
  the wall of Babylon has fallen.

45 Come out of her, my people!
  Save your lives, each of you,
  from the fierce anger of the LORD!
46 Do not be fainthearted or fearful
  at the rumors heard in the land—
one year one rumor comes,
  the next year another,
rumors of violence in the land
  and of ruler against ruler.

47 Assuredly, the days are coming
  when I will punish the images of Babylon;
her whole land shall be put to shame,
  and all her slain shall fall in her midst.
48 Then the heavens and the earth,
  and all that is in them,
shall shout for joy over Babylon;
  for the destroyers shall come against them out
      of the north,
                              says the LORD.
49 Babylon must fall for the slain of Israel,
  as the slain of all the earth have fallen
      because of Babylon.

50 You survivors of the sword,
  go, do not linger!
Remember the LORD in a distant land,
  and let Jerusalem come into your mind:
51 We are put to shame, for we have heard insults;
  dishonor has covered our face,
for aliens have come
  into the holy places of the LORD's house.

52 Therefore the time is surely coming, says the
      LORD,
  when I will punish her idols,
and through all her land

---

a *Sheshach* is a cryptogram for *Babel*, Babylon

the wounded shall groan.

53 Though Babylon should mount up to heaven,
and though she should fortify her strong
height,
from me destroyers would come upon her,
says the Lord.

54 Listen!—a cry from Babylon!
A great crashing from the land of the
Chaldeans!

55 For the Lord is laying Babylon waste,
and stilling her loud clamor.
Their waves roar like mighty waters,
the sound of their clamor resounds;

56 for a destroyer has come against her,
against Babylon;
her warriors are taken,
their bows are broken;
for the Lord is a God of recompense,
he will repay in full.

57 I will make her officials and her sages drunk,
also her governors, her deputies, and her
warriors;
they shall sleep a perpetual sleep and never
wake,
says the King, whose name is the Lord of
hosts.

58 Thus says the Lord of hosts:
The broad wall of Babylon
shall be leveled to the ground,
and her high gates
shall be burned with fire.
The peoples exhaust themselves for nothing,
and the nations weary themselves only for
fire.ᵃ

Jeremiah's Command to Seraiah

59 The word that the prophet Jeremiah commanded Seraiah son of Neriah son of Mahseiah,
when he went with King Zedekiah of Judah to
Babylon, in the fourth year of his reign. Seraiah
was the quartermaster. 60Jeremiah wrote in aᵇ
scroll all the disasters that would come on Babylon, all these words that are written concerning
Babylon. 61And Jeremiah said to Seraiah: "When
you come to Babylon, see that you read all these
words, 62and say, 'O Lord, you yourself threatened to destroy this place so that neither human
beings nor animals shall live in it, and it shall
be desolate forever.' 63When you finish reading
this scroll, tie a stone to it, and throw it into the
middle of the Euphrates, 64and say, 'Thus shall
Babylon sink, to rise no more, because of the disasters that I am bringing on her.' "ᶜ
Thus far are the words of Jeremiah.

The Destruction of Jerusalem Reviewed

52 Zedekiah was twenty-one years old when
he began to reign; he reigned eleven years
in Jerusalem. His mother's name was Hamutal
daughter of Jeremiah of Libnah. 2He did what
was evil in the sight of the Lord, just as Jehoiakim had done. 3Indeed, Jerusalem and Judah so
angered the Lord that he expelled them from his
presence.

Zedekiah rebelled against the king of Babylon.
4And in the ninth year of his reign, in the tenth
month, on the tenth day of the month, King
Nebuchadrezzar of Babylon came with all his
army against Jerusalem, and they laid siege to it;
they built siegeworks against it all around. 5So the
city was besieged until the eleventh year of King
Zedekiah. 6On the ninth day of the fourth month
the famine became so severe in the city that there
was no food for the people of the land. 7Then a
breach was made in the city wall;ᵈ and all the
soldiers fled and went out from the city by night
by the way of the gate between the two walls, by
the king's garden, though the Chaldeans were
all around the city. They went in the direction
of the Arabah. 8But the army of the Chaldeans
pursued the king, and overtook Zedekiah in the
plains of Jericho; and all his army was scattered,
deserting him. 9Then they captured the king, and
brought him up to the king of Babylon at Riblah
in the land of Hamath, and he passed sentence
on him. 10The king of Babylon killed the sons of
Zedekiah before his eyes, and also killed all the
officers of Judah at Riblah. 11He put out the eyes
of Zedekiah, and bound him in fetters, and the
king of Babylon took him to Babylon, and put
him in prison until the day of his death.

12 In the fifth month, on the tenth day of the
month—which was the nineteenth year of King
Nebuchadrezzar, king of Babylon—Nebuzaradan the captain of the bodyguard who served the
king of Babylon, entered Jerusalem. 13He burned
the house of the Lord, the king's house, and all
the houses of Jerusalem; every great house he
burned down. 14All the army of the Chaldeans,
who were with the captain of the guard, broke
down all the walls around Jerusalem. 15Nebuzar-
adan the captain of the guard carried into exile
some of the poorest of the people and the rest
of the people who were left in the city and the
deserters who had defected to the king of Babylon, together with the rest of the artisans. 16But

---

a Gk Syr Compare Hab 2.13: Heb *and the nations for fire, and they
are weary*   b Or *one*   c Gk: Heb *on her. And they shall weary
themselves*   d Heb lacks *wall*

Nebuzaradan the captain of the guard left some of the poorest people of the land to be vinedressers and tillers of the soil.

17 The pillars of bronze that were in the house of the LORD, and the stands and the bronze sea that were in the house of the LORD, the Chaldeans broke in pieces, and carried all the bronze to Babylon. [18]They took away the pots, the shovels, the snuffers, the basins, the ladles, and all the vessels of bronze used in the temple service. [19]The captain of the guard took away the small bowls also, the firepans, the basins, the pots, the lampstands, the ladles, and the bowls for libation, both those of gold and those of silver. [20]As for the two pillars, the one sea, the twelve bronze bulls that were under the sea, and the stands,[a] which King Solomon had made for the house of the LORD, the bronze of all these vessels was beyond weighing. [21]As for the pillars, the height of the one pillar was eighteen cubits, its circumference was twelve cubits; it was hollow and its thickness was four fingers. [22]Upon it was a capital of bronze; the height of the capital was five cubits; latticework and pomegranates, all of bronze, encircled the top of the capital. And the second pillar had the same, with pomegranates. [23]There were ninety-six pomegranates on the sides; all the pomegranates encircling the latticework numbered one hundred.

24 The captain of the guard took the chief priest Seraiah, the second priest Zephaniah, and the three guardians of the threshold; [25]and from the city he took an officer who had been in command of the soldiers, and seven men of the king's council who were found in the city; the secretary of the commander of the army who mustered the people of the land; and sixty men of the people of the land who were found inside the city. [26]Then Nebuzaradan the captain of the guard took them, and brought them to the king of Babylon at Riblah. [27]And the king of Babylon struck them down, and put them to death at Riblah in the land of Hamath. So Judah went into exile out of its land.

28 This is the number of the people whom Nebuchadrezzar took into exile: in the seventh year, three thousand twenty-three Judeans; [29]in the eighteenth year of Nebuchadrezzar he took into exile from Jerusalem eight hundred thirty-two persons; [30]in the twenty-third year of Nebuchadrezzar, Nebuzaradan the captain of the guard took into exile of the Judeans seven hundred forty-five persons; all the persons were four thousand six hundred.

Jehoiachin Favored in Captivity

31 In the thirty-seventh year of the exile of King Jehoiachin of Judah, in the twelfth month, on the twenty-fifth day of the month, King Evil-merodach of Babylon, in the year he began to reign, showed favor to King Jehoiachin of Judah and brought him out of prison; [32]he spoke kindly to him, and gave him a seat above the seats of the other kings who were with him in Babylon. [33]So Jehoiachin put aside his prison clothes, and every day of his life he dined regularly at the king's table. [34]For his allowance, a regular daily allowance was given him by the king of Babylon, as long as he lived, up to the day of his death.

---

a Cn: Heb that were under the stands

If someone close to you has died, you know that the grief and sadness can be almost too much for words. At such times of deep emotion, many people resort to poetry or song to try to express their feelings. Written during the Babylonian Exile, the Book of Lamentations poetically expresses the overwhelming grief the Israelites felt over the loss of their homes, their freedom, their capital, and their Temple. Through its passages, the Book of Lamentations gives us insight into how devastating and destructive those days actually were.

At a Glance

- Chapter 1. a description of the desolation of Mount Zion and Jerusalem
- Chapter 2. a discussion of God's wrath upon Jerusalem
- Chapter 3. an account moving from grief to memory to hope
- Chapter 4. a revisitation of Jerusalem
- Chapter 5. a prayer of the people

Quick Facts

Period Covered: the Babylonian Exile, from 587 to 538 BC
Inspired Authors: unknown
Theme: poems of grief over the destruction of Jerusalem and the hardships of the Exile

In Depth

The Book of Lamentations is a collection of five poem songs, each a separate chapter in the book. If you take a quick look, you will notice that each poem has twenty-two verses, except the third, which has sixty-six. This is not an accident. In the original Hebrew language, each verse of the first, second, and fourth poems begins with successive letters of the Hebrew alphabet, which has twenty-two letters. In the third poem, every set of three verses begins with a different letter of the alphabet. This poetic structure, called acrostic, cannot be successfully translated into English. It is found in several poetic sections of the Old Testament, including Psalm 119.

We are not sure why the Lamentation poems were written in this fashion. It may be because the structure made them easier to memorize. Some scholars believe that it may have been a mystical sign of order and completeness. Another possibility is that the poem's structure helped to give form to the people's grief, which is important because uncontrollable grief can keep people from moving on in life. Knowing that the poem had a definite end may have reminded them that their sorrow would also come to an end.

Through these beautiful poems, Israelites were able to grieve and acknowledge the sin that led to their destruction. By recalling their experience of the goodness of God in the past, they were also able to hope for the day when God would lead them back to their land to rebuild their lives in faithfulness to the covenant.

The Book of Lamentations

Lamentations

The Deserted City

1 How lonely sits the city
    that once was full of people!
How like a widow she has become,
    she that was great among the nations!
She that was a princess among the provinces
    has become a vassal.

2 She weeps bitterly in the night,
    with tears on her cheeks;
among all her lovers
    she has no one to comfort her;
all her friends have dealt treacherously with her,
    they have become her enemies.

3 Judah has gone into exile with suffering
    and hard servitude;
she lives now among the nations,
    and finds no resting place;
her pursuers have all overtaken her
    in the midst of her distress.

4 The roads to Zion mourn,
    for no one comes to the festivals;
all her gates are desolate,
    her priests groan;
her young girls grieve,[a]
    and her lot is bitter.

5 Her foes have become the masters,
    her enemies prosper,
because the LORD has made her suffer
for the multitude of her transgressions;
her children have gone away,
    captives before the foe.

6 From daughter Zion has departed
    all her majesty.
Her princes have become like stags
    that find no pasture;
they fled without strength
    before the pursuer.

7 Jerusalem remembers,
    in the days of her affliction and wandering,
all the precious things
    that were hers in days of old.
When her people fell into the hand of the foe,
    and there was no one to help her,
the foe looked on mocking
    over her downfall.

8 Jerusalem sinned grievously,
    so she has become a mockery;
all who honored her despise her,
    for they have seen her nakedness;
she herself groans,
    and turns her face away.

9 Her uncleanness was in her skirts;
    she took no thought of her future;
her downfall was appalling,
    with none to comfort her.

a Meaning of Heb uncertain

"O Lord, look at my affliction,
   for the enemy has triumphed!"

10 Enemies have stretched out their hands
   over all her precious things;
she has even seen the nations
   invade her sanctuary,
those whom you forbade
   to enter your congregation.

11 All her people groan
   as they search for bread;
they trade their treasures for food
   to revive their strength.
Look, O Lord, and see
   how worthless I have become.

12 Is it nothing to you,[a] all you who pass by?
   Look and see
if there is any sorrow like my sorrow,
   which was brought upon me,
which the Lord inflicted
   on the day of his fierce anger.

13 From on high he sent fire;
   it went deep into my bones;
he spread a net for my feet;
   he turned me back;
he has left me stunned,
   faint all day long.

14 My transgressions were bound[a] into a yoke;
   by his hand they were fastened together;
they weigh on my neck,
   sapping my strength;
the Lord handed me over
   to those whom I cannot withstand.

15 The Lord has rejected
   all my warriors in the midst of me;
he proclaimed a time against me
   to crush my young men;
the Lord has trodden as in a wine press
   the virgin daughter Judah.

16 For these things I weep;
   my eyes flow with tears;
for a comforter is far from me,
   one to revive my courage;
my children are desolate,
   for the enemy has prevailed.

17 Zion stretches out her hands,
   but there is no one to comfort her;
the Lord has commanded against Jacob
   that his neighbors should become his foes;

Jerusalem has become
   a filthy thing among them.

18 The Lord is in the right,
   for I have rebelled against his word;
but hear, all you peoples,
   and behold my suffering;
my young women and young men
   have gone into captivity.

19 I called to my lovers
   but they deceived me;
my priests and elders
   perished in the city
while seeking food
   to revive their strength.

20 See, O Lord, how distressed I am;
   my stomach churns,
my heart is wrung within me,
   because I have been very rebellious.
In the street the sword bereaves;
   in the house it is like death.

21 They heard how I was groaning,
   with no one to comfort me.
All my enemies heard of my trouble;
   they are glad that you have done it.
Bring on the day you have announced,
   and let them be as I am.

22 Let all their evil doing come before you;
   and deal with them
as you have dealt with me
   because of all my transgressions;
for my groans are many
   and my heart is faint.

God's Warnings Fulfilled

2 How the Lord in his anger
   has humiliated[a] daughter Zion!
He has thrown down from heaven to earth
   the splendor of Israel;
he has not remembered his footstool
   in the day of his anger.

2 The Lord has destroyed without mercy
   all the dwellings of Jacob;
in his wrath he has broken down
   the strongholds of daughter Judah;
he has brought down to the ground in
   dishonor
   the kingdom and its rulers.

a Meaning of Heb uncertain

L
A
M

Violence in Our City Streets

Poetic language is often used in the Bible to express the depth of human emotion that the author either feels or is trying to convey. When reading the Scriptures, we should be aware that poetic language often does not lend itself to a literal interpretation. Instead, we should open ourselves up to the spiritual and emotional truth this poetry contains.

The Book of Lamentations is a book of poetry that helps us reflect on the feelings and thoughts of the Jewish people in exile, who were suffering from the loss of their homes, freedom, security, and so much more. Verses 12 and 19 of the poem in chapter 2 of Lamentations both mention hunger and violence in the streets. Are things much different in our streets? In our own time, children are hungry, and people are being killed and violated. Our voice echoes the voice of this ancient prayer, calling out for God's mercy.

When will the violence stop, Lord? How many will die today from drug overdose and domestic abuse? How many children will go hungry because nobody took the time to care for them? Have mercy on your people, Lord!

▶ **Lamentations, chapter 2**

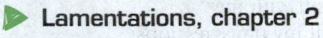

3 He has cut down in fierce anger
　　all the might of Israel;
he has withdrawn his right hand from them
　　in the face of the enemy;
he has burned like a flaming fire in Jacob,
　　consuming all around.

4 He has bent his bow like an enemy,
　　with his right hand set like a foe;
he has killed all in whom we took pride
　　in the tent of daughter Zion;
he has poured out his fury like fire.

5 The Lord has become like an enemy;
　　he has destroyed Israel.
He has destroyed all its palaces,
　　laid in ruins its strongholds,
and multiplied in daughter Judah
　　mourning and lamentation.

6 He has broken down his booth like a garden,
　　he has destroyed his tabernacle;
the Lord has abolished in Zion
　　festival and sabbath,
and in his fierce indignation has spurned
　　king and priest.

7 The Lord has scorned his altar,
　　disowned his sanctuary;
he has delivered into the hand of the enemy
　　the walls of her palaces;
a clamor was raised in the house of the Lord
　　as on a day of festival.

8 The Lord determined to lay in ruins
　　the wall of daughter Zion;
he stretched the line;
　　he did not withhold his hand from
　　　　destroying;
he caused rampart and wall to lament;
　　they languish together.

9 Her gates have sunk into the ground;
　　he has ruined and broken her bars;
her king and princes are among the nations;
　　guidance is no more,
and her prophets obtain
　　no vision from the Lord.

10 The elders of daughter Zion
　　sit on the ground in silence;
they have thrown dust on their heads
　　and put on sackcloth;
the young girls of Jerusalem
　　have bowed their heads to the ground.

11 My eyes are spent with weeping;
　　my stomach churns;
my bile is poured out on the ground
　　because of the destruction of my people,
because infants and babes faint
　　in the streets of the city.

12 They cry to their mothers,
　　"Where is bread and wine?"
as they faint like the wounded
　　in the streets of the city,
as their life is poured out
　　on their mothers' bosom.

13 What can I say for you, to what compare you,
    O daughter Jerusalem?
To what can I liken you, that I may comfort you,
    O virgin daughter Zion?
For vast as the sea is your ruin;
    who can heal you?

14 Your prophets have seen for you
    false and deceptive visions;
they have not exposed your iniquity
    to restore your fortunes,
but have seen oracles for you
    that are false and misleading.

15 All who pass along the way
    clap their hands at you;
they hiss and wag their heads
    at daughter Jerusalem;
"Is this the city that was called
    the perfection of beauty,
    the joy of all the earth?"

16 All your enemies
    open their mouths against you;
they hiss, they gnash their teeth,
    they cry: "We have devoured her!
Ah, this is the day we longed for;
    at last we have seen it!"

17 The LORD has done what he purposed,
    he has carried out his threat;
as he ordained long ago,
    he has demolished without pity;
he has made the enemy rejoice over you,
    and exalted the might of your foes.

18 Cry aloud*a* to the Lord!
    O wall of daughter Zion!
Let tears stream down like a torrent
    day and night!
Give yourself no rest,
    your eyes no respite!

19 Arise, cry out in the night,
    at the beginning of the watches!
Pour out your heart like water
    before the presence of the Lord!
Lift your hands to him
    for the lives of your children,
who faint for hunger
    at the head of every street.

20 Look, O LORD, and consider!
    To whom have you done this?
Should women eat their offspring,
    the children they have borne?

Should priest and prophet be killed
    in the sanctuary of the Lord?

21 The young and the old are lying
    on the ground in the streets;
my young women and my young men
    have fallen by the sword;
in the day of your anger you have killed them,
    slaughtering without mercy.

22 You invited my enemies from all around
    as if for a day of festival;
and on the day of the anger of the LORD
    no one escaped or survived;
those whom I bore and reared
    my enemy has destroyed.

God's Steadfast Love Endures

3 I am one who has seen affliction
    under the rod of God's*b* wrath;
2 he has driven and brought me
    into darkness without any light;
3 against me alone he turns his hand,
    again and again, all day long.

4 He has made my flesh and my skin waste away,
    and broken my bones;
5 he has besieged and enveloped me

---

a Cn: Heb *Their heart cried*   *b* Heb *his*

2:10

with bitterness and tribulation;
6 he has made me sit in darkness
    like the dead of long ago.

7 He has walled me about so that I cannot
        escape;
    he has put heavy chains on me;
8 though I call and cry for help,
    he shuts out my prayer;
9 he has blocked my ways with hewn stones,
    he has made my paths crooked.

10 He is a bear lying in wait for me,
    a lion in hiding;
11 he led me off my way and tore me to pieces;
    he has made me desolate;
12 he bent his bow and set me
    as a mark for his arrow.

13 He shot into my vitals
    the arrows of his quiver;
14 I have become the laughingstock of all my
        people,
    the object of their taunt-songs all day long.
15 He has filled me with bitterness,
    he has sated me with wormwood.

Each New Day

The poems in Lamentations also have their hopeful side. They acknowledge that God's love never ceases (see 3:22) and that the Israelites will not experience God's rejection forever (see verse 31). Verse 23 reminds the people that God's love is there each new day.

Imagine that at the beginning of each day, you are given $86,400. You have the whole day to spend every last penny any way you want. Does that sound exciting? Well, God gives you 86,400 seconds every day to use however you like. Try making a one-day budget of the best ways to spend your 86,400 seconds. Remember, each day is a new gift filled with God's love. Make the most of it, and do so for God!

▶ Lam 3:22–33

16 He has made my teeth grind on gravel,
    and made me cower in ashes;
17 my soul is bereft of peace;
    I have forgotten what happiness is;
18 so I say, "Gone is my glory,
    and all that I had hoped for from the
        LORD."

19 The thought of my affliction and my
        homelessness
    is wormwood and gall!
20 My soul continually thinks of it
    and is bowed down within me.
21 But this I call to mind,
    and therefore I have hope:

22 The steadfast love of the LORD never ceases,[a]
    his mercies never come to an end;
23 they are new every morning;
    great is your faithfulness.
24 "The LORD is my portion," says my soul,
    "therefore I will hope in him."

25 The LORD is good to those who wait for him,
    to the soul that seeks him.
26 It is good that one should wait quietly
    for the salvation of the LORD.
27 It is good for one to bear
    the yoke in youth,
28 to sit alone in silence
    when the Lord has imposed it,
29 to put one's mouth to the dust
    (there may yet be hope),
30 to give one's cheek to the smiter,
    and be filled with insults.

31 For the Lord will not
    reject forever.
32 Although he causes grief, he will have
        compassion
    according to the abundance of his steadfast
        love;
33 for he does not willingly afflict
    or grieve anyone.

34 When all the prisoners of the land
    are crushed under foot,
35 when human rights are perverted
    in the presence of the Most High,
36 when one's case is subverted
    —does the Lord not see it?

37 Who can command and have it done,
    if the Lord has not ordained it?

a Syr Tg: Heb LORD, we are not cut off

38 Is it not from the mouth of the Most High
　　that good and bad come?
39 Why should any who draw breath complain
　　about the punishment of their sins?

40 Let us test and examine our ways,
　　and return to the Lord.
41 Let us lift up our hearts as well as our hands
　　to God in heaven.
42 We have transgressed and rebelled,
　　and you have not forgiven.

43 You have wrapped yourself with anger and
　　　　pursued us,
　　killing without pity;
44 you have wrapped yourself with a cloud
　　so that no prayer can pass through.
45 You have made us filth and rubbish
　　among the peoples.

46 All our enemies
　　have opened their mouths against us;
47 panic and pitfall have come upon us,
　　devastation and destruction.
48 My eyes flow with rivers of tears
　　because of the destruction of my people.

49 My eyes will flow without ceasing,
　　without respite,
50 until the Lord from heaven
　　looks down and sees.
51 My eyes cause me grief
　　at the fate of all the young women in my
　　　　city.

52 Those who were my enemies without cause
　　have hunted me like a bird;
53 they flung me alive into a pit
　　and hurled stones on me;
54 water closed over my head;
　　I said, "I am lost."

55 I called on your name, O Lord,
　　from the depths of the pit;
56 you heard my plea, "Do not close your ear
　　to my cry for help, but give me relief!"
57 You came near when I called on you;
　　you said, "Do not fear!"

58 You have taken up my cause, O Lord,
　　you have redeemed my life.
59 You have seen the wrong done to me, O
　　　　Lord;
　　judge my cause.
60 You have seen all their malice,
　　all their plots against me.

61 You have heard their taunts, O Lord,
　　all their plots against me.
62 The whispers and murmurs of my assailants
　　are against me all day long.
63 Whether they sit or rise—see,
　　I am the object of their taunt-songs.

64 Pay them back for their deeds, O Lord,
　　according to the work of their hands!
65 Give them anguish of heart;
　　your curse be on them!
66 Pursue them in anger and destroy them
　　from under the Lord's heavens.

The Punishment of Zion

4 How the gold has grown dim,
　　how the pure gold is changed!
The sacred stones lie scattered
　　at the head of every street.

2 The precious children of Zion,
　　worth their weight in fine gold—
how they are reckoned as earthen pots,
　　the work of a potter's hands!

3 Even the jackals offer the breast
　　and nurse their young,
but my people has become cruel,
　　like the ostriches in the wilderness.

4 The tongue of the infant sticks
　　to the roof of its mouth for thirst;
the children beg for food,
　　but no one gives them anything.

5 Those who feasted on delicacies
　　perish in the streets;
those who were brought up in purple
　　cling to ash heaps.

6 For the chastisement[a] of my people has been
　　　　greater
　　than the punishment[b] of Sodom,
which was overthrown in a moment,
　　though no hand was laid on it.[c]

7 Her princes were purer than snow,
　　whiter than milk;
their bodies were more ruddy than coral,
　　their hair[c] like sapphire.[d]

8 Now their visage is blacker than soot;
　　they are not recognized in the streets.

---

a Or iniquity　b Or sin　c Meaning of Heb uncertain
d Or lapis lazuli

Growing Through Loss

One purpose of the poems in Lamentations is to help the ancient Israelites heal from the horrible tragedy of their loss. The poems accomplish this in three ways. First, in describing Israel's present loss and tragedy, they acknowledge that grief and mourning are needed. Second, they challenge Israel to look at its past, both to accept responsibility for its sin and to remember its great blessings from God. Finally, they encourage Israel to have hope for the future. In image after image, Israel is assured that the door to God's mercy is still open, in spite of great pain and loss.

So too must we allow ourselves to grieve when we have experienced the loss of someone we love. If we wall up our grief—and perhaps our guilt, because guilt often accompanies such a loss—we may at the same time shut out those who can help us heal. We must surround ourselves with family and friends who can be a source of comfort and support. We must also reclaim our memories of the person we lost, celebrating those of good times and healing those of hurtful times. Finally, as difficult as it may seem, we must open ourselves to the future, for God's love continues to be there for us, calling us to new life.

Their skin has shriveled on their bones;
  it has become as dry as wood.

⁹ Happier were those pierced by the sword
  than those pierced by hunger,
whose life drains away, deprived
  of the produce of the field.

¹⁰ The hands of compassionate women
  have boiled their own children;
they became their food
  in the destruction of my people.

¹¹ The Lᴏʀᴅ gave full vent to his wrath;
  he poured out his hot anger,

and kindled a fire in Zion
  that consumed its foundations.

¹² The kings of the earth did not believe,
  nor did any of the inhabitants of the world,
that foe or enemy could enter
  the gates of Jerusalem.

¹³ It was for the sins of her prophets
  and the iniquities of her priests,
who shed the blood of the righteous
  in the midst of her.

¹⁴ Blindly they wandered through the streets,
  so defiled with blood
that no one was able
  to touch their garments.

¹⁵ "Away! Unclean!" people shouted at them;
  "Away! Away! Do not touch!"
So they became fugitives and wanderers;
  it was said among the nations,
  "They shall stay here no longer."

¹⁶ The Lᴏʀᴅ himself has scattered them,
  he will regard them no more;
no honor was shown to the priests,
  no favor to the elders.

¹⁷ Our eyes failed, ever watching
  vainly for help;
we were watching eagerly
  for a nation that could not save.

¹⁸ They dogged our steps
  so that we could not walk in our streets;
our end drew near; our days were numbered;
  for our end had come.

¹⁹ Our pursuers were swifter
  than the eagles in the heavens;
they chased us on the mountains,
  they lay in wait for us in the wilderness.

²⁰ The Lᴏʀᴅ's anointed, the breath of our life,
  was taken in their pits—
the one of whom we said, "Under his shadow
  we shall live among the nations."

²¹ Rejoice and be glad, O daughter Edom,
  you that live in the land of Uz;
but to you also the cup shall pass;
  you shall become drunk and strip yourself bare.

²² The punishment of your iniquity, O daughter
  Zion, is accomplished,

he will keep you in exile no longer;
but your iniquity, O daughter Edom, he will
  punish,
he will uncover your sins.

A Plea for Mercy

5 Remember, O Lord, what has befallen us;
  look, and see our disgrace!
2 Our inheritance has been turned over to
    strangers,
  our homes to aliens.
3 We have become orphans, fatherless;
  our mothers are like widows.
4 We must pay for the water we drink;
  the wood we get must be bought.
5 With a yoke*a* on our necks we are hard driven;
  we are weary, we are given no rest.
6 We have made a pact with*b* Egypt and Assyria,
  to get enough bread.
7 Our ancestors sinned; they are no more,
  and we bear their iniquities.
8 Slaves rule over us;
  there is no one to deliver us from their hand.
9 We get our bread at the peril of our lives,
  because of the sword in the wilderness.
10 Our skin is black as an oven
  from the scorching heat of famine.
11 Women are raped in Zion,
  virgins in the towns of Judah.

12 Princes are hung up by their hands;
  no respect is shown to the elders.
13 Young men are compelled to grind,
  and boys stagger under loads of wood.
14 The old men have left the city gate,
  the young men their music.
15 The joy of our hearts has ceased;
  our dancing has been turned to mourning.
16 The crown has fallen from our head;
  woe to us, for we have sinned!
17 Because of this our hearts are sick,
  because of these things our eyes have grown
    dim:
18 because of Mount Zion, which lies desolate;
  jackals prowl over it.

19 But you, O Lord, reign forever;
  your throne endures to all generations.
20 Why have you forgotten us completely?
  Why have you forsaken us these many
    days?
21 Restore us to yourself, O Lord, that we may be
    restored;
  renew our days as of old—
22 unless you have utterly rejected us,
  and are angry with us beyond measure.

---

a Symmachus: Heb lacks *With a yoke*   b Heb *have given the hand to*

LAM

The Book of Baruch

Perhaps you've seen them on the news—long lines of refugees leaving war-torn countries. Or the camps where they set up temporary homes, waiting to return to their homeland. The sad truth is many of them can never return home. They are faced with the difficult task of building new homes in a foreign land. The Book of Baruch was written in such a situation—after many Israelites were forced to relocate following the Babylonian invasion in 587 BC.

At a Glance

- **1:1—3:8.** an introduction and a penitential prayer
- **3:9—4:4.** a poem on wisdom
- **4:5—5:9.** words of comfort for believers
- **Chapter 6.** a letter from Jeremiah against idolatry

Quick Facts

Period Covered: The setting is after the Babylonian Exile. The time of the author is probably from the second to the first centuries BC.

Inspired Author: an unknown compiler who attributed the book to Baruch, Jeremiah's secretary

Theme: Even in foreign lands, God's People can live faithful lives and find hope in God's promises.

Of Note: Baruch is not found in every version of the Old Testament (see "The Case of the Missing Books," near Tob 1:16).

In Depth

In the ancient world, it was not uncommon for people to write books and letters in the name of famous ancestors or historical figures. Several Old and New Testament books, including Baruch, were written in this manner. An anonymous person collected a variety of independent writings and named them for Baruch, the famous secretary of the prophet Jeremiah, in order to emphasize their link with Jeremiah's tradition of prophecy.

The short Book of Baruch recalls the Babylonian conquest of Jerusalem in the sixth century BC. In doing so, it points out these lessons to be learned from the painful past:

- We do not gain anything when we sin. Instead, we invite suffering into our lives.

- No matter how difficult life gets, we can always rely on God's goodness.

- Believers can always approach God in prayer, even when their situation seems impossibly painful.

- The traditions we have inherited from our ancestors are a reliable guide in facing life's challenges.

- We should resist all cultural pressures to act in violation of God's will.

- God can return Diaspora Jews to the holy land just as God returned the Babylonian exiles.

The core truth Baruch addresses is that no matter where they are, God's People can lead happy and holy lives by admitting their sinfulness and committing themselves to the Lord. This is an important lesson for all believers to learn. Unless we learn from history, we will repeat its mistakes.

Baruch

Baruch and the Jews in Babylon

1 These are the words of the book that Baruch son of Neriah son of Mahseiah son of Zedekiah son of Hasadiah son of Hilkiah wrote in Babylon, ²in the fifth year, on the seventh day of the month, at the time when the Chaldeans took Jerusalem and burned it with fire.

3 Baruch read the words of this book to Jeconiah son of Jehoiakim, king of Judah, and to all the people who came to hear the book, ⁴and to the nobles and the princes, and to the elders, and to all the people, small and great, all who lived in Babylon by the river Sud.

5 Then they wept, and fasted, and prayed before the Lord; ⁶they collected as much money as each could give, ⁷and sent it to Jerusalem to the high priest*a* Jehoiakim son of Hilkiah son of Shallum, and to the priests, and to all the people who were present with him in Jerusalem. ⁸At the same time, on the tenth day of Sivan, Baruch*b* took the vessels of the house of the Lord, which had been carried away from the temple, to return them to the land of Judah—the silver vessels that Zedekiah son of Josiah, king of Judah, had made, ⁹after King Nebuchadnezzar of Babylon had carried away from Jerusalem Jeconiah and the princes and the prisoners and the nobles and the people of the land, and brought them to Babylon.

A Letter to Jerusalem

10 They said: Here we send you money; so buy with the money burnt offerings and sin offerings and incense, and prepare a grain offering, and offer them on the altar of the Lord our God; ¹¹and pray for the life of King Nebuchadnezzar of Babylon, and for the life of his son Belshazzar, so that their days on earth may be like the days of heaven. ¹²The Lord will give us strength, and light to our eyes; we shall live under the protection*c* of King Nebuchadnezzar of Babylon, and under the protection of his son Belshazzar, and we shall serve them many days and find favor in their sight. ¹³Pray also for us to the Lord our God, for we have sinned against the Lord our God, and to this day the anger of the Lord and his wrath have not turned away from us. ¹⁴And you shall read aloud this scroll that we are sending you, to make your confession in the house of the Lord on the days of the festivals and at appointed seasons.

Confession of Sins

15 And you shall say: The Lord our God is in the right, but there is open shame on us today, on the people of Judah, on the inhabitants of Jerusalem, ¹⁶and on our kings, our rulers, our priests, our prophets, and our ancestors, ¹⁷because we have sinned before the Lord. ¹⁸We have disobeyed him, and have not heeded the voice of the Lord our God, to walk in the statutes of the Lord that he set before us. ¹⁹From the time when the Lord brought our ancestors out of the land of Egypt until today, we have been disobedient to the Lord our God, and we have been negligent,

a Gk the priest   b Gk he   c Gk in the shadow

in not heeding his voice. ²⁰So to this day there have clung to us the calamities and the curse that the Lord declared through his servant Moses at the time when he brought our ancestors out of the land of Egypt to give to us a land flowing with milk and honey. ²¹We did not listen to the voice of the Lord our God in all the words of the prophets whom he sent to us, ²²but all of us followed the intent of our own wicked hearts by serving other gods and doing what is evil in the sight of the Lord our God.

2 So the Lord carried out the threat he spoke against us: against our judges who ruled Israel, and against our kings and our rulers and the people of Israel and Judah. ²Under the whole heaven there has not been done the like of what he has done in Jerusalem, in accordance with the threats that were^a written in the law of Moses. ³Some of us ate the flesh of their sons and others the flesh of their daughters. ⁴He made them subject to all the kingdoms around us, to be an object of scorn and a desolation among all the surrounding peoples, where the Lord has scattered them. ⁵They were brought down and not raised up, because our nation^b sinned against the Lord our God, in not heeding his voice.

6 The Lord our God is in the right, but there is open shame on us and our ancestors this very day. ⁷All those calamities with which the Lord threatened us have come upon us. ⁸Yet we have not entreated the favor of the Lord by turning away, each of us, from the thoughts of our wicked hearts. ⁹And the Lord has kept the calamities ready, and the Lord has brought them upon us, for the Lord is just in all the works that he has commanded us to do. ¹⁰Yet we have not obeyed his voice, to walk in the statutes of the Lord that he set before us.

Prayer for Deliverance

11 And now, O Lord God of Israel, who brought your people out of the land of Egypt with a mighty hand and with signs and wonders and with great power and outstretched arm, and made yourself a name that continues to this day, ¹²we have sinned, we have been ungodly, we have done wrong, O Lord our God, against all your ordinances. ¹³Let your anger turn away from us, for we are left, few in number, among the nations where you have scattered us. ¹⁴Hear, O Lord, our prayer and our supplication, and for your own sake deliver us, and grant us favor in the sight of those who have carried us into exile; ¹⁵so that all the earth may know that you are the Lord our God, for Israel and his descendants are called by your name.

16 O Lord, look down from your holy dwelling, and consider us. Incline your ear, O Lord, and hear; ¹⁷open your eyes, O Lord, and see, for the dead who are in Hades, whose spirit has been taken from their bodies, will not ascribe glory or justice to the Lord; ¹⁸but the person who is deeply grieved, who walks bowed and feeble, with failing eyes and famished soul, will declare your glory and righteousness, O Lord.

19 For it is not because of any righteous deeds of our ancestors or our kings that we bring before you our prayer for mercy, O Lord our God. ²⁰For you have sent your anger and your wrath upon us, as you declared by your servants the prophets, saying: ²¹Thus says the Lord: Bend your shoulders and serve the king of Babylon, and you will remain in the land that I gave to your ancestors. ²²But if you will not obey the voice of the Lord and will not serve the king of Babylon, ²³I will make to cease from the towns of Judah and from the region around Jerusalem the voice of mirth and the voice of gladness, the voice of the bridegroom and the voice of the bride, and the whole land will be a desolation without inhabitants.

24 But we did not obey your voice, to serve the king of Babylon; and you have carried out your threats, which you spoke by your servants the prophets, that the bones of our kings and the bones of our ancestors would be brought out of their resting place; ²⁵and indeed they have been thrown out to the heat of day and the frost of night. They perished in great misery, by famine and sword and pestilence. ²⁶And the house that is called by your name you have made as it is today, because of the wickedness of the house of Israel and the house of Judah.

God's Promise Recalled

27 Yet you have dealt with us, O Lord our God, in all your kindness and in all your great compassion, ²⁸as you spoke by your servant Moses on the day when you commanded him to write your law in the presence of the people of Israel, saying, ²⁹"If you will not obey my voice, this very great multitude will surely turn into a small number among the nations, where I will scatter them. ³⁰For I know that they will not obey me, for they are a stiff-necked people. But in the land of their exile they will come to themselves ³¹and know that I am the Lord their God. I will give them a heart that obeys and ears that hear; ³²they will praise me in the land of their exile, and will remember my name ³³and turn from their stubbornness and their wicked deeds; for

---

a Gk in accordance with what is b Gk because we

they will remember the ways of their ancestors, who sinned before the Lord. ³⁴I will bring them again into the land that I swore to give to their ancestors, to Abraham, Isaac, and Jacob, and they will rule over it; and I will increase them, and they will not be diminished. ³⁵I will make an everlasting covenant with them to be their God and they shall be my people; and I will never again remove my people Israel from the land that I have given them."

3 O Lord Almighty, God of Israel, the soul in anguish and the wearied spirit cry out to you. ²Hear, O Lord, and have mercy, for we have sinned before you. ³For you are enthroned forever, and we are perishing forever. ⁴O Lord Almighty, God of Israel, hear now the prayer of the people[a] of Israel, the children of those who sinned before you, who did not heed the voice of the Lord their God, so that calamities have clung to us. ⁵Do not remember the iniquities of our ancestors, but in this crisis remember your power and your name. ⁶For you are the Lord our God, and it is you, O Lord, whom we will praise. ⁷For you have put the fear of you in our hearts so that we would call upon your name; and we will praise you in our exile, for we have put away from our hearts all the iniquity of our ancestors who sinned against you. ⁸See, we are today in our exile where you have scattered us, to be reproached and cursed and punished for all the iniquities of our ancestors, who forsook the Lord our God.

In Praise of Wisdom

⁹ Hear the commandments of life, O Israel;
　　give ear, and learn wisdom!
¹⁰ Why is it, O Israel, why is it that you are in the
　　　land of your enemies,
　　that you are growing old in a foreign country,
　　that you are defiled with the dead,
¹¹　　that you are counted among those in Hades?
¹² You have forsaken the fountain of wisdom.
¹³ If you had walked in the way of God,
　　you would be living in peace forever.
¹⁴ Learn where there is wisdom,
　　where there is strength,
　　where there is understanding,
　　so that you may at the same time discern
　　where there is length of days, and life,
　　where there is light for the eyes, and peace.

¹⁵ Who has found her place?
　　And who has entered her storehouses?
¹⁶ Where are the rulers of the nations,
　　and those who lorded it over the animals on
　　　earth;

¹⁷ those who made sport of the birds of the air,
　　and who hoarded up silver and gold
　in which people trust,
　　and there is no end to their getting;
¹⁸ those who schemed to get silver, and were
　　　anxious,
　　but there is no trace of their works?
¹⁹ They have vanished and gone down to Hades,
　　and others have arisen in their place.

²⁰ Later generations have seen the light of day,
　　and have lived upon the earth;
　but they have not learned the way to knowledge,
　　nor understood her paths,
　　nor laid hold of her.
²¹ Their descendants have strayed far from her[b] way.
²² She has not been heard of in Canaan,
　　or seen in Teman;
²³ the descendants of Hagar, who seek for
　　　understanding on the earth,
　　the merchants of Merran and Teman,
　　the story-tellers and the seekers for
　　　understanding,
　have not learned the way to wisdom,
　　or given thought to her paths.

²⁴ O Israel, how great is the house of God,
　　how vast the territory that he possesses!
²⁵ It is great and has no bounds;
　　it is high and immeasurable.
²⁶ The giants were born there, who were famous of
　　　old,
　　great in stature, expert in war.
²⁷ God did not choose them,
　　or give them the way to knowledge;
²⁸ so they perished because they had no wisdom,
　　they perished through their folly.

²⁹ Who has gone up into heaven, and taken her,
　　and brought her down from the clouds?
³⁰ Who has gone over the sea, and found her,
　　and will buy her for pure gold?
³¹ No one knows the way to her,
　　or is concerned about the path to her.
³² But the one who knows all things knows her,
　　he found her by his understanding.
　The one who prepared the earth for all time
　　filled it with four-footed creatures;
³³ the one who sends forth the light, and it goes;
　　he called it, and it obeyed him, trembling;
³⁴ the stars shone in their watches, and were glad;
　　he called them, and they said, "Here we are!"
　　They shone with gladness for him who made
　　　them.

---

a Gk *dead*　b Other ancient authorities read *their*

35 This is our God;
   no other can be compared to him.
36 He found the whole way to knowledge,
   and gave her to his servant Jacob
   and to Israel, whom he loved.
37 Afterward she appeared on earth
   and lived with humankind.

4 She is the book of the commandments of God,
   the law that endures forever.
   All who hold her fast will live,
   and those who forsake her will die.
2 Turn, O Jacob, and take her;
   walk toward the shining of her light.
3 Do not give your glory to another,
   or your advantages to an alien people.

The House of God

It is a warm, clear summer night. You and a good friend are sitting outside talking about the struggles both of you have been having with parents. Suddenly, you see a shooting star. Both of you spend a few moments gazing at the sky and marveling at how many stars there are and how clear the night is. The problems you were just discussing seem to pale in significance next to the vastness of the universe. And you realize that the two of you are seeing only one corner of the universe, "the house of God" (Bar 3:24). You both feel a connection with the stars and the sky and with the God who created it all.

The author of Baruch 3:24–37 seems to be having a similar moment. This writer describes God's wisdom as vast and endless (see verse 25) and beyond any person's grasp (see verse 29), but given to Israel for salvation (see verse 36). The author is saying: "Be at ease. God is bigger than your problems and in control."

When struggling with life's problems, recall the beauty of the night sky in order to put them in perspective. Spend a few moments gazing at the stars, and remember who's really in control.

▶ **Bar 3:24–37**

4 Happy are we, O Israel,
   for we know what is pleasing to God.

Encouragement for Israel

5 Take courage, my people,
   who perpetuate Israel's name!
6 It was not for destruction
   that you were sold to the nations,
   but you were handed over to your enemies
   because you angered God.
7 For you provoked the one who made you
   by sacrificing to demons and not to God.
8 You forgot the everlasting God, who brought
   you up,
   and you grieved Jerusalem, who reared you.
9 For she saw the wrath that came upon you from
   God,
   and she said:
   Listen, you neighbors of Zion,
   God has brought great sorrow upon me;
10 for I have seen the exile of my sons and
   daughters,
   which the Everlasting brought upon them.
11 With joy I nurtured them,
   but I sent them away with weeping and
   sorrow.
12 Let no one rejoice over me, a widow
   and bereaved of many;
   I was left desolate because of the sins of my
   children,
   because they turned away from the law of
   God.
13 They had no regard for his statutes;
   they did not walk in the ways of God's
   commandments,
   or tread the paths his righteousness showed
   them.
14 Let the neighbors of Zion come;
   remember the capture of my sons and
   daughters,
   which the Everlasting brought upon them.
15 For he brought a distant nation against them,
   a nation ruthless and of a strange language,
   which had no respect for the aged
   and no pity for a child.
16 They led away the widow's beloved sons,
   and bereaved the lonely woman of her
   daughters.
17 But I, how can I help you?
18 For he who brought these calamities upon you
   will deliver you from the hand of your
   enemies.
19 Go, my children, go;
   for I have been left desolate.
20 I have taken off the robe of peace

BAR

and put on sackcloth for my supplication;
   I will cry to the Everlasting all my days.

21 Take courage, my children, cry to God,
   and he will deliver you from the power and
      hand of the enemy.
22 For I have put my hope in the Everlasting to
     save you,
   and joy has come to me from the Holy One,
   because of the mercy that will soon come
     to you
   from your everlasting savior.[a]
23 For I sent you out with sorrow and weeping,
   but God will give you back to me with joy
     and gladness forever.
24 For as the neighbors of Zion have now seen
     your capture,
   so they soon will see your salvation by God,
   which will come to you with great glory
   and with the splendor of the Everlasting.
25 My children, endure with patience the wrath
     that has come upon you from God.
   Your enemy has overtaken you,
   but you will soon see their destruction
   and will tread upon their necks.
26 My pampered children have traveled rough
     roads;
   they were taken away like a flock carried off
     by the enemy.
27 Take courage, my children, and cry to God,
   for you will be remembered by the one who
     brought this upon you.
28 For just as you were disposed to go astray from
     God,
   return with tenfold zeal to seek him.
29 For the one who brought these calamities
     upon you
   will bring you everlasting joy with your
     salvation.

Jerusalem Is Assured of Help

30 Take courage, O Jerusalem,
   for the one who named you will
     comfort you.
31 Wretched will be those who mistreated you
   and who rejoiced at your fall.
32 Wretched will be the cities that your children
    served as slaves;
   wretched will be the city that received your
     offspring.
33 For just as she rejoiced at your fall
   and was glad for your ruin,
   so she will be grieved at her own desolation.
34 I will take away her pride in her great
     population,
   and her insolence will be turned to grief.

Stand Up!

The poem that begins with Baruch 4:5 has the nation of Israel speaking to the Jews in exile. After recalling that their disobedience brought on the exile, the author of the poem calls them to conversion. Worried that they may start worshiping the false gods of their new neighbors, the writer reminds them that if they are faithful to God, God will not abandon them.

It can be said that as Christians, we too live in a culture that is in some ways foreign to our values and beliefs. How easy is it to stand up against the pressures of peers, media values, and social standards that go against Christian values and beliefs? Are you confident enough to do what's right if others do not? It is important to find friends who share your values and look to your faith community for strength and courage.

▶ Bar 4:17–19

35 For fire will come upon her from the Everlasting
     for many days,
   and for a long time she will be inhabited by
     demons.

36 Look toward the east, O Jerusalem,
   and see the joy that is coming to you from
     God.

37 Look, your children are coming, whom you sent
     away;
   they are coming, gathered from east and west,
   at the word of the Holy One,
   rejoicing in the glory of God.

5 Take off the garment of your sorrow and
     affliction, O Jerusalem,
   and put on forever the beauty of the glory
     from God.
2 Put on the robe of the righteousness that comes
     from God;
   put on your head the diadem of the glory of
     the Everlasting;

---

a Or from the Everlasting, your savior

3 for God will show your splendor everywhere
 under heaven.
4 For God will give you evermore the name,
 "Righteous Peace, Godly Glory."

5 Arise, O Jerusalem, stand upon the height;
 look toward the east,
and see your children gathered from west and
  east
 at the word of the Holy One,
 rejoicing that God has remembered them.
6 For they went out from you on foot,
 led away by their enemies;
but God will bring them back to you,
 carried in glory, as on a royal throne.
7 For God has ordered that every high mountain
  and the everlasting hills be made low
 and the valleys filled up, to make level
  ground,
 so that Israel may walk safely in the glory of
  God.
8 The woods and every fragrant tree
 have shaded Israel at God's command.
9 For God will lead Israel with joy,
 in the light of his glory,
 with the mercy and righteousness that come
  from him.

The Letter of Jeremiah

6 [a] A copy of a letter that Jeremiah sent to those who were to be taken to Babylon as exiles by the king of the Babylonians, to give them the message that God had commanded him.

The People Face a Long Captivity

2 Because of the sins that you have committed before God, you will be taken to Babylon as exiles by Nebuchadnezzar, king of the Babylonians. 3Therefore when you have come to Babylon you will remain there for many years, for a long time, up to seven generations; after that I will bring you away from there in peace. 4Now in Babylon you will see gods made of silver and gold and wood, which people carry on their shoulders, and which cause the heathen to fear. 5So beware of becoming at all like the foreigners or of letting fear for these gods[b] possess you 6when you see the multitude before and behind them worshiping them. But say in your heart, "It is you, O Lord, whom we must worship." 7For my angel is with you, and he is watching over your lives.

The Helplessness of Idols

8 Their tongues are smoothed by the carpenter, and they themselves are overlaid with gold and silver; but they are false and cannot speak. 9People[c] take gold and make crowns for the heads of their gods, as they might for a girl who loves ornaments. 10Sometimes the priests secretly take gold and silver from their gods and spend it on themselves, 11or even give some of it to the prostitutes on the terrace. They deck their gods[d] out with garments like human beings— these gods of silver and gold and wood 12that cannot save themselves from rust and corrosion. When they have been dressed in purple robes, 13their faces are wiped because of the dust from the temple, which is thick upon them. 14One of them holds a scepter, like a district judge, but is unable to destroy anyone who offends it. 15Another has a dagger in its right hand, and an ax, but cannot defend itself from war and robbers. 16From this it is evident that they are not gods; so do not fear them.

17 For just as someone's dish is useless when it is broken, 18so are their gods when they have been set up in the temples. Their eyes are full of the dust raised by the feet of those who enter. And just as the gates are shut on every side against anyone who has offended a king, as though under sentence of death, so the priests make their temples secure with doors and locks and bars, in order that they may not be plundered by robbers. 19They light more lamps for them than they light for themselves, though their gods[e] can see none of them. 20They are[f] just like a beam of the temple, but their hearts, it is said, are eaten away when crawling creatures from the earth devour them and their robes. They do not notice 21when their faces have been blackened by the smoke of the temple. 22Bats, swallows, and birds alight on their bodies and heads; and so do cats. 23From this you will know that they are not gods; so do not fear them.

24 As for the gold that they wear for beauty— it[g] will not shine unless someone wipes off the tarnish; for even when they were being cast, they did not feel it. 25They are bought without regard to cost, but there is no breath in them. 26Having no feet, they are carried on the shoulders of others, revealing to humankind their worthlessness. And those who serve them are put to shame 27because, if any of these gods falls[h] to the ground, they themselves must pick it up. If anyone sets it upright, it cannot move itself; and if it is tipped

---

a The King James Version (like the Latin Vulgate) prints The Letter of Jeremiah as Chapter 6 of the Book of Baruch, and the chapter and verse numbers are here retained. In the Greek Septuagint, the Letter is separated from Baruch by the Book of Lamentations. b Gk for them   c Gk They   d Gk them   e Gk they   f Gk It is g Lat Syr: Gk they   h Gk if they fall over, it cannot straighten itself. Gifts are placed before them just as before the dead. ²⁸The priests sell the sacrifices that are offered to these gods*a* and use the money themselves. Likewise their wives preserve some of the meat*b* with salt, but give none to the poor or helpless. ²⁹Sacrifices to them may even be touched by women in their periods or at childbirth. Since you know by these things that they are not gods, do not fear them.

30 For how can they be called gods? Women serve meals for gods of silver and gold and wood; ³¹and in their temples the priests sit with their clothes torn, their heads and beards shaved, and their heads uncovered. ³²They howl and shout before their gods as some do at a funeral banquet. ³³The priests take some of the clothing of their gods*c* to clothe their wives and children. ³⁴Whether one does evil to them or good, they will not be able to repay it. They cannot set up a king or depose one. ³⁵Likewise they are not able to give either wealth or money; if one makes a vow to them and does not keep it, they will not require it. ³⁶They cannot save anyone from death or rescue the weak from the strong. ³⁷They cannot restore sight to the blind; they cannot rescue one who is in distress. ³⁸They cannot take pity on a widow or do good to an orphan. ³⁹These things that are made of wood and overlaid with gold and silver are like stones from the mountain, and those who serve them will be put to shame. ⁴⁰Why then must anyone think that they are gods, or call them gods?

The Foolishness of Worshiping Idols

Besides, even the Chaldeans themselves dishonor them; for when they see someone who cannot speak, they bring Bel and pray that the mute may speak, as though Bel*d* were able to understand! ⁴¹Yet they themselves cannot perceive this and abandon them, for they have no sense. ⁴²And the women, with cords around them, sit along the passageways, burning bran for incense. ⁴³When one of them is led off by one of the passers-by and is taken to bed by him, she derides the woman next to her, because she was not as attractive as herself and her cord was not broken. ⁴⁴Whatever is done for these idols*e* is false. Why then must anyone think that they are gods, or call them gods?

45 They are made by carpenters and goldsmiths; they can be nothing but what the artisans wish them to be. ⁴⁶Those who make them will certainly not live very long themselves; ⁴⁷how then can the things that are made by them be gods? They have left only lies and reproach for those who come after. ⁴⁸For when war or

Pray It!

Lucky Charms?

The whole sixth chapter of Baruch points out the foolishness of people who worship statues of gods and goddesses. Some ancient peoples felt these images gave them luck or fertility or health. The author of this chapter is warning, "Just because you are in a foreign land, don't take up silly superstitions!"

Sometimes, modern people like to carry a special lucky charm in the belief that it will protect them or bring them good luck. Do you carry a rabbit's foot, wear a special piece of clothing for big events, or use some other good luck charm? If so, why?

Dear Lord, sometimes, when I feel like I can use every bit of luck I can get, a "lucky" object can be a comfort. Help me to remember, though, the true power over my life that comes from you.

▶ **Baruch, chapter 6**

calamity comes upon them, the priests consult together as to where they can hide themselves and their gods.*e* ⁴⁹How then can one fail to see that these are not gods, for they cannot save themselves from war or calamity? ⁵⁰Since they are made of wood and overlaid with gold and silver, it will afterward be known that they are false. ⁵¹It will be manifest to all the nations and kings that they are not gods but the work of human hands, and that there is no work of God in them. ⁵²Who then can fail to know that they are not gods?*f*

53 For they cannot set up a king over a country or give rain to people. ⁵⁴They cannot judge their own cause or deliver one who is wronged, for they have no power; ⁵⁵they are like crows between heaven and earth. When fire breaks out in a temple of wooden gods overlaid with gold or silver, their priests will flee and escape, but the gods*g* will be burned up like timbers. ⁵⁶Besides, they can offer no resistance to king or enemy.

---

a Gk *to them*   *b* Gk *of them*   *c* Gk *some of their clothing*
d Gk *he*   *e* Gk *them*   *f* Meaning of Gk uncertain   *g* Gk *they*

B
A
R

Why then must anyone admit or think that they are gods?

57 Gods made of wood and overlaid with silver and gold are unable to save themselves from thieves or robbers. [58]Anyone who can will strip them of their gold and silver and of the robes they wear, and go off with this booty, and they will not be able to help themselves. [59]So it is better to be a king who shows his courage, or a household utensil that serves its owner's need, than to be these false gods; better even the door of a house that protects its contents, than these false gods; better also a wooden pillar in a palace, than these false gods.

60 For sun and moon and stars are bright, and when sent to do a service, they are obedient. [61]So also the lightning, when it flashes, is widely seen; and the wind likewise blows in every land. [62]When God commands the clouds to go over the whole world, they carry out his command. [63]And the fire sent from above to consume mountains and woods does what it is ordered. But these idols[a] are not to be compared with them in appearance or power. [64]Therefore one must not think that they are gods, nor call them gods, for they are not able either to decide a case or to do good to anyone. [65]Since you know then that they are not gods, do not fear them.

66 They can neither curse nor bless kings; [67]they cannot show signs in the heavens for the nations, or shine like the sun or give light like the moon. [68]The wild animals are better than they are, for they can flee to shelter and help themselves. [69]So we have no evidence whatever that they are gods; therefore do not fear them.

70 Like a scarecrow in a cucumber bed, which guards nothing, so are their gods of wood, overlaid with gold and silver. [71]In the same way, their gods of wood, overlaid with gold and silver, are like a thornbush in a garden on which every bird perches; or like a corpse thrown out in the darkness. [72]From the purple and linen[b] that rot upon them you will know that they are not gods; and they will finally be consumed themselves, and be a reproach in the land. [73]Better, therefore, is someone upright who has no idols; such a person will be far above reproach.

a Gk these things   b Cn: Gk marble, Syr silk

Four-headed creatures, a strange craft made up of wheels within wheels, a being of light that appears out of the sky—the first chapter of the Book of Ezekiel sounds like a preview for a science fiction movie. Ezekiel, more than any other prophet, proclaims astonishing visions that are filled with bizarre images, symbols, and creatures.

At a Glance

- **Chapters 1–3.** Ezekiel's call
- **Chapters 4–24.** visions and prophecies about Jerusalem
- **Chapters 25–32.** oracles against foreign nations
- **Chapters 33–39.** oracles of the restoration of Judah and Jerusalem
- **Chapters 40–48.** visions of a new Temple and a new worship

Quick Facts

Period Covered: from 593 to 573 BC

Inspired Authors: Ezekiel, and the scribes who recorded his words and actions

Themes: Jerusalem is being punished for its sin. God's glory will be known to all the nations. God will restore the Temple.

In Depth

Ezekiel lived during the last days of Judah, just before it was destroyed by the Babylonians. He was probably among an early group of captives sent into exile in Babylon before Judah and the city of Jerusalem were demolished in 587 BC (see the timeline at the back of this Bible). He began his prophetic ministry in 593 BC, when he received a fantastic vision and call, described in chapters 1–3 of his book. We know that Ezekiel came from a priestly family (see 1:3) and that he was married (see 24:16–18).

Ezekiel preached many of the traditional themes of the other prophets but in a unique way. Note these examples:

The Lord's presence in the Temple. Possibly because of Ezekiel's priestly heritage, he gave God's presence—or lack of presence—in the Temple a more central role than did the other prophets. In his vision, the Temple will be the center of the new Israel, and a great priest will rule instead of a king.

The awesomeness of God. For Ezekiel, the Lord did not appear as a parent or someone to be argued with; rather, God was awesome and overpowering, beyond human explanations. Ezekiel often spoke of God's glory and holiness.

Personal responsibility. Ezekiel did not condemn the previous generation for the destruction of Judah, but preached that every generation is responsible for its own acts. Each individual can direct his or her life according to God's will.

Apocalyptic prophecy. Some of Ezekiel's prophecies take the form of symbolic images. The images are so mysterious they require special explanation by heavenly beings. The Books of Daniel and Revelation continue this type of writing, which is called apocalyptic literature.

The Book of Ezekiel

Ezekiel

Chapter 2

The Vision of the Chariot

1 In the thirtieth year, in the fourth month, on the fifth day of the month, as I was among the exiles by the river Chebar, the heavens were opened, and I saw visions of God. ²On the fifth day of the month (it was the fifth year of the exile of King Jehoiachin), ³the word of the LORD came to the priest Ezekiel son of Buzi, in the land of the Chaldeans by the river Chebar; and the hand of the LORD was on him there.

4 As I looked, a stormy wind came out of the north: a great cloud with brightness around it and fire flashing forth continually, and in the middle of the fire, something like gleaming amber. ⁵In the middle of it was something like four living creatures. This was their appearance: they were of human form. ⁶Each had four faces, and each of them had four wings. ⁷Their legs were straight, and the soles of their feet were like the sole of a calf's foot; and they sparkled like burnished bronze. ⁸Under their wings on their four sides they had human hands. And the four had their faces and their wings thus: ⁹their wings touched one another; each of them moved straight ahead, without turning as they moved. ¹⁰As for the appearance of their faces: the four had the face of a human being, the face of a lion on the right side, the face of an ox on the left side, and the face of an eagle; ¹¹such were their faces. Their wings were spread out above; each creature had two wings, each of which touched the wing of another, while two covered their bodies. ¹²Each moved straight ahead; wherever the spirit would go, they went, without turning as they went. ¹³In the middle of*ᵃ* the living creatures there was something that looked like burning coals of fire, like torches moving to and fro among the living creatures; the fire was bright, and lightning issued from the fire. ¹⁴The living creatures darted to and fro, like a flash of lightning.

15 As I looked at the living creatures, I saw a wheel on the earth beside the living creatures, one for each of the four of them.*ᵇ* ¹⁶As for the appearance of the wheels and their construction: their appearance was like the gleaming of beryl; and the four had the same form, their construction being something like a wheel within a wheel. ¹⁷When they moved, they moved in any of the four directions without veering as they moved. ¹⁸Their rims were tall and awesome, for the rims of all four were full of eyes all around. ¹⁹When the living creatures moved, the wheels moved beside them; and when the living creatures rose from the earth, the wheels rose. ²⁰Wherever the spirit would go, they went, and the wheels rose along with them; for the spirit of the living creatures was in the wheels. ²¹When they moved, the others moved; when they stopped, the others stopped; and when they rose from the earth, the wheels rose along with them; for the spirit of the living creatures was in the wheels.

22 Over the heads of the living creatures there

---

a Gk OL: Heb *And the appearance of*   *b* Heb *of their faces* was something like a dome, shining like crystal,[a] spread out above their heads. 23Under the dome their wings were stretched out straight, one toward another; and each of the creatures had two wings covering its body. 24When they moved, I heard the sound of their wings like the sound of mighty waters, like the thunder of the Almighty,[b] a sound of tumult like the sound of an army; when they stopped, they let down their wings. 25And there came a voice from above the dome over their heads; when they stopped, they let down their wings.

26 And above the dome over their heads there was something like a throne, in appearance like sapphire;[c] and seated above the likeness of a throne was something that seemed like a human form. 27Upward from what appeared like the loins I saw something like gleaming amber, something that looked like fire enclosed all around; and downward from what looked like the loins I saw something that looked like fire, and there was a splendor all around. 28Like the bow in a cloud on a rainy day, such was the appearance of the splendor all around. This was the appearance of the likeness of the glory of the LORD.

When I saw it, I fell on my face, and I heard the voice of someone speaking.

The Vision of the Scroll

2 He said to me: O mortal,[d] stand up on your feet, and I will speak with you. 2And when he spoke to me, a spirit entered into me and set me on my feet; and I heard him speaking to me. 3He said to me, Mortal, I am sending you to the people of Israel, to a nation[e] of rebels who have rebelled against me; they and their ancestors have transgressed against me to this very day. 4The descendants are impudent and stubborn. I am sending you to them, and you shall say to them, "Thus says the Lord GOD." 5Whether they hear or refuse to hear (for they are a rebellious house), they shall know that there has been a prophet among them. 6And you, O mortal, do not be afraid of them, and do not be afraid of their words, though briers and thorns surround you and you live among scorpions; do not be afraid of their words, and do not be dismayed at their looks, for they are a rebellious house. 7You shall speak my words to them, whether they hear or refuse to hear; for they are a rebellious house.

8 But you, mortal, hear what I say to you; do not be rebellious like that rebellious house; open your mouth and eat what I give you. 9I looked, and a hand was stretched out to me, and a written scroll was in it. 10He spread it before me; it had writing on the front and on the back, and

Live It!

The Word Is Sweet

God called Ezekiel to speak God's word to the people. It was a tough job, for God's people weren't always willing to listen. But Ezekiel opened his mouth to receive the scroll containing God's word, and the scroll was sweet (see Ezek 3:3).

God gave Ezekiel words to eat, nourishing Ezekiel so that he could carry out his calling. In the same way, God gives us the Word to eat and nourishes us to carry out our calling. Jesus is often called the Word of God (see "The 'Cosmic Christ,'" near Jn 1:1–18).

At the Eucharist, we receive not only the Word of God when the Scriptures are proclaimed but also the Body of Christ when we come forward for Communion. With both Word and Sacrament, we are called to share the Good News of our faith with others.
- What are some ways we can bring this Good News to others?
- What are some things we might say or do to share our faith with the people we know?

▶ **Ezek 2:1—3:11**

written on it were words of lamentation and mourning and woe.

3 He said to me, O mortal, eat what is offered to you; eat this scroll, and go, speak to the house of Israel. 2So I opened my mouth, and he gave me the scroll to eat. 3He said to me, Mortal, eat this scroll that I give you and fill your stomach with it. Then I ate it; and in my mouth it was as sweet as honey.

4 He said to me: Mortal, go to the house of Israel and speak my very words to them. 5For you are not sent to a people of obscure speech and difficult language, but to the house of Israel— 6not to many peoples of obscure speech and difficult language, whose words you cannot understand. Surely, if I sent you to them, they

a Gk: Heb *like the awesome crystal* b Traditional rendering of Heb *Shaddai* c Or *lapis lazuli* d Or *son of man*; Heb *ben adam* (and so throughout the book when Ezekiel is addressed) e Syr: Heb *to nations*

E Z E K

would listen to you. 7But the house of Israel will not listen to you, for they are not willing to listen to me; because all the house of Israel have a hard forehead and a stubborn heart. 8See, I have made your face hard against their faces, and your forehead hard against their foreheads. 9Like the hardest stone, harder than flint, I have made your forehead; do not fear them or be dismayed at their looks, for they are a rebellious house. 10He said to me: Mortal, all my words that I shall speak to you receive in your heart and hear with your ears; 11then go to the exiles, to your people, and speak to them. Say to them, "Thus says the Lord God"; whether they hear or refuse to hear.

Ezekiel at the River Chebar

12 Then the spirit lifted me up, and as the glory of the Lord rose*a* from its place, I heard behind me the sound of loud rumbling; 13it was the sound of the wings of the living creatures brushing against one another, and the sound of the wheels beside them, that sounded like a loud rumbling. 14The spirit lifted me up and bore me away; I went in bitterness in the heat of my spirit, the hand of the Lord being strong upon me. 15I came to the exiles at Tel-abib, who lived by the river Chebar.*b* And I sat there among them, stunned, for seven days.

16 At the end of seven days, the word of the Lord came to me: 17Mortal, I have made you a sentinel for the house of Israel; whenever you hear a word from my mouth, you shall give them warning from me. 18If I say to the wicked, "You shall surely die," and you give them no warning, or speak to warn the wicked from their wicked way, in order to save their life, those wicked persons shall die for their iniquity; but their blood I will require at your hand. 19But if you warn the wicked, and they do not turn from their wickedness, or from their wicked way, they shall die for their iniquity; but you will have saved your life. 20Again, if the righteous turn from their righteousness and commit iniquity, and I lay a stumbling block before them, they shall die; because you have not warned them, they shall die for their sin, and their righteous deeds that they have done shall not be remembered; but their blood I will require at your hand. 21If, however, you warn the righteous not to sin, and they do not sin, they shall surely live, because they took warning; and you will have saved your life.

Ezekiel Isolated and Silenced

22 Then the hand of the Lord was upon me there; and he said to me, Rise up, go out into the valley, and there I will speak with you. 23So I rose up and went out into the valley; and the glory of the Lord stood there, like the glory that I had seen by the river Chebar; and I fell on my face. 24The spirit entered into me, and set me on my feet; and he spoke with me and said to me: Go, shut yourself inside your house. 25As for you, mortal, cords shall be placed on you, and you shall be bound with them, so that you cannot go out among the people; 26and I will make your tongue cling to the roof of your mouth, so that you shall be speechless and unable to reprove them; for they are a rebellious house. 27But when I speak with you, I will open your mouth, and you shall say to them, "Thus says the Lord God";

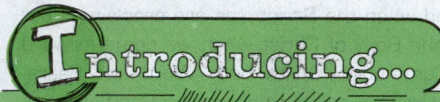

Ezekiel

E zekiel's name means "God strengthens." He was a complex person: priest and prophet, poet and teacher, tender and angry. He experienced God in mysterious ways, often through visions that greatly influenced his life and prophetic ministry.

Ezekiel's vision of creatures from heaven in chapters 1–3 of his book was the basis for his call and prophetic ministry. His vision of the defilement of the Temple in chapters 8–11 was a major conversion experience. He, along with most of Israel, believed that God's glory resided in the Temple and that nothing could ever change that. The vision revealed corruption in Jerusalem and that the glory of God had left the Temple and had come to Babylon. His vision of dry bones coming to life in chapter 37 helped him understand that God would breathe new life into Israel. His final visions of a new Temple in chapters 40, 43, and 47 told him that God would restore Jerusalem and the Temple.

Besides having symbolic visions, Ezekiel also performed many dramatic, symbolic actions (see "Street Theater," near Ezek 4:1—5:4). These were designed to catch people's attention and transmit God's message.

EZEK

a Cn: Heb *and blessed be the glory of the* Lord   b Two Mss Syr: Heb *Chebar, and to where they lived.* Another reading is *Chebar, and I sat where they sat*

let those who will hear, hear; and let those who refuse to hear, refuse; for they are a rebellious house.

The Siege of Jerusalem Portrayed

4 And you, O mortal, take a brick and set it before you. On it portray a city, Jerusalem; ²and put siegeworks against it, and build a siege wall against it, and cast up a ramp against it; set camps also against it, and plant battering rams against it all around. ³Then take an iron plate and place it as an iron wall between you and the city; set your face toward it, and let it be in a state of siege, and press the siege against it. This is a sign for the house of Israel.

4 Then lie on your left side, and place the punishment of the house of Israel upon it; you shall bear their punishment for the number of the days that you lie there. ⁵For I assign to you a number of days, three hundred ninety days, equal to the number of the years of their punishment; and so you shall bear the punishment of the house of Israel. ⁶When you have completed these, you shall lie down a second time, but on your right side, and bear the punishment of the house of Judah; forty days I assign you, one day for each year. ⁷You shall set your face toward the siege of Jerusalem, and with your arm bared you shall prophesy against it. ⁸See, I am putting cords on you so that you cannot turn from one side to the other until you have completed the days of your siege.

9 And you, take wheat and barley, beans and lentils, millet and spelt; put them into one vessel, and make bread for yourself. During the number of days that you lie on your side, three hundred ninety days, you shall eat it. ¹⁰The food that you eat shall be twenty shekels a day by weight; at fixed times you shall eat it. ¹¹And you shall drink water by measure, one-sixth of a hin; at fixed times you shall drink. ¹²You shall eat it as a barley-cake, baking it in their sight on human dung. ¹³The LORD said, "Thus shall the people of Israel eat their bread, unclean, among the nations to which I will drive them." ¹⁴Then I said, "Ah Lord GOD! I have never defiled myself; from my youth up until now I have never eaten what died of itself or was torn by animals, nor has carrion flesh come into my mouth." ¹⁵Then he said to me, "See, I will let you have cow's dung instead of human dung, on which you may prepare your bread."

16 Then he said to me, Mortal, I am going to break the staff of bread in Jerusalem; they shall eat bread by weight and with fearfulness; and they shall drink water by measure and in dismay. ¹⁷Lacking bread and water, they will look at one

Live It!

Street Theater

Look over what the prophet does in Ezekiel, chapters 3–5, to get people's attention before the fall of Jerusalem in 587 BC. He is speechless (see 3:22–27) as a sign that the people are rebellious and unwilling to hear God's word. He lies on his left side for days, and then his right (see 4:4–5), as a sign of the number of years the two kingdoms Israel and Judah will be in exile. He eats small amounts of food cooked on dung (see verses 10–15) as a sign of the shortage of food during the siege of the city. Ezekiel's "street theater" is a good way of making a point that everyone can understand.

Christians today need to use creative means to raise consciousness about the ways society violates human life and harms our world. Radio and television, the Internet, public prayer services, and rallies all help people get the message out. What does your church do to raise consciousness and move people to change their ways? What can you do?

▶ **Ezek 4:1—5:4**

E Z E K

another in dismay, and waste away under their punishment.

A Sword against Jerusalem

5 And you, O mortal, take a sharp sword; use it as a barber's razor and run it over your head and your beard; then take balances for weighing, and divide the hair. ²One third of the hair you shall burn in the fire inside the city, when the days of the siege are completed; one third you shall take and strike with the sword all around the city;ᵃ and one third you shall scatter to the wind, and I will unsheathe the sword after them. ³Then you shall take from these a small number, and bind them in the skirts of your robe. ⁴From these, again, you shall take some, throw them into the fire and burn them up; from there a fire will come out against all the house of Israel.

a Heb it

5 Thus says the Lord GOD: This is Jerusalem; I have set her in the center of the nations, with countries all around her. ⁶But she has rebelled against my ordinances and my statutes, becoming more wicked than the nations and the countries all around her, rejecting my ordinances and not following my statutes. ⁷Therefore thus says the Lord GOD: Because you are more turbulent than the nations that are all around you, and have not followed my statutes or kept my ordinances, but have acted according to the ordinances of the nations that are all around you; ⁸therefore thus says the Lord GOD: I, I myself, am coming against you; I will execute judgments among you in the sight of the nations. ⁹And because of all your abominations, I will do to you what I have never yet done, and the like of which I will never do again. ¹⁰Surely, parents shall eat their children in your midst, and children shall eat their parents; I will execute judgments on you, and any of you who survive I will scatter to every wind. ¹¹Therefore, as I live, says the Lord GOD, surely, because you have defiled my sanctuary with all your detestable things and with all your abominations—therefore I will cut you down;ᵃ my eye will not spare, and I will have no pity. ¹²One third of you shall die of pestilence or be consumed by famine among you; one third shall fall by the sword around you; and one third I will scatter to every wind and will unsheathe the sword after them.

13 My anger shall spend itself, and I will vent my fury on them and satisfy myself; and they shall know that I, the LORD, have spoken in my jealousy, when I spend my fury on them. ¹⁴Moreover I will make you a desolation and an object of mocking among the nations around you, in the sight of all that pass by. ¹⁵You shall beᵇ a mockery and a taunt, a warning and a horror, to the nations around you, when I execute judgments on you in anger and fury, and with furious punishments—I, the LORD, have spoken— ¹⁶when I loose against youᶜ my deadly arrows of famine, arrows for destruction, which I will let loose to destroy you, and when I bring more and more famine upon you, and break your staff of bread. ¹⁷I will send famine and wild animals against you, and they will rob you of your children; pestilence and bloodshed shall pass through you; and I will bring the sword upon you. I, the LORD, have spoken.

Judgment on Idolatrous Israel

6 The word of the LORD came to me: ²O mortal, set your face toward the mountains of Israel, and prophesy against them, ³and say, You

mountains of Israel, hear the word of the Lord GOD! Thus says the Lord GOD to the mountains and the hills, to the ravines and the valleys: I, I myself will bring a sword upon you, and I will destroy your high places. ⁴Your altars shall become desolate, and your incense stands shall be broken; and I will throw down your slain in front of your idols. ⁵I will lay the corpses of the people of Israel in front of their idols; and I will scatter your bones around your altars. ⁶Wherever you live, your towns shall be waste and your high places ruined, so that your altars will be waste and ruined,ᵈ your idols broken and destroyed, your incense stands cut down, and your works wiped out. ⁷The slain shall fall in your midst; then you shall know that I am the LORD.

8 But I will spare some. Some of you shall escape the sword among the nations and be scattered through the countries. ⁹Those of you who escape shall remember me among the nations where they are carried captive, how I was crushed by their wanton heart that turned away from me, and their wanton eyes that turned after their idols. Then they will be loathsome in their own sight for the evils that they have committed, for all their abominations. ¹⁰And they shall know that I am the LORD; I did not threaten in vain to bring this disaster upon them.

11 Thus says the Lord GOD: Clap your hands and stamp your foot, and say, Alas for all the vile abominations of the house of Israel! For they shall fall by the sword, by famine, and by pestilence. ¹²Those far off shall die of pestilence; those nearby shall fall by the sword; and any who are left and are spared shall die of famine. Thus I will spend my fury upon them. ¹³And you shall know that I am the LORD, when their slain lie among their idols around their altars, on every high hill, on all the mountain tops, under every green tree, and under every leafy oak, wherever they offered pleasing odor to all their idols. ¹⁴I will stretch out my hand against them, and make the land desolate and waste, throughout all their settlements, from the wilderness to Riblah.ᵉ Then they shall know that I am the LORD.

Impending Disaster

7 The word of the LORD came to me: ²You, O mortal, thus says the Lord GOD to the land of Israel:

An end! The end has come
　upon the four corners of the land.

ᵃ Another reading is *I will withdraw*　ᵇ Gk Syr Vg Tg: Heb *It shall be*　ᶜ Heb *them*　ᵈ Syr Vg Tg: Heb *and be made guilty*　ᵉ Another reading is *Diblah*

³ Now the end is upon you,
   I will let loose my anger upon you;
I will judge you according to your ways,
   I will punish you for all your abominations.
⁴ My eye will not spare you, I will have no pity.
   I will punish you for your ways,
   while your abominations are among you.
Then you shall know that I am the Lord.
   5 Thus says the Lord God:
Disaster after disaster! See, it comes.
⁶   An end has come, the end has come.
It has awakened against you; see, it comes!
⁷ Your doom*a* has come to you,
   O inhabitant of the land.
The time has come, the day is near—
   of tumult, not of reveling on the mountains.
⁸ Soon now I will pour out my wrath upon you;
   I will spend my anger against you.
I will judge you according to your ways,
   and punish you for all your abominations.
⁹ My eye will not spare; I will have no pity.
   I will punish you according to your ways,
   while your abominations are among you.
Then you shall know that it is I the Lord who
strike.
¹⁰ See, the day! See, it comes!
   Your doom*a* has gone out.
The rod has blossomed, pride has budded.
¹¹   Violence has grown into a rod of wickedness.
None of them shall remain,
   not their abundance, not their wealth;
   no pre-eminence among them.*a*
¹² The time has come, the day draws near;
   let not the buyer rejoice, nor the seller mourn,
   for wrath is upon all their multitude.
¹³For the sellers shall not return to what has
been sold as long as they remain alive. For the
vision concerns all their multitude; it shall not
be revoked. Because of their iniquity, they cannot
maintain their lives.*a*
¹⁴ They have blown the horn and made everything
      ready;
   but no one goes to battle,
   for my wrath is upon all their multitude.
¹⁵ The sword is outside, pestilence and famine are
      inside;
   those in the field die by the sword;
   those in the city—famine and pestilence
   devour them.
¹⁶ If any survivors escape,
   they shall be found on the mountains
   like doves of the valleys,
all of them moaning over their iniquity.
¹⁷ All hands shall grow feeble,
   all knees turn to water.
¹⁸ They shall put on sackcloth,

horror shall cover them.
Shame shall be on all faces,
   baldness on all their heads.
¹⁹ They shall fling their silver into the streets,
   their gold shall be treated as unclean.
Their silver and gold cannot save them on the
day of the wrath of the Lord. They shall not satisfy their hunger or fill their stomachs with it.
For it was the stumbling block of their iniquity.
²⁰From their*b* beautiful ornament, in which they
took pride, they made their abominable images,
their detestable things; therefore I will make of it
an unclean thing to them.
²¹ I will hand it over to strangers as booty,
   to the wicked of the earth as plunder;
   they shall profane it.
²² I will avert my face from them,
   so that they may profane my treasured*c* place;
the violent shall enter it,
   they shall profane it.
²³ Make a chain!*a*
For the land is full of bloody crimes;
   the city is full of violence.
²⁴ I will bring the worst of the nations
   to take possession of their houses.
I will put an end to the arrogance of the strong,
   and their holy places shall be profaned.
²⁵ When anguish comes, they will seek peace,
   but there shall be none.
²⁶ Disaster comes upon disaster,
   rumor follows rumor;
they shall keep seeking a vision from the
      prophet;
   instruction shall perish from the priest,
   and counsel from the elders.
²⁷ The king shall mourn,
   the prince shall be wrapped in despair,
   and the hands of the people of the land shall
      tremble.
According to their way I will deal with them;
   according to their own judgments I will judge
      them.
And they shall know that I am the Lord.

Abominations in the Temple

8 In the sixth year, in the sixth month, on the
fifth day of the month, as I sat in my house,
with the elders of Judah sitting before me, the
hand of the Lord God fell upon me there. ²I
looked, and there was a figure that looked like
a human being;*d* below what appeared to be
its loins it was fire, and above the loins it was
like the appearance of brightness, like gleaming

---

a Meaning of Heb uncertain   *b* Syr Symmachus: Heb *its*
c Or *secret*   *d* Gk: Heb *like fire*

amber. [3]It stretched out the form of a hand, and took me by a lock of my head; and the spirit lifted me up between earth and heaven, and brought me in visions of God to Jerusalem, to the entrance of the gateway of the inner court that faces north, to the seat of the image of jealousy, which provokes to jealousy. [4]And the glory of the God of Israel was there, like the vision that I had seen in the valley.

5 Then God[a] said to me, "O mortal, lift up your eyes now in the direction of the north." So I lifted up my eyes toward the north, and there, north of the altar gate, in the entrance, was this image of jealousy. [6]He said to me, "Mortal, do you see what they are doing, the great abominations that the house of Israel are committing here, to drive me far from my sanctuary? Yet you will see still greater abominations."

7 And he brought me to the entrance of the court; I looked, and there was a hole in the wall. [8]Then he said to me, "Mortal, dig through the wall"; and when I dug through the wall, there was an entrance. [9]He said to me, "Go in, and see the vile abominations that they are committing here." [10]So I went in and looked; there, portrayed on the wall all around, were all kinds of creeping things, and loathsome animals, and all the idols of the house of Israel. [11]Before them stood seventy of the elders of the house of Israel, with Jaazaniah son of Shaphan standing among them. Each had his censer in his hand, and the fragrant cloud of incense was ascending. [12]Then he said to me, "Mortal, have you seen what the elders of the house of Israel are doing in the dark, each in his room of images? For they say, 'The LORD does not see us, the LORD has forsaken the land.'" [13]He said also to me, "You will see still greater abominations that they are committing."

14 Then he brought me to the entrance of the north gate of the house of the LORD; women were sitting there weeping for Tammuz. [15]Then he said to me, "Have you seen this, O mortal? You will see still greater abominations than these."

16 And he brought me into the inner court of the house of the LORD; there, at the entrance of the temple of the LORD, between the porch and the altar, were about twenty-five men, with their backs to the temple of the LORD, and their faces toward the east, prostrating themselves to the sun toward the east. [17]Then he said to me, "Have you seen this, O mortal? Is it not bad enough that the house of Judah commits the abominations done here? Must they fill the land with violence, and provoke my anger still further? See, they are putting the branch to their nose! [18]Therefore I will act in wrath; my eye will not spare, nor

will I have pity; and though they cry in my hearing with a loud voice, I will not listen to them."

The Slaughter of the Idolaters

9 Then he cried in my hearing with a loud voice, saying, "Draw near, you executioners of the city, each with his destroying weapon in his hand." [2]And six men came from the direction of the upper gate, which faces north, each with his weapon for slaughter in his hand; among them was a man clothed in linen, with a writing case at his side. They went in and stood beside the bronze altar.

3 Now the glory of the God of Israel had gone up from the cherub on which it rested to the threshold of the house. The LORD called to the man clothed in linen, who had the writing case at his side; [4]and said to him, "Go through the city, through Jerusalem, and put a mark on the foreheads of those who sigh and groan over all the abominations that are committed in it." [5]To the others he said in my hearing, "Pass through the city after him, and kill; your eye shall not spare, and you shall show no pity. [6]Cut down old men, young men and young women, little children and women, but touch no one who has the mark. And begin at my sanctuary." So they began with the elders who were in front of the house. [7]Then he said to them, "Defile the house, and fill the courts with the slain. Go!" So they went out and killed in the city. [8]While they were killing, and I was left alone, I fell prostrate on my face and cried out, "Ah Lord GOD! will you destroy all who remain of Israel as you pour out your wrath upon Jerusalem?" [9]He said to me, "The guilt of the house of Israel and Judah is exceedingly great; the land is full of bloodshed and the city full of perversity; for they say, 'The LORD has forsaken the land, and the LORD does not see.' [10]As for me, my eye will not spare, nor will I have pity, but I will bring down their deeds upon their heads."

11 Then the man clothed in linen, with the writing case at his side, brought back word, saying, "I have done as you commanded me."

God's Glory Leaves Jerusalem

10 Then I looked, and above the dome that was over the heads of the cherubim there appeared above them something like a sapphire,[b] in form resembling a throne. [2]He said to the man clothed in linen, "Go within the wheelwork underneath the cherubim; fill your hands with burning coals from among the cherubim,

---

a Heb *he* b Or *lapis lazuli*

and scatter them over the city." He went in as I looked on. ³Now the cherubim were standing on the south side of the house when the man went in; and a cloud filled the inner court. ⁴Then the glory of the LORD rose up from the cherub to the threshold of the house; the house was filled with the cloud, and the court was full of the brightness of the glory of the LORD. ⁵The sound of the wings of the cherubim was heard as far as the outer court, like the voice of God Almighty[a] when he speaks.

6 When he commanded the man clothed in linen, "Take fire from within the wheelwork, from among the cherubim," he went in and stood beside a wheel. ⁷And a cherub stretched out his hand from among the cherubim to the fire that was among the cherubim, took some of it and put it into the hands of the man clothed in linen, who took it and went out. ⁸The cherubim appeared to have the form of a human hand under their wings.

9 I looked, and there were four wheels beside the cherubim, one beside each cherub; and the appearance of the wheels was like gleaming beryl. ¹⁰And as for their appearance, the four looked alike, something like a wheel within a wheel. ¹¹When they moved, they moved in any of the four directions without veering as they moved; but in whatever direction the front wheel faced, the others followed without veering as they moved. ¹²Their entire body, their rims, their spokes, their wings, and the wheels—the wheels of the four of them—were full of eyes all around. ¹³As for the wheels, they were called in my hearing "the wheelwork." ¹⁴Each one had four faces: the first face was that of the cherub, the second face was that of a human being, the third that of a lion, and the fourth that of an eagle.

15 The cherubim rose up. These were the living creatures that I saw by the river Chebar. ¹⁶When the cherubim moved, the wheels moved beside them; and when the cherubim lifted up their wings to rise up from the earth, the wheels at their side did not veer. ¹⁷When they stopped, the others stopped, and when they rose up, the others rose up with them; for the spirit of the living creatures was in them.

18 Then the glory of the LORD went out from the threshold of the house and stopped above the cherubim. ¹⁹The cherubim lifted up their wings and rose up from the earth in my sight as they went out with the wheels beside them. They stopped at the entrance of the east gate of the house of the LORD; and the glory of the God of Israel was above them. 20 These were the living creatures that I saw

underneath the God of Israel by the river Chebar; and I knew that they were cherubim. ²¹Each had four faces, each four wings, and underneath their wings something like human hands. ²²As for what their faces were like, they were the same faces whose appearance I had seen by the river Chebar. Each one moved straight ahead.

Judgment on Wicked Counselors

11 The spirit lifted me up and brought me to the east gate of the house of the LORD, which faces east. There, at the entrance of the gateway, were twenty-five men; among them I saw Jaazaniah son of Azzur, and Pelatiah son of Benaiah, officials of the people. ²He said to me, "Mortal, these are the men who devise iniquity and who give wicked counsel in this city; ³they say, 'The time is not near to build houses; this city is the pot, and we are the meat.' ⁴Therefore prophesy against them; prophesy, O mortal."

5 Then the spirit of the LORD fell upon me, and he said to me, "Say, Thus says the LORD: This is what you think, O house of Israel; I know the things that come into your mind. ⁶You have killed many in this city, and have filled its streets with the slain. ⁷Therefore thus says the Lord GOD: The slain whom you have placed within it are the meat, and this city is the pot; but you shall be taken out of it. ⁸You have feared the sword; and I will bring the sword upon you, says the Lord GOD. ⁹I will take you out of it and give you over to the hands of foreigners, and execute judgments upon you. ¹⁰You shall fall by the sword; I will judge you at the border of Israel. And you shall know that I am the LORD. ¹¹This city shall not be your pot, and you shall not be the meat inside it; I will judge you at the border of Israel. ¹²Then you shall know that I am the LORD, whose statutes you have not followed, and whose ordinances you have not kept, but you have acted according to the ordinances of the nations that are around you."

13 Now, while I was prophesying, Pelatiah son of Benaiah died. Then I fell down on my face, cried with a loud voice, and said, "Ah Lord GOD! will you make a full end of the remnant of Israel?"

God Will Restore Israel

14 Then the word of the LORD came to me: ¹⁵Mortal, your kinsfolk, your own kin, your fellow exiles,[b] the whole house of Israel, all of them, are those of whom the inhabitants of Jerusalem

---

a Traditional rendering of Heb *El Shaddai* b Gk Syr: Heb *people of your kindred*

have said, "They have gone far from the Lord; to us this land is given for a possession." ¹⁶Therefore say: Thus says the Lord God: Though I removed them far away among the nations, and though I scattered them among the countries, yet I have been a sanctuary to them for a little while[a] in the countries where they have gone. ¹⁷Therefore say: Thus says the Lord God: I will gather you from the peoples, and assemble you out of the countries where you have been scattered, and I will give you the land of Israel. ¹⁸When they come there, they will remove from it all its detestable things and all its abominations. ¹⁹I will give them one[b] heart, and put a new spirit within them; I will remove the heart of stone from their flesh and give them a heart of flesh, ²⁰so that they may follow my statutes and keep my ordinances and obey them. Then they shall be my people, and I will be their God. ²¹But as for those whose heart goes after their detestable things and their abominations,[c] I will bring their deeds upon their own heads, says the Lord God.

22 Then the cherubim lifted up their wings, with the wheels beside them; and the glory of the God of Israel was above them. ²³And the glory of the Lord ascended from the middle of the city, and stopped on the mountain east of

Have a Heart!

The Old Testament prophets are concerned about people's hearts. The ancient Israelites understood the heart as the center of intelligence, feelings, and human will. Jeremiah says the New Covenant will be written on people's hearts (see Jer 31:33), and Ezekiel says God will take away their stony hearts and give them natural hearts (see Ezek 11:19).

In your prayer, reflect or journal on the following questions:

● What's the difference between having a natural, fleshy heart and a cold, stony heart?
● Why would a natural heart lead to obeying God (see verse 20)?
● When does your heart feel natural? When does it feel stony?

▶ **Ezek 11:19–20**

the city. ²⁴The spirit lifted me up and brought me in a vision by the spirit of God into Chaldea, to the exiles. Then the vision that I had seen left me. ²⁵And I told the exiles all the things that the Lord had shown me.

Judah's Captivity Portrayed

12 The word of the Lord came to me: ²Mortal, you are living in the midst of a rebellious house, who have eyes to see but do not see, who have ears to hear but do not hear; ³for they are a rebellious house. Therefore, mortal, prepare for yourself an exile's baggage, and go into exile by day in their sight; you shall go like an exile from your place to another place in their sight. Perhaps they will understand, though they are a rebellious house. ⁴You shall bring out your baggage by day in their sight, as baggage for exile; and you shall go out yourself at evening in their sight, as those do who go into exile. ⁵Dig through the wall in their sight, and carry the baggage through it. ⁶In their sight you shall lift the baggage on your shoulder, and carry it out in the dark; you shall cover your face, so that you may not see the land; for I have made you a sign for the house of Israel.

7 I did just as I was commanded. I brought out my baggage by day, as baggage for exile, and in the evening I dug through the wall with my own hands; I brought it out in the dark, carrying it on my shoulder in their sight.

8 In the morning the word of the Lord came to me: ⁹Mortal, has not the house of Israel, the rebellious house, said to you, "What are you doing?" ¹⁰Say to them, "Thus says the Lord God: This oracle concerns the prince in Jerusalem and all the house of Israel in it." ¹¹Say, "I am a sign for you: as I have done, so shall it be done to them; they shall go into exile, into captivity." ¹²And the prince who is among them shall lift his baggage on his shoulder in the dark, and shall go out; he[d] shall dig through the wall and carry it through; he shall cover his face, so that he may not see the land with his eyes. ¹³I will spread my net over him, and he shall be caught in my snare; and I will bring him to Babylon, the land of the Chaldeans, yet he shall not see it; and he shall die there. ¹⁴I will scatter to every wind all who are around him, his helpers and all his troops; and I will unsheathe the sword behind them. ¹⁵And they shall know that I am the Lord, when I disperse them among the nations and scatter

---

a Or to some extent   b Another reading is a new   c Cn: Heb
And to the heart of their detestable things and their abominations
their heart goes   d Gk Syr: Heb they

E
Z
E
K

them through the countries. ¹⁶But I will let a few of them escape from the sword, from famine and pestilence, so that they may tell of all their abominations among the nations where they go; then they shall know that I am the LORD.

Judgment Not Postponed

17 The word of the LORD came to me: ¹⁸Mortal, eat your bread with quaking, and drink your water with trembling and with fearfulness; ¹⁹and say to the people of the land, Thus says the Lord GOD concerning the inhabitants of Jerusalem in the land of Israel: They shall eat their bread with fearfulness, and drink their water in dismay, because their land shall be stripped of all it contains, on account of the violence of all those who live in it. ²⁰The inhabited cities shall be laid waste, and the land shall become a desolation; and you shall know that I am the LORD.

21 The word of the LORD came to me: ²²Mortal, what is this proverb of yours about the land of Israel, which says, "The days are prolonged, and every vision comes to nothing"? ²³Tell them therefore, "Thus says the Lord GOD: I will put an end to this proverb, and they shall use it no more as a proverb in Israel." But say to them, The days are near, and the fulfillment of every vision. ²⁴For there shall no longer be any false vision or flattering divination within the house of Israel. ²⁵But I the LORD will speak the word that I speak, and it will be fulfilled. It will no longer be delayed; but in your days, O rebellious house, I will speak the word and fulfill it, says the Lord GOD.

26 The word of the LORD came to me: ²⁷Mortal, the house of Israel is saying, "The vision that he sees is for many years ahead; he prophesies for distant times." ²⁸Therefore say to them, Thus says the Lord GOD: None of my words will be delayed any longer, but the word that I speak will be fulfilled, says the Lord GOD.

False Prophets Condemned

13 The word of the LORD came to me: ²Mortal, prophesy against the prophets of Israel who are prophesying; say to those who prophesy out of their own imagination: "Hear the word of the LORD!" ³Thus says the Lord GOD, Alas for the senseless prophets who follow their own spirit, and have seen nothing! ⁴Your prophets have been like jackals among ruins, O Israel. ⁵You have not gone up into the breaches, or repaired a wall for the house of Israel, so that it might stand in battle on the day of the LORD. ⁶They have envisioned falsehood and lying divination; they say, "Says the LORD," when the LORD has not sent them, and yet they wait for the fulfillment of

their word! ⁷Have you not seen a false vision or uttered a lying divination, when you have said, "Says the LORD," even though I did not speak?

8 Therefore thus says the Lord GOD: Because you have uttered falsehood and envisioned lies, I am against you, says the Lord GOD. ⁹My hand will be against the prophets who see false visions and utter lying divinations; they shall not be in the council of my people, nor be enrolled in the register of the house of Israel, nor shall they enter the land of Israel; and you shall know that I am the Lord GOD. ¹⁰Because, in truth, because they have misled my people, saying, "Peace," when there is no peace; and because, when the people build a wall, these prophets*a* smear whitewash on it. ¹¹Say to those who smear whitewash on it that it shall fall. There will be a deluge of rain,*b* great hailstones will fall, and a stormy wind will break out. ¹²When the wall falls, will it not be said to you, "Where is the whitewash you smeared on it?" ¹³Therefore thus says the Lord GOD: In my wrath I will make a stormy wind break out, and in my anger there shall be a deluge of rain, and hailstones in wrath to destroy it. ¹⁴I will break down the wall that you have smeared with whitewash, and bring it to the ground, so that its foundation will be laid bare; when it falls, you shall perish within it; and you shall know that I am the LORD. ¹⁵Thus I will spend my wrath upon the wall, and upon those who have smeared it with whitewash; and I will say to you, The wall is no more, nor those who smeared it— ¹⁶the prophets of Israel who prophesied concerning Jerusalem and saw visions of peace for it, when there was no peace, says the Lord GOD.

17 As for you, mortal, set your face against the daughters of your people, who prophesy out of their own imagination; prophesy against them ¹⁸and say, Thus says the Lord GOD: Woe to the women who sew bands on all wrists, and make veils for the heads of persons of every height, in the hunt for human lives! Will you hunt down lives among my people, and maintain your own lives? ¹⁹You have profaned me among my people for handfuls of barley and for pieces of bread, putting to death persons who should not die and keeping alive persons who should not live, by your lies to my people, who listen to lies.

20 Therefore thus says the Lord GOD: I am against your bands with which you hunt lives;*c* I will tear them from your arms, and let the lives go free, the lives that you hunt down like birds. ²¹I will tear off your veils, and save my people from your hands; they shall no longer be prey

EZEK

a Heb *they*   *b* Heb *rain and you*   *c* Gk Syr: Heb *lives for birds*

in your hands; and you shall know that I am the LORD. ²²Because you have disheartened the righteous falsely, although I have not disheartened them, and you have encouraged the wicked not to turn from their wicked way and save their lives; ²³therefore you shall no longer see false visions or practice divination; I will save my people from your hand. Then you will know that I am the LORD.

God's Judgments Justified

14 Certain elders of Israel came to me and sat down before me. ²And the word of the LORD came to me: ³Mortal, these men have taken their idols into their hearts, and placed their iniquity as a stumbling block before them; shall I let myself be consulted by them? ⁴Therefore speak to them, and say to them, Thus says the Lord GOD: Any of those of the house of Israel who take their idols into their hearts and place their iniquity as a stumbling block before them, and yet come to the prophet—I the LORD will answer those who come with the multitude of their idols, ⁵in order that I may take hold of the hearts of the house of Israel, all of whom are estranged from me through their idols.

6 Therefore say to the house of Israel, Thus says the Lord GOD: Repent and turn away from your idols; and turn away your faces from all your abominations. ⁷For any of those of the house of Israel, or of the aliens who reside in Israel, who separate themselves from me, taking their idols into their hearts and placing their iniquity as a stumbling block before them, and yet come to a prophet to inquire of me by him, I the LORD will answer them myself. ⁸I will set my face against them; I will make them a sign and a byword and cut them off from the midst of my people; and you shall know that I am the LORD.

9 If a prophet is deceived and speaks a word, I, the LORD, have deceived that prophet, and I will stretch out my hand against him, and will destroy him from the midst of my people Israel. ¹⁰And they shall bear their punishment—the punishment of the inquirer and the punishment of the prophet shall be the same— ¹¹so that the house of Israel may no longer go astray from me, nor defile themselves any more with all their transgressions. Then they shall be my people, and I will be their God, says the Lord GOD.

12 The word of the LORD came to me: ¹³Mortal, when a land sins against me by acting faithlessly, and I stretch out my hand against it, and break its staff of bread and send famine upon it, and cut off from it human beings and animals, ¹⁴even if Noah, Daniel,[a] and Job, these three,

were in it, they would save only their own lives by their righteousness, says the Lord GOD. ¹⁵If I send wild animals through the land to ravage it, so that it is made desolate, and no one may pass through because of the animals; ¹⁶even if these three men were in it, as I live, says the Lord GOD, they would save neither sons nor daughters; they alone would be saved, but the land would be desolate. ¹⁷Or if I bring a sword upon that land and say, "Let a sword pass through the land," and I cut off human beings and animals from it; ¹⁸though these three men were in it, as I live, says the Lord GOD, they would save neither sons nor daughters, but they alone would be saved. ¹⁹Or if I send a pestilence into that land, and pour out my wrath upon it with blood, to cut off humans and animals from it; ²⁰even if Noah, Daniel,[a] and Job were in it, as I live, says the Lord GOD, they would save neither son nor daughter; they would save only their own lives by their righteousness.

21 For thus says the Lord GOD: How much more when I send upon Jerusalem my four deadly acts of judgment, sword, famine, wild animals, and pestilence, to cut off humans and animals from it! ²²Yet, survivors shall be left in it, sons and daughters who will be brought out; they will come out to you. When you see their ways and their deeds, you will be consoled for the evil that I have brought upon Jerusalem, for all that I have brought upon it. ²³They shall console you, when you see their ways and their deeds; and you shall know that it was not without cause that I did all that I have done in it, says the Lord GOD.

The Useless Vine

15 The word of the LORD came to me: ²O mortal, how does the wood of the vine surpass all other wood—
    the vine branch that is among the trees of the forest?
3 Is wood taken from it to make anything?
    Does one take a peg from it on which to hang any object?
4 It is put in the fire for fuel;
    when the fire has consumed both ends of it
    and the middle of it is charred,
    is it useful for anything?
5 When it was whole it was used for nothing;
    how much less—when the fire has consumed it,
    and it is charred—
    can it ever be used for anything!
6 Therefore thus says the Lord GOD: Like the wood of the vine among the trees of the forest,

---

a Or, as otherwise read, *Danel*

which I have given to the fire for fuel, so I will give up the inhabitants of Jerusalem. 7I will set my face against them; although they escape from the fire, the fire shall still consume them; and you shall know that I am the LORD, when I set my face against them. 8And I will make the land desolate, because they have acted faithlessly, says the Lord GOD.

God's Faithless Bride

16 The word of the LORD came to me: 2Mortal, make known to Jerusalem her abominations, 3and say, Thus says the Lord GOD to Jerusalem: Your origin and your birth were in the land of the Canaanites; your father was an Amorite, and your mother a Hittite. 4As for your birth, on the day you were born your navel cord was not cut, nor were you washed with water to cleanse you, nor rubbed with salt, nor wrapped in cloths. 5No eye pitied you, to do any of these things for you out of compassion for you; but you were thrown out in the open field, for you were abhorred on the day you were born.

6 I passed by you, and saw you flailing about in your blood. As you lay in your blood, I said to you, "Live! 7and grow up*a* like a plant of the field." You grew up and became tall and arrived at full womanhood;*b* your breasts were formed, and your hair had grown; yet you were naked and bare.

8 I passed by you again and looked on you; you were at the age for love. I spread the edge of my cloak over you, and covered your nakedness: I pledged myself to you and entered into a covenant with you, says the Lord GOD, and you became mine. 9Then I bathed you with water and washed off the blood from you, and anointed you with oil. 10I clothed you with embroidered cloth and with sandals of fine leather; I bound you in fine linen and covered you with rich fabric.*c* 11I adorned you with ornaments: I put bracelets on your arms, a chain on your neck, 12a ring on your nose, earrings in your ears, and a beautiful crown upon your head. 13You were adorned with gold and silver, while your clothing was of fine linen, rich fabric,*c* and embroidered cloth. You had choice flour and honey and oil for food. You grew exceedingly beautiful, fit to be a queen. 14Your fame spread among the nations on account of your beauty, for it was perfect because of my splendor that I had bestowed on you, says the Lord GOD.

15 But you trusted in your beauty, and played the whore because of your fame, and lavished your whorings on any passer-by.*d* 16You took some of your garments, and made for yourself colorful shrines, and on them played the whore; nothing like this has ever been or ever shall be.*c* 17You also took your beautiful jewels of my gold and my silver that I had given you, and made for yourself male images, and with them played the whore; 18and you took your embroidered garments to cover them, and set my oil and my incense before them. 19Also my bread that I gave you—I fed you with choice flour and oil and honey—you set it before them as a pleasing odor; and so it was, says the Lord GOD. 20You took your sons and your daughters, whom you had borne to me, and these you sacrificed to them to be devoured. As if your whorings were not enough! 21You slaughtered my children and delivered them up as an offering to them. 22And in all your abominations and your whorings you did not remember the days of your youth, when you were naked and bare, flailing about in your blood.

23 After all your wickedness (woe, woe to you! says the Lord GOD), 24you built yourself a platform and made yourself a lofty place in every square; 25at the head of every street you built your lofty place and prostituted your beauty, offering yourself to every passer-by, and multiplying your whoring. 26You played the whore with the Egyptians, your lustful neighbors, multiplying your whoring, to provoke me to anger. 27Therefore I stretched out my hand against you, reduced your rations, and gave you up to the will of your enemies, the daughters of the Philistines, who were ashamed of your lewd behavior. 28You played the whore with the Assyrians, because you were insatiable; you played the whore with them, and still you were not satisfied. 29You multiplied your whoring with Chaldea, the land of merchants; and even with this you were not satisfied.

30 How sick is your heart, says the Lord GOD, that you did all these things, the deeds of a brazen whore; 31building your platform at the head of every street, and making your lofty place in every square! Yet you were not like a whore, because you scorned payment. 32Adulterous wife, who receives strangers instead of her husband! 33Gifts are given to all whores; but you gave your gifts to all your lovers, bribing them to come to you from all around for your whorings. 34So you were different from other women in your whorings: no one solicited you to play the whore; and you gave payment, while no payment was given to you; you were different.

EZEK

---

a Gk Syr: Heb *Live! I made you a myriad*   *b* Cn: Heb *ornament of ornaments*   *c* Meaning of Heb uncertain   *d* Heb adds *let it be his*

35 Therefore, O whore, hear the word of the LORD: ³⁶Thus says the Lord GOD, Because your lust was poured out and your nakedness uncovered in your whoring with your lovers, and because of all your abominable idols, and because of the blood of your children that you gave to them, ³⁷therefore, I will gather all your lovers, with whom you took pleasure, all those you loved and all those you hated; I will gather them against you from all around, and will uncover your nakedness to them, so that they may see all your nakedness. ³⁸I will judge you as women who commit adultery and shed blood are judged, and bring blood upon you in wrath and jealousy. ³⁹I will deliver you into their hands, and they shall throw down your platform and break down your lofty places; they shall strip you of your clothes and take your beautiful objects and leave you naked and bare. ⁴⁰They shall bring up a mob against you, and they shall stone you and cut you to pieces with their swords. ⁴¹They shall burn your houses and execute judgments on you in the sight of many women; I will stop you from playing the whore, and you shall also make no more payments. ⁴²So I will satisfy my fury on you, and my jealousy shall turn away from you; I will be calm, and will be angry no longer. ⁴³Because you have not remembered the days of your youth, but have enraged me with all these things; therefore, I have returned your deeds upon your head, says the Lord GOD.

Have you not committed lewdness beyond all your abominations? ⁴⁴See, everyone who uses proverbs will use this proverb about you, "Like mother, like daughter." ⁴⁵You are the daughter of your mother, who loathed her husband and her children; and you are the sister of your sisters, who loathed their husbands and their children. Your mother was a Hittite and your father an Amorite. ⁴⁶Your elder sister is Samaria, who lived with her daughters to the north of you; and your younger sister, who lived to the south of you, is Sodom with her daughters. ⁴⁷You not only followed their ways, and acted according to their abominations; within a very little time you were more corrupt than they in all your ways. ⁴⁸As I live, says the Lord GOD, your sister Sodom and her daughters have not done as you and your daughters have done. ⁴⁹This was the guilt of your sister Sodom: she and her daughters had pride, excess of food, and prosperous ease, but did not aid the poor and needy. ⁵⁰They were haughty, and did abominable things before me; therefore I removed them when I saw it. ⁵¹Samaria has not committed half your sins; you have committed more abominations than they, and have made

your sisters appear righteous by all the abominations that you have committed. ⁵²Bear your disgrace, you also, for you have brought about for your sisters a more favorable judgment; because of your sins in which you acted more abominably than they, they are more in the right than you. So be ashamed, you also, and bear your disgrace, for you have made your sisters appear righteous.

53 I will restore their fortunes, the fortunes of Sodom and her daughters and the fortunes of Samaria and her daughters, and I will restore your own fortunes along with theirs, ⁵⁴in order that you may bear your disgrace and be ashamed of all that you have done, becoming a consolation to them. ⁵⁵As for your sisters, Sodom and her daughters shall return to their former state, Samaria and her daughters shall return to their former state, and you and your daughters shall return to your former state. ⁵⁶Was not your sister Sodom a byword in your mouth in the day of your pride, ⁵⁷before your wickedness was uncovered? Now you are a mockery to the daughters of Aram^a and all her neighbors, and to the daughters of the Philistines, those all around who despise you. ⁵⁸You must bear the penalty of your lewdness and your abominations, says the LORD.

An Everlasting Covenant

59 Yes, thus says the Lord GOD: I will deal with you as you have done, you who have despised the oath, breaking the covenant; ⁶⁰yet I will remember my covenant with you in the days of your youth, and I will establish with you an everlasting covenant. ⁶¹Then you will remember your ways, and be ashamed when I^b take your sisters, both your elder and your younger, and give them to you as daughters, but not on account of my^c covenant with you. ⁶²I will establish my covenant with you, and you shall know that I am the LORD, ⁶³in order that you may remember and be confounded, and never open your mouth again because of your shame, when I forgive you all that you have done, says the Lord GOD.

The Two Eagles and the Vine

17 The word of the LORD came to me: ²O mortal, propound a riddle, and speak an allegory to the house of Israel. ³Say: Thus says the Lord GOD:

A great eagle, with great wings and long pinions,
   rich in plumage of many colors,
   came to the Lebanon.
He took the top of the cedar,

---

a Another reading is *Edom*   b Syr: Heb *you*   c Heb lacks *my*

4 broke off its topmost shoot;
　he carried it to a land of trade,
　　set it in a city of merchants.
5 Then he took a seed from the land,
　placed it in fertile soil;
a plant[a] by abundant waters,
　he set it like a willow twig.
6 It sprouted and became a vine
　spreading out, but low;
its branches turned toward him,
　its roots remained where it stood.
So it became a vine;
　it brought forth branches,
　put forth foliage.

7 There was another great eagle,
　with great wings and much plumage.
And see! This vine stretched out
　its roots toward him;
it shot out its branches toward him,
　so that he might water it.
From the bed where it was planted
8 　it was transplanted
to good soil by abundant waters,
　so that it might produce branches
　and bear fruit
　and become a noble vine.
9 Say: Thus says the Lord GOD:
　Will it prosper?
Will he not pull up its roots,
　cause its fruit to rot[a] and wither,
　its fresh sprouting leaves to fade?
No strong arm or mighty army will be needed
　to pull it from its roots.
10 When it is transplanted, will it thrive?
　When the east wind strikes it,
　will it not utterly wither,
　wither on the bed where it grew?

11 Then the word of the LORD came to me:
12 Say now to the rebellious house: Do you not
know what these things mean? Tell them: The
king of Babylon came to Jerusalem, took its king
and its officials, and brought them back with
him to Babylon. 13 He took one of the royal offspring and made a covenant with him, putting
him under oath (he had taken away the chief
men of the land), 14 so that the kingdom might
be humble and not lift itself up, and that by
keeping his covenant it might stand. 15 But he
rebelled against him by sending ambassadors to
Egypt, in order that they might give him horses
and a large army. Will he succeed? Can one escape who does such things? Can he break the
covenant and yet escape? 16 As I live, says the Lord
GOD, surely in the place where the king resides
who made him king, whose oath he despised,

and whose covenant with him he broke—in
Babylon he shall die. 17 Pharaoh with his mighty
army and great company will not help him in
war, when ramps are cast up and siege walls built
to cut off many lives. 18 Because he despised the
oath and broke the covenant, because he gave
his hand and yet did all these things, he shall not
escape. 19 Therefore thus says the Lord GOD: As I
live, I will surely return upon his head my oath
that he despised, and my covenant that he broke;
20 I will spread my net over him, and he shall be
caught in my snare; I will bring him to Babylon
and enter into judgment with him there for the
treason he has committed against me. 21 All the
pick[b] of his troops shall fall by the sword, and
the survivors shall be scattered to every wind; and
you shall know that I, the LORD, have spoken.

Israel Exalted at Last

22 Thus says the Lord GOD:
I myself will take a sprig
　from the lofty top of a cedar;
　I will set it out.
I will break off a tender one
　from the topmost of its young twigs;
I myself will plant it
　on a high and lofty mountain.
23 On the mountain height of Israel
　I will plant it,
in order that it may produce boughs and bear
　　fruit,
　and become a noble cedar.
Under it every kind of bird will live;
　in the shade of its branches will nest
　winged creatures of every kind.
24 All the trees of the field shall know
　that I am the LORD.
I bring low the high tree,
　I make high the low tree;
I dry up the green tree
　and make the dry tree flourish.
I the LORD have spoken;
　I will accomplish it.

Individual Retribution

18 The word of the LORD came to me: 2 What
do you mean by repeating this proverb
concerning the land of Israel, "The parents have
eaten sour grapes, and the children's teeth are
set on edge"? 3 As I live, says the Lord GOD, this
proverb shall no more be used by you in Israel.
4 Know that all lives are mine; the life of the parent as well as the life of the child is mine: it is
only the person who sins that shall die.

a Meaning of Heb uncertain　b Another reading is fugitives

EZEK

5 If a man is righteous and does what is lawful and right— 6if he does not eat upon the mountains or lift up his eyes to the idols of the house of Israel, does not defile his neighbor's wife or approach a woman during her menstrual period, 7does not oppress anyone, but restores to the debtor his pledge, commits no robbery, gives his bread to the hungry and covers the naked with a garment, 8does not take advance or accrued interest, withholds his hand from iniquity, executes true justice between contending parties, 9follows my statutes, and is careful to observe my ordinances, acting faithfully—such a one is righteous; he shall surely live, says the Lord God.

10 If he has a son who is violent, a shedder of blood, 11who does any of these things (though his father[a] does none of them), who eats upon the mountains, defiles his neighbor's wife, 12oppresses the poor and needy, commits robbery, does not restore the pledge, lifts up his eyes to the idols, commits abomination, 13takes advance or accrued interest; shall he then live? He shall not. He has done all these abominable things; he shall surely die; his blood shall be upon himself.

14 But if this man has a son who sees all the sins that his father has done, considers, and does not do likewise, 15who does not eat upon the mountains or lift up his eyes to the idols of the house of Israel, does not defile his neighbor's wife, 16does not wrong anyone, exacts no pledge, commits no robbery, but gives his bread to the hungry and covers the naked with a garment, 17withholds his hand from iniquity,[b] takes no advance or accrued interest, observes my ordinances, and follows my statutes; he shall not die for his father's iniquity; he shall surely live. 18As for his father, because he practiced extortion, robbed his brother, and did what is not good among his people, he dies for his iniquity.

19 Yet you say, "Why should not the son suffer for the iniquity of the father?" When the son has done what is lawful and right, and has been careful to observe all my statutes, he shall surely live. 20The person who sins shall die. A child shall not suffer for the iniquity of a parent, nor a parent suffer for the iniquity of a child; the righteousness of the righteous shall be his own, and the wickedness of the wicked shall be his own.

21 But if the wicked turn away from all their sins that they have committed and keep all my statutes and do what is lawful and right, they shall surely live; they shall not die. 22None of the transgressions that they have committed shall be remembered against them; for the righteousness that they have done they shall live. 23Have I any pleasure in the death of the wicked, says the Lord God, and not rather that they should turn from their ways and live? 24But when the righteous turn away from their righteousness and commit iniquity and do the same abominable things that the wicked do, shall they live? None of the righteous deeds that they have done shall be remembered; for the treachery of which they are guilty and the sin they have committed, they shall die.

25 Yet you say, "The way of the Lord is unfair." Hear now, O house of Israel: Is my way unfair? Is it not your ways that are unfair? 26When the righteous turn away from their righteousness and commit iniquity, they shall die for it; for the iniquity that they have committed they shall die. 27Again, when the wicked turn away from the wickedness they have committed and do what is lawful and right, they shall save their life. 28Because they considered and turned away from all the transgressions that they had committed, they shall surely live; they shall not die. 29Yet the house of Israel says, "The way of the Lord is unfair." O house of Israel, are my ways unfair? Is it not your ways that are unfair?

30 Therefore I will judge you, O house of Israel, all of you according to your ways, says the Lord God. Repent and turn from all your transgressions; otherwise iniquity will be your ruin.[c] 31Cast away from you all the transgressions that you have committed against me, and get yourselves a new heart and a new spirit! Why will you die, O house of Israel? 32For I have no pleasure in the death of anyone, says the Lord God. Turn, then, and live.

Israel Degraded

19 As for you, raise up a lamentation for the princes of Israel, 2and say:
What a lioness was your mother
  among lions!
She lay down among young lions,
  rearing her cubs.
3 She raised up one of her cubs;
  he became a young lion,
and he learned to catch prey;
  he devoured humans.
4 The nations sounded an alarm against him;
  he was caught in their pit;
and they brought him with hooks
  to the land of Egypt.
5 When she saw that she was thwarted,
  that her hope was lost,

---

a Heb he   b Gk: Heb the poor   c Or so that they shall not be a stumbling block of iniquity to you

she took another of her cubs
  and made him a young lion.
6 He prowled among the lions;
  he became a young lion,
  and he learned to catch prey;
  he devoured people.
7 And he ravaged their strongholds,*a*
  and laid waste their towns;
the land was appalled, and all in it,
  at the sound of his roaring.
8 The nations set upon him
  from the provinces all around;
they spread their net over him;
  he was caught in their pit.
9 With hooks they put him in a cage,
  and brought him to the king of Babylon;
  they brought him into custody,
so that his voice should be heard no more
  on the mountains of Israel.
10 Your mother was like a vine in a vineyard*b*
  transplanted by the water,
fruitful and full of branches
  from abundant water.
11 Its strongest stem became
  a ruler's scepter;*c*
  it towered aloft
  among the thick boughs;
  it stood out in its height
  with its mass of branches.
12 But it was plucked up in fury,
  cast down to the ground;
  the east wind dried it up;
  its fruit was stripped off,
  its strong stem was withered;
  the fire consumed it.
13 Now it is transplanted into the wilderness,
  into a dry and thirsty land.
14 And fire has gone out from its stem,
  has consumed its branches and fruit,
so that there remains in it no strong stem,
  no scepter for ruling.

This is a lamentation, and it is used as a lamentation.

Israel's Continuing Rebellion

20 In the seventh year, in the fifth month, on the tenth day of the month, certain elders of Israel came to consult the Lord, and sat down before me. 2And the word of the Lord came to me: 3Mortal, speak to the elders of Israel, and say to them: Thus says the Lord God: Why are you coming? To consult me? As I live, says the Lord God, I will not be consulted by you. 4Will you judge them, mortal, will you judge them? Then let them know the abominations of their

ancestors, 5and say to them: Thus says the Lord God: On the day when I chose Israel, I swore to the offspring of the house of Jacob—making myself known to them in the land of Egypt—I swore to them, saying, I am the Lord your God. 6On that day I swore to them that I would bring them out of the land of Egypt into a land that I had searched out for them, a land flowing with milk and honey, the most glorious of all lands. 7And I said to them, Cast away the detestable things your eyes feast on, every one of you, and do not defile yourselves with the idols of Egypt; I am the Lord your God. 8But they rebelled against me and would not listen to me; not one of them cast away the detestable things their eyes feasted on, nor did they forsake the idols of Egypt.

Then I thought I would pour out my wrath upon them and spend my anger against them in the midst of the land of Egypt. 9But I acted for the sake of my name, that it should not be profaned in the sight of the nations among whom they lived, in whose sight I made myself known to them in bringing them out of the land of Egypt. 10So I led them out of the land of Egypt and brought them into the wilderness. 11I gave them my statutes and showed them my ordinances, by whose observance everyone shall live. 12Moreover I gave them my sabbaths, as a sign between me and them, so that they might know that I the Lord sanctify them. 13But the house of Israel rebelled against me in the wilderness; they did not observe my statutes but rejected my ordinances, by whose observance everyone shall live; and my sabbaths they greatly profaned.

Then I thought I would pour out my wrath upon them in the wilderness, to make an end of them. 14But I acted for the sake of my name, so that it should not be profaned in the sight of the nations, in whose sight I had brought them out. 15Moreover I swore to them in the wilderness that I would not bring them into the land that I had given them, a land flowing with milk and honey, the most glorious of all lands, 16because they rejected my ordinances and did not observe my statutes, and profaned my sabbaths; for their heart went after their idols. 17Nevertheless my eye spared them, and I did not destroy them or make an end of them in the wilderness.

18 I said to their children in the wilderness, Do not follow the statutes of your parents, nor observe their ordinances, nor defile yourselves with their idols. 19I the Lord am your God; follow my statutes, and be careful to observe my

a Heb his widows   b Cn: Heb in your blood   c Heb Its strongest stems became rulers' scepters

E
Z
E
K

ordinances, 20and hallow my sabbaths that they may be a sign between me and you, so that you may know that I the LORD am your God. 21But the children rebelled against me; they did not follow my statutes, and were not careful to observe my ordinances, by whose observance everyone shall live; they profaned my sabbaths.

Then I thought I would pour out my wrath upon them and spend my anger against them in the wilderness. 22But I withheld my hand, and acted for the sake of my name, so that it should not be profaned in the sight of the nations, in whose sight I had brought them out. 23Moreover I swore to them in the wilderness that I would scatter them among the nations and disperse them through the countries, 24because they had not executed my ordinances, but had rejected my statutes and profaned my sabbaths, and their eyes were set on their ancestors' idols. 25Moreover I gave them statutes that were not good and ordinances by which they could not live. 26I defiled them through their very gifts, in their offering up all their firstborn, in order that I might horrify them, so that they might know that I am the LORD.

27 Therefore, mortal, speak to the house of Israel and say to them, Thus says the Lord GOD: In this again your ancestors blasphemed me, by dealing treacherously with me. 28For when I had brought them into the land that I swore to give them, then wherever they saw any high hill or any leafy tree, there they offered their sacrifices and presented the provocation of their offering; there they sent up their pleasing odors, and there they poured out their drink offerings. 29(I said to them, What is the high place to which you go? So it is called Bamah*a* to this day.) 30Therefore say to the house of Israel, Thus says the Lord GOD: Will you defile yourselves after the manner of your ancestors and go astray after their detestable things? 31When you offer your gifts and make your children pass through the fire, you defile yourselves with all your idols to this day. And shall I be consulted by you, O house of Israel? As I live, says the Lord GOD, I will not be consulted by you.

32 What is in your mind shall never happen— the thought, "Let us be like the nations, like the tribes of the countries, and worship wood and stone."

God Will Restore Israel

33 As I live, says the Lord GOD, surely with a mighty hand and an outstretched arm, and with wrath poured out, I will be king over you. 34I will bring you out from the peoples and gather you out of the countries where you are scattered, with a mighty hand and an outstretched arm, and with wrath poured out; 35and I will bring you into the wilderness of the peoples, and there I will enter into judgment with you face to face. 36As I entered into judgment with your ancestors in the wilderness of the land of Egypt, so I will enter into judgment with you, says the Lord GOD. 37I will make you pass under the staff, and will bring you within the bond of the covenant. 38I will purge out the rebels among you, and those who transgress against me; I will bring them out of the land where they reside as aliens, but they shall not enter the land of Israel. Then you shall know that I am the LORD.

39 As for you, O house of Israel, thus says the Lord GOD: Go serve your idols, every one of you now and hereafter, if you will not listen to me; but my holy name you shall no more profane with your gifts and your idols.

40 For on my holy mountain, the mountain height of Israel, says the Lord GOD, there all the house of Israel, all of them, shall serve me in the land; there I will accept them, and there I will require your contributions and the choicest of your gifts, with all your sacred things. 41As a pleasing odor I will accept you, when I bring you out from the peoples, and gather you out of the countries where you have been scattered; and I will manifest my holiness among you in the sight of the nations. 42You shall know that I am the LORD, when I bring you into the land of Israel, the country that I swore to give to your ancestors. 43There you shall remember your ways and all the deeds by which you have polluted yourselves; and you shall loathe yourselves for all the evils that you have committed. 44And you shall know that I am the LORD, when I deal with you for my name's sake, not according to your evil ways, or corrupt deeds, O house of Israel, says the Lord GOD.

A Prophecy against the Negeb

45 *b* The word of the LORD came to me: 46Mortal, set your face toward the south, preach against the south, and prophesy against the forest land in the Negeb; 47say to the forest of the Negeb, Hear the word of the LORD: Thus says the Lord GOD, I will kindle a fire in you, and it shall devour every green tree in you and every dry tree; the blazing flame shall not be quenched, and all faces from south to north shall be scorched by it. 48All flesh shall see that I the LORD have kindled it; it shall not be quenched. 49Then I said,

---

a That is *High Place*   b Ch 21.1 in Heb

E Z E K

"Ah Lord God! they are saying of me, 'Is he not a maker of allegories?' "

The Drawn Sword of God

21 [a] The word of the Lord came to me: [2]Mortal, set your face toward Jerusalem and preach against the sanctuaries; prophesy against the land of Israel [3]and say to the land of Israel, Thus says the Lord: I am coming against you, and will draw my sword out of its sheath, and will cut off from you both righteous and wicked. [4]Because I will cut off from you both righteous and wicked, therefore my sword shall go out of its sheath against all flesh from south to north; [5]and all flesh shall know that I the Lord have drawn my sword out of its sheath; it shall not be sheathed again. [6]Moan therefore, mortal; moan with breaking heart and bitter grief before their eyes. [7]And when they say to you, "Why do you moan?" you shall say, "Because of the news that has come. Every heart will melt and all hands will be feeble, every spirit will faint and all knees will turn to water. See, it comes and it will be fulfilled," says the Lord God.

8 And the word of the Lord came to me: [9]Mortal, prophesy and say: Thus says the Lord; Say:

A sword, a sword is sharpened,
  it is also polished;
[10] it is sharpened for slaughter,
  honed to flash like lightning!
How can we make merry?
  You have despised the rod,
  and all discipline.[b]
[11] The sword[c] is given to be polished,
  to be grasped in the hand;
it is sharpened, the sword is polished,
  to be placed in the slayer's hand.
[12] Cry and wail, O mortal,
  for it is against my people;
it is against all Israel's princes;
  they are thrown to the sword,
  together with my people.
Ah! Strike the thigh!
[13]For consider: What! If you despise the rod, will it not happen?[b] says the Lord God.
[14] And you, mortal, prophesy;
strike hand to hand.
Let the sword fall twice, thrice;
  it is a sword for killing.
A sword for great slaughter—
  it surrounds them;
[15] therefore hearts melt
  and many stumble.
At all their gates I have set
  the point[b] of the sword.

Ah! It is made for flashing,
  it is polished[d] for slaughter.
[16] Attack to the right!
  Engage to the left!
  —wherever your edge is directed.
[17] I too will strike hand to hand,
  I will satisfy my fury;
  I the Lord have spoken.

18 The word of the Lord came to me: [19]Mortal, mark out two roads for the sword of the king of Babylon to come; both of them shall issue from the same land. And make a signpost, make it for a fork in the road leading to a city; [20]mark out the road for the sword to come to Rabbah of the Ammonites or to Judah and to[e] Jerusalem the fortified. [21]For the king of Babylon stands at the parting of the way, at the fork in the two roads, to use divination; he shakes the arrows, he consults the teraphim,[f] he inspects the liver. [22]Into his right hand comes the lot for Jerusalem, to set battering rams, to call out for slaughter, for raising the battle cry, to set battering rams against the gates, to cast up ramps, to build siege towers. [23]But to them it will seem like a false divination; they have sworn solemn oaths; but he brings their guilt to remembrance, bringing about their capture.

24 Therefore thus says the Lord God: Because you have brought your guilt to remembrance, in that your transgressions are uncovered, so that in all your deeds your sins appear—because you have come to remembrance, you shall be taken in hand.[g]
[25] As for you, vile, wicked prince of Israel,
  you whose day has come,
  the time of final punishment,
[26] thus says the Lord God:
Remove the turban, take off the crown;
  things shall not remain as they are.
Exalt that which is low,
  abase that which is high.
[27] A ruin, a ruin, a ruin—
  I will make it!
  (Such has never occurred.)
Until he comes whose right it is;
  to him I will give it.

28 As for you, mortal, prophesy, and say, Thus says the Lord God concerning the Ammonites, and concerning their reproach; say:
A sword, a sword! Drawn for slaughter,
  polished to consume,[h] to flash like lightning.
[29] Offering false visions for you,

---

a Ch 21.6 in Heb   b Meaning of Heb uncertain   c Heb It
d Tg: Heb wrapped up   e Gk Syr: Heb Judah in   f Or the
household gods   g Or be taken captive   h Cn: Heb to contain

divining lies for you,
they place you over the necks
    of the vile, wicked ones—
those whose day has come,
    the time of final punishment.
[30] Return it to its sheath!
In the place where you were created,
    in the land of your origin,
    I will judge you.
[31] I will pour out my indignation upon you,
    with the fire of my wrath
    I will blow upon you.
I will deliver you into brutish hands,
    those skillful to destroy.
[32] You shall be fuel for the fire;
    your blood shall enter the earth;
you shall be remembered no more,
    for I the LORD have spoken.

The Bloody City

22 The word of the LORD came to me: [2]You, mortal, will you judge, will you judge the bloody city? Then declare to it all its abominable deeds. [3]You shall say, Thus says the Lord GOD: A city! Shedding blood within itself; its time has come; making its idols, defiling itself. [4]You have become guilty by the blood that you have shed, and defiled by the idols that you have made; you have brought your day near, the appointed time of your years has come. Therefore I have made you a disgrace before the nations, and a mockery to all the countries. [5]Those who are near and those who are far from you will mock you, you infamous one, full of tumult.

6 The princes of Israel in you, everyone according to his power, have been bent on shedding blood. [7]Father and mother are treated with contempt in you; the alien residing within you suffers extortion; the orphan and the widow are wronged in you. [8]You have despised my holy things, and profaned my sabbaths. [9]In you are those who slander to shed blood, those in you who eat upon the mountains, who commit lewdness in your midst. [10]In you they uncover their fathers' nakedness; in you they violate women in their menstrual periods. [11]One commits abomination with his neighbor's wife; another lewdly defiles his daughter-in-law; another in you defiles his sister, his father's daughter. [12]In you, they take bribes to shed blood; you take both advance interest and accrued interest, and make gain of your neighbors by extortion; and you have forgotten me, says the Lord GOD.

13 See, I strike my hands together at the dishonest gain you have made, and at the blood that has been shed within you. [14]Can your courage endure, or can your hands remain strong in the days when I shall deal with you? I the LORD have spoken, and I will do it. [15]I will scatter you among the nations and disperse you through the countries, and I will purge your filthiness out of you. [16]And I[a] shall be profaned through you in the sight of the nations; and you shall know that I am the LORD.

17 The word of the LORD came to me: [18]Mortal, the house of Israel has become dross to me; all of them, silver,[b] bronze, tin, iron, and lead. In the smelter they have become dross. [19]Therefore thus says the Lord GOD: Because you have all become dross, I will gather you into the midst of Jerusalem. [20]As one gathers silver, bronze, iron, lead, and tin into a smelter, to blow the fire upon them in order to melt them; so I will gather you in my anger and in my wrath, and I will put you in and melt you. [21]I will gather you and blow upon you with the fire of my wrath, and you shall be melted within it. [22]As silver is melted in a smelter, so you shall be melted in it; and you shall know that I the LORD have poured out my wrath upon you.

23 The word of the LORD came to me: [24]Mortal, say to it: You are a land that is not cleansed, not rained upon in the day of indignation. [25]Its princes[c] within it are like a roaring lion tearing the prey; they have devoured human lives; they have taken treasure and precious things; they have made many widows within it. [26]Its priests have done violence to my teaching and have profaned my holy things; they have made no distinction between the holy and the common, neither have they taught the difference between the unclean and the clean, and they have disregarded my sabbaths, so that I am profaned among them. [27]Its officials within it are like wolves tearing the prey, shedding blood, destroying lives to get dishonest gain. [28]Its prophets have smeared whitewash on their behalf, seeing false visions and divining lies for them, saying, "Thus says the Lord GOD," when the LORD has not spoken. [29]The people of the land have practiced extortion and committed robbery; they have oppressed the poor and needy, and have extorted from the alien without redress. [30]And I sought for anyone among them who would repair the wall and stand in the breach before me on behalf of the land, so that I would not destroy it; but I found no one. [31]Therefore I have poured out my indignation upon them; I have consumed them with the fire of my wrath; I have returned their conduct upon their heads, says the Lord GOD.

---

a Gk Syr Vg: Heb *you*   b Transposed from the end of the verse; compare verse 20   c Gk: Heb *indignation*. 25*A conspiracy of its prophets*

Oholah and Oholibah

23 The word of the LORD came to me: [2]Mortal, there were two women, the daughters of one mother; [3]they played the whore in Egypt; they played the whore in their youth; their breasts were caressed there, and their virgin bosoms were fondled. [4]Oholah was the name of the elder and Oholibah the name of her sister. They became mine, and they bore sons and daughters. As for their names, Oholah is Samaria, and Oholibah is Jerusalem.

5 Oholah played the whore while she was mine; she lusted after her lovers the Assyrians, warriors[a] [6]clothed in blue, governors and commanders, all of them handsome young men, mounted horsemen. [7]She bestowed her favors upon them, the choicest men of Assyria all of them; and she defiled herself with all the idols of everyone for whom she lusted. [8]She did not give up her whorings that she had practiced since Egypt; for in her youth men had lain with her and fondled her virgin bosom and poured out their lust upon her. [9]Therefore I delivered her into the hands of her lovers, into the hands of the Assyrians, for whom she lusted. [10]These uncovered her nakedness; they seized her sons and her daughters; and they killed her with the sword. Judgment was executed upon her, and she became a byword among women.

11 Her sister Oholibah saw this, yet she was more corrupt than she in her lusting and in her whorings, which were worse than those of her sister. [12]She lusted after the Assyrians, governors and commanders, warriors[a] clothed in full armor, mounted horsemen, all of them handsome young men. [13]And I saw that she was defiled; they both took the same way. [14]But she carried her whorings further; she saw male figures carved on the wall, images of the Chaldeans portrayed in vermilion, [15]with belts around their waists, with flowing turbans on their heads, all of them looking like officers—a picture of Babylonians whose native land was Chaldea. [16]When she saw them she lusted after them, and sent messengers to them in Chaldea. [17]And the Babylonians came to her into the bed of love, and they defiled her with their lust; and after she defiled herself with them, she turned from them in disgust. [18]When she carried on her whorings so openly and flaunted her nakedness, I turned in disgust from her, as I had turned from her sister. [19]Yet she increased her whorings, remembering the days of her youth, when she played the whore in the land of Egypt [20]and lusted after her paramours there, whose members were like those

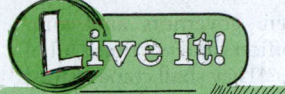

Irresponsible Children

Raising children is a demanding job. In teaching their children about life, parents try to help them be responsible—to accept the consequences of their actions. For example, a parent might say: "You threw the ball and broke the window. The wind had nothing to do with it! Now, what are you going to do about it?"

Chapters 13–24 of Ezekiel contain prophecies, allegories, fables, and symbolic actions, all intended to encourage the people of Judah to take responsibility for their sinful actions. In a graphic allegory in chapter 23, the northern and southern kingdoms are compared to promiscuous daughters who will sleep with almost anyone who comes their way. God is using just about every possible means to say, "Take responsibility for your actions, my children, and live with the consequences!"

We are all like little children in that we are often tempted to ignore the consequences of our actions. For instance, we may think of cheating on homework as just a little wrong. But that wrong will catch up with us. It will lead to more cheating, in bigger things. By then, our "little" wrong could mean losing a job or destroying a relationship. If you want to please God, be honest in looking at the consequences of your actions and choose responsibly!

▶ Ezek 23:1–21

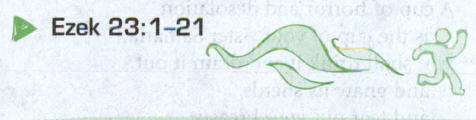

of donkeys, and whose emission was like that of stallions. [21]Thus you longed for the lewdness of your youth, when the Egyptians[b] fondled your bosom and caressed[c] your young breasts.

22 Therefore, O Oholibah, thus says the Lord GOD: I will rouse against you your lovers from whom you turned in disgust, and I will bring them against you from every side: [23]the Babylonians and all the Chaldeans, Pekod and Shoa and Koa, and all the Assyrians with them,

---

a Meaning of Heb uncertain   b Two Mss: MT *from Egypt*
c Cn: Heb *for the sake of*

EZEK

handsome young men, governors and commanders all of them, officers and warriors,[a] all of them riding on horses. 24They shall come against you from the north[b] with chariots and wagons and a host of peoples; they shall set themselves against you on every side with buckler, shield, and helmet, and I will commit the judgment to them, and they shall judge you according to their ordinances. 25I will direct my indignation against you, in order that they may deal with you in fury. They shall cut off your nose and your ears, and your survivors shall fall by the sword. They shall seize your sons and your daughters, and your survivors shall be devoured by fire. 26They shall also strip you of your clothes and take away your fine jewels. 27So I will put an end to your lewdness and your whoring brought from the land of Egypt; you shall not long for them, or remember Egypt any more. 28For thus says the Lord GOD: I will deliver you into the hands of those whom you hate, into the hands of those from whom you turned in disgust; 29and they shall deal with you in hatred, and take away all the fruit of your labor, and leave you naked and bare, and the nakedness of your whorings shall be exposed. Your lewdness and your whorings 30have brought this upon you, because you played the whore with the nations, and polluted yourself with their idols. 31You have gone the way of your sister; therefore I will give her cup into your hand.
32Thus says the Lord GOD:

You shall drink your sister's cup,
    deep and wide;
you shall be scorned and derided,
    it holds so much.
33 You shall be filled with drunkenness and sorrow.
A cup of horror and desolation
    is the cup of your sister Samaria;
34 you shall drink it and drain it out,
    and gnaw its sherds,
    and tear out your breasts;

for I have spoken, says the Lord GOD. 35Therefore thus says the Lord GOD: Because you have forgotten me and cast me behind your back, therefore bear the consequences of your lewdness and whorings.

36 The LORD said to me: Mortal, will you judge Oholah and Oholibah? Then declare to them their abominable deeds. 37For they have committed adultery, and blood is on their hands; with their idols they have committed adultery; and they have even offered up to them for food the children whom they had borne to me. 38Moreover this they have done to me: they have defiled my sanctuary on the same day and profaned my sabbaths. 39For when they had slaughtered their children for their idols, on the same day they came into my sanctuary to profane it. This is what they did in my house.

40 They even sent for men to come from far away, to whom a messenger was sent, and they came. For them you bathed yourself, painted your eyes, and decked yourself with ornaments; 41you sat on a stately couch, with a table spread before it on which you had placed my incense and my oil. 42The sound of a raucous multitude was around her, with many of the rabble brought in drunken from the wilderness; and they put bracelets on the arms[c] of the women, and beautiful crowns upon their heads.

43 Then I said, Ah, she is worn out with adulteries, but they carry on their sexual acts with her. 44For they have gone in to her, as one goes in to a whore. Thus they went in to Oholah and to Oholibah, wanton women. 45But righteous judges shall declare them guilty of adultery and of bloodshed; because they are adulteresses and blood is on their hands.

46 For thus says the Lord GOD: Bring up an assembly against them, and make them an object of terror and of plunder. 47The assembly shall stone them and with their swords they shall cut them down; they shall kill their sons and their daughters, and burn up their houses. 48Thus will I put an end to lewdness in the land, so that all women may take warning and not commit lewdness as you have done. 49They shall repay you for your lewdness, and you shall bear the penalty for your sinful idolatry; and you shall know that I am the Lord GOD.

The Boiling Pot

24 In the ninth year, in the tenth month, on the tenth day of the month, the word of the LORD came to me: 2Mortal, write down the name of this day, this very day. The king of Babylon has laid siege to Jerusalem this very day. 3And utter an allegory to the rebellious house and say to them, Thus says the Lord GOD:

Set on the pot, set it on,
    pour in water also;
4 put in it the pieces,
    all the good pieces, the thigh and the shoulder;
    fill it with choice bones.
5 Take the choicest one of the flock,
    pile the logs[d] under it;
boil its pieces,[e]
    seethe[f] also its bones in it.

---

a Compare verses 6 and 12: Heb *officers and called ones*
b Gk: Meaning of Heb uncertain   c Heb *hands*   d Compare verse 10: Heb *the bones*   e Two Mss: Heb *its boilings*
f Cn: Heb *its bones seethe*

6 Therefore thus says the Lord GOD:
Woe to the bloody city,
   the pot whose rust is in it,
   whose rust has not gone out of it!
Empty it piece by piece,
   making no choice at all.[a]
7 For the blood she shed is inside it;
   she placed it on a bare rock;
she did not pour it out on the ground,
   to cover it with earth.
8 To rouse my wrath, to take vengeance,
   I have placed the blood she shed
   on a bare rock,
   so that it may not be covered.
9 Therefore thus says the Lord GOD:
Woe to the bloody city!
   I will even make the pile great.
10 Heap up the logs, kindle the fire;
   boil the meat well, mix in the spices,
   let the bones be burned.
11 Stand it empty upon the coals,
   so that it may become hot, its copper glow,
   its filth melt in it, its rust be consumed.
12 In vain I have wearied myself;[b]
   its thick rust does not depart.
   To the fire with its rust![c]
13 Yet, when I cleansed you in your filthy lewdness,
   you did not become clean from your filth;
you shall not again be cleansed
   until I have satisfied my fury upon you.
14 I the LORD have spoken; the time is coming, I will act. I will not refrain, I will not spare, I will not relent. According to your ways and your doings I will judge you, says the Lord GOD.

Ezekiel's Bereavement

15 The word of the LORD came to me: 16 Mortal, with one blow I am about to take away from you the delight of your eyes; yet you shall not mourn or weep, nor shall your tears run down. 17 Sigh, but not aloud; make no mourning for the dead. Bind on your turban, and put your sandals on your feet; do not cover your upper lip or eat the bread of mourners.[d] 18 So I spoke to the people in the morning, and at evening my wife died. And on the next morning I did as I was commanded.

19 Then the people said to me, "Will you not tell us what these things mean for us, that you are acting this way?" 20 Then I said to them: The word of the LORD came to me: 21 Say to the house of Israel, Thus says the Lord GOD: I will profane my sanctuary, the pride of your power, the delight of your eyes, and your heart's desire; and your sons and your daughters whom you left behind shall fall by the sword. 22 And you shall do as I have done; you shall not cover your upper lip or eat the bread of mourners.[d] 23 Your turbans shall be on your heads and your sandals on your feet; you shall not mourn or weep, but you shall pine away in your iniquities and groan to one another. 24 Thus Ezekiel shall be a sign to you; you shall do just as he has done. When this comes, then you shall know that I am the Lord GOD.

25 And you, mortal, on the day when I take from them their stronghold, their joy and glory, the delight of their eyes and their heart's affection, and also[e] their sons and their daughters, 26 on that day, one who has escaped will come to you to report to you the news. 27 On that day your mouth shall be opened to the one who has escaped, and you shall speak and no longer be silent. So you shall be a sign to them; and they shall know that I am the LORD.

Proclamation against Ammon

25 The word of the LORD came to me: 2 Mortal, set your face toward the Ammonites and prophesy against them. 3 Say to the Ammonites, Hear the word of the Lord GOD: Thus says the Lord GOD, Because you said, "Aha!" over my sanctuary when it was profaned, and over the land of Israel when it was made desolate, and over the house of Judah when it went into exile; 4 therefore I am handing you over to the people of the east for a possession. They shall set their encampments among you and pitch their tents in your midst; they shall eat your fruit, and they shall drink your milk. 5 I will make Rabbah a pasture for camels and Ammon a fold for flocks. Then you shall know that I am the LORD. 6 For thus says the Lord GOD: Because you have clapped your hands and stamped your feet and rejoiced with all the malice within you against the land of Israel, 7 therefore I have stretched out my hand against you, and will hand you over as plunder to the nations. I will cut you off from the peoples and will make you perish out of the countries; I will destroy you. Then you shall know that I am the LORD.

Proclamation against Moab

8 Thus says the Lord GOD: Because Moab[f] said, The house of Judah is like all the other nations, 9 therefore I will lay open the flank of Moab from the towns[g] on its frontier, the glory of the country, Beth-jeshimoth, Baal-meon, and Kiriathaim. 10 I will give it along with Ammon to the people

---

a Heb *piece, no lot has fallen on it*   b Cn: Meaning of Heb uncertain   c Meaning of Heb uncertain   d Vg Tg: Heb of *men*   e Heb lacks *and also*   f Gk Old Latin: Heb *Moab and Seir*   g Heb *towns from its towns*

of the east as a possession. Thus Ammon shall be remembered no more among the nations, ¹¹and I will execute judgments upon Moab. Then they shall know that I am the LORD.

Proclamation against Edom

12 Thus says the Lord GOD: Because Edom acted revengefully against the house of Judah and has grievously offended in taking vengeance upon them, ¹³therefore thus says the Lord GOD, I will stretch out my hand against Edom, and cut off from it humans and animals, and I will make it desolate; from Teman even to Dedan they shall fall by the sword. ¹⁴I will lay my vengeance upon Edom by the hand of my people Israel; and they shall act in Edom according to my anger and according to my wrath; and they shall know my vengeance, says the Lord GOD.

Proclamation against Philistia

15 Thus says the Lord GOD: Because with unending hostilities the Philistines acted in vengeance, and with malice of heart took revenge in destruction; ¹⁶therefore thus says the Lord GOD, I will stretch out my hand against the Philistines, cut off the Cherethites, and destroy the rest of the seacoast. ¹⁷I will execute great vengeance on them with wrathful punishments. Then they shall know that I am the LORD, when I lay my vengeance on them.

Proclamation against Tyre

26 In the eleventh year, on the first day of the month, the word of the LORD came to me: ²Mortal, because Tyre said concerning Jerusalem,

"Aha, broken is the gateway of the peoples;
    it has swung open to me;
I shall be replenished,
    now that it is wasted,"

³therefore, thus says the Lord GOD:
See, I am against you, O Tyre!
    I will hurl many nations against you,
        as the sea hurls its waves.
⁴ They shall destroy the walls of Tyre
    and break down its towers.
I will scrape its soil from it
    and make it a bare rock.
⁵ It shall become, in the midst of the sea,
    a place for spreading nets.
I have spoken, says the Lord GOD.
    It shall become plunder for the nations,
⁶   and its daughter-towns in the country
        shall be killed by the sword.
Then they shall know that I am the LORD.

7 For thus says the Lord GOD: I will bring against Tyre from the north King Nebuchadrezzar of Babylon, king of kings, together with horses, chariots, cavalry, and a great and powerful army.
⁸ Your daughter-towns in the country
    he shall put to the sword.
He shall set up a siege wall against you,
    cast up a ramp against you,
    and raise a roof of shields against you.
⁹ He shall direct the shock of his battering rams
        against your walls
    and break down your towers with his axes.
¹⁰ His horses shall be so many
    that their dust shall cover you.
At the noise of cavalry, wheels, and chariots
    your very walls shall shake,
when he enters your gates
    like those entering a breached city.
¹¹ With the hoofs of his horses
    he shall trample all your streets.
He shall put your people to the sword,
    and your strong pillars shall fall to the
        ground.
¹² They will plunder your riches
    and loot your merchandise;
they shall break down your walls
    and destroy your fine houses.
Your stones and timber and soil
    they shall cast into the water.
¹³ I will silence the music of your songs;
    the sound of your lyres shall be heard no more.
¹⁴ I will make you a bare rock;
    you shall be a place for spreading nets.
You shall never again be rebuilt,
    for I the LORD have spoken,
        says the Lord GOD.

15 Thus says the Lord GOD to Tyre: Shall not the coastlands shake at the sound of your fall, when the wounded groan, when slaughter goes on within you? ¹⁶Then all the princes of the sea shall step down from their thrones; they shall remove their robes and strip off their embroidered garments. They shall clothe themselves with trembling, and shall sit on the ground; they shall tremble every moment, and be appalled at you. ¹⁷And they shall raise a lamentation over you, and say to you:

How you have vanished*ᵃ* from the seas,
    O city renowned,
once mighty on the sea,
    you and your inhabitants,*ᵇ*
who imposed your*ᶜ* terror
    on all the mainland!*ᵈ*

---

a Gk OL Aquila: Heb *have vanished, O inhabited one,*   b Heb *it and its inhabitants*   c Heb *their*   d Cn: Heb *its inhabitants*

18 Now the coastlands tremble
  on the day of your fall;
the coastlands by the sea
  are dismayed at your passing.

19 For thus says the Lord GOD: When I make you a city laid waste, like cities that are not inhabited, when I bring up the deep over you, and the great waters cover you, 20then I will thrust you down with those who descend into the Pit, to the people of long ago, and I will make you live in the world below, among primeval ruins, with those who go down to the Pit, so that you will not be inhabited or have a place*a* in the land of the living. 21I will bring you to a dreadful end, and you shall be no more; though sought for, you will never be found again, says the Lord GOD.

Lamentation over Tyre

27 The word of the LORD came to me: 2Now you, mortal, raise a lamentation over Tyre, 3and say to Tyre, which sits at the entrance to the sea, merchant of the peoples on many coastlands, Thus says the Lord GOD:

O Tyre, you have said,
  "I am perfect in beauty."
4 Your borders are in the heart of the seas;
  your builders made perfect your beauty.
5 They made all your planks
  of fir trees from Senir;
they took a cedar from Lebanon
  to make a mast for you.
6 From oaks of Bashan
  they made your oars;
they made your deck of pines*b*
  from the coasts of Cyprus,
  inlaid with ivory.
7 Of fine embroidered linen from Egypt
  was your sail,
  serving as your ensign;
blue and purple from the coasts of Elishah
  was your awning.
8 The inhabitants of Sidon and Arvad
  were your rowers;
skilled men of Zemer*c* were within you,
  they were your pilots.
9 The elders of Gebal and its artisans were within
  you,
  caulking your seams;
all the ships of the sea with their mariners were
  within you,
  to barter for your wares.
10 Paras*d* and Lud and Put
  were in your army,
  your mighty warriors;
they hung shield and helmet in you;
  they gave you splendor.

11 Men of Arvad and Helech*e*
  were on your walls all around;
men of Gamad were at your towers.
They hung their quivers all around your walls;
  they made perfect your beauty.

12 Tarshish did business with you out of the abundance of your great wealth; silver, iron, tin, and lead they exchanged for your wares. 13Javan, Tubal, and Meshech traded with you; they exchanged human beings and vessels of bronze for your merchandise. 14Beth-togarmah exchanged for your wares horses, war horses, and mules. 15The Rhodians*f* traded with you; many coastlands were your own special markets; they brought you in payment ivory tusks and ebony. 16Edom*g* did business with you because of your abundant goods; they exchanged for your wares turquoise, purple, embroidered work, fine linen, coral, and rubies. 17Judah and the land of Israel traded with you; they exchanged for your merchandise wheat from Minnith, millet,*h* honey, oil, and balm. 18Damascus traded with you for your abundant goods—because of your great wealth of every kind—wine of Helbon, and white wool. 19Vedan and Javan from Uzal*h* entered into trade for your wares; wrought iron, cassia, and sweet cane were bartered for your merchandise. 20Dedan traded with you in saddlecloths for riding. 21Arabia and all the princes of Kedar were your favored dealers in lambs, rams, and goats; in these they did business with you. 22The merchants of Sheba and Raamah traded with you; they exchanged for your wares the best of all kinds of spices, and all precious stones, and gold. 23Haran, Canneh, Eden, the merchants of Sheba, Asshur, and Chilmad traded with you. 24These traded with you in choice garments, in clothes of blue and embroidered work, and in carpets of colored material, bound with cords and made secure; in these they traded with you.*i* 25The ships of Tarshish traveled for you in your trade.

So you were filled and heavily laden
  in the heart of the seas.
26 Your rowers have brought you
  into the high seas.
The east wind has wrecked you
  in the heart of the seas.
27 Your riches, your wares, your merchandise,
  your mariners and your pilots,
your caulkers, your dealers in merchandise,
  and all your warriors within you,

---

a Gk: Heb *I will give beauty*   b Or *boxwood*   c Cn Compare Gen 10.18: Heb *your skilled men, O Tyre*   d Or *Persia*   e Or *and your army*   f Gk: Heb *The Dedanites*   g Another reading is *Aram*   h Meaning of Heb uncertain   i Cn: Heb *in your market*

EZEK

with all the company
    that is with you,
sink into the heart of the seas
    on the day of your ruin.
28 At the sound of the cry of your pilots
    the countryside shakes,
29 and down from their ships
    come all that handle the oar.
The mariners and all the pilots of the sea
    stand on the shore
30 and wail aloud over you,
    and cry bitterly.
They throw dust on their heads
    and wallow in ashes;
31 they make themselves bald for you,
    and put on sackcloth,
and they weep over you in bitterness of soul,
    with bitter mourning.
32 In their wailing they raise a lamentation for you,
    and lament over you:
"Who was ever destroyed[a] like Tyre
    in the midst of the sea?
33 When your wares came from the seas,
    you satisfied many peoples;
with your abundant wealth and merchandise
    you enriched the kings of the earth.
34 Now you are wrecked by the seas,
    in the depths of the waters;
your merchandise and all your crew
    have sunk with you.
35 All the inhabitants of the coastlands
    are appalled at you;
and their kings are horribly afraid,
    their faces are convulsed.
36 The merchants among the peoples hiss at you;
    you have come to a dreadful end
    and shall be no more forever."

Proclamation against the King of Tyre

28 The word of the Lord came to me: 2Mortal, say to the prince of Tyre, Thus says the Lord God:
Because your heart is proud
    and you have said, "I am a god;
I sit in the seat of the gods,
    in the heart of the seas,"
yet you are but a mortal, and no god,
    though you compare your mind
    with the mind of a god.
3 You are indeed wiser than Daniel;[b]
    no secret is hidden from you;
4 by your wisdom and your understanding
    you have amassed wealth for yourself,
and have gathered gold and silver
    into your treasuries.
5 By your great wisdom in trade

you have increased your wealth,
    and your heart has become proud in your
    wealth.
6 Therefore thus says the Lord God:
Because you compare your mind
    with the mind of a god,
7 therefore, I will bring strangers against you,
    the most terrible of the nations;
they shall draw their swords against the beauty
    of your wisdom
    and defile your splendor.
8 They shall thrust you down to the Pit,
    and you shall die a violent death
    in the heart of the seas.
9 Will you still say, "I am a god,"
    in the presence of those who kill you,
though you are but a mortal, and no god,
    in the hands of those who wound you?
10 You shall die the death of the uncircumcised
    by the hand of foreigners;
for I have spoken, says the Lord God.

Lamentation over the King of Tyre

11 Moreover the word of the Lord came to me: 12Mortal, raise a lamentation over the king of Tyre, and say to him, Thus says the Lord God:
You were the signet of perfection,[c]
    full of wisdom and perfect in beauty.
13 You were in Eden, the garden of God;
    every precious stone was your covering,
carnelian, chrysolite, and moonstone,
    beryl, onyx, and jasper,
sapphire,[d] turquoise, and emerald;
    and worked in gold were your settings
    and your engravings.[c]
On the day that you were created
    they were prepared.
14 With an anointed cherub as guardian I placed
    you;[c]
    you were on the holy mountain of God;
    you walked among the stones of fire.
15 You were blameless in your ways
    from the day that you were created,
    until iniquity was found in you.
16 In the abundance of your trade
    you were filled with violence, and you sinned;
so I cast you as a profane thing from the
      mountain of God,
    and the guardian cherub drove you out
    from among the stones of fire.
17 Your heart was proud because of your beauty;
    you corrupted your wisdom for the sake of
    your splendor.

---

a Tg Vg: Heb *like silence*   b Or, as otherwise read, *Danel*
c Meaning of Heb uncertain   d Or *lapis lazuli*

I cast you to the ground;
I exposed you before kings,
to feast their eyes on you.
18 By the multitude of your iniquities,
in the unrighteousness of your trade,
you profaned your sanctuaries.
So I brought out fire from within you;
it consumed you,
and I turned you to ashes on the earth
in the sight of all who saw you.
19 All who know you among the peoples
are appalled at you;
you have come to a dreadful end
and shall be no more forever.

Proclamation against Sidon

20 The word of the Lord came to me: 21Mortal, set your face toward Sidon, and prophesy against it, 22and say, Thus says the Lord God:
I am against you, O Sidon,
and I will gain glory in your midst.
They shall know that I am the Lord
when I execute judgments in it,
and manifest my holiness in it;
23 for I will send pestilence into it,
and bloodshed into its streets;
and the dead shall fall in its midst,
by the sword that is against it on every side.
And they shall know that I am the Lord.

24 The house of Israel shall no longer find a pricking brier or a piercing thorn among all their neighbors who have treated them with contempt. And they shall know that I am the Lord God.

Future Blessing for Israel

25 Thus says the Lord God: When I gather the house of Israel from the peoples among whom they are scattered, and manifest my holiness in them in the sight of the nations, then they shall settle on their own soil that I gave to my servant Jacob. 26They shall live in safety in it, and shall build houses and plant vineyards. They shall live in safety, when I execute judgments upon all their neighbors who have treated them with contempt. And they shall know that I am the Lord their God.

Proclamation against Egypt

29 In the tenth year, in the tenth month, on the twelfth day of the month, the word of the Lord came to me: 2Mortal, set your face against Pharaoh king of Egypt, and prophesy against him and against all Egypt; 3speak, and say, Thus says the Lord God:
I am against you,
Pharaoh king of Egypt,
the great dragon sprawling

in the midst of its channels,
saying, "My Nile is my own;
I made it for myself."
4 I will put hooks in your jaws,
and make the fish of your channels stick to
your scales.
I will draw you up from your channels,
with all the fish of your channels
sticking to your scales.
5 I will fling you into the wilderness,
you and all the fish of your channels;
you shall fall in the open field,
and not be gathered and buried.
To the animals of the earth and to the birds of
the air
I have given you as food.
6 Then all the inhabitants of Egypt shall know
that I am the Lord
because you*ᵃ* were a staff of reed
to the house of Israel;
7 when they grasped you with the hand, you broke,
and tore all their shoulders;
and when they leaned on you, you broke,
and made all their legs unsteady.*ᵇ*

8 Therefore, thus says the Lord God: I will bring a sword upon you, and will cut off from you human being and animal; 9and the land of Egypt shall be a desolation and a waste. Then they shall know that I am the Lord.

Because you*ᶜ* said, "The Nile is mine, and I made it," 10therefore, I am against you, and against your channels, and I will make the land of Egypt an utter waste and desolation, from Migdol to Syene, as far as the border of Ethiopia.*ᵈ* 11No human foot shall pass through it, and no animal foot shall pass through it; it shall be uninhabited forty years. 12I will make the land of Egypt a desolation among desolated countries; and her cities shall be a desolation forty years among cities that are laid waste. I will scatter the Egyptians among the nations, and disperse them among the countries.

13 Further, thus says the Lord God: At the end of forty years I will gather the Egyptians from the peoples among whom they were scattered; 14and I will restore the fortunes of Egypt, and bring them back to the land of Pathros, the land of their origin; and there they shall be a lowly kingdom. 15It shall be the most lowly of the kingdoms, and never again exalt itself above the nations; and I will make them so small that they will never again rule over the nations. 16The Egyptians*ᵉ* shall never again be the reliance of

EZEK

---

a Gk Syr Vg: Heb *they*   *b* Syr: Heb *stand*   *c* Gk Syr Vg: Heb *he*
d Or *Nubia;* Heb *Cush*   *e* Heb *It*

the house of Israel; they will recall their iniquity, when they turned to them for aid. Then they shall know that I am the Lord GOD.

Babylonia Will Plunder Egypt

17 In the twenty-seventh year, in the first month, on the first day of the month, the word of the LORD came to me: 18Mortal, King Nebuchadrezzar of Babylon made his army labor hard against Tyre; every head was made bald and every shoulder was rubbed bare; yet neither he nor his army got anything from Tyre to pay for the labor that he had expended against it. 19Therefore thus says the Lord GOD: I will give the land of Egypt to King Nebuchadrezzar of Babylon; and he shall carry off its wealth and despoil it and plunder it; and it shall be the wages for his army. 20I have given him the land of Egypt as his payment for which he labored, because they worked for me, says the Lord GOD.

21 On that day I will cause a horn to sprout up for the house of Israel, and I will open your lips among them. Then they shall know that I am the LORD.

Lamentation for Egypt

30 The word of the LORD came to me: 2Mortal, prophesy, and say, Thus says the Lord GOD:
Wail, "Alas for the day!"
3 For a day is near,
   the day of the LORD is near;
   it will be a day of clouds,
   a time of doom*a* for the nations.
4 A sword shall come upon Egypt,
   and anguish shall be in Ethiopia,*b*
   when the slain fall in Egypt,
   and its wealth is carried away,
   and its foundations are torn down.
5Ethiopia,*b* and Put, and Lud, and all Arabia, and Libya,*c* and the people of the allied land*d* shall fall with them by the sword.

6 Thus says the LORD:
   Those who support Egypt shall fall,
   and its proud might shall come down;
   from Migdol to Syene
   they shall fall within it by the sword,
   says the Lord GOD.
7 They shall be desolated among other desolated
      countries,
   and their cities shall lie among cities laid waste.
8 Then they shall know that I am the LORD,
   when I have set fire to Egypt,
   and all who help it are broken.
9 On that day, messengers shall go out from

me in ships to terrify the unsuspecting Ethiopians;*e* and anguish shall come upon them on the day of Egypt's doom;*f* for it is coming!

10 Thus says the Lord GOD:
I will put an end to the hordes of Egypt,
   by the hand of King Nebuchadrezzar of
      Babylon.
11 He and his people with him, the most terrible of
      the nations,
   shall be brought in to destroy the land;
and they shall draw their swords against Egypt,
   and fill the land with the slain.
12 I will dry up the channels,
   and will sell the land into the hand of evildoers;
I will bring desolation upon the land and
      everything in it
   by the hand of foreigners;
I the LORD have spoken.

13 Thus says the Lord GOD:
I will destroy the idols
   and put an end to the images in Memphis;
there shall no longer be a prince in the land of
      Egypt;
so I will put fear in the land of Egypt.
14 I will make Pathros a desolation,
   and will set fire to Zoan,
   and will execute acts of judgment on Thebes.
15 I will pour my wrath upon Pelusium,
   the stronghold of Egypt,
   and cut off the hordes of Thebes.
16 I will set fire to Egypt;
   Pelusium shall be in great agony;
Thebes shall be breached,
   and Memphis face adversaries by day.
17 The young men of On and of Pi-beseth shall fall
      by the sword;
   and the cities themselves*g* shall go into
      captivity.
18 At Tehaphnehes the day shall be dark,
   when I break there the dominion of Egypt,
and its proud might shall come to an end;
   the city*h* shall be covered by a cloud,
   and its daughter-towns shall go into captivity.
19 Thus I will execute acts of judgment on Egypt.
   Then they shall know that I am the LORD.

Proclamation against Pharaoh

20 In the eleventh year, in the first month, on the seventh day of the month, the word of the LORD came to me: 21Mortal, I have broken the arm

---

a Heb lacks *of doom*   b Or *Nubia*; Heb *Cush*   c Compare Gk Syr Vg: Heb *Cub*   d Meaning of Heb uncertain   e Or *Nubians*; Heb *Cush*   f Heb *the day of Egypt*   g Heb *and they*   h Heb *she*

of Pharaoh king of Egypt; it has not been bound up for healing or wrapped with a bandage, so that it may become strong to wield the sword. 22Therefore thus says the Lord God: I am against Pharaoh king of Egypt, and will break his arms, both the strong arm and the one that was broken; and I will make the sword fall from his hand. 23I will scatter the Egyptians among the nations, and disperse them throughout the lands. 24I will strengthen the arms of the king of Babylon, and put my sword in his hand; but I will break the arms of Pharaoh, and he will groan before him with the groans of one mortally wounded. 25I will strengthen the arms of the king of Babylon, but the arms of Pharaoh shall fall. And they shall know that I am the Lord, when I put my sword into the hand of the king of Babylon. He shall stretch it out against the land of Egypt, 26and I will scatter the Egyptians among the nations and disperse them throughout the countries. Then they shall know that I am the Lord.

The Lofty Cedar

31 In the eleventh year, in the third month, on the first day of the month, the word of the Lord came to me: 2Mortal, say to Pharaoh king of Egypt and to his hordes:

Whom are you like in your greatness?
3 Consider Assyria, a cedar of Lebanon,
with fair branches and forest shade,
and of great height,
its top among the clouds.*a*
4 The waters nourished it,
the deep made it grow tall,
making its rivers flow*b*
around the place it was planted,
sending forth its streams
to all the trees of the field.
5 So it towered high
above all the trees of the field;
its boughs grew large
and its branches long,
from abundant water in its shoots.
6 All the birds of the air
made their nests in its boughs;
under its branches all the animals of the field
gave birth to their young;
and in its shade
all great nations lived.
7 It was beautiful in its greatness,
in the length of its branches;
for its roots went down
to abundant water.
8 The cedars in the garden of God could not
rival it,
nor the fir trees equal its boughs;

the plane trees were as nothing
compared with its branches;
no tree in the garden of God
was like it in beauty.
9 I made it beautiful
with its mass of branches,
the envy of all the trees of Eden
that were in the garden of God.

10 Therefore thus says the Lord God: Because it*c* towered high and set its top among the clouds,*a* and its heart was proud of its height, 11I gave it into the hand of the prince of the nations; he has dealt with it as its wickedness deserves. I have cast it out. 12Foreigners from the most terrible of the nations have cut it down and left it. On the mountains and in all the valleys its branches have fallen, and its boughs lie broken in all the watercourses of the land; and all the peoples of the earth went away from its shade and left it.
13 On its fallen trunk settle
all the birds of the air,
and among its boughs lodge
all the wild animals.
14All this is in order that no trees by the waters may grow to lofty height or set their tops among the clouds,*a* and that no trees that drink water may reach up to them in height.

For all of them are handed over to death,
to the world below;
along with all mortals,
with those who go down to the Pit.

15 Thus says the Lord God: On the day it went down to Sheol I closed the deep over it and covered it; I restrained its rivers, and its mighty waters were checked. I clothed Lebanon in gloom for it, and all the trees of the field fainted because of it. 16I made the nations quake at the sound of its fall, when I cast it down to Sheol with those who go down to the Pit; and all the trees of Eden, the choice and best of Lebanon, all that were well watered, were consoled in the world below. 17They also went down to Sheol with it, to those killed by the sword, along with its allies,*d* those who lived in its shade among the nations.

18 Which among the trees of Eden was like you in glory and in greatness? Now you shall be brought down with the trees of Eden to the world below; you shall lie among the uncircumcised, with those who are killed by the sword. This is Pharaoh and all his horde, says the Lord God.

---

a Gk: Heb *thick boughs*   *b* Gk: Heb *rivers going*   *c* Syr Vg: Heb *you*   *d* Heb *its arms*

Lamentation over Pharaoh and Egypt

32 In the twelfth year, in the twelfth month, on the first day of the month, the word of the Lord came to me: [2]Mortal, raise a lamentation over Pharaoh king of Egypt, and say to him:

You consider yourself a lion among the nations,
  but you are like a dragon in the seas;
you thrash about in your streams,
  trouble the water with your feet,
  and foul your[a] streams.
[3] Thus says the Lord God:
In an assembly of many peoples
I will throw my net over you;
  and I[b] will haul you up in my dragnet.
[4] I will throw you on the ground,
  on the open field I will fling you,
and will cause all the birds of the air to settle on
    you,
  and I will let the wild animals of the whole
    earth gorge themselves with you.
[5] I will strew your flesh on the mountains,
  and fill the valleys with your carcass.[c]
[6] I will drench the land with your flowing blood
  up to the mountains,
  and the watercourses will be filled with you.
[7] When I blot you out, I will cover the heavens,
  and make their stars dark;
I will cover the sun with a cloud,
  and the moon shall not give its light.
[8] All the shining lights of the heavens
  I will darken above you,
  and put darkness on your land,
                says the Lord God.
[9] I will trouble the hearts of many peoples,
  as I carry you captive[d] among the nations,
  into countries you have not known.
[10] I will make many peoples appalled at you;
  their kings shall shudder because of you.
When I brandish my sword before them,
  they shall tremble every moment
for their lives, each one of them,
  on the day of your downfall.
[11] For thus says the Lord God:
The sword of the king of Babylon shall come
  against you.
[12] I will cause your hordes to fall
  by the swords of mighty ones,
  all of them most terrible among the nations.
They shall bring to ruin the pride of Egypt,
  and all its hordes shall perish.
[13] I will destroy all its livestock
  from beside abundant waters;
and no human foot shall trouble them any
  more,

nor shall the hoofs of cattle trouble them.
[14] Then I will make their waters clear,
  and cause their streams to run like oil, says
    the Lord God.
[15] When I make the land of Egypt desolate
  and when the land is stripped of all that
    fills it,
when I strike down all who live in it,
  then they shall know that I am the Lord.
[16] This is a lamentation; it shall be chanted.
  The women of the nations shall chant it.
Over Egypt and all its hordes they shall chant it,
  says the Lord God.

Dirge over Egypt

17 In the twelfth year, in the first month,[e] on the fifteenth day of the month, the word of the Lord came to me: [18] Mortal, wail over the hordes of Egypt,
  and send them down,
with Egypt[f] and the daughters of majestic
    nations,
  to the world below,
  with those who go down to the Pit.
[19] "Whom do you surpass in beauty?
  Go down! Be laid to rest with the
    uncircumcised!"
[20]They shall fall among those who are killed by the sword. Egypt[g] has been handed over to the sword; carry away both it and its hordes. [21]The mighty chiefs shall speak of them, with their helpers, out of the midst of Sheol: "They have come down, they lie still, the uncircumcised, killed by the sword."

22 Assyria is there, and all its company, their graves all around it, all of them killed, fallen by the sword. [23]Their graves are set in the uttermost parts of the Pit. Its company is all around its grave, all of them killed, fallen by the sword, who spread terror in the land of the living.

24 Elam is there, and all its hordes around its grave; all of them killed, fallen by the sword, who went down uncircumcised into the world below, who spread terror in the land of the living. They bear their shame with those who go down to the Pit. [25]They have made Elam[f] a bed among the slain with all its hordes, their graves all around it, all of them uncircumcised, killed by the sword; for terror of them was spread in the land of the living, and they bear their shame with those who go down to the Pit; they are placed among the slain.

---

a Heb *their* b Gk Vg: Heb *they* c Symmachus Syr Vg: Heb *your height* d Gk: Heb *bring your destruction* e Gk: Heb lacks *in the first month* f Heb *it* g Heb *It*

26 Meshech and Tubal are there, and all their multitude, their graves all around them, all of them uncircumcised, killed by the sword; for they spread terror in the land of the living. 27And they do not lie with the fallen warriors of long ago[a] who went down to Sheol with their weapons of war, whose swords were laid under their heads, and whose shields[b] are upon their bones; for the terror of the warriors was in the land of the living. 28So you shall be broken and lie among the uncircumcised, with those who are killed by the sword.

29 Edom is there, its kings and all its princes, who for all their might are laid with those who are killed by the sword; they lie with the uncircumcised, with those who go down to the Pit.

30 The princes of the north are there, all of them, and all the Sidonians, who have gone down in shame with the slain, for all the terror that they caused by their might; they lie uncircumcised with those who are killed by the sword, and bear their shame with those who go down to the Pit.

31 When Pharaoh sees them, he will be consoled for all his hordes—Pharaoh and all his army, killed by the sword, says the Lord God. 32For he[c] spread terror in the land of the living; therefore he shall be laid to rest among the uncircumcised, with those who are slain by the sword—Pharaoh and all his multitude, says the Lord God.

Ezekiel Israel's Sentry

33 The word of the Lord came to me: 2O Mortal, speak to your people and say to them, If I bring the sword upon a land, and the people of the land take one of their number as their sentinel; 3and if the sentinel sees the sword coming upon the land and blows the trumpet and warns the people; 4then if any who hear the sound of the trumpet do not take warning, and the sword comes and takes them away, their blood shall be upon their own heads. 5They heard the sound of the trumpet and did not take warning; their blood shall be upon themselves. But if they had taken warning, they would have saved their lives. 6But if the sentinel sees the sword coming and does not blow the trumpet, so that the people are not warned, and the sword comes and takes any of them, they are taken away in their iniquity, but their blood I will require at the sentinel's hand.

7 So you, mortal, I have made a sentinel for the house of Israel; whenever you hear a word from my mouth, you shall give them warning from me. 8If I say to the wicked, "O wicked ones, you shall surely die," and you do not speak to warn the wicked to turn from their ways, the wicked shall die in their iniquity, but their blood I will require at your hand. 9But if you warn the wicked to turn from their ways, and they do not turn from their ways, the wicked shall die in their iniquity, but you will have saved your life.

God's Justice and Mercy

10 Now you, mortal, say to the house of Israel, Thus you have said: "Our transgressions and our sins weigh upon us, and we waste away because of them; how then can we live?" 11Say to them, As I live, says the Lord God, I have no pleasure in the death of the wicked, but that the wicked turn from their ways and live; turn back, turn back from your evil ways; for why will you die, O house of Israel? 12And you, mortal, say to your people, The righteousness of the righteous shall not save them when they transgress; and as for the wickedness of the wicked, it shall not make them stumble when they turn from their wickedness; and the righteous shall not be able to live by their righteousness[d] when they sin. 13Though I say to the righteous that they shall surely live, yet if they trust in their righteousness and commit iniquity, none of their righteous deeds shall be remembered; but in the iniquity that they have committed they shall die. 14Again, though I say to the wicked, "You shall surely die," yet if they turn from their sin and do what is lawful and right— 15if the wicked restore the pledge, give back what they have taken by robbery, and walk in the statutes of life, committing no iniquity— they shall surely live, they shall not die. 16None of the sins that they have committed shall be remembered against them; they have done what is lawful and right, they shall surely live.

17 Yet your people say, "The way of the Lord is not just," when it is their own way that is not just. 18When the righteous turn from their righteousness, and commit iniquity, they shall die for it.[e] 19And when the wicked turn from their wickedness, and do what is lawful and right, they shall live by it.[e] 20Yet you say, "The way of the Lord is not just." O house of Israel, I will judge all of you according to your ways!

The Fall of Jerusalem

21 In the twelfth year of our exile, in the tenth month, on the fifth day of the month, someone who had escaped from Jerusalem came to me and said, "The city has fallen." 22Now the hand

EZEK

of the LORD had been upon me the evening before the fugitive came; but he had opened my mouth by the time the fugitive came to me in the morning; so my mouth was opened, and I was no longer unable to speak.

The Survivors in Judah

23 The word of the LORD came to me: 24Mortal, the inhabitants of these waste places in the land of Israel keep saying, "Abraham was only one man, yet he got possession of the land; but we are many; the land is surely given us to possess." 25Therefore say to them, Thus says the Lord GOD: You eat flesh with the blood, and lift up your eyes to your idols, and shed blood; shall you then possess the land? 26You depend on your swords, you commit abominations, and each of you defiles his neighbor's wife; shall you then possess the land? 27Say this to them, Thus says the Lord GOD: As I live, surely those who are in the waste places shall fall by the sword; and those who are in the open field I will give to the wild animals to be devoured; and those who are in strongholds and in caves shall die by pestilence. 28I will make the land a desolation and a waste, and its proud might shall come to an end; and the mountains of Israel shall be so desolate that no one will pass through. 29Then they shall know that I am the LORD, when I have made the land a desolation and a waste because of all their abominations that they have committed.

30 As for you, mortal, your people who talk together about you by the walls, and at the doors of the houses, say to one another, each to a neighbor, "Come and hear what the word is that comes from the LORD." 31They come to you as people come, and they sit before you as my people, and they hear your words, but they will not obey them. For flattery is on their lips, but their heart is set on their gain. 32To them you are like a singer of love songs,a one who has a beautiful voice and plays well on an instrument; they hear what you say, but they will not do it. 33When this comes—and come it will!—then they shall know that a prophet has been among them.

Israel's False Shepherds

34 The word of the LORD came to me: 2Mortal, prophesy against the shepherds of Israel: prophesy, and say to them—to the shepherds: Thus says the Lord GOD: Ah, you shepherds of Israel who have been feeding yourselves! Should not shepherds feed the sheep? 3You eat the fat, you clothe yourselves with the wool, you slaughter the fatlings; but you do not feed the sheep. 4You have not strengthened the weak, you have not healed the sick, you have not bound up the injured, you have not brought back the strayed, you have not sought the lost, but with force and harshness you have ruled them. 5So they were scattered, because there was no shepherd; and scattered, they became food for all the wild animals. 6My sheep were scattered, they wandered over all the mountains and on every high hill; my sheep were scattered over all the face of the earth, with no one to search or seek for them.

7 Therefore, you shepherds, hear the word of the LORD: 8As I live, says the Lord GOD, because my sheep have become a prey, and my sheep have become food for all the wild animals, since there was no shepherd; and because my shepherds have not searched for my sheep, but the shepherds have fed themselves, and have not fed my sheep; 9therefore, you shepherds, hear the word of the LORD: 10Thus says the Lord GOD, I am against the shepherds; and I will demand my sheep at their hand, and put a stop to their feeding the sheep; no longer shall the shepherds feed themselves. I will rescue my sheep from their mouths, so that they may not be food for them.

God, the True Shepherd

11 For thus says the Lord GOD: I myself will search for my sheep, and will seek them out. 12As shepherds seek out their flocks when they are among their scattered sheep, so I will seek out my sheep. I will rescue them from all the places to which they have been scattered on a day of clouds and thick darkness. 13I will bring them out from the peoples and gather them from the countries, and will bring them into their own land; and I will feed them on the mountains of Israel, by the watercourses, and in all the inhabited parts of the land. 14I will feed them with good pasture, and the mountain heights of Israel shall be their pasture; there they shall lie down in good grazing land, and they shall feed on rich pasture on the mountains of Israel. 15I myself will be the shepherd of my sheep, and I will make them lie down, says the Lord GOD. 16I will seek the lost, and I will bring back the strayed, and I will bind up the injured, and I will strengthen the weak, but the fat and the strong I will destroy. I will feed them with justice.

17 As for you, my flock, thus says the Lord GOD: I shall judge between sheep and sheep, between rams and goats: 18Is it not enough for you to feed on the good pasture, but you must tread down with your feet the rest of your pasture? When you drink of clear water, must you foul

a Cn: Heb *like a love song*

the rest with your feet? ¹⁹And must my sheep eat what you have trodden with your feet, and drink what you have fouled with your feet?

20 Therefore, thus says the Lord GOD to them: I myself will judge between the fat sheep and the lean sheep. ²¹Because you pushed with flank and shoulder, and butted at all the weak animals with your horns until you scattered them far and wide, ²²I will save my flock, and they shall no longer be ravaged; and I will judge between sheep and sheep.

23 I will set up over them one shepherd, my servant David, and he shall feed them: he shall feed them and be their shepherd. ²⁴And I, the LORD, will be their God, and my servant David shall be prince among them; I, the LORD, have spoken.

25 I will make with them a covenant of peace and banish wild animals from the land, so that they may live in the wild and sleep in the woods securely. ²⁶I will make them and the region around my hill a blessing; and I will send down the showers in their season; they shall be showers of blessing. ²⁷The trees of the field shall yield their fruit, and the earth shall yield its increase. They shall be secure on their soil; and they shall know that I am the LORD, when I break the bars of their yoke, and save them from the hands of those who enslaved them. ²⁸They shall no more be plunder for the nations, nor shall the animals of the land devour them; they shall live in safety, and no one shall make them afraid. ²⁹I will provide for them a splendid vegetation so that they shall no more be consumed with hunger in the land, and no longer suffer the insults of the nations. ³⁰They shall know that I, the LORD their God, am with them, and that they, the house of Israel, are my people, says the Lord GOD. ³¹You are my sheep, the sheep of my pasture*a* and I am your God, says the Lord GOD.

Judgment on Mount Seir

35 The word of the LORD came to me: ²Mortal, set your face against Mount Seir, and prophesy against it, ³and say to it, Thus says the Lord GOD:

I am against you, Mount Seir;
  I stretch out my hand against you
  to make you a desolation and a waste.
⁴ I lay your towns in ruins;
  you shall become a desolation,
  and you shall know that I am the LORD.
⁵Because you cherished an ancient enmity, and gave over the people of Israel to the power of the sword at the time of their calamity, at the time of their final punishment; ⁶therefore, as I live, says

Pray It!

The Good Shepherd

The theme of the good shepherd is common in the Bible. Psalm 23 compares God to a protective shepherd. Ezekiel, chapter 34, describes bad shepherds and contrasts them with God, the true shepherd, who feeds the flock with justice. In John 10:1–18, Jesus compares himself to a good shepherd.

God, the true shepherd, thank you for your care and protection. Today, I will do what I can to help your work. Make me aware of the people in my life who are weak, injured, straying, or lost. With your help, I will do what I can to strengthen them, heal them, and bring them back to you. Help me to be more like a shepherd than like a sheep that merely follows!

▶ **Ezekiel, chapter 34**

the Lord GOD, I will prepare you for blood, and blood shall pursue you; since you did not hate bloodshed, bloodshed shall pursue you. ⁷I will make Mount Seir a waste and a desolation; and I will cut off from it all who come and go. ⁸I will fill its mountains with the slain; on your hills and in your valleys and in all your watercourses those killed with the sword shall fall. ⁹I will make you a perpetual desolation, and your cities shall never be inhabited. Then you shall know that I am the LORD.

10 Because you said, "These two nations and these two countries shall be mine, and we will take possession of them,"—although the LORD was there— ¹¹therefore, as I live, says the Lord GOD, I will deal with you according to the anger and envy that you showed because of your hatred against them; and I will make myself known among you *b* when I judge you. ¹²You shall know that I, the LORD, have heard all the abusive speech that you uttered against the mountains of Israel, saying, "They are laid desolate, they are given us to devour." ¹³And you magnified yourselves against me with your mouth, and multiplied your words against me; I heard it. ¹⁴Thus says

a Gk OL: Heb *pasture, you are people*   *b* Gk: Heb *them*

EZEK

the Lord God: As the whole earth rejoices, I will make you desolate. ¹⁵As you rejoiced over the inheritance of the house of Israel, because it was desolate, so I will deal with you; you shall be desolate, Mount Seir, and all Edom, all of it. Then they shall know that I am the Lord.

Blessing on Israel

36 And you, mortal, prophesy to the mountains of Israel, and say: O mountains of Israel, hear the word of the Lord. ²Thus says the Lord God: Because the enemy said of you, "Aha!" and, "The ancient heights have become our possession," ³therefore prophesy, and say: Thus says the Lord God: Because they made you desolate indeed, and crushed you from all sides, so that you became the possession of the rest of the nations, and you became an object of gossip and slander among the people; ⁴therefore, O mountains of Israel, hear the word of the Lord God: Thus says the Lord God to the mountains and the hills, the watercourses and the valleys, the desolate wastes and the deserted towns, which have become a source of plunder and an object of derision to the rest of the nations all around; ⁵therefore thus says the Lord God: I am speaking in my hot jealousy against the rest of the nations, and against all Edom, who, with wholehearted joy and utter contempt, took my land as their possession, because of its pasture, to plunder it. ⁶Therefore prophesy concerning the land of Israel, and say to the mountains and hills, to the watercourses and valleys, Thus says the Lord God: I am speaking in my jealous wrath, because you have suffered the insults of the nations; ⁷therefore thus says the Lord God: I swear that the nations that are all around you shall themselves suffer insults.

8 But you, O mountains of Israel, shall shoot out your branches, and yield your fruit to my people Israel; for they shall soon come home. ⁹See now, I am for you; I will turn to you, and you shall be tilled and sown; ¹⁰and I will multiply your population, the whole house of Israel, all of it; the towns shall be inhabited and the waste places rebuilt; ¹¹and I will multiply human beings and animals upon you. They shall increase and be fruitful; and I will cause you to be inhabited as in your former times, and will do more good to you than ever before. Then you shall know that I am the Lord. ¹²I will lead people upon you—my people Israel—and they shall possess you, and you shall be their inheritance. No longer shall you bereave them of children.

13 Thus says the Lord God: Because they say to you, "You devour people, and you bereave your nation of children," ¹⁴therefore you shall no longer devour people and no longer bereave your nation of children, says the Lord God; ¹⁵and no longer will I let you hear the insults of the nations, no longer shall you bear the disgrace of the peoples; and no longer shall you cause your nation to stumble, says the Lord God.

The Renewal of Israel

16 The word of the Lord came to me: ¹⁷Mortal, when the house of Israel lived on their own soil, they defiled it with their ways and their deeds; their conduct in my sight was like the uncleanness of a woman in her menstrual period. ¹⁸So I poured out my wrath upon them for the blood that they had shed upon the land, and for the idols with which they had defiled it. ¹⁹I scattered them among the nations, and they were dispersed through the countries; in accordance with their conduct and their deeds I judged them. ²⁰But when they came to the nations, wherever they came, they profaned my holy name, in that it was said of them, "These are the people of the Lord, and yet they had to go out of his land." ²¹But I had concern for my holy name, which the house of Israel had profaned among the nations to which they came.

22 Therefore say to the house of Israel, Thus says the Lord God: It is not for your sake, O house of Israel, that I am about to act, but for the sake of my holy name, which you have profaned among the nations to which you came. ²³I will sanctify my great name, which has been profaned among the nations, and which you have profaned among them; and the nations shall know that I am the Lord, says the Lord God, when through you I display my holiness before their eyes. ²⁴I will take you from the nations, and gather you from all the countries, and bring you into your own land. ²⁵I will sprinkle clean water upon you, and you shall be clean from all your uncleannesses, and from all your idols I will cleanse you. ²⁶A new heart I will give you, and a new spirit I will put within you; and I will remove from your body the heart of stone and give you a heart of flesh. ²⁷I will put my spirit within you, and make you follow my statutes and be careful to observe my ordinances. ²⁸Then you shall live in the land that I gave to your ancestors; and you shall be my people, and I will be your God. ²⁹I will save you from all your uncleannesses, and I will summon the grain and make it abundant and lay no famine upon you. ³⁰I will make the fruit of the tree and the produce of the field abundant, so that you may never again suffer the disgrace of famine among the nations.

EZEK

Cultural Connection

You Will Be Cleansed

The sweat lodge ceremony is a Native American tradition that is still used today. It is performed whenever there is a need to be purified in order to prepare for God's blessings or ask for God's help.

This ceremony is held in a shelter of poles and blankets that is made over a pit, with the door flap facing west, the direction the rains come from. Heated rocks fill the pit, and steam is formed when water is poured on the rocks. The ceremony consists of entering the shelter and sitting in a circle, passing a pipe, making steam, and praying toward the four directions for guidance and blessings and for maintaining an attitude of thankfulness.

This tradition ritualizes the cleansing and conversion Ezekiel proclaims in Ezekiel 36:25–26.

It reflects a faith that the Great Spirit, or God, will cleanse us with waters and give us a new heart and spirit.

▶ Ezek 36:25–26

31Then you shall remember your evil ways, and your dealings that were not good; and you shall loathe yourselves for your iniquities and your abominable deeds. 32It is not for your sake that I will act, says the Lord GOD; let that be known to you. Be ashamed and dismayed for your ways, O house of Israel.

33 Thus says the Lord GOD: On the day that I cleanse you from all your iniquities, I will cause the towns to be inhabited, and the waste places shall be rebuilt. 34The land that was desolate shall be tilled, instead of being the desolation that it was in the sight of all who passed by. 35And they will say, "This land that was desolate has become like the garden of Eden; and the waste and desolate and ruined towns are now inhabited and fortified." 36Then the nations that are left all around you shall know that I, the LORD, have rebuilt the ruined places, and replanted that which was desolate; I, the LORD, have spoken, and I will do it.

37 Thus says the Lord GOD: I will also let the house of Israel ask me to do this for them: to increase their population like a flock. 38Like the flock for sacrifices,*a* like the flock at Jerusalem during her appointed festivals, so shall the ruined towns be filled with flocks of people. Then they shall know that I am the LORD.

The Valley of Dry Bones

37 The hand of the LORD came upon me, and he brought me out by the spirit of the LORD and set me down in the middle of a valley; it was full of bones. 2He led me all around them; there were very many lying in the valley, and they were very dry. 3He said to me, "Mortal, can these bones live?" I answered, "O Lord GOD, you know." 4Then he said to me, "Prophesy to these bones, and say to them: O dry bones, hear the word of the LORD. 5Thus says the Lord GOD to these bones: I will cause breath*b* to enter you, and you shall live. 6I will lay sinews on you, and will cause flesh to come upon you, and cover you with skin, and put breath*b* in you, and you shall live; and you shall know that I am the LORD."

7 So I prophesied as I had been commanded; and as I prophesied, suddenly there was a noise, a rattling, and the bones came together, bone to its bone. 8I looked, and there were sinews on them, and flesh had come upon them, and skin had covered them; but there was no breath in them. 9Then he said to me, "Prophesy to the breath, prophesy, mortal, and say to the breath:*c* Thus says the Lord GOD: Come from the four winds, O breath,*c* and breathe upon these slain, that they may live." 10I prophesied as he commanded me, and the breath came into them, and they lived, and stood on their feet, a vast multitude.

11 Then he said to me, "Mortal, these bones are the whole house of Israel. They say, 'Our bones are dried up, and our hope is lost; we are cut off completely.' 12Therefore prophesy, and say to them, Thus says the Lord GOD: I am going to open your graves, and bring you up from your graves, O my people; and I will bring you back to the land of Israel. 13And you shall know that I am the LORD, when I open your graves, and bring you up from your graves, O my people. 14I will

---

a Heb *flock of holy things*   *b* Or *spirit*   *c* Or *wind* or *spirit*

EZEK

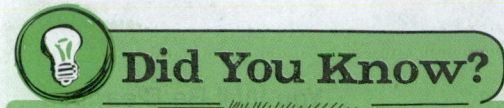

Did You Know?

Wind, Breath, and Spirit

In English, the words *wind*, *breath*, and *spirit* have three different meanings. Hebrew has only one word for all three meanings: *ruah.* The "wind from God [that] swept over the face of the waters" at Creation (Gen 1:2) is *ruah.* The "breath of life" that God blows into the lifeless clay of the first human (Gen 2:7) is *ruah.* And the "spirit of the Lᴏʀᴅ [that] came mightily upon David" at his anointing (1 Sam 16:13) is *ruah.*

In Ezekiel 37:1–14, all three meanings of the word *ruah* come into play. Ezekiel cries out, "Thus says the Lord Gᴏᴅ: Come from the four winds, O breath [or spirit], and breathe upon these slain, that they may live" (verse 9). In the prophet's vision, the bones scattered across the battlefield are the exiled people of God, who have experienced the "death" of defeat and humiliation. God promises that the spirit *(ruah)* of God (see verse 14) will bring the people of Israel back from the Exile and restore them to their land.

▶ **Ezek 37:1–14**

put my spirit within you, and you shall live, and I will place you on your own soil; then you shall know that I, the Lᴏʀᴅ, have spoken and will act, says the Lᴏʀᴅ."

The Two Sticks

15 The word of the Lᴏʀᴅ came to me: [16]Mortal, take a stick and write on it, "For Judah, and the Israelites associated with it"; then take another stick and write on it, "For Joseph (the stick of Ephraim) and all the house of Israel associated with it"; [17]and join them together into one stick, so that they may become one in your hand. [18]And when your people say to you, "Will you not show us what you mean by these?" [19]say to them, Thus says the Lord Gᴏᴅ: I am about to take the stick of Joseph (which is in the hand of Ephraim) and the tribes of Israel associated with it; and I will put the stick of Judah upon it,[a] and make them one stick, in order that they may be one in my hand. [20]When the sticks on which you write are in your hand before their eyes, [21]then say to them, Thus says the Lord Gᴏᴅ: I will take the people of Israel from the nations among

which they have gone, and will gather them from every quarter, and bring them to their own land. [22]I will make them one nation in the land, on the mountains of Israel; and one king shall be king over them all. Never again shall they be two nations, and never again shall they be divided into two kingdoms. [23]They shall never again defile themselves with their idols and their detestable things, or with any of their transgressions. I will save them from all the apostasies into which they have fallen,[b] and will cleanse them. Then they shall be my people, and I will be their God.

24 My servant David shall be king over them; and they shall all have one shepherd. They shall follow my ordinances and be careful to observe my statutes. [25]They shall live in the land that I gave to my servant Jacob, in which your ancestors lived; they and their children and their children's children shall live there forever; and my servant David shall be their prince forever. [26]I will make a covenant of peace with them; it shall be an everlasting covenant with them; and I will bless[c] them and multiply them, and will set my sanctuary among them forevermore. [27]My dwelling place shall be with them; and I will be their God, and they shall be my people. [28]Then the nations shall know that I the Lᴏʀᴅ sanctify Israel, when my sanctuary is among them forevermore.

Invasion by Gog

38 The word of the Lᴏʀᴅ came to me: [2]Mortal, set your face toward Gog, of the land of Magog, the chief prince of Meshech and Tubal. Prophesy against him [3]and say: Thus says the Lord Gᴏᴅ: I am against you, O Gog, chief prince of Meshech and Tubal; [4]I will turn you around and put hooks into your jaws, and I will lead you out with all your army, horses and horsemen, all of them clothed in full armor, a great company, all of them with shield and buckler, wielding swords. [5]Persia, Ethiopia,[d] and Put are with them, all of them with buckler and helmet; [6]Gomer and all its troops; Beth-togarmah from the remotest parts of the north with all its troops—many peoples are with you.

7 Be ready and keep ready, you and all the companies that are assembled around you, and hold yourselves in reserve for them. [8]After many days you shall be mustered; in the latter years you shall go against a land restored from war, a land where people were gathered from many nations on the mountains of Israel, which had long

---

a Heb *I will put them upon it* b Another reading is *from all the settlements in which they have sinned* c Tg: Heb *give* d Or *Nubia*; Heb *Cush*

lain waste; its people were brought out from the nations and now are living in safety, all of them. ⁹You shall advance, coming on like a storm; you shall be like a cloud covering the land, you and all your troops, and many peoples with you.

10 Thus says the Lord God: On that day thoughts will come into your mind, and you will devise an evil scheme. ¹¹You will say, "I will go up against the land of unwalled villages; I will fall upon the quiet people who live in safety, all of them living without walls, and having no bars or gates"; ¹²to seize spoil and carry off plunder; to assail the waste places that are now inhabited, and the people who were gathered from the nations, who are acquiring cattle and goods, who live at the center*ᵃ* of the earth. ¹³Sheba and Dedan and the merchants of Tarshish and all its young warriors*ᵇ* will say to you, "Have you come to seize spoil? Have you assembled your horde to carry off plunder, to carry away silver and gold, to take away cattle and goods, to seize a great amount of booty?"

14 Therefore, mortal, prophesy, and say to Gog: Thus says the Lord God: On that day when my people Israel are living securely, you will rouse yourself*ᶜ* ¹⁵and come from your place out of the remotest parts of the north, you and many peoples with you, all of them riding on horses, a great horde, a mighty army; ¹⁶you will come up against my people Israel, like a cloud covering the earth. In the latter days I will bring you against my land, so that the nations may know me, when through you, O Gog, I display my holiness before their eyes.

Judgment on Gog

17 Thus says the Lord God: Are you he of whom I spoke in former days by my servants the prophets of Israel, who in those days prophesied for years that I would bring you against them? ¹⁸On that day, when Gog comes against the land of Israel, says the Lord God, my wrath shall be aroused. ¹⁹For in my jealousy and in my blazing wrath I declare: On that day there shall be a great shaking in the land of Israel; ²⁰the fish of the sea, and the birds of the air, and the animals of the field, and all creeping things that creep on the ground, and all human beings that are on the face of the earth, shall quake at my presence, and the mountains shall be thrown down, and the cliffs shall fall, and every wall shall tumble to the ground. ²¹I will summon the sword against Gog*ᵈ* in*ᵉ* all my mountains, says the Lord God; the swords of all will be against their comrades. ²²With pestilence and bloodshed I will enter into judgment with him; and I will pour down

torrential rains and hailstones, fire and sulfur, upon him and his troops and the many peoples that are with him. ²³So I will display my greatness and my holiness and make myself known in the eyes of many nations. Then they shall know that I am the Lord.

Gog's Armies Destroyed

39 And you, mortal, prophesy against Gog, and say: Thus says the Lord God: I am against you, O Gog, chief prince of Meshech and Tubal! ²I will turn you around and drive you forward, and bring you up from the remotest parts of the north, and lead you against the mountains of Israel. ³I will strike your bow from your left hand, and will make your arrows drop out of your right hand. ⁴You shall fall on the

---

a Heb *navel*   *b* Heb *young lions*   *c* Gk: Heb *will you not know?*
d Heb *him*   *e* Heb *to* or *for*

Bone Dry

When have you felt dry and lifeless, like the collection of dry bones Ezekiel sees in his vision in Ezekiel 37:1–2? What helps you to re-energize, to put muscle and flesh back on your tired bones? What winds blow life through you to give you breath again, to make you new again?

Bones are our body's support structure, and prayer is our soul's support structure. In verse 14, God's Spirit brings life. We need to pray for God's Spirit—the Holy Spirit—to fill us in order to avoid shriveling up and becoming parched and lifeless. And we need to share God's Spirit with others, to breathe life into the dry bones around us—the people who seem to have no energy or hope.

What are the dry bones in your life? What can you do to be re-energized by God when you feel like dry bones? How can you help to energize others who seem dry and lifeless?

▶ **Ezekiel, chapter 37**

mountains of Israel, you and all your troops and the peoples that are with you; I will give you to birds of prey of every kind and to the wild animals to be devoured. 5You shall fall in the open field; for I have spoken, says the Lord GOD. 6I will send fire on Magog and on those who live securely in the coastlands; and they shall know that I am the LORD.

7 My holy name I will make known among my people Israel; and I will not let my holy name be profaned any more; and the nations shall know that I am the LORD, the Holy One in Israel. 8It has come! It has happened, says the Lord GOD. This is the day of which I have spoken.

9 Then those who live in the towns of Israel will go out and make fires of the weapons and burn them—bucklers and shields, bows and arrows, handpikes and spears—and they will make fires of them for seven years. 10They will not need to take wood out of the field or cut down any trees in the forests, for they will make their fires of the weapons; they will despoil those who despoiled them, and plunder those who plundered them, says the Lord GOD.

The Burial of Gog

11 On that day I will give to Gog a place for burial in Israel, the Valley of the Travelers*a* east of the sea; it shall block the path of the travelers, for there Gog and all his horde will be buried; it shall be called the Valley of Hamon-gog.*b* 12Seven months the house of Israel shall spend burying them, in order to cleanse the land. 13All the people of the land shall bury them; and it will bring them honor on the day that I show my glory, says the Lord GOD. 14They will set apart men to pass through the land regularly and bury any invaders*c* who remain on the face of the land, so as to cleanse it; for seven months they shall make their search. 15As the searchers*c* pass through the land, anyone who sees a human bone shall set up a sign by it, until the buriers have buried it in the Valley of Hamon-gog.*b* 16(A city Hamonah*d* is there also.) Thus they shall cleanse the land.

17 As for you, mortal, thus says the Lord GOD: Speak to the birds of every kind and to all the wild animals: Assemble and come, gather from all around to the sacrificial feast that I am preparing for you, a great sacrificial feast on the mountains of Israel, and you shall eat flesh and drink blood. 18You shall eat the flesh of the mighty, and drink the blood of the princes of the earth—of rams, of lambs, and of goats, of bulls, all of them fatlings of Bashan. 19You shall eat fat until you are filled, and drink blood until you are drunk, at the sacrificial feast that I am preparing

for you. 20And you shall be filled at my table with horses and charioteers,*e* with warriors and all kinds of soldiers, says the Lord GOD.

Israel Restored to the Land

21 I will display my glory among the nations; and all the nations shall see my judgment that I have executed, and my hand that I have laid on them. 22The house of Israel shall know that I am the LORD their God, from that day forward. 23And the nations shall know that the house of Israel went into captivity for their iniquity, because they dealt treacherously with me. So I hid my face from them and gave them into the hand of their adversaries, and they all fell by the sword. 24I dealt with them according to their uncleanness and their transgressions, and hid my face from them.

25 Therefore thus says the Lord GOD: Now I will restore the fortunes of Jacob, and have mercy on the whole house of Israel; and I will be jealous for my holy name. 26They shall forget*f* their shame, and all the treachery they have practiced against me, when they live securely in their land with no one to make them afraid, 27when I have brought them back from the peoples and gathered them from their enemies' lands, and through them have displayed my holiness in the sight of many nations. 28Then they shall know that I am the LORD their God because I sent them into exile among the nations, and then gathered them into their own land. I will leave none of them behind; 29and I will never again hide my face from them, when I pour out my spirit upon the house of Israel, says the Lord GOD.

The Vision of the New Temple

40 In the twenty-fifth year of our exile, at the beginning of the year, on the tenth day of the month, in the fourteenth year after the city was struck down, on that very day, the hand of the LORD was upon me, and he brought me there. 2He brought me, in visions of God, to the land of Israel, and set me down upon a very high mountain, on which was a structure like a city to the south. 3When he brought me there, a man was there, whose appearance shone like bronze, with a linen cord and a measuring reed in his hand; and he was standing in the gateway. 4The man said to me, "Mortal, look closely and listen attentively, and set your mind upon all that I shall show you, for you were brought here

---

a Or of the Abarim   *b* That is, *the Horde of Gog*
c Heb *travelers*   *d* That is *The Horde*   *e* Heb *chariots*
f Another reading is *They shall bear*

in order that I might show it to you; declare all that you see to the house of Israel."

5 Now there was a wall all around the outside of the temple area. The length of the measuring reed in the man's hand was six long cubits, each being a cubit and a handbreadth in length; so he measured the thickness of the wall, one reed; and the height, one reed. ⁶Then he went into the gateway facing east, going up its steps, and measured the threshold of the gate, one reed deep.^a There were ⁷recesses, and each recess was one reed wide and one reed deep; and the space between the recesses, five cubits; and the threshold of the gate by the vestibule of the gate at the inner end was one reed deep. ⁸Then he measured the inner vestibule of the gateway, one cubit. ⁹Then he measured the vestibule of the gateway, eight cubits; and its pilasters, two cubits; and the vestibule of the gate was at the inner end. ¹⁰There were three recesses on either side of the east gate; the three were of the same size; and the pilasters on either side were of the same size. ¹¹Then he measured the width of the opening of the gateway, ten cubits; and the width of the gateway, thirteen cubits. ¹²There was a barrier before the recesses, one cubit on either side; and the recesses were six cubits on either side. ¹³Then he measured the gate from the back^b of the one recess to the back^b of the other, a width of twenty-five cubits, from wall to wall.^c ¹⁴He measured^d also the vestibule, twenty cubits; and the gate next to the pilaster on every side of the court.^e ¹⁵From the front of the gate at the entrance to the end of the inner vestibule of the gate was fifty cubits. ¹⁶The recesses and their pilasters had windows, with shutters^e on the inside of the gateway all around, and the vestibules also had windows on the inside all around; and on the pilasters were palm trees.

17 Then he brought me into the outer court; there were chambers there, and a pavement, all around the court; thirty chambers fronted on the pavement. ¹⁸The pavement ran along the side of the gates, corresponding to the length of the gates; this was the lower pavement. ¹⁹Then he measured the distance from the inner front of^f the lower gate to the outer front of the inner court, one hundred cubits.^g

20 Then he measured the gate of the outer court that faced north—its depth and width. ²¹Its recesses, three on either side, and its pilasters and its vestibule were of the same size as those of the first gate; its depth was fifty cubits, and its width twenty-five cubits. ²²Its windows, its vestibule, and its palm trees were of the same size as those of the gate that faced toward the east. Seven steps led up to it; and its vestibule was on the inside.^h

²³Opposite the gate on the north, as on the east, was a gate to the inner court; he measured from gate to gate, one hundred cubits.

24 Then he led me toward the south, and there was a gate on the south; and he measured its pilasters and its vestibule; they had the same dimensions as the others. ²⁵There were windows all around in it and in its vestibule, like the windows of the others; its depth was fifty cubits, and its width twenty-five cubits. ²⁶There were seven steps leading up to it; its vestibule was on the inside.^h It had palm trees on its pilasters, one on either side. ²⁷There was a gate on the south of the inner court; and he measured from gate to gate toward the south, one hundred cubits.

28 Then he brought me to the inner court by the south gate, and he measured the south gate; it was of the same dimensions as the others. ²⁹Its recesses, its pilasters, and its vestibule were of the same size as the others; and there were windows all around in it and in its vestibule; its depth was fifty cubits, and its width twenty-five cubits. ³⁰There were vestibules all around, twenty-five cubits deep and five cubits wide. ³¹Its vestibule faced the outer court, and palm trees were on its pilasters, and its stairway had eight steps.

32 Then he brought me to the inner court on the east side, and he measured the gate; it was of the same size as the others. ³³Its recesses, its pilasters, and its vestibule were of the same

---

a Heb *deep, and one threshold, one reed deep*   b Gk: Heb *roof*
c Heb *opening facing opening*   d Heb *made*   e Meaning of Heb
uncertain   f Compare Gk: Heb *from before*   g Heb adds *the east
and the north*   h Gk: Heb *before them*

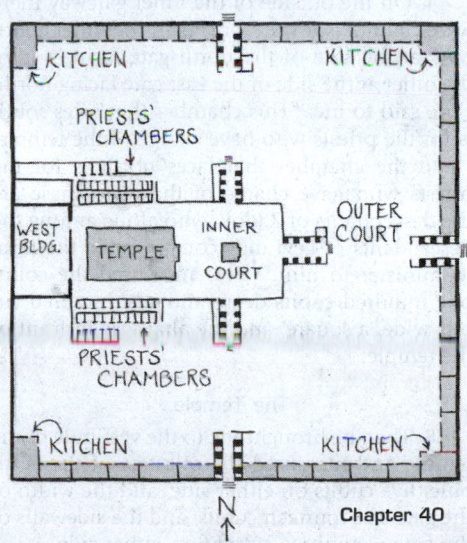

N

Chapter 40

E
Z
E
K

dimensions as the others; and there were windows all around in it and in its vestibule; its depth was fifty cubits, and its width twenty-five cubits. [34]Its vestibule faced the outer court, and it had palm trees on its pilasters, on either side; and its stairway had eight steps.

35 Then he brought me to the north gate, and he measured it; it had the same dimensions as the others. [36]Its recesses, its pilasters, and its vestibule were of the same size as the others;[a] and it had windows all around. Its depth was fifty cubits, and its width twenty-five cubits. [37]Its vestibule[b] faced the outer court, and it had palm trees on its pilasters, on either side; and its stairway had eight steps.

38 There was a chamber with its door in the vestibule of the gate,[c] where the burnt offering was to be washed. [39]And in the vestibule of the gate were two tables on either side, on which the burnt offering and the sin offering and the guilt offering were to be slaughtered. [40]On the outside of the vestibule[d] at the entrance of the north gate were two tables; and on the other side of the vestibule of the gate were two tables. [41]Four tables were on the inside, and four tables on the outside of the side of the gate, eight tables, on which the sacrifices were to be slaughtered. [42]There were also four tables of hewn stone for the burnt offering, a cubit and a half long, and one cubit and a half wide, and one cubit high, on which the instruments were to be laid with which the burnt offerings and the sacrifices were slaughtered. [43]There were pegs, one handbreadth long, fastened all around the inside. And on the tables the flesh of the offering was to be laid.

44 On the outside of the inner gateway there were chambers for the singers in the inner court, one[e] at the side of the north gate facing south, the other at the side of the east gate facing north. [45]He said to me, "This chamber that faces south is for the priests who have charge of the temple, [46]and the chamber that faces north is for the priests who have charge of the altar; these are the descendants of Zadok, who alone among the descendants of Levi may come near to the Lord to minister to him." [47]He measured the court, one hundred cubits deep, and one hundred cubits wide, a square; and the altar was in front of the temple.

The Temple

48 Then he brought me to the vestibule of the temple and measured the pilasters of the vestibule, five cubits on either side; and the width of the gate was fourteen cubits; and the sidewalls of the gate were three cubits[f] on either side. [49]The depth of the vestibule was twenty cubits, and the width twelve[g] cubits; ten steps led up[h] to it; and there were pillars beside the pilasters on either side.

41 Then he brought me to the nave, and measured the pilasters; on each side six cubits was the width of the pilasters.[i] [2]The width of the entrance was ten cubits; and the sidewalls of the entrance were five cubits on either side. He measured the length of the nave, forty cubits, and its width, twenty cubits. [3]Then he went into the inner room and measured the pilasters of the entrance, two cubits; and the width of the entrance, six cubits; and the sidewalls[j] of the entrance, seven cubits. [4]He measured the depth of the room, twenty cubits, and its width, twenty cubits, beyond the nave. And he said to me, This is the most holy place.

5 Then he measured the wall of the temple, six cubits thick; and the width of the side chambers, four cubits, all around the temple. [6]The side chambers were in three stories, one over another, thirty in each story. There were offsets[k] all around the wall of the temple to serve as supports for the side chambers, so that they should not be supported by the wall of the temple. [7]The passageway[l] of the side chambers widened from story to story; for the structure was supplied with a stairway all around the temple. For this reason the structure became wider from story to story. One ascended from the bottom story to the uppermost story by way of the middle one. [8]I saw also that the temple had a raised platform all around; the foundations of the side chambers measured a full reed of six long cubits. [9]The thickness of the outer wall of the side chambers was five cubits; and the free space between the side chambers of the temple [10]and the chambers of the court was a width of twenty cubits all around the temple on every side. [11]The side chambers opened onto the area left free, one door toward the north, and another door toward the south; and the width of the part that was left free was five cubits all around.

12 The building that was facing the temple yard on the west side was seventy cubits wide; and the wall of the building was five cubits thick all around, and its depth ninety cubits.

13 Then he measured the temple, one hundred

a One Ms: Compare verses 29 and 33: MT lacks were of the same size as the others   b Gk Vg Compare verses 26, 31, 34: Heb pilasters   c Cn: Heb at the pilasters of the gates   d Cn: Heb to him who goes up   e Heb lacks one   f Gk: Heb and the width of the gate was three cubits   g Gk: Heb eleven   h Gk: Heb and by steps that went up   i Compare Gk: Heb tent   j Gk: Heb width   k Gk Compare 1 Kings 6.6: Heb they entered   l Cn: Heb it was surrounded

cubits deep; and the yard and the building with its walls, one hundred cubits deep; [14]also the width of the east front of the temple and the yard, one hundred cubits.

15 Then he measured the depth of the building facing the yard at the west, together with its galleries[a] on either side, one hundred cubits.

The nave of the temple and the inner room and the outer[b] vestibule [16]were paneled,[c] and, all around, all three had windows with recessed[d] frames. Facing the threshold the temple was paneled with wood all around, from the floor up to the windows (now the windows were covered), [17]to the space above the door, even to the inner room, and on the outside. And on all the walls all around in the inner room and the nave there was a pattern.[e] [18]It was formed of cherubim and palm trees, a palm tree between cherub and cherub. Each cherub had two faces: [19]a human face turned toward the palm tree on the one side, and the face of a young lion turned toward the palm tree on the other side. They were carved on the whole temple all around; [20]from the floor to the area above the door, cherubim and palm trees were carved on the wall.[f]

21 The doorposts of the nave were square. In front of the holy place was something resembling [22]an altar of wood, three cubits high, two cubits long, and two cubits wide;[g] its corners, its base,[h] and its walls were of wood. He said to me, "This is the table that stands before the LORD." [23]The nave and the holy place had each a double door. [24]The doors had two leaves apiece, two swinging leaves for each door. [25]On the doors of the nave were carved cherubim and palm trees, such as were carved on the walls; and there was a canopy of wood in front of the vestibule outside. [26]And there were recessed windows and palm trees on either side, on the sidewalls of the vestibule.[i]

The Holy Chambers and the Outer Wall

42 Then he led me out into the outer court, toward the north, and he brought me to the chambers that were opposite the temple yard and opposite the building on the north. [2]The length of the building that was on the north side[j] was[k] one hundred cubits, and the width fifty cubits. [3]Across the twenty cubits that belonged to the inner court, and facing the pavement that belonged to the outer court, the chambers rose[l] gallery[m] by gallery[m] in three stories. [4]In front of the chambers was a passage on the inner side, ten cubits wide and one hundred cubits deep,[n] and its[o] entrances were on the north. [5]Now the upper chambers were narrower, for the galleries[m] took more away from them than from the lower

and middle chambers in the building. [6]For they were in three stories, and they had no pillars like the pillars of the outer[p] court; for this reason the upper chambers were set back from the ground more than the lower and the middle ones. [7]There was a wall outside parallel to the chambers, toward the outer court, opposite the chambers, fifty cubits long. [8]For the chambers on the outer court were fifty cubits long, while those opposite the temple were one hundred cubits long. [9]At the foot of these chambers ran a passage that one entered from the east in order to enter them from the outer court. [10]The width of the passage[q] was fixed by the wall of the court.

On the south[r] also, opposite the vacant area and opposite the building, there were chambers [11]with a passage in front of them; they were similar to the chambers on the north, of the same length and width, with the same exits[s] and arrangements and doors. [12]So the entrances of the chambers to the south were entered through the entrance at the head of the corresponding passage, from the east, along the matching wall.[m]

13 Then he said to me, "The north chambers and the south chambers opposite the vacant area are the holy chambers, where the priests who approach the LORD shall eat the most holy offerings; there they shall deposit the most holy offerings—the grain offering, the sin offering, and the guilt offering—for the place is holy. [14]When the priests enter the holy place, they shall not go out of it into the outer court without laying there the vestments in which they minister, for these are holy; they shall put on other garments before they go near to the area open to the people."

15 When he had finished measuring the interior of the temple area, he led me out by the gate that faces east, and measured the temple area all around. [16]He measured the east side with the measuring reed, five hundred cubits by the measuring reed. [17]Then he turned and measured[t] the north side, five hundred cubits by the measuring reed. [18]Then he turned and measured[t] the south side, five hundred cubits by the measuring reed. [19]Then he turned to the west side and measured, five hundred cubits by the measuring reed. [20]He measured it on the four sides. It had a wall

a Cn: Meaning of Heb uncertain   b Gk: Heb of the court
c Gk: Heb the thresholds   d Cn Compare Gk 1 Kings 6.4:
Meaning of Heb uncertain   e Heb measures   f Cn Compare
verse 25: Heb and the wall   g Gk: Heb lacks two cubits wide
h Gk: Heb length   i Cn: Heb vestibule. And the side chambers
of the temple and the canopies   j Gk: Heb door   k Gk: Heb
before the length   l Heb lacks the chambers rose   m Meaning of
Heb uncertain   n Gk Syr: Heb a way of one cubit   o Heb their
p Gk: Heb lacks outer   q Heb lacks of the passage   r Gk: Heb
east   s Heb and all their exits   t Gk: Heb measuring reed all
around. He measured

around it, five hundred cubits long and five hundred cubits wide, to make a separation between the holy and the common.

The Divine Glory Returns to the Temple

43 Then he brought me to the gate, the gate facing east. [2]And there, the glory of the God of Israel was coming from the east; the sound was like the sound of mighty waters; and the earth shone with his glory. [3]The[a] vision I saw was like the vision that I had seen when he came to destroy the city, and[b] like the vision that I had seen by the river Chebar; and I fell upon my face. [4]As the glory of the Lord entered the temple by the gate facing east, [5]the spirit lifted me up, and brought me into the inner court; and the glory of the Lord filled the temple.

6 While the man was standing beside me, I heard someone speaking to me out of the temple. [7]He said to me: Mortal, this is the place of my throne and the place for the soles of my feet, where I will reside among the people of Israel forever. The house of Israel shall no more defile my holy name, neither they nor their kings, by their whoring, and by the corpses of their kings at their death.[c] [8]When they placed their threshold by my threshold and their doorposts beside my doorposts, with only a wall between me and them, they were defiling my holy name by their abominations that they committed; therefore I have consumed them in my anger. [9]Now let them put away their idolatry and the corpses of their kings far from me, and I will reside among them forever.

10 As for you, mortal, describe the temple to the house of Israel, and let them measure the pattern; and let them be ashamed of their iniquities. [11]When they are ashamed of all that they have done, make known to them the plan of the temple, its arrangement, its exits and its entrances, and its whole form—all its ordinances and its entire plan and all its laws; and write it down in their sight, so that they may observe and follow the entire plan and all its ordinances. [12]This is the law of the temple: the whole territory on the top of the mountain all around shall be most holy. This is the law of the temple.

The Altar

13 These are the dimensions of the altar by cubits (the cubit being one cubit and a handbreadth): its base shall be one cubit high,[d] and one cubit wide, with a rim of one span around its edge. This shall be the height of the altar: [14]From the base on the ground to the lower ledge, two cubits, with a width of one cubit; and from the smaller ledge to the larger ledge, four cubits, with a width of one cubit; [15]and the altar hearth, four cubits; and from the altar hearth projecting upward, four horns. [16]The altar hearth shall be square, twelve cubits long by twelve wide. [17]The ledge also shall be square, fourteen cubits long by fourteen wide, with a rim around it half a cubit wide, and its surrounding base, one cubit. Its steps shall face east.

18 Then he said to me: Mortal, thus says the Lord God: These are the ordinances for the altar: On the day when it is erected for offering burnt offerings upon it and for dashing blood against it, [19]you shall give to the levitical priests of the family of Zadok, who draw near to me to minister to me, says the Lord God, a bull for a sin offering. [20]And you shall take some of its blood, and put it on the four horns of the altar, and on the four corners of the ledge, and upon the rim all around; thus you shall purify it and make

God's Dwelling Place

Ezekiel's vision of God returning to the Temple in Ezekiel 43:1–5 completes the circle of his prophecy. Earlier, as described in chapter 10, he had a unique vision of God's glory leaving the Temple and coming to rest in Babylon. For Ezekiel, the Temple represents the heart of Israel's relationship with God, and it is important that God's presence will return to it. This probably explains why Ezekiel carefully records the specifics of the new Temple in the remaining chapters of his book—to help make it more real.

The early Christians learned from Jesus that God's presence isn't limited to the Temple. The good news is that God is present in every person! First Corinthians 3:16 says, "Do you not know that you are God's temple and that God's Spirit dwells in you?" The basis for our self-worth should be knowing that God's Spirit dwells within us. If that doesn't make us special, what will?

▶ Ezek 43:1–5

atonement for it. [21]You shall also take the bull of the sin offering, and it shall be burnt in the appointed place belonging to the temple, outside the sacred area.

22 On the second day you shall offer a male goat without blemish for a sin offering; and the altar shall be purified, as it was purified with the bull. [23]When you have finished purifying it, you shall offer a bull without blemish and a ram from the flock without blemish. [24]You shall present them before the Lord, and the priests shall throw salt on them and offer them up as a burnt offering to the Lord. [25]For seven days you shall provide daily a goat for a sin offering; also a bull and a ram from the flock, without blemish, shall be provided. [26]Seven days shall they make atonement for the altar and cleanse it, and so consecrate it. [27]When these days are over, then from the eighth day onward the priests shall offer upon the altar your burnt offerings and your offerings of well-being; and I will accept you, says the Lord God.

The Closed Gate

44 Then he brought me back to the outer gate of the sanctuary, which faces east; and it was shut. [2]The Lord said to me: This gate shall remain shut; it shall not be opened, and no one shall enter by it; for the Lord, the God of Israel, has entered by it; therefore it shall remain shut. [3]Only the prince, because he is a prince, may sit in it to eat food before the Lord; he shall enter by way of the vestibule of the gate, and shall go out by the same way.

Admission to the Temple

4 Then he brought me by way of the north gate to the front of the temple; and I looked, and lo! the glory of the Lord filled the temple of the Lord; and I fell upon my face. [5]The Lord said to me: Mortal, mark well, look closely, and listen attentively to all that I shall tell you concerning all the ordinances of the temple of the Lord and all its laws; and mark well those who may be admitted to[a] the temple and all those who are to be excluded from the sanctuary. [6]Say to the rebellious house,[b] to the house of Israel, Thus says the Lord God. O house of Israel, let there be an end to all your abominations [7]in admitting foreigners, uncircumcised in heart and flesh, to be in my sanctuary, profaning my temple when you offer to me my food, the fat and the blood. You[c] have broken my covenant with all your abominations. [8]And you have not kept charge of my sacred offerings; but you have appointed foreigners[d] to act for you in keeping my charge in my sanctuary.

9 Thus says the Lord God: No foreigner, uncircumcised in heart and flesh, of all the foreigners who are among the people of Israel, shall enter my sanctuary. [10]But the Levites who went far from me, going astray from me after their idols when Israel went astray, shall bear their punishment. [11]They shall be ministers in my sanctuary, having oversight at the gates of the temple, and serving in the temple; they shall slaughter the burnt offering and the sacrifice for the people, and they shall attend on them and serve them. [12]Because they ministered to them before their idols and made the house of Israel stumble into iniquity, therefore I have sworn concerning them, says the Lord God, that they shall bear their punishment. [13]They shall not come near to me, to serve me as priest, nor come near any of my sacred offerings, the things that are most sacred; but they shall bear their shame, and the consequences of the abominations that they have committed. [14]Yet I will appoint them to keep charge of the temple, to do all its chores, all that is to be done in it.

The Levitical Priests

15 But the levitical priests, the descendants of Zadok, who kept the charge of my sanctuary when the people of Israel went astray from me, shall come near to me to minister to me; and they shall attend me to offer me the fat and the blood, says the Lord God. [16]It is they who shall enter my sanctuary, it is they who shall approach my table, to minister to me, and they shall keep my charge. [17]When they enter the gates of the inner court, they shall wear linen vestments; they shall have nothing of wool on them, while they minister at the gates of the inner court, and within. [18]They shall have linen turbans on their heads, and linen undergarments on their loins; they shall not bind themselves with anything that causes sweat. [19]When they go out into the outer court to the people, they shall remove the vestments in which they have been ministering, and lay them in the holy chambers; and they shall put on other garments, so that they may not communicate holiness to the people with their vestments. [20]They shall not shave their heads or let their locks grow long; they shall only trim the hair of their heads. [21]No priest shall drink wine when he enters the inner court. [22]They shall not marry a widow, or a divorced woman, but only a virgin of the stock of the house of Israel, or a widow who is the widow of a priest. [23]They shall

---

a Cn: Heb *the entrance of*   b Gk: Heb lacks *house*   c Gk Syr Vg: Heb *They*   d Heb lacks *foreigners*

teach my people the difference between the holy and the common, and show them how to distinguish between the unclean and the clean. [24]In a controversy they shall act as judges, and they shall decide it according to my judgments. They shall keep my laws and my statutes regarding all my appointed festivals, and they shall keep my sabbaths holy. [25]They shall not defile themselves by going near to a dead person; for father or mother, however, and for son or daughter, and for brother or unmarried sister they may defile themselves. [26]After he has become clean, they shall count seven days for him. [27]On the day that he goes into the holy place, into the inner court, to minister in the holy place, he shall offer his sin offering, says the Lord GOD.

28 This shall be their inheritance: I am their inheritance; and you shall give them no holding in Israel; I am their holding. [29]They shall eat the grain offering, the sin offering, and the guilt offering; and every devoted thing in Israel shall be theirs. [30]The first of all the first fruits of all kinds, and every offering of all kinds from all your offerings, shall belong to the priests; you shall also give to the priests the first of your dough, in order that a blessing may rest on your house. [31]The priests shall not eat of anything, whether bird or animal, that died of itself or was torn by animals.

The Holy District

45 When you allot the land as an inheritance, you shall set aside for the LORD a portion of the land as a holy district, twenty-five thousand cubits long and twenty[a] thousand cubits wide; it shall be holy throughout its entire extent. [2]Of this, a square plot of five hundred by five hundred cubits shall be for the sanctuary, with fifty cubits for an open space around it. [3]In the holy district you shall measure off a section twenty-five thousand cubits long and ten thousand wide, in which shall be the sanctuary, the most holy place. [4]It shall be a holy portion of the land; it shall be for the priests, who minister in the sanctuary and approach the LORD to minister to him; and it shall be both a place for their houses and a holy place for the sanctuary. [5]Another section, twenty-five thousand cubits long and ten thousand cubits wide, shall be for the Levites who minister at the temple, as their holding for cities to live in.[b]

6 Alongside the portion set apart as the holy district you shall assign as a holding for the city an area five thousand cubits wide, and twenty-five thousand cubits long; it shall belong to the whole house of Israel.

7 And to the prince shall belong the land on both sides of the holy district and the holding of the city, alongside the holy district and the holding of the city, on the west and on the east, corresponding in length to one of the tribal portions, and extending from the western to the eastern boundary [8]of the land. It is to be his property in Israel. And my princes shall no longer oppress my people; but they shall let the house of Israel have the land according to their tribes.

9 Thus says the Lord GOD: Enough, O princes of Israel! Put away violence and oppression, and do what is just and right. Cease your evictions of my people, says the Lord GOD.

Weights and Measures

10 You shall have honest balances, an honest ephah, and an honest bath.[c] [11]The ephah and the bath shall be of the same measure, the bath containing one-tenth of a homer, and the ephah one-tenth of a homer; the homer shall be the standard measure. [12]The shekel shall be twenty gerahs. Twenty shekels, twenty-five shekels, and fifteen shekels shall make a mina for you.

Offerings

13 This is the offering that you shall make: one-sixth of an ephah from each homer of wheat, and one-sixth of an ephah from each homer of barley, [14]and as the fixed portion of oil,[d] one-tenth of a bath from each cor (the cor,[e] like the homer, contains ten baths); [15]and one sheep from every flock of two hundred, from the pastures of Israel. This is the offering for grain offerings, burnt offerings, and offerings of well-being, to make atonement for them, says the Lord GOD. [16]All the people of the land shall join with the prince in Israel in making this offering. [17]But this shall be the obligation of the prince regarding the burnt offerings, grain offerings, and drink offerings, at the festivals, the new moons, and the sabbaths, all the appointed festivals of the house of Israel: he shall provide the sin offerings, grain offerings, the burnt offerings, and the offerings of well-being, to make atonement for the house of Israel.

Festivals

18 Thus says the Lord GOD: In the first month, on the first day of the month, you shall take a young bull without blemish, and purify the sanctuary. [19]The priest shall take some of the blood

---

a Gk: Heb ten   b Gk: Heb as their holding, twenty chambers
c A Heb measure of volume   d Cn: Heb oil, the bath the oil
e Vg: Heb homer

of the sin offering and put it on the doorposts of the temple, the four corners of the ledge of the altar, and the posts of the gate of the inner court. [20]You shall do the same on the seventh day of the month for anyone who has sinned through error or ignorance; so you shall make atonement for the temple.

21 In the first month, on the fourteenth day of the month, you shall celebrate the festival of the passover, and for seven days unleavened bread shall be eaten. [22]On that day the prince shall provide for himself and all the people of the land a young bull for a sin offering. [23]And during the seven days of the festival he shall provide as a burnt offering to the LORD seven young bulls and seven rams without blemish, on each of the seven days; and a male goat daily for a sin offering. [24]He shall provide as a grain offering an ephah for each bull, an ephah for each ram, and a hin of oil to each ephah. [25]In the seventh month, on the fifteenth day of the month and for the seven days of the festival, he shall make the same provision for sin offerings, burnt offerings, and grain offerings, and for the oil.

Miscellaneous Regulations

46 Thus says the Lord GOD: The gate of the inner court that faces east shall remain closed on the six working days; but on the sabbath day it shall be opened and on the day of the new moon it shall be opened. [2]The prince shall enter by the vestibule of the gate from outside, and shall take his stand by the post of the gate. The priests shall offer his burnt offering and his offerings of well-being, and he shall bow down at the threshold of the gate. Then he shall go out, but the gate shall not be closed until evening. [3]The people of the land shall bow down at the entrance of that gate before the LORD on the sabbaths and on the new moons. [4]The burnt offering that the prince offers to the LORD on the sabbath day shall be six lambs without blemish and a ram without blemish; [5]and the grain offering with the ram shall be an ephah, and the grain offering with the lambs shall be as much as he wishes to give, together with a hin of oil to each ephah. [6]On the day of the new moon he shall offer a young bull without blemish, and six lambs and a ram, which shall be without blemish; [7]as a grain offering he shall provide an ephah with the bull and an ephah with the ram, and with the lambs as much as he wishes, together with a hin of oil to each ephah. [8]When the prince enters, he shall come in by the vestibule of the gate, and he shall go out by the same way.

9 When the people of the land come before the LORD at the appointed festivals, whoever enters by the north gate to worship shall go out by the south gate; and whoever enters by the south gate shall go out by the north gate: they shall not return by way of the gate by which they entered, but shall go out straight ahead. [10]When they come in, the prince shall come in with them; and when they go out, he shall go out.

11 At the festivals and the appointed seasons the grain offering with a young bull shall be an ephah, and with a ram an ephah, and with the lambs as much as one wishes to give, together with a hin of oil to an ephah. [12]When the prince provides a freewill offering, either a burnt offering or offerings of well-being as a freewill offering to the LORD, the gate facing east shall be opened for him; and he shall offer his burnt offering or his offerings of well-being as he does on the sabbath day. Then he shall go out, and after he has gone out the gate shall be closed.

13 He shall provide a lamb, a yearling, without blemish, for a burnt offering to the LORD daily; morning by morning he shall provide it. [14]And he shall provide a grain offering with it morning by morning regularly, one-sixth of an ephah, and one-third of a hin of oil to moisten the choice flour, as a grain offering to the LORD; this is the ordinance for all time. [15]Thus the lamb and the grain offering and the oil shall be provided, morning by morning, as a regular burnt offering.

16 Thus says the Lord GOD: If the prince makes a gift to any of his sons out of his inheritance,[a] it shall belong to his sons, it is their holding by inheritance. [17]But if he makes a gift out of his inheritance to one of his servants, it shall be his to the year of liberty; then it shall revert to the prince; only his sons may keep a gift from his inheritance. [18]The prince shall not take any of the inheritance of the people, thrusting them out of their holding; he shall give his sons their inheritance out of his own holding, so that none of my people shall be dispossessed of their holding.

19 Then he brought me through the entrance, which was at the side of the gate, to the north row of the holy chambers for the priests; and there I saw a place at the extreme western end of them. [20]He said to me, "This is the place where the priests shall boil the guilt offering and the sin offering, and where they shall bake the grain offering, in order not to bring them out into the outer court and so communicate holiness to the people."

21 Then he brought me out to the outer court, and led me past the four corners of the court; and

---

a Gk: Heb it is his inheritance

in each corner of the court there was a court—²²in the four corners of the court were small[a] courts, forty cubits long and thirty wide; the four were of the same size. ²³On the inside, around each of the four courts[b] was a row of masonry, with hearths made at the bottom of the rows all around. ²⁴Then he said to me, "These are the kitchens where those who serve at the temple shall boil the sacrifices of the people."

Water Flowing from the Temple

47 Then he brought me back to the entrance of the temple; there, water was flowing from below the threshold of the temple toward the east (for the temple faced east); and the water was flowing down from below the south end of the threshold of the temple, south of the altar. ²Then he brought me out by way of the north gate, and led me around on the outside to the outer gate that faces toward the east;[c] and the water was coming out on the south side.

3 Going on eastward with a cord in his hand, the man measured one thousand cubits, and then led me through the water; and it was ankle-deep. ⁴Again he measured one thousand, and led me through the water; and it was knee-deep. Again he measured one thousand, and led me through the water; and it was up to the waist. ⁵Again he measured one thousand, and it was a river that I could not cross, for the water had risen; it was deep enough to swim in, a river that could not be crossed. ⁶He said to me, "Mortal, have you seen this?"

Then he led me back along the bank of the river. ⁷As I came back, I saw on the bank of the river a great many trees on the one side and on the other. ⁸He said to me, "This water flows toward the eastern region and goes down into the Arabah; and when it enters the sea, the sea of stagnant waters, the water will become fresh. ⁹Wherever the river goes,[d] every living creature that swarms will live, and there will be very many fish, once these waters reach there. It will become fresh; and everything will live where the river goes. ¹⁰People will stand fishing beside the sea[e] from En-gedi to En-eglaim; it will be a place for the spreading of nets; its fish will be of a great many kinds, like the fish of the Great Sea. ¹¹But its swamps and marshes will not become fresh; they are to be left for salt. ¹²On the banks, on both sides of the river, there will grow all kinds of trees for food. Their leaves will not wither nor their fruit fail, but they will bear fresh fruit every month, because the water for them flows from the sanctuary. Their fruit will be for food, and their leaves for healing."

The New Boundaries of the Land

13 Thus says the Lord God: These are the boundaries by which you shall divide the land for inheritance among the twelve tribes of Israel. Joseph shall have two portions. ¹⁴You shall divide it equally; I swore to give it to your ancestors, and this land shall fall to you as your inheritance.

15 This shall be the boundary of the land: On the north side, from the Great Sea by way of Hethlon to Lebo-hamath, and on to Zedad,[f] ¹⁶Berothah, Sibraim (which lies between the border of Damascus and the border of Hamath), as far as Hazer-hatticon, which is on the border of Hauran. ¹⁷So the boundary shall run from the sea to Hazar-enon, which is north of the border of Damascus, with the border of Hamath to the north.[c] This shall be the north side.

18 On the east side, between Hauran and Damascus; along the Jordan between Gilead and the land of Israel; to the eastern sea and as far as Tamar.[g] This shall be the east side.

19 On the south side, it shall run from Tamar as far as the waters of Meribath-kadesh, from there along the Wadi of Egypt[h] to the Great Sea. This shall be the south side.

20 On the west side, the Great Sea shall be the boundary to a point opposite Lebo-hamath. This shall be the west side.

21 So you shall divide this land among you according to the tribes of Israel. ²²You shall allot it as an inheritance for yourselves and for the aliens who reside among you and have begotten children among you. They shall be to you as citizens of Israel; with you they shall be allotted an inheritance among the tribes of Israel. ²³In whatever tribe aliens reside, there you shall assign them their inheritance, says the Lord God.

The Tribal Portions

48 These are the names of the tribes: Beginning at the northern border, on the Hethlon road,[i] from Lebo-hamath, as far as Hazar-enon (which is on the border of Damascus, with Hamath to the north), and[j] extending from the east side to the west,[k] Dan, one portion. ²Adjoining the territory of Dan, from the east side to the west, Asher, one portion. ³Adjoining the territory of Asher, from the east side

---

a Gk Syr Vg: Meaning of Heb uncertain　b Heb *the four of them* c Meaning of Heb uncertain　d Gk Syr Vg Tg: Heb *the two rivers go*　e Heb *it*　f Gk: Heb *Lebo-zedad*, ¹⁶*Hamath*　g Compare Syr: Heb *you shall measure*　h Heb lacks *of Egypt*　i Compare 47.15: Heb *by the side of the way*　j Cn: Heb *and they shall be his*　k Gk Compare verses 2-8: Heb *the east side the west*

to the west, Naphtali, one portion. [4]Adjoining the territory of Naphtali, from the east side to the west, Manasseh, one portion. [5]Adjoining the territory of Manasseh, from the east side to the west, Ephraim, one portion. [6]Adjoining the territory of Ephraim, from the east side to the west, Reuben, one portion. [7]Adjoining the territory of Reuben, from the east side to the west, Judah, one portion.

8 Adjoining the territory of Judah, from the east side to the west, shall be the portion that you shall set apart, twenty-five thousand cubits in width, and in length equal to one of the tribal portions, from the east side to the west, with the sanctuary in the middle of it. [9]The portion that you shall set apart for the LORD shall be twenty-five thousand cubits in length, and twenty[a] thousand in width. [10]These shall be the allotments of the holy portion: the priests shall have an allotment measuring twenty-five thousand cubits on the northern side, ten thousand cubits in width on the western side, ten thousand in width on the eastern side, and twenty-five thousand in length on the southern side, with the sanctuary of the LORD in the middle of it. [11]This shall be for the consecrated priests, the descendants[b] of Zadok, who kept my charge, who did not go astray when the people of Israel went astray, as the Levites did. [12]It shall belong to them as a special portion from the holy portion of the land, a most holy place, adjoining the territory of the Levites. [13]Alongside the territory of the priests, the Levites shall have an allotment twenty-five thousand cubits in length and ten thousand in width. The whole length shall be twenty-five thousand cubits and the width twenty[c] thousand. [14]They shall not sell or exchange any of it; they shall not transfer this choice portion of the land, for it is holy to the LORD.

15 The remainder, five thousand cubits in width and twenty-five thousand in length, shall be for ordinary use for the city, for dwellings and for open country. In the middle of it shall be the city; [16]and these shall be its dimensions: the north side four thousand five hundred cubits, the south side four thousand five hundred, the east side four thousand five hundred, and the west side four thousand five hundred. [17]The city shall have open land: on the north two hundred fifty cubits, on the south two hundred fifty, on the east two hundred fifty, on the west two hundred fifty. [18]The remainder of the length alongside the holy portion shall be ten thousand cubits to the east, and ten thousand to the west, and it shall be alongside the holy portion. Its produce shall be food for the workers of the city. [19]The workers

of the city, from all the tribes of Israel, shall cultivate it. [20]The whole portion that you shall set apart shall be twenty-five thousand cubits square, that is, the holy portion together with the property of the city.

21 What remains on both sides of the holy portion and of the property of the city shall belong to the prince. Extending from the twenty-five thousand cubits of the holy portion to the east border, and westward from the twenty-five thousand cubits to the west border, parallel to the tribal portions, it shall belong to the prince. The holy portion with the sanctuary of the temple in the middle of it, [22]and the property of the Levites and of the city, shall be in the middle of that which belongs to the prince. The portion of the prince shall lie between the territory of Judah and the territory of Benjamin.

23 As for the rest of the tribes: from the east side to the west, Benjamin, one portion. [24]Adjoining the territory of Benjamin, from the east side to the west, Simeon, one portion. [25]Adjoining the territory of Simeon, from the east side to the west, Issachar, one portion. [26]Adjoining the territory of Issachar, from the east side to the west, Zebulun, one portion. [27]Adjoining the territory of Zebulun, from the east side to the west, Gad, one portion. [28]And adjoining the territory of Gad to the south, the boundary shall run from Tamar to the waters of Meribath-kadesh, from there along the Wadi of Egypt[d] to the Great Sea. [29]This is the land that you shall allot as an inheritance among the tribes of Israel, and these are their portions, says the Lord GOD.

30 These shall be the exits of the city: On the north side, which is to be four thousand five hundred cubits by measure, [31]three gates, the gate of Reuben, the gate of Judah, and the gate of Levi, the gates of the city being named after the tribes of Israel. [32]On the east side, which is to be four thousand five hundred cubits, three gates, the gate of Joseph, the gate of Benjamin, and the gate of Dan. [33]On the south side, which is to be four thousand five hundred cubits by measure, three gates, the gate of Simeon, the gate of Issachar, and the gate of Zebulun. [34]On the west side, which is to be four thousand five hundred cubits, three gates,[e] the gate of Gad, the gate of Asher, and the gate of Naphtali. [35]The circumference of the city shall be eighteen thousand cubits. And the name of the city from that time on shall be, The LORD is There.

---

a Compare 45.1: Heb *ten*   b One Ms Gk: Heb *of the descendants*   c Gk: Heb *ten*   d Heb lacks *of Egypt*   e One Ms Gk Syr: MT *their gates three*

Do you have a favorite superhero from television or comic books? One characteristic of these larger-than-life heroes is their commitment to their own values and to saving victims of injustice. The Book of Daniel portrays just such a hero. Daniel's powers are his courage to remain faithful to God despite the threat of punishment, and his special visions, which foresee how things will turn out good even though the present situation seems far from hopeful. These powers enable him to lead his people on the right path in a foreign land filled with persecution and idolatry.

At a Glance

■ Chapters 1–6. stories of Daniel at the Babylonian court

■ Chapters 7–12. apocalyptic visions of Daniel

■ Chapters 13–14. stories about Daniel that were added later

Quick Facts

Period Covered: from the Babylonian Exile in the sixth century to the second century BC

Inspired Author: unknown, writing around 164 BC, during the persecution of Israel by Antiochus IV Epiphanes

Theme: God's reign will ultimately triumph; hope for those experiencing oppression and persecution

In Depth

Daniel represents the ideal leader with the spiritual and prophetic insight to lead people through troubled times. Scholars question whether he was an actual person. If he was, he lived in the sixth century BC—but the Book of Daniel was written four hundred years later, during the reign of an evil Greek-Syrian king, Antiochus IV Epiphanes. This was also the time of the Maccabean revolt told about in First and Second Maccabees (see the timeline at the back of this Bible). King Antiochus desecrated the Temple and attempted to erase many of Israel's religious practices. To many in Israel, this seemed like the end of the world.

The author of the Book of Daniel writes about the great hero Daniel to give the people hope during this persecution. Chapters 1–6 present six stories of Daniel and three friends living their faith during the Babylonian Exile. Chapters 7–12 tell of Daniel's four visions about the empires that dominated Israel after the Exile: Media, Persia, and Greece. The visions are full of strange symbols meant to be understood by the Israelites but not the Greek rulers of the author's time.

As you read the Book of Daniel, you will find themes familiar from other biblical books. Like Baruch, it describes living faithfully in a strange land. Like First and Second Maccabees, the book shows the courage of Israelites willing to die for their beliefs. And it declares even more clearly than Second Maccabees and Wisdom of Solomon the belief in life after death. Daniel is shown as the ideal Jew—the embodiment of all the best of the people in exile. In the face of unjust persecution and oppression, he leads his people in faithfulness to God, even through death itself.

Daniel

Four Young Israelites at the Babylonian Court

1 In the third year of the reign of King Jehoiakim of Judah, King Nebuchadnezzar of Babylon came to Jerusalem and besieged it. ²The Lord let King Jehoiakim of Judah fall into his power, as well as some of the vessels of the house of God. These he brought to the land of Shinar,ᵃ and placed the vessels in the treasury of his gods.

3 Then the king commanded his palace master Ashpenaz to bring some of the Israelites of the royal family and of the nobility, ⁴young men without physical defect and handsome, versed in every branch of wisdom, endowed with knowledge and insight, and competent to serve in the king's palace; they were to be taught the literature and language of the Chaldeans. ⁵The king assigned them a daily portion of the royal rations of food and wine. They were to be educated for three years, so that at the end of that time they could be stationed in the king's court. ⁶Among them were Daniel, Hananiah, Mishael, and Azariah, from the tribe of Judah. ⁷The palace master gave them other names: Daniel he called Belteshazzar, Hananiah he called Shadrach, Mishael he called Meshach, and Azariah he called Abednego.

8 But Daniel resolved that he would not defile himself with the royal rations of food and wine; so he asked the palace master to allow him not to defile himself. ⁹Now God allowed Daniel to receive favor and compassion from the palace master. ¹⁰The palace master said to Daniel, "I am afraid of my lord the king; he has appointed your food and your drink. If he should see you in poorer condition than the other young men of your own age, you would endanger my head with the king." ¹¹Then Daniel asked the guard whom the palace master had appointed over Daniel, Hananiah, Mishael, and Azariah: ¹²"Please test your servants for ten days. Let us be given vegetables to eat and water to drink. ¹³You can then compare our appearance with the appearance of the young men who eat the royal rations, and deal with your servants according to what you observe." ¹⁴So he agreed to this proposal and tested them for ten days. ¹⁵At the end of ten days it was observed that they appeared better and fatter than all the young men who had been eating the royal rations. ¹⁶So the guard continued to withdraw their royal rations and the wine they were to drink, and gave them vegetables. ¹⁷To these four young men God gave knowledge and skill in every aspect of literature and wisdom; Daniel also had insight into all visions and dreams.

18 At the end of the time that the king had set for them to be brought in, the palace master brought them into the presence of Nebuchadnezzar, ¹⁹and the king spoke with them. And among them all, no one was found to compare with Daniel, Hananiah, Mishael, and Azariah; therefore they were stationed in the king's court. ²⁰In every matter of wisdom and understanding concerning which the king inquired of them, he found them ten times better than all the magicians and

ᵃ Gk Theodotion: Heb adds *to the house of his own gods*

enchanters in his whole kingdom. ²¹And Daniel continued there until the first year of King Cyrus.

Nebuchadnezzar's Dream

2 In the second year of Nebuchadnezzar's reign, Nebuchadnezzar dreamed such dreams that his spirit was troubled and his sleep left him. ²So the king commanded that the magicians, the enchanters, the sorcerers, and the Chaldeans be summoned to tell the king his dreams. When they came in and stood before the king, ³he said to them, "I have had such a dream that my spirit is troubled by the desire to understand it." ⁴The Chaldeans said to the king (in Aramaic),ᵃ "O king, live forever! Tell your servants the dream, and we will reveal the interpretation." ⁵The king answered the Chaldeans, "This is a public decree: if you do not tell me both the dream and its interpretation, you shall be torn limb from limb, and your houses shall be laid in ruins. ⁶But if you do tell me the dream and its interpretation, you shall receive from me gifts and rewards and great honor. Therefore tell me the dream and its interpretation." ⁷They answered a second time, "Let the king first tell his servants the dream, then we can give its interpretation." ⁸The king answered, "I know with certainty that you are trying to gain time, because you see I have firmly decreed: ⁹if you do not tell me the dream, there is but one verdict for you. You have agreed to speak lying and misleading words to me until things take a turn. Therefore, tell me the dream, and I shall know that you can give me its interpretation." ¹⁰The Chaldeans answered the king, "There is no one on earth who can reveal what the king demands! In fact no king, however great and powerful, has ever asked such a thing of any magician or enchanter or Chaldean. ¹¹The thing that the king is asking is too difficult, and no one can reveal it to the king except the gods, whose dwelling is not with mortals."

12 Because of this the king flew into a violent rage and commanded that all the wise men of Babylon be destroyed. ¹³The decree was issued, and the wise men were about to be executed; and they looked for Daniel and his companions, to execute them. ¹⁴Then Daniel responded with prudence and discretion to Arioch, the king's chief executioner, who had gone out to execute the wise men of Babylon; ¹⁵he asked Arioch, the royal official, "Why is the decree of the king so urgent?" Arioch then explained the matter to Daniel. ¹⁶So Daniel went in and requested that the king give him time and he would tell the king the interpretation.

God Reveals Nebuchadnezzar's Dream

17 Then Daniel went to his home and informed his companions, Hananiah, Mishael, and Azariah, ¹⁸and told them to seek mercy from the God of heaven concerning this mystery, so that Daniel and his companions with the rest of the wise men of Babylon might not perish. ¹⁹Then the mystery was revealed to Daniel in a vision of the night, and Daniel blessed the God of heaven.

²⁰ Daniel said:

"Blessed be the name of God from age to age,
    for wisdom and power are his.
²¹ He changes times and seasons,
    deposes kings and sets up kings;
he gives wisdom to the wise
    and knowledge to those who have
        understanding.
²² He reveals deep and hidden things;
    he knows what is in the darkness,
    and light dwells with him.
²³ To you, O God of my ancestors,
    I give thanks and praise,
for you have given me wisdom and power,
    and have now revealed to me what we asked
        of you,
    for you have revealed to us what the king
        ordered."

Daniel Interprets the Dream

24 Therefore Daniel went to Arioch, whom the king had appointed to destroy the wise men of Babylon, and said to him, "Do not destroy the wise men of Babylon; bring me in before the king, and I will give the king the interpretation."

25 Then Arioch quickly brought Daniel before the king and said to him: "I have found among the exiles from Judah a man who can tell the king the interpretation." ²⁶The king said to Daniel, whose name was Belteshazzar, "Are you able to tell me the dream that I have seen and its interpretation?" ²⁷Daniel answered the king, "No wise men, enchanters, magicians, or diviners can show to the king the mystery that the king is asking, ²⁸but there is a God in heaven who reveals mysteries, and he has disclosed to King Nebuchadnezzar what will happen at the end of days. Your dream and the visions of your head as you lay in bed were these: ²⁹To you, O king, as you lay in bed, came thoughts of what would be hereafter, and the revealer of mysteries disclosed to you what is to be. ³⁰But as for me, this mystery

---

a The text from this point to the end of chapter 7 is in Aramaic, except for 3.24-91a, the text of which is in Greek

has not been revealed to me because of any wisdom that I have more than any other living being, but in order that the interpretation may be known to the king and that you may understand the thoughts of your mind.

31 "You were looking, O king, and lo! there was a great statue. This statue was huge, its brilliance extraordinary; it was standing before you, and its appearance was frightening. ³²The head of that statue was of fine gold, its chest and arms of silver, its middle and thighs of bronze, ³³its legs of iron, its feet partly of iron and partly of clay. ³⁴As you looked on, a stone was cut out, not by human hands, and it struck the statue on its feet of iron and clay and broke them in pieces. ³⁵Then the iron, the clay, the bronze, the silver, and the gold, were all broken in pieces and became like the chaff of the summer threshing floors; and the wind carried them away, so that not a trace of them could be found. But the stone that struck the statue became a great mountain and filled the whole earth.

36 "This was the dream; now we will tell the king its interpretation. ³⁷You, O king, the king of kings—to whom the God of heaven has given the kingdom, the power, the might, and the glory, ³⁸into whose hand he has given human beings, wherever they live, the wild animals of the field, and the birds of the air, and whom he has established as ruler over them all—you are the head of gold. ³⁹After you shall arise another kingdom inferior to yours, and yet a third kingdom of bronze, which shall rule over the whole earth. ⁴⁰And there shall be a fourth kingdom, strong as iron; just as iron crushes and smashes everything,ᵃ it shall crush and shatter all these. ⁴¹As you saw the feet and toes partly of potter's clay and partly of iron, it shall be a divided kingdom; but some of the strength of iron shall be in it, as you saw the iron mixed with the clay. ⁴²As the toes of the feet were part iron and part clay, so the kingdom shall be partly strong and partly brittle. ⁴³As you saw the iron mixed with clay, so will they mix with one another in marriage,ᵇ but they will not hold together, just as iron does not mix with clay. ⁴⁴And in the days of those kings the God of heaven will set up a kingdom that shall never be destroyed, nor shall this kingdom be left to another people. It shall crush all these kingdoms and bring them to an end, and it shall stand forever; ⁴⁵just as you saw that a stone was cut from the mountain not by hands, and that it crushed the iron, the bronze, the clay, the silver, and the gold. The great God has informed the king what shall be hereafter. The dream is certain, and its interpretation trustworthy."

Daniel and His Friends Promoted

46 Then King Nebuchadnezzar fell on his face, worshiped Daniel, and commanded that a grain offering and incense be offered to him. ⁴⁷The king said to Daniel, "Truly, your God is God of gods and Lord of kings and a revealer of mysteries, for you have been able to reveal this mystery!" ⁴⁸Then the king promoted Daniel, gave him many great gifts, and made him ruler over the whole province of Babylon and chief prefect over all the wise men of Babylon. ⁴⁹Daniel made a request of the king, and he appointed Shadrach, Meshach, and Abednego over the affairs of the province of Babylon. But Daniel remained at the king's court.

The Golden Image

3 King Nebuchadnezzar made a golden statue whose height was sixty cubits and whose width was six cubits; he set it up on the plain of Dura in the province of Babylon. ²Then King Nebuchadnezzar sent for the satraps, the prefects, and the governors, the counselors, the treasurers, the justices, the magistrates, and all the officials of the provinces, to assemble and come to the dedication of the statue that King Nebuchadnezzar had set up. ³So the satraps, the prefects, and the governors, the counselors, the treasurers, the justices, the magistrates, and all the officials of the provinces, assembled for the dedication of the statue that King Nebuchadnezzar had set up. When they were standing before the statue that Nebuchadnezzar had set up, ⁴the herald proclaimed aloud, "You are commanded, O peoples, nations, and languages, ⁵that when you hear the sound of the horn, pipe, lyre, trigon, harp, drum, and entire musical ensemble, you are to fall down and worship the golden statue that King Nebuchadnezzar has set up. ⁶Whoever does not fall down and worship shall immediately be thrown into a furnace of blazing fire." ⁷Therefore, as soon as all the peoples heard the sound of the horn, pipe, lyre, trigon, harp, drum, and entire musical ensemble, all the peoples, nations, and languages fell down and worshiped the golden statue that King Nebuchadnezzar had set up.

8 Accordingly, at this time certain Chaldeans came forward and denounced the Jews. ⁹They said to King Nebuchadnezzar, "O king, live forever! ¹⁰You, O king, have made a decree, that everyone who hears the sound of the horn, pipe, lyre, trigon, harp, drum, and entire

ᵃ Gk Theodotion Syr Vg: Aram adds *and like iron that crushes*
ᵇ Aram *by human seed*

Doing the Right Thing

Chapter 3 of Daniel tells us of Shadrach, Meshach, and Abednego, three companions of Daniel's who refuse to compromise their religious beliefs. Even in the face of death, they will not denounce the Lord and worship the god of Nebuchadnezzar (also called Nebuchadrezzar).

The pressure to do what we know is wrong takes many forms. For teens in particular, numerous temptations—drugs, alcohol, sex, shoplifting, and many more—can create an overwhelming amount of pressure in their lives. Caving in to that pressure typically leads people to suffering, because by definition, sin leads to unhappy and unhealthy consequences. It may offer some short-term satisfaction, but denying what we know is right is ultimately denying God and the fullness of life God has planned for us.

Follow Shadrach, Meshach, and Abednego's example and stand up for what is right. Stand up for God!

▶ Dan 3:1–24

musical ensemble, shall fall down and worship the golden statue, 11and whoever does not fall down and worship shall be thrown into a furnace of blazing fire. 12There are certain Jews whom you have appointed over the affairs of the province of Babylon: Shadrach, Meshach, and Abednego. These pay no heed to you, O king. They do not serve your gods and they do not worship the golden statue that you have set up."

13 Then Nebuchadnezzar in furious rage commanded that Shadrach, Meshach, and Abednego be brought in; so they brought those men before the king. 14Nebuchadnezzar said to them, "Is it true, O Shadrach, Meshach, and Abednego, that you do not serve my gods and you do not worship the golden statue that I have set up? 15Now if you are ready when you hear the sound of the horn, pipe, lyre, trigon, harp, drum, and entire musical ensemble to fall down and worship the statue that I have made, well and good.*a* But if you do not worship, you shall immediately be thrown into a furnace of blazing fire, and who is the god that will deliver you out of my hands?"

16 Shadrach, Meshach, and Abednego answered the king, "O Nebuchadnezzar, we have no need to present a defense to you in this matter. 17If our God whom we serve is able to deliver us from the furnace of blazing fire and out of your hand, O king, let him deliver us.*b* 18But if not, be it known to you, O king, that we will not serve your gods and we will not worship the golden statue that you have set up."

The Fiery Furnace

19 Then Nebuchadnezzar was so filled with rage against Shadrach, Meshach, and Abednego that his face was distorted. He ordered the furnace heated up seven times more than was customary, 20and ordered some of the strongest guards in his army to bind Shadrach, Meshach, and Abednego and to throw them into the furnace of blazing fire. 21So the men were bound, still wearing their tunics,*c* their trousers,*c* their hats, and their other garments, and they were thrown into the furnace of blazing fire. 22Because the king's command was urgent and the furnace was so overheated, the raging flames killed the men who lifted Shadrach, Meshach, and Abednego. 23But the three men, Shadrach, Meshach, and Abednego, fell down, bound, into the furnace of blazing fire.

The Prayer of Azariah in the Furnace

24 They walked around in the midst of the flames, singing hymns to God and blessing the Lord. 25Then Azariah stood still in the fire and prayed aloud:

26 "Blessed are you, O Lord, God of our ancestors,
　　and worthy of praise;
　　and glorious is your name forever!
27 For you are just in all you have done;
　　all your works are true and your ways right,
　　and all your judgments are true.
28 You have executed true judgments in all you
　　have brought upon us
　　and upon Jerusalem, the holy city of our
　　ancestors;
　　by a true judgment you have brought all this
　　upon us because of our sins.
29 For we have sinned and broken your law in
　　turning away from you;
　　in all matters we have sinned grievously.
30 We have not obeyed your commandments,
　　we have not kept them or done what you
　　have commanded us for our own good.

a Aram lacks *well and good*　*b* Or *If our God whom we serve is able to deliver us, he will deliver us from the furnace of blazing fire and out of your hand, O king.*　*c* Meaning of Aram word uncertain

31 So all that you have brought upon us,
   and all that you have done to us,
   you have done by a true judgment.

32 You have handed us over to our enemies,
   lawless and hateful rebels,
   and to an unjust king, the most wicked in all
     the world.

33 And now we cannot open our mouths;
   we, your servants who worship you, have
     become a shame and a reproach.

34 For your name's sake do not give us up forever,
   and do not annul your covenant.

35   Do not withdraw your mercy from us,
   for the sake of Abraham your beloved
   and for the sake of your servant Isaac
   and Israel your holy one,

36 to whom you promised
   to multiply their descendants like the stars of
     heaven
   and like the sand on the shore of the sea.

37 For we, O Lord, have become fewer than any
     other nation,
   and are brought low this day in all the world
     because of our sins.

38 In our day we have no ruler, or prophet, or
     leader,
   no burnt offering, or sacrifice, or oblation, or
     incense,
   no place to make an offering before you and
     to find mercy.

39 Yet with a contrite heart and a humble spirit
     may we be accepted,

40   as though it were with burnt offerings of rams
     and bulls,
   or with tens of thousands of fat lambs;
   such may our sacrifice be in your sight
     today,
   and may we unreservedly follow you,[a]
   for no shame will come to those who trust in
     you.

41 And now with all our heart we follow you;
   we fear you and seek your presence.

42 Do not put us to shame,
   but deal with us in your patience
   and in your abundant mercy.

43 Deliver us in accordance with your marvelous
     works,
   and bring glory to your name, O Lord.

44 Let all who do harm to your servants be put to
     shame;
   let them be disgraced and deprived of all
     power,
   and let their strength be broken.

45 Let them know that you alone are the Lord
     God,
   glorious over the whole world."

The Song of the Three Jews

46 Now the king's servants who threw them in kept stoking the furnace with naphtha, pitch, tow, and brushwood. 47 And the flames poured out above the furnace forty-nine cubits, 48 and spread out and burned those Chaldeans who were caught near the furnace. 49 But the angel of the Lord came down into the furnace to be with Azariah and his companions, and drove the fiery flame out of the furnace, 50 and made the inside of the furnace as though a moist wind were whistling through it. The fire did not touch them at all and caused them no pain or distress.

51 Then the three with one voice praised and glorified and blessed God in the furnace:

52 "Blessed are you, O Lord, God of our ancestors,
   and to be praised and highly exalted forever;
  And blessed is your glorious, holy name,
   and to be highly praised and highly exalted
     forever.

53 Blessed are you in the temple of your holy glory,
   and to be extolled and highly glorified
     forever.

54 Blessed are you who look into the depths from
     your throne on the cherubim,
   and to be praised and highly exalted forever.

55 Blessed are you on the throne of your kingdom,
   and to be extolled and highly exalted forever.

56 Blessed are you in the firmament of heaven,
   and to be sung and glorified forever.

57 "Bless the Lord, all you works of the Lord;
   sing praise to him and highly exalt him
     forever.

58 Bless the Lord, you heavens;
   sing praise to him and highly exalt him
     forever.

59 Bless the Lord, you angels of the Lord;
   sing praise to him and highly exalt him
     forever.

60 Bless the Lord, all you waters above the heavens;
   sing praise to him and highly exalt him
     forever.

61 Bless the Lord, all you powers of the Lord;
   sing praise to him and highly exalt him
     forever.

62 Bless the Lord, sun and moon;
   sing praise to him and highly exalt him
     forever.

63 Bless the Lord, stars of heaven;
   sing praise to him and highly exalt him
     forever.

---

a Meaning of Gk uncertain

64 "Bless the Lord, all rain and dew;
 sing praise to him and highly exalt him
  forever.
65 Bless the Lord, all you winds;
 sing praise to him and highly exalt him
  forever.
66 Bless the Lord, fire and heat;
 sing praise to him and highly exalt him
  forever.
67 Bless the Lord, winter cold and summer heat;
 sing praise to him and highly exalt him
  forever.
68 Bless the Lord, dews and falling snow;
 sing praise to him and highly exalt him
  forever.
69 Bless the Lord, ice and cold;
 sing praise to him and highly exalt him
  forever.
70 Bless the Lord, frosts and snows;
 sing praise to him and highly exalt him
  forever.
71 Bless the Lord, nights and days;
 sing praise to him and highly exalt him
  forever.
72 Bless the Lord, light and darkness;
 sing praise to him and highly exalt him
  forever.
73 Bless the Lord, lightnings and clouds;
 sing praise to him and highly exalt him
  forever.

74 "Let the earth bless the Lord;
 let it sing praise to him and highly exalt him
  forever.
75 Bless the Lord, mountains and hills;
 sing praise to him and highly exalt him
  forever.
76 Bless the Lord, all that grows in the ground;
 sing praise to him and highly exalt him
  forever.
77 Bless the Lord, you springs;
 sing praise to him and highly exalt him
  forever.
78 Bless the Lord, seas and rivers;
 sing praise to him and highly exalt him
  forever.
79 Bless the Lord, you whales and all that swim in
 the waters;
 sing praise to him and highly exalt him
  forever.
80 Bless the Lord, all birds of the air;
 sing praise to him and highly exalt him
  forever.
81 Bless the Lord, all wild animals and cattle;
 sing praise to him and highly exalt him
  forever.

82 "Bless the Lord, all people on earth;
 sing praise to him and highly exalt him
  forever.
83 Bless the Lord, O Israel;
 sing praise to him and highly exalt him
  forever.
84 Bless the Lord, you priests of the Lord;
 sing praise to him and highly exalt him
  forever.
85 Bless the Lord, you servants of the Lord;
 sing praise to him and highly exalt him
  forever.
86 Bless the Lord, spirits and souls of the righteous;
 sing praise to him and highly exalt him
  forever.
87 Bless the Lord, you who are holy and humble in
 heart;
 sing praise to him and highly exalt him
  forever.

88 "Bless the Lord, Hananiah, Azariah, and
 Mishael;
 sing praise to him and highly exalt him
  forever.
For he has rescued us from Hades and saved us
 from the power[a] of death,
and delivered us from the midst of the
 burning fiery furnace;
from the midst of the fire he has delivered us.
89 Give thanks to the Lord, for he is good,
 for his mercy endures forever.
90 All who worship the Lord, bless the God of
 gods,
 sing praise to him and give thanks to him,
 for his mercy endures forever."

91 Hearing them sing, and amazed at seeing them alive, King Nebuchadnezzar rose up quickly. He said to his counselors, "Was it not three men that we threw bound into the fire?" They answered the king, "True, O king." 92He replied, "But I see four men unbound, walking in the middle of the fire, and they are not hurt; and the fourth has the appearance of a god."[b] 93Nebuchadnezzar then approached the door of the furnace of blazing fire and said, "Shadrach, Meshach, and Abednego, servants of the Most High God, come out! Come here!" So Shadrach, Meshach, and Abednego came out from the fire. 94And the satraps, the prefects, the governors, and the king's counselors gathered together and saw that the fire had not had any power over the bodies of those men; the hair of their heads was not singed, their tunics[c] were not harmed,

---

a Gk hand b Aram a son of the gods c Meaning of Aram word uncertain

and not even the smell of fire came from them. ⁹⁵Nebuchadnezzar said, "Blessed be the God of Shadrach, Meshach, and Abednego, who has sent his angel and delivered his servants who trusted in him. They disobeyed the king's command and yielded up their bodies rather than serve and worship any god except their own God. ⁹⁶Therefore I make a decree: Any people, nation, or language that utters blasphemy against the God of Shadrach, Meshach, and Abednego shall be torn limb from limb, and their houses laid in ruins; for there is no other god who is able to deliver in this way." ⁹⁷Then the king promoted Shadrach, Meshach, and Abednego in the province of Babylon.

Nebuchadnezzar's Second Dream

4 ᵃ King Nebuchadnezzar to all peoples, nations, and languages that live throughout the earth: May you have abundant prosperity! ²The signs and wonders that the Most High God has worked for me I am pleased to recount.

³ How great are his signs,
　how mighty his wonders!
His kingdom is an everlasting kingdom,
　and his sovereignty is from generation to
　　generation.

4 ᵇ I, Nebuchadnezzar, was living at ease in my home and prospering in my palace. ⁵I saw a dream that frightened me; my fantasies in bed and the visions of my head terrified me. ⁶So I made a decree that all the wise men of Babylon should be brought before me, in order that they might tell me the interpretation of the dream. ⁷Then the magicians, the enchanters, the Chaldeans, and the diviners came in, and I told them the dream, but they could not tell me its interpretation. ⁸At last Daniel came in before me—he who was named Belteshazzar after the name of my god, and who is endowed with a spirit of the holy godsᶜ—and I told him the dream: ⁹"O Belteshazzar, chief of the magicians, I know that you are endowed with a spirit of the holy godsᶜ and that no mystery is too difficult for you. Hearᵈ the dream that I saw; tell me its interpretation.

¹⁰ ᵉ Upon my bed this is what I saw;
　there was a tree at the center of the earth,
　and its height was great.
¹¹ The tree grew great and strong,
　its top reached to heaven,
　and it was visible to the ends of the whole
　　earth.
¹² Its foliage was beautiful,
　its fruit abundant,
　and it provided food for all.
The animals of the field found shade under it,

　the birds of the air nested in its branches,
　and from it all living beings were fed.

13 "I continued looking, in the visions of my head as I lay in bed, and there was a holy watcher, coming down from heaven. ¹⁴He cried aloud and said:

'Cut down the tree and chop off its branches,
　strip off its foliage and scatter its fruit.
Let the animals flee from beneath it
　and the birds from its branches.
¹⁵ But leave its stump and roots in the ground,

---

a Ch 3.31 in Aram　b Ch 4.1 in Aram　c Or a holy, divine spirit
d Theodotion: Aram The visions of　e Theodotion Syr Compare
Gk: Aram adds The visions of my head

with a band of iron and bronze,
    in the tender grass of the field.
Let him be bathed with the dew of heaven,
    and let his lot be with the animals of the field
    in the grass of the earth.
[16] Let his mind be changed from that of a human,
    and let the mind of an animal be given to
      him.
    And let seven times pass over him.
[17] The sentence is rendered by decree of the
      watchers,
    the decision is given by order of the holy
      ones,
in order that all who live may know
    that the Most High is sovereign over the
      kingdom of mortals;
he gives it to whom he will
    and sets over it the lowliest of human beings.'

18 "This is the dream that I, King Nebuchadnezzar, saw. Now you, Belteshazzar, declare the interpretation, since all the wise men of my kingdom are unable to tell me the interpretation. You are able, however, for you are endowed with a spirit of the holy gods."[a]

Daniel Interprets the Second Dream

19 Then Daniel, who was called Belteshazzar, was severely distressed for a while. His thoughts terrified him. The king said, "Belteshazzar, do not let the dream or the interpretation terrify you." Belteshazzar answered, "My lord, may the dream be for those who hate you, and its interpretation for your enemies! [20]The tree that you saw, which grew great and strong, so that its top reached to heaven and was visible to the end of the whole earth, [21]whose foliage was beautiful and its fruit abundant, and which provided food for all, under which animals of the field lived, and in whose branches the birds of the air had nests— [22]it is you, O king! You have grown great and strong. Your greatness has increased and reaches to heaven, and your sovereignty to the ends of the earth. [23]And whereas the king saw a holy watcher coming down from heaven and saying, 'Cut down the tree and destroy it, but leave its stump and roots in the ground, with a band of iron and bronze, in the grass of the field; and let him be bathed with the dew of heaven, and let his lot be with the animals of the field, until seven times pass over him'— [24]this is the interpretation, O king, and it is a decree of the Most High that has come upon my lord the king: [25]You shall be driven away from human society, and your dwelling shall be with the wild animals. You shall be made to eat grass like oxen,

you shall be bathed with the dew of heaven, and seven times shall pass over you, until you have learned that the Most High has sovereignty over the kingdom of mortals, and gives it to whom he will. [26]As it was commanded to leave the stump and roots of the tree, your kingdom shall be re-established for you from the time that you learn that Heaven is sovereign. [27]Therefore, O king, may my counsel be acceptable to you: atone for[b] your sins with righteousness, and your iniquities with mercy to the oppressed, so that your prosperity may be prolonged."

Nebuchadnezzar's Humiliation

28 All this came upon King Nebuchadnezzar. [29]At the end of twelve months he was walking on the roof of the royal palace of Babylon, [30]and the king said, "Is this not magnificent Babylon, which I have built as a royal capital by my mighty power and for my glorious majesty?" [31]While the words were still in the king's mouth, a voice came from heaven: "O King Nebuchadnezzar, to you it is declared: The kingdom has departed from you! [32]You shall be driven away from human society, and your dwelling shall be with the animals of the field. You shall be made to eat grass like oxen, and seven times shall pass over you, until you have learned that the Most High has sovereignty over the kingdom of mortals and gives it to whom he will." [33]Immediately the sentence was fulfilled against Nebuchadnezzar. He was driven away from human society, ate grass like oxen, and his body was bathed with the dew of heaven, until his hair grew as long as eagles' feathers and his nails became like birds' claws.

Nebuchadnezzar Praises God

34 When that period was over, I, Nebuchadnezzar, lifted my eyes to heaven, and my reason returned to me.

I blessed the Most High,
    and praised and honored the one who lives
      forever.
For his sovereignty is an everlasting sovereignty,
    and his kingdom endures from generation to
      generation.
[35] All the inhabitants of the earth are accounted as
      nothing,
    and he does what he wills with the host of
      heaven
    and the inhabitants of the earth.
There is no one who can stay his hand
    or say to him, "What are you doing?"
[36]At that time my reason returned to me; and my

---

a Or a holy, divine spirit b Aram break off

majesty and splendor were restored to me for the glory of my kingdom. My counselors and my lords sought me out, I was re-established over my kingdom, and still more greatness was added to me. [37]Now I, Nebuchadnezzar, praise and extol and honor the King of heaven,

for all his works are truth,
and his ways are justice;
and he is able to bring low
those who walk in pride.

Belshazzar's Feast

5 King Belshazzar made a great festival for a thousand of his lords, and he was drinking wine in the presence of the thousand.

2 Under the influence of the wine, Belshazzar commanded that they bring in the vessels of gold and silver that his father Nebuchadnezzar had taken out of the temple in Jerusalem, so that the king and his lords, his wives, and his concubines might drink from them. [3]So they brought in the vessels of gold and silver[a] that had been taken out of the temple, the house of God in Jerusalem, and the king and his lords, his wives, and his concubines drank from them. [4]They drank the wine and praised the gods of gold and silver, bronze, iron, wood, and stone.

The Writing on the Wall

5 Immediately the fingers of a human hand appeared and began writing on the plaster of the wall of the royal palace, next to the lampstand. The king was watching the hand as it wrote. [6]Then the king's face turned pale, and his thoughts terrified him. His limbs gave way, and his knees knocked together. [7]The king cried aloud to bring in the enchanters, the Chaldeans, and the diviners; and the king said to the wise men of Babylon, "Whoever can read this writing and tell me its interpretation shall be clothed in purple, have a chain of gold around his neck, and rank third in the kingdom." [8]Then all the king's wise men came in, but they could not read the writing or tell the king the interpretation. [9]Then King Belshazzar became greatly terrified and his face turned pale, and his lords were perplexed.

10 The queen, when she heard the discussion of the king and his lords, came into the banqueting hall. The queen said, "O king, live forever! Do not let your thoughts terrify you or your face grow pale. [11]There is a man in your kingdom who is endowed with a spirit of the holy gods.[b] In the days of your father he was found to have enlightenment, understanding, and wisdom like the wisdom of the gods. Your father, King Nebuchadnezzar, made him chief of the magicians,

enchanters, Chaldeans, and diviners,[c] [12]because an excellent spirit, knowledge, and understanding to interpret dreams, explain riddles, and solve problems were found in this Daniel, whom the king named Belteshazzar. Now let Daniel be called, and he will give the interpretation."

The Writing on the Wall Interpreted

13 Then Daniel was brought in before the king. The king said to Daniel, "So you are Daniel, one of the exiles of Judah, whom my father the king brought from Judah? [14]I have heard of you that a spirit of the gods[d] is in you, and that enlightenment, understanding, and excellent wisdom are found in you. [15]Now the wise men, the enchanters, have been brought in before me to read this writing and tell me its interpretation, but they were not able to give the interpretation of the matter. [16]But I have heard that you can give interpretations and solve problems. Now if you are able to read the writing and tell me its interpretation, you shall be clothed in purple, have a chain of gold around your neck, and rank third in the kingdom."

17 Then Daniel answered in the presence of the king, "Let your gifts be for yourself, or give your rewards to someone else! Nevertheless I will read the writing to the king and let him know the interpretation. [18]O king, the Most High God gave your father Nebuchadnezzar kingship, greatness, glory, and majesty. [19]And because of the greatness that he gave him, all peoples, nations, and languages trembled and feared before him. He killed those he wanted to kill, kept alive those he wanted to keep alive, honored those he wanted to honor, and degraded those he wanted to degrade. [20]But when his heart was lifted up and his spirit was hardened so that he acted proudly, he was deposed from his kingly throne, and his glory was stripped from him. [21]He was driven from human society, and his mind was made like that of an animal. His dwelling was with the wild asses, he was fed grass like oxen, and his body was bathed with the dew of heaven, until he learned that the Most High God has sovereignty over the kingdom of mortals, and sets over it whomever he will. [22]And you, Belshazzar his son, have not humbled your heart, even though you knew all this! [23]You have exalted yourself against the Lord of heaven! The vessels of his temple have been brought in before you, and you and your lords, your wives and your concubines have been drinking wine from them.

You have praised the gods of silver and gold, of bronze, iron, wood, and stone, which do not see or hear or know; but the God in whose power is your very breath, and to whom belong all your ways, you have not honored.

24 "So from his presence the hand was sent and this writing was inscribed. 25And this is the writing that was inscribed: MENE, MENE, TEKEL, and PARSIN. 26This is the interpretation of the matter: MENE, God has numbered the days of[a] your kingdom and brought it to an end; 27TEKEL, you have been weighed on the scales and found wanting; 28PERES,[b] your kingdom is divided and given to the Medes and Persians."

29 Then Belshazzar gave the command, and Daniel was clothed in purple, a chain of gold was put around his neck, and a proclamation was made concerning him that he should rank third in the kingdom.

30 That very night Belshazzar, the Chaldean king, was killed. 31[c] And Darius the Mede received the kingdom, being about sixty-two years old.

The Plot against Daniel

6 It pleased Darius to set over the kingdom one hundred twenty satraps, stationed throughout the whole kingdom, 2and over them three presidents, including Daniel; to these the satraps gave account, so that the king might suffer no loss. 3Soon Daniel distinguished himself above all the other presidents and satraps because an excellent spirit was in him, and the king planned to appoint him over the whole kingdom. 4So the presidents and the satraps tried to find grounds for complaint against Daniel in connection with the kingdom. But they could find no grounds for complaint or any corruption, because he was faithful, and no negligence or corruption could be found in him. 5The men said, "We shall not find any ground for complaint against this Daniel unless we find it in connection with the law of his God."

6 So the presidents and satraps conspired and came to the king and said to him, "O King Darius, live forever! 7All the presidents of the kingdom, the prefects and the satraps, the counselors and the governors are agreed that the king should establish an ordinance and enforce an interdict, that whoever prays to anyone, divine or human, for thirty days, except to you, O king, shall be thrown into a den of lions. 8Now, O king, establish the interdict and sign the document, so that it cannot be changed, according to the law of the Medes and the Persians, which cannot be revoked." 9Therefore King Darius signed the document and interdict.

Daniel in the Lions' Den

10 Although Daniel knew that the document had been signed, he continued to go to his house, which had windows in its upper room open toward Jerusalem, and to get down on his knees three times a day to pray to his God and praise him, just as he had done previously. 11The conspirators came and found Daniel praying and seeking mercy before his God. 12Then they approached the king and said concerning the interdict, "O king! Did you not sign an interdict, that anyone who prays to anyone, divine or human, within thirty days except to you, O king, shall be thrown into a den of lions?" The king answered, "The thing stands fast, according to the law of the Medes and Persians, which cannot be revoked." 13Then they responded to the king, "Daniel, one of the exiles from Judah, pays no attention to you, O king, or to the interdict you have signed, but he is saying his prayers three times a day."

14 When the king heard the charge, he was very much distressed. He was determined to save Daniel, and until the sun went down he made every effort to rescue him. 15Then the conspirators came to the king and said to him, "Know, O king, that it is a law of the Medes and Persians that no interdict or ordinance that the king establishes can be changed."

16 Then the king gave the command, and Daniel was brought and thrown into the den of lions. The king said to Daniel, "May your God, whom you faithfully serve, deliver you!" 17A stone was brought and laid on the mouth of the den, and the king sealed it with his own signet and with the signet of his lords, so that nothing might be changed concerning Daniel. 18Then the king went to his palace and spent the night fasting; no food was brought to him, and sleep fled from him.

Daniel Saved from the Lions

19 Then, at break of day, the king got up and hurried to the den of lions. 20When he came near the den where Daniel was, he cried out anxiously to Daniel, "O Daniel, servant of the living God, has your God whom you faithfully serve been able to deliver you from the lions?" 21Daniel then said to the king, "O king, live forever! 22My God sent his angel and shut the lions' mouths so that they would not hurt me, because I was found blameless before him; and also before you, O king, I have done no wrong."

a Aram lacks the days of   b The singular of Parsin   c Ch 6.1 in Aram

[23]Then the king was exceedingly glad and commanded that Daniel be taken up out of the den. So Daniel was taken up out of the den, and no kind of harm was found on him, because he had trusted in his God. [24]The king gave a command, and those who had accused Daniel were brought and thrown into the den of lions—they, their children, and their wives. Before they reached the bottom of the den the lions overpowered them and broke all their bones in pieces.

25 Then King Darius wrote to all peoples and nations of every language throughout the whole world: "May you have abundant prosperity! [26]I make a decree, that in all my royal dominion people should tremble and fear before the God of Daniel:

For he is the living God,
    enduring forever.
His kingdom shall never be destroyed,
    and his dominion has no end.
[27] He delivers and rescues,
    he works signs and wonders in heaven and on
        earth;
for he has saved Daniel
    from the power of the lions."

[28]So this Daniel prospered during the reign of Darius and the reign of Cyrus the Persian.

Visions of the Four Beasts

7 In the first year of King Belshazzar of Babylon, Daniel had a dream and visions of his head as he lay in bed. Then he wrote down the dream:[a] [2,b] Daniel, saw in my vision by night the four winds of heaven stirring up the great sea, [3]and four great beasts came up out of the sea, different from one another. [4]The first was like a lion and had eagles' wings. Then, as I watched, its wings were plucked off, and it was lifted up from the ground and made to stand on two feet like a human being; and a human mind was given to it. [5]Another beast appeared, a second one, that looked like a bear. It was raised up on one side, had three tusks[c] in its mouth among its teeth and was told, "Arise, devour many bodies!" [6]After this, as I watched, another appeared, like a leopard. The beast had four wings of a bird on its back and four heads; and dominion was given to it. [7]After this I saw in the visions by night a fourth beast, terrifying and dreadful and exceedingly strong. It had great iron teeth and was devouring, breaking in pieces, and stamping what was left with its feet. It was different from all the beasts that preceded it, and it had ten horns. [8]I was considering the horns, when another horn appeared, a little one coming up among them; to make room for it, three of the earlier horns were plucked up by the roots. There were eyes like human eyes in this horn, and a mouth speaking arrogantly.

Judgment before the Ancient One

[9] As I watched,
    thrones were set in place,
        and an Ancient One[d] took his throne,
    his clothing was white as snow,
        and the hair of his head like pure wool;
    his throne was fiery flames,
        and its wheels were burning fire.
[10] A stream of fire issued
        and flowed out from his presence.
    A thousand thousands served him,
        and ten thousand times ten thousand stood
            attending him.
    The court sat in judgment,
        and the books were opened.

[11]I watched then because of the noise of the arrogant words that the horn was speaking. And as I watched, the beast was put to death, and its body destroyed and given over to be burned with fire. [12]As for the rest of the beasts, their dominion was taken away, but their lives were prolonged for a season and a time. [13]As I watched in the night visions,

I saw one like a human being[e]
    coming with the clouds of heaven.
And he came to the Ancient One[f]
    and was presented before him.
[14] To him was given dominion
        and glory and kingship,
    that all peoples, nations, and languages
        should serve him.
    His dominion is an everlasting dominion
        that shall not pass away,
    and his kingship is one
        that shall never be destroyed.

Daniel's Visions Interpreted

15 As for me, Daniel, my spirit was troubled within me,[g] and the visions of my head terrified me. [16]I approached one of the attendants to ask him the truth concerning all this. So he said that he would disclose to me the interpretation of the matter: [17]"As for these four great beasts, four kings shall arise out of the earth. [18]But the holy ones of the Most High shall receive the kingdom and possess the kingdom forever—forever and ever."

19 Then I desired to know the truth concerning

---

a Q Ms Theodotion: MT adds *the beginning of the words; he said*
b Theodotion: Aram *Daniel answered and said, I*   c Or *ribs*
d Aram *an Ancient of Days*   e Aram *one like a son of man*
f Aram *the Ancient of Days*   g Aram *troubled in its sheath*

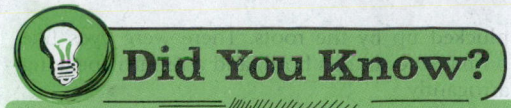

Apocalyptic Literature

As you read chapters 7–10 of Daniel, you might ask, What's with the four beasts in chapter 7, and the goat with the horn in chapter 8, and the man with a face like lightning in chapter 10? These are all examples of apocalyptic literature. *Apocalypse* is a Greek word meaning "to uncover or reveal." Apocalyptic literature is written to sound like an attempt to foretell the future by using symbols and visions. But the symbols are often codes for people and events in the present. This type of literature frequently is produced during a time of persecution, when using real names could get a person into trouble or even killed. Apocalyptic literature developed in Israel around 200 BC when the country was enduring great persecution and suffering. The Book of Revelation in the New Testament is another example of apocalyptic literature.

The Book of Daniel contains some explanation of the visions it describes. But sometimes, you will have to consult a good Bible commentary (a book that gives additional background on Bible passages) to completely understand the symbols. For instance, you might need help recognizing that the four beasts in chapter 7 are symbols for Babylon, Media, Persia, and Greece—the four nations that ruled over Israel but would pass away. Or that the arrogant eleventh horn on the fourth beast's head is a symbol for Antiochus IV Epiphanes, the king who persecuted the Jews during the time Daniel was written.

Apocalyptic literature assured the people of Israel that God would triumph and the present evil would eventually pass away. It was one more way to reinforce the belief that evil would be punished and good rewarded, even when it didn't look that way at the moment.

▶ Daniel, chapters 7–10

the fourth beast, which was different from all the rest, exceedingly terrifying, with its teeth of iron and claws of bronze, and which devoured and broke in pieces, and stamped what was left with its feet; 20and concerning the ten horns that were on its head, and concerning the other horn, which came up and to make room for which three of them fell out—the horn that had eyes and a mouth that spoke arrogantly, and that seemed greater than the others. 21As I looked, this horn made war with the holy ones and was prevailing over them, 22until the Ancient One[a] came; then judgment was given for the holy ones of the Most High, and the time arrived when the holy ones gained possession of the kingdom.

23 This is what he said: "As for the fourth beast,

there shall be a fourth kingdom on earth
    that shall be different from all the other
        kingdoms;
it shall devour the whole earth,
    and trample it down, and break it to pieces.
24 As for the ten horns,
    out of this kingdom ten kings shall arise,
    and another shall arise after them.
This one shall be different from the former ones,
    and shall put down three kings.
25 He shall speak words against the Most High,
    shall wear out the holy ones of the Most
        High,
    and shall attempt to change the sacred
        seasons and the law;
and they shall be given into his power
    for a time, two times,[b] and half a time.
26 Then the court shall sit in judgment,
    and his dominion shall be taken away,
    to be consumed and totally destroyed.
27 The kingship and dominion
    and the greatness of the kingdoms under the
        whole heaven
    shall be given to the people of the holy ones
        of the Most High;
their kingdom shall be an everlasting kingdom,
    and all dominions shall serve and obey
        them."

28 Here the account ends. As for me, Daniel, my thoughts greatly terrified me, and my face turned pale; but I kept the matter in my mind.

Vision of a Ram and a Goat

8 In the third year of the reign of King Belshazzar a vision appeared to me, Daniel, after the one that had appeared to me at first. 2In the vision I was looking and saw myself in Susa the capital, in the province of Elam,[c] and I was by the river Ulai.[d] 3I looked up and saw a ram standing beside the river.[e] It had two horns. Both horns were long, but one was longer than the other,

a Aram *the Ancient of Days*   b Aram *a time, times*
c Gk Theodotion: MT Q Ms repeat *in the vision I was looking*
d Or *the Ulai Gate*   e Or *gate*

and the longer one came up second. [4]I saw the ram charging westward and northward and southward. All beasts were powerless to withstand it, and no one could rescue from its power; it did as it pleased and became strong.

5 As I was watching, a male goat appeared from the west, coming across the face of the whole earth without touching the ground. The goat had a horn[a] between its eyes. [6]It came toward the ram with the two horns that I had seen standing beside the river,[b] and it ran at it with savage force. [7]I saw it approaching the ram. It was enraged against it and struck the ram, breaking its two horns. The ram did not have power to withstand it; it threw the ram down to the ground and trampled upon it, and there was no one who could rescue the ram from its power. [8]Then the male goat grew exceedingly great; but at the height of its power, the great horn was broken, and in its place there came up four prominent horns toward the four winds of heaven.

9 Out of one of them came another[c] horn, a little one, which grew exceedingly great toward the south, toward the east, and toward the beautiful land. [10]It grew as high as the host of heaven. It threw down to the earth some of the host and some of the stars, and trampled on them. [11]Even against the prince of the host it acted arrogantly; it took the regular burnt offering away from him and overthrew the place of his sanctuary. [12]Because of wickedness, the host was given over to it together with the regular burnt offering;[d] it cast truth to the ground, and kept prospering in what it did. [13]Then I heard a holy one speaking, and another holy one said to the one that spoke, "For how long is this vision concerning the regular burnt offering, the transgression that makes desolate, and the giving over of the sanctuary and host to be trampled?"[d] [14]And he answered him,[e] "For two thousand three hundred evenings and mornings; then the sanctuary shall be restored to its rightful state."

Gabriel Interprets the Vision

15 When I, Daniel, had seen the vision, I tried to understand it. Then someone appeared standing before me, having the appearance of a man, [16]and I heard a human voice by the Ulai, calling, "Gabriel, help this man understand the vision." [17]So he came near where I stood; and when he came, I became frightened and fell prostrate. But he said to me, "Understand, O mortal,[f] that the vision is for the time of the end."

18 As he was speaking to me, I fell into a trance, face to the ground; then he touched me and set me on my feet. [19]He said, "Listen, and I will tell you what will take place later in the period of wrath; for it refers to the appointed time of the end. [20]As for the ram that you saw with the two horns, these are the kings of Media and Persia. [21]The male goat[g] is the king of Greece, and the great horn between its eyes is the first king. [22]As for the horn that was broken, in place of which four others arose, four kingdoms shall arise from his[h] nation, but not with his power.
23 At the end of their rule,

> when the transgressions have reached their
>   full measure,
> a king of bold countenance shall arise,
>   skilled in intrigue.
24 He shall grow strong in power,[i]
>   shall cause fearful destruction,
>   and shall succeed in what he does.
> He shall destroy the powerful
>   and the people of the holy ones.
25 By his cunning
>   he shall make deceit prosper under his hand,
>   and in his own mind he shall be great.
> Without warning he shall destroy many
>   and shall even rise up against the Prince of
>   princes.
> But he shall be broken, and not by human
>   hands.
26The vision of the evenings and the mornings that has been told is true. As for you, seal up the vision, for it refers to many days from now."

27 So I, Daniel, was overcome and lay sick for some days; then I arose and went about the king's business. But I was dismayed by the vision and did not understand it.

Daniel's Prayer for the People

9 In the first year of Darius son of Ahasuerus, by birth a Mede, who became king over the realm of the Chaldeans— [2]in the first year of his reign, I, Daniel, perceived in the books the number of years that, according to the word of the LORD to the prophet Jeremiah, must be fulfilled for the devastation of Jerusalem, namely, seventy years.

3 Then I turned to the Lord God, to seek an answer by prayer and supplication with fasting and sackcloth and ashes. [4]I prayed to the LORD my God and made confession, saying,

"Ah, Lord, great and awesome God, keeping covenant and steadfast love with those who love

---

a Theodotion: Gk *one horn*; Heb *a horn of vision*   b Or *gate*
c Cn Compare 7.8: Heb *one*   d Meaning of Heb uncertain   e Gk Theodotion Syr Vg: Heb *me*   f Heb *son of man*   g Or *shaggy male goat*   h Gk Theodotion Vg: Heb *the*
i Theodotion and one Gk Ms: Heb repeats (from 8.22) *but not with his power*

you and keep your commandments, 5we have sinned and done wrong, acted wickedly and rebelled, turning aside from your commandments and ordinances. 6We have not listened to your servants the prophets, who spoke in your name to our kings, our princes, and our ancestors, and to all the people of the land.

7 "Righteousness is on your side, O Lord, but open shame, as at this day, falls on us, the people of Judah, the inhabitants of Jerusalem, and all Israel, those who are near and those who are far away, in all the lands to which you have driven them, because of the treachery that they have committed against you. 8Open shame, O LORD, falls on us, our kings, our officials, and our ancestors, because we have sinned against you. 9To the Lord our God belong mercy and forgiveness, for we have rebelled against him, 10and have not obeyed the voice of the LORD our God by following his laws, which he set before us by his servants the prophets.

11 "All Israel has transgressed your law and turned aside, refusing to obey your voice. So the curse and the oath written in the law of Moses, the servant of God, have been poured out upon us, because we have sinned against you. 12He has confirmed his words, which he spoke against us

A Closer Look

Let's look closely at the prayer in chapter 9 of Daniel. Here, the prophet uses four types of prayer:

- *intercession*, because he prays on behalf of the people
- *praise*, because he proclaims God to be awesome and great
- *sorrow*, because he expresses sadness for past sinfulness and asks for forgiveness
- *petition*, because he asks God for help

Daniel gives us a great example of the various ways we can pray to God. When you have a moment, pray by yourself or with a friend, trying to incorporate all four of these types into your prayer.

▶ **Daniel, chapter 9**

and against our rulers, by bringing upon us a calamity so great that what has been done against Jerusalem has never before been done under the whole heaven. 13Just as it is written in the law of Moses, all this calamity has come upon us. We did not entreat the favor of the LORD our God, turning from our iniquities and reflecting on his*a* fidelity. 14So the LORD kept watch over this calamity until he brought it upon us. Indeed, the LORD our God is right in all that he has done; for we have disobeyed his voice.

15 "And now, O Lord our God, who brought your people out of the land of Egypt with a mighty hand and made your name renowned even to this day—we have sinned, we have done wickedly. 16O Lord, in view of all your righteous acts, let your anger and wrath, we pray, turn away from your city Jerusalem, your holy mountain; because of our sins and the iniquities of our ancestors, Jerusalem and your people have become a disgrace among all our neighbors. 17Now therefore, O our God, listen to the prayer of your servant and to his supplication, and for your own sake, Lord,*b* let your face shine upon your desolated sanctuary. 18Incline your ear, O my God, and hear. Open your eyes and look at our desolation and the city that bears your name. We do not present our supplication before you on the ground of our righteousness, but on the ground of your great mercies. 19O Lord, hear; O Lord, forgive; O Lord, listen and act and do not delay! For your own sake, O my God, because your city and your people bear your name!"

The Seventy Weeks

20 While I was speaking, and was praying and confessing my sin and the sin of my people Israel, and presenting my supplication before the LORD my God on behalf of the holy mountain of my God— 21while I was speaking in prayer, the man Gabriel, whom I had seen before in a vision, came to me in swift flight at the time of the evening sacrifice. 22He came*c* and said to me, "Daniel, I have now come out to give you wisdom and understanding. 23At the beginning of your supplications a word went out, and I have come to declare it, for you are greatly beloved. So consider the word and understand the vision:

24 "Seventy weeks are decreed for your people and your holy city: to finish the transgression, to put an end to sin, and to atone for iniquity, to bring in everlasting righteousness, to seal both vision and prophet, and to anoint a

DAN

most holy place.[a] 25 Know therefore and understand: from the time that the word went out to restore and rebuild Jerusalem until the time of an anointed prince, there shall be seven weeks; and for sixty-two weeks it shall be built again with streets and moat, but in a troubled time. 26 After the sixty-two weeks, an anointed one shall be cut off and shall have nothing, and the troops of the prince who is to come shall destroy the city and the sanctuary. Its[b] end shall come with a flood, and to the end there shall be war. Desolations are decreed. 27 He shall make a strong covenant with many for one week, and for half of the week he shall make sacrifice and offering cease; and in their place[c] shall be an abomination that desolates, until the decreed end is poured out upon the desolator."

Conflict of Nations and Heavenly Powers

10 In the third year of King Cyrus of Persia a word was revealed to Daniel, who was named Belteshazzar. The word was true, and it concerned a great conflict. He understood the word, having received understanding in the vision.

2 At that time I, Daniel, had been mourning for three weeks. 3 I had eaten no rich food, no meat or wine had entered my mouth, and I had not anointed myself at all, for the full three weeks. 4 On the twenty-fourth day of the first month, as I was standing on the bank of the great river (that is, the Tigris), 5 I looked up and saw a man clothed in linen, with a belt of gold from Uphaz around his waist. 6 His body was like beryl, his face like lightning, his eyes like flaming torches, his arms and legs like the gleam of burnished bronze, and the sound of his words like the roar of a multitude. 7 I, Daniel, alone saw the vision; the people who were with me did not see the vision, though a great trembling fell upon them, and they fled and hid themselves. 8 So I was left alone to see this great vision. My strength left me, and my complexion grew deathly pale, and I retained no strength. 9 Then I heard the sound of his words; and when I heard the sound of his words, I fell into a trance, face to the ground.

10 But then a hand touched me and roused me to my hands and knees. 11 He said to me, "Daniel, greatly beloved, pay attention to the words that I am going to speak to you. Stand on your feet, for I have now been sent to you." So while he was speaking this word to me, I stood up trembling. 12 He said to me, "Do not fear, Daniel, for from the first day that you set your mind to gain understanding and to humble yourself before your God, your words have been heard, and I have come because of your words. 13 But the prince of the kingdom of Persia opposed me twenty-one days. So Michael, one of the chief princes, came to help me, and I left him there with the prince of the kingdom of Persia,[d] 14 and have come to help you understand what is to happen to your people at the end of days. For there is a further vision for those days."

15 While he was speaking these words to me, I turned my face toward the ground and was speechless. 16 Then one in human form touched my lips, and I opened my mouth to speak, and said to the one who stood before me, "My lord, because of the vision such pains have come upon me that I retain no strength. 17 How can my lord's servant talk with my lord? For I am shaking,[e] no strength remains in me, and no breath is left in me."

18 Again one in human form touched me and strengthened me. 19 He said, "Do not fear, greatly beloved, you are safe. Be strong and courageous!" When he spoke to me, I was strengthened and said, "Let my lord speak, for you have strengthened me." 20 Then he said, "Do you know why I have come to you? Now I must return to fight against the prince of Persia, and when I am through with him, the prince of Greece will come. 21 But I am to tell you what is inscribed in the book of truth. There is no one with me who contends against these princes except Michael,

11 your prince. 1 As for me, in the first year of Darius the Mede, I stood up to support and strengthen him.

2 "Now I will announce the truth to you. Three more kings shall arise in Persia. The fourth shall be far richer than all of them, and when he has become strong through his riches, he shall stir up all against the kingdom of Greece. 3 Then a warrior king shall arise, who shall rule with great dominion and take action as he pleases. 4 And while still rising in power, his kingdom shall be broken and divided toward the four winds of heaven, but not to his posterity, nor according to the dominion with which he ruled; for his kingdom shall be uprooted and go to others besides these.

5 "Then the king of the south shall grow strong, but one of his officers shall grow stronger than he and shall rule a realm greater than his own realm. 6 After some years they shall make an alliance, and the daughter of the king of the south shall come to the king of the north to

---

a Or thing or one   b Or His   c Cn: Meaning of Heb uncertain
d Gk Theodotion: Heb I was left there with the kings of Persia
e Gk: Heb from now

ratify the agreement. But she shall not retain her power, and his offspring shall not endure. She shall be given up, she and her attendants and her child and the one who supported her.

"In those times [7]a branch from her roots shall rise up in his place. He shall come against the army and enter the fortress of the king of the north, and he shall take action against them and prevail. [8]Even their gods, with their idols and with their precious vessels of silver and gold, he shall carry off to Egypt as spoils of war. For some years he shall refrain from attacking the king of the north; [9]then the latter shall invade the realm of the king of the south, but will return to his own land.

10 "His sons shall wage war and assemble a multitude of great forces, which shall advance like a flood and pass through, and again shall carry the war as far as his fortress. [11]Moved with rage, the king of the south shall go out and do battle against the king of the north, who shall muster a great multitude, which shall, however, be defeated by his enemy. [12]When the multitude has been carried off, his heart shall be exalted, and he shall overthrow tens of thousands, but he shall not prevail. [13]For the king of the north shall again raise a multitude, larger than the former, and after some years[a] he shall advance with a great army and abundant supplies.

14 "In those times many shall rise against the king of the south. The lawless among your own people shall lift themselves up in order to fulfill the vision, but they shall fail. [15]Then the king of the north shall come and throw up siegeworks, and take a well-fortified city. And the forces of the south shall not stand, not even his picked troops, for there shall be no strength to resist. [16]But he who comes against him shall take the actions he pleases, and no one shall withstand him. He shall take a position in the beautiful land, and all of it shall be in his power. [17]He shall set his mind to come with the strength of his whole kingdom, and he shall bring terms of peace[b] and perform them. In order to destroy the kingdom,[c] he shall give him a woman in marriage; but it shall not succeed or be to his advantage. [18]Afterward he shall turn to the coastlands, and shall capture many. But a commander shall put an end to his insolence; indeed,[d] he shall turn his insolence back upon him. [19]Then he shall turn back toward the fortresses of his own land, but he shall stumble and fall, and shall not be found.

20 "Then shall arise in his place one who shall send an official for the glory of the kingdom; but within a few days he shall be broken, though not in anger or in battle. [21]In his place shall arise a contemptible person on whom royal majesty had not been conferred; he shall come in without warning and obtain the kingdom through intrigue. [22]Armies shall be utterly swept away and broken before him, and the prince of the covenant as well. [23]And after an alliance is made with him, he shall act deceitfully and become strong with a small party. [24]Without warning he shall come into the richest parts[e] of the province and do what none of his predecessors had ever done, lavishing plunder, spoil, and wealth on them. He shall devise plans against strongholds, but only for a time. [25]He shall stir up his power and determination against the king of the south with a great army, and the king of the south shall wage war with a much greater and stronger army. But he shall not succeed, for plots shall be devised against him [26]by those who eat of the royal rations. They shall break him, his army shall be swept away, and many shall fall slain. [27]The two kings, their minds bent on evil, shall sit at one table and exchange lies. But it shall not succeed, for there remains an end at the time appointed. [28]He shall return to his land with great wealth, but his heart shall be set against the holy covenant. He shall work his will, and return to his own land.

29 "At the time appointed he shall return and come into the south, but this time it shall not be as it was before. [30]For ships of Kittim shall come against him, and he shall lose heart and withdraw. He shall be enraged and take action against the holy covenant. He shall turn back and pay heed to those who forsake the holy covenant. [31]Forces sent by him shall occupy and profane the temple and fortress. They shall abolish the regular burnt offering and set up the abomination that makes desolate. [32]He shall seduce with intrigue those who violate the covenant; but the people who are loyal to their God shall stand firm and take action. [33]The wise among the people shall give understanding to many; for some days, however, they shall fall by sword and flame, and suffer captivity and plunder. [34]When they fall victim, they shall receive a little help, and many shall join them insincerely. [35]Some of the wise shall fall, so that they may be refined, purified, and cleansed,[f] until the time of the end, for there is still an interval until the time appointed.

36 "The king shall act as he pleases. He shall exalt himself and consider himself greater than

---

a Heb *and at the end of the times years*　*b* Gk; Heb *kingdom, and upright ones with him*　*c* Heb *it*　*d* Meaning of Heb uncertain　*e* Or *among the richest men*　*f* Heb *made them white*

any god, and shall speak horrendous things against the God of gods. He shall prosper until the period of wrath is completed, for what is determined shall be done. ³⁷He shall pay no respect to the gods of his ancestors, or to the one beloved by women; he shall pay no respect to any other god, for he shall consider himself greater than all. ³⁸He shall honor the god of fortresses instead of these; a god whom his ancestors did not know he shall honor with gold and silver, with precious stones and costly gifts. ³⁹He shall deal with the strongest fortresses by the help of a foreign god. Those who acknowledge him he shall make more wealthy, and shall appoint them as rulers over many, and shall distribute the land for a price.

The Time of the End

40 "At the time of the end the king of the south shall attack him. But the king of the north shall rush upon him like a whirlwind, with chariots and horsemen, and with many ships. He shall advance against countries and pass through like a flood. ⁴¹He shall come into the beautiful land, and tens of thousands shall fall victim, but Edom and Moab and the main part of the Ammonites shall escape from his power. ⁴²He shall stretch out his hand against the countries, and the land of Egypt shall not escape. ⁴³He shall become ruler of the treasures of gold and of silver, and all the riches of Egypt; and the Libyans and the Ethiopiansᵃ shall follow in his train. ⁴⁴But reports from the east and the north shall alarm him, and he shall go out with great fury to bring ruin and complete destruction to many. ⁴⁵He shall pitch his palatial tents between the sea and the beautiful holy mountain. Yet he shall come to his end, with no one to help him.

The Resurrection of the Dead

12 "At that time Michael, the great prince, the protector of your people, shall arise. There shall be a time of anguish, such as has never occurred since nations first came into existence. But at that time your people shall be delivered, everyone who is found written in the book. ²Many of those who sleep in the dust of the earthᵇ shall awake, some to everlasting life, and some to shame and everlasting contempt. ³Those who are wise shall shine like the brightness of the sky,ᶜ and those who lead many to righteousness, like the stars forever and ever. ⁴But you, Daniel, keep the words secret and the book sealed until the time of the end. Many shall be running back and forth, and evilᵈ shall increase."

5 Then I, Daniel, looked, and two others

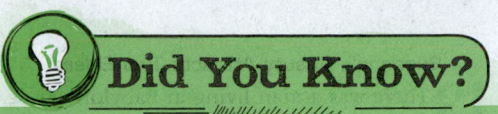

Did You Know?

Resurrection

Most of the Old Testament contains no indication of a belief in life after death. Daniel, however, speaks of individual resurrection, or rising to life from death. This goes beyond the less specific belief in life after death expressed in the Wisdom of Solomon 5:15 and is similar to the belief expressed in 2 Maccabees 7:23. The understanding of personal resurrection developed quite late in Israel's existence. It is described as the complete transformation of the human being, body and spirit, after death. Daniel 12:3 says the resurrected will shine like stars.

▶ **Dan 12:1–3**

appeared, one standing on this bank of the stream and one on the other. ⁶One of them said to the man clothed in linen, who was upstream, "How long shall it be until the end of these wonders?" ⁷The man clothed in linen, who was upstream, raised his right hand and his left hand toward heaven. And I heard him swear by the one who lives forever that it would be for a time, two times, and half a time,ᵉ and that when the shattering of the power of the holy people comes to an end, all these things would be accomplished. ⁸I heard but could not understand; so I said, "My lord, what shall be the outcome of these things?" ⁹He said, "Go your way, Daniel, for the words are to remain secret and sealed until the time of the end. ¹⁰Many shall be purified, cleansed, and refined, but the wicked shall continue to act wickedly. None of the wicked shall understand, but those who are wise shall understand. ¹¹From the time that the regular burnt offering is taken away and the abomination that desolates is set up, there shall be one thousand two hundred ninety days. ¹²Happy are those who persevere and attain the thousand three hundred thirty-five days. ¹³But you, go your way,ᶠ and rest; you shall rise for your reward at the end of the days."

DAN

ᵃ Or *Nubians*; Heb *Cushites*   ᵇ Or *the land of dust*   ᶜ Or *dome*
ᵈ Cn Compare Gk: Heb *knowledge*   ᵉ Heb *a time, times, and a half*   ᶠ Gk Theodotion: Heb adds *to the end*

Susanna's Beauty Attracts Two Elders

13 There was a man living in Babylon whose name was Joakim. ²He married the daughter of Hilkiah, named Susanna, a very beautiful woman and one who feared the Lord. ³Her parents were righteous, and had trained their daughter according to the law of Moses. ⁴Joakim was very rich, and had a fine garden adjoining his house; the Jews used to come to him because he was the most honored of them all.

5 That year two elders from the people were appointed as judges. Concerning them the Lord had said: "Wickedness came forth from Babylon, from elders who were judges, who were supposed to govern the people." ⁶These men were frequently at Joakim's house, and all who had a case to be tried came to them there.

7 When the people left at noon, Susanna would go into her husband's garden to walk. ⁸Every day the two elders used to see her, going in and walking about, and they began to lust for her. ⁹They suppressed their consciences and turned away their eyes from looking to Heaven or remembering their duty to administer justice. ¹⁰Both were overwhelmed with passion for her,

but they did not tell each other of their distress, ¹¹for they were ashamed to disclose their lustful desire to seduce her. ¹²Day after day they watched eagerly to see her.

13 One day they said to each other, "Let us go home, for it is time for lunch." So they both left and parted from each other. ¹⁴But turning back, they met again; and when each pressed the other for the reason, they confessed their lust. Then together they arranged for a time when they could find her alone.

The Elders Attempt to Seduce Susanna

15 Once, while they were watching for an opportune day, she went in as before with only two maids, and wished to bathe in the garden, for it was a hot day. ¹⁶No one was there except the two elders, who had hidden themselves and were watching her. ¹⁷She said to her maids, "Bring me olive oil and ointments, and shut the garden doors so that I can bathe." ¹⁸They did as she told them: they shut the doors of the garden and went out by the side doors to bring what they had been commanded; they did not see the elders, because they were hiding.

19 When the maids had gone out, the two elders got up and ran to her. ²⁰They said, "Look, the garden doors are shut, and no one can see us. We are burning with desire for you; so give your consent, and lie with us. ²¹If you refuse, we will testify against you that a young man was with you, and this was why you sent your maids away."

22 Susanna groaned and said, "I am completely trapped. For if I do this, it will mean death for me; if I do not, I cannot escape your hands. ²³I choose not to do it; I will fall into your hands, rather than sin in the sight of the Lord."

24 Then Susanna cried out with a loud voice, and the two elders shouted against her. ²⁵And one of them ran and opened the garden doors. ²⁶When the people in the house heard the shouting in the garden, they rushed in at the side door to see what had happened to her. ²⁷And when the elders told their story, the servants felt very much ashamed, for nothing like this had ever been said about Susanna.

The Elders Testify against Susanna

28 The next day, when the people gathered at the house of her husband Joakim, the two elders came, full of their wicked plot to have Susanna put to death. In the presence of the people they said, ²⁹"Send for Susanna daughter of Hilkiah, the wife of Joakim." ³⁰So they sent for her. And she came with her parents, her children, and all her relatives.

Pray It!

Susanna

Daniel is called the hero of chapter 13 of his book. But don't forget Susanna. A real hero, Susanna chooses to risk death rather than submitting to sin. Her prayer demanding God's justice causes the Holy Spirit to stir Daniel into action.

Through prayer, we have a similar opportunity to cry out to God for justice. Every day, the news is filled with stories of violence, injustice, and oppression. Although we typically can't directly change these situations, we can offer our prayers up to God in solidarity with those who suffer, hoping that the Holy Spirit will inspire a just response to these social sins.

● What injustices might you pray about?
● Whose attention do you need to get?

▶ Daniel, chapter 13

31 Now Susanna was a woman of great refinement and beautiful in appearance. ³²As she was veiled, the scoundrels ordered her to be unveiled, so that they might feast their eyes on her beauty. ³³Those who were with her and all who saw her were weeping.

34 Then the two elders stood up before the people and laid their hands on her head. ³⁵Through her tears she looked up toward Heaven, for her heart trusted in the Lord. ³⁶The elders said, "While we were walking in the garden alone, this woman came in with two maids, shut the garden doors, and dismissed the maids. ³⁷Then a young man, who was hiding there, came to her and lay with her. ³⁸We were in a corner of the garden, and when we saw this wickedness we ran to them. ³⁹Although we saw them embracing, we could not hold the man, because he was stronger than we, and he opened the doors and got away. ⁴⁰We did, however, seize this woman and asked who the young man was, ⁴¹but she would not tell us. These things we testify."

Because they were elders of the people and judges, the assembly believed them and condemned her to death.

42 Then Susanna cried out with a loud voice, and said, "O eternal God, you know what is secret and are aware of all things before they come to be; ⁴³you know that these men have given false evidence against me. And now I am to die, though I have done none of the wicked things that they have charged against me!"

44 The Lord heard her cry. ⁴⁵Just as she was being led off to execution, God stirred up the holy spirit of a young lad named Daniel, ⁴⁶and he shouted with a loud voice, "I want no part in shedding this woman's blood!"

Daniel Rescues Susanna

47 All the people turned to him and asked, "What is this you are saying?" ⁴⁸Taking his stand among them he said, "Are you such fools, O Israelites, as to condemn a daughter of Israel without examination and without learning the facts? ⁴⁹Return to court, for these men have given false evidence against her."

50 So all the people hurried back. And the rest of the*ᵃ* elders said to him, "Come, sit among us and inform us, for God has given you the standing of an elder." ⁵¹Daniel said to them, "Separate them far from each other, and I will examine them."

52 When they were separated from each other, he summoned one of them and said to him, "You old relic of wicked days, your sins have now come home, which you have committed in the past, ⁵³pronouncing unjust judgments, condemning the innocent and acquitting the guilty, though the Lord said, 'You shall not put an innocent and righteous person to death.' ⁵⁴Now then, if you really saw this woman, tell me this: Under what tree did you see them being intimate with each other?" He answered, "Under a mastic tree."*ᵇ* ⁵⁵And Daniel said, "Very well! This lie has cost you your head, for the angel of God has received the sentence from God and will immediately cut*ᵇ* you in two."

56 Then, putting him to one side, he ordered them to bring the other. And he said to him, "You offspring of Canaan and not of Judah, beauty has beguiled you and lust has perverted your heart. ⁵⁷This is how you have been treating the daughters of Israel, and they were intimate with you through fear; but a daughter of Judah would not tolerate your wickedness. ⁵⁸Now then, tell me: Under what tree did you catch them being intimate with each other?" He answered, "Under an evergreen oak."*ᶜ* ⁵⁹Daniel said to him, "Very well! This lie has cost you also your head, for the angel of God is waiting with his sword to split*ᶜ* you in two, so as to destroy you both."

60 Then the whole assembly raised a great shout and blessed God, who saves those who hope in him. ⁶¹And they took action against the two elders, because out of their own mouths Daniel had convicted them of bearing false witness; they did to them as they had wickedly planned to do to their neighbor. ⁶²Acting in accordance with the law of Moses, they put them to death. Thus innocent blood was spared that day.

63 Hilkiah and his wife praised God for their daughter Susanna, and so did her husband Joakim and all her relatives, because she was found innocent of a shameful deed. ⁶⁴And from that day onward Daniel had a great reputation among the people.

Daniel and the Priests of Bel

14 When King Astyages was laid to rest with his ancestors, Cyrus the Persian succeeded to his kingdom. ²Daniel was a companion of the king, and was the most honored of all his Friends.

3 Now the Babylonians had an idol called Bel, and every day they provided for it twelve bushels of choice flour and forty sheep and six measures*ᵈ* of wine. ⁴The king revered it and went

---

a Gk lacks *rest of the*   *b* The Greek words for *mastic tree* and *cut* are similar, thus forming an ironic wordplay   *c* The Greek words for *evergreen oak* and *split* are similar, thus forming an ironic wordplay   *d* A little more than fifty gallons

Cultural Connection

The following excerpt from *Prophetic Voices* reveals how Hispanic young people express their prophetic mission:

As Hispanic young people, as members of the Catholic Church, we wish to raise our prophetic voice in order to announce the values of the Gospel, to denounce sin, to invite all youth to struggle for the Kingdom of God.

First of all, we announce the option for peace as against violence (see Mt 26:51–52, 2 Cor 5:18); for love as against injustice (see Jn 15:17); for good as against evil (see Deut 30:15); for the family as a fundamental value through which faith is transmitted (see Eph 6:4); and for maintaining one's own culture.

Likewise, we denounce materialism, which leads us to believe that the important thing in life is to have more and more in contrast to the teachings of the Gospel (see Mt 6:25–30; *Populorum Progressio* 19).

We denounce the injustice and oppression that Latin America suffers as a result of the cultural, economic, military, and political intervention of wealthy nations. . . .

We denounce the Melting Pot theory and make an option for learning the culture of this country without forgetting our own (*Evangelii Nuntiandi* 20). We denounce abortion, the abuse of drugs and alcohol, and the negative and manipulative influence of commercial propaganda that creates false needs.

We do not just denounce these injustices, we also feel ourselves called to struggle for peace in the world, to live a more simple life-style in solidarity with our poor brothers and sisters. . . .

Let us be aware that we can change the world with our way of life today.

(Secretariat for Hispanic Affairs, p. 12)

every day to worship it. But Daniel worshiped his own God.

So the king said to him, "Why do you not worship Bel?" [5]He answered, "Because I do not revere idols made with hands, but the living God, who created heaven and earth and has dominion over all living creatures."

6 The king said to him, "Do you not think that Bel is a living god? Do you not see how much he eats and drinks every day?" [7]And Daniel laughed, and said, "Do not be deceived, O king, for this thing is only clay inside and bronze outside, and it never ate or drank anything."

8 Then the king was angry and called the priests of Bel[a] and said to them, "If you do not tell me who is eating these provisions, you shall die. [9]But if you prove that Bel is eating them, Daniel shall die, because he has spoken blasphemy against Bel." Daniel said to the king, "Let it be done as you have said."

10 Now there were seventy priests of Bel, besides their wives and children. So the king went with Daniel into the temple of Bel. [11]The priests of Bel said, "See, we are now going outside; you yourself, O king, set out the food and prepare the wine, and shut the door and seal it with your signet. [12]When you return in the morning, if you do not find that Bel has eaten it all, we will die;

otherwise Daniel will, who is telling lies about us." [13]They were unconcerned, for beneath the table they had made a hidden entrance, through which they used to go in regularly and consume the provisions. [14]After they had gone out, the king set out the food for Bel. Then Daniel ordered his servants to bring ashes, and they scattered them throughout the whole temple in the presence of the king alone. Then they went out, shut the door and sealed it with the king's signet, and departed. [15]During the night the priests came as usual, with their wives and children, and they ate and drank everything.

16 Early in the morning the king rose and came, and Daniel with him. [17]The king said, "Are the seals unbroken, Daniel?" He answered, "They are unbroken, O king." [18]As soon as the doors were opened, the king looked at the table, and shouted in a loud voice, "You are great, O Bel, and in you there is no deceit at all!"

19 But Daniel laughed and restrained the king from going in. "Look at the floor," he said, "and notice whose footprints these are." [20]The king said, "I see the footprints of men and women and children."

21 Then the king was enraged, and he arrested

a Gk *his priests*

the priests and their wives and children. They showed him the secret doors through which they used to enter to consume what was on the table. 22 Therefore the king put them to death, and gave Bel over to Daniel, who destroyed it and its temple.

Daniel Kills the Dragon

23 Now in that place[a] there was a great dragon, which the Babylonians revered. 24 The king said to Daniel, "You cannot deny that this is a living god; so worship him." 25 Daniel said, "I worship the Lord my God, for he is the living God. 26 But give me permission, O king, and I will kill the dragon without sword or club." The king said, "I give you permission."

27 Then Daniel took pitch, fat, and hair, and boiled them together and made cakes, which he fed to the dragon. The dragon ate them, and burst open. Then Daniel said, "See what you have been worshiping!"

28 When the Babylonians heard about it, they were very indignant and conspired against the king, saying, "The king has become a Jew; he has destroyed Bel, and killed the dragon, and slaughtered the priests." 29 Going to the king, they said, "Hand Daniel over to us, or else we will kill you and your household." 30 The king saw that they were pressing him hard, and under compulsion he handed Daniel over to them.

Daniel in the Lions' Den

31 They threw Daniel into the lions' den, and he was there for six days. 32 There were seven lions in the den, and every day they had been given two human bodies and two sheep; but now they were given nothing, so that they would devour Daniel.

33 Now the prophet Habakkuk was in Judea; he had made a stew and had broken bread into a bowl, and was going into the field to take it to the reapers. 34 But the angel of the Lord said to Habakkuk, "Take the food that you have to Babylon, to Daniel, in the lions' den." 35 Habakkuk said, "Sir, I have never seen Babylon, and I know nothing about the den." 36 Then the angel of the Lord took him by the crown of his head and carried him by his hair; with the speed of the wind[b] he set him down in Babylon, right over the den.

37 Then Habakkuk shouted, "Daniel, Daniel! Take the food that God has sent you." 38 Daniel said, "You have remembered me, O God, and have not forsaken those who love you." 39 So Daniel got up and ate. And the angel of God immediately returned Habakkuk to his own place.

40 On the seventh day the king came to mourn for Daniel. When he came to the den he looked in, and there sat Daniel! 41 The king shouted with a loud voice, "You are great, O Lord, the God of Daniel, and there is no other besides you!" 42 Then he pulled Daniel[c] out, and threw into the den those who had attempted his destruction, and they were instantly eaten before his eyes.

---

a Other ancient authorities lack *in that place* b Or *by the power of his spirit* c Gk *him*

Go marry a prostitute. Say what, God? A picture is worth a thousand words, and Hosea's family life was a living picture of Israel's infidelity and God's continuing faithfulness. The Book of Hosea captures this faithful prophet's commitment to God and his loving faithfulness to his straying wife.

At a Glance

- **Chapters 1–3.** descriptions of Hosea's marriage and family
- **Chapters 4–14.** Hosea's speeches

Quick Facts

Period Covered: from 750 to after 732 BC

Inspired Authors: Hosea and later scribes

Themes: God's faithful love for Israel, the image of God as a loving parent

In Depth

Hosea preached to the northern kingdom of Israel before it was conquered by the Assyrians in 721 BC. As we learn from Hosea's speeches, the situation in the northern kingdom was not good. Over twenty-five years, Hosea saw seven kings come and go, most of them corrupt (see the timeline at the back of this Bible, and 2 Kings 14:23—17:23). Pursuing their own greedy ends and trying to play power politics, the ruling class overlooked the poor and the needy in their midst and led the people into idolatry. Through Hosea, God proclaimed, "I have been the LORD your God / ever since the land of Egypt" (Hos 13:4).

Even more powerful than Hosea's words was the living symbol of his marriage. Early in Hosea's preaching, God commanded him to marry a prostitute and have children by her. Hosea remained faithful to her, loving her even when she wandered to other men. Hosea used the image of his own marriage to preach his message to Israel. As Hosea's wife was unfaithful to him, so too was Israel unfaithful to God, wandering off in worship of other gods. However, just as Hosea was faithful to his wife and awaited her return, so too God was faithful to Israel and awaited its return from the distractions of power, wealth, and other gods.

Hosea and Amos were prophets in the northern kingdom at about the same time. But Amos had come from the southern kingdom and was more distant and cynical in describing the sins of the ruling class (see his description of well-off women in Am 4:1–3). Hosea was from the northern kingdom—these people were his people! He took their sins personally and passionately. Initially, he had hopes that the people would repent and return to God (see 2:16–23). But after a succession of selfish and violent rulers, he prophesied against his people with all the passion of a scorned lover (see Hos 13:7–11). Still, at the end, he hoped for Israel's return to God (see 14:1–2).

The Book of **Hosea**

Hosea

1 The word of the LORD that came to Hosea son of Beeri, in the days of Kings Uzziah, Jotham, Ahaz, and Hezekiah of Judah, and in the days of King Jeroboam son of Joash of Israel.

The Family of Hosea

2 When the LORD first spoke through Hosea, the LORD said to Hosea, "Go, take for yourself a wife of whoredom and have children of whoredom, for the land commits great whoredom by forsaking the LORD." ³So he went and took Gomer daughter of Diblaim, and she conceived and bore him a son.

4 And the LORD said to him, "Name him Jezreel;*a* for in a little while I will punish the house of Jehu for the blood of Jezreel, and I will put an end to the kingdom of the house of Israel. ⁵On that day I will break the bow of Israel in the valley of Jezreel."

6 She conceived again and bore a daughter. Then the LORD said to him, "Name her Lo-ruhamah,*b* for I will no longer have pity on the house of Israel or forgive them. ⁷But I will have pity on the house of Judah, and I will save them by the LORD their God; I will not save them by bow, or by sword, or by war, or by horses, or by horsemen."

8 When she had weaned Lo-ruhamah, she conceived and bore a son. ⁹Then the LORD said, "Name him Lo-ammi,*c* for you are not my people and I am not your God."*d*

The Restoration of Israel

10 *e* Yet the number of the people of Israel shall be like the sand of the sea, which can be neither measured nor numbered; and in the place where it was said to them, "You are not my people," it shall be said to them, "Children of the living God." ¹¹The people of Judah and the people of Israel shall be gathered together, and they shall appoint for themselves one head; and they shall take possession of*f* the land, for great shall be the day of Jezreel.

2 *g* Say to your brother,*h* Ammi,*i* and to your sister,*j* Ruhamah.*k*

Israel's Infidelity, Punishment, and Redemption

² Plead with your mother, plead—
    for she is not my wife,
    and I am not her husband—
  that she put away her whoring from her face,
    and her adultery from between her breasts,
³ or I will strip her naked
    and expose her as in the day she was born,
  and make her like a wilderness,
    and turn her into a parched land,
    and kill her with thirst.
⁴ Upon her children also I will have no pity,
    because they are children of whoredom.
⁵ For their mother has played the whore;
    she who conceived them has acted shamefully.
  For she said, "I will go after my lovers;
    they give me my bread and my water,
    my wool and my flax, my oil and my drink."

a That is *God sows*   *b* That is *Not pitied*   *c* That is *Not my people*   *d* Heb *I am not yours*   *e* Ch 2.1 in Heb   *f* Heb *rise up from*   *g* Ch 2.3 in Heb   *h* Gk: Heb *brothers*   *i* That is *My people*   *j* Gk Vg: Heb *sisters*   *k* That is *Pitied*

6 Therefore I will hedge up her[a] way with thorns;
   and I will build a wall against her,
   so that she cannot find her paths.
7 She shall pursue her lovers,
   but not overtake them;
 and she shall seek them,
   but shall not find them.
 Then she shall say, "I will go
   and return to my first husband,
   for it was better with me then than now."
8 She did not know
   that it was I who gave her
   the grain, the wine, and the oil,
 and who lavished upon her silver
   and gold that they used for Baal.
9 Therefore I will take back
   my grain in its time,
   and my wine in its season;
 and I will take away my wool and my flax,
   which were to cover her nakedness.
10 Now I will uncover her shame
   in the sight of her lovers,
   and no one shall rescue her out of my hand.
11 I will put an end to all her mirth,
   her festivals, her new moons, her sabbaths,
   and all her appointed festivals.
12 I will lay waste her vines and her fig trees,
   of which she said,
 "These are my pay,
   which my lovers have given me."
 I will make them a forest,
   and the wild animals shall devour them.
13 I will punish her for the festival days of the Baals,
   when she offered incense to them
 and decked herself with her ring and jewelry,
   and went after her lovers,
   and forgot me, says the LORD.

14 Therefore, I will now allure her,
   and bring her into the wilderness,
   and speak tenderly to her.
15 From there I will give her her vineyards,
   and make the Valley of Achor a door of hope.
 There she shall respond as in the days of her
   youth,
   as at the time when she came out of the land
   of Egypt.
16 On that day, says the LORD, you will call me,
"My husband," and no longer will you call me,
"My Baal."[b] 17 For I will remove the names of the
Baals from her mouth, and they shall be mentioned by name no more. 18 I will make for you[c]
a covenant on that day with the wild animals,
the birds of the air, and the creeping things of the
ground; and I will abolish[d] the bow, the sword,
and war from the land; and I will make you lie

down in safety. 19 And I will take you for my
wife forever; I will take you for my wife in righteousness and in justice, in steadfast love, and in
mercy. 20 I will take you for my wife in faithfulness; and you shall know the LORD.
21 On that day I will answer, says the LORD,
   I will answer the heavens
   and they shall answer the earth;
22 and the earth shall answer the grain, the wine,
     and the oil,
   and they shall answer Jezreel;[e]
23   and I will sow him[f] for myself in the land.
 And I will have pity on Lo-ruhamah,[g]
   and I will say to Lo-ammi,[h] "You are my
     people";
   and he shall say, "You are my God."

Further Assurances of God's Redeeming Love

3 The LORD said to me again, "Go, love a
woman who has a lover and is an adulteress,
just as the LORD loves the people of Israel, though
they turn to other gods and love raisin cakes."
2 So I bought her for fifteen shekels of silver and
a homer of barley and a measure of wine.[i] 3 And I
said to her, "You must remain as mine for many
days; you shall not play the whore, you shall not
have intercourse with a man, nor I with you."
4 For the Israelites shall remain many days without king or prince, without sacrifice or pillar,
without ephod or teraphim. 5 Afterward the Israelites shall return and seek the LORD their God,
and David their king; they shall come in awe to
the LORD and to his goodness in the latter days.

God Accuses Israel

4 Hear the word of the LORD, O people of Israel;
   for the LORD has an indictment against the
     inhabitants of the land.
 There is no faithfulness or loyalty,
   and no knowledge of God in the land.
2 Swearing, lying, and murder,
   and stealing and adultery break out;
   bloodshed follows bloodshed.
3 Therefore the land mourns,
   and all who live in it languish;
 together with the wild animals
   and the birds of the air,
   even the fish of the sea are perishing.

4 Yet let no one contend,
   and let none accuse,
   for with you is my contention, O priest.[j]

---

a Gk Syr: Heb your   b That is, "My master"   c Heb them
d Heb break   e That is God sows   f Cn: Heb her   g That is
Not pitied   h That is Not my people   i Gk: Heb a homer of
barley and a lethech of barley   j Cn: Meaning of Heb uncertain

5 You shall stumble by day;
    the prophet also shall stumble with you by
        night,
    and I will destroy your mother.
6 My people are destroyed for lack of knowledge;
    because you have rejected knowledge,
    I reject you from being a priest to me.
    And since you have forgotten the law of your God,
    I also will forget your children.

7 The more they increased,
    the more they sinned against me;
    they changed*a* their glory into shame.
8 They feed on the sin of my people;
    they are greedy for their iniquity.
9 And it shall be like people, like priest;
    I will punish them for their ways,
    and repay them for their deeds.
10 They shall eat, but not be satisfied;
    they shall play the whore, but not multiply;
    because they have forsaken the Lord
    to devote themselves to 11whoredom.

The Idolatry of Israel

Wine and new wine
    take away the understanding.
12 My people consult a piece of wood,
    and their divining rod gives them oracles.
For a spirit of whoredom has led them astray,
    and they have played the whore, forsaking
        their God.
13 They sacrifice on the tops of the mountains,
    and make offerings upon the hills,
under oak, poplar, and terebinth,
    because their shade is good.

Therefore your daughters play the whore,
    and your daughters-in-law commit adultery.
14 I will not punish your daughters when they play
    the whore,
    nor your daughters-in-law when they commit
        adultery;
for the men themselves go aside with whores,
    and sacrifice with temple prostitutes;
thus a people without understanding comes to
        ruin.

15 Though you play the whore, O Israel,
    do not let Judah become guilty.
Do not enter into Gilgal,
    or go up to Beth-aven,
    and do not swear, "As the Lord lives."
16 Like a stubborn heifer,
    Israel is stubborn;
can the Lord now feed them
    like a lamb in a broad pasture?

17 Ephraim is joined to idols—
    let him alone.
18 When their drinking is ended, they indulge in
        sexual orgies;
    they love lewdness more than their
        glory.*b*
19 A wind has wrapped them*c* in its wings,
    and they shall be ashamed because of their
        altars.*d*

Impending Judgment on Israel and Judah

5 Hear this, O priests!
    Give heed, O house of Israel!
Listen, O house of the king!
    For the judgment pertains to you;
for you have been a snare at Mizpah,
    and a net spread upon Tabor,

Live It!

Unconditional Faithfulness

We don't know all the details of Hosea's relationship with his wife, Gomer. But most people understand Hosea 3:1–3 to mean that Hosea accepted her back after she was unfaithful to him. We can only hope that Gomer was so touched by Hosea's unconditional forgiveness that she turned her life around and was faithful to him in return.

It is hard to be faithful to someone who is unfaithful to you. The other person doesn't have to be an adulterous spouse. She or he can be a friend who starts spending time with someone else instead of you, or a family member who keeps breaking promises to be with you. A natural reaction is to return the hurt in some way. How much harder—and more Christlike—it is to keep being faithful and friendly.

● Have you ever been hurt by someone's unfaithful behavior? If so, how did you react?
● How can you address a friend's or family member's unfaithful behavior and still remain faithful and loving yourself?

▶ Hos 3:1–3

HOS

2 and a pit dug deep in Shittim;[a]
   but I will punish all of them.

3 I know Ephraim,
   and Israel is not hidden from me;
for now, O Ephraim, you have played the
      whore;
   Israel is defiled.
4 Their deeds do not permit them
   to return to their God.
For the spirit of whoredom is within them,
   and they do not know the LORD.

5 Israel's pride testifies against him;
   Ephraim[b] stumbles in his guilt;
   Judah also stumbles with them.
6 With their flocks and herds they shall go
   to seek the LORD,
but they will not find him;
   he has withdrawn from them.
7 They have dealt faithlessly with the LORD;
   for they have borne illegitimate children.
Now the new moon shall devour them along
      with their fields.

8 Blow the horn in Gibeah,
   the trumpet in Ramah.
Sound the alarm at Beth-aven;
   look behind you, Benjamin!
9 Ephraim shall become a desolation
   in the day of punishment;
among the tribes of Israel
   I declare what is sure.
10 The princes of Judah have become
   like those who remove the landmark;
on them I will pour out
   my wrath like water.
11 Ephraim is oppressed, crushed in judgment,
   because he was determined to go after
      vanity.[c]
12 Therefore I am like maggots to Ephraim,
   and like rottenness to the house of Judah.
13 When Ephraim saw his sickness,
   and Judah his wound,
then Ephraim went to Assyria,
   and sent to the great king.[d]
But he is not able to cure you
   or heal your wound.
14 For I will be like a lion to Ephraim,
   and like a young lion to the house of Judah.
I myself will tear and go away;
   I will carry off, and no one shall rescue.
15 I will return again to my place
   until they acknowledge their guilt and seek
      my face.
   In their distress they will beg my favor:

A Call to Repentance

6 "Come, let us return to the LORD;
   for it is he who has torn, and he will heal us;
   he has struck down, and he will bind us up.
2 After two days he will revive us;
   on the third day he will raise us up,
   that we may live before him.
3 Let us know, let us press on to know the LORD;
   his appearing is as sure as the dawn;
he will come to us like the showers,
   like the spring rains that water the earth."

Impenitence of Israel and Judah

4 What shall I do with you, O Ephraim?
   What shall I do with you, O Judah?
Your love is like a morning cloud,
   like the dew that goes away early.
5 Therefore I have hewn them by the prophets,
   I have killed them by the words of my mouth,
   and my[e] judgment goes forth as the light.
6 For I desire steadfast love and not sacrifice,
   the knowledge of God rather than burnt
      offerings.

7 But at[f] Adam they transgressed the covenant;
   there they dealt faithlessly with me.
8 Gilead is a city of evildoers,
   tracked with blood.
9 As robbers lie in wait[a] for someone,
   so the priests are banded together;[g]
they murder on the road to Shechem,
   they commit a monstrous crime.
10 In the house of Israel I have seen a horrible
      thing;
   Ephraim's whoredom is there, Israel is
      defiled.

11 For you also, O Judah, a harvest is appointed.

When I would restore the fortunes of my people,
7 when I would heal Israel,
   the corruption of Ephraim is revealed,
   and the wicked deeds of Samaria;
for they deal falsely,
   the thief breaks in,
   and the bandits raid outside.
2 But they do not consider
   that I remember all their wickedness.
Now their deeds surround them,
   they are before my face.
3 By their wickedness they make the king glad,

a Cn: Meaning of Heb uncertain   b Heb Israel and Ephraim
c Gk: Meaning of Heb uncertain   d Cn: Heb to a king who will
contend   e Gk Syr: Heb your   f Cn: Heb like   g Syr: Heb are
a company

HOS

and the officials by their treachery.
⁴ They are all adulterers;
   they are like a heated oven,
whose baker does not need to stir the fire,
   from the kneading of the dough until it is
      leavened.
⁵ On the day of our king the officials
   became sick with the heat of wine;
   he stretched out his hand with mockers.
⁶ For they are kindled[a] like an oven, their heart
      burns within them;
   all night their anger smolders;
   in the morning it blazes like a flaming fire.
⁷ All of them are hot as an oven,
   and they devour their rulers.
All their kings have fallen;
   none of them calls upon me.

⁸ Ephraim mixes himself with the peoples;
   Ephraim is a cake not turned.
⁹ Foreigners devour his strength,
   but he does not know it;
gray hairs are sprinkled upon him,
   but he does not know it.
¹⁰ Israel's pride testifies against[b] him;
   yet they do not return to the LORD their
      God,
   or seek him, for all this.

Futile Reliance on the Nations

¹¹ Ephraim has become like a dove,
   silly and without sense;
   they call upon Egypt, they go to Assyria.
¹² As they go, I will cast my net over them;
   I will bring them down like birds of the air;
   I will discipline them according to the report
      made to their assembly.[c]
¹³ Woe to them, for they have strayed from me!
   Destruction to them, for they have rebelled
      against me!
I would redeem them,
   but they speak lies against me.

¹⁴ They do not cry to me from the heart,
   but they wail upon their beds;
they gash themselves for grain and wine;
   they rebel against me.
¹⁵ It was I who trained and strengthened their
      arms,
   yet they plot evil against me.
¹⁶ They turn to that which does not profit;[d]
   they have become like a defective bow;
their officials shall fall by the sword
   because of the rage of their tongue.
So much for their babbling in the land of
      Egypt.

Israel's Apostasy

8 Set the trumpet to your lips!
   One like a vulture[c] is over the house of the
      LORD,
   because they have broken my covenant,
      and transgressed my law.
² Israel cries to me,
   "My God, we—Israel—know you!"
³ Israel has spurned the good;
   the enemy shall pursue him.

⁴ They made kings, but not through me;
   they set up princes, but without my
      knowledge.
With their silver and gold they made idols
   for their own destruction.
⁵ Your calf is rejected, O Samaria.
   My anger burns against them.
How long will they be incapable of innocence?
⁶   For it is from Israel,
an artisan made it;
   it is not God.
The calf of Samaria
   shall be broken to pieces.[e]

⁷ For they sow the wind,
   and they shall reap the whirlwind.
The standing grain has no heads,
   it shall yield no meal;
if it were to yield,
   foreigners would devour it.
⁸ Israel is swallowed up;
   now they are among the nations
   as a useless vessel.
⁹ For they have gone up to Assyria,
   a wild ass wandering alone;
   Ephraim has bargained for lovers.
¹⁰ Though they bargain with the nations,
   I will now gather them up.
They shall soon writhe
   under the burden of kings and princes.

¹¹ When Ephraim multiplied altars to expiate sin,
   they became to him altars for sinning.
¹² Though I write for him the multitude of my
      instructions,
   they are regarded as a strange thing.
¹³ Though they offer choice sacrifices,[d]
      though they eat flesh,
   the LORD does not accept them.
Now he will remember their iniquity,

---

a Gk Syr: Heb brought near   b Or humbles   c Meaning of Heb uncertain   d Cn: Meaning of Heb uncertain   e Or shall go up in flames

Reaping the Whirlwind

Hosea uses lots of metaphors, or symbols, in describing Israel's relationship with God. Hosea 8:7 gives one of those metaphors, saying the Israelites have sowed the wind and will reap the whirlwind. The wind is their political scheming, injustice, and idolatry; the whirlwind is violence and injustice that will destroy the whole country.

Like Israel, we are free to reject or accept God, but we will have to reap the consequences of our choices.

In your prayer, reflect or journal on the following questions:

- What significant decisions have you made recently?
- What consequences are likely to follow as a result of each decision?
- Were your choices the ones that God wanted you to make? How do you know this?

▶ Hos 8:7

and punish their sins;
   they shall return to Egypt.
14 Israel has forgotten his Maker,
   and built palaces;
and Judah has multiplied fortified cities;
   but I will send a fire upon his cities,
   and it shall devour his strongholds.

Punishment for Israel's Sin

9 Do not rejoice, O Israel!
   Do not exult[a] as other nations do;
for you have played the whore, departing from
      your God.
   You have loved a prostitute's pay
   on all threshing floors.
2 Threshing floor and wine vat shall not feed
      them,
   and the new wine shall fail them.
3 They shall not remain in the land of the Lord;
   but Ephraim shall return to Egypt,
   and in Assyria they shall eat unclean food.

4 They shall not pour drink offerings of wine to
      the Lord,

and their sacrifices shall not please him.
   Such sacrifices shall be like mourners' bread;
   all who eat of it shall be defiled;
for their bread shall be for their hunger only;
   it shall not come to the house of the Lord.

5 What will you do on the day of appointed
      festival,
   and on the day of the festival of the Lord?
6 For even if they escape destruction,
   Egypt shall gather them,
   Memphis shall bury them.
Nettles shall possess their precious things of
      silver;[b]
   thorns shall be in their tents.

7 The days of punishment have come,
   the days of recompense have come;
   Israel cries,[c]
"The prophet is a fool,
   the man of the spirit is mad!"
Because of your great iniquity,
   your hostility is great.
8 The prophet is a sentinel for my God over
      Ephraim,
   yet a fowler's snare is on all his ways,
   and hostility in the house of his God.
9 They have deeply corrupted themselves
   as in the days of Gibeah;
he will remember their iniquity,
   he will punish their sins.

10 Like grapes in the wilderness,
   I found Israel.
Like the first fruit on the fig tree,
   in its first season,
   I saw your ancestors.
But they came to Baal-peor,
   and consecrated themselves to a thing of
      shame,
   and became detestable like the thing they
      loved.
11 Ephraim's glory shall fly away like a bird—
   no birth, no pregnancy, no conception!
12 Even if they bring up children,
   I will bereave them until no one is left.
Woe to them indeed
   when I depart from them!
13 Once I saw Ephraim as a young palm planted in
      a lovely meadow,[b]
   but now Ephraim must lead out his children
      for slaughter.
14 Give them, O Lord—

a Gk: Heb To exultation   b Meaning of Heb uncertain
c Cn Compare Gk: Heb shall know

what will you give?
Give them a miscarrying womb
  and dry breasts.

15 Every evil of theirs began at Gilgal;
  there I came to hate them.
Because of the wickedness of their deeds
  I will drive them out of my house.
I will love them no more;
  all their officials are rebels.

16 Ephraim is stricken,
  their root is dried up,
  they shall bear no fruit.
Even though they give birth,
  I will kill the cherished offspring of their
    womb.
17 Because they have not listened to him,
  my God will reject them;
  they shall become wanderers among the
    nations.

Israel's Sin and Captivity

10 Israel is a luxuriant vine
  that yields its fruit.
The more his fruit increased
  the more altars he built;
as his country improved,
  he improved his pillars.
2 Their heart is false;
  now they must bear their guilt.
The Lord[a] will break down their altars,
  and destroy their pillars.

3 For now they will say:
  "We have no king,
for we do not fear the Lord,
  and a king—what could he do for us?"
4 They utter mere words;
  with empty oaths they make covenants;
so litigation springs up like poisonous weeds
  in the furrows of the field.
5 The inhabitants of Samaria tremble
  for the calf[b] of Beth-aven.
Its people shall mourn for it,
  and its idolatrous priests shall wail[c] over it,
  over its glory that has departed from it.
6 The thing itself shall be carried to Assyria
  as tribute to the great king.[d]
Ephraim shall be put to shame,
  and Israel shall be ashamed of his idol.[e]

7 Samaria's king shall perish
  like a chip on the face of the waters.
8 The high places of Aven, the sin of Israel,
  shall be destroyed.

Thorn and thistle shall grow up
  on their altars.
They shall say to the mountains, Cover us,
  and to the hills, Fall on us.

9 Since the days of Gibeah you have sinned,
    O Israel;
  there they have continued.
  Shall not war overtake them in Gibeah?
10 I will come[f] against the wayward people to
    punish them;
  and nations shall be gathered against them
  when they are punished[g] for their double
    iniquity.

11 Ephraim was a trained heifer
  that loved to thresh,
  and I spared her fair neck;
but I will make Ephraim break the ground;
  Judah must plow;
  Jacob must harrow for himself.
12 Sow for yourselves righteousness;
  reap steadfast love;
  break up your fallow ground;
for it is time to seek the Lord,
  that he may come and rain righteousness
    upon you.

13 You have plowed wickedness,
  you have reaped injustice,
  you have eaten the fruit of lies.
Because you have trusted in your power
  and in the multitude of your warriors,
14 therefore the tumult of war shall rise against
    your people,
  and all your fortresses shall be destroyed,
as Shalman destroyed Beth-arbel on the day of
    battle
  when mothers were dashed in pieces with
    their children.
15 Thus it shall be done to you, O Bethel,
  because of your great wickedness.
At dawn the king of Israel
  shall be utterly cut off.

God's Compassion Despite Israel's Ingratitude

11 When Israel was a child, I loved him,
  and out of Egypt I called my son.
2 The more I[h] called them,
  the more they went from me;[i]
they kept sacrificing to the Baals,
  and offering incense to idols.

---

a Heb *he*   b Gk Syr: Heb *calves*   c Cn: Heb *exult*   d Cn: Heb
to a king who will contend   e Cn: Heb *counsel*   f Cn Compare
Gk: Heb *In my desire*   g Gk: Heb *bound*   h Gk: Heb *they*
i Gk: Heb *them*

A Parent's Love

Hosea, chapter 11, describes God as a loving parent. This is one of the most touching passages of the Old Testament. Despite God's tenderness and care, Israel behaves as a rebellious child. God is heartbroken by Israel's rejection, but is compassionate in calling for its return.

God, loving father and mother, thank you for your generous and unconditional love. Let me remember that you always love me, even when I have done something wrong. Help me to return your love by living in a way that is pleasing to you. Amen.

▶ Hos 11:1–7

3 Yet it was I who taught Ephraim to walk,
    I took them up in my[a] arms;
      but they did not know that I healed them.
4 I led them with cords of human kindness,
    with bands of love.
  I was to them like those
    who lift infants to their cheeks.[b]
    I bent down to them and fed them.

5 They shall return to the land of Egypt,
    and Assyria shall be their king,
      because they have refused to return to me.
6 The sword rages in their cities,
    it consumes their oracle-priests,
    and devours because of their schemes.
7 My people are bent on turning away from me.
    To the Most High they call,
      but he does not raise them up at all.[c]

8 How can I give you up, Ephraim?
    How can I hand you over, O Israel?
  How can I make you like Admah?
    How can I treat you like Zeboiim?
  My heart recoils within me;
    my compassion grows warm and tender.
9 I will not execute my fierce anger;
    I will not again destroy Ephraim;
  for I am God and no mortal,
    the Holy One in your midst,
    and I will not come in wrath.[c]

10 They shall go after the LORD,
    who roars like a lion;
  when he roars,
    his children shall come trembling from the west.
11 They shall come trembling like birds from Egypt,
    and like doves from the land of Assyria;
    and I will return them to their homes, says the LORD.

12 [d] Ephraim has surrounded me with lies,
    and the house of Israel with deceit;
  but Judah still walks[e] with God,
    and is faithful to the Holy One.

12 Ephraim herds the wind,
    and pursues the east wind all day long;
  they multiply falsehood and violence;
    they make a treaty with Assyria,
    and oil is carried to Egypt.

The Long History of Rebellion

2 The LORD has an indictment against Judah,
    and will punish Jacob according to his ways,
    and repay him according to his deeds.
3 In the womb he tried to supplant his brother,
    and in his manhood he strove with God.
4 He strove with the angel and prevailed,
    he wept and sought his favor;
  he met him at Bethel,
    and there he spoke with him.[f]
5 The LORD the God of hosts,
    the LORD is his name!
6 But as for you, return to your God,
    hold fast to love and justice,
    and wait continually for your God.

7 A trader, in whose hands are false balances,
    he loves to oppress.
8 Ephraim has said, "Ah, I am rich,
    I have gained wealth for myself;
  in all of my gain
    no offense has been found in me
    that would be sin."[c]
9 I am the LORD your God
    from the land of Egypt;
  I will make you live in tents again,
    as in the days of the appointed festival.

10 I spoke to the prophets;
    it was I who multiplied visions,
    and through the prophets I will bring destruction.

---

a Gk Syr Vg: Heb *his*   b Or *who ease the yoke on their jaws*
c Meaning of Heb uncertain   d Ch 12.1 in Heb   e Heb *roams* or *rules*   f Gk Syr: Heb *us*

HOS

Cultural Connection

I Therefore Commit

This prayer from Elizabeth S. Tapia of the Philippines could have been written in response to Hosea's call to live justly, to live the spirit of being a holy people of God:

> We should not oppress children, indigenous people, women, the homeless, refugees and victims of war.
> We need to live in defense of peoples and creation.
> For I believe in the interwovenness of life.
> Creator and Creatures. Cosmic and Individual.
> West, North, East, South. Rest and Prayer.
> Food and Freedom. Theology and Ecology.
> I therefore commit myself, together with you, to take care of mother earth.
> To advocate for peace and justice.
> To choose and celebrate life!
> These things I believe. Amen. ("Earth Credo," from *A Time to Speak*)

▶ Hos 12:2–6

---

¹¹ In Gilead*a* there is iniquity,
    they shall surely come to nothing.
In Gilgal they sacrifice bulls,
    so their altars shall be like stone heaps
    on the furrows of the field.
¹² Jacob fled to the land of Aram,
    there Israel served for a wife,
    and for a wife he guarded sheep.*b*
¹³ By a prophet the LORD brought Israel up from
    Egypt,
    and by a prophet he was guarded.
¹⁴ Ephraim has given bitter offense,
    so his Lord will bring his crimes down on
    him
    and pay him back for his insults.

Relentless Judgment on Israel

13 When Ephraim spoke, there was trembling;
    he was exalted in Israel;
    but he incurred guilt through Baal and died.
² And now they keep on sinning
    and make a cast image for themselves,
idols of silver made according to their
    understanding,
    all of them the work of artisans.
"Sacrifice to these," they say.*c*
    People are kissing calves!
³ Therefore they shall be like the morning mist
    or like the dew that goes away early,
like chaff that swirls from the threshing floor
    or like smoke from a window.

⁴ Yet I have been the LORD your God
    ever since the land of Egypt;
you know no God but me,
    and besides me there is no savior.

⁵ It was I who fed*d* you in the wilderness,
    in the land of drought.
⁶ When I fed*e* them, they were satisfied;
    they were satisfied, and their heart was proud;
    therefore they forgot me.
⁷ So I will become like a lion to them,
    like a leopard I will lurk beside the way.
⁸ I will fall upon them like a bear robbed of her
    cubs,
    and will tear open the covering of their heart;
there I will devour them like a lion,
    as a wild animal would mangle them.

⁹ I will destroy you, O Israel;
    who can help you?*f*
¹⁰ Where now is*g* your king, that he may save you?
    Where in all your cities are your rulers,
of whom you said,
    "Give me a king and rulers"?
¹¹ I gave you a king in my anger,
    and I took him away in my wrath.

¹² Ephraim's iniquity is bound up;
    his sin is kept in store.
¹³ The pangs of childbirth come for him,
    but he is an unwise son;
for at the proper time he does not present
    himself
    at the mouth of the womb.

¹⁴ Shall I ransom them from the power of Sheol?
    Shall I redeem them from Death?

---

a Compare Syr: Heb *Gilead*   b Heb lacks *sheep*   c Cn Compare Gk: Heb *To these they say sacrifices of people*   d Gk Syr: Heb *knew*   e Cn: Heb *according to their pasture*   f Gk Syr: Heb *for in me is your help*   g Gk Syr Vg: Heb *I will be*

HOS

O Death, where are[a] your plagues?
O Sheol, where is[a] your destruction?
Compassion is hidden from my eyes.

[15] Although he may flourish among rushes,[b]
the east wind shall come, a blast from the
Lord,
rising from the wilderness;
and his fountain shall dry up,
his spring shall be parched.
It shall strip his treasury
of every precious thing.
[16] [c] Samaria shall bear her guilt,
because she has rebelled against her God;
they shall fall by the sword,
their little ones shall be dashed in pieces,
and their pregnant women ripped open.

> "Return, O Israel, to the
> Lord your God,
> for you have stumbled
> because of your iniquity."
>
> (Hos 14:1)

A Plea for Repentance

14 Return, O Israel, to the Lord your God,
for you have stumbled because of your
iniquity.
[2] Take words with you
and return to the Lord;
say to him,
"Take away all guilt;
accept that which is good,

and we will offer
the fruit[d] of our lips.
[3] Assyria shall not save us;
we will not ride upon horses;
we will say no more, 'Our God,'
to the work of our hands.
In you the orphan finds mercy."

Assurance of Forgiveness

[4] I will heal their disloyalty;
I will love them freely,
for my anger has turned from them.
[5] I will be like the dew to Israel;
he shall blossom like the lily,
he shall strike root like the forests of
Lebanon.[e]
[6] His shoots shall spread out;
his beauty shall be like the olive tree,
and his fragrance like that of Lebanon.
[7] They shall again live beneath my[f] shadow,
they shall flourish as a garden;[g]
they shall blossom like the vine,
their fragrance shall be like the wine of
Lebanon.

[8] O Ephraim, what have I[h] to do with idols?
It is I who answer and look after you.[i]
I am like an evergreen cypress;
your faithfulness[j] comes from me.
[9] Those who are wise understand these things;
those who are discerning know them.
For the ways of the Lord are right,
and the upright walk in them,
but transgressors stumble in them.

a Gk Syr: Heb *I will be*   b Or *among brothers*   c Ch 14.1 in
Heb   d Gk Syr: Heb *bulls*   e Cn: Heb *like Lebanon*   f Heb *his*
g Cn: Heb *they shall grow grain*   h Or *What more has Ephraim*
i Heb *him*   j Heb *your fruit*

You're just cruising along, in the groove, and everything is going your way. Then it happens. You hit a major bump in the road, and everything starts falling apart. This appears to have been the situation in Joel's time, when a major plague of locusts was causing widespread destruction. Joel took it as a wake-up sign, calling Israel to rely totally on God no matter what happened.

At a Glance

- 1:1—2:17. a discussion of a plague of locusts and the day of the Lord
- 2:18—3:21. several prophecies promising God's salvation for Israel

Quick Facts

Period Covered: after the re-building of the Temple (515 BC) and before the destruction of Sidon (343 BC)

Inspired Authors: Joel and scribes, writing around 400 BC

Theme: a plague of locusts as an occasion to call for Israel to repent and turn to the Lord

In Depth

The Book of Joel does not state clearly when it was written, but it gives several clues that lead biblical scholars to believe it was written after the Babylonian Exile. During this time, Israel was ruled by the Greeks and did not have a king. The Temple and Jerusalem had been rebuilt, and Israel enjoyed relative peace, along with a growing expectancy for the coming of a messiah, a savior.

In this period, a natural disaster, perhaps a plague of locusts, occurred. In the first part of the book, Joel uses this tragedy to call Israel's attention toward God and renew its faith. He compares the plague of locusts to an invading army that brings devastation to a city. Eventually, prayer and penance end the plague and bring rain for new crops. More important, the gift of the Spirit renews the people of God (see Joel 2:28–29).

A major element of this book is a warrior-type song in which Joel speaks of the coming of the day of the Lord (see 2:1–17). He describes this as the day when judgment will be delivered against the nations that have destroyed Israel. The day of the Lord is a theme that runs throughout the Bible. It is sometimes described as a joyful time of celebration (see Isa 9:3), and other times as a day of punishment and destruction (see Am 5:18–24). Initially, writers of the Scriptures applied the term *day of the Lord* only to Israel; Joel applied it to all nations. Gradually, it became connected to the final judgment (see Mt 25:31–46).

The Book of Joel ends by affirming that the Lord dwells in Zion (Jerusalem) and the land will be fruitful once more. This is Joel's central message: Despite plagues and even war, God is present in Judah, and there is reason for hope.

The Book of Joel

1041

Joel

1 The word of the LORD that came to Joel son of Pethuel:

Lament over the Ruin of the Country

2 Hear this, O elders,
    give ear, all inhabitants of the land!
Has such a thing happened in your days,
    or in the days of your ancestors?
3 Tell your children of it,
    and let your children tell their children,
    and their children another generation.

4 What the cutting locust left,
    the swarming locust has eaten.
What the swarming locust left,
    the hopping locust has eaten,
and what the hopping locust left,
    the destroying locust has eaten.

5 Wake up, you drunkards, and weep;
    and wail, all you wine-drinkers,
over the sweet wine,
    for it is cut off from your mouth.
6 For a nation has invaded my land,
    powerful and innumerable;
its teeth are lions' teeth,
    and it has the fangs of a lioness.
7 It has laid waste my vines,
    and splintered my fig trees;
it has stripped off their bark and thrown it down;
    their branches have turned white.

8 Lament like a virgin dressed in sackcloth
    for the husband of her youth.
9 The grain offering and the drink offering are
    cut off
    from the house of the LORD.
The priests mourn,
    the ministers of the LORD.
10 The fields are devastated,
    the ground mourns;
for the grain is destroyed,
    the wine dries up,
    the oil fails.

11 Be dismayed, you farmers,
    wail, you vinedressers,
over the wheat and the barley;
    for the crops of the field are ruined.
12 The vine withers,
    the fig tree droops.
Pomegranate, palm, and apple—
    all the trees of the field are dried up;
surely, joy withers away
    among the people.

A Call to Repentance and Prayer

13 Put on sackcloth and lament, you priests;
    wail, you ministers of the altar.
Come, pass the night in sackcloth,
    you ministers of my God!
Grain offering and drink offering
    are withheld from the house of your God.

14 Sanctify a fast,
    call a solemn assembly.
Gather the elders
    and all the inhabitants of the land
to the house of the Lord your God,
    and cry out to the Lord.

15 Alas for the day!
For the day of the Lord is near,
    and as destruction from the Almighty[a] it comes.
16 Is not the food cut off
    before our eyes,
joy and gladness
    from the house of our God?

17 The seed shrivels under the clods,[b]
    the storehouses are desolate;
the granaries are ruined
    because the grain has failed.
18 How the animals groan!
    The herds of cattle wander about
because there is no pasture for them;
    even the flocks of sheep are dazed.[c]

19 To you, O Lord, I cry.
For fire has devoured
    the pastures of the wilderness,
and flames have burned
    all the trees of the field.
20 Even the wild animals cry to you
    because the watercourses are dried up,
and fire has devoured
    the pastures of the wilderness.

2 Blow the trumpet in Zion;
    sound the alarm on my holy mountain!
Let all the inhabitants of the land tremble,
    for the day of the Lord is coming, it is near—
2 a day of darkness and gloom,
    a day of clouds and thick darkness!
Like blackness spread upon the mountains
    a great and powerful army comes;
their like has never been from of old,
    nor will be again after them
    in ages to come.

3 Fire devours in front of them,
    and behind them a flame burns.
Before them the land is like the garden of Eden,
    but after them a desolate wilderness,
    and nothing escapes them.

4 They have the appearance of horses,
    and like war-horses they charge.
5 As with the rumbling of chariots,
    they leap on the tops of the mountains,

like the crackling of a flame of fire
    devouring the stubble,
like a powerful army
    drawn up for battle.

6 Before them peoples are in anguish,
    all faces grow pale.[b]
7 Like warriors they charge,
    like soldiers they scale the wall.
Each keeps to its own course,
    they do not swerve from[d] their paths.
8 They do not jostle one another,
    each keeps to its own track;
they burst through the weapons
    and are not halted.
9 They leap upon the city,
    they run upon the walls;
they climb up into the houses,
    they enter through the windows like a thief.

10 The earth quakes before them,
    the heavens tremble.
The sun and the moon are darkened,
    and the stars withdraw their shining.
11 The Lord utters his voice
    at the head of his army;
how vast is his host!
    Numberless are those who obey his
       command.
Truly the day of the Lord is great;
    terrible indeed—who can endure it?

12 Yet even now, says the Lord,
    return to me with all your heart,
with fasting, with weeping, and with mourning;
13   rend your hearts and not your clothing.
Return to the Lord, your God,
    for he is gracious and merciful,
slow to anger, and abounding in steadfast love,
    and relents from punishing.
14 Who knows whether he will not turn and relent,
    and leave a blessing behind him,
a grain offering and a drink offering
    for the Lord, your God?

15 Blow the trumpet in Zion;
    sanctify a fast;
call a solemn assembly;
16   gather the people.
Sanctify the congregation;
    assemble the aged;
gather the children,

---

a Traditional rendering of Heb *Shaddai* b Meaning of Heb
uncertain c Compare Gk Syr Vg: Meaning of Heb uncertain
d Gk Syr Vg: Heb *they do not take a pledge along*

Cultural Connection

Vision Quest

Joel 2:28 mentions young men having visions. Vision quests are a Native American tradition. A young man with only a blanket is led by a holy person to a hill to be on his own for several days. During that time, he refrains from eating and drinking and tries to focus on being very still, believing he will receive a personal vision. That vision will give shape to his life and help him know his place in the world. The key is in the wait-ing. When the young man returns from his vision quest, he is consid-ered a man and can become the person he is destined to become. He now has a vision to live out.

Jesus went on something like a vision quest before he began his public ministry. He went into the wilderness, fasted, and wrestled with the demons.

Joel 2:28–29 is read at Pen-tecost—the Church feast day that celebrates the coming of the Holy Spirit. You can let the Holy Spirit help you discern the path for your life through a personal retreat, guided by a spiritual director in the Christian tradition.

▶ **Joel 2:28–29**

even infants at the breast.
Let the bridegroom leave his room,
   and the bride her canopy.

17 Between the vestibule and the altar
   let the priests, the ministers of the Lᴏʀᴅ, weep.
Let them say, "Spare your people, O Lᴏʀᴅ,
   and do not make your heritage a mockery,
   a byword among the nations.
Why should it be said among the peoples,
   'Where is their God?' "

God's Response and Promise

18 Then the Lᴏʀᴅ became jealous for his land,
   and had pity on his people.
19 In response to his people the Lᴏʀᴅ said:
I am sending you
   grain, wine, and oil,
   and you will be satisfied;
and I will no more make you
   a mockery among the nations.

20 I will remove the northern army far from you,
   and drive it into a parched and desolate land,
its front into the eastern sea,
   and its rear into the western sea;
its stench and foul smell will rise up.
   Surely he has done great things!

21 Do not fear, O soil;
   be glad and rejoice,
   for the Lᴏʀᴅ has done great things!
22 Do not fear, you animals of the field,
   for the pastures of the wilderness are green;

the tree bears its fruit,
   the fig tree and vine give their full yield.

23 O children of Zion, be glad
   and rejoice in the Lᴏʀᴅ your God;
for he has given the early rainᵃ for your
   vindication,
   he has poured down for you abundant rain,
   the early and the later rain, as before.
24 The threshing floors shall be full of grain,
   the vats shall overflow with wine and oil.

25 I will repay you for the years
   that the swarming locust has eaten,
the hopper, the destroyer, and the cutter,
   my great army, which I sent against you.

26 You shall eat in plenty and be satisfied,
   and praise the name of the Lᴏʀᴅ your God,
   who has dealt wondrously with you.
And my people shall never again be put to
      shame.
27 You shall know that I am in the midst of Israel,
   and that I, the Lᴏʀᴅ, am your God and there
      is no other.
And my people shall never again be put to
      shame.

God's Spirit Poured Out

28ᵇ Then afterward
   I will pour out my spirit on all flesh;
   your sons and your daughters shall prophesy,

───────────────

ᵃ Meaning of Heb uncertain   ᵇ Ch 3.1 in Heb

your old men shall dream dreams,
   and your young men shall see visions.
29 Even on the male and female slaves,
   in those days, I will pour out my spirit.

30 I will show portents in the heavens and on
the earth, blood and fire and columns of smoke.
31The sun shall be turned to darkness, and the
moon to blood, before the great and terrible
day of the LORD comes. 32Then everyone who
calls on the name of the LORD shall be saved;
for in Mount Zion and in Jerusalem there shall
be those who escape, as the LORD has said, and
among the survivors shall be those whom the
LORD calls.

3 a For then, in those days and at that time,
   when I restore the fortunes of Judah and
Jerusalem, 2I will gather all the nations and
bring them down to the valley of Jehoshaphat,
and I will enter into judgment with them there,
on account of my people and my heritage Israel,
because they have scattered them among the nations. They have divided my land, 3and cast lots
for my people, and traded boys for prostitutes,
and sold girls for wine, and drunk it down.

4 What are you to me, O Tyre and Sidon,
and all the regions of Philistia? Are you paying
me back for something? If you are paying me
back, I will turn your deeds back upon your own
heads swiftly and speedily. 5For you have taken
my silver and my gold, and have carried my rich
treasures into your temples.b 6You have sold the
people of Judah and Jerusalem to the Greeks,
removing them far from their own border. 7But
now I will rouse them to leave the places to
which you have sold them, and I will turn your
deeds back upon your own heads. 8I will sell
your sons and your daughters into the hand of
the people of Judah, and they will sell them to
the Sabeans, to a nation far away; for the LORD
has spoken.

Judgment in the Valley of Jehoshaphat

9 Proclaim this among the nations:
Prepare war,c
   stir up the warriors.
Let all the soldiers draw near,
   let them come up.
10 Beat your plowshares into swords,
   and your pruning hooks into spears;
   let the weakling say, "I am a warrior."

11 Come quickly,d
   all you nations all around,
   gather yourselves there.

Bring down your warriors, O LORD.
12 Let the nations rouse themselves,
   and come up to the valley of Jehoshaphat;
for there I will sit to judge
   all the neighboring nations.

13 Put in the sickle,
   for the harvest is ripe.
Go in, tread,
   for the wine press is full.
The vats overflow,
   for their wickedness is great.

14 Multitudes, multitudes,
   in the valley of decision!
For the day of the LORD is near
   in the valley of decision.

15 The sun and the moon are darkened,
   and the stars withdraw their shining.

16 The LORD roars from Zion,
   and utters his voice from Jerusalem,
   and the heavens and the earth shake.
But the LORD is a refuge for his people,
   a stronghold for the people of Israel.

The Glorious Future of Judah

17 So you shall know that I, the LORD your God,
   dwell in Zion, my holy mountain.
And Jerusalem shall be holy,
   and strangers shall never again pass through it.

18 In that day
the mountains shall drip sweet wine,
   the hills shall flow with milk,
and all the stream beds of Judah
   shall flow with water;
a fountain shall come forth from the house of
      the LORD
   and water the Wadi Shittim.

19 Egypt shall become a desolation
   and Edom a desolate wilderness,
because of the violence done to the people of
      Judah,
   in whose land they have shed innocent blood.
20 But Judah shall be inhabited forever,
   and Jerusalem to all generations.
21 I will avenge their blood, and I will not clear the
      guilty,e
   for the LORD dwells in Zion.

---

a Ch 4.1 in Heb   b Or palaces   c Heb sanctify war
d Meaning of Heb uncertain   e Gk Syr: Heb I will hold innocent
their blood that I have not held innocent

You've probably run across people who bluntly state what they see going on. They don't seem to care too much about what other people think. They say, "I just tell it like it is." The prophet Amos was like that. He didn't pull any punches in describing the wealthy class's sins or the destruction that God had planned for Israel. He was a powerful voice calling for justice in God's plan of salvation.

At a Glance

- 1:1—2:3. a condemnation of Israel's neighbors
- 2:4—9:8. a proclamation of the destruction of the northern kingdom, Israel
- 9:9-15. a word of hope, probably added by a later editor

Quick Facts

Period Covered: from 760 to 750 BC

Inspired Authors: Amos and later scribes

Theme: God's destruction of Israel because of the injustice and hypocrisy of the wealthy and the ruling class

In Depth

Amos lived when there were two separate kingdoms of Israelites: a northern kingdom, named Israel, and a southern kingdom, named Judah. He was born in the southern kingdom and worked as a shepherd and tree trimmer (see Am 7:14). But God called him to preach to the northern kingdom. Amos was not an official prophet of the king's court, so he was free to speak against the king and the court and to be brutally honest in delivering God's message.

Among the Old Testament prophecies, Amos's are the least hopeful. Amos stresses that Israel's destruction, complete and total, is certain. He condemns Israel for its failure to be faithful to the covenant, but he has a special anger toward the king, the priests, and the wealthy class. He accuses them of being hypocrites who lead the people of Israel astray while pretending to be faithful themselves.

What was Amos's evidence? First, the covenant demanded special care for the poor, the outcast, and the marginalized. The king, the wealthy, and some of the priests were ignoring this demand. Instead of caring for the poor and the lowly, the wealthy were cheating them and treating them unjustly (see 2:6–8).

Second, with the monies they cheated out of the poor, the ruling class and the wealthy staged lavish ceremonies to God that were modeled on ceremonies honoring foreign gods. They went through the motions of worshiping God, but they ignored the demand to care for their neighbor (see 5:21–24). For Amos, this was the heart of Israel's hypocrisy—its sinful habit of separating its religious rituals from concern for its citizens. This phoniness was repulsive to God, and because of Israel's sin, God would bring it to destruction. Amos is rightly called the prophet of the Lord's justice.

The Book of **Amos**

Amos

1 The words of Amos, who was among the shepherds of Tekoa, which he saw concerning Israel in the days of King Uzziah of Judah and in the days of King Jeroboam son of Joash of Israel, two years[a] before the earthquake.

Judgment on Israel's Neighbors

2 And he said:

The LORD roars from Zion,
and utters his voice from Jerusalem;
the pastures of the shepherds wither,
and the top of Carmel dries up.

3 Thus says the LORD:
For three transgressions of Damascus,
and for four, I will not revoke the
punishment;[b]
because they have threshed Gilead
with threshing sledges of iron.
4 So I will send a fire on the house of Hazael,
and it shall devour the strongholds of Ben-
hadad.
5 I will break the gate bars of Damascus,
and cut off the inhabitants from the Valley of
Aven,
and the one who holds the scepter from
Beth-eden;
and the people of Aram shall go into exile to
Kir,
says the LORD.

6 Thus says the LORD:
For three transgressions of Gaza,

and for four, I will not revoke the
punishment;[b]
because they carried into exile entire
communities,
to hand them over to Edom.
7 So I will send a fire on the wall of Gaza,
fire that shall devour its strongholds.
8 I will cut off the inhabitants from Ashdod,
and the one who holds the scepter from
Ashkelon;
I will turn my hand against Ekron,
and the remnant of the Philistines shall perish,
says the Lord GOD.

9 Thus says the LORD:
For three transgressions of Tyre,
and for four, I will not revoke the
punishment;[b]
because they delivered entire communities over
to Edom,
and did not remember the covenant of
kinship.
10 So I will send a fire on the wall of Tyre,
fire that shall devour its strongholds.

11 Thus says the LORD:
For three transgressions of Edom,
and for four, I will not revoke the
punishment;[b]
because he pursued his brother with the sword
and cast off all pity;

---

a Or *during two years* b Heb *cause it to return*

he maintained his anger perpetually,[a]
  and kept his wrath[b] forever.
12 So I will send a fire on Teman,
  and it shall devour the strongholds of Bozrah.

13 Thus says the LORD:
For three transgressions of the Ammonites,
  and for four, I will not revoke the
    punishment;[c]
because they have ripped open pregnant women
    in Gilead
  in order to enlarge their territory.
14 So I will kindle a fire against the wall of
    Rabbah,
  fire that shall devour its strongholds,
with shouting on the day of battle,
  with a storm on the day of the whirlwind;
15 then their king shall go into exile,
  he and his officials together,
                                    says the LORD.

2 Thus says the LORD:
For three transgressions of Moab,
  and for four, I will not revoke the
    punishment;[c]
because he burned to lime
  the bones of the king of Edom.
2 So I will send a fire on Moab,
  and it shall devour the strongholds of
    Kerioth,
and Moab shall die amid uproar,
  amid shouting and the sound of the trumpet;
3 I will cut off the ruler from its midst,
  and will kill all its officials with him,
                                    says the LORD.

Judgment on Judah

4 Thus says the LORD:
For three transgressions of Judah,
  and for four, I will not revoke the
    punishment;[c]
because they have rejected the law of the LORD,
  and have not kept his statutes,
but they have been led astray by the same lies
  after which their ancestors walked.
5 So I will send a fire on Judah,
  and it shall devour the strongholds of
    Jerusalem.

Judgment on Israel

6 Thus says the LORD:
For three transgressions of Israel,
  and for four, I will not revoke the
    punishment;[c]
because they sell the righteous for silver,
  and the needy for a pair of sandals—

7 they who trample the head of the poor into the
    dust of the earth,
  and push the afflicted out of the way;
father and son go in to the same girl,
  so that my holy name is profaned;
8 they lay themselves down beside every altar
  on garments taken in pledge;
and in the house of their God they drink
  wine bought with fines they imposed.

9 Yet I destroyed the Amorite before them,
  whose height was like the height of cedars,
  and who was as strong as oaks;
I destroyed his fruit above,
  and his roots beneath.
10 Also I brought you up out of the land of Egypt,
  and led you forty years in the wilderness,
  to possess the land of the Amorite.
11 And I raised up some of your children to be
    prophets
  and some of your youths to be nazirites.[d]
  Is it not indeed so, O people of Israel?
                                    says the LORD.

12 But you made the nazirites[d] drink wine,
  and commanded the prophets,
  saying, "You shall not prophesy."

13 So, I will press you down in your place,
  just as a cart presses down
  when it is full of sheaves.[e]
14 Flight shall perish from the swift,
  and the strong shall not retain their
    strength,
  nor shall the mighty save their lives;
15 those who handle the bow shall not stand,
  and those who are swift of foot shall not save
    themselves,
  nor shall those who ride horses save their
    lives;
16 and those who are stout of heart among the
    mighty
  shall flee away naked in that day,
                                    says the LORD.

Israel's Guilt and Punishment

3 Hear this word that the LORD has spoken
against you, O people of Israel, against the
whole family that I brought up out of the land
of Egypt:
  2 You only have I known
    of all the families of the earth;

---

a Syr Vg: Heb and his anger tore perpetually   b Gk Syr Vg: Heb
and his wrath kept   c Heb cause it to return   d That is, those
separated or those consecrated   e Meaning of Heb uncertain

therefore I will punish you
  for all your iniquities.

3 Do two walk together
  unless they have made an appointment?
4 Does a lion roar in the forest,
  when it has no prey?
Does a young lion cry out from its den,
  if it has caught nothing?
5 Does a bird fall into a snare on the earth,
  when there is no trap for it?
Does a snare spring up from the ground,
  when it has taken nothing?
6 Is a trumpet blown in a city,
  and the people are not afraid?
Does disaster befall a city,
  unless the LORD has done it?
7 Surely the Lord GOD does nothing,
  without revealing his secret
  to his servants the prophets.
8 The lion has roared;
  who will not fear?
The Lord GOD has spoken;
  who can but prophesy?

9 Proclaim to the strongholds in Ashdod,
  and to the strongholds in the land of Egypt,
and say, "Assemble yourselves on Mount*a*
  Samaria,
  and see what great tumults are within it,
  and what oppressions are in its midst."
10 They do not know how to do right, says the LORD,
  those who store up violence and robbery in
  their strongholds.
11 Therefore thus says the Lord GOD:
An adversary shall surround the land,
  and strip you of your defense;
  and your strongholds shall be plundered.

12 Thus says the LORD: As the shepherd rescues from the mouth of the lion two legs, or a
piece of an ear, so shall the people of Israel who
live in Samaria be rescued, with the corner of a
couch and part*b* of a bed.

13 Hear, and testify against the house of Jacob,
  says the Lord GOD, the God of hosts:
14 On the day I punish Israel for its transgressions,
  I will punish the altars of Bethel,
and the horns of the altar shall be cut off
  and fall to the ground.
15 I will tear down the winter house as well as the
  summer house;
and the houses of ivory shall perish,
and the great houses*c* shall come to an end,
  says the LORD.

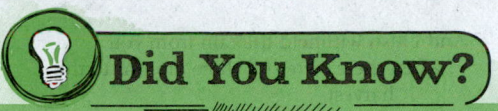

Did You Know?

The Remnant

Does Amos feel that Israel is so corrupt that
God will destroy it entirely? Apparently not,
because he refers in several places to a tiny portion that will be saved (see Am 3:12). The idea
that God will save a remnant—a small part—of
the Jewish people gets picked up by others who
prophesy after Amos (see Isa 10:20–22, Jer
23:3, Mic 5:7–8, Zeph 3:13).

The remnant that will be saved becomes an
important biblical symbol of God's plan not to let
Israel be completely destroyed. It will be known
as a holy group because of its faith, repentance,
purification, and willingness to be God's servant.

▶ Am 3:12

4 Hear this word, you cows of Bashan
  who are on Mount Samaria,
who oppress the poor, who crush the needy,
  who say to their husbands, "Bring something
  to drink!"
2 The Lord GOD has sworn by his holiness:
  The time is surely coming upon you,
when they shall take you away with hooks,
  even the last of you with fishhooks.
3 Through breaches in the wall you shall leave,
  each one straight ahead;
and you shall be flung out into Harmon,*b*
                              says the LORD.

4 Come to Bethel—and transgress;
  to Gilgal—and multiply transgression;
bring your sacrifices every morning,
  your tithes every three days;
5 bring a thank offering of leavened bread,
  and proclaim freewill offerings, publish
  them;
for so you love to do, O people of Israel!
                              says the Lord GOD.

Israel Rejects Correction

6 I gave you cleanness of teeth in all your cities,
  and lack of bread in all your places,
yet you did not return to me,
                              says the LORD.

---

a Gk Syr: Heb *the mountains of*   *b* Meaning of Heb uncertain
c Or *many houses*

7 And I also withheld the rain from you
 when there were still three months to the
 harvest;
I would send rain on one city,
 and send no rain on another city;
one field would be rained upon,
 and the field on which it did not rain withered;
8 so two or three towns wandered to one town
 to drink water, and were not satisfied;
yet you did not return to me,
                              says the LORD.

9 I struck you with blight and mildew;
 I laid waste[a] your gardens and your vineyards;
 the locust devoured your fig trees and your
  olive trees;
yet you did not return to me,
                              says the LORD.

10 I sent among you a pestilence after the manner
  of Egypt;
 I killed your young men with the sword;
I carried away your horses;[b]
 and I made the stench of your camp go up
  into your nostrils;
yet you did not return to me,
                              says the LORD.

11 I overthrew some of you,
 as when God overthrew Sodom and Gomorrah,
 and you were like a brand snatched from the
  fire;
yet you did not return to me,
                              says the LORD.

12 Therefore thus I will do to you, O Israel;
 because I will do this to you,
 prepare to meet your God, O Israel!

13 For lo, the one who forms the mountains,
  creates the wind,
 reveals his thoughts to mortals,
makes the morning darkness,
 and treads on the heights of the earth—
 the LORD, the God of hosts, is his name!

A Lament for Israel's Sin

5 Hear this word that I take up over you in
 lamentation, O house of Israel:
2 Fallen, no more to rise,
 is maiden Israel;
forsaken on her land,
 with no one to raise her up.

3 For thus says the Lord GOD:
The city that marched out a thousand

shall have a hundred left,
and that which marched out a hundred
 shall have ten left.[c]

4 For thus says the LORD to the house of Israel:
Seek me and live;
5 but do not seek Bethel,
and do not enter into Gilgal
 or cross over to Beer-sheba;
for Gilgal shall surely go into exile,
 and Bethel shall come to nothing.

6 Seek the LORD and live,
 or he will break out against the house of
  Joseph like fire,
 and it will devour Bethel, with no one to
  quench it.
7 Ah, you that turn justice to wormwood,
 and bring righteousness to the ground!

8 The one who made the Pleiades and Orion,
 and turns deep darkness into the morning,
 and darkens the day into night,
who calls for the waters of the sea,
 and pours them out on the surface of the
  earth,
the LORD is his name,
9 who makes destruction flash out against the
  strong,
 so that destruction comes upon the fortress.

10 They hate the one who reproves in the gate,
 and they abhor the one who speaks the truth.
11 Therefore because you trample on the poor
 and take from them levies of grain,
you have built houses of hewn stone,
 but you shall not live in them;
you have planted pleasant vineyards,
 but you shall not drink their wine.
12 For I know how many are your transgressions,
 and how great are your sins—
you who afflict the righteous, who take a bribe,
 and push aside the needy in the gate.
13 Therefore the prudent will keep silent in such a
  time;
 for it is an evil time.

14 Seek good and not evil,
 that you may live;
and so the LORD, the God of hosts, will be with
  you,
 just as you have said.
15 Hate evil and love good,

---

a Cn: Heb *the multitude of*   b Heb *with the captivity of your
horses*   c Heb adds *to the house of Israel*

and establish justice in the gate;
it may be that the Lord, the God of hosts,
    will be gracious to the remnant of Joseph.

16 Therefore thus says the Lord, the God of hosts,
    the Lord:
In all the squares there shall be wailing;
    and in all the streets they shall say, "Alas!
      alas!"
They shall call the farmers to mourning,
    and those skilled in lamentation, to wailing;
17 in all the vineyards there shall be wailing,
    for I will pass through the midst of you,
                         says the Lord.

The Day of the Lord a Dark Day

18 Alas for you who desire the day of the Lord!
    Why do you want the day of the Lord?
It is darkness, not light;
19   as if someone fled from a lion,
    and was met by a bear;
or went into the house and rested a hand against
    the wall,
    and was bitten by a snake.
20 Is not the day of the Lord darkness, not light,
    and gloom with no brightness in it?

21 I hate, I despise your festivals,
    and I take no delight in your solemn
      assemblies.
22 Even though you offer me your burnt offerings
      and grain offerings,
    I will not accept them;
and the offerings of well-being of your fatted
    animals
    I will not look upon.
23 Take away from me the noise of your songs;
    I will not listen to the melody of your harps.
24 But let justice roll down like waters,
    and righteousness like an ever-flowing stream.

> **"Let justice roll down like**
> **waters,**
> **and righteousness like an**
> **ever-flowing stream."**
> (Am 5:24)

25 Did you bring to me sacrifices and offerings the forty years in the wilderness, O house of Israel? 26 You shall take up Sakkuth your king, and Kaiwan your star-god, your images,ᵃ which you made for yourselves; 27 therefore I will take

Pray It!

Prayer That Does Justice

In Amos 5:21–24, Amos again has harsh words, this time for the people who attend lavish religious ceremonies but don't practice justice in their life. To God and the prophets, justice is about living in right relationship with our fellow brothers and sisters, making sure that the dignity of all is protected and that the basic needs of all are met. Without a commitment to justice, the people's festivals, assemblies, and offerings will remain meaningless noise to God.

Amos's harsh words challenge us too. What does it mean to act justly as a teenager in today's world? Think about how you treat other people, especially people who are in need. How are you responding to these needs? Have you ever been wasteful, or consumed too much while others go in need of basic resources? What changes can you make in your life in order to live more justly? Pray today for all those who suffer from injustice in our world, and for the courage to personally respond by acting more justly in your own life.

▶ **Am 5:21–24**

you into exile beyond Damascus, says the Lord, whose name is the God of hosts.

Complacent Self-Indulgence Will Be Punished

6 Alas for those who are at ease in Zion,
    and for those who feel secure on Mount
      Samaria,
the notables of the first of the nations,
    to whom the house of Israel resorts!
2 Cross over to Calneh, and see;
    from there go to Hamath the great;
    then go down to Gath of the Philistines.
Are you betterᵇ than these kingdoms?
    Or is yourᶜ territory greater than theirᵈ
      territory,
3 O you that put far away the evil day,
    and bring near a reign of violence?

---

a Heb *your images, your star-god*   *b* Or *Are they better*
c Heb *their*   *d* Heb *your*

4 Alas for those who lie on beds of ivory,
   and lounge on their couches,
   and eat lambs from the flock,
   and calves from the stall;
5 who sing idle songs to the sound of the harp,
   and like David improvise on instruments of
      music;
6 who drink wine from bowls,
   and anoint themselves with the finest oils,
   but are not grieved over the ruin of Joseph!
7 Therefore they shall now be the first to go into
      exile,
   and the revelry of the loungers shall pass
      away.

8 The Lord God has sworn by himself
   (says the Lord, the God of hosts):
   I abhor the pride of Jacob
      and hate his strongholds;
   and I will deliver up the city and all that is
      in it.

9 If ten people remain in one house, they shall die. 10And if a relative, one who burns the dead,*a* shall take up the body to bring it out of the house, and shall say to someone in the innermost parts of the house, "Is anyone else with you?" the answer will come, "No." Then the relative*b* shall say, "Hush! We must not mention the name of the Lord."

11 See, the Lord commands,
   and the great house shall be shattered to bits,
   and the little house to pieces.
12 Do horses run on rocks?
   Does one plow the sea with oxen?*c*
   But you have turned justice into poison
   and the fruit of righteousness into
      wormwood—
13 you who rejoice in Lo-debar,*d*
   who say, "Have we not by our own strength
   taken Karnaim*e* for ourselves?"
14 Indeed, I am raising up against you a nation,
   O house of Israel, says the Lord, the God of
      hosts,
   and they shall oppress you from Lebo-hamath
   to the Wadi Arabah.

Locusts, Fire, and a Plumb Line

7 This is what the Lord God showed me: he was forming locusts at the time the latter growth began to sprout (it was the latter growth after the king's mowings). 2When they had finished eating the grass of the land, I said,
   "O Lord God, forgive, I beg you!
   How can Jacob stand?

He is so small!"
3 The Lord relented concerning this;
   "It shall not be," said the Lord.

4 This is what the Lord God showed me: the Lord God was calling for a shower of fire,*f* and it devoured the great deep and was eating up the land. 5Then I said,
   "O Lord God, cease, I beg you!
   How can Jacob stand?
   He is so small!"
6 The Lord relented concerning this;
   "This also shall not be," said the Lord God.

7 This is what he showed me: the Lord was standing beside a wall built with a plumb line, with a plumb line in his hand. 8And the Lord said to me, "Amos, what do you see?" And I said, "A plumb line." Then the Lord said,
   "See, I am setting a plumb line
   in the midst of my people Israel;
   I will never again pass them by;
9 the high places of Isaac shall be made desolate,
   and the sanctuaries of Israel shall be laid
      waste,
   and I will rise against the house of Jeroboam
      with the sword."

Amaziah Complains to the King

10 Then Amaziah, the priest of Bethel, sent to King Jeroboam of Israel, saying, "Amos has conspired against you in the very center of the house of Israel; the land is not able to bear all his words. 11For thus Amos has said,
   'Jeroboam shall die by the sword,
   and Israel must go into exile
   away from his land.' "

12And Amaziah said to Amos, "O seer, go, flee away to the land of Judah, earn your bread there, and prophesy there; 13but never again prophesy at Bethel, for it is the king's sanctuary, and it is a temple of the kingdom."

14 Then Amos answered Amaziah, "I am*g* no prophet, nor a prophet's son; but I am*g* a herdsman, and a dresser of sycamore trees, 15and the Lord took me from following the flock, and the Lord said to me, 'Go, prophesy to my people Israel.'
16 "Now therefore hear the word of the Lord.
   You say, 'Do not prophesy against Israel,
   and do not preach against the house of Isaac.'

---

a Or who makes a burning for him   b Heb he   c Or Does one plow them with oxen   d Or in a thing of nothingness   e Or horns   f Or for a judgment by fire   g Or was

Catholic Social Teaching

Stand Up and Be Counted!

A
M

In a small-town newspaper's opinion page, a reader complains about homeless people on the streets of his town. The reader writes: "These people are ruining our quality of life. They should get a job and get off our streets! Stand up and be counted and do not let this happen anymore in our town!"

Amos would have had a harsh reply for the author of that letter. Read 8:4–10 for his words condemning the people of his time who had no care or thought for the poor. Amos says that the more we choose to think of ourselves, rather than those who are needy, the closer we come to our own destruction. Jesus later echoes Amos in teaching that God's Reign of peace and justice will come through our efforts to support the weaker and less fortunate people in our world (see "Jesus' Preference for the Poor" near Lk 6:17–49). It is our responsibility as Christians to care for and protect those who are most in need in our world.

Let's be examples of God's care for those who are poor, until all opinion-page letters read: "Stand up and be counted! Let's work to end poverty and until then welcome the people who are poor among us!"

▶ **Am 8:4–10**
Option for the Poor and Vulnerable

---

17 Therefore thus says the LORD:
'Your wife shall become a prostitute in the city,
    and your sons and your daughters shall fall
        by the sword,
    and your land shall be parceled out by line;
you yourself shall die in an unclean land,
    and Israel shall surely go into exile away from
        its land.' "

The Basket of Fruit

8 This is what the Lord GOD showed me—a basket of summer fruit.*a* ²He said, "Amos, what do you see?" And I said, "A basket of summer fruit."*a* Then the LORD said to me,
"The end*b* has come upon my people Israel;
    I will never again pass them by.
3 The songs of the temple*c* shall become wailings
    in that day,"
                            says the Lord GOD;
"the dead bodies shall be many,
    cast out in every place. Be silent!"

4 Hear this, you that trample on the needy,
    and bring to ruin the poor of the land,
5 saying, "When will the new moon be over
    so that we may sell grain;
and the sabbath,
    so that we may offer wheat for sale?
We will make the ephah small and the shekel
        great,
    and practice deceit with false balances,
6 buying the poor for silver

and the needy for a pair of sandals,
    and selling the sweepings of the wheat."

7 The LORD has sworn by the pride of Jacob:
    Surely I will never forget any of their deeds.
8 Shall not the land tremble on this account,
    and everyone mourn who lives in it,
and all of it rise like the Nile,
    and be tossed about and sink again, like the
        Nile of Egypt?

9 On that day, says the Lord GOD,
    I will make the sun go down at noon,
    and darken the earth in broad daylight.
10 I will turn your feasts into mourning,
    and all your songs into lamentation;
I will bring sackcloth on all loins,
    and baldness on every head;
I will make it like the mourning for an only son,
    and the end of it like a bitter day.

11 The time is surely coming, says the Lord GOD,
    when I will send a famine on the land;
not a famine of bread, or a thirst for water,
    but of hearing the words of the LORD.
12 They shall wander from sea to sea,
    and from north to east;
they shall run to and fro, seeking the word of
        the LORD,
    but they shall not find it.

---

a Heb *qayits*   *b* Heb *qets*   *c* Or *palace*

13 In that day the beautiful young women and the
     young men
   shall faint for thirst.
14 Those who swear by Ashimah of Samaria,
   and say, "As your god lives, O Dan,"
   and, "As the way of Beer-sheba lives"—
   they shall fall, and never rise again.

The Destruction of Israel

9 I saw the Lord standing beside*a* the altar, and
   he said:
Strike the capitals until the thresholds shake,
   and shatter them on the heads of all the
     people;*b*
and those who are left I will kill with the sword;
   not one of them shall flee away,
   not one of them shall escape.

2 Though they dig into Sheol,
   from there shall my hand take them;
though they climb up to heaven,
   from there I will bring them down.
3 Though they hide themselves on the top of
     Carmel,
   from there I will search out and take them;
and though they hide from my sight at the
     bottom of the sea,
   there I will command the sea-serpent, and it
     shall bite them.
4 And though they go into captivity in front of
     their enemies,
   there I will command the sword, and it shall
     kill them;
and I will fix my eyes on them
   for harm and not for good.

5 The Lord, God of hosts,
   he who touches the earth and it melts,
   and all who live in it mourn,
and all of it rises like the Nile,
   and sinks again, like the Nile of Egypt;
6 who builds his upper chambers in the heavens,
   and founds his vault upon the earth;
who calls for the waters of the sea,
   and pours them out upon the surface of the
     earth—
the Lord is his name.

7 Are you not like the Ethiopians*c* to me,
   O people of Israel? says the Lord.

Did I not bring Israel up from the land of Egypt,
   and the Philistines from Caphtor and the
     Arameans from Kir?
8 The eyes of the Lord God are upon the sinful
     kingdom,
   and I will destroy it from the face of the earth
   —except that I will not utterly destroy the
     house of Jacob,
                              says the Lord.

9 For lo, I will command,
   and shake the house of Israel among all the
     nations
as one shakes with a sieve,
   but no pebble shall fall to the ground.
10 All the sinners of my people shall die by the
     sword,
   who say, "Evil shall not overtake or meet us."

The Restoration of David's Kingdom

11 On that day I will raise up
   the booth of David that is fallen,
and repair its*d* breaches,
   and raise up its*e* ruins,
   and rebuild it as in the days of old;
12 in order that they may possess the remnant of
     Edom
   and all the nations who are called by my name,
   says the Lord who does this.

13 The time is surely coming, says the Lord,
   when the one who plows shall overtake the
     one who reaps,
   and the treader of grapes the one who sows
     the seed;
the mountains shall drip sweet wine,
   and all the hills shall flow with it.
14 I will restore the fortunes of my people Israel,
   and they shall rebuild the ruined cities and
     inhabit them;
they shall plant vineyards and drink their wine,
   and they shall make gardens and eat their
     fruit.
15 I will plant them upon their land,
   and they shall never again be plucked up
   out of the land that I have given them,
                         says the Lord your God.

---

a Or *on*   *b* Heb *all of them*   *c* Or *Nubians*; Heb *Cushites*
d Gk: Heb *their*   *e* Gk: Heb *his*

A betrayal is always difficult, and a betrayal by someone who is related to you is a particularly hard pill to swallow. This is perhaps most true in abusive relationships where one person, through his or her words and actions, mistreats another. It can take a long time to heal these divisions and restore a sense of trust in the relationship. The Book of Obadiah has angry words against the nation of Edom, whose people were related to the Israelites. It should remind us that when the people we expect to care for us instead take advantage of us, the wound is especially painful.

Quick Facts

Period Covered: after the Babylonian Exile, sometime in the fifth century BC
Inspired Author: Obadiah
Theme: God will punish Edom for its abuse of Judah.
Of Note: *Obadiah* means "servant" or "worshiper of the Lord."

In Depth

The Book of Genesis records a conflict between Jacob (the father of the nation of Israel) and his brother Esau (the father of the nation of Edom, later called Idumea). Hundreds of years later, the Israelites still fought with the Edomites (see map 4, "The Kingdom Years"). In the Book of Obadiah, the bitterness deepens.

In 587 BC, Jerusalem was destroyed by the Babylonians. Apparently, the Edomites not only did not aid their "brother" (Obadiah, verse 10) but took advantage of Israel's situation by gloating (see verse 12), looting (see verse 13), and raiding its territory (see verse 14). Because of the Edomites' cruelty, the prophet Obadiah prophesied the destruction of Edom by another country (see verse 15).

Like many of the Old Testament prophets, Obadiah ultimately saw a hopeful future for Israel. All Israel's enemies would wither before the strong arm of the Lord. And there would come a day— "the day of the LORD" (verse 15)—when all Jews would unite and return to Mount Zion (the place where the Temple stood in Jerusalem). Mount Zion would "rule Mount Esau" and that new "kingdom shall be the LORD's" (verse 21).

We are given no clues about the identity or life of the prophet Obadiah. We know only that he wrote the shortest book in the Old Testament— just one chapter long.

The Book of **Obadiah**

Obadiah

Proud Edom Will Be Brought Low

1 The vision of Obadiah.

Thus says the Lord God concerning Edom:
We have heard a report from the Lord,
   and a messenger has been sent among the
      nations:
"Rise up! Let us rise against it for battle!"
2 I will surely make you least among the nations;
   you shall be utterly despised.
3 Your proud heart has deceived you,
   you that live in the clefts of the rock,[a]
   whose dwelling is in the heights.
You say in your heart,
   "Who will bring me down to the ground?"
4 Though you soar aloft like the eagle,
   though your nest is set among the stars,
   from there I will bring you down,
             says the Lord.

Pillage and Slaughter Will Repay Edom's Cruelty

5 If thieves came to you,
   if plunderers by night
   —how you have been destroyed!—
   would they not steal only what they wanted?
If grape-gatherers came to you,
   would they not leave gleanings?
6 How Esau has been pillaged,
   his treasures searched out!
7 All your allies have deceived you,
   they have driven you to the border;
your confederates have prevailed against you;

those who ate[b] your bread have set a trap for
   you—
there is no understanding of it.
8 On that day, says the Lord,
   I will destroy the wise out of Edom,
   and understanding out of Mount Esau.
9 Your warriors shall be shattered, O Teman,
   so that everyone from Mount Esau will be cut
      off.

Edom Mistreated His Brother

10 For the slaughter and violence done to your
      brother Jacob,
shame shall cover you,
   and you shall be cut off forever.
11 On the day that you stood aside,
   on the day that strangers carried off his wealth,
and foreigners entered his gates
   and cast lots for Jerusalem,
   you too were like one of them.
12 But you should not have gloated[c] over[d] your
      brother
   on the day of his misfortune;
you should not have rejoiced over the people of
      Judah
   on the day of their ruin;
you should not have boasted
   on the day of distress.
13 You should not have entered the gate of my
      people

---

a Or *clefts of Sela* b Cn: Heb lacks *those who ate* c Heb *But do not gloat* (and similarly through verse 14) d Heb *on the day of*

Catholic Social Teaching

What Goes Around

"**W**hat goes around comes around." Have you ever heard that saying? Isn't that exactly what Obadiah is saying in verse 15 when he states, "Your deeds shall return on your own head"?

Whatever you do comes back to affect you eventually. This is especially true when we consider our care for God's creation. Catholic social teaching reminds us that we have a moral obligation to protect the earth on which we live. Care for the earth is a *responsibility* of our faith, not an option we can choose to ignore. God has made us co-creators, entrusted with the stewardship of all that God has created. To be good stewards, we must work to create a world where God's creation is always respected and protected. This means speaking out against individuals, governments, and corporations that pollute and destroy our environment. In a more personal way, it means we must never litter and must be committed to recycling and reducing consumption.

The ongoing destruction of our environment may not ever affect our lives directly, but it will negatively affect the lives of our children and grandchildren, and the generations that follow them. In this way, the decisions we make today will come back around to impact both our family and the larger human family.

Think about what individual changes you can make to be a better steward of the environment.

● In what ways are you being wasteful with the world's natural resources?

● How can you show more concern in your life for the gift of God's creation?

▶ **Obadiah, verse 15**
Care for God's Creation

---

on the day of their calamity;
you should not have joined in the gloating over
    Judah's[a] disaster
  on the day of his calamity;
you should not have looted his goods
  on the day of his calamity.
14 You should not have stood at the crossings
    to cut off his fugitives;
you should not have handed over his survivors
  on the day of distress.

15 For the day of the LORD is near against all the
    nations.
As you have done, it shall be done to you;
  your deeds shall return on your own head.
16 For as you have drunk on my holy mountain,
  all the nations around you shall drink;
they shall drink and gulp down [b]
  and shall be as though they had never been.

Israel's Final Triumph

17 But on Mount Zion there shall be those that
    escape,
  and it shall be holy;
and the house of Jacob shall take possession of
    those who dispossessed them.

18 The house of Jacob shall be a fire,
  the house of Joseph a flame,
  and the house of Esau stubble;
they shall burn them and consume them,
  and there shall be no survivor of the house of
    Esau;
      for the LORD has spoken.
19 Those of the Negeb shall possess Mount Esau,
  and those of the Shephelah the land of the
    Philistines;
they shall possess the land of Ephraim and the
    land of Samaria,
  and Benjamin shall possess Gilead.
20 The exiles of the Israelites who are in Halah[c]
  shall possess[d] Phoenicia as far as
    Zarephath;
and the exiles of Jerusalem who are in
    Sepharad
  shall possess the towns of the Negeb.
21 Those who have been saved[e] shall go up to
    Mount Zion
  to rule Mount Esau;
  and the kingdom shall be the LORD's.

---

a Heb *his* b Meaning of Heb uncertain c Cn: Heb *in this army*
d Cn: Meaning of Heb uncertain e Or *Saviors*

You're watching a comedy show where someone dressed like a doctor starts making outrageous comments about a person's health. You laugh, not because sickness is funny, but because doctors are supposed to be sensitive and caring. That's the basis of satire—that someone or something that is supposed to act one way acts another way. You're about to read a biblical satire about Jonah the prophet. The Book of Jonah uses humor to make an important point—God is the God of all people, even those we consider our enemies.

In Depth

This story was written after the Jews returned from their exile in Babylon. Jewish leaders encouraged Jewish people to stay away from non-Jewish people (see Ezra, chapter 9) in order to avoid falling into idolatry again. A result was a religious bigotry against other nations—a belief that God was against every nation that opposed Israel. The Book of Jonah was written to correct that narrow attitude. Through satire, this fictional short story gently pokes fun at Israel's religious self-righteousness.

How is the book funny? Well, right off the bat, Jonah is called by God and immediately takes off in the opposite direction (see Jon 1:1–3). What kind of prophet is this? When God tries to get his attention with a storm, it's the non-Jewish sailors who get the point (see verse 14). Just as the reader is probably wondering how God is going to get Jonah to Nineveh, along comes a taxi in the form of a large fish's stomach (see verse 17).

At a Glance

- **1:1–16. Jonah's being sent by God to Nineveh**
- **1:17—2:10. Jonah in the belly of a large fish**
- **Chapter 3. the Ninevites' conversion**
- **Chapter 4. Jonah's anger outside of Nineveh**

Quick Facts

Period Covered: eighth century BC
Inspired Author: unknown, probably writing in the fifth century BC
Theme: a fictional short story showing that God cares for all people, including Israel's enemies

There's more. Readers from the author's time would have expected Jonah to be ignored at best, more likely beaten or killed by the people of Nineveh. After all, these were Israel's mortal enemies. Instead, the Ninevites immediately respond to Jonah's message and repent, even the animals (see 3:8)! At this point, the reader is giggling at the goofiness of pigs and sheep in sackcloth, but getting the message about God's salvation being for all nations.

Jonah is angry and upset. He didn't expect the Ninevites to convert—he wanted them punished. He goes outside the city to mope, and his favorite tree dies. The book ends with God's chiding Jonah for his bigoted anger. If Jonah is so concerned for his little tree (see 4:6–8), shouldn't God be concerned for the great city of Nineveh with its thousands of people (see verse 11)? The point is driven home, and the humor has helped to make a challenging message easier to accept.

The Book of **Jonah**

Jonah

Jonah Tries to Run Away from God

1 Now the word of the Lord came to Jonah son of Amittai, saying, ²"Go at once to Nineveh, that great city, and cry out against it; for their wickedness has come up before me." ³But Jonah set out to flee to Tarshish from the presence of the Lord. He went down to Joppa and found a ship going to Tarshish; so he paid his fare and went on board, to go with them to Tarshish, away from the presence of the Lord.

4 But the Lord hurled a great wind upon the sea, and such a mighty storm came upon the sea that the ship threatened to break up. ⁵Then the mariners were afraid, and each cried to his god. They threw the cargo that was in the ship into the sea, to lighten it for them. Jonah, meanwhile, had gone down into the hold of the ship and had lain down, and was fast asleep. ⁶The captain came and said to him, "What are you doing sound asleep? Get up, call on your god! Perhaps the god will spare us a thought so that we do not perish."

7 The sailors*a* said to one another, "Come, let us cast lots, so that we may know on whose account this calamity has come upon us." So they cast lots, and the lot fell on Jonah. ⁸Then they said to him, "Tell us why this calamity has come upon us. What is your occupation? Where do you come from? What is your country? And of what people are you?" ⁹"I am a Hebrew," he replied. "I worship the Lord, the God of heaven, who made the sea and the dry land." ¹⁰Then the men were even more afraid, and said to him, "What is this that you have done!" For the men knew that he was fleeing from the presence of the Lord, because he had told them so.

11 Then they said to him, "What shall we do to you, that the sea may quiet down for us?" For the sea was growing more and more tempestuous. ¹²He said to them, "Pick me up and throw me into the sea; then the sea will quiet down for you; for I know it is because of me that this great storm has come upon you." ¹³Nevertheless the men rowed hard to bring the ship back to land, but they could not, for the sea grew more and more stormy against them. ¹⁴Then they cried out to the Lord, "Please, O Lord, we pray, do not let us perish on account of this man's life. Do not make us guilty of innocent blood; for you, O Lord, have done as it pleased you." ¹⁵So they picked Jonah up and threw him into the sea; and the sea ceased from its raging. ¹⁶Then the men feared the Lord even more, and they offered a sacrifice to the Lord and made vows.

17 *b* But the Lord provided a large fish to swallow up Jonah; and Jonah was in the belly of the fish three days and three nights.

A Psalm of Thanksgiving

2 Then Jonah prayed to the Lord his God from the belly of the fish, ²saying,

"I called to the Lord out of my distress,
    and he answered me;
out of the belly of Sheol I cried,

---

a Heb *They*   *b* Ch 2.1 in Heb

Jesus and Jonah

Do you see any similarities between Jonah and Jesus? Jonah is in the darkness of a fish's belly for three days before the Lord commands the fish to spit him out. Jesus experiences the darkness of death for three days before he bursts from the tomb in resurrected glory. In Matthew 16:4 and Luke 11:29, Jesus even refers to "the sign of Jonah" in relation to his own ministry.

Jonah's prayer in Jonah 2:2–10 could well have been Jesus' prayer before his death. It reminds us that salvation comes from God when we are experiencing dark times. When you are going through a difficult time, use Jonah's prayer as a model for writing your own prayer of trust. Describe your difficulties and your situation, and end by expressing your ultimate trust in God. Then say your prayer until the difficulty passes. It could make a difference!

▶ **Jon 2:2–10**

and you heard my voice.
³ You cast me into the deep,
    into the heart of the seas,
    and the flood surrounded me;
all your waves and your billows
    passed over me.
⁴ Then I said, 'I am driven away
    from your sight;
how*ᵃ* shall I look again
    upon your holy temple?'
⁵ The waters closed in over me;
    the deep surrounded me;
weeds were wrapped around my head
⁶   at the roots of the mountains.
I went down to the land
    whose bars closed upon me forever;
yet you brought up my life from the Pit,
    O Lᴏʀᴅ my God.

⁷ As my life was ebbing away,
    I remembered the Lᴏʀᴅ;
and my prayer came to you,
    into your holy temple.
⁸ Those who worship vain idols
    forsake their true loyalty.
⁹ But I with the voice of thanksgiving
    will sacrifice to you;
what I have vowed I will pay.
    Deliverance belongs to the Lᴏʀᴅ!"

¹⁰Then the Lᴏʀᴅ spoke to the fish, and it spewed Jonah out upon the dry land.

Conversion of Nineveh

3 The word of the Lᴏʀᴅ came to Jonah a second time, saying, ²"Get up, go to Nineveh, that great city, and proclaim to it the message that I tell you." ³So Jonah set out and went to Nineveh, according to the word of the Lᴏʀᴅ. Now Nineveh was an exceedingly large city, a three days' walk across. ⁴Jonah began to go into the city, going a day's walk. And he cried out, "Forty days more, and Nineveh shall be overthrown!" ⁵And the people of Nineveh believed God; they proclaimed a fast, and everyone, great and small, put on sackcloth.

6 When the news reached the king of Nineveh, he rose from his throne, removed his robe, covered himself with sackcloth, and sat in ashes. ⁷Then he had a proclamation made in Nineveh: "By the decree of the king and his nobles: No human being or animal, no herd or flock, shall taste anything. They shall not feed, nor shall they drink water. ⁸Human beings and animals shall be covered with sackcloth, and they shall cry mightily to God. All shall turn from their evil ways and from the violence that is in their hands. ⁹Who knows? God may relent and change his mind; he may turn from his fierce anger, so that we do not perish."

10 When God saw what they did, how they turned from their evil ways, God changed his mind about the calamity that he had said he would bring upon them; and he did not do it.

Jonah's Anger

4 But this was very displeasing to Jonah, and he became angry. ²He prayed to the Lᴏʀᴅ and said, "O Lᴏʀᴅ! Is not this what I said while I was still in my own country? That is why I fled to

---

a Theodotion: Heb *surely*

Tarshish at the beginning; for I knew that you are a gracious God and merciful, slow to anger, and abounding in steadfast love, and ready to relent from punishing. ³And now, O Lord, please take my life from me, for it is better for me to die than to live." ⁴And the Lord said, "Is it right for you to be angry?" ⁵Then Jonah went out of the city and sat down east of the city, and made a booth for himself there. He sat under it in the shade, waiting to see what would become of the city.

6 The Lord God appointed a bush,ᵃ and made it come up over Jonah, to give shade over his head, to save him from his discomfort; so Jonah was very happy about the bush. ⁷But when dawn came up the next day, God appointed a worm that attacked the bush, so that it withered. ⁸When the sun rose, God prepared a sultry east wind, and the sun beat down on the head of Jonah so that he was faint and asked that he might die. He said, "It is better for me to die than to live."

Jonah Is Reproved

9 But God said to Jonah, "Is it right for you to be angry about the bush?" And he said, "Yes, angry enough to die." ¹⁰Then the Lord said, "You are concerned about the bush, for which you did not labor and which you did not grow; it came into being in a night and perished in a night. ¹¹And should I not be concerned about Nineveh, that great city, in which there are more than a hundred and twenty thousand persons who do not know their right hand from their left, and also many animals?"

---

a Heb *qiqayon*, possibly *the castor bean plant*

Live It!

Mistaken Loyalties

When God spares Nineveh, Jonah is angry! He is so angry he is willing to let his anger destroy him. And all because of mistaken loyalty. Jonah thought he was loyal to God (which is funny because at first, he tried to run away from God), and he feels that God is being disloyal to him by not destroying Nineveh. Jonah lacks empathy. He does not—or will not—understand that God's loyalty is to the whole human race, not just to Jonah's desires.

Are you ever angry with God because things don't go your way? Maybe your anger is about mistaken loyalties. If you didn't get picked for the lead part, that doesn't mean God is being disloyal to you. God is God over everyone—which sometimes means that you will not get what you want so that other people can receive what they need. We must never be selfish, striving instead to have empathy—true understanding of another—at all times.

The next time you are angry at God, ask yourself: Am I willing to see things from a large enough perspective? Am I expecting to receive God's favor at someone else's expense?

 Jon 4:1–8

Oftentimes it takes someone from outside our local community to help us see things from a new perspective. We are so used to seeing things as they are that we sometimes fail to envision what could be until a new voice with unique insights comes along. Indeed, people who visit the places we live in often see things we have overlooked or taken for granted. The prophet Micah was like such a visitor. His home was a small village, but he prophesied in the big capital city of Jerusalem. God uses Micah's unique perspective to communicate warnings and promises to the people of Israel and to us.

In Depth

The Book of Micah is a collection of oracles (poemlike prophetic messages) taking different forms. Some of the oracles are harsh judgments (see 1:8—2:11), some are comforting promises that God will not desert the people (see chapter 4), and some are the prophet's own confessions of faith (see 3:8, 7:7). The Book of Micah shows us a God who is passionate for justice and fairness (see 3:9).

Perhaps because of his rural background, the prophet Micah has a special connection to the land and the people who work it. He speaks against those who covet and seize fields and homes (see 2:2). He describes the destruction of Zion (Jerusalem) as plowing a field (see 3:12). He represents the Ideal Kingdom as a place where all the people have their own grapevines and fig trees (see 4:4).

The Book of Micah shows signs of being extensively edited and revised to keep the prophet's message relevant during changing times. This is particularly true in chapters 4 and 5, which were added after the Babylonian Exile to give hope following the nation's great tragedy. In 4:3, the prophet envisions a day when nations will "beat their swords into plowshares" and when "nation shall not lift up sword against nation, / neither shall they learn war any more."

Micah prophesied at about the same time as First Isaiah (see the timeline at the back of this Bible), during the days of Kings Jotham, Ahaz, and Hezekiah (see 2 Chr 27:1—31:21). But whereas Isaiah was a member of the upper class, defending the rights of the poor, Micah was a poor person, suffering with the poor. That is why he speaks so passionately about their mistreatment (see Mic 3:1–3). Even though his message went unheeded at the time, he models for us trust in the Lord's saving power (see 7:7).

At a Glance

- **Chapters 1–2.** a judgment against Israel and Judah, and promise
- **3:1—5:9.** a judgment against rulers, prophets, and priests, and promise
- **5:10—6:8.** a judgment against foreign religions, and a plea for justice
- **6:9—7:20.** a judgment against the people, and message of God's compassion

Quick Facts

Period Covered: late eighth century BC

Inspired Authors: Micah and later editors

Themes: warnings against injustice and idolatry, promises of a new future, God's faithfulness to the covenant

The Book of

Micah

Micah

1 The word of the LORD that came to Micah of Moresheth in the days of Kings Jotham, Ahaz, and Hezekiah of Judah, which he saw concerning Samaria and Jerusalem.

Judgment Pronounced against Samaria

2 Hear, you peoples, all of you;
  listen, O earth, and all that is in it;
and let the Lord GOD be a witness against you,
  the Lord from his holy temple.
3 For lo, the LORD is coming out of his place,
  and will come down and tread upon the high
    places of the earth.
4 Then the mountains will melt under him
  and the valleys will burst open,
like wax near the fire,
  like waters poured down a steep place.
5 All this is for the transgression of Jacob
  and for the sins of the house of Israel.
What is the transgression of Jacob?
  Is it not Samaria?
And what is the high place^a of Judah?
  Is it not Jerusalem?
6 Therefore I will make Samaria a heap in the open
    country,
  a place for planting vineyards.
I will pour down her stones into the valley,
  and uncover her foundations.
7 All her images shall be beaten to pieces,
  all her wages shall be burned with fire,
  and all her idols I will lay waste;
for as the wages of a prostitute she gathered
    them,

and as the wages of a prostitute they shall
  again be used.

The Doom of the Cities of Judah

8 For this I will lament and wail;
  I will go barefoot and naked;
I will make lamentation like the jackals,
  and mourning like the ostriches.
9 For her wound^b is incurable.
  It has come to Judah;
it has reached to the gate of my people,
  to Jerusalem.

10 Tell it not in Gath,
  weep not at all;
in Beth-leaphrah
  roll yourselves in the dust.
11 Pass on your way,
  inhabitants of Shaphir,
  in nakedness and shame;
the inhabitants of Zaanan
  do not come forth;
Beth-ezel is wailing
  and shall remove its support from you.
12 For the inhabitants of Maroth
  wait anxiously for good,
yet disaster has come down from the LORD
  to the gate of Jerusalem.
13 Harness the steeds to the chariots,
  inhabitants of Lachish;
it was the beginning of sin

---

a Heb *what are the high places*   b Gk Syr Vg: Heb *wounds*

Did You Know?

Micah Challenges Us to Fight Injustice

In chapter 2, the prophet Micah challenges the people to take an honest look at their behavior. In harsh images and language, he articulates how greed and injustice have destroyed the well-being of the nation. In verse 3, Micah implies that because of their injustice, the people will be like oxen whose necks are confined to yokes that hold their heads down in shame. Micah's message is that injustice forces all in the community and nation to carry a heavy burden.

This theme of examining injustices in the world has been repeated numerous times throughout the Scriptures. And to this very day, we continue to hear similar teachings coming out of the Church. What are we doing in our communities and in our country to fight against modern instances of injustice, such as racism, hunger, poverty, abortion, capital punishment, violence, and destruction of the natural environment? What injustices do you see in your own actions and in your own community? What can you do to stop injustices from happening so that our communities and nation can live freely in peace?

▶ **Micah, chapter 2**

to daughter Zion,
for in you were found
the transgressions of Israel.
14 Therefore you shall give parting gifts
to Moresheth-gath;
the houses of Achzib shall be a deception
to the kings of Israel.
15 I will again bring a conqueror upon you,
inhabitants of Mareshah;
the glory of Israel
shall come to Adullam.
16 Make yourselves bald and cut off your hair
for your pampered children;
make yourselves as bald as the eagle,
for they have gone from you into exile.

Social Evils Denounced

2 Alas for those who devise wickedness
and evil deeds[a] on their beds!
When the morning dawns, they perform it,

because it is in their power.
2 They covet fields, and seize them;
houses, and take them away;
they oppress householder and house,
people and their inheritance.
3 Therefore thus says the LORD:
Now, I am devising against this family an evil
from which you cannot remove your necks;
and you shall not walk haughtily,
for it will be an evil time.
4 On that day they shall take up a taunt song
against you,
and wail with bitter lamentation,
and say, "We are utterly ruined;
the LORD[b] alters the inheritance of my people;
how he removes it from me!
Among our captors[c] he parcels out our fields."
5 Therefore you will have no one to cast the line
by lot
in the assembly of the LORD.

6 "Do not preach"—thus they preach—
"one should not preach of such things;
disgrace will not overtake us."
7 Should this be said, O house of Jacob?
Is the LORD's patience exhausted?
Are these his doings?
Do not my words do good
to one who walks uprightly?
8 But you rise up against my people[d] as an enemy;
you strip the robe from the peaceful,[e]
from those who pass by trustingly
with no thought of war.
9 The women of my people you drive out
from their pleasant houses;
from their young children you take away
my glory forever.
10 Arise and go;
for this is no place to rest,
because of uncleanness that destroys
with a grievous destruction.[f]
11 If someone were to go about uttering empty
falsehoods,
saying, "I will preach to you of wine and
strong drink,"
such a one would be the preacher for this
people!

A Promise for the Remnant of Israel

12 I will surely gather all of you, O Jacob,
I will gather the survivors of Israel;
I will set them together

---

a Cn: Heb *work evil*   b Heb *he*   c Cn: Heb *the rebellious*
d Cn: Heb *But yesterday my people rose*   e Cn: Heb *from before
a garment*   f Meaning of Heb uncertain

like sheep in a fold,
  like a flock in its pasture;
  it will resound with people.
13 The one who breaks out will go up before them;
  they will break through and pass the gate,
  going out by it.
Their king will pass on before them,
  the LORD at their head.

Wicked Rulers and Prophets

3 And I said:
Listen, you heads of Jacob
  and rulers of the house of Israel!
Should you not know justice?—
2   you who hate the good and love the evil,
who tear the skin off my people,[a]
  and the flesh off their bones;
3 who eat the flesh of my people,
  flay their skin off them,
break their bones in pieces,
  and chop them up like meat[b] in a kettle,
  like flesh in a caldron.

4 Then they will cry to the LORD,
  but he will not answer them;
he will hide his face from them at that time,
  because they have acted wickedly.

5 Thus says the LORD concerning the prophets
  who lead my people astray,
who cry "Peace"
  when they have something to eat,
but declare war against those
  who put nothing into their mouths.
6 Therefore it shall be night to you, without vision,
  and darkness to you, without revelation.
The sun shall go down upon the prophets,
  and the day shall be black over them;
7 the seers shall be disgraced,
  and the diviners put to shame;
they shall all cover their lips,
  for there is no answer from God.
8 But as for me, I am filled with power,
  with the spirit of the LORD,
  and with justice and might,
to declare to Jacob his transgression
  and to Israel his sin.

9 Hear this, you rulers of the house of Jacob
  and chiefs of the house of Israel,
who abhor justice
  and pervert all equity,
10 who build Zion with blood
  and Jerusalem with wrong!
11 Its rulers give judgment for a bribe,
  its priests teach for a price,

its prophets give oracles for money;
yet they lean upon the LORD and say,
  "Surely the LORD is with us!
  No harm shall come upon us."
12 Therefore because of you
  Zion shall be plowed as a field;
Jerusalem shall become a heap of ruins,
  and the mountain of the house a wooded
    height.

Peace and Security through Obedience

4 In days to come
  the mountain of the LORD's house
shall be established as the highest of the
    mountains,
  and shall be raised up above the hills.
Peoples shall stream to it,
2   and many nations shall come and say:
"Come, let us go up to the mountain of the
    LORD,
  to the house of the God of Jacob;
that he may teach us his ways
  and that we may walk in his paths."
For out of Zion shall go forth instruction,
  and the word of the LORD from Jerusalem.
3 He shall judge between many peoples,
  and shall arbitrate between strong nations far
    away;
they shall beat their swords into plowshares,
  and their spears into pruning hooks;
nation shall not lift up sword against nation,
  neither shall they learn war any more;
4 but they shall all sit under their own vines and
    under their own fig trees,
  and no one shall make them afraid;
for the mouth of the LORD of hosts has
    spoken.

5 For all the peoples walk,
  each in the name of its god,
but we will walk in the name of the LORD
    our God
  forever and ever.

Restoration Promised after Exile

6 In that day, says the LORD,
  I will assemble the lame
and gather those who have been driven away,
  and those whom I have afflicted.
7 The lame I will make the remnant,
  and those who were cast off, a strong nation;
and the LORD will reign over them in Mount
    Zion
  now and forevermore.

8 And you, O tower of the flock,
 hill of daughter Zion,
to you it shall come,
 the former dominion shall come,
 the sovereignty of daughter Jerusalem.

9 Now why do you cry aloud?
 Is there no king in you?
Has your counselor perished,
 that pangs have seized you like a woman in
  labor?
10 Writhe and groan,*a* O daughter Zion,
 like a woman in labor;
for now you shall go forth from the city
 and camp in the open country;
 you shall go to Babylon.
There you shall be rescued,
 there the LORD will redeem you
 from the hands of your enemies.

11 Now many nations
 are assembled against you,

saying, "Let her be profaned,
 and let our eyes gaze upon Zion."
12 But they do not know
 the thoughts of the LORD;
they do not understand his plan,
 that he has gathered them as sheaves to the
  threshing floor.
13 Arise and thresh,
 O daughter Zion,
for I will make your horn iron
 and your hoofs bronze;
you shall beat in pieces many peoples,
 and shall*b* devote their gain to the LORD,
 their wealth to the Lord of the whole earth.

5 *c* Now you are walled around with a wall;*d*
 siege is laid against us;
with a rod they strike the ruler of Israel
 upon the cheek.

The Ruler from Bethlehem

2 *e* But you, O Bethlehem of Ephrathah,
 who are one of the little clans of Judah,
from you shall come forth for me
 one who is to rule in Israel,
whose origin is from of old,
 from ancient days.
3 Therefore he shall give them up until the
  time
 when she who is in labor has brought forth;
then the rest of his kindred shall return
 to the people of Israel.
4 And he shall stand and feed his flock in the
  strength of the LORD,
 in the majesty of the name of the LORD his
  God.
And they shall live secure, for now he shall be
  great
 to the ends of the earth;
5 and he shall be the one of peace.

 If the Assyrians come into our land
  and tread upon our soil,*f*
we will raise against them seven shepherds
 and eight installed as rulers.
6 They shall rule the land of Assyria with the
  sword,
 and the land of Nimrod with the drawn
  sword;*g*
they*h* shall rescue us from the Assyrians
 if they come into our land
 or tread within our border.

From Humble Beginnings

As a country boy, Micah has a different vision than do some of the other prophets. He doesn't see the Ideal Ruler coming out of a big city like Jerusalem. No, he sees this great person coming from Bethlehem—a tiny, insignificant city, but also a place free from political corruption. The Gospel of Matthew shows Micah's prophecy being fulfilled in the birth of Jesus (see Mt 2:5–6).

Often in the Bible, we hear of God's accomplishing huge feats with small and humble people and things. In your prayer, reflect or journal on the following questions:

● What famous people started from humble beginnings?
● Why does God often use small and hidden people or things to accomplish God's purposes?
● What small or hidden gifts do you have to offer God to work with?

▶ Mic 5:2–5

---

a Meaning of Heb uncertain   b Gk Syr Tg: Heb *and I will*
c Ch 4.14 in Heb   d Cn Compare Gk: Meaning of Heb uncertain
e Ch 5.1 in Heb   f Gk: Heb *in our palaces*   g Cn: Heb *in its
entrances*   h Heb *he*

The Future Role of the Remnant

7 Then the remnant of Jacob,
　　surrounded by many peoples,
　shall be like dew from the Lord,
　　like showers on the grass,
　which do not depend upon people
　　or wait for any mortal.
8 And among the nations the remnant of Jacob,
　　surrounded by many peoples,
　shall be like a lion among the animals of the
　　　　forest,
　　like a young lion among the flocks of sheep,
　which, when it goes through, treads down
　　and tears in pieces, with no one to deliver.
9 Your hand shall be lifted up over your
　　　adversaries,
　　and all your enemies shall be cut off.

10 In that day, says the Lord,
　　I will cut off your horses from among you
　　and will destroy your chariots;
11 and I will cut off the cities of your land
　　and throw down all your strongholds;
12 and I will cut off sorceries from your hand,
　　and you shall have no more soothsayers;
13 and I will cut off your images
　　and your pillars from among you,
　and you shall bow down no more
　　to the work of your hands;
14 and I will uproot your sacred poles*a* from
　　　among you
　　and destroy your towns.
15 And in anger and wrath I will execute vengeance
　　on the nations that did not obey.

God Challenges Israel

6 Hear what the Lord says:
　　Rise, plead your case before the mountains,
　　and let the hills hear your voice.
2 Hear, you mountains, the controversy of the
　　　Lord,
　　and you enduring foundations of the earth;
　for the Lord has a controversy with his people,
　　and he will contend with Israel.

3 "O my people, what have I done to you?
　　In what have I wearied you? Answer me!
4 For I brought you up from the land of Egypt,
　　and redeemed you from the house of slavery;
　and I sent before you Moses,
　　Aaron, and Miriam.
5 O my people, remember now what King Balak
　　　of Moab devised,
　　what Balaam son of Beor answered him,
　and what happened from Shittim to Gilgal,

that you may know the saving acts of the
　Lord."

What God Requires

6 "With what shall I come before the Lord,
　　and bow myself before God on high?
　Shall I come before him with burnt offerings,
　　with calves a year old?
7 Will the Lord be pleased with thousands of
　　　rams,
　　with ten thousands of rivers of oil?
　Shall I give my firstborn for my transgression,
　　the fruit of my body for the sin of my soul?"
8 He has told you, O mortal, what is good;
　　and what does the Lord require of you
　but to do justice, and to love kindness,
　　and to walk humbly with your God?

> **"He has told you, O mortal,**
> **what is good;**
> **and what does the Lord**
> **require of you**
> **but to do justice,**
> **and to love kindness,**
> **and to walk humbly**
> **with your God?"**
>
> [Mic 6:8]

Cheating and Violence to Be Punished

9 The voice of the Lord cries to the city
　　(it is sound wisdom to fear your name):
　Hear, O tribe and assembly of the city!*b*
10 　Can I forget*c* the treasures of wickedness in
　　　the house of the wicked,
　　and the scant measure that is accursed?
11 Can I tolerate wicked scales
　　and a bag of dishonest weights?
12 Your*d* wealthy are full of violence;
　　your*e* inhabitants speak lies,
　　with tongues of deceit in their mouths.
13 Therefore I have begun*f* to strike you down,
　　making you desolate because of your sins.
14 You shall eat, but not be satisfied,
　　and there shall be a gnawing hunger within
　　　you;

MIC

---

a Heb *Asherim*　b Cn Compare Gk: Heb *tribe, and who
has appointed it yet?*　c Cn: Meaning of Heb uncertain
d Heb *Whose*　e Heb *whose*　f Gk Syr Vg: Heb *have made sick*

Catholic Social Teaching

"To Love Kindness"

Perhaps you have heard the expression, "Perform a random act of kindness." This statement is commonly seen as an invitation to do something nice and unexpected for another person. Kindness, however, shouldn't be a random thing we do; rather, kindness is something that should be integrated into our lives at all times, not just at random moments. Imagine what our world would be like if every day, each of us were consistently kind to each person we encountered, whether we knew the person or not. Imagine if kindness were seen as a responsibility of all people, and not just as something done randomly!

Just as violence leads to more violence, so also can kindness create more kindness. This is why Micah includes kindness in his simple formula for doing God's will—it is not meant to be a random choice, but a human responsibility.

Consider these questions:
● What are some of the specific responsibilities all people have in our world today?
● Whom or what are we responsible for?
● When, if ever, does our responsibility to the rest of the world end?

 **Mic 6:8**

Rights and Responsibilities

---

you shall put away, but not save,
    and what you save, I will hand over to the
      sword.
15 You shall sow, but not reap;
    you shall tread olives, but not anoint
      yourselves with oil;
    you shall tread grapes, but not drink wine.
16 For you have kept the statutes of Omri*a*
    and all the works of the house of Ahab,
    and you have followed their counsels.
Therefore I will make you a desolation, and
    your*b* inhabitants an object of hissing;
so you shall bear the scorn of my people.

The Total Corruption of the People

7 Woe is me! For I have become like one who,
    after the summer fruit has been gathered,
    after the vintage has been gleaned,
finds no cluster to eat;
    there is no first-ripe fig for which I hunger.
2 The faithful have disappeared from the land,
    and there is no one left who is upright;
they all lie in wait for blood,
    and they hunt each other with nets.
3 Their hands are skilled to do evil;
    the official and the judge ask for a bribe,
and the powerful dictate what they desire;
    thus they pervert justice.*c*
4 The best of them is like a brier,
    the most upright of them a thorn hedge.
The day of their*d* sentinels, of their*d* punishment,
    has come;

now their confusion is at hand.
5 Put no trust in a friend,
    have no confidence in a loved one;
guard the doors of your mouth
    from her who lies in your embrace;
6 for the son treats the father with contempt,
    the daughter rises up against her mother,
the daughter-in-law against her mother-in-law;
    your enemies are members of your own
      household.
7 But as for me, I will look to the Lord,
    I will wait for the God of my salvation;
    my God will hear me.

Penitence and Trust in God

8 Do not rejoice over me, O my enemy;
    when I fall, I shall rise;
when I sit in darkness,
    the Lord will be a light to me.
9 I must bear the indignation of the Lord,
    because I have sinned against him,
until he takes my side
    and executes judgment for me.
He will bring me out to the light;
    I shall see his vindication.
10 Then my enemy will see,
    and shame will cover her who said to me,
    "Where is the Lord your God?"

---

a Gk Syr Vg Tg: Heb *the statutes of Omri are kept*   b Heb *its*
c Cn: Heb *they weave it*   d Heb *your*

My eyes will see her downfall;*a*
  now she will be trodden down
  like the mire of the streets.

A Prophecy of Restoration

11 A day for the building of your walls!
  In that day the boundary shall be far
    extended.
12 In that day they will come to you
  from Assyria to*b* Egypt,
and from Egypt to the River,
  from sea to sea and from mountain to
    mountain.
13 But the earth will be desolate
  because of its inhabitants,
  for the fruit of their doings.

14 Shepherd your people with your staff,
  the flock that belongs to you,
which lives alone in a forest
  in the midst of a garden land;
let them feed in Bashan and Gilead
  as in the days of old.
15 As in the days when you came out of the land of
  Egypt,
  show us*c* marvelous things.
16 The nations shall see and be ashamed

of all their might;
  they shall lay their hands on their mouths;
  their ears shall be deaf;
17 they shall lick dust like a snake,
  like the crawling things of the earth;
they shall come trembling out of their fortresses;
  they shall turn in dread to the Lord our God,
  and they shall stand in fear of you.

God's Compassion and Steadfast Love

18 Who is a God like you, pardoning iniquity
  and passing over the transgression
  of the remnant of your*d* possession?
He does not retain his anger forever,
  because he delights in showing clemency.
19 He will again have compassion upon us;
  he will tread our iniquities under foot.
You will cast all our*e* sins
  into the depths of the sea.
20 You will show faithfulness to Jacob
  and unswerving loyalty to Abraham,
as you have sworn to our ancestors
  from the days of old.

---

a Heb lacks *downfall* *b* One Ms: MT *Assyria and cities of*
c Cn: Heb *I will show him* *d* Heb *his* *e* Gk Syr Vg Tg: Heb
their

Devastation, desolation, and destruction! If the Book of Nahum were made into a movie, it would have to be rated R for graphic violence. You are about to read some angry words. They portray a vengeful God bringing destruction upon Israel's enemies. What could make the prophet Nahum so angry? What could make God so angry?

At a Glance

- **1:1–11. the coming of the Lord in judgment**
- **1:12–15. good news for Judah**
- **Chapters 2–3. the destruction of Nineveh**

Quick Facts

Period Covered: from 622 to 609 BC
Inspired Author: Nahum
Theme: God will avenge Israel and destroy its cruel enemies, the Assyrians.

In Depth

At the time Nahum was written, the Assyrian Empire had been the terror of the Middle East for several centuries. In 721 BC, it destroyed the northern part of Israel, called Israel. In 701 BC, it invaded the southern part of Israel, called Judah, and laid siege to Jerusalem (see the timeline and map 5, "The Assyrian Empire," at the back of this Bible). The siege broke off, and Jerusalem did not fall, but the Chosen People of God got a gruesome taste of Assyria's savage cruelty.

The sole concern of the prophet Nahum is the destruction of this evil world power. In the first chapter of his book, he declares the coming wrath of God, and in chapters 2–3, he describes the destruction of Nineveh (the Assyrian capital). We shouldn't be too surprised that when Assyria falls in 612 BC, Nahum sees the justice of God being worked out: the Assyrians are finally getting a taste of their own medicine! Nahum seems almost to be gloating in 3:19:

> All who hear the news about you
>   clap their hands over you.
> For who has ever escaped
>   your endless cruelty?

Hidden among the threats and violence against Assyria, we also find words of comfort for God's Chosen People: the awesome war with which God will avenge them because their enemies are God's enemies (see 1:2); good news and peace are coming for Judah (see 2:1); the Lord will restore Israel to its original majesty (see 2:3). We even find some wonderful reminders of God's love and protection, which balance the image of the God of vengeance and destruction: "The LORD is slow to anger but great in power" (1:3); "The LORD is good" (1:7); God is "a stronghold in a day of trouble" (1:7); God "protects those who take refuge in him" (1:7). Nahum reminds us that God has many sides and is always more than we can imagine.

The Book of **Nahum**

Nahum

1 An oracle concerning Nineveh. The book of the vision of Nahum of Elkosh.

The Consuming Wrath of God

2 A jealous and avenging God is the LORD,
  the LORD is avenging and wrathful;
the LORD takes vengeance on his adversaries
  and rages against his enemies.
3 The LORD is slow to anger but great in power,
  and the LORD will by no means clear the
    guilty.

His way is in whirlwind and storm,
  and the clouds are the dust of his feet.
4 He rebukes the sea and makes it dry,
  and he dries up all the rivers;
Bashan and Carmel wither,
  and the bloom of Lebanon fades.
5 The mountains quake before him,
  and the hills melt;
the earth heaves before him,
  the world and all who live in it.

6 Who can stand before his indignation?
  Who can endure the heat of his anger?
His wrath is poured out like fire,
  and by him the rocks are broken in pieces.
7 The LORD is good,
  a stronghold in a day of trouble;
he protects those who take refuge in him,
8   even in a rushing flood.
He will make a full end of his adversaries,[a]
  and will pursue his enemies into darkness.

9 Why do you plot against the LORD?
  He will make an end;
  no adversary will rise up twice.
10 Like thorns they are entangled,
  like drunkards they are drunk;
  they are consumed like dry straw.
11 From you one has gone out
  who plots evil against the LORD,
  one who counsels wickedness.

Good News for Judah

12 Thus says the LORD,
"Though they are at full strength and many,[b]
  they will be cut off and pass away.
Though I have afflicted you,
  I will afflict you no more.
13 And now I will break off his yoke from you
  and snap the bonds that bind you."

14 The LORD has commanded concerning you:
  "Your name shall be perpetuated no longer;
from the house of your gods I will cut off
  the carved image and the cast image.
I will make your grave, for you are worthless."

15 [c] Look! On the mountains the feet of one
  who brings good tidings,
  who proclaims peace!
Celebrate your festivals, O Judah,
  fulfill your vows,

---

a Gk: Heb *of her place*   b Meaning of Heb uncertain   c Ch 2.1
in Heb

for never again shall the wicked invade you;
   they are utterly cut off.

The Destruction of the Wicked City

2 A shatterer*ᵃ* has come up against you.
   Guard the ramparts;
     watch the road;

Images of God

"**P**iles of dead, / heaps of corpses, / dead bodies without end . . ." (Nah 3:3). The descriptions of God's vengeance on the Assyrians throughout chapters 2 and 3 of Nahum seem contradictory to Jesus' command to love one's enemies (see Mt 5:43–48). Was God different back in Old Testament times? or was Nahum just mistaken? These are difficult but important questions!

In understanding Nahum's message, it helps to keep in mind three things. First, throughout the Bible, there is a strong theme of divine hatred for all sin. In the New Testament, though, a distinction emerges that although God hates the sin, God still loves the sinner. Nahum doesn't make that distinction.

Second, Christians today make a distinction between God's directly causing something to happen and God's allowing something to occur—usually as a result of human limitations, people's poor choices, or natural phenomena. Again, Nahum doesn't make this distinction—for Nahum, if something happens, God is the direct cause.

Finally, we have to keep in mind that all our attempts to understand God will fall short. God is beyond human understanding. That is why the Bible's authors, including Nahum, describe God in many different—and often seemingly contradictory—ways.

How do you see God? as a vengeful fire (see Nah 1:6) or as a stronghold of protection (see verse 7)? Are you comfortable imagining God in different—even opposite—ways?

▶ Nah 2:1—3:3

gird your loins;
   collect all your strength.

² (For the Lᴏʀᴅ is restoring the majesty of Jacob,
   as well as the majesty of Israel,
though ravagers have ravaged them
   and ruined their branches.)

³ The shields of his warriors are red;
   his soldiers are clothed in crimson.
The metal on the chariots flashes
   on the day when he musters them;
    the chargers*ᵇ* prance.
⁴ The chariots race madly through the streets,
   they rush to and fro through the squares;
their appearance is like torches,
   they dart like lightning.
⁵ He calls his officers;
   they stumble as they come forward;
they hasten to the wall,
   and the mantelet*ᶜ* is set up.
⁶ The river gates are opened,
   the palace trembles.
⁷ It is decreed*ᶜ* that the city*ᵈ* be exiled,
   its slave women led away,
moaning like doves
   and beating their breasts.
⁸ Nineveh is like a pool
   whose waters*ᵉ* run away.
"Halt! Halt!"—
   but no one turns back.
⁹ "Plunder the silver,
   plunder the gold!
There is no end of treasure!
   An abundance of every precious thing!"

¹⁰ Devastation, desolation, and destruction!
   Hearts faint and knees tremble,
all loins quake,
   all faces grow pale!
¹¹ What became of the lions' den,
   the cave*ᶠ* of the young lions,
where the lion goes,
   and the lion's cubs, with no one to disturb
      them?
¹² The lion has torn enough for his whelps
   and strangled prey for his lionesses;
he has filled his caves with prey
   and his dens with torn flesh.

13 See, I am against you, says the Lᴏʀᴅ of hosts, and I will burn your*ᵍ* chariots in smoke, and

---

a Cn: Heb *scatterer* *b* Cn Compare Gk Syr: Heb *cypresses*
c Meaning of Heb uncertain *d* Heb *it* *e* Cn Compare Gk: Heb
a pool, from the days that she has become, and they *f* Cn: Heb
pasture *g* Heb *her*

the sword shall devour your young lions; I will cut off your prey from the earth, and the voice of your messengers shall be heard no more.

Ruin Imminent and Inevitable

3 Ah! City of bloodshed,
    utterly deceitful, full of booty—
    no end to the plunder!
2 The crack of whip and rumble of wheel,
    galloping horse and bounding chariot!
3 Horsemen charging,
    flashing sword and glittering spear,
piles of dead,
    heaps of corpses,
dead bodies without end—
    they stumble over the bodies!
4 Because of the countless debaucheries of the
        prostitute,
gracefully alluring, mistress of sorcery,
who enslaves[a] nations through her debaucheries,
    and peoples through her sorcery,
5 I am against you,
    says the Lord of hosts,
    and will lift up your skirts over your face;
and I will let nations look on your nakedness
    and kingdoms on your shame.
6 I will throw filth at you
    and treat you with contempt,
    and make you a spectacle.
7 Then all who see you will shrink from you and say,
    "Nineveh is devastated; who will bemoan her?"
    Where shall I seek comforters for you?

8 Are you better than Thebes[b]
    that sat by the Nile,
with water around her,
    her rampart a sea,
    water her wall?
9 Ethiopia[c] was her strength,
    Egypt too, and that without limit;
    Put and the Libyans were her[d] helpers.

10 Yet she became an exile,
    she went into captivity;
even her infants were dashed in pieces
    at the head of every street;
lots were cast for her nobles,
    all her dignitaries were bound in fetters.
11 You also will be drunken,
    you will go into hiding;[e]
you will seek
    a refuge from the enemy.
12 All your fortresses are like fig trees
    with first-ripe figs—
if shaken they fall
    into the mouth of the eater.

13 Look at your troops:
    they are women in your midst.
The gates of your land
    are wide open to your foes;
    fire has devoured the bars of your gates.

14 Draw water for the siege,
    strengthen your forts;
trample the clay,
    tread the mortar,
    take hold of the brick mold!
15 There the fire will devour you,
    the sword will cut you off.
    It will devour you like the locust.

Multiply yourselves like the locust,
    multiply like the grasshopper!
16 You increased your merchants
    more than the stars of the heavens.
    The locust sheds its skin and flies away.
17 Your guards are like grasshoppers,
    your scribes like swarms[e] of locusts
settling on the fences
    on a cold day—
when the sun rises, they fly away;
    no one knows where they have gone.

18 Your shepherds are asleep,
    O king of Assyria;
    your nobles slumber.
Your people are scattered on the mountains
    with no one to gather them.
19 There is no assuaging your hurt,
    your wound is mortal.
All who hear the news about you
    clap their hands over you.
For who has ever escaped
    your endless cruelty?

---

a Heb *sells*   b Heb *No-amon*   c Or *Nubia*; Heb *Cush*
d Gk: Heb *your*   e Meaning of Heb uncertain

Chapter 2

God, why aren't you answering our cries for help? How long must we endure this trial? Most people have wondered this at times. Why does our good, all-powerful God let suffering or injustice go on? The prophet Habakkuk struggled with these same painful and disturbing questions. His hope in God's justice is a model of faith amid doubt.

At a Glance

- **1:1—2:5.** Habakkuk's complaints and God's responses
- **2:6–20.** five warnings against wicked people
- **Chapter 3.** Habakkuk's prayer of confidence

Quick Facts

Period Covered: probably the reign of King Jehoiakim, from 605 to 597 BC (2 Kings 23:36—24:7)

Inspired Author: Habakkuk

Theme: The answer to evil is faith in God's justice.

In Depth

Habakkuk was the first prophet who dared to ask God about God's behavior. He looked around at all the terrible things that were happening to his people and cried out: God, where are you? Do you even care about us? Why do you allow evil people to oppress us?

We know little about Habakkuk except that he was a prophet in the southern kingdom of Judah in the late seventh century BC. The Chaldeans (another name for the Babylonians) and the corrupt king of Judah, Jehoiakim, were causing so much trouble that Habakkuk was ready to despair. God answered him in a most surprising way, saying that the Chaldeans—as bad as they were—were chosen as God's instrument to punish the wicked all over the earth. Habakkuk was not satisfied. He asked why God was silent while the wicked destroyed the righteous. God then spoke to him in a vision (see Hab 2:2), saying that justice would come to the wicked in its own time, but the "righteous live by their faith" (Hab 2:4). Later, Paul would use these same words to describe the Christians (see Rom 1:17, Gal 3:11). For Habakkuk, faith in God and hope in God's justice were the same thing.

The short Book of Habakkuk is unique among the prophetic books in the variety of its writings. Its reflections about the problem of evil in the world resemble the wisdom literature. Its dialogues with God (see 1:2) are similar to Jeremiah's confessions (see Jer 12:6). Habakkuk, chapter 3 is a canticle (song).

The prophet's concluding canticle is a prayer of confidence in God's power to save the people. We too can pray in confidence because God is just and will save us in our time of need.

The Book of
Habakkuk

Habakkuk

1 The oracle that the prophet Habakkuk saw.

The Prophet's Complaint

2 O LORD, how long shall I cry for help,
  and you will not listen?
Or cry to you "Violence!"
  and you will not save?
3 Why do you make me see wrongdoing
  and look at trouble?
Destruction and violence are before me;
  strife and contention arise.
4 So the law becomes slack
  and justice never prevails.
The wicked surround the righteous—
  therefore judgment comes forth perverted.

5 Look at the nations, and see!
  Be astonished! Be astounded!
For a work is being done in your days
  that you would not believe if you were told.
6 For I am rousing the Chaldeans,
  that fierce and impetuous nation,
who march through the breadth of the earth
  to seize dwellings not their own.
7 Dread and fearsome are they;
  their justice and dignity proceed from
    themselves.
8 Their horses are swifter than leopards,
  more menacing than wolves at dusk;
  their horses charge.
Their horsemen come from far away;
  they fly like an eagle swift to devour.

9 They all come for violence,
  with faces pressing[a] forward;
  they gather captives like sand.
10 At kings they scoff,
  and of rulers they make sport.
They laugh at every fortress,
  and heap up earth to take it.
11 Then they sweep by like the wind;
  they transgress and become guilty;
  their own might is their god!

12 Are you not from of old,
  O LORD my God, my Holy One?
  You[b] shall not die.
O LORD, you have marked them for judgment;
  and you, O Rock, have established them for
    punishment.
13 Your eyes are too pure to behold evil,
  and you cannot look on wrongdoing;
why do you look on the treacherous,
  and are silent when the wicked swallow
  those more righteous than they?
14 You have made people like the fish of the sea,
  like crawling things that have no ruler.

15 The enemy[c] brings all of them up with a hook;
  he drags them out with his net,
he gathers them in his seine;
  so he rejoices and exults.
16 Therefore he sacrifices to his net

---

a Meaning of Heb uncertain   b Ancient Heb tradition: MT *We*
c Heb *He*

and makes offerings to his seine;
for by them his portion is lavish,
    and his food is rich.
17 Is he then to keep on emptying his net,
    and destroying nations without mercy?

God's Reply to the Prophet's Complaint

2 I will stand at my watchpost,
    and station myself on the rampart;
I will keep watch to see what he will say to me,
    and what he[d] will answer concerning my
        complaint.
2 Then the LORD answered me and said:
Write the vision;

Now!

“❝I want it all, and I want it now!” That statement could sum up the ambitions of a lot
of people. It is how they define success. The key
word in their goal is now. They don't like to wait
in lines; they want instant service and immediate
gratification. Think about your own frustration if
the internet connection you're using is too slow,
or if you can't immediately reach a friend on her
or his cell phone. We have grown used to getting
things right away, and become impatient when
our expectations are not met.

There is a temptation to apply this goal to our
spiritual lives, hoping for an immediate and fulfilling relationship with God. But the spiritual life
does not work that way. Recall these words from
the Book of Ecclesiastes: “For everything there
is a season, and a time for every matter under
heaven” (3:1). We have to remind ourselves that
many valuable things take time. Our growth in
faith will take time. We need to be open, patient,
and trusting. As God reminds Habakkuk in his
vision in Habakkuk 2:3, “If it seems to tarry, wait
for it; / it will surely come, it will not delay.”

Consider these questions:
● What are your goals for your relationship with
  God?
● How patient are you with your spiritual growth?
  How do you nurture it day by day?

▶ **Hab 2:3**

make it plain on tablets,
    so that a runner may read it.
3 For there is still a vision for the appointed time;
    it speaks of the end, and does not lie.
If it seems to tarry, wait for it;
    it will surely come, it will not delay.
4 Look at the proud!
    Their spirit is not right in them,
    but the righteous live by their faith.[b]
5 Moreover, wealth[c] is treacherous;
    the arrogant do not endure.
They open their throats wide as Sheol;
    like Death they never have enough.
They gather all nations for themselves,
    and collect all peoples as their own.

The Woes of the Wicked

6 Shall not everyone taunt such people and,
with mocking riddles, say about them,
    “Alas for you who heap up what is not your own!”
    How long will you load yourselves with
        goods taken in pledge?
7 Will not your own creditors suddenly rise,
    and those who make you tremble wake up?
    Then you will be booty for them.
8 Because you have plundered many nations,
    all that survive of the peoples shall plunder
        you—
because of human bloodshed, and violence to
        the earth,
    to cities and all who live in them.

9 “Alas for you who get evil gain for your house,
    setting your nest on high
    to be safe from the reach of harm!”
10 You have devised shame for your house
    by cutting off many peoples;
    you have forfeited your life.
11 The very stones will cry out from the wall,
    and the plaster[d] will respond from the
        woodwork.

12 “Alas for you who build a town by bloodshed,
    and found a city on iniquity!”
13 Is it not from the LORD of hosts
    that peoples labor only to feed the flames,
    and nations weary themselves for nothing?
14 But the earth will be filled
    with the knowledge of the glory of the LORD,
    as the waters cover the sea.

15 “Alas for you who make your neighbors drink,
    pouring out your wrath[e] until they are drunk,

in order to gaze on their nakedness!"

16 You will be sated with contempt instead of glory.
  Drink, you yourself, and stagger!*a*
The cup in the Lord's right hand
  will come around to you,
  and shame will come upon your glory!
17 For the violence done to Lebanon will
    overwhelm you;
  the destruction of the animals will terrify
    you—*b*
because of human bloodshed and violence to
    the earth,
  to cities and all who live in them.

18 What use is an idol
  once its maker has shaped it—
  a cast image, a teacher of lies?
For its maker trusts in what has been made,
  though the product is only an idol that
    cannot speak!
19 Alas for you who say to the wood, "Wake up!"
  to silent stone, "Rouse yourself!"
  Can it teach?
See, it is gold and silver plated,
  and there is no breath in it at all.

20 But the Lord is in his holy temple;
  let all the earth keep silence before him!

3 A prayer of the prophet Habakkuk according
to Shigionoth.

The Prophet's Prayer

2 O Lord, I have heard of your renown,
  and I stand in awe, O Lord, of your work.
In our own time revive it;
  in our own time make it known;
  in wrath may you remember mercy.
3 God came from Teman,
  the Holy One from Mount Paran.   Selah
His glory covered the heavens,
  and the earth was full of his praise.
4 The brightness was like the sun;
  rays came forth from his hand,
  where his power lay hidden.
5 Before him went pestilence,
  and plague followed close behind.
6 He stopped and shook the earth;
  he looked and made the nations tremble.
The eternal mountains were shattered;
  along his ancient pathways
  the everlasting hills sank low.
7 I saw the tents of Cushan under affliction;
  the tent-curtains of the land of Midian
    trembled.
8 Was your wrath against the rivers,*c* O Lord?

Or your anger against the rivers,*c*
  or your rage against the sea,*d*
when you drove your horses,
  your chariots to victory?
9 You brandished your naked bow,
  sated*e* were the arrows at your command.*f*
       Selah
You split the earth with rivers.
10 The mountains saw you, and writhed;
  a torrent of water swept by;
the deep gave forth its voice.
  The sun*g* raised high its hands;
11 the moon*h* stood still in its exalted place,
  at the light of your arrows speeding by,
  at the gleam of your flashing spear.
12 In fury you trod the earth,
  in anger you trampled nations.
13 You came forth to save your people,
  to save your anointed.
You crushed the head of the wicked house,
  laying it bare from foundation to roof.*f*   Selah
14 You pierced with their*i* own arrows the head*j* of
    his warriors,*k*
  who came like a whirlwind to scatter us,*l*
  gloating as if ready to devour the poor who
    were in hiding.
15 You trampled the sea with your horses,
  churning the mighty waters.

16 I hear, and I tremble within;
  my lips quiver at the sound.
Rottenness enters into my bones,
  and my steps tremble*m* beneath me.
I wait quietly for the day of calamity
  to come upon the people who attack us.

Trust and Joy in the Midst of Trouble

17 Though the fig tree does not blossom,
  and no fruit is on the vines;
though the produce of the olive fails,
  and the fields yield no food;
though the flock is cut off from the fold,
  and there is no herd in the stalls,
18 yet I will rejoice in the Lord;
  I will exult in the God of my salvation.
19 God, the Lord, is my strength;
  he makes my feet like the feet of a deer,
  and makes me tread upon the heights.*n*

To the leader: with stringed*o* instruments.

---

a Q Ms Gk: MT *be uncircumcised*   b Gk Syr: Meaning of Heb
uncertain   c Or *against River*   d Or *against Sea*   e Cn: Heb
oaths   f Meaning of Heb uncertain   g Heb *It*   h Heb *sun,
moon*   i Heb *his*   j Or *leader*   k Vg Compare Gk Syr: Meaning
of Heb uncertain   l Heb *me*   m Cn Compare Gk: Meaning of
Heb uncertain   n Heb *my heights*   o Heb *my stringed*

During childhood, we usually have to clean up messes, take time-outs, or lose privileges as consequences for poor choices we have made. As we get older, we learn that our wrongdoing has more personal and painful consequences: perhaps a parent's refusal to trust us, a friend's anger, or pain after hurting someone we love. The prophet Zephaniah warned the people of Judah of the severe consequences of their sin against the Lord.

The Book of Zephaniah

🟢 At a Glance

- **Chapter 1.** a warning about Judah's idolatry
- **2:1—3:7.** a discussion of the destruction of the nations and the corrupt nature of Jerusalem
- **3:8–20.** a message about the conversion of the nations and salvation for Jerusalem

⭐ Quick Facts

Period Covered: approximately 630 BC
Inspired Author: Zephaniah (and perhaps a later editor)
Theme: Judah and its neighbors will experience the consequences of their sinfulness.

In Depth

The Book of Zephaniah gives us few clues about the prophet Zephaniah's identity. We do know that he preached in the southern kingdom of Judah during the reign of King Josiah (see 2 Chronicles, chapters 34–35), around 630 BC. He followed First Isaiah and Micah, and came a little before Habakkuk, during the time of Nahum.

Zephaniah follows the footsteps of the classical Old Testament prophets in denouncing the wrongdoing of society. His main contribution is considering pride (see 1:6, 2:10, 3:11) as the source of problems such as smugness (see 1:12), rebellion (see 3:2), and treachery (see 3:11). All these attitudes toward God lead to idolatry and social sin. Although all people sin, leaders have a greater responsibility, and their sins will provoke a harsh judgment during the coming day of the Lord (see 1:14). Only those who worship God humbly and who seek justice will be spared. Zephaniah calls them the remnant (see 3:12–13), meaning "a little piece that is left over." They are the ones who will stay faithful to God through both good times and bad.

The book ends with a song of joy reassuring the people of Jerusalem that God still loves them and will save them in the end. We are not sure whether the song is from Zephaniah himself or is the addition of a later editor. It is as if the writer knows that when people are experiencing the negative results of sinful actions, they need to be reassured they are still loved. God's punishment is to teach us, not to destroy us. Therefore, God's People should not despair but keep their trust in God.

Zephaniah

1 The word of the LORD that came to Zephaniah son of Cushi son of Gedaliah son of Amariah son of Hezekiah, in the days of King Josiah son of Amon of Judah.

The Coming Judgment on Judah

2 I will utterly sweep away everything
　from the face of the earth, says the LORD.
3 I will sweep away humans and animals;
　I will sweep away the birds of the air
　and the fish of the sea.
I will make the wicked stumble.*a*
　I will cut off humanity
from the face of the earth, says the LORD.
4 I will stretch out my hand against Judah,
　and against all the inhabitants of Jerusalem;
and I will cut off from this place every remnant
　　of Baal
　and the name of the idolatrous priests;*b*
5 those who bow down on the roofs
　to the host of the heavens;
those who bow down and swear to the LORD,
　but also swear by Milcom;*c*
6 those who have turned back from following the
　　LORD,
who have not sought the LORD or inquired of
　him.

7 Be silent before the Lord GOD!
　For the day of the LORD is at hand;
the LORD has prepared a sacrifice,
　he has consecrated his guests.
8 And on the day of the LORD's sacrifice

I will punish the officials and the king's sons
　and all who dress themselves in foreign
　　attire.
9 On that day I will punish
　all who leap over the threshold,
who fill their master's house
　with violence and fraud.

10 On that day, says the LORD,
　a cry will be heard from the Fish Gate,
a wail from the Second Quarter,
　a loud crash from the hills.
11 The inhabitants of the Mortar wail,
　for all the traders have perished;
　all who weigh out silver are cut off.
12 At that time I will search Jerusalem with
　　lamps,
　and I will punish the people
who rest complacently*d* on their dregs,
　those who say in their hearts,
"The LORD will not do good,
　nor will he do harm."
13 Their wealth shall be plundered,
　and their houses laid waste.
Though they build houses,
　they shall not inhabit them;
though they plant vineyards,
　they shall not drink wine from them.

---

a Cn: Heb *sea, and those who cause the wicked to stumble*
b Compare Gk: Heb *the idolatrous priests with the priests*
c Gk Mss Syr Vg: Heb *Malcam* (or, *their king*)　d Heb *who thicken*

1079

The Great Day of the Lord

14 The great day of the Lord is near,
      near and hastening fast;
   the sound of the day of the Lord is bitter,
      the warrior cries aloud there.
15 That day will be a day of wrath,
      a day of distress and anguish,
   a day of ruin and devastation,
      a day of darkness and gloom,
   a day of clouds and thick darkness,
16   a day of trumpet blast and battle cry
   against the fortified cities
      and against the lofty battlements.

17 I will bring such distress upon people
      that they shall walk like the blind;
   because they have sinned against the Lord,
   their blood shall be poured out like dust,
      and their flesh like dung.
18 Neither their silver nor their gold
      will be able to save them
   on the day of the Lord's wrath;
   in the fire of his passion
      the whole earth shall be consumed;
   for a full, a terrible end
      he will make of all the inhabitants of the
      earth.

Judgment on Israel's Enemies

2 Gather together, gather,
      O shameless nation,
2 before you are driven away
      like the drifting chaff,*a*
   before there comes upon you
      the fierce anger of the Lord,
   before there comes upon you
      the day of the Lord's wrath.
3 Seek the Lord, all you humble of the land,
      who do his commands;
   seek righteousness, seek humility;
      perhaps you may be hidden
   on the day of the Lord's wrath.
4 For Gaza shall be deserted,
      and Ashkelon shall become a desolation;
   Ashdod's people shall be driven out at noon,
      and Ekron shall be uprooted.

5 Ah, inhabitants of the seacoast,
      you nation of the Cherethites!
   The word of the Lord is against you,
      O Canaan, land of the Philistines;
   and I will destroy you until no inhabitant is
      left.
6 And you, O seacoast, shall be pastures,
      meadows for shepherds

and folds for flocks.
7 The seacoast shall become the possession
      of the remnant of the house of Judah,
      on which they shall pasture,
   and in the houses of Ashkelon
      they shall lie down at evening.
   For the Lord their God will be mindful of them
      and restore their fortunes.

8 I have heard the taunts of Moab
      and the revilings of the Ammonites,
   how they have taunted my people
      and made boasts against their territory.
9 Therefore, as I live, says the Lord of hosts,
      the God of Israel,
   Moab shall become like Sodom
      and the Ammonites like Gomorrah,
   a land possessed by nettles and salt pits,
      and a waste forever.
   The remnant of my people shall plunder them,
      and the survivors of my nation shall possess
         them.
10 This shall be their lot in return for their pride,
      because they scoffed and boasted
      against the people of the Lord of hosts.
11 The Lord will be terrible against them;
      he will shrivel all the gods of the earth,
   and to him shall bow down,
      each in its place,
   all the coasts and islands of the nations.

12 You also, O Ethiopians,*b*
      shall be killed by my sword.

13 And he will stretch out his hand against the
      north,
      and destroy Assyria;
   and he will make Nineveh a desolation,
      a dry waste like the desert.
14 Herds shall lie down in it,
      every wild animal;*c*
   the desert owl*d* and the screech owl*d*
      shall lodge on its capitals;
   the owl*e* shall hoot at the window,
      the raven*f* croak on the threshold;
      for its cedar work will be laid bare.
15 Is this the exultant city
      that lived secure,
   that said to itself,
      "I am, and there is no one else"?
   What a desolation it has become,
      a lair for wild animals!

---

a Cn Compare Gk Syr: Heb *before a decree is born; like
chaff a day has passed away*   b Or Nubians; Heb *Cushites*
c Tg Compare Gk: Heb *nation*   d Meaning of Heb uncertain
e Cn: Heb *a voice*   f Gk Vg: Heb *desolation*

Cultural Connection

Material Poverty and Spiritual Poverty

In the Bible, God is always opposed to material poverty and misery. Over and over in the Old Testament, wealth is called a blessing and poverty a curse. The laws of the covenant assert that poverty should not exist in Israel. Rich people are commanded to periodically forgive the debts of the poor and return land taken as payment of debt to the land's original owners (see Lev 25:8). Selfishness leads to injustice, and injustice leads to tragedy, violence, and despair.

Zephaniah gives a spiritual connotation to the word *poor* (translated as "lowly" in Zephaniah 3:12). He relates poverty to humility. In this sense, to be poor is to be empty of egoism and pride, and therefore open to God's action in us. Zephaniah believes a small group of spiritually poor people, known as the remnant of Israel or the poor of God, will keep the covenant alive.

Hispanic spirituality is deeply rooted in this concept of the poor, and the Virgin Mary is the culture's supreme example of it. To be spiritually poor is to be receptive to the Holy Spirit, to be generous with others, to trust in God's providence, and to accept suffering without losing hope.

● How will you live out the call to be spiritually poor, free of material goods beyond what is necessary to live?

● Ask God to give you the strength to respond to this call, which is so necessary in this world of pride, injustice, and materialism.

▶ **Zeph 3:11–13**

Everyone who passes by it
  hisses and shakes the fist.

The Wickedness of Jerusalem

3 Ah, soiled, defiled,
  oppressing city!
2 It has listened to no voice;
  it has accepted no correction.
It has not trusted in the LORD;
  it has not drawn near to its God.

3 The officials within it
  are roaring lions;
its judges are evening wolves
  that leave nothing until the morning.
4 Its prophets are reckless,
  faithless persons;
its priests have profaned what is sacred,
  they have done violence to the law.
5 The LORD within it is righteous;
  he does no wrong.
Every morning he renders his judgment,
  each dawn without fail;
  but the unjust knows no shame.

6 I have cut off nations;
  their battlements are in ruins;
I have laid waste their streets
  so that no one walks in them;
their cities have been made desolate,

without people, without inhabitants.
7 I said, "Surely the city[a] will fear me,
  it will accept correction;
it will not lose sight[b]
  of all that I have brought upon it."
But they were the more eager
  to make all their deeds corrupt.

Punishment and Conversion of the Nations

8 Therefore wait for me, says the LORD,
  for the day when I arise as a witness.
For my decision is to gather nations,
  to assemble kingdoms,
to pour out upon them my indignation,
  all the heat of my anger;
for in the fire of my passion
  all the earth shall be consumed.

9 At that time I will change the speech of the
    peoples
  to a pure speech,
that all of them may call on the name of the
    LORD
  and serve him with one accord.
10 From beyond the rivers of Ethiopia[c]
  my suppliants, my scattered ones,
  shall bring my offering.

a Heb *it*   b Gk Syr: Heb *its dwelling will not be cut off*
c Or *Nubia*; Heb *Cush*

11 On that day you shall not be put to shame
  because of all the deeds by which you have
    rebelled against me;
  for then I will remove from your midst
    your proudly exultant ones,
  and you shall no longer be haughty
    in my holy mountain.
12 For I will leave in the midst of you
    a people humble and lowly.
  They shall seek refuge in the name of the LORD—
13   the remnant of Israel;
  they shall do no wrong
    and utter no lies,
  nor shall a deceitful tongue
    be found in their mouths.
  Then they will pasture and lie down,
    and no one shall make them afraid.

A Song of Joy

14 Sing aloud, O daughter Zion;
    shout, O Israel!
  Rejoice and exult with all your heart,
    O daughter Jerusalem!
15 The LORD has taken away the judgments against
      you,
    he has turned away your enemies.
  The king of Israel, the LORD, is in your midst;

    you shall fear disaster no more.
16 On that day it shall be said to Jerusalem:
  Do not fear, O Zion;
    do not let your hands grow weak.
17 The LORD, your God, is in your midst,
    a warrior who gives victory;
  he will rejoice over you with gladness,
    he will renew you[a] in his love;
  he will exult over you with loud singing
18   as on a day of festival.[b]
  I will remove disaster from you,[c]
    so that you will not bear reproach for it.
19 I will deal with all your oppressors
    at that time.
  And I will save the lame
    and gather the outcast,
  and I will change their shame into praise
    and renown in all the earth.
20 At that time I will bring you home,
    at the time when I gather you;
  for I will make you renowned and praised
    among all the peoples of the earth,
  when I restore your fortunes
    before your eyes, says the LORD.

a Gk Syr: Heb *he will be silent*   b Gk Syr: Meaning of Heb
uncertain   c Cn: Heb *I will remove from you; they were*

ZEPH

Imagine that you've been saving for months for a new stereo system. Just when you are about to purchase it, a good friend's family has a major house fire. Unfortunately, they were not insured, so the community is taking up a collection to help them rebuild. Now you are faced with a decision: Will you buy the new stereo or help your friend's family? The Jews at the time of the prophet Haggai faced an even more difficult decision: Returning to Jerusalem after the Babylonian Exile, which would they rebuild first—their homes or God's Temple?

At a Glance

- **Chapter 1.** a command to rebuild the Temple
- **2:1–19.** a description of the future glory of God's Temple and the future prosperity of God's People
- **2:20–23.** a message about the future nation of Judah and its king

Quick Facts

Period Covered: approximately 520 BC
Inspired Author: Haggai
Theme: Rebuilding God's Temple

In Depth

When the people of ancient Judah lost their Temple in 587 BC and were deported to a strange land, they experienced a crisis in faith. Had God abandoned them? Were they no longer God's People? Was God punishing them for their sins? Some of them dreamed of a time when they could return to their land and rebuild God's Temple. However, when they finally were able to return in 538 BC, things weren't as easy as they had hoped. Suffering from poverty, droughts, and crop failures (see Hag 1:10–11), they put off rebuilding the Temple. Into this scene came the prophet Haggai. He told the people that God was still with them, and life was so difficult because they didn't seem to care that God's house was in ruins (see verse 9). They had to get their priorities in order!

The people heard God's Word spoken through Haggai and immediately began working on the Temple. In their minds, they knew the new Temple would never be as beautiful as the original one (see 2:3). Haggai used this opportunity to prophesy about a future Temple that would be filled with God's glory (see verse 7), a time when God would again bless these people and make their offerings holy. God would establish Judah as a powerful nation, and Zerubbabel (a descendant of David) would be its anointed king.

The Book of **Haggai**

1083

Haggai

Chapter 2

The Command to Rebuild the Temple

1 In the second year of King Darius, in the sixth month, on the first day of the month, the word of the LORD came by the prophet Haggai to Zerubbabel son of Shealtiel, governor of Judah, and to Joshua son of Jehozadak, the high priest: ²Thus says the LORD of hosts: These people say the time has not yet come to rebuild the LORD's house. ³Then the word of the LORD came by the prophet Haggai, saying: ⁴Is it a time for you yourselves to live in your paneled houses, while this house lies in ruins? ⁵Now therefore thus says the LORD of hosts: Consider how you have fared. ⁶You have sown much, and harvested little; you eat, but you never have enough; you drink, but you never have your fill; you clothe yourselves, but no one is warm; and you that earn wages earn wages to put them into a bag with holes.

7 Thus says the LORD of hosts: Consider how you have fared. ⁸Go up to the hills and bring wood and build the house, so that I may take pleasure in it and be honored, says the LORD. ⁹You have looked for much, and, lo, it came to little; and when you brought it home, I blew it away. Why? says the LORD of hosts. Because my house lies in ruins, while all of you hurry off to your own houses. ¹⁰Therefore the heavens above you have withheld the dew, and the earth has withheld its produce. ¹¹And I have called for a drought on the land and the hills, on the grain, the new wine, the oil, on what the soil produces, on human beings and animals, and on all their labors.

12 Then Zerubbabel son of Shealtiel, and Joshua son of Jehozadak, the high priest, with all the remnant of the people, obeyed the voice of the LORD their God, and the words of the prophet Haggai, as the LORD their God had sent him; and the people feared the LORD. ¹³Then Haggai, the messenger of the LORD, spoke to the people with the LORD's message, saying, I am with you, says the LORD. ¹⁴And the LORD stirred up the spirit of Zerubbabel son of Shealtiel, governor of Judah, and the spirit of Joshua son of Jehozadak, the high priest, and the spirit of all the remnant of the people; and they came and worked on the house of the LORD of hosts, their God, ¹⁵on the twenty-fourth day of the month, in the sixth month.

The Future Glory of the Temple

2 In the second year of King Darius, ¹in the seventh month, on the twenty-first day of the month, the word of the LORD came by the prophet Haggai, saying: ²Speak now to Zerubbabel son of Shealtiel, governor of Judah, and to Joshua son of Jehozadak, the high priest, and to the remnant of the people, and say, ³Who is left among you that saw this house in its former glory? How does it look to you now? Is it not in your sight as nothing? ⁴Yet now take courage, O Zerubbabel, says the LORD; take courage, O Joshua, son of Jehozadak, the high priest; take courage, all you people of the land, says the LORD; work, for I am with you, says the LORD of hosts, ⁵according to the promise that I made you when you came out of Egypt. My spirit abides among you; do not fear. ⁶For thus says the LORD of hosts: Once again, in a little while, I will shake the heavens and the earth and the sea and the dry land; ⁷and I will shake all the nations, so that the treasure of all nations shall come, and I will fill this house with splendor, says the LORD of hosts. ⁸The silver is mine, and the gold is mine, says the LORD of hosts. ⁹The latter splendor of this house shall be greater than the former, says the LORD of hosts; and in this place I will give prosperity, says the LORD of hosts.

A Rebuke and a Promise

10 On the twenty-fourth day of the ninth month, in the second year of Darius, the word of the LORD came by the prophet Haggai, saying: ¹¹Thus says the LORD of hosts: Ask the priests for a ruling: ¹²If one carries consecrated meat in the fold of one's garment, and with the fold touches bread, or stew, or wine, or oil, or any kind of food, does it become holy? The priests answered, "No." ¹³Then Haggai said, "If one who is unclean by contact with a dead body touches any of these, does it become unclean?" The priests answered, "Yes, it becomes unclean." ¹⁴Haggai then said, So is it with this people, and with this nation before me, says the LORD; and so with every work of their hands; and what they offer there is unclean. ¹⁵But now, consider what will come to pass from this day on. Before a stone was placed upon a stone in the LORD's temple, ¹⁶how did you fare?ᵃ When one came to a heap of twenty measures, there were but ten; when one came to the wine vat to draw fifty measures, there were but twenty. ¹⁷I struck you and all the products of your toil with blight and mildew and hail; yet you did not return to me, says the LORD. ¹⁸Consider from this day on, from the twenty-fourth day of the ninth month. Since the day that the foundation of the LORD's temple was laid, consider: ¹⁹Is there any seed left in the barn? Do the vine, the fig tree, the pomegranate, and the olive tree still yield nothing? From this day on I will bless you.

God's Promise to Zerubbabel

20 The word of the LORD came a second time to Haggai on the twenty-fourth day of the month: ²¹Speak to Zerubbabel, governor of Judah, saying, I am about to shake the heavens

Pray It!

God at the Center

The people of Haggai's time thought they did not have enough wealth to rebuild the Temple (see Hag 1:2). God told them they were poor and unsuccessful because they had not rebuilt it (see verse 9). They needed to trust that if they put their priorities in the right order, God would provide.

Perhaps Haggai's people had forgotten what the true riches in life are. One of the first things many poor European immigrants settling in the United States did was to build a church (and often a school). They did this at a great sacrifice of time and materials. The church was more than a building; it was a symbol of their willingness to work together and a symbol of their common faith. It is in things like this that true wealth is found.

God, help me and my family, friends, and community to put you and the building of your Reign first in our lives. Give us the true wealth that comes from working with others for the good of all. Amen.

▶ **Haggai, chapter 1**

and the earth, ²²and to overthrow the throne of kingdoms; I am about to destroy the strength of the kingdoms of the nations, and overthrow the chariots and their riders; and the horses and their riders shall fall, every one by the sword of a comrade. ²³On that day, says the LORD of hosts, I will take you, O Zerubbabel my servant, son of Shealtiel, says the LORD, and make you like a signet ring; for I have chosen you, says the LORD of hosts.

---

a Gk: Heb *since they were*

H A G

What do you do when life is difficult and things seem to just be getting worse? Some people dream about the future. They imagine a time when all their troubles have ended and life is happy again. If their trouble is caused by certain people, they may imagine how these people eventually pay for their wrong-doing. The Book of Zechariah looks at Israel's future in exactly these two ways.

The Book of

Zechariah

At a Glance

■ **Chapters 1–6.** Zechariah's visions

■ **Chapters 7–8.** a discussion of fasting and God's promises

■ **Chapters 9–10.** a description of the King of Peace and the evil shepherds of Judah

■ **Chapters 11–14.** a message of the day of God's judgment and the final war

Quick Facts

Period Covered: First Zechariah around 520 BC, Second Zechariah sometime after 333 BC
Inspired Authors: the original Zechariah, and an unknown prophet or prophets writing much later
Themes: a command to rebuild the Temple, the message that God will win the final victory
Of Note: The prophecies of Zechariah are quoted in the New Testament because they were understood by the early Church to have been fulfilled in Jesus Christ.

In Depth

Like the Book of Isaiah, the Book of Zechariah was written by at least two prophets. The original Zechariah—we'll call him First Zechariah—lived around the same time as Haggai, after the exiled Israelites returned to Jerusalem from Babylon (see the timeline at the back of this Bible). Second Zechariah, who may have been one or more prophets, wrote about two hundred years later.

The optimistic message of the first prophet in chapters 1–8 of Zechariah is centered on two concerns: the rebuilding of the Temple and the end of time. First Zechariah saw that a rebuilt Temple was needed to restore the people's unity, identity, and relationship with God. Through a series of visions (see "Apocalyptic Literature," near Daniel, chapters 7–10), he announced his message: under the guidance of the priest Joshua and the prince Zerubbabel (a descendant of King David), Israel would be restored. It would become a nation of justice, faith, love, mercy, and truth where the Lord would dwell. Even the Gentiles (non-Jews) would come from faraway lands to worship God.

Second Zechariah wrote later, when Israel was under Greek domination (see the timeline at the back of this Bible). He preached not through visions, but through oracles (prophetic speeches) of warning, violence, and also promise. He talked about a great battle that was about to take place between the forces of good and the forces of evil. This was the final war, which would bring an end to the present-day evil and corrupt world. But Second Zechariah also proclaimed the coming of a humble king who would bring peace to all nations. Jerusalem would be purified and would become victorious as the city where God reigns as the highest power for good.

Israel Urged to Repent

1 In the eighth month, in the second year of Darius, the word of the Lord came to the prophet Zechariah son of Berechiah son of Iddo, saying: [2] The Lord was very angry with your ancestors. [3] Therefore say to them, Thus says the Lord of hosts: Return to me, says the Lord of hosts, and I will return to you, says the Lord of hosts. [4] Do not be like your ancestors, to whom the former prophets proclaimed, "Thus says the Lord of hosts, Return from your evil ways and from your evil deeds." But they did not hear or heed me, says the Lord. [5] Your ancestors, where are they? And the prophets, do they live forever? [6] But my words and my statutes, which I commanded my servants the prophets, did they not overtake your ancestors? So they repented and said, "The Lord of hosts has dealt with us according to our ways and deeds, just as he planned to do."

First Vision: The Horsemen

7 On the twenty-fourth day of the eleventh month, the month of Shebat, in the second year of Darius, the word of the Lord came to the prophet Zechariah son of Berechiah son of Iddo; and Zechariah[a] said, [8] In the night I saw a man riding on a red horse! He was standing among the myrtle trees in the glen; and behind him were red, sorrel, and white horses. [9] Then I said, "What are these, my lord?" The angel who talked with me said to me, "I will show you what they are." [10] So the man who was standing among the myrtle trees answered, "They are those whom the Lord has sent to patrol the earth." [11] Then they spoke to the angel of the Lord who was standing among the myrtle trees, "We have patrolled the earth, and lo, the whole earth remains at peace." [12] Then the angel of the Lord said, "O Lord of hosts, how long will you withhold mercy from Jerusalem and the cities of Judah, with which you have been angry these seventy years?" [13] Then the Lord replied with gracious and comforting words to the angel who talked with me. [14] So the angel who talked with me said to me, Proclaim this message: Thus says the Lord of hosts; I am very jealous for Jerusalem and for Zion. [15] And I am extremely angry with the nations that are at ease; for while I was only a little angry, they made the disaster worse. [16] Therefore, thus says the Lord, I have returned to Jerusalem with compassion; my house shall be built in it, says the Lord of hosts, and the measuring line shall be stretched out over Jerusalem. [17] Proclaim further: Thus says the Lord of hosts: My cities shall again overflow with prosperity; the Lord will again comfort Zion and again choose Jerusalem.

Second Vision: The Horns and the Smiths

18 [b] And I looked up and saw four horns. [19] I asked the angel who talked with me, "What are these?" And he answered me, "These are the horns that have scattered Judah, Israel, and Jerusalem." [20] Then the Lord showed me four blacksmiths.

a Heb *and he* b Ch 2.1 in Heb

1087

Cultural Connection

Four Winds, Four Directions

To many Native American peoples, the repeated emphasis on the number four in the visions of Zechariah could have a special meaning. In these visions are four horns representing the nations that oppressed Israel (see Zech 1:18), four blacksmiths to beat those horns down (see verse 20), and four chariots sent out to the four directions of the world (see 6:1–8).

Native Americans see the number four as special because it is repeated often in nature. There are four compass directions, four chambers of the human heart, four seasons, four phases of human life (child, youth, adult, and elder), and four basic elements (fire, water, rock, and air).

When Native Americans offer a formal prayer, they often do so facing the four directions, each with its own traditional color and emphasis:

- east (yellow), where the sun rises; the direction of light and wisdom
- south (white), where the warmth is; the direction of life
- west (black), where the sun sets; the direction of water and cleansing
- north (red), where the cold is; the direction of strength in hardship

Sometimes, two more directions are added: up, toward Father Sky (blue), and down, toward Mother Earth (green).

▶ **Zech 1:18–21**

21 And I asked, "What are they coming to do?" He answered, "These are the horns that scattered Judah, so that no head could be raised; but these have come to terrify them, to strike down the horns of the nations that lifted up their horns against the land of Judah to scatter its people."[a]

Third Vision: The Man with a Measuring Line

2[b] I looked up and saw a man with a measuring line in his hand. 2 Then I asked, "Where are you going?" He answered me, "To measure Jerusalem, to see what is its width and what is its length." 3 Then the angel who talked with me came forward, and another angel came forward to meet him, 4 and said to him, "Run, say to that young man: Jerusalem shall be inhabited like villages without walls, because of the multitude of people and animals in it. 5 For I will be a wall of fire all around it, says the LORD, and I will be the glory within it."

Interlude: An Appeal to the Exiles

6 Up, up! Flee from the land of the north, says the LORD; for I have spread you abroad like the four winds of heaven, says the LORD. 7 Up! Escape to Zion, you that live with daughter Babylon. 8 For thus said the LORD of hosts (after his glory[c] sent me) regarding the nations that plundered you: Truly, one who touches you touches the apple of my eye.[d] 9 See now, I am going to raise[e] my hand against them, and they shall become plunder for their own slaves. Then you will know that the LORD of hosts has sent me. 10 Sing and rejoice, O daughter Zion! For lo, I will come and dwell in your midst, says the LORD. 11 Many nations shall join themselves to the LORD on that day, and shall be my people; and I will dwell in your midst. And you shall know that the LORD of hosts has sent me to you. 12 The LORD will inherit Judah as his portion in the holy land, and will again choose Jerusalem.

13 Be silent, all people, before the LORD; for he has roused himself from his holy dwelling.

Fourth Vision: Joshua and Satan

3 Then he showed me the high priest Joshua standing before the angel of the LORD, and Satan[f] standing at his right hand to accuse him. 2 And the LORD said to Satan,[f] "The LORD rebuke you, O Satan![f] The LORD who has chosen Jerusalem rebuke you! Is not this man a brand plucked from the fire?" 3 Now Joshua was dressed with filthy clothes as he stood before the angel. 4 The angel said to those who were standing before him, "Take off his filthy clothes." And to him he said, "See, I have taken your guilt away from you, and I will clothe you with festal apparel."

a Heb it   b Ch 2.5 in Heb   c Cn: Heb after glory he   d Heb his eye   e Or wave   f Or the Accuser; Heb the Adversary

5And I said, "Let them put a clean turban on his head." So they put a clean turban on his head and clothed him with the apparel; and the angel of the LORD was standing by.

6 Then the angel of the LORD assured Joshua, saying 7"Thus says the LORD of hosts: If you will walk in my ways and keep my requirements, then you shall rule my house and have charge of my courts, and I will give you the right of access among those who are standing here. 8Now listen, Joshua, high priest, you and your colleagues who sit before you! For they are an omen of things to come: I am going to bring my servant the Branch. 9For on the stone that I have set before Joshua, on a single stone with seven facets, I will engrave its inscription, says the LORD of hosts, and I will remove the guilt of this land in a single day. 10On that day, says the LORD of hosts, you shall invite each other to come under your vine and fig tree."

Fifth Vision: The Lampstand and Olive Trees

4 The angel who talked with me came again, and wakened me, as one is wakened from sleep. 2He said to me, "What do you see?" And I said, "I see a lampstand all of gold, with a bowl on the top of it; there are seven lamps on it, with seven lips on each of the lamps that are on the top of it. 3And by it there are two olive trees, one on the right of the bowl and the other on its left." 4I said to the angel who talked with me, "What are these, my lord?" 5Then the angel who talked with me answered me, "Do you not know what these are?" I said, "No, my lord." 6He said to me, "This is the word of the LORD to Zerubbabel: Not by might, nor by power, but by my spirit, says the LORD of hosts. 7What are you, O great mountain? Before Zerubbabel you shall become a plain; and he shall bring out the top stone amid shouts of 'Grace, grace to it!' "

8 Moreover the word of the LORD came to me, saying, 9"The hands of Zerubbabel have laid the foundation of this house; his hands shall also complete it. Then you will know that the LORD of hosts has sent me to you. 10For whoever has despised the day of small things shall rejoice, and shall see the plummet in the hand of Zerubbabel.

"These seven are the eyes of the LORD, which range through the whole earth." 11Then I said to him, "What are these two olive trees on the right and the left of the lampstand?" 12And a second time I said to him, "What are these two branches of the olive trees, which pour out the oila through the two golden pipes?" 13He said to me, "Do you not know what these are?" I said,

"No, my lord." 14Then he said, "These are the two anointed ones who stand by the Lord of the whole earth."

Sixth Vision: The Flying Scroll

5 Again I looked up and saw a flying scroll. 2And he said to me, "What do you see?" I answered, "I see a flying scroll; its length is twenty cubits, and its width ten cubits." 3Then he said to me, "This is the curse that goes out over the face of the whole land; for everyone who steals shall be cut off according to the writing on one side, and everyone who swears falselyb shall be cut off according to the writing on the other side. 4I have sent it out, says the LORD of hosts, and it shall enter the house of the thief, and the house of anyone who swears falsely by my name; and it shall abide in that house and consume it, both timber and stones."

Seventh Vision: The Woman in a Basket

5 Then the angel who talked with me came forward and said to me, "Look up and see what this is that is coming out." 6I said, "What is it?" He said, "This is a basketc coming out." And he said, "This is their iniquityd in all the land." 7Then a leaden cover was lifted, and there was a woman sitting in the basket!c 8And he said, "This is Wickedness." So he thrust her back into the basket,c and pressed the leaden weight down on its mouth. 9Then I looked up and saw two women coming forward. The wind was in their wings; they had wings like the wings of a stork, and they lifted up the basketc between earth and sky. 10Then I said to the angel who talked with me, "Where are they taking the basket?"c 11He said to me, "To the land of Shinar, to build a house for it; and when this is prepared, they will set the basketc down there on its base."

Eighth Vision: Four Chariots

6 And again I looked up and saw four chariots coming out from between two mountains— mountains of bronze. 2The first chariot had red horses, the second chariot black horses, 3the third chariot white horses, and the fourth chariot dappled graye horses. 4Then I said to the angel who talked with me, "What are these, my lord?" 5The angel answered me, "These are the four windsf of heaven going out, after presenting themselves before the Lord of all the earth. 6The chariot with the black horses goes toward the north country,

---

a Cn: Heb gold b The word falsely added from verse 4
c Heb ephah d Gk Compare Syr: Heb their eye e Compare Gk: Meaning of Heb uncertain f Or spirits

the white ones go toward the west country,[a] and the dappled ones go toward the south country." [7]When the steeds came out, they were impatient to get off and patrol the earth. And he said, "Go, patrol the earth." So they patrolled the earth. [8]Then he cried out to me, "Lo, those who go toward the north country have set my spirit at rest in the north country."

The Coronation of the Branch

9 The word of the LORD came to me: [10]Collect silver and gold[b] from the exiles—from Heldai, Tobijah, and Jedaiah—who have arrived from Babylon; and go the same day to the house of Josiah son of Zephaniah. [11]Take the silver and gold and make a crown,[c] and set it on the head of the high priest Joshua son of Jehozadak; [12]say to him: Thus says the LORD of hosts: Here is a man whose name is Branch: for he shall branch out in his place, and he shall build the temple of the LORD. [13]It is he that shall build the temple of the LORD; he shall bear royal honor, and shall sit upon his throne and rule. There shall be a priest by his throne, with peaceful understanding between the two of them. [14]And the crown[d] shall be in the care of Heldai,[e] Tobijah, Jedaiah, and Josiah[f] son of Zephaniah, as a memorial in the temple of the LORD.

15 Those who are far off shall come and help to build the temple of the LORD; and you shall know that the LORD of hosts has sent me to you. This will happen if you diligently obey the voice of the LORD your God.

Hypocritical Fasting Condemned

7 In the fourth year of King Darius, the word of the LORD came to Zechariah on the fourth day of the ninth month, which is Chislev. [2]Now the people of Bethel had sent Sharezer and Regemmelech and their men, to entreat the favor of the

6:1

ZECH

LORD, [3]and to ask the priests of the house of the LORD of hosts and the prophets, "Should I mourn and practice abstinence in the fifth month, as I have done for so many years?" [4]Then the word of the LORD of hosts came to me: [5]Say to all the people of the land and the priests: When you fasted and lamented in the fifth month and in the seventh, for these seventy years, was it for me that you fasted? [6]And when you eat and when you drink, do you not eat and drink only for yourselves? [7]Were not these the words that the LORD proclaimed by the former prophets, when Jerusalem was inhabited and in prosperity, along with the towns around it, and when the Negeb and the Shephelah were inhabited?

Punishment for Rejecting God's Demands

8 The word of the LORD came to Zechariah, saying: [9]Thus says the LORD of hosts: Render true judgments, show kindness and mercy to one another; [10]do not oppress the widow, the orphan, the alien, or the poor; and do not devise evil in your hearts against one another. [11]But they refused to listen, and turned a stubborn shoulder, and stopped their ears in order not to hear. [12]They made their hearts adamant in order not to hear the law and the words that the LORD of hosts had sent by his spirit through the former prophets. Therefore great wrath came from the LORD of hosts. [13]Just as, when I[g] called, they would not hear, so, when they called, I would not hear, says the LORD of hosts, [14]and I scattered them with a whirlwind among all the nations that they had not known. Thus the land they left was desolate, so that no one went to and fro, and a pleasant land was made desolate.

God's Promises to Zion

8 The word of the LORD of hosts came to me, saying: [2]Thus says the LORD of hosts: I am jealous for Zion with great jealousy, and I am jealous for her with great wrath. [3]Thus says the LORD: I will return to Zion, and will dwell in the midst of Jerusalem; Jerusalem shall be called the faithful city, and the mountain of the LORD of hosts shall be called the holy mountain. [4]Thus says the LORD of hosts: Old men and old women shall again sit in the streets of Jerusalem, each with staff in hand because of their great age. [5]And the streets of the city shall be full of boys and girls playing in its streets. [6]Thus says the LORD of hosts: Even though it seems impossible

---

a Cn: Heb go after them   b Cn Compare verse 11: Heb lacks *silver and gold*   c Gk Mss Syr Tg: Heb *crowns*   d Gk Syr: Heb *crowns*   e Syr Compare verse 10: Heb *Helem*   f Syr Compare verse 10: Heb *Hen*   g Heb *he*

to the remnant of this people in these days, should it also seem impossible to me, says the LORD of hosts? [7]Thus says the LORD of hosts: I will save my people from the east country and from the west country; [8]and I will bring them to live in Jerusalem. They shall be my people and I will be their God, in faithfulness and in righteousness.

9 Thus says the LORD of hosts: Let your hands be strong—you that have recently been hearing these words from the mouths of the prophets who were present when the foundation was laid for the rebuilding of the temple, the house of the LORD of hosts. [10]For before those days there were no wages for people or for animals, nor was there any safety from the foe for those who went out or came in, and I set them all against one another. [11]But now I will not deal with the remnant of this people as in the former days, says the LORD of hosts. [12]For there shall be a sowing of peace; the vine shall yield its fruit, the ground shall give its produce, and the skies shall give their dew; and I will cause the remnant of this people to possess all these things. [13]Just as you have been a cursing among the nations, O house of Judah and house of Israel, so I will save you and you shall be a blessing. Do not be afraid, but let your hands be strong.

14 For thus says the LORD of hosts: Just as I purposed to bring disaster upon you, when your ancestors provoked me to wrath, and I did not relent, says the LORD of hosts, [15]so again I have purposed in these days to do good to Jerusalem and to the house of Judah; do not be afraid. [16]These are the things that you shall do: Speak the truth to one another, render in your gates judgments that are true and make for peace, [17]do not devise evil in your hearts against one another, and love no false oath; for all these are things that I hate, says the LORD.

Joyful Fasting

18 The word of the LORD of hosts came to me, saying: [19]Thus says the LORD of hosts: The fast of the fourth month, and the fast of the fifth, and the fast of the seventh, and the fast of the tenth, shall be seasons of joy and gladness, and cheerful festivals for the house of Judah: therefore love truth and peace.

Many Peoples Drawn to Jerusalem

20 Thus says the LORD of hosts: Peoples shall yet come, the inhabitants of many cities; [21]the inhabitants of one city shall go to another, saying, "Come, let us go to entreat the favor of the LORD, and to seek the LORD of hosts; I myself am going." [22]Many peoples and strong nations shall come to

Thumbs Up!

"I will save you and you shall be a blessing. Do not be afraid, but let your hands be strong" (Zech 8:13). These words are a promise that God will bring the people of Israel out of hard times into good times. They are also an encouragement to us.

A young woman named Ana was in a car accident in which the driver lost control and three people were killed. Ana was severely hurt and faced months of rehabilitation. Ana, who once hoped to play college softball, now needed to learn to walk and talk again.

Ana knew that for some reason, God spared her life. She knew that her rehabilitation was not going to be easy and would take hard work. She was motivated by her faith and the feeling that God was there helping her. Her attitude and ambition came out every time she was asked how she was doing. She raised her hand and lifted her thumb and said faintly, "Thumbs up."
- How would you react in a situation like this?
- How can you be more like Ana?

▶ **Zech 8:9–17**

seek the LORD of hosts in Jerusalem, and to entreat the favor of the LORD. [23]Thus says the LORD of hosts: In those days ten men from nations of every language shall take hold of a Jew, grasping his garment and saying, "Let us go with you, for we have heard that God is with you."

Judgment on Israel's Enemies

9
An Oracle.

The word of the LORD is against the land of Hadrach
  and will rest upon Damascus.
For to the LORD belongs the capital[a] of Aram,[b]
  as do all the tribes of Israel;
[2] Hamath also, which borders on it,
  Tyre and Sidon, though they are very wise.
[3] Tyre has built itself a rampart,

---

a Heb eye   *b* Cn: Heb *of Adam* (or *of humankind*)

and heaped up silver like dust,
and gold like the dirt of the streets.
⁴ But now, the Lord will strip it of its possessions
and hurl its wealth into the sea,
and it shall be devoured by fire.

⁵ Ashkelon shall see it and be afraid;
Gaza too, and shall writhe in anguish;
Ekron also, because its hopes are withered.
The king shall perish from Gaza;
Ashkelon shall be uninhabited;
⁶ a mongrel people shall settle in Ashdod,
and I will make an end of the pride of
Philistia.
⁷ I will take away its blood from its mouth,
and its abominations from between its teeth;
it too shall be a remnant for our God;
it shall be like a clan in Judah,
and Ekron shall be like the Jebusites.
⁸ Then I will encamp at my house as a guard,
so that no one shall march to and fro;
no oppressor shall again overrun them,
for now I have seen with my own eyes.

The Coming Ruler of God's People

⁹ Rejoice greatly, O daughter Zion!
Shout aloud, O daughter Jerusalem!
Lo, your king comes to you;
triumphant and victorious is he,
humble and riding on a donkey,
on a colt, the foal of a donkey.
¹⁰ He[a] will cut off the chariot from Ephraim
and the war-horse from Jerusalem;
and the battle bow shall be cut off,
and he shall command peace to the nations;
his dominion shall be from sea to sea,
and from the River to the ends of the earth.

¹¹ As for you also, because of the blood of my
covenant with you,
I will set your prisoners free from the
waterless pit.
¹² Return to your stronghold, O prisoners of hope;
today I declare that I will restore to you
double.
¹³ For I have bent Judah as my bow;
I have made Ephraim its arrow.
I will arouse your sons, O Zion,
against your sons, O Greece,
and wield you like a warrior's sword.

¹⁴ Then the Lord will appear over them,
and his arrow go forth like lightning;
the Lord God will sound the trumpet
and march forth in the whirlwinds of the
south.

¹⁵ The Lord of hosts will protect them,
and they shall devour and tread down the
slingers;[b]
they shall drink their blood[c] like wine,
and be full like a bowl,
drenched like the corners of the altar.
¹⁶ On that day the Lord their God will save them
for they are the flock of his people;
for like the jewels of a crown
they shall shine on his land.
¹⁷ For what goodness and beauty are his!
Grain shall make the young men flourish,
and new wine the young women.

Restoration of Judah and Israel

10 Ask rain from the Lord
in the season of the spring rain,
from the Lord who makes the storm clouds,
who gives showers of rain to you,[d]
the vegetation in the field to everyone.
² For the teraphim[e] utter nonsense,
and the diviners see lies;
the dreamers tell false dreams,
and give empty consolation.
Therefore the people wander like sheep;
they suffer for lack of a shepherd.

³ My anger is hot against the shepherds,
and I will punish the leaders;[f]
for the Lord of hosts cares for his flock, the
house of Judah,
and will make them like his proud war-horse.
⁴ Out of them shall come the cornerstone,
out of them the tent peg,
out of them the battle bow,
out of them every commander.
⁵ Together they shall be like warriors in battle,
trampling the foe in the mud of the streets;
they shall fight, for the Lord is with them,
and they shall put to shame the riders on
horses.

⁶ I will strengthen the house of Judah,
and I will save the house of Joseph.
I will bring them back because I have
compassion on them,
and they shall be as though I had not rejected
them;
for I am the Lord their God and I will answer
them.
⁷ Then the people of Ephraim shall become like
warriors,

---

a Gk: Heb I b Cn: Heb *the slingstones* c Gk: Heb *shall drink*
d Heb *them* e Or *household gods* f Or *male goats*

Cultural Connection

The Principle of *Umoja*

Chapter 11 of Zechariah contains several allegorical images that represent the breakdown of the Israelite nation. In one, a shepherd's staff named Unity (see verse 7) is broken—symbolizing that the people have lost the unity that bound them together.

Unity is vital to the success of any people. For example, African Americans rely on the Kwanzaa principle of unity, called *umoja* (see "Kwanzaa as a Way of Life," near Deut 10:12–22). *Umoja* signifies unity in the family, community, nation, and race. This unity keeps brothers from killing brothers and

sisters from killing sisters. This unity keeps families together even when the going gets tough.

Any race or culture can and often does experience difficulty maintaining and promoting *umoja*, especially a race or culture facing injustice, racism, or prejudice. With these elements present, a race or culture can be negatively affected as individuals, young and old, are tempted to come together in attitudes and behaviors that are selfish and destructive.

All of us are called to live in unity. All of us are called to foster unity and to direct our efforts

toward bringing our families, communities, races, and nations together.

Keep the Kwanzaa principle of *umoja* alive! Be united in making the honor roll. Be united in respecting and protecting one another. Be united in putting an end to the problems that plague our cities and nation. Be united in being the best you can be!

▶ **Zech 11:4–17**

and their hearts shall be glad as with wine.
Their children shall see it and rejoice,
their hearts shall exult in the LORD.

8 I will signal for them and gather them in,
for I have redeemed them,
and they shall be as numerous as they were before.
9 Though I scattered them among the nations,
yet in far countries they shall remember me,
and they shall rear their children and return.
10 I will bring them home from the land of Egypt,
and gather them from Assyria;
I will bring them to the land of Gilead and to Lebanon,
until there is no room for them.
11 They[a] shall pass through the sea of distress,
and the waves of the sea shall be struck down,
and all the depths of the Nile dried up.
The pride of Assyria shall be laid low,
and the scepter of Egypt shall depart.
12 I will **make them strong in the LORD**,
and they shall walk in his name,
says the LORD.

11 Open your doors, O Lebanon,
so that fire may devour your cedars!
2 Wail, O cypress, for the cedar has fallen,
for the glorious trees are ruined!

Wail, oaks of Bashan,
for the thick forest has been felled!
3 Listen, the wail of the shepherds,
for their glory is despoiled!
Listen, the roar of the lions,
for the thickets of the Jordan are destroyed!

Two Kinds of Shepherds

4 Thus said the LORD my God: Be a shepherd of the flock doomed to slaughter. 5 Those who buy them kill them and go unpunished; and those who sell them say, "Blessed be the LORD, for I have become rich"; and their own shepherds have no pity on them. 6 For I will no longer have pity on the inhabitants of the earth, says the LORD. I will cause them, every one, to fall each into the hand of a neighbor, and each into the hand of the king; and they shall devastate the earth, and I will deliver no one from their hand.

7 So, on behalf of the sheep merchants, I became the shepherd of the flock doomed to slaughter. I took two staffs; one I named Favor, the other I named Unity, and I tended the sheep. 8 In one month I disposed of the three shepherds, for I had become impatient with them, and they also detested me. 9 So I said, "I will not be your shepherd. What is to die, let it die; what is to be

a Gk: Heb He

ZECH

destroyed, let it be destroyed; and let those that are left devour the flesh of one another!" [10]I took my staff Favor and broke it, annulling the covenant that I had made with all the peoples. [11]So it was annulled on that day, and the sheep merchants, who were watching me, knew that it was the word of the LORD. [12]I then said to them, "If it seems right to you, give me my wages; but if not, keep them." So they weighed out as my wages thirty shekels of silver. [13]Then the LORD said to me, "Throw it into the treasury"[a]—this lordly price at which I was valued by them. So I took the thirty shekels of silver and threw them into the treasury[a] in the house of the LORD. [14]Then I broke my second staff Unity, annulling the family ties between Judah and Israel.

15 Then the LORD said to me: Take once more the implements of a worthless shepherd. [16]For I am now raising up in the land a shepherd who does not care for the perishing, or seek the wandering,[b] or heal the maimed, or nourish the healthy,[c] but devours the flesh of the fat ones, tearing off even their hoofs.

[17] Oh, my worthless shepherd,
    who deserts the flock!
May the sword strike his arm
    and his right eye!
Let his arm be completely withered,
    his right eye utterly blinded!

Jerusalem's Victory

12

        An Oracle.

The word of the LORD concerning Israel: Thus says the LORD, who stretched out the heavens and founded the earth and formed the human spirit within: [2]See, I am about to make Jerusalem a cup of reeling for all the surrounding peoples; it will be against Judah also in the siege against Jerusalem. [3]On that day I will make Jerusalem a heavy stone for all the peoples; all who lift it shall grievously hurt themselves. And all the nations of the earth shall come together against it. [4]On that day, says the LORD, I will strike every horse with panic, and its rider with madness. But on the house of Judah I will keep a watchful eye, when I strike every horse of the peoples with blindness. [5]Then the clans of Judah shall say to themselves, "The inhabitants of Jerusalem have strength through the LORD of hosts, their God."

6 On that day I will make the clans of Judah like a blazing pot on a pile of wood, like a flaming torch among sheaves; and they shall devour to the right and to the left all the surrounding peoples, while Jerusalem shall again be inhabited in its place, in Jerusalem.

7 And the LORD will give victory to the tents of Judah first, that the glory of the house of David and the glory of the inhabitants of Jerusalem may not be exalted over that of Judah. [8]On that day the LORD will shield the inhabitants of Jerusalem so that the feeblest among them on that day shall be like David, and the house of David shall be like God, like the angel of the LORD, at their head. [9]And on that day I will seek to destroy all the nations that come against Jerusalem.

Mourning for the Pierced One

10 And I will pour out a spirit of compassion and supplication on the house of David and the inhabitants of Jerusalem, so that, when they look on the one[d] whom they have pierced, they shall

Did You Know?

Prophecies of God's Victory

Zechariah, chapters 12–14, has several of Second Zechariah's prophecies on the final judgment, the restoration of Israel, and the Reign of God. Many of these prophecies were applied to Jesus by the first Christians.

For example, Zechariah foretells a time of mourning for "one whom they have pierced" (Zech 12:10); the Gospel of John applies this verse to Jesus' death on the cross (see Jn 19:37). Zechariah says the sheep will be dispersed when the shepherd is struck (see Zech 13:7); the Gospel of Matthew uses this verse to describe the disciples' deserting Jesus (see Mt 26:31). And passages from Zechariah's description of the day of the Lord (see Zech 14:6–9) show up in the Book of Revelation's description of the new Jerusalem (see Rev 11:15, 21:23).

These beautiful prophecies assured Israel's people of God's love and mercy. For Christians, they have additional meaning. They also describe Jesus Christ, whose death is our salvation and whose Resurrection is the promise of the fullness of God's Reign!

▶ **Zechariah, chapters 12–14**

Z E C H

---

a Syr: Heb *it to the potter*   b Syr Compare Gk Vg: Heb *the youth*
c Meaning of Heb uncertain   d Heb *on me*

mourn for him, as one mourns for an only child, and weep bitterly over him, as one weeps over a firstborn. ¹¹On that day the mourning in Jerusalem will be as great as the mourning for Hadad-rimmon in the plain of Megiddo. ¹²The land shall mourn, each family by itself; the family of the house of David by itself, and their wives by themselves; the family of the house of Nathan by itself, and their wives by themselves; ¹³the family of the house of Levi by itself, and their wives by themselves; the family of the Shimeites by itself, and their wives by themselves; ¹⁴and all the families that are left, each by itself, and their wives by themselves.

13 On that day a fountain shall be opened for the house of David and the inhabitants of Jerusalem, to cleanse them from sin and impurity.

Idolatry Cut Off

2 On that day, says the LORD of hosts, I will cut off the names of the idols from the land, so that they shall be remembered no more; and also I will remove from the land the prophets and the unclean spirit. ³And if any prophets appear again, their fathers and mothers who bore them will say to them, "You shall not live, for you speak lies in the name of the LORD"; and their fathers and their mothers who bore them shall pierce them through when they prophesy. ⁴On that day the prophets will be ashamed, every one, of their visions when they prophesy; they will not put on a hairy mantle in order to deceive, ⁵but each of them will say, "I am no prophet, I am a tiller of the soil; for the land has been my possession*ᵃ* since my youth." ⁶And if anyone asks them, "What are these wounds on your chest?"*ᵇ* the answer will be "The wounds I received in the house of my friends."

The Shepherd Struck, the Flock Scattered

7 "Awake, O sword, against my shepherd,
   against the man who is my associate,"
                    says the LORD of hosts.
Strike the shepherd, that the sheep may be
      scattered;
   I will turn my hand against the little ones.
8 In the whole land, says the LORD,
   two-thirds shall be cut off and perish,
   and one-third shall be left alive.
9 And I will put this third into the fire,
   refine them as one refines silver,
   and test them as gold is tested.
They will call on my name,
   and I will answer them.
I will say, "They are my people";
   and they shall say, "The LORD is our God."

Future Warfare and Final Victory

14 See, a day is coming for the LORD, when the plunder taken from you will be divided in your midst. ²For I will gather all the nations against Jerusalem to battle, and the city shall be taken and the houses looted and the women raped; half the city shall go into exile, but the rest of the people shall not be cut off from the city. ³Then the LORD will go forth and fight against those nations as when he fights on a day of battle. ⁴On that day his feet shall stand on the Mount of Olives, which lies before Jerusalem on the east; and the Mount of Olives shall be split in two from east to west by a very wide valley; so that one half of the Mount shall withdraw northward, and the other half southward. ⁵And you shall flee by the valley of the LORD's mountain,*ᶜ* for the valley between the mountains shall reach to Azal;*ᵈ* and you shall flee as you fled from the earthquake in the days of King Uzziah of Judah. Then the LORD my God will come, and all the holy ones with him.

6 On that day there shall not be*ᵉ* either cold or frost.*ᶠ* ⁷And there shall be continuous day (it is known to the LORD), not day and not night, for at evening time there shall be light.

8 On that day living waters shall flow out from Jerusalem, half of them to the eastern sea and half of them to the western sea; it shall continue in summer as in winter.

9 And the LORD will become king over all the earth; on that day the LORD will be one and his name one.

10 The whole land shall be turned into a plain from Geba to Rimmon south of Jerusalem. But Jerusalem shall remain aloft on its site from the Gate of Benjamin to the place of the former gate, to the Corner Gate, and from the Tower of Hananel to the king's wine presses. ¹¹And it shall be inhabited, for never again shall it be doomed to destruction; Jerusalem shall abide in security.

12 This shall be the plague with which the LORD will strike all the peoples that wage war against Jerusalem: their flesh shall rot while they are still on their feet; their eyes shall rot in their sockets, and their tongues shall rot in their mouths. ¹³On that day a great panic from the LORD shall fall on them, so that each will seize the hand of a neighbor, and the hand of the one will be raised against the hand of the other; ¹⁴even Judah will fight at Jerusalem. And the wealth of

---

a Cn: Heb *for humankind has caused me to possess*
b Heb *wounds between your hands* *c* Heb *my mountains*
d Meaning of Heb uncertain *e* Cn: Heb *there shall not be light*
f Compare Gk Syr Vg Tg: Meaning of Heb uncertain

all the surrounding nations shall be collected—gold, silver, and garments in great abundance. [15]And a plague like this plague shall fall on the horses, the mules, the camels, the donkeys, and whatever animals may be in those camps.

16 Then all who survive of the nations that have come against Jerusalem shall go up year after year to worship the King, the LORD of hosts, and to keep the festival of booths.[a] [17]If any of the families of the earth do not go up to Jerusalem to worship the King, the LORD of hosts, there will be no rain upon them. [18]And if the family of Egypt do not go up and present themselves, then on them shall[b] come the plague that the LORD inflicts on the nations that do not go up to keep the festival of booths.[a] [19]Such shall be the

punishment of Egypt and the punishment of all the nations that do not go up to keep the festival of booths.[a]

20 On that day there shall be inscribed on the bells of the horses, "Holy to the LORD." And the cooking pots in the house of the LORD shall be as holy as[c] the bowls in front of the altar; [21]and every cooking pot in Jerusalem and Judah shall be sacred to the LORD of hosts, so that all who sacrifice may come and use them to boil the flesh of the sacrifice. And there shall no longer be traders[d] in the house of the LORD of hosts on that day.

a Or tabernacles; Heb succoth b Gk Syr: Heb shall not
c Heb shall be like d Or Canaanites

"You promised me!" These three words speak volumes when they're used against us. A promise is a sacred thing, and breaking promises hurts and destroys relationships. The last book of the Old Testament, Malachi, focuses on promises with God that have been broken. At the time of its writing, priests had broken the covenant by offering inferior sacrifices, and men had broken the covenant by marrying foreign women and divorcing their Jewish wives. The prophet Malachi predicts that someone is coming who will purify the people, punishing the wicked and rewarding the righteous.

In Depth

The author of the Book of Malachi wrote just before the reforms of Ezra and Nehemiah, starting around 458 BC (see the timeline at the back of this Bible). The Temple had been rebuilt (see the Books of Haggai and Zechariah), and Temple worship had been restored, but serious violations of the covenantal law existed.

The Book of Malachi addresses two main problems. The first is the failure of Israel's priests to provide good leadership. Through a series of questions and answers, the prophet Malachi speaks harsh words against the priests of the Temple for failing to live up to their calling to honor God. They offer inferior sacrifices on the altar of the Temple, thinking that God won't notice. The prophet compares these priests with their ancestor Levi, who offered only the finest gifts to God. Levi was a good and honest man who kept God's Covenant; these priests are not.

The second problem has to do with marriage and divorce. Evidently, many men are marrying non-Jewish women and divorcing their Jewish wives. It's not clear why they are doing this, but maybe they are trying to climb the social ladder. The prophet challenges the people to be faithful to one another because their marriages are a reminder of God's Covenant with the people of Judah.

The book ends with a prophecy that forms a bridge to the New Testament and the coming of Jesus. It says that God will send a messenger, the prophet Elijah, before the day of judgment. His job will be to prepare the way for God. Those who repent will enjoy God's blessings; those who do not will be punished by God. New Testament writers saw this prophecy fulfilled by John the Baptist, who prepared the way for the coming of the Messiah, Jesus of Nazareth.

At a Glance

- **1:1—2:9.** a message of God's love for Israel and of the sins of the priests
- **2:10—16.** call for faithfulness in marriage
- **2:17—4:3.** prophecies about God's messenger and God's judgment
- **4:4—6.** God's promise to send the prophet Elijah

Quick Facts

Period Covered: around 455 BC
Inspired Author: unknown
Theme: calls for priestly reform and faithfulness in marriage; God sends his messenger to prepare the way for the Savior

The Book of Malachi

Malachi

1 An oracle. The word of the LORD to Israel by Malachi.[a]

Israel Preferred to Edom

2 I have loved you, says the LORD. But you say, "How have you loved us?" Is not Esau Jacob's brother? says the LORD. Yet I have loved Jacob ³but I have hated Esau; I have made his hill country a desolation and his heritage a desert for jackals. ⁴If Edom says, "We are shattered but we will rebuild the ruins," the LORD of hosts says: They may build, but I will tear down, until they are called the wicked country, the people with whom the LORD is angry forever. ⁵Your own eyes shall see this, and you shall say, "Great is the LORD beyond the borders of Israel!"

Corruption of the Priesthood

6 A son honors his father, and servants their master. If then I am a father, where is the honor due me? And if I am a master, where is the respect due me? says the LORD of hosts to you, O priests, who despise my name. You say, "How have we despised your name?" ⁷By offering polluted food on my altar. And you say, "How have we polluted it?"[b] By thinking that the LORD's table may be despised. ⁸When you offer blind animals in sacrifice, is that not wrong? And when you offer those that are lame or sick, is that not wrong? Try presenting that to your governor; will he be pleased with you or show you favor? says the LORD of hosts. ⁹And now implore the favor of God, that he may be gracious to us. The fault is yours. Will he show favor to any of you? says the LORD of hosts. ¹⁰Oh, that someone among you would shut the temple[c] doors, so that you would not kindle fire on my altar in vain! I have no pleasure in you, says the LORD of hosts, and I will not accept an offering from your hands. ¹¹For from the rising of the sun to its setting my name is great among the nations, and in every place incense is offered to my name, and a pure offering; for my name is great among the nations, says the LORD of hosts. ¹²But you profane it when you say that the Lord's table is polluted, and the food for it[d] may be despised. ¹³"What a weariness this is," you say, and you sniff at me,[e] says the LORD of hosts. You bring what has been taken by violence or is lame or sick, and this you bring as your offering! Shall I accept that from your hand? says the LORD. ¹⁴Cursed be the cheat who has a male in the flock and vows to give it, and yet sacrifices to the Lord what is blemished; for I am a great King, says the LORD of hosts, and my name is reverenced among the nations.

2 And now, O priests, this command is for you. ²If you will not listen, if you will not lay it to heart to give glory to my name, says the LORD of hosts, then I will send the curse on you and I will curse your blessings; indeed I have already cursed them,[f] because you do not lay it to heart. ³I will

---

a Or *by my messenger*   b Gk: Heb *you*   c Heb lacks *temple*
d Compare Syr Tg: Heb *its fruit, its food*   e Another reading is *at it*   f Heb *it*

rebuke your offspring, and spread dung on your faces, the dung of your offerings, and I will put you out of my presence.[a]

4 Know, then, that I have sent this command to you, that my covenant with Levi may hold, says the LORD of hosts. [5]My covenant with him was a covenant of life and well-being, which I gave him; this called for reverence, and he revered me and stood in awe of my name. [6]True instruction was in his mouth, and no wrong was found on his lips. He walked with me in integrity and uprightness, and he turned many from iniquity. [7]For the lips of a priest should guard knowledge, and people should seek instruction from his mouth, for he is the messenger of the LORD of hosts. [8]But you have turned aside from the way; you have caused many to stumble by your instruction; you have corrupted the covenant of Levi, says the LORD of hosts, [9]and so I make you despised and abased before all the people, inasmuch as you have not kept my ways but have shown partiality in your instruction.

The Covenant Profaned by Judah

10 Have we not all one father? Has not one God created us? Why then are we faithless to one another, profaning the covenant of our ancestors? [11]Judah has been faithless, and abomination has been committed in Israel and in Jerusalem; for Judah has profaned the sanctuary of the LORD, which he loves, and has married the daughter of a foreign god. [12]May the LORD cut off from the tents of Jacob anyone who does this— any to witness[b] or answer, or to bring an offering to the LORD of hosts.

13 And this you do as well: You cover the LORD's altar with tears, with weeping and groaning because he no longer regards the offering or accepts it with favor at your hand. [14]You ask, "Why does he not?" Because the LORD was a witness between you and the wife of your youth, to whom you have been faithless, though she is your companion and your wife by covenant. [15]Did not one God make her?[c] Both flesh and spirit are his.[d] And what does the one God[e] desire? Godly offspring. So look to yourselves, and do not let anyone be faithless to the wife of his youth. [16]For I hate[f] divorce, says the LORD, the God of Israel, and covering one's garment with violence, says the LORD of hosts. So take heed to yourselves and do not be faithless.

17 You have wearied the LORD with your words. Yet you say, "How have we wearied him?" By saying, "All who do evil are good in the sight of the LORD, and he delights in them." Or by asking, "Where is the God of justice?"

The Coming Messenger

3 See, I am sending my messenger to prepare the way before me, and the Lord whom you seek will suddenly come to his temple. The messenger of the covenant in whom you delight— indeed, he is coming, says the LORD of hosts. [2]But who can endure the day of his coming, and who can stand when he appears?

For he is like a refiner's fire and like fullers' soap; [3]he will sit as a refiner and purifier of silver, and he will purify the descendants of Levi and refine them like gold and silver, until they present offerings to the LORD in righteousness.[g] [4]Then the offering of Judah and Jerusalem will be pleasing to the LORD as in the days of old and as in former years.

5 Then I will draw near to you for judgment; I will be swift to bear witness against the sorcerers, against the adulterers, against those who swear falsely, against those who oppress the hired workers in their wages, the widow and the orphan, against those who thrust aside the alien, and do not fear me, says the LORD of hosts.

6 For I the LORD do not change; therefore you, O children of Jacob, have not perished. [7]Ever since the days of your ancestors you have turned aside from my statutes and have not kept them. Return to me, and I will return to you, says the LORD of hosts. But you say, "How shall we return?"

Do Not Rob God

8 Will anyone rob God? Yet you are robbing me! But you say, "How are we robbing you?" In your tithes and offerings! [9]You are cursed with a curse, for you are robbing me—the whole nation of you! [10]Bring the full tithe into the storehouse, so that there may be food in my house, and thus put me to the test, says the LORD of hosts; see if I will not open the windows of heaven for you and pour down for you an overflowing blessing. [11]I will rebuke the locust[h] for you, so that it will not destroy the produce of your soil; and your

> "See, I am sending my messenger. . . . Who can endure the day of his coming?"
>
> (Mal 3:1–2)

---

a Cn Compare Gk Syr: Heb *and he shall bear you to it*
b Cn Compare Gk: Heb *arouse*   c Or *Has he not made one?*
d Cn: Heb *and a remnant of spirit was his*   e Heb *he*   f Cn: Heb
he hates   g Or *right offerings to the LORD*   h Heb *devourer*

Prepare the Way

Malachi 3:1–2 talks about the sending of a messenger to prepare for God's coming. That arrival will mark a day of purification, when anything that isn't of value will be burnt away. In Matthew's Gospel, Jesus states that it is John the Baptist who fulfills this prophecy (see Mt 11:10–14). What does that have to do with you? Well, John the Baptist wasn't the only one entrusted with the task of preparing for the Lord's coming. As followers of Christ, we all continue to share in that role today.

So how do we do this? Where do we start? We start by listening to Jesus and nurturing our relationship with God through prayer and the sacraments. We must also share what we believe with others so that they too can find their way. By growing in faith and helping others to do the same, we will be a light for the world, preparing the way for Christ's return.

▶ **Mal 3:1–7**

vine in the field shall not be barren, says the Lord of hosts. 12Then all nations will count you happy, for you will be a land of delight, says the Lord of hosts.

13 You have spoken harsh words against me, says the Lord. Yet you say, "How have we spoken against you?" 14You have said, "It is vain to serve God. What do we profit by keeping his command or by going about as mourners before the Lord of hosts? 15Now we count the arrogant happy; evildoers not only prosper, but when they put God to the test they escape."

The Reward of the Faithful

16 Then those who revered the Lord spoke with one another. The Lord took note and listened, and a book of remembrance was written before him of those who revered the Lord and thought on his name. 17They shall be mine, says the Lord of hosts, my special possession on the day when I act, and I will spare them as parents spare their children who serve them. 18Then once more you shall see the difference between the righteous and the wicked, between one who serves God and one who does not serve him.

The Great Day of the Lord

4 *a* See, the day is coming, burning like an oven, when all the arrogant and all evildoers will be stubble; the day that comes shall burn them up, says the Lord of hosts, so that it will leave them neither root nor branch. 2But for you who revere my name the sun of righteousness shall rise, with healing in its wings. You shall go out leaping like calves from the stall. 3And you shall tread down the wicked, for they will be ashes under the soles of your feet, on the day when I act, says the Lord of hosts.

4 Remember the teaching of my servant Moses, the statutes and ordinances that I commanded him at Horeb for all Israel.

5 Lo, I will send you the prophet Elijah before the great and terrible day of the Lord comes. 6He will turn the hearts of parents to their children and the hearts of children to their parents, so that I will not come and strike the land with a curse.*b*

---

a Ch 4.1-6 are Ch 3.19-24 in Heb   *b* Or a ban of utter destruction

The
New Testament

Introduction to the
Gospels and the
Acts of the Apostles

If you have ever written a research paper for a class project, you know how important it is to have good sources. You want sources that have the most insight into your chosen topic, sources that provide inspiration. The books of the New Testament are those sources for the Christian faith. The Gospels of Matthew, Mark, Luke, and John lay the foundation for understanding the message and the mission of Jesus, the center of the Christian faith. The Acts of the Apostles continues with an inspiring account of how the earliest Christians continued Jesus' mission despite conflicts and persecution. The Good News in these books invites a response from us: to accept Jesus as the promised Messiah, the Son of God, the Savior of the world.

In Depth

The books of the New Testament continue the Old Testament's revelation of God's saving work in the world. Their focus is on Jesus Christ—the hoped-for Messiah, the Savior. Jesus Christ is revealed as God's Son, being both fully human and fully divine. In Jesus, God's promises to Abraham, Moses, and David were fulfilled. In Jesus, God's covenant is expanded beyond Judaism to include all peoples. In Jesus lie the forgiveness of sins and a new life of love and freedom for anyone who believes.

The New Testament tells of this Good News through four different types of books: (1) four similar but unique views of Jesus' life and teaching in books called Gospels, (2) stories on how the Apostles spread the Good News of Jesus in the Acts of the Apostles, (3) letters from early Christian leaders to the first Christians and Christian communities, and (4) apocalyptic writings in the Book of Revelation. This introduction covers the four Gospels and the Acts of the Apostles; another introduction will give further background on the letters and Revelation.

The Gospels of Matthew, Mark, Luke, and John tell the story of Jesus from four different perspectives. They are not historical biographies or documentaries like you might read today. They grew out of the teaching and preaching about Jesus in different early Christian communities. They reflect these early Christian communities' beliefs about Jesus, but they do not tell us exactly what Jesus said and did in his life on earth. Inspired by God, the authors of the Gospels arranged the stories to bring out a particular understanding of Jesus that had great importance in their Christian communities. Because of God's inspiration, the Gospels are without error in teaching us the truth about Christ's message, mission, and identity.

The Gospels of Matthew, Mark, and Luke are similar in their style and share much of the same content. They are called synoptic (from a Greek word that means "seeing the whole together") Gospels. It is likely that Mark was written first and the authors of Matthew and Luke used Mark as a source in creating their own Gospels (Lk 1:1

mentions other accounts of Jesus). The Gospel of John is quite different from the synoptic Gospels. It was written later and is more symbolic in its expression of who Jesus is.

The Acts of the Apostles is a continuation of Luke's Gospel (Acts 1:1). However, it is not itself a Gospel. It picks up where the Gospel of Luke ends, telling the story of the origins of Christianity after the death and Resurrection of Jesus, covering the period from about AD 30 to 64. Although Acts gives us a good deal of information about early Church leaders like Peter and Paul, its purpose is not to tell us their biographies. Rather, it gives us an interpretation of the events of the beginnings of Christianity that emphasizes God's saving purpose. The Book of Acts explains how Christianity, which began as an offshoot of the Jewish faith, gradually spread beyond Judaism into the Gentile, or non-Jewish, world.

The original Greek word for *gospel* is *euangelion,* which means "big or important news" (sometimes translated as "good news"). The authors of the Gospels wanted to share with others the important news of Jesus Christ. When you read these powerful stories of faith, let God use them to inspire and strengthen your faith in Jesus.

Other Background

▶ The Gospel of Matthew emphasizes Jesus as the promised Messiah of the Jewish people. Jesus is portrayed as the greatest prophet, teaching the New Law and calling people to be faithful to God.

▶ The Gospel of Mark was probably the first of the four Gospels to be written. It portrays Jesus as an active healer and miracle worker who accepts loneliness and suffering as the cost of obedience to God's will.

▶ The Gospel of Luke is a clear, orderly presentation of Jesus' mission to all people, Jews and Gentiles. This Gospel emphasizes Jesus' mercy, compassion, and concern for poor people.

▶ The Gospel of John was the last Gospel written and seeks to show Jesus as the unique Son of God. This Gospel portrays Jesus as noble and powerful, fully in control of his own destiny.

▶ The Acts of the Apostles was written by the author of the Gospel of Luke. It shows God at work in the growth of the early Christian communities, particularly through the efforts of Peter and Paul.

Does your family have a traditional way of celebrating a holiday? Family traditions are usually handed down from one generation to the next. They give meaning to our special celebrations and help us know where we came from. The Gospel of Matthew presents Jesus as the promised Messiah and highlights Jesus' Jewish origins. The author wanted Jewish-Christian readers to know that believing in Jesus as the Son of God was not a break with their tradition but the fulfillment of it.

In Depth

The author of Matthew was probably a Jewish Christian writing for a community of Jewish Christians. This community's main mission was to bring the gospel message to its Jewish brothers and sisters (see 10:6) but there are also indications that this mission was beginning to be spread to the Gentile world (see 4:12–25). In defense of the community's belief in Jesus, the Gospel of Matthew links Jesus to important Jewish traditions and gives them new meanings. The Gospel begins with a list of Jesus' Jewish ancestors, connecting Jesus to Abraham, the father of Judaism, and David, Israel's greatest king. Then it makes frequent references to Old Testament laws, prophecies, and events that Jesus fulfills or completes.

The author of Matthew also wanted to show how Jesus broke with certain Jewish beliefs—no doubt to help explain why his community of Jewish Christians was protesting against the Jewish religious establishment that it considered corrupt and wayward. So in the Sermon on the Mount (see 5:1–7:29), the Gospel has Jesus giving a deeper interpretation to Jewish laws. And Jesus is frequently in conflict with the scribes and Pharisees over things like healing on the Sabbath (see 12:9–14). Such incidents probably reflect the experience of the author's community with Jewish leaders as much as Jesus' own conflicts.

Gradually, the Gospel of Matthew paints a picture of Jesus as the promised Son of David who would reign as king forever and a prophet / teacher like Moses, the true law giver. He is the Messiah, the fulfillment of all that the Jewish people have been waiting for, the one who will bring their liberation and salvation. This Good News should be proclaimed to Jews and non-Jews alike. And so the Gospel ends with the risen Jesus telling his disciples, "Go therefore and make disciples of all nations" (28:19).

◉ At a Glance

- **1:1—4:17.** the birth of Jesus and the beginning of Jesus' ministry
- **4:18—9:38.** the Sermon on the Mount and miracles in Galilee
- **10:1—12:50.** teaching on mission and rejection
- **13:1—18:35.** Jesus, the Kingdom, and the Church
- **19:1—25:46.** Jesus' ministry in Judea and Jerusalem
- **26:1—28:20.** Jesus' death and Resurrection

✪ Quick Facts

Inspired Author: unknown; traditionally associated with the Apostle Matthew
Date Written: approximately AD 85
Audience: Christian Jews
Image of Jesus: the greatest prophet, who brings the New Law

Matthew

The Genealogy of Jesus the Messiah

1 An account of the genealogy[a] of Jesus the Messiah,[b] the son of David, the son of Abraham.

2 Abraham was the father of Isaac, and Isaac the father of Jacob, and Jacob the father of Judah and his brothers, ³and Judah the father of Perez and Zerah by Tamar, and Perez the father of Hezron, and Hezron the father of Aram, ⁴and Aram the father of Aminadab, and Aminadab the father of Nahshon, and Nahshon the father of Salmon, ⁵and Salmon the father of Boaz by Rahab, and Boaz the father of Obed by Ruth, and Obed the father of Jesse, ⁶and Jesse the father of King David.

And David was the father of Solomon by the wife of Uriah, ⁷and Solomon the father of Rehoboam, and Rehoboam the father of Abijah, and Abijah the father of Asaph,[c] ⁸and Asaph[c] the father of Jehoshaphat, and Jehoshaphat the father of Joram, and Joram the father of Uzziah, ⁹and Uzziah the father of Jotham, and Jotham the father of Ahaz, and Ahaz the father of Hezekiah, ¹⁰and Hezekiah the father of Manasseh, and Manasseh the father of Amos,[d] and Amos[d] the father of Josiah, ¹¹and Josiah the father of Jechoniah and his brothers, at the time of the deportation to Babylon.

12 And after the deportation to Babylon: Jechoniah was the father of Salathiel, and Salathiel the father of Zerubbabel, ¹³and Zerubbabel the father of Abiud, and Abiud the father of Eliakim, and Eliakim the father of Azor, ¹⁴and Azor the father of Zadok, and Zadok the father of Achim, and Achim the father of Eliud, ¹⁵and Eliud the father of Eleazar, and Eleazar the father of Matthan, and Matthan the father of Jacob, ¹⁶and Jacob the father of Joseph the husband of Mary, of whom Jesus was born, who is called the Messiah.[e]

17 So all the generations from Abraham to David are fourteen generations; and from David to the deportation to Babylon, fourteen generations; and from the deportation to Babylon to the Messiah,[e] fourteen generations.

The Birth of Jesus the Messiah

18 Now the birth of Jesus the Messiah[b] took place in this way. When his mother Mary had been engaged to Joseph, but before they lived together, she was found to be with child from the Holy Spirit. ¹⁹Her husband Joseph, being a righteous man and unwilling to expose her to public disgrace, planned to dismiss her quietly. ²⁰But just when he had resolved to do this, an angel of the Lord appeared to him in a dream and said, "Joseph, son of David, do not be afraid to take Mary as your wife, for the child conceived in her is from the Holy Spirit. ²¹She will bear a son, and you are to name him Jesus, for he will save his people from their sins." ²²All this took place to fulfill what had been spoken by the Lord through the prophet:

---

a Or birth   b Or Jesus Christ   c Other ancient authorities read Asa   d Other ancient authorities read Amon   e Or the Christ
f Or Jesus Christ

23 "Look, the virgin shall conceive and bear a son,
  and they shall name him Emmanuel,"
which means, "God is with us." 24When Joseph
awoke from sleep, he did as the angel of the Lord
commanded him; he took her as his wife, 25but
had no marital relations with her until she had
borne a son;*a* and he named him Jesus.

The Visit of the Wise Men

2 In the time of King Herod, after Jesus was
born in Bethlehem of Judea, wise men*b* from
the East came to Jerusalem, 2asking, "Where is
the child who has been born king of the Jews?
For we observed his star at its rising,*c* and have
come to pay him homage." 3When King Herod
heard this, he was frightened, and all Jerusalem
with him; 4and calling together all the chief
priests and scribes of the people, he inquired of
them where the Messiah*d* was to be born. 5They
told him, "In Bethlehem of Judea; for so it has
been written by the prophet:

6 'And you, Bethlehem, in the land of Judah,
  are by no means least among the rulers of
    Judah;
for from you shall come a ruler
  who is to shepherd*e* my people Israel.' "

7 Then Herod secretly called for the wise
men*b* and learned from them the exact time
when the star had appeared. 8Then he sent them
to Bethlehem, saying, "Go and search diligently
for the child; and when you have found him,
bring me word so that I may also go and pay him
homage." 9When they had heard the king, they
set out; and there, ahead of them, went the star
that they had seen at its rising,*c* until it stopped
over the place where the child was. 10When they
saw that the star had stopped,*f* they were overwhelmed with joy. 11On entering the house, they
saw the child with Mary his mother; and they
knelt down and paid him homage. Then, opening their treasure chests, they offered him gifts
of gold, frankincense, and myrrh. 12And having
been warned in a dream not to return to Herod,
they left for their own country by another road.

The Escape to Egypt

13 Now after they had left, an angel of the
Lord appeared to Joseph in a dream and said,

---

a Other ancient authorities read *her firstborn son*
b Or *astrologers;* Gk *magi* c Or *in the East* d Or *the Christ*
e Or *rule* f Gk *saw the star*

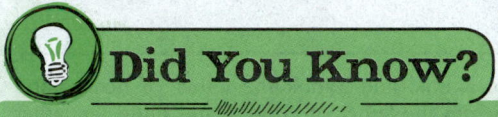

Jesus' Family Tree

In the first two chapters of Matthew, the
author begins to reveal the unique focus of
the Gospel. He starts by tracing Jesus' family
tree, making his case that Jesus was the Messiah who would restore the covenant promised
to Abraham, the father of the Jewish people.
He also traces Jesus' ancestry back to David to
show that Jesus is the fulfillment of the promises
made to David (see 2 Samuel, chapter 7).

Things get even more interesting with a closer
look at all the people mentioned in the list. There
is a wide assortment of groups and social classes: patriarchs and slaves, kings and peasants,
men and women, Jews and non-Jews. This genealogy is based on clan relations where non-
Jews are included because they have been incor-
porated into the clan that traces itself back to
David and Abraham. Essentially, this genealogy
demonstrates that God has been at work from
the call of Abraham, the "father" of Judaism,
through the high point of their history (David),
and even through their darkest times (the Babylonian Exile). And "God is with us" still in Jesus
(Mt 1:23).

▶ Mt 1:1–17

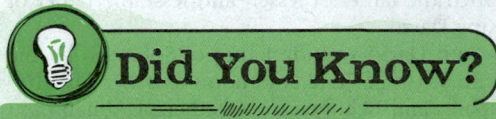

Jesus, Emmanuel

In announcing Jesus' birth, the Gospel of Matthew quotes Isaiah 7:14, in which Isaiah tells
King Ahaz that his young wife will conceive a son
and they will name him Emmanuel, which means
"God is with us" (Mt 1:23). This is the perfect
description for Jesus, the Son of God, who fully
shares our humanity. The Gospel ends with the
same promise, when the risen Jesus tells his
disciples, "I am with you always" (28:20).

▶ Mt 1:23

Cultural Connection

Jesus Brought the Good News of Salvation to People of All Races

The wise men from another culture, who came to offer Jesus gifts for a royal messiah, symbolize that Jesus came as the savior of all races and cultures. Matthew 2:1–12 is the biblical basis for the religious feast day of Epiphany, which officially is January 6 but is celebrated on the first Sunday after the New Year.

In some Latin American traditions, children receive gifts on Epiphany, in remembrance of the gifts the wise men offered to Jesus. The evening before, at parties celebrated in homes and offices, a special bread is shared, known as *La Rosca*, that has a figure of the baby Jesus baked inside of it. Whoever finds the figure of the baby Jesus in a piece of bread has to host a party to celebrate Jesus' presentation in the Temple (see Lk 2:22–24). The Church celebrates this feast on February 2.

- How do you accept and celebrate people of different cultures?
- Think of spiritual gifts you have received from other people. Express your gratitude to God for those gifts.

▶ Mt 2:1–12

"Get up, take the child and his mother, and flee to Egypt, and remain there until I tell you; for Herod is about to search for the child, to destroy him." [14]Then Joseph[a] got up, took the child and his mother by night, and went to Egypt, [15]and remained there until the death of Herod. This was to fulfill what had been spoken by the Lord through the prophet, "Out of Egypt I have called my son."

The Massacre of the Infants

16 When Herod saw that he had been tricked by the wise men,[b] he was infuriated, and he sent and killed all the children in and around Bethlehem who were two years old or under, according to the time that he had learned from the wise men.[b] [17]Then was fulfilled what had been spoken through the prophet Jeremiah:
[18] "A voice was heard in Ramah,
    wailing and loud lamentation,
Rachel weeping for her children;
    she refused to be consoled, because they are
        no more."

The Return from Egypt

19 When Herod died, an angel of the Lord suddenly appeared in a dream to Joseph in Egypt and said, [20]"Get up, take the child and his mother, and go to the land of Israel, for those who were seeking the child's life are dead." [21]Then Joseph[a] got up, took the child and his mother, and went to the land of Israel. [22]But when he heard that Archelaus was ruling over Judea in place of his father Herod, he was afraid to go there. And after being warned in a dream, he went away to the district of Galilee. [23]There he made his home in a town called Nazareth, so that what had been spoken through the prophets might be fulfilled, "He will be called a Nazorean."

The Proclamation of John the Baptist

3 In those days John the Baptist appeared in the wilderness of Judea, proclaiming, [2]"Repent, for the kingdom of heaven has come near."[c] [3]This is the one of whom the prophet Isaiah spoke when he said,

"The voice of one crying out in the wilderness:
 'Prepare the way of the Lord,
    make his paths straight.' "
[4]Now John wore clothing of camel's hair with a leather belt around his waist, and his food was locusts and wild honey. [5]Then the people of Jerusalem and all Judea were going out to him, and all the region along the Jordan, [6]and they were baptized by him in the river Jordan, confessing their sins.

7 But when he saw many Pharisees and Sadducees coming for baptism, he said to them, "You brood of vipers! Who warned you to flee from the wrath to come? [8]Bear fruit worthy of repentance. [9]Do not presume to say to yourselves, 'We have Abraham as our ancestor'; for I tell you, God is able from these stones to raise up children to Abraham. [10]Even now the ax is lying at the root of the trees; every tree therefore that

---

a Gk he   *b* Or astrologers; Gk magi   *c* Or is at hand

Catholic Social Teaching — The Slaughter of the Innocents

The event described in Matthew 2:16–18 is often called the Slaughter of the Innocents. In many circumstances in history, innocent people, including infants and young children, have been victims of war and other acts of violence. Today, abortion has unfortunately continued this trend, prematurely ending the lives of innocent children. To many people, abortion is a simple solution to an unwanted pregnancy. The Church teaches, however, that human life begins at the moment of con-ception, and that these lives, no matter how small, are sacred and must always be protected. Abortion, therefore, is wrong in all circumstances.

Catholic social teaching extends this belief in the dignity of human life from "womb to tomb" to numerous other life issues, including capital punishment, war, and euthanasia. We, in turn, must reflect this consistent ethic of life in all that we believe, say, and do, working hard to ensure that human dignity is always upheld.

● How might we as individuals or communities support pregnant women to ensure they do not choose abortion?
● How difficult is it to have a truly consistent ethic of life in our world today?

▶ **Mt 2:16–18**

Life and Dignity of the Human Person

does not bear good fruit is cut down and thrown into the fire.

11 "I baptize you with*a* water for repentance, but one who is more powerful than I is coming after me; I am not worthy to carry his sandals. He will baptize you with*a* the Holy Spirit and fire. [12]His winnowing fork is in his hand, and he will clear his threshing floor and will gather his wheat into the granary; but the chaff he will burn with unquenchable fire."

The Baptism of Jesus

13 Then Jesus came from Galilee to John at the Jordan, to be baptized by him. [14]John would have prevented him, saying, "I need to be baptized by you, and do you come to me?" [15]But Jesus answered him, "Let it be so now; for it is proper for us in this way to fulfill all righteousness." Then he consented. [16]And when Jesus had been baptized, just as he came up from the water, suddenly the heavens were opened to him and he saw the Spirit of God descending like a dove and alighting on him. [17]And a voice from heaven said, "This is my Son, the Beloved,*b* with whom I am well pleased."

The Temptation of Jesus

4 Then Jesus was led up by the Spirit into the wilderness to be tempted by the devil. [2]He fasted forty days and forty nights, and afterwards he was famished. [3]The tempter came and said to him, "If you are the Son of God, command these stones to become loaves of bread." [4]But he answered, "It is written,

'One does not live by bread alone,
    but by every word that comes from the mouth
        of God.' "

5 Then the devil took him to the holy city and placed him on the pinnacle of the temple, [6]saying to him, "If you are the Son of God, throw yourself down; for it is written,

'He will command his angels concerning you,'
    and 'On their hands they will bear you up,
    so that you will not dash your foot against a
        stone.' "

[7]Jesus said to him, "Again it is written, 'Do not put the Lord your God to the test.' "

8 Again, the devil took him to a very high mountain and showed him all the kingdoms of the world and their splendor; [9]and he said to him, "All these I will give you, if you will fall down and worship me." [10]Jesus said to him, "Away with you, Satan! for it is written,

'Worship the Lord your God,
    and serve only him.' "

[11]Then the devil left him, and suddenly angels came and waited on him.

Jesus Begins His Ministry in Galilee

12 Now when Jesus*c* heard that John had been arrested, he withdrew to Galilee. [13]He left Nazareth and made his home in Capernaum by

a Or in   b Or my beloved Son   c Gk he

the sea, in the territory of Zebulun and Naphtali, ¹⁴so that what had been spoken through the prophet Isaiah might be fulfilled:

¹⁵ "Land of Zebulun, land of Naphtali,
   on the road by the sea, across the Jordan,
       Galilee of the Gentiles—
¹⁶ the people who sat in darkness
   have seen a great light,
   and for those who sat in the region and shadow
       of death
   light has dawned."

¹⁷From that time Jesus began to proclaim, "Repent, for the kingdom of heaven has come near."ᵃ

Jesus' Family Lives as Immigrants

Following an angel's order and facing the massacre of all boys under age two, Joseph takes Mary and Jesus to Egypt to protect them from Herod's threats. They become immigrants to avoid persecution.

Every year, millions of people in the world become immigrants, fleeing their countries because of hunger, poverty, or persecution. Often, they find themselves feeling like unwelcome strangers, not able to communicate in the language of their new land and even persecuted by its inhabitants—many who believe that these immigrants have come simply to take advantage of services provided by the government. Christians, however, should have a special compassion for immigrants because Jesus told us to love everyone, especially those who suffer. By honoring the plight of today's immigrants, we honor the Holy Family.

- Imagine Jesus, Mary, and Joseph exiled in this country. How would you treat them?
- What is your attitude toward refugees and immigrants in our country?
- Ask God to bless legislators with the love and wisdom to welcome immigrants, and to give your generation a courageous heart to seek justice and peace in the world.

▶ Mt 2:13

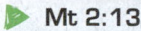

Jesus Calls the First Disciples

18 As he walked by the Sea of Galilee, he saw two brothers, Simon, who is called Peter, and Andrew his brother, casting a net into the

---

a Or is at hand

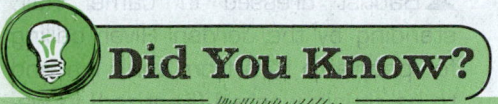

Pharisees, Sadducees, and Scribes

In Jesus' day, several groups of Jews held positions of status or leadership. The *Pharisees* were devoted laymen who were scholars of the Law of Moses and experts at interpreting it, so as many as possible could obey it. People looked up to them for guidance about how they should live as good Jews. The Pharisees believed in the resurrection of the body at the end time. The *Sadducees* were associated with the Temple and the ruling class. They thought the well-being of the Jewish people was dependent on proper operation and support of the Temple. They did not believe in the resurrection of body as the Pharisees did. The *scribes* were skilled at reading and writing, and most likely performed those services for the ruling class and those who were able to pay them. Scribes were not a religious group within Judaism, but they would have been familiar with the Torah and other aspects of religious practice because they worked as secretaries for the Pharisees and Sadducees. Scribes probably were involved in copying some of the Old Testament manuscripts.

The negative reaction of John the Baptist to the Pharisees and Sadducees is typical in Matthew. But in general, the Pharisees, the Sadducees, and scribes were respected leaders during Jesus' time. The persecution later experienced by the community in which the author of Matthew lived probably affected his portrayal of them. (See "Introducing Jewish Sects," near the end of Second Maccabees, for more information on these groups.)

▶ Mt 3:7

✝ Catholic Connection

Baptism

Imagine the scene . . . John the Baptist dressed in camel hair, standing by the Jordan River calling for people to turn from their sin and to be ritually washed (baptized) in water as a sign of their conversion. And who steps forward? Jesus, the Son of God, who is without sin! Jesus convinces John to baptize him as a sign of how fully Jesus embraces his humanity. As Jesus comes out of the water, God reveals Jesus' true identity to the world—"This is my Son, the Beloved, with whom I am well pleased" (Mt 3:17)—thus beginning Jesus' public ministry leading toward his Passion, death, and Resurrection.

The sacrament of Baptism also serves as a beginning for all Catholics. As the first of the three sacraments of initiation, Baptism establishes our identity as adopted sons or daughters of God and makes us members of the Christian community.

Although many Catholics are baptized as infants, some young people and adults, referred to as catechumens, are baptized at the Easter Vigil each year. During the Baptism ritual, the person is immersed in water or has water poured over his or her head three times with the words: "I baptize you in the name of the Father, and of the Son, and of the Holy Spirit" (*Rite of Christian Initiation of Adults*, no. 226). By being washed in water, the person dies to sin and rises freed from sin, both original sin and personal sin, as a new creation in Christ. The individual is then anointed with chrism (sacred oil) to strengthen him or her to "remain for ever a member of Christ" (no. 228), who was anointed priest, prophet, and king. (In the Old Testament, such oil was used to anoint priests, prophets, and kings for service.) Afterward, a white garment is put on the newly baptized person, signifying his or her new life in Christ, and a candle is given to the person, calling him or her to always walk in the light of Christ and be a light to the world.

Together the sacraments of Baptism, Confirmation, and the Eucharist are a person's initiation into the Christian community. They call Christians to continual conversion in following Jesus.

▶ **Mt 3:13–17**
Catechism, nos. 1213–1284

sea—for they were fishermen. [19]And he said to them, "Follow me, and I will make you fish for people." [20]Immediately they left their nets and followed him. [21]As he went from there, he saw two other brothers, James son of Zebedee and his brother John, in the boat with their father Zebedee, mending their nets, and he called them. [22]Immediately they left the boat and their father, and followed him.

Jesus Ministers to Crowds of People

23 Jesus[a] went throughout Galilee, teaching in their synagogues and proclaiming the good news[b] of the kingdom and curing every disease and every sickness among the people. [24]So his fame spread throughout all Syria, and they brought to him all the sick, those who were afflicted with various diseases and pains, demoniacs, epileptics, and paralytics, and he cured them. [25]And great crowds followed him from Galilee, the Decapolis, Jerusalem, Judea, and from beyond the Jordan.

Jesus' Temptations, My Temptations

" **C**ommand these stones to become loaves of bread" (4:3).

Jesus, you trusted God to provide your material needs. Help me to avoid placing my priorities on material things.

"Throw yourself down; for it is written, . . . 'you will not dash your foot against a stone'" (verse 6).

Jesus, you resisted using your power for vain and foolish reasons. Help me to resist doing foolish things only to impress others.

"All these I will give you, if you will fall down and worship me" (verse 9).

Jesus, you refused to cooperate with the devil to achieve status and power. Help me to refuse to cooperate with evil and injustice in achieving my life's goals.

▶ Mt 4:1–11

The Beatitudes

5 When Jesus[c] saw the crowds, he went up the mountain; and after he sat down, his disciples came to him. [2]Then he began to speak, and taught them, saying:

3 "Blessed are the poor in spirit, for theirs is the kingdom of heaven.

4 "Blessed are those who mourn, for they will be comforted.

5 "Blessed are the meek, for they will inherit the earth.

6 "Blessed are those who hunger and thirst for righteousness, for they will be filled.

7 "Blessed are the merciful, for they will receive mercy.

8 "Blessed are the pure in heart, for they will see God.

9 "Blessed are the peacemakers, for they will be called children of God.

10 "Blessed are those who are persecuted for righteousness' sake, for theirs is the kingdom of heaven.

11 "Blessed are you when people revile you and persecute you and utter all kinds of evil against you falsely[d] on my account. [12]Rejoice and be glad, for your reward is great in heaven, for in the same way they persecuted the prophets who were before you.

Salt and Light

13 "You are the salt of the earth; but if salt has lost its taste, how can its saltiness be restored? It

---

a Gk He   b Gk gospel   c Gk he   d Other ancient authorities lack falsely

Follow Me

As the first disciples chose to follow Jesus, what did they leave behind? Nets, boats, even parents—the very things they depended on for life and security! Knowing what you know of Jesus, what are you ready to "leave behind" in order to follow him and continue his mission?

▶ Mt 4:18–22

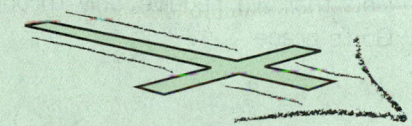

✚ Catholic Connection

The Beatitudes

Have you ever thought if you only had the latest technology, or if only you were more popular, then you would be happy? Those feelings are natural, but in the Sermon on the Mount, Jesus offers a radically different view of true happiness. Jesus provides a list of attitudes, called the Beatitudes, that will bring us happiness. This list has nothing to do with material goods or popularity contests but focuses instead on our response to God's love and our love of neighbor. True happiness is found not here on earth, but in the gift of eternal reward in the kingdom of heaven.

Our desire for happiness was placed within us by God and can only be satisfied by loving God and doing God's will. Real happiness is attained not through the accumulation of possessions, but through the moral choices we make. The Beatitudes call us to turn from our desire for false or temporary happiness to seek the eternal happiness only God can give. By focusing on heaven, the decisions we make and the trials we endure on a daily basis are seen in a new light—the light of Christ's Passion and Resurrection.

Having heaven as our goal enables us to . . .

- realize that heaven is a gift from God that we receive only through God's grace

- find comfort when we mourn the loss of a loved one

- be humble

- desire righteousness (a right relationship with God and others) with every ounce of our being

- be merciful when others offend or harm us

- purify our heart so that we only desire God

- seek peace when conflict arises

- stick to our convictions when it is a question of right and wrong

- endure being made fun of or threatened because of our faith in Jesus Christ

Each and every day, God calls us to seek happiness by loving God and others generously, compassionately, humbly, with a hunger for justice, with a pure heart, and in a desire for peace. Make the Beatitudes part of your daily prayer, and know that you are not alone in the pursuit of happiness. You walk this journey with the Church, with Mary and the saints, who encourage you along the way!

▶ **Mt 5:1–12**
Catechism, nos. 1716–1729

Catholic Social Teaching

An Upside-Down Kingdom

Read Matthew 5:1–12. These familiar words of Jesus, called the Beatitudes, begin what is called the Sermon on the Mount. In chapters 5–7, Jesus speaks about life in a way that challenged the attitudes of his listeners. Many thought it was enough to follow the letter of the law by performing minimal acts of caring for the poor, burying the dead, and giving alms. Jesus, however, turns their worldview upside down, asserting that they should do these things generously, compassionately, and humbly, with a hunger for justice, with a pure heart, and in a desire for peace.

Catholic social teaching promotes this same message, reminding us that God has a special love for those who are poor and those who are oppressed. If we are to be authentic Christians, we must show a similar love for those who are most in need in our world. Thankfully, our world has been blessed with numerous modern-day prophets who have shown us what it truly means to love and care for the poor. People like Archbishop Oscar Romero of El Salvador, who risked and eventually lost his own life because he was unafraid to speak out against the grave injustices being inflicted

upon the poor in his country. Or Dorothy Day, who founded the Catholic Worker movement and devoted her adult life to promoting peace while serving the most poor and destitute. With these people and so many others as examples for us to follow, we too must always opt to love and serve the poor in our midst.

▶ **Mt 5:1–12**

Option for the Poor and Vulnerable

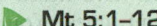

---

is no longer good for anything, but is thrown out and trampled under foot.

14 "You are the light of the world. A city built on a hill cannot be hid. 15No one after lighting a lamp puts it under the bushel basket, but on the lampstand, and it gives light to all in the house. 16In the same way, let your light shine before others, so that they may see your good works and give glory to your Father in heaven.

The Law and the Prophets

17 "Do not think that I have come to abolish the law or the prophets; I have come not to abolish but to fulfill. 18For truly I tell you, until heaven and earth pass away, not one letter,*a* not one stroke of a letter, will pass from the law until all is accomplished. 19Therefore, whoever breaks*b* one of the least of these commandments, and teaches others to do the same, will be called least in the kingdom of heaven; but whoever does them and teaches them will be called great in the kingdom of heaven. 20For I tell you, unless your righteousness exceeds that of the scribes and Pharisees, you will never enter the kingdom of heaven.

Concerning Anger

21 "You have heard that it was said to those of ancient times, 'You shall not murder'; and

'whoever murders shall be liable to judgment.' 22But I say to you that if you are angry with a brother or sister,*c* you will be liable to judgment; and if you insult*d* a brother or sister,*e* you will be liable to the council; and if you say, 'You fool,' you will be liable to the hell*f* of fire. 23So when you are offering your gift at the altar, if you remember that your brother or sister*g* has something against you, 24leave your gift there before the altar and go; first be reconciled to your brother or sister,*g* and then come and offer your gift. 25Come to terms quickly with your accuser while you are on the way to court*h* with him, or your accuser may hand you over to the judge, and the judge to the guard, and you will be thrown into prison. 26Truly I tell you, you will never get out until you have paid the last penny.

Concerning Adultery

27 "You have heard that it was said, 'You shall not commit adultery.' 28But I say to you that everyone who looks at a woman with lust has already committed adultery with her in his heart. 29If your right eye causes you to sin, tear it

---

a Gk *one iota* *b* Or *annuls* *c* Gk *a brother*; other ancient authorities add *without cause* *d* Gk *say Raca to* (an obscure term of abuse) *e* Gk *a brother* *f* Gk *Gehenna* *g* Gk *your brother* *h* Gk lacks *to court*

out and throw it away; it is better for you to lose one of your members than for your whole body to be thrown into hell.*a* 30And if your right hand causes you to sin, cut it off and throw it away; it is better for you to lose one of your members than for your whole body to go into hell.*a*

Concerning Divorce

31 "It was also said, 'Whoever divorces his wife, let him give her a certificate of divorce.' 32But I say to you that anyone who divorces his wife, except on the ground of unchastity, causes her to commit adultery; and whoever marries a divorced woman commits adultery.

Concerning Oaths

33 "Again, you have heard that it was said to those of ancient times, 'You shall not swear

Christians and Revenge

For Jesus one way to love our enemies is to refuse to take revenge on those who have wronged us. Is this really possible to do?

Consider the case of a young woman named Julie Welch who was killed by a terrorist bombing in Oklahoma City. Julie's father worked unceasingly against the death penalty for the man responsible for the bombing. He knew that revenge would not bring his daughter back or make him feel better. He believed that Christians are obligated to always assume that for even the most heinous criminal, reconciliation and remorse are possible. Although his stance was not easy or popular, it illustrates what this passage teaches.

In your prayer, reflect or journal on the following questions:
● Who are your enemies?
● When they or someone else hurts you, what is your usual reaction?
● How hard is it to forgive someone who has hurt you?
● What is the greatest challenge for you in living out this teaching from Jesus?

▶ Mt 5:38–48

falsely, but carry out the vows you have made to the Lord.' 34But I say to you, Do not swear at all, either by heaven, for it is the throne of God, 35or by the earth, for it is his footstool, or by Jerusalem, for it is the city of the great King. 36And do not swear by your head, for you cannot make one hair white or black. 37Let your word be 'Yes, Yes' or 'No, No'; anything more than this comes from the evil one.*b*

Concerning Retaliation

38 "You have heard that it was said, 'An eye for an eye and a tooth for a tooth.' 39But I say to you, Do not resist an evildoer. But if anyone strikes you on the right cheek, turn the other also; 40and if anyone wants to sue you and take your coat, give your cloak as well; 41and if anyone forces you to go one mile, go also the second mile. 42Give to everyone who begs from you, and do not refuse anyone who wants to borrow from you.

Love for Enemies

43 "You have heard that it was said, 'You shall love your neighbor and hate your enemy.' 44But I say to you, Love your enemies and pray for those who persecute you, 45so that you may be children of your Father in heaven; for he makes his sun rise on the evil and on the good, and sends rain on the righteous and on the unrighteous. 46For if you love those who love you, what reward do you have? Do not even the tax collectors do the same? 47And if you greet only your brothers and sisters,*c* what more are you doing than others? Do not even the Gentiles do the same? 48Be perfect, therefore, as your heavenly Father is perfect.

Concerning Almsgiving

6 "Beware of practicing your piety before others in order to be seen by them; for then you have no reward from your Father in heaven.

2 "So whenever you give alms, do not sound a trumpet before you, as the hypocrites do in the synagogues and in the streets, so that they may be praised by others. Truly I tell you, they have received their reward. 3But when you give alms, do not let your left hand know what your right hand is doing, 4so that your alms may be done in secret; and your Father who sees in secret will reward you.*d*

Concerning Prayer

5 "And whenever you pray, do not be like the hypocrites; for they love to stand and pray in the

a Gk *Gehenna*   *b* Or *evil*   *c* Gk *your brothers*   *d* Other ancient authorities add *openly*

A Lord's Prayer Reflection

In the Book of Matthew, Jesus teaches his followers the Lord's Prayer as an alternative to hypocritical and empty prayer. Most of us have memorized the Lord's Prayer. But although we know it by heart, we do not always pray it from the heart. It can easily become "empty phrases" (6:7). Let this reflection help you to pray the Lord's Prayer thoughtfully:

Our Father in heaven,
  hallowed be your name.

(Verse 9)

How do I honor God as creator of all things? How do I honor God in my thoughts, my words, and my actions?

Your kingdom come.
Your will be done,
  on earth as it is in heaven.

(Verse 10)

How does my life reflect God's Reign of love, justice, and peace? Am I putting too much emphasis on material things?

Give us this day our daily bread. (Verse 11)

Can I trust God to provide for my daily physical, emotional, and spiritual needs?

And forgive us our debts,
  as we also have forgiven our debtors.

(Verse 12)

When I have sinned, do I admit my wrong, ask God's forgiveness, and start anew? When people have wronged me, do I hold a grudge? Am I able to forgive them as God forgives me?

And do not bring us to the time of trial,
  but rescue us from the evil one.

(Verse 13)

What are the temptations I face in life? How do I rely on God for the strength to resist them?

▶ Mt 6:5–15

synagogues and at the street corners, so that they may be seen by others. Truly I tell you, they have received their reward. 6But whenever you pray, go into your room and shut the door and pray to your Father who is in secret; and your Father who sees in secret will reward you.*a*

7 "When you are praying, do not heap up empty phrases as the Gentiles do; for they think that they will be heard because of their many words. 8Do not be like them, for your Father knows what you need before you ask him.

9 "Pray then in this way:
  Our Father in heaven,
    hallowed be your name.
10   Your kingdom come.
  Your will be done,

---

a Other ancient authorities add *openly*

Ash Wednesday

Matthew 6:1–18 is read on Ash Wednesday, the beginning of Lent. Lent is traditionally a forty-day period to examine and renew our spiritual lives. It is a time of prayer, service, and fasting. The forty days recall the forty years that the people of Israel wandered in the wilderness before arriving at the Promised Land and the forty days that Jesus spent in the wilderness after being baptized.

On Ash Wednesday, we receive ashes that remind us of our nature as created beings (see Gen 3:19). This practice echoes the Old Testament tradition of wearing ashes as a sign of anguish and repentance (see Jdt 4:11). As the ash cross is made on our foreheads, we hear words that echo John the Baptist's call to conversion: "Repent, and believe in the Gospel" (*Roman Missal*). We respond "Amen," meaning "So be it."

When Lent begins again, how will you use the forty days to strengthen your spiritual life? Make a special commitment and ask God for the grace to grow from it.

▶ Mt 6:1–18

on earth as it is in heaven.

11   Give us this day our daily bread.[a]

12   And forgive us our debts,
        as we also have forgiven our debtors.

13   And do not bring us to the time of trial,[b]
        but rescue us from the evil one.[c]

[14]For if you forgive others their trespasses, your heavenly Father will also forgive you; [15]but if you do not forgive others, neither will your Father forgive your trespasses.

Concerning Fasting

16   "And whenever you fast, do not look dismal, like the hypocrites, for they disfigure their faces so as to show others that they are fasting. Truly I tell you, they have received their reward. [17]But when you fast, put oil on your head and wash your face, [18]so that your fasting may be seen not by others but by your Father who is in secret; and your Father who sees in secret will reward you.[d]

Concerning Treasures

19   "Do not store up for yourselves treasures on earth, where moth and rust[e] consume and where thieves break in and steal; [20]but store up for yourselves treasures in heaven, where neither moth nor rust[e] consumes and where thieves do not break in and steal. [21]For where your treasure is, there your heart will be also.

The Sound Eye

22   "The eye is the lamp of the body. So, if your eye is healthy, your whole body will be full of light; [23]but if your eye is unhealthy, your whole body will be full of darkness. If then the light in you is darkness, how great is the darkness!

Serving Two Masters

24   "No one can serve two masters; for a slave will either hate the one and love the other, or be devoted to the one and despise the other. You cannot serve God and wealth.[f]

Do Not Worry

25   "Therefore I tell you, do not worry about your life, what you will eat or what you will drink,[g] or about your body, what you will wear. Is not life more than food, and the body more than clothing? [26]Look at the birds of the air; they neither sow nor reap nor gather into barns, and yet your heavenly Father feeds them. Are you not of more value than they? [27]And can any of you by worrying add a single hour to your span of life?[h] [28]And why do you worry about clothing?

Consider the lilies of the field, how they grow; they neither toil nor spin, [29]yet I tell you, even Solomon in all his glory was not clothed like one of these. [30]But if God so clothes the grass of the field, which is alive today and tomorrow is thrown into the oven, will he not much more clothe you—you of little faith? [31]Therefore do not worry, saying, 'What will we eat?' or 'What will we drink?' or 'What will we wear?' [32]For it is the Gentiles who strive for all these things; and indeed your heavenly Father knows that you need all these things. [33]But strive first for the kingdom of God[i] and his[j] righteousness, and all these things will be given to you as well.

34   "So do not worry about tomorrow, for tomorrow will bring worries of its own. Today's trouble is enough for today.

Judging Others

7 "Do not judge, so that you may not be judged. [2]For with the judgment you make you will be judged, and the measure you give will be the measure you get. [3]Why do you see the speck in your neighbor's[k] eye, but do not notice the log in your own eye? [4]Or how can you say to your neighbor,[l] 'Let me take the speck out of your eye,' while the log is in your own eye? [5]You hypocrite, first take the log out of your own eye, and then you will see clearly to take the speck out of your neighbor's[k] eye.

Profaning the Holy

6   "Do not give what is holy to dogs; and do not throw your pearls before swine, or they will trample them under foot and turn and maul you.

Ask, Search, Knock

7   "Ask, and it will be given you; search, and you will find; knock, and the door will be opened for you. [8]For everyone who asks receives, and everyone who searches finds, and for everyone who knocks, the door will be opened. [9]Is there anyone among you who, if your child asks for bread, will give a stone? [10]Or if the child asks for a fish, will give a snake? [11]If you then, who are evil, know how to give good gifts to your children, how much more will your Father in heaven give good things to those who ask him!

---

a Or our bread for tomorrow   b Or us into temptation
c Or from evil. Other ancient authorities add, in some form,
For the kingdom and the power and the glory are yours forever.
Amen.   d Other ancient authorities add openly   e Gk eating
f Gk mammon   g Other ancient authorities lack or what you
will drink   h Or add one cubit to your height   i Other ancient
authorities lack of God   j Or its   k Gk brother's   l Gk brother

The Golden Rule

12 "In everything do to others as you would have them do to you; for this is the law and the prophets.

The Narrow Gate

13 "Enter through the narrow gate; for the gate is wide and the road is easy[a] that leads to destruction, and there are many who take it. [14]For the gate is narrow and the road is hard that leads to life, and there are few who find it.

A Tree and Its Fruit

15 "Beware of false prophets, who come to you in sheep's clothing but inwardly are ravenous wolves. [16]You will know them by their fruits. Are grapes gathered from thorns, or figs from thistles? [17]In the same way, every good tree bears good fruit, but the bad tree bears bad fruit. [18]A good tree cannot bear bad fruit, nor can a bad tree bear good fruit. [19]Every tree that does not bear good fruit is cut down and thrown into the fire. [20]Thus you will know them by their fruits.

Concerning Self-Deception

21 "Not everyone who says to me, 'Lord, Lord,' will enter the kingdom of heaven, but only the one who does the will of my Father in heaven. [22]On that day many will say to me, 'Lord, Lord, did we not prophesy in your name, and cast out demons in your name, and do many deeds of power in your name?' [23]Then I will declare to them, 'I never knew you; go away from me, you evildoers.'

Hearers and Doers

24 "Everyone then who hears these words of mine and acts on them will be like a wise man who built his house on rock. [25]The rain fell, the floods came, and the winds blew and beat on that house, but it did not fall, because it had been founded on rock. [26]And everyone who hears these words of mine and does not act on them will be like a foolish man who built his house on sand. [27]The rain fell, and the floods came, and the winds blew and beat against that house, and it fell—and great was its fall!"

28 Now when Jesus had finished saying these things, the crowds were astounded at his teaching, [29]for he taught them as one having authority, and not as their scribes.

Jesus Cleanses a Leper

8 When Jesus[b] had come down from the mountain, great crowds followed him; [2]and

The Gospel Call to Conversion

In closing the Sermon on the Mount, Jesus calls people to conversion. It is not enough to talk the talk; you must also walk the walk. As part of our conversion, Jesus commands the following:

- Those who are rich need to share their wealth with those who are poor.
- Those who have power need to serve those who do not have power.
- Priests need to serve all people without prejudice.
- Politicians need to govern with justice, taking into account the needs of people, especially those who are poor and powerless.
- Wise people need to express their knowledge in ways everyone can understand.

In your prayer, reflect or journal on the following:

- In the above list, what are some of the most needed areas of conversion in society today? in your local community? in your life?
- List some concrete ways you can make those conversions real.

▶ Mt 7:21–27

there was a leper[c] who came to him and knelt before him, saying, "Lord, if you choose, you can make me clean." [3]He stretched out his hand and touched him, saying, "I do choose. Be made clean!" Immediately his leprosy[c] was cleansed. [4]Then Jesus said to him, "See that you say nothing to anyone; but go, show yourself to the priest, and offer the gift that Moses commanded, as a testimony to them."

Jesus Heals a Centurion's Servant

5 When he entered Capernaum, a centurion came to him, appealing to him [6]and saying, "Lord, my servant is lying at home paralyzed, in terrible distress." [7]And he said to him, "I will come and cure him." [8]The centurion answered,

a Other ancient authorities read *for the road is wide and easy*
b Gk *he*   c The terms *leper* and *leprosy* can refer to several diseases

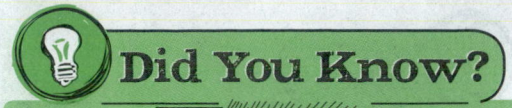

Did You Know?

Miracles and the Reign of God

Matthew, chapters 8–9, describes ten miracles of Jesus intended as signs of the coming of the Reign of God. Most of Jesus' miracles are healings, but some also show his power over demons and nature. The Gospel of Mark records the most miracles (twenty-one), and the Gospel of John, the least (eight).

People today tend to view reports of miracles with suspicion. That's because our scientific minds want to believe that everything has a rational explanation. Because of this, we miss the point. People in Jesus' time were more concerned about what the miracle revealed than in the miracle itself or even the miracle worker. Other people besides Jesus were known to perform miracles. In fact, Jesus' healing miracles were not taken as proof of his divinity, only that he worked by the power of God.

In curing people of their illnesses and driving out demons, Jesus was revealing that the Reign of God is a place where suffering and evil are banished. By curing sinners, women, and foreigners, he showed that the Reign of God is also open to all, especially outcasts.

Miracles—then and now—point to God. Whether they are easily explained or beyond reasonable explanation does not matter. What matters is that they make us aware of God's loving presence in our lives. If we look at the events in our lives and ask ourselves what they point to and what they tell us about God's presence in the world, we might find ourselves utterly surrounded by miracles.

▶ Mt 8:1—9:34

"Lord, I am not worthy to have you come under my roof; but only speak the word, and my servant will be healed. 9For I also am a man under authority, with soldiers under me; and I say to one, 'Go,' and he goes, and to another, 'Come,' and he comes, and to my slave, 'Do this,' and the slave does it." 10When Jesus heard him, he was amazed and said to those who followed him, "Truly I tell you, in no one[a] in Israel have I found such faith. 11I tell you, many will come from east and west

and will eat with Abraham and Isaac and Jacob in the kingdom of heaven, 12while the heirs of the kingdom will be thrown into the outer darkness, where there will be weeping and gnashing of teeth." 13And to the centurion Jesus said, "Go; let it be done for you according to your faith." And the servant was healed in that hour.

Jesus Heals Many at Peter's House

14 When Jesus entered Peter's house, he saw his mother-in-law lying in bed with a fever; 15he touched her hand, and the fever left her, and she got up and began to serve him. 16That evening they brought to him many who were possessed with demons; and he cast out the spirits with a word, and cured all who were sick. 17This was to fulfill what had been spoken through the prophet Isaiah, "He took our infirmities and bore our diseases."

Would-Be Followers of Jesus

18 Now when Jesus saw great crowds around him, he gave orders to go over to the other side. 19A scribe then approached and said, "Teacher, I will follow you wherever you go." 20And Jesus said to him, "Foxes have holes, and birds of the air have nests; but the Son of Man has nowhere to lay his head." 21Another of his disciples said to him, "Lord, first let me go and bury my father." 22But Jesus said to him, "Follow me, and let the dead bury their own dead."

Jesus Stills the Storm

23 And when he got into the boat, his disciples followed him. 24A windstorm arose on the sea, so great that the boat was being swamped by the waves; but he was asleep. 25And they went and woke him up, saying, "Lord, save us! We are perishing!" 26And he said to them, "Why are you afraid, you of little faith?" Then he got up and rebuked the winds and the sea; and there was a dead calm. 27They were amazed, saying, "What sort of man is this, that even the winds and the sea obey him?"

Jesus Heals the Gadarene Demoniacs

28 When he came to the other side, to the country of the Gadarenes,[b] two demoniacs coming out of the tombs met him. They were so fierce that no one could pass that way. 29Suddenly they shouted, "What have you to do with us, Son of God? Have you come here to torment us before the time?" 30Now a large herd

---

a Other ancient authorities read *Truly I tell you, not even*
b Other ancient authorities read *Gergesenes*; others, *Gerasenes*

of swine was feeding at some distance from them. ³¹The demons begged him, "If you cast us out, send us into the herd of swine." ³²And he said to them, "Go!" So they came out and entered the swine; and suddenly, the whole herd rushed down the steep bank into the sea and perished in the water. ³³The swineherds ran off, and on going into the town, they told the whole story about what had happened to the demoniacs. ³⁴Then the whole town came out to meet Jesus; and when they saw him, they begged

9 him to leave their neighborhood. ¹And after getting into a boat he crossed the sea and came to his own town.

Jesus Heals a Paralytic

2 And just then some people were carrying a paralyzed man lying on a bed. When Jesus saw their faith, he said to the paralytic, "Take heart, son; your sins are forgiven." ³Then some of the scribes said to themselves, "This man is blaspheming." ⁴But Jesus, perceiving their thoughts, said, "Why do you think evil in your hearts? ⁵For which is easier, to say, 'Your sins are forgiven,' or to say, 'Stand up and walk'? ⁶But so that you may know that the Son of Man has authority on earth to forgive sins"—he then said to the paralytic— "Stand up, take your bed and go to your home." ⁷And he stood up and went to his home. ⁸When the crowds saw it, they were filled with awe, and they glorified God, who had given such authority to human beings.

The Call of Matthew

9 As Jesus was walking along, he saw a man called Matthew sitting at the tax booth; and he said to him, "Follow me." And he got up and followed him.

10 And as he sat at dinner*ᵃ* in the house, many tax collectors and sinners came and were sitting*ᵇ* with him and his disciples. ¹¹When the Pharisees saw this, they said to his disciples, "Why does your teacher eat with tax collectors and sinners?" ¹²But when he heard this, he said, "Those who are well have no need of a physician, but those who are sick. ¹³Go and learn what this means, 'I desire mercy, not sacrifice.' For I have come to call not the righteous but sinners."

The Question about Fasting

14 Then the disciples of John came to him, saying, "Why do we and the Pharisees fast often,*ᶜ* but your disciples do not fast?" ¹⁵And Jesus said to them, "The wedding guests cannot mourn as long as the bridegroom is with them, can they? The days will come when the bridegroom is

Pray It!

Spiritual Paralysis

Jesus, healer, like the man you healed spiritually and physically, I too have experienced paralysis. Not a physical paralysis, but a spiritual paralysis that keeps me from walking with you.

This paralysis happens at times in school and in my neighborhood, when I know what the right thing to do is, but I am afraid to do it. I see someone discriminating against or abusing another person, but I stand by and do nothing. By my silence, I give my approval, but I am afraid to risk ridicule and rejection.

Forgive me of my sin of silence, Lord. Help me to overcome my fears so that I can stand up for what is right. Heal me of my spiritual paralysis so that I may walk with you. Amen.

▶ **Mt 9:1–8**

taken away from them, and then they will fast. ¹⁶No one sews a piece of unshrunk cloth on an old cloak, for the patch pulls away from the cloak, and a worse tear is made. ¹⁷Neither is new wine put into old wineskins; otherwise, the skins burst, and the wine is spilled, and the skins are destroyed; but new wine is put into fresh wineskins, and so both are preserved."

A Girl Restored to Life and a Woman Healed

18 While he was saying these things to them, suddenly a leader of the synagogue*ᵈ* came in and knelt before him, saying, "My daughter has just died; but come and lay your hand on her, and she will live." ¹⁹And Jesus got up and followed him, with his disciples. ²⁰Then suddenly a woman who had been suffering from hemorrhages for twelve years came up behind him and touched the fringe of his cloak, ²¹for she said to herself, "If I only touch his cloak, I will be made well." ²²Jesus turned, and seeing her he said, "Take heart, daughter; your faith has made you well." And instantly the woman was made well. ²³When Jesus came to the leader's house and saw the flute players and the crowd making a commotion, ²⁴he

---

a Gk *reclined*   *b* Gk *were reclining*   *c* Other ancient authorities lack *often*   *d* Gk lacks *of the synagogue*

said, "Go away; for the girl is not dead but sleeping." And they laughed at him. 25But when the crowd had been put outside, he went in and took her by the hand, and the girl got up. 26And the report of this spread throughout that district.

Jesus Heals Two Blind Men

27 As Jesus went on from there, two blind men followed him, crying loudly, "Have mercy on us, Son of David!" 28When he entered the house, the blind men came to him; and Jesus said to them, "Do you believe that I am able to do this?" They said to him, "Yes, Lord." 29Then he touched their eyes and said, "According to your faith let it be done to you." 30And their eyes were opened. Then Jesus sternly ordered them, "See that no one knows of this." 31But they went away and spread the news about him throughout that district.

Jesus Heals One Who Was Mute

32 After they had gone away, a demoniac who was mute was brought to him. 33And when the demon had been cast out, the one who had been mute spoke; and the crowds were amazed and said, "Never has anything like this been seen in Israel." 34But the Pharisees said, "By the ruler of the demons he casts out the demons."a

The Harvest Is Great, the Laborers Few

35 Then Jesus went about all the cities and villages, teaching in their synagogues, and proclaiming the good news of the kingdom, and curing every disease and every sickness. 36When he saw the crowds, he had compassion for them, because they were harassed and helpless, like sheep without a shepherd. 37Then he said to his disciples, "The harvest is plentiful, but the laborers are few; 38therefore ask the Lord of the harvest to send out laborers into his harvest."

The Twelve Apostles

10 Then Jesusb summoned his twelve disciples and gave them authority over unclean spirits, to cast them out, and to cure every disease and every sickness. 2These are the names of the twelve apostles: first, Simon, also known as Peter, and his brother Andrew; James son of Zebedee, and his brother John; 3Philip and Bartholomew; Thomas and Matthew the tax collector; James son of Alphaeus, and Thaddaeus;c 4Simon the Cananaean, and Judas Iscariot, the one who betrayed him.

The Mission of the Twelve

5 These twelve Jesus sent out with the following instructions: "Go nowhere among the Gentiles, and enter no town of the Samaritans, 6but go rather to the lost sheep of the house of Israel. 7As you go, proclaim the good news, 'The kingdom of heaven has come near.'d 8Cure the sick, raise the dead, cleanse the lepers,e cast out demons. You received without payment; give without payment. 9Take no gold, or silver, or copper in your belts, 10no bag for your journey, or two tunics, or sandals, or a staff; for laborers deserve their food. 11Whatever town or village you enter, find out who in it is worthy, and stay there until you leave. 12As you enter the house, greet it. 13If the house is worthy, let your peace come upon it; but if it is not worthy, let your peace return to you. 14If anyone will not welcome you or listen to your words, shake off the dust from your feet as you leave that house or town. 15Truly I tell you, it will be more tolerable for the land of Sodom and Gomorrah on the day of judgment than for that town.

Coming Persecutions

16 "See, I am sending you out like sheep into the midst of wolves; so be wise as serpents and innocent as doves. 17Beware of them, for they will hand you over to councils and flog you in their synagogues; 18and you will be dragged before governors and kings because of me, as a testimony to them and the Gentiles. 19When they hand you over, do not worry about how you are to speak or what you are to say; for what you are to say will be given to you at that time; 20for it is not you who speak, but the Spirit of your Father speaking through you. 21Brother will betray brother to death, and a father his child, and children will rise against parents and have them put to death; 22and you will be hated by all because of my name. But the one who endures to the end will be saved. 23When they persecute you in one town, flee to the next; for truly I tell you, you will not have gone through all the towns of Israel before the Son of Man comes.

24 "A disciple is not above the teacher, nor a slave above the master; 25it is enough for the disciple to be like the teacher, and the slave like the master. If they have called the master of the house Beelzebul, how much more will they malign those of his household!

Whom to Fear

26 "So have no fear of them; for nothing is covered up that will not be uncovered, and

---

a Other ancient authorities lack this verse   b Gk he   c Other ancient authorities read *Lebbaeus*, or *Lebbaeus called Thaddaeus* d Or *is at hand*   e The terms *leper* and *leprosy* can refer to several diseases

nothing secret that will not become known. [27]What I say to you in the dark, tell in the light; and what you hear whispered, proclaim from the housetops. [28]Do not fear those who kill the body but cannot kill the soul; rather fear him who can destroy both soul and body in hell.[a] [29]Are not two sparrows sold for a penny? Yet not one of them will fall to the ground apart from your Father. [30]And even the hairs of your head are all counted. [31]So do not be afraid; you are of more value than many sparrows.

[32] "Everyone therefore who acknowledges me before others, I also will acknowledge before my Father in heaven; [33]but whoever denies me before others, I also will deny before my Father in heaven.

Not Peace, but a Sword

[34] "Do not think that I have come to bring peace to the earth; I have not come to bring peace, but a sword.

[35] For I have come to set a man against his father,
   and a daughter against her mother,
   and a daughter-in-law against her mother-in-law;
[36] and one's foes will be members of one's own
      household.

[37]Whoever loves father or mother more than me is not worthy of me; and whoever loves son or daughter more than me is not worthy of me; [38]and whoever does not take up the cross and follow me is not worthy of me. [39]Those who find their life will lose it, and those who lose their life for my sake will find it.

Rewards

[40] "Whoever welcomes you welcomes me, and whoever welcomes me welcomes the one who sent me. [41]Whoever welcomes a prophet in the name of a prophet will receive a prophet's reward; and whoever welcomes a righteous person in the name of a righteous person will receive the reward of the righteous; [42]and whoever gives even a cup of cold water to one of these little ones in the name of a disciple—truly I tell you, none of these will lose their reward."

11 Now when Jesus had finished instructing his twelve disciples, he went on from there to teach and proclaim his message in their cities.

Messengers from John the Baptist

[2] When John heard in prison what the Messiah[b] was doing, he sent word by his[c] disciples [3]and said to him, "Are you the one who is to come, or are we to wait for another?" [4]Jesus answered them, "Go and tell John what you hear

A Violent Jesus?

Jesus says a curious thing as he prepares the Twelve for their mission: "I have not come to bring peace, but a sword" [Mt 10:34]. This is one of the many hard sayings attributed to Jesus in the Gospels. Jesus is speaking metaphorically to emphasize the extreme demands of discipleship. He is not advocating violence but simply predicting how people will react to the new values and way of life of his followers. The author of Matthew lived in a community that knew living as Jesus' disciples is not always simple or easy. The people wished for peace, but living by Jesus' words brought them hatred and conflict with people in power.

At the time Matthew was written, Christians needed to be able to give up everything, including family attachments, in order to follow Jesus. Is it any different today? What attachments would it be difficult for you to leave behind?

▶ **Mt 10:34–39**

and see: [5]the blind receive their sight, the lame walk, the lepers[d] are cleansed, the deaf hear, the dead are raised, and the poor have good news brought to them. [6]And blessed is anyone who takes no offense at me."

Jesus Praises John the Baptist

[7] As they went away, Jesus began to speak to the crowds about John: "What did you go out into the wilderness to look at? A reed shaken by the wind? [8]What then did you go out to see? Someone[e] dressed in soft robes? Look, those who wear soft robes are in royal palaces. [9]What then did you go out to see? A prophet?[f] Yes, I tell you, and more than a prophet. [10]This is the one about whom it is written,

'See, I am sending my messenger ahead of you,
   who will prepare your way before you.'

---

a Gk *Gehenna*   b Or *the Christ*   c Other ancient authorities read *two of his*   d The terms *leper* and *leprosy* can refer to several diseases   e Or *Why then did you go out?* To see someone f Other ancient authorities read *Why then did you go out? To see a prophet?*

MT

[11]Truly I tell you, among those born of women no one has arisen greater than John the Baptist; yet the least in the kingdom of heaven is greater than he. [12]From the days of John the Baptist until now the kingdom of heaven has suffered violence,[a] and the violent take it by force. [13]For all the prophets and the law prophesied until John came; [14]and if you are willing to accept it, he is Elijah who is to come. [15]Let anyone with ears[b] listen!

16 "But to what will I compare this generation? It is like children sitting in the marketplaces and calling to one another,

[17] 'We played the flute for you, and you did not
      dance;
    we wailed, and you did not mourn.'

[18]For John came neither eating nor drinking, and they say, 'He has a demon'; [19]the Son of Man came eating and drinking, and they say, 'Look, a glutton and a drunkard, a friend of tax collectors and sinners!' Yet wisdom is vindicated by her deeds."[c]

Woes to Unrepentant Cities

20 Then he began to reproach the cities in which most of his deeds of power had been done, because they did not repent. [21]"Woe to you, Chorazin! Woe to you, Bethsaida! For if the deeds of power done in you had been done in Tyre and Sidon, they would have repented long ago in sackcloth and ashes. [22]But I tell you, on the day of judgment it will be more tolerable for Tyre and Sidon than for you. [23]And you, Capernaum,

    will you be exalted to heaven?

No, you will be brought down to Hades.
For if the deeds of power done in you had been done in Sodom, it would have remained until this day. [24]But I tell you that on the day of judgment it will be more tolerable for the land of Sodom than for you."

Jesus Thanks His Father

25 At that time Jesus said, "I thank[d] you, Father, Lord of heaven and earth, because you have hidden these things from the wise and the intelligent and have revealed them to infants; [26]yes, Father, for such was your gracious will.[e] [27]All things have been handed over to me by my Father; and no one knows the Son except the Father, and no one knows the Father except the Son and anyone to whom the Son chooses to reveal him.

28 "Come to me, all you that are weary and are carrying heavy burdens, and I will give you rest. [29]Take my yoke upon you, and learn from me; for I am gentle and humble in heart, and you will find rest for your souls. [30]For my yoke is easy, and my burden is light."

Plucking Grain on the Sabbath

12 At that time Jesus went through the grainfields on the sabbath; his disciples were hungry, and they began to pluck heads of grain and to eat. [2]When the Pharisees saw it, they said to him, "Look, your disciples are doing what is not lawful to do on the sabbath." [3]He said to them, "Have you not read what David did when he and his companions were hungry? [4]He entered the house of God and ate the bread of the Presence, which it was not lawful for him or his companions to eat, but only for the priests. [5]Or have you not read in the law that on the sabbath the priests in the temple break the sabbath and yet are guiltless? [6]I tell you, something greater than the temple is here. [7]But if you had known what this means, 'I desire mercy and not sacrifice,' you would not have condemned the guiltless. [8]For the Son of Man is lord of the sabbath."

The Man with a Withered Hand

9 He left that place and entered their synagogue; [10]a man was there with a withered hand, and they asked him, "Is it lawful to cure on the sabbath?" so that they might accuse him. [11]He said to them, "Suppose one of you has only one sheep and it falls into a pit on the sabbath; will you not lay hold of it and lift it out? [12]How much more valuable is a human being than a sheep! So it is lawful to do good on the sabbath." [13]Then he said to the man, "Stretch out your hand." He stretched it out, and it was restored, as sound as the other. [14]But the Pharisees went out and conspired against him, how to destroy him.

God's Chosen Servant

15 When Jesus became aware of this, he departed. Many crowds[f] followed him, and he cured all of them, [16]and he ordered them not to make him known. [17]This was to fulfill what had been spoken through the prophet Isaiah:

[18] "Here is my servant, whom I have chosen,
      my beloved, with whom my soul is well
        pleased.
    I will put my Spirit upon him,
      and he will proclaim justice to the Gentiles.
[19] He will not wrangle or cry aloud,
      nor will anyone hear his voice in the streets.
[20] He will not break a bruised reed
      or quench a smoldering wick

---

a Or *has been coming violently*   b Other ancient authorities add *to hear*   c Other ancient authorities read *children*   d Or *praise*   e Or *for so it was well-pleasing in your sight*   f Other ancient authorities lack *crowds*

until he brings justice to victory.
21   And in his name the Gentiles will hope."

Jesus and Beelzebul

22 Then they brought to him a demoniac who was blind and mute; and he cured him, so that the one who had been mute could speak and see. 23All the crowds were amazed and said, "Can this be the Son of David?" 24But when the Pharisees heard it, they said, "It is only by Beelzebul, the ruler of the demons, that this fellow casts out the demons." 25He knew what they were thinking and said to them, "Every kingdom divided against itself is laid waste, and no city or house divided against itself will stand. 26If Satan casts out Satan, he is divided against himself; how then will his kingdom stand? 27If I cast out demons by Beelzebul, by whom do your own exorcists*a* cast them out? Therefore they will be your judges. 28But if it is by the Spirit of God that I cast out demons, then the kingdom of God has come to you. 29Or how can one enter a strong man's house and plunder his property, without first tying up the strong man? Then indeed the house can be plundered. 30Whoever is not with me is against me, and whoever does not gather with me scatters. 31Therefore I tell you, people will be forgiven for every sin and blasphemy, but blasphemy against the Spirit will not be forgiven. 32Whoever speaks a word against the Son of Man will be forgiven, but whoever speaks against the Holy Spirit will not be forgiven, either in this age or in the age to come.

A Tree and Its Fruit

33 "Either make the tree good, and its fruit good; or make the tree bad, and its fruit bad; for the tree is known by its fruit. 34You brood of vipers! How can you speak good things, when you are evil? For out of the abundance of the heart the mouth speaks. 35The good person brings good things out of a good treasure, and the evil person brings evil things out of an evil treasure. 36I tell you, on the day of judgment you will have to give an account for every careless word you utter; 37for by your words you will be justified, and by your words you will be condemned."

The Sign of Jonah

38 Then some of the scribes and Pharisees said to him, "Teacher, we wish to see a sign from you." 39But he answered them, "An evil and adulterous generation asks for a sign, but no sign will be given to it except the sign of the prophet Jonah. 40For just as Jonah was three days and three nights in the belly of the sea monster, so for three days and three nights the Son of Man will be in the heart of the earth. 41The people of Nineveh will rise up at the judgment with this generation and condemn it, because they repented at the proclamation of Jonah, and see, something greater than Jonah is here! 42The queen of the South will rise up at the judgment with this generation and condemn it, because she came from the ends of the earth to listen to the wisdom of Solomon, and see, something greater than Solomon is here!

The Return of the Unclean Spirit

43 "When the unclean spirit has gone out of a person, it wanders through waterless regions looking for a resting place, but it finds none. 44Then it says, 'I will return to my house from which I came.' When it comes, it finds it empty, swept, and put in order. 45Then it goes and brings along seven other spirits more evil than itself, and they enter and live there; and the last state of that person is worse than the first. So will it be also with this evil generation."

---

a Gk *sons*

Tripping over My Tongue

Just as a tree's fruit reveals whether the tree is good or bad, so also our words reveal much about our individual character. Unfortunately, swearing is all too common among young people today. For many it has become a habitual sin—a sin that is committed so frequently and casually that those who commit it sometimes don't even realize they're doing it! Yet, the words we choose to use say much about the person we are and the values that are at the core of our lives. When we swear, we carelessly neglect to honor the goodness that is inherent in our hearts, a goodness that has been within us since the moment we were created. Thus, we must strive to expand our vocabulary, choosing words that more fully reflect the treasure that is our life.

▶ Mt 12:33–37

The True Kindred of Jesus

46 While he was still speaking to the crowds, his mother and his brothers were standing outside, wanting to speak to him. [47]Someone told him, "Look, your mother and your brothers are standing outside, wanting to speak to you."[a] [48]But to the one who had told him this, Jesus[b] replied, "Who is my mother, and who are my brothers?" [49]And pointing to his disciples, he said, "Here are my mother and my brothers! [50]For whoever does the will of my Father in heaven is my brother and sister and mother."

The Parable of the Sower

13 That same day Jesus went out of the house and sat beside the sea. [2]Such great crowds gathered around him that he got into a boat and sat there, while the whole crowd stood on the beach. [3]And he told them many things in parables, saying: "Listen! A sower went out to sow. [4]And as he sowed, some seeds fell on the path, and the birds came and ate them up. [5]Other seeds fell on rocky ground, where they did not have much soil, and they sprang up quickly, since they had no depth of soil. [6]But when the sun rose, they were scorched; and since they had no root, they withered away. [7]Other seeds fell among thorns, and the thorns grew up and choked them. [8]Other seeds fell on good soil and brought forth grain, some a hundredfold, some sixty, some thirty. [9]Let anyone with ears[c] listen!"

The Purpose of the Parables

10 Then the disciples came and asked him, "Why do you speak to them in parables?" [11]He answered, "To you it has been given to know the secrets[d] of the kingdom of heaven, but to them

---

a Other ancient authorities lack verse 47   *b* Gk *he*   *c* Other ancient authorities add *to hear*   *d* Or *mysteries*

The Kingdom Is Like . . .

In trying to get people to understand something as mystifying and overwhelming as the kingdom of heaven, Jesus used ordinary objects, like seeds and light, salt and yeast. He chose everyday actions like farming, fishing, and baking. And in doing so, he helped the people of his time to understand the new life that comes with the kingdom of heaven. Using these metaphors, Jesus is also clear that the kingdom of heaven is not a place we are trying to get to but a reality we have to work to create here on earth. Heaven is living in perfect communion with Christ and all who believe in him forever.

What does the kingdom mean to you? Based on what you read in Matthew 13:10–53, meditate on the following questions:

- What would our world look like if it truly reflected Jesus' vision for the kingdom of heaven?
- What object, action, or image best describes your understanding of the kingdom of heaven?

End your meditation with a prayer that your life will be a living sign to help others understand what the kingdom of heaven is all about.

▶ **Mt 13:10–53**

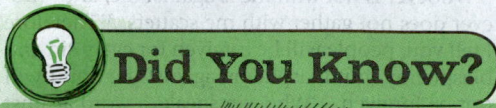

Parables

The Gospels frequently describe Jesus' teaching in parables. A parable is a literary form that uses a fictional story to make a point.

Many of Jesus' parables are like riddles. They have surprising or shocking endings designed to tease the people of his time into examining certain beliefs they took for granted. Unfortunately, the surprise of Jesus' parables is hard for some of us to understand today because we may be unfamiliar with the examples he used: baking bread, planting crops, herding sheep, or fishing for our supper.

Jesus also used parables to teach about God's Reign. These were often in the form of analogies comparing God's Reign to common things or events: "The kingdom of heaven is like . . ." Using parables, Jesus challenged powerful and educated people but was also understood by common people.

▶ **Mt 13:10**

it has not been given. [12]For to those who have, more will be given, and they will have an abundance; but from those who have nothing, even what they have will be taken away. [13]The reason I speak to them in parables is that 'seeing they do not perceive, and hearing they do not listen, nor do they understand.' [14]With them indeed is fulfilled the prophecy of Isaiah that says:

'You will indeed listen, but never understand,
    and you will indeed look, but never perceive.
[15] For this people's heart has grown dull,
    and their ears are hard of hearing,
    and they have shut their eyes;
     so that they might not look with their eyes,
    and listen with their ears,
and understand with their heart and turn—
    and I would heal them.'

[16]But blessed are your eyes, for they see, and your ears, for they hear. [17]Truly I tell you, many prophets and righteous people longed to see what you see, but did not see it, and to hear what you hear, but did not hear it.

The Parable of the Sower Explained

[18] "Hear then the parable of the sower. [19]When anyone hears the word of the kingdom and does not understand it, the evil one comes and snatches away what is sown in the heart; this is what was sown on the path. [20]As for what was sown on rocky ground, this is the one who hears the word and immediately receives it with joy; [21]yet such a person has no root, but endures only for a while, and when trouble or persecution arises on account of the word, that person immediately falls away.[a] [22]As for what was sown among thorns, this is the one who hears the word, but the cares of the world and the lure of wealth choke the word, and it yields nothing. [23]But as for what was sown on good soil, this is the one who hears the word and understands it, who indeed bears fruit and yields, in one case a hundredfold, in another sixty, and in another thirty."

The Parable of Weeds among the Wheat

[24] He put before them another parable: "The kingdom of heaven may be compared to someone who sowed good seed in his field; [25]but while everybody was asleep, an enemy came and sowed weeds among the wheat, and then went away. [26]So when the plants came up and bore grain, then the weeds appeared as well. [27]And the slaves of the householder came and said to him, 'Master, did you not sow good seed in your field? Where, then, did these weeds come from?' [28]He answered, 'An enemy has done this.' The slaves said to him, 'Then do you want us to go and gather them?' [29]But he replied, 'No; for in gathering the weeds you would uproot the wheat along with them. [30]Let both of them grow together until the harvest; and at harvest time I will tell the reapers, Collect the weeds first and bind them in bundles to be burned, but gather the wheat into my barn.' "

The Parable of the Mustard Seed

[31] He put before them another parable: "The kingdom of heaven is like a mustard seed that someone took and sowed in his field; [32]it is the smallest of all the seeds, but when it has grown it is the greatest of shrubs and becomes a tree, so that the birds of the air come and make nests in its branches."

The Parable of the Yeast

[33] He told them another parable: "The kingdom of heaven is like yeast that a woman took and mixed in with[b] three measures of flour until all of it was leavened."

The Use of Parables

[34] Jesus told the crowds all these things in parables; without a parable he told them nothing. [35]This was to fulfill what had been spoken through the prophet:[c]

"I will open my mouth to speak in parables;
   I will proclaim what has been hidden from
     the foundation of the world."[d]

Jesus Explains the Parable of the Weeds

[36] Then he left the crowds and went into the house. And his disciples approached him, saying, "Explain to us the parable of the weeds of the field." [37]He answered, "The one who sows the good seed is the Son of Man; [38]the field is the world, and the good seed are the children of the kingdom; the weeds are the children of the evil one, [39]and the enemy who sowed them is the devil; the harvest is the end of the age, and the reapers are angels. [40]Just as the weeds are collected and burned up with fire, so will it be at the end of the age. [41]The Son of Man will send his angels, and they will collect out of his kingdom all causes of sin and all evildoers, [42]and they will throw them into the furnace of fire, where there will be weeping and gnashing of teeth. [43]Then the righteous will shine like the sun in the kingdom of their Father. Let anyone with ears[e] listen!

---

a Gk stumbles   b Gk hid in   c Other ancient authorities read the prophet Isaiah   d Other ancient authorities lack of the world   e Other ancient authorities add to hear

Cultural Connection

The Carpenter's Son

In Matthew 13:55, Jesus is called the carpenter's son. The carpenter is Saint Joseph, who has two feast days attributed to him—May 1 and March 19. In Sicily, there is a custom called Saint Joseph's Altar. The custom began during a time of severe drought and famine in the Middle Ages. The Sicilian people offered intercessory prayers to Saint Joseph for rain so that their crops would grow. Eventually, their prayers were answered, the crops grew, and they harvested grains, fruits, and vegetables in abundance. In thanksgiving to Saint Joseph, the people gathered to share their harvest with the poor people of the area. Bread, wine, vegetables, fruits, eggs, and fish were placed on an altar and then distributed to those in need. The altar filled with the harvest came to be known as Saint Joseph's Altar.

This event is now celebrated annually in Sicily on March 19. Throughout the year, Sicilians also direct many other intercessions toward Saint Joseph, their patron saint. The Sicilians pray not only for good weather and crops but also for health, for family members and friends, and for all kinds of other personal intentions. On March 19, they show their gratitude to Saint Joseph by preparing a Saint Joseph's Altar and by celebrating their good fortune with one another and the community.

▶ Mt 13:55

Three Parables

44 "The kingdom of heaven is like treasure hidden in a field, which someone found and hid; then in his joy he goes and sells all that he has and buys that field.

45 "Again, the kingdom of heaven is like a merchant in search of fine pearls; 46on finding one pearl of great value, he went and sold all that he had and bought it.

47 "Again, the kingdom of heaven is like a net that was thrown into the sea and caught fish of every kind; 48when it was full, they drew it ashore, sat down, and put the good into baskets but threw out the bad. 49So it will be at the end of the age. The angels will come out and separate the evil from the righteous 50and throw them into the furnace of fire, where there will be weeping and gnashing of teeth.

Treasures New and Old

51 "Have you understood all this?" They answered, "Yes." 52And he said to them, "Therefore every scribe who has been trained for the kingdom of heaven is like the master of a household who brings out of his treasure what is new and what is old." 53When Jesus had finished these parables, he left that place.

The Rejection of Jesus at Nazareth

54 He came to his hometown and began to teach the people*a* in their synagogue, so that they were astounded and said, "Where did this man get this wisdom and these deeds of power? 55Is not this the carpenter's son? Is not his mother called Mary? And are not his brothers James and Joseph and Simon and Judas? 56And are not all his sisters with us? Where then did this man get all this?" 57And they took offense at him. But Jesus said to them, "Prophets are not without honor except in their own country and in their own house." 58And he did not do many deeds of power there, because of their unbelief.

The Death of John the Baptist

14 At that time Herod the ruler*b* heard reports about Jesus; 2and he said to his servants, "This is John the Baptist; he has been raised from the dead, and for this reason these powers are at work in him." 3For Herod had arrested John, bound him, and put him in prison on account

a Gk them *b* Gk tetrarch

14:1–12

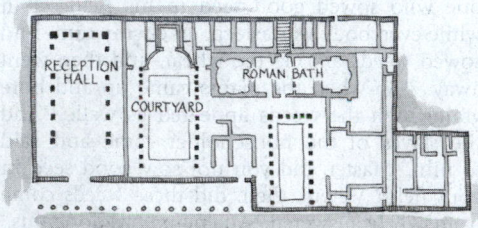

Herod's winter palace

of Herodias, his brother Philip's wife,[a] [4]because John had been telling him, "It is not lawful for you to have her." [5]Though Herod[b] wanted to put him to death, he feared the crowd, because they regarded him as a prophet. [6]But when Herod's birthday came, the daughter of Herodias danced before the company, and she pleased Herod [7]so much that he promised on oath to grant her whatever she might ask. [8]Prompted by her mother, she said, "Give me the head of John the Baptist here on a platter." [9]The king was grieved, yet out of regard for his oaths and for the guests, he commanded it to be given; [10]he sent and had John beheaded in the prison. [11]The head was brought on a platter and given to the girl, who brought it to her mother. [12]His disciples came and took the body and buried it; then they went and told Jesus.

Feeding the Five Thousand

13 Now when Jesus heard this, he withdrew from there in a boat to a deserted place by himself. But when the crowds heard it, they followed him on foot from the towns. [14]When he went ashore, he saw a great crowd; and he had compassion for them and cured their sick. [15]When it was evening, the disciples came to him and said, "This is a deserted place, and the hour is now late; send the crowds away so that they may go into the villages and buy food for themselves." [16]Jesus said to them, "They need not go away; you give them something to eat." [17]They replied, "We have nothing here but five loaves and two fish." [18]And he said, "Bring them here to me." [19]Then he ordered the crowds to sit down on the grass. Taking the five loaves and the two fish, he looked up to heaven, and blessed and broke the loaves, and gave them to the disciples, and the disciples gave them to the crowds. [20]And all ate and were filled; and they took up what was left over of the broken pieces, twelve baskets full. [21]And those who ate were about five thousand men, besides women and children.

Jesus Walks on the Water

22 Immediately he made the disciples get into the boat and go on ahead to the other side, while he dismissed the crowds. [23]And after he had dismissed the crowds, he went up the mountain by himself to pray. When evening came, he was there alone, [24]but by this time the boat, battered by the waves, was far from the land,[c] for the wind was against them. [25]And early in the morning he came walking toward them on the sea. [26]But when the disciples saw him walking on the sea, they were terrified, saying, "It is a ghost!" And they cried out

in fear. [27]But immediately Jesus spoke to them and said, "Take heart, it is I; do not be afraid."

28 Peter answered him, "Lord, if it is you, command me to come to you on the water." [29]He said, "Come." So Peter got out of the boat, started walking on the water, and came toward Jesus. [30]But when he noticed the strong wind,[d] he became frightened, and beginning to sink, he cried out, "Lord, save me!" [31]Jesus immediately reached out his hand and caught him, saying to him, "You of little faith, why did you doubt?"

---

a Other ancient authorities read *his brother's wife*   b Gk *he*   c Other ancient authorities read *was out on the sea*   d Other ancient authorities read *the wind*

Do You Trust Jesus?

At this point in the Gospel of Matthew, different groups are beginning to line up for or against Jesus. The Pharisees, Sadducees, and scribes do not trust him. The disciples still follow Jesus, but they do not yet understand who he really is. In chapters 14–17, through several signs and wonders, the true identity of Jesus is revealed to the disciples. Peter in particular is being prepared for his role as leader.

Of the four Gospels, only Matthew includes the story of Peter's walking on the water. If you have gotten acquainted with Peter (see "Introducing Peter the Rock," near Mt 16:13–20), it will not surprise you that he was willing to take the risk. But why does Peter start to sink? When he is focused on Jesus, everything is fine. It is when he takes his eyes off Jesus, noticing the fierce wind, that he begins to sink.

Jesus invites you to risk a relationship with him. You have to step out in faith, maybe leaving some old ways of life behind. Learn from Peter to keep your focus on Jesus. As the disciples learned, this is no ordinary man but the Son of God! Following Jesus might get scary or difficult at times, but all great adventures involve some risk.

▶ Mt 14:22–33

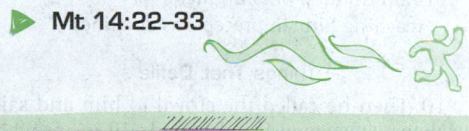

Cultural Connection

A Prayer for Healing Humankind

In Matthew 15:1–20, Jesus addresses the hypocrisy of the Jewish leaders who manipulate the Law to their own good. They and the people who follow them are blind to the results of their evil intentions. In this prayer, the Ojibwa (or Anishinabe) recognize the need for humans to overcome the evil that resides within the human heart:

Grandfather,
Look at our brokenness.
We know that in all creation
Only the human family
Has strayed from the Sacred
  Way.
We know that we are the
  ones
Who must come back
  together
To walk in the Sacred Way.
Grandfather,
Sacred One,

Teach us love, compassion,
  and honor
That we may heal the earth
And heal each other.

▶ Mt 15:1–20

32When they got into the boat, the wind ceased. 33And those in the boat worshiped him, saying, "Truly you are the Son of God."

Jesus Heals the Sick in Gennesaret

34 When they had crossed over, they came to land at Gennesaret. 35After the people of that place recognized him, they sent word throughout the region and brought all who were sick to him, 36and begged him that they might touch even the fringe of his cloak; and all who touched it were healed.

The Tradition of the Elders

15 Then Pharisees and scribes came to Jesus from Jerusalem and said, 2"Why do your disciples break the tradition of the elders? For they do not wash their hands before they eat." 3He answered them, "And why do you break the commandment of God for the sake of your tradition? 4For God said,*a* 'Honor your father and your mother,' and, 'Whoever speaks evil of father or mother must surely die.' 5But you say that whoever tells father or mother, 'Whatever support you might have had from me is given to God,'*b* then that person need not honor the father.*c* 6So, for the sake of your tradition, you make void the word*d* of God. 7You hypocrites! Isaiah prophesied rightly about you when he said:

8 'This people honors me with their lips,
    but their hearts are far from me;
9 in vain do they worship me,
    teaching human precepts as doctrines.' "

Things That Defile

10 Then he called the crowd to him and said to them, "Listen and understand: 11it is not what goes into the mouth that defiles a person, but it is what comes out of the mouth that defiles." 12Then the disciples approached and said to him, "Do you know that the Pharisees took offense when they heard what you said?" 13He answered, "Every plant that my heavenly Father has not planted will be uprooted. 14Let them alone; they are blind guides of the blind.*e* And if one blind person guides another, both will fall into a pit." 15But Peter said to him, "Explain this parable to us." 16Then he said, "Are you also still without understanding? 17Do you not see that whatever goes into the mouth enters the stomach, and goes out into the sewer? 18But what comes out of the mouth proceeds from the heart, and this is what defiles. 19For out of the heart come evil intentions, murder, adultery, fornication, theft, false witness, slander. 20These are what defile a person, but to eat with unwashed hands does not defile."

The Canaanite Woman's Faith

21 Jesus left that place and went away to the district of Tyre and Sidon. 22Just then a Canaanite woman from that region came out and started shouting, "Have mercy on me, Lord, Son of David; my daughter is tormented by a demon." 23But he did not answer her at all. And his disciples came and urged him, saying, "Send her away, for she keeps shouting after us." 24He answered, "I was sent only to the lost sheep of the house of Israel." 25But she came and knelt before him, saying, "Lord, help me." 26He answered, "It

---

a Other ancient authorities read *commanded, saying*   b Or *is an offering*   c Other ancient authorities add *or the mother*   d Other ancient authorities read *law*; others, *commandment*   e Other ancient authorities lack *of the blind*

is not fair to take the children's food and throw it to the dogs." ²⁷She said, "Yes, Lord, yet even the dogs eat the crumbs that fall from their masters' table." ²⁸Then Jesus answered her, "Woman, great is your faith! Let it be done for you as you wish." And her daughter was healed instantly.

Jesus Cures Many People

29 After Jesus had left that place, he passed along the Sea of Galilee, and he went up the mountain, where he sat down. ³⁰Great crowds came to him, bringing with them the lame, the maimed, the blind, the mute, and many others. They put them at his feet, and he cured them, ³¹so that the crowd was amazed when they saw the mute speaking, the maimed whole, the lame walking, and the blind seeing. And they praised the God of Israel.

Feeding the Four Thousand

32 Then Jesus called his disciples to him and said, "I have compassion for the crowd, because they have been with me now for three days and have nothing to eat; and I do not want to send them away hungry, for they might faint on the way." ³³The disciples said to him, "Where are we to get enough bread in the desert to feed so great a crowd?" ³⁴Jesus asked them, "How many loaves have you?" They said, "Seven, and a few small fish." ³⁵Then ordering the crowd to sit down on the ground, ³⁶he took the seven loaves and the fish; and after giving thanks he broke them and gave them to the disciples, and the disciples gave them to the crowds. ³⁷And all of them ate and were filled; and they took up the broken pieces left over, seven baskets full. ³⁸Those who had eaten were four thousand men, besides women and children. ³⁹After sending away the crowds, he got into the boat and went to the region of Magadan.ᵃ

The Demand for a Sign

16 The Pharisees and Sadducees came, and to test Jesusᵇ they asked him to show them a sign from heaven. ²He answered them, "When it is evening, you say, 'It will be fair weather, for the sky is red.' ³And in the morning, 'It will be stormy today, for the sky is red and threatening.' You know how to interpret the appearance of the sky, but you cannot interpret the signs of the times.'ᶜ ⁴An evil and adulterous generation asks for a sign, but no sign will be given to it except the sign of Jonah." Then he left them and went away.

The Yeast of the Pharisees and Sadducees

5 When the disciples reached the other side, they had forgotten to bring any bread. ⁶Jesus said

to them, "Watch out, and beware of the yeast of the Pharisees and Sadducees." ⁷They said to one another, "It is because we have brought no bread." ⁸And becoming aware of it, Jesus said, "You of little faith, why are you talking about having no bread? ⁹Do you still not perceive? Do you not remember the five loaves for the five thousand, and how many baskets you gathered? ¹⁰Or the seven loaves for the four thousand, and how many baskets you gathered? ¹¹How could you fail to perceive that I was not speaking about bread? Beware of the yeast of the Pharisees and

---

a Other ancient authorities read *Magdala* or *Magdalan*   b Gk *him*
c Other ancient authorities lack ²*When it is . . . of the times*

Peter the Rock

What images does the name Saint Peter bring to your mind? The simple fisherman named Simon who was among the first disciples called by Jesus (see Mt 4:18, Mk 1:16; Lk 5:10)? the hopeful believer who first recognized Jesus as the Messiah (see Mt 16:16, Mk 8:29, Lk 9:20)? the fearful friend who denied Jesus three times (see Mt 26:69–74, Mk 14:66–72, Lk 22:54–61, Jn 18:15–27)? the leader of the early Church, whom we recognize as the first Pope (see Jn 21:15, Acts 2:14)? Peter is all these things and more. The Bible paints a picture of a very human leader with sins and weaknesses along with many gifts and great faith.

The author of Matthew uses a play on words to make a statement about Peter as the foundation of the Church. The new name Jesus gives him—Peter—means "rock." So Jesus is saying, "You are a rock, and on this rock I will build my church" (see Mt 16:18). The Catholic Church uses this Scripture passage as support for its teaching on the Pope's position as the spiritual leader and highest authority of the Church. Peter's primacy as the first of Jesus' Apostles is understood to be passed on to the current Pope, through the succession of popes who go back to the beginnings of the Church at Rome.

▶ **Mt 16:13–20**

✝ Catholic Connection

The Church

Even after Jesus has been teaching and performing miracles for a while, people are still confused about his identity. So Jesus turns to the disciples and asks, "Who do you say that I am?" (Mt 16:15). Peter alone answers correctly, saying Jesus is the Messiah. As a result, Jesus tells Peter that he is clearly blessed and then proceeds to tell Peter that he will build the Church upon him and give him the keys to the kingdom of heaven!

Two thousand years later, the Catholic Church still recognizes the authority of Peter through Peter's successor the Pope, the Bishop of Rome. Just as Peter was the leader and sign of unity for the disciples, the Pope serves as the leader and sign of unity for the bishops and all the faithful. As the leader, the Pope has ultimate authority over the Church as both pastor and teacher. The Pope is also blessed just like Peter. For example, when the Pope makes an official declaration of doctrine addressing faith and morals, God ensures the truth of the doctrine. We call this papal infallibility.

As the Pope is the successor of Peter, the bishops are the successors of the Apostles. Each bishop is responsible for leading and ministering to the people within their own area, called a diocese. Under the authority of the bishop are the priests and deacons who aid him in his duties to care for the faithful. The bishops also work together in union with the Pope to address issues concerning the wider Church.

In addition to those already mentioned, the Catholic Church consists of people living a consecrated life. Those in consecrated life are not ordained but have dedicated their lives to a unique form of service to the Lord. Among them are nuns and brothers who have taken various vows, or promises, to live a certain lifestyle dedicated to Christ.

Finally, the main body of the Church, or the largest group, is the laity. The laity are those members who are not ordained or living a consecrated life. The laity has its own role to play in the mission of the Church. These individuals are called to seek the Reign of God in their everyday lives at school, work, or with family. They are called to proclaim the Good News and often may be the first or only ones able to bring the Good News to someone. By virtue of their Baptism, the laity are also able to bless the world by uniting their everyday lives to the sacrifice Christ made on the cross and by offering their lives to God.

Together all the different roles in the Church work together as one to bear witness that Jesus is the Son of God, the Messiah.

▶ **Mt 16:13–20**
Catechism, nos. 871–945

Cultural Connection

The Principle of *Ujamaa*

A man who won't die for something is not fit to live. [Martin Luther King Jr.]

Jesus tells us that we need to leave behind our old lives of selfishness and embrace a new way of life marked by caring about the needs of others. Only then can the Spirit of the Lord abound. Martin Luther King Jr. practiced this new way of life in his dream for a better day for African Americans—a dream he was willing to work and die for.

The Kwanzaa principle of *ujamaa*, or cooperative economics, requires this kind of selfless love for others. To practice *ujamaa* means to share resources with our brothers and sisters, to support one another's businesses, and to live so that everybody receives what they need to prosper. Jesus' words challenge us to build up our communities, preserving the gains we have made and laying foundations for the success of those who come after us. The

cost is our me-first attitudes, but the reward is a new life of justice and freedom.

Dear God, my humanness wants to hoard myself; my spirit wants to give!

▶ **Mt 16:25**

M
T

Sadducees!" ¹²Then they understood that he had not told them to beware of the yeast of bread, but of the teaching of the Pharisees and Sadducees.

Peter's Declaration about Jesus

13 Now when Jesus came into the district of Caesarea Philippi, he asked his disciples, "Who do people say that the Son of Man is?" ¹⁴And they said, "Some say John the Baptist, but others Elijah, and still others Jeremiah or one of the prophets." ¹⁵He said to them, "But who do you say that I am?" ¹⁶Simon Peter answered, "You are the Messiah,ᵃ the Son of the living God." ¹⁷And Jesus answered him, "Blessed are you, Simon son of Jonah! For flesh and blood has not revealed this to you, but my Father in heaven. ¹⁸And I tell you, you are Peter,ᵇ and on this rockᶜ I will build my church, and the gates of Hades will not prevail against it. ¹⁹I will give you the keys of the kingdom of heaven, and whatever you bind on earth will be bound in heaven, and whatever you loose on earth will be loosed in heaven." ²⁰Then he sternly ordered the disciples not to tell anyone that he wasᵈ the Messiah.ᵃ

Jesus Foretells His Death and Resurrection

21 From that time on, Jesus began to show his disciples that he must go to Jerusalem and undergo great suffering at the hands of the elders and chief priests and scribes, and be killed, and on the third day be raised. ²²And Peter took him aside and began to rebuke him, saying, "God forbid it, Lord! This must never happen to you."

²³But he turned and said to Peter, "Get behind me, Satan! You are a stumbling block to me; for you are setting your mind not on divine things but on human things."

The Cross and Self-Denial

24 Then Jesus told his disciples, "If any want to become my followers, let them deny themselves and take up their cross and follow me. ²⁵For those who want to save their life will lose it, and those who lose their life for my sake will find it. ²⁶For what will it profit them if they gain the whole world but forfeit their life? Or what will they give in return for their life?

27 "For the Son of Man is to come with his angels in the glory of his Father, and then he will repay everyone for what has been done. ²⁸Truly I tell you, there are some standing here who will not taste death before they see the Son of Man coming in his kingdom."

The Transfiguration

17 Six days later, Jesus took with him Peter and James and his brother John and led them up a high mountain, by themselves, ²And he was transfigured before them, and his face shone like the sun, and his clothes became dazzling white. ³Suddenly there appeared to them Moses and Elijah, talking with him. ⁴Then Peter said to Jesus, "Lord, it is good for us to be here;

---

a Or *the Christ*   *b* Gk *Petros*   *c* Gk *petra*   *d* Other ancient authorities add *Jesus*

✝ Catholic Connection

The Old Testament and the New Testament

The word *old* can often be taken to mean "outdated" or "no longer useful." Unfortunately, some people assume those meanings when they hear the words *Old Testament*. But the Gospel of Matthew is very clear that the Old Testament is indeed relevant (see 5:17–20) and that Jesus is its fulfillment.

Consider the story of the Transfiguration in Matthew's Gospel, which is packed with allusions and references to the Old Testament. According to the Gospel, the event took place on a mountain, which immediately calls to mind Moses' meeting with God and establishing the covenant on Mount Sinai (see Ex 24:12–18). The Gospel of Matthew also says that Moses (who represents the law) and Elijah (who represents the prophets) appeared with Jesus on the mountain; their presence highlights how Jesus' work is in agreement with the Old Testament law and prophets. Another allusion can be found in the cloud that accompanies God's presence during the scene, a cloud much like the one that led the Israelites during their wanderings in the desert (see Ex 40:34–37). A final reference to the Old Testament can be found in God's words commanding the disciples to listen to Jesus. This fulfills a prophecy in Deuteronomy, which states that God would deliver a prophet who would speak God's words and all are called to listen to him (see Deut 18:15–22).

From apostolic times to the present, the Catholic Church has continued to affirm the relevance and importance of the Old Testament. The Church teaches that from the beginning of creation to the sending of Jesus and the Holy Spirit, God gradually revealed himself and his plan for our salvation. Because God's one plan spans both the Old and New Testaments, the Church accepts and honors the natural unity of the two testaments. The Old Testament lays the foundation and prophesies the coming of Christ. The New Testament is the fulfillment of the prophecies and contains the story and teachings of Jesus Christ. Together the two testaments are read in light of each other, meaning we need to study both to fully understand God's plan for our salvation.

▶ **Mt 17:1–13**
Catechism, nos. 120–137

if you wish, I[a] will make three dwellings[b] here, one for you, one for Moses, and one for Elijah." [5]While he was still speaking, suddenly a bright cloud overshadowed them, and from the cloud a voice said, "This is my Son, the Beloved;[c] with him I am well pleased; listen to him!" [6]When the disciples heard this, they fell to the ground and were overcome by fear. [7]But Jesus came and touched them, saying, "Get up and do not be afraid." [8]And when they looked up, they saw no one except Jesus himself alone.

9 As they were coming down the mountain, Jesus ordered them, "Tell no one about the vision until after the Son of Man has been raised from the dead." [10]And the disciples asked him, "Why, then, do the scribes say that Elijah must come first?" [11]He replied, "Elijah is indeed coming and will restore all things; [12]but I tell you that Elijah has already come, and they did not recognize him, but they did to him whatever they pleased. So also the Son of Man is about to suffer at their hands." [13]Then the disciples understood that he was speaking to them about John the Baptist.

Jesus Cures a Boy with a Demon

14 When they came to the crowd, a man came to him, knelt before him, [15]and said, "Lord, have mercy on my son, for he is an epileptic and he suffers terribly; he often falls into the fire and often into the water. [16]And I brought him to your disciples, but they could not cure him." [17]Jesus answered, "You faithless and perverse generation, how much longer must I be with you? How much longer must I put up with you? Bring him here to me." [18]And Jesus rebuked the demon,[d] and it[e] came out of him, and the boy was cured instantly. [19]Then the disciples came to Jesus privately and said, "Why could we not cast it out?" [20]He said to them, "Because of your little faith. For truly I tell you, if you have faith the size of a[f] mustard seed, you will say to this mountain, 'Move from here to there,' and it will move; and nothing will be impossible for you."[g]

Jesus Again Foretells His Death and Resurrection

22 As they were gathering[h] in Galilee, Jesus said to them, "The Son of Man is going to be betrayed into human hands, [23]and they will kill him, and on the third day he will be raised." And they were greatly distressed.

Jesus and the Temple Tax

24 When they reached Capernaum, the collectors of the temple tax[i] came to Peter and said, "Does your teacher not pay the temple tax?"[i]

[25]He said, "Yes, he does." And when he came home, Jesus spoke of it first, asking, "What do you think, Simon? From whom do kings of the earth take toll or tribute? From their children or from others?" [26]When Peter[j] said, "From others," Jesus said to him, "Then the children are free. [27]However, so that we do not give offense to them, go to the sea and cast a hook; take the first fish that comes up; and when you open its mouth, you will find a coin;[k] take that and give it to them for you and me."

True Greatness

18 At that time the disciples came to Jesus and asked, "Who is the greatest in the kingdom of heaven?" [2]He called a child, whom he put among them, [3]and said, "Truly I tell you, unless you change and become like children, you will never enter the kingdom of heaven. [4]Whoever becomes humble like this child is the greatest in the kingdom of heaven. [5]Whoever welcomes one such child in my name welcomes me.

Temptations to Sin

6 "If any of you put a stumbling block before one of these little ones who believe in me, it would be better for you if a great millstone were fastened around your neck and you were drowned in the depth of the sea. [7]Woe to the world because of stumbling blocks! Occasions for stumbling are bound to come, but woe to the one by whom the stumbling block comes!

8 "If your hand or your foot causes you to stumble, cut it off and throw it away; it is better for you to enter life maimed or lame than to have two hands or two feet and to be thrown into the eternal fire. [9]And if your eye causes you to stumble, tear it out and throw it away; it is better for you to enter life with one eye than to have two eyes and to be thrown into the hell[l] of fire.

The Parable of the Lost Sheep

10 "Take care that you do not despise one of these little ones; for, I tell you, in heaven their angels continually see the face of my Father in heaven.[m] [12]What do you think? If a shepherd has a hundred sheep, and one of them has gone astray, does he not leave the ninety-nine on the mountains and go in search of the one that went

a Other ancient authorities read we   b Or tents   c Or my beloved Son   d Gk it or him   e Gk the demon   f Gk faith as a grain of   g Other ancient authorities add verse 21, But this kind does not come out except by prayer and fasting   h Other ancient authorities read living   i Gk didrachma   j Gk he   k Gk stater; the stater was worth two didrachmas   l Gk Gehenna   m Other ancient authorities add verse 11, For the Son of Man came to save the lost

Cultural Connection

Santo Niño

The feast of Santo Niño, which means "Holy Child," is celebrated in the Philippines on the Sunday after the feast of the Baptism of the Lord. The beginning of chapter 18 of Matthew is one of the readings you might hear at Mass that day. The feast of Santo Niño celebrates Jesus as a child and is associated with a special statue. The statue portrays the child Jesus wearing a crown, red pants, and a white robe with a large triangular red collar flaring out from the shoulders. The statue can be found in many Philippine churches and on many car dashboards.

The original Santo Niño statue was made in Belgium and sent to a girl in the Philippines as a gift for her Baptism. Then it was lost for twenty-four years, until, during a battle, a soldier found it unharmed in the flaming ruins of a house. Folklore says that the statue once protected the island of Cebu from English invaders and that when the statue was placed in the sea during a drought, it miraculously began to rain.

The devotion to Santo Niño can help us to remember that Jesus was once a child who was taught and cared for by loving parents. In the spirit of Santo Niño, why not surprise a parent or grandparent with a love letter thanking him or her for all he or she has done for you?

 Mt 18:1–10

---

astray? [13]And if he finds it, truly I tell you, he rejoices over it more than over the ninety-nine that never went astray. [14]So it is not the will of your[a] Father in heaven that one of these little ones should be lost.

Reproving Another Who Sins

[15] "If another member of the church[b] sins against you,[c] go and point out the fault when the two of you are alone. If the member listens to you, you have regained that one.[d] [16]But if you are not listened to, take one or two others along with you, so that every word may be confirmed by the evidence of two or three witnesses. [17]If the member refuses to listen to them, tell it to the church; and if the offender refuses to listen even to the church, let such a one be to you as a Gentile and a tax collector. [18]Truly I tell you, whatever you bind on earth will be bound in heaven, and whatever you loose on earth will be loosed in heaven. [19]Again, truly I tell you, if two of you agree on earth about anything you ask, it will be done for you by my Father in heaven. [20]For where two or three are gathered in my name, I am there among them."

Forgiveness

[21] Then Peter came and said to him, "Lord, if another member of the church[e] sins against me, how often should I forgive? As many as seven times?" [22]Jesus said to him, "Not seven times, but, I tell you, seventy-seven[f] times.

The Parable of the Unforgiving Servant

[23] "For this reason the kingdom of heaven may be compared to a king who wished to settle accounts with his slaves. [24]When he began the reckoning, one who owed him ten thousand talents[g] was brought to him; [25]and, as he could not pay, his lord ordered him to be sold, together with his wife and children and all his possessions, and payment to be made. [26]So the slave fell on his knees before him, saying, 'Have patience with me, and I will pay you everything.' [27]And out of pity for him, the lord of that slave released him and forgave him the debt. [28]But that same slave, as he went out, came upon one of his fellow slaves who owed him a hundred denarii;[h] and seizing him by the throat, he said, 'Pay what you owe.' [29]Then his fellow slave fell down and pleaded with him, 'Have patience with me, and I will pay you.' [30]But he refused; then he went and threw him into prison until he would pay the debt. [31]When his fellow slaves saw what had happened, they were greatly distressed, and they went and reported to their lord all that had taken place. [32]Then his lord summoned him and said to him, 'You wicked slave! I forgave you all

---

a Other ancient authorities read *my* b Gk *If your brother*
c Other ancient authorities lack *against you* d Gk *the brother*
e Gk *if my brother* f Or *seventy times seven* g A talent was worth more than fifteen years' wages of a laborer h The denarius was the usual day's wage for a laborer

Old Testament Biblical Images

This statue of Ramses III, an **Egyptian Pharaoh,** was found in the ancient Canaanite city of Bet She'an, located on the Jordon River. The Egyptian Empire controlled Palestine for many centuries before the Kingdom of Israel was formed.

The **Sinai Desert** is on a triangle-shaped peninsula located between the Mediterranean Sea and the Red Sea. In the Scriptures it is often referred to as Horeb, meaning waste or wilderness (Ex 17:6). Moses and the Israelites wandered in the desert for forty years before reaching the Promised Land.

This massive stone structure was discovered in recent excavations of the **City of David.** Dating back to around the 10th century BCE, it is possibly a public building that existed during the time of the united kingdom of David and Solomon (2 Sam 5:6–10).

During Hezekiah's reforms all **high places** and **pagan altars,** similar to the one pictured in the photo were destroyed (1 Kings 18:1–4; 2 Chr 31:1).

In anticipation of the Assyrian assault on Jerusalem, Hezekiah had a tunnel cut through solid rock from outside the city walls to bring water into the city. This photo shows the entrance to **Hezekiah's tunnel** at the **Spring of Gihon** (2 Chr 32:30).

During the reign of Zedekiah, Nebuchadrezzar and his army destroyed the Temple and the city of Jerusalem and exiled the Israelites to Babylon, where they remained in **Babylonian captivity** for over a generation (Jer 52:1–30).

New Testament Biblical Images

The **Sea of Galilee** is where Jesus began his ministry and first called his disciples (Mt 4:12–22).

The Second **Temple** is presented here in a scale model as it would have appeared in Jerusalem at about the year AD 20. The Second Temple is where Mary and Joseph found the twelve-year-old Jesus conversing with the teachers (Lk 2:41–52) and where Jesus upset the trading of the money changers and the vendors (Mt 21:12–17; Mk 11:15–19; Lk 19:45–47; Jn 2:12–25). It was built to replace Solomon's Temple when the people of Israel returned from exile.

The **Mount of Olives** is directly across the Kidron Valley from the City of Jerusalem. This is where Jesus went to pray with his disciples before his arrest (Mt 26:36–46; Mk 14:32–42; Lk 22:39–46).

An **ablution basin** was used for ritual washing. This basin is in the Church of Saint Peter in Gallicantu on Mount Zion outside Jerusalem. Gallicantu is Latin for "cock crow". The church commemorates Peter's denial of Jesus and his subsequent repentance. How do you express sorrow for your sins?

This ancient **amphitheater at Caesarea** was built by Herod the Great and had a seating capacity of 3,500. All that remains is the seating and backstage area of this once magnificent theatre. But these were so well constructed that it is used for performances today! Caesarea was the center of Roman government in Palestine for over six hundred years. Both Philip and Peter preached the message of Jesus Christ to the people of Caesarea (Acts 8:40; 10:1—11:18).

This is an entrance to a **burial tomb** carved out of rock. The round stone is rolled in front of the opening to seal the tomb. The tomb Jesus was buried in was probably similar to this (Mt 27:57–61).

Titles of Jesus of Nazareth

Christology attempts to give language to the great mystery of Jesus, the Christ. Those who wrote the Gospels hoped to honor him with names, words, and titles that speak to our faith in Jesus.

Title	Significance and Reference
Jesus	*Yeshua* (or Joshua) in Hebrew, it means "God saves" (Mt 1:21; Lk 1:31).
Son of Mary	Identifies Jesus as born of woman and fully human (Mt 1:18; Lk 1:26–31)
Rabbi or Rabbouni	Jesus was a Jewish wisdom teacher, healer, and scholar of the Torah. His disciples honored him as Master (Mk 9:5; 10:51; Jn 3:2; 20:16).
Carpenter	Jesus was a craftsman who served with his father Joseph (Mt 13:55; Mk 6:3).
Messiah (Christ in Greek)	Christ (*Mashia* in Hebrew) means "anointed one" and is a title used for kings, prophets, and war heroes. Jesus was the Messiah who freed humanity from the bondage of slavery and from the pain and despair of sin. Over the centuries, this title honored Jesus' divinity (Mt 1:1,18; 16:16; Mk 1:1; 8:29; Jn 4:25–26; Acts 2:38).
King of the Jews	Jesus was born of David's royal line. Angels, shepherds, and the Magi adored the newborn king. Pilate mocked him with this title that he nailed to the cross of Christ (Mt 2:2; Mk 15:2; Lk 23:38; Jn 19:19).
Son (Root) of David	Jesus is a descendant of Israel's great King David, the fulfillment of the prophecy of Nathan who said the Covenant would remain with the house of David (2 Sam 7:11–16; Mt 1:1; 12:23; Lk 18:38; Rev 5:5).
Son of Abraham	Jesus is the descendant of Israel's great patriarch and shares in the election of Israel and the eternal covenant (Mt 1:1; Lk 3:34; Jn 8:58).
Son of Man Bar Nasa	*Bar Nasa* is Aramaic for Son of Man. Jesus and the evangelists of the Gospels used this divine title to describe Jesus' triune relationship in God (Mt 12:8; 16:13–16; Lk 6:5).
	Jesus used this title for himself when he spoke of his mission and of his Passion to come (Mt 8:20; 17:9; 19:28; Lk 9:22,58; 18:8).
	The Son of Man came as the "human one" from heaven with the authority to forgive sin (Mt 9:6; 12:32; Mk 2:10; Lk 5:24; 12:10; Jn 3:13).
	The Son of Man will be betrayed and handed over (Mt 17:12,22–23; 26:24).
	The Son of Man will be condemned, die, be buried, and offer his life to redeem many (Mt 20:18–19,28; Mk 9:31).
	The Son of Man will rise from the dead (Mk 9:9).
	There will be signs of the coming of the Son of Man (Mt 24:27,37,39,44).
	The Son of Man will be glorified, honored before angels, and send angels to earth (Mt 13:41; 16:27; 25:31; Lk 12:8; Jn 1:51; 12:23; 13:31).
	The Son of Man will judge the living and the dead and herald in a new age in glory (Mt 19:28, 26:64; Lk 22:69; Jn 5:26–29).
Son of God	Jesus is the Incarnation of the divine—Son of the Most High (Mt 4:3; 14:33; 27:54; Mk 3:11; Lk 1:32; Jn 20:31).
Savior	Jesus is savior of the world; the one who releases humanity from bondage, from sin and death, a form of Messiah or Christ (Lk 2:11; Jn 4:42).
	Israel's deliverer; the Redeemer; the God of history and of Israel revealed in Christ (Acts 13:23).
	As savior, Jesus grants forgiveness of sin (Acts 5:31).
The Lord; I am	Jesus Christ is Lord, the Glory of God, the manifestation of Yahweh among us. Jesus is the perfect image of true humanity. The one who calls us into eternal life (Mt 1:23; Lk 1:66; Jn 11:25–27; 20:28–29; Acts 2:36; Col 2:9–10; Phil 2:11).
	Jesus is the "I am" of Yahweh; the bread of life; the light of the world; the door, the gate; the Good Shepherd; the resurrection and life; the way, the truth, and the life (Jn 6:35; 8:12; 10:7,11; 11:25; 14:6).
Lamb of God	The worthy sacrifice who frees humanity from sin, who was slain, and who takes away grief (Jn 1:29,36; Rev 5:6; 17:14)
Word of God	Jesus is the word (logos) of God in the flesh. Jesus is the alpha and the omega; the beginning and end of all creation, the pre-existent one (Jn 1:1–3; Rev 19:13; 21:6).

Gospel Comparisons

	Mark	Matthew	Luke	John
Writer	Mark: A second generation Christian, possibly a follower of Peter; traditionally the John Mark of Acts	Matthew: An unknown Jewish Christian, traditionally the Apostle Matthew	Luke: A Gentile Christian, traditionally Luke the physician and Paul's traveling companion	John: The beloved disciple, the Apostle John, or his disciple
Date Written	65–70 CE	75–80 CE	80–85 CE	90–110 CE
Images of Christ	The suffering servant of God, Son of Man, Son of God, Messiah, and Lord	Teacher and prophet like Moses, Son of God, Son of Man, Messiah, and Lord	Great healer, merciful, compassion for the poor, Son of God, Son of Man, Messiah, and Lord	Logos, word of God, Son of God, Son of Man, lamb of God, Redeemer, Messiah, and Lord
The Author's Community	A Gentile Christian community in Rome undergoing persecution	A Jewish Christian community in Antioch, Syria	Written to Theophilus (meaning "lover of God"), who possibly represents any Christian (Greece)	Community of Jews, Gentiles, and Samaritans of Ephesus in Turkey
Theological Themes	Jesus shows that the suffering in our lives can be a source of grace when united to the sufferings of Christ	Jesus teaches what it means to be a member of the Kingdom of heaven. He prepares his followers to continue his teaching and ministry.	Jesus heals long-standing divisions among people. He calls his followers to have a special compassion for those excluded from wealth and power.	Jesus is the divine Son of God, the image of God in flesh. Salvation is available for those who believe in Jesus and commit their lives to him.
Historical Situation	The Romans subdue armed Jewish rebellions. Christians experience persecution in Rome.	Written after Romans had destroyed all of Jerusalem, including the Temple of Herod	Written when the persecution of Jews and Christians was intensifying	Emperor Domitian deified himself and mandated that all people worship him. Jewish leaders banned Christians from the synagogues.
Caesars	Nero (54–68 CE)	Vespasian and Titus (70–81 CE)	Domitian (81–96 CE)	Domitian (81–96 CE), Nerva (96–98 CE), Trajan (98–117 CE)

that debt because you pleaded with me. ³³Should you not have had mercy on your fellow slave, as I had mercy on you?' ³⁴And in anger his lord handed him over to be tortured until he would pay his entire debt. ³⁵So my heavenly Father will also do to every one of you, if you do not forgive your brother or sister*ᵃ* from your heart."

Teaching about Divorce

19 When Jesus had finished saying these things, he left Galilee and went to the region of Judea beyond the Jordan. ²Large crowds followed him, and he cured them there.

3 Some Pharisees came to him, and to test him they asked, "Is it lawful for a man to divorce his wife for any cause?" ⁴He answered, "Have you not read that the one who made them at the beginning 'made them male and female,' ⁵and said, 'For this reason a man shall leave his father and mother and be joined to his wife, and the two shall become one flesh'? ⁶So they are no longer two, but one flesh. Therefore what God has joined together, let no one separate." ⁷They said to him, "Why then did Moses command us to give a certificate of dismissal and to divorce her?" ⁸He said to them, "It was because you were so hard-hearted that Moses allowed you to divorce your wives, but from the beginning it was not so. ⁹And I say to you, whoever divorces his wife, except for unchastity, and marries another commits adultery."*ᵇ*

10 His disciples said to him, "If such is the case of a man with his wife, it is better not to marry." ¹¹But he said to them, "Not everyone can accept this teaching, but only those to whom it is given. ¹²For there are eunuchs who have been so from birth, and there are eunuchs who have been made eunuchs by others, and there are eunuchs who have made themselves eunuchs for the sake of the kingdom of heaven. Let anyone accept this who can."

Jesus Blesses Little Children

13 Then little children were being brought to him in order that he might lay his hands on them and pray. The disciples spoke sternly to those who brought them; ¹⁴but Jesus said, "Let the little children come to me, and do not stop them; for it is to such as these that the kingdom of heaven belongs." ¹⁵And he laid his hands on them and went on his way.

The Rich Young Man

16 Then someone came to him and said, "Teacher, what good deed must I do to have eternal life?" ¹⁷And he said to him, "Why do you ask me about what is good? There is only one who is good. If you wish to enter into life, keep the commandments." ¹⁸He said to him, "Which ones?" And Jesus said, "You shall not murder; You shall not commit adultery; You shall not steal; You shall not bear false witness; ¹⁹Honor your father and mother; also, You shall love your neighbor as yourself." ²⁰The young man said to him, "I have kept all these;*ᶜ* what do I still lack?" ²¹Jesus said to him, "If you wish to be perfect, go, sell your possessions, and give the money*ᵈ* to the poor, and you will have treasure in heaven; then come, follow me." ²²When the young man heard this word, he went away grieving, for he had many possessions.

23 Then Jesus said to his disciples, "Truly I tell you, it will be hard for a rich person to enter the kingdom of heaven. ²⁴Again I tell you, it is easier for a camel to go through the eye of a needle than for someone who is rich to enter the kingdom of God." ²⁵When the disciples heard this, they were greatly astounded and said, "Then who can be saved?" ²⁶But Jesus looked at them and said, "For mortals it is impossible, but for God all things are possible."

---

a Gk *brother*   *b* Other ancient authorities read *except on the ground of unchastity, causes her to commit adultery*; others add at the end of the verse *and he who marries a divorced woman commits adultery*   *c* Other ancient authorities add *from my youth*   *d* Gk *lacks the money*

Forgive Us Our Debts

The parable of the unforgiving servant spells out clearly (and a bit harshly) what it means to ask God to "forgive us our debts, / as we also have forgiven our debtors" (Mt 6:12).

Bring to mind a person who has hurt you or made you angry lately. Hold this person's image in your thoughts, and realize that Jesus is calling you to forgive her or him. Now, tell this person in your thoughts how she or he has hurt you. Finally, offer your forgiveness to the person so that you can let go of the burden of your hurt.

When you are done, imagine Jesus in your prayer and share with him something you have done that has hurt another person. Let Jesus forgive you in the same way you just forgave.

▶ Mt 18:21–35

MT

27 Then Peter said in reply, "Look, we have left everything and followed you. What then will we have?" ²⁸Jesus said to them, "Truly I tell you, at the renewal of all things, when the Son of Man is seated on the throne of his glory, you who have followed me will also sit on twelve thrones, judging the twelve tribes of Israel. ²⁹And everyone who has left houses or brothers or sisters or father or mother or children or fields, for my name's sake, will receive a hundredfold,ᵃ and will inherit eternal life. ³⁰But many who are first will be last, and the last will be first.

The Laborers in the Vineyard

20 "For the kingdom of heaven is like a land-owner who went out early in the morning to hire laborers for his vineyard. ²After agreeing

with the laborers for the usual daily wage,ᵇ he sent them into his vineyard. ³When he went out about nine o'clock, he saw others standing idle in the marketplace; ⁴and he said to them, 'You also go into the vineyard, and I will pay you whatever is right.' So they went. ⁵When he went out again about noon and about three o'clock, he did the same. ⁶And about five o'clock he went out and found others standing around; and he said to them, 'Why are you standing here idle all day?' ⁷They said to him, 'Because no one has hired us.' He said to them, 'You also go into the vineyard.' ⁸When evening came, the owner of the vineyard said to his manager, 'Call the laborers and give them their pay, beginning with the last and then

---

a Other ancient authorities read *manifold*   b Gk a *denarius*

Are You for Real?

Read Matthew 20:1–16 as an introduction to this prayer:

Lord, could you really be such a generous God? I have heard that you offer the same welcome to the sinner as to the saint. That you walk with the angry as well as the joyful, and can embrace the hurtful as well as the helpful. That you even offer the exact same love for the last to turn to you as you do for the first.

That's just not the way it is done around here, God, so excuse me if I have a hard time believing. But then, I've heard it said that you are as patient with the doubtful as you are with the faithful.

If you are this type of God, then please be with me right now. I need to talk to someone who understands and loves me despite my doubts and sin. I need a God who breaks the rules to let me know how much I am loved.

If you are indeed this kind of God, thanks! Thanks for being so crazy with your love that you would allow someone like me to hang around you. Promise to stay with me as I learn to trust in you and your acceptance of all people. Amen.

▶ Mt 20:1–16

True Greatness

What good parent does not want his or her son or daughter to find success in life? Like most people at the time of Jesus, the mother of James and John is confused about the Kingdom that Jesus had come to establish. She lobbies for her sons (see Mt 20:21), hoping they might be made "senior vice presidents" of the new "firm."

The resulting confusion and anger among the disciples allows Jesus the opportunity to remind them of how God defined true greatness. Jesus turns the tables on them by asking in a veiled way, "Are you able to drink the cup that I am about to drink?" (verse 22). He reminds them—and reminds us today—that true greatness is gained in serving others (see verses 26–27).

When you are in a position of leadership, do you see it as a chance to control others in order to gain power or social status, or do you see it as a chance to serve others and help them obtain what they need to live full and healthy lives? Why is it that wanting power for ourselves so often gets in the way of wanting to serve the needs of others?

▶ Mt 20:20–28

Catholic Social Teaching

A Living Wage

In this parable, Jesus tells the story of a landowner who agrees on a daily wage with his workers and then pays them that established wage at the end of their work day. Because different workers were paid the same amount for varying amounts of work, some of the workers found the wage to be unfair, even though they received the amount they had agreed to when they were hired. Therein lies the difference between God's notion of fairness and justice. Fairness would mean paying the workers based on the hours they worked. Justice, however, means providing all people with what they need, as God, the landowner in this story, does. Such is the radical grace of God!

Throughout our world, many workers toil for long hours under brutal conditions for a wage that is not just. Even in the United States, a person working forty hours per week at minimum wage will rarely earn enough to cover all of life's basic needs—food, shelter, clothing, utilities, transportation, medical insurance—especially when caring for a family. Often, women and children suffer the most from unjust wage practices.

This is why Catholic social teaching asserts that we must advocate for a living wage for all workers. A living wage is the minimum hourly wage necessary for a person to achieve a basic standard of living above the poverty line. Paying higher wages is sometimes difficult for small business owners who fear it may raise operating costs and put them out of business. However, it is certainly no excuse for failing to give workers the wages they need to adequately survive.

 Mt 20:1–16

The Dignity of Work and the Rights of Workers

---

going to the first.' ⁹When those hired about five o'clock came, each of them received the usual daily wage.ᵃ ¹⁰Now when the first came, they thought they would receive more; but each of them also received the usual daily wage.ᵃ ¹¹And when they received it, they grumbled against the landowner, ¹²saying, 'These last worked only one hour, and you have made them equal to us who have borne the burden of the day and the scorching heat.' ¹³But he replied to one of them, 'Friend, I am doing you no wrong; did you not agree with me for the usual daily wage?ᵃ ¹⁴Take what belongs to you and go; I choose to give to this last the same as I give to you. ¹⁵Am I not allowed to do what I choose with what belongs to me? Or are you envious because I am generous?'ᵇ ¹⁶So the last will be first, and the first will be last."ᶜ

A Third Time Jesus Foretells His Death and Resurrection

17 While Jesus was going up to Jerusalem, he took the twelve disciples aside by themselves, and said to them on the way, ¹⁸"See, we are going up to Jerusalem, and the Son of Man will be handed over to the chief priests and scribes, and they will condemn him to death; ¹⁹then they will hand him over to the Gentiles to be mocked and flogged and crucified; and on the third day he will be raised."

The Request of the Mother of James and John

20 Then the mother of the sons of Zebedee came to him with her sons, and kneeling before him, she asked a favor of him. ²¹And he said to her, "What do you want?" She said to him, "Declare that these two sons of mine will sit, one at your right hand and one at your left, in your kingdom." ²²But Jesus answered, "You do not know what you are asking. Are you able to drink the cup that I am about to drink?"ᵈ They said to him, "We are able." ²³He said to them, "You will indeed drink my cup, but to sit at my right hand and at my left, this is not mine to grant, but it is for those for whom it has been prepared by my Father."

24 When the ten heard it, they were angry with the two brothers. ²⁵But Jesus called them to him and said, "You know that the rulers of the Gentiles lord it over them, and their great ones are tyrants over them. ²⁶It will not be so among you; but whoever wishes to be great among you

---

ᵃ Gk a denarius   ᵇ Gk is your eye evil because I am good?
ᶜ Other ancient authorities add *for many are called but few are chosen*   ᵈ Other ancient authorities add *or to be baptized with the baptism that I am baptized with?*

must be your servant, ²⁷and whoever wishes to be first among you must be your slave; ²⁸just as the Son of Man came not to be served but to serve, and to give his life a ransom for many."

Jesus Heals Two Blind Men

29 As they were leaving Jericho, a large crowd followed him. ³⁰There were two blind men sitting by the roadside. When they heard that Jesus was passing by, they shouted, "Lord,*a* have mercy on us, Son of David!" ³¹The crowd sternly ordered them to be quiet; but they shouted even more loudly, "Have mercy on us, Lord, Son of David!" ³²Jesus stood still and called them, saying, "What do you want me to do for you?" ³³They said to him, "Lord, let our eyes be opened." ³⁴Moved with compassion, Jesus touched their eyes. Immediately they regained their sight and followed him.

Jesus' Triumphal Entry into Jerusalem

21 When they had come near Jerusalem and had reached Bethphage, at the Mount of Olives, Jesus sent two disciples, ²saying to them, "Go into the village ahead of you, and immediately you will find a donkey tied, and a colt with her; untie them and bring them to me. ³If anyone says anything to you, just say this, 'The Lord needs them.' And he will send them immediately.*b*" ⁴This took place to fulfill what had been spoken through the prophet, saying,

⁵ "Tell the daughter of Zion,

Look, your king is coming to you,

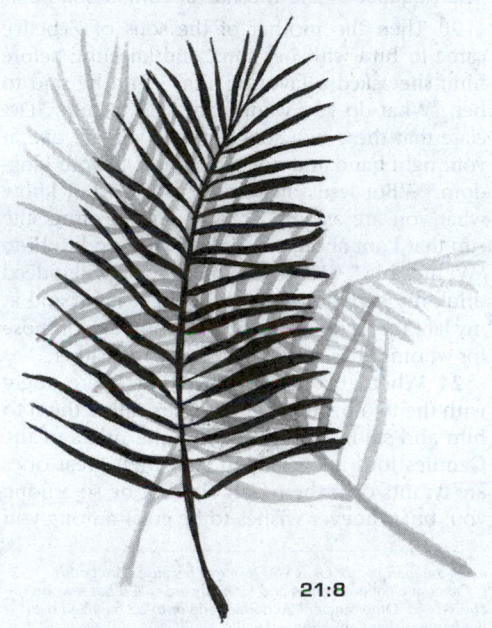

21:8

humble, and mounted on a donkey,

and on a colt, the foal of a donkey."

⁶The disciples went and did as Jesus had directed them; ⁷they brought the donkey and the colt, and put their cloaks on them, and he sat on them. ⁸A very large crowd*c* spread their cloaks on the road, and others cut branches from the trees and spread them on the road. ⁹The crowds that went ahead of him and that followed were shouting,

"Hosanna to the Son of David!

Blessed is the one who comes in the name of the Lord!

Hosanna in the highest heaven!"

¹⁰When he entered Jerusalem, the whole city was in turmoil, asking, "Who is this?" ¹¹The crowds were saying, "This is the prophet Jesus from Nazareth in Galilee."

Jesus Cleanses the Temple

12 Then Jesus entered the temple*d* and drove out all who were selling and buying in the temple, and he overturned the tables of the money changers and the seats of those who sold doves. ¹³He said to them, "It is written,

'My house shall be called a house of prayer';

but you are making it a den of robbers."

14 The blind and the lame came to him in the temple, and he cured them. ¹⁵But when the chief priests and the scribes saw the amazing things that he did, and heard*e* the children crying out in the temple, "Hosanna to the Son of David," they became angry ¹⁶and said to him, "Do you hear what these are saying?" Jesus said to them, "Yes; have you never read,

'Out of the mouths of infants and nursing babies you have prepared praise for yourself'?"

¹⁷He left them, went out of the city to Bethany, and spent the night there.

Jesus Curses the Fig Tree

18 In the morning, when he returned to the city, he was hungry. ¹⁹And seeing a fig tree by the side of the road, he went to it and found nothing at all on it but leaves. Then he said to it, "May no fruit ever come from you again!" And the fig tree withered at once. ²⁰When the disciples saw it, they were amazed, saying, "How did the fig tree wither at once?" ²¹Jesus answered them, "Truly I tell you, if you have faith and do not doubt, not only will you do what has been done to the fig tree, but even if you say to this

---

a Other ancient authorities lack *Lord*   *b* Or *'The Lord needs them and will send them back immediately.'*   *c* Or *Most of the crowd*   *d* Other ancient authorities add *of God*   *e* Gk lacks *heard*

mountain, 'Be lifted up and thrown into the sea,' it will be done. ²²Whatever you ask for in prayer with faith, you will receive."

The Authority of Jesus Questioned

23 When he entered the temple, the chief priests and the elders of the people came to him as he was teaching, and said, "By what authority are you doing these things, and who gave you this authority?" ²⁴Jesus said to them, "I will also ask you one question; if you tell me the answer, then I will also tell you by what authority I do these things. ²⁵Did the baptism of John come from heaven, or was it of human origin?" And they argued with one another, "If we say, 'From heaven,' he will say to us, 'Why then did you not believe him?' ²⁶But if we say, 'Of human origin,' we are afraid of the crowd; for all regard John as a prophet." ²⁷So they answered Jesus, "We do not know." And he said to them, "Neither will I tell you by what authority I am doing these things.

The Parable of the Two Sons

28 "What do you think? A man had two sons; he went to the first and said, 'Son, go and work in the vineyard today.' ²⁹He answered, 'I will not'; but later he changed his mind and went. ³⁰The father*ᵃ* went to the second and said the same; and he answered, 'I go, sir'; but he did not go. ³¹Which of the two did the will of his father?" They said, "The first." Jesus said to them, "Truly I tell you, the tax collectors and the prostitutes are going into the kingdom of God ahead of you. ³²For John came to you in the way of righteousness and you did not believe him, but the tax collectors and the prostitutes believed him; and even after you saw it, you did not change your minds and believe him.

The Parable of the Wicked Tenants

33 "Listen to another parable. There was a landowner who planted a vineyard, put a fence around it, dug a wine press in it, and built a watchtower. Then he leased it to tenants and went to another country. ³⁴When the harvest time had come, he sent his slaves to the tenants to collect his produce. ³⁵But the tenants seized his slaves and beat one, killed another, and stoned another. ³⁶Again he sent other slaves, more than the first; and they treated them in the same way. ³⁷Finally he sent his son to them, saying, 'They will respect my son.' ³⁸But when the tenants saw the son, they said to themselves, 'This is the heir; come, let us kill him and get his inheritance.' ³⁹So they seized him, threw him out of the vineyard, and killed him. ⁴⁰Now when the owner of the vineyard comes, what will he do to

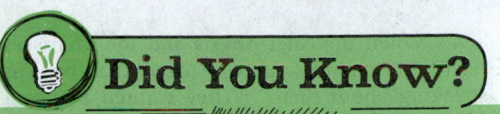

Did You Know?

Jesus and Civil Disobedience

The cleansing of the Temple is one of the few stories that occurs in all four Gospels. To fully understand Jesus' anger in this situation, we need to remember that the Jews were required to offer sacrificial animals as part of their religious obligation. Money exchange was a very necessary service for the proper operation of the Temple. Pilgrims needed Jewish coinage to pay the Temple tax. Likewise, buying animals for sacrifice at the Temple ensured that only the best would be offered to God. Jesus was angry because the religious and civil leaders were too concerned about these things, failing to remember that the Temple is God's house.

Jesus' clearing of the Temple was an act of religious and civil disobedience, challenging the highest members of Jewish society. His actions would have been viewed as an attack on the Temple. The Gospels of Luke and Mark both say that immediately after this event, Jewish leaders began looking for a way to kill Jesus. They waited because Jesus was so popular with the people (see Mk 11:18–19 and Lk 19:47–48). Jesus knew that his actions and teachings made these corrupt leaders angry and would ultimately lead to his death (see Mt 20:17–19).

▶ Mt 21:12–13

those tenants?" ⁴¹They said to him, "He will put those wretches to a miserable death, and lease the vineyard to other tenants who will give him the produce at the harvest time."

42 Jesus said to them, "Have you never read in the scriptures:

'The stone that the builders rejected
   has become the cornerstone;*ᵇ*
this was the Lord's doing,
   and it is amazing in our eyes'?

⁴³Therefore I tell you, the kingdom of God will be taken away from you and given to a people that produces the fruits of the kingdom.*ᶜ* ⁴⁴The one who falls on this stone will be broken to pieces; and it will crush anyone on whom it falls."*ᵈ*

---

a Gk *He*   *b* Or *keystone*   *c* Gk *the fruits of it*   *d* Other ancient authorities lack verse 44

MT

45 When the chief priests and the Pharisees heard his parables, they realized that he was speaking about them. 46They wanted to arrest him, but they feared the crowds, because they regarded him as a prophet.

The Parable of the Wedding Banquet

22 Once more Jesus spoke to them in parables, saying: 2"The kingdom of heaven may be compared to a king who gave a wedding banquet for his son. 3He sent his slaves to call those who had been invited to the wedding banquet, but they would not come. 4Again he sent other slaves, saying, 'Tell those who have been invited: Look, I have prepared my dinner, my oxen and my fat calves have been slaughtered, and everything is ready; come to the wedding banquet.' 5But they made light of it and went away, one to his farm, another to his business, 6while the rest seized his slaves, mistreated them, and killed them. 7The king was enraged. He sent his troops, destroyed those murderers, and

The Perfect Plan

Can you imagine a world where every person lives according to the two commandments Jesus gives in Matthew 22:34–40? where every word, thought, and action is motivated by a deep love for God and by a desire for the well-being of others? Sounds a bit like the Garden of Eden! Libraries are filled with volumes describing philosophies for achieving the ideal human society, yet Jesus articulates the perfect plan in a few short sentences. In fact, these two commands summarize the Ten Commandments and were long considered a summary of Mosaic Law.

The message of these two great commandments obviously remains real and relevant for us today. Following in the footsteps of the Apostles who first heard Jesus' words, it is now our responsibility to live out these commandments in our world—becoming living, breathing examples of what it means to love God, neighbor, and self.

▶ Mt 22:34–40

burned their city. 8Then he said to his slaves, 'The wedding is ready, but those invited were not worthy. 9Go therefore into the main streets, and invite everyone you find to the wedding banquet.' 10Those slaves went out into the streets and gathered all whom they found, both good and bad; so the wedding hall was filled with guests.

11 "But when the king came in to see the guests, he noticed a man there who was not wearing a wedding robe, 12and he said to him, 'Friend, how did you get in here without a wedding robe?' And he was speechless. 13Then the king said to the attendants, 'Bind him hand and foot, and throw him into the outer darkness, where there will be weeping and gnashing of teeth.' 14For many are called, but few are chosen."

The Question about Paying Taxes

15 Then the Pharisees went and plotted to entrap him in what he said. 16So they sent their disciples to him, along with the Herodians, saying, "Teacher, we know that you are sincere, and teach the way of God in accordance with truth, and show deference to no one; for you do not regard people with partiality. 17Tell us, then, what you think. Is it lawful to pay taxes to the emperor, or not?" 18But Jesus, aware of their malice, said, "Why are you putting me to the test, you hypocrites? 19Show me the coin used for the tax." And they brought him a denarius. 20Then he said to them, "Whose head is this, and whose title?" 21They answered, "The emperor's." Then he said to them, "Give therefore to the emperor the things that are the emperor's, and to God the things that are God's." 22When they heard this, they were amazed; and they left him and went away.

The Question about the Resurrection

23 The same day some Sadducees came to him, saying there is no resurrection;[a] and they asked him a question, saying, 24"Teacher, Moses said, 'If a man dies childless, his brother shall marry the widow, and raise up children for his brother.' 25Now there were seven brothers among us; the first married, and died childless, leaving the widow to his brother. 26The second did the same, so also the third, down to the seventh. 27Last of all, the woman herself died. 28In the resurrection, then, whose wife of the seven will she be? For all of them had married her."

29 Jesus answered them, "You are wrong, because you know neither the scriptures nor the power of God. 30For in the resurrection they

---

a Other ancient authorities read *who say that there is no resurrection* neither marry nor are given in marriage, but are like angels[a] in heaven. [31]And as for the resurrection of the dead, have you not read what was said to you by God, [32]'I am the God of Abraham, the God of Isaac, and the God of Jacob'? He is God not of the dead, but of the living." [33]And when the crowd heard it, they were astounded at his teaching.

The Greatest Commandment

34 When the Pharisees heard that he had silenced the Sadducees, they gathered together, [35]and one of them, a lawyer, asked him a question to test him. [36]"Teacher, which commandment in the law is the greatest?" [37]He said to him, "'You shall love the Lord your God with all your heart, and with all your soul, and with all your mind.' [38]This is the greatest and first commandment. [39]And a second is like it: 'You shall love your neighbor as yourself.' [40]On these two commandments hang all the law and the prophets."

The Question about David's Son

41 Now while the Pharisees were gathered together, Jesus asked them this question: [42]"What do you think of the Messiah?[b] Whose son is he?" They said to him, "The son of David." [43]He said to them, "How is it then that David by the Spirit[c] calls him Lord, saying,

[44] 'The Lord said to my Lord,

"Sit at my right hand,

    until I put your enemies under your feet"' ?

[45]If David thus calls him Lord, how can he be his son?" [46]No one was able to give him an answer, nor from that day did anyone dare to ask him any more questions.

Jesus Denounces Scribes and Pharisees

23 Then Jesus said to the crowds and to his disciples, [2]"The scribes and the Pharisees sit on Moses' seat; [3]therefore, do whatever they teach you and follow it; but do not do as they do, for they do not practice what they teach. [4]They tie up heavy burdens, hard to bear,[d] and lay them on the shoulders of others; but they themselves are unwilling to lift a finger to move them. [5]They do all their deeds to be seen by others; for they make their phylacteries broad and their fringes long. [6]They love to have the place of honor at banquets and the best seats in the synagogues, [7]and to be greeted with respect in the marketplaces, and to have people call them rabbi. [8]But you are not to be called rabbi, for you have one teacher, and you are all students.[e] [9]And call no one your father on earth, for you have

one Father—the one in heaven. [10]Nor are you to be called instructors, for you have one instructor, the Messiah.[b] [11]The greatest among you will be

a Other ancient authorities add *of God*   b Or *Christ*   c Gk *in spirit*   d Other ancient authorities lack *hard to bear*   e Gk *brothers*

No Respect

The "woe" statements of Jesus in Matthew 23:1–36 may be his harshest words in all the Gospels. Scholars think the community in which the author of Matthew lived may have had negative experiences with certain Jewish leaders (see "Pharisees, Sadducees, and Scribes," near Mt 3:7), and their hard feelings are reflected in Jesus' words. We should take Matthew 23:3–24 not as a condemnation of Jewish people but as a call to do the following:

- practice what we preach (see verse 3)
- show compassion; don't burden others (see verse 4)
- practice religion not to look important but as an expression of faith (see verses 5–7)
- humbly respect the people who follow us (see verses 8–15)
- be guided by mercy and justice in our understanding of law (see verses 23–24)

Jesus' sharpest criticism here and in many other places in the Gospels is directed against hypocrisy—the act of pretending to be holy and just while actually doing sinful things.

In your prayer, reflect or journal on the following questions:

- How have I expressed my faith in my spoken words as well as in my inner thoughts?
- When has my life demonstrated what my faith is all about?
- When have I asked others to do something I was not willing to do myself? Why did I do that?
- When have I used any power or influence I might have in a way that was humble and served the needs of others? How did I do that?

Try looking at these same questions each week or month, and see if your answers change over time.

▶ Mt 23:1–36

MT

your servant. ¹²All who exalt themselves will be humbled, and all who humble themselves will be exalted.

13 "But woe to you, scribes and Pharisees, hypocrites! For you lock people out of the kingdom of heaven. For you do not go in yourselves, and when others are going in, you stop them.ᵃ ¹⁵Woe to you, scribes and Pharisees, hypocrites! For you cross sea and land to make a single convert, and you make the new convert twice as much a child of hellᵇ as yourselves.

16 "Woe to you, blind guides, who say, 'Whoever swears by the sanctuary is bound by nothing, but whoever swears by the gold of the sanctuary is bound by the oath.' ¹⁷You blind fools! For which is greater, the gold or the sanctuary that has made the gold sacred? ¹⁸And you say, 'Whoever swears by the altar is bound by nothing, but whoever swears by the gift that is on the altar is bound by the oath.' ¹⁹How blind you are! For which is greater, the gift or the altar that makes the gift sacred? ²⁰So whoever swears by the altar, swears by it and by everything on it; ²¹and whoever swears by the sanctuary, swears by it and by the one who dwells in it; ²²and whoever swears by heaven, swears by the throne of God and by the one who is seated upon it.

23 "Woe to you, scribes and Pharisees, hypocrites! For you tithe mint, dill, and cummin, and have neglected the weightier matters of the law: justice and mercy and faith. It is these you ought to have practiced without neglecting the others. ²⁴You blind guides! You strain out a gnat but swallow a camel!

25 "Woe to you, scribes and Pharisees, hypocrites! For you clean the outside of the cup and of the plate, but inside they are full of greed and self-indulgence. ²⁶You blind Pharisee! First clean the inside of the cup,ᶜ so that the outside also may become clean.

27 "Woe to you, scribes and Pharisees, hypocrites! For you are like whitewashed tombs, which on the outside look beautiful, but inside they are full of the bones of the dead and of all kinds of filth. ²⁸So you also on the outside look righteous to others, but inside you are full of hypocrisy and lawlessness.

29 "Woe to you, scribes and Pharisees, hypocrites! For you build the tombs of the prophets and decorate the graves of the righteous, ³⁰and you say, 'If we had lived in the days of our ancestors, we would not have taken part with them in shedding the blood of the prophets.' ³¹Thus you testify against yourselves that you are descendants of those who murdered the prophets. ³²Fill up, then, the measure of your ancestors. ³³You

snakes, you brood of vipers! How can you escape being sentenced to hell?ᵇ ³⁴Therefore I send you prophets, sages, and scribes, some of whom you will kill and crucify, and some you will flog in your synagogues and pursue from town to town, ³⁵so that upon you may come all the righteous blood shed on earth, from the blood of righteous Abel to the blood of Zechariah son of Barachiah, whom you murdered between the sanctuary and the altar. ³⁶Truly I tell you, all this will come upon this generation.

The Lament over Jerusalem

37 "Jerusalem, Jerusalem, the city that kills the prophets and stones those who are sent to it! How often have I desired to gather your children together as a hen gathers her brood under her wings, and you were not willing! ³⁸See, your house is left to you, desolate.ᵈ ³⁹For I tell you, you will not see me again until you say, 'Blessed is the one who comes in the name of the Lord.' "

The Destruction of the Temple Foretold

24 As Jesus came out of the temple and was going away, his disciples came to point out to him the buildings of the temple. ²Then he asked them, "You see all these, do you not? Truly I tell you, not one stone will be left here upon another; all will be thrown down."

Signs of the End of the Age

3 When he was sitting on the Mount of Olives, the disciples came to him privately, saying, "Tell us, when will this be, and what will be the sign of your coming and of the end of the age?" ⁴Jesus answered them, "Beware that no one leads you astray. ⁵For many will come in my name, saying, 'I am the Messiah!'ᵉ and they will lead many astray. ⁶And you will hear of wars and rumors of wars; see that you are not alarmed; for this must take place, but the end is not yet. ⁷For nation will rise against nation, and kingdom against kingdom, and there will be faminesᶠ and earthquakes in various places: ⁸all this is but the beginning of the birth pangs.

Persecutions Foretold

9 "Then they will hand you over to be tortured and will put you to death, and you will be

---

a Other authorities add here (or after verse 12) verse 14, *Woe to you, scribes and Pharisees, hypocrites! For you devour widows' houses and for the sake of appearance you make long prayers; therefore you will receive the greater condemnation* b Gk *Gehenna* c Other ancient authorities add *and of the plate* d Other ancient authorities lack *desolate* e Or *the Christ* f Other ancient authorities add *and pestilences*

hated by all nations because of my name. [10]Then many will fall away,[a] and they will betray one another and hate one another. [11]And many false prophets will arise and lead many astray. [12]And because of the increase of lawlessness, the love of many will grow cold. [13]But the one who endures to the end will be saved. [14]And this good news[b] of the kingdom will be proclaimed throughout the world, as a testimony to all the nations; and then the end will come.

The Desolating Sacrilege

15 "So when you see the desolating sacrilege standing in the holy place, as was spoken of by the prophet Daniel (let the reader understand), [16]then those in Judea must flee to the mountains; [17]the one on the housetop must not go down to take what is in the house; [18]the one in the field must not turn back to get a coat. [19]Woe to those who are pregnant and to those who are nursing infants in those days! [20]Pray that your flight may not be in winter or on a sabbath. [21]For at that time there will be great suffering, such as has not been from the beginning of the world until now, no, and never will be. [22]And if those days had not been cut short, no one would be saved; but for the sake of the elect those days will be cut short. [23]Then if anyone says to you, 'Look! Here is the Messiah!'[c] or 'There he is!'—do not believe it. [24]For false messiahs[d] and false prophets will appear and produce great signs and omens, to lead astray, if possible, even the elect. [25]Take note, I have told you beforehand. [26]So, if they say to you, 'Look! He is in the wilderness,' do not go out. If they say, 'Look! He is in the inner rooms,' do not believe it. [27]For as the lightning comes from the east and flashes as far as the west, so will be the coming of the Son of Man. [28]Wherever the corpse is, there the vultures will gather.

The Coming of the Son of Man

29 "Immediately after the suffering of those days

the sun will be darkened,
and the moon will not give its light;
the stars will fall from heaven,
and the powers of heaven will be shaken.
[30]Then the sign of the Son of Man will appear in heaven, and then all the tribes of the earth will mourn, and they will see 'the Son of Man coming on the clouds of heaven' with power and great glory. [31]And he will send out his angels with a loud trumpet call, and they will gather his elect from the four winds, from one end of heaven to the other.

The Lesson of the Fig Tree

32 "From the fig tree learn its lesson: as soon as its branch becomes tender and puts forth its leaves, you know that summer is near. [33]So also, when you see all these things, you know that he[e] is near, at the very gates. [34]Truly I tell you, this generation will not pass away until all these things have taken place. [35]Heaven and earth will pass away, but my words will not pass away.

The Necessity for Watchfulness

36 "But about that day and hour no one knows, neither the angels of heaven, nor the Son,[f] but only the Father. [37]For as the days of Noah were, so will be the coming of the Son of

---

a Or *stumble* b Or *gospel* c Or *the Christ* d Or *christs*
e Or *it* h Other ancient authorities lack *nor the Son*

Look Busy!

Cardinal Francis Spellman, former archbishop of New York, was in his office when the phone rang. It was a receptionist from the chancery lobby who said, "Cardinal, there is a man here in the lobby claiming to be Jesus Christ. What should I do?" The Cardinal responded, "Look busy!"

Though the cardinal's response was meant to be a humorous one, the message should resonate with all of us. If Jesus were to return today, what would he say about our lives? What would he say about our world? Are we truly awake and ready for Jesus' return?

In this final teaching in Matthew, Jesus is speaking of the final coming of God. The Gospel reminds us that no one knows when Christ will come for us. Thus, it is foolish and dangerous to put off living a life committed to Christ. Instead, we should "look busy" every day of our lives, working hard to ensure that we are living as true disciples of Christ. We never know when that "unexpected hour" may arrive!

▶ Mt 24:36–44

Man. [38]For as in those days before the flood they were eating and drinking, marrying and giving in marriage, until the day Noah entered the ark, [39]and they knew nothing until the flood came and swept them all away, so too will be the coming of the Son of Man. [40]Then two will be in the field; one will be taken and one will be left. [41]Two women will be grinding meal together; one will be taken and one will be left. [42]Keep awake therefore, for you do not know on what day[a] your Lord is coming. [43]But understand this: if the owner of the house had known in what part of the night the thief was coming, he would have stayed awake and would not have let his house be broken into. [44]Therefore you also must be ready, for the Son of Man is coming at an unexpected hour.

The Faithful or the Unfaithful Slave

45 "Who then is the faithful and wise slave, whom his master has put in charge of his household, to give the other slaves[b] their allowance of food at the proper time? [46]Blessed is that slave whom his master will find at work when he arrives. [47]Truly I tell you, he will put that one in charge of all his possessions. [48]But if that wicked slave says to himself, 'My master is delayed,' [49]and he begins to beat his fellow slaves, and eats and drinks with drunkards, [50]the master of that slave will come on a day when he does not expect him and at an hour that he does not know. [51]He will cut him in pieces[c] and put him with the hypocrites, where there will be weeping and gnashing of teeth.

Pray It!

When Are You Coming?

I have accepted your invitation, Lord.
    But when are you coming?
I need to be ready, Lord.
    But when are you coming?
I want to share your love with others, Lord.
    But when are you coming?
I will be prepared, Lord.
    No matter when you are
    coming.

▶ Mt 25:1–13

The Parable of the Ten Bridesmaids

25 "Then the kingdom of heaven will be like this. Ten bridesmaids[d] took their lamps and went to meet the bridegroom.[e] [2]Five of them were foolish, and five were wise. [3]When the foolish took their lamps, they took no oil with them; [4]but the wise took flasks of oil with their lamps. [5]As the bridegroom was delayed, all of them became drowsy and slept. [6]But at midnight there was a shout, 'Look! Here is the bridegroom! Come out to meet him.' [7]Then all those bridesmaids[d] got up and trimmed their lamps. [8]The foolish said to the wise, 'Give us some of your oil, for our lamps are going out.' [9]But the wise replied, 'No! there will not be enough for you and for us; you had better go to the dealers and buy some for yourselves.' [10]And while they went to buy it, the bridegroom came, and those who were ready went with him into the wedding banquet; and the door was shut. [11]Later the other bridesmaids[d] came also, saying, 'Lord, lord, open to us.' [12]But he replied, 'Truly I tell you, I do not know you.' [13]Keep awake therefore, for you know neither the day nor the hour.[f]

The Parable of the Talents

14 "For it is as if a man, going on a journey, summoned his slaves and entrusted his property to them; [15]to one he gave five talents,[g] to another two, to another one, to each according to his ability. Then he went away. [16]The one who had received the five talents went off at once and traded with them, and made five more talents. [17]In the same way, the one who had the two talents made two more talents. [18]But the one who had received the one talent went off and dug a hole in the ground and hid his master's money. [19]After a long time the master of those slaves came and settled accounts with them. [20]Then the one who had received the five talents came forward, bringing five more talents, saying, 'Master, you handed over to me five talents; see, I have made five more talents.' [21]His master said to him, 'Well done, good and trustworthy slave; you have been trustworthy in a few things, I will put you in charge of many things; enter into the joy of your master.' [22]And the one with the two talents also came forward, saying, 'Master, you handed over to me two talents; see, I have made two more talents.' [23]His master said to him, 'Well

---

a Other ancient authorities read at what hour   b Gk to give them   c Or cut him off   d Gk virgins   e Other ancient authorities add and the bride   f Other ancient authorities add in which the Son of Man is coming   g A talent was worth more than fifteen years' wages of a laborer

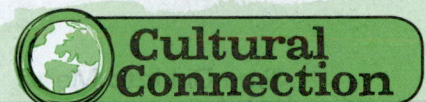

Cultural Connection

The Principle of *Kuumba*

I wish I had a great singing voice. I often daydream about belting out songs with the vocal power of the sister of soul, Aretha Franklin. Sure, I have other gifts, but more than anything else, I wish I could sing. Here I go again, neglecting what I do have as I yearn for what I lack. Why do I do that?

This attitude sounds a bit like that of the servant Jesus speaks of in Matthew 25:14–30, the parable of the talents, doesn't it? In the parable, the master gives the third servant a talent, but the servant keeps it hidden. And precisely because he keeps it hidden, the timid servant loses the one talent he does have.

Although a talent is actually a very large sum of money, many contemporary commentaries associate the word with abilities. God has given us our talents and abilities. The Kwanzaa principle of *kuumba* (creativity) calls us to use our talents creatively and boldly in the service of God. Don't second-guess the Lord by wanting something you do not have. Trust that God has blessed you with the gifts you need, and use them!

Dear God, thank you for what I have. Help me to use it to your glory. Amen.

 Mt 25:14–30

done, good and trustworthy slave; you have been trustworthy in a few things, I will put you in charge of many things; enter into the joy of your master.' ²⁴Then the one who had received the one talent also came forward, saying, 'Master, I knew that you were a harsh man, reaping where you did not sow, and gathering where you did not scatter seed; ²⁵so I was afraid, and I went and hid your talent in the ground. Here you have what is yours.' ²⁶But his master replied, 'You wicked and lazy slave! You knew, did you, that I reap where I did not sow, and gather where I did not scatter? ²⁷Then you ought to have invested my money with the bankers, and on my return I would have received what was my own with interest. ²⁸So take the talent from him, and give it to the one with the ten talents. ²⁹For to all those who have, more will be given, and they will have an abundance; but from those who have nothing, even what they have will be taken away. ³⁰As for this worthless slave, throw him into the outer darkness, where there will be weeping and gnashing of teeth.'

The Judgment of the Nations

31 "When the Son of Man comes in his glory, and all the angels with him, then he will sit on the throne of his glory. ³²All the nations will be gathered before him, and he will separate people one from another as a shepherd separates the sheep from the goats, ³³and he will put the sheep at his right hand and the goats at the left.

³⁴Then the king will say to those at his right hand, 'Come, you that are blessed by my Father, inherit the kingdom prepared for you from the foundation of the world; ³⁵for I was hungry and you gave me food, I was thirsty and you gave me something to drink, I was a stranger and you welcomed me, ³⁶I was naked and you gave me clothing, I was sick and you took care of me, I was in prison and you visited me.' ³⁷Then the righteous will answer him, 'Lord, when was it that we saw you hungry and gave you food, or thirsty and gave you something to drink? ³⁸And when was it that we saw you a stranger and welcomed you, or naked and gave you clothing? ³⁹And when was it that we saw you sick or in prison and visited you?' ⁴⁰And the king will answer them, 'Truly I tell you, just as you did it to one of the least of these who are members of my family,ᵃ you did it to me.' ⁴¹Then he will say to those at his left hand, 'You that are accursed, depart from me into the eternal fire prepared for the devil and his angels; ⁴²for I was hungry and you gave me no food, I was thirsty and you gave me nothing to drink, ⁴³I was a stranger and you did not welcome me, naked and you did not give me clothing, sick and in prison and you did not visit me.' ⁴⁴Then they also will answer, 'Lord, when was it that we saw you hungry or thirsty or a stranger or naked or sick or in prison, and did not take care of you?' ⁴⁵Then he will answer them, 'Truly I tell

a Gk these my brothers

Catholic Social Teaching

"You Did It to Me"

We have all heard excuses for not helping those in need: "He got what he deserved!" "She is not my problem!" "If only they would have done this or that, they wouldn't be in the mess they're in!" These common misconceptions pacify the consciences of many people. Instead, Jesus says we shouldn't let people suffer; we must reach out to them. He is neither suggesting that we respond nor encouraging us to; he is demanding that we do. He also states quite clearly that we will be judged by God as to how well we care for those who are disadvantaged because that is where we encounter and minister to Christ.

Catholic social teaching teaches that all human beings have basic rights that need to be protected at all times. The United Nations'

"Universal Declaration of Human Rights" gives a good starting point in determining what these basic rights might be, listing thirty human rights that should always be guaranteed for all members of the human family. These rights include the right to work, education, fair legal treatment, and ownership of property.

Corresponding to these rights are certain responsibilities, similar to what Jesus outlines for his disciples in this challenging passage—feeding the hungry, welcoming the stranger, clothing the naked, tending to the sick, and supporting those who have been imprisoned. These are the demands of our faith, if we want to call ourselves disciples. There is no option, only an obligation, as Jesus makes abundantly clear.

How does your local community

respond to Jesus' call? Can hungry people get a free meal somewhere? Does your school or parish have food or clothing drives? How are shut-ins and terminally ill people cared for? Who visits or writes to the prisoners in the county jail? How does your community, school, or parish respond to refugees or immigrants? Who are the hungry, the thirsty, the strangers, the naked, the sick, or the imprisoned in your neighborhood or community? What can you do to help minister to them?

 **Mt 25:31–46**

Rights and Responsibilities

you, just as you did not do it to one of the least of these, you did not do it to me.' [46]And these will go away into eternal punishment, but the righteous into eternal life."

The Plot to Kill Jesus

26 When Jesus had finished saying all these things, he said to his disciples, [2]"You know that after two days the Passover is coming, and the Son of Man will be handed over to be crucified."

3 Then the chief priests and the elders of the people gathered in the palace of the high priest, who was called Caiaphas, [4]and they conspired to arrest Jesus by stealth and kill him. [5]But they said, "Not during the festival, or there may be a riot among the people."

The Anointing at Bethany

6 Now while Jesus was at Bethany in the house of Simon the leper,[a] [7]a woman came to him with an alabaster jar of very costly ointment, and she poured it on his head as he sat at the table. [8]But when the disciples saw it, they were angry and said, "Why this waste? [9]For this ointment could have been sold for a large sum, and the money given to the poor." [10]But Jesus, aware of this, said to them, "Why do you trouble the woman? She has performed a good service for me. [11]For you always have the poor with you, but you will not always have me. [12]By pouring this ointment on my body she has prepared me for burial. [13]Truly I tell you, wherever this good news[b] is proclaimed in the whole world, what she has done will be told in remembrance of her."

Judas Agrees to Betray Jesus

14 Then one of the twelve, who was called Judas Iscariot, went to the chief priests [15]and said, "What will you give me if I betray him to you?"

a The terms *leper* and *leprosy* can refer to several diseases
b Or *gospel*

They paid him thirty pieces of silver. ¹⁶And from that moment he began to look for an opportunity to betray him.

The Passover with the Disciples

17 On the first day of Unleavened Bread the disciples came to Jesus, saying, "Where do you want us to make the preparations for you to eat the Passover?" ¹⁸He said, "Go into the city to a certain man, and say to him, 'The Teacher says, My time is near; I will keep the Passover at your house with my disciples.' " ¹⁹So the disciples did as Jesus had directed them, and they prepared the Passover meal.

20 When it was evening, he took his place with the twelve;ᵃ ²¹and while they were eating, he said, "Truly I tell you, one of you will betray me." ²²And they became greatly distressed and began to say to him one after another, "Surely not I, Lord?" ²³He answered, "The one who has dipped his hand into the bowl with me will betray me. ²⁴The Son of Man goes as it is written of him, but woe to that one by whom the Son of Man is betrayed! It would have been better for that one not to have been born." ²⁵Judas, who betrayed him, said, "Surely not I, Rabbi?" He replied, "You have said so."

The Institution of the Lord's Supper

26 While they were eating, Jesus took a loaf of bread, and after blessing it he broke it, gave it to the disciples, and said, "Take, eat; this is my body." ²⁷Then he took a cup, and after giving thanks he gave it to them, saying, "Drink from it, all of you; ²⁸for this is my blood of theᵇ covenant, which is poured out for many for the forgiveness of sins. ²⁹I tell you, I will never again drink of this fruit of the vine until that day when I drink it new with you in my Father's kingdom."

30 When they had sung the hymn, they went out to the Mount of Olives.

Peter's Denial Foretold

31 Then Jesus said to them, "You will all become desertersᶜ because of me this night; for it is written,

'I will strike the shepherd,
   and the sheep of the flock will be scattered.'

³²But after I am raised up, I will go ahead of you to Galilee." ³³Peter said to him, "Though all become deserters because of you, I will never desert you." ³⁴Jesus said to him, "Truly I tell you, this very night, before the cock crows, you will deny me three times." ³⁵Peter said to him, "Even though I must die with you, I will not deny you." And so said all the disciples.

Jesus Prays in Gethsemane

36 Then Jesus went with them to a place called Gethsemane; and he said to his disciples, "Sit here while I go over there and pray." ³⁷He took with him Peter and the two sons of Zebedee, and began to be grieved and agitated. ³⁸Then he said to them, "I am deeply grieved, even to death; remain here, and stay awake with me." ³⁹And going a little farther, he threw himself on the ground and prayed, "My Father, if it is possible, let this cup pass from me; yet not what I want but what you want." ⁴⁰Then he came to the disciples and found them sleeping; and he said to Peter, "So, could you not stay awake with me one hour? ⁴¹Stay awake and pray that you may not come into the time of trial;ᶜ the spirit indeed is willing, but the flesh is weak." ⁴²Again he went away for the second time and prayed, "My Father, if this cannot pass unless I drink it, your will be done." ⁴³Again he came and found them sleeping, for their eyes were heavy. ⁴⁴So leaving them again, he went away and prayed for the third time, saying the same words. ⁴⁵Then he came to the disciples and said to them, "Are you still sleeping and taking your rest? See, the hour is at hand, and the Son of Man is betrayed into the hands of sinners. ⁴⁶Get up, let us be going. See, my betrayer is at hand."

The Betrayal and Arrest of Jesus

47 While he was still speaking, Judas, one of the twelve, arrived; with him was a large crowd with swords and clubs, from the chief priests and the elders of the people. ⁴⁸Now the betrayer had given them a sign, saying, "The one I will kiss is the man; arrest him." ⁴⁹At once he came up to Jesus and said, "Greetings, Rabbi!" and kissed him. ⁵⁰Jesus said to him, "Friend, do what you are here to do." Then they came and

---

a Other ancient authorities add *disciples*   b Other ancient authorities add *new*   c Or *into temptation*

26:26

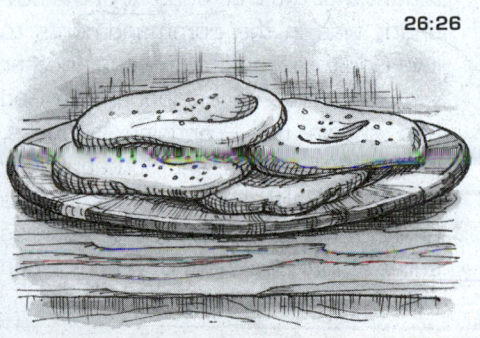

✝ Catholic Connection

The New Covenant

Covenant is such a key theme throughout the Scriptures that the Bible itself is often called the Old and New Covenants or *Testaments,* which is the Latin word for *covenant.* The word *covenant* is used to express the unique relationship between God and God's people. In the Old Testament, the laws and worship practices of the Israelites were a sign of this covenant relationship (see "Covenant," near Gen 17:1–27.) But during the Last Supper, Jesus catapults humanity into a new and dynamic dimension of the covenant relationship with God when he shares the cup and says, "Drink from it, all of you; for this is my blood of the covenant" (Mt 26:27–28). In Luke's Gospel, Jesus calls it "the new covenant in my blood" (Lk 22:20). Through Jesus' selfless love shown on the cross, our relationship with God is restored fully and completely and a new, eternal covenant is established with God.

Jesus Christ, the Word made flesh, initiated the New Covenant through his life offered up in sacrifice for all. In his teaching and ministry, Jesus reinterpreted the life of a covenant people. He taught that the true content of the covenant was in the commandments to love God totally and to love one another with the same unconditional love God has shown us. Practicing kindness, justice, forgiveness, and righteousness are the qualities that constitute the heart of the covenant. Jesus' disciples entered into this New Covenant when they partook of the Body and Blood of Christ at the Last Supper and actually became the Body of Christ, entering into the deepest kind of communion (relationship) with God.

This communion in the Body of Christ also speaks of the communion of all believers to one another—no matter how different we may be from one another in nationality, race, culture, or social status. Our communion as Christians, the covenant people of God, transcends any and all human division. As often as we partake in the Eucharist, we reaffirm the New Covenant in Jesus. Our hearts are cleansed and renewed by Jesus' self-offering upon the cross; and we pledge to share our lives together as a Christian community, to be an example for the world.

The covenant, which began with Abraham and was fully revealed in Jesus, is God's way of bringing us back to the source of our lives in God and into unity with one another. We enter into this New and Eternal Covenant through Baptism and keep it by remaining faithful to Christ. In the Eucharist, we are brought more deeply into communion with God and with one another and, through the power of the Holy Spirit, we are able to go forth and live the New Covenant.

▶ **Mt 26:26–29**

Catechism, nos. 68–73, 610, 613, 1365, 1405

laid hands on Jesus and arrested him. [51]Suddenly, one of those with Jesus put his hand on his sword, drew it, and struck the slave of the high priest, cutting off his ear. [52]Then Jesus said to him, "Put your sword back into its place; for all who take the sword will perish by the sword. [53]Do you think that I cannot appeal to my Father, and he will at once send me more than twelve legions of angels? [54]But how then would the scriptures be fulfilled, which say it must happen in this way?" [55]At that hour Jesus said to the crowds, "Have you come out with swords and clubs to arrest me as though I were a bandit? Day after day I sat in the temple teaching, and you did not arrest me. [56]But all this has taken place, so that the scriptures of the prophets may be fulfilled." Then all the disciples deserted him and fled.

Jesus before the High Priest

[57] Those who had arrested Jesus took him to Caiaphas the high priest, in whose house the scribes and the elders had gathered. [58]But Peter was following him at a distance, as far as the courtyard of the high priest; and going inside, he sat with the guards in order to see how this would end. [59]Now the chief priests and the whole council were looking for false testimony against Jesus so that they might put him to death, [60]but they found none, though many false witnesses came forward. At last two came forward [61]and said, "This fellow said, 'I am able to destroy the temple of God and to build it in three days.' " [62]The high priest stood up and said, "Have you no answer? What is it that they testify against you?" [63]But Jesus was silent. Then the high priest said to him, "I put you under oath before the living God, tell us if you are the Messiah,[a] the Son of God." [64]Jesus said to him, "You have said so. But I tell you,

> From now on you will see the Son of Man
> seated at the right hand of Power
> and coming on the clouds of heaven."

[65]Then the high priest tore his clothes and said, "He has blasphemed! Why do we still need witnesses? You have now heard his blasphemy. [66]What is your verdict?" They answered, "He deserves death." [67]Then they spat in his face and struck him; and some slapped him, [68]saying, "Prophesy to us, you Messiah![a] Who is it that struck you?"

Peter's Denial of Jesus

[69] Now Peter was sitting outside in the courtyard. A servant-girl came to him and said, "You also were with Jesus the Galilean." [70]But he

Live It!

Jesus' Imperfect Friends

Imagine that you are in the middle of a crisis and ask your best friends to stay with you while you prepare to face the situation. They all promise to be there for you. But one friend after another fails to come through, and you are left to face the predicament alone.

The friends of Jesus were no different. They were well intentioned and meant to stay awake with him. But in their tiredness, they let him down.

We recognize that the friends of Jesus, the Apostles in particular, were special and holy, but they were also human and had their own weaknesses. Even Peter, one of the greatest heroes of Christianity, lacked the courage to admit he knew Jesus, as we read in Matthew 26:69–75. Yet, Jesus loved his disciples despite their failings and even when they were disloyal.

● Is it easy for you to stay friends with those who let you down?
● Can you follow the example of Jesus?

▶ Mt 26:36–45

denied it before all of them, saying, "I do not know what you are talking about." [71]When he went out to the porch, another servant-girl saw him, and she said to the bystanders, "This man was with Jesus of Nazareth."[b] [72]Again he denied it with an oath, "I do not know the man." [73]After a little while the bystanders came up and said to Peter, "Certainly you are also one of them, for your accent betrays you." [74]Then he began to curse, and he swore an oath, "I do not know the man!" At that moment the cock crowed. [75]Then Peter remembered what Jesus had said: "Before the cock crows, you will deny me three times." And he went out and wept bitterly.

Jesus Brought before Pilate

27 When morning came, all the chief priests and the elders of the people conferred together against Jesus in order to bring about

a Or Christ   *b* Gk the Nazorean

his death. ²They bound him, led him away, and handed him over to Pilate the governor.

The Suicide of Judas

3 When Judas, his betrayer, saw that Jesus*a* was condemned, he repented and brought back the thirty pieces of silver to the chief priests and the elders. ⁴He said, "I have sinned by betraying innocent*b* blood." But they said, "What is that to us? See to it yourself." ⁵Throwing down the pieces of silver in the temple, he departed; and he went and hanged himself. ⁶But the chief priests, taking the pieces of silver, said, "It is not lawful to put them into the treasury, since they are blood money." ⁷After conferring together,

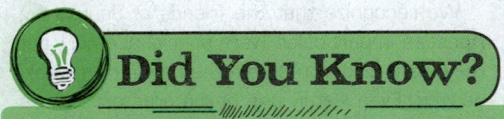

Did You Know?

Judas's Suicide

The Gospel of Matthew presents Judas's suicide as the fulfillment of some Old Testament prophecies, but it does not tell us why Judas killed himself. We don't know the historical circumstances around this event, nor do we know what was in Judas's mind or what motivated him to do this or how this event would have been perceived at a different time and in a culture very different from our own. But some teenagers think suicide will end their pain, using it as a way out.

Unfortunately, suicide ends everything; not just the current pain but future possibilities for healing, for growth, for new relationships and good times. Consider that both Judas and Peter betrayed Jesus. But Judas ended his life, and Peter trusted in God's love and forgiveness and went on to become a great hero. Nothing you can do is so terrible that your only option is taking your life.

Do you ever have thoughts of suicide? If so, talk about them with someone you trust. Speak with a priest, a parent, a youth minister, a school counselor, a coach, or a trusted friend. Caring people will help you. Seeking their help is a better way out. (For more on suicide, see "Suicide Is Not an Answer," near 1 Sam 31:1–6.)

▶ Mt 27:3–10

they used them to buy the potter's field as a place to bury foreigners. ⁸For this reason that field has been called the Field of Blood to this day. ⁹Then was fulfilled what had been spoken through the prophet Jeremiah,*c* "And they took*d* the thirty pieces of silver, the price of the one on whom a price had been set,*e* on whom some of the people of Israel had set a price, ¹⁰and they gave*f* them for the potter's field, as the Lord commanded me."

Pilate Questions Jesus

11 Now Jesus stood before the governor; and the governor asked him, "Are you the King of the Jews?" Jesus said, "You say so." ¹²But when he was accused by the chief priests and elders, he did not answer. ¹³Then Pilate said to him, "Do you not hear how many accusations they make against you?" ¹⁴But he gave him no answer, not even to a single charge, so that the governor was greatly amazed.

Barabbas or Jesus?

15 Now at the festival the governor was accustomed to release a prisoner for the crowd, anyone whom they wanted. ¹⁶At that time they had a notorious prisoner, called Jesus*g* Barabbas. ¹⁷So after they had gathered, Pilate said to them, "Whom do you want me to release for you, Jesus*g* Barabbas or Jesus who is called the Messiah?"*h* ¹⁸For he realized that it was out of jealousy that they had handed him over. ¹⁹While he was sitting on the judgment seat, his wife sent word to him, "Have nothing to do with that innocent man, for today I have suffered a great deal because of a dream about him." ²⁰Now the chief priests and the elders persuaded the crowds to ask for Barabbas and to have Jesus killed. ²¹The governor again said to them, "Which of the two do you want me to release for you?" And they said, "Barabbas." ²²Pilate said to them, "Then what should I do with Jesus who is called the Messiah?"*h* All of them said, "Let him be crucified!" ²³Then he asked, "Why, what evil has he done?" But they shouted all the more, "Let him be crucified!"

Pilate Hands Jesus over to Be Crucified

24 So when Pilate saw that he could do nothing, but rather that a riot was beginning, he took some water and washed his hands before the crowd, saying, "I am innocent of this man's

---

a Gk *he* b Other ancient authorities read *righteous* c Other ancient authorities read *Zechariah* or *Isaiah* d Or *I took*
e Or *the price of the precious One* f Other ancient authorities read *I gave* g Other ancient authorities lack *Jesus* h Or *the Christ*

blood;*a* see to it yourselves." 25Then the people as a whole answered, "His blood be on us and on our children!" 26So he released Barabbas for them; and after flogging Jesus, he handed him over to be crucified.

The Soldiers Mock Jesus

27 Then the soldiers of the governor took Jesus into the governor's headquarters,*b* and they gathered the whole cohort around him. 28They stripped him and put a scarlet robe on him, 29and after twisting some thorns into a crown, they put it on his head. They put a reed in his right hand and knelt before him and mocked him, saying, "Hail, King of the Jews!" 30They spat on him, and took the reed and struck him on the head. 31After mocking him, they stripped him of the robe and put his own clothes on him. Then they led him away to crucify him.

The Crucifixion of Jesus

32 As they went out, they came upon a man from Cyrene named Simon; they compelled this man to carry his cross. 33And when they came to a place called Golgotha (which means Place of a Skull), 34they offered him wine to drink, mixed with gall; but when he tasted it, he would not drink it. 35And when they had crucified him, they divided his clothes among themselves by casting lots;*c* 36then they sat down there and kept watch over him. 37Over his head they put the charge against him, which read, "This is Jesus, the King of the Jews."

38 Then two bandits were crucified with him, one on his right and one on his left. 39Those who passed by derided*d* him, shaking their heads 40and saying, "You who would destroy the temple and build it in three days, save yourself! If you are the Son of God, come down from the cross." 41In the same way the chief priests also, along with the scribes and elders, were mocking him, saying, 42"He saved others; he cannot save himself.*e* He is the King of Israel; let him come down from the cross now, and we will believe

---

a Other ancient authorities read *this righteous blood,* or *this righteous man's blood*   *b* Gk the praetorium   *c* Other ancient authorities add *in order that what had been spoken through the prophet might be fulfilled, "They divided my clothes among themselves, and for my clothing they cast lots."*   *d* Or *blasphemed*   *e* Or *is he unable to save himself?*

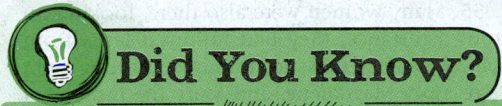

Did You Know?

The Dawn of a New Age

According to the Gospel of Matthew, some strange things happened when Jesus died. Each event tells us something about Jesus. The darkness that covered the land (see Mt 27:45) and the earthquake (see verse 51) show that all creation was aware that something significant had happened, a new age was dawning. The splitting of the sanctuary veil (see verse 51), which is the barrier that separated the holiest part of the Temple (where God was thought to dwell) from the rest of the Temple area, symbolizes that now God would be directly accessible to the people. And the dead saints who came out of their tombs to walk in the city symbolize God's triumph over death. These are all Old Testament signs of the end times (see Isa 26:19, Ezek 37:12, Joel 2:10, Nah 1:5–6).

▶ Mt 27:45–54

Pray It!

Suffering Prayer

Jesus, anointed one, everyone endures some suffering in life. Some suffer in silence. Some loudly complain, making it known to all. Some bitterly blame everyone around them. You suffered ridicule, betrayal, persecution, Crucifixion, and death. Your burden was so great, yet you endured. Glorifying God, your sacrifice gives us the hope of eternal life.

Strengthen me to withstand the suffering I must face in my life. When I feel that I have more than I can take, fortify me with the endurance of Job. Give me the patience to suffer injustices without lashing out at others. Fill me with mercy to forgive those who persecute me. Fill me with your loving presence to be a faithful witness to the glory of God and to the promise of eternal life. Amen.

▶ Mt 27:27–44

Cultural Connection

Jesus Died on the Cross Because He Loves Us

Hispanics often identify more with the suffering and crucified Christ than with the risen Christ because of how much they and their ancestors have suffered oppression. In the cross, Hispanics find God's immense love for them. It is a redemptive love, one that brings peace and the strength to accept what cannot be changed and to continue the struggle out of poverty and oppression.

Hispanic young people learn from their families and culture that there is always suffering in life. When this suffering is not ac-

cepted, it is even worse. In contrast, when we accept suffering, it is bearable, and we have the inner peace needed to continue living and working for a better life. Suffering achieves its highest meaning when it is accepted out of love. That Jesus is capable of suffering gives witness to God's special love for those who suffer.

Finding God's life in the midst of suffering leads to generous sacrifices that are a source of life for those we love. Let's pray:

Jesus, help us to always remember that your commitment to your

mission led to your death. Help us to understand that true life is always achieved through love. Help us to have love at the core of all we think and do. And help us to share your love, especially with those who need it the most, those who are poor and marginalized. Amen.

▶ **Mt 27:24–56**

---

in him. ⁴³He trusts in God; let God deliver him now, if he wants to; for he said, 'I am God's Son.'" ⁴⁴The bandits who were crucified with him also taunted him in the same way.

The Death of Jesus

45 From noon on, darkness came over the whole land[a] until three in the afternoon. ⁴⁶And about three o'clock Jesus cried with a loud voice, "Eli, Eli, lema sabachthani?" that is, "My God, my God, why have you forsaken me?" ⁴⁷When some of the bystanders heard it, they said, "This man is calling for Elijah." ⁴⁸At once one of them ran and got a sponge, filled it with sour wine, put it on a stick, and gave it to him to drink. ⁴⁹But the others said, "Wait, let us see whether Elijah will come to save him."[b] ⁵⁰Then Jesus cried again with a loud voice and breathed his last.[c] ⁵¹At that moment the curtain of the temple was torn in two, from top to bottom. The earth shook, and the rocks were split. ⁵²The tombs also were opened, and many bodies of the saints who had fallen asleep were raised. ⁵³After his resurrection they came out of the tombs and entered the holy city and appeared to many. ⁵⁴Now when the centurion and those with him, who were keeping watch over Jesus, saw the earthquake and what took place, they were terrified and said, "Truly this man was God's Son!"[d]

55 Many women were also there, looking on from a distance; they had followed Jesus from Galilee and had provided for him. ⁵⁶Among them were Mary Magdalene, and Mary the mother of James and Joseph, and the mother of the sons of Zebedee.

The Burial of Jesus

57 When it was evening, there came a rich man from Arimathea, named Joseph, who was also a disciple of Jesus. ⁵⁸He went to Pilate and asked for the body of Jesus; then Pilate ordered it to be given to him. ⁵⁹So Joseph took the body and wrapped it in a clean linen cloth ⁶⁰and laid it in his own new tomb, which he had hewn in the rock. He then rolled a great stone to the door of the tomb and went away. ⁶¹Mary Magdalene and the other Mary were there, sitting opposite the tomb.

The Guard at the Tomb

62 The next day, that is, after the day of Preparation, the chief priests and the Pharisees gathered before Pilate ⁶³and said, "Sir, we remember what that impostor said while he was still alive,

---

a Or earth   b Other ancient authorities add *And another took a spear and pierced his side, and out came water and blood*
c Or *gave up his spirit*   d Or *a son of God*

'After three days I will rise again.' ⁶⁴Therefore command the tomb to be made secure until the third day; otherwise his disciples may go and steal him away, and tell the people, 'He has been raised from the dead,' and the last deception would be worse than the first." ⁶⁵Pilate said to them, "You have a guard*ᵃ* of soldiers; go, make it as secure as you can."*ᵇ* ⁶⁶So they went with the guard and made the tomb secure by sealing the stone.

The Resurrection of Jesus

28 After the sabbath, as the first day of the week was dawning, Mary Magdalene and the other Mary went to see the tomb. ²And suddenly there was a great earthquake; for an angel of the Lord, descending from heaven, came and rolled back the stone and sat on it. ³His appearance was like lightning, and his clothing white as snow. ⁴For fear of him the guards shook and became like dead men. ⁵But the angel said to the women, "Do not be afraid; I know that you are looking for Jesus who was crucified. ⁶He is not here; for he has been raised, as he said. Come, see the place where he*ᶜ* lay. ⁷Then go quickly and tell his disciples, 'He has been raised from the dead,*ᵈ* and indeed he is going ahead of you to Galilee; there you will see him.' This is my message for you." ⁸So they left the tomb quickly with fear and great joy, and ran to tell his disciples. ⁹Suddenly Jesus met them and said, "Greetings!" And they came to him, took hold of his feet, and worshiped him. ¹⁰Then Jesus said to them, "Do not be afraid; go and tell my brothers to go to Galilee; there they will see me."

The Report of the Guard

11 While they were going, some of the guard went into the city and told the chief priests everything that had happened. ¹²After the priests*ᵉ* had assembled with the elders, they devised a plan to give a large sum of money to the soldiers, ¹³telling them, "You must say, 'His disciples came by night and stole him away while we were asleep.' ¹⁴If this comes to the governor's ears, we

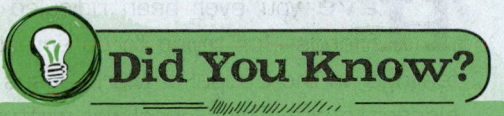

Did You Know?

Jesus Prays Psalm 22

The Gospel writer tells us that before Jesus gave up his spirit and breathed his last breath, he cried out, "My God, my God, why have you forsaken me?" Jesus was actually reciting and praying the opening lines of Psalm 22. This psalm begins in despair but ends in triumph and confidence through God's saving help. With this prayer to God, Jesus invites all people gathered at the Crucifixion to pray the entire psalm—not just the first words of despair but also the concluding words of hope.

▶ Mt 27:46

will satisfy him and keep you out of trouble." ¹⁵So they took the money and did as they were directed. And this story is still told among the Jews to this day.

The Commissioning of the Disciples

16 Now the eleven disciples went to Galilee, to the mountain to which Jesus had directed them. ¹⁷When they saw him, they worshiped him; but some doubted. ¹⁸And Jesus came and said to them, "All authority in heaven and on earth has been given to me. ¹⁹Go therefore and make disciples of all nations, baptizing them in the name of the Father and of the Son and of the Holy Spirit, ²⁰and teaching them to obey everything that I have commanded you. And remember, I am with you always, to the end of the age."*ᶠ*

---

a Or *Take a guard*   *b* Gk *you know how*   *c* Other ancient authorities read *the Lord*   *d* Other ancient authorities lack *from the dead*   *e* Gk *they*   *f* Other ancient authorities add *Amen*

MT

Have you ever been ridiculed or rejected by others—maybe even your friends—for trying to do something good? Jesus would understand your feelings. In the Gospel of Mark, Jesus is misunderstood and abandoned by those closest to him. This Gospel was written for early Christians experiencing persecution or death for their faith. The author is reminding them and us to put our total trust in God as Jesus did, despite whatever difficulties we encounter in being a Christian.

In Depth

The Gospel of Mark is the shortest of the four Gospels and can be easily read in one sitting. It portrays Jesus as a man of action—human in his feelings, and always on the move fulfilling his mission. This Gospel answers two fundamental questions: Who is this Jesus called the Christ? and What does it mean to be his disciple? Because the people hearing this Gospel were being persecuted for believing in Jesus, those questions were a matter of life and death.

At a Glance

- **1:1–15.** John the Baptist's announcement of Jesus' ministry
- **1:16—8:21.** Jesus' preaching and miracles in Galilee
- **8:22—10:52.** Jesus' teaching and healing on the way to Jerusalem
- **Chapters 11–13.** Jesus' teaching in Jerusalem
- **Chapters 14–16.** Jesus' death and Resurrection

Quick Facts

Inspired Author: a Gentile Christian, traditionally thought to be a disciple of Peter named John Mark

Date Written: from approximately AD 65 to 70; this was the first written Gospel

Audience: non-Jewish Christians (in Rome?) who were experiencing persecution because of their belief in Jesus

Image of Jesus: healer and miracle worker who accepts suffering as the cost for following God's will

To answer the first question, the Gospel of Mark tells stories about Jesus' power to heal and about his compassion for suffering people. It tells about his conflicts with demons and with religious and civil authorities and how he was misunderstood by his own disciples. Through these stories, the reader learns that Jesus is the Son of God, the favored one who acts with God's authority because he is obedient to God's will. Jesus did not come as the victorious king as many Jews expected. Instead, he accepted the suffering that comes with doing God's will. His painful and shameful death was needed before his glory could be seen. Can we believe in a despised, suffering Messiah?

Mark answers the second question in surprising ways. The disciples Jesus called were initially eager to follow him, but they quickly became fearful. They wanted to be powerful and important, and they wanted the approval of their peers. Even when Jesus was arrested, they were so fearful that they ran away and left Jesus alone. But Jesus did not abandon them. After he was raised from the dead, he sent them a message that he would meet them again in Galilee. The Gospel of Mark also tells stories about a blind man, a leper, and Gentiles (non-Jews), all of whom were Jesus' disciples because they placed their total trust in him. Whether gradually or quickly, can we place our complete faith in Jesus, becoming his disciples?

Mark

The Proclamation of John the Baptist

1 The beginning of the good news[a] of Jesus Christ, the Son of God.[b]

2 As it is written in the prophet Isaiah,[c]

"See, I am sending my messenger ahead of
you,[d]
who will prepare your way;
3 the voice of one crying out in the wilderness:
'Prepare the way of the Lord,
make his paths straight,' "

4 John the baptizer appeared[e] in the wilderness, proclaiming a baptism of repentance for the forgiveness of sins. 5 And people from the whole Judean countryside and all the people of Jerusalem were going out to him, and were baptized by him in the river Jordan, confessing their sins. 6 Now John was clothed with camel's hair, with a leather belt around his waist, and he ate locusts and wild honey. 7 He proclaimed, "The one who is more powerful than I is coming after me; I am not worthy to stoop down and untie the thong of his sandals. 8 I have baptized you with[f] water; but he will baptize you with[f] the Holy Spirit."

The Baptism of Jesus

9 In those days Jesus came from Nazareth of Galilee and was baptized by John in the Jordan. 10 And just as he was coming up out of the water, he saw the heavens torn apart and the Spirit descending like a dove on him. 11 And a voice came from heaven, "You are my Son, the Beloved;[g] with you I am well pleased."

The Temptation of Jesus

12 And the Spirit immediately drove him out into the wilderness. 13 He was in the wilderness forty days, tempted by Satan; and he was with the wild beasts; and the angels waited on him.

The Beginning of the Galilean Ministry

14 Now after John was arrested, Jesus came to Galilee, proclaiming the good news[a] of God,[h] 15 and saying, "The time is fulfilled, and the kingdom of God has come near;[i] repent, and believe in the good news."[a]

Jesus Calls the First Disciples

16 As Jesus passed along the Sea of Galilee, he saw Simon and his brother Andrew casting a net into the sea—for they were fishermen. 17 And Jesus said to them, "Follow me and I will make you fish for people." 18 And immediately they left their nets and followed him. 19 As he went a little farther, he saw James son of Zebedee and his brother John, who were in their boat mending the nets. 20 Immediately he called them; and they left their father Zebedee in the boat with the hired men, and followed him.

---

a Or *gospel*   b Other ancient authorities lack *the Son of God*
c Other ancient authorities read *in the prophets*   d Gk *before your face*   e Other ancient authorities read *John was baptizing*   f Or *in* g Or *my beloved Son*   h Other ancient authorities read *of the kingdom*   i Or *is at hand*

Cultural Connection

Spirits

Most Native American peoples would not be surprised by all the angels and spirits in the first chapter of Mark. Many Native American cultures believe in the presence of good and bad spirits in the world. They view good spirits as personal helpers and message bearers, like the angels who take care of Jesus in verse 13. They believe that spirits often appear as animals, much as the Holy Spirit appears as a dove in verse 10. And many believe that bad spirits influence and control people, just as the unclean spirit does in verse 23.

Isn't it interesting that different cultures can develop such parallel religious beliefs? Whether we call them angels and demons or good and bad spirits, we share a common understanding about unseen powers influencing our lives. It is an understanding of the world that is often rejected in our scientific, technology-filled culture.

▶ **Mk 1:9–39**

The Man with an Unclean Spirit

21 They went to Capernaum; and when the sabbath came, he entered the synagogue and taught. 22They were astounded at his teaching, for he taught them as one having authority, and not as the scribes. 23Just then there was in their synagogue a man with an unclean spirit, 24and he cried out, "What have you to do with us, Jesus of Nazareth? Have you come to destroy us? I know who you are, the Holy One of God." 25But Jesus rebuked him, saying, "Be silent, and come out of him!" 26And the unclean spirit, convulsing him and crying with a loud voice, came out of him. 27They were all amazed, and they kept on asking one another, "What is this? A new teaching—with authority! He*a* commands even the unclean spirits, and they obey him." 28At once his fame began to spread throughout the surrounding region of Galilee.

Jesus Heals Many at Simon's House

29 As soon as they*b* left the synagogue, they entered the house of Simon and Andrew, with James and John. 30Now Simon's mother-in-law was in bed with a fever, and they told him about her at once. 31He came and took her by the hand and lifted her up. Then the fever left her, and she began to serve them.

32 That evening, at sunset, they brought to him all who were sick or possessed with demons. 33And the whole city was gathered around the door. 34And he cured many who were sick with various diseases, and cast out many demons; and he would not permit the demons to speak, because they knew him.

A Preaching Tour in Galilee

35 In the morning, while it was still very dark, he got up and went out to a deserted place, and there he prayed. 36And Simon and his companions hunted for him. 37When they found him, they said to him, "Everyone is searching for you." 38He answered, "Let us go on to the neighboring towns, so that I may proclaim the message there also; for that is what I came out to do." 39And he went throughout Galilee, proclaiming the message in their synagogues and casting out demons.

Jesus Cleanses a Leper

40 A leper*c* came to him begging him, and kneeling*d* he said to him, "If you choose, you can make me clean." 41Moved with pity,*e* Jesus*f* stretched out his hand and touched him, and said to him, "I do choose. Be made clean!" 42Immediately the leprosy*c* left him, and he was made clean. 43After sternly warning him he sent him away at once, 44saying to him, "See that you say nothing to anyone; but go, show yourself to the priest, and offer for your cleansing what Moses commanded, as a testimony to them." 45But he went out and began to proclaim it freely, and to spread the word, so that Jesus*f* could no longer go into a town openly, but stayed out in the country; and people came to him from every quarter.

a Or *A new teaching! With authority he*　*b* Other ancient authorities read *he*　*c* The terms *leper* and *leprosy* can refer to several diseases　*d* Other ancient authorities lack *kneeling*　*e* Other ancient authorities read *anger*　*f* Gk *he*

Jesus Heals a Paralytic

2 When he returned to Capernaum after some days, it was reported that he was at home. ²So many gathered around that there was no longer room for them, not even in front of the door; and he was speaking the word to them. ³Then some peopleᵃ came, bringing to him a paralyzed man, carried by four of them. ⁴And when they could not bring him to Jesus because of the crowd, they removed the roof above him; and after having dug through it, they let down the mat on which the paralytic lay. ⁵When Jesus saw their faith, he said to the paralytic, "Son, your sins are forgiven." ⁶Now some of the scribes were sitting there, questioning in their hearts, ⁷"Why

does this fellow speak in this way? It is blasphemy! Who can forgive sins but God alone?" ⁸At once Jesus perceived in his spirit that they were discussing these questions among themselves; and he said to them, "Why do you raise such questions in your hearts? ⁹Which is easier, to say to the paralytic, 'Your sins are forgiven,' or to say, 'Stand up and take your mat and walk'? ¹⁰But so that you may know that the Son of Man has authority on earth to forgive sins"—he said to the paralytic— ¹¹"I say to you, stand up, take your mat and go to your home." ¹²And he stood up, and immediately took the mat and went out before all of them; so that they were all amazed and glorified God, saying, "We have never seen anything like this!"

a Gk they

Called to Follow Jesus

The response of Peter, Andrew, James, and John to Jesus is an example of obedience to God's call. Jesus calls them because he loves them and trusts them to share in his mission.

The Catholic Church believes that through Baptism, all Christians are called to be Jesus' disciples (followers) in whatever path their lives take. Most people are called to mission as laypersons. A few are called to serve through the priesthood, diaconate, or religious life. So whether you end up a priest or a plumber, married or single, poor or rich, faithfulness to God's call is the most important loyalty you can have.

It might be hard to imagine how school or a fast-food job is part of your call to follow Jesus. But attitude is everything! Do you see school as a necessary evil to get a high-paying job? or do you see it as preparation for a career that will allow you to serve others and contribute to society? If you work, do you approach your job halfheartedly, or are you enthusiastic, always giving your best effort? Do you treat coworkers and customers with warmth and respect? Jesus is calling you to be his disciple wherever you are and in whatever you might be doing.

▶ Mk 1:16–20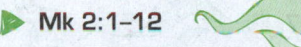

Sacramental Healing

The physical healing Jesus provides for the paralytic in this story is considered miraculous, and rightly so. What shouldn't get lost in the story, however, is that along with his physical healing, Jesus offers this man spiritual healing: the forgiveness of his sins. Imagine the sense of comfort this man must have felt as he walked away, his heart cleansed and his spirit lifted!

Reflecting the actions of Jesus in this story, the Catholic Church has two sacraments dedicated to healing. The sacrament of Penance and Reconciliation offers us personal healing if we are willing to be honest about the sinfulness in our lives. The sacrament of Anointing of the Sick offers hope, strength, and spiritual comfort to the seriously ill and aged. Each sacrament is a tangible sign of God's love for those who suffer in body and spirit, and is meant to empower us to share in Jesus' ministry of healing.

- When have you reconciled with those who are in need of forgiveness?
- In what ways can you bring comfort and hope to those who are in need of healing, either in body or spirit?

▶ Mk 2:1–12

MK

Jesus Calls Levi

13 Jesus[a] went out again beside the sea; the whole crowd gathered around him, and he taught them. [14]As he was walking along, he saw Levi son of Alphaeus sitting at the tax booth, and he said to him, "Follow me." And he got up and followed him.

15 And as he sat at dinner[b] in Levi's[c] house, many tax collectors and sinners were also sitting[d] with Jesus and his disciples—for there were many who followed him. [16]When the scribes of[e] the Pharisees saw that he was eating with sinners and tax collectors, they said to his disciples, "Why does he eat[f] with tax collectors and sinners?" [17]When Jesus heard this, he said to them, "Those who are well have no need of a physician, but those who are sick; I have come to call not the righteous but sinners."

The Question about Fasting

18 Now John's disciples and the Pharisees were fasting; and people[g] came and said to him, "Why do John's disciples and the disciples of the Pharisees fast, but your disciples do not fast?" [19]Jesus said to them, "The wedding guests cannot fast while the bridegroom is with them, can they? As long as they have the bridegroom with them, they cannot fast. [20]The days will come when the bridegroom is taken away from them, and then they will fast on that day.

21 "No one sews a piece of unshrunk cloth on an old cloak; otherwise, the patch pulls away from it, the new from the old, and a worse tear is made. [22]And no one puts new wine into old wineskins; otherwise, the wine will burst the skins, and the wine is lost, and so are the skins; but one puts new wine into fresh wineskins."[h]

Pronouncement about the Sabbath

23 One sabbath he was going through the grainfields; and as they made their way his disciples began to pluck heads of grain. [24]The Pharisees said to him, "Look, why are they doing what is not lawful on the sabbath?" [25]And he said to them, "Have you never read what David did when he and his companions were hungry and in need of food? [26]He entered the house of God, when Abiathar was high priest, and ate the bread of the Presence, which it is not lawful for any but the priests to eat, and he gave some to his companions." [27]Then he said to them, "The sabbath was made for humankind, and not humankind for the sabbath; [28]so the Son of Man is lord even of the sabbath."

The Man with a Withered Hand

3 Again he entered the synagogue, and a man was there who had a withered hand. [2]They watched him to see whether he would cure him on the sabbath, so that they might accuse him. [3]And he said to the man who had the withered hand, "Come forward." [4]Then he said to them, "Is it lawful to do good or to do harm on the sabbath, to save life or to kill?" But they were

MK

Getting Personal

It is one thing to be seen hanging out with certain groups of people, but it is another to be seen eating with them. Jesus was often criticized for eating with the wrong kind of people, a charge he answers in Mark 2:13–17. He knew that the only way to help someone grow was to get to know him or her personally. This is why he consistently invited people to sit down and share a meal with him, in the same way we share meals with our family and friends.

Jesus' "meal ministry" throughout the Gospels is a reminder to us that we too must live in solidarity and friendship with all people in our world, especially those who are most in need. It did not matter to Jesus whether a person was rich or poor, well known or unknown, regarded as a saint or as a sinner. It did not matter to him whether a person was black or white, male or female, young or old. What did matter to Jesus was whether the person he approached was interested in getting to know him—and his heavenly Father—personally.

Are you ready to get to know Jesus personally? If so, take a few minutes to close your eyes and think about what this passage says. Talk to Jesus about what is going on in your life and in your family's life. When you are done talking, spend some time quietly listening for what Jesus has to say to you—personally.

▶ Mk 2:13–17

silent. ⁵He looked around at them with anger; he was grieved at their hardness of heart and said to the man, "Stretch out your hand." He stretched it out, and his hand was restored. ⁶The Pharisees went out and immediately conspired with the Herodians against him, how to destroy him.

A Multitude at the Seaside

7 Jesus departed with his disciples to the sea, and a great multitude from Galilee followed him; ⁸hearing all that he was doing, they came to him in great numbers from Judea, Jerusalem, Idumea, beyond the Jordan, and the region around Tyre and Sidon. ⁹He told his disciples to have a boat ready for him because of the crowd, so that they would not crush him; ¹⁰for he had cured many, so that all who had diseases pressed upon him to touch him. ¹¹Whenever the unclean spirits saw him, they fell down before him and shouted, "You are the Son of God!" ¹²But he sternly ordered them not to make him known.

Jesus Appoints the Twelve

13 He went up the mountain and called to him those whom he wanted, and they came to him. ¹⁴And he appointed twelve, whom he also named apostles,ᵃ to be with him, and to be sent out to proclaim the message, ¹⁵and to have authority to cast out demons. ¹⁶So he appointed the twelve:ᵇ Simon (to whom he gave the name Peter); ¹⁷James son of Zebedee and John the brother of James (to whom he gave the name Boanerges, that is, Sons of Thunder); ¹⁸and Andrew, and Philip, and Bartholomew, and Matthew, and Thomas, and James son of Alphaeus, and Thaddaeus, and Simon the Cananaean, ¹⁹and Judas Iscariot, who betrayed him.

Jesus and Beelzebul

Then he went home; ²⁰and the crowd came together again, so that they could not even eat. ²¹When his family heard it, they went out to restrain him, for people were saying, "He has gone out of his mind." ²²And the scribes who came down from Jerusalem said, "He has Beelzebul, and by the ruler of the demons he casts out demons." ²³And he called them to him, and spoke to them in parables, "How can Satan cast out Satan? ²⁴If a kingdom is divided against itself, that kingdom cannot stand. ²⁵And if a house is divided against itself, that house will not be able to stand. ²⁶And if Satan has risen up against himself and is divided, he cannot stand, but his end has come. ²⁷But no one can enter a strong man's house and plunder his property without first

Live It!

Trusting God

In Mark 3:1–6, among those gathered in the synagogue is a man with a withered hand. There is no indication that he is seeking out Jesus or that he commands any special attention. Jesus notices him and invites him to come forward. Jesus then asks the man to stretch out his disfigured hand for all to see. The man, we might guess, probably did not feel proud of his hand. It certainly would be understandable if, when invited by Jesus to stretch out his hand for all to see, the man had stormed out of the synagogue in anger and shame. Instead, he did what Jesus asked, and through his trust in Jesus, his hand was restored to wholeness.

We are all "disfigured" in some way—whether physically, emotionally, or spiritually. We may feel a sense of shame or embarrassment at our imperfections and come to think of ourselves as less than what we were created to be. Jesus, however, invites us into relationship with him despite our limitations, offering us compassion, love, and mercy if we are willing to put our trust in him.

- What source of pain or shame in your own life might Jesus be inviting you to share with him?
- Can you risk becoming vulnerable and trusting him with it?

▶ Mk 3:1–6

tying up the strong man; then indeed the house can be plundered.

28 "Truly I tell you, people will be forgiven for their sins and whatever blasphemies they utter; ²⁹but whoever blasphemes against the Holy Spirit can never have forgiveness, but is guilty of an eternal sin"— ³⁰for they had said, "He has an unclean spirit."

The True Kindred of Jesus

31 Then his mother and his brothers came; and standing outside, they sent to him and called

---

ᵃ Other ancient authorities lack *whom he also named apostles*
ᵇ Other ancient authorities lack *So he appointed the twelve*

MK

✝ Catholic Connection

Holy Orders

God has a plan for each of us, if we just have the courage to follow it. Look at the Twelve Apostles Christ called to join him on the mountain. Each had the choice to go up the mountain or not, and each chose to go. Once on the mountain, Christ appointed them Apostles (which means "sent") to continue his mission. If the Apostles had answered "no" to Jesus' call, they may have been spared the heartbreak of witnessing the Crucifixion, but they also would have missed the joy of seeing Jesus after the Resurrection!

All God's people are invited to share in Christ's mission through the sacrament of Baptism in what is called the common priesthood. This means that all Christians are called to share in Christ's priesthood by living holy lives and spreading God's message of love. But just as Jesus singled out the Twelve Apostles to carry on his mission as leaders in the Church, some men are also invited to participate in the mission of Christ by answering the call to the ministerial priesthood. This differs from the common priesthood in that the ministerial priesthood is given a sacred power to serve the Church by helping all the faithful to live out their baptismal calling. Men who answer "yes" to the ministerial priesthood are ordained by receiving the sacrament of Holy Orders.

Through the sacrament, a man enters into one of three forms of ministry, becoming a bishop, priest, or deacon. Through the grace of ordination, bishops are the direct successors of the Apostles. Out of their love for Christ, they work with the Pope to lead, teach, and celebrate the sacraments. Priests are ordained as co-workers of the bishop and serve the Church especially through teaching the faithful and sacramental ministry. Deacons are ordained as helpers to the bishop, proclaiming the word and performing acts of charity. Together, through these three forms of ministry, these men show their love for Christ and through their work Christ shows his love for the Church.

The celebration of the sacrament of Holy Orders is always administered by a bishop and varies depending on the ministry the man is entering. During the rite, the men becoming bishops and priests are anointed with sacred chrism (oil) as a sign of the Holy Spirit who empowers them to fulfill their ministry. During the ordination of a deacon, the man has hands laid upon him by the bishop, who then prays for the gift of the Holy Spirit to empower and guide the new deacon's ministry.

▶ Mk 3:13–19

Catechism, nos. 1533–1600

Cultural Connection

Jesus Teaches Us Through Stories

In Mark, chapter 4, Jesus teaches about God's Reign through parables (see "Parables," near Mt 13:10). In some Hispanic families, it is customary for young people to hear their *abuelita* (grandmother) tell stories about their family history, traditions, and faith. Many of the stories are true; others may be created to give a moral teaching, like the parables.

Here is a true story: A little girl's father died, leaving her family in extreme poverty. Her mother never lost faith in God, daily prayed to the Divine Providence, and asked other people to pray with her. Her prayers were always answered: food appeared miraculously in front of the family's door, and her six children were accepted free in Catholic schools.

Eventually, the mother married a creative businessman. When the business prospered, she remembered the way God had moved the hearts of people so that her family could have food and education, and with great confidence in God, she started a boarding school for boys. Whenever there was not enough food, she prayed and invited other people to pray. The Divine Providence always responded. The school has sheltered and educated two hundred boys each year for the last seventy years.

- Which stories of faith, love, and service have marked the history of your family?
- How are you honoring your family's tradition of bringing the Gospel to people in need?

▶ Mk 4:1–34

him. ³²A crowd was sitting around him; and they said to him, "Your mother and your brothers and sisters[a] are outside, asking for you." ³³And he replied, "Who are my mother and my brothers?" ³⁴And looking at those who sat around him, he said, "Here are my mother and my brothers! ³⁵Whoever does the will of God is my brother and sister and mother."

The Parable of the Sower

4 Again he began to teach beside the sea. Such a very large crowd gathered around him that he got into a boat on the sea and sat there, while the whole crowd was beside the sea on the land. ²He began to teach them many things in parables, and in his teaching he said to them: ³"Listen! A sower went out to sow. ⁴And as he sowed, some seed fell on the path, and the birds came and ate it up. ⁵Other seed fell on rocky ground, where it did not have much soil, and it sprang up quickly, since it had no depth of soil. ⁶And when the sun rose, it was scorched; and since it had no root, it withered away. ⁷Other seed fell among thorns, and the thorns grew up and choked it, and it yielded no grain. ⁸Other seed fell into good soil and brought forth grain, growing up and increasing and yielding thirty and sixty and a hundredfold." ⁹And he said, "Let anyone with ears to hear listen!"

The Purpose of the Parables

10 When he was alone, those who were around him along with the twelve asked him about the parables. ¹¹And he said to them, "To you has been given the secret[b] of the kingdom of God, but for those outside, everything comes in parables; ¹²in order that

'they may indeed look, but not perceive,
and may indeed listen, but not understand;
so that they may not turn again and be forgiven.' "

13 And he said to them, "Do you not understand this parable? Then how will you understand all the parables? ¹⁴The sower sows the word. ¹⁵These are the ones on the path where the word is sown: when they hear, Satan immediately comes and takes away the word that is sown in them. ¹⁶And these are the ones sown on rocky ground: when they hear the word, they immediately receive it with joy. ¹⁷But they have no root, and endure only for a while; then, when trouble or persecution arises on account of the word, immediately they fall away.[c] ¹⁸And others are those sown among the thorns: these are the ones who hear the word, ¹⁹but the cares of the world, and

---

a Other ancient authorities lack *and sisters* b Or *mystery*
c Or *stumble*

the lure of wealth, and the desire for other things come in and choke the word, and it yields nothing. ²⁰And these are the ones sown on the good soil: they hear the word and accept it and bear fruit, thirty and sixty and a hundredfold."

A Lamp under a Bushel Basket

21 He said to them, "Is a lamp brought in to be put under the bushel basket, or under the bed, and not on the lampstand? ²²For there is nothing hidden, except to be disclosed; nor is anything secret, except to come to light. ²³Let anyone with ears to hear listen!" ²⁴And he said to them, "Pay attention to what you hear; the measure you give will be the measure you get, and still more will be given you. ²⁵For to those who have, more will be given; and from those who have nothing, even what they have will be taken away."

The Parable of the Growing Seed

26 He also said, "The kingdom of God is as if someone would scatter seed on the ground, ²⁷and would sleep and rise night and day, and the seed would sprout and grow, he does not know how. ²⁸The earth produces of itself, first the stalk, then the head, then the full grain in the head. ²⁹But when the grain is ripe, at once he goes in with his sickle, because the harvest has come."

The Parable of the Mustard Seed

30 He also said, "With what can we compare the kingdom of God, or what parable will we use for it? ³¹It is like a mustard seed, which, when sown upon the ground, is the smallest of all the seeds on earth; ³²yet when it is sown it grows up and becomes the greatest of all shrubs, and puts forth large branches, so that the birds of the air can make nests in its shade."

The Use of Parables

33 With many such parables he spoke the word to them, as they were able to hear it; ³⁴he

did not speak to them except in parables, but he explained everything in private to his disciples.

Jesus Stills a Storm

35 On that day, when evening had come, he said to them, "Let us go across to the other side." ³⁶And leaving the crowd behind, they took him with them in the boat, just as he was. Other boats were with him. ³⁷A great windstorm arose, and the waves beat into the boat, so that the boat was already being swamped. ³⁸But he was in the stern, asleep on the cushion; and they woke him up and said to him, "Teacher, do you not care that we are perishing?" ³⁹He woke up and rebuked the wind, and said to the sea, "Peace! Be still!" Then the wind ceased, and there was a dead calm. ⁴⁰He said to them, "Why are you

Life's Storms

Storms on the Sea of Galilee are a common occurrence. They are a fisher's nightmare, and the one described in Mark 4:35–41 was really bad! It is no wonder the Apostles felt fearful and powerless. As part of your prayer, try this meditation:

Begin by closing your eyes and relaxing. Then visualize yourself standing on the beach with Jesus and the disciples. Join them as they board the boat. When the squall comes, experience the rocking of the boat, the waves crashing on deck, and the winds blowing. Feel the disciples' anxiety and fear as the boat is tossed and water pours into the boat. Go with the disciples to wake Jesus, and watch as Jesus calms the storm. Now, experience the peacefulness and tranquility of the miracle you have witnessed.

All of us have storms we must face—that is, parts of our lives that are filled with anxiety or fear. Think about your life. What are the storms that batter and rock your world? Who in your family or in your community can calm your fears? How would you respond to Jesus' question, "Have you still no faith?" (Mk 4:40).

▶ Mk 4:35–41

4:30–32

afraid? Have you still no faith?" ⁴¹And they were filled with great awe and said to one another, "Who then is this, that even the wind and the sea obey him?"

Jesus Heals the Gerasene Demoniac

5 They came to the other side of the sea, to the country of the Gerasenes.ᵃ ²And when he had stepped out of the boat, immediately a man out of the tombs with an unclean spirit met him. ³He lived among the tombs; and no one could restrain him any more, even with a chain; ⁴for he had often been restrained with shackles and chains, but the chains he wrenched apart, and the shackles he broke in pieces; and no one had the strength to subdue him. ⁵Night and day among the tombs and on the mountains he was always howling and bruising himself with stones. ⁶When he saw Jesus from a distance, he ran and bowed down before him; ⁷and he shouted at the top of his voice, "What have you to do with me, Jesus, Son of the Most High God? I adjure you by God, do not torment me." ⁸For he had said to him, "Come out of the man, you unclean spirit!" ⁹Then Jesusᵇ asked him, "What

is your name?" He replied, "My name is Legion; for we are many." ¹⁰He begged him earnestly not to send them out of the country. ¹¹Now there on the hillside a great herd of swine was feeding; ¹²and the unclean spiritsᶜ begged him, "Send us into the swine; let us enter them." ¹³So he gave them permission. And the unclean spirits came out and entered the swine; and the herd, numbering about two thousand, rushed down the steep bank into the sea, and were drowned in the sea.

14 The swineherds ran off and told it in the city and in the country. Then people came to see what it was that had happened. ¹⁵They came to Jesus and saw the demoniac sitting there, clothed and in his right mind, the very man who had had the legion; and they were afraid. ¹⁶Those who had seen what had happened to the demoniac and to the swine reported it. ¹⁷Then they began to beg Jesusᵈ to leave their neighborhood. ¹⁸As

---

a Other ancient authorities read *Gergesenes*; others, *Gadarenes*
b Gk *he*   c Gk *they*   d Gk *him*

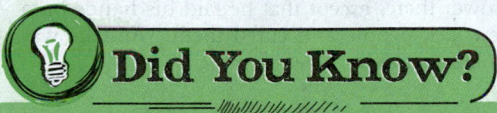

Did You Know?

Demon Possession

The Gospels of Matthew, Mark, and Luke all have stories about Jesus' curing people of unclean spirits, or demons. Many cultures believe in spirits, both good and bad (see "Spirits," near Mk 1:9–39), which can influence or even control people's decisions and actions. The first time a demon is mentioned in the Bible is in the Book of Tobit; however, the concept of demons is much older. Demons represented evil—mysterious powers hostile to God, health, and goodness. Jesus' ability to free people of demonic influence was a sign of the arrival of the Reign of God (see "Miracles and the Reign of God," near Mt 8:1—9:34).

The ancients believed that illness was caused by evil spirits. We don't hold that view today, but we do recognize that illness is a part of the spiritual reality that affects our lives.

▶ Mk 1:23–34, 5:1–20

Everyone's Welcome!

In Mark, chapters 5–8, Jesus expands his mission into Gentile territory, the region on the eastern side of the Sea of Galilee. Three miraculous healings of Gentiles—the Gerasene demoniac (see 5:1–13), the Syrophoenician's daughter (see 7:24–30), and the deaf man from Tyre (see 7:31–37)—extend the promises of the Reign of God to all who have faith in Jesus. In arranging these stories, the author of the Gospel emphasizes that God's salvation is available to everyone, not just to the Jews.

In your prayer, reflect or journal on the following questions:
- How do you treat people from a different race, culture, or religion?
- How could you be more welcoming toward them, more like Jesus?

Write a prayer expressing your desire to be more like Jesus.

▶ Mk 5:1—8:30

he was getting into the boat, the man who had been possessed by demons begged him that he might be with him. [19]But Jesus*a* refused, and said to him, "Go home to your friends, and tell them how much the Lord has done for you, and what mercy he has shown you." [20]And he went away and began to proclaim in the Decapolis how much Jesus had done for him; and everyone was amazed.

A Girl Restored to Life and a Woman Healed

21 When Jesus had crossed again in the boat*b* to the other side, a great crowd gathered around him; and he was by the sea. [22]Then one of the leaders of the synagogue named Jairus came and, when he saw him, fell at his feet [23]and begged him repeatedly, "My little daughter is at the point of death. Come and lay your hands on her, so that she may be made well, and live." [24]So he went with him.

And a large crowd followed him and pressed in on him. [25]Now there was a woman who had been suffering from hemorrhages for twelve years. [26]She had endured much under many physicians, and had spent all that she had; and she was no better, but rather grew worse. [27]She had heard about Jesus, and came up behind him in the crowd and touched his cloak, [28]for she said, "If I but touch his clothes, I will be made well." [29]Immediately her hemorrhage stopped; and she felt in her body that she was healed of her disease. [30]Immediately aware that power had gone forth from him, Jesus turned about in the crowd and said, "Who touched my clothes?" [31]And his disciples said to him, "You see the crowd pressing in on you; how can you say, 'Who touched me?'" [32]He looked all around to see who had done it. [33]But the woman, knowing what had happened to her, came in fear and trembling, fell down before him, and told him the whole truth. [34]He said to her, "Daughter, your faith has made you well; go in peace, and be healed of your disease."

35 While he was still speaking, some people came from the leader's house to say, "Your daughter is dead. Why trouble the teacher any further?" [36]But overhearing*c* what they said, Jesus said to the leader of the synagogue, "Do not fear, only believe." [37]He allowed no one to follow him except Peter, James, and John, the brother of James. [38]When they came to the house of the leader of the synagogue, he saw a commotion, people weeping and wailing loudly. [39]When he had entered, he said to them, "Why do you make a commotion and weep? The child is not dead but sleeping." [40]And they laughed at him. Then he put them all outside, and took the child's father and mother and those who were with him, and went in where the child was. [41]He took her by the hand and said to her, "Talitha cum," which means, "Little girl, get up!" [42]And immediately the girl got up and began to walk about (she was twelve years of age). At this they were overcome with amazement. [43]He strictly ordered them that no one should know this, and told them to give her something to eat.

The Rejection of Jesus at Nazareth

6 He left that place and came to his hometown, and his disciples followed him. [2]On the sabbath he began to teach in the synagogue, and many who heard him were astounded. They said, "Where did this man get all this? What is this wisdom that has been given to him? What deeds of power are being done by his hands! [3]Is not this the carpenter, the son of Mary*d* and brother of James and Joses and Judas and Simon, and are not his sisters here with us?" And they took offense*e* at him. [4]Then Jesus said to them, "Prophets are not without honor, except in their hometown, and among their own kin, and in their own house." [5]And he could do no deed of power there, except that he laid his hands on a few sick people and cured them. [6]And he was amazed at their unbelief.

The Mission of the Twelve

Then he went about among the villages teaching. [7]He called the twelve and began to send them out two by two, and gave them authority over the unclean spirits. [8]He ordered them to take nothing for their journey except a staff; no bread, no bag, no money in their belts; [9]but to wear sandals and not to put on two tunics. [10]He said to them, "Wherever you enter a house, stay there until you leave the place. [11]If any place will not welcome you and they refuse to hear you, as you leave, shake off the dust that is on your feet as a testimony against them." [12]So they went out and proclaimed that all should repent. [13]They cast out many demons, and anointed with oil many who were sick and cured them.

The Death of John the Baptist

14 King Herod heard of it, for Jesus'*f* name had become known. Some were*g* saying, "John the baptizer has been raised from the dead; and for this reason these powers are at work in him."

---

a Gk *he* *b* Other ancient authorities lack *in the boat* *c* Or *ignoring*; other ancient authorities read *hearing* *d* Other ancient authorities read *son of the carpenter and of Mary* *e* Or *stumbled* *f* Gk *his* *g* Other ancient authorities read *He was*

Catholic Social Teaching

"The Carpenter?"

"Is not this the carpenter?" (Mk 6:3). The people of Nazareth were astounded by how a man, who in their minds was merely a carpenter, could speak and act with such wisdom and power. Perhaps they had low expectations of Jesus, given that his work was a humble trade, one that certainly was not associated with great wealth or prestige. Jesus shows us, however, that all workers, even those who engage in simple, unassuming work, are capable of great things.

This unique glimpse of Jesus, as the worker, is a reminder to us that Jesus was both a laborer and a minister to his people. We have a similar vocational call to be workers and ministers, no matter what kind of work we do. As Jesus did, we must ensure that the work we do is focused not on the acquisition of wealth, power, or social status but on the preservation of justice, fairness, and the dignity of all people. Catholic social teaching reminds us that all work inherently has dignity and

that, consequently, all those who work deserve to be treated with dignity, whether that worker is an underpaid factory worker, an overworked migrant farmer, or even a humble carpenter.

▶ **Mk 6:1–6**
The Dignity of Work and the Rights of Workers

**M
K**

---

¹⁵But others said, "It is Elijah." And others said, "It is a prophet, like one of the prophets of old." ¹⁶But when Herod heard of it, he said, "John, whom I beheaded, has been raised."

17 For Herod himself had sent men who arrested John, bound him, and put him in prison on account of Herodias, his brother Philip's wife, because Herod*ᵃ* had married her. ¹⁸For John had been telling Herod, "It is not lawful for you to have your brother's wife." ¹⁹And Herodias had a grudge against him, and wanted to kill him. But she could not, ²⁰for Herod feared John, knowing that he was a righteous and holy man, and he protected him. When he heard him, he was greatly perplexed;*ᵇ* and yet he liked to listen to him. ²¹But an opportunity came when Herod on his birthday gave a banquet for his courtiers and officers and for the leaders of Galilee. ²²When his daughter Herodias*ᶜ* came in and danced, she pleased Herod and his guests; and the king said to the girl, "Ask me for whatever you wish, and I will give it." ²³And he solemnly swore to her, "Whatever you ask me, I will give you, even half of my kingdom." ²⁴She went out and said to her mother, "What should I ask for?" She replied, "The head of John the baptizer." ²⁵Immediately she rushed back to the king and requested, "I want you to give me at once the head of John the Baptist on a platter." ²⁶The king was deeply grieved; yet out of regard for his oaths and for the guests, he did not want to refuse her.

²⁷Immediately the king sent a soldier of the guard with orders to bring John's*ᵈ* head. He went and beheaded him in the prison, ²⁸brought his head on a platter, and gave it to the girl. Then the girl gave it to her mother. ²⁹When his disciples heard about it, they came and took his body, and laid it in a tomb.

Feeding the Five Thousand

30 The apostles gathered around Jesus, and told him all that they had done and taught. ³¹He said to them, "Come away to a deserted place all by yourselves and rest a while." For many were coming and going, and they had no leisure even to eat. ³²And they went away in the boat to a deserted place by themselves. ³³Now many saw them going and recognized them, and they hurried there on foot from all the towns and arrived ahead of them. ³⁴As he went ashore, he saw a great crowd; and he had compassion for them, because they were like sheep without a shepherd; and he began to teach them many things. ³⁵When it grew late, his disciples came to him and said, "This is a deserted place, and the hour is now very late; ³⁶send them away so that they may go into the surrounding country and villages and buy something for themselves

---

a Gk *he*   *b* Other ancient authorities read *he did many things*
c Other ancient authorities read *the daughter of Herodias herself*
d Gk *his*

Did You Know?

Those Thickheaded Disciples

The disciples in the Gospel of Mark seem unable to do anything right. During a storm at sea, they fail to put their trust in Jesus (see Mk 4:35–41). Then they cannot understand about the miracle of the bread because their hearts are hardened (see 6:52). When Jesus gives them private tutoring sessions, they still fail to understand his teachings. Later, Peter proclaims that Jesus is the Messiah, but he ends up arguing with him after Jesus tells him that he will be a suffering Messiah (see 8:27–33). Finally, when Jesus is arrested, the disciples all desert him (see 14:50).

The author of Mark intentionally emphasizes the lack of faith of the original disciples in order to contrast it with the unexpected faith of people like the Syrophoenician woman in 7:24–30. The Gospel makes the point that Jesus' true disciples are the ones who hear Jesus and place their faith in him. But don't count out the original disciples. Their journey is like most of ours, a lifelong experience of growing in faith and understanding. The Acts of the Apostles tells how they fearlessly preached the news about the risen Christ. Despite their human weakness, God works through them. That goes for us too!

▶ Mk 6:30–52

to eat." ³⁷But he answered them, "You give them something to eat." They said to him, "Are we to go and buy two hundred denarii*a* worth of bread, and give it to them to eat?" ³⁸And he said to them, "How many loaves have you? Go and see." When they had found out, they said, "Five, and two fish." ³⁹Then he ordered them to get all the people to sit down in groups on the green grass. ⁴⁰So they sat down in groups of hundreds and of fifties. ⁴¹Taking the five loaves and the two fish, he looked up to heaven, and blessed and broke the loaves, and gave them to his disciples to set before the people; and he divided the two fish among them all. ⁴²And all ate and were filled; ⁴³and they took up twelve baskets full of broken pieces and of the fish. ⁴⁴Those who had eaten the loaves numbered five thousand men.

Jesus Walks on the Water

45 Immediately he made his disciples get into the boat and go on ahead to the other side, to Bethsaida, while he dismissed the crowd. ⁴⁶After saying farewell to them, he went up on the mountain to pray.

47 When evening came, the boat was out on the sea, and he was alone on the land. ⁴⁸When he saw that they were straining at the oars against an adverse wind, he came towards them early in the morning, walking on the sea. He intended to pass them by. ⁴⁹But when they saw him walking on the sea, they thought it was a ghost and cried out; ⁵⁰for they all saw him and were terrified. But immediately he spoke to them and said, "Take heart, it is I; do not be afraid." ⁵¹Then he got into the boat with them and the wind ceased. And they were utterly astounded, ⁵²for they did not understand about the loaves, but their hearts were hardened.

Healing the Sick in Gennesaret

53 When they had crossed over, they came to land at Gennesaret and moored the boat. ⁵⁴When they got out of the boat, people at once recognized him, ⁵⁵and rushed about that whole region and began to bring the sick on mats to wherever they heard he was. ⁵⁶And wherever he went, into villages or cities or farms, they laid the sick in the marketplaces, and begged him that they might touch even the fringe of his cloak; and all who touched it were healed.

The Tradition of the Elders

7 Now when the Pharisees and some of the scribes who had come from Jerusalem gathered around him, ²they noticed that some of his disciples were eating with defiled hands, that is, without washing them. ³(For the Pharisees, and all the Jews, do not eat unless they thoroughly wash their hands,*b* thus observing the tradition of the elders; ⁴and they do not eat anything from the market unless they wash it;*c* and there are also many other traditions that they observe, the washing of cups, pots, and bronze kettles.*d*) ⁵So the Pharisees and the scribes asked him, "Why do your disciples not live*e* according to the tradition of the elders, but eat with defiled hands?" ⁶He said to them, "Isaiah prophesied rightly about you hypocrites, as it is written,

a The denarius was the usual day's wage for a laborer
b Meaning of Gk uncertain   c Other ancient authorities read *and when they come from the marketplace, they do not eat unless they purify themselves*   d Other ancient authorities add *and beds*
e Gk *walk*

'This people honors me with their lips,
　　but their hearts are far from me;
7 in vain do they worship me,
　　teaching human precepts as doctrines.'
8You abandon the commandment of God and hold to human tradition."

9 Then he said to them, "You have a fine way of rejecting the commandment of God in order to keep your tradition! 10For Moses said, 'Honor your father and your mother'; and, 'Whoever speaks evil of father or mother must surely die.' 11But you say that if anyone tells father or mother, 'Whatever support you might have had from me is Corban' (that is, an offering to God*a*)— 12then you no longer permit doing anything for a father or mother, 13thus making void the word of God through your tradition that you have handed on. And you do many things like this."

14 Then he called the crowd again and said to them, "Listen to me, all of you, and understand: 15there is nothing outside a person that by going in can defile, but the things that come out are what defile."*b*

17 When he had left the crowd and entered the house, his disciples asked him about the parable. 18He said to them, "Then do you also fail to understand? Do you not see that whatever goes into a person from outside cannot defile, 19since it enters, not the heart but the stomach, and goes out into the sewer?" (Thus he declared all foods clean.) 20And he said, "It is what comes out of a person that defiles. 21For it is from within, from the human heart, that evil intentions come: fornication, theft, murder, 22adultery, avarice, wickedness, deceit, licentiousness, envy, slander, pride, folly. 23All these evil things come from within, and they defile a person."

The Syrophoenician Woman's Faith

24 From there he set out and went away to the region of Tyre.*c* He entered a house and did not want anyone to know he was there. Yet he could not escape notice, 25but a woman whose little daughter had an unclean spirit immediately heard about him, and she came and bowed down at his feet. 26Now the woman was a Gentile, of Syrophoenician origin. She begged him to cast the demon out of her daughter. 27He said to her, "Let the children be fed first, for it is not fair to take the children's food and throw it to the dogs." 28But she answered him, "Sir,*d* even the dogs under the table eat the children's crumbs." 29Then he said to her, "For saying that, you may go—the demon has left your daughter." 30So she went home, found the child lying on the bed, and the demon gone.

Jesus Cures a Deaf Man

31 Then he returned from the region of Tyre, and went by way of Sidon towards the Sea of Galilee, in the region of the Decapolis. 32They brought to him a deaf man who had an impediment in his speech; and they begged him to lay his hand on him. 33He took him aside in private, away from the crowd, and put his fingers into his ears, and he spat and touched his tongue. 34Then looking up to heaven, he sighed and said to him, "Ephphatha," that is, "Be opened." 35And immediately his ears were opened, his tongue was released, and he spoke plainly. 36Then Jesus*e* ordered them to tell no one; but the more he ordered them, the more zealously they proclaimed it. 37They were astounded beyond measure, saying, "He has done everything well; he even makes the deaf to hear and the mute to speak."

Feeding the Four Thousand

8 In those days when there was again a great crowd without anything to eat, he called his disciples and said to them, 2"I have compassion for the crowd, because they have been with me now for three days and have nothing to eat. 3If I

---

a Gk lacks *to God*　　b Other ancient authorities add verse 16, *"Let anyone with ears to hear listen"*　　c Other ancient authorities add *and Sidon*　　d Or *Lord*; other ancient authorities prefix *Yes*　　e Gk *he*

Sin's Source

Some people believe that spiritual depth is measured by how well certain rules or religious practices are followed. Jesus reminds us in Mark 7:14–15 that our greater concern ought to be with what is in our heart, because it is from there that both our good and bad actions originate. Ultimately, what is in our heart should have a greater effect on our spiritual lives than should outside sources, even though these external influences can often be powerful forces.

● What outside sources have the potential to negatively affect your spiritual life?

▶ Mk 7:14–23

send them away hungry to their homes, they will faint on the way—and some of them have come from a great distance." [4]His disciples replied, "How can one feed these people with bread here in the desert?" [5]He asked them, "How many loaves do you have?" They said, "Seven." [6]Then he ordered the crowd to sit down on the ground; and he took the seven loaves, and after giving thanks he broke them and gave them to his disciples to distribute; and they distributed them to the crowd. [7]They had also a few small fish; and after blessing them, he ordered that these too should be distributed. [8]They ate and were filled; and they took up the broken pieces left over, seven baskets full. [9]Now there were about four thousand people. And he sent them away. [10]And immediately he got into the boat with his disciples and went to the district of Dalmanutha.[a]

The Demand for a Sign

11 The Pharisees came and began to argue with him, asking him for a sign from heaven, to test him. [12]And he sighed deeply in his spirit and said, "Why does this generation ask for a sign? Truly I tell you, no sign will be given to this generation." [13]And he left them, and getting into the boat again, he went across to the other side.

The Yeast of the Pharisees and of Herod

14 Now the disciples[b] had forgotten to bring any bread; and they had only one loaf with them in the boat. [15]And he cautioned them, saying, "Watch out—beware of the yeast of the Pharisees and the yeast of Herod."[c] [16]They said to one another, "It is because we have no bread." [17]And becoming aware of it, Jesus said to them, "Why are you talking about having no bread? Do you still not perceive or understand? Are your hearts hardened? [18]Do you have eyes, and fail to see? Do you have ears, and fail to hear? And do you not remember? [19]When I broke the five loaves

8:8

for the five thousand, how many baskets full of broken pieces did you collect?" They said to him, "Twelve." [20]"And the seven for the four thousand, how many baskets full of broken pieces did you collect?" And they said to him, "Seven." [21]Then he said to them, "Do you not yet understand?"

Jesus Cures a Blind Man at Bethsaida

22 They came to Bethsaida. Some people[d] brought a blind man to him and begged him to touch him. [23]He took the blind man by the hand and led him out of the village; and when he had put saliva on his eyes and laid his hands on him, he asked him, "Can you see anything?" [24]And

*a Other ancient authorities read Mageda or Magdala   b Gk they
c Other ancient authorities read the Herodians   d Gk They*

Total Commitment

In Mark 8:34–38, Jesus calls for a total commitment requiring great sacrifice. He tells the disciples that to be truly alive, they must be willing to deny themselves and take up their own crosses. The cross symbolizes denying the way of the world and embracing the way of Jesus. It means tough self-sacrifice and, at times, a willingness to suffer for what is right.

But what does it mean to deny ourselves and take up our own crosses? When we deny ourselves, it means we cannot be fooled by what the world says about being truly alive. The world tells us to buy our happiness with wealth, power, prestige, or selfish pleasure. But those things actually make us feel less alive and more anxious.

Taking up our own crosses means being willing to cling to the right things—forgiveness, justice, service, and compassion for those who are poor and those who are unpopular—even if it brings us suffering and pain. Being committed to Jesus and these virtues or "right things" will bring us real life, true freedom, joy, and inner peace.

The way of the cross is the path to resurrection and eternal life.

▶ Mk 8:34–38

the man[a] looked up and said, "I can see people, but they look like trees, walking." 25Then Jesus[a] laid his hands on his eyes again; and he looked intently and his sight was restored, and he saw everything clearly. 26Then he sent him away to his home, saying, "Do not even go into the village."[b]

Peter's Declaration about Jesus

27 Jesus went on with his disciples to the villages of Caesarea Philippi; and on the way he asked his disciples, "Who do people say that I am?" 28And they answered him, "John the Baptist; and others, Elijah; and still others, one of the prophets." 29He asked them, "But who do you say that I am?" Peter answered him, "You are the Messiah."[c] 30And he sternly ordered them not to tell anyone about him.

Jesus Foretells His Death and Resurrection

31 Then he began to teach them that the Son of Man must undergo great suffering, and be rejected by the elders, the chief priests, and the scribes, and be killed, and after three days rise again. 32He said all this quite openly. And Peter took him aside and began to rebuke him. 33But turning and looking at his disciples, he rebuked Peter and said, "Get behind me, Satan! For you are setting your mind not on divine things but on human things."

34 He called the crowd with his disciples, and said to them, "If any want to become my followers, let them deny themselves and take up their cross and follow me. 35For those who want to save their life will lose it, and those who lose their life for my sake, and for the sake of the gospel,[d] will save it. 36For what will it profit them to gain the whole world and forfeit their life? 37Indeed, what can they give in return for their life? 38Those who are ashamed of me and of my words[e] in this adulterous and sinful generation, of them the Son of Man will also be ashamed when he comes in the glory of his Father with the holy angels."

9 1And he said to them, "Truly I tell you, there are some standing here who will not taste death until they see that the kingdom of God has come with[f] power."

The Transfiguration

2 Six days later, Jesus took with him Peter and James and John, and led them up a high mountain apart, by themselves. And he was transfigured before them, 3and his clothes became dazzling white, such as no one[g] on earth could bleach them. 4And there appeared to them Elijah with Moses, who were talking with Jesus. 5Then Peter said to Jesus, "Rabbi, it is good for

---

The Transfiguration: On Top of the World

The story of the Transfiguration takes place after Jesus tells his disciples about his coming suffering, death, and Resurrection (see Mk 8:31). They need hope and a boost of faith. Jesus takes three disciples to a mountaintop to see the Reign of God coming in power. The three disciples see Jesus in a glorious state talking with Moses and Elijah.

God revealed the secret about Jesus to three of his disciples. The two Old Testament figures are key symbols: Moses represents the law, and Elijah, the prophets. The message is clear: Jesus is the person who fulfills the law and who realizes God's promises to the prophets. It was a profound religious experience. The disciples glimpsed Jesus' glory, but they could not understand it. Understanding came only after Jesus' Resurrection.

It is understandable to want to found our faith on mountaintop experiences (see "Spiritual Highs," near Lk 9:28–36). But though profound religious experiences enliven our faith, listening and following Jesus' words daily are what really fortify our faith and give us new life.

▶ **Mk 9:2–8**

---

us to be here; let us make three dwellings,[h] one for you, one for Moses, and one for Elijah." 6He did not know what to say, for they were terrified. 7Then a cloud overshadowed them, and from the cloud there came a voice, "This is my Son, the Beloved;[i] listen to him!" 8Suddenly when they looked around, they saw no one with them any more, but only Jesus.

The Coming of Elijah

9 As they were coming down the mountain, he ordered them to tell no one about what they had seen, until after the Son of Man had risen

---

MK

from the dead. [10]So they kept the matter to themselves, questioning what this rising from the dead could mean. [11]Then they asked him, "Why do the scribes say that Elijah must come first?" [12]He said to them, "Elijah is indeed coming first to restore all things. How then is it written about the Son of Man, that he is to go through many sufferings and be treated with contempt? [13]But I tell you that Elijah has come, and they did to him whatever they pleased, as it is written about him."

The Healing of a Boy with a Spirit

14 When they came to the disciples, they saw a great crowd around them, and some scribes arguing with them. [15]When the whole crowd saw him, they were immediately overcome with awe, and they ran forward to greet him. [16]He asked them, "What are you arguing about with them?" [17]Someone from the crowd answered him, "Teacher, I brought you my son; he has a spirit that makes him unable to speak; [18]and whenever it seizes him, it dashes him down; and he foams and grinds his teeth and becomes rigid; and I asked your disciples to cast it out, but they could not do so." [19]He answered them, "You faithless generation, how much longer must I be among you? How much longer must I put up with you? Bring him to me." [20]And they brought the boy[a] to him. When the spirit saw him, immediately

it convulsed the boy,[a] and he fell on the ground and rolled about, foaming at the mouth. [21]Jesus[b] asked the father, "How long has this been happening to him?" And he said, "From childhood. [22]It has often cast him into the fire and into the water, to destroy him; but if you are able to do anything, have pity on us and help us." [23]Jesus said to him, "If you are able!—All things can be done for the one who believes." [24]Immediately the father of the child cried out,[c] "I believe; help my unbelief!" [25]When Jesus saw that a crowd came running together, he rebuked the unclean spirit, saying to it, "You spirit that keeps this boy from speaking and hearing, I command you, come out of him, and never enter him again!" [26]After crying out and convulsing him terribly, it came out, and the boy was like a corpse, so that most of them said, "He is dead." [27]But Jesus took him by the hand and lifted him up, and he was able to stand. [28]When he had entered the house, his disciples asked him privately, "Why could we not cast it out?" [29]He said to them, "This kind can come out only through prayer."[d]

Jesus Again Foretells His Death and Resurrection

30 They went on from there and passed through Galilee. He did not want anyone to know it; [31]for he was teaching his disciples, saying to them, "The Son of Man is to be betrayed into human hands, and they will kill him, and three days after being killed, he will rise again." [32]But they did not understand what he was saying and were afraid to ask him.

Who Is the Greatest?

33 Then they came to Capernaum; and when he was in the house he asked them, "What were you arguing about on the way?" [34]But they were silent, for on the way they had argued with one another who was the greatest. [35]He sat down, called the twelve, and said to them, "Whoever wants to be first must be last of all and servant of all." [36]Then he took a little child and put it among them; and taking it in his arms, he said to them, [37]"Whoever welcomes one such child in my name welcomes me, and whoever welcomes me welcomes not me but the one who sent me."

Another Exorcist

38 John said to him, "Teacher, we saw someone[e] casting out demons in your name, and we

Pray It!

"I Believe; Help My Unbelief!"

Saying that we believe in something may not be enough to prove that we truly believe. Faith in God means knowing that God is totally with us even when it doesn't seem that way!

When we have nagging doubts whether even God can help us in a particular situation—like the father in Mark 9:24—we can turn to God by praying for faith. We don't have to have our faith or our lives perfectly together before we ask God for help. The test of faith is trusting that God cares for us and provides what we need, even when our prayers are not answered in the way we desire.

▶ Mk 9:14–29

---

a Gk *him*   b Gk *He*   c Other ancient authorities add *with tears*
d Other ancient authorities add *and fasting*   e Other ancient authorities add *who does not follow us*

tried to stop him, because he was not following us." [39]But Jesus said, "Do not stop him; for no one who does a deed of power in my name will be able soon afterward to speak evil of me. [40]Whoever is not against us is for us. [41]For truly I tell you, whoever gives you a cup of water to drink because you bear the name of Christ will by no means lose the reward.

Temptations to Sin

42 "If any of you put a stumbling block before one of these little ones who believe in me,[a] it would be better for you if a great millstone were hung around your neck and you were thrown into the sea. [43]If your hand causes you to stumble, cut it off; it is better for you to enter life maimed than to have two hands and to go to hell,[b] to the unquenchable fire.[c] [45]And if your foot causes you to stumble, cut it off; it is better for you to enter life lame than to have two feet and to be thrown into hell.[b,c] [47]And if your eye causes you to stumble, tear it out; it is better for you to enter the kingdom of God with one eye than to have two eyes and to be thrown into hell,[b] [48]where their worm never dies, and the fire is never quenched.

49 "For everyone will be salted with fire.[d] [50]Salt is good; but if salt has lost its saltiness, how can you season it?[e] Have salt in yourselves, and be at peace with one another."

Teaching about Divorce

10 He left that place and went to the region of Judea and[f] beyond the Jordan. And crowds again gathered around him; and, as was his custom, he again taught them.

2 Some Pharisees came, and to test him they asked, "Is it lawful for a man to divorce his wife?" [3]He answered them, "What did Moses command you?" [4]They said, "Moses allowed a man to write a certificate of dismissal and to divorce her." [5]But Jesus said to them, "Because of your hardness of heart he wrote this commandment for you. [6]But from the beginning of creation, 'God made them male and female.' [7]For this reason a man shall leave his father and mother and be joined to his wife,[g] [8]and the two shall become one flesh.' So they are no longer two, but one flesh. [9]Therefore what God has joined together, let no one separate."

10 Then in the house the disciples asked him again about this matter. [11]He said to them, "Whoever divorces his wife and marries another commits adultery against her; [12]and if she divorces her husband and marries another, she commits adultery."

Jesus Blesses Little Children

13 People were bringing little children to him in order that he might touch them; and the disciples spoke sternly to them. [14]But when Jesus saw this, he was indignant and said to them, "Let the little children come to me; do not stop them; for it is to such as these that the kingdom of God belongs. [15]Truly I tell you, whoever does not receive the kingdom of God as a little child will never enter it." [16]And he took them up in his arms, laid his hands on them, and blessed them.

The Rich Man

17 As he was setting out on a journey, a man ran up and knelt before him, and asked him, "Good Teacher, what must I do to inherit eternal life?" [18]Jesus said to him, "Why do you call me good? No one is good but God alone. [19]You know the commandments: 'You shall not murder; You shall not commit adultery; You shall not steal; You shall not bear false witness; You shall not defraud; Honor your father and mother.' " [20]He said to him, "Teacher, I have kept all these since my youth." [21]Jesus, looking at him, loved him and said, "You lack one thing; go, sell what you own, and give the money[h] to the poor, and you will have treasure in heaven; then come, follow me." [22]When he heard this, he was shocked and went away grieving, for he had many possessions.

23 Then Jesus looked around and said to his disciples, "How hard it will be for those who have wealth to enter the kingdom of God!" [24]And the disciples were perplexed at these words. But Jesus said to them again, "Children, how hard it is[i] to enter the kingdom of God! [25]It is easier for a camel to go through the eye of a needle than for someone who is rich to enter the kingdom of God." [26]They were greatly astounded and said to one another,[j] "Then who can be saved?" [27]Jesus looked at them and said, "For mortals it is impossible, but not for God; for God all things are possible."

28 Peter began to say to him, "Look, we have left everything and followed you." [29]Jesus said, "Truly I tell you, there is no one who has left house or brothers or sisters or mother or father or children or fields, for my sake and for the sake of the good news,[k] [30]who will not receive a

---

a Other ancient authorities lack *in me*　b Gk *Gehenna*　c Verses 44 and 46 (which are identical with verse 48) are lacking in the best ancient authorities　d Other ancient authorities either add or substitute *and every sacrifice will be salted with salt*　e Or *how can you restore its saltiness?*　f Other ancient authorities lack *and*　g Other ancient authorities lack *and be joined to his wife*　h Gk lacks *the money*　i Other ancient authorities add *for those who trust in riches*　j Other ancient authorities read *to him*　k Or *gospel*

✚ Catholic Connection

Marriage

Jesus always has a great way of seeing the good in everything. For example, when the Pharisees try to test Jesus with a question about divorce, Jesus speaks about marriage. Rather than focus on the negative, Jesus turns everyone's attention to the positive—the beauty of two people who "are no longer two, but one flesh" (Mk 10:8).

The Catholic Church shares Jesus' positive view of marriage and celebrates it in the sacrament of Matrimony, one of the seven official sacraments of the Church. The Church teaches that through the sacrament, the couple's love for one another is sealed by God and actually becomes a part of God's love. As a result, the sacrament provides the couple with the grace necessary to love one another fully as God intends; helps them to welcome children joyfully as a gift from God; and gives them the strength to overcome the challenges that their life together may bring. The Church believes that in a Christian marriage, God's love and grace are present in a special way (see Eph 5:21–33).

When two Catholics are joined in Matrimony, it is usually celebrated during a Mass. When a Catholic mar-

ries a Christian of another faith or an unbaptized person, it is usually celebrated within the context of the liturgy of the word and prayer. During the liturgical celebration, the couple is questioned by the celebrant (either a priest or deacon) after the homily as to their desire to be married and to ensure that they are freely choosing to enter into this special union. Then the couple exchanges vows before God and the community, declaring their undying love and commitment to one another. During this exchange, the couple actually confers the sacrament upon one another, with the celebrant there as a witness for the Church. Afterwards, the celebrant declares, as Christ did, that what has been joined by God shall not be separated. The couple then exchanges rings as a sign of their everlasting commitment to one another. Finally, toward the conclusion of the liturgical celebration, the celebrant offers the nuptial blessing which calls upon the Lord to watch over and guide the new couple as they begin their new life together as one.

▶ **Mk 10:1–12**
Catechism, nos. 1601–1666

hundredfold now in this age—houses, brothers and sisters, mothers and children, and fields, with persecutions—and in the age to come eternal life. [31]But many who are first will be last, and the last will be first."

A Third Time Jesus Foretells His Death and Resurrection

32 They were on the road, going up to Jerusalem, and Jesus was walking ahead of them; they were amazed, and those who followed were afraid. He took the twelve aside again and began to tell them what was to happen to him, [33]saying, "See, we are going up to Jerusalem, and the Son of Man will be handed over to the chief priests and the scribes, and they will condemn him to death; then they will hand him over to the Gentiles; [34]they will mock him, and spit upon him, and flog him, and kill him; and after three days he will rise again."

The Request of James and John

35 James and John, the sons of Zebedee, came forward to him and said to him, "Teacher, we want you to do for us whatever we ask of you." [36]And he said to them, "What is it you want me to do for you?" [37]And they said to him, "Grant us to sit, one at your right hand and one at your left, in your glory." [38]But Jesus said to them, "You do not know what you are asking. Are you able to drink the cup that I drink, or be baptized with the baptism that I am baptized with?" [39]They replied, "We are able." Then Jesus said to them, "The cup that I drink you will drink; and with the baptism with which I am baptized, you will be baptized; [40]but to sit at my right hand or at my left is not mine to grant, but it is for those for whom it has been prepared."

41 When the ten heard this, they began to be angry with James and John. [42]So Jesus called them and said to them, "You know that among the Gentiles those whom they recognize as their rulers lord it over them, and their great ones are tyrants over them. [43]But it is not so among you; but whoever wishes to become great among you must be your servant, [44]and whoever wishes to be first among you must be slave of all. [45]For the Son of Man came not to be served but to serve, and to give his life a ransom for many."

The Healing of Blind Bartimaeus

46 They came to Jericho. As he and his disciples and a large crowd were leaving Jericho, Bartimaeus son of Timaeus, a blind beggar, was sitting by the roadside. [47]When he heard that it was Jesus of Nazareth, he began to shout out and

say, "Jesus, Son of David, have mercy on me!" [48]Many sternly ordered him to be quiet, but he cried out even more loudly, "Son of David, have mercy on me!" [49]Jesus stood still and said, "Call him here." And they called the blind man, saying to him, "Take heart; get up, he is calling you." [50]So throwing off his cloak, he sprang up and came to Jesus. [51]Then Jesus said to him, "What do you want me to do for you?" The blind man said to him, "My teacher,[a] let me see again." [52]Jesus said to him, "Go; your faith has made you well." Immediately he regained his sight and followed him on the way.

Jesus' Triumphal Entry into Jerusalem

11 When they were approaching Jerusalem, at Bethphage and Bethany, near the Mount of Olives, he sent two of his disciples [2]and said to them, "Go into the village ahead of you, and immediately as you enter it, you will find tied there a colt that has never been ridden; untie it and bring it. [3]If anyone says to you, 'Why are you doing this?' just say this, 'The Lord needs it and will send it back here immediately.' " [4]They went away and found a colt tied near a door, outside in the street. As they were untying it, [5]some of the bystanders said to them, "What are you doing, untying the colt?" [6]They told them what Jesus had said; and they allowed them to take it. [7]Then they brought the colt to Jesus and threw their cloaks on it; and he sat on it. [8]Many people spread their cloaks on the road, and others spread leafy branches that they had cut in the fields. [9]Then those who went ahead and those who followed were shouting,

"Hosanna!
Blessed is the one who comes in the name of
　the Lord!
[10]　Blessed is the coming kingdom of our
　ancestor David!
Hosanna in the highest heaven!"

11 Then he entered Jerusalem and went into the temple; and when he had looked around at everything, as it was already late, he went out to Bethany with the twelve.

Jesus Curses the Fig Tree

12 On the following day, when they came from Bethany, he was hungry. [13]Seeing in the distance a fig tree in leaf, he went to see whether perhaps he would find anything on it. When he came to it, he found nothing but leaves, for it was not the season for figs. [14]He said to it, "May no one ever eat fruit from you again." And his disciples heard it.

a Aramaic *Rabbouni*

Unanswered Prayer

Did you ever want something so badly that you prayed for it?

Sometimes, when things turn out the way we want, we say that God has answered our prayers. But when things don't turn out the way we want, we say that God didn't answer our prayers.

In Mark 11:24, it seems that we have the power to obtain what we want from God just by stating our wishes. This is a dangerous thought, though, especially when someone else might be praying for the exact opposite of what we're praying for. Why should God answer our prayers and not someone else's? In addition, when something horrible happens despite all our prayers, it is incorrect to think that God willed such pain and suffering. For example, sometimes we hear people saying, "God must have wanted me to learn some lesson from this tragedy." God never causes tragedy. Tragedy just happens. Saying that such things are "God's will" or part of "God's plan" is dangerous, and not an accurate representation of the God we know—a God who loves us intimately and hates to see us suffering or in pain.

People often ask, and we may be asking ourselves, Why pray at all if it isn't going to change anything? God wants only the best for us and knows what we need before we ask. But God also waits for us to ask because of the freedom he has given us. In freedom we ask, and in love we await God's response.

▶ Mk 11:24

Jesus Cleanses the Temple

15 Then they came to Jerusalem. And he entered the temple and began to drive out those who were selling and those who were buying in the temple, and he overturned the tables of the money changers and the seats of those who sold doves; [16]and he would not allow anyone to carry anything through the temple. [17]He was teaching and saying, "Is it not written,

'My house shall be called a house of prayer for all the nations'?

But you have made it a den of robbers."
[18]And when the chief priests and the scribes heard it, they kept looking for a way to kill him; for they were afraid of him, because the whole crowd was spellbound by his teaching. [19]And when evening came, Jesus and his disciples[a] went out of the city.

The Lesson from the Withered Fig Tree

20 In the morning as they passed by, they saw the fig tree withered away to its roots. [21]Then Peter remembered and said to him, "Rabbi, look! The fig tree that you cursed has withered." [22]Jesus answered them, "Have[b] faith in God. [23]Truly I tell you, if you say to this mountain, 'Be taken up and thrown into the sea,' and if you do not doubt in your heart, but believe that what you say will come to pass, it will be done for you. [24]So I tell you, whatever you ask for in prayer, believe that you have received[c] it, and it will be yours.

25 "Whenever you stand praying, forgive, if you have anything against anyone; so that your Father in heaven may also forgive you your trespasses."[d]

Jesus' Authority Is Questioned

27 Again they came to Jerusalem. As he was walking in the temple, the chief priests, the scribes, and the elders came to him [28]and said, "By what authority are you doing these things? Who gave you this authority to do them?" [29]Jesus said to them, "I will ask you one question; answer me, and I will tell you by what authority I do these things. [30]Did the baptism of John come from heaven, or was it of human origin? Answer me." [31]They argued with one another, "If we say, 'From heaven,' he will say, 'Why then did you not believe him?' [32]But shall we say, 'Of human origin'?"—they were afraid of the crowd, for all regarded John as truly a prophet. [33]So they answered Jesus, "We do not know." And Jesus said to them, "Neither will I tell you by what authority I am doing these things."

The Parable of the Wicked Tenants

12 Then he began to speak to them in parables. "A man planted a vineyard, put a fence around it, dug a pit for the wine press, and built a watchtower; then he leased it to tenants

---

a Gk they: other ancient authorities read he   b Other ancient authorities read "If you have   c Other ancient authorities read are receiving   d Other ancient authorities add verse 26, "But if you do not forgive, neither will your Father in heaven forgive your trespasses."

and went to another country. ²When the season came, he sent a slave to the tenants to collect from them his share of the produce of the vineyard. ³But they seized him, and beat him, and sent him away empty-handed. ⁴And again he sent another slave to them; this one they beat over the head and insulted. ⁵Then he sent another, and that one they killed. And so it was with many others; some they beat, and others they killed. ⁶He had still one other, a beloved son. Finally he sent him to them, saying, 'They will respect my son.' ⁷But those tenants said to one another, 'This is the heir; come, let us kill him, and the inheritance will be ours.' ⁸So they seized him, killed him, and threw him out of the vineyard. ⁹What then will the owner of the vineyard do? He will come and destroy the tenants and give the vineyard to others. ¹⁰Have you not read this scripture:

'The stone that the builders rejected
    has become the cornerstone;ᵃ
¹¹ this was the Lord's doing,
    and it is amazing in our eyes'?"

12 When they realized that he had told this parable against them, they wanted to arrest him, but they feared the crowd. So they left him and went away.

The Question about Paying Taxes

13 Then they sent to him some Pharisees and some Herodians to trap him in what he said. ¹⁴And they came and said to him, "Teacher, we know that you are sincere, and show deference to no one; for you do not regard people with partiality, but teach the way of God in accordance with truth. Is it lawful to pay taxes to the emperor, or not? ¹⁵Should we pay them, or should we not?" But knowing their hypocrisy, he said to them, "Why are you putting me to the test? Bring me a denarius and let me see it." ¹⁶And they brought one. Then he said to them, "Whose head is this, and whose title?" They answered, "The emperor's." ¹⁷Jesus said to them, "Give to the emperor the things that are the emperor's, and to God the things that are God's." And they were utterly amazed at him.

The Question about the Resurrection

18 Some Sadducees, who say there is no resurrection, came to him and asked him a question, saying, ¹⁹"Teacher, Moses wrote for us that if a man's brother dies, leaving a wife but no child, the manᵇ shall marry the widow and raise up children for his brother. ²⁰There were seven brothers; the first married and, when he died, left no children; ²¹and the second married the widowᶜ and died, leaving no children; and the third likewise;

²²none of the seven left children. Last of all the woman herself died. ²³In the resurrectionᵈ whose wife will she be? For the seven had married her."

24 Jesus said to them, "Is not this the reason you are wrong, that you know neither the scriptures nor the power of God? ²⁵For when they rise from the dead, they neither marry nor are given in marriage, but are like angels in heaven. ²⁶And as for the dead being raised, have you not read in the book of Moses, in the story about the bush, how God said to him, 'I am the God of Abraham, the God of Isaac, and the God of Jacob'? ²⁷He is God not of the dead, but of the living; you are quite wrong."

The First Commandment

28 One of the scribes came near and heard them disputing with one another, and seeing that

---

ᵃ Or *keystone*   ᵇ Gk *his brother*   ᶜ Gk *her*   ᵈ Other ancient authorities add *when they rise*

What Do You Want from Me?

Dear God, Jesus tells us to give to you what is yours. What do you want from me, God? What can I give to you?

As a young person still growing and developing, I don't have much to offer financially. I can make a small financial contribution to the church, to poor people, . . . but is it enough, Lord? What more can I give?

I can offer my time and talents to serve my faith community. I can sing, play an instrument, draw posters, greet visitors, clean, decorate, organize, cook, bake, and make phone calls. I can help teach children, lector, or usher, . . . but is it enough, Lord? What more can I give?

I can reach out to serve and share your love at home, in my neighborhood, my school, my community, . . . but is it enough, Lord? What more can I give?

I want to serve you better, Lord. Speak to me, and I will listen. Amen.

▶ Mk 12:13–17

Cultural Connection

Sacrificial Giving

Native Americans can appreciate the widow's offering in Mark 12:41–44. For example, the Lakota tribe has a custom called *otuhan*, or "giveaway." During important occasions, a person honors the other members of the tribe by giving away much of what she or he has. Sometimes, everything is given away. To be called stingy is the worst insult.

Think about your own circumstances. How easy would it be to share or give away your favorite possessions? Could you give away something you really value? Why or why not?

Many Native Americans believe that all we have belongs to the Great Spirit and is a gift to be shared with others. Make a decision! Follow the example of the widow, and be generous to others to the point of sacrifice.

▶ Mk 12:41–44

---

he answered them well, he asked him, "Which commandment is the first of all?" 29Jesus answered, "The first is, 'Hear, O Israel: the Lord our God, the Lord is one; 30you shall love the Lord your God with all your heart, and with all your soul, and with all your mind, and with all your strength.' 31The second is this, 'You shall love your neighbor as yourself.' There is no other commandment greater than these." 32Then the scribe said to him, "You are right, Teacher; you have truly said that 'he is one, and besides him there is no other'; 33and 'to love him with all the heart, and with all the understanding, and with all the strength,' and 'to love one's neighbor as oneself,'—this is much more important than all whole burnt offerings and sacrifices." 34When Jesus saw that he answered wisely, he

12:41–44

said to him, "You are not far from the kingdom of God." After that no one dared to ask him any question.

The Question about David's Son

35 While Jesus was teaching in the temple, he said, "How can the scribes say that the Messiah[a] is the son of David? 36David himself, by the Holy Spirit, declared,

'The Lord said to my Lord,
"Sit at my right hand,
    until I put your enemies under your feet." '
37David himself calls him Lord; so how can he be his son?" And the large crowd was listening to him with delight.

Jesus Denounces the Scribes

38 As he taught, he said, "Beware of the scribes, who like to walk around in long robes, and to be greeted with respect in the marketplaces, 39and to have the best seats in the synagogues and places of honor at banquets! 40They devour widows' houses and for the sake of appearance say long prayers. They will receive the greater condemnation."

The Widow's Offering

41 He sat down opposite the treasury, and watched the crowd putting money into the treasury. Many rich people put in large sums. 42A poor widow came and put in two small copper coins, which are worth a penny. 43Then he called his disciples and said to them, "Truly I tell you, this poor widow has put in more than all those who are contributing to the treasury. 44For all of

a Or the Christ

them have contributed out of their abundance; but she out of her poverty has put in everything she had, all she had to live on."

The Destruction of the Temple Foretold

13 As he came out of the temple, one of his disciples said to him, "Look, Teacher, what large stones and what large buildings!" ²Then Jesus asked him, "Do you see these great buildings? Not one stone will be left here upon another; all will be thrown down."

3 When he was sitting on the Mount of Olives opposite the temple, Peter, James, John, and Andrew asked him privately, ⁴"Tell us, when will this be, and what will be the sign that all these things are about to be accomplished?" ⁵Then Jesus began to say to them, "Beware that no one leads you astray. ⁶Many will come in my name and say, 'I am he!'ᵃ and they will lead many astray. ⁷When you hear of wars and rumors of wars, do not be alarmed; this must take place, but the end is still to come. ⁸For nation will rise against nation, and kingdom against kingdom; there will be earthquakes in various places; there will be famines. This is but the beginning of the birth pangs.

Persecution Foretold

9 "As for yourselves, beware; for they will hand you over to councils; and you will be beaten in synagogues; and you will stand before governors and kings because of me, as a testimony to them. ¹⁰And the good newsᵇ must first be proclaimed to all nations. ¹¹When they bring you to trial and hand you over, do not worry beforehand about what you are to say; but say whatever is given you at that time, for it is not you who speak, but the Holy Spirit. ¹²Brother will betray brother to death, and a father his child, and children will rise against parents and have them put to death; ¹³and you will be hated by all because of my name. But the one who endures to the end will be saved.

The Desolating Sacrilege

14 "But when you see the desolating sacrilege set up where it ought not to be (let the reader understand), then those in Judea must flee to the mountains; ¹⁵the one on the housetop must not go down or enter the house to take anything away; ¹⁶the one in the field must not turn back to get a coat. ¹⁷Woe to those who are pregnant and to those who are nursing infants in those days! ¹⁸Pray that it may not be in winter. ¹⁹For in those days there will be suffering, such as has not been from the beginning of the creation that God

created until now, no, and never will be. ²⁰And if the Lord had not cut short those days, no one would be saved; but for the sake of the elect, whom he chose, he has cut short those days. ²¹And if anyone says to you at that time, 'Look! Here is the Messiah!'ᶜ or 'Look! There he is!'—do not believe it. ²²False messiahsᵈ and false prophets will appear and produce signs and omens, to lead astray, if possible, the elect. ²³But be alert; I have already told you everything.

The Coming of the Son of Man

24 "But in those days, after that suffering,
the sun will be darkened,
and the moon will not give its light,
²⁵ and the stars will be falling from heaven,
and the powers in the heavens will be shaken.
²⁶Then they will see 'the Son of Man coming in clouds' with great power and glory. ²⁷Then he will send out the angels, and gather his elect from the four winds, from the ends of the earth to the ends of heaven.

---

a Gk *I am*   b Gk *gospel*   c Or *the Christ*   d Or *christs*

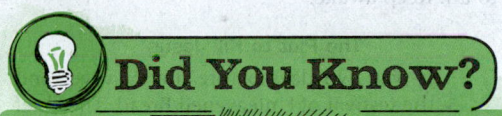

Signs and Omens

The community for which the author of Mark's Gospel wrote saw its sufferings as part of the troubles that would come with the end time. However, the author didn't intend that his readers take Jesus' signs and omens of wars and earthquakes to mean that the end of the world was literally at hand; rather, these descriptions were used symbolically (see "Apocalyptic Literature," near Daniel, chapters 7–10) to help the community make sense of its persecutions. The message of this Gospel is that Christians who were getting beaten up and thrown in jail would be saved by God. And ultimately, human history would climax in the perfect Reign of God. It was their job to hang on and endure to the end. All they had to worry about was spreading the Good News of Jesus Christ, and God would take care of the rest.

▶ **Mark, chapter 13**

The Lesson of the Fig Tree

28 "From the fig tree learn its lesson: as soon as its branch becomes tender and puts forth its leaves, you know that summer is near. 29So also, when you see these things taking place, you know that he[a] is near, at the very gates. 30Truly I tell you, this generation will not pass away until all these things have taken place. 31Heaven and earth will pass away, but my words will not pass away.

The Necessity for Watchfulness

32 "But about that day or hour no one knows, neither the angels in heaven, nor the Son, but only the Father. 33Beware, keep alert;[b] for you do not know when the time will come. 34It is like a man going on a journey, when he leaves home and puts his slaves in charge, each with his work, and commands the doorkeeper to be on the watch. 35Therefore, keep awake—for you do not know when the master of the house will come, in the evening, or at midnight, or at cockcrow, or at dawn, 36or else he may find you asleep when he comes suddenly. 37And what I say to you I say to all: Keep awake."

The Plot to Kill Jesus

14 It was two days before the Passover and the festival of Unleavened Bread. The chief priests and the scribes were looking for a way to arrest Jesus[c] by stealth and kill him; 2for they said, "Not during the festival, or there may be a riot among the people."

The Anointing at Bethany

3 While he was at Bethany in the house of Simon the leper,[d] as he sat at the table, a woman came with an alabaster jar of very costly ointment of nard, and she broke open the jar and poured the ointment on his head. 4But some were there who said to one another in anger, "Why was the ointment wasted in this way? 5For this ointment could have been sold for more than three hundred denarii,[e] and the money given to the poor." And they scolded her. 6But Jesus said, "Let her alone; why do you trouble her? She has performed a good service for me. 7For you always have the poor with you, and you can show kindness to them whenever you wish; but you will not always have me. 8She has done what she could; she has anointed my body beforehand for its burial. 9Truly I tell you, wherever the good news[f] is proclaimed in the whole world, what she has done will be told in remembrance of her."

Judas Agrees to Betray Jesus

10 Then Judas Iscariot, who was one of the twelve, went to the chief priests in order to betray him to them. 11When they heard it, they were greatly pleased, and promised to give him money. So he began to look for an opportunity to betray him.

The Passover with the Disciples

12 On the first day of Unleavened Bread, when the Passover lamb is sacrificed, his disciples said to him, "Where do you want us to go and make the preparations for you to eat the Passover?" 13So he sent two of his disciples, saying to them, "Go into the city, and a man carrying a jar of water will meet you; follow him, 14and wherever he enters, say to the owner of the house, 'The Teacher asks, Where is my guest room where I may eat the Passover with my disciples?' 15He will show you a large room upstairs, furnished and ready. Make preparations for us there." 16So the disciples set out and went to the city, and found everything as he had told them; and they prepared the Passover meal.

17 When it was evening, he came with the twelve. 18And when they had taken their places and were eating, Jesus said, "Truly I tell you, one of you will betray me, one who is eating with me." 19They began to be distressed and to say to him one after another, "Surely, not I?" 20He said to them, "It is one of the twelve, one who is dipping bread[g] into the bowl[h] with me. 21For the Son of Man goes as it is written of him, but woe to that one by whom the Son of Man is betrayed! It would have been better for that one not to have been born."

The Institution of the Lord's Supper

22 While they were eating, he took a loaf of bread, and after blessing it he broke it, gave it to them, and said, "Take; this is my body." 23Then he took a cup, and after giving thanks he gave it to them, and all of them drank from it. 24He said to them, "This is my blood of the[i] covenant, which is poured out for many. 25Truly I tell you, I will never again drink of the fruit of the vine until that day when I drink it new in the kingdom of God."

Peter's Denial Foretold

26 When they had sung the hymn, they went out to the Mount of Olives. 27And Jesus said to

---

a Or it   b Other ancient authorities add and pray   c Gk him
d The terms leper and leprosy can refer to several diseases
e The denarius was the usual day's wage for a laborer
f Or gospel   g Gk lacks bread   h Other ancient authorities read same bowl   i Other ancient authorities add new

them, "You will all become deserters; for it is written,

'I will strike the shepherd,
and the sheep will be scattered.'

[28]But after I am raised up, I will go before you to Galilee." [29]Peter said to him, "Even though all become deserters, I will not." [30]Jesus said to him, "Truly I tell you, this day, this very night, before the cock crows twice, you will deny me three times." [31]But he said vehemently, "Even though I must die with you, I will not deny you." And all of them said the same.

Jesus Prays in Gethsemane

32 They went to a place called Gethsemane; and he said to his disciples, "Sit here while I pray." [33]He took with him Peter and James and John, and began to be distressed and agitated. [34]And he said to them, "I am deeply grieved, even to death; remain here, and keep awake." [35]And going a little farther, he threw himself on the ground and prayed that, if it were possible, the hour might pass from him. [36]He said, "Abba,[a] Father, for you all things are possible; remove this cup from me; yet, not what I want, but what you want." [37]He came and found them sleeping; and he said to Peter, "Simon, are you asleep? Could you not keep awake one hour? [38]Keep awake and pray that you may not come into the time of trial;[b] the spirit indeed is willing, but the flesh is weak." [39]And again he went away and prayed, saying the same words. [40]And once more he came and found them sleeping, for their eyes were very heavy; and they did not know what to say to him. [41]He came a third time and said to them, "Are you still sleeping and taking your rest? Enough! The hour has come; the Son of Man is betrayed into the hands of sinners. [42]Get up, let us be going. See, my betrayer is at hand."

The Betrayal and Arrest of Jesus

43 Immediately, while he was still speaking, Judas, one of the twelve, arrived; and with him there was a crowd with swords and clubs, from the chief priests, the scribes, and the elders. [44]Now the betrayer had given them a sign, saying, "The one I will kiss is the man; arrest him and lead him away under guard." [45]So when he came, he went up to him at once and said, "Rabbi!" and kissed him. [46]Then they laid hands on him and arrested him. [47]But one of those who stood near drew his sword and struck the slave of the high priest, cutting off his ear. [48]Then Jesus said to them, "Have you come out with swords and clubs to arrest me as though I were a bandit?

Mass Prayer

"Take; this is my body. . . . This is my blood." Reading those words may sometimes make us feel guilty because we should be hearing them at Mass, and we are often good at finding excuses not to go to Mass: the church pews are uncomfortable, we'd rather sleep late, we don't like the music or the homily, it is too nice outside, it's boring.

Amidst the busyness of our lives and the excuses we make up, it is easy to forget that Jesus gave us a special invitation to share in the Eucharistic meal. Regularly celebrating the Eucharist gives us an opportunity to participate in Jesus' death and Resurrection, strengthen our faith, and renew our hope of sharing in God's Reign. It is a privilege to be invited to the Eucharistic table, to be nourished by Christ, and to connect with both the present Church and all the saints of the past who have shared this sacred meal. Although it's usually easier to make excuses, it is important for each of us to make Mass a priority in our lives. (For more on the Eucharist, see "The New Covenant," near Mt 26:26–29; "The Eucharist," near Lk 22:14–20; and "Feast of the Passover," near Jn 13:1–20.)

▶ **Mk 14:22–25**

[49]Day after day I was with you in the temple teaching, and you did not arrest me. But let the scriptures be fulfilled." [50]All of them deserted him and fled.

51 A certain young man was following him, wearing nothing but a linen cloth. They caught hold of him, [52]but he left the linen cloth and ran off naked.

Jesus before the Council

53 They took Jesus to the high priest; and all the chief priests, the elders, and the scribes were assembled. [54]Peter had followed him at a distance, right into the courtyard of the high priest;

---

a Aramaic for *Father*   *b* Or *into temptation*

and he was sitting with the guards, warming himself at the fire. ⁵⁵Now the chief priests and the whole council were looking for testimony against Jesus to put him to death; but they found none. ⁵⁶For many gave false testimony against him, and their testimony did not agree. ⁵⁷Some stood up and gave false testimony against him, saying, ⁵⁸"We heard him say, 'I will destroy this temple that is made with hands, and in three days I will build another, not made with hands.' " ⁵⁹But even on this point their testimony did not agree. ⁶⁰Then the high priest stood up before them and asked Jesus, "Have you no answer? What is it that they testify against you?" ⁶¹But he was silent and did not answer. Again the high priest asked him, "Are you the Messiah,ᵃ the Son of the Blessed One?" ⁶²Jesus said, "I am; and

'you will see the Son of Man
seated at the right hand of the Power,'
and 'coming with the clouds of heaven.' "

Facing the Hard Times

Lord, you really do know what it is like to be beaten, teased, pushed around, and rejected. If you could put up with this torment, then maybe there is hope for others who feel the same way at times. Like when we are made fun of or rejected because of the way we look or act or for what we believe in. Or when we feel all alone or that no one understands what we are feeling.

But now I know that you understand, Lord. You took these difficult steps even before we did. You have been there. You show us a way through these tough times.

Teach me to pray as you did: "Abba, Father, for you all things are possible; remove this cup [suffering] from me; yet, not what I want, but what you want" (Mk 14:36). Give me the strength to overcome my despair. Give me faith to abandon myself in God's hands as you did. Give me hope to see a new life beyond these moments of pain and hopelessness. Amen.

▶ Mk 15:16–20

⁶³Then the high priest tore his clothes and said, "Why do we still need witnesses? ⁶⁴You have heard his blasphemy! What is your decision?" All of them condemned him as deserving death. ⁶⁵Some began to spit on him, to blindfold him, and to strike him, saying to him, "Prophesy!" The guards also took him over and beat him.

Peter Denies Jesus

66 While Peter was below in the courtyard, one of the servant-girls of the high priest came by. ⁶⁷When she saw Peter warming himself, she stared at him and said, "You also were with Jesus, the man from Nazareth." ⁶⁸But he denied it, saying, "I do not know or understand what you are talking about." And he went out into the forecourt.ᵇ Then the cock crowed.ᶜ ⁶⁹And the servant-girl, on seeing him, began again to say to the bystanders, "This man is one of them." ⁷⁰But again he denied it. Then after a little while the bystanders again said to Peter, "Certainly you are one of them; for you are a Galilean." ⁷¹But he began to curse, and he swore an oath, "I do not know this man you are talking about." ⁷²At that moment the cock crowed for the second time. Then Peter remembered that Jesus had said to him, "Before the cock crows twice, you will deny me three times." And he broke down and wept.

Jesus before Pilate

15 As soon as it was morning, the chief priests held a consultation with the elders and scribes and the whole council. They bound Jesus, led him away, and handed him over to Pilate. ²Pilate asked him, "Are you the King of the Jews?" He answered him, "You say so." ³Then the chief priests accused him of many things. ⁴Pilate asked him again, "Have you no answer? See how many charges they bring against you." ⁵But Jesus made no further reply, so that Pilate was amazed.

Pilate Hands Jesus over to Be Crucified

6 Now at the festival he used to release a prisoner for them, anyone for whom they asked. ⁷Now a man called Barabbas was in prison with the rebels who had committed murder during the insurrection. ⁸So the crowd came and began to ask Pilate to do for them according to his custom. ⁹Then he answered them, "Do you want me to release for you the King of the Jews?" ¹⁰For he realized that it was out of jealousy that

---

ᵃ Or the Christ ᵇ Or gateway ᶜ Other ancient authorities lack Then the cock crowed

Cultural Connection

According to Mark 15:21, the Roman soldiers compelled a North African black man from Cyrene by the name of Simon, a passerby, to carry the cross of Jesus. We do not know anything more about Simon of Cyrene, except that Mark identifies him as the father of Alexander and Rufus. The reference to Simon's sons by name and the possibility that Rufus is the same person Paul greets in Romans 16:13 indicate that they were known among the early Christians. This is significant for African Americans because it is evidence of the prominence and influence of African people in the early Christian Church.

African people were there from the beginning of Christianity (see also Acts 8:26–40). They were not latecomers to the Christian faith. Thank God, somebody always remembers! African Americans and other people who have experienced oppression are in danger of forgetting who they are and where they come from—not because they are forgetful peoples, but because the oppressors have tried to erase their culture and identity to cripple and control them. Yet despite all this, somebody always remembers.

We praise you, God, for having African people there to minister to Jesus in his time of need. We praise you in knowing that people of all races will be with you at the end. Hallelujah. Amen!

▶ **Mk 15:21**

the chief priests had handed him over. ¹¹But the chief priests stirred up the crowd to have him release Barabbas for them instead. ¹²Pilate spoke to them again, "Then what do you wish me to do*ᵃ* with the man you call*ᵇ* the King of the Jews?" ¹³They shouted back, "Crucify him!" ¹⁴Pilate asked them, "Why, what evil has he done?" But they shouted all the more, "Crucify him!" ¹⁵So Pilate, wishing to satisfy the crowd, released Barabbas for them; and after flogging Jesus, he handed him over to be crucified.

The Soldiers Mock Jesus

16 Then the soldiers led him into the courtyard of the palace (that is, the governor's headquarters*ᶜ*); and they called together the whole cohort. ¹⁷And they clothed him in a purple cloak; and after twisting some thorns into a crown, they put it on him. ¹⁸And they began saluting him, "Hail, King of the Jews!" ¹⁹They struck his head with a reed, spat upon him, and knelt down in homage to him. ²⁰After mocking him, they stripped him of the purple cloak and put his own clothes on him. Then they led him out to crucify him.

The Crucifixion of Jesus

21 They compelled a passer-by, who was coming in from the country, to carry his cross; it was Simon of Cyrene, the father of Alexander and Rufus. ²²Then they brought Jesus*ᵈ* to the place called Golgotha (which means the place of a skull). ²³And they offered him wine mixed with myrrh; but he did not take it. ²⁴And they crucified him, and divided his clothes among them, casting lots to decide what each should take.

25 It was nine o'clock in the morning when they crucified him. ²⁶The inscription of the charge against him read, "The King of the Jews." ²⁷And with him they crucified two bandits, one on his right and one on his left.*ᵉ* ²⁹Those who passed by derided*ᶠ* him, shaking their heads and saying, "Aha! You who would destroy the temple

a Other ancient authorities read *what should I do*   *b* Other ancient authorities lack *the man you call*   *c* Gk *the praetorium*   *d* Gk *him*   *e* Other ancient authorities add verse 28, *And the scripture was fulfilled that says, "And he was counted among the lawless."*   *f* Or *blasphemed*

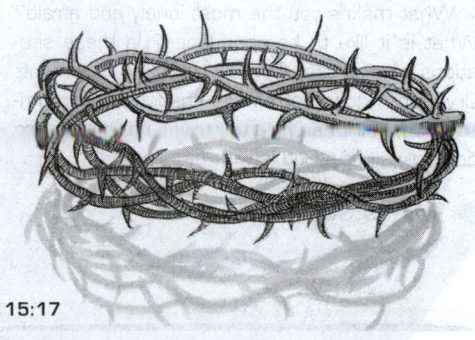

15:17

MK

and build it in three days, ³⁰save yourself, and come down from the cross!" ³¹In the same way the chief priests, along with the scribes, were also mocking him among themselves and saying, "He saved others; he cannot save himself. ³²Let the Messiah,ᵃ the King of Israel, come down from the cross now, so that we may see and believe." Those who were crucified with him also taunted him.

The Death of Jesus

33 When it was noon, darkness came over the whole landᵇ until three in the afternoon. ³⁴At three o'clock Jesus cried out with a loud voice, "Eloi, Eloi, lema sabachthani?" which means, "My God, my God, why have you forsaken me?"ᶜ ³⁵When some of the bystanders heard it, they said, "Listen, he is calling for Elijah." ³⁶And someone ran, filled a sponge with sour wine, put it on a stick, and gave it to him to drink, saying, "Wait, let us see whether Elijah

Alone!

Have you ever felt lost, afraid, or abandoned? Sometimes, we may actually be physically lost or abandoned, but more often these feelings are deeply emotional or spiritual as we struggle to find our way, feeling that there is no one in our lives who can fully help and support us.

Jesus may have had similar feelings. He may have felt lost, and he may have felt completely abandoned by his friends and even by God. He had to face his death alone. Can you imagine anything more lonely? His prayers did not change his circumstances but gave him a way to lament, to cry out to God to express his distress.

What makes you the most lonely and afraid? What is it like to be abandoned? In these situations of distress, it is always okay to lament. Crying out does not always change our circumstances, but it can help to remind us that we are not truly alone—God is with us.

▶ Mk 15:33–34

will come to take him down." ³⁷Then Jesus gave a loud cry and breathed his last. ³⁸And the curtain of the temple was torn in two, from top to bottom. ³⁹Now when the centurion, who stood facing him, saw that in this way heᵈ breathed his last, he said, "Truly this man was God's Son!"ᵉ

40 There were also women looking on from a distance; among them were Mary Magdalene, and Mary the mother of James the younger and of Joses, and Salome. ⁴¹These used to follow him and provided for him when he was in Galilee; and there were many other women who had come up with him to Jerusalem.

The Burial of Jesus

42 When evening had come, and since it was the day of Preparation, that is, the day before the sabbath, ⁴³Joseph of Arimathea, a respected member of the council, who was also himself waiting expectantly for the kingdom of God, went boldly to Pilate and asked for the body of Jesus. ⁴⁴Then Pilate wondered if he were already dead; and summoning the centurion, he asked him whether he had been dead for some time. ⁴⁵When he learned from the centurion that he was dead, he granted the body to Joseph. ⁴⁶Then Josephᶠ bought a linen cloth, and taking down the body,ᵍ wrapped it in the linen cloth, and laid it in a tomb that had been hewn out of the rock. He then rolled a stone against the door of the tomb. ⁴⁷Mary Magdalene and Mary the mother of Joses saw where the bodyᵍ was laid.

The Resurrection of Jesus

16 When the sabbath was over, Mary Magdalene, and Mary the mother of James, and Salome bought spices, so that they might go and anoint him. ²And very early on the first day of the week, when the sun had risen, they went to the tomb. ³They had been saying to one another, "Who will roll away the stone for us from the entrance to the tomb?" ⁴When they looked up, they saw that the stone, which was very large, had already been rolled back. ⁵As they entered the tomb, they saw a young man, dressed in a white robe, sitting on the right side; and they were alarmed. ⁶But he said to them, "Do not be alarmed; you are looking for Jesus of Nazareth, who was crucified. He has been raised; he is not here. Look, there is the place they laid him. ⁷But

---

ᵃ Or *the Christ*   ᵇ Or *earth*   ᶜ Other ancient authorities read *made me a reproach*   ᵈ Other ancient authorities add *cried out and*   ᵉ Or *a son of God*   ᶠ Gk *he*   ᵍ Gk *it*

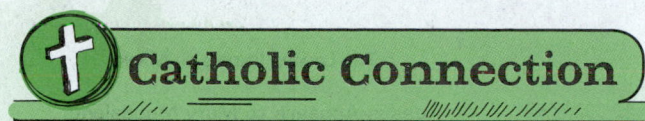

Catholic Connection

Faith and Reason

When we hear a person make some incredible claim on television, we often want to see proof that the claim is true. This was also the case for the disciples after Jesus rose from the dead. Some saw the risen Lord and believed, but others refused to believe because they had not witnessed the risen Lord with their own eyes (see Mk 16:9–12). Jesus scolds these disciples for their lack of faith (see verse 14). If the disciples who were with Jesus throughout his ministry were slow to believe, how difficult then would it be for the rest of the world to believe? Perhaps that is why Mark's Gospel concludes by saying that Jesus himself confirms the message of the Good News with signs like healings and miracles.

Although that is the end of Mark's Gospel, the story has fortunately continued for over two thousand years. Countless people have come to faith in Jesus Christ through the ongoing preaching of the Good News and the signs that confirm Christ's message. Through this combination of the message and signs, we begin to see the natural relationship that exists between faith and reason.

To understand this relationship, we must begin by examining the Church's understanding of faith. First and foremost, faith is a gift from God. Through God's grace and the help of the Holy Spirit, our heart is turned toward God. Through this change, God then opens our minds so that we may accept and believe the truth. We too play an active role in receiving the gift of faith by welcoming God's grace and accepting the truth.

Our acceptance of the truth is not by blind faith; it involves our use of reason. And because God created everything, including both faith and reason, he did not create them to contradict one another but to work together to arrive at the truth. Therefore, God provides external proofs like the signs and miracles mentioned in the Gospel. But God also provides other more ordinary proofs like the existence and growth of the Church or the daily lives of saints and people of faith.

When our faith and reason work together, an interesting thing can occur. Our faith leads us to desire and know God better, so we then use our reason to learn more about God. Once we learn more about God, our faith is deepened and we then desire to know God even more! The use of faith and reason becomes a never ending circle that continues to draw us closer and closer to the God who we love and who loves us.

▶ **Mk 16:20**

Catechism, nos. 156–159

Jesus Strengthens Our Faith

A group of faithful women accompany Jesus from afar when he dies on the cross, and they look to see where he is buried (see Mk 15:40–47). They are witnesses to the terrible violence of Jesus' death. Two days later, after the Sabbath, three of the women go to the tomb to anoint Jesus' body, giving him a proper burial. When they receive the news that Jesus is alive, they flee from the tomb terrified and amazed.

This is where the original Gospel of Mark ends. Immediately we want to ask lots of questions. What happened to the disciples? Did they go to Galilee? How did the word get out that Jesus had risen from the dead? Apparently, early Christians found this abrupt ending troublesome, so they added other endings similar to those of the other Gospels.

These additions, starting at Mark 16:9, emphasize the surprise of the disciples. It seems as if they are paralyzed. Only a strong scolding by Jesus and being commissioned to proclaim the Good News to the whole creation brings them around.

How do doubts and confusion paralyze you in living your faith? Pay attention to Jesus! Hear his voice! He is telling you to carry his message of love to other people. By doing so, you will strengthen your faith, and your life will be full of joy!

▶ Mk 16:1–20

go, tell his disciples and Peter that he is going ahead of you to Galilee; there you will see him, just as he told you." [8]So they went out and fled from the tomb, for terror and amazement had seized them; and they said nothing to anyone, for they were afraid.[a]

THE SHORTER ENDING OF MARK

‖And all that had been commanded them they told briefly to those around Peter. And afterward Jesus himself sent out through them, from east to west, the sacred and imperishable proclamation ·ernal salvation.[b] ‖

THE LONGER ENDING OF MARK

Jesus Appears to Mary Magdalene

[9] ‖Now after he rose early on the first day of the week, he appeared first to Mary Magdalene, from whom he had cast out seven demons. [10]She went out and told those who had been with him, while they were mourning and weeping. [11]But when they heard that he was alive and had been seen by her, they would not believe it.

Jesus Appears to Two Disciples

[12] After this he appeared in another form to two of them, as they were walking into the country. [13]And they went back and told the rest, but they did not believe them.

Jesus Commissions the Disciples

[14] Later he appeared to the eleven themselves as they were sitting at the table; and he upbraided them for their lack of faith and stubbornness, because they had not believed those who saw him after he had risen.[c] [15]And he said to them, "Go into all the world and proclaim the good news[d] to the whole creation. [16]The one who believes and is baptized will be saved; but the one who does not believe will be condemned. [17]And these signs will accompany those who believe: by using my name they will cast out demons; they will speak in new tongues; [18]they will pick up snakes in their hands,[e] and if they drink any deadly thing, it will not hurt them; they will lay their hands on the sick, and they will recover."

The Ascension of Jesus

[19] So then the Lord Jesus, after he had spoken to them, was taken up into heaven and sat down at the right hand of God. [20]And they went out and proclaimed the good news everywhere, while the Lord worked with them and confirmed the message by the signs that accompanied it.[b] ‖

---

a Some of the most ancient authorities bring the book to a close at the end of verse 8. One authority concludes the book with the shorter ending; others include the shorter ending and then continue with verses 9-20. In most authorities verses 9-20 follow immediately after verse 8, though in some of these authorities the passage is marked as being doubtful.   *b* Other ancient authorities add *Amen*   *c* Other ancient authorities add, in whole or in part, *And they excused themselves, saying, "This age of lawlessness and unbelief is under Satan, who does not allow the truth and power of God to prevail over the unclean things of the spirits. Therefore reveal your righteousness now"—thus they spoke to Christ. And Christ replied to them, "The term of years of Satan's power has been fulfilled, but other terrible things draw near. And for those who have sinned I was handed over to death, that they may return to the truth and sin no more, that they may inherit the spiritual and imperishable glory of righteousness that is in heaven."*   *d* Or *gospel*   *e* Other ancient authorities lack *in their hands*

Black and white. Male and female. Rich and poor. In our world today, we often divide ourselves into distinct categories instead of focusing on what unites us. These divisions can lead to discrimination, inequality, and injustice as one group is considered "less than" another. In the Gospel of Luke, Jesus asserts that such divisions have no place in the Kingdom of God. Outcasts, sinners, women, those who are poor—all are compassionately welcomed to be disciples.

At a Glance

- **Chapters 1–2.** introduction; stories about Jesus' birth and early childhood

- **3:1—9:50.** Jesus' ministry in Galilee

- **9:51—19:27.** parables and miracles on the way to Jerusalem

- **19:28—21:38.** Jesus in Jerusalem: conflict with the religious authorities

- **Chapters 22–24.** stories about Jesus' death, Resurrection, and Ascension

Quick Facts

Inspired Author: a Gentile Christian named Luke, traditionally thought to be a disciple of Paul (see Col 4:14)
Date Written: from approximately AD 80 to 90
Audience: Gentile (Greek) Christians represented by Theophilus (see Lk 1:3)
Of Note: Luke also wrote the Acts of the Apostles.
Image of Jesus: merciful, compassionate, with a special concern for poor people, women, and non-Jews

In Depth

The author of the Gospel of Luke was a Gentile (non-Jewish) convert to Christianity. So one of Luke's important concerns is to show how Gentiles came to be included in God's plan of salvation and among God's elect, which first belonged to the Jews alone. In Luke's Gospel, Jesus praises the faith of a centurion (see 7:1–10), who is a Gentile. Jesus also makes a Samaritan (Samaritans were considered foreigners by other Jews) the hero of a parable (see 10:25–37).

Other in-groups for Jesus in Luke's Gospel are women and poor people. Most women had little status in society at the time. But Luke includes many stories about women, including Mary's visit to her cousin Elizabeth before the births of their sons, Jesus and John the Baptist (see 1:39–66). This Gospel also shows how Jesus loved the poor and scolded the rich for their lack of concern for the poor. For example, it includes a story about a poor man named Lazarus, who begged for food at a rich man's door. God honored Lazarus with a special place in Abraham's bosom (Heaven) when he died (see 16:19–31), whereas the rich man suffered in Hades.

Finally, Luke's Gospel shows Jesus' compassion and forgiveness for outcasts and sinners. It includes stories about the tax collector Zacchaeus, who climbs a tree to see Jesus (see 19:1–10), the good Samaritan (see 10:25–37), and the penitent sinner who was crucified beside Jesus (see 23:39–43). In the Gospel of Luke, Jesus is also the prophet par excellence who will be rejected by his own people (see 4:16–30). The Gospel presents a vivid picture of how Jesus made the Reign of God present, inspiring his disciples to take the Gospel message to other lands and cultures.

The Gospel According to **Luke**

Luke

Dedication to Theophilus

1 Since many have undertaken to set down an orderly account of the events that have been fulfilled among us, ²just as they were handed on to us by those who from the beginning were eyewitnesses and servants of the word, ³I too decided, after investigating everything carefully from the very first,*a* to write an orderly account for you, most excellent Theophilus, ⁴so that you may know the truth concerning the things about which you have been instructed.

The Birth of John the Baptist Foretold

5 In the days of King Herod of Judea, there was a priest named Zechariah, who belonged to the priestly order of Abijah. His wife was a descendant of Aaron, and her name was Elizabeth. ⁶Both of them were righteous before God, living blamelessly according to all the commandments and regulations of the Lord. ⁷But they had no children, because Elizabeth was barren, and both were getting on in years.

8 Once when he was serving as priest before God and his section was on duty, ⁹he was chosen by lot, according to the custom of the priesthood, to enter the sanctuary of the Lord and offer incense. ¹⁰Now at the time of the incense offering, the whole assembly of the people was praying outside. ¹¹Then there appeared to him an angel of the Lord, standing at the right side of the altar of incense. ¹²When Zechariah saw him, he was terrified; and fear overwhelmed him. ¹³But the angel said to him, "Do not be afraid, Zechariah, for your prayer has been heard. Your wife Elizabeth will bear you a son, and you will name him John. ¹⁴You will have joy and gladness, and many will rejoice at his birth, ¹⁵for he will be great in the sight of the Lord. He must never drink wine or strong drink; even before his birth he will be filled with the Holy Spirit. ¹⁶He will turn many of the people of Israel to the Lord their God. ¹⁷With the spirit and power of Elijah he will go before him, to turn the hearts of parents to their children, and the disobedient to the wisdom of the righteous, to make ready a people prepared for the Lord." ¹⁸Zechariah said to the angel, "How will I know that this is so? For I am an old man, and my wife is getting on in years." ¹⁹The angel replied, "I am Gabriel. I stand in the presence of God, and I have been sent to speak to you and to bring you this good news. ²⁰But now, because you did not believe my words, which will be fulfilled in their time, you will become mute, unable to speak, until the day these things occur."

21 Meanwhile the people were waiting for Zechariah, and wondered at his delay in the sanctuary. ²²When he did come out, he could not speak to them, and they realized that he had seen a vision in the sanctuary. He kept motioning to them and remained unable to speak. ²³When his time of service was ended, he went to his home.

24 After those days his wife Elizabeth conceived, and for five months she remained in

---

a Or for a long time

seclusion. She said, [25]"This is what the Lord has done for me when he looked favorably on me and took away the disgrace I have endured among my people."

The Birth of Jesus Foretold

26 In the sixth month the angel Gabriel was sent by God to a town in Galilee called Nazareth, [27]to a virgin engaged to a man whose name was Joseph, of the house of David. The virgin's name was Mary. [28]And he came to her and said, "Greetings, favored one! The Lord is with you."[a] [29]But she was much perplexed by his words and pondered what sort of greeting this might be. [30]The angel said to her, "Do not be afraid, Mary, for you have found favor with God. [31]And now, you will conceive in your womb and bear a son, and you will name him Jesus. [32]He will be great, and will be called the Son of the Most High, and the Lord God will give to him the throne of his ancestor David. [33]He will reign over the house of Jacob forever, and of his kingdom there will be no end." [34]Mary said to the angel, "How can this be, since I am a virgin?"[b] [35]The angel said to her, "The Holy Spirit will come upon you, and the power of the Most High will overshadow you; therefore the child to be born[c] will be holy; he will be called Son of God. [36]And now, your relative Elizabeth in her old age has also conceived a son; and this is the sixth month for her who was said to be barren. [37]For nothing will be impossible with God." [38]Then Mary said, "Here am I, the servant of the Lord; let it be with me according to your word." Then the angel departed from her.

Mary Visits Elizabeth

39 In those days Mary set out and went with haste to a Judean town in the hill country, [40]where she entered the house of Zechariah and greeted Elizabeth. [41]When Elizabeth heard Mary's greeting, the child leaped in her womb. And Elizabeth was filled with the Holy Spirit [42]and exclaimed with a loud cry, "Blessed are you among women, and blessed is the fruit of your womb. [43]And why has this happened to me, that the mother of my Lord comes to me? [44]For as soon as I heard the sound of your greeting, the child in my womb leaped for joy. [45]And blessed is she who believed that there would be[d] a fulfillment of what was spoken to her by the Lord."

Mary's Song of Praise

46 And Mary[e] said,
"My soul magnifies the Lord,
[47]   and my spirit rejoices in God my Savior,

[48] for he has looked with favor on the lowliness of
     his servant.
   Surely, from now on all generations will call
     me blessed;

---

a Other ancient authorities add *Blessed are you among women*
b Gk *I do not know a man*   c Other ancient authorities add *of you*   d Or *believed, for there will be*   e Other ancient authorities read *Elizabeth*

Mary of Nazareth

Luke's Gospel makes it clear that Mary of Nazareth has a special place in God's plan of salvation. Beginning with Mary's humble acceptance of God's will revealed by the angel Gabriel (see Lk 1:26–38), Mary is presented as the true, first disciple who does the will of God. Her yes to God leads to Jesus' presence among us. She follows Jesus to the cross and is with the disciples in the upper room during the coming of the Holy Spirit (see Acts 1:14). Mary reveals to us the meaning of true faith—a willingness to accept God's call and to gradually discover the full meaning of God's will.

In choosing Mary to be the mother of Jesus, God selects not a rich queen but a poor young girl open to the action of the Holy Spirit in her life. In Mary, Luke emphasizes God's preference for the poor and the little ones (see "The *Magnificat*: The Prayer of the Poor" near Lk 1:39–56).

Besides being the mother of Jesus, Mary is presented in the Bible as the mother of the Church (see Jn 19:25–27). For this reason, Catholic Christians have a special devotion to Mary. They celebrate her virginal conception of Jesus on the feast of the Annunciation (March 25). They believe Mary was born free from original sin, and they celebrate this on the feast of the Immaculate Conception (December 8). They also believe she was taken into heaven, body and soul, at the end of her life, and they celebrate this on the feast of the Assumption (August 15). Catholics also have a special prayer form honoring Mary, called the rosary.

▶ Lk 1:26–56

LK

Cultural Connection

The *Magnificat*: The Prayer of the Poor

Mary gives a testimony of her faith right after she receives the news that she will be the mother of God. During her visit to her cousin Elizabeth, she sings of God's salvation in a song known as the *Magnificat*, which means "[my soul] praises." This prayer is mainly made up of verses taken from the Psalms and the prophets. Mary first sings of her salvation; then she sings of God's salvation brought to the humble, the poor, and the hungry; and she finishes by singing of the salvation brought to all the people of God as promised to Abraham.

The *Magnificat* is an important prayer for Hispanic people. It is the song of the poor of God, those who expected salvation from God, not from people in power or through wars and conquests. The social consequences of God's salvation are clearly revealed in Mary's song. The prayer is directed to God and talks about God's care for the poor. Jesus is the one who acts as God's agent, accomplishing these things on God's behalf; he raises up the lowly and brings down the powerful to build the Reign of God.

● In a world marked by huge gaps between rich people and poor people, is it clear that Christians are in solidarity with the poor?

● How are you helping the poor now, and how are you planning to do so as an adult?

● Pray the *Magnificat* slowly, savoring what it says, letting it move to the core of your heart.

▶ Lk 1:39–56

---

49 for the Mighty One has done great things
    for me,
  and holy is his name.
50 His mercy is for those who fear him
  from generation to generation.
51 He has shown strength with his arm;
  he has scattered the proud in the thoughts of
    their hearts.
52 He has brought down the powerful from their
    thrones,
  and lifted up the lowly;
53 he has filled the hungry with good things,
  and sent the rich away empty.
54 He has helped his servant Israel,
  in remembrance of his mercy,
55 according to the promise he made to our
    ancestors,
  to Abraham and to his descendants forever."

56 And Mary remained with her about three months and then returned to her home.

The Birth of John the Baptist

57 Now the time came for Elizabeth to give birth, and she bore a son. 58Her neighbors and relatives heard that the Lord had shown his great mercy to her, and they rejoiced with her.

59 On the eighth day they came to circumcise the child, and they were going to name him Zechariah after his father. 60But his mother said, "No; he is to be called John." 61They said to her, "None of your relatives has this name." 62Then they began motioning to his father to find out what name he wanted to give him. 63He asked for a writing tablet and wrote, "His name is John." And all of them were amazed. 64Immediately his mouth was opened and his tongue freed, and he began to speak, praising God. 65Fear came over all their neighbors, and all these things were talked about throughout the entire hill country of Judea. 66All who heard them pondered them and said, "What then will this child become?" For, indeed, the hand of the Lord was with him.

Zechariah's Prophecy

67 Then his father Zechariah was filled with the Holy Spirit and spoke this prophecy:
68 "Blessed be the Lord God of Israel,
  for he has looked favorably on his people and
    redeemed them.
69 He has raised up a mighty savior[a] for us
  in the house of his servant David,
70 as he spoke through the mouth of his holy
    prophets from of old,
71   that we would be saved from our enemies
  and from the hand of all who hate us.
72 Thus he has shown the mercy promised to our
    ancestors,

---

a Gk a horn of salvation

Cultural Connection

O Christmas Tree

Did you ever wonder where the tradition of the Christmas tree came from? It began in Germany, the country that also gave us the beautiful song "Silent Night." For hundreds of years, the Christmas tree has been the focal point and symbol of the Christmas season for the people of Germany.

In the year AD 350, Pope Julius declared December 25, which had been the day of the pagan feast of the sun god, a feast day in observance of the birth of the Son of God. Prior to AD 350,

the German people had a tradition of keeping evergreen branches in the house to ward off evil spirits. This pagan tradition was exchanged for a Christian tradition of having branches in the house to symbolize the life that Jesus brought to the world. After some time, the branches themselves were exchanged for entire trees, which were brought into homes and decorated with candles. Centuries later, as the German people immigrated into North America, especially to the U.S. and Canada,

they brought the lovely tradition of the Christmas tree with them.

Today, the Christmas tree is a central symbol of Christmas in the United States. Adding lights and decorations helps us to celebrate the birth of Jesus, the light of the world.

▶ Lk 2:1–14

---

and has remembered his holy covenant,
⁷³ the oath that he swore to our ancestor Abraham,
to grant us ⁷⁴that we, being rescued from the hands of our enemies,
might serve him without fear, ⁷⁵in holiness and righteousness
before him all our days.
⁷⁶ And you, child, will be called the prophet of the Most High;
for you will go before the Lord to prepare his ways,
⁷⁷ to give knowledge of salvation to his people by the forgiveness of their sins.
⁷⁸ By the tender mercy of our God,
the dawn from on high will break upon^a us,
⁷⁹ to give light to those who sit in darkness and in the shadow of death,
to guide our feet into the way of peace."
⁸⁰ The child grew and became strong in spirit, and he was in the wilderness until the day he appeared publicly to Israel.

The Birth of Jesus

2 In those days a decree went out from Emperor Augustus that all the world should be registered. ²This was the first registration and was taken while Quirinius was governor of Syria. ³All went to their own towns to be registered. ⁴Joseph also went from the town of Nazareth in Galilee to Judea, to the city of David called Bethlehem, because he was descended from the house and family of David. ⁵He went to be registered with

Mary, to whom he was engaged and who was expecting a child. ⁶While they were there, the time came for her to deliver her child. ⁷And she gave birth to her firstborn son and wrapped him in bands of cloth, and laid him in a manger, because there was no place for them in the inn.

The Shepherds and the Angels

⁸ In that region there were shepherds living in the fields, keeping watch over their flock by night. ⁹Then an angel of the Lord stood before them, and the glory of the Lord shone around them, and they were terrified. ¹⁰But the angel said to them, "Do not be afraid; for see—I am bringing you good news of great joy for all the people: ¹¹to you is born this day in the city of David a Savior, who is the Messiah,^b the Lord. ¹²This will be a sign for you: you will find a child wrapped in bands of cloth and lying in a manger." ¹³And suddenly there was with the angel a multitude of the heavenly host,^c praising God and saying,
¹⁴ "Glory to God in the highest heaven,
and on earth peace among those whom he favors!"^d

¹⁵ When the angels had left them and gone into heaven, the shepherds said to one another, "Let us go now to Bethlehem and see this thing that has taken place, which the Lord has made

---

^a Other ancient authorities read *has broken upon*   ^b Or *the Christ*   ^c Gk *army*   ^d Other ancient authorities read *peace, goodwill among people*

Jesus' Birth: Good News to the Poor

On December 25, we celebrate Christmas, the birth of Jesus. We recall the moment of God's entering our world—a defining moment in the history of salvation. As Luke records the moment of the birth of the Messiah, who are the stars of the show? To whom do the angels appear to announce this remarkable event, this "good news of great joy for all the people" (Lk 2:10)? the high priest? the rich and important residents of Bethlehem? No. The announcement is made to shepherds, poor workers living in the fields nearby.

Like Mary the shepherds are people of little power and significance. Luke makes the point that sometimes what the world sees as unimportant, God honors. This is the justice of God. It is the same today. The poorest in our world, the most hidden people who have no power, hold a special place in the heart of God. And, like the shepherds, those who are poor often know God better than those who are rich or powerful by this world's standards.

This truth is a challenge but also good news for all of us, rich and poor alike. How do your attitudes and actions—even the way you celebrate Christmas—reflect God's special attention to those who are poor?

▶ Lk 2:8–20

known to us." 16So they went with haste and found Mary and Joseph, and the child lying in the manger. 17When they saw this, they made known what had been told them about this child; 18and all who heard it were amazed at what the shepherds told them. 19But Mary treasured all these words and pondered them in her heart. 20The shepherds returned, glorifying and praising God for all they had heard and seen, as it had been told them.

Jesus Is Named

21 After eight days had passed, it was time to circumcise the child; and he was called Jesus, the name given by the angel before he was conceived in the womb.

Jesus Is Presented in the Temple

22 When the time came for their purification according to the law of Moses, they brought him up to Jerusalem to present him to the Lord 23(as it is written in the law of the Lord, "Every firstborn male shall be designated as holy to the Lord"), 24and they offered a sacrifice according to what is stated in the law of the Lord, "a pair of turtledoves or two young pigeons."

25 Now there was a man in Jerusalem whose name was Simeon;[a] this man was righteous and devout, looking forward to the consolation of Israel, and the Holy Spirit rested on him. 26It had been revealed to him by the Holy Spirit that he would not see death before he had seen the Lord's Messiah.[b] 27Guided by the Spirit, Simeon[c] came into the temple; and when the parents brought in the child Jesus, to do for him what was customary under the law, 28Simeon[d] took him in his arms and praised God, saying,

29 "Master, now you are dismissing your servant[e] in peace,
    according to your word;
30 for my eyes have seen your salvation,
31   which you have prepared in the presence of all peoples,
32 a light for revelation to the Gentiles
    and for glory to your people Israel."

33 And the child's father and mother were amazed at what was being said about him. 34Then Simeon[a] blessed them and said to his mother Mary, "This child is destined for the falling and the rising of many in Israel, and to be a sign that will be opposed 35so that the inner thoughts of many will be revealed—and a sword will pierce your own soul too."

36 There was also a prophet, Anna[f] the daughter of Phanuel, of the tribe of Asher. She was of a great age, having lived with her husband seven years after her marriage, 37then as a widow to the age of eighty-four. She never left the temple but worshiped there with fasting and prayer night and day. 38At that moment she came, and began to praise God and to speak about the child[g] to all who were looking for the redemption of Jerusalem.

The Return to Nazareth

39 When they had finished everything required by the law of the Lord, they returned to

---

a Gk Symeon   b Or the Lord's Christ   c Gk In the Spirit, he
d Gk he   e Gk slave   f Gk Hanna   g Gk him

Galilee, to their own town of Nazareth. ⁴⁰The child grew and became strong, filled with wisdom; and the favor of God was upon him.

The Boy Jesus in the Temple

41 Now every year his parents went to Jerusalem for the festival of the Passover. ⁴²And when he was twelve years old, they went up as usual for the festival. ⁴³When the festival was ended and they started to return, the boy Jesus stayed behind in Jerusalem, but his parents did not know it. ⁴⁴Assuming that he was in the group of travelers, they went a day's journey. Then they started to look for him among their relatives and friends. ⁴⁵When they did not find him, they returned to Jerusalem to search for him. ⁴⁶After three days they found him in the temple, sitting among the teachers, listening to them and asking them questions. ⁴⁷And all who heard him were amazed at his understanding

and his answers. ⁴⁸When his parents*a* saw him they were astonished; and his mother said to him, "Child, why have you treated us like this? Look, your father and I have been searching for you in great anxiety." ⁴⁹He said to them, "Why were you searching for me? Did you not know that I must be in my Father's house?"*b* ⁵⁰But they did not understand what he said to them. ⁵¹Then he went down with them and came to Nazareth, and was obedient to them. His mother treasured all these things in her heart.

52 And Jesus increased in wisdom and in years,*c* and in divine and human favor.

The Proclamation of John the Baptist

3 In the fifteenth year of the reign of Emperor Tiberius, when Pontius Pilate was governor

---

a Gk they   b Or be about my Father's interests?   c Or in stature

The Holy Family

On the first Sunday after Christmas, the Catholic Church celebrates the feast of the Holy Family: Jesus, Mary, and Joseph. The Bible does not tell us a lot about the Holy Family. We know that Joseph was a kind and compassionate man, eager to do God's will. He raised Jesus as his own son, even though he was not Jesus' biological father. Jesus was raised in a home in which love and faith were the norm.

We can be sure that the Holy Family had their moments of conflict and crisis—all families do. Luke's story of Jesus' getting separated from his parents demonstrates that. But we can also be sure that their love and faith helped them to survive such conflicts and grow stronger because of them. The Church holds the Holy Family up as a model of respect, compassion, love, and faith in family life.

How does your family express love and respect for one another? What crises and conflicts have you and your family survived? What can you do to bring the qualities of the Holy Family more fully into your family's life?

▶ Lk 2:41–52

Jesus Grows in Age and Wisdom

Luke is the only New Testament Gospel that has any stories of Jesus' childhood. When Jesus was twelve, he came to Jerusalem with his family to celebrate the pilgrimage festival of Passover. He was left behind, and when Mary and Joseph searched for him, they found him in the Temple. At the Temple, Jesus listened to and questioned the teachers, trying to understand his faith better. His questions and his understanding—and, we can presume, his sincerity—amazed all who heard him.

Adolescence is an important time for exploring life's questions—including life's religious questions. Sometimes, young people are led to believe they shouldn't have any questions—which is a sad statement about adult leaders and teachers. Wise teachers—like those the young Jesus met in the Temple—welcome and encourage your questions, even your religious questions. So ask yourself: How well do I know my faith? What are my main questions? Who are the wise teachers I can go to for help in searching out the answers?

▶ Lk 2:41–52

of Judea, and Herod was ruler*a* of Galilee, and his brother Philip ruler*a* of the region of Ituraea and Trachonitis, and Lysanias ruler*a* of Abilene, ²during the high priesthood of Annas and Caiaphas, the word of God came to John son of Zechariah in the wilderness. ³He went into all the region around the Jordan, proclaiming a baptism of repentance for the forgiveness of sins, ⁴as it is written in the book of the words of the prophet Isaiah,

"The voice of one crying out in the wilderness:
'Prepare the way of the Lord,
　make his paths straight.

Introducing...

John the Baptist

Picture a man living in the desert, eating grasshoppers and wild honey, and wearing a camel hair coat. Does this sound like the person Jesus described as "among those born of women no one is greater than John" (Lk 7:28)? The person Jesus is talking about is John the Baptist, and he plays an important role in all four Gospels. John is portrayed like an Old Testament prophet, calling people to repentance for their sins. Indeed, his ministry was so similar to Jesus' ministry that after Herod had John killed (see Mt 14:1–12), he thought that Jesus might have been John raised from the dead (see Lk 9:7–9). The power of John's preaching is demonstrated by Jesus' disciples still encountering John's followers years after John's death (see Acts 19:1–7).

John the Baptist was Jesus' cousin, and the Gospel of Luke presents many parallels between the two men. John's preaching gives us a preview into Jesus' message. John was preparing the way for Jesus. He was a humble servant "not worthy to untie the thong of [Jesus'] sandals" (Lk 3:16). He described his baptism as a baptism of water in contrast with Jesus' baptism with "the Holy Spirit and fire" (verse 16).

John the Baptist is the model of how Christians should perform their prophetic mission, pointing others toward Jesus with passion and humility.

▶ Lk 3:1–20

⁵ Every valley shall be filled,
　and every mountain and hill shall be made low,
　and the crooked shall be made straight,
　　and the rough ways made smooth;
⁶ and all flesh shall see the salvation of God.' "

7 John said to the crowds that came out to be baptized by him, "You brood of vipers! Who warned you to flee from the wrath to come? ⁸Bear fruits worthy of repentance. Do not begin to say to yourselves, 'We have Abraham as our ancestor'; for I tell you, God is able from these stones to raise up children to Abraham. ⁹Even now the ax is lying at the root of the trees; every tree therefore that does not bear good fruit is cut down and thrown into the fire."

10 And the crowds asked him, "What then should we do?" ¹¹In reply he said to them, "Whoever has two coats must share with anyone who has none; and whoever has food must do likewise." ¹²Even tax collectors came to be baptized, and they asked him, "Teacher, what should we do?" ¹³He said to them, "Collect no more than the amount prescribed for you." ¹⁴Soldiers also asked him, "And we, what should we do?" He said to them, "Do not extort money from anyone by threats or false accusation, and be satisfied with your wages."

15 As the people were filled with expectation, and all were questioning in their hearts concerning John, whether he might be the Messiah,*b* ¹⁶John answered all of them by saying, "I baptize

---

a Gk tetrarch   *b* Or the Christ

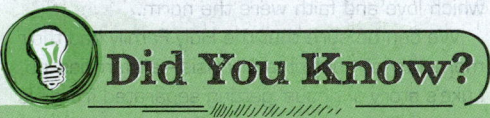

Did You Know?

The Liturgical Year

The story of Jesus' baptism is one of the readings for the feast of the Baptism of the Lord. The feast days and holy days celebrated by Catholics and other Christians follow a yearly pattern. This pattern is called the liturgical year; it is not the same as the calendar year. You can read more about Church feast days and see a diagram of the liturgical calendar on pages 1522–1523.

▶ Lk 3:15–22

Cultural Connection

Free . . . to Be Tempted

African Americans have been struggling for freedom for a long time. They have sung about freedom. They have written poems about it. And they have had demonstrations over it. For most African Americans, freedom is the Promised Land, a place overflowing with milk and honey, a place like heaven where there is justice and peace.

After Jesus' baptism, he went out into the wilderness to be alone so he could discern what God wanted him to do. While he was out there, he realized he could still be tempted to make selfish choic-es. Read Luke 4:1–13. Imagine how tempting it might have been for Jesus to use his power to prove to the world how great he was, instead of how great and loving God is. But he never gave in!

Many people throughout history have faced the choice of using their newly won freedom for their own selfish interests or for the good of others. After securing their freedom, some slaves, like Harriet Tubman, decided to spend their lives helping others become free—often at great risk and sacrifice to themselves. You can be sure they were tempted to choose an easier and safer life.

If we want to be free, we will face temptation. And if we want to remain free, we must resist the temptation to choose selfishly. Once we give in to selfishness, we become less free to resist it the next time around. And before long, we will become slaves again—slaves to our own desires.

▶ Lk 4:1–13

you with water; but one who is more powerful than I is coming; I am not worthy to untie the thong of his sandals. He will baptize you with[a] the Holy Spirit and fire. [17]His winnowing fork is in his hand, to clear his threshing floor and to gather the wheat into his granary; but the chaff he will burn with unquenchable fire."

18 So, with many other exhortations, he proclaimed the good news to the people. [19]But Herod the ruler,[b] who had been rebuked by him because of Herodias, his brother's wife, and because of all the evil things that Herod had done, [20]added to them all by shutting up John in prison.

The Baptism of Jesus

21 Now when all the people were baptized, and when Jesus also had been baptized and was praying, the heaven was opened, [22]and the Holy Spirit descended upon him in bodily form like a dove. And a voice came from heaven, "You are my Son, the Beloved;[c] with you I am well pleased."[d]

The Ancestors of Jesus

[23] Jesus was about thirty years old when he began his work. He was the son (as was thought) of Joseph son of Heli, [24]son of Matthat, son of Levi, son of Melchi, son of Jannai, son of Joseph, [25]son of Mattathias, son of Amos, son of Nahum, son of Esli, son of Naggai, [26]son of Maath, son of Mattathias, son of Semein, son of Josech, son of Joda, [27]son of Joanan, son of Rhesa, son of Zerubbabel, son of Shealtiel,[e] son of Neri, [28]son of Melchi, son of Addi, son of Cosam, son of El-madam, son of Er, [29]son of Joshua, son of Eliezer, son of Jorim, son of Matthat, son of Levi, [30]son of Simeon, son of Judah, son of Joseph, son of Jo-nam, son of Eliakim, [31]son of Melea, son of Men-na, son of Mattatha, son of Nathan, son of David, [32]son of Jesse, son of Obed, son of Boaz, son of Sala,[f] son of Nahshon, [33]son of Amminadab, son of Admin, son of Arni,[g] son of Hezron, son of Pe-rez, son of Judah, [34]son of Jacob, son of Isaac, son of Abraham, son of Terah, son of Nahor, [35]son of Serug, son of Reu, son of Peleg, son of Eber, son of Shelah, [36]son of Cainan, son of Arphaxad, son of Shem, son of Noah, son of Lamech, [37]son of Methuselah, son of Enoch, son of Jared, son of Mahalaleel, son of Cainan, [38]son of Enos, son of Seth, son of Adam, son of God.

The Temptation of Jesus

4 Jesus, full of the Holy Spirit, returned from the Jordan and was led by the Spirit in the wilderness, [2]where for forty days he was tempted by the devil. He ate nothing at all during those

---

a Or in   b Gk tetrarch   c Or my beloved Son   d Other ancient authorities read You are my Son, today I have begotten you   e Gk Salathiel   f Other ancient authorities read Salmon g Other ancient authorities read Amminadab, son of Aram; others vary widely

✝ Catholic Connection

The Bible, Tradition, and Magisterium

Knowing the Scriptures and applying them to our lives is essential as Christians. Jesus himself often quoted the Sacred Scriptures during his ministry. In the story of Jesus' temptation in the wilderness, Jesus quotes the Scriptures several times as a means to refute the devil and his temptations. But the devil also quotes the Scriptures in an effort to lead Jesus astray. The confrontation ends with the departure of the devil and Jesus' holding fast to the truth of God's Revelation and, ultimately, his role as the obedient Son of God.

We should always be careful about misinterpreting the Bible. That is why the Catholic Church teaches that our faith is based on both the Bible and the Sacred Tradition handed down by the Apostles. The Sacred Scriptures are the inspired word of God—inspired in the sense that the Holy Spirit guided the many authors who wrote and compiled the books of both the Old and New Testaments. When we are interpreting the Scriptures, we must be mindful of what the human authors intended—which requires learning about the history, culture, literary expressions, and language of the time. In this way, we learn what God wanted communicated through the Scriptures.

Sacred Tradition is rooted in the teachings of the Apostles, refined and passed on through the teaching authority of the Church. It includes development of doctrine and morals. Together, Scripture and Tradition form the one sacred deposit of the word of God for the salvation of God's people.

The role of the Magisterium, or teaching authority of the Church, is to act as shepherd in service of the word of God (Scripture and Tradition). Under the guidance of the Holy Spirit, the bishops, in communion with the Pope, are entrusted with teaching what has been handed on through the Scriptures and Tradition.

Together the Bible, Tradition, and Magisterium help us discern God's Revelation in the world. All three are essential guides in our efforts to know Christ and our role as Christians.

▶ **Lk 4:1–13**

Catechism, nos. 74–141

Catholic Social Teaching

Jesus Liberates People from Oppression

In the Gospel of Luke, Jesus begins his mission by referring to Isaiah's prophecy (see Isa 61:1). In the Gospel, we see Jesus fulfilling this prophecy by:

- healing the sick, whose sickness is viewed as caused by demon possession
- touching and curing lepers, who are separated from the rest of society
- speaking to and spending time with Samaritans, who are looked down upon and rejected by the Jews
- accepting as disciples women, who are generally not accepted as equals, socially and religiously
- forgiving and eating with sinners, who are put down and discriminated against by leaders of the Temple

Throughout his ministry, Jesus treats with great respect all whom he encounters. He recognizes that all people possess dignity and that their lives, even when afflicted by sin, sickness, or poverty, are a reflection of God's own self. Catholic social teaching urges us to do the same in our world today. We must never discriminate against or marginalize someone because of his or her race, gender, health, or social status; rather, our actions must be directed toward protecting and enhancing the dignity that all have been blessed with from the moment of creation.

Consider these questions:

- How and where is human dignity being diminished in our world?
- Where is human dignity being uplifted and protected?
- How can we work to ensure the enhancement of the dignity of all people?

▶ **Lk 4:14–30**

Life and Dignity of the Human Person

L
K

---

days, and when they were over, he was famished. ³The devil said to him, "If you are the Son of God, command this stone to become a loaf of bread." ⁴Jesus answered him, "It is written, 'One does not live by bread alone.' "

5 Then the devil[a] led him up and showed him in an instant all the kingdoms of the world. ⁶And the devil[a] said to him, "To you I will give their glory and all this authority; for it has been given over to me, and I give it to anyone I please. ⁷If you, then, will worship me, it will all be yours." ⁸Jesus answered him, "It is written,

'Worship the Lord your God,
    and serve only him.' "

9 Then the devil[a] took him to Jerusalem, and placed him on the pinnacle of the temple, saying to him, "If you are the Son of God, throw yourself down from here, ¹⁰for it is written,

'He will command his angels concerning you,
    to protect you,'

¹¹and

'On their hands they will bear you up,
    so that you will not dash your foot against a
        stone.' "

¹²Jesus answered him, "It is said, 'Do not put the Lord your God to the test.' " ¹³When the devil had finished every test, he departed from him until an opportune time.

The Beginning of the Galilean Ministry

14 Then Jesus, filled with the power of the Spirit, returned to Galilee, and a report about him spread through all the surrounding country. ¹⁵He began to teach in their synagogues and was praised by everyone.

The Rejection of Jesus at Nazareth

16 When he came to Nazareth, where he had been brought up, he went to the synagogue on the sabbath day, as was his custom. He stood up to read, ¹⁷and the scroll of the prophet Isaiah was given to him. He unrolled the scroll and found the place where it was written:

¹⁸ "The Spirit of the Lord is upon me,
    because he has anointed me
        to bring good news to the poor.
He has sent me to proclaim release to the
        captives
    and recovery of sight to the blind,
        to let the oppressed go free,
¹⁹ to proclaim the year of the Lord's favor."

²⁰And he rolled up the scroll, gave it back to the attendant, and sat down. The eyes of all in the synagogue were fixed on him. ²¹Then he

---

a Gk *he*

began to say to them, "Today this scripture has been fulfilled in your hearing." [22]All spoke well of him and were amazed at the gracious words that came from his mouth. They said, "Is not this Joseph's son?" [23]He said to them, "Doubtless you will quote to me this proverb, 'Doctor, cure yourself!' And you will say, 'Do here also in your hometown the things that we have heard you did at Capernaum.' " [24]And he said, "Truly I tell you, no prophet is accepted in the prophet's hometown. [25]But the truth is, there were many widows in Israel in the time of Elijah, when the heaven was shut up three years and six months, and there was a severe famine over all the land; [26]yet Elijah was sent to none of them except to a widow at Zarephath in Sidon. [27]There were also many lepers[a] in Israel in the time of the prophet Elisha, and none of them was cleansed except Naaman the Syrian." [28]When they heard this, all in the synagogue were filled with rage. [29]They got up, drove him out of the town, and led him to the brow of the hill on which their town was built, so that they might hurl him off the cliff. [30]But he passed through the midst of them and went on his way.

The Man with an Unclean Spirit

31 He went down to Capernaum, a city in Galilee, and was teaching them on the sabbath. [32]They were astounded at his teaching, because he spoke with authority. [33]In the synagogue there was a man who had the spirit of an unclean demon, and he cried out with a loud voice, [34]"Let us alone! What have you to do with us, Jesus of Nazareth? Have you come to destroy us? I know who you are, the Holy One of God." [35]But Jesus rebuked him, saying, "Be silent, and come out of him!" When the demon had thrown him down before them, he came out of him without having done him any harm. [36]They were all amazed and kept saying to one another, "What kind of utterance is this? For with authority and power he commands the unclean spirits, and out they come!" [37]And a report about him began to reach every place in the region.

Healings at Simon's House

38 After leaving the synagogue he entered Simon's house. Now Simon's mother-in-law was suffering from a high fever, and they asked him about her. [39]Then he stood over her and rebuked the fever, and it left her. Immediately she got up and began to serve them.

40 As the sun was setting, all those who had any who were sick with various kinds of diseases brought them to him; and he laid his hands on each of them and cured them. [41]Demons also came out of many, shouting, "You are the Son of God!" But he rebuked them and would not allow them to speak, because they knew that he was the Messiah.[b]

Jesus Preaches in the Synagogues

42 At daybreak he departed and went into a deserted place. And the crowds were looking for him; and when they reached him, they wanted to prevent him from leaving them. [43]But he said to them, "I must proclaim the good news of the kingdom of God to the other cities also; for I was sent for this purpose." [44]So he continued proclaiming the message in the synagogues of Judea.[c]

Jesus Calls the First Disciples

5 Once while Jesus[d] was standing beside the lake of Gennesaret, and the crowd was pressing in on him to hear the word of God, [2]he saw two boats there at the shore of the lake; the fishermen had gone out of them and were washing their nets. [3]He got into one of the boats, the one belonging to Simon, and asked him to put out a little way from the shore. Then he sat down and taught the crowds from the boat. [4]When he had finished speaking, he said to Simon, "Put out into the deep water and let down your nets for a catch." [5]Simon answered, "Master, we have worked all night long but have caught nothing. Yet if you say so, I will let down the nets." [6]When they had done this, they caught so many fish that their nets were beginning to break. [7]So they signaled their partners in the other boat to come and help them. And they came and filled both boats, so that they began to sink. [8]But when Simon Peter saw it, he fell down at Jesus' knees, saying, "Go away from me, Lord, for I am a sinful man!" [9]For he and all who were with him were amazed at the catch of fish that they had taken; [10]and so also were James and John, sons of Zebedee, who were partners with Simon. Then Jesus said to Simon, "Do not be afraid; from now on you will be catching people." [11]When they had brought their boats to shore, they left everything and followed him.

Jesus Cleanses a Leper

12 Once, when he was in one of the cities, there was a man covered with leprosy.[a] When he saw Jesus, he bowed with his face to the ground

---

a The terms *leper* and *leprosy* can refer to several diseases
b Or *the Christ*   c Other ancient authorities read *Galilee*
d Gk *he*

and begged him, "Lord, if you choose, you can make him clean." [13]Then Jesus[a] stretched out his hand, touched him, and said, "I do choose. Be made clean." Immediately the leprosy[b] left him. [14]And he ordered him to tell no one. "Go," he said, "and show yourself to the priest, and, as Moses commanded, make an offering for your cleansing, for a testimony to them." [15]But now more than ever the word about Jesus[c] spread abroad; many crowds would gather to hear him and to be cured of their diseases. [16]But he would withdraw to deserted places and pray.

Jesus Heals a Paralytic

17 One day, while he was teaching, Pharisees and teachers of the law were sitting near by (they had come from every village of Galilee and Judea and from Jerusalem); and the power of the Lord was with him to heal.[d] [18]Just then some men came, carrying a paralyzed man on a bed. They were trying to bring him in and lay him before Jesus;[c] [19]but finding no way to bring him in because of the crowd, they went up on the roof and let him down with his bed through the tiles into the middle of the crowd[e] in front of Jesus. [20]When he saw their faith, he said, "Friend,[f] your sins are forgiven you." [21]Then the scribes and the Pharisees began to question, "Who is this who is speaking blasphemies? Who can forgive sins but God alone?" [22]When Jesus perceived their questionings, he answered them, "Why do you raise such questions in your hearts? [23]Which is easier, to say, 'Your sins are forgiven you,' or to say, 'Stand up and walk'? [24]But so that you may know that the Son of Man has authority on earth to forgive sins"—he said to the one who was paralyzed—"I say to you, stand up and take your bed and go to your home." [25]Immediately he stood up before them, took what he had been lying on, and went to his home, glorifying God. [26]Amazement seized all of them, and they glorified God and were filled with awe, saying, "We have seen strange things today."

Jesus Calls Levi

27 After this he went out and saw a tax collector named Levi, sitting at the tax booth; and he said to him, "Follow me." [28]And he got up, left everything, and followed him.

29 Then Levi gave a great banquet for him in his house, and there was a large crowd of tax collectors and others sitting at the table[g] with them. [30]The Pharisees and their scribes were complaining to his disciples, saying, "Why do you eat and drink with tax collectors and sinners?" [31]Jesus answered, "Those who are well have no need

Do Not Be Afraid

How would you respond if someone walked into the room right now and announced that God wanted to see you in the next room in five minutes? As astonishing as that would be, few of us would probably be anxious about running right in to see God. We would probably want a little more time to get some things in our lives "straightened out"!

The Gospel of Luke reveals something interesting when it describes a miraculous catch of fish and the call of the first disciples. Upon seeing the miraculous catch, Peter knows he is in the presence of God. He asks Jesus to leave because Peter is overwhelmed by his own sinfulness and he knows that no one can see the face of God and live (see Lk 5:8).

If we found ourselves in a boat with God, we might respond the same way. Jesus reassures Peter, uttering words so important that they are repeated six times in Luke: "Do not be afraid." God knows we are sinners too. Jesus came not to condemn us but to save us and to make God's love known to us. Jesus is also saying to us: "Do not be afraid. Come, follow me!"

▶ Lk 5:1–11

of a physician, but those who are sick; [32]I have come to call not the righteous but sinners to repentance."

The Question about Fasting

33 Then they said to him, "John's disciples, like the disciples of the Pharisees, frequently fast and pray, but your disciples eat and drink." [34]Jesus said to them, "You cannot make wedding guests fast while the bridegroom is with them, can you? [35]The days will come when the bridegroom will be taken away from them, and then they will fast in those days." [36]He also told them a parable: "No one tears a piece from a new

---

a Gk he   b The terms *leper* and *leprosy* can refer to several diseases   c Gk *him*   d Other ancient authorities *was present to heal them*   e Gk *into the midst*   f Gk *Man*   g Gk *reclining*

garment and sews it on an old garment; otherwise the new will be torn, and the piece from the new will not match the old. 37And no one puts new wine into old wineskins; otherwise the new wine will burst the skins and will be spilled, and the skins will be destroyed. 38But new wine must be put into fresh wineskins. 39And no one after drinking old wine desires new wine, but says, 'The old is good.'"a

The Question about the Sabbath

6 One sabbathb while Jesusc was going through the grainfields, his disciples plucked some heads of grain, rubbed them in their hands, and ate them. 2But some of the Pharisees said, "Why are you doing what is not lawfuld on the sabbath?" 3Jesus answered, "Have you not read what David did when he and his companions were hungry? 4He entered the house of God and took and ate the bread of the Presence, which it is not lawful for any but the priests to eat, and gave some to his companions?" 5Then he said to them, "The Son of Man is lord of the sabbath."

The Man with a Withered Hand

6 On another sabbath he entered the synagogue and taught, and there was a man there whose right hand was withered. 7The scribes and the Pharisees watched him to see whether he would cure on the sabbath, so that they might find an accusation against him. 8Even though he knew what they were thinking, he said to the man who had the withered hand, "Come and stand here." He got up and stood there. 9Then Jesus said to them, "I ask you, is it lawful to do good or to do harm on the sabbath, to save life or to destroy it?" 10After looking around at all of them, he said to him, "Stretch out your hand." He did so, and his hand was restored. 11But they were filled with fury and discussed with one another what they might do to Jesus.

Jesus Chooses the Twelve Apostles

12 Now during those days he went out to the mountain to pray; and he spent the night in prayer to God. 13And when day came, he called his disciples and chose twelve of them, whom he also named apostles: 14Simon, whom he named Peter, and his brother Andrew, and James, and John, and Philip, and Bartholomew, 15and Matthew, and Thomas, and James son of Alphaeus, and Simon, who was called the Zealot, 16and Judas son of James, and Judas Iscariot, who became a traitor.

Jesus Teaches and Heals

17 He came down with them and stood on a level place, with a great crowd of his disciples and a great multitude of people from all Judea, Jerusalem, and the coast of Tyre and Sidon. 18They had come to hear him and to be healed of their diseases; and those who were troubled with unclean spirits were cured. 19And all in the crowd were trying to touch him, for power came out from him and healed all of them.

Blessings and Woes

20 Then he looked up at his disciples and said:

Jesus' Preference for the Poor

In the Gospel of Luke, Jesus gives the Sermon on the Plain, which parallels the Sermon on the Mount in Matthew. Even more clearly than Matthew, Luke makes the point that God's justice has a preference for the poor and the little ones. So it's not surprising that the four Beatitudes (blessings) in Luke are balanced by four woes ("Woe!" is like saying, "Trouble ahead!"). For example, "Blessed are you who are poor" (Lk 6:20) is countered by "Woe to you who are rich" (verse 24). Jesus shows his care for both those who are rich and those who are poor by calling the rich to practice justice and the poor to have hope.

Unlike Matthew, Luke does not "spiritualize" the Beatitudes. Matthew says, "Blessed are the poor in spirit" (5:3), but Luke simply says, "Blessed are you who are poor" (6:20), meaning materially poor. Matthew is concerned for people's salvation; Luke is concerned about their salvation and their material needs.

How do you show special concern for those who are poor? Pray that God helps us to share God's love with those caught in the struggles of life.

▶ Lk 6:17–49

a Other ancient authorities read *better*; others lack verse 39
b Other ancient authorities read *On the second first sabbath*
c Gk *he*   d Other ancient authorities add *to do*

"Blessed are you who are poor,
  for yours is the kingdom of God.
21 "Blessed are you who are hungry now,
  for you will be filled.
"Blessed are you who weep now,
  for you will laugh.
22 "Blessed are you when people hate you, and when they exclude you, revile you, and defame you[a] on account of the Son of Man. 23 Rejoice in that day and leap for joy, for surely your reward is great in heaven; for that is what their ancestors did to the prophets.
24 "But woe to you who are rich,
  for you have received your consolation.
25 "Woe to you who are full now,
  for you will be hungry.
"Woe to you who are laughing now,
  for you will mourn and weep.
26 "Woe to you when all speak well of you, for that is what their ancestors did to the false prophets.

Love for Enemies

27 "But I say to you that listen, Love your enemies, do good to those who hate you, 28 bless those who curse you, pray for those who abuse you. 29 If anyone strikes you on the cheek, offer the other also; and from anyone who takes away your coat do not withhold even your shirt. 30 Give to everyone who begs from you; and if anyone takes away your goods, do not ask for them again. 31 Do to others as you would have them do to you.
32 "If you love those who love you, what credit is that to you? For even sinners love those who love them. 33 If you do good to those who do good to you, what credit is that to you? For even sinners do the same. 34 If you lend to those from whom you hope to receive, what credit is that to you? Even sinners lend to sinners, to receive as much again. 35 But love your enemies, do good, and lend, expecting nothing in return.[b] Your reward will be great, and you will be children of the Most High; for he is kind to the ungrateful and the wicked. 36 Be merciful, just as your Father is merciful.

Judging Others

37 "Do not judge, and you will not be judged; do not condemn, and you will not be condemned. Forgive, and you will be forgiven; 38 give, and it will be given to you. A good measure, pressed down, shaken together, running over, will be put into your lap; for the measure you give will be the measure you get back."
39 He also told them a parable: "Can a blind person guide a blind person? Will not both fall into a pit? 40 A disciple is not above the teacher, but everyone who is fully qualified will be like the teacher. 41 Why do you see the speck in your neighbor's[c] eye, but do not notice the log in your own eye? 42 Or how can you say to your neighbor,[d] 'Friend,[d] let me take out the speck in your eye,' when you yourself do not see the log in your own eye? You hypocrite, first take the log out of your own eye, and then you will see clearly to take the speck out of your neighbor's[c] eye.

A Tree and Its Fruit

43 "No good tree bears bad fruit, nor again does a bad tree bear good fruit; 44 for each tree is known by its own fruit. Figs are not gathered from thorns, nor are grapes picked from a bramble bush. 45 The good person out of the good treasure of the heart produces good, and the evil person out of evil treasure produces evil; for it is out of the abundance of the heart that the mouth speaks.

The Two Foundations

46 "Why do you call me 'Lord, Lord,' and do not do what I tell you? 47 I will show you what someone is like who comes to me, hears my words, and acts on them. 48 That one is like a man building a house, who dug deeply and laid the foundation on rock; when a flood arose, the river burst against that house but could not shake it, because it had been well built.[e] 49 But the one who hears and does not act is like a man who built a house on the ground without a foundation. When the river burst against it, immediately it fell, and great was the ruin of that house."

Jesus Heals a Centurion's Servant

7 After Jesus[f] had finished all his sayings in the hearing of the people, he entered Capernaum. 2 A centurion there had a slave whom he valued highly, and who was ill and close to death. 3 When he heard about Jesus, he sent some Jewish elders to him, asking him to come and heal his slave. 4 When they came to Jesus, they appealed to him earnestly, saying, "He is worthy of having you do this for him, 5 for he loves our people, and it is he who built our synagogue for us." 6 And Jesus went with them, but when he was not far from the house, the centurion sent friends to say to him, "Lord, do not trouble yourself, for I am not worthy to have you come under my roof; 7 therefore I did not presume to come to

---

a Gk cast out your name as evil   b Other ancient authorities read despairing of no one   c Gk brother's   d Gk brother   e Other ancient authorities read founded upon the rock   f Gk he

Cultural Connection

The Reunion Dinner

The words of the centurion in Luke 7:6–7 are the basis for the words Catholics say before receiving the Holy Eucharist: "Lord, I am not worthy that you should enter under my roof, but only say the word and my soul shall be healed" (*Roman Missal*). These words indicate our humility and our willingness to accept God's forgiveness and healing in our lives. They remind us to receive Jesus in a state of peace with God and one another, especially by seeking reconciliation with family and friends.

The Chinese New Year's celebration includes a "reunion dinner." The whole family gathers at the home of the eldest family member. People travel from faraway cities, and even from other countries, to be together. The meal is not eaten until everyone is present, and no one eats until any disagreement or hurt is forgiven, and the family is at peace.

▶ Lk 7:1–10

you. But only speak the word, and let my servant be healed. [8]For I also am a man set under authority, with soldiers under me; and I say to one, 'Go,' and he goes, and to another, 'Come,' and he comes, and to my slave, 'Do this,' and the slave does it." [9]When Jesus heard this he was amazed at him, and turning to the crowd that followed him, he said, "I tell you, not even in Israel have I found such faith." [10]When those who had been sent returned to the house, they found the slave in good health.

Jesus Raises the Widow's Son at Nain

11 Soon afterwards[a] he went to a town called Nain, and his disciples and a large crowd went with him. [12]As he approached the gate of the town, a man who had died was being carried out. He was his mother's only son, and she was a widow; and with her was a large crowd from the town. [13]When the Lord saw her, he had compassion for her and said to her, "Do not weep." [14]Then he came forward and touched the bier, and the bearers stood still. And he said, "Young man, I say to you, rise!" [15]The dead man sat up and began to speak, and Jesus[b] gave him to his mother. [16]Fear seized all of them; and they glorified God, saying, "A great prophet has risen among us!" and "God has looked favorably on his people!" [17]This word about him spread throughout Judea and all the surrounding country.

Messengers from John the Baptist

18 The disciples of John reported all these things to him. So John summoned two of his disciples [19]and sent them to the Lord to ask, "Are you the one who is to come, or are we to wait for another?" [20]When the men had come to him, they said, "John the Baptist has sent us to you to ask, 'Are you the one who is to come, or are we to wait for another?'" [21]Jesus[c] had just then cured many people of diseases, plagues, and evil spirits, and had given sight to many who were blind. [22]And he answered them, "Go and tell John what you have seen and heard: the blind receive their sight, the lame walk, the lepers[d] are cleansed, the deaf hear, the dead are raised, the poor have good news brought to them. [23]And blessed is anyone who takes no offense at me."

24 When John's messengers had gone, Jesus[b] began to speak to the crowds about John:[e] "What did you go out into the wilderness to look at? A reed shaken by the wind? [25]What then did you go out to see? Someone[f] dressed in soft robes? Look, those who put on fine clothing and live in luxury are in royal palaces. [26]What then did you go out to see? A prophet? Yes, I tell you, and more than a prophet. [27]This is the one about whom it is written,

'See, I am sending my messenger ahead of you,
    who will prepare your way before you.'

[28]I tell you, among those born of women no one is greater than John; yet the least in the kingdom of God is greater than he." [29](And all the people who heard this, including the tax collectors, acknowledged the justice of God,[g] because they had been baptized with John's baptism. [30]But by refusing to be baptized by him, the Pharisees

a Other ancient authorities read *Next day*   b Gk *he*   c Gk *He*
d The terms *leper* and *leprosy* can refer to several diseases
e Gk *him*   f Or *Why then did you go out? To see someone*
g Or *praised God*

and the lawyers rejected God's purpose for themselves.)

31 "To what then will I compare the people of this generation, and what are they like? [32]They are like children sitting in the marketplace and calling to one another,

'We played the flute for you, and you did not dance;

we wailed, and you did not weep.'

[33]For John the Baptist has come eating no bread and drinking no wine, and you say, 'He has a demon'; [34]the Son of Man has come eating and drinking, and you say, 'Look, a glutton and a drunkard, a friend of tax collectors and sinners!' [35]Nevertheless, wisdom is vindicated by all her children."

A Sinful Woman Forgiven

36 One of the Pharisees asked Jesus[a] to eat with him, and he went into the Pharisee's house and took his place at the table. [37]And a woman in the city, who was a sinner, having learned that he was eating in the Pharisee's house, brought an alabaster jar of ointment. [38]She stood behind him at his feet, weeping, and began to bathe his feet with her tears and to dry them with her hair. Then she continued kissing his feet and anointing them with the ointment. [39]Now when the Pharisee who had invited him saw it, he said to himself, "If this man were a prophet, he would have known who and what kind of woman this is who is touching him—that she is a sinner." [40]Jesus spoke up and said to him, "Simon, I have something to say to you." "Teacher," he replied, "speak." [41]"A certain creditor had two debtors; one owed five hundred denarii,[b] and the other fifty. [42]When they could not pay, he canceled the debts for both of them. Now which of them will love him more?" [43]Simon answered, "I suppose the one for whom he canceled the greater debt." And Jesus[c] said to him, "You have judged rightly." [44]Then turning toward the woman, he said to Simon, "Do you see this woman? I entered your house; you gave me no water for my feet, but she has bathed my feet with her tears and dried them with her hair. [45]You gave me no kiss, but from the time I came in she has not stopped kissing my feet. [46]You did not anoint my head with oil, but she has anointed my feet with ointment. [47]Therefore, I tell you, her sins, which were many, have been forgiven; hence she has shown great love. But the one to whom little is forgiven, loves little." [48]Then he said to her, "Your sins are forgiven." [49]But those who were at the table with him began to say among themselves, "Who is this who even forgives sins?" [50]And he said to the woman, "Your faith has saved you; go in peace."

Some Women Accompany Jesus

8 Soon afterwards he went on through cities and villages, proclaiming and bringing the good news of the kingdom of God. The twelve were with him, [2]as well as some women who had been cured of evil spirits and infirmities: Mary, called Magdalene, from whom seven demons had gone out, [3]and Joanna, the wife of Herod's steward Chuza, and Susanna, and many others, who provided for them[d] out of their resources.

The Parable of the Sower

4 When a great crowd gathered and people from town after town came to him, he said in a parable: [5]"A sower went out to sow his seed;

---

a Gk *him*   b The denarius was the usual day's wage for a laborer
c Gk *he*   d Other ancient authorities read *him*

8:4–8

and as he sowed, some fell on the path and was trampled on, and the birds of the air ate it up. ⁶Some fell on the rock; and as it grew up, it withered for lack of moisture. ⁷Some fell among thorns, and the thorns grew with it and choked it. ⁸Some fell into good soil, and when it grew, it produced a hundredfold." As he said this, he called out, "Let anyone with ears to hear listen!"

The Purpose of the Parables

9 Then his disciples asked him what this parable meant. ¹⁰He said, "To you it has been given to know the secrets*a* of the kingdom of God; but to others I speak*b* in parables, so that

'looking they may not perceive,
　　and listening they may not understand.'

The Parable of the Sower Explained

11 "Now the parable is this: The seed is the word of God. ¹²The ones on the path are those who have heard; then the devil comes and takes away the word from their hearts, so that they may not believe and be saved. ¹³The ones on the rock are those who, when they hear the word, receive it with joy. But these have no root; they believe only for a while and in a time of testing fall away. ¹⁴As for what fell among the thorns, these are the ones who hear; but as they go on their way, they are choked by the cares and riches and pleasures of life, and their fruit does not mature. ¹⁵But as for that in the good soil, these are the ones who, when they hear the word, hold it fast in an honest and good heart, and bear fruit with patient endurance.

A Lamp under a Jar

16 "No one after lighting a lamp hides it under a jar, or puts it under a bed, but puts it on a lampstand, so that those who enter may see the light. ¹⁷For nothing is hidden that will not be disclosed, nor is anything secret that will not become known and come to light. ¹⁸Then pay attention to how you listen; for to those who have, more will be given; and from those who do not have, even what they seem to have will be taken away."

The True Kindred of Jesus

19 Then his mother and his brothers came to him, but they could not reach him because of the crowd. ²⁰And he was told, "Your mother and your brothers are standing outside, wanting to see you." ²¹But he said to them, "My mother and my brothers are those who hear the word of God and do it."

Jesus Calms a Storm

22 One day he got into a boat with his disciples, and he said to them, "Let us go across to the other side of the lake." So they put out, ²³and while they were sailing he fell asleep. A windstorm swept down on the lake, and the boat was filling with water, and they were in danger. ²⁴They went to him and woke him up, shouting, "Master, Master, we are perishing!" And he woke up and rebuked the wind and the raging waves; they ceased, and there was a calm. ²⁵He said to them, "Where is your faith?" They were afraid and amazed, and said to one another, "Who then is this, that he commands even the winds and the water, and they obey him?"

Jesus Heals the Gerasene Demoniac

26 Then they arrived at the country of the Gerasenes,*c* which is opposite Galilee. ²⁷As he stepped out on land, a man of the city who had demons met him. For a long time he had worn*d* no clothes, and he did not live in a house but in the tombs. ²⁸When he saw Jesus, he fell down before him and shouted at the top of his voice, "What have you to do with me, Jesus, Son of the Most High God? I beg you, do not torment me"— ²⁹for Jesus*e* had commanded the unclean spirit to come out of the man. (For many times it had seized him; he was kept under guard and bound with chains and shackles, but he would break the bonds and be driven by the demon into the wilds.) ³⁰Jesus then asked him, "What is your name?" He said, "Legion"; for many demons had entered him. ³¹They begged him not to order them to go back into the abyss.

32 Now there on the hillside a large herd of swine was feeding; and the demons*f* begged Jesus*g* to let them enter these. So he gave them permission. ³³Then the demons came out of the man and entered the swine, and the herd rushed down the steep bank into the lake and was drowned.

34 When the swineherds saw what had happened, they ran off and told it in the city and in the country. ³⁵Then people came out to see what had happened, and when they came to Jesus, they found the man from whom the demons had gone sitting at the feet of Jesus, clothed and in his right mind. And they were afraid. ³⁶Those who had seen it told them how the one who had been possessed by demons had been healed. ³⁷Then all the people of the surrounding country

---

a Or *mysteries*　*b* Gk lacks *I speak*　*c* Other ancient authorities read *Gadarenes*; others, *Gergesenes*　*d* Other ancient authorities read *a man of the city who had had demons for a long time met him. He wore*　*e* Gk *he*　*f* Gk *they*　*g* Gk *him*

of the Gerasenes*a* asked Jesus*b* to leave them; for they were seized with great fear. So he got into the boat and returned. 38The man from whom the demons had gone begged that he might be with him; but Jesus*c* sent him away, saying, 39"Return to your home, and declare how much God has done for you." So he went away, proclaiming throughout the city how much Jesus had done for him.

A Girl Restored to Life and a Woman Healed

40 Now when Jesus returned, the crowd welcomed him, for they were all waiting for him. 41Just then there came a man named Jairus, a leader of the synagogue. He fell at Jesus' feet and begged him to come to his house, 42for he had an only daughter, about twelve years old, who was dying.

As he went, the crowds pressed in on him. 43Now there was a woman who had been suffering from hemorrhages for twelve years; and though she had spent all she had on physicians,*d* no one could cure her. 44She came up behind him and touched the fringe of his clothes, and immediately her hemorrhage stopped. 45Then Jesus asked, "Who touched me?" When all denied it, Peter*e* said, "Master, the crowds surround you and press in on you." 46But Jesus said, "Someone touched me; for I noticed that power had gone out from me." 47When the woman saw that she could not remain hidden, she came trembling; and falling down before him, she declared in the presence of all the people why she had touched him, and how she had been immediately healed. 48He said to her, "Daughter, your faith has made you well; go in peace."

49 While he was still speaking, someone came from the leader's house to say, "Your daughter is dead; do not trouble the teacher any longer." 50When Jesus heard this, he replied, "Do not fear. Only believe, and she will be saved." 51When he came to the house, he did not allow anyone to enter with him, except Peter, John, and James, and the child's father and mother. 52They were all weeping and wailing for her; but he said, "Do not weep; for she is not dead but sleeping." 53And they laughed at him, knowing that she was dead. 54But he took her by the hand and called out, "Child, get up!" 55Her spirit returned, and she got up at once. Then he directed them to give her something to eat. 56Her parents were astounded; but he ordered them to tell no one what had happened.

The Mission of the Twelve

9 Then Jesus*c* called the twelve together and gave them power and authority over all

Live It!

Mission Possible

Just like the director of operations in the movie *Mission Impossible*, Jesus, in Luke 9:1–6, seems to say to the disciples, "Your mission, should you choose to accept it. . . ." The director in the movie labeled his missions as impossible, but Jesus knew *his* missions were possible—though, in some cases, not always popular (see 10:10–11).

We too are asked to share in Jesus' mission. Sound easy? We know it is not. Doing what Jesus would do may mean sticking our necks out rather than following the crowd. The hardest part? Letting people know that the reason for our actions is our faith in Jesus Christ. It's not impossible, but it's certainly a challenge! Are you up to it? If you trust in God, you will be!

▶ **Lk 9:1–6**

demons and to cure diseases, 2and he sent them out to proclaim the kingdom of God and to heal. 3He said to them, "Take nothing for your journey, no staff, nor bag, nor bread, nor money—not even an extra tunic. 4Whatever house you enter, stay there, and leave from there. 5Wherever they do not welcome you, as you are leaving that town shake the dust off your feet as a testimony against them." 6They departed and went through the villages, bringing the good news and curing diseases everywhere.

Herod's Perplexity

7 Now Herod the ruler*f* heard about all that had taken place, and he was perplexed, because it was said by some that John had been raised from the dead, 8by some that Elijah had appeared, and by others that one of the ancient prophets had arisen. 9Herod said, "John I beheaded; but who is this about whom I hear such things?" And he tried to see him.

---

a Other ancient authorities read *Gadarenes*; others, *Gergesenes* *b* Gk *him* *c* Gk *he* *d* Other ancient authorities lack *and though she had spent all she had on physicians* *e* Other ancient authorities add *and those who were with him* *f* Gk *tetrarch*

L
K

Feeding the Five Thousand

10 On their return the apostles told Jesus[a] all they had done. He took them with him and withdrew privately to a city called Bethsaida. [11]When the crowds found out about it, they followed him; and he welcomed them, and spoke to them about the kingdom of God, and healed those who needed to be cured.

12 The day was drawing to a close, and the twelve came to him and said, "Send the crowd away, so that they may go into the surrounding villages and countryside, to lodge and get provisions; for we are here in a deserted place." [13]But

Spiritual Highs

Have you ever been on a great retreat, camping trip, or service trip? If so, you may have felt really close to God and to others who shared that experience with you. You may have even wished the experience did not have to end.

Peter, James, and John must have felt that way when they saw Jesus in his glory talking with Moses and Elijah on the mountaintop. Peter wanted to stay up on the mountain, but it quickly became clear that he could not do so.

Faith has its high moments as well as its low moments. It is unrealistic to think we can maintain some kind of spiritual high all the time—doing so may even be dangerous. The faith of those who depend on mountaintop experiences often fizzles out. The better challenge is to learn what it means to live as a Christian down in the thick of life. Remember, our faith is more than feelings. God's love and mercy do not depend on our ability to feel "warm fuzzies," as nice as those may be.

Recall a special time in your life when you felt on top of the world. Relive the moment in your mind, this time looking for how God was present in that experience. What direction was God inviting you to go after it was over? Are you there yet?

▶ Lk 9:28–36

he said to them, "You give them something to eat." They said, "We have no more than five loaves and two fish—unless we are to go and buy food for all these people." [14]For there were about five thousand men. And he said to his disciples, "Make them sit down in groups of about fifty each." [15]They did so and made them all sit down. [16]And taking the five loaves and the two fish, he looked up to heaven, and blessed and broke them, and gave them to the disciples to set before the crowd. [17]And all ate and were filled. What was left over was gathered up, twelve baskets of broken pieces.

Peter's Declaration about Jesus

18 Once when Jesus[b] was praying alone, with only the disciples near him, he asked them, "Who do the crowds say that I am?" [19]They answered, "John the Baptist; but others, Elijah; and still others, that one of the ancient prophets has arisen." [20]He said to them, "But who do you say that I am?" Peter answered, "The Messiah[c] of God."

Jesus Foretells His Death and Resurrection

21 He sternly ordered and commanded them not to tell anyone, [22]saying, "The Son of Man must undergo great suffering, and be rejected by the elders, chief priests, and scribes, and be killed, and on the third day be raised."

23 Then he said to them all, "If any want to become my followers, let them deny themselves and take up their cross daily and follow me. [24]For those who want to save their life will lose it, and those who lose their life for my sake will save it. [25]What does it profit them if they gain the whole world, but lose or forfeit themselves? [26]Those who are ashamed of me and of my words, of them the Son of Man will be ashamed when he comes in his glory and the glory of the Father and of the holy angels. [27]But truly I tell you, there are some standing here who will not taste death before they see the kingdom of God."

The Transfiguration

28 Now about eight days after these sayings Jesus[b] took with him Peter and John and James, and went up on the mountain to pray. [29]And while he was praying, the appearance of his face changed, and his clothes became dazzling white. [30]Suddenly they saw two men, Moses and Elijah, talking to him. [31]They appeared in glory and were speaking of his departure, which he was about to accomplish at Jerusalem. [32]Now Peter and his companions were weighed down with

a Gk him   b Gk he   c Or The Christ

✝ Catholic Connection

The Messiah

Have you ever noticed that when a dramatic event takes place, people want to gather and talk about it? The same was probably true when Jesus walked the earth teaching and performing miracles. It is not difficult to imagine people talking over dinner or in the public square about Jesus and the things he was doing. Jesus was probably aware of the talk when he turned to the disciples and asked them what the crowds were saying about him. The disciples replied that the people thought Jesus was John the Baptist or some other great hero brought back to life. The crowds were on the right track thinking Jesus was someone special, but only the disciples realized his true identity as the Messiah.

Ever since sin entered the world with Adam and Eve, humankind anxiously awaited the arrival of the Messiah. Throughout the Old Testament, God was laying the foundation for the coming of the Messiah. The prophecies in Isaiah tell us a lot about the identity and role of the Messiah. In Isaiah, the Messiah is described as fully possessing the gifts of the Holy Spirit (see "The Gifts of the Holy Spirit," near Isa 11:1–2). The Messiah is the one who will usher in an era of peace that will be evident in all of God's creation (the lamb will lie down with the wolf), as it was intended before Adam and Eve fell into sin. In chapter 53 of Isaiah, the Messiah is described as God's servant who, even though he was without sin, willingly takes on the punishment for the sins of the world. His suffering and death would restore humankind's relationship with God.

Although Jesus is the Messiah hoped for in the Old Testament, many did not recognize him because they mistakenly thought the messiah was going to be a king who would establish his rule over Israel like Kings David and Solomon. They wanted a messiah who would do battle with earthly powers and save them from oppressive rulers. Jesus showed the world that the messiah was a king, but one who would usher in the Reign of God. Jesus is the Messiah, the Christ or anointed one, who must suffer and die for the sins of all just as Isaiah had prophesied. And when the time was right, Jesus willfully suffered Crucifixion and offered his life on our behalf. He did battle with the powers of darkness and saved us from oppression to sin. Jesus' death and Resurrection opened up for us the way to heaven, where the lamb and the wolf will lie together in peace.

▶ **Lk 9:18–20**

Catechism, nos. 436–440, 711–716

sleep; but since they had stayed awake,[a] they saw his glory and the two men who stood with him. [33]Just as they were leaving him, Peter said to Jesus, "Master, it is good for us to be here; let us make three dwellings,[b] one for you, one for Moses, and one for Elijah"—not knowing what he said. [34]While he was saying this, a cloud came and overshadowed them; and they were terrified as they entered the cloud. [35]Then from the cloud came a voice that said, "This is my Son, my Chosen;[c] listen to him!" [36]When the voice had spoken, Jesus was found alone. And they kept silent and in those days told no one any of the things they had seen.

Jesus Heals a Boy with a Demon

[37] On the next day, when they had come down from the mountain, a great crowd met him. [38]Just then a man from the crowd shouted, "Teacher, I beg you to look at my son; he is my only child. [39]Suddenly a spirit seizes him, and all at once he[d] shrieks. It convulses him until he foams at the mouth; it mauls him and will scarcely leave him. [40]I begged your disciples to cast it out, but they could not." [41]Jesus answered, "You faithless and perverse generation, how much longer must I be with you and bear with you? Bring your son here." [42]While he was coming, the demon dashed him to the ground in convulsions. But Jesus rebuked the unclean spirit, healed the boy, and gave him back to his father. [43]And all were astounded at the greatness of God.

Jesus Again Foretells His Death

While everyone was amazed at all that he was doing, he said to his disciples, [44]"Let these words sink into your ears: The Son of Man is going to be betrayed into human hands." [45]But they did not understand this saying; its meaning was concealed from them, so that they could not perceive it. And they were afraid to ask him about this saying.

True Greatness

[46] An argument arose among them as to which one of them was the greatest. [47]But Jesus, aware of their inner thoughts, took a little child and put it by his side, [48]and said to them, "Whoever welcomes this child in my name welcomes me, and whoever welcomes me welcomes the one who sent me; for the least among all of you is the greatest."

Another Exorcist

[49] John answered, "Master, we saw someone casting out demons in your name, and we tried to stop him, because he does not follow with us." [50]But Jesus said to him, "Do not stop him; for whoever is not against you is for you."

A Samaritan Village Refuses to Receive Jesus

[51] When the days drew near for him to be taken up, he set his face to go to Jerusalem. [52]And he sent messengers ahead of him. On their way they entered a village of the Samaritans to make ready for him; [53]but they did not receive him, because his face was set toward Jerusalem. [54]When his disciples James and John saw it, they said, "Lord, do you want us to command fire to come down from heaven and consume them?"[e] [55]But he turned and rebuked them. [56]Then[f] they went on to another village.

Would-Be Followers of Jesus

[57] As they were going along the road, someone said to him, "I will follow you wherever you go." [58]And Jesus said to him, "Foxes have holes, and birds of the air have nests; but the Son of Man has nowhere to lay his head." [59]To another he said, "Follow me." But he said, "Lord, first let me go and bury my father." [60]But Jesus[g] said to him, "Let the dead bury their own dead; but as for you, go and proclaim the kingdom of God." [61]Another said, "I will follow you, Lord; but let me first say farewell to those at my home." [62]Jesus said to him, "No one who puts a hand to the plow and looks back is fit for the kingdom of God."

The Mission of the Seventy

10 After this the Lord appointed seventy[h] others and sent them on ahead of him in pairs to every town and place where he himself intended to go. [2]He said to them, "The harvest is plentiful, but the laborers are few; therefore ask the Lord of the harvest to send out laborers into his harvest. [3]Go on your way. See, I am sending you out like lambs into the midst of wolves. [4]Carry no purse, no bag, no sandals; and greet no one on the road. [5]Whatever house you enter, first say, 'Peace to this house!' [6]And if anyone is there who shares in peace, your peace will rest on that person; but if not, it will return to you. [7]Remain in the same house, eating and drinking whatever they provide, for the laborer deserves to be paid. Do not move about from house to house. [8]Whenever you enter a town and its people welcome

a Or but when they were fully awake   b Or tents   c Other ancient authorities read my Beloved   d Or it   e Other ancient authorities add as Elijah did   f Other ancient authorities read rebuked them, and said, "You do not know what spirit you are of, [56]for the Son of Man has not come to destroy the lives of human beings but to save them." Then   g Gk he   h Other ancient authorities read seventy-two

Catholic Social Teaching

Discrimination in Jesus' Time

The good Samaritan is a popular Bible story with an obvious message: We must not only help others but also love the ones who hate us. In Jesus' day, the Samaritans were despised by Jews and vice versa, even though Abraham was the father of faith for both groups. Jesus' making a Samaritan the hero of the story would have given the lawyer and other people listening to Jesus something to think about.

The parable itself is told as a response to the question posed of Jesus, "Who is my neighbor?" The answer to this question? Everyone! Jesus reminds us that we are called to live in solidarity with all people, no matter what their race, religion, ethnicity, gender, or social status. We are also called to treat all people with great compassion, loving our neighbor as ourselves and welcoming the stranger into our midst.

Catholic social teaching further reminds us that we are, in fact, our brother's keeper, and that we have been entrusted with the responsibility of taking care of one another. Indeed, we are all called to stand united as one human family, even though we are often used to thinking in terms of what divides us rather than what brings us together.

Imagine that this story takes place in your community.

- Who are the Samaritans in your community—that is, the culture or people that others judge and reject?
- How does this reflection affect your understanding of discrimination and racism?
- What can you do to better live in solidarity with all people in your community?

▶ **Lk 10:25–37**

Solidarity

L
K

---

you, eat what is set before you; [9]cure the sick who are there, and say to them, 'The kingdom of God has come near to you.'[a] [10]But whenever you enter a town and they do not welcome you, go out into its streets and say, [11]'Even the dust of your town that clings to our feet, we wipe off in protest against you. Yet know this: the kingdom of God has come near.'[b] [12]I tell you, on that day it will be more tolerable for Sodom than for that town.

Woes to Unrepentant Cities

13 "Woe to you, Chorazin! Woe to you, Bethsaida! For if the deeds of power done in you had been done in Tyre and Sidon, they would have repented long ago, sitting in sackcloth and ashes. [14]But at the judgment it will be more tolerable for Tyre and Sidon than for you. [15]And you, Capernaum,

will you be exalted to heaven?

No, you will be brought down to Hades.

16 "Whoever listens to you listens to me, and whoever rejects you rejects me, and whoever rejects me rejects the one who sent me."

The Return of the Seventy

17 The seventy[c] returned with joy, saying, "Lord, in your name even the demons submit to us!" [18]He said to them, "I watched Satan fall from heaven like a flash of lightning. [19]See, I have given you authority to tread on snakes and scorpions, and over all the power of the enemy; and nothing will hurt you. [20]Nevertheless, do not rejoice at this, that the spirits submit to you, but rejoice that your names are written in heaven."

Jesus Rejoices

21 At that same hour Jesus[d] rejoiced in the Holy Spirit[e] and said, "I thank[f] you, Father, Lord of heaven and earth, because you have hidden these things from the wise and the intelligent and have revealed them to infants; yes, Father, for such was your gracious will.[g] [22]All things have been handed over to me by my Father; and no one knows who the Son is except the Father, or who the Father is except the Son and anyone to whom the Son chooses to reveal him."

23 Then turning to the disciples, Jesus[d] said to them privately, "Blessed are the eyes that see what you see! [24]For I tell you that many prophets and kings desired to see what you see, but did not see it, and to hear what you hear, but did not hear it."

---

a Or is at hand for you   b Or is at hand   c Other ancient authorities read seventy-two   d Gk he   e Other authorities read in the spirit   f Or praise   g Or for so it was well-pleasing in your sight

The Parable of the Good Samaritan

25 Just then a lawyer stood up to test Jesus.[a] "Teacher," he said, "what must I do to inherit eternal life?" [26]He said to him, "What is written in the law? What do you read there?" [27]He answered, "You shall love the Lord your God with all your heart, and with all your soul, and with all your strength, and with all your mind; and your neighbor as yourself." [28]And he said to him, "You have given the right answer; do this, and you will live."

29 But wanting to justify himself, he asked Jesus, "And who is my neighbor?" [30]Jesus replied, "A man was going down from Jerusalem to Jericho, and fell into the hands of robbers, who stripped him, beat him, and went away, leaving him half dead. [31]Now by chance a priest was going down that road; and when he saw him, he passed by on the other side. [32]So likewise a Levite, when he came to the place and saw him, passed by on the other side. [33]But a Samaritan while traveling came near him; and when he saw him, he was moved with pity. [34]He went to him and bandaged his wounds, having poured oil and wine on them. Then he put him on his own animal, brought him to an inn, and took care of him. [35]The next day he took out two denarii,[b] gave them to the innkeeper, and said, 'Take care of him; and when I come back, I will repay you whatever more you spend.' [36]Which of these three, do you think, was a neighbor to the man who fell into the hands of the robbers?" [37]He said, "The one who showed him mercy." Jesus said to him, "Go and do likewise."

Too Busy to Be Still

Help me to slow down, Lord, right now, before I think of something else that I should be doing—as if it really is more important than you. Let me sit in the quiet peace of your presence and soak up all that you have to say to me. Give me the patience and perception to do nothing else for these next few moments except to be totally, completely, and wonderfully centered on you!

▶ Lk 10:38–42

Jesus Visits Martha and Mary

38 Now as they went on their way, he entered a certain village, where a woman named Martha welcomed him into her home. [39]She had a sister named Mary, who sat at the Lord's feet and listened to what he was saying. [40]But Martha was distracted by her many tasks; so she came to him and asked, "Lord, do you not care that my sister has left me to do all the work by myself? Tell her then to help me." [41]But the Lord answered her, "Martha, Martha, you are worried and distracted by many things; [42]there is need of only one thing.[c] Mary has chosen the better part, which will not be taken away from her."

The Lord's Prayer

11 He was praying in a certain place, and after he had finished, one of his disciples said to him, "Lord, teach us to pray, as John taught his disciples." [2]He said to them, "When you pray, say:

Father,[d] hallowed be your name.
　　Your kingdom come.[e]
3　　Give us each day our daily bread.[f]
4　　And forgive us our sins,
　　　　for we ourselves forgive everyone indebted
　　　　　to us.
　　And do not bring us to the time of trial."[g]

Perseverance in Prayer

5 And he said to them, "Suppose one of you has a friend, and you go to him at midnight and say to him, 'Friend, lend me three loaves of bread; [6]for a friend of mine has arrived, and I have nothing to set before him.' [7]And he answers from within, 'Do not bother me; the door has already been locked, and my children are with me in bed; I cannot get up and give you anything.' [8]I tell you, even though he will not get up and give him anything because he is his friend, at least because of his persistence he will get up and give him whatever he needs.

9 "So I say to you, Ask, and it will be given you; search, and you will find; knock, and the door will be opened for you. [10]For everyone who asks receives, and everyone who searches finds, and for everyone who knocks, the door will be opened. [11]Is there anyone among you who, if

a Gk him   b The denarius was the usual day's wage for a laborer
c Other ancient authorities read few things are necessary, or only
one   d Other ancient authorities read Our Father in heaven   e A
few ancient authorities read Your Holy Spirit come upon us and
cleanse us. Other ancient authorities add Your will be done, on
earth as in heaven   f Or our bread for tomorrow   g Or us into
temptation. Other ancient authorities add but rescue us from the
evil one (or from evil)

✝ Catholic Connection

The Lord's Prayer

Sometimes, asking the simplest question can make all the difference! The disciples had been traveling with Jesus for some time and no doubt began to notice how frequently Jesus prayed, especially before important events, like the Transfiguration. So, it is no wonder that after hearing Jesus pray to the Father about how only the Son can reveal the Father to the world that the disciples ask Jesus a simple question: Can you teach us how to pray? Jesus responds by teaching them the Lord's Prayer, also called the Our Father.

The disciples' simple question led to what is now the model for all Christian prayer. It is the perfect prayer in that it covers everything regarding our relationship with God and our needs as God's children. The structure of the prayer even helps us to put our lives in proper order. The prayer can be broken down into the opening address and seven petitions as follows:

Our Father who art in heaven,

1. hallowed be thy name.

2. Thy kingdom come.

3. Thy will be done, on earth as it is in heaven.

4. Give us this day our daily bread.

5. And forgive us our trespasses, as we forgive those who trespass against us.

6. And lead us not into temptation,

7. but deliver us from evil.

We begin with the opening address, by calling God "Father," which reflects our own identity as adopted daughters and sons of God through our Baptism. Then we focus our first three petitions on God: we acknowledge God's holiness, we express a desire for his Kingdom, and we seek to unite our will with God's. By placing our attention on God, we draw closer to God and begin to leave behind all that would hold us back from loving God. The final four petitions acknowledge our own weaknesses and call on God's mercy. They address our basic human need for nourishment, both physical and spiritual, and for forgiveness, for both ourselves and others. They also focus on our struggle to resist sin, our need for God's grace to persevere, and our hope in deliverance from all that would keep us from the eternal life already won by Christ. The Lord's Prayer teaches us how to love God and gives us the words to express and deepen that love. As followers of Jesus, we are called to not only pray the Lord's Prayer frequently but also to live it!

▶ Lk 11:1–4
Catechism, nos. 2759–2776

Ask and You Shall Receive

Have you ever determinedly asked your parents for something? They may have replied, "Will you stop asking me?!"

This is one response you will never hear from God. In fact, Jesus tells us to always be persistent with God. God wants to hear from us! Too often we hesitate to bring everything inside of us to God. We sort through what we think God wants to hear. Don't be selective! Bring it *all* to God—the big stuff as well as the little stuff. Be persistent and relentless. God doesn't mind at all.

▶ **Lk 11:5–13**

your child asks for[a] a fish, will give a snake instead of a fish? 12 Or if the child asks for an egg, will give a scorpion? 13 If you then, who are evil, know how to give good gifts to your children, how much more will the heavenly Father give the Holy Spirit[b] to those who ask him!"

Jesus and Beelzebul

14 Now he was casting out a demon that was mute; when the demon had gone out, the one who had been mute spoke, and the crowds were amazed. 15 But some of them said, "He casts out demons by Beelzebul, the ruler of the demons." 16 Others, to test him, kept demanding from him a sign from heaven. 17 But he knew what they were thinking and said to them, "Every kingdom divided against itself becomes a desert, and house falls on house. 18 If Satan also is divided against himself, how will his kingdom stand? —for you say that I cast out the demons by Beelzebul. 19 Now if I cast out the demons by Beelzebul, by whom do your exorcists[c] cast them out? Therefore they will be your judges. 20 But if it is by the finger of God that I cast out the demons, then the kingdom of God has come to you. 21 When a strong man, fully armed, guards his castle, his property is safe. 22 But when one stronger than he attacks him and overpowers him, he takes away his armor in which he trusted and divides his plunder. 23 Whoever is not with me is against me, and whoever does not gather with me scatters.

The Return of the Unclean Spirit

24 "When the unclean spirit has gone out of a person, it wanders through waterless regions looking for a resting place, but not finding any, it says, 'I will return to my house from which I came.' 25 When it comes, it finds it swept and put in order. 26 Then it goes and brings seven other spirits more evil than itself, and they enter and live there; and the last state of that person is worse than the first."

True Blessedness

27 While he was saying this, a woman in the crowd raised her voice and said to him, "Blessed is the womb that bore you and the breasts that nursed you!" 28 But he said, "Blessed rather are those who hear the word of God and obey it!"

The Sign of Jonah

29 When the crowds were increasing, he began to say, "This generation is an evil generation; it asks for a sign, but no sign will be given to it except the sign of Jonah. 30 For just as Jonah became a sign to the people of Nineveh, so the Son of Man will be to this generation. 31 The queen of the South will rise at the judgment with the people of this generation and condemn them, because she came from the ends of the earth to listen to the wisdom of Solomon, and see, something greater than Solomon is here! 32 The people of Nineveh will rise up at the judgment with this generation and condemn it, because they repented at the proclamation of Jonah, and see, something greater than Jonah is here!

The Light of the Body

33 "No one after lighting a lamp puts it in a cellar,[d] but on the lampstand so that those who enter may see the light. 34 Your eye is the lamp of your body. If your eye is healthy, your whole body is full of light; but if it is not healthy, your body is full of darkness. 35 Therefore consider whether the light in you is not darkness. 36 If then your whole body is full of light, with no part of it in darkness, it will be as full of light as when a lamp gives you light with its rays."

Jesus Denounces Pharisees and Lawyers

37 While he was speaking, a Pharisee invited him to dine with him; so he went in and took his place at the table. 38 The Pharisee was amazed

---

a Other ancient authorities add *bread, will give a stone; or if your child asks for*   b Other ancient authorities read *the Father give the Holy Spirit from heaven*   c Gk *sons*   d Other ancient authorities add *or under the bushel basket*

to see that he did not first wash before dinner. [39]Then the Lord said to him, "Now you Pharisees clean the outside of the cup and of the dish, but inside you are full of greed and wickedness. [40]You fools! Did not the one who made the outside make the inside also? [41]So give for alms those things that are within; and see, everything will be clean for you.

[42] "But woe to you Pharisees! For you tithe mint and rue and herbs of all kinds, and neglect justice and the love of God; it is these you ought to have practiced, without neglecting the others. [43]Woe to you Pharisees! For you love to have the seat of honor in the synagogues and to be greeted with respect in the marketplaces. [44]Woe to you! For you are like unmarked graves, and people walk over them without realizing it."

[45] One of the lawyers answered him, "Teacher, when you say these things, you insult us too." [46]And he said, "Woe also to you lawyers! For you load people with burdens hard to bear, and you yourselves do not lift a finger to ease them. [47]Woe to you! For you build the tombs of the prophets whom your ancestors killed. [48]So you are witnesses and approve of the deeds of your ancestors; for they killed them, and you build their tombs. [49]Therefore also the Wisdom of God said, 'I will send them prophets and apostles, some of whom they will kill and persecute,' [50]so that this generation may be charged with the blood of all the prophets shed since the foundation of the world, [51]from the blood of Abel to the blood of Zechariah, who perished between the altar and the sanctuary. Yes, I tell you, it will be charged against this generation. [52]Woe to you lawyers! For you have taken away the key of knowledge; you did not enter yourselves, and you hindered those who were entering."

[53] When he went outside, the scribes and the Pharisees began to be very hostile toward him and to cross-examine him about many things, [54]lying in wait for him, to catch him in something he might say.

A Warning against Hypocrisy

12 Meanwhile, when the crowd gathered by the thousands, so that they trampled on one another, he began to speak first to his disciples, "Beware of the yeast of the Pharisees, that is, their hypocrisy. [2]Nothing is covered up that will not be uncovered, and nothing secret that will not become known. [3]Therefore whatever you have said in the dark will be heard in the light, and what you have whispered behind closed doors will be proclaimed from the housetops.

Exhortation to Fearless Confession

[4] "I tell you, my friends, do not fear those who kill the body, and after that can do nothing more. [5]But I will warn you whom to fear: fear him who, after he has killed, has authority[a] to cast into hell.[b] Yes, I tell you, fear him! [6]Are not five sparrows sold for two pennies? Yet not one of them is forgotten in God's sight. [7]But even the hairs of your head are all counted. Do not be afraid; you are of more value than many sparrows.

[8] "And I tell you, everyone who acknowledges me before others, the Son of Man also will acknowledge before the angels of God; [9]but whoever denies me before others will be denied before the angels of God. [10]And everyone who speaks a word against the Son of Man will be forgiven; but whoever blasphemes against the Holy Spirit will not be forgiven. [11]When they bring you before the synagogues, the rulers, and the authorities, do not worry about how[c] you are to defend yourselves or what you are to say; [12]for the Holy Spirit will teach you at that very hour what you ought to say."

The Parable of the Rich Fool

[13] Someone in the crowd said to him, "Teacher, tell my brother to divide the family inheritance with me." [14]But he said to him, "Friend, who set me to be a judge or arbitrator over you?" [15]And he said to them, "Take care! Be on your guard against all kinds of greed; for one's life does not consist in the abundance of possessions." [16]Then he told them a parable: "The land of a rich man produced abundantly. [17]And he thought to himself, 'What should I do, for I have no place to store my crops?' [18]Then he said, 'I will do this: I will pull down my barns and build larger ones, and there I will store all my grain and my goods. [19]And I will say to my soul, Soul, you have ample goods laid up for many years; relax, eat, drink, be merry.' [20]But God said to him, 'You fool! This very night your life is being demanded of you. And the things you have prepared, whose will they be?' [21]So it is with those who store up treasures for themselves but are not rich toward God."

Do Not Worry

[22] He said to his disciples, "Therefore I tell you, do not worry about your life, what you will eat, or about your body, what you will wear. [23]For life is more than food, and the body more than

---

a Or power   b Gk Gehenna   c Other ancient authorities add or what

clothing. 24Consider the ravens: they neither sow nor reap, they have neither storehouse nor barn, and yet God feeds them. Of how much more value are you than the birds! 25And can any of you by worrying add a single hour to your span of life?*a 26If then you are not able to do so small a thing as that, why do you worry about the rest? 27Consider the lilies, how they grow: they neither toil nor spin;*b yet I tell you, even Solomon in all his glory was not clothed like one of these. 28But if God so clothes the grass of the field, which is alive today and tomorrow is thrown into the oven, how much more will he clothe you—you of little faith! 29And do not keep striving for what you are to eat and what you are to drink, and do not keep worrying. 30For it is the nations of the world that strive after all these things, and your Father knows that you need them. 31Instead, strive for his*c kingdom, and these things will be given to you as well.

The Greed Trap

It is easy to regard possessions as treasures and to find so much pleasure in them that we want more and more. This is the greed trap Jesus warns against in Luke 12:13–21. How do we let ourselves fall into this trap? Certainly, advertisements play a role in convincing us we need to own everything that is new and improved (see "New and Improved!" near Eccl 1:1–11). Our own insecurities also play a role—the more we possess, the more important we tend to think we are. But as Luke 12:18 indicates, greed is a sin that is addictive. Instead of feeling fulfilled by attaining the thing we crave, we feel that what we have still isn't enough. It is a vicious cycle.

The solution to greed is simple. It's sharing—that value we learned when we were very small. Sharing our time and possessions makes us "rich toward God" (verse 21). Where do you see the sin of greed at work in your world? Where and when could you, your friends, and your family share more? Don't fall into the greed trap. Share!

▶ Lk 12:13–21

32 "Do not be afraid, little flock, for it is your Father's good pleasure to give you the kingdom. 33Sell your possessions, and give alms. Make purses for yourselves that do not wear out, an unfailing treasure in heaven, where no thief comes near and no moth destroys. 34For where your treasure is, there your heart will be also.

Watchful Slaves

35 "Be dressed for action and have your lamps lit; 36be like those who are waiting for their master to return from the wedding banquet, so that they may open the door for him as soon as he comes and knocks. 37Blessed are those slaves whom the master finds alert when he comes; truly I tell you, he will fasten his belt and have them sit down to eat, and he will come and serve them. 38If he comes during the middle of the night, or near dawn, and finds them so, blessed are those slaves.

39 "But know this: if the owner of the house had known at what hour the thief was coming, he*d would not have let his house be broken into. 40You also must be ready, for the Son of Man is coming at an unexpected hour."

The Faithful or the Unfaithful Slave

41 Peter said, "Lord, are you telling this parable for us or for everyone?" 42And the Lord said, "Who then is the faithful and prudent manager whom his master will put in charge of his slaves, to give them their allowance of food at the proper time? 43Blessed is that slave whom his master will find at work when he arrives. 44Truly I tell you, he will put that one in charge of all his possessions. 45But if that slave says to himself, 'My master is delayed in coming,' and if he begins to beat the other slaves, men and women, and to eat and drink and get drunk, 46the master of that slave will come on a day when he does not expect him and at an hour that he does not know, and will cut him in pieces,*e and put him with the unfaithful. 47That slave who knew what his master wanted, but did not prepare himself or do what was wanted, will receive a severe beating. 48But the one who did not know and did what deserved a beating will receive a light beating. From everyone to whom much has been given, much will be required; and from the one to whom much has been entrusted, even more will be demanded.

a Or add a cubit to your stature   b Other ancient authorities read Consider the lilies; they neither spin nor weave   c Other ancient authorities read God's   d Other ancient authorities add would have watched and   e Or cut him off

Jesus the Cause of Division

49 "I came to bring fire to the earth, and how I wish it were already kindled! [50]I have a baptism with which to be baptized, and what stress I am under until it is completed! [51]Do you think that I have come to bring peace to the earth? No, I tell you, but rather division! [52]From now on five in one household will be divided, three against two and two against three; [53]they will be divided:

father against son
 and son against father,
mother against daughter
 and daughter against mother,
mother-in-law against her daughter-in-law
 and daughter-in-law against mother-in-law."

Interpreting the Time

54 He also said to the crowds, "When you see a cloud rising in the west, you immediately say, 'It is going to rain'; and so it happens. [55]And when you see the south wind blowing, you say, 'There will be scorching heat'; and it happens. [56]You hypocrites! You know how to interpret the appearance of earth and sky, but why do you not know how to interpret the present time?

Settling with Your Opponent

57 "And why do you not judge for yourselves what is right? [58]Thus, when you go with your accuser before a magistrate, on the way make an effort to settle the case,[a] or you may be dragged before the judge, and the judge hand you over to the officer, and the officer throw you in prison. [59]I tell you, you will never get out until you have paid the very last penny."

Repent or Perish

13 At that very time there were some present who told him about the Galileans whose blood Pilate had mingled with their sacrifices. [2]He asked them, "Do you think that because these Galileans suffered in this way they were worse sinners than all other Galileans? [3]No, I tell you; but unless you repent, you will all perish as they did. [4]Or those eighteen who were killed when the tower of Siloam fell on them—do you think that they were worse offenders than all the others living in Jerusalem? [5]No, I tell you; but unless you repent, you will all perish just as they did."

The Parable of the Barren Fig Tree

6 Then he told this parable: "A man had a fig tree planted in his vineyard; and he came looking for fruit on it and found none. [7]So he said

The Anxiety Trap

Doesn't it seem a little naive to assume that if we just trust God, we will get what we need and that we shouldn't worry about the everyday things like clothing, food, and shelter, or even things like work, our grades in school, and relationships? That certainly seems risky.

Indeed, putting our faith in God is a risk, but it's one that comes with the potential for great reward. Jesus tells us to not worry so much about everyday needs. Instead, we should look around for the simple signs that show God's care for us. Of course we also need to recognize that God intends we use the gifts, creativity, and freedom he has given us to meet those needs. If we do so, we won't fail to notice the many ways God is already working in our lives. Life will surely be so much calmer and less stressful if we heed Jesus' message. Try it!

▶ **Lk 12:22–34**

to the gardener, 'See here! For three years I have come looking for fruit on this fig tree, and still I find none. Cut it down! Why should it be wasting the soil?' [8]He replied, 'Sir, let it alone for one more year, until I dig around it and put manure on it. [9]If it bears fruit next year, well and good; but if not, you can cut it down.' "

Jesus Heals a Crippled Woman

10 Now he was teaching in one of the synagogues on the sabbath. [11]And just then there appeared a woman with a spirit that had crippled her for eighteen years. She was bent over and was quite unable to stand up straight. [12]When Jesus saw her, he called her over and said, "Woman, you are set free from your ailment." [13]When he laid his hands on her, immediately she stood up straight and began praising God. [14]But the leader of the synagogue, indignant because Jesus had cured on the sabbath, kept saying to the crowd, "There are six days on which work ought to be done; come on those days and be cured, and not on the sabbath day." [15]But the Lord answered

a Gk settle with him

him and said, "You hypocrites! Does not each of you on the sabbath untie his ox or his donkey from the manger, and lead it away to give it water? ¹⁶And ought not this woman, a daughter of Abraham whom Satan bound for eighteen long years, be set free from this bondage on the sabbath day?" ¹⁷When he said this, all his opponents were put to shame; and the entire crowd was rejoicing at all the wonderful things that he was doing.

The Parable of the Mustard Seed

18 He said therefore, "What is the kingdom of God like? And to what should I compare it? ¹⁹It is like a mustard seed that someone took and sowed in the garden; it grew and became a tree, and the birds of the air made nests in its branches."

The Parable of the Yeast

20 And again he said, "To what should I compare the kingdom of God? ²¹It is like yeast that a woman took and mixed in with^a three measures of flour until all of it was leavened."

The Narrow Door

22 Jesus^b went through one town and village after another, teaching as he made his way to Jerusalem. ²³Someone asked him, "Lord, will only a few be saved?" He said to them, ²⁴"Strive to enter through the narrow door; for many, I tell you, will try to enter and will not be able. ²⁵When once the owner of the house has got up and shut the door, and you begin to stand outside and to knock at the door, saying, 'Lord, open to us,' then in reply he will say to you, 'I do not know where you come from.' ²⁶Then you will begin to say, 'We ate and drank with you, and you taught in our streets.' ²⁷But he will say, 'I do not know where you come from; go away from me, all you evildoers!' ²⁸There will be weeping and gnashing of teeth when you see Abraham and Isaac and Jacob and all the prophets in the kingdom of God, and you yourselves thrown out. ²⁹Then people will come from east and west, from north and south, and will eat in the kingdom of God. ³⁰Indeed, some are last who will be first, and some are first who will be last."

The Lament over Jerusalem

31 At that very hour some Pharisees came and said to him, "Get away from here, for Herod wants to kill you." ³²He said to them, "Go and tell that fox for me,^{c} 'Listen, I am casting out demons and performing cures today and tomorrow, and on the third day I finish my work. ³³Yet today, tomorrow, and the next day I must be on my way, because it is impossible for a prophet to be killed outside of Jerusalem.' ³⁴Jerusalem, Jerusalem, the city that kills the prophets and stones those who are sent to it! How often have I desired to gather your children together as a hen gathers her brood under her wings, and you were not willing! ³⁵See, your house is left to you. And I tell you, you will not see me until the time comes when^d you say, 'Blessed is the one who comes in the name of the Lord.' "

Jesus Heals the Man with Dropsy

14 On one occasion when Jesus^e was going to the house of a leader of the Pharisees to eat a meal on the sabbath, they were watching him closely. ²Just then, in front of him, there was a man who had dropsy. ³And Jesus asked the lawyers and Pharisees, "Is it lawful to cure people on the sabbath, or not?" ⁴But they were silent. So Jesus^e took him and healed him, and sent him away. ⁵Then he said to them, "If one of you has a child^f or an ox that has fallen into a well, will you not immediately pull it out on a sabbath day?" ⁶And they could not reply to this.

Humility and Hospitality

7 When he noticed how the guests chose the places of honor, he told them a parable. ⁸"When you are invited by someone to a wedding banquet, do not sit down at the place of honor, in case someone more distinguished than you has been invited by your host; ⁹and the host who

God's Invitation List

Jesus uses the image of a banquet to describe the Reign of God. Jesus' point is not about what is on the menu but who is on the invitation list: the weak, the poor, and the little ones. Who is on your "invitation list"—who are the people you reach out to and serve?

▶ Lk 14:7–24

---

a Gk *hid in* b Gk *He* c Gk lacks *for me* d Other ancient authorities lack *the time comes when* e Gk *he* f Other ancient authorities read *a donkey*

invited both of you may come and say to you, 'Give this person your place,' and then in disgrace you would start to take the lowest place. [10]But when you are invited, go and sit down at the lowest place, so that when your host comes, he may say to you, 'Friend, move up higher'; then you will be honored in the presence of all who sit at the table with you. [11]For all who exalt themselves will be humbled, and those who humble themselves will be exalted."

12 He said also to the one who had invited him, "When you give a luncheon or a dinner, do not invite your friends or your brothers or your relatives or rich neighbors, in case they may invite you in return, and you would be repaid. [13]But when you give a banquet, invite the poor, the crippled, the lame, and the blind. [14]And you will be blessed, because they cannot repay you, for you will be repaid at the resurrection of the righteous."

The Parable of the Great Dinner

15 One of the dinner guests, on hearing this, said to him, "Blessed is anyone who will eat bread in the kingdom of God!" [16]Then Jesus[a] said to him, "Someone gave a great dinner and invited many. [17]At the time for the dinner he sent his slave to say to those who had been invited, 'Come; for everything is ready now.' [18]But they all alike began to make excuses. The first said to him, 'I have bought a piece of land, and I must go out and see it; please accept my regrets.' [19]Another said, 'I have bought five yoke of oxen, and I am going to try them out; please accept my regrets.' [20]Another said, 'I have just been married, and therefore I cannot come.' [21]So the slave returned and reported this to his master. Then the owner of the house became angry and said to his slave, 'Go out at once into the streets and lanes of the town and bring in the poor, the crippled, the blind, and the lame.' [22]And the slave said, 'Sir, what you ordered has been done, and there is still room.' [23]Then the master said to the slave, 'Go out into the roads and lanes, and compel people to come in, so that my house may be filled. [24]For I tell you,[b] none of those who were invited will taste my dinner.' "

The Cost of Discipleship

25 Now large crowds were traveling with him; and he turned and said to them, [26]"Whoever comes to me and does not hate father and mother, wife and children, brothers and sisters, yes, and even life itself, cannot be my disciple. [27]Whoever does not carry the cross and follow me cannot be my disciple. [28]For which of you,

LK

intending to build a tower, does not first sit down and estimate the cost, to see whether he has enough to complete it? [29]Otherwise, when he has laid a foundation and is not able to finish, all who see it will begin to ridicule him, [30]saying, 'This fellow began to build and was not able to finish.' [31]Or what king, going out to wage war against another king, will not sit down first and consider whether he is able with ten thousand to oppose the one who comes against him with twenty thousand? [32]If he cannot, then, while the other is still far away, he sends a delegation and asks for the terms of peace. [33]So therefore, none of you can become my disciple if you do not give up all your possessions.

About Salt

34 "Salt is good; but if salt has lost its taste, how can its saltiness be restored?[c] [35]It is fit neither for the soil nor for the manure pile; they throw it away. Let anyone with ears to hear listen!"

The Parable of the Lost Sheep

15 Now all the tax collectors and sinners were coming near to listen to him. [2]And the Pharisees and the scribes were grumbling and saying, "This fellow welcomes sinners and eats with them."

3 So he told them this parable: [4]"Which one of you, having a hundred sheep and losing one

---

a Gk *he*   *b* The Greek word for *you* here is plural   *c* Or *how can it be used for seasoning?*

of them, does not leave the ninety-nine in the wilderness and go after the one that is lost until he finds it? [5]When he has found it, he lays it on his shoulders and rejoices. [6]And when he comes home, he calls together his friends and neighbors, saying, 'Rejoice with me, for I have found my sheep that was lost.' [7]Just so, I tell you, there will be more joy in heaven over one sinner who repents than over ninety-nine righteous persons who need no repentance.

The Parable of the Lost Coin

8 "Or what woman having ten silver coins,[a] if she loses one of them, does not light a lamp, sweep the house, and search carefully until she finds it? [9]When she has found it, she calls together her friends and neighbors, saying, 'Rejoice with me, for I have found the coin that I had lost.' [10]Just so, I tell you, there is joy in the presence of the angels of God over one sinner who repents."

The Parable of the Prodigal and His Brother

11 Then Jesus[b] said, "There was a man who had two sons. [12]The younger of them said to his father, 'Father, give me the share of the property that will belong to me.' So he divided his property between them. [13]A few days later the younger son gathered all he had and traveled to a distant country, and there he squandered his property in dissolute living. [14]When he had spent everything, a severe famine took place throughout that country, and he began to be in need. [15]So he went and hired himself out to one of the citizens of

15:1–7

that country, who sent him to his fields to feed the pigs. [16]He would gladly have filled himself with[c] the pods that the pigs were eating; and no one gave him anything. [17]But when he came to himself he said, 'How many of my father's hired hands have bread enough and to spare, but here I am dying of hunger! [18]I will get up and go to my father, and I will say to him, "Father, I have sinned against heaven and before you; [19]I am no longer worthy to be called your son; treat me like one of your hired hands."' [20]So he set off and went to his father. But while he was still far off, his father saw him and was filled with compassion; he ran and put his arms around him and kissed him. [21]Then the son said to him, 'Father, I have sinned against heaven and before you; I am no longer worthy to be called your son.'[d] [22]But the father said to his slaves, 'Quickly, bring out a robe—the best one—and put it on him; put a ring on his finger and sandals on his feet. [23]And get the fatted calf and kill it, and let us eat and celebrate; [24]for this son of

---

a Gk *drachmas*, each worth about a day's wage for a laborer b Gk *he* c Other ancient authorities read *filled his stomach with* d Other ancient authorities add *Treat me like one of your hired servants*

Lost and Found

Who hasn't been lost at some point in life? Everyone can identify with the frustration, fear, and loneliness that come with being lost . . . which means everyone can also identify with being found! What a wonderful feeling it is to finally see the familiar landmark or to make the right turn to the main road or to have someone help you get your life back on track.

If you identify with that lone sheep who strayed from the flock (see Lk 15:1–7), remember that God never stops looking for you. Maybe all you need to do is stop and listen for God's call so God can embrace you and celebrate your return.

Talk to God now about the recent experiences that have led you astray and have made you feel lost. Let God hold you tight and lift you high as the divine shepherd celebrates your return.

▶ Lk 15:1–7

mine was dead and is alive again; he was lost and is found!' And they began to celebrate.

25 "Now his elder son was in the field; and when he came and approached the house, he heard music and dancing. ²⁶He called one of the slaves and asked what was going on. ²⁷He

God's Limitless Love

We have all heard the story of the lost son (prodigal son). We have all heard about the older brother's envious reaction to his father's generosity. And it seems clear that the forgiving father represents God and the sons represent each of us at different points in our lives.

On second thought, perhaps there is more to this familiar parable than meets the eye. Think about the story for a moment. What does it really say about God? Not only is the father not upset about his son's wasting all his money, but the father is incredibly happy to see his son return home. He runs to meet him! Picture it—this man so eager to welcome his son that he runs down the road toward him and then hugs and kisses him. Doesn't this seem a bit excessive?

But it doesn't end there. Despite the son's apology, which the father ignores, the father tells his servants to throw a huge party, to go all out for his son. This seems almost too much to believe, doesn't it? Music, dancing, expensive robes and rings, and a feast for everyone! What's going on here?

Luke is trying to show us, in the most visual way possible, that there is simply no limit to God's love for us. It is not a conditional love. It is an extravagant, outrageous love. God doesn't hold back. How can we refuse such boundless love? How can we hold back from such divine eagerness? The next time you think you have separated yourself from God's love, picture yourself walking down a road, God running toward you with open arms. What is your response?

▶ Lk 15:11–32

replied, 'Your brother has come, and your father has killed the fatted calf, because he has got him back safe and sound.' ²⁸Then he became angry and refused to go in. His father came out and began to plead with him. ²⁹But he answered his father, 'Listen! For all these years I have been working like a slave for you, and I have never disobeyed your command; yet you have never given me even a young goat so that I might celebrate with my friends. ³⁰But when this son of yours came back, who has devoured your property with prostitutes, you killed the fatted calf for him!' ³¹Then the father*a* said to him, 'Son, you are always with me, and all that is mine is yours. ³²But we had to celebrate and rejoice, because this brother of yours was dead and has come to life; he was lost and has been found.' "

The Parable of the Dishonest Manager

16 Then Jesus*a* said to the disciples, "There was a rich man who had a manager, and charges were brought to him that this man was squandering his property. ²So he summoned

---

a Gk *he*

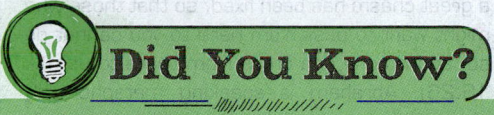

Understanding Parables

In some of Jesus' parables, the characters represent someone else. For example, in the parable of the prodigal son (see Lk 15:11–32), the forgiving father represents God. In other parables, the characters are examples for us to follow, as in the parable of the good Samaritan (see 10:29–37). However, in some parables, the characters neither represent God nor are role models for us.

For example, in the parable of the dishonest manager (see 16:1–13), the master doesn't represent God. And Jesus is not encouraging us to be dishonest like the manager. Jesus is simply saying that we need to be even more clever than dishonest people in using our money and talents for the sake of the Gospel.

(For more on understanding the parables, see "Parables," near Mt 13:10.)

▶ Lk 16:1–13

him and said to him, 'What is this that I hear about you? Give me an accounting of your management, because you cannot be my manager any longer.' ³Then the manager said to himself, 'What will I do, now that my master is taking the position away from me? I am not strong enough to dig, and I am ashamed to beg. ⁴I have decided what to do so that, when I am dismissed as manager, people may welcome me into their homes.' ⁵So, summoning his master's debtors one by one, he asked the first, 'How much do you owe my master?' ⁶He answered, 'A hundred jugs of olive oil.' He said to him, 'Take your bill, sit down quickly, and make it fifty.' ⁷Then he asked another, 'And how much do you owe?' He replied,

The Great Chasm

In this famous parable about the rich man and poor Lazarus, Luke puts the following words in the mouth of Abraham: "Between you and us a great chasm has been fixed, so that those who might want to pass from here to you cannot do so, and no one can cross from there to us" (Lk 16:26). Abraham is speaking metaphorically about heaven and hell, but he could just as easily be speaking about the gap between the "haves" and the "have-nots."

In our society and across the globe, the gap between those who are wealthy and those who are poor is indeed becoming a great chasm. It grows more and more difficult for those who are poor and destitute to improve their lot in life. Yet, we hear about millionaires becoming billionaires, many of whom seem to have little or no regard for the millions of people who go without in the world.

This parable speaks volumes to the inequities in our world and to our responsibility to be concerned for all the Lazaruses at our door.

● What are we doing now for those who are poor? What more could we be doing?
● How can we become more sensitive to the needs of those who are poor?

▶ Lk 16:19–31

'A hundred containers of wheat.' He said to him, 'Take your bill and make it eighty.' ⁸And his master commended the dishonest manager because he had acted shrewdly; for the children of this age are more shrewd in dealing with their own generation than are the children of light. ⁹And I tell you, make friends for yourselves by means of dishonest wealth*a* so that when it is gone, they may welcome you into the eternal homes.*b*

10 "Whoever is faithful in a very little is faithful also in much; and whoever is dishonest in a very little is dishonest also in much. ¹¹If then you have not been faithful with the dishonest wealth,*a* who will entrust to you the true riches? ¹²And if you have not been faithful with what belongs to another, who will give you what is your own? ¹³No slave can serve two masters; for a slave will either hate the one and love the other, or be devoted to the one and despise the other. You cannot serve God and wealth."*a*

The Law and the Kingdom of God

14 The Pharisees, who were lovers of money, heard all this, and they ridiculed him. ¹⁵So he said to them, "You are those who justify yourselves in the sight of others; but God knows your hearts; for what is prized by human beings is an abomination in the sight of God.

16 "The law and the prophets were in effect until John came; since then the good news of the kingdom of God is proclaimed, and everyone tries to enter it by force.*c* ¹⁷But it is easier for heaven and earth to pass away, than for one stroke of a letter in the law to be dropped.

18 "Anyone who divorces his wife and marries another commits adultery, and whoever marries a woman divorced from her husband commits adultery.

The Rich Man and Lazarus

19 "There was a rich man who was dressed in purple and fine linen and who feasted sumptuously every day. ²⁰And at his gate lay a poor man named Lazarus, covered with sores, ²¹who longed to satisfy his hunger with what fell from the rich man's table; even the dogs would come and lick his sores. ²²The poor man died and was carried away by the angels to be with Abraham.*d* The rich man also died and was buried. ²³In Hades, where he was being tormented, he looked up and saw Abraham far away with Lazarus by his side.*e* ²⁴He called out, 'Father Abraham, have mercy on me, and send Lazarus to dip the tip of

---

a Gk mammon   *b* Gk tents   *c* Or everyone is strongly urged to enter it   *d* Gk to Abraham's bosom   *e* Gk in his bosom

his finger in water and cool my tongue; for I am in agony in these flames.' 25But Abraham said, 'Child, remember that during your lifetime you received your good things, and Lazarus in like manner evil things; but now he is comforted here, and you are in agony. 26Besides all this, between you and us a great chasm has been fixed, so that those who might want to pass from here to you cannot do so, and no one can cross from there to us.' 27He said, 'Then, father, I beg you to send him to my father's house— 28for I have five brothers—that he may warn them, so that they will not also come into this place of torment.' 29Abraham replied, 'They have Moses and the prophets; they should listen to them.' 30He said, 'No, father Abraham; but if someone goes to them from the dead, they will repent.' 31He said to him, 'If they do not listen to Moses and the prophets, neither will they be convinced even if someone rises from the dead.' "

Some Sayings of Jesus

17 Jesus*a* said to his disciples, "Occasions for stumbling are bound to come, but woe to anyone by whom they come! 2It would be better for you if a millstone were hung around your neck and you were thrown into the sea than for you to cause one of these little ones to stumble. 3Be on your guard! If another disciple*b* sins, you must rebuke the offender, and if there is repentance, you must forgive. 4And if the same person sins against you seven times a day, and turns back to you seven times and says, 'I repent,' you must forgive."

5 The apostles said to the Lord, "Increase our faith!" 6The Lord replied, "If you had faith the size of a*c* mustard seed, you could say to this mulberry tree, 'Be uprooted and planted in the sea,' and it would obey you.

7 "Who among you would say to your slave who has just come in from plowing or tending sheep in the field, 'Come here at once and take your place at the table'? 8Would you not rather say to him, 'Prepare supper for me, put on your apron and serve me while I eat and drink; later you may eat and drink'? 9Do you thank the slave for doing what was commanded? 10So you also, when you have done all that you were ordered to do, say, 'We are worthless slaves; we have done only what we ought to have done!' "

Jesus Cleanses Ten Lepers

11 On the way to Jerusalem Jesus*d* was going through the region between Samaria and Galilee. 12As he entered a village, ten lepers*e* approached him. Keeping their distance, 13they

called out, saying, "Jesus, Master, have mercy on us!" 14When he saw them, he said to them, "Go and show yourselves to the priests." And as they went, they were made clean. 15Then one of them, when he saw that he was healed, turned back, praising God with a loud voice. 16He prostrated himself at Jesus'*f* feet and thanked him. And he was a Samaritan. 17Then Jesus asked, "Were not ten made clean? But the other nine, where are they? 18Was none of them found to return and give praise to God except this foreigner?" 19Then he said to him, "Get up and go on your way; your faith has made you well."

The Coming of the Kingdom

20 Once Jesus*d* was asked by the Pharisees when the kingdom of God was coming, and he answered, "The kingdom of God is not coming with things that can be observed; 21nor will they say, 'Look, here it is!' or 'There it is!' For, in fact, the kingdom of God is among*g* you."

22 Then he said to the disciples, "The days are coming when you will long to see one of the days of the Son of Man, and you will not see it. 23They will say to you, 'Look there!' or 'Look here!' Do not go, do not set off in pursuit. 24For as the lightning flashes and lights up the sky from one side to the other, so will the Son of Man be in his day.*h* 25But first he must endure much suffering and be rejected by this generation. 26Just as it was in the days of Noah, so too it will be in the days of the Son of Man. 27They were eating and drinking, and marrying and being given in marriage, until the day Noah entered the ark, and the flood came and destroyed all of them. 28Likewise, just as it was in the days of Lot: they were eating and drinking, buying and selling, planting and building, 29but on the day that Lot left Sodom, it rained fire and sulfur from heaven and destroyed all of them 30—it will be like that on the day that the Son of Man is revealed. 31On that day, anyone on the housetop who has belongings in the house must not come down to take them away; and likewise anyone in the field must not turn back. 32Remember Lot's wife. 33Those who try to make their life secure will lose it, but those who lose their life will keep it. 34I tell you, on that night there will be two in one bed; one will be taken and the other left. 35There will be two women grinding meal together; one will be taken and the other left."*i* 37Then they asked him,

---

a Gk He   b Gk your brother   c Gk faith as a grain of   d Gk he
e The terms leper and leprosy can refer to several diseases
f Gk his   g Or within   h Other ancient authorities lack in his day   i Other ancient authorities add verse 36, "Two will be in the field; one will be taken and the other left."

"Where, Lord?" He said to them, "Where the corpse is, there the vultures will gather."

The Parable of the Widow and the Unjust Judge

18 Then Jesus[a] told them a parable about their need to pray always and not to lose heart. [2]He said, "In a certain city there was a judge who neither feared God nor had respect for people. [3]In that city there was a widow who kept coming to him and saying, 'Grant me justice against my opponent.' [4]For a while he refused; but later he said to himself, 'Though I have no fear of God and no respect for anyone, [5]yet because this widow keeps bothering me, I will grant her justice, so that she may not wear me out by continually coming.'"[b] [6]And the Lord said, "Listen to what the unjust judge says. [7]And will not God grant justice to his chosen ones who cry to him day and night? Will he delay long in helping them? [8]I tell you, he will quickly grant justice to them. And yet, when the Son of Man comes, will he find faith on earth?"

The Parable of the Pharisee and the Tax Collector

[9] He also told this parable to some who trusted in themselves that they were righteous and regarded others with contempt: [10]"Two men went up to the temple to pray, one a Pharisee and the other a tax collector. [11]The Pharisee, standing by himself, was praying thus, 'God, I thank you that I am not like other people: thieves, rogues, adulterers, or even like this tax collector. [12]I fast twice a week; I give a tenth of all my income.' [13]But the tax collector, standing far off, would not even look up to heaven, but was beating his breast and saying, 'God, be merciful to me, a sinner!' [14]I tell you, this man went down to his home justified rather than the other; for all who exalt themselves will be humbled, but all who humble themselves will be exalted."

Jesus Blesses Little Children

[15] People were bringing even infants to him that he might touch them; and when the disciples saw it, they sternly ordered them not to do it. [16]But Jesus called for them and said, "Let the little children come to me, and do not stop them; for it is to such as these that the kingdom of God belongs. [17]Truly I tell you, whoever does not receive the kingdom of God as a little child will never enter it."

The Rich Ruler

[18] A certain ruler asked him, "Good Teacher, what must I do to inherit eternal life?" [19]Jesus said to him, "Why do you call me good? No one is good but God alone. [20]You know the commandments: 'You shall not commit adultery; You shall not murder; You shall not steal; You shall not bear false witness; Honor your father and mother.'" [21]He replied, "I have kept all these since my youth." [22]When Jesus heard this, he said to him, "There is still one thing lacking. Sell all that you own and distribute the money[c] to the poor, and you will have treasure in heaven; then come, follow me." [23]But when he heard this, he became sad; for he was very rich. [24]Jesus looked at him and said, "How hard it is for those who have wealth to enter the kingdom of God! [25]Indeed, it is easier for a camel to go through the eye of a needle than for someone who is rich to enter the kingdom of God."

[26] Those who heard it said, "Then who can be saved?" [27]He replied, "What is impossible for mortals is possible for God."

[28] Then Peter said, "Look, we have left our homes and followed you." [29]And he said to them, "Truly I tell you, there is no one who has left house or wife or brothers or parents or children, for the sake of the kingdom of God, [30]who will not get back very much more in this age, and in the age to come eternal life."

Pray It!

Can You Hear Me, Lord?

Dear God, Jesus had to remind people to pray always and not to lose hope when faced with injustice. I need to hear that too. Sometimes it seems like I pray and pray, but you are not answering.

I know I have to be willing to look and listen for your response. I know I have to pray always, not just in times of need. I know I need to share my daily life with you. Help me to do these things I know I need to do. Help me to pray, Lord. Amen.

▶ Lk 18:1–8

---

a Gk he b Or so that she may not finally come and slap me in the face c Gk lacks the money

A Third Time Jesus Foretells His Death and Resurrection

31 Then he took the twelve aside and said to them, "See, we are going up to Jerusalem, and everything that is written about the Son of Man by the prophets will be accomplished. ³²For he will be handed over to the Gentiles; and he will be mocked and insulted and spat upon. ³³After they have flogged him, they will kill him, and on the third day he will rise again." ³⁴But they understood nothing about all these things; in fact, what he said was hidden from them, and they did not grasp what was said.

Jesus Heals a Blind Beggar Near Jericho

35 As he approached Jericho, a blind man was sitting by the roadside begging. ³⁶When he heard a crowd going by, he asked what was happening. ³⁷They told him, "Jesus of Nazareth[a] is passing by." ³⁸Then he shouted, "Jesus, Son of David, have mercy on me!" ³⁹Those who were in front sternly ordered him to be quiet; but he shouted even more loudly, "Son of David, have mercy on me!" ⁴⁰Jesus stood still and ordered the man to be brought to him; and when he came near, he asked him, ⁴¹"What do you want me to do for you?" He said, "Lord, let me see again." ⁴²Jesus said to him, "Receive your sight; your faith has saved you." ⁴³Immediately he regained his sight and followed him, glorifying God; and all the people, when they saw it, praised God.

Jesus and Zacchaeus

19 He entered Jericho and was passing through it. ²A man was there named Zacchaeus; he was a chief tax collector and was rich.

a Gk the Nazorean

The Loaded Question

If you ask a loaded question, you should expect a loaded answer, especially if you're asking God! Picture the rich ruler in Luke 18:18–30, who devoutly followed the Commandments all his life. After hearing Jesus talk about the Reign of God, he eagerly asks Jesus, "What must I do to inherit eternal life?"

Jesus' answer, "Sell all that you own and distribute the money to the poor" (verse 22), must have been like a blow. Jesus asked for a radical commitment from this rich ruler, just as Jesus asks for a radical commitment from us. As often happens in Luke's portrayal of Jesus, that radical commitment has something to do with wealth and those who are poor. If we dare to ask the loaded question—What must I do?—we must be prepared to unload something too. Our human tendency is to hoard our money and our material goods. But with God's help (see verse 27), we can become generous with those in need.

▶ Lk 18:18–30

Look Up!

Jesus looked up. With this simple act, Jesus changed a man's life, inviting him down from the tree and into relationship with him. Why would Jesus choose Zacchaeus, who was hated and despised as a tax collector, to become a disciple? Besides that, he was pretty short and did not stand out in a crowd. Perhaps Luke is trying to tell us that our physical attributes, our past history, and other people's perceptions do not figure into God's equation.

When Jesus looks up and notices Zacchaeus, Zacchaeus ends up not only believing in Jesus but also doing something surprising. He gives away half of his money and possessions, perhaps to make up for all the times he cheated people. This is what conversion is—a change of heart and behavior. Conversion calls us to act in ways we would not have acted before.

● Jesus has been with you from the moment of your conception. How have you tried to know him better?

● How do you feel knowing that Jesus sees past externals and loves you for who you truly are?

● Whom in your own life have you been failing to notice by not taking the time to look up?

▶ Lk 19:1–10

LK

Cultural Connection

Jesus Goes to Jerusalem as the Messiah

As Jesus enters Jerusalem to celebrate the Passover, the crowd joyfully hails him as the king and Messiah returning to the City of David. He is the prophet who brings new hope and calls people to conversion.

On Palm Sunday—also known as Passion Sunday—we begin our preparation for Holy Week. At Mass we receive blessed branches of palms to symbolize our profession of Jesus as the Messiah, king of peace. In some Hispanic communities, the palms are woven into beautiful braids, crosses, and flowers. In others, people receive a small donkey made of palm leaves, as a remembrance of Jesus' riding the donkey into Jerusalem. Often, Jesus' entrance into Jerusalem is re-enacted. Hispanics use art, song, and drama to celebrate and express their faith.

● Picture yourself in the crowd welcoming Jesus. Does Jesus' arrival fill you with joy and hope?

● Next Palm Sunday, find a special place for your palm. Think of a concrete way you will live out your calling as a disciple of Jesus in the coming year. Each time you see the palm, remember your call, and pray for help to respond to it.

▶ Lk 19:28–40

³He was trying to see who Jesus was, but on account of the crowd he could not, because he was short in stature. ⁴So he ran ahead and climbed a sycamore tree to see him, because he was going to pass that way. ⁵When Jesus came to the place, he looked up and said to him, "Zacchaeus, hurry and come down; for I must stay at your house today." ⁶So he hurried down and was happy to welcome him. ⁷All who saw it began to grumble and said, "He has gone to be the guest of one who is a sinner." ⁸Zacchaeus stood there and said to the Lord, "Look, half of my possessions, Lord, I will give to the poor; and if I have defrauded anyone of anything, I will pay back four times as much." ⁹Then Jesus said to him, "Today salvation has come to this house, because he too is a son of Abraham. ¹⁰For the Son of Man came to seek out and to save the lost."

The Parable of the Ten Pounds

11 As they were listening to this, he went on to tell a parable, because he was near Jerusalem, and because they supposed that the kingdom of God was to appear immediately. ¹²So he said, "A nobleman went to a distant country to get royal power for himself and then return. ¹³He summoned ten of his slaves, and gave them ten pounds,ᵃ and said to them, 'Do business with these until I come back.' ¹⁴But the citizens of his country hated him and sent a delegation after him, saying, 'We do not want this man to rule over us.' ¹⁵When he returned, having received royal power, he ordered these slaves, to whom he had given the money, to be summoned so that he might find out what they had gained by trading. ¹⁶The first came forward and said, 'Lord, your pound has made ten more pounds.' ¹⁷He said to him, 'Well done, good slave! Because you have been trustworthy in a very small thing, take charge of ten cities.' ¹⁸Then the second came, saying, 'Lord, your pound has made five pounds.' ¹⁹He said to him, 'And you, rule over five cities.' ²⁰Then the other came, saying, 'Lord, here is your pound. I wrapped it up in a piece of cloth, ²¹for I was afraid of you, because you are a harsh man; you take what you did not deposit, and reap what you did not sow.' ²²He said to him, 'I will judge you by your own words, you wicked slave! You knew, did you, that I was a harsh man, taking what I did not deposit and reaping what I did not sow? ²³Why then did you not put my money into the bank? Then when I returned, I could have collected it with interest.' ²⁴He said to the bystanders, 'Take the pound from him and give it to the one who has ten pounds.' ²⁵(And they said to him, 'Lord, he has ten pounds!') ²⁶'I tell you, to all those who have, more will be given; but from those who have nothing, even what they have will be taken away. ²⁷But as for these enemies of mine who did not want me to be king over them—bring them here and slaughter them in my presence.'"

a The mina, rendered here by *pound*, was about three months' wages for a laborer

Jesus' Triumphal Entry into Jerusalem

28 After he had said this, he went on ahead, going up to Jerusalem.

29 When he had come near Bethphage and Bethany, at the place called the Mount of Olives, he sent two of the disciples, 30saying, "Go into the village ahead of you, and as you enter it you will find tied there a colt that has never been ridden. Untie it and bring it here. 31If anyone asks you, 'Why are you untying it?' just say this, 'The Lord needs it.'" 32So those who were sent departed and found it as he had told them. 33As they were untying the colt, its owners asked them, "Why are you untying the colt?" 34They said, "The Lord needs it." 35Then they brought it to Jesus; and after throwing their cloaks on the colt, they set Jesus on it. 36As he rode along, people kept spreading their cloaks on the road. 37As he was now approaching the path down from the Mount of Olives, the whole multitude of the disciples began to praise God joyfully with a loud voice for all the deeds of power that they had seen, 38saying,

"Blessed is the king
　who comes in the name of the Lord!
Peace in heaven,
　and glory in the highest heaven!"

39Some of the Pharisees in the crowd said to him, "Teacher, order your disciples to stop." 40He answered, "I tell you, if these were silent, the stones would shout out."

Jesus Weeps over Jerusalem

41 As he came near and saw the city, he wept over it, 42saying, "If you, even you, had only recognized on this day the things that make for peace! But now they are hidden from your eyes. 43Indeed, the days will come upon you, when your enemies will set up ramparts around you and surround you, and hem you in on every side. 44They will crush you to the ground, you and your children within you, and they will not leave within you one stone upon another; because you did not recognize the time of your visitation from God."a

Jesus Cleanses the Temple

45 Then he entered the temple and began to drive out those who were selling things there; 46and he said, "It is written,

'My house shall be a house of prayer';
　but you have made it a den of robbers."

47 Every day he was teaching in the temple. The chief priests, the scribes, and the leaders of the people kept looking for a way to kill him; 48but they did not find anything they could do, for all the people were spellbound by what they heard.

The Authority of Jesus Questioned

20 One day, as he was teaching the people in the temple and telling the good news, the chief priests and the scribes came with the elders 2and said to him, "Tell us, by what authority are you doing these things? Who is it who gave you this authority?" 3He answered them, "I will also ask you a question, and you tell me: 4Did the baptism of John come from heaven, or was it of human origin?" 5They discussed it with one another, saying, "If we say, 'From heaven,' he will say, 'Why did you not believe him?' 6But if we say, 'Of human origin,' all the people will stone us; for they are convinced that John was a prophet." 7So they answered that they did not know where it came from. 8Then Jesus said to them, "Neither will I tell you by what authority I am doing these things."

---

a Gk lacks *from God*

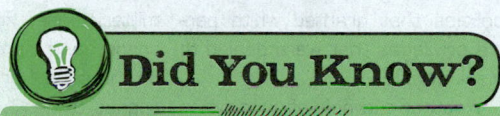

Did You Know?

The Human Jesus

Have you ever been so disappointed in something that you just sat down and wept? That's what happened to Jesus. In Luke 19:41–42, we hear of his great disappointment and frustration that he cannot help Jerusalem and its people. The people of Jerusalem do not accept his message of justice and peace, so the Temple and Jerusalem are to be destroyed again. Jesus is so upset that he weeps.

We often forget that, although Jesus is fully God, he is also fully human and experienced all the things that normal people experience. He enjoyed excitement, laughter, and fun times with friends. He also experienced fear, sadness, and frustration. He was completely human in all things but sin.

● What does it mean to you that Jesus shares our humanity?
● Why is Jesus' humanity an important part of the Christian message?

▶ Lk 19:41–42

Catholic Social Teaching

Sit and Stand Against Injustice

Jesus not only claimed to be God's son but also took an active stand against injustice, greed, and religious hypocrisy. This outraged the leaders of his time and put his life in danger.

Despite the risks, other people have followed Jesus' example of civil disobedience. On February 1, 1960, in Greensboro, North Carolina, four first-year college students began a sit-in at a diner that did not allow black people to eat there. These students' actions against injustice sparked similar sit-ins across the country. Thousands of courageous people protested against unfair and cruel policies that granted white people privileges that were denied to black people.

Another example of uncommon bravery occurred on December 1, 1955, in Selma, Alabama. Rosa Parks, a black woman, boarded a public bus and sat in one of the seats toward the front, where only white people were allowed to sit. For her bravery, she was arrested, jailed, and fined. This event triggered a bus boycott that lasted for months and finally put an end to that policy.

Civil disobedience continues today. Every year, busloads of people travel to Fort Benning, Georgia, to protest a U.S. military facility nicknamed "The School of the Assassins." This school teaches methods of torture and terrorism. Over the years, peaceful protesters have poured water on the grounds of the military base, held candles, sung songs, and sprawled themselves on the school grounds to re-enact scenes of death inflicted upon victims of the school's graduates. The protestors often end up in jail.

Catholic social teaching asserts that every person has a right and a duty to participate actively in shaping society and to promote the well-being of all, especially the poor and vulnerable. Not every Christian is called to participate in acts of civil disobedience, but we are all called to be aware of and speak out against situations that are racist, sexist, or unjust. As Jesus shows us, silence is not an acceptable option in the face of injustice.

▶ **Lk 19:45–48**

Call to Family, Community, and Participation

The Parable of the Wicked Tenants

9 He began to tell the people this parable: "A man planted a vineyard, and leased it to tenants, and went to another country for a long time. [10]When the season came, he sent a slave to the tenants in order that they might give him his share of the produce of the vineyard; but the tenants beat him and sent him away empty-handed. [11]Next he sent another slave; that one also they beat and insulted and sent away empty-handed. [12]And he sent still a third; this one also they wounded and threw out. [13]Then the owner of the vineyard said, 'What shall I do? I will send my beloved son; perhaps they will respect him.' [14]But when the tenants saw him, they discussed it among themselves and said, 'This is the heir; let us kill him so that the inheritance may be ours.' [15]So they threw him out of the vineyard and killed him. What then will the owner of the vineyard do to them? [16]He will come and destroy those tenants and give the vineyard to others."

When they heard this, they said, "Heaven forbid!" [17]But he looked at them and said, "What then does this text mean:

'The stone that the builders rejected
    has become the cornerstone'?[a]

[18]Everyone who falls on that stone will be broken to pieces; and it will crush anyone on whom it falls." [19]When the scribes and chief priests realized that he had told this parable against them, they wanted to lay hands on him at that very hour, but they feared the people.

The Question about Paying Taxes

20 So they watched him and sent spies who pretended to be honest, in order to trap him by what he said, so as to hand him over to the jurisdiction and authority of the governor. [21]So they asked him, "Teacher, we know that you are right in what you say and teach, and you show deference to no one, but teach the way of God

a Or keystone

in accordance with truth. ²²Is it lawful for us to pay taxes to the emperor, or not?" ²³But he perceived their craftiness and said to them, ²⁴"Show me a denarius. Whose head and whose title does it bear?" They said, "The emperor's." ²⁵He said to them, "Then give to the emperor the things that are the emperor's, and to God the things that are God's." ²⁶And they were not able in the presence of the people to trap him by what he said; and being amazed by his answer, they became silent.

The Question about the Resurrection

27 Some Sadducees, those who say there is no resurrection, came to him ²⁸and asked him a question, "Teacher, Moses wrote for us that if a man's brother dies, leaving a wife but no children, the man*a* shall marry the widow and raise up children for his brother. ²⁹Now there were seven brothers; the first married, and died childless; ³⁰then the second ³¹and the third married her, and so in the same way all seven died childless. ³²Finally the woman also died. ³³In the resurrection, therefore, whose wife will the woman be? For the seven had married her."

34 Jesus said to them, "Those who belong to this age marry and are given in marriage; ³⁵but those who are considered worthy of a place in that age and in the resurrection from the dead neither marry nor are given in marriage. ³⁶Indeed they cannot die anymore, because they are like angels and are children of God, being children of the resurrection. ³⁷And the fact that the dead are raised Moses himself showed, in the story about the bush, where he speaks of the Lord as the God of Abraham, the God of Isaac, and the God of Jacob. ³⁸Now he is God not of the dead, but of the living; for to him all of them are alive." ³⁹Then some of the scribes answered, "Teacher, you have spoken well." ⁴⁰For they no longer dared to ask him another question.

The Question about David's Son

41 Then he said to them, "How can they say that the Messiah*b* is David's son? ⁴²For David himself says in the book of Psalms,

'The Lord said to my Lord,

"Sit at my right hand,

⁴³   until I make your enemies your footstool." '

⁴⁴David thus calls him Lord; so how can he be his son?"

Jesus Denounces the Scribes

45 In the hearing of all the people he said to the*c* disciples, ⁴⁶"Beware of the scribes, who like to walk around in long robes, and love to be greeted with respect in the marketplaces, and to have the best seats in the synagogues and places of honor at banquets. ⁴⁷They devour widows' houses and for the sake of appearance say long prayers. They will receive the greater condemnation."

The Widow's Offering

21 He looked up and saw rich people putting their gifts into the treasury; ²he also saw a poor widow put in two small copper coins. ³He said, "Truly I tell you, this poor widow has put in more than all of them; ⁴for all of them have contributed out of their abundance, but she out of her poverty has put in all she had to live on."

The Destruction of the Temple Foretold

5 When some were speaking about the temple, how it was adorned with beautiful stones and gifts dedicated to God, he said, ⁶"As for these things that you see, the days will come when not

---

a Gk his brother   *b* Or the Christ   *c* Other ancient authorities read *his*

Stewardship: Making a Contribution

In Luke 21:1–4, Jesus notices that the rich people gave from their excess wealth, but the widow gave from her limited budget. She actually contributed more meaningfully because she gave from what little she had.

God calls us to be contributing members of the faith community and the human family—even to the point of sacrifice. We are called to stewardship, which means giving our time, talents, and treasure to support the Church's mission to spread the Good News of Jesus Christ. We should also support other organizations that contribute to the positive welfare of people in need.

How are you responding to God's call to give? Pray for the generosity of the poor widow as you discern how much of your time, talents, and treasure you are being called to give.

▶ Lk 21:1–4

one stone will be left upon another; all will be thrown down."

Signs and Persecutions

7 They asked him, "Teacher, when will this be, and what will be the sign that this is about to take place?" [8]And he said, "Beware that you are not led astray; for many will come in my name and say, 'I am he!'[a] and, 'The time is near!'[b] Do not go after them.

9 "When you hear of wars and insurrections, do not be terrified; for these things must take place first, but the end will not follow immediately." [10]Then he said to them, "Nation will rise against nation, and kingdom against kingdom; [11]there will be great earthquakes, and in various places famines and plagues; and there will be dreadful portents and great signs from heaven.

12 "But before all this occurs, they will arrest you and persecute you; they will hand you over to synagogues and prisons, and you will be brought before kings and governors because of my name. [13]This will give you an opportunity to testify. [14]So make up your minds not to prepare your defense in advance; [15]for I will give you words[c] and a wisdom that none of your opponents will be able to withstand or contradict. [16]You will be betrayed even by parents and brothers, by relatives and friends; and they will put some of you to death. [17]You will be hated by all because of my name. [18]But not a hair of your head will perish. [19]By your endurance you will gain your souls.

The Destruction of Jerusalem Foretold

20 "When you see Jerusalem surrounded by armies, then know that its desolation has come near.[d] [21]Then those in Judea must flee to the mountains, and those inside the city must leave it, and those out in the country must not enter it; [22]for these are days of vengeance, as a fulfillment of all that is written. [23]Woe to those who are pregnant and to those who are nursing infants in those days! For there will be great distress on the earth and wrath against this people; [24]they will fall by the edge of the sword and be taken away as captives among all nations; and Jerusalem will be trampled on by the Gentiles, until the times of the Gentiles are fulfilled.

The Coming of the Son of Man

25 "There will be signs in the sun, the moon, and the stars, and on the earth distress among nations confused by the roaring of the sea and the waves. [26]People will faint from fear and foreboding of what is coming upon the world, for the powers of the heavens will be shaken. [27]Then they will see 'the Son of Man coming in a cloud' with power and great glory. [28]Now when these things begin to take place, stand up and raise your heads, because your redemption is drawing near."

The Lesson of the Fig Tree

29 Then he told them a parable: "Look at the fig tree and all the trees; [30]as soon as they sprout leaves you can see for yourselves and know that summer is already near. [31]So also, when you see these things taking place, you know that the kingdom of God is near. [32]Truly I tell you, this generation will not pass away until all things have taken place. [33]Heaven and earth will pass away, but my words will not pass away.

Exhortation to Watch

34 "Be on guard so that your hearts are not weighed down with dissipation and drunkenness and the worries of this life, and that day does not catch you unexpectedly, [35]like a trap. For it will come upon all who live on the face of the whole earth. [36]Be alert at all times, praying that you may have the strength to escape all these things that will take place, and to stand before the Son of Man."

37 Every day he was teaching in the temple, and at night he would go out and spend the night on the Mount of Olives, as it was called. [38]And all the people would get up early in the morning to listen to him in the temple.

The Plot to Kill Jesus

22 Now the festival of Unleavened Bread, which is called the Passover, was near. [2]The chief priests and the scribes were looking for a way to put Jesus[e] to death, for they were afraid of the people.

3 Then Satan entered into Judas called Iscariot, who was one of the twelve; [4]he went away and conferred with the chief priests and officers of the temple police about how he might betray him to them. [5]They were greatly pleased and agreed to give him money. [6]So he consented and began to look for an opportunity to betray him to them when no crowd was present.

The Preparation of the Passover

7 Then came the day of Unleavened Bread, on which the Passover lamb had to be sacrificed. [8]So Jesus[f] sent Peter and John, saying, "Go and

---

a Gk *I am*   b Or *at hand*   c Gk *a mouth*   d Or *is at hand*
e Gk *him*   f Gk *he*

prepare the Passover meal for us that we may eat it." ⁹They asked him, "Where do you want us to make preparations for it?" ¹⁰"Listen," he said to them, "when you have entered the city, a man carrying a jar of water will meet you; follow him into the house he enters ¹¹and say to the owner of the house, 'The teacher asks you, "Where is the guest room, where I may eat the Passover with my disciples?" ' ¹²He will show you a large room upstairs, already furnished. Make preparations for us there." ¹³So they went and found everything as he had told them; and they prepared the Passover meal.

The Institution of the Lord's Supper

14 When the hour came, he took his place at the table, and the apostles with him. ¹⁵He said to them, "I have eagerly desired to eat this Passover with you before I suffer; ¹⁶for I tell you, I will not eat it*a* until it is fulfilled in the kingdom of God." ¹⁷Then he took a cup, and after giving thanks he said, "Take this and divide it among yourselves; ¹⁸for I tell you that from now on I will not drink of the fruit of the vine until the kingdom of God comes." ¹⁹Then he took a loaf of bread, and when he had given thanks, he broke it and gave it to them, saying, "This is my body, which is given for you. Do this in remembrance of me." ²⁰And he did the same with the cup after supper, saying, "This cup that is poured out for you is the new covenant in my blood.*b* ²¹But see, the one who betrays me is with me, and his hand is on the table. ²²For the Son of Man is going as it has been determined, but woe to that one by whom he is betrayed!" ²³Then they began to ask one another which one of them it could be who would do this.

The Dispute about Greatness

24 A dispute also arose among them as to which one of them was to be regarded as the greatest. ²⁵But he said to them, "The kings of the Gentiles lord it over them; and those in authority over them are called benefactors. ²⁶But not so with you; rather the greatest among you must become like the youngest, and the leader like one who serves. ²⁷For who is greater, the one who is at the table or the one who serves? Is it not the one at the table? But I am among you as one who serves.

28 "You are those who have stood by me in my trials; ²⁹and I confer on you, just as my Father has conferred on me, a kingdom, ³⁰so that you may eat and drink at my table in my kingdom, and you will sit on thrones judging the twelve tribes of Israel.

Jesus Predicts Peter's Denial

31 "Simon, Simon, listen! Satan has demanded*c* to sift all of you like wheat, ³²but I have prayed for you that your own faith may not fail; and you, when once you have turned back, strengthen your brothers." ³³And he said to him, "Lord, I am ready to go with you to prison and to death!" ³⁴Jesus*d* said, "I tell you, Peter, the cock will not crow this day, until you have denied three times that you know me."

Purse, Bag, and Sword

35 He said to them, "When I sent you out without a purse, bag, or sandals, did you lack anything?" They said, "No, not a thing." ³⁶He said to them, "But now, the one who has a purse must take it, and likewise a bag. And the one who has no sword must sell his cloak and buy one. ³⁷For I tell you, this scripture must be fulfilled in me, 'And he was counted among the lawless'; and indeed what is written about me is being fulfilled." ³⁸They said, "Lord, look, here are two swords." He replied, "It is enough."

Jesus Prays on the Mount of Olives

39 He came out and went, as was his custom, to the Mount of Olives; and the disciples

---

a Other ancient authorities read *never eat it again*   *b* Other ancient authorities lack, in whole or in part, verses 19b-20 (*which is given . . . in my blood*)   *c* Or *has obtained permission*   *d* Gk *He*

Prayer of a Servant Leader

Dear Jesus, you made it clear that those who are greatest are the ones who serve, not the ones who have fame, fortune, or authority. Help me to adjust my priorities to put others first. Place within me a genuine desire to serve. Enable me to recognize the daily opportunities I have to reach out to those in need in my family, in my school, and in my community. Guide me as I strive to follow your example to become a servant leader. Amen.

▶ Lk 22:24–27

✝ Catholic Connection

The Eucharist

In Luke's Gospel, Jesus' words from the Last Supper, "Do this in remembrance of me" (22:19), invite us to enter into the mystery of Jesus' life, Passion, death, and Resurrection. These are not just separate events in Jesus' life but rather essential parts of the whole mystery of Christ's redemption and salvation, known as the Paschal mystery. Each Sunday, Catholics gather together with their parish community, the assembled Body of Christ, to celebrate this core mystery of our faith during the Eucharist.

To share in this mystery means we take on the pattern of Jesus' life, Passion, death, and Resurrection as the pattern for our own lives. When we celebrate the Eucharist, we are truly sharing in the sacrifice of Christ. Everything that happens in our lives we take with us to the Eucharist and offer up in the gifts of bread and wine. As the bread and wine become the Body and Blood of Christ, so are our lives transformed by the Spirit of God. As we leave Mass, we enter back into our everyday world more prepared to be Christ's presence for others.

To celebrate the Eucharist is to commit ourselves to a way of life based on the Paschal mystery. Over and over again, we commit ourselves to dying to self and living for others, to putting to death our old ways of sin and living a life of holiness, to embracing the cross so that we might be raised to new life in Christ. Each week, we strive to enter more fully into the Paschal mystery by pledging to live more like Christ the rest of the week ahead. That is why we need to celebrate and attend Mass every week. Each week, as the mystery of God's Revelation is shared and unpacked, we come to a deeper understanding of how pain and death, lovingly embraced, can result in growth and new life. This contradicts the cultural message that we should avoid pain at all costs. We cannot afford to delude ourselves into thinking that growth should be easy, that love should be painless, and that happiness should be constant. By embracing the Paschal mystery as a way of life, we will, more and more, come to live a life of real love.

For the short period of time we gather at the Eucharist each week, we are given time away from "practicing our faith" in order to just *be* the Body of Christ. It is the other 167 hours of the week that we are called to put into practice what we are when we are assembled at Mass. The Eucharist ends with a reminder of our purpose in life—to love and serve God by loving and serving one another as Christ did. Thus, the Eucharist never really ends, for we are always called to be a Eucharistic people.

▶ **Lk 22:14–20**

Catechism, nos. 787–796, 1329, 1396

followed him. ⁴⁰When he reached the place, he said to them, "Pray that you may not come into the time of trial."ᵃ ⁴¹Then he withdrew from them about a stone's throw, knelt down, and prayed, ⁴²"Father, if you are willing, remove this cup from me; yet, not my will but yours be done." ⟦⁴³Then an angel from heaven appeared to him and gave him strength. ⁴⁴In his anguish he prayed more earnestly, and his sweat became like great drops of blood falling down on the ground.⟧ᵇ ⁴⁵When he got up from prayer, he came to the disciples and found them sleeping because of grief, ⁴⁶and he said to them, "Why are you sleeping? Get up and pray that you may not come into the time of trial."ᵃ

The Betrayal and Arrest of Jesus

47 While he was still speaking, suddenly a crowd came, and the one called Judas, one of the twelve, was leading them. He approached Jesus to kiss him; ⁴⁸but Jesus said to him, "Judas, is it with a kiss that you are betraying the Son of Man?" ⁴⁹When those who were around him saw what was coming, they asked, "Lord, should we strike with the sword?" ⁵⁰Then one of them struck the slave of the high priest and cut off his right ear. ⁵¹But Jesus said, "No more of this!" And he touched his ear and healed him. ⁵²Then Jesus said to the chief priests, the officers of the temple police, and the elders who had come for him, "Have you come out with swords and clubs as if I were a bandit? ⁵³When I was with you day after day in the temple, you did not lay hands on me. But this is your hour, and the power of darkness!"

Peter Denies Jesus

54 Then they seized him and led him away, bringing him into the high priest's house. But Peter was following at a distance. ⁵⁵When they had kindled a fire in the middle of the courtyard and sat down together, Peter sat among them. ⁵⁶Then a servant-girl, seeing him in the firelight, stared at him and said, "This man also was with him." ⁵⁷But he denied it, saying, "Woman, I do not know him." ⁵⁸A little later someone else, on seeing him, said, "You also are one of them." But Peter said, "Man, I am not!" ⁵⁹Then about an hour later still another kept insisting, "Surely this man also was with him; for he is a Galilean." ⁶⁰But Peter said, "Man, I do not know what you are talking about!" At that moment, while he was still speaking, the cock crowed. ⁶¹The Lord turned and looked at Peter. Then Peter remembered the word of the Lord, how he had said to him, "Before the cock crows today, you will deny

me three times." ⁶²And he went out and wept bitterly.

The Mocking and Beating of Jesus

63 Now the men who were holding Jesus began to mock him and beat him; ⁶⁴they also blindfolded him and kept asking him, "Prophesy! Who is it that struck you?" ⁶⁵They kept heaping many other insults on him.

Jesus before the Council

66 When day came, the assembly of the elders of the people, both chief priests and scribes, gathered together, and they brought him to their council. ⁶⁷They said, "If you are the Messiah,ᶜ tell us." He replied, "If I tell you, you will not believe; ⁶⁸and if I question you, you will not answer. ⁶⁹But from now on the Son of Man will be seated at the right hand of the power of God." ⁷⁰All of them asked, "Are you, then, the Son of God?" He said to them, "You say that I am." ⁷¹Then they said, "What further testimony do we need? We have heard it ourselves from his own lips!"

Jesus before Pilate

23 Then the assembly rose as a body and brought Jesusᵈ before Pilate. ²They began to accuse him, saying, "We found this man perverting our nation, forbidding us to pay taxes to

---

a Or *into temptation*   b Other ancient authorities lack verses 43 and 44   c Or *the Christ*   d Gk *him*

22:39

Did You Know?

Luke's Account of Jesus' Death

The stories of Jesus' Passion—the name Christians use to describe his suffering and death—differ in all four Gospels. By comparing these stories, we get insight into the authors' portrayal of Jesus. Let's take a closer look at the perspective in the Gospel of Luke.

First, in Jesus' Passion, Luke describes the openness of Gentiles to Jesus' message of salvation. The Roman centurion who praises God at the moment of Jesus' death (see Lk 23:47) is an example.

Second, Luke emphasizes Jesus' compassion and forgiveness, even during his greatest suffering. While carrying the cross, Jesus shows his concern for the women who are following him (see verses 28–31). As he is nailed to the cross, he forgives those responsible (see verse 34). And when one of the criminals asks for Jesus to remember him, Jesus goes beyond that to promise him the first place in Paradise (see verse 43).

Third, whereas Mark portrays Jesus as abandoned in his Passion (see Mk 15:34), Luke surrounds Jesus with sympathetic people: a crowd including the women of Jerusalem (see Lk 23:27), the good thief (see verses 40–41), and the centurion (see verse 47). In Mark, Jesus feels God's absence (see Mk 15:34), but Luke presents Jesus as obedient even at his death, handing his spirit over to God (see Lk 23:46). Mark's emphasis is on Jesus' suffering and loss because he is writing to a community of Christians who are being persecuted. Luke's emphasis is on Jesus' obedience and love for those on the fringe of society because Luke's audience consists of Gentiles, considered outcasts in Jewish tradition. Luke is making it clear in his portrayal of Jesus' Passion that Jesus is the loving, forgiving savior of all humankind.

▶ Lk 22:47—23:56

the emperor, and saying that he himself is the Messiah, a king."*a* *3*Then Pilate asked him, "Are you the king of the Jews?" He answered, "You say so." *4*Then Pilate said to the chief priests and the crowds, "I find no basis for an accusation against this man." *5*But they were insistent and said, "He stirs up the people by teaching throughout all Judea, from Galilee where he began even to this place."

Jesus before Herod

6 When Pilate heard this, he asked whether the man was a Galilean. *7*And when he learned that he was under Herod's jurisdiction, he sent him off to Herod, who was himself in Jerusalem at that time. *8*When Herod saw Jesus, he was very glad, for he had been wanting to see him for a long time, because he had heard about him and was hoping to see him perform some sign. *9*He questioned him at some length, but Jesus*b* gave him no answer. *10*The chief priests and the scribes stood by, vehemently accusing him. *11*Even Herod with his soldiers treated him with contempt and mocked him; then he put an elegant robe on him, and sent him back to Pilate. *12*That same day Herod and Pilate became friends with each other; before this they had been enemies.

Jesus Sentenced to Death

13 Pilate then called together the chief priests, the leaders, and the people, *14*and said to them, "You brought me this man as one who was perverting the people; and here I have examined him in your presence and have not found this man guilty of any of your charges against him. *15*Neither has Herod, for he sent him back to us. Indeed, he has done nothing to deserve death. *16*I will therefore have him flogged and release him."*c*

18 Then they all shouted out together, "Away with this fellow! Release Barabbas for us!" *19*(This was a man who had been put in prison for an insurrection that had taken place in the city, and for murder.) *20*Pilate, wanting to release Jesus, addressed them again; *21*but they kept shouting, "Crucify, crucify him!" *22*A third time he said to them, "Why, what evil has he done? I have found in him no ground for the sentence of death; I will therefore have him flogged and then release him." *23*But they kept urgently demanding with loud shouts that he should be crucified; and their voices prevailed. *24*So Pilate gave his verdict that their demand should be granted. *25*He released

a Or *is an anointed king*   *b* Gk *he*   *c* Here, or after verse 19, other ancient authorities add verse 17, *Now he was obliged to release someone for them at the festival*

Cultural Connection

Salubong

In the Philippines, Catholics celebrate the *Salubong*, the encounter between the risen Jesus and his sorrowful mother on Easter morning. This is based on a tradition that Mary was with the women mentioned in Luke 23:27,55; 24:1,10.

On the day of *Salubong*, at dawn, two groups of worshipers begin walking in two different directions. One group carries a statue of Jesus, and the other group carries a statue of Mary. Both statues are draped in black capes. The people walk through the town and meet on a main street, usually under an arch. A little robed "angel" (a small girl or boy) then removes the sorrowful black capes to reveal joyful white or golden robes on each statue, symbolizing the joy and glory of the Resurrection. Then the entire assembly returns to the church, and Easter Mass begins.

▶ **Lk 23:26–31**

the man they asked for, the one who had been put in prison for insurrection and murder, and he handed Jesus over as they wished.

The Crucifixion of Jesus

26 As they led him away, they seized a man, Simon of Cyrene, who was coming from the country, and they laid the cross on him, and made him carry it behind Jesus. 27A great number of the people followed him, and among them were women who were beating their breasts and wailing for him. 28But Jesus turned to them and said, "Daughters of Jerusalem, do not weep for me, but weep for yourselves and for your children. 29For the days are surely coming when they will say, 'Blessed are the barren, and the wombs that never bore, and the breasts that never nursed.' 30Then they will begin to say to the mountains, 'Fall on us'; and to the hills, 'Cover us.' 31For if they do this when the wood is green, what will happen when it is dry?"

32 Two others also, who were criminals, were led away to be put to death with him. 33When they came to the place that is called The Skull, they crucified Jesus*a* there with the criminals, one on his right and one on his left. ⟦34Then Jesus said, "Father, forgive them; for they do not know what they are doing."⟧*b* And they cast lots to divide his clothing. 35And the people stood by, watching, but the leaders scoffed at him, saying, "He saved others; let him save himself if he is the Messiah*c* of God, his chosen one!" 36The soldiers also mocked him, coming up and offering him sour wine, 37and saying, "If you are the King of the Jews, save yourself!" 38There was also an inscription over him,*d* "This is the King of the Jews."

39 One of the criminals who were hanged there kept deriding*e* him and saying, "Are you not the Messiah?*c* Save yourself and us!" 40But the other rebuked him, saying, "Do you not fear God, since you are under the same sentence of condemnation? 41And we indeed have been condemned justly, for we are getting what we deserve for our deeds, but this man has done nothing wrong." 42Then he said, "Jesus, remember me when you come into*f* your kingdom." 43He replied, "Truly I tell you, today you will be with me in Paradise."

The Death of Jesus

44 It was now about noon, and darkness came over the whole land*g* until three in the afternoon, 45while the sun's light failed;*h* and the curtain of the temple was torn in two. 46Then Jesus, crying with a loud voice, said, "Father, into your hands I commend my spirit." Having said this, he breathed his last. 47When the centurion saw what had taken place, he praised God and said, "Certainly this man was innocent."*i* 48And when all the crowds who had gathered there for this spectacle saw what had taken place, they returned home, beating their breasts. 49But all his acquaintances, including the women who had followed him from Galilee, stood at a distance, watching these things.

---

a Gk *him*   *b* Other ancient authorities lack the sentence *Then Jesus . . . what they are doing*   *c* Or *the Christ*   *d* Other ancient authorities add *written in Greek and Latin and Hebrew* (that is, *Aramaic*)   *e* Or *blaspheming*   *f* Other ancient authorities read *in*   *g* Or *earth*   *h* Or *the sun was eclipsed.* Other ancient authorities read *the sun was darkened*   *i* Or *righteous*

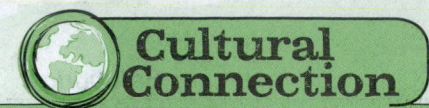

Cultural Connection

Waiting in Darkness

The darkness before Jesus died symbolizes the coming of the day of the Lord (see the introduction to Joel). This Iroquois prayer expresses the feeling of that moment:

We wait in the darkness!
Come, all ye who listen,
Help in our night journey:
Now no sun is shining;
Now no star is glowing;

Come show us the pathway:
The night is not friendly;
The moon has forgot us,
We wait in the darkness!

▶ **Lk 23:44–46**

The Burial of Jesus

50 Now there was a good and righteous man named Joseph, who, though a member of the council, [51]had not agreed to their plan and action. He came from the Jewish town of Arimathea, and he was waiting expectantly for the kingdom of God. [52]This man went to Pilate and asked for the body of Jesus. [53]Then he took it down, wrapped it in a linen cloth, and laid it in a rock-hewn tomb where no one had ever been laid. [54]It was the day of Preparation, and the sabbath was beginning.[a] [55]The women who had come with him from Galilee followed, and they saw the tomb and how his body was laid. [56]Then they returned, and prepared spices and ointments.

On the sabbath they rested according to the commandment.

The Resurrection of Jesus

24 But on the first day of the week, at early dawn, they came to the tomb, taking the spices that they had prepared. [2]They found the stone rolled away from the tomb, [3]but when they went in, they did not find the body.[b] [4]While they were perplexed about this, suddenly two men in dazzling clothes stood beside them. [5]The women[c] were terrified and bowed their faces to the ground, but the men[d] said to them, "Why do you look for the living among the dead? He is not here, but has risen.[e] [6]Remember how he told you, while he was still in Galilee, [7]that the Son of Man must be handed over to sinners, and be crucified, and on the third day rise again." [8]Then they remembered his words, [9]and returning from the tomb, they told all this to the eleven and to all the rest. [10]Now it was Mary Magdalene, Joanna, Mary the mother of James, and the other women with them who told this to the apostles. [11]But these words seemed to them an idle tale, and they did not believe them. [12]But Peter got up and ran to the tomb; stooping and looking in, he saw the linen cloths by themselves; then he went home, amazed at what had happened.[f]

The Walk to Emmaus

13 Now on that same day two of them were going to a village called Emmaus, about seven miles[g] from Jerusalem, [14]and talking with each other about all these things that had happened. [15]While they were talking and discussing, Jesus himself came near and went with them, [16]but their eyes were kept from recognizing him. [17]And he said to them, "What are you discussing with each other while you walk along?" They stood still, looking sad.[h] [18]Then one of them, whose name was Cleopas, answered him, "Are you the only stranger in Jerusalem who does not know the things that have taken place there in these days?" [19]He asked them, "What things?" They replied, "The things about Jesus of Nazareth,[i] who was a prophet mighty in deed and word before God and all the people, [20]and how our chief priests and leaders handed him over to be condemned to death and crucified him. [21]But we had hoped that he was the one to redeem Israel.[j] Yes, and besides all this, it is now the third day since these things took place. [22]Moreover, some women of our group astounded us. They were at the tomb early this morning, [23]and when they

---

a Gk *was dawning*   b Other ancient authorities add *of the Lord Jesus*   c Gk *They*   d Gk *but they*   e Other ancient authorities lack *He is not here, but has risen*   f Other ancient authorities lack verse 12   g Gk *sixty stadia*; other ancient authorities read *a hundred sixty stadia*   h Other ancient authorities read *walk along, looking sad?"*   i Other ancient authorities read *Jesus the Nazorean*   j Or *to set Israel free*

did not find his body there, they came back and told us that they had indeed seen a vision of angels who said that he was alive. ²⁴Some of those who were with us went to the tomb and found it just as the women had said; but they did not see him." ²⁵Then he said to them, "Oh, how foolish you are, and how slow of heart to believe all that the prophets have declared! ²⁶Was it not necessary that the Messiah[a] should suffer these things and then enter into his glory?" ²⁷Then beginning with Moses and all the prophets, he interpreted to them the things about himself in all the scriptures.

28 As they came near the village to which they were going, he walked ahead as if he were going on. ²⁹But they urged him strongly, saying, "Stay with us, because it is almost evening and the day is now nearly over." So he went in to stay with them. ³⁰When he was at the table with them, he took bread, blessed and broke it, and gave it to them. ³¹Then their eyes were opened, and they recognized him; and he vanished from their sight. ³²They said to each other, "Were not our hearts burning within us[b] while he was talking

a Or *the Christ*   b Other ancient authorities lack *within us*

Jesus Is with Us!

A young man was at Mass when he heard Luke 24:13–35. "Pretty strange!" he thought. "Those two guys did not recognize Jesus after they had been with him for three years. I wonder if he looked different after the Resurrection. If I had been walking on the road to Emmaus, I wonder if I would have recognized him. I wonder if people would recognize him today if he came among us." He continued to ponder these thoughts as the Mass continued. He remembered his mother saying that Jesus is present among us every day—in the people we meet, when we gather to pray, and in the Eucharist.

Suddenly, the young man was aware of what the priest was saying: "This is my body which will be given up for you. This is the cup of my blood . . . it will be shed for you and for all. Do this in memory of me."

He looked around the church, noticing people he had not paid attention to before: the family who were refugees from a war-torn country, the little baby who had been born with severe disabilities, the woman who lived alone at ninety-six years old, some other teenagers who were sitting together in the front of church. Somehow, all these different people found love and acceptance in the parish family. "I think I understand now," he thought. "Jesus does look different, but he is here!"

When Jesus joined the disciples at their table and broke the bread, they recognized him. It was at the Eucharist that this young man recognized the presence of Jesus alive today. How about you? When and where do you recognize Jesus? Who in your community reminds you of him the most? How hard is it to recognize Jesus' presence in all people today?

▶ Lk 24:13–35

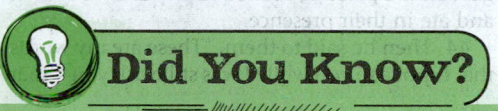

Resurrection Hope

Think about a time when you felt hopeless. Were you depressed? lonely? angry? afraid? These were probably some of the feelings of the women who approached Jesus' tomb on the Sunday morning after his death. Their leader, their teacher, their Lord had just been horribly executed before a huge crowd, and his wonderful vision of love, justice, and forgiveness had been shattered.

But what they encountered in that tomb likely changed their lives forever. The tomb was empty. Two dazzling men appeared and spoke to them. Jesus had indeed risen!

When you think that a situation is hopeless, that no end is in sight, that evil is winning out, remember this story. Along with the Resurrection stories in the other three Gospels, this story is proof that despair and death do not win, that God is at work in the most hopeless situations!

▶ Lk 24:1–12

to us on the road, while he was opening the scriptures to us?" [33]That same hour they got up and returned to Jerusalem; and they found the eleven and their companions gathered together. [34]They were saying, "The Lord has risen indeed, and he has appeared to Simon!" [35]Then they told what had happened on the road, and how he had been made known to them in the breaking of the bread.

Jesus Appears to His Disciples

36 While they were talking about this, Jesus himself stood among them and said to them, "Peace be with you."[a] [37]They were startled and terrified, and thought that they were seeing a ghost. [38]He said to them, "Why are you frightened, and why do doubts arise in your hearts? [39]Look at my hands and my feet; see that it is I myself. Touch me and see; for a ghost does not have flesh and bones as you see that I have." [40]And when he had said this, he showed them his hands and his feet.[b] [41]While in their joy they were disbelieving and still wondering, he said to them, "Have you anything here to eat?" [42]They gave him a piece of broiled fish, [43]and he took it and ate in their presence.

44 Then he said to them, "These are my words that I spoke to you while I was still with you—that everything written about me in the law of Moses, the prophets, and the psalms must be fulfilled." [45]Then he opened their minds to understand the scriptures, [46]and he said to them, "Thus it is written, that the Messiah[c] is to suffer and to rise from the dead on the third day, [47]and that repentance and forgiveness of sins is to be proclaimed in his name to all nations, beginning from Jerusalem. [48]You are witnesses[d] of these things. [49]And see, I am sending upon you what my Father promised; so stay here in the city until you have been clothed with power from on high."

The Ascension of Jesus

50 Then he led them out as far as Bethany, and, lifting up his hands, he blessed them. [51]While he was blessing them, he withdrew from them and was carried up into heaven.[e] [52]And they worshiped him, and[f] returned to Jerusalem with great joy; [53]and they were continually in the temple blessing God.[g]

---

a Other ancient authorities lack *and said to them, "Peace be with you."*   b Other ancient authorities lack verse 40   c Or *the Christ*   d Or *nations. Beginning from Jerusalem* [48]*you are witnesses*   e Other ancient authorities lack *and was carried up into heaven*   f Other ancient authorities lack *worshiped him, and*   g Other ancient authorities add *Amen*

"We are like two peas in a pod." "She's a great shoulder to cry on." "Our friendship is as solid as a rock." People often use analogies or symbolic images in describing their closest relationships. The author of the Gospel of John does this. Throughout the Gospel, symbolic imagery is used to describe the Christian believer's relationship with Jesus. Very different in style from the other Gospels, John's Gospel also gives us the clearest picture of Jesus' unique relationship with God the Father.

At a Glance

- **1:1–18.** prologue: a poem about the Word of God

- **1:19—12:50.** the Book of Signs: Jesus' miracles and teachings, disputes with "the Jews"

- **Chapters 13–20.** the Book of Glory: the Last Supper, and Jesus' suffering, death, and Resurrection

- **Chapter 21.** epilogue: another appearance of the risen Jesus

Quick Facts

Inspired Author: a member of a Christian community possibly founded by the Beloved Disciple
Date Written: most likely from AD 90 to 100
Audience: a Jewish Christian community that may have admitted Gentiles and Samaritans
Image of Jesus: noble and powerful, one with the Father; fully in control of his destiny

In Depth

The Gospel of John begins with symbolic language describing Jesus as the Word, who was with God in the beginning of Creation and who became flesh to live among us. The author goes on to describe Jesus as the light that overcomes darkness. Those who believe in Jesus walk in the light—their lives have meaning and direction. Those who do not believe stumble in the darkness of confusion and sin. John is clear that Jesus is the divine Son of God and that to belong to God, we have to follow Jesus.

In addition to its symbolic language and stress on Jesus' unique relationship with God the Father, John's Gospel differs from the synoptic Gospels—Matthew, Mark, and Luke—in other ways:

In the synoptic Gospels, Jesus' teaching focuses on the Kingdom (or Reign) of God. In John's Gospel, Jesus' teaching stresses relationships: Jesus' relationship with God the Father and our relationship with Jesus.

In the synoptic Gospels, Jesus teaches with parables and performs many healings and miracles. In the Gospel of John, Jesus does not teach by parables. Instead, Jesus performs seven miraculous signs and teaches in long discourses.

John's Gospel has several passages about the role of the Holy Spirit. The synoptic Gospels hardly mention the Holy Spirit.

John's story of Jesus climaxes with the coming of Jesus' "hour," a symbol for Jesus' death and execution. But in the Gospel of John, Jesus' death is not tragic at all—it is his glorious return to the Father. This Gospel assures us that trust in God will pay off in the end: "I will come again and will take you to myself, so that where I am, there you may be also" (14:3).

The Gospel According to **John**

John

The Word Became Flesh

1 In the beginning was the Word, and the Word was with God, and the Word was God. ²He was in the beginning with God. ³All things came into being through him, and without him not one thing came into being. What has come into being ⁴in him was life,ᵃ and the life was the light of all people. ⁵The light shines in the darkness, and the darkness did not overcome it.

6 There was a man sent from God, whose name was John. ⁷He came as a witness to testify to the light, so that all might believe through him. ⁸He himself was not the light, but he came to testify to the light. ⁹The true light, which enlightens everyone, was coming into the world.ᵇ

10 He was in the world, and the world came into being through him; yet the world did not know him. ¹¹He came to what was his own,ᶜ and his own people did not accept him. ¹²But to all who received him, who believed in his name, he gave power to become children of God, ¹³who were born, not of blood or of the will of the flesh or of the will of man, but of God.

14 And the Word became flesh and lived among us, and we have seen his glory, the glory as of a father's only son,ᵈ full of grace and truth. ¹⁵(John testified to him and cried out, "This was he of whom I said, 'He who comes after me ranks ahead of me because he was before me.' ") ¹⁶From his fullness we have all received, grace upon grace. ¹⁷The law indeed was given through Moses; grace and truth came through Jesus Christ. ¹⁸No one has ever seen God. It is God the only Son,ᵉ who is close to the Father's heart,ᶠ who has made him known.

The Testimony of John the Baptist

19 This is the testimony given by John when the Jews sent priests and Levites from Jerusalem to ask him, "Who are you?" ²⁰He confessed and did not deny it, but confessed, "I am not the Messiah."ᵍ ²¹And they asked him, "What then? Are you Elijah?" He said, "I am not." "Are you the prophet?" He answered, "No." ²²Then they said to him, "Who are you? Let us have an answer for those who sent us. What do you say about yourself?" ²³He said,

"I am the voice of one crying out in the
    wilderness,
'Make straight the way of the Lord,' "

as the prophet Isaiah said.

24 Now they had been sent from the Pharisees. ²⁵They asked him, "Why then are you baptizing if you are neither the Messiah,ᵍ nor Elijah, nor the prophet?" ²⁶John answered them, "I baptize with water. Among you stands one whom you do not know, ²⁷the one who is coming after me; I am not worthy to untie the thong of his sandal." ²⁸This took place in Bethany across the Jordan where John was baptizing.

---

a Or ³through him. And without him not one thing came into being that has come into being. ⁴In him was life b Or He was the true light that enlightens everyone coming into the world c Or to his own home d Or the Father's only Son e Other ancient authorities read It is an only Son, God, or It is the only Son f Gk bosom g Or the Christ

The Lamb of God

29 The next day he saw Jesus coming toward him and declared, "Here is the Lamb of God who takes away the sin of the world! [30]This is he of whom I said, 'After me comes a man who ranks ahead of me because he was before me.' [31]I myself did not know him; but I came baptizing with water for this reason, that he might be revealed to Israel." [32]And John testified, "I saw the Spirit descending from heaven like a dove, and it remained on him. [33]I myself did not know him, but the one who sent me to baptize with water said to me, 'He on whom you see the Spirit descend and remain is the one who baptizes with the Holy Spirit.' [34]And I myself have seen and have testified that this is the Son of God."[a]

The First Disciples of Jesus

35 The next day John again was standing with two of his disciples, [36]and as he watched Jesus walk by, he exclaimed, "Look, here is the Lamb of God!" [37]The two disciples heard him say this, and they followed Jesus. [38]When Jesus turned and saw them following, he said to them, "What are you looking for?" They said to him, "Rabbi" (which translated means Teacher), "where are you staying?" [39]He said to them, "Come and see." They came and saw where he was staying, and they remained with him that day. It was about four o'clock in the afternoon. [40]One of the two who heard John speak and followed him was Andrew, Simon Peter's brother. [41]He first found his brother Simon and said to him, "We have found the Messiah" (which is translated Anointed[b]). [42]He brought Simon[c] to Jesus, who looked at him and said, "You are Simon son of John. You are to be called Cephas" (which is translated Peter[d]).

Jesus Calls Philip and Nathanael

43 The next day Jesus decided to go to Galilee. He found Philip and said to him, "Follow me." [44]Now Philip was from Bethsaida, the city of Andrew and Peter. [45]Philip found Nathanael and said to him, "We have found him about whom Moses in the law and also the prophets wrote, Jesus son of Joseph from Nazareth." [46]Nathanael said to him, "Can anything good come out of Nazareth?" Philip said to him, "Come and see." [47]When Jesus saw Nathanael coming toward him, he said of him, "Here is truly an Israelite in whom there is no deceit!" [48]Nathanael asked him, "Where did you get to know me?" Jesus answered, "I saw you under the fig tree before Philip called you." [49]Nathanael replied, "Rabbi,

Live It!

The "Cosmic Christ"

Science fiction or fantasy movies and books often include important eternal beings or powers. The Star Wars series has "the Force." The Chronicles of Narnia, a fantasy series by C. S. Lewis, has Aslan, the noble lion who is the creator and savior of Narnia.

The poem that begins the Gospel of John reads like something from a great science fiction classic. Only in this case, the story is not fiction but God's Revelation! The poem presents Jesus as the Word, who has existed from all time, the one through whom all things came into being. The Scriptures tell us a great mystery here: the man named Jesus, who lived in Nazareth some two thousand years ago, is the creative power of God, who "became flesh and lived among us" (Jn 1:14). No one has ever seen God. But Jesus, the revealer of God, "has made him known" (verse 18) in flesh and blood.

Many people in the Gospel of John do not recognize or accept Jesus, and many people still do not today.

● What does it mean for you to accept Jesus?
● Who or what has helped you to recognize or accept Jesus?

▶ Jn 1:1–18

you are the Son of God! You are the King of Israel!" [50]Jesus answered, "Do you believe because I told you that I saw you under the fig tree? You will see greater things than these." [51]And he said to him, "Very truly, I tell you,[e] you will see heaven opened and the angels of God ascending and descending upon the Son of Man."

The Wedding at Cana

2 On the third day there was a wedding in Cana of Galilee, and the mother of Jesus was there. [2]Jesus and his disciples had also been invited to the wedding. [3]When the wine gave out, the mother of Jesus said to him, "They have no

a Other ancient authorities read *is God's chosen one*   b Or *Christ*
c Gk *him*   d From the word for *rock* in Aramaic (*kepha*) and
Greek (*petra*), respectively   e Both instances of the Greek word
for *you* in this verse are plural

wine." ⁴And Jesus said to her, "Woman, what concern is that to you and to me? My hour has not yet come." ⁵His mother said to the servants, "Do whatever he tells you." ⁶Now standing there were six stone water jars for the Jewish rites of purification, each holding twenty or thirty gallons. ⁷Jesus said to them, "Fill the jars with water." And they filled them up to the brim. ⁸He said to them, "Now draw some out, and take it to the chief steward." So they took it. ⁹When the steward tasted the water that had become wine, and did not know where it came from (though the servants who had drawn the water knew), the steward called the bridegroom ¹⁰and said to him, "Everyone serves the good wine first, and then the inferior wine after the guests have become drunk. But you have kept the good wine until now." ¹¹Jesus did this, the first of his signs, in

The First Sign

If there is one day that people want to go exactly as planned, it's usually a wedding day. Months of planning, and usually lots of money, go into ensuring the big day will go smoothly. Imagine if there wasn't enough food to feed everyone! How embarrassing! Imagine if the cake never arrived, or if there wasn't enough wine for all the guests!

This is exactly what happens at the wedding at Cana. Jesus is there, along with his followers and his mother, Mary. Mary mentions to Jesus that they are running out of wine. Take a moment to study Jesus' reaction to his mother's comment. Does it seem a bit strange? Why do you think Jesus hesitates? Why does Mary persist?

In the Gospel of John, this is the first of seven miracles, or as John calls them, signs, that Jesus performs. Why do you think this one is first? What happens because of this miracle? What might it be a sign of? As you read further in John's Gospel, pay attention to what each of Jesus' seven miracles teaches us about Jesus and his mission.

▶ Jn 2:1–11

Cana of Galilee, and revealed his glory; and his disciples believed in him.

12 After this he went down to Capernaum with his mother, his brothers, and his disciples; and they remained there a few days.

Jesus Cleanses the Temple

13 The Passover of the Jews was near, and Jesus went up to Jerusalem. ¹⁴In the temple he found people selling cattle, sheep, and doves, and the money changers seated at their tables. ¹⁵Making a whip of cords, he drove all of them out of the temple, both the sheep and the cattle. He also poured out the coins of the money changers and overturned their tables. ¹⁶He told those who were selling the doves, "Take these things out of here! Stop making my Father's house a marketplace!" ¹⁷His disciples remembered that it was written, "Zeal for your house will consume me." ¹⁸The Jews then said to him, "What sign can you show us for doing this?" ¹⁹Jesus answered them, "Destroy this temple, and in three days I will raise it up." ²⁰The Jews then said, "This temple has been under construction for forty-six years, and will you raise it up in three days?" ²¹But he was speaking of the temple of his body. ²²After he was raised from the dead, his disciples remembered that he had said this; and they believed the scripture and the word that Jesus had spoken.

23 When he was in Jerusalem during the Passover festival, many believed in his name because they saw the signs that he was doing. ²⁴But Jesus on his part would not entrust himself to them,

2:1–12

because he knew all people ²⁵and needed no one to testify about anyone; for he himself knew what was in everyone.

Nicodemus Visits Jesus

3 Now there was a Pharisee named Nicodemus, a leader of the Jews. ²He came to Jesus*a* by night and said to him, "Rabbi, we know that you are a teacher who has come from God; for no one can do these signs that you do apart from the presence of God." ³Jesus answered him, "Very truly, I tell you, no one can see the kingdom of God without being born from above."*b* ⁴Nicodemus said to him, "How can anyone be born after having grown old? Can one enter a second time into the mother's womb and be born?" ⁵Jesus answered, "Very truly, I tell you, no one can enter the kingdom of God without being born of water and Spirit. ⁶What is born of the flesh is flesh, and what is born of the Spirit is spirit.*c* ⁷Do not be astonished that I said to you, 'You*d* must be born from above.'*e* ⁸The wind*c* blows where it chooses, and you hear the sound of it, but you do not know where it comes from or where it goes. So it is with everyone who is born of the Spirit." ⁹Nicodemus said to him, "How can these things be?" ¹⁰Jesus answered him, "Are you a teacher of Israel, and yet you do not understand these things?

11 "Very truly, I tell you, we speak of what we know and testify to what we have seen; yet you*f* do not receive our testimony. ¹²If I have told you about earthly things and you do not believe, how can you believe if I tell you about heavenly things? ¹³No one has ascended into heaven except the one who descended from heaven, the Son of Man.*g* ¹⁴And just as Moses lifted up the serpent in the wilderness, so must the Son of Man be lifted up, ¹⁵that whoever believes in him may have eternal life.*h*

16 "For God so loved the world that he gave his only Son, so that everyone who believes in him may not perish but may have eternal life.

17 "Indeed, God did not send the Son into the world to condemn the world, but in order that the world might be saved through him. ¹⁸Those who

---

a Gk *him*   *b* Or *born anew*   *c* The same Greek word means both *wind* and *spirit*   *d* The Greek word for *you* here is plural   *e* Or *anew*   *f* The Greek word for *you* here and in verse 12 is plural   *g* Other ancient authorities add *who is in heaven*   *h* Some interpreters hold that the quotation concludes with verse 15

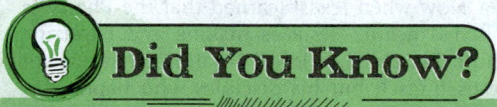

"The Jews" in the Gospel of John

When you read the Gospel of John, you may notice that the Gospel writer often makes references to "the Jews." They are often portrayed questioning (see Jn 2:18) or challenging Jesus. Around the time John was written, Christian Jews were being forcibly removed from Jewish synagogues (see 16:1–4). With this rivalry in the background, the Gospel writer sometimes lumps all Jews together, portraying them as the "bad guys." Christian churches teach that we should not take John's references to "the Jews" as a basis for prejudice or anger against Jewish people.

▶ Jn 2:18–20

Nic at Night

Nicodemus, a Jewish teacher with a high position of leadership, is meeting secretly with Jesus. Nicodemus has been waiting for a sign that God's promise of salvation through a savior will happen in his lifetime. He senses that maybe Jesus is this savior. But he does not yet believe in Jesus, as is emphasized by his coming to Jesus "by night" (Jn 3:2). Speaking symbolically, Jesus outlines what it takes for salvation: to believe in Jesus as the one sent by God and to be born again through baptism and the Holy Spirit. The same is true for people today.

Nicodemus most likely knew that to accept Jesus publicly would put him in bad standing with the other Jewish leaders. Sometimes, we must make choices that might make us look foolish to others.

- How hard would it be for you to express belief in Jesus publicly?
- Are you a believer in the night or in the light?

▶ Jn 3:1–21

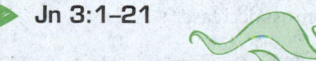

Cultural Connection

This Is Christmas

This poem, by Masao and Fumiko Takenaka of Japan, is a reflection on Jesus as "living water" (Jn 4:10):

> One who said I am the
>   eternal water
> Dwelt among us
> Living with us
> Sustaining us

This is Christmas.
To receive a cup of living
    water
Is not only to cleanse
    ourselves
But also to cleanse all the
    waters,
River and well, lake and
    ocean,

And to share them with all.
This is Christmas.

[From Tirabassi and Eddy, editors, *Gifts of Many Cultures*, p. 144]

▶ Jn 4:1–15

---

believe in him are not condemned; but those who do not believe are condemned already, because they have not believed in the name of the only Son of God. [19]And this is the judgment, that the light has come into the world, and people loved darkness rather than light because their deeds were evil. [20]For all who do evil hate the light and do not come to the light, so that their deeds may not be exposed. [21]But those who do what is true come to the light, so that it may be clearly seen that their deeds have been done in God."[a]

Jesus and John the Baptist

[22] After this Jesus and his disciples went into the Judean countryside, and he spent some time there with them and baptized. [23]John also was baptizing at Aenon near Salim because water was abundant there; and people kept coming and were being baptized [24]—John, of course, had not yet been thrown into prison.

[25] Now a discussion about purification arose between John's disciples and a Jew.[b] [26]They came to John and said to him, "Rabbi, the one who was with you across the Jordan, to whom you testified, here he is baptizing, and all are going to him." [27]John answered, "No one can receive anything except what has been given from heaven. [28]You yourselves are my witnesses that I said, 'I am not the Messiah,[c] but I have been sent ahead of him.' [29]He who has the bride is the bridegroom. The friend of the bridegroom, who stands and hears him, rejoices greatly at the bridegroom's voice. For this reason my joy has been fulfilled. [30]He must increase, but I must decrease."[d]

The One Who Comes from Heaven

[31] The one who comes from above is above all; the one who is of the earth belongs to the earth and speaks about earthly things. The one who comes from heaven is above all. [32]He testifies to what he has seen and heard, yet no one accepts his testimony. [33]Whoever has accepted his testimony has certified[e] this, that God is true. [34]He whom God has sent speaks the words of God, for he gives the Spirit without measure. [35]The Father loves the Son and has placed all things in his hands. [36]Whoever believes in the Son has eternal life; whoever disobeys the Son will not see life, but must endure God's wrath.

Jesus and the Woman of Samaria

[4] Now when Jesus[f] learned that the Pharisees had heard, "Jesus is making and baptizing more disciples than John" [2]—although it was not Jesus himself but his disciples who baptized— [3]he left Judea and started back to Galilee. [4]But he had to go through Samaria. [5]So he came to a Samaritan city called Sychar, near the plot of ground that Jacob had given to his son Joseph. [6]Jacob's well was there, and Jesus, tired out by his journey, was sitting by the well. It was about noon.

[7] A Samaritan woman came to draw water, and Jesus said to her, "Give me a drink." [8](His disciples had gone to the city to buy food.) [9]The Samaritan woman said to him, "How is it that you, a Jew, ask a drink of me, a woman of Samaria?" (Jews do not share things in common with Samaritans.)[g] [10]Jesus answered her, "If you knew the gift of God, and who it is that is saying to you, 'Give me a drink,' you would have

---

a Some interpreters hold that the quotation concludes with verse 15   *b* Other ancient authorities read *the Jews*   *c* Or *the Christ* *d* Some interpreters hold that the quotation continues through verse 36   *e* Gk *set a seal to*   *f* Other ancient authorities read *the Lord* *g* Other ancient authorities lack this sentence

asked him, and he would have given you living water." ¹¹The woman said to him, "Sir, you have no bucket, and the well is deep. Where do you get that living water? ¹²Are you greater than our ancestor Jacob, who gave us the well, and with his sons and his flocks drank from it?" ¹³Jesus said to her, "Everyone who drinks of this water will be thirsty again, ¹⁴but those who drink of the water that I will give them will never be thirsty. The water that I will give will become in them a spring of water gushing up to eternal life." ¹⁵The woman said to him, "Sir, give me this water, so that I may never be thirsty or have to keep coming here to draw water."

16 Jesus said to her, "Go, call your husband, and come back." ¹⁷The woman answered him, "I have no husband." Jesus said to her, "You are right in saying, 'I have no husband'; ¹⁸for you have had five husbands, and the one you have now is not your husband. What you have said is true!" ¹⁹The woman said to him, "Sir, I see that you are a prophet. ²⁰Our ancestors worshiped on this mountain, but you*a* say that the place where people must worship is in Jerusalem." ²¹Jesus said to her, "Woman, believe me, the hour is coming when you will worship the Father neither on this mountain nor in Jerusalem. ²²You worship what you do not know; we worship what we know, for salvation is from the Jews. ²³But the hour is coming, and is now here, when the true worshipers will worship the Father in spirit and truth, for the Father seeks such as these to worship him. ²⁴God is spirit, and those who worship him must worship in spirit and truth." ²⁵The woman said to him, "I know that Messiah is coming" (who is called Christ). "When he comes, he will proclaim all things to us." ²⁶Jesus said to her, "I am he,*b* the one who is speaking to you."

27 Just then his disciples came. They were astonished that he was speaking with a woman,

---

a The Greek word for *you* here and in verses 21 and 22 is plural
b Gk *I am*

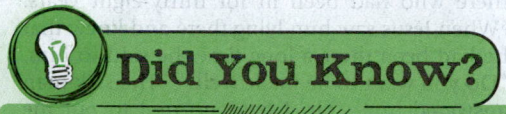

Did You Know?

Why Are the Disciples Surprised?

The disciples "were astonished that he [Jesus] was speaking with a woman" (Jn 4:27). For several reasons, it was unusual for Jesus to be talking to her. First, in first-century Israel, men did not talk to women, especially strangers, in public places. Second, Jews did not talk to Samaritans (see "Who Belongs and Who Does Not?" near Ezra, chapters 9–10, and "Discrimination in Jesus' Time," near Lk 10:25–37), who were not considered to be real Jews (see Jn 4:20). And finally, the woman with whom Jesus was speaking was accused of having had five husbands. Some scholars think that "five husbands" is symbolic of the five books of the Torah that the Samaritans revered. On the other hand, most first-century women did not have the right to divorce, only their husbands did. So it may be that she was just terribly unlucky having been widowed or dismissed numerous times and now taken in as a servant in someone's household.

This episode is one more example in the Gospel of John that shows Jesus is not bound by customs and stereotypes when the message of the Gospel is at stake.

▶ Jn 4:1–42

Pray It!

How Deep Is Your Well?

In John 4:1–42, Jesus engages a Samaritan woman in conversation. She has no idea who Jesus is and what living water he is referring to, but she stands and listens. She is changed as a result. She comes to believe in Jesus and goes to tell others about the Messiah. John uses her as a role model for those who believe.

Look inside the well of faith within you. How deep is that well? Do you thirst for a deeper relationship with Jesus? Are you ready to share the Good News with others? Jesus invites each of us to join with him in a personal relationship. All we have to do is ask. Begin your relationship with Jesus by praying:

Jesus, you are the Messiah, the anointed one. I am thirsty. Quench my thirst.

▶ Jn 4:1–42

but no one said, "What do you want?" or, "Why are you speaking with her?" ²⁸Then the woman left her water jar and went back to the city. She said to the people, ²⁹"Come and see a man who told me everything I have ever done! He cannot be the Messiah,ᵃ can he?" ³⁰They left the city and were on their way to him.

31 Meanwhile the disciples were urging him, "Rabbi, eat something." ³²But he said to them, "I have food to eat that you do not know about." ³³So the disciples said to one another, "Surely no one has brought him something to eat?" ³⁴Jesus said to them, "My food is to do the will of him who sent me and to complete his work. ³⁵Do you not say, 'Four months more, then comes the harvest'? But I tell you, look around you, and see how the fields are ripe for harvesting. ³⁶The reaper is already receivingᵇ wages and is gathering fruit for eternal life, so that sower and reaper may rejoice together. ³⁷For here the saying holds true, 'One sows and another reaps.' ³⁸I sent you to reap that for which you did not labor. Others have labored, and you have entered into their labor."

39 Many Samaritans from that city believed in him because of the woman's testimony, "He told me everything I have ever done." ⁴⁰So when the Samaritans came to him, they asked him to stay with them; and he stayed there two days. ⁴¹And many more believed because of his word. ⁴²They said to the woman, "It is no longer because of what you said that we believe, for we have heard for ourselves, and we know that this is truly the Savior of the world."

Jesus Returns to Galilee

43 When the two days were over, he went from that place to Galilee ⁴⁴(for Jesus himself had testified that a prophet has no honor in the prophet's own country). ⁴⁵When he came to Galilee, the Galileans welcomed him, since they had seen all that he had done in Jerusalem at the festival; for they too had gone to the festival.

Jesus Heals an Official's Son

46 Then he came again to Cana in Galilee where he had changed the water into wine. Now there was a royal official whose son lay ill in Capernaum. ⁴⁷When he heard that Jesus had come from Judea to Galilee, he went and begged him to come down and heal his son, for he was at the point of death. ⁴⁸Then Jesus said to him, "Unless youᶜ see signs and wonders you will not believe." ⁴⁹The official said to him, "Sir, come down before my little boy dies." ⁵⁰Jesus said to him, "Go; your son will live." The man believed the word

that Jesus spoke to him and started on his way. ⁵¹As he was going down, his slaves met him and told him that his child was alive. ⁵²So he asked them the hour when he began to recover, and they said to him, "Yesterday at one in the afternoon the fever left him." ⁵³The father realized that this was the hour when Jesus had said to him, "Your son will live." So he himself believed, along with his whole household. ⁵⁴Now this was the second sign that Jesus did after coming from Judea to Galilee.

Jesus Heals on the Sabbath

5 After this there was a festival of the Jews, and Jesus went up to Jerusalem.

2 Now in Jerusalem by the Sheep Gate there is a pool, called in Hebrewᵈ Beth-zatha,ᵉ which has five porticoes. ³In these lay many invalids— blind, lame, and paralyzed.ᶠ ⁵One man was there who had been ill for thirty-eight years. ⁶When Jesus saw him lying there and knew that he had been there a long time, he said to him, "Do you want to be made well?" ⁷The sick man answered him, "Sir, I have no one to put me into the pool when the water is stirred up; and while I am making my way, someone else steps down ahead of me." ⁸Jesus said to him, "Stand up, take your mat and walk." ⁹At once the man was made well, and he took up his mat and began to walk.

Now that day was a sabbath. ¹⁰So the Jews said to the man who had been cured, "It is the sabbath; it is not lawful for you to carry your mat." ¹¹But he answered them, "The man who made me well said to me, 'Take up your mat and walk.'" ¹²They asked him, "Who is the man who said to you, 'Take it up and walk'?" ¹³Now the man who had been healed did not know who it was, for Jesus had disappeared inᵍ the crowd that was there. ¹⁴Later Jesus found him in the temple and said to him, "See, you have been made well! Do not sin any more, so that nothing worse happens to you." ¹⁵The man went away and told the Jews that it was Jesus who had made him well. ¹⁶Therefore the Jews started persecuting Jesus, because he was doing such things on the sabbath. ¹⁷But Jesus answered them, "My Father is still working, and

a Or the Christ b Or ³⁵. . . the fields are already ripe for harvesting. ³⁶The reaper is receiving c Both instances of the Greek word for you in this verse are plural d That is, Aramaic
e Other ancient authorities read Bethesda, others Bethsaida
f Other ancient authorities add, wholly or in part, waiting for the stirring of the water; ⁴for an angel of the Lord went down at certain seasons into the pool, and stirred up the water; whoever stepped in first after the stirring of the water was made well from whatever disease that person had. g Or had left because of

I also am working." [18]For this reason the Jews were seeking all the more to kill him, because he was not only breaking the sabbath, but was also calling God his own Father, thereby making himself equal to God.

The Authority of the Son

19 Jesus said to them, "Very truly, I tell you, the Son can do nothing on his own, but only what he sees the Father doing; for whatever the Father[a] does, the Son does likewise. [20]The Father loves the Son and shows him all that he himself is doing; and he will show him greater works than these, so that you will be astonished. [21]Indeed, just as the Father raises the dead and gives them life, so also the Son gives life to whomever he wishes. [22]The Father judges no one but has given all judgment to the Son, [23]so that all may honor the Son just as they honor the Father. Anyone who does not honor the Son does not honor the Father who sent him. [24]Very truly, I tell you, anyone who hears my word and believes him who sent me has eternal life, and does not come under judgment, but has passed from death to life.

25 "Very truly, I tell you, the hour is coming, and is now here, when the dead will hear the voice of the Son of God, and those who hear will live. [26]For just as the Father has life in himself, so he has granted the Son also to have life in himself; [27]and he has given him authority to execute judgment, because he is the Son of Man. [28]Do not be astonished at this; for the hour is coming when all who are in their graves will hear his voice [29]and will come out—those who have done good, to the resurrection of life, and those who have done evil, to the resurrection of condemnation.

Witnesses to Jesus

30 "I can do nothing on my own. As I hear, I judge; and my judgment is just, because I seek to do not my own will but the will of him who sent me.

31 "If I testify about myself, my testimony is not true. [32]There is another who testifies on my behalf, and I know that his testimony to me is true. [33]You sent messengers to John, and he testified to the truth. [34]Not that I accept such human testimony, but I say these things so that you may be saved. [35]He was a burning and shining lamp, and you were willing to rejoice for a while in his light. [36]But I have a testimony greater than John's. The works that the Father has given me to complete, the very works that I am doing, testify on my behalf that the Father has sent me. [37]And

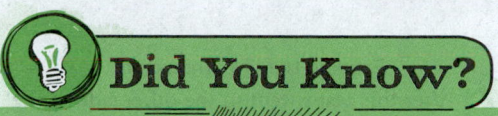

Did You Know?

"I Am" Sayings of Jesus

The Gospel of John contains a whole series of "I am" sayings as a way for Jesus to explain his role as the Messiah. For example:

- "I am the bread of life" (6:35).
- "I am the light of the world" (8:12).
- "I am the gate for the sheep" (10:7).
- "I am the good shepherd" (10:11).
- "I am the resurrection and the life" (11:25).
- "I am the way, and the truth, and the life" (14:6).
- "I am the vine, you are the branches" (15:5).

The "I am" sayings are also a means of establishing the divine nature of Jesus. Jesus' use of "I am" is similar to the revelation of God's name to Moses at the burning bush (see Ex 3:14). Ironically, in John, the Jewish leaders are correct in thinking that Jesus is equating himself with God (see 5:18). But they are wrong in not recognizing that Jesus is right!

▶ Jn 5:16–18

JN

the Father who sent me has himself testified on my behalf. You have never heard his voice or seen his form, [38]and you do not have his word abiding in you, because you do not believe him whom he has sent.

39 "You search the scriptures because you think that in them you have eternal life; and it is they that testify on my behalf. [40]Yet you refuse to come to me to have life. [41]I do not accept glory from human beings. [42]But I know that you do not have the love of God in[b] you. [43]I have come in my Father's name, and you do not accept me; if another comes in his own name, you will accept him. [44]How can you believe when you accept glory from one another and do not seek the glory that comes from the one who alone is God? [45]Do not think that I will accuse you before the Father; your accuser is Moses, on whom you have set your hope. [46]If you believed Moses, you would believe me, for he wrote about me. [47]But if you do not believe what he wrote, how will you believe what I say?"

---

a Gk that one *b* Or among

Feeding the Five Thousand

6 After this Jesus went to the other side of the Sea of Galilee, also called the Sea of Tiberias.[a] ²A large crowd kept following him, because they saw the signs that he was doing for the sick. ³Jesus went up the mountain and sat down there with his disciples. ⁴Now the Passover, the festival of the Jews, was near. ⁵When he looked up and saw a large crowd coming toward him, Jesus said to Philip, "Where are we to buy bread for these people to eat?" ⁶He said this to test him, for he himself knew what he was going to do. ⁷Philip answered him, "Six months' wages[b] would not buy enough bread for each of them to get a little." ⁸One of his disciples, Andrew, Simon Peter's brother, said to him, ⁹"There is a boy here who has five barley loaves and two fish. But what are they among so many people?" ¹⁰Jesus said, "Make the people sit down." Now there was a

Pray It!

A Little Gift Goes a Long Way

God, could you use me like the boy who helped feed the five thousand? Out of the thousands of people gathered to see you, you chose a young person, took his five loaves and two fish, and made sure thousands had more than their fill to eat (see Jn 6:1–13).

I wonder how those people felt when that little bit of food was offered by a youth? Were they embarrassed by the boy's foolishness? Or did they feel guilty that they had not offered their own food? Regardless, you accepted the gift and did fantastic things with it.

Could you do the same with me? Could you take my simple gifts and do wondrous things with them? I'm just afraid that my gifts will be rejected.

Help me to take the risk and let you use the gifts I have, trusting that it doesn't matter what other people think. Even if things don't work out as I plan, I'll trust that you are in charge and know better than I do. Amen.

▶ **Jn 6:1–14**

great deal of grass in the place; so they[c] sat down, about five thousand in all. ¹¹Then Jesus took the loaves, and when he had given thanks, he distributed them to those who were seated; so also the fish, as much as they wanted. ¹²When they were satisfied, he told his disciples, "Gather up the fragments left over, so that nothing may be lost." ¹³So they gathered them up, and from the fragments of the five barley loaves, left by those who had eaten, they filled twelve baskets. ¹⁴When the people saw the sign that he had done, they began to say, "This is indeed the prophet who is to come into the world."

15 When Jesus realized that they were about to come and take him by force to make him king, he withdrew again to the mountain by himself.

Jesus Walks on the Water

16 When evening came, his disciples went down to the sea, ¹⁷got into a boat, and started across the sea to Capernaum. It was now dark, and Jesus had not yet come to them. ¹⁸The sea became rough because a strong wind was blowing. ¹⁹When they had rowed about three or four miles,[d] they saw Jesus walking on the sea and coming near the boat, and they were terrified. ²⁰But he said to them, "It is I;[e] do not be afraid." ²¹Then they wanted to take him into the boat, and immediately the boat reached the land toward which they were going.

The Bread from Heaven

22 The next day the crowd that had stayed on the other side of the sea saw that there had been only one boat there. They also saw that Jesus had not got into the boat with his disciples, but that his disciples had gone away alone. ²³Then some boats from Tiberias came near the place where they had eaten the bread after the Lord had given thanks.[f] ²⁴So when the crowd saw that neither Jesus nor his disciples were there, they themselves got into the boats and went to Capernaum looking for Jesus.

25 When they found him on the other side of the sea, they said to him, "Rabbi, when did you come here?" ²⁶Jesus answered them, "Very truly, I tell you, you are looking for me, not because you saw signs, but because you ate your fill of the loaves. ²⁷Do not work for the food that perishes, but for the food that endures for eternal life, which the Son of Man will give you. For it is on him that God the Father has set his

---

a Gk of Galilee of Tiberias   b Gk Two hundred denarii; the denarius was the usual day's wage for a laborer   c Gk the men d Gk about twenty-five or thirty stadia   e Gk I am   f Other ancient authorities lack *after the Lord had given thanks*

JN

seal." ²⁸Then they said to him, "What must we do to perform the works of God?" ²⁹Jesus answered them, "This is the work of God, that you believe in him whom he has sent." ³⁰So they said to him, "What sign are you going to give us then, so that we may see it and believe you? What work are you performing? ³¹Our ancestors ate the manna in the wilderness; as it is written, 'He gave them bread from heaven to eat.'" ³²Then Jesus said to them, "Very truly, I tell you, it was not Moses who gave you the bread from heaven, but it is my Father who gives you the true bread from heaven. ³³For the bread of God is that which*ᵃ* comes down from heaven and gives life to the world." ³⁴They said to him, "Sir, give us this bread always."

35 Jesus said to them, "I am the bread of life. Whoever comes to me will never be hungry, and whoever believes in me will never be thirsty. ³⁶But I said to you that you have seen me and yet do not believe. ³⁷Everything that the Father gives me will come to me, and anyone who comes to me I will never drive away; ³⁸for I have come down from heaven, not to do my own will, but the will of him who sent me. ³⁹And this is the will of him who sent me, that I should lose nothing of all that he has given me, but raise it up on the last day. ⁴⁰This is indeed the will of my Father, that all who see the Son and believe in him may have eternal life; and I will raise them up on the last day."

41 Then the Jews began to complain about him because he said, "I am the bread that came down from heaven." ⁴²They were saying, "Is not this Jesus, the son of Joseph, whose father and mother we know? How can he now say, 'I have come down from heaven'?" ⁴³Jesus answered them, "Do not complain among yourselves. ⁴⁴No one can come to me unless drawn by the Father who sent me; and I will raise that person up on the last day. ⁴⁵It is written in the prophets, 'And they shall all be taught by God.' Everyone who has heard and learned from the Father comes to me. ⁴⁶Not that anyone has seen the Father except the one who is from God; he has seen the Father. ⁴⁷Very truly, I tell you, whoever believes has eternal life. ⁴⁸I am the bread of life. ⁴⁹Your ancestors ate the manna in the wilderness, and they died. ⁵⁰This is the bread that comes down from heaven, so that one may eat of it and not die. ⁵¹I am the living bread that came down from heaven. Whoever eats of this bread will live forever; and the bread that I will give for the life of the world is my flesh."

52 The Jews then disputed among themselves, saying, "How can this man give us his flesh to eat?" ⁵³So Jesus said to them, "Very truly, I tell you, unless you eat the flesh of the Son of Man and drink his blood, you have no life in you. ⁵⁴Those who eat my flesh and drink my blood have eternal life, and I will raise them up on the last day; ⁵⁵for my flesh is true food and my blood is true drink. ⁵⁶Those who eat my flesh and drink my blood abide in me, and I in them. ⁵⁷Just as the living Father sent me, and I live because of the Father, so whoever eats me will live because of me. ⁵⁸This is the bread that came down from

Pray It!

The Eucharist

Jesus calls himself the "bread of life" [Jn 6:35]. Some type of bread is part of the basic diet of almost every culture. Thus, in a symbolic way, Jesus is telling us that he is part of the basic diet for spiritual life. And just as bread is shared and valued in every culture, Jesus shares himself with all people who are willing to believe.

Many of Jesus' early followers were troubled when he taught that they must eat his flesh and drink his blood in order to have true life (see verses 56–60). The confusion and arguing among his listeners are understandable; his words must have sounded strange. Yet, this teaching about the Body and Blood of Christ (which is portrayed in the Last Supper in Matthew, Mark, and Luke) is central to the Catholic faith. Catholics believe that Jesus is really present with us and nourishes us when we celebrate the Eucharist together, the bread and wine being changed into the Body and Blood of Christ.

In your prayer, reflect or journal on the following questions:

● How is Jesus a source of nourishment for you?

● How does celebrating the Eucharist help you to recognize more clearly Jesus' presence?

● How are you called to be the Body and Blood of Christ to the world around you?

▶ John, chapter 6

ᵃ Or he who

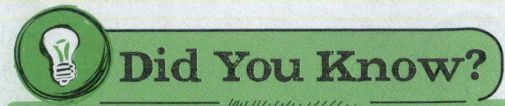

Did You Know?

Jesus Fulfills Jewish Feasts

In John, chapters 5–10, several references are made to four Old Testament feasts, which are also called festivals. On each feast, the author of John has Jesus say or do something that cleverly indicates he is the fulfillment of the feast's intent.

In chapter 5, after healing on the *Sabbath*, Jesus says, "My Father is still working, and I also am working" (verse 17). Essentially, he is declaring himself equal to God. In chapter 6, near the feast of the *Passover* (see "The Passover," near Ex 12:14–28), Jesus feeds five thousand people and teaches that he is the bread of life. The implication is that although Moses gave the Israelites manna during the Exodus, God gives a greater gift in Jesus, who is the bread of everlasting life—the Eucharist.

Chapters 7–9 of John refer to the *feast of Booths*, also called Tabernacles. This is a harvest festival that lasts a whole week. Two of the main symbols of the feast of Booths are water and light. Jesus proclaims himself living water (see 7:38) and the light of the world (see 8:12).

Finally, the *feast of the Dedication*, sometimes called Hanukkah (see "Hanukkah," near 1 Macc 4:52–59), is mentioned in chapter 10. During this festival, which celebrates the dedication of the Temple, Jesus claims to be the one who is consecrated and sent into the world (see verse 36). In fulfilling these feasts, Jesus' saving mission is made clear. But his actions also lead to continued conflicts with the Jewish leaders.

▶ John, chapters 5–10

heaven, not like that which your ancestors ate, and they died. But the one who eats this bread will live forever." ⁵⁹He said these things while he was teaching in the synagogue at Capernaum.

The Words of Eternal Life

60 When many of his disciples heard it, they said, "This teaching is difficult; who can accept it?" ⁶¹But Jesus, being aware that his disciples were complaining about it, said to them, "Does this offend you? ⁶²Then what if you were to see the Son of Man ascending to where he was before? ⁶³It is the spirit that gives life; the flesh is useless. The words that I have spoken to you are spirit and life. ⁶⁴But among you there are some who do not believe." For Jesus knew from the first who were the ones that did not believe, and who was the one that would betray him. ⁶⁵And he said, "For this reason I have told you that no one can come to me unless it is granted by the Father."

66 Because of this many of his disciples turned back and no longer went about with him. ⁶⁷So Jesus asked the twelve, "Do you also wish to go away?" ⁶⁸Simon Peter answered him, "Lord, to whom can we go? You have the words of eternal life. ⁶⁹We have come to believe and know that you are the Holy One of God."ᵃ ⁷⁰Jesus answered them, "Did I not choose you, the twelve? Yet one of you is a devil." ⁷¹He was speaking of Judas son of Simon Iscariot,ᵇ for he, though one of the twelve, was going to betray him.

The Unbelief of Jesus' Brothers

7 After this Jesus went about in Galilee. He did not wishᶜ to go about in Judea because the Jews were looking for an opportunity to kill him. ²Now the Jewish festival of Boothsᵈ was near. ³So his brothers said to him, "Leave here and go to Judea so that your disciples also may see the works you are doing; ⁴for no one who wantsᵉ to be widely known acts in secret. If you do these things, show yourself to the world." ⁵(For not even his brothers believed in him.) ⁶Jesus said to them, "My time has not yet come, but your time is always here. ⁷The world cannot hate you, but it hates me because I testify against it that its works are evil. ⁸Go to the festival yourselves. I am notᶠ going to this festival, for my time has not yet fully come." ⁹After saying this, he remained in Galilee.

Jesus at the Festival of Booths

10 But after his brothers had gone to the festival, then he also went, not publicly but as it wereᵍ in secret. ¹¹The Jews were looking for him at the festival and saying, "Where is he?" ¹²And there was considerable complaining about him among the crowds. While some were saying, "He is a good man," others were saying, "No, he is

---

a Other ancient authorities read *the Christ, the Son of the living God*   b Other ancient authorities read *Judas Iscariot son of Simon;* others, *Judas son of Simon from Karyot* (Kerioth)   c Other ancient authorities read *was not at liberty*   d Or *Tabernacles*   e Other ancient authorities read *wants it*   f Other ancient authorities add *yet*   g Other ancient authorities lack *as it were*

deceiving the crowd." [13]Yet no one would speak openly about him for fear of the Jews.

14　About the middle of the festival Jesus went up into the temple and began to teach. [15]The Jews were astonished at it, saying, "How does this man have such learning,[a] when he has never been taught?" [16]Then Jesus answered them, "My teaching is not mine but his who sent me. [17]Anyone who resolves to do the will of God will know whether the teaching is from God or whether I am speaking on my own. [18]Those who speak on their own seek their own glory; but the one who seeks the glory of him who sent him is true, and there is nothing false in him.

19　"Did not Moses give you the law? Yet none of you keeps the law. Why are you looking for an opportunity to kill me?" [20]The crowd answered, "You have a demon! Who is trying to kill you?" [21]Jesus answered them, "I performed one work, and all of you are astonished. [22]Moses gave you circumcision (it is, of course, not from Moses, but from the patriarchs), and you circumcise a man on the sabbath. [23]If a man receives circumcision on the sabbath in order that the law of Moses may not be broken, are you angry with me because I healed a man's whole body on the sabbath? [24]Do not judge by appearances, but judge with right judgment."

Is This the Christ?

25　Now some of the people of Jerusalem were saying, "Is not this the man whom they are trying to kill? [26]And here he is, speaking openly, but they say nothing to him! Can it be that the authorities really know that this is the Messiah?[b] [27]Yet we know where this man is from; but when the Messiah[b] comes, no one will know where he is from." [28]Then Jesus cried out as he was teaching in the temple, "You know me, and you know where I am from. I have not come on my own. But the one who sent me is true, and you do not know him. [29]I know him, because I am from him, and he sent me." [30]Then they tried to arrest him, but no one laid hands on him, because his hour had not yet come. [31]Yet many in the crowd believed in him and were saying, "When the Messiah[b] comes, will he do more signs than this man has done?"[c]

Officers Are Sent to Arrest Jesus

32　The Pharisees heard the crowd muttering such things about him, and the chief priests and Pharisees sent temple police to arrest him. [33]Jesus then said, "I will be with you a little while longer, and then I am going to him who sent me. [34]You will search for me, but you will not find me; and where I am, you cannot come." [35]The Jews said

to one another, "Where does this man intend to go that we will not find him? Does he intend to go to the Dispersion among the Greeks and teach the Greeks? [36]What does he mean by saying, 'You will search for me and you will not find me' and 'Where I am, you cannot come'?"

Rivers of Living Water

37　On the last day of the festival, the great day, while Jesus was standing there, he cried out, "Let anyone who is thirsty come to me, [38]and let the one who believes in me drink. As[d] the scripture has said, 'Out of the believer's heart[e] shall flow rivers of living water.'" [39]Now he said this about the Spirit, which believers in him were to receive; for as yet there was no Spirit,[f] because Jesus was not yet glorified.

Division among the People

40　When they heard these words, some in the crowd said, "This is really the prophet." [41]Others said, "This is the Messiah."[b] But some asked, "Surely the Messiah[b] does not come from Galilee, does he? [42]Has not the scripture said that the Messiah[b] is descended from David and comes from Bethlehem, the village where David lived?" [43]So there was a division in the crowd because of him. [44]Some of them wanted to arrest him, but no one laid hands on him.

The Unbelief of Those in Authority

45　Then the temple police went back to the chief priests and Pharisees, who asked them, "Why did you not arrest him?" [46]The police answered, "Never has anyone spoken like this!" [47]Then the Pharisees replied, "Surely you have not been deceived too, have you? [48]Has any one of the authorities or of the Pharisees believed in him? [49]But this crowd, which does not know the law—they are accursed." [50]Nicodemus, who had gone to Jesus[g] before, and who was one of them, asked, [51]"Our law does not judge people without first giving them a hearing to find out what they are doing, does it?" [52]They replied, "Surely you are not also from Galilee, are you? Search and you will see that no prophet is to arise from Galilee."

The Woman Caught in Adultery

8 [53]Then each of them went home, [1]while Jesus went to the Mount of Olives. [2]Early in the morning he came again to the temple. All the

---

a Or this man know his letters　b Or the Christ　c Other ancient authorities read is doing　d Or come to me and drink. [38]The one who believes in me, as　e Gk out of his belly　f Other ancient authorities read for as yet the Spirit (others, Holy Spirit) had not been given　g Gk him

people came to him and he sat down and began to teach them. ³The scribes and the Pharisees brought a woman who had been caught in adultery; and making her stand before all of them, ⁴they said to him, "Teacher, this woman was caught in the very act of committing adultery. ⁵Now in the law Moses commanded us to stone such women. Now what do you say?" ⁶They said this to test him, so that they might have some charge to bring against him. Jesus bent down and wrote with his finger on the ground. ⁷When they kept on questioning him, he straightened up and said to them, "Let anyone among you who is without sin be the first to throw a stone at her." ⁸And once again he bent down and wrote on the ground.ᵃ ⁹When they heard it, they went away, one by one, beginning with the elders; and Jesus was left alone with the woman standing before him. ¹⁰Jesus straightened up and said to

Divine Compassion

Jesus was great at turning the tables on those who considered themselves his enemies. In John 8:2–11, the scribes and Pharisees think they have come up with a perfect trap. They want Jesus to save the woman from being stoned by giving a "wrong" interpretation of the Law. Making such a wrong judgment publicly would cause Jesus to lose his credibility quickly.

With one amazing sentence, Jesus redefines the game. The focus moves away from the woman and onto the accusers, who cannot deny that they too are guilty of sin. The trap fails miserably, and the humbled religious leaders leave in silence.

We are often quick to notice the sinfulness of others while minimizing our own guilt. Jesus reminds us to be compassionate toward the sins of others. And notice how tenderly Christ dealt with the woman, whose dignity and reputation had been trampled on. When you recognize your own guilt and stand exposed and shamed before God and others, remember that God is just as tender and compassionate toward you.

▶ Jn 8:2–11

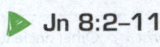

her, "Woman, where are they? Has no one condemned you?" ¹¹She said, "No one, sir."ᵇ And Jesus said, "Neither do I condemn you. Go your way, and from now on do not sin again."‖ᶜ

Jesus the Light of the World

12 Again Jesus spoke to them, saying, "I am the light of the world. Whoever follows me will never walk in darkness but will have the light of life." ¹³Then the Pharisees said to him, "You are testifying on your own behalf; your testimony is not valid." ¹⁴Jesus answered, "Even if I testify on my own behalf, my testimony is valid because I know where I have come from and where I am going, but you do not know where I come from or where I am going. ¹⁵You judge by human standards;ᵈ I judge no one. ¹⁶Yet even if I do judge, my judgment is valid; for it is not I alone who judge, but I and the Fatherᵉ who sent me. ¹⁷In your law it is written that the testimony of two witnesses is valid. ¹⁸I testify on my own behalf, and the Father who sent me testifies on my behalf." ¹⁹Then they said to him, "Where is your Father?" Jesus answered, "You know neither me nor my Father. If you knew me, you would know my Father also." ²⁰He spoke these words while he was teaching in the treasury of the temple, but no one arrested him, because his hour had not yet come.

Jesus Foretells His Death

21 Again he said to them, "I am going away, and you will search for me, but you will die in your sin. Where I am going, you cannot come." ²²Then the Jews said, "Is he going to kill himself? Is that what he means by saying, 'Where I am going, you cannot come'?" ²³He said to them, "You are from below, I am from above; you are of this world, I am not of this world. ²⁴I told you that you would die in your sins, for you will die in your sins unless you believe that I am he."ᶠ ²⁵They said to him, "Who are you?" Jesus said to them, "Why do I speak to you at all?ᵍ ²⁶I have much to say about you and much to condemn; but the one who sent me is true, and I declare to the world what I have heard from him." ²⁷They did not understand that he was speaking to them about the Father. ²⁸So Jesus said, "When you have lifted up the Son of Man, then you will realize that I am he,ᶠ and that I do nothing on

---

ᵃ Other ancient authorities add *the sins of each of them*
ᵇ Or *Lord*   ᶜ The most ancient authorities lack 7.53–8.11; other authorities add the passage here or after 7.36 or after 21.25 or after Luke 21.38, with variations of text; some mark the passage as doubtful.   ᵈ Gk *according to the flesh*   ᵉ Other ancient authorities read *he*   ᶠ Gk *I am*   ᵍ Or *What I have told you from the beginning*

Cultural Connection

The Sun Gives Life

The Sun, the Light of the world,
I hear Him coming,
I see His Face as He comes.
He makes the beings on earth happy,
And they rejoice.
O Wakan-Tanka, I offer to You this world of
   light . . .
I offer all to You. . . .
May all be attentive and behold! . . . that they
   may live.

(In Brown, *The Sacred Pipe*,
University of Oklahoma Press)

▶ Jn 8:12–20

For many Native Americans, the sun is a symbol of the Great Spirit, or *Wakan-Tanka*. Black Elk's poem prayer has a strong parallel in the Gospel of John. When Jesus reveals that he is "the light of the world" (8:12), he is saying that those who walk in the light (believe) enjoy eternal life and those who walk in darkness or avoid the light (refuse to believe) are condemned. In Christian spirituality, Jesus is sometimes called the Sun (or Son) of Righteousness.

---

my own, but I speak these things as the Father instructed me. ²⁹And the one who sent me is with me; he has not left me alone, for I always do what is pleasing to him." ³⁰As he was saying these things, many believed in him.

True Disciples

31 Then Jesus said to the Jews who had believed in him, "If you continue in my word, you are truly my disciples; ³²and you will know the truth, and the truth will make you free." ³³They answered him, "We are descendants of Abraham and have never been slaves to anyone. What do you mean by saying, 'You will be made free'?"

34 Jesus answered them, "Very truly, I tell you, everyone who commits sin is a slave to sin. ³⁵The slave does not have a permanent place in the household; the son has a place there forever. ³⁶So if the Son makes you free, you will be free indeed. ³⁷I know that you are descendants of Abraham; yet you look for an opportunity to kill me, because there is no place in you for my word. ³⁸I declare what I have seen in the Father's presence; as for you, you should do what you have heard from the Father."[a]

Jesus and Abraham

39 They answered him, "Abraham is our father." Jesus said to them, "If you were Abraham's children, you would be doing[b] what Abraham did, ⁴⁰but now you are trying to kill me, a man who has told you the truth that I heard from God. This is not what Abraham did. ⁴¹You are indeed doing what your father does." They said to him, "We are not illegitimate children; we have

one father, God himself." ⁴²Jesus said to them, "If God were your Father, you would love me, for I came from God and now I am here. I did not come on my own, but he sent me. ⁴³Why do you not understand what I say? It is because you cannot accept my word. ⁴⁴You are from your father the devil, and you choose to do your father's desires. He was a murderer from the beginning and does not stand in the truth, because there is no truth in him. When he lies, he speaks according to his own nature, for he is a liar and the father of lies. ⁴⁵But because I tell the truth, you do not believe me. ⁴⁶Which of you convicts me of sin? If I tell the truth, why do you not believe me? ⁴⁷Whoever is from God hears the words of God. The reason you do not hear them is that you are not from God."

48 The Jews answered him, "Are we not right in saying that you are a Samaritan and have a demon?" ⁴⁹Jesus answered, "I do not have a demon; but I honor my Father, and you dishonor me. ⁵⁰Yet I do not seek my own glory; there is one who seeks it and he is the judge. ⁵¹Very truly, I tell you, whoever keeps my word will never see death." ⁵²The Jews said to him, "Now we know that you have a demon. Abraham died, and so did the prophets; yet you say, 'Whoever keeps my word will never taste death.' ⁵³Are you greater than our father Abraham, who died? The prophets also died. Who do you claim to be?" ⁵⁴Jesus answered, "If I glorify myself, my glory is

---

a Other ancient authorities read *you do what you have heard from your father* b Other ancient authorities read *If you are Abraham's children, then do*

Cultural Connection

Jesus Is the Light of Life

Once again, the Gospel of John creates a sharp distinction between light and darkness, belief and unbelief. Those who follow Jesus will never walk in darkness but will have the light of life. Light is a symbol of belief that results in life, happiness, and the joy of salvation and liberation in Christ. Darkness is a symbol of unbelief that results in death, disgrace, and condemnation.

Hispanics have a long tradition of lighting candles in church, at home, and at job sites. The candles symbolize the light that comes from Christ and guides us to true life.

We need the light of Christ to live with wholeness and integrity, and to give a proper value and place to material things and human activities. The light of Christ can direct us in our journey to God. Religious symbols and rituals are privileged means to help us to remember the Gospel, to give witness of the Gospel with our own lives, and to radiate God's love to those around us.

- How do you transmit the light of Christ to others today?
- Where in your life do you need the light of Christ?
- Give thanks to Jesus for inviting you to share in the life of God.

▶ **Jn 8:12–59**

nothing. It is my Father who glorifies me, he of whom you say, 'He is our God,' [55]though you do not know him. But I know him; if I would say that I do not know him, I would be a liar like you. But I do know him and I keep his word. [56]Your ancestor Abraham rejoiced that he would see my day; he saw it and was glad." [57]Then the Jews said to him, "You are not yet fifty years old, and have you seen Abraham?"[a] [58]Jesus said to them, "Very truly, I tell you, before Abraham was, I am." [59]So they picked up stones to throw at him, but Jesus hid himself and went out of the temple.

A Man Born Blind Receives Sight

9 As he walked along, he saw a man blind from birth. [2]His disciples asked him, "Rabbi, who sinned, this man or his parents, that he was born blind?" [3]Jesus answered, "Neither this man nor his parents sinned; he was born blind so that God's works might be revealed in him. [4]We[b] must work the works of him who sent me[c] while it is day; night is coming when no one can work. [5]As long as I am in the world, I am the light of the world." [6]When he had said this, he spat on the ground and made mud with the saliva and spread the mud on the man's eyes, [7]saying to him, "Go, wash in the pool of Siloam" (which means Sent). Then he went and washed and came back able to see. [8]The neighbors and those who had seen him before as a beggar began to ask, "Is this not the man who used to sit and beg?" [9]Some were saying, "It is he." Others were saying, "No, but it is someone like him." He kept saying, "I am the man." [10]But they kept asking him, "Then how were your eyes opened?" [11]He answered, "The man called Jesus made mud, spread it on my eyes, and said to me, 'Go to Siloam and wash.' Then I went and washed and received my sight." [12]They said to him, "Where is he?" He said, "I do not know."

The Pharisees Investigate the Healing

13 They brought to the Pharisees the man who had formerly been blind. [14]Now it was a sabbath day when Jesus made the mud and opened his eyes. [15]Then the Pharisees also began to ask him how he had received his sight. He said to them, "He put mud on my eyes. Then I washed, and now I see." [16]Some of the Pharisees said, "This man is not from God, for he does not observe the sabbath." But others said, "How can a man who is a sinner perform such signs?" And they were divided. [17]So they said again to the blind man, "What do you say about him? It was your eyes he opened." He said, "He is a prophet."

18 The Jews did not believe that he had been blind and had received his sight until they called the parents of the man who had received his sight [19]and asked them, "Is this your son, who you say was born blind? How then does he now see?" [20]His parents answered, "We know that this is our son, and that he was born blind; [21]but we

---

a Other ancient authorities read *has Abraham seen you?* *b* Other ancient authorities read *I* *c* Other ancient authorities read *us*

do not know how it is that now he sees, nor do we know who opened his eyes. Ask him; he is of age. He will speak for himself." 22His parents said this because they were afraid of the Jews; for the Jews had already agreed that anyone who confessed Jesus*a* to be the Messiah*b* would be put out of the synagogue. 23Therefore his parents said, "He is of age; ask him."

24 So for the second time they called the man who had been blind, and they said to him, "Give glory to God! We know that this man is a sinner." 25He answered, "I do not know whether he is a sinner. One thing I do know, that though I was blind, now I see." 26They said to him, "What did he do to you? How did he open your eyes?" 27He answered them, "I have told you already, and you would not listen. Why do you want to hear it again? Do you also want to become his disciples?" 28Then they reviled him, saying, "You are his disciple, but we are disciples of Moses. 29We know that God has spoken to Moses, but as for this man, we do not know where he comes from." 30The man answered, "Here is an astonishing thing! You do not know where he comes from, and yet he opened my eyes. 31We know that God does not listen to sinners, but he does listen to one who worships him and obeys his will. 32Never since the world began has it been heard that anyone opened the eyes of a person born blind. 33If this man were not from God, he could do nothing." 34They answered him, "You were born entirely in sins, and are you trying to teach us?" And they drove him out.

Spiritual Blindness

35 Jesus heard that they had driven him out, and when he found him, he said, "Do you believe in the Son of Man?"*c* 36He answered, "And who is he, sir?*d* Tell me, so that I may believe in him." 37Jesus said to him, "You have seen him, and the one speaking with you is he." 38He said, "Lord,*d* I believe." And he worshiped him. 39Jesus said, "I came into this world for judgment so that those who do not see may see, and those who do see may become blind." 40Some of the Pharisees near him heard this and said to him, "Surely we are not blind, are we?" 41Jesus said to them, "If you were blind, you would not have sin. But now that you say, 'We see,' your sin remains.

Jesus the Good Shepherd

10 "Very truly, I tell you, anyone who does not enter the sheepfold by the gate but climbs in by another way is a thief and a bandit. 2The one who enters by the gate is the shepherd of the sheep. 3The gatekeeper opens the gate for

him, and the sheep hear his voice. He calls his own sheep by name and leads them out. 4When he has brought out all his own, he goes ahead of them, and the sheep follow him because they know his voice. 5They will not follow a stranger, but they will run from him because they do not know the voice of strangers." 6Jesus used this figure of speech with them, but they did not understand what he was saying to them.

7 So again Jesus said to them, "Very truly, I tell you, I am the gate for the sheep. 8All who came before me are thieves and bandits; but the sheep did not listen to them. 9I am the gate. Whoever enters by me will be saved, and will come in and go out and find pasture. 10The thief comes only to steal and kill and destroy. I came that they may have life, and have it abundantly.

11 "I am the good shepherd. The good

---

a Gk *him*   *b* Or *the Christ*   *c* Other ancient authorities read *the Son of God*   *d* *Sir* and *Lord* translate the same Greek word

Seeing with God's Eyes

Lord, can you fix my eyesight like you did for the blind man?

I want to see with your eyes those who are teased for being different at school.

I want to see with your eyes the homeless person on a park bench.

I want to see with your eyes people from other races and cultures.

I want to see more than people who think that being thinner or stronger makes you more lovable.

I want to see more than people who look at wealth and think that's what life is all about.

Help me to see with your eyes, Lord! Blind me to the way the world sees so that I won't give in to judging people on their looks or skin color or possessions or personality.

Help me to see, and to love, as you love, Lord—with eyes so wide open that they see past the outside and right into the heart of another.

▶ **John, chapter 9**

Jesus, the Good Shepherd

The theme of shepherds and sheep is a recurring one in the Bible. In the Old Testament, God is sometimes portrayed as a shepherd. For example, see Psalm 23 and Ezekiel, chapter 34. David, the greatest king of Israel, is also portrayed as a shepherd in Psalm 78:70–72. In passages like Jeremiah 23:1–6, God promises to raise up new shepherds who will follow in David's legacy. So it is natural that Jesus compares himself to a shepherd in John 10:1–18.

Being a shepherd is not an easy job. Sheep are pretty defenseless creatures, and shepherds have to protect them from predators like lions and wolves. Sheep also have a tendency to stray from the flock, making them especially vulnerable. Shepherds endure the hardships of being away from their homes and putting up with simple food and harsh weather while pasturing sheep. Their lives can be endangered when confronted by desperate predators. Sheep learn to recognize their shepherd's voice, which makes it easier to separate different flocks when flocks are mixed together for grazing or protection.

In your prayer, reflect or journal on the following questions:

● How do you relate to Jesus as the good shepherd?

● When is it reassuring to know that Jesus is watching out for you? How do you see yourself helping to "shepherd" other people as a follower of Jesus?

▶ Jn 10:1–18

shepherd lays down his life for the sheep. ¹²The hired hand, who is not the shepherd and does not own the sheep, sees the wolf coming and leaves the sheep and runs away—and the wolf snatches them and scatters them. ¹³The hired hand runs away because a hired hand does not care for the sheep. ¹⁴I am the good shepherd. I know my own and my own know me, ¹⁵just as the Father knows me and I know the Father. And I lay down my life for the sheep. ¹⁶I have other sheep that do not belong to this fold. I

must bring them also, and they will listen to my voice. So there will be one flock, one shepherd. ¹⁷For this reason the Father loves me, because I lay down my life in order to take it up again. ¹⁸No one takes[a] it from me, but I lay it down of my own accord. I have power to lay it down, and I have power to take it up again. I have received this command from my Father."

19 Again the Jews were divided because of these words. ²⁰Many of them were saying, "He has a demon and is out of his mind. Why listen to him?" ²¹Others were saying, "These are not the words of one who has a demon. Can a demon open the eyes of the blind?"

Jesus Is Rejected by the Jews

22 At that time the festival of the Dedication took place in Jerusalem. It was winter, ²³and Jesus was walking in the temple, in the portico of Solomon. ²⁴So the Jews gathered around him and said to him, "How long will you keep us in suspense? If you are the Messiah,[b] tell us plainly." ²⁵Jesus answered, "I have told you, and you do not believe. The works that I do in my Father's name testify to me; ²⁶but you do not believe, because you do not belong to my sheep. ²⁷My sheep hear my voice. I know them, and they follow me. ²⁸I give them eternal life, and they will never perish. No one will snatch them out of my hand. ²⁹What my Father has given me is greater than all else, and no one can snatch it out of the Father's hand.[c] ³⁰The Father and I are one."

31 The Jews took up stones again to stone him. ³²Jesus replied, "I have shown you many good works from the Father. For which of these are you going to stone me?" ³³The Jews answered, "It is not for a good work that we are going to stone you, but for blasphemy, because you, though only a human being, are making yourself God." ³⁴Jesus answered, "Is it not written in your law,[d] 'I said, you are gods'? ³⁵If those to whom the word of God came were called 'gods'—and the scripture cannot be annulled—³⁶can you say that the one whom the Father has sanctified and sent into the world is blaspheming because I said, 'I am God's Son'? ³⁷If I am not doing the works of my Father, then do not believe me. ³⁸But if I do them, even though you do not believe me, believe the works, so that you may know and understand[e] that the Father is in me

a Other ancient authorities read has taken   b Or the Christ
c Other ancient authorities read My Father who has given them to me is greater than all, and no one can snatch them out of the Father's hand   d Other ancient authorities read in the law
e Other ancient authorities lack and understand; others read and believe

and I am in the Father." ³⁹Then they tried to arrest him again, but he escaped from their hands.

40 He went away again across the Jordan to the place where John had been baptizing earlier, and he remained there. ⁴¹Many came to him, and they were saying, "John performed no sign, but everything that John said about this man was true." ⁴²And many believed in him there.

The Death of Lazarus

11 Now a certain man was ill, Lazarus of Bethany, the village of Mary and her sister Martha. ²Mary was the one who anointed the Lord with perfume and wiped his feet with her hair; her brother Lazarus was ill. ³So the sisters sent a message to Jesus,ᵃ "Lord, he whom you love is ill." ⁴But when Jesus heard it, he said, "This illness does not lead to death; rather it is for God's glory, so that the Son of God may be glorified through it." ⁵Accordingly, though Jesus loved Martha and her sister and Lazarus, ⁶after having heard that Lazarusᵇ was ill, he stayed two days longer in the place where he was.

7 Then after this he said to the disciples, "Let us go to Judea again." ⁸The disciples said to him, "Rabbi, the Jews were just now trying to stone you, and are you going there again?" ⁹Jesus answered, "Are there not twelve hours of daylight? Those who walk during the day do not stumble, because they see the light of this world. ¹⁰But those who walk at night stumble, because the light is not in them." ¹¹After saying this, he told them, "Our friend Lazarus has fallen asleep, but I am going there to awaken him." ¹²The disciples said to him, "Lord, if he has fallen asleep, he will be all right." ¹³Jesus, however, had been speaking about his death, but they thought that he was referring merely to sleep. ¹⁴Then Jesus told them plainly, "Lazarus is dead. ¹⁵For your sake I am glad I was not there, so that you may believe. But let us go to him." ¹⁶Thomas, who was called the Twin,ᶜ said to his fellow disciples, "Let us also go, that we may die with him."

Jesus the Resurrection and the Life

17 When Jesus arrived, he found that Lazarusᵇ had already been in the tomb four days. ¹⁸Now Bethany was near Jerusalem, some two milesᵈ away, ¹⁹and many of the Jews had come to Martha and Mary to console them about their brother. ²⁰When Martha heard that Jesus was coming, she went and met him, while Mary stayed at home. ²¹Martha said to Jesus, "Lord, if you had been here, my brother would not have died. ²²But even now I know that God will give you whatever you ask of him." ²³Jesus said to

her, "Your brother will rise again." ²⁴Martha said to him, "I know that he will rise again in the resurrection on the last day." ²⁵Jesus said to her, "I am the resurrection and the life.ᵉ Those who believe in me, even though they die, will live, ²⁶and everyone who lives and believes in me will never die. Do you believe this?" ²⁷She said to him, "Yes, Lord, I believe that you are the Messiah,ᶠ the Son of God, the one coming into the world."

---

a Gk *him*   b Gk *he*   c Gk *Didymus*   d Gk *fifteen stadia*
e Other ancient authorities lack *and the life*   f Or *the Christ*

Alive Again!

"**J**esus began to weep" (Jn 11:35). Why does Jesus weep? Scholars are not exactly sure what causes Jesus to weep. But it might be plausible that when Jesus sees his dear friend Mary crying because of the death of her brother Lazarus, Jesus cannot help himself and cries too, expressing both compassion for Mary and his own grief at the loss of his friend Lazarus. What a beautiful, powerful expression of Jesus' humanity!

What follows next is a powerful expression of Jesus' impending death and Resurrection—his glorification. It is the seventh and final sign in John's Gospel. What a dramatic moment, as Jesus steps into the tomb of a man who has been dead for four days. He calls to Lazarus and asks him to come out—and Lazarus, bound in burial cloth, indeed comes out! He is alive again. Imagine how astonished the onlookers must have been and how grateful Martha and Mary would have been to have their brother alive again.

It does make one wonder what it would feel like to be alive again after being in the grave for four days. How do people react to this man who is alive once again? Why do you think John chose this as the last sign of Jesus' power? Notice that this event occurs about a week before the last days of Jesus' life. Why is this sign such a threat to the ruling officials of Jerusalem?

▶ Jn 11:1–44

Jesus Weeps

28 When she had said this, she went back and called her sister Mary, and told her privately, "The Teacher is here and is calling for you." [29]And when she heard it, she got up quickly and went to him. [30]Now Jesus had not yet come to the village, but was still at the place where Martha had met him. [31]The Jews who were with her in the house, consoling her, saw Mary get up quickly and go out. They followed her because they thought that she was going to the tomb to weep there. [32]When Mary came where Jesus was and saw him, she knelt at his feet and said to him, "Lord, if you had been here, my brother would not have died." [33]When Jesus saw her weeping, and the Jews who came with her also weeping, he was greatly disturbed in spirit and deeply moved. [34]He said, "Where have you laid him?" They said to him, "Lord, come and see." [35]Jesus began to weep. [36]So the Jews said, "See how he loved him!" [37]But some of them said, "Could not he who opened the eyes of the blind man have kept this man from dying?"

Jesus Raises Lazarus to Life

38 Then Jesus, again greatly disturbed, came to the tomb. It was a cave, and a stone was lying against it. [39]Jesus said, "Take away the stone." Martha, the sister of the dead man, said to him, "Lord, already there is a stench because he has been dead four days." [40]Jesus said to her, "Did I not tell you that if you believed, you would see the glory of God?" [41]So they took away the stone. And Jesus looked upward and said, "Father, I thank you for having heard me. [42]I knew that you always hear me, but I have said this for the sake of the crowd standing here, so that they may believe that you sent me." [43]When he had said this, he cried with a loud voice, "Lazarus, come out!" [44]The dead man came out, his hands and feet bound with strips of cloth, and his face wrapped in a cloth. Jesus said to them, "Unbind him, and let him go."

The Plot to Kill Jesus

45 Many of the Jews therefore, who had come with Mary and had seen what Jesus did, believed in him. [46]But some of them went to the Pharisees and told them what he had done. [47]So the chief priests and the Pharisees called a meeting of the council, and said, "What are we to do? This man is performing many signs. [48]If we let him go on like this, everyone will believe in him, and the Romans will come and destroy both our holy place[a] and our nation." [49]But one of them, Caiaphas, who was high priest that year, said to them, "You know nothing at all! [50]You do not understand that it is better for you to have one man die for the people than to have the whole nation destroyed." [51]He did not say this on his own, but being high priest that year he prophesied that Jesus was about to die for the nation, [52]and not for the nation only, but to gather into one the dispersed children of God. [53]So from that day on they planned to put him to death.

54 Jesus therefore no longer walked about openly among the Jews, but went from there to a town called Ephraim in the region near the wilderness; and he remained there with the disciples.

55 Now the Passover of the Jews was near, and many went up from the country to Jerusalem before the Passover to purify themselves. [56]They were looking for Jesus and were asking one another as they stood in the temple, "What do you think? Surely he will not come to the festival, will he?" [57]Now the chief priests and the Pharisees had given orders that anyone who knew where Jesus[b] was should let them know, so that they might arrest him.

Mary Anoints Jesus

12 Six days before the Passover Jesus came to Bethany, the home of Lazarus, whom he had raised from the dead. [2]There they gave a dinner for

Pray It!

A God Who Cries

*L*ord, have I ever made you cry? angry enough to yell? tickled enough to laugh? proud enough to burst? I hope so. I hope you know me so well that my every movement, my every breath, is noticed by you. I want to believe that about you, Jesus, because that is the image of you I can talk to—the image of a God who can relate to me and accept me in all that I do, a God who understands the real emotions I feel, a God who knows what it means to be human, a God who is not afraid to cry. Amen.

▶ Jn 11:35

a Or our temple; Greek our place   b Gk he

him. Martha served, and Lazarus was one of those at the table with him. ³Mary took a pound of costly perfume made of pure nard, anointed Jesus' feet, and wiped them*ᵃ* with her hair. The house was filled with the fragrance of the perfume. ⁴But Judas Iscariot, one of his disciples (the one who was about to betray him), said, ⁵"Why was this perfume not sold for three hundred denarii*ᵇ* and the money given to the poor?" ⁶(He said this not because he cared about the poor, but because he was a thief; he kept the common purse and used to steal what was put into it.) ⁷Jesus said, "Leave her alone. She bought it*ᶜ* so that she might keep it for the day of my burial. ⁸You always have the poor with you, but you do not always have me."

The Plot to Kill Lazarus

9 When the great crowd of the Jews learned that he was there, they came not only because of Jesus but also to see Lazarus, whom he had raised from the dead. ¹⁰So the chief priests planned to put Lazarus to death as well, ¹¹since it was on account of him that many of the Jews were deserting and were believing in Jesus.

Jesus' Triumphal Entry into Jerusalem

12 The next day the great crowd that had come to the festival heard that Jesus was coming to Jerusalem. ¹³So they took branches of palm trees and went out to meet him, shouting,

"Hosanna!
Blessed is the one who comes in the name of the Lord—
    the King of Israel!"

¹⁴Jesus found a young donkey and sat on it; as it is written:

¹⁵ "Do not be afraid, daughter of Zion.
Look, your king is coming,
    sitting on a donkey's colt!"

¹⁶His disciples did not understand these things at first; but when Jesus was glorified, then they remembered that these things had been written of him and had been done to him. ¹⁷So the crowd that had been with him when he called Lazarus out of the tomb and raised him from the dead continued to testify.*ᵈ* ¹⁸It was also because they heard that he had performed this sign that the crowd went to meet him. ¹⁹The Pharisees then said to one another, "You see, you can do nothing. Look, the world has gone after him!"

Some Greeks Wish to See Jesus

20 Now among those who went up to worship at the festival were some Greeks. ²¹They came to Philip, who was from Bethsaida in Galilee, and said to him, "Sir, we wish to see Jesus."

Dying for New Life

In John 12:24–26, Jesus is describing what Christians call the *Paschal mystery*. It is the belief that God brings new life out of suffering and death. The ultimate expression of the Paschal mystery is Jesus' own death and Resurrection. God used Christ's sacrifice to free us from the bonds of sin, and Christ's Resurrection to open the path to new life. This belief that new life can come out of sin and death is a continuously unfolding mystery that no one can fully explain, and yet it is perhaps the most essential foundation of our faith.

Like the grain of wheat in this Gospel passage, in death we bear the fruit of new life. The path to new life is through sacrifice and death. By dying to our selfishness and focusing on loving others, we experience the fullness of life in Christ Jesus.

In your prayer, reflect or journal on the following questions:
● What does the Paschal mystery mean to you?
● What kinds of attitudes, desires, or actions must be let go of in your life?

Write a prayer asking God to give you the courage to let go of the things that keep you from fullness of life.

▶ Jn 12:24–26

²²Philip went and told Andrew; then Andrew and Philip went and told Jesus. ²³Jesus answered them, "The hour has come for the Son of Man to be glorified. ²⁴Very truly, I tell you, unless a grain of wheat falls into the earth and dies, it remains just a single grain; but if it dies, it bears much fruit. ²⁵Those who love their life lose it, and those who hate their life in this world will keep it for eternal life. ²⁶Whoever serves me must follow me, and where I am, there will my servant be also. Whoever serves me, the Father will honor.

a Gk *his feet*   *b* Three hundred denarii would be nearly a year's wages for a laborer   *c* Gk lacks *She bought it*   *d* Other ancient authorities read *with him* began to testify that he had called . . . *from the dead*

Jesus Speaks about His Death

27 "Now my soul is troubled. And what should I say—'Father, save me from this hour'? No, it is for this reason that I have come to this hour. ²⁸Father, glorify your name." Then a voice came from heaven, "I have glorified it, and I will glorify it again." ²⁹The crowd standing there heard it and said that it was thunder. Others said, "An angel has spoken to him." ³⁰Jesus answered, "This voice has come for your sake, not for mine. ³¹Now is the judgment of this world; now the ruler of this world will be driven out. ³²And I, when I am lifted up from the earth, will draw all people[a]

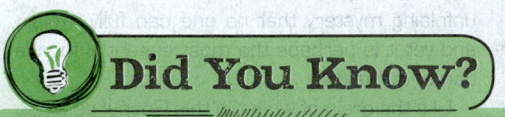

Did You Know?

Feast of the Passover

Chapter 13 is the beginning of the second part of the Gospel of John, sometimes called the Book of Glory. Its central theme is how Jesus is glorified through his Passion, death, and Resurrection. It begins with Jesus' washing the disciples' feet at the Last Supper, before the Passover.

The Jewish feast of Passover, also called the feast of Unleavened Bread, reminds us of how God rescued the Israelites from slavery in Egypt by killing the firstborn Egyptians and "passing over" the homes of the Israelites (about 1250 BC). The feast was traditionally celebrated with a meal of lamb, bitter herbs, and unleavened bread (see "The Passover," near Ex 12:14–28). It was the blood of a lamb, smeared on the doorposts of the Israelites' houses, that signaled the angel of death to spare the firstborn of God's people.

In the other Gospels, the last meal that Jesus shares with his disciples is the Passover meal. However, in the Gospel of John, Jesus is arrested before Passover. He is crucified on the preparation day of the feast of Unleavened Bread, at the same time that the lambs are being sacrificed in the Temple. The symbolism would not be missed by the readers of John: Jesus is the new and perfect Passover lamb.

▶ Jn 13:1–20

to myself." ³³He said this to indicate the kind of death he was to die. ³⁴The crowd answered him, "We have heard from the law that the Messiah[b] remains forever. How can you say that the Son of Man must be lifted up? Who is this Son of Man?" ³⁵Jesus said to them, "The light is with you for a little longer. Walk while you have the light, so that the darkness may not overtake you. If you walk in the darkness, you do not know where you are going. ³⁶While you have the light, believe in the light, so that you may become children of light."

The Unbelief of the People

After Jesus had said this, he departed and hid from them. ³⁷Although he had performed so many signs in their presence, they did not believe in him. ³⁸This was to fulfill the word spoken by the prophet Isaiah:

"Lord, who has believed our message,
    and to whom has the arm of the Lord been revealed?"

³⁹And so they could not believe, because Isaiah also said,

⁴⁰ "He has blinded their eyes
    and hardened their heart,
so that they might not look with their eyes,
    and understand with their heart and turn—
    and I would heal them."

⁴¹Isaiah said this because[c] he saw his glory and spoke about him. ⁴²Nevertheless many, even of the authorities, believed in him. But because of the Pharisees they did not confess it, for fear that they would be put out of the synagogue; ⁴³for they loved human glory more than the glory that comes from God.

Summary of Jesus' Teaching

44 Then Jesus cried aloud: "Whoever believes in me believes not in me but in him who sent me. ⁴⁵And whoever sees me sees him who sent me. ⁴⁶I have come as light into the world, so that everyone who believes in me should not remain in the darkness. ⁴⁷I do not judge anyone who hears my words and does not keep them, for I came not to judge the world, but to save the world. ⁴⁸The one who rejects me and does not receive my word has a judge; on the last day the word that I have spoken will serve as judge, ⁴⁹for I have not spoken on my own, but the Father who sent me has himself given me a commandment about what to say and what to speak. ⁵⁰And I know that his commandment is eternal life. What I speak, therefore, I speak just as the Father has told me."

---

a Other ancient authorities read *all things*   b Or *the Christ*
c Other ancient witnesses read *when*

Cultural Connection

The *Indriappam*

In the province of Kerala, in India, about 80 percent of the population is Catholic and celebrates the Lord's Passion with special time-honored customs. One such custom takes place on Holy Thursday. On that day, nearly all the villagers or townspeople attend morning Mass. During the Eucharist, the ritual of foot washing occurs, the priest washing the feet of twelve children chosen from among those who are poor. Then, after dinner that evening, the people gather again for the stations of the cross and prayers. They return home around nine or ten o'clock for a special Passover meal.

The Passover meal consists of bread baked only on Holy Thursday and a special drink of coconut milk mixed with brown sugar and spices. This Passover bread, or *indriappam*, is baked with a cross of palm on top, which is placed there by the oldest woman of the family. At the meal, the oldest man cuts the bread and passes a piece to each person, beginning with the oldest and working down to the youngest. Often, families visit one another and share this tradition throughout the evening. And if a death has occurred in any family that year, the other households of the village provide the *indriappam* for them.

On Good Friday, which is a national holiday in India despite the fact that India is a primarily Hindu country, the leftover bread and milk are served to the servants and those of the village who are poor and needy. This custom of *indriappam* combines devotion to Christ in the Eucharist with a reminder of the service we are obliged to offer to those who are needy and poor.

● What customs and traditions does your family or parish take part in to commemorate the gift of the Eucharist given at the Last Supper?

▶ Jn 13:1–13

Jesus Washes the Disciples' Feet

13 Now before the festival of the Passover, Jesus knew that his hour had come to depart from this world and go to the Father. Having loved his own who were in the world, he loved them to the end. [2]The devil had already put it into the heart of Judas son of Simon Iscariot to betray him. And during supper [3]Jesus, knowing that the Father had given all things into his hands, and that he had come from God and was going to God, [4]got up from the table,[a] took off his outer robe, and tied a towel around himself. [5]Then he poured water into a basin and began to wash the disciples' feet and to wipe them with the towel that was tied around him. [6]He came to Simon Peter, who said to him, "Lord, are you going to wash my feet?" [7]Jesus answered, "You do not know now what I am doing, but later you will understand." [8]Peter said to him, "You will never wash my feet." Jesus answered, "Unless I wash you, you have no share with me." [9]Simon Peter said to him, "Lord, not my feet only but also my hands and my head!" [10]Jesus said to him, "One who has bathed does not need to wash, except for the feet,[b] but is entirely clean.

And you[c] are clean, though not all of you." [11]For he knew who was to betray him; for this reason he said, "Not all of you are clean."

12 After he had washed their feet, had put on his robe, and had returned to the table, he said to them, "Do you know what I have done to you? [13]You call me Teacher and Lord—and you are right, for that is what I am. [14]So if I, your Lord and Teacher, have washed your feet, you also ought to wash one another's feet. [15]For I have set you an example, that you also should do as I have done to you. [16]Very truly, I tell you, servants[d] are not greater than their master, nor are messengers greater than the one who sent them. [17]If you know these things, you are blessed if you do them. [18]I am not speaking of all of you; I know whom I have chosen. But it is to fulfill the scripture, 'The one who ate my bread[e] has lifted his heel against me.' [19]I tell you this now, before it occurs, so that when it does occur, you may believe that I am he.[f] [20]Very truly, I tell you, whoever receives one whom I

---

a Gk *from supper*   b Other ancient authorities lack *except for the feet*   c The Greek word for *you* here is plural   d Gk *slaves*
e Other ancient authorities read *ate bread with me*   f Gk *I am*

send receives me; and whoever receives me receives him who sent me."

Jesus Foretells His Betrayal

21 After saying this Jesus was troubled in spirit, and declared, "Very truly, I tell you, one of you will betray me." [22]The disciples looked at one another, uncertain of whom he was speaking. [23]One of his disciples—the one whom Jesus loved—was reclining next to him; [24]Simon Peter therefore motioned to him to ask Jesus of whom he was speaking. [25]So while reclining next to Jesus, he asked him, "Lord, who is it?" [26]Jesus answered, "It is the one to whom I give this piece of bread when I have dipped it in the dish."[a] So when he had dipped the piece of bread, he gave it to Judas son of Simon Iscariot.[b] [27]After he received the piece of bread,[c] Satan entered into him. Jesus said to him, "Do quickly what you are going to do." [28]Now no one at the table knew why he said this to him. [29]Some thought that, because Judas had the common purse, Jesus was telling him, "Buy what we need for the festival"; or, that he should give something to the poor. [30]So, after receiving the piece of bread, he immediately went out. And it was night.

The New Commandment

31 When he had gone out, Jesus said, "Now the Son of Man has been glorified, and God has been glorified in him. [32]If God has been glorified in him,[d] God will also glorify him in himself and will glorify him at once. [33]Little children, I am with you only a little longer. You will look for me; and as I said to the Jews so now I say to you, 'Where I am going, you cannot come.' [34]I give you a new commandment, that you love one another. Just as I have loved you, you also should love one another. [35]By this everyone will know that you are my disciples, if you have love for one another."

---

a Gk *dipped it*   b Other ancient authorities read *Judas Iscariot son of Simon*; others, *Judas son of Simon from Karyot* (Kerioth)   c Gk *After the piece of bread*   d Other ancient authorities lack *If God has been glorified in him*

The Beloved Disciple

In the Last Supper scene, we are introduced to a mysterious character found only in the Gospel of John, described as the disciple "whom Jesus loved" (Jn 13:23). He is mentioned several more times in John: at the foot of the cross with Jesus' mother (see 19:25–27), on Easter morning when he enters the empty tomb with Peter (see 20:2–12), and after the Resurrection when he identifies Jesus from the boat (see 21:7,20). He is always with Peter or where Peter should be (at the cross).

So who is the mystery man? Traditionally, he has been identified as John, the son of Zebedee and one of the Twelve Apostles, and as the writer of the Gospel of John. But if that is true, why does he refer to himself so strangely? Many scholars today believe that the Beloved Disciple was a lesser-known follower of Jesus who was the founder of the Christian community that ultimately produced the Gospel of John. They think his eyewitness accounts (see 21:24) were passed on and are the basis for the Gospel we have today.

▶ **Jn 13:23–25**

Jesus Models Service to Others

In Matthew, Mark, and Luke, the focus of the Last Supper is on the institution of the Eucharist. But in John, the focus is on Jesus' washing his disciples' feet (see 13:1–17). John makes the point that serving others is at the heart of being a follower of Jesus. In Holy Thursday Mass, we celebrate both traditions, indicating that service is a necessary part of living the Paschal mystery that we celebrate in the Eucharist.

● Read John 13:1–17. Reflect on and listen to Jesus' message to you.
● How is Jesus calling you to serve others, humbly and compassionately?

For more on the Eucharist, see "The New Covenant," near Matthew 26:26–29; "The Eucharist," near Luke 22:14–20; and "Feast of the Passover," near John 13:1–20.

▶ **Jn 13:1–17**

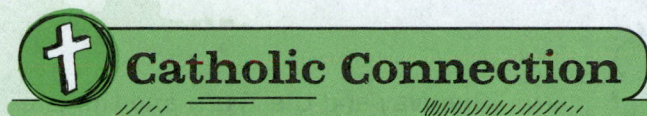

Catholic Connection

Easter Triduum

In the Gospel of John, the beloved disciple was with Jesus in the upper room at the Last Supper, stood at the foot of the cross during Jesus' Crucifixion (see Jn 19:26), and was there to examine the empty tomb (see 20:1–10). It is no surprise then that roughly more than a third of the Gospel of John is devoted to detailing the events in the upper room and the subsequent Passion, death, and Resurrection of Jesus. John's Gospel progressively reveals the glory of God's only Son, who reveals the Father and then reveals the disciples' place in God's plan of salvation. These events changed our world and our relationship with God.

The importance and meaning of these events also serve as the focus for the greatest feast in the liturgical year, the Easter Triduum. The Easter Triduum consists of three holy days that celebrate Jesus' Passion, death, and Resurrection. The Triduum begins on Holy Thursday, the Thursday before Easter. The reading for the day recounts the Last Supper and Christ's humility when washing the disciples' feet (see 13:1–15). Holy Thursday is followed by Good Friday, during which John's account of Jesus' Passion (see chapters 18–19) is read. In the course of the service, Catholics vener-

ate (honor) the cross, recalling Jesus' painful sacrifice that opened the way to our salvation.

The climax of the Triduum is the Easter Vigil held on Saturday evening, beginning after nightfall. This celebration incorporates a dramatic ceremony of light in which the Easter fire is lit, followed by the lighting of the Paschal (Jesus) candle and a candle for every person in the church. During the Mass, seven readings from the Old Testament and one epistle from the New Testament are proclaimed. These readings highlight important events that have shaped our salvation history. The readings culminate with a reading from John's Gospel that recounts the story of Jesus' Resurrection (see 20:1–9). Then those who have been preparing to join the church are baptized, confirmed, and welcomed to receive the Eucharist.

The Easter Triduum, although celebrated over three days, is actually one celebration, from the opening song on Holy Thursday to the closing song of the Easter Vigil.

▶ **Jn 13:1—20:18**
Catechism, nos. 1168–1171

Cultural Connection

The Way and the Truth and the Life

Catholics from the country of Laos often point to John 14:6 as a significant connection between the Buddhist faith and their Catholic faith. There is a Buddhist tradition of honoring the way and the truth. Becoming a Catholic and knowing the risen Christ bring a deeper appreciation of everlasting life. This completes the triangle of "the way and the truth and the life."

▶ Jn 14:6–7

Jesus Foretells Peter's Denial

36 Simon Peter said to him, "Lord, where are you going?" Jesus answered, "Where I am going, you cannot follow me now; but you will follow afterward." 37Peter said to him, "Lord, why can I not follow you now? I will lay down my life for you." 38Jesus answered, "Will you lay down your life for me? Very truly, I tell you, before the cock crows, you will have denied me three times.

Jesus the Way to the Father

14 "Do not let your hearts be troubled. Believe[a] in God, believe also in me. 2In my Father's house there are many dwelling places. If it were not so, would I have told you that I go to prepare a place for you?[b] 3And if I go and prepare a place for you, I will come again and will take you to myself, so that where I am, there you may be also. 4And you know the way to the place where I am going."[c] 5Thomas said to him, "Lord, we do not know where you are going. How can we know the way?" 6Jesus said to him, "I am the way, and the truth, and the life. No one comes to the Father except through me. 7If you know me, you will know[d] my Father also. From now on you do know him and have seen him."

8 Philip said to him, "Lord, show us the Father, and we will be satisfied." 9Jesus said to him, "Have I been with you all this time, Philip, and you still do not know me? Whoever has seen me has seen the Father. How can you say, 'Show us the Father'? 10Do you not believe that I am in the Father and the Father is in me? The words that I say to you I do not speak on my own; but the Father who dwells in me does his works. 11Believe me that I am in the Father and the Father is in me; but if you do not, then believe me because of the works themselves. 12Very truly, I tell you, the one who believes in me will also do the works that I do and, in fact, will do greater works than

these, because I am going to the Father. 13I will do whatever you ask in my name, so that the Father may be glorified in the Son. 14If in my name you ask me[e] for anything, I will do it.

The Promise of the Holy Spirit

15 "If you love me, you will keep[f] my commandments. 16And I will ask the Father, and he will give you another Advocate,[g] to be with you forever. 17This is the Spirit of truth, whom the world cannot receive, because it neither sees him nor knows him. You know him, because he abides with you, and he will be in[h] you.

18 "I will not leave you orphaned; I am coming to you. 19In a little while the world will no longer see me, but you will see me; because I live, you also will live. 20On that day you will know that I am in my Father, and you in me, and I in you. 21They who have my commandments and keep them are those who love me; and those who love me will be loved by my Father, and I will love them and reveal myself to them." 22Judas (not Iscariot) said to him, "Lord, how is it that you will reveal yourself to us, and not to the world?" 23Jesus answered him, "Those who love me will keep my word, and my Father will love them, and we will come to them and make our home with them. 24Whoever does not love me does not keep my words; and the word that you hear is not mine, but is from the Father who sent me.

25 "I have said these things to you while I am still with you. 26But the Advocate,[g] the Holy Spirit, whom the Father will send in my name, will teach you everything, and remind you of all

---

a Or *You believe*   b Or *If it were not so, I would have told you; for I go to prepare a place for you*   c Other ancient authorities read *Where I am going you know, and the way you know*
d Other ancient authorities read *If you had known me, you would have known*   e Other ancient authorities lack *me*   f Other ancient authorities read *me, keep*   g Or *Helper*   h Or *among*

JN

that I have said to you. ²⁷Peace I leave with you; my peace I give to you. I do not give to you as the world gives. Do not let your hearts be troubled, and do not let them be afraid. ²⁸You heard me say to you, 'I am going away, and I am coming to you.' If you loved me, you would rejoice that I am going to the Father, because the Father is greater than I. ²⁹And now I have told you this before it occurs, so that when it does occur, you may believe. ³⁰I will no longer talk much with you, for the ruler of this world is coming. He has no power over me; ³¹but I do as the Father has commanded me, so that the world may know that I love the Father. Rise, let us be on our way.

Jesus the True Vine

15 "I am the true vine, and my Father is the vinegrower. ²He removes every branch in me that bears no fruit. Every branch that bears fruit he prunes^a to make it bear more fruit. ³You have already been cleansed^a by the word that I have spoken to you. ⁴Abide in me as I abide in you. Just as the branch cannot bear fruit by itself unless it abides in the vine, neither can you unless you abide in me. ⁵I am the vine, you are the branches. Those who abide in me and I in them bear much fruit, because apart from me you can do nothing. ⁶Whoever does not abide in me is thrown away like a branch and withers; such branches are gathered, thrown into the fire, and burned. ⁷If you abide in me, and my words abide in you, ask for whatever you wish, and it will be done for you. ⁸My Father is glorified by this, that you bear much fruit and become^b my disciples. ⁹As the Father has loved me, so I have loved you; abide in my love. ¹⁰If you keep my commandments, you will abide in my love, just as I have kept my Father's commandments and abide in his love. ¹¹I have said these things to you so that my joy may be in you, and that your joy may be complete.

12 "This is my commandment, that you love one another as I have loved you. ¹³No one has greater love than this, to lay down one's life for one's friends. ¹⁴You are my friends if you do what I command you. ¹⁵I do not call you servants^c any longer, because the servant^d does not know what the master is doing; but I have called you friends, because I have made known to you everything that I have heard from my Father. ¹⁶You did not choose me but I chose you. And I appointed you to go and bear fruit, fruit that will last, so that the Father will give you whatever you ask him in my

---

^a The same Greek root refers to pruning and cleansing ^b Or be ^c Gk *slaves* ^d Gk *slave*

The Holy Spirit Guides Us into All Truth

Jesus told his disciples that after his death, God would send the Spirit of Truth to be with them forever. Jesus calls the Holy Spirit the Advocate (see Jn 16:7), the one who defends us from sin. The Holy Spirit also guides us into all Truth, helping us to grasp the meaning of Jesus' words, actions, and miracles. As we live out our faith, it is the Spirit that animates us as disciples, empowering us to use our unique gifts to make a difference in our world.

- Jesus promises his followers that the Holy Spirit will abide in us (see 14:17). How are you aware of the Holy Spirit's presence in your life?
- Place yourself in the hands of the Most Holy Trinity and call upon the Holy Spirit to protect you from all sin and evil and to bring you peace.

▶ Jn 14:15–31; 16:5–15

Make Your Home with Jesus

Jesus calls himself the true vine, and us the branches (see Jn 15:5). What does this mean for us? First, it means that apart from Jesus, we can produce no fruit—that is, we have nothing of ultimate value to offer others. It also means that to stay alive, we must "abide" in Jesus (verse 4). To abide, in this sense, means to stay or make our home with. How at home are you with Jesus?

▶ Jn 15:1–11

name. ¹⁷I am giving you these commands so that you may love one another.

The World's Hatred

18 "If the world hates you, be aware that it hated me before it hated you. ¹⁹If you belonged to the world,*a* the world would love you as its own. Because you do not belong to the world, but I have chosen you out of the world—therefore the world hates you. ²⁰Remember the word that I said to you, 'Servants*b* are not greater than their master.' If they persecuted me, they will persecute you; if they kept my word, they will keep yours also. ²¹But they will do all these things to you on account of my name, because they do not know him who sent me. ²²If I had not come and spoken to them, they would not have sin; but now they have no excuse for their sin.

²³Whoever hates me hates my Father also. ²⁴If I had not done among them the works that no one else did, they would not have sin. But now they have seen and hated both me and my Father. ²⁵It was to fulfill the word that is written in their law, 'They hated me without a cause.'

26 "When the Advocate*c* comes, whom I will send to you from the Father, the Spirit of truth who comes from the Father, he will testify on my behalf. ²⁷You also are to testify because you have been with me from the beginning.

16 "I have said these things to you to keep you from stumbling. ²They will put you out of the synagogues. Indeed, an hour is coming when those who kill you will think that by doing so they are offering worship to God. ³And they will do this because they have not known the Father or me. ⁴But I have said these things to you so that when their hour comes you may remember that I told you about them.

The Work of the Spirit

"I did not say these things to you from the beginning, because I was with you. ⁵But now I am going to him who sent me; yet none of you asks me, 'Where are you going?' ⁶But because I have said these things to you, sorrow has filled your hearts. ⁷Nevertheless I tell you the truth: it is to your advantage that I go away, for if I do not go away, the Advocate*c* will not come to you; but if I go, I will send him to you. ⁸And when he comes, he will prove the world wrong about*d* sin and righteousness and judgment: ⁹about sin, because they do not believe in me; ¹⁰about righteousness, because I am going to the Father and you will see me no longer; ¹¹about judgment, because the ruler of this world has been condemned.

12 "I still have many things to say to you, but you cannot bear them now. ¹³When the Spirit of truth comes, he will guide you into all the truth; for he will not speak on his own, but will speak whatever he hears, and he will declare to you the things that are to come. ¹⁴He will glorify me, because he will take what is mine and declare it to you. ¹⁵All that the Father has is mine. For this reason I said that he will take what is mine and declare it to you.

Sorrow Will Turn into Joy

16 "A little while, and you will no longer see me, and again a little while, and you will see me." ¹⁷Then some of his disciples said to one another, "What does he mean by saying to us, 'A

Pray It!

Not of This World

It is easy to get caught up in the pressures put on us by our society. It seems that we have to dress a certain way, have certain possessions, and live in a certain kind of house just to be considered average. People who resist those pressures are often labeled weird or different. They often feel out of place, not of this world.

The community from which the Gospel of John emerged did not feel at home in the world either. Their message of the divine Jesus had been rejected by Jews, Gentiles, and perhaps even other early Christians. No wonder the author has Jesus emphasize, "Because you do not belong to the world, . . . therefore the world hates you" (15:19).

In your prayer, reflect or journal on the following questions:

- How might Christians today be considered not of this world?
- What societal pressures do you need to resist?
- How does Jesus' warning to his disciples about the world's hatred (see verses 18–25) apply to Christians today?

▶ Jn 15:18–25

---

a Gk *were of the world*   *b* Gk *Slaves*   *c* Or *Helper*
d Or *convict the world of*

Cultural Connection

Christ Lives in Us Through the Holy Spirit

In his farewell speech to his disciples, Jesus tells them he will return to the Father but will not leave them orphaned (see Jn 14:18). The Father will give them another Advocate—the Holy Spirit. We also receive the Holy Spirit, through our Baptism and our Confirmation. Hispanic spirituality emphasizes the Spirit's gifts of love, freedom, truth, life, and hope.

- *Love* lets us find joy in the midst of suffering and pain. Christ did not end human suffering; instead, he showed how suffering for those we love can bring new life to them.
- *Freedom* from material goods, false gratification, and addictions nurtures the lifestyle we adopt as disciples of Jesus.
- *Truth* about God, us, and history can be achieved only through God's Revelation. The Spirit gives us the light to discover this truth and the strength to direct our lives by it.
- *God's life* in us helps us to overcome prejudices, promote reconciliation, foster unity in diversity, and work for justice and peace.
- *Hope* in being forever with God and the people we love is continuously nourished by the Spirit, who gives us a glimpse of the glory to come despite our earthly limitations.

▶ Jn 14:12–21, 16:12–15

---

little while, and you will no longer see me, and again a little while, and you will see me'; and 'Because I am going to the Father'?" 18They said, "What does he mean by this 'a little while'? We do not know what he is talking about." 19Jesus knew that they wanted to ask him, so he said to them, "Are you discussing among yourselves what I meant when I said, 'A little while, and you will no longer see me, and again a little while, and you will see me'? 20Very truly, I tell you, you will weep and mourn, but the world will rejoice; you will have pain, but your pain will turn into joy. 21When a woman is in labor, she has pain, because her hour has come. But when her child is born, she no longer remembers the anguish because of the joy of having brought a human being into the world. 22So you have pain now; but I will see you again, and your hearts will rejoice, and no one will take your joy from you. 23On that day you will ask nothing of me.ᵃ Very truly, I tell you, if you ask anything of the Father in my name, he will give it to you.ᵇ 24Until now you have not asked for anything in my name. Ask and you will receive, so that your joy may be complete.

Peace for the Disciples

25 "I have said these things to you in figures of speech. The hour is coming when I will no longer speak to you in figures, but will tell you plainly of the Father. 26On that day you will ask in my name. I do not say to you that I will ask the Father on your behalf; 27for the Father himself loves you, because you have loved me and have believed that I came from God.ᶜ 28I came from the Father and have come into the world; again, I am leaving the world and am going to the Father."

29 His disciples said, "Yes, now you are speaking plainly, not in any figure of speech! 30Now we know that you know all things, and do not need to have anyone question you; by this we believe that you came from God." 31Jesus answered them, "Do you now believe? 32The hour is coming, indeed it has come, when you will be scattered, each one to his home, and you will leave me alone. Yet I am not alone because the Father is with me. 33I have said this to you, so that in me you may have peace. In the world you face persecution. But take courage; I have conquered the world!"

Jesus Prays for His Disciples

17 After Jesus had spoken these words, he looked up to heaven and said, "Father, the hour has come; glorify your Son so that the Son may glorify you, 2since you have given him authority over all people,ᵈ to give eternal life to all whom you have given him. 3And this is eternal life, that they may know you, the only true God,

---

ᵃ Or *will ask me no question*   ᵇ Other ancient authorities read *Father, he will give it to you in my name*   ᶜ Other ancient authorities read *the Father*   ᵈ Gk *flesh*

and Jesus Christ whom you have sent. ⁴I glorified you on earth by finishing the work that you gave me to do. ⁵So now, Father, glorify me in your own presence with the glory that I had in your presence before the world existed.

6 "I have made your name known to those whom you gave me from the world. They were yours, and you gave them to me, and they have kept your word. ⁷Now they know that everything you have given me is from you; ⁸for the words that you gave to me I have given to them, and they have received them and know in truth that I came from you; and they have believed that you sent me. ⁹I am asking on their behalf; I am not asking on behalf of the world, but on behalf of those whom you gave me, because they are yours. ¹⁰All mine are yours, and yours are mine; and I have been glorified in them. ¹¹And now I am no longer in the world, but they are in the world, and I am coming to you. Holy Father, protect them in your name that you have given

me, so that they may be one, as we are one. ¹²While I was with them, I protected them in your name that*ᵃ* you have given me. I guarded them, and not one of them was lost except the one destined to be lost,ᵇ so that the scripture might be fulfilled. ¹³But now I am coming to you, and I speak these things in the world so that they may have my joy made complete in themselves.ᶜ ¹⁴I have given them your word, and the world has hated them because they do not belong to the world, just as I do not belong to the world. ¹⁵I am not asking you to take them out of the world, but I ask you to protect them from the evil one.ᵈ ¹⁶They do not belong to the world, just as I do not belong to the world. ¹⁷Sanctify them in the truth; your word is truth. ¹⁸As you have sent me into the world, so I have sent them into the world. ¹⁹And for their sakes I sanctify myself, so that they also may be sanctified in truth.

20 "I ask not only on behalf of these, but also on behalf of those who will believe in me through their word, ²¹that they may all be one. As you, Father, are in me and I am in you, may they also be in us,ᵉ so that the world may believe that you have sent me. ²²The glory that you have given me I have given them, so that they may be one, as we are one, ²³I in them and you in me, that they may become completely one, so that the world may know that you have sent me and have loved them even as you have loved me. ²⁴Father, I desire that those also, whom you have given me, may be with me where I am, to see my glory, which you have given me because you loved me before the foundation of the world.

25 "Righteous Father, the world does not know you, but I know you; and these know that you have sent me. ²⁶I made your name known to them, and I will make it known, so that the love with which you have loved me may be in them, and I in them."

The Betrayal and Arrest of Jesus

18 After Jesus had spoken these words, he went out with his disciples across the Kidron valley to a place where there was a garden, which he and his disciples entered. ²Now Judas, who betrayed him, also knew the place, because Jesus often met there with his disciples. ³So Judas brought a detachment of soldiers together with police from the chief priests and the Pharisees, and they came there with lanterns and torches and weapons. ⁴Then Jesus, knowing all

Pray It!

A Prayer for Friends

In John, chapter 17, Jesus prays for his friends, the disciples. And he also prays for us, his future disciples (see verse 20)! Here is a prayer you can say for your friends:

Dear Jesus, thank you for my true friends. They accept me for who I am. With them, I don't have to pretend to be someone else. They support me when I feel that the world is crumbling around me. They are honest with me even if what they say is not what I want to hear. They offer their sense of humor so that we can laugh together.

Spirit of Jesus, watch over these friends just as you watch over me. Show them your loving acceptance and support. Help them to honestly look at themselves and the decisions they are making. If they experience pain, frustration, or failure, give them strength to lean on you. Fill their days with laughter and love. Protect them and keep them safe all the days of their lives. Amen.

▶ John, chapter 17

ᵃ Other ancient authorities read *protected in your name those whom*   ᵇ Gk *except the son of destruction*   ᶜ Or *among themselves*   ᵈ Or *from evil*   ᵉ Other ancient authorities read *be one in us*

Cultural Connection

Race Relations

On April 4, 2001, the thirty-third anniversary of the death of Martin Luther King Jr., Cardinal George of the Archdiocese of Chicago published a letter to the faithful, titled "Dwell in My Love." In it Cardinal George challenges us to look at John 15:7–10, in which Jesus invites us to dwell in his love. Cardinal George makes the point that all people, races, cultures, and nationalities are part of the human family and that Jesus invites us to be unified in his love.

Race is a gift from God that underscores our uniqueness. It is important for us to celebrate our differences in a way that brings us together as followers of Jesus. The bottom line of Cardinal George's letter is that our diversity enriches us, making life more full and interesting.

Think of all the ways in which people of different races, cultures, and nationalities have brought richness to your community, family, parish, and school.

▶ Jn 15:7–10

---

that was to happen to him, came forward and asked them, "Whom are you looking for?" ⁵They answered, "Jesus of Nazareth."ᵃ Jesus replied, "I am he."ᵇ Judas, who betrayed him, was standing with them. ⁶When Jesusᶜ said to them, "I am he,"ᵇ they stepped back and fell to the ground. ⁷Again he asked them, "Whom are you looking for?" And they said, "Jesus of Nazareth."ᵃ ⁸Jesus answered, "I told you that I am he.ᵇ So if you are looking for me, let these men go." ⁹This was to fulfill the word that he had spoken, "I did not lose a single one of those whom you gave me." ¹⁰Then Simon Peter, who had a sword, drew it, struck the high priest's slave, and cut off his right ear. The slave's name was Malchus. ¹¹Jesus said to Peter, "Put your sword back into its sheath. Am I not to drink the cup that the Father has given me?"

Jesus before the High Priest

12 So the soldiers, their officer, and the Jewish police arrested Jesus and bound him. ¹³First they took him to Annas, who was the father-in-law of Caiaphas, the high priest that year. ¹⁴Caiaphas was the one who had advised the Jews that it was better to have one person die for the people.

Peter Denies Jesus

15 Simon Peter and another disciple followed Jesus. Since that disciple was known to the high priest, he went with Jesus into the courtyard of the high priest, ¹⁶but Peter was standing outside at the gate. So the other disciple, who was known to the high priest, went out, spoke to the woman who guarded the gate, and brought Peter in.

¹⁷The woman said to Peter, "You are not also one of this man's disciples, are you?" He said, "I am not." ¹⁸Now the slaves and the police had made a charcoal fire because it was cold, and they were standing around it and warming themselves. Peter also was standing with them and warming himself.

The High Priest Questions Jesus

19 Then the high priest questioned Jesus about his disciples and about his teaching. ²⁰Jesus answered, "I have spoken openly to the world; I have always taught in synagogues and in the temple, where all the Jews come together. I have said nothing in secret. ²¹Why do you ask me? Ask those who heard what I said to them; they know what I said." ²²When he had said this, one of the police standing nearby struck Jesus on the face, saying, "Is that how you answer the high priest?" ²³Jesus answered, "If I have spoken wrongly, testify to the wrong. But if I have spoken rightly, why do you strike me?" ²⁴Then Annas sent him bound to Caiaphas the high priest.

Peter Denies Jesus Again

25 Now Simon Peter was standing and warming himself. They asked him, "You are not also one of his disciples, are you?" He denied it and said, "I am not." ²⁶One of the slaves of the high priest, a relative of the man whose ear Peter had cut off, asked, "Did I not see you in the garden with him?" ²⁷Again Peter denied it, and at that moment the cock crowed.

---

a Gk the Nazorean   b Gk I am   c Gk he

✝ Catholic Connection

The Trinity

If you knew you were about to die, how would you spend your final moments with your friends? The Gospel of John (see 13:1—17:26) gives us a window into Jesus' final moments with his disciples right before his arrest and Crucifixion. During his time with them, Jesus washes their feet, tells them about the promise of the Holy Spirit, and shares his hopes for them. Jesus concludes his last moments with them with a prayer that reveals and reflects on the unity that exists between Jesus, God the Father, and his disciples. The unity between the Father and the Son, which Jesus refers to in his prayer, points to one of the greatest mysteries of the Christian faith: that there is only one God in three persons—the Father, the Son, and the Holy Spirit. We call this mystery the Trinity.

This mystery is known only because God chose to reveal it to the world. A glimpse of it can be seen in God's actions over the course of salvation history. In the Old Testament, God revealed himself as the Father of all creation. In the New Testament, God revealed himself as Father in relationship to the Son, as Son in the person of Jesus Christ, and as Holy Spirit sent from the Father and the Son. United as one God, the Father, Son, and Holy Spirit worked together to bring about our salvation.

The Church teaches that each person of the Trinity—Father, Son, and Holy Spirit—is fully divine in and of themselves. In other words, the Father is God, Jesus is God, and the Holy Spirit is God, and together they are the one God. The Church also teaches that each person of the Trinity is truly distinct from the others and each person's true distinction lies in the relationship among all three as Father, Son, and Holy Spirit—meaning they are not just a way to name the different ways God acts in the world. Because of their unity, each person of the Trinity is entirely in the other two and all work together. For example, when we follow the Son, we are doing so because the Father invited us and the Holy Spirit moved us to do so.

Jesus' prayer calls us to share in and reflect the unity that exists in the Trinity. When we are baptized in the name of the Father, Son, and Holy Spirit, we enter into the life and mystery of the Trinity. Every time we make the sign of the cross, we are reminded of the Trinity. As believers in the Triune God, we are called to reflect God's unity in our relationships with one another by working together to help all people find salvation in God the Father, Son, and Holy Spirit.

▶ **Jn 17:20–26**
Catechism, nos. 232–267

Jesus before Pilate

28 Then they took Jesus from Caiaphas to Pilate's headquarters.*a* It was early in the morning. They themselves did not enter the headquarters,*a*

Did You Know?

The Triumph of Jesus

The Gospel of John most closely resembles the other three Gospels in its stories of Jesus' trial, death, and Resurrection. But even here, John's unique portrayal of Jesus is seen. The most obvious difference is that in John, Jesus is clearly in charge and in his glory from the moment he is arrested. There is no agony in the garden. When the soldiers and police come to arrest Jesus, they fall to the ground as he speaks (see Jn 18:6). He teaches Pilate about his identity and mission, in essence putting Pilate on trial (see verses 33–38). Jesus brings together his mother and the Beloved Disciple (see 19:26–27). Jesus is not the victim; rather, he decides the moment of his death when he gives up his spirit (see verse 30).

John is also careful to show in detail the ways Jesus' Crucifixion fulfills Old Testament prophecies of the Messiah. He identifies Jesus with the just man who was persecuted in Psalms 22 and 69. He does this by connecting the gambling for Jesus' seamless tunic (see Jn 19:24) with Psalm 22:18, and the offering of sour wine (see Jn 19:29) with Psalm 69:21. Jesus' unbroken legs (see Jn 19:33) are a reference to the Paschal lamb in Exodus 12:46, and his pierced side (see Jn 19:34) is seen as the fulfillment of Zechariah 12:10.

John wants us to know that these events are the central "Hour" in the world's history and the time of Jesus' triumph. For the author of John, Jesus is clearly the divine Son of God, and by Jesus' self-sacrifice, God brings salvation to the entire world. The author of John wants us to focus not on the tragedy but on God's power at work in Jesus.

▶ **John, chapters 18–19**

so as to avoid ritual defilement and to be able to eat the Passover. 29So Pilate went out to them and said, "What accusation do you bring against this man?" 30They answered, "If this man were not a criminal, we would not have handed him over to you." 31Pilate said to them, "Take him yourselves and judge him according to your law." The Jews replied, "We are not permitted to put anyone to death." 32(This was to fulfill what Jesus had said when he indicated the kind of death he was to die.)

33 Then Pilate entered the headquarters*a* again, summoned Jesus, and asked him, "Are you the King of the Jews?" 34Jesus answered, "Do you ask this on your own, or did others tell you about me?" 35Pilate replied, "I am not a Jew, am I? Your own nation and the chief priests have handed you over to me. What have you done?" 36Jesus answered, "My kingdom is not from this world. If my kingdom were from this world, my followers would be fighting to keep me from being handed over to the Jews. But as it is, my kingdom is not from here." 37Pilate asked him, "So you are a king?" Jesus answered, "You say that I am a king. For this I was born, and for this I came into the world, to testify to the truth. Everyone who belongs to the truth listens to my voice." 38Pilate asked him, "What is truth?"

Jesus Sentenced to Death

After he had said this, he went out to the Jews again and told them, "I find no case against him. 39But you have a custom that I release someone for you at the Passover. Do you want me to release for you the King of the Jews?" 40They shouted in reply, "Not this man, but Barabbas!" Now Barabbas was a bandit.

19 Then Pilate took Jesus and had him flogged. 2And the soldiers wove a crown of thorns and put it on his head, and they dressed him in a purple robe. 3They kept coming up to him, saying, "Hail, King of the Jews!" and striking him on the face. 4Pilate went out again and said to them, "Look, I am bringing him out to you to let you know that I find no case against him." 5So Jesus came out, wearing the crown of thorns and the purple robe. Pilate said to them, "Here is the man!" 6When the chief priests and the police saw him, they shouted, "Crucify him! Crucify him!" Pilate said to them, "Take him yourselves and crucify him; I find no case against him." 7The Jews answered him, "We have a law, and according to that law he ought to die because he has claimed to be the Son of God."

J
N

---

a Gk *the praetorium*

8 Now when Pilate heard this, he was more afraid than ever. 9He entered his headquarters[a] again and asked Jesus, "Where are you from?" But Jesus gave him no answer. 10Pilate therefore said to him, "Do you refuse to speak to me? Do you not know that I have power to release you, and power to crucify you?" 11Jesus answered him, "You would have no power over me unless it had been given you from above; therefore the one who handed me over to you is guilty of a greater sin." 12From then on Pilate tried to release him, but the Jews cried out, "If you release this man, you are no friend of the emperor. Everyone who claims to be a king sets himself against the emperor."

13 When Pilate heard these words, he brought Jesus outside and sat[b] on the judge's bench at a place called The Stone Pavement, or in Hebrew[c] Gabbatha. 14Now it was the day of Preparation for the Passover; and it was about noon. He said to the Jews, "Here is your King!" 15They cried out, "Away with him! Away with him! Crucify him!" Pilate asked them, "Shall I crucify your King?" The chief priests answered, "We have no king but the emperor." 16Then he handed him over to them to be crucified.

The Crucifixion of Jesus

So they took Jesus; 17and carrying the cross by himself, he went out to what is called The Place of the Skull, which in Hebrew[c] is called Golgotha.

19:2

18There they crucified him, and with him two others, one on either side, with Jesus between them. 19Pilate also had an inscription written and put on the cross. It read, "Jesus of Nazareth,[d] the King of the Jews." 20Many of the Jews read this inscription, because the place where Jesus was crucified was near the city; and it was written in Hebrew,[c] in Latin, and in Greek. 21Then the chief priests of the Jews said to Pilate, "Do not write, 'The King of the Jews,' but, 'This man said, I am King of the Jews.' " 22Pilate answered,

---

a Gk *the praetorium*   b Or *seated him*   c That is, *Aramaic*
d Gk *the Nazorean*

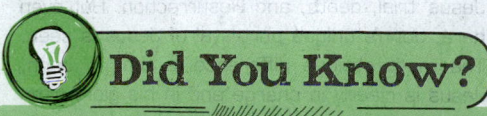

Did You Know?

The Words on the Cross

In the Gospel of John, Pontius Pilate acts as a mediator between two worlds—the outside world of darkness and unbelief and the inner world of light and truth. During Jesus' trial, Pilate goes back and forth between the Jewish religious authorities who are outside (in the dark) and Jesus, who is inside Pilate's headquarters (in the light).

Does Pilate know the truth about Jesus? When he writes out the charges to be placed on the cross, "the Jews" (see "'The Jews' in the Gospel of John," near Jn 2:18–20) argue with him about the wording. He answers by saying, "What I have written I have written" (19:22)—that is, "These words are the truth about Jesus." The words he writes are "Jesus of Nazareth, the King of the Jews" (verse 19). In Latin, they read, *Iesus Nazarenus Rex Iudaeorum.* When artists draw or sculpt the Crucifixion scene, they often include this Latin phrase in abbreviated form above the cross: *INRI.*

In another of the Gospel's ironies, Pilate recognizes what the Jewish leaders rejected—Jesus Christ is a king. Christians believe a deeper truth—Christ is king of not only the Jews but of all creation! On the last Sunday of the liturgical year, the Catholic Church celebrates this in the feast of Christ the King.

▶ Jn 19:19–22

Cultural Connection

Our Mother of Guadalupe: A Gift from God

Devotion to Mary as mother of God and mother of the Church has been a consistent dimension of Christian faith. From Jesus' words on the cross in John 19:25–27, Christians have identified with the Beloved Disciple and seen Mary as their mother. This experience has led Catholics of many countries to name Mary as their patroness (advocate, protector, supporter, mother): for instance, they call her Virgin of the Immaculate Conception in the United States and Chile, Virgin of Lourdes in France, and Virgin of Fátima in Portugal. The strong devotion of Latin American countries to Mary as a mother who protects and assists her children is revealed in their titles for her: Our Lady of Mercy in the Dominican Republic, Our Lady of Caridad del Cobre (charity) in Cuba, Our Lady of Divine Providence in Puerto Rico, and Our Lady of Help in Guatemala, to name a few.

But Mexico developed the strongest devotion to Mary as mother of a nation. The Virgin of Guadalupe appeared to Saint Juan Diego, a humble native from Tenochtitlán, near Mexico City. She had the face of the mestizo people (the descendants of native and Spanish peoples), and her words to Juan Diego were those of a caring mother, especially for her children who are suffering, poor, or oppressed:

Here I wish to hear and help you, and all who dwell in this land and all those who love me, and invoke and place their confidence in me; and to hear your complaints and remedy all your sorrows, hardships, and suffering. . . .

Listen and understand well my son, smallest of all, that you have no cause to be frightened. . . . Is this not your mother here next to you? Are you not here in the shelter of my loving shadow? . . . Let nothing worry or afflict you further. . . . (Office of Religious Education, *A Handbook on Guadalupe*, pp. 148, 152)

▶ Jn 19:25–27

"What I have written I have written." 23When the soldiers had crucified Jesus, they took his clothes and divided them into four parts, one for each soldier. They also took his tunic; now the tunic was seamless, woven in one piece from the top. 24So they said to one another, "Let us not tear it, but cast lots for it to see who will get it." This was to fulfill what the scripture says,

"They divided my clothes among themselves,
    and for my clothing they cast lots."

25And that is what the soldiers did.

Meanwhile, standing near the cross of Jesus were his mother, and his mother's sister, Mary the wife of Clopas, and Mary Magdalene. 26When Jesus saw his mother and the disciple whom he loved standing beside her, he said to his mother, "Woman, here is your son." 27Then he said to the disciple, "Here is your mother." And from that hour the disciple took her into his own home.

28 After this, when Jesus knew that all was now finished, he said (in order to fulfill the scripture), "I am thirsty." 29A jar full of sour wine was standing there. So they put a sponge full of the wine on a branch of hyssop and held it to his mouth. 30When Jesus had received the wine, he said, "It is finished." Then he bowed his head and gave up his spirit.

Jesus' Side Is Pierced

31 Since it was the day of Preparation, the Jews did not want the bodies left on the cross during the sabbath, especially because that sabbath was a day of great solemnity. So they asked Pilate to have the legs of the crucified men broken and the bodies removed. 32Then the soldiers came and broke the legs of the first and of the other who had been crucified with him. 33But when they came to Jesus and saw that he was already dead, they did not break his legs. 34Instead, one of the soldiers pierced his side with a spear, and at once blood and water came out. 35(He who saw this has testified so that you also may believe. His testimony is true, and he knows[a] that he tells the truth.) 36These things occurred so that the scripture might be fulfilled, "None of his bones shall be broken." 37And again another passage of scripture says, "They will look on the one whom they have pierced."

---

a Or there is one who knows

The Burial of Jesus

38 After these things, Joseph of Arimathea, who was a disciple of Jesus, though a secret one because of his fear of the Jews, asked Pilate to let him take away the body of Jesus. Pilate gave him permission; so he came and removed his body. 39Nicodemus, who had at first come to Jesus by night, also came, bringing a mixture of myrrh and aloes, weighing about a hundred pounds. 40They took the body of Jesus and wrapped it with the spices in linen cloths, according to the burial custom of the Jews. 41Now there was a garden in the place where he was crucified, and in the garden there was a new tomb in which no one had ever been laid. 42And so, because it was the Jewish day of Preparation, and the tomb was nearby, they laid Jesus there.

The Resurrection of Jesus

20 Early on the first day of the week, while it was still dark, Mary Magdalene came

Introducing...

Mary Magdalene

Like the Samaritan woman, who is the first to spread the word that Jesus is the Messiah (see Jn 4:1–42), Mary Magdalene is the first to announce that Jesus has been raised from the dead. She comes to the tomb while it is still dark (symbolizing unbelief). Later, she encounters the risen Jesus and begins to see with eyes of faith. Belief prompts her to action, and so she goes to tell the others, "I have seen the Lord" (20:18).

Mary Magdalene is first in every listing of Jesus' female disciples (see Mt 27:55–56, Mk 15:40–41, Lk 8:2–3). She seems to have been the leader of a group of women who followed Jesus from the beginning of his ministry, through his death and beyond. Luke indicates that Jesus cured her of seven demons (see Lk 8:2). All four Gospels name her as one of the first eyewitnesses of Jesus' Resurrection. From all this, we can presume that she was a special friend and disciple of Jesus and an important leader among the first Christians.

▶ Jn 20:1–18

to the tomb and saw that the stone had been removed from the tomb. 2So she ran and went to Simon Peter and the other disciple, the one whom Jesus loved, and said to them, "They have taken the Lord out of the tomb, and we do not know where they have laid him." 3Then Peter and the other disciple set out and went toward the tomb. 4The two were running together, but the other disciple outran Peter and reached the tomb first. 5He bent down to look in and saw the linen wrappings lying there, but he did not go in. 6Then Simon Peter came, following him, and went into the tomb. He saw the linen wrappings lying there, 7and the cloth that had been on Jesus' head, not lying with the linen wrappings but rolled up in a place by itself. 8Then the other disciple, who reached the tomb first, also went in, and he saw and believed; 9for as yet they did not understand the scripture, that he must rise from the dead. 10Then the disciples returned to their homes.

Jesus Appears to Mary Magdalene

11 But Mary stood weeping outside the tomb. As she wept, she bent over to look*a* into the tomb; 12and she saw two angels in white, sitting where the body of Jesus had been lying, one at the head and the other at the feet. 13They said to her, "Woman, why are you weeping?" She said to them, "They have taken away my Lord, and I do not know where they have laid him." 14When she had said this, she turned around and saw Jesus standing there, but she did not know that it was Jesus. 15Jesus said to her, "Woman, why are you weeping? Whom are you looking for?" Supposing him to be the gardener, she said to him, "Sir, if you have carried him away, tell me where you have laid him, and I will take him away." 16Jesus said to her, "Mary!" She turned and said to him in Hebrew,*b* "Rabbouni!" (which means Teacher). 17Jesus said to her, "Do not hold on to me, because I have not yet ascended to the Father. But go to my brothers and say to them, 'I am ascending to my Father and your Father, to my God and your God.' " 18Mary Magdalene went and announced to the disciples, "I have seen the Lord"; and she told them that he had said these things to her.

Jesus Appears to the Disciples

19 When it was evening on that day, the first day of the week, and the doors of the house where the disciples had met were locked for fear

---

a Gk lacks *to look*   *b* That is, *Aramaic*

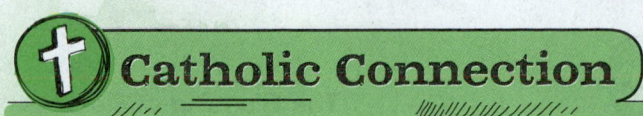

Catholic Connection

Sacrament of Penance and Reconciliation

Imagine the disciples locked in a room, full of fear. Then Jesus miraculously appears, showing them that neither fear nor human obstacles can keep out Christ and his offer of peace. The disciples' fear is suddenly turned into rejoicing. Jesus hands on his mission to the disciples and gives them the Holy Spirit so that they may reconcile people to the Father by forgiving sins in God's name just as Jesus had done.

The Church continues Jesus' ministry of reconciling people to God in a special way through the sacrament of Penance and Reconciliation. Although Baptism takes away original sin, it does not remove its effects, namely our tendency to sin. Because we are members of the Church, our sin not only offends God but also harms the community. Therefore, we need to be reconciled to God and the Church. Celebrating the sacrament of Penance and Reconciliation helps us to do that.

The sacrament of Penance and Reconciliation, which is sometimes called Confession, because a person confesses his or her sins, is generally administered by a priest who represents Christ and the Church. As Christ's representative, the priest acts as the servant of God's mercy and forgiveness. Through the actions of the priest, the individual receiving the sacrament truly experiences the peace of Christ's redeeming love.

The sacrament takes place between a baptized individual (penitent) and a priest. The rite begins with the priest's greeting the penitent and the penitent's responding by making the sign of the cross. The priest invites the penitent to trust in God's mercy and may choose to read a passage from the Scriptures. Then the penitent confesses his or her sins and the priest gives him or her a penance. A penance is something the penitent will later say or do that will help to repair the harm his or her sins have caused. It also can strengthen the penitent and help him or her to avoid the sin in the future. Next, the penitent will say an Act of Contrition—a prayer that admits guilt and expresses the penitent's desire to do better with God's help. The priest, in the name of Christ and his Church, then offers a prayer of absolution, which frees the penitent from all sin and reconciles him or her to God and the Church. Concluding the sacrament, the penitent gives praise to God for his mercy, and the priest tells the penitent to go forth in peace.

When was the last time you experienced God's love and mercy in the sacrament of Penance and Reconciliation? Even if it has been a while, God and the Church are always there waiting with open arms. So consider making time this week to be reconciled and renewed.

▶ **Jn 20:19–23**
Catechism, nos. 1420–1470

JN

Cultural Connection

The Blessing of Baskets

It's early Holy Saturday morning, and the priest of the parish arrives to open the church for a special event. As he draws near the front door, the smell of eggs, sausages, freshly baked bread, and other breakfast foods wafts from the baskets of those already gathered. As people enter the church, they place their baskets on a table before the altar. The priest begins Mass with a prayer and then blesses the baskets of food with holy water and the sign of the cross:

Blessed are you, O God! In your bounty you provide for your people. As we prepare to celebrate the Resurrection of your Son, bless these Easter foods, and strengthen your people that they may be true witnesses to the new life offered in Christ Jesus, our Lord. Amen.

This custom originated in Eastern Europe and can be found today in many churches around the world. The blessing of baskets reminds us that Jesus' death and Resurrection should touch every aspect of the lives of the faithful. Especially after a long Lent of fasting and self-denial, the rich foods of the Easter table call to mind that Good Friday's sacrifice culminated in Easter glory—a time for celebration and feasting.

▶ Jn 21:1–14

---

of the Jews, Jesus came and stood among them and said, "Peace be with you." 20After he said this, he showed them his hands and his side. Then the disciples rejoiced when they saw the Lord. 21Jesus said to them again, "Peace be with you. As the Father has sent me, so I send you." 22When he had said this, he breathed on them and said to them, "Receive the Holy Spirit. 23If you forgive the sins of any, they are forgiven them; if you retain the sins of any, they are retained."

Jesus and Thomas

24 But Thomas (who was called the Twin[a]), one of the twelve, was not with them when Jesus came. 25So the other disciples told him, "We have seen the Lord." But he said to them, "Unless I see the mark of the nails in his hands, and put my finger in the mark of the nails and my hand in his side, I will not believe."

26 A week later his disciples were again in the house, and Thomas was with them. Although the doors were shut, Jesus came and stood among them and said, "Peace be with you." 27Then he said to Thomas, "Put your finger here and see my hands. Reach out your hand and put it in my side. Do not doubt but believe." 28Thomas answered him, "My Lord and my God!" 29Jesus said to him, "Have you believed because you have seen me? Blessed are those who have not seen and yet have come to believe."

The Purpose of This Book

30 Now Jesus did many other signs in the presence of his disciples, which are not written in this book. 31But these are written so that you may come to believe[b] that Jesus is the Messiah,[c] the Son of God, and that through believing you may have life in his name.

Jesus Appears to Seven Disciples

21 After these things Jesus showed himself again to the disciples by the Sea of Tiberias; and he showed himself in this way. 2Gathered there together were Simon Peter, Thomas called the Twin,[a] Nathanael of Cana in Galilee, the sons of Zebedee, and two others of his disciples. 3Simon Peter said to them, "I am going fishing." They said to him, "We will go with you." They went out and got into the boat, but that night they caught nothing.

4 Just after daybreak, Jesus stood on the beach; but the disciples did not know that it was Jesus. 5Jesus said to them, "Children, you have no fish, have you?" They answered him, "No." 6He said to them, "Cast the net to the right side of the boat, and you will find some." So they cast it, and now they were not able to haul it in because there were so many fish. 7That disciple whom Jesus loved said to Peter, "It is the Lord!" When Simon Peter

---

a Gk *Didymus*   b Other ancient authorities read *may continue to believe*   c Or *the Christ*

heard that it was the Lord, he put on some clothes, for he was naked, and jumped into the sea. [8]But the other disciples came in the boat, dragging the net full of fish, for they were not far from the land, only about a hundred yards[a] off.

9 When they had gone ashore, they saw a charcoal fire there, with fish on it, and bread. [10]Jesus said to them, "Bring some of the fish that you have just caught." [11]So Simon Peter went aboard and hauled the net ashore, full of large fish, a hundred fifty-three of them; and though there were so many, the net was not torn. [12]Jesus said to them, "Come and have breakfast." Now none of the disciples dared to ask him, "Who are you?" because they knew it was the Lord. [13]Jesus came and took the bread and gave it to them, and did the same with the fish. [14]This was now the third time that Jesus appeared to the disciples after he was raised from the dead.

Jesus and Peter

15 When they had finished breakfast, Jesus said to Simon Peter, "Simon son of John, do you love me more than these?" He said to him, "Yes, Lord; you know that I love you." Jesus said to him, "Feed my lambs." [16]A second time he said to him, "Simon son of John, do you love me?" He said to him, "Yes, Lord; you know that I love you." Jesus said to him, "Tend my sheep." [17]He said to him the third time, "Simon son of John, do you love me?" Peter felt hurt because he said to him the third time, "Do you love me?" And he said to him, "Lord, you know everything; you know that I love you." Jesus said to him, "Feed my sheep. [18]Very truly, I tell you, when you were younger, you used to fasten your own belt and to go wherever you wished. But when you grow old, you will stretch out your hands, and someone else will fasten a belt around you and take you where you do not wish to go." [19](He said this to indicate the kind of death by which he would glorify God.) After this he said to him, "Follow me."

Jesus and the Beloved Disciple

20 Peter turned and saw the disciple whom Jesus loved following them; he was the one who had reclined next to Jesus at the supper and had said, "Lord, who is it that is going to betray you?" [21]When Peter saw him, he said to Jesus, "Lord, what about him?" [22]Jesus said to him, "If it is my

---

a Gk *two hundred cubits*

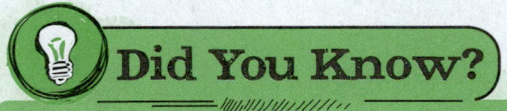

Did You Know?

Resurrection Stories

There are fourteen stories about Jesus' Resurrection in the four Gospels. None of the stories describes the actual Resurrection or the physical appearance of the resurrected Christ. Matthew emphasizes God's power with dramatic symbols like earthquakes and lightning (see Mt 28:2–3). Mark, in its original ending, focuses on the empty tomb (see Mk 16:1–8). Luke emphasizes the living presence of Jesus in the Scriptures and the Eucharist (see Lk 24:13–35). John brings out the authority of the leaders of the early Church, especially Peter's role as shepherd of the Church (see Jn 20:19–23, 21:15–19).

Together, all these stories convey the faith of the disciples that Jesus is alive. Through God's power, life has triumphed over death. The disciples' mission is to communicate this Good News. And that's our mission too!

▶ Jn 21:15–19

The Gospel According To . . .

The Gospel of John ends by saying that if everything Jesus did were to be written down, the entire world could not contain it. Sounds like a challenge, doesn't it? Perhaps the author was thinking of all the things the risen Christ continues to do in the lives of believers. If you were to write your own Gospel story, one based on the risen Jesus at work in your life, what marvelous stories would it hold? What messages and teachings would you offer to the people of today? How has your life revealed and reflected the Good News of Jesus?

▶ Jn 21:24–25

will that he remain until I come, what is that to you? Follow me!" [23]So the rumor spread in the community[a] that this disciple would not die. Yet Jesus did not say to him that he would not die, but, "If it is my will that he remain until I come, what is that to you?"[b]

24 This is the disciple who is testifying to these things and has written them, and we know that his testimony is true. [25]But there are also many other things that Jesus did; if every one of them were written down, I suppose that the world itself could not contain the books that would be written.

---

a Gk *among the brothers*   *b* Other ancient authorities lack *what is that to you*

In your history classes in school, you probably studied stories about the heroic men and women who helped create the United States: George Washington, Benjamin Franklin, Harriet Tubman, Susan B. Anthony, and Harry S. Truman to name a few. The stories about these famous people are an important part of our national identity. The Acts of the Apostles is a book containing stories like these. It continues the account of salvation history by telling about the beginnings of the Christian movement, primarily through stories about two of its most important missionaries, Peter and Paul.

At a Glance

- **1:1—6:7.** the new Pentecost, the mission in Jerusalem

- **6:8—9:43.** the martyrdom of Stephen, the spread of the mission outside Jerusalem, Paul's conversion

- **10:1—15:35.** continuing the spread of the mission to the Gentiles, the Council of Jerusalem

- **15:36—28:31.** Paul's mission to the ends of the earth

Quick Facts

Inspired Author: often identified as Luke, who also wrote the Gospel of Luke
Date Written: approximately AD 80
Audience: Gentile (Greek) Christians represented by Theophilus (Acts 1:1)

In Depth

The Acts of the Apostles—sometimes simply called Acts—was written by the same author as the Gospel of Luke. So Acts is really the second volume of a two-volume history. Like the Gospels, it is not a history in the sense of an eyewitness account of the beginnings of Christianity; rather, it is an interpretation of this history, explaining how Christianity spread outside of Judaism to the Gentile world under the direction of the Holy Spirit.

Lots of great stories are in the Acts of the Apostles. We read about the descent of the Holy Spirit on the Apostles (see 2:1–41), Paul's conversion to the Christian way (see 9:1–19), and some miraculous escapes from prisons and riots (see 12:6–11, 16:16–40). We learn about the first church council in Jerusalem, where a decision was made to accept Gentiles (non-Jews) as Christians without requiring that they also become practicing Jews (see 15:1–35). Acts continuously emphasizes how faith in Christ is shared and supported through Christian community.

The Acts of the Apostles gives us information about how Christians lived in the years after Jesus' Resurrection and Ascension. We learn how the believers celebrated the Eucharist together and shared their belongings (see 2:42–47). We learn how the Gospel message was preached, first to Jews in the synagogues and later to Gentiles. We learn how traveling missionaries like Paul went on long journeys and suffered many hardships to form new groups of believers across the Roman Empire. Under the guidance of the Holy Spirit, the church miraculously went from a small group of disciples in Jerusalem to a movement spreading across the entire Roman Empire, even to Rome itself.

The Acts of the **Apostles**

Acts

The Promise of the Holy Spirit

1 In the first book, Theophilus, I wrote about all that Jesus did and taught from the beginning ²until the day when he was taken up to heaven, after giving instructions through the Holy Spirit to the apostles whom he had chosen. ³After his suffering he presented himself alive to them by many convincing proofs, appearing to them during forty days and speaking about the kingdom of God. ⁴While staying*a* with them, he ordered them not to leave Jerusalem, but to wait there for the promise of the Father. "This," he said, "is what you have heard from me; ⁵for John baptized with water, but you will be baptized with*b* the Holy Spirit not many days from now."

The Ascension of Jesus

6 So when they had come together, they asked him, "Lord, is this the time when you will restore the kingdom to Israel?" ⁷He replied, "It is not for you to know the times or periods that the Father has set by his own authority. ⁸But you will receive power when the Holy Spirit has come upon you; and you will be my witnesses in Jerusalem, in all Judea and Samaria, and to the ends of the earth." ⁹When he had said this, as they were watching, he was lifted up, and a cloud took him out of their sight. ¹⁰While he was going and they were gazing up toward heaven, suddenly two men in white robes stood by them. ¹¹They said, "Men of Galilee, why do you stand looking up toward heaven? This Jesus, who has been taken up from you into heaven, will come in the same way as you saw him go into heaven."

Matthias Chosen to Replace Judas

12 Then they returned to Jerusalem from the mount called Olivet, which is near Jerusalem, a sabbath day's journey away. ¹³When they had entered the city, they went to the room upstairs where they were staying, Peter, and John, and James, and Andrew, Philip and Thomas, Bartholomew and Matthew, James son of Alphaeus, and Simon the Zealot, and Judas son of*c* James. ¹⁴All these were constantly devoting themselves to prayer, together with certain women, including Mary the mother of Jesus, as well as his brothers.

15 In those days Peter stood up among the believers*d* (together the crowd numbered about one hundred twenty persons) and said, ¹⁶"Friends,*e* the scripture had to be fulfilled, which the Holy Spirit through David foretold concerning Judas, who became a guide for those who arrested Jesus— ¹⁷for he was numbered among us and was allotted his share in this ministry." ¹⁸(Now this man acquired a field with the reward of his wickedness; and falling headlong,*f* he burst open in the middle and all his bowels gushed out. ¹⁹This became known to all the residents of Jerusalem, so that the field was called in their language Hakeldama, that is, Field of Blood.) ²⁰"For it is written in the book of Psalms,

a Or *eating*   *b* Or *by*   *c* Or *the brother of*   *d* Gk *brothers*
e Gk *Men, brothers*   *f* Or *swelling up*

'Let his homestead become desolate,
   and let there be no one to live in it';
and
'Let another take his position of overseer.'
²¹So one of the men who have accompanied us during all the time that the Lord Jesus went in and out among us, ²²beginning from the baptism of John until the day when he was taken up from us—one of these must become a witness with us to his resurrection." ²³So they proposed two, Joseph called Barsabbas, who was also known as Justus, and Matthias. ²⁴Then they prayed and said, "Lord, you know everyone's heart. Show us which one of these two you have chosen ²⁵to take the place*a* in this ministry and apostleship from which Judas turned aside to go to his own place." ²⁶And they cast lots for them, and the lot fell on Matthias; and he was added to the eleven apostles.

The Coming of the Holy Spirit

2 When the day of Pentecost had come, they were all together in one place. ²And suddenly from heaven there came a sound like the rush of a violent wind, and it filled the entire house where they were sitting. ³Divided tongues, as of fire, appeared among them, and a tongue rested on each of them. ⁴All of them were filled with the Holy Spirit and began to speak in other languages, as the Spirit gave them ability.

5 Now there were devout Jews from every nation under heaven living in Jerusalem. ⁶And at this sound the crowd gathered and was bewildered, because each one heard them speaking in the native language of each. ⁷Amazed and astonished, they asked, "Are not all these who are speaking Galileans? ⁸And how is it that we hear, each of us, in our own native language? ⁹Parthians, Medes, Elamites, and residents of Mesopotamia, Judea and Cappadocia, Pontus and Asia, ¹⁰Phrygia and Pamphylia, Egypt and the parts of Libya belonging to Cyrene, and visitors from Rome, both Jews and proselytes, ¹¹Cretans and Arabs—in our own languages we hear them speaking about God's deeds of power." ¹²All were amazed and perplexed, saying to one another, "What does this mean?" ¹³But others sneered and said, "They are filled with new wine."

Peter Addresses the Crowd

14 But Peter, standing with the eleven, raised his voice and addressed them, "Men of Judea and all who live in Jerusalem, let this be known to you, and listen to what I say. ¹⁵Indeed, these are not drunk, as you suppose, for it is only nine

Pray It!

Send Us Your Spirit

After Jesus was taken up to heaven, the Apostles, Mary, and other women and men gathered to pray together. They knew they needed the Holy Spirit, promised by Jesus, to begin the difficult task of giving witness to the Reign of God. Today, we continue to pray:

Jesus, send us your Spirit, and renew the face of the earth. You know our strengths and weaknesses. Transform us into messengers of your Gospel for those who yearn for you.

Jesus, send us your Spirit, and renew the face of the earth. You know our history, with its beautiful and painful experiences. Help us to be untiring promoters of a society based on love, justice, and peace.

Jesus, send us your Spirit, and renew the face of the earth. You know our longing for love and community. Make us instruments of unity and service, especially for those who are weak and those who are lonely. Amen.

▶ **Acts 1:1–11**

o'clock in the morning. ¹⁶No, this is what was spoken through the prophet Joel:
¹⁷ 'In the last days it will be, God declares,
   that I will pour out my Spirit upon all flesh,
      and your sons and your daughters shall
         prophesy,
   and your young men shall see visions,
      and your old men shall dream dreams.
¹⁸ Even upon my slaves, both men and women,
      in those days I will pour out my Spirit;
         and they shall prophesy.
¹⁹ And I will show portents in the heaven above
      and signs on the earth below,
         blood, and fire, and smoky mist.
²⁰ The sun shall be turned to darkness
      and the moon to blood,
         before the coming of the Lord's great and
            glorious day.
²¹ Then everyone who calls on the name of the
      Lord shall be saved.'

---

a Other ancient authorities read *the share*

✝ Catholic Connection

Confirmation

After Jesus' Ascension, the Apostles eagerly awaited the promised arrival of the Holy Spirit. What an arrival it was! The loud noise and tongues of fire were only the beginning of the amazing work the Holy Spirit initiated that day. Filled with the Holy Spirit, the Apostles suddenly had abilities and courage they never had before. The Holy Spirit began to guide and empower each of them, leading the Apostles to proclaim Christ's Resurrection to all who had ears to hear.

Following Pentecost, the Apostles began to baptize and lay hands on each new convert so that they too could receive the gift of the Holy Spirit. The laying on of hands and the prayer for the Holy Spirit was a part of one's initiation into the Church and continues to be celebrated in the sacrament of Confirmation today. The Church teaches that through the sacrament of Confirmation, one is given a special outpouring of the Holy Spirit and is thereby given special strength (see "The Gifts of the Holy Spirit," near Isa 11:1–2) to spread the Gospel.

Confirmation is ordinarily administered by a bishop as a sign of the connection between the Apostles' experience of receiving the Holy Spirit and the recipient's initiation into the Church. During the rite, the bishop extends his hands over the candidates and prays for the coming of the Holy Spirit. Then each candidate is presented to the bishop by her or his sponsor, who is a representative from the Catholic community. The bishop uses chrism (sacred oil) and traces the sign of the cross on the candidate's forehead with the words, "Be sealed with the gift of the Holy Spirit." The candidate responds "Amen" (*Rite of Confirmation*, no. 27). Then the bishop and candidate exchange an offering of Christ's peace to each other. The rite ends with a final blessing, asking God to keep the Spirit active in the hearts of all believers so they will never be ashamed to proclaim Christ to the world.

Together the sacraments of Baptism, Confirmation, and the Eucharist are a person's initiation into the Church.

▶ **Acts 2:1–13**
Catechism, nos. 1285–1321

ACTS

22 "You that are Israelites,*a* listen to what I have to say: Jesus of Nazareth,*b* a man attested to you by God with deeds of power, wonders, and signs that God did through him among you, as you yourselves know— 23 this man, handed over to you according to the definite plan and foreknowledge of God, you crucified and killed by the hands of those outside the law. 24 But God raised him up, having freed him from death,*c* because it was impossible for him to be held in its power. 25 For David says concerning him,

'I saw the Lord always before me,
    for he is at my right hand so that I will not be shaken;
26 therefore my heart was glad, and my tongue rejoiced;
    moreover my flesh will live in hope.
27 For you will not abandon my soul to Hades,
    or let your Holy One experience corruption.
28 You have made known to me the ways of life;
    you will make me full of gladness with your presence.'

29 "Fellow Israelites,*d* I may say to you confidently of our ancestor David that he both died and was buried, and his tomb is with us to this day. 30 Since he was a prophet, he knew that God had sworn with an oath to him that he would put one of his descendants on his throne. 31 Foreseeing this, David*e* spoke of the resurrection of the Messiah,*f* saying,

'He was not abandoned to Hades,
    nor did his flesh experience corruption.'

32 This Jesus God raised up, and of that all of us are witnesses. 33 Being therefore exalted at*g* the right hand of God, and having received from the Father the promise of the Holy Spirit, he has poured out this that you both see and hear. 34 For David did not ascend into the heavens, but he himself says,

'The Lord said to my Lord,
    "Sit at my right hand,
35   until I make your enemies your footstool." '

36 Therefore let the entire house of Israel know with certainty that God has made him both Lord and Messiah,*h* this Jesus whom you crucified."

The First Converts

37 Now when they heard this, they were cut to the heart and said to Peter and to the other apostles, "Brothers,*d* what should we do?" 38 Peter said to them, "Repent, and be baptized every one of you in the name of Jesus Christ so that your sins may be forgiven; and you will receive the gift of the Holy Spirit. 39 For the promise is for you, for your children, and for all who are far away, everyone whom the Lord our God calls to him."

40 And he testified with many other arguments and exhorted them, saying, "Save yourselves from this corrupt generation." 41 So those who welcomed his message were baptized, and that day about three thousand persons were added. 42 They devoted themselves to the apostles' teaching and fellowship, to the breaking of bread and the prayers.

Life among the Believers

43 Awe came upon everyone, because many wonders and signs were being done by the apostles. 44 All who believed were together and had all things in common; 45 they would sell their possessions and goods and distribute the proceeds*i* to all, as any had need. 46 Day by day, as they spent much time together in the temple, they broke bread at home*j* and ate their food with glad and generous*k* hearts, 47 praising God and having the goodwill of all the people. And day by day the Lord added to their number those who were being saved.

Peter Heals a Crippled Beggar

3 One day Peter and John were going up to the temple at the hour of prayer, at three o'clock in the afternoon. 2 And a man lame from birth was being carried in. People would lay him daily at the gate of the temple called the Beautiful Gate so that he could ask for alms from those entering the temple. 3 When he saw Peter and John about to go into the temple, he asked them for alms. 4 Peter looked intently at him, as did John, and said, "Look at us." 5 And he fixed his attention on them, expecting to receive something from them. 6 But Peter said, "I have no silver or gold, but what I have I give you; in the name of Jesus Christ of Nazareth,*b* stand up and walk." 7 And he took him by the right hand and raised him up; and immediately his feet and ankles were made strong. 8 Jumping up, he stood and began to walk, and he entered the temple with them, walking and leaping and praising God. 9 All the people saw him walking and praising God, 10 and they recognized him as the one who used to sit and ask for alms at the Beautiful Gate of the temple; and they were filled with wonder and amazement at what had happened to him.

Peter Speaks in Solomon's Portico

11 While he clung to Peter and John, all the people ran together to them in the portico called

---

a Gk *Men, Israelites*   *b* Gk *the Nazorean*   *c* Gk *the pains of death*   *d* Gk *Men, brothers*   *e* Gk *he*   *f* Or *the Christ*   *g* Or *by*   *h* Or *Christ*   *i* Gk *them*   *j* Or *from house to house*   *k* Or *sincere*

✝ Catholic Connection

Pentecost

Another promise kept. On Pentecost, fifty days after his Resurrection, Jesus fulfilled his promise to his disciples by sending the Holy Spirit, or the Advocate (see Jn 14:26). Before returning to his father, Jesus told his followers that the Holy Spirit would guide them in truth and give them power from heaven. The dramatic descent of the Holy Spirit on Pentecost brought about more than the disciples could have ever imagined. The Spirit enabled them to speak in languages that everyone could understand and transformed their fears so they were able to proclaim God's salvation in Jesus Christ with courage, confidence, and zeal. And that was just on day one!

The descent of the Holy Spirit on Pentecost also brought about several interesting events in the history of the world. First, Pentecost marks the day the Trinity was made fully known. Second, it marks the day the Reign of God was first made available to all who believed in Jesus Christ. And finally, in a sense, the world entered into what is called the time of the Church or final days when God's Reign is, in part, here on earth.

By ushering in the time of the Church, Pentecost is considered the birthday of the Christian Church. The Catholic Church traditionally celebrates the feast of Pentecost on the second Sunday after Ascension Thursday, which is approximately fifty days after Easter (the term *pente* means "fifty"). It continues to be an important feast to celebrate the unity of all Christians.

Since Pentecost, the Holy Spirit has been guiding the Church in carrying out its mission to lead people to salvation through Jesus Christ for over two thousand years. At Mass it is the Holy Spirit who prepares those gathered to receive Christ, transforms the bread and wine into the Body and Blood of Jesus Christ, and transforms the community in the process. It is through the prompting of the Holy Spirit that the Church and its members are formed in a life of prayer. The Holy Spirit also guides the Church so that it can teach about faith and morals without error.

The Holy Spirit that worked wonders through the disciples and continues to guide the Church today can also work wonders through each of us. Through the power of the Holy Spirit, we too can find the courage, confidence, and zeal to boldly share our faith and follow God's will. All we need to do is ask, knowing that Jesus always keeps his promises, often in ways we never could have dreamed!

▶ **Acts 2:1–13**
Catechism, nos. 731–741, 1108–1112

Catholic Social Teaching

Christian Community

In the famous passage of Acts of the Apostles 2:42–47, the ideal Christian community is portrayed as open to the Holy Spirit. The people shared everything in common, including prayer, meals, and possessions. No one went in need. Sound impossible?

One of the principles of Catholic social teaching, *Call to Family, Community, and Participation*, invites us to be mindful of the fact that families are at the heart of the community. Programs and policies of our society should demonstrate support and respect for the family. The U.S. bishops call us to be concerned for those who are at risk and vulnerable, not only in our own country but also in the global community. They speak about the importance of supporting policies that address the needs of families, specifically the rights of children, who often are the most vulnerable, to adequate food, shelter, healthcare, quality education, and a safe environment in which to flourish.

Our faith teaches us to respect the dignity of the human person. This passage from Acts of the Apostles reminds us that the early Christian community tried very hard to live as a community that cared for one another and made sure that everyone felt respected and had their basic needs met.

We are also called to be participants in helping to promote this reality in the world today. It is not always easy, but we can find ways to do what we can to share in that vision.

● What do you think society would be like today if everyone lived as the early Christian community tried to live?

▶ **Acts 2:42–47**
Call to Family, Community, and Participation

Solomon's Portico, utterly astonished. [12]When Peter saw it, he addressed the people, "You Israelites,[a] why do you wonder at this, or why do you stare at us, as though by our own power or piety we had made him walk? [13]The God of Abraham, the God of Isaac, and the God of Jacob, the God of our ancestors has glorified his servant[b] Jesus, whom you handed over and rejected in the presence of Pilate, though he had decided to release him. [14]But you rejected the Holy and Righteous One and asked to have a murderer given to you, [15]and you killed the Author of life, whom God raised from the dead. To this we are witnesses. [16]And by faith in his name, his name itself has made this man strong, whom you see and know; and the faith that is through Jesus[c] has given him this perfect health in the presence of all of you.

[17] "And now, friends,[d] I know that you acted in ignorance, as did also your rulers. [18]In this way God fulfilled what he had foretold through all the prophets, that his Messiah[e] would suffer. [19]Repent therefore, and turn to God so that your sins may be wiped out, [20]so that times of refreshing may come from the presence of the Lord, and that he may send the Messiah[f] appointed for you, that is, Jesus, [21]who must remain in heaven until the time of universal restoration that God announced long ago through his holy prophets.

[22]Moses said, 'The Lord your God will raise up for you from your own people[d] a prophet like me. You must listen to whatever he tells you. [23]And it will be that everyone who does not listen to that prophet will be utterly rooted out of the people.' [24]And all the prophets, as many as have spoken, from Samuel and those after him, also predicted these days. [25]You are the descendants of the prophets and of the covenant that God gave to your ancestors, saying to Abraham, 'And in your descendants all the families of the earth shall be blessed.' [26]When God raised up his servant,[b] he sent him first to you, to bless you by turning each of you from your wicked ways."

Peter and John before the Council

4 While Peter and John[g] were speaking to the people, the priests, the captain of the temple, and the Sadducees came to them, [2]much annoyed because they were teaching the people and proclaiming that in Jesus there is the resurrection of the dead. [3]So they arrested them and put them in custody until the next day, for it was already evening. [4]But many of those who heard

A
C
T
S

---

a Gk *Men, Israelites*   b Or *child*   c Gk *him*   d Gk *brothers*
e Or *his Christ*   f Or *the Christ*   g Gk *While they*

the word believed; and they numbered about five thousand.

5 The next day their rulers, elders, and scribes assembled in Jerusalem, [6]with Annas the high priest, Caiaphas, John,[a] and Alexander, and all who were of the high-priestly family. [7]When they had made the prisoners[b] stand in their midst, they inquired, "By what power or by what name did you do this?" [8]Then Peter, filled with the Holy Spirit, said to them, "Rulers of the people and elders, [9]if we are questioned today because of a good deed done to someone who was sick and are asked how this man has been healed, [10]let it be known to all of you, and to all the people of Israel, that this man is standing before you in good health by the name of Jesus Christ of Nazareth,[c] whom you crucified, whom God raised from the dead. [11]This Jesus[d] is

'the stone that was rejected by you, the builders;
    it has become the cornerstone.'[e]

[12]There is salvation in no one else, for there is no other name under heaven given among mortals by which we must be saved."

Live It!

Share Christ

As is true in our own cities today, it was not uncommon to encounter beggars on the streets in Jerusalem during the first century. And probably, like today, some people averted their eyes and walked by while others stopped to offer a few coins.

When Peter and John encounter a beggar in Acts of the Apostles 3:3, they don't have a whole lot of money to share with him, but they stop just the same. Looking him in the eye, Peter offers the lame man the one thing of value he does have: the powerful gift of healing found in the name of Jesus Christ.

You may not have the gift of healing or lots of extra money to give to those in need. But Peter and John remind us that knowing Jesus is the greatest treasure one can acquire in life, and that this treasure has been given to us freely. Don't forget to share it with others!

▶ Acts 3:1–10

13 Now when they saw the boldness of Peter and John and realized that they were uneducated and ordinary men, they were amazed and recognized them as companions of Jesus. [14]When they saw the man who had been cured standing

---

a Other ancient authorities read *Jonathan*   *b* Gk *them*   *c* Gk *the Nazorean*   *d* Gk *This*   *e* Or *keystone*

Pray It!

I Believe! The Apostles' Creed

In Acts of the Apostles 4:5–12, Peter stands up before the Jewish rulers and elders of the Temple and boldly proclaims his faith in Jesus as healer and Messiah. Every Sunday at Mass, Catholic Christians also profess their faith when they pray the Nicene Creed. (A creed is a type of prayer that expresses faith beliefs.) Did you know there is also a shorter creed called the Apostles' Creed? The Apostles' Creed is based on the teachings and beliefs of the earliest Christians.

Take a moment to pray the Apostles' Creed:

I believe in God, the Father almighty, Creator of heaven and earth, and in Jesus Christ, his only Son, our Lord, who was conceived by the Holy Spirit, born of the Virgin Mary, suffered under Pontius Pilate, was crucified, died and was buried; he descended into hell; on the third day he rose again from the dead; he ascended into heaven, and is seated at the right hand of God the Father almighty; from there he will come to judge the living and the dead. I believe in the Holy Spirit, the holy catholic Church, the communion of saints, the forgiveness of sins, the resurrection of the body, and life everlasting. Amen.

Then reflect or journal on the following questions:

● Which statements of the creed do you have questions about?
● How hard would it be for you to express your faith beliefs to people who don't believe in Jesus?
● To what actions does a faith like this call us?

▶ Acts 4:5–12

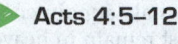

beside them, they had nothing to say in opposition. ¹⁵So they ordered them to leave the council while they discussed the matter with one another. ¹⁶They said, "What will we do with them? For it is obvious to all who live in Jerusalem that a notable sign has been done through them; we cannot deny it. ¹⁷But to keep it from spreading further among the people, let us warn them to speak no more to anyone in this name." ¹⁸So they called them and ordered them not to speak or teach at all in the name of Jesus. ¹⁹But Peter and John answered them, "Whether it is right in God's sight to listen to you rather than to God, you must judge; ²⁰for we cannot keep from speaking about what we have seen and heard." ²¹After threatening them again, they let them go, finding no way to punish them because of the people, for all of them praised God for what had happened. ²²For the man on whom this sign of healing had been performed was more than forty years old.

The Believers Pray for Boldness

23 After they were released, they went to their friends[a] and reported what the chief priests and the elders had said to them. ²⁴When they heard it, they raised their voices together to God and said, "Sovereign Lord, who made the heaven and the earth, the sea, and everything in them, ²⁵it is you who said by the Holy Spirit through our ancestor David, your servant:[b]

'Why did the Gentiles rage,
    and the peoples imagine vain things?
²⁶ The kings of the earth took their stand,
    and the rulers have gathered together
      against the Lord and against his Messiah.'[c]

²⁷For in this city, in fact, both Herod and Pontius Pilate, with the Gentiles and the peoples of Israel, gathered together against your holy servant[b] Jesus, whom you anointed, ²⁸to do whatever your hand and your plan had predestined to take place. ²⁹And now, Lord, look at their threats, and grant to your servants[d] to speak your word with all boldness, ³⁰while you stretch out your hand to heal, and signs and wonders are performed through the name of your holy servant[b] Jesus." ³¹When they had prayed, the place in which they were gathered together was shaken; and they were all filled with the Holy Spirit and spoke the word of God with boldness.

The Believers Share Their Possessions

32 Now the whole group of those who believed were of one heart and soul, and no one claimed private ownership of any possessions, but everything they owned was held in common. ³³With

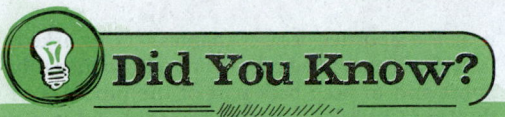

Did You Know?

Stewardship

Acts of the Apostles 4:32–37 describes the value of stewardship. Stewardship involves sharing the gifts of time, talents, and treasure that God has placed in your care (see "Stewardship: Making a Contribution," near Lk 21:1–4). It is key to the life of any Christian community.

Sharing our treasure and giving money are the most obvious ways of sharing. Consider the disciple named in the passage, Joseph Barnabas. How did he share? Can you think of things you spend money on—a CD, new jeans, a movie—and make a commitment to give some of that money to a charitable organization?

But giving money isn't the only way to share with others. Think about your own gifts. What are you good at that you could share with your parish, school, or community? Do not discount even the simplest ability. For example, maybe you are persistent; this talent can help with the success of any project. Or perhaps you love children and can baby-sit for overwhelmed parents.

How are you a good steward of your time, talents, and treasure? Think about it!

▶ Acts 4:32–37

great power the apostles gave their testimony to the resurrection of the Lord Jesus, and great grace was upon them all. ³⁴There was not a needy person among them, for as many as owned lands or houses sold them and brought the proceeds of what was sold. ³⁵They laid it at the apostles' feet, and it was distributed to each as any had need. ³⁶There was a Levite, a native of Cyprus, Joseph, to whom the apostles gave the name Barnabas (which means "son of encouragement"). ³⁷He sold a field that belonged to him, then brought the money, and laid it at the apostles' feet.

Ananias and Sapphira

5 But a man named Ananias, with the consent of his wife Sapphira, sold a piece of property; ²with his wife's knowledge, he kept back some of the proceeds, and brought only a part and laid

---

a Gk *their own*   *b* Or *child*   *c* Or *his Christ*   *d* Gk *slaves*

it at the apostles' feet. ³"Ananias," Peter asked, "why has Satan filled your heart to lie to the Holy Spirit and to keep back part of the proceeds of the land? ⁴While it remained unsold, did it not remain your own? And after it was sold, were not the proceeds at your disposal? How is it that you have contrived this deed in your heart? You did not lie to us*ᵃ* but to God!" ⁵Now when Ananias heard these words, he fell down and died. And great fear seized all who heard of it. ⁶The young men came and wrapped up his body,*ᵇ* then carried him out and buried him.

7 After an interval of about three hours his wife came in, not knowing what had happened. ⁸Peter said to her, "Tell me whether you and your husband sold the land for such and such a price." And she said, "Yes, that was the price." ⁹Then Peter said to her, "How is it that you have agreed together to put the Spirit of the Lord to the test? Look, the feet of those who have buried your husband are at the door, and they will carry you out." ¹⁰Immediately she fell down at his feet and died. When the young men came in they found her dead, so they carried her out and buried her

Pop Quiz

The scene. The disciples, who are spreading the Good News of Jesus Christ, are taken before the Jewish council to explain their motives and reasons for this work.

The test. Gamaliel, a wise Jewish leader, talks the rest of the council out of killing the disciples, whose profession of faith in Jesus was considered blasphemy, by using the following reasoning: If the disciples' mission is from God, it will succeed despite anything the council does. But if it is not of God's design, it will fail and Jesus' followers will eventually disappear anyway.

The question. If you were brought before a similar council, would your life's mission pass or fail this test? Would your words and actions in the past week reflect Jesus' attitudes, actions, and mission?

▶ **Acts 5:27–39**

beside her husband. ¹¹And great fear seized the whole church and all who heard of these things.

The Apostles Heal Many

12 Now many signs and wonders were done among the people through the apostles. And they were all together in Solomon's Portico. ¹³None of the rest dared to join them, but the people held them in high esteem. ¹⁴Yet more than ever believers were added to the Lord, great numbers of both men and women, ¹⁵so that they even carried out the sick into the streets, and laid them on cots and mats, in order that Peter's shadow might fall on some of them as he came by. ¹⁶A great number of people would also gather from the towns around Jerusalem, bringing the sick and those tormented by unclean spirits, and they were all cured.

The Apostles Are Persecuted

17 Then the high priest took action; he and all who were with him (that is, the sect of the Sadducees), being filled with jealousy, ¹⁸arrested the apostles and put them in the public prison. ¹⁹But during the night an angel of the Lord opened the prison doors, brought them out, and said, ²⁰"Go, stand in the temple and tell the people the whole message about this life." ²¹When they heard this, they entered the temple at daybreak and went on with their teaching.

When the high priest and those with him arrived, they called together the council and the whole body of the elders of Israel, and sent to the prison to have them brought. ²²But when the temple police went there, they did not find them in the prison; so they returned and reported, ²³"We found the prison securely locked and the guards standing at the doors, but when we opened them, we found no one inside." ²⁴Now when the captain of the temple and the chief priests heard these words, they were perplexed about them, wondering what might be going on. ²⁵Then someone arrived and announced, "Look, the men whom you put in prison are standing in the temple and teaching the people!" ²⁶Then the captain went with the temple police and brought them, but without violence, for they were afraid of being stoned by the people.

27 When they had brought them, they had them stand before the council. The high priest questioned them, ²⁸saying, "We gave you strict orders not to teach in this name,*ᶜ* yet here you have filled Jerusalem with your teaching and

---

a Gk *to men*   *b* Meaning of Gk uncertain   *c* Other ancient authorities read *Did we not give you strict orders not to teach in this name?*

you are determined to bring this man's blood on us." [29]But Peter and the apostles answered, "We must obey God rather than any human authority.[a] [30]The God of our ancestors raised up Jesus, whom you had killed by hanging him on a tree. [31]God exalted him at his right hand as Leader and Savior that he might give repentance to Israel and forgiveness of sins. [32]And we are witnesses to these things, and so is the Holy Spirit whom God has given to those who obey him."

33 When they heard this, they were enraged and wanted to kill them. [34]But a Pharisee in the council named Gamaliel, a teacher of the law, respected by all the people, stood up and ordered the men to be put outside for a short time. [35]Then he said to them, "Fellow Israelites,[b] consider carefully what you propose to do to these men. [36]For some time ago Theudas rose up, claiming to be somebody, and a number of men, about four hundred, joined him; but he was killed, and all who followed him were dispersed and disappeared. [37]After him Judas the Galilean rose up at the time of the census and got people to follow him; he also perished, and all who followed him were scattered. [38]So in the present case, I tell you, keep away from these men and let them alone; because if this plan or this undertaking is of human origin, it will fail; [39]but if it is of God, you will not be able to overthrow them—in that case you may even be found fighting against God!"

They were convinced by him, [40]and when they had called in the apostles, they had them flogged. Then they ordered them not to speak in the name of Jesus, and let them go. [41]As they left the council, they rejoiced that they were considered worthy to suffer dishonor for the sake of the name. [42]And every day in the temple and at home[c] they did not cease to teach and proclaim Jesus as the Messiah.[d]

Seven Chosen to Serve

6 Now during those days, when the disciples were increasing in number, the Hellenists complained against the Hebrews because their widows were being neglected in the daily distribution of food. [2]And the twelve called together the whole community of the disciples and said, "It is not right that we should neglect the word of God in order to wait on tables.[e] [3]Therefore, friends,[f] select from among yourselves seven men of good standing, full of the Spirit and of wisdom, whom we may appoint to this task, [4]while we, for our part, will devote ourselves to prayer and to serving the word." [5]What they said pleased the whole community, and they chose

Stephen, a man full of faith and the Holy Spirit, together with Philip, Prochorus, Nicanor, Timon, Parmenas, and Nicolaus, a proselyte of Antioch. [6]They had these men stand before the apostles, who prayed and laid their hands on them.

7 The word of God continued to spread; the number of the disciples increased greatly in Jerusalem, and a great many of the priests became obedient to the faith.

The Arrest of Stephen

8 Stephen, full of grace and power, did great wonders and signs among the people. [9]Then some of those who belonged to the synagogue of the Freedmen (as it was called), Cyrenians, Alexandrians, and others of those from Cilicia and Asia, stood up and argued with Stephen. [10]But they could not withstand the wisdom and the Spirit[g] with which he spoke. [11]Then they secretly instigated some men to say, "We have heard him speak blasphemous words against Moses and God." [12]They stirred up the people as well as the elders and the scribes; then they suddenly confronted him, seized him, and brought him before the council. [13]They set up false witnesses who said, "This man never stops saying things against this holy place and the law; [14]for we have heard him say that this Jesus of Nazareth[h] will destroy this place and will change the customs that Moses handed on to us." [15]And all who sat in the council looked intently at him, and they saw that his face was like the face of an angel.

Stephen's Speech to the Council

7 Then the high priest asked him, "Are these things so?" [2]And Stephen replied:

"Brothers[i] and fathers, listen to me. The God of glory appeared to our ancestor Abraham when he was in Mesopotamia, before he lived in Haran, [3]and said to him, 'Leave your country and your relatives and go to the land that I will show you.' [4]Then he left the country of the Chaldeans and settled in Haran. After his father died, God had him move from there to this country in which you are now living. [5]He did not give him any of it as a heritage, not even a foot's length, but promised to give it to him as his possession and to his descendants after him, even though he had no child. [6]And God spoke in these terms, that his descendants would be resident aliens in a country belonging to others, who would enslave them and mistreat them during four

---

a Gk than men   b Gk Men, Israelites   c Or from house to house   d Or the Christ   e Or keep accounts   f Gk brothers g Or spirit   h Gk the Nazorean   i Gk Men, brothers

Cultural Connection

Don't Forget the Shoulders You Stand On

Take a few minutes to read about the martyrdom of Stephen, in Acts of the Apostles 6:8—7:60. There is perhaps no more touching story in the New Testament than this young man's brave defense of his faith as he followed in his Lord's footsteps. He knew his history and his ancestors, and they gave him divine courage in the face of death.

People of all ages and cultures need to respect and honor the faith and sacrifices of their ancestors. For example, the *Eyes on the Prize* video series is a reminder for all Americans of the debt owed to African Americans of a previous generation. This documentation of the civil rights movement immortalizes the faith of countless people who were brave enough to protest the injustice of racism.

Today is a gift from them. Somebody died so that all Americans might live freely. Somebody suffered so that all Americans could enjoy civil rights. Somebody accepted persecution to call all Americans to respect God's justice.

How many youth today would be willing to make similar sacrifices in the struggle for freedom and equality—signs of the Reign of God?

Dear God, help me to treasure my ancestors' sacrifice and bravery. Help me to follow their example in working for justice with love and courage. Amen.

▶ **Acts 6:8—7:60**

---

hundred years. [7]'But I will judge the nation that they serve,' said God, 'and after that they shall come out and worship me in this place.' [8]Then he gave him the covenant of circumcision. And so Abraham[a] became the father of Isaac and circumcised him on the eighth day; and Isaac became the father of Jacob, and Jacob of the twelve patriarchs.

9 "The patriarchs, jealous of Joseph, sold him into Egypt; but God was with him, [10]and rescued him from all his afflictions, and enabled him to win favor and to show wisdom when he stood before Pharaoh, king of Egypt, who appointed him ruler over Egypt and over all his household. [11]Now there came a famine throughout Egypt and Canaan, and great suffering, and our ancestors could find no food. [12]But when Jacob heard that there was grain in Egypt, he sent our ancestors there on their first visit. [13]On the second visit Joseph made himself known to his brothers, and Joseph's family became known to Pharaoh. [14]Then Joseph sent and invited his father Jacob and all his relatives to come to him, seventy-five in all; [15]so Jacob went down to Egypt. He himself died there as well as our ancestors, [16]and their bodies[b] were brought back to Shechem and laid in the tomb that Abraham had bought for a sum of silver from the sons of Hamor in Shechem.

17 "But as the time drew near for the fulfillment of the promise that God had made to Abraham, our people in Egypt increased and multiplied [18]until another king who had not known Joseph ruled over Egypt. [19]He dealt craftily with our race and forced our ancestors to abandon their infants so that they would die. [20]At this time Moses was born, and he was beautiful before God. For three months he was brought up in his father's house; [21]and when he was abandoned, Pharaoh's daughter adopted him and brought him up as her own son. [22]So Moses was instructed in all the wisdom of the Egyptians and was powerful in his words and deeds.

23 "When he was forty years old, it came into his heart to visit his relatives, the Israelites.[c] [24]When he saw one of them being wronged, he defended the oppressed man and avenged him by striking down the Egyptian. [25]He supposed that his kinsfolk would understand that God through him was rescuing them, but they did not understand. [26]The next day he came to some of them as they were quarreling and tried to reconcile them, saying, 'Men, you are brothers; why do you wrong each other?' [27]But the man who was wronging his neighbor pushed Moses[d] aside, saying, 'Who made you a ruler and a judge over us? [28]Do you want to kill me as you killed the Egyptian yesterday?' [29]When he heard this, Moses fled and became a resident alien in the

---

a Gk he   b Gk they   c Gk his brothers, the sons of Israel
d Gk him

ACTS

land of Midian. There he became the father of two sons.

30 "Now when forty years had passed, an angel appeared to him in the wilderness of Mount Sinai, in the flame of a burning bush. [31]When Moses saw it, he was amazed at the sight; and as he approached to look, there came the voice of the Lord: [32]'I am the God of your ancestors, the God of Abraham, Isaac, and Jacob.' Moses began to tremble and did not dare to look. [33]Then the Lord said to him, 'Take off the sandals from your feet, for the place where you are standing is holy ground. [34]I have surely seen the mistreatment of my people who are in Egypt and have heard their groaning, and I have come down to rescue them. Come now, I will send you to Egypt.'

35 "It was this Moses whom they rejected when they said, 'Who made you a ruler and a judge?' and whom God now sent as both ruler and liberator through the angel who appeared to him in the bush. [36]He led them out, having performed wonders and signs in Egypt, at the Red Sea, and in the wilderness for forty years. [37]This is the Moses who said to the Israelites, 'God will raise up a prophet for you from your own people[a] as he raised me up.' [38]He is the one who was in the congregation in the wilderness with the angel who spoke to him at Mount Sinai, and with our ancestors; and he received living oracles to give to us. [39]Our ancestors were unwilling to obey him; instead, they pushed him aside, and in their hearts they turned back to Egypt, [40]saying to Aaron, 'Make gods for us who will lead the way for us; as for this Moses who led us out from the land of Egypt, we do not know what has happened to him.' [41]At that time they made a calf, offered a sacrifice to the idol, and reveled in the works of their hands. [42]But God turned away from them and handed them over to worship the host of heaven, as it is written in the book of the prophets:

'Did you offer to me slain victims and sacrifices
   forty years in the wilderness, O house of
      Israel?
[43] No; you took along the tent of Moloch,
   and the star of your god Rephan,
      the images that you made to worship;
so I will remove you beyond Babylon.'

44 "Our ancestors had the tent of testimony in the wilderness, as God[b] directed when he spoke to Moses, ordering him to make it according to the pattern he had seen. [45]Our ancestors in turn brought it in with Joshua when they dispossessed the nations that God drove out before our ancestors. And it was there until the time of David, [46]who found favor with God and

asked that he might find a dwelling place for the house of Jacob.[c] [47]But it was Solomon who built a house for him. [48]Yet the Most High does not dwell in houses made with human hands;[d] as the prophet says,

[49] 'Heaven is my throne,

---

a Gk your brothers   *b* Gk he   *c* Other ancient authorities read
for the God of Jacob   *d* Gk with hands

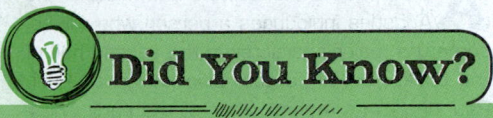

Martyrs

The stoning of Stephen is a turning point in Luke's account of the first Christians. Symbolically, Stephen marks the beginning of the phenomenon of martyrdom—dying for one's faith—but historically, we don't actually know that he was the first martyr. Luke makes it clear that Stephen's death, rather than causing the Christian movement to fall apart now that the stakes were higher, actually strengthened the Church. His heroic sacrifice is even presented as a model for Christians—notice all the similarities between his death and Jesus'.

It is easy for North Americans to assume that religious persecution does not exist today. We do not normally hear stories of people being killed for their beliefs in Jesus or Christianity. Not so for people on other continents. All around the world, including places close to home, people are mistreated, and even killed, because of their religious beliefs.

For example, Archbishop Oscar Romero of El Salvador was shot to death because he challenged the wealthy and powerful people in his country to change their ways so the poor people could have a better quality of life. Archbishop Romero, like Stephen, was killed for being a faithful Christian.

Stephen was convinced that following the teachings of Jesus was the most important way to live. He died for his beliefs, and the Church became stronger because of his faith and heroism. What would you die for?

▶ Acts 6:8—8:1

and the earth is my footstool.
What kind of house will you build for me, says
the Lord,

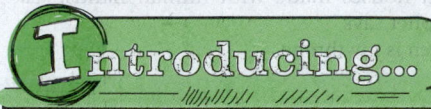

Saint Paul

As Stephen is stoned to death, Acts of the Apostles introduces a person who will become the major character in the second half of the book, Saul of Tarsus, also known as Paul. Paul begins as a persecutor of the early Christians. He is a member of the Pharisees, a group that holds to a rigid interpretation of Jewish Law (see Acts 26:4–5). He probably sees the Christians as a threat to the Jewish faith. But after a profound experience of the risen Christ, Paul is converted to the Christian faith. Paul is initially distrusted by other Christians who remember his persecution of them. However, another early Christian leader, Barnabas, becomes Paul's companion and advocate (see 9:27).

Paul's major insight is that God has made salvation available to everyone, Jews and Gentiles alike. He also knows that God's offer of salvation is a free gift, that no one could do anything to actually earn it. But many of the early Christians, who are former Jews, disagree with him. This conflict comes to a head at the Council of Jerusalem (see Acts of the Apostles, chapter 15), where Paul stands toe to toe with Peter and James (see Gal 2:1–10) and argues that the Gentiles can become Christians without following Jewish laws and customs, including circumcision.

Paul took it upon himself to spread the Good News of God's salvation in Jesus to the Gentiles. During three different missionary journeys, he was instrumental in founding new Christian communities in what is now the Middle East and Western Europe. He stayed in touch with those communities through letters, some of which are included as books in the New Testament. Paul's impact in spreading Christianity was so great that he is sometimes called the second founder of Christianity.

▶ Acts 8:1–3

or what is the place of my rest?
50 Did not my hand make all these things?'

51 "You stiff-necked people, uncircumcised in heart and ears, you are forever opposing the Holy Spirit, just as your ancestors used to do. 52Which of the prophets did your ancestors not persecute? They killed those who foretold the coming of the Righteous One, and now you have become his betrayers and murderers. 53You are the ones that received the law as ordained by angels, and yet you have not kept it."

The Stoning of Stephen

54 When they heard these things, they became enraged and ground their teeth at Stephen.[a] 55But filled with the Holy Spirit, he gazed into heaven and saw the glory of God and Jesus standing at the right hand of God. 56"Look," he said, "I see the heavens opened and the Son of Man standing at the right hand of God!" 57But they covered their ears, and with a loud shout all rushed together against him. 58Then they dragged him out of the city and began to stone him; and the witnesses laid their coats at the feet of a young man named Saul. 59While they were stoning Stephen, he prayed, "Lord Jesus, receive my spirit." 60Then he knelt down and cried out in a loud voice, "Lord, do not hold this sin against them." When he had said this, he died.[b] 8 1And Saul approved of their killing him.

Saul Persecutes the Church

That day a severe persecution began against the church in Jerusalem, and all except the apostles were scattered throughout the countryside of Judea and Samaria. 2Devout men buried Stephen and made loud lamentation over him. 3But Saul was ravaging the church by entering house after house; dragging off both men and women, he committed them to prison.

Philip Preaches in Samaria

4 Now those who were scattered went from place to place, proclaiming the word. 5Philip went down to the city[c] of Samaria and proclaimed the Messiah[d] to them. 6The crowds with one accord listened eagerly to what was said by Philip, hearing and seeing the signs that he did, 7for unclean spirits, crying with loud shrieks, came out of many who were possessed; and many others who were paralyzed or lame were cured. 8So there was great joy in that city.

9 Now a certain man named Simon had

ACTS

a Gk him   b Gk fell asleep   c Other ancient authorities read a city   d Or the Christ

previously practiced magic in the city and amazed the people of Samaria, saying that he was someone great. [10]All of them, from the least to the greatest, listened to him eagerly, saying, "This man is the power of God that is called Great." [11]And they listened eagerly to him because for a long time he had amazed them with his magic. [12]But when they believed Philip, who was proclaiming the good news about the kingdom of God and the name of Jesus Christ, they were baptized, both men and women. [13]Even Simon himself believed. After being baptized, he stayed constantly with Philip and was amazed when he saw the signs and great miracles that took place.

14 Now when the apostles at Jerusalem heard that Samaria had accepted the word of God, they sent Peter and John to them. [15]The two went down and prayed for them that they might receive the Holy Spirit [16](for as yet the Spirit had not come[a] upon any of them; they had only been baptized in the name of the Lord Jesus). [17]Then Peter and John[b] laid their hands on them, and they received the Holy Spirit. [18]Now when Simon saw that the Spirit was given through the laying on of the apostles' hands, he offered them money, [19]saying, "Give me also this power so that anyone on whom I lay my hands may receive the Holy Spirit." [20]But Peter said to him, "May your silver perish with you, because you thought you could obtain God's gift with money! [21]You have no part or share in this, for your heart is not right before God. [22]Repent therefore of this wickedness of yours, and pray to the Lord that, if possible, the intent of your heart may be forgiven you. [23]For I see that you are in the gall of bitterness and the chains of wickedness." [24]Simon answered, "Pray for me to the Lord, that nothing of what you[c] have said may happen to me."

25 Now after Peter and John[d] had testified and spoken the word of the Lord, they returned to Jerusalem, proclaiming the good news to many villages of the Samaritans.

Philip and the Ethiopian Eunuch

26 Then an angel of the Lord said to Philip, "Get up and go toward the south[e] to the road that goes down from Jerusalem to Gaza." (This is a wilderness road.) [27]So he got up and went. Now there was an Ethiopian eunuch, a court official of the Candace, queen of the Ethiopians, in charge of her entire treasury. He had come to Jerusalem to worship [28]and was returning home; seated in his chariot, he was reading the prophet Isaiah. [29]Then the Spirit said to Philip, "Go over to this chariot and join it." [30]So Philip ran up to it and heard him reading the prophet Isaiah. He

asked, "Do you understand what you are reading?" [31]He replied, "How can I, unless someone guides me?" And he invited Philip to get in and sit beside him. [32]Now the passage of the scripture that he was reading was this:

"Like a sheep he was led to the slaughter,
  and like a lamb silent before its shearer,
    so he does not open his mouth.
[33] In his humiliation justice was denied him.
  Who can describe his generation?
    For his life is taken away from the earth."

[34]The eunuch asked Philip, "About whom, may I ask you, does the prophet say this, about himself or about someone else?" [35]Then Philip began to speak, and starting with this scripture, he proclaimed to him the good news about Jesus. [36]As they were going along the road, they came to some water; and the eunuch said, "Look, here is water! What is to prevent me from being baptized?"[f] [38]He commanded the chariot to stop, and both of them, Philip and the eunuch, went down into the water, and Philip[g] baptized him. [39]When they came up out of the water, the Spirit of the Lord snatched Philip away; the eunuch saw him no more, and went on his way rejoicing. [40]But Philip found himself at Azotus, and as he was passing through the region, he proclaimed the good news to all the towns until he came to Caesarea.

---

a Gk fallen   b Gk they   c The Greek word for *you* and the verb *pray* are plural   d Gk *after they*   e Or *go at noon*   f Other ancient authorities add all or most of verse 37, *And Philip said, "If you believe with all your heart, you may." And he replied, "I believe that Jesus Christ is the Son of God."*   g Gk *he*

Chapter 8

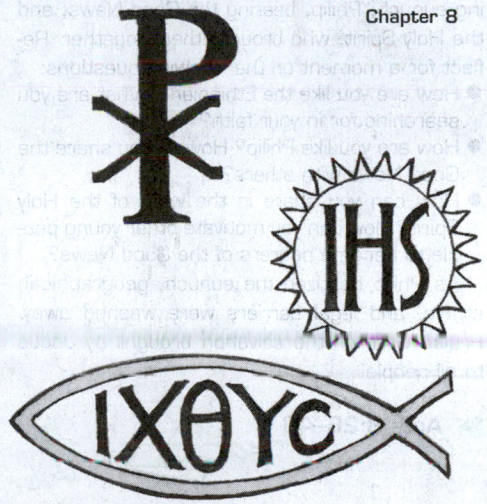

Early Christian symbols representing Jesus Christ

The Conversion of Saul

9 Meanwhile Saul, still breathing threats and murder against the disciples of the Lord, went to the high priest ²and asked him for letters to the synagogues at Damascus, so that if he found any who belonged to the Way, men or women, he might bring them bound to Jerusalem. ³Now as he was going along and approaching Damascus, suddenly a light from heaven flashed around him. ⁴He fell to the ground and heard a voice saying to him, "Saul, Saul, why do you persecute me?" ⁵He asked, "Who are you,

Bearing Good News

A cts of the Apostles 8:26–40 tells the story of an Ethiopian (African) eunuch. A eunuch is a man who has been castrated, either by accident or by design. Eunuchs often served as guards of the harems of kings. This eunuch was reading a text from Isaiah while returning from a visit to Jerusalem. The Holy Spirit moved the missionary Philip to explain to him how Isaiah's prophecies pointed to Jesus. And the eunuch believed and was baptized. From a cultural point of view, this story is significant because the eunuch was presumably African.

The eunuch's faith was dependent on the interaction of three characters: himself, the searching eunuch; Philip, bearing the Good News; and the Holy Spirit, who brought them together. Reflect for a moment on the following questions:

- How are you like the Ethiopian? What are you searching for in your faith?
- How are you like Philip? How do you share the Good News with others?
- How can you share in the work of the Holy Spirit? How can you motivate other young people to become bearers of the Good News?

As Philip baptized the eunuch, geographical, ethnic, and legal barriers were washed away. Praise God for the salvation brought by Jesus to all people!

▶ **Acts 8:26–40**

Conversion

S aul (or Paul) experienced some dramatic events that converted him from a persecutor of Christians to a believer in Jesus Christ. He had a powerful experience of the risen Christ during which he was blinded. His physical blindness is symbolic of his previous spiritual blindness. For three days, Paul was practically lifeless—not seeing, not eating, not drinking. This period reminds us of Jesus' three days in the tomb. In many ways, going through a conversion is like dying—dying to old ways of thinking and acting. But after three days, Paul's blindness was lifted, and he was filled with the Holy Spirit.

No longer a persecutor of Christians, Paul was a new person. He now felt compelled to learn more about Jesus and to share the Good News with other people. Paul's change told the early Christians that even the most unlikely person can be called by God and radically changed.

In our own lives, conversions can also happen in more subtle, ordinary ways. Sometimes, in the midst of our days, we come to a new realization about how we should live as Jesus did, or how we might be kinder to others or sacrifice some of our needs to help someone else—even when that may seem difficult.

In your prayer, reflect or journal on the following questions:

- Have you ever been suddenly aware of God's presence and calling in your life?
- What plans do you think God might have for your life?
- How will you respond?

Then close with these words:

Dear Jesus, following you is a lifelong journey where we come to learn more about how we can follow your ways. Sometimes, it is an easy journey; sometimes, it is a struggle. Help me to be open to your light in the Scriptures, in others, and within myself. Amen.

▶ **Acts 9:1–19**

ACTS

Lord?" The reply came, "I am Jesus, whom you are persecuting. 6But get up and enter the city, and you will be told what you are to do." 7The men who were traveling with him stood speechless because they heard the voice but saw no one. 8Saul got up from the ground, and though his eyes were open, he could see nothing; so they led him by the hand and brought him into Damascus. 9For three days he was without sight, and neither ate nor drank.

10 Now there was a disciple in Damascus named Ananias. The Lord said to him in a vision, "Ananias." He answered, "Here I am, Lord." 11The Lord said to him, "Get up and go to the street called Straight, and at the house of Judas look for a man of Tarsus named Saul. At this moment he is praying, 12and he has seen in a vision*a* a man named Ananias come in and lay his hands on him so that he might regain his sight." 13But Ananias answered, "Lord, I have heard from many about this man, how much evil he has done to your saints in Jerusalem; 14and here he has authority from the chief priests to bind all who invoke your name." 15But the Lord said to him, "Go, for he is an instrument whom I have chosen to bring my name before Gentiles and kings and before the people of Israel; 16I myself will show him how much he must suffer for the sake of my name." 17So Ananias went and entered the house. He laid his hands on Saul*b* and said, "Brother Saul, the Lord Jesus, who appeared to you on your way here, has sent me so that you may regain your sight and be filled with the Holy Spirit." 18And immediately something like scales fell from his eyes, and his sight was restored. Then he got up and was baptized, 19and after taking some food, he regained his strength.

Saul Preaches in Damascus

For several days he was with the disciples in Damascus, 20and immediately he began to proclaim Jesus in the synagogues, saying, "He is the Son of God." 21All who heard him were amazed and said, "Is not this the man who made havoc in Jerusalem among those who invoked this name? And has he not come here for the purpose of bringing them bound before the chief priests?" 22Saul became increasingly more powerful and confounded the Jews who lived in Damascus by proving that Jesus*c* was the Messiah.*d*

Saul Escapes from the Jews

23 After some time had passed, the Jews plotted to kill him, 24but their plot became known to Saul. They were watching the gates day and night so that they might kill him; 25but his disciples took him by night and let him down through an opening in the wall,*e* lowering him in a basket.

Saul in Jerusalem

26 When he had come to Jerusalem, he attempted to join the disciples; and they were all afraid of him, for they did not believe that he was a disciple. 27But Barnabas took him, brought him to the apostles, and described for them how on the road he had seen the Lord, who had spoken to him, and how in Damascus he had spoken boldly in the name of Jesus. 28So he went in and out among them in Jerusalem, speaking boldly in the name of the Lord. 29He spoke and argued with the Hellenists; but they were attempting to kill him. 30When the believers*f* learned of it, they brought him down to Caesarea and sent him off to Tarsus.

31 Meanwhile the church throughout Judea, Galilee, and Samaria had peace and was built up. Living in the fear of the Lord and in the comfort of the Holy Spirit, it increased in numbers.

The Healing of Aeneas

32 Now as Peter went here and there among all the believers,*g* he came down also to the saints living in Lydda. 33There he found a man named Aeneas, who had been bedridden for eight years, for he was paralyzed. 34Peter said to him, "Aeneas, Jesus Christ heals you; get up and make your bed!" And immediately he got up. 35And all the residents of Lydda and Sharon saw him and turned to the Lord.

Peter in Lydda and Joppa

36 Now in Joppa there was a disciple whose name was Tabitha, which in Greek is Dorcas.*h* She was devoted to good works and acts of charity. 37At that time she became ill and died. When they had washed her, they laid her in a room upstairs. 38Since Lydda was near Joppa, the disciples, who heard that Peter was there, sent two men to him with the request, "Please come to us without delay." 39So Peter got up and went with them; and when he arrived, they took him to the room upstairs. All the widows stood beside him, weeping and showing tunics and other clothing that Dorcas had made while she was with them. 40Peter put all of them outside, and then he knelt down and prayed. He turned to the body and said, "Tabitha, get up." Then she opened her eyes, and seeing Peter, she sat up. 41He gave

---

a Other ancient authorities lack *in a vision*   b Gk *him*
c Gk *that this*   d Or *the Christ*   e Gk *through the wall*
f Gk *brothers*   g Gk *all of them*   h The name Tabitha in
Aramaic and the name Dorcas in Greek mean *a gazelle*

her his hand and helped her up. Then calling the saints and widows, he showed her to be alive. ⁴²This became known throughout Joppa, and many believed in the Lord. ⁴³Meanwhile he stayed in Joppa for some time with a certain Simon, a tanner.

Peter and Cornelius

10 In Caesarea there was a man named Cornelius, a centurion of the Italian Cohort, as it was called. ²He was a devout man who feared God with all his household; he gave alms generously to the people and prayed constantly to God. ³One afternoon at about three o'clock he had a vision in which he clearly saw an angel of God coming in and saying to him, "Cornelius." ⁴He stared at him in terror and said, "What is it, Lord?" He answered, "Your prayers and your alms have ascended as a memorial before God. ⁵Now send men to Joppa for a certain Simon who is called Peter; ⁶he is lodging with Simon, a tanner, whose house is by the seaside." ⁷When the angel who spoke to him had left, he called two of his slaves and a devout soldier from the ranks of those who served him, ⁸and after telling them everything, he sent them to Joppa.

9 About noon the next day, as they were on their journey and approaching the city, Peter went up on the roof to pray. ¹⁰He became hungry and wanted something to eat; and while it was being prepared, he fell into a trance. ¹¹He saw the heaven opened and something like a large sheet coming down, being lowered to the ground by its four corners. ¹²In it were all kinds of four-footed creatures and reptiles and birds of the air. ¹³Then he heard a voice saying, "Get up, Peter; kill and eat." ¹⁴But Peter said, "By no means, Lord; for I have never eaten anything that is profane or unclean." ¹⁵The voice said to him again, a second time, "What God has made clean, you must not call profane." ¹⁶This happened three times, and the thing was suddenly taken up to heaven.

17 Now while Peter was greatly puzzled about what to make of the vision that he had seen, suddenly the men sent by Cornelius appeared. They were asking for Simon's house and were standing by the gate. ¹⁸They called out to ask whether Simon, who was called Peter, was staying there. ¹⁹While Peter was still thinking about the vision, the Spirit said to him, "Look, three*a* men are searching for you. ²⁰Now get up, go down, and go with them without hesitation; for I have sent them." ²¹So Peter went down to the men and said, "I am the one you are looking for; what is the reason for your coming?" ²²They answered, "Cornelius, a centurion, an upright and God-

fearing man, who is well spoken of by the whole Jewish nation, was directed by a holy angel to send for you to come to his house and to hear what you have to say." ²³So Peter*b* invited them in and gave them lodging.

The next day he got up and went with them, and some of the believers*c* from Joppa accompanied him. ²⁴The following day they came to Caesarea. Cornelius was expecting them and had called together his relatives and close friends. ²⁵On Peter's arrival Cornelius met him, and falling at his feet, worshiped him. ²⁶But Peter made him get up, saying, "Stand up; I am only a mortal." ²⁷And as he talked with him, he went in and found that many had assembled; ²⁸and he said to them, "You yourselves know that it is unlawful for a Jew to associate with or to visit a Gentile; but God has shown me that I should not call anyone profane or unclean. ²⁹So when I was sent for, I came without objection. Now may I ask why you sent for me?"

30 Cornelius replied, "Four days ago at this very hour, at three o'clock, I was praying in my house when suddenly a man in dazzling clothes stood before me. ³¹He said, 'Cornelius, your prayer has been heard and your alms have been remembered before God. ³²Send therefore to Joppa and ask for Simon, who is called Peter; he is staying in the home of Simon, a tanner, by the sea.' ³³Therefore I sent for you immediately, and you have been kind enough to come. So now all of us are here in the presence of God to listen to all that the Lord has commanded you to say."

Gentiles Hear the Good News

34 Then Peter began to speak to them: "I truly understand that God shows no partiality, ³⁵but in every nation anyone who fears him and does what is right is acceptable to him. ³⁶You know the message he sent to the people of Israel, preaching peace by Jesus Christ—he is Lord of all. ³⁷That message spread throughout Judea, beginning in Galilee after the baptism that John announced: ³⁸how God anointed Jesus of Nazareth with the Holy Spirit and with power; how he went about doing good and healing all who were oppressed by the devil, for God was with him. ³⁹We are witnesses to all that he did both in Judea and in Jerusalem. They put him to death by hanging him on a tree; ⁴⁰but God raised him on the third day and allowed him to appear, ⁴¹not to all the people but to us who were chosen by God as witnesses, and

Cultural Connection

Here Comes Everybody

The word *catholic* means "universal." Someone once described being Catholic as, "Here comes everybody!"

In Acts of the Apostles 10:34–36, we hear that God shows no partiality; neither should we. Even so, it is sometimes easier to stick with people who are similar to us. They understand us and know where we are coming from. There's less explaining to do. Right?

But being catholic means reaching out of our familiar circle of friends and including in our group people of different cultures and religions.

Have you ever seen a Native American blanket? Threads of various colors are woven together to form an intricate, new pattern. Each blanket is completely different from every other blanket. By building relationships with people of different cultures and embrac-

ing their diversity, we become like one of the threads in such a blanket, weaving our uniquenesses in a new and beautiful pattern. The result is different and enriching, and then we become truly catholic.

▶ **Acts 10:34–36**

---

who ate and drank with him after he rose from the dead. ⁴²He commanded us to preach to the people and to testify that he is the one ordained by God as judge of the living and the dead. ⁴³All the prophets testify about him that everyone who believes in him receives forgiveness of sins through his name."

Gentiles Receive the Holy Spirit

44 While Peter was still speaking, the Holy Spirit fell upon all who heard the word. ⁴⁵The circumcised believers who had come with Peter were astounded that the gift of the Holy Spirit had been poured out even on the Gentiles, ⁴⁶for they heard them speaking in tongues and extolling God. Then Peter said, ⁴⁷"Can anyone withhold the water for baptizing these people who have received the Holy Spirit just as we have?" ⁴⁸So he ordered them to be baptized in the name of Jesus Christ. Then they invited him to stay for several days.

Peter's Report to the Church at Jerusalem

11 Now the apostles and the believers[a] who were in Judea heard that the Gentiles had also accepted the word of God. ²So when Peter went up to Jerusalem, the circumcised believers[b] criticized him, ³saying, "Why did you go to uncircumcised men and eat with them?" ⁴Then Peter began to explain it to them, step by step, saying, ⁵"I was in the city of Joppa praying, and in a trance I saw a vision. There was something like a large sheet coming down from heaven, being lowered by its four corners; and it came

close to me. ⁶As I looked at it closely I saw four-footed animals, beasts of prey, reptiles, and birds of the air. ⁷I also heard a voice saying to me, 'Get up, Peter; kill and eat.' ⁸But I replied, 'By no means, Lord; for nothing profane or unclean has ever entered my mouth.' ⁹But a second time the voice answered from heaven, 'What God has made clean, you must not call profane.' ¹⁰This happened three times; then everything was pulled up again to heaven. ¹¹At that very moment three men, sent to me from Caesarea, arrived at the house where we were. ¹²The Spirit told me to go with them and not to make a distinction between them and us.[c] These six brothers also accompanied me, and we entered the man's house. ¹³He told us how he had seen the angel standing in his house and saying, 'Send to Joppa and bring Simon, who is called Peter; ¹⁴he will give you a message by which you and your entire household will be saved.' ¹⁵And as I began to speak, the Holy Spirit fell upon them just as it had upon us at the beginning. ¹⁶And I remembered the word of the Lord, how he had said, 'John baptized with water, but you will be baptized with the Holy Spirit.' ¹⁷If then God gave them the same gift that he gave us when we believed in the Lord Jesus Christ, who was I that I could hinder God?" ¹⁸When they heard this, they were silenced. And they praised God, saying, "Then God has given even to the Gentiles the repentance that leads to life."

---

a Gk *brothers*   *b* Gk lacks *believers*   *c* Or *not to hesitate*

ACTS

The Church in Antioch

19 Now those who were scattered because of the persecution that took place over Stephen traveled as far as Phoenicia, Cyprus, and Antioch, and they spoke the word to no one except Jews. 20But among them were some men of Cyprus and Cyrene who, on coming to Antioch, spoke to the Hellenists*a* also, proclaiming the Lord Jesus. 21The hand of the Lord was with them, and a great number became believers and turned to the Lord. 22News of this came to the ears of the church in Jerusalem, and they sent Barnabas to Antioch. 23When he came and saw the grace of God, he rejoiced, and he exhorted them all to remain faithful to the Lord with steadfast devotion; 24for he was a good man, full of the Holy Spirit and of faith. And a great many people were brought to the Lord. 25Then Barnabas went to Tarsus to look for Saul, 26and when he had found him, he brought him to Antioch. So it was that for an entire year they met with*b* the church and taught a great many people, and it was in Antioch that the disciples were first called "Christians."

27 At that time prophets came down from Jerusalem to Antioch. 28One of them named Agabus stood up and predicted by the Spirit that there would be a severe famine over all the world; and this took place during the reign of Claudius. 29The disciples determined that according to their ability, each would send relief to the believers*c* living in Judea; 30this they did, sending it to the elders by Barnabas and Saul.

James Killed and Peter Imprisoned

12 About that time King Herod laid violent hands upon some who belonged to the church. 2He had James, the brother of John, killed with the sword. 3After he saw that it pleased the Jews, he proceeded to arrest Peter also. (This was during the festival of Unleavened Bread.) 4When he had seized him, he put him in prison and handed him over to four squads of soldiers to guard him, intending to bring him out to the people after the Passover. 5While Peter was kept in prison, the church prayed fervently to God for him.

Peter Delivered from Prison

6 The very night before Herod was going to bring him out, Peter, bound with two chains, was sleeping between two soldiers, while guards in front of the door were keeping watch over the prison. 7Suddenly an angel of the Lord appeared and a light shone in the cell. He tapped Peter on the side and woke him, saying, "Get up quickly." And the chains fell off his wrists. 8The angel said to him, "Fasten your belt and put on your sandals." He did so. Then he said to him, "Wrap your cloak around you and follow me." 9Peter*d* went out and followed him; he did not realize that what was happening with the angel's help was real; he thought he was seeing a vision. 10After they had passed the first and the second guard, they came before the iron gate leading into the city. It opened for them of its own accord, and they went outside and walked along a lane, when suddenly the angel left him. 11Then Peter came to himself and said, "Now I am sure that the Lord has sent his angel and rescued me from the hands of Herod and from all that the Jewish people were expecting."

12 As soon as he realized this, he went to the house of Mary, the mother of John whose other name was Mark, where many had gathered and

Barnabas

We first met Barnabas defending Paul after Paul's conversion in Acts of the Apostles, chapter 9. Now, in chapter 11, we are told that Barnabas "was a good man, full of the Holy Spirit and of faith" (verse 24). Barnabas's name literally means "son of encouragement." And encouraging others seemed to be Barnabas's gift. He recognized Paul's gifts and brought Paul to Antioch to minister to the new Christians there when no one else trusted Paul. Later, Barnabas reached out to Mark, disagreeing with Paul on whether to give Mark a second chance to travel with them (see 15:36–39). Barnabas sounds like the friend we would all like to have, someone who would believe in us through good times and bad.

Have you had a Barnabas in your life, someone who encouraged you and believed in you even after you made mistakes? Can you be that kind of encouraging friend to others?

▶ **Acts 11:19–26**

A
C
T
S

---

a Other ancient authorities read *Greeks*   *b* Or *were guests of*
c Gk *brothers*   *d* Gk *He*

were praying. ¹³When he knocked at the outer gate, a maid named Rhoda came to answer. ¹⁴On recognizing Peter's voice, she was so overjoyed that, instead of opening the gate, she ran in and announced that Peter was standing at the gate. ¹⁵They said to her, "You are out of your mind!" But she insisted that it was so. They said, "It is his angel." ¹⁶Meanwhile Peter continued knocking; and when they opened the gate, they saw him and were amazed. ¹⁷He motioned to them with his hand to be silent, and described for them how the Lord had brought him out of the prison. And he added, "Tell this to James and to the believers."ᵃ Then he left and went to another place.

18 When morning came, there was no small commotion among the soldiers over what had become of Peter. ¹⁹When Herod had searched for him and could not find him, he examined the guards and ordered them to be put to death. Then he went down from Judea to Caesarea and stayed there.

The Death of Herod

20 Now Herodᵇ was angry with the people of Tyre and Sidon. So they came to him in a body; and after winning over Blastus, the king's chamberlain, they asked for a reconciliation, because their country depended on the king's country for food. ²¹On an appointed day Herod put on his royal robes, took his seat on the platform, and delivered a public address to them. ²²The people kept shouting, "The voice of a god, and not of a mortal!" ²³And immediately, because he had not given the glory to God, an angel of the Lord struck him down, and he was eaten by worms and died.

24 But the word of God continued to advance and gain adherents. ²⁵Then after completing their mission Barnabas and Saul returned toᶜ Jerusalem and brought with them John, whose other name was Mark.

Barnabas and Saul Commissioned

13 Now in the church at Antioch there were prophets and teachers: Barnabas, Simeon who was called Niger, Lucius of Cyrene, Manaen a member of the court of Herod the ruler,ᵈ and Saul. ²While they were worshiping the Lord and fasting, the Holy Spirit said, "Set apart for me Barnabas and Saul for the work to which I have called them." ³Then after fasting and praying they laid their hands on them and sent them off.

The Apostles Preach in Cyprus

4 So, being sent out by the Holy Spirit, they went down to Seleucia; and from there they sailed to Cyprus. ⁵When they arrived at Salamis, they proclaimed the word of God in the synagogues of the Jews. And they had John also to assist them. ⁶When they had gone through the whole island as far as Paphos, they met a certain magician, a Jewish false prophet, named Bar-Jesus. ⁷He was with the proconsul, Sergius Paulus, an intelligent man, who summoned Barnabas and Saul and wanted to hear the word of God. ⁸But the magician Elymas (for that is the translation of his name) opposed them and tried to turn the proconsul away from the faith. ⁹But Saul, also known as Paul, filled with the Holy Spirit, looked intently at him ¹⁰and said, "You son of the devil, you enemy of all righteousness, full of all deceit and villainy, will you not stop making crooked the straight paths of the Lord? ¹¹And now listen—the hand of the Lord is against you, and you will be blind for a while, unable to see the sun." Immediately mist and darkness came over him, and he went about groping for someone to lead him by the hand. ¹²When the proconsul saw what had happened, he believed, for he was astonished at the teaching about the Lord.

Paul and Barnabas in Antioch of Pisidia

13 Then Paul and his companions set sail from Paphos and came to Perga in Pamphylia. John, however, left them and returned to Jerusalem; ¹⁴but they went on from Perga and came to Antioch in Pisidia. And on the sabbath day they

Pray It!

What Imprisons You?

Holy Spirit, come! Open my mind to seek the truth. Break down the barriers that imprison me. Empower me to overcome any guilt by asking for forgiveness. Enable me to forgive others and release my past hurt and anger. Open my eyes to vices, habits, and attitudes that are destructive to me and to others. Guide me to true freedom with your word. Amen.

▶ **Acts 12:6–19**

A C T S

ᵃ Gk brothers   ᵇ Gk he   ᶜ Other ancient authorities read from
ᵈ Gk tetrarch

went into the synagogue and sat down. ¹⁵After the reading of the law and the prophets, the officials of the synagogue sent them a message, saying, "Brothers, if you have any word of exhortation for the people, give it." ¹⁶So Paul stood up and with a gesture began to speak:

"You Israelites,ᵃ and others who fear God, listen. ¹⁷The God of this people Israel chose our ancestors and made the people great during their stay in the land of Egypt, and with uplifted arm he led them out of it. ¹⁸For about forty years he put up withᵇ them in the wilderness. ¹⁹After he had destroyed seven nations in the land of Canaan, he gave them their land as an inheritance ²⁰for about four hundred fifty years. After that he gave them judges until the time of the prophet Samuel. ²¹Then they asked for a king; and God gave them Saul son of Kish, a man of the tribe of Benjamin, who reigned for forty years. ²²When he had removed him, he made David their king. In his testimony about him he said, 'I have found David, son of Jesse, to be a man after my heart, who will carry out all my wishes.' ²³Of this man's posterity God has brought to Israel a Savior, Jesus, as he promised; ²⁴before his coming John had already proclaimed a baptism of repentance to all the people of Israel. ²⁵And as John was finishing his work, he said, 'What do you suppose that I am? I am not he. No, but one is coming after me; I am not worthy to untie the thong of the sandalsᶜ on his feet.'

26 "My brothers, you descendants of Abraham's family, and others who fear God, to usᵈ the message of this salvation has been sent. ²⁷Because the residents of Jerusalem and their leaders did not recognize him or understand the words of the prophets that are read every sabbath, they fulfilled those words by condemning him. ²⁸Even though they found no cause for a sentence of death, they asked Pilate to have him killed. ²⁹When they had carried out everything that was written about him, they took him down from the tree and laid him in a tomb. ³⁰But God raised him from the dead; ³¹and for many days he appeared to those who came up with him from Galilee to Jerusalem, and they are now his witnesses to the people. ³²And we bring you the good news that what God promised to our ancestors ³³he has fulfilled for us, their children, by raising Jesus; as also it is written in the second psalm,

'You are my Son;
    today I have begotten you.'

³⁴As to his raising him from the dead, no more to return to corruption, he has spoken in this way,

'I will give you the holy promises made to
    David.'

³⁵Therefore he has also said in another psalm,

'You will not let your Holy One experience
    corruption.'

³⁶For David, after he had served the purpose of God in his own generation, died,ᵉ was laid beside his ancestors, and experienced corruption; ³⁷but he whom God raised up experienced no corruption. ³⁸Let it be known to you therefore, my brothers, that through this man forgiveness of sins is proclaimed to you; ³⁹by this Jesusᶠ everyone who believes is set free from all those sinsᵍ from which you could not be freed by the law of Moses. ⁴⁰Beware, therefore, that what the prophets said does not happen to you:

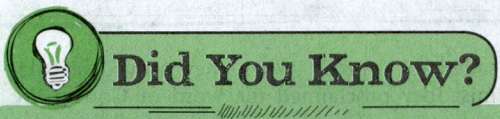

Did You Know?

The Journeys of Paul

According to the way Luke constructed Paul's story, Paul made three missionary journeys over a ten-year period to spread the Gospel message. The details of his first journey are covered in chapters 13–14. The second journey is reported in chapters 16–18. The third journey is described in chapters 19–21. Paul himself may have seen these not as three separate journeys but as one continuous missionary activity. On these journeys, Paul made converts and started Christian communities. On the second and third journeys, he also visited established communities to give them guidance and support. See maps 8 and 9 for the routes of Paul's journeys.

Paul's third journey landed him back in Jerusalem, where some Jews had him arrested. On the basis of his Roman citizenship, Paul appealed to the emperor. So he was transported to Rome (this trip is referred to as his fourth journey). He probably died there as a martyr around AD 65. Some traditions say that Paul wasn't martyred there but went on to evangelize in Spain.

▶ Acts of the Apostles,
    chapters 13–21

ᵃ Gk Men, Israelites   ᵇ Other ancient authorities read cared for   ᶜ Gk untie the sandals   ᵈ Other ancient authorities read you   ᵉ Gk fell asleep   ᶠ Gk this   ᵍ Gk all

41 'Look, you scoffers!
　Be amazed and perish,
　for in your days I am doing a work,
　　a work that you will never believe, even if
　　　someone tells you.' "

42 As Paul and Barnabas[a] were going out, the people urged them to speak about these things again the next sabbath. 43When the meeting of the synagogue broke up, many Jews and devout converts to Judaism followed Paul and Barnabas, who spoke to them and urged them to continue in the grace of God.

44 The next sabbath almost the whole city gathered to hear the word of the Lord.[b] 45But when the Jews saw the crowds, they were filled with jealousy; and blaspheming, they contradicted what was spoken by Paul. 46Then both Paul and Barnabas spoke out boldly, saying, "It was necessary that the word of God should be spoken first to you. Since you reject it and judge yourselves to be unworthy of eternal life, we are now turning to the Gentiles. 47For so the Lord has commanded us, saying,

'I have set you to be a light for the Gentiles,
　so that you may bring salvation to the ends of
　　the earth.' "

48 When the Gentiles heard this, they were glad and praised the word of the Lord; and as many as had been destined for eternal life became believers. 49Thus the word of the Lord spread throughout the region. 50But the Jews incited the devout women of high standing and the leading men of the city, and stirred up persecution against Paul and Barnabas, and drove them out of their region. 51So they shook the dust off their feet in protest against them, and went to Iconium. 52And the disciples were filled with joy and with the Holy Spirit.

Paul and Barnabas in Iconium

14 The same thing occurred in Iconium, where Paul and Barnabas[a] went into the Jewish synagogue and spoke in such a way that a great number of both Jews and Greeks became believers. 2But the unbelieving Jews stirred up the Gentiles and poisoned their minds against the brothers. 3So they remained for a long time, speaking boldly for the Lord, who testified to the word of his grace by granting signs and wonders to be done through them. 4But the residents of the city were divided; some sided with the Jews, and some with the apostles. 5And when an attempt was made by both Gentiles and Jews, with their rulers, to mistreat them and to stone them, 6the apostles[a] learned of it and fled to Lystra and Derbe, cities of Lycaonia, and to the surrounding

Live It!

A Courageous Stance

One thing is clear about taking a stand and spreading the Gospel—it takes great courage. The story of Paul and Barnabas in Iconium is further evidence of how the early disciples risked their own lives to preach the Good News. It seems the Good News is not easy for some people to hear or accept.

In your prayer, reflect or journal on the following questions:

● In what ways is God inviting you to speak and act boldly to spread the Good News in your school? your home? your neighborhood and community?
● What keeps you from responding?

▶ **Acts 14:1–7**

country; 7and there they continued proclaiming the good news.

Paul and Barnabas in Lystra and Derbe

8 In Lystra there was a man sitting who could not use his feet and had never walked, for he had been crippled from birth. 9He listened to Paul as he was speaking. And Paul, looking at him intently and seeing that he had faith to be healed, 10said in a loud voice, "Stand upright on your feet." And the man[c] sprang up and began to walk. 11When the crowds saw what Paul had done, they shouted in the Lycaonian language, "The gods have come down to us in human form!" 12Barnabas they called Zeus, and Paul they called Hermes, because he was the chief speaker. 13The priest of Zeus, whose temple was just outside the city,[d] brought oxen and garlands to the gates; he and the crowds wanted to offer sacrifice. 14When the apostles Barnabas and Paul heard of it, they tore their clothes and rushed out into the crowd, shouting, 15"Friends,[e] why are you doing this? We are mortals just like you, and we bring you good news, that you should turn from these worthless things to the living God, who made the heaven and the earth and the sea and all that is in them. 16In past generations he

---

a Gk they　b Other ancient authorities read God　c Gk he
d Or The priest of Zeus-Outside-the-City　e Gk Men

allowed all the nations to follow their own ways; [17]yet he has not left himself without a witness in doing good—giving you rains from heaven and fruitful seasons, and filling you with food and your hearts with joy." [18]Even with these words, they scarcely restrained the crowds from offering sacrifice to them.

19 But Jews came there from Antioch and Iconium and won over the crowds. Then they stoned Paul and dragged him out of the city, supposing that he was dead. [20]But when the

Unity in Faith and Love

When Paul and Barnabas were in Antioch, a controversy arose regarding the need for Gentiles to be circumcised and to follow certain Jewish laws and holidays. The earliest Christians were Jews. They believed in Jesus and continued to follow the rules of the Jewish faith as a sign that they were a covenant people. But with Gentiles becoming Christians, new questions were raised: Do Gentiles have to follow all the Jewish rules? Do Gentiles need to be circumcised as a sign of the covenant? Circumcision is the surgical removal of the foreskin from the penis, and the Gentile converts did not see the need for it.

Paul and Barnabas insisted that Christians were free from such Jewish laws; they went to Jerusalem to meet with the other Apostles to defend their position. With Peter's support, the community decided that Paul and Barnabas were right. And so the Apostles at the council agreed that the center of the Christian faith was believing in the risen Christ, not conforming to specific Jewish rituals. This meeting of the Apostles is called the Council of Jerusalem and was a pivotal point in the history of the Church.

How does your youth group or parish handle conflict? Does it handle it better when members remind themselves that they are united by their faith in Jesus?

▶ **Acts 15:1–35**

disciples surrounded him, he got up and went into the city. The next day he went on with Barnabas to Derbe.

The Return to Antioch in Syria

21 After they had proclaimed the good news to that city and had made many disciples, they returned to Lystra, then on to Iconium and Antioch. [22]There they strengthened the souls of the disciples and encouraged them to continue in the faith, saying, "It is through many persecutions that we must enter the kingdom of God." [23]And after they had appointed elders for them in each church, with prayer and fasting they entrusted them to the Lord in whom they had come to believe.

24 Then they passed through Pisidia and came to Pamphylia. [25]When they had spoken the word in Perga, they went down to Attalia. [26]From there they sailed back to Antioch, where they had been commended to the grace of God for the work[a] that they had completed. [27]When they arrived, they called the church together and related all that God had done with them, and how he had opened a door of faith for the Gentiles. [28]And they stayed there with the disciples for some time.

The Council at Jerusalem

15 Then certain individuals came down from Judea and were teaching the brothers, "Unless you are circumcised according to the custom of Moses, you cannot be saved." [2]And after Paul and Barnabas had no small dissension and debate with them, Paul and Barnabas and some of the others were appointed to go up to Jerusalem to discuss this question with the apostles and the elders. [3]So they were sent on their way by the church, and as they passed through both Phoenicia and Samaria, they reported the conversion of the Gentiles, and brought great joy to all the believers.[b] [4]When they came to Jerusalem, they were welcomed by the church and the apostles and the elders, and they reported all that God had done with them. [5]But some believers who belonged to the sect of the Pharisees stood up and said, "It is necessary for them to be circumcised and ordered to keep the law of Moses."

6 The apostles and the elders met together to consider this matter. [7]After there had been much debate, Peter stood up and said to them, "My brothers,[c] you know that in the early days God made a choice among you, that I should be the

a Or committed in the grace of God to the work   b Gk brothers
c Gk Men, brothers

✝ Catholic Connection

Ministry in the Church

This was not your typical road trip! Paul and Barnabas had been sent forth by the Church in Antioch to spread the Gospel message. While traveling and preaching about Jesus, they were persecuted, falsely worshiped as gods, and nearly stoned to death! But that did not stop them. They bravely returned to each city to encourage those who had converted and to appoint elders, or presbyters. These leaders were selected through prayers and fasting to lead the community and guard against those who would twist and distort the Gospel. At the conclusion of their trip, Paul and Barnabas returned home to share the joys of their success and the thrills of a few heroic moments.

Paul and Barnabas's journeys to local churches give us great insight into the origins and development of ministry within the Catholic Church. From the leaders or overseers (see Acts 20:28) Paul and Barnabas appointed to guard and teach the faith, we get a glimpse at the origins of the role of bishops, the successors of the Apostles. The leaders who assisted the bishops became known as priests, or presbyters. Finally, those who were specifically set aside for service to the community and who aided the bishops and priests were called deacons (see 1 Tim 3:8–13).

There are numerous ways a person can answer her or his baptismal call to serve and take part in the ministry of the Church today. Some men choose to answer the call through ordained ministry as bishops, priests, or deacons. Other women and men may discern a call to the religious life as sisters or brothers. Finally, some men and women choose to use their gifts to serve the community as lay ecclesial ministers. Lay ecclesial ministry is very broad and includes youth ministers, catechists, liturgical ministers, outreach ministers, and so on. All the various ministries work together under the direction of the bishop and pastors. By using all the various gifts of its members, the Church is able to spread the Gospel with courage and perseverance as Paul and Barnabas did so long ago.

▶ **Acts 14:21–28**
Catechism, nos. 871–945

ACTS

one through whom the Gentiles would hear the message of the good news and become believers. [8]And God, who knows the human heart, testified to them by giving them the Holy Spirit, just as he did to us; [9]and in cleansing their hearts by faith he has made no distinction between them and us. [10]Now therefore why are you putting God to the test by placing on the neck of the disciples a yoke that neither our ancestors nor we have been able to bear? [11]On the contrary, we believe that we will be saved through the grace of the Lord Jesus, just as they will."

12 The whole assembly kept silence, and listened to Barnabas and Paul as they told of all the signs and wonders that God had done through them among the Gentiles. [13]After they finished speaking, James replied, "My brothers,[a] listen to me. [14]Simeon has related how God first looked favorably on the Gentiles, to take from among them a people for his name. [15]This agrees with the words of the prophets, as it is written,

[16] 'After this I will return,
    and I will rebuild the dwelling of David, which
        has fallen;
    from its ruins I will rebuild it,
        and I will set it up,
[17] so that all other peoples may seek the Lord—
    even all the Gentiles over whom my name
        has been called.
    Thus says the Lord, who has been making
        these things [18]known from long ago.'[b]

[19]Therefore I have reached the decision that we should not trouble those Gentiles who are turning to God, [20]but we should write to them to abstain only from things polluted by idols and from fornication and from whatever has been strangled[c] and from blood. [21]For in every city, for generations past, Moses has had those who proclaim him, for he has been read aloud every sabbath in the synagogues."

The Council's Letter to Gentile Believers

22 Then the apostles and the elders, with the consent of the whole church, decided to choose men from among their members[d] and to send them to Antioch with Paul and Barnabas. They sent Judas called Barsabbas, and Silas, leaders among the brothers, [23]with the following letter: "The brothers, both the apostles and the elders, to the believers[e] of Gentile origin in Antioch and Syria and Cilicia, greetings. [24]Since we have heard that certain persons who have gone out from us, though with no instructions from us, have said things to disturb you and have unsettled your minds,[f] [25]we have decided unanimously to choose representatives[g] and send them to

you, along with our beloved Barnabas and Paul, [26]who have risked their lives for the sake of our Lord Jesus Christ. [27]We have therefore sent Judas and Silas, who themselves will tell you the same things by word of mouth. [28]For it has seemed good to the Holy Spirit and to us to impose on you no further burden than these essentials: [29]that you abstain from what has been sacrificed to idols and from blood and from what is strangled[h] and from fornication. If you keep yourselves from these, you will do well. Farewell."

30 So they were sent off and went down to Antioch. When they gathered the congregation together, they delivered the letter. [31]When its members[i] read it, they rejoiced at the exhortation. [32]Judas and Silas, who were themselves prophets, said much to encourage and strengthen the believers.[e] [33]After they had been there for some time, they were sent off in peace by the believers[e] to those who had sent them.[j] [35]But Paul and Barnabas remained in Antioch, and there, with many others, they taught and proclaimed the word of the Lord.

Paul and Barnabas Separate

36 After some days Paul said to Barnabas, "Come, let us return and visit the believers[e] in every city where we proclaimed the word of the Lord and see how they are doing." [37]Barnabas wanted to take with them John called Mark. [38]But Paul decided not to take with them one who had deserted them in Pamphylia and had not accompanied them in the work. [39]The disagreement became so sharp that they parted company; Barnabas took Mark with him and sailed away to Cyprus. [40]But Paul chose Silas and set out, the believers[e] commending him to the grace of the Lord. [41]He went through Syria and Cilicia, strengthening the churches.

Timothy Joins Paul and Silas

16 Paul[k] went on also to Derbe and to Lystra, where there was a disciple named Timothy, the son of a Jewish woman who was a believer; but his father was a Greek. [2]He was well spoken of by the believers[e] in Lystra and Iconium. [3]Paul wanted Timothy to accompany him; and he took him and had him circumcised because of the Jews who were in those places,

a Gk Men, brothers   b Other ancient authorities read things. [18]Known to God from of old are all his works.'   c Other ancient authorities lack and from whatever has been strangled   d Gk from among them   e Gk brothers   f Other ancient authorities add saying, 'You must be circumcised and keep the law,'   g Gk men   h Other ancient authorities lack and from what is strangled   i Gk When they   j Other ancient authorities add verse 34, But it seemed good to Silas to remain there   k Gk He

for they all knew that his father was a Greek. [4]As they went from town to town, they delivered to them for observance the decisions that had been reached by the apostles and elders who were in Jerusalem. [5]So the churches were strengthened in the faith and increased in numbers daily.

Paul's Vision of the Man of Macedonia

[6] They went through the region of Phrygia and Galatia, having been forbidden by the Holy Spirit to speak the word in Asia. [7]When they had come opposite Mysia, they attempted to go into Bithynia, but the Spirit of Jesus did not allow them; [8]so, passing by Mysia, they went down to Troas. [9]During the night Paul had a vision: there stood a man of Macedonia pleading with him and saying, "Come over to Macedonia and help us." [10]When he had seen the vision, we immediately tried to cross over to Macedonia, being convinced that God had called us to proclaim the good news to them.

The Conversion of Lydia

[11] We set sail from Troas and took a straight course to Samothrace, the following day to Neapolis, [12]and from there to Philippi, which is a leading city of the district[a] of Macedonia and a Roman colony. We remained in this city for some days. [13]On the sabbath day we went outside the gate by the river, where we supposed there was a place of prayer; and we sat down and spoke to the women who had gathered there. [14]A certain woman named Lydia, a worshiper of God, was listening to us; she was from the city of Thyatira and a dealer in purple cloth. The Lord opened her heart to listen eagerly to what was said by Paul. [15]When she and her household were baptized, she urged us, saying, "If you have judged me to be faithful to the Lord, come and stay at my home." And she prevailed upon us.

Paul and Silas in Prison

[16] One day, as we were going to the place of prayer, we met a slave-girl who had a spirit of divination and brought her owners a great deal of money by fortune-telling. [17]While she followed Paul and us, she would cry out, "These men are slaves of the Most High God, who proclaim to you[b] a way of salvation." [18]She kept doing this for many days. But Paul, very much annoyed, turned and said to the spirit, "I order you in the name of Jesus Christ to come out of her." And it came out that very hour.

[19] But when her owners saw that their hope of making money was gone, they seized Paul and Silas and dragged them into the marketplace

Introducing...

Lydia and Priscilla

Women were a crucial part of Christianity from its beginnings. The Acts of the Apostles names two women who were instrumental in Paul's missionary journeys: Lydia and Priscilla. Lydia (see Acts 16:11–15) was Paul's first convert in Philippi, which is part of modern-day Europe. She was a textile merchant and was wealthy enough to support a household and open her home to Paul and Silas to stay for an extended time.

In chapter 18, we meet Priscilla and her husband, Aquila. This family hosted Paul in Corinth. Later, they accompanied him from Corinth to Antioch. While there they instructed Apollos in the "Way of God" (18:26). Luke's inclusion of these women indicates that women were active in the early Church, not only supporting the missionary work of Paul but also leading and teaching.

▶ **Acts 16:14–15, 18:1–26**

before the authorities. [20]When they had brought them before the magistrates, they said, "These men are disturbing our city; they are Jews [21]and are advocating customs that are not lawful for us as Romans to adopt or observe." [22]The crowd joined in attacking them, and the magistrates had them stripped of their clothing and ordered them to be beaten with rods. [23]After they had given them a severe flogging, they threw them into prison and ordered the jailer to keep them securely. [24]Following these instructions, he put them in the innermost cell and fastened their feet in the stocks.

[25] About midnight Paul and Silas were praying and singing hymns to God, and the prisoners were listening to them. [26]Suddenly there was an earthquake, so violent that the foundations of the prison were shaken; and immediately all the doors were opened and everyone's chains were unfastened. [27]When the jailer woke up and saw the prison doors wide open, he drew his sword and was about to kill himself, since he supposed

A C T S

---

a Other authorities read *a city of the first district*   b Other ancient authorities read *to us* that the prisoners had escaped. 28But Paul shouted in a loud voice, "Do not harm yourself, for we are all here." 29The jailer[a] called for lights, and rushing in, he fell down trembling before Paul and Silas. 30Then he brought them outside and said, "Sirs, what must I do to be saved?" 31They answered, "Believe on the Lord Jesus, and you will be saved, you and your household." 32They spoke the word of the Lord[b] to him and to all who were in his house. 33At the same hour of the night he took them and washed their wounds; then he and his entire family were baptized without delay. 34He brought them up into the house and set food before them; and he and his entire household rejoiced that he had become a believer in God.

35 When morning came, the magistrates sent the police, saying, "Let those men go." 36And the jailer reported the message to Paul, saying, "The magistrates sent word to let you go; therefore come out now and go in peace." 37But Paul replied, "They have beaten us in public, uncondemned, men who are Roman citizens, and have thrown us into prison; and now are they going to discharge us in secret? Certainly not! Let them come and take us out themselves." 38The police reported these words to the magistrates, and they were afraid when they heard that they were Roman citizens; 39so they came and apologized to them. And they took them out and asked them to leave the city. 40After leaving the prison they went to Lydia's home; and when they had seen and encouraged the brothers and sisters[c] there, they departed.

The Uproar in Thessalonica

17 After Paul and Silas[d] had passed through Amphipolis and Apollonia, they came to Thessalonica, where there was a synagogue of the Jews. 2And Paul went in, as was his custom, and on three sabbath days argued with them from the scriptures, 3explaining and proving that it was necessary for the Messiah[e] to suffer and to rise from the dead, and saying, "This is the Messiah,[e] Jesus whom I am proclaiming to you." 4Some of them were persuaded and joined Paul and Silas, as did a great many of the devout Greeks and not a few of the leading women. 5But the Jews became jealous, and with the help of some ruffians in the marketplaces they formed a mob and set the city in an uproar. While they were searching for Paul and Silas to bring them out to the assembly, they attacked Jason's house. 6When they could not find them, they dragged Jason and some believers[c] before the city authorities,[f] shouting, "These people who have been turning the world upside down have come here also, 7and Jason has entertained them as guests. They are all acting contrary to the decrees of the emperor, saying that there is another king named Jesus." 8The people and the city officials were disturbed when they heard this, 9and after they had taken bail from Jason and the others, they let them go.

Paul and Silas in Beroea

10 That very night the believers[c] sent Paul and Silas off to Beroea; and when they arrived, they went to the Jewish synagogue. 11These Jews were more receptive than those in Thessalonica, for they welcomed the message very eagerly and examined the scriptures every day to see whether these things were so. 12Many of them therefore believed, including not a few Greek women and men of high standing. 13But when the Jews of Thessalonica learned that the word of God had been proclaimed by Paul in Beroea as well, they came there too, to stir up and incite the crowds. 14Then the believers[c] immediately sent Paul away to the coast, but Silas and Timothy remained behind. 15Those who conducted Paul brought him as far as Athens; and after receiving instructions to have Silas and Timothy join him as soon as possible, they left him.

Paul in Athens

16 While Paul was waiting for them in Athens, he was deeply distressed to see that the city was full of idols. 17So he argued in the synagogue with the Jews and the devout persons, and also in the marketplace[g] every day with those who happened to be there. 18Also some Epicurean and Stoic philosophers debated with him. Some said, "What

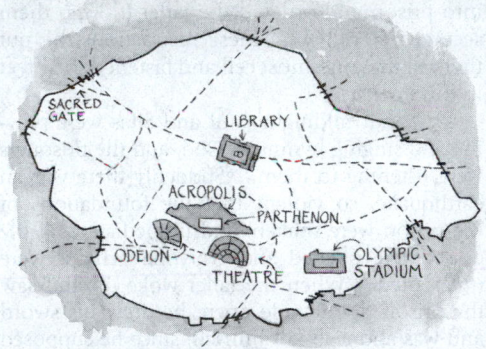

SACRED GATE

LIBRARY

ACROPOLIS

PARTHENON

ODEION

THEATRE

OLYMPIC STADIUM

- - - ROADS
- -╪- GATES

17:16–34

Map of first-century Athens

---

a Gk *He*   *b* Other ancient authorities read *word of God*
c Gk *brothers*   *d* Gk *they*   *e* Or *the Christ*   *f* Gk *politarchs*
g Or *civic center;* Gk *agora*

ACTS

does this babbler want to say?" Others said, "He seems to be a proclaimer of foreign divinities." (This was because he was telling the good news about Jesus and the resurrection.) ¹⁹So they took him and brought him to the Areopagus and asked him, "May we know what this new teaching is that you are presenting? ²⁰It sounds rather strange to us, so we would like to know what it means." ²¹Now all the Athenians and the foreigners living there would spend their time in nothing but telling or hearing something new.

22 Then Paul stood in front of the Areopagus and said, "Athenians, I see how extremely religious you are in every way. ²³For as I went through the city and looked carefully at the objects of your worship, I found among them an altar with the inscription, 'To an unknown god.' What therefore you worship as unknown, this I proclaim to you. ²⁴The God who made the world and everything in it, he who is Lord of heaven and earth, does not live in shrines made by human hands, ²⁵nor is he served by human hands, as though he needed anything, since he himself gives to all mortals life and breath and all things. ²⁶From one ancestor*a* he made all nations to inhabit the whole earth, and he allotted the times of their existence and the boundaries of the places where they would live, ²⁷so that they would search for God*b* and perhaps grope for him and find him—though indeed he is not far from each one of us. ²⁸For 'In him we live and move and have our being'; as even some of your own poets have said,

'For we too are his offspring.'

²⁹Since we are God's offspring, we ought not to think that the deity is like gold, or silver, or stone, an image formed by the art and imagination of mortals. ³⁰While God has overlooked the times of human ignorance, now he commands all people everywhere to repent, ³¹because he has fixed a day on which he will have the world judged in righteousness by a man whom he has appointed, and of this he has given assurance to all by raising him from the dead."

32 When they heard of the resurrection of the dead, some scoffed; but others said, "We will hear you again about this." ³³At that point Paul left them. ³⁴But some of them joined him and became believers, including Dionysius the Areopagite and a woman named Damaris, and others with them.

Paul in Corinth

18 After this Paul*c* left Athens and went to Corinth. ²There he found a Jew named Aquila, a native of Pontus, who had recently

Help Us to Evangelize

Paul was wonderfully gifted for his work as an evangelist. He had the ability to communicate with both common people and intellectuals. He was familiar with three cultures—Jewish, Greek, and Roman—and proclaimed the Gospel message in ways all three could understand. He was skilled at building Christian communities. And he was absolutely fearless in preaching about Jesus Christ. Let's pray for these gifts in ourselves so that we can continue the Church's mission of evangelization, particularly to young people.

O God, how I admire Paul! I too want to share your Good News with others. So let your Holy Spirit bless me with the gift of evangelization. Help me to reach out to other young people no matter what clique or group they belong to. Help me to bring out the best in our culture and to challenge that which is wrong or misleading. Give me courage to speak fearlessly about my faith in Jesus when it is right to do so. And let me be your instrument in building communities of faith, hope, and love. Amen.

▶ **Acts of the Apostles, chapter 17**

come from Italy with his wife Priscilla, because Claudius had ordered all Jews to leave Rome. Paul*d* went to see them, ³and, because he was of the same trade, he stayed with them, and they worked together—by trade they were tentmakers. ⁴Every sabbath he would argue in the synagogue and would try to convince Jews and Greeks.

5 When Silas and Timothy arrived from Macedonia, Paul was occupied with proclaiming the word,*e* testifying to the Jews that the Messiah*f* was Jesus. ⁶When they opposed and reviled him, in protest he shook the dust from his clothes*g* and said to them, "Your blood be

---

a Gk *From one*; other ancient authorities read *From one blood*
b Other ancient authorities read *the Lord*   *c* Gk *he*   *d* Gk *He*
e Gk *with the word*   *f* Or *the Christ*   *g* Gk *reviled him, he shook out his clothes*

on your own heads! I am innocent. From now on I will go to the Gentiles." [7]Then he left the synagogue[a] and went to the house of a man named Titius[b] Justus, a worshiper of God; his house was next door to the synagogue. [8]Crispus, the official of the synagogue, became a believer in the Lord, together with all his household; and many of the Corinthians who heard Paul became believers and were baptized. [9]One night the Lord said to Paul in a vision, "Do not be afraid, but speak and do not be silent; [10]for I am with you, and no one will lay a hand on you to harm you, for there are many in this city who are my people." [11]He stayed there a year and six months, teaching the word of God among them.

[12] But when Gallio was proconsul of Achaia, the Jews made a united attack on Paul and brought him before the tribunal. [13]They said, "This man is persuading people to worship God in ways that are contrary to the law." [14]Just as Paul was about to speak, Gallio said to the Jews, "If it were a matter of crime or serious villainy, I would be justified in accepting the complaint of you Jews; [15]but since it is a matter of questions about words and names and your own law, see to it yourselves; I do not wish to be a judge of these matters." [16]And he dismissed them from the tribunal. [17]Then all of them[c] seized Sosthenes, the official of the synagogue, and beat him in front of the tribunal. But Gallio paid no attention to any of these things.

Paul's Return to Antioch

[18] After staying there for a considerable time, Paul said farewell to the believers[d] and sailed for Syria, accompanied by Priscilla and Aquila. At Cenchreae he had his hair cut, for he was under a vow. [19]When they reached Ephesus, he left them there, but first he himself went into the synagogue and had a discussion with the Jews. [20]When they asked him to stay longer, he declined; [21]but on taking leave of them, he said, "I[e] will return to you, if God wills." Then he set sail from Ephesus.

[22] When he had landed at Caesarea, he went up to Jerusalem[f] and greeted the church, and then went down to Antioch. [23]After spending some time there he departed and went from place to place through the region of Galatia[g] and Phrygia, strengthening all the disciples.

Ministry of Apollos

[24] Now there came to Ephesus a Jew named Apollos, a native of Alexandria. He was an eloquent man, well-versed in the scriptures. [25]He had been instructed in the Way of the Lord; and he spoke with burning enthusiasm and taught accurately the things concerning Jesus, though he knew only the baptism of John. [26]He began to speak boldly in the synagogue; but when Priscilla and Aquila heard him, they took him aside and explained the Way of God to him more accurately. [27]And when he wished to cross over to Achaia, the believers[d] encouraged him and wrote to the disciples to welcome him. On his arrival he greatly helped those who through grace had become believers, [28]for he powerfully refuted the Jews in public, showing by the scriptures that the Messiah[h] is Jesus.

Paul in Ephesus

19 While Apollos was in Corinth, Paul passed through the interior regions and came to Ephesus, where he found some disciples. [2]He said to them, "Did you receive the Holy Spirit when you became believers?" They replied, "No, we have not even heard that there is a Holy Spirit." [3]Then he said, "Into what then were you baptized?" They answered, "Into John's baptism." [4]Paul said, "John baptized with the baptism of repentance, telling the people to believe in the one who was to come after him, that is, in Jesus." [5]On hearing this, they were baptized in the name of the Lord Jesus. [6]When Paul had laid his hands on them, the Holy Spirit came upon them, and they spoke in tongues and prophesied— [7]altogether there were about twelve of them.

[8] He entered the synagogue and for three months spoke out boldly, and argued persuasively about the kingdom of God. [9]When some stubbornly refused to believe and spoke evil of the Way before the congregation, he left them, taking the disciples with him, and argued daily in the lecture hall of Tyrannus.[i] [10]This continued for two years, so that all the residents of Asia, both Jews and Greeks, heard the word of the Lord.

The Sons of Sceva

[11] God did extraordinary miracles through Paul, [12]so that when the handkerchiefs or aprons that had touched his skin were brought to the sick, their diseases left them, and the evil spirits came out of them. [13]Then some

---

a Gk *left there*   *b* Other ancient authorities read *Titus*   *c* Other ancient authorities read *all the Greeks*   *d* Gk *brothers*   *e* Other ancient authorities read *I must at all costs keep the approaching festival in Jerusalem, but I*   *f* Gk *went up*   *g* Gk *the Galatian region*   *h* Or *the Christ*   *i* Other ancient authorities read *of a certain Tyrannus, from eleven o'clock in the morning to four in the afternoon*

itinerant Jewish exorcists tried to use the name of the Lord Jesus over those who had evil spirits, saying, "I adjure you by the Jesus whom Paul proclaims." ¹⁴Seven sons of a Jewish high priest named Sceva were doing this. ¹⁵But the evil spirit said to them in reply, "Jesus I know, and Paul I know; but who are you?" ¹⁶Then the man with the evil spirit leaped on them, mastered them all, and so overpowered them that they fled out of the house naked and wounded. ¹⁷When this became known to all residents of Ephesus, both Jews and Greeks, everyone was awestruck; and the name of the Lord Jesus was praised. ¹⁸Also many of those who became believers confessed and disclosed their practices. ¹⁹A number of those who practiced magic collected their books and burned them publicly; when the value of these booksᵃ was calculated, it was found to come to fifty thousand silver coins. ²⁰So the word of the Lord grew mightily and prevailed.

The Riot in Ephesus

21 Now after these things had been accomplished, Paul resolved in the Spirit to go through Macedonia and Achaia, and then to go on to Jerusalem. He said, "After I have gone there, I must also see Rome." ²²So he sent two of his helpers, Timothy and Erastus, to Macedonia, while he himself stayed for some time longer in Asia.

23 About that time no little disturbance broke out concerning the Way. ²⁴A man named Demetrius, a silversmith who made silver shrines of Artemis, brought no little business to the artisans. ²⁵These he gathered together, with the workers of the same trade, and said, "Men, you know that we get our wealth from this business. ²⁶You also see and hear that not only in Ephesus but in almost the whole of Asia this Paul has persuaded and drawn away a considerable number of people by saying that gods made with hands are not gods. ²⁷And there is danger not only that this trade of ours may come into disrepute but also that the temple of the great goddess Artemis will be scorned, and she will be deprived of her majesty that brought all Asia and the world to worship her."

28 When they heard this, they were enraged and shouted, "Great is Artemis of the Ephesians!" ²⁹The city was filled with the confusion; and peopleᵇ rushed together to the theater, dragging with them Gaius and Aristarchus, Macedonians who were Paul's travel companions. ³⁰Paul wished to go into the crowd, but the disciples would not let him; ³¹even some officials of the province of Asia,ᶜ who were

friendly to him, sent him a message urging him not to venture into the theater. ³²Meanwhile, some were shouting one thing, some another; for the assembly was in confusion, and most of them did not know why they had come together. ³³Some of the crowd gave instructions to Alexander, whom the Jews had pushed forward. And Alexander motioned for silence and tried to make a defense before the people. ³⁴But when they recognized that he was a Jew, for about two hours all of them shouted in unison, "Great is Artemis of the Ephesians!" ³⁵But when the town clerk had quieted the crowd, he said, "Citizens of Ephesus, who is there that does not know that the city of the Ephesians is the temple keeper of the great Artemis and of the statue that fell from heaven?ᵈ ³⁶Since these things cannot be denied, you ought to be quiet and do nothing rash. ³⁷You have brought these men here who are neither temple robbers nor blasphemers of ourᵉ goddess. ³⁸If therefore Demetrius and the artisans with him have a complaint against anyone, the courts are open, and there are proconsuls; let them bring charges there against one another. ³⁹If there is anything furtherᶠ you want to know, it must be settled in the regular assembly. ⁴⁰For we are in danger of being charged with rioting today, since there is no cause that we can give to justify this commotion." ⁴¹When he had said this, he dismissed the assembly.

Paul Goes to Macedonia and Greece

20 After the uproar had ceased, Paul sent for the disciples; and after encouraging them and saying farewell, he left for Macedonia. ²When he had gone through those regions and had given the believersᵍ much encouragement,

---

ᵃ Gk them ᵇ Gk they ᶜ Gk some of the Asiarchs ᵈ Meaning of Gk uncertain ᵉ Other ancient authorities read your ᶠ Other ancient authorities read about other matters ᵍ Gk given them

19:23–40

The temple of the goddess Artemis

he came to Greece, [3]where he stayed for three months. He was about to set sail for Syria when a plot was made against him by the Jews, and so he decided to return through Macedonia. [4]He was accompanied by Sopater son of Pyrrhus from Beroea, by Aristarchus and Secundus from Thessalonica, by Gaius from Derbe, and by Timothy, as well as by Tychicus and Trophimus from Asia. [5]They went ahead and were waiting for us in Troas; [6]but we sailed from Philippi after the days of Unleavened Bread, and in five days we joined them in Troas, where we stayed for seven days.

Paul's Farewell Visit to Troas

7 On the first day of the week, when we met to break bread, Paul was holding a discussion with them; since he intended to leave the next day, he continued speaking until midnight. [8]There were many lamps in the room upstairs where we were meeting. [9]A young man named Eutychus, who was sitting in the window, began to sink off into a deep sleep while Paul talked still longer. Overcome by sleep, he fell to the ground three floors below and was picked up dead. [10]But Paul went down, and bending over him took him in his arms, and said, "Do not be alarmed, for his life is in him." [11]Then Paul went upstairs, and after he had broken bread and eaten, he continued to converse with them until dawn; then he left. [12]Meanwhile they had taken the boy away alive and were not a little comforted.

The Voyage from Troas to Miletus

13 We went ahead to the ship and set sail for Assos, intending to take Paul on board there; for he had made this arrangement, intending to go by land himself. [14]When he met us in Assos, we took him on board and went to Mitylene. [15]We sailed from there, and on the following day we arrived opposite Chios. The next day we touched at Samos, and[a] the day after that we came to Miletus. [16]For Paul had decided to sail past Ephesus, so that he might not have to spend time in Asia; he was eager to be in Jerusalem, if possible, on the day of Pentecost.

Paul Speaks to the Ephesian Elders

17 From Miletus he sent a message to Ephesus, asking the elders of the church to meet him. [18]When they came to him, he said to them:

"You yourselves know how I lived among you the entire time from the first day that I set foot in Asia, [19]serving the Lord with all humility and with tears, enduring the trials that came to me through the plots of the Jews. [20]I did not shrink from doing anything helpful, proclaiming the message to you and teaching you publicly and from house to house, [21]as I testified to both Jews and Greeks about repentance toward God and faith toward our Lord Jesus. [22]And now, as a captive to the Spirit,[b] I am on my way to Jerusalem, not knowing what will happen to me there, [23]except that the Holy Spirit testifies to me in every city that imprisonment and persecutions are waiting for me. [24]But I do not count my life of any value to myself, if only I may finish my course and the ministry that I received from the Lord Jesus, to testify to the good news of God's grace.

25 "And now I know that none of you, among whom I have gone about proclaiming the kingdom, will ever see my face again. [26]Therefore I declare to you this day that I am not responsible for the blood of any of you, [27]for I did not shrink from declaring to you the whole purpose of God. [28]Keep watch over yourselves and over all the flock, of which the Holy Spirit has made you overseers, to shepherd the church of God[c] that he obtained with the blood of his own Son.[d] [29]I know that after I have gone, savage wolves will come in among you, not sparing the flock. [30]Some even from your own group will come distorting the truth in order to entice the disciples to follow them. [31]Therefore be alert, remembering that for three years I did not cease night or day to warn everyone with tears. [32]And now I commend you to God and to the message of his grace, a message that is able to build you up and to give you the inheritance among all who are sanctified. [33]I coveted no one's silver or gold or clothing. [34]You know for yourselves that I worked with my own hands to support myself and my companions. [35]In all this I have given you an example that by such work we must support the weak, remembering the words of the Lord Jesus, for he himself said, 'It is more blessed to give than to receive.' "

36 When he had finished speaking, he knelt down with them all and prayed. [37]There was much weeping among them all; they embraced Paul and kissed him, [38]grieving especially because of what he had said, that they would not see him again. Then they brought him to the ship.

Paul's Journey to Jerusalem

21 When we had parted from them and set sail, we came by a straight course to Cos,

---

a Other ancient authorities add *after remaining at Trogyllium*
b Or *And now, bound in the spirit*   c Other ancient authorities read *of the Lord*   d Or *with his own blood*; Gk *with the blood of his Own*

and the next day to Rhodes, and from there to Patara.*ᵃ* ²When we found a ship bound for Phoenicia, we went on board and set sail. ³We came in sight of Cyprus; and leaving it on our left, we sailed to Syria and landed at Tyre, because the ship was to unload its cargo there. ⁴We looked up the disciples and stayed there for seven days. Through the Spirit they told Paul not to go on to Jerusalem. ⁵When our days there were ended, we left and proceeded on our journey; and all of them, with wives and children, escorted us outside the city. There we knelt down on the beach and prayed ⁶and said farewell to one another. Then we went on board the ship, and they returned home.

7 When we had finished*ᵇ* the voyage from Tyre, we arrived at Ptolemais; and we greeted the believers*ᶜ* and stayed with them for one day. ⁸The next day we left and came to Caesarea; and we went into the house of Philip the evangelist, one of the seven, and stayed with him. ⁹He had four unmarried daughters*ᵈ* who had the gift of prophecy. ¹⁰While we were staying there for several days, a prophet named Agabus came down from Judea. ¹¹He came to us and took Paul's belt, bound his own feet and hands with it, and said, "Thus says the Holy Spirit, 'This is the way the Jews in Jerusalem will bind the man who owns this belt and will hand him over to the Gentiles.'" ¹²When we heard this, we and the people there urged him not to go up to Jerusalem. ¹³Then Paul answered, "What are you doing, weeping and breaking my heart? For I am ready not only to be bound but even to die in Jerusalem for the name of the Lord Jesus." ¹⁴Since he would not be persuaded, we remained silent except to say, "The Lord's will be done."

15 After these days we got ready and started to go up to Jerusalem. ¹⁶Some of the disciples from Caesarea also came along and brought us to the house of Mnason of Cyprus, an early disciple, with whom we were to stay.

Paul Visits James at Jerusalem

17 When we arrived in Jerusalem, the brothers welcomed us warmly. ¹⁸The next day Paul went with us to visit James; and all the elders were present. ¹⁹After greeting them, he related one by one the things that God had done among the Gentiles through his ministry. ²⁰When they heard it, they praised God. Then they said to him, "You see, brother, how many thousands of believers there are among the Jews, and they are all zealous for the law. ²¹They have been told about you that you teach all the Jews living

Pray It!

Good-Bye to a Friend

As Paul prepares to leave Ephesus in Acts of the Apostles 20:36–38, we hear that the members of the Christian community there are experiencing feelings of sadness as they say good-bye to Paul. He has been an important person in their lives, and they have come to depend on him. Their grief overwhelms them, and they all experience great pain over his departure.

When we have to say good-bye to someone we care for deeply, we go through a grieving process. We feel sad and mad at the same time. Even after our friend has been gone for a long time, our heart has an empty space that our friend used to fill.

Lord, it is so difficult to say good-bye to my friend. We have shared so much together. I thank you for blessing me with this friendship. As we depart in separate directions, be our constant guardian and companion. Guide each of us safely to our destination. And until our paths cross again, surround us with your loving and protective embrace. Amen.

▶ **Acts 20:36–38**

among the Gentiles to forsake Moses, and that you tell them not to circumcise their children or observe the customs. ²²What then is to be done? They will certainly hear that you have come. ²³So do what we tell you. We have four men who are under a vow. ²⁴Join these men, go through the rite of purification with them, and pay for the shaving of their heads. Thus all will know that there is nothing in what they have been told about you, but that you yourself observe and guard the law. ²⁵But as for the Gentiles who have become believers, we have sent a letter with our judgment that they should abstain from what has been sacrificed to idols and from blood and

---

ᵃ Other ancient authorities add *and Myra*   *ᵇ* Or *continued*
ᶜ Gk *brothers*   *ᵈ* Gk *four daughters, virgins,*

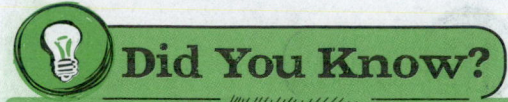

Did You Know?

Who Are Paul's Opponents?

As you read about Paul's return to Jerusalem, it may become confusing to keep track of the main characters. To help you keep it straight, here are some clues:

● One group is the Jewish Christians, represented by James and the elders (see Acts 21:17–26). Although the Jewish Christians might be suspicious of Paul's defense of the Gentile Christians, they support Paul and come up with a plan for him to try to prove his Jewish loyalty.

● Another group is the Jews who don't believe in Jesus. These Jews see the rise of the Jesus movement as a threat to Judaism, and Paul is the most well-known representative of that movement. They attempt to arrest him and have him killed in a mob scene (see verses 27–36).

● The third group is the Roman rulers. The Romans probably have no interest in this conflict except to keep the peace. The Roman tribune (governor) thinks he can keep the Jews happy by having Paul flogged (see 22:22–29). But surprise! Paul is a Roman citizen and has civil rights that the tribune must honor.

So who are Paul's—and Christianity's—opponents? Luke tells us that at first they are the Jewish Christians. Later, they are the Jews who don't believe in Jesus. Still later—after this story occurs—they will be the Romans. Luke knows all this in hindsight and brings all of Paul's opponents into play in describing Paul's arrest and imprisonment.

▶ **Acts 21:17–26**

from what is strangled[a] and from fornication." [26]Then Paul took the men, and the next day, having purified himself, he entered the temple with them, making public the completion of the days of purification when the sacrifice would be made for each of them.

Paul Arrested in the Temple

27 When the seven days were almost completed, the Jews from Asia, who had seen him in the temple, stirred up the whole crowd.

They seized him, [28]shouting, "Fellow Israelites, help! This is the man who is teaching everyone everywhere against our people, our law, and this place; more than that, he has actually brought Greeks into the temple and has defiled this holy place." [29]For they had previously seen Trophimus the Ephesian with him in the city, and they supposed that Paul had brought him into the temple. [30]Then all the city was aroused, and the people rushed together. They seized Paul and dragged him out of the temple, and immediately the doors were shut. [31]While they were trying to kill him, word came to the tribune of the cohort that all Jerusalem was in an uproar. [32]Immediately he took soldiers and centurions and ran down to them. When they saw the tribune and the soldiers, they stopped beating Paul. [33]Then the tribune came, arrested him, and ordered him to be bound with two chains; he inquired who he was and what he had done. [34]Some in the crowd shouted one thing, some another; and as he could not learn the facts because of the uproar, he ordered him to be brought into the barracks. [35]When Paul[b] came to the steps, the violence of the mob was so great that he had to be carried by the soldiers. [36]The crowd that followed kept shouting, "Away with him!"

Paul Defends Himself

37 Just as Paul was about to be brought into the barracks, he said to the tribune, "May I say something to you?" The tribune[c] replied, "Do you know Greek? [38]Then you are not the Egyptian who recently stirred up a revolt and led the four thousand assassins out into the wilderness?" [39]Paul replied, "I am a Jew, from Tarsus in Cilicia, a citizen of an important city; I beg you, let me speak to the people." [40]When he had given him permission, Paul stood on the steps and motioned to the people for silence; and when there was a great hush, he addressed them in the Hebrew[d] language, saying:

22 "Brothers and fathers, listen to the defense that I now make before you."

2 When they heard him addressing them in Hebrew,[d] they became even more quiet. Then he said:

3 "I am a Jew, born in Tarsus in Cilicia, but brought up in this city at the feet of Gamaliel, educated strictly according to our ancestral law, being zealous for God, just as all of you are

---

a Other ancient authorities lack *and from what is strangled*
b Gk *he*   c Gk *He*   d That is, *Aramaic*

today. ⁴I persecuted this Way up to the point of death by binding both men and women and putting them in prison, ⁵as the high priest and the whole council of elders can testify about me. From them I also received letters to the brothers in Damascus, and I went there in order to bind those who were there and to bring them back to Jerusalem for punishment.

Paul Tells of His Conversion

6 "While I was on my way and approaching Damascus, about noon a great light from heaven suddenly shone about me. ⁷I fell to the ground and heard a voice saying to me, 'Saul, Saul, why are you persecuting me?' ⁸I answered, 'Who are you, Lord?' Then he said to me, 'I am Jesus of Nazareth*a* whom you are persecuting.' ⁹Now those who were with me saw the light but did not hear the voice of the one who was speaking to me. ¹⁰I asked, 'What am I to do, Lord?' The Lord said to me, 'Get up and go to Damascus; there you will be told everything that has been assigned to you to do.' ¹¹Since I could not see because of the brightness of that light, those who were with me took my hand and led me to Damascus.

12 "A certain Ananias, who was a devout man according to the law and well spoken of by all the Jews living there, ¹³came to me; and standing beside me, he said, 'Brother Saul, regain your sight!' In that very hour I regained my sight and saw him. ¹⁴Then he said, 'The God of our ancestors has chosen you to know his will, to see the Righteous One and to hear his own voice; ¹⁵for you will be his witness to all the world of what you have seen and heard. ¹⁶And now why do you delay? Get up, be baptized, and have your sins washed away, calling on his name.'

Paul Sent to the Gentiles

17 "After I had returned to Jerusalem and while I was praying in the temple, I fell into a trance ¹⁸and saw Jesus*b* saying to me, 'Hurry and get out of Jerusalem quickly, because they will not accept your testimony about me.' ¹⁹And I said, 'Lord, they themselves know that in every synagogue I imprisoned and beat those who believed in you. ²⁰And while the blood of your witness Stephen was shed, I myself was standing by, approving and keeping the coats of those who killed him.' ²¹Then he said to me, 'Go, for I will send you far away to the Gentiles.' "

Paul and the Roman Tribune

22 Up to this point they listened to him, but then they shouted, "Away with such a fellow from the earth! For he should not be allowed to live." ²³And while they were shouting, throwing off their cloaks, and tossing dust into the air, ²⁴the tribune directed that he was to be brought into the barracks, and ordered him to be examined by flogging, to find out the reason for this outcry against him. ²⁵But when they had tied him up with thongs,*c* Paul said to the centurion who was standing by, "Is it legal for you to flog a Roman citizen who is uncondemned?" ²⁶When the centurion heard that, he went to the tribune and said to him, "What are you about to do? This man is a Roman citizen." ²⁷The tribune came and asked Paul,*b* "Tell me, are you a Roman citizen?" And he said, "Yes." ²⁸The tribune answered, "It cost me a large sum of money to

---

a Gk the Nazorean   *b* Gk him   *c* Or up for the lashes

Sharing Your Story

Have you ever heard a dramatic conversion story? Sometimes, on religious television programs or at large youth rallies, individuals share personal stories of their belief in God helping them to overcome addictions, terrible problems, or great sin. Or they tell of how they came to recognize and accept God in their lives as a result of a serious illness or the death of a close friend or family member. Listening to these dramatic stories may make us feel that our own journey as a follower of Jesus—our own story—does not quite measure up. Nothing could be further from the truth in God's eyes.

We all have our own conversion stories—those moments of turning to God, of receiving a special call to serve others. And though our personal story might not be as dramatic as other people's stories, God will use it to encourage others to put their faith in Christ and dedicate their lives to his mission. Are you willing to share your story of faith with others?

▶ **Acts 22:6–16**

get my citizenship." Paul said, "But I was born a citizen." ²⁹Immediately those who were about to examine him drew back from him; and the tribune also was afraid, for he realized that Paul was a Roman citizen and that he had bound him.

Paul before the Council

30 Since he wanted to find out what Paul[a] was being accused of by the Jews, the next day he released him and ordered the chief priests and the entire council to meet. He brought Paul down and had him stand before them.

23 While Paul was looking intently at the council he said, "Brothers,[b] up to this day I have lived my life with a clear conscience before God." ²Then the high priest Ananias ordered those standing near him to strike him on the mouth. ³At this Paul said to him, "God will strike you, you whitewashed wall! Are you sitting there to judge me according to the law, and yet in violation of the law you order me to be struck?" ⁴Those standing nearby said, "Do you dare to insult God's high priest?" ⁵And Paul said, "I did not realize, brothers, that he was high priest; for it is written, 'You shall not speak evil of a leader of your people.' "

6 When Paul noticed that some were Sadducees and others were Pharisees, he called out in the council, "Brothers, I am a Pharisee, a son of Pharisees. I am on trial concerning the hope of the resurrection[c] of the dead." ⁷When he said this, a dissension began between the Pharisees and the Sadducees, and the assembly was divided. ⁸(The Sadducees say that there is no resurrection, or angel, or spirit; but the Pharisees acknowledge all three.) ⁹Then a great clamor arose, and certain scribes of the Pharisees' group stood up and contended, "We find nothing wrong with this man. What if a spirit or an angel has spoken to him?" ¹⁰When the dissension became violent, the tribune, fearing that they would tear Paul to pieces, ordered the soldiers to go down, take him by force, and bring him into the barracks.

11 That night the Lord stood near him and said, "Keep up your courage! For just as you have testified for me in Jerusalem, so you must bear witness also in Rome."

The Plot to Kill Paul

12 In the morning the Jews joined in a conspiracy and bound themselves by an oath neither to eat nor drink until they had killed Paul. ¹³There were more than forty who joined in this conspiracy. ¹⁴They went to the chief priests and elders and said, "We have strictly bound ourselves by an oath to taste no food until we have killed Paul. ¹⁵Now then, you and the council must notify the tribune to bring him down to you, on the pretext that you want to make a more thorough examination of his case. And we are ready to do away with him before he arrives."

16 Now the son of Paul's sister heard about the ambush; so he went and gained entrance to the barracks and told Paul. ¹⁷Paul called one of the centurions and said, "Take this young man to the tribune, for he has something to report to him." ¹⁸So he took him, brought him to the tribune, and said, "The prisoner Paul called me and asked me to bring this young man to you; he has something to tell you." ¹⁹The tribune took him by the hand, drew him aside privately, and asked, "What is it that you have to report to me?"

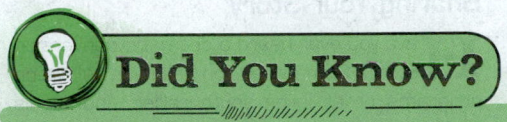

Did You Know?

What About the Jews?

The earliest Christians were Jews. It was agonizing to them that so many of their Jewish friends wouldn't believe in Jesus. Indeed, not only did those friends not believe in Jesus, but some tried to stop the spread of Christianity because they viewed Christian beliefs as blasphemy. Acts of the Apostles, chapters 22–28, tells of Jewish attacks against Paul, which ultimately end with Paul's traveling to Rome to make his case before the emperor.

But the questions remain: If the Jews are God's People, why don't they believe that Jesus was the Jewish Messiah? Couldn't God make it easier for them to believe? Does God cause their lack of faith in Jesus? Who is ultimately responsible for anyone's faith? If you are interested, read Romans, chapters 9–11, where Paul tries to answer those questions.

▶ **Acts 22:30—28:31**

---

a Gk *he*   *b* Gk *Men, brothers*   *c* Gk *concerning hope and resurrection*

²⁰He answered, "The Jews have agreed to ask you to bring Paul down to the council tomorrow, as though they were going to inquire more thoroughly into his case. ²¹But do not be persuaded by them, for more than forty of their men are lying in ambush for him. They have bound themselves by an oath neither to eat nor drink until they kill him. They are ready now and are waiting for your consent." ²²So the tribune dismissed the young man, ordering him, "Tell no one that you have informed me of this."

Paul Sent to Felix the Governor

23 Then he summoned two of the centurions and said, "Get ready to leave by nine o'clock tonight for Caesarea with two hundred soldiers, seventy horsemen, and two hundred spearmen. ²⁴Also provide mounts for Paul to ride, and take him safely to Felix the governor." ²⁵He wrote a letter to this effect:

26 "Claudius Lysias to his Excellency the governor Felix, greetings. ²⁷This man was seized by the Jews and was about to be killed by them, but when I had learned that he was a Roman citizen, I came with the guard and rescued him. ²⁸Since I wanted to know the charge for which they accused him, I had him brought to their council. ²⁹I found that he was accused concerning questions of their law, but was charged with nothing deserving death or imprisonment. ³⁰When I was informed that there would be a plot against the man, I sent him to you at once, ordering his accusers also to state before you what they have against him.ᵃ"

31 So the soldiers, according to their instructions, took Paul and brought him during the night to Antipatris. ³²The next day they let the horsemen go on with him, while they returned to the barracks. ³³When they came to Caesarea and delivered the letter to the governor, they presented Paul also before him. ³⁴On reading the letter, he asked what province he belonged to, and when he learned that he was from Cilicia, ³⁵he said, "I will give you a hearing when your accusers arrive." Then he ordered that he be kept under guard in Herod's headquarters.ᵇ

Paul before Felix at Caesarea

24 Five days later the high priest Ananias came down with some elders and an attorney, a certain Tertullus, and they reported their case against Paul to the governor. ²When Paulᶜ had been summoned, Tertullus began to accuse him, saying:

"Your Excellency,ᵈ because of you we have long enjoyed peace, and reforms have been made for this people because of your foresight. ³We welcome this in every way and everywhere with utmost gratitude. ⁴But, to detain you no further, I beg you to hear us briefly with your customary graciousness. ⁵We have, in fact, found this man a pestilent fellow, an agitator among all the Jews throughout the world, and a ringleader of the sect of the Nazarenes.ᵉ ⁶He even tried to profane the temple, and so we seized him.ᶠ ⁸By examining him yourself you will be able to learn from him concerning everything of which we accuse him."

9 The Jews also joined in the charge by asserting that all this was true.

Paul's Defense before Felix

10 When the governor motioned to him to speak, Paul replied:

"I cheerfully make my defense, knowing that for many years you have been a judge over this nation. ¹¹As you can find out, it is not more than twelve days since I went up to worship in Jerusalem. ¹²They did not find me disputing with anyone in the temple or stirring up a crowd either in the synagogues or throughout the city. ¹³Neither can they prove to you the charge that they now bring against me. ¹⁴But this I admit to you, that according to the Way, which they call a sect, I worship the God of our ancestors, believing everything laid down according to the law or written in the prophets. ¹⁵I have a hope in God— a hope that they themselves also accept—that there will be a resurrection of bothᵍ the righteous and the unrighteous. ¹⁶Therefore I do my best always to have a clear conscience toward God and all people. ¹⁷Now after some years I came to bring alms to my nation and to offer sacrifices. ¹⁸While I was doing this, they found me in the temple, completing the rite of purification, without any crowd or disturbance. ¹⁹But there were some Jews from Asia—they ought to be here before you to make an accusation, if they have anything against me. ²⁰Or let these men here tell what crime they had found when I stood before the council, ²¹unless it was this one sentence that I called out while standing before them, 'It is about the resurrection of the dead that I am on trial before you today.' "

22 But Felix, who was rather well informed

---

a Other ancient authorities add *Farewell*   b Gk *praetorium*
c Gk *he*   d Gk lacks *Your Excellency*   e Gk *Nazoreans*
f Other ancient authorities add *and we would have judged him according to our law.* ⁷*But the chief captain Lysias came and with great violence took him out of our hands,* ⁸*commanding his accusers to come before you.*   g Other ancient authorities read *of the dead, both of*

ACTS

about the Way, adjourned the hearing with the comment, "When Lysias the tribune comes down, I will decide your case." 23Then he ordered the centurion to keep him in custody, but to let him have some liberty and not to prevent any of his friends from taking care of his needs.

Paul Held in Custody

24 Some days later when Felix came with his wife Drusilla, who was Jewish, he sent for Paul and heard him speak concerning faith in Christ Jesus. 25And as he discussed justice, self-control, and the coming judgment, Felix became frightened and said, "Go away for the present; when I have an opportunity, I will send for you." 26At the same time he hoped that money would be given him by Paul, and for that reason he used to send for him very often and converse with him.

27 After two years had passed, Felix was succeeded by Porcius Festus; and since he wanted to grant the Jews a favor, Felix left Paul in prison.

Paul Appeals to the Emperor

25 Three days after Festus had arrived in the province, he went up from Caesarea to Jerusalem 2where the chief priests and the leaders of the Jews gave him a report against Paul. They appealed to him 3and requested, as a favor to them against Paul,*a* to have him transferred to Jerusalem. They were, in fact, planning an ambush to kill him along the way. 4Festus replied that Paul was being kept at Caesarea, and that he himself intended to go there shortly. 5"So," he said, "let those of you who have the authority come down with me, and if there is anything wrong about the man, let them accuse him."

6 After he had stayed among them not more than eight or ten days, he went down to Caesarea; the next day he took his seat on the tribunal and ordered Paul to be brought. 7When he arrived, the Jews who had gone down from Jerusalem surrounded him, bringing many serious charges against him, which they could not prove. 8Paul said in his defense, "I have in no way committed an offense against the law of the Jews, or against the temple, or against the emperor." 9But Festus, wishing to do the Jews a favor, asked Paul, "Do you wish to go up to Jerusalem and be tried there before me on these charges?" 10Paul said, "I am appealing to the emperor's tribunal; this is where I should be tried. I have done no wrong to the Jews, as you very well know. 11Now if I am in the wrong and have committed something for which I deserve

to die, I am not trying to escape death; but if there is nothing to their charges against me, no one can turn me over to them. I appeal to the emperor." 12Then Festus, after he had conferred with his council, replied, "You have appealed to the emperor; to the emperor you will go."

Festus Consults King Agrippa

13 After several days had passed, King Agrippa and Bernice arrived at Caesarea to welcome Festus. 14Since they were staying there several days, Festus laid Paul's case before the king, saying, "There is a man here who was left in prison by Felix. 15When I was in Jerusalem, the chief priests and the elders of the Jews informed me about him and asked for a sentence against him. 16I told them that it was not the custom of the Romans to hand over anyone before the accused had met the accusers face to face and had been given an opportunity to make a defense against the charge. 17So when they met here, I lost no time, but on the next day took my seat on the tribunal and ordered the man to be brought. 18When the accusers stood up, they did not charge him with any of the crimes*b* that I was expecting. 19Instead they had certain points of disagreement with him about their own religion and about a certain Jesus, who had died, but whom Paul asserted to be alive. 20Since I was at a loss how to investigate these questions, I asked whether he wished to go to Jerusalem and be tried there on these charges.*c* 21But when Paul had appealed to be kept in custody for the decision of his Imperial Majesty, I ordered him to be held until I could send him to the emperor." 22Agrippa said to Festus, "I would like to hear the man myself." "Tomorrow," he said, "you will hear him."

Paul Brought before Agrippa

23 So on the next day Agrippa and Bernice came with great pomp, and they entered the audience hall with the military tribunes and the prominent men of the city. Then Festus gave the order and Paul was brought in. 24And Festus said, "King Agrippa and all here present with us, you see this man about whom the whole Jewish community petitioned me, both in Jerusalem and here, shouting that he ought not to live any longer. 25But I found that he had done nothing deserving death; and when he appealed to his Imperial Majesty, I decided to send him. 26But I have nothing definite to write to our sovereign about him. Therefore I have brought him before all of

---

a Gk *him*   *b* Other ancient authorities read *with anything*
c Gk *on them*

Cultural Connection

Paul Teaches Us How to Live Our Faith

Reporters *Marisa and Ricardo.* [Speaking into their microphones] We're here, live, in Caesarea, where Paul of Tarsus has just spoken with King Agrippa and Governor Festus. Here comes Paul now. Let's see what he has to say. Paul, why has your message caused so much controversy?

Paul. It was never my intention to cause strife or conflict. But I must speak the truth, and the truth is that God has revealed his salvation for us in Jesus Christ. In Jesus, salvation is available to everyone—Jews and Gentiles, slaves and free people, men and women—and we are all equal as sons and daughters of God. Unfortunately, this truth is upsetting to some people, and they have gone to great lengths to try to get rid of me.

Marisa and Ricardo. But hasn't your message been well received by many people—including many different types of people?

Paul. Yes, it has. I think this is because Jesus taught us always to respect every person as a son or daughter of God regardless of his or her culture or social class. Under the guidance of the Holy Spirit, Christian communities allow for diversity while keeping a common unity in Jesus Christ. I think people are hungry for this.

Marisa and Ricardo. Soon you will be heading for Rome, where you will be on trial for alleged crimes against the empire. Are you worried?

Paul. [Smiling] Why be worried? No one has ultimate power over me except my Lord Jesus Christ. I only need to be faithful to my calling, and I will receive my prize—eternal life with God. Plus I have the prayers and support of many close friends. But thank you for your concern. God's grace and peace be with you.

Marisa and Ricardo. And thank you, Paul.

▶ **Acts of the Apostles, chapter 26**

you, and especially before you, King Agrippa, so that, after we have examined him, I may have something to write— [27] for it seems to me unreasonable to send a prisoner without indicating the charges against him."

Paul Defends Himself before Agrippa

26 Agrippa said to Paul, "You have permission to speak for yourself." Then Paul stretched out his hand and began to defend himself:

2 "I consider myself fortunate that it is before you, King Agrippa, I am to make my defense today against all the accusations of the Jews, [3] because you are especially familiar with all the customs and controversies of the Jews; therefore I beg of you to listen to me patiently.

4 "All the Jews know my way of life from my youth, a life spent from the beginning among my own people and in Jerusalem. [5] They have known for a long time, if they are willing to testify, that I have belonged to the strictest sect of our religion and lived as a Pharisee. [6] And now I stand here on trial on account of my hope in the promise made by God to our ancestors, [7] a promise that our twelve tribes hope to attain, as they earnestly worship day and night. It is for this hope, your Excellency,[a] that I am accused by Jews! [8] Why is it thought incredible by any of you that God raises the dead?

9 "Indeed, I myself was convinced that I ought to do many things against the name of Jesus of Nazareth.[b] [10] And that is what I did in Jerusalem; with authority received from the chief priests, I not only locked up many of the saints in prison, but I also cast my vote against them when they were being condemned to death. [11] By punishing them often in all the synagogues I tried to force them to blaspheme; and since I was so furiously enraged at them, I pursued them even to foreign cities.

a Gk O king   *b* Gk the Nazorean

A
C
T
S

Paul Tells of His Conversion

12 "With this in mind, I was traveling to Damascus with the authority and commission of the chief priests, [13]when at midday along the road, your Excellency,[a] I saw a light from heaven, brighter than the sun, shining around me and my companions. [14]When we had all fallen to the ground, I heard a voice saying to me in the Hebrew[b] language, 'Saul, Saul, why are you persecuting me? It hurts you to kick against the goads.' [15]I asked, 'Who are you, Lord?' The Lord answered, 'I am Jesus whom you are persecuting. [16]But get up and stand on your feet; for I have appeared to you for this purpose, to appoint you to serve and testify to the things in which you have seen me[c] and to those in which I will appear to you. [17]I will rescue you from your people and from the Gentiles—to whom I am sending you [18]to open their eyes so that they may turn from darkness to light and from the power of Satan to God, so that they may receive forgiveness of sins and a place among those who are sanctified by faith in me.'

Paul Tells of His Preaching

19 "After that, King Agrippa, I was not disobedient to the heavenly vision, [20]but declared first to those in Damascus, then in Jerusalem and throughout the countryside of Judea, and also to the Gentiles, that they should repent and turn to God and do deeds consistent with repentance. [21]For this reason the Jews seized me in the temple and tried to kill me. [22]To this day I have had help from God, and so I stand here, testifying to both small and great, saying nothing but what the prophets and Moses said would take place: [23]that the Messiah[d] must suffer, and that, by being the first to rise from the dead, he would proclaim light both to our people and to the Gentiles."

Paul Appeals to Agrippa to Believe

24 While he was making this defense, Festus exclaimed, "You are out of your mind, Paul! Too much learning is driving you insane!" [25]But Paul said, "I am not out of my mind, most excellent Festus, but I am speaking the sober truth. [26]Indeed the king knows about these things, and to him I speak freely; for I am certain that none of these things has escaped his notice, for this was not done in a corner. [27]King Agrippa, do you believe the prophets? I know that you believe." [28]Agrippa said to Paul, "Are you so quickly persuading me to become a Christian?"[e] [29]Paul replied, "Whether quickly or not, I pray to God that not only you but also all who are listening to me today might become such as I am—except for these chains."

30 Then the king got up, and with him the governor and Bernice and those who had been seated with them; [31]and as they were leaving, they said to one another, "This man is doing nothing to deserve death or imprisonment." [32]Agrippa said to Festus, "This man could have been set free if he had not appealed to the emperor."

Paul Sails for Rome

27 When it was decided that we were to sail for Italy, they transferred Paul and some other prisoners to a centurion of the Augustan Cohort, named Julius. [2]Embarking on a ship of Adramyttium that was about to set sail to the ports along the coast of Asia, we put to sea, accompanied by Aristarchus, a Macedonian from Thessalonica. [3]The next day we put in at Sidon; and Julius treated Paul kindly, and allowed him to go to his friends to be cared for. [4]Putting out to sea from there, we sailed under the lee of Cyprus, because the winds were against us. [5]After we had sailed across the sea that is off Cilicia and Pamphylia, we came to Myra in Lycia. [6]There the centurion found an Alexandrian ship bound for Italy and put us on board. [7]We sailed slowly for a number of days and arrived with difficulty off Cnidus, and as the wind was against us, we sailed under the lee of Crete off Salmone. [8]Sailing past it with difficulty, we came to a place called Fair Havens, near the city of Lasea.

9 Since much time had been lost and sailing was now dangerous, because even the Fast had already gone by, Paul advised them, [10]saying, "Sirs, I can see that the voyage will be with danger and much heavy loss, not only of the cargo and the ship, but also of our lives." [11]But the centurion paid more attention to the pilot and to the owner of the ship than to what Paul said. [12]Since the harbor was not suitable for spending the winter, the majority was in favor of putting to sea from there, on the chance that somehow they could reach Phoenix, where they could spend the winter. It was a harbor of Crete, facing southwest and northwest.

The Storm at Sea

13 When a moderate south wind began to blow, they thought they could achieve their

---

a Gk O king   b That is, Aramaic   c Other ancient authorities read *the things that you have seen*   d Or *the Christ*   e Or *Quickly you will persuade me to play the Christian*

purpose; so they weighed anchor and began to sail past Crete, close to the shore. ¹⁴But soon a violent wind, called the northeaster, rushed down from Crete.ᵃ ¹⁵Since the ship was caught and could not be turned head-on into the wind, we gave way to it and were driven. ¹⁶By running under the lee of a small island called Caudaᵇ we were scarcely able to get the ship's boat under control. ¹⁷After hoisting it up they took measuresᶜ to undergird the ship; then, fearing that they would run on the Syrtis, they lowered the sea anchor and so were driven. ¹⁸We were being pounded by the storm so violently that on the next day they began to throw the cargo overboard, ¹⁹and on the third day with their own hands they threw the ship's tackle overboard. ²⁰When neither sun nor stars appeared for many days, and no small tempest raged, all hope of our being saved was at last abandoned.

21 Since they had been without food for a long time, Paul then stood up among them and said, "Men, you should have listened to me and not have set sail from Crete and thereby avoided this damage and loss. ²²I urge you now to keep up your courage, for there will be no loss of life among you, but only of the ship. ²³For last night there stood by me an angel of the God to whom I belong and whom I worship, ²⁴and he said, 'Do not be afraid, Paul; you must stand before the emperor; and indeed, God has granted safety to all those who are sailing with you.' ²⁵So keep up your courage, men, for I have faith in God that it will be exactly as I have been told. ²⁶But we will have to run aground on some island."

27 When the fourteenth night had come, as we were drifting across the sea of Adria, about midnight the sailors suspected that they were nearing land. ²⁸So they took soundings and found twenty fathoms; a little farther on they took soundings again and found fifteen fathoms. ²⁹Fearing that we might run on the rocks, they let down four anchors from the stern and prayed for day to come. ³⁰But when the sailors tried to escape from the ship and had lowered the boat into the sea, on the pretext of putting out anchors from the bow, ³¹Paul said to the centurion and the soldiers, "Unless these men stay in the ship, you cannot be saved." ³²Then the soldiers cut away the ropes of the boat and set it adrift.

33 Just before daybreak, Paul urged all of them to take some food, saying, "Today is the fourteenth day that you have been in suspense and remaining without food, having eaten nothing. ³⁴Therefore I urge you to take some

Pray It!

When the Waves Get Too Rough

It is not easy to be courageous when you face danger. When you find yourself in situations where things are beyond your control, like Paul caught in a storm at sea, turn to God. After all, isn't faith for the times when you feel the most helpless and out of control?

Help, Lord, I'm lost at sea! When I started this journey of life, I thought I knew where I was headed, but then a few waves started to rock the boat, and I became frightened.

Next, the wind picked up, and my fear turned into confusion. Then the night fell, and my confusion turned into despair. And now I am lost and need you to help calm the waves in my life and stand beside me until the night turns into day.

Help me to find my bearings again, Lord. And when this storm is over, gift me with the wisdom to learn from this experience—to go back and make right what was wrong, not to lose hope at the first sign of trouble, and to hang on to you, my anchor, when life gets rough. Amen.

▶ **Acts 27:21–25**

food, for it will help you survive; for none of you will lose a hair from your heads." ³⁵After he had said this, he took bread; and giving thanks to God in the presence of all, he broke it and began to eat. ³⁶Then all of them were encouraged and took food for themselves. ³⁷(We were in all two hundred seventy-sixᵈ persons in the ship.) ³⁸After they had satisfied their hunger, they lightened the ship by throwing the wheat into the sea.

The Shipwreck

39 In the morning they did not recognize the land, but they noticed a bay with a beach, on which they planned to run the ship ashore, if they could. ⁴⁰So they cast off the anchors and left

---

a Gk *it*   b Other ancient authorities read *Clauda*   c Gk *helps*
d Other ancient authorities read *seventy-six*; others, *about seventy-six*

ACTS

them in the sea. At the same time they loosened the ropes that tied the steering-oars; then hoisting the foresail to the wind, they made for the beach. ⁴¹But striking a reef,^a they ran the ship aground; the bow stuck and remained immovable, but the stern was being broken up by the force of the waves. ⁴²The soldiers' plan was to kill the prisoners, so that none might swim away and escape; ⁴³but the centurion, wishing to save Paul, kept them from carrying out their plan. He ordered those who could swim to jump overboard first and make for the land, ⁴⁴and the rest to follow, some on planks and others on pieces of the ship. And so it was that all were brought safely to land.

Paul on the Island of Malta

28 After we had reached safety, we then learned that the island was called Malta. ²The natives showed us unusual kindness. Since it had begun to rain and was cold, they kindled a fire and welcomed all of us around it. ³Paul had gathered a bundle of brushwood and was putting it on the fire, when a viper, driven out by the heat, fastened itself on his hand. ⁴When the natives saw the creature hanging from his hand, they said to one another, "This man must be a murderer; though he has escaped from the sea, justice has not allowed him to live." ⁵He, however, shook off the creature into the fire and suffered no harm. ⁶They were expecting him to swell up or drop dead, but after they had waited a long time and saw that nothing unusual had happened to him, they changed their minds and began to say that he was a god.

7 Now in the neighborhood of that place were lands belonging to the leading man of the island, named Publius, who received us and entertained us hospitably for three days. ⁸It so happened that the father of Publius lay sick in bed with fever and dysentery. Paul visited him and cured him by praying and putting his hands on him. ⁹After this happened, the rest of the people on the island who had diseases also came and were cured. ¹⁰They bestowed many honors on us, and when we were about to sail, they put on board all the provisions we needed.

Paul Arrives at Rome

11 Three months later we set sail on a ship that had wintered at the island, an Alexandrian ship with the Twin Brothers as its figurehead. ¹²We put in at Syracuse and stayed there for three days; ¹³then we weighed anchor and came to Rhegium. After one day there a south wind

sprang up, and on the second day we came to Puteoli. ¹⁴There we found believers^b and were invited to stay with them for seven days. And so we came to Rome. ¹⁵The believers^b from there, when they heard of us, came as far as the Forum of Appius and Three Taverns to meet us. On seeing them, Paul thanked God and took courage.

16 When we came into Rome, Paul was allowed to live by himself, with the soldier who was guarding him.

Paul and Jewish Leaders in Rome

17 Three days later he called together the local leaders of the Jews. When they had assembled, he said to them, "Brothers, though I had done nothing against our people or the customs of our ancestors, yet I was arrested in Jerusalem and handed over to the Romans. ¹⁸When they had examined me, the Romans^c wanted to release me, because there was no reason for the death penalty in my case. ¹⁹But when the Jews objected, I was compelled to appeal to the emperor—even though I had no charge to bring against my nation. ²⁰For this reason therefore I have asked to see you and speak with you,^d since it is for the sake of the hope of Israel that I am bound with this chain." ²¹They replied, "We have received no letters from Judea about you, and none of the brothers coming here has reported or spoken anything evil about you. ²²But we would like to hear from you what you think, for with regard to this sect we know that everywhere it is spoken against."

Paul Preaches in Rome

23 After they had set a day to meet with him, they came to him at his lodgings in great numbers. From morning until evening he explained the matter to them, testifying to the kingdom of God and trying to convince them about Jesus both from the law of Moses and from the prophets. ²⁴Some were convinced by what he had said, while others refused to believe. ²⁵So they disagreed with each other; and as they were leaving, Paul made one further statement: "The Holy Spirit was right in saying to your ancestors through the prophet Isaiah,

26 'Go to this people and say,

You will indeed listen, but never understand,
    and you will indeed look, but never perceive.
²⁷ For this people's heart has grown dull,
    and their ears are hard of hearing,
    and they have shut their eyes;

_a Gk *place of two seas*   _b Gk *brothers*   _c Gk *they*   _d Or *I have asked you to see me and speak with me*

so that they might not look with their eyes,
        and listen with their ears,
    and understand with their heart and turn—
        and I would heal them.'

28 Let it be known to you then that this salvation of God has been sent to the Gentiles; they will listen."*a*

30 He lived there two whole years at his own expense*b* and welcomed all who came to him, 31 proclaiming the kingdom of God and teaching about the Lord Jesus Christ with all boldness and without hindrance.

---

a Other ancient authorities add verse 29, *And when he had said these words, the Jews departed, arguing vigorously among themselves*   *b* Or *in his own hired dwelling*

Introduction to the
Letters and Revelation

Despite the popularity of e-mailing, writing letters with pen and paper is still alive today. In letters, people often express themselves more clearly than they do in person, and say things that are difficult to say face-to-face. Perhaps you've been lucky enough to receive some special letters. Letters between parents and children, engaged couples, and even pen pals are often saved to be read again and again. They are treasured for their stories, their advice, and their expressions of love. The next twenty-one books of the New Testament are also treasured letters. Their stories, their advice, and their confidence in God's loving guidance have inspired generations of Christians.

In Depth

When you read someone else's mail, you see only one side of the conversation. So you have to do some reading between the lines to understand the issues being addressed. This is also true of the New Testament letters. But when you do this, they give you a firsthand look at the first Christian communities and what they believed. In fact, the letters written by Paul are the oldest Christian documents we have, written even before the four Gospels. Paul's earliest letter, First Thessalonians, was probably written around AD 50. That's just a little over twenty years after the death and Resurrection of Jesus!

These letters follow a common pattern. They usually begin with (1) a greeting from the sender to the receiver or receivers. Next is (2) a prayer, most often of thanksgiving. This is followed by (3) the body of the letter, which addresses whatever issues the author wants to discuss; often, it includes general advice about Christian living. The letters close with (4) greetings and instructions to specific people and a final blessing.

There are exceptions to this pattern. The Books of Hebrews and First John do not have all four of these features and are more like essays about faith. The Book of James has more of the features but reads like a good sermon rather than a letter.

Saint Paul was the most prolific writer of the letters. At one time, it was thought that he produced thirteen of the twenty-one. However, modern scholars believe that some of the letters traditionally attributed to Paul were actually written by associates or later followers. Scholars have reached this conclusion because of differences in writing style, vocabulary, and thought. Those associates or followers of Paul applied his teaching to new situations faced by the early Christian communities. Similarly, the letters bearing the names of James, Peter, and John were probably written by associates or later followers of those men.

To a modern person, that might seem like forgery. But in the ancient world, it was not uncommon for followers of an important person to write in the person's name after her or his death. It was a way of honoring the person and keeping her or his traditions alive.

Although the Book of Revelation is grouped together with the letters in this introduction, it really is not a letter at all. Revelation was written as a series of visions to a disciple named John. The visions are filled with dramatic imagery and events. Some people interpret them as prophecies about the way the world will end, but for the most part, they are really coded messages about events happening in John's own time. Ultimately, the Book of Revelation is a hopeful message to persecuted Christians that God is in control and that goodness and justice will triumph.

As you explore these letters and the Book of Revelation, you'll see the church at its best: the miraculous growth, the Spirit-filled enthusiasm, and the deep love the early Christians had for one another and for Jesus. You'll also see how the early church was threatened by intense disagreements, jealousy, and scandals. Through it all, the authors reveal a deep faith and missionary spirit. They focus again and again on the death and Resurrection of Jesus and on the mystery of the church as the living Body of Christ acting in the world through the power of the Holy Spirit. These letters had a specific audience in the first century AD, but because God inspired them, their words are for you too!

Other Background

▶ There are nine letters by Paul or his followers named for the communities in which the recipient churches were located: Romans, First and Second Corinthians, Galatians, Ephesians (called a captivity letter because it is attributed to Paul writing from jail), Philippians (also a captivity letter), Colossians (also a captivity letter), and First and Second Thessalonians.

▶ There are four letters by Paul or his followers named for the individuals to whom they were sent: First and Second Timothy and Titus (called pastoral letters), and Philemon (a captivity letter).

▶ Hebrews is named for the Christian Jews for whom it was intended.

▶ There are seven catholic letters named after their stated authors: James; First and Second Peter; First, Second, and Third John; and Jude. They are called catholic because they are general letters to all Christians.

▶ The Book of Revelation is not a letter. It is a collection of the prophecies and visions of John of Patmos, a Christian prophet.

Have you ever wondered what it is like to be loved unconditionally? This was the message Saint Paul was trying to convey to the people of Rome—God loves us unconditionally. In his Letter to the Romans, Paul addresses some important questions of life and faith. Paul wanted to share his understanding that although we may not always do what is right, God still desires a relationship with us through Jesus. We are justified—made right with God—by faith in Jesus Christ.

In Depth

Many people consider the Letter to the Romans the deepest expression of Paul's thinking. This was the only letter Paul wrote to a community he had not yet visited. At the time, he was planning to go to Rome and was trying to prepare the way by explaining his teaching on justification (or righteousness) and faith. Paul's message is that only God can acquit humanity of its sin so it can be restored to right relationship with God. His ideas are summed up in a verse from the first chapter: "For I am not ashamed of the gospel; it is the power of God for salvation to everyone who has faith" (verse 16).

Romans is not easy reading. Paul often makes his case by using arguments that might seem strange to us today. Some of his main points are these:

🟩 Justification (or being made right with God) is available to both Jews and Gentiles (non-Jews).

🟩 Because all people have sinned, no one has "earned" justification.

🟩 Justification and salvation come through faith in Jesus Christ, not through following the Jewish religious law.

🟩 Even though the Gospel has come to the Gentiles, God has not abandoned the Jews.

The Letter to the Romans contains many wonderfully comforting words. It tells us that when we don't know how to pray, God prays for us "with sighs too deep for words" (8:26)! And it says that "all things work together for good for those who love God" (verse 28). And it asks, "If God is for us, who is against us?" (verse 31).

So as you read this powerful letter, let go of your fears. Even though you're not perfect, God will never leave you. As Paul says, "I am convinced that neither death, nor life, nor angels, nor rulers, nor things present, nor things to come, nor powers, nor height, nor depth, nor anything else in all creation, will be able to separate us from the love of God in Christ Jesus our Lord" (verses 38–39).

🟢 At a Glance

- **1:1–15.** a greeting and thanks
- **1:16—4:25.** the lesson that humanity was once under the power of sin but is now justified
- **Chapters 5–8.** a description of the life of the justified
- **Chapters 9–11.** a discussion of Judaism's place in God's plan of salvation
- **Chapters 12–16.** moral advice, personal notes, and blessings

⭐ Quick Facts

Inspired Author: Paul
Date Written: from AD 56 to 58
Audience: Jewish and Gentile Christians in Rome

The Letter to the Romans

Romans

Salutation

1 Paul, a servant^a of Jesus Christ, called to be an apostle, set apart for the gospel of God, ²which he promised beforehand through his prophets in the holy scriptures, ³the gospel concerning his Son, who was descended from David according to the flesh ⁴and was declared to be Son of God with power according to the spirit^b of holiness by resurrection from the dead, Jesus Christ our Lord, ⁵through whom we have received grace and apostleship to bring about the obedience of faith among all the Gentiles for the sake of his name, ⁶including yourselves who are called to belong to Jesus Christ,

7 To all God's beloved in Rome, who are called to be saints:

Grace to you and peace from God our Father and the Lord Jesus Christ.

Prayer of Thanksgiving

8 First, I thank my God through Jesus Christ for all of you, because your faith is proclaimed throughout the world. ⁹For God, whom I serve with my spirit by announcing the gospel^c of his Son, is my witness that without ceasing I remember you always in my prayers, ¹⁰asking that by God's will I may somehow at last succeed in coming to you. ¹¹For I am longing to see you so that I may share with you some spiritual gift to strengthen you— ¹²or rather so that we may be mutually encouraged by each other's faith, both yours and mine. ¹³I want you to know, brothers

and sisters,^d that I have often intended to come to you (but thus far have been prevented), in order that I may reap some harvest among you as I have among the rest of the Gentiles. ¹⁴I am a debtor both to Greeks and to barbarians, both to the wise and to the foolish ¹⁵—hence my eagerness to proclaim the gospel to you also who are in Rome.

The Power of the Gospel

16 For I am not ashamed of the gospel; it is the power of God for salvation to everyone who has faith, to the Jew first and also to the Greek. ¹⁷For in it the righteousness of God is revealed through faith for faith; as it is written, "The one who is righteous will live by faith."^e

The Guilt of Humankind

18 For the wrath of God is revealed from heaven against all ungodliness and wickedness of those who by their wickedness suppress the truth. ¹⁹For what can be known about God is plain to them, because God has shown it to them. ²⁰Ever since the creation of the world his eternal power and divine nature, invisible though they are, have been understood and seen through the things he has made. So they are without excuse; ²¹for though they knew God, they did not honor him as God or give thanks to him, but they became futile in their thinking, and their senseless minds were darkened.

---

a Gk *slave*   b Or *Spirit*   c Gk *my spirit in the gospel*
d Gk *brothers*   e Or *The one who is righteous through faith will live*

²²Claiming to be wise, they became fools; ²³and they exchanged the glory of the immortal God for images resembling a mortal human being or birds or four-footed animals or reptiles.

24 Therefore God gave them up in the lusts of their hearts to impurity, to the degrading of their bodies among themselves, ²⁵because they exchanged the truth about God for a lie and worshiped and served the creature rather than the Creator, who is blessed forever! Amen.

26 For this reason God gave them up to degrading passions. Their women exchanged natural intercourse for unnatural, ²⁷and in the same way also the men, giving up natural intercourse with women, were consumed with passion for one another. Men committed shameless acts with men and received in their own persons the due penalty for their error.

28 And since they did not see fit to acknowledge God, God gave them up to a debased mind and to things that should not be done. ²⁹They were filled with every kind of wickedness, evil, covetousness, malice. Full of envy, murder, strife, deceit, craftiness, they are gossips, ³⁰slanderers,

God-haters,ᵃ insolent, haughty, boastful, inventors of evil, rebellious toward parents, ³¹foolish, faithless, heartless, ruthless. ³²They know God's decree, that those who practice such things deserve to die—yet they not only do them but even applaud others who practice them.

The Righteous Judgment of God

2 Therefore you have no excuse, whoever you are, when you judge others; for in passing judgment on another you condemn yourself, because you, the judge, are doing the very same things. ²You say,ᵇ "We know that God's judgment on those who do such things is in accordance with truth." ³Do you imagine, whoever

---

a Or *God-hated*   b Gk lacks *You say*

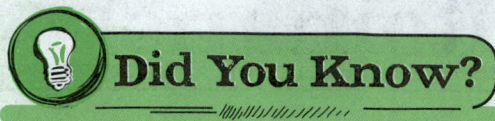

Did You Know?

The Many Meanings of *Gospel*

The word *gospel* is the best translation of the Greek word *euangelion*, which was used in Romans 1:16. *Gospel* comes from the old English word *godspel*, which means "good news." From *euangelion*, we get the word *evangelize*, which means "to share the good news."

In the New Testament, the meaning of the word *Gospel* goes through an evolution. For Paul, whose writings are the earliest in the New Testament, *Gospel* referred to the good news of salvation for all who believe. Paul associated the Gospel directly with Jesus himself, centering on his death and Resurrection.

As Christian faith developed, the understanding of *Gospel* expanded to include the Reign (Kingdom) of God that Jesus preached. The Gospel was not just associated with Jesus' saving death and Resurrection, but included all his teachings, miracles, promises, and demands. After the original Apostles died or were killed, Christian communities desired a record of their teachings about Jesus, and the Gospel message was written down. So *Gospel* came also to refer to the writings named for Matthew, Mark, Luke, and John.

▶ Rom 1:16

TIBER RIVER

FORUM

APPIAN WAY

SEVEN HILLS OF ROME
- QUIRINAL
- VIMINAL
- ESQUILINE
TIBER RIVER
- CAPITOL
- PALATINE
- CAELIAN
- AVENTINE

--- ROADS
⌃ HILLS

1:1-7

Map illustrating first-century Rome

R O M

you are, that when you judge those who do such things and yet do them yourself, you will escape the judgment of God? ⁴Or do you despise the riches of his kindness and forbearance and patience? Do you not realize that God's kindness is meant to lead you to repentance? ⁵But by your hard and impenitent heart you are storing up wrath for yourself on the day of wrath, when God's righteous judgment will be revealed. ⁶For he will repay according to each one's deeds: ⁷to those who by patiently doing good seek for glory and honor and immortality, he will give eternal life; ⁸while for those who are self-seeking and who obey not the truth but wickedness, there will be wrath and fury. ⁹There will be anguish

and distress for everyone who does evil, the Jew first and also the Greek, ¹⁰but glory and honor and peace for everyone who does good, the Jew first and also the Greek. ¹¹For God shows no partiality.

12 All who have sinned apart from the law will also perish apart from the law, and all who have sinned under the law will be judged by the law. ¹³For it is not the hearers of the law who are righteous in God's sight, but the doers of the law who will be justified. ¹⁴When Gentiles, who do not possess the law, do instinctively what the law requires, these, though not having the law, are a law to themselves. ¹⁵They show that what the law requires is written on their hearts, to which their own conscience also bears witness; and their conflicting thoughts will accuse or perhaps

Homosexuality and AIDS

In making his case that all people are in need of salvation, Paul talks about the sinfulness of humankind in Romans 1:18–32. As a specific example of what happens when people refuse to acknowledge God as God and Creator and instead worship created things, homosexual activity is discussed in verses 26–27.

Some people interpret these verses to mean that Paul is condemning homosexual persons. But this is a serious misinterpretation of Paul's words. Why? First, look at the context. After this specific example in verses 26–27, Paul lists all kinds of sinful behaviors in verses 28–32. He is not picking on homosexuals; rather, he is showing that all people are guilty of sin.

Most important, notice that Paul never condemns people; he condemns sinful behavior. The Catholic Church does the same. The Church teaches that homosexual orientation is not sinful, but it also states that any sexual activity outside of marriage is wrong.

Romans 1:18–32 has also been used wrongly against AIDS victims. Some of them have been told that their horrible disease is a result of God's vengeance against homosexual behavior. Our loving God would never use AIDS, or any other disease, to punish people.

▶ Rom 1:18–32

Examination of Conscience

God of love and forgiveness, help me to be aware of those times when I begin to think I've earned the right to judge others. Paul reminds us that we are all guilty of sin. I have no right to judge others.

Direct me to turn my attention to examining my own conscience:

Have I been patient with those around me?

Have I offered forgiveness to those who have hurt me?

Have I had the courage to admit when I am wrong?

Have I treated my parents and siblings with respect?

Have I been sensitive to the feelings and needs of those around me?

Have I made an effort to become more aware of how my actions contribute to larger social problems such as hunger, poverty, and global warming?

Forgive me, God, for I have sinned. Help me to recognize the generosity of your forgiveness and love. Help me also to have the strength and courage to follow the ways of your Son Jesus. Amen.

▶ Rom 2:1–4

ROM

excuse them ¹⁶on the day when, according to my gospel, God, through Jesus Christ, will judge the secret thoughts of all.

The Jews and the Law

17 But if you call yourself a Jew and rely on the law and boast of your relation to God ¹⁸and know his will and determine what is best because you are instructed in the law, ¹⁹and if you are sure that you are a guide to the blind, a light to those who are in darkness, ²⁰a corrector of the foolish, a teacher of children, having in the law the embodiment of knowledge and truth, ²¹you, then, that teach others, will you not teach yourself? While you preach against stealing, do you steal? ²²You that forbid adultery, do you commit adultery? You that abhor idols, do you rob temples? ²³You that boast in the law, do you dishonor God by breaking the law? ²⁴For, as it is written, "The name of God is blasphemed among the Gentiles because of you."

25 Circumcision indeed is of value if you

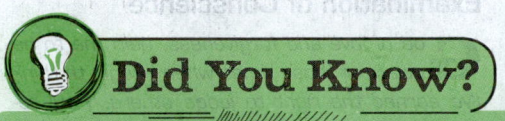

Did You Know?

Circumcision, the Law, and Faith

Circumcision is the surgical removal of the foreskin from a male's penis. It was the sign of the covenant (agreement) between Israel and God (see Gen 17:2). As Gentiles became Christians, many Jewish Christians claimed they had to live by Jewish religious laws, including circumcision.

Paul consistently insists that such rituals are not necessary for Gentile converts. He says that "real circumcision is a matter of the heart" (Rom 2:29), which leads to "faith working through love" (Gal 5:6). In Romans, chapter 4, Paul sheds further light on this by considering the case of Abraham. Abraham was considered the father of the Jewish faith. He was made righteous by God before he was circumcised (see verse 10). Why? Because of his strong and heroic faith in God. Christians are called to this kind of faith in God, whose plan of salvation is now fully revealed in Jesus Christ.

▶ Rom 2:25–29

obey the law; but if you break the law, your circumcision has become uncircumcision. ²⁶So, if those who are uncircumcised keep the requirements of the law, will not their uncircumcision be regarded as circumcision? ²⁷Then those who are physically uncircumcised but keep the law will condemn you that have the written code and circumcision but break the law. ²⁸For a person is not a Jew who is one outwardly, nor is true circumcision something external and physical. ²⁹Rather, a person is a Jew who is one inwardly, and real circumcision is a matter of the heart—it is spiritual and not literal. Such a person receives praise not from others but from God.

3 Then what advantage has the Jew? Or what is the value of circumcision? ²Much, in every way. For in the first place the Jews^a were entrusted with the oracles of God. ³What if some were unfaithful? Will their faithlessness nullify the faithfulness of God? ⁴By no means! Although everyone is a liar, let God be proved true, as it is written,

"So that you may be justified in your words,
　　and prevail in your judging."^b

⁵But if our injustice serves to confirm the justice of God, what should we say? That God is unjust to inflict wrath on us? (I speak in a human way.) ⁶By no means! For then how could God judge the world? ⁷But if through my falsehood God's truthfulness abounds to his glory, why am I still being condemned as a sinner? ⁸And why not say (as some people slander us by saying that we say), "Let us do evil so that good may come"? Their condemnation is deserved!

None Is Righteous

9 What then? Are we any better off?^c No, not at all; for we have already charged that all, both Jews and Greeks, are under the power of sin, ¹⁰as it is written:
"There is no one who is righteous, not even one;
¹¹　there is no one who has understanding,
　　there is no one who seeks God.
¹² All have turned aside, together they have
　　become worthless;
　there is no one who shows kindness,
　　there is not even one."
¹³ "Their throats are opened graves;
　they use their tongues to deceive."
"The venom of vipers is under their lips."
¹⁴　"Their mouths are full of cursing and
　　bitterness."
¹⁵ "Their feet are swift to shed blood;

R
O
M

16   ruin and misery are in their paths,
17 and the way of peace they have not known."
18   "There is no fear of God before their eyes."

The Law, Faith, and Justification

Throughout much of Romans, Paul is explaining the relationship between the law, faith, and justification (righteousness). At the end of Romans, chapter 2, and the beginning of chapter 3, he shows that the Jewish Law of the Old Testament cannot save us from the effect of sin. But he recognizes the value of the law (see 3:31). The law was the expression of the Jewish people's response of faith to God's covenant. It expressed their covenant relationship with God and one another.

We often think of sin as breaking God's law. But at its core, sin is really breaking our relationship with God and distancing ourselves from God. Remember what Adam and Eve did after their first sin? They hid from God, ashamed of their action. Paul is clear that we are all guilty of sin. Separated from God, the source of all life, we would eventually perish without God's help. But God is always seeking us out. In the ultimate act of love, God sent Jesus to restore the break in our relationship caused by sin. Jesus' life, death, Resurrection, and Ascension show us that God's great love is far more powerful than any sin we can commit.

Paul uses the word *justification* (righteousness) to explain the process that brings us back into a good relationship with God. It is a state of being right with God, of not being separated from God.

How are we justified or considered righteous? Not by our ability to keep any laws but by God, as a free gift to those who have faith in Jesus Christ. God's gift of grace also helps us respond to his call to live the Gospel message. The effect of justification by God is opposite that of sin. Where sin creates distance, Christ draws us close. Where sin kills, Christ gives life. Where sin produces hate and misery, Christ brings love and peace.

▶ Rom 3:1–31

19 Now we know that whatever the law says, it speaks to those who are under the law, so that every mouth may be silenced, and the whole world may be held accountable to God. 20For "no human being will be justified in his sight" by deeds prescribed by the law, for through the law comes the knowledge of sin.

Righteousness through Faith

21 But now, apart from law, the righteousness of God has been disclosed, and is attested by the law and the prophets, 22the righteousness of God through faith in Jesus Christ*a* for all who believe. For there is no distinction, 23since all have sinned and fall short of the glory of God; 24they are now justified by his grace as a gift, through the redemption that is in Christ Jesus, 25whom God put forward as a sacrifice of atonement*b* by his blood, effective through faith. He did this to show his righteousness, because in his divine forbearance he had passed over the sins previously committed; 26it was to prove at the present time that he himself is righteous and that he justifies the one who has faith in Jesus.*c*

27 Then what becomes of boasting? It is excluded. By what law? By that of works? No, but by the law of faith. 28For we hold that a person is justified by faith apart from works prescribed by the law. 29Or is God the God of Jews only? Is he not the God of Gentiles also? Yes, of Gentiles also, 30since God is one; and he will justify the circumcised on the ground of faith and the uncircumcised through that same faith. 31Do we then overthrow the law by this faith? By no means! On the contrary, we uphold the law.

The Example of Abraham

4 What then are we to say was gained by*d* Abraham, our ancestor according to the flesh? 2For if Abraham was justified by works, he has something to boast about, but not before God. 3For what does the scripture say? "Abraham believed God, and it was reckoned to him as righteousness." 4Now to one who works, wages are not reckoned as a gift but as something due. 5But to one who without works trusts him who justifies the ungodly, such faith is reckoned as righteousness. 6So also David speaks of the blessedness of those to whom God reckons righteousness apart from works:
7 "Blessed are those whose iniquities are forgiven,
       and whose sins are covered;

---

a Or *through the faith of Jesus Christ*   *b* Or *a place of atonement*
c Or *who has the faith of Jesus*   *d* Other ancient authorities read *say about*

⁸ blessed is the one against whom the Lord will
  not reckon sin."

9 Is this blessedness, then, pronounced only
on the circumcised, or also on the uncircumcised? We say, "Faith was reckoned to Abraham
as righteousness." ¹⁰How then was it reckoned to
him? Was it before or after he had been circumcised? It was not after, but before he was circumcised. ¹¹He received the sign of circumcision as
a seal of the righteousness that he had by faith
while he was still uncircumcised. The purpose
was to make him the ancestor of all who believe
without being circumcised and who thus have
righteousness reckoned to them, ¹²and likewise
the ancestor of the circumcised who are not only
circumcised but who also follow the example of
the faith that our ancestor Abraham had before
he was circumcised.

God's Promise Realized through Faith

13 For the promise that he would inherit
the world did not come to Abraham or to his

Trusting the Grace of God

A grandmother pushes her grandson out of
the path of a speeding car, but she is hit
by the car and dies. A stranger jumps into a
surging river to save a young girl, but he loses
his own life. A firefighter is killed battling a blaze
to rescue three trapped people. Their concern
for others leads these real-life heroes to make
the ultimate sacrifice.

Like the grandson, the young girl, and the
three trapped people, we too have been saved
from death at a great cost—Jesus' loving sacrifice in obedience to God's will. Paul reminds
us that our justification—our reconciliation and
peace with God—is not a reward we deserve for
being good. It is God's free gift of love despite
our weakness and sin. And that is grace. Put
your faith not in your own ability to please God,
but in God's abundant grace. It is God's grace
that will give you the strength you need to reach
out in loving service to others.

▶ Rom 5:1–11

descendants through the law but through the
righteousness of faith. ¹⁴If it is the adherents of
the law who are to be the heirs, faith is null and
the promise is void. ¹⁵For the law brings wrath;
but where there is no law, neither is there violation.

16 For this reason it depends on faith, in order that the promise may rest on grace and be
guaranteed to all his descendants, not only to
the adherents of the law but also to those who
share the faith of Abraham (for he is the father
of all of us, ¹⁷as it is written, "I have made you
the father of many nations")—in the presence
of the God in whom he believed, who gives life
to the dead and calls into existence the things
that do not exist. ¹⁸Hoping against hope, he
believed that he would become "the father of
many nations," according to what was said, "So
numerous shall your descendants be." ¹⁹He did
not weaken in faith when he considered his
own body, which was already*a* as good as dead
(for he was about a hundred years old), or when
he considered the barrenness of Sarah's womb.
²⁰No distrust made him waver concerning the
promise of God, but he grew strong in his faith
as he gave glory to God, ²¹being fully convinced
that God was able to do what he had promised.
²²Therefore his faith*b* "was reckoned to him as
righteousness." ²³Now the words, "it was reckoned to him," were written not for his sake
alone, ²⁴but for ours also. It will be reckoned
to us who believe in him who raised Jesus our
Lord from the dead, ²⁵who was handed over to
death for our trespasses and was raised for our
justification.

Results of Justification

5 Therefore, since we are justified by faith,
we*c* have peace with God through our Lord
Jesus Christ, ²through whom we have obtained
access*d* to this grace in which we stand; and
we*e* boast in our hope of sharing the glory of
God. ³And not only that, but we*e* also boast in
our sufferings, knowing that suffering produces
endurance, ⁴and endurance produces character,
and character produces hope, ⁵and hope does
not disappoint us, because God's love has been
poured into our hearts through the Holy Spirit
that has been given to us.

6 For while we were still weak, at the right
time Christ died for the ungodly. ⁷Indeed, rarely
will anyone die for a righteous person—though

---

a Other ancient authorities lack *already*   b Gk *Therefore
it*   c Other ancient authorities read *let us*   d Other ancient
authorities add *by faith*   e Or *let us*

Catholic Practices and Prayers

Being Catholic

There are an estimated one billion Catholics living in the world. That is about 17 percent of the world's population. There are more Catholics than there are people in any other Christian denomination. There are also more Catholics than there are Jews, Hindus, or Buddhists—only Muslims have more members. The great number of Catholics in the world testifies to Catholicism's universal appeal and to the power that the Catholic faith has in people's lives.

This section of The Catholic Youth Bible® provides only a quick view of Catholic beliefs, practices, and attitudes. It does not offer in-depth explanation as to why Catholics believe or practice what they do. For an in-depth exploration of the Catholic faith, you may wish to purchase The Catholic Faith Handbook for Youth, Second Edition, by Brian Singer-Towns (Saint Mary's Press, 2008) from which the content of this section has been adapted.

Core Catholic Beliefs

- God created human beings to be in perfect union with God and one another. However, the sin of our first parents—original sin—deprived the human race of our original holiness and justice.

- Throughout human history, God worked to restore the relationship of love and trust that was lost through original sin. God did this by entering into covenants—

Core Catholic Spirituality and Prayers

Two Great Commandments

- "You shall love the Lord your God with all your heart, with all your soul, and all your mind, and with all your strength."

- "You shall love your neighbor as yourself."

(Mt 22:37–40, Mk 12:29–31, Lk 10:27)

Ten Commandments

1. I am the Lord your God: you shall not have strange gods before me.

2. You shall not take the name of the Lord, your God, in vain.

3. Remember to keep holy the Lord's Day.

4. Honor your father and mother.

5. You shall not kill.

6. You shall not commit adultery.

7. You shall not steal.

8. You shall not bear false witness against your neighbor.

9. You shall not covet your neighbor's wife.

10. You shall not covet your neighbor's goods.

Beatitudes

- Blessed are the poor in spirit, the kingdom of heaven is theirs.

- Blessed are they who mourn, they will be comforted.

- Blessed are the meek, they will inherit the earth.

- Blessed are they who hunger and thirst for righteousness, they will be satisfied.

- Blessed are the merciful, they will be shown mercy.

- Blessed are the clean of heart, they will see God.

- Blessed are the peacemakers, they will be called children of God.

- Blessed are they who are persecuted for the sake of righteousness, the kingdom of heaven is theirs.

Corporal Works of Mercy

- Feed the hungry.
- Give drink to the thirsty.
- Shelter the homeless.
- Clothe the naked.
- Care for the sick.
- Help the imprisoned.
- Bury the dead.

Spiritual Works of Mercy

- Share knowledge.
- Give advice to those who need it.
- Comfort those who suffer.
- Be patient with others.
- Forgive those who hurt you.
- Give correction to those who need it.
- Pray for the living and the dead.

Theological Virtues

- Faith
- Hope
- Love

Cardinal Virtues

- Prudence
- Justice
- Fortitude
- Temperance

Seven Gifts of the Holy Spirit

- Wisdom
- Understanding
- Right judgment
- Courage
- Knowledge
- Reverence
- Wonder and awe

Fruits of the Holy Spirit

- Charity
- Joy
- Peace
- Patience
- Goodness
- Kindness
- Long suffering
- Humility
- Faithfulness
- Modesty
- Continence
- Chastity

Four Marks of the Catholic Church

- One
- Holy
- Catholic
- Apostolic

Seven Sacraments

- Baptism
- Confirmation
- The Eucharist
- Penance and Reconciliation
- Anointing of the Sick
- Matrimony
- Holy Orders

Precepts of the Church

1. To keep holy the day of the Lord's Resurrection; to worship God by participating in Mass every Sunday and on the holy days of obligation; to avoid those activities that would hinder renewal of the soul and body on the Sabbath (for example, needless work or unnecessary shopping).
2. To lead a sacramental life; to receive Holy Communion frequently and the sacrament of Penance and Reconciliation regularly—minimally, to receive the sacrament of Penance and Reconciliation at least once a year (annual confession is obligatory only if serious sin is involved); minimally also, to receive Holy Communion at least once a year between the first Sunday of Lent and Trinity Sunday.
3. To study Catholic teaching in preparation for the sacrament of Confirmation, to be confirmed, and then to continue to study and advance the cause of Christ.
4. To observe the marriage laws of the Church; to give religious training, by example and word, to one's children; to use parish schools and catechetical programs.
5. To strengthen and support the Church—one's own parish community and parish priests, the worldwide Church, and the Pope.
6. To do penance, including abstaining from meat and fasting from food on the appointed days.
7. To join in the missionary spirit and apostolate (work) of the Church.

Holy Days of Obligation

- Christmas (December 25)
- Solemnity of the Blessed Virgin Mary, the Mother of God (January 1)
- Ascension of the Lord (the Sunday that follows forty days after Easter)
- Assumption of the Blessed Virgin Mary (August 15)
- All Saints (November 1)
- Immaculate Conception of the Blessed Virgin Mary (December 8)

Catholic Prayers and Devotions

Act of Contrition

My God, I am sorry for my sins
with all my heart, and I detest them.
In choosing to do wrong and failing to
do good, I have sinned against you,
whom I should love above all things.
I firmly intend, with your help,
to do penance, to sin no more,
and to avoid whatever
leads me to sin.
Our savior Jesus Christ
suffered and died for us.
In his name, my God,
have mercy.

Act of Faith

My God, I firmly believe you are one God in three Divine Persons, Father, Son, and Holy Spirit.

I believe in Jesus Christ, your son, who became man and died for our sins, and who will come to judge the living and the dead.

I believe these and all the truths which the Holy Catholic Church teaches, because you have revealed them, who can neither deceive nor be deceived. Amen.

Act of Hope

O my God, trusting in your infinite goodness and promises, I hope to obtain pardon of my sins, the help of your grace, and life everlasting, through the merits of Jesus Christ, my Lord and redeemer. Amen.

Act of Love

My God, I love you above all things, with my whole heart and soul, because you are all-good and worthy of all my love. I love my neighbor as myself for love of you. I forgive all who have injured me, and I ask pardon of all whom I have injured. Amen.

Apostles' Creed

I believe in God, the Father almighty, Creator of heaven and earth, and in Jesus Christ, his only Son, our Lord, who was conceived by the Holy Spirit, born of the Virgin Mary, suffered under Pontius Pilate, was crucified, died and was buried; he descended into hell; on the third day he rose again from the dead; he ascended into heaven, and is seated at the right hand of God the Father almighty; from there he will come to judge the living and the dead.

I believe in the Holy Spirit, the holy catholic Church, the communion of saints, the forgiveness of sins, the resurrection of the body, and life everlasting. Amen.

Glory Be

Glory be to the Father, and to the Son, and to the Holy Spirit, as it was in the beginning, is now, and will be forever. Amen.

Grace After Meals

We give you thanks, almighty God, for these and all your gifts which we have received through Christ our Lord. Amen.

The Lord's Prayer (also called the Our Father)

Our Father who art in heaven, hallowed be thy name. Thy kingdom come. Thy will be done, on earth as it is in heaven. Give us this day our daily bread, and forgive us our trespasses, as we forgive those who trespass against us, and lead us not into temptation, but deliver us from evil. Amen.

Grace Before Meals

Bless us, O Lord, and these your gifts, which we are about to receive from your bounty, through Christ our Lord. Amen.

Hail Mary

Hail Mary, full of grace, the Lord is with you; blessed are you among women, and blessed is the fruit of your womb, Jesus.

Holy Mary, Mother of God, pray for us sinners now and at the hour of our death. Amen.

Mysteries of the Rosary

Joyful Mysteries
- The Annunciation
- The Visitation
- The Birth of Our Lord
- The Presentation of Jesus in the Temple
- The Finding of Jesus in the Temple

(continued on next page)

(Mysteries of the Rosary continued)

Sorrowful Mysteries
- The Agony of Jesus in the Garden
- The Scourging at the Pillar
- The Crowning of Thorns
- The Carrying of the Cross
- The Crucifixion

Glorious Mysteries
- The Resurrection of Jesus
- The Ascension of Jesus into Heaven
- The Descent of the Holy Spirit on the Apostles (Pentecost)
- The Assumption of Mary into Heaven
- The Crowning of Mary as Queen of Heaven

Luminous Mysteries
- The Baptism of Jesus
- Jesus Reveals Himself in the Miracle at Cana
- Jesus Proclaims the Good News of the Kingdom of God
- The Transfiguration of Jesus
- The Institution of the Eucharist

Prayer to the Holy Spirit

Come, Holy Spirit, fill the hearts of your faithful. Enkindle in them the fire of your love. Send forth your Spirit, and they will be created. And you will renew the face of the earth.

Let us pray:
Lord, by the light of the Holy Spirit, you have taught the hearts of the faithful. In the same Spirit, help to us relish what is right and always rejoice in your consolation. We ask this through Christ our Lord. Amen.

Stations of the Cross

1. Jesus is condemned to death.
2. Jesus takes up his cross.
3. Jesus falls the first time.
4. Jesus meets his mother.
5. Simon helps Jesus carry the cross.
6. Veronica wipes the face of Jesus.
7. Jesus falls the second time.
8. Jesus meets the women of Jerusalem.
9. Jesus falls the third time.
10. Jesus is stripped of his garments.
11. Jesus is nailed to the cross.
12. Jesus dies on the cross.
13. Jesus is taken down from the cross.
14. Jesus is laid in the tomb.

✚ Catholic Connection

The Holy Spirit

Do you allow the Holy Spirit to lead your life? The Letter to the Romans reminds us that through the gift of the Holy Spirit, we are all children of God, and as his children we are called to live a life of love according to God's will. The same Spirit that makes us children of God is the one that helps us to live out God's will individually and collectively as a Church.

On a personal level, God's Spirit is at work in many different ways in our lives. At Baptism we receive the Holy Spirit and become temples, or homes, for God's Spirit. As we grow in faith, the Holy Spirit is there guiding us and interceding for us when we pray. During the sacrament of Confirmation, the grace of Baptism is completed with a special outpouring of the Holy Spirit, giving us the gifts we need to live and spread the Gospel message.

Throughout the Scriptures, there are many symbols for the Holy Spirit that can help us to understand how the Spirit can guide us in our daily lives. For example:

- The Holy Spirit in the form of a **dove** recalls the end of the flood during the time of Noah (see Gen 8:8—12) and the descent of God's Spirit after Jesus was baptized (see Mt 3:16). It can serve as a reminder of our own Baptism and that we are called to live as followers of Christ.

- The Holy Spirit in the form of a **cloud**, who led the Israelites on their jour-

ney out of slavery toward the Promised Land (see Ex 40:34–38) and overshadowed Mary when the angel told her she would be the Mother of God's Son (see Lk 1:35), can remind us that God's Spirit can give us clarity when we have tough decisions to make and can guide us on our journey through life.

- The Holy Spirit in the form of **fire**, who descended on the disciples at Pentecost and transformed all who were present, can serve as a reminder that God's Spirit is present and is transforming our lives today (see Acts 2:3–12).

The same Spirit who is at work in our lives individually is also active in helping and guiding the Church. The Holy Spirit inspired the writing of the Scriptures and guides the Church in its understanding of them. God's Spirit continues to guide the Pope and bishops (the Magisterium) as they lead the Church and teach about the faith. (see "The Bible, Tradition, and Magisterium," near Lk 4:1–13.) And it is the Holy Spirit that unites us as the Body of Christ and empowers us to bring Christ's message to the world.

- How is the Holy Spirit present and actively working in your life? in the lives of your family and friends? in your community? in the world?

▶ **Rom 8:1–17**

Catechism, nos. 683–747

...eive New Life!

...ans, Paul tells us that ...eceive new life in Jesus ...e forgiveness of all sin ...d. By participating in the ..."Dying for New Life," near ... Baptism, we are no lon-

...life. For the wages of sin ...e gift of God is eternal life ...Lord" (Rom 6:22–23). Let ...passage fill you. Feel God's ...ou. Never forget that God ...d you to right relationship

...ss that I have sinned. My ac-...s hurt me and others. Help ...learn from my mistakes, and ...n the ways of Jesus. I ...ow to understand more ...s you have ...person of

...3

...efore we have been buried with ...into death, so that, just as Christ ...the dead by the glory of the Fa-...night walk in newness of life. ...ave been united with him in a ...we will certainly be united with ...ction like his. [6]We know that our ...cified with him so that the body ...destroyed, and we might no lon-...to sin. [7]For whoever has died is ...[8]But if we have died with Christ, ...we will also live with him. [9]We ...rist, being raised from the dead, ...gain; death no longer has domin-...[10]The death he died, he died to sin, ...t the life he lives, he lives to God. ...must consider yourselves dead to ...o God in Christ Jesus. ...re, do not let sin exercise dominion

> Or righteousness

in your mortal bodies, to make you obey their passions. 13No longer present your members to sin as instruments[a] of wickedness, but present yourselves to God as those who have been brought from death to life, and present your members to God as instruments[a] of righteousness. 14For sin will have no dominion over you, since you are not under law but under grace.

Slaves of Righteousness

15 What then? Should we sin because we are not under law but under grace? By no means! 16Do you not know that if you present yourselves to anyone as obedient slaves, you are slaves of the one whom you obey, either of sin,

Pray It!

I'm Not Perfect

Some people today think, If God has already forgiven me, why should I be concerned about sinning? Evidently, some people in Paul's time thought that too (see Rom 6:15). Paul reminds them, and us, that faith in Christ should be a matter of the heart, not simply a mechanical commitment. Like a married couple's love calls them to commit to each other (see 7:2), so our love for Christ should make us want to live in the light, free from sin. Why would we want to return to the things that bring death to the soul (see 6:21)?

But even when we commit to follow Christ, sin is a constant challenge. Paul encourages us, in the face of temptation, to maintain our focus on God and refrain from sin.

Jesus, you experienced temptation throughout your ministry. Yet, you always made the decision to avoid sin and live in the light.

I have made the commitment to follow you. Give me the strength to overcome temptations and avoid sin. If in my weaknesses I allow my sin and passions to steer me in the wrong direction, please forgive me and help me to find the right path again.
Amen.

▶ Rom 6:15—7:6

ROM

which leads ... part from ... came, sin leads to right ... command- that you, hav ... death to become obed ... the com- teaching to wh ... it killed you, having b ... mandment slaves of righ ... man terms be ... eath to me? For just as you ... eath in me slaves to impu ... in might be iquity, so now ... nmandment righteousness ... re.

20 When yo ... in regard to ri ... did you then ... piritual; but I now are ashar ... nder sin.[a] 15I death. 22But no ... For I do not sin and enslav ... thing I hate. is sanctification ... agree that the wages of sin is ... nger I that do eternal life in C ... 18For I know ... me, that is, in

An A...

7 Do you not ... nt, but the evil I am speaki ... w if I do what I that the law is ... t do it, but sin that person's lif ... bound by the la ... when I want to lives; but if her ... at hand. 22For I from the law c ... nmost self, 23but ingly, she will b ... y at war with the with another ma ... tive to the law of if her husband di ... 24Wretched man she marries anot ... rom this body of ... ugh Jesus Christ

4 In the sam ... died to the law that you may be ... a slave to the law been raised from ... am a slave to the bear fruit for Go ... flesh, our sinful ... rit were at work in ... death. 6But now ... condemnation for dead to that whic ... sus. 2For the law of slaves not under ... us has set you[c] free new life of the Sp ... eath. 3For God has ... d by the flesh, could ... on in the likeness of

7 What then s ... sin,[d] he condemned sin? By no means ... just requirement of law, I would not ... us, who walk not ac- have known wha ... ording to the Spirit.[b] not said, "You sh ... ding to the flesh set an opportunity in ... f the flesh, but those in me all kinds o ... pirit[b] set their minds ... 6To set the mind on

a Or weapons   b Gk th

Live It!

Our Inner Struggle

In Romans 7:15–16, Paul reveals his own struggle to do what is right. It seems there's a part of us that wants to do right, and another part that wants to do wrong. Even when we try to be good, "evil lies close at hand" (verse 21), ready to have its way.

Paul uses the words *spirit* and *flesh* to describe this struggle. He says our flesh tempts us to do wrong, and our spirit wants us to do right. Paul does not mean that our physical bodies are evil and the source of sin; rather, he is warning us that it is difficult to always do good, and many things around us can lead us astray.

Sin is hard to resist at times. To do what is right requires us to stop and think clearly about our choices and actively select good over sin. The good news is that God, the understanding forgiver, is on our side in the struggle. Thanks be to God!

▶ Rom 7:13–25

the flesh is death, but to set the mind on the Spirit[b] is life and peace. 7For this reason the mind that is set on the flesh is hostile to God; it does not submit to God's law—indeed it cannot, 8and those who are in the flesh cannot please God.

9 But you are not in the flesh; you are in the Spirit,[b] since the Spirit of God dwells in you. Anyone who does not have the Spirit of Christ does not belong to him. 10But if Christ is in you, though the body is dead because of sin, you, though the body is dead because of sin, the Spirit[a] is life because of righteousness. 11If the Spirit of him who raised Jesus from the dead dwells in you, he who raised Christ[e] from the dead will give life to your mortal bodies also through[f] his Spirit that dwells in you.

12 So then, brothers and sisters,[g] we are debtors, not to the flesh, to live according to the flesh, flesh— 13for if you live according to the flesh,

a Gk *sold under sin*   b Or *spirit*   c Here the Greek word *you* is singular number; other ancient authorities read *me* or *us*   d Or *and as a sin offering*   e Other ancient authorities read *the Christ* or *Christ Jesus* or *Jesus Christ*   f Other ancient authorities read *on account of*   g Gk *brothers*

ROM

you will die; but if by the Spirit you put to death the deeds of the body, you will live. [14]For all who are led by the Spirit of God are children of God. [15]For you did not receive a spirit of slavery to fall back into fear, but you have received a spirit of adoption. When we cry, "Abba![a] Father!" [16]it is that very Spirit bearing witness[b] with our spirit that we are children of God, [17]and if children, then heirs, heirs of God and joint heirs with Christ—if, in fact, we suffer with him so that we may also be glorified with him.

Future Glory

18 I consider that the sufferings of this present time are not worth comparing with the glory about to be revealed to us. [19]For the creation waits with eager longing for the revealing of the children of God; [20]for the creation was subjected to futility, not of its own will but by the will of the one who subjected it, in hope [21]that the creation itself will be set free from its bondage to decay and will obtain the freedom of the glory of the children of God. [22]We know that the whole creation has been groaning in labor pains until now; [23]and not only the creation, but we ourselves, who have the first fruits of the Spirit, groan inwardly while we wait for adoption, the redemption of our bodies. [24]For in[c] hope we were saved. Now hope that is seen is not hope. For who hopes[d] for what is seen? [25]But if we hope for what we do not see, we wait for it with patience.

26 Likewise the Spirit helps us in our weakness; for we do not know how to pray as we ought, but that very Spirit intercedes[e] with sighs too deep for words. [27]And God,[f] who searches the heart, knows what is the mind of the Spirit, because the Spirit[g] intercedes for the saints according to the will of God.[h]

> "We know that all things work together for good for those who love God, who are called according to his purpose."
>
> (Rom 8:28)

28 We know that all things work together for good[i] for those who love God, who are called according to his purpose. [29]For those whom he foreknew he also predestined to be conformed to the image of his Son, in order that he might be the firstborn within a large family.[j] [30]And

those whom he predestined he also called; and those whom he called he also justified; and those whom he justified he also glorified.

God's Love in Christ Jesus

31 What then are we to say about these things? If God is for us, who is against us? [32]He who did not withhold his own Son, but gave him up for all of us, will he not with him also give us everything else? [33]Who will bring any charge against God's elect? It is God who justifies. [34]Who is to condemn? It is Christ Jesus, who died, yes, who

<hr>

[a] Aramaic for *Father*   [b] Or [15a] *spirit of adoption, by which we cry, "Abba! Father!"* [16]*The Spirit itself bears witness*   [c] Or *by*   [d] Other ancient authorities read *awaits*   [e] Other ancient authorities add *for us*   [f] Gk *the one*   [g] Gk *he* or *it*   [h] Gk *according to God*   [i] Other ancient authorities read *God makes all things work together for good,* or *in all things God works for good*   [j] Gk *among many brothers*

Absolutely Nothing!

G od, what could separate me from your love?

Not a failed test or a broken promise or a hurtful word.

What could tear you from me?

Not the lure of power or immediate gratification or unnatural highs.

If you, God, are on my side, who could be against me?

Not a vengeful peer or an uncaring date or someone whose relationship with me has gone sour.

What situation could divide you and me, God?

Not depression over a loss or anger over being laughed at or guilt from being caught red-handed.

No, in all these things, I know that I am never alone, because you, God, conquered sin, despair, and even death itself through your endless love, a love that showed itself through your Son. I am convinced, Lord, that nothing, absolutely nothing, will ever separate me from your love . . . ever!

Amen.

▶ Rom 8:31–39

R
O
M

was raised, who is at the right hand of God, who indeed intercedes for us.[a] 35Who will separate us from the love of Christ? Will hardship, or distress, or persecution, or famine, or nakedness, or peril, or sword? 36As it is written,

Did You Know?

The Fate of Israel

In Romans, chapters 9–11, Paul takes on a difficult question: What will happen to Israel (the Jews), God's Chosen People, if they reject Jesus? For the early Jewish Christians, who probably had friends and maybe had family members who didn't believe in Jesus, this was an important question.

To respond, Paul makes several points. In the beginning of chapter 9, he affirms Israel's special place in God's plan of salvation. But the people's righteousness (see "The Law, Faith, and Justification," near Rom 3:1–31) is based on faith, not on fulfilling the law. In chapter 10, Paul notes that justification is available for all. The Jewish people are not left out if they call on the name of the Lord. But Israel's rejection of Jesus is good news for the Gentiles who have come to believe.

In chapter 11, Paul uses the analogy of grafting branches onto a tree. The Gentiles were grafted onto the original tree, which is Israel. Paul warns the Gentile Christians not to think they are better than the Jews. God grafted the Gentiles onto the tree; he can just as easily remove them. Paul says the Jews can be grafted back onto that tree (see verse 23). In fact, he ends with the hopeful promise that after the salvation of the Gentiles, all Israel will be saved (see verse 26)!

Christians recognize Jewish people as their spiritual ancestors. Christians have inherited from the Jews part of their Scriptures and a rich spiritual tradition. They respect the Jews' faith and their relationship with God. They pray for the Jews' salvation and their own, in the hope that Paul's promise will come to pass.

▶ **Romans, chapters 9–11**

"For your sake we are being killed all day long;
    we are accounted as sheep to be slaughtered."
37No, in all these things we are more than conquerors through him who loved us. 38For I am convinced that neither death, nor life, nor angels, nor rulers, nor things present, nor things to come, nor powers, 39nor height, nor depth, nor anything else in all creation, will be able to separate us from the love of God in Christ Jesus our Lord.

God's Election of Israel

9 I am speaking the truth in Christ—I am not lying; my conscience confirms it by the Holy Spirit— 2I have great sorrow and unceasing anguish in my heart. 3For I could wish that I myself were accursed and cut off from Christ for the sake of my own people,[b] my kindred according to the flesh. 4They are Israelites, and to them belong the adoption, the glory, the covenants, the giving of the law, the worship, and the promises; 5to them belong the patriarchs, and from them, according to the flesh, comes the Messiah,[c] who is over all, God blessed forever.[d] Amen.

6 It is not as though the word of God had failed. For not all Israelites truly belong to Israel, 7and not all of Abraham's children are his true descendants; but "It is through Isaac that descendants shall be named for you." 8This means that it is not the children of the flesh who are the children of God, but the children of the promise are counted as descendants. 9For this is what the promise said, "About this time I will return and Sarah shall have a son." 10Nor is that all; something similar happened to Rebecca when she had conceived children by one husband, our ancestor Isaac. 11Even before they had been born or had done anything good or bad (so that God's purpose of election might continue, 12not by works but by his call) she was told, "The elder shall serve the younger." 13As it is written,

"I have loved Jacob,
    but I have hated Esau."

14 What then are we to say? Is there injustice on God's part? By no means! 15For he says to Moses,

"I will have mercy on whom I have mercy,
    and I will have compassion on whom I have
        compassion."
16So it depends not on human will or exertion, but on God who shows mercy. 17For the scripture says to Pharaoh, "I have raised you up for the very purpose of showing my power in you,

a Or Is it Christ Jesus . . . for us?   b Gk my brothers   c Or the Christ   d Or Messiah, who is God over all, blessed forever; or Messiah. May he who is God over all be blessed forever so that my name may be proclaimed in all the earth." [18]So then he has mercy on whomever he chooses, and he hardens the heart of whomever he chooses.

God's Wrath and Mercy

19 You will say to me then, "Why then does he still find fault? For who can resist his will?" [20]But who indeed are you, a human being, to argue with God? Will what is molded say to the one who molds it, "Why have you made me like this?" [21]Has the potter no right over the clay, to make out of the same lump one object for special use and another for ordinary use? [22]What if God, desiring to show his wrath and to make known his power, has endured with much patience the objects of wrath that are made for destruction; [23]and what if he has done so in order to make known the riches of his glory for the objects of mercy, which he has prepared beforehand for glory— [24]including us whom he has called, not from the Jews only but also from the Gentiles? [25]As indeed he says in Hosea,

"Those who were not my people I will call 'my people,'
    and her who was not beloved I will call 'beloved.' "
[26] "And in the very place where it was said to them, 'You are not my people,'
    there they shall be called children of the living God."

27 And Isaiah cries out concerning Israel, "Though the number of the children of Israel were like the sand of the sea, only a remnant of them will be saved; [28]for the Lord will execute his sentence on the earth quickly and decisively."[a] [29]And as Isaiah predicted,

"If the Lord of hosts had not left survivors[b] to us,
    we would have fared like Sodom
    and been made like Gomorrah."

Israel's Unbelief

30 What then are we to say? Gentiles, who did not strive for righteousness, have attained it, that is, righteousness through faith; [31]but Israel, who did strive for the righteousness that is based on the law, did not succeed in fulfilling that law. [32]Why not? Because they did not strive for it on the basis of faith, but as if it were based on works. They have stumbled over the stumbling stone, [33]as it is written,

"See, I am laying in Zion a stone that will make people stumble, a rock that will make them fall,
    and whoever believes in him[c] will not be put to shame."

10 Brothers and sisters,[d] my heart's desire and prayer to God for them is that they may be saved. [2]I can testify that they have a zeal for God, but it is not enlightened. [3]For, being ignorant of the righteousness that comes from God, and seeking to establish their own, they have not submitted to God's righteousness. [4]For Christ is the end of the law so that there may be righteousness for everyone who believes.

Salvation Is for All

5 Moses writes concerning the righteousness that comes from the law, that "the person who does these things will live by them." [6]But the righteousness that comes from faith says, "Do not say in your heart, 'Who will ascend into heaven?' " (that is, to bring Christ down) [7]"or 'Who will descend into the abyss?' " (that is, to bring Christ up from the dead). [8]But what does it say?

"The word is near you,
    on your lips and in your heart"
(that is, the word of faith that we proclaim); [9]because[e] if you confess with your lips that Jesus is Lord and believe in your heart that God raised him from the dead, you will be saved. [10]For one believes with the heart and so is justified, and one confesses with the mouth and so is saved. [11]The scripture says, "No one who believes in him will be put to shame." [12]For there is no distinction between Jew and Greek; the same Lord is Lord of all and is generous to all who call on him. [13]For, "Everyone who calls on the name of the Lord shall be saved."

14 But how are they to call on one in whom they have not believed? And how are they to believe in one of whom they have never heard? And how are they to hear without someone to proclaim him? [15]And how are they to proclaim him unless they are sent? As it is written, "How beautiful are the feet of those who bring good news!" [16]But not all have obeyed the good news;[f] for Isaiah says, "Lord, who has believed our message?" [17]So faith comes from what is heard, and what is heard comes through the word of Christ.[g]

18 But I ask, have they not heard? Indeed they have; for

"Their voice has gone out to all the earth,
    and their words to the ends of the world."

---

a Other ancient authorities read *for he will finish his work and cut it short in righteousness, because the Lord will make the sentence shortened on the earth*   b Or *descendants; Gk seed*   c Or *trusts in it*   d Gk *Brothers*   e Or *namely, that*   f Or *gospel*   g Or *about Christ; other ancient authorities read of God*

¹⁹Again I ask, did Israel not understand? First Moses says,

"I will make you jealous of those who are not a nation;

with a foolish nation I will make you angry."

²⁰Then Isaiah is so bold as to say,

"I have been found by those who did not seek me;

I have shown myself to those who did not ask for me."

²¹But of Israel he says, "All day long I have held out my hands to a disobedient and contrary people."

Are Your Feet Beautiful?

Have you ever been drawn to buy something new after seeing a really clever commercial on TV? Companies trying to sell a product develop amazing ways of grabbing our attention. Without this effort, they will reach few people and fail in their mission.

The Church has undoubtedly the most important mission of all—to share with others the saving power that comes from faith in Jesus Christ. The promise in Romans 10:11–15 is that all who know and call on the name of Jesus will be saved. God is great!

How do others hear about this Good News? Paul says only through us. And he adds, "How beautiful are the feet of those who bring good news!" (verse 15). In other words, action, not just words, is needed to spread the Gospel message.

In your prayer, reflect or journal on the following questions:

● Who are some of the people who first helped you to know Jesus and how did they do that?
● In what ways can you show others how important your faith is to you?
● Which of your friends need to hear this Good News about Jesus? How can you share your faith with them, perhaps through a message of hope, forgiveness, healing, or encouragement?

▶ Rom 10:11–15

Israel's Rejection Is Not Final

11 I ask, then, has God rejected his people? By no means! I myself am an Israelite, a descendant of Abraham, a member of the tribe of Benjamin. ²God has not rejected his people whom he foreknew. Do you not know what the scripture says of Elijah, how he pleads with God against Israel? ³"Lord, they have killed your prophets, they have demolished your altars; I alone am left, and they are seeking my life." ⁴But what is the divine reply to him? "I have kept for myself seven thousand who have not bowed the knee to Baal." ⁵So too at the present time there is a remnant, chosen by grace. ⁶But if it is by grace, it is no longer on the basis of works, otherwise grace would no longer be grace.ᵃ

7 What then? Israel failed to obtain what it was seeking. The elect obtained it, but the rest were hardened, ⁸as it is written,

"God gave them a sluggish spirit,

eyes that would not see

and ears that would not hear,

down to this very day."

⁹And David says,

"Let their table become a snare and a trap,

a stumbling block and a retribution for them;

¹⁰ let their eyes be darkened so that they cannot see,

and keep their backs forever bent."

The Salvation of the Gentiles

11 So I ask, have they stumbled so as to fall? By no means! But through their stumblingᵇ salvation has come to the Gentiles, so as to make Israelᶜ jealous. ¹²Now if their stumblingᵇ means riches for the world, and if their defeat means riches for Gentiles, how much more will their full inclusion mean!

13 Now I am speaking to you Gentiles. Inasmuch then as I am an apostle to the Gentiles, I glorify my ministry ¹⁴in order to make my own peopleᵈ jealous, and thus save some of them. ¹⁵For if their rejection is the reconciliation of the world, what will their acceptance be but life from the dead! ¹⁶If the part of the dough offered as first fruits is holy, then the whole batch is holy; and if the root is holy, then the branches also are holy.

17 But if some of the branches were broken off, and you, a wild olive shoot, were grafted in their place to share the rich rootᵉ of the olive tree, ¹⁸do not boast over the branches. If you do

---

a Other ancient authorities add *But if it is by works, it is no longer on the basis of grace, otherwise work would no longer be work* b Gk *transgression*   c Gk *them*   d Gk *my flesh*   e Other ancient authorities read *the richness*

boast, remember that it is not you that support the root, but the root that supports you. ¹⁹You will say, "Branches were broken off so that I might be grafted in." ²⁰That is true. They were broken off because of their unbelief, but you stand only through faith. So do not become proud, but stand in awe. ²¹For if God did not spare the natural branches, perhaps he will not spare you.ᵃ ²²Note then the kindness and the severity of God: severity toward those who have fallen, but God's kindness toward you, provided you continue in his kindness; otherwise you also will be cut off. ²³And even those of Israel,ᵇ if they do not persist in unbelief, will be grafted in, for God has the power to graft them in again. ²⁴For if you have been cut from what is by nature a wild olive tree and grafted, contrary to nature, into a cultivated olive tree, how much more will these natural branches be grafted back into their own olive tree.

All Israel Will Be Saved

25 So that you may not claim to be wiser than you are, brothers and sisters,ᶜ I want you to understand this mystery: a hardening has come upon part of Israel, until the full number of the Gentiles has come in. ²⁶And so all Israel will be saved; as it is written,

"Out of Zion will come the Deliverer;
   he will banish ungodliness from Jacob."
²⁷ "And this is my covenant with them,
   when I take away their sins."
²⁸As regards the gospel they are enemies of Godᵈ for your sake; but as regards election they are beloved, for the sake of their ancestors; ²⁹for the gifts and the calling of God are irrevocable. ³⁰Just as you were once disobedient to God but have now received mercy because of their disobedience, ³¹so they have now been disobedient in order that, by the mercy shown to you, they too may nowᵉ receive mercy. ³²For God has imprisoned all in disobedience so that he may be merciful to all.

33 O the depth of the riches and wisdom and knowledge of God! How unsearchable are his judgments and how inscrutable his ways!
³⁴ "For who has known the mind of the Lord?
   Or who has been his counselor?"
³⁵ "Or who has given a gift to him,
   to receive a gift in return?"
³⁶For from him and through him and to him are all things. To him be the glory forever. Amen.

The New Life in Christ

12 I appeal to you therefore, brothers and sisters,ᶜ by the mercies of God, to present your bodies as a living sacrifice, holy and

Live It!

We Are the Body of Christ

According to Romans 12:1–8, we are the Body of Christ! Just thinking about this beautiful and powerful image fills us with energy. Imagine the power if all Christians really behaved as the living Body of Christ in their home, church, neighborhood, country, and world.

In verse 1, Paul calls us to present our bodies to God as a living, holy, and acceptable sacrifice. The best thing that we can offer to God is our whole life—all we are and all we do. When we worship God by doing this, our prayer and rituals are real and meaningful.

In verse 2, Paul calls us not to be conformed to this world but to be transformed. We are transformed by renewing our mind. We are intelligent people. God gave us the power to discern what is good and evil, true and false, in agreement with or against God's loving plan for humanity.

We must think and act according to the measure of faith and the different gifts we have received for the service of others (charisms). So we, who are many, may become one Body in Christ and be better collaborators in Jesus' mission.

▶ Rom 12:1–8

acceptable to God, which is your spiritualᶠ worship. ²Do not be conformed to this world,ᵍ but be transformed by the renewing of your minds, so that you may discern what is the will of God— what is good and acceptable and perfect.ʰ

3 For by the grace given to me I say to everyone among you not to think of yourself more highly than you ought to think, but to think with sober judgment, each according to the measure of faith that God has assigned. ⁴For as in one body we have many members, and not all the members

---

a Other ancient authorities read *neither will he spare you*   b Gk lacks *of Israel*   c Gk *brothers*   d Gk lacks *of God*   e Other ancient authorities lack *now*   f Or *reasonable*   g Gk *age*   h Or *what is the good and acceptable and perfect will of God*

have the same function, [5]so we, who are many, are one body in Christ, and individually we are members one of another. [6]We have gifts that differ according to the grace given to us: prophecy, in proportion to faith; [7]ministry, in ministering; the teacher, in teaching; [8]the exhorter, in exhortation; the giver, in generosity; the leader, in diligence; the compassionate, in cheerfulness.

Marks of the True Christian

9 Let love be genuine; hate what is evil, hold fast to what is good; [10]love one another with mutual affection; outdo one another in showing honor. [11]Do not lag in zeal, be ardent in spirit, serve the Lord.[a] [12]Rejoice in hope, be patient in suffering, persevere in prayer. [13]Contribute to the needs of the saints; extend hospitality to strangers.

14 Bless those who persecute you; bless and do not curse them. [15]Rejoice with those who rejoice,

Becoming a Peacemaker

A common response when someone mistreats us is to seek revenge. But in Romans 12:17–19, Paul tells us we should never try to avenge wrong against us—God will take care of it in God's own time. He goes on to remind us of Jesus' teaching to treat our enemies with kindness. That is certainly easier said than done! It is difficult to respond with goodwill when we are hurt.

Nevertheless, real people have tried to embody the idea of living peaceably—Martin Luther King Jr., Mother Teresa, Bishop Desmond Tutu, and the Dalai Lama are some examples. But there are also countless unnamed persons in our world who respond to hurt with love, respond to assault with peace. Perhaps you know people in your own community who have made similar commitments.

● Think of the people you know. Who is a peacemaker in your life?
● What can you do to be a peacemaker in your family, school, or community?

▶ Rom 12:17–19

weep with those who weep. [16]Live in harmony with one another; do not be haughty, but associate with the lowly;[b] do not claim to be wiser than you are. [17]Do not repay anyone evil for evil, but take thought for what is noble in the sight of all. [18]If it is possible, so far as it depends on you, live peaceably with all. [19]Beloved, never avenge yourselves, but leave room for the wrath of God;[c] for it is written, "Vengeance is mine, I will repay, says the Lord." [20]No, "if your enemies are hungry, feed them; if they are thirsty, give them something to drink; for by doing this you will heap burning coals on their heads." [21]Do not be overcome by evil, but overcome evil with good.

Being Subject to Authorities

13 Let every person be subject to the governing authorities; for there is no authority except from God, and those authorities that exist have been instituted by God. [2]Therefore whoever resists authority resists what God has appointed, and those who resist will incur judgment. [3]For rulers are not a terror to good conduct, but to bad. Do you wish to have no fear of the authority? Then do what is good, and you will receive its approval; [4]for it is God's servant for your good. But if you do what is wrong, you should be afraid, for the authority[d] does not bear the sword in vain! It is the servant of God to execute wrath on the wrongdoer. [5]Therefore one must be subject, not only because of wrath but also because of conscience. [6]For the same reason you also pay taxes, for the authorities are God's servants, busy with this very thing. [7]Pay to all what is due them—taxes to whom taxes are due, revenue to whom revenue is due, respect to whom respect is due, honor to whom honor is due.

Love for One Another

8 Owe no one anything, except to love one another; for the one who loves another has fulfilled the law. [9]The commandments, "You shall not commit adultery; You shall not murder; You shall not steal; You shall not covet"; and any other commandment, are summed up in this word, "Love your neighbor as yourself." [10]Love does no wrong to a neighbor; therefore, love is the fulfilling of the law.

An Urgent Appeal

11 Besides this, you know what time it is, how it is now the moment for you to wake from sleep.

---

a Other ancient authorities read *serve the opportune time*
b Or *give yourselves to humble tasks*   c Gk *the wrath*   d Gk *it*

For salvation is nearer to us now than when we became believers; ¹²the night is far gone, the day is near. Let us then lay aside the works of darkness and put on the armor of light; ¹³let us live honorably as in the day, not in reveling and drunkenness, not in debauchery and licentiousness, not in quarreling and jealousy. ¹⁴Instead, put on the Lord Jesus Christ, and make no provision for the flesh, to gratify its desires.

Do Not Judge Another

14 Welcome those who are weak in faith,[a] but not for the purpose of quarreling over opinions. ²Some believe in eating anything, while the weak eat only vegetables. ³Those who eat must not despise those who abstain, and those who abstain must not pass judgment on those who eat; for God has welcomed them. ⁴Who are you to pass judgment on servants of another? It is before their own lord that they stand or fall. And they will be upheld, for the Lord[b] is able to make them stand.

5 Some judge one day to be better than another, while others judge all days to be alike. Let all be fully convinced in their own minds. ⁶Those who observe the day, observe it in honor of the Lord. Also those who eat, eat in honor of the Lord, since they give thanks to God; while those who abstain, abstain in honor of the Lord and give thanks to God.

Pray It!

A Real Love

Lord, why is it so hard to love? Love is mentioned so much in the Bible that it makes me wonder why we don't get it. It seems that we do a good job of talking love and a poor job of doing love. We can point out where there is no love, but it sure is hard to bring love to where it is needed.

Jesus, fill me with your love to share with others. The kind of love that changes people forever. The kind of love that breaks down barriers and overcomes fears. The love that gives without counting the costs. Amen.

▶ Rom 13:8–10

7 We do not live to ourselves, and we do not die to ourselves. ⁸If we live, we live to the Lord, and if we die, we die to the Lord; so then, whether we live or whether we die, we are the Lord's. ⁹For to this end Christ died and lived again, so that he might be Lord of both the dead and the living.

10 Why do you pass judgment on your brother or sister?[c] Or you, why do you despise your

---

a Or *conviction*   b Other ancient authorities read *for God*
c Gk *brother*

Respecting Differences

If you have traveled to different parts of the United States, you may have discovered that people call similar drinks and sandwiches by different names, depending on what city you are in. Some people talk about soda and others call it pop. Still others call it a soft drink. So too with sandwiches. You may order a hoagie in one town, but it's called a submarine sandwich or grinder in a different part of the country.

In the same way that people from different parts of our country disagree over the "best" names for their favorite food or drink, Christians have different ideas about what to believe and how to act. In this passage, Paul has heard that the Christians in Rome disagree about what to eat (see Rom 14:2) and what days to hold holy (see verse 5). He tells them not to quarrel over these differences. Whatever they do, they should do it "in honor of the Lord" (verse 6). The Church would be shamed if these minor differences became a stumbling block to someone's faith.

The fullness of God's truth exists in a unique way in the Catholic Church, but we respect God's truth where it is found in other Christian Churches. Christians of all denominations should rejoice in their common faith, respect and learn from their differences, and work together "in honor of the Lord."

▶ Rom 14:1–23

R
O
M

brother or sister?[a] For we will all stand before the judgment seat of God.[b] [11]For it is written,

"As I live, says the Lord, every knee shall bow
    to me,
    and every tongue shall give praise to[c] God."
[12]So then, each of us will be accountable to God.[d]

Do Not Make Another Stumble

13 Let us therefore no longer pass judgment on one another, but resolve instead never to put a stumbling block or hindrance in the way of another.[e] [14]I know and am persuaded in the Lord Jesus that nothing is unclean in itself; but it is unclean for anyone who thinks it unclean. [15]If your brother or sister[a] is being injured by what you eat, you are no longer walking in love. Do not let what you eat cause the ruin of one for whom Christ died. [16]So do not let your good be spoken of as evil. [17]For the kingdom of God is not food and drink but righteousness and peace and joy in the Holy Spirit. [18]The one who thus serves Christ is acceptable to God and has human approval. [19]Let us then pursue what makes for peace and for mutual upbuilding. [20]Do not, for the sake of food, destroy the work of God. Everything is indeed clean, but it is wrong for you to make others fall by what you eat; [21]it is good not to eat meat or drink wine or do anything that makes your brother or sister[a] stumble.[f] [22]The faith that you have, have as your own conviction before God. Blessed are those who have no reason to condemn themselves because of what they approve. [23]But those who have doubts are condemned if they eat, because they do not act from faith;[g] for whatever does not proceed from faith[g] is sin.[h]

Please Others, Not Yourselves

15 We who are strong ought to put up with the failings of the weak, and not to please ourselves. [2]Each of us must please our neighbor for the good purpose of building up the neighbor. [3]For Christ did not please himself; but, as it is written, "The insults of those who insult you have fallen on me." [4]For whatever was written in former days was written for our instruction, so that by steadfastness and by the encouragement of the scriptures we might have hope. [5]May the God of steadfastness and encouragement grant you to live in harmony with one another, in accordance with Christ Jesus, [6]so that together you may with one voice glorify the God and Father of our Lord Jesus Christ.

The Gospel for Jews and Gentiles Alike

7 Welcome one another, therefore, just as Christ has welcomed you, for the glory of God.

[8]For I tell you that Christ has become a servant of the circumcised on behalf of the truth of God in order that he might confirm the promises given to the patriarchs, [9]and in order that the Gentiles might glorify God for his mercy. As it is written,

"Therefore I will confess[i] you among the
    Gentiles,
    and sing praises to your name";
[10]and again he says,
"Rejoice, O Gentiles, with his people";
[11]and again,
"Praise the Lord, all you Gentiles,
    and let all the peoples praise him";
[12]and again Isaiah says,
"The root of Jesse shall come,
    the one who rises to rule the Gentiles;
in him the Gentiles shall hope."
[13]May the God of hope fill you with all joy and peace in believing, so that you may abound in hope by the power of the Holy Spirit.

Paul's Reason for Writing So Boldly

14 I myself feel confident about you, my brothers and sisters,[j] that you yourselves are full of goodness, filled with all knowledge, and able to instruct one another. [15]Nevertheless on some points I have written to you rather boldly by way of reminder, because of the grace given me by God [16]to be a minister of Christ Jesus to the Gentiles in the priestly service of the gospel of God, so that the offering of the Gentiles may be acceptable, sanctified by the Holy Spirit. [17]In Christ Jesus, then, I have reason to boast of my work for God. [18]For I will not venture to speak of anything except what Christ has accomplished[k] through me to win obedience from the Gentiles, by word and deed, [19]by the power of signs and wonders, by the power of the Spirit of God,[l] so that from Jerusalem and as far around as Illyricum I have fully proclaimed the good news[m] of Christ. [20]Thus I make it my ambition to proclaim the good news,[m] not where Christ has already been named, so that I do not build on someone else's foundation, [21]but as it is written,

"Those who have never been told of him shall
    see,
    and those who have never heard of him shall
    understand."

---

a Gk brother   b Other ancient authorities read of Christ
c Or confess   d Other ancient authorities lack to God   e Gk of
a brother   f Other ancient authorities add or be upset or be
weakened   g Or conviction   h Other authorities, some ancient,
add here 16.25-27   i Or thank   j Gk brothers   k Gk speak of
those things that Christ has not accomplished   l Other ancient
authorities read of the Spirit or of the Holy Spirit   m Or gospel

Paul's Plan to Visit Rome

22 This is the reason that I have so often been hindered from coming to you. 23But now, with no further place for me in these regions, I desire, as I have for many years, to come to you 24when I go to Spain. For I do hope to see you on my journey and to be sent on by you, once I have enjoyed your company for a little while. 25At present, however, I am going to Jerusalem in a ministry to the saints; 26for Macedonia and Achaia have been pleased to share their resources with the poor among the saints at Jerusalem. 27They were pleased to do this, and indeed they owe it to them; for if the Gentiles have come to share in their spiritual blessings, they ought also to be of service to them in material things. 28So, when I have completed this, and have delivered to them what has been collected,*a* I will set out by way of you to Spain; 29and I know that when I come to you, I will come in the fullness of the blessing*b* of Christ.

30 I appeal to you, brothers and sisters,*c* by our Lord Jesus Christ and by the love of the Spirit, to join me in earnest prayer to God on my behalf, 31that I may be rescued from the unbelievers in Judea, and that my ministry*d* to Jerusalem may be acceptable to the saints, 32so that by God's will I may come to you with joy and be refreshed in your company. 33The God of peace be with all of you.*e* Amen.

Personal Greetings

16 I commend to you our sister Phoebe, a deacon*f* of the church at Cenchreae, 2so that you may welcome her in the Lord as is fitting for the saints, and help her in whatever she may require from you, for she has been a benefactor of many and of myself as well.

3 Greet Prisca and Aquila, who work with me in Christ Jesus, 4and who risked their necks for my life, to whom not only I give thanks, but also all the churches of the Gentiles. 5Greet also the church in their house. Greet my beloved Epaenetus, who was the first convert*g* in Asia for Christ. 6Greet Mary, who has worked very hard among you. 7Greet Andronicus and Junia,*h* my relatives*i* who were in prison with me; they are prominent among the apostles, and they were in Christ before I was. 8Greet Ampliatus, my beloved in the Lord. 9Greet Urbanus, our co-worker in Christ, and my beloved Stachys. 10Greet Apelles, who is approved in Christ. Greet those who belong to the family of Aristobulus. 11Greet my relative*j* Herodion. Greet those in the Lord who belong to the family of Narcissus. 12Greet those workers

in the Lord, Tryphaena and Tryphosa. Greet the beloved Persis, who has worked hard in the Lord. 13Greet Rufus, chosen in the Lord; and greet his mother—a mother to me also. 14Greet Asyncritus, Phlegon, Hermes, Patrobas, Hermas, and the brothers and sisters*c* who are with them. 15Greet Philologus, Julia, Nereus and his sister, and Olympas, and all the saints who are with them. 16Greet one another with a holy kiss. All the churches of Christ greet you.

Final Instructions

17 I urge you, brothers and sisters,*c* to keep an eye on those who cause dissensions and offenses, in opposition to the teaching that you have learned; avoid them. 18For such people do not serve our Lord Christ, but their own appetites,*k*

---

a Gk *have sealed to them this fruit*   *b* Other ancient authorities add *of the gospel*   *c* Gk *brothers*   *d* Other ancient authorities read *my bringing of a gift*   *e* One ancient authority adds 16.25-27 here   *f* Or *minister*   *g* Gk *first fruits*   *h* Or *Junias*; other ancient authorities read *Julia*   *i* Or *compatriots*   *j* Or *compatriot*   *k* Gk *their own belly*

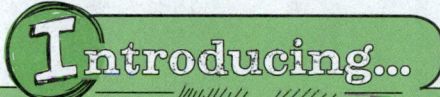

Introducing...

Phoebe and Junia

In Romans 16:1–16, Paul greets almost thirty people and their families in Rome—more people than he greets in any of his other letters. It is thought that perhaps he is trying to establish a connection among the Christians in Rome by mentioning mutual acquaintances. About a third of the people he greets are women, highlighting the important role women played in Paul's ministry and in the leadership of the early Church.

Of particular interest are Paul's comments about Phoebe, whom he calls a deacon, and Junia (also called Julia), whom he declares "prominent among the apostles" (verse 7). In Paul's time, deacons were usually associated with a ministry of service, and apostles with a ministry of leadership. Even though women were not allowed to fill official positions in government or society, the early Church recognized them as being as important as men in service, leadership, and bringing the Gospel to others.

▶ Rom 16:1–16

and by smooth talk and flattery they deceive the hearts of the simple-minded. [19]For while your obedience is known to all, so that I rejoice over you, I want you to be wise in what is good and guileless in what is evil. [20]The God of peace will shortly crush Satan under your feet. The grace of our Lord Jesus Christ be with you.[a]

21 Timothy, my co-worker, greets you; so do Lucius and Jason and Sosipater, my relatives.[b]

22 I Tertius, the writer of this letter, greet you in the Lord.[c]

23 Gaius, who is host to me and to the whole church, greets you. Erastus, the city treasurer, and our brother Quartus, greet you.[d]

Final Doxology

25 Now to God[e] who is able to strengthen you according to my gospel and the proclamation of Jesus Christ, according to the revelation of the mystery that was kept secret for long ages [26]but is now disclosed, and through the prophetic writings is made known to all the Gentiles, according to the command of the eternal God, to bring about the obedience of faith— [27]to the only wise God, through Jesus Christ, to whom[f] be the glory forever! Amen.[g]

---

a Other ancient authorities lack this sentence b Or *compatriots* c Or *I Tertius, writing this letter in the Lord, greet you* d Other ancient authorities add verse 24, *The grace of our Lord Jesus Christ be with all of you. Amen.* e Gk *the one* f Other ancient authorities lack *to whom.* The verse then reads, *to the only wise God be the glory through Jesus Christ forever. Amen.* g Other ancient authorities lack 16.25-27 or include it after 14.23 or 15.33; others put verse 24 after verse 27

Churches have problems. Sometimes parishes harbor power struggles, sex scandals, troubled marriages, bitter disagreements, alcohol abuse, and even disorderly worship. Maybe you know of Christian communities that have had some of these difficulties. The early church in Corinth had them all. In his first letter to the Corinthians, Paul gave them guidance and encouragement. This letter can teach churches in all times to more faithfully follow Christ.

In Depth

Corinth was an important seaport city in what is now southern Greece. It was a center of commerce for people from many cultures. It also had quite a reputation for sexual immorality. Paul established the Christian church there around AD 51 and spent about eighteen months with its converts. After Paul left, a man named Apollos came to help the young church grow.

Later, when Paul was in Ephesus, he got a letter from the Corinthian church (see 1 Cor 7:1) and a report from others about them (see 1:11). The church there was having problems. The problems were natural in a young Christian community whose members included both Jewish Christians and Gentile (non-Jewish) converts. The community was divided into groups with different leaders. There were some disagreements on how to worship properly. And there were different opinions about eating meat that had been sacrificed to pagan idols. In addition, some of the wealthy Christians were ignoring those who were poorer. And those with certain spiritual gifts were claiming to be more important than other people.

In response to all these divisions and various questions, Paul gives the Corinthians good, practical advice. At the same time, he reminds them of what is truly important for Christian believers: the death and Resurrection of Jesus is central to faith; human wisdom is foolish when measured against God's wisdom; others' needs and concerns must always be put before their own; and love should be the primary focus in everything they do and say.

To this divided, confused community, Paul offers a picture of unity: we are all different parts of the same Body of Christ (see 12:12–26). Paul celebrates our diversity and insists on our unity. The advice and teaching he gives in this letter are good for Christians of any time or place to take to heart.

 At a Glance

- **1:1–9.** a greeting and thanks

- **1:10—4:21.** a discussion of divisions in the church and their implications for the Gospel

- **Chapters 5–11.** advice and answers to some questions

- **Chapters 12–14.** an explanation of spiritual gifts and the primacy of love

- **Chapter 15.** Paul's teaching about the resurrection of the body

- **Chapter 16.** Paul's plans and final blessing

⭐ Quick Facts

Inspired Author: Paul
Date Written: AD 56
Audience: the mainly Gentile church at Corinth

The First Letter to the Corinthians

1 Corinthians

Salutation

1 Paul, called to be an apostle of Christ Jesus by the will of God, and our brother Sosthenes,

2 To the church of God that is in Corinth, to those who are sanctified in Christ Jesus, called to be saints, together with all those who in every place call on the name of our Lord Jesus Christ, both their Lord[a] and ours:

3 Grace to you and peace from God our Father and the Lord Jesus Christ.

4 I give thanks to my[b] God always for you because of the grace of God that has been given you in Christ Jesus, [5]for in every way you have been enriched in him, in speech and knowledge of every kind— [6]just as the testimony of[c] Christ has been strengthened among you— [7]so that you are not lacking in any spiritual gift as you wait for the revealing of our Lord Jesus Christ. [8]He will also strengthen you to the end, so that you may be blameless on the day of our Lord Jesus Christ. [9]God is faithful; by him you were called into the fellowship of his Son, Jesus Christ our Lord.

Divisions in the Church

10 Now I appeal to you, brothers and sisters,[d] by the name of our Lord Jesus Christ, that all of you be in agreement and that there be no divisions among you, but that you be united in the same mind and the same purpose. [11]For it has been reported to me by Chloe's people that there are quarrels among you, my brothers and sisters.[e]

[12]What I mean is that each of you says, "I belong to Paul," or "I belong to Apollos," or "I belong to Cephas," or "I belong to Christ." [13]Has Christ been divided? Was Paul crucified for you? Or were you baptized in the name of Paul? [14]I thank God[f] that I baptized none of you except Crispus and Gaius, [15]so that no one can say that you were baptized in my name. [16](I did baptize also the household of Stephanas; beyond that, I do not know whether I baptized anyone else.) [17]For Christ did not send me to baptize but to proclaim the gospel, and not with eloquent wisdom, so that the cross of Christ might not be emptied of its power.

Christ the Power and Wisdom of God

18 For the message about the cross is foolishness to those who are perishing, but to us who are being saved it is the power of God. [19]For it is written,

"I will destroy the wisdom of the wise,
  and the discernment of the discerning I will
    thwart."

[20]Where is the one who is wise? Where is the scribe? Where is the debater of this age? Has not God made foolish the wisdom of the world? [21]For since, in the wisdom of God, the world did not know God through wisdom, God decided, through the foolishness of our proclamation, to save those who believe. [22]For Jews demand signs

---

a Gk *theirs*   *b* Other ancient authorities lack *my*   *c* Or *to*
d Gk *brothers*   *e* Gk *my brothers*   *f* Other ancient authorities
read *I am thankful*

and Greeks desire wisdom, [23]but we proclaim Christ crucified, a stumbling block to Jews and foolishness to Gentiles, [24]but to those who are the called, both Jews and Greeks, Christ the power of God and the wisdom of God. [25]For God's foolishness is wiser than human wisdom, and God's weakness is stronger than human strength.

[26] Consider your own call, brothers and sisters:[a] not many of you were wise by human standards,[b] not many were powerful, not many were of noble birth. [27]But God chose what is foolish in the world to shame the wise; God chose what

is weak in the world to shame the strong; [28]God chose what is low and despised in the world, things that are not, to reduce to nothing things that are, [29]so that no one[c] might boast in the presence of God. [30]He is the source of your life in Christ Jesus, who became for us wisdom from God, and righteousness and sanctification and redemption, [31]in order that, as it is written, "Let the one who boasts, boast in[d] the Lord."

Proclaiming Christ Crucified

2 When I came to you, brothers and sisters,[a] I did not come proclaiming the mystery[e] of God to you in lofty words or wisdom. [2]For I decided to know nothing among you except Jesus Christ, and him crucified. [3]And I came to you in weakness and in fear and in much trembling. [4]My speech and my proclamation were not with plausible words of wisdom,[f] but with a demonstration of the Spirit and of power, [5]so that your faith might rest not on human wisdom but on the power of God.

The True Wisdom of God

[6] Yet among the mature we do speak wisdom, though it is not a wisdom of this age or of the rulers of this age, who are doomed to perish. [7]But we speak God's wisdom, secret and hidden, which God decreed before the ages for our glory. [8]None of the rulers of this age understood this; for if they had, they would not have crucified the Lord of glory. [9]But, as it is written,

"What no eye has seen, nor ear heard,
    nor the human heart conceived,
what God has prepared for those who love
        him"—

[10]these things God has revealed to us through the Spirit; for the Spirit searches everything, even the

Divisions in the Church

At a family reunion to honor his grandfather's eighty-fifth birthday, Tyrone brags about his school's victory over his cousin Martin's school in a recent football game. Martin counters that the referees overlooked a crucial penalty. Before long, the entire gathering is fighting about which team was the best. The birthday party is ruined.

This is similar to what happened to the Christians in Corinth. They were divided over which missionary was the best and which leaders to follow. Paul challenges them to get over this foolish division and focus on the important thing they share—the love of God and their salvation through the cross of Christ.

Christians today continue to struggle with Paul's challenge to be united. Even though the gift of unity has been given to the Church by Christ, the Church is called to work toward that unity by living holy lives, through public and private prayer, and in service to others. Knowing this, we look for those shared beliefs and practices that unite us, while respectfully talking about the sometimes significant differences that exist between different Christian Churches. In this way, all Catholics look to build unity and communion with other Christians.

▶ 1 Cor 1:10–17

---

a Gk *brothers*   b Gk *according to the flesh*   c Gk *no flesh*
d Or *of*   e Other ancient authorities read *testimony*   f Other
ancient authorities read *the persuasiveness of wisdom*

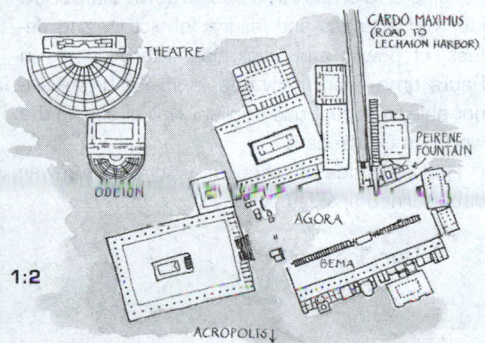

Artist's rendition of city plans for first-century Corinth

depths of God. [11]For what human being knows what is truly human except the human spirit that is within? So also no one comprehends what is truly God's except the Spirit of God. [12]Now we have received not the spirit of the world, but the Spirit that is from God, so that we may understand the gifts bestowed on us by God. [13]And we speak of these things in words not taught by human wisdom but taught by the Spirit, interpreting spiritual things to those who are spiritual.[a]

14 Those who are unspiritual[b] do not receive the gifts of God's Spirit, for they are foolishness to them, and they are unable to understand them because they are spiritually discerned. [15]Those who are spiritual discern all things, and they are themselves subject to no one else's scrutiny.

[16] "For who has known the mind of the Lord
    so as to instruct him?"
But we have the mind of Christ.

On Divisions in the Corinthian Church

3 And so, brothers and sisters,[c] I could not speak to you as spiritual people, but rather as people of the flesh, as infants in Christ. [2]I fed you with milk, not solid food, for you were not ready for solid food. Even now you are still not ready, [3]for you are still of the flesh. For as long as there is jealousy and quarreling among you, are you

---

a Or *interpreting spiritual things in spiritual language,* or *comparing spiritual things with spiritual*   b Or *natural*   c Gk *brothers*

God's Wisdom and Ours

What is the difference between a smart person and a wise person? Many smart people excel in a subject in school or a skill at work. A person has to be very smart to run an illegal drug ring or to make a nuclear bomb. But being smart in these ways does not make a person wise in the ways of God.

Paul reminds the Corinthians that the central Christian message—that Christ was crucified for our salvation—seems foolish to many wise people of their time. The Greeks of this period pride themselves on their wisdom. And the Jews hope for signs of a kingly messiah who will make the nation strong. Both the Jews and the Greeks think the idea of a crucified messiah, or a god who can suffer and die, is foolish.

There is great mystery here: The foolishness of God is wiser than the greatest wisdom of the world. Our ways are not God's ways. Christ's hanging on a cross turns upside down the world's ideas of success and failure, of victory and defeat, of power and weakness. Many people in Paul's time—and many people in our time—are not able to accept this "foolish" way of seeing the world as God sees it.

Has your idea of success, victory, and power been turned upside down by the cross?

▶ 1 Cor 1:18–31

We Are God's Servants, Who Share a Common Mission

Sometimes, Christians engage in destructive competition or are motivated by personal pride. Paul says clearly that all Christians are God's servants, should work together, and should have a common purpose—God's purpose. Whatever we do for the Gospel is part of Jesus' mission and has the same value for God. Paul uses two images to tell us this: "Neither the one who plants nor the one who waters is anything, but only God who gives the growth" (1 Cor 3:7) and "Like a skilled master builder I laid a foundation, and someone else is building on it. . . . For no one can lay any foundation other than the one that has been laid; that foundation is Jesus Christ" (verses 10–11).

● As a young person, how can you work cooperatively with other young people and with the adult community?

● Express your gratitude for the building of the Church done by previous generations of Christians. Pray that young Christians will embrace Jesus' mission with passion and with the global perspective needed at this time in history.

▶ 1 Cor 3:1–15

1
C
O
R

not of the flesh, and behaving according to human inclinations? [4]For when one says, "I belong to Paul," and another, "I belong to Apollos," are you not merely human?

5 What then is Apollos? What is Paul? Servants through whom you came to believe, as the Lord assigned to each. [6]I planted, Apollos watered, but God gave the growth. [7]So neither the one who plants nor the one who waters is anything, but only God who gives the growth. [8]The one who plants and the one who waters

have a common purpose, and each will receive wages according to the labor of each. [9]For we are God's servants, working together; you are God's field, God's building.

10 According to the grace of God given to me, like a skilled master builder I laid a foundation, and someone else is building on it. Each builder must choose with care how to build on it. [11]For no one can lay any foundation other than the one that has been laid; that foundation is Jesus Christ. [12]Now if anyone builds on the foundation with gold, silver, precious stones, wood, hay, straw— [13]the work of each builder will become visible, for the Day will disclose it, because it will be revealed with fire, and the fire will test what sort of work each has done. [14]If what has been built on the foundation survives, the builder will receive a reward. [15]If the work is burned up, the builder will suffer loss; the builder will be saved, but only as through fire.

16 Do you not know that you are God's temple and that God's Spirit dwells in you?[a] [17]If anyone destroys God's temple, God will destroy

---

a In verses 16 and 17 the Greek word for *you* is plural

From the Bottom Up

The most important part of a building is its foundation. If the foundation is built well and with care, what is placed on it will last. And so it is with people. We all have before us a wide variety of construction materials—values, beliefs, and principles—to use in building the foundation of our lives. Initially, our foundation is built through our family, using the values taught in schools and churches. In our adolescent years, most of us discover that other materials are available and that we must choose which ones to add to our foundation.

In 1 Corinthians 3:10–17, Paul tells the people of Corinth that whatever they choose to use in building their foundation will show itself in the end. A poor foundation will lead to a poor end. He also reminds them that they are living temples of God, to be filled with the Holy Spirit. Even though Paul was referring to Christ as the foundation of the Church, each of us as individuals is also called to build our lives on Christ.

In your prayer, reflect or journal on the following questions:

- How is Christ the foundation you build your life on?
- What kind of person do you want to be remembered as when you are gone?
- What qualities, values, and virtues do you want to have? How can these be a sign of the Holy Spirit living within you?

▶ 1 Cor 3:10–17

We Are God's Temple

We are God's temple.
  We are rich, we are poor,
We are young, we are old,
We are male, we are female,
We are disabled, we are sick, we are healthy,
We are unborn,
We are all races and cultures.
O God,
Fill us with your spirit of unity.
Abolish the destructive forces of hate:
  prejudice, racism, physical and verbal abuse,
  abortion, murder, and euthanasia.
Break down the barriers that divide us.
Fill us with your loving spirit and an
appreciation for the value of each and
every life. Amen.

▶ 1 Cor 3:16–17

that person. For God's temple is holy, and you are that temple.

18 Do not deceive yourselves. If you think that you are wise in this age, you should become fools so that you may become wise. [19]For the wisdom of this world is foolishness with God. For it is written,

"He catches the wise in their craftiness,"

[20]and again,

"The Lord knows the thoughts of the wise,
      that they are futile."

[21]So let no one boast about human leaders. For all things are yours, [22]whether Paul or Apollos or Cephas or the world or life or death or the present or the future—all belong to you, [23]and you belong to Christ, and Christ belongs to God.

The Ministry of the Apostles

4 Think of us in this way, as servants of Christ and stewards of God's mysteries. [2]Moreover, it is required of stewards that they be found trustworthy. [3]But with me it is a very small thing that I should be judged by you or by any human court. I do not even judge myself. [4]I am not aware of anything against myself, but I am not thereby acquitted. It is the Lord who judges me. [5]Therefore do not pronounce judgment before the time, before the Lord comes, who will bring to light the things now hidden in darkness and will disclose the purposes of the heart. Then each one will receive commendation from God.

6 I have applied all this to Apollos and myself for your benefit, brothers and sisters,[a] so that you may learn through us the meaning of the saying, "Nothing beyond what is written," so that none of you will be puffed up in favor of one against another. [7]For who sees anything different in you?[b] What do you have that you did not receive? And if you received it, why do you boast as if it were not a gift?

8 Already you have all you want! Already you have become rich! Quite apart from us you have become kings! Indeed, I wish that you had become kings, so that we might be kings with you! [9]For I think that God has exhibited us apostles as last of all, as though sentenced to death, because we have become a spectacle to the world, to angels and to mortals. [10]We are fools for the sake of Christ, but you are wise in Christ. We are weak, but you are strong. You are held in honor, but we are in disrepute. [11]To the present hour we are hungry and thirsty, we are poorly clothed and beaten and homeless, [12]and we grow weary from the work of our own hands. When reviled, we bless; when persecuted, we endure; [13]when slandered, we speak kindly. We have become like the rubbish of the world, the dregs of all things, to this very day.

Fatherly Admonition

14 I am not writing this to make you ashamed, but to admonish you as my beloved children. [15]For though you might have ten thousand guardians in Christ, you do not have many fathers. Indeed, in Christ Jesus I became your father through the gospel. [16]I appeal to you, then, be imitators of me. [17]For this reason I sent[c] you Timothy, who is my beloved and faithful child in the Lord, to remind you of my ways in Christ Jesus, as I teach them everywhere in every church. [18]But some of you, thinking that I am not coming to you, have become arrogant. [19]But I will come to you soon, if the Lord wills, and I will find out not the talk of these arrogant people but their power. [20]For the kingdom of God depends not on talk but on power. [21]What would you prefer? Am I to come to you with a stick, or with love in a spirit of gentleness?

Sexual Immorality Defiles the Church

5 It is actually reported that there is sexual immorality among you, and of a kind that is not found even among pagans; for a man is living with his father's wife. [2]And you are arrogant! Should you not rather have mourned, so that he who has done this would have been removed from among you?

3 For though absent in body, I am present in spirit; and as if present I have already pronounced judgment [4]in the name of the Lord Jesus on the man who has done such a thing.[d] When you are assembled, and my spirit is present with the power of our Lord Jesus, [5]you are to hand this man over to Satan for the destruction of the flesh, so that his spirit may be saved in the day of the Lord.[e]

6 Your boasting is not a good thing. Do you not know that a little yeast leavens the whole batch of dough? [7]Clean out the old yeast so that you may be a new batch, as you really are unleavened. For our paschal lamb, Christ, has been sacrificed. [8]Therefore, let us celebrate the festival, not with the old yeast, the yeast of malice and evil, but with the unleavened bread of sincerity and truth.

Sexual Immorality Must Be Judged

9 I wrote to you in my letter not to associate with sexually immoral persons— [10]not

---

a Gk brothers   b Or Who makes you different from another?
c Or am sending   d Or on the man who has done such a thing in the name of the Lord Jesus   e Other ancient authorities add Jesus

at all meaning the immoral of this world, or the greedy and robbers, or idolaters, since you would then need to go out of the world. ¹¹But now I am writing to you not to associate with anyone who bears the name of brother or sister*a* who is sexually immoral or greedy, or is an idolater, reviler, drunkard, or robber. Do not even eat with such a one. ¹²For what have I to do with judging those outside? Is it not those who are inside that you are to judge? ¹³God will judge those outside. "Drive out the wicked person from among you."

Lawsuits among Believers

6 When any of you has a grievance against another, do you dare to take it to court before the unrighteous, instead of taking it before the saints? ²Do you not know that the saints will judge the world? And if the world is to be judged by you, are you incompetent to try trivial cases? ³Do you not know that we are to judge angels—to say nothing of ordinary matters? ⁴If you have ordinary cases, then, do you appoint as judges those who have no standing in the church? ⁵I say this to your shame. Can it be that there is no one among you wise enough to decide between one believer*a* and another, ⁶but a believer*a* goes to court against a believer*a*—and before unbelievers at that?

7 In fact, to have lawsuits at all with one another is already a defeat for you. Why not rather be wronged? Why not rather be defrauded? ⁸But you yourselves wrong and defraud—and believers*b* at that.

9 Do you not know that wrongdoers will not inherit the kingdom of God? Do not be deceived! Fornicators, idolaters, adulterers, male prostitutes, sodomites, ¹⁰thieves, the greedy, drunkards, revilers, robbers—none of these will inherit the kingdom of God. ¹¹And this is what some of you used to be. But you were washed, you were sanctified, you were justified in the name of the Lord Jesus Christ and in the Spirit of our God.

Glorify God in Body and Spirit

12 "All things are lawful for me," but not all things are beneficial. "All things are lawful for me," but I will not be dominated by anything. ¹³"Food is meant for the stomach and the stomach for food,"*c* and God will destroy both one and the other. The body is meant not for fornication but for the Lord, and the Lord for the body. ¹⁴And God raised the Lord and will also raise us by his power. ¹⁵Do you not know that your bodies are members of Christ? Should

Living Well

Some people think that God or the Christian religion is primarily interested in preventing us from doing fun things. They imagine the Bible as a book of thou-shalt-nots, and the church as a place where they are told to avoid enjoying themselves!

Paul helps us to understand that God's desire is for us to live well. All good gifts from God, including food and sexuality, are meant to be enjoyed to the fullest. But they also can be misused, and if they are, we miss out on the joy and purpose intended by God.

For example, in 1 Corinthians 6:12–20, Paul affirms that sexual intercourse is meant to bond a man and a woman for life. Fornication—sexual intercourse between people who are not married—defeats its true purpose. Fornication diminishes the full joy and beauty of sexual intimacy as intended by God.

God created our sexuality. Our sexual desires—felt keenly during adolescence!—are not sinful but a normal part of being human. As the author of our sexuality, God wants us not to be hurt by this gift but instead to experience its fullness in marriage.

▶ 1 Cor 6:12–20

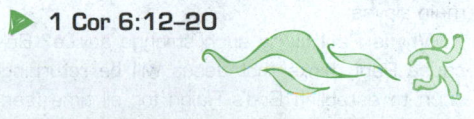

I therefore take the members of Christ and make them members of a prostitute? Never! ¹⁶Do you not know that whoever is united to a prostitute becomes one body with her? For it is said, "The two shall be one flesh." ¹⁷But anyone united to the Lord becomes one spirit with him. ¹⁸Shun fornication! Every sin that a person commits is outside the body; but the fornicator sins against the body itself. ¹⁹Or do you not know that your body is a temple*d* of the Holy Spirit within you, which you have from God, and that you are not your own? ²⁰For you were bought with a price; therefore glorify God in your body.

---

a Gk *brother*   *b* Gk *brothers*   *c* The quotation may extend to the word *other*   *d* Or *sanctuary*

Directions concerning Marriage

7 Now concerning the matters about which you wrote: "It is well for a man not to touch a woman." ²But because of cases of sexual immorality, each man should have his own wife and each woman her own husband. ³The husband should give to his wife her conjugal rights, and likewise the wife to her husband. ⁴For the wife does not have authority over her own body, but the husband does; likewise the husband does not have authority over his own body, but the wife does. ⁵Do not deprive one another except perhaps by agreement for a set time, to devote yourselves to prayer, and then come together again, so that Satan may not tempt you because of your lack of self-control. ⁶This I say by way of concession, not of command. ⁷I wish that all were as I myself am. But each has a particular gift from God, one having one kind and another a different kind.

8 To the unmarried and the widows I say that it is well for them to remain unmarried as I am. ⁹But if they are not practicing self-control, they should marry. For it is better to marry than to be aflame with passion.

10 To the married I give this command—not I but the Lord—that the wife should not separate from her husband ¹¹(but if she does separate, let her remain unmarried or else be reconciled to her husband), and that the husband should not divorce his wife.

12 To the rest I say—I and not the Lord—that if any believer*a* has a wife who is an unbeliever, and she consents to live with him, he should not divorce her. ¹³And if any woman has a husband who is an unbeliever, and he consents to live with her, she should not divorce him. ¹⁴For the unbelieving husband is made holy through his wife, and the unbelieving wife is made holy through her husband. Otherwise, your children would be unclean, but as it is, they are holy. ¹⁵But if the unbelieving partner separates, let it be so; in such a case the brother or sister is not bound. It is to peace that God has called you.*b* ¹⁶Wife, for all you know, you might save your husband. Husband, for all you know, you might save your wife.

The Life that the Lord Has Assigned

17 However that may be, let each of you lead the life that the Lord has assigned, to which God called you. This is my rule in all the churches. ¹⁸Was anyone at the time of his call already circumcised? Let him not seek to remove the marks of circumcision. Was anyone at the time of his call uncircumcised? Let him not seek circumcision. ¹⁹Circumcision is nothing, and uncircumcision is nothing; but obeying the commandments of God is everything. ²⁰Let each of you remain in the condition in which you were called.

21 Were you a slave when called? Do not be concerned about it. Even if you can gain your freedom, make use of your present condition now more than ever.*c* ²²For whoever was called in the Lord as a slave is a freed person belonging to the Lord, just as whoever was free when called is a slave of Christ. ²³You were bought with a price; do not become slaves of human masters. ²⁴In whatever condition you were called, brothers and sisters,*d* there remain with God.

The Unmarried and the Widows

25 Now concerning virgins, I have no command of the Lord, but I give my opinion as one

---

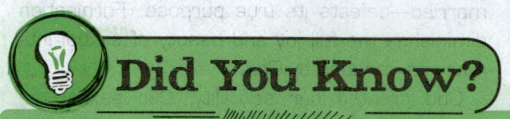

Did You Know?

Strange Advice!?

First Corinthians, chapter 7, says people shouldn't marry, uncircumcised people shouldn't get circumcised, and slaves should remain slaves.

Why is Paul giving such strange advice? Because Paul thinks that Jesus will be returning soon to establish God's Reign for all time (see verse 31). So he advises the Corinthians to remain in whatever condition they were called, in order to keep their focus on preparing for Christ's return, rather than be distracted with other cares.

But Jesus didn't come back during Paul's time. In fact, we are still waiting for his return. When is Jesus going to come again? Don't try to figure it out. Jesus told us we will never know (see Mt 24:36–44). But whatever our state of life is, or will become, we would be wise to follow Paul's intent "to promote good order and unhindered devotion to the Lord" (1 Cor 7:35).

▶ **1 Corinthians, chapter 7**

---

a Gk *brother*   *b* Other ancient authorities read *us*   *c* Or *avail yourself of the opportunity*   *d* Gk *brothers*

who by the Lord's mercy is trustworthy. [26] I think that, in view of the impending[a] crisis, it is well for you to remain as you are. [27] Are you bound to a wife? Do not seek to be free. Are you free from a wife? Do not seek a wife. [28] But if you marry, you do not sin, and if a virgin marries, she does not sin. Yet those who marry will experience distress in this life,[b] and I would spare you that. [29] I mean, brothers and sisters,[c] the appointed time has grown short; from now on, let even those who have wives be as though they had none, [30] and those who mourn as though they were not mourning, and those who rejoice as though they were not rejoicing, and those who buy as though they had no possessions, [31] and those who deal with the world as though they had no dealings with it. For the present form of this world is passing away.

32 I want you to be free from anxieties. The unmarried man is anxious about the affairs of the Lord, how to please the Lord; [33] but the married man is anxious about the affairs of the world, how to please his wife, [34] and his interests are divided. And the unmarried woman and the virgin are anxious about the affairs of the Lord, so that they may be holy in body and spirit; but the married woman is anxious about the affairs of the world, how to please her husband. [35] I say this for your own benefit, not to put any restraint upon you, but to promote good order and unhindered devotion to the Lord.

36 If anyone thinks that he is not behaving properly toward his fiancée,[d] if his passions are strong, and so it has to be, let him marry as he wishes; it is no sin. Let them marry. [37] But if someone stands firm in his resolve, being under no necessity but having his own desire under control, and has determined in his own mind to keep her as his fiancée,[d] he will do well. [38] So then, he who marries his fiancée[d] does well; and he who refrains from marriage will do better.

39 A wife is bound as long as her husband lives. But if the husband dies,[e] she is free to marry anyone she wishes, only in the Lord. [40] But in my judgment she is more blessed if she remains as she is. And I think that I too have the Spirit of God.

Food Offered to Idols

8 Now concerning food sacrificed to idols, we know that "all of us possess knowledge." Knowledge puffs up, but love builds up. [2] Anyone who claims to know something does not yet have the necessary knowledge; [3] but anyone who loves God is known by him.

4 Hence, as to the eating of food offered to

Live It!

Restrain Your Ego!

Maria's parents have stopped drinking alcohol. Not that they ever drank to excess. But for months, Maria bugged them, saying, "If I can't drink, then why do you?" Because she accepted none of their arguments, they agreed that they would stop until she reached legal age.

Crazy? Not according to Paul. He recommends something similar. Paul recognizes that it is not necessarily wrong for some members of the community of Christians in Corinth to eat meat sacrificed to idols, or pagan gods, because they don't believe in those gods. Still, he recommends that they not do it, because some members of the community find it upsetting. For Paul, paying attention to the welfare of everyone in the community is more important than always "being right."

Do you ever do things that aren't necessarily wrong just because it's your right? like whistle around a sibling who cannot stand it? or pick a sweater for the family picture that doesn't match anyone else's? or, when your younger brothers and sisters are around, watch a television show that's okay for you but not for them? When you find yourself doing something like this, think about Paul's advice. Are you making your ego more important than other people's feelings?

▶ **1 Cor 8:1–13**

idols, we know that "no idol in the world really exists," and that "there is no God but one." [5] Indeed, even though there may be so-called gods in heaven or on earth—as in fact there are many gods and many lords— [6] yet for us there is one God, the Father, from whom are all things and for whom we exist, and one Lord, Jesus Christ, through whom are all things and through whom we exist.

7 It is not everyone, however, who has this knowledge. Since some have become so

---

a Or present   b Gk in the flesh   c Gk brothers   d Gk virgin
e Gk falls asleep

accustomed to idols until now, they still think of the food they eat as food offered to an idol; and their conscience, being weak, is defiled. 8"Food will not bring us close to God."*a* We are no worse off if we do not eat, and no better off if we do. 9But take care that this liberty of yours does not somehow become a stumbling block to the weak. 10For if others see you, who possess knowledge, eating in the temple of an idol, might they not, since their conscience is weak, be encouraged to the point of eating food sacrificed to idols? 11So by your knowledge those weak believers for whom Christ died are destroyed.*b* 12But when you thus sin against members of your family,*c* and wound their conscience when it is weak, you sin against Christ. 13Therefore, if food is a cause of their falling,*d* I will never eat meat, so that I may not cause one of them*e* to fall.

The Rights of an Apostle

9 Am I not free? Am I not an apostle? Have I not seen Jesus our Lord? Are you not my work in the Lord? 2If I am not an apostle to

Spiritual Perseverance

Did you know that Michael Jordan—once the points leader of the record-setting Chicago Bulls—had difficulty making his high school varsity basketball team the first year he tried out? He could have quit trying, but he set a goal for himself and made practicing a priority for his daily life. Not only did he finally make the team, he broke state scoring records and was named all-state. And that was just the beginning!

Perseverance means setting priorities, sticking to them even when you get discouraged, and trying over and over to accomplish your goals. For the next six months, set yourself a goal that will help you to grow closer to God. What will you have to do to accomplish it? What priorities must you establish? As 1 Corinthians 9:24–27 says, run your race by staying focused on your goal!

▶ 1 Cor 9:24–27

others, at least I am to you; for you are the seal of my apostleship in the Lord.

3 This is my defense to those who would examine me. 4Do we not have the right to our food and drink? 5Do we not have the right to be accompanied by a believing wife,*f* as do the other apostles and the brothers of the Lord and Cephas? 6Or is it only Barnabas and I who have no right to refrain from working for a living? 7Who at any time pays the expenses for doing military service? Who plants a vineyard and does not eat any of its fruit? Or who tends a flock and does not get any of its milk?

8 Do I say this on human authority? Does not the law also say the same? 9For it is written in the law of Moses, "You shall not muzzle an ox while it is treading out the grain." Is it for oxen that God is concerned? 10Or does he not speak entirely for our sake? It was indeed written for our sake, for whoever plows should plow in hope and whoever threshes should thresh in hope of a share in the crop. 11If we have sown spiritual good among you, is it too much if we reap your material benefits? 12If others share this rightful claim on you, do not we still more?

Nevertheless, we have not made use of this right, but we endure anything rather than put an obstacle in the way of the gospel of Christ. 13Do you not know that those who are employed in the temple service get their food from the temple, and those who serve at the altar share in what is sacrificed on the altar? 14In the same way, the Lord commanded that those who proclaim the gospel should get their living by the gospel.

15 But I have made no use of any of these rights, nor am I writing this so that they may be applied in my case. Indeed, I would rather die than that—no one will deprive me of my ground for boasting! 16If I proclaim the gospel, this gives me no ground for boasting, for an obligation is laid on me, and woe to me if I do not proclaim the gospel! 17For if I do this of my own will, I have a reward; but if not of my own will, I am entrusted with a commission. 18What then is my reward? Just this: that in my proclamation I may make the gospel free of charge, so as not to make full use of my rights in the gospel.

19 For though I am free with respect to all, I have made myself a slave to all, so that I might win more of them. 20To the Jews I became as a Jew, in order to win Jews. To those under the law I became as one under the law (though I myself

---

a The quotation may extend to the end of the verse   *b* Gk *the weak brother . . . is destroyed*   *c* Gk *against the brothers*
d Gk *my brother's falling*   *e* Gk *cause my brother*   *f* Gk *a sister as wife*

am not under the law) so that I might win those under the law. ²¹To those outside the law I became as one outside the law (though I am not free from God's law but am under Christ's law) so that I might win those outside the law. ²²To the weak I became weak, so that I might win the weak. I have become all things to all people, that I might by all means save some. ²³I do it all for the sake of the gospel, so that I may share in its blessings.

24 Do you not know that in a race the runners all compete, but only one receives the prize? Run in such a way that you may win it. ²⁵Athletes exercise self-control in all things; they do it to receive a perishable wreath, but we an imperishable one. ²⁶So I do not run aimlessly, nor do I box as though beating the air; ²⁷but I punish my body and enslave it, so that after proclaiming to others I myself should not be disqualified.

Warnings from Israel's History

10 I do not want you to be unaware, brothers and sisters,[a] that our ancestors were all under the cloud, and all passed through the sea, ²and all were baptized into Moses in the cloud and in the sea, ³and all ate the same spiritual food, ⁴and all drank the same spiritual drink. For they drank from the spiritual rock that followed them, and the rock was Christ. ⁵Nevertheless, God was not pleased with most of them, and they were struck down in the wilderness.

6 Now these things occurred as examples for us, so that we might not desire evil as they did. ⁷Do not become idolaters as some of them did; as it is written, "The people sat down to eat and drink, and they rose up to play." ⁸We must not indulge in sexual immorality as some of them did, and twenty-three thousand fell in a single day. ⁹We must not put Christ[b] to the test, as some of them did, and were destroyed by serpents. ¹⁰And do not complain as some of them did, and were destroyed by the destroyer. ¹¹These things happened to them to serve as an example, and they were written down to instruct us, on whom the ends of the ages have come. ¹²So if you think you are standing, watch out that you do not fall. ¹³No testing has overtaken you that is not common to everyone. God is faithful, and he will not let you be tested beyond your strength, but with the testing he will also provide the way out so that you may be able to endure it.

14 Therefore, my dear friends,[c] flee from the worship of idols. ¹⁵I speak as to sensible people; judge for yourselves what I say. ¹⁶The cup of blessing that we bless, is it not a sharing in the blood of Christ? The bread that we break, is it not

Live It!

Addictive Behavior

How do you spend the bulk of your free time? Talking with your friends on the phone? playing video games? listening to your favorite music? If you discover that you have become obsessed with a particular activity, maybe it has become addictive. Although perhaps your obsession is not a true addiction—like those caused by drugs, alcohol, gambling, or eating disorders—it still might have more control over your life than it should have.

Paul reminds the Corinthians that they should put God at the center of their lives. He points out that they will always be tempted to replace God with something else—which is called idolatry— like the ancient Israelites were tempted. Paul is also introducing his teaching on participation in the Eucharist as a way of turning one's back on this old way of life and committing oneself to a new way of life.

How about us today? We may not worship foreign gods or eat meat sacrificed to idols. But in many ways, our addictive behaviors are like idolatry. They consume our thoughts and time and can even lead us away from God.

Addictive behaviors are hard to break. And true addictions are very difficult to control. But you have the promise that God "will not let you be tested beyond your strength" (1 Cor 10:13). If you think you may have an addiction, talk to a parent or school counselor or minister. Participating in the Eucharist is also a good way to express your desire to live the life God is calling you to.

▶ **1 Cor 10:6–14**

a sharing in the body of Christ? ¹⁷Because there is one bread, we who are many are one body, for we all partake of the one bread. ¹⁸Consider the people of Israel;[d] are not those who eat the sacrifices partners in the altar? ¹⁹What do I imply

---

a Gk *brothers*   b Other ancient authorities read *the Lord*
c Gk *my beloved*   d Gk *Israel according to the flesh*

Cultural Connection

Food and Gratitude

Have you ever considered eating and drinking for the glory of God? Paul tells the Corinthians that it is more important to respect the conscience of their dining partners than to worry about where the meat came from. By appreciating what they have been given to eat, they show respect for the people who have prepared the food.

Native Americans have that same sense of appreciation—not just for the people they share meals with but for the animals and plants that provide the food. When they kill an animal to eat, they pray to its spirit for forgiveness. Everything from the animal is put to good use, because wasting any part of it would be an insult to its honor.

This Native American meal blessing is an expression of thanks:

Now that I am about to eat, O great Spirit, give my thanks to the beasts and birds whom You have provided for my hunger, and pray deliver my sorrow that living things must make a sacrifice for my comfort and well-being. Let the feather of corn spring up in its time and let it not wither but make full grains for the fires of our cooking pots, now that I am about to eat.

▶ **1 Cor 10:23–33**

---

then? That food sacrificed to idols is anything, or that an idol is anything? 20No, I imply that what pagans sacrifice, they sacrifice to demons and not to God. I do not want you to be partners with demons. 21You cannot drink the cup of the Lord and the cup of demons. You cannot partake of the table of the Lord and the table of demons. 22Or are we provoking the Lord to jealousy? Are we stronger than he?

Do All to the Glory of God

23 "All things are lawful," but not all things are beneficial. "All things are lawful," but not all things build up. 24Do not seek your own advantage, but that of the other. 25Eat whatever is sold in the meat market without raising any question on the ground of conscience, 26for "the earth and its fullness are the Lord's." 27If an unbeliever invites you to a meal and you are disposed to go, eat whatever is set before you without raising any question on the ground of conscience. 28But if someone says to you, "This has been offered in sacrifice," then do not eat it, out of consideration for the one who informed you, and for the sake of conscience— 29I mean the other's conscience, not your own. For why should my liberty be subject to the judgment of someone else's conscience? 30If I partake with thankfulness, why should I be denounced because of that for which I give thanks?

> "Do everything for the glory of God."
>
> (1 Cor 10:31)

31 So, whether you eat or drink, or whatever you do, do everything for the glory of God. 32Give no offense to Jews or to Greeks or to the church of God, 33just as I try to please everyone in everything I do, not seeking my own advantage, but that of many, so that they may be saved. 1Be imitators of me, as I am of Christ.

Head Coverings

2 I commend you because you remember me in everything and maintain the traditions just as I handed them on to you. 3But I want you to understand that Christ is the head of every man, and the husband*a* is the head of his wife,*b* and God is the head of Christ. 4Any man who prays or prophesies with something on his head disgraces his head, 5but any woman who prays or prophesies with her head unveiled disgraces her head—it is one and the same thing as having her head shaved. 6For if a woman will not veil herself, then she should cut off her hair; but if it is disgraceful for a woman to have her hair cut off or to be shaved, she should wear a veil. 7For a man ought not to have his head veiled, since he is the image and reflection*c* of God; but woman is the reflection*c* of man. 8Indeed, man was not made from woman, but

a The same Greek word means man or husband   b Or head of the woman   c Or glory

Cultural Connection

In China and Singapore, when people meet up with friends, they ask whether the friends have eaten a meal yet. This custom dates back to the great famine of China in the 1950s, when there was so little food that people were starving and a friend's last meal might have been a day or two ago. So whatever food someone had, he or she shared it with friends. Such generosity is truly a sign of God's love and justice.

Paul had to remind the Corinthians about God's love and justice when they gathered in their homes to talk about their faith, share a meal, and celebrate the Eucharist. In 1 Corinthians 11:17–22, Paul tells the Corinthians that when the wealthy humiliate the poor by not allowing them to share equally in the meal, they are abusing the purpose of the Lord's Supper. To celebrate the Lord's Supper is to partake in the Body and Blood of Christ, and it is impossible to do this if they do not live out the values of Christ.

In your prayer, journal or reflect on the following questions:
● What might Paul say to your church community if he sat with you during Sunday Mass?
● How do you share with people who have little or nothing?
● What can you do in your community so that the celebration of the Lord's Supper is more truly a sign of generosity, justice, and love?

▶ **1 Cor 11:17–33**

---

woman from man. ⁹Neither was man created for the sake of woman, but woman for the sake of man. ¹⁰For this reason a woman ought to have a symbol of[a] authority on her head,[b] because of the angels. ¹¹Nevertheless, in the Lord woman is not independent of man or man independent of woman. ¹²For just as woman came from man, so man comes through woman; but all things come from God. ¹³Judge for yourselves: is it proper for a woman to pray to God with her head unveiled? ¹⁴Does not nature itself teach you that if a man wears long hair, it is degrading to him, ¹⁵but if a woman has long hair, it is her glory? For her hair is given to her for a covering. ¹⁶But if anyone is disposed to be contentious—we have no such custom, nor do the churches of God.

Abuses at the Lord's Supper

17 Now in the following instructions I do not commend you, because when you come together it is not for the better but for the worse. ¹⁸For, to begin with, when you come together as a church, I hear that there are divisions among you; and to some extent I believe it. ¹⁹Indeed, there have to be factions among you, for only so will it become clear who among you are genuine. ²⁰When you come together, it is not really to eat the Lord's supper. ²¹For when the time comes to eat, each of you goes ahead with your own supper, and one goes hungry and another becomes drunk. ²²What! Do you not have homes to eat and drink in? Or do you show contempt for the church of God and humiliate those who have nothing? What should I say to you? Should I commend you? In this matter I do not commend you!

The Institution of the Lord's Supper

23 For I received from the Lord what I also handed on to you, that the Lord Jesus on the night when he was betrayed took a loaf of bread, ²⁴and when he had given thanks, he broke it and said, "This is my body that is for[c] you. Do this in remembrance of me." ²⁵In the same way he took the cup also, after supper, saying, "This cup is the new covenant in my blood. Do this, as often as you drink it, in remembrance of me." ²⁶For as often as you eat this bread and drink the cup, you proclaim the Lord's death until he comes.

Partaking of the Supper Unworthily

27 Whoever, therefore, eats the bread or drinks the cup of the Lord in an unworthy manner will be answerable for the body and blood of the Lord. ²⁸Examine yourselves, and only then eat of the bread and drink of the cup, ²⁹For all who eat and drink[d] without discerning the body,[e] eat and drink judgment against themselves. ³⁰For

---

a Gk lacks a symbol of　b Or have freedom of choice regarding her head　c Other ancient authorities read is broken for
d Other ancient authorities add in an unworthy manner,　e Other ancient authorities read the Lord's body

1
C
O
R

✚ Catholic Connection

Real Presence

If Jesus were standing in the room, would you be acting any differently? Paul could have posed this question to the Church in Corinth. In his letter, Paul scolds the people for getting drunk while letting others continue to starve, all during the celebration of the Lord's Supper! The Corinthians had forgotten that Jesus Christ is really present during the Eucharistic celebration.

The Church teaches that Christ is present in various ways every time we celebrate the Mass. Christ is present in the word when it is proclaimed, in the assembly gathered, in the priest who is presiding, and, most important, in the consecrated bread and wine.

The Church teaches that Christ, his soul and divinity, is truly and completely present in the Eucharist. We call this "real presence." Through the power of Christ's words from the Last Supper and the workings of the Holy Spirit, the bread and wine become the Body and Blood of Christ. They may look and taste like bread and wine, but in substance they have been changed into Christ's Body and Blood. The Church calls this *transubstantiation.* The Church also teaches that Christ's Body cannot be divided and is therefore fully present in both the bread and the wine, even in the smallest crumb or drop of the Eucharist!

Through Christ's real presence in the Eucharist, we are able to celebrate and renew the new and everlasting covenant that Christ established with the sacrifice of his own Body and Blood. By celebrating the Eucharist, we as a community and as individuals are transformed to love others as Christ has loved us. So next time you are at Mass, reflect on the many ways Christ is making himself present to you and give thanks for the gift of his real presence that he is offering to you in the Eucharist. Then go forth to be Christ's presence in the world.

▶ **1 Cor 11:23–26**
Catechism, nos. 1373–1377

Cultural Connection

The Body of Christ

As Christians we are called to work together within the Body of Christ. Read 1 Corinthians 12:12–31. Here Paul says that God has given us different gifts.

A long time ago, Booker T. Washington realized that everyone can make a contribution to the world, regardless of his or her status or possessions. He wrote, "No race can prosper till it learns that there is as much dignity in tilling a field as in writing a poem." This is the Kwanzaa principle of *umoja,* or unity [see "Kwanzaa as a Way of Life," near Deut 10:12–22].

Paul proclaims that each part of the Body of Christ—not only each person, but each diverse culture and race—is needed for the Church to function properly. Many look at the most visible people in the Church and conclude that they are more important than others. Remember that God sees differently. Often, important things are done by quiet people with little fanfare, but God always notices.

Can you focus on the success of the whole rather than on what you have or do not have?

Dear God, free me from excessive worry about what someone else has or is able to do. Place my mind on unity and community. Amen.

▶ 1 Cor 12:12–31

---

this reason many of you are weak and ill, and some have died.*a* 31But if we judged ourselves, we would not be judged. 32But when we are judged by the Lord, we are disciplined*b* so that we may not be condemned along with the world.

33 So then, my brothers and sisters,*c* when you come together to eat, wait for one another. 34If you are hungry, eat at home, so that when you come together, it will not be for your condemnation. About the other things I will give instructions when I come.

Spiritual Gifts

12 Now concerning spiritual gifts,*d* brothers and sisters,*c* I do not want you to be uninformed. 2You know that when you were pagans, you were enticed and led astray to idols that could not speak. 3Therefore I want you to understand that no one speaking by the Spirit of God ever says "Let Jesus be cursed!" and no one can say "Jesus is Lord" except by the Holy Spirit.

4 Now there are varieties of gifts, but the same Spirit; 5and there are varieties of services, but the same Lord; 6and there are varieties of activities, but it is the same God who activates all of them in everyone. 7To each is given the manifestation of the Spirit for the common good. 8To one is given through the Spirit the utterance of wisdom, and to another the utterance of knowledge according to the same Spirit, 9to another faith by the same Spirit, to another gifts of healing by the one Spirit, 10to another the working of miracles, to another prophecy, to another the discernment of spirits, to another various kinds of tongues, to another the interpretation of tongues. 11All these are activated by one and the same Spirit, who allots to each one individually just as the Spirit chooses.

One Body with Many Members

12 For just as the body is one and has many members, and all the members of the body, though many, are one body, so it is with Christ. 13For in the one Spirit we were all baptized into one body—Jews or Greeks, slaves or free—and we were all made to drink of one Spirit.

14 Indeed, the body does not consist of one member but of many. 15If the foot would say, "Because I am not a hand, I do not belong to the body," that would not make it any less a part of the body. 16And if the ear would say, "Because I am not an eye, I do not belong to the body," that would not make it any less a part of the body. 17If the whole body were an eye, where would the hearing be? If the whole body were hearing, where would the sense of smell be? 18But as it is, God arranged the members in the body, each one of them, as he chose. 19If all were a single member, where would the body be? 20As it is, there are many members, yet one body. 21The eye cannot say to the hand, "I have no need of you," nor again the head to the feet, "I have no need

---

a Gk *fallen asleep*   *b* Or *When we are judged, we are being disciplined by the Lord*   *c* Gk *brothers*   *d* Or *spiritual persons*

1 COR

of you." 22On the contrary, the members of the body that seem to be weaker are indispensable, 23and those members of the body that we think less honorable we clothe with greater honor, and our less respectable members are treated with greater respect; 24whereas our more respectable members do not need this. But God has so arranged the body, giving the greater honor to the inferior member, 25that there may be no dissension within the body, but the members may have the same care for one another. 26If one member suffers, all suffer together with it; if one member is honored, all rejoice together with it.

27 Now you are the body of Christ and individually members of it. 28And God has

appointed in the church first apostles, second prophets, third teachers; then deeds of power, then gifts of healing, forms of assistance, forms of leadership, various kinds of tongues. 29Are all apostles? Are all prophets? Are all teachers? Do all work miracles? 30Do all possess gifts of healing? Do all speak in tongues? Do all interpret? 31But strive for the greater gifts. And I will show you a still more excellent way.

The Gift of Love

13 If I speak in the tongues of mortals and of angels, but do not have love, I am a noisy gong or a clanging cymbal. 2And if I have prophetic powers, and understand all mysteries and all knowledge, and if I have all faith, so as to remove mountains, but do not have love, I am nothing. 3If I give away all my possessions, and if I hand over my body so that I may boast,*a* but do not have love, I gain nothing.

4 Love is patient; love is kind; love is not envious or boastful or arrogant 5or rude. It does not insist on its own way; it is not irritable or resentful; 6it does not rejoice in wrongdoing, but rejoices in the truth. 7It bears all things, believes all things, hopes all things, endures all things.

8 Love never ends. But as for prophecies, they will come to an end; as for tongues, they will cease; as for knowledge, it will come to an end. 9For we know only in part, and we prophesy only in part; 10but when the complete comes, the partial will come to an end. 11When I was a child, I spoke like a child, I thought like a child, I reasoned like a child; when I became an adult, I put an end to childish ways. 12For now we see in a mirror, dimly,*b* but then we will see face to face. Now I know only in part; then I will know fully, even as I have been fully known. 13And now faith, hope, and love abide, these three; and the greatest of these is love.

Gifts of Prophecy and Tongues

14 Pursue love and strive for the spiritual gifts, and especially that you may prophesy. 2For those who speak in a tongue do not speak to other people but to God; for nobody understands them, since they are speaking mysteries in the Spirit. 3On the other hand, those who prophesy speak to other people for their upbuilding and encouragement and consolation. 4Those who speak in a tongue build up themselves, but those who prophesy build up the church. 5Now I would like all of you to speak in

Pray It!

Loving Others

Read 1 Corinthians 13:1–13. It is a beautiful description of the spiritual gift Paul wants the Christian community to strive for—love. You may want to reflect in your journal upon some experiences you have had with the kind of love Paul speaks about:

- When have you seen a love that is patient and kind, and is not boastful or arrogant or resentful?
- Consider people you know who share their love in this way and imagine how you might grow to love others as Jesus loved us.

Often this passage is read at weddings as a model for the new couple and how they might love each other, but we are all invited to stretch in our capacity to love. Love is much more complicated and expansive than the kind of romantic love we most often hear about.

Dear Lord, help me to recognize the people in my life who share their love with me as you call us to do. Please help me to grow in my understanding of the fullness of love so that I may express this love to my family and friends, and most especially to those who I often find most difficult to love. Amen.

▶ **1 Corinthians, chapter 13**

a Other ancient authorities read *body to be burned*   b Gk *in a riddle*

tongues, but even more to prophesy. One who prophesies is greater than one who speaks in tongues, unless someone interprets, so that the church may be built up.

6 Now, brothers and sisters,[a] if I come to you speaking in tongues, how will I benefit you unless I speak to you in some revelation or knowledge or prophecy or teaching? [7]It is the same way with lifeless instruments that produce sound, such as the flute or the harp. If they do not give distinct notes, how will anyone know what is being played? [8]And if the bugle gives an indistinct sound, who will get ready for battle? [9]So with yourselves; if in a tongue you utter speech that is not intelligible, how will anyone know what is being said? For you will be speaking into the air. [10]There are doubtless many different kinds of sounds in the world, and nothing is without sound. [11]If then I do not know the meaning of a sound, I will be a foreigner to the speaker and the speaker a foreigner to me. [12]So with yourselves; since you are eager for spiritual gifts, strive to excel in them for building up the church.

13 Therefore, one who speaks in a tongue should pray for the power to interpret. [14]For if I pray in a tongue, my spirit prays but my mind is unproductive. [15]What should I do then? I will pray with the spirit, but I will pray with the mind also; I will sing praise with the spirit, but I will sing praise with the mind also. [16]Otherwise, if you say a blessing with the spirit, how can anyone in the position of an outsider say the "Amen" to your thanksgiving, since the outsider does not know what you are saying? [17]For you may give thanks well enough, but the other person is not built up. [18]I thank God that I speak in tongues more than all of you; [19]nevertheless, in church I would rather speak five words with my mind, in order to instruct others also, than ten thousand words in a tongue.

20 Brothers and sisters,[a] do not be children in your thinking; rather, be infants in evil, but in thinking be adults. [21]In the law it is written,

"By people of strange tongues
   and by the lips of foreigners
I will speak to this people;
   yet even then they will not listen to me,"

says the Lord. [22]Tongues, then, are a sign not for believers but for unbelievers, while prophecy is not for unbelievers but for believers. [23]If, therefore, the whole church comes together and all speak in tongues, and outsiders or unbelievers enter, will they not say that you are out of your mind? [24]But if all prophesy, an unbeliever or outsider who enters is reproved by all and called to account by all. [25]After the secrets of the

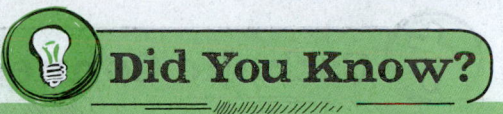

Did You Know?

God's Love

Greek, the language of the New Testament, has several words for love. There are words for parental love, romantic love, and love between friends or relatives. The Greek word Paul uses in 1 Corinthians, chapter 13—*agape*—is reserved for a special kind of love.

Agape (ah-GAH-pay) is love without conditions or motivations. It is there no matter who you are or what you do. It willingly chooses to serve without expectation of service in return. The Bible tells us that God is *agape* (see 1 Jn 4:16). The source of *agape* is the unconditional love of God. God's *agape* is revealed to us in Jesus Christ. Through the Holy Spirit, we become a channel for communicating this wonderful love to others.

We are created in God's image. God wants us to love one another with the *agape* that Paul describes in chapter 13. It's a wonderful challenge!

 1 Corinthians, chapter 13

unbeliever's heart are disclosed, that person will bow down before God and worship him, declaring, "God is really among you."

Orderly Worship

26 What should be done then, my friends?[a] When you come together, each one has a hymn, a lesson, a revelation, a tongue, or an interpretation. Let all things be done for building up. [27]If anyone speaks in a tongue, let there be only two or at most three, and each in turn; and let one interpret. [28]But if there is no one to interpret, let them be silent in church and speak to themselves and to God. [29]Let two or three prophets speak, and let the others weigh what is said. [30]If a revelation is made to someone else sitting nearby, let the first person be silent. [31]For you can all prophesy one by one, so that all may learn and all be encouraged. [32]And the spirits of prophets are subject to the prophets, [33]for God is a God not of disorder but of peace.

a Gk brothers

✝ Catholic Connection

The Theological Virtues

Have you ever witnessed one group of students putting down another group of students for some reason? Well, Paul was addressing a similar problem in his Letter to the Corinthians. People in the community were claiming that their particular spiritual gift made them superior to others in the community. Paul challenges the Corinthians to be unified as one community and to respect their diversity of gifts. To put it all in perspective, Paul calls them to seek something even greater: faith, hope, and love.

Together faith, hope, and love (also called charity) are what the Church calls theological virtues. These virtues are attitudes or habits that direct our hearts and minds toward God and strengthen our relationship with God. They help open our hearts to living according to God's will and serve as a basis for all our actions. Ultimately, they help us to live as children of God.

Faith. Faith is the virtue that helps us to believe in God and all that God has revealed. Through faith we give over our lives to God and actively seek to do God's will. For our faith to be truly alive, it must be evident in the love we show others and in the good works we do. We are called to not only have and live faith but also to confidently share our faith in God with others.

Hope. Hope is the virtue that helps us to keep our hearts and minds focused on the goal, eternal life with God in heaven. Through hope our actions take on a new direction and purpose, namely building up the Reign of God. By placing our hope in God's plan for our lives, our daily struggles and sufferings take on new meaning. Hope gives us the strength to endure what previously seemed impossible. Jesus' teachings on the Beatitudes and the Lord's Prayer express the fullness of what is hoped for.

Love (charity). Paul leaves no doubt that love is the most important of the theological virtues. Love is the virtue that helps us to fulfill the two greatest commandments: to love God with our whole heart and to love others as we love ourselves. Jesus showed us just how much God loves us not only by his words and deeds but also by his dying for us despite our sinfulness. Jesus calls us to love God and one another with the same limitless love.

All three of these virtues are essential to our lives in Christ but, as Paul points out, without love everything else is worth nothing.

- Where in your life is God calling you to: put your faith into action? be filled with hope? love others as God has loved you?

▶ **1 Cor 13:13**
Catechism, nos. 1812–1841

1 COR

(As in all the churches of the saints, 34women should be silent in the churches. For they are not permitted to speak, but should be subordinate, as the law also says. 35If there is anything they desire to know, let them ask their husbands at home. For it is shameful for a woman to speak in church.a 36Or did the word of God originate with you? Or are you the only ones it has reached?)

37 Anyone who claims to be a prophet, or to have spiritual powers, must acknowledge that what I am writing to you is a command of the Lord. 38Anyone who does not recognize this is not to be recognized. 39So, my friends,b be eager to prophesy, and do not forbid speaking in tongues; 40but all things should be done decently and in order.

The Resurrection of Christ

15 Now I would remind you, brothers and sisters,c of the good newsd that I proclaimed to you, which you in turn received, in which also you stand, 2through which also you are being saved, if you hold firmly to the message that I proclaimed to you—unless you have come to believe in vain.

3 For I handed on to you as of first importance what I in turn had received: that Christ died for our sins in accordance with the scriptures, 4and that he was buried, and that he was raised on the third day in accordance with the scriptures, 5and that he appeared to Cephas, then to the twelve. 6Then he appeared to more than five hundred brothers and sistersc at one time, most of whom are still alive, though some have died.e 7Then he appeared to James, then to all the apostles. 8Last of all, as to one untimely born, he appeared also to me. 9For I am the least of the apostles, unfit to be called an apostle, because I persecuted the church of God. 10But by the grace of God I am what I am, and his grace toward me has not been in vain. On the contrary, I worked harder than any of them—though it was not I, but the grace of God that is with me. 11Whether then it was I or they, so we proclaim and so you have come to believe.

The Resurrection of the Dead

12 Now if Christ is proclaimed as raised from the dead, how can some of you say there is no resurrection of the dead? 13If there is no resurrection of the dead, then Christ has not been raised; 14and if Christ has not been raised, then our proclamation has been in vain and your faith has been in vain. 15We are even found to be misrepresenting God, because we testified of God that he raised Christ—whom he did not

raise if it is true that the dead are not raised. 16For if the dead are not raised, then Christ has not been raised. 17If Christ has not been raised, your faith is futile and you are still in your sins. 18Then those also who have diede in Christ have perished. 19If for this life only we have hoped in Christ, we are of all people most to be pitied.

20 But in fact Christ has been raised from the dead, the first fruits of those who have died.e 21For since death came through a human being, the resurrection of the dead has also come through a human being; 22for as all die in Adam, so all will be made alive in Christ. 23But each

---

a Other ancient authorities put verses 34-35 after verse 40
b Gk *my brothers*   c Gk *brothers*   d Or *gospel*   e Gk *fallen asleep*

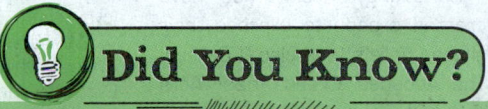

Did You Know?

What's Going On?

In 1 Corinthians 14:34, Paul says women should be silent in church. Yet, in 11:5 he implies that women can pray and prophesy in church, and throughout his life, he supported and worked closely with many different women (see "Introducing Lydia and Priscilla," near Acts 16:14–15, 18:1–26 and "Introducing Phoebe and Junia," near Rom 16:1–16).

What explains Paul's turnaround? It appears that 1 Corinthians 14:34–36, was added to Paul's original letter by a later writer. Perhaps someone copying Paul's letters needed to show that Christianity was not a movement that would disrupt the social order by allowing women to speak in public. It is important to note that this cultural expectation in the ancient world is not directly transferable to our contemporary setting.

Like Paul, the Catholic Church today values women's participation in worship. Women are cantors, musicians, lectors, and Eucharistic ministers. But like the later editor of 1 Corinthians, chapter 14, the Church insists on a certain order in worship and limits women's roles because the Church seeks to remain faithful to Christ's original design of the ministry of the Apostles.

▶ 1 Cor 14:34–36

1
C
O
R

Cultural Connection — The First Creed and a Contemporary Creed

In 1 Corinthians 15:3–11 is an early creed written in the Scriptures. It expresses the fundamental aspects of the Christian faith and is made up of historic facts and faith statements such as the following:

● Christ died for our sins, according to the Scriptures (see Isaiah, chapter 53).
● Christ was buried.
● Christ rose on the third day.

Christians of all times have created creeds to express their shared beliefs (see also "I Believe! The Apostles' Creed," near Acts 4:5–12). Some Christian communities create their own particular creedal statements based on the foundations of the Christian faith and their experience of God. Here are some extracts from a credo created by Hispanics during their Third Encuentro Nacional de Pastoral, in 1985:

We believe in the most Holy Trinity, God the Father, Son, and Holy Spirit. We sense his powerful work in our people, and we see it as a model to be followed. . . .

We believe in our identification with Christ, as the suffering people we are. We believe, . . . as he did, in the divinity of all human beings and in their liberation through love. . . .

We believe in the Catholic Church, which is integrated in Christ by means of the communion we, as laity, share with bishops, priests, and men and women religious. . . .

We have faith in our people because we know that God, who abides in a special manner and forever among us, has raised it [our people] up. . . .

We believe in the gift of being a prophetic voice as something given by God to our people and as a means of promoting the unity and love that are necessary for the building of the Kingdom. . . .

We believe in Mary, our Mother, who has taken our Hispanic culture under her protection, and who has accompanied us and will accompany us always in our journey as she works to carry the message of Jesus to the whole world. . . .

Amen.

(Secretariat for Hispanic Affairs, *Prophetic Voices,* pp. 17–18)

▶ **1 Cor 15:3–11**

in his own order: Christ the first fruits, then at his coming those who belong to Christ. 24Then comes the end,*a* when he hands over the kingdom to God the Father, after he has destroyed every ruler and every authority and power. 25For he must reign until he has put all his enemies under his feet. 26The last enemy to be destroyed is death. 27For "God*b* has put all things in subjection under his feet." But when it says, "All things are put in subjection," it is plain that this does not include the one who put all things in subjection under him. 28When all things are subjected to him, then the Son himself will also be subjected to the one who put all things in subjection under him, so that God may be all in all.

29 Otherwise, what will those people do who receive baptism on behalf of the dead? If the dead are not raised at all, why are people baptized on their behalf?

30 And why are we putting ourselves in danger every hour? 31I die every day! That is as certain, brothers and sisters,*c* as my boasting of

you—a boast that I make in Christ Jesus our Lord. 32If with merely human hopes I fought with wild animals at Ephesus, what would I have gained by it? If the dead are not raised,

"Let us eat and drink,
    for tomorrow we die."

33Do not be deceived:

"Bad company ruins good morals."

34Come to a sober and right mind, and sin no more; for some people have no knowledge of God. I say this to your shame.

The Resurrection Body

35 But someone will ask, "How are the dead raised? With what kind of body do they come?" 36Fool! What you sow does not come to life unless it dies. 37And as for what you sow, you do not sow the body that is to be, but a bare seed, perhaps of wheat or of some other grain. 38But God gives it a body as he has chosen, and

a Or Then come the rest   b Gk he   c Gk brothers

Live It!

Life After Death

During childhood, reality and fantasy are often confused. We might believe in Santa Claus, the Easter Bunny, the Tooth Fairy, even a monster living under our bed. We may imagine heaven as having pearly gates, golden streets, and angels flying around with harps. As we grow older, some of us exchange this fantastic image for a more mature belief in the mystery of the Resurrection. But many adult Christians simply do not know what to believe about life after death.

Christians from Corinth also had problems with the concept of resurrection of the body. Common ideas influenced by Greek philosophy made it difficult for them to think of a body's returning to life after death. They believed body and soul were separate. The soul was immortal and continued living after the body died.

In contrast, the Hebrews saw a unity between the spiritual and material aspects of the human person. When the prophets, such as Daniel, envisaged a blessed life after death, they did not think in terms of a soul freed from the body but in terms of a body filled once more with life (see "Resurrection," near Dan 12:1–3).

Believing in the resurrection of the body is essential in the Christian faith. The Gospel writers describe the risen Jesus as different from the Jesus who died on the cross; the disciples did not recognize him at first sight; they knew him only through their faith.

Paul gets right to the point: Jesus' followers need to believe in their own resurrection of the body, otherwise the belief that Christ was raised from death is in vain. Paul explains that in the resurrection, our earthly body will be transformed—it will become a glorious, imperishable, and immortal body. We will not be disembodied spirits or souls when we have eternal life in communion with God. And we will be made alive in Christ, whether our mind can comprehend that idea or not. Our end is not death, but eternal life with Christ!

▶ 1 Cor 15:35–58

to each kind of seed its own body. ³⁹Not all flesh is alike, but there is one flesh for human beings, another for animals, another for birds, and another for fish. ⁴⁰There are both heavenly bodies and earthly bodies, but the glory of the heavenly is one thing, and that of the earthly is another. ⁴¹There is one glory of the sun, and another glory of the moon, and another glory of the stars; indeed, star differs from star in glory.

42 So it is with the resurrection of the dead. What is sown is perishable, what is raised is imperishable. ⁴³It is sown in dishonor, it is raised in glory. It is sown in weakness, it is raised in power. ⁴⁴It is sown a physical body, it is raised a spiritual body. If there is a physical body, there is also a spiritual body. ⁴⁵Thus it is written, "The first man, Adam, became a living being"; the last Adam became a life-giving spirit. ⁴⁶But it is not the spiritual that is first, but the physical, and then the spiritual. ⁴⁷The first man was from the earth, a man of dust; the second man is*a* from heaven. ⁴⁸As was the man of dust, so are those who are of the dust; and as is the man of heaven, so are those who are of heaven. ⁴⁹Just as we have borne the image of the man of dust, we will*b* also bear the image of the man of heaven.

50 What I am saying, brothers and sisters,*c* is this: flesh and blood cannot inherit the kingdom of God, nor does the perishable inherit the imperishable. ⁵¹Listen, I will tell you a mystery! We will not all die,*d* but we will all be changed, ⁵²in a moment, in the twinkling of an eye, at the last trumpet. For the trumpet will sound, and the dead will be raised imperishable, and we will be changed. ⁵³For this perishable body must put on imperishability, and this mortal body must put on immortality. ⁵⁴When this perishable body puts on imperishability, and this mortal body puts on immortality, then the saying that is written will be fulfilled:

"Death has been swallowed up in victory."
⁵⁵ "Where, O death, is your victory?
        Where, O death, is your sting?"
⁵⁶The sting of death is sin, and the power of sin is the law. ⁵⁷But thanks be to God, who gives us the victory through our Lord Jesus Christ.

58 Therefore, my beloved,*e* be steadfast, immovable, always excelling in the work of the Lord, because you know that in the Lord your labor is not in vain.

a Other ancient authorities add *the Lord*   b Other ancient authorities read *let us*   c Gk *brothers*   d Gk *fall asleep* e Gk *beloved brothers*

1
C
O
R

The Collection for the Saints

16 Now concerning the collection for the saints: you should follow the directions I gave to the churches of Galatia. ²On the first day of every week, each of you is to put aside and save whatever extra you earn, so that collections need not be taken when I come. ³And when I arrive, I will send any whom you approve with letters to take your gift to Jerusalem. ⁴If it seems advisable that I should go also, they will accompany me.

Plans for Travel

5 I will visit you after passing through Macedonia—for I intend to pass through Macedonia— ⁶and perhaps I will stay with you or even spend the winter, so that you may send me on my way, wherever I go. ⁷I do not want to see you now just in passing, for I hope to spend some time with you, if the Lord permits. ⁸But I will stay in Ephesus until Pentecost, ⁹for a wide door for effective work has opened to me, and there are many adversaries.

10 If Timothy comes, see that he has nothing to fear among you, for he is doing the work of the Lord just as I am; ¹¹therefore let no one despise him. Send him on his way in peace, so that he may come to me; for I am expecting him with the brothers.

12 Now concerning our brother Apollos, I strongly urged him to visit you with the other brothers, but he was not at all willing*a* to come now. He will come when he has the opportunity.

Final Messages and Greetings

13 Keep alert, stand firm in your faith, be courageous, be strong. ¹⁴Let all that you do be done in love.

15 Now, brothers and sisters,*b* you know that members of the household of Stephanas were the first converts in Achaia, and they have devoted themselves to the service of the saints; ¹⁶I urge you to put yourselves at the service of such people, and of everyone who works and toils with them. ¹⁷I rejoice at the coming of Stephanas and Fortunatus and Achaicus, because they have made up for your absence; ¹⁸for they refreshed my spirit as well as yours. So give recognition to such persons.

19 The churches of Asia send greetings. Aquila and Prisca, together with the church in their house, greet you warmly in the Lord. ²⁰All the brothers and sisters*b* send greetings. Greet one another with a holy kiss.

21 I, Paul, write this greeting with my own hand. ²²Let anyone be accursed who has no love for the Lord. Our Lord, come!*c* ²³The grace of the Lord Jesus be with you. ²⁴My love be with all of you in Christ Jesus.*d*

---

a Or *it was not at all God's will for him*   *b* Gk *brothers*
c Gk *Marana tha.* These Aramaic words can also be read *Maran atha,* meaning *Our Lord has come*   *d* Other ancient authorities add *Amen*

Unfortunately, you probably know all too well what it's like to be criticized. It's no fun to be under attack. Our instinct is to get defensive and strike back. But in his Second Letter to the Corinthians, Paul shows us how God helps us rise above our instincts. Paul responds to personal attacks with directness and honesty. He demonstrates how to witness to Jesus—even when we are in the middle of conflict.

In Depth

The relationship between Paul and the Corinthians deteriorated after Paul wrote First Corinthians. Apparently, some other traveling missionaries came to Corinth and undermined Paul's credibility. They attacked him as a person (see 2 Cor 10:10), implied that he was mentally imbalanced (see 5:13), and criticized him as a speaker (see 10:10). They even suggested that Paul was not trustworthy about money (see 8:20–21).

As part of these attacks, some people claimed that Paul couldn't make up his mind about returning to visit Corinth; they said he kept changing between yes and no. In defending himself, Paul skillfully changes the focus and says that in Jesus, we always find a yes. In Jesus, every one of God's promises is a yes (see 1:19–20). And whereas Paul's opponents make boastful claims for themselves, Paul realizes that God's grace is all he needs. In fact, he says, "I will boast all the more gladly of my weaknesses, so that the power of Christ may dwell in me" (12:9). Paul's decision not to return is also an attempt to avoid causing the community any more pain as a result of another conflict that happened within the Corinthian community (see 2:1–11).

With breathtaking insight, Paul puts all the conflicts into perspective. "From now on, therefore, we regard no one from a human point of view. . . . So if anyone is in Christ, there is a new creation" (5:16–17). Knowing Christ changes everything! Through Christ, we are reconciled with God, meaning God overcomes the sin and weakness that separate us from God's love. We should also become ambassadors for Christ, reconciling with one another and announcing to all that they are reconciled with God.

Scholars see evidence that several original letters were combined to form Second Corinthians. For example, Paul's concerns seem to be resolved in chapter 7, but then chapters 10–13 pick up those concerns again. And chapters 8 and 9 each describe a collection being taken up for the Christians in Jerusalem without making any connection between the two collections. Despite its uneven flow, the letter reveals a personal look into Paul's life and ministry.

At a Glance

- **1:1–11.** greetings
- **1:12—7:16.** a description of how Paul and the Corinthians resolve their conflict; teaching on the nature of Paul's ministry
- **Chapters 8–9.** a discussion of a collection for the church at Jerusalem
- **10:1—13:10.** a defense of Paul's ministry as an Apostle
- **13:11–13.** a final greeting and a blessing

Quick Facts

Inspired Author: Paul
Date Written: around AD 57
Audience: the mainly Gentile (non-Jewish) church in Corinth

The Second Letter to the **Corinthians**

2 Corinthians

Salutation

1 Paul, an apostle of Christ Jesus by the will of God, and Timothy our brother,

To the church of God that is in Corinth, including all the saints throughout Achaia:

2 Grace to you and peace from God our Father and the Lord Jesus Christ.

Paul's Thanksgiving after Affliction

3 Blessed be the God and Father of our Lord Jesus Christ, the Father of mercies and the God of all consolation, ⁴who consoles us in all our affliction, so that we may be able to console those who are in any affliction with the consolation with which we ourselves are consoled by God. ⁵For just as the sufferings of Christ are abundant for us, so also our consolation is abundant through Christ. ⁶If we are being afflicted, it is for your consolation and salvation; if we are being consoled, it is for your consolation, which you experience when you patiently endure the same sufferings that we are also suffering. ⁷Our hope for you is unshaken; for we know that as you share in our sufferings, so also you share in our consolation.

8 We do not want you to be unaware, brothers and sisters,ᵃ of the affliction we experienced in Asia; for we were so utterly, unbearably crushed that we despaired of life itself. ⁹Indeed, we felt that we had received the sentence of death so that we would rely not on ourselves but on God who raises the dead. ¹⁰He who rescued us from so

deadly a peril will continue to rescue us; on him we have set our hope that he will rescue us again, ¹¹as you also join in helping us by your prayers, so that many will give thanks on ourᵇ behalf for the blessing granted us through the prayers of many.

The Postponement of Paul's Visit

12 Indeed, this is our boast, the testimony of our conscience: we have behaved in the world with franknessᶜ and godly sincerity, not by earthly wisdom but by the grace of God—and all the more toward you. ¹³For we write you nothing other than what you can read and also understand; I hope you will understand until the end— ¹⁴as you have already understood us in part—that on the day of the Lord Jesus we are your boast even as you are our boast.

15 Since I was sure of this, I wanted to come to you first, so that you might have a double favor;ᵈ ¹⁶I wanted to visit you on my way to Macedonia, and to come back to you from Macedonia and have you send me on to Judea. ¹⁷Was I vacillating when I wanted to do this? Do I make my plans according to ordinary human standards,ᵉ ready to say "Yes, yes" and "No, no" at the same time? ¹⁸As surely as God is faithful, our word to you has not been "Yes and No." ¹⁹For the Son of God, Jesus Christ, whom we proclaimed

---

a Gk *brothers* b Other ancient authorities read *your* c Other ancient authorities read *holiness* d Other ancient authorities read *pleasure* e Gk *according to the flesh*

among you, Silvanus and Timothy and I, was not "Yes and No"; but in him it is always "Yes." [20]For in him every one of God's promises is a "Yes." For this reason it is through him that we say the "Amen," to the glory of God. [21]But it is God who establishes us with you in Christ and has anointed us, [22]by putting his seal on us and giving us his Spirit in our hearts as a first installment.

23 But I call on God as witness against me: it was to spare you that I did not come again to Corinth. [24]I do not mean to imply that we lord it over your faith; rather, we are workers with you for your joy, because you stand firm in the faith. **2** [1]So I made up my mind not to make you another painful visit. [2]For if I cause you pain, who is there to make me glad but the one whom I have pained? [3]And I wrote as I did, so that when I came, I might not suffer pain from those who should have made me rejoice; for I am confident about all of you, that my joy would be the joy of all of you. [4]For I wrote you out of much distress and anguish of heart and with many tears, not to cause you pain, but to let you know the abundant love that I have for you.

Forgiveness for the Offender

5 But if anyone has caused pain, he has caused it not to me, but to some extent—not to exaggerate it—to all of you. [6]This punishment by the majority is enough for such a person; [7]so now instead you should forgive and console him, so that he may not be overwhelmed by excessive sorrow. [8]So I urge you to reaffirm your love for him. [9]I wrote for this reason: to test you and to know whether you are obedient in everything. [10]Anyone whom you forgive, I also forgive. What I have forgiven, if I have forgiven anything, has been for your sake in the presence of Christ. [11]And we do this so that we may not be outwitted by Satan; for we are not ignorant of his designs.

Paul's Anxiety in Troas

12 When I came to Troas to proclaim the good news of Christ, a door was opened for me in the Lord; [13]but my mind could not rest because I did not find my brother Titus there. So I said farewell to them and went on to Macedonia.

14 But thanks be to God, who in Christ always leads us in triumphal procession, and through us spreads in every place the fragrance that comes from knowing him. [15]For we are the aroma of Christ to God among those who are being saved and among those who are perishing; [16]to the one a fragrance from death to death, to the other a fragrance from life to life. Who is sufficient for these things? [17]For we are not peddlers of God's word like so many;[a] but in Christ we speak as persons of sincerity, as persons sent from God and standing in his presence.

---

a Other ancient authorities read *like the others*

The Presence of God

Carlos is an undocumented worker at a chicken processing plant, that is until he and many others are apprehended by Immigration Services and brought to a detention center where they will be processed before being returned to Mexico. The workers' spirits are low. Many of them have children in school and in child care. They suffer uncertainty over knowing when they might be reunited with their families.

Then Carlos hears Marisol, a grandmother who works with him, call out to the group: "We are not alone, and we have not been abandoned. God has been with us every minute through this ordeal. I pray every morning and every night in thanksgiving for that presence. It is on my worst days that I most strongly feel the presence of God." Carlos finds consolation in Marisol's words.

When we are suffering, we too can feel alone and abandoned—sometimes even by God. But Paul emphasizes that God is always present, consoling us in our affliction. It is sometimes difficult to experience this presence because we are caught up in the pain and hurt of the situation, as Carlos was in his captivity. How do you experience God's presence or absence during times of pain and suffering?

Paul also says that the support of the Christian community can help us to get through our pain. The comfort of friends and relatives during difficult times can help us to recognize that God is with us. Is there someone you can comfort who is going through a hard time?

▶ **2 Cor 1:3–11**

2 COR

Cultural Connection

Yes, Yes, May We Not Fail

Paul ensures the people of Corinth that he has not wavered in his commitment to them. In a similar manner, Saint Andrew Dung-Lac and the Vietnamese martyrs were unwavering in their commitment to the Gospels. These martyrs consisted of 117 people who died for their faith in nineteenth-century Vietnam. Saint Andrew was a priest in Vietnam, and many of the other 117 martyrs were Catholic laypeople. Pope John Paul II made them all saints of the Church on June 19, 1988.

Vietnam is a country that has been rocked by many bloody wars, run by ruthless dictators, and overrun by rampant violence through many of the years of its history as a country. Despite such extreme social conditions, and in the midst of such horrible violence, these martyrs and many like them had the courage to preach the Gospel and live as disciples of Christ.

Take a few moments to reflect on the lives of these martyrs.

▶ **2 Cor 1:15–22**

Ministers of the New Covenant

3 Are we beginning to commend ourselves again? Surely we do not need, as some do, letters of recommendation to you or from you, do we? ²You yourselves are our letter, written on our*ᵃ* hearts, to be known and read by all; ³and you show that you are a letter of Christ, prepared by us, written not with ink but with the Spirit of the living God, not on tablets of stone but on tablets of human hearts.

4 Such is the confidence that we have through Christ toward God. ⁵Not that we are competent of ourselves to claim anything as coming from us; our competence is from God, ⁶who has made us competent to be ministers of a new covenant, not of letter but of spirit; for the letter kills, but the Spirit gives life.

7 Now if the ministry of death, chiseled in letters on stone tablets,*ᵇ* came in glory so that the people of Israel could not gaze at Moses' face because of the glory of his face, a glory now set aside, ⁸how much more will the ministry of the Spirit come in glory? ⁹For if there was glory in the ministry of condemnation, much more does the ministry of justification abound in glory! ¹⁰Indeed, what once had glory has lost its glory because of the greater glory; ¹¹for if what was set aside came through glory, much more has the permanent come in glory!

12 Since, then, we have such a hope, we act with great boldness, ¹³not like Moses, who put a veil over his face to keep the people of Israel from gazing at the end of the glory that*ᶜ* was being set aside. ¹⁴But their minds were hardened.

Indeed, to this very day, when they hear the reading of the old covenant, that same veil is still there, since only in Christ is it set aside. ¹⁵Indeed, to this very day whenever Moses is read, a veil lies over their minds; ¹⁶but when one turns to the Lord, the veil is removed. ¹⁷Now the Lord is the Spirit, and where the Spirit of the Lord is, there is freedom. ¹⁸And all of us, with unveiled faces, seeing the glory of the Lord as though reflected in a mirror, are being transformed into the same image from one degree of glory to another; for this comes from the Lord, the Spirit.

Treasure in Clay Jars

4 Therefore, since it is by God's mercy that we are engaged in this ministry, we do not lose heart. ²We have renounced the shameful things that one hides; we refuse to practice cunning or to falsify God's word; but by the open statement of the truth we commend ourselves to the conscience of everyone in the sight of God. ³And even if our gospel is veiled, it is veiled to those who are perishing. ⁴In their case the god of this world has blinded the minds of the unbelievers, to keep them from seeing the light of the gospel of the glory of Christ, who is the image of God. ⁵For we do not proclaim ourselves; we proclaim Jesus Christ as Lord and ourselves as your slaves for Jesus' sake. ⁶For it is the God who said, "Let light shine out of darkness," who has shone in our hearts to give the light of the knowledge of the glory of God in the face of Jesus Christ.

a Other ancient authorities read *your*   *b* Gk *on stones*   *c* Gk *of what*

2 COR

7 But we have this treasure in clay jars, so that it may be made clear that this extraordinary power belongs to God and does not come from us. ⁸We are afflicted in every way, but not crushed; perplexed, but not driven to despair; ⁹persecuted, but not forsaken; struck down, but not destroyed; ¹⁰always carrying in the body the death of Jesus, so that the life of Jesus may also be made visible in our bodies. ¹¹For while we live, we are always being given up to death for Jesus' sake, so that the life of Jesus may be made visible in our mortal flesh. ¹²So death is at work in us, but life in you.

13 But just as we have the same spirit of faith that is in accordance with scripture—"I believed, and so I spoke"—we also believe, and so we speak, ¹⁴because we know that the one who raised the Lord Jesus will raise us also with Jesus, and will bring us with you into his presence. ¹⁵Yes, everything is for your sake, so that grace, as it extends to more and more people, may increase thanksgiving, to the glory of God.

Living by Faith

16 So we do not lose heart. Even though our outer nature is wasting away, our inner nature is being renewed day by day. ¹⁷For this slight momentary affliction is preparing us for an eternal weight of glory beyond all measure, ¹⁸because we look not at what can be seen but at what cannot be seen; for what can be seen is temporary, but what cannot be seen is eternal.

5 For we know that if the earthly tent we live in is destroyed, we have a building from God, a house not made with hands, eternal in the heavens. ²For in this tent we groan, longing to be clothed with our heavenly dwelling— ³if indeed, when we have taken it off[a] we will not be found naked. ⁴For while we are still in this tent, we groan under our burden, because we wish not to be unclothed but to be further clothed, so that what is mortal may be swallowed up by life. ⁵He who has prepared us for this very thing is God, who has given us the Spirit as a guarantee.

6 So we are always confident; even though we know that while we are at home in the body we are

---

a Other ancient authorities read *put it on*

Live It!

Christ in Us

It is sometimes tempting to take ourselves a bit too seriously, to feel too self-important. When given a particular responsibility at school, home, or church, we may begin to act as though we are what is important, rather than the task.

The same is true when we accept our calling as a disciple of Christ. Feelings of self-righteousness or pride can creep in, leading to what friends might call a holier-than-thou attitude. Paul reminds us that "we do not proclaim ourselves; we proclaim Jesus Christ as Lord" (2 Cor 4:5). We are simply fragile clay jars that hold a great treasure to be shared with all. What a wonderful and awesome responsibility we have been given: to share, with our lives and our words, what Jesus has done in us, giving him the glory and not seeking it for ourselves.

▶ 2 Cor 4:5–10

Pray It!

Hopeless and Hurting

Sometimes, life can be filled with despair and discouragement. We can get down in the dumps and feel like everything is a waste of our time and energy. Paul encourages us not to lose hope but to keep our hearts and minds very much alive. Paul connects our moments of despair to Jesus' suffering on the cross. Jesus never lost hope. He believed to the end and then was raised from the dead to new life to show the world that his suffering and death had a hopeful outcome. God promises us this same hopeful outcome of being raised up.

Try this exercise: Re-read 2 Corinthians 4:7–18 in a prayerful way, perhaps while listening to some reflective music. Then write a few thoughts of your own in a journal, or write your own prayer about suffering and despair. Don't forget to mention hope at the end of your prayer, because, ultimately, that was Jesus' message.

▶ 2 Cor 4:7–18

2 COR

away from the Lord— ⁷for we walk by faith, not by sight. ⁸Yes, we do have confidence, and we would rather be away from the body and at home with the Lord. ⁹So whether we are at home or away, we make it our aim to please him. ¹⁰For all of us must appear before the judgment seat of Christ, so that each may receive recompense for what has been done in the body, whether good or evil.

The Ministry of Reconciliation

11 Therefore, knowing the fear of the Lord, we try to persuade others; but we ourselves are

It's What's Inside That Counts

Television, magazines, and advertising show the ideal person as skinny, well developed, muscular, clear complexioned, tall, and with perfect features. Very few people fit that image. Many of those who don't fit that image feel insecure and inadequate. Some people try desperately to measure up to that standard with crash diets, workouts at fitness centers, weight training, steroids, or plastic surgery. Some people even end up with eating disorders like bulimia and anorexia.

In 2 Corinthians 5:1–5, Paul reminds us that our earthly body is a temporary dwelling. It is important for us to take care of this earthly "tent" with a healthy diet and regular exercise. But our desire for our heavenly dwelling should cause us to focus on our inner appearance more than our outer appearance.

In your prayer, reflect on the following questions:

● Are you satisfied with your physical appearance? Why or why not?

● Do you spend as much time working on your inner appearance—by developing virtues like compassion, generosity, mercy, and patience—as you do on your outer appearance?

Write a prayer asking God for the grace (gift) to feel secure in your outward appearance. Listen for God's response.

▶ **2 Cor 5:1–5**

well known to God, and I hope that we are also well known to your consciences. ¹²We are not commending ourselves to you again, but giving you an opportunity to boast about us, so that you may be able to answer those who boast in outward appearance and not in the heart. ¹³For if we are beside ourselves, it is for God; if we are in our right mind, it is for you. ¹⁴For the love of Christ urges us on, because we are convinced that one has died for all; therefore all have died. ¹⁵And he died for all, so that those who live might live no longer for themselves, but for him who died and was raised for them.

16 From now on, therefore, we regard no one from a human point of view;ᵃ even though we once knew Christ from a human point of view,ᵃ we know him no longer in that way. ¹⁷So if anyone is in Christ, there is a new creation: everything old has passed away; see, everything has become new! ¹⁸All this is from God, who reconciled us to himself through Christ, and has given us the ministry of reconciliation; ¹⁹that is, in Christ God was reconciling the world to himself,ᵇ not counting their trespasses against them, and entrusting the message of reconciliation to us. ²⁰So we are ambassadors for Christ, since God is making his appeal through us; we entreat you on behalf of Christ, be reconciled to God. ²¹For our sake he made him to be sin who knew no sin, so that in him we might become the righteousness of God.

> **"So if anyone is in Christ, there is a new creation."**
> (2 Cor 5:17)

6 As we work together with him,ᶜ we urge you also not to accept the grace of God in vain. ²For he says,

"At an acceptable time I have listened to you,
    and on a day of salvation I have helped you."

See, now is the acceptable time; see, now is the day of salvation! ³We are putting no obstacle in anyone's way, so that no fault may be found with our ministry, ⁴but as servants of God we have commended ourselves in every way: through great endurance, in afflictions, hardships, calamities, ⁵beatings, imprisonments, riots, labors, sleepless nights, hunger; ⁶by purity, knowledge, patience, kindness, holiness of spirit, genuine love, ⁷truthful speech, and the power of God;

---

a Gk according to the flesh   b Or God was in Christ reconciling the world to himself   c Gk As we work together

with the weapons of righteousness for the right hand and for the left; [8]in honor and dishonor, in ill repute and good repute. We are treated as impostors, and yet are true; [9]as unknown, and yet are well known; as dying, and see—we are alive; as punished, and yet not killed; [10]as sorrowful, yet always rejoicing; as poor, yet making many rich; as having nothing, and yet possessing everything.

11 We have spoken frankly to you Corinthians; our heart is wide open to you. [12]There is no restriction in our affections, but only in yours. [13]In return—I speak as to children—open wide your hearts also.

The Temple of the Living God

14 Do not be mismatched with unbelievers. For what partnership is there between righteousness and lawlessness? Or what fellowship is there between light and darkness? [15]What agreement does Christ have with Beliar? Or what does a believer share with an unbeliever? [16]What agreement has the temple of God with idols? For we[a] are the temple of the living God; as God said,

"I will live in them and walk among them,
    and I will be their God,
    and they shall be my people.
[17] Therefore come out from them,
    and be separate from them, says the Lord,
    and touch nothing unclean;

---

a Other ancient authorities read *you*

Ambassadors for Christ

The title *ambassador* is usually used by people who are authorized to represent their country while living as a resident in a foreign nation. For example, the U.S. ambassador to Mexico is an official representative of the United States who lives in Mexico and speaks for the U.S. government in Mexico.

Paul tells us that we are reconciled—that is, united—with God through Christ, and that God has now entrusted us with the ministry of helping others to be reconciled through Christ. This is our mission today. We are ambassadors for Christ! Of all the ways God could be made known in the world, God chooses to use us. We are authorized representatives. We are God's messengers.

That might sound a bit intimidating! We might naturally wonder how we, broken and imperfect people, are supposed to represent God, who is completely holy and just. The reality is that God wants to use us, flaws and all. God does not need perfect people—just willing people! Spend some time in prayer, and share with God your thoughts, feelings, and fears about being invited to take on this great role of ambassador for Christ.

▶ 2 Cor 5:17–21

Shine Like a Star

Second Corinthians 6:14 makes a sudden transition; 6:14—7:1 may even be a fragment from another letter. We are not sure what kind of behavior or problem Paul is talking about here. But it does seem clear that Paul is cautioning the Corinthians against being too closely influenced by non-Christians—unbelievers. Paul doesn't want the Corinthians to return to sinful behaviors.

Christians in the United States are also surrounded by many unhealthy and unholy choices. Our words and behaviors should show that "we are the temple of the living God" (6:16). We must be careful of friendships and media influences that might tempt us to start thinking that wrong is right. This doesn't mean we should be arrogant and separate ourselves from others. Remember that Jesus sometimes hung around with sinners. But he didn't share in their sins. He was a light for them.

As Paul says in Philippians 2:15, we are "children of God" in a "perverse generation," where we shine "like stars in the world."

▶ 2 Cor 6:14–18

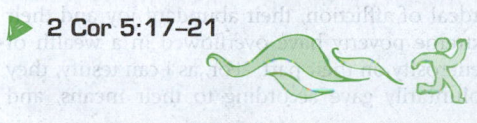

Cultural Connection

An "Anyway" God

We serve an "anyway" God. Impediments, hurdles, and obstacles are part of our inheritance, yet we excel anyway. Some of us were kidnapped from Africa, enslaved and shackled, stripped of our culture, robbed of our native language, and torn from our family, yet today, we thrive anyway.

Surely, the Lord was in the midst of the African Americans' past, ushering them on to a better day. The evidence that the Lord walked with them through horrific conditions is simply too great to deny. Yet, as a people, they can identify with Paul's words in 2 Corinthians 6:1–10—their struggles have only made them stronger.

Even today, life for most of us is no cakewalk, but our ability to walk at all comes from God, who conquers all. Can you recognize God's grace and mercy and celebrate the presence of God in your good and bad times?

Dear God, no matter how high the odds are stacked against me, I can overcome them with your grace and mercy, and survive. Amen.

▶ 2 Cor 6:1–10

---

then I will welcome you,
18 and I will be your father,
 and you shall be my sons and daughters,
 says the Lord Almighty."

7 Since we have these promises, beloved, let us cleanse ourselves from every defilement of body and of spirit, making holiness perfect in the fear of God.

Paul's Joy at the Church's Repentance

2 Make room in your hearts*a* for us; we have wronged no one, we have corrupted no one, we have taken advantage of no one. ³I do not say this to condemn you, for I said before that you are in our hearts, to die together and to live together. ⁴I often boast about you; I have great pride in you; I am filled with consolation; I am overjoyed in all our affliction.

5 For even when we came into Macedonia, our bodies had no rest, but we were afflicted in every way—disputes without and fears within. ⁶But God, who consoles the downcast, consoled us by the arrival of Titus, ⁷and not only by his coming, but also by the consolation with which he was consoled about you, as he told us of your longing, your mourning, your zeal for me, so that I rejoiced still more. ⁸For even if I made you sorry with my letter, I do not regret it (though I did regret it, for I see that I grieved you with that letter, though only briefly). ⁹Now I rejoice, not because you were grieved, but because your grief led to repentance; for you felt a godly grief, so that you were not harmed in any way by us. ¹⁰For godly grief produces a repentance that leads to salvation and brings no regret, but worldly grief produces death. ¹¹For see what earnestness this godly grief has produced in you, what eagerness to clear yourselves, what indignation, what alarm, what longing, what zeal, what punishment! At every point you have proved yourselves guiltless in the matter. ¹²So although I wrote to you, it was not on account of the one who did the wrong, nor on account of the one who was wronged, but in order that your zeal for us might be made known to you before God. ¹³In this we find comfort.

In addition to our own consolation, we rejoiced still more at the joy of Titus, because his mind has been set at rest by all of you. ¹⁴For if I have been somewhat boastful about you to him, I was not disgraced; but just as everything we said to you was true, so our boasting to Titus has proved true as well. ¹⁵And his heart goes out all the more to you, as he remembers the obedience of all of you, and how you welcomed him with fear and trembling. ¹⁶I rejoice, because I have complete confidence in you.

Encouragement to Be Generous

8 We want you to know, brothers and sisters,*b* about the grace of God that has been granted to the churches of Macedonia; ²for during a severe ordeal of affliction, their abundant joy and their extreme poverty have overflowed in a wealth of generosity on their part. ³For, as I can testify, they voluntarily gave according to their means, and

---

a Gk lacks *in your hearts*   b Gk *brothers*

2
COR

Cultural Connection

Christians Share Their Money out of Solidarity

In chapters 8–9 of Second Corinthians, Paul encourages the Corinthians to give generously to a collection for the poor Christians of Jerusalem. In a similar way, Hispanics in the United States often generously collect and share the money they earn with their families in Latin America.

"I cannot fail my mother," Anita said. "I always try to send her at least a hundred dollars a month because she depends on me." Anita, who lives in Minneapolis with her husband and children, has been sending money to her mother in central Mexico since Anita came to the United States eight years ago. Anita and other Hispanics share the money they make in the United States with their families in Latin America in the spirit of solidarity. "It is something that we have to do," a Central American immigrant tells us. "It is part of our culture. It is the responsibility of all adult children to help our families, even if we don't make much money."

● How are you generous with your money? What financial sacrifices can you make this week for the sake of family members or others you know who are as poor or poorer than you?

● Ask the Holy Spirit for the gift of generosity for yourself and for other young Catholics. Pray that a willingness to share the resources God has blessed you with becomes a lifelong habit.

▶ **2 Corinthians, chapters 8–9**

even beyond their means, [4]begging us earnestly for the privilege[a] of sharing in this ministry to the saints— [5]and this, not merely as we expected; they gave themselves first to the Lord and, by the will of God, to us, [6]so that we might urge Titus that, as he had already made a beginning, so he should also complete this generous undertaking[b] among you. [7]Now as you excel in everything—in faith, in speech, in knowledge, in utmost eagerness, and in our love for you[c]—so we want you to excel also in this generous undertaking.[b]

8 I do not say this as a command, but I am testing the genuineness of your love against the earnestness of others. [9]For you know the generous act[d] of our Lord Jesus Christ, that though he was rich, yet for your sakes he became poor, so that by his poverty you might become rich. [10]And in this matter I am giving my advice: it is appropriate for you who began last year not only to do something but even to desire to do something— [11]now finish doing it, so that your eagerness may be matched by completing it according to your means. [12]For if the eagerness is there, the gift is acceptable according to what one has—not according to what one does not have. [13]I do not mean that there should be relief for others and pressure on you, but it is a question of a fair balance between [14]your present abundance and their need, so that their abundance may be for your need, in order that there may be a fair balance. [15]As it is written,

"The one who had much did not have too
    much,
    and the one who had little did not have too
    little."

Commendation of Titus

16 But thanks be to God who put in the heart of Titus the same eagerness for you that I myself have. [17]For he not only accepted our appeal, but since he is more eager than ever, he is going to you of his own accord. [18]With him we are sending the brother who is famous among all the churches for his proclaiming the good news;[e] [19]and not only that, but he has also been appointed by the churches to travel with us while we are administering this generous undertaking[b] for the glory of the Lord himself[f] and to show our goodwill. [20]We intend that no one should blame us about this generous gift that we are administering, [21]for we intend to do what is right not only in the Lord's sight but also in the sight of others. [22]And with them we are sending our brother whom we have often tested and found eager in many matters, but who is now more eager than ever because of his great confidence in you. [23]As for Titus, he is my partner and co-worker in your service; as for our brothers, they are messengers[g] of the churches, the glory of

a Gk grace b Gk this grace c Other ancient authorities read your love for us d Gk the grace e Or the gospel f Other ancient authorities lack himself g Gk apostles

2 COR

Christ. 24Therefore openly before the churches, show them the proof of your love and of our reason for boasting about you.

The Collection for Christians at Jerusalem

9 Now it is not necessary for me to write you about the ministry to the saints, 2for I know your eagerness, which is the subject of my boasting about you to the people of Macedonia, saying that Achaia has been ready since last year; and your zeal has stirred up most of them. 3But I am sending the brothers in order that our boasting about you may not prove to have been empty in this case, so that you may be ready, as I said you would be; 4otherwise, if some Macedonians come with me and find that you are not ready, we would be humiliated—to say nothing of you—in this undertaking.a 5So I thought it necessary to urge the brothers to go on ahead to you, and arrange in advance for this bountiful gift that you have promised, so that it may be ready as a voluntary gift and not as an extortion.

6 The point is this: the one who sows sparingly will also reap sparingly, and the one who sows bountifully will also reap bountifully. 7Each of you must give as you have made up your mind, not reluctantly or under compulsion, for God loves a cheerful giver. 8And God is able to provide you with every blessing in abundance, so that by always having enough of everything, you may share abundantly in every good work. 9As it is written,

"He scatters abroad, he gives to the poor;
     his righteousnessb endures forever."

10He who supplies seed to the sower and bread for food will supply and multiply your seed for sowing and increase the harvest of your righteousness.b 11You will be enriched in every way for your great generosity, which will produce thanksgiving to God through us; 12for the rendering of this ministry not only supplies the needs of the saints but also overflows with many thanksgivings to God. 13Through the testing of this ministry you glorify God by your obedience to the confession of the gospel of Christ and by the generosity of your sharing with them and with all others, 14while they long for you and pray for you because of the surpassing grace of God that he has given you. 15Thanks be to God for his indescribable gift!

Paul Defends His Ministry

10 I myself, Paul, appeal to you by the meekness and gentleness of Christ—I who am humble when face to face with you, but bold toward you when I am away!— 2I ask that when

I am present I need not show boldness by daring to oppose those who think we are acting according to human standards.c 3Indeed, we live as human beings,d but we do not wage war according to human standards;c 4for the weapons of our warfare are not merely human,e but they have divine power to destroy strongholds. We destroy arguments 5and every proud obstacle raised up against the knowledge of God, and we take every thought captive to obey Christ. 6We are ready to punish every disobedience when your obedience is complete.

7 Look at what is before your eyes. If you are confident that you belong to Christ, remind yourself of this, that just as you belong to Christ, so also do we. 8Now, even if I boast a little too much of our authority, which the Lord gave for building you up and not for tearing you down, I will not be ashamed of it. 9I do not want to seem as though I am trying to frighten you with my letters. 10For they say, "His letters are weighty and strong, but his bodily presence is weak, and his speech contemptible." 11Let such people understand that what we say by letter when absent, we will also do when present.

12 We do not dare to classify or compare ourselves with some of those who commend themselves. But when they measure themselves by one another, and compare themselves with one another, they do not show good sense. 13We, however, will not boast beyond limits, but will keep within the field that God has assigned to us, to reach out even as far as you. 14For we were not overstepping our limits when we reached you; we were the first to come all the way to you with the good newsf of Christ. 15We do not boast beyond limits, that is, in the labors of others; but our hope is that, as your faith increases, our sphere of action among you may be greatly enlarged, 16so that we may proclaim the good newsf in lands beyond you, without boasting of work already done in someone else's sphere of action. 17"Let the one who boasts, boast in the Lord." 18For it is not those who commend themselves that are approved, but those whom the Lord commends.

Paul and the False Apostles

11 I wish you would bear with me in a little foolishness. Do bear with me! 2I feel a divine jealousy for you, for I promised you in marriage to one husband, to present you as a

---

a Other ancient authorities add of boasting   b Or benevolence   c Gk according to the flesh   d Gk in the flesh   e Gk fleshly   f Or the gospel

chaste virgin to Christ. ³But I am afraid that as the serpent deceived Eve by its cunning, your thoughts will be led astray from a sincere and pure*a* devotion to Christ. ⁴For if someone comes and proclaims another Jesus than the one we proclaimed, or if you receive a different spirit from the one you received, or a different gospel from the one you accepted, you submit to it readily enough. ⁵I think that I am not in the least inferior to these super-apostles. ⁶I may be untrained in speech, but not in knowledge; certainly in every way and in all things we have made this evident to you.

7 Did I commit a sin by humbling myself so that you might be exalted, because I proclaimed God's good news*b* to you free of charge? ⁸I robbed other churches by accepting support from them in order to serve you. ⁹And when I was with you and was in need, I did not burden anyone, for my needs were supplied by the friends*c* who came from Macedonia. So I refrained and will continue to refrain from burdening you in any way. ¹⁰As the truth of Christ is in me, this boast of mine will not be silenced in the regions of Achaia. ¹¹And why? Because I do not love you? God knows I do!

12 And what I do I will also continue to do, in order to deny an opportunity to those who want an opportunity to be recognized as our equals in what they boast about. ¹³For such boasters are false apostles, deceitful workers, disguising themselves as apostles of Christ. ¹⁴And no wonder! Even Satan disguises himself as an angel of light. ¹⁵So it is not strange if his ministers also disguise themselves as ministers of righteousness. Their end will match their deeds.

Paul's Sufferings as an Apostle

16 I repeat, let no one think that I am a fool; but if you do, then accept me as a fool, so that I too may boast a little. ¹⁷What I am saying in regard to this boastful confidence, I am saying not with the Lord's authority, but as a fool; ¹⁸since many boast according to human standards,*d* I will also boast. ¹⁹For you gladly put up with fools, being wise yourselves! ²⁰For you put up with it when someone makes slaves of you, or preys upon you, or takes advantage of you, or puts on airs, or gives you a slap in the face. ²¹To my shame, I must say, we were too weak for that!

But whatever anyone dares to boast of—I am speaking as a fool—I also dare to boast of that. ²²Are they Hebrews? So am I. Are they Israelites? So am I. Are they descendants of Abraham? So am I. ²³Are they ministers of Christ? I am talking like a madman—I am a better one: with far greater labors, far more imprisonments, with countless floggings, and often near death. ²⁴Five times I have received from the Jews the forty lashes minus one. ²⁵Three times I was beaten with rods. Once I received a stoning. Three times I was shipwrecked; for a night and a day I was adrift at sea; ²⁶on frequent journeys, in danger from rivers, danger from bandits, danger from my own people, danger from Gentiles, danger in the city, danger in the wilderness, danger at sea, danger from false brothers and sisters;*c* ²⁷in toil and hardship, through many a sleepless night, hungry and thirsty, often without food, cold and naked. ²⁸And, besides other things, I am under daily pressure because of my anxiety for all the churches. ²⁹Who is weak, and I am not weak? Who is made to stumble, and I am not indignant?

30 If I must boast, I will boast of the things that show my weakness. ³¹The God and Father of the Lord Jesus (blessed be he forever!) knows that I do not lie. ³²In Damascus, the governor*e* under King Aretas guarded the city of Damascus in order to*f* seize me, ³³but I was let down in a basket through a window in the wall,*g* and escaped from his hands.

Paul's Visions and Revelations

12 It is necessary to boast; nothing is to be gained by it, but I will go on to visions and revelations of the Lord. ²I know a person in Christ who fourteen years ago was caught up to the third heaven—whether in the body or out of the body I do not know; God knows. ³And I know that such a person—whether in the body or out of the body I do not know; God knows— ⁴was caught up into Paradise and heard things that are not to be told, that no mortal is permitted to repeat. ⁵On behalf of such a one I will boast, but on my own behalf I will not boast, except of my weaknesses. ⁶But if I wish to boast, I will not be a fool, for I will be speaking the truth. But I refrain from it, so that no one may think better of me than what is seen in me or heard from me, ⁷even considering the exceptional character of the revelations. Therefore, to keep*h* me from being too elated, a thorn was given me in the flesh, a messenger of Satan to torment me, to keep me from being too elated.*i* ⁸Three times I appealed to the Lord about this, that it

---

a Other ancient authorities lack *and pure*   b Gk *the gospel of God*   c Gk *brothers*   d Gk *according to the flesh*
e Gk *ethnarch*   f Other ancient authorities read *and wanted to*
g Gk *through the wall*   h Other ancient authorities read *To keep*
i Other ancient authorities lack *to keep me from being too elated*

would leave me, ⁹but he said to me, "My grace is sufficient for you, for power*a* is made perfect in weakness." So, I will boast all the more gladly of my weaknesses, so that the power of Christ may dwell in me. ¹⁰Therefore I am content with weaknesses, insults, hardships, persecutions, and calamities for the sake of Christ; for whenever I am weak, then I am strong.

Paul's Concern for the Corinthian Church

11 I have been a fool! You forced me to it. Indeed you should have been the ones commending me, for I am not at all inferior to these super-apostles, even though I am nothing. ¹²The signs of a true apostle were performed among you with utmost patience, signs and wonders and mighty works. ¹³How have you been worse off than the other churches, except that I myself did not burden you? Forgive me this wrong!

14 Here I am, ready to come to you this third time. And I will not be a burden, because I do not want what is yours but you; for children ought not to lay up for their parents, but parents for their children. ¹⁵I will most gladly spend and be spent for you. If I love you more, am I to be loved less? ¹⁶Let it be assumed that I did not burden you. Nevertheless (you say) since I was crafty, I took you in by deceit. ¹⁷Did I take advantage of you through any of those whom I sent to you? ¹⁸I urged Titus to go, and sent the brother with him. Titus did not take advantage of you, did he? Did we not conduct ourselves with the same spirit? Did we not take the same steps?

19 Have you been thinking all along that we

---

a Other ancient authorities read *my power*

When I Am Weak, Then I Am Strong!

Sensible people go to a physician when they are suffering from an illness or injury. Smart students seek help from a teacher when they are stumped by an assignment. Honest people admit when they have failed. Humble people are not afraid to apologize. Admitting we are sick or need help with a problem or have failed or been wrong is a sign not of weakness but a sign of wisdom and maturity.

Paul mentions a mysterious affliction he had to suffer—a "thorn . . . in the flesh" (2 Cor 12:7)—and how desperately he wanted to be rid of it. When he asked God to remove the "thorn," God chose to let it remain in Paul's life.

Paul wanted to be strong on his own, but his experience of struggling with this thorn reminded him that he needed to depend completely on the grace of God. Recognizing that we need God, admitting that we cannot make it on our own—that is a sign of true strength!

▶ 2 Cor 12:1–10

A Spiritual Checkup

STOP! How often do you take a break from all the activities in your life to do a spiritual checkup on your relationships with God, other people, and yourself? In 2 Corinthians 13:5–7, Paul suggests that the Corinthians give themselves a spiritual self-check. This is good advice for us today as well.

A stop sign is a good guiding image for a spiritual checkup. It signals you to interrupt the motion of life and look at what's going on around you. Each letter of the sign can be a reminder to check a different area of your spiritual life:

- *S* can stand for "seek." Do you seek information, counsel, and help when facing difficult or confusing situations and choices?
- *T* can stand for "think." Do you honestly think about how your actions and behaviors affect you, others, and your relationship with God?
- *O* can stand for "others." Do you make it a priority to reach out and support others—particularly those in great need? Are you there for your family and friends?
- *P* can stand for "pray." Do you turn to God for guidance in your life? for the strength to do what is right? Do you thank God for your blessings and the struggles that make you stronger?

▶ 2 Cor 13:5–7

have been defending ourselves before you? We are speaking in Christ before God. Everything we do, beloved, is for the sake of building you up. [20]For I fear that when I come, I may find you not as I wish, and that you may find me not as you wish; I fear that there may perhaps be quarreling, jealousy, anger, selfishness, slander, gossip, conceit, and disorder. [21]I fear that when I come again, my God may humble me before you, and that I may have to mourn over many who previously sinned and have not repented of the impurity, sexual immorality, and licentiousness that they have practiced.

Further Warning

13 This is the third time I am coming to you. "Any charge must be sustained by the evidence of two or three witnesses." [2]I warned those who sinned previously and all the others, and I warn them now while absent, as I did when present on my second visit, that if I come again, I will not be lenient— [3]since you desire proof that Christ is speaking in me. He is not weak in dealing with you, but is powerful in you. [4]For he was crucified in weakness, but lives by the power of God. For we are weak in him,[a] but in dealing with you we will live with him by the power of God.

5 Examine yourselves to see whether you are living in the faith. Test yourselves. Do you not realize that Jesus Christ is in you?—unless, indeed, you fail to meet the test! [6]I hope you will find out that we have not failed. [7]But we pray to God that you may not do anything wrong—not that we may appear to have met the test, but that you may do what is right, though we may seem to have failed. [8]For we cannot do anything against the truth, but only for the truth. [9]For we rejoice when we are weak and you are strong. This is what we pray for, that you may become perfect. [10]So I write these things while I am away from you, so that when I come, I may not have to be severe in using the authority that the Lord has given me for building up and not for tearing down.

Final Greetings and Benediction

11 Finally, brothers and sisters,[b] farewell.[c] Put things in order, listen to my appeal,[d] agree with one another, live in peace; and the God of love and peace will be with you. [12]Greet one another with a holy kiss. All the saints greet you.

13 The grace of the Lord Jesus Christ, the love of God, and the communion of[e] the Holy Spirit be with all of you.

---

a Other ancient authorities read *with him* b Gk *brothers*
c Or *rejoice* d Or *encourage one another* e Or *and the sharing in*

Do you ever scan a letter before you start to read, to see what mood the writer was in? Try it with Galatians. Notice that Paul is angry and upset. He was weak and sick when he founded the church in Galatia. Now, everything is falling apart. He feels like a mother who has to give birth to her children all over again (see 4:12–20). Why? Paul is afraid the Galatians are trading in the true Gospel, based on faith in Jesus, for a false gospel based on Jewish rules and customs.

In Depth

Jesus, the disciples, and most of the first Christians were Jewish. When Gentiles (non-Jews) started to become Christians, a question came up that almost split the early Christian community: Do Gentiles have to become Jewish before they can become Christian? The whole debate soon centered around the Jewish ritual of circumcision. (Circumcision is the surgical removal of the foreskin of a male's penis, which for Jews is the mark of the covenant.)

Paul insisted that circumcision—and all the other Jewish ceremonial laws—had nothing to do with faith in Jesus and was unnecessary for Gentile Christians. At the Council of Jerusalem (see Acts of the Apostles, chapter 15), the other Apostles reluctantly agreed with Paul. But the argument wasn't over. Other Christian missionaries came to Galatia after Paul left the Christian community there. They implied that faith in Christ wasn't enough and insisted that Gentile Christians must be circumcised. The Galatian churches seemed to have agreed because they accepted this difficult teaching quickly.

When Paul heard of this, he was mad! In his Letter to the Galatians, he doesn't even include his typical thanksgiving at the end of his greeting but launches right into his concern. He starts by defending his apostleship. He goes on to tell how the other Apostles at the Council of Jerusalem had agreed with him that the Gentiles do not need to be circumcised. He states how he later challenged Peter personally when Peter allowed himself to be influenced by missionaries preaching something else.

In his fervor, Paul confronts the Galatians: "I am afraid that my work for you may have been wasted" (4:11). He condemns the false missionaries: "If anyone proclaims to you a gospel contrary to what you received, let that one be accursed!" (1:9). Paul is defending the freedom of Gentile Christians from having to obey Jewish religious laws. He is writing the Christians' declaration of independence: "Christ has set us free" (5:1).

🔵 At a Glance

- **1:1–5.** a greeting

- **1:6–10.** Paul's complaint against the Galatian churches

- **1:11—2:14.** Paul's defense of his right to be called an apostle; his encounter with Cephas

- **2:15–21.** Paul's teaching on being made right with God, justification by faith

- **3:1—5:1.** "proofs" in support of his teaching on justification by faith

- **5:2—6:10.** advice on Christian living

- **6:11–18.** final words and a blessing

⭐ Quick Facts

Inspired Author: Paul
Date: from AD 54 to 55
Audience: Gentile Christian churches, probably in northern Galatia

Galatians

Salutation

1 Paul an apostle—sent neither by human commission nor from human authorities, but through Jesus Christ and God the Father, who raised him from the dead— ²and all the members of God's family*a* who are with me,

To the churches of Galatia:

3 Grace to you and peace from God our Father and the Lord Jesus Christ, ⁴who gave himself for our sins to set us free from the present evil age, according to the will of our God and Father, ⁵to whom be the glory forever and ever. Amen.

There Is No Other Gospel

6 I am astonished that you are so quickly deserting the one who called you in the grace of Christ and are turning to a different gospel— ⁷not that there is another gospel, but there are some who are confusing you and want to pervert the gospel of Christ. ⁸But even if we or an angel*b* from heaven should proclaim to you a gospel contrary to what we proclaimed to you, let that one be accursed! ⁹As we have said before, so now I repeat, if anyone proclaims to you a gospel contrary to what you received, let that one be accursed!

10 Am I now seeking human approval, or God's approval? Or am I trying to please people? If I were still pleasing people, I would not be a servant*c* of Christ.

Paul's Vindication of His Apostleship

11 For I want you to know, brothers and sisters,*d* that the gospel that was proclaimed by me is not of human origin; ¹²for I did not receive it from a human source, nor was I taught it, but I received it through a revelation of Jesus Christ.

13 You have heard, no doubt, of my earlier life in Judaism. I was violently persecuting the church of God and was trying to destroy it. ¹⁴I advanced in Judaism beyond many among my people of the same age, for I was far more zealous for the traditions of my ancestors. ¹⁵But when God, who had set me apart before I was born and called me through his grace, was pleased ¹⁶to reveal his Son to me,*e* so that I might proclaim him among the Gentiles, I did not confer with any human being, ¹⁷nor did I go up to Jerusalem to those who were already apostles before me, but I went away at once into Arabia, and afterwards I returned to Damascus.

18 Then after three years I did go up to Jerusalem to visit Cephas and stayed with him fifteen days; ¹⁹but I did not see any other apostle except James the Lord's brother. ²⁰In what I am writing to you, before God, I do not lie! ²¹Then I went into the regions of Syria and Cilicia, ²²and I was still unknown by sight to the churches of Judea that are in Christ; ²³they only heard it said, "The one who formerly was persecuting us is now proclaiming the faith he once tried to destroy." ²⁴And they glorified God because of me.

---

a Gk *all the brothers*   *b* Or *a messenger*   *c* Gk *slave*
d Gk *brothers*   *e* Gk *in me*

Paul and the Other Apostles

2 Then after fourteen years I went up again to Jerusalem with Barnabas, taking Titus along with me. [2]I went up in response to a revelation. Then I laid before them (though only in a private meeting with the acknowledged leaders) the gospel that I proclaim among the Gentiles, in order to make sure that I was not running, or had not run, in vain. [3]But even Titus, who was with me, was not compelled to be circumcised, though he was a Greek. [4]But because of false believers[a] secretly brought in, who slipped in to spy on the freedom we have in Christ Jesus, so that they might enslave us— [5]we did not submit to them even for a moment, so that the truth of the gospel might always remain with you. [6]And from those who were supposed to be acknowledged leaders (what they actually were makes no difference to me; God shows no partiality)—those leaders contributed nothing to me. [7]On the contrary, when they saw that I had been entrusted with the gospel for the uncircumcised, just as Peter had been entrusted with the gospel for the circumcised [8](for he who worked through Peter making him an apostle to the circumcised also worked through me in sending me to the Gentiles), [9]and when James and Cephas and John, who were acknowledged pillars, recognized the grace that had been given to me, they gave to Barnabas and me the right hand of fellowship, agreeing that we should go to the Gentiles and they to the circumcised. [10]They asked only one thing, that we remember the poor, which was actually what I was[b] eager to do.

Paul Rebukes Peter at Antioch

11 But when Cephas came to Antioch, I opposed him to his face, because he stood self-condemned; [12]for until certain people came from James, he used to eat with the Gentiles. But after they came, he drew back and kept himself separate for fear of the circumcision faction. [13]And the other Jews joined him in this hypocrisy, so that even Barnabas was led astray by their hypocrisy. [14]But when I saw that they were not acting consistently with the truth of the gospel, I said to Cephas before them all, "If you, though a Jew, live like a Gentile and not like a Jew, how can you compel the Gentiles to live like Jews?"[c]

Jews and Gentiles Are Saved by Faith

15 We ourselves are Jews by birth and not Gentile sinners; [16]yet we know that a person is justified[d] not by the works of the law but through faith in Jesus Christ.[e] And we have come to believe in Christ Jesus, so that we might be justified by faith in Christ,[f] and not by doing the works of the law, because no one will be justified by the works of the law. [17]But if, in our effort to be justified in Christ, we ourselves have been found to be sinners, is Christ then a servant of sin? Certainly not! [18]But if I build up again the very things that I once tore down, then I demonstrate that I am a transgressor. [19]For through the law I died to the law, so that I might live to God. I have

Live It!

Consistent and Trustworthy

At the beginning of Galatians, chapter 2, Paul describes what went on at the Council of Jerusalem. The Council established that Gentile Christians do not have to become Jews by following certain Jewish laws, such as circumcision and dietary regulations, to gain admission to the Christian community. Paul emphasizes that a person is made right with God (justified) not through the law but through faith in Jesus Christ.

In Antioch, when Peter (Cephas) stops eating with Gentile Christians under pressure from Jewish Christians, Paul challenges him. He points out that Peter's behavior is not consistent with the truth of the Gospel and that this inconsistency is misleading and confusing to the Christian community.

A credible Christian seeks to be consistent in word and deed. Unfortunately, Peter's actions speak much louder than his words. And, like Peter, when our actions do not match our words, people stop trusting us. And then we too begin to feel like hypocrites and lose our self-esteem.

Take some time to reflect on how consistently your actions reflect your words. Consider ways you can improve. When your actions match your words, people will recognize you as a person of integrity and place their trust in you.

▶ Gal 2:11–14

been crucified with Christ; 20and it is no longer I who live, but it is Christ who lives in me. And the life I now live in the flesh I live by faith in the Son of God,*a* who loved me and gave himself for me. 21I do not nullify the grace of God; for if justification*b* comes through the law, then Christ died for nothing.

Law or Faith

3 You foolish Galatians! Who has bewitched you? It was before your eyes that Jesus Christ was publicly exhibited as crucified! 2The only thing I want to learn from you is this: Did you receive the Spirit by doing the works of the law or by believing what you heard? 3Are you so foolish? Having started with the Spirit, are you now ending with the flesh? 4Did you experience so much for nothing?—if it really was for nothing. 5Well then, does God*c* supply you with the Spirit and work miracles among you by your doing the works of the law, or by your believing what you heard?

6 Just as Abraham "believed God, and it was reckoned to him as righteousness," 7so, you see, those who believe are the descendants of Abraham. 8And the scripture, foreseeing that God would justify the Gentiles by faith, declared the gospel beforehand to Abraham, saying, "All the Gentiles shall be blessed in you." 9For this reason, those who believe are blessed with Abraham who believed.

10 For all who rely on the works of the law are under a curse; for it is written, "Cursed is everyone who does not observe and obey all the things written in the book of the law." 11Now it is evident that no one is justified before God by the law; for "The one who is righteous will live by faith."*d* 12But the law does not rest on faith; on the contrary, "Whoever does the works of the law*e* will live by them." 13Christ redeemed us from the curse of the law by becoming a curse for us—for it is written, "Cursed is everyone who hangs on a tree"— 14in order that in Christ Jesus the blessing of Abraham might come to the Gentiles, so that we might receive the promise of the Spirit through faith.

The Promise to Abraham

15 Brothers and sisters,*f* I give an example from daily life: once a person's will*g* has been ratified, no one adds to it or annuls it. 16Now the promises were made to Abraham and to his offspring;*h* it does not say, "And to offsprings,"*i* as of many; but it says, "And to your offspring,"*h* that is, to one person, who is Christ. 17My point is this: the law, which came four hundred thirty

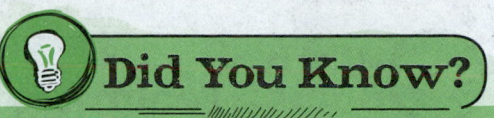

Did You Know?

Justified in Christ

Throughout Galatians, Paul speaks about the difference between being justified by faith and being justified through the law. Christians believe they are justified—made right with God—not through a perfect keeping of religious laws, but through God's free gift to those who have faith in Christ. Christ's saving sacrifice alone will set them free from their sin. Their trust must be in him and not in their own ability to please God. God gives us the grace needed to live as children of God.

▶ **Gal 3:1—4:7**

years later, does not annul a covenant previously ratified by God, so as to nullify the promise. 18For if the inheritance comes from the law, it no longer comes from the promise; but God granted it to Abraham through the promise.

The Purpose of the Law

19 Why then the law? It was added because of transgressions, until the offspring*h* would come to whom the promise had been made; and it was ordained through angels by a mediator. 20Now a mediator involves more than one party; but God is one.

21 Is the law then opposed to the promises of God? Certainly not! For if a law had been given that could make alive, then righteousness would indeed come through the law. 22But the scripture has imprisoned all things under the power of sin, so that what was promised through faith in Jesus Christ*j* might be given to those who believe.

23 Now before faith came, we were imprisoned and guarded under the law until faith would be revealed. 24Therefore the law was our disciplinarian until Christ came, so that we might be justified by faith. 25But now that faith has come, we are no longer subject to a disciplinarian, 26for in Christ Jesus you are all children of God through faith. 27As many of you as were baptized into Christ have clothed yourselves

---

a Or by the faith of the Son of God   b Or righteousness
c Gk he   d Or The one who is righteous through faith will live
e Gk does them   f Gk Brothers   g Or covenant (as in verse 17)
h Gk seed   i Gk seeds   j Or through the faith of Jesus Christ

GAL

GAL

Catholic Social Teaching

Radical Equality

Galatians 3:28 may have been an early baptismal formula. In it Paul makes a radical statement: The source of our equality as humans is Jesus Christ! (Note that the word *radical* means both "root" and "extreme"—and that Paul's statement is both fundamental to Christian belief and a great expression of that belief.)

This passage is a source of hope for all who have at times been made to feel as if they are not fully human. In Baptism we become one in Christ and, as part of the Christian community, are called to respect the equality of all living persons. This may not seem

like a radical idea in our contemporary culture, but throughout history people have not always been treated as full human persons. Even today in many parts of the world there are people who find themselves treated as "less than" because of their race, ethnic background, religion, or gender.

The principles of Catholic social teaching call us to respect the dignity of all human persons and to be in solidarity with others, especially those who live on the margins. Being in solidarity means that we help to create a world in which basic human needs like

food, housing, healthcare, and religious freedom are met and justice and peace are available to all.

Is Paul's vision of equality a reality in the world around you? Are all the people in your school or community regarded as equally valuable? What can you do to help create a world where all people live in solidarity?

▶ **Gal 3:28**

Solidarity

---

with Christ. 28There is no longer Jew or Greek, there is no longer slave or free, there is no longer male and female; for all of you are one in Christ Jesus. 29And if you belong to Christ, then you are Abraham's offspring,[a] heirs according to the promise.

4 My point is this: heirs, as long as they are minors, are no better than slaves, though they are the owners of all the property; 2but they remain under guardians and trustees until the date set by the father. 3So with us; while we were minors, we were enslaved to the elemental spirits[b] of the world. 4But when the fullness of time had come, God sent his Son, born of a woman, born under the law, 5in order to redeem those who were under the law, so that we might receive adoption as children. 6And because you are children, God has sent the Spirit of his Son into our[c] hearts, crying, "Abba![d] Father!" 7So you are no longer a slave but a child, and if a child then also an heir, through God.[e]

Paul Reproves the Galatians

8 Formerly, when you did not know God, you were enslaved to beings that by nature are

> "There is no longer Jew or Greek, there is no longer slave or free, there is no longer male and female; for all of you are one in Christ Jesus."
>
> (Gal 3:28)

not gods. 9Now, however, that you have come to know God, or rather to be known by God, how can you turn back again to the weak and beggarly elemental spirits?[f] How can you want to be enslaved to them again? 10You are observing special days, and months, and seasons, and years. 11I am afraid that my work for you may have been wasted.

12 Friends,[g] I beg you, become as I am, for I also have become as you are. You have done me no wrong. 13You know that it was because of a physical infirmity that I first announced the gospel to you; 14though my condition put you to the test, you did not scorn or despise me, but welcomed me as an angel of God, as Christ Jesus. 15What has become of the goodwill you felt? For I testify that, had it been possible, you would have torn out your eyes and given them to me. 16Have I now become your enemy by telling you

a Gk *seed*   b Or *the rudiments*   c Other ancient authorities read *your*   d Aramaic for *Father*   e Other ancient authorities read *an heir of God through Christ*   f Or *beggarly rudiments*   g Gk *Brothers*

the truth? [17]They make much of you, but for no good purpose; they want to exclude you, so that you may make much of them. [18]It is good to be made much of for a good purpose at all times, and not only when I am present with you. [19]My little children, for whom I am again in the pain of childbirth until Christ is formed in you, [20]I wish I were present with you now and could change my tone, for I am perplexed about you.

The Allegory of Hagar and Sarah

21 Tell me, you who desire to be subject to the law, will you not listen to the law? [22]For it is written that Abraham had two sons, one by a slave woman and the other by a free woman. [23]One, the child of the slave, was born according to the flesh; the other, the child of the free woman, was born through the promise. [24]Now this is an allegory: these women are two covenants. One woman, in fact, is Hagar, from Mount Sinai, bearing children for slavery. [25]Now Hagar is Mount Sinai in Arabia[a] and corresponds to the present Jerusalem, for she is in slavery with her children. [26]But the other woman corresponds to the Jerusalem above; she is free, and she is our mother. [27]For it is written,

"Rejoice, you childless one, you who bear no
    children,
    burst into song and shout, you who endure
    no birth pangs;
for the children of the desolate woman are more
    numerous
    than the children of the one who is married."
[28]Now you,[b] my friends,[c] are children of the promise, like Isaac. [29]But just as at that time the child who was born according to the flesh persecuted the child who was born according to the Spirit, so it is now also. [30]But what does the scripture say? "Drive out the slave and her child; for the child of the slave will not share the inheritance with the child of the free woman." [31]So then, friends,[c] we are children, not of the slave but of the free woman. [1]For freedom Christ has set us free. Stand firm, therefore, and do not submit again to a yoke of slavery.

The Nature of Christian Freedom

2 Listen! I, Paul, am telling you that if you let yourselves be circumcised, Christ will be of no benefit to you. [3]Once again I testify to every man who lets himself be circumcised that he is obliged to obey the entire law. [4]You who want to be justified by the law have cut yourselves off from Christ; you have fallen away from grace. [5]For through the Spirit, by faith, we eagerly wait for the hope of righteousness. [6]For in Christ Jesus

neither circumcision nor uncircumcision counts for anything; the only thing that counts is faith working[d] through love.

7 You were running well; who prevented you from obeying the truth? [8]Such persuasion does not come from the one who calls you. [9]A little yeast leavens the whole batch of dough. [10]I am confident about you in the Lord that you will not think otherwise. But whoever it is that is

---

a Other ancient authorities read *For Sinai is a mountain in Arabia*
b Other ancient authorities read *we*   *c* Gk *brothers*   *d* Or *made effective*

Fill Me, Lord

Fill me with the fruits of your Spirit, Lord. Fill me with love, so that I seek to understand and appreciate the rich variety and diversity of life that surrounds me.

Fill me with joy, so that I celebrate your presence in each and every moment I am on this earth.

Fill me with peace, so that I know how to ease those angry and sometimes violent urges that well up inside of me.

Fill me with patience, so that I stop rushing long enough to witness your miraculous work taking place all around me (and within me!).

Fill me with kindness, so that I take the extra time to help the one in need, even when it isn't convenient for me.

Fill me with faithfulness, so that I place my mind, heart, and all that I do in the service of your Gospel.

Fill me with gentleness, so that others know that I believe in a God who loves and cares for all people.

Fill me with self-control, so that I act not on my impulses and urges, but rather on my beliefs and values, which are rooted in you.

Fill me with these fruits of your spirit, Lord! Amen

▶ Gal 5:22–26

Cultural Connection

The Principle of *Imani*

Be not discouraged. There is a future for you. . . . The resistance encountered now predicates hope. . . . Only as we rise . . . do we encounter opposition.

These words by Frederick Douglass in 1892 encouraged African Americans not to abandon their struggle for equality. It seemed that the more they struggled, the more pain was inflicted on them. In the face of certain suffering, Douglass urged them to look toward the promise of living as equals under the law.

They knew that God was their liberator and justice giver. God made them brave in the face of danger and capable of dying for the cause they embraced. They looked to God and saw their future. They took the words of Galatians 6:9 seriously: "Let us not grow weary in doing what is right."

Today, we don't face slave masters and live on plantations as servants in fetters, but we do endure other situations equally as dangerous. Let us not grow weary

or lose heart. We must practice the Kwanzaa principle of *imani*, or "faith" (see "Kwanzaa as a Way of Life," near Deut 10:12–22). Our God is still in the saving business.

Dear God, my future is in your hands. Lead me to it with your power. Amen.

▶ **Gal 6:9**

---

confusing you will pay the penalty. [11]But my friends,[a] why am I still being persecuted if I am still preaching circumcision? In that case the offense of the cross has been removed. [12]I wish those who unsettle you would castrate themselves!

13 For you were called to freedom, brothers and sisters;[a] only do not use your freedom as an opportunity for self-indulgence,[b] but through love become slaves to one another. [14]For the whole law is summed up in a single commandment, "You shall love your neighbor as yourself." [15]If, however, you bite and devour one another, take care that you are not consumed by one another.

The Works of the Flesh

16 Live by the Spirit, I say, and do not gratify the desires of the flesh. [17]For what the flesh desires is opposed to the Spirit, and what the Spirit desires is opposed to the flesh; for these are opposed to each other, to prevent you from doing what you want. [18]But if you are led by the Spirit, you are not subject to the law. [19]Now the works of the flesh are obvious: fornication, impurity, licentiousness, [20]idolatry, sorcery, enmities, strife, jealousy, anger, quarrels, dissensions, factions, [21]envy,[c] drunkenness, carousing, and things like these. I am warning you, as I warned you before: those who do such things will not inherit the kingdom of God.

The Fruit of the Spirit

22 By contrast, the fruit of the Spirit is love, joy, peace, patience, kindness, generosity, faithfulness, [23]gentleness, and self-control. There is no law against such things. [24]And those who belong to Christ Jesus have crucified the flesh with its passions and desires. [25]If we live by the Spirit, let us also be guided by the Spirit. [26]Let us not become conceited, competing against one another, envying one another.

Bear One Another's Burdens

6 My friends,[d] if anyone is detected in a transgression, you who have received the Spirit should restore such a one in a spirit of gentleness. Take care that you yourselves are not tempted. [2]Bear one another's burdens, and in this way you will fulfill[e] the law of Christ. [3]For if those who are nothing think they are something, they deceive themselves. [4]All must test their own work; then that work, rather than their neighbor's work, will become a cause for pride. [5]For all must carry their own loads.

6 Those who are taught the word must share in all good things with their teacher.

7 Do not be deceived; God is not mocked,

---

a Gk brothers   b Gk the flesh   c Other ancient authorities add murder   d Gk Brothers   e Other ancient authorities read in this way fulfill for you reap whatever you sow. [8]If you sow to your own flesh, you will reap corruption from the flesh; but if you sow to the Spirit, you will reap eternal life from the Spirit. [9]So let us not grow weary in doing what is right, for we will reap at harvest time, if we do not give up. [10]So then, whenever we have an opportunity, let us work for the good of all, and especially for those of the family of faith.

Final Admonitions and Benediction

[11] See what large letters I make when I am writing in my own hand! [12]It is those who want to make a good showing in the flesh that try to compel you to be circumcised—only that they may not be persecuted for the cross of Christ. [13]Even the circumcised do not themselves obey the law, but they want you to be circumcised so that they may boast about your flesh. [14]May I never boast of anything except the cross of our Lord Jesus Christ, by which[a] the world has been crucified to me, and I to the world. [15]For[b] neither circumcision nor uncircumcision is anything; but a new creation is everything! [16]As for those who will follow this rule—peace be upon them, and mercy, and upon the Israel of God.

17 From now on, let no one make trouble for me; for I carry the marks of Jesus branded on my body.

18 May the grace of our Lord Jesus Christ be with your spirit, brothers and sisters.[c] Amen.

---

a Or *through whom*   *b* Other ancient authorities add *in Christ Jesus*   *c* Gk *brothers*

What's the purpose of life? Why am I alive? What's the point of it all anyway? You may have asked questions like these out of simple curiosity, or during a time when life wasn't going so well. In either case, God has an answer for you tucked away inside the Letter to the Ephesians. This letter talks about God's plan to save us for a life in union with God and one another, both now and for all eternity!

In Depth

Three times in the poetic opening chapter, the writer of Ephesians tells us that we are here because we have been chosen by God! In this beautiful prayer of praise for the Father (see verses 3–6), the Son (see verse 12), and the Holy Spirit (see verses 13–14), we are told that that's why we're alive!

This letter has hardly any of the personal greeting you'd expect in a communication to a specific group of people. Also, the reference to Ephesus in the first verse doesn't appear in some of the earliest copies we have of the letter. For these reasons, many scholars believe that this letter was intended to be circulated among various churches and that the author was addressing the universal church with Christ as its head, unlike Paul who talks about the individual or local church. Most scholars also believe that the Letter to the Colossians was used as a pattern for this letter.

Ephesians emphasizes unity among Christians. It especially emphasizes that Gentile (non-Jewish) Christians are one with Jewish Christians, for Christ "has made both groups into one and has broken down the dividing wall" (2:14). It explains that it is the early Christians' job—as it is our job—to treat one another with love, "making every effort to maintain the unity" (4:3). The image of the church as Christ's body is used here, as it is in 1 Corinthians, chapter 12, to emphasize our unity (4:15–16).

Ephesians also talks about the place of good works in the life of a Christian. Good works can be thought of as living a moral life, or as following moral rules. The author of this letter has made clear that we are not saved by the law. So, does this mean we can do anything we want? The letter explains that we are saved not *by doing* good works but *in order to do* good works.

The letter ends with some practical advice for living out the faith on a daily basis. There are rules for moral living. There are instructions for Christian family life. There is an analogy for putting on the "armor of God" to resist evil in all its forms. As long as we keep in mind that this letter is written for a culture that was different from ours, the advice will serve us well too!

At a Glance

- **1:1–2.** a greeting
- **1:3–23.** a benediction, and prayer for the community
- **Chapters 2–3.** a discussion of unity in Christ and the mystery of the gospel
- **4:1—6:20.** advice for Christian living
- **6:21–24.** a final message and a blessing

Quick Facts

Inspired Author: a follower of Paul (see "Introduction to the Letters and Revelation")
Date Written: after Paul's death, from AD 90 to 100
Audience: Gentile churches, possibly in Asia Minor

Ephesians

Salutation

1 Paul, an apostle of Christ Jesus by the will of God,

To the saints who are in Ephesus and are faithful[a] in Christ Jesus:

2 Grace to you and peace from God our Father and the Lord Jesus Christ.

Spiritual Blessings in Christ

3 Blessed be the God and Father of our Lord Jesus Christ, who has blessed us in Christ with every spiritual blessing in the heavenly places, [4]just as he chose us in Christ[b] before the foundation of the world to be holy and blameless before him in love. [5]He destined us for adoption as his children through Jesus Christ, according to the good pleasure of his will, [6]to the praise of his glorious grace that he freely bestowed on us in the Beloved. [7]In him we have redemption through his blood, the forgiveness of our trespasses, according to the riches of his grace [8]that he lavished on us. With all wisdom and insight [9]he has made known to us the mystery of his will, according to his good pleasure that he set forth in Christ, [10]as a plan for the fullness of time, to gather up all things in him, things in heaven and things on earth. [11]In Christ we have also obtained an inheritance,[c] having been destined according to the purpose of him who accomplishes all things according to his counsel and will, [12]so that we, who were the first to set our hope on Christ, might live for the praise of his glory. [13]In him you also, when you had heard the word of truth, the gospel of your salvation, and had believed in him, were marked with the seal of the promised Holy Spirit; [14]this[d] is the pledge of our inheritance toward redemption as God's own people, to the praise of his glory.

Paul's Prayer

15 I have heard of your faith in the Lord Jesus and your love[e] toward all the saints, and for this reason [16]I do not cease to give thanks for you as I remember you in my prayers. [17]I pray that the God of our Lord Jesus Christ, the Father of glory, may give you a spirit of wisdom and revelation as you come to know him, [18]so that, with the eyes of your heart enlightened, you may know what is the hope to which he has called you, what are

---

a Other ancient authorities lack *in Ephesus*, reading *saints who are also faithful* b Gk *in him* c Or *been made a heritage* d Other ancient authorities read *who* e Other ancient authorities lack *and your love*

1:1

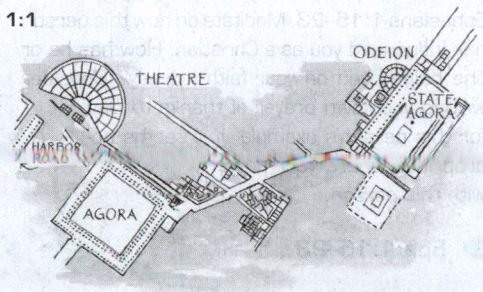

Artist's rendition of the city plan for first-century Ephesus

the riches of his glorious inheritance among the saints, [19]and what is the immeasurable greatness of his power for us who believe, according to the working of his great power. [20]God[a] put this power to work in Christ when he raised him from the dead and seated him at his right hand in the heavenly places, [21]far above all rule and authority and power and dominion, and above every name that is named, not only in this age but also in the age to come. [22]And he has put all things under his feet and has made him the head over all things for the church, [23]which is his body, the fullness of him who fills all in all.

From Death to Life

2 You were dead through the trespasses and sins [2]in which you once lived, following the course of this world, following the ruler of the power of the air, the spirit that is now at work among those who are disobedient. [3]All of us once lived among them in the passions of our flesh, following the desires of flesh and senses, and we were by nature children of wrath, like everyone else. [4]But God, who is rich in mercy, out of the great love with which he loved us [5]even when we were dead through our trespasses, made us alive together with Christ[b]—by grace you have been saved— [6]and raised us up with him and seated us with him in the heavenly places in Christ Jesus, [7]so that in the ages to come he might show

the immeasurable riches of his grace in kindness toward us in Christ Jesus. [8]For by grace you have been saved through faith, and this is not your own doing; it is the gift of God— [9]not the result of works, so that no one may boast. [10]For we are what he has made us, created in Christ Jesus for good works, which God prepared beforehand to be our way of life.

One in Christ

11 So then, remember that at one time you Gentiles by birth,[c] called "the uncircumcision" by those who are called "the circumcision"—a physical circumcision made in the flesh by human hands— [12]remember that you were at that time without Christ, being aliens from the commonwealth of Israel, and strangers to the covenants of promise, having no hope and without God in the world. [13]But now in Christ Jesus you who once were far off have been brought near by the blood of Christ. [14]For he is our peace; in his flesh he has made both groups into one and has broken down the dividing wall, that is, the hostility

---

a Gk He   b Other ancient authorities read *in Christ*   c Gk *in the flesh*

P ray It!

I Give God Thanks for You!

T hink of people in your family, community, school, and church who are living out the Gospel message. Who is honestly striving to live her or his Christian faith? A parent or guardian? a friend? a neighbor? a teacher? a minister?

Hold this person in your heart as you read Ephesians 1:15–23. Meditate on how this person has influenced you as a Christian. How has he or she helped you on your faith journey? Consider writing your own prayer of thanks to God for this person's example. If it seems appropriate, share your prayer with this person.

▶ **Eph 1:15–23**

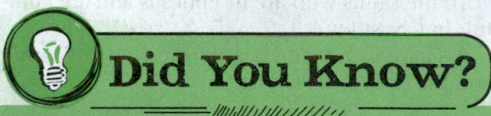

Did You Know?

Faith Versus Good Works

E phesians 2:1–10 deals with the question of faith versus good works (good works are moral living and Gospel-motivated works of service, justice, courage, and so on). This issue has divided Christians since the early Church and was a major issue at the time of the Protestant Reformation. Some say we are saved by our good works. Others say that good works are irrelevant and that we are saved only through our faith in Christ.

The writer of Ephesians makes it clear that both those statements are incomplete. The core Christian belief is this: We are saved by God's grace through faith in Jesus Christ. We were saved not *by doing* good works but *in order to do* good works. Our salvation is God's gift to us; how we live is our gift to God.

▶ **Eph 2:1–10**

Cultural Connection

Rooted in Love

Read the prayer in Ephesians 3:14–21. Then reflect on the prayer below from Christians in the Philippines, which also talks about roots and love.

Lord,
make us realize that our Chris-
tianity is like a rice field:
when it is newly planted the
paddies are prominent,
but as the plants take root
and grow taller;

these divided paddies gradu-
ally vanish,
and soon there appears only
one vast continuous field.
So give us roots that love,
and help us grow in Christian
fellowship and service,
that thy will be done in our
lives,
through our Savior, Jesus
Christ.

(From *Your Will Be Done*, p. 145)

Finally, personalize the prayer in 3:14–21 by changing *you* to *I* or *we*, and *your* to *my* or *our*. Kneel and pray this prayer, knowing that God is indeed listening to you at this very moment.

▶ **Eph 3:14–21**

E
P
H

---

between us. [15]He has abolished the law with its commandments and ordinances, that he might create in himself one new humanity in place of the two, thus making peace, [16]and might reconcile both groups to God in one body[a] through the cross, thus putting to death that hostility through it.[b] [17]So he came and proclaimed peace to you who were far off and peace to those who were near; [18]for through him both of us have access in one Spirit to the Father. [19]So then you are no longer strangers and aliens, but you are citizens with the saints and also members of the household of God, [20]built upon the foundation of the apostles and prophets, with Christ Jesus himself as the cornerstone.[c] [21]In him the whole structure is joined together and grows into a holy temple in the Lord; [22]in whom you also are built together spiritually[d] into a dwelling place for God.

Paul's Ministry to the Gentiles

3 This is the reason that I Paul am a prisoner for[e] Christ Jesus for the sake of you Gentiles— [2]for surely you have already heard of the commission of God's grace that was given me for you, [3]and how the mystery was made known to me by revelation, as I wrote above in a few words, [4]a reading of which will enable you to perceive my understanding of the mystery of Christ. [5]In former generations this mystery[f] was not made known to humankind, as it has now been revealed to his holy apostles and prophets by the Spirit: [6]that is, the Gentiles have become fellow heirs, members of the same body, and sharers in the promise in Christ Jesus through the gospel.

7 Of this gospel I have become a servant according to the gift of God's grace that was given me by the working of his power. [8]Although I am the very least of all the saints, this grace was given to me to bring to the Gentiles the news of the boundless riches of Christ, [9]and to make everyone see[g] what is the plan of the mystery hidden for ages in[h] God who created all things; [10]so that through the church the wisdom of God in its rich variety might now be made known to the rulers and authorities in the heavenly places. [11]This was in accordance with the eternal purpose that he has carried out in Christ Jesus our Lord, [12]in whom we have access to God in boldness and confidence through faith in him.[i] [13]I pray therefore that you[j] may not lose heart over my sufferings for you; they are your glory.

Prayer for the Readers

14 For this reason I bow my knees before the Father,[k] [15]from whom every family[l] in heaven and on earth takes its name. [16]I pray that, according to the riches of his glory, he may grant that you may be strengthened in your inner being with power through his Spirit, [17]and that Christ may dwell in your hearts through faith, as you are being rooted and grounded in love. [18]I pray that you may have the power to comprehend, with all the saints, what is the breadth and length and height and depth, [19]and to know the love of

---

a Or *reconcile both of us in one body for God*   b Or *in him*, or *in himself*   c Or *keystone*   d Gk *in the Spirit*   e Or *of*   f Gk *it*   g Other ancient authorities read *to bring to light*   h Or *by*   i Or *the faith of him*   j Or *I*   k Other ancient authorities add *of our Lord Jesus Christ*   l Gk *fatherhood*

Cultural Connection

Weave for Us a Garment

The prayer in Ephesians 4:1–6 is a prayer of unity, a prayer for us to live as one—one faith, one Baptism, one God, one body, one Spirit, one hope. This Native American prayer is also a prayer of unity, a prayer for us to live in a world where all people, all creation, are woven into one garment. May we walk in such a world. May we be part of creating such a world.

Weave for us a garment of brightness;
May the warp be the white light of morning,
May the weft be the red light of evening,

May the fringes be the falling rain,
May the border be the standing rainbow.
Thus weave for us a garment of brightness,
That we may walk fittingly where birds sing,
That we may walk fittingly where grass is green,
O our Mother the Earth, O our Father the Sky.

▶ **Eph 4:1–6**

Christ that surpasses knowledge, so that you may be filled with all the fullness of God.

20 Now to him who by the power at work within us is able to accomplish abundantly far more than all we can ask or imagine, ²¹to him be glory in the church and in Christ Jesus to all generations, forever and ever. Amen.

Unity in the Body of Christ

4 I therefore, the prisoner in the Lord, beg you to lead a life worthy of the calling to which you have been called, ²with all humility and gentleness, with patience, bearing with one another in love, ³making every effort to maintain the unity of the Spirit in the bond of peace. ⁴There is one body and one Spirit, just as you were called to the one hope of your calling, ⁵one Lord, one faith, one baptism, ⁶one God and Father of all, who is above all and through all and in all.

7 But each of us was given grace according to the measure of Christ's gift. ⁸Therefore it is said,

"When he ascended on high he made captivity
    itself a captive;
    he gave gifts to his people."

⁹(When it says, "He ascended," what does it mean but that he had also descended*a* into the lower parts of the earth? ¹⁰He who descended is the same one who ascended far above all the heavens, so that he might fill all things.) ¹¹The gifts he gave

were that some would be apostles, some prophets, some evangelists, some pastors and teachers, ¹²to equip the saints for the work of ministry, for building up the body of Christ, ¹³until all of us come to the unity of the faith and of the knowledge of the Son of God, to maturity, to the measure of the full stature of Christ. ¹⁴We must no longer be children, tossed to and fro and blown about by every wind of doctrine, by people's trickery, by their craftiness in deceitful scheming. ¹⁵But speaking the truth in love, we must grow up in every way into him who is the head, into Christ, ¹⁶from whom the whole body, joined and knit together by every ligament with which it is equipped, as each part is working properly, promotes the body's growth in building itself up in love.

The Old Life and the New

17 Now this I affirm and insist on in the Lord: you must no longer live as the Gentiles live, in the futility of their minds. ¹⁸They are darkened in their understanding, alienated from the life of God because of their ignorance and hardness of heart. ¹⁹They have lost all sensitivity and have abandoned themselves to licentiousness, greedy to practice every kind of impurity. ²⁰That is not the way you learned Christ! ²¹For surely you have heard about him and were taught in him, as truth is in Jesus. ²²You were taught to put away

> "There is one body and one Spirit, just as you were called to the one hope of your calling, one Lord, one faith, one baptism, one God and Father of all."
>
> (Eph 4:4–6)

a Other ancient authorities add *first*

Cultural Connection

Prophets of Hope, Youth on a Mission

Ephesians 4:17–32 has some teachings about the Christian way of life that uses baptismal imagery. Those who are trying to follow Jesus want to be prophets of hope, as expressed in this song written for Hispanic youth:

> We're Prophets of Hope, youth on a mission, spreading the Gospel of Christ.
> We're Prophets of Hope, issuing the challenge: to build the Reign of God.
>
> Pilgrims on a journey, marching towards our goal.
> Led by the Spirit, strengthened by the Lord.
> We bear each other's burdens and give each other hope.
> Following our savior we press on towards our goal.
>
> We come from towns and cities.
> We are immigrants and natives,
> laborers and students who want a better life.

> We want to be successful, but not at any cost.
> Unless we work for justice humanity is lost.
>
> We face discrimination, poverty and drugs.
> The values of our culture are all under attack.
> But we have faith in Jesus; he will give us strength.
> Together we will struggle to build a better world.
>
> The Gospel is our road map, the Church is our guide.
> We're Catholic Latinos, youth who take a stand.
> Leaders in our churches, reflecting as we go.
> Learning from our set-backs, we never give up hope.

(Jose Antonio Rubio)

▶ Eph 4:17–32

---

your former way of life, your old self, corrupt and deluded by its lusts, 23and to be renewed in the spirit of your minds, 24and to clothe yourselves with the new self, created according to the likeness of God in true righteousness and holiness.

Rules for the New Life

25 So then, putting away falsehood, let all of us speak the truth to our neighbors, for we are members of one another. 26Be angry but do not sin; do not let the sun go down on your anger, 27and do not make room for the devil. 28Thieves must give up stealing; rather let them labor and work honestly with their own hands, so as to have something to share with the needy. 29Let no evil talk come out of your mouths, but only what is useful for building up,*a* as there is need, so that your words may give grace to those who hear. 30And do not grieve the Holy Spirit of God, with which you were marked with a seal for the day of redemption. 31Put away from you all bitterness and wrath and anger and wrangling and slander, together with all malice, 32and be kind to one another, tenderhearted, forgiving one another, as God in Christ has forgiven you.*b*

5 1Therefore be imitators of God, as beloved children, 2and live in love, as Christ loved us*c* and gave himself up for us, a fragrant offering and sacrifice to God.

Renounce Pagan Ways

3 But fornication and impurity of any kind, or greed, must not even be mentioned among you, as is proper among saints. 4Entirely out of place is obscene, silly, and vulgar talk; but instead, let there be thanksgiving. 5Be sure of this, that no fornicator or impure person, or one who is greedy (that is, an idolater), has any inheritance in the kingdom of Christ and of God.

6 Let no one deceive you with empty words, for because of these things the wrath of God comes on those who are disobedient. 7Therefore do not be associated with them. 8For once you were darkness, but now in the Lord you are light. Live as children of light— 9for the fruit of the light is found in all that is good and right and true. 10Try to find out what is pleasing to the Lord. 11Take no part in the unfruitful works of darkness, but instead expose them. 12For it is shameful even to mention what such people do secretly; 13but everything exposed by the light becomes visible, 14for everything that becomes visible is light. Therefore it says,

> "Sleeper, awake!
>   Rise from the dead,
>   and Christ will shine on you."

---

a Other ancient authorities read *building up faith*   *b* Other ancient authorities read *us*   *c* Other ancient authorities read *you*

15 Be careful then how you live, not as unwise people but as wise, [16]making the most of the time, because the days are evil. [17]So do not be foolish, but understand what the will of the Lord is. [18]Do not get drunk with wine, for that is debauchery; but be filled with the Spirit, [19]as you sing psalms and hymns and spiritual songs among yourselves, singing and making melody to the Lord in your hearts, [20]giving thanks to God the Father at all times and for everything in the name of our Lord Jesus Christ.

The Christian Household

21 Be subject to one another out of reverence for Christ.

22 Wives, be subject to your husbands as you are to the Lord. [23]For the husband is the head of the wife just as Christ is the head of the church,

the body of which he is the Savior. [24]Just as the church is subject to Christ, so also wives ought to be, in everything, to their husbands.

25 Husbands, love your wives, just as Christ loved the church and gave himself up for her, [26]in order to make her holy by cleansing her with the washing of water by the word, [27]so as to present the church to himself in splendor, without a spot or wrinkle or anything of the kind—yes, so that she may be holy and without blemish. [28]In the same way, husbands should love their wives as they do their own bodies. He who loves his wife loves himself. [29]For no one ever hates his own body, but he nourishes and tenderly cares for it, just as Christ does for the church, [30]because we are members of his body.[a] [31]"For this reason a man will leave his father and mother

a Other ancient authorities add *of his flesh and of his bones*

Alcohol

The author of Ephesians 5:10–20 does not mince words. This passage encourages the early Christians, and us, to wake up and find out what pleases God. It calls them to avoid participating in actions they would be ashamed of if the actions were exposed in the light. Its tone is not of scolding but rather of passionate encouragement, wanting the best for each of us.

Although the use of alcohol is singled out in this passage, drinking is not the only substance abuse issue young people face during adolescence. Many young people are pressured by friends, the media, or family members to participate in drinking, smoking, and using drugs. Abuse of these substances prevents us from being filled with the Spirit. As the author of Ephesians advises, making wise choices about these substances is important.

Take some time to reflect on your own life.
● What temptations do you face in this regard?
● What choices can you make that would please God and allow you to enjoy the fullness of life in the Spirit?
● Who can help you to make the correct decisions and help you to stick to them?

▶ Eph 5:10–20

Family Relationships

When Ephesians 5:21—6:4 comes up in the Sunday readings, it sometimes causes confusion. People wonder how the Bible can teach that a wife should be subject to her husband. This is another case where we must take into account the cultural context of the biblical writer in order to properly interpret the passage. At the time the Letter to the Ephesians was written, males were dominant in society. Wives and children were considered men's property. The letter's challenge to a man to love his wife and to treat his children respectfully was probably viewed as a radical statement by people at the time.

Our culture is different. Just as we should not interpret 6:5–9 as giving permission to own slaves, we should not interpret 5:21—6:4 as commanding submissive behavior of married women today. Understanding this, we can appreciate the passage as it was intended: a practical guide for a family life where love is the rule (see "The Christian Family," near Col 3:18—4:1).

▶ Eph 5:21—6:4

and be joined to his wife, and the two will become one flesh." [32]This is a great mystery, and I am applying it to Christ and the church. [33]Each of you, however, should love his wife as himself, and a wife should respect her husband.

Children and Parents

6 Children, obey your parents in the Lord,[a] for this is right. [2]"Honor your father and mother"—this is the first commandment with a promise: [3]"so that it may be well with you and you may live long on the earth."

4 And, fathers, do not provoke your children to anger, but bring them up in the discipline and instruction of the Lord.

Slaves and Masters

5 Slaves, obey your earthly masters with fear and trembling, in singleness of heart, as you obey Christ; [6]not only while being watched, and in order to please them, but as slaves of Christ, doing the will of God from the heart. [7]Render service with enthusiasm, as to the Lord and not to men and women, [8]knowing that whatever good we do, we will receive the same again from the Lord, whether we are slaves or free.

9 And, masters, do the same to them. Stop threatening them, for you know that both of you have the same Master in heaven, and with him there is no partiality.

The Whole Armor of God

10 Finally, be strong in the Lord and in the strength of his power. [11]Put on the whole armor of God, so that you may be able to stand against the wiles of the devil. [12]For our[b] struggle is not against enemies of blood and flesh, but against the rulers, against the authorities, against the cosmic powers of this present darkness, against the spiritual forces of evil in the heavenly places. [13]Therefore take up the whole armor of God, so that you may be able to withstand on that evil day, and having done everything, to stand firm. [14]Stand therefore, and fasten the belt of truth around your waist, and put on the breastplate of righteousness. [15]As shoes for your feet put on whatever will make you ready to proclaim the gospel of peace. [16]With all of these,[c] take the shield of faith, with which you will be able to quench all the flaming arrows of the evil one. [17]Take the helmet of salvation, and the sword of the Spirit, which is the word of God.

18 Pray in the Spirit at all times in every prayer and supplication. To that end keep alert and always persevere in supplication for all the saints. [19]Pray also for me, so that when I speak,

Pray It!

The "Peace Prayer" of Saint Francis of Assisi

Ephesians 6:10–17 is a poetic passage encouraging us to resist evil. The "Peace Prayer" of Saint Francis of Assisi tells us how to do this—without using the imagery of warfare. After you read each line of this powerful prayer, close your eyes to meditate on its meaning for your life. What is one way you can live out each line of this prayer?

> Lord, make me an instrument of your peace;
> where there is hatred, let me sow love;
> where there is injury, pardon;
> where there is doubt, faith;
> where there is despair, hope;
> where there is darkness, light;
> and where there is sadness, joy.
> Grant that I may not so much seek
> to be consoled as to console;
> to be understood as to understand,
> to be loved as to love;
> for it is in giving that we receive,
> it is in pardoning that we are pardoned,
> and it is in dying that we
>   are born to eternal life.

▶ Eph 6:10–17

a message may be given to me to make known with boldness the mystery of the gospel,[d] [20]for which I am an ambassador in chains. Pray that I may declare it boldly, as I must speak.

Personal Matters and Benediction

21 So that you also may know how I am and what I am doing, Tychicus will tell you everything. He is a dear brother and a faithful minister in the Lord. [22]I am sending him to you for this very purpose, to let you know how we are, and to encourage your hearts.

23 Peace be to the whole community,[e] and love with faith, from God the Father and the Lord Jesus Christ [24]Grace be with all who have an undying love for our Lord Jesus Christ.[f]

---

a Other ancient authorities lack *in the Lord* b Other ancient authorities read *your* c Or *In all circumstances* d Other ancient authorities lack *of the gospel* e Gk *to the brothers* f Other ancient authorities add *Amen*

EPH

"To be, or not to be: that is the question." In this line from Shakespeare's *Hamlet*, Hamlet wonders which is better for him—to live or to die. He doesn't want to live and suffer, but he's afraid the "sleep of death" may be worse. Either way, he loses. In the Letter to the Philippians, Paul struggles with a similar question. But Paul wants to die to be with God. His desire to stay is to later serve the church.

In Depth

When Paul wrote this letter, he was imprisoned facing a charge that might end in his death. He wrote it either near the end of his life when he was under house arrest in Rome or, more likely, during an earlier imprisonment in Ephesus (see 1 Cor 15:32, 2 Cor 1:8).

Like Hamlet, Paul is torn: "I am hard pressed between" life and death (Phil 1:23). But unlike Hamlet, Paul feels he'll win either way: "For to me, living is Christ and dying is gain" (verse 21). In addition, Paul believes this imprisonment will not end with his death, because he is still needed to support the new churches he helped start.

Incredibly, even in prison, Paul exhibits a spirit of hope and encouragement. In this short letter, he uses the words *rejoice* and *joy* fifteen times! Living in Christ doesn't mean everything will always go wonderfully. But it does mean that God can get you through the good times and the difficult times with joy.

At a Glance

- **1:1–26.** a greeting, thanks, and a discussion of Paul's imprisonment
- **1:27—2:18.** advice to imitate Christ
- **2:19—3:1.** plans for Timothy and Epaphroditus
- **3:2—4:9.** warning against false teachers and advice for Christian living
- **4:10–23.** thanks, a final greeting, and a blessing

Quick Facts

Inspired Author: Paul
Date Written: AD 55 if from Ephesus, from AD 59 to 63 if from Rome
Audience: the church in Philippi

In this letter, Paul asks the Philippians—and us—to imitate Christ. Imitating Christ is to think and act as Christ did even when things aren't going our way. Paul quotes an early Christian song (see 2:6–11) to the Philippians to show what imitating Christ means. The song praises our Lord Jesus, who chose to humble himself, chose to become a servant, and was "obedient to the point of death" (verse 8). Therefore God exalted him above all things.

It is clear from this letter that Paul had a close relationship with the Philippians. No doubt, they were upset for him. Paul wanted them to rejoice in Christ and in their suffering, and to stop worrying (see 4:4–6). He encouraged them to present their concerns—all of them—to God in prayer. And he pointed out that if they did so, "the peace of God, which surpasses all understanding, will guard your hearts and your minds in Christ Jesus" (verse 7). What marvelous advice and comfort for people of all times and ages.

The Letter to the

Philippians

Philippians

Salutation

1 Paul and Timothy, servants*a* of Christ Jesus,
To all the saints in Christ Jesus who are in Philippi, with the bishops*b* and deacons:*c*

2 Grace to you and peace from God our Father and the Lord Jesus Christ.

Friendship

In Philippians 1:3–11, Paul writes beautifully of his love for and friendship with the people living in Philippi. We need to remember that Paul—and the other people who wrote the inspired words of the Scriptures—was a real person with problems and needs. He had some dear friends in Philippi, and his words to them provide a great model of true friendship: sharing the ups and downs, being committed to one another, being thankful for one another, and wanting the best for one another. Friendship in Christ is like that!

Who are true friends for you? To whom are you a true friend? How can you keep Christ at the center of your friendships?

▶ Phil 1:3–11

Paul's Prayer for the Philippians

3 I thank my God every time I remember you, [4]constantly praying with joy in every one of my prayers for all of you, [5]because of your sharing in the gospel from the first day until now. [6]I am confident of this, that the one who began a good work among you will bring it to completion by the day of Jesus Christ. [7]It is right for me to think this way about all of you, because you hold me in your heart,*d* for all of you share in God's grace*e* with me, both in my imprisonment and in the defense and confirmation of the gospel. [8]For God is my witness, how I long for all of you with the compassion of Christ Jesus. [9]And this is my prayer, that your love may overflow more and more with knowledge and full insight [10]to help you to determine what is best, so that in the day of Christ you may be pure and blameless, [11]having produced the harvest of righteousness that comes through Jesus Christ for the glory and praise of God.

Paul's Present Circumstances

12 I want you to know, beloved,*f* that what has happened to me has actually helped to spread the gospel, [13]so that it has become known throughout the whole imperial guard*g* and to everyone else that my imprisonment is for Christ; [14]and

---

a Gk *slaves*   *b* Or *overseers*   *c* Or *overseers and helpers*   *d* Or *because I hold you in my heart*   *e* Gk *in grace*   *f* Gk *brothers*   *g* Gk *whole praetorium*

most of the brothers and sisters,[a] having been made confident in the Lord by my imprisonment, dare to speak the word[b] with greater boldness and without fear.

15 Some proclaim Christ from envy and rivalry, but others from goodwill. [16]These proclaim Christ out of love, knowing that I have been put here for the defense of the gospel; [17]the others proclaim Christ out of selfish ambition, not sincerely but intending to increase my suffering in my imprisonment. [18]What does it matter? Just this, that Christ is proclaimed in every way, whether out of false motives or true; and in that I rejoice.

Yes, and I will continue to rejoice, [19]for I know that through your prayers and the help of the Spirit of Jesus Christ this will turn out for my deliverance. [20]It is my eager expectation and hope that I will not be put to shame in any way, but that by my speaking with all boldness, Christ will be exalted now as always in my body, whether by life or by death. [21]For to me, living is Christ and dying is gain. [22]If I am to live in the flesh, that means fruitful labor for me; and I do not know which I prefer. [23]I am hard pressed between the two: my desire is to depart and be with Christ, for that is far better; [24]but to remain in the flesh is more necessary for you. [25]Since I am convinced of this, I know that I will remain and continue with all of you for your progress and joy in faith, [26]so that I may share abundantly in your boasting in Christ Jesus when I come to you again.

27 Only, live your life in a manner worthy of the gospel of Christ, so that, whether I come and see you or am absent and hear about you, I know that you are standing firm in one spirit, striving side by side with one mind for the faith of the gospel, [28]and are in no way intimidated by your opponents. For them this is evidence of their destruction, but of your salvation. And this is God's doing. [29]For he has graciously granted you the privilege not only of believing in Christ, but of suffering for him as well— [30]since you are having the same struggle that you saw I had and now hear that I still have.

Imitating Christ's Humility

2 If then there is any encouragement in Christ, any consolation from love, any sharing in the Spirit, any compassion and sympathy, [2]make my joy complete: be of the same mind, having the same love, being in full accord and of one mind. [3]Do nothing from selfish ambition or conceit, but in humility regard others as better than yourselves. [4]Let each of you look not to your own interests, but to the interests of others. [5]Let the same mind be in you that was[c] in Christ Jesus,

6 who, though he was in the form of God,
    did not regard equality with God
    as something to be exploited,
7 but emptied himself,
    taking the form of a slave,
    being born in human likeness.
And being found in human form,
8   he humbled himself
    and became obedient to the point of death—
    even death on a cross.

9 Therefore God also highly exalted him
    and gave him the name

Divine Humility, Cosmic Glory

Mention the name Jesus, or the title Christ, and many images spring to mind. That is good, because no single image can capture Jesus' true nature completely.

In Philippians 2:6–11, borrowing from a hymn sung in the earliest days of the Church, Paul explains how the community should be of the same mind as Jesus Christ. Jesus gave up equality with God as his right (see verse 6) and entered our world as a human being. He lived in utter humility, from his simple birth to his Crucifixion. Because of his humility and obedience, Jesus' name is exalted by God so that Jesus Christ is now Lord of all and worshiped by all creation!

To be the loving people God calls us to be, we must imitate Christ's humility in our love for one another. Most of us are used to seeing those who are "powerful" in this world being served by others. But Paul reminds us it is the nature of Jesus to serve. Christians are called to be powerful in a radically different way—to see humble service as their basic call and the path to true glory—with the "same mind . . . that was in Christ Jesus" (verse 5).

▶ **Phil 2:1–11**

---

a Gk brothers   b Other ancient authorities read *word of God*
c Or *that you have*

that is above every name,
10 so that at the name of Jesus
     every knee should bend,
     in heaven and on earth and under the earth,
11 and every tongue should confess
     that Jesus Christ is Lord,
     to the glory of God the Father.

Shining as Lights in the World

12 Therefore, my beloved, just as you have always obeyed me, not only in my presence, but much more now in my absence, work out your own salvation with fear and trembling; 13for it is God who is at work in you, enabling you both to will and to work for his good pleasure.

14 Do all things without murmuring and arguing, 15so that you may be blameless and innocent, children of God without blemish in the midst of a crooked and perverse generation, in which you shine like stars in the world. 16It is by your holding fast to the word of life that I can boast on the day of Christ that I did not run in vain or labor in vain. 17But even if I am being poured out as a libation over the sacrifice and the offering of your faith, I am glad and rejoice with all of you— 18and in the same way you also must be glad and rejoice with me.

Timothy and Epaphroditus

19 I hope in the Lord Jesus to send Timothy to you soon, so that I may be cheered by news of you. 20I have no one like him who will be genuinely concerned for your welfare. 21All of them are seeking their own interests, not those of Jesus Christ. 22But Timothy's[a] worth you know, how like a son with a father he has served with me in the work of the gospel. 23I hope therefore to send him as soon as I see how things go with me; 24and I trust in the Lord that I will also come soon.

25 Still, I think it necessary to send to you Epaphroditus—my brother and co-worker and fellow soldier, your messenger[b] and minister to my need; 26for he has been longing for[c] all of you, and has been distressed because you heard that he was ill. 27He was indeed so ill that he nearly died. But God had mercy on him, and not only on him but on me also, so that I would not have one sorrow after another. 28I am the more eager to send him, therefore, in order that you may rejoice at seeing him again, and that I may be less anxious. 29Welcome him then in the Lord with all joy, and honor such people, 30because he came close to death for the work of Christ,[d] risking his life to make up for those services that you could not give me.

3 Finally, my brothers and sisters,[e] rejoice[f] in the Lord.

Breaking with the Past

To write the same things to you is not troublesome to me, and for you it is a safeguard.

2 Beware of the dogs, beware of the evil workers, beware of those who mutilate the flesh![g] 3For it is we who are the circumcision, who worship in the Spirit of God[h] and boast in Christ Jesus and have no confidence in the flesh— 4even though I, too, have reason for confidence in the flesh.

If anyone else has reason to be confident in the flesh, I have more: 5circumcised on the eighth day, a member of the people of Israel, of the tribe of Benjamin, a Hebrew born of Hebrews; as to the law, a Pharisee; 6as to zeal, a persecutor of the church; as to righteousness under the law, blameless.

7 Yet whatever gains I had, these I have come to regard as loss because of Christ. 8More than that, I regard everything as loss because of the surpassing value of knowing Christ Jesus my Lord. For his sake I have suffered the loss of all things, and I regard them as rubbish, in order that I may gain Christ 9and be found in him, not

---

a Gk *his*   b Gk *apostle*   c Other ancient authorities read *longing to see*   d Other ancient authorities read *of the Lord*   e Gk *my brothers*   f Or *farewell*   g Gk *the mutilation*   h Other ancient authorities read *worship God in spirit*

Commitment to the Ultimate Goal

In what ways have you become more mature in the last five years? How do other people recognize that you are maturing?

In Philippians 3:12–16, Paul describes one measure of maturity—the ability to keep a commitment to the ultimate goal of God's call in Christ Jesus. Mature people—whether sixteen or sixty—are always striving to perfect themselves in pursuit of their goals.

Paul says the goal that guides his life is "to know Christ and the power of his resurrection" (verse 10). Is knowing Christ and the power of his Resurrection the goal that guides your life?

▶ Phil 3:12–16

Cultural Connection

The Beauty of Creation

Paul ends his message to the Philippians by encouraging them to keep their minds on things that are true, humble, just, pure, lovely, and gracious. This would certainly include the wonder and beauty of creation, something Native Americans are deeply aware of. Let this Navajo prayer in praise of creation inspire you to keep focused on the beauty God has provided in the world around us:

I walk with beauty before me
I walk with beauty behind me
I walk with beauty above me
I walk with beauty below me
Beauty has been restored
from the East
Beauty has been restored
from the South
Beauty has been restored
from the West
Beauty has been restored
from the North
Beauty has been restored
from the sky-top
Beauty has been restored

from the earth-bottom
Beauty has been restored
from all around me
(From Michael F. Steltenkamp,
The Sacred Vision, p. 92)

▶ **Phil 4:8–9**

---

having a righteousness of my own that comes from the law, but one that comes through faith in Christ,[a] the righteousness from God based on faith. [10]I want to know Christ[b] and the power of his resurrection and the sharing of his sufferings by becoming like him in his death, [11]if somehow I may attain the resurrection from the dead.

Pressing toward the Goal

12 Not that I have already obtained this or have already reached the goal;[c] but I press on to make it my own, because Christ Jesus has made me his own. [13]Beloved,[d] I do not consider that I have made it my own;[e] but this one thing I do: forgetting what lies behind and straining forward to what lies ahead, [14]I press on toward the goal for the prize of the heavenly[f] call of God in Christ Jesus. [15]Let those of us then who are mature be of the same mind; and if you think differently about anything, this too God will reveal to you. [16]Only let us hold fast to what we have attained.

17 Brothers and sisters,[d] join in imitating me, and observe those who live according to the example you have in us. [18]For many live as enemies of the cross of Christ; I have often told you of them, and now I tell you even with tears. [19]Their end is destruction; their god is the belly; and their glory is in their shame; their minds are set on earthly things. [20]But our citizenship[g] is in heaven, and it is from there that we are expecting a Savior, the Lord Jesus Christ. [21]He will

> "Rejoice in the Lord always; again I will say, Rejoice."
> (Phil 4:4)

transform the body of our humiliation[h] that it may be conformed to the body of his glory,[i] by the power that also enables him to make all things **4** subject to himself. [1]Therefore, my brothers and sisters,[j] whom I love and long for, my joy and crown, stand firm in the Lord in this way, my beloved.

Exhortations

2 I urge Euodia and I urge Syntyche to be of the same mind in the Lord. [3]Yes, and I ask you also, my loyal companion,[k] help these women, for they have struggled beside me in the work of the gospel, together with Clement and the rest of my co-workers, whose names are in the book of life.

4 Rejoice[l] in the Lord always; again I will say, Rejoice.[l] [5]Let your gentleness be known to everyone. The Lord is near. [6]Do not worry about anything, but in everything by prayer and supplication with thanksgiving let your requests be made known to God. [7]And the peace of God, which surpasses all understanding, will guard your hearts and your minds in Christ Jesus.

---

a Or through the faith of Christ   b Gk him   c Or have already been made perfect   d Gk Brothers   e Other ancient authorities read my own yet   f Gk upward   g Or commonwealth h Or our humble bodies   i Or his glorious body   j Gk my brothers   k Or loyal Syzygus   l Or Farewell

8 Finally, beloved,[a] whatever is true, whatever is honorable, whatever is just, whatever is pure, whatever is pleasing, whatever is commendable, if there is any excellence and if there is anything worthy of praise, think about[b] these things. [9]Keep on doing the things that you have learned and received and heard and seen in me, and the God of peace will be with you.

Acknowledgment of the Philippians' Gift

10 I rejoice[c] in the Lord greatly that now at last you have revived your concern for me; indeed, you were concerned for me, but had no opportunity to show it.[d] [11]Not that I am referring to being in need; for I have learned to be content with whatever I have. [12]I know what it is to have little, and I know what it is to have plenty. In any and all circumstances I have learned the secret of being well-fed and of going hungry, of having plenty and of being in need. [13]I can do all things through him who strengthens me. [14]In any case, it was kind of you to share my distress.

15 You Philippians indeed know that in the early days of the gospel, when I left Macedonia, no church shared with me in the matter of giving and receiving, except you alone. [16]For even when I was in Thessalonica, you sent me help for my needs more than once. [17]Not that I seek the gift, but I seek the profit that accumulates to your account. [18]I have been paid in full and have more than enough; I am fully satisfied, now that I have received from Epaphroditus the gifts you sent, a fragrant offering, a sacrifice acceptable and pleasing to God. [19]And my God will fully satisfy every need of yours according to his riches in glory in Christ Jesus. [20]To our God and Father be glory forever and ever. Amen.

Final Greetings and Benediction

21 Greet every saint in Christ Jesus. The friends[a] who are with me greet you. [22]All the saints greet you, especially those of the emperor's household.

23 The grace of the Lord Jesus Christ be with your spirit.[e]

---

a Gk brothers   b Gk take account of   c Gk I rejoiced
d Gk lacks to show it   e Other ancient authorities add Amen

Every now and then, we hear about some latest secular fads being applied to Christianity. It is not unusual to hear of a minister of some megachurch applying an entertainment model to ministry or preaching that Christians will be rewarded with prosperity, reflecting the comfort and ease of contemporary suburban life. Although those fads may be popular, they do not accurately reflect the Christian message. This is not a new phenomenon, even in first-century Colossae. There was a group who was applying pagan religious practices and beliefs from Greek philosophy to the Christian community. The author's advice in the Letter to the Colossians is pretty direct: Stay focused on Christ and the authentic Gospel message!

In Depth

This letter attacks a group that was teaching a weird mixture of ideas. It insisted on Jewish rituals (see 2:16) and regulations (see verse 22), severe treatment of one's own body (see verse 23), and a philosophy that included "the elemental spirits of the universe" (verse 8) mixed with pagan religious practices. These teachers probably had Jewish roots, because they observed the Sabbath and other Jewish feasts (see verse 16). But it appears they were teaching that Jesus was a first-born creature, although lower than the angels.

At a Glance

- **1:1–2.** a greeting
- **1:3–23.** a thanksgiving and hymn of praise of Christ as the first of creation and Lord of all
- **1:24—2:23.** relations with the community and warnings against false teachers
- **3:1—4:6.** advice for Christian living
- **4:7–18.** final greetings

Quick Facts

Inspired Author: Paul or more likely a follower of Paul (see "Introduction to the Letters and Revelation")
Date Written: around AD 61 if by Paul; if by a follower, approximately AD 80
Audience: the Christian community at Colossae

Against the backdrop of all this thinking, the author—who may not have been Paul but a disciple of Paul—declares the supreme mystery of Christ. Quoting a Christian hymn (see 1:15–20), the writer says Christ is honored not only as the first-born of creation but also as the one through whom everything was created and who holds everything together. He is above everything that is!

Christians believe Jesus is more than just a great teacher; they believe Jesus is God, who chose to become human and live with us. This letter gives us an early statement of that belief: "In [Christ] the whole fullness of deity dwells bodily" (2:9).

The Letter to the Colossians also offers comforting words about our God. God has given us life and forgiveness. God erased the record of our sins and set it aside, "nailing it to the cross" (verse 14). Unlike those teachers who burden their followers with guilt and impossible rules, our God frees us from guilt and gives us life! As you read this letter, you will find these and many other words to live by: "God's chosen ones . . . forgive each another . . . clothe yourselves with love . . . And let the peace of Christ rule in your hearts" (3:12–15).

The Letter to the
Colossians

With gratitude sing songs to God.

Colossians

Salutation

1 Paul, an apostle of Christ Jesus by the will of God, and Timothy our brother,

2 To the saints and faithful brothers and sisters*a* in Christ in Colossae:

Grace to you and peace from God our Father.

Paul Thanks God for the Colossians

3 In our prayers for you we always thank God, the Father of our Lord Jesus Christ, 4for we have heard of your faith in Christ Jesus and of the love that you have for all the saints, 5because of the hope laid up for you in heaven. You have heard of this hope before in the word of the truth, the gospel 6that has come to you. Just as it is bearing fruit and growing in the whole world, so it has been bearing fruit among yourselves from the day you heard it and truly comprehended the grace of God. 7This you learned from Epaphras, our beloved fellow servant.*b* He is a faithful minister of Christ on your*c* behalf, 8and he has made known to us your love in the Spirit.

9 For this reason, since the day we heard it, we have not ceased praying for you and asking that you may be filled with the knowledge of God's*d* will in all spiritual wisdom and understanding, 10so that you may lead lives worthy of the Lord, fully pleasing to him, as you bear fruit in every good work and as you grow in the knowledge of God. 11May you be made strong with all the strength that comes from his glorious power, and may you be prepared to endure everything with

patience, while joyfully 12giving thanks to the Father, who has enabled*e* you*f* to share in the inheritance of the saints in the light. 13He has rescued us from the power of darkness and transferred us into the kingdom of his beloved Son, 14in whom we have redemption, the forgiveness of sins.*g*

The Supremacy of Christ

15 He is the image of the invisible God, the firstborn of all creation; 16for in*h* him all things in heaven and on earth were created, things visible and invisible, whether thrones or dominions or rulers or powers—all things have been created through him and for him. 17He himself is before all things, and in*h* him all things hold together. 18He is the head of the body, the church; he is the beginning, the firstborn from the dead, so that he might come to have first place in everything. 19For in him all the fullness of God was pleased to dwell, 20and through him God was pleased to reconcile to himself all things, whether on earth or in heaven, by making peace through the blood of his cross.

21 And you who were once estranged and hostile in mind, doing evil deeds, 22he has now reconciled*i* in his fleshly body*j* through death, so as to present you holy and blameless and irreproachable before him— 23provided that you continue securely established and steadfast in the

---

a Gk *brothers*   *b* Gk *slave*   *c* Other ancient authorities read *our*   *d* Gk *his*   *e* Other ancient authorities read *called*   *f* Other ancient authorities read *us*   *g* Other ancient authorities add *through his blood*   *h* Or *by*   *i* Other ancient authorities read *you have now been reconciled*   *j* Gk *in the body of his flesh*

faith, without shifting from the hope promised by the gospel that you heard, which has been proclaimed to every creature under heaven. I, Paul, became a servant of this gospel.

Paul's Interest in the Colossians

24 I am now rejoicing in my sufferings for your sake, and in my flesh I am completing what is lacking in Christ's afflictions for the sake of his body, that is, the church. [25] I became its servant according to God's commission that was given to me for you, to make the word of God fully known, [26] the mystery that has been hidden throughout the ages and generations but has now been revealed to his saints. [27] To them God chose to make known how great among the Gentiles are the riches of the glory of this mystery, which is Christ in you, the hope of glory. [28] It is he whom we proclaim, warning everyone and teaching everyone in all wisdom, so that we may present everyone mature in Christ. [29] For this I toil and struggle with all the energy that he powerfully inspires within me.

2 For I want you to know how much I am struggling for you, and for those in Laodicea, and for all who have not seen me face to face. [2] I want their hearts to be encouraged and united in love, so that they may have all the riches of assured understanding and have the knowledge of God's mystery, that is, Christ himself,[a] [3] in whom are hidden all the treasures of wisdom and knowledge. [4] I am saying this so that no one may deceive you with plausible arguments. [5] For though I am absent in body, yet I am with you in spirit, and I rejoice to see your morale and the firmness of your faith in Christ.

Fullness of Life in Christ

6 As you therefore have received Christ Jesus the Lord, continue to live your lives[b] in him, [7] rooted and built up in him and established in the faith, just as you were taught, abounding in thanksgiving.

---

a Other ancient authorities read *of the mystery of God, both of the Father and of Christ* b Gk *to walk*

The Image of God

It is possible to describe God by naming certain characteristics. We can say God is all-powerful, all-knowing, and eternal. But knowing about God is not the same as knowing God. So how can we really understand the mysterious, invisible, eternal God?

The author of Colossians gives us a clue. This writer calls Jesus "the image of the invisible God" (Col 1:15). If we want to know about God, who is hidden from us in mystery, we look at Christ. Christ has existed for all eternity; through Christ, all things were created; and in Christ, all things continue to "hold together" (verse 17). God chose to use Christ as the way in which all creation would be reconciled to God (see verse 20).

Is there still the unknown? Yes. We cannot comprehend God completely. But we can understand more about God by getting to know more about Jesus Christ.

▶ **Col 1:15–20**

Where Are Your Roots?

What is one thing that motivates you, that keeps you going? Is it a special friendship or a close family? the drive to succeed or to be the best? Maybe it's having a car or holding down a job.

Colossians 2:7 says that we should be "rooted and built up in [Christ]." Where you have your roots is where you get your nourishment to keep going. Think again about what motivates you. Is it enough to nourish a full, rich life?

In your prayer, journal or reflect on the following questions:

● What things are most important in your life right now? Where is God in each of those things?
● What do you need to reorder so that Christ "might come to have first place" (1:18) in your life?

▶ **Col 2:6–7**

8 See to it that no one takes you captive through philosophy and empty deceit, according to human tradition, according to the elemental spirits of the universe,*a* and not according to Christ. ⁹For in him the whole fullness of deity dwells bodily, ¹⁰and you have come to fullness in him, who is the head of every ruler and authority. ¹¹In him also you were circumcised with a spiritual circumcision,*b* by putting off the body of the flesh in the circumcision of Christ; ¹²when you were buried with him in baptism, you were also raised with him through faith in the power of God, who raised him from the dead. ¹³And when you were dead in trespasses and the uncircumcision of your flesh, God*c* made you*d* alive together with him, when he forgave us all our trespasses, ¹⁴erasing the record that stood against us with its legal demands. He set this aside, nailing it to the cross. ¹⁵He disarmed*e* the rulers and authorities and made a public example of them, triumphing over them in it.

16 Therefore do not let anyone condemn you in matters of food and drink or of observing festivals, new moons, or sabbaths. ¹⁷These are only a shadow of what is to come, but the substance belongs to Christ. ¹⁸Do not let anyone disqualify you, insisting on self-abasement and worship of angels, dwelling*f* on visions,*g* puffed up without cause by a human way of thinking,*h* ¹⁹and not holding fast to the head, from whom the whole body, nourished and held together by its ligaments and sinews, grows with a growth that is from God.

Warnings against False Teachers

20 If with Christ you died to the elemental spirits of the universe,*a* why do you live as if you still belonged to the world? Why do you submit to regulations, ²¹"Do not handle, Do not taste, Do not touch"? ²²All these regulations refer to things that perish with use; they are simply human commands and teachings. ²³These have indeed an appearance of wisdom in promoting self-imposed piety, humility, and severe treatment of the body, but they are of no value in checking self-indulgence.*i*

The New Life in Christ

3 So if you have been raised with Christ, seek the things that are above, where Christ is, seated at the right hand of God. ²Set your minds on things that are above, not on things that are on earth, ³for you have died, and your life is hidden with Christ in God. ⁴When Christ who is your*j* life is revealed, then you also will be revealed with him in glory.

A Top-Shelf Life

In stores, the best product is often put on the top shelf, for all to see. It is also usually priced higher than other products, and therefore is not purchased by everyone. Colossians 3:1 calls us to "seek the things that are above, where Christ is"—in other words, to live a top-shelf life.

Living a top-shelf life means living a moral life, free from sin. It means ridding ourselves of "anger, wrath, malice, slander, and abusive language" (verse 8). It means avoiding "fornication, impurity, . . . strife, jealousy, anger, quarrels, dissensions, factions, envy, drunkenness, carousing" (Gal 5:19–21). It also means living with "compassion, kindness, humility, meekness, and patience," and forgiving one another and clothing ourselves with love (Col 3:12–14). Paul and the other authors of the letters focus on moral living because it is what God wants for us. How could we claim to have faith in Jesus Christ and choose to live in sin?

Living a moral life, a top-shelf life, isn't always easy. But it is the way to true happiness, holiness, and health. This is the witness of the Church and generations of Christian believers. Why settle for less?

▶ **Col 3:1–4**

5 Put to death, therefore, whatever in you is earthly: fornication, impurity, passion, evil desire, and greed (which is idolatry). ⁶On account of these the wrath of God is coming on those who are disobedient.*k* ⁷These are the ways you also once followed, when you were living that life.*l* ⁸But now you must get rid of all such things—anger, wrath, malice, slander, and abusive*m* language from your mouth. ⁹Do not lie to one another, seeing that you have stripped off the old self with its practices

---

a Or *the rudiments of the world*   *b* Gk *a circumcision made without hands*   *c* Gk *he*   *d* Other ancient authorities read *made us*; others, *made*   *e* Or *divested himself of*   *f* Other ancient authorities read *not dwelling*   *g* Meaning of Gk uncertain   *h* Gk *by the mind of his flesh*   *i* Or *are of no value, serving only to indulge the flesh*   *j* Other authorities read *our*   *k* Other ancient authorities lack *on those who are disobedient* (Gk *the children of disobedience*)   *l* Or *living among such people*   *m* Or *filthy*

COL

Catholic Social Teaching

The Christian Family

The rules for Christian families in chapter 3 of Colossians seem a little strange in our culture. But Colossians is simply calling families to be rooted in loving relationships (see also "Family Relationships," near Eph 5:21—6:4). A family is God's gift. It is a community where an atmosphere of mutual love and respect exists between its members, both young and old. It is a community we can turn to for comfort and support. The Catholic Church calls families the domestic church, meaning that they are the primary place where people learn about God and God's love. Catholic social teaching says that the family is the foundation on which communal life is built.

Being the domestic church doesn't just happen, however. Every member of a family must make an effort. That means taking time to listen to one another, to help one another out, and to respect each person in the family. Sometimes, selfishness gets in the way of making God's love real. At those times, family members must try even harder. Taking time to pray together, and to read and talk about the Bible together, can help a family focus on God's presence in their lives. The bishops understand that families face many challenges today, and they invite all of us to help families find the support they need to stay together as loving communities.

How is your family life? Is love the guiding rule? Does everyone take time to pray together? Do you support and participate in family activities and chores willingly? How does your parish or community serve as a source of support for your family?

▶ **Col 3:18—4:1**

Call to Family, Community, and Participation

10and have clothed yourselves with the new self, which is being renewed in knowledge according to the image of its creator. 11In that renewal*a* there is no longer Greek and Jew, circumcised and uncircumcised, barbarian, Scythian, slave and free; but Christ is all and in all!

12 As God's chosen ones, holy and beloved, clothe yourselves with compassion, kindness, humility, meekness, and patience. 13Bear with one another and, if anyone has a complaint against another, forgive each other; just as the Lord*b* has forgiven you, so you also must forgive. 14Above all, clothe yourselves with love, which binds everything together in perfect harmony. 15And let the peace of Christ rule in your hearts, to which indeed you were called in the one body. And be thankful. 16Let the word of Christ*c* dwell in you richly; teach and admonish one another in all wisdom; and with gratitude in your hearts sing psalms, hymns, and spiritual songs to God.*d* 17And whatever you do, in word or deed, do everything in the name of the Lord Jesus, giving thanks to God the Father through him.

Rules for Christian Households

18 Wives, be subject to your husbands, as is fitting in the Lord. 19Husbands, love your wives and never treat them harshly.

20 Children, obey your parents in everything, for this is your acceptable duty in the Lord. 21Fathers, do not provoke your children, or they may lose heart. 22Slaves, obey your earthly masters*e* in everything, not only while being watched and in order to please them, but wholeheartedly, fearing the Lord.*e* 23Whatever your task, put yourselves into it, as done for the Lord and not for your masters,*f* 24since you know that from the Lord you will receive the inheritance as your reward; you serve*g* the Lord Christ. 25For the wrongdoer will be paid back for whatever wrong has been done, and there is no partiality. 1Masters, treat your slaves justly and fairly, for you know that you also have a Master in heaven.

Further Instructions

2 Devote yourselves to prayer, keeping alert in it with thanksgiving. 3At the same time pray for us as well that God will open to us a door for the word, that we may declare the mystery of Christ, for which I am in prison, 4so that I may reveal it clearly, as I should.

---

a Gk *its creator,* 11*where*   *b* Other ancient authorities read *just as Christ*   *c* Other ancient authorities read *of God,* or *of the Lord*   *d* Other ancient authorities read *to the Lord*   *e* In Greek the same word is used for *master* and *Lord*   *f* Gk *not for men*   *g* Or *you are slaves of,* or *be slaves of*

5 Conduct yourselves wisely toward outsiders, making the most of the time.[a] 6Let your speech always be gracious, seasoned with salt, so that you may know how you ought to answer everyone.

Final Greetings and Benediction

7 Tychicus will tell you all the news about me; he is a beloved brother, a faithful minister, and a fellow servant[b] in the Lord. 8I have sent him to you for this very purpose, so that you may know how we are[c] and that he may encourage your hearts; 9he is coming with Onesimus, the faithful and beloved brother, who is one of you. They will tell you about everything here.

10 Aristarchus my fellow prisoner greets you, as does Mark the cousin of Barnabas, concerning whom you have received instructions—if he comes to you, welcome him. 11And Jesus who is called Justus greets you. These are the only ones of the circumcision among my co-workers for the kingdom of God, and they have been a comfort to me. 12Epaphras, who is one of you, a servant[b] of Christ Jesus, greets you. He is always wrestling in his prayers on your behalf, so that you may stand mature and fully assured in everything that God wills. 13For I testify for him that he has worked hard for you and for those in Laodicea and in Hierapolis. 14Luke, the beloved physician, and Demas greet you. 15Give my greetings to the brothers and sisters[d] in Laodicea, and to Nympha and the church in her house. 16And when this letter has been read among you, have it read also in the church of the Laodiceans; and see that you read also the letter from Laodicea. 17And say to Archippus, "See that you complete the task that you have received in the Lord."

18 I, Paul, write this greeting with my own hand. Remember my chains. Grace be with you.[e]

a Or *opportunity*   b Gk *slave*   c Other authorities read *that I may know how you are*   d Gk *brothers*   e Other ancient authorities add *Amen*

C
O
L

You're about to read what is probably the oldest book in the New Testament. It was written a little over twenty years after Jesus' death and Resurrection, by a man named Paul. It is the very first Christian letter that we still have! In it, Paul answers some questions that were on people's minds back then. Even though it was written so long ago, you might have some of the same questions.

At a Glance

- **Chapter 1.** a greeting and thanksgiving

- **Chapters 2–3.** a discussion of Paul's ministry in Thessalonica and Timothy's report

- **4:1–12.** advice about the Christian life

- **4:13—5:11.** teaching about the end times

- **5:12–28.** final advice and a blessing

Quick Facts

Inspired Author: Paul
Date Written: AD 51
Audience: the mainly Gentile church in Thessalonica

In Depth

Thessalonica was the capital of a Roman province called Macedonia. Today, that area is in northern Greece (see map 8, "Paul's First and Second Journeys"). Acts of the Apostles, chapter 17, tells us that Paul spent three weeks in Thessalonica preaching about Jesus Christ. Because of his preaching, many people, mainly Gentiles (non-Jews), became Christians. After Paul left the city, he worried about the new Christian community, so he sent his coworker Timothy back to check things out. When Timothy rejoined Paul, he had some great news. Even though the Thessalonians were being persecuted, they were staying strong in their "faith and love" (1 Thess 3:6).

When you read this letter, you can tell that Paul is thankful that the church is thriving! Four different times he expresses his gratitude. But he also apparently feels the need to defend himself against some critics. So he reminds everyone that he has been genuine and has cared for them "like a nurse tenderly caring for her own children" (2:7).

After reassuring the Thessalonians that the persecution they are suffering is to be expected (see 3:3–4), Paul takes the time to answer some questions about the coming of the Lord at the end of time. Apparently, some of the Thessalonians are concerned about their friends who have already died. Will they join the living when Christ returns again?

Paul tells them they don't have to worry about those who die before Jesus returns; the dead will be raised first and join the living, to "be with the Lord forever" (4:17). When will that happen? they ask. No one knows, Paul says, but Christians don't have to be afraid of that day. Their job is to stay alert and clothe themselves with "faith and love . . . and . . . hope" (5:8).

The First Letter to the **Thessalonians**

1 Thessalonians

Salutation

1 Paul, Silvanus, and Timothy,
To the church of the Thessalonians in God the Father and the Lord Jesus Christ:
Grace to you and peace.

The Thessalonians' Faith and Example

2 We always give thanks to God for all of you and mention you in our prayers, constantly ³remembering before our God and Father. your work of faith and labor of love and steadfastness of hope in our Lord Jesus Christ. ⁴For we know, brothers and sisters*a* beloved by God, that he has chosen you, ⁵because our message of the gospel came to you not in word only, but also in power and in the Holy Spirit and with full conviction; just as you know what kind of persons we proved to be among you for your sake. ⁶And you became imitators of us and of the Lord, for in spite of persecution you received the word with joy inspired by the Holy Spirit, ⁷so that you became an example to all the believers in Macedonia and in Achaia. ⁸For the word of the Lord has sounded forth from you not only in Macedonia and Achaia, but in every place your faith in God has become known, so that we have no need to speak about it. ⁹For the people of those regions*b* report about us what kind of welcome we had among you, and how you turned to God from idols, to serve a living and true God, ¹⁰and to wait for his Son from heaven, whom he raised from the dead—Jesus, who rescues us from the wrath that is coming.

Paul's Ministry in Thessalonica

2 You yourselves know, brothers and sisters,*a* that our coming to you was not in vain, ²but though we had already suffered and been shamefully mistreated at Philippi, as you know, we had courage in our God to declare to you the gospel of God in spite of great opposition. ³For our appeal does not spring from deceit or impure motives or trickery, ⁴but just as we have been approved by God to be entrusted with the message of the gospel, even so we speak, not to please mortals, but to please God who tests our hearts. ⁵As you know and as God is our witness, we never came with words of flattery or with a pretext for greed; ⁶nor did we seek praise from mortals, whether from you or from others, ⁷though we might have made demands as apostles of Christ. But we were gentle*c* among you, like a nurse tenderly caring for her own children. ⁸So deeply do we care for you that we are determined to share with you not only the gospel of God but also our own selves, because you have become very dear to us.

9 You remember our labor and toil, brothers and sisters;*a* we worked night and day, so that we might not burden any of you while we proclaimed to you the gospel of God. ¹⁰You are witnesses, and God also, how pure, upright, and blameless our conduct was toward you believers.

---

a Gk brothers   *b* Gk For they   *c* Other ancient authorities read infants

[11]As you know, we dealt with each one of you like a father with his children, [12]urging and encouraging you and pleading that you lead a life worthy of God, who calls you into his own kingdom and glory.

13 We also constantly give thanks to God for this, that when you received the word of God that you heard from us, you accepted it not as a human word but as what it really is, God's word, which is also at work in you believers. [14]For you, brothers and sisters,[a] became imitators of the churches of God in Christ Jesus that are in Judea, for you suffered the same things from your own compatriots as they did from the Jews, [15]who killed both the Lord Jesus and the prophets,[b] and drove us out; they displease God and oppose everyone [16]by hindering us from speaking to the Gentiles so that they may be saved. Thus they have constantly been filling up the measure of their sins; but God's wrath has overtaken them at last.[c]

Paul's Desire to Visit the Thessalonians Again

17 As for us, brothers and sisters,[a] when, for a short time, we were made orphans by being separated from you—in person, not in heart—we longed with great eagerness to see you face to face. [18]For we wanted to come to you—certainly I, Paul, wanted to again and again—but Satan blocked our way. [19]For what is our hope or joy or crown of boasting before our Lord Jesus at his coming? Is it not you? [20]Yes, you are our glory and joy!

---

a Gk *brothers*   b Other ancient authorities read *their own prophets*   c Or *completely* or *forever*

True Love Waits

The Church has taught from its beginning that fornication, including premarital sex, is wrong. Paul's teaching in 1 Thessalonians 4:1–8 clearly explains why. If we get involved in a sexual relationship outside of marriage, we are exploiting another person (see verse 6)—even if that person is a willing partner. God intends sexual intercourse to create a lifelong bond between a man and a woman for the creation of a family. Sexual expression outside of marriage diminishes the beautiful purpose of sexual intimacy.

Paul reminds the Thessalonians to live in ways pleasing to God. To behave contrary to God's purpose is to say no to the gift of the Holy Spirit and to the holiness God wants for us. In our culture, sex is often portrayed as a recreational activity, violating the gift of sexuality God created within us! God's message in the Bible and the Church calls us to take a stand that is unpopular with some people—to support sexual abstinence until marriage.

Valuing our gift of sexuality and expressing it as God intended is not always easy. However, this old idea has a new slogan and campaign today: True love waits. Think about it!

▶ 1 Thess 4:1–8

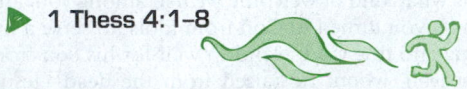

Encouragement

Sometimes, we feel alone in our faith. We wonder if anyone feels, thinks, or prays the way we do. As a first missionary of the faith, Paul must have experienced his share of dark days when he wondered if the people would really accept the Good News. He must have been so encouraged when Timothy returned to tell him of the "faith and love" of the Thessalonians (1 Thess 3:6).

The Christian faith is never meant to be held privately. We don't grow in our faith, hope, and love by being isolated from other people. Like Paul, we need the encouragement and challenge of other people: our family, friends, and the entire Christian community.

In your prayer, reflect or journal on the following questions:

● How do you encourage others to grow in Christ?
● How do others encourage or challenge you to grow in faith, hope, and love?

▶ 1 Thess 3:6–13

Cultural Connection

Iroquois Prayer of Thanksgiving

This Iroquois prayer—although clearly not addressed to the one God who is creator of all—is still a beautiful expression of thankfulness for the wonders of the natural world. It can remind us of Paul's instruction to the Thessalonians (1 Thess 5:16–24) to give thanks without ceasing.

> We return thanks to our mother,
>   the earth, which sustains us.
> We return thanks to the rivers and streams,
>   which supply us with water.
> We return thanks to all herbs,
>   which furnish medicines for the cure to our
>   diseases.
> We return thanks to the corn, and to her
>   sisters,
>   the beans and squashes,
>   which give us life.
> We return thanks to the bushes and trees,
>   which provide us with fruit.
> We return thanks to the wind,

> which, moving in the air, has banished
>   diseases.
> We return thanks to the moon and stars,
>   which have given to us their light
>   when the sun was gone.
> We return thanks to our grandfather Hé-no,
>   that he has protected his grandchildren
>   from witches and reptiles,
>   and has given to us his rain.
> We return thanks to the sun,
>   that he has looked upon the earth
>   with a beneficent eye.
> Lastly, we return thanks to the Great Spirit,
>   in whom is embodied all goodness,
>   and who directs all things
>   for the good of his children.

▶ 1 Thess 5:16–24

3 Therefore when we could bear it no longer, we decided to be left alone in Athens; ²and we sent Timothy, our brother and co-worker for God in proclaiming*ᵃ* the gospel of Christ, to strengthen and encourage you for the sake of your faith, ³so that no one would be shaken by these persecutions. Indeed, you yourselves know that this is what we are destined for. ⁴In fact, when we were with you, we told you beforehand that we were to suffer persecution; so it turned out, as you know. ⁵For this reason, when I could bear it no longer, I sent to find out about your faith; I was afraid that somehow the tempter had tempted you and that our labor had been in vain.

Timothy's Encouraging Report

6 But Timothy has just now come to us from you, and has brought us the good news of your faith and love. He has told us also that you always remember us kindly and long to see us—just as we long to see you. ⁷For this reason, brothers and sisters,*ᵇ* during all our distress and persecution we have been encouraged about you through your faith. ⁸For we now live, if you continue to stand firm in the Lord. ⁹How can we thank God enough for you in return for all the joy that we feel before our God because of you? ¹⁰Night and day we pray most earnestly that we

may see you face to face and restore whatever is lacking in your faith.

11 Now may our God and Father himself and our Lord Jesus direct our way to you. ¹²And may the Lord make you increase and abound in love for one another and for all, just as we abound in love for you. ¹³And may he so strengthen your hearts in holiness that you may be blameless before our God and Father at the coming of our Lord Jesus with all his saints.

A Life Pleasing to God

4 Finally, brothers and sisters,*ᵇ* we ask and urge you in the Lord Jesus that, as you learned from us how you ought to live and to please God (as, in fact, you are doing), you should do so more and more. ²For you know what instructions we gave you through the Lord Jesus. ³For this is the will of God, your sanctification: that you abstain from fornication; ⁴that each one of you know how to control your own body*ᶜ* in holiness and honor, ⁵not with lustful passion, like the Gentiles who do not know God; ⁶that no one wrong or exploit a brother or sister*ᵈ* in this matter, because the Lord is an avenger in all these things, just as we have already told

---

a Gk lacks *proclaiming*   *b* Gk *brothers*   *c* Or *how to take a wife for himself*   *d* Gk *brother*

Cultural Connection

Give Thanks at All Times

Gratitude is an essential element of the Christian faith for Hispanic people. We turn to the Scriptures and Tradition for examples of gratitude in all things. Mary, the mother of Jesus, personified this gratitude when she accepted the responsibility of bearing the Son of God in her womb. Paul continually promoted gratitude in his letters to the first Christians.

To be grateful, we must humbly open up to receiving and acknowledging God's many gifts to us. When we do this, we express our gratitude for God's gifts by loving God and neighbor. Expressing love is an automatic response for someone who is grateful.

Juan Diego, a sixteenth-century Mexican man, opened up to the love and message of Our Lady of Guadalupe, who appeared to him on Tepeyac Hill, today located within Mexico City. In the spirit of gratitude, Juan Diego wanted to share the news of this loving appearance. After persistently speaking about it and eventually providing proof of the appearance to his local bishop, he was finally listened to and believed. For hundreds of years, a church, which is now a basilica, has stood on Tepeyac Hill. Mary had asked Juan Diego to see that a church was built there.

Juan Diego's message and Mary's message to him continue to be spread today in the lives of Mexicans and Mexican Americans. Because Juan Diego's gratitude was so great and because he shared his gratitude with so many others, Pope John Paul II declared him a saint on July 31, 2002.

▶ 1 Thess 5:18

---

you beforehand and solemnly warned you. ⁷For God did not call us to impurity but in holiness. ⁸Therefore whoever rejects this rejects not human authority but God, who also gives his Holy Spirit to you.

9 Now concerning love of the brothers and sisters,ᵃ you do not need to have anyone write to you, for you yourselves have been taught by God to love one another; ¹⁰and indeed you do love all the brothers and sistersᵃ throughout Macedonia. But we urge you, beloved,ᵃ to do so more and more, ¹¹to aspire to live quietly, to mind your own affairs, and to work with your hands, as we directed you, ¹²so that you may behave properly toward outsiders and be dependent on no one.

The Coming of the Lord

13 But we do not want you to be uninformed, brothers and sisters,ᵃ about those who have died,ᵇ so that you may not grieve as others do who have no hope. ¹⁴For since we believe that Jesus died and rose again, even so, through Jesus, God will bring with him those who have died.ᵇ ¹⁵For this we declare to you by the word of the Lord, that we who are alive, who are left until the coming of the Lord, will by no means precede those who have died.ᵇ ¹⁶For the Lord himself, with a cry of command, with the archangel's call and with the sound of God's trumpet, will descend from heaven, and the dead in Christ will rise first. ¹⁷Then we who are alive, who are left, will be caught up in the clouds together with them to meet the Lord in the air; and so we will be with the Lord forever. ¹⁸Therefore encourage one another with these words.

5 Now concerning the times and the seasons, brothers and sisters,ᵃ you do not need to have anything written to you. ²For you yourselves know very well that the day of the Lord will come like a thief in the night. ³When they say, "There is peace and security," then sudden destruction will come upon them, as labor pains come upon a pregnant woman, and there will be no escape! ⁴But you, beloved,ᵃ are not in darkness, for that day to surprise you like a thief; ⁵for you are all children of light and children of the day; we are not of the night or of darkness. ⁶So then let us not fall asleep as others do, but let us keep awake and be sober; ⁷for those who sleep sleep at night, and those who are drunk get drunk at night. ⁸But since we belong to the day, let us be sober, and put on the breastplate of faith and love, and for a helmet the hope of salvation. ⁹For God has destined us not for wrath but for obtaining salvation through our Lord Jesus Christ, ¹⁰who died for

---

a Gk brothers   b Gk fallen asleep

us, so that whether we are awake or asleep we may live with him. ¹¹Therefore encourage one another and build up each other, as indeed you are doing.

Final Exhortations, Greetings, and Benediction

12 But we appeal to you, brothers and sisters,ᵃ to respect those who labor among you, and have charge of you in the Lord and admonish you; ¹³esteem them very highly in love because of their work. Be at peace among yourselves. ¹⁴And we urge you, beloved,ᵃ to admonish the idlers, encourage the fainthearted, help the weak, be patient with all of them. ¹⁵See that none of you repays evil for evil, but always seek to do good to one another and to all. ¹⁶Rejoice always, ¹⁷pray without ceasing, ¹⁸give thanks in all circumstances; for this is the will of God in Christ Jesus for you. ¹⁹Do not

quench the Spirit. ²⁰Do not despise the words of prophets,ᵇ ²¹but test everything; hold fast to what is good; ²²abstain from every form of evil.

23 May the God of peace himself sanctify you entirely; and may your spirit and soul and body be kept soundᶜ and blameless at the coming of our Lord Jesus Christ. ²⁴The one who calls you is faithful, and he will do this.

25 Beloved,ᵈ pray for us.

26 Greet all the brothers and sistersᵃ with a holy kiss. ²⁷I solemnly command you by the Lord that this letter be read to all of them.ᵉ

28 The grace of our Lord Jesus Christ be with you.ᶠ

> "Test everything; hold fast to what is good; abstain from every form of evil."
>
> (1 Thess 5:21–22)

---

a Gk brothers b Gk despise prophecies c Or complete d Gk Brothers e Gk to all the brothers f Other ancient authorities add Amen

Thessalonians

Has a parent or other adult ever said to you, "You know, when I was your age . . ." and launched into some story about how hard it was in the "good old days"? It seems all past generations, including those who lived in biblical times, had their struggles and challenges. When the Thessalonians were going through some really tough times, Paul's second letter to them promised that if they continued to trust God and endure, they would give glory to God and receive salvation.

At a Glance

- **1:1–4.** a greeting and thanksgiving
- **1:5—2:17.** information about the day of judgment
- **3:1–15.** a prayer request, and warning against idleness
- **3:16–18.** a final greeting and blessing

Quick Facts

Inspired Author: possibly Paul, but more likely a disciple of Paul (see "Introduction to the Letters and Revelation")

Date Written: after AD 51 if by Paul, from AD 90 to 100 if by a disciple

Audience: the mainly Gentile (non-Jewish) church in Thessalonica

In Depth

From the short Second Letter to the Thessalonians, it appears the Thessalonians were experiencing two problems. First, they were being persecuted by non-Christians. Second, some of them were becoming confused over "the coming of our Lord Jesus Christ" (2:1), sometimes called the second coming. Word was being spread that Jesus had already come again (see verse 2)! They were becoming fearful that they hadn't seen the signs of the end times or properly interpreted them.

This letter speaks to the Thessalonians, using apocalyptic language (see "Apocalyptic Literature," near Daniel, chapters 7–10, and the introduction to Revelation), which means it is rich in cosmic symbolism. It tells the Thessalonians to have peace and not let themselves be deceived, because "all who have not believed the truth but took pleasure in unrighteousness will be condemned" (2:12). It also tells them to have hope because at the end time, Christ will overcome all evil and will destroy the lawless one (see 2:8).

This letter is not as warm and personal as First Thessalonians. Perhaps that's because it's filled with the sobering awareness that more suffering is to come before the end time. In such an environment, the letter advises the Thessalonians—and us—to "stand firm and hold fast to the traditions that you were taught" (2:15).

2 Thessalonians

Salutation

1 Paul, Silvanus, and Timothy,
To the church of the Thessalonians in God our Father and the Lord Jesus Christ:

2 Grace to you and peace from God our*a* Father and the Lord Jesus Christ.

Thanksgiving

3 We must always give thanks to God for you, brothers and sisters,*b* as is right, because your faith is growing abundantly, and the love of every one of you for one another is increasing. 4Therefore we ourselves boast of you among the churches of God for your steadfastness and faith during all your persecutions and the afflictions that you are enduring.

The Judgment at Christ's Coming

5 This is evidence of the righteous judgment of God, and is intended to make you worthy of the kingdom of God, for which you are also suffering. 6For it is indeed just of God to repay with affliction those who afflict you, 7and to give relief to the afflicted as well as to us, when the Lord Jesus is revealed from heaven with his mighty angels 8in flaming fire, inflicting vengeance on those who do not know God and on those who do not obey the gospel of our Lord Jesus. 9These will suffer the punishment of eternal destruction, separated from the presence of the Lord and from the glory of his might, 10when he comes to be glorified by his saints and to be marveled at on that day among all who have believed, because our testimony to you was believed. 11To this end we always pray for you, asking that our God will make you worthy of his call and will fulfill by his power every good resolve and work of faith, 12so that the name of our Lord Jesus may be glorified in you, and you in him, according to the grace of our God and the Lord Jesus Christ.

The Man of Lawlessness

2 As to the coming of our Lord Jesus Christ and our being gathered together to him, we beg you, brothers and sisters,*b* 2not to be quickly shaken in mind or alarmed, either by spirit or by word or by letter, as though from us, to the effect that the day of the Lord is already here. 3Let no one deceive you in any way; for that day will not come unless the rebellion comes first and the lawless one*c* is revealed, the one destined for destruction.*d* 4He opposes and exalts himself above every so-called god or object of worship, so that he takes his seat in the temple of God, declaring himself to be God. 5Do you not remember that I told you these things when I was still with you? 6And you know what is now restraining him, so that he may be revealed when his time comes. 7For the mystery of lawlessness is already at work, but only until the one who now restrains it is removed. 8And then the lawless one will be

---

a Other ancient authorities read *the*   *b* Gk *brothers*   *c* Gk *the man of lawlessness*; other ancient authorities read *the man of sin*   *d* Gk *the son of destruction*

revealed, whom the Lord Jesus[a] will destroy[b] with the breath of his mouth, annihilating him by the manifestation of his coming. [9]The coming of the lawless one is apparent in the working of Satan, who uses all power, signs, lying wonders, [10]and every kind of wicked deception for those who are perishing, because they refused to love the truth and so be saved. [11]For this reason God sends them a powerful delusion, leading them to believe what is false, [12]so that all who have not believed the truth but took pleasure in unrighteousness will be condemned.

Chosen for Salvation

13 But we must always give thanks to God for you, brothers and sisters[c] beloved by the Lord, because God chose you as the first fruits[d] for salvation through sanctification by the Spirit and through belief in the truth. [14]For this purpose he called you through our proclamation of the good news,[e] so that you may obtain the glory of our Lord Jesus Christ. [15]So then, brothers and sisters,[c] stand firm and hold fast to the traditions that you were taught by us, either by word of mouth or by our letter.

16 Now may our Lord Jesus Christ himself and God our Father, who loved us and through grace gave us eternal comfort and good hope, [17]comfort your hearts and strengthen them in every good work and word.

Request for Prayer

3 Finally, brothers and sisters,[c] pray for us, so that the word of the Lord may spread rapidly and be glorified everywhere, just as it is among you, [2]and that we may be rescued from wicked and evil people; for not all have faith. [3]But the Lord is faithful; he will strengthen you and guard you from the evil one.[f] [4]And we have confidence

---

a Other ancient authorities lack *Jesus*   b Other ancient authorities read *consume*   c Gk *brothers*   d Other ancient authorities read *from the beginning*   e Or *through our gospel*   f Or *from evil*

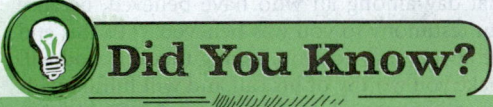

Did You Know?

The Parousia

After Jesus' death and Resurrection, the early Christians start to wait for his Second Coming, also called the Parousia. They think Jesus will return soon in glory to judge the living and the dead and to bring to complete fulfillment the Reign of God. They even see some signs of his imminent arrival and express an urgent call to be prepared. Paul seems to expect Christ's return in the near future but insists that nobody can predict when. He emphasizes the importance of living the Gospel and always being prepared for "our being gathered together to him" (2 Thess 2:1).

The important message for us today is that our history has meaning and purpose and that Christ ultimately triumphs over sin and death. The various descriptions of the signs preceding the end time are intended not to predict the future but rather to encourage us to live the Gospel as we wait in hope for Christ's glorious return.

▶ **2 Thess 1:5—2:17**

Live It!

Laziness

How well do you balance work—the things you are expected to do in your home, school, job, or community—with leisure? Workaholics find it hard to relax and just do nothing. Others find it easy to loosen up and recreate, and need a little push to get back to their responsibilities.

Evidently, some of the early Thessalonians are determined to avoid work altogether (see 2 Thess 3:6) because they thought the end time had already come. The author of Second Thessalonians sees this idleness as destructive for the Church. His answer is simple: no work, no food (see verse 10).

Christ invites us not to a life of laziness, where we take advantage of the kindness of others, but to an active life. Our work ought to be an expression of who we are and should contribute something meaningful and positive to the world.

▶ **2 Thess 3:6–13**

✚ Catholic Connection

Revelation and the Apostolic Tradition

What are some of your favorite family traditions? The traditions you celebrate when you gather with your relatives say something about who you are as a family. The same is true for Christianity. The Second Letter to the Thessalonians emphasizes the importance of the traditions about Jesus Christ that had been handed on to the church in Thessalonica through the Apostles' preaching and written letters (see 2 Thess 2:15).

Like the Thessalonians, we too are called by God to know Jesus Christ. Yet even before the coming of Christ, God had been slowly revealing himself through words, as when God spoke to Moses out of the burning bush (see Ex 3:1–22) and deeds, as when God led the Israelites across the Red Sea (see Ex 14:1–31). These words and deeds laid the foundation for the ultimate and final revelation of God in the Word made flesh, Jesus Christ. It is through knowing Jesus Christ, the Son of God, that we come to know God the Father and find salvation.

The Church teaches that, through the guidance of the Holy Spirit, the Apostles went forth as Jesus commanded and spread the Gospel, in both written and spoken word. The writings of the Apostles were preserved for the benefit of all generations in Sacred Scripture. The spoken words and actions of the Apostles, which reflect the growth and development of the Church's understanding and teachings about Jesus Christ, have also been preserved in what is known as the Apostolic Tradition. Both Sacred Scripture and Tradition have the same goal, yet they are distinct from one another (see "The Bible, Tradition, and Magisterium," near Lk 4:1–13). As successors to the Apostles, bishops have been entrusted with handing on the Apostolic Tradition through the Church's doctrines, worship, and life.

The Apostolic Tradition, big-T Tradition, should not be confused with what is called ecclesial tradition, small-t tradition. Small-t traditions are the customs and rituals that help Catholics live out their faith in their own particular time and locale. These traditions are influenced by history and culture and account for the rich variety of faith expressions in the Universal Church. They can also be changed or eliminated over time. Ecclesial traditions are important and good, as long as they help us to live out the mission and teachings of Jesus embodied in Sacred Scripture and Tradition.

● What big-T Traditions or small-t traditions of the Church have been important to you? Ask the same question of a parent, a grandparent, or someone from a previous generation and compare your answers.

▶ **2 Thess 2:13–17**
Catechism, nos. 74–83

in the Lord concerning you, that you are doing and will go on doing the things that we command. [5]May the Lord direct your hearts to the love of God and to the steadfastness of Christ.

Warning against Idleness

6 Now we command you, beloved,[a] in the name of our Lord Jesus Christ, to keep away from believers who are[b] living in idleness and not according to the tradition that they[c] received from us. [7]For you yourselves know how you ought to imitate us; we were not idle when we were with you, [8]and we did not eat anyone's bread without paying for it; but with toil and labor we worked night and day, so that we might not burden any of you. [9]This was not because we do not have that right, but in order to give you an example to imitate. [10]For even when we were with you, we gave you this command: Anyone unwilling to work should not eat. [11]For we hear that some of you are living in idleness, mere busybodies, not doing any work. [12]Now such persons we command and exhort in the Lord Jesus Christ to do their work quietly and to earn their own living. [13]Brothers and sisters,[d] do not be weary in doing what is right.

14 Take note of those who do not obey what we say in this letter; have nothing to do with them, so that they may be ashamed. [15]Do not regard them as enemies, but warn them as believers.[e]

Final Greetings and Benediction

16 Now may the Lord of peace himself give you peace at all times in all ways. The Lord be with all of you.

17 I, Paul, write this greeting with my own hand. This is the mark in every letter of mine; it is the way I write. [18]The grace of our Lord Jesus Christ be with all of you.[f]

---

a Gk *brothers*   b Gk *from every brother who is*   c Other ancient authorities read *you*   d Gk *Brothers*   e Gk *a brother*   f Other ancient authorities add *Amen*

Imagine you are a bishop writing a letter to the new priests, deacons, and lay ministers in your diocese. How do you encourage them? What do you warn them about? The two Letters to Timothy and the Letter to Titus are such letters, written to give good, practical advice to the leaders of the early church.

At a Glance

- **1 Tim 1:1–2.** a greeting
- **1 Tim 1:3—2:15.** warnings about false teachers; advice on prayer
- **1 Tim 3:1–13.** qualifications of bishops and deacons
- **1 Tim 3:14—6:19.** rules for Christian living
- **1 Tim 6:20–21.** final advice and a blessing
- **2 Tim 1:1–2.** a greeting
- **2 Tim 1:3–18.** thanksgiving and words of encouragement
- **2 Tim 2:1—3:9.** how to be a good teacher; examples of true and false teaching
- **2 Tim 3:10—4:22.** last words of advice, final greeting, and blessing
- **Titus 1:1–4.** greeting
- **Titus 1:5–16.** appointing church leaders; dealing with false teachers
- **Titus 2:1—3:11.** teachings about the Christian life
- **Titus 3:12–15.** final greeting and blessing

Quick Facts

Inspired Authors: followers of Paul (see "Introduction to the Letters and Revelation")
Date Written: around AD 100
Audience: leaders of the early churches

In Depth

The Letters to Timothy and Titus are called the pastoral letters because they were written to church leaders, or pastors. These letters sound as if they were written by Paul. But evidence suggests they may have been written by later disciples of Paul, adapting Paul's teaching and advice to the situation of the churches a generation later.

The First Letter to Timothy addresses practical issues the churches needed to deal with in order to achieve stability and respond to new challenges as Christianity became more visible in society: How should the churches deal with people teaching false beliefs? What qualities should church leaders have? Who deserves financial help from the community? How should Christians view success?

The Second Letter to Timothy presents Paul as being close to his execution. As you read this letter, you will experience his sadness at death, hear his reflections on his life and ministry, and see a man who feels deserted by many. This letter tells Timothy—who stands for all faithful Christians—that he needs to endure suffering with hope. Doing the right thing often means more pain than popularity. But even when other people desert us, God "remains faithful— / for he cannot deny himself" (2:13).

The Letter to Titus gives advice for elders, bishops, older men, older women, slaves, younger men, and younger women. It also offers repeated warnings to guard against temptations and false teachings and to be self-controlled.

The pastoral letters give us a picture of the church moving into a new phase. The church seems to have more structure, leadership roles are becoming more defined, and the people are more concerned about its public appearance. Like Christians today, the early Christians struggled to be faithful in applying Jesus' teachings to their culture and time.

The Pastoral Letters

1 Timothy

Salutation

1 Paul, an apostle of Christ Jesus by the command of God our Savior and of Christ Jesus our hope,

2 To Timothy, my loyal child in the faith:

Grace, mercy, and peace from God the Father and Christ Jesus our Lord.

Warning against False Teachers

3 I urge you, as I did when I was on my way to Macedonia, to remain in Ephesus so that you may instruct certain people not to teach any different doctrine, 4and not to occupy themselves with myths and endless genealogies that promote speculations rather than the divine training*a* that is known by faith. 5But the aim of such instruction is love that comes from a pure heart, a good conscience, and sincere faith. 6Some people have deviated from these and turned to meaningless talk, 7desiring to be teachers of the law, without understanding either what they are saying or the things about which they make assertions.

8 Now we know that the law is good, if one uses it legitimately. 9This means understanding that the law is laid down not for the innocent but for the lawless and disobedient, for the godless and sinful, for the unholy and profane, for those who kill their father or mother, for murderers, 10fornicators, sodomites, slave traders, liars, perjurers, and whatever else is contrary to the sound teaching 11that conforms to the glorious gospel of the blessed God, which he entrusted to me.

Gratitude for Mercy

12 I am grateful to Christ Jesus our Lord, who has strengthened me, because he judged me faithful and appointed me to his service, 13even though I was formerly a blasphemer, a persecutor, and a man of violence. But I received mercy because I had acted ignorantly in unbelief, 14and the grace of our Lord overflowed for me with the faith and love that are in Christ Jesus. 15The saying is sure and worthy of full acceptance, that Christ Jesus came into the world to save sinners—of whom I am the foremost. 16But for that very reason I received mercy, so that in me, as the foremost, Jesus Christ might display the utmost patience, making me an example to those who would come to believe in him for eternal life. 17To the King of the ages, immortal, invisible, the only God, be honor and glory forever and ever.*b* Amen.

18 I am giving you these instructions, Timothy, my child, in accordance with the prophecies made earlier about you, so that by following them you may fight the good fight, 19having faith and a good conscience. By rejecting conscience, certain persons have suffered shipwreck in the faith; 20among them are Hymenaeus and Alexander, whom I have turned over to Satan, so that they may learn not to blaspheme.

---

a Or *plan* *b* Gk *to the ages of the ages*

Instructions concerning Prayer

2 First of all, then, I urge that supplications, prayers, intercessions, and thanksgivings be made for everyone, [2]for kings and all who are in high positions, so that we may lead a quiet and peaceable life in all godliness and dignity. [3]This is right and is acceptable in the sight of God our Savior, [4]who desires everyone to be saved and to come to the knowledge of the truth. [5]For

there is one God;
> there is also one mediator between God and
>   humankind,
> Christ Jesus, himself human,
[6]   who gave himself a ransom for all

—this was attested at the right time. [7]For this I was appointed a herald and an apostle (I am

Conscience: God in the Gut

Do you ever wonder where God is during those really difficult moments of decision? Like when you're with some friends and someone proposes you all do something exciting but dangerous, and you feel caught in the middle. Or when an entire group is taking advantage of a teacher who has left the room during a test. Or when a new kid trips and falls in the cafeteria and no one makes a move to help.

One of the best places to look for God's direction is that feeling in the center of your stomach when you are faced with life's dilemmas. That feeling may be a sign of your conscience prompting you to act.

In 1 Timothy 1:19, Timothy is told to have "faith and a good conscience." A good conscience is based on reason and love and is developed through a commitment to make good and thoughtful moral decisions. It also means acting in a way that is true to your faith. In other words, Timothy is supposed to be a model of sound teaching and moral action that corresponds to it.

Take time to develop your conscience by studying moral issues and the Church's teaching on them. The more you develop your conscience, the more you will experience God's speaking to you and the more you will be empowered to live your faith.

▶ **1 Tim 1:18–19**

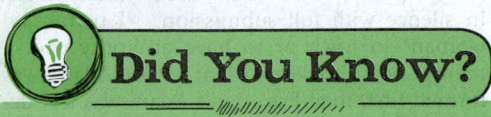

Women and Cultural Roles

A modern person reading 1 Timothy 2:8–15 may be shocked by the teaching there. A passage like this can be easily misunderstood and even misused against women. It is very important to realize that it is a reflection of women's roles in the ancient world. Whatever her religious background—Jewish, Christian, or pagan—a woman's place was in the home. Women generally married young, had no education, and were not allowed to hold a position of public authority.

The earliest Christian communities gathered in members' homes. In this less public arena, women taught and performed other ministries. As Christianity became more widely accepted, concern for how the Church appeared to outsiders grew—including concern about drunken bishops, immodest dress, and women teaching in public. That is probably why the author of First Timothy says, "I permit no woman to teach" (2:12).

Are things different for women in contemporary Christianity? Yes! Society has changed. Today, people in the United States are not scandalized if a woman manages a business, runs for public office, or leads a private foundation. Today, if you ask people to name influential Church leaders, Mother Teresa almost always comes up. Think of women you know who are involved in Church life. In your own parish or community, for example, there are probably women who are religious education directors, coordinators of youth ministry, or pastoral ministers.

▶ **1 Tim 2:8–15**

telling the truth,[a] I am not lying), a teacher of the Gentiles in faith and truth.

8 I desire, then, that in every place the men should pray, lifting up holy hands without anger or argument; [9]also that the women should dress themselves modestly and decently in suitable clothing, not with their hair braided, or with gold, pearls, or expensive clothes, [10]but with good works, as is proper for women who profess reverence for God. [11]Let a woman[b] learn in silence with full submission. [12]I permit no woman[b] to teach or to have authority over a man;[c] she is to keep silent. [13]For Adam was formed first, then Eve; [14]and Adam was not deceived, but the woman was deceived and became a transgressor. [15]Yet she will be saved through childbearing, provided they continue in faith and love and holiness, with modesty.

Qualifications of Bishops

3 The saying is sure:[d] whoever aspires to the office of bishop[e] desires a noble task. [2]Now a bishop[f] must be above reproach, married only once,[g] temperate, sensible, respectable, hospitable, an apt teacher, [3]not a drunkard, not violent but gentle, not quarrelsome, and not a lover of money. [4]He must manage his own household well, keeping his children submissive and respectful in every way— [5]for if someone does not know how to manage his own household, how can he take care of God's church? [6]He must not be a recent convert, or he may be puffed up with conceit and fall into the condemnation of the devil. [7]Moreover, he must be well thought of by

3:1–13

outsiders, so that he may not fall into disgrace and the snare of the devil.

Qualifications of Deacons

8 Deacons likewise must be serious, not double-tongued, not indulging in much wine, not greedy for money; [9]they must hold fast to the mystery of the faith with a clear conscience. [10]And let them first be tested; then, if they prove themselves blameless, let them serve as deacons. [11]Women[h] likewise must be serious, not slanderers, but temperate, faithful in all things. [12]Let deacons be married only once,[g] and let them manage their children and their households well; [13]for those who serve well as deacons gain a good standing for themselves and great boldness in the faith that is in Christ Jesus.

The Mystery of Our Religion

14 I hope to come to you soon, but I am writing these instructions to you so that, [15]if I am delayed, you may know how one ought to behave in the household of God, which is the church of the living God, the pillar and bulwark of the truth. [16]Without any doubt, the mystery of our religion is great:

He[i] was revealed in flesh,
  vindicated[j] in spirit,[k]
  seen by angels,
proclaimed among Gentiles,
  believed in throughout the world,
  taken up in glory.

False Asceticism

4 Now the Spirit expressly says that in later[l] times some will renounce the faith by paying attention to deceitful spirits and teachings of demons, [2]through the hypocrisy of liars whose consciences are seared with a hot iron. [3]They forbid marriage and demand abstinence from foods, which God created to be received with thanksgiving by those who believe and know the truth. [4]For everything created by God is good, and nothing is to be rejected, provided it is received with thanksgiving; [5]for it is sanctified by God's word and by prayer.

A Good Minister of Jesus Christ

6 If you put these instructions before the brothers and sisters,[m] you will be a good

---

a Other ancient authorities add *in Christ* *b* Or *wife* *c* Or *her husband* *d* Some interpreters place these words at the end of the previous paragraph. Other ancient authorities read *The saying is commonly accepted* *e* Or *overseer* *f* Or *an overseer* *g* Gk *the husband of one wife* *h* Or *Their wives,* or *Women deacons* *i* Gk *Who*; other ancient authorities read *God*; others, *Which* *j* Or *justified* *k* Or *by the Spirit* *l* Or *the last* *m* Gk *brothers*

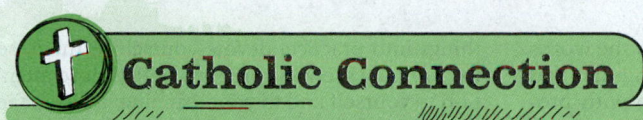

Catholic Connection

The Incarnation

Being new at something can be difficult, and it helps to have someone experienced show you the way. This is what Paul was doing for Timothy in his first letter. Timothy was new at leading his local church and was apparently facing some difficulties with people promoting false beliefs about Jesus Christ. To help, Paul provides Timothy with a brief summary of beliefs and acknowledges that faith in Christ involves mystery, or things that go beyond understanding. In this brief summary, Paul mentions that Jesus "was revealed in flesh" (1 Tim 3:16). This verse points to the mystery that Jesus is both fully divine and fully human.

Similar to the challenges that Timothy faced, the Church has also had to address those who preached false beliefs. During its first five hundred years, the Church struggled to clarify and explain the mystery of the relationship between Jesus' divinity and humanity. Some falsely said Jesus was created by God and therefore only semi-divine. Others falsely said the two natures remained totally separate in Jesus. And still others falsely claimed Jesus' human nature ceased to exist once it was assumed by Christ when he came in the flesh.

The Scriptures provide evidence of the presence and role of both a divine and human nature united in one person, Jesus Christ. We see that Jesus is truly human, for he had to learn and grow (see Lk 2:52), he experienced emotions (see Jn 11:28–37), and he faced temptations just like we do (see Mt 4:1–11). We also see that Jesus is truly divine, for he could read the heart of those he encountered (see Jn 4:5–42) and performed many miracles (see Mt 9:18–26).

After much effort, this mysterious relationship is now understood through the Church's teaching called the Incarnation. The Incarnation is the belief that Jesus is truly divine and assumed a truly human nature when he became man. The Church teaches that, with the exception of sinning, Jesus is just like each one of us in every way. By becoming human, Jesus showed us how God would live and act. He showed us how to live totally obedient to the Father's will. Through his love and service to others, he showed us how much God loves us and how much we should love others. By becoming human, Jesus revealed to us our true nature as sons and daughters of God.

▶ **1 Tim 3:14–16**
Catechism, nos. 456–483

servant[a] of Christ Jesus, nourished on the words of the faith and of the sound teaching that you have followed. [7]Have nothing to do with profane myths and old wives' tales. Train yourself in godliness, [8]for, while physical training is of some value, godliness is valuable in every way, holding promise for both the present life and the life to come. [9]The saying is sure and worthy of full acceptance. [10]For to this end we toil and struggle,[b] because we have our hope set on the living God, who is the Savior of all people, especially of those who believe.

11 These are the things you must insist on and teach. [12]Let no one despise your youth, but set the believers an example in speech and conduct, in love, in faith, in purity. [13]Until I arrive, give attention to the public reading of scripture,[c] to exhorting, to teaching. [14]Do not neglect the gift that is in you, which was given to you through prophecy with the laying on of hands by the council of elders.[d] [15]Put these

> "Let no one despise your youth, but set the believers an example in speech and conduct."
>
> (1 Tim 4:12)

things into practice, devote yourself to them, so that all may see your progress. [16]Pay close attention to yourself and to your teaching; continue in these things, for in doing this you will save both yourself and your hearers.

Duties toward Believers

5 Do not speak harshly to an older man,[e] but speak to him as to a father, to younger men as brothers, [2]to older women as mothers, to younger women as sisters—with absolute purity.

3 Honor widows who are really widows. [4]If a widow has children or grandchildren, they should first learn their religious duty to their own family and make some repayment to their parents; for this is pleasing in God's sight. [5]The real widow, left alone, has set her hope on God and continues in supplications and prayers night and day; [6]but the widow[f] who lives for pleasure is dead even while she lives. [7]Give these commands as well, so that they may be above reproach. [8]And whoever does not provide for relatives, and especially for family members, has denied the faith and is worse than an unbeliever.

9 Let a widow be put on the list if she is not less than sixty years old and has been married only once;[g] [10]she must be well attested for her good works, as one who has brought up children, shown hospitality, washed the saints' feet, helped the afflicted, and devoted herself to doing good in every way. [11]But refuse to put younger widows on the list; for when their sensual desires alienate them from Christ, they want to marry, [12]and so they incur condemnation for having violated their first pledge. [13]Besides that, they learn to be idle, gadding about from house to house; and they are not merely idle, but also gossips and busybodies, saying what they should not say. [14]So I would have younger widows marry, bear children, and manage their households, so as to give the adversary no occasion to revile us. [15]For some have already turned away to follow Satan. [16]If any believing woman[h] has relatives who are really widows, let her assist them; let the church not be burdened, so that it can assist those who are real widows.

L ive It!

Training for Christ

We spend countless hours in training to become better athletes, musicians, scientists, teachers, electricians; you name it, we train for it if we want to be good at it. Paul says the soul needs that same kind of training.

In your journal or on a piece of paper, make two columns—one to list the ways you train for your sporting event or other activity and the other to list ways you might train your soul to become a more loving person, in the image of Jesus. Once you have completed your lists, put them in a place where you can see them every day. Use them as a guide and as a reminder to continue in your efforts to train for Christ. You may also find that you need to keep adding to your soul-training list as your training starts to pay off!

▶ 1 Tim 4:6–10

---

a Or *deacon*   b Other ancient authorities read *suffer reproach*   c Gk *to the reading*   d Gk *by the presbytery*   e Or an elder, *a presbyter*   f Gk *she*   g Gk the *wife of one husband*   h Other ancient authorities read *believing man or woman*; others, *believing man*

17 Let the elders who rule well be considered worthy of double honor,[a] especially those who labor in preaching and teaching; [18]for the scripture says, "You shall not muzzle an ox while it is treading out the grain," and, "The laborer deserves to be paid." [19]Never accept any accusation against an elder except on the evidence of two or three witnesses. [20]As for those who persist in sin, rebuke them in the presence of all, so that the rest also may stand in fear. [21]In the presence of God and of Christ Jesus and of the elect angels, I warn you to keep these instructions without prejudice, doing nothing on the basis of partiality. [22]Do not ordain[b] anyone hastily, and do not participate in the sins of others; keep yourself pure.

23 No longer drink only water, but take a little wine for the sake of your stomach and your frequent ailments.

24 The sins of some people are conspicuous and precede them to judgment, while the sins of others follow them there. [25]So also good works are conspicuous; and even when they are not, they cannot remain hidden.

6 Let all who are under the yoke of slavery regard their masters as worthy of all honor, so that the name of God and the teaching may not be blasphemed. [2]Those who have believing masters must not be disrespectful to them on the ground that they are members of the church;[c] rather they must serve them all the more, since those who benefit by their service are believers and beloved.[d]

False Teaching and True Riches

Teach and urge these duties. [3]Whoever teaches otherwise and does not agree with the sound words of our Lord Jesus Christ and the teaching that is in accordance with godliness, [4]is conceited, understanding nothing, and has a morbid craving for controversy and for disputes about words. From these come envy, dissension, slander, base suspicions, [5]and wrangling among those who are depraved in mind and bereft of the truth, imagining that godliness is a means of gain.[e] [6]Of course, there is great gain in godliness combined with contentment; [7]for we brought nothing into the world, so that[f] we can take nothing out of it; [8]but if we have food and clothing, we will be content with these. [9]But those who want to be rich fall into temptation and are trapped by many senseless and harmful desires that plunge people into ruin and destruction. [10]For the love of money is a root of all kinds of evil, and in their eagerness to be rich some have wandered away from the faith and pierced themselves with many pains.

Dangers of Money

We live in a culture that glorifies material things, money, and consumption. People are generally thought to be successful if they have great riches and all the luxury items to prove it to their neighbors. There is a bumper sticker that reads, "The one who dies with the most toys wins!" Even when individuals or families have the essential things to live comfortably, many are driven to acquire more.

An important truth found many places in the Scriptures (see, for example, Lk 12:20) is repeated here: You can't take it with you. The Scriptures warn about something that most of us know deep down but often ignore: "The love of money is a root of all kinds of evil" (1 Tim 6:10). In our eagerness to become financially rich, we can lose sight of God and become entangled in all kinds of senseless distractions.

All of us need the basic stuff of life: food, clothing, and shelter. God wants us to have these things—and more! Ultimately, real riches or success will not be measured by bank accounts or material things, but by the love and generosity with which we have lived. How rich are you becoming in these things?

▶ 1 Tim 6:6–10

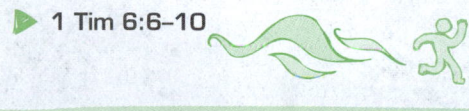

The Good Fight of Faith

11 But as for you, man of God, shun all this; pursue righteousness, godliness, faith, love, endurance, gentleness. [12]Fight the good fight of the faith; take hold of the eternal life, to which you were called and for which you made[g] the good confession in the presence of many witnesses. [13]In the presence of God, who gives life to all things, and of Christ Jesus, who in his testimony before Pontius Pilate made the good confession,

---

a Or compensation   b Gk Do not lay hands on   c Gk are brothers   d Or since they are believers and beloved, who devote themselves to good deeds   e Other ancient authorities add Withdraw yourself from such people   f Other ancient authorities read world—it is certain that   g Gk confessed

I charge you [14]to keep the commandment without spot or blame until the manifestation of our Lord Jesus Christ, [15]which he will bring about at the right time—he who is the blessed and only Sovereign, the King of kings and Lord of lords. [16]It is he alone who has immortality and dwells in unapproachable light, whom no one has ever seen or can see; to him be honor and eternal dominion. Amen.

17 As for those who in the present age are rich, command them not to be haughty, or to set their hopes on the uncertainty of riches, but rather on God who richly provides us with everything for our enjoyment. [18]They are to do good, to be rich in good works, generous, and ready to share, [19]thus storing up for themselves the treasure of a good foundation for the future, so that they may take hold of the life that really is life.

Personal Instructions and Benediction

20 Timothy, guard what has been entrusted to you. Avoid the profane chatter and contradictions of what is falsely called knowledge; [21]by professing it some have missed the mark as regards the faith.

Grace be with you.[a]

---

a The Greek word for *you* here is plural; in other ancient authorities it is singular. Other ancient authorities add *Amen*

2 Timothy

Salutation

1 Paul, an apostle of Christ Jesus by the will of God, for the sake of the promise of life that is in Christ Jesus,

2 To Timothy, my beloved child:

Grace, mercy, and peace from God the Father and Christ Jesus our Lord.

Thanksgiving and Encouragement

3 I am grateful to God—whom I worship with a clear conscience, as my ancestors did—when I remember you constantly in my prayers night and day. 4Recalling your tears, I long to see you so that I may be filled with joy. 5I am reminded of your sincere faith, a faith that lived first in your grandmother Lois and your mother Eunice and now, I am sure, lives in you. 6For this reason I remind you to rekindle the gift of God that is within you through the laying on of my hands; 7for God did not give us a spirit of cowardice, but rather a spirit of power and of love and of self-discipline.

8 Do not be ashamed, then, of the testimony about our Lord or of me his prisoner, but join with me in suffering for the gospel, relying on the power of God, 9who saved us and called us with a holy calling, not according to our works but according to his own purpose and grace. This grace was given to us in Christ Jesus before the ages began, 10but it has now been revealed through the appearing of our Savior Christ Jesus, who abolished death and brought life and immortality to light through the gospel. 11For this gospel

I was appointed a herald and an apostle and a teacher,*a* 12and for this reason I suffer as I do. But I am not ashamed, for I know the one in whom I have put my trust, and I am sure that he is able to guard until that day what I have entrusted to him.*b* 13Hold to the standard of sound teaching that you have heard from me, in the faith and love that are in Christ Jesus. 14Guard the good treasure entrusted to you, with the help of the Holy Spirit living in us.

15 You are aware that all who are in Asia have turned away from me, including Phygelus and Hermogenes. 16May the Lord grant mercy to the household of Onesiphorus, because he often refreshed me and was not ashamed of my chain; 17when he arrived in Rome, he eagerly*c* searched for me and found me 18—may the Lord grant that he will find mercy from the Lord on that day! And you know very well how much service he rendered in Ephesus.

A Good Soldier of Christ Jesus

2 You then, my child, be strong in the grace that is in Christ Jesus; 2and what you have heard from me through many witnesses entrust to faithful people who will be able to teach others as well. 3Share in suffering like a good soldier of Christ Jesus. 4No one serving in the army gets entangled in everyday affairs; the soldier's aim is to please the enlisting officer. 5And in the case of

---

a Other ancient authorities add *of the Gentiles* *b* Or *what has been entrusted to me* *c* Or *promptly*

an athlete, no one is crowned without competing according to the rules. ⁶It is the farmer who does the work who ought to have the first share of the crops. ⁷Think over what I say, for the Lord will give you understanding in all things.

8 Remember Jesus Christ, raised from the dead, a descendant of David—that is my gospel, ⁹for which I suffer hardship, even to the point of being chained like a criminal. But the word of God is not chained. ¹⁰Therefore I endure everything for the sake of the elect, so that they may also obtain the salvation that is in Christ Jesus, with eternal glory. ¹¹The saying is sure:

If we have died with him, we will also live with
    him;
¹² if we endure, we will also reign with him;
    if we deny him, he will also deny us;
¹³ if we are faithless, he remains faithful—
    for he cannot deny himself.

A Worker Approved by God

14 Remind them of this, and warn them before God[a] that they are to avoid wrangling over words, which does no good but only ruins those who are listening. ¹⁵Do your best to present yourself to God as one approved by him, a worker who has no need to be ashamed, rightly explaining the word of truth. ¹⁶Avoid profane chatter, for it will lead people into more and more impiety, ¹⁷and their talk will spread like gangrene. Among them are Hymenaeus and Philetus, ¹⁸who have swerved from the truth by claiming that the resurrection has already taken place. They are upsetting the faith of some. ¹⁹But God's firm foundation stands, bearing this inscription: "The Lord knows those who are his," and, "Let everyone who calls on the name of the Lord turn away from wickedness."

20 In a large house there are utensils not only of gold and silver but also of wood and clay, some for special use, some for ordinary. ²¹All who cleanse themselves of the things I have mentioned[b] will become special utensils, dedicated and useful to the owner of the house, ready for every good work. ²²Shun youthful passions and pursue righteousness, faith, love, and peace, along with those who call on the Lord from a pure heart. ²³Have nothing to do

---

a Other ancient authorities read *the Lord*   b Gk *of these things*

Do Not Be Ashamed

Terry is a popular guy in the senior class. He is on the basketball and track teams and served on student council. He is extremely friendly and never says anything bad about anyone. Everyone likes him.

Terry is also very active in his church's youth group. He is not afraid to let others know that church is important to him. He never preaches religion, but he lets people know that church and Jesus are central to his life.

The author of Second Timothy encourages today's readers, "Do not be ashamed, then, of the testimony about our Lord" (1:8). You do not have to announce your faith from mountaintops or from street corners, but like Terry, you should not be afraid to admit that God is important to you. You will likely discover that others admire you for your faith and commitment.

▶ 2 Tim 1:6–18

Teaching Others

Have you ever tried to explain to someone something about your faith? That can be challenging. Second Timothy 2:22–26 contains some tips on sharing faith with others: live a good moral life, do good works, and have a pure heart. Be kind, patient, and gentle. And be an apt teacher, someone who is qualified or prepared.

Imagine that you are helping to teach a group of younger people about their faith. What do you want to say about God? How do you explain Jesus' love? How do you show your patience and gentleness? If you can answer these questions, maybe you should volunteer to help with your church's religious education program!

▶ 2 Tim 2:22–26

with stupid and senseless controversies; you know that they breed quarrels. 24And the Lord's servant[a] must not be quarrelsome but kindly to everyone, an apt teacher, patient, 25correcting opponents with gentleness. God may perhaps grant that they will repent and come to know the truth, 26and that they may escape from the snare of the devil, having been held captive by him to do his will.[b]

Godlessness in the Last Days

3 You must understand this, that in the last days distressing times will come. 2For people will be lovers of themselves, lovers of money, boasters, arrogant, abusive, disobedient to their parents, ungrateful, unholy, 3inhuman, implacable, slanderers, profligates, brutes, haters of good, 4treacherous, reckless, swollen with conceit, lovers of pleasure rather than lovers of God, 5holding to the outward form of godliness but

"All scripture is inspired by God and is useful for teaching, for reproof, for correction, and for training in righteousness."
(2 Tim 3:16)

denying its power. Avoid them! 6For among them are those who make their way into households and captivate silly women, overwhelmed by their sins and swayed by all kinds of desires, 7who are always being instructed and can never arrive at a knowledge of the truth. 8As Jannes and Jambres opposed Moses, so these people, of corrupt mind and counterfeit faith, also oppose the truth. 9But they will not make much progress, because, as in the case of those two men,[c] their folly will become plain to everyone.

Paul's Charge to Timothy

10 Now you have observed my teaching, my conduct, my aim in life, my faith, my patience, my love, my steadfastness, 11my persecutions, and my suffering the things that happened to me in Antioch, Iconium, and Lystra. What persecutions I endured! Yet the Lord rescued me from all of them. 12Indeed, all who want to live a godly life in Christ Jesus will be persecuted. 13But wicked people and impostors will go from bad to worse, deceiving others and being deceived. 14But as for you, continue in what you have learned and firmly believed, knowing from whom you learned it, 15and how from childhood you have known the sacred writings that are able to instruct you for salvation through faith in Christ Jesus. 16All scripture is inspired by God and is[d] useful for teaching, for reproof, for correction, and for training in righteousness, 17so that everyone who belongs to God may be proficient, equipped for every good work.

4 In the presence of God and of Christ Jesus, who is to judge the living and the dead, and in view of his appearing and his kingdom, I solemnly urge you: 2proclaim the message; be persistent whether the time is favorable or unfavorable; convince, rebuke, and encourage, with the utmost patience in teaching. 3For the time is coming when people will not put up with sound doctrine, but having itching ears, they will accumulate for themselves teachers to suit their own desires, 4and will turn away from listening to the truth and wander away to myths. 5As for you, always be sober, endure suffering, do the work of an evangelist, carry out your ministry fully.

6 As for me, I am already being poured out

Misleading Messages

Sticking with something can be difficult. When things get tough, many people are tempted to quit or walk away. If swim practice is boring, they drop off the team. If homework is too complicated, they just don't finish it. If one of their friends starts to annoy them, they stop hanging around with her or him. We are surrounded by messages like "If it feels good, do it" and "You should have whatever your heart desires," and "Life will be great if you wear these clothes" or "Drink this beverage" or "Hang out with these people."

But reaching this worthy goal often requires hard choices and hard work. Second Timothy 4:1–5 warns us against being taken in by deceptive messages that suit our own desires—like cultural teachings that life should always be easy and pleasurable. Such messages water down the real challenge of living as a follower of Jesus Christ! If we are not finding life to be challenging, maybe we have tuned in to these misleading messages.

▶ **2 Tim 4:1–5**

as a libation, and the time of my departure has come. [7]I have fought the good fight, I have finished the race, I have kept the faith. [8]From now on there is reserved for me the crown of righteousness, which the Lord, the righteous judge, will give me on that day, and not only to me but also to all who have longed for his appearing.

Personal Instructions

9 Do your best to come to me soon, [10]for Demas, in love with this present world, has deserted me and gone to Thessalonica; Crescens has gone to Galatia,[a] Titus to Dalmatia. [11]Only Luke is with me. Get Mark and bring him with you, for he is useful in my ministry. [12]I have sent Tychicus to Ephesus. [13]When you come, bring the cloak that I left with Carpus at Troas, also the books, and above all the parchments. [14]Alexander the coppersmith did me great harm; the Lord will pay him back for his deeds. [15]You also must beware of him, for he strongly opposed our message.

16 At my first defense no one came to my support, but all deserted me. May it not be counted against them! [17]But the Lord stood by me and gave me strength, so that through me the message might be fully proclaimed and all the Gentiles might hear it. So I was rescued from the lion's mouth. [18]The Lord will rescue me from every evil attack and save me for his heavenly kingdom. To him be the glory forever and ever. Amen.

Final Greetings and Benediction

19 Greet Prisca and Aquila, and the household of Onesiphorus. [20]Erastus remained in Corinth; Trophimus I left ill in Miletus. [21]Do your best to come before winter. Eubulus sends greetings to you, as do Pudens and Linus and Claudia and all the brothers and sisters.[b]

22 The Lord be with your spirit. Grace be with you.[c]

---

a Other ancient authorities read *Gaul*   *b* Gk *all the brothers*
c The Greek word for *you* here is plural. Other ancient authorities add *Amen*

For background on this letter, see the introduction to the pastoral letters, before 1 Timothy.

Titus

Salutation

1 Paul, a servant[a] of God and an apostle of Jesus Christ, for the sake of the faith of God's elect and the knowledge of the truth that is in accordance with godliness, [2] in the hope of eternal life that God, who never lies, promised before the ages began— [3] in due time he revealed his word through the proclamation with which I have been entrusted by the command of God our Savior,

4 To Titus, my loyal child in the faith we share:

Grace[b] and peace from God the Father and Christ Jesus our Savior.

Titus in Crete

5 I left you behind in Crete for this reason, so that you should put in order what remained to be done, and should appoint elders in every town, as I directed you: [6] someone who is blameless, married only once,[c] whose children are believers, not accused of debauchery and not rebellious. [7] For a bishop,[d] as God's steward, must be blameless; he must not be arrogant or quick-tempered or addicted to wine or violent or greedy for gain; [8] but he must be hospitable, a lover of goodness, prudent, upright, devout, and self-controlled. [9] He must have a firm grasp of the word that is trustworthy in accordance with the teaching, so that he may be able both to preach with sound doctrine and to refute those who contradict it.

10 There are also many rebellious people, idle talkers and deceivers, especially those of the circumcision; [11] they must be silenced, since they are upsetting whole families by teaching for sordid gain what it is not right to teach. [12] It was one of them, their very own prophet, who said,

"Cretans are always liars, vicious brutes, lazy
    gluttons."

[13] That testimony is true. For this reason rebuke them sharply, so that they may become sound in the faith, [14] not paying attention to Jewish myths or to commandments of those who reject the truth. [15] To the pure all things are pure, but to the corrupt and unbelieving nothing is pure. Their very minds and consciences are corrupted. [16] They profess to know God, but they deny him by their actions. They are detestable, disobedient, unfit for any good work.

Teach Sound Doctrine

2 But as for you, teach what is consistent with sound doctrine. [2] Tell the older men to be temperate, serious, prudent, and sound in faith, in love, and in endurance.

3 Likewise, tell the older women to be reverent in behavior, not to be slanderers or slaves to drink; they are to teach what is good, [4] so that they may encourage the young women to love their husbands, to love their children, [5] to be self-controlled, chaste, good managers of the household, kind, being submissive to their husbands, so that the word of God may not be discredited.

---

a Gk *slave*   b Other ancient authorities read *Grace, mercy,*
c Gk *husband of one wife*   d Or *an overseer*

Christian Leadership

Leadership is an esteemed but difficult calling. Church leaders in particular must earn the respect of others through the integrity of their lifestyle and their commitment and service to the values of Jesus Christ. Good leaders also know how to motivate others to grow and to serve.

Maybe you too possess leadership qualities and wish to pursue a leadership position in the Church or in another field. Make a list of the values you think a leader should have. How closely does your list match the characteristics of a good leader in Titus 1:5–9? When you are ready to lead, review the list from verses 5–9, and remember the importance of living a life of character and leading others to positions of leadership.

As you discern your own leadership potential, look to others who you feel possess good leadership qualities. Which leaders in your school or youth program do you admire the most? What qualities make them good leaders? How do these leaders stack up against the good-leader characteristics you listed?

▶ Titus 1:5–9

6 Likewise, urge the younger men to be self-controlled. [7]Show yourself in all respects a model of good works, and in your teaching show integrity, gravity, [8]and sound speech that cannot be censured; then any opponent will be put to shame, having nothing evil to say of us.

9 Tell slaves to be submissive to their masters and to give satisfaction in every respect; they are not to talk back, [10]not to pilfer, but to show complete and perfect fidelity, so that in everything they may be an ornament to the doctrine of God our Savior.

11 For the grace of God has appeared, bringing salvation to all,[a] [12]training us to renounce impiety and worldly passions, and in the present age to live lives that are self-controlled, upright, and godly, [13]while we wait for the blessed hope and the manifestation of the glory of our great God and Savior,[b] Jesus Christ. [14]He it is who gave himself for us that he might redeem us from all iniquity and purify for himself a people of his own who are zealous for good deeds.

15 Declare these things; exhort and reprove with all authority.[c] Let no one look down on you.

Maintain Good Deeds

3 Remind them to be subject to rulers and authorities, to be obedient, to be ready for every good work, [2]to speak evil of no one, to avoid quarreling, to be gentle, and to show every courtesy to everyone. [3]For we ourselves were once foolish, disobedient, led astray, slaves to various passions and pleasures, passing our days in

a Or has appeared to all, bringing salvation   b Or of the great God and our Savior   c Gk commandment

Sioux Prayer for Transformation

I come before thee as one of thy many children. See, I am small and weak; I need thy strength and wisdom. Grant me to walk in beauty and that my eyes may ever behold the crimson sunset. May my hands treat with respect the things which thou hast created, may my ears hear thy voice!

Make me wise, that I may understand the things which thou hast taught my people, which thou hast hidden in every leaf and every rock. I long for strength, not in order that I may overreach my brother but to fight my greatest enemy—myself. Make me ever ready to come to thee with pure hands

and candid eyes, so that my spirit, when life disappears like the setting sun, may stand unashamed before thee.

▶ Titus 3:3–7

TITUS

malice and envy, despicable, hating one another. [4]But when the goodness and loving kindness of God our Savior appeared, [5]he saved us, not because of any works of righteousness that we had done, but according to his mercy, through the water[a] of rebirth and renewal by the Holy Spirit. [6]This Spirit he poured out on us richly through Jesus Christ our Savior, [7]so that, having been justified by his grace, we might become heirs according to the hope of eternal life. [8]The saying is sure.

I desire that you insist on these things, so that those who have come to believe in God may be careful to devote themselves to good works; these things are excellent and profitable to everyone. [9]But avoid stupid controversies, genealogies, dissensions, and quarrels about the law, for they are unprofitable and worthless. [10]After a first and second admonition, have nothing more to do with anyone who causes divisions, [11]since you know that such a person is perverted and sinful, being self-condemned.

Final Messages and Benediction

12 When I send Artemas to you, or Tychicus, do your best to come to me at Nicopolis, for I have decided to spend the winter there. [13]Make every effort to send Zenas the lawyer and Apollos on their way, and see that they lack nothing. [14]And let people learn to devote themselves to good works in order to meet urgent needs, so that they may not be unproductive.

15 All who are with me send greetings to you. Greet those who love us in the faith.

Grace be with all of you.[b]

---

a Gk *washing* b Other ancient authorities add *Amen*

The brief Letter to Philemon is about slavery. It may surprise you that it doesn't condemn slavery outright. In fact, other parts of the Bible take the idea of human slavery for granted! How can the Bible not challenge something we think is wrong? Seeking to understand this puzzling question gives us a key to understanding God's Revelation in the Bible.

In Depth

One key to understanding God's message in the Bible is to understand the beliefs of the authors and the first readers. The Letter to Philemon is addressed to a slave owner named Philemon, a woman named Apphia, and a soldier named Archippus, who all lived in Colossae. Philemon's slave, Onesimus, ran away, wound up in prison with Paul, and became a Christian. Now, Paul is sending him back to Philemon, as the law requires. That same law gives Philemon the right to punish Onesimus for escaping. But Paul asks—indirectly, but clearly enough—for Onesimus's freedom. Paul also asks for something far more challenging—that Philemon, Apphia, and Archippus accept Onesimus as "a beloved brother" (verse 16) in Christ.

We see in this letter the beginning of a new attitude toward slavery. Recall Paul's basic statement on Christian freedom in Galatians 3:28: "There is no longer Jew or Greek, there is no longer slave or free, there is no longer male and female; for all of you are one in Christ Jesus." However, slavery was an integral part of life during Paul's time. This is probably why he never directly challenged the institution of slavery.

Paul may not have been a social revolutionary by our standards, but he did believe the Christian community ought to live by a higher standard than other people. This letter is a masterpiece of persuasion as it urges Philemon and the church community in Colossae to accept Onesimus as a beloved brother in Christ. It uses flattery (see verses 4–7), a veiled reference to Paul's authority (see verses 8–9), Paul's personal relationship with everyone involved (see verses 12–17), and maybe even a little guilt in Paul's offer to pay for anything Onesimus stole (see verses 18–19). Paul's message to the household of Philemon and to us is this: We must get beyond whatever cultural boundaries prevent us from treating one another as brothers and sisters in Christ!

At a Glance

- **Verses 1–7.** a greeting and gratitude for Philemon
- **Verses 8–22.** Paul's request
- **Verses 23–25.** final greetings and a blessing

Quick Facts

Inspired Author: Paul
Date Written: from AD 54 to 56 if from Ephesus, from AD 61 to 63 if from Rome
Audience: Philemon and his household

The Letter to

Philemon

Philemon

Salutation

1 Paul, a prisoner of Christ Jesus, and Timothy our brother,[a]

To Philemon our dear friend and co-worker, [2]to Apphia our sister,[b] to Archippus our fellow soldier, and to the church in your house:

3 Grace to you and peace from God our Father and the Lord Jesus Christ.

Philemon's Love and Faith

4 When I remember you[c] in my prayers, I always thank my God [5]because I hear of your love for all the saints and your faith toward the Lord Jesus. [6]I pray that the sharing of your faith may become effective when you perceive all the good that we[d] may do for Christ. [7]I have indeed received much joy and encouragement from your love, because the hearts of the saints have been refreshed through you, my brother.

Paul's Plea for Onesimus

8 For this reason, though I am bold enough in Christ to command you to do your duty, [9]yet I would rather appeal to you on the basis of love— and I, Paul, do this as an old man, and now also as a prisoner of Christ Jesus.[e] [10]I am appealing to you for my child, Onesimus, whose father I have become during my imprisonment. [11]Formerly he was useless to you, but now he is indeed useful[f] both to you and to me. [12]I am sending him, that is, my own heart, back to you. [13]I wanted to keep him with me, so that he might be of service to

Live It!

Rethinking Social Structures

In sending Onesimus back to Philemon, Paul asked Philemon not only to forgive his runaway slave but to rethink his relationship with him. Paul's plea to Philemon and the Church in Colossae to look on Onesimus as a brother in Christ was radical for the time. People expected runaway slaves to be punished severely. Accepting Onesimus as a Christian would be a sign that Paul truly intended that his notion of the Church as one body in Christ should be lived out in concrete ways!

- What commonly accepted social structures in our day might need a fresh look?
- Might any privileges that we take for granted actually prevent true equality in Christ?

▶ Philemon, verses 8–21

---

a Gk *the brother*   b Gk *the sister*   c From verse 4 through verse 21, *you* is singular   d Other ancient authorities read *you* (plural)
e Or *as an ambassador of Christ Jesus, and now also his prisoner*
f The name Onesimus means *useful* or (compare verse 20) *beneficial*

me in your place during my imprisonment for the gospel; [14]but I preferred to do nothing without your consent, in order that your good deed might be voluntary and not something forced. [15]Perhaps this is the reason he was separated from you for a while, so that you might have him back forever, [16]no longer as a slave but more than a slave, a beloved brother—especially to me but how much more to you, both in the flesh and in the Lord.

17 So if you consider me your partner, welcome him as you would welcome me. [18]If he has wronged you in any way, or owes you anything, charge that to my account. [19]I, Paul, am writing this with my own hand: I will repay it. I say nothing about your owing me even your own self. [20]Yes, brother, let me have this benefit from you in the Lord! Refresh my heart in Christ. [21]Confident of your obedience, I am writing to you, knowing that you will do even more than I say.

22 One thing more—prepare a guest room for me, for I am hoping through your prayers to be restored to you.

Final Greetings and Benediction

23 Epaphras, my fellow prisoner in Christ Jesus, sends greetings to you,[a] [24]and so do Mark, Aristarchus, Demas, and Luke, my fellow workers.

25 The grace of the Lord Jesus Christ be with your spirit.[b]

---

a Here *you* is singular b Other ancient authorities add *Amen*

Have you ever wondered why it makes sense to believe that Jesus is the Savior of all humanity? It's an honest question. Evidently, some early Christians asked it. The Letter to the Hebrews is a sermon—to them and to us—to strengthen our faith and belief in Jesus Christ, the Son of God and our "great high priest" (4:14).

At a Glance

- **Chapters 1–2.** an introduction, and a message that Christ is greater than the angels

- **Chapters 3–7.** Christ is greater than Moses, Melchizedek, and the priests of the Temple.

- **8:1—10:18.** Christ offers the perfect sacrifice of the New Covenant.

- **10:19—12:29.** call to perseverance, list of heroes of the faith, the example of Christ, warnings based on Old Testament stories

- **13:1–19.** exhortations to right behavior

- **13:20–25.** blessing and final greeting

Quick Facts

Inspired Author: unknown
Date Written: from approximately AD 80 to 90
Audience: Hellenistic (Greek-speaking) Christians and possibly Jewish Christians

In Depth

The Letter to the Hebrews gives us almost no information about its author and the community it is addressed to. But it appears that some members of the community are in danger of giving up their faith—and this is happening after the group has already survived a period of persecution. The letter encourages them to be strong in their faith and seeks to give a sound foundation for believing in Jesus Christ. It is a statement on the saving power of Christ's sacrificial death and his unique role as High Priest of the New Covenant.

The letter presents Christ as the divine Son of God, through whom the world was created, superior to any angel, and the culmination of all the promises and expectations of the Old Testament. In explaining Christ's importance, the letter uses a type of argument called "from the lesser to the greater." This type of argument is based on the idea that if you accept something as true in a lesser situation, then it is certainly true in a greater situation. The author uses it to show that Christ's sacrifice is far greater than the sacrifices offered by the priests in the Temple. As the perfect high priest, Christ offers the perfect sacrifice—his death on the cross—through which God saves us once and for all from sin.

This letter reads like one long sermon made up of interconnecting parts. Begin by reading the whole thing out loud to truly appreciate its power and wording. Then look up some of its references to people and events in the Old Testament to better appreciate its inspired explanation of Christ's nature and mission.

The Letter to the Hebrews

Hebrews

God Has Spoken by His Son

1 Long ago God spoke to our ancestors in many and various ways by the prophets, ²but in these last days he has spoken to us by a Son,ᵃ whom he appointed heir of all things, through whom he also created the worlds. ³He is the reflection of God's glory and the exact imprint of God's very being, and he sustainsᵇ all things by his powerful word. When he had made purification for sins, he sat down at the right hand of the Majesty on high, ⁴having become as much superior to angels as the name he has inherited is more excellent than theirs.

The Son Is Superior to Angels

5 For to which of the angels did God ever say,

"You are my Son;
    today I have begotten you"?

Or again,

"I will be his Father,
    and he will be my Son"?

⁶And again, when he brings the firstborn into the world, he says,

"Let all God's angels worship him."

⁷Of the angels he says,

"He makes his angels winds,
    and his servants flames of fire."

⁸But of the Son he says,

"Your throne, O God, isᶜ forever and ever,
    and the righteous scepter is the scepter of
        yourᵈ kingdom.

⁹ You have loved righteousness and hated
        wickedness;
therefore God, your God, has anointed you
    with the oil of gladness beyond your
        companions."

¹⁰And,

"In the beginning, Lord, you founded the earth,
    and the heavens are the work of your hands;
¹¹ they will perish, but you remain;
    they will all wear out like clothing;
¹² like a cloak you will roll them up,
    and like clothingᵉ they will be changed.
But you are the same,
    and your years will never end."

¹³But to which of the angels has he ever said,

"Sit at my right hand
    until I make your enemies a footstool for your
        feet"?

¹⁴Are not all angelsᶠ spirits in the divine service, sent to serve for the sake of those who are to inherit salvation?

Warning to Pay Attention

2 Therefore we must pay greater attention to what we have heard, so that we do not drift away from it. ²For if the message declared through angels was valid, and every transgression or disobedience received a just penalty, ³how can we escape if we neglect so great a salvation? It was

---

a Or *the Son*   b Or *bears along*   c Or *God is your throne*
d Other ancient authorities read *his*   e Other ancient authorities
lack *like clothing*   f Gk *all of them*

declared at first through the Lord, and it was attested to us by those who heard him, [4]while God added his testimony by signs and wonders and various miracles, and by gifts of the Holy Spirit, distributed according to his will.

Exaltation through Abasement

5 Now God[a] did not subject the coming world, about which we are speaking, to angels. [6]But someone has testified somewhere,

"What are human beings that you are mindful
    of them,[b]
  or mortals, that you care for them?[c]
[7] You have made them for a little while lower[d]
      than the angels;
  you have crowned them with glory and honor,[e]
[8]   subjecting all things under their feet."

Now in subjecting all things to them, God[a] left nothing outside their control. As it is, we do not yet see everything in subjection to them, [9]but we do see Jesus, who for a little while was made lower[f] than the angels, now crowned with glory and honor because of the suffering of death, so that by the grace of God[g] he might taste death for everyone.

10 It was fitting that God,[a] for whom and through whom all things exist, in bringing many children to glory, should make the pioneer of their salvation perfect through sufferings. [11]For the one who sanctifies and those who are sanctified all have one Father.[h] For this reason Jesus[a] is not ashamed to call them brothers and sisters,[i] [12]saying,

"I will proclaim your name to my brothers and
    sisters,[i]
  in the midst of the congregation I will praise
    you."
[13]And again,
"I will put my trust in him."
And again,
"Here am I and the children whom God has
    given me."

14 Since, therefore, the children share flesh and blood, he himself likewise shared the same things, so that through death he might destroy the one who has the power of death, that is, the devil, [15]and free those who all their lives were held in slavery by the fear of death. [16]For it is clear that he did not come to help angels, but the descendants of Abraham. [17]Therefore he had to become like his brothers and sisters[i] in every respect, so that he might be a merciful and faithful high priest in the service of God, to make a sacrifice of atonement for the sins of the people. [18]Because he himself was tested by what he suffered, he is able to help those who are being tested.

Moses a Servant, Christ a Son

3 Therefore, brothers and sisters,[i] holy partners in a heavenly calling, consider that Jesus, the apostle and high priest of our confession, [2]was faithful to the one who appointed him, just as Moses also "was faithful in all[j] God's[k] house." [3]Yet Jesus[l] is worthy of more glory than Moses, just as the builder of a house has more honor than the house itself. [4](For every house is built by someone, but the builder of all things is God.) [5]Now Moses was faithful in all God's[k] house as a servant, to testify to the things that would be spoken later. [6]Christ, however, was faithful over God's[k] house as a son, and we are his house if

---

a Gk he   b Gk *What is man that you are mindful of him?*
c Gk *or the son of man that you care for him?* In the Hebrew of Psalm 8.4-6 both *man* and *son of man* refer to all humankind
d Or *them only a little lower*   e Other ancient authorities add *and set them over the works of your hands*   f Or *who was made a little lower*   g Other ancient authorities read *apart from God*
h Gk *are all of one*   i Gk *brothers*   j Other ancient authorities lack *all*   k Gk *his*   l Gk *this one*

"The Exact Imprint"

Throughout history there have been many opinions about who Jesus of Nazareth was. Some have called him a great teacher, some a prophet, some a charismatic preacher, and others a worker of miracles. Christians believe Jesus was all of these and more—much more.

The Letter to the Hebrews makes a bold claim about Jesus. It says the historical human being from Nazareth named Jesus is the perfect human image of God. Jesus reflects God's glory and is "the exact imprint of God's very being" (1:3). In other words, although a human being like us, Jesus is God.

This astonishing claim is central to the Christian faith. If you accept it as true, it will change your life. And if you are to believe it, you need to know the whole story behind it and all the evidence that supports it. The best place to start is with the book in your hands right now. Read on!

▶ Heb 1:1–14

we hold firm*a* the confidence and the pride that belong to hope.

Warning against Unbelief

7 Therefore, as the Holy Spirit says,

"Today, if you hear his voice,
8 do not harden your hearts as in the rebellion,
    as on the day of testing in the wilderness,
9 where your ancestors put me to the test,
    though they had seen my works 10for forty
        years.
Therefore I was angry with that generation,
    and I said, 'They always go astray in their hearts,
    and they have not known my ways.'
11 As in my anger I swore,
    'They will not enter my rest.' "

12Take care, brothers and sisters,*b* that none of you may have an evil, unbelieving heart that turns away from the living God. 13But exhort one another every day, as long as it is called "today," so that none of you may be hardened by the deceitfulness of sin. 14For we have become partners of Christ, if only we hold our first confidence firm to the end. 15As it is said,

Approach God Boldly!

Have you ever believed you did something God could never forgive? Or do you ever have thoughts that make you feel so ashamed you do not dare talk with God about them?

Hebrews 4:14–16 reminds us of a remarkable truth: Jesus, though fully divine, was also fully human. And though he never sinned, this Scripture passage tells us that he was tempted, as we are, in every respect. Think about that! Jesus was once fourteen years old. He was once seventeen. He was once twenty-two. There is no temptation that you have considered that Jesus cannot understand. And that is why you can approach him in any circumstance—even your deepest trouble—and find compassion and grace.

Remember: (1) you cannot hide from God, and (2) you don't have to!

▶ Heb 4:14–16

"Today, if you hear his voice,
    do not harden your hearts as in the rebellion."
16Now who were they who heard and yet were rebellious? Was it not all those who left Egypt under the leadership of Moses? 17But with whom was he angry forty years? Was it not those who sinned, whose bodies fell in the wilderness? 18And to whom did he swear that they would not enter his rest, if not to those who were disobedient? 19So we see that they were unable to enter because of unbelief.

The Rest That God Promised

4 Therefore, while the promise of entering his rest is still open, let us take care that none of you should seem to have failed to reach it. 2For indeed the good news came to us just as to them; but the message they heard did not benefit them, because they were not united by faith with those who listened.*c* 3For we who have believed enter that rest, just as God*d* has said,

"As in my anger I swore,
    'They shall not enter my rest,' "
though his works were finished at the foundation of the world. 4For in one place it speaks about the seventh day as follows, "And God rested on the seventh day from all his works." 5And again in this place it says, "They shall not enter my rest." 6Since therefore it remains open for some to enter it, and those who formerly received the good news failed to enter because of disobedience, 7again he sets a certain day— "today"—saying through David much later, in the words already quoted,

"Today, if you hear his voice,
    do not harden your hearts."
8For if Joshua had given them rest, God*d* would not speak later about another day. 9So then, a sabbath rest still remains for the people of God; 10for those who enter God's rest also cease from their labors as God did from his. 11Let us therefore make every effort to enter that rest, so that no one may fall through such disobedience as theirs.

> "The word of God is living
> and active."
>
> (Heb 4:12)

12 Indeed, the word of God is living and active, sharper than any two-edged sword, piercing

a Other ancient authorities add *to the end*   b Gk *brothers*
c Other ancient authorities read *it did not meet with faith in those who listened*   d Gk *he*

until it divides soul from spirit, joints from marrow; it is able to judge the thoughts and intentions of the heart. ¹³And before him no creature is hidden, but all are naked and laid bare to the eyes of the one to whom we must render an account.

Jesus the Great High Priest

14 Since, then, we have a great high priest who has passed through the heavens, Jesus, the Son of God, let us hold fast to our confession. ¹⁵For we do not have a high priest who is unable to sympathize with our weaknesses, but we have one who in every respect has been tested*a* as we are, yet without sin. ¹⁶Let us therefore approach the throne of grace with boldness, so that we may receive mercy and find grace to help in time of need.

5 Every high priest chosen from among mortals is put in charge of things pertaining to God on their behalf, to offer gifts and sacrifices for sins. ²He is able to deal gently with the ignorant and wayward, since he himself is subject to weakness; ³and because of this he must offer sacrifice for his own sins as well as for those of the people. ⁴And one does not presume to take this honor, but takes it only when called by God, just as Aaron was.

5 So also Christ did not glorify himself in becoming a high priest, but was appointed by the one who said to him,

"You are my Son,
      today I have begotten you";

⁶as he says also in another place,

"You are a priest forever,
      according to the order of Melchizedek."

7 In the days of his flesh, Jesus*b* offered up prayers and supplications, with loud cries and tears, to the one who was able to save him from death, and he was heard because of his reverent submission. ⁸Although he was a Son, he learned obedience through what he suffered; ⁹and having been made perfect, he became the source of eternal salvation for all who obey him, ¹⁰having been designated by God a high priest according to the order of Melchizedek.

Warning against Falling Away

11 About this we have much to say that is hard to explain, since you have become dull in understanding. ¹²For though by this time you ought to be teachers, you need someone to teach you again the basic elements of the oracles of God. You need milk, not solid food; ¹³for everyone who lives on milk, being still an infant, is unskilled in the word of righteousness. ¹⁴But

solid food is for the mature, for those whose faculties have been trained by practice to distinguish good from evil.

a Or tempted   b Gk he   c Or him

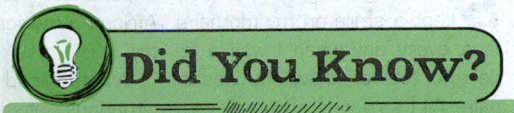

Did You Know?

The Priesthood and Christ's Sacrifice

In the Old Testament, the priesthood evolved after Israel became a nation, and it underwent a long process of development. Priests were not ordained; the priesthood was considered hereditary within the tribe of Levi. After the Exile, three classes of clergy emerged: high priests, priests, and Levites. Priestly functions included maintaining religion as the center of Israel's life, taking care of the Temple of Jerusalem, and interpreting and teaching the Scriptures. In a special way, the priests of Israel represented the people before God by offering prayer and sacrifices for the forgiveness of sin. Their sacrifices foreshadowed the sacrifice of Jesus, the only sacrifice truly capable of reconciling a broken relationship with God caused by sin.

In the New Testament, Christ made the Apostles co-ministers in his saving mission, including a special participation in his high priesthood—the high priesthood described in Hebrews 4:14—5:10. Today, the bishops, as successors of the Apostles, continue the Apostolic Tradition. They ordain priests to assist in their responsibilities as pastors of the faithful, preachers of God's word, and celebrants of Christian worship (see "Holy Orders," near Mk 3:13–19).

Catholic bishops and priests exercise their special participation in Christ's priesthood while presiding at the Eucharist. Acting in Christ's name and in communion with the assembly, they celebrate a memorial of Jesus' life, death, and Resurrection. In the celebration of the Eucharist, Christ's sacrifice on the cross is "re-presented"—that is, Jesus' sacrifice for the forgiveness of sins is made real and present.

▶ Heb 4:14—5:10

H E B

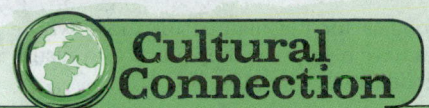

Cultural Connection

Anchor of the Soul

Something mighty powerful kept a smile on my mother's face every day when I was a little girl. I never knew she was in pain. All I saw was a woman with a demeanor of hope and a purpose in life.

I did not know it back then, but she was enduring racial harassment at her job. There was unceasing verbal hate toward African Americans. As I have matured, I have learned that her harassment was not unique. It was a common experience for many African Americans in this country.

When faced with oppressive situations, let us be thankful for a God who continuously fills us with hope. Without hope, oppression is lethal. Hope keeps us moving forward when we are about to give up. Hope makes us smile at tomorrow, even though today is a bitter pill.

Hope is "a sure and steadfast anchor of the soul" (Heb 6:19). A hopeless soul is a major threat to our faith. Is your hope anchored in the Lord?

Dear God, give me hope when I face oppression. Amen.

▶ Heb 6:19–20

The Peril of Falling Away

6 Therefore let us go on toward perfection,[a] leaving behind the basic teaching about Christ, and not laying again the foundation: repentance from dead works and faith toward God, [2]instruction about baptisms, laying on of hands, resurrection of the dead, and eternal judgment. [3]And we will do[b] this, if God permits. [4]For it is impossible to restore again to repentance those who have once been enlightened, and have tasted the heavenly gift, and have shared in the Holy Spirit, [5]and have tasted the goodness of the word of God and the powers of the age to come, [6]and then have fallen away, since on their own they are crucifying again the Son of God and are holding him up to contempt. [7]Ground that drinks up the rain falling on it repeatedly, and that produces a crop useful to those for whom it is cultivated, receives a blessing from God. [8]But if it produces thorns and thistles, it is worthless and on the verge of being cursed; its end is to be burned over.

9 Even though we speak in this way, beloved, we are confident of better things in your case, things that belong to salvation. [10]For God is not unjust; he will not overlook your work and the love that you showed for his sake[c] in serving the saints, as you still do. [11]And we want each one of you to show the same diligence so as to realize the full assurance of hope to the very end, [12]so that you may not become sluggish, but imitators of those who through faith and patience inherit the promises.

The Certainty of God's Promise

13 When God made a promise to Abraham, because he had no one greater by whom to swear, he swore by himself, [14]saying, "I will surely bless you and multiply you." [15]And thus Abraham,[d] having patiently endured, obtained the promise. [16]Human beings, of course, swear by someone greater than themselves, and an oath given as confirmation puts an end to all dispute. [17]In the same way, when God desired to show even more clearly to the heirs of the promise the unchangeable character of his purpose, he guaranteed it by an oath, [18]so that through two unchangeable things, in which it is impossible that God would prove false, we who have taken refuge might be strongly encouraged to seize the hope set before us. [19]We have this hope, a sure and steadfast anchor of the soul, a hope that enters the inner shrine behind the curtain, [20]where Jesus, a forerunner on our behalf, has entered, having become a high priest forever according to the order of Melchizedek.

The Priestly Order of Melchizedek

7 This "King Melchizedek of Salem, priest of the Most High God, met Abraham as he was returning from defeating the kings and blessed him"; [2]and to him Abraham apportioned "one-tenth of everything." His name, in the first place,

---

a Or *toward maturity*   b Other ancient authorities read *let us do*
c Gk *for his name*   d Gk *he*

means "king of righteousness"; next he is also king of Salem, that is, "king of peace." ³Without father, without mother, without genealogy, having neither beginning of days nor end of life, but resembling the Son of God, he remains a priest forever.

4 See how great he is! Even[a] Abraham the patriarch gave him a tenth of the spoils. ⁵And those descendants of Levi who receive the priestly office have a commandment in the law to collect tithes[b] from the people, that is, from their kindred,[c] though these also are descended from Abraham. ⁶But this man, who does not belong to their ancestry, collected tithes[b] from Abraham and blessed him who had received the promises. ⁷It is beyond dispute that the inferior is blessed by the superior. ⁸In the one case, tithes are received by those who are mortal; in the other, by one of whom it is testified that he lives. ⁹One might even say that Levi himself, who receives tithes, paid tithes through Abraham, ¹⁰for he was still in the loins of his ancestor when Melchizedek met him.

Another Priest, Like Melchizedek

11 Now if perfection had been attainable through the levitical priesthood—for the people received the law under this priesthood—what further need would there have been to speak of another priest arising according to the order of Melchizedek, rather than one according to the order of Aaron? ¹²For when there is a change in the priesthood, there is necessarily a change in the law as well. ¹³Now the one of whom these things are spoken belonged to another tribe, from which no one has ever served at the altar. ¹⁴For it is evident that our Lord was descended from Judah, and in connection with that tribe Moses said nothing about priests.

15 It is even more obvious when another priest arises, resembling Melchizedek, ¹⁶one who has become a priest, not through a legal requirement concerning physical descent, but through the power of an indestructible life. ¹⁷For it is attested of him,

"You are a priest forever,
    according to the order of Melchizedek."

¹⁸There is, on the one hand, the abrogation of an earlier commandment because it was weak and ineffectual ¹⁹(for the law made nothing perfect); there is, on the other hand, the introduction of a better hope, through which we approach God.

20 This was confirmed with an oath; for others who became priests took their office without an oath, ²¹but this one became a priest with an oath, because of the one who said to him,

"The Lord has sworn
    and will not change his mind,
'You are a priest forever' "—

²²accordingly Jesus has also become the guarantee of a better covenant.

23 Furthermore, the former priests were many in number, because they were prevented by death from continuing in office; ²⁴but he holds his priesthood permanently, because he continues forever. ²⁵Consequently he is able for all time to save[d] those who approach God through him, since he always lives to make intercession for them.

26 For it was fitting that we should have such a high priest, holy, blameless, undefiled, separated from sinners, and exalted above the heavens. ²⁷Unlike the other[e] high priests, he has no need to offer sacrifices day after day, first for his own sins, and then for those of the people; this he did once for all when he offered himself. ²⁸For the law appoints as high priests those who are subject to weakness, but the word of the oath, which came later than the law, appoints a Son who has been made perfect forever.

Mediator of a Better Covenant

8 Now the main point in what we are saying is this: we have such a high priest, one who is seated at the right hand of the throne of the Majesty in the heavens, ²a minister in the sanctuary

---

a Other ancient authorities lack *Even*   b Or *a tenth*
c Gk *brothers*   d Or *able to save completely*   e Gk lacks *other*

Be pleased to look upon these offerings . . . , and to accept them, as you were pleased to accept the gifts of your servant Abel the just, the sacrifice of Abraham, our father in faith, and the offering of your high priest Melchizedek.

(Roman Missal)

and the true tent[a] that the Lord, and not any mortal, has set up. [3]For every high priest is appointed to offer gifts and sacrifices; hence it is necessary for this priest also to have something to offer. [4]Now if he were on earth, he would not be a priest at all, since there are priests who offer gifts according to the law. [5]They offer worship in a sanctuary that is a sketch and shadow of the heavenly one; for Moses, when he was about to erect the tent,[a] was warned, "See that you make everything according to the pattern that was shown you on the mountain." [6]But Jesus[b] has now obtained a more excellent ministry, and to that degree he is the mediator of a better covenant, which has been enacted through better promises. [7]For if that first covenant had been faultless, there would have been no need to look for a second one.

[8] God[c] finds fault with them when he says:
"The days are surely coming, says the Lord,
    when I will establish a new covenant with the
        house of Israel
    and with the house of Judah;
[9] not like the covenant that I made with their
        ancestors,
    on the day when I took them by the hand to
        lead them out of the land of Egypt;
for they did not continue in my covenant,
    and so I had no concern for them, says the
        Lord.
[10] This is the covenant that I will make with the
        house of Israel
    after those days, says the Lord:
I will put my laws in their minds,
    and write them on their hearts,
and I will be their God,
    and they shall be my people.
[11] And they shall not teach one another
    or say to each other, 'Know the Lord,'
for they shall all know me,
    from the least of them to the greatest.
[12] For I will be merciful toward their iniquities,
    and I will remember their sins no more."

[13]In speaking of "a new covenant," he has made the first one obsolete. And what is obsolete and growing old will soon disappear.

The Earthly and the Heavenly Sanctuaries

9 Now even the first covenant had regulations for worship and an earthly sanctuary. [2]For a tent[a] was constructed, the first one, in which were the lampstand, the table, and the bread of the Presence;[d] this is called the Holy Place. [3]Behind the second curtain was a tent[a] called the Holy of Holies. [4]In it stood the golden altar of incense and the ark of the covenant overlaid on all sides with gold, in which there were a golden urn holding the manna, and Aaron's rod that budded, and the tablets of the covenant; [5]above it were the cherubim of glory overshadowing the mercy seat.[e] Of these things we cannot speak now in detail.

6 Such preparations having been made, the priests go continually into the first tent[a] to carry out their ritual duties; [7]but only the high priest goes into the second, and he but once a year, and not without taking the blood that he offers for himself and for the sins committed unintentionally by the people. [8]By this the Holy Spirit indicates that the way into the sanctuary has not yet been disclosed as long as the first tent[a] is still standing. [9]This is a symbol[f] of the present time, during which gifts and sacrifices are offered that cannot perfect the conscience of the worshiper, [10]but deal only with food and drink and various baptisms, regulations for the body imposed until the time comes to set things right.

11 But when Christ came as a high priest of the good things that have come,[g] then through the greater and perfect[h] tent[a] (not made with hands, that is, not of this creation), [12]he entered once for all into the Holy Place, not with the blood of goats and calves, but with his own blood, thus obtaining eternal redemption. [13]For if the blood of goats and bulls, with the sprinkling of the ashes of a heifer, sanctifies those who have been defiled so that their flesh is purified, [14]how much more will the blood of Christ, who through the eternal Spirit[i] offered himself without blemish to God, purify our[j] conscience from dead works to worship the living God!

15 For this reason he is the mediator of a new covenant, so that those who are called may receive the promised eternal inheritance, because a death has occurred that redeems them from the transgressions under the first covenant.[k] [16]Where a will[k] is involved, the death of the one who made it must be established. [17]For a will[k] takes effect only at death, since it is not in force as long as the one who made it is alive. [18]Hence not even the first covenant was inaugurated without blood. [19]For when every commandment had been told to all the people by Moses in accordance with the law, he took the blood of calves and goats,[l] with water and scarlet wool and hyssop, and sprinkled both the scroll itself and all

---

a Or tabernacle   b Gk he   c Gk He   d Gk the presentation of the loaves   e Or the place of atonement   f Gk parable   g Other ancient authorities read good things to come   h Gk more perfect   i Other ancient authorities read Holy Spirit   j Other ancient authorities read your   k The Greek word used here means both covenant and will   l Other ancient authorities lack and goats

the people, ²⁰saying, "This is the blood of the covenant that God has ordained for you." ²¹And in the same way he sprinkled with the blood both the tent^a and all the vessels used in worship. ²²Indeed, under the law almost everything is purified with blood, and without the shedding of blood there is no forgiveness of sins.

Christ's Sacrifice Takes Away Sin

23 Thus it was necessary for the sketches of the heavenly things to be purified with these rites, but the heavenly things themselves need better sacrifices than these. ²⁴For Christ did not enter a sanctuary made by human hands, a mere copy of the true one, but he entered into heaven itself, now to appear in the presence of God on our behalf. ²⁵Nor was it to offer himself again and again, as the high priest enters the Holy Place year after year with blood that is not his own; ²⁶for then he would have had to suffer again and again since the foundation of the world. But as it is, he has appeared once for all at the end of the age to remove sin by the sacrifice of himself. ²⁷And just as it is appointed for mortals to die once, and after that the judgment, ²⁸so Christ, having been offered once to bear the sins of many, will appear a second time, not to deal with sin, but to save those who are eagerly waiting for him.

Christ's Sacrifice Once for All

10 Since the law has only a shadow of the good things to come and not the true form of these realities, it^b can never, by the same sacrifices that are continually offered year after year, make perfect those who approach. ²Otherwise, would they not have ceased being offered, since the worshipers, cleansed once for all, would no longer have any consciousness of sin? ³But in these sacrifices there is a reminder of sin year after year. ⁴For it is impossible for the blood of bulls and goats to take away sins. ⁵Consequently, when Christ^c came into the world, he said,

"Sacrifices and offerings you have not desired,
　but a body you have prepared for me;
⁶ in burnt offerings and sin offerings
　you have taken no pleasure.
⁷ Then I said, 'See, God, I have come to do your
　will, O God'
　(in the scroll of the book^d it is written of
　me).''

⁸When he said above, "You have neither desired nor taken pleasure in sacrifices and offerings and burnt offerings and sin offerings" (these are offered according to the law), ⁹then he added, "See, I have come to do your will." He abolishes

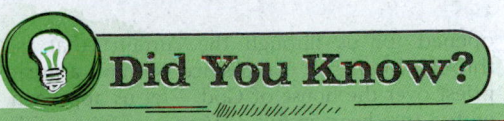
the first in order to establish the second. ¹⁰And it is by God's will^e that we have been sanctified through the offering of the body of Jesus Christ once for all.

11 And every priest stands day after day at his service, offering again and again the same sacrifices that can never take away sins. ¹²But when Christ^f had offered for all time a single sacrifice for sins, "he sat down at the right hand of God," ¹³and since then has been waiting "until his enemies would be made a footstool for his feet." ¹⁴For by a single offering he has perfected for all time those who are sanctified. ¹⁵And the Holy Spirit also testifies to us, for after saying,

¹⁶ "This is the covenant that I will make with them
　after those days, says the Lord:
I will put my laws in their hearts,
　and I will write them on their minds,"
¹⁷he also adds,
"I will remember^g their sins and their lawless
　deeds no more."
¹⁸Where there is forgiveness of these, there is no longer any offering for sin.

A Call to Persevere

19 Therefore, my friends,^h since we have confidence to enter the sanctuary by the blood of Jesus, ²⁰by the new and living way that he

---

a Or *tabernacle*　*b* Other ancient authorities read *they*　*c* Gk *he*　*d* Meaning of Gk uncertain　*e* Gk *by that will*　*f* Gk *this one*　*g* Gk *on their minds and I will remember*　*h* Gk *Therefore, brothers*

HEB

opened for us through the curtain (that is, through his flesh), 21and since we have a great priest over the house of God, 22let us approach with a true heart in full assurance of faith, with our hearts sprinkled clean from an evil conscience and our bodies washed with pure water. 23Let us hold fast to the confession of our hope without wavering, for he who has promised is faithful. 24And let us consider how to provoke one another to love and good deeds, 25not neglecting to meet together, as is the habit of some, but encouraging one another, and all the more as you see the Day approaching.

26 For if we willfully persist in sin after having received the knowledge of the truth, there no longer remains a sacrifice for sins, 27but a fearful prospect of judgment, and a fury of fire that will consume the adversaries. 28Anyone who has violated the law of Moses dies without mercy "on the testimony of two or three witnesses." 29How much worse punishment do you think will be deserved by those who have spurned the Son of God, profaned the blood of the covenant by which they were sanctified, and outraged the Spirit of grace? 30For we know the one who said, "Vengeance is mine, I will repay." And again, "The Lord will judge his people." 31It is a fearful thing to fall into the hands of the living God.

32 But recall those earlier days when, after you had been enlightened, you endured a hard struggle with sufferings, 33sometimes being publicly exposed to abuse and persecution, and sometimes being partners with those so treated. 34For you had compassion for those who were in prison, and you cheerfully accepted the plundering of your possessions, knowing that you yourselves possessed something better and more lasting. 35Do not, therefore, abandon that confidence of yours; it brings a great reward. 36For you need endurance, so that when you have done the will of God, you may receive what was promised. 37For yet

"in a very little while,
　　the one who is coming will come and will not
　　　delay;
38 but my righteous one will live by faith.
　　My soul takes no pleasure in anyone who
　　　shrinks back."

39But we are not among those who shrink back and so are lost, but among those who have faith and so are saved.

The Meaning of Faith

11 Now faith is the assurance of things hoped for, the conviction of things not seen. 2Indeed, by faith*a* our ancestors received approval.

3By faith we understand that the worlds were prepared by the word of God, so that what is seen was made from things that are not visible.*b*

The Examples of Abel, Enoch, and Noah

4 By faith Abel offered to God a more acceptable*c* sacrifice than Cain's. Through this he received approval as righteous, God himself giving approval to his gifts; he died, but through his faith*d* he still speaks. 5By faith Enoch was taken so that he did not experience death; and "he was not found, because God had taken him." For it was attested before he was taken away that "he had pleased God." 6And without faith it is impossible to please God, for whoever would approach him must believe that he exists and that he rewards those who seek him. 7By faith Noah, warned by God about events as yet unseen, respected the warning and built an ark to save his household; by this he condemned the world and became an heir to the righteousness that is in accordance with faith.

The Faith of Abraham

8 By faith Abraham obeyed when he was called to set out for a place that he was to receive as an inheritance; and he set out, not knowing where he was going. 9By faith he stayed for a time in the land he had been promised, as in a foreign land, living in tents, as did Isaac and Jacob, who were heirs with him of the same promise. 10For he looked forward to the city that has foundations, whose architect and builder is God. 11By faith he received power of procreation, even though he was too old—and Sarah herself was barren—because he considered him faithful who had promised.*e* 12Therefore from one person, and this one as good as dead, descendants were born, "as many as the stars of heaven and as the innumerable grains of sand by the seashore."

13 All of these died in faith without having received the promises, but from a distance they saw and greeted them. They confessed that they were strangers and foreigners on the earth, 14for people who speak in this way make it clear that they are seeking a homeland. 15If they had been thinking of the land that they had left behind, they would have had opportunity to return. 16But as it is, they desire a better country, that is, a heavenly one. Therefore God is not ashamed to be called their God; indeed, he has prepared a city for them.

---

a Gk by this　b Or was not made out of visible things
c Gk greater　d Gk through it　e Or By faith Sarah herself, though barren, received power to conceive, even when she was too old, because she considered him faithful who had promised.

17 By faith Abraham, when put to the test, offered up Isaac. He who had received the promises was ready to offer up his only son, [18]of whom he had been told, "It is through Isaac that descendants shall be named for you." [19]He considered the fact that God is able even to raise someone from the dead—and figuratively speaking, he did receive him back. [20]By faith Isaac invoked blessings for the future on Jacob and Esau. [21]By faith Jacob, when dying, blessed each of the sons of Joseph, "bowing in worship over the top of his staff." [22]By faith Joseph, at the end of his life, made mention of the exodus of the Israelites and gave instructions about his burial.[a]

The Faith of Moses

23 By faith Moses was hidden by his parents for three months after his birth, because they saw that the child was beautiful; and they were not afraid of the king's edict.[b] [24]By faith Moses, when he was grown up, refused to be called a son of Pharaoh's daughter, [25]choosing rather to share ill-treatment with the people of God than to enjoy the fleeting pleasures of sin. [26]He considered abuse suffered for the Christ[c] to be greater wealth than the treasures of Egypt, for he was looking ahead to the reward. [27]By faith he left Egypt, unafraid of the king's anger; for he persevered as though[d] he saw him who is invisible. [28]By faith he kept the Passover and the sprinkling of blood, so that the destroyer of the firstborn would not touch the firstborn of Israel.[e]

The Faith of Other Israelite Heroes

29 By faith the people passed through the Red Sea as if it were dry land, but when the Egyptians attempted to do so they were drowned. [30]By faith the walls of Jericho fell after they had been encircled for seven days. [31]By faith Rahab the prostitute did not perish with those who were disobedient,[f] because she had received the spies in peace.

32 And what more should I say? For time would fail me to tell of Gideon, Barak, Samson, Jephthah, of David and Samuel and the prophets— [33]who through faith conquered kingdoms, administered justice, obtained promises, shut the mouths of lions, [34]quenched raging fire, escaped the edge of the sword, won strength out of weakness, became mighty in war, put foreign armies to flight. [35]Women received their dead by resurrection. Others were tortured, refusing to accept release, in order to obtain a better resurrection. [36]Others suffered mocking and flogging, and even chains and imprisonment. [37]They were stoned to death, they were sawn in two,[g] they were killed by the sword; they went about in skins of sheep and goats, destitute, persecuted, tormented— [38]of whom the world was not worthy. They wandered in deserts and mountains, and in caves and holes in the ground.

39 Yet all these, though they were commended for their faith, did not receive what was promised, [40]since God had provided something better so that they would not, apart from us, be made perfect.

The Example of Jesus

12 Therefore, since we are surrounded by so great a cloud of witnesses, let us also lay aside every weight and the sin that clings so closely,[h] and let us run with perseverance the race that is set before us, [2]looking to Jesus the pioneer and perfecter of our faith, who for the sake of[i] the joy that was set before him endured the cross, disregarding its shame, and has taken his seat at the right hand of the throne of God.

3 Consider him who endured such hostility against himself from sinners,[j] so that you may not grow weary or lose heart. [4]In your struggle against sin you have not yet resisted to the point of shedding your blood. [5]And you have forgotten the exhortation that addresses you as children—

"My child, do not regard lightly the discipline of
   the Lord,
  or lose heart when you are punished by him;
[6] for the Lord disciplines those whom he loves,
  and chastises every child whom he accepts."

[7]Endure trials for the sake of discipline. God is treating you as children; for what child is there whom a parent does not discipline? [8]If you do not have that discipline in which all children share, then you are illegitimate and not his children. [9]Moreover, we had human parents to discipline us, and we respected them. Should we not be even more willing to be subject to the Father of spirits and live? [10]For they disciplined us for a short time as seemed best to them, but he disciplines us for our good, in order that we may share his holiness. [11]Now, discipline always seems painful rather than pleasant at the time, but later it yields the peaceful fruit of righteousness to those who have been trained by it.

12 Therefore lift your drooping hands and strengthen your weak knees, [13]and make straight

---

a Gk his bones   b Other ancient authorities add *By faith Moses, when he was grown up, killed the Egyptian, because he observed the humiliation of his people* (Gk *brothers*)   c Or *the Messiah*   d Or *because*   e Gk *would not touch them*   f Or *unbelieving*   g Other ancient authorities add *they were tempted*   h Other ancient authorities read *sin that easily distracts*   i Or *who* instead of   j Other ancient authorities read *such hostility from sinners against themselves*

paths for your feet, so that what is lame may not be put out of joint, but rather be healed.

Warnings against Rejecting God's Grace

14 Pursue peace with everyone, and the holiness without which no one will see the Lord. ¹⁵See to it that no one fails to obtain the grace of God; that no root of bitterness springs up and causes trouble, and through it many become defiled. ¹⁶See to it that no one becomes like Esau, an immoral and godless person, who sold his birthright for a single meal. ¹⁷You know that later, when he wanted to inherit the blessing, he was rejected, for he found no chance to repent,ᵃ even though he sought the blessingᵇ with tears.

18 You have not come to somethingᶜ that can be touched, a blazing fire, and darkness, and gloom, and a tempest, ¹⁹and the sound of a trumpet, and a voice whose words made the hearers beg that not another word be spoken to them. ²⁰(For they could not endure the order that was given, "If even an animal touches the mountain, it shall be stoned to death." ²¹Indeed, so terrifying was the sight that Moses said, "I tremble with fear.") ²²But you have come to Mount Zion and to the city of the living God, the heavenly Jerusalem, and to innumerable angels in festal gathering, ²³and to the assemblyᵈ of the firstborn who are enrolled in heaven, and to God the judge of all, and to the spirits of the righteous made perfect, ²⁴and to Jesus, the mediator of a new covenant, and to the sprinkled blood that speaks a better word than the blood of Abel.

25 See that you do not refuse the one who is speaking; for if they did not escape when they refused the one who warned them on earth, how much less will we escape if we reject the one who warns from heaven! ²⁶At that time his voice shook the earth; but now he has promised, "Yet once more I will shake not only the earth but also the heaven." ²⁷This phrase, "Yet once more," indicates the removal of what is shaken—that is, created things—so that what cannot be shaken may remain. ²⁸Therefore, since we are receiving a kingdom that cannot be shaken, let us give thanks, by which we offer to God an acceptable worship with reverence and awe; ²⁹for indeed our God is a consuming fire.

Service Well-Pleasing to God

13 Let mutual love continue. ²Do not neglect to show hospitality to strangers, for by doing that some have entertained angels without knowing it. ³Remember those who are in prison, as though you were in prison with them; those who are being tortured, as though you yourselves were being tortured.ᵉ ⁴Let marriage be held in honor by all, and let the marriage bed be kept undefiled; for God will judge fornicators and adulterers. ⁵Keep your lives free from the love of money, and be content with what you have; for he has said, "I will never leave you or forsake you." ⁶So we can say with confidence,

"The Lord is my helper;
   I will not be afraid.
What can anyone do to me?"

7 Remember your leaders, those who spoke the word of God to you; consider the outcome of their way of life, and imitate their faith. ⁸Jesus Christ is the same yesterday and today and forever. ⁹Do not be carried away by all kinds of

Entertaining Angels

The subject of angels has always fascinated the media, especially filmmakers and television show producers. They often develop stories around the idea from the Letter to the Hebrews that people sometimes encounter angels and that angels are sent to rescue people caught in dire or tragic circumstances.

We know God has created a category of beings that is made up of pure spirits without bodies. These beings act as God's messengers and serve as spiritual guardians for humans. Their mission is to bring God's word to those who are open to hear it and respond to it with faith and humility.

Will we ever have the opportunity to entertain angels in human disguise? We may never know the answer to this question, but we should entertain this truth in our hearts and minds: God guides the world and has sent messengers and guardians—angels—whose mysterious presence offers support, protection, and intercession for those who believe in God and seek the face of God.

▶ Heb 13:1–5

ᵃ Or no chance to change his father's mind   ᵇ Gk it   ᶜ Other ancient authorities read a mountain   ᵈ Or angels, and to the festal gathering ²³and assembly   ᵉ Gk were in the body

strange teachings; for it is well for the heart to be strengthened by grace, not by regulations about food,[a] which have not benefited those who observe them. [10]We have an altar from which those who officiate in the tent[b] have no right to eat. [11]For the bodies of those animals whose blood is brought into the sanctuary by the high priest as a sacrifice for sin are burned outside the camp. [12]Therefore Jesus also suffered outside the city gate in order to sanctify the people by his own blood. [13]Let us then go to him outside the camp and bear the abuse he endured. [14]For here we have no lasting city, but we are looking for the city that is to come. [15]Through him, then, let us continually offer a sacrifice of praise to God, that is, the fruit of lips that confess his name. [16]Do not neglect to do good and to share what you have, for such sacrifices are pleasing to God.

17 Obey your leaders and submit to them, for they are keeping watch over your souls and will give an account. Let them do this with joy and not with sighing—for that would be harmful to you.

18 Pray for us; we are sure that we have a clear conscience, desiring to act honorably in all things. [19]I urge you all the more to do this, so that I may be restored to you very soon.

Benediction

20 Now may the God of peace, who brought back from the dead our Lord Jesus, the great shepherd of the sheep, by the blood of the eternal covenant, [21]make you complete in everything good so that you may do his will, working among us[c] that which is pleasing in his sight, through Jesus Christ, to whom be the glory forever and ever. Amen.

Final Exhortation and Greetings

22 I appeal to you, brothers and sisters,[d] bear with my word of exhortation, for I have written to you briefly. [23]I want you to know that our brother Timothy has been set free; and if he comes in time, he will be with me when I see you. [24]Greet all your leaders and all the saints. Those from Italy send you greetings. [25]Grace be with all of you.[e]

---

a Gk *not by foods*   b Or *tabernacle*   c Other ancient authorities read *you*   d Gk *brothers*   e Other ancient authorities add *Amen*

Have you ever noticed how a kite strains at the string as it soars in the sky? It seems to want to be free of the string that ties it down, free to fly on its own. But if that string does break, the kite flounders and crashes. The kite has the freedom to fly only as long as it's tied to something. That's the way we are under the New Covenant in Christ. We may think we're free to do whatever we want, but if we break from a faithful response to God's love for us, we flounder and crash. The Letter of James provides guidance for living "the law of liberty" (1:25), which leads to real freedom.

At a Glance

- **Chapter 1.** proverbs for Christian living
- **2:1–13.** a discussion of discrimination within the Christian community
- **2:14–26.** a message that faith without works is dead
- **3:1–12.** warnings about controlling the tongue
- **3:13—5:20.** more advice for Christian living

Quick Facts

Inspired Author: possibly James the relative of Jesus, but most likely a later admirer of James
Date Written: from AD 57 to 62 if by James, from AD 70 to 110 if by a later admirer
Audience: Christians in Palestine, Syria, or Rome

In Depth

Defining the literary form (structure) of James is a little difficult. It opens like the other letters but lacks the typical closing. In ways, it is similar to the wisdom literature of the Old Testament. It provides practical advice for how wise people ought to live. It is also similar to Greek moral teaching, which used famous people as models for how we ought to live. This has led scholars to think the book might have been written by an educated Jewish Christian, possibly living in Jerusalem. The author could have been an admirer of James, the first leader of the early church in Jerusalem.

The letter addresses several issues in Christian living. It warns that rich people should not discriminate against poor people. It insists that Christians' actions must reflect their beliefs. It cautions against careless speech and a poorly controlled tongue. It encourages believers to patiently endure suffering.

James also addresses a misunderstanding of Paul's teaching that "a person is justified by faith apart from works prescribed by the law" (Rom 3:28). Using Abraham and Rahab as examples, the author of James declares, "A person is justified by works and not by faith alone" (Jas 2:24). After all, "faith by itself, if it has no works, is dead" (2:17). To say you love Jesus, and then do unloving things, makes no sense; it's just plain hypocritical.

But, if we act on God's word and live our faith intensely from the heart, as the Letter of James instructs, we will keep from floundering and be able to soar in the freedom of God's love!

James

Salutation

1 James, a servant[a] of God and of the Lord Jesus Christ,

To the twelve tribes in the Dispersion:

Greetings.

Faith and Wisdom

2 My brothers and sisters,[b] whenever you face trials of any kind, consider it nothing but joy, ³because you know that the testing of your faith produces endurance; ⁴and let endurance have its full effect, so that you may be mature and complete, lacking in nothing.

5 If any of you is lacking in wisdom, ask God, who gives to all generously and ungrudgingly, and it will be given you. ⁶But ask in faith, never doubting, for the one who doubts is like a wave of the sea, driven and tossed by the wind; ⁷, ⁸for the doubter, being double-minded and unstable in every way, must not expect to receive anything from the Lord.

Poverty and Riches

9 Let the believer[c] who is lowly boast in being raised up, ¹⁰and the rich in being brought low, because the rich will disappear like a flower in the field. ¹¹For the sun rises with its scorching heat and withers the field; its flower falls, and its beauty perishes. It is the same way with the rich; in the midst of a busy life, they will wither away.

Trial and Temptation

12 Blessed is anyone who endures temptation. Such a one has stood the test and will receive the crown of life that the Lord[d] has promised to those who love him. ¹³No one, when tempted, should say, "I am being tempted by God"; for God cannot be tempted by evil and he himself tempts no one. ¹⁴But one is tempted by one's own desire, being lured and enticed by it; ¹⁵then, when that desire has conceived, it gives birth to sin, and that sin, when it is fully grown, gives birth to death. ¹⁶Do not be deceived, my beloved.[e]

17 Every generous act of giving, with every perfect gift, is from above, coming down from the Father of lights, with whom there is no variation or shadow due to change.[f] ¹⁸In fulfillment of his own purpose he gave us birth by the word of truth, so that we would become a kind of first fruits of his creatures.

Hearing and Doing the Word

19 You must understand this, my beloved:[e] let everyone be quick to listen, slow to speak, slow to anger; ²⁰for your anger does not produce God's righteousness. ²¹Therefore rid yourselves of all sordidness and rank growth of wickedness, and

---

a Gk *slave*   *b* Gk *brothers*   *c* Gk *brother*   *d* Gk *he*; other ancient authorities read *God*   *e* Gk *my beloved brothers*   *f* Other ancient authorities read *variation due to a shadow of turning*

welcome with meekness the implanted word that has the power to save your souls.

22 But be doers of the word, and not merely hearers who deceive themselves. [23]For if any are hearers of the word and not doers, they are like those who look at themselves[a] in a mirror; [24]for they look at themselves and, on going away, immediately forget what they were like. [25]But those who look into the perfect law, the law of liberty, and persevere, being not hearers who forget but doers who act—they will be blessed in their doing.

26 If any think they are religious, and do not bridle their tongues but deceive their hearts, their religion is worthless. [27]Religion that is pure and undefiled before God, the Father, is this: to care for orphans and widows in their distress, and to keep oneself unstained by the world.

Warning against Partiality

2 My brothers and sisters,[b] do you with your acts of favoritism really believe in our glorious Lord Jesus Christ?[c] [2]For if a person with gold rings and in fine clothes comes into your assembly, and if a poor person in dirty clothes also comes in, [3]and if you take notice of the one wearing the fine clothes and say, "Have a seat here, please," while to the one who is poor you say, "Stand there," or, "Sit at my feet,"[d] [4]have you not made distinctions among yourselves, and become judges with evil thoughts? [5]Listen, my beloved brothers and sisters.[e] Has not God chosen the poor in the world to be rich in faith and to be heirs of the kingdom that he has promised to those who love him? [6]But you have dishonored the poor. Is it not the rich who oppress you? Is it

a Gk at the face of his birth   b Gk My brothers   c Or hold the faith of our glorious Lord Jesus Christ without acts of favoritism   d Gk Sit under my footstool   e Gk brothers

Meditation on the Walk of Faith

Relax. Clear your mind. Read and reflect on this meditation:

Imagine yourself on your favorite stretch of road. Look back along the road as if it represents your life so far. You have traveled this road all your life to get to where you are standing right now. What obstacles and temptations to your faith have you encountered? Which ones have you stumbled over? Which ones have you overcome?

You see a figure approaching. You strain to see who it is. It gets close enough to recognize. It is Jesus! Jesus sits down with you and asks about the trials you have encountered on your journey. Talk to Jesus about how they have given you the opportunity to grow. Talk to him about the many choices you have made, the good and the bad.

Leave with Jesus to continue forward on the journey. With Jesus, you can joyfully accept the tests of faith that lie ahead, knowing that each is an opportunity to build endurance "so that you may be mature and complete, lacking in nothing" (Jas 1:4).

▶ **Jas 1:2–18**

Faith and Works

A person who insists that faith alone is necessary for our salvation might think: "I don't have to demonstrate my faith with action at all. I just have to believe in Jesus, and then I can do anything I want." Such an attitude isn't very faithful, mature, or helpful.

Yet a person who insists that particular actions alone are necessary for our salvation might think: "I don't have to really believe in what I'm doing. I'll just go through the motions of faith, and that way I'll play it safe." This attitude is not very faithful, mature, or helpful either.

James is saying, "Show me a person who has real faith, and I will show you a person doing good works."

Faith and works are discussed at length in two letters from Paul: Romans 3:21–31 (see also "The Law, Faith, and Justification," near Rom 3:1–31) and Galatians 2:15—3:14 (see also "Justified in Christ," near Gal 3:1—4:7).

▶ **Jas 2:14–26**

Catholic Social Teaching

Playing Favorites

Many of us have had the experience of watching someone else receive special treatment. It doesn't seem fair when a person gets singled out because of his or her looks, money, athletic ability, or some other reason. Too often it makes others feel hurt and diminished. In James 2:1–13, the author clearly spells out where God stands on the issue of favoritism and partiality. God's response is to turn things upside down by raising up the poor and the lowly (see verse 5). The Catholic Church refers to this response as a preferential option or love for the poor, which means always giving priority to the needs of those who are poor and vulnerable when setting policies, providing benefits, and so on.

In our world, there is a big difference between rich and poor, top and bottom, included and excluded. God needs us to respond to this injustice by recognizing that we have a special responsibility to care for those who are struggling the most just to live. If we do not give those living in poverty opportunities to live in justice and equality, and if we do not challenge the people in power to live according to God's justice, who will? And if we don't reach out to those students at school who seem to be the least popular or least favorite, who will?

▶ **Jas 2:1–13**

Option for the Poor and Vulnerable

J A S

---

not they who drag you into court? ⁷Is it not they who blaspheme the excellent name that was invoked over you?

8 You do well if you really fulfill the royal law according to the scripture, "You shall love your neighbor as yourself." ⁹But if you show partiality, you commit sin and are convicted by the law as transgressors. ¹⁰For whoever keeps the whole law but fails in one point has become accountable for all of it. ¹¹For the one who said, "You shall not commit adultery," also said, "You shall not murder." Now if you do not commit adultery but if you murder, you have become a transgressor of the law. ¹²So speak and so act as those who are to be judged by the law of liberty. ¹³For judgment will be without mercy to anyone who has shown no mercy; mercy triumphs over judgment.

Faith without Works Is Dead

14 What good is it, my brothers and sisters,[a] if you say you have faith but do not have works? Can faith save you? ¹⁵If a brother or sister is naked and lacks daily food, ¹⁶and one of you says to them, "Go in peace; keep warm and eat your fill," and yet you do not supply their bodily needs, what is the good of that? ¹⁷So faith by itself, if it has no works, is dead.

18 But someone will say, "You have faith and I have works." Show me your faith apart from your works, and I by my works will show you my faith. ¹⁹You believe that God is one; you do well.

Even the demons believe—and shudder. ²⁰Do you want to be shown, you senseless person, that faith apart from works is barren? ²¹Was not our ancestor Abraham justified by works when he offered his son Isaac on the altar? ²²You see that faith was active along with his works, and faith was brought to completion by the works. ²³Thus the scripture was fulfilled that says, "Abraham believed God, and it was reckoned to him as righteousness," and he was called the friend of God. ²⁴You see that a person is justified by works and not by faith alone. ²⁵Likewise, was not Rahab the prostitute also justified by works when she welcomed the messengers and sent them out by another road? ²⁶For just as the body without the spirit is dead, so faith without works is also dead.

Taming the Tongue

3 Not many of you should become teachers, my brothers and sisters,[a] for you know that we who teach will be judged with greater strictness. ²For all of us make many mistakes. Anyone who makes no mistakes in speaking is perfect, able to keep the whole body in check with a bridle. ³If we put bits into the mouths of horses to make them obey us, we guide their whole bodies. ⁴Or look at ships: though they are so large that it takes strong winds to drive them, yet they

a Gk brothers

are guided by a very small rudder wherever the will of the pilot directs. [5]So also the tongue is a small member, yet it boasts of great exploits.

How great a forest is set ablaze by a small fire! [6]And the tongue is a fire. The tongue is placed among our members as a world of iniquity; it stains the whole body, sets on fire the cycle of nature,[a] and is itself set on fire by hell.[b] [7]For every species of beast and bird, of reptile and sea creature, can be tamed and has been tamed by the human species, [8]but no one can tame the tongue—a restless evil, full of deadly poison. [9]With it we bless the Lord and Father, and with it we curse those who are made in the likeness of God. [10]From the same mouth come blessing and cursing. My brothers and sisters,[c] this ought not to be so. [11]Does a spring pour forth from the same opening both fresh and brackish water?

The Tongue: Friend or Foe?

Sometimes, we are advised to hold it. Other times, we are ordered to bite it. Try as we might to keep this counsel, our tongue often proves to be much stronger than our will to control it.

All of us have said things we have later regretted. Frequently against our better judgment, we find ourselves speaking in ways that hurt or offend others and God. People are injured by what others say to—or about—them far more often than by physical attack. The scars left by hurtful words can last a lifetime, destroying families and ruining friendships.

Have you spoken words that are hurtful to another person, directly or behind the person's back? How might you use your tongue to begin to heal someone's hurts? Apologies, compliments, and affirmations—the tongue can utter these things too! It is a mark of maturity and confidence when we are able to ask forgiveness or affirm others. Christians are called to this kind of courage and maturity.

Use your tongue to speak positively to others today!

▶ Jas 3:1–12

[12]Can a fig tree, my brothers and sisters,[d] yield olives, or a grapevine figs? No more can salt water yield fresh.

Two Kinds of Wisdom

13 Who is wise and understanding among you? Show by your good life that your works are done with gentleness born of wisdom. [14]But if you have bitter envy and selfish ambition in your hearts, do not be boastful and false to the truth. [15]Such wisdom does not come down from above, but is earthly, unspiritual, devilish. [16]For where there is envy and selfish ambition, there will also be disorder and wickedness of every kind. [17]But the wisdom from above is first pure, then peaceable, gentle, willing to yield, full of mercy and good fruits, without a trace of partiality or hypocrisy. [18]And a harvest of righteousness is sown in peace for[e] those who make peace.

Friendship with the World

4 Those conflicts and disputes among you, where do they come from? Do they not come from your cravings that are at war within you? [2]You want something and do not have it; so you commit murder. And you covet[f] something and cannot obtain it; so you engage in disputes and conflicts. You do not have, because you do not ask. [3]You ask and do not receive, because you ask wrongly, in order to spend what you get on your pleasures. [4]Adulterers! Do you not know that friendship with the world is enmity with God? Therefore whoever wishes to be a friend of the world becomes an enemy of God. [5]Or do you suppose that it is for nothing that the scripture says, "God[g] yearns jealously for the spirit that he has made to dwell in us"? [6]But he gives all the more grace; therefore it says,

"God opposes the proud,
 but gives grace to the humble."

> "Draw near to God, and he will draw near to you."
>
> (Jas 4:8)

[7]Submit yourselves therefore to God. Resist the devil, and he will flee from you. [8]Draw near to God, and he will draw near to you. Cleanse your hands, you sinners, and purify your hearts, you double-minded. [9]Lament and mourn and weep.

---

a Or *wheel of birth*   b Gk *Gehenna*   c Gk *My brothers*
d Gk *my brothers*   e Or *by*   f Or *you murder and you covet*
g Gk *He*

Let your laughter be turned into mourning and your joy into dejection. [10]Humble yourselves before the Lord, and he will exalt you.

Warning against Judging Another

11 Do not speak evil against one another, brothers and sisters.[a] Whoever speaks evil against another or judges another, speaks evil against the law and judges the law; but if you judge the law, you are not a doer of the law but a judge. [12]There is one lawgiver and judge who is able to save and to destroy. So who, then, are you to judge your neighbor?

Boasting about Tomorrow

13 Come now, you who say, "Today or tomorrow we will go to such and such a town and spend a year there, doing business and making money." [14]Yet you do not even know what tomorrow will bring. What is your life? For you are a mist that appears for a little while and then vanishes. [15]Instead you ought to say, "If the Lord wishes, we will live and do this or that." [16]As it is, you boast in your arrogance; all such boasting is evil. [17]Anyone, then, who knows the right thing to do and fails to do it, commits sin.

---

a Gk brothers

Justice for Those Who Are Poor

Warnings to the rich are common in the Bible and should be of concern for Christians living in a wealthy nation like the United States. Here are two tough questions to consider: First, in what do we put our trust—the comfort and pleasure that can be had in wealth and material possessions, or God? And second, how does our lifestyle—including the way we spend money, the choices we make about our future work, and the way we use our time—affect the poor people of this world?

God's justice requires that Christians care about the abuse of poor people for the benefit of rich people. God does not want us to become paralyzed with guilt because we are wealthy compared with the poorest of the earth. But the Scriptures remind us that the life choices we make matter, and that those choices may either contribute to a more just world, or support a status quo that keeps rich people comfortable and poor people down. To make good life choices, we must educate ourselves about the situations that cause poverty, examine how our own lifestyle or beliefs might unintentionally contribute to the misery of those who are poor, and actively work to alleviate the suffering of others. That is hard work—perhaps work we would rather avoid. But ignoring the plight of poor people is exactly what the Scriptures warn us against! Money in itself is not evil; it's what we do (or don't do) with it that can be sinful.

▶ **Jas 5:1–6**

The Making of a Prayer

Have you ever been in a prayer rut? It happens when you get stuck on saying the same prayer every time, no matter what the situation. It becomes a habit, and like all habits, after a while, you may stop thinking about why you are even doing it.

James offers some advice in 5:13–18 that can help you to get out of such a rut and back on track with your prayer life. This passage says to think about the needs and feelings you have at any given moment of the day and turn them into a prayer. Feeling down? Tell God about it. Just had the best day of your life? Share it with God. Want to get even with a person who hurt you? Let God know about it. In fact, there is nothing you can't tell God—even if you are mad and God is the one you are mad at.

Get in touch with what is occupying your mind the most right now—good, bad, or ordinary—and turn it into a prayer by sharing it with the God who is always ready to hear what you have to say.

▶ **Jas 5:13–18**

✝ Catholic Connection

Anointing of the Sick

Have you or a loved one ever been seriously ill? It can be a scary time. Yet, it is in the midst of fear and suffering that Jesus' followers are called to bring compassion and healing. In the Letter of James, the author talks about how Christians are called to care for those who are sick by praying over them and anointing them with oil. As a result, the sick will be helped and strengthened by Christ and have their sins forgiven.

Caring for those who are ill, as expressed in the Letter of James, is still practiced in the Catholic Church today through the sacrament of the Anointing of the Sick. Through prayers and anointing with sacred oil, those who are seriously ill are entrusted to God's merciful love and the physical and spiritual struggles that their illness brings are addressed. Physically, the sick are strengthened by the sacrament and, if God wills, find healing. Spiritually, the sick receive special graces from the Holy Spirit. These graces help the sick unite their own sufferings with those of Christ, free them from their sins, and give them the courage they need to face the challenges and fear illness brings.

The sacrament may be celebrated within Mass or outside of Mass, with a large group of those who are ill or with an individual sick person. No matter how it is celebrated, it is always administered by a priest or bishop and has the same three basic parts. During the first part, **the prayer of faith**, the priest, family, friends, and others from the community who are gathered confidently ask God to help those who are sick. The second part is the **laying on of hands**, where the priest, like Jesus often did, lays his hands upon those who are sick. Through this gesture, the priest shows that the prayers the community is offering are directed toward the sick. It is a sign of blessing as the community prays for God's healing grace so those who are sick can be healed and strengthened. The laying on of hands is also a plea for the Holy Spirit to descend upon those who are ill. The third part is the **anointing with oil**. The sacred oil signifies the presence of the Holy Spirit, whose power can bring strength and healing both physically and spiritually.

So, if you or a loved one is faced with a serious illness, remember that the Church is there to relieve your fears and suffering through the sacrament of the Anointing of the Sick.

▶ **Jas 5:13–15**
Catechism, nos. 1499–1532

Warning to Rich Oppressors

5 Come now, you rich people, weep and wail for the miseries that are coming to you. ²Your riches have rotted, and your clothes are moth-eaten. ³Your gold and silver have rusted, and their rust will be evidence against you, and it will eat your flesh like fire. You have laid up treasure*a* for the last days. ⁴Listen! The wages of the laborers who mowed your fields, which you kept back by fraud, cry out, and the cries of the harvesters have reached the ears of the Lord of hosts. ⁵You have lived on the earth in luxury and in pleasure; you have fattened your hearts in a day of slaughter. ⁶You have condemned and murdered the righteous one, who does not resist you.

Patience in Suffering

7 Be patient, therefore, beloved,*b* until the coming of the Lord. The farmer waits for the precious crop from the earth, being patient with it until it receives the early and the late rains. ⁸You also must be patient. Strengthen your hearts, for the coming of the Lord is near.*c* ⁹Beloved,*d* do not grumble against one another, so that you may not be judged. See, the Judge is standing at the doors! ¹⁰As an example of suffering and patience, beloved,*b* take the prophets who spoke in the name of the Lord. ¹¹Indeed we call blessed those who showed endurance. You have heard of the endurance of Job, and you have seen the purpose of the Lord, how the Lord is compassionate and merciful.

12 Above all, my beloved,*b* do not swear, either by heaven or by earth or by any other oath, but let your "Yes" be yes and your "No" be no, so that you may not fall under condemnation.

The Prayer of Faith

13 Are any among you suffering? They should pray. Are any cheerful? They should sing songs of praise. ¹⁴Are any among you sick? They should call for the elders of the church and have them pray over them, anointing them with oil in the name of the Lord. ¹⁵The prayer of faith will save the sick, and the Lord will raise them up; and anyone who has committed sins will be forgiven. ¹⁶Therefore confess your sins to one another, and pray for one another, so that you may be healed. The prayer of the righteous is powerful and effective. ¹⁷Elijah was a human being like us, and he prayed fervently that it might not rain, and for three years and six months it did not rain on the earth. ¹⁸Then he prayed again, and the heaven gave rain and the earth yielded its harvest.

19 My brothers and sisters,*e* if anyone among you wanders from the truth and is brought back by another, ²⁰you should know that whoever brings back a sinner from wandering will save the sinner's*f* soul from death and will cover a multitude of sins.

a Or will eat your flesh, since you have stored up fire b Gk brothers c Or is at hand d Gk Brothers e Gk My brothers f Gk his

Close friends refuse to speak to you after you challenge them about shoplifting. Students make fun of classmates who are trying to start a prayer group before school. Citizens break windows in the homes of Christian leaders who have spoken out publicly against racist attitudes. It's enough to make some Christians ask, Is living our faith worth this persecution and separation? This is a major concern addressed by the First Letter of Peter.

At a Glance

- **1:1–2.** a greeting and thanksgiving

- **1:3—2:10.** the message that Christians are called to be a chosen race and a royal priesthood

- **2:11—3:12.** a description of the Christian way of life

- **3:13—5:11.** a discussion of Christian suffering

- **5:12–14.** a closing

Quick Facts

Inspired Author: possibly Peter, but most likely a later disciple of Peter

Date Written: from AD 60 to 63 if by Peter, from AD 70 to 90 if by a later disciple

Audience: a Gentile (non-Jewish) Christian community

In Depth

The First Letter of Peter was written to a Christian community that was alienated and persecuted because of its Christian lifestyle. Its members were ridiculed, treated as evildoers, and insulted by unbelieving neighbors who did not understand their faith or their moral code of behavior. The author—who may have been Peter but was more likely a later disciple of his—wants to console them and help them make sense of what they're going through.

The author of the First Letter of Peter says that Christ suffered, and therefore we should expect to suffer too. The writer also says that suffering purifies our faith and makes it more genuine (see 1 Pet 1:7). When we suffer, we are united with all the world's people who are suffering (see 5:9). And no matter how great our suffering is, we should be hopeful, and we should be willing to witness to our hope. Then our persecutors will be ashamed and will repent of their wrongdoing (see 3:14–16). We cannot avoid suffering, but when we follow in the footsteps of Jesus, we can make it result in something good.

Despite all this attention to suffering, First Peter is a hope-filled letter. It offers constant reminders of the wonderful things God has done—and will do—for us. When you are going through a hard time, turn to this letter for hope and encouragement. "After you have suffered for a little while, the God of all grace, who has called you to his eternal glory in Christ, will himself restore, support, strengthen, and establish you" (5:10).

The First Letter of

Peter

1 Peter

Salutation

1 Peter, an apostle of Jesus Christ,

To the exiles of the Dispersion in Pontus, Galatia, Cappadocia, Asia, and Bithynia, ²who have been chosen and destined by God the Father and sanctified by the Spirit to be obedient to Jesus Christ and to be sprinkled with his blood:

May grace and peace be yours in abundance.

A Living Hope

3 Blessed be the God and Father of our Lord Jesus Christ! By his great mercy he has given us a new birth into a living hope through the resurrection of Jesus Christ from the dead, ⁴and into an inheritance that is imperishable, undefiled, and unfading, kept in heaven for you, ⁵who are being protected by the power of God through faith for a salvation ready to be revealed in the last time. ⁶In this you rejoice,ᵃ even if now for a little while you have had to suffer various trials, ⁷so that the genuineness of your faith—being more precious than gold that, though perishable, is tested by fire—may be found to result in praise and glory and honor when Jesus Christ is revealed. ⁸Although you have not seenᵇ him, you love him; and even though you do not see him now, you believe in him and rejoice with an indescribable and glorious joy, ⁹for you are receiving the outcome of your faith, the salvation of your souls.

10 Concerning this salvation, the prophets who prophesied of the grace that was to be yours made careful search and inquiry, ¹¹inquiring about the person or time that the Spirit of Christ within them indicated when it testified in advance to the sufferings destined for Christ and the subsequent glory. ¹²It was revealed to them that they were serving not themselves but you, in regard to the things that have now been announced to you through those who brought you good news by the Holy Spirit sent from heaven—things into which angels long to look!

A Call to Holy Living

13 Therefore prepare your minds for action;ᶜ discipline yourselves; set all your hope on the grace that Jesus Christ will bring you when he is revealed. ¹⁴Like obedient children, do not be conformed to the desires that you formerly had in ignorance. ¹⁵Instead, as he who called you is holy, be holy yourselves in all your conduct; ¹⁶for it is written, "You shall be holy, for I am holy."

17 If you invoke as Father the one who judges all people impartially according to their deeds, live in reverent fear during the time of your exile. ¹⁸You know that you were ransomed from the futile ways inherited from your ancestors, not with perishable things like silver or gold, ¹⁹but with the precious blood of Christ, like that of a lamb without defect or blemish. ²⁰He was destined before the foundation of the world, but was revealed at the end of the ages for your sake. ²¹Through him you have come to trust in God, who raised him

---

a Or *Rejoice in this*   *b* Other ancient authorities read *known*
c Gk *gird up the loins of your mind*

Cultural Connection

Saint Lucy

December 13 marks the feast day of Saint Lucy. Little is known about Saint Lucy except that she was martyred in Sicily early in the fourth century.

In Scandinavia, however, Saint Lucy is a very important part of the Christmas celebration. By tradition, the feast of Santa Lucia marks the longest night of the year. And keep in mind that winter nights are very long there because of the northern location.

The tradition goes that the oldest daughter in each home dresses in white with a red ribbon tied around her waist and wears on her head a wreath with candles. She then rises early in the morning to serve the family hot chocolate and cinnamon rolls. This is done in commemoration of the legend that Saint Lucy brought food and water to the early Christians who were hiding from their Roman persecutors. Despite the risk of suffering and persecution, Lucy was committed to living her faith by serving others.

This Scandinavian tradition is a beautiful reminder of how, even in the midst of darkness, Christians can bring the light of hope and nourishment to one another. To whom can you bring the light of hope today?

▶ **1 Pet 1:3–9**

---

from the dead and gave him glory, so that your faith and hope are set on God.

22 Now that you have purified your souls by your obedience to the truth[a] so that you have genuine mutual love, love one another deeply[b] from the heart.[c] 23 You have been born anew, not of perishable but of imperishable seed, through the living and enduring word of God.[d] 24 For

"All flesh is like grass
　　and all its glory like the flower of grass.
The grass withers,
　　and the flower falls,
25 but the word of the Lord endures forever."

That word is the good news that was announced to you.

The Living Stone and a Chosen People

2 Rid yourselves, therefore, of all malice, and all guile, insincerity, envy, and all slander. 2 Like newborn infants, long for the pure, spiritual milk, so that by it you may grow into salvation— 3 if indeed you have tasted that the Lord is good.

4 Come to him, a living stone, though rejected by mortals yet chosen and precious in God's sight, and 5 like living stones, let yourselves be built[e] into a spiritual house, to be a holy priesthood, to offer spiritual sacrifices acceptable to God through Jesus Christ. 6 For it stands in scripture:

"See, I am laying in Zion a stone,
　　a cornerstone chosen and precious;

Pray It!

Live the Belief

Holy God,
　　You invite me to live the Gospel message, not just hear and accept it. It is not enough to say I believe. I am called to live that belief.
I want to lovingly serve you, God, and all my brothers and sisters.
I want to seek knowledge of your word and follow it faithfully.
I want to exercise self-control and avoid temptations.
I want to build endurance to stand firm against life's trials.
I want to value truth and goodness.
Provide me with the fruits of your Spirit to sustain me for my journey, as I work to imitate your Son, Jesus Christ. Amen.

▶ **1 Pet 1:13–25**

---

a Other ancient authorities add *through the Spirit*
b Or *constantly*　c Other ancient authorities read *a pure heart*
d Or *through the word of the living and enduring God*　e Or *you yourselves are being built*

and whoever believes in him[a] will not be put to shame."

[7] To you then who believe, he is precious; but for those who do not believe,

"The stone that the builders rejected
has become the very head of the corner,"

[8] and

"A stone that makes them stumble,
and a rock that makes them fall."

They stumble because they disobey the word, as they were destined to do.

[9] But you are a chosen race, a royal priesthood, a holy nation, God's own people,[b] in order that you may proclaim the mighty acts of him who called you out of darkness into his marvelous light.

[10] Once you were not a people,
but now you are God's people;
once you had not received mercy,
but now you have received mercy.

Live as Servants of God

11 Beloved, I urge you as aliens and exiles to abstain from the desires of the flesh that wage

a Or it   b Gk a people for his possession

The Priesthood of the Faithful

In the New Testament, the only person, other than the Jewish priests, who is actually called a priest is Jesus. In the Letter to the Hebrews, the efficacy, or effectiveness, of Jesus as High Priest is proclaimed—a new priesthood has been born in Christ, one that surpasses the priesthood of the Old Testament.

Did you know that every baptized Christian shares in Christ's priesthood as well? Although it is different from hierarchical or ordained priesthood, the priesthood of each baptized person is recognized in their participating in the mission of Christ. Every Christian is to offer her or his life as a living sacrifice and to intercede on behalf of the Church and the world with the Father.

The priesthood of the faithful is part of our baptismal responsibility to proclaim what God has done for his people and to live a life consecrated by faith and hope in Christ crucified and risen. Because we share in the priesthood of the Son through Baptism, we have access to the divine through him. We are consecrated, put aside for the work of salvation.

We live this priesthood by offering ourselves to God. When we do so, we align ourselves to the way of Christ and live as lights for the world. We live for others and thus become instruments in the hand of God. Remember the words of 1 Peter 2:9: "You are a chosen race, a royal priesthood, a holy nation, God's own people."

▶ 1 Pet 2:1–10

Part of the Family

All of us come from and belong to a family. Some families are large and some small, some have two parents and others one, and some include aunts, uncles, or grandparents. Every family is unique.

Christians belong to a family that extends well beyond the relationships of blood or adoption. As followers of Christ, they make up a "royal priesthood" and a "holy nation," and are called "God's own people" (1 Pet 2:9). That is pretty lofty language! What does it mean?

First, it means that our faith is not just between us and God but is shared with others. Yes, there is something personal about our relationship with the Lord, but in addition, we are called by God into a community of disciples who share a common faith. Second, God has chosen us to live together in such a way that others who see our example will see something so good that they want to be a part of it.

In your prayer, reflect or journal on the following questions:

● How connected do you feel to the Christian family?
● What kind of support would you like to receive from other believers? What kind of support can you give?

▶ 1 Pet 2:9–17

war against the soul. ¹²Conduct yourselves honorably among the Gentiles, so that, though they malign you as evildoers, they may see your honorable deeds and glorify God when he comes to judge.ᵃ

13 For the Lord's sake accept the authority of every human institution,ᵇ whether of the emperor as supreme, ¹⁴or of governors, as sent by him to punish those who do wrong and to praise those who do right. ¹⁵For it is God's will that by doing right you should silence the ignorance of the foolish. ¹⁶As servantsᶜ of God, live as free people, yet do not use your freedom as a pretext for evil. ¹⁷Honor everyone. Love the family of believers.ᵈ Fear God. Honor the emperor.

The Example of Christ's Suffering

18 Slaves, accept the authority of your masters with all deference, not only those who are kind and gentle but also those who are harsh. ¹⁹For it is a credit to you if, being aware of God, you endure pain while suffering unjustly. ²⁰If you endure when you are beaten for doing wrong, what credit is that? But if you endure when you do right and suffer for it, you have God's approval. ²¹For to this you have been called, because Christ also suffered for you, leaving you an example, so that you should follow in his steps. ²² "He committed no sin,
    and no deceit was found in his mouth."
²³When he was abused, he did not return abuse; when he suffered, he did not threaten; but he entrusted himself to the one who judges justly. ²⁴He himself bore our sins in his body on the cross,ᵉ so that, free from sins, we might live for righteousness; by his woundsᶠ you have been healed. ²⁵For you were going astray like sheep, but now you have returned to the shepherd and guardian of your souls.

Wives and Husbands

3 Wives, in the same way, accept the authority of your husbands, so that, even if some of them do not obey the word, they may be won over without a word by their wives' conduct, ²when they see the purity and reverence of your lives. ³Do not adorn yourselves outwardly by braiding your hair, and by wearing gold ornaments or fine clothing; ⁴rather, let your adornment be the inner self with the lasting beauty of a gentle and quiet spirit, which is very precious in God's sight. ⁵It was in this way long ago that the holy women who hoped in God used to adorn themselves by accepting the authority of their husbands. ⁶Thus Sarah obeyed Abraham and called him lord. You have become her daughters as long as you do what is good and never let fears alarm you.

7 Husbands, in the same way, show consideration for your wives in your life together, paying honor to the woman as the weaker sex,ᵍ since they too are also heirs of the gracious gift of life—so that nothing may hinder your prayers.

Suffering for Doing Right

8 Finally, all of you, have unity of spirit, sympathy, love for one another, a tender heart, and a humble mind. ⁹Do not repay evil for evil or abuse for abuse; but, on the contrary, repay with a blessing. It is for this that you were called—that you might inherit a blessing. ¹⁰For
"Those who desire life
    and desire to see good days,
let them keep their tongues from evil
    and their lips from speaking deceit;
¹¹ let them turn away from evil and do good;
    let them seek peace and pursue it.
¹² For the eyes of the Lord are on the righteous,
    and his ears are open to their prayer.
But the face of the Lord is against those who do
    evil."

13 Now who will harm you if you are eager to do what is good? ¹⁴But even if you do suffer for doing what is right, you are blessed. Do not fear what they fear,ʰ and do not be intimidated, ¹⁵but in your hearts sanctify Christ as Lord. Always be ready to make your defense to anyone who demands from you an accounting for the hope that is in you; ¹⁶yet do it with gentleness and reverence.ⁱ Keep your conscience clear, so that, when you are maligned, those who abuse you for your good conduct in Christ may be put to shame. ¹⁷For it is better to suffer for doing good, if suffering should be God's will, than to suffer for doing evil. ¹⁸For Christ also sufferedʲ for sins once for all, the righteous for the unrighteous, in order to bring youᵏ to God. He was put to death in the flesh, but made alive in the spirit, ¹⁹in which also he went and made a proclamation to the spirits

> "You are a
> chosen race,
> a royal priesthood,
> a holy nation, God's
> own people."
>
> (1 Pet 2:9)

Cultural Connection

Living Gospel Values Even If It Demands Suffering

Many Hispanic teenagers and young adults in the United States send money to parents in Latin America. Others work to sustain the education of younger brothers and sisters here. Many times they are criticized because they are unable to continue their own studies and advance in society.

Other young people, of any culture, also suffer for living the Gospel. Those who want to leave a gang are harassed by gang members. Young women and men who want to maintain their virginity are made fun of. Young people who start participating in church programs are not understood by their friends. The commitment of young leaders sometimes is misinterpreted by their parents as a way of escaping their duties at home.

These behaviors cause suffering because Gospel values are conflicting with the mainstream culture within our society. In today's First World, particularly in the United States, blending into the surrounding society is pushed by the media and is almost an ideal set by society.

● How does a true Christian lifestyle cause conflict with mainstream culture within our society? How can young Hispanics keep their values of love, generosity, and solidarity with their families while continuing their own personal development?

● Think of Peter's advice to the early Christian communities. Remember Jesus' suffering, and offer yours together with his so that you and all young people may share Christ's new life.

▶ **1 Pet 3:13–22**

---

in prison, 20who in former times did not obey, when God waited patiently in the days of Noah, during the building of the ark, in which a few, that is, eight persons, were saved through water. 21And baptism, which this prefigured, now saves you—not as a removal of dirt from the body, but as an appeal to God for*a* a good conscience, through the resurrection of Jesus Christ, 22who has gone into heaven and is at the right hand of God, with angels, authorities, and powers made subject to him.

Good Stewards of God's Grace

4 Since therefore Christ suffered in the flesh,*b* arm yourselves also with the same intention (for whoever has suffered in the flesh has finished with sin), 2so as to live for the rest of your earthly life*c* no longer by human desires but by the will of God. 3You have already spent enough time in doing what the Gentiles like to do, living in licentiousness, passions, drunkenness, revels, carousing, and lawless idolatry. 4They are surprised that you no longer join them in the same excesses of dissipation, and so they blaspheme.*d* 5But they will have to give an accounting to him who stands ready to judge the living and the dead. 6For this is the reason the gospel was proclaimed even to the dead, so that, though they had been judged in the flesh as everyone is judged, they might live in the spirit as God does.

7 The end of all things is near;*e* therefore be serious and discipline yourselves for the sake of your prayers. 8Above all, maintain constant love for one another, for love covers a multitude of sins. 9Be hospitable to one another without complaining. 10Like good stewards of the manifold grace of God, serve one another with whatever gift each of you has received. 11Whoever speaks must do so as one speaking the very words of God; whoever serves must do so with the strength that God supplies, so that God may be glorified in all things through Jesus Christ. To him belong the glory and the power forever and ever. Amen.

Suffering as a Christian

12 Beloved, do not be surprised at the fiery ordeal that is taking place among you to test you, as though something strange were happening to you. 13But rejoice insofar as you are sharing Christ's sufferings, so that you may also be glad and shout for joy when his glory is revealed. 14If you are reviled for the name of Christ, you are

---

a Or a pledge to God from   b Other ancient authorities add for us; others, for you   c Gk rest of the time in the flesh   d Or they malign you   e Or is at hand

blessed, because the spirit of glory,[a] which is the Spirit of God, is resting on you.[b] 15But let none of you suffer as a murderer, a thief, a criminal, or even as a mischief maker. 16Yet if any of you suffers as a Christian, do not consider it a disgrace, but glorify God because you bear this name. 17For the time has come for judgment to begin with the household of God; if it begins with us, what will be the end for those who do not obey the gospel of God? 18And

> "If it is hard for the righteous to be saved,
>> what will become of the ungodly and the sinners?"

19Therefore, let those suffering in accordance with God's will entrust themselves to a faithful Creator, while continuing to do good.

Shout for Joy!

No healthy person likes to suffer. Yet, when we suffer for resisting evil and doing good—like being identified as a follower of Christ or defending someone who is under attack by others—First Peter calls us blessed. God notices when we are mocked or ridiculed for our faith. We are challenged to rejoice when we experience such treatment, rather than take it as a sign of failure. Didn't Christ suffer for doing good? Won't he be with us when we suffer for his name? The Gospel has a strange way of turning things upside down—it says that instead of causing suffering, these things should bring us joy!

The Bible has a lot more to say on the topic of suffering. See the "Life and Faith Issues" index to locate other passages.

▶ 1 Pet 4:12–19

Tending the Flock of God

5 Now as an elder myself and a witness of the sufferings of Christ, as well as one who shares in the glory to be revealed, I exhort the elders among you 2to tend the flock of God that is in your charge, exercising the oversight,[c] not under compulsion but willingly, as God would have you do it[d]—not for sordid gain but eagerly. 3Do not lord it over those in your charge, but be examples to the flock. 4And when the chief shepherd appears, you will win the crown of glory that never fades away. 5In the same way, you who are younger must accept the authority of the elders.[e] And all of you must clothe yourselves with humility in your dealings with one another, for

"God opposes the proud,
but gives grace to the humble."

6 Humble yourselves therefore under the mighty hand of God, so that he may exalt you in due time. 7Cast all your anxiety on him, because he cares for you. 8Discipline yourselves, keep alert.[f] Like a roaring lion your adversary the devil prowls around, looking for someone to devour. 9Resist him, steadfast in your faith, for you know that your brothers and sisters[g] in all the world are undergoing the same kinds of suffering. 10And after you have suffered for a little while, the God of all grace, who has called you to his eternal glory in Christ, will himself restore, support, strengthen, and establish you. 11To him be the power forever and ever. Amen.

Final Greetings and Benediction

12 Through Silvanus, whom I consider a faithful brother, I have written this short letter to encourage you and to testify that this is the true grace of God. Stand fast in it. 13Your sister church[h] in Babylon, chosen together with you, sends you greetings; and so does my son Mark. 14Greet one another with a kiss of love.

Peace to all of you who are in Christ.[i]

---

a Other ancient authorities add and of power   b Other ancient authorities add On their part he is blasphemed, but on your part he is glorified   c Other ancient authorities lack exercising the oversight   d Other ancient authorities lack as God would have you do it   e Or of those who are older   f Or be vigilant   g Gk your brotherhood   h Gk She who is   i Other ancient authorities add Amen

What happens to us when we die? What is heaven like? Does God even care what happens to us? Many people believe there is no heaven, no hell, and no God. Some say that when we die, our bodies simply decay and we no longer exist in any form. They say there is no life after death, no punishment, and no reward. But the Bible tells us differently. Second Peter was written to reassure believers that God does indeed care, and that they will be rewarded for leading faithful and virtuous lives.

At a Glance

- **Chapter 1.** a greeting, and encouragement to lead a holy life
- **Chapter 2.** a warning to beware of false teachers
- **Chapter 3.** a message that the day of God's judgment is coming

Quick Facts

Inspired Author: an unknown person writing in Peter's name
Date Written: from approximately AD 100 to 125
Audience: a community of both Jewish and Gentile (non-Jewish) Christians

In Depth

Bible scholars have convincing evidence that Second Peter is one of the latest books in the New Testament. The letter appears to have been written by someone who is appealing to the authority of the dead Apostle Peter (see "Introduction to the Letters and Revelation"). At the time of its writing—perhaps as many as one hundred years after Jesus' death and Resurrection—some Christians were starting to wonder if what they believed was true. People were even teaching that there would be no reward or punishment after death. So why not live any way you wanted to?

The author of the Second Letter of Peter is arguing against these false teachers. This writer uses famous examples from the Old Testament to remind readers how God has acted through history. And the author promises that those who have chosen to separate themselves from God in their lifetime will experience the fullness of separation from God in death—a separation that Christians call hell. Those who have stayed faithful to God's calling will enjoy eternal life in union with God—a life that Christians call heaven. Why? Because God is good and just.

Tied to this argument is another concern. Many of the earliest Christians believed Christ would return soon after his Resurrection, probably within their lifetime, to establish God's Reign once and for all (see "The Parousia," near 2 Thess 1:5—2:17). When generations had passed and Christ had not yet returned, false teachers claimed he would never return. The author of Second Peter reminds readers that God's time is not our time—Christ is simply waiting so more people have a chance to repent of their sins before he comes for judgment (see 2 Pet 3:9).

The Second Letter of Peter

2 Peter

Salutation

1 Simeon[a] Peter, a servant[b] and apostle of Jesus Christ,

To those who have received a faith as precious as ours through the righteousness of our God and Savior Jesus Christ:[c]

2 May grace and peace be yours in abundance in the knowledge of God and of Jesus our Lord.

The Christian's Call and Election

3 His divine power has given us everything needed for life and godliness, through the knowledge of him who called us by[d] his own glory and goodness. [4]Thus he has given us, through these things, his precious and very great promises, so that through them you may escape from the corruption that is in the world because of lust, and may become participants of the divine nature. [5]For this very reason, you must make every effort to support your faith with goodness, and goodness with knowledge, [6]and knowledge with self-control, and self-control with endurance, and endurance with godliness, [7]and godliness with mutual[e] affection, and mutual[e] affection with love. [8]For if these things are yours and are increasing among you, they keep you from being ineffective and unfruitful in the knowledge of our Lord Jesus Christ. [9]For anyone who lacks these things is short-sighted and blind, and is forgetful of the cleansing of past sins. [10]Therefore, brothers and sisters,[f] be all the more eager to confirm your call and election, for if you do this, you will never stumble. [11]For in this way, entry into the eternal kingdom of our Lord and Savior Jesus Christ will be richly provided for you.

12 Therefore I intend to keep on reminding you of these things, though you know them already and are established in the truth that has come to you. [13]I think it right, as long as I am in this body,[g] to refresh your memory, [14]since I know that my death[h] will come soon, as indeed our Lord Jesus Christ has made clear to me. [15]And I will make every effort so that after my departure you may be able at any time to recall these things.

Eyewitnesses of Christ's Glory

16 For we did not follow cleverly devised myths when we made known to you the power and coming of our Lord Jesus Christ, but we had been eyewitnesses of his majesty. [17]For he received honor and glory from God the Father when that voice was conveyed to him by the Majestic Glory, saying, "This is my Son, my Beloved,[i] with whom I am well pleased." [18]We ourselves heard this voice come from heaven, while we were with him on the holy mountain.

19 So we have the prophetic message more fully confirmed. You will do well to be attentive to this as to a lamp shining in a dark place,

---

a Other ancient authorities read *Simon*   b Gk *slave*   c Or *of our God and the Savior Jesus Christ*   d Other ancient authorities read *through*   e Gk *brotherly*   f Gk *brothers*   g Gk *tent*   h Gk *the putting off of my tent*   i Other ancient authorities read *my beloved Son*

until the day dawns and the morning star rises in your hearts. [20]First of all you must understand this, that no prophecy of scripture is a matter of one's own interpretation, [21]because no prophecy ever came by human will, but men and women moved by the Holy Spirit spoke from God.[a]

False Prophets and Their Punishment

2 But false prophets also arose among the people, just as there will be false teachers among you, who will secretly bring in destructive opinions. They will even deny the Master who bought them—bringing swift destruction on themselves. [2]Even so, many will follow their licentious ways, and because of these teachers[b] the way of truth will be maligned. [3]And in their greed they will exploit you with deceptive words. Their condemnation, pronounced against them long ago, has not been idle, and their destruction is not asleep.

4 For if God did not spare the angels when they sinned, but cast them into hell[c] and committed them to chains[d] of deepest darkness to be kept until the judgment; [5]and if he did not spare the ancient world, even though he saved Noah, a herald of righteousness, with seven others, when he brought a flood on a world of the ungodly; [6]and if by turning the cities of Sodom and Gomorrah to ashes he condemned them to extinction[e] and made them an example of what is coming to the ungodly;[f] [7]and if he rescued Lot, a righteous man greatly distressed by the licentiousness of the lawless [8](for that righteous man, living among them day after day, was tormented in his righteous soul by their lawless deeds that he saw and heard), [9]then the Lord knows how to rescue the godly from trial, and to keep the unrighteous under punishment until the day of judgment [10]—especially those who indulge their flesh in depraved lust, and who despise authority.

Bold and willful, they are not afraid to slander the glorious ones,[g] [11]whereas angels, though greater in might and power, do not bring against them a slanderous judgment from the Lord.[h] [12]These people, however, are like irrational animals, mere creatures of instinct, born to be caught and killed. They slander what they do not understand, and when those creatures are destroyed,[i] they also will be destroyed, [13]suffering[j] the penalty for doing wrong. They count it a pleasure to revel in the daytime. They are blots and blemishes, reveling in their dissipation[k] while they feast with you. [14]They have eyes full of adultery, insatiable for sin. They entice unsteady souls. They have hearts trained in greed.

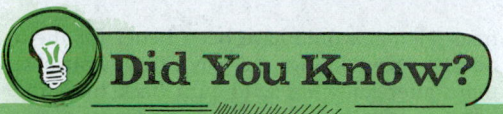

Did You Know?

Identifying False Prophets

Many times throughout history, people have misled others in the name of God. Adolf Hitler is probably the best known such leader in the twentieth century. Some of these leaders have even convinced their followers to commit mass suicide as part of their beliefs. These extreme examples show how people can be misguided by false prophets.

In 2 Peter 2:1–3, the author gives guidelines for identifying false prophets, explaining that false prophets use secrets, propose destructive opinions, deny God's teachings, twist the truth to their needs, and exploit their followers. Beware of any leader, religious or nonreligious, who uses these techniques. As Second Peter says, they malign the way of truth.

▶ **2 Pet 2:1–3**

Accursed children! [15]They have left the straight road and have gone astray, following the road of Balaam son of Bosor,[l] who loved the wages of doing wrong, [16]but was rebuked for his own transgression; a speechless donkey spoke with a human voice and restrained the prophet's madness.

17 These are waterless springs and mists driven by a storm; for them the deepest darkness has been reserved. [18]For they speak bombastic nonsense, and with licentious desires of the flesh they entice people who have just[m] escaped from those who live in error. [19]They promise them freedom, but they themselves are slaves of corruption; for people are slaves to whatever masters them. [20]For if, after they have escaped the defilements of the world through the knowledge of our Lord and Savior Jesus Christ, they are again entangled in them and overpowered, the last state has become worse for them than the

a Other ancient authorities read *but moved by the Holy Spirit saints of God spoke*   b Gk *because of them*   c Gk *Tartaros*   d Other ancient authorities read *pits*   e Other ancient authorities lack *to extinction*   f Other ancient authorities read *an example to those who were to be ungodly*   g Or *angels*; Gk *glories*   h Other ancient authorities read *before the Lord*; others lack the phrase   i Gk *in their destruction*   j Other ancient authorities read *receiving*   k Other ancient authorities read *love-feasts*   l Other ancient authorities read *Beor*   m Other ancient authorities read *actually*

first. ²¹For it would have been better for them never to have known the way of righteousness than, after knowing it, to turn back from the holy commandment that was passed on to them. ²²It has happened to them according to the true proverb,

"The dog turns back to its own vomit,"

and,

"The sow is washed only to wallow in the mud."

The Promise of the Lord's Coming

3 This is now, beloved, the second letter I am writing to you; in them I am trying to arouse your sincere intention by reminding you ²that you should remember the words spoken in the past by the holy prophets, and the commandment of the Lord and Savior spoken through your apostles. ³First of all you must understand this, that in the last days scoffers will come,

Seeing God

A frustrated and frazzled New York City tour guide is trying to get her group through a maze of homeless people and panhandlers outside the great Saint Patrick's Cathedral. After the group has safely entered the cathedral, she exclaims, with arms outstretched, "God is definitely here!" A young girl whose gaze lingers on the people outside asks, with all seriousness, "Why won't they let him out?"

The early readers of Second Peter were confused that Jesus Christ had not yet returned again (see "The Parousia," near 2 Thess 1:5—2:17). They wondered, "Where is God?" The author reminds them not to apply human limits to God's response.

Sometimes, when we pray for something, it seems like God keeps us waiting for an eternity. We want something to happen quickly—but God is on a different schedule. You might say the only limits we have in seeing God's actions are the ones we establish. What prevents you from seeing God in your life?

▶ **2 Pet 3:9**

scoffing and indulging their own lusts ⁴and saying, "Where is the promise of his coming? For ever since our ancestors died,ᵃ all things continue as they were from the beginning of creation!" ⁵They deliberately ignore this fact, that by the word of God heavens existed long ago and an earth was formed out of water and by means of water, ⁶through which the world of that time was deluged with water and perished. ⁷But by the same word the present heavens and earth have been reserved for fire, being kept until the day of judgment and destruction of the godless.

8 But do not ignore this one fact, beloved, that with the Lord one day is like a thousand years, and a thousand years are like one day. ⁹The Lord is not slow about his promise, as some think of slowness, but is patient with you,ᵇ not wanting any to perish, but all to come to repentance. ¹⁰But the day of the Lord will come like a thief, and then the heavens will pass away with a loud noise, and the elements will be dissolved with fire, and the earth and everything that is done on it will be disclosed.ᶜ

11 Since all these things are to be dissolved in this way, what sort of persons ought you to be in leading lives of holiness and godliness, ¹²waiting for and hasteningᵈ the coming of the day of God, because of which the heavens will be set ablaze and dissolved, and the elements will melt with fire? ¹³But, in accordance with his promise, we wait for new heavens and a new earth, where righteousness is at home.

Final Exhortation and Doxology

14 Therefore, beloved, while you are waiting for these things, strive to be found by him at peace, without spot or blemish; ¹⁵and regard the patience of our Lord as salvation. So also our beloved brother Paul wrote to you according to the wisdom given him, ¹⁶speaking of this as he does in all his letters. There are some things in them hard to understand, which the ignorant and unstable twist to their own destruction, as they do the other scriptures. ¹⁷You therefore, beloved, since you are forewarned, beware that you are not carried away with the error of the lawless and lose your own stability. ¹⁸But grow in the grace and knowledge of our Lord and Savior Jesus Christ. To him be the glory both now and to the day of eternity. Amen.ᵉ

---

a Gk *our fathers fell asleep*　b Other ancient authorities read *on your account*　c Other ancient authorities read *will be burned up*　d Or *earnestly desiring*　e Other ancient authorities lack *Amen*

Betrayal is painful. Unfortunately, most of us have experienced it at one time or another. It often begins with a misunderstanding. Sometimes harsh words are exchanged, and people part ways feeling sad and bitter. The community addressed by the Letters of John had experienced sharp division and conflict. It is impossible to avoid the author's feeling of betrayal as you read these letters.

In Depth

All three Letters of John were probably written by the same person, the elder referred to in the second and third letters. This writer probably belonged to the community for which the Gospel of John was written. He saw himself and his community as being faithful to the true meaning of John's Gospel. Now, others who had once belonged to this community had abandoned it in its time of need. They too read the Gospel of John, but they interpreted it very differently. The disagreement between these two groups resulted in a bitter conflict.

At a Glance

- **1 Jn 1:1–4.** an introduction
- **1 Jn 1:5—3:10.** a message that God is light, and we must walk in the light
- **1 Jn 3:11—5:12.** a message that those who are God's children show it by their love
- **1 Jn 5:13–21.** a conclusion
- **2 Jn.** a warning about the false message of some deceivers
- **3 Jn.** a letter to Gaius, a man who provides hospitality to missionaries

Quick Facts

Inspired Author: an unknown person associated with the community that produced the Gospel of John
Date Written: approximately AD 100
Audience: Christians who were suffering from a split in their community

Even after careful study of the first letter, it is difficult to determine exactly what the disagreement was about. One issue seems to have been the proper understanding of Jesus' humanity. Apparently, the deceivers did not fully believe in Jesus' humanity and its connection to salvation through Jesus' death and Resurrection. To emphasize Jesus' humanity, the author several times mentions that Jesus came "in the flesh" and comments on the saving power of the "blood of Jesus."

The author also challenges the deceivers' claims that they were free to do anything they wanted and still love God. If they truly loved God, they would also love their brothers and sisters and would not have abandoned the community.

The Second Letter of John is brief and seems to be a follow-up to the first letter addressed to the same community. The Third Letter of John is also brief. It is addressed to a man named Gaius, and in it the elder is complaining about a church leader named Diotrephes who refused to provide hospitality to some missionaries sent by the elder.

Through these letters, God reminds today's Christians that believers will inevitably have profoundly different understandings about what they believe. Conflict and disagreement will occur even within the Christian community. Can Christians handle such discord with love and respect?

The First, Second, and Third Letters of **John**

1 John

 4:7

The Word of Life

1 We declare to you what was from the beginning, what we have heard, what we have seen with our eyes, what we have looked at and touched with our hands, concerning the word of life— ²this life was revealed, and we have seen it and testify to it, and declare to you the eternal life that was with the Father and was revealed to us— ³we declare to you what we have seen and heard so that you also may have fellowship with us; and truly our fellowship is with the Father and with his Son Jesus Christ. ⁴We are writing these things so that our*ª* joy may be complete.

God Is Light

5 This is the message we have heard from him and proclaim to you, that God is light and in him there is no darkness at all. ⁶If we say that we have fellowship with him while we are walking in darkness, we lie and do not do what is true; ⁷but if we walk in the light as he himself is in the light, we have fellowship with one another, and the blood of Jesus his Son cleanses us from all sin. ⁸If we say that we have no sin, we deceive ourselves, and the truth is not in us. ⁹If we confess our sins, he who is faithful and just will forgive us our sins and cleanse us from all unrighteousness. ¹⁰If we say that we have not sinned, we make him a liar, and his word is not in us.

Christ Our Advocate

2 My little children, I am writing these things to you so that you may not sin. But if anyone does sin, we have an advocate with the Father, Jesus Christ the righteous; ²and he is the atoning sacrifice for our sins, and not for ours only but also for the sins of the whole world.

3 Now by this we may be sure that we know him, if we obey his commandments. ⁴Whoever

---

Live It!

Live in the Light

Do you ever find it hard to decide whether something is right or wrong? Instead of the sharp distinction between light and darkness described in First John, you might see a lot of shades of gray. But be careful; you might simply be seeing what you want to see! Remember, "If we say that we have no sin, we deceive ourselves" (1 Jn 1:8). There are times when our choices aren't clear, but usually they are. Listen to your inner voice of honesty and integrity, and courageously choose to live in the light!

▶ 1 Jn 1:5–10

---

a Other ancient authorities read your

1466

Cultural Connection

Sometimes, it's hardest to show your love to the people you are closest to. Maybe you get along great with all your friends but are always arguing with your brother or sister. Or in your youth group, you are always tense around that one person with whom you had angry words several months ago.

The author of First John tells us we cannot ignore a relationship with a brother or sister in the Lord who has been upset. The Hmong culture has the same tradition. If you frighten or hurt or offend someone, you have created an imbalance of spirits. It is your responsibility to go back and seek to re-establish harmony. It is the Hmong custom to go to a shaman (an elder of the community, a holy person) for advice and to perform a ritual for reconciliation.

The Catholic Tradition has the sacrament of Penance and Reconciliation for the same purpose: to admit that the imbalance in a relationship has been caused by sin, discuss ways to make things right, express sorrow, and celebrate God's forgiveness and love.

▶ **1 Jn 2:7–11**

---

says, "I have come to know him," but does not obey his commandments, is a liar, and in such a person the truth does not exist; [5]but whoever obeys his word, truly in this person the love of God has reached perfection. By this we may be sure that we are in him: [6]whoever says, "I abide in him," ought to walk just as he walked.

A New Commandment

7 Beloved, I am writing you no new commandment, but an old commandment that you have had from the beginning; the old commandment is the word that you have heard. [8]Yet I am writing you a new commandment that is true in him and in you, because[a] the darkness is passing away and the true light is already shining. [9]Whoever says, "I am in the light," while hating a brother or sister,[b] is still in the darkness. [10]Whoever loves a brother or sister[c] lives in the light, and in such a person[d] there is no cause for stumbling. [11]But whoever hates another believer[e] is in the darkness, walks in the darkness, and does not know the way to go, because the darkness has brought on blindness.

12 I am writing to you, little children,
    because your sins are forgiven on account of
       his name.
13 I am writing to you, fathers,
    because you know him who is from the
       beginning.
  I am writing to you, young people,
    because you have conquered the evil one.
14 I write to you, children,
    because you know the Father.
  I write to you, fathers,

because you know him who is from the
       beginning.
  I write to you, young people,
    because you are strong
  and the word of God abides in you,
    and you have overcome the evil one.

15 Do not love the world or the things in the world. The love of the Father is not in those who love the world; [16]for all that is in the world—the desire of the flesh, the desire of the eyes, the pride in riches—comes not from the Father but from the world. [17]And the world and its desire[f] are passing away, but those who do the will of God live forever.

Warning against Antichrists

18 Children, it is the last hour! As you have heard that antichrist is coming, so now many antichrists have come. From this we know that it is the last hour. [19]They went out from us, but they did not belong to us; for if they had belonged to us, they would have remained with us. But by going out they made it plain that none of them belongs to us. [20]But you have been anointed by the Holy One, and all of you have knowledge.[g] [21]I write to you, not because you do not know the truth, but because you know it, and you know that no lie comes from the truth. [22]Who is the liar but the one who denies that Jesus is the Christ?[h] This is the antichrist, the one who denies the Father and

---

a Or that   b Gk hating a brother   c Gk loves a brother
d Or in it   e Gk hates a brother   f Or the desire for it   g Other
ancient authorities read you know all things   h Or the Messiah

the Son. ²³No one who denies the Son has the Father; everyone who confesses the Son has the Father also. ²⁴Let what you heard from the beginning abide in you. If what you heard from the beginning abides in you, then you will abide in the Son and in the Father. ²⁵And this is what he has promised us,ᵃ eternal life.

26 I write these things to you concerning those who would deceive you. ²⁷As for you, the anointing that you received from him abides in you, and so you do not need anyone to teach you. But as his anointing teaches you about all things, and is true and is not a lie, and just as it has taught you, abide in him.ᵇ

28 And now, little children, abide in him, so that when he is revealed we may have confidence and not be put to shame before him at his coming.

> "Let us love, not in word or speech, but in truth and action."
> (1 Jn 3:18)

Children of God

29 If you know that he is righteous, you may be sure that everyone who does right has been **3** born of him. ¹See what love the Father has given us, that we should be called children of God; and that is what we are. The reason the world does not know us is that it did not know him. ²Beloved, we are God's children now; what

Pray It!

Love in Action

Clear your mind of all thoughts and concerns. Help your body and mind relax with some deep breaths. Now read 1 John 3:18 several times until you can say it by heart. Reflect on its meaning. Think about how you have lived and acted during this past week. Have you shown love in truth and action? by word or speech?

Ask God to forgive you for any situations in which you failed to act lovingly. Pray for the gift of being able to put your love in action in your daily life. Throughout the remainder of this day, remind yourself of this prayer by calling to mind verse 18.

▶ **1 Jn 3:18**

we will be has not yet been revealed. What we do know is this: when heᵇ is revealed, we will be like him, for we will see him as he is. ³And all who have this hope in him purify themselves, just as he is pure.

4 Everyone who commits sin is guilty of lawlessness; sin is lawlessness. ⁵You know that he was revealed to take away sins, and in him there is no sin. ⁶No one who abides in him sins; no one who sins has either seen him or known him. ⁷Little children, let no one deceive you. Everyone who does what is right is righteous, just as he is righteous. ⁸Everyone who commits sin is a child of the devil; for the devil has been sinning from the beginning. The Son of God was revealed for this purpose, to destroy the works of the devil. ⁹Those who have been born of God do not sin, because God's seed abides in them;ᶜ they cannot sin, because they have been born of God. ¹⁰The children of God and the children of the devil are revealed in this way: all who do not do what is right are not from God, nor are those who do not love their brothers and sisters.ᵈ

Love One Another

11 For this is the message you have heard from the beginning, that we should love one another. ¹²We must not be like Cain who was from the evil one and murdered his brother. And why did he murder him? Because his own deeds were evil and his brother's righteous. ¹³Do not be astonished, brothers and sisters,ᵈ that the world hates you. ¹⁴We know that we have passed from death to life because we love one another. Whoever does not love abides in death. ¹⁵All who hate a brother or sisterᵉ are murderers, and you know that murderers do not have eternal life abiding in them. ¹⁶We know love by this, that he laid down his life for us—and we ought to lay down our lives for one another. ¹⁷How does God's love abide in anyone who has the world's goods and sees a brother or sisterᶠ in need and yet refuses help?

18 Little children, let us love, not in word or speech, but in truth and action. ¹⁹And by this we will know that we are from the truth and will reassure our hearts before him ²⁰whenever our hearts condemn us; for God is greater than our hearts, and he knows everything. ²¹Beloved, if

---

ᵃ Other ancient authorities read *you* ᵇ Or *it* ᶜ Or *because the children of God abide in him* ᵈ Gk *his brother* ᵉ Gk *brothers* ᶠ Gk *brother*

Testing Spirits

Ancient peoples believed in different kinds of spirits that could affect the way things happened in the world. The First Letter of John talks about two kinds of spirit: that which comes from God and that which does not come from God. This letter gives us two ways for testing whether something comes from God: The first has to do with whether our actions reflect love for God and love for our brothers and sisters (see 1 Jn 3:18). The second has to do with our beliefs about Jesus Christ. To understand this, let's look closer at the controversy that prompted the author of this letter to offer these two tests.

The author of First John says of those who left their community—he calls them antichrists—that they do not believe that Jesus is the Christ and they do not confess the Father and the Son (see 2:22). But this cannot be the end of the story because they are Jesus' followers just like the author. The key to the problem is 1 John 4:2, but the meaning of this verse in its original Greek language is not clear. Even Bible scholars don't know how to translate it. Luckily they could go to Second John, verse 7, where the letter writes more clearly about the same issue. These deceivers do not believe that Jesus Christ came in the flesh. They believe in Jesus Christ and that he came to live among us, but they do not believe he actually became one of us and suffered and died like we do. After all, who could possibly imagine God doing such a thing? But this is what the author of First John believed and what Christians today believe. This is what we mean when we talk about the Incarnation—God takes on flesh and becomes like us.

You can apply this letter's two tests to just about any spiritual idea or practice you come across. Ask yourself: Does this help me to love God and other people? Does this support the Christian belief that Jesus Christ is fully God and fully human, and that faith in him is necessary for salvation? If you cannot answer yes to both of these questions, stay away!

▶ 1 Jn 4:1–21

our hearts do not condemn us, we have boldness before God; 22and we receive from him whatever we ask, because we obey his commandments and do what pleases him.

23 And this is his commandment, that we should believe in the name of his Son Jesus Christ and love one another, just as he has commanded us. 24All who obey his commandments abide in him, and he abides in them. And by this we know that he abides in us, by the Spirit that he has given us.

Testing the Spirits

4 Beloved, do not believe every spirit, but test the spirits to see whether they are from God; for many false prophets have gone out into the world. 2By this you know the Spirit of God: every spirit that confesses that Jesus Christ has come in the flesh is from God, 3and every spirit that does not confess Jesus*a* is not from God. And this is the spirit of the antichrist, of which you have heard that it is coming; and now it is already in the world. 4Little children, you are from God, and have conquered them; for the one who is in you is greater than the one who is in the world. 5They are from the world; therefore what they say is from the world, and the world listens to them. 6We are from God. Whoever knows God listens to us, and whoever is not from God does not listen to us. From this we know the spirit of truth and the spirit of error.

God Is Love

7 Beloved, let us love one another, because love is from God; everyone who loves is born of God and knows God. 8Whoever does not love does not know God, for God is love. 9God's love was revealed among us in this way: God sent his only Son into the world so that we might live through him. 10In this is love, not that we loved God but that he loved us and sent his Son to be the atoning sacrifice for our sins. 11Beloved, since God loved us so much, we also ought to love one another. 12No one has ever seen God; if we love one another, God lives in us, and his love is perfected in us.

13 By this we know that we abide in him and he in us, because he has given us of his Spirit. 14And we have seen and do testify that the Father has sent his Son as the Savior of the world. 15God abides in those who confess that Jesus is the Son of God, and they abide in God. 16So we have known and believe the love that God has for us.

---

a Other ancient authorities read *does away with Jesus* (Gk *dissolves Jesus*)

Understanding Love

Some of the most beautiful prose and poetry written about love are contained in the Bible. First John 4:7–21 is a particularly eloquent piece that captures the heart of the Good News: God has loved us in Christ Jesus, who came as the Savior of the world. Now, we have been given the Spirit of God, and we are commanded to love others as we have been loved by God.

It is easy to say we love God. But First John tells us that our love for God is shown in our love for one another. Loving one another is much harder than simply saying, "I love God." What does this love for God look like? It is not the romantic love or sentimental affection the world usually presents to us. Read Matthew 25:31–36 or 1 Corinthians, chapter 13, for some ideas.

▶ 1 Jn 4:7–21

God is love, and those who abide in love abide in God, and God abides in them. [17]Love has been perfected among us in this: that we may have boldness on the day of judgment, because as he is, so are we in this world. [18]There is no fear in love, but perfect love casts out fear; for fear has to do with punishment, and whoever fears has not reached perfection in love. [19]We love[a] because he first loved us. [20]Those who say, "I love God," and hate their brothers or sisters,[b] are liars; for those who do not love a brother or sister[c] whom they have seen, cannot love God whom they have not seen. [21]The commandment we have from him is this: those who love God must love their brothers and sisters[b] also.

Faith Conquers the World

5 Everyone who believes that Jesus is the Christ[d] has been born of God, and everyone who loves the parent loves the child. [2]By this we know that we love the children of God, when we love God and obey his commandments. [3]For the love of God is this, that we obey his commandments. And his commandments are not burdensome, [4]for whatever is born of God conquers the world. And this is the victory that conquers the world, our faith. [5]Who is it that conquers the world but the one who believes that Jesus is the Son of God?

Testimony concerning the Son of God

6 This is the one who came by water and blood, Jesus Christ, not with the water only but with the water and the blood. And the Spirit is the one that testifies, for the Spirit is the truth. [7]There are three that testify:[e] [8]the Spirit and the water and the blood, and these three agree. [9]If we receive human testimony, the testimony of God is greater; for this is the testimony of God that he has testified to his Son. [10]Those who believe in the Son of God have the testimony in their hearts. Those who do not believe in God[f] have made him a liar by not believing in the testimony that God has given concerning his Son. [11]And this is the testimony: God gave us eternal life, and this life is in his Son. [12]Whoever has the Son has life; whoever does not have the Son of God does not have life.

Epilogue

13 I write these things to you who believe in the name of the Son of God, so that you may know that you have eternal life.

14 And this is the boldness we have in him, that if we ask anything according to his will, he hears us. [15]And if we know that he hears us in whatever we ask, we know that we have obtained the requests made of him. [16]If you see your brother or sister[g] committing what is not a mortal sin, you will ask, and God[h] will give life to such a one—to those whose sin is not mortal. There is sin that is mortal; I do not say that you should pray about that. [17]All wrongdoing is sin, but there is sin that is not mortal.

18 We know that those who are born of God do not sin, but the one who was born of God protects them, and the evil one does not touch them. [19]We know that we are God's children, and that the whole world lies under the power of the evil one. [20]And we know that the Son of God has come and has given us understanding so that we may know him who is true;[i] and we are in him who is true, in his Son Jesus Christ. He is the true God and eternal life.

21 Little children, keep yourselves from idols.[j]

---

a Other ancient authorities add *him*; others add *God*
b Gk *brothers*   c Gk *brother*   d Or *the Messiah*   e A few other ancient authorities read (with variations) [7]*There are three that testify in heaven, the Father, the Word, and the Holy Spirit, and these three are one.* [8]*And there are three that testify on earth:*   f Other ancient authorities read *in the Son*   g Gk *your brother*   h Gk *he* i Other ancient authorities read *know the true God*   j Other ancient authorities add *Amen*

For background on this letter, see the introduction to 1, 2, and 3 John before 1 John.

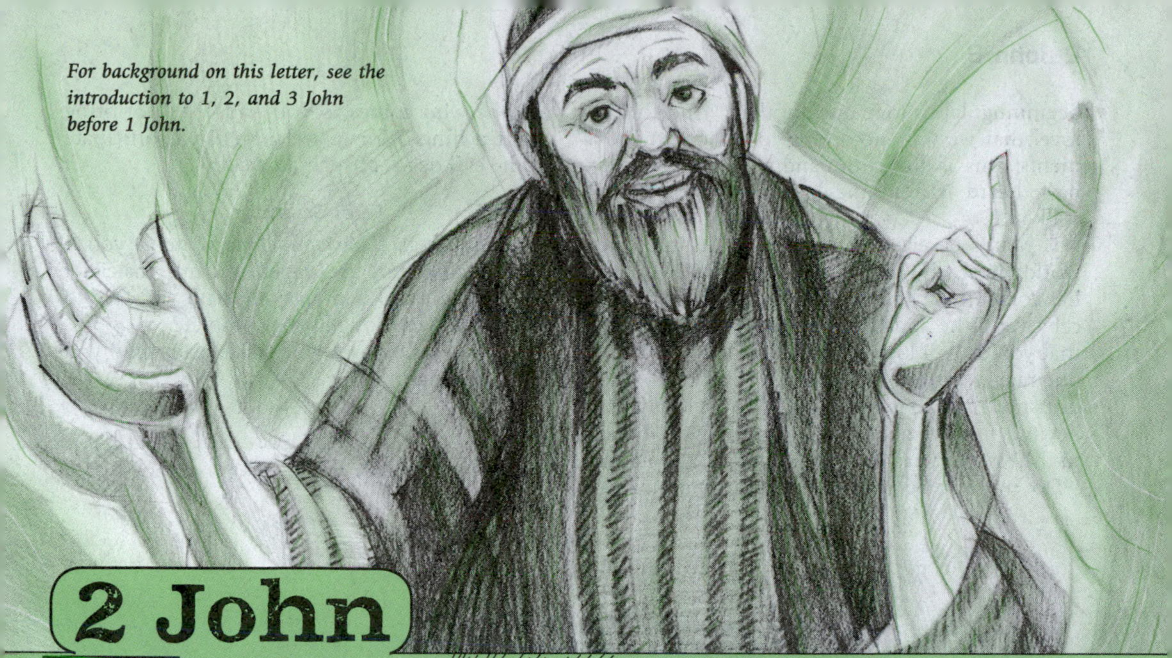

2 John

Salutation

1 The elder to the elect lady and her children,
whom I love in the truth, and not only I but also
all who know the truth, 2because of the truth that
abides in us and will be with us forever:
3 Grace, mercy, and peace will be with us
from God the Father and from[a] Jesus Christ, the
Father's Son, in truth and love.

Truth and Love

4 I was overjoyed to find some of your children walking in the truth, just as we have been
commanded by the Father. 5But now, dear lady, I
ask you, not as though I were writing you a new
commandment, but one we have had from the

a Other ancient authorities add *the Lord*

Live It!

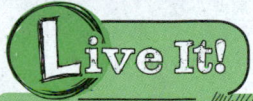

Unwelcome Guests

The author of Second John is warning a Christian community—called the elect lady and her children—about the false message of some "deceivers" (see the introduction to First, Second, and Third John, before First John). The author cautions the community not to have anything to do with such people, not even to let them into their homes (see 2 Jn, verses 10–11). Although the words sound harsh, the reasoning is sound.

Every day, we could be letting people with false messages into our homes "virtually" through television, books, music, the Internet, and magazines. Their false messages promote values and behaviors that are contrary to a healthy and holy way of life. Can these "guests" affect our attitudes and choices? They sure can, especially if we welcome them blindly without thinking about the impact of their messages.

- On a piece of paper or in your journal, identify the television shows, magazines, radio stations, and Internet sites that regularly visit your home. List the positive values and behaviors these guests display. Now list the negative ones. How do the lists compare?
- How can you manage your media exposure wisely in order to resist its negative influence?

beginning, let us love one another. [6]And this is love, that we walk according to his commandments; this is the commandment just as you have heard it from the beginning—you must walk in it.

7 Many deceivers have gone out into the world, those who do not confess that Jesus Christ has come in the flesh; any such person is the deceiver and the antichrist! [8]Be on your guard, so that you do not lose what we[a] have worked for, but may receive a full reward. [9]Everyone who does not abide in the teaching of Christ, but goes beyond it, does not have God; whoever abides in the teaching has both the Father and the Son. [10]Do not receive into the house or welcome anyone who comes to you and does not bring this teaching; [11]for to welcome is to participate in the evil deeds of such a person.

Final Greetings

12 Although I have much to write to you, I would rather not use paper and ink; instead I hope to come to you and talk with you face to face, so that our joy may be complete.

13 The children of your elect sister send you their greetings.[b]

---

a Other ancient authorities read *you*   b Other ancient authorities add *Amen*

3 John

For background on this letter, see the introduction to 1, 2, and 3 John before 1 John.

Live It!

Supporting the Ministry of Others

Gaius was a man of faith who opened his home to missionaries who were passing through his city. Though Gaius did not personally know these missionaries, he provided hospitality for them because he knew they were helping to spread the Good News. In Third John, the elder appeals to him to welcome his messenger, Demetrius, even when others refuse to do so.

Christians find many needs they cannot respond to by themselves. The story of Gaius shows how you can become a co-missionary with Christians who are ministering in some way you cannot. These may be ministers in your own parish or diocese, or a religious group that sends missionaries to other countries. You can offer them your hospitality, support them financially, or promote their work in your parish or community. Consider talking with your family about a specific ministry or missionary activity you can support together.

Salutation

1 The elder to the beloved Gaius, whom I love in truth.

Gaius Commended for His Hospitality

2 Beloved, I pray that all may go well with you and that you may be in good health, just as it is well with your soul. ³I was overjoyed when some of the friends*ᵃ* arrived and testified to your faithfulness to the truth, namely how you walk in the truth. ⁴I have no greater joy than this, to hear that my children are walking in the truth.

5 Beloved, you do faithfully whatever you do for the friends,*ᵃ* even though they are strangers to you; ⁶they have testified to your love before the church. You will do well to send them on in a manner worthy of God; ⁷for they began their journey for the sake of Christ,*ᵇ* accepting no support from non-believers.*ᶜ* ⁸Therefore we ought to support such people, so that we may become co-workers with the truth.

Diotrephes and Demetrius

9 I have written something to the church; but Diotrephes, who likes to put himself first, does not acknowledge our authority. ¹⁰So if I come, I will call attention to what he is doing in spreading false charges against us. And not content with

---

a Gk brothers   *b* for the sake of the name   *c* Gk the Gentiles

1473

those charges, he refuses to welcome the friends,[a] and even prevents those who want to do so and expels them from the church.

11 Beloved, do not imitate what is evil but imitate what is good. Whoever does good is from God; whoever does evil has not seen God. [12]Everyone has testified favorably about Demetrius, and so has the truth itself. We also testify for him,[b] and you know that our testimony is true.

Final Greetings

13 I have much to write to you, but I would rather not write with pen and ink; [14]instead I hope to see you soon, and we will talk together face to face.

15 Peace to you. The friends send you their greetings. Greet the friends there, each by name.

---

a Gk brothers   b Gk lacks for him

They pretend to be part of your group, but all they really do is cause trouble. They claim to have all the right answers, but they won't listen to other people's opinions. They flatter people to get what they want, but then they grumble and complain behind people's backs. They cause division wherever they go. Do you know people like this? Maybe you even find yourself acting like them sometimes. The Letter of Jude has some things to say about "these people."

At a Glance

- **Verses 1–2.** an opening
- **Verses 3–23.** warnings about judgment
- **Verses 24–25.** a closing

Quick Facts

Inspired Author: unknown, traditionally thought to be Jude, the brother of James
Date Written: maybe from AD 80 to 90
Audience: unknown

In Depth

The purpose of the Letter of Jude is to warn churches about false teachers who come into the Christian community with lies and tricks, making trouble wherever they go. The author recalls stories from the past in which God punished such people: stories about the Egyptians who opposed God's plan to bring the Hebrew people to the Promised Land; the immoral people of Sodom and Gomorrah; the angels who revolted against God; and Cain, who killed his brother. The author also encourages people to build themselves in the faith. Finally, the author cautions Christians to ignore ungodly people—unless those people truly want to change, in which case, Christians should be examples of the mercy of Jesus Christ.

Notice that this letter includes some terms that are unfamiliar to modern Christians or that have different meanings today. For instance, the term *holy ones* refers to the members of the Christian community, and a *love feast* is a celebration of the Eucharist.

The message of the Letter of Jude is difficult to understand for many reasons. We know almost nothing about who wrote it, to whom it was written, when it was written, and what it is really addressing—except from hints in the letter itself. Tradition says that the author is Jude, the brother of James and Jesus as mentioned in Mark 6:3 (the name Jude is a form of Judas). The word *brother* was used to express the relationship between a close sibling, a cousin, or other clan member, and even a spiritual relationship with someone of the same religion.

Jude

Salutation

1 Jude,*a* a servant*b* of Jesus Christ and brother of James,

To those who are called, who are beloved*c* in*d* God the Father and kept safe for*d* Jesus Christ:

2 May mercy, peace, and love be yours in abundance.

Occasion of the Letter

3 Beloved, while eagerly preparing to write to you about the salvation we share, I find it necessary to write and appeal to you to contend for the faith that was once for all entrusted to the saints. *4*For certain intruders have stolen in among you, people who long ago were designated for this condemnation as ungodly, who pervert the grace of our God into licentiousness and deny our only Master and Lord, Jesus Christ.*e*

Judgment on False Teachers

5 Now I desire to remind you, though you are fully informed, that the Lord, who once for all saved*f* a people out of the land of Egypt, afterward destroyed those who did not believe. *6*And the angels who did not keep their own position, but left their proper dwelling, he has kept in eternal chains in deepest darkness for the judgment of the great day. *7*Likewise, Sodom and Gomorrah and the surrounding cities, which, in the same manner as they, indulged in sexual immorality and pursued unnatural lust,*g* serve as an example by undergoing a punishment of eternal fire.

8 Yet in the same way these dreamers also defile the flesh, reject authority, and slander the glorious ones.*h* *9*But when the archangel Michael contended with the devil and disputed about the body of Moses, he did not dare to bring a condemnation of slander*i* against him, but said, "The Lord rebuke you!" *10*But these people slander whatever they do not understand, and they are destroyed by those things that, like irrational animals, they know by instinct. *11*Woe to them! For they go the way of Cain, and abandon themselves to Balaam's error for the sake of gain, and perish in Korah's rebellion. *12*These are blemishes*j* on your love-feasts, while they feast with you without fear, feeding themselves.*k* They are waterless clouds carried along by the winds; autumn trees without fruit, twice dead, uprooted; *13*wild waves of the sea, casting up the foam of their own shame; wandering stars, for whom the deepest darkness has been reserved forever.

14 It was also about these that Enoch, in the seventh generation from Adam, prophesied, saying, "See, the Lord is coming*l* with ten thousands of his holy ones, *15*to execute judgment on all, and to convict everyone of all the deeds of ungodliness that they have committed in such an ungodly way, and of all the harsh things that ungodly

---

a Gk *Judas* *b* Gk *slave* *c* Other ancient authorities read *sanctified* *d* Or *by* *e* Or *the only Master and our Lord Jesus Christ* *f* Other ancient authorities read *though you were once for all fully informed, that Jesus* (or *Joshua*) *who saved* *g* Gk *went after other flesh* *h* Or *angels*; Gk *glories* *i* Or *condemnation for blasphemy* *j* Or *reefs* *k* Or *without fear. They are shepherds who care only for themselves* *l* Gk *came*

sinners have spoken against him." [16]These are grumblers and malcontents; they indulge their own lusts; they are bombastic in speech, flattering people to their own advantage.

Warnings and Exhortations

17 But you, beloved, must remember the predictions of the apostles of our Lord Jesus Christ; [18]for they said to you, "In the last time there will be scoffers, indulging their own ungodly lusts." [19]It is these worldly people, devoid of the Spirit, who are causing divisions. [20]But you, beloved, build yourselves up on your most holy faith; pray in the Holy Spirit; [21]keep yourselves in the love of God; look forward to the mercy of our Lord Jesus Christ that leads to[a] eternal life. [22]And have mercy on some who are wavering; [23]save others by snatching them out of the fire; and have mercy on still others with fear, hating even the tunic defiled by their bodies.[b]

Benediction

24 Now to him who is able to keep you from falling, and to make you stand without blemish in the presence of his glory with rejoicing, [25]to the only God our Savior, through Jesus Christ our Lord, be glory, majesty, power, and authority, before all time and now and forever. Amen.

---

a Gk *Christ to*   b Gk *by the flesh*. The Greek text of verses 22–23 is uncertain at several points

Have you ever shown people a text message from a friend and they just couldn't seem to understand it? You may understand it perfectly, but others cannot because they weren't part of your conversation. Similarly, it is also hard to understand the message in the Book of Revelation. The symbols and visions that appear in this book are not always clear. Some people mistakenly think it is a frightening book about the end of the world. However, for the early Christian community and the Church today, the Book of Revelation is a message of hope that proclaims God's ultimate triumph over evil in history.

The Revelation to John

At a Glance

- **Chapters 1–3.** an introduction, and letters to the seven churches

- **Chapters 4–11.** visions of God's throne, the Lamb, the seven seals, and the seven trumpets

- **Chapters 12–14.** visions of the dragon and the two beasts

- **Chapters 15–18.** visions of the seven plagues, and the fall of Babylon (Rome)

- **Chapters 19–22.** visions of the victory of Christ and the end of history

Quick Facts

Inspired Author: a Jewish-Christian prophet named John
Date: probably from AD 92 to 96
Audience: Christian churches in Asia Minor during a time of Roman persecution

In Depth

This book is unique in that the author, who calls himself John, received a series of visions from God that form most of the content. The recorded visions take the form of apocalyptic literature (see "Apocalyptic Literature," near Daniel, chapters 7–10) and are full of symbols. These symbols are like the language of a secret club. You use it when you want to keep people who do not belong to your club from understanding what you are saying.

Why was it important that the meaning of the visions be known to the Christian communities only? Because the Christians still remembered their persecution under the Roman emperor Nero Caesar (AD 54–68) and were suffering a new persecution under the Roman emperor Domitian (AD 81–96). This "coded language" allowed John to criticize the Roman emperor and empire without necessarily putting his readers at risk of persecution or even death. John himself was exiled to an island off Asia Minor for preaching the Gospel (see Rev 1:9).

Once the symbols are understood, it is clear that the Book of Revelation offers hope to a church under persecution. It expresses belief in God's justice and God's victory over evil—an evil that at John's time was embodied in the Roman Empire. But it also expresses the great Christian belief that God will ultimately be victorious, at the end of time, when Christ will come again in his full glory and power. It is a mistake for Christians to try to decipher Revelation as a prediction as to when and how that final coming will occur. But they can take great joy and hope in the promise of a new world where God will wipe away every tear, and suffering and death will be no more (see 21:4).

Revelation

Introduction and Salutation

1 The revelation of Jesus Christ, which God gave him to show his servants[a] what must soon take place; he made[b] it known by sending his angel to his servant[c] John, [2]who testified to the word of God and to the testimony of Jesus Christ, even to all that he saw.

[3] Blessed is the one who reads aloud the words of the prophecy, and blessed are those who hear and who keep what is written in it; for the time is near.

[4] John to the seven churches that are in Asia:

Grace to you and peace from him who is and who was and who is to come, and from the seven spirits who are before his throne, [5]and from Jesus Christ, the faithful witness, the firstborn of the dead, and the ruler of the kings of the earth.

To him who loves us and freed[d] us from our sins by his blood, [6]and made[b] us to be a kingdom, priests serving[e] his God and Father, to him be glory and dominion forever and ever. Amen.

[7] Look! He is coming with the clouds;
    every eye will see him,
    even those who pierced him;
        and on his account all the tribes of the earth
            will wail.
So it is to be. Amen.

[8] "I am the Alpha and the Omega," says the Lord God, who is and who was and who is to come, the Almighty.

A Vision of Christ

[9] I, John, your brother who share with you in Jesus the persecution and the kingdom and the patient endurance, was on the island called Patmos because of the word of God and the testimony of Jesus.[f] [10]I was in the spirit[g] on the Lord's day, and I heard behind me a loud voice like a trumpet [11]saying, "Write in a book what you see and send it to the seven churches, to Ephesus, to Smyrna, to Pergamum, to Thyatira, to Sardis, to Philadelphia, and to Laodicea."

[12] Then I turned to see whose voice it was that spoke to me, and on turning I saw seven golden lampstands, [13]and in the midst of the lampstands I saw one like the Son of Man, clothed with a long robe and with a golden sash across his chest. [14]His head and his hair were white as white wool, white as snow; his eyes were like a flame of fire, [15]his feet were like burnished bronze, refined as in a furnace, and his voice was like the sound of many waters. [16]In his right hand he held seven stars, and from his mouth came a sharp, two-edged sword, and his face was like the sun shining with full force.

[17] When I saw him, I fell at his feet as though dead. But he placed his right hand on me, saying, "Do not be afraid; I am the first and the last, [18]and

---

a Gk slaves   b Gk and he made   c Gk slave   d Other ancient authorities read washed   e Gk priests to   f Or testimony to Jesus   g Or in the Spirit

the living one. I was dead, and see, I am alive forever and ever; and I have the keys of Death and of Hades. 19Now write what you have seen, what is, and what is to take place after this. 20As for the mystery of the seven stars that you saw in my right hand, and the seven golden lampstands: the seven stars are the angels of the seven churches, and the seven lampstands are the seven churches.

The Message to Ephesus

2 "To the angel of the church in Ephesus write: These are the words of him who holds the

The Alpha and the Omega

In the first chapter of Revelation, John introduces God's message to the seven churches in Asia. After explaining that he received the message through a vision and that an angel instructed him to communicate it to them, John describes a vision of Christ.

A vision is like a dream. It cannot be interpreted literally; we must seek its deep meaning and be open to its message. For example, in the vision of Revelation 1:12–16, a magnificently robed Christ stands amid seven lampstands. The deeper meaning is that the resurrected Jesus in all his glory and power is watching over the seven churches. Here's another example: Revelation 1:8 has God saying, "I am the Alpha and the Omega." In the Greek alphabet, *alpha* is the first letter, and *omega* is the last letter. This passage is telling us that God and Jesus are in control of all history, from its beginning to its end.

In your prayer, think of any current event that frightens you or any harassments you experience because of your faith or moral principles. See the image of the risen Christ described by John. Feel Jesus lovingly touching your head. Hear Jesus telling you that history is always in God's hands. Let God strengthen your faith and renew your hope with this wonderful revelation of God's love.

▶ Rev 1:7–20

seven stars in his right hand, who walks among the seven golden lampstands:

2 "I know your works, your toil and your patient endurance. I know that you cannot tolerate evildoers; you have tested those who claim to be apostles but are not, and have found them to be false. 3I also know that you are enduring patiently and bearing up for the sake of my name, and that you have not grown weary. 4But I have this against you, that you have abandoned the love you had at first. 5Remember then from what you have fallen; repent, and do the works you did at first. If not, I will come to you and remove your lampstand from its place, unless you repent. 6Yet this is to your credit: you hate the works of the Nicolaitans, which I also hate. 7Let anyone who has an ear listen to what the Spirit is saying to the churches. To everyone who conquers, I will give permission to eat from the tree of life that is in the paradise of God.

The Message to Smyrna

8 "And to the angel of the church in Smyrna write: These are the words of the first and the last, who was dead and came to life:

9 "I know your affliction and your poverty, even though you are rich. I know the slander on the part of those who say that they are Jews and are not, but are a synagogue of Satan. 10Do not fear what you are about to suffer. Beware, the devil is about to throw some of you into prison so that you may be tested, and for ten days you will have affliction. Be faithful until death, and I will give you the crown of life. 11Let anyone who has an ear listen to what the Spirit is saying to the churches. Whoever conquers will not be harmed by the second death.

The Message to Pergamum

12 "And to the angel of the church in Pergamum write: These are the words of him who has the sharp two-edged sword:

13 "I know where you are living, where Satan's throne is. Yet you are holding fast to my name, and you did not deny your faith in me[a] even in the days of Antipas my witness, my faithful one, who was killed among you, where Satan lives. 14But I have a few things against you: you have some there who hold to the teaching of Balaam, who taught Balak to put a stumbling block before the people of Israel, so that they would eat food sacrificed to idols and practice fornication. 15So you also have some who hold to the teaching of the Nicolaitans. 16Repent then. If not,

a Or deny my faith

I will come to you soon and make war against them with the sword of my mouth. [17]Let anyone who has an ear listen to what the Spirit is saying to the churches. To everyone who conquers I will give some of the hidden manna, and I will give a white stone, and on the white stone is written a new name that no one knows except the one who receives it.

The Message to Thyatira

18 "And to the angel of the church in Thyatira write: These are the words of the Son of God, who has eyes like a flame of fire, and whose feet are like burnished bronze:

19 "I know your works—your love, faith, service, and patient endurance. I know that your last works are greater than the first. [20]But I have this against you: you tolerate that woman Jezebel, who calls herself a prophet and is teaching and beguiling my servants[a] to practice fornication and to eat food sacrificed to idols. [21]I gave her time to repent, but she refuses to repent of her fornication. [22]Beware, I am throwing her on a bed, and those who commit adultery with her I am throwing into great distress, unless they repent of her doings; [23]and I will strike her children dead. And all the churches will know that I am the one who searches minds and hearts, and I will give to each of you as your works deserve. [24]But to the rest of you in Thyatira, who do not hold this teaching, who have not learned what some call 'the deep things of Satan,' to you I say, I do not lay on you any other burden; [25]only hold fast to what you have until I come. [26]To everyone who conquers and continues to do my works to the end,

I will give authority over the nations;
[27] to rule[b] them with an iron rod,
    as when clay pots are shattered—
[28]even as I also received authority from my Father. To the one who conquers I will also give the morning star. [29]Let anyone who has an ear listen to what the Spirit is saying to the churches.

The Message to Sardis

3 "And to the angel of the church in Sardis write: These are the words of him who has the seven spirits of God and the seven stars:

"I know your works; you have a name of being alive, but you are dead. [2]Wake up, and strengthen what remains and is on the point of death, for I have not found your works perfect in the sight of my God. [3]Remember then what you received and heard; obey it, and repent. If you do not wake up, I will come like a thief, and you will not know at what hour I will come to you. [4]Yet you have still

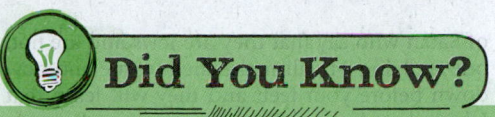

Did You Know?

The Seven Churches

The messages addressed to the seven churches in Asia Minor (modern Greece and Turkey) are not predictions of the future. Like the prophets of the Old Testament who called Israel to return to the Covenant, John calls these communities to deeper faith. Two churches are praised (Smyrna and Philadelphia), two are scolded (Sardis and Laodicea), and the remaining three receive both praise and criticism. The churches are scolded because they have tolerated leaders whose teaching contradicts the true Gospel message and because their faith has become "lukewarm," lacking the devotion it had when they first became Christians.

If the author of Revelation wrote such a prophecy to your local church, what would he praise and what would he criticize? Is your community on fire in living the Gospel, or is it lukewarm in its commitment?

▶ **Rev 2:1—3:22**

a few persons in Sardis who have not soiled their clothes; they will walk with me, dressed in white, for they are worthy. [5]If you conquer, you will be clothed like them in white robes, and I will not blot your name out of the book of life; I will confess your name before my Father and before his angels. [6]Let anyone who has an ear listen to what the Spirit is saying to the churches.

The Message to Philadelphia

7 "And to the angel of the church in Philadelphia write:
These are the words of the holy one, the true
    one,
    who has the key of David,
    who opens and no one will shut,
        who shuts and no one opens:
8 "I know your works. Look, I have set before you an open door, which no one is able to shut. I know that you have but little power, and yet you have kept my word and have not denied my name. [9]I will make those of the synagogue

a Gk *slaves*   b Or *to shepherd*

of Satan who say that they are Jews and are not, but are lying—I will make them come and bow down before your feet, and they will learn that I have loved you. [10]Because you have kept my word of patient endurance, I will keep you from the hour of trial that is coming on the whole world to test the inhabitants of the earth. [11]I am coming soon; hold fast to what you have, so that no one may seize your crown. [12]If you conquer, I will make you a pillar in the temple of my God; you will never go out of it. I will write on you the name of my God, and the name of the city of my God, the new Jerusalem that comes down from my God out of heaven, and my own new name. [13]Let anyone who has an ear listen to what the Spirit is saying to the churches.

The Message to Laodicea

14 "And to the angel of the church in Laodicea write: The words of the Amen, the faithful and true witness, the origin[a] of God's creation:

15 "I know your works; you are neither cold nor hot. I wish that you were either cold or hot. [16]So, because you are lukewarm, and neither cold nor hot, I am about to spit you out of my mouth. [17]For you say, 'I am rich, I have

prospered, and I need nothing.' You do not realize that you are wretched, pitiable, poor, blind, and naked. [18]Therefore I counsel you to buy from me gold refined by fire so that you may be rich; and white robes to clothe you and to keep the shame of your nakedness from being seen; and salve to anoint your eyes so that you may see. [19]I reprove and discipline those whom I love. Be earnest, therefore, and repent. [20]Listen! I am standing at the door, knocking; if you hear my voice and open the door, I will come in to you and eat with you, and you with me. [21]To the one

---

a Or *beginning*

Jesus Christ Is the Lord of History

After the messages to the churches in Asia, John presents several visions that reveal God's action in history. Read Revelation 4:1–11. The vision of God's throne is the background of the whole Book of Revelation. It symbolizes God's authority over history. The vision is enhanced by a heavenly worship in which God is proclaimed and praised:

> "Holy, holy, holy,
>   the Lord God the Almighty,
>   who was and is and is to come."
>
>   (Rev 4:8)

Read 5:1–14. The vision continues. Two symbols stand out: a sealed scroll and a lamb. God holds a scroll, whose meaning was hidden to the Christian communities in their persecution. A lamb appears. It is the risen Jesus, carrying in his body the signs of his Passion. He receives the scroll from God. He is the only one who can open the scroll and reveal the mystery of death and life.

Read both visions again and experience the honor, glory, and power of Christ. Let these visions reinforce your faith and renew your hope every time you wonder about the meaning of an event you cannot make sense of.

▶ **Revelation, chapters 4–5**

Opening the Door

The image in Revelation 3:20 inspired an artist to depict our relationship with Christ in a popular painting. The painting shows a door overgrown with vines. The door obviously has not been opened in a long time. As you examine it, you realize it has no outside latch or knob—it can be opened only from the inside. At the door stands Jesus, knocking—not pounding, just knocking patiently.

What is your relationship with Christ like right now? Is the door of your life open to let Christ in, or has it been closed for a while? Jesus will not force his way into your life. Jesus seeks a close friendship with you, and real friendship—real love—always involves a free choice. No one can choose to open the door but you.

▶ **Rev 3:14–22**

who conquers I will give a place with me on my throne, just as I myself conquered and sat down with my Father on his throne. ²²Let anyone who has an ear listen to what the Spirit is saying to the churches."

The Heavenly Worship

4 After this I looked, and there in heaven a door stood open! And the first voice, which I had heard speaking to me like a trumpet, said, "Come up here, and I will show you what must take place after this." ²At once I was in the spirit,ᵃ and there in heaven stood a throne, with one seated on the throne! ³And the one seated there looks like jasper and carnelian, and around the throne is a rainbow that looks like an emerald. ⁴Around the throne are twenty-four thrones, and seated on the thrones are twenty-four elders, dressed in white robes, with golden crowns on their heads. ⁵Coming from the throne are flashes of lightning, and rumblings and peals of thunder, and in front of the throne burn seven flaming torches, which are the seven spirits of God; ⁶and in front of the throne there is something like a sea of glass, like crystal.

Around the throne, and on each side of the throne, are four living creatures, full of eyes in front and behind: ⁷the first living creature like a lion, the second living creature like an ox, the third living creature with a face like a human face, and the fourth living creature like a flying eagle. ⁸And the four living creatures, each of them with six wings, are full of eyes all around and inside. Day and night without ceasing they sing,

"Holy, holy, holy,
  the Lord God the Almighty,
    who was and is and is to come."

⁹And whenever the living creatures give glory and honor and thanks to the one who is seated on the throne, who lives forever and ever, ¹⁰the twenty-four elders fall before the one who is seated on the throne and worship the one who lives forever and ever; they cast their crowns before the throne, singing,

¹¹ "You are worthy, our Lord and God,
  to receive glory and honor and power,
  for you created all things,
    and by your will they existed and were
      created."

The Scroll and the Lamb

5 Then I saw in the right hand of the one seated on the throne a scroll written on the inside and on the back, sealedᵇ with seven seals; ²and I saw a mighty angel proclaiming with a loud voice, "Who is worthy to open the scroll and

break its seals?" ³And no one in heaven or on earth or under the earth was able to open the scroll or to look into it. ⁴And I began to weep bitterly because no one was found worthy to open the scroll or to look into it. ⁵Then one of the elders said to me, "Do not weep. See, the Lion of the tribe of Judah, the Root of David, has conquered, so that he can open the scroll and its seven seals."

6 Then I saw between the throne and the four living creatures and among the elders a Lamb standing as if it had been slaughtered, having seven horns and seven eyes, which are the seven spirits of God sent out into all the earth. ⁷He went and took the scroll from the right hand of

---

ᵃ Or *in the Spirit*   ᵇ Or *written on the inside, and sealed on the back*

Enthusiastic Praise!

Over and over in John's vision of heaven, we find enthusiastic praise being offered to God, or to the Lamb of God, who is Christ Jesus. There are angels, incense, fantastic creatures, jewels, gold, elders, white-robed martyrs, and a crowd too great to number. The scenes of this vision inspire us to add our voice to theirs, to praise the majesty of God and the saving sacrifice of Jesus Christ.

In some Christian traditions, including some Catholic traditions, loud, spontaneous praise of God is common. However, for other Catholics and Christians, praise is also expressed through more solemn prayers and music. Whatever our expression, we should be enthusiastic with our praise!

How does the vision of the "thousands, singing with full voice" in Revelation 5:11–12 encourage you to be more bold in your praise of God? Can you sing out more loudly in Mass? Can you participate more from your heart in saying common prayers with others? In your private prayer, can you praise God without asking for anything or using memorized prayers?

▶ **Rev 4:1—5:14**

the one who was seated on the throne. [8]When he had taken the scroll, the four living creatures and the twenty-four elders fell before the Lamb, each holding a harp and golden bowls full of incense, which are the prayers of the saints. [9]They sing a new song:

"You are worthy to take the scroll
   and to open its seals,
for you were slaughtered and by your blood you
     ransomed for God
   saints from[a] every tribe and language and
      people and nation;
[10] you have made them to be a kingdom and
   priests serving[b] our God,
   and they will reign on earth."

11 Then I looked, and I heard the voice of many angels surrounding the throne and the living creatures and the elders; they numbered myriads of myriads and thousands of thousands, [12]singing with full voice,

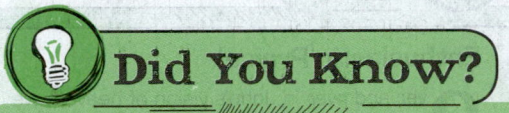

Did You Know?

Symbolic Numbers and Colors

To understand the Book of Revelation, we need to understand the symbolism of its numbers and colors. The numbers seven and twelve symbolize fullness or perfection. The number four symbolizes universality (as in the four compass directions). The number one thousand symbolizes a multitude or a quantity too big to count. Thus, the twenty-four elders (see Rev 4:4) represent the perfection of the twelve Tribes of Israel and the Twelve Apostles. The Lamb with horns and eyes (see 5:6) represents the risen Christ, who has the fullness of power (seven horns) and perfect knowledge (seven eyes). The 144,000 who will be saved (see 7:4) represent a chosen multitude too big to count, because 144,000 equals 12 times 12 times 1,000.

The color white symbolizes victory, and red symbolizes bloodshed. Thus, the people who are slaughtered and given white robes (see 6:9–11) are the martyrs, who gave up their lives for their faith. They are victorious in martyrdom because God raised them to eternal life.

▶ Rev 4:1—7:17

"Worthy is the Lamb that was slaughtered
   to receive power and wealth and wisdom and
     might
   and honor and glory and blessing!"
[13]Then I heard every creature in heaven and on earth and under the earth and in the sea, and all that is in them, singing,

"To the one seated on the throne and to the
   Lamb
   be blessing and honor and glory and might
   forever and ever!"
[14]And the four living creatures said, "Amen!" And the elders fell down and worshiped.

The Seven Seals

6 Then I saw the Lamb open one of the seven seals, and I heard one of the four living creatures call out, as with a voice of thunder, "Come!"[c] [2]I looked, and there was a white horse! Its rider had a bow; a crown was given to him, and he came out conquering and to conquer.

3 When he opened the second seal, I heard the second living creature call out, "Come!"[c] [4]And out came[d] another horse, bright red; its rider was permitted to take peace from the earth, so that people would slaughter one another; and he was given a great sword.

5 When he opened the third seal, I heard the third living creature call out, "Come!"[c] I looked, and there was a black horse! Its rider held a pair of scales in his hand, [6]and I heard what seemed to be a voice in the midst of the four living creatures saying, "A quart of wheat for a day's pay,[e] and three quarts of barley for a day's pay,[e] but do not damage the olive oil and the wine!"

7 When he opened the fourth seal, I heard the voice of the fourth living creature call out, "Come!"[c] [8]I looked and there was a pale green horse! Its rider's name was Death, and Hades followed with him; they were given authority over a fourth of the earth, to kill with sword, famine, and pestilence, and by the wild animals of the earth.

9 When he opened the fifth seal, I saw under the altar the souls of those who had been slaughtered for the word of God and for the testimony they had given; [10]they cried out with a loud voice, "Sovereign Lord, holy and true, how long will it be before you judge and avenge our blood on the inhabitants of the earth?" [11]They were each given a white robe and told to rest a little longer, until the number would be complete

a Gk ransomed for God from   b Gk priests to   c Or "Go!"
d Or went   e Gk a denarius

both of their fellow servants[a] and of their brothers and sisters,[b] who were soon to be killed as they themselves had been killed.

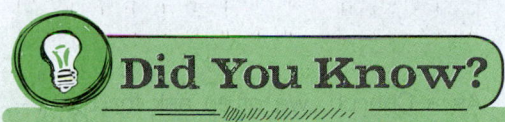

Did You Know?

The Seven Seals and Seven Trumpets

The vision continues. In chapters 6–8 of Revelation, the Lamb opens the seven seals on the scroll and thus reveals the great forces in salvation history. The opening of the first four seals reveals the four horses of the apocalypse that bring conquest, strife, famine, and plagues. These are the things that throughout history have made people yearn for God's salvation.

The opening of the fifth seal reveals the souls of the martyrs, who demand justice. Their white robes indicate that they are already with the risen Christ. They are waiting for other martyrs, but this stage will end soon.

The opening of the sixth seal reveals how God will get justice for the martyrs. History will change, and all people, even the powerful, will suffer. The visions of the census and of the great crowd in 7:1–17 reveal the destiny of Christians. The vision contains many reminders of the Exodus story. After this, a multitude that cannot be counted, from all nations, tribes, peoples, and languages, will experience God's salvation and sing of God's glory.

Finally, the Lamb opens the last seal. Seven more trumpets are revealed. When they are blown by angels, a new series of plagues is released (see 8:6—9:21). One-third of the people are destroyed by these plagues so that those remaining might repent. But in spite of these warnings, many people do not change.

Apocalyptic writing, as in the Book of Revelation, used symbolic language because it was addressed to Christians who were being persecuted. Its meaning could not be taken at face value but held a deeper meaning for those who believed. This vision tells us that no matter what evil besets us, God saves the faithful.

▶ Revelation, chapters 6–9

12 When he opened the sixth seal, I looked, and there came a great earthquake; the sun became black as sackcloth, the full moon became like blood, [13]and the stars of the sky fell to the earth as the fig tree drops its winter fruit when shaken by a gale. [14]The sky vanished like a scroll rolling itself up, and every mountain and island was removed from its place. [15]Then the kings of the earth and the magnates and the generals and the rich and the powerful, and everyone, slave and free, hid in the caves and among the rocks of the mountains, [16]calling to the mountains and rocks, "Fall on us and hide us from the face of the one seated on the throne and from the wrath of the Lamb; [17]for the great day of their wrath has come, and who is able to stand?"

The 144,000 of Israel Sealed

7 After this I saw four angels standing at the four corners of the earth, holding back the four winds of the earth so that no wind could blow on earth or sea or against any tree. [2]I saw another angel ascending from the rising of the sun, having the seal of the living God, and he called with a loud voice to the four angels who had been given power to damage earth and sea, [3]saying, "Do not damage the earth or the sea or the trees, until we have marked the servants[a] of our God with a seal on their foreheads."

4 And I heard the number of those who were sealed, one hundred forty-four thousand, sealed out of every tribe of the people of Israel:

5 From the tribe of Judah twelve thousand sealed,

from the tribe of Reuben twelve thousand,
from the tribe of Gad twelve thousand,

6 from the tribe of Asher twelve thousand,
from the tribe of Naphtali twelve thousand,
from the tribe of Manasseh twelve thousand,

7 from the tribe of Simeon twelve thousand,
from the tribe of Levi twelve thousand,
from the tribe of Issachar twelve thousand,

8 from the tribe of Zebulun twelve thousand,
from the tribe of Joseph twelve thousand,
from the tribe of Benjamin twelve thousand sealed.

The Multitude from Every Nation

9 After this I looked, and there was a great multitude that no one could count, from every nation, from all tribes and peoples and languages, standing before the throne and before the Lamb, robed in white, with palm branches

---

a Gk *slaves*   *b* Gk *brothers*

✝ Catholic Connection

The Communion of Saints

What do you do when things get really difficult? John is answering that question for his readers. John describes a looming ordeal and how the faithful will be marked on the forehead as a sign of God's protection. This sign does not remove them from the trials ahead but calls them to trust in God during the trials. John then describes a multitude in heaven that have already survived the ordeal and remained faithful to God. The important message for John's audience is how those in heaven survived. The angel says that they were made pure through the blood of the Lamb. That is, they united their lives with the Passion, death, and Resurrection of Jesus Christ and remained faithful throughout.

It is the union of those on earth facing life's ordeals and those already in heaven, along with those who have died and are being purified, that make up the Church. The Church refers to this body of believers as the communion of saints. As a communion of saints, we are all united to one another, and the good that any one of us does benefits all of us. Therefore, our prayers for the dead are effective, just as the prayers of those in heaven help us on earth.

As a Church, we often ask for the prayers of those in heaven, especially the saints—those who have been canonized or officially recognized by the Church. These women and men lived extraordinary, often heroic, lives of faith. The process of canonization can take many years, even centuries. During the process, the Church investigates the individual's life, writings, and any miracles attributed to her or him. If there is sufficient evidence of the person's holiness, the Church beatifies the individual, which is an intermediate step toward canonization. Then over time, if there are more confirmed miracles, the Church may then decide to canonize the person, making her or him an official saint.

The saints also serve as models for how we are to face trials and remain faithful throughout our lives. Just like the saints and the faithful in John's vision, we too are called to resist sin and offer our lives to God, even if it means facing the discipline of suffering. We are called to be the new generation of witnesses—the saints of our day whose example calls and strengthens others on the journey.

▶ **Rev 7:2–14**
Catechism, nos. 946–962

in their hands. ¹⁰They cried out in a loud voice, saying,

"Salvation belongs to our God who is seated on
the throne, and to the Lamb!"

¹¹And all the angels stood around the throne and around the elders and the four living creatures, and they fell on their faces before the throne and worshiped God, ¹²singing,

"Amen! Blessing and glory and wisdom
and thanksgiving and honor
and power and might
be to our God forever and ever! Amen."

13 Then one of the elders addressed me, saying, "Who are these, robed in white, and where have they come from?" ¹⁴I said to him, "Sir, you are the one that knows." Then he said to me, "These are they who have come out of the great ordeal; they have washed their robes and made them white in the blood of the Lamb.

¹⁵ For this reason they are before the throne of
God,
and worship him day and night within his
temple,
and the one who is seated on the throne will
shelter them.

¹⁶ They will hunger no more, and thirst no more;
the sun will not strike them,
nor any scorching heat;

¹⁷ for the Lamb at the center of the throne will be
their shepherd,
and he will guide them to springs of the water
of life,
and God will wipe away every tear from their
eyes."

The Seventh Seal and the Golden Censer

8 When the Lamb opened the seventh seal, there was silence in heaven for about half an hour. ²And I saw the seven angels who stand before God, and seven trumpets were given to them.

3 Another angel with a golden censer came and stood at the altar; he was given a great quantity of incense to offer with the prayers of all the saints on the golden altar that is before the throne. ⁴And the smoke of the incense, with the prayers of the saints, rose before God from the hand of the angel. ⁵Then the angel took the censer and filled it with fire from the altar and threw it on the earth; and there were peals of thunder, rumblings, flashes of lightning, and an earthquake.

The Seven Trumpets

6 Now the seven angels who had the seven trumpets made ready to blow them.

Pray It!

Sing God's Glory

The Book of Revelation contains beautiful prayers of praise. Among them are the hymn to the Lamb (see 5:9–14), the hymn of the multitude from every nation (see 7:10–17), the song of the Lamb (see 15:3–4), and the victory song (see 19:1–8).

In your prayer, read these prayers slowly and carefully. Imagine the awe-inspiring scenes of God's glory they describe. Quietly reflect on how you have experienced the glory and power of God in your life. Look at the events you experience day to day; can you find the extraordinary in the ordinary? End your reflection by letting these songs inspire your own prayer of praise to God.

▶ **Rev 7:10–17**

7 The first angel blew his trumpet, and there came hail and fire, mixed with blood, and they were hurled to the earth; and a third of the earth was burned up, and a third of the trees were burned up, and all green grass was burned up.

8 The second angel blew his trumpet, and something like a great mountain, burning with fire, was thrown into the sea. ⁹A third of the sea became blood, a third of the living creatures in the sea died, and a third of the ships were destroyed.

10 The third angel blew his trumpet, and a great star fell from heaven, blazing like a torch, and it fell on a third of the rivers and on the springs of water. ¹¹The name of the star is Wormwood. A third of the waters became wormwood, and many died from the water, because it was made bitter.

12 The fourth angel blew his trumpet, and a third of the sun was struck, and a third of the moon, and a third of the stars, so that a third of their light was darkened; a third of the day was kept from shining, and likewise the night.

13 Then I looked, and I heard an eagle crying with a loud voice as it flew in midheaven, "Woe, woe, woe to the inhabitants of the earth, at the blasts of the other trumpets that the three angels are about to blow!"

9 And the fifth angel blew his trumpet, and I saw a star that had fallen from heaven to earth, and he was given the key to the shaft of the bottomless pit; ²he opened the shaft of the bottomless pit, and from the shaft rose smoke like the smoke of a great furnace, and the sun and the air were darkened with the smoke from the shaft. ³Then from the smoke came locusts on the earth, and they were given authority like the authority of scorpions of the earth. ⁴They were told not to damage the grass of the earth or any green growth or any tree, but only those people who do not have the seal of God on their foreheads. ⁵They were allowed to torture them for five months, but not to kill them, and their torture was like the torture of a scorpion when it stings someone. ⁶And in those days people will seek death but will not find it; they will long to die, but death will flee from them.

7 In appearance the locusts were like horses equipped for battle. On their heads were what looked like crowns of gold; their faces were like human faces, ⁸their hair like women's hair, and their teeth like lions' teeth; ⁹they had scales like iron breastplates, and the noise of their wings was like the noise of many chariots with horses rushing into battle. ¹⁰They have tails like scorpions, with stingers, and in their tails is their power to harm people for five months. ¹¹They have as king over them the angel of the bottomless pit; his name in Hebrew is Abaddon,ᵃ and in Greek he is called Apollyon.ᵇ

12 The first woe has passed. There are still two woes to come.

13 Then the sixth angel blew his trumpet, and I heard a voice from the fourᶜ horns of the golden altar before God, ¹⁴saying to the sixth angel who had the trumpet, "Release the four angels who are bound at the great river Euphrates." ¹⁵So the four angels were released, who had been held ready for the hour, the day, the month, and the year, to kill a third of humankind. ¹⁶The number of the troops of cavalry was two hundred million; I heard their number. ¹⁷And this was how I saw the horses in my vision: the riders wore breastplates the color of fire and of sapphireᵈ and of sulfur; the heads of the horses were like lions' heads, and fire and smoke and sulfur came out of their mouths. ¹⁸By these three plagues a third of humankind was killed, by the fire and smoke and sulfur coming out of their mouths. ¹⁹For the power of the horses is in their mouths and in their tails; their tails are like serpents, having heads; and with them they inflict harm.

20 The rest of humankind, who were not killed by these plagues, did not repent of the works of their hands or give up worshiping demons and idols of gold and silver and bronze and stone and wood, which cannot see or hear or walk. ²¹And they did not repent of their murders or their sorceries or their fornication or their thefts.

The Angel with the Little Scroll

10 And I saw another mighty angel coming down from heaven, wrapped in a cloud, with a rainbow over his head; his face was like the sun, and his legs like pillars of fire. ²He held a little scroll open in his hand. Setting his right foot on the sea and his left foot on the land, ³he gave a great shout, like a lion roaring. And when he shouted, the seven thunders sounded. ⁴And when the seven thunders had sounded, I was about to write, but I heard a voice from heaven saying, "Seal up what the seven thunders have said, and do not write it down." ⁵Then the angel whom I saw standing on the sea and the land

raised his right hand to heaven

6 and swore by him who lives forever and ever, who created heaven and what is in it, the earth and what is in it, and the sea and what is in it: "There will be no more delay, ⁷but in the days when the seventh angel is to blow his trumpet, the mystery of God will be fulfilled, as he announced to his servantsᵉ the prophets."

8 Then the voice that I had heard from heaven spoke to me again, saying, "Go, take the scroll that is open in the hand of the angel who is standing on the sea and on the land." ⁹So I went to the angel and told him to give me the little scroll; and he said to me, "Take it, and eat; it will be bitter to your stomach, but sweet as honey in your mouth." ¹⁰So I took the little scroll from the hand of the angel and ate it; it was sweet as honey in my mouth, but when I had eaten it, my stomach was made bitter.

11 Then they said to me, "You must prophesy again about many peoples and nations and languages and kings."

The Two Witnesses

11 Then I was given a measuring rod like a staff, and I was told, "Come and measure the temple of God and the altar and those who worship there, ²but do not measure the court outside the temple; leave that out, for it is given over to the nations, and they will trample over the holy city for forty-two months. ³And I will grant my two witnesses authority to prophesy for

---

ᵃ That is, *Destruction*   ᵇ That is, *Destroyer*   ᶜ Other ancient authorities lack *four*   ᵈ Gk *hyacinth*   ᵉ Gk *slaves*

one thousand two hundred sixty days, wearing sackcloth."

4 These are the two olive trees and the two lampstands that stand before the Lord of the earth. [5]And if anyone wants to harm them, fire pours from their mouth and consumes their foes; anyone who wants to harm them must be killed in this manner. [6]They have authority to shut the sky, so that no rain may fall during the days of their prophesying, and they have authority over the waters to turn them into blood, and to strike the earth with every kind of plague, as often as they desire.

7 When they have finished their testimony, the beast that comes up from the bottomless pit will make war on them and conquer them and kill them, [8]and their dead bodies will lie in the street of the great city that is prophetically[a] called Sodom and Egypt, where also their Lord was crucified. [9]For three and a half days members of the peoples and tribes and languages and nations will gaze at their dead bodies and refuse to let them be placed in a tomb; [10]and the inhabitants of the earth will gloat over them and celebrate and exchange presents, because these two prophets had been a torment to the inhabitants of the earth.

11 But after the three and a half days, the breath[b] of life from God entered them, and they stood on their feet, and those who saw them were terrified. [12]Then they[c] heard a loud voice from heaven saying to them, "Come up here!" And they went up to heaven in a cloud while their enemies watched them. [13]At that moment there was a great earthquake, and a tenth of the city fell; seven thousand people were killed in the earthquake, and the rest were terrified and gave glory to the God of heaven.

14 The second woe has passed. The third woe is coming very soon.

The Seventh Trumpet

15 Then the seventh angel blew his trumpet, and there were loud voices in heaven, saying,

"The kingdom of the world has become the
    kingdom of our Lord
    and of his Messiah,[d]
and he will reign forever and ever."

16 Then the twenty-four elders who sit on their thrones before God fell on their faces and worshiped God, [17]singing,

"We give you thanks, Lord God Almighty,
    who are and who were,
for you have taken your great power
    and begun to reign.

18 The nations raged,

Live It!

God in Control

The world is a wonderful place, full of life and hope. At the same time, it is full of pain and suffering, illness and death. It can seem frightening and out of control. Wars break out, a drought threatens the lives of millions, a friend dies in a senseless car accident, terrorists attack and kill innocent people, global warming threatens the existence of life as we know it. We can be left wondering why God allows such things.

The Book of Revelation was written to encourage the people of John's time that despite the evil that happens, God is in control. It can do the same for us too. The song in 11:15–18 reminds us that there will come a time when the just will be rewarded and the wicked punished. And although God's Reign is not yet fully realized, as members of God's family, we are called to be people of justice, peace, and hope to a world desperately seeking these things.

▶ **Rev 11:15–18**

---

but your wrath has come,
    and the time for judging the dead,
for rewarding your servants,[e] the prophets
    and saints and all who fear your name,
    both small and great,
and for destroying those who destroy the earth."

19 Then God's temple in heaven was opened, and the ark of his covenant was seen within his temple; and there were flashes of lightning, rumblings, peals of thunder, an earthquake, and heavy hail.

The Woman and the Dragon

12 A great portent appeared in heaven: a woman clothed with the sun, with the moon under her feet, and on her head a crown of twelve stars. [2]She was pregnant and was crying out in birth pangs, in the agony of giving birth. [3]Then another portent appeared in heaven: a great red dragon, with seven heads and ten horns,

---

a Or *allegorically*; Gk *spiritually*   b Or *the spirit*   c Other ancient authorities read *I*   d Gk *Christ*   e Gk *slaves*

and seven diadems on his heads. [4]His tail swept down a third of the stars of heaven and threw them to the earth. Then the dragon stood before the woman who was about to bear a child, so that he might devour her child as soon as it was born. [5]And she gave birth to a son, a male child, who is to rule[a] all the nations with a rod of iron. But her child was snatched away and taken to God and to his throne; [6]and the woman fled into the wilderness, where she has a place prepared by God, so that there she can be nourished for one thousand two hundred sixty days.

Michael Defeats the Dragon

7 And war broke out in heaven; Michael and his angels fought against the dragon. The dragon and his angels fought back, [8]but they were defeated, and there was no longer any place for them in heaven. [9]The great dragon was thrown down, that ancient serpent, who is called the Devil and Satan, the deceiver of the whole world—he was thrown down to the earth, and his angels were thrown down with him.

10 Then I heard a loud voice in heaven, proclaiming,

"Now have come the salvation and the power
  and the kingdom of our God
  and the authority of his Messiah,[b]
for the accuser of our comrades[c] has been
    thrown down,
  who accuses them day and night before our
    God.
[11] But they have conquered him by the blood of
    the Lamb
  and by the word of their testimony,
for they did not cling to life even in the face of
    death.
[12] Rejoice then, you heavens
  and those who dwell in them!
But woe to the earth and the sea,
  for the devil has come down to you
with great wrath,
  because he knows that his time is short!"

The Dragon Fights Again on Earth

13 So when the dragon saw that he had been thrown down to the earth, he pursued[d] the woman who had given birth to the male child. [14]But the woman was given the two wings of the great eagle, so that she could fly from the serpent into the wilderness, to her place where she is nourished for a time, and times, and half a time. [15]Then from his mouth the serpent poured water like a river after the woman, to sweep her away with the flood. [16]But the earth came to the help of the woman; it opened its mouth and swallowed the river that the dragon had poured from his mouth. [17]Then the dragon was angry with the woman, and went off to make war on the rest of her children, those who keep the commandments of God and hold the testimony of Jesus.

The First Beast

18 Then the dragon[e] took his stand on the
13 sand of the seashore. [1]And I saw a beast rising out of the sea, having ten horns and seven heads; and on its horns were ten diadems, and on its heads were blasphemous names. [2]And the beast that I saw was like a leopard, its feet were like a bear's, and its mouth was like a lion's mouth. And the dragon gave it his power and his throne and great authority. [3]One of its heads seemed to

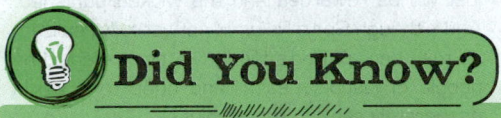

Did You Know?

The Woman and the Dragon

The vision in chapter 12 of Revelation symbolizes the great battle between Christ and Satan. In the opening scene, the pregnant woman represents Israel, from which the Messiah will come. The dragon waiting to devour her child is a symbol for Satan (see verse 9). This child, who will rule all the nations, is the Messiah, Jesus Christ. Therefore, the woman has also been equated with Mary, the mother of Jesus.

The conflict moves from heaven to earth when Satan fails to devour the child and is thrown down from his place in heaven. The dragon continues his pursuit of the woman on earth. The woman now represents the Church. The "rest of her children" (verse 17) represent its members whom the dragon angrily persecutes because he did not succeed in devouring her child. In this vision, John is telling the persecuted Christians of his time to have hope because in the end, Christ will totally and completely destroy Satan (see also 20:1–10).

▶ **Rev 12:1–18**

---

a Or to shepherd   b Gk Christ   c Gk brothers
d Or persecuted   e Gk Then he; other ancient authorities read
Then I stood

Cultural Connection

Mary Has a Vital Mission in Salvation History

The New Testament links Mary's mission intimately to the mystery of Christ. In Luke 1:38, Mary's yes to the angel Gabriel allows the Son of God to enter the world as a human being. At a wedding in Cana (see Jn 2:1–11), Mary is a model for the Church as she intercedes before Jesus, has faith in him, points to him as the source of life, and leads others to follow his words. Jesus' words to Mary and the Beloved Disciple at the cross (see Jn 19:26–27) name Mary mother of the universal Church, which is symbolized by the Beloved Disciple.

Over the centuries, some Christians have seen in the unnamed woman mentioned in chapter 12 of Revelation representations of Mary and the Church, who both share in Jesus' messianic mission. For Catholics on the feast of the Assumption, this passage is one of the readings that celebrates Mary's entrance into heaven as the first disciple. Mary is a symbol of the triumphant Church that awaits and intercedes for us, the pilgrim Church.

Catholics of Latino origin have a long tradition of linking Mary to their history of salvation. She is their companion on their journey of faith and a very dear member of their community. Hispanic popular piety draws strength from Mary's example in daily life, in situations of need and suffering, and in times of celebration.

Reflect on the ways Mary teaches us to be servants of the Reign of God. Pray that we are as willing to fulfill our mission in salvation history as she is.

▶ **Revelation, chapter 12**

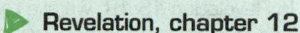

have received a death-blow, but its mortal wound[a] had been healed. In amazement the whole earth followed the beast. [4]They worshiped the dragon, for he had given his authority to the beast, and they worshiped the beast, saying, "Who is like the beast, and who can fight against it?"

5 The beast was given a mouth uttering haughty and blasphemous words, and it was allowed to exercise authority for forty-two months. [6]It opened its mouth to utter blasphemies against God, blaspheming his name and his dwelling, that is, those who dwell in heaven. [7]Also it was allowed to make war on the saints and to conquer them.[b] It was given authority over every tribe and people and language and nation, [8]and all the inhabitants of the earth will worship it, everyone whose name has not been written from the foundation of the world in the book of life of the Lamb that was slaughtered.[c]

9 Let anyone who has an ear listen:

[10] If you are to be taken captive,
   into captivity you go;
 if you kill with the sword,
   with the sword you must be killed.

Here is a call for the endurance and faith of the saints.

The Second Beast

11 Then I saw another beast that rose out of the earth; it had two horns like a lamb and it spoke like a dragon. [12]It exercises all the authority of the first beast on its behalf, and it makes the earth and its inhabitants worship the first beast, whose mortal wound[d] had been healed. [13]It performs great signs, even making fire come down from heaven to earth in the sight of all; [14]and by the signs that it is allowed to perform on behalf of the beast, it deceives the inhabitants of earth, telling them to make an image for the beast that had been wounded by the sword[e] and yet lived; [15]and it was allowed to give breath[f] to the image of the beast so that the image of the beast could even speak and cause those who would not worship the image of the beast to be killed. [16]Also it causes all, both small and great, both rich and poor, both free and slave, to be marked on the right hand or the forehead, [17]so that no one can buy or sell who does not have the mark, that is, the name of the beast or the number of its name. [18]This calls for wisdom: let anyone with understanding calculate the number of the beast, for it is the number of a person. Its number is six hundred sixty-six.[g]

---

a Gk the plague of its death   b Other ancient authorities lack this sentence   c Or written in the book of life of the Lamb that was slaughtered from the foundation of the world   d Gk whose plague of its death   e Or that had received the plague of the sword
f Or spirit   g Other ancient authorities read six hundred sixteen

Did You Know?

The Number of the Beast

The vision of the two beasts in chapter 13 of Revelation is a continuation of the vision about the woman and the dragon in chapter 12. The beasts represent the Roman Empire and its emperor, which at the time threatened the true practice of Christianity. Roman leaders expected all citizens, including Christians, to offer sacrifices to the Roman gods and to worship the emperor as though he were a god. This may have been especially true in the cities in Asia Minor, which were trying to prove their loyalty to the Roman emperor.

In Revelation 13:18, we are told that the number of the second beast is 666. Most scholars believe that this stands for Nero Caesar, who was the emperor of Rome from AD 54 to 68. Their reasoning is that when you convert the Greek letters for Nero's name and title into Hebrew letters, which also stand for numbers, and then add them up, you get the number 666. Six is one less than seven, the perfect number, so 666 represents something less than perfect or evil itself. Nero was responsible for some especially vicious attacks on Christians in Rome. The Book of Revelation was written after Nero committed suicide, but many people thought that he had not died and had come out of hiding in the East to lead this new wave of persecution against Christians (see verse 3).

▶ Revelation, chapter 13

The Lamb and the 144,000

14 Then I looked, and there was the Lamb, standing on Mount Zion! And with him were one hundred forty-four thousand who had his name and his Father's name written on their foreheads. ²And I heard a voice from heaven like the sound of many waters and like the sound of loud thunder; the voice I heard was like the sound of harpists playing on their harps, ³and they sing a new song before the throne and before the four living creatures and before the elders. No one could learn that song except the one hundred forty-four thousand who have been redeemed from the earth. ⁴It is these who have not defiled themselves with women, for they are virgins; these follow the Lamb wherever he goes. They have been redeemed from humankind as first fruits for God and the Lamb, ⁵and in their mouth no lie was found; they are blameless.

The Messages of the Three Angels

6 Then I saw another angel flying in midheaven, with an eternal gospel to proclaim to those who live*d* on the earth—to every nation and tribe and language and people. ⁷He said in a loud voice, "Fear God and give him glory, for the hour of his judgment has come; and worship him who made heaven and earth, the sea and the springs of water."

8 Then another angel, a second, followed, saying, "Fallen, fallen is Babylon the great! She has made all nations drink of the wine of the wrath of her fornication."

9 Then another angel, a third, followed them, crying with a loud voice, "Those who worship the beast and its image, and receive a mark on their foreheads or on their hands, ¹⁰they will also drink the wine of God's wrath, poured unmixed into the cup of his anger, and they will be tormented with fire and sulfur in the presence of the holy angels and in the presence of the Lamb. ¹¹And the smoke of their torment goes up forever and ever. There is no rest day or night for those who worship the beast and its image and for anyone who receives the mark of its name."

12 Here is a call for the endurance of the saints, those who keep the commandments of God and hold fast to the faith of*b* Jesus.

13 And I heard a voice from heaven saying, "Write this: Blessed are the dead who from now on die in the Lord." "Yes," says the Spirit, "they will rest from their labors, for their deeds follow them."

Reaping the Earth's Harvest

14 Then I looked, and there was a white cloud, and seated on the cloud was one like the Son of Man, with a golden crown on his head, and a sharp sickle in his hand! ¹⁵Another angel came out of the temple, calling with a loud voice to the one who sat on the cloud, "Use your sickle and reap, for the hour to reap has come, because the harvest of the earth is fully ripe." ¹⁶So the one who sat on the cloud swung his sickle over the earth, and the earth was reaped.

17 Then another angel came out of the temple in heaven, and he too had a sharp sickle.

a Gk sit *b Or to their faith in*

¹⁸Then another angel came out from the altar, the angel who has authority over fire, and he called with a loud voice to him who had the sharp sickle, "Use your sharp sickle and gather the clusters of the vine of the earth, for its grapes are ripe." ¹⁹So the angel swung his sickle over the earth and gathered the vintage of the earth, and he threw it into the great wine press of the wrath of God. ²⁰And the wine press was trodden outside the city, and blood flowed from the wine press, as high as a horse's bridle, for a distance of about two hundred miles.ᵃ

The Angels with the Seven Last Plagues

15 Then I saw another portent in heaven, great and amazing: seven angels with seven plagues, which are the last, for with them the wrath of God is ended.

2 And I saw what appeared to be a sea of glass mixed with fire, and those who had conquered the beast and its image and the number of its name, standing beside the sea of glass with harps of God in their hands. ³And they sing the song of Moses, the servantᵇ of God, and the song of the Lamb:

"Great and amazing are your deeds,
    Lord God the Almighty!
Just and true are your ways,
    King of the nations!ᶜ
⁴ Lord, who will not fear
    and glorify your name?
For you alone are holy.
    All nations will come
    and worship before you,
for your judgments have been revealed."

5 After this I looked, and the temple of the tentᵈ of witness in heaven was opened, ⁶and out of the temple came the seven angels with the seven plagues, robed in pure bright linen,ᵉ with golden sashes across their chests. ⁷Then one of the four living creatures gave the seven angels seven golden bowls full of the wrath of God, who lives forever and ever; ⁸and the temple was filled with smoke from the glory of God and from his power, and no one could enter the temple until the seven plagues of the seven angels were ended.

The Bowls of God's Wrath

16 Then I heard a loud voice from the temple telling the seven angels, "Go and pour out on the earth the seven bowls of the wrath of God."

2 So the first angel went and poured his bowl on the earth, and a foul and painful sore came on those who had the mark of the beast and who worshiped its image.

3 The second angel poured his bowl into the sea, and it became like the blood of a corpse, and every living thing in the sea died.

4 The third angel poured his bowl into the rivers and the springs of water, and they became blood. ⁵And I heard the angel of the waters say,

"You are just, O Holy One, who are and were,
    for you have judged these things;
⁶ because they shed the blood of saints and
        prophets,
    you have given them blood to drink.
It is what they deserve!"
⁷And I heard the altar respond,
    "Yes, O Lord God, the Almighty,
    your judgments are true and just!"

8 The fourth angel poured his bowl on the sun, and it was allowed to scorch people with fire; ⁹they were scorched by the fierce heat, but they cursed the name of God, who had authority over these plagues, and they did not repent and give him glory.

10 The fifth angel poured his bowl on the throne of the beast, and its kingdom was plunged into darkness; people gnawed their tongues in agony, ¹¹and cursed the God of heaven because of their pains and sores, and they did not repent of their deeds.

12 The sixth angel poured his bowl on the great river Euphrates, and its water was dried up in order to prepare the way for the kings from the east. ¹³And I saw three foul spirits like frogs coming from the mouth of the dragon, from the mouth of the beast, and from the mouth of the false prophet. ¹⁴These are demonic spirits, performing signs, who go abroad to the kings of the whole world, to assemble them for battle on the great day of God the Almighty. ¹⁵("See, I am coming like a thief! Blessed is the one who stays awake and is clothed,ᶠ not going about naked and exposed to shame.") ¹⁶And they assembled them at the place that in Hebrew is called Harmagedon.

17 The seventh angel poured his bowl into the air, and a loud voice came out of the temple, from the throne, saying, "It is done!" ¹⁸And there came flashes of lightning, rumblings, peals of thunder, and a violent earthquake, such as had not occurred since people were upon the earth, so violent was that earthquake. ¹⁹The great city was split into three parts, and the cities of the

---

a Gk one thousand six hundred stadia   b Gk slave   c Other ancient authorities read the ages   d Or tabernacle   e Other ancient authorities read stone   f Gk and keeps his robes

REV

nations fell. God remembered great Babylon and gave her the wine-cup of the fury of his wrath. 20And every island fled away, and no mountains were to be found; 21and huge hailstones, each weighing about a hundred pounds,*a* dropped from heaven on people, until they cursed God for the plague of the hail, so fearful was that plague.

The Sins of Empires

In John's coded language, the whore called Babylon in chapter 17 is Rome, a city built on seven hills. She is dressed in colors that symbolize her royalty (purple) and her obscene and immoral behavior (scarlet). Her gold and pearls are signs of her wealth and excessive luxury. The blasphemous names on her forehead are the titles that should be given to God but are given to the emperor instead. By calling her Babylon, John is creating a tie with the capital of another evil empire from the Old Testament (see "The Fall of Jerusalem," near 2 Kings 25:1–21).

The whore is drunk on the blood of the saints she killed because of their faith. John indicates that her evil is caused by her unrestrained desire for wealth and luxury and her abuse of power (see Rev 18:3–19). He tells his Christian readers that they can be hopeful, even amid so much suffering, because in the end, the Lamb (Christ) will conquer the beast (see 17:14).

Since Revelation was written, many other countries have abused their power, including the United States. Consider, for example, its treatment of Native Americans, practice of slavery, and lack of care for the environment.

Reflect for a moment.

● In what areas does your country need to take more responsibility to ensure justice for all people? Where has the desire for wealth and luxury gone too far?

● What can you do locally to take greater responsibility in these areas?

▶ **Revelation, chapter 17**

The Great Whore and the Beast

17 Then one of the seven angels who had the seven bowls came and said to me, "Come, I will show you the judgment of the great whore who is seated on many waters, 2with whom the kings of the earth have committed fornication, and with the wine of whose fornication the inhabitants of the earth have become drunk." 3So he carried me away in the spirit*b* into a wilderness, and I saw a woman sitting on a scarlet beast that was full of blasphemous names, and it had seven heads and ten horns. 4The woman was clothed in purple and scarlet, and adorned with gold and jewels and pearls, holding in her hand a golden cup full of abominations and the impurities of her fornication; 5and on her forehead was written a name, a mystery: "Babylon the great, mother of whores and of earth's abominations." 6And I saw that the woman was drunk with the blood of the saints and the blood of the witnesses to Jesus.

When I saw her, I was greatly amazed. 7But the angel said to me, "Why are you so amazed? I will tell you the mystery of the woman, and of the beast with seven heads and ten horns that carries her. 8The beast that you saw was, and is not, and is about to ascend from the bottomless pit and go to destruction. And the inhabitants of the earth, whose names have not been written in the book of life from the foundation of the world, will be amazed when they see the beast, because it was and is not and is to come.

9 "This calls for a mind that has wisdom: the seven heads are seven mountains on which the woman is seated; also, they are seven kings, 10of whom five have fallen, one is living, and the other has not yet come; and when he comes, he must remain only a little while. 11As for the beast that was and is not, it is an eighth but it belongs to the seven, and it goes to destruction. 12And the ten horns that you saw are ten kings who have not yet received a kingdom, but they are to receive authority as kings for one hour, together with the beast. 13These are united in yielding their power and authority to the beast; 14they will make war on the Lamb, and the Lamb will conquer them, for he is Lord of lords and King of kings, and those with him are called and chosen and faithful."

15 And he said to me, "The waters that you saw, where the whore is seated, are peoples and multitudes and nations and languages. 16And the ten horns that you saw, they and the beast will

a Gk *weighing about a talent*   *b* Or *in the Spirit*

hate the whore; they will make her desolate and naked; they will devour her flesh and burn her up with fire. ¹⁷For God has put it into their hearts to carry out his purpose by agreeing to give their kingdom to the beast, until the words of God will be fulfilled. ¹⁸The woman you saw is the great city that rules over the kings of the earth."

The Fall of Babylon

18 After this I saw another angel coming down from heaven, having great authority; and the earth was made bright with his splendor. ²He called out with a mighty voice,

"Fallen, fallen is Babylon the great!
　　It has become a dwelling place of demons,
　a haunt of every foul spirit,
　　a haunt of every foul bird,
　　a haunt of every foul and hateful beast.^a
³ For all the nations have drunk^b
　　of the wine of the wrath of her fornication,
　and the kings of the earth have committed
　　　fornication with her,
　　and the merchants of the earth have grown
　　　rich from the power^c of her luxury."

⁴ Then I heard another voice from heaven saying,

"Come out of her, my people,
　　so that you do not take part in her sins,
　and so that you do not share in her plagues;
⁵ for her sins are heaped high as heaven,
　　and God has remembered her iniquities.
⁶ Render to her as she herself has rendered,
　　and repay her double for her deeds;
　　mix a double draught for her in the cup she
　　　mixed.
⁷ As she glorified herself and lived luxuriously,
　　so give her a like measure of torment and
　　　grief.
Since in her heart she says,
　'I rule as a queen;
I am no widow,
　and I will never see grief,'
⁸ therefore her plagues will come in a single day—
　　pestilence and mourning and famine—
　and she will be burned with fire;
　　for mighty is the Lord God who judges her."

⁹ And the kings of the earth, who committed fornication and lived in luxury with her, will weep and wail over her when they see the smoke of her burning; ¹⁰they will stand far off, in fear of her torment, and say,

"Alas, alas, the great city,
　　Babylon, the mighty city!
For in one hour your judgment has come."

¹¹ And the merchants of the earth weep and mourn for her, since no one buys their cargo

anymore, ¹²cargo of gold, silver, jewels and pearls, fine linen, purple, silk and scarlet, all kinds of scented wood, all articles of ivory, all articles of costly wood, bronze, iron, and marble, ¹³cinnamon, spice, incense, myrrh, frankincense, wine, olive oil, choice flour and wheat, cattle and sheep, horses and chariots, slaves—and human lives.^d

¹⁴ "The fruit for which your soul longed
　　has gone from you,
　and all your dainties and your splendor
　　are lost to you,
　　never to be found again!"

¹⁵The merchants of these wares, who gained wealth from her, will stand far off, in fear of her torment, weeping and mourning aloud,

¹⁶ "Alas, alas, the great city,
　　clothed in fine linen,
　　　in purple and scarlet,
　　adorned with gold,
　　　with jewels, and with pearls!
¹⁷ For in one hour all this wealth has been laid
　　　waste!"

And all shipmasters and seafarers, sailors and all whose trade is on the sea, stood far off ¹⁸and cried out as they saw the smoke of her burning,

"What city was like the great city?"
¹⁹And they threw dust on their heads, as they wept and mourned, crying out,

"Alas, alas, the great city,
　　where all who had ships at sea
　　grew rich by her wealth!
For in one hour she has been laid waste."

²⁰ Rejoice over her, O heaven, you saints and apostles and prophets! For God has given judgment for you against her.

²¹ Then a mighty angel took up a stone like a great millstone and threw it into the sea, saying,

"With such violence Babylon the great city
　　will be thrown down,
　　and will be found no more;
²² and the sound of harpists and minstrels and of
　　　flutists and trumpeters
　　will be heard in you no more;
　and an artisan of any trade
　　will be found in you no more;
　and the sound of the millstone
　　will be heard in you no more;
²³ and the light of a lamp
　　will shine in you no more;
　and the voice of bridegroom and bride

---

a Other ancient authorities lack the words *a haunt of every foul beast* and attach the words *and hateful* to the previous line so as to read *a haunt of every foul and hateful bird*　*b* Other ancient authorities read *She has made all nations drink*　*c* Or *resources*　*d* Or *chariots, and human bodies and souls*

will be heard in you no more;
for your merchants were the magnates of the
earth,
and all nations were deceived by your sorcery.
24 And in you*a* was found the blood of prophets
and of saints,
and of all who have been slaughtered on
earth."

The Rejoicing in Heaven

19 After this I heard what seemed to be the
loud voice of a great multitude in heaven,
saying,
"Hallelujah!
Salvation and glory and power to our God,
2   for his judgments are true and just;
he has judged the great whore
who corrupted the earth with her fornication,
and he has avenged on her the blood of his
servants."*b*
³Once more they said,
"Hallelujah!
The smoke goes up from her forever and ever."
⁴And the twenty-four elders and the four living
creatures fell down and worshiped God who is
seated on the throne, saying,
"Amen. Hallelujah!"
5 And from the throne came a voice saying,
"Praise our God,
all you his servants,*b*
and all who fear him,
small and great."
⁶Then I heard what seemed to be the voice of a
great multitude, like the sound of many waters
and like the sound of mighty thunderpeals, crying out,
"Hallelujah!
For the Lord our God
the Almighty reigns.
7 Let us rejoice and exult
and give him the glory,
for the marriage of the Lamb has come,
and his bride has made herself ready;
8 to her it has been granted to be clothed
with fine linen, bright and pure"—
for the fine linen is the righteous deeds of the
saints.
9 And the angel said*c* to me, "Write this:
Blessed are those who are invited to the marriage
supper of the Lamb." And he said to me, "These
are true words of God." ¹⁰Then I fell down at
his feet to worship him, but he said to me, "You
must not do that! I am a fellow servant*d* with you
and your comrades*e* who hold the testimony of
Jesus.*f* Worship God! For the testimony of Jesus*f*
is the spirit of prophecy."

The Rider on the White Horse

11 Then I saw heaven opened, and there was
a white horse! Its rider is called Faithful and
True, and in righteousness he judges and makes
war. ¹²His eyes are like a flame of fire, and on
his head are many diadems; and he has a name
inscribed that no one knows but himself. ¹³He is
clothed in a robe dipped in*g* blood, and his name
is called The Word of God. ¹⁴And the armies
of heaven, wearing fine linen, white and pure,
were following him on white horses. ¹⁵From his
mouth comes a sharp sword with which to strike
down the nations, and he will rule*h* them with
a rod of iron; he will tread the wine press of the
fury of the wrath of God the Almighty. ¹⁶On his
robe and on his thigh he has a name inscribed,
"King of kings and Lord of lords."

The Beast and Its Armies Defeated

17 Then I saw an angel standing in the sun,
and with a loud voice he called to all the birds
that fly in midheaven, "Come, gather for the
great supper of God, ¹⁸to eat the flesh of kings,
the flesh of captains, the flesh of the mighty, the
flesh of horses and their riders—flesh of all, both
free and slave, both small and great." ¹⁹Then I
saw the beast and the kings of the earth with their
armies gathered to make war against the rider on
the horse and against his army. ²⁰And the beast
was captured, and with it the false prophet who
had performed in its presence the signs by which
he deceived those who had received the mark of
the beast and those who worshiped its image.
These two were thrown alive into the lake of fire
that burns with sulfur. ²¹And the rest were killed
by the sword of the rider on the horse, the sword
that came from his mouth; and all the birds were
gorged with their flesh.

The Thousand Years

20 Then I saw an angel coming down from
heaven, holding in his hand the key to
the bottomless pit and a great chain. ²He seized
the dragon, that ancient serpent, who is the Devil
and Satan, and bound him for a thousand years,
³and threw him into the pit, and locked and
sealed it over him, so that he would deceive the
nations no more, until the thousand years were
ended. After that he must be let out for a little
while.
4 Then I saw thrones, and those seated on

---

a Gk *her*   *b* Gk *slaves*   *c* Gk *he said*   *d* Gk *slave*
e Gk *brothers*   *f* Or *to Jesus*   *g* Other ancient authorities read
sprinkled with   *h* Or *will shepherd*

them were given authority to judge. I also saw the souls of those who had been beheaded for their testimony to Jesus[a] and for the word of God. They had not worshiped the beast or its image and had not received its mark on their foreheads or their hands. They came to life and reigned with Christ a thousand years. [5](The rest of the dead did not come to life until the thousand years were ended.) This is the first resurrection. [6]Blessed and holy are those who share in the first resurrection. Over these the second death has no power, but they will be priests of God and of Christ, and they will reign with him a thousand years.

Satan's Doom

7 When the thousand years are ended, Satan will be released from his prison [8]and will come out to deceive the nations at the four corners of the earth, Gog and Magog, in order to gather them for battle; they are as numerous as the sands of the sea. [9]They marched up over the breadth of the earth and surrounded the camp of the saints and the beloved city. And fire came down from heaven[b] and consumed them. [10]And the devil who had deceived them was thrown into the lake of fire and sulfur, where the beast and the false prophet were, and they will be tormented day and night forever and ever.

The Dead Are Judged

11 Then I saw a great white throne and the one who sat on it; the earth and the heaven fled from his presence, and no place was found for them. [12]And I saw the dead, great and small, standing before the throne, and books were opened. Also another book was opened, the book of life. And the dead were judged according to their works, as recorded in the books. [13]And the sea gave up the dead that were in it, Death and Hades gave up the dead that were in them, and all were judged according to what they had done. [14]Then Death and Hades were thrown into the lake of fire. This is the second death, the lake of fire; [15]and anyone whose name was not found written in the book of life was thrown into the lake of fire.

The New Heaven and the New Earth

21 Then I saw a new heaven and a new earth; for the first heaven and the first earth had passed away, and the sea was no more. [2]And I saw the holy city, the new Jerusalem, coming down out of heaven from God, prepared as a bride adorned for her husband. [3]And I heard a loud voice from the throne saying,

The New Jerusalem

The last three chapters of Revelation contain John's visions of the Reign of God, the end of history, and eternal life. In chapter 20, Satan is alive but has limited power. This is symbolized by the dragon's thousand-year imprisonment, during which the martyrs reign with Christ. The thousand-year reign has been interpreted in many different ways over the centuries, but no one knows its true significance. At the end of the thousand years, Satan is defeated, and Christ sits in final judgment over all the dead.

In chapter 21, John describes a new heaven and a new earth. The Bible begins in Genesis with the story of the creation of a world in which everything is good. It ends in Revelation with a new creation where God's goodness again overflows. A holy city, the New Jerusalem, comes down out of heaven. The New Jerusalem is described as a beautiful bride who is preparing to marry Jesus Christ. John tells his Christian readers that they should look forward to the time of this new city with joy, because when it comes, God and Christ will live in their midst. The whole city will be God's temple. The sun will always shine, a river of living water will flow from God's throne, and the trees will produce fruit year-round recalling the Garden of Eden where Adam and Eve lived before their sin. The New Jerusalem is a symbol for the new world that God will establish when evil is destroyed and suffering is banished.

These visions helped Christians at the end of the first century to maintain their hope by focusing on the glorious victory of God in history. They can also help us to renew our commitment to Christ and keep our hope alive, especially when we are misunderstood or harassed because of our faith.

▶ Rev 20:1–22:5

"See, the home*a* of God is among mortals.
He will dwell*b* with them;
they will be his peoples,*c*
and God himself will be with them;*d*
4 he will wipe every tear from their eyes.
Death will be no more;
mourning and crying and pain will be no more,
for the first things have passed away."

5 And the one who was seated on the throne said, "See, I am making all things new." Also he said, "Write this, for these words are trustworthy and true." 6Then he said to me, "It is done! I am the Alpha and the Omega, the beginning and the end. To the thirsty I will give water as a gift from the spring of the water of life. 7Those who conquer will inherit these things, and I will be their God and they will be my children. 8But as for the cowardly, the faithless,*e* the polluted, the murderers, the fornicators, the sorcerers, the

Come, Lord Jesus!

Most young children want immediate gratification. Waiting for Christmas or a birthday is nearly impossible. Saving a piece of candy for after dinner is downright torture. And a long trip in a car produces a familiar and persistent question: Are we there yet?

The Bible tells us that Jesus will return. In the creed, Christians proclaim, "He will come again in glory to judge the living and the dead and his kingdom will have no end" (*Roman Missal*). When will this happen? Like impatient children, some people have tried to predict the Lord's Second Coming. "But about that day and hour no one knows, . . . only the Father" (Mt 24:36).

Can we say, with John, "Amen! Come, Lord Jesus!" (Rev 22:20) and really hope that Jesus will come today? We may hesitate, wanting to hang on to the life we know here and now. Yet, the coming of Christ will be the most glorious event imaginable for those who have put their trust in God. So keep preparing and praying for the return of Christ!

▶ **Rev 22:7–21**

idolaters, and all liars, their place will be in the lake that burns with fire and sulfur, which is the second death."

Vision of the New Jerusalem

9 Then one of the seven angels who had the seven bowls full of the seven last plagues came and said to me, "Come, I will show you the bride, the wife of the Lamb." 10And in the spirit*f* he carried me away to a great, high mountain and showed me the holy city Jerusalem coming down out of heaven from God. 11It has the glory of God and a radiance like a very rare jewel, like jasper, clear as crystal. 12It has a great, high wall with twelve gates, and at the gates twelve angels, and on the gates are inscribed the names of the twelve tribes of the Israelites; 13on the east three gates, on the north three gates, on the south three gates, and on the west three gates. 14And the wall of the city has twelve foundations, and on them are the twelve names of the twelve apostles of the Lamb.

15 The angel*g* who talked to me had a measuring rod of gold to measure the city and its gates and walls. 16The city lies foursquare, its length the same as its width; and he measured the city with his rod, fifteen hundred miles;*h* its length and width and height are equal. 17He also measured its wall, one hundred forty-four cubits*i* by human measurement, which the angel was using. 18The wall is built of jasper, while the city is pure gold, clear as glass. 19The foundations of the wall of the city are adorned with every jewel; the first was jasper, the second sapphire, the third agate, the fourth emerald, 20the fifth onyx, the sixth carnelian, the seventh chrysolite, the eighth beryl, the ninth topaz, the tenth chrysoprase, the eleventh jacinth, the twelfth amethyst. 21And the twelve gates are twelve pearls, each of the gates is a single pearl, and the street of the city is pure gold, transparent as glass.

22 I saw no temple in the city, for its temple is the Lord God the Almighty and the Lamb. 23And the city has no need of sun or moon to shine on it, for the glory of God is its light, and its lamp is the Lamb. 24The nations will walk by its light, and the kings of the earth will bring their glory into it. 25Its gates will never be shut by day—and there will be no night there. 26People will bring into it the glory and the honor of the nations. 27But nothing unclean will enter it, nor anyone who practices abomination or falsehood, but only those who are written in the Lamb's book of life.

a Gk *the tabernacle*   *b* Gk *will tabernacle*   *c* Other ancient authorities read *people*   *d* Other ancient authorities add *and be their God*   *e* Or *the unbelieving*   *f* Or *in the Spirit*   *g* Gk *He*   *h* Gk *twelve thousand stadia*   *i* That is, almost seventy-five yards

The River of Life

22 Then the angel[a] showed me the river of the water of life, bright as crystal, flowing from the throne of God and of the Lamb [2]through the middle of the street of the city. On either side of the river is the tree of life[b] with its twelve kinds of fruit, producing its fruit each month; and the leaves of the tree are for the healing of the nations. [3]Nothing accursed will be found there any more. But the throne of God and of the Lamb will be in it, and his servants[c] will worship him; [4]they will see his face, and his name will be on their foreheads. [5]And there will be no more night; they need no light of lamp or sun, for the Lord God will be their light, and they will reign forever and ever.

6 And he said to me, "These words are trustworthy and true, for the Lord, the God of the spirits of the prophets, has sent his angel to show his servants[c] what must soon take place."

7 "See, I am coming soon! Blessed is the one who keeps the words of the prophecy of this book."

Epilogue and Benediction

8 I, John, am the one who heard and saw these things. And when I heard and saw them, I fell down to worship at the feet of the angel who showed them to me; [9]but he said to me, "You must not do that! I am a fellow servant[d] with you and your comrades[e] the prophets, and with those who keep the words of this book. Worship God!"

10 And he said to me, "Do not seal up the words of the prophecy of this book, for the time is near. [11]Let the evildoer still do evil, and the filthy still be filthy, and the righteous still do right, and the holy still be holy."

12 "See, I am coming soon; my reward is with me, to repay according to everyone's work. [13]I am the Alpha and the Omega, the first and the last, the beginning and the end."

14 Blessed are those who wash their robes,[f] so that they will have the right to the tree of life and may enter the city by the gates. [15]Outside are the dogs and sorcerers and fornicators and murderers and idolaters, and everyone who loves and practices falsehood.

16 "It is I, Jesus, who sent my angel to you with this testimony for the churches. I am the root and the descendant of David, the bright morning star."

[17] The Spirit and the bride say, "Come."
And let everyone who hears say, "Come."

And let everyone who is thirsty come.
Let anyone who wishes take the water of life as a gift.

18 I warn everyone who hears the words of the prophecy of this book: if anyone adds to them, God will add to that person the plagues described in this book; [19]if anyone takes away from the words of the book of this prophecy, God will take away that person's share in the tree of life and in the holy city, which are described in this book.

20 The one who testifies to these things says, "Surely I am coming soon."
Amen. Come, Lord Jesus!

21 The grace of the Lord Jesus be with all the saints. Amen.[g]

---

a Gk he   *b* Or the Lamb. [2]In the middle of the street of the city, and on either side of the river, is the tree of life   *c* Gk slaves   *d* Gk slave   *e* Gk brothers   *f* Other ancient authorities read do his commandments   *g* Other ancient authorities lack all; others lack the saints; others lack Amen

---

AMEN!

In Hebrew, *amen* means "so be it" or "yes, it is true." So saying "Amen" in your prayers is the same as saying, "Yes, I believe!" It is an appropriate way to conclude the last book of the Bible, and it should not be said lightly. Are you able to say "Amen" to all you have read, prayed, and reflected on in this Bible? Have the stories and the poems, the teachings and the parables, the songs and the sayings led you to believe in a God who is with you every step of your journey, every minute of the day and night?

Each of us is invited to join the great Amen, to say: "Yes, I believe in a loving God who is father and mother to us all! Yes, I believe in God's Son, Jesus Christ, who is my Lord and Savior! Yes, I believe in the Holy Spirit, who will help me to continue Jesus' mission of justice, reconciliation, and love!" But these words remain just words until people with courage and conviction take the risk to live them out in their own corner of the world. Take the risk; heaven awaits you! Amen!

▶ **Rev 22:20**

Where Do I Find It?

Events, People, and Teachings

Old Testament Stories

These stories are listed in the order in which they first appear in the Bible.

Creation, *Gen, chs 1–2*
original sin and its punishment, *Gen, ch 3*
Cain and Abel, *Gen 4:1–16*
Noah and the Great Flood, *Gen, chs 6–9*
God's covenant with Abraham, *Gen 17:1—18:15*
God's command to sacrifice Isaac, *Gen 22:1–19*
Isaac's blessing of Jacob, *Gen 27:1–29*
Jacob's dream, *Gen 28:10–22*
Joseph and his brothers, *Gen, chs 37–46*
birth and youth of Moses, *Ex 2:1–10*
Moses at the burning bush, *Ex 3:1–12*
plagues on Egypt, *Ex, chs 7–12*
Passover and the Exodus, *Ex, chs 12–-14*
Ten Commandments, *Ex 20:1–17*
destruction of Jericho, *Josh 5:13—6:27*
Gideon and the sign of the fleece, *Judg 6:36–40*
Samson, *Judg, chs 13–16*
Samuel's birth and calling, *1 Sam, chs 1–3*
David and Goliath, *1 Sam, ch 17*
David and Bathsheba, *2 Sam, ch 11*
Solomon's wisdom, *1 Kings, ch 3*
Elijah's triumph over the priests of Baal, *1 Kings 18:20–40*
miracles of Elisha, *2 Kings 4:1—6:23*
end of the Babylonian captivity, *Ezra, ch 1*
battles of Judas Maccabeus, *1 Macc, chs 3–5*
Ezekiel and the valley of dry bones, *Ezek 37:1–14*
Daniel, *Dan, chs 1–6*
Jonah and the Ninevites, *Jon, chs 1–3*

New Testament Stories

These stories are listed in the order in which they first appear in the Bible.

birth of Jesus, *Mt 1:18—2:12; Lk, chs 1–2*
baptism of Jesus, *Mt 3:13–17; Mk 1:9–11; Lk 3:21–22*
temptation of Jesus, *Mt 4:1–11; Mk 1:12–13; Lk 4:1–13*
Peter's declaration about Jesus, *Mt 16:13–20; Mk 8:27–30; Lk 9:18–20*
Transfiguration of Jesus, *Mt 17:1–13; Mk 9:2–13; Lk 9:28–36*
Jesus' triumphal entry into Jerusalem, *Mt 21:1–11; Mk 11:1–11; Lk 19:28–40; Jn 12:12–19*
Jesus in the Temple, *Mt 21:12–17; Mk 11:15–19; Lk 19:45–48; Jn 2:13–16*
Judas's betrayal of Jesus, *Mt 26:14–16,47–56; Mk 14:10–11,43–52; Lk 22:1–53; Jn 13:21–30; 18:1–5*
Last Supper, *Mt 26:17–30; Mk 14:12–25; Lk 22:7–38; 1 Cor 11:23–26*
Jesus at Gethsemane, *Mt 26:36–56; Mk 14:32–51; Lk 22:39–53*
Peter's denial of Christ, *Mt 26:69–75; Mk 14:66–72; Lk 22:54–62; Jn 18:15–18,25–27*
Crucifixion, *Mt 27:32–56; Mk 15:21–41; Lk 23:26–49; Jn 19:16–30*
Resurrection and appearances, *Mt, ch 28; Mk, ch 16; Lk, ch 24; Jn, chs 20–21; Acts 1:1–11*
Jesus washing his disciples' feet, *Jn 13:1–17*
Holy Spirit at Pentecost, *Acts 2:1–42*
stoning of Stephen, *Acts, chs 6–7*
conversion of Saul, *Acts 9:1–31*
Peter's escape from prison, *Acts 12:1–19*
Paul and Silas's escape from prison, *Acts 16:16–40*
Paul's journey to Rome for his trial, *Acts, chs 27–28*

People

Each person entry is followed by a page number or numbers that lead you to an "Introducing . . ." article or other articles in which the person is featured.

Abraham, *2, 3, 4, 19, 22, 23, 24, 25, 26, 29, 32, 34, 56*

Barnabas, *1294, 1297, 1298*

Beloved Disciple, *1258*

David, *35, 271, 288, 289, 291, 295, 301, 302, 304, 308, 312, 313, 315, 321, 325*

Elijah, *354, 360, 1169*

Elisha, *354, 363*

Ezekiel, *964*

First Isaiah, *841*

Holy Family, *1191*

Jacob, *2, 4, 29, 32, 33, 34, 35, 37, 38, 41, 42, 47, 56*

Jeremiah, *886*

John the Baptist, *1110, 1192*

Joseph, *3, 4, 33, 35, 46, 47, 54, 56*

Junia, *1339*

Lady Wisdom, *699, 757*

Lydia, *1301*

Mary Magdalene, *1270*

Mary, mother of Jesus, *824, 1187, 1238, 1269, 1491*

Moses, *3, 67, 80, 183, 212, 224, 1169*

Nicodemus, *1239*

Paul, *1288, 1290, 1296, 1297, 1298, 1344*

Peter, *1127, 1129, 1149, 1197*

Phoebe, *1339*

Priscilla, *1301*

Samson, *255, 258*

Sarah, *3, 4, 19, 23, 24, 28, 56*

Satan, *573, 1490*

Solomon, *332, 334*

Stephen, *1286, 1287*

Prayers

These prayers are listed in the order in which they first appear in the Bible.

The Lord bless you and keep you, *Num 6:24–27*

Hannah's prayer, *1 Sam 2:1–10*

Speak, Lord, for your servant is listening, *1 Sam 3:9–10*

Blessed be the Lord, *1 Kings 8:56–61*

Tobit's thanksgiving, *Tob, ch 13*

Judith's hymn of praise, *Jdt 16:1–17*

The Lord is my shepherd, *Ps 23*

Have mercy on me, O God, *Ps 51*

O Lord, you have searched me and known me, *Ps 139*

Holy, Holy, Holy (Hosanna), *Isa 6:3; Mt 21:9; Mk 11:9–10; Lk 19:38; Jn 12:13; Rev 4:8*

Lord's Prayer, *Mt 6:9–15; Lk 11:2–4*

Lord, I am not worthy, *Mt 8:8*

Jesus' prayer for deliverance, *Mt 26:39; Mk 14:36; Lk 22:42*

Mary's song of praise, *Lk 1:46–55*

Zechariah's prophecy, *Lk 1:68–79*

Glory to God in the highest, *Lk 2:14*

Simeon's prayer, *Lk 2:29–32*

God, be merciful to me, a sinner!, *Lk 18:13*

Lamb of God, *Jn 1:29*

Jesus' prayer for his disciples, *Jn, ch 17*

Paul's prayer for the Ephesians, *Eph 3:14–21*

Amen, *1 Pet 5:11; Jude, v 25; Rev 1:6–7; 3:14*

Miracles of Jesus

These miracle stories are listed in the order in which they first appear in the Bible.

Healing Individuals

leper, *Mt 8:1–4; Mk 1:40–45; Lk 5:12–16*

centurion's servant, *Mt 8:5–13; Lk 7:1–10*

many at Peter's house, *Mt 8:14–17; Mk 1:29–34; Lk 4:38–41*

Gadarene (Gerasene) demoniacs, *Mt 8:28–34; Mk 5:1–20; Lk 8:26–39*

paralytic, *Mt 9:1–8; Mk 2:1–12; Lk 5:17–26*

woman with bleeding, *Mt 9:20–22; Mk 5:25–34; Lk 8:43–48*

two blind men, *Mt 9:27–31*

mute man, *Mt 9:32–34*

man with a withered hand, *Mt 12:9–13; Mk 3:1–5; Lk 6:6–11*

blind, mute, and possessed man, *Mt 12:22*

Canaanite woman's daughter, *Mt 15:21–28; Mk 7:24–30*

boy with a demon, *Mt 17:14–21; Mk 9:14–29; Lk 9:37–43*

blind Bartimaeus, *Mt 20:29–34; Mk 10:46–52; Lk 18:35–43*

man with an unclean spirit, *Mk 1:21–28; Lk 4:31–37*

deaf man, *Mk 7:31–37*

blind man at Bethsaida, *Mk 8:22–26*

crippled woman, *Lk 13:11–13*

man with dropsy, *Lk 14:1–4*

ten lepers, *Lk 17:11–19*

high priest's servant, *Lk 22:50–51*

official's son, *Jn 4:46–54*

man at the pool of Beth-zatha, *Jn 5:1–9*

Controlling Nature

stilling the storm, Mt 8:23–27; Mk 4:35–41; Lk 8:22–25

feeding five thousand, Mt 14:13–21; Mk 6:30–44; Lk 9:10–17; Jn 6:1–15

walking on water, Mt 14:22–33; Mk 6:45–52; Jn 6:16–21

feeding four thousand, Mt 15:32–39; Mk 8:1–10

fish with a coin, Mt 17:24–27

fig tree withers, Mt 21:18–22; Mk 11:12–14,20–25

huge catch of fish, Lk 5:1–11; Jn 21:1–11

turning water into wine, Jn 2:1–11

Raising the Dead

Jairus's daughter, Mt 9:18–19,23–26; Mk 5:21–24,35–43; Lk 8:40–42,49–56

widow's son at Nain, Lk 7:11–17

Lazarus, Jn 11:1–44

Parables of Jesus

These parables are listed in alphabetical order.

barren fig tree, Lk 13:6–9

canceled debts, Lk 7:41–43

cost of discipleship, Lk 14:25–33

dishonest manager, Lk 16:1–8

faithful or unfaithful slave, Mt 24:45–51; Lk 12:42–48

fig tree, Mt 24:32–35; Mk 13:28–31; Lk 21:29–33

good Samaritan, Lk 10:30–37

great dinner, Lk 14:16–24

growing seed, Mk 4:26–29

hidden treasure and pearl, Mt 13:44–46

honor at a banquet, Lk 14:7–14

laborers in the vineyard, Mt 20:1–16

light of the world, Mt 5:14–16

lost coin, Lk 15:8–10

lost sheep, Mt 18:12–14; Lk 15:3–7

mustard seed, Mt 13:31–32; Mk 4:30–32; Lk 13:18–19

net, Mt 13:47–50

new wine in old wineskins, Mt 9:16–17; Mk 2:21–22; Lk 5:36–39

persistent friend, Lk 11:5–8

persistent widow, Lk 18:2–8

Pharisee and the tax collector, Lk 18:10–14

prodigal son, Lk 15:11–32

rich fool, Lk 12:16–21

rich man and Lazarus, Lk 16:19–31

salt, Mt 5:13; Mk 9:50; Lk 14:34–35

sheep and the goats, Mt 25:31–46

sower, Mt 13:3–8,18–23; Mk 4:3–9,14–20; Lk 8:5–8,11–15

talents, Mt 25:14–30

ten bridesmaids, Mt 25:1–13

ten pounds, Lk 19:11–27

two sons, Mt 21:28–31

unforgiving servant, Mt 18:23–35

watchful slaves, Lk 12:35–40

wedding banquet, Mt 22:1–14

weeds among the wheat, Mt 13:24–30,36–43

wicked tenants, Mt 21:33–44; Mk 12:1–12; Lk 20:9–18

wise and foolish builders, Mt 7:24–27; Lk 6:47–49

worthless slaves, Lk 17:7–10

yeast, Mt 13:33; Lk 13:20–21

Teachings of Jesus

These teachings are listed in alphabetical order.

Beatitudes, Mt 5:1–12; Lk 6:20–26

born from above, Jn 3:1–21

bread of life, Jn 6:25–59

children, Mk 10:13–16

discipleship, Lk 14:25–33

do not worry, Mt 6:19–21,25–34; Lk 12:22–34

golden rule, Mt 7:12; Lk 6:31

good shepherd, Jn 10:1–21

greatest commandment, Mt 22:34–40; Mk 12:28–34; Lk 10:25–28

living water, Jn 4:1–26

Lord's Prayer, Mt 6:9–13; Lk 11:2–4

mission of the twelve Apostles, Mt 10:1–15

paying taxes, Mt 22:15–22; Mk 12:13–17; Lk 20:20–26

rich young man, Mt 19:16–30; Mk 10:17–31; Lk 18:18–30

Sermon on the Mount, Mt, chs 5–7

Sermon on the Plain, Lk 6:17–49

vine and branches, Jn 15:1–17

"the way, the truth, and the life," Jn 14:1–14

"where two or three are gathered," Mt 18:20

Catholic Connections

Creed

Bible, Tradition, and Magisterium, Lk 4:1–13, *Catechism*, nos. 74–141, 1194

Church, Mt 16:13–20, *Catechism*, nos. 871–945, p. 1130

Communion of Saints, Rev 7:2–14, *Catechism*, nos. 946–962, p. 1486

Eucharist, Lk 22:14–20, *Catechism*, nos. 787–796, pp. 1329, 1396, 1228

Faith and Reason, Mk 16:20, *Catechism*, nos. 156–159, p. 1183

Final Judgment, 2 Macc 12:38–45, *Catechism*, nos. 1020–1060, p. 562

God the Father, Ex 3:13–15, *Catechism*, nos. 232–243, p. 66

Holy Spirit, Rom 8:1–17, *Catechism*, nos. 683–747, p. 1330

Incarnation, 1 Tim 3:14–16, *Catechism*, nos. 456–483, p. 1419

Mary, Isa 7:14, *Catechism*, nos. 484–511, 721–726, 963–975, p. 824

Messiah, Lk 9:18–20, *Catechism*, nos. 436–440, 711–716, p. 1205

Ministry in the Church, Acts 14:21–28, *Catechism*, nos. 871–945, p. 1299

New Covenant, Mt 26:26–29, *Catechism*, nos. 68–73, pp. 610, 613, 1365, 1405, 1148

Old Testament and the New Testament, Mt 17:1–13, *Catechism*, nos. 120–137, p. 1132

Original Sin, Gen 3:1–24, *Catechism*, nos. 369–421, p. 10

Pentecost, Acts 2:1–13, *Catechism*, nos. 731–741, 1108–1112, p. 1280

Revelation and the Apostolic Tradition, 2 Thess 2:13–17, *Catechism*, nos. 74–83, p. 1413

Trinity, Jn 17:20–26, *Catechism*, nos. 232–267, p. 1266

Morality

Beatitudes, Mt 5:1–12, *Catechism*, nos. 1716–1729, p. 1112

Cardinal Virtues, Wis 8:7, *Catechism*, nos. 1803–1811, p. 747

Corporal and Spiritual Works of Mercy, Isa 58:1–9, *Catechism*, nos. 2443–2449, p. 873

Gifts of the Holy Spirit, Isa 11:1–2, *Catechism*, nos. 1830–1832, p. 829

Sin and Moral Decision Making, Sir 22:27—23:6, *Catechism*, nos. 1749–1761, 1846–1864, p. 784

Sources of Moral Truth, Prov 2:1–22, *Catechism*, nos. 1949–1986, p. 694

Ten Commandments, Deut 5:1–21, *Catechism*, nos. 2052–2082, p. 183

Theological Virtues, 1 Cor 13:13, *Catechism*, nos. 1812–1841, p. 1358

Prayer

Lord's Prayer, Lk 11:1–4, *Catechism*, nos. 2759–2776, p. 1209

Prayer, Ps 130:1–8, *Catechism*, nos. 2558–2567, 2650–2662, p. 680

Types of Prayer, 1 Chr 16:37–42, *Catechism*, nos. 2623–2649, 2697–2758, p. 401

Sacraments

Anointing of the Sick, Jas 5:13–15, *Catechism*, nos. 1499–1532, p. 1452

Baptism, Mt 3:13–17, *Catechism*, nos. 1213–1284, p. 1110

Confirmation, Acts 2:1–13, *Catechism*, nos. 1285–1321, p. 1278

Easter Triduum, Jn 13:1—20:18, *Catechism*, nos. 1168–1171, p. 1259

Eucharist, Lk 22:14–20, *Catechism*, nos. 787–796, 1329, 1396, p. 1228

Holy Orders, Mk 3:13–19, *Catechism*, nos. 1533–1600, p. 1160

Liturgical Year, Isa 35:1–10, *Catechism*, nos. 1163–1173, p. 850

Marriage, Mk 10:1–12, *Catechism*, nos. 1601–1666, p. 1172

New Covenant, Mt 26:26–29, *Catechism*, nos. 68–73, 610, 613, 1365, 1405, p. 1148

Parts of the Mass, Josh 8:30–35, *Catechism*, nos. 1345–1355, p. 224

Pentecost, Acts 2:1–13, *Catechism*, nos. 731–741, 1108–1112, p. 1280

Real Presence, 1 Cor 11:23–26, *Catechism*, nos. 1373–1377, p. 1354

Sacrament of Penance and Reconciliation, Jn 20:19–23, *Catechism*, nos. 1420–1470, p. 1271

Sacramental Symbols, Gen 14:17–20, *Catechism*, nos. 1145–1152, p. 21

Sacrament Connections

These are some passages that can help us understand God's action in the sacraments. It is not meant to be a complete list of all the biblical connections for all seven sacraments.

Baptism

Isa 43:1
Mt 3:13–17; 28:19–20
Mk 1:9–11
Lk 3:21–22
Jn 1:29–34; 3:5
Acts 2:37–41
Rom 6:3–4

Confirmation

Isa 11:2; 61:1
Mt 3:13–17
Jn 1:33–34; 14:15–31; 16:5–15
Acts 2:1–4; 8:14–17
2 Cor 1:21–22
Gal 5:22–23

Eucharist

Gen 14:17–20
Ex 12:1–28; 24:1–8
Mt 14:13–21; 26:17–29
Mk 6:30–44; 14:12–25
Lk 9:10–17; 22:14–20; 24:13–35
Jn 6:1–13,25–59
1 Cor 11:17–34

Reconciliation (penance)

Gen 45:1–15
Joel 2:12–13
Mt 5:21–26,38–48; 18:23–35
Mk 2:1–12
Lk 15:11–32
Jn 20:19–23
Rom, ch 6

Anointing

Ps 23
Mk 6:7–13
Lk 13:10–13
2 Tim 2:11–12
Jas 5:14–16

Holy Orders

Deut 18:1–5
Ps 110:1–4
Mt 10:1–4
Mk 3:14–19
Lk 6:12–16
Jn 13:1–14
Rom 12:1–8
1 Tim 3:1–13
Titus 1:5–9
Heb 4:14—5:10

Marriage

Gen 2:18–25
Song 8:6–7
Mt 19:1–12
Mk 10:2–12
Jn 2:1–11
1 Cor, ch 13
Eph 5:21–33
1 Jn 4:4–16

Seven Themes of Catholic Social Teaching

Here is an index to articles on seven significant themes that summarize much of Catholic social teaching, which is rooted in the Scriptures and Tradition and should be woven into the biblical principles that every disciple lives by. For a fuller description/ see page C24.

Life and Dignity of the Human Person

12, 650, 1108, 1195

Call to Family, Community, and Participation

238, 1224, 1281, 1402

Rights and Responsibilities

461, 838, 1068, 1146

Option for the Poor and Vulnerable

88, 1053, 1113, 1449

The Dignity of Work and the Rights of Workers

68, 750, 1137, 1165

Solidarity

269, 505, 1207, 1380

Care for God's Creation

7, 663, 689, 1057

Life and Faith Issues

Here are some passages that can give you comfort or direction. There are many other passages in the Bible that also address these and other topics.

Anger

Mt 5:21–24
Jn 2:13–17
Eph 4:25–27,31–32
Jas 1:19–21

Call

Gen 12:1–9
1 Sam, chs 1–3
Isa 6:1–8
Jer 1:4–10
Mt 4:18–22; 28:16–20
Mk 1:16–20
Lk 5:1–11

Commitment

Num 30:2–4
Deut 6:1–9; 11:8–9
Josh 24:14–15
Mk 8:34–38

Courage

Josh 1:9
1 Sam, ch 17
Ps 31

Discipleship

Mk 8:34–38
Lk 9:1–6
Jn 4:1–42

Family

Gen 4:9; 12:10–20
Sir 3:1–16
Eph 5:21—6:4

Fear

Ps 27, 91
Zeph 3:14–20
Mt 14:22–33

Mk 4:35–41
Lk 22:54–62

Forgiveness

Gen 33:1–17
Ps 51
Mt 18:21–35
Lk 6:27–36; 23:34
Jn 8:2–11

Friendship

Ruth 1:1–19
1 Sam, ch 20
Sir 6:5–17
Jn 15:12–17

Friendship with God

Gen 28:10–22
Mic 6:8
Jn 15:12–17

Giving

2 Chr 31:2–10
Ezra 1:6–11
Mk 12:41–44
Lk 21:1–4

Happiness

Sir 25:1–11
Lk 12:22–34
Phil 4:4–9

Honesty with God

Gen 18:22–33
Jer 12:1–16
Mk 14:32–42

Hope

Eccl 3:1–8
Lam 3:22–26
Rom 8:18–30

Hypocrisy

Mt 6:1–6; 23:1–36
Lk 18:9–14
Jas 1:22—2:4

Images of God

Gen 1:26–27;
    32:22–32
Ps 23
Jer 18:1–11

Judgment of Others

Mt 7:1–5
Rom 14:1–12
Gal 3:26–28

Loneliness and Abandonment

Ps 22:1–12
Mk 15:33–34
2 Tim 4:9–18

Love

Song 8:6–7
Mt 5:43–48
Mk 12:28–34
1 Cor, ch 13

Peace

Isa 11:1–9
Mic 4:1–5
Jn 14:25–31

Persistence

Lk 11:5–8; 18:1–8

Popularity

Mk 9:33–37
1 Cor 3:1–9
Phil 2:1–11

Presence of God

Gen 15:7
Ex 3:1–6; 33:17–23
Mt 18:20

Promises of God

Ex 6:1–9
Jer 29:11
Lk 4:14–30

Repentance

1 Chr 21:1–17
Joel 2:12–18
Lk 15:11–32

Responsibility

Sir 15:11–20
Ezek, ch 18

Service

Isa 42:1–6
Mt 20:20–28; 25:31–46
Mk 10:35–45
Jn 13:1–17

Sexuality

Gen 1:26–31
Tob 8:4–9
Song of Solomon
Eph 5:1–14
1 Thess 4:3–8

Suffering

Job 1:13–21
Ps 22
Mt 5:1–12
1 Pet 3:13–18

Temptation

Gen, ch 3
Mt 4:1–11
Mk 1:12–13; 7:14–23
Lk 4:1–13

Trust in God

Ps 62
Isa 43:1–5
Mt 11:28–30
Mk 10:46–52

Vocation (*See* call; discipleship)

Wisdom

2 Chr 1:7–13
Prov 8:1–21
Wis, ch 7

Article Subject Index

This subject index is not an index to the Bible itself (sometimes called a concordance). Rather, it is an index to the subjects covered in the various articles in The Catholic Youth Bible. *But because most articles are based on a Bible passage, this index will also help you find Bible passages related to these topics.*

A

abortion
685

Abraham
2, 3, 4, 19, 22, 23, 24, 25, 26, 29, 34, 35, 56

addiction
1351

Adonai
65, 66

Advocate
See Holy Spirit

African American articles
78, 187, 190, 336, 493, 640, 643, 732, 926, 1093, 1131, 1145, 1181, 1193, 1265, 1286, 1355, 1370, 1382

aging
729

AIDS
650, 1323

alcohol
496, 792, 1390

amen, meaning of
1499

angels
478, 1444

anger
661

Anointing of the Sick, sacrament of
21, 1157, 1452

anxiety
1162, 1213

apocryphal books
473

Apostles
1160, 1194, 1278, 1413, 1437

Apostles' Creed
6, 1282

Apostolic Tradition
1413

ark of the Covenant
103, 107, 183

Ash Wednesday
1115

Asian articles
58, 64, 82, 107, 132, 411, 476, 553, 666, 724, 766, 874, 1039, 1134, 1257, 1260, 1353, 1366, 1387

Assyrian Empire
376

authority
243

awe
64

B

Babel, tower of
17

Babylonian Exile
3, 384

Baptism, sacrament of
10, 21, 1110, 1157

Barnabas
1294, 1297, 1298

Beatitudes
1112, 1198

belief
608, 1170, 1456

Beloved Disciple
1258

betrayal
258

birthright
35

blessings
21, 35, 41, 995

Body of Christ
1148, 1228, 1335

bread and wine
224

brothers and sisters
11, 22, 33, 505

C

capital punishment
12, 1114

challenges
41

charisms
1335

childbirth
119

choices
128

Christmas
1189, 1190, 1240

Church
1130

circumcision
23, 24, 1298, 1324

civil disobedience
1139

commitment
169, 1168, 1395, 1424

Communion of Saints
1486

sin offering
111

Sinai Covenant
2, 85, 110

solidarity
269, 360, 505, 1028, 1158,
1380

Solomon
332, 334

Song at the Sea
79

spirits
411, 1156, 1469

spiritual growth
363

spiritual leaders
67, 1336

spiritual writings
381

Stephen
1286, 1287

stewardship
1225, 1283

stories
3, 313

suffering
572, 573, 599, 604, 1151, 1152,
1365, 1459, 1460

suffering servant
111

suicide
301, 1150

sweatshops
68

symbols, biblical
41, 1177, 1482, 1484, 1485,
1490

symbols, Native American
1249

symbols, sacramental
21

T

Temple
1002

temptation
1111, 1436

Ten Commandments
85, 86, 183, 918

testing God
248

thankfulness
401, 666, 671, 995, 1352, 1386,
1407, 1408

theological virtues
1358

tithing
437

Torah
3

Transfiguration
1132, 1169, 1204

transubstantiation
1354

Trinity
See Holy Trinity

trust in God
25, 29, 248, 258, 831, 926, 1127,
1159, 1213

Truth
1261

Truth, Sojourner
493

U

unity
238, 1093, 1343

Unleavened Bread, feast of
See Passover

V

values
190, 1262

violence
12, 244, 245, 315, 830

visions
46, 1480, 1482, 1485, 1497

W

war
141, 244, 245
See also violence

water
15, 242

Way and the Truth and the Life
1260

wealth
725

Weeks, feast of
101

wisdom
334, 644, 713, 745

women
244, 245, 507, 1359, 1390,
1417

works
1386, 1448

wrestling with God
41

Y

Yahweh
2, 65, 66

youth
728

Z

Zacchaeus
1221

Acknowledgments

Third edition focus group members: Jane Angha, Kelsey Denzer, Jacob DeMarais, Elizabeth Kilkus, Rebecca Otte, Elizabeth Perkins, Margaret Scannell, Larry Schatz, FSC, Sarah Schrupp, James Spillman, Jocelyn Stage, Dan Streefland

Second edition writers: Tony Tamberino, Victor Valenzuela, Larry Schatz, FSC, Lisa-Marie Calderone-Stewart, and Vikki Shepp

First Edition article and introduction writers: Eduardo Arnouil; Lisa-Marie Calderone-Stewart; Carmen Maria Cervantes; Catherine Cory; Gary Dreier; Karen Emmerich; Carole Goodwin; Ron Kenney; Edward P. Kunzman; Judi Lanciotti; Joseph A. Morris, CM; Daniel Ponsetto; Rosa Sanchez; Larry Schatz, FSC; Valerie Shields; Brian Singer-Towns; and Michael Theisen

Consultants: Barbara Allaire, Mary Lee Becker, Philip J. Calderone, Brian K. Johnson, Carl Koch, Stephan Nagel, Pheme Perkins, and Kevin Schneider

The Catholic Youth Bible NRSV Publishing Team: Brian Singer-Towns, general editor; Carmen María Cervantes, Shirley Kelter, and Robert P. Stamschror, consulting editors; Lynn Riska Dahdal, production editor; Cheryl Drivdahl and Mary Duerson, copy editors; Hollace Storkel, article typesetter; Auto-Graphics, Scripture typesetters; Peachtree Editorial and Proofreading Service, Scripture proofreaders; Maurine R. Twait, art director; Stephan Nagel, art director and cover designer; Sue Campbell, Carol Evans-Smith, Kent Linder, and Cindi Ramm, designers; Alan S. Hanson, prepress specialist; Gary J. Boisvert and Alan S. Hanson, illustration colorizers; Michael O. McGrath, illustrator

The Catholic Youth Bible NAB Publishing team: Steven Roe development editor; Beverly DeGeorge, managing editor; Don Curtin, marketing coordinator; Bill Northam, printing coordinator; Stephan Nagel and Brian Singer-Towns, consulting editors; Cindi Ramm, consulting cover designer; Lynn Riska, consultant for typesetting and project management; Gabrielle Koenig and Brooke E. Saron, editorial assistance; Genevieve Nagel, photo and illustration acquisition editor; James Koenig and Alan S. Hanson, technical assistance; Cären Yang, contributing graphic designer; The Livingstone Corporation, article and Scripture typesetter, copy editor, cover design adaptation, and project management; Peachtree Editorial and Proofreading Service, Scripture and article proofreaders; Michael O. McGrath, illustrator

The Catholic Youth Bible, Revised, Publishing Team: Steven Roe and Brian Singer-Towns, development editors; Heather Sutton, marketing director; Bill Northam, printing coordinator; Jim Gurley and Cären Yang, production editors; Andy Palmer, designer; Lynn Riska, consultant for typesetting; Brooke E. Saron and Paul Grass, FSC, copy editors; Genevieve Nagel, photo and illustration acquisitions editor; James Koenig, technical consultant; Alan S. Hanson, prepress specialist; The Livingstone Corporation, article and Scripture typesetter and project management; Peachtree Editorial and Proofreading Service, Scripture and article proofreaders. We extend a special thank-you to our student article reviewers, for their time, enthusiasm, invaluable comments, and recommendations. The student article review team included Renea Carlson, Neal Frantzen, Joshua Hamann, Aubrey Hollnagel, William Jaspers, Benjamin Leist, Megan Leopold, Kendall Marsden, and Brenda Maurer.

A special thank-you to the members of the original *Catholic Youth Bible* focus group: Catherine Cory; Carole Goodwin; Maryann Hakowski; Shirley Kelter; Marilyn Kielbasa; Joseph A. Morris, CM; Daniel Ponsetto; Pat Rinker; Virginia Smith; Carleen Suttman; and especially Robert P. Stamschror for his work in starting this project.

Finally, we are very grateful for the many young people, youth leaders, and teachers who helped as reviewers and consultants through the duration of this project.

Notes

Notes

Notes

Study Aids

The Church Year

The Feast Days and Holy Days celebrated by Catholics and other Christians follow a yearly pattern. This pattern is called the liturgical year; it is different from the calendar year. Here is a description of the major seasons in the liturgical year. It might help you if you also take a look at the circular diagram of the liturgical year, found on the next page.

Advent begins the liturgical year four Sundays before Christmas. It is a time of preparation for the coming of Christ. The Advent season can be found on the liturgical year wheel in November and December. It is represented by the small graphic of an Advent wreath.

The **Christmas** season lasts twelve days, beginning with Christmas Day and concluding with the feast of the Baptism of the Lord. This season is found at the top part of the liturgical year wheel. The cross reminds us that the wood of the manger becomes the wood of the cross.

Lent begins with Ash Wednesday and lasts forty days. It is a solemn time of fasting, prayer, and almsgiving in preparation for Easter. The small picture of the palms and cross in the liturgical year wheel symbolizes all of Lent as a journey toward Palm Sunday, when the same crowd that waves palms and yells "Hosanna!" ends up waving angry fists and shouting "Crucify him!"

The **Easter Triduum** is the celebration of Holy Thursday, Good Friday, and the Easter Vigil on Holy Saturday. At this one, continuous, three-day liturgy, Christians remember the Lord's Supper, Christ's Passion and death, and his Resurrection. These feasts are at the heart of the liturgical year. They are represented by the picture of the Easter candle, which makes its appearance in the darkness of the Easter Vigil. The vestments and altar cloths seen are red on Good Friday and white on the other two days.

The **Easter** Season lasts fifty days, beginning with Easter Sunday and ending with the feast of Pentecost. The symbol of the lamb represents Jesus, the innocent sacrificial lamb of God. The symbol of the Holy Spirit reminds us that the Holy Spirit came to the disciples, in the rush of wind and tongues of fire. The altar cloths and vestments are white throughout the Easter season, and then red on Pentecost. Red is the color of the Holy Spirit (as in Confirmation Mass) and of the celebration of feast days associated with martyrs, people killed for their faith (such as the feast of Saints Peter and Paul).

The season of **Ordinary Time** is made up of the days between Christmas and Lent, and the days between Easter and Advent. The bread and wine show us that the main focus of Ordinary Time is the ministry of Jesus, represented by the grapes and bread of communion. There are some special feast days during Ordinary Time that are not celebrated with green vestments and altar cloths, such as Trinity Sunday and the Feast of the Body and Blood of Christ, the first two Sundays after Pentecost, and the Feast of Christ the King, the last Sunday before Advent. You'll see white on all three of those days. The particular dates and days these feasts fall upon vary from year to year.

Christmas is always December 25, so counting backwards four Sundays shows the four Sundays of Advent. Sometimes Advent includes Thanksgiving weekend, and sometimes it doesn't, depending on which day of the week Christmas is.

Easter is always the first Sunday after the first full moon in the spring. Counting backwards six Sundays and then one Wednesday shows when Ash Wednesday and Lent begin. Sometimes Easter is in March, and sometimes it is in April.

On page 1524, you will find a Bible reading plan that corresponds to the readings of the Bible heard on Sundays throughout these seasons. That is an excellent way to get to know the Bible and the liturgical year at the same time.

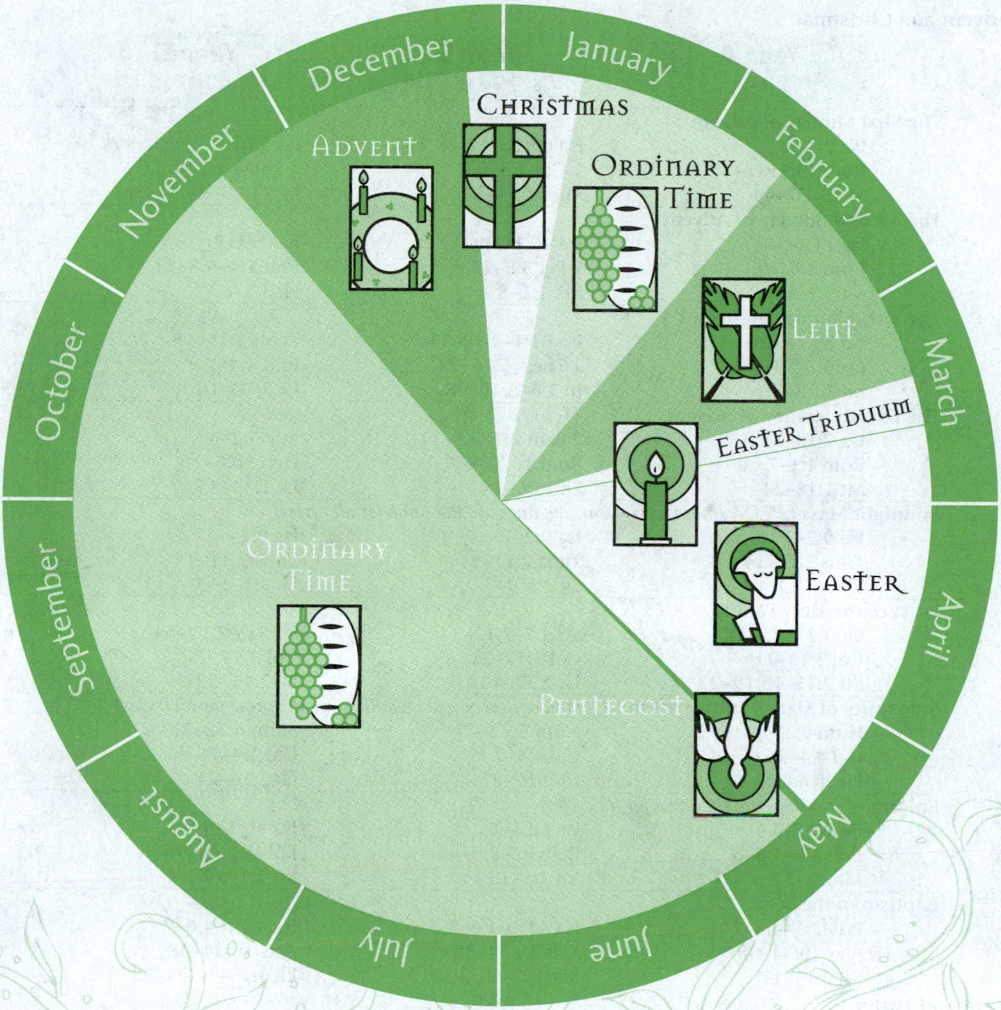
January
February
March
April
May
June
July
August
September
October
November
December
Advent
Christmas
Ordinary Time
Lent
Easter Triduum
Easter
Pentecost
Ordinary Time

Sunday Readings

Reading the Bible with the Church

This reading plan lists the Sunday readings for the liturgical year. The Scripture passages listed in the following table reflect those found in the official Catholic Lectionary for Mass, which uses the New American Bible translation.

Advent and Christmas

Year A 2010, 2013, 2016	Year B 2011, 2014, 2017	Year C 2009, 2012, 2015
The First Sunday of Advent		
Isa 2:1–5	Isa 63:16–17; 64:1–8	Jer 33:14–16
Rom 13:11–14	1 Cor 1:3–9	1 Thess 3:12—4:2
Mt 24:37–44	Mk 13:33–37	Lk 21:25–28,34–36
The Second Sunday of Advent		
Isa 11:1–10	Isa 40:1–5,9–11	Bar 5:1–9
Rom 15:4–9	2 Pet 3:8–14	Phil 1:4–6,8–11
Mt 3:1–12	Mk 1:1–8	Lk 3:1–6
The Third Sunday of Advent		
Isa 35:1–6,10	Isa 61:1–2,10–11	Zeph 3:14–18
Jas 5:7–10	1 Thess 5:16–24	Phil 4:4–7
Mt 11:2–11	Jn 1:6–8,19–28	Lk 3:10–18
The Fourth Sunday of Advent		
Isa 7:10–14	2 Sam 7:1–5,8–11,14,16	Mic 5:2–4
Rom 1:1–7	Rom 16:25–27	Heb 10:5–10
Mt 1:18–24	Lk 1:26–38	Lk 1:39–45
Midnight Mass *(25 December, every year, readings are the same for all cycles)*		
Isa 9:2–7	Isa 9:2–7	Isa 9:2–7
Titus 2:11–14	Titus 2:11–14	Titus 2:11–14
Lk 2:1–14	Lk 2:1–14	Lk 2:1–14
Feast of the Holy Family		
Sir 3:2–7,12–14	Sir 3:2–7,12–14	Sir 3:2–7,12–14
Col 3:12–21	Col 3:12–21	Col 3:12–21
Mt 2:13–15,19–23	Lk 2:22–40	Lk 2:41–52
Solemnity of Mary, Mother of God *(1 January, every year, readings are the same for all cycles)*		
Num 6:22–27	Num 6:22–27	Num 6:22–27
Gal 4:4–7	Gal 4:4–7	Gal 4:4–7
Lk 2:16–21	Lk 2:16–21	Lk 2:16–21
Epiphany *(readings are the same for all cycles)*		
Isa 60:1–6	Isa 60:1–6	Isa 60:1–6
Eph 3:2–3,5–6	Eph 3:2–3,5–6	Eph 3:2–3,5–6
Mt 2:1–12	Mt 2:1–12	Mt 2:1–12
Baptism of the Lord		
Isa 42:1–4,6–7	Isa 42:1–4,6–7	Isa 42:1–4,6–7
Acts 10:34–38	Acts 10:34–38	Acts 10:34–38
Mt 3:13–17	Mk 1:7–11	Lk 3:15–16,21–22

Lent and Easter

Year A 2011, 2014, 2017	Year B 2012, 2015, 2018	Year C 2010, 2013, 2016
Ash Wednesday *(readings are the same for all cycles)*		
Joel 2:12–18	Joel 2:12–18	Joel 2:12–18
2 Cor 5:20—6:2	2 Cor 5:20—6:2	2 Cor 5:20—6:2
Mt 6:1–6,16–18	Mt 6:1–6,16–18	Mt 6:1–6,16–18

Lent and Easter *(continued)*

Year A 2011, 2014, 2017	Year B 2012, 2015, 2018	Year C 2010, 2013, 2016
The First Sunday of Lent		
Gen 2:7–9; 3:1–7	Gen 9:8–15	Deut 26:4–10
Rom 5:12–19	1 Pet 3:18–22	Rom 10:8–13
Mt 4:1–11	Mk 1:12–15	Lk 4:1–13
The Second Sunday of Lent		
Gen 12:1–4	Gen 22:1–2,9,10–13,15–18	Gen 15:5–12,17–18
2 Tim 1:8–10	Rom 8:31–34	Phil 3:17—4:1
Mt 17:1–9	Mk 9:2–10	Lk 9:28–36
The Third Sunday of Lent		
Ex 17:3–7	Ex 20:1–17	Ex 3:1–8,13–15
Rom 5:1–2,5–8	1 Cor 1:22–25	1 Cor 10:1–6,10–12
Jn 4:5–42	Jn 2:13–25	Lk 13:1–9
The Fourth Sunday of Lent		
1 Sam 16:1,6–7,10–13	2 Chr 36:14–17,19–23	Josh 5:9,10–12
Eph 5:8–14	Eph 2:4–10	2 Cor 5:17–21
Jn 9:1–41	Jn 3:14–21	Lk 15:1–3,11–32
The Fifth Sunday of Lent		
Ezek 37:12–14	Jer 31:31–34	Isa 43:16–21
Rom 8:8–11	Heb 5:7–9	Phil 3:8–14
Jn 11:1–45	Jn 12:20–33	Jn 8:1–11
Passion Sunday (Palm Sunday)		
Isa 50:4–7	Isa 50:4–7	Isa 50:4–7
Phil 2:6–11	Phil 2:6–11	Phil 2:6–11
Mt 26:14—27:66	Mk 14:1—15:47	Lk 22:14—23:56
Holy Thursday *(readings are the same for all cycles)*		
Ex 12:1–8,11–14	Ex 12:1–8,11–14	Ex 12:1–8,11–14
1 Cor 11:23–26	1 Cor 11:23–26	1 Cor 11:23–26
Jn 13:1–15	Jn 13:1–15	Jn 13:1–15
Good Friday *(readings are the same for all cycles)*		
Isa 52:13—53:12	Isa 52:13—53:12	Isa 52:13—53:12
Heb 4:14–16; 5:7–9	Heb 4:14–16; 5:7–9	Heb 4:14–16; 5:7–9
Jn 18:1—19:42	Jn 18:1—19:42	Jn 18:1—19:42
Easter Sunday *(readings are the same for all cycles)*		
Acts 10:34,37–43	Acts 10:34,37–43	Acts 10:34,37–43
Col 3:1–4 or 1 Cor 5:6–8	Col 3:1–4 or 1 Cor 5:6–8	Col 3:1–4 or 1 Cor 5:6–8
Jn 20:1–9	Jn 20:1–9	Jn 20:1–9
Second Sunday of Easter		
Acts 2:42–47	Acts 4:32–35	Acts 5:12–16
1 Pet 1:3–9	1 Jn 5:1–6	Rev 1:9–19
Jn 20:19–31	Jn 20:19–31	Jn 20:19–31
Third Sunday of Easter		
Acts 2:14,22–28	Acts 3:13–19	Acts 5:27–32,40–41
1 Pet 1:17–21	1 Jn 2:1–5	Rev 5:11–14
Lk 24:13–35	Lk 24:35–48	Jn 21:1–19
Fourth Sunday of Easter		
Acts 2:14,36–41	Acts 4:8–12	Acts 13:14,43–52
1 Pet 2:20–25	1 Jn 3:1–2	Rev 7:9,14–17
Jn 10:1–10	Jn 10:11–18	Jn 10:27–30
Fifth Sunday of Easter		
Acts 6:1–7	Acts 9:26–31	Acts 14:21–27
1 Pet 2:4–9	1 Jn 3:18–24	Rev 21:1–5
Jn 14:1–12	Jn 15:1–8	Jn 13:31–35
Sixth Sunday of Easter		
Acts 8:5–8,14–17	Acts 10:25–26,34–35,44–48	Acts 15:1–2,22–29
1 Pet 3:15–18	1 Jn 4:7–10	Rev 21:10–14,22–23
Jn 14:15–21	Jn 15:9–17	Jn 14:23–29

Lent and Easter *(continued)*

Year A 2011, 2014, 2017	Year B 2012, 2015, 2018	Year C 2010, 2013, 2016
Seventh Sunday of Easter		
Acts 1:12–14	Acts 1:15–17,20–26	Acts 7:55–60
1 Pet 4:13–16	1 Jn 4:11–16	Rev 22:12–14,16–17,20
Jn 17:1–11	Jn 17:11–19	Jn 17:20–26
Pentecost Sunday *(readings are the same for all cycles)*		
Acts 2:1–11	Acts 2:1–11	Acts 2:1–11
1 Cor 12:3–7,12–13	1 Cor 12:3–7,12–13	1 Cor 12:3–7,12–13
Jn 20:19–23	Jn 20:19–23	Jn 20:19–23

Ordinary Time

Year A 2011, 2014, 2017	Year B 2012, 2015, 2018	Year C 2010, 2013, 2016
The First Sunday in Ordinary Time		
(see the Feast of the Baptism of the Lord under "Advent and Christmas")		
The Second Sunday in Ordinary Time		
Isa 49:3,5–6	1 Sam 3:3b–10,19	Isa 62:1–5
1 Cor 1:1–3	1 Cor 6:13c–15a,17–20	1 Cor 12:4–11
Jn 1:29–34	Jn 1:35–42	Jn 2:1–11
The Third Sunday in Ordinary Time		
Isa 8:23—9:3	Jon 3:1–5,10	Neh 8:2–4a,5–6,8–10
1 Cor 1:10–13,17	1 Cor 7:29–31	1 Cor 12:12–30
Mt 4:12–23	Mk 1:14–20	Lk 1:1–4; 4:14–21
The Fourth Sunday in Ordinary Time		
Zeph 2:3; 3:12–13	Deut 18:15–20	Jer 1:4–5,17–19
1 Cor 1:26–31	1 Cor 7:32–35	1 Cor 12:31—13:13
Mt 5:1–12a	Mk 1:21–28	Lk 4:21–30
The Fifth Sunday in Ordinary Time		
Isa 58:7–10	Job 7:1–4,6–7	Isa 6:1–2a,3–8
1 Cor 2:1–5	1 Cor: 9,16–19,22–23	1 Cor 15:1–11
Mt 5:13–16	Mk 1:29–39	Lk 5:1–11
The Sixth Sunday in Ordinary Time		
Sir 15:15–20	Lev 13:1–2,45–46	Jer 17:5–8
1 Cor 2:6–10	1 Cor 10:31—11:1	1 Cor 15:12,16–20
Mt 5:17–37	Mk 1:40–45	Lk 6:17,20–26
The Seventh Sunday in Ordinary Time		
Lev 19:1–2,17–18	Isa 43:18–19,21–22,24b–25	1 Sam 26:2,7–9,12–13,22–23
1 Cor 3:16–23	2 Cor 1:18–22	1 Cor 15:45–49
Mt 5:38–48	Mk 2:1–12	Lk 6:27–38
The Eighth Sunday in Ordinary Time		
Isa 49:14–15	Hos 2:16b,17b,21–22	Sir 27:4–7
1 Cor 4:1–5	2 Cor 3:1b–6	1 Cor 15:54–58
Mt 6:24–34	Mk 2:18–22	Lk 6:39–45
The Ninth Sunday in Ordinary Time		
Deut 11:18,26–28,32	Deut 5:12–15	1 Kings 8:41–43
Rom 3:21–25a,28	2 Cor 4:6–11	Gal 1:1–2,6–10
Mt 7:21–27	Mk 2:23—3:6	Lk 7:1–10
The Tenth Sunday in Ordinary Time		
Hos 6:3–6	Gen 3:9–15	1 Kings 17:17–24
Rom 4:18–25	2 Cor 4:13—5:1	Gal 1:11–19
Mt 9:9–13	Mk 3:20–35	Lk 7:11–17
The Eleventh Sunday in Ordinary Time		
Ex 19:2–6a	Ezek 17:22–24	2 Sam 12:7–10,13
Rom 5:6–11	2 Cor 5:6–10	Gal 2:16,19–21
Mt 9:36—10:8	Mk 4:26–34	Lk 7:36—8:3

Year A 2011, 2014, 2017	**Year B** 2012, 2015, 2018	**Year C** 2010, 2013, 2016
The Twelfth Sunday in Ordinary Time		
Jer 20:10–13	Job 38:1,8–11	Zech 12:10–11; 13:1
Rom 5:12–15	2 Cor 5:14–17	Gal 3:26–29
Mt 10:26–33	Mk 4:35–41	Lk 9:18–24
The Thirteenth Sunday in Ordinary Time		
2 Kings 4:8–11,14–16a	Wis 1:13–15; 2:23–24	1 Kings 19:16b,19–21
Rom 6:3–4,8–11	2 Cor 8:7,9,13–15	Gal 5:1,13–18
Mt 10:37–42	Mk 5:21–43	Lk 9:51–62
The Fourteenth Sunday in Ordinary Time		
Zech 9:9–10	Ezek 2:2–5	Isa 66:10–14c
Rom 8:9,11–13	2 Cor 12:7–10	Gal 6:14–18
Mt 11:25–30	Mk 6:1–6	Lk 10:1–12,17–20
The Fifteenth Sunday in Ordinary Time		
Isa 55:10–11	Am 7:12–15	Deut 30:10–14
Rom 8:18–23	Eph 1:3–14	Col 1:15–20
Mt 13:1–23	Mk 6:7–13	Lk 10:25–37
The Sixteenth Sunday in Ordinary Time		
Wis 12:13,16–19	Jer 23:1–6	Gen 18:1–10a
Rom 8:26–27	Eph 2:13–18	Col 1:24–28
Mt 13:24–43	Mk 6:30–34	Lk 10:38–42
The Seventeenth Sunday in Ordinary Time		
1 Kings 3:5,7–12	2 Kings 4:42–44	Gen 18:20–32
Rom 8:28–30	Eph 4:1–6	Col 2:12–14
Mt 13:44–52	Jn 6:1–15	Lk 11:1–13
The Eighteenth Sunday in Ordinary Time		
Isa 55:1–3	Ex 16:2–4,12–15	Eccl 1:2; 2:21–23
Rom 8:35,37–39	Eph 4:17,20–24	Col 3:1–5,9–11
Mt 14:13–21	Jn 6:24–35	Lk 12:13–21
The Nineteenth Sunday in Ordinary Time		
1 Kings 19:9a,11–13a	1 Kings 19:4–8	Wis 18:6–9
Rom 9:1–5	Eph 4:30—5:2	Heb 11:1–2,8–19
Mt 14:22–33	Jn 6:41–51	Lk 12:32–48
The Twentieth Sunday in Ordinary Time		
Isa 56:1,6–7	Prov 9:1–6	Jer 38:4–6,8–10
Rom 11:13–15,29–32	Eph 5:15–20	Heb 12:1–4
Mt 15:21–28	Jn 6:51–58	Lk 12:49–53
The Twenty-First Sunday in Ordinary Time		
Isa 22:19–23	Josh 24:1–2a,15–17,18b	Isa 66:18–21
Rom 11:33–36	Eph 5:21–32	Heb 12:5–7,11–13
Mt 16:13–20	Jn 6:60–69	Lk 13:22–30
The Twenty-Second Sunday in Ordinary Time		
Jer 20:7–9	Deut 4:1–2,6–8	Sir 3:17–18,20,28–29
Rom 12:1–2	Jas 1:17–18,21b–22,27	Heb 12:18–19,22–24a
Mt 16:21–27	Mk 7:1–8,14–15,21–23	Lk 14:1,7–14
The Twenty-Third Sunday in Ordinary Time		
Ezek 33:7–9	Isa 35:4–7a	Wis 9:13–18b
Rom 13:8–10	Jas 2:1–5	Philem 9–10,12–17
Mt 18:15–20	Mk 7:31–37	Lk 14:25–33
The Twenty-Fourth Sunday in Ordinary Time		
Isa 55:6–9	Isa 50:5–9a	Ex 32:7–11,13–14
Rom 14:7–9	Jas 2:14–18	1 Tim 1:12–17
Mt 18:21–35	Mk 8:27–35	Lk 15:1–32
The Twenty-Fifth Sunday in Ordinary Time		
Acts 2:14,22–28	Wis 2:12,17–20	Am 8:4–7
Phil 1:20c–24,27a	Jas 3:16—4:3	1 Tim 2:1–8
Mt 20:1–16a	Mk 9:30–37	Lk 16:1–13

Year A 2011, 2014, 2017	**Year B** 2012, 2015, 2018	**Year C** 2010, 2013, 2016
The Twenty-Sixth Sunday in Ordinary Time		
Ezek 18:25–28	Num 11:25–29	Am 6:1a,4–7
Phil 2:1–11	Jas 5:1–6	1 Tim 6:11–16
Mt 21:28–32	Mk 9:38–43,45,47–48	Lk 16:19–31
The Twenty-Seventh Sunday in Ordinary Time		
Isa 5:1–7	Gen 2:18–24	Hab 1:2–3; 2:2–4
Phil 4:6–9	Heb 2:9–11	2 Tim 1:6–8,13–14
Mt 21:33–43	Mk 10:2–16	Lk 17:5–10
The Twenty-Eighth Sunday in Ordinary Time		
Isa 25:6–10a	Wis 7:7–11	2 Kings 5:14–17
Phil 4:12–14,19–20	Heb 4:12–13	2 Tim 2:8–13
Mt 22:1–14	Mk 10:17–30	Lk 17:11–19
The Twenty-Ninth Sunday in Ordinary Time		
Isa 45:1,4–6	Isa 52:10–11	Ex 17:8–13
1 Thess 1:1–5b	Heb 4:14–16	2 Tim 3:14—4:2
Mt 22:15–21	Mk 10:35–45	Lk 18:1–8
The Thirtieth Sunday in Ordinary Time		
Ex 22:20–26	Jer 31:7–9	Sir 35:12–14,16–18
1 Thess 1:5c–10	Heb 5:1–6	2 Tim 4:6–8,16–18
Mt 22:34–40	Mk 10:46–52	Lk 18:9–14
The Thirty-First Sunday in Ordinary Time		
Mal 1:14b—2:2b,8–10	Deut 6:2–6	Wis 11:22—12:2
1 Thess 2:7b–9,13	Heb 7:23–28	2 Thess 1:11—2:2
Mt 23:1–12	Mk 12:28b–34	Lk 19:1–10
The Thirty-Second Sunday in Ordinary Time		
Wis 6:12–16	1 Kings 17:10–16	2 Macc 7:1–2,9–14
1 Thess 5:1–6	Heb 9:24–28	2 Thess 2:16—3:5
Mt 25:14–30	Mk 12:38–44	Lk 20:27–38
The Thirty-Third Sunday in Ordinary Time		
Prov 31:10–13,19–20,30–31	Dan 12:1–3	Mal 4:1–2
Rom 8:35,37–39	Heb 10:11–14,18	2 Thess 3:7–12
Mt 14:13–21	Mk 13:24–32	Lk 21:5–19
The Thirty-Fourth Sunday in Ordinary Time (*The Solemnity of Our Lord Jesus Christ the King*)		
Ezek 34:11–12,15–17	Dan 7:13–14	2 Sam 5:1–3
1 Cor 15:20–26,28	Rev 1:5–8	Col 1:12–20
Mt 25:31–46	Jn 18:33b–37	Lk 23:35–43

Glossary

A

abba

From Aramaic—a language spoken in Palestine at the time of Jesus—*abba*, meaning "father," was used by children in addressing their fathers. Jesus used the word *abba* to express his relationship with God (see Mk 14:36) and taught his disciples to pray to God as a loving and loveable parent.

Adam

Related to the Hebrew *adamah*, meaning "ground," this name signifies "one formed from the earth." According to the Book of Genesis, Adam was the first man to be formed; he was the husband of Eve and the father of Cain and Abel. Christ is sometimes called the "new Adam" or the "second Adam," as Christ initiated the new or second creation by restoring the divine friendship that had been lost by original sin.

allegory

This is a literary form in which something is said to be like something else. Allegories are often used to communicate a hidden or symbolic meaning commonly understood by the people it is addressed to. The Bible often uses allegories to explain spiritual reality. For example, Jesus is called the Lamb of God (see Jn 1:29), an allegory symbolizing that Jesus was the sacrifice for our sins.

alleluia

From the Hebrew meaning "praise to Yahweh" or "praise to God," *alleluia* is an exclamation that is used in the Christian liturgy as a way of praising God, especially during the Easter season.

amen

This Hebrew word means "let it be so" or "let it be done." As a conclusion to prayer, it represents the agreement by the person praying to what has been said in the prayer.

angel

This word is based on a word meaning "messenger," a personal and immortal creature, with intelligence and free will, who constantly glorifies God and serves as a messenger of God to humans in order to carry out God's saving plan.

anointing

This word (from the Latin *in-ungere*, meaning "to smear" or "rub on" oil or ointment for medicinal purposes) refers to an act of applying oil in a religious ceremony or as part of a blessing. In the Old Testament, kings, priests, and prophets were anointed as sign of their divine mission. Today, anointing is part of the sacraments of Baptism, Confirmation, Holy Orders, and Anointing of the Sick.

Antichrist

This word from the Greek literally means "against Christ," thus an adversary of Christ. In the New Testament, the Antichrist is a deceitful figure associated with the mystery of iniquity that is to precede the Second Coming of Christ. In modern usage, the term Antichrist describes both those who falsely claim to speak in the name of Christ and those who are enemies of Christ.

apocalypse

This word (from the Greek *apocalypses*, meaning "revelation" or "unveiling" or "uncovering"), in a general sense, refers to the end of the world when God will destroy the forces of evil. In the Scriptures, the Apocalypse or Book of Revelation, which is the last book of the New Testament, describes the conflict between good and evil, the end of the world and heaven.

apocalyptic literature

Having roots in both Jewish and Christian tradition, this genre of literature appears in the books of Ezekiel, Daniel, and Revelation. It is associated with the end-times or the last things and anticipates the time of Last Judgment when Jesus returns and the world as we know it disappears. Frequently referred to as "crisis literature," it generally appears in the context of historical, political, or religious turmoil and is characterized by symbols and images used to communicate a message to the intended audience while preventing the enemies of faith from understanding its true meaning.

Apocryphal Books

In the first centuries of Christianity, a great number of books and letters written by Christians did not become part of the Bible. These writings were not included in the New Testament because they were not in complete agreement theologically with the Apostolic Tradition. They are called apocryphal writings, and they include such works as the gospels of Thomas, Peter, and Mary Magdalene, the Epistle of Barnabas, the Acts of John and Paul, and the Shepherd of Hermas.

Some of the images in apocryphal writings are quite beautiful, some are Gnostic (an early Christian heresy), and some are just strange. With the exception of Thomas, most were written in the second through the fourth centuries AD. Apocryphal writings provide a resource that helps scholars reconstruct and understand the diversity of the early Christian period, but they are not inspired Scripture, and they are theologically in error. See *canon of Scripture, deuterocanonical books*.

apostle

The general term *apostle* means "one who is sent" and can be used in reference to any missionary of the Church during the New Testament period. In reference to the twelve companions chosen by Jesus, also known as "the Twelve," the term refers to those special witnesses of Jesus on whose ministry the early Church was built, and whose successors are the bishops.

Apostolic Tradition

See *Tradition*.

ark of the Covenant

In the Old Testament, this sacred chest housed the holy presence of God. The Book of Exodus contains the details of its construction (see 25:10–22, 37:1–9, 39:16–21). In the time of Moses, the ark was carried during the desert wanderings (1250 BC) and kept in the Tent of Meeting. In the period of the kings (about 1000 BC), it was placed in the holy of holies in the Temple (see 1 Kings 8:6–8). It held the tablets of the Law of Moses, manna from heaven, and the rod of Aaron. It was also called the ark of God (see 1 Sam 3:3).

Ascension

This is the "going up" into heaven of the risen Christ forty days after his Resurrection (see Mk 16:19, Lk 24:50–53).

B

Baal

This generic Semitic word means "master," "owner," "husband," or "lord." The word could be used to refer to Yahweh or to the master of a slave (see Hos 2:16). However, in the Scriptures, the word Baal most often refers to the practices of idolatry or the worship of gods other than Yahweh. Baal was both the name of a specific god and a generic title that could refer to any number of gods such as Baal Peor or Baal of Hermon. Often, the religion included the use of Temple prostitutes and even demanded human sacrifice, especially of infants. The worshipers of Baal were generally seen as the enemies of the Israelites (see 1 Kings 18:20–40).

Babylonian captivity

Babylon pillaged Judah three times, eventually causing the demise of the holy city, Jerusalem. In 587 BC, King Nebuchadnezzar murdered thousands of Israelites, destroyed the Temple, stole anything of value, burned Jerusalem to the ground, and enslaved a large portion of the population, sending them into exile in Babylon.

The captivity resulted in the deaths of multitudes, destruction of the land, devastation of the nation, loss of national identity, and infliction of hopelessness. The captivity lasted an entire generation (586–539 BC) until Cyrus the Persian, the king of Elam, conquered the Babylonians and let the Israelite people return home to Jerusalem (see Ezra, chapter 1). See *Diaspora, exile*.

ban, the

This was God's command that the Israelites destroy all the inhabitants, animals, and material possessions of the towns that they conquered. The ban first appears in the Book of Deuteronomy and is included partly as a warning to God's people against taking up the immoral practices of other religions, which included Temple prostitution and human sacrifice.

Beatitudes

The Beatitudes are the blessings enunciated by Jesus as part of the Sermon on the Mount (see Mt 5:3–12) and as part of the Sermon on the Plain (see Lk 6:20–26). The Beatitudes are often considered to represent the heart of the preaching of Jesus.

Bible

This word (derived from the Greek *biblia*, meaning "books") refers to the collection of Jewish and Christian writings that are considered inspired and normative for belief. The Hebrew Bible contains many of the works of what Christians call the Old Testament; the Christian Bible also includes writings known as the New Testament. See *New Testament, Old Testament*.

biblical criticism

This term (from the Greek *kritikos*, meaning "able to judge") refers to two different approaches to studying the Bible: (1) "lower criticism" attempts to reconstruct the original biblical text (because none of the original manuscripts have survived), and (2) "higher criticism" compares this reconstructed text with other documents of the time.

biblical interpretation

This kind of Scripture study looks at not only what the human authors intended to say but also at what God reveals to humans through their words. Criteria for interpreting the Scriptures are (1) considering the kind of writing—that is, the literary form—in which a particular passage appears, (2) considering the context of each author's historical time and the presumptions the author and the audience shared, and (3) considering the context of the process of revelation that occurred over time. Early insights often represent one step in understanding a mystery, not the fullness of revelation. The Scriptures should be read and understood within the living Tradition of the Church.

C

canon of Scripture

The canon of Scripture is the official list of the books of the Bible regarded as sacred because they are inspired; the list of books accepted by Catholic and Orthodox Churches includes some books and parts of books not accepted as inspired by most Protestant Churches.

Chosen People

According to the Old Testament, God chose Abraham and his descendants to be the recipients of Divine Revelation and so to play a unique role in salvation history; thus, their descendants, the Jewish people, are God's Chosen People.

Christian

According to the Acts of the Apostles (see 11:26), the disciples of Jesus were first called Christians in Antioch. In accord with the Greek word *christos* (meaning the "anointed one"), a Christian is a person who has been anointed at Baptism and Confirmation. In contemporary usage, all those who profess to follow Christ are called Christians.

church

In common Christian usage, the term *church* is used in three related ways: (1) to mean the entire people of God throughout the world, (2) to mean the diocese, which is also known as the local church, and (3) to mean the assembly of believers gathered for celebration of the liturgy, especially the Eucharist. In the creed, the Church is recognized as one, holy, catholic, and apostolic—traits that together are referred to as "marks of the Church."

circumcision

This is the act of surgically removing the foreskin of males; according to Jewish Law, males are to be circumcised eight days after birth (see Gen 17:12–14, Lev 12:3).

cities of refuge

These are cities that were designated as safe places where an individual who had accidentally caused the death of another could seek protection from the victim's family members who were seeking revenge for the killing. Initially the accused would seek safety by clinging to the horns of the altar in the sanctuary. Later on, various cities in strategic locations were set aside as safe havens. Offering sanctuary was a humanitarian effort to protect people who were falsely accused and prevent blood feuds between families that would continue until one family was completely annihilated. Still practiced today, sanctuary is often in the form of aid to the homeless and persecuted.

Commandments of God

The Commandments of God are the ten laws, or Decalogue, given by God to Moses on Mount Sinai (see Ex 20:2–17, Deut 5:6–21) as the fundamental rules of conduct for the Chosen People. These com-

mandments, also called the Law of Moses, were given in the books of Exodus, Leviticus, Numbers, and Deuteronomy. The first three of the Ten Commandments concern the love of God; the other seven commandments concern the love of neighbor.

contextualist

A contextualist is a person who interprets biblical passages by considering the literary and historical context and the whole process of revelation in order to correctly understand what the Bible is teaching.

council of the Church

An official assembly of Church leaders, this body gathers often for the purpose of discernment and decision making about particular issues. When represented by and concerned with the entire Church, it is called ecumenical, from a word meaning "the whole wide world." Councils can also be regional or local. The Jerusalem Council in chapter 15 of the Acts of the Apostles is considered the first council of the Church.

covenant

In general, a covenant is a solemn agreement between human beings or between God and a human being in which mutual commitments are recognized. A covenant can also be called a testament. In the Bible, two covenants are central: (1) the covenant between God and the ancient people of Israel established in God's Sinai Covenant with Moses, also called the Old Testament or Old Covenant; and (2) the New Covenant established by Jesus through his sacrificial death and Resurrection, also called the New Testament. The term testament has come to be associated primarily with the

Sacred Scriptures that record the history and meaning of the two biblical covenants.

Creation accounts

Genesis, the first book of the Bible presents two different accounts of God's Creation of all things (see 1:1—2:4, 2:4—3:24). Although different in their details, both accounts present Creation as a divine action that affirms the goodness of all creatures; in particular, humans were created in the image of God (see Gen 1:27) and called to live in mutual and life-giving friendships (see 2:18–22).

D

Day of Judgment

This is the biblical name for the time when God's justice will prevail, also known as the Day of the Lord or the Day of Wrath. In the Old Testament, the prophets proclaimed a Day of the Lord, in which all of humanity will share the bounty of the earth and "beat their swords into plowshares" and make war no more (Isa 2:2–4). The prophets also declared that the Day of the Lord was a time when God's wrath would be brought against those who practiced idolatry and injustice (see Zeph 2:1–3).

In the New Testament, the Day of Judgment came to mean the Last Judgment, when Jesus Christ will judge each person (see Mt 10:15; 12:36).

Dead Sea Scrolls

From the time of King David (1000 BC), Jewish rebels and refugees sought shelter in the caves cut into the limestone cliffs along the left bank of the Dead Sea. The site had been a ruin since the Romans destroyed Jerusalem in AD 68–70. In the spring of 1947, Bedouin shepherds found clay jars filled with ancient writings hidden by a group we call the Essenes. The find included the Dead Sea Scrolls, a Hebrew canon of Scripture (except Esther) from 250 BC, older than any Old Testament in existence by one thousand years. The Dead Sea Scroll collection also included Essene writings in Hebrew, Aramaic, and Greek. See *Essenes*.

deuterocanonical books

These are seven books that are part of the Catholic Old Testament but are not included in many Protestant Bibles. The deuterocanonical books were part of a Greek-language collection of the Jewish Scriptures called the Septuagint. The Catholic Church uses this collection of the Jewish Scriptures as the basis for the Old Testament. The seven deuterocanonical books in the Old Testament canon are Tobit, Judith, First Maccabees, Second Maccabees, Sirach, Baruch, and Wisdom of Solomon, along with parts of Esther and Daniel. Catholics believe them to be the inspired word of God.

deuteronomist

This term is used for the person or group responsible for writing the histories contained in the Old Testament books of Deuteronomy through Second Kings. The deuteronomist emphasized that God's just punishment occurred whenever the people sinned and broke their covenant with God. The deuteronomist also emphasized that if the people repented and returned to obedience to the Law of Moses, God's favor would return.

devil; demon

A devil or demon is a fallen angel—one created naturally good but who has sinned against God by refusing to accept God's Reign. The term devil refers to Satan, Lucifer, or the Evil One, the chief of the fallen angels; demon refers to an agent of the Evil One.

Diaspora

This word (from the Greek *diaspeirein*, meaning "to scatter") refers to a community of people who live in exile from their native land. In the Old Testament, the Diaspora of the Jewish people began in 587 BC when the Temple in Jerusalem was destroyed and many Jews were taken into exile in Babylon.

disciple

A disciple is a follower of Christ. It is based on a word for "pupil" or "student" and is used to designate both those who learned from and followed Jesus in New Testament times (the disciples) as well as those who commit to follow him today.

dispersion

See *Diaspora*.

E

Elohim

Elohim is one of the names for God in the Old Testament. Some scholars translate the word in the plural to mean "divinities" or "host of heaven"; other scholars consider Elohim a "majestic plural."

Elohist

The scribes who wrote of Elohim were the Elohists. They lived in seventh to sixth centuries BC. Later writers edited the Elohists' writings into sections of the Pentateuch. The scribes portray God as a humanlike figure who appears in person at different events and who is capable of regret. This is referred to by scholars as the E Tradition.

Emmanuel

This word from the Hebrew means "God with us." Matthew's Gospel calls Jesus by the name Emmanuel (see 1:23).

epistle

This word refers to the letters written by Church leaders in the first two centuries AD, especially those letters that are included in the New Testament and read during the celebration of the Mass and other sacraments.

Essenes

The Essenes were a group of pious, ultraconservative Jews who left the Temple of Jerusalem and began a community beside the Dead Sea that was known as Qumran. Originating in 100 BC, the Essenes thrived until AD 70, when the Romans violently put down a Jewish rebellion. The Essene community copied, wrote, and preserved the library of texts known today as the Dead Sea Scrolls.

E Tradition

See *Elohist*.

Eucharist, the

Also called the Mass or Lord's Supper, the term Eucharist is based on a word for "thanksgiving." It is the central Christian liturgical celebration, established by Jesus at the Last Supper. In the Eucharist, the sacrificial death and Resurrection of Jesus are both remembered ("Do this in memory of me") and renewed ("This is my body, given for you"). The Sunday celebration of the Eucharist is considered the heart of the Church's life and worship, and participation in it is expected of all Catholics of the age and ability to do so.

evangelist

Based on a word for "good news," evangelist describes anyone who actively works to spread the Gospel of Jesus; more commonly and specifically, evangelist refers to one of the persons traditionally recognized as an author of the four Gospels, Matthew, Mark, Luke, and John.

Eve

This name (related to the Hebrew *hawwah*, meaning "a living being") was given to the first woman, who was the partner of Adam and the mother of Cain and Abel. Mary is sometimes called the "new Eve" or the "second Eve," because, as mother of God, she was instrumental in initiating the new or second creation.

exegesis

The writers and editors of the Bible lived in various countries and cultures, wrote in several different languages, and wrote about events that spanned thousands of years. Faithful scholars have dedicated their lives to understanding the languages, symbols, culture, history, and meanings intended by those who wrote the Bible. The search into the Scriptures is called by the Greek word *exegesis*, which means "to draw out" or "to explain." The work of scholars assists Church leaders in their interpretation. Catholics interpret the Scriptures in union with the Tradition and the Magisterium of the Church.

Modern scholars use a number of methods to deepen understanding of the Bible. These methods are often called criticisms, not in the sense of being critically negative, but in the sense of taking a disciplined approach to the Bible as literature. See *form criticism, historical critical method, literary criticism, redaction criticism, source criticism, textual criticism*.

exile

This word (from the Latin *exilium*, meaning "banishment") refers to an absence from one's native land; sometimes this separation is forced, but other times it is self-imposed or voluntary. The Babylonian Exile (587–539 BC) was a particularly symbolic part of Jewish history; the Church today considers itself in exile until the coming of the risen Lord. See *Babylonian captivity, Diaspora*.

Exodus

This Greek word meaning "going out" is the name given the second book of the Bible, which describes the departure of the Israelites from Egypt under the leadership of Moses. The Exodus is celebrated at Passover as the liberation of the Chosen People.

F

Fall, the

Also called the fall from grace, the Fall is the biblical revelation about the origins of sin and evil in the world, expressed figuratively in the story of Adam and Eve in Genesis. See *Original Sin*.

Father

Like many other religions, Christianity looks upon God as a Father. Jesus called God abba (Father) and taught his disciples to pray to God as "Our Father."

form criticism

Form criticism is a method of studying the literary forms of a document in order to ascertain the background of a particular passage. For example, biblical form criticism studies such forms as parables, proverbs, and poems in order to discover the origin and history of a particular scriptural text.

fundamentalism

This is an interpretation of the Bible and Christian doctrine that is based on the literal meaning of the words and without regard to the historical setting in which the writings or teachings were first developed. A person who holds such a perspective is called a fundamentalist.

G

Gehenna
This word (from the Hebrew *Ge Hinnom*, meaning the "Valley of Hinnom") is the name of the place where children were once sacrificed to *Moloch (Baal)* (see Jer 19:5); Jesus spoke of Gehenna as a place of punishment for those who refused to repent and be converted.

genre
A genre is a category of literature, art, or music. Genres in the Scriptures include prose, poetry, myth, law codes, historical narrative, didactic (teaching) narrative, parable, and miracle stories. The first step in correctly interpreting a Scripture passage is to know its genre.

Gentile
This word (from the Latin *gens*, meaning "race" or "clan") is usually used in the New Testament to designate a person who is not Jewish; sometimes the word is used to refer to a person who is not Christian.

Gospel
Most basically, *Gospel* means "the Good News" of the Revelation of God in and through Jesus Christ, proclaimed initially by him, then by the Apostles, and now by the Church. The term also refers to those four books of the New Testament that focus on the person, life, teachings, death, and Resurrection of Jesus.

H

heaven
From the Old English meaning "home of God," *heaven* has various meanings: (1) in the ancient world, heaven was often identified with the sky or firmament and considered the dwelling place of the divine; (2) in Judaism, because of the reluctance to pronounce the name of God, heaven was sometimes used as a substitute for God's name; (3) among Christians, heaven represents the final goal of all Christians, where they are definitively united with God and reunited with their fellow Christians.

Hebrew
This word of Hebrew origin seemingly meant "one from the other side" or possibly "immigrant." The term *Hebrew* can refer to either the Israelite people or their language.

Hebrew Scriptures
See *Old Testament*.

hermeneutics
This word (from the Greek *hermeneus*, meaning "interpreter") refers to the study of the interpretation of texts, especially the study of the theory and method of biblical interpretation.

high place
Both the Hebrews and the Canaanites established places of worship on high ground (see Gen 12:7–8, 1 Kings 13:32). The Caananite high places often included practices of the fertility rites and human sacrifices offered to Baal Molech and Asherah. Over the centuries, the Hebrews destroyed the high places of the Canaanites (see Deut 12:2–3).

historical books
These writings make up a continuous narrative of Israel's history from the conquest of the land of Canaan to the rebuilding of Jerusalem after the Babylonian Exile. They include the books of Joshua, Judges, Ruth, First and Second Samuel, First and Second Kings, First and Second Chronicles, Ezra, Nehemiah, Tobit, Judith, Esther, and First and Second Maccabees.

historical critical method
This term (from the Greek *historia*, meaning "record" or "account," and *kritikos*, meaning "able to judge") refers to a method of studying texts, especially the Bible. The historical critical method considers the historical context, the philosophical presuppositions, and the theological perspective of a particular passage. See *biblical criticism*.

Holiness Code
This is a collection of teachings found in the Book of Leviticus, chapters 17–26, that remind God's people that true worship is more than following prescribed rituals or saying the right prayers. Love of God is demonstrated in the just and compassionate ways others are treated. Many of the precepts show great sensitivity to those who are poor and to the understanding of social justice.

holy of holies
The holy of holies, the innermost part of the Temple in Jerusalem, was the repository for the ark of the Covenant. Only the high priest was permitted to enter the holy of holies and then only once a year.

Holy Spirit
This word (from the Latin *spiritus*, meaning "breath" or "soul") refers to the third person of the Trinity, the Paraclete divinely sent to teach and guide the Church to the end of times. See *Paraclete*.

I

I AM
"I AM WHO I AM" was the name God called himself when talking to Moses from the burning bush (see Ex 3:14). It expressed that God simply is, God has no beginning and no end, and everything else exists because of God. Yahweh, the most common name for God in the Old Testament, was probably based on that phrase.

The New Testament contained suggestions of this title in connection with Jesus. Jesus asked Peter, "Who do you say that I am?" And Peter said, "You are the Messiah, the Son of the living God" (Mt 16:16).

idolatry

Idolatry is worship of other beings, creatures, or material goods in a way that is fitting for God alone. It is a violation of the first commandment (see Ex 20:3, Deut 5:7).

Incarnation, the

Based on words meaning "in flesh," the Incarnation refers to the mystery and Church dogma that the Son of God assumed human nature and "became flesh" in the person of Jesus of Nazareth (Jn 1:14). The Incarnation means that Jesus, the Son of God and second person of the Trinity, is both fully God and fully human.

inerrancy

This term, as related to the Scriptures, means that the books of the Bible are free from error regarding the spiritual and religious truth that God wishes to reveal through them for the sake of our salvation. See also *inspiration, biblical; Tradition.*

inspiration, biblical

This term refers to the guidance of the Holy Spirit in the development of the Scriptures, whereby the Spirit guided the human authors to teach without error those truths of God that are necessary for our salvation. It is on the basis of inspiration that we can call the Bible the word of God.

Israel

This name comes from Jacob's experience of "wrestling with God" (see Gen 32:28) and is used in different ways: (1) the twelve Tribes of Israel as descendants of the twelve sons of Jacob, (2) the Chosen People or Jewish People as a whole, (3) the northern kingdom (Israel) in contrast to the southern kingdom (Judah), (4) the modern nation of Israel.

Israelites

The Israelites were the Chosen People of God; members of the twelve Tribes of Israel descended from Jacob, who inhabited the land of Israel during biblical times.

J

Jesus Christ

In Hebrew *Jesus* means "God saves" and was the name given the historical Jesus at the Annunciation. Christ comes from the Greek *christos*, meaning the "anointed one" and translates the Hebrew word *messiah*. In the Old Testament, kings, priests, and prophets were anointed; in giving Jesus the title *Christ*, the New Testament indicates that Jesus fulfilled the messianic hope of Israel through his threefold office of king, prophet, and priest.

J Tradition

See *Yahwist.*

jubilee

This word comes from the sound of the ram's horn trumpet, the shofar. When blown, the shofar's sound signified the heavens' opening and the presence of God made near. According to the Law of Moses, every fiftieth year was proclaimed a jubilee, a year of repentance, and the people were to place their focus on the redistribution of wealth and property to the poor and dispossessed. During the jubilee, the land was to rest. Only gleaning of the fields was permitted. All landed property was returned to its original owners, slaves were set free, and all debts were erased (see Lev 25:8–55). The jubilee created a society of justice in which the bounty and the land were shared. It prevented abject poverty and erased lines between rich and poor. It corrected societal injustices and restored God's intended equality to human relationships.

Judah, Judea

These words come from the Hebrew word *Yehudah*, meaning "praise the Lord." Judah was a son of Jacob and Leah, a patriarch and founder of one of the twelve Tribes of Israel. The tribe of Judah became the most powerful of the twelve Tribes of Israel. Judah became a place-name of the southern territory of Palestine. Judah and its capital city, Jerusalem, were the headquarters for the administration of the nation of Israel, the location of religious life via the Temple, and dwelling place of the royal family of David. After the civil war at the end of Solomon's reign, the northern tribes separated and became known as the kingdom of Israel, and the southern tribes became known as the kingdom of Judah. For centuries the Temple priests and Judean kings ruled Judah. In the time of Roman rule, the area was called Judea.

Judaism

This word, which has been traced to Judah, the fourth son of Jacob and the tribe descended from him, refers to the monotheistic religion of the Jewish people who trace their origin to Abraham and whose religious observance is based on the Torah and the Talmud.

Judge

Judges were men and women who served the Hebrew people as tribal leaders and military commanders. The judges settled disputes and proclaimed the will of God. They were not judges as we understand that role today, presiding over legal cases. Instead, they were charismatic leaders whom the Holy Spirit inspired to lead the Israelites when they were a loosely knit federation of tribes (1200–1000 BC). The judges were clan heroes who empowered the faith of the people in times of crisis and focused their attention on the promises of the covenant.

K

Kingdom of God

Also referred to as the Reign of God, this term refers to the reign or rule of God over the hearts of people and, as a consequence of that, the development of a new social order based on unconditional love.

kingdom of heaven

The Gospel of Matthew uses this phrase, which seemingly reflects the Jewish custom of not speaking directly about God or the Kingdom of God.

L

Last Supper

During the Jewish celebration of Passover, this was the last meal Jesus shared with his disciples before being handed over for Crucifixion. It is remembered by Catholics as the occasion of the first Eucharist and is commemorated by believers on Holy Thursday.

law (biblical)

The Law, or Torah, which consists of the first five books of the Bible, is contrasted with the books of the prophets and the other writings. In the New Testament, Jesus often referred to "the Law and the Prophets." See *Tanak*.

Law (New)

This is the law of the Gospel of Jesus Christ, a law of love, grace, and freedom. It is distinguished from the Old Law, or the Law of Moses.

Law (Old)

This is the Law of Moses, the Ten Commandments. It contrasts the New Law of the Gospel. See *Torah, Pentatuech, law (biblical)*.

lectio divina

This is a form of meditative prayer, usually focused on a passage from the Scriptures, that involves repetitive readings and periods of reflection. Lectio divina can serve as either private or communal prayer.

Levi, Levite

Levi was one of Leah's sons fathered by Jacob (see Gen 29:34). He became a patriarch of Israel and the head of the tribe that carried his name, the Levites. Moses and Aaron were descendants of Levi (see Ex 2:1). According to the command of God, only Aaron and his sons could serve as priests (see 28:1). Thus, the Levites became the tribe entrusted with sacred ministries, the caretakers of the tabernacle and the Temple (see Num 1:48–54). See *priest, sacrifice*.

literal sense

This term (from the Latin *litera*, meaning "letter") refers to a form of biblical interpretation that translates a text word-for-word and emphasizes the explicit meaning of biblical texts. See *senses of the Scriptures*.

literary criticism

This term refers to a method of studying the Scriptures that looks at the text and seeks to understand it as a work of literature. Literary criticism considers what literary form (poetry, letter, story, and so on) or device (pun, parable, exaggeration, and so on) was used and how the particular literary forms or devices function in an ancient society. See *exegesis*.

literary forms

Literary forms are categories of smaller units of text that can be used within a particular genre. For example, the newspaper genre contains many literary forms, including national news stories, editorials, obituaries, sports stories, and classified ads.

Lord

This is the Old Testament name for God that in speaking or reading aloud was automatically substituted for the name Yahweh, which was considered too sacred to be spoken. In the New Testament, Lord is used for both God the Father and, on occasion, for Jesus, to reflect awareness of Jesus' identity as the Son of God.

M

Maccabees

This refers to a family whose real name was the Hasmoneans but became known after the most famous son, Judas Maccabeus. Maccabeus was probably his nickname, meaning "the hammer." The Maccabees became the political and religious leaders of the Jewish people in the second and first centuries before Christ.

Magisterium

This is the name given the official teaching authority of the Church, whose task is to interpret and preserve the truths of the Church revealed in both the Scriptures and Tradition.

messiah

This word comes from the Hebrew *mashah*, meaning "anoint" and was later translated into Greek as *christos* and into English as *Christ*. Many of the Jewish contemporaries of Jesus were awaiting the arrival of a messiah to deliver them from oppression.

metaphor

This word (from the Greek *metaphora*, meaning "transfer") refers to a literary comparison that compares and contrasts two things that are basically different. The parables of Jesus, for example, describe the Kingdom of God by using human examples that are different from, but simultaneously suggest the uniqueness of, the Kingdom.

monotheism

This is the belief in and worship of one true God. The Israelites were unique in their monotheism; other peoples in biblical times were polytheistic, believing in many gods and goddesses.

Mosaic Law

See *Law (Old)*.

Mount Zion

This is the hill on which the citadel of David and the city of Jerusalem stood. On Zion, David built his palace, and Solomon later built the Temple of Jerusalem. The city of Jerusalem came to represent the people and faith of Israel (see Pss 87:2, 149:2). In the Scriptures, the use of the phrase "virgin Zion" represents the ideal, pure relationship between the people of Israel and God (see 2 Kings 19:21, Lam 2:13–22). During the Babylonian captivity (586–539 BC), the prophets promised a time when God would make his home again in Zion (see Zech 2:10–11). In the Book of Revelation, Jesus Christ, the lamb of God, appears on Mount Zion (see 14:1).

myth

This word (from the Greek *mythos*, meaning "story" or "speech") is used in a variety of ways: (1) originally a myth was a story about the gods or heavenly beings and usually taught a moral lesson, (2) theologians sometimes contrast fact and myth understood as a story that is not factual but artificially contrived to teach a lesson, (3) myth has been understood as a story of ultimate significance that treats the origin, purpose, and end of creatures and creation.

N

natural law

This is our God-given instinct to be in right relationship with God, other people, the world, and ourselves. The basis for natural law is our participation in God's wisdom and goodness because we are created in the divine likeness. The fundamental expressions of natural law remain fixed and unchanging, which is why natural law is the foundation for both personal morality and civil norms.

New Covenant

This term refers to the covenant or law established by God in order to fulfill and perfect the Old Covenant or Mosaic Law. The Second Vatican Council emphasized that the New Covenant does not replace the Old Covenant, much less does it oppose the Old Covenant; rather it brings the Old Covenant to completion. See *Law (New)*, *Law (Old)*, *Old Covenant*.

New Testament

This is the name of the twenty-seven books of the Bible written during the early years of the Church in response to the life, mission, death, and Resurrection of Jesus. It is also another name for the New Covenant established between God and humanity by Jesus.

northern kingdom

See *Israel*.

O

Old Covenant

This term refers to the covenant or law that was given by God to Moses on Mount Sinai for the Chosen People. Although Christians consider the Old Law a preparation for the New Covenant or New Law given by Christ, the Old Covenant has never been revoked. See *Law (New)*, *Law (Old)*, *New Covenant*.

Old Testament

This is the name of the forty-six books of the Bible that record the history of salvation from Creation, through the story of ancient Israel, and up to the time of Jesus. It also refers to the Old Covenant established between God and the people of Israel in God's encounter with Moses on Mount Sinai. See *Septuagint*, *Tanak*.

oral tradition

In the ancient world, storytellers preserved the sacred wisdom, parables, regulations, and rules of life revealed to the ancestors and passed down across the ages. By telling these stories around campfires and at religious festivals, the sacred wisdom was passed from one generation to the next, until later scribes wrote it down. Many of the stories and teachings in both the Old and New Testaments were passed on by oral tradition for a generation or more before they were written down.

original sin

This term refers to the sin of the first human beings who disobeyed God's command and thereby lost their original holiness and became subject to death. Original sin affects every person born into the world.

P

parable

A parable is a story intended to convey a religious truth or particular teaching through the use of metaphors. Parables are a central feature of Jesus' teaching ministry.

Paraclete

This is a name for the Holy Spirit, based on a word for "helper" or "advocate." See *Holy Spirit*.

paradise

This word refers both to the Garden of Eden in the Book of Genesis and also to the New Jerusalem in the Book of Revelation. It has come to be identified with heaven.

Parousia

This is the Second Coming of Christ, when his Kingdom will be fully established and his triumph over evil will be complete.

Paschal lamb

This is a name for Jesus, whose death and Resurrection redeemed humanity. The name is associated with Passover, a commemoration of the deliverance of the Jewish people from Egypt. To avoid the slaughter of first-born sons by the Egyptian army, the Jews sprinkled the blood of a lamb on their doorposts. See *Passover; Eucharist, the*.

Passion of Christ

This term refers to the sufferings of Jesus during the final days in his life: his agony in the garden at Gethsemane, his trial, and his Crucifixion. Contemporary theologians often relate the Passion of Christ to the present-day suffering of people, especially those who are needy and marginalized.

Passover

This is the Jewish feast that memorializes the Exodus from Egypt when the Hebrews sacrificed a lamb; smeared its blood on their doorposts; prepared unleavened bread, bitter herbs, and the wine of blessing; and shared the sacred seder meal as family. That night the Lord passed over the houses of Egypt, and in all the houses not marked with the blood of the lamb, the first-born children and animals died (see Ex 21:29–30). Pharaoh sent the Israelites away. They crossed the Red Sea and became a free people.

The Passover festival, with its seder meal and its Paschal lamb, commemorates the creation of a new people, a society of justice based on a sacred trust between Yahweh and Israel. Passover honors a God who heard the cries of his people and responded with miraculous power to free them from a terrible oppressor. Jesus gathered his disciples together on Passover to celebrate the seder and offer them the bread of life (see Mt 26:17–30; Mk 14:12–26; Lk 22:7–23; 1 Cor 10:1, 11:23–26). See *Eucharist, the; Exodus; Last Supper; Paschal lamb*.

patriarch (Old Testament)

This word (from the Greek *patriarches*, meaning "chief" or "head of a family") is a title given to the fathers of the Old Testament, such as Abraham, Isaac, and Jacob, who were divinely selected to guide the Chosen People.

Pentateuch

This word (from the Greek *pente*, meaning "five," and *teuchos*, meaning "vessels" or "containers for scrolls") is a name given to the Torah, the first five books of the Hebrew Scriptures: Genesis, Exodus, Leviticus, Numbers, and Deuteronomy. See *Old Testament, Torah*.

Pentecost

This is the biblical event that followed the Resurrection and Ascension of Jesus at which the Holy Spirit was poured out on his disciples. The first Pentecost is often identified as the birth of the Church (see Acts 2:1–13). In the Christian liturgical year, the feast of Pentecost recalls the biblical event and is celebrated fifty days after Easter.

People of God

This is the biblical image for the Church, referring to those who share in Christ's mission as priest, prophet, and king.

Pharisees

The Pharisees were a Jewish sect during the time of Jesus. They were known for their strict adherence to the law and their concern with superficial matters.

priest

This word (from the Greek *presbyter*, meaning "elder") in the Scriptures designates one who offers sacrifice to God on behalf of the people. The first priestly man in the Hebrew tradition was Melchizedek of Salem. With Abraham he offered bread and wine and was a "priest of God Most High" (Gen 14:18). As part of the Sinai Covenant, God instituted an order of priests that began with Aaron and his sons. Because they were of the tribe of Levi, the Levites became known as the priestly class. As the Israelites settled Palestine, they built local temples at which the priests led the community in prayer and offered required animal sacrifices.

Once the Temple was built in Jerusalem, religious observances became centered there. All local temples were destroyed, and the priests were all moved to Jerusalem, where they assisted with worship and sacrifice in the Temple. The high priest was the chief priest and led all the major religious rituals in the Temple. The priesthood of Christ fulfills the expectations of the Old Testament priesthood through Christ's perfect sacrifice on the cross (see Heb 7:1–28). See *Levi, Levite*.

Priestly Tradition

This particular theological tradition present in the Pentateuch is the work of priestly scribes who hoped to restore the memory of the divided kingdoms of Israel and Judah and restore focus on the Sinai Covenant. Commonly known by scholars as the P Tradition, this tradition involved the scribes' blending the sacred names from northern Israel and southern Judah into a unified title for the Holy, which in English translates as "Lord God." God is portrayed as transcendent and distant, thus the need for priestly intercession.

Promised Land

This term refers to the land that God promised to the descendants of Abraham (see Genesis, chapter 12), the land of Canaan or Palestine.

prophet

This word (from the Greek *prophetes*, meaning "interpreter" or "spokesperson") refers to a person chosen by God to communicate a salvific message. A biblical prophet was primarily a communicator of a divine message of repentance to the Chosen People and not necessarily a person who predicted the future. Prophecy refers to the messages communicated by prophets on behalf of God. Seventeen prophets had books in the Bible named after them. Known as the prophetic books, they include Isaiah, Jeremiah, Baruch, Ezekiel, Daniel, Hosea, Joel, Amos, Obadiah, Jonah, Micah, Nahum, Habakkuk, Zephaniah, Haggai, Zechariah, and Malachi. The author of the book of Lamentations is unknown. The prophecies of other prophets, such as Moses, Deborah, Nathan, Elijah, Elisha, and Anna, were recorded in other books. Isaiah, Jeremiah, and Ezekiel are called the major prophets because so much of their prophecies were written down.

proverb

This word (from the Latin *proverbium*, meaning "common saying") refers to any short saying that has been orally passed down as advice from generation to generation. The Book of Proverbs in the Old Testament contains many examples of such wisdom sayings, which provide an understanding of human experience from a religious perspective.

psalm, psalter

The word *psalm* refers to a hymn or song of prayer that expresses praise, thanksgiving, petition, lamentation, or a historical memory of God's actions on behalf of the Chosen People. The word *psalter* refers to the Book of Psalms in the Old Testament that contains 150 psalms.

P Tradition

See *Priestly Tradition*.

R

redaction criticism

This refers to the process of editing or revising a text. Redaction criticism is the technical effort to determine the editorial history of a particular text, especially in biblical studies.

redemption, Redeemer

Redemption is the process by which we are "bought back" (the meaning of *redeem*) from slavery to sin into a right relationship with God. We are redeemed by the grace of God and through the life, death, and Resurrection of Jesus Christ. As the agent of redemption, Jesus is called the Redeemer.

Reign of God

See *Kingdom of God*.

Resurrection of Christ

This is the passage of Jesus from death to life "on the third day" after his Crucifixion. This is the heart of the Paschal mystery and the basis of our hope in the resurrection of the dead.

resurrection of the dead

This is the Christian dogma that all those deemed righteous by God will be raised and will live forever with God in heaven. It is the conviction that not only our souls but also our transformed bodies will live on after death ("I believe in the resurrection of the body").

revelation

This is God's self-communication and disclosure of the divine plan to humankind through creation, events, persons, and, most fully, in Jesus Christ.

S

Sabbath, *Shabbath*

In the Old Testament, this is the "seventh day" on which God rested after the work of Creation was completed. In Jewish Law, this is the weekly day of rest to remember God's work through private prayer, communal worship, and spiritual disciplines such as fasting. For Catholics, this is Sunday, the day on which Jesus was raised, which we are to observe with participation in the Eucharist in fulfillment of the commandment to "keep holy the Sabbath."

sacrifice

This word (from the Latin *sacer*, meaning "sacred," and *facere*, meaning "to make") refers to an offering made to God by a priest on behalf of the people as a sign of adoration, thanksgiving, petition, and communion (see Leviticus, chapters 1–7). In the Old Testament, a sacrifice was needed as atonement—that is, a healing rite that restored holiness by cleansing the people from infractions of the law. Sacrifices also reconciled their covenant relationship with God (see Ps 51:1–17). The only perfect sacrifice is that offered by Christ on the cross (see Heb 7:22–28).

salvation
Salvation is liberation from sin and eternal union with God in heaven. Salvation is accomplished by God alone through the Paschal mystery—the dying and rising of Jesus Christ.

salvation history
The pattern of events in human history that exemplify God's presence and saving actions. In Catholic thought, all of history is salvation history, even though God's presence may not be recognized.

Samaria
This territory, whose name comes from Shemer, the owner of the hill on which the town was originally constructed (see 1 Kings 16:24), consisted, at the time of Jesus, of the region south of Galilee and north of Judea—that is, the region between Nazareth and Jerusalem.

Samaritans
This term refers to the inhabitants of Samaria. The Samaritans rejected the Jerusalem Temple and worshiped at Mount Gerizim. The New Testament describes the Jewish rejection of Samaritans in both the parable of the good Samaritan (see Lk 10:29–37) and the account of Jesus' speaking with the Samaritan woman at the well (see Jn 4:1–42).

Satan
This Hebrew word, meaning "adversary," refers to the fallen angel or spirit of evil, who is the enemy of God and a continuing

instigator of temptation and sin in the world.

Savior
This word (from the Latin *salvator*, meaning "saver" or "preserver") is a title appropriately given to Jesus, whose Hebrew name means "God saves."

scribes
In Jewish history, these were government officials and scholars of the Law of Moses. They enforced the requirements of the law.

Scriptures
In general this is the term for any sacred writing. For Christians it refers to the Old and New Testaments that make up the Bible and are recognized as the word of God.

Semitic
The ancient language, culture, and various racial groups that make up the Middle East all have a common Semitic ancestry. The Hebrew, Aramaic, Arabic, and Akkadian languages, as well as the lost Hyksos language of Egypt, all have a Semitic source or root.

senses of the Scriptures
This term indicates that every text is open to a variety of interpretations or senses. In the history of Christian biblical interpretation, the following meanings or senses of the Scriptures have been proposed: (1) the literal sense seeks the word-for-word meaning of a text, (2) the allegorical sense seeks the symbolic meaning behind the text, (3) the anagogical sense seeks the spiritual meaning of a text, (4) the tropological sense searches for the ethical implications of a text, (5) the typological sense shows how the Old Testament prefigured the New Testament.

Septuagint
This term (from the Latin *septuaginta*, meaning "seventy") is

the name given to the Greek translation of the Hebrew Bible that was widely used among Hellenized Jews at the time of Jesus. According to a popular legend, a group of seventy (or seventy-two) Jewish scholars, working independently, produced the identically same translation in seventy (or seventy-two) days; hence the name Septuagint (seventy). See *Old Testament, Torah*.

Shema
The prayer known as the Shema has been said by observant Jews three times a day for thousands of years to honor the unity of God. In essence, it calls the faithful across the centuries to "Hear, O Israel: the LORD [Yahweh] is our God [Elohim], the LORD alone" (Deut 6:4). It leads the faithful to love the Lord with a whole heart, mind, and soul, and to love others as one loves oneself (see 6:5, 11:13–21). Jesus used the Shema to summarize the law and the faith of Moses into the two great commandments (see Mt 22:36–40).

source criticism
This term refers to the method of studying the Scriptures that identifies other writings outside of the Scriptures known in the ancient cultures that influenced the writer of a specific passage. It considers whether the writers build on an existing story, myth, or other literature as a basis for their work and whether the theology or justice ethic of the biblical version varies from that of the cultural source. See *exegesis*.

southern kingdom
See *Judah*.

suffering servant
The prophets revealed that the people of Israel were God's suffering servant who endured the pain of alienation and grief across history. Yet, the prophets also proclaimed that one to

come, the promised one of God, would suffer as a result of his compassion for humanity. He was to be Emmanuel—God with us. The suffering servant of Yahweh would be one with the people and would be one who knew suffering. He would bear our sufferings and bring us redemption (see Isa 52:13—53:12).

synagogue

This Greek word, meaning "meeting" or "assembly," refers to the worship assemblies of Jews, who lived outside of Jerusalem, to celebrate the Sabbath. Jesus is depicted in the Gospel of Luke (see 4:14–30) as beginning his Galilean ministry in the synagogue at Nazareth.

synoptic Gospels

This term (from the Greek *syn*, meaning "seen together," refers to the fact that the Gospels of Matthew, Mark, and Luke follow a similar pattern in both their overall structure and their individual narratives.

T

tabernacle

The receptacle in a church in which the consecrated bread and wine of the Eucharist is reserved for Communion for the sick and dying. The tabernacle is sometimes the focus of private and communal prayer and adoration. It was originally the portable Dwelling carried by the Israelites in their wilderness wandering (see Ex 25:8–9).

Talmud

This Hebrew word meaning "instruction" refers to the collection of rabbinic writings that constitute the basic religious authority in Judaism.

Tanak

This word is an acronym that refers to the major divisions of the Hebrew Scriptures: Torah (Law–T), Nebi'im (Prophets–N), and Ketubim (Writings–K).

temples

This biblical term refers to the various temples mentioned in the Old Testament. The Jewish people built temples on Mount Moriah, which is believed to be the place where Abraham went to sacrifice Isaac (see Genesis, chapter 22). The so-called First Temple period (1006–586 BC) began with David's occupation of Jerusalem and was followed by Solomon's building the First Temple. This period ended with the Babylonian Exile. The Second Temple period (536 BC–AD 70) began with the return of the Jewish exiles and culminated in the building of a new Temple by Herod shortly before the birth of Jesus. This Temple was destroyed by the Romans about four decades after the death of Jesus.

Ten Commandments

See *Commandments of God.*

testament

This word (from the Latin *testamentum*, meaning "will") describes the two parts of the Bible, the Old Testament and the New Testament, both of which are covenants offered by God.

textual criticism

This term refers to a method of studying the Scriptures that compares and contrasts various translations of the Scriptures to more clearly understand the meaning of a given passage. It considers whether the modern translations are in union with the oldest versions of the Scriptures available. See *exegesis.*

Torah

This word (from the Hebrew *torah*, meaning "law" or "instruc-

tion") refers to the Pentateuch or the Mosaic Law, which includes the first five books of the Hebrew Scriptures: Genesis, Exodus, Leviticus, Numbers, and Deuteronomy. See *Old Testament, Tanak.*

Tradition

Based on a word meaning "to hand on," Tradition is the central content of Catholic faith contained in both the Scriptures and in Church doctrines and dogmas, as well as the process by which that content is faithfully passed on from generation to generation, under the guidance of the Holy Spirit.

twelve Tribes

The twelve Tribes were a confederation of twelve Hebrew tribes that traced their origin to the patriarch Jacob. The Pentateuch stories tell how God renewed with Jacob the promises of the covenant he had originally made with Abraham (see Gen 28:10–17). Jacob then went on to have twelve sons by his two wives, Leah and Rachel, and their two maidservants, Zilpah and Bilhah. Leah bore six sons—Reuben, Simeon, Levi, Judah, Issachar, and Zebulun—and one daughter, Dinah. Leah's slave Zilpah bore Gad and Asher. Rachel, Jacob's beloved, gave birth to Joseph and Benjamin. Rachel's slave Bilhah mothered two more sons. Rachel named them Dan and Naphtali (see Gen 35:22–26).

After Jacob's first eleven sons were born, God renamed Jacob Israel (see Gen 32:28). Thus, the descendants of Jacob / Israel's sons became the Israelites, God's Chosen People. Their names came to symbolize the twelve Tribes that settled in the Promised Land.

W

wisdom

This word (from the Old English "aware" or "cunning") has several meanings: (1) Wisdom is one of the books of the Old Testament; (2) in the Hebrew Scriptures, wisdom is depicted as the action of God in the world; (3) in Christian theology, wisdom is one of the seven gifts of the Holy Spirit and enables a person to know God's divine plan of salvation.

wisdom literature

This is a genre of ancient literature that extolled the virtue of wisdom and gave practical advice on what it meant to be wise. In the Old Testament, the books of Proverbs, Job, Ecclesiastes, Sirach, and the Wisdom of Solomon are wisdom literature. Sections of other books (see Genesis, chapters 37–50) and certain psalms (see Psalm 37) also have traits of wisdom literature. The Song of Songs, a collection of love songs, is also included with the wisdom books. Typical themes in these books were the value of wisdom, self-control, patience, honesty, diligence, and respect for elders. A theme in several of the books was wisdom personified as a woman, Lady Wisdom (see Prov 1:1–36, Wis 6:12–25).

Wisdom literature in the Bible has certain characteristics. There is little mention of Israelite history, the Law of Moses, or the covenant. The emphasis is on what can be learned by experience and applied in daily life. The writing is often somewhat poetic; an idea is stated and then repeated in a slightly different way in the next line. See *wisdom*.

word of God

God's word is the power through which God created all that is (see Ps 33:6). The Bible is called the word of God because it has the power to create new life within the soul, to renew spirits, to teach, and to give hope (see 2 Tim 3:14–16). The Revelation contained in the Bible is inspired by the Holy Spirit to be without error in teaching the religious truth people need for salvation.

Jesus is also called the Word of God—the *Logos* in Greek (see Jn 1:1, Rev 19:13). This title describes the divine nature of Christ: "The Word was with God, and the Word was God" (Jn 1:1). See *Bible*.

Y

Yahweh

This word represents the four consonants, usually transcribed YHWH, used in the Hebrew Scriptures to indicate the name for God. Modern biblical scholars have reconstructed the word as *Yahweh*, though some have transcribed the Hebrew letters as JHVH and pronounce the name as "Jehovah." The meaning of YHWH is often translated as "I am who I am" (Ex 3:14).

Yahwist

This is a particular school of writing woven throughout the Pentateuch, attributed to the Yahwist authors or Yahwist school. This is the oldest literary source in the Pentateuch. It is sometimes called the J Tradition because the scholars who first noticed this were German, and in German, Yahweh is spelled *Jahweh*. This J Tradition was probably written by unknown scribes from Judah who, in 950 BC, wrote sections of the books of Genesis through Numbers. God to the Yahwist had human, or anthropomorphic, qualities. This God walked in the Garden (see Gen 3:8), sculpted humanity with divine hands (see 2:7), planted groves of trees (see 2:8), and grieved at the human beings who were lost among the trees or idols.

Yom Kippur

Yom Kippur is a Jewish holy day that is also referred to as the Day of Atonement, which falls on the tenth day of Tishri and is observed with prayer and fasting in accord with Leviticus (see chapter 16).

Z

zealots

This word refers to a Jewish group at the beginning of the first century AD who sought religious and political independence from the Romans and rose up in open rebellion. After their defeat, they carried on guerrilla warfare against the Romans.

Notes

Notes

Notes

Notes

Notes

Notes

Notes

Notes

THE WORLD OF THE PATRIARCHS map

Grid references (top): 1 · 2 · 3

Labels on map:

GOMER

LUD (Lydia)

JAVAN (Greeks)

ASHKENAZ (Scythians)

MADAI (Medes)

ELAM (Persia)

Persian Gulf

ARPHAXAD

River Tigris

River Euphrates

ASSHUR (Assyria)

TOGARMAH

HITTITES

KITTIM (Cyprus)

The Great Sea (Mediterranean Sea)

ARAM (Syria)

AMORITES

CANAAN

PHILISTINES

JOKTAN (Arabia)

Red Sea

MIZRAIM (Egypt)

PUT

River Nile

Place names:

Ur · Babylon · Mari · Haran · *Paddan-Aram* · Damascus · Penuel · Shechem · Hebron · Beersheba · Gaza · Zoan · On

Callout boxes:

Abraham and Sarah's original home (Gen 11:28)

Abraham and Lot first settle (Gen 11:31).

Jacob meets Leah and Rachel (Gen, ch 29).

Jacob wrestles with God (Gen 32:22–32).

Abraham and Sarah's burial site (Gen 25:9–10)

Joseph is sold into slavery in Egypt (Gen, ch 37).

Legend:

Map 1: **THE WORLD OF THE PATRIARCHS**

JAVAN — Descendants of Japheth (Gen 10:2–5)

PUT — Descendants of Ham (Gen 10:6–20)

LUD — Descendants of Shem (Gen 10:21–31)

(Egypt) — Later biblical name

→ Abraham's route

Scale: 200 miles / 200 kilometers

©2001 by Thomas Nelson, Inc. and Saint Mary's Press

maps.com

1543

Map 2:
THE EXODUS FROM EGYPT

↑ Route of the Exodus

▨ Alternate routes of Red Sea crossing

⬆ Unsuccessful invasion of Canaan (Num 14:39–45)

– – Trade routes

? Exact location questionable

0 — 75 miles

0 — 75 kilometers

Moses' death (Deut, ch 34)

Desert wandering (Deut, ch 2)

God gives the Ten Commandments (Ex, ch 20).

Miracles of manna and quail (Ex, ch 16)

Ammon

River Arnon

Moab

Brook Zered

MT. NEBO +

Dead Sea (Salt Sea)

Zoar

Punon

Edom

Hebron

Arad

Beersheba

Gaza

Wilderness of Zin

Kadesh Barnea

Arabah

Ezion Geber

Midian

Gulf of Aqaba

Wilderness of Paran

The Great Sea (Mediterranean Sea)

Way of the Philistines

Way of Shur

Route from Egypt to Arabia

MT. SINAI + HOREB

Red Sea

Marah?

Elim?

Baal Zephon

Avaris

Qantir

Pithom

Succoth

Land of Goshen

Memphis

River Nile

River Nile

35°

33°

31°E

31°N

29°

© 2001 by Thomas Nelson, Inc., and Saint Mary's Press

maps.com

1544

Map 3:
JACOB'S CHILDREN IN PALESTINE

+ Mount Hermon

• Tyre

DAN

Mediterranean Sea

ASHER

NAPHTALI

• Hazor

GESHUR

Sea of Galilee (Kinnereth)

ZEBULUN

• Megiddo

ISSACHAR

• Hepher

MANESSEH

Jordan River

GAD

Jabbok River

• Aphek

EPHRAIM

Bethel •

• Jericho

DAN

• Gezer

BENJAMIN

• Jerusalem

+ Pisgah Peak

JUDAH

REUBEN

Lachish •

• Hebron

Dead Sea

Arnon River

THE JORDAN VALLEY

JUDEAN DESERT

SIMEON

THE NEGEV

| 0 | 20 Mi. |

| 0 | 20 Km. |

Mount Halak +

©Saint Mary's Press

Map 10:
THE HOLY LAND IN MODERN TIMES

Area occupied by Israel since June 1967

0 — 75 miles
0 — 75 kilometers

LEBANON

SYRIA

Tripoli

Beirut

34°N

Sidon

Damascus

LEBANON MOUNTAINS

BEKAA VALLEY

ANTI-LEBANON MOUNTAINS

Tyre

Dan

Qiryat Shemona

*The Great Sea
(Mediterranean Sea)*

Nahariyya

Quneitra

**GOLAN
HEIGHTS**

33°

Akko

Safad

Haifa

1973 Line
1967 Cease-Fire Line

Tiberias

*Sea of
Galilee*

Nazareth

Dera

Afula

Ramtha

Beth Shean

Hadera

Netanya

Jarash

Tulkarm

Nablus

Herzliyya

**WEST
BANK**

River Jordan

Tel Aviv
Yafo

Petah
Tiqwa

Rishon le Zion

Lod

32°

Ramla

Ramalah

Amman

Ashdod

Jericho

Jerusalem

Ashqelon

Bethlehem

Madaba

Gaza

Qiryat
Gat

Hebron

Dhiban

**GAZA
STRIP**

En Gedi

*Dead Sea
(Salt Sea)*

Beersheba

31°

Al-Arish

Karak

ISRAEL

JORDAN

EGYPT

Negev

Arabah

Sinai

30°

**SAUDI
ARABIA**

Elat

Aqaba

© 2001 by Thomas Nelson, Inc.

maps.com

1550

Old Testament Figures and Events

Earthly Paradise (panel), Brueghel, Jan the Younger (1601-78)/Galerie de Jonckheere, Paris, France/ The Bridgeman Art Library

The Covenant of Yahweh with Noah, a detail from Noah and the Flood Scroll, 1996 (acrylic on canvas), Laura James (Contemporary Artist), Private Collection

Adam and Eve

(See Gen 3:1–24) By Jan Brueghel the Younger, Flemish 17th century. In this painting Adam and Eve are being escorted from the Garden of Eden by an angel. In contrast to the beauty and richness of God's creation all around them, Adam and Eve have clothed themselves in an attempt to hide their shame in having disobeyed God. In what ways do people today still try to cover up and hide their sinfulness?

Noah's Ark

(See Gen 5:32—9:29), by the contemporary American artist Laura James. The artist captures the energy of Noah's family as they load the ark with supplies. The Book of Genesis has many stories about families. When has your family worked together to accomplish an important goal?

© Saint Mary's Press/Brian Singer-Towns

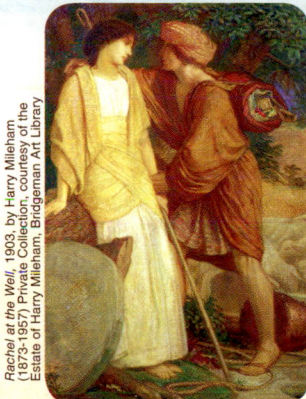

Rachel at the Well, 1903, by Harry Mileham (1873–1957) Private Collection, courtesy of the Estate of Harry Mileham, Bridgeman Art Library

Rachel at the well

(See Gen 29:1–30), by Harry Mileham, England, 1903. Jacob fell in love with Rachel at the well and served her father for fourteen years in order to marry her. Notice how young they look. What would you do for someone you loved?

Moses with the Tablets of the Law

(See Ex 20:1–21, 32:15–20) This depiction of Moses holding a stone tablet on top of Mount Sinai appears in the chapel of Moses in the Church of the Transfiguration on Mount Tabor. The tablets always symbolize the Ten Commandments. Do you think images of the tablets should be allowed in public places?

© Saint Mary's Press/Brian Singer-Towns

Ruth Gleaning the Field

(See Ruth, chapter 2; Lev 23:22) This depiction of Ruth holding a sheaf of grain is one of six women from the Old Testament surrounding Jesus in a mosaic that appears in the Church of the Dormition on Mount Zion in Jerusalem. Ruth is a foreigner from the land of Moab who becomes the great-grandmother of King David, an ancestor of Jesus.

© Saint Mary's Press/Brian Singer-Towns

David and Goliath

(See 1 Sam 17:1–51) This statue, which stands in the Tower of David Museum in the Old City of Jerusalem, depicts David's victory over Goliath, a Philistine warrior who challenged God's People to a fight and threatened to enslave them. David's faith in God helped him defeat the giant. In your life, what Goliaths do you need God's help to face?

New Testament Figures and Events

© Saint Mary's Press/Brian Singer-Towns

Courtesy of Stony Point Center, Stony Point, New York

Wise Men from the East
(See Mt 2:1–12) By Iranian artist Agha Behzad, 1958. This painting, from Iran, of the Nativity does not contain images of angels or the star of Bethlehem. Why do some paintings emphasize the human nature of Jesus' birth while other paintings emphasize his divine nature?

Mary Greets Elizabeth
(See Lk 1:39–56) This statue of Mary greeting her cousin Elizabeth appears in the courtyard of the Church of the Visitation on the hillside of Ein Kerem in Jerusalem. When Elizabeth heard Mary's greeting, the child within her leapt for joy. How do you react when hearing the Good News of the Gospel?

Jesus Calms the Storm, 1995 (acrylic on canvas) James, Laura (Contemporary Artist)/ Private Collection/The Bridgeman Art Library

© Saint Mary's Press/Brian Singer-Towns

The Escape to Egypt and the Slaughter of the Innocents
(See Mt 2:13–18) This mural, found in the Orthodox Church of the Annunciation in Nazareth, depicts the flight of the Holy Family into Egypt when King Herod threatened to destroy the child Jesus and ordered the massacre of all boys two years old and younger. Who or what threatens the lives of innocent people today?

Calming the Storm
(See Mt 8:23–27, Mk 4:35–41, Lk 8:22–25), by the contemporary American artist Laura James. The artist reflects both the humanity of the Apostles and the divinity of Jesus. Imagine being on that boat.

Jesus' Body is Removed from the Cross
(See Mt 27:57–61, Mk 15:42–47, Lk 23:50–55, Jn 19:38–42) This painting of Jesus' family and friends removing his body from the cross is from the Church of the Holy Sepulcher in Jerusalem, built on what is believed to be the site of Jesus' tomb. Imagine the sorrow Jesus' family and friends must have been feeling. How would you have reacted to Jesus' death?

© Saint Mary's Press/Brian Singer-Towns

Encounters with Jesus

Madonna and Child

This mosaic of Mary holding the child Jesus is from Japan and hangs in the Basilica of the Annunciation in Nazareth. Why do you think it is important to view images of Christ from different cultural perspectives?

Jesus Teaches the Crowds

(See Mt 5:1–11, Lk 6:20–26) By French artist James Tissot, 1836–1902. This painting depicts Jesus teaching the crowds. One of the most important teachings Jesus shared with his followers was the Beatitudes, rules for living that will bring true happiness. What has given you true happiness?

Jesus prays in the Garden at Gethsemane

(See Mt 26:36–46, Mk 14:32–42, Lk 22:39–46), from the Mafa Life of Jesus series, late twentieth century. This painting reflects the West-African vision of a garden. Notice how rocky it is and how short the trees are. How do you envision the Garden at Gethsemane?

Jesus Holding the Word

(See Jn 6:60–69) This mosaic of Jesus holding the word is in the Church of the Dormition on Mount Zion in Jerusalem. Jesus offers his followers the words of eternal life. Will you believe and follow?

Lamb of God

(See Jn 1:29; Rev 5:1–14) Found in the Church of the Visitation in Jerusalem, this mosaic of the Lamb of God symbolizes Jesus' sacrifice in redeeming the sins of the world. What sacrifice are you willing to make for others?

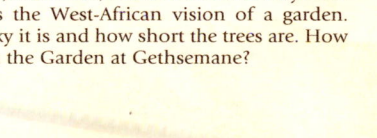

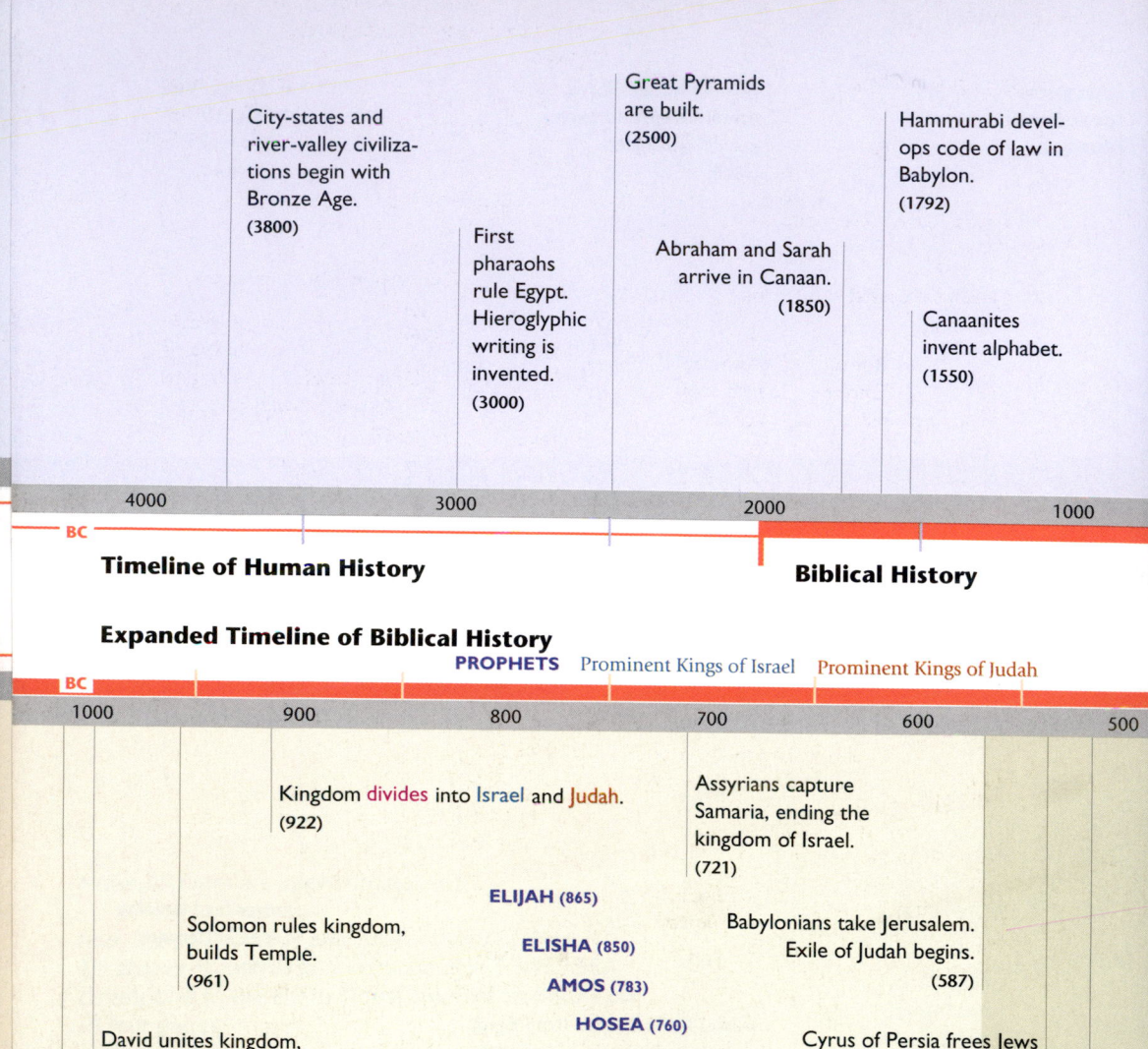

Timeline of Human History

City-states and river-valley civilizations begin with Bronze Age. (3800)

First pharaohs rule Egypt. Hieroglyphic writing is invented. (3000)

Great Pyramids are built. (2500)

Abraham and Sarah arrive in Canaan. (1850)

Hammurabi develops code of law in Babylon. (1792)

Canaanites invent alphabet. (1550)

BC · 4000 · 3000 · 2000 · 1000

Biblical History

Expanded Timeline of Biblical History

PROPHETS · Prominent Kings of Israel · Prominent Kings of Judah

BC · 1000 · 900 · 800 · 700 · 600 · 500

Kingdom divides into Israel and Judah. (922)

Solomon rules kingdom, builds Temple. (961)

David unites kingdom, takes Jerusalem as capital. (1000)

Saul is named first king of Israel. (1020)

ELIJAH (865)

ELISHA (850)

AMOS (783)

HOSEA (760)

FIRST ISAIAH (740)

MICAH (720)

NAHUM (663)

ZEPHANIAH (630)

JEREMIAH (626)

HABAKKUK (609)

EZEKIEL (593)

OBADIAH (586)

Assyrians capture Samaria, ending the kingdom of Israel. (721)

Babylonians take Jerusalem. Exile of Judah begins. (587)

Cyrus of Persia frees Jews to return to Judah. (538)

People of Judah rebuild Temple. (515)

SECOND ISAIAH (540)

ZECHARIAH (520)

HAGGAI (520)

TIME OF THE KINGS AND PROPHETS

UNITED KINGDOM · DIVIDED KINGDOM · PERSIAN DOMINATION

Saul · David · Solomon

Jeroboam I (922)
Ahab (869)
Ahaziah (850)
Jeroboam II (786)
Hoshea (732)

Rehoboam (922)
Ahaziah (842)
Jehoash (837)
Uzziah (783)
Hezekiah (715)
Josiah (640)
Jehoiachin (598)
Zedekiah (597)

1556

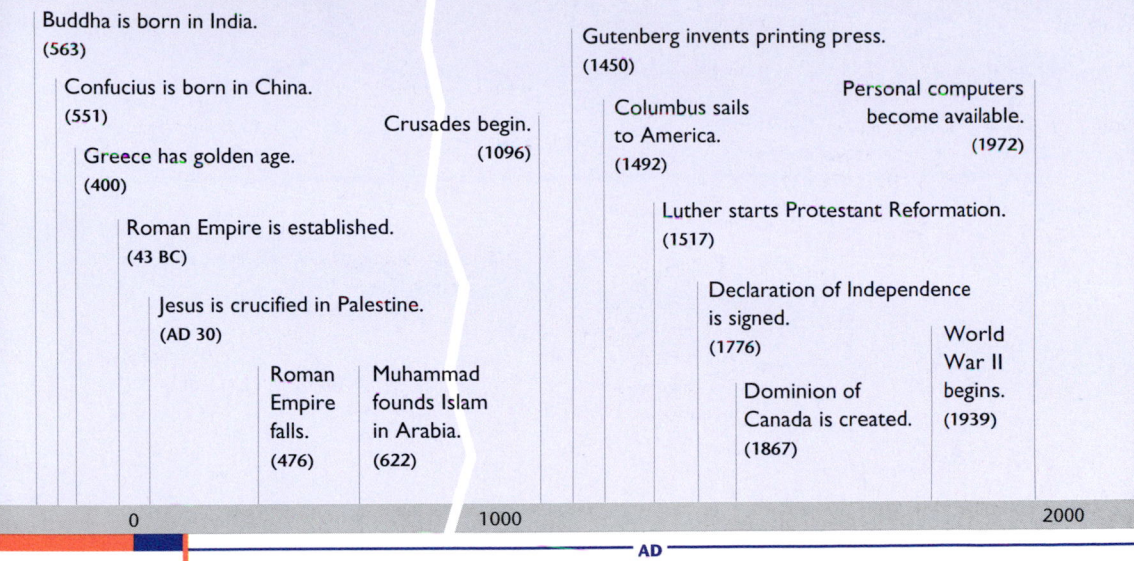

Timeline of Human History

Buddha is born in India. (563)

Confucius is born in China. (551)

Greece has golden age. (400)

Roman Empire is established. (43 BC)

Jesus is crucified in Palestine. (AD 30)

Roman Empire falls. (476)

Muhammad founds Islam in Arabia. (622)

Crusades begin. (1096)

Gutenberg invents printing press. (1450)

Columbus sails to America. (1492)

Luther starts Protestant Reformation. (1517)

Declaration of Independence is signed. (1776)

Dominion of Canada is created. (1867)

Personal computers become available. (1972)

World War II begins. (1939)

0   1000   2000

AD

Expanded Timeline of Biblical History

New Testament Books

BC   AD

400   300   200   100   0   100

Revolt against Greeks by Maccabees begins. (166)

Greeks conquer Holy Land. (332)

Temple is rededicated. (165)

Ezra brings Torah to Jerusalem. (398)

Simon, Jonathan's brother, establishes Hasmonean dynasty. (142)

Nehemiah becomes governor of Judah, starts renewal. (445)

Romans conquer Holy Land. (63)

Jesus is born. (5 BC)

Jesus is crucified. (AD 30)

Saul is converted. (31)

James is martyred. (61)

Nero persecutes Christians. Peter and Paul are martyred. (64 68)

Romans destroy Jerusalem Temple. (70)

MALACHI (458)

JOEL (400)

1 Thess (51), Paul's major letters (mid- to late 50s)

Colossians, Philemon (early 60s)

Gospel of Mark (mid-60s)

Gospels of Matthew and Luke, Acts of the Apostles, Hebrews (70s to 80s)

Gospel of John; 1, 2, and 3 John; and Revelation (90s); 2 Peter (after 100)

TIME OF FOREIGN DOMINATION

TIME OF NEW TESTAMENT

GREEK DOMINATION

HASMONEAN DYNASTY (FREE FROM FOREIGN DOMINATION)

ROMAN DOMINATION

Nehemiah   Ezra   The Maccabees

Domitian persecutes Christians. (95)

Alphabetical List of Bible Books and Abbreviations

Book	Abbreviation	Page	Book	Abbreviation	Page
Acts	Acts	1275	1 Kings	1 Kings	329
Amos	Am	1046	2 Kings	2 Kings	359
Baruch	Bar	952	Lamentations	Lam	943
1 Chronicles	1 Chr	386	Leviticus	Lev	108
2 Chronicles	2 Chr	413	Luke	Lk	1185
Colossians	Col	1398	1 Maccabees	1 Macc	514
1 Corinthians	1 Cor	1341	2 Maccabees	2 Macc	543
2 Corinthians	2 Cor	1363	Malachi	Mal	1097
Daniel	Dan	1008	Mark	Mk	1154
Deuteronomy	Deut	176	Matthew	Mt	1104
Ecclesiastes	Eccl	720	Micah	Mic	1062
Ephesians	Eph	1384	Nahum	Nah	1070
Esther	Esth	501	Nehemiah	Neh	457
Exodus	Ex	61	Numbers	Num	138
Ezekiel	Ezek	961	Obadiah	Ob	1055
Ezra	Ezra	445	1 Peter	1 Pet	1454
Galatians	Gal	1376	2 Peter	2 Pet	1461
Genesis	Gen	4	Philemon	Philem	1430
Habakkuk	Hab	1074	Philippians	Phil	1392
Haggai	Hag	1083	Proverbs	Prov	691
Hebrews	Heb	1433	Psalms	Ps	601
Hosea	Hos	1030	Revelation	Rev	1478
Isaiah	Isa	816	Romans	Rom	1320
James	Jas	1446	Ruth	Ruth	265
Jeremiah	Jer	883	1 Samuel	1 Sam	271
Job	Job	570	2 Samuel	2 Sam	302
Joel	Joel	1041	Sirach	Sir	762
1 John	1 Jn	1465	Song of Solomon	Song	730
2 John	2 Jn	1471	1 Thessalonians	1 Thess	1404
3 John	3 Jn	1473	2 Thessalonians	2 Thess	1410
John	Jn	1235	1 Timothy	1 Tim	1415
Jonah	Jon	1058	2 Timothy	2 Tim	1423
Joshua	Josh	216	Titus	Titus	1427
Jude	Jude	1475	Tobit	Tob	471
Judges	Judg	240	Wisdom of Solomon	Wis	739
Judith	Jdt	486	Zechariah	Zech	1086
			Zephaniah	Zeph	1078

All scripture is inspired by God and is useful for teaching, for reproof, for correction, and for training in righteousness, so that everyone who belongs to God may be proficient, equipped for every good work.
(2 Tim 3:16–17)